TWENTY-THIRD EDITION

KOVELS'
Antiques &
Collectibles
PRICE LIST

For the 1991 Market

ILLUSTRATED

Crown Publishers, Inc.
New York

D PRICES

the only newsworthy piece of furni-
records. A pier table, c.1775, by
Apn; a Chippendale tea table, c.1760-
765 $1.2 million; a Chippendale carved
00; $418,000; a mirror labeled John
ez, -paw foot firescreen, c.1770, at-
0. But eighteenth-century pieces
an Belter parlor suite auctioned
nch, made in 1907, brought
irror was $22,000; and a John
rprised bidders at $27,500.
to rise. Teco pottery seems
igned by Fritz Albert about
tied later in the year by a
prices were much higher
any records. Ohr pottery
zed, twisted-neck vase
by Wilhelmina Post,
lehead pottery vase,
ase decorated with
vl pattern charger

A Bonnin and
Losanti por-
d note other
e for a G.
wing the
tion fig-

enth-
ught
land
thr
ing
$58,

BOOKS BY RALPH AND TERRY KOVEL

American Country Furniture 1780–1875
Dictionary of Marks—Pottery & Porcelain
Kovels' Advertising Collectibles Price List
Kovels' American Silver Marks
Kovels' Antiques & Collectibles Price List
Kovels' Antiques & Collectible Fix-It Source Book
Kovels' Book of Antique Labels
Kovels' Bottles Price List
Kovels' Collector's Guide to American Art Pottery
Kovels' Collector's Source Book
Kovels' Depression Glass & American Dinnerware Price List
Kovels' Guide to Selling Your Antiques & Collectibles
Kovels' Illustrated Price Guide to Royal Doulton
Kovels' Know Your Antiques
Kovels' Know Your Collectibles
Kovels' New Dictionary of Marks—Pottery & Porcelain
Kovels' Organizer for Collectors
Kovels' Price Guide for Collector Plates, Figurines, Paperweights,
    and Other Limited Editions

Published by Crown Publishers, Inc., 201 East 50th Street,
New York, New York 10022
CROWN is a trademark of Crown Publishers, Inc.
Manufactured in the U.S.A.
Library of Congress Catalog Card Number: 83-643618

ISBN: 0-517-58095-0
10 9 8 7 6 5 4 3 2 1
First Edition

School lamp, c.1913, was $55,000, and a Karl Kipp and Roycroft lamp was $63,800.

And, of course, toys, folk art, and other collectibles continued to set records. A Tanneau perpetual calendar wristwatch was $539,000; a National pedal car shaped like a fire truck was $77,000; and a tin Coca-Cola sign with Hilda Clark, 1899, was $23,650. Carousel figure records include a deer for $34,000, a horse for $121,000, and a full carousel by Dentzel company, c.1920, for $1,424,500. There were several auctions of important toy collections and many records were set. An Arcade Chevrolet sedan was $17,050; a Francis, Fields and Francis paddlewheel tin boat went for $35,000; a Charles hose reel toy was $125,000; a Girl Skipping Rope mechanical bank was $19,800; and a yellow cast-iron Arcade Baby dump truck was $15,950. Even recent toys set records. A No. 2 Barbie doll brought $3,500, and a Thunder Robot was $9,020.

But the unusual collectibles are those that surprise. A feather golf ball sold for $11,550; and a Brown patent golf club, c.1900, sold for $90,000. A Hammonia typewriter, made in 1882, sold for $23,000; and a copper and zinc J. Howard & Co. horse-and-rider weather vane, complete with bullet holes, was $770,000. An American Indian, First Phase, Navajo man's wearing blanket, c.1850, was $522,500; and a jeweled presentation sword given to General Grant was $330,000. Smallest record setter of the year, a tiny heart-shaped willowware Shaker box for $2,860.

The prices in this book are reports of the general antiques market, not the recordsetting examples. Each year every price in the book is new. We do *not* estimate or "update" prices. Prices are the actual asking price, although the buyer may have negotiated to a lower figure. No price is an estimate. *We do not ask dealers and writers to estimate prices.* Experience has shown that a collector of one type of antique is prejudiced in favor of that item, and prices are usually high or low, but rarely a true report. If a price range is given, it is because at least two identical items were offered for sale at different times. The computer records prices and prints the high and low figures. Price ranges are found only in categories like "Pressed Glass," where identical items can be identified. Some prices in *Kovels' Antiques & Collectibles Price List* may seem high, and some may seem low because of regional variations. But each price is one you could have paid for the object.

If you are selling your collection, do *not* expect to get retail value unless you are a dealer. Wholesale prices for antiques are from 20 to 50 percent less than retail. Remember, the antiques dealer must make a profit or go out of business.

HOW TO USE THIS BOOK

There are a few rules for using this book. Each listing is arranged in the following manner: CATEGORY (such as pressed glass or furniture), OB-

JECT (such as vase), DESCRIPTION (as much information as possible about size, age, color and pattern). Some types of glass are exceptions to this rule. These are listed CATEGORY, PATTERN, OBJECT, DESCRIPTION. All items are presumed to be in good condition, undamaged, unless otherwise noted.

Several special categories were formed to make a more sensible listing possible. For instance, "Tool" includes special equipment, because the casual collector might not know the proper name for an "adze." Masonic has been put into the larger category "Fraternal." New categories include "Consolidated Glass," "Credit Cards," "Franciscan," and "Gustavsberg." The index can help you locate items.

Several idiosyncrasies of style appear because the book is printed by computer. Everything is listed according to the computer alphabetizing system. This means words such as "Mt." are alphabetized as "M-T," not as "M-O-U-N-T." All numerals are before all letters, thus 2 comes before A. A quick glance will make this clear, as it is consistent throughout the book.

We made several editorial decisions. A bowl is a "bowl" and not a dish, unless it is a special dish, such as a pickle dish. A butter dish is a "butter." A salt dish is called a "salt" to differentiate it from a saltshaker. It is always "sugar and creamer," never "creamer and sugar." Where one dimension is given, it is the height; or, if the object is round, the dimension is the diameter. The height of a picture is listed before width. Glass is clear unless a color is indicated.

Every entry is listed alphabetically, but the problem of language remains. Some antiques terms, like "Sheffield" or "snow baby," have two meanings. Be sure to read the paragraph headings to determine the meaning used. All category headings are based on the language of the average person at an average show, and we use terms like "mud figures" even if they are not technically correct.

This book does not include price listings of fine art paintings, books, comic books, stamps, coins, and a few other special categories.

All pictures in *Kovels' Antiques & Collectibles Price List* are listed with the prices asked by the seller. "Illus" (illustrated on the page) is part of the description if a picture is shown.

There have been misinformed comments about how this book is written. We *do* use the computer. It alphabetizes, ranges prices, sets type, and does other time-consuming jobs. Because of the computer, the book can be produced quickly. The last entries are added in June; the book is available in October. This is six months faster than would be possible any other way. But it is human help that finds prices and checks accuracy. We read everything at least twice, sometimes more. We edit 100,000 entries to the 50,000 entries found here. We correct spelling, remove incorrect data, write category headings, and decide on new categories. We sometimes make errors.

Prices are reported from all parts of the United States and Canada (translated to U.S. dollars at the rate of 75¢ U.S. to $1 Canadian) between June 1989 and June 1990. A few prices are from auctions, most are from shops and shows. Every price is checked for accuracy, but we are not responsible for errors.

It is unprofessional for an appraiser to set a value for an unseen item. Because of this we cannot answer your letters asking for specific price information. But please write if you have any requests for categories to be included in future editions.

When you see us at the shows, stop and say hello. Since our television show has been on The Discovery Channel in all parts of the country, we find we can no longer be anonymous buyers. It may mean the dealers know us before we ask a price, but it has been wonderful to meet all of you. Don't be surprised if we ask for your suggestions for the next edition of *Kovels' Antiques & Collectibles Price List*. Or you can write us at P.O. Box 22200, Beachwood, Ohio 44122.

Ralph & Terry Kovel
Senior Members, American Society of Appraisers
July 1990

ACKNOWLEDGMENTS

Special thanks should go to those who helped us with pictures and deeds: Neal Alford, Robert Anderson, Frank H. Boos Gallery, Christie's, Irene Davis, DuMouchelle Art Galleries, Glass-Works Auctions, Morton M. Goldberg Auction Galleries, Gene Harris, Willis Henry, Leslie Hindman Auctioneers, Richard Oliver, Skinner, Inc., Sotheby's, Swann Galleries, Theriault's, and Wolf's. Lee Markley and Rachel Davis gave special help.

To the others in the antiques trade who knowingly or unknowingly contributed prices or pictures to this book, we say "Thank You!" We could not do it without you. Some of you are: Terry & Evelyn Adams, Albert's Collectables, The Aluminist, American Pin Collection, American Spoon Collectors, Dianne Anglin, Antiquaria, Antique Bottle & Glass Collector, Arman Absentee Auctions, Avon Times, Jeffrey W. Baker, Noel Barrett, Lloyd R. Bauman, Dorothy Becker, 3 Behrs, Robin Bellamy, Bill's Classic Cyclery, Blair Museum, Stanley A. Block, Bobin's Antiques, Ronald Bourgeault, Richard A. Boune Co. Inc., Brillscote Farm Auction, Don & Bonnie Bull, Butterfield & Butterfield, Butterfly Net, Cambridge Crystal Ball, Cel-ebration!, Cerebro, Christie's East, Coin-Op Newsletter, Collectors' Classified, Mr. Condom, Credit Card Collector, The Crown Point,

Dairy & Country Collectibles (Fay & John Shaw), DeFina Auctions, J.C. Devine Inc., Doll Times, Eagles, G. I. Joe Action Figure Exahnge, Garth's Auctions, Inc., Tony Goodstone, Walt Grace, Graybird Publishing, Guernsey's, Norman Heckler, Heisey News, H. T. Hicks, Hobstar, Holiday Antiques (Shannon P. Riggs), Horsin' Around, Horst Auctions (C. E. Spohn), Howard's Sports Collectibles, Hummel Collector's Club, Inc. (Dorothy Dous), Jack & Scottie Imrie, The Indian Trader, Michael Ivankovich Antiques, Just Kids Nostalgia, George Kamm, Karen's Cookie Jars, William H. Kenney, Kevin Francis, Ltd., Lladro Collectors Society, Lyons Ltd. Antique Prints, Mike & Donna Marsh, Mike's General Store, Moore's Antiques, Mouse Man Ink (Robert Crooker), The New Glaze, The O. J. Club, The Old House, Old Sleepy Eye, Old Storefront Antiques, Richard Opfer Auctioneering, Inc., Paper Pile Quarterly, Phillips, Photique, David Rago, Lloyd Ralston Toys, Riba Auctions Inc., Charles G. & Lillian C. Richardson, Ronin Gallery, Sandy Rosnik, The Salt & Pepper Man, Kenneth E. Scheneringer, Jack Seiderman, George Shaw, Bill Shawver, R. H. Stevens, Team Antiques, Barry Thomsen, Time Will Tell, Sylvia P. Tompkins & Associates, Inc., Tool Ads, Toothick Bulletin (Judy Terlingo), Toy Scouts, Don Treadway, Treasure House, The TV Collector, Vollmar's Park Auction (David A. Norton), Larry Wells, Western World Avon Club, Whirligig Antiques, Robert Wieland, Anne D. Williams, Robert Wing, Tom Witte's Antiques, Woody Auction Company.

MORE ANTIQUE PRICE NEWS

Need to know the latest prices? We write a newsletter for collectors who want to know the latest news, trends, and prices for the antiques and collectibles market. *Kovels on Antiques and Collectibles* is an easy-to-read, 12-page, picture-filled newsletter about antiques of interest to collectors and dealers. It includes sale reports, reviews of price books, information about what to buy and sell, and articles on marks, fakes, care, security, and more. For more information about *Kovels on Antiques and Collectibles*, send a double-stamped, self-addressed envelope to Kovels, P.O. Box 22200-K, Beachwood, Ohio 44122.

Our TV series, "Collector's Journal with Ralph and Terry Kovel," can be seen on The Discovery Channel. The show includes news, prices, and information. Watch us to see collectors and collections.

Almaric Walter made pate–de–verre glass under contract at the Daum glassworks from 1908 to 1914. He started his own firm in Nancy, France, in 1919. Pieces made before 1914 are signed "Daum, Nancy" with a cross. After 1919 the signature is "A. Walter Nancy."

A.WALTER, Dish, 2 Interlocking Fish, Pate–De–Verre, C.1925, 5 3/4 In. 6350.00
Dish, Amber Bumblebee, Pate–De–Verre, C.1925, 9 1/8 In. 8470.00
Dish, Insect, Black Body, Turquoise, Pate–De–Verre, C.1925, 4 In. 2390.00
Dish, Rust & Black Beetle, Pate–De–Verre, C.1925, 5 1/4 In. 3395.00
Figurine, Nude Woman, Reclining, Head Tilted Backward, 8 1/2 In. 4250.00
Figurine, Women Sitting On Bench, Grecian Dresses, Signed, 8 In. 2950.00
Inkwell, Domed Cover, Berried Branches, 3 Bees, C.1925, 3 1/2 In. 5500.00
Paperweight, Japanese Beetle On Rock, Oval, Signed, 3 1/2 In. 4950.00
Pendant, Moth, Turquoise & White Ground, Marked, 2 1/2 In. 1100.00
Vase, Stylized Geometric Leaf, Pate–De–Verre, Signed, 5 1/2 In. 4400.00
Vase, Trailing Buds & Vines, Pate–De–Verre, Signed, 6 3/4 In. 5500.00

ABC plates, or children's alphabet plates, were most popular from 1780 to 1860, but are still being made. The letters on the plate were meant as teaching aids for children learning to read. The plates were made of pottery, porcelain, metal, or glass.

ABC, Bowl, Little Bo Peep, Glass 35.00
Dish, Child's, Feeding, Little Red Riding Hood 50.00
Feeding Dish, Looney Tunes 8.00
Mug, Etched Farm Animals, Sterling Silver 150.00
Mug, Little Jack Horner, Staffordshire 125.00
Mug, Seashore Scene, 4 Children, Silver Plate 150.00
Plate & Bowl, Raggedy Ann & Andy, 1969 .... 10.00
Plate, "F" Is For Frank Who A Sailor Would Be, 7 3/4 In. 125.00
Plate, 2 Little Boys In Sailor Hats, Fishing, Staffordshire 110.00
Plate, 2 Little Boys In Soldier Hats, Playing Cards, Staffordshire 110.00
Plate, 3 Black People In Rowboat, Fishing, Staffordshire, 6 1/8 In. 165.00
Plate, Baker, Putting Bread In Brick Oven, Staffordshire, 7 In. 135.00
Plate, Best For Bobby's Breakfast, Bessie's Bread & Milk 95.00
Plate, Black Transfer Scenes, French & English Captions, 6 In., 6 Pc. 570.00
Plate, Brownies, Tin 150.00
Plate, Children Playing Leap Frog, Staffordshire, 6 1/4 In. 125.00
Plate, Clock Center, Crystal, 6 In. 55.00
Plate, Clock, Amethyst, 8 In. 45.00
Plate, Coal Burning Train 145.00
Plate, Cock Robin, Alphabet, Tin, 8 In. 65.00
Plate, Crusoe Discovers Friday, 7 In. 95.00
Plate, Egg, Eye & Eel, Black Transfer, Staffordshire, 6 3/4 In. 100.00
Plate, Elephant, Howdah Riders, Alphabet Border, Glass, 6 In. 150.00
Plate, Flowers That Never Fade, Enameling, Staffordshire, 6 In. 30.00
Plate, Franklin Proverb, Embossed Alphabet Rim, 6 In. 85.00
Plate, General McClellan, Greeting To Civil War Soldiers 155.00
Plate, General McClellan, On Horseback, Union Troops, 7 In. 225.00
Plate, Harvest Home, 5 In. .... 50.00 To 65.00
Plate, House That Jack Built, 7 In. 55.00
Plate, How Glorious Is Our Heavenly King, 7 In. 65.00
Plate, Hunters, Polychrome Enameling, Staffordshire, 6 3/4 In. 100.00
Plate, Jumbo, Tin 32.00
Plate, Maiden All Forlorn, Germany, 7 In. 15.00
Plate, Mary Had A Little Lamb, Tin 150.00
Plate, Niagara, From Edge of American Falls, Staffordshire, 7 1/4 In. 125.00
Plate, Philadelphia, Raised Alphabet On Rim, 8 1/4 In. 72.00
Plate, Punch & Judy, Allerton & Sons, 7 1/2 In. 115.00
Plate, Reflections On The Beauty of Nature 95.00
Plate, Robinson Crusoe Building Boat, 7 In. 125.00
Plate, Roosters, 6 1/2 In. 12.00
Plate, Stork, Carnival Glass, Marigold 65.00
Plate, Stork, Crystal, Frosted, 6 In. 65.00
Plate, Thousand Eye, Clock Center, Amber, 6 In. 65.00

Abingdon Pottery was established in 1934 by Raymond E. Bidwell as the Abingdon Sanitary Manufacturing Company. The company made art pottery and other wares. Sixteen varieties of cookie jars are known. The factory ceased production of art pottery in 1950.

ABINGDON, Bookends, Horsehead, Black	65.00
Bookends, Horsehead, White .... 42.00 To 50.00	
Bookends, Horsehead, Yellow	35.00
Bowl, No.544, Rectangular	15.00
Cookie Jar, Hobby Horse	125.00
Cookie Jar, Humpty Dumpty	70.00
Cookie Jar, Little Bo Peep .... 95.00 To 125.00	
Cookie Jar, Little Miss Muffet	95.00
Cookie Jar, Mary Had A Little Lamb .... 162.00 To 170.00	
Cookie Jar, Money Sack, White	70.00
Cookie Jar, Mother Goose	200.00
Cookie Jar, Three Bears .... 68.00 To 125.00	
Cookie Jar, Train .... 75.00 To 88.00	
Cornucopia, Double, Pink Matte	15.00
Figurine, Peacock, Ivory	50.00
Figurine, Shepherdess & Fawn, No.3906	158.00
Planter, Basket, Star	35.00
Vase, Blue Seagulls, 7 1/2 In.	25.00
Vase, Blue, 8 1/2 In.	5.00
Vase, Scroll, Green, 15 In.	22.00
Vase, Seagull, White & Blue, 7 3/4 In.	12.50
Wall Pocket, Apron, Black & Pink	75.00

 Adams china was made by William Adams and Sons of Staffordshire, England. The firm was founded in 1769 and is still working. All types of tablewares and useful wares have been made through the years. Other pieces of Adams will be found listed under Flow Blue.

ADAMS, Cup & Saucer, Handleless, Nesting Birds, Pair	55.00
Cup & Saucer, Rose, Blue Sponged Florets	80.00
Cup & Saucer, Rose, Spatter, Blue Bowknot Border	250.00
Humidor, Dr. Syntax Transfer, Marked Adam's Tunstall, 5 In.	40.00
Mug, Oliver Twist	99.00
Plate, Prince of Wales Entry Into London, Shakespeare	30.00
Plate, Rose, 10 1/2 In.	150.00
Plate, Rose, Green Bowknot Border, Red Band, 5 3/4 In.	50.00
Plate, Shylock, Shakespeare	30.00
Plate, St. Paul's School, London, 7 3/4 In.	105.00
Platter, Blue Feather Edge, 17 1/2 In.	50.00
Platter, Dr. Syntax, Blue & White, Small	75.00
Soup, Dish, Scene of Cattle, 10 /4 In.	45.00

The old country store with the crackers in a barrel and a potbellied stove is a symbol of an earlier, less hectic time. The advertisements, containers, and products sold in these stores are now all collectibles. We have tried to list items in the logical places, so large store fixtures will be found under the Architectural category, enameled tin dishes under Graniteware, etc. Listed here are many of the advertising items. Other similar pieces may be found under the product name such as Planters Peanuts.

ADVERTISING, see also Paper

ADVERTISING, Ashtray, Allison Air, Metal, May 1947	10.00
Ashtray, Breyer's Ice Cream, 5 In.	20.00
Ashtray, Breyers, 95th Anniversary	22.00
Ashtray, Camel A Real Cigarette, Camel Center, Tin, Small	16.00
Ashtray, Carter Hall Smoking Tobacco, Metal	3.00
Ashtray, Diamond Tire, Blue Embossed Glass Insert, 1905	50.00
Ashtray, Figural, Steel Worker, Lebanon Beer, 3 3/4 In.	55.00
Ashtray, Firestone, Copper Tire	10.00

Ashtray, Firestone, Tire, Art Deco Insert	16.00
Ashtray, Fleer Dubble Bubble Gum	15.00
Ashtray, General Tire	10.00 To 15.00
Ashtray, Goodrich Silvertown, Green Insert	25.00
Ashtray, Griesedieck Brewery, Cardinal's Baseball Glove	48.00
Ashtray, Iron Fireman	16.00
Ashtray, Knobby Tire, Blue Embossed Glass Insert, 1905	50.00
Ashtray, Levy's Bread, Black Boy	35.00
Ashtray, Lucky Strike, Pocket	22.00
Ashtray, Master Ball Bearings, Metal	11.00
Ashtray, Mohawk Tire Co.	12.00 To 15.00
Ashtray, Moxie	60.50
Ashtray, Panther Oil & Grease Co., Panther Jumping Over Moon	20.00
Ashtray, Philco Radio, Havana Convention, Stoneware, 1936	150.00
Ashtray, Playboy Club, Orange Glass, Black Semi-Nude, 3 3/4 In.	8.00
Ashtray, Reddy Kilowatt, Red On White China, Gold Rim, 1957	11.00
Ashtray, St. Louis Malleable, Bathing Beauty, Bronze, 6 In.	75.00
Ashtray, Top Hat, Lowell Hand Cream	25.00
Ashtray, Western Holly Gas Ranges, Graniteware, Yellow	28.00
Bag, Feed, E. Mensch, March 2, 1868, Coarse Linen, 19 X 49 In.	15.00
Bag, Feed, Johannes Mohring Von Meisheim, Tools, 24 X 58 In.	250.00
Bag, Gold Medal Flour, With Flour, Salesman's Sample, 2 3/4 In.	10.00
Bag, Shopping, Iroquois Beer, Indian, 1930s	10.00
Bag, Tobacco, Oceanic, Cloth	5.00
Bank, Delivery Truck, Pet Milk	20.00
Bank, Green Giant, Musical	85.00
Bank, Razor Blade, Frog, Listerine	35.00
Bank, Razor, Gillette, Donkey	10.00
Bank, Telephone, Pillsbury Doughboy	75.00
Banner, Cetacolor, Gay 90's Woman, Linen, Colors, 24 X 35 In.	175.00
Banner, Dupont Five Star Antifreeze, Canvas, 36 X 56 In.	50.00
Banner, Plymouth Show, Lawrence Welk, Pink, 40 X 58 In.	25.00
Banner, Sparrows Empress Chocolates, 8 Ft.	55.00
Banner, Sweet Caporal, Canvas, Red, White, Green, 3 X 5 Ft.	18.00
Barrel, Dad's Old Fashioned Root Beer, Soda Fountain, C.1920	200.00
Bean Pot, Chisholm's Hardware, Gary, Minn., Pottery	145.00
Bean Pot, Hancock Market, Pottery	145.00
Bean Pot, Julius Jetka Hardware, Little Falls, Minn., Pottery	145.00
Bean Pot, Winnebago Co-Op Creamery Assoc., Buttermilk, Pottery	145.00
Beater Jar, Wesson Oil, Stoneware	67.50
Belt Buckle, Champion Spark Plug, Airplane In Flight	10.00
Bill Hook, Hirsch Brothers Whip Powder, Celluloid	35.00
Bin, Blankes Expo Brand Coffee, Wooden	395.00
Bin, Edwards Cloves	525.00
Bin, Lorillard's Rose Leaf Tobacco, Cardboard, Wood Top	125.00
Bin, Mellow Mint	50.00
Bin, Red Band Scrap, Tobacco	450.00
Bin, Shure Shot Tobacco, Pictures Indian	425.00
Bin, Sweet Burley Tobacco, Yellow, Round	65.00
Bin, Sweet Cuba Tobacco, Slant Front, Small	65.00
Bin, Sweet Cuba, Lift Top, Lady's Face On Front, 8 X 8 X 11 In.	44.00
Bin, Use Only Lion Coffee, Red Paint, 19th Century, 33 In.	375.00
Binoculars, Kellogg, Premium	45.00
Blackboard, Kayo, Metal, 27 X 14 In.	85.00
Blanket, TWA, Black & Red	75.00
Blotter, Beich Whiz Chocolate, 5 Cent, Candy Picture	12.00
Blotter, Effervescent Tablets, Sea Diving, 1930s, 4 X 8 In.	3.00
Blotter, State Mill & Elevator Co., 5 Flour Bags, 1930s	5.00
Bonnet, Puritan Flour, Bakery, 1900	13.00
ADVERTISING, BOOK, see Paper, Book	
Booklet, Dandy Duck, Uncut Cloth, Kellogg, 1935	60.00
Booklet, Fun Book, Elsie The Cow, 1950s	25.00
Booklet, Jell-O, 1917, O'Neill Page, Kewpies Mother	20.00
Booklet, Magic Parasol, Palmolive, Child's Story, 1928	18.00

To cover a scratch in a piece of furniture made of dark wood, rub a walnut, Brazil nut or butternut into the scratch. Eyebrow pencil or shoe polish in a matching shade will also work.

Advertising, Cabinet, Diamond Dyes,
Children Playing

Booklet, Old Dutch	12.00
Booklet, Secret Patrol, Uncle Don, Bond Bread, 1936	20.00
Booklet, Wheaties, Want To Be A Basketball Champion, 1945	7.00
Boot, Rubber, U.S. Rubber, Oversize, 36 In.	550.00
ADVERTISING, BOTTLE, see Bottle	
ADVERTISING, BOTTLE OPENER, see Bottle Opener	
Bowl, Skippy, Orange Beetleware, 1933	20.00
Bowl, Wheaties, Milk Glass, 1939	42.00
ADVERTISING, BOX, see also Box	
Box Opener, Iron Hatchet, Hirsch's Happy Boy Peanut Cake, 7 In.	18.00
Box, 7–Up, Dovetailed Wood, Label, 17 X 9 In.	40.00
Box, Angelus Marshmallows, Cherubs, Oval, 2 1/2 In.	49.00
Box, Arm & Hammer Baking Soda, Sample	20.00 To 30.00
Box, Baker's Condition Powders, Cover, 1930s, 15 X 9 In.	30.00
Box, Beauty, Gloria Swanson, 1922, 8 In.	35.00
Box, Cascarets Laxative, Cherub, On Chamber Pot, Round, 2 In.	44.00
Box, Champ Prophylactics, 4 Different Scene Packages	125.00
Box, Cigar, Tabacalera, Hinged, Phillipine Wood, Center Tray	25.00
Box, Cigar, Two Birds, Cartoon Roosters, 1909 Stamp	30.00
Box, Cooper Underwear, Black, White Cat, Oval, 3 In.	35.00
Box, Desk, Figural, Victor Adding Machine, Copper	20.00
Box, Display, The Standard Baseballs For Sale Here, Shelves	341.00
Box, Domino Sugar, 1 Lb.	8.00
Box, Egg, Wooden, H.C. Gerhart, 1900–10	65.00
Box, Elk Drugs Borax Soap, Elk Picture, Unopened	20.00
Box, Fanny Farmer, Calendar Box of Good Dinners, Oak, 1913	75.00
Box, Florida Queen Projecto Cigar	8.00
Box, Gold Dust Washing Powder, 2 Black Boys, Unopened, 9 In.	38.00
Box, Green Tree Beer, 1910	49.00
Box, Hatchet Brand Spaghetti, Contents, L Lb.	8.00
Box, Ivory Snow Soap, 1940s	9.00
Box, Ivory Snow, Unopened, 1963	8.00
Box, Jack Sprat Cheese, Wooden, 2 Lb.	15.00
Box, Keebler–Weyl Baking Co., Brass, Glass, 11 1/2 X 10 In.	98.00
Box, Kodak Film, 3–Dimensional, Checkerboard Design, Metal	650.00
Box, Lady Luxury Toilet Water, Empty, C.1900	10.00
Box, Lux Soap, 1940s	9.00
Box, Nature's Remedy, Face, With Pill, Round, 2 In.	45.00
Box, Old King Cole Drinking Straws, Colorful	15.00
Box, Premium No.1 Chocolate, Wooden Dovetailed, Pioneer Woman	45.00
Box, Ralston Cereal, Boy Picture, Checkerboard Design, Sample	25.00
Box, Regal Brand Oats, Indianapolis, 1 Lb.	12.00

Box, Seed, D.M. Ferry & Co., Dovetailed, Picture Inside Cover 60.00
Box, Seed, Mandeville Triple Tested, Oak, 15 X 8 X 4 1/2 In. 65.00
Box, Silver–Tex Prophylactics 15.00
Box, Stenciled, R. Scheetz Gro., Wire Bail, Wooden Handle, 11 In 265.00
Box, Sweetheart Straws, Kids Pictures, 1000 Piece 95.00
Box, Telephone Cigarettes, General Talking, Girlfriend, Full 30.00
Box, Washing Powder, Fun To Wash 55.00
Box, Woven Straw, Sparrow's Holly Chocolate, Attached Tip Tray 120.00
Broom Holder, Consumer's Power Co. 22.50
Broom Holder, Heins Superette 6.00
Cabinet, A.H. Rice & Co., Oak, Silk & Twist, Mirror, 39 X 14 In. 330.00
Cabinet, Angel Dainty Dye, 17 X 16 X 6 In. 150.00
Cabinet, Belding, Paul & Co. Ltd., Calendar Clock, 29 X 21 In. 1650.00
Cabinet, Diamond Dyes, Children Jumping Rope, 30 X 23 X 10 In. 1550.00
Cabinet, Diamond Dyes, Children Playing ....*Illus* 700.00
Cabinet, Diamond Dyes, Children With Balloon, Tin, 24 X 15 In. 550.00
Cabinet, Diamond Dyes, Court Jester Scene, 27 X 21 X 9 1/2 In. 1450.00
Cabinet, Display, Oak, Union Made, 8 Ft.4 In.X 8 Ft. X 17 In. 3900.00
Cabinet, Dr. Daniel's, Tin Front, 26 1/2 X 21 In. 250.00
Cabinet, Dr. Lesures Remedies, Oak, Horse Picture, 27 X 21 In. 625.00
Cabinet, Heminway & Sons Spool Silk, Oak, 36 Drawers, 72 In. 3500.00
Cabinet, Humphreys Specifics Dye, Oak, Tin, 28 X 22 X 10 In. 295.00
Cabinet, Morrison's English Remedies, Veterinary, 28 X 16 In. 880.00
Cabinet, Pearl Lustre Dyes, Wood, Tin Front, 22 X 17 X 7 In. 935.00
Cabinet, Peerless Dyes, Tin, 25 X 19 X 10 In. 5500.00
Cabinet, Pratt Food Veterinarian, Tin Front, Horse, 33 X 17 In. 660.00
Cabinet, Putnam Dye, Pine, Red, Tin Litho Front, Hinged Lid 200.00
Cabinet, Red Squirrel Nut Co., Glass Front, 6 Back Bins, 17 In. 95.00
Cabinet, Spool, Coats & Clark Thread, Metal 60.00
Cabinet, Spool, Corticelli, Cylinder, Roll Glass Door 285.00
Cabinet, Spool, Corticelli, Ribbon, Mirrored Center Door, Walnut 1400.00
Cabinet, Spool, J.P. Coats Cotton 575.00
Cabinet, Spool, J.P. Coats, 3 Drawers, Glass Panels, Logo 250.00
Cabinet, Straight Razors, Winchester, Simmons 295.00
Cabinet, Tin Chuck Wagon, Complete 495.00
Cabinet, Whillemores Shoe Polish, Oak, Stepback, Glass, 56 In. 660.00
     ADVERTISING, CANISTER, see Advertising, Tin
Card Game, Sarsaparilla Flag 28.00
Card, Diamond Dye, 3 Black Children, Framed, 7 1/2 X 7 1/2 In. 495.00
Carrier, Bottle, 7–Up, 1940 .... 45.00
Case, Belding Bros., & Co., Spool, Counter Top Display, 42 In. 675.00
Case, Display, Bakers Extracts, Slant Front, 24 X 24 X 15 In. 715.00
Case, Display, Fleer's Pepsin Gum, Oak, Tin Front, 15 X 7 In. 1000.00
Case, Display, J.P. Primley's Cal. Fruit & Pepsin Chewing Gum 450.00
Case, Display, Wear–Ever Fountain Pens 90.00
Case, Esterbrook Pens, Drawer, Rounded Glass, Holds 2 Doz. 98.00
Case, Sauer's Extract, Etched Glass, Oak, 15 X 10 In. 685.00
Case, Up To Date Remedies, Black Person, Wood, 30 X 13 In. 750.00
Case, West Hair Nets, Tin, Lift Lid, 2 Drawers, Square, 1918 .... 200.00
Case, Winchester, Glass Front, Wood, 18 X 14 X 7 1/2 In. 225.00
     ADVERTISING, CHANGE RECEIVER, see also Advertising, Tip Tray
Change Receiver, Boston Herald, Newsboy In Knickers, 3 1/2 In. 94.00
Change Receiver, Doublewear Spinner, 4 Horses, 4 In. 28.00
Change Receiver, LaPalina Cigars, Glass 75.00
Change Receiver, Old Reliable Coffee, Woman, 5 In. 42.00
Change Receiver, Thomson Bros., Romanesque Woman, 4 In. 44.00
Charger, Home of Falstaff, Tavern Scene, Tin, Round, 24 In. 150.00
Checkerboard, Standard Oil, Checkers 35.00
Cigar Cutter, Boy Thumbing Nose On Handle, Iron, 12 1/2 In. 65.00
Cigar Cutter, Brighton Little Imp, Iron 75.00
Cigar Cutter, Dawson's Scot, Pocket 15.00
Cigar Cutter, Keywind, Harvard, Iron 300.00
Cigar Cutter, Peter Schuyler, Wood Base, Glass Top, 8 1/2 In. 66.00
Clicker, Old Time Coffee 25.00

Clicker, Poll Parrot	10.00
Clicker, Quaker State Oil	14.00
Clock, Bottle Cap, Dr Pepper, Metal	95.00
Coal Sack, Paper, Red Lodge, MT., Bear Picture, Unused	15.00
Coaster, Melrose Whiskeys, Tin	12.50
ADVERTISING, COFFEE GRINDER, see Coffee Grinder	
Coffee–Tap, Bing Crosby, Box	35.00
Comb, Ronald McDonald, Rattail	7.50
Counter, Arctic Soda Water, 1880–1890, 30 X 16 X 44in.	660.00
Coupon, Aunt Jemima Pancake Flour, 1929	10.00
Cream Separator, DeLaval, Electric, Table Top, With Book, 22 In.	65.00
Creamer, Homestead	17.00
Creamer, Jersey Pride	15.00
Creamer, Kellogg's, Clear	11.00
Creamer, Kellogg's, Perfect Measure, Glass, 1920s	9.00
Creamer, Meadow Gold, Shield, 1/2 Oz.	12.50
Creamer, Plainview Farms, Green Script, 3/4 Oz.	12.50
Creamer, Schmidt Guernsey Beaver Dams, 1 Oz.	29.00
Crock, Ferndell Brand Mince Meat, White & Brown, Lid, 9 In.	39.00
Crock, Heinz Mustard, Blue & White, Black Stencil, 4 1/2 In.	90.00
Crock, Virol Bone Marrow, Stoneware, Ideal Cat Food	45.00
Cup & Saucer, Horlicks, 1930–40	18.50
Cup & Saucer, Red Tea Rose, Fortune Telling, Bone China	16.00
Cup, Armour's Vigoral, China	20.00
Cup, Hershey 1934 Chocolate Cookbook Scene	15.00
Cup, Maytag, Miniature	20.00
Cup, Measuring, Figural, Quaker Oats Man, Celluloid, 3 1/2 In.	30.00
Cup, Michelin Tires	12.50
Cup, Solitaire Coffee, Tin	25.00
Cutter, Cigar, Harvard, Boy Picture, Windup, 7 X 9 In.	132.00
Cutter, Cookie Set, Borden, Elsie, Beulah, Pair	25.00
Cutter, Plug Tobacco, Star, Iron, Dated 1885	65.00
Decals, Li'l Abner, Orange Crush Giveaway, Envelope	18.00
Dish, Compliments of Empire Cream Separator Co., Brass, 5 In.	1100.00
Dish, Sundae, Vortex, For Use With Paper Liner, Pat. Jan.2, 1923	8.50
Dish, Teaberry Gum, Vaseline Glass, Pedestal	53.00
Dispenser, Alka–Seltzer, Celluloid	30.00
Dispenser, Anheuser–Busch, Crockery, Dated 1919	750.00
Dispenser, Baby Ruth Hot Fudge	95.00
Dispenser, Brown Crock, Breakfast Cheer Tea	45.00
Dispenser, Buckeye Root Beer Syrup, Pump, Dancing Devils	1750.00
Dispenser, Buckeye Root Beer, Log, Brown China	650.00
Dispenser, Buffalo Brand Peanut, Jar, 21 1/2 In.	605.00
Dispenser, Cherry Drip, Pump, 15 In.	5200.00
Dispenser, Cherry Smash, Porcelain, White, Round Shape	1300.00
Dispenser, Cherry Smash, With Glass, 5 Cents In Middle	2500.00
Dispenser, Collar Button, Price Collar Button Mach. Co., 12in.	500.00
Dispenser, Cone, I.C., Plated, 38 In.	410.00
Dispenser, Copenhagen Snuff, Wall, Tin Lithograph, Product	75.00
Dispenser, Dad's Old Fashioned Root Beer, Oak Barrel, 1930s	200.00
Dispenser, Drink Fan–Jaz, Baseball Shape	4500.00
Dispenser, Fowler's Cherry Smash	1500.00
Dispenser, Grape Crush, Purple Glass, Pump Barrel Shape, 15 In.	1650.00
Dispenser, Hires Root Beer	1600.00
Dispenser, Hires Syrup, Hires It Is Pure, Waisted, Pump, 14 In.	300.00
Dispenser, Hires, Fountain, Hourglass Shape, Pump, 15 In.	578.00
Dispenser, Magnus Root Beer, Barrel, Blue Bands & Lettering	300.00
Dispenser, Mahogany, Silver Plate, Victorian, 6 Taps, 31 In.	440.00
Dispenser, Middleby Root Beer	350.00
Dispenser, Middleby, Root Beer, Glass	575.00
Dispenser, Middleby, Syrup, Brown Glass, RB	650.00
Dispenser, Mission Orange, Lights Up, Glass & Metal	650.00
Dispenser, Mission Orange, Pink Barrel	200.00
Dispenser, Mission Orange, Tin, Orange & Black	575.00

Dispenser, Mission Real Fruit, Green 175.00
Dispenser, Mission Real Fruit, Pink 150.00
Dispenser, Moxie, Cardboard Surround For Syrup Bottle 600.00
Dispenser, Nestea, White Letters On Green, Spigot 98.00
Dispenser, Nut, 3 Glass Containers, 17 X 21 In. 198.00
Dispenser, Potato Chip, Amusement Park 300.00
Dispenser, Right Cut Chewing Tobacco, Wall, Tin, 4 1/2 X 11 In. 285.00
Dispenser, Shot, Wooden, Glass, 8 Sections, Oak, 25 X 12 X 10 In. 330.00
Dispenser, Shotwell's Marshmallow 50.00
Dispenser, Soda, Bigelow Supply Co., Silver Plated, 1865, Pair 2000.00
Dispenser, Straw, Velvet Ice Cream 190.00
Dispenser, Ward's Lemon Crush, Porcelain, 9 X 3 1/2 In. 485.00
Dispenser, Ward's Orange Crush .... 300.00 To 425.00
Display Cabinet, Eveready Flashlight Batteries, Tin 125.00
Display Case, Boye Needle Co., Shuttle Display, Drawer, Wooden 135.00
Display Case, Corina Larks Cigars, 15 Cents, Metal & Glass 36.50
Display Case, J.P. Priwley Fruit & Pepsin Gum, Curved Glass 650.00
Display Shelf, Sunshine Biscuit, Metal 25.00
Display, Chandler's Chewing Laxative, 24 Packets, 9 X 11 In. 15.50
Display, Figural, Dutch Boy, Heineken, For The Bar 85.00
Display, Giant Thread, Wood Store Box 45.00
Display, Hadacol, Mechanized, Family, On Carousel, 1950s, Box 195.00
Display, Kellogg's Cereal, C-3PO 80.00
Display, Kiwi Boot Polish, Metal 35.00
Display, McDonald's, Star Trek 100.00
Display, P. Lorillar & Co., Wooden, 1760-1886, 33 X 40 X 3 In. 660.00
Display, Ward's Cake, Tin, Glass, Children, 20 X 17 X 13 In. 2750.00
Display, Wise Potato Chips, Cardboard, Easel, 1949, 21 X 27 In. 120.00
Dog, RCA Nipper, Stuffed, 1940s, Large 150.00
Dominoes, Marlboro Cigarettes, 18 Piece 25.00
Dominoes, Wooden, Lord Calvert Whiskey 25.00
Door Push, Biltrite, Porcelain, Silhouette of Man At Anvil 80.00
Door Push, Canada Dry, Tin 18.00
Door Push, Crescent Flour, Flour Sack, Tin 85.00
Door Push, Ex-Lax, Porcelain, Pair 75.00
Door Push, Kool Cigarettes, Tin, 1940s 25.00
Door Push, Major's China Cement, Porcelain 110.00
Door Push, Munsingware, Man On 1, Girl On Other, Pair 1000.00
Door Push, Read The Toronto Star, Porcelain 52.00
Door Push, Red Rose Tea, Tin, Blue, Red & White 50.00
Door Push, Robin Hood Flour, Porcelain, Red & White 48.00
Door Push, Salada Tea, Porcelain, Yellow, Red 65.00
Door Push, Sunspot Orange Drink, Picture of Bottle 75.00
Door Push, Texas Punch, Tin 20.00
Driver's Patch, Hires, Colorful, Large 24.00
Earrings, Reddy Kilowatt 35.00
Emblem, Hat, Gulf, Silver Trim-Like Wings 30.00
　　　　ADVERTISING, FAN, see Fan, Advertising
Figure, Battery, Car, Firestone 50.00
Figure, Dachshund, Frankenmuth Beer, Dog Gone Good, Chalkware 45.00
Figure, Dog, RCA, Chalkware, 5 1/2 In. 20.00
Figure, Eagle, White Eagle Oil Co., Cast Iron, 34 In. 900.00
Figure, Indian, Reclining, Ohio Match Co., Plaster, 24 In. 200.00
Figure, Johnnie Walker, Plastic Molded, 28 In. 185.00
Figure, Little Man, Playing Flute, Pfeiffer's Beer, 8 In. 35.00
Figure, Lollipop Holder, Bulldog, Morses Pure Pops 75.00
Figure, Nipper, RCA Dog, Canadian, Hard Rubber, 32 In. 1100.00
Figure, Parrot, Poll Parrot Shoes, On Stand, 8 In. 75.00
Figure, Philip Morris, Chalkware, 1934 .... 40.00
Figure, Pig, Glass, Best Pig Forceps, 6 X 5 In. 225.00
Figure, Skippy, Bisque, 1930s, 5 In. 55.00
Figure, Waiter, With Apron, Schmidt's Beer, 6 In. 25.00
Figure, Woman Holding Bottle of Moxie, 29 3/4 In. 3025.00
Figurine, Bovril, England, Mache Black Automation, 23 In. 2700.00

Flashlight, Schlitz Beer, Bottle Shape 14.00
Flashlight, Shamrock Oil Co., Green 15.00
Flip Book, Bromo Seltzer, Arthur Murray, Missing Back Cover 10.00
Fly Swatter, Dutch Club Beer, Penna. 25.00
Foam Scraper, Num–Hum Pretzel 35.00
Foam Scraper, Old Clarke Bourbon, Celluloid 35.00
Fork, Pickle & Olive, Jewel Tea Co. 32.00
Glass, Beer, Grand Prize, Texas 35.00
Glass, Beer, Premium Atlantic Beer 30.00
Glass, Milwaukee Brewing Co., Etched 115.00
Glass, Moxie, Embossed, Straight Sides 50.00
Glass, Schlitz, Etched 54.00
Goblet, Figural, Crow, Old Crow Whiskey 35.00
Hairnet, Invisible, Silk, Colorful Envelope, 1960 .... 6.00
Hat, Sample, Stetson, Tiny 20.00
Hat, Soda Jerk, Curtiss Candies, Baby Ruth 15.00
Holder, Foam Scraper, Piel's Bros., 2 Elves On Front, Metal 65.00
Holder, Kiwi Shoe Polish, Revolving, Tin, Kiwi On Top, 36 In. 50.00
Holder, Needle, General Electric, Vacuum Cleaner, 2 In. 30.00
Holder, Paper Roll, Sensible Tobacco, Nickel Plated 100.00
Holder, Pin, Dorothy Vernon, Jennings Co., Perfumers, 2 3/4 In. 11.00
Holder, Pin, Kemp & Burpee Mfg. Co. 33.00
Holder, Straw, Fluted Glass, Nickel Over Brass Top, Base, 13 In. 358.00
Holder, Straw, Green Fluted Glass, Nickel Cover, 11 In. 468.00
Humidor, Briggs Tobacco, Wooden Barrel, 7 1/4 In. .... 20.00 To 25.00
Humidor, Cremo Cigars, Store Bin 98.00
Humidor, Imperial Cube Cut Tobacco, Pressed Glass, Cover, 8 In. 94.00
Humidor, Tobacco, Imperial Cube Cut, Cover, 7 In. 12.00
Jar, Adams Chewing Gum 100.00
Jar, Borden's Milk, Fluted Glass, Nickel Cover, 6 1/2 In. 215.00
Jar, Buffalo Brand Peanut, Buffalo, Aluminum Cover, 10 In. 230.00
Jar, Gum, Adams Tutti–Frutti, Paper Label 400.00
Jar, Gum, Kis–Me, Kis–Me, 9 1/2 In. 44.00
Jar, Horlick's Malted Milk, Tin Lid, Miniature 25.00
Jar, Kimball–Rochester, NY, Amber, Cover, 7 X 5 In. 29.00
Jar, Kis–Me Gum, Louisville, Ky. 45.00
Jar, La Palina–Quality Cigars, 16–Sided Glass, 6 X 7 In. 50.00
Jar, Lance, Embossed Glass Lid, Large 27.00
Jar, Malted Milk, Thompson 35.00
Jar, National Biscuit Co., Cover, 12 In. 116.00
Jar, National Biscuit Co., General Store, Flint Glaze 675.00
Jar, Nut House Nuts, Store Counter, Embossed 185.00
Jar, Rochester Candy Works, Royal Marshmallows, 9 In. 94.00
Jar, Shaving Compound, W.C. Taylor's, Porcelain 66.00
Jar, Squirrel Nut, Label, Cover, 14 In. 132.00
Jar, Straw, Manhatten 325.00
Jar, Straw, Sunshine, Art Deco 35.00
Jar, Teaberry Gum, Yellow Glass 95.00
Jar, Vaaser Chocolate, Makes Life Sweeter, Brass Lid 95.00
Jar, W & S Cough Drops, Embossed Base & Cover 35.00
Kit, Cutex Manicuring, Tin, Hinged Lid, Containers, 1920s 14.00
Knife, Anheuser–Busch, German Silver Handle 66.00
Knife, Chickering Grand Pianos, Brass & Enamel, Pen 22.50
Knife, Drink He–Hi, Remington Gun Co., 3 1/4 In. 78.00
Knife, Goodwill Shoes, Blade, Holliston, Mass, Mfg., 2 3/4 In. 83.00
Knife, Mitchell Seed Co., Budding, Celluloid Handle 35.00
Knife, Pocket, Nehi Soda 40.00
Knife, West End Brewing, Boot Shape 65.00
Label, Alphabetical, Boy Playing With Blocks, Orange, 1930 .... 125.00
Label, Altissimo, Pink Mountains, Orange, 1920 .... 3.00
Label, Atlas, Atlas With Globe On Back, Orange, 1930 .... 24.50
Label, Best Strike, Baseball Player, 1920 .... 45.00
Label, Boyhood, Smiling Boy Driving Mule Cart, 1920 .... 95.00

Label, California Beauty, Bouquet of Roses, Pear, 1930 .... 3.75
Label, California Dream, Gold Peacock, Orange, 1920 .... 16.75
Label, Chanticleer Brand, Image of Chicken, Cape Cod 8.00
Label, Daisy, Large White Flower, 1930 .... 3.00
Label, Du Pont Golden Pheasant Powder 25.00
Label, Du Pont Indian Rifle Powder 20.00
Label, Fontana Girl, Girl Drinking Lemonade, 1918 .... 50.00
Label, Good Cheer Inn, Christmas Holly, Horse & Carriage, 1947 .... 4.75
Label, Hi–Goal, Polo Player Ready To Hit Ball, 1940 .... 5.50
Label, Holiday Brand, Child With Toys Under Christmas Tree 15.00
Label, K–O, Boxing Glove 7.50
Label, Keeper, 2 Gold Keys, 1940 .... 2.00
Label, Luna, Orange With Moon Face 150.00
Label, Merry–Mount, Indian In Canoe 4.00
Label, Pala Brave, Indian Chief, 1930 .... 4.00
Label, Pocahontas, Bust of Indian Maid, 1930 .... 55.00
Label, Pride of The River, Mississippi River Boat, 1930 .... 6.50
Label, Rosa De Oro, Oranges Orchard Scene, Mission, 1930 .... 12.00
Label, Sawmill Peak, View of Mountain, Dammed River, 1940 .... 1.00
Label, Sea Bound, Clipper Ship At Sea, 1937 .... 12.00
Label, Shipping, United States Express Co., 1890s 1.50
Label, Tie–It–On, Running Dog, Apple Tied To Tail, 1930 .... 5.50
Label, Tit Willow, Family Having Picnic, Birds 5.00
Label, Washington, General On White Horse 8.00
Lamp, Pabst Blue Ribbon Beer, Boxer 75.00
Lamp, Shade, Leaded, John McCormick Cigars, Hanging 3495.00
License Plate Attachment, Squeeze Soda, Tin 65.00
      ADVERTISING, LUNCH BOX, see Lunch Box
Match Holder, Cochran's Ginger Ale, 3 Inch Glass Balls 45.00
Match Holder, Dr. Pepper, Tin, Green, Logo, 1940s 50.00
Match Holder, Kool Cigarettes 25.00
Menu Board, Drink Barq's, It's Good, Chalkboard, Tin, 20 X 28 In 50.00
Milkshake Maker, Hamilton Beach, 3–Station 90.00

     Pocket mirrors range in size from 1 1/2 to 5 inches in diameter.
     Most of these mirrors were given away as advertising promotions.

Mirror, 3–20–8 Cigars, Pocket 50.00
Mirror, 7–Up, Octagonal 85.00
Mirror, Alber's Cereals & Flours, 3 3/8 In. 150.00
Mirror, Anheuser–Busch, Clydesdales, Late 1970s 25.00
Mirror, Beautyskin, Chichester Chemical Co., Lady, Pocket, Oval 75.00
Mirror, Beehive Overalls, Pocket 275.00
Mirror, Big Joe Flour, Pocket 25.00
Mirror, Borden's Evaporated Milk, Oval, Pocket 250.00
Mirror, Bradford Wholesale Furniture Mfg. Co., 2 3/4 In. 8.00
Mirror, Bradley & Vrooman Co., Cottage Colors, 2 In. 16.50
Mirror, Brotherhood American Yeomen, Building, Des Moines, 1912 .... 35.00
Mirror, Brotherhood Overalls, Victorian Nude, Pocket 60.00
Mirror, Buckeye Grain Drills, Pocket 35.00
Mirror, Budweiser Beer, Reverse Glass, Team of Clydesdales 60.00
Mirror, Buy White Cat Union Suits, Cooper Underwear, Pocket 30.00
Mirror, Cabett's System Regulator, Pocket 12.50
Mirror, Caf–Fee–No, Baltimore, 2 3/4 In. 440.00
Mirror, Carmen Complexion Powder, Pretty Woman, Pocket 35.00
Mirror, Carnation Mush, 3 3/8 In. 66.00
Mirror, Cascarets, Cherub On Pot, Pocket .... 30.00 To 65.00
Mirror, Ceresota Flour, Pocket .... 83.00 To 95.00
Mirror, Chew White's Yucatan Gum, Pocket 20.00
Mirror, Chicago Tailoring Co., 2 3/4 In. 11.00
Mirror, Continental Tobacco, Pocket 275.00
Mirror, Cooper Underwear Co., Pocket 75.00
Mirror, Dockash Stoves & Ranges, Black & White, Pocket 35.00
Mirror, Drewers & Flick Shoes Sales, 2 3/4 In. 68.00

Mirror, Duffy's Malt Chemist, Pocket 75.00
Mirror, Duffy's Pure Malt Whiskey, Pocket 40.00
Mirror, Eagle Lye, Picture of Can, Pocket 35.00
Mirror, Elsie The Cow, Borden's Ice Cream Flavors Listed 25.00
Mirror, Emerson–Brantingham, Beveled, Pocket 75.00
Mirror, Ericsson Line, 2 3/4 In. 16.50
Mirror, Gates Hats, Chicago, Pocket 35.00
Mirror, Gavitt's System Regulator, Metal Rim, Pocket 12.00
Mirror, Granite Building, Barber Shop, Pocket 35.00
Mirror, Great Western Separator, Pocket 55.00
Mirror, Gussard Corset, 2 3/4 In. 88.00
Mirror, Haines, Shoe Wizard, Makes Wonderful Prices, Pocket 30.00
Mirror, Henry Whiskey, Richmond, Va., Pocket, Late 19th Century 85.00
Mirror, High Button Shoe, Boot & Shoe Worker's Union, Pocket 35.00
Mirror, Huyler's Candy, 2 3/4 In. 55.00
Mirror, International Tailoring Co., Bead Game, 1 7/8 In. 5.50
Mirror, J.I. Case Threshing Machine Co., 2 3/4 In. 95.00
Mirror, Kleinert's Dress Shields, Pocket 37.50
Mirror, Lee Line Steamers, 2 3/4 In. 16.50
Mirror, Maccabees Insurance Co., Baby Picture, Pocket .... 35.00 To 45.00
Mirror, Majestic Range, 1 3/4 In. 16.50
Mirror, Maryland Casualty Insurance, Pocket 18.00
Mirror, Massachusetts Breweries Co., 2 In. 12.00
Mirror, Mennen's Violet Talcum Powder, Oval, Pocket 45.00
Mirror, Merode Underwear, Celluloid, Pocket 17.00
Mirror, Merrian & Millard Grain Co., Omaha 25.00
Mirror, Morton's Salt, Pocket 20.00
Mirror, Mother Hubbard Flour, Reverse Back Lit 150.00
Mirror, New King Snuff, Pocket, Rectangular 37.50
Mirror, Noxall Clothing, Pocket 20.00
Mirror, Ohio Blue Tip Matches, 3 1/2 In. .... 45.00 To 85.00
Mirror, Old Reliable Coffee, 2 In. 25.00
Mirror, Polar Bear Fur Cleaner, Orange Printing, Pocket 20.00
Mirror, Queen Shoes, Pocket 75.00
Mirror, Reliable Coffee, Pocket, 1 3/4 In. 40.00
Mirror, Royal Blend Coffee, 2 3/4 In. 50.00
Mirror, Sani–Tubes Restroom, Prevent Infection, Pocket 80.00
Mirror, Schell's Beer, Pocket 110.00
Mirror, Shawmut Rubbers, Pocket 58.00
Mirror, Shawmut Rubbers, Rain Wear, Skowhegan, Maine, Pocket 28.00
Mirror, Sherwin Williams, Pocket .... 20.00 To 35.00
Mirror, Shulman's Standard System, Suit & Overcoat, Pocket 24.00
Mirror, Socony Motor Gasoline, Tin Lithograph, Pocket 100.00
Mirror, Stacy's Chocolates, Rochester, N.Y., Seascape, Pocket 20.00
Mirror, Starrett Tools, Gold & Red, Architect's Tools, Pocket 37.50
Mirror, State Life Insurance Co., Baby's Photograph, Pocket 22.00
Mirror, Sterling Range, 2 1/4 In. 110.00
Mirror, Strunk & Moyer Pigeon & Poultry Supply House, 2 In. 33.00
Mirror, Studebaker Vehicle, Wagon Carriage Factory, Pocket 195.00
Mirror, Traymore Tailoring Co., Philadelphia, Pa., Jewel, Pocket 45.00
Mirror, Twin City Barber College, Photograph Prof. Gilsdor 28.00
Mirror, Valley Forge Special, Pictures Beer Bottle, Pocket 45.00
Mirror, Waterloo Street Fair, Souvenir, 1 3/4 In. 50.00
Mirror, Wheeler Publishing Co., Wag & Puff, 2 In. 60.00
Mirror, White Rock Table Water, 1 7/8 In. 16.50
Mirror, Widows & Orphans Home, Ben Avon, Penna., 1915, Pocket 20.00
Mirror, Wilbur's Chocolate, 2 In. 110.00
Mortar & Pestle, KLM Airlines, Brass 25.00
Mug, Baltimore Dairy Lunch, 3 1/4 In. 60.00
Mug, Beer, Winston Cigarettes, Glass, Fluted 20.00
Mug, Bovox Makes Real Strength, 3 5/8 In. 5.50
Mug, Buckeye Root Beer, Stoneware 75.00
Mug, Carter Carburetor, Stoneware 15.00
Mug, Dad's Root Beer, Embossed 5.00

Mug, Doe–Wah–Jack 110.00
Mug, Dr. Swetts Root Beer 195.00
Mug, Goetz Beer, Brick–Type 45.00
Mug, Hires Root Beer, Ceramic 145.00
Mug, Kayo Hot Chcolate, 1950s 30.00
Mug, Kodak, Plastic, 1880–1980 .... 10.00
Mug, Magnus Root Beer 35.00
Mug, Papst Beer, Milwaukee, 4 In. 50.00
Mug, Quaker Oats, Celluloid 18.00
Mug, Rochester Root Beer, Glass 12.50
Mug, Twin Kiss Root Beer 22.00
Mug, Van Houten's Hot Chocolate, 1908 .... 45.00
Mug, White Castle 12.00
Mug, XXX Root Beer, White Porcelain, Barrel Shape, 4 Piece 145.00
Note Pad, Buckingham Bros. Cigars, Celluloid, 1900, 2 X 5 In. 85.00
Note Pad, Rock Crystal Salt, Celluloid 20.00
Pail, Armour Mincemeat, 1 1/2 Lb. 35.00
Pail, Baby Snooks Pops, Fanny Brice, 3 In. 400.00
Pail, Black Hawk Lard, Indian 20.00
Pail, Buffalo Brand Peanut Butter, Tin 175.00
Pail, Dixie Queen, Tin 125.00
Pail, Home Brand Coffee, 5 Lb. 48.00
Pail, Jolly Time Popcorn 160.00
Pail, Liberty Bell Candy 275.00
Pail, Lutters Lard, Tin, Mammy With Spatula 45.00
Pail, May's Creamer, Paper Label, 10 In. 137.00
Pail, Morris Supreme Peanut Butter 250.00
Pail, Nigger Hair Tobacco 195.00
Pail, Ojibwa Tobacco 185.00
Pail, Pickaninny Brand Salted Peanuts, Tin, 1 Lb. 225.00
Pail, Pickwick Peanut Butter, Tin, 1 Lb. 60.00
Pail, School Boy, Peanut Butter, Tin, 2 Lb. 340.00
Pail, Squirrel Peanut Butter, 2 Lb. 100.00
Pail, Sultana Peanut Butter 50.00
Pail, Swift & Company, Leaf Lard, Tin, 5 1/2 In. 16.00
Pail, Triangle Club Peanut Butter 145.00
Pail, Veribest Mincemeat, Tin 67.50
Pail, Yum–Yum Tobacco, Black Boy, 8 In. 310.00
Paperweight, Chicago, Milwaukee & St. Paul R.R. Bear 65.00
Paperweight, Hagerstown Brewing Co., C.1900, 3 1/2 In. 125.00
Paperweight, Hartford Fire Insurance, Bronze, 1921 .... 45.00
Paperweight, Holt Motors, Figural, Iron 25.00
Paperweight, Kellogg's, Vitrolite, Girl Holding Box, C.1905 .... 450.00
Paperweight, Macbeth Evans Glass Co., Glass Blower 17.50
Paperweight, Maytag, Cast Iron 30.00
Paperweight, Pig, Best Pig Forceps, 6 In. 95.00
Paperweight, Read Radio News, Shape of Radio, Cast Iron 80.00
Paperweight, Wolff American Cycles, Scenic 40.00
Pencil Clip, Bakers Chocolate 13.00
Pennant, Telling's Ice Cream, Kids Making Ice Cream 85.00
Pez, Dispenser, Angel 15.00
Pez, Dispenser, Betsy Ross 22.00
Pez, Dispenser, Casper 70.00
Pez, Dispenser, Cockatoo, Blue Face, Red Beak 35.00
Pez, Dispenser, Creature From Black Lagoon 155.00
Pez, Dispenser, Indian Squaw 30.00
Pez, Dispenser, Ringmaster, Gray Hat 30.00
Pez, Dispenser, Roar The Lion 13.00
Pez, Dispenser, Snowman 20.00
Pez, Dispenser, Uncle Sam 13.00
Pez, Dispenser, Whistle, Purple & Orange 2.00
Pin Tray, Prudential Insurance 15.00
Pin, Columbia Broadcasting, Kitty Kelly 7.50
Pin, Hohner Harmonica, Enameled Brass 10.00

Pin, Sharples Separator, Mother & Child	22.50
Pitcher, Crawford Cooking Ranges, Flow Blue, 5 In.	175.00
Pitcher, Cross Country Motor Oil	145.00
Pitcher, Dr. Harter's Wild Cherry Bitters, 13 In.	325.00
Pitcher, Fish, Figural, Plymouth Gin, England, 10 In.	55.00
Plaque, Man In The Moon, Climax Cigars, Chalkware, 11 X 19 In.	200.00
Plaque, Mutual Ins., Washington's Birthday, 1732–1932, 8 In.	10.00
Plate, Anger Baking Co., Portrait, Child's Head, 10 In.	50.00
Plate, Anheuser–Busch, Tin Lithograph, 1905, 10 In.	95.00
Plate, Fanny Farmer, 1944	45.00
Plate, Holiday Inn, Woman At Typewriter	15.00
Plate, Krug Brewery, Brewery & Owner	95.00
Plate, Moxie Girl, Flowered Border	45.00
Plate, Woman, Anheuser–Busch's Malt Nutrine, Tin, Wagner, 1905	135.00
Platter, Michigan Condensed Milk Co., White, 12 X 17 In.	50.00
Postcard, Anheuser–Busch Brewery, Power Plant, Brew House, 1904	12.00
Postcard, Kinsey Pure Rye Whiskey, Hunting Scene, 1906	15.00
Postcard, Millstadt Brewery Co., Millstadt, Ill.	12.00
Postcard, Rockford Watches, 1910	12.50
Potholder, Hotpoint Stoves	10.00
Pouch, Marilyn Club Tobacco, Silk	20.00
Powder Puff, Betty Lou, Package, 3 Piece	3.00
Puzzle, Baby Ruth, Jigsaw	25.00
Puzzle, Box, Baser's Root Beer, Reading, Pa., 2 1/2 In.	60.00
Puzzle, Kellogg's For Crispness, Cardboard, Girl, 1933, 6 X 8 In.	38.00
Puzzle, McDonald's, 1973	3.50
Rack, Beechnut Chewing Gum, 4 Tier, Picture On Top	145.00
Rack, Carters Ink, Oak, 46 In.	450.00
Rack, Keen Kutter Knife Display	95.00
Rack, National Biscuit, Oak, 4 Shelves, Logo, 47 X 56 X 15 In.	495.00
Rack, Wrigley Gum, Elf–Like Figure, Celluloid Face	295.00
Ring, Andy Pafco, Ball & Strike Baseball, Premium, 1949	45.00
Ring, Post Toasties, Felix The Cat, Tin Lithograph,, 1949	40.00
Ruler, Townsend Grace Co., Straw Hat, Size Chart, Celluloid	10.00
ADVERTISING, SALT & PEPPER, see Salt & Pepper	
ADVERTISING, SCALE, see Scale	
School Multiplier, Rex Bitters, Chicago, 4 3/4 In.	90.00
Scissors, Star Brand Shoes Are Better	19.50
Scoop, Icypi Ice Cream, Sandwich	145.00
Sewing Kit, Lydia Pinkham, Metal Tube	10.00
Shade, Pull, Aunt Jemima	35.00
Shoe Brush, Port Washington Brewery	45.00
Shot Glass, Cabin Still, Gold Painted	6.00
Shot Glass, Jack Daniel's No.7, Gold Painted	6.00
Shot Glass, Sunny Brook Pure Food Whiskey, Etched, Inspector	17.00
Shot Glass, Teapot Whiskey, Charleston, Etched, Teapot	17.00
Sign, 7–Up, Porcelain, White, Green & Red, 17 X 19 In.	36.00
Sign, A.W. Faber Pencils, Tin Lithograph, 1920's, 2 X 7 In.	65.00
Sign, Admiration Cigars, Pottery, 12 X 16 In.	175.00
Sign, Admiration Cigars, Tin Lithograph, 5 1/2 X 7 1/2 In.	90.00
Sign, All Jacks Hard To Beat, 4 Jacks, Tin, 10 X 14 In.	60.00
Sign, Anheuser–Busch, Custer's Last Fight, 1958, 21 X 29 In.	25.00
Sign, Anheuser–Busch, Custer's Last Stand, Cardboard, 46 In.	215.00
Sign, Barber's, Straight Edge Razor, Tin Blade, Wood, 17 In.	305.00
Sign, Bavis & Son Grocers, West India Goods, 71 X 31 In.	9900.00
Sign, Beacon Farms Eggs, Tin, Lighthouse, Blue, 14 X 19 In.	75.00
Sign, Beechnut Chewing Tobacco, Factory, Employees, 26 X 36 In.	225.00
Sign, Berghoff Beer, Tin Lithograph, Bird, Dogs, 21 X 13 In.	125.00
Sign, Berina Malted Milk, Porcelain, 24 X 60 In.	450.00
Sign, Blackhawk Brewing, Print, Chief, Framed, 22 X 24 In.	75.00
Sign, Bludwine, Metal, Flange, 5 Cent, 12 1/2 X 9 1/2 In.	275.00
Sign, Borden's Ice Cream, Open Or Closed, Clocks, 9 X 14 In.	65.00
Sign, Borden's, With Elsie, Metal, 36 In. Diam.	275.00
Sign, Boshee's German Syrup, August Flower, Tin, 20 X 14 In.	2000.00

Sign, Braem's Bitters, Bottle Picture, Tin, 13 X 7 In. 45.00
Sign, British Navy Chewing Tobacco, Sailor, 1900s, 9 X 16 In. 90.00
Sign, Bromo Seltzer Bottle, Glass, Dispenser, Metal, 9 X 20 In. 200.00
Sign, Brown's Iron Bitters, Girl, Paper, 14 7/8 In. ....:...................... 400.00
Sign, Buffalo Brewing, Tin, Self-Framed, 29 X 22 In. 850.00
Sign, Buick, Porcelain, Round, 42 In. 345.00
Sign, C.F. Porter Co., B. 42nd, Ohio, Wooden, 9 3/4 X 13 3/4 In. 65.00
Sign, Caille, W.L. Masters & Co., Embossed Tin, 23 X 11 In. 650.00
Sign, California Sunkist Oranges, Tin, 38 X 15 In. 155.00
Sign, Carey Board, For Better Building, Porcelain, 28 X 12 In. 60.00
Sign, Chesterfield Cigarettes, Stand–Up, Crosby & Como 165.00
Sign, Chesterfield Cigarettes, Tin Lithograph, 24 X 30 In. 85.00
Sign, Clarke's Rye, Man & Bottles, Wooden, 10 X 14 In. 55.00
Sign, Coles Peruvian, Enamel On Metal, 6 X 16 In. 350.00
Sign, Columbia Healing Powders 1 Side, Gall Salve Other, 14 In. 445.00
Sign, Common Sense Exterminator Kills Rats, 7 X 8 In. 165.00
Sign, Concordia Fire Insurance Co., Porcelain, 20 X 14 In. 85.00
Sign, Cook's Beer, 2 Sides, Tin, 1940s, 14 X 28 In. 35.00
Sign, Crescent Beverages, Embossed Tin, 1940s, 14 X 20 In. 30.00
Sign, Crown Cola, Santa Claus, Cardboard, 1950s, 30 X 10 In. 35.00
Sign, Davis Carriage, Everything To Ride In, 1906, 7 X 20 In. 155.00
Sign, Dealer, Gorham, Town & Country, 3 X 3 In. 25.00
Sign, DeLaval Cream Separator, Girl, Cow, 40 1/2 X 28 1/2 In. 750.00
Sign, DeLaval Separator, Yellow Letters On Blue, 12 X 16 In. 60.00
Sign, DeLaval, Girl, Cow, Green, Tin, 41 X 30 In. 3000.00
Sign, Dr Pepper, Bottle & Clock, 18 X 54 In. 125.00
Sign, Dr. Jayne's, Reverse On Glass, 12 1/2 In. 850.00
Sign, Drink Grain Belt Beer, Friendly, Porcelain, 4 X 3 In. 475.00
Sign, Dub–L–Value Root Beer, Embossed Tin, 1930s, 11 X 18 In. 30.00
Sign, Ferris Maternity Corsets, Tin, 1920s, 15 1/2 X 19 In. 300.00
Sign, Fish Shape, Says Lures, Wooden, Old Paint, 35 In. 350.00
Sign, Fish Shape, Shiners 1 Side, Minnows Other, Wooden, 20 In. 150.00
Sign, Foster Hose Supporters, Celluloid, Cardboard, 9 X 17 In. 198.00
Sign, Gem Razors, Paperboard, Framed, 15 X 22 In. 85.00
Sign, General Motors, Vertical Letters, Metal, 29 X 3 In. 75.00
Sign, Gilbey's Wines, Enameled, 2 Sides, 16 X 21 In. 66.00
Sign, Girard Fire & Marine Ins., Reverse Glass, 32 X 22 In. 650.00
Sign, Glendora Coffee, 1 Lb. Tin Shape, 14 X 9 In. 88.00
Sign, Goodyear Service Station, Tire, Earth, Porcelain, 6 X 2 Ft 575.00
Sign, Grape–Nuts, Tin, Self–Framed, 31 X 20 In. 2200.00
Sign, Grapette Soda, Neon, 12 X 22 In. 1400.00
Sign, Green River Whiskey, Self–Framed, 22 X 28 1/2 In. 795.00
Sign, Gulfpride, Metal, 24 X 48 In. 165.00
Sign, Ham Bone Cigar, Black Man In Airplane, Round, 7 In. 45.00
Sign, Harp Shape, Wooden, Gold On Brown, 55 In. 3500.00
Sign, Havana Ribbon Cigars, Store Indian, Cardboard, 18 In. 275.00
Sign, Hires To Your Health, Tin, 19 1/2 X 27 1/2 In. 8250.00
Sign, Hires, 2 1/2 Ft. Circle 65.00
Sign, Hoehner's Harmonicas, 3–Dimensional, 24 X 6 1/2 In. 195.00
Sign, Hoof, Johnson's Patent Pad, Horseshoe, Embossed, 9 1/2 In. 345.00
Sign, Horseshoes, Blacksmith, Silver & Black, Iron, 20 1/4 In. 150.00
Sign, Hot Barbecue, Blue & Yellow Letters, Wooden, 60 1/2 In. 125.00
Sign, Howe Scales, Porcelain, Yellow, Gray & Black, 9 X 40 In. 70.00
Sign, Hudson Insurance Co., Early Ship, Metal, 20 X 14 In. 50.00
Sign, Hudson River Dayline, Gateway To Happiness, 8 1/2 In. 55.00
Sign, Jewelry Store, Figural Pocket Watch, Iron, 26 X 18 In. 700.00
Sign, John Deere, Buck Running, 2 Sides, 2 /2 X 5 Ft. 785.00
Sign, Jos. A. Enzler, Trunk, Factory, Leather Goods, 61 X 42 In. 1925.00
Sign, Just Suits Tobacco, Porcelain, 8 X 12 In. 125.00
Sign, K.C. Baking Powder, 2 Sides, Tin, 1930's, 12 X 28 In. 45.00
Sign, Kodak Film, Checkerboad Design, Box of Film, 28 In. 375.00
Sign, Komo Metal Paste, Porcelain, England, 1920s, 30 X 24 In. 300.00
Sign, La Deva, Havana Cigar, Woman, Tin, Framed, 11 X 17 In. 1200.00
Sign, LaReine, Rex Shoes, Metal, Crimped, C.1910, 13 X 20 In. 165.00

Sign, Lincoln Seed Dealer, Lincoln's Picture, 24 X 36 In.	75.00
Sign, Lord Calvert Whiskey, Ruffled Collar, Tin, 10 X 13 In.	35.00
Sign, Loutz Naphtha Soap, Tin Litho, Black, Yellow, 18 X 12 In.	45.00
Sign, M.Wings Inn, Wingsdale, N.Y., 65 1/2 X 50 1/2 In.	3500.00
Sign, Manitou Table Water, Indian, Scenes, Framed, 35 X 27 In.	450.00
Sign, Mayo's Cock O'The Walk, Rooster, Porcelain, 13 X 6 In.	90.00
Sign, Miller High Life, Electric, Red & White, 6 X 22 In.	10.00
Sign, Millinery, Yellow & White Letters, Black, 8 X 36 In.	175.00
Sign, Mobil Gas Flying Horse, Porcelain Over Metal, 7 X 6 Ft.	500.00
Sign, Monarch Bicycles, Wooden, Black, Gold Letters, 42 X 5 In.	385.00
Sign, Monito Silk Hosiery, Brass, 6 In.	25.00
Sign, Moxie, Oval, Tin, 1905, 41 1/2 In.	195.00
Sign, Moxieland, Cardboard, 28 1/2 X 39 In.	137.50
Sign, Mt. Kinco Ginger Ale, Embossed, 1940s, 12 X 24 In.	30.00
Sign, Mule–Hide Roofs, Flange, 4–Color Enamel, Mule, 21 In.	435.00
Sign, Munsing Twins, Tin, Self–Framed, 38 X 26 In.	3500.00
Sign, Munsing Union Suits, Kids In Car, 16 1/4 X 12 In.	1250.00
Sign, Murad The Turkish Cigarette, Tin, Early 1900s, 2 X 6 In.	95.00
Sign, Muriel Cigars, Edie Adams, Figural	35.00
Sign, Natural Chilean Soda, Uncle Natchel, Tin, 22 X 15 In.	275.00
Sign, Nichol 5 Cent Kola, Multicolor, Tin, 1930s, 12 X 36 In.	100.00
Sign, Nichol Cola, Pictures Bottle & Soldier, Tin, 1930s, 30 In.	36.00
Sign, Nu–Grape, Tin, Yellow, Red & Black, 19 X 27 In.	42.00
Sign, Old Gold Cigarettes, Football Player, Standup, Cardboard	325.00
Sign, Old Virginia Cheroots, Framed, 20 X 20 In.	55.00
Sign, Oliver Plow, Wooden, 14 X 15 In.	475.00
Sign, Orange Crush, Metal, Flange, 14 X 22 In.	150.00
Sign, Orange Crush, Natural Flavor, Tin, 3 1/4 X 26 1/2 In.	30.00
Sign, Pabst Beer, 2 Bottles & Schooner, Framed, 21 X 24 In.	350.00
Sign, Pacific Liver Pills, Gold Leaf Type Frame, 2 1/2 X 5 Ft.	395.00
Sign, Packers Tar Soap, With Soap, Tin, 2 1/2 X 3 1/2 In.	75.00
Sign, Padlock, Souvenir Marquette Prison, 12 X 7 3/4 In.	250.00
Sign, Paine's Celery Compound, Tin, 14 X 10 In.	325.00
Sign, Perry's Beverages, Embossed Tin, 1940s, 14 X 20 In.	35.00
Sign, Pittsburgh Paints, Standup, Girl Waxing Floor, 4 Ft.	45.00
Sign, Polar Bear Flour, Rainbow Colors, Tin, 13 X 35 In.	125.00
Sign, Powerine, Porcelain, 20 X 28 In.	150.00
Sign, Red Goose Shoes, Light–Up, Wood & Celluloid	465.00
Sign, Red Goose Shoes, Porcelain & Neon, 3 Ft.	750.00
Sign, Red Goose Shoes, Sulphur Lick, Ky., Tin, 13 X 18 In.	130.00
Sign, Red Jacket Tobacco, Baseball, Cardboard, 22 X 28 In.	130.00
Sign, Red Man, Package, Tin, 1950s, 14 X 4 1/2 In.	28.00
Sign, Red Raven, Girl Hugging Giant Bird, Metal, 1900	1500.00
Sign, Red Seal Battery, Porcelain, Battery Shape	95.00
Sign, Red Wing Shoes, Embossed Metal, 23 X 18 In.	100.00
Sign, Rich Valley Ice Cream, Yellow, Red, 1940s, 9 In. Diam.	40.00
Sign, Round Oak Stoves, Indian, 33 X 21 In.	350.00
Sign, Salada Tea, Porcelain, Purple, Yellow & Black, 3 X 15 In.	100.00
Sign, Schlitz Beer, Winged Nymph, Paper Lithograph, 18 X 26 In.	825.00
Sign, Schlitz Foam Scraper With 4 Tumblers, 27 X 18 In.	145.00
Sign, Schlitz, Diecut Cardboard, 36 In. Bottle, Glass	145.00
Sign, Seagrams, Store Hours, Chain, Leather	22.50
Sign, Sealy Mattress, Die Cut, Black In Cotton Field, 72 In.	3500.00
Sign, Seneca Cameras, Grand Ledge, Mich., Indian, 11 X 35 In.	150.00
Sign, Sharples Separator, 12 X 18 In.	125.00
Sign, Silver Gem Chewing Gum, Tin Lithograph, 5 X 7 In.	85.00
Sign, Sinclair Opaline, Porcelain, 15 X 60 In.	120.00
Sign, Sinclair Opaline, Porcelain, 2 Sides, Round, 24 In.	185.00
Sign, Snap–On–Tools, Reverse On Glass, Framed, 1920 Auto, 19 In.	27.50
Sign, Sparrow's Chocolates, Tin, Self Frame, 15 X 22 In.	550.00
Sign, Sterling Super–Bru Beer, Circus, 1938, 20 3/4 X 27 In.	400.00
Sign, Sterling, Linen Collars, Reverse On Glass, 22 X 12 In.	225.00
Sign, Strohs Beer, Cherubic Man In Hat, Tin, 14 X 20 In.	250.00
Sign, Sun Crest, Bottle, Tin, 7 X 20 In.	65.00

Sign, Sunshine Soda Cracker, Tin, Embossed, 28 X 10 In. 413.00
Sign, Texaco Fire Chief, Porcelain .... 30.00 To 65.00
Sign, Texaco Motor Oil Insulated, Tin, 22 X 11 In. 45.00
Sign, Tin Horse & Typewriter, Embossed, Smith Bros., 12 In. 750.00
Sign, Toledo Scales, No Springs, Honest Weight, Tin, 11 X 16 In. 125.00
Sign, Tom Sawyer Apparel For Real Boys, Graphics, 7 X 21 In. 150.00
Sign, Top Hat, Iron Glove Hangs Below, Sheet Metal, Black 2310.00
Sign, Trade, Ingersoll Dollar Watch, Pocket Watch Shape 470.00
Sign, Trade, Tobacconist, Pipe, Iron Frame, Large 1500.00
Sign, True Fruit, Self-Framed, Tin, 24 X 36 In. 300.00
Sign, Trunk Factory, 3 Sided Trunk 1925.00
Sign, Tuttle's Elixir, Tin, 4 1/4 X 19 3/4 In. 210.00
Sign, Tweddle's Chickens, Order Here, Tin, 1940s, 19 X 27 In. 48.00
Sign, U.S. Cartridge Co., Climax Smokeless Powder, 46 In. 450.00
Sign, Utica Fishing Tackle, Tin, Trout In Basket, 8 In. 75.00
Sign, Velvet Tobacco, Porcelain, C.1915, 12 X 39 In. 200.00
Sign, Vermo Stomach Bitters, Tin, 6 1/2 X 9 1/4 In. 160.00
Sign, Victor Beer, Jeannette, Penna., Wood Frame, 5 X 10 Ft. 350.00
Sign, Vitalis Aftershave, Cardboard, 26 X 18 In. 40.00
Sign, We Sell & Repair, Shoe Shape, Wooden, 2 Sides, 31 X 16 In. 468.00
Sign, We Serve Ives Delicious Ice Cream, 2-Sided, 20 X 28 In. 90.00
Sign, White Label Cigars, Embossed Tin, 14 X 10 In. 49.00
Sign, Willard Battery Cable, Pictures Battery, 12 X 17 In. 45.00
Sign, Winchester Rifle, Repairs & Sales, C.1898, 11 Ft. 1500.00
Sign, Winchester Western, Classic Horse, Rider, Round, 30 In. 325.00
Sign, Yankee Girl, Standup, Cardboard, 1930s, 7 X 10 In. 20.00
Spittoon, Redskin Brand Chewing Tobacco & Cut Plug, Brass 35.00
Spoon, Baby's, Gerber, Original Envelope, Dated 1949 .... 55.00
Spoon, Calumet, Silver, Indian On Handle 28.00
Spoon, Decker's Ice Cream, Soda 12.00
Spoon, Golden Sun Coffee, Navarre Steel Cut, Tin Litho 65.00
Spoon, Log Cabin Syrup, Towle 32.00
Spoon, Round Oak Stoves, Full Indian Handle, Silver Plate 25.00
Spoon, Tony The Tiger, 1965, 6 In. 10.00
Stickpin, Indian, Round Oak Range, Gilt 15.00
Stickpin, Leica In Script, Red Enameled Ground 25.00
Stickpin, Oak Stove, Round 25.00
Stickpin, P & O Plows 30.00
Sugar & Creamer, Lipton Tea, Yellow 12.50
Sugar & Creamer, Purinton, Apple 15.00
Syrup, S & H Rootbeer, Stoneware, Blue Printing, 12 In. 77.00
Tank Head, Helium, Ronald McDonald 215.00
Tap Knob, Dubois Beer, Black Hard Rubber, Yellow & Gold Face 27.50
Teapot, Sanka, Restaurant 12.00

ADVERTISING, THERMOMETER, see Thermometer

The English language is sometimes confusing. Tin cans or canisters were first used commercially in the United States in 1819 and were called "tins." Today the word "tin" is used by most collectors to describe many types of containers, including food tins, biscuit boxes, roly poly tobacco containers, gunpowder cans, talcum powder sprinkle-top cans, cigarette flat-fifty tins, and more. Beer cans are listed in their own section. Things made of undecorated tin are listed under Tinware.

Tin, Abbey Tobacco, Blue, 8 In. 110.00
Tin, Alex Parsons Carbolic Tooth Powder 400.00
Tin, American Ideal Talcum, California Perfume 135.00
Tin, Ansonia, Pocket Watch, Factory, Pat. April 23, 1878, 2 In. 285.00
Tin, Army & Navy Coffee, N. Martin & Co., Chicago, 5 X 3 In. 275.00
Tin, Artex Oil, 2 Gal. 25.00
Tin, Avon Perfection Mothocide 30.00
Tin, B.F. Graveley's Cut Plug, Hinged Lid, 4 1/2 X 3 1/2 In. 33.00
Tin, B.F. Gravely & Sons Special Pipe Tobacco, Pocket, 4 In. 715.00
Tin, Baking Powder, Alspice, Revolves, Base Opening, 12 X 9 In. 295.00

Tin, Berma Coffee, Screw Top, 1 Lb. 35.00
Tin, Bickmore Gall Salve, Sample 10.00
Tin, Blue Boar Tobacco, Cylindrical, 5 X 3 In. 25.00
Tin, Bob White Tobacco, 7 1/2 X 8 In. 275.00
Tin, Bokar Coffee Supreme, A & P, 1 Lb. 25.00
Tin, Brotherhood Tobacco, 6 X 5 X 4 In. 125.00
Tin, Browne's Pedigreed Salted Peanuts, , 10 Lb. 175.00
Tin, Buckingham Tobacco, Pocket ....40.00 To 100.00
Tin, Buckingham Tobacco, Sample 85.00
Tin, Bulldog, Upright, Pocket 200.00
Tin, Bunnies Salted Peanuts, Uncle Wiggley Type Rabbit, 10 Lb. 325.00
Tin, Burley Boy Tobacco, Rolltop 1400.00
Tin, Burley Boy, Pocket 850.00
Tin, Cadette Baby Talc, Soldier Shape 110.00
Tin, California Perfume Co., Vernaflear Powder 30.00
Tin, Calirox Cookies, Capistrano Scenes, 1930s, 2 1/2 Lb. 45.00
Tin, Calumet, Red, Indian 13.00
Tin, Capitol Square Oil, 2 Gal. 35.00
Tin, Central Union Tobacco, Pocket 120.00
Tin, Century Tobacco, Flat Pocket 850.00
Tin, Chariots Prophylactics 125.00
Tin, Charm of The West Tobacco, Pocket, 7 In. 150.00
Tin, Checkers Tobacco, Upright, Pocket 225.00
Tin, Clark's Peanut Butter, 1 Lb. 300.00
Tin, Clark's Peanut Butter, Pictures Indian, Little Boy 375.00
Tin, Coach & Four Tobacco, Pocket 93.00
Tin, Coffee, Ivanhoe, Castle, 1 Lb. 55.00
Tin, Coffee, Luzianne Mammy, Sample 125.00
Tin, Colgate Talcum Powder, Baby 125.00
Tin, Continental Cubes Tobacco, Upright, 8 1/2 In. .... 250.00 To 350.00
Tin, Credo Peanut Butter 45.00
Tin, Crescent Peanuts, 10 Lb. 450.00
Tin, Dad's Root Beer Syrup, 5 Gal. 42.00
Tin, Daddy's Choice Coffee 450.00
Tin, Delco Shock Fluid, 1 Gal. 25.00
Tin, Detroit Club Tobacco, Rolltop 550.00
Tin, DeVoe's Sweet Smoke, Pocket, 7 1/2 In. .... 250.00 To 325.00
Tin, Dixie Queen Plug Cut, Portrait of Woman, 6 X 4 X 3 In. 225.00
Tin, Doughboy Prophylactic Kit 5.00
Tin, Dr. Hand's Chafing Powder 275.00
Tin, Dunhill's Pipe Bowl Preservative, Sample 10.00
Tin, Dunnsboro Tobacco, Pocket 795.00
Tin, Eden Tobacco, Hinged Lid, Pocket, 3 3/4 In. 293.00
Tin, Edgeworth Tobacco, 3 1/4 X 4 1/2 In. 12.00
Tin, Ensign Tobacco, Indian, Pocket 90.00
Tin, Epicure Tobacco, Pocket 115.00
Tin, Euclid Tobacco, Upright, Pocket 195.00
Tin, Eve Tobacco, Nude Eve, With Leaf, Pocket, 3 1/4 In. 83.00
Tin, Everyday Tobacco, Pocket, 9 In. 650.00
Tin, Express Tobacco, Pie Shape, 2 X 8 In. 750.00
Tin, Fehr's Talcum 375.00
Tin, Forest & Stream Tobacco, Double Fisherman .... 175.00 To 225.00
Tin, Forest & Stream, With Duck, Pocket 80.00
Tin, Forsters Peanut Butter, Kid, Dog 30.00
Tin, Four Roses Tobacco, Pocket 65.00
Tin, Franklin Coffee, 3 Lb. 1200.00
Tin, Full Dress Tobacco, Canister 210.00
Tin, Gardenia Talcum, 4 Oz. 5.00
Tin, Gems Prophylactics 50.00
Tin, Genesco Prophylactics 100.00
Tin, Giant Salted Peanuts, Tin, 10 Lb. 350.00
Tin, Globe Soap, Blue, Dancing Figures 22.50
Tin, Gold Medal Coffee, 3 Lb. 70.00
Tin, Gold Shore Tobacco, Pocket, 7 1/2 In. 310.00

Tin, Gold Trojan Prophylactics 90.00
Tin, Good Luck Baking Powder, Horseshoe, Clover, Red, 1901 .... 25.00
Tin, Goodyear French Talc 32.50
Tin, Granulated 54 Tobacco, Pocket 75.00
Tin, Greyhound Typewriter, Dog Bus Logo Look–A–Like 15.00
Tin, Guide Tobacco, Pocket .... 165.00 To 195.00
Tin, Half & Half Tobacco, Sample 65.00
Tin, Hi–Grade Tobacco, Green, Pocket, 8 1/2 In. 750.00
Tin, Hi–Plane Tobacco, 2 Engines, Pocket 60.00
Tin, Hi–Plane Tobacco, 4 Engines, Pocket .... 265.00 To 495.00
Tin, Hiawatha Tobacco, Pocket 85.00
Tin, High Grade Tobacco, Green, Pocket ....795.00 To 1000.00
Tin, High Hat Face Powder, Contents 5.00
Tin, Honest Labor Tobacco, Pictures Arm & Hammer 35.00
Tin, Honeymoon Rum Flavored Tobacco, Pocket 100.00
Tin, Huberd's Show Oil, Man's Face On Boot 25.00
Tin, Hudson Bay Tea, 6 X 6 X 8 1/2 In. 70.00
Tin, Huntley & Palmers, Bell, When You Ring, I Sing 90.00
Tin, Huntley & Palmers, Lantern Lighthouse Shape 125.00
Tin, Huntley & Palmers, Oriental Vase 85.00
Tin, Indian Head Brake Fluid, Chief, 5 Gal. 65.00
Tin, Instant Postum 19.00
Tin, Ivin's Cookies, Cracker, Child's Drum Form 33.00
Tin, Jada Talc 150.00
Tin, Jam Boy Coffee 350.00
Tin, Jayne's Nervo Pills 200.00
Tin, Jim Dandie Peanuts 150.00
Tin, Johnson & Johnson Perfect Mustard Plasters 40.00
Tin, Johnson's Wax, Woman Vacuuming, 1932, 1 Lb. 13.00
Tin, Jolly Time Popcorn ....35.00 To 160.00
Tin, Kaffee Hag Coffee, Pry Lid, 1927, 1 Lb. 75.00
Tin, Kamel's Prophylactics 70.00
Tin, Kig's Gunpowder, Sample 350.00
Tin, King Edward Tobacco, Rolltop 400.00
Tin, King Parcot Peanut Butter, 3 Gal. 20.00
Tin, Knighthood Coffee, Key Lid, 1 Lb. 28.00
Tin, Kohr's Crown Lard, Red, 6 1/2 X 12 In. 15.00
Tin, Koin Pack Prophylactics 40.00
Tin, Kools, Flat, 50's 69.00
Tin, La Parot Hi Life Hair Dressing 13.00
Tin, La Parot Talc 17.50
Tin, Laymon's Aspirin Tablets, Blue, Small, 6 .... 5.00
Tin, Lipton Tea, East Indian Women Tea Pickers, 9 X 6 X 6 In. 130.00
Tin, Log Cabin Syrup, 12 Oz. 50.00
Tin, Log Cabin Syrup, Free Sample, Lable, C.1914 .... 255.00
Tin, Log Cabin Syrup, Frontier Jail, 4 In. 150.00
Tin, Log Cabin Syrup, Towle's, 5 Lb. 125.00
Tin, Log Cabin, Syrup, Red, 5 Lbs. 65.00
Tin, Lotus Peanuts, 10 Lbs. 115.00
Tin, Lucky Strike, Pocket, Sample ....59.00 To 70.00
Tin, Luzianne Coffee, Red, Contents, 1 Lb. 45.00
Tin, Madame Butterfly Cigar 75.00
Tin, Mammoth Brand Peanuts, Elephant, Gigantic Tusks, 10 Lb. 145.00
Tin, Maryland Club Tobacco, Flat Top, Pocket 350.00
Tin, Maryland Club Tobacco, Rolltop 450.00
Tin, Maryland Club Tobacco, Slip Lid 225.00
Tin, Master Mason Tobacco, Pocket 1200.00
Tin, May Queen Tobacco, Flat, Pocket 1000.00
Tin, Merry Widows Condoms 20.00
Tin, Mohawk Chief Cigars, Oval 550.00
Tin, Monarch Teenie Weenie Peanut Butter, 1 Lb. 150.00
Tin, Monopol London Club Tobacco, 6 X 4 X 1 In. 15.00
Tin, Morris Supreme Peanut Butter, Child At Beach, 1 Lb. 250.00
Tin, Mother's Joy Coffee, Screw Lid, 1 Lb. 35.00

Tin, Natoma Rose Talc, Indian Maiden	750.00
Tin, Navy Tobacco, Pocket, 3 X 5 In.	80.00
Tin, Neubert Oyster, Mermaid	50.00
Tin, New Bachelor Cigar	150.00
Tin, Nigger Hair Tobacco, Brown	150.00
Tin, North Pole Tobacco, Oval Top, Bears, 4 X 6 X 5 1/2 In.	137.00
Tin, O–Cedar Polish, Art Deco, 1920s	30.00
Tin, Oakhill Coffee, Farm Scene, 1 Lb.	50.00
Tin, Ocean Queen Coffee, Ship Graphics	65.00
Tin, Octagon Cleanser	12.00
Tin, Old Dutch Cleanser, Sample, Unopened	35.00
Tin, Old Reliable Peanuts, 10 Lb.	200.00
Tin, Ontario Peanut Butter, L Lb.	125.00
Tin, Orion Talcum	40.00
Tin, Paul Jones Tobacco, Blue, Pocket	250.00
Tin, Paul Jones Tobacco, Rolltop, Blue	1400.00
Tin, Peacock Condoms	32.00 To 40.00
Tin, Pencil Case, A.W. Faber, Tin, Graphics, 1911	45.00
Tin, Pete Rose Chocolate Soda, Contents	28.00
Tin, Peter Pan Peanut Butter	24.00
Tin, Pic–O–Bac Tobacco, 2 X 3 In.	14.00
Tin, Pioneer Coffee, 1 Lb,	175.00
Tin, Pipe Major Tobacco, Pocket, 4 1/4 In.	275.00
Tin, Piper Heidsieck Chewing Tobacco, Pocket	6.00
Tin, Player's Gold Leaf Navy Cigarettes, 4 X 3 1/2 In.	30.00
Tin, Powow Brand Salted Peanuts, Indian, Green, 10 Lb.	715.00
Tin, Prairie Flower Tobacco, Flat, Pocket	1500.00
Tin, Prince Albert Tobacco, July 30, 1907	6.00
Tin, Prince Albert, Cut–Off, Sample	20.00
Tin, R.A. Patterson Tobacco Co., Lucky Strike, Pocket	45.00
Tin, Raco Lard, 1 Lb.	35.00
Tin, Realeaf Aspirin Tablets, Red, Brown, Small	6.00
Tin, Red Indian, Tin, Blue, Gold, Canister, 7 In.	247.00
Tin, Red Jacket Tobacco, Pocket, 4 1/2 In.	28.00
Tin, Repeater Tobacco, Pocket	85.00
Tin, Revelation Tobacco, Sample	70.00
Tin, Rock City Chewing Tobacco, Chicago Cubs, Pocket	295.00
Tin, Roly Poly, Barnett's Man From Scotland Yard	1100.00
Tin, Roly Poly, Bartender, Mayo	375.00
Tin, Roly Poly, Dutchman	175.00
Tin, Roly Poly, Keystone Cop, Blue Suit & Hat, Germany	395.00
Tin, Roly Poly, Mayos Tobacco, Dutchman, With Pipe	605.00
Tin, Roly Poly, Mayos Tobacco, Mammy, Smoking Pipe	495.00
Tin, Roly Poly, Satisfied Customer	225.00
Tin, Roly Poly, Singing Waiter, Mayo	585.00
Tin, Roly Poly, Storekeeper, Mayo	225.00 To 660.00
Tin, Saf–T–Way Prophylactics	75.00
Tin, Safe Owl Paprika, Picture of Owl	20.00
Tin, Sambo Axle Grease, Boy In Overalls, 1 Lb.	85.00
Tin, Satyr Maid Salted Peantus, 10 Lb.	65.00
Tin, Savage Gunpowder, Pictures Rifles	575.00
Tin, Scissors Tobacco, Rolltop	575.00
Tin, Seidlity Powders, Owl Drug	110.00
Tin, Sheik Condoms, Dated 1931	25.00 To 50.00
Tin, Shot Plug Cut, Green, Square, Pocket	90.00
Tin, Silk Skin Prophylactics	100.00
Tin, Smith Brothers Cough Drops	125.00
Tin, Smith Typewriters, Horse & Typewriter, C.1900	800.00
Tin, Snowdrift Coconut, Red & Yellow, Round, 6 1/2 X 12 In.	42.00
Tin, Southern States Special Oil, 2 Gal.	45.00
Tin, Stanwix Tobacco, Blue, Upright Pocket	395.00
Tin, Star Safety Razor, Green, No Razor, Rectangular	65.00
Tin, Sterling Brand Thyme, Blue Label, 1 1/2 Oz.	4.00
Tin, Sterling Fine Cut Tobacco, Tartan Plaid, Pocket	75.00

Tin, Stollwerck Cocoa 65.00
Tin, Sugardale Lard, Blue, 50 Lb. 22.00
Tin, Sultana Peanut Butter, Blue, 1 Lb. 125.00
Tin, Sunbrite Cleanser 12.00
Tin, Sunset Trail Cigars 185.00
Tin, Superior Salted Nuts, Picture of Tropical Scene, 10 Lb. 50.00
Tin, Sweet Burley Tobacco, Red Letters, Yellow, 5 Lb. 55.00
Tin, Sweet's Snowflake Marshmallows, 4 Oz. 60.00
Tin, Sylvan Carnation Talc 33.00
Tin, Three Feathers Tobacco, Pocket .... 220.00 To 325.00
Tin, Three Flowers Talcum, Richard Hudnut, Bell Shape 75.00
Tin, Tidex Oil, 2 Gal. 45.00
Tin, Tiger Chewing Tobacco, P. Lorillard Co., Pocket 45.00
Tin, Times Square Tobacco, Contents, Pocket 250.00
Tin, Tom Moore Cigar, Hinged Lid, Souvenir, 4 1/2 X 3 1/2 In. 17.00
Tin, Toyland Peanut Butter 80.00
Tin, Tried & True Brand Coffee, 1930s, 1 Lb. 12.00
Tin, Trojan Prophylactics 25.00
Tin, Turkey Coffee, 3 Lb. 1500.00
Tin, Tuxedo Tobacco, Man With Pipe, Pocket 30.00
Tin, Twin Oaks Tobacco, Casket 85.00
Tin, Twin Oaks Tobacco, Flat Lid, Pocket 120.00
Tin, Twin Oaks Tobacco, Flip Lid, Pocket 45.00
Tin, Twin Oaks Tobacco, Sample 120.00
Tin, U.S. Marine Tobacco, Pocket, 8 1/2 In. 225.00
Tin, Uncle Daniel Tobacco, Pie–Shaped, Early 1900s, 1 Lb. 195.00
Tin, Uniform Tobacco, 4 X 6 In. 125.00
Tin, Vanko Cigars, 5 Cents, Label 95.00
Tin, Victoria Tea, 5 Lb. 150.00
Tin, White Bear Coffee, 4 1/2 X 3 X 6 In. 55.00
Tin, White Lilac Coffee, 1920s, 1 Lb. 60.00
Tin, White Manor Tobacco, Pocket 250.00
Tin, White Rose Coffee, Key Lid, 1 Lb. 16.00
Tin, Whitman's Instantaneous Sweet Chocolate, Black & White 95.00
Tin, Winola Peanuts, Indian Maiden, 10 Lb. 400.00
Tin, Yankee Boy, Blonde Boy, Pocket 1000.00
Tin, Yankee Boy, Brunette Boys, Pocket 495.00

A tip tray is a decorated metal tray less than 5 inches in diameter. It was placed on the table or counter to hold either the bill or the coins that were left as a tip. A change receiver could be made of glass, plastic, or metal. It was kept on the counter near the cash register and held the money passed back and forth by the cashier.

ADVERTISING, TIP TRAY, see also Advertising, Change Receiver

Tip Tray, Apollinaris, 1920s 32.00
Tip Tray, Bailey's Whiskey 60.00
Tip Tray, Bartels Lager, Ale & Porter 80.00
Tip Tray, Bartholomay 115.00
Tip Tray, C.D. Kenney, George Washington On Front 85.00
Tip Tray, Corbys, Full Color, 4 In. 55.00
Tip Tray, Cottolene, Blacks Picking Cotton 95.00
Tip Tray, Dallas Brewery Home Beer 65.00
Tip Tray, De Laval Cream Separator 77.50
Tip Tray, De Laval Cream Separator, Lady, Farmyard Scene, 4 In. 110.00
Tip Tray, Dixie Loan Co., Logo, Gold Letters, Woman 75.00
Tip Tray, Dr.Pepper, Kittens 165.00
Tip Tray, El Verso, Cole Phillips Lithograph 85.00
Tip Tray, Fairy Soap .... 35.00 To 60.00
Tip Tray, Fraternal Life & Accident Ins. Co., Des Moines 65.00
Tip Tray, Globe Wernecke Sectional Bookcase 85.00
Tip Tray, Hiroller Whiskey, Fancy Dude, 1910 .... 100.00
Tip Tray, Home Like, Gas Stove, Woman In Kitchen, Baby, Blocks 125.00
Tip Tray, Hurd Truman Superiority Cigars, Sacramento 35.00
Tip Tray, Hydroler Whiskey, Man In Evening Clothes, 1900s 40.00

Tip Tray, Jenny Aiero Gasoline, Airplane 35.00
Tip Tray, Kenney, Thanksgiving Greetings, 4 1/4 In. 18.00
Tip Tray, King's Pure Malt, Panama Pacific Expo Seal, 6 In. 55.00
Tip Tray, Lewardo's, Cat With Chicks, Porcelain 125.00
Tip Tray, Marilyn Monroe, Nude 32.00
Tip Tray, Montgomery Ward 50.00
Tip Tray, Moxie 93.50
Tip Tray, Our Brands National Cigar Co., Lovely Woman 60.00
Tip Tray, Peter Doelger Bottled Beer 28.00
Tip Tray, Phil Schneider Brewing Co., Trinidad, Colo., Drinkers 25.00
Tip Tray, Prudential Life Insurance Co., 1920s 20.00
Tip Tray, Pulver's Cocoa, 4 1/2 In. 340.00
Tip Tray, Quick Meal Ranges, St. Louis, Mo., Baby Chicks 77.50
Tip Tray, Red Earl Cigars, Cavalier 120.00
Tip Tray, Rockford Watches, Girl, Sitting, 1900s .... 50.00 To 75.00
Tip Tray, S & H Green Stamps, Art Nouveau Lady Bust 60.00
Tip Tray, Success Manure Spreader 110.00
Tip Tray, Sun Light Oil Co. 30.00
Tip Tray, Wagner Shoes, 6 In. 120.00
Tip Tray, Welsbach, Family Scene, 1900s 45.00
Tip Tray, Yeomen, Des Moines, Iowa 35.00
Tobacco Cutter, Countertop, Lettering Star, Iron, 8 X 20 In. 75.00
Tobacco Cutter, Countertop, Peter C. Beck Co., Cast Iron, 9 In. 100.00
Tobacco Cutter, Iron, Griswold, 20 In. 125.00
Tobacco Cutter, Lorillard's Tomahawk, Iron .... 45.00 To 70.00
Tobacco Cutter, Master Workman, Iron 100.00
Tooth Powder, Colgate, WWII 16.50
Toothbrush, Doctor West Miracle Tuft, 18 In. 125.00
Tray, Akron Brewery, Scene 550.00
Tray, Anheuser-Busch Beer, Factory Scene 325.00
Tray, Arctic Ice Cream, Square, 13 In. .... 100.00 To 195.00
Tray, Beer, Enterprise Brewing, Poinsettias On Front 75.00
Tray, Bettendorf Steel Gear Wagon, Davenport, Iowa, Tin 195.00
Tray, Bevo Beverage, Team of Horses, Wood Grain Border, 1900s 125.00
Tray, Bimbo Beer, Elephant In Bellboy Outfit, 1940s 65.00
Tray, Boy Angel With Maiden, Serving, Tin, Oval, 14 X 17 In. 60.00
Tray, Budweiser, 5 Redcoats 37.50
Tray, Budweiser, Hunting Dog, Men At Fireside, 1920s 75.00
Tray, Budweiser, Men In Tavern, Rectangular 55.00
Tray, Central Brewing Co., Bright Colors, 16 1/2 In. 1320.00
Tray, Chattanooga Girl, Map, Picture 1150.00
Tray, Christian Feighn-Span Beer, Woman, 13 1/4 In. .... 85.00 To 100.00
Tray, Cincinnati Creammunchener Beer & Black Pirate Ale 100.00
Tray, Cold Spring Brewing, Oval, 13 In. 425.00
Tray, Crescent Brewing Co., Nampa, Idaho, Pretty Girl 87.50
Tray, Detroit Brewing Co., C.1910 .... 75.00
Tray, Dr Pepper, Oval, Reclining Lion, Bottle 500.00
Tray, Edelweiss Beer, Pretty Girl, Round, 13 In. 165.00
Tray, Ehret's Hell Gate Brewery, Round 75.00
Tray, Fairy Soap, 13 In. 110.00
Tray, Falstaff, Maiden Pouring Beer, Castle, Round, 24 In. 110.00
Tray, General Tires, 1917 Packard, Metal 20.00
Tray, Ginger Ale, Frank's 69.00
Tray, Goebel Beer, Detroit, Michigan, Dutch Girl 110.00
Tray, Golden West Brewery Scene 450.00
Tray, Haeusermann, Lion, Oval 55.00
Tray, Hampden Beer, Waiter, Round, Comical 100.00
Tray, Heim Brewery, Scene of Kansas City 625.00
Tray, Henley's Connoisseur, 12 In. 175.00
Tray, Hires, Girl In White Oval Center, Tin, 10 X 13 In. 209.00
Tray, Humbolt Brewing Co., Beautiful Woman 70.00
Tray, Koch's Beer, Dunkirk, New York 25.00
Tray, LaVerdo Cigars 160.00
Tray, Liberty Ice Cream, Pictures Liberty Bell, Papier-Mache 25.00

Tray, Merrigan's Ice Cream, 2 Kids, Beach Umbrella, 1925, 8 In. 300.00
Tray, Merrigan's Ice Cream, When Dreams Come True, 8 In. 250.00
Tray, Miller Brewing Co., Milwaukee, Wisconsin, Girl On Moon 35.00
Tray, Muehlebach Brewing Co., Kansas City, Missouri 17.50
Tray, Neef Bros., Denver, 3 Dogs Playing Cards 850.00
Tray, Old Pepper Whiskey, Bottle & Continental Soldiers, Tin 550.00
Tray, Orange Crush, Pictures Crushy, Rectangular, 1929 .... 140.00
Tray, Pabst Beer, Man Pouring From Bottle 65.00
Tray, Pacific Beer, Wood Grain Ground, M.T. Tacoma, 1930s, Round 100.00
Tray, Quinlan's Butter Pretzels, Victorian Woman, Boy On Back 25.00
Tray, Quiri & Casey, Home of Good Shoes, Metal, 4 1/2 X 4 In. 35.00
Tray, RCA Needle, Porcelain, Heart Shape 35.00
Tray, Robin Brand Ice Cream, 10 Kids At Table 750.00
Tray, Ruhstaller's Beer, Girl Strolling On Boulevard 145.00
Tray, Schaefer Beer 7.50
Tray, Schell's Beer, Deer Head 95.00
Tray, Schmidts Budweiser, Indianapolis, Etched Ruby Glass 175.00
Tray, Schneider Brewing Co., Trinidad, Colorado, Oval 127.50
Tray, Snow White, Dwarfs, Ohio Art, 1937 .... 35.00
Tray, Sparrow's Chocolate, Girl Standing On Chair, 8 X 6 In. 440.00
Tray, Storz Brewing Co., Omaha, Nebraska 37.50
Tray, T.V., Falls City Beer 25.00
Tray, Texatone, 1899 .... 225.00
       ADVERTISING, TRAY, TIP, see Advertising, Tip Tray
Tray, Use Fleischmann & Co's Compressed Yeast, Tin, Round 650.00
Tray, Wilson's Invalid's Port Wine, Woman In Gown 165.00
Tray, Wm. Ohlhaver Co. Ice Creamer, 1915 .... 250.00
Tray, Zipps Cherri-O, Parrot Drinking From Glass 675.00
Tumbler, Beer, Ober Beer, Embossed 275.00
Tumbler, Bevo Soda, 1920s 35.00
Tumbler, Birelys Soda 12.00
Tumbler, Dr. Pepper, Star Trek, Captain Kirk, 1975 .... 12.00
Tumbler, Flintstone, Welch's 5.00
Tumbler, Fountain, Cheer-Up 16.50
Tumbler, Fountain, Squirt, With Boy, 1949 .... 18.50
Tumbler, German Brewing Co., Cumberland, Maryland, Union Made 22.50
Tumbler, Hires Root Beer, Enameled, Syrup Line, 10 Oz. 25.00
Tumbler, Hires Soda 14.00
Tumbler, L. Hoster Brewing Co., Etched 60.00
Tumbler, Measuring, Red Owl 12.50
Tumbler, Moxie, Embossed, Straight Sides 50.00
Tumbler, Phillips 66 .... 10.00
Tumbler, Quality Checked Ice Cream, Rootbeer Float 6.00
Tumbler, Soda, Moxie, Embossed, Straight-Sided 50.00
Tumbler, Uneeda Milk Biscuit, Carmel Glass 165.00
Tumbler, Welch's, Fred & Barney, Flintstones, Baseball, 1964 .... 8.00
Tumbler, Whistle Soda 12.00
Wagon, Good-Will Soap, 2 Small, 2 Large Wheels, 27 X 13 In. 1320.00
Wheel, Geography, Tip Top Bread, Mechanical, USA, 1944 .... 10.00
Whistle, Hires, Blue, Pink, 3 Finger Holes Top, 4 1/2 In. 18.00
Whistle, Yellow Cab, Tin 10.00

Agata glass was made by Joseph Locke of the New England Glass Company of Cambridge, Massachusetts, after 1885. A metallic stain was applied to New England Peachblow and the mottled design characteristic of agata appeared.

AGATA, Bowl, Gray, Grayish Green, White, 5 3/4 In. 160.00
Bowl, Rose To Pale Pink, Spotted Design, Ruffled Rim, 5 1/2 In. 525.00
Finger Bowl, Dark Mottling, Golden Tracery, Fluted Rim 685.00
Teapot, Brown, Cream, Square Pot, Short Feet, Embossed Spout, 5 In. 6300.00
Tumbler, Lemonade, Handle, Peachblow, New England, 5 1/8 In. 1250.00
Vase, Rose To White, Gold & Lavender Spotted Design, 4 In. 825.00

Akro agate glass was made in Clarksburg, West Virginia, from 1932 to 1951. Before that time, the firm made children's glass marbles. Most of the glass is marked with a crow flying through the letter A.

AKRO AGATE, Ashtray, Atlantic Foundry, Hexagonal, 4 1/2 In. 7.50
Ashtray, Ellipsoid, Marbelized, 5 In. 8.50
Ashtray, Green, Square, 3 In. 4.00
Ashtray, Match Holder, Green, Hotel Lincoln Advertising 45.00
Ashtray, Pumpkin, Square, 3 In. 7.00
Ashtray, Turquoise, Square, 3 In. 6.00
Bowl, Child's, Octagonal, Closed Handles, Blue 10.00
Bowl, Scalloped, 3–Footed, Blue, 5 1/4 In. 50.00
Bowl, Scalloped, 3–Footed, Pumpkin, 5 1/4 In. 45.00
Bowl, Stacked Disc, Green 35.00
Bowl, Stacked Disc, Yellow 35.00
Box, Cigarette, White, 3 1/2 X 4 In. 12.50
Box, Scottie Dog, Pink, Cover 95.00
Candlestick, Blue, Pair 165.00
Candlestick, Pumpkin, Pair 145.00
Coaster, Blue, Westite 90.00
Cornucopia, Orange 4.00
Creamer, Child's, Blue, Interior Panel 21.00
Creamer, Child's, Raised Daisy, Opaque Blue, 1 3/16 In. 18.00
Cup & Saucer, Child's, Yellow 11.00
Cup, Child's, Blue, Marble 7.00
Cup, Child's, Concentric Ring, Pumpkin 15.00
Cup, Child's, Concentric Ring, Purple 25.00
Cup, Child's, Interior Panel, Pink 11.00
Cup, Child's, Raised Daisy, Opaque Yellow, 1 3/16 In. 13.00
Cup, Pink, Demitasse 6.00
Flowerpot, Banded Darts, Green, 4 In. 35.00
Flowerpot, Banded Darts, Pumpkin, 2 1/2 In. 35.00
Flowerpot, Banded Darts, Turquoise, 2 1/2 In. 35.00
Flowerpot, Banded Darts, Yellow, 4 In. 40.00
Flowerpot, Blue, 5 1/2 In. 85.00
Flowerpot, Hand Fluted, Cobalt & Pumpkin, 5 1/4 In. 10.00
Flowerpot, Ribbed Top, Black Amethyst, 4 In. 15.00
Jar, Apothecary, Black Amethyst 65.00
Jar, Apothecary, Powder Blue 95.00
Jardiniere, Bell Shape, Rectangular Top, Yellow, 4 3/4 In. 8.00
Jardiniere, Graduated Darts, Smooth Top, Green, 5 In. 5.00
Lamp, Wall, With Akro Shade, Marbelized Green 35.00
Lamp, With Akro Shade, Marbelized Green 40.00
Marbles, Box, Set of 100 .... 12.50
Match Holder, Marbelized, 3 In. 5.00
Mortar & Pestle, Powder Blue 16.00
Planter, Scalloped, Oval, Cobalt Blue, 6 In. 2.50
Plate, Blue, White Agate Interior, 9 3/4 In. 22.50

To remove a stubborn stain from the outside of a bottle, try this. Fill a bucket with soft sand. Push the bottle in and out of the sand, rotate it, and try to loosen the stain. Then wash in clean water. To remove a stain inside a bottle, put a handful of gravel in the bottle and shake vigorously.

Alabaster, Figurine, Child, Crying,
Injured Bird, 21 In.

Plate, Red, 10 1/4 In.	50.00
Powder Bowl, Scotty Cover, Allover Embossed Scotties, Blue	55.00
Powder Box, Colonial Lady, Light Blue	22.00
Powder Box, Colonial Lady, Lime Green	50.00
Powder Box, Scotty Dog, Lime Green	60.00
Powder Box, Scotty Dog, Transparent Color	75.00
Powder Jar, Colonial Lady, Lime Green	225.00
Powder Jar, Colonial Lady, Pink	68.00
Powder Jar, Mexicalli With Hat, Blue & White	25.00
Saucer, Child's, Chiquita, Green	3.00
Saucer, Childs, Stacked Disc, Pink	4.50
Shaving Mug, Black Amethyst, Ring Handle	65.00
Soup, Dish, Yellow, 10 1/4 In.	45.00
Sugar, Child's, Interior Panel, Blue	21.00
Sugar, Cover, Child's, Raised Daisy, Light Blue, 1 3/16 In.	18.00
Tea Set, Child's, Amber, Stippled Band, 16 Piece	285.00
Tea Set, Child's, Chiquita, Green, 22 Piece	155.00
Tea Set, Child's, Interior Panel, Pink, 16 Piece	325.00
Tea Set, Child's, Stacked Disc, Green, 8 Piece	60.00
Teapot, Wire Handle, Wooden Grip & Cover Knob, Red, 5 3/4 In.	75.00
Tumbler, Child's, Raised Daisy, Yellow, 2 In.	15.00
Tumbler, Child's, Stacked Disc & Interior Panel, Green	15.00
Vase, Blue, Scalloped, 3–Footed, 6 In.	90.00
Vase, Ribs & Flutes, Lime Green, 8 In.	125.00
Vase, Ribs & Flutes, Marbelized, 8 In.	12.50
Vase, Ribs & Flutes, Pumpkin, 8 In.	125.00
Vase, Tab Handle, Green, 6 1/4 In.	40.00
Vase, Tab Handle, Orange, 6 1/4 In.	45.00
Vase, Tab Handle, Pumpkin, 6 1/4 In.	45.00
Water Set, Child's, Green, Box, 7 Piece	85.00

 Alabaster is a very soft form of gypsum, a stone that resembles marble. It was often carved into vases or statues in Victorian times. There are alabaster carvings being made even today. Because the alabaster is very porous, it will dissolve if kept in water, so do not use alabaster vases for flowers.

ALABASTER, Bust, Beatrice, Head Wrapped In Scarf, Red Dress, C.1900, 15 In.	665.00
Bust, Victorian Woman, Ruffled Hat, A. Cipriani, 18 In.	250.00
Buts, Young Victorian Woman, Scarf On Head, M. Luti, 14 1/2 In.	225.00
Clock, Stepped Cornice, 1/2 Hour Strike, Kuhling, 11 1/2 In.	110.00
Figurine, Child, Crying, Injured Bird, 21 In. ....*Illus*	715.00
Figurine, La Piccola, Young Girl, Pedestal, 1904, 65 In.	1925.00

Lamp, 3 Cherubs On Base, Globular Carved Shade, Electric, 25 In.	385.00
Lamp, Art Deco 3 Winged Women's Heads, Scroll Feet, 15 X 18 In.	1450.00
Lamp, Women's Heads Around Rim, Framed By Wings, 18 In.	1750.00
Urn, Classical, Band of Warriors, Heroes, Gods, 15 1/4 In., Pair	2100.00

Alexandrite is a name with many meanings. It is a form of the mineral chrysoberyl that changes from green to red under artificial light. A man–made version of this mineral is sold in Mexico today. It changes from deep purple to aquamarine blue under artificial light. The Alexandrite listed here is glass made in the late nineteenth and twentieth centuries. Thomas Webb & Sons sold their transparent glass shaded from yellow to rose to blue under the name Alexandrite. Stevens and Williams had a cased Alexandrite of yellow, rose, and blue. A. Douglas Nash Corporation made an amethyst–colored Alexandrite. Several American glass companies of the 1920s made a glass that changed color under electric lights and these were called Alexandrite too.

ALEXANDRITE, Bowl, Ribbed, 4 1/2 X 6 1/2 In.	185.00
Pitcher, Petal–Shaped Top, Amber To Lavender, 5 1/2 In.	1700.00
Vase, 2 Morning Glory Shapes, Triangular Base, 9 X 8 1/2 In.	1500.00
Vase, Elongated Leaves, Webb, Metal Triangular 8 1/2 X 9 In.	1500.00
Vase, Jack–In–The–Pulpit, Allover Honeycomb, 4 X 3 1/2 In.	925.00

Alhambra is a pattern of tableware made in Vienna, Austria, in the twentieth century. The geometric designs are in applied gold, red, and dark green. Full sets of dishes can be found in this pattern.

ALHAMBRA, Chocolate Set, 6 Piece	295.00
Coffeepot, Goose Neck Spout, Demitasse, 9 1/2 In.	175.00
Cup & Saucer, Bouillon, Double Handle	48.00
Pitcher, 8 In.	190.00

Aluminum was more expensive than gold or silver until the 1850s. Chemists learned how to refine bauxite to get aluminum. Jewelry and other small objects were made of the valuable metal until 1914 when an inexpensive smelting process was invented. The aluminum collected today dates from the 1930s through 1950s. Hand–hammered pieces are the most popular.

ALUMINUM, Basket, Fruit & Flowers, Turned–Up Sides, Cromwell	17.50
Basket, Rose Pattern, Knotted Handle, World Hand Forged	12.00
Bowl, Flower & Ribbon Handles, Rodney Kent	20.00
Casserole, Baking Dish Inset, Rose Pattern, Everlast	20.00
Casserole, Glass Lid, Guardian	10.00
Casserole, No.1058, Continental	12.50
Coaster, Flower Pattern, Holder, Everlast, 8 Piece	20.00
Coaster, Kensington, 4 In.	4.00
Coffeepot, Chrysanthemum, Electric, Lucite Handles, Continental	95.00
Compote, Ribbon & Flower Strips On Stand, Rodney Kent	25.00
Juicer, Crank	10.00
Mold, Cake, Santa In Chimney, 2 Piece	15.00
Salt & Pepper, Kensington, 2 3/4 In.	15.00
Server, Cromwell Pattern, Curled Handles, 3 Sections	7.50
Server, Wildflower Pattern, 3–Tiered, Gailstyn	22.00
Silent Butler, Pine Pattern, Everlast	10.00
Tray, 3 Sectioned Glass Inset, Everlast, Square, 12 In.	12.00
Tray, Cromwell, 10 X 15 In.	10.00
Tray, Flowers, Imperial Chantilly, 22K White Gold, Farberware	28.00
Tray, Flowers, Swirled Ridges On Flange, Everlast, Square, 12 In.	32.00
Tray, Handle, Round, Buenilum, 11 In.	10.00
Tray, Heart Shape, Bakelite Handle, Chase Brass	22.00
Tray, Leaf Shape, Everlast, 4 X 6 1/2 In., 5 Piece	12.00
Tray, Morning Glory, Farberware, 11 1/2 In.	8.00
Tray, No.1128, Basketweave Glass Insert, Everlast, 12 In.	12.00
Tray, Sebring Insert, Handles, Farberware	17.50
Water Set, Colored, 1950s, 7 Piece	12.00

AMBER, see Jewelry

Amber glass is the name of any glassware with the proper yellow–brown shading. It was a popular color just after the Civil War and many pressed glass pieces were made of amber glass. Depression glass of the 1930s–1950s was also made in shades of amber glass. All types are being reproduced.

AMBER GLASS, Bottle, Barber, Inverted Thumbprint, Enameled, 8 In.	155.00
Candy Dish, Lace Edge, Footed, Square	15.00
Compote, Goddess of Liberty	75.00
Creamer, Mayfair, Federal	5.00
Cruet, Stars & Bars, Stopper	55.00
Goblet, Hourglass	30.00
Goblet, Orion	30.00
Goblet, Spirea Band	25.00
Goblet, Valencia Waffle	30.00
Liqueur Set, 3 Bottles, 9 Mugs, Gazebo Shaped Metal Holder	510.00
Tray, Asparagus, Daisy & Button	30.00

AMBERETTE, see Pressed Glass, Klondike

Amberina is a two–toned glassware made from 1883 to about 1900. It was patented by Joseph Locke of the New England Glass Company. The glass shades from red to amber.

AMBERINA, see also Baccarat; Plated Amberina

AMBERINA, Bottle, Depose, Draped Curtain, Blown, 11 In.	98.00
Bowl, Square, 8 1/2 X 8 In.	395.00
Bowl, Venetian Diamond, Ruffled Rim, 5 X 7 In.	275.00
Bride's Basket, Inverted Thumbprint, Scalloped Rim	595.00
Candlestick, Eiffel Tower, 10 3/4 In., Pair	140.00
Candlestick, Twisted Stem, Plated Fittings, 9 1/2 In., Pair	975.00
Castor, Inverted Thumbprint, Footed Frame, Bow On Handle, 10 In.	885.00
Celery Vase, 6 1/2 In.	510.00
Celery Vase, Frosted, Scalloped Rim, 10 In.	295.00
Celery Vase, Moon & Star, Fluted, Footed, 5 3/4 In.	265.00
Celery, Diamond Pattern, Fuchsia, Scalloped Edge, 6 1/4 In.	400.00
Celery, Diamond–Quilted, 7 In.	235.00
Celery, New England, Fuchsia, 6 1/4 In.	400.00
Celery, New England, Inverted Thumbprint, Square Top, 6 1/2 In.	375.00
Compote, Diamond Hobnail, Footed, Square, 5 1/2 In.	210.00
Cordial, 4 1/2 In.	475.00
Creamer, Victorian, Wide Optic, 3 1/2 In.	75.00
Cruet, Inverted Thumbprint, Amber Stopper & Handle	300.00
Cruet, Trefoil Spout, Handle, Stopper, New England	385.00
Decanter, Wine, Pedestal Foot, Flattened Stopper, 12 1/4 In.	245.00
Dish, Cheese, Hobnail, Expanded Hobnails On Base, 9 1/2 In.	395.00
Finger Bowl, Reverse Quilted	130.00
Lamp, Hall, Diamond–Quilted, Pear Shape	495.00
Pitcher, Applied Handle, Blown, 6 X 5 1/4 In.	135.00
Pitcher, Crackle, Amber Handle, 8 In.	375.00
Pitcher, Crimped Top, New England, Small	225.00
Pitcher, Inverted Baby Thumbprint, Handle, Squared Rim, 7 1/2 In.	325.00
Pitcher, Inverted Thumbprint, Quatrefoil Top, Bulbous	235.00
Pitcher, New England, Swirl, 8 In.	200.00
Pitcher, Water, Child's, Hobnail, Square Mouth, 3 3/4 In.	195.00
Punch Cup, Inverted Baby Thumbprint, Amber Handle	90.00
Punch Cup, Inverted Optic, Scrolled Handle	55.00
Punch Cup, Wheeling	50.00
Spooner, Inverted Thumbprint, Scalloped Edge	175.00
Sugar, Daisy & Button, Tabs In Base Fit Into Notched Lid	535.00
Syrup, Inverted Baby Thumbprint, Tuft's Collar & Underplate	750.00
Toothpick, Daisy & Button	180.00 To 385.00
Toothpick, Diamond–Quilted	190.00
Toothpick, Faceted Amber Body	185.00
Toothpick, Venetian Diamond, Urn Shape	180.00

Tumbler, 4 1/2 In.	70.00
Tumbler, Baby Thumbprint, Enameled	100.00
Tumbler, Fuchsia Shades To Cream Lower, Optic Ribs, New England	1550.00
Tumbler, Inverted Thumbprint .... 50.00 To 90.00
Vase, Applied Amber Edge, Swirl, 10 In.	275.00
Vase, Free Blown, Shaded Yellow To Deep Fuchsia, Bulbous, 16 In.	95.00
Vase, Inverted Thumbprint, Rigaree Neck, Mt. Washington, 3 In.	225.00
Vase, Jack-In-The-Pulpit, Swirl Body, Amber Feet, 12 In.	440.00
Vase, Lily, 8 In.	275.00
Vase, Ruffled Top, Amber Feet, 11 1/4 In., Pair	350.00
Vase, Swirled Rib, Bulbous Mushroom Base, 10 In.	350.00

Amethyst glass is any of the many glasswares made in the dark purple color of the gemstone called amethyst. Included in this section are many pieces made in the nineteenth and twentieth centuries. Very dark pieces are called black amethyst and are listed under that heading.

AMETHYST GLASS, Bottle, Barber, Enameled Flowers, 7 3/4 In.	155.00
Bowl, Dragon, Lotus, Footed	65.00
Candlestick, Hexagonal, Socket, Pair	1400.00
Compote, Loop Pattern, Medium	4000.00
Figurine, Duck, Milk Glass Head, Atterbury	225.00
Pitcher, Water, Paneled Forget-Me-Not	175.00
Toothpick, Monkey	325.00

AMPHORA, see Teplitz
ANDIRON AND RELATED FIREPLACE ITEMS, see Fireplace

Stuffed animals or fish, rugs made of animal skins, and other similar collectibles are listed in this section. Collectors should be aware of the endangered species laws that make it illegal to buy and sell some of these items. Any eagle feathers, many types of cats, such as leopard, and many forms of tortoiseshell can be confiscated if discovered by the government.

ANIMAL TROPHY, Bear, Black, Standing, Naturalistic Platform	2750.00
Bear, Brown, 6 Ft.	3850.00
Birds, Nest, Beetles, Victorian, Dome Case, C.1860	650.00
Black Bear, Rug, Full Head, Open Mouth, 6 Ft.	1500.00
Black Bear, Walking Mount, Full Body, 45 In.	275.00
Brown Bear, Mounted, Full Size, European, 6 Ft.	3500.00
Buffalo Skull, 24 In.	48.00
Buffalo, Full Body, Mounted	4950.00
Cape Buffalo	895.00
Caribou, Mounted	350.00
Elephant Tusk, Carved, African	950.00
Lap Robe, Buggy, Horsehide, 5 X 5 Ft.	35.00
Moose Head, Mounted .... 650.00 To 750.00
Muskie Fish	29.50
Stone Sheep, Skull & Horse, 24 In.	150.00
Whitetail Buck, 10 Point, Full Body, 5 Ft. X 5 Ft. 1 In.	170.00

Dust trophies at least every other week. Dust and dirt damage the animal skin. Always dust from the head to the back, in the direction of the fur or feathers. Vacuum animals once every three years. Never vacuum a bird. Wash gently with mild soap and water every five years.

Animation cels are painted drawings on celluloid that are needed to make an animated cartoon. Hundreds of cels are made, then photographed in sequence to make a cartoon showing moving figures. Early examples made by the Walt Disney Studios are popular with collectors today.

ANIMATION ART, Cel, 101 Dalmatians 2250.00
Cel, Alice In Wonderland 1750.00
Cel, Baby Pegasus, Airborne, Fantasia, 1940 .... 1100.00
Cel, Baby Pegasus, Free Falling, Fantasia, 1940, 7 X 9 In. 935.00
Cel, Baloo, Full Figure, Background 450.00
Cel, Bambi 2250.00
Cel, Bambi & Thumper On Ice, 1942, 5 X 7 In. 1430.00
Cel, Bambi, Background 1600.00
Cel, Big Mama, Fox & The Hound, 1/2 Figure, 1981 .... 125.00
Cel, Brer Fox Frightening Brer Rabbit, 1946, 8 X 10 In. 2860.00
Cel, Briar Rose, Owl, Sleeping Beauty, Disney 1800.00
Cel, Briar Rose, Singing To Forest Owl, 1959, 8 1/2 X 9 In. 2000.00
Cel, Captain Crunch, Hand Inked, Matted, Jay Ward 110.00
Cel, Centaurette, Riding Attire, 7 X 8 In. 600.00
Cel, Christmas Carol, Jiminy Cricket On Table 500.00
Cel, Christmas Carol, Scrooge Quaking In His Spats 500.00
Cel, Cinderella, Fairy Godmother, Limited Edition, 1970 .... 1000.00
Cel, Cinderella, Reading Book, 1949, 11 X 13 In. 2860.00
Cel, Cruella De Vil, 100 and 1 Dalmations, 1961, 9 X 7 In. 990.00
Cel, Daffy Duck, In Trench Coat 250.00
Cel, Daisy Duck, Purple Dress, Mickey's Christmas Carol 625.00
Cel, Donald Duck, As Bell Hop, 9 1/2 X 12 1/2 In. 880.00
Cel, Donald Duck, From 1941 Cartoon, A Good Time For A Dime 215.00
Cel, Donald Duck, Full Body, Cymbals, Mickey Mouse Club 650.00
Cel, Donald Duck, Mickey's Fire Brigade, 1935, 9 X 12 In. 1200.00
Cel, Donald's Nephew, Dressed As Zorroduck, Hand Inked 275.00
Cel, Dumbo & Timothy Mouse, 1941, 8 X 10 In. 1750.00
Cel, Edgar, The Aristocats, Full Figure, Puts On Pants, 1970 .... 325.00
Cel, Ferdinand The Bull, Sniffing Flowers, 1939 .... 1320.00
Cel, Floyd Gottfredson, Mickey Comic Strip, Goofy, Inked 275.00
Cel, Fox & Hound, Looking At Disgruntled Badger 300.00
Cel, Fred Flintstone, Dressed As Santa Claus, Framed 125.00
Cel, Fred Flintstone, Wilma, Betty & Barney, Framed 275.00
Cel, Friar Tuck, Robin Hood, Waist Up, 1973 .... 125.00
Cel, Great Mouse Detective, Basil, Olivia, Looking For Clues 275.00
Cel, Harpies, Fantasia 1875.00
Cel, Heffalumps & Woozles, Winnie The Pooh, 1968 .... 55.00
Cel, Jiminy Cricket, From Christmas Carol, Framed 525.00
Cel, Jiminy Cricket, I'M No Fool, 1950s .... 200.00 To 250.00
Cel, Jose Carioca, Jose With Cigar & Umbrella 300.00
Cel, Lady & Tramp, Canine Cutups, 1955 .... 1760.00
Cel, Lady and The Tramp, 1955, 10 3/4 X 12 1/2 In. 605.00
Cel, Ludwig Von Drake, Full Figured, 1960 .... 175.00
Cel, Madame Medusa, Water Skiing On Alligator's Back 175.00
Cel, Magilla Gorilla, In Clover, Talking To Leprechaun 60.00
Cel, Medusa & Mr. Snoops 375.00
Cel, Medusa & Mr. Snoops, The Rescuers, 1977, 7 X 11 In. 425.00
Cel, Mickey Mouse, In Tuxedo, 1988 Academy Awards 1100.00
Cel, Mickey Mouse, Pluto & Little Whirlwind, 60th Birthday 2500.00
Cel, Mickey Mouse, Sorcerer's Apprentice, 8 X 12 In. 2200.00
Cel, Mickey Mouse, Wearing Mexican Hat, Dancing, 9 X 7 In. 1210.00
Cel, Mickey's Rival, Mickey, Minnie & Mortimer 1100.00
Cel, Mole, Mickey's Christmas Carol, Money Bag In Pants, 1983 .... 300.00
Cel, Mr. Codfish, Swimming, Holding Trophy, Bubbles, 1971 .... 400.00
Cel, Pastoral Symphony, Fantasia, 1940, 12 X 15 In. 775.00
Cel, Pedro The Chihuahua, Lady & The Tramp, 1955 .... 175.00 To 250.00
Cel, Penny, Carried In Brutus' Teeth, The Rescuers, 1977 .... 650.00

Cel, Peter Pan, Fighting Hook, Lithograph Background 1100.00
Cel, Peter Pan, Sitting Cross–Legged, Indian Headdress, 1953 .... 825.00
Cel, Pinocchio, Glancing Down, 1939, 5 3/4 X 5 3/4 In. 3950.00
Cel, Pixie, Boo Boo, Yogi Bear, Huckleberry Hound, 9 X 11 In. 660.00
Cel, Pluto, Toby Tortoise On Beach, 1947, 8 X 12 In. 2650.00
Cel, Pongo, 101 Dalmatians, Holds Roger's Hat, 1961, 8 X 9 In. 1800.00
Cel, Popeye Close–Up, Matted, Large 225.00
Cel, Prince Charming Walking Down Stairs, 1950, 8 X 6 In. 715.00
Cel, Prince, Briar Rose Embracing, Sleeping Beauty, 4 X 3 In. 880.00
Cel, Sea Scouts, Donald Duck & Nephews 1150.00
Cel, Sleeping Beauty, View From Cottage Scene 800.00
Cel, Snow White & Seven Dwarfs, 1937, 9 X 12 In. 1540.00
Cel, Song of The South, Close–Up of Brer Bear 295.00
Cel, Tigger, Eyes Closed, Full Figure, 1970 .... 145.00
Cel, Tinkerbell, Trail of Star Dust, 1953, 11 X 15 In. 1325.00
Cel, Toad, Fox & The Hound, 10 X 4 In. 125.00
Cel, Toad, Fox & The Hound, 3/4 Figure, 1981 .... 125.00
Cel, Tom & Jerry, Straw Hats & Canes, TV, 1960s, Pair 495.00
Cel, Toucan Sam, Flying Over Police Car, Hand Inked 85.00
Cel, Wile E. Coyote, In Desert, 8 X 11 In. 1320.00
Cel, Winnie The Pooh, 4 Scenes of Piglet Doing Chores 350.00
Cel, Witch Holding Apple, Snow White, 1947, 10 X 12 In. 4400.00
Cel, Wizard of Oz, All Characters, Matted, 1973 .... 225.00
Cel, Wynken, Blynken and Nod, 1938, 7 X 8 In. 1100.00

APPLE PEELER, see Kitchen, Peeler, Apple

 This section includes a variety of collectibles, usually very large, that have been removed from buildings. Hardware, backbars, doors, paneling, and even old bathtubs are now wanted by collectors. Pieces of the Victorian, Art Nouveau, and Art Deco styles are in greatest demand.

ARCHITECTURAL, Backbar, 4 Columns, Brunswick–Galke Callonder Co., 18 Ft. 8500.00
Backbar, 7 Stools, Ice Cream Parlor, Quarter Sawed Oak, 7 Ft. 2750.00
Backbar, Ice Cream Parlor, Mirrored, Oak, 2 Stools 2600.00
Backbar, Rococo, 11 Beveled & Scalloped Mirrors, Mahogany 3750.00
Bathtub, Folding, Kerosene Burner, Can Be Wheeled From Room 475.00
Bathtub, Porcelain, Claw Footed 275.00
Bathtub, The Ebinger Sanitary Mfg. Co., Salesman's Sample 23.00
Bathtub, Tin, Cast Iron Legs 150.00
Birdbath, Scalloped Shell, Iron 900.00
Box, 2 Windows, Post Office, 64 Call Windows, 8 X 4 Ft. 1375.00
Capital, Corinthian, Terra–Cotta, 18 In. 660.00
Capital, Ionic, Carved & Painted, 20 In., Pair 1210.00
Column, Colonial, Fluted, Sandstone Base, 16 Ft.2 In. 750.00
Commode, Oak Tank & Seat 175.00
Counter, Grain, 31 Drawers, Oak, 16 Ft. 2400.00
Counter, Grain, 6 Drawers, Oak, 5 Ft. 6 In. 700.00
Cupboard, Corner, Open Top, 2 Paneled Doors, 105 X 51 In. 5500.00
Door Knocker, Lion Head, Victorian, Gilded Bronze, 9 In. 200.00
Door Strap, Scrolled Foliage Design, Iron, 31 1/2 In., Pair 70.00
Door, Chevrons, Nickled Bronze, C.1930, 7 Ft. 2 1/8 In., Pair 5500.00

To remove the remains of sticky glue and tape from antiques, try rubbing peanut butter on the sticky area until the glue is gone. Do not use this method on porous materials where the oil from the peanut butter could leave a stain.

Door, French, Leaded, Grape Clusters On Transom, 48 X 24 In. 3000.00
Door, Library, Dutch, Rollers, Oak, 8 X 4 Ft., Pair 500.00
Doorbell, Pull Type, Spring Operated, Nickel Plated, 1855 .... 40.00
Doorknob & Escutcheon, L. Sullivan, With Lockset, 11 In., Pr. 2170.00
Doorway, Federal Style, Painted & Carved 660.00
Drinking Fountain, Brass Hardware 500.00
Drugstore Soda Room, Tables, Seats, Mirror, 10 X 16 Ft. 7500.00
Element, Copper Plated Cast Iron, L. Sullivan, 1895, 10 In. 2425.00
Elevator Cage, English Oak, Cut Crystal 1650.00
Fan, Over The Door, White Paint, Poplar, 41 1/2 In., Pair 935.00
Fence, With Gate & Posts, Iron, C.1865, 66 Ft. 2200.00
Fence, Wrought Iron, With Gate, Calais, Me., 1872, Over 200 Ft. 5700.00
Fence, Yard, Iron, 18 5–Ft. Links, 90 Ft. 500.00
Figure, Angel, Kneeling, Stone Carving, France, 19th Century 1800.00
Figure, Dove, In Wreath, From Fence, Iron, 16 In., Pair 850.00
Fireplug, Bunker Hill Air Force Base, Iron 35.00
Foot Rail, Brass, 18 Ft. 200.00
Fountain, Figural, Nude Maiden, Marble, Bronze, Mosaic, 21 In. 3520.00
Fountain, Garden, Pelicans Base, Cherub Supports, Lead, 70 In. 3000.00
Furnace Damper, Doe Wah Jack 50.00
Garden Urn, Plinth Base, Cast Iron 275.00
Gate & Posts, Cast Iron, J.J. Reichert, Pat. 1869 .... 1000.00
Gazebo, 6 Posts, Foliate Devices, Cast Iron, 12 Ft. 5500.00
Jockey, Lawn, Cast Metal, Electric, 46 In. 302.00
Lavatory, Brass & Porcelain Handled Faucets 500.00
Lavatory, Brass Mixer Set 600.00
Lavatory, Porcelain Pedestal, China Cross–Arm Handles 700.00
Log Cabin, Knockdown & Numbered, 16 X 24 Ft. 3200.00
Mail Slot, Door Installation, Spring Hinged, Brass, 10 In. 38.00
Mailbox Cluster, Country Store, Bronze, 32 U.S. Doors, 1920s 495.00
Mantel & Mirror, Chinese Chippendale, Pine, 5 Ft. 5 In. 9350.00
Mantel, Carved, Portrait Center, Grapes, Floral, Painted, 1890s 3700.00
Mantel, Federal, Fluting & Stop Fluting, Poplar, 69 1/4 In. 600.00
Mantel, Fireplace, With Dressing Mirror, Cherry 450.00
Mantel, Pine, Still Life By H. Mann Livers, 1800s 200.00
Monument, Cemetery, Zinc, White Bronze Co., 1885, 18 1/4 In. 325.00
Ornament, American Eagle, Outspread Wings, Copper, 42 In. 1210.00
Post Office Unit, 1911, Small 500.00
Post Office, 4 Sections, 3 Window Stations, Oak, 1896, 32 Ft. 8000.00
Roof Finial, Wrought Iron, 28 In., Pair 880.00
Saloon Backbar, Mahogany, Marble, Brass Hardware, 10 Ft. 3300.00
Seat Ends, Theater, Art Nouveau, Heywood Wakefield, Iron, Pair 65.00
Sink, Porcelain, Brass Legs, Feeds & Faucets, Oval 595.00
Soda Fountain, Manitoba, Marble, J.W. Tuft's, 4 Ft. 10 In. 9500.00
Soda Room, Drug Store, Oak, Built–In Tables, 1927, 10 X 16 In. 7500.00
Spire, Gothic, Gray & Red & Gilt, Wooden, 20 In., 3 Piece 225.00
Street Light, 2–Light, Acorn Globe, Cast Iron, 1900s, 22 Ft. 1650.00
Sundial, Atlas Holding World On Shoulders, Metal, 12 In. 500.00
Teller's Cage, Oak, Iron, Ornate, 25 Ft. 6500.00
Tub & Pedestal Sink, Claw Foot, 2 Piece 135.00
U.S. Post Office Interior, 36 Units, With Drop 605.00
Water Pump, Wooden, Wooden Handle 195.00

> Arequipa Pottery was produced from 1911 to 1918 by the patients of the Arequipa Sanitorium in Marin County Hills, California.

AREQUIPA, Bowl, Applied Seashells, Luster Glaze, 2 X 6 In. 350.00
Vase, Green Lava Glaze, Rhead Period Mark, 8 In. 695.00
Vase, Landscape, 9 In. 550.00
Vase, Lava Glaze, Green, 8 In. 625.00
Vase, Light Bulb Shape, Matte Green, Marked, 5 In. 300.00
     ARGY–ROUSSEAU, see G. Argy–Rousseau

Art Deco, or Art Moderne, a style started at the Paris Exposition of 1925, is characterized by linear, geometric designs. All types of furniture and decorative arts, jewelry, book bindings, and even games were designed in this style.

ART DECO, Ashtray, Chrome, World, Encircling Orb, Copper Stars .... 24.00 To 25.00
Ashtray, Floor, Black, Chrome Ball, Electrolier Co., 24 In. 460.00
Ashtray, Greyhound Handle, Standing, Iron 39.00
Bottle, French Priest, Hat Stopper, Robj, 10 1/4 In. 335.00
Bottle, Napoleon, Hat Stopper, Robj, 10 In. 335.00
Bowl, Matte Glaze, Base Seal, MW 22, 7 1/2 In. 1250.00
Bowl, Matte Glaze, Base Seal, MW, C.1921, 6 1/2 In. 875.00
Box, Cigarette, Piano Shape, Musical, Bakelite, 5 1/4 X 8 In. 115.00
Coaster, Scotty, Metal, In Holder 28.00
Figure, Minerva, Cast, Marble Base, 11 In. 275.00
Frame, Cherubs & Seahorse, Iron–Bronze Coated, 12 In. 40.00
Goblet, Nude Figural Stem, Gold, Frosted Crystal, France, 7 1/4 In. 55.00
Ice Crusher, Rocket Ship Shape, Silvery Metal 15.00
Incense Burner, Egyptian Figure, Metal, Vantines, France, 6 1/2 In. 200.00
Knife Rest, Green Grasshopper, Signed Vallauri, Box 140.00
Lamp, Lady On Back, Legs Up, Holding Ball, Green Shade, 22 In. 350.00
Pitcher, Orange & Yellow Flowers, Charlotte Rhead, 9 3/8 In. 195.00
Vase, Orange & Green Leaves, Flowers, Charlotte Rhead, 8 5/8 In. 195.00

Art glass means any of the many forms of glassware made during the late nineteenth century or early twentieth century. These wares were expensive and production was limited. Art glass is not the typical commercial glass that was made in large quantities, and most of the art glass was produced by hand methods.

ART GLASS, see also separate headings such as Burmese; Cameo Glass; Tiffany; etc.
ART GLASS, Basket, Blue, Vaseline Band, Orange Enameled, Thorn Handle, 7 In. 350.00
Basket, Rainbow, Coinspot Exterior, Loop Handle, 7 1/2 In. 415.00
Bowl, Brown, Lithyalin, Polished Agate, Eggermann, 1835, 3 In. 385.00
Bowl, Fern, Black, Silver Floral, Footed, L.E. Smith, 5 1/2 In. 20.00
Bowl, Frosted Flowers, St. Helaire, 6 3/4 In. 330.00
Bowl, Reclining Nude, On Large Curled Leaf, Malachite, 8 In. 110.00
Candleholder, Pink On White Cased Top, Base, Clear Stem, 8 In. 275.00
Candlestick, Green, 6 Points, Silver Overlay Flame, St. Graal, Pr. 60.00
Cruet, Faceted Stopper, Opaque Green 785.00
Cuspidor, Allover Chipped Ice, Rolled Over Top, 4 1/4 X 7 In. 125.00
Ewer, Lava, Colored Slashes, Black Ground, Frederick Shirley 1675.00
Figurine, 2 Horse, 1 Rider, Tarnish Tinge, Jon Cerny, 4 X 4 In. 150.00
Hanging, Dragonfly, Mottled & Textured, 24 In. Diam. 385.00
Pitcher, Water, Pink, Molded Drapery, Beaded Neck, 9 1/2 In. 250.00
Rose Bowl, Overlay of Bronze Chestnuts, Austrian, 4 1/2 In. 165.00
Sculpture, Black Exterior, White Interior, 18 In. 100.00
Shade, Chipped Ice, Scenic, 5 1/2 In. 350.00
Shade, Gold Iridescent, Ruffled, 6 In. 66.00
Shade, Reverse Painted Scene, Chipped Ice, 5 1/2 In. 150.00
Spooner, Green Opaque, Gold Border, New England, 3 3/4 In. 945.00
Tray, Silver Overlay Flowers & Leaves & Scalloped Rim, 13 In. 45.00
Vase, 3 Bacchantes & Grapevines, Malachite Glass, 8 1/2 In., Pair 100.00
Vase, 3 Standing Nude Woman, Fluted, A.C. Remington 350.00
Vase, 6 Standing Nudes, Malachite, 1920, 5 In. 265.00
Vase, Bacchus, Stylized Poses, Gilt & Enamel, Heiligenstein, 8 In. 4400.00
Vase, Black Squares, Wiener Werkstatte, 8 3/4 In. 1320.00
Vase, Clear Icicles, Amethyst Body, 4–Footed, 8 3/4 In. 880.00
Vase, Clear, Yellow Orange Interior, R. Jolley, 10 In. 225.00
Vase, Cluthra, Swirled Mauve & White, Kimball, 4 1/2 In. 625.00

Vase, Enameled Birds In Trees, Gilt, Marcel Goupy, 1925, 8 1/4 In. 1925.00
Vase, Figural, Mother & Child, Orange, Marcel Goupy, C.1925, 7 In. 3850.00
Vase, Green, Gold, Possibly Trevaise, 9 1/4 In. 1100.00
Vase, Hounds Chasing Gazelles, Marcel Goupy, C.1920, 6 3/4 In. 4400.00
Vase, King Tut, Gold, Turquoise Stripes, Cobalt Ground, 8 In. 400.00
Vase, Leaf Design, Red Flowers, C.Lotton, 8 3/4 In. 357.00
Vase, Maroon Pulled Feather, Green Interior, Vandermark, 7 In. 125.00
Vase, Murano, Venetian, Barovier & Tosco 75.00
Vase, Nicolas, 19 1/2 In. 7500.00
Vase, Opaque Top, Yellow, Cone Shape, Leerdam UNICA, 8 In. 250.00
Vase, Trumpet, Orange To Clear, Yellow Flowers, Signed, 18 In. 350.00
Vase, Woman's Portrait, Green Overlay, Gold Trim, 13 1/2 In., Pair 650.00
Vase, Zigzag Loops At Shoulder, Green, Austrian, C.1900, 5 1/4 In. 1450.00

 Art Nouveau is a style of design that was at its most popular from 1895 to 1905. Famous designers, including Rene Lalique and Emile Galle, produced furniture, glass, silver, metalwork, and buildings in the new style. Ladies with long flowing hair and elongated bodies were among the more easily recognized design elements. Copies of this style are being made today. Many modern pieces of jewelry can be found.

ART NOUVEAU, see also Furniture; various glass categories; etc.
ART NOUVEAU, Box, Blue & White, Porcelain, Brass Trim 500.00
Box, Leatherette, 12 In. 99.00
Box, Lingerie, Woman's Picture, Early 1900s 20.00
Casket, Jewel, Gilt, Footed, Taffeta Lined 7.50
Frame, Iron, Floral, Oval, 12 X 12 In. 45.00
Holder, Cigarette, Date 25.00
Mirror, Dresser, & Comb, Hope Silver Co., Beveled Edge 20.00
Plaque, Woman's Head, Border, Silver Plate Over Pewter, 20 In. 1250.00
Vase, Bronze, Flower Form, Applied Leaves, Flowers, 1890, 23 In. 1430.00
Vase, Flower Form, Gnarled Roots & Vine, Woman, A. Inrep, 12 In. 455.00
Vase, Grape Clusters, 13 In. ....*Illus* 130.00
Vase, Hunter, Black Vines, Handles, 1890, Forester & Sons, 9 In. 195.00

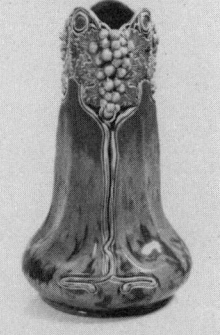 The first American art pottery was made in Cincinnati, Ohio, during the 1870s. The pieces were hand thrown and hand decorated. The art pottery tradition continued until the 1920s when studio potters began making the more artistic wares.

ART POTTERY, see also under factory name
ART POTTERY, Bookends, Bear, California Faience, 4 1/2 X 6 In. 500.00
Bowl, Mottled Pink, Ruskin, 8 In. 120.00

Do not put water in a pottery container with an unglazed interior. The water will be absorbed and eventually stain the container.

Art Nouveau, Vase, Grape Clusters, 13 In.

Chamberstick, Squeeze Bag Design, Wardle, C.1905, 15 In. 192.50
Charger, Spotted Glaze, Buff Rim, Maija Grotell, 12 1/2 In. 1575.00
Dish, Orange & Brown Pitted Glaze, Natzler, C.1948, 4 3/4 In. 1450.00
Dish, Red & Salmon, Natzler, 6 In. 2050.00
Jug, Grotesque, Devil–Like Mask, American, C.1890, 19 In. 660.00
Lamp Base, 3 Rabbits In Various Positions, Blue, 6 In. 250.00
Mug, Monk Playing Violin, Trenton 80.00
Pitcher, Cherokee, Mauve, 6 In. 55.00
Pitcher, Lemonade, Band of Water Lilies, Allover Roses, Osborne 230.00
Pitcher, Paneled Rim, Serpent Handle, Poillon, C.1910, 9 In. 55.00
Pitcher, Saguaro, Turquoise Glaze, DeGrazia, 9 In. 500.00
Pitcher, Walrath, 5 In. 750.00
Vase, Blue Drip, Over Brown Crystalline, Pierrefonds, 3 In. 80.00
Vase, Brownish Copper, Grand Feu, C.1916, 8 In. 1800.00
Vase, Celadon, Kentucky Bybee Pottery, 8 In. 22.50
Vase, English Country Scene, Bretby, C.1883, 8 1/2 In. 60.00
Vase, Foliate, Seed Form, Gilded Stand, Montieres, 5 1/4 In. 302.00
Vase, Matte Mauve Glaze, Buff Base, C.F. Binns, 1915, 8 1/2 In. 4235.00
Vase, Mission Glaze, Brauckman, 7 3/4 In. 1800.00
Vase, Oriental, David Leach, 7 In. 150.00
Vase, Purple & Blue Crackle, Durant Kilns, 1917, 8 In. 750.00
Vase, Scrolled Lines, Circles, W. Werkstatte, C.1910, 7 1/4 In. 825.00
Vase, Swastika Keramos, Stylized Landscape, 9 In. 800.00
Vase, Trefoil, Purple Grape Clusters, Austrian, 13 In. 130.00
Vase, Urn Shape, Sepia & Brown, C.F. Binns, 1927, 11 1/2 In. 7260.00
Vase, Volcanic Glaze, Beatrice Wood, C.1967, 12 1/2 In. 1085.00
Vase, Yellow Glaze, Natzler, 5 X 4 1/4 In. 795.00

Aurene glass was made by Frederick Carder of New York about
1904. It is an iridescent gold or blue glass, usually marked "Aurene"
or "Steuben."

AURENE, Basket, Gold, Ormolu Frame & Handle, F. Carder, 14 In. 2600.00
Bowl, Blue, 3 1/2 X 6 In. 675.00
Bowl, Blue, Signed, 9 In. 522.00
Bowl, Calcite, 12 In. 495.00
Bowl, Crimped Rim, Calcite, Silver Holder 225.00
Bowl, Gold & Calcite, 2 3/4 X 6 1/4 In. 180.00
Bowl, Gold, 4 1/4 In. 400.00
Bowl, Gold, 10 In. 350.00
Candleholder, Blue Over Calcite, Monogram, Revere Plated 325.00
Candleholder, Flattened Mushroom Form, 6 1/4 In. 935.00
Candlestick, Gold, Twisted Stem, Signed, C.1925, 10 In., Pair 2100.00
Cigarette Holder, Blue, 4 1/4 In. 350.00
Compote, Blue, Calcite, 3 X 6 In. 600.00
Compote, Underplate, Gold, Calcite 175.00
Console Set, Blue, Twisted Candleholders, 10–In. Bowl 2950.00
Goblet, Blue, Pedestal, Bulbous Center, Royal Blue Interior 450.00
Goblet, Royal Blue Interior, Pedestal, Signed 450.00
Perfume Bottle, Blue, Pedestal, Teardrop Stopper, Signed, 8 In. 595.00
Perfume Bottle, Blue, Stopper, 4 1/2 In. 325.00
Perfume Bottle, Gold, Melon Ribbed, Signed, 5 1/2 In. 495.00
Perfume Bottle, Gold, Teardrop Stopper, 10 1/2 In. 750.00
Perfume Bottle, Melon Ribbed, Signed, 5 1/2 In. 495.00
Shot Glass, Gold, 2 1/2 In. 335.00
Vase, 8 In. 395.00
Vase, Blue, 8 In. .... 1200.00 To 1250.00
Vase, Blue, 9 1/4 In. 950.00
Vase, Blue, 12 In. 1500.00
Vase, Blue, Ribbed, 6 In. 700.00
Vase, Blue, Ruffled Top, 8 In. 985.00
Vase, Blue, Urn Shape, Flared Collar, 8 1/2 In. 1295.00
Vase, Bud, 3 Tree Trunks, Gold, Signed, 6 In. 725.00
Vase, Gold, Iridescent, Ovoid, Rolled Lip, Signed, 10 In. 880.00

Vase, Gold, Ribbed, Reddish–Purple Highlights, 3 3/4 In. 725.00
Vase, Gold, Signed & Numbered 1682, 10 X 31 In. 3500.00
Vase, Gold, Signed, 10 In. 1200.00
Vase, Hunter, Landscape, Signed, C.1920, 10 1/8 In. 2300.00
Vase, Ruffled Trumpet Shape, Signed, C.1915, 9 In. .... 1095.00 To 1395.00
Vase, Stick, Gold 350.00
Vase, Tree Stump, 3 Prongs, Green, 6 In. 125.00
Vase, Trumpet, Gold, Calcite, 6 X 5 In. 305.00
Wine, Amber, Stemmed, Footed, Signed, 6 1/2 In. 195.00
    AUSTRIA, see Royal Dux; Kauffmann; Porcelain

    Auto parts and accessories are collectors' items today. Gas pump
globes and license plates are part of this specialty. Prices are
determined by age, rarity, and condition.

AUTO, Alarm System, Automatic Devil Dog, 1950s 20.00
  Book, Auto Electrician's Guide, 100 Pages of Diagrams, 1906–1919 Cars 25.00
  Book, Auto Storage Battery, 1918, 284 Pages 10.00
  Book, Studebaker, Care of Truck In Wartime, World War II 45.00
  Bulb Kit, Spare, Packard, Tin Container 45.00
  Cable Box, Model T, Dovetailed Wood 18.50
  Clock, Oldsmobile, 1912 .... 95.00
  Clock, Waltham, 7 Jewels, 8–Day, C.1922 .... 65.00
  Container, Car Battery Shape, Firestone 50.00
  Cushion, Auto, Conoco Gas, Colored, 1930s 20.00
  Display Case, Trico Windshield Wipers, On Wheels 125.00
  Filmstrip, Chrysler Promotional, Full Line, 1955 .... 18.00
  Gas Pump Globe, Aladdin Gasoline, Illinois Farm Service, Red Plastic 125.00
  Gas Pump Globe, American Gas, Blue, White Lettering, Metal Ring 295.00
  Gas Pump Globe, Atlantic Refining Company 1550.00
  Gas Pump Globe, Bartles Sweney Gasoline, Milk Glass, Embossed Letters 350.00
  Gas Pump Globe, Canfield Oil, 1920s, 10 Ft. 1200.00
  Gas Pump Globe, Clock Face, Correct Measure 1000.00
  Gas Pump Globe, Essolene, Metal Frame, Glass Inserts, 1920s 165.00
  Gas Pump Globe, Fire Chief, Texaco, Restored, 1940s 2500.00
  Gas Pump Globe, Gulf White Marine 325.00
  Gas Pump Globe, Mobil, Metal Frame, Inserts, 15 In. 195.00
  Gas Pump Globe, Mobiloil, Gargoyle 800.00
  Gas Pump Globe, Multipower, 3 Piece 150.00
  Gas Pump Globe, Red Crown Gas, Embossed Crown 275.00
  Gas Pump Globe, Red Crown, Metal Band 800.00
  Gas Pump Globe, Sinclair Dino 525.00
  Gas Pump Globe, Standard Oil, Crown 225.00
  Gas Pump Globe, Standard Oil, Flames 195.00
  Gas Pump Globe, Texaco, Milk Glass, Lenses Attach Metal Ring, 1 Piece 350.00
  Gas Pump Globe, White Crown, Base 185.00
  Gas Pump, Globe, Phillips 66, Orange & Black Paint, 10 Ft. 1560.00
  Gauntlets, Driving, Leather 55.00
  Grinder, Valve, Model T .... 23.00 To 35.00
  Headlight, Hupmobile, Brass, Pair 250.00
  Headlight, Model A Ford, Pair 50.00
  Hood Ormamemt, Superman, Chrome Plated White Metal 1100.00
    AUTO, HOOD ORNAMENT, see also Lalique
  Hood Ornament, Bulldog, Mack Truck, Chrome .... 30.00 To 85.00
  Hood Ornament, Butterfly, With Auto–Con–Den–So–Meter, Nickel Plated 225.00
  Hood Ornament, Horse, 1950s 30.00
  Hood Ornament, Hudson, 1949 .... 85.00
  Hood Ornament, Indian Head, Pontiac, 1930 .... 55.00
  Hood Ornament, Kewpie Doll 1210.00
  Hood Ornament, Leaping Greyhound, Ford 100.00
  Hood Ornament, Nude Woman, Graham Paige, 1927 .... 40.00
  Hood Ornament, Spirit of The Wind, Bust of Goddess, Blowing Hair 1045.00
  Hood Ornament, Viking, Chevrolet, 1929 .... 125.00
  Horn, Boa Constrictor Shape, Rubber Squeeze Bulb, Glass Eyes, Metal 2600.00
  Horn, Model T, Brass, 4 Tubes 45.00

Horn, Pontiac, 1958	12.00
Hubcap, Buick, 5 In., Pair	10.00
Hubcap, Chevrolet, 1957	15.00
Hubcap, Ford, Model B, Brass	30.00
Hubcap, Plymouth, Ship	15.00
Kit, Standard Oil, Salesman's Sample, 15 Vials, 5 Jars, Grease, 1890s	95.00
Knob, Gearshift, Green & Cream Swirl Glass	20.00
Knob, Steering Wheel, Blue & White Swirl	58.00
License Plate Attachment, State Farm, Metal	15.00
License Plate, California, 1935	4.50
License Plate, Connecticut, 1911, Porcelain	95.00
License Plate, Idaho, 1924	10.00
License Plate, Idaho, 1937	14.00
License Plate, Idaho, Potato, 1928	75.00
License Plate, Illinois, 1936	18.00
License Plate, Indiana, 1916, Pair	25.00
License Plate, Massachusetts, 1915, Porcelain	50.00
License Plate, Massachusetts, 1919	10.00
License Plate, Michigan, 1939, Original Wrapper, Pair ...	32.00
License Plate, Michigan, 1953, Original Wrapper	15.00
License Plate, Missouri, 1929	30.00
License Plate, New Hampshire, 1915, Porcelain	50.00
License Plate, New Jersey, 1908, Pair	350.00
License Plate, New Jersey, 1913, Porcelain	75.00
License Plate, New York, 1912, Porcelain	95.00
License Plate, North Dakota, 1933, Original Wrapper, Pair ...	32.00
License Plate, Oregon, 1923	10.00
License Plate, Pennsylvania, 1914, Porcelain	50.00
License Plate, Wartime Soybean, 1944	10.00
License Plate, Wisconsin, 1929	10.00
Luggage Carrier, Running Board, For Model T	26.00
Manual, Owner's, Buick, 1969	12.00
Radiator Cap, Chevrolet, 1932	75.00
Radiator Cap, Chevrolet, Viking, 1929	175.00
Ratchet Set, For Cole 8 Touring Car, Fitted Box	585.00
Screwdriver, Overland Willys Knight	20.00
Spotlight, Hudson	40.00
Tire Gauge, Schrader, Lee Tires, Conshohocken, Nickel Over Brass ...	10.00
Tire Pump, Cast Iron, 1926 .... 22.00 To 28.00
Tire Pump, Model T, Running Board	55.00
Vase, Floral Design, Clear	125.00
Vase, Frosted Glass, Design, Pair	50.00
Vase, Rolls–Royce, C.1915, 10 In.	37.50
Wheel Cover Spinner, For Rambler Classic, Unused, Set of 4 ...	45.00
Wrench, Adjustable, Marked Ford USA	12.00
Wrench, Lug, Ford Motor Co., 1920s	25.00
Wrench, Model T, Lug & Spark Plug	5.00

Autumn Leaf pattern china was made for the Jewel Tea Company beginning in 1933. Hall China Company of East Liverpool, Ohio, Crooksville China Company of Crooksville, Ohio, Harker Potteries of Chester, West Virginia, and Paden City Pottery, Paden City, West Virginia, made dishes with this design. Autumn Leaf has remained popular and was made by Hall China Company until 1978. Some other pieces in the Autumn Leaf pattern are still being made.

AUTUMN LEAF, Baker, Cover, Hall	25.00
Baker, Open, Jewel Tea	22.00
Bean Pot, 1 Handle, Hall	195.00
Bowl Set, Stacking, 3 Piece	58.00
Bowl, Jewel Tea, 6 1/4 In.	7.50
Bowl, Set, Nesting, 1978, 3 Piece	55.00
Bowl, Vegetable, Jewel Tea, 9 In.	55.00
Bowl, Vegetable, Oval	14.50

Cake Lifter, Hall 185.00
Cake Plate, Metal Stand 100.00
Card, Playing, Pinochle 185.00
Casserole, Cover, Jewel Tea, 8 1/2 In. 30.00
Clock, Electric 425.00
Coaster, Jewel Tea .... 4.00 To 8.00
Coffee Server, Jewel Tea, 9 Cup .... 20.00 To 45.00
Coffeepot, Drip, China Insert 185.00
Coffeepot, Percolator, Electric, Hall 275.00
Cookie Jar, Jewel Tea 50.00
Cookie Jar, Tab Handles, Jewel Tea 145.00
Cookie Jar, Tootsie 90.00
Cup & Saucer, Jewel Tea .... 4.00 To 9.00
Custard, Hall ....4.00 To 11.00
Gravy Boat 18.00
Grease Cover, Hall 8.00
Grease Pot, Tab Handle Cover, Hall 9.00
Jar, Grease, Jewel Tea .... 15.00 To 17.50
Jug, Ball, Hall 30.00
Jug, Ball, Ice Lip, Hall 11.00
Mug, Irish Coffee, Jewel Tea 60.00
Pie Baker 10.00
Pitcher, Ice Lip, Jewel Tea, Globular 20.00
Pitcher, Tilt, Hall 19.00
Pitcher, Utility 15.00
Plate, 6 In. 4.00
Plate, 9 In. 8.00
Platter, Large 12.00
Salt & Pepper, Jewel Tea, Range 15.00
Soup, Cream 20.00
Soup, Dish 10.00
Stack Set .... 50.00 To 65.00
Sugar & Creamer, Hall 20.00
Tablecloth, Jewel Tea, 54 X 72 In. 95.00
Teapot, Aladdin, Jewel Tea .... 39.75 To 50.00
Tray, Jewel Tea, Tin, Oval 45.00

AVON, see Bottle, Avon

Baccarat glass was made in France by La Compagnie des Cristalleries de Baccarat, located 150 miles from Paris. The factory was started in 1765. The firm went bankrupt and began operating again about 1822. Cane and millefiori paperweights were made during the 1860 to 1880 period. The firm is still working near Paris making paperweights and glasswares.

BACCARAT, Biscuit Jar, Cranberry 675.00
Bowl, Swirl, Depose, 9 In. 92.50
Bust, Woman, Flowing Hair, Draped From Head Over Shoulders 195.00
Castor, Pickle, Heavy Swirl, Reed & Barton Frame, 3 1/2 In. 85.00
Castor, Pickle, Swirl, Ornamented, Signed 225.00
Celery Tray, Rose Teinte Swirl, 9 1/2 In. .... 52.00 To 78.00
Compote, Aqua, Gold Trim 30.00
Dish, Rose Teinte Swirl, Pedestal, Signed, 5 1/2 In. 70.00
Figurine, Porcupine, Crystal, Signed 155.00
Figurine, Wild Boar, Crystal, Signed .... 125.00 To 145.00
Goblet, Upper Half Clear, Lower Half 8 Cut Panels, 6 Piece 150.00
Lamp, Hurricane, Amberina, Prisms, Etched Shade, 21 1/2 In., Pair 1000.00
Lamp, Piano, Twist Fluted Design, Prism Pendants, 37 In. 1000.00
Paperweight, Butterfly 1540.00
Paperweight, Butterfly & White Clematis 8100.00
Paperweight, Millefiori, 6 Different Animals, Multicolored Canes 1975.00
Paperweight, Millefiori, Animals & Flower Design, 2 In. ....Illus 450.00
Paperweight, Pansy 2255.00
Paperweight, Scattered Millefiori, Lacy Ground, Miniature 950.00
Paperweight, Sulfide, Adlai Stevenson, Tangerine .... 50.00 To 95.00

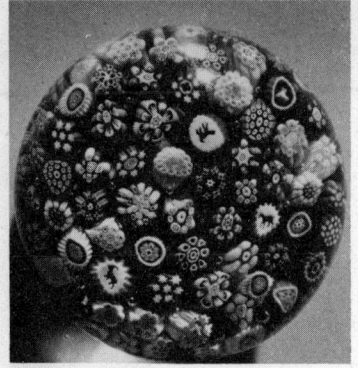

If using a glass shelf to display a paperweight collection, be sure it is strong enough. Ideal size is 18 inches long, 4 inches deep, ¼ inch thick. Paperweights are very heavy and collectors tend to add "just one more" and overload a shelf. Glass will become more fragile with age.

Baccarat, Paperweight, Millefiori, Animals & Flower Design, 2 In.

Paperweight, Sulfide, Andrew Jackson, Green	200.00
Paperweight, Sulfide, Buccaneer, Red	140.00
Paperweight, Sulfide, Eleanor Roosevelt, Amethyst, Star Cut	200.00
Paperweight, Sulfide, Harry Truman, Yellow	80.00
Paperweight, Sulfide, Herbert Hoover, Cobalt Blue	100.00
Paperweight, Sulfide, John F. Kennedy, White, Red Ground	275.00
Paperweight, Sulfide, Martin Luther King Jr., Gold, Teal Ground	160.00
Paperweight, Sulfide, Patrick Henry, White, Green Ground	75.00
Paperweight, Sulfide, Pope John XXIII, White, Amber Ground	375.00
Paperweight, Sulfide, Theodore Roosevelt, Amethyst	200.00
Paperweight, Sulfide, Thomas Paine, White, Azure Ground	75.00
Paperweight, Sulfide, Thomas Paine, White, Clear Ground	250.00
Paperweight, Sulfide, Woodrow Wilson, Aqua, Star Cut	80.00
Paperweight, Victorian Vase, Crystal, Controlled Bubble, Red	110.00
Paperweight, Wheat Flower, Yellow, Brown	2300.00
Paperweight, White Dahlia, Blue Ground	350.00
Perfume Bottle, Geometric Cut Crystal, Art Deco, 8 In.	115.00
Perfume Bottle, Houbigant, Colonial Scene	185.00
Perfume Bottle, L'Heure Bleu, Box	75.00
Perfume Bottle, Rose Amber To Clear, 5 1/2 In.	80.00
Perfume Bottle, Signed, 4 1/2 In.	40.00
Rose Bowl, Herringbone	360.00
Tumbler, Bluish Green, Signed	135.00
Vase, Bamboo Branch Form, Crawling Insect, Signed, 1890, 8 1/2 In.	450.00
Vase, Fan, Raised Butterflies, Flowers, Trees, 5 1/2 In.	150.00
Vase, Milk Glass, Hand Painted Songbird, Crescent Moon, 9 3/4 In.	110.00

 Badges have been used since before the Civil War. Collectors search for examples of all types, including law enforcement and company identification badges. Well-known prison or law enforcement badges are most desirable. Most are made of nickel or brass. Many recent reproductions have been made.

BADGE, American Bureau of Shipping, Surveyor, Brass	32.00
Bill Hickok, Raisin Bran	7.50
Cap, St. Louis Public Service Co., City Transit, Enameled, 1920s	7.50
Census, United States, Eagle On Top, 1910, 1 3/4 In.	30.00
Chauffeur, California, 1931	6.00
Chauffeur, Colorado, 1954	20.00
Chauffeur, Indiana, 1927, Brass	10.00
Chauffeur, Minnesota, 1934	23.00
Deputy Forest Warden, Rhode Island	60.00
Deputy Sheriff, Massachusetts, Blue & Gold Cloisonne	35.00

Deputy Special Officer, Bureau of Indian Affairs, Shield–Type	50.00
Detective Post J.D.C., Nickel Plated Brass	12.00
G.A.R., Wisconsin State Encampment, May 20–22, 1896, Package	20.00
Horse Racing, Patrol, American Jockey Club, 1900	62.00
Illinois Federation of Labor, Ribbon, 1909	15.00
Illinois State Fair, Brass, Golden Jubilee, 1902	15.00
Infantry, Cap, Crossed Rifles, Gilt, U.S. Model 1896	8.95
LaCienega Gun Club, 1941	22.00
Mail Handlers, Frisco, Nickel Plated	50.00
Membership, Society of Cincinnati, Silversmiths, Enameled Gold	3250.00
Military, Souvenir 1914 Encampment, Detroit	20.00
Miner's, Eldorado Mining Beaverlodge, Brass	5.00
Night Watchman's, Larkin Co., 1900	50.00
Patrolman, Mt. Vernon, Ohio, Chrome Plate, Screw Back	40.00
Police, Chicago, Pie Plate	75.00
Police, Indian Territory, 19th Century	150.00
Police, Special, Glenns Falls, New York, Silver Plate	35.00
Postmasters' Convention, 1906	50.00
Railroad, Road & Track Supply Assoc., Metal, 2 Part, 1910	15.00
Scandinavian Fraternity of America, Ribbon	17.00
Southwest Security, Inc., Special Officer, 6–Point Star	35.00
Spanish–American War Veteran, Eagle, Wreath, Guns, 1898–1902, 5 In.	65.00
Women's Western Gold Association, Low Net, Brass	10.00
Yellow Cab, Chrome, Yellow, Black, Fifth Avenue Uniform Co., Chicago	55.00

BAG, BEADED, see Purse

Metal banks have been made since 1868. There are still banks, mechanical banks, and registering banks (those which show the total money deposited on the face of the bank). Many old banks have been reproduced since the 1950s in iron or plastic.

BANK, 3 Wise Monkeys, Cast Iron, 3 1/4 X 3 1/2 In.	225.00
8 O'Clock Coffee, Red, Tin	8.00 To 10.00
Abe Lincoln, Lincoln Foods, Unslit Metal Cap, Glass, 9 In.	30.00
Acorn Shape, Blue, Cherokee Pottery	68.00
Acorn Stoves, Stoneware	4.00
Acorn, Black Barnyard Scene, 7 1/2 In.	185.00
Addams Family Thing, Box	95.00
Airplane, P–38, Hubley, 9 In.	45.00
Alice In Wonderland, Disney	85.00
Andy Gump, Thrift, Pocket	345.00
Andy Panda, Lantz	59.00
Apple, Cast Iron	750.00 To 775.00
Atlas Preserve Jar, Miniature	12.00
Bank of Industry, Blacksmith On Front, Kenton	575.00
Barney & Bam Bam, Plastic, Hanna Barbera Prod., Large	35.00
Barrel Shape, Stoneware, Brown Glaze	48.00
Basket, Woven, Cast Iron	110.00
Battleship Maine	360.00
Bear, Celluloid, 7 In.	16.00
Bear, Holding Tray, Cast Iron	150.00
Bear, On Hind Legs, Painted Cast Iron, Slot On Head, 6 1/4 In.	66.00
Bear, Snow Crest, Refrigerator Bottle, Glass, 8 In.	30.00
Bear, Teddy In Overalls Pushing Flowered Cart, Porcelain, 7 X 7 In.	35.00
Beauty, Arcade, 4 3/4 In.	50.00
Beaver, Chalkware	12.00
Beehive, Cast Iron, Gold Paint, 2 3/8 In.	65.00
Beehive, Whiting No.169, 7 In.	200.00
Benjamin Franklin Thrift, Marx	55.00 To 80.00
Betsy Ross Tea, Tin	8.00
Big Boy, Doll Shape, Package, 1973	10.00 To 25.00
Big Boy, Vinyl, 9 In.	5.00
Billiken, On Throne	75.00 To 95.00
Black Boy, Nodder, Composition, Germany	450.00
Black Girl, 2 Faces	125.00

Black On Watermelon, Nodder, Wearing Straw Hat 50.00
Black, Sharecropper, Iron, 5 1/2 In. 155.00
Bluebird, Cast Iron 295.00
Book, Franklin Savings Institution, Greenfield, Mass, Red, 4 1/2 In. 65.00
Book, Frigidaire 40.00
Book, Key, California Western State Life Insurance 65.00
Book, Savings For Baby, Toys & Stork Holding Baby, Metal 55.00
Bosco, Glass Bottom, Clown Top 14.00
Buffalo, Brown & White Sponged, Pottery 145.00
Building, Flat Iron, Cast Iron 350.00
Building, Gothic Style, Cast Iron 95.00
Building, Home Bank, Polychrome Paint, Cast Iron, 5 1/4 In. 700.00
Building, Home Savings, Whiting No.279, 3 1/2 In. 75.00
Building, Independence Hall Tower, Cast Iron 220.00
Building, Independence Hall, Philadelphia, Glass, 1876, 5 1/2 In. 500.00
Building, Jefferson County Bank, Jefferson, Wisc. 50.00
Building, Slot In Chimney, Whiting No.300, 3 In. 200.00
Building, Whiting No.424, 3 X 2 In. 45.00
Building, Woolworth, Whiting No.386, 8 In. 75.00
Bust of Franklin D. Roosevelt, Metal 50.00
Buster Brown, Cast Iron 175.00
Cabin, Cast Iron 200.00
Calumet, Paper Litho & Tin, 5 1/2 In. 66.00
Camel, A.C. Williams, Cast Iron, 1920s, 7 1/4 X 6 1/4 In. 265.00
Camel, Cast Iron, 1900, 7 In. 315.00
Camel, Cast Iron, Whiting, No.201, Large 100.00
Campbell Kids, A.C. Williams, 3 5/16 In. 225.00
Captain Kidd, 5 5/8 X 4 1/8 In. .... 295.00 To 350.00
Car, Chevrolet, Convertible, Promotional, 1954 .... 65.00
Car, Chevrolet, Ivory Over Turquoise, Verse On Bottom 60.00
Car, Flintmobile, Box 30.00
Car, Ford, Model T, Banthrico, Metal 25.00
Car, Nash, Rush Motors, Columbus, Ohio, 1949 .... 65.00
Castle, Cast Iron, Late 1800s 65.00
Cat's Head, Porcelain, 2 1/4 In. 235.00
Cat, Arcade, Cast Iron, 1912 .... 110.00
Charlie Chaplin, Glass 175.00
Chocolat Menier Savings, Vending, Tin Litho, 10 In. 198.00
Church Towers, Cast Iron .... 525.00 To 550.00
Church, Tin, Chein 25.00
Cleves National Bank, Glass, Metal 5.00
Clock, Street, Cast Iron 300.00
Clown, Chalkware, 13 In. 45.00
Clown, Chein, Tin, 5 In. 40.00
Clown, Riding Spotted Pig, Chalkware, Dated 1949, 10 1/2 In. 45.00
Columbus Safe, Iron 125.00
Cosmos Spar Varnish, Tin 20.00
Cottage, Staffordshire 135.00
Cow, Holstein, Cast Iron 145.00
Cow, Standing, Cast Iron, Gilt Paint, 5 1/2 In. 195.00
Cowboy On Horse, Cragstan, Tin 140.00
Crazy Mouse, Graduation Dress, Standing On Pile of Books 30.00
Cupid, Chalkware 25.00
Cutie, Hubley, 3 7/8 In. 50.00
Darth Vader, Plastic, Box 25.00
Decker's Iowana Pig, Gold Paint, Cast Iron 275.00
Devil, 2 Faces.Cast Iron 450.00
Dime Register, 3 Coin, Recordo Coin Safe, Fidelity Investment Assoc. 22.50
Dime Register, City Deposit, Chrome 3.00
Dime Register, Clock Shape, Notre Dame Logo, Opens At 10.00, 7 1/2 In. 135.00
Dime Register, Lucky, Tin 35.00
Dime Register, Piggy, Opens At 5.00, 1950s 15.00
Dime Register, Snow White, 1939 ....90.00 To 160.00
Dime Register, Superman 55.00

Dime Register, Uncle Sam, 3 Coin 35.00
Dino, Sinclair 20.00
Dog, Basset Hound, 3 1/8 In. 950.00
Dog, Boston Bull Terrier, Painted Cast Iron, 5 1/2 In. 110.00
Dog, Boxer, Hubley, 4 1/2 X 3 7/8 In. 50.00
Dog, Bulldog With Bee, Cast Iron 58.00
Dog, Bulldog, Painted Cast Iron, 4 1/4 In. 38.50
Dog, Fido Pup, Bee On Bottom 85.00
Dog, Fido, White Paint, Cast Iron, 5 In. 49.50
Dog, I Hear A Call, Cast Iron 75.00
Dog, On Tub, Cast Iron .... 100.00 To 130.00
Dog, Retriever With Bundle, Gold Harness, Cast Iron, 3 3/4 In. 45.00
Dog, Scotty, Seated, White Metal, 6 In. 75.00
Dog, Scotty, Standing, Cast Iron, 3 5/16 In. 100.00
Dog, Snoopy, Glass 13.00
Dog, Spaniel With Trap, Hubley, Cast Iron, 3 3/4 In. 115.00
Dog, Spaniel, Cast Iron, 9 1/2 In. 70.00
Dog, St. Bernard With Pack, Cast Iron, 3 3/4 X 5 1/2 In. 45.00
Dog, With Backpack, Cast Iron, 5 1/2 In. 75.00
Dog, With Pack, Whiting 225.00
Donkey, Arcade, Cast Iron, 4 5/8 In. 85.00
Donkey, White Blanket, Red Border, Iron Saddle, 3 1/2 In. 125.00
Doughboy, Soldier, Grey Iron Casting Co. 450.00
Dove, Polychrome Paint, Chalk, 11 In. 350.00
Dr. Ross Dog Food, Can Shape, 1950s 4.00
Dr. Zaius, Planet of The Apes 20.00
Dutch Boy, Cast Iron 65.00
Electrolux Refrigerator, Tin 25.00
Electrolux, Cast Iron 28.00
Elephant With Howdah, Cast Iron, 6 3/8 In. 60.00
Elephant, Chein 50.00
Elephant, Gray, Cast Iron 50.00
Elephant, On Tub, Cast Iron 130.00
Elephant, On Wheels, Painted Cast Iron, 4 In. 88.00
Elephant, Painted Cast Iron, Swivel Trunk, 3 1/2 In. 132.00
Elephant, Seated, Trumpeting, White Metal, 5 In. 35.00
Elf, Cast Iron 180.00
Elmer Fudd, Cast Iron .... 145.00 To 200.00
Emerson Radio, Bakelite 29.00
Emigrant Industrial Savings Bank, Eagle 12.00
Fairy Godmother, Pottery, Disney 25.00
Ferdinand Bull, Composition 150.00
Ferry Boat, Cast Iron 300.00
Flintstones, Wilma & Fred, Pottery 85.00
Fortune Ship, Cast Iron, 5 3/48 In. 600.00
Frankenstein, Box 18.00
Fred Flintstone, Plastic, Hanna Barbera Prod., Large 35.00
Furnace, Gem Heaters Save Money, Cast Iron, 5 In. .... 140.00 To 220.00
General Pershing, Bronze Electroplate, 7 3/4 In. 125.00
General Pershing, Cast Iron .... 125.00 To 160.00
Girl, With Sheep, Cast Iron 120.00
Give Me A Penny, Cast Iron .... 165.00 To 200.00
Globe, Depositors Savings, Litho Paper On Metal, Akron, Oh., 4 In. 88.00
Globe, On Stand, Cast Iron, 5 1/4 In. 110.00
Globe, Tin, Chein 9.00
Goodyear Blimp, Pottery 45.00
Gorilla, Seated, Brass, 4 In. 40.00
Green Giant, Musical 85.00
Happy Days, Chein, Tin 15.00
Hen On Nest, Brown Comb, Cream Ground, Pottery, 3 1/2 In. 5.00
Hippo, Windup, Hippo Swallows Coin In Mouth, 1960s 70.00
Honey Bear, Cast Iron .... 775.00 To 850.00
Horse & Wagon, Montgomery Ward, No.4 .... 10.00
Horse, Gold & White Paint, Cast Iron, 4 In. 100.00

Horse, On Hind Legs, Cast Iron 95.00
Horse, On Tub, A.C. Williams, 1920s, 5 5/16 In. 125.00
Horse, Prancing, Oval Base, Cast Iron 100.00
House, Cast Iron, Small 30.00
Humble Oil, Tiger 20.00
Ice Cream Freezer, Save Your Money Freeze It 250.00
Indian Chief, Bust, Cast Iron, Gold, 5 In. 60.00
Indian Head, Cast Iron, 5 In. 65.00
Indian Head, Painted, Redware, 5 1/2 In. 20.00
Indian, Cast Iron, 6 In. ....90.00 To 150.00
Joe Louis, Jar, Nash's Mustard 14.00
John Deere, Centennial, Tin, 1940 .... 35.00 To 68.50
Judd Clock, Cast Iron 300.00
Jug, Dixon National Bank, Dixon, Illinois, Stoneware 495.00
Junior Cash Register, Nickeled Cast Iron, 4 1/4 In. 93.50
Kodak, Nickeled Cast Iron, 5 In. 330.00
Kyser & Rex, Small House, Cast Iron, 1880 .... 175.00
Land of Israel, Tin, Map Picture 15.00
Li'L Abner, Windup 395.00
Liberty Bell, Cast Iron .... 65.00 To 75.00
Liberty Bell, Whiting No.279, 3 1/2 In. 45.00
Liberty Bell, With Yoke, Arcade, 1925, 3 1/2 In. 25.00
Lincoln Log Cabin, Van Dyke Teas 125.00
Lion & Cub, Papier–Mache, 5 1/2 In. 15.00
Lion, On Tub, Gold Paint, Cast Iron 55.00
Little Lulu, 8 In. ....8.00 To 18.00
Little Max's Lunch, Plastic 10.00
Log Cabin, Milk Glass ....45.00 To 100.00
Log Cabin, Syrup, Tin 595.00
Lucky Joe, Nash's Prepared Mustard, Chicago On Metal Cap, Glass, 4 In. 17.50
Lyons Tea, Tin 800.00
Magician, Cast Iron 2300.00
Main Street Trolley, Cast Iron, 3 X 6 3/4 In. 275.00
Mama Squirrel, Reading To Baby On Log, Chalkware 22.50
Mammy, Cast Iron .... 120.00 To 170.00
Man, Hands On Hips, Cast Iron 125.00
Mary & Lamb, Cast Iron .... 375.00 To 400.00

 Mechanical banks were first made about 1870. Any bank with moving parts is considered mechanical. The metal banks made before World War I are the most desirable. Copies and new designs of mechanical banks have been made in metal or plastic since the 1920s.

Mechanical, 2 Frogs, Cast Iron 650.00
Mechanical, Acrobat, Iron 550.00
Mechanical, Artillery 1750.00
Mechanical, Astro World, Rocket Ship 60.00
Mechanical, Baseball Pitcher, To Batter, To Catcher, Book of Knowledge 125.00
Mechanical, Boy On Trapeze, Cast Iron, Restored, 9 1/4 In. 825.00
Mechanical, Building, U.S. Bank, Cast Iron 6750.00
Mechanical, Bulldog 1350.00
Mechanical, Cabin, Darkie In Door, 4 3/16 In. .... 400.00 To 875.00
Mechanical, Cabin, Painted Cast Iron, 4 1/4 In. 121.00
Mechanical, Cat & Mouse 2750.00
Mechanical, Clown 325.00
Mechanical, Clown, On Ball, Cast Iron 2000.00
Mechanical, Darktown Battery, Cast Iron, 9 7/8 In. 1100.00
Mechanical, Eagle & Eaglets, Painted Cast Iron, 6 3/4 In. .... 495.00 To 775.00
Mechanical, Elephant, 3 Stars, Push Tail, Trunk Throws Coin Into Head 650.00
Mechanical, Elephant, Howdah, Man Pops Out, Painted Iron, 6 3/4 In. 425.00
Mechanical, Fortune Teller, Savings Bank, Cast Iron, 5 1/2 In. 385.00
Mechanical, Frog, Polychrome Paint, Cast Iron, 4 1/4 In. 85.00
Mechanical, Hall's Excelsior, 1869, 5 1/8 In. 495.00
Mechanical, I Always Dis 'Spise A Mule, Boy On Bench, 10 1/16 In. 1850.00

Mechanical, Jolly Minstrel 145.00
Mechanical, Jolly Nigger, Aluminum 135.00
Mechanical, Jolly Nigger, Cast Iron, 1882 .... 225.00 To 385.00
Mechanical, Jolly Nigger, With Top Hat, Aluminum 115.00
Mechanical, Liberty Bell Memorial, Painted Iron, Brass Bell, 6 In. 450.00
Mechanical, Mammy & Child, Cast Iron, 7 1/2 In. 2100.00
Mechanical, Mammy & Child, Pat. 1884 .... 6750.00
Mechanical, Mammy, With Spatula, Cast Iron 75.00
Mechanical, Mason, Painted Cast Iron, 7 1/2 In. 2200.00
Mechanical, Mule Entering Barn, Cast Iron, Pat. 1880, 8 1/2 In. 1500.00
Mechanical, Organ Grinder & Monkey .... 250.00 To 595.00
Mechanical, Organ Playing Monkey, 2 Dancers, Book of Knowledge, Iron 150.00
Mechanical, Paddy & His Pig, 1882 Pat. 525.00
Mechanical, Paddy & Pig, Cast Iron, 7 In. 1350.00
Mechanical, Punch & Judy, Book of Knowledge, Iron, 1950 .... 85.00
Mechanical, Punch & Judy, Cast Iron, Painted, 7 1/2 In. 2200.00
Mechanical, Rocket Ship, Strato Moon 50.00
Mechanical, Rocket, Metal, Duro–Mold, Box 75.00
Mechanical, Scotsman, Painted Cast Iron, Nods Head, 7 3/4 In. 192.00
Mechanical, Southern Comfort 50.00
Mechanical, Stump Speaker, Painted, Cast Iron, 10 In. .... 425.00 To 775.00
Mechanical, Tammany Hall, Cast Iron, Polychrome, Dated 1879 .... 300.00 To 365.00
Mechanical, Teddy & Bear, Cast Iron, 10 1/8 In. .... 1100.00 To 3250.00
Mechanical, Trick Dog, 6 Part Base, 8 3/4 In. 935.00
Mechanical, Uncle Sam, Cast Iron, 10 5/8 In. 125.00
Mechanical, Uncle Sam, Satchel & Umbrella 1800.00
Mechanical, Uncle Sam, Shepard Hardware .... 2150.00 To 2500.00
Mechanical, Watch Me Grow, Tin Litho, Apex, 6 In. 38.50
Mechanical, William Tell, Cast Iron .... 750.00 To 1250.00
Merry–Go–Round, Semi–Mechanical, Meyers No.158 .... 250.00
Middy, Gold, Whiting No.26, 5 1/4 In. 150.00
Minnie Mouse, Illco Toy Co., 11 1/2 In. 15.00
Minute Man, Cast Iron 275.00
Monkey, Ceramic, Brown Glaze 185.00
Monkeys, 3, Cast Iron 225.00
Moose, Antlers, Plastic 25.00
Mosque, Cast Iron, Whiting No.416, 4 1/2 In. .... 65.00 To 85.00
Mr. Peanut, 1950s 13.00
Mr. Peanut, Red, Box, 1938 .... 475.00
Mr. Peanut, Yellow, Box, 1938 .... 475.00
Mutt & Jeff, Cast Iron, 5 1/4 In. .... 125.00 To 250.00
Nodder, Black, On Watermelon 50.00
Oilcan Harry, 1950 .... 185.00
Oliver Hardy, Plastic, 1974 .... 40.00
Owl, Be Wise, Save Money, Painted Cast Iron, 5 In. .... 85.00 To 150.00
Pass Around The Hat, Cast Iron 75.00
Phillips 66, Oil For Your Motor, Tin 30.00
Phillips Premium Gasoline, Plastic 10.00
Pig, Brown Sponging, White, Pottery, 5 3/4 In. 35.00
Pig, Christmas Roast, Cast Iron 150.00
Pig, Decker's Iowana, Cast Iron, 4 1/2 In. 75.00
Pig, Howdy Doody On Pig's Back, Ceramic 250.00
Pig, Marbelized Glaze, Pottery, 5 In. 35.00
Pig, Pink, For My Cadillac 30.00
Pig, Save With Marathon, Ohio Oil Co., Amber Glass 22.00
Pig, Seated, This Is Pete, Be Fed Coins, Mission To Lepers, 4 7/8 In. 45.00
Pig, Sitting, Cast Iron 85.00
Pig, The Wise 165.00
Pig, White Clay, Rockingham Glaze, 5 5/8 In. 25.00
Pig, Wise, Hubley, C.1930, 6 5/8 In. 25.00
Piggy, Cream With Brown Spots, Ceramic 35.00
Piggy, Green & White, Spongeware, 3 1/4 X 5 1/2 In. 175.00
Pinocchio, Bronze Cast Metal 20.00
Pirate, On Chest, Cast Iron 50.00

Planet of The Apes, Galen, 1974, 10 3/4 In. 20.00
Planters Peanuts, Figural, 8 1/2 In. 22.00
Policeman, Cast Iron ....95.00 To 125.00
Poll–Parrot, Tin 15.00
Popeye, Animated, Knockout, Metal 950.00
Radiator Cap, Model T, Red Goose Shoes 300.00
Radio, Tin, Marx 15.00
RCA Nipper, Dog, Snow Dome 35.00
Red Goose Shoes, Cast Iron .... 125.00 To 150.00
Refrigerator, GE, Cast Iron 58.00
Refrigerator, Servel Electrolux, Cast Iron 22.50
Remember Pearl Harbor 55.00
Rival Dog Food, Tin 10.00
Rocket, Jupiter, Box, 1950s 40.00
Rocket, Metal, 1960s, Large 35.00
Rooster, Pea Necklace, Pennsylvania German, Pottery 495.00
Saddle Horse, A.C. Williams, Cast Iron, 2 3/4 X 3 3/16 In. .... 150.00 To 360.00
Safe, Columbus, Cast Iron, 5 In. 85.00
Safe, Daisy, Tin 30.00
Safe, Floral, Cast Iron 100.00
Safe, Ideal, Cast Iron, 5 X 6 1/2 In. 120.00
Safe, National Bank, Cast Iron 60.00
Safe, Tiny Mite, Metal 20.00
Safety Deposit, Alarm, Night Light 165.00
Santa Claus, Asleep In Chair, Pot Metal 60.00
Santa Claus, Chalkware, 15 In. 25.00
Santa Claus, On Roof, Ringing Bell, Battery Operated, Tin ....85.00 To 125.00
Santa Claus, Painted Chalkware, 11 In. 132.50
Santa Claus, Sitting In Rocker, Tin 65.00
Santa Claus, Somerset Savings Bank, Mass., 1910, 8 In. 110.00
Santa Claus, Stoneware, Austria, 1918 .... 200.00
Santa Claus, Toys, Fireplace, Reindeer, Tin, 4 X 3 In. .... 195.00 To 225.00
Save For A Rainy Day Umbrella, Silver Plate, Napier, 6 In. 55.00
Seaman's Service, With Bag Over Shoulder, Pottery 30.00
Service Station, Tin Litho 15.00
Skeleton, Windup, Tin 35.00
Slot Machine, Cast Iron, 10 X 7 In. 500.00
Smokey The Bear, 1972 .... 35.00
Snoopy, Silver Plate 7.00
Soldier, Minuteman, Hubley, 1905, ... 325.00
State, Whiting No.442, Small 125.00
Stove, Mellow Furnace Co., Cast Iron 65.00
Streetcar, Cast Iron .... 300.00 To 325.00
Sunbonnet Sue, Cast Iron, 7 1/2 In. 75.00
Sunoco Gasoline, Plastic 10.00
Tally–Ho, Cast Iron 150.00
Tank, World War I, Cast Iron 90.00
Teddy, A.C. Williams, 1919, 3 1/2 In. 175.00
Telephone, Nickel Plated, Meyers No.227 .... 350.00
Telephone, Wall, Tin 42.00
Time Safe, Cast Iron 350.00
Tom Sawyer & Huckleberry Finn, Cast Iron 80.00
Top Hat, Steel Bank, Pass Around The Hat, Cast Iron 85.00
Treasure Chest, Sheet Metal 20.00
Truck, Armored, Brinks, Combination Lock, 1940s 200.00
Truck, Delivery, Servco Gas, The Tank Is Bank 35.00
Truck, Winn Dixie 16.50
U.S. Mail, Cast Iron, Green, 3 1/2 In. 65.00
Uncle Sam, Roseville 75.00
W.C. Fields, Plaster, 11 In. 60.00
Washington Monument, Whiting No.360, Cast Iron, 6 In. 125.00
Washington, Bust, Pedestal, Cast Iron 175.00
White City Puzzle Savings, Nickeled Cast Iron, 2 5/8 In. 77.00
Young Negro, Painted Cast Iron, 4 1/2 In. 145.00

There is much confusion about the terms Banko, Korean ware, and Sumida. We are using the terms in the way most often used by antiques dealers and collectors. Korean ware is now called "Sumida Gawa" and is listed in this book under that heading. Banko is a group of rustic Japanese wares made in the nineteenth and twentieth centuries. Some pieces are made of mosaics of colored clay, some are fanciful teapots. Redware and other materials were also used.

BANKO, Creamer, Floral, 4 In.	45.00
Cup, Gray	50.00
Tea Set, Flying Crane Design, Yellow Enamel, 3 Piece	95.00 To 135.00
Teapot, Child's, 1875	100.00
Teapot, Elephant	85.00
Teapot, Floral, Raffia Handle, 4 In.	55.00
Teapot, Marbelized, White Glaze, Molded With 5 Masks, 1870	450.00
Vase, Tea House, Waterfall, Mezzo–Relievo, 5 In., Pair	125.00

Barbershop collectibles range from the popular red and white striped pole that used to be found in front of every shop to the small scissors and tools of the trade. Barber chairs are wanted, especially the older models with elaborate iron trim.

BARBER, Back Bar, 3 Stations, Marble Top, Koken, Walnut, 7 X 11 Ft.	4500.00
Brush, Shaving, Blue–Green Marbelized Bakelite Handle, Box	15.00
Chair, Child's, Pedal Car Design	1250.00
Chair, Child's, Philadelphia Toboggan Co., Horse Head	1700.00
Chair, Child's, Victorian, Walnut	550.00
Chair, Columbia, Brass & Hand Carved Wood	900.00
Chair, Kochs, Hydraulic, Brass Base, Oak, Green Velvet Upholstery	2000.00
Chair, Koken & Boppert, Reclining, Walnut, Dated 1881	625.00
Chair, Koken, Art Deco	550.00
Chair, Koken, Rechromed	350.00
Chair, Koken, Walnut	850.00 To 1000.00
Chair, Round Seat, Porcelain	200.00
Chair, Velvet Cover, Walnut, 1870s	1500.00
Dispenser, Brylcreem, White Letters, Black Glass, 8 Sides	255.00
Display Case, 3 Glass Shelves, Glass Doors, Maple, 60 X 52 In.	650.00
Globe, Hair Bobbing, Double Sides, Milk Glass, Etched Letters, 12 In.	285.00
Pole, Black & White Geometric Paint, Wooden, Acorn Ends, 34 In.	1200.00
Pole, Koken, Art Glass, Inside Light, 1930	3500.00
Pole, Koken, Leaded Glass, 1890s	350.00
Pole, Koken, Wall Mounted, Fluted	650.00 To 900.00
Pole, Light–Up, Molded 1 Piece, Red, White & Blue, 15 In.	385.00
Pole, Turned Wood, Kingston Mines, Illinois, 39 In.	85.00
Pole, Wall Mount, Red, White & Blue, Metal, Electrified	175.00
Pole, Wall Mount, Stars In Lower Section, Electrified	450.00
Pole, Wall Mount, Wooden, 30 In.	375.00
Razor Blade Bank, Listerine	16.00
Razor Strop, U.S. Cavalry	125.00
Shaving Brush, Yellow Bakelite Handle, 1950s, Box	15.00
Sign, Barber Science Shop Personality Haircuts, Cardboard, 1940s	15.00
Sign, Barbers Union Shop, Metal, 9 X 7 In.	15.00

Barometers are used to forecast the weather. Antique barometers with elaborate wooden cases and brass trim are the most desirable. Mercury column barometers are popular with collectors. It is difficult to find someone to repair a broken example, so be sure your barometer is in working condition.

BAROMETER, Carved Oak, Torricelli	1300.00
Convex Mirror, Silvered Dials, Wood Veneer, 38 In.	375.00
Georgian, Brass Finial, Inlaid Mahogany, 1800, 38 1/2 In.	2200.00
Hagger & Brothers, Baltimore, Early 19th Century	7700.00
Hygrodeik, Edson, Measures Relative Humidity, 1865–70	770.00
Mercury, Porcelain Face, Engish, C.1880	775.00
Silvered Brass Face, Rosewood, Woodruff's, 1860, 37 1/2 In.	400.00

Stick, Federal, Brass Bezel, Haggar & Bros., Mahogany, 36 In. 7800.00
Wheel, George III, Ebony & Satinwood Banded, Convex Glass, 46 In. 885.00
With Thermometer, Charles E. Yarge, Storm Glass, 8 3/4 In. 225.00

Basalt is a special type of ceramic invented by Josiah Wedgwood in the eighteenth century. It is a fine-grained, unglazed stoneware.

BASALT, Ashtray, Spade, Wedgwood, Black 25.00
Charger, Plain, Rolled Edge, Wedgwood, Black, 12 In. 95.00
Coffeepot, Black, Embossed Design, Dome Lid, 10 1/4 In. 300.00
Medallion, White Bust of Gentleman, Oval 35.00
Plaque, Classically Draped Figures, Oval, Framed, 8 X 11 In., Pr. 750.00
Spill Holder, Embossed Cherubs, Copper Luster Interior, 4 3/4 In. 200.00
Urn, Amphora, Scrolled Legs, Tripod Pedestal, Wedgwood, Black, 7 In. 1000.00
Urn, Black, White Design, Dancing Girls, Classical, 12 In., Pair 180.00
Urn, Floral, Wedgwood, Black, 15 1/2 In. 1650.00
BASEBALL CARDS, see Card, Baseball

Baskets of all types are popular with collectors. Indian, Japanese, African, Shaker, and many other kinds of baskets can be found. Of course, baskets are still being made; so the collector must learn to tell the age and style of the basket to determine the value.

BASKET, 4-Pocket, Splint, Painted, Wall, Handle Top 3200.00
Apple, Iron Hook 155.00
Bee Skep, Hive Shape, Small Opening On Top 95.00
Buttocks, Single Arched Handle, 6 X 8 X 10 In. 85.00
Buttocks, Woven Reed & Cane, Handle, 5 In. 60.00
Buttocks, Woven Splint, 9 3/4 X 16 1/2 X 18 In. 145.00
Buttocks, Woven Splint, Bentwood Handle, 13 X 13 1/2 X 8 In. 150.00
Buttocks, Woven Splint, Bentwood Handle, 7 1/2 In. 175.00
Buttocks, Woven Splint, Bentwood Handle, 7 1/2 X 12 X 18 In. 125.00
Buttocks, Woven Splint, Blue & Pink Paint, 5 In. 85.00
Buttocks, Woven Splint, Gray Finish, 8 1/2 X 15 X 15 In. 25.00
Buttocks, Woven Splint, Rope Twist Handle, Handmade, 9 3/4 In. 100.00
Cheese, Woven Splint, Gray Scrubbed Finish, Blue Paint, 24 In. 475.00
Clam, Brass Wire, Bent Oak Rim & Handle, John Furlow, 14 In. 351.00
Coiled, Rye-Straw, Openwork Rim, Loop, Flat Bottom, 8 3/8 X 3 In. 1225.00
Dough Rising, Pennsylvania, Coiled Rye, Wire Bound 195.00
Egg, Woven Splint, Radiating Ribs, Eye of God At Handle, 4 1/2 In. 135.00
Gathering, Flat Form, Black Paint, 30 X 18 In. 325.00
Gathering, Oak Splint, Stationary Wooden Handle, 12 In. 150.00
Gathering, Woven Splint, Worn Blue Paint, Woven Handle, 12 X 13 In. 175.00
Goose, Woven Splint, Colored Stripes, 23 In. 90.00
Half, Woven Splint, Bentwood Handle, 10 X 5 In. 65.00
Harvest, Grape, Italian, Wooden 165.00
Laundry, Woven Splint, Bentwood Rim Handles, 21 1/2 In. 120.00
Masai, Kenya, 4 5/8 X 6 1/4 In. 175.00
Masai, Kenya, Bamboo Reed & Red & Black Leather, 17 1/2 In. 105.00
Nantucket Lightship, Ferdinand Sylvaro, Label, 13 In. 1331.00
Nantucket, Lightship, Swing Handle, 7 1/2 In. 850.00
Nantucket, Oak Rim, Rattan Body, Swing Handle, L.H. Macy, 8 1/2 In. 2300.00
Nantucket, Oak Rim, Rattan Body, Swing Handle, Oval, 11 1/2 X 8 In. 335.00
Nantucket, Pocketbook Shape, Ivory Whale On Cover, C.1953 .... 675.00
Nantucket, Woven Rattan, Oak Rim, A.D. Williams, 5 X 11 X 7 3/4 In. 1100.00
Oak Splint, 2 Carved Handles, Hand Made, C.1890, 26 X 21 X 12 In. 150.00
Oak Splint, Rib Type, Stationary Wrapped Handle, 11 X 7 X 4 In. 250.00
Papago Indian, 2 Colors, 4 1/2 In. 50.00
Peach, Wide Splint, Slant Sided, Copper Fasteners, 1/2 Bushel 250.00
Picnic, Splint Bottom, Wicker Sides, 2 Lids Open From Center 60.00
Picnic, Woven Splint & Cane, Wooden Lid, Gray Paint, 5 X 7 In. 85.00
Purse, Rice Straw, Lid & Handles, Floral Design On Lid, Chinese, 4 In 180.00
Red & Green Stained Splints, Oak Handle, 8 X 8 1/2 In. 85.00
Rye Straw, 3 3/4 X 4 1/4 In. 25.00
Rye Straw, Brown Varnish, 3 1/2 X 8 3/4 In. 55.00
Rye Straw, Round, 5 1/2 In. 25.00

Sewing, Wicker, Lined, Embroidered, Net Skirt, 1890s, 16 X 15 X 3 In. 40.00
Splint, Bentwood Handle, 1/2 Bushel 55.00
Splint, Bentwood Handles, 17 X 24 X 12 In. 49.50
Splint, Potato Stamped Design, 2 Wooden Handles, 13 1/2 X 11 X 6 In 150.00
Tray, Coiled, Rye–Straw, Round, 2 1/4 X 19 3/4 In. Diam. 55.00
Wash, Round, Woven Vine, Handles, 10 In. 145.00
Wash, Woven Splint, Bentwood Rim Handles, 10 1/2 X 21 In. 55.00
Wash, Woven Splint, Bentwood Rim Handles, 11 In. 95.00
Wash, Woven Splint, Bentwood Rim Handles, 21 1/2 X 31 1/2 In. 200.00
Weaver's, Woven Splint, Bundled Grass Rim, 9 X 9 In. 55.00
Wicker, Glass Bottom Insert, Dried Butterfly & Flowers, 1935 .... 40.00
Woven Oak Splint, Swing Handle, 19th Century, 7 1/2 In. 195.00
Woven Reed, Folding Lid, Bentwood Handle, 8 1/2 In. 45.00
Woven Reed, Polychrome Floral, Oriental Export, Oval, 12 In. 45.00
Woven Splint & Sweet Grass, Melon Ribs, Eye of God Design, 10 In. 135.00
Woven Splint, Bentwood Handle, 2–Tone, 10 1/2 X 6 In. 85.00
Woven Splint, Bentwood Handle, 4 1/2 X 8 1/2 X 9 In. 25.00
Woven Splint, Bentwood Handle, 5 1/2 X 12 1/2 X 20 1/2 In. 45.00
Woven Splint, Bentwood Handle, 7 X 10 In. ....45.00 To 250.00
Woven Splint, Bentwood Handle, 8 1/2 In. ....65.00 To 450.00
Woven Splint, Bentwood Handle, Egg 125.00
Woven Splint, Bentwood Handle, Gray Scrubbed Finial, 9 In. 55.00
Woven Splint, Bentwood Handle, Green Stripes, 9 X 10 1/4 X 18 In. 30.00
Woven Splint, Bentwood Handle, Oblong, 14 X 21 In. 85.00
Woven Splint, Bentwood Handle, Oblong, 7 1/2 X 12 1/2 X 19 In. 55.00
Woven Splint, Bentwood Handle, Radiating Ribs, 11 3/4 X 18 1/2 In. 125.00
Woven Splint, Bentwood Handle, Radiating Ribs, 7 X 15 In. 75.00
Woven Splint, Bentwood Handle, Radiating Ribs, 9 X 15 In. 45.00
Woven Splint, Bentwood Handle, Red & Blue, 8 1/4 X 12 In. 115.00
Woven Splint, Bentwood Handle, Red Woven Design, Oblong, 15 X 23 In. 115.00
Woven Splint, Bentwood Handle, Reddish Brown Paint, 10 1/2 X 15 In. 115.00
Woven Splint, Bentwood Handle, Round, 7 X 13 In. 65.00
Woven Splint, Bentwood Handle, Square Base, Circular Rim, 11 X 6 In. 80.00
Woven Splint, Bentwood Handle, Vertical Shape, 8 1/2 In. 450.00
Woven Splint, Bentwood Handle, Weathered Finish, 8 X 12 X 18 In. 95.00
Woven Splint, Bentwood Rim Handles, 18 1/2 X 23 In. 55.00
Woven Splint, Bentwood Rim Handles, Oblong, 11 X 20 X 27 In. 45.00
Woven Splint, Bentwood Rim Handles, Round, 19 In. 40.00
Woven Splint, Bentwood Swivel Handle, Round, 9 X 15 In. 55.00
Woven Splint, Bundled Grass Rim, Bentwood Handle, Square, 10 1/2 In. 10.00
Woven Splint, Curlicues, Oval, 6 1/4 X 11 1/2 In. 35.00
Woven Splint, Dark Patina, Bentwood Handle, 9 In. 65.00
Woven Splint, Green, Bentwood Handle, 8 3/4 X 8 In. 75.00
Woven Splint, Loom, Green & Yellow, 9 1/2 X 9 1/2 In. 65.00
Woven Splint, Melon Rib, Eye of God Design, Bentwood Handle, 9 In. 95.00
Woven Splint, Melon Rib, Rim Handles, 8 3/4 X 16 X 18 In. 225.00
Woven Splint, Melon Rib, Woven Handle, 7 X 12 X 13 In. 75.00
Woven Splint, Oval, Red, Blue, Natural, 5 In. 65.00
Woven Splint, Potato Print Design, Cover, 9 1/2 In. 150.00
Woven Splint, Round, Curlicues On Lid, 7 1/2 In. 65.00
Woven Splint, Rye Straw Rim, Ovoid, 14 In. 25.00
Woven Splint, Signed, W.D. Hunter, 7 X 11 X 16 1/2 In. 25.00
Woven Splint, Square, Signed, 4 1/4 In. 165.00
Woven Splint, Wire Reinforced Where Handle Joins Rim, 13 In. 165.00

BATCHELDER Ernest Batchelder made ceramic and copper items in Los Angeles,
LOS ANGELES California. He died in 1957.

BATCHELDER, Tile, Stylized Ivy, Tan, Blue, Matte, 7 In. 45.00
Vase, Blue High Glaze, Omar Khayyam Pottery, 3 X 4 In. 300.00

Batman and Robin are characters from a comic strip by Bob Kane
that started in 1939. In 1966, the characters became part of a
popular television series. There have been radio and movie serials
that featured the pair. In 1989 a full–length movie was made.

BATMAN, Alarm Clock, Talking, Equity 50.00
Album, Batman Theme, Marketts, Warner Bros., 1966 .... 25.00
Album, Jan & Dean Meet Batman, Liberty 5.00
Badge, Batman & Robin Society, Charter Member 32.00
Bank, Bust of Batman, Plastic, 1974, Mego, 9 In. 45.00
Bank, Hard Plastic, Blue Cape, Transogram Co., 19 In. 43.00
Banner, Versus Joker, Cloth, 1966 .... 165.00
Bat Belt & Mask, Sealed Package, 1950s 28.00
Batcopter, Corgi Jr., Mettoy, Package, 1978 .... 15.00
Batcopter, Super Powers, Box, 1985 .... 95.00
Batmemos, Notepad Pictures Batman, 1960s, 7 X 10 In. 25.00
Batmobile, Battery Operated, Batman & Robin, Blue, Tin 250.00
Batmobile, Child's Size, Marx 150.00
Batmobile, Corgi Jr., Mettoy Co., Package, 1978 .... 15.00
Batmobile, Kenner, 1984, Box 50.00
Batmobile, Magicar, Quick–Change, Plastic, 1966, 5 In. 145.00
Batmobile, Plastic, Kenner, 1984 .... 12.00 To 15.00
Batmobile, Red Tin Lithographed, Box, 1970s, 11 1/2 In. 125.00
Batmobile, Slot Car, With Batman & Robin, Plastic, 1966, 3 In. 125.00
Batmobile, With Batman & Robin, Simms 40.00
Batmobile, With Batman & Robin, Worchester, No.17, 1966, 9 In. 105.00
Bicycle Ornament, Batman, Figural, Plastic, Empire, 1966, 8 In. 65.00
Bicycle Siren, Super Sonic, Empire, 1978 .... 25.00
Bicycle, 20 In.–Wheel 1500.00
Book Bag, Red Canvas, Batman & Robin, Dated 1982 .... 45.00
Book, Batman's Head Shape, 1967 .... 25.00
Book, Cheetah Caper, Big Little Book, 1969 .... 8.00
Book, Comic, No.110, 1957 .... 25.00
Book, Paint By Number Book, Whitman, 1966 .... 20.00
Box, Candy, The Joker, Phoenix Candy, 1966, 3 1/2 X 4 In. 15.00
Box, Slam Bang Ice Cream, Batman & Robin In Action, 1966, 1/2 Gal. 25.00
Bracelet, Charm, Gold, Batman, Robin, Joker, Penguin, Riddler, 1966 .... 65.00
Brooch, Figural, Enameled, On Card, 1966 .... 45.00
Brush, Avon, Box, 1976 .... 20.00
Button, Batman & Robin Society, Celluloid, 3 1/2 In. 10.00
Card Game, Cards, Chips, Board, 1966, Ideal 35.00
Case, Pencil, Shaped Like Car 20.00
Chair, Inflatable, 1977 .... 40.00
Cigarette Box, Candy, Cavenham Confectionery, England, 1966, 2 X 3 In 65.00
Clock, Talking Alarm, No.77 .... 125.00
Clock, Talking, With Robin, Janex Corp., 1974 .... 65.00
Colorform Secret Putty & Print Set, On Card, 1966 .... 75.00 To 90.00
Communications Console, 1976, Mego 85.00
Compass, On Card, 1966 .... 25.00
Costume & Mask, Box 15.00
Costume, Halloween, No Mask, Ben Copper Cardboard Hanger, 1976 .... 25.00
Cowl, Felt, Sticker Logo, 1973 .... 12.00
Cup, Milk Glass, 1966 .... 15.00
Display, Stand Up, Cardboard, Batman With Hands On Hips, 1966 .... 225.00
Doll, Box, 12 1/2 In. 50.00
Doll, Mego, 8 In. 25.00
Doll, Plastic, Blue Molded, Red Cape, 1966, 8 In. 45.00
Executive Set, Calendar, Pencil Sharpener, Stapler, Janex Corp, 1977 .... 115.00
Figure, Batman, Action, Mego, Unused, 8 In. 40.00
Figure, Comic Action Hero, Robin, Mego, 3 3/4 In. 50.00
Figure, Robin, Action, Mego, Unused, 8 In. 30.00
Game, Adventures of The Caped Crusader, Box, 1973 .... 20.00
Game, Batman & Robin, Hasbro, 1965 .... 25.00
Game, Batman Electronic Quiz, 1966 .... 58.00
Game, Board, Hasbro, 1978 .... 40.00
Gun, Ray, Box 40.00
Gun, Squirt, Emblem On Side, 1978 .... 5.00
Hairbrush, Avon, 1976 .... 20.00
Hand Puppet, Vinyl Body & Head, 1966 .... 25.00

Ice Cream Container, Unused, 1966 .... 65.00
Jokermobile, Van, Green, Red, Plastic, Mego, 1975, 8 In. 125.00
Lamp, Desk, 1977 .... 45.00
License Plate, Package, 1966, Miniature 28.00
Lobby Card, Batman & Robin Reading Message In Batcave, 11 X 14 In. 65.00
Lunch Box, Thermos, 1966 .... 85.00 To 95.00
Mask, Flip, & Robin 10.00
Metal Tab, Black Bat Symbol, White Ground, 1 1/2 In. 3.50
Model Kit, Batmobile, Aurora, Box, 1966 .... 350.00
Model Kit, Robin, Aurora, Box, 1966 .... 45.00
Mug, 1966 .... 15.00 To 20.00
Napkin, Paper, Package, Sealed, 1966, 7 X 7 In., 8 Piece 15.00
Night-Light, Figural, Batman's Face, Snapit, 1966 .... 25.00
Night-Light, Graphic Figural, Riddler, 9 In. 75.00
Night-Light, Snap It Mfg., Original Package, 1966 .... 25.00
Pencil Sharpener, Battery, 1977 .... 35.00
Penguinmobile, Metal Car, Penguin Driving, Corgi, 1978 .... 35.00
Photograph, TV Series, Black & White 2.50
Picture, 3 Color Airbrush Acetate Overlay, B. Wrightson, Framed 350.00
Pinball, Bagatelle, Marx, 1966, 24 X 12 In. 150.00
Pogo Stick 135.00
Poster, Movie, Batman & Robin, Bat Badguys, 1966, 14 X 22 In. 125.00
Puzzle, Batman, Robin & Villain, Watkins-Strathmore Co., 1966 .... 25.00
Race Car Set, Box 125.00
Radio, 1978 .... 80.00 To 175.00
Record Set, Batman Book, 1976 .... 3.00
Record, Batman & Robin, Die-Cut Sleeve, Pair 20.00
Record, Book, Stacked Cards, 45 RPM, Power Records, 1975 .... 5.00
Record, Robin, Die-Cut Sleeve, Pair 20.00
Record, Scarecrow's Miracle, Power Records, 45 RPM, 1975 .... 5.00
Reel, Viewmaster, Reel L, 1966 .... 5.00
Ring 18.00
Robin Slippers, Olive Green, Suede, R On Each Boot, 1960s 65.00
Roller Skates, 1979, Larami 20.00
Roller Skates, Batman's Face On Front of Skates, 1966 .... 20.00 To 30.00
Shooting Gallery, 1966, Marx 215.00
Spoon & Fork, Imperial 45.00
Squirt Gun, Bat Emblem, Azrak-Hamway Intl., 1978 .... 5.00
Table Cover, Paper, Amscan, Package, 1972 .... 20.00
Toy, Batman On String, Looks & Feels Alive, Rubber, 1966, 4 In. 45.00
Toy, Batman Scope, Black Plastic, Mirrors, Glass, Park Plastics, 1966 .... 63.00
Toy, Batmobile, Battery Operated, Tin, Japan, 12 In. 250.00
Toy, Squeeze, Batman Super Jr., Package, 1983 .... 17.00
Toy, Zoom Cycle, With Power Pack, Box, 1977 .... 35.00
Tumbler, Batman, Pepsi-Cola Collector's Series, 1966 .... 22.00
Tumbler, Batman, Pepsi-Cola Super Series, 1976 .... 18.00
Walkie-Talkie, 1976, Mego 130.00
Wallpaper, Crown, England, Package, 56 Square Ft. 100.00

J.A. Bauer moved his Kentucky pottery to Los Angeles, California, in 1909. The company made art pottery after 1912 and dinnerwares after 1929. The factory went out of business around 1958.

BAUER, Ashtray, Pinched 165.00
Bowl, Mixing, Yellow Ring, 11 In. 14.00
Bowl, Salad, Yellow, 9 1/2 In. 25.00
Butter, Cover, Cobalt Blue Ring 87.50
Butter, Cover, Ring, Round, Green 35.00
Chop Plate, LaLinda, 12 In. 12.00
Chop Plate, Ring, Blue, 12 1/2 In. 28.00
Coffee Server, Turquoise, Copper Handle 25.00

Coffee Server, Wooden Handle 22.00
Gravy Boat, Monterey, Cobalt Blue 40.00
Mug, Coffee, Wooden Handle, Orange 15.00
Mug, Coffee, Wooden Handle, Turquoise 15.00
Pitcher, Cal–Art, 10 In. 25.00
Pitcher, Ring, Cobalt Blue, 2 Qt. 30.00
Plate, Ring, Yellow, 9 1/2 In. 12.00
Platter, Orange, Oval, 12 1/2 In. 15.00

Porcelains of all types were made in the region known as Bavaria. In the nineteenth century, the mark often included the word "Bavaria." After 1871, the words "Bavaria, Germany" were used. Listed here are pieces that include the name Bavaria in some form, but major porcelain makers such as Rosenthal are listed in their own categories.

BAVARIA, Box, Powder, Figural, Pink Rose, Yellow & Black Butterfly Top 65.00
Cake Plate, Purple Flowers, Turquoise Luster, Gold Trim, Handles 32.00
Cup & Saucer, Painted, Black, Heavy Gold, After Dinner, Eberthal 20.00
Fish Set, Cobalt Blue, Gold Rim, 6 Plates, 14 X 9 In., Platter, 9 Pc. 125.00
Luncheon Set, Luster, Blue & Gold Trim, 12 Piece 65.00
Pitcher Set, Cider, Tumblers & Tray 650.00
Pitcher, Mother–of–Pearl Luster Trim At Top, 5 1/4 In. 30.00
Plate, Child's, Girls Hanging Out Wash, Schoolbook, 7 In. 25.00
Sugar, Scrolled Spray, Blue & Orange, Gold Trim 15.00

The Beatles became a famous music group in the 1960s. They first appeared on American network television in 1964. The group disbanded in 1971. Collectors search for any items picturing the four members of the group or any recordings. Because these items are so new, the condition is very important and top prices are paid only for items in mint condition.

BEATLES, Album, Record, Hear The Beatles Tell All, Vee–Jay Records 45.00
Album, Sgt. Pepper's Lonely Hearts Club Band, Cutout Cards 75.00
Bandage, Promotional, Help 8.00
Bank, Register, Nems Enterprises 20.00
Bank, Yellow Submarine, Paul, Pride Creations, 8 In. 185.00
Beach Towel 100.00
Belt 80.00
Book, Beatles Official Coloring Book, Saalfield, 1964 .... 25.00
Book, Coloring, 1964, 9 X 11 In. 35.00
Book, Diary, Pictures, Bios, Color Photos, Vinyl Cover, 1965 .... 15.00
Book, Pop–Out, Yellow Submarine, 1968, 9 1/2 X 15 In. 10.00
Book, True Story of The Beatles, Bantam, Paperback, 1964 .... 12.00 To 15.00
Bottle, Blowing Bubbles 19.00
Brunch Bag 275.00
Bubble Bath, Ringo 60.00
Calendar, 1964 .... 50.00
Candy Box, George, Yellow, Picturing George, Cartoon, 1 X 2 1/2 In. 125.00
Candy Box, Ringo, Blue, Picturing Ringo, Cartoon, 1 X 2 1/2 In. 125.00
Comic Book, Yellow Submarine, With Poster 30.00
Doll Set, Remco, With Instruments, 4 Piece 300.00
Doll Set, Rooted Hair, Instrument Strapped Around Neck, 1964, 4 Pc. 250.00
Doll, Bobbin Head, 1964, Set of 4 ....Illus 300.00
Doll, George Harrison, Inflatable 25.00
Doll, Nodder, Box, 1960s, 8 In., 4 Piece 640.00
Game, Flip Your Wig, Milton Bradley, 1964 .... 75.00 To 110.00
Game, Magnetic Hair Styles 205.00
Glass, Pictures The Beatles On Front, Plastic 125.00
Guitar, Pop, Red, Beatles, On Front, Mastro, 21 In. 385.00
Guitar, Sound, Orange & White, Selcor, English, 22 In. 325.00
Headband, Package 30.00
Jelly Jar, Ringo, Glass 125.00
Lunch Box, Blue .... 150.00 To 200.00
Lunch Box, Yellow Submarine, 1968 .... 100.00 To 125.00

Magazine, All About The Beatles, No.1, 1964 .... 22.00
Magazine, Fan Club, Tour, Black & White Pictures, 1964 .... 12.50
Magazine, Life, 1968 .... 30.00
Magazine, Meet The Beatles, 1963 .... 22.00
Mirror, Pocket, Yellow Submarine, 2 In., 4 Piece 11.00
Model Kit, John, Plastic, Unassembled, Box 110.00
Model, Ringo, Painted Boots, Revell, 1964 .... 175.00
Mug, Picture of John, Paul, George, Ringo, Broadhurst Bros., Ceramic 125.00
Pen Holder, 1964 .... 35.00
Pillow, John, Paul, George, Ringo On Front, Blue Back 125.00
Pin, Guitar, John, On Card .... 15.00 To 35.00
Postcard, German, John, Paul, George, Ringo, 6 X 8 In. 15.00
Poster, San Fran. Candlestick Park, Psychedelic Rock, Wilson, 1966 .... 1000.00
Puppet, Pelham, Box 200.00
Puzzle, Yellow Submarine, Blue Meanies Attack, 650 Pcs., 12 In. 65.00
Ring, Plastic, Lennon Photo 12.00
Scarf, Beatles Images, White, Black Logo, Unused 40.00
Scarf, Pictures, Signatures & Song Titles, 1964 .... 11.00
School Tablet, Colored Cover 29.00
Sheet Music, I'Ll Follow The Sun, Black & White 15.00
Sheet Music, Revolution, Picture of The Beatles 15.00
Sneakers, Wing Dings, Box 150.00
Stationery, Yellow Submarine, Unicorn Creations 25.00
Suit, Geo. Harrison, From Hard Day's Night, Gray, Velvet Collar 2200.00
Thermos, Blue 45.00
Ticket, Suffolk Downs, Aug.18, 1966, Unused 65.00
Tie Tack Set, Raised Faces, 1964, 4 Piece 20.00
Tray, Metal, Color, England, 13 X 13 In. 12.00
Tray, Serving, Metal, Great Britain 35.00
Wallet, Each Has Different Beatle Picture, Set of 4, Miniature 12.50
Wig, Original Package, 1964 .... 35.00

"Beehive, Austria," or "Beehive, Vienna," are terms used in English-speaking countries to refer to the many types of decorated porcelain bearing a mark that looks like a beehive. The mark is actually a shield, viewed upside down. It was first used in 1744 by the Royal Porcelain Manufactory of Vienna. The firm made porcelains, called "Royal Vienna" by collectors, until it closed in 1864. Many other German, Austrian, and Japanese factories have reproduced Royal Vienna wares, complete with the original shield or "beehive" mark. This listing includes the expensive, original Royal Vienna porcelains and many other types of beehive porcelain. The Royal Vienna pieces include that name in the description.

BEEHIVE, Bowl, With Portraits, Austria, 7 In. 95.00
Box, Woman & Cherub Scene, Red & Blue Ground, 4 1/2 X 6 1/4 In. 350.00
Chocolate Pot, Cherub Scene, Gold Handle, Royal Vienna 250.00
Cracker Jar, Pearlized Porcelain, Floral Design, Royal Vienna 160.00
Cup & Saucer, Enameled Garlands & Floral, Allover Gilt, 6 3/4 In. 400.00
Pitcher, Portrait, 12 In. 700.00
Plate, 2 Maidens In Garden, O. & C. Larsson, Royal Vienna, 15 In. 165.00
Plate, Amorosa Center, Maroon, Gold Tracery, Royal Vienna, 8 In. 55.00
Plate, Lattice, Royal Vienna, 4 3/4 In. 45.00
Plate, Melon Boys, Dice Players, Royal Vienna, 12 1/2 In. 225.00
Plate, Portrait, Garden Scene, Gold Edge, Royal Vienna, 12 In. 49.00
Plate, Prince & Princess, Marked, 9 3/4 In. 85.00
Stein, Hand Painted, Royal Vienna, C.1780 .... 1500.00
Urn, Portrait, Austria 145.00
Urn, Portrait, Panels of Nymphs & Cherubs, 11 In. 275.00
Vase, Blown Out Tulip, Gold, Tulip Handle, Royal Vienna, 8 In. 500.00

Beatles, Doll, Bobbin Head, 1964, Set of 4

Vase, Blue, Raised Gold Flowers, Woman, Red Hair, Royal Vienna, 9 In. 695.00
Vase, Portrait, Austria, 4 In. 85.00
Vase, Woman, Flowing Red Hair Medallion, Royal Vienna, 11 1/2 In. 695.00
     BEER BOTTLE, see Bottle, Beer

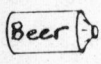

Beer was sold in kegs or returnable bottles until 1934. The first patent for a can was issued to the American Can Company in September of that year; and Gotfried Kruger Brewing Company, Newark, New Jersey, was the first to use the can. The cone–top can was first made in 1935, the aluminum pop–top in 1962. Collectors should look for cans in good condition, with no dents or rust. Serious collectors prefer cans that have been opened from the bottom.

BEER CAN, ABC Ale, Stainless Steel 75
    Andy's Series, Blue 1.00
    Ballantine Draft, Brewed 75
    Base Brau, Red, White & Blue, Stainless Steel, 1978 ....   1.00
    Bavarian Club, Huber, Stainless Steel 2.00
    Billy Beer, Air Filled, Unopened, 6 Pack 25.00
    Bounty Hunger, River City, 1983 ....   1.50
    Champagne Velvet, 1930s 85.00
    Colt 45 Malt Lager, 8 Oz. 1.50
    Coors Light, Silver, 16 Oz. 75
    Coors Original Draft, Aluminum, 16 Oz. 75
    Dakota 12.00
    DuBois, Cone Top 25.00
    Elks Beer, 100th Anniversary, ...   1.00
    Frankenmuth Mel–O–Dry, Black & Yellow, Man In Top Hat 35.00
    Genesee, Aluminum, 16 Oz. 75
    Genesee, Flat Top, Gold, Red Letters 85.00
    Hanley, Cone Top 50.00
    Hudepohl Pure Grain, Cincinnati, Stainless Steel 10.00
    Iron City, 1975 Steelers, Stainless Steel, 16 Oz. 1.00
    Iron City, Christmas Scene, Bridge, Stainless Steel 2.00
    Iron City, Defense Helmets, Stainless Steel, 16 Oz. 10.00
    Iron City, Mel Blount 75
    King Cobra Malt Liquor, Aluminum, 12 Oz. 1.00
    Miller, Aluminum, 16 Oz. 2.00
    Miller, Flat Top, Red, 12 Oz. 50.00
    National Bohemian Pale, Cone Top, 1903 ....   40.00
    Near Beer, Flat Top, 12 Oz. 12.00
    Olde Frothingslosh, Maroon, Stainless Steel 1.50

Pabst Blue Ribbon, Newark, N.J., Flat Top	17.00
Pearl, 16 Oz.	2.00
Piels Real Draft, Aluminum, 16 Oz.	.75
Red Bull Malt Liquor, Aluminum, 16 Oz.	.75
Red Top Ale, Cone Top	20.00
Rheingold, Stainless Steel, 16 Oz.	2.00
Schell's, Multicolor, Stainless Steel, 16 Oz.	5.00
Schlitz Commemorative, Tampa, Stainless Steel, Bank, 16 Oz.	4.00
Schlitz, Steel	5.00
Schmidt's, Metallic, Aluminum, 16 Oz.	.75
St. Urho's Day, Steel, Sealed, 1975	1.00

Bells have been made of porcelain, china, or metal through the centuries. All types are collected. Favorites include glass bells, figural bells, school bells, and cowbells. Be careful not to buy a bell made from an old glass goblet.

BELL, Amish Man, Brass	15.00
Call, Brass, Red Granite Base, 6 1/4 In.	25.00
Camel, Brass	75.00
Carriage, Floor Mounted	115.00
Cow, Iron	12.00
Desk, Hotel	7.00
Dinner Gong, Hung From Wooden Frame, L. & J.G. Stickley, 1912	7000.00
Dinner, Farm, Iron	75.00
Embossed Northwood Lucky Bell, Brass, 4 1/2 In., Pair	150.00
Hindu, Wind God, Monkey Handle, Brass	75.00
Horse, Circus, Double Clappers, 5 Piece	200.00
Owl, Brass, Tap To Ring, 7 1/2 In.	25.00
School, Brass, 1910, 13 In.	150.00
School, Frame, Cast Iron, 250 Lbs.	475.00
Ship's, Aimee, Brass, 1967, 12 In.	175.00
Ship's, Andros, Texas, Brass, 12 In.	425.00
Ship's, Brass, Wall Mounted, 7 3/4 In.	25.00
Ship's, Gulfa Hansa, Brass, 1962, 10 In.	475.00
Sleigh, 39 Steel, Leather Strap	200.00
Sleigh, Brass, Shiny, On Strap	155.00
Sleigh, Graduated, 90–In. Leather Strap, 29 Bells, 1870s	300.00
Smoke, Cream Glass	12.50

Belleek china is made in Ireland, other European countries, and the United States. The glaze is creamy yellow and appears wet. The first Belleek was made in 1857. All pieces listed here are Irish Belleek. The mark changed through the years. The first mark, black, dates from 1863 to 1890. The second mark, black, dates from 1891 to 1926 and includes the words "Co. Fermanagh, Ireland." The third mark, black, dates from 1926 to 1946 and has the words "Deanta in Eirinn." The fourth mark, same as the third mark but green, dates from 1946 to 1955. The fifth mark, green, dates from 1955 to 1965 and has an R in a circle added in the upper right. The sixth mark, green, dates after 1965 and the words "Co. Fermanagh" have been omitted. The seventh mark, gold, was used after 1980 and omits the words "Deanta in Eirinn."

BELLEEK, see also Ceramic Art Co.; Haviland; Lenox; Ott & Brewer; Willets

BELLEEK, Basket, 3 Strand Basketweave, Henshalls, C.1880, 9 X 10 3/4 In.	385.00
Basket, 3 Strand Weave, 3 Shamrocks On Rim	535.00
Blotter, Rose Garlands, Cream, Rocker Type, Ornate Handle, 5 3/4 In.	150.00
Bowl, Bamboo, Green Mark, 5 In.	48.00
Bowl, Heart, 2nd Black Mark, Pink, 5 In.	70.00

Bowl, Heart, Pink, 5 In. 80.00
Creamer, Scale, 1st Black Mark 80.00
Creamer, Toy, Yellow, 2nd Black Mark 60.00
Creamer, Tridacna, 2nd Black Mark, Large 65.00
Creamer, White, Twig Shaped Base, Handles, FBM, 1860 .... 165.00
Cup & Saucer, Institute, White & Pink, Gold Trim, 1st Black Mark 165.00
Cup & Saucer, Limpet, 1st Green Mark 60.00
Cup & Saucer, Neptune, 2nd Black Mark 75.00
Cup & Saucer, Shamrock, 3rd Black Mark .... 48.00 To 80.00
Cup & Saucer, Tridacna, 3rd Black Mark .... 65.00 To 78.00
Dish, Heart Shape, Pink Edging, Cream, 3rd Black Mark 95.00
Dish, Shell, 1st Black Mark, 7 In. 65.00
Eggcup Set, Holder, Hand Finial, 1st Black Mark, 5 1/2 In., 6 Pc. 1195.00
Eggcup, Sidney, Green, Holder 195.00
Figurine, Griffin On Clam Shell, 1st Black Mark 1400.00
Figurine, Irish Terrier, 3 In. 48.00
Figurine, Meditation, 3rd Black Mark 750.00
Figurine, Pig, 2nd Green Mark 70.00
Figurine, Swan, Gold At Neck, Orange Bill, Gray Head, 2nd Green Mark 75.00
Honey Pot, Grassware, Stand 425.00
Jam Jar, Shamrock & Basket Weave, 2nd Green Mark 135.00
Jardiniere, 1st Black Mark, 18 In. 2000.00
Mug, Shamrock, 3rd Black Mark, 6 In. 95.00
Panel, Alms Giver, Lithophane 225.00
Pitcher, Basket Weave, Shamrock, 2nd Green Mark, 6 In. 75.00
Pitcher, Florence, Pink Trim, Gold Mark, 6 1/2 In. 95.00
Pitcher, Milk, Berry & Leaf, Twisted Vine Handle, Marked, 6 1/4 In. 95.00
Plate, Limpet, 3rd Black Amrk, 7 In. 52.00
Plate, Limpet, Green, Pearlized Trim, 8 In. 25.00
Plate, Limpet, Pearlized Trim, 3rd Black Mark, 8 1/4 In. 35.00
Plate, Limpet, Plain Rim, 3rd Black Mark 35.00
Plate, Mask, 4 Handles, 3rd Black Mark, 6 In. 60.00
Plate, Neptune, 2nd Black Mark 27.50
Plate, Shamrock, 3rd Black Mark, 8 In. 45.00
Plate, Shamrock, Basket Weave, 2nd Black Mark, 6 1/4 In. 70.00
Plate, Shamrock, Basket Weave, 3rd Black Mark, 8 1/2 In. 500.00
Plate, Shamrock, Basket Weave, Green Mark, 10 1/7 In. 42.50
Plate, Tridacna, 2nd Black Mark, 5 1/2 In. 27.50
Plate, Tridacna, Green, Gold Trim, 2nd Black Mark, 6 In. 20.00
Shell, Cardium, On Coral Base, 2nd Black Mark 475.00
Spill, Owl, 5th Green Mark 60.00
Sugar & Creamer, Ivy, 1st Green Mark 35.00
Sugar & Creamer, Lily, 1st Green Mark 95.00
Sugar & Creamer, Lily-of-The-Valley, 2nd Green Mark 65.00
Sugar & Creamer, Lotus, 3rd Black Mark 125.00
Sugar & Creamer, Ribbon, 1st Green Mark 110.00
Sugar & Creamer, Rose Garlands, Blue, Gold, Signed Madalin Land 225.00
Sugar & Creamer, Shamrock, 3rd Black Mark 125.00
Sugar & Creamer, Tridacna, 3rd Black Mark 125.00
Sugar Bowl, Lotus, Pink Trim, 3rd Black Mark 35.00
Sugar, Cover, Tridacna, 3rd Black Mark 65.00
Sugar, Shamrock, Basket Weave Design, 2nd Black Mark 85.00
Tea Kettle, Tridacna, 2nd Black Mark 300.00
Tea Kettle, Tridacna, Pink, 2nd Black Mark 325.00
Tea Set, Shamrock, 2nd Green Mark, Service For 4 .... 510.00
Teapot, Neptune, Yellow, 2nd Black Mark 300.00
Teapot, Tridacna, 2nd Black Mark, Large 275.00
Toothpick, Sawtooth Rim, Allover Leaves & Flowers, 2nd Black Mark 125.00
Vase, Flying Fish, Pink Trim, 2nd Black Mark, 4 3/8 In. 425.00
Vase, Lily-of-The-Valley, 3rd Green Mark, 6 1/2 In. 40.00
Vase, Peacocks, 9 In. 175.00
Vase, Princess, Applied Flowers, 2nd Black Mark, 9 In. 795.00
Vase, Shamrock, Pierced, 3rd Green Mark, 7 1/2 In. 78.00
Vase, Swirled Shell, Ruffled Rim, 4 1/2 In. 60.00

Bennington ware was the product of two factories working in Bennington, Vermont. Both firms were out of business by 1896. The wares include brown and yellow mottled pottery, Parian, scroddled ware, stoneware, graniteware, yellowware, and Staffordshirelike vases.

BENNINGTON, Candlestick, 8 In.	500.00
Candlestick, Brown, Free–Form, Square, S. Ballard, Pair	32.00
Candlestick, Flint Enamel, 8 1/4 In.	475.00
Candlestick, Flint Enamel, 9 1/2 In.	750.00
Candlestick, Rockingham Glaze, 8 3/8 In.	100.00
Churn, Peacock On Stump, 2 Gal.	775.00
Crock, Eared, Floral, 3 Gal.	275.00
Custard Set, Spongeware, 7 Piece	135.00
Jar, Crossed Birds	1525.00
Jug, Batter, Bail, White	45.00
Jug, Floral, 3 Gal.	225.00
Match Box, Blue, White Parian, Vintage On Lid, 3 5/8 In.	45.00
Pie Plate, 9 1/2 In.	50.00
Pipkin, Alternate Rib Pattern, Rockingham Glaze, 7 1/2 In.	650.00
Pitcher, Deer & Eagle	200.00
Pitcher, Paneled, Marked, 1849, 12 1/2 In.	800.00
Pitcher, Peacock On Fence	95.00
Spittoon, Shell Pattern, 8 1/2 In.	60.00
Spittoon, Shell, Murray & Co., Glasgow	80.00
Spittoon, Shell, Side Vents, 8 1/2 In.	90.00
Teapot, Toby, Riding Elephant, 9 1/2 In.	850.00
Wash Bowl, In Wooden Frame, Brown & Cream Marbelized, 26 In.	570.00
Washboard	395.00

Berlin, a German porcelain factory, was started in 1751 by Wilhelm Kaspar Wegely. In 1763, the factory was taken over by Frederick the Great and became the Royal Berlin Porcelain Manufactory. It is still in operation today. Pieces have been marked in a variety of ways.

BERLIN, Plaque, Child, Carrying Plate of Food, Marked, 9 1/4 X 6 1/2 In.	4950.00
Plaque, Madonna & Child, 2 Saints, Marked, 1860s, 13 1/4 X 11 1/4 In.	2200.00
Plaque, Madonna & Child, Marked, C.1880, 17 In.	5500.00
Plaque, Maiden, Dark Flowing Hair, Marked, 1880x, 9 1/4 X 6 1/4 In.	2750.00
Plaque, Man In Chains, Bearded Prisoner, Marked, C.1880, 9 In.	1100.00
Plaque, Nude Water Nymph, Marked, C.1900, 10 X 7 1/2 In.	6650.00

Berlin, Urn, Garden Scene, Rams' Heads,
18 1/2 In., Pair

Don't store dishes for long periods of time in old newspaper wrappings. The ink can make indelible stains on china.

Plaque, Penitent Magdalene, Marked, C.1880, 7 1/2 X 10 1/2 In.	2750.00
Plaque, Psyche, Kneeling, Looking Into Lake, C.1900, 11 X 8 3/4 In.	3850.00
Plaque, Water Nymphs, Tempting Robed Figure, Marked, 13 X 10 1/2 In.	4675.00
Plaque, Young Woman, Framed, Scepter Mark, 6 1/4 X 8 3/4 In.	3800.00
Urn, Garden Scene, Rams' Heads, 18 1/2 In., Pair ....*Illus*	1210.00

John Beswick started making earthenware in Staffordshire, England, in 1936. The company is now part of Royal Doulton Tableware, Ltd. Figurines of animals, especially dogs and horses, Beatrix Potter animals, and other wares are still being made.

BESWICK, Ashtray, 3 Dogs, No.916	30.00
Cheese Keeper, Green	25.00
Figurine, Appaloosa Horse, Large	125.00
Figurine, Bobwhite Quail, 5 1/4 In.	55.00
Figurine, Collie, 5 1/2 In.	40.00
Figurine, Dachshund	40.00
Figurine, Dog, Collie, Lochinvar of Ladypark, 5 1/2 In.	35.00
Figurine, Sheep Dog, No.2232	75.00
Mug, Christmas, 1975	65.00
Mug, Christmas, 1978	65.00
Mug, Pecksniff	30.00
Toby, Scrooge, No. 372 .... 60.00 To 75.00
Vase, Landscape, 10 In.	85.00

Betty Boop, the cartoon figure, first appeared on the screen in 1931. Her face was modeled after the famous singer Helen Kane and her body after Mae West. In 1935 a comic strip was started. Although the Betty Boop cartoons were ended by 1938, there has been a revival of interest in the Betty Boop image in the 1980s and new pieces are being made.

BETTY BOOP, Ashtray, Betty Boop & Bimbo, Glazed	70.00
Card, Playing	20.00
Clock, Alarm	37.00
Cookie Jar, King Features	300.00
Coverlet	85.00
Dinner Set, Box	495.00
Doll, Chalkware, Small	22.50
Doll, Clothes, Colorforms, 1978, 17 In.	34.00
Doll, Jointed, Bynal, Box, 1986, 11 1/2 In.	34.00
Doll, Romper, Matching Bonnet, 10 1/2 In.	12.00
Doll, Wooden, Black Dress, Kallus, Label	850.00
Marble, Picture	15.00
Perfume Bottle, Red Heart Label Says Dada, Contents, 3 5/8 In.	25.00
Planter	75.00
Salt & Pepper, Bimbo In Bumper Car, Betty As Waitress	18.00
Salt & Pepper, With Dog Bimbo, In Wooden Boat	15.00
Soap, Box	45.00
Toy, Head Nods, Celluloid, Japan, Box, 7 In.	1100.00
Wall Pocket, With Bimbo, Lustre, Fleischer Studios	95.00
Whistle, Japan	40.00

The bicycle was invented in 1839. The first manufactured bicycle was made in 1861. Special ladies' bicycles were made after 1874. The modern safety bicycle was not produced until 1885. Collectors search for all types of bicycles and tricycles. Bicycle–related items are also listed here.

BICYCLE, Columbia, Model 65	600.00
Crescent, Woman's, C.1895	150.00
Flint Flyer, Flint, Michigan	285.00
Frame, Cannondale, 60 Centimeters	150.00
Gas Light	62.50

Hawthorn Flyer, All Original, 1930s 850.00
High Wheel, 56 In. 2475.00
High Wheel, Boston 1800.00
Ice Cream Vendor's, Attached Cart 450.00
King, 1888 .... 250.00
Lamp, Balaco, Carbide 60.00
Motorcycle, Humbell Ltd., 1922 .... 8800.00
Motorcycle, Indian, 1920 .... 6050.00 To 8250.00
Motorcycle, Moto Guzzi, Flacone, Italy, 1948 .... 8800.00
Motorcycle, Scott, Flying Squirrel, 1939 .... 6050.00
Otto, 42–In. Front Wheel 1850.00
Roadmaster, 2 Wheels, Spiderman, Graphics 125.00
Schwinn, Black Phantom 800.00
Schwinn, Cycle Truck, Painted, Pin Striping, All Original 450.00
Schwinn, Men's Springer Balloon Tank, Pee Wee Herman Style 1200.00
Sherrell, Custom Made 1800.00
Tricycle, Air Flow, Headlight 425.00
Tricycle, Carved Wooden Horse, Hair Tail, Glass Eyes, Saddle 1250.00
Tricycle, Horse Form, American, 19th Century 1350.00
Tricycle, Wooden, Leather Seat, 1860s 1250.00
Velocipede, Whitney Read, Horse 2650.00
Victor, High Wheel 1800.00
Woman's, Crescent, 1895 .... 1200.00

Bing and Grondahl is a famous Danish factory making fine porcelains from 1853 to the present. Underglaze blue decoration was started in 1886. The annual Christmas plate series was introduced in 1895. Dinnerwares, stoneware, and figurines are still being made today. The firm has used the initials B & G and a stylized castle as part of the mark since 1898.

BING & GRONDAHL, Cruet, White Seagull, Gold Trim 65.00
Figurine, Boy Kissing Girl, Youthful Boldness, No.2162 .... 125.00
Figurine, Boy, Accordion, Merry Sailor, No.1661, 9 In. 175.00
Figurine, Boy, With Duck, No.1836 .... 125.00
Figurine, Boy, With Puppy, Ole, No.1747 .... 115.00
Figurine, Boy, With Sandals, Pink, No.1671 .... 225.00
Figurine, Boy, With Skis, No.2358, 8 1/2 In. 260.00
Figurine, Bulldog Pup, Sitting, 5 In. 185.00
Figurine, Bunny, White Rabbit Standing, No.2443, 5 In. 75.00
Figurine, Cat, No.1801, 5 1/2 In. 125.00
Figurine, Dancing Children, No.1885 .... 160.00
Figurine, Dog, Collie, Lying, 11 In. 450.00
Figurine, Dog, Shepherd, Lying, 9 1/2 In. 350.00
Figurine, Eskimo, Sitting On Pond, 13 In. 650.00
Figurine, Girl Kissing Boy, Love Refused, No.1614 .... 135.00
Figurine, Girl With Kitten, One Drop, No.1745 .... 165.00
Figurine, Girl With Puppy & Kitten, Make Friends, No.2333 .... 125.00
Figurine, Girl, Holding Butterfly, Pink, No.2185 .... 270.00
Figurine, Girl, Little Girl With Doll, No.1526 .... 125.00
Figurine, Girl, Mending, No.1879, 7 3/4 In. 160.00
Figurine, Girl, Spilt Milk, No.2246 .... 120.00 To 240.00
Figurine, Kingfisher, No.1885 .... 98.00
Figurine, Kitten, Standing, White, No.2506 .... 70.00
Figurine, News Boy, No.2148 .... 150.00
Figurine, Nurse, No.2379, 9 In. 225.00
Figurine, Squirrel With Acorn, No.2177 .... 75.00
Figurine, Tennis Girl, No.2364, 8 In. 235.00
Figurine, Woman With Guitar Player, No.1684, 10 In. 245.00
Plaque, Expo Universelle Paris, Half Shell Shape, 6 In. 650.00
Plate, Christmas, 1904, View of Copenhagen 109.00
Plate, Christmas, 1907, Little Match Girl 85.00
Plate, Christmas, 1922, Star of Bethlehem 52.00
Plate, Christmas, 1952, Old Copenhagen Canals 59.00
Plate, Christmas, 1972, In Greenland 30.00

Plate, Christmas, 1978, A Christmas Tale 30.00
Plate, Christmas, 1987, Christmas Remembered 49.00
Plate, Jubilee, 1895–1970 .... 35.00
Plate, Mother's Day, 1968 .... 300.00
Plate, Mother's Day, 1969, Dog & Puppies 250.00
Plate, Mother's Day, 1975, Carl Larsson 8.00
Plate, Mother's Day, 1982, Lioness & Cubs 13.00
Vase, Cherubs At Neck, Flowers, Silver Overlay, 8 In., Pair 195.00
Vase, Cover, Mushrooms, Cluster of Leaves Handle, 10 In. 2400.00
Vase, Lorelei, 7 1/4 In. 75.00
Vase, Seagulls, 5 In. 25.00

All types of old binoculars are wanted by collectors. Those made in the eighteenth and nineteenth centuries are favored by serious collectors. The small, attractive binoculars called opera glasses are listed in their own section.

BINOCULARS, Bardou & Sons, Paris .... 45.00 To 55.00
French, Enamel 375.00
Ostrich Leather Case 125.00
Tiffany, Young & Ellis, Black, Gold Trim 70.00

Old birdcages are collected for use as homes for pet birds and as decorative objects of folk art. Elaborate wooden cages of the past centuries can still be found. The brass or wicker cages of the 1930s are popular with bird owners.

BIRDCAGE, 2–Story Building Form, Applied Designs, Wood & Wire, 25 X 25 In. 610.00
All Glass, Signed 125.00
Hanger & Pedestal, Wire & Tin, Early 1800s 165.00
Hanging, Wood & Wire, White Paint, 16 In. 155.00
Hendryx, Brass, 16 In. 85.00
Pagoda, Meissen Feeders 165.00
Parrot, Victorian, Brass Stand 125.00
Semicircular, Wire Base, Tin Back, Tole, 18 1/2 In. 200.00
Shaped As A House, Double Roof, Wood & Wire, Large 140.00
Wire, Tin Floor, Cutout Music Notes On Door 30.00
Wirework, Curbed Top, Wood Framed Bottom, Wheel & Feeders 95.00
Wooden Finial, 4 Tin Feet, Orange & Beige Paint, Hendryx, Small 75.00

Bisque is an unglazed baked porcelain. Finished bisque has a slightly sandy texture with a dull finish. Some of it may be decorated with various colors. Bisque gained favor during the late Victorian era when thousands of bisque figurines were made. It is still being made.

BISQUE, see also named porcelain factories
BISQUE, Box, White, Free–Hanging Rings Finial & Handle, French, 1950s 150.00
Bust, Spring & Autumn, Floral Spray In Hair, L.Kley, 10 In., Pair 325.00
Cornucopia, Cherub, Large 145.00
Figurine, Baby Girl, Flower Container Each Side, 10 1/2 In. 125.00
Figurine, Boy, With Puggs, Germany, 7 1/2 In. 175.00
Figurine, Classical Maiden, Turned Stands, Pastel, 13 In., Pair 55.00
Figurine, Girl, Blond, Germany, 7 1/2 In. 375.00
Figurine, Girl, With Rose, Germany, 10 In. 175.00
Figurine, Romeo & Juliet, Standing Figures, 13 In. 275.00
Figurine, Shelf Sitter, Black Boy, Green Hat, Fishing Pole, Germany ..../......... 65.00
Figurine, St.Anthony, Holding Child Jesus, Painted, 9 In. 25.50
Toothpick, Little Girl, Basket On Back, Germany, 4 In. 75.00

Black amethyst glass appears black until it is held to the light, then a dark purple can be seen. It has been made in many factories from 1860 to the present.

BLACK AMETHYST, Ashtray, Cloverleaf 50.00
Ashtray, Elephant 10.00
Bowl, Acid Etched, Gold Design, 12 In. 195.00
Box, Patch, Enameled Florals On Top, Dots At Base, 1 X 2 In. 100.00

Candleholder, Double, Silver Overlay, Pair	35.00
Candlestick, 7 In.	28.00
Clock, Mantel, Tambour, McKee	375.00
Cuspidor, Woman's	28.00
Dish, Elephant Cover	65.00
Loving Cup, Dancing Girls, 7 In.	27.50
Pomade, Bear, Sandwich, 3 3/4 In.	250.00
Powder Jar, Monkey	8.00
Salt & Pepper, Art Deco	20.00
Salt, Hobnail, Master	15.00
Spice Set, Rounded, 5 Piece	65.00
Vase, Art Deco, 8 In.	36.00

Black memorabilia has become an important area of collecting since the 1970s. Any piece that pictures a black person is included in this category and objects range from sheet music to salt and pepper shakers. The best material dates from past centuries, but many recent items are of interest even if not yet expensive.

BLACK, Advertising Box, Sun-X Bleach	15.00
Apron, Aunt Jemima	25.00
Ashtray, Boy & Donkey	20.00
Automaton, Black Man, Wearing Pork-Pie Hat, Papier-Mache, 32 In.	1925.00
Banner, Aunt Jemima, Kiwanis Pancake Day, Printed Cloth, 3 X 5 Ft.	350.00
Bean Bag, Felt Face, Round, 4 In.	15.00
Beer Stein, Moretti Boot Shape, Black Cartoon Boxers	30.00
Biscuit Jar, Butler	165.00
Black, Sign, Fern Glen Rye, Tin Litho, Self Framed	4500.00
Book, Black Dynamite, Story of Negro In Boxing, N.Fleischer, 1938	15.00
Book, Bones, His Gags & Stump Speeches, 1879, 64 Pages	15.00
Book, Burnt Cork Or The Amateur Minstrel, F.Dumont, 1881, 132 Pages	150.00
Book, Little Black Sambo, 1931	85.00
Book, Little Black Sambo, 1948	20.00
Book, Little Black Sambo, 1961	22.00
Book, Little Black Sambo, Whitman, 1959	18.50
Book, Tambo, His Jokes & Funny Sayings, Minstrel, Wehman Bros., 1879	10.00
Bottle, Blacks Playing Drum Decanter, Italy	135.00
Bottle, Butler Holding Decanter	100.00
Bottle, Figural, Mammy, Soda, 1920s, 60 Oz., 14 In.	150.00
Box, Candy, Amos & Andy	200.00
Bust, Girl & Boy, With Watermelon, Chalkware	25.00
Bust, Man, Ceramic, 7 X 8 1/2 In.	28.00
Calendar, Girl Feeding Bottle To Black Doll, Stockton, Calif., 1951	135.00
Cigarette Holder, Mammy Holding Basket, Ashtrays	86.00
Cookie Jar, 2-Sets Salt & Pepper, Mammy & Chef, Pearl China, 6 Piece	850.00
Cookie Jar, Chef, Pearl China	285.00
Cookie Jar, Chef, Striped Pants, Blue Buttons, White Ground	225.00
Crate, Packing, Aunt Jemima, Cardboard, Held 24 Package Pancake Flour	125.00
Cruet Set, Oil & Vinegar, Ceramic, Figural, Mammy & Chef, Plastic	85.00
Display, Die-Cut, Stylized French Art Deco, 16 In.	25.00
Doll, Articulated Limbs, Button Eyes, White Wool Hair, 9 1/2 In.	115.00
Doll, Aunt Jemima, Plastic, Fillable	15.00
Doll, Aunt Jemima, Uncle Moses, Diana & Wade, Oilcloth, 4 Piece	150.00
Doll, Baby, Bisque, Little Tufts of Hair, Japan, 1 1/2 In.	20.00
Doll, Baby, Jointed, Celluloid, 5 In.	15.00
Doll, Baby, Windup, Celluloid, Jointed, 3 In.	250.00
Doll, Black Sambo, Inflatable, Winking, Package, 1960s	15.00
Doll, Celluloid, With Feathers, 6 1/2 In.	15.00
Doll, Dancin' Dina, Jointed Wood	95.00
Doll, Flip Wilson-Geraldine, Mute, Box	115.00
Doll, Gerber, 1979, 19 In.	59.00
Doll, Girl, On Stand, Basket On Head, Jewelry, Brazil, 10 In.	35.00
Doll, Golliwog, Red Dress, 5 In.	195.00
Doll, Jackie Robinson, Composition, 14 In. ....*Illus*	825.00
Doll, Mammy, Rag, 11 In.	12.00

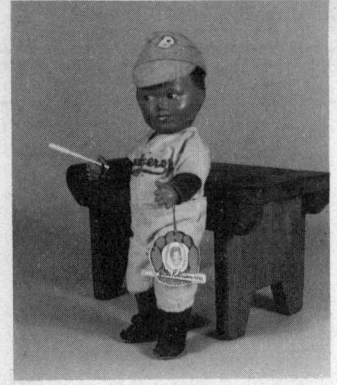

If you bought a Cabbage Patch doll as an investment, it is best to keep it mint in the box. Save all papers, correspondence, and even newspaper clippings telling about the 1983 Christmas season sellouts.

Black, Doll, Jackie Robinson, Composition,
14 In.

Doll, Man, Crocheted, Anatomically, Correct	175.00
Doll, Painted Nut Head, Black Wool Hair, Wood & Cloth, 7 1/2 In.	25.00
Doll, Praline Mammy, Hand Painted, 8 In.	15.00
Doll, Rag, Smiling, With Teeth, Wooden Nose Through Cloth, 25 In.	595.00
Doll, Red & White Polka Dot Dress & Scarf, Paper Eyes, 11 1/2 In.	42.00
Doll, Red Flowered Dress, Beecher Type	4250.00
Doll, Sunbabe So–Wee, 1957, 10 In.	20.00
Doll, Sunshine Family, Box	35.00
Doll, Toaster, Cover	16.50
Doll, Vinyl, Colonial Dress Costume	45.00
Egg Timer, Figural, Chef, Porcelain, Germany	49.00
Figurine, Bar, Native Bartender, Ceramic, Red Duck Lips, Implements	50.00
Figurine, Black Boy, Eating Watermelon, Ceramic, 4 X 3 1/2 In.	65.00
Figurine, Black Ned, Standing Under Bower, Hat In Hand	3025.00
Figurine, Black, Holding Hot Air Balloon	104.50
Figurine, Boy, With Watermelon, Bisque, 2 In.	6.00
Figurine, Outhouse, One Moment Please, Japan, Bisque	28.00
Game, Dart, Sambo, Tin	95.00
Game, Nodding Nancy, Mammy Pipe Toss, Parker Bros., Complete	225.00
Garden Ornament, Boy, Chalkware	55.00
Gum Wrapper, Black Joe, Early 1900s	6.75
Head, Parade, Dandy, With Top Hat, Papier–Mache, 24 In.	250.00
Holder, Note, Chef, Plaster	52.50
Holder, String, Mammy	110.00
Holder, String, Porter, Fredicksburg	125.00
Joke Book, Coon Jokes No.1, 64 Pages, 1907	35.00
Joke Book, Darkey Jokes & Funny Stories, Color Cover, 1916	25.00
Laundry Bag, Mammy, Unused, 1930	95.00
Mammy, Pot Holder, Embroidered Cloth	30.00
Mannequin, Black Boy, Millinery	50.00
Match Holder, Mammy With Laundry Basket	40.00
Memo Holder, Chef, Chalkware, 1947	45.00
Memo, Mammy, Finger To Forehead, Reckon Ah Needs	28.00
Menu, Coon Chicken Inn, Small	35.00
Nodder, Baby, Straw Hat, Holding Fruit, 8 In.	34.00
Nodder, Black Boy, Occupied Japan	95.00
Noisemaker, Black Man Caricature, Tin	10.00
Noisemaker, Black Musician Figures, Tin, Germany	62.00
Nose Maker, Black Mammy Face, Pressed Cardboard, Germany, 6 1/2 In.	44.00
Note Pad Holder, Aunt Jemima, Hanging	25.00
Paperweight, Aunt Jemima, Snow Scene	75.00
Perfume Bottle, Figural, Black Boy, Glass, Germany, Miniature	26.00

Perfume Bottle, Golliwog, Fur Cap, Partial Label, 5 1/2 In. 45.00
Pie Bird, Chef 52.00
Pie Bird, Mammy 46.00
Pinback, Little Black Sambo, Pull String, Eyes Roll, 1910, 2 1/2 In. 40.00
Pincushion Doll, Mammy, Calico Prints, On Log Slice, 1930s, 7 In. 125.00
Pincushion, Mammy, Large 40.00
Pipe, Black Man, Gouda, Clay 115.00
Place Mat, Aunt Jemima Family Restaurant, Paper 45.00
Place Mat, Coon Chicken Inn 20.00
Plaque, Mammy Face, With Hook, Plaster, 1950s, 5 X 6 In. 30.00
Plaque, Wall, Girl, Googly Eyes, Under Umbrella, Chalkware 15.00
Plate, Coon Chicken Inn, 5 1/2 In., 4 Piece 380.00
Plate, Painted Child Eating Slice of Watermelon, Wooden 165.00
Platter, Coon Chicken Inn, Large Head, 11 In. 300.00
Postcard, Child, Pops Out of Basket When Card Turned, 1908 .... 8.00
Poster, Lime Kiln Club, Blacks, 24 X 36 In. 935.00
Poster, Negro American League, K.C.Monarchs, Harlem Stars, 1940s 95.00
Potholder, Boy & Girl Eating Watermelon 24.00
Potholder, Chef & Mammy, Pair 25.00
Print, Fortune Teller, Original Frame 325.00
Print, Last One In's A Nigger, 1898 .... 150.00 To 245.00
Print, Washday Blues, Black Baby, Sacra, Framed, 14 X 18 In. 125.00
Puppet, Black Ventriloquist's Dummy, Wooden Hands, Dressed, 1900s 3500.00
Puzzle, Little Black Sambo, Box, 1940s 17.50
Record, Little Black Sambo, 78 RPM, Listen–Look Book, 1941 .... 65.00
Salt & Pepper, Aunt Jemima & Uncle Mose, 5 In. 35.00
Salt & Pepper, Aunt Jemima & Uncle Mose, Plastic, F&F Mold, 3 1/2 In. 25.00
Salt & Pepper, Aunt Jemima, Range Set, With Grease Container 75.00
Salt & Pepper, Black Boy & Dog, Van Tellingen 20.00
Salt & Pepper, Black Boy Holding Slice of Watermelon 55.00
Salt & Pepper, Black Man & Woman, Valentine 95.00
Salt & Pepper, Black Waiters, 4 1/2 In. 18.00
Salt & Pepper, Black Woman, Baby In Lap 45.00
Salt & Pepper, Butler 52.50
Salt & Pepper, Chef Winking, Mammy Poking Tongue 49.00
Salt & Pepper, Mammy & Chef, Pearl China, Large 75.00
Salt & Pepper, Mammy & Chef, Pearl China, Small 50.00
Saucer, Coon Chicken Inn 55.00
Shaker, Boy On Eggplant, Ceramic 25.00
Sheet Music, Amos 'N' Andy, Perfect Song, Pepsodent Premium, 1935 .... 10.00
Sheet Music, Aunt Jemima's Picnic Day, 1914 .... 20.00
Sign, Cream of Wheat, Black Schoolmaster, Students, 1917, 9 X 12 In. 27.50
Sign, German Mixed Pickles, Mammy, White, Black Baby, Man, 12 X 24 In. 1650.00
Sign, Goetz Brewing Co., Jerry's Smile, Self Framed, 3 X 2 Ft. 3000.00
String Holder, Black Mammy, Pottery 95.00
String Holder, Butler 95.00
String Holder, Mammy, Checkered Dress, Hole In Flowerpot, Pottery 110.00
Sugar & Creamer, Mammy, Cover, F & S 85.00
Syrup, Aunt Jemima 42.50
Tablecloth, Black Boy, Watermelon, Farmer, Hoe, Printed, 48 X 54 In. 55.00
Tablecloth, Embroidered Black Child & Woman Corners 65.00
Tea Cozy, Black Mammy 36.00
Teapot, Black Man Clown, Pottery 30.00
Tin, Aunt Jemima Salad Oil, 1 Qt. 375.00
Tin, Golliwog 65.00
Tin, Luzianne Mammy Coffee, Salesman's Sample 125.00
Tin, Mason's Stove Polish 43.00
Tin, Picture of Black, Rapid Cleanser, It Sure Do Clean 35.00
Tin, Sambo Axle Grease 95.00
Toothpick, Cotton Bale, 2 Men, Metal 125.00
Towel Set, Mammy, Embroidered, 7 Days of The Week, Unused, 7 Piece 185.00
Towel, Mammy, Washing Floor 39.00
Toy, Alligator, With Native On Back, Tin, Windup, Chein 270.00
Toy, Amos & Andy Walkers, Tin Litho, Mechanical, Blinking Eyes, 11 In. 2090.00

Toy, Black Dancing Man, On Stick, Uncle Charlie, 1951 .... 75.00
Toy, Black Man & Mule, Animated, Pull 295.00
Toy, Black Native Face, Tin Litho, String Toy, Germany, 2 1/2 In. 115.00
Toy, Chicken Snatcher, Tin, Windup, Man Running, Chicken In Hand, Dog 1285.00
Toy, Dancing Dan, Box 465.00
Toy, Darkie & Dog, Tin Litho, Mechanical, Touched Up Paint, 6 1/2 In. 220.00
Toy, Darkie & Dog, Windup, Tin Litho, Germany, 6 3/4 In. 247.50
Toy, Doll, Squeeze, Painted Composition, Bellows For Mouth, 12 In. 275.00
Toy, Ham & Sam, Tin, Windup, Strauss Co. 700.00
Toy, Hey–Hey, Chicken Snatcher, Mechanical, Tin Litho, Marx, 8 1/2 In. 577.50
Toy, Jazzbo Jim, Mechanical, Tin Litho, Strauss, 10 In. 302.50
Toy, Jazzbo Jim, Standing On House 450.00
Toy, Jazzbo Jim, Tin Litho, Mechanical, Unique, Box, 10 1/2 In. 445.00
Toy, Jazzbo Jim, Windup 675.00
Toy, Mammy & Broom, Mechanical, Tin Litho, Lindstrom, 8 In. 176.00
Toy, Man, Walker, Tin Litho, Mechanical, Blinking Eyes, Marx, 11 In. 440.00
Toy, Porter, Tip Top, Tin, Windup, Box 450.00
Toy, Rollo–Chair, Man, Pushes Chair, Tin, Mechanical, Strauss, 6 In. 2500.00
Toy, Spic & Span, Mechanical, Tin Litho, Marx, 10 In. 1875.00
Toy, Sweeping Mammy, Tin Litho, Mechanical, Box, Lindstrom, 8 In. 445.00
Toy, Tom Tom Jungle Boy, Tin Litho, Cloth, Louis Marx, Box, 7 In. 159.00
Toy, Xylophone Player, Mechanical, Painted Tin, Fabric, Germany, 10 In. 415.00
Voucher, Southern Express Pay, Illiterate Porter, X, 1918, 4 X 9 In. 15.00

Blown glass was formed by forcing air through a rod into molten glass. Early glass and some forms of art glass were hand blown. Other types of glass were molded or pressed.

BLOWN GLASS, Bottle, Globular, Aqua, Twenty-Four Swirled Ribs, 8 1/4 In. 145.00
Canister, Blue Finial, Cobalt Blue Rings, 9 3/4 In. 585.00
Canister, Cover, Applied Rings, 10 3/8 In. 55.00
Canister, Oversize Tin Lid, 6 3/4 In. 85.00
Canister, Tin Lid, Aqua, 7 In. 225.00
Compote, Amber, Applied Foot, Wafer Stem, 3 1/2 In. 1400.00
Compote, Pillar Mold, Applied Foot, 8 Ribs, Folded Rim, 7 In. 295.00
Compote, Teardrop Center Stem, 7 3/8 In. 25.00
Creamer, 12 Vertical Ribs, Folded Lip, 5 1/2 In. 105.00
Creamer, 16 Vertical Ribs, Cobalt Blue, 3 3/4 In. 150.00
Creamer, Applied Foot & Handle, Rigaree Attachment, 3 7/8 In. 150.00
Creamer, Ear Handle, Deep Blue, 1830–50, 3 3/4 In. 500.00
Creamer, Golden Amber, Ten Swirled Ribs, Applied Handle, 3 In. 25.00
Cruet, 16 Vertical Ribs, Hollow Handle, 7 1/4 In. 45.00
Cruet, Vertical Ribs, Hollow Handles, Ribbed Stopper, 8 In. 150.00
Cuspidor, Invalid's, Folded Lip, Amber, C.1830, 5 1/4 In. 245.00
Darning Egg, End of Day, Multicolored, 3 X 4 1/2 In. 175.00
Decanter, 3 Applied Rings & Peacock Eye, Stopper, 6 3/4 In. 270.00
Decanter, 4 Vertical Ribs, Sterling Silver Stopper, 10 1/4 In. 75.00
Decanter, Cranberry, Clear Stopper & Handle 275.00
Decanter, Geometric Pattern, 3 Mold 385.00
Decanter, Rigaree Handles, 2 Pouring Lips, Emerald, 7 1/2 In. 125.00
Decanter, Windmills, Applied Rigaree, Clear, 9 1/2 In. 30.00
Firing Glass, Teadrop & Crimped Base, Pair 125.00
Flask, Chestnut, Amber, Twenty-Four Swirled Ribs, 4 3/4 In. 275.00
Goblet, Cut Floral Design, 5 1/2 In. 50.00
Goblet, Thumbprint Design, Hexagonal, Amethyst, 6 3/8 In. 65.00
Jar, Iridescent, Flecks, Blue Interior, Eickholt, 1977, 8 1/2 In. 125.00
Jigger, Pittsburgh, Sapphire Blue, Six Panels, 2 1/4 In. 20.00
Lamp, Hand, Purple–Blue, Applied Handle, 19th Century, 3 1/8 In. 2000.00
Pitcher, Applied Handle, 5 1/4 In. 165.00
Pitcher, Green, Open Pontil, Reed Handle, Gold Design 50.00
Pitcher, Pillar Mold, Applied Handle, Ground Pontil, 9 In. 375.00
Pitcher, Tooled Foot & Lip, Amber, 6 In. 325.00
Sugar, Cover, Applied Font & Finial, Sapphire Blue, 7 1/4 In. 275.00
Sugar, Cover, Cobalt Blue, 7 In. 300.00
Sugar, Knop Finial, Folded Rim, Bell Shape, 7 5/8 In. 325.00

Tumbler, Aqua, Applied Handle, 5 In. 1150.00
Tumbler, Footed, Cut Panels, 3 1/4 In., Pair 140.00
Vase, Baluster Stem & Bowl, 12 Arched Panels, 9 1/8 In. 175.00
Vase, Copper Wheel Engraved Bowl, Clear, 8 In. 100.00
Vase, Horse Chestnut Pattern, Vaseline Opalescent, 8 1/2 In. 255.00
Whimsey, Pregnant Pig, Clear, 2 Piglets Inside Her, 4 1/2 In. 105.00
Whimsy, Apple, 19th Century 280.00
Wine, Applied Foot & Knop Stem, Amethyst, 4 3/8 In. 75.00
    BLUE AMBERINA, see Bluerina
    BLUE GLASS, see Cobalt Blue
    BLUE ONION, see Onion

 Blue Willow pattern has been made in England since 1780. The pattern has been copied by factories in many countries, including Germany, Japan, and the United States. It is still being made. Willow was named for a pattern that pictures a bridge, birds, willow trees, and a Chinese landscape.

BLUE WILLOW, Bowl, Johnson Bros., 5 In. 4.00
Bowl, Vegetable, Cover, Dudson, Wilcox, 9 1/2 In. 45.00
Bread Plate, Japan 1.50
Cake Lifter 49.50
Canister, Cover, Oval, Small 49.50
Children's Set, 21 Piece 165.00
Clock, Wall, Seth Thomas 500.00
Coffeepot, Japan, 7 1/2 In. 50.00
Cracker Jar, Cover, Metal Top Rim, Handle 189.00
Creamer, Japan 5.00
Cruet Set 105.00
Cup & Saucer, Child's 6.50
Cup & Saucer, Homer Laughlin 8.00
Cup & Saucer, Johnson Bros. 8.00
Cup Plate, Japan 3.00
Cup Plate, Purple Luster Rim, 4 In. 75.00
Cup, Geisha Lithophane In Bottom 25.00
Cup, Japan 3.50
Eggcup 10.00
Grill Plate, Child's 45.00
Grill Plate, Japan, 10 In. 12.00
Grill Plate, Moriyama 19.00
Jug, Batter, Cover, Paneled 128.00
Lamp, Kerosene, 8 1/2 In. 50.00
Mixing Bowl Set, Moriyama 500.00
Pitcher, Milk, Newport, England 85.00
Plate, Child's 7.00
Plate, Dinner, Homer Laughlin 8.00
Plate, Dinner, Japan 4.00
Plate, Homer Laughlin, 6 In. 3.00
Plate, Hot Water, C.1840 .... 225.00
Plate, Johnson Bros.8 In. 5.00
Plate, Staffordshire, 8 1/4 In. 25.00
Platter, Allerton 75.00
Platter, Homer Laughlin, 13 1/2 In. 20.00
Platter, Ironstone, Staffordshire, 15 In. 100.00
Platter, Johnson Bros., 14 In. 25.00
Salt Box, Wooden Cover, Japan 60.00
Saucer, Japan 1.00
Scoop, Ice Cream, China Handle 25.00
Sugar & Creamer, Child's 12.50
Sugar & Creamer, Cover, Homer Laughlin 20.00
Sugar & Creamer, Peacock & Urn 35.00
Tablecloth, 54 X 54 In. 28.50
Tea Set, Child's, 2 Place Settings 95.00
Teapot, Child's, Large 17.50
Thimble 20.00

The Boch Freres factory was founded in 1841 in La Louviere in eastern Belgium. The wares resemble the work of Villeroy & Boch. The factory is still in business.

BOCH FRERES, Pitcher, Art Deco, Large	225.00
Vase, Gourd Shape, Foliage, C.1925, 11 3/8 In.	265.00
Vase, Yellow Crackle, Ovoid, 12 1/2 In.	150.00

Osso China Company was reorganized as Edward Marshall Boehm, Inc., in 1953. The company is still working in England and New Jersey. In the early days of the factory, dishes were made, but the elaborate and lifelike bird figurines are the best known ware. Edward Marshall Boehm, the founder, died in 1961; but the firm has continued to design and produce porcelain. Today, the firm makes both limited and unlimited editions of figurines and plates.

BOEHM, Figurine, American Bald Eagle	1260.00
Figurine, Canada Geese, Pair	675.00
Figurine, Canada Goose With Goslings, No.408	690.00
Figurine, Dog, Brindle Boxer, 5 X 4 1/2 In.	200.00
Figurine, Dog, Bulldog Head, White	375.00
Figurine, Fledgling Bluebird, No.442	195.00
Figurine, Fledgling Bluejay, No.436	175.00
Figurine, Fledgling Chickadee, No.461	195.00
Figurine, Fledgling Crested Flycatcher, No.458	195.00
Figurine, Fledgling Robin	175.00
Figurine, Grosbeak, All White, C.1953, 6 X 9 In.	450.00
Figurine, Hummingbird & Cactus	950.00
Figurine, Lion & Lamb	295.00
Figurine, Madonna, 11 1/2 In.	225.00
Figurine, Mallards In Flight, No.406, 11 In., Pair	2050.00
Letter Opener, Eagle, Porcelain Handle, Bicentennial, 1976	95.00

Bohemian glass is an ornate overlay or flashed glass made during the Victorian era. It has been reproduced in Bohemia, which is now a part of Czechoslovakia. Glass made from 1875 to 1900 is preferred by collectors.

BOHEMIAN GLASS, Bowl, Cobalt Blue, Cut Hobstars & Diamonds, 5 In.	75.00
Cruet, Deer & Castle, Ruby	85.00
Decanter, 2 Stemmed Goblets, Vintage, Green To Clear, 15 In.	185.00
Decanter, Deer & Cottage, Stopper	125.00
Decanter, Ruby, Matching Stopper, Deer & Bird, 11 In.	115.00
Goblet, Cut & Engraved, Ruby Flashed, 7 7/8 In.	25.00
Goblet, Ruby & Clear Panels, Gilt Accents, 7 1/2 In., 10 Pc.	415.00
Jar, Dresser, Frosted Flowers, Gold Trim, 6 1/2 In., Pair	100.00
Lamp, Deer & Castle, 20 In.	350.00
Perfume Bottle, Red Cut To White, Triple Overlay, Brass Top	345.00
Powder Jar, Cover, Red, Etched Birds & Deer, 4 In.	75.00
Syrup, Floradora, Gold Trim	125.00
Tumbler, Etched Grapes & Leaves, Ruby To Clear	35.00
Vase, Bird & Castle, Balluster, 12 In.	180.00
Vase, Clear Diamond Panels, Ruby Cutout Panels, 10 1/2 In.	475.00
Vase, Gold Salmander Handles, Green, Purple, Marked, 10 In.	350.00
Wine, Deer & Cottage	27.00
Wine, Grape	35.00

Bone dishes were considered a necessary part of a table setting for the Victorian table. The crescent–shaped dish was kept at the edge of the dinner plate so the bones removed from the fish could be stored away from the uneaten food. Some bone dishes were made in more fanciful shapes and many resemble fish.

BONE DISH, Flow Blue, Lorraine 25.00
   Flow Blue, Martha 25.00
   Tonquin, Clarice Cliff 10.00

Bookends have probably been used since books became inexpensive. Early libraries kept books in cupboards, not on open shelves. By the 1870s bookends appear, especially homemade fretcarved wooden examples. Most bookends listed in this book date from the twentieth century.

BOOKENDS, Abraham Lincoln, Sitting On Bench, Bronze Finish 30.00
   Abraham Lincoln, Standing By Chair, Bronze, 1923 .... 35.00
   Black Cat, Ceramic, 6 In. 20.00
   Black Farmer & Wife, Cast Iron 30.00
   Brass, Inset With Jade, China 53.00
   Bust of Indian Chief, Bronzed, 4 In. 19.00
   Canterbury Cathedral, Bronze, 1928 .... 40.00
   Cat, Crouching, Cast Metal, Brass Finish, 5 1/2 In. 45.00
   Cat, Siamese, Brass, Omnibus Paper Label, 6 In. 45.00
   Caterpillar Bulldozer, With Man 75.00
   Cats, Crouched Down, Rears Up In Air, Brass, 6 1/2 In. 48.00
   Circus, Elephants Pushing Wagon, Wooden, 8 1/2 In. 55.00
   Covered Wagon, Oxen, Figures, Bronze Finish, Signed 45.00
   Dog Next To Fence, Syroco Wood 15.00
   Dog, German Shepherd, Bronze .... 50.00 To 95.00
   Dog, Scotty, Pressed Wood 25.00
   Ducklings, Bronze 75.00
   Eagle Head Rising From Base, Word Courage, Bronze, 1930, 5 5/8 In. 60.00
   End of Trail, Cast Iron 12.50
   End of Trail, White Metal 20.00
   Expandable, Applied Brass Trim, Arts & Crafts 100.00
   Flower Vine, Bronze & Sterling Silver, Art Deco, Patent 1912 .... 85.00
   Football Players, Cast Iron 60.00
   Gazelle In Relief, Frosted Clear Glass 85.00
   George Washington, Cast Iron, 1928, 5 In. 45.00
   Girl, Sitting With Book In Lap, Medieval, Bronze, 6 X 6 In. 250.00
   Goose Girl, Glass 25.00
   Hartford Fire Insurance Co., Bronze, Dated 1935 .... 100.00
   Horse At Stall Door, Hubley 125.00
   Horse, Jumping, American Glass 80.00
   Horse, Rearing, Policeman, Penna.State Police, Brass, 8 In. 60.00
   Horsehead, Frankart, Art Deco 75.00
   Indian Head, Brass, 1920s 50.00
   Kopper Kraft, Mission, Small 45.00
   Liberty Bell, Bronze Finish 20.00
   Lion, Bradley & Hubbard 26.00
   Male, Nude, Playing Cello, Bronze, Pompeian Bronze 45.00
   Monks Reading, Bronze Finish, 1922 .... 14.00
   Nude Holding Tambourine, Art Deco, Armor Bronze, 1927, Pair 275.00
   Nude, Winged Fairy, Frog Among Flowers, Art Nouveau, Metal 150.00
   Owl, Cast Iron, Original Paint 55.00
   Owls, Expansion, Brass 38.00
   Praying Hands & Bible, Plaster 6.00
   Sailing Ship, Jadite 50.00
   Scenic, Bradley & Hubbard 50.00
   Scotty, Full Figure, Frankart 25.00
   Scotty, Full Figure, Onyx Base, Spelter 60.00
   Ship, Cast Iron 14.00
   Stag, Hartford Insurance Co., Bronze 55.00
   Storm, Bronzed Metal, 1928 .... 15.00
   Thinker, Brass 12.00
   Thinker, Bronze 80.00
   Thinker, Bronze Finish 18.00
   Thinker, Cast Iron 8.00
   Trooper On Horse, Pennsylvania, State Police, Brass, 1921 .... 45.00

Bookmarks were originally made of parchment, cloth, or leather. Soon woven silk ribbon, thin cardboard, celluloid, wood, silver, tortoiseshell, and metals were used. Examples made before 1850 are scarce, but there are many to be found dating before 1920.

BOOKMARK, 23rd Psalm, Celluloid, Floral Design, 1912, 1 1/2 X 5 In. 4.00
  Auld Lang Syne, Engraved, Silver 45.00
  Beaded, Native American 38.00
  Brass Wash 12.00
  Cleveland, Stevenson, Marked 1893–97 .... 35.00
  Dog, Tin 17.00
  Eastman's Extract Wild Roses, Girl In Roses, 1888, 2 X 7 1/4 In. 8.50
  Golfer, Knickers & Cap, Art Deco, Enameled Brass 90.00
  Happy May Thy Birthday Be 65.00
  Hoyt's Perfume, Die Cut 17.00
  J.Hayden Muzzle Loading Shotguns, Oxford, Ohio 25.00
  Mark Estey Organ, Piano Co., Baby, 2 Sides, 1890, 2 1/4 X 6 In. 8.50
  National Geographic, Balloon, 1935, 2 1/4 X 7 In. 75.00
  Pear's Soap, Die Cut 18.00
  Presbyterian Sabbath School, Sailing Front, 1880, 1 1/2 X 5 In. 4.50
  Stouwerk Chocolate, Celluloid 24.00
      BOSTON & SANDWICH CO., see Sandwich Glass; Lutz

As soon as the commercial bottle was invented, the opener to be used with the new types of closures became a necessity. Many types of bottle openers can be found, most dating from the twentieth century. Collectors prize advertising and comic openers.

BOTTLE OPENER, 4–Eyed Man, Cast Iron 32.00
  4–Eyed Woman, Cast Iron 54.00
  Alligator & Boy, Cast Iron 160.00
  Alligator, Cast Iron ....65.00 To 140.00
  Amish Man, Cast Iron, Wall Mount, Wilton Products 500.00
  Auto Jack, Duff, Norton, Jacks, Wall Mount, Box 60.50
  Bear, Cast Iron, Brown, Wall Mount, John Wright Co. 99.00
  Beaver, Brass 115.00
  Billy Goat, Black, Cast Iron 45.00
  Billy Goat, White, Cast Iron 70.00
  Bird, Copper 137.50
  Buffalo Brewing Co., Bohemian, Sacramento, Calif. 15.00
  Cathy Coed, Girl, Carrying Books, L & L Favors, Cast Iron 710.00
  Charleston Beer Is Good, Kanawha Brewing Company 19.00
  Cockatoo, On Perch, Cast Iron, 5 In. 40.00
  Compliments of Grand Rapids Brewing Co., Silver Foam 21.00
  Cowboy & Cactus, Cast Iron 165.00
  Cowboy, Aluminum 5.00
  Cowboy, With Guitar, Cast Iron 150.00
  Decoy, Cast Iron 60.00
  Devil, Reclining, Aluminum 250.00
  Dodo Bird, Aluminum 31.50
  Dog, Bulldog, Cast Iron 125.00
  Dog, Cocker Spaniel, Cast Iron 15.00
  Dog, Dachshund, Brass 32.50
  Dog, Spaniel, Cast Iron 75.00
  Dolphin, Chrome–Plated, Double, Germany 25.00
  Donkey, Cast Iron ....25.00 To 60.00
  Drink Reisch's Gold Top Bohemian 10.50
  Drink Tiger Brew, South Bend Brewing Assn. 20.00
  Drunk At Lamp Post, Bent Post, Brass, England 45.00
  Drunk At Lamp Post, Leg Up, Green Post, Cast Iron 10.00
  Drunk At Lamp Post, Leg Up, Spats, Black Post, Dalecraft 125.00
  Drunk At Lamp Post, Tux, Spats, Green Post, John Wright Co. 20.00
  Drunk On Palm Tree, Cast Iron 125.00
  Elephant, Cast Iron ....40.00 To 65.00

Elephant, Pink, Seated, Upturned Trunk	35.00
Enterprise Brewing Co., Ale–Lager, Fall River, Mass.	16.00
Fish, Abalone Flat, Stands Alone	28.00
Fish, Aluminum, Large	26.00
Flamingo, Hollow Blown Mold, John Wright	80.00
Flamingo, Hollow Blown Mold, Wilton Products	50.00
Foundryman, Aluminum	22.00
Foundryman, White Pants, Cast Iron	106.00
Freddie Frosh, Pledge Dance 1955, Red Sweater, L & L Favors	400.00
Goat, Brass	135.00
Goat, Cast Iron	45.00
Golf Club	20.00
Handy Hans, Beta Sigma Rho, Pledge Formal, L & L Favors	140.00
Heart Design, Sterling Silver	47.50
Horse's Rear, Cast Iron	35.00
Ice Cream Slicer, Peerless Ice Cream, 11–24–14	12.00
Iron Worker, Cast Iron, 3 1/8 In.	185.00
Johnny Walker, Miniature	10.00
Key To Voight's Beer & Nurshin–Malt, Detroit	17.00
Key, Brass	14.00 To 60.00
Man, Blowing Horn, Brass	15.00
Nude Woman, Arms Over Head, Brass, 4 In.	16.00
Nude, Brass, Cap Lifter–Corkscrew, 6 1/2 In.	30.00
Nude, Copper Plated, 8 3/4 In.	30.00
Nude, Gilt, 4 1/2 In.	19.00
Ocean Liner France, Metal, Embossed Ship, In French, 1962	14.00
Old Man, Top Hat, Cast Iron	35.00
Old Snifter, Brass	20.00
Oriental Clown, Aluminum	45.00
Parrot, Bronze, Large	36.00
Parrot, Cast Iron	35.00 To 48.00
Parrot, Feathers On Neck, Wilton Products	26.00
Parrot, On Bottle Cap, Aluminum, Gold Paint	37.00
Parrot, On Ornate Perch, Painted Cast Iron	375.00
Parrot, Painted, John Wright Co.	110.00
Patty Pep, Yellow Hat, Skirt, Women's Weekend, '55	780.00
Peacock, Brass, Canada	45.00
Pelican, Cast Iron	60.00 To 65.00
Pelican, Copper, 8 On Bottom	159.00
Pelican, Painted, Cast Iron, John Wright	235.00
Pelican, Painted, Cast Iron, Wilton Products	46.00
Pheasant, Cast Iron, Life–Size Head	25.00
Pie Server, Eat The Best, Mrs.Wagner's Pies	15.00
Pumpkin Head, Aluminum	45.00
Pumpkin, Wall Mount, Cast Iron	50.00
Rolling Pin Lady, Copper, Hollow	12.00
Rooster, Cast Iron	40.00 To 75.00
S.S.Constitution, Brass, England	10.00
Sammy Samoa, Native Boy, Wearing 3 Leaves, L & L Favors	595.00
Sea Horse, Cast Iron	15.00
Seagull, Cast Iron	35.00 To 65.00
Shalom With Menorah Design	8.00
Skeleton, Aluminum	45.00
Skull, Cast Iron, White Paint, Wall Mount	725.00
Squirrel, Cast Iron	28.00 To 52.00
Stag Handle	20.00
Sterling Silver, Rugged Handle, 5 3/4 In.	35.00
Teeth, Patented	20.00
Tennis Racquet, Brass	20.00
Trout, Cast Iron	50.00
Uncle Sam, Wall Mount, Cast Iron	30.00

Bottle collecting has become a major American hobby. There are several general categories of bottles, such as historic flasks, bitters, household, and figural. For modern bottle prices and more old bottle prices, see the book "The Kovels' Bottles Price List" by Ralph and Terry Kovel.

BOTTLE, Apothecary, Metal Frame, Wall Mount Bracket, 1879	275.00
Apothecary, Pepto Bismol, Enamel Label	85.00

Avon started in 1886 as the California Perfume Company. It was not until 1929 that the name Avon was used. In 1939, it became Avon Products, Inc. Each year Avon sells figural bottles filled with cosmetic products. Ceramic, plastic, and glass bottles are made in limited editions.

Avon, Avon Calling 1905, 1973	10.00
Avon, Black Lady, Club, 1984	15.00
Avon, Electric Charger Car, 1970	3.00
Avon, Five Presidents, White, 1973	10.00
Avon, Pheasant, 1972	4.00
Avon, Toilet Water, Apple Blossom, 1941, Box	12.00
Avon, Toilet Water, Flower Time, 1948, Box	9.00
Avon, Volkswagen, Lotion, Box	10.00
Bar, Blown, Kent, Ohio, Globular	3700.00
Barber, Blown Glass, Deep Purple, White Enameled Scenes, Bulbous, Pr.	295.00
Barber, Clambroth, 8 In.	75.00
Barber, Clear, White Ceramic Stopper, 9 1/2 In.	10.00
Barber, Cobalt Blue, Hand Painted Flowers, 8 In.	95.00
Barber, Cranberry Crackle Glass, Polished Pontil, Pewter Top	145.00
Barber, Daisy & Fern, Cranberry	150.00
Barber, Geo.C.Mager, Ribbed, Blue, Stopper, 11 1/2 In.	87.50
Barber, Le Varns Hair Tonic, Label, Glass	68.00
Barber, Lion, Amber	12.00
Barber, Onion Shape, 12–Sided At Base, Enameled Design Base	65.00
Barber, Seafoam Label, Milk Glass, 12 In.	75.00
Barber, Stars & Stripes, Cranberry	325.00
Barber, T.Noonan & Co., Light Green	55.00
Barber, White Stars, Stripes, Tooled Mouth, Ground Pontil, C.1900	325.00
Barber, Wildroot Hair Tonic, For Professional Use Only, Label, 1940s	15.00
Barber, Witch Hazel, Milk Glass, Stopper	45.00
Barber, Woman's Face, Geo.C.Mager, Ribbed, Milk Glass, Stopper, 11 In.	87.50

Beam bottles are made to hold Kentucky Straight Bourbon, made by the James B. Beam Distilling Company. The Beam series of ceramic bottles began in 1953.

Beam, Ford Coupe	65.00
Beam, Miss Pumper	75.00
Beam, Model T, Box, Filled, 1974	200.00
Beam, Red Caboose	59.00
Beam, Train Set, Engine, Coal Car, Caboose, Track, 8 Piece	200.00
Beer, Demott's Porter & Ale, Light Blue–Green	35.00
Beer, Geo.A.Ticoulet, Split, Amber, Crown Top, Blown In Mold	22.00
Beer, Heidelbrau, Windber, Pa., Label	10.00
Beer, Pabst, Milwaukee, Amber, 7 1/2 In.	5.50
Beer, Porter & Ale, Embossed Star, Yellow–Lime Green, Iron Pontil	190.00
Beer, Sunshine, Green, Grinning Boy Picture	10.00
Bitters, Baker's Orange Grove, 98% Label, Yellow	425.00
Bitters, Bourbon Whiskey, Barrel, Washington, Taylor, Cobalt Blue	2750.00
Bitters, Brown's Celebrated Indian Herb, Patented 1867, Amber	375.00
Bitters, Dr. J. Hostetter's Stomach, Yellow, Olive Cast	325.00
Bitters, Dr. Walkinshaw's Curative, Batavia, N.Y., Label, Amber	450.00
Bitters, Drake's Plantation, Amber, 10 In. .... 38.00 To 52.00
Bitters, Greeley's, Barrel, Olive Green	575.00
Bitters, Holtzermann's Patent Stomach, Applied Mouth, Medium Amber	625.00
Bitters, Loveridges Wahoo, Buffalo, N.Y., Salt Glaze	825.00

Bitters, Mishler's Herb, Amber, 8 1/2 In. 28.00
Bitters, Old Quaker Bourbon 9.00
Bitters, Seaworth Bitters Co., Figural, Lighthouse, Cape May, 1870 .... 2860.00
Bitters, Tippecanoe 50.00
Bitters, Woodcock Pepsin, Amber, 8 In. 49.50
Bluing, Sawyer's Crystal Bluing, 10 Oz. 8.00
Bromo Seltzer, On Dispenser Stand 145.00
Brooks, F.O.E. Eagle, Decanter, 1979 .... 12.00
Brooks, Owl, Decanter 40.00
Brooks, Shrine, Clown, Decanter 10.00
Canteen Shape, Grant On 1 Side, Lee On Other, G.A.R., Pottery 225.00
Casper Co., Lowest Price Whiskey, Wire Bail, Pottery, 1 Gal. 95.00
Catsup, Knox 7.50
Chlorine, Platt's, Aqua, 1913, 1 Qt. 12.00
  BOTTLE, COCA-COLA, see Coca-Cola, Bottle
Cologne, Gothic Arches, Blue Overlay, 9 In. 220.00
Cologne, Petticoat Form, Clear To Cobalt Blue, 7 1/4 In. 330.00
Cosmetic, Massage Cream, California Perfume Co., 1916 .... 120.00
Cosmetic, Professor Woods Hair Restorative, Aqua, 1 Qt., 9 In. 475.00
Cosmetics, Toilet Water, Devonshire Violets, Barrel Shape 15.00
Cough Syrup, Cauvins, 5 3/4 In. 7.00
Cure, Sanford's Radical Cure, Cobalt, 1860, Rectangular, 7 1/2 In. 40.00
Decanter, McK G II-7, Barrel, 3-Mold, Aqua, 1820 .... 2860.00
Decanter, McK G III-02, Stopper, Clear, 1830, 1 Qt. 495.00
Drug, Davis & Miller Druggists, Baltimore, 9 In. 110.00
Drug, Volina Cordial Drug Co., Baltimore, Md., Amber, 10 In. 8.00
Figural, Bob Fitzsimmons, Prizefighter 1150.00
Figural, Cologne, Jester, Butterfly On Chest, Dog Between Legs, 7 In. 60.00
Figural, Fat Man, Label On Stomach, 7 In. 90.00
Figural, Fish, Silver-Plated, Towle 75.00
Figural, Gold, 19th Hole, 1930s 85.00
Figural, Indian Queen, Shampoo, Clear, 1920s, 13 In. 75.00
Figural, Indian, Mohawk Pure Rye, Amber, Pat. Feb. 1868, 12 1/2 In. 2425.00
Figural, Man In The Moon, Amber, Green Base, Shot Glass, 13 In. 1900.00
Figural, Matador, Clear, 11 3/4 In. 30.00
Figural, Old Jalopy, Store Display, 1920, Large 165.00
Figural, Owl, Shot Glass Stopper, Marshall Field Label, 9 1/4 In. 40.00
Figural, Pineapple, A.L. Lacroix, Pat. October 1st, 1870 .... 2530.00
Figural, Pineapple, W & Co., N.Y., 1860 .... 990.00
Figural, Pistol, Eagle, 13 Stars, Brass 200.00
Figural, Senorita, Clear, 12 1/2 In. 30.00
Flask, Clasped Hands, Union, Aqua, 1860 .... 500.00
Flask, Cornucopia, Urn, Lancaster Glass Works, N.Y., Ice Blue, 1 Qt. 1150.00
Flask, For Pike's Peak, Prospector, Eagle, Golden Amber, 1 Pt. 775.00
Flask, General Washington, Eagle, Colorless, 1820-40 .... 1265.00
Flask, Keene, Marlboro Street, Amber Neck, Yellow-Green, 1820-40 .... 3850.00
Flask, Lafayette, De Witt Clinton, Coventry, Ct., Open Pontil, Yellow 500.00
Flask, McK G II-1, Eagle, Aqua, Sheared Lip, OP, Seed Bubbles, 1 Pt. 140.00
Flask, McK G II-60, Eagle, Charter Oak, Amber, 1820, 1/2 Pt. 350.00
Flask, McK G IV-28A, Masonic, Peacock Green 550.00
Flask, McK G VIII-04, E.G. Booz's Old Cabin Whiskey, Amber 1 Qt. 1265.00
Flask, McK G X-1, Pike's Peak, Aqua, 1/2 Pt. 145.00
Flask, McK G XI-27, Pike's Peak, 1 Pt. 125.00
Flask, McK G XI-53, Pike's Peak, Green, C.1870, 1 Pt. 1650.00
Flask, McK G XII-10, Sunburst, Keene, Light Olive, Pontil, 1/2 Pt. 275.00
Flask, Newburgh Glass Co., Patent Feb. 27th, 1866, Olive Green, 1 Pt. 550.00
Flask, Painted Design, Oval Portrait, Olive Green, Demijohn 350.00
Flask, Sheaf of Grain, 5-Pointed Star, Open Pontil, Green 475.00
Flask, Washington Monument, Corn For The World, Blue, 1 Qt. 2800.00
Flask, Whiskey, Grand Army of The Republic 95.00
Flask, Whiskey, Prohibition Secret, Doughnut Shape 75.00
Food, Brer Rabbit Molasses, Cartoon Label, Sample 20.00
Fruit Jar, Amazon Swift Seal, Aqua 12.50
Fruit Jar, Atlas E-Z, Aqua, 58 Oz. 35.00

Fruit Jar, Atlas Good Luck, 1/2 Pt.	12.00
Fruit Jar, Ball Ideal, Glass Lid, Aqua, 1908, Pt.	5.00
Fruit Jar, Ball Mason, Aqua, Pat. 1858, 1/2 Gal.	5.00
Fruit Jar, Helmes, Lorrilord Co., Amber, 1 Qt.	18.00
Fruit Jar, J.D. Willoughby, Inverted Base, Iron Pontil, 6 3/4 In.	165.00
Fruit Jar, Kerr Anniversary, Amber, 1 Qt.	30.00
Fruit Jar, Lockport, Blue, 1 Pt.	35.00
Fruit Jar, Mason, Maltese Cross, 1858, 1/2 Gal.	5.00
Fruit Jar, Medford Preserved Fruit, Cornflower Blue, 2 Qt.	240.00
Fruit Jar, Osotite, Diamond On Side, Fairfield, Iowa, 1924, 1 Qt.	85.00
Fruit Jar, Root Mason, Aqua, 1/2 Gal.	5.00
Fruit Jar, Swayzee's Improved Mason, Aqua, 1/2 Gal.	5.00
Fruit Jar, Victory, Clear, 1 Pt.	25.00
Fruit Jar, Wan–Eta Cocoa, Amber, 1 Qt.	38.00
Fruit, Pacific Mason, Clear, 1 Qt.	30.00
General Taylor, Monument Portrait, Bright Green, 1830, 1 Pt.	1500.00
Humphrey's Veterinary Specifics, Horsehead Circle, Cork, 3 1/2 In.	22.00
Ink, Carter's, Cathedral, Light Cobalt Blue, 1 Pt.	75.00
Ink, Carter's, Gothic Arch, Paper Labels, Pewter Cap, 8 3/4 In.	25.00
Ink, Harrison's Columbian Ink, Open Pontil, Cobalt Blue, 4 5/8 In.	500.00
Ink, Jacobs & Brown, Hamilton, Ohio, 12 Sides, Pale Green, 2 1/2 In.	375.00
Ink, Pitkin–Type, Swirled Rib	525.00
Ink, R.B. Snow, St.Louis, 12 Sides, Open Pontil, Aqua, 1 7/8 In.	400.00
Ink, Tangerine Form, Light Olive–Amber	475.00
Ink, Teakettle, Smooth Base, Sheared & Ground Lip, Amber, 2 1/8 In.	750.00
Ink, Umbrella, 8 Sides, Smooth Base, Folded Lip, Cobalt Blue	450.00
Ink, Wheeler's Premium Ink, Jet Black, Paper Litho, Green, 9 In.	77.00
Ink, Wm. Allen & Co., Ledger Inks, Stoneware, Pouring Spout, 8 In.	45.00
Lancaster Glass Works, Cobalt, Iron Pontil	70.00
Medicine, Bennett's Magic Cure, Smooth Base, Cobalt Blue, 5 1/4 In.	400.00
Medicine, Boracetanile, John Wyeth & Bros. Mfg. Chemists, 9 1/2 In.	10.00
Medicine, Davis Botanic Cholagogue, Open Pontil, Aqua, 6 1/8 In.	325.00
Medicine, Dr. Craig's Cough & Consumption Cure, Orange Amber, 8 In.	625.00
Medicine, Dr. J.S. Wood's Elixir, Albany, N.Y., Green, 8 3/4 In.	1100.00
Medicine, Dr. Porter, New York, Open Pontil, 6 In.	38.00
Medicine, Dr. Scholl's Bunion Remover, 1913	20.00
Medicine, Dr.Jones Liniment, Cork Top, Embossed Beaver, Aqua	20.00
Medicine, Dr.King's Croup & Cough Syrup, Aqua, 5 1/2 In.	140.00
Medicine, Ferro Salicylata Liquid, Label, Square, 8 In.	10.00
Medicine, For Health Sake Drink Peptolac	235.00
Medicine, Friend's Rheumatic Dispeller, Open Pontil, Aqua, 6 5/8 In.	450.00
Medicine, Hair Restorer, Martha Washington, 7 In.	160.00
Medicine, MacArthur's Genuine Yankee Liniment, Aqua, 7 5/16 In.	400.00
Medicine, Otto's Cure For Throat & Lungs, Aqua	14.00
Medicine, Race's Indian Blood Remedy, Aqua, Applied Top, 9 In.	45.00
Medicine, Robert Gibson Tables, Manchester, England, Aqua, 13 In.	12.00
Medicine, Schenck's Pulmonic Syrup, Phila., 8 Sides, Open Pontil	45.00
Medicine, Sweet's Black Oil, Rochester, N.Y., Open Pontil, Green	875.00
Medicine, W.W. Huff's Liniment, Open Pontil, Emerald Green, 5 In.	1950.00
Medicine, Warner's Safe Diabetes Cure	75.00
Milk, Ayrhill Farms, Adams, Mass., 1 Qt.	7.00
Milk, Borden's, Elsie The Cow Painted On Side, 1/2 Pt.	15.00
Milk, Brookfield Dairy, Baby Face, 1/2 Pt.	55.00
Milk, Butler Dairy, Willimantic, Conn., 1 Qt.	12.00
Milk, Canyon Creek Dairy Co., Purple, 1 Qt.	10.00
Milk, Cream Valley Dairy, Woodstown, N.J., 1 Qt.	8.00
Milk, Farrell's Dairy, Bradford, Pa., 1/2 Pt.	5.50
Milk, Hendrick's Dairy, Perkasie, Pa., Red Pyro, Cream Top, 1 Qt.	23.00
Milk, Indianhills Farms, Indian On Front & Back	12.50
Milk, Jersey, Red Painted Label, Cow's Head Center, 1 Qt.	5.00
Milk, Maplewood Dairy, Fairhaven, Vt. & Hudson Falls, Amber, 1 Qt.	10.00
Milk, Mt. Ararat Farms, Maryland, Cream Top, 1 Qt.	35.00
Milk, Pemrick's Dairy, Cambridge, N.Y., 1 Qt.	6.00
Milk, Rosebud Creamery, Red Painted Label, Plattsburg, N.Y., 1/2 Pt.	2.00

Milk, Rosebud Dairy, 2 In.	8.00
Milk, Seeger's Dairy, Merrill, Wisc., 1/2 Pt.	5.00
Milk, Tenny Wayside, Greenfield, Mass., 1 Qt.	6.00
Milk, Thatcher Farm, Cream Top, 1 Qt.	12.00
Milk, Wilson's Dairy, Grenwich, N.Y., 1 Qt.	6.00
Mineral Water, Avon Spring Water, Olive Green, 1 Qt.	500.00
Mineral Water, Darien Mineral Springs, Tifft & Perry, Aqua, 1 Pt.	450.00
Mineral Water, Lynch & Clarke, N.Y., Pontil Base, Olive Amber, 1 Pt.	210.00
Mineral Water, Missisquoi Springs, Embossed Squaw, Olive Green	400.00
Mineral Water, Richfield Springs, Sulphur Water, Green, 1 Pt.	375.00
Mineral Water, Superior, Morristown, N.J., Emerald Green, Mug Base	195.00
Mineral Water, Washington Springs, Bust of Washington, Green, 1 Pt.	425.00
Naval Jelly, Figural, Nude, Frosted, 10 1/2 In.	85.00
Nurser, Cat, With Kittens	8.00
Nurser, Evenflo	4.50
Nurser, Kittens	5.00
Nurser, Perma, Vantines Since 1866, Baby Bottle Top	4.00
Nurser, Saratoga, With Brush, Box	30.00
Nurser, Sonny Boy, Embossed Baby, Lying On Bottle, 5 In.	16.00
Nursing, South Jersey, Nailsea Design, Crystal Body	95.00
Oil, F.S. Pease Sewing Machine Oil, Cornflower Blue, 5 3/4 In.	300.00
Oil, Mastic Spout, 1 Qt.	25.00
Onion, Black Glass, Handle, England	3900.00
BOTTLE, PERFUME, see Perfume Bottle	
Pickle, Iron Pontil, Paneled Shoulders, Aqua, 11 3/8 In.	85.00
Pickle, Wm. Underwood & Co., Boston, Iron Pontil, Aqua, 11 1/2 In.	650.00
Pinch, Milk Glass, Yellow, Mushroom Stopper, 9 1/2 X 3 3/4 In.	450.00
Poison, Champion Embalming Fluid, Aqua	45.00
Poison, Coffin Shaped Bottle, Coffin Shaped Tablets, 3 5/8 In.	210.00
Poison, Coffin, Cobalt Blue, Embossed, Blown In Mold, 3 1/2 In.	90.00
Poison, John Hulle, 8 Sides, Cobalt Blue, 3 In.	150.00
Poison, John Irving & Son, Brisbane, Diamond Shape, Amber, 8 1/2 In.	125.00
Poison, Label Under Glass, Ground Stopper, 7 1/2 In.	83.00
Sarsaparilla, Dr. Townsend's, Emerald Green, Iron Pontil	195.00
Seltzer, Home Town Beer & Soda Distributors, With Pump, 12 In.	40.00
Ski Country, Black Swan	55.00
Ski Country, Duck, Red Head	65.00
Ski Country, Jaguar, Decanter	70.00
Ski Country, Majestic Eagle, 1 Gal.	2000.00
Snuff, Allover Carved Cinnabar	95.00
Snuff, Erotic Scenes, Jade Top, Wooden Spoon, Oriental	75.00
Snuff, Lorilards, Macoby, Green, 1845–60, 4 1/2 In.	75.00
Snuff, Metallic Gold Boar, Blue Ground, Red Top	55.00
Snuff, Pilgrim, Flask Shape, Green Hardstone Stopper, 2 1/2 In.	1300.00
Soda, Donal & McShane, Emerald Green	60.00
Soda, F. Gleason, Sarsaparilla & Lemon, Rochester, Sapphire Blue	375.00
Soda, Ginger Ale, Carse & Ohlweiler Co., 7 In.	45.00
Soda, Gleason's Mineral Water, 10–Pin Shape, Cobalt Blue	525.00
Soda, Grimes Kola, 5 Cents, 12 Oz.	24.00
Soda, J & A Dearborn, N.Y., Cobalt Blue, 7 1/4 In.	450.00
Soda, Jas. McDonough, Geneva, N.Y., Iron Pontil, Cobalt Blue	240.00
Soda, Knicker Bocker Soda Water, 8 Sides, Iron Pontil, Teal Blue	375.00
Soda, Owen Casey Eagle Soda Works, Medium Green, Blob Top	35.00
Soda, Royal Crown Cola, Dated 1936	25.00
Soda, S. Smith, Auburn, N.Y., 1857, 10 Sides, Cobalt Blue	425.00
Soda, S.H. Boughton, Root Porter, Iron Pontil, Cobalt Blue	325.00
Syrup, Polar Bear, Paper Label, 6 1/4 In.	22.00
Water, Spring, Congress & Empire Spring Co., Emerald, 9 In.	38.00
Whiskey, A Wee Scotch, Brown, Miniature	85.00
Whiskey, Bale of Cotton, Embossed Shryock & Rowland, 8 1/2 In.	500.00
Whiskey, Belle of Anderson, White Milk Glass, 8 1/2 In.	80.00
Whiskey, Black Bull, Pottery, Box, 4/5 Qt.	27.50
Whiskey, Black Cat Rare & Old Whiskey, Seated Cat, 1870–1900, 1 Qt.	1700.00
Whiskey, Donkey Canteen Shape, Blue Porcelain, Cognac, 1914	35.00

Whiskey, Drinkometer, Brown, Miniature 65.00
Whiskey, Flask, Horseshoe, Brown, Miniature 55.00
Whiskey, Flask, Sewer Tile, A Good Sip, Miniature 85.00
Whiskey, Foghorn Leghorn, Sealed, Miniature 25.00
Whiskey, Hi Road 21, Strawberry Malt Liquor, Label, Canada, 1 Pt. 1.00
Whiskey, Lord Calvert, Canada Goose .... 35.00 To 85.00
Whiskey, Lord Calvert, Wood Duck 85.00
Whiskey, McK GVII–03, E.G.Booz's, Amber, 7 3/4 In. 900.00
Whiskey, Old Kentucky Bourbon, A.M. Bininger & Co., Amber, 8 In. 190.00
Whiskey, Seagram's Frost, White, Unopened, 1972 .... 400.00
Whiskey, The Duffy Malt Whiskey Co., Baltimore, 10 In. 19.00
Whiskey, Topic, Leadville, Colo., Strap Sides, Magnesium Top, 1/2 Pt. 200.00
Whiskey, Wild Turkey, No.3 .... 85.00
Wild Turkey, Fighting Gamecock 125.00
Wild Turkey, Horned Owl 1100.00
Wild Turkey, Lionstone Fireman, No. 1 Red Hat 125.00
Wild Turkey, Mountain Goat 800.00
Wine, Wistarburg, Painted Floral, Jared Irwin, 1770–90, 7 3/4 In. 1595.00
Zanesville, 24 Ribs, Swirl, Bright Citron, 1800–35, 7 1/2 In. 2860.00

Boxes of all kinds are collected. They were made of thin strips of inlaid wood, metal, tortoiseshell, embroidery, or other material.

BOX, see also Advertising, Box; Ivory, Box; Porcelain, Box; Shaker, Box; and various Porcelain categories.

BOX, American Eagle On Cover, From 1 Piece of Walnut, 4 3/4 X 8 In. 175.00
Apothecary, Late–Georgian, Mahogany Base, 2 Bottles, Early–19th Century 302.00
Ballot, Wooden Handle 20.00
Bats & Clouds, Natural Half Pearls, Chinese, Bronze & Coral, 4 In. 635.00
BOX, BATTERSEA, see Battersea, Box
Bentwood Band, Wallpaper Cover, Oblong, White Design, Brown, 13 In. 175.00
Bentwood, 3 Fingers On Base, Green Paint, Cover, 7 5/8 In. 525.00
Bentwood, 3 Sides Shape, Floral Design, Stripes Gold, Black, Blue, 7 In. 1300.00
Bentwood, Gold Stenciled Design, Brown Ground, Oval, 5 1/2 In. 500.00
Bentwood, Laced Seams, Oval, 14 1/2 In. 155.00
Bentwood, Lapped Seams, Red Varnish Finish, Round, 6 In. 25.00
Bentwood, Round Cover Has Scene of Ship, Hinged, 4 In. 225.00
Bentwood, Round, 2 Branded Labels On Cover, Dark Patina, 6 3/4 In. 125.00
Bentwood, Single Finger Construction, Copper Tacks, Oval, 5 3/8 In. 150.00
Bentwood, Spring Latch Cover, Lapped Seam, Copper Tacks, 7 1/2 In. 45.00
Bentwood, Stenciled Label On Cover, Round, 12 X 15 In. 35.00
Bentwood, Storage, Round, Varnish Finish, 15 1/2 In. X 9 3/4 In. 175.00
Bentwood, Storage, Round, Varnish Finish, Impressed Label, 11 X 5 In. 155.00
Bible, Incised, Iron Key, England, Oak, Branded R.P., 17th Century 355.00
Bible, Oak, Iron Lock, Hasp, & Strap Hinges, Cover, 21 3/4 In. 150.00
Bible, Wooden, Paint Design, Cover 550.00
Bird's–Eye Veneer, Filled With Checkers, 4 In. 85.00
Book Shape, Chip Carved Pine, 5 In. 50.00
Book Shape, Primitive, Snake Pops Out, Brown Finish, 5 1/2 In. 250.00
Book, Oak, Dark Finish, Primitive, 15 1/2 In. 150.00
Book, Spruce Gum, Carved, Slide Cover Top & Base, 3 X 5 In. 325.00
Bride's, Decoupage Scene On Cover, Floral Design, Stipes, Oval, 18 In. 500.00
Bride's, Hand Painted Angel Cover, Brown, Oval, 17 3/8 X 10 1/2 X 6 In. 1150.00
Bride's, Polychrome Floral Design, Bentwood Sides, Pine, 16 1/2 In. 750.00
Burl Walnut, 2 Blown Glass Decanters, England, 5 1/2 X 5 1/2 X 3 In. 440.00
Candle, Bittersweet Paint, Slide Cover, 5 1/2 X 6 X 14 In. 350.00
Candle, Dovetailed Walnut, Slide Cover, 14 In. 120.00
Candle, Hanging, 1 Drawer, Pine, 15 1/2 In. 400.00
Candle, Hanging, Hinged Cover, 2 Section Interior, Pine, 12 3/4 In. 275.00
Candle, Hanging, Slide Cover, English, Oak, 19 1/2 In. 105.00
Candle, Hanging, Spoon Rack, Pine, Natural Finish, 20 In. 250.00
Candle, Pin Striping, Painted Eagle & Shield Emblem On Cover, C.1830 .... 600.00
Candle, Pine, Green Paint, Black Stenciled Stylized Flowers, 15 In. 300.00
Candle, Shield Back, 2 Wire Hangers, Cylindrical, 12 1/2 In. 265.00
Candle, Tin, Cylindrical, Hinged Cover, 1 7/8 In. 400.00

Candle, Top Opening, Long Drawer Beneath, English, Oak, C.1780 .... 360.00
Candle, Wooden, Finger Grip, Red, Hand Painted Stars, 18 X 19 In. 9750.00
Candle, Wooden, Sliding Lid, Red & White Tulip, Dots, 9 X 4 X 3 In. 150.00
Candle, Wooden, Sliding Lid, Stenciled Floral, Brown, 12 X 5 X 4 3/4 In. 525.00
Cardboard, Floral Design, Wallpaper Covered, Oblong, Beige, 12 In. 300.00
Cardboard, Wallpaper Cover, Rectangular, Gray-Blue, Castles, 8 In. 300.00
Cedar, Tree Trunk Shape, Brand Band, Small 15.00
Chalk, Sliding Cover, Mortised Poplar, 13 X 3 3/4 In. 75.00
Cherry, Dovetailed Drawer, 17 1/2 In. 325.00
Cigar, Verse To Mother On Cover, Wooden 25.00
Cigar, Zinc Liner, Oak 25.00
Cigarette, Art Deco, Piano Shape, Gilded Metal, Bakelite Cover, 8 In. 75.00
Coffer, Neoclassical, Scrolling Designs, C.1900, 33 1/2 In. 110.00
Collar, Inside Mirror, Silver Inset On Top, Walnut, Dated 1877 .... 95.00
Cutlery, Georgian Provincial, Mahogany, Scalloped, Handle, 9 X 18 In. 2000.00
Desk, English, Oak, Dark Finish, 1699, 24 X 16 X 12 In. 800.00
Desk, Table Top, Pine, Dovetailed, 3 Interior Drawers, 17 X 17 X 7 In. 175.00
Ditty, Engraved & Polychrome Panbone, 19th Century, 8 In. 7150.00
Document, Center Landscape, Church, Hinged Cover, 13 X 8 1/2 In. 1650.00
Document, Design On Domed Top, Red, Green Leaves On Silver, 2 X 3 In. 175.00
Document, George III, Mahogany, Hinged Cover, Base, 7 X 16 X 7 In. 249.00
Document, Mustard Paint, Scalloped Design, 19th Century, 24 X 13 In. 350.00
Document, Painted Scroll On Lid, Grain Painted Sides, 8 1/4 X 17 In. 165.00
Document, Velvet Interior, Rosewood, French, 4 1/2 X 12 In. 715.00
Document, Walnut, English, Rosettes, Pinwheels, 20 1/2 In. 275.00
Dome Top, Dovetailed, Garden Scenes, Dancing Bears, Dueling, 9 In. 200.00
Dome Top, Floral, Geometric Design, Green, Blue, Black, Red, 30 3/4 In. 6100.00
Dome Top, Hinged, Grain Painted, B. Tilden, C.1830, 14 1/2 X 30 1/8 In. 935.00
Dome Top, Leaf-Type Designs, Several Coats of Varnish 605.00
Dome Top, Poplar, Black Paint, Star Flowers, Leather Handle, 16 In. 200.00
Dome Top, Poplar, Green Paint, Black Rectangles, Floral Design, 19 In. 325.00
Dome Top, Tole, Brown Japanning, Floral Design, 4 1/4 In. 90.00
Dough, Chip-Carved Edge, White Paint, Poplar, 8 3/4 X 15 In. 100.00
Dovetailed, 2 Drawers, Poplar, 7 1/4 In. 425.00
Dovetailed, Cherry & Poplar, Sliding Cover, 2 1/4 In. 65.00
Dovetailed, Mahogany, 2 Drawers, Oriental, 15 In. 50.00
Dovetailed, Painted Pine, Curved, Cutout Apron, Diamond Lid, 11 In. 175.00
Dovetailed, Pine With Walnut, Shield Shape Medallion, 31 1/4 X 21 In. 140.00
Dovetailed, Poplar, Red & Black Flame Graining, Iron Lock, 19 In. 450.00
Dresser, Malachite, Art Deco Bows, High Relief Sides & Top, 4 In. 68.00
Dresser, Puffy, Blown, Green, Floral Trace Enameled, Brass Collar, 4 In. 72.00
English Pine, Natural, Applied Cover & Base Molding, 16 1/2 In. 175.00
Figural, Duck, Curled Wings, Golden Tiger Eye, 4 X 5 1/2 In., Pair 650.00
Figures & Houses, Brass Fittings, Camphorwood, Chinese, 5 1/2 X 10 In. 75.00
Floral Printed Designs, Wallpaper Cover, Oval, 4 3/8 In. 305.00
Game Board, Cribbage, Walnut, 5 In. 65.00
Handkerchief, Woman Golfer Burned, Wooden 42.00
Hanging, Pine, 2 Sections, Crest, Hinged Cover, 9 1/2 In. 135.00
Hanging, Scalloped Front Edge, Pine, 6 X 14 In. 55.00
Hanging, Tin, Beaded Brass Trim, Hinged Lid, 4 1/4 In. 55.00
Hanging, Wooden, Hinged Drop Front Door, 4 Drawers, Black, Streaks, 16 In 775.00
Hardwood, Sliding Cover, 3 Inside Sections, 16 1/2 In. 75.00
Hat, Scenes of General Taylor On Horseback, Wallpaper, 12 1/2 X 15 In. 2300.00
Hat, Wooden, Red Paint, Primitive Design, Large 360.00
House, Cream, Painted Fruit Cluster, Hinged Cover, 1840, 6 X 6 X 10 In. 6000.00
Interior Till, Exterior Drawer, Pine, 17 1/2 In. 155.00
Jewelry, Carved Design On Cover, Charles Rohlfs, Oak, 1902, 12 1/2 In. 1815.00
Jewelry, Carved Oak, Hinged, Velvet Lining, 3 X 5 In. 20.00
Jewelry, Filigree Silver, Glass, Hinged, 1900s, 3 X 4 In. 55.00
Knife, Carved Handle, Cut-Out Heart, Cherry & Pine, 7 1/2 X 12 In. 155.00
Knife, Dovetailed, Bird's-Eye Walnut, 9 1/4 X 15 In. 800.00
Knife, Dovetailed, Poplar, 2 Sliding Covers, Compartments, 12 X 14 In. 125.00
Knife, Foliage Design, Brown & Green Paint, 9 X 13 In. 95.00
Knife, George III, Mahogany, Slant Hinge, Serpentine, 14 X 9 X 12 In. 385.00

Knife, George III, Slant Top, Fitted Interior, Irish, 15 1/2 X 16 In. 3300.00
Knife, Hepplewhite, Figured Mahogany, Star Inlay On Cover, 14 1/2 In. 250.00
Knife, Walnut, Divided, Cutout Handle, 9 1/2 X 13 1/4 In. 75.00
Lacquer, Gifts From Overseas, Russian, 4 1/2 X 3 In. 225.00
Lacquer, Hand Painted Pastel Nature Scene, Russian, 3 1/2 X 5 1/4 In. 225.00
Lacquer, Oval, Russian, Shalnev, 3 X 4 1/2 In. 245.00
Lacquer, Sivka–Burko–Magic Horse, Russian, 3 X 3 1/2 In. 200.00
Letter, Inlaid Oak, Sloped Hinge, Calendar, England, 10 X 11 X 6 In. 440.00
Metal Hopper, Dovetailed Drawer, Dated 1844, Square, 6 In. 225.00
Molded Top & Base, Green Paint, Stenciled, Initials, 1835, Small 300.00
Nesting, Bentwood, Lapped Seams, Iron Tacks, 5 3/4 To 10 1/4 In., 4 Pc. 180.00
Oak Graining, Strap Hinges, Brass Handle, 1851, 10 1/2 X 10 1/2 In. 85.00
Oak, Relief Carved, Iron Lock, Hasp, Hinges, England, 26 3/4 In. 325.00
Paint, Artist's, Unused, 1897 .... 20.00
Pantry, Wood Cover, Bail Handle, Oak, 6 1/2 X 11 1/2 In. 165.00
Pine, Burnt Orange Paint, Oak Leaf Border, 2 Dovetailed Trays, 12 In. 950.00
Pine, Gray Paint, Interlaced Wooden Bands, Round, 7 In. 325.00
Pine, Red Paint, Black Graining, Sliding Cover, 2 X 5 X 5 3/8 In. 275.00
Pine, Sliding Cover, Divided Interior, 5 3/4 X 16 X 16 In. 45.00
Pipe, Hanging, Carved Star In Arched Panel, Walnut, 13 X 7 In. 400.00
Polychrome Floral Design, Stripes, Polka Dots, Wooden Hinges, 12 In. 1000.00
Poplar, Flame Graining, Green, Yellow Striping, Cover, 9 1/2 In. 170.00
Poplar, Green Paint, 29 1/2 In. 250.00
Poplar, Sliding Cover, Green Paint, 24 1/2 In. 225.00
Prayer, Egyptian, Brass Life & Death Symbols, C.1900, 10 X 7 In. 125.00
Prison, Inlaid Cover & 3 Sides, Berks County, Nailed, 8 1/2 X 6 X 4 In. 200.00
Relief Carved Scenes, Black Cut To Red, Round, 7 1/2 In. 75.00
Salt, Hanging, Pine, Natural Patina, Branded Design, Dated, 10 3/4 In. 130.00
Salt, Slant Cover, Carved Front Panel, English, Oak, 9 3/4 In. 200.00
Sewing, Musical, Inlaid Walnut, Fitted, 1850, 7 X 14 X 10 In. 990.00
Snuff, Dr.Syntax, Shooting Pony, Yellow & Black Transfer, Papier–Mache 130.00
Spice, Hanging, Poplar, Red, Drawer Has 4 Compartments, 11 X 7 In. 200.00
Spice, Red Paint, 3 Sections, Sliding Cover, 10 In. 195.00
Spice, Toleware, 6 Interior Canisters & Grater, Stenciled Labels, 7 In. 85.00
Storage, Carved Compass Star Design On Cover, Bentwood, 10 1/4 In. 100.00
Storage, Red Paint, Bentwood, 4 X 9 1/2 In. 75.00
Storage, Stave Constructed, Wood Bands, Copper Tacks, E.W. Royce, 17 In. 50.00
Sugar, Twist–Off Cover, Arched Handle, Red & Black, Wooden, Round, 8 In. 325.00
   BOX, TEA CADDY, see Tea Caddy
Theorem, Fruit, Embossed Red Cardboard, 5 X 2 3/4 In. 55.00
Theorem, Pincushion Cover, Forget–Me–Not, Cardboard, Paper, 4 X 3 In. 40.00
Ties, Pyrographic, 11 In. 11.00
Tinder, Striker & Flint Inside Cover, Tin, Wooden Handle, 4 In. 522.50
Tobacco, Engraved Inscription, Animals, Horses, Copper & Tin, 6 1/4 In. 85.00
Trinket, Walnut Inlay, Sliding Cover, Diamond Design, 6 1/2 X 4 X 3 In. 100.00
Trinket, Wooden, Painted Tulip & Floral Cover & Sides, 4 X 2 5/8 In. 225.00
Vanity, Woman's, Brass Bound, Bottles & Manicure Set, Rosewood, C.1830 .... 575.00
Wallpaper, Blue & Black Floral, Yellow, Cardboard, Round, 3 X 1 3/4 In. 150.00

If you have an instant-on television set, beware! The instant-on works because a current is always running through the set, even when it is off. This means more power is used, the set wears out faster, and most serious for the collector, there is a greater risk of fire. Next time the set needs repair, ask the service man to remove the instant-on feature. If you use a remote unit to turn off the set, the same dangers exist. While on vacation, if your microwave oven has a clock, unplug it, as well as your instant-on TV.

Wallpaper, Marbelized Paper Cover, Newspaper Lining, 2 5/8 X 2 In. 375.00
Wallpaper, Vining Foliage & Lattice, Cover, Oct. 28, '96, 4 X 6 In. 250.00
Walnut, Dovetailed, Original Lock, Ivory Escutcheon, 12 In. 175.00
Walnut, Dovetailed, Overlapping Drawer, 2 Sections, 12 3/4 In. 200.00
Walnut, Hinged Cover, With Lock, Marquetry Inlay, 12 3/8 X 8 1/2 In. 425.00
Walnut, Raised Medallion On Cover, Dark Finish, 16 In. 110.00
Walnut, Wooden Latch & Hinges, Tapestry Lining, 8 5/8 In. 40.00
Writing, Burl & Bands of Marquetry Inlay, Fitted, 11 3/4 In. 325.00
Writing, Ebonized Molding, Brass Trim, Oak Veneer, English, 9 3/4 In. 85.00
Writing, Plover On Cover, Inner Chrysanthemums, Black & Gold Lacquer 1100.00
Writing, Poplar, Alligatored Red Paint, Striped, Crest, 12 3/4 In. 100.00
Writing, Primitive Landscape Scene, Dovetailed Drawer, 18 In. 3200.00

The Boy Scout movement in the United States started in 1910. The first Jamboree was held in 1937. Collectors search for any material related to scouting, including patches, manuals, and uniforms. Girl Scouts are listed under their own heading.

BOY SCOUT, Award, Silver Beaver, Sterling Silver 150.00
Ax, Official, Cover 18.00
Bank, Figural, Painted Cast Iron, 5 3/4 In. 132.00
Book, Boy Hikers Doing Their Bit For Uncle Sam, 1918 .... 6.00
Book, Golden Anniversary, R.D. Bezucha, Rockwell, 165 Pages, 1959 .... 40.00
Book, Pets, 1930 .... 7.50
Book, Test of Courage, A.L. Fletcher, M.A. Donohue Co., 1913 .... 6.00
Bugle, Rexcraft, Red Tassel, Case 95.00
Calendar, 1928, Brown & Bigelow 50.00
Calendar, 1937, Norman Rockwell, Full Pad, 14 X 7 1/2 In. 40.00
Calendar, 1945, Paper 12.00
Calendar, 1949, Norman Rockwell 30.00
Calendar, 1966, Norman Rockwell, Full Pad, 14 X 7 1/2 In. 30.00
Catalog, Boy Scouts of America Equipment, 78 Pages, 1941 .... 25.00
Diary, 1914 .... 22.00
Doorknob Hanger, Vote, November 6, 1956, Liberty Bell Shape 5.00
Figurine, Boy Scout, In Shorts, Silver Plated, 4 1/2 In. 27.50
Figurine, Saluting, Boy Scout Award, 19 In. 100.00
Flashlight 12.50
Handbook, 1930 .... 35.00
Handbook, 1938, Scoutmaster 10.00
Kerchief, Jamboree, 1935 .... 20.00
Knife, Remington ....85.00 To 100.00
Magazine, Life, Boy Scout Jamboree, 1950 .... 12.50
Match Holder, Hangs From Belt 15.00
Medal, 1910 .... 8.00
Medal, 1917, Liberty Loan 22.00
Pamphlet, First Boy Scout Jamboree, 1937 .... 5.00
Paperweight, Hat, Metal 8.00
Paperweight, Sequoia Council, Blue & Gold 40.00
Print, Anniversary, 1910–1960, Rockwell, 11 X 14 In. 7.50
Ring, Sterling Silver 16.00
Sash, Merit Badges, 15 Badges, 1950s 20.00
Scarf, National Jamboree, 1969 .... 15.00
Signal Set, Instructions, Box ....20.00 To 35.00
Tumbler, Half–Century Jubilee 5.00
Wristwatch, 1930s 200.00

Bradley & Hubbard Manufacturing Company made lamps and other metalwork in Meriden, Connecticut, from the 1840s. Their lamps are especially prized by collectors.

BRADLEY & HUBBARD, Andirons, Sunburst, C.1886 .... 3900.00
Chamberstick, Arts & Crafts 30.00
Chamberstick, Bronze & Copper, Lily Pad, Frogs, 7 In. 275.00
Desk Set, Black Textured Metal, Brass Corners 195.00
Humidor, Brass, Small 38.00
Inkstand, Milk Glass Insert, Art Deco, Brass, 8 1/2 In. 85.00

Lamp, 1–Light, 8 Carmel Slag Panels, Marked, 20 1/2 In.	335.00
Lamp, 3–Light, No.303b	130.00
Lamp, 3–Light, No.304	160.00
Lamp, 8 Curved Panels, Reverse Painted, Flowers, 24 In.	995.00
Lamp, Hanging, Milk Glass Shade, Electrified	475.00
Lamp, Kerosene, Brass, Hanging, Wall Bracket, Signed	160.00
Lamp, Oil, Onyx, Rococo, Frosted Shade, Electrified, 34 In.	575.00
Lamp, Reverse Painted Shade, Blossoms, 24 In. ....*Illus*	990.00
Lamp, Slag Glass, 6 Panels, Signed	300.00
Lamp, Table, Lakeside Scene, Pink & Yellow	1295.00
Lamp, Tulips, Green Ground, 18 In. ....:..........*Illus*	2500.00
Lamp, White Slag, Metal Shade, Gold Color, 14 In.	125.00
Mirror, Bacchus Head, Scrolls, Bronze Finish, 9 X 14 In.	95.00
Mirror, Father Neptune Head, Scrollwork, 14 X 16 In.	125.00
Pen Tray, Greek Key Border, Brass	18.50
Shade, Threaded, Band of Gold Flowers, Blue Ground	395.00
Tray, Pen, Greek Key Border, Copper	23.00
Tray, Pink, 3 Sitting Kittens, Signed, Marked, 5 X 7 In.	57.00

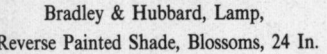 Brass has been used for decorative pieces and useful tablewares since ancient times. It is an alloy of copper, zinc, and other metals.

BRASS, see also Bell; Tool; Trivet; etc.

BRASS, Bed Warmer, Brass, Wooden Handle	275.00
Bed Warmer, Pierced Lid, Turned Handle, 58 In.	150.00
Bed Warmer, Tooled Design On Lid, Wooden Handle, 43 In.	320.00
Bed Warmer, Turned Cherry Handle, Engraved Flowers, 43 In.	500.00
Bowl, Footed, Dutch, Late 17th Century, 4 X 7 In.	385.00
Box, Hanging, Embossed Floral Design, 6 3/4 In.	25.00
Box, Sailing Ship On High Seas On Lid, George W. Frost, 6 1/4 In.	225.00
Box, Stamp, Double Pocket, Hinged Lid	28.50
Bucket, Coal, Victorian, Helmet Shape, 19th Century, 18 In.	50.00
Candle Lighter, Sliding Wick, 10 1/2 In.	195.00

Bradley & Hubbard, Lamp,
Reverse Painted Shade, Blossoms, 24 In.

Bradley & Hubbard, Lamp, Tulips,
Green Ground, 18 In.

Candle Sconce, Removable S Scroll Arms, 8 1/2 In., Pair 3100.00
Candleholder, Blue & White Latticino Swirl Shade, 5 In. 340.00
Candleholder, Fluted Columns, Bobeches, 18th Century, Signed E.K., Pr. 2600.00
   BRASS, CANDLESTICK, see Candlestick
Chamberstick, Push–Up, 3 3/4 In. 105.00
Chamberstick, Push–Up, Stamped Patent Secured, 3 1/4 In. 45.00
Chandelier, 4–Light, Crimped Pan, Hanging Loop, Dark Patina 205.00
Cigar Cutter, Figural, Horse, Germany, 11 1/2 In. 55.00
Cigar Cutter, Pilot's Wheel, 7–In. Base 95.00
Cigar Cutter, Rook, Put Cigar In Eye, Beak Scissors Cut, 19th Century 395.00
Cigar Wick Cutter, Scissors & Stand, Brass 65.00
Coffee Urn Set, Coronet, Art Deco, Chase, No.90121 .... 400.00
Coffeepot, Queen Anne, Long Straight Wooden Handle 2200.00
Compass, U.S. Army, Dated 1918 .... 75.00
Compass, Vernier, Surveyor's, Sights & Swing Needle 135.00
Compote, Black Bristol Glass Insert, White Flowers, 9 1/2 In. 75.00
Compote, Classical Scene of Satyr Center, 7 3/4 X 12 1/4 In. 20.00
Dish, Alms, Repousse & Hammered Floral Design, German, 15 1/8 In. 445.00
Door Knocker, Anchor, Signed Rostand 20.00
Door Knocker, Cartouche–Form Backplate, Poppy, England, 10 In. 225.00
Figurine, Art Deco Gymnast, 18 In. 105.00
Figurine, Boy, With Sailboat, Ladies of GAR, 1933, 3 1/4 In. 455.00
Figurine, Buddha, On Lotus Throne, Turquoise & Lapis, 6 3/8 In. 115.00
Frame, Picture, 3 1/2 Lb. 75.00
Graphometer, Surveyor's, France, 1770, 7 1/4 In. 1295.00
Humidor, La Palina, Chase 15.00
Incense Burner, Foo Dog, Teakwood Base, Marked 200.00
Inkwell, Sphinx 50.00
Inkwell, Temple Script 135.00
Kettle, Jam, Wrought Iron Bail, 12 X 7 In. 250.00
Magazine Rack, Crossed Golf Clubs, Victorian, 3 Footed 1100.00
Mortar & Pestle, 6 X 6 In. 100.00
Pail, Iron Bail Handle, Spun, 14 3/4 In. 75.00
Plaque, Reticulated, Floral Design, Hanging Chains, 6 In., Pair 82.50
Pot, Pounce, Cover, 3 1/2 In. 85.00
Sack Set, Electric, Chase, No.90093 .... 85.00
Salver, Persian Inscriptions In Silver, 18 In. 105.00
Samovar, Russian, 25 In. ....50.00 To 125.00
Samovar, Tray & Drip Receptacle 165.00
Samovar, Tray, Russia, 25 1/2 In. 390.00
Sconce, 2–Light, Early 1920s, Pair 85.00
Sconce, 2–Light, Lyre Form, Scrolled Arms, Baroque, 8 In., Pair 275.00
Sconce, Wall, Scrolled, 19th Century, 12 In., Pair 99.00
Spitton, Turtle, Brass Plated 475.00
Stand, Plant, Allover Open Carved, 19 X 11 In. 65.00
Stand, Shoeshine 65.00
Teakettle, Brass, Swing Handle, Dutch 650.00
Teapot, In Brass Frame, Warmer 165.00
Tieback, Gilt, Mid–19th Century, Set of 12 .... 1700.00
Tray, Engraved Fruit & Dragon, Made In China, 25 In. 30.00
Tray, Oriental Dragons, 12 3/8 X 17 7/8 In. 95.00
Vase, Applied Dragon, China, 7 In. 65.00
Watch Holder, Figural, Man Bagpiper, Seated, Dog, Continental, 8 In. 110.00
Watch Holder, Rococo, Father Time, Cupids, Late 19th Century, 13 In. 120.00
Watch Holder, Rococo, Scroll, Leaf & Floral Design, 8 1/2 In. 175.00
Wick Trimmer, Patent 1857 .... 50.00
   BREAD PLATE, see various Pressed Glass patterns

Glass bride's baskets or bride's bowls were usually one–of–a–kind
novelties made in American and European glass factories. They were
especially popular about 1880 when the decorated basket was often
given as a wedding gift. Cut glass baskets were popular after 1890.
All bride's baskets lost favor about 1905.

BRIDE'S BASKET, Birds In Ornaments, Plated Holder, 10 3/4 In. 85.00

Cranberry Overlay 50.00
Enameled Flowers, Tufted, Pink To White, Plated Holder 225.00
Figural Hands & Fruit On Handle, Wilcox 65.00
Hummingbirds, Silver Plate, Meriden 58.00
Loetz-Type Insert, Flowers, Lilies On Frame, 12 1/2 In. 495.00
Mauve, Green & Yellow, Brass Footed Holder, France 350.00
Pink & White Fluted Glass Edge, Silver Plated Base 225.00
Pink, Amber Rim, Flowers, 12 In. ....*Illus* 450.00
Ruffled, Enameled Forget-Me-Nots, Meriden Frame 495.00
Scalloped, Red To Yellow, Footed 195.00
Scrolled Blue Garlands, White Satin Glass, 5 1/4 X 11 In. 75.00
Tapestry Herringbone, Mother-of-Pearl, Thorn Handle, C.1812 .... 1250.00
Tufted Sides, Ruffled Rim, Enameled Flowers, Silver Frame 275.00
BRIDE'S BOWL, Aventurine 295.00
Enameled, Brass Stand, Germany, 8 In. 125.00
Maroon To Yellow-Green Overlay, Aurora Silver Plate, 11 In. 375.00
Mother-of-Pearl Opalescent, Enameled Floral, 8 1/4 In. 155.00
Mother-of-Pearl, Pink Satin, Herringbone, Webb 950.00
Pigeon Blood, Scalloped, Pleated, 11 In. 75.00
Pleated Rim, Aventurine 295.00
Portrait Center, Flowers, Ruffled, Cased Pink & White 195.00
Stylized Peacocks, Box Pleated Top, Swirl Pattern, 11 1/2 In. 395.00
White Opalescent Ribs, Fluted Ruffles, 11 1/4 In. 65.00

Bristol glass was made in Bristol, England, after the 1700s. The Bristol glass most often seen today is a Victorian, lightweight opaque glass that is often blue. Some of the glass was decorated with enamels.

BRISTOL, Biscuit Jar, Allover Enameled Flowers, Silver-Plated Lid, Handle 145.00
Box, Jewelry, Enamel Florals, Ball Feet, 5 X 5 1/4 In. 375.00
Box, Lift-Off Lid, Gold Bands, Flowers, Enameled Dots, 2 1/4 In. 85.00
Cracker Jar, Pansies, Burmese Ground, Signed A.J. Hall 175.00
Cup & Saucer, Floral Design With Gilt, Blue Mark 95.00
Decanter Set, Cobalt Blue, Sheffield Holder, 1880s, 3 Piece 895.00
Decanter, Old Design, Twig Handles 245.00
Flowerpot, Enamel Flowers 150.00
Lamp, Fragonard Painting, Tulip Form Shades, 3 Cased, 20 In., Pair 750.00
Lamp, Opaque Blue Base, Clambroth Font, Pewter Collar, 11 1/2 In. 85.00
Perfume Bottle, Enameled Flowers, Gold Trim, Crimped, 11 In. 195.00
Perfume Bottle, Gold Panels, Leaves, Flowers, Blue, 3 3/4 In. 85.00
Perfume Bottle, Raised White Flowers, Gold Trim, Blue 50.00
Perfume Bottle, Silver Plated Meriden Stand 225.00

Floodlights facing toward the house are better protection than floodlights facing away from the house. Moving figures and shadows can be seen more easily.

Bride's Basket, Pink, Amber Rim, Flowers,
12 In.

Salt & Pepper, Enameled Floral 65.00
Teapot, Polychrome Floral Enameling, Porcelain, 5 3/4 In. 425.00
Vase, Baluster Shape, Red Roses, Straight Neck, 14 1/2 In. 225.00
Vase, Botanical Design, Pink Overlay, 10 1/2 In. 85.00
Vase, Cherubs, Raised Enameled Scroll, Pale Cream, 10 In., Pair 130.00
Vase, Children, Ormolu Feet & Handles, Green, 6 1/2 In., Pair 175.00
Vase, Enameled Cherubs, 7 1/4 In., Pair 150.00
Vase, Enameled Classical Figure In Garden, Ovoid, 10 In. 35.00
Vase, Enameled Flowers, Beading, Silver-Plated Holder, 14 1/2 In. 250.00
Vase, Floral Design, Shaded Peach To Ivory, 12 In. 45.00
Vase, Gold Bands, Yellow & Gold Flowers, Turquoise, 5 1/8 In., Pair ... 125.00
Vase, Green & Brown Leaves, Ruffled, 11 1/4 In. 95.00
Vase, Hand Painted Flowers, White, 7 1/2 In. 45.00
Vase, Hand Painted Spidermums, Red & Green, 18 1/2 In. 425.00
Vase, Hand Painted, Enameled, Pink Fluted Top, 14 1/2 In., Pair 595.00
Vase, Light Green, Iris, 14 1/2 In., Pair 180.00
Vase, Pink Overlay, Botanical Design, 10 1/2 In. 85.00
Vase, Raised Gold Trim, Pink, 10 In. 65.00
BRITANNIA, see Pewter

Bronze is an alloy of copper, tin, and other metals. It is used to
make figurines, lamps, and other decorative objects.

BRONZE, Bowl, Relief Dragon Form Handles, Japanese, 17 1/2 In. 2420.00
Bust, Bernard, Man & Woman, Red Marble Base, Signed, 1900, 19 3/4 In. 2750.00
Bust, Copeland, Veiled Bride, C.1875, 15 In. 1500.00
Bust, Febrari, Young Girl, Bonnet, 24 In. 2100.00
Bust, James MacDonald, George Washington, C.1900, 18 In. 885.00
Bust, Paul Silvestre, Woman, Stylized Hair, C.1920, 17 1/4 In. 2425.00
Bust, Rembrandt, 30 In. 1210.00
Bust, S.Watrin, Young Woman, White Marble Face, 21 1/2 X 22 1/2 In. 2100.00
Bust, Villanis, Diana, Head Turned, C.1900, 22 3/4 In. 735.00
Candelabra, 5-Light, Man Holding Wheel, H.Maras 625.00
Dresser Set, Glass Lined Powder & Jewelry Box, Apollo, 3 Piece 295.00
Figure, Sino-Tibetan, Goddess, Lotus Base, 56 In. 200.00
Figure, Venus De Milo, 24 In. 175.00
Figurine, Aizelin, Young Water Maiden, C.1880, 31 1/4 In. 3300.00
Figurine, Alonzo, Young Girl, Ivory Face, Marble Socle, 9 1/8 In. 1320.00
Figurine, Aphrodite, Bowl of Fruit, Ivory Head & Body, 8 5/8 In. 4950.00
Figurine, Austria, Bearded Collie, 2 1/2 X 3 In. .... 250.00 To 265.00
Figurine, Barbedienne, Diana, With Stag, 23 1/2 In. 2310.00
Figurine, Barbedienne, Panther, 7 3/4 In. 250.00
Figurine, Barrias, Nature Revealing Herself Before Science, 25 In. 6000.00
Figurine, Barye, Greyhound & Hare, Signed, C.1880, 8 1/4 In. 1430.00
Figurine, Bergman, Vienna, Soldier, 4 In. 475.00
Figurine, Borglum, Solon H., Blizzard, Dated 1900, 6 In. 8000.00
Figurine, Boucher, Peasant Woman, Long Skirt, Clogs, 1880s, 22 3/4 In. 2970.00
Figurine, Bouraine, Female Archer, C.1925, 19 In. 990.00
Figurine, Cain, Bull, Tiffany Foundry Mark, 19th Century 5500.00
Figurine, Cambos, Scribe, Seated, At Work, 1870, 19 1/2 In. 880.00
Figurine, Canova, Napoleon, Standing, Long Coat, 1950s, 27 1/2 In. 1760.00
Figurine, Cat, Sitting, Licking Front Paw, 3 3/4 X 2 3/4 In. 195.00
Figurine, Chinese, Buddha, Legs Crossed, Holds Cup, Gilt, 12 In. 605.00
Figurine, Chiparus, Innocence, Female Figure, Gilt, 14 5/8 In. 4950.00
Figurine, Chiparus, Woman In Coat, Ivory Head, 1925, 7 3/8 In. 2640.00
Figurine, Classical Woman, Reclining, Art Nouveau, Over Plaster, 7 In 75.00
Figurine, Clerget, Woman, Loose Robe, Reading Book, C.1900, 13 1/4 In. 715.00
Figurine, Cormier, Seated Discus Thrower, C.1930, 13 1/2 In. 1100.00
Figurine, Croisy, Romeo & Juliet, Dated 1878, 28 1/2 In. 1900.00
Figurine, David, With Head of Goliath, 7 3/4 In. 155.00
Figurine, Delabriere, Grouse, On Rock Formation, 7 1/2 X 6 In. 310.00
Figurine, Descomps, Dancing Lady, Ivory Face, Hands, 1925, 18 3/8 In. 8800.00
Figurine, Descomps, Diana, Ivory Head, Onyx Base, 16 1/2 In. 3850.00
Figurine, Devriez, Dancing Woman, Ruffled Skirt, Pants, 1930, 17 In. 3145,00
Figurine, Drouoet, Classical Female, 33 In. 1000.00

Figurine, Dutch Boy, 1–In. Base, 5 5/8 In. 225.00
Figurine, Egret, Japan, 13 In., Pair 225.00
Figurine, Female Archer, Nude, Ready To Pull Bow, C.1920, 17 In. 990.00
Figurine, Fratin, Horse, Standing, Cheval De Chasse, 13 In. 1100.00
Figurine, Fremiet, Bear Cub Thief, C.1875, Signed, 10 7/8 In. 1275.00
Figurine, God of War, Kuan Ti Seated With Lance, 16 In. 125.00
Figurine, Goddess & Mercury, Art Deco, Black Marble Base, 35 In., Pr. 2500.00
Figurine, Golfer, Action, Knickers, Germany, 10 In. 400.00
Figurine, Grevin, Girl, Seated, Rabbit Costume, C.1880, 11 1/2 In. 770.00
Figurine, Hagenaur, Giraffe, 3 1/2 In. 110.00
Figurine, Harlequin & Dancer, Ivory Faces, C.1920, 16 1/4 In. 2090.00
Figurine, Herzel, German Shepherd, 8 1/2 In. 390.00
Figurine, Jackson, Two Bulls, Greenish–Brown Patina, 14 X 33 In. 5000.00
Figurine, John Ball, Swinging Golf Club, 7 1/2 In. 2200.00
Figurine, Kauba, Indian Brace, Shooting Bow & Arrow, 7 1/2 In. 500.00
Figurine, Kauba, Indian Chief, Little Soldier, 7 1/2 In. 550.00
Figurine, Konti, Isidore, Seated Nude, Marble Base, Signed, 11 5/8 In. 2500.00
Figurine, Lady Dancer, White Face, Dress, Green Onyx Base 225.00
Figurine, Laroff, Polar Bear, C.1925, 17 3/8 In. 4000.00
Figurine, Lion, Arrow Under Paw, 9 3/8 X 16 In. 880.00
Figurine, Lorenzl, Woman With Parrot, Ivory Head, C.1925, 12 3/8 In. 5500.00
Figurine, Lorenzo Medici, Battle Armor, Paris, Red Marble, 38 In. 2450.00
Figurine, MacMonnies, Young Faun & Heron, 1890, 27 In. 7500.00
Figurine, Marx, Group, Cat & Monkey, On Rock, C.1900, 19 In. 1925.00
Figurine, Metal Forger At Work, Johnson Bronze Co., 6 1/2 In. 95.00
Figurine, Molins, Dancing Girl, Cat Costume, Ivory Face, 16 In. 7700.00
Figurine, Monteverde, Cherub Seated On Pedestal, 23 In. 745.00
Figurine, Moreau, Girl On Pillow, Marble Mount, 14 In. 1800.00
Figurine, Nude Slave Girl, Standing, Signed, 34 3/4 In. 1600.00
Figurine, Philippe, Nude Maiden, Arms On Chest, C.1920, 25 1/2 In. 1320.00
Figurine, Philippe, Russian Dancer, Outspread Arms, 1920, 23 3/4 In. 1540.00
Figurine, Pierrot, Baggy Pants, Ivory Face & Hands, 1925, 13 3/4 In. 2750.00
Figurine, Pierrot, Flower Seller, Ivory Head, Bouquet, C.1925, 15 In. 2750.00
Figurine, Preiss, Dancing Girl, Onyx Base, 9 7/8 In. 4620.00
Figurine, Remington, Indian Warrior On Horseback, 23 In. 550.00
Figurine, Richard, Woman, Flowing Veil Held By Flowers, 20 In. 1950.00
Figurine, Rodin, Head of Lust, 14 1/2 In. 7500.00
Figurine, Sage, Holding Book, Tiger, Rosewood Stand, 9 1/2 In. 895.00
Figurine, Sandoz, Puppy, Paw Raised, Looking At Insect, 1910, 5 In. 1760.00
Figurine, Stuck & Leyrer, Male Athlete, Holding Ball, 26 In. 4400.00
Figurine, Turtle, Signed Scippa, 4 3/4 In. 105.00
Figurine, Villanis, Sappho, Flowing Costume, Head Turned, 1900, 22 In. 1650.00
Figurine, Woman Playing Flute, Ivory Head, Arms & Legs, 1925, 14 In. 5500.00
Figurine, Zach, Flapper, Bow–Tied Garters, Signed, C.1925, 24 1/2 In. 8250.00
Figurine, Zach, Indian On Horseback, Polychromed, C.1930, 15 7/8 In. 4400.00
Figurine, Zach, Man Smoking, Jacket, Ascot, Signed, C.1930, 16 1/4 In. 3300.00
Group, Barye, Lapith Slaying Centaur, Marked, 13 3/8 In. 4400.00
Group, Barye, Lion Crushes Serpent Under Paw, Signed, 8 7/8 In. 2475.00
Group, Bergman, Slave Dealer, Woman On Rug, 7 X 8 1/2 In. 665.00
Group, Carles, Woman, Flowing Robes, Before Tablet, 26 In. 825.00
Group, Eberlein, Tango Couple, C.1920, 21 1/2 In. .... 8000.00 To 9680.00
Group, Lipchutz, Woman & Parrot, Ivory Head, Hands, Bird, 1925, 19 In. 5500.00
Group, Mene, L'Accolade, 2 Horses Over Each Other, 1900, 26 3/4 In. 4730.00
Group, Moigniez, Pheasant Hen & Chicks, 19th Century, 4 1/4 In. 825.00
Group, Rivoire, Woman & Hound, Nude, C.1925, 21 7/8 In. 4400.00
Group, Spaniel Pointing At Rabbit, Signed, 4 1/2 In. 1550.00
Group, Woman & Dog, On Rococo–Style Chair, C.1900, 15 X 13 1/4 In. 1650.00
Group, Woman & Peacock, Ivory Head, Feet & Arms, 1920, 13 In. 2850.00
Group, Zach, Embracing Couple, Dancing, Signed, C.1930, 11 1/2 In. 2475.00
Handle, Lion's Head Shape, Roman 450.00
Incense Burner, Elephant Head Handles, Dog Finial 175.00
Incense Burner, Louis Philippe, Acanthus Leaf Design, 8 3/8 In. 220.00
Incense Burner, Winged Caryatids Supports, Gilded, 7 1/2 In., Pair 192.50
Inkwell, Figural, Neptune, Shells Are Wells, C.1900, 15 1/2 In. 1650.00

Inkwell, Korschamm, Shepherdess, 2 Sheep, 6 3/4 X 8 1/2 In. 650.00
Inkwell, Urn Mounted On Tray, Pierced Clover Leaves, Pottery Insert 95.00
Mortar & Pestle, Mortar Engraved, 3 3/4 In. 185.00
Pen Holder, Fish, Leaping Out of Water, 4 X 4 In. 75.00
Plaque, Christ Brought Before Pontius Pilate, 31 X 23 1/2 In. 325.00
Plaque, George Washington & Troops Crossing Delaware, 9 X 7 In. 115.00
Plaque, Quan Yin, Phoenix Headdress, Chinese, 18 X 13 In. 82.50
Plate, Christmas, 8 Figures In Design, Gorham, 1925, 7 In. 125.00
Seal, Foo Dog, 19th Century, 1 5/8 X 2 In., Pair 125.00
Smoke Stand, Parlor Putter, Golf 528.00
Spurs, Hercules Bronze, Horseheads On Sides 175.00
Sundial, Indian, Hermphriess, 18 In. 6800.00
Sundial, Zodiac, Corner Fleur-De-Lis, Square, 14 In. 250.00
Tray, Leaf Shape, 8 In. 48.00
Urn, Hawk On Domed Cover, Ovoid, Hawk & Tree Handles, Japan, 39 In. 2550.00
Urn, Iris, Oriental, 11 In. 350.00
Urn, Japanese, Dragon, Phoenix, 5 In., Pair 350.00
Urn, Louis XVI, White Marble, Cover, Ram's Head Handles, 20 In., Pair 2650.00
Urn, Rococo Style, Young Boy Below Urn, 19th Century, 16 1/2 In. 655.00
Urn, Square Stepped Pedestal, Mounted As Lamps, 13 1/2 In., Pair 2225.00
Vase, Gustav Gurschner, Bands of Scrolls, Parcel Gilt, 2 1/2 In. 445.00
Vase, Phoenix Birds, Rope Swags, Baluster, 1900, Japan, 25 In., Pair 3100.00
Vase, Relief Birds, Flowering Trees, Pedestal, Globular, Japan, 35 In. 995.00
Vase, Relief Woman & Flowers, Art Nouveau, 17 In. 140.00
Vase, Sorensen, Verdigris Finish, Gilt Stripes, 5 1/2 In.' 75.00
Vase, Tied Bundle of Wheat Shape, Meiji Period, 13 1/4 In. 2000.00

Brownies were first drawn in 1883 by Palmer Cox. They are characterized by large round eyes, downturned mouths, and skinny legs. Toys, books, dinnerware, and other objects were made with the Brownies as part of the design.

BROWNIES, Book, Brownies' The Land of The Lost Toys, J.H. Ewing, 1910 .... 10.00
Book, Their Book, Palmer Cox, 1915 .... 125.00
Candlestick, Figural, Palmer Cox, Majolica 145.00
Candy Container, Little Boy, Marked Halloween, 1911, Germany, 6 In. 115.00
Cup & Plate, Palmer Cox, China 70.00
Doll, Cloth, Pat.1892 .... 125.00
Doll, Effanbee, 1966, 8 In. 30.00
Game, Auto Race, Brownie, Palmer Cox, Tin 65.00
Napkin Ring, Brownie Climbs Up Side, Silver Plated 175.00
Runner, Paper, Brownies At Halloween, 1920s, 72 X 20 In. 85.00
Sheet Music, Dance of The Brownies 25.00
Tray, Pin, Palmer Cox, Pairpoint 125.00
Whistle, Palmer Cox 150.00

George Brush started working in 1901 in Zanesville, Ohio. He started his own pottery in 1907, but it burned to the ground and he joined McCoy in 1909. After a series of name changes, the company became The Brush Pottery in 1925. Collectors favor the figural cookie jars made by this company.

BRUSH, Cookie Jar, Boy, Barefoot 295.00
Cookie Jar, Bunny, Gray 125.00
Cookie Jar, Cinderella's Pumpkin .... 45.00 To 98.00
Cookie Jar, Clown, Blue & Yellow .... 70.00 To 85.00
Cookie Jar, Covered Wagon 185.00
Cookie Jar, Cow .... 55.00 To 125.00
Cookie Jar, Cow, Kitten On Back, Tan .... 59.00 To 70.00
Cookie Jar, Hippo, Green 125.00
Cookie Jar, Humpty Dumpty 80.00
Cookie Jar, Humpty Dumpty, With Beanie 60.00
Cookie Jar, Old Woman In A Shoe .... 70.00 To 75.00
Cookie Jar, Peter Pan 280.00
Cookie Jar, Peter Pumpkin 125.00
Cookie Jar, Shoe .... 45.00 To 49.00

Cookie Jar, Squirrel On Log .... 28.00 To 65.00
Juicer, Clown, 2 Piece 25.00
Pitcher, Avenue Trees 52.00

BRUSH MCCOY, see McCoy

Buck Rogers was the first American science fiction comic strip. It started in 1929 and continued until 1965. Buck has also appeared in comic books, movies, and, in the 1980s, in a television series. Any memorabilia connected with the character Buck Rogers is collectible.

BUCK ROGERS, Atomic Pistol, Gold Color, Daisy, 1930s, 9 1/4 In. .... 110.00 To 185.00
Atomic Pistol, U–235, Box 185.00
Badge, Solar Scout .... 65.00 To 95.00
Balsa Kit, 1934, 11 X 17 In. 125.00
Belt & Buckle, Silver, 2 Rocket Shapes, 1930 .... 425.00
Belt, Official Utility, Remco, 1979, Box 15.00
Book, A Dangerous Mission, Pop–Up, 1934 .... 60.00
Book, Big Little Book, City Below The Sea, 1934 .... 22.00
Book, Big Little Book, Doom Comet 65.00
Book, Big Little Book, Moons of Saturn 65.00
Book, Big, Big Book, Adventures of Buck Rogers, 1934 .... 96.00
Book, Buck Rogers In 25th Century, Kellogg Co., 1933 .... 100.00
Comic Book, Famous Funnies, 1st Issue, Early 1940s 775.00
Comic Book, Issue No.100, 1951 .... 90.00
Doll, 1979, Box, 12 In. 35.00
Doll, Space Outfits, Mego, 12 In. 10.00
Flashlight, Space Patrol, Silver, Ray–O–Vac, 10 In. 125.00
Game, Adventures In 25th Century, Milton Bradley, 1979, Box 7.00
Game, Buck Rogers Adventures In 25th Century, Transogram 35.00
Gun, Disintegrator, 1936 .... 95.00
Knife, Pocket 130.00
Lunch Box .... 25.00 To 45.00
Pencil Box, 1936 .... 95.00
Pistol, Liquid Helium 225.00
Robot, Twiki, Walks, Box, 8 In. 40.00
Shaker Maker Set, Buck Rogers In 25th Century, Ideal, 1980 .... 30.00
Sonic Ray Gun, Multicolored Plastic, Battery Operated, 1950 .... 125.00
Space Ranger Kit, Unpunched & Complete, Sylvania 135.00
Spaceship, Tin Litho 295.00
Totem Head, Chex Cereal Premium, Man From Mars, Unpunched 345.00
Toy, Battle Cruiser, Tootsietoy, 1937 .... 70.00
Toy, Buck Rogers Patrol, Tin Litho, Mechanical, Marx, 12 In. 160.00
Toy, Starfighter, Corgi, On Card, 1979, 3 In. .... 5.00 To 20.00

Buffalo Pottery Deldare, Bowl, Ye Village Tavern, 9 1/2 In., Candlestick, 9 In., Pair
Mug, Ye Lion Inn, 4 1/2 In., Plate, Evening At Ye Lion Inn, 14 In.

Watch, Pocket, Artwork Face, Engraved Back, Ingraham 577.00
Water Gun, Giant, On Card, 1979 .... 25.00

 Buffalo pottery was made in Buffalo, New York, after 1902. The company was established by the Larkin Company, famous manufacturers of soap. The wares are marked with a picture of a buffalo and the date of manufacture. Deldare ware is the most famous pottery made at the factory. It is khaki–colored transfer–decorated ware.

BUFFALO POTTERY DELDARE, Bowl, Popcorn, Ye Village Tavern 500.00
Bowl, Ye Village Tavern, 1908, 9 In. .... 350.00 To 475.00
Bowl, Ye Village Tavern, 9 1/2 In. ....*Illus* 275.00
Candlestick, 9 In., Pair ....*Illus* 385.00
Candlestick, Figural Design, Hexagonal, 9 In., Pair 385.00
Charger, The Start, 1908 .... 450.00
Fernery, Ye Village Street, Signed, 8 In. 450.00
Humidor, Seamen 850.00
Humidor, Ye Lion Inn, Octagonal, 7 In. 725.00
Mug, At Three Pigeons, 1909, 4 1/2 In. .... 250.00 To 350.00
Mug, Fallowfield Hunt, 4 1/2 In. .... 225.00 To 400.00
Mug, Ye Lion Inn, 4 1/2 In. ....*Illus* 220.00
Pitcher, Fallowfield Hunt, Octagonal, Dated 1908 .... 400.00
Pitcher, Great Controversy, 1909, 12 In. 330.00
Pitcher, Hunt Supper, 12 1/2 In. .... 1000.00 To 1100.00
Pitcher, Manner of Telling Stories .... 395.00 To 475.00
Pitcher, To Spare An Old Broken Soldier, 1908 .... 425.00
Plaque, At Three Pigeons, 1908, 12 In. 375.00
Plaque, Ye Lion Inn, 1908, 12 In. .... 375.00 To 410.00
Plate, At Three Pigeons, 12 1/2 In. 430.00
Plate, Calendar, 1910 ....850.00 To 1800.00
Plate, Evening At Ye Lion Inn, 14 In. ....*Illus* 385.00
Plate, Fallowfield Hunt, 9 1/2 In. .... 150.00 To 210.00
Plate, Ye Lion Inn, 6 1/2 In. .... 60.00 To 65.00
Plate, Ye Olden Times, 9 1/2 In. .... 125.00 To 195.00
Plate, Ye Village Gossips, 1909, 10 In. 130.00
Powder Box, Ye Village Street 395.00
Saucer, Ye Olden Days, 1908 .... 50.00
Tankard, Great Controversy, 12 1/2 In. 695.00
Tobacco Jar, Ye Lion Inn 595.00
Tray, Dancing Ye Minuet, 1909, 12 In. .... 450.00 To 475.00
Tray, Tea, Heirlooms 575.00
Vase, Kingfisher, With Iris, 8 In. 1500.00
BUFFALO POTTERY, Butter Tub, 1916 .... 30.00 To 35.00
Chamber Pot, Yellow & Pink Roses 75.00
Creamer, Restaurant 12.00
Hair Receiver, Ships, Abino, 4 1/4 In. 225.00
Pitcher, Bluebird, 7 In. 110.00
Pitcher, Buffalo Hunt, 6 In. 250.00
Pitcher, Cinderella, 1907 .... 225.00
Pitcher, George Washington 395.00
Pitcher, Holland Scene, 1907 .... 225.00
Pitcher, Hounds & Stag, 6 1/2 In. 195.00
Pitcher, New Bedford Whaling, 1908, 6 In. 250.00
Pitcher, Pilgrim, 1908, 9 In. .... 500.00 To 600.00
Pitcher, Rip Van Winkle, 6 1/2 In. 490.00
Pitcher, Robin Hood, 8 1/4 In. .... 275.00 To 350.00
Pitcher, Tea Rose 95.00
Plate, Christmas, 1950, 9 1/2 In. 60.00
Plate, Niagara Falls, 1907, 7 In. 35.00
Plate, Washington's Home At Mt. Vernon, Signed, 7 1/2 In. 60.00
Platter, Blue Willow, 15 In. 55.00
Platter, Deer Scene, Artist Signed, Marked, Large 115.00
Shaving Mug, Double Cup, Wild Root Hair Tonic 125.00
Soap Dish, Red Flowers, Gold Trim, White 25.00

Sugar, Blue Willow, Dated 1911 .... 75.00
Teapot, Argyle Pattern, Blue, Dated 1914 .... 165.00
Teapot, Blue Willow 140.00
Tray, Sailboats, Abino, 1912, 12 X 9 1/4 In. 950.00

Burmese glass was developed by Frederick Shirley at the Mt. Washington Glass Works in New Bedford, Massachusetts, in 1885. It is a two–toned glass, shading from peach to yellow. Some have a pattern mold design. A few Burmese pieces were decorated with pictures or applied glass flowers of colored Burmese glass.

BURMESE, see also Gunderson
BURMESE, Cruet, Chrysanthemum, Coral Striped Mushroom Stopper, 6 1/2 In. 2750.00
Epergne, 1–Trumpet, Silver Plated Holder, 8 In. 395.00
Finger Bowl, Fluted, Mt. Washington, 5 3/4 In. 245.00
Lamp, Fairy, Pleated Skirt, Clarke Insert, 4 1/2 X 5 1/4 In. 685.00
Lamp, Fairy, Porcelain Base, Bands of Gold & Silver Florals 850.00
Lamp, Fairy, Silver Floral Design, 3 Bud Vases Around, 4 7/8 In. 850.00
Lamp, Fairy, Tunnicliffe Pottery Base, Ivy Leaves On Shade, 4 In. 510.00
Mustard, Metal Collar, Hinged Lid, Marked 1334 .... 285.00
Perfume Bottle, Double Gourd Form, Deep Rose, Yellow Stopper, 4 In. 375.00
Perfume Bottle, Lay–Down, Mistletoe Branch, Berries, 4 7/8 In. 1250.00
Pitcher, Tankard, Shiny, Mt. Washington, 10 In. 785.00
Scent Bottle, Yellow Ribbons Around, Stopper, Mt. Washington, 4 In. 750.00
Sugar & Creamer, No Design 750.00
Sugar & Creamer, Open, Applied Yellow Handle, Mt. Washington 750.00
Toothpick, 6–Point Crimped Rim 140.00
Toothpick, Blackberry & Leaves, New England Glass 200.00
Toothpick, Diamond–Quilted, Bulbous, Square Mouth, 2 1/2 In. 300.00
Toothpick, Floral Design, Hand Painted, Hexagonal Top 300.00
Toothpick, Floral Design, Pink 465.00
Tumbler, Diamond–Quilted, 2 3/4 In. 395.00
Tumbler, Lemonade, Mt. Washington, 4 3/4 In. 330.00
Tumbler, Swag of Blue Forget–Me–Nots, 3 3/4 In. 885.00
Vase, Bud, Floral Design, Silver–Plated Frame, 8 1/4 In. 510.00
Vase, Enameled Pine Bough, Flared Crimped Rim, 4 1/2 In. 195.00
Vase, Jack–In–The–Pulpit, Crimped Yellow Rim, 7 3/4 In. 325.00
Vase, Pine Bough Enamel Design, Satin Body, Flared, Crimped, 5 In. 175.00
Vase, Prunus Blossom, White Beaded Lip, Mt. Washington, 6 In. 745.00
Vase, Yellow–Orange, 10 In. 725.00
BURMESE, WEBB, see Webb Burmese

Buster Brown, the comic strip, first appeared in color in 1902. Buster and his dog Tige remained a popular comic and soon became even more famous as the emblem for a shoe company, a textile firm, and others. The strip was discontinued in 1920, but some of the advertising is still in use.

BUSTER BROWN, Badge, Secret Service 20.00
Bank, Figural, Buster Brown & Tige, Painted Cast Iron, 5 In. 132.00
Bill Hook, Celluloid, 1946 .... 7.50
Book, Comic, Buster & His Pets, Color 50.00
Book, Me In My Bubble, R.F. Outcault, 1903 .... 210.00
Box, Pencil, Pencil Shape 35.00
Carousel, 6 Wooden Pedal Ponies, Buster's Decal On All, 1940s 1475.00
Chair, Beach, Child's 395.00
Clock, Electric, Buster Brown & Tige, Advertising 75.00
Cup & Saucer, Pottery 45.00
Dictionary, 1927 .... 12.00
Figure, Buster Brown & Tige, Chalkware, 8 In. 25.00
Figure, Shoes On Back, 2 3/4 In. 95.00
Figure, Store Display, & Tige, Red Velvet Suit & Hat, 28 In. 350.00
Figurine, Buster Brown, Bisque, 8 In. 25.00
Flashlight, Health Shoes 30.00
Game Box, Carrying Case, Andy Devine Picture, 10 X 6 X 3 In. 50.00
Gyroscope, Box 25.00

Hobby Horse	225.00
Mirror, With Tige, Pocket, 1946	22.50
Pen, Figure of Buster, Red & White	30.00
Pencil Case, Oversized Fountain Pen	45.00
Pin, Buster Brown Bread	27.50
Pitcher & Plate, With Tige, 3 1/4 In.	60.00
Plaque, For Boys & Girls, Cast Iron, Round, 18 In.	395.00
Plate	65.00
Playing Cards	20.00
Postcard, Buster Brown, & Black Boy, Outcault, 1906 Postmark	25.00
Postcard, Valentine, Unused	15.00
Printing Blocks, Inserts, Box	65.00
Ring, With Tige	35.00
Scissors, With Tige, Characters Both Sides, Germany	35.00
Shoe Horn, Metal	15.00
Whistle, Shoes	15.00
Whistle, Wooden	52.50

BUTTER MOLD, see Kitchen, Mold, Butter
BUTTERMILK GLASS, see Custard Glass

 Buttons have been known throughout the centuries, and there are millions of styles. Gold, silver, or precious stones were used for the best buttons, but most were made of natural materials like bone or shell, or from inexpensive metals. Only a few types are listed for comparison.

BUTTON, Crowns, Latin Inscription & 1776, Brass, 11 Piece	25.00
Eagle, Art Nouveau, Paris	1.50
Gibson Girl	15.00
Jet, Faceted, Floral, Scenic, Goldstone, 97 Piece	45.00
Lady's Garden, 5–Color, Scroll Border, 1 1/8 In.	57.00
Lucky Day, White	3.00
Mother–of–Pearl, Paste Sapphires, 18th Century	270.00
Multicolor, Latest In Buttons, Czechslovakia, Card	3.00
Paperweight, Pink & Blue Flowers, Green Leaves, Germany, 3/8 In.	2.50
Pearl, Davenport, Yellow & Green, Card	3.00
Pewter, Bronze Sculpture of Maude Adams, As Peter Pan, 1907, 1 In.	22.50
Quality Pearl, Yellow	3.00
Stud, Porcelain, Raised Floral, Gold Trim, Hand Painted, 4 Piece	50.00
Uniform, Royal Air Force, Brass, Embossed Wings & Crown, W.W. II	2.00
Yellow, Red Roses, Hand Painted, Limoges, 5 Piece	85.00

 Buttonhooks have been a popular collectible in England for many years but only recently have gained the attention of American collectors. The buttonhooks were made to help fasten the many buttons of the old–fashioned high–button shoes and other items of apparel.

BUTTONHOOK, Art Nouveau, Repousse, Dated 1893, 6 1/4 In.	67.50
Bone Handle, 2 1/2 In.	13.00
Brass Leg	23.00
Chas. Rathke Shoes, Clintonville, Wisconsin, 3 1/2 In.	10.00
Figural, Jockey Handle	65.00
Glove, Mother–of–Pearl Handle	25.00
J.C. Penney	4.00
Mother–of–Pearl Handle .... 15.00 To 35.00
Pear Shaped Handle, Sterling Silver, 8 In.	45.00
Raised Florals, Sterling Silver Handle	35.00
Shoe, Engraved Handle, Silver, England	25.00
Silver, 2 Hooks Fold Into Handle	75.00
Sterling Silver, Folding Knife, 2 In.	20.00

 Calendars made to hang on the wall or to be displayed on a desk top have been popular since the last quarter of the nineteenth century. Many were printed with advertising as part of the artwork and were given away as premiums. Calendars with gun or gunpowder or Coca–Cola advertising are most prized.

CALENDAR PAPER, 1876, Home Insurance 50.00
1883, Patton Bros., Catlettsburg, Kentucky 15.00
1883, T. Ehrenberg, Loom Maker 16.00
1884, Maud Humphrey, 12 Illustrated Pages, 9 X 11 In. 75.00
1885, Case Farm Machinery, Framed 500.00
1890, Hood's Sarsaparilla 40.00
1890, Sulphur Bitters 30.00
1892, A & P, Drummer Boy, Gilt Frame 125.00
1892, Golden Days, E. Nister, Illustrations, 4 X 3 In. 37.50
1892, Val Blatz Brewing Co., Lithograph Girl 500.00
1893, Metropolitan Life Insurance Co. 33.00
1894, Garland of The Year, Illustrated Pages With Poems 35.00
1895, Phoenix Mutual Life, Victorian Children, 4 Pages 48.00
1895, Trailing Arbutus 50.00
1895, W.E. Hoyt & Co., Perfumed 12.00
1896, W.W. Johnson & Co., Redistillers, Cincinnati, Ohio 85.00
1898, Girl Front, Scalloped Edges, Ornate Design, 6 X 3 In. 11.00
1900, Frisco Railroad, Black Man, Son, Hunters 12.50
1900, Penfield Golf 6050.00
1900–04, Beautiful Women 15.00
1901, Fairbanks, Fairy 65.00
1901, Laflin & Rand Powder, 7 Pages 200.00
1902, Youth's Companion, Die Cut 185.00
1903, Lowel Fertilizer, Harvesting Scene 275.00
1904, Charles Dana Gibson, 13 Sheets 250.00
1904, Equitable Insurance, Children, Maude Humphrey 125.00
1904, Youth's Companion, 4 Pages 6.00
1905, New Home Sewing Machine 27.50
1906, Deering Harvester, Pretty Girl, 20 X 13 In. 65.00
1906, Peters Cartridge Co., Hunters Carrying Moose 1150.00
1906, Where Violets Blow 15.00
1907, Continental Fire Ins. Co. 42.50
1908, Harry Roseland McCormick, Fortuneteller 275.00
1909, Abraham Lincoln Centennial 24.00
1909, T.J. Hitchcock, Lumber, Lime, Hard & Soft Coal, With Pad 20.00
1910, Golfing Woman, Chromolithograph 1100.00
1910, Sherman E. Pate, Grains, Seeds, Flour, Farm Scene, Pad 20.00
1911, Zula Kenyoin, 1 Page Each 2 Months 250.00
1914, Hercules Powder Co. 350.00
1915, Continental Fire Ins. 12.00
1915, Prudential Insurance 32.00
1915, Valley Lumber Co., Young Girl, 4 1/2 X 10 In. 9.00
1918, Armour Meats, Interior Grocery Store 275.00
1918, DeLaval, Girl, Horse, Pastoral Scene 250.00
1921, H.W. Ross Lumber Co. 47.50
1921, Winchester, U.S. Cartridge 450.00
1922, Pompeian Beauty, Gene Pressler, 7 1/2 X 13 1/2 In. 35.00
1923, Mazda, Lithograph On Paper, Cole Phillips 850.00
1923, Wrigley's Gum, 3 1/2 X 5 1/2 In. 10.00
1924, Hupmobile 175.00
1925, Dodge, Parrish, With Box 125.00
1926, Orange Crush 400.00
1926, Parrish, Calendar of Friendship, 53 Pages 17.00

1927, Chero–Cola, Woman Sitting On Boat At Beach 245.00
1927, Nehi, Woman At Beach, Bottle 225.00
1927, U.S. Cartridge Co. 385.00
1927, Wrigley's Gum, Sample Card 15.00
1928, Dodge 48.00
1928, Hercules Powder Co., Sports 385.00
1931, Mazda, Parrish 275.00
1933, Kenyon Superior Weekly Memo 12.00
1933, Winchester Wester 80.00
1936, Denver & Santa Fe Railroad 30.00
1937, DeLaval, Iowa 28.00
1937, Hercules Powder Co. 145.00
1938, Kellogg Bros. Lumber Co., 12 Pages, 13 X 19 In. 4.00
1938, Nicholas Marr, Coal, Coke, Wood, Pocket, Unused 15.00
1939, Boys In Swimming Hole, Rockwell 35.00
1939, Goodyear Tires, Father & Son Looking At Old Cars 35.00
1941, July 4th Children's Parade, F.T. Hunter 12.00
1941, Nervine, Anti–Pain Pills, Cartoon–Style Characters 30.00
1942, Texaco, Zoe Mozert 75.00
1946, Esquire Varga, Original Envelope ....75.00 To 125.00
1946, Rolf Armstrong, I'Ll Say So, Bowling, 10 X 17 In. 27.00
1947, Armstrong Construction Co., Here's Our Number 36.00
1947, Elvgreen, Nude Front Plate, 12 Different Pictures 150.00
1947, Purina, Animals & Children 8.00
1948, DuPont, Dog 40.00
1948, Harness Racing Champions, 14 X 22 In. 15.00
1948, Varga, Envelope 55.00
1950, Brown & Bigelow, Path To Home, Parrish, Medium 115.00
1950, MacPherson, Colored Pinup Girls 30.00
1951, Esquire, Al Moore, Original Envelope 30.00
1951, Studio Setting, Armitage, Karmelkorn Shop, Partial Pad 28.00
1952, Budweiser, Clydesdales 150.00
1952, Studio Secrets, Girlie 15.00
1953, Moorman's Feed 5.00
1955, Marilyn Monroe 35.00
1957, Esquire Girl, Desk, Leatherette 35.00
1965, Will Rogers 12.50
1966, Union Pacific R.R. 5.00
1977, Frazetta 25.00
1978, Star Wars 50.00
1981, California Southern R.R. 8.00
1981, Miss Piggy Covergirl 10.00

Calendar plates were very popular in the United States from 1906 to 1929. Since then, plates have been made every year. A calendar and the name of a store, a picture of flowers, a girl, or a scene were featured on the plate.

CALENDAR PLATE, 1908, Lake Scene 27.00
1909, A.C. Brower, Fruit & Flowers, Calendar On Rim, 7 In. 25.00
1909, Gibson Girl ....15.00 To 30.00
1909, Horse 23.00
1909, Indian 18.00
1909, Queen Louise 23.00
1910, Cupid Center 28.00
1910, Gibson Girl 15.00
1910, High School Center, Bell Border 32.00
1910, Ole Swimmin' Hole 33.00
1910, Victorian Woman 40.00
1910, Victory, Orion, Illinois 25.00
1911, Bradford, Iowa 28.00
1911, Deer In Meadow, Animal Panels Between Months 28.00
1912, Indian Maiden 37.00
1913, Irises 28.00
1914, Flower Vase Center, Blue & Gold Edge, 8 1/2 In. 24.00

1915, Boy & Girl, Wicker Basket of Apples, 7 1/2 In.	25.00
1915, Panama Canal	28.00 To 35.00
1919, Betsy Ross Sewing Flag	38.00
1919, Ship	25.00
1920, Victory, Globe	34.00 To 35.00
1921, Peace, Dove, Flags	35.00
1924, Rockford, Illinois	50.00
1929, Automobile	28.00
1953, Jubilee, 10 In.	18.00
1957, Gold Zodiac, Blue	8.00
1968, Sports Activities	12.00
1976, Bicentennial	15.00

Camark Pottery started in 1924 in Camden, Arkansas. Jack Carnes founded the firm and made many types of glazes and wares. The company was bought by Mary Daniel, who still owns the firm. Production was halted in 1983.

CAMARK, Figurine, Cat, Pink	25.00
Pitcher, Milk, Parrot Handle, Green, Signed	45.00
Pitcher, Parrot Handle, Blue, Gold Mark, 6 In.	25.00
Vase, Corn, 8 In.	48.00
Vase, Pink & Blue, 5 1/2 In.	15.00
Wall Pocket, 16 In.	26.00

Cambridge art pottery was made in Cambridge, Ohio, from about 1895 until World War I. The factory made brown glazed decorated wares with a variety of marks including an acorn, the name "Cambridge," the name "Oakwood," or the name "Terrhea."

CAMBRIDGE POTTERY, Tile, Portrait, High Glaze, 4 In.	90.00

Cambridge Glass Company was founded in 1901 in Cambridge, Ohio. The company closed in 1954, reopened briefly, and closed again in 1958. The firm made all types of glass. Their early wares included heavy pressed glass with the mark "Near Cut." Later wares included Crown Tuscan, etched stemware, clear and colored glass. The firm used a C in a triangle mark after 1920.

CAMBRIDGE, see also Depression Glass

CAMBRIDGE, Alpine, Caprice, Bowl, 4–Footed, Fluted, Blue, 12 In.	65.00
Alpine, Caprice, Torte Plate, 14 In.	62.00
Alpine, Caprice, Tumbler, Footed, 5 Oz.	30.00
Apple Blossom, Candlestick, 3 Light, Black, Silver	85.00
Apple Blossom, Console Set, 1 Light Keyhole, Oval, 3 Piece	135.00
Apple Blossom, Goblet	22.50
Apple Blossom, Pitcher, Ball, Yellow	210.00
Apple Blossom, Plate, 6 In.	10.00
Apple Blossom, Plate, Yellow, 8 1/2 In.	16.00
Apple Blossom, Relish, 5 Sections, Gold Plated Stand, 12 1/4 In.	75.00
Apple Blossom, Salt, Flat	75.00
Apple Blossom, Sherbet, Yellow, Tall	19.00
Apple Blossom, Tumbler, Yellow, 12 Oz.	32.50
Aurora, Goblet, Carmen	20.00
Aurora, Sherbet, Green	10.00
Bashful Charlotte, Flower Block, Crystal	88.00
Bashful Charlotte, Flower Frog, Crystal, 8 1/2 In.	13.00
Bashful Charlotte, Flower Frog, Pink, 7 In.	40.00
Bashful Charlotte, Flower Frog, Pink, 11 In.	195.00
Blue Jay, Flower Frog	80.00
Calla Lily, Candlestick, 6 1/2 In., Pair	75.00
Candlelight, Mayonaise Set, 3 Piece	48.00
Caprice, Ashtray, Attached Place Cardholder, Individual	7.50
Caprice, Ashtray, Blue, 5 In.	15.00
Caprice, Bonbon, Blue, 4 1/4 In.	20.00
Caprice, Bowl, 4–Footed, 13 In.	30.00
Caprice, Bowl, 4–Footed, Cupped, Silver Deposit, 13 1/2 In.	60.00

Caprice, Bowl, 4–Footed, Oval, 13 In. 70.00
Caprice, Bowl, Blue, 13 In. 60.00
Caprice, Bowl, Footed, 10 In. 17.00
Caprice, Bowl, Ruffled, Green, 14 In. 40.00
Caprice, Box, Cigarette, Cover, Blue 12.00
Caprice, Box, Cigarette, Dolphin–Footed, Blue 45.00
Caprice, Candleholder, Light Green, Pair 85.00
Caprice, Candlestick, Blue, 7 In., Pair 70.00
Caprice, Candy Dish, Cover, Footed, 6 In. 42.00
Caprice, Creamer 10.00
Caprice, Cup 11.00
Caprice, Cup & Saucer 15.00
Caprice, Cup & Saucer, Amber 50.00
Caprice, Cup & Saucer, Blue 30.00
Caprice, Goblet 16.00
Caprice, Goblet, Blue 40.00
Caprice, Goblet, Water, 9 Oz. 14.00
Caprice, Goblet, Water, Stem, 10 Oz. 20.00
Caprice, Ice Bucket 42.00
Caprice, Ice Bucket, Crystal 20.00
Caprice, Mayonnaise Set, Blue, 6 1/2 In., 3 Piece ....70.00 To 110.00
Caprice, Plate, 4–Footed, 13 1/2 In. 30.00
Caprice, Plate, 6 1/4 In. 6.00
Caprice, Plate, 7 In. 7.50
Caprice, Plate, 8 1/2 In. 10.00
Caprice, Plate, 9 1/2 In. 34.00
Caprice, Plate, Amber, 8 1/2 In. 18.00
Caprice, Plate, Divided, Blue, Small 47.00
Caprice, Rose Bowl, Blue 50.00
Caprice, Salt & Pepper, Tray 18.00
Caprice, Sherbet, 6 Oz. 10.00
Caprice, Sherbet, Blue, 4 3/8 In. 27.00
Caprice, Sherbet, Blue, Tall 17.00
Caprice, Sugar ....7.00 To 10.00
Caprice, Sugar, Individual, Blue 14.00
Caprice, Torte Plate, 14 In. 28.50
Caprice, Tumbler, Blue, Footed, 5 1/2 In. 26.00
Caprice, Tumbler, Ice Tea, 12 Oz. 18.00
Caprice, Tumbler, Juice, Blue, Mushroom 30.00
Cascade, Bowl, 12 1/2 In. 35.00
Cascade, Vase, Mandarin Gold, 9 1/2 In. 40.00
Chantilly, Bottle, French Dressing, Sterling Top & Base 100.00
Chantilly, Cake Plate, Martha, Footed, 13 In. 80.00
Chantilly, Candy Dish, Cover, 3 Sections, Sterling Base 125.00
Chantilly, Coaster, Sterling Base 25.00
Chantilly, Cocktail Shaker, Chrome Top 95.00
Chantilly, Cruet, Oil & Vinegar, Sterling Top & Base 90.00
Chantilly, Mayonnaise Bowl, Sterling Base 35.00
Chantilly, Saltshaker, Footed, Handle 18.00
Chantilly, Vase, Sterling Silver Band, 10 1/4 In. 90.00
Cleo, Candlestick, 1–Light, Green, Gold, Pair 40.00
Cleo, Compote, Decagon, 11 1/2 In. 50.00
Cleo, Cup & Saucer, Green 16.00
Cleo, Plate, 2 Handles, Green, 6 1/2 In. 20.00
Cleo, Plate, Amber, 9 1/2 In. 28.00
Cleo, Plate, Blue, 9 In. 39.00
Cleo, Plate, Decagon, Yellow, 10 In. 48.00
Cleo, Plate, Yellow, 9 1/2 In. 48.00
Cleo, Sugar & Creamer 30.00
Colonial, Spooner, Child's, Cobalt Blue 20.00
Colonial, Toothpick, Crystal 4.00
Corinth, Juice Set, Yellow Gyro Optic, 6 Piece 95.00
Crown Tuscan, Bowl, Gold Trim, Footed, 6 X 5 1/2 In. 55.00
Crown Tuscan, Candlestick, Dolphin, Pair 345.00

Crown Tuscan, Candlestick, Ram's Head, Pair 85.00
Crown Tuscan, Candy Dish, 3 Sections, Pink, 8 In. 45.00
Crown Tuscan, Candy Dish, Cover, 3 Sections 80.00
Crown Tuscan, Compote, Nude, 5 1/2 In. 110.00
Crown Tuscan, Compote, Shell, Footed, 7 In. 44.00
Crown Tuscan, Cruet, Green, 7 3/4 In. 75.00
Crown Tuscan, Swan, 3 1/2 In. .... 35.00 To 65.00
Crown Tuscan, Vase, Shell, Roses & Gold, 8 In. 195.00
Decagon, Bonbon, Amber, Handle, 7 In. 12.00
Decagon, Bowl, Black Ebony, Handles, 7 1/2 In., Pair 36.00
Decagon, Ice Bucket, Blue, Handle 55.00
Decagon, Sugar, Creamer & Tray, Green .... 32.00 To 33.00
Diane, Candy Dish, Cover, 3 Sections, 8 In. 20.00
Diane, Candy Dish, Cover, Footed 90.00
Diane, Compote, 5 3/4 In. 40.00
Diane, Jug, Ball, 80 Oz. 150.00
Diane, Lamp, Gold Encrusted, Red, 14 1/2 In., Pair 375.00
Diane, Relish, 3 Sections, 10 In. 28.0
Doric Column, Candlestick, Ebony, Gold Painted, 9 In., Pair 75.00
Draped Lady, Cocktail, Silver Overlay 85.00
Draped Lady, Flower Frog, 9 3/4 In. 225.00
Draped Lady, Flower Frog, Mandolin Lady, Bent Back, Green, 9 In. 395.00
Draped Lady, Flower Frog, Moonlight Blue Satin, 6 In. 300.00
Draped Lady, Flower Frog, Pink, 13 1/2 In. 225.00
Draped Lady, Flower Frog, Rose Lady, Amber 225.00
Draped Lady, Flower Frog, Yellow, 8 1/2 In. 250.00
Draped Lady, Vase, 8 1/2 In. 115.00
Elaine, Jug, Ball & 3 Tumblers 155.00
Elaine, Plate, Handles, 14 In. 35.00
Elaine, Sugar & Creamer 30.00
Everglade, Plate, 16 In. 35.00
Fernland, Butter, Cover, Child's, Cobalt Blue 50.00
Fernland, Creamer, Child's, Cobalt Blue 45.00
Frogs, Flower Frog 80.00
Gadroon, Relish, 3 Sections 10.00
Gadroon, Urn, Cover, Amethyst, 10 In. 105.00
Georgian, Candy Dish, Cover, Light Green & Mandarin Gold 40.00
Gloria, Bowl, Yellow, 13 In. 55.00
Heatherbloom, Jug, Ball, 80 Oz. 195.00
Heatherbloom, Sandwich Plate, Yellow, Tab Handle, 11 1/2 In. 80.00
Heirloom, Bowl, Footed, 10 In. 21.00
Heirloom, Creamer 10.00
Helio, Compote, 5 X 10 In. 180.00
Heron, Flower Frog 65.00
Keyhole, Tray, Handle, Amber 22.50
Krystol, Candlestick, Gold, Pair 30.00
LaRosa, Cake Stand 42.00
Lynbrok, Plate, 7 1/2 In. 5.00
Manor, Cordial, Cut 15.00
Marjorie, Tumbler, 8 Oz, 8 Piece 96.00
Martha, Cheese & Cracker Set, Floral Etch, 2 Piece 43.00
Moonlight, Smoking Set, Box & 3 Ashtrays, Blue 28.00
Mt.Vernon, Sherbet 15.00
Mt.Vernon, Toothpick, 2 1/4 In. 28.00
Near Cut, Coaster, 6 Piece 25.00
Near Cut, Ice Bucket, Amber 25.00
Nude Stem, Cocktail, Amber 95.00
Nude Stem, Cocktail, Amethyst 95.00
Nude Stem, Cocktail, Cobalt Blue 125.00
Nude Stem, Cocktail, Emerald Green 95.00
Nude Stem, Compote, Amethyst Bowl, Farber Ware Holder 95.00
Nude Stem, Compote, Carmen, 7 In. 160.00
Nude Stem, Compote, Chantilly Insert, Farber Ware 70.00
Nude Stem, Compote, Cupped, Carmen Top, 8 In. 145.00

Nude Stem, Compote, Cupped, Royal Blue Top 250.00
Nude, Compote, Crown Tuscan, 5 1/2 In. 110.00
Nursery Rhyme, Butter, Cover, Child's 85.00
Nursery Rhyme, Sugar, Cover, Child's 75.00
Peacock & Rose, Plate, Scalloped, Etched, Pink, 10 1/2 In. 30.00
Portia, Platter, Round, 14 In. 45.00
Ribbon Candy, Salt & Pepper 62.50
Rooster, Muddler 30.00
Rose Point, Basket, Handles, 4 In. 125.00
Rose Point, Bowl, 2 Handles, 8 1/2 In. 49.50
Rose Point, Bowl, Footed, 11 1/2 In. 85.00
Rose Point, Bowl, Handle, 5 In. 38.00
Rose Point, Butter, Cover 165.00
Rose Point, Candleholder, 2–Light, Pair 85.00
Rose Point, Candlestick, 3–Light, Pair 125.00
Rose Point, Candy Dish, Cover, 3 Sections, 8 In. 68.00
Rose Point, Candy Dish, Floral Cover, Sapphire Blue, 6 1/2 In. 35.00
Rose Point, Celery, 11 In. 55.00
Rose Point, Cheese & Cracker 65.00
Rose Point, Claret, Stemmed 30.00
Rose Point, Cocktail, Oyster 25.00
Rose Point, Cruet 60.00
Rose Point, Cup & Saucer 39.00
Rose Point, Dish, Pickle, 9 1/2 In. 25.00
Rose Point, Goblet, 10 Oz. .... 20.00 To 27.75
Rose Point, Ice Bucket, Chrome Handle, 5 3/4 In. 95.00
Rose Point, Nappy, 3 Sections 28.00
Rose Point, Nut Cup, 12 Piece 600.00
Rose Point, Plate, 8 1/4 In. 20.00
Rose Point, Plate, 10 In. 115.00
Rose Point, Relish .... 25.00 To 50.00
Rose Point, Salt & Pepper 68.00
Rose Point, Sherbet, Low, 6 Oz. 23.00
Rose Point, Sugar & Creamer .... 30.00 To 55.00
Rose Point, Tray, 5 Sections, 12 In. 45.00
Rose Point, Tray, Center Handle, 10 In. 87.50
Rose Point, Tumbler, Footed, 12 Oz. 30.00
Rose Point, Underplate, 2 Handles, Gold Edge, 7 3/4 In. 24.50
Rose Point, Vase, Gold Encrusted, Crown Tuscan, 10 In. 85.00
Rose Point, Wine, Stemmed 35.00
Roxbury, Wine, Cut, 2 1/2 Oz. 15.00
Seagull, Flower Frog .... 40.00 To 50.00
Starlight, Cocktail, Cut, Label 9.00
Swan, Crystal, 8 In. 38.00
Swan, Green, 3 1/2 In. .... 25.00 To 38.00
Sweetheart, Table Set, Child's, 4 Piece 65.00
Tally–Ho, Cup & Saucer, Amethyst 21.50
Tally–Ho, Goblet, Amber, 14 Oz. 15.00
Tally–Ho, Mug, Carmen 28.00
Tally–Ho, Oyster Cocktail, Cobalt Blue 26.00
Tally–Ho, Punch Set, Red, 13 Piece 650.00
Tally–Ho, Sugar & Creamer, Red 35.00
Virginian, Sherbet 8.00
Virginian, Tumbler, Water 11.00
Wildflower, Bowl, 12 In. 35.00
Wildflower, Butter, Cover, Round 75.00
Wildflower, Candy Dish, Cover, 4–Footed, Gold Trim 68.00
Wildflower, Celery, 3 Sections 50.00
Wildflower, Plate, 7 1/2 In. 10.00
Wildflower, Relish, 3 Sections, 2 Handles 35.00
Wildflower, Salt & Pepper 27.50
Wildflower, Sherbet, 5 In. .... 10.00 To 15.00
Wildflower, Sugar, Gold Trim 12.00

Cameo glass was made in much the same manner as a cameo in jewelry. Parts of the top layer of glass were cut away to reveal a different colored glass beneath. The most famous cameo glass was made during the nineteenth century.

CAMEO GLASS, see also under factory names

CAMEO GLASS, Bowl, Poppies, Emerald Green Blown Glass, Lorraine, 12 X 6 In.	1200.00
Bowl, Stylized Design, Red To Cream, St. Louis, 7 X 12 In.	950.00
Dish, Sweetmeat, English, Red Floral, Silver–Plated Fittings	1100.00
Flask, Bamboo & Leaves, Butterflies On Back, English, 5 1/2 In.	2750.00
Inkwell, Silver Mounted, Blossoms, Grass, English, 4 3/4 In.	2200.00
Jam Jar, White Flowers, Medium Blue, English, 5 1/4 In.	1620.00
Lamp, Domed Shade, Stylized Flowers, Iron Mounts, French, 19 In.	2750.00
Perfume Bottle, Flowers On Clear Glass, English, 3 1/2 In.	1000.00
Perfume Bottle, Lay–Down, Sterling Top, English, 1896, 5 In.	1325.00
Perfume Bottle, Mustard Yellow, Silver Mount, English, Bulbous	1400.00
Rose Bowl, Paisley Cutting, White On Blue, English, 4 1/2 In.	750.00
Vase, 2 Cut Continous Landscape, Michel De Nancy, 12 1/2 In.	950.00
Vase, 3 Colors, Goldberg, 10 1/2 In.	950.00
Vase, Acid Cut, Devianne, 11 In.	575.00
Vase, Applied Glass Serpent, Lemaitre, C.1925, 17 In.	660.00
Vase, Autumn Leaves, Gray Frosted Ground, Bulbous, Arsall, 7 In.	575.00
Vase, Blossoms, Flying Insects, George Woodall, 5 In.	2860.00
Vase, Bud, Rampant Lion Holder, Gilt Mount, 5 X 2 3/4 In.	1835.00
Vase, Elephant, Amber, Gold Finish, 13 In.	3025.00
Vase, Flowering Branch & Grasses, English, C.1900, 4 5/8 In.	275.00
Vase, Flowers & Leaves, Butterfly On Back, English, 6 1/2 In.	1395.00
Vase, Gold Enameled Floral, Frosted Ground, St. Denis, 6 In.	295.00
Vase, Gold Enameled Floral, Pinched Sides, St. Denis, 6 In.	450.00
Vase, Holly Design, Richard, 5 In.	875.00
Vase, Landscape Scene, Brown Cut To Peach, Barz, 10 1/4 In.	295.00
Vase, Lavender Clematis, Burgun & Schverer, 1900, 10 In.	1100.00
Vase, Leaves & Berries, Rust & Green, Arsall, 6 X 6 1/4 In.	950.00
Vase, Mountains, Trees, Lake, Amber & Purple, La Rochere	795.00
Vase, Orchids, Leaves, Burgun & Schverer, C.1900, 3 1/2 In.	995.00
Vase, Primrose Blossoms, Burgun & Schverer, C.1895, 7 3/4 In.	7800.00
Vase, Purple Leafage, Chrysanthemums, Purple Ground, Weis, 6 In.	1000.00
Vase, Ruffled Rim, Exotic Birds, Blossoms, English, 4 1/4 In.	2200.00
Vase, Rust, Green, Frosted Amber, Modified Bowl, Arsall, 6 In.	1250.00
Vase, Sailboats, Brown On Yellow, J.Michel, 10 In.	895.00
Vase, Stick, Cut Branches & Leaves, DeLianne, 13 In.	565.00
Vase, Sweet Peas, Hammered Frost, Conical, St.Denis, 9 3/4 In.	325.00
Vase, White Leaves, Flowers, Citron & White, English, 3 3/4 In.	850.00
Vase, 2 Continuous Landscapes, Michel De Nancy, 12 1/2 In.	1150.00
Vase, Cinnamon, Allover Flowers, Leaves, Rolled Out Collar, 4 1/2 In.	975.00

CAMPAIGN, see Political

The Campbell Kids were first used as part of an advertisement for the Campbell Soup Company in 1906. The kids were created by Grace Drayton, a popular illustrator of the day. The kids were used in magazine and newspaper ads until about 1951. They were presented again in 1966; and in 1983, they were redesigned with a slimmer, more contemporary appearance.

CAMPBELL KIDS, Bank, Campbell Soup	15.00
Bank, Figural, Painted Cast Iron, 3 1/4 In.	297.00
Calendar, 1899	15.00
Cup, Silver Plate	35.00
Dish, Child's, Buffalo Pottery	60.00
Doll, Bisque, Blue Outfit, Germany, 5 In.	275.00
Doll, Bisque, Pink Outfit, Germany, 7 1/2 In.	375.00
Doll, Black, Vinyl, Eugene Co., Box, 1984, 17 In., Pr. ....75.00 To	120.00
Doll, Cloth, 1973, 16 1/2 In., Pair	25.00
Doll, Composition, Effanbee, 1948	175.00

Doll, Horsman, 1948	195.00
Feeding Dish, Signed Drayton, Buffalo Pottery, 8 In.	50.00
Photograph, Girl, Campbell Kids Doll, Framed, 1920, 8 X 10 In.	27.50
Puzzle, Jaymar, 13 X 10 In.	45.00
Salt & Pepper	45.00
Spoon, Girl	28.00
Spoon, Soup, Silver Plate	18.00
Toy, Farm Truck, Fisher-Price	55.00

Camphor glass is a cloudy white glass that has been blown or pressed. It was made by many factories in the Midwest during the mid-nineteenth century.

CAMPHOR GLASS, Basket, Ruffled, Handle, 6 In.	30.00
Bookends, Sailing Ship	25.00
Plate, Dog, 7 In.	25.00
Powder Jar, Pink	55.00
Toothpick, Elf, Basket	55.00

CANARY GLASS, see Vaseline Glass

A candlestick is designed to hold one candle; a candelabrum has more than one arm and holds many candles. The eccentricity of the English language makes the plural of candelabrum into candelabra.

CANDELABRUM, 2-Light, Adjustable Screen, Gilt Metal, 18 In.	195.00
2-Light, Silver Plate, Pair	225.00
2-Light, Silver Plate, Scrolled, Sheffield, 22 In., Pair	800.00
2-Light, Sterling Silver, Gadrooned, Scrolled, 15 1/2 In., Pair	715.00
3-Light, Pressed Glass, Prisms, Flared Foot, 17 In., Pair	400.00
3-Light, Russian Cut, Clear Buttons, 17 1/2 X 14 In.	525.00
5-Light, Etched Design, Chinese, C.1930, 12 In., Pair	95.00
5-Light, Man Holding Wheel, H.Maras, Bronze Patina, 15 In.	575.00
6-Light, Continental Ormolu, Scroll Arms, Crystal, Pedestal, Pr.	1500.00
Porcelain, Gilt Trim, 1 3/4 In., Pair	35.00

Candlesticks were made of brass, pewter, Sandwich glass, sterling silver, plated silver, and all types of pottery and porcelain. The earliest candlesticks, dating from the sixteenth century, held the candle on a pricket (sharp pointed spike). These lost favor because in times of strife the large church candlesticks with prickets became formidable weapons, so the socket was mandated. Candlesticks changed in style through the centuries and designs range from classic to rococo to Art Nouveau to Art Deco.

CANDLESTICK, Brass, Altar, Pricket, 3 Faces On Base, 17 In., Pair	375.00
Brass, Baluster-Shaped Stem, Mid-Drip Pan, Europe, 7 In.	440.00
Brass, Capstan, 4 5/8 In.	325.00
Brass, Capstan, Tall Stem With Socket, 10 1/4 In.	1000.00
Brass, Cast Iron Fleur-De-Lis Shaped Push-Up, 7 In.	25.00
Brass, Conical Socket, Short Neck, Jarvie, C.1910, 6 In., Pair	440.00
Brass, Diamond-Quilted, Push-Up, England, 11 In.	60.00
Brass, Domed Base, 8 In.	350.00
Brass, Domed Base, Baluster-Shaped Stem, Holland, 17th Century	880.00
Brass, English, Air Twist, C.1880, 12 In., Pair	450.00
Brass, Flat Rim, Trumpet Form, Preston, 1920s, 14 In., Pair	1100.00
Brass, Glass Flowers On Brass Leaves, French, Brass, 14 In., Pr.	155.00
Brass, Octagonal Base, 5 1/2 In.	300.00
Brass, Push-Up, Victorian, 11 In., Pair	170.00
Brass, Push-Up, Victorian, 11 3/4 In., Pair	150.00
Brass, Push-Up, Victorian, 7 7/8 In., Pair	110.00
Brass, Queen Anne, 7 1/4 In.	350.00
Brass, Saucer Base, Side Pushup, 8 1/8 In.	115.00
Brass, Scalloped Mid-Drip Pan, 11 In.	325.00
Brass, Square Base, Short Stem, 3 3/4 In.	100.00
Brass, Square Bass, Paw Feet, 6 In.	250.00
Brass, Victorian, Push-Up, 10 In., Pair	130.00
Bronze, Altar, Baroque Foliate, Griffins Form Feet, 27 In., Pair	360.00

Copper, 2 Flaring Stems, Square Base, Karl Kipp, 1930, 6 7/8 In. 225.00
Copper, Double Gourd Shape, Jarvie 4950.00
Ebony, Silver Socket, Drip Pan, Birmingham Hallmarks, 2 7/8 In. 115.00
Gilded Bronze, Empire, Cut Sawtooth Pattern, 8 1/2 In., Pair 687.50
Hog Scraper, Push–Up, Lip Hanger, Marked Shaw Birm, Iron, 7 In. 185.00
Hunting Horn, 1810, Pair 1450.00
Iron, Hog Scraper, Push–Up, Shaws, 7 In. 115.00
Iron, Ivy Design, 4 1/2 In. 100.00
Oak, Dutch Twist, Pair 225.00
Silver On Brass, Continental Gothic, 7 In., Pair 500.00
Tin, Hog Scraper, Finger Hold & Lift, 6 1/2 In. 100.00
Tin, Hog Scraper, Push–Up, Shaw's, Birm., 7 In. 85.00
Wooden, Beehive Type, Early 19th Century, 16 In. 225.00
    CANDLEWICK, see Imperial; Pressed Glass

 Candy containers have been popular since the late Victorian era. Collectors have long favored the glass containers; but now all types, including tin and papier–mache, are collected. Probably the earliest glass container sold commercially was the Liberty Bell made in 1876 for sale at the Centennial Exposition. Thousands of designs were made until the cost became too high in the 1960s. By the late 1970s, reproductions were being made and sold without the candy. Containers listed here are glass unless otherwise described.

CANDY CONTAINER, Airplane, Army Bomber, 4 1/8 In. .... 21.00 To 22.00
  Airplane, Spirit of Goodwill, 4 3/8 In. .... 100.00 To 150.00
  Airplane, Spirit of Goodwill, Tin Cap, 5 In. .... 116.00 To 150.00
  Angel's Head, Bisque, Cotton Robe, Stars, 8 In. 110.00
  Auto, Bottle Sedan, Volkswagen, 6 1/8 In. 30.00
  Auto, Hearse No.2, Tassels, Original Candy, 4 3/8 In. 150.00
  Auto, Limousine, Rear Trunk & Tire, 4 13/16 In. .... 165.00 To 175.00
  Auto, Racer No.12, 5 3/8 In. 275.00
  Auto, Sedan, 4 Doors, Tin Wheels, 4 1/4 In. 125.00
  Auto, Sedan, 6 Vents, Green Glass, Original Candy 125.00
  Auto, Station Wagon, 4 7/8 In. .... 35.00 To 40.00
  Bank, Clock, Dime, Kiddie, Original Candy, 2 In. 15.00
  Baseball Bank, Frosted Glass, 3 1/4 In. 75.00
  Baseball Player On Base, With Glove, Original Paint, 5 In. 900.00
  Baseball Player, With Bat, Barrel, 3 1/4 In. 600.00
  Baseball, Paper, Germany, 1920s 90.00
  Basket, Hanging, Grape Design, Milk Glass, Chain, 2 3/8 In. 100.00
  Bell, Cotton Rabbit & Chick On Each Side, Purple, 5 In. 30.00
  Bell, Liberty No.3, Amber, 4 1/8 In. 60.00
  Bird Cage, 4 1/2 In. 150.00
  Bird On Stump, Wood, Compositon & Chalk, 5 In. 25.00
  Boat, Battleship, On Waves, 5 1/4 In. 75.00
  Boy, Happifats On Drum, 4 3/8 In. 75.00
  Brownie In Egg, Painted Papier–Mache, 4 1/2 In. 38.50
  Bucket, Ye Old Oaken Bucket, Tin Lid, Milk Glass, 4 1/4 In. 75.00
  Bull, Papier–Mache 375.00
  Bunny, Driving Firetruck, Papier–Mache, Egg, 6 In. 66.00
  Bunny, Egg, Papier–Mache, 4 1/2 In. 57.00
  Bunny, Girl, Fur Covered, Neck Closure, Germany, 5 1/2 In. 185.00
  Bus, Greyhound, No.1, Original Wheels, 5 In. 400.00
  Bus, Jitney, Black & Gold 450.00
  Bus, Victory Lines Special, 4 7/8 In. 30.00
  Camera, On Tripod, 5 1/2 In. .... 150.00 To 395.00
  Cane, 4 5/8 In. 25.00
  Cannon, U.S., Defense Field Gun, No.17, Barrel, 4 1/4 In. 400.00
  Cart, Pulled By Rabbit Container, Glass Eyes, 14 3/4 In. 155.00
  Cat, Black, Glass Eyes 85.00
  Cat, Painted Composition, 4 1/2 In. 75.00
  Cherry Tree, Paper Leaves, Composition Cherries, 7 1/2 In. 28.00
  Chick, In Eggshell Auto, Replaced Closure 275.00
  Chick, Standing, Original Paint & Closure, Candy, 2 1/4 In. 120.00

Chicken Hawk, Mechanical, Paper Box, Germany, 6 In. 325.00
Chicken, Crowing Rooster, Original Candy, 5 In. 275.00
Chicken, On Nest, 4 5/8 In. 20.00
Chicken, On Oblong Basket, 3 In. 45.00
Chicken, On Oblong Basket, Original Candy, 3 In. 75.00
Chicken, On Sagging Basket, Original Candy, 3 1/8 In. 75.00
Child In Sleigh, Bisque, Cotton 350.00
Clock, Happy Time, Tin 165.00
Clock, Mantel, 3 3/4 In. 175.00
Clock, White Milk Glass, Oval, Painted 175.00
Clown Rabbit, Composition, Germany, 5 In. 225.00
Dirigible, Los Angeles, 5 3/4 In. 80.00
Dog, Bulldog, Round Base, Black, Glass, Sitting, 4 1/2 In. 50.00
Dog, By Barrel, Glass Eyes, Original Candy, 2 1/8 In. 350.00
Dog, Hound Pup, Small Glass Hat, Original Candy, 3 1/2 In. 30.00
Dog, Puppy, Papier-Mache, Black Muzzle, 2 1/2 In. 30.00
Doll, Glass Eyes, Straw Stuffed, 9 1/2 In. 82.50
Drum, Candy Filled Bank, Opal Glass, 2 15/16 In. 525.00
Duck, Large Bill, Green Paint, Ugly Duckling, 3 1/4 In. 125.00
Duck, On Rope, Top Basket, Glass, 3 1/4 In. 50.00
Duck, White Compostion, Neck Closure, 5 In. 165.00
Duck, With Large Bill, Ugly Ducking, Candy, 3 1/4 In. 160.00
Elephant, Amber Glass, Trunk Up, 1930s, 7 1/2 In. 65.00
Father Christmas, Lavender, Mica Covered, Germany, 10 In. 895.00
Fire Engine, 1914, Stough, Original Wheels, 5 In. 200.00
Fire Engine, Ladder Truck, Original Wheels, 5 In. 250.00
Fire Engine, V.G. Co., 4 1/4 In. 65.00
Football Player, Jointed Limbs, Composition, 8 1/2 In. 495.00
Football, Tin Lithograph, Germany .... 18.00 To 25.00
George Washington, Horse, Bisque Head, Wire Frame, 14 In. 1000.00
Girl, With 2 Geese, Glass, 3 3/8 In. 30.00
Gun, Indian Head Revolver, Glass, 5 3/8 In. 75.00
Gun, Millstein's, Plastic, Original Candy 45.00
Halloween, Mushroom, Orange Stem, Painted Face, 4 In. 165.00
Hen, On Easter Egg, Tin, Chein 69.00
Horn, Stough's Musical Toy No.2, Original Candy 25.00
Horn, Trumpet, Milk Glass, Tin Closure 95.00
Horse, Brown, Black Mane & Tail, 6 X 5 1/2 In. 210.00
Horse, Spark Plug, Glass, 3 In. .... 50.00 To 100.00
House, All Glass, Original Candy, 2 3/8 In. 150.00
House, Gel Windows, Back Closure, Green, Orange, 4 In. 22.00
House, Green Cottage, Dark Roof, 3 X 3 In. 30.00
House, Red Brick, Back Closure, 4 X 3 In. 30.00
House, Red, Brown, Snow Covered Roof, Tree, 7 In. 40.00
Independence Hall, 7 3/16 In. .... 325.00 To 400.00
Irish Fighter, Germany, 10 In. 300.00
Irish Gentleman, Composition, On Papier-Mache, 6 In. 230.00
Irish Girl, White & Green Dress, Bonnet, On Box, 4 In. 45.00
Iron, Electic, With Cord & Plug, Original Candy, 4 1/2 In. 65.00
Jackie Coogan, No.2, Orginal Candy, 5 In. 1200.00
Jeep, Scout Car, 4 3/8 In. 25.00
Jitney Bus, Tin Top & Wheels, 3 X 4 1/2 In. 275.00
Kewpie By Barrel, Original Candy, 3 In. 125.00
Lamp, Hobnail, Orignal Candy, 5 In. 100.00
Lamp, Kerosene, Original Candy, 4 5/8 In. 75.00
Lantern, Barn Type No.3, Original Bail 100.00
Lantern, Barn Type, Ruby Glass, Souvenir, Harrisburg, Bail 100.00
Lantern, Beveled Panel, Square,, Original Candy, 4 1/8 In. 100.00
Lantern, Oval Panels, Medallion Center, Green, 4 1/16 In. 35.00
Lantern, Souvenir of Thousand Islands, 6 1/2 In. 1100.00
Lighthouse, Cork Closure, Clear, 6 In. 27.50
Locomotive, 888, Pink Glass 39.50
Locomotive, Open Bottom, Amethyst 120.00
Locomotive, Tin Closure Back, M.C.R.R., 3 X 4 1/2 In. 138.00

Locomotive, Victorian, Red Closure, Long 50.00
Mailbox, Souvenir, Monroe, N.Y., Silver Paint, 3 1/4 In. 225.00
Man On Motorcycle, With Sidecar, 5 1/8 In. .... 468.00 To 550.00
Mr.Chicken, Red Vest, Black Top Hat, Lead Feet, 7 In. 110.00
Mug, Drum, With Eagle, 2 1/4 In. 60.00
Mule Pulling 2-Wheeled Barrel, Driver, 4 1/2 In. .... 65.00 To 100.00
Naked Child With Derby, Original Candy, 4 3/8 In. 50.00
Naked Child, Victory Glass, Orginal Candy, 3 5/8 In. 80.00
Opera Glasses, Ruby Glass, Souvenir, Gettysburg, 1863 .... 135.00
Opera Glasses, Souvenir, Providence, Metal Cap, 3 In. 55.00
Owl, 4 3/8 In. .... 20.00 To 55.00
Peanut, Embossed Cardboard, Celluloid Baby Inside 40.00
Phonograph, Tin Horn & Bottom, Glass, 5 In. 308.00
Pig, Flocked, Green, Neck Closure, 2 1/2 In. 48.00
Prime Rib Roast, Bottom Closure, Germany, 8 X 10 In. 125.00
Rabbit Hunter, Papier-Mache, Jointed Arms, 11 In. 935.00
Rabbit, & Cart, Glass Eyes, Neck Closure, 7 1/2 X 12 In. 225.00
Rabbit, & Cart, Green Moss, 7-In.Rabbit, 11-In.Cart, Germany 175.00
Rabbit, & Wooden Cart, Brown, 13 1/2 X 8 1/2 In. 225.00
Rabbit, Eating Carrot, 4 3/8 In. .... 22.00 To 40.00
Rabbit, Eating Carrot, Original Candy, 4 3/8 In. 75.00
Rabbit, Fur Covered, Composition, Carrot In Mouth, 6 In. 165.00
Rabbit, Fur Covered, Germany, 1910-20, 8 7/16 In. 85.00
Rabbit, In Car, Blue & Red Outfit, Papier-Mache, 5 In. 75.00
Rabbit, Nodder, 10 1/2 In. 600.00
Rabbit, Papier-Mache, Glass Eyes, Brown, Cream, 8 1/2 In. 110.00
Rabbit, Peter Rabbit, Marked J.H. Millstein Co., 6 1/4 In. 35.00
Rabbit, Pressed Cardboard, 8 In. 20.00
Rabbit, Pushing Chick In Wheelbarrow, Candy, 4 In. 500.00
Rabbit, Pushing Twig Wheelbarrow, Glass, Germany, 9 In. 275.00
Rabbit, Seated, Glass, 6 1/4 In. 25.00
Rabbit, Sitting Up, Wooden Legs & Arms, Germany, 9 In. 90.00
Rabbit, Twig Cart, Papier-Mache, Brown, Cream, 6 In. 220.00
Rabbit, With Laid Back Ears, J.H. Millstein Co., 4 1/4 In. 35.00
Reindeer, Glass Eyes, Neck Closure, Brown, 6 X 5 In. 295.00
Rocking Horse, 4 1/2 In. 245.00
Rocking Horse, Clown Rider, Blue Glass, 4 3/4 In. 250.00
Roly Poly, Yellow Clown, Pressed Cardboard 100.00
Rooster, With Feather Tail, On Candy Box 150.00
Santa Claus, & Sleigh, With Reindeer, Germany, 10 In. 1390.00
Santa Claus, Banded Coat, Original Candy, 5 1/4 In. 225.00
Santa Claus, Climbing Down Chimney, Glass, 5 In. 120.00
Santa Claus, Double Cuff, Original Candy, 4 3/8 In. 125.00
Santa Claus, Feather Tree In Hand, Germany, 11 In. 575.00
Santa Claus, Green Moss Over Cardboard, Wheels, 5 1/2 In. 775.00
Santa Claus, In Boot, Mesh Bag, Japan, 6 In. 105.00
Santa Claus, Leaving Chimney, Original Candy, 5 1/16 In. 110.00
Santa Claus, On Log Sleigh, Feather Tree, Germany, 5 In. 465.00
Santa Claus, Papier-Mache, Japan, 5 1/2 In. 30.00
Santa Claus, Plastic Head, Jeannette Label, 5 5/8 In. 45.00
Santa Claus, Plastic Head, Sticker, Candy, 5 5/8 In. 100.00
Santa Claus, Pulls Apart At Waist, Germany, 11 In. 695.00
Santa Claus, Red Felt Coat, Rabbit Fur Beard, 1950s, 10 In. 95.00
Santa On Reindeer, Celluloid, 9 In. 14.00
Sheep, Wooly, Blue Paper Collar, Glass Eyes, Germany, 4 In. 175.00
Shoe, Lady's, Cardboard, Fabric Covered, 3 1/2 In. 121.00
Skookum, By Tree Stump, Original Candy, 3 5/8 In. 400.00
Snowman, Red & Black, Papier-Mache, 6 3/4 In. 25.00
Stork, 10 In. 45.00
Stork, Cotton Over Paper, Wire Legs, Wood Beak, Glass Eyes 95.00
Suitcase, 1/2 In. 65.00
Suitcase, Dresden, Red Trim, Gold Lock, 2 1/2 X 4 In. 125.00
Suitcase, Milk Glass, Original Bail, 2 1/2 In. 150.00
Tank, World War I, 4 3/8 In. 120.00

Tank, World War I, Painted, Replaced Closure, 4 3/8 In. 90.00
Telephone, Box Opens, Wooden Receiver, 6 X 3 In. 95.00
Telephone, Millsteins Tot, Original Candy, 3 In. 45.00
Telephone, Wall, Wooden Receiver, Hello Central, 6 In. 50.00
Telephone, Wooden Receiver, Victory Glass, 5 In. 45.00
Toonerville Trolley, 3 1/2 In. .... 600.00 To 900.00
Trunk, With Round Top, Milk Glass, 3 In. 95.00
Turkey, Composition, Bottom Close, Germany, 3 1/2 In. 45.00
Turkey, Cooked, Germany, 5 In. 50.00
Turkey, Papier–Mache, Green, Black, Red, 4 1/2 In. 20.00
Vegetable Witch, Red & Yellow Dress, Stands On Box, 4 In. 100.00
Vegetable Witch, Squash Body, Pickle Arms, 5 In. 90.00
Village Building, Bank, Tin, 3 In. 125.00
Village Building, Bungalow, Tin, 2 1/2 In. 400.00
Village Building, Church With Steeple, Tin, 3 1/2 In. 150.00
Village Building, Church, With Cross, Tin, 3 1/2 In. 125.00
Village Building, City Garage, Tin, 2 7/8 In. 65.00
Village Building, Confectionery, Tin, 2 7/8 In. 50.00
Village Building, Drug Store, Tin, 2 7/8 In. 35.00
Village Building, Engine Vp/ No.23, 2 7/8 In. 35.00
Village Building, English Cottage, Tin, 3 In. 400.00
Village Building, Log Cabin, Tin, 3 In. 400.00
Village Building, Princess Theatre, Tin, 2 7/8 In. 50.00
Village Building, Schoolhouse, With Flag, Tin, 2 3/4 In. 75.00
Village Building, Two Story House, Tin, 3 1/8 In. 35.00
Wagon, Stage Coach, Metal Top, 3 3/8 On. 75.00
Wagon, U.S. Express, West Bros., 4 In. 150.00
Watch, Pocket, Tin Back, Wire Handle, 2 3/4 In. 110.00
Watch, With Fob, Original Candy, 2 3/4 In. 150.00
Wheelbarrow, 6 In. 100.00
Wheelbarrow, Straw, Twig, 6 X 3 In. 40.00
White Chalet, Jesso Rose Bush, German, 2 X 3 In. 45.00
Windmill, Tin Arms, Clear Glass, 4 7/8 In. 38.50
Witch, Compostion Face, Paper Cape & Clothes, 5 1/2 In. 350.00
Witch, Pumpkin Head, Straw Hair & Broom, 7 In. 345.00
Woman's Shoe, Cardboard, Fabric, Germany, 3 1/2 In. 121.00
World Globe, On Stand, 4 1/4 In. 585.00

Canes and walking sticks were used by every well–dressed man in the nineteenth century, but by World War I the style had changed. Today canes are used by few but the infirm. Collectors prize old canes made with special features such as hidden swords, whiskey flasks, or risque pictures seen through peepholes. Examples with solid gold heads or made from exotic materials such as walrus vertebrae are among the higher priced canes.

CANE, Antler Bone Handle, Twig, 30 1/4 In. 17.50
Antler Handle, Malacca, Metal Eyelets For Cord, Silver Ferrule 60.00
Antler Handle, Malacca, Stiletto, Brass Ferrule, 26 3/4 In. 150.00
Ash Tree, Turned Ball Handle, Tied Branch, Kenneth Young, 58 In. 50.00
Ash, Inscribed Holsteins For Profit Burnt On Handle 6.00
Bamboo, Ivory Handle, Engraved MDB, Sterling Ferrule, 1902 .... 190.00
Bird's Head Handle, Carved Ropelike Shaft 125.00
Blackthorn, Engraved D.W.T. Taylor, Round Cap Type Handle, Sterling 25.00
Blackthorn, Shaft & Handle, Carved Head of Bird 185.00
Bone Hand, Ebonized, Carved Shield, 34 1/2 In. 32.50
Brass Handle, Glass Vial Inside, Oak 60.00
Briar Wood, Shaft & Handle, Ivory Bulldog Insert 675.00
Cap Gun, National 45.00
Cap Shooter, Iron Bird's Head Handle, Child's 65.00
Carved & Incised With Masonic Devices, Painted Yellow, 38 In. 115.00
Carved Bull & Bullfighter, 3 Scenes, Wooden, Green, Brown, Gold, Red, Tan 35.00
Carved Bullfighter, Black Paint, Red, Green & Gold On Carvings 45.00
Carved Dog Handle, Glass Eyes, Malacca Shaft 160.00
Carved Handle, Malacca, Silver Ferrule, Trip Lock To Open, 23 In. 500.00

Carved Old Man's Head, Black Walnut Shaft, Folk Art 400.00
Cobra Snake Head, With Body The Shaft, Rosewood, 1 Piece 240.00
Concealed Whiskey Flask, Southern Comfort 325.00
Deer's Foot Handle, Leather Ferrule, Rope Type Strips, On Pine Shaft 60.00
Dog Head Handle, Celluloid, Glass Eyes 50.00
Dog Head Handle, Malacca, Sterling Ferrule, Glass Eyes, Metal Tip 160.00
Dog Head Handle, Wooden, Glass Eyes, Bamboo Bottom 60.00
Egyptian Head Handle, Wooden Shaft, Black, Trip For Releasing Sword 150.00
Glass, Burgundy Swirl Stripes, Baton Top, 58 In. 225.00
Glass, Latticino With Pink & White Swirls, Baton Top, 36 In. 235.00
Gold Handle, 3 Sections With Gold Bands, Medicine Bottle Top 1000.00
Gold Handle, Ebony, Inscribed Lentz & Co., Dated Oct. 18, 1881 .... 155.00
Gold Handle, Inscribed Rev. Al Dobbs, Dec. 25, 1881, Black Lacquered 130.00
Gold Knopped Head, 9K, Foliate Design, Name & Date, 35 1/2 In. 330.00
Grant's Head Metal Handle, Ash, 26th Annl. Encampment, 1892 .... 155.00
Ivory Ball-Type Handle, Bone Shaft 240.00
Ivory Derby-Shaped Handle, Cherry Wood Shaft, Brass Tip 70.00
Ivory Derby-Shaped Handle, Ebony, D.S. Richmond, Silver Ferrule 55.00
Ivory Dog Head Handle, Maple, Gold Ferrule, Brass Tip, Rubber Cap 375.00
Ivory Handle, Rosewood, 7 1/2-In. Stiletto, Ferrule Release Blade 170.00
Ivory Horsehead Handle, Black Painted Wood, Ebony Type 180.00
Ivory Ringed Handle, Curly Maple Shaft, Octagon 45.00
Ivory Tip & Handle, Gold Ferrule, Presentation Dated 1872, 32 1/2 In. 105.00
Maple, Inscribed St. Paul Hydraulic 7.50
McKinley's Head, 25th Pres. Wm. McKinley, Campaign, Wooden 290.00
Native Head, Teakwood, Alligator Crawling Up Shaft, Tapered Handle 40.00
Oak, King Midas Flour 25.00
Political, Parade, Carved Court Jester's Head, Polychrome 1900.00
Ribbed Handle, Square Body, Corkscrew Bottom, Glass, 33 In. 195.00
Riding Crop, Carved Ivory Dog's Head Handle 90.00
Riding Crop, Spelter Rabbit's Head Handle 85.00
Rosewood, 18K Gold Trim, Tiffany 190.00
Seat, Folk Art, Scrimshaw-Type Man, Woman, Dogs & Dates 1836-1896 .... 3600.00
Silver Head, Knopped & Reeded, Horn Tip, 19th Century, 33 1/2 In. 250.00
Snake Swallowing Cane Handle, Reptile & Snakes Wrapped Around Shaft 55.00
T-Shaped Handle, Black Walnut, Inside Patterns of Squares 120.00
Tree Root Shaft, Head of African Native, Brass Tip 95.00
Walking Stick, Blackthorn, Mother-of-Pearl Raised Inlay 70.00
Walking Stick, Carved Bird Grip, Painted, Wooden, 36 1/2 In. 495.00
Walking Stick, Carved Man's Head, Beard Handle, Silver Collar, 1849 .... 190.00
Walking Stick, Carved, Oriental Figures, 36 In. 100.00
Walking Stick, Composition Ivory Handle, Stag & Dogs, 34 3/4 In. 65.00
Walking Stick, Ebonized, Turned Bone Handle, 32 1/4 In. 12.50
Walking Stick, Face, Spade, Hearts & Eagle, Walnut, 35 1/4 In. 175.00
Walking Stick, Folk Art Handle, Old Man, Mustache, Black Walnut 400.00
Walking Stick, Hand Holding Sphere Grip, Winding Serpent, Maple 990.00
Walking Stick, In Honor of Reunion At Gettysburg, 1913, 36 1/2 In. 2600.00
Walking Stick, Soldier & Rope Carved Shaft, Brown Finish, 38 In. 1100.00
Walking Stick, Southern Comfort Handle, Opens To 5 Vials 250.00
Walking Stick, Tiger Maple, Inlaid Knob Handle, Tapered, 33 In. 85.00
Walking Stick, Totem Pole, Carved 14.00
Walking Stick, Twisted Wooden, Horn Handle & Tip 180.00
Wm. Henry Harrison's Head In Metal, Black, Wooden Shaft 400.00
Wm. J. Bryan Head, Our Next President, Metal, Free Coinage 400.00
Wooden Shaft & Handle, Carved Bird, Brass Tip 300.00
Zebra Type Stripes, Black, Great Lakes Expo, 1936 .... 20.00

Canton china is blue-and-white ware made near Canton, China, from about 1785 to 1895. It is hand decorated with Chinese scenes.

CANTON, Bowl, Hexagonal Scalloped Form, Canton Scene, Cloud Rim, 9 1/2 In. 550.00
Bowl, Salad, Shaped Rim, Blue & White, 19th Century, 9 1/2 In. 825.00
Bowl, Scalloped Rim, Blue & White, 10 5/8 In. 285.00
Bowl, Square, 8 In. 140.00
Bowl, Vegetable, Pine Cone Finial, Domed Lid, Canton Scene, 9 1/2 In. 385.00
Canister, Tea, Cover, Square, Blue & White, 19th Century, 5 1/2 In. 2300.00
Creamer, Helmet–Shaped, 5 1/8 In. 200.00
Cup & Saucer 325.00
Dish, Serving, Cover, Landscape, 11 1/2 In. 550.00
Dish, Vegetable, Cover, Acorn Finial, 19th Century, 8 1/4 X 9 1/4 In. 250.00
Ginger Jar, Bulbous, 19th Century, 8 1/4 In. 365.00
Plate, Chop, Blue & White, 19th Century, 14 1/2 In. 1045.00
Plate, Syllabub 192.50
Platter, Central Canton Scene, Rain & Clouds Rim, 18 1/4 X 15 In. 550.00
Platter, Cut Corners, Blue & White, 15 1/2 X 19 In. 425.00
Platter, Landscape, Blue & White, 17 In. 440.00
Platter, Meat, With Strainer 1210.00
Platter, Oval, Blue & White, 14 1/2 X 18 In. 550.00
Tea Caddy, Cover, Hexagonal, Blue & White, 6 In., Pair .... 5750.00 To 6325.00
Teapot, Domed Cover, Ball Finial, Blue & White, 8 1/2 In. 1200.00
Teapot, Drum Shape, Cover 275.00
Tureen, Cover, Boar Handles, Blue & White, 19th Century, 13 In. 725.00
Tureen, Landscape, Boar's Head Handle, 13 In. 715.00

Capo–di–Monte porcelain was first made in Naples, Italy, from 1743 to 1759. The factory moved near Madrid, Spain, reopened in 1771, and worked to 1834. Since that time the Doccia factory of Italy acquired the molds and is using the N and crown mark. Societe Richard Ceramica is a modern–day firm often referred to as Ginori or Capo–di–Monte. This company uses the crown and N mark.

CAPO–DI–MONTE, Box, Cherubs, 7 1/4 X 4 1/2 X 5 In. 85.00
Box, Cover, Paw Feet, Children, Trees, Fruit, 7 In. 75.00
Box, Dresser, Bonbon, Greek Mythology, Serpentine, 10 In. 1500.00
Box, Jewelry, Bouquet Cover, Rose Bouquet Inside, 8 1/2 In. 80.00
Box, Musicians & Cherubs, Lozenge Form, 9 In. 110.00
Box, Relief Putti, Porcelain, Rectangular, 3 X 7 X 6 1/2 In. 110.00
Cup & Saucer, Harvest & Other Scenes, Demitasse, 12 Sets 312.00
Figurine, African Crowned Crane, Water Plants, 14 In. 150.00
Figurine, Aristocratic Woman With Flowers, 1900, 10 In. 85.00
Figurine, Beauties, Girl In Green Dress, Dog On Leash, 10 In. 225.00
Figurine, Beauties, Girls Next To Tree, Marked, 10 In. 225.00
Figurine, Boy Flutist, Early Mark 55.00
Figurine, Chestnut Vendor, Woman, In Front of Stove, 10 In. 250.00
Figurine, Clown, Standing On Drum, Gold Cymbals, 12 In. 75.00
Figurine, Dandy, Long Blue Coat, Striped Trousers, 8 In. 160.00
Figurine, Fisherman, Man Smoking Pipe, 10 1/2 In. 250.00
Figurine, Last Cab, 9 X 17 In. 350.00
Figurine, Man With Top Hat, Green Coat, Posies, 8 In. 160.00
Figurine, Masked Jester, Holding Sword, 5 In. 95.00
Figurine, Pan, Gold Horns, Seated, Goat Head, 8 1/2 In. 325.00
Figurine, Pearl Fisherman, 9 1/2 X 7 1/2 In. 174.00
Figurine, Photographer, Young Boy, Kneeling, Camera, 9 1/2 In. 125.00
Figurine, Seesaw, Pink Dress, Blue Trousers, 11 In. 150.00
Group, Woman, Man, Bench, Flower Jug, Crown N Mark, 8 1/2 In. 195.00
Lamp, Urn, Cupids, Forest Green, Dolphin Feet, 16 In., Pair 165.00
Perfume Bottle, Signed 45.00
Plate, Border of Rollicking Cherubs, Blue Mark, 9 In. 45.00
Triptych, Coronation of Charlemagne, Hinged, 16 1/4 X 20 In. 1350.00
Tureen, Soup, Marked, 1840, 13 X 12 In. 1000.00
Urn, Classical Ladies, Flower Swags, Loop Handles, 8 1/2 In. 50.00
Urn, Cover, Cherubs, Grapes, Bacchus Head Handles, 15 In., Pair 450.00
Urn, Molded Body of Cherubs, Bacchus Handles, 18 In., Pair 425.00
Vase, Square Pedestal, 9 1/4 In. 100.00

Captain Marvel was introduced in February 1940 in Whiz comic books. An orphan named Billy Batson met the wizard Shazam and whenever he said the magic word he was transformed into a superhero. A movie serial was released in 1940. The comic was discontinued in 1954. A second Captain Marvel appeared in 1966, a third in 1967. Only the original was transformed by shouting "Shazam."

CAPTAIN MARVEL, Book, No.11	12.00
Toy, Punch Out, Ski Jump Action, Envelope	18.00
Wristwatch, 1948	230.00

Captain Midnight began as a radio show in September 1940. The first comic book appeared in July 1941. Captain Midnight was really the aviator Captain Albright, who was to defeat the Nazis. A movie serial was made in 1942 and a comic strip was published for a short time. The comic book Captain Midnight ended his career in 1948. The radio premiums are the prized collector memorabilia today.

CAPTAIN MIDNIGHT, Book, Joyce of Secret Squadron, Hardback	18.00
Code–O–Graph & Magnifier	65.00
Decoder, Secret Squadron Plane Puzzle, 1955–56	50.00
Decoder, Silver Dart Secret Squadron, 1957	35.00
Figure, Skelly	12.00
Magnifier & Decoder, Secret Squadron, 1945	75.00
Manual, Official Secret Code Book, 1940	125.00
Mug, Ovaltine, 1953	27.50
Photo, Black, White, Cap'T Patsy & Chuck	25.00
Pin, Skelly Flight Patrol	50.00
Postcard, Premium, Be A Secret Squadron Flight Commander	35.00
Record Set, Longines Symphonette, Captain Cover	65.00
Ring, Flight Commander	45.00
Token, Membership	10.00

CARAMEL SLAG, see Chocolate Glass

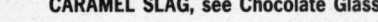

The cards listed here include advertising cards, greeting cards, baseball cards, playing cards, valentines, and others. Color pictures were rare in the nineteenth century, so companies gave away colorful cards with pictures of children, flowers, products, or related scenes that promoted the company name. These were often collected and stored in albums. Greeting cards are also a nineteenth–century idea that has remained popular. Baseball cards also date from the nineteenth century when they were used by tobacco companies as giveaways. The gum cards were started in 1933, but it was not until after World War II that the bubble gum cards favored today were produced. Today over 1,000 cards are issued each year by the gum companies.

CARD, see also Postcard

CARD, Advertising, Air Raid Tips, Churchman's Cigarettes, 1938, 48 Pieces	40.00
Advertising, Arbuckle's Ariosia Coffee, 49 of 50 States	100.00
Advertising, Bird Series, Arm & Hammer, 1922, Small	2.00
Advertising, Blatz Gum, Wilen Movie Stars Pictures, 20 Piece	50.00
Advertising, Bunker Hill Harness Oil, Geis Litho, 1880s	10.00
Advertising, Clark's Thread, Ladies, Uncle Sam Sewing, Pocket Calendar	15.00
Advertising, Coats Thread, We Never Fade, Black Boy, 1885, 4 X 3 In.	15.00
Advertising, Dry Goods Store, Lady In U.S. Flag, 1882, 4 1/2 X 3 In.	8.50
Advertising, Durham Tobacco, Tilden–Grant Metamorphic	25.00
Advertising, Estey Organs, Brownies	4.00
Advertising, Fairy Soap, M.F. Fairbank, Calendar, 1904, 2 1/2 X 2 In.	5.00
Advertising, Gold Baking Powder, French Franc, 1888, 2 3/4 X 3 1/2 In.	12.50
Advertising, Gypsy Queen Cigarettes, 1896	2.00
Advertising, Hold To Light, Wm. Penn, Holding Quaker Oats, 1890	20.00
Advertising, Luca's Co., Paints, Varnishes, Factory Pictures	6.00
Advertising, Lux Soap, Cardboard, Color Litho, 22 X 13 1/2 In.	78.00
Advertising, Mack's Milk Chocolate	2.00

Advertising, McCormick Farm Machinery, Turnover Card, 1890	20.00
Advertising, Merrick's Thread, Search of No. Pole, 1885, 2 1/2 X 4 In.	7.50
Advertising, Old Kentucky Distillery, Monkeys, Cats, 1898	20.00
Advertising, Pear's Soap, Baby, 8 3/4 X 5 3/4 In.	10.00
Advertising, RAF At Work, Churchman's Cigarettes, 1937, 48 Piece	75.00
Advertising, Rubifoam For The Teeth	3.00
Advertising, Saratoga Cooking Stove, Mfg. By Peckham, 1880	10.00
Advertising, Soapine, Girl, Doll, 7 1/4 X 5 1/2 In.	7.00
Advertising, Standard Plumbing Fixtures, Early 1900s, 11 X 21 In.	20.00
Advertising, Sterling Pianos, Twelvetrees Drawings, 4 Piece	20.00
Advertising, Swan Soap, 5 X 7 1/2 In.	12.00
Advertising, Turkish Trophies Cigarette, H. King, 1 Framed, 4 Piece	75.00
Advertising, Velvet Whiskey, Flip-Top	12.00
Advertising, When Babe Ruth Comes Home, Fro-Jay Ice Cream, 1928	90.00
Baseball Set, Topps, 1981, 12 Month Series	75.00
Baseball Set, Topps, 1985, 12 Month Series	85.00
Baseball, Brooks Robinson, No.550, Topps, 1972	7.50
Baseball, Campanella, Red Man Tobacco, 1953	35.00
Baseball, Carl Yastrzemski, No.250, Topps, 1968	24.00
Baseball, Charles "Old Hoss" Radbourne, 1888	605.00
Baseball, Duke Snider, Red Man Tobacco	28.00
Baseball, Duke Snider, Topps, 1964	10.00
Baseball, Ed Matthews, No.120, Topps, 1961	10.00
Baseball, Ed Matthews, Topps, 1956	25.00
Baseball, Eric Davis, Topps, 1985	15.00
Baseball, Hand Aaron, Topps, 1962	52.00
Baseball, Harmon Killebrew, Topps, 1958	14.00
Baseball, Harry Brecheen, Topps, 1954	7.00
Baseball, Johnny Bench, RC, 1968	225.00
Baseball, Kelly, Boston, Old Judge & Gypsy Queen Cigarettes, 1888	1600.00
Baseball, Pee Wee Reese, Red Man Tobacco	30.00
Baseball, Pete Rose, No.580, Topps, 1970	62.00
Baseball, Pete Rose, Topps, 1964	175.00
Baseball, Phil Rizzuto, Red Man Tobacco	25.00
Baseball, Robin Roberts, Topps, 1959	7.50
Baseball, Sandy Koufax, Topps, 1957	65.00
Baseball, Stan Musial, Red Man Tobacco	75.00
Baseball, Ted Williams, 1971	4.00
Baseball, Willie Mays, Topps, 1956	125.00
Birthday, Floral Design 2 Sides, Silk Fringed, 1890, 6 X 4 1/2 In.	13.50
Birthday, Wishing Happy Returns, Prang, Shell Design, 1879, 5 X 3 In.	15.00
Christmas, Bell Shape, Sol Strauss, Leading Clothier, Dayton, 1880, 4 In	. 7.50
Christmas, Christmas Morn, Brown & Bigelow, Parrish	12.00
Christmas, Cloth & Paper, Red Tassel, Framed, 9 1/2 X 8 1/4 In.	5.00
Christmas, Eventide, Parrish, 1942, 6 X 7 1/2 In.	20.00
Christmas, Floral, Black Ground, Litho, Prang, 2 1/2 X 5 1/4 In.	20.00
Christmas, Victorian Children, Decorated Tree, 3 X 5 In.	8.00
Gum, Yellow Kid, Adam's Yellow Kid Chewing Gum, 1896	87.50
Lobby, Beat Generation, 1959, Lou Armstrong, All-Stars, 11 X 14 In.	35.00
Lobby, Big Shot, Humphrey Bogart, 1942	200.00
Lobby, Breakfast In Hollywood, Spike Jones & Band, 1946	20.00
Lobby, Easter Parade, Judy Garland, Fred Astaire, 1948, 14 X 22 In.	37.50
Lobby, Flashing Guns, Johnny Mack Brown, 1947	6.00
Lobby, Grand Slam, Loretta Young, In Closeup, First National, 1933	15.00
Lobby, Key Largo, Humphrey Bogart, 1948	200.00
Lobby, Last Hurrah, Spencer Tracy, Pat O'Brien, 1958	15.00
Lobby, Laugh Clown Laugh, Lon Chaney	800.00
Lobby, Law of The Lash, Lash LaRue, On Horseback, 1947	6.00
Lobby, Mark of Zorro, Fairbanks Portrait, 14 X 22 In.	1000.00
Lobby, P.T. 109, Cliff Robertson As John F. Kennedy, 1963	20.00
Lobby, Rebel Without A Cause, James Dean	50.00
Lobby, Rock Around The Clock, 1956, Alan Freed, 11 X 14 In.	15.00
Lobby, Temptation, Merle Oberon, Paul Lukas, 1946	6.00
Lobby, That Girl From Paris, Jack Oakie, Lily Pons, 1936	15.00

Lobby, Wagons Roll At Night, Humphrey Bogart, 1941 .... 225.00
Mechanical, Cafe Advertising, Back Reads White Help Only 20.00
Mother's Day, Sip of Tea, Framed, 5 X 6 In. 95.00
New Years, Chinese–U.S.Flag, Color, In Chinese, Unused, 1940 .... 7.50
Playing, Allied Van Lines, Unopened 10.00
Playing, Arrow Beer, 1935 .... 20.00
Playing, Braille, Marked Metal Box 38.00
Playing, Contentment, Maxfield Parrish .... 125.00 To 225.00
Playing, Egypt, Box, 1922 .... 275.00
Playing, Elvgren, 52 Different Pinup Girls 75.00
Playing, Fish Tire 25.00
Playing, In The Mountains, Parrish 40.00
Playing, Kuhn's Northside Chevrolet 16.00
Playing, Oriental Lady, Cho Cho San 14.00
Playing, Pennsylvania R.R., Double Deck 70.00
Playing, Reveries, Box 175.00
Playing, Royal Deal Cigars 55.00
Playing, TWA, Box 5.00
Playing, Tydol Flying A Gas, Box, 2 Decks 45.00
Valentine, Boy & Girl, Sewing Machine, 5 1/2 In. 9.00
Valentine, Boy, Chalkboard, Hand Moves & Erases Message 10.00
Valentine, Dancing Boy, I'M No Jitterbug, Pullout, Unused, 1930s 4.00
Valentine, Flowers, Children, Lacy, 1896 .... 25.00
Valentine, Honeycomb, Large 12.00
Valentine, Mechanical, Snow White 15.00
Valentine, Pickaninny, Tuck 20.00
Valentine, Popeye, 1929 .... 17.00
Valentine, Rocking Horse, Boy & Girl, Moving 25.00
Valentine, Sailing Ship, Honeycomb Paper, 3D, 12 1/2 X 14 In. 95.00
Valentine, Wheel of Love, Fold–Out, Beistle 14.00
Valentine, Wizard of Oz, Dorothy & Tin Man, 1939 .... 40.00
Valentine, Woman Wearing Pink Pansy Hat, Parchment Paper, 11 1/2 In. 45.00
    CARDER, see Aurene; Steuben

Carlsbad, Germany, is a mark found on china made by several factories in Germany. Most of the pieces available today were made after 1891.

CARLSBAD, Ewer, Classical Scene, Gold Handle, Tracery, 9 1/2 In. 125.00
Pitcher, Gray & Green Leave, Gold Veining, White Ground, 7 1/2 In. 65.00
Rose Bowl, 12 Crimps, Yellow Roses, Brown Leaves, Raised Gold 85.00
Tray, Pink, Blue & Orchid Flowers, Gold, Oval, 17 In. 95.00
Vase, Burmese, Birds, Foliage, Moon, Flask Shape, Signed, 12 1/2 In. 500.00
Vase, Flowers, Gourd Shape, 12 1/2 In. 225.00
Vase, Grecian Figures On Center Panel, Handles, 9 1/2 In. 48.00
Vase, Grecian Figures, Blue Green, Cream, Ornate Handles, 9 In. 75.00
Vase, Pink Flowers, 2 Handles, Worn Gold, Ovoid Flat, 5 3/4 In. 35.00

Carlton ware was made at the Carlton Works of Stoke–on–Trent, England, about 1890. The firm traded as Wiltshaw & Robinson until 1957. It was renamed Carlton Ware Ltd. in 1958.

CARLTON WARE, Biscuit Jar, Blue Willow Pattern, C.1890 .... 225.00
Fruit Bowl, Yellow & Brown Bananas, Green, Footed, 9 In. 48.00
Jar, Oriental Design, Yellow Ground, W & R, 9 5/8 In. 80.00
Pitcher, Australian Design, 7 1/2 In. 38.00
Salad Set, Pedestal Bowl, Flowers In & Out, Beige, 9 3/4 In. 385.00

Carnival, or taffeta, glass was an inexpensive, pressed, iridescent glass made from about 1907 to about 1925. Over 1,000 different patterns are known. Carnival glass is currently being reproduced.

    CARNIVAL GLASS, see also Northwood
CARNIVAL GLASS, Acanthus, Plate, Smoky, 10 In. 275.00
    ACORN BURRS & BARK, see Acorn Burrs
Acorn Burrs, Butter, Cover, Amethyst .... 195.00 To 210.00
Acorn Burrs, Pitcher, Water, Marigold 200.00

Acorn Burrs, Punch Set, Marigold, 8 Piece 675.00
Acorn Burrs, Sugar & Creamer, Marigold 85.00
Acorn Burrs, Tumbler, Amethyst 40.00
Acorn Burrs, Tumbler, Marigold 60.00
Acorn Burrs, Water Set, Marigold, 5 Piece 650.00
Acorn, Bowl, Blue, 6 In. 45.00
Acorn, Bowl, Blue, 7 In. 65.00
Acorn, Bowl, Red 695.00
    AMARYLLIS, see Tiger Lily
    AMERICAN BEAUTY ROSES, see Wreath of Roses
Apple Blossoms, Bowl, Marigold, 7 1/2 In. 30.00
Apple Tree, Pitcher, Marigold 150.00
Apple Tree, Tumbler, White 170.00
Apple Tree, Water Set, White, 7 Piece 1100.00
April Showers, Vase, Blue, 8 In. 50.00
Arched Flute, Toothpick, Marigold 75.00
    AURORA, see Flowers
    BASKETWEAVE & CABLE BAND, see Basketweave & Cable
Basketweave & Cable, Creamer, Marigold 47.00
Basketweave & Cable, Creamer, Purple 38.00
    BATTENBURG LACE NO.1, see Hearts & Flowers
    BATTENBURG LACE NO.2, see Captive Rose
    BATTENBURG LACE NO.3, see Fanciful
Beaded Cable, Rose Bowl, Aqua .... 250.00 To 335.00
Beaded Shell, Carnival, Tumbler, Amethyst 65.00
Beaded Shell, Creamer, Marigold 40.00
Beaded Shell, Mug, Amethyst 85.00
Big Fish, Bowl, Marigold, 9 In. 350.00
Birds & Cherries, Compote, Amethyst 40.00
    BIRDS ON BOUGH, see Birds & Cherries
    BLACKBERRY & CHECKERBOARD, see Blackberry Block
    BLACKBERRY A., see Blackberry
    BLACKBERRY B., see Blackberry Spray
Blackberry Block, Water Set, Marigold, 7 Piece 495.00
Blackberry Bramble, Compote, Marigold .... 35.00 To 70.00
Blackberry Spray, Hat, Red 345.00
Blackberry Spray, Hat, Vaseline 95.00
Blackberry Wreath, Bowl, Amethyst, 7 In. 55.00
Blackberry, Compote, Blue, Miniature 75.00
Blackberry, Compote, Jelly, Purple 4 1/2 In. 35.00
Blossom Time, Bonbon, Footed, Purple 175.00
Blossoms & Spears, Plate, Marigold, 8 In. 30.00
Bouquet, Tumbler, Marigold 35.00
Brocaded Acorns, Cake Stand, Open Handle, Ice Blue, 12 In. 75.00
Brocaded Acorns, Candlestick, Ice Blue, Pair 55.00
Brocaded Acorns, Tumbler, Ice Blue 70.00
Brocaded Daffodils, Plate, Hexagonal, Pink, 8 1/2 In. 70.00
Brocaded Summer Garden, Plate, Center Handle, White 125.00
Butterfly & Berry, Bowl, 3–Footed, Marigold, 5 In. 25.00
Butterfly & Berry, Bowl, Footed, Blue, 10 In. 150.00
Butterfly & Berry, Bowl, Marigold, 9 In. 60.00
Butterfly & Berry, Pitcher, Water, Blue 275.00
Butterfly & Berry, Spooner, Blue 75.00

Candle drippings can be removed from fabric or furniture with the help of ice cubes. Rub the wax with the ice until the wax hardens. Scrape off the hard wax with a credit card or stiff cardboard. If some wax remains, put a blotter over the wax, then iron with a cool iron.

Butterfly & Berry, Tumbler, Blue .... 45.00 To 50.00
Butterfly & Berry, Tumbler, Marigold .... 20.00 To 30.00
Butterfly & Berry, Water Set, Amethyst, 7 Piece 495.00
Butterfly & Berry, Water Set, Marigold, 7 Piece 375.00
 BUTTERFLY & CABLE, see Springtime
Butterfly & Fern, Tumbler, Amethyst 40.00
Butterfly & Fern, Water Set, Blue, 7 Piece 650.00
Butterfly & Fern, Water Set, Green, 7 Piece 695.00
 BUTTERFLY & GRAPE, see Butterfly & Berry
 BUTTERFLY & PLUME, see Butterfly & Fern
 BUTTERFLY & STIPPLED RAYS, see Butterfly
Butterfly, Bonbon, 2 Handles, Purple 65.00
Butterfly, Bonbon, Green 45.00
Buzz Saw, Cruet, Green, 4 In. 400.00
 CACTUS LEAF RAYS, see Leaf Rays
Cannon Ball, Water Set, Blue, 7 Piece 150.00
Captive Rose, Bowl, Amethyst, 9 In. .... 35.00 To 50.00
Captive Rose, Plate, Blue, 9 In. .... 155.00 To 225.00
Captive Rose, Plate, Marigold, 9 In. 275.00
Carolina Dogwood, Bowl, Blue Opalescent, 8 In. 315.00
 CATTAILS & WATER LILY, see Water Lily & Cattails
 CHERRIES & MUMS, see Mikado
Cherry Chain, Bowl, Marigold, 10 In. .... 40.00 To 42.50
Cherry Circle, Bowl, Handles, Blue, 7 1/2 In. 60.00
 CHERRY WREATHED, see Wreathed Cherry

Put a piece of cardboard between the back of the plate and the wire plate holder to keep the back from scratching.

Cherry, Banana Boat, Amethyst 150.00
Cherry, Bowl, Footed, Fluted, Marigold, 8 1/2 In. 65.00
Cherry, Bowl, Ice Cream, Green, 10 In. 135.00
Cherry, Spooner, Green 65.00
 CHRISTMAS CACTUS, see Thistle
 CHRISTMAS PLATE, see Poinsettia
 CHRISTMAS ROSE & POPPY, see Six-Petals
 CHRYSANTHEMUM WREATH, see Ten Mums
Chrysanthemum, Bowl, Collar Base, Red, 9 1/2 In. 3600.00
Chrysanthemum, Bowl, Footed, Green, 10 In. 250.00
Chrysanthemum, Bowl, Footed, Marigold, 10 In. 60.00
Coin Dot, Bowl, Amethyst, 9 1/2 In. .... 60.00 To 68.00
Coin Dot, Bowl, Marigold, 9 1/2 In. 35.00
Coral, Plate, Marigold 900.00
Corinth, Banana Boat, Amber 55.00
Corinth, Bowl, Aqua, 7 In. 85.00
Cornucopia, Vase, Marigold, 5 In. 75.00
Cosmos & Cane, Bowl, White, 5 In. 40.00
Cosmos & Cane, Bowl, White, 8 In. 95.00
Cosmos & Cane, Tumbler, Marigold 85.00
Cosmos, Bowl, Amethyst, 9 3/4 In. 70.00
Crab Claw, Water Set, Marigold, 7 Piece 950.00
Crackle, Tumbler, Green 40.00
Crackle, Water Set, Marigold, 7 Piece .... 82.00 To 100.00
Dahlia, Berry Set, Marigold, 5 Piece 295.00
Dahlia, Table Set, White, 4 Piece 1150.00
Daisies & Drape, Vase, Aqua Opalescent 600.00
Daisy & Cane, Bowl, White, 8 1/4 In. 125.00
 DAISY & LATTICE BAND, see Lattice & Daisy
 DAISY BAND & DRAPE, see Daisies & Drape
 DANDELION VARIANT, see Paneled Dandelion

Dandelion, Mug, Marigold 350.00
Dandelion, Pitcher, Green 985.00
Dandelion, Tumbler, Amethyst 65.00
Dandelion, Tumbler, Marigold 50.00
    DIAMOND & CABLE, see Fentonia
Diamond & File, Vase, Purple, 10 1/2 In. 45.00
Diamond & Rib, Vase, Aqua, 11 In. 45.00
Diamond & Rib, Vase, Green, 11 In. 30.00
Diamond & Sunburst, Wine, Marigold 22.00
    DIAMOND BAND, see Diamond
Diamond Lace, Bowl, Marigold, 5 In. 25.00
Diamond Lace, Pitcher, Amethyst 125.00
Diamond Lace, Tumbler, Purple .... 40.00 To 55.00
    DIAMOND POINT & DAISY, see Cosmos & Cane
Diamond Point, Vase, Amethyst, 9 In. 55.00
Diamond Point, Vase, Ice Green, 10 1/2 In. 195.00
Diamond Point, Vase, White, 10 1/2 In. 115.00
    DOGWOOD & MARSH LILY, see Two Flowers
Dogwood Spray, Bowl, Collar Base, Peach, 7 In. 60.00
Double Dutch, Bowl, 3–Footed, Marigold, 9 In. 45.00
Double Star, Tumbler, Green 30.00
Double–Stem Rose, Bowl, Amethyst, 8 In. .... 68.00 To 75.00
Double–Stem Rose, Bowl, Footed, Marigold, 9 In. 32.00
Dragon & Lotus, Bowl, Blue, 9 In. .... 75.00 To 90.00
Dragon & Lotus, Bowl, Green, 9 In. 65.00
Dragon & Lotus, Bowl, Red, 9 In. 900.00

Smoking is bad for the health of your antiques! Smoke causes discoloration; weakens textiles. Another reason to stop smoking!

Drapery, Rose Bowl, Aqua .... 280.00 To 325.00
Dutch Twins, Ashtray, Marigold 25.00
    DUTCHMAN, see Sailing Ship
    EGYPTIAN BAND, see Round–Up
    EMALINE, see Zippered Loop Lamp
Embroidered Mums, Bowl, Ice Blue 1050.00
Embroidered Mums, Plate, Ice Green 1500.00
    FAN & ARCH, see Persian Garden
Fanciful, Plate, Ruffled, White, 9 1/2 In. 275.00
    FANTASY, see Question Marks
Fashion, Bowl, Fruit, Marigold, 2 Piece 95.00
Fashion, Creamer, Marigold 18.00
Fashion, Punch Cup, Marigold 11.00
Fashion, Punch Set, Marigold, 5 Piece 200.00
Fashion, Tumbler, Marigold 20.00
    FEATHER & HOBSTAR, see Inverted Feather
Feather Stitch, Bowl, Blue, 8 In. 70.00
    FEATHERED SCROLL, see Feathered Serpent
Feathered Serpent, Bowl, Amethyst, 10 In. 70.00
Feathered Serpent, Bowl, Purple, 5 In. 30.00
    FENTON'S BUTTERFLY, see Butterfly
Fentonia, Berry Set, Marigold, 5 Piece .... 150.00 To 195.00
    FIELD ROSE, see Rambler Rose
Fieldflower, Tumbler, Amethyst 30.00
Fieldflower, Tumbler, Blue 60.00
Fine Cut & Roses, Candy Dish, Footed, Green .... 60.00 To 85.00
Fine Cut & Roses, Candy Dish, White 95.00
Fine Cut & Roses, Dish, 3–Footed, Purple 45.00
Fine Cut & Roses, Rose Bowl, Amethyst 65.00
Fine Cut & Roses, Rose Bowl, Aqua 1000.00
Fine Cut & Roses, Rose Bowl, Purple 95.00
Fine Rib, Vase, Marigold, 12 In. 28.00

FINECUT & STAR, see Star & File
FISH & FLOWERS, see Trout & Fly
FISHERMAN'S NET, see Treebark
Fleur De Lis, Bowl, Marigold, 10 In. 150.00
FLORAL & DIAMOND POINT, see Fine Cut & Roses
Floral & Grape, Pitcher, Blue 265.00
Floral & Grape, Tumbler, Amethyst 50.00
Floral & Grape, Tumbler, Blue 28.00
Floral & Grape, Water Set, Marigold, 7 Piece 200.00
FLORAL & GRAPEVINE, see Floral & Grape
Flowers, Nut Bowl, Amethyst, 5 In. 125.00
FLUFFY BIRD, see Peacock
Fluffy Peacock, Pitcher, Purple 625.00
Fluffy Peacock, Pitcher, Water, Blue 650.00
Fluffy Peacock, Tumbler, Marigold 70.00
Flute, Berry Bowl, Signed, Amethyst 65.00
Flute, Punch Set, Amethyst, 14 Piece 850.00
Flute, Toothpick, Amethyst 65.00

> Scratches can be rubbed off the mirror glass by using a piece of felt and polishing rouge from a paint store.

French Knots, Candy Dish, Cobalt Blue 48.00
Fruits & Flowers, Bonbon, Pedestal Base, Marigold, 9 In. 90.00
Fruits & Flowers, Bowl, Amethyst, 9 1/2 In. 50.00
Fruits & Flowers, Plate, Amber, 7 In. 165.00
Garland, Rose Bowl, Marigold .... 45.00 To 48.00
Good Luck, Bowl, Amethyst 285.00
Good Luck, Bowl, Blue 95.00
Good Luck, Bowl, Marigold 135.00
Good Luck, Bowl, Ruffled, Blue, 8 In. 250.00
Good Luck, Bowl, Stippled, Blue 225.00
Grape & Cable, Banana Boat, Footed, Amethyst 220.00
Grape & Cable, Banana Boat, White .... 595.00 To 675.00
Grape & Cable, Berry Set, Amethyst, 7 Piece 100.00
Grape & Cable, Bonbon, 2 Handles, White 750.00
Grape & Cable, Bonbon, Marigold 35.00
Grape & Cable, Bonbon, Stippled, Green 100.00
Grape & Cable, Bowl, Aqua, 7 In. 300.00
Grape & Cable, Bowl, Cobalt Blue, 12 In. 195.00
Grape & Cable, Bowl, Flared, Purple, 6 In. 22.00
Grape & Cable, Bowl, Fluted, Blue, 11 In. .... 165.00 To 195.00
Grape & Cable, Bowl, Fluted, White, 10 1/2 In. 395.00
Grape & Cable, Bowl, Footed, Green, Fenton, 8 In. 175.00
Grape & Cable, Bowl, Ice Cream, White 250.00
Grape & Cable, Bowl, Marigold, 9 In. 95.00
Grape & Cable, Bowl, Ruffled, Purple, 5 1/2 In. 30.00
Grape & Cable, Butter, Cover, Amethyst .... 125.00 To 150.00
Grape & Cable, Butter, Cover, Marigold 210.00
Grape & Cable, Butter, Cover, Purple 30.00
Grape & Cable, Candlestick, Green, Pair 75.00
Grape & Cable, Cracker Jar, Marigold 295.00
Grape & Cable, Cracker Jar, Purple 50.00
Grape & Cable, Fernery, Ice Blue 1300.00
Grape & Cable, Hatpin Holder, Green 190.00
Grape & Cable, Hatpin Holder, Purple 145.00
Grape & Cable, Lamp Shade, Marigold 275.00
Grape & Cable, Lamp, Candle, Shade & Metal Holder, Amethyst 600.00
Grape & Cable, Orange Bowl, Blue 350.00
Grape & Cable, Orange Bowl, Green 235.00
Grape & Cable, Orange Bowl, White 765.00
Grape & Cable, Perfume Bottle, Marigold 150.00

Grape & Cable, Perfume Bottle, Purple, Pair 475.00
Grape & Cable, Pitcher, Water, Amethyst 250.00
Grape & Cable, Pitcher, Water, Purple 525.00
Grape & Cable, Plate, 3–Toed, Marigold, 9 In. .... 60.00 To 65.00
Grape & Cable, Powder Jar, Purple 125.00
Grape & Cable, Punch Cup, Green, 6 Piece 225.00
Grape & Cable, Punch Cup, Purple, 2 3/4 In. 28.00
Grape & Cable, Punch Set, Amethyst, 8 Piece 475.00
Grape & Cable, Sauce, Fluted, Marigold, 6 In. 20.00
Grape & Cable, Sherbet, Footed, Amethyst 40.00
Grape & Cable, Sweetmeat, Purple 275.00
Grape & Cable, Tray, Dresser, Purple 275.00
Grape & Cable, Tumbler, Amethyst .... 22.00 To 50.00
Grape & Cable, Water Set, Amethyst, 7 Piece 475.00
Grape & Gothic Arches, Bowl, Blue, 5 In. 30.00
Grape & Gothic Arches, Bowl, Green, 4 1/2 In. 75.00
Grape & Gothic Arches, Spooner, Blue 65.00
Grape & Gothic Arches, Tumbler, Holmes County, Blue 40.00
Grape & Lattice, Tumbler, Marigold 40.00
Grape Arbor, Orange Bowl, Footed, Marigold 145.00
Grape Arbor, Tankard, Purple 300.00
Grape Arbor, Tumbler, Marigold 30.00
Grape Arbor, Tumbler, Purple 55.00
  GRAPE DELIGHT, see Vintage
Grape, Bowl, Amber, 1906, 12 In. 375.00
Grape, Punch Cup, Marigold 15.00
Grape, Punch Set, Green, 12 Piece 225.00
Grape, Tumbler, Amethyst 45.00
Grape, Tumbler, Marigold, 6 Piece 90.00
Grape, Wine, Green 11.00
  GRAPEVINE DIAMONDS, see Grapevine Lattice
Grapevine Lattice, Plate, Ruffled, White 50.00
Grapevine Lattice, Tankard, Marigold 245.00
Grapevine Lattice, Tumbler, Marigold 50.00
Hattie, Bowl, Marigold, 8 In. 35.00
Heart & Vine, Bowl, Green, 8 3/8 In. 48.00
Heart & Vine, Plate, Blue 350.00
Hearts & Flowers, Compote, Purple 210.00
Heavy Grape, Berry Set, Purple, 7 Piece 165.00
Heavy Grape, Bowl, Amethyst, 4 In. 25.00
Heavy Grape, Bowl, Purple, 10 In. 225.00
Heavy Grape, Chop Plate, Smoky 950.00
Heavy Grape, Plate, Amber, 7 In. 45.00
Heavy Grape, Plate, Marigold, 8 In. 90.00
Heavy Iris, Tumbler, White 200.00
  HERON & RUSHES, see Stork & Rushes
Herringbone & Iris, Plate, Marigold, 11 3/4 In. 20.00
  HOBNAIL, see also Hobnail category
Hobnail, Butter, Cover, Purple 850.00
Hobstar & Arches, Bowl, Clambroth, 9 In. 20.00
Hobstar & Feather, Punch Set, Marigold, 7 Piece 1250.00
  HOBSTAR & TORCH, see Double Star
Hobstar, Table Set, Marigold, 4 Piece 235.00

Wear rubber gloves when handling bleaching materials, strong solvents,
or other harsh chemicals.

  HOLLY SPRAY, see Holly Sprig
Holly Sprig, Bonbon, Green 65.00
Holly Sprig, Bowl, Amethyst, 8 1/4 In. 50.00
Holly Sprig, Card Tray, Handles, Purple 65.00
Holly Sprig, Compote, Marigold, 4 1/2 In. 25.00

Holly, Bowl, Blue, 9 In. 45.00
Holly, Bowl, Green, 8 In. 60.00
Holly, Bowl, Marigold, 10 In. 110.00
Holly, Bowl, White, 9 1/2 In. 125.00
Holly, Compote, Marigold .... 28.00 To 30.00
Holly, Hat, Red .... 375.00 To 550.00
Holly, Tumbler 22.00
    HORN OF PLENTY, see Cornucopia
    HORSE MEDALLIONS, see Horses' Heads
Horses' Heads, Bowl, Marigold, 7 1/2 In. 70.00
Horses' Heads, Rose Bowl, Blue 150.00
Imperial Grape, Bottle, Water, Amethyst .... 190.00 To 225.00
Imperial Grape, Bottle, Water, Purple .... 200.00 To 250.00
Imperial Grape, Bowl, Green, 6 1/2 In. 75.00
Imperial Grape, Decanter Set, Stopper, Amethyst, 7 Piece 400.00
Imperial Grape, Decanter, Stopper, Green 160.00
Imperial Grape, Decanter, Stopper, Purple 145.00
Imperial Grape, Pitcher, Water, Amber 625.00
Imperial Grape, Pitcher, Water, Green 98.00
Imperial Grape, Pitcher, Water, Marigold .... 80.00 To 90.00
Imperial Grape, Plate, Green, 6 In. 50.00
Imperial Grape, Plate, Marigold, 6 1/2 In. 35.00
Imperial Grape, Wine, Marigold 30.00
    INTAGLIO, see Hobstar & Feather
    INTERIOR OF CHERRIES & MUMS, see Mikado
Inverted Feather, Cracker Jar, Green .... 185.00 To 225.00
Inverted Feather, Parfait, Marigold 50.00
Inverted Strawberry, Powder Jar, Green 170.00
Inverted Strawberry, Table Set, Marigold 1000.00
Iris, Goblet, Amethyst 65.00
Iris, Tankard, Marigold 290.00
Iris, Tumbler, Amethyst 85.00
    IRISH LACE, see Louisa
Kingfisher, Bowl, Purple, 9 1/4 In. 100.00
Kingfisher, Sauce, Marigold 42.00
Kittens, Bowl, Marigold, 3 1/2 In. 140.00
    LABELLE ELAINE, see Primrose
    LABELLE POPPY, see Poppy Show
    LABELLE ROSE, see Rose Show

Buy a paint-by-number kit to get an inexpensive assortment of paint colors to use for touch-ups and restorations for paintings and furniture.

Late Thistle, Water Set, Amethyst, 7 Piece 3500.00
Lattice & Daisy, Tumbler, Marigold 40.00
Lattice & Daisy, Water Set, Marigold, 7 Piece 360.00
Lattice & Grape, Tumbler, Marigold .... 15.00 To 22.00
Lattice & Grape, Water Set, Blue, 7 Piece 595.00
    LATTICE & GRAPEVINE, see Lattice & Grape
Leaf & Beads, Rose Bowl, Aqua 400.00
Leaf & Beads, Rose Bowl, Blue 325.00
Leaf & Beads, Rose Bowl, Green 75.00
Leaf & Beads, Rose Bowl, Marigold ....80.00 To 125.00
Leaf & Beads, Rose Bowl, Purple 88.00
Leaf Chain, Bowl, Blue, 7 In. 65.00
    LEAF MEDALLION, see Leaf Chain
    LEAF PINWHEEL & STAR FLOWER, see Whirling Leaves
Leaf Rays, Bonbon, Marigold 18.00
Leaf Rays, Nappy, Amethyst 35.00
Leaf Rays, Nappy, Marigold .... 17.00 To 25.00
Leaf Rays, Nappy, Peach 20.00
Lily of The Valley, Tumbler, Blue 300.00

Little Fishes, Bowl, 3–Footed, Blue, 10 In. 250.00
Little Flowers, Bowl, Crimped, Marigold, 8 3/4 In. 50.00
   LOOP & COLUMN, see Pulled Loop
   LOOPED PETALS, see Scales
Lotus & Grape, Bonbon, 2 Handles, Marigold .... 55.00 To 58.00
Louisa, Bowl, Footed, Green, 7 In. 45.00
Louisa, Bowl, Purple, 9 In. .... 40.00 To 45.00
Louisa, Nut Bowl, Amethyst 60.00
Louisa, Rose Bowl, Amethyst 65.00
Lustre Flute, Hat, Amethyst 40.00
Lustre Rose, Bowl, Footed, Marigold 10 In. 45.00
Lustre Rose, Bowl, Marigold, 8 In. .... 30.00 To 50.00
Lustre Rose, Bowl, Ruffled, Footed, Purple, 11 In. 650.00
Lustre Rose, Butter, Marigold 35.00
Lustre Rose, Table Set, Marigold, 4 Piece 175.00
Lustre Rose, Tumbler, Marigold 15.00
Lustre Rose, Tumbler, Purple 70.00
Lustre Rose, Water Set, Marigold, 7 Piece 125.00
Lustre Rose, Water Set, Purple, 5 Piece 700.00
   MAGNOLIA & POINSETTIA, see Water Lily
Maple Leaf, Bowl, Ice Cream, Footed, Marigold, 4 1/2 In. 55.00
Maple Leaf, Butter, Cover, Purple 195.00
Maple Leaf, Ice Cream Set, Blue, 7 Piece 250.00
Maple Leaf, Water Set, Amethyst, 7 Piece 550.00
   MARYLAND, see Rustic
Mayan, Bowl, Green, 8 1/4 In. 85.00
   MELINDA, see Wishbone
Memphis, Cup, Marigold 30.00
Mikado, Compote, Marigold, 10 In. 133.00
Milady, Tumbler, Blue 85.00
Milady, Tumbler, Purple 70.00
   MUMS & GREEK KEY, see Embroidered Mums
Nautilus, Dish, Flattened Boat Shape, Peach, 7 1/2 X 6 In. 295.00
   NESTING SWAN, see Swan, Carnival
   OAK LEAF & ACORN, see Acorn
   OAK LEAF BROCADE, see Brocaded Acorns
Octagon, Decanter, Marigold, Stopper 85.00
Octagon, Pitcher, Water, Marigold 100.00
   OLD FASHION FLAG, see Iris
Open Rose, Berry Set, Marigold, 7 Piece 125.00
Orange Tree, Bowl, 3–Footed, Marigold, 10 In. 95.00
Orange Tree, Bowl, Green, 8 1/2 In. 150.00
Orange Tree, Bowl, Marigold, 9 In. 95.00
Orange Tree, Butter, Cover, Cobalt Blue 210.00
Orange Tree, Compote, Marigold, 5 In. 45.00
Orange Tree, Dish, Ice Cream, White, 8 1/2 In. 145.00
Orange Tree, Hatpin Holder, Blue 250.00
Orange Tree, Loving Cup, Blue 185.00
Orange Tree, Loving Cup, Green 350.00
Orange Tree, Loving Cup, Marigold 87.50
Orange Tree, Mug, Amethyst 30.00
Orange Tree, Mug, Blue .... 30.00 To 60.00
Orange Tree, Mug, Marigold 35.00
Orange Tree, Mug, Red .... 445.00 To 495.00

"A stitch in time" helps with repairs, too. If, while you are cleaning it, a small piece of veneer falls from a piece of furniture, put it in an envelope immediately, mark where it came from, and put it in the drawer (or tape it to the piece), to be reglued when you have time. Reglue as soon as possible.

Orange Tree, Plate, Blue, 9 1/4 In. 290.00
Orange Tree, Powder Jar, Cover, Cobalt Blue .... 75.00 To 85.00
Orange Tree, Powder Jar, Marigold .... 55.00 To 75.00
Orange Tree, Punch Set, Blue, 7 Piece 425.00
Orange Tree, Punch Set, White, 7 Piece 650.00
Orange Tree, Spooner, Footed, White 95.00
Orange Tree, Tumbler, Cobalt Blue, 4 3/8 In. 40.00
Oriental Poppy, Pitcher, Water, Marigold 345.00
Oriental Poppy, Pitcher, Water, Purple 750.00
Oriental Poppy, Tumbler, Marigold 38.00
Oriental Poppy, Tumbler, Purple 40.00
Oriental Poppy, Water Set, White, 7 Piece 1990.00
   PANELED BACHELOR BUTTONS, see Milady
Panelled Dandelion, Tumbler, Purple 35.00
Panelled Dandelion, Water Set, Marigold, 7 Piece 385.00
Panelled Holly, Bonbon, Marigold 40.00
Pansy, Nappy, Green 28.00
Pansy, Pickle, Amethyst 48.00
Pansy, Relish, Marigold 40.00
Panther, Berry Set, Marigold, 7 Piece .... 400.00 To 550.00
Panther, Bowl, Footed, Marigold, 5 In. .... 45.00 To 95.00
   PARROT TULIP SWIRL, see Acanthus
Peacock & Grape, Bowl, Marigold, 9 In. 50.00
Peacock & Urn, Bowl, Amethyst, 8 1/2 In. 185.00
Peacock & Urn, Bowl, White, 10 In. 275.00
Peacock & Urn, Chop Plate, Marigold 1600.00
Peacock & Urn, Compote, Green 1100.00
Peacock & Urn, Compote, Marigold .... 45.00 To 95.00
Peacock At The Fountain, Butter, Cover, Purple 235.00
Peacock At The Fountain, Orange Bowl, Blue 900.00
Peacock At The Fountain, Punch Cup, Blue 32.00
Peacock At The Fountain, Punch Cup, White 55.00
Peacock At The Fountain, Tumbler, Amethyst 45.00
Peacock At The Fountain, Tumbler, Blue 45.00
Peacock At The Fountain, Water Set, Blue, 7 Piece .... 600.00 To 775.00
   PEACOCK EYE & GRAPE, see Vineyard
   PEACOCK ON FENCE, see Peacock
Peacock Tail, Berry Set, Green, 5 Piece 140.00
Peacock Tail, Bonbon, 2 Handles, Marigold 20.00
Peacock Tail, Bonbon, Amethyst 42.00
Peacock, Plate, Marigold, 9 In. 310.00
Peacock, Plate, Stippled Ground, Blue, 9 In. 545.00
Persian Garden, Plate, Marigold, 6 1/2 In. 150.00
Persian Garden, Plate, Marigold, 6 In. 65.00
Persian Garden, Plate, White, 6 1/2 In. 110.00
Persian Medallion, Bonbon, 2 Handles, Blue .... 48.00 To 65.00
Persian Medallion, Bonbon, Amethyst 60.00
Persian Medallion, Bonbon, Red .... 650.00 To 1150.00
Persian Medallion, Bowl, Blue, 8 In. .... 50.00 To 68.00
Persian Medallion, Bowl, Marigold, 5 In. 35.00
Persian Medallion, Chop Plate, Blue, 11 In. .... 300.00 To 600.00
Persian Medallion, Nappy, Marigold 45.00
Persian Medallion, Plate, Marigold, 6 1/2 In. 60.00
Persian Medallion, Rose Bowl, Marigold 65.00
Petal & Fan, Berry Set, Peach, 7 Piece 395.00
Pillow & Sunburst, Dish, Ruffled, Purple, 8 In. 35.00
   PINE CONE WREATH, see Pine Cone
Pine Cone, Plate, Blue, 6 1/2 In. 70.00
Pine Cone, Plate, Blue, 6 In. 57.50
Pods & Posies, Plate, Purple, 9 In. 500.00
   POINSETTIA & LATTICE, see Poinsettia
Poinsettia, Pitcher, Milk, Marigold, 6 1/2 In. 95.00

Pond Lily, Bonbon, Cobalt Blue 35.00
PONY ROSETTE, see Pony
Pony, Bowl, Marigold, 8 1/2 In. 115.00
Pony, Bowl, Marigold, 9 In. 100.00
POPLAR TREE, see Feathers
POPPY SCROLL, see Poppy
Poppy Show, Bowl, White 390.00
Poppy Show, Plate, Ice Blue 1500.00
Poppy, Dish, Pickle, Amber 225.00
Primrose, Bowl, Amethyst, 9 1/2 In. 125.00
PRINCESS LACE, see Octagon
Prism & Daisy Band, Berry Set, Marigold, 5 Piece 115.00
Puzzle, Bonbon, Marigold 25.00
Question Marks, Bonbon, Amethyst 48.00
Question Marks, Bonbon, Footed, Peach 85.00
Question Marks, Bonbon, Marigold .... 30.00 To 40.00
Rambler Rose, Tumbler, Amethyst 35.00
Rambler Rose, Water Set, Purple, 7 Piece 595.00
Raspberry, Pitcher, Milk, Green .... 265.00 To 275.00
Raspberry, Pitcher, Purple 175.00
Raspberry, Tumbler, Ice Blue 100.00
Raspberry, Tumbler, Purple 30.00
Raspberry, Water Set, Green, 7 Piece 650.00
ROBIN RED BREAST, see Robin
Robin, Mug, Marigold 50.00
Rococo, Candy Dish, Smoky 35.00
ROSE & RUFFLES, see Open Rose
Rose Show, Bowl, Ice Green 1400.00
Rose Show, Bowl, Marigold 425.00
Rose Show, Bowl, White, 8 3/4 In. 200.00
Rose Show, Plate, Ice Blue 2000.00
Roses & Fruit, Compote, Amethyst 1450.00
ROSES & LOOPS, see Double–Stem Rose
ROSETTE & PRISMS, see Rosette
Rosette, Bowl, Green, Footed 65.00
Round–Up, Plate, Purple 225.00
Rustic, Vase, Amethyst, 12 In. 35.00
SAILBOAT & WINDMILL, see Sailboats
Sailboats, Compote, Marigold 50.00
Sailboats, Wine, Cobalt Blue 95.00
Sailboats, Wine, Marigold .... 30.00 To 50.00
Sailing Ship, Plate, Amber, 8 In. 75.00
Satin Jewels, Tumbler, Amethyst 80.00
Scales, Finger Bowl, Purple, 5 In. 12.00
Scarab, Hatpin, Purple 27.50
Scroll Embossed, Plate, Ruffled, Amethyst, 5 3/4 In. 95.00
SEA LANES, see Little Fishes
Seaweed, Lamp, Marigold 195.00
SHELL & SAND, see Shell, Carnival
SHELL & WILD ROSE, see Wild Rose
Shell, Carnival, Bowl, Stippled, Green, 7 3/4 In. 60.00
Singing Birds, Berry Set, Green, 7 Piece 395.00
Singing Birds, Creamer, Marigold 40.00
Singing Birds, Mug, Blue 175.00
Singing Birds, Mug, Marigold .... 48.00 To 95.00
Singing Birds, Mug, Purple 59.00
Singing Birds, Tumbler, Purple 60.00
Singing Birds, Water Set, Purple, 7 Piece 795.00
Six–Petals, Bowl, Dome Foot, Peach, 9 In. 70.00

To clean carnival glass, try using a mixture of ½ cup ammonia and ⅛ cup white vinegar.

Ski Star, Bowl, Peach, 10 1/2 In. 85.00
Smooth Rays, Bowl, Aqua, 8 1/2 In. 28.00
Smooth Rays, Bowl, Green, 8 In. 35.00
Smooth Rays, Bowl, Purple, 6 In. 25.00
Smooth Rays, Plate, White, 9 In. 40.00
SPRING FLOWERS, see Bouquet
Springtime, Butter, Cover, Green 285.00
Springtime, Spooner, Green 145.00
Springtime, Tumbler, Marigold 45.00
Stag & Holly, Bowl, 3-Footed, Aqua, 10 1/2 In. 485.00
Stag & Holly, Bowl, Footed, Amethyst, 9 In. 135.00
Stag & Holly, Bowl, Footed, Cobalt Blue, 11 In. .... 215.00 To 250.00
Stag & Holly, Bowl, Footed, Marigold, 9 1/2 In. 85.00
Stag & Holly, Bowl, Footed, Scalloped, Marigold, 10 1/2 In. 105.00
Star & File, Bowl, Marigold, 6 1/2 In. 40.00
Star & File, Dish, Pickle, Marigold 30.00
Star Medallion, Bowl, Marigold, 6 In. 20.00
Star Medallion, Pitcher, Milk, Marigold 45.00
Star of David & Bows, Bowl, Footed, Amethyst, 7 In. 75.00
Star of David & Bows, Bowl, Footed, Purple, 8 In. 80.00
STAR OF DAVID MEDALLION, see Star of David & Bows
Starfish, Compote, Peach, 6 In. 78.00
STIPPLED DIAMOND & FLOWER, see Little Flowers
Stippled Flower, Bowl, Fluted, Peach, 7 1/2 In. 50.00
STIPPLED LEAF & BEADS, see leaf & Beads
STIPPLED POSY & PODS, see Four Flowers
Stippled Rays, Bowl, Green, 5 In. 30.00
Stippled Rays, Bowl, Marigold, 9 1/2 In. 35.00
Stippled Rays, Purple, 9 In. 50.00
Stork & Rushes, Mug, Amethyst 270.00
Stork & Rushes, Mug, Marigold 42.00
Stork & Rushes, Punch Cup, Marigold .... 15.00 To 16.00
Stork & Rushes, Tumbler, Marigold .... 20.00 To 29.00
STRAWBERRY, see Wild Strawberry
Strawberry Scroll, Tumbler, Blue 95.00
Strawberry Scroll, Tumbler, Marigold 150.00
Strawberry, Bonbon, Blue 48.00
Strawberry, Bowl, Basketweave, Amethyst, 8 1/2 In. 50.00
Strawberry, Bowl, Ruffled, Basketweave, Marigold, 10 In. 95.00
Strawberry, Dish, Green, 8 1/2 In. 75.00
SUNFLOWER, see Dandelion
SUNFLOWER & WHEAT, see Fieldflower
SUNFLOWER-WHEAT-CLOVER, see Harvest Flower
Swan, Bowl, Ruffled Edge, Australian, Purple, 9 In. 165.00
Swan, Carnival, Bowl, Amethyst, 9 1/2 In. 200.00
Swirl Hobnail, Rose Bowl, Amethyst 325.00
Swirl Hobnail, Rose Bowl, Marigold .... 195.00 To 275.00
Target, Vase, White, 11 In. 95.00
Ten Mums, Bowl, Green, 10 In. 185.00
Ten Mums, Pitcher, Water, Blue 265.00
Ten Mums, Pitcher, Water, Marigold 135.00
Thin Rib, Plate, Marigold, 9 1/2 In. 50.00
Thin Rib, Vase, Green, 8 In. 30.00
Thistle & Thorn, Creamer, Footed, Marigold 75.00
Thistle & Thorn, Sugar, Cover, Marigold, 6 In. 75.00
Thistle, Banana Boat, Cobalt Blue .... 275.00 To 350.00
Thistle, Banana Boat, Green 350.00

In snowy weather make tracks both in and out of your door. One set of tracks leaving the house is an invitation to an intruder. Or perhaps you could walk out of the house backward.

Thistle, Banana Boat, Marigold .... 195.00 To 235.00
Three Fruits, Bowl, Dome–Footed, Green, 8 1/2 In. 55.00
Three Fruits, Bowl, Purple, 8 1/2 In. 60.00
Three Fruits, Bowl, Ruffled, Footed, Green, 9 In. 60.00
Three Fruits, Plate, Blue, 9 In. 75.00
Three Fruits, Plate, Green 1500.00
Three Fruits, Plate, Stippled, Amethyst 150.00
Three Fruits, Plate, Stippled, Aqua 2700.00
Tiger Lily, Pitcher, Green 150.00
Tiger Lily, Tumbler, Amethyst 70.00
Tiger Lily, Tumbler, Marigold 30.00
Tiger Lily, Tumbler, Purple 60.00
Tobacco Leaf, Champagne, Louisville & Pittsburg, White, 1909 .... 90.00
Tree Trunk, Vase, Funeral, Cobalt Blue, 20 In. 1300.00
Tree Trunk, Vase, Funeral, Purple, 12 1/2 In. 1300.00
Tree Trunk, Vase, Funeral, White, 17 In. 1000.00
Treebark, Lemonade Set, Margiold, 7 Piece 185.00
Treebark, Vase, Marigold, 8 In. 15.00
Treebark, Water Set, Marigold, 7 Piece .... 75.00 To 100.00
Trout & Fly, Bowl, Candy Ribbon Edge, Marigold 275.00
Twins, Bowl, Green, 5 In. 40.00
Twins, Bowl, Marigold, 10 In. 35.00
Two Flowers, Bowl, Amber, 8 In. 1920.00
Two Flowers, Bowl, Footed, Purple, 11 In. 110.00
Two Flowers, Bowl, Ruffled, Footed, Purple, 11 In. 750.00
Two Flowers, Rose Bowl, Marigold 95.00
Venetian, Rose Bowl, Green 800.00
Victorian, Bowl, Fluted, Purple, 11 In. 245.00
Vineyard, Pitcher, Bulbous, Marigold 95.00
Vineyard, Tumbler, Marigold 30.00
Vintage, Berry Set, Cobalt Blue, 5 Piece .... 395.00 To 450.00
Vintage, Bowl, Blue, 10 In. .... 65.00 To 75.00
Vintage, Compote, Green 45.00
Vintage, Epergne, 1 Lily, Green 145.00
Vintage, Fernery, Blue 65.00
Vintage, Plate, Amethyst, 7 In. 110.00
    WAFFLE BAND, see Lustre Flute
Water Lily & Cattails, Tumbler, Marigold .... 25.00 To 65.00
Water Lily, Bonbon, 3–Footed, Blue 55.00
Water Lily, Bowl, Footed, Green, 10 In. 115.00
Water Lily, Bowl, Ice Cream, Footed, Marigold, 10 In. 68.50
Water Lily, Bowl, Marigold, 10 In. .... 55.00 To 60.00
Whirling Leaves, Bowl, Marigold, 10 In. 85.00
Whirling Star, Punch Set, Marigold, 8 Piece 130.00
Wide Panel, Goblet, Green 50.00
Wild Rose, Bowl, Footed, Green, 6 In. 75.00
Wild Rose, Bowl, Footed, Marigold, 7 In. 23.00
Wild Strawberry, Bowl, Basketweave, Marigold, 9 In. 115.00
Wild Strawberry, Bowl, Ice Green, 10 In. 1750.00
Wild Strawberry, Bowl, Marigold, 7 In. 85.00
Windflower, Nappy, Handle, Marigold 35.00
    WINDMILL MEDALLION, see Windmill
Windmill, Tumbler, Green 40.00
Wishbone, Bowl, Amethyst, 10 In. 195.00
Wishbone, Bowl, Footed, Amethyst, 8 In. 90.00
Wishbone, Bowl, Footed, Marigold, 9 In. 70.00
Wishbone, Epergne, 1 Lily, Amethyst 450.00
Wishbone, Epergne, 1 Lily, Green 675.00
Wishbone, Epergne, 1 Lily, Marigold .... 395.00 To 450.00
Wishbone, Epergne, Purple 475.00

Never leave your housekeys on the car ring when you park the car with an attendant.

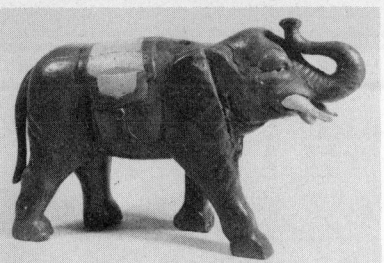

Carousel, Elephant, Gray,
Red & Orange Trim, 42 In.

If you have a battery-operated
1940s toy like "smoking
grandpa," you might want to re-
plenish the smoke-maker when it
wears out. Just put a few drops of
sewing machine oil into the smoking tube. An electric spark in the
toy causes the oil to smoke, and
allows the toy to puff on a cigarette, pipe, or cigar.

Carousel, Horse, Dapple Gray,
Brown & Red Trim, 54 In.

Wishbone, Pitcher, Marigold	110.00
Wishbone, Plate, Footed, Amethyst, 8 1/4 In.	275.00
Wreath of Roses, Bonbon, Footed, Marigold	50.00
Wreath of Roses, Compote, Green	50.00
Wreathed Cherry, Bowl, Amethyst, Oval, 5 In.	35.00
Wreathed Cherry, Bowl, Amethyst, Oval, 12 In.	130.00
Wreathed Cherry, Pitcher, Gold Cherries, White	550.00
Wreathed Cherry, Tumbler, Marigold	35.00
Zippered Loop Lamp, Lamp, Marigold	895.00

 The first carousel or merry–go–round figures carved in the United
States were made in 1867 by Gustav Dentzel. Collectors discovered
the charm of the hand–carved figures in the 1970s and they were
soon classed as folk art. Most desirable are the figures other than
horses, such as pigs, camels, lions, or dogs. A jumper is a figure
that was made to move up and down on a pole, a stander was
placed in a stationary position.

CAROUSEL, Camel, Inside Row	7000.00
Camel, Original & Worn Paint	7700.00
Camel, Original Paint, 4 Ft.	3000.00
Chariot Side, Salon Carousel, Heyn	4645.00
Chariot, Norseman & Sea Dragon, Seats 4, Herschell–Spillman	1550.00
Dog, Herschell–Spillman, Painted Pine, Black Saddle, 54 X 30 In.	4100.00
Donkey, Heyn	4645.00
Elephant, Gray, Red & Orange Trim, 42 In. ....*Illus*	675.00
Elephant, Wooden, 31 In.	495.00
Giraffe, Carved Wood	4500.00
Hare, Hubner	2965.00
Hippocampus, Mythical Sea Creature, Outside Row	6000.00
Horse, Baby Parker	4500.00
Horse, Cast Aluminum, Polychrome Paint, 44 In.	100.00

Horse, Child's Ride, Cast Iron 200.00
Horse, Dapple Gray, Brown & Red Trim, 54 In. ....*Illus* 2300.00
Horse, Herschell–Spillman, All Wood 3500.00
Horse, Jumper, Gilt Wind–Blown Mane, Miniature, 28 X 34 In. 467.50
Horse, Jumper, Herschell–Spillman, 20 Jewels 3750.00
Horse, Jumper, Parker, Signed 5500.00
Horse, Parker–Type, Cast Aluminum, 1930s 1250.00
Horse, Prancer, Herschell–Spillman, Hair Tail, Glass Eyes 5000.00
Horse, Standing, Stein & Goldstein, Restored, 1911 .... 3500.00
Peacock, Spinner, Lakin 1161.00
Pig, Limonaire 2157.00
Pig, Single Iron Pole 1760.00
Rooster, French 2300.00
Shield, Silver Band of Stars, Vertical Bars, 24 1/2 In. 525.00
Swan, Devos 3484.00
Turkey, Spinner, Kalin 4645.00

The word "carriage" has several meanings, so this section lists baby carriages, buggies for adults, horse–drawn sleighs, and even strollers. Doll–sized carriages are listed under "toy."

CARRIAGE, Baby Buggy, Bentwood, Victorian 575.00
Baby Buggy, Canvas, Folds Flat, 1930s 125.00
Baby Buggy, Hide Cover, Wood Horse, Fur Lined, 66 In. 2400.00
Baby Buggy, Metal Wheels, Push Bar, Window Openings In Hood 195.00
Baby Buggy, Wicker, Heywood Wakefield 675.00
Buggy Steps, Henney Buggy Co., Pair 24.00
Buggy, Child's, Wicker, Iron Wheel, Open 295.00
Buggy, Surrey Top, Red & Gold Stenciled Design 605.00
Doctor's Carriage, 2 Leather Seats & Top, Restored, 1890 .... 3200.00
Goat Cart, Iron Rimmed Spoke Wheels 350.00
Goat Cart, Yellow, Red Pinstriped, Stenciled 825.00
Governess Cart, Wickerwork, C.1915 .... 2500.00
Hearse, Horse Drawn 3100.00
Phaeton, Woman's, Wicker, Fringed Parasol, A.T. Demarest & Co. 4000.00
Pull Cart, Newspaper Delivery, St. Louis Post Dispatch 395.00
Sleigh, Push, Carved, Painted Wood, Dutch 2600.00
Wagon, Farm, Studebaker 5000.00

An eye on the cash was a necessity in stores of the nineteenth century, too. The cash register was invented in 1884. John and James Ritty invented a large clocklike model that kept a record of the dollars and cents exchanged in the store. John Patterson improved the cash register with a paper roll to record the money. By the early 1900s, elaborate brass registers were made. About World War I, the fancy case was exchanged for the more modern types.

CASH REGISTER, Eagle, Rotate Wooden Knob, Clock–Like Numbered Dial, Wooden 995.00
National, Floor Model, Brass, 9 Drawers 1250.00
National, Model 2, Devil's Head Door Pull, Brass 350.00
National, Model 8, Clock, 1900 .... 1800.00
National, Model 30, Brass Raised Letters On Rear Door 895.00
National, Model 50, Copley Square Hotel, 16 X 16 X 10 In. 2255.00
National, Model 130, Barber Shop, Keyed From 5 Cents To 1.00 .... 475.00
National, Model 311, Candy Store, Brass 1050.00
National, Model 313, Candy Store, 10 In. 600.00
National, Model 327, Barber Shop, Extended Base 850.00
National, Model 333, Ornate Brass, 14 In. 350.00
National, Model 452–2, Crank–Style, 2 Drawers, Oak Base 700.00
National, Model 542–4C, Brass 1050.00
National, Model 572–4F, Floor Model, Quartersawn Oak 1200.00
National, Model 582–5E, 9 Drawers, Bronze Case, Paneled Oak 850.00
National, Woodie 2200.00
Standard, No.1, Oak 450.00
Standard, Oak 375.00

Castor sets holding just salt and pepper castors were used in the seventeenth century. The sugar castor, mustard pot, spice dredger, bottles for vinegar and oil, and other spice holders became popular by the eighteenth century. These sets were usually made of sterling silver. The American Victorian castor set, the type most collected today, was made of silver–plated Britannia metal. Colored glass bottles were introduced after the Civil War. The sets were out of fashion by World War I. Be careful when buying sets with colored bottles; many are reproductions.

CASTOR SET, see also various Porcelain and Glass categories

CASTOR SET, 4–Bottle, Ruby Thumbprint, Frame	350.00
4–Bottle, Unusual Wooden Lacquered Holder	60.00
4–Cup, For Eggs, Salt & Pepper, 4 Spoons	110.00
6–Bottle, Kate Greenway–Type Girl On Handle, Silver Plate	48.00
Venecia, Rubina, Salt, Pepper, Mustard & Cruet, Glass Frame	100.00

The pickle castor was a glass jar about six inches in height, held in a special metal holder. It became a popular dinner table accessory about 1890. The jar had a top that was usually silver or silver plate. The frame, also of a silver metal, had a handle that arched above the jar and a hook that held a pair of tongs. By 1900, the pickle castor was out of fashion. Many examples found today have reproduced glass jars in old holders.

CASTOR, PICKLE, see also various Glass categories

CASTOR, Pickle, Amber Insert, Inverted Thumbprint, Blown–Out Center Band	325.00
Pickle, Birds & Flowers On Silver Holder, Cranberry, 13 1/2 In.	450.00
Pickle, Blue Daisy & Button Insert	185.00
Pickle, Blue Embossed Blocks, D–Cover, Signed, Tongs	155.00
Pickle, Blue Inverted Thumbprint Insert, Quadruplated Frame, Tongs	295.00
Pickle, Coreopsis, Ruby, White Enamel, Silver Frame	365.00
Pickle, Cranberry Glass, Inverted Thumbprint, Silver–Plated Holder	785.00
Pickle, Daisy & Button, Original Frame, Tongs & Cover	175.00
Pickle, Daisy & Button, Top Ornament, Topaz	175.00
Pickle, Enameled Cranberry, Silver Stand & Tongs	295.00
Pickle, Figural, Strawberry, Bird Finial On Lid, Sawtooth Insert	175.00
Pickle, Flowers & Leaves, Satin Glass Jar	400.00
Pickle, Flowers On Panels, Gold Around Top, Beaded, Cranberry, 11 In.	450.00
Pickle, Gold Flowers, Leaves, Blue Jar, Reed & Barton, 8 5/8 In.	275.00
Pickle, Hobnail Insert, Meriden Frame	295.00
Pickle, Inverted Thumbprint Insert, Enameled Design, Cranberry	295.00
Pickle, Inverted Thumbprint, Blue Insert, Fork, Silver–Plated Holder	295.00
Pickle, Inverted Thumbprint, Cranberry, Floral Enameled	150.00
Pickle, Inverted Thumbprint, Embossed, Tongs & Cover, Meridan	285.00
Pickle, Inverted Thumbprint, Enameled Flowers, Tongs, Blue, 11 In.	250.00
Pickle, Melon Ribbed, Enameled Flowers, Cranberry Jar	350.00
Pickle, Rubina Inserts, Enameled Flowers, Double, Meriden Holder	195.00
Pickle, Sapphire Blue, Bulbous, Allover Gold Floral, Frame & Cover	395.00
Pickle, Strawberry & Diamond Point, Fan, Silver–Plated Frame, Tongs	105.00
Pickle, Tongs, Allover Enameled Flowers, Tall Plated Frame	400.00
Pickle, Vasa Murrhina, Mica Flake, Frame, Cover & Tongs	325.00
Pickle, Zipper Insert, Footed, Tongs, Silver Plated	125.00

CATALOG, see Paper, Catalog
CAUGHLEY, see Salopian

The firm Cauldon Limited worked in Staffordshire, Great Britain, and went through many name changes. John Ridgway made porcelain at Cauldon Place, Hanley, until 1855. The firm of John Ridgway, Bates and Co. of Cauldon Place worked from 1856 to 1859. It became Bates, Brown–Westhead, Moore and Co. from 1859 to 1862. Brown–Westhead, Moore and Co. worked from 1862 to

1904. About 1890, this firm started using the words "Cauldon" or "Cauldon ware" as part of the mark. Cauldon Ltd. worked from 1905 to 1920, Cauldon Potteries from 1920 to 1962.

CAULDON, see also Indian Tree

CAULDON, Plate, Hunt Scene, Staffordshire	35.00

Celadon is a Chinese porcelain having a velvet–textured green–gray glaze. Japanese, Korean, and other factories also made a celadon–colored glaze.

CELADON, Bowl, Large Crackle, 19th Century, 7 In.	465.00
Jardiniere, Chinese, 16 In, Pair	825.00
Teapot, Cat Shape, 6 In.	100.00
Urn, Cachet, White & Cobalt Blue Birds & Clouds, 10 X 10 In.	250.00
Vase, Rose Mandarin Design, Gilt Dragon Handles, 16 1/2 In.	495.00
Vase, Trailing Floral Design, Lamp, Baluster Form, 20 In., Pair	308.00

Celluloid is a trademark for a plastic developed in 1868 by John W. Hyatt. Celluloid Manufacturing Company, the Celluloid Novelty Company, Celluloid Fancy Goods Company, and American Xylonite Company all used Celluloid to make jewelry, games, sewing equipment, false teeth, and piano keys. Eventually, the Hyatt Company became the American Celluloid and Chemical Manufacturing Company—the Celanese Corporation. The name "Celluloid" was often used to identify any similar plastic. Celluloid toys are listed under toys.

CELLULOID, Belt Buckle, Art Deco, Black, Yellow Design	10.00
Box, Boy Picture, Dated 1897	20.00
Box, Collar, River Scene	45.00
Box, Comb & Brush, Ship Picture	20.00
Box, Jewelry, Round, Signed, 3 1/2 In.	13.00
Button, Thousand Island House, Alexandria Bay, N.Y.1895, 1 1/4 In	22.50
Dresser Set, Ivory, 7 Piece	20.00
Dresser Set, Ivory, 9 Piece	30.00
Dresser Set, Mauve, 8 Piece	25.00
Dresser Set, Pearlized Green, Black Case, 12 Piece	115.00
Dresser Set, Tray, Mirror, Hair Receiver, Shaker, French, 6 Piece	65.00
Dresser Set, Turquoise & Amber, Glass, Mirror, 3 Piece	37.50
Dresser Set, Victorian, Enameled, Plush Box, Complete	50.00
Glove Stretcher	12.00
Knife Sharpener, National Hog Compound	24.00
Manicure Set, Box, 4 Piece	20.00
Mirror, Beveled, 3–Way, Gibson Girl	125.00
Multi-Sheet, Peter Pan, Tinkerbell Flying, 1953, 13 X 15 In.	2475.00
Napking Ring, Food Pusher, Spoon & Fork, Athoware, 4 Piece	35.00
Pin, Scotty Dog, With Clubs	65.00
Rattle, Santa Claus & Sleigh, 6 Reindeer, Harnesses & Bells	110.00
Rattle, Ship With Boy On Deck	95.00
Rattle, Turtle	18.00
Spoon & Fork, Child's, Teddy Bear, Athoware, Unused, Box	30.00
Toy, Donkey, Gray, Red & White Saddle Blanket On Back	8.00
Toy, Roly Poly, Kitty, Sitting On Ball, Japan, 1920s, 1 1/2 In.	8.50
Travel Kit, Tortoise, Monogram, 1930s, 11 Piece	65.00

The Ceramic Art Company of Trenton, New Jersey, was established in 1889 by J. Coxon and W. Lenox and was an early producer of American Belleek porcelain. Pieces made by this company are listed here. Do not confuse this ware with the pottery made by the Ceramic Arts Studio of Madison, Wisconsin, from 1941 to 1957.

CERAMIC ART CO., Bowl, Design, Dated 1905	125.00
Mug, Pink, Coral & Plum Pomegranates, Marked, 5 1/2 In.	165.00
Pitcher, Cider	50.00
Vase, Swans, Dark Green Ground, Green Palette Mark, 12 In.	575.00

Chalkware is really plaster of Paris decorated with watercolors. One type was molded from Staffordshire and other porcelain models and painted and sold as inexpensive decorations in the nineteenth century. Figures of plaster, made from about 1910 to 1940 for use as prizes at carnivals, are also known as chalkware.

CHALKWARE, Bank, Collie	32.00
Bank, Dog, 6 3/4 In.	450.00
Bank, Pug Dog	35.00
CHALKWARE, FIGURINE, see also Kewpie	
Figurine, Bingo	35.00
Figurine, Carousel Horses, Large	30.00
Figurine, Cat, Sitting, Hollow	50.00
Figurine, Cats, Sleeping, 1890	40.00
Figurine, Colonial Woman & Man, Soft Blue & Rose, 16 In., Pair	65.00
Figurine, Deer, Reddish Paint, Black Trim, 10 1/2 In.	250.00
Figurine, Dog, At Wall, German Shepherd	12.00
Figurine, Dog, Boston Bull, Red, White & Black Paint, 8 1/2 In.	150.00
Figurine, Dog, Collie	12.00
Figurine, Dog, Spaniel, Flat Back, 5 1/2 In.	20.00
Figurine, Elephant, Red	7.00
Figurine, Foxy Grandpa, 11 In.	75.00
Figurine, Girl, 14 In.	35.00
Figurine, Horse, Brown & Green Paint, 10 3/8 In.	900.00
Figurine, Indian Chief, Arms Crossed, Headdress, 30 In.	22.50
Figurine, Indian, Carnival	16.00
Figurine, Indian, Reclining	50.00
Figurine, Lamb, Bucks County, Penna., Late 1900s, 9 X 7 In.	625.00
Figurine, Mae West	40.00
Figurine, Mrs. Rabbit, Pushing Pink Buggy, Baby	20.00
Figurine, Nude Hawaiian Girl	35.00
Figurine, Porky Pig	22.50
Figurine, Rabbit, Driving Green Car, With Baby Bird In Back	20.00
Figurine, Santa Claus, 3 Ft.	110.00
Figurine, Scotty Dog, Holds Comb & Brush	10.00
Figurine, Squirrel, Eating Nut, Brown, Textured Tail, 6 1/2 In.	275.00
Figurine, Stella Strawberry, Pee Dee, Dated 1949	20.00
Figurine, Victorian Boy, With Basket	45.00
Figurine, W.C.Fields	36.00
Humidor, 3 Indian Faces	100.00
Plaque, Dutch Boy & Girl, Artistic Royalties, 1968, Pair	45.00
String Holder, French Chef	20.00
Wall Pocket, Comedy & Tragedy, 1915, Pair	30.00

Charlie Chaplin, the famous comic and actor, lived from 1889 to 1977. He made his first movie in 1913. He did the movie "The Tramp" in 1915. The character of the Tramp has remained famous and is in use today in a series of television commercials for computers. Dolls, candy containers, and all sorts of memorabilia picture Charlie Chaplin. Pieces are being made even today.

CHARLIE CHAPLIN, Bank, Glass, 1920s	175.00
Book, Cartoon, 1917, 9 3/4 X 16 In.	120.00
Bottle, Whiskey, Musical, Plays How Dry I Am, China	35.00
Candy Cantainer, Borgfeldt, Original Candy	150.00
Candy Container, Painted, Cane Broken, Smith	330.00
Cane, With 2-In. Lead Figure, Colored, 3 Ft.	25.00
Card, Advertising, Bicycle, Mechanical, Changing Picture	20.00
Card, Peep Show, 10 Different Scenes, Uncut, 14 X 2 1/2 In.	15.00
Comic Page, From Danish Magazine, Matted, 1926, 7 X 9 In.	15.00
Doll, Bubbles, Cadeax, 1972, Box, 17 In.	75.00
Doll, Little Tramp, World, 19 In.	65.00
Figurine, Plaster, Chas. Chaplin On Base, 9 In.	225.00
Figurine, Wax, 7 In.	45.00
Figurine, With Cane, Plaster, Base, 4 3/4 In.	55.00

Match Holder, Figural, With Barrel, Glass, 3 3/4 In. 85.00
Paper Doll, 1941, Uncut 400.00
Pencil Box, Tin, 1920s 30.00
Poster, Cantilever Shoes, 1927, 24 1/2 X 19 In. 90.00
Poster, Movie, The Bank, Sketch of Chaplin 9350.00
Toy, Charlie, Walking, Tin Litho, Mechanical, 8 1/2 In. 770.00
Toy, Mechanical, Twirls Cane, Cloth Cover, Shuco, 6 1/2 In. 2400.00
Toy, Pull Toy, Flipping Hat, 4 In. 125.00
Toy, Squeeze, Tin, Nods Head, Plays Cymbals, J.D.N., 7 In. 1980.00

Charlie McCarthy was the ventriloquist's dummy used by Edgar Bergen from the 1930s. He was famous for his work in radio, movies, and television. The act was retired in the 1970s.

CHARLIE MCCARTHY, Benzine Buggy, Tin Litho, Mechanical, Marx, 7 1/4 In. 880.00
Clock, Alarm, Mouth Moves Up & Down, Gilbert Clock Corp. 1200.00
Doll, 28 In. 18.00
Doll, Mortimer Snerd 55.00
Doll, Stuffed, Composition Head 18.00
Dummy, 1970, Box 75.00
Figure, Cardboard, Semi-Mechanical, 20 In. 22.00
Figure, Chalkware 15.00
Game, Bingo 25.00
Mask, Rubber, 1930s 85.00
Paper Doll 25.00
Puppet, Movable Mouth, Top Hat 109.00
Radio Party, Spinner, 21 Figures, 1938 .... 65.00
Toy, Buggy, Venzine, Windup, Marx 475.00
Toy, Charlie In Auto, Windup, Tin Litho, Marx, 7 1/2 In. 165.00
Toy, Crazy Car 550.00
Toy, Walker, Windup 375.00

Chelsea grape pattern was made before 1840. A small bunch of grapes in a raised design, colored with purple or blue luster, is on the border of the white plate. Most of the pieces are unmarked. The pattern is sometimes called "Aynsley" or "Grandmother." Chelsea sprig is similar but has a sprig of flowers instead of the bunch of grapes. Chelsea thistle has a raised thistle pattern.

CHELSEA GRAPE, Coffeepot 150.00
Creamer 50.00
Cup & Saucer 35.00
Pitcher, 6 In. 55.00
Plate, 9 In. 25.00
    CHELSEA KERAMIC ART WORKS, see Dedham
CHELSEA SPRIG, Bowl, 6 In. 18.00
Cup & Saucer 27.50
Plate, 10 In. 25.00
Plate, Cake 45.00
Tea Set, Grandmother's Ware, 20 Piece 145.00
CHELSEA THISTLE, Butter Pat 12.00
Cup & Saucer 27.50
Teapot 125.00

Chelsea porcelain was made in the Chelsea area of London from about 1745 to 1784. Ceramic designs were borrowed from the Meissen models of the day. Pieces were made of soft paste. The gold anchor was used as the mark but it has been copied by many other factories. Recent copies of Chelsea have been made from the original molds.

CHELSEA, Bowl, Scalloped Rim, Embossed Swirled Ribs, Foliage Design, 9 In. 575.00
Cup & Saucer, Tulips, Leaves, Lilies, Gold Rim, 1760 .... 350.00
Figurine, Lamb, Lying Down, Flowers On Base, 4 In. Wide 1000.00
Figurine, Shepherdess Holding Flowers, 1775, 8 In. 350.00
Perfume Bottle, Pug Dog, Leaves, 1775, 2 1/2 In. 3500.00
Plate, Embossed Scalloped Rim, Floral Enameling, Porcelain, 8 In. 450.00

Plate, Flowers, Sprigs, 1775, 8 In. 500.00
Tea Bowl & Saucer, Octagonal, Flowers, C.1760 .... 1200.00
Teapot, Polychrome Floral Enameling, 6 1/4 In. 750.00

Chinese export porcelain comprises all the many kinds of porcelain made in China for export to America and Europe in the eighteenth and nineteenth centuries.

CHINESE EXPORT, see also Canton; Celadon; Nanking; Rose Medallion
CHINESE EXPORT, Basket, Famille Verte, Reticulated, Porcelain, 8 In. 2500.00
Bowl, Figural Frieze, Porcelain, Famille Rose, 14 In. 110.00
Bowl, Floral Border & Spray, Late 19th Century, 12 In. 120.00
Bowl, Floral, Figural Scenes, 7 5/8 In. Diam. 825.00
Bowl, From East India Trading Ship, Sunk 1613, 8 In. 575.00
Bowl, Mandarin Palette, 10 1/4 In. 935.00
Bowl, Rose Mandarin, Continous Courtyard Scene, 6 3/4 In. 445.00
Candle Lamp, Pink, Blue, Reticulated Hexagon, 8 1/2 In., Pair 350.00
Charger, Pastel Flowers, White, 10 1/4 In. 95.00
Charger, Rose Mandarin, Scholar, Courtyard, 13 1/2 In., Pair 1225.00
Compote, Navy Band, Florals, Gold Leaf, C.1740, 13 In., Pair 4000.00
Creamer, Helmet Form, Bough Handle, 5 5/8 In. 175.00
Cup & Saucer, Diaper Border, Family Gathering Scenes 355.00
Cup, Cover, Oriental Court Scene, C.1760, 12 1/2 In., Pair 6875.00
Dish, Vegetable, Cover, Fitzhugh, C.1800, 12 1/4 In. 1100.00
Garden Seat, Blue & White, Early 19th Century 1200.00
Garden Seat, Rose Verte, Yongzheng Period 3000.00
Garniture Set, Flattened Shape, Court Scenes, 14 1/2 In., 3 .... 4450.00
Ginger Jar, Blue, 6 1/2 In. 475.00
Gravy Boat, Undertray, Basket of Flowers, 7 1/2 In. 305.00
Jar, Blue & White, Vessels, 10 In. 160.00
Jar, Famille Verte, Birds, Flowers, Mounted As Lamp, 15 In. 715.00
Jug, Cider, Cover, Entwined Handle, Fitzhugh, C.1800 .... 3000.00
Panel, Famille Rose, 9 X 12 In., Pair 165.00
Plate, Allover Rose Canton, Gilt Ground, 9 3/4 In. 225.00
Plate, Arm, Cross & H, Royal Blue & Gold, 9 3/4 In. 150.00
Plate, Butterfly, Pomegranate Rim, 9 1/4 In., Pr. 400.00
Plate, Imari, 8 3/4 In., 6 Piece 995.00
Platter, Arm, Cross & H, Royal Blue & Gold, 13 1/8 In. 260.00
Platter, Coat of Arms, Lion, 18 1/2 In. 1595.00
Platter, Famille Rose, Inglis De Cramond Arms, 13 In., Pr. 3750.00
Platter, Fishing Scene, Mountain, 11 1/2 X 14 3/4 In. 775.00
Platter, Fitzhugh, Center Medallion, 1800, 12 X 14 1/2 In. 935.00
Platter, Flowers & Insects, Vine Border, Puce, 13 X 16 In. 885.00
Pot, Hot Water, Village Scene, C.1800, 9 1/2 In. 650.00
Punch Bowl, Dragon, Medallion Center, Pink, C.1880, 16 In. 1550.00
Punch Bowl, Polychrome Design, C.1790 .... 1875.00
Rose, Bowl, Figural Cartouche, Floral Border, Famille Rose 660.00
Tankard, Bat Designs, Figural Scene, Gilt Ground, 4 3/4 In. 495.00
Teapot, Cover, Figure Panel, Loop Handle, Silver Spout, 6 In. 247.50
Tureen, Cover, Famille Rose, Hare's Head Handles, 12 1/8 In. 7000.00
Tureen, Cover, Nanking, Blue & White, C.1800, 14 In. 350.00
Tureen, Soup, Bead & Garland Design, 9 1/2 X 13 1/2 In. 775.00
Tureen, Soup, Undertray, Peacock 9100.00
Tureen, Tobacco Leaf, Lotus Bud Finial, Tray, 7 X 14 In. 495.00
Umbrella Stand, Famille Verte, 18 1/2 In. 340.00
Umbrella Stand, Figural Reserves, Famille Rose, 18 In. 132.00
Vase, Bladder, Famille Rose, Seated People, 16 In., Pair 450.00
Vase, Chinese Scenes, C.1770, 14 1/2 In., Pair 7500.00
Vase, Elephant Handles, Landscape, Floral, Famille Rose, Pair 605.00
Vase, Famille Rose, Bird of Paradise, Rocks, C.1850, 14 In. 1200.00
Vase, Famille Verte, Phoenix Birds On Branch, C.1905, 12 In. 125.00
Vase, Lamp, Famille Verte, Landscape Reserves, Green, 27 In. 125.00
Vase, Mantel, Chocolate Trees, Crackle Glaze, 8 1/2 In., Pair 175.00

Chocolate glass, sometimes mistakenly called caramel slag, was made by the Indiana Tumbler and Goblet Company of Greentown, Indiana, from 1900 to 1903. Fenton Art Glass Co. also made chocolate glass from about 1907 to 1915. A few recent reproductions have been made.

CHOCOLATE GLASS, Berry Set, Leaf Bracket, 7 Piece 300.00
Bowl, Geneva, 8 3/8 In. 185.00
Bowl, Geneva, Oval, 8 1/4 In. 95.00
Bowl, Windmill Scene, 8 In. 25.00
Butter, Cover, Geneva 345.00
Butter, Cover, Leaf Bracket 125.00
Cake Stand, Cactus 795.00
Celery, Leaf Bracket 90.00
Compote, Jelly, Cactus, 5 1/4 In. 145.00
Compote, Melrose, Scalloped Rim, 4 3/4 X 6 In. 195.00
Creamer, Cactus 80.00
Creamer, Child's 150.00
Creamer, Leaf Bracket 95.00
Cruet, Cactus 190.00
Cruet, Cord Drapery 100.00
Cruet, Dewey, Stopper 1650.00
Cruet, Leaf Bracket 175.00
Cruet, Wild Rose With Bowknot .... 350.00 To 365.00
Dish, Cat On Hamper, Low 300.00
Dish, Dolphin Cover, Sawtooth Edge 100.00
Dish, Fish Cover, 7 In. 395.00
Hatpin Holder, Orange Tree 150.00
Lamp, Wild Rose With Bowknot, Greentown 525.00
Mug, Herringbone 52.00
Mug, Indoor Drinking Scene, 5 1/2 In. 150.00
Nappy, Leaf Bracket, 4 In. 45.00
Pitcher, Milk, Feather 425.00
Pitcher, Water, Deer & Doe 350.00
Planter, Jefferson Davis Medallion, Square 28.00
Punch Bowl Set, Child's, 4 Cups 75.00
Punch Cup, Shuttle .... 35.00 To 85.00
Relish, Leaf Bracket, Oval, 4 1/2 X 7 1/4 In. 65.00
Saltshaker, Cactus 55.00
Sauce, Leaf Bracket, Footed, 4 In. 35.00
Sauce, Wild Rose With Bowknot 60.00
Spooner, Cover, Leaf Bracket 125.00
Spooner, Geneva 95.00
Spooner, Shuttle 175.00
Sugar & Creamer, Geneva 145.00
Sugar, Cover, Cactus 175.00
Sugar, Cover, Leaf Bracket .... 110.00 To 140.00
Syrup, Cactus, Red Agate Edge & Base 145.00
Syrup, Cord Drapery 195.00
Syrup, Herringbone Buttress 185.00
Table Set, Leaf Bracket, 4 Piece .... 400.00 To 425.00
Toothpick, Cactus .... 45.00 To 65.00
Toothpick, Dolphins & Shells 45.00
Toothpick, Geneva 375.00
Toothpick, Hand & Barrel 40.00
Tray, Wild Rose With Bowknot, 8 X 10 1/4 In. 225.00
Tumbler, Cactus .... 55.00 To 65.00
Tumbler, Geneva 110.00
Tumbler, Leaf Bracket 45.00
Tumbler, Sawtooth .... 75.00 To 85.00
Tumbler, Uneeda Milk Biscuit, Greentown .... 85.00 To 135.00

The first decorated Christmas tree in America is claimed by many states, including Pennsylvania (1747), Massachusetts (1832), Illinois (1833), Ohio (1838), and Iowa (1845). The first glass ornaments were imported from Germany about 1860. Dresden ornaments were made about 100 years ago of paper and tinsel. Manufacturers in the United States were making ornaments in the early 1870s. Electric lights were first used on a Christmas tree in 1882. Character light bulbs became popular in the 1920s, bubble lights in the 1940s, twinkle bulbs in the 1950s, plastic bulbs by 1955. In this book a Christmas light is a holder for a candle used on the tree. Other forms of lighting include light bulbs.

CHRISTMAS TREE, Base, Attached Picket Fence, Pine, 19 1/2 X 19 1/2 In. 75.00
Candle Clip, Oak Leaf & Acorn, Lithographed Tin, 2 In. 95.00
Feather, 13 Tiers, White Berries, Goose Feathers, 60 In. 785.00
Feather, 2-Tone Green, Berries, Stenciled Base, Box, 52 In. 625.00
Feather, 22 In. 235.00
Feather, 48 In. .... 200.00 To 400.00
Feather, Arched Gates, 8 Sections, Berries, Germany, Box 585.00
Feather, Berries & Clips, Turned Base, 26 In. 245.00
Feather, Blue & Green, 22 In. 85.00
Feather, Dark Green, Lighter Green Branch Tips, 36 In. 325.00
Feather, Dark Green, Red, Green Square Base, Stencils, 48 In. 275.00
Feather, Green, Red Berries, Wood Base, Germany, 32 In., Pair 300.00
Feather, Green, Red Berries, Wooden Base, 24 In. 160.00
Feather, Red Berries, 32 In. 190.00
Feather, Red Berries, 4 In. 400.00
Feather, Red Berries, Germany, 52 In. 365.00
Feather, Red Berries, Red & White Base, Germany, 23 In. 185.00
Feather, Wooden Base, Germany, 40 In. 350.00
Fence, 14 Sections, 2 Gates, 13 Posts, Brass, 157 1/4 In. 200.00
Fence, 6 Sections, Double Door Gate, Green, Gold Trim, 80 In. 225.00
Fence, Double Gate, Red & Green, Accordion Type, 36 In. 85.00
Fence, Green Wicker, Red Post, Gates, Hazelton, Pa., 36 In. 225.00
Fence, Green, Red Posts, 5 Sections Gate, Tin, 55 In. 175.00
Fence, Picket, Swinging Gate, Square, 18 In. 110.00
Fence, Square Pickets, Corner Posts, Wood, Square, 30 In. 90.00
Fence, Twig, With Gate, 15-In. Sections, Germany 30.00
Fence, Twig, With Gate, Germany, Square, 36 In. 75.00
Fence, Wire & Wood Rails, Green, Red Posts, 24 In. 70.00
Fence, Wooden, Red & Green, Folding, Double Gate, 3 X 36 In. 79.00
Garland, Tinsel, 8 Ft. 8.00
Light Bulb, Angel, Holds Candle, Noma, Box, 7 In. 5.00
Light Bulb, Bird, Cardinal, Red, Glass 20.00
Light Bulb, Bluebird, Celluloid 12.50
Light Bulb, Bubble, Royal, Red Shell Pattern 7.00
Light Bulb, Candle 12.50
Light Bulb, Cat, Wearing Tuxedo, Playing Mandolin 25.00
Light Bulb, Chinese Lantern 15.00
Light Bulb, Cottage 1.50
Light Bulb, Dog, Sandy 45.00
Light Bulb, Glo Lite, Series, Santa Box 18.00
Light Bulb, Glo-Ray, Ball-Type, Noma, Box, 1946 .... 20.00
Light Bulb, Goldfinch 18.00
Light Bulb, Grapes 20.00
Light Bulb, Lantern, Snow Covered, Green & White 5.00
Light Bulb, Lion, With Tennis Racket 17.50
Light Bulb, Noma, Bubble, C-6's, Box 38.00
Light Bulb, Parrot 15.00
Light Bulb, Prism, Star, Red, Green Jewel Center, Glass 15.00
Light Bulb, Santa Claus, 2 Sides 25.00
Light Bulb, Santa Claus, 8 In. 65.00
Light Bulb, Santa Claus, Felt Lined, Hanging 17.50
Light Bulb, Santa Claus, Milk Glass, 4 In. 19.50

Light Bulb, Santa Claus, Plastic, 3 In. 25.00
Light Bulb, Santa Claus, Tin, Back Hangs On Wall 18.00
Light Bulb, Silly Symphony, Walt Disney, Box, Set 75.00
Light Bulb, Snowman, Milk Glass, 3 In. 17.50
Light Bulb, Star, Tin, 5 Glass Points, White 8.00
Light Bulb, Street Lamp 12.50
Light Bulb, Zeppelin Shape, Red, Green, & White, 3 In. 38.00
Light, Diamond Point, Victorian, 2 3/8 X 3 3/4 In. 36.00
Ornament, Airship, Santa Claus, Cotton, Wire Propeller, 3 In. 175.00
Ornament, Angel, Giving Girl A Doll, Paper, Tinsel, 4 X 6 In. 32.00
Ornament, Angel, Red & Gold, Embossed Paper Wings, 5 In. 250.00
Ornament, Angel, Tree Top, 1950s 10.00
Ornament, Angel, With Tree, Die Cut, 1880, 5 1/2 In. 9.00
Ornament, Baby In Cradle, Rattle, Paper Canopy, 6 1/4 In. 475.00
Ornament, Baby In Cradle, Wire Wrapped, Crepe, 3 1/2 X 5 In. 150.00
Ornament, Baby, Die Cut, Tinsel Around Baby & Hanger 30.00
Ornament, Baby, In Shoe, Red & Gold, 3 1/2 In. 125.00
Ornament, Ball, Litho Paper, 3 1/4 In. 22.00
Ornament, Basket of Roses, Blown Glass 12.50
Ornament, Basket, Metal, Victorian 15.00
Ornament, Beads, Glass, Green, Silver, Czechoslovakia 15.00
Ornament, Beads, Glass, Multicolored, Czechoslovakia 12.00
Ornament, Bear, With Mandolin, Gold Trim 95.00
Ornament, Bee & Flower, Molded Glass, 2 3/4 In. 27.50
Ornament, Bell, Mercury Glass 20.00
Ornament, Bell, With Santa Claus Head, Red Chenille, Tassels 45.00
Ornament, Belsnickle, Gold Face, White Trim, 5 1/4 In. 375.00
Ornament, Belsnickle, Green, Gold Mica, Black Feet, 2 3/4 In. 85.00
Ornament, Bird, Cotton, Paper Wings & Tail 24.00
Ornament, Bird, Pink Wings, Spun Glass Tail, Clip 15.00
Ornament, Black Boy, White, Silver & Red, 3 1/2 In. 225.00
Ornament, Blackberry Cluster, Gold 10.00
Ornament, Bottle, Molded Glass, Nier Steiner, 5 In. 33.00
Ornament, Boy, Girl, Holding Parasol, Die Cut, 4 1/2 In. 35.00
Ornament, Bunny, With Carrot, Pressed Cotton, Germany 20.00
Ornament, Butterfly On Ball, Blown Glass 95.00
Ornament, Canary In Cage 65.00
Ornament, Church, Blown Glass 27.50
Ornament, Clock, Glass, Clip-On 15.00
Ornament, Clown Head, Tin Cap, White Head, 4 In. 200.00
Ornament, Clown, Chubby, Glass 45.00
Ornament, Clown, Pearl Silver, Navy Cap 65.00
Ornament, Clown, Pot Belly, Pink, Green & Silver, 4 1/2 In. 45.00
Ornament, Clown, Roly Poly, 3 1/4 In. 135.00
Ornament, Cockatoo, On Clip, Glass 22.00
Ornament, Cowl, Black, White, 3 In. 10.00
Ornament, Dancing Mouse, Blue, Gold, Italy, 5 In. 10.00
Ornament, Deer, Laying, Cast, Germany, 6 X 5 In. 58.00
Ornament, Deer, Metal, Germany, 3 In. 20.00
Ornament, Devil Clown, Molded Glass, 3 In. 121.00
Ornament, Devil's Head, Molded Glass, 4 In. 303.00
Ornament, Devil's Head, Silvered, 3 In. 150.00
Ornament, Dog, Brown, Tan, Celluloid, 6 In. 12.00
Ornament, Dracula, Papier-Mache, 1939, 4 In. 5.00
Ornament, Elf In Pinecone, White Beard, 3 3/4 In. 65.00
Ornament, Elf, Under Mushroom, On Clip, 3 1/4 In. 85.00
Ornament, Father Christmas, Blue Cape, Red Lining, 3 1/2 In. 40.00
Ornament, Fish, Blown Glass 150.00
Ornament, Fish, Opalescent & Blue, Nygren, 2 In. 85.00
Ornament, Flower Basket, Glass, Pink, Gold, Feather Fern 35.00
Ornament, Flower, Pink Celluloid, Die Cut, Wire Wrap, 5 In. 42.00
Ornament, Foxy Grandpa, Silvered, Black Glasses, 4 In. 120.00
Ornament, Frog, Glass 35.00
Ornament, Girl, In Basket of Daisies, Blue & Gold, 2 1/2 In. 65.00

Ornament, Girl, Painted Plaster, Fabric Cover, 6 In. 55.00
Ornament, Goat, Flocked, Udders, Tan, Brown, Putz, 3 1/2 In. 42.00
Ornament, Goose, Embossed Cardboard, 3 In. 55.00
Ornament, Grape Cluster, Glass, 2 1/2 In. 80.00
Ornament, Hanging Lantern, Red, Blue, Dresden, 4 X 5 In. 195.00
Ornament, Head, Christ Child 70.00
Ornament, Horse, Mercury Glass, Primitive, Germany 150.00
Ornament, Hot Air Balloon, Blue, Die Cut of Elf & Package 50.00
Ornament, Hummingbird, Blown Glass 30.00
Ornament, Hummingbird, Spun Glass Wings 25.00
Ornament, Hunting Horn, Blue 14.00
Ornament, Hurricane Lamp, Glass, Pink, White Stripes, 1950s 7.00
Ornament, Indian Head, Blown Glass 500.00
Ornament, Lemon, Blown Glass 95.00
Ornament, Little Red Riding Hood, Glass Eyes, 3 In. 65.00
Ornament, Mandolin, Wire Wrapped, Blown Glass 175.00
Ornament, Medallion, 12 Days, Christmas, Sterling, Towle, 1973 .... 30.00
Ornament, Medallion, Dove, Sterling Silver, Wallace, 1972 .... 25.00
Ornament, Monkey, Glass 40.00
Ornament, Monkey, Pink, Snow Covered Hat, Painted Eyes, 5 In. 25.00
Ornament, Moose, Dresden 95.00
Ornament, Mouse, Dancing, Blue Suit, Gold Hat, Italy 20.00
Ornament, Mushroom, Glass, Clip–On 15.00
Ornament, Orange, Blown Glass 125.00
Ornament, Orange, Spun Cotton 23.00
Ornament, Owl, Glass 22.00
Ornament, Peach, Blown Glass 125.00
Ornament, Peacock, Clip–On, Blown Glass 45.00
Ornament, Pickle, Curved, Light Green, 4 1/2 In. 90.00
Ornament, Pig, Standing, Pink Matte, Red Trim, 3 3/4 In. 165.00
Ornament, Pipe, Molded Glass, 4 1/2 In. 11.00
Ornament, Policeman, Molded Glass, 4 1/2 In. 132.00
Ornament, Popcorn Head, Red Trim, On Clip, 4 1/4 In. 425.00
Ornament, Rabbit, Eating Carrot, 4 In. 145.00
Ornament, Rabbit, Glass, 4 1/2 In. 33.00
Ornament, Reindeer, Pulling Sleigh, Silvered, Germany 30.00
Ornament, Reindeer, White, On Clip 95.00
Ornament, Robot, In Rocket, Italy, 1950s, 9 In. 25.00
Ornament, Sailboat, Wire Wrapped 38.00
Ornament, Santa Claus Head, Glass 30.00
Ornament, Santa Claus, Blown Glass 25.00
Ornament, Santa Claus, Head, Annalee, 1960s, 2 1/2 In. 15.00
Ornament, Santa Claus, Holding Tree, Glass 35.00
Ornament, Santa Claus, In Sleigh, Pack Open, Mercury Glass 35.00
Ornament, Santa Claus, On Sleigh, Wood & Cloth, 5 3/4 In. 95.00
Ornament, Santa Claus, Sitting, Pressed Cotton, 1940s 10.00
Ornament, Santa Claus, Sleigh, Red, White, Green, Celluloid 40.00
Ornament, Santa Claus, Tree, Molded Glass, 3 3/4 In. 28.00
Ornament, Santa Claus, With Pack, Molded Glass, 4 1/2 In. 55.00
Ornament, Sheep, White, Wooly, Blue Neck Ring, 3 1/2 X 4 In. 48.00
Ornament, Snow Girl, On Block of Snow, Bisque, 2 In. 18.00
Ornament, Snowball, Holly & Berries, Cotton, 3 In. 25.00
Ornament, Snowflake, Sterling Silver, Gorham, 1977 .... 30.00
Ornament, Snowman With Broom, Blown Glass 125.00
Ornament, Starburst, Eagle Center, Tin 65.00
Ornament, Stocking, Glass, Clip–On, 5 In. 45.00
Ornament, Stork, 7 1/2 In. 95.00
Ornament, Table Lamp, Blown Glass 25.00
Ornament, Tree Top, Angel, China Head, Feather Body 14.00
Ornament, Tree Top, Paper Angel Face, Spun Glass 9.00
Ornament, Turnip, Spun Cotton, Mica Covered 222.00
Ornament, Umbrella, Closed, Glass, 5 In. 35.00
Ornament, Umbrella, Closed, Glass, 10 In. 45.00
Ornament, Umbrella, Wire Wrapped 26.00

Ornament, Violin, Glass	12.00
Ornament, Watermelon Slice, Red & Black, 4 1/2 In.	195.00
Reflector, Snowflake, Metal, 11 Piece	17.00
Stand, Cast Iron	75.00
Stand, Lithographed Tin & Iron, Bulbs In Base, 14 1/2 In.	275.00
Stand, Metal, Green, 4–Footed, 3 In. Opening, 4 X 11 In.	48.00

Almost anything connected with Christmas is collected. Ornaments, feather trees, tree stands, santa claus figures, special dishes, even games and wrapping paper. A Belsnickle is a nineteenth–century figure of Father Christmas.

CHRISTMAS, Advertising, Mechanical Santa Claus, Longines Watches, 21 In.	150.00
Angel, Brown Hair, Spun Glass Wings, Dresden, Wax, 4 In.	50.00
Bank, Father Christmas, Cast Iron	15.00
Belsnickle, Chalkware, Germany, 5 In.	60.00
Belsnickle, Grey–White, Red Piping On Hood, 9 1/2 In.	695.00
Belsnickle, Mica Coat, Feather Branch, Papier–Mache, 10 1/2 In.	465.00
Belsnickle, Mica Face, Red Chenille Trim, Early 1900s, 9 1/2 In.	595.00
Belsnickle, Papier–Mache, Red, Germany, 12 In.	800.00
Belsnickle, Polychrome Face, Tree In Arm, Papier–Mache, 6 1/4 In.	400.00
Belsnickle, Silver Gray, Beard, Red Chenille Trim, 9 1/2 In.	795.00
Belsnickle, Tree, Red Coat, Black Boot Base, Gold Mica, 6 In.	330.00
Blotter, Santa Claus, Bischoff Surgical Co., 1930, 3 1/2 X 6 In.	4.50
Book, Merry Christmas, W.B. Conkey & Co., 1909	38.00
Book, Night Before Christmas, M.A. Donohue	35.00
Book, Santa Claus Big Picture, M.A. Donahue	40.00
Booklet, Christmas Seals, Currier & Ives, 4 X 5 In., 120 Piece	7.50
Cake Tin, Santa Claus, 9 In.	83.00
Cardholder, Santa Claus, 1981, 29 In.	165.00
Chimes, Angels, Electric, 6 Bulb	95.00
Church, Red Paper Windows, Glitter Allover, 16 In.	60.00
Creche Scene, Twig Stable, 8 Papier–Mache Figures, Germany	95.00
Display, Santa Claus Head, Mica Covered Beard, Plaster, 17 Lb.	595.00
House, Cardboard, With Fences & Trees	16.00
House, Red Roof, Cellophane Windows, Fence, China Santa, 3 X 6 In.	46.00
Kugel, Embossed Cap, Gold, 5 In.	50.00
Kugel, Green, Brass Fastener, France Label, 7 1/2 In.	475.00
Kugel, Green, Embossed Cap, 4 In.	60.00
Kugel, Silver, Embossed Cap, 2 1/2 In.	25.00
Label, Crate, Santa, Sunkist, 1928, 12 1/2 X 9 In.	20.00
Lamp, Santa Claus, U.S. Glass, Screw On Base	675.00
Lantern, Glass Santa With Tree Light Cover	70.00
Lantern, Noel, Green Wreath, Ribbon, Milk Glass, Battery Operated	45.00
Lantern, Snowman, Milk Glass, Battery Operated, Box	55.00
Letter Holder, Santa Claus, Die–Cut	45.00
Nativity Set, 24 X 25 In. Stable, 22 Figure, Glass Eyes, 7 In.	675.00
Nodder, Donkey, With Santa On Back, Platform With Wheels, Basket	995.00
CHRISTMAS, PLATE, see Collector Plate	
Puzzle, Santa Claus, McLoughlin Bros., Litho, Framed, 11 X 13 In.	77.00
Santa Claus, Cardboard Easel, Flocked, 12 In.	18.00
Santa Claus, Chalkware, Red Suit, Sinister Smile, 1940s, 24 In.	78.00
Santa Claus, Chimney, Chalkware, S.A.N.Co., 1935, 11 In.	125.00
Santa Claus, Composition Face, Hands, Boots	75.00
Santa Claus, Feather Tree, Sleigh, Fur Beard, Germany, 5 In.	95.00
Santa Claus, Felt, Japan, 9 In.	95.00
Santa Claus, Holding Knapsack & Switches, Felt, Germany, 15 In.	155.00
Santa Claus, Hunched–Back, Rabbit Fur Beard, Lantern, Tree	650.00
Santa Claus, In Sleigh, Celluloid, Japan, 2 Piece	27.50
Santa Claus, Key Wound Clockwork Reindeer, 19–In. Wicker Sleigh	1700.00
Santa Claus, On Skis, Red, White, Flesh Face, Cast Metal, 3 In.	45.00
Santa Claus, Painted Plaster, Flat Back, 8 1/2 In.	44.00
Santa Claus, Pull–Apart, Felt, Fur Beard, Molded Pants, Germany	450.00
Santa Claus, Roly Poly, Celluloid, Japan, 5 1/2 In.	52.50
Santa Claus, Satin Suit, Mask Face, 30 In.	125.00

Santa Claus, Sleigh, Toy Filled, C.1920, 17 1/2 In. 2450.00
Santa Claus, White Paper Sleigh, Celluloid Reindeer 165.00
Santa Claus, Wooden Sled, Fur Beard & Hat, Germany, 11–In. Santa 950.00
Shaker, Snow, Santa & Snowman 10.00
Sheep, Green Glass Eyes, Red Saddle, Stake Legs, Wheels, 7 In. 295.00
Shepherd & Sheep, Wood Legs, Papier–Mache, Metal Crook, 4 In. 75.00
Sign, Santa Claus' Face, Holly Border, Lights Up, 17 X 15 X 4 In. 27.00
St. Nick, Long Coat, Holding Lantern, 5 In. 40.00
Stocking, Celluloid Toys, Red Net 25.00
Stocking, Red, White, Stencils of Santa, Sleigh, Roof, 15 In. 12.00
Toy, Balloon Santa, Alps, Box 100.00
Toy, Santa Claus In Sled, Tin Litho, Mechanical, Strauss, 11 In. 1650.00
Toy, Santa Claus, Holds Book, Lifts Pages, Windup, Tin, 8 In. 65.00
Toy, Santa Claus, In Chimney, Picks Up Presents, Windup, Box 135.00
Toy, Santa Claus, On Reindeer, Windup 85.00
Toy, Santa Claus, Windup, Bell, Flexible Arms, Box 130.00
Toy, Surprise Santa, Windup, Bell, Pulls Package From Bag, Box 185.00
Wall Decoration, Santa, Sleigh, Brown Reindeer, Germany, 10 In. 40.00
Wreath, Blinking, Paper, Box 20.00

Art Deco chrome items became popular in the 1930s. Collectors are most interested in high–style pieces made by the Connecticut firms of Chase Brass and Copper Company and Manning Bowman.

CHROME, Ashtray, 2 Monkeys Holds Spinning Bullet Shaped Vessel, Art Deco 40.00
Ashtray, Attached Airplane On Stand, Air Force One Convair 225.00
Ashtray, Attached Airplane On Stand, Swissair 707 .... 185.00

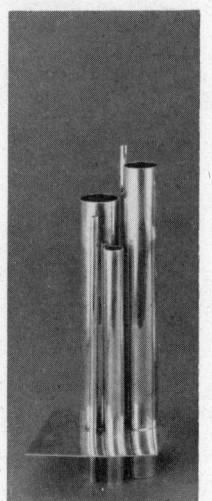

Chrome, Vase, Bell Form, Coils, Brandt,
C.1935, 10 1/2 In.

Chrome, Wine Cooler, Chase, Rockwell Kent Design,
9 In.

Chrome, Vase, Bell Form, Edgar Brandt,
C.1935, Rockwell, 10 1/2 In.

Clean brass regularly with a solution of liquid dishwashing detergent and warm water. Rinse in warm water. Dry.

Ashtray, Attached Airplane On Stand, Swissair, 4 Engine Prop	195.00
Ashtray, Toucan, Pair	25.00
Bowl, Child's, Uncle Wiggily, Farberware, 1924	175.00
Box, American Airlines, Wrigley Gum, Chase	100.00
Candleholder, U Shape, Split Level Tubes, Chase, 9 1/4 In., Pair	350.00
Candlestick, Farber Bros., 8 1/2 In., Pair	85.00
Case, Cigarette, Flying Eagle On Side	10.00
Cocktail Set, Skyscraper, Revere Brass & Copper, 6 Piece	1210.00
Cocktail Shaker, Butterscotch Handle, Knob, Spout Cover, Farberware	20.00
Cocktail Shaker, Farberware	40.00
Coffee Set, Art Deco, Wooden, King's Port	65.00
Coffee Set, Diplomat, Chase Brass, White Handles, 3 Piece	450.00
Coffee Set, Farberware, 4 Piece	36.00
Coffee Set, Royal Rochester, Robeson, 4 Piece	50.00
Coffee Set, Sugar, Creamer & Tray, Manning Bowman, Rosewood Handles	75.00
Coffee Urn, Coronet, Chase	500.00
Group, Jazz Musicians, Hagenauer, 3 Piece	4250.00
Ice Bucket, Penguin, Westbend	15.00
Pitcher, Cocktail, Bakelite Handle, Krome Kraft	25.00
Pitcher, Martini, Musical, Red Bakelite Handle	30.00
Pitcher, Normandie, P. Peter Muller–Munk, C.1935, 12 In.	2450.00
Rolling Pin, Red Handles, Box	45.00
Server, Snack, Electric, Chase Brass	180.00
Silent Butler, Wood Handle, Amber Insert, Farberware	50.00
Tea Set, Electric, Teapot, Sugar, Creamer & Tray, Chase	95.00
Tray, Fold–Down, Celluloid Handles, Embossed Foods	55.00
Vase, Band of Spheres, E. Brandt & G. Bastard, C.1935, 10 1/2 In.	2750.00
Vase, Bell Form, Coils, Brandt, C.1935, 10 1/2 In. ....Illus	2200.00
Vase, Bell Form, Edgar Brandt, C.1935, Rockwell, 10 1/2 In. ....Illus	2200.00
Wine Cooler, Chase, Rockwell Kent Design, 9 In. ....Illus	880.00

Carved wooden or cast iron figures were used as advertisements in front of the Victorian cigar store. The carved figures are now collected as folk art. They range in size from counter type, about three feet, to over eight feet high.

CIGAR STORE FIGURE, Indian, Headdress, Straddling Tobacco Keg, 47 3/4 In.	2750.00
Jack Tar, Painted Pine, Wide Brimmed Lead Hat, 63 In.	8000.00
Seated Man, Full Round, Holding Cigars, C.1900, 52 In.	775.00

Cinnabar is a vermilion or red lacquer. Some pieces are made with hundreds of thicknesses of the lacquer that is later carved.

CINNABAR, Box, Carved, Cover, 4 X 2 In.	70.00

Civil War mementos are important collectors' items. Most of the pieces are military items used from 1861 to 1865.

CIVIL WAR, Ambrotype, Armed Soldier, Full Case, 1/2 Plate	325.00
Badge, G.A.R., Face of A. Lincoln	50.00
Bayonette, Enfield	45.00
Belt, Sergeant's, Marine	192.50
Bible, 1850, 11 1/2 X 9 1/2 In.	40.00
Bible, 1856, 5 1/2 X 3 1/2 In.	40.00
Bible, 1864, 5 1/2 X 4 1/2 In.	50.00
Book, Songs & Ballads of The Blue & Gray, 215 Pages, 1905	5.00
Buckle, N.Y. In Raised Letters	85.00
Buckle, U.S. Federal	75.00
Button, GAR, Copper	25.00
Button, Home For Confederate Woman, C.S.A. Flag, Pinback	5.00
Cane, Ivory Ball Top	125.00
Cane, Silver Nickel	85.00
Canteen, Confederate	375.00
Canteen, Kansas, 1891, 2 1/4 In.	55.00
Canteen, Red Cloth Cover, Leather Strap, Tin	85.00
Canteen, Screw Spout, Tin	40.00

Canteen, Union 25.00
Case, Document, Tin 95.00
Casket, Jewelry, G.A.R., Pittsburgh 1884 .... 70.00
Chair, Camp, Officer's, Fold–Up Style, Carpet Seat & Back, Cherry 145.00
Chair, Camp, Seat & Back Is Carpet Material, Fold–Up Style 145.00
Coat, Sergeant's, Marine Regiment 1650.00
Cutlass, Brass Hilt, Dated 1827 .... 70.00
Drum, Eagle .... 3000.00 To 5500.00
Fork & Spoon, Folding, Union Knife 28.00
Frock Coat, Union Infantry Captain's, Crimson Sash 1650.00
Handcuffs, Numbered Key 90.00
Holster, Cylinder, Copper 550.00
Knife, Bloodletting, Bone Handle 28.00
Lamp, Mess Kit, Alcohol Burners, Wicks, Tin, 2 1/2 X 5 1/2 In. 95.00
Lantern, Hand, Tin 125.00
Medal, G.A.R. 28.00
Mug, Bumper To The Flag, Union Forever, Handle 235.00
Photograph, Carte De Viste, General A. Burnsides, Bust 8.00
Photograph, Union Soldier & Surgeon, Signed, 3 1/2 X 2 1/2 In. 200.00
Poster, Memorial, 46th Illinois 275.00
Razor, Wade & Butcher, Wooden Box .... 25.00 To 35.00
Ribbon, Veterans', 45th Illinois, Rockford, Ill., 1888 .... 30.00
Rosette, Brass, Embossed Heart of Union Army 5th Corps, 2 1/4 In 18.00
Saber, Cavalry, Model 1913, Marked Lf+1918 .... 225.00
Saber, Wrist Breaker, Cavalry, 1840 .... 325.00
Saddle, Used By Man From Elgin, Illinois 585.00
Scale, Platform, Portable, Folding, Recruiting Office 195.00
Soap Dish, Cover, Brass, 20 Corps Badge Wooden Top 35.00
Soap Dish, Cover, Brass, Wood & 2nd Corps Badge Top 35.00
Song Sheet, When This Cruel War Is Over 25.00
Sword, Foot Officer's, Black Leather Scabbard, Brass Fittings 525.00
Sword, Model 1840, NCO 85.00
Sword, Musician's, 1855 .... 145.00
Sword, Navy Officer's, E.E. Braine, Jr., Leather Scabbard 375.00
Sword, Officer's, U.S. Regulation Type, Knot, Box 85.00
Sword, Staff & Field Officers, No.1860, Clam Shell Guard 325.00
Sword, U.S. Marine Officer's, Model 1902, Black Leather Scabbard 325.00
  CKAW, see Dedham

Clambroth glass, popular in the Victorian era, is a grayish color and is semiopaque like clambroth.

CLAMBROTH, Basket, Waffle Block, Tall Handle, 10 In. 35.00

Clarice Cliff, Dinner Set, Black, Red,
Orange On Ivory, Set of 12

Box, Cigarette, Art Deco, Black Dots On Dice 12.00
Butter, Cover, Block, Green 165.00
Candlestick, Fluted Column, Petal Top, Pair 300.00
Ewer, Green Applied Handle & Band, Pewter Fittings, 10 7/8 In. 55.00
Lamp, Ripley, Double Wedding 1750.00
Paperweight, Buddha, Gillinder 65.00
Pitcher, Art Glass, Enameled 40.00
Toothpick, Buttons & Arches 20.00
Toothpick, Souvenir, Erickson, Nebraska 17.50

Clarice Cliff
NEWPORT POTTERY
ENGLAND

Clarice Cliff was a designer who worked in several English factories after the 1920s. She died in 1972.

CLARICE CLIFF, Biscuit Barrel, Celtic Harvest 150.00
Bone Dish, Tonquin, Green .... 10.00 To 12.00
Bowl, Salad, Celtic Harvest 250.00
Breakfast Set, Autumn Crocus, Pitcher & Teapot, 14 Piece 1200.00
Dinner Set, Black, Red, Orange On Ivory, Set of 12 ....*Illus* 3400.00
Dinner Set, Coral Fir, With Candleholders, Service For 6 .... 1850.00
Dinner Set, Tonquin, Purple, 69 Piece 475.00
Dish, Bone, Tonquin, Green .... 12.50 To 18.50
Gravy Boat, Attached Underplate, 8 In. 23.00
Honey Pot, Beehive, Bizarre, Crocus 125.00
Jam Jar, Celtic Harvest 110.00
Jam Jar, Corn, Fruit 30.00
Jardiniere, Bizarre 850.00
Jug, My Garden, Flower Handle, Delicia Glaze 195.00
Match Holder, Toby Seated, Jug O Knee, 2 1/4 In. 135.00
Mustard, Bizarre, Blue, Green, 3 1/2 In. 160.00
Plate, Queen Elizabeth, 10 1/2 In. 25.00
Platter, Tonquin, Plum, 11 1/2 In. 22.00
Sauceboat, Tonquin, Brown, Underplate 20.00
Service For 16, Tonquin, Complete, 1944–52 .... 1200.00
Soup, Dish, Devonshire 12.50
Sugar & Creamer, Bizarre 100.00
Sugar, Cover, Rural Scenes 12.00
Vase, Bull's Eye Blossoms, Fantasque, Black Branches, 6 In. 3800.00
Vase, Trumpet, Sculpted Floral, 7 In. 150.00
Waste Plate, Tonquin, Purple, Pair 32.00

Clewell ware was made in limited quantities by Charles Walter Clewell of Canton, Ohio, from 1902 to 1955. Pottery was covered with a thin coating of bronze, then treated to make the bronze turn different colors. Pieces covered with copper, brass, or silver were also made. Mr. Clewell's secret formula for blue patina bronze was burned when he died in 1965.

CLEWELL, Bowl, Copper Pattern, 3 In. 135.00
Pot, Orange & Green Patina, 8 In. 880.00
Vase, Bronze Skin Cover, Free–Form Design, Marked, 19 In. 1695.00
Vase, Brown Patina, Green Foot, 8 1/2 In. 500.00
Vase, Brown, Green Patina, 6 1/2 In., Pair 350.00
Vase, Orange & Green Patina, 9 In. 1050.00
Vase, Ovoid Form, Green Patina, Signed, 5 1/2 In. 250.00
Vase, Seed Form, Green, Brown Patina, Signed, 6 In. 230.00
Vase, Streaked Green Patina, 7 1/2 In. 500.00
Vase, Trumpet Form, Flared Rim, C.1910, Marked, 8 In., Pair 600.00

Clews pottery was made by George Clews & Co. of Brownhill Pottery, Tunstall, England, from 1806 to 1861.

CLEWS, see also Flow Blue
CLEWS, Cup & Saucer, Handleless, Coronation, Blue 250.00
Latter, View of Detroit, 18 1/2 In. 5600.00
Plate, America & Independence Series, 2 Story House, Blue 215.00
Plate, Sancho Panza & Priest, Dark Blue, 7 1/2 In. 225.00
Platter, Newburg On Hudson, Black, On White, C.1820 .... 375.00

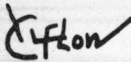

Clifton Pottery was founded by William Long in Clifton, New Jersey, in 1905. He worked there until 1908 making a line called "Crystal Patina." Clifton Pottery made art pottery. Another firm, Chesapeake Pottery, sold majolica marked "Clifton ware."

CLIFTON, Dish, Begonia Leaf, Brown, Gold, Pink & Green, 7 In.	32.00
Dish, Begonia Leaf, Yellow, Aqua, Brown & Pink, 8 In.	60.00
Plate, Blackberry, 8 In.	85.00
Teapot, Indian Ware, 1 Up	65.00
Vase, Bulbous Bottom, Stick Neck, Crystal, 1906, 9 1/2 In.	290.00
Vase, Crystalline, 1906, 7 In.	120.00
Vase, Indian Ware, S–Curve Design, Incised Mississippi, 3 1/2 In.	50.00

Clocks of all types have always been popular with collectors. The eighteenth–century tall case, or grandfather's clock, was designed to house a works with a long pendulum. In 1816, Eli Terry patented a new, smaller works for a clock; and the case became smaller. The clock could be kept on a shelf instead of on the floor. By 1840, coiled springs were used and even smaller clocks were made. Battery–powered electric clocks were made in the 1870s.

CLOCK, Advertising, 7–Up	15.00
Advertising, AC Sparkplug, Electric	45.00 To 75.00
Advertising, American Express	125.00
Advertising, Ancient Age Bourbon, Light Up, Glass Front	95.00
Advertising, Baird's Jolly Tar, 1890s	825.00
Advertising, Beeline Fashions, Electric	45.00
Advertising, Budweiser Beer, Ceiling, Chain	75.00
Advertising, Buster Brown, Pam Electric, Wall Type	190.00
Advertising, Calumet, Regulator	525.00 To 600.00
Advertising, Canada Dry, Plastic Face, Metal Frame, 16 X 16 In.	38.00
Advertising, Cat's Paw, Shoe Repairing, Lights Up	165.00
Advertising, Chantilly, 3 Putti, Flowers, Electric, 11 X 11 1/2 In.	225.00
Advertising, Clapperton Spool Silks, Baird	1000.00
Advertising, Diet Rite, PAM, Illuminated, 17 In.	75.00
Advertising, Dr Pepper, Metal Rim	135.00
Advertising, Dr Pepper, Neon	1500.00
Advertising, Duquesne Pilsner Beer, Light–Up	75.00
Advertising, Ever–Ready Safety Razor, Wood, Man Shaving, 22 X 18 In.	815.00
Advertising, Four Roses Whiskey, Electric, 13 In.	40.00
Advertising, Frostie Root Beer, Metal, Fluorescent Bulb	150.00
Advertising, G.E. Refrigerator, With Salt & Pepper	155.00
Advertising, Garfield Tea & Syrup	775.00
Advertising, Hartford Fire Insurance, Bronze & Oak, Wall Plaque, 1909	125.00
Advertising, Heinz Aristocrat Tomatoes, Man Talking Alarm	65.00
Advertising, Heinz, Mr. Tomato, Given To Retirees	75.00
Advertising, Hires, Glass Face, Cover, Electric, Round, 1950s	95.00
Advertising, Hornung Beer, Light–Up, Glass & Metal, 1934	345.00
Advertising, Hostetter's Stomach Bitters	1095.00
Advertising, International Harvester, Neon	275.00
Advertising, Jeweler, Ogdensburg, N.Y., Wall, Electric	50.00
Advertising, Kodak Film, Electric, Tin, 1920s	100.00
Advertising, Merrick's Spool Cotton	995.00 To 1695.00
Advertising, Mr. Peanut, Battery Operated	35.00
Advertising, National Cash Register, Electric, 1939	300.00
Advertising, Nu Grape, Bottles, Light–Up	150.00
Advertising, Old Character Whiskey, Sirocco Wood	75.00
Advertising, Old Mr. Boston Bottle, Windup, Metal, 22 In.	950.00
Advertising, Orange Crush	1395.00
Advertising, Osh Kosh B'Gosh, Neon	70.00
Advertising, Pabst Beer	45.00 To 50.00
Advertising, Pepsi–Cola, Lights Up, Plastic & Metal, Round, 16 In.	160.00
Advertising, Pierce's Lignite Floor Varnish	1095.00
Advertising, Pillsbury, Neon	365.00
Advertising, Pure Spring, Wood, Tin, Plastic, 16 X 16 In.	75.00

Advertising, RCA Nipper	150.00
Advertising, RCA Records, Light–Up, Electric, Nipper The Dog	375.00
Advertising, Reeds Tonic, Pendulum, Reverse Paintings, 24 X 10 In.	1450.00
Advertising, Regal Beer, Illuminated, 14 In.	35.00
Advertising, Ronald McDonald, Wall, Wristwatch–Style, Electric	35.00
Advertising, Royal Crown Cola, Tin Face, Wooden Frame, Electric	250.00
Advertising, Sauer's Extract, New Haven	950.00
Advertising, Sauer's Extract, Reverse Painting On Glass	1975.00
Advertising, Schaefer Beer, Art Deco, Lights, Boat Shape	75.00
Advertising, Schmidts Beer, Sheet Metal, Chain For Hanging	75.00
Advertising, Session, Mohawk Tires, Table Model	65.00
Advertising, Shell Oil, Shell Globe Shape, Key Wind, Pendulum, Wood	2795.00
Advertising, Sprite Soda	35.00 To 45.00
Advertising, Squirt, Glass Cover, Face, Square, 1950s	75.00
Advertising, St. Joseph Aspirin, Neon	300.00
Advertising, Sun Crest, Metal & Glass, 13 X 16 In.	58.00
Advertising, Traveler's Express, Greyhound Lines, Electric, 15 In.	150.00
Advertising, Valvoline Oil	75.00
Advertising, Ward's Orange Crush, Key Wind, Wood Frame, 14 In.	600.00
Advertising, Watch & Clock Repairs, Neon, Hanging, 34 X 48 X 15 In.	1800.00
Advertising, Winchester Cartridge Board	3995.00
Advertising, Wings Perfume, Detroit, Iron, Ornate, 10 Bottles, 14 In.	295.00
Alarm, Animated, Big Bad Wolf, Box	1850.00
Alarm, Bank, Robert Shaw Controls, Night–Light, Battery Operated	350.00
Alarm, Metal, Plays Some Enchanted Evening, Germany, 5 In.	65.00
Alarm, Raggedy Ann & Raggedy Andy, Talking	25.00
Animated, Cat, Moving Eyes	275.00
Animated, Dog, Eyes Tell Time, Carved Wood	395.00
Animated, Felix, Eyes & Tail Move	165.00
Animated, Guitar, Band Conductor	295.00
Animated, Haddon, Woman Rocks In Chair, 1955	47.00
Animated, Kit–Kat, Black, Eyes Move, Tail Wags	20.00 To 25.00
Animated, Spirit of U.S., Roosevelt	125.00
Ansonia, 8–Day, Time & Strike, 11 In.	225.00
Ansonia, Art & Commerce, Double Statue	1195.00
Ansonia, Boar Hunter, Eureka Base	1700.00
Ansonia, Brass, Enameled, Wall, Roman Numerals, Square, 20 X 18 In.	165.00
Ansonia, Cobalt Blue, Royal Bonn Case	650.00
Ansonia, Figural, Cavalier, Bronze	775.00
Ansonia, Gallery, 8–Day, Time & Strike, 11 In.	225.00
Ansonia, Huntress, Swinger	1450.00
Ansonia, Kitchen, Reverse Painted Glass, Oak	325.00
Ansonia, Mirror Side, Walnut	350.00
Ansonia, Pink China, Case	450.00
Ansonia, Queen Elizabeth, Wall, Time & Strike, Walnut Case	700.00
Ansonia, Regulator, School, Double Time	425.00
Ansonia, School, Oak, Short Drop, Time Only, Paper Inside	175.00
Ansonia, Statue, Mercury	375.00
Art Deco, Round, Dragonflies Sides, Marble, Bronze, 3 Piece	925.00
Art Deco, Windup, Cut Glass Case, Red Mirror Face, 7 In.	185.00
Atkins, Gallery, Double Fusee, 8–Sided, Rosewood	900.00
Augustin & Paris, French, Mantel, Louis XVI, Bisque, 16 1/2 In.	1300.00
Automaton, Potato Eater Figure, Black Forest, Walnut, 21 In.	3500.00
Banjo, Chelsea, Mahogany, 20th Century, 29 1/2 In.	600.00
Banjo, Giltwood & Mahogany, Reverse Painted, 8–Day, 1820, 29 1/2 In.	1400.00
Banjo, Lynn, Gilt Front, C.1825	3500.00
Banjo, New England, Eglomise Panels	2800.00
Banjo, Willard Type, Mahogany, Parcel Gilt, Eglomise Panels, 34 In.	1500.00
Bradley, Alarm, Star Wars	35.00 To 40.00
Carriage, French, Brass, Leather Carrying Case	385.00
Century, Huckleberry Finn, Fish On Line Motion, Bronzed Metal	65.00
Chauncey Ives, Pillar & Scroll, Brass Finials, Mahogany, 31 1/4 In.	425.00
Courtyard, Iron, Painted Dial Over Lion Mask, Continental, 38 In.	385.00
Cuckoo, Black Forest, 30–Hour, 3 Weights, Germany, Instructions, 1914	335.00

Cuckoo, Black Forest, Carved Bird & Leaves, 3 Weights, 1914	400.00
Cuckoo, Oil Painting On Front of Tiger, Glass Eyes Move, C.1880	1000.00
Dewey, Brass Over Iron	450.00
Double Steeple, Wagon Spring Movement	2090.00
Dutch, Brass Works, Wooden, Weight & Pendulum, 29 In.	325.00
Edward Grudy, Banjo, Lyre, Gilded Mahogany	7150.00
Eiffel Tower, Bronze, C.1900, 45 In.	1400.00
Elgin, Travel, Rhinestone Edges, Germany	25.00
Elgin, Wall, Cinderella, 1960s	35.00
Eli Terry, Pillar & Scroll, Brass Finials, Mahgonay, 1815, 31 In.	1780.00
Eli Terry, Pillar & Scroll, Original Wooden Works	2400.00
Eli Terry, Pillar & Scroll, Reverse Painted Lower Panel	4290.00
Eli Terry, Pillar & Scroll, Shelf, Brass Finials, Glazed Door, C.1830	1045.00
Elmer Stennes, Tall Case, Bird's-Eye, Tiger Maple, C.1975, 86 1/2 In.	2100.00
Ephraim Downes, Pillar & Scroll, Reverse Painted Glass	2500.00
European, Cherubs Holding Items, Representing Arts, Bronze, 27 In.	4100.00
Falling Ball, Sir Francis Drake, 7-Day Movement, Mahogany, 30 In.	750.00
Franklin Delano Roosevelt, Standing By Ship's Wheel Clock	125.00
French, Birds, Butterflies, Sanskrit Numbers, Candelabras, Bronze	4500.00
French, Mantel, Bacchic Figural Group, Putti Over Case, Bronze, 21 In.	1100.00
French, Mantel, Bell Form, Brass, 19th Century	325.00
French, Mantel, Figure Beside Group of Soldiers, Bronze, 22 In.	1485.00
French, Mantel, Seated Figure, Bronze & Marble, 12 X 16 1/2 In.	550.00
French, Mantel, Tambour, Porcelain Dial, 8-Day, Open Escapement, 11 In.	900.00
French, Robinson Crusoe & Friday, Gilt-Bronze, Empire	7975.00
French, Tall Case, Bronze Repousse Face, Walnut, 102 In.	2300.00
G. Votti, Regulator, Giltwood, Wall, Pendulum, 1884, 57 In.	2600.00
G.S. Bellerose, Tall Case, Three Rivers, Early 19th Century	8200.00
Garniture, Carved Pine, Birds, Foliage Over Fox, Bavaria, 28 In., 3 Pc.	1450.00
Garniture, French, Onyx Clock, 2 5-Light Candelabrum, 17 In.	2200.00
General Electric, Electric, Ivory	20.00
General Electric, Mirrored, Peach	55.00
General Electric, Power Station, Pyrex Crystal, Round, 8 In.	85.00
General Electric, Refrigerator, Coil On Top, 1931	125.00
General Electric, Wrought Iron, Black, 9 1/2 In.	20.00
Geo. Levely, Bracket, Painted Face	1530.00
George III, Painted, Act of Parliament, Pendulum Drawer, 47 X 20 In.	1045.00
Gilbert, Calendar, Perpetual, Walnut, Burl, 33 X 19 In.	1705.00
Gilbert, Mantel, 8 Day, Alarm, Dated 1896	125.00
Gilbert, Perpetual Calendar, Walnut, Newsstand Reverse Glass, 33 In.	1705.00
Gilbert, Regulator, No. 3, Office, Rosewood, 1870	850.00
Gilbert, Regulator, No. 9	2800.00
Gilbert, Regulator, No.14	1050.00
Gilbert, Regulator, Store, Walnut Finish Case, 35 X 17 1/2 In.	260.00
Gilbert, School, Oak, Fancy, Long Drop	275.00
Gilbert, School, Time & Strike, Paper Inside	200.00
Gousset A Pontivy, Tall Case, Oak, Pendulum, Weights, 85 In.	800.00
Gustav Becker, Regulator, 2-Weight	775.00
Hanson Clock Co., Westminster, Wall, 1920	250.00
Henry Thornton, Tall Case, Calendar, Mahogany, C.1780, 6 Ft. 9 1/4 In.	3850.00
Herschede, Grandmother's, Mahogany, Chime & Strike, 70 1/4 In.	1100.00
Herschede, Tall Case, 9-Tube, Mahogany, C.1962, 81 In.	4500.00
Hoadley, Grained Case, Cream & Green Sponged Door	5000.00
Hoadley, Transition, Stenciled Eagle Splat, 25 X 13 In.	2250.00
Howard & Davis, Banjo, No.2	4750.00
Howard, Banjo, Figure-Eight, 8-Day, Weight Driven, 1857, 44 In.	4000.00
Howard, Banjo, No.40	4750.00
Howard, Banjo, No.59, Cherry	3750.00
Howard, Regulator, 59 X 18 X 7 In.	1900.00
Howard, Tall Case, Federal, 8-Day, Weight Driven, Mahogany, 92 In.	5600.00
Ingraham, Admiral Dewey, 8-Day, Time & Strike, Oak	350.00
Ingraham, Animated Cowboy, Riding The Plains, Metal	145.00
Ingraham, Banjo, Yankee Clipper, 8-Day, Strike Pendulum	190.00
Ingraham, Grecian, 8-Day, Time & Strike, Label	240.00

Ingraham, Mantel, Dark Wood 22.50
Ingraham, Roy Rogers & Trigger, Motion 225.00
International, Battery Wind Pendulum, 2 Weight, Railroad, 1915, 6 Ft. 700.00
International, Time, Carved & Inlaid 330.00
Isaac Brokaw, Tall Case, Bridgetown, N.J., Mahogany, 18th Century 7040.00
Ithaca, Calendar, Farmers With Pillars, No.10, Walnut, 25 In. 1000.00
Ithaca, Calendar, Model 3 1/2, Leaf & Flower Crest, Mahogany, C.1880 .... 2090.00
Ithaca, Mantel, Walnut, Ebony, Double Dial, 20 1/2 In. 2800.00
Ithaca, Shelf, No.2, Regulator, 2 Faces 3000.00
J. Gulliford, Lantern, George II, Brass, Arbor Pediment, 1740, 15 In. 1200.00
Japanese, Hardwood, Brass, Glazed Hood, Silver & Gold Design, 44 In. 1100.00
Jerome & Darrow, Shelf, Bouquet, Black & Gold, 35 In. 325.00
John Brown, Bracket, Ebonized, Brass Handle, English, C.1790 .... 5750.00
John Monk, Water, Brass, 24–Hour Dial, England, 1474, 29 In. 357.00
John S. Krause, Tall Case, 8–Day, Moon Phase, C.1800, 96 In. 5200.00
Josa. Lockwood, Tall Case, Damp–Dry Dial, South Carolina, 1887, 95 In. 6250.00
Joshua Wilder, Banjo, Reverse Painted On Throat & Tablet 1250.00
Junghans, Mantel, 8–Day, Westminster Chimes 595.00
Junghans, Musical, Walnut Case, 1900–10, 6 X 4 1/2 In. 1000.00
Kalex, World Time, Brass Dial, Leather Case, Electric 85.00
Kroeber, Marine, Dial With Seconds, Time & Strike, Label 265.00
L. Watson, Tall Case, Wooden Face, Cherry, 89 In. 1300.00
Lamp, Art Deco, 2 Women Hold Clock, Globe Shade, Electric, 10 X 11 In. 145.00
Lantern, Jacobean, Brass, 30–Hour, Floral & Leaf Design, 16 In. 522.00
Lavroff, Gilt–Bronze & Marble, Nude Figure Lying On Top, 20 1/4 In. 4950.00
Lenzkirch, Regulator, Vienna, No.18, 2–Weight 1250.00
Limoges, Desk, Bronze & Marble, Hunter, Stag, 7 In. ....*Illus* 525.00
Louis–Phillipe, Papier–Mache, Wall, Polychromed, 1840–50 .... 300.00
Lux, Alarm, Frown Face 45.00
Lux, Bird, Swinging, Box 75.00
Lux, Cat, Brown, With Tail .... 150.00 To 160.00
Lux, Chrome, Good Luck, Horseshoe, Art Deco 150.00
Lux, Clown With Seals, Animated 375.00
Lux, Clown With Tie, Pendulette 495.00
Lux, Cuckoo 35.00
Lux, Dutch Cottage, 30 Hour, Papers, Box .... 155.00 To 195.00
Lux, Girl On Swing, Electric 40.00
Lux, Honey Bunny, Lavender 250.00
Lux, Kitty Kat Over Fence 375.00
Lux, Red Petunia, Box 210.00
Lux, Schmoo, Pendulette, Pink 150.00
Lux, Ship's Wheel, Brown .... 150.00 To 175.00
Lux, Showboat, Animated 50.00
Lux, Sunflower, Pendulum 225.00
Lux, Windmill 80.00
Mantel, Chromed Square Face, Marble, Onyx, Oval Plinth, Key, 10 In. 1760.00
Mantel, Continental, Neoclassical Ormolu, Mahogany, 26 In. 4000.00
Mantel, French Empire, Gilt Bronze, 4 Columns, Roman Dial, 17 In. 1210.00
Mantel, French, Brass Works, Gilt Bronze Mountings, Walnut, C.1830 .... 1800.00
Mantel, Gilt Bronze & Marble, Enamel Dial, French, 15 In. 550.00
Mantel, Parian Group of Lovers, Walnut Base, 19th Century, 20 1/2 In. 225.00
Mantel, Regency, Balloon Form, Painted Satinwood, 1802, 20 1/2 In. 7000.00
Mantel, Tabernacle, Geometric, Strike & Repeat, Austrian, 1800, 6 In. 55.00
Mantel, Tortoiseshell, Ormolu Floral & Scroll Design, 1855, 11 In. 4100.00
Mantel, Yankee Clipper, Chrome Sails, Walnut 110.00
Mission, Wall, 8–Day, Time & Strike, Pendulum 150.00
Morbier, 8–Day Time & Strike, Pressed Brass, France, 1850, 56 In. 225.00
Mouse, Travels Up & Down To Indicate Time, 1910, 43 In. 500.00
Movado, Black Enamel Case Which Winds Clock, Tiffany 4200.00
Mystery, Jefferson, Gold Chrome, Art Deco, Golden Hour, Floating Dial 45.00
Napoleon III, Bronze Dore, Fluted Marble Ring & Snake, 1875 .... 5750.00
New Haven, Banjo, 2 Ships, Eagle Finial, Key Wind, 36 In. 475.00
New Haven, Banjo, 8–Day, Time & Strike, 38 In. 400.00
New Haven, Banjo, Mahogany Veneer, Windsor Model, 20th Century 100.00

Clock, Limoges, Desk, Bronze & Marble,
Hunter, Stag, 7 In.

Clock, Tall Case, English,
Mahogany, 83 In.

Clock, Tall Case, Farm Scene,
Broken Arch, C.1800

Clock, Tall Case, Federal, Mahogany, C.1800

Clock, Tall Case, Walnut,
Roman Numerals, 86 In.

New Haven, Banjo, Westminster 350.00
New Haven, Banjo, Willard Style, 30–Day 475.00
New Haven, Bronze, Sevres Painting 600.00
New Haven, Gallery, Hanging, 12–In. Dial 125.00
New Haven, Keyhole, Chauncey Jerome, 15 1/2 In. 1350.00
New Haven, Regulator, Saturn, Weight Driven, Railroad 600.00
New Haven, Ripple Front, Double Fussee Mechanism, Jerome, 21 1/2 In. 1650.00
Paperweight, Sun & Moon, Piccadilly Circus, Desk, Swiss Movement 425.00
Porcelain, Enameled & Ormolu Trim, France, 11 In. 150.00
Puiforcat, Silver Plated, Marble, Rectangular Plinth, 1932, 10 1/4 In. 8500.00
R. Street, Tall Case, George III, Oak, Roman Numerals, 30–Hour, 77 In. 1100.00
Raingo Freres, Mantel, Louis XVI, Ormolu, Putti, Floral Flags, 14 In. 2300.00
Regulator, 8–Day Fusee, Striking, England, 1870, 14 In. 2300.00
Roper Ashwick, Tall Case, Swan Neck Pediment, Mahogany, 1800, 80 In. 1760.00
S. Hoadley, Tall Case, Hepplewhite, Cherry, Inladi, Bonnet Top, 1825 .... 6750.00
Samuel Abbot, Mirror, Original Gilt, Boston, 1815 .... 9500.00
Sessions, Banjo, 8–Day, Ship & Lighthouse, 36 In. 185.00
Sessions, Mantel, Lion Head, Black, C.1904 .... 35.00
Sessons, Golden Girl, Nude 250.00
Seth Thomas, 1 Weight, Railroad Station, 68 In. 1400.00
Seth Thomas, Banjo, Eagle Finial, Walnut 115.00
Seth Thomas, Banjo, Time & Strike, Pendulum 375.00
Seth Thomas, Bracket, Mahogany, 1/4–Hour Westminster Chimes 200.00
Seth Thomas, Cottage, Time & Strike, Rosewood Veneer, 14 In. 75.00
Seth Thomas, Gallery, Time & Strike, 11 In.–Dial 150.00
Seth Thomas, Lobby, Dial With Seconds, Mahogany Finish, 38 X 25 In. 885.00
Seth Thomas, Mantel, Rectangular Window, G. Stickley, C.1912 .... 7865.00
Seth Thomas, Peach Mirrored Glass, 5 3/4 X 7 In. 40.00
Seth Thomas, Pillar & Scroll, C.1930, Full Size 785.00
Seth Thomas, Railroad Station, Time Only, 68 In. 1400.00
Seth Thomas, Regulator, Jeweler's, Bracket Dead Beat 500.00
Seth Thomas, Regulator, No.2, 8–Day, Walnut 625.00
Seth Thomas, Regulator, Pagoda Gilded Top, Pendulum, 1868, 2 Doors 750.00
Seth Thomas, School, Rosewood Case, Short Drop, Time Only 350.00
Seth Thomas, School, Strike, Walnut, 9 In. 400.00
Seth Thomas, Shelf, Restoration, 8–Day, Gilded Half Columns, Glass 475.00
Seth Thomas, Wall, No.9, Walnut, Double Dial, Weight Driven, 6 Ft. 4500.00
Seth Thomas, Watchman's, 1899 Special, Nickel Trim, 4 1/2 In. 995.00
Sevres Style, Birds, Ram's Head Mount, Porcelain, Cobalt Blue, 19 In. 400.00
Shelf, Federal, Farm Scene, Mahogany, C.1830, 17 1/4 In. 1045.00
Ship, Wooden, Chrome Sails, 18 In. 95.00
Skeleton, Single Train, Fusee, English 700.00
Skeleton, With Gothic Plates, England, 8–Day, Fusee Movement, 10 In. 1200.00
Sonara, Porcelain Dial, Time & Stike, 4–Bell 475.00
Spartus, Trotter Harness Racehorse, Clock Center of Wheel, Electric 175.00
Stennes, Banjo, Boston State House Glasses 1800.00
Stetson, Mantel, Black, Lion's Heads, Round Clock Center, 3 Columns 135.00
Stromberg, Regulator, Beveled Glass, Oak 600.00
Tall Case, 30–Hour, Broken Arch Bonnet, Walnut, Painted Face, 91 In. 1600.00
Tall Case, 5–Tube, American, 1920, 6 1/2 In. 1300.00
Tall Case, 8 Day, Weight Driven, Bird's–Eye Maple, C.1800, 86 In. 2100.00
Tall Case, Arts & Crafts, Oak, Arabic Numerals, Weights, 1910, 75 In. 515.00
Tall Case, Brass Works, Metal Face, Rocking Ship, Handmade, 59 3/4 In. 1000.00
Tall Case, Brass Works, Painted Metal Face, Oak & Mahogany, 88 In. 800.00
Tall Case, Cherry, Arched Door In Waist, Flat Top, Brass Gears, 89 In. 1100.00
Tall Case, Chinoiserie, Red & Gold Lacquer, English, C.1830 .... 9000.00
Tall Case, Chippendale, Gilt Dial, New England, Cherry, C.1790, 87 In. 6650.00
Tall Case, English, Inlaid Case, C.1880, 8 Ft.4 1/2 In. 6200.00
Tall Case, English, Mahogany, 83 In. ....*Illus* 1650.00
Tall Case, English, Sphinx Head Carvings, 9–Tube 995.00
Tall Case, Face Depicting Lord Nelson Death At Sea 5500.00
Tall Case, Farm Scene, Broken Arch, C.1800 ....*Illus* 1000.00
Tall Case, Federal, Mahogany, C.1800 ....*Illus* 1650.00
Tall Case, Fluted Columns In Molding, English, Oak, 86 1/2 In. 1000.00

Tall Case, George III, Inlaid Mahogany, Rocking Ship Dial, 81 In.	3700.00
Tall Case, Georgian, Mahogany, 4 Seasons Painted Dial, 8–Day, 95 In.	825.00
Tall Case, Glazed Door, Brass Dial, Oak, C.1920, 80 1/2 In.	385.00
Tall Case, Hamered Copper Dial, Oak, C.1910, 6 Ft.11 In.	1500.00
Tall Case, Mahogany, 8–Day, Weight Driven, Time & Strike, England	2800.00
Tall Case, Mahogany, Dome Top, Maple, London, Brass Dial, 80 In.	1300.00
Tall Case, Mercury Pendulum, 9–Tube, Sphinx Carved	9350.00
Tall Case, Morbier, Enameled Dial, Banjo Case, Signed Bailly, 94 In.	4200.00
Tall Case, Mural Face, Scotland, C.1775	2400.00
Tall Case, Oak Inlaid, Eglomise Black & Gold Panel, England, 91 In.	2200.00
Tall Case, Painted Face, Finmore Works, Date, C.1790	3500.00
Tall Case, Turned Rosettes, Painted Metal Face, Cherry, 97 In.	800.00
Tall Case, Wag–On–Wall Works, Brass Gears, Walnut, 94 In.	1625.00
Tall Case, Walnut, Roman Numerals, 86 In. ....*Illus*	850.00
Tall Case, Waterbury, Oak, Carved Shells, Columns, 75 In.	1450.00
Tall Case, Wooden Dial, 8–Day Metal Works, Pennsylvania, C.1830	3450.00
Tall, Calendar Movement, Moon Dial, Scotland, 1835, 7 1/2 Ft.	3500.00
Teeter–Totter, Boy & Girl Go Up & Down	135.00
Telechron, Alarm, Electric, 1927	35.00
Telechron, Electric, Lucite, 1950s	25.00
Thos. Sturgeon, Tall Case, Pineapple 1/2 Columns, Cherry, 103 In.	5500.00
CLOCK, TIFFANY, see Tiffany, Clock	
Tift, Banjo, 8–Day, Brass Movement	2300.00
Vienna, Regulator, Enameled Plaque Inserts, Ebonized, 46 In.	2400.00
W. & Hinsch, Mantel, Time & Strike	610.00
W.M. Whitburn, Tall Case, Metal Face, Figures of 4 Seasons, 83 In.	2750.00
Wag–On–Wall, Engraved Brass Dial, Brass Spandrels, 17th Century	665.00
Wag–On–Wall, Wooden Plates, Brass Gears, 7 1/4 X 5 1/2 In.	200.00
Waltham, Banjo, Mahogany, Crossbanded Veneer, 20th Century, 42 In.	1300.00
Waltham, Banjo, Reverse Painted Boston State House, 42 In.	1300.00
Waltham, Regulator, Railroad, 1 Weight	2500.00
Waterbury, Carriage, Time & Strike	100.00
Waterbury, Cast Iron Front, 1860	100.00
Waterbury, Mantel, Porcelain Dial, 8–Day, Time & Strike	85.00
Waterbury, Pillar & Scroll, Mark Leavenworth	2530.00
Waterbury, Regulator, Cartier's Watch & Ring House, Oak, No.9	269.00
Waterbury, School, Time & Calendar, Oak	400.00
Welch, Double Spring Drive, 30–Day, 31 In.	425.00
Welch, Gingerbread, Time & Strike, Alarm	150.00
Welch, School, Short Drop, Advertising On Dial	250.00
Welch, Wall, Figure 8 Shape, Time Only, August 30, 1870	350.00
Westclox, Paperweight, Midnight Sky, Stars, Encircling World	300.00
Wightman & Yark, Tall Case, Tortoiseshell Japanned, 1800, 8 Ft. 3 In.	4950.00
Willard, Banjo, 30–Day, 44 In.	395.00
Willard, Banjo, Gilt Wood, Mahogany, 8–Day, Restored, 29 1/2 In.	1400.00
Willard, Banjo, Reverse Painted Glass, U.S. Seal, Naval Action	1100.00
Willard, Banjo, Sailing Ships Base	3100.00
William Brenneiser, Tall Case, Iron Moon Phase Dial, Mahogany, 99 In.	2865.00

Cloisonne enamel was developed during the tenth century. A glass enamel was applied between small ribbonlike pieces of metal on a metal base. Most cloisonne is Chinese or Japanese. Pieces marked "China" are twentieth–century examples.

CLOISONNE, Bottle, Snuff, Panels of Multicolored Flowers, 3 In.	75.00
Bowl, Incurved Rim, Black, Brass Wirework, 8 In.	150.00
Bowl, Polychrome Floral Design, Red Ground, 8 In.	85.00
Buckle, Shoe, Vines, Leaves, Openwork, 1920s, Oversize, Pair	65.00
Burner, Incense, Footed, 19th Century, 5 In.	65.00
Figurine, Crane, Holding Vine, Candle Cups, 14 In., Pair	2095.00
Figurine, Crane, Standing On Rockwork With Deer, Chinese, 19 In.	410.00
Flask, Moon, 5–Toed Dragons Amid Clouds, Early 19th Century	770.00
Jar, Brass Foo Dog Finial, Floral Design On Blue, 4 1/2 In.	55.00
Jar, Cover, Rust Ground, Colored Blossoms, 3 In.	45.00
Jar, Ginger, Cover, Magenta, 7 In.	35.00

Jar, Ginger, Multicolored Flowers, Black Ground, Marked	140.00
Jar, Ginger, Mums, Black Ground, Marked, 7 In.	145.00
Match Holder, Pink Flowers, Wine Ground	35.00
Napkin Ring, Berries, Flowers, On Black, Turquoise Inside	55.00
Panel, 2 Figures Beside Lake, Framed, 11 1/2 X 12 1/2 In.	3000.00
Plate, Bird, Flowers, Turquoise Center, 9 1/2 In.	195.00
Plate, Butterflies, Fancy Border, 9 3/4 In.	110.00
Teapot, Goldstones, Butterflies	210.00
Tray, Scene of Piano Recital, Brass Feet, C.1900, 17 In.	3025.00
Tumbler, Multicolored Dragon, Black Ground, 3 3/4 In.	125.00
Vase, 3 Butterflies, C.1880, 3 3/4 In.	1400.00
Vase, Bluebirds, Clouds, 10 1/2 In., Pair	600.00
Vase, Dragon, Black, 10 In., Pair	450.00
Vase, Dragon, C.1880, 4 7/8 In.	900.00
Vase, Dragons, Black & Gold, 6 1/ 2in.	45.00
Vase, Gold Flecks, Black Floral, 7 In.	225.00
Vase, Hu Shape, Ring Handles, Blue Ground, Chinese, 16 In.	770.00
Vase, Multicolored Flowers, Butterfly, Cobalt Ground, 8 In., Pair	245.00
Vase, Pear Form, Hydrangeas, Drilled For Lamp, 1920, 11 In., Pair	2800.00
Vase, Shields, Phoenix Birds, Scrolls Inside, 15 X 19 In.	1000.00
Vase, Warrior, Sparrow & Floral, 4–Sided, C.1880, 9 1/2 In.	2500.00
Vase, Writhing Double Dragons, Butterflies, C.1875, 12 1/2 In.	800.00

Antique and collectible clothes of all types are listed in this section. Dresses, hats, shoes, underwear and more are found here. Other textiles are to be found in the Textile, World War I, World War II, Quilt, and Coverlet sections.

CLOTHING, Apron, Body, Bar Print, White Linen, Crocheted Trim	18.00
Apron, Crochet Filet Trim, Irish Linen, Pocket	12.00
Apron, Tea, Embroidered Violets, Lace Trim, Pink Silk	15.00
Bathing Suit, Woman's, Hawaiian Print, 1940s, Size 7, 3 Piece	15.00
Beanie, Propeller, 1940s	20.00
Bloomers, Trimmed With Red Embroidery, White	35.00
Blouse, Beaded & Sequined Front, High Neck, Ivory Silk, Medium	15.00
Blouse, Black Lace, 1920s, Small	24.00
Blouse, Leg–of–Mutton Sleeves, Jet Bead Trim, Size 6	25.00
Blouse, Silk, Formal Bodice, Tucked, C.1890	5.00
Blouse, White Nylon, Satin Trim, 1930s	10.00
Bonnet, Black, C.1895	20.00
Bonnet, Child's, Civil War, Quilted, Lavender Lace	40.00
Bonnet, Quilted Brown Wool, Linen	135.00
Bonnet, Satin Ribbons, Lace, Black Net	20.00
Booties, Child's, Leather, Blue	30.00
Boots, Moon, 1969	20.00
Camisole, Black	5.00
Camisole, Crocheted Yoke	12.50
Camisole, Hand Crocheted	15.00
Cape, Black Curly Fur	45.00
Cape, Black Plush, Monkey Fur Trim	40.00
Cape, Ecclesiastical, Silver Metallic Thread Embroidery	270.00
Cape, Opera, Black, Black Beading, Fancy, Short	85.00
Cloche, Brown, 1920s	28.00
Clogs, Child's, Wooden, Tipped Soles, Leather, Silver Buckles, 6 In.	200.00
Coat, Baby's, Pink Silk, Pearl Buttons	35.00
Coat, Bear	65.00
Coat, Black Mink	825.00
Coat, Child's, Silk, 1920s	55.00
Coat, Child's, White Wool, Linen Embroidery, 1915	45.00
Coat, Christening, Ruffled High Neck, Embroidered, Cape, Ecru	28.00
Coat, Lynx Fur, Leather, 3/4 Length, Size 12	350.00
Coat, Racoon, Woman's	100.00
Coat, Sheepskin, Dark Brown, Long, Medium	32.00
Coat, Toddler's, Pique, C.1920	15.00
Coat, Woman's, Victorian, Black Velvet, Brown Fur Collar & Cuffs	125.00

Collar, Embroidered, Black Silk, India	25.00
Collar, Mink, Pastel	10.00
Collar, Stand–Up, Arrow, Box, 1910, 6 In Box	15.00
Collar, Studded With Rhinestones, Beads & Pearls, Black Velvet	28.00
Collar, White Beaded, 1930s	12.00
Dress & Apron, Girl's, Amish	22.00
Dress, Battenburg Lace, Cream, C.1930	240.00
Dress, Black & White Stripes, C.1912	45.00
Dress, Black Velvet, C.1920	22.50
Dress, Brown Lace, Bias Cut, 1930s, Size 7–8	175.00
Dress, Child's, Green Velvet, Victorian, Size 4	125.00
Dress, Child's, Linen, Red Embroidery, Size 8	35.00
Dress, Child's, Smocking, Tucks, Lace, Ribbon Trim, Size 8	35.00
Dress, Child's, Victorian, Dropped Waist, Green Velvet, Size 3	125.00
Dress, Chinese Silk, Mandarin Neck, Raspberry, Black, Size 7–9	25.00
Dress, Christening, Cape, Cutwork, Handmade, C.1850	125.00
Dress, Christening, Dimity, Pleated Bodice, Lace Trim	44.00
Dress, Christening, Pintuck Yoke, Lace Trim	45.00
Dress, Christening, Yoke, Ruffle, 1920s	55.00
Dress, Church Apron, Amish, Girl's	45.00
Dress, Drop Waist, Jewel Neck, Bow Trim, Ivory, Size 6	24.00
Dress, Edwardian, Silk Brocade, Robin's Egg Blue, Lace Trim	675.00
Dress, Edwardian, Silk Twill, Green & Coral Floral Accents	65.00
Dress, Evening, Sleeveless, Backless, Gold & Lilac Print, 1920s	40.00
Dress, Flapper, Beaded, Red	47.50
Dress, Flapper, Overall Beading, Black Chiffon	75.00
Dress, Handmade Lace Trim, Ivory Silk	200.00
Dress, Jacket, Taffeta, Full–Length, Jonathan Logan, 1940s	20.00
Dress, Middy, Black, Original White Blouse	25.00
Dress, Silk, Brown Plaid, Matching Cape, Velvet Trim, Civil War	140.00
Dress, Victorian, Peach Lace	90.00
Dress, Victorian, White Lingerie, 18–In. Waist	250.00
Dress, Wedding, Beaded Crown, Lace	75.00
Dress, Wedding, Victorian, High Neck, Lace & Tucking, 2 Piece	30.00
Dress, Wedding, Victorian, Petticoat, Ivory Silk	120.00
Dress, White Embroidery & Cutwork, White Batiste, C.1915	50.00
Duster, Belted Back, Pockets, Ecru Linen, Size M	35.00
Evening Coat, Black Velvet, Long	98.00
Fur Piece, Marten, Hooks In Front	25.00
Glove, Woman's, Amish, Hand Knitted	65.00
Gloves, Sleigh, Horsehair	20.00
Handkerchief, White Voile, 2 Rows Embroidered Hearts, 1930, 11 In.	4.00
Hat, Baby's, Crocheted, Cloth Lined, Hand Stitched	5.00
Hat, Beaver, Lincoln	65.00
Hat, Black Ostrich Feathers	275.00
Hat, Brown Felt, 1930s	24.00
Hat, Feathered, 1930s	15.00
Hat, Man's, Black Derby, Box	65.00
Hat, Man's, High, Beaver	35.00
Hat, Man's, Straw, 1920s	15.00
Hat, Mink, Black, Small Visor, Small	16.00
Hat, Straw, Rose, Silk Trim, Matching Ostrich Plume	60.00
Hat, Straw, Wide Brim, Flowers	28.00
Hat, Top, Beaver, 5th Avenue Dobbs, Brush, Size 7	350.00
Hat, Woman's, Black Ostrich Feathers	275.00
Headdress & Sash, Girl's, Balkan, 19th Centennial	100.00
Headdress, Flapper, Indian Type, 1920	39.50
Infant Outfit, Amish, Black Dress, White Pinafore, Prayer Cap	50.00
Jacket, Army Fatigue, Olive Cotton	38.00
Jacket, Edwardian, Battenburg, Silk, Toast Collar, Rust Lining	75.00
Jacket, Kimono–Type, Multi–Flower, Black, Chinese	135.00
Jacket, Label Bielfeld, Black, 1894, Size 14	45.00
Jacket, Lynx Fur, Medium	500.00

Jacket, Moxie Advertising	175.00
Jacket, Smoking, Man's, Blue & Gold Paisley	20.00
Jacket, Woman's, Green, Velvet Trim, 1895	65.00
Kimono, Embroidered Dragons, Black, Lined	28.00 To 35.00
Kimono, Man's, Tabi Length, Mt. Fuji On Back	225.00
Kimono, Wedding, Embroidered Cranes & Pines On Red, Japanese	145.00
Kimono, Wedding, Embroidered Gold Kiku & Cranes, Japanese, Silk	210.00
Kimono, Wedding, With Tabi & Shoes, Japan, 1973	950.00
Leggings, Child's, Black Knit	8.00
Mittens, Man's, Black & White Stripes, C.1830	65.00
Muff, Black Fur	12.00
Muff, Down–Filled Sealskin	55.00
Muff, Rabbit Fur, Box	35.00
Nightcap, Pale Blue Silk, Net Ruffle,	20.00
Nightgown, Peach Lace, 1930s	26.00
Nightgown, Woman's, Crocheted Yoke	8.00
Nightgown, Woman's, White, Eyelet Yoke	45.00
Obi, Silk, Bird & Floral Pattern, Gold Thread, 1900s, 28 X 166 In.	225.00
Outfit, Man's, Amish, Frock Coat, Vest, Shirt, Trousers	90.00
Pajamas, Lounging, Oriental	16.00 To 20.00
Pantalettes, Split Legs, White Cotton	25.00
Pantaloons, Child's, White Cotton, Victorian	25.00
Pantaloons, Tucked, Embroidered Legs, 30 In.	22.00
Petticoat, Cotton Quilted, White, Crocheted Hem	80.00
Petticoat, Cotton, Lace Trim	14.00
Petticoat, Drawstring, Double Ruffles Flounce	35.00
Petticoat, Victorian, Crocheted Yoke, Tucks, Lace Bottom, Short	27.50
Petticoat, Wool Flannel, Lace Trim	12.00
Robe, Cotton, Embroidery At Shoulders, Hausa, Nigeria	85.00
Robe, Cut Velvet Peony & Bamboo Design, Red Silk, Chinese	125.00
Robe, Embroidered Butterflies On Sleeve Bands, Blue Silk, Chinese	125.00
Robe, Embroidered In Gold, Rose & Blue Threads, Persian, 56 In.	500.00
Sash, Floral Design, Japanese, 120 In.	35.00
Sash, Gold Metallic Floral Design, Oriental, 140 In.	25.00
Shawl, Amish, Heavy Black Wool, Square, Large	45.00
Shawl, Coptic, Silver & White Mesh	200.00
Shawl, Embroidered Silk, White, Grape Vines, Fringe, 1900	195.00
Shawl, Floral Design, Silk, Full Fringe, 3 X 6 Ft.	30.00
Shawl, Maroon & Gold Floral Design, Machine Woven, 60 X 60 In.	30.00
Shawl, Woven Paisley, 61 X 66 In.	62.50
Shirt & Trousers, Boy's, Amish, Broadfall, 2 Piece	29.00
Shirt, Hawaiian Print, 1950s	20.00 To 65.00
Shirt, Man's, Quad Ruffled Front, Lace Inserts, Dart Back	25.00
Shoes, Child's, High Button, Black	50.00
Shoes, Child's, Tan Leather, Silk Ribbon	75.00
Skirt, Black Lace, Lined, 3/4 Sleeve, 1940s	20.00
Skirt, Floor Length, Flounce, 26–In. Waist, 1800	35.00
Skirt, Floor Length, Flounce, 40–In. Waist, 1800s	18.00
Skirt, Pleated Front, 1940s	12.00
Slip, Full, Acetate, Rayon, Shapely Romance, Size 44	9.00
Slip, Girl's, Tucking, Lace Trim	15.00
Slip, Half, Lace Trim, White	32.00
Slip, White Cotton, Full–Length	17.50
Spats, Man's, Pair	13.50
Stole, Mink, Medium, 1960s	150.00
Stole, Peach Machine Knit, Floral, Long Fringe, 1940s	20.00
Suit, Baby's, C.1895	40.00
Suit, Walking, Woman's, Edwardian, Navy Wool	935.00
Suit, White Tie & Tails, Man's	15.00
Teddy, Pink Silk Crepe	15.00
Teddy, Rose Print On White, French Lace Yoke	20.00
Trousers & Shirt, Amish, Boy's, Broadfall	30.00
Underwear, Knit, Thigh Length, Buttons On Side	7.00

Underwear, Long, Bassett–Walker	12.00
Uniform, Portland Policeman, 1940s, 7 Piece	165.00
Vest, Woman's, Patchwork, Medium	25.00
Waistcoat, Mutton Sleeves, Silk	85.00
Wedding Dress, Cream Lace, Separate Slip, 1930s	250.00
Wedding Dress, Irish Lace Crocheted	1100.00
Wedding Dress, Lace, Cream Color, 1930s, Small	250.00
Wedding Dress, Silk, 1911, 2 Piece	70.00
Wedding Gown, Crocheted, Irish Lace Trim	1100.00
Wrapper, White Batiste, Waist Length, Lace Edges, Embroidered	32.00

Cluthra glass is a two–layered glass with small air pockets that form white spots. The Steuben Glass Works of Corning, New York, made it after 1903. Kimball Glass Company of Vineland, New Jersey, made Cluthra from about 1925. Victor Durand signed some pieces with his name.

CLUTHRA, see also Steuben

CLUTHRA, Bowl, Blue To White Rim, Steuben, 12 1/2 In.	550.00
Bowl, Bubbled, Blue, Steuben, 4 X 12 In.	610.00
Bowl, Center, Blue To White, Steuben, 12 1/2 In.	500.00
Bowl, Strawberry, Steuben, 4 X 12 In.	450.00
Plate, Amethyst, Steuben, 3 1/2 In.	400.00
Spittoon, Woman's	285.00
Vase, Blue & White, Drilled For Lamp, Steuben, 11 In.	785.00
Vase, Blue, Steuben, 12 In.	2500.00
Vase, Dark Blue, Steuben, 6 In.	1350.00
Vase, Urn Shape, Lavendar, Steuben, 9 In.	1200.00
Vase, White, Fleu–De–Lis Mark, Steuben, 8 In.	1300.00

Coalbrookdale was made by the Coalport porcelain factory of England during the Victorian period. Pieces are decorated with floral encrustations.

COALBROOKDALE, Basket, Pierced Lid, Flowers & Foliage, Handle, 4 3/4 In.	225.00
Dish, Leaf, Chamberstick Form, Encrusted Flowers, 8 1/2 In.	250.00
Dish, Underplate, Sweetmeat, Insects, Twig Handles, 5 1/2 In.	495.00
Ewer, Applied Flowers, Leaves, Vines, 8 In.	300.00
Jar, Pomander, Pierced Cover, In Molded Saucer, 6 3/4 In.	335.00
Jar, Sweetmeat, Cover, Polychrome Flowers, 4 3/4 In.	380.00
Pitcher, Trumpet Form, Leaf Handle, 8 In., Pair	1500.00

Coalport ware has been made by the Coalport Porcelain Works of England from 1795 to the present time. Early pieces were unmarked. About 1810–1825 the pieces were marked with the name "Coalport" in various forms. Later pieces also had the name "John Rose" in the mark. The crown mark has been used with variations since 1881.

BONE CHINA
COALPORT
MADE IN ENGLAND
EST.1750

COALPORT, Cup & Saucer, Allover Gold Design, Yellow Ground, Cup, 1 In.	100.00
Cup & Saucer, Bluebirds & Floral, Gold Trim	20.00
Cup & Saucer, Indian Tree, Miniature	35.00
Dessert Set, Botanical, Blue, C.1840, 19 Piece	5800.00
Figurine, Miss Prudence	95.00
Plate, Bust of Dewey, Rope Border, Manila, May 1898, 10 1/2 In.	95.00
Plate, Indian Tree, Handles, Square, 9 In.	45.00
Toast Holder, Roman Key Edge, Floral, Marked	35.00

Cobalt blue glass was made using oxide of cobalt. The characteristic bright dark blue identifies it for the collector. Most cobalt glass found today was made after the Civil War.

COBALT BLUE, Bowl, Grape & Cable, 12 In.	195.00
Bowl, Ruffled, 10 In.	55.00
Candlestick, 8 1/2 In., Pair	125.00
Console Set, Large Bowl, 6–In. Candleholder, 3 Piece	135.00
Cruet, Pressed Glass	49.00
Cup & Saucer, Demitasse	35.00

Decanter Set, Silver Overlay, 7 Piece	525.00
Decanter, Scotch, Silver Resist Thistle Design, 10 1/2 In.	50.00
Jug, Incised Tulip, Ribbed Neck, Ovoid, Handle, 14 1/2 In.	1300.00
Mug, King's, Grapevine	35.00
Mustard, Spoon, Tin Lid, Round, 3 1/4 In.	18.00
Swizzle Stick, Glass, Pair	10.00
Tumbler, 9 Oz.	18.00
Tumbler, Art Deco, Chrome Holder, 2 3/4 In., Set of 7	52.00

Coca–Cola was first served in 1886 in Atlanta, Georgia. It was advertised through signs, newspaper ads, coupons, bottles, trays, calendars, and even lamps and clocks. Collectors want anything with the word "Coca–Cola," including a few rare products like gum wrappers and cigar bands. The famous trademark was patented in 1893, the "Coke" mark in 1945. Many modern items and reproductions are being made.

COCA–COLA, Apron, Change, Cloth, Coca–Cola In Bottles	10.00
Ashtray, Metal, 1940	135.00
Bank, Vending Machine, Plastic, 1950	50.00
Barrel, Syrup, 1940s, 5 Gal.	100.00
Baseball Bat	64.00
Billfold, Shows 1915 Bottle, Envelope	85.00
Blotter, 1915	75.00
Blotter, 1956	5.00
Bookmark, Owl, Celluloid, 1906	775.00
Bottle Opener, Drink Coca–Cola, Stationary	2.00
Bottle Opener, World's Fair, 1982	8.00
Bottle, Amber, Pittsburg, Pa., 6 1/2 Oz.	66.00
Bottle, Salida, Colo.	25.00
Bottle, Soda Water, Crown Top, Gulfport, Miss., Aqua, 1926	35.00
Bottle, Soda Water, Embossed Flowers, Green Aqua, Crown Top, 1926	35.00
Bottle, Syrup, Shield Shape Applied Label, 12 In.	50.00
Calendar, 1931, Paper, Norman Rockwell	350.00
Calendar, 1933, Paper	300.00
Calendar, 1935, Rockwell	250.00
Calendar, 1960, Red Disc, 6 In.	50.00
Calendar, 1963, With Sign	55.00
Card Set, Nature Series, Coke Bottle & Logo, 1920s, 12 Piece	10.00
Card Table, 1940s	125.00
Card, Baseball, Del Pratt Swinging A Bat, 1916, 5 X 7 In.	12.00
Card, Playing, 1938	62.00
Card, Playing, Air Force Girl, Graphics, 1943	60.00
Card, Playing, Box, 1956	20.00
Card, Playing, Hund & Eger Bottling Co.	60.00
Card, Playing, Unopened, 1943	85.00
Carrier, Wooden, Christmas Bottle On Ends, 1930s	65.00
Case, Train, 1908	225.00
Changer, Wall, Vendo	350.00
Clock, Drink Coca–Cola, Round, Dated 1951	155.00
Clock, Gilbert, Electric, 1931	495.00
Clock, Light–Up, 1956	95.00
Clock, Neon, Octagonal	7795.00
Clock, Plastic, Glass Face, 1950s	68.00
Coaster, 6 Different Delivery Trucks, Metal, Square, 4 In., 6 Pc.	14.50
Coin–Operated Machine, 10 Cent, 1952	1800.00
Coin–Operated Machine, Bottle Storage, 10 Cent, 3 X 1 1/2 Ft.	350.00
Coin–Operated Machine, Jacob No.26	500.00
Coin–Operated Machine, Vendo 44	950.00
Cooler, 1950s, 2 X 3 Ft.	75.00
Cooler, Arrow, Aluminum, 1940s	250.00
Cooler, Educational Cards, Salesman's Sample, 12 X 7 X 10 In.	1650.00
Cooler, Glasscock Jr., Floor Model, Square, 17 In.	1500.00
Cooler, Junior, Dated 1930	995.00
Cooler, Picnic, 1950s	75.00

Cooler, Radio, 1949, 7 X 12 X 9 1/2 In.	695.00
Cooler, Salesman's Sample, 1934 Model, 8 1/2 X 9 X 11 In.	2800.00
Cooler, Wooden, 1920s	150.00
Coupon, With 1909 Calendar Pad, 1904	550.00
Critter, Penguin, Stuffed, 9 In.	13.00
Cuff Links, Red, White, 1950s	25.00
Dish, Pretzel, 3 Bottle Legs	95.00
Dish, Pretzel, Aluminum, 1930s	150.00
Dispenser, Soda Fountain, Counter	245.00
Display, Bottle, With Cap, Dec. 25, 1923, 20 In.	250.00
Doll, Santa Claus, Rubber Face & Hands, Holds Bottle, 12 In.	250.00
Door Push, Porcelain, Come In Have A Coca–Cola, 11 X 3 1/2 In.	335.00
Door Push, Porcelain, French, 1930s, 11 X 4 In.	100.00
Fan, 1920s	25.00
Flag, Truck, 1950s, 12 X 18 In.	75.00
Fly Swatter	7.00
Folder, Progress of Electricity, 22 X 32 In., 4 Different Scenes	10.00
Game, Bingo	60.00
Game, Dominoes, 19 Piece	55.00
Ice Scoop	6.00
Ingot, 75th Anniversary Bottling Plants, Silver	25.00
Jackknife, Brass, 1903	125.00
Jar, Gum, 1908	595.00
Jug, Syrup, 1940s, 1 Gal.	50.00
Knife, Bread, French Ivory Handle, Red Printing, 1900	20.00
Knife, Cornwall Knife Co., Box	35.00
Knife, Pocket, Chicago World's Fair, 1933	27.50
Knife, World's Fair, 5 Cent, 1933	30.00
Lighter, Cigarette, Bottle Shape, Metal Cap, 2 1/2 In.	15.00 To 25.00
Magazine, Coca–Cola Red Barrel, No.9, 1949	8.00
Magazine, Trade, Red Barrel, 1926	25.00
Mat, Autumn Girl, Cloth, Round, 1943	135.00
Matchbook Cover, 1930s	2.00
Menu, Lillian, 1904	650.00
Mirror, 1905, Pocket, Juanita	275.00
Mirror, 1906, Pocket, Relieves Fatigue	375.00 To 585.00
Mirror, 1909, Pocket, Coca–Cola Girl	565.00
Mirror, 1911, Pocket, Coca–Cola Girl	175.00 To 225.00
Mirror, 1917, Pocket, Elaine	180.00 To 200.00
Mold, Bottle, Non–Returnable Bottles	135.00
Neckerchief, Kit Carson	9.00
Notepad, Celluloid, 1903	625.00
Paperweight, Calendar, Mid–Atlantic	20.00
Pencil Sharpener, Figural, Cast Iron, Painted, Germany, 1930	75.00
Penholder, Music Box, Miniature Cooler	125.00
Pin, Official Olympic International Flag, Box, Set of 50	345.00
Ping–Pong Set	55.00
Plaque, Award, Atlanta, Plant's 1st 50 Years, Bronze, 14 X 18 In.	675.00
Plate, Knowles China Co., 7 1/4 In.	235.00
Plate, Vienna Art, Tin, 1905	300.00
Poster, Empire Strikes Back, 1980, 24 X 33 In.	12.00
Pushbar, Expandable, Tin, Red, Yellow, White, 3 X 30 In.	85.00
Rack, 6–Pack, Tin Sign Top, 6 For 25 Cents, Iron Base, 53 In.	150.00
Radio, Bottle Shape	35.00 To 95.00
Recipe Book, 1951	8.00
Sign, 2 Sides, Coca–Cola Dispenser, Porcelain, 16 X 16 In.	193.00
Sign, 3 Girls, Cardboard, 1942, 56 X 27 1/2 In.	225.00
Sign, 5 Cent Coke, Tin, 1922, 6 X 23 In.	350.00
Sign, 5–Color, Bottom Slotted Ribs, Bottle In Circle, 20 X 24 In.	275.00
Sign, 6 Pack, 1937, 54 X 18 In.	225.00
Sign, Bottle In Sun, Tin & Masonite, 1940, 19 X 28 In.	250.00
Sign, Bottle Shape, 6 Ft.	575.00
Sign, Bottle Shape, Cutout, Tin, 1950, 3 Ft.	350.00
Sign, Canadian, Red, Yellow, Green, White, 31 X 12 In.	175.00

Sign, Canadian, Red, Yellow, White, 1946, 12 X 29 In. 70.00
Sign, Cardboard, 1946, 29 X 50 In. 350.00
Sign, Charm of Coca–Cola, Soda Fountain, Sepia, Barclay, 12 In. 20.00
Sign, Coca–Cola In Bottles 5 Cents, Tin, 1920s 395.00
Sign, Drink Coca–Cola, Fountain Service, Both Sides, 63 X 42 In. 400.00
Sign, Fishtail, 1960s, 26 X 56 In. 100.00
Sign, Fountain Service, Porcelain, 1950s, 12 X 28 In. 195.00
Sign, Fountain Service, Porcelain, 1950s, 22 X 26 In. 850.00
Sign, Girl With Bottle, 1941, 20 X 28 In. 225.00
Sign, Ice Cold Coca–Cola Sold Here, 5 Colors, Tin 295.00
Sign, Porcelain, Script, 1929, 10 X 28 In. 475.00
Sign, Santa Claus, Cardboard, Easel Back, 54 In. 150.00
Sign, Sidewalk, 6 For 25 Cents, 1930s, 19 X 28 In. 295.00
Sign, Sidewalk, Take Home A Carton, 1950s, 19 X 28 In. 250.00
Sign, Things Go Better With Coke, Button, Bottle, 17 1/2 X 54 In. 85.00
Sign, Triangle Shape, Original Bracket, 1930s 795.00
Sign, Truck, Sign of Good Taste, Metal, Button, 16 In. 150.00
Sign, Turtle, Embossed, 20 X 15 In., 1920s 1350.00
Sign, With Bottle, Flange, 1948 .... 275.00
Sign, Woman & Bottle, Tin, November 1940 .... 400.00
Sign, World War II Nurse, Gold Frame, 55 X 36 In. 150.00
Stamp Book, Our America, Complete, 1945 .... 6.50
Stamp Holder, With Calendar, Celluloid, 1900 .... 750.00
Stand, Place Empties Here 65.00
Street Marker, Brass, Alabama Foundry, Safety Drink First 125.00
String Holder, Red Button On Panels, 1930s, 14 X 16 In. 450.00
Tally Card, Whist 3.00
Teaching Kit, Our America Series, Making Motion Pictures, 1943 .... 300.00
Telephone, Bottle 45.00
Thermometer, 2 Bottles, Tin, 1941, 15 1/2 X 7 In. 176.00
Thermometer, Bottle Shape, 1950, 10 In. 50.00
Thermometer, Bottle Shape, Tin, 1929, 17 In. 110.00
Thermometer, Cigar Shape, 1950s 75.00
Thermometer, Coke, Gold Bottle 125.00
Thermometer, Enameled, Girl Picture Base, 6 X 18 In. 335.00
Thermometer, Gold Bottle, 1938, 16 In. 125.00
Thermometer, In Bottles, Round, 1950 .... 65.00
Thermometer, Red, Round, 1950s 85.00
Thermometer, Silhouette Girl, Canadian, 1940, 18 X 16 In. 225.00
Thermometer, Silhouette, 1940s 140.00
Tip Tray, 1900, Hilda Clark, 5 5/8 In. 1925.00
Tip Tray, 1912, Hamilton King Girl 160.00
Tip Tray, 1914, Betty ....95.00 To 165.00
Tip Tray, 1917, Elaine, 6 In. ....116.00 To 150.00
Tip Tray, 1920, Garden Girl 285.00
Tip Tray, 1926, Golfers 550.00
Toy, Yo–Yo, 1930s 150.00
Training Film, Christmas Campaign, Gift For Thirst, Profit, 1953 .... 35.00
Trash Can 225.00
Tray, 1909, Hamilton King Girl 95.00
Tray, 1914, Betty 250.00
Tray, 1917, Elaine 125.00
Tray, 1920, Garden Girl 385.00
Tray, 1921, Summer Girl ....125.00 To 225.00
Tray, 1922, Autumn Girl ....325.00 To 375.00
Tray, 1923, Flapper Girl 225.00
Tray, 1924, Smiling Girl ....265.00 To 350.00
Tray, 1925, Girl At Party ....165.00 To 176.00
Tray, 1926, Sports Couple, Golfers 550.00
Tray, 1929, Girl In Swimsuit ....155.00 To 215.00
Tray, 1931, Farm Boy With Dog, Rockwell 750.00
Tray, 1936, Hostess 120.00
Tray, 1937, Running Girl ....85.00 To 125.00
Tray, 1938, Girl In The Afternoon ....55.00 To 145.00

Tray, 1939, Springboard Girl	75.00 To 135.00
Tray, 1940, Sailor Girl	87.00 To 110.00
Tray, 1941, Girl Ice Skater	155.00
Tray, 1942, Two Girls At Car	85.00
Tray, 1950, Girl With Menu, French	30.00
Tray, 1976, Montreal Olympics	125.00 To 135.00
Tumbler, Gold Cover, 1950s, 10 Oz.	50.00
Tumbler, Santa Claus	4.00
Wallet, Pigskin, 1950s	35.00
Watch Fob, Brass	295.00
Watch Fob, Celluloid, 1911	650.00
Watch, Pocket	135.00
Whistle, Purest Sunlight, Wooden, 1930s	75.00

Coffee grinders of home size were first made about 1894. They lost favor by the 1930s. Large floor–standing or counter model coffee grinders were used in the nineteenth–century country store. The renewed interest in fresh–ground coffee has produced many modern electric and hand grinders, and reproductions of the old styles are being made.

COFFEE GRINDER, Arcade, Glass Top & Tumbler, Crank Handle, 19 In.	175.00
Arcade, No.3, Crystal	75.00
Arcade, No.4, Wall Mount	145.00
Arcade, Telephone Mill	395.00
Brass Hopper, Iron & Wood Handle, Wooden, 9 In.	85.00
Charles Parker, Wall, Hinged Lid, Crank Handle, Tin & Iron	85.00
Elgin Mfg., Hand Crank, Iron Stand, Red, Gold Trim, 65 In.	1350.00
Enterprise, 8 1/2.–In. Wheel	375.00
Enterprise, Award Winning, 1876, 24 In.	850.00
Enterprise, Double Wheel, 1873, 8 3/4–In. Wheel	150.00
Enterprise, Model 0, Clamp On Table Model	60.00
Enterprise, No. 2, 2 Wheels, Iron Drawer, 12 In.	623.00
Enterprise, No.750, Single Wheel, 17 In.	100.00
Golden Rule, Wall Mount, See Through Window	190.00 To 250.00
Kar–A–Van, Lithographed Tin, Camels, Color	875.00
Landers Ferry & Clark, No.20, 2 Wheels, Wood Base, 12 In.	660.00
Lap, Walnut Box, Metal Hopper, Dovetailed Drawer, 1844, 6 In.	225.00
Oster, Glass Top, Counter Top, Electric	40.00
Parker, Crank Handle, No.90, 10 X 18 In.	175.00
Persepolis, Counter	275.00
Pine, Dovetailed, Box, Square, 6 In.	97.50
Steinfeld, Glass Top, Cast Iron, Wall	45.00
Swift Mill, Lane Bros., Red, Blue & Gold Paint, 18 In.	605.00
T. & C. Clark, Lap, Iron Body & Drawer, Brass Cup	130.00
Universal, Metal, 7 In.	35.00
Universal, Model 012, Cast Iron & Tin	40.00
Wilson's Improved, Wall Mounted, Cast Iron, Brass Insert	35.00

Coin spot is a glass pattern that was named by the collectors. It features coinlike spots as part of the glass. Colored, clear, and opalescent glass was made with the spots. Many companies used the design in the 1870–90 period. It is so popular that reproductions are still being made.

COIN SPOT, Banana Boat, Ruffle Trim, Green	65.00
Castor, Pickle, Tongs, Enameled Flowers, Plated Holder	475.00
Creamer, Cranberry	35.00
Finger Lamp, Hobbs, Cranberry Opalescent	425.00
Muffineer, Green	85.00
Pitcher, Clear Handle, Crimped Top, Cranberry	160.00
Pitcher, Ribbed Handle, Vaseline, 8 1/2 In.	85.00
Pitcher, Water, Green	135.00
Shade, White Opalescent, 4 3/4 X 8 3/4 In.	85.00
Sugar Shaker, Cranberry	110.00
Syrup, 9 Panel, Blue Opalescent	90.00

Syrup, Clear & Opalescent, Swirl	85.00
Syrup, Nine Panel, Green	135.00
Tumbler, Water, Mother–of–Pearl, Rose To White, 3 5/8 In.	110.00
Vase, Narrow Neck, Fluted, Large	75.00

The vending machine is an ancient invention dating back to 200 B.C. when holy water was dispensed in a coin–operated vase. Smokers in seventeenth–century England could buy tobacco from a coin–operated box. It was not until after the Civil War that the technology made modern coin–operated games and vending machines plentiful. Slot machines, arcade games, and dispensers are all collected.

COIN–OPERATED MACHINE, Baseball, Daval, Miniature	770.00
Baseball, Hi–Fly, Central	330.00
Baseball, Skill Game	225.00
Baseball, Slugger, Marvel, 5 Cent, 1930s	250.00
Booz Barometer, Counter Top, 5 Cent	75.00
Candy, Abbey, With Tray	60.00
Candy, Brice Williams, Slug Rejector	435.00
Candy, Zeno, Wood	250.00
Cigarette, Buckley Cent–A–Pack, 1 Cent	375.00
Claw, Candy, Digger, Exhibit Rotary	1500.00
Coin Changer, Hopkins & Robinson, 1883	2500.00
Coin Counter, Standard Johnson, 1900s	125.00
Digger, Electro–Hoist, Floor Model, 5 Cent	2000.00
Digger, Erie, Claw	1100.00
Digger, Mutoscope, Iron Claw, Floor Model, Walnut	2500.00
Digger, Steam Shovel, Chicago Coin	600.00
Fortune–Teller, Ask Grandma, Life Size, Moving	5500.00
Fortune–Teller, Ask The Pharaoh	825.00
Fortune–Teller, Berger, 1 Cent	2800.00
Fortune–Teller, Card Vendor, Cards, Hand Painted	650.00
Fortune–Teller, Exhibit Supply Co.	225.00
Fortune–Teller, Horoscopes, Watling, 1 Cent	1200.00
Fortune–Teller, Wizard, 1 Cent, Oak, 16 1/2 X 13 In.	220.00
Golf, Pen–Nee	500.00
Gum, Adams, Chrome Plated, 1 Cent	125.00
Gum, D'Lish–Us, Bottle Shape, Cast Iron	4400.00
Gum, Dentyne & Stick, Wall, 5 Cent	100.00
Gum, Ford, 1 Cent, 1950 ....60.00 To	125.00
Gum, Mansfields Automatic Clerk, 5 Cent, 12 In.	550.00
Gum, Pulver, 3 Selections, Yellow, Mirror In Top	175.00
Gum, Pulver, Cop Directing Traffic, Porcelain Case	750.00
Gum, Zeno, Yellow Porcelain	425.00
Gumball, Atlas Masters	37.50
Gumball, Auto Sales	675.00
Gumball, B & D, Hit The Target, Penny Drop, Key, 1950	175.00
Gumball, Bally, Double Bell, 5 Cent–25 Cent	3000.00
Gumball, Bally, Poker Spinner	2000.00
Gumball, Burnham & Mills, 1 Cent	1250.00
Gumball, Caille, Center Pull, 1 Cent	1150.00
Gumball, Captain America, Box, 1984	50.00
Gumball, Columbus, 1 Cent, Label, 17 In.	293.00
Gumball, Columbus, 8–Sided Globe, Barrel Lock, 1928	275.00
Gumball, E–Z, Cast Aluminum Base, 18 In.	116.00
Gumball, Ford, Pat.1919	200.00
Gumball, Jennings, In The Bag	295.00
Gumball, Masters, 1923	160.00
Gumball, Masters, 5 Cent, Gooseneck	275.00
Gumball, Mills Sega, Columbia, Cast Iron	475.00
Gumball, Northwestern Moon Rocket, 1 Cent	195.00
Gumball, Oak Acorn, 1950s	50.00
Gumball, Peanut, Acorn, Tall Glass Globe, 1950s	50.00
Gumball, Rock–Ola, Horse Race	875.00

Gumball, Silver King	65.00
Gumball, Victor Topper, 1 Cent, 1950	65.00
Gumball, Victor Universal	65.00
Gumball, Victor Vending, Super V, 1954	75.00
Gumball, Victor, Halfback, 1950 .... 25.00 To 40.00	
Gumball, Victor, Vendorama, 1 Cent	25.00
Horoscope, Filled With Original Horoscopes, 1950s	45.00
Horse Race, 25–Cent Payout, 60 X 47 In.	3500.00
Horse Race, Derby, 1 Cent	1350.00
Legal Target Penny Flip	1100.00
Lighter Fluid, Mixed Metals, 1 Cent, 19 In.	109.00
Love Tester, Munves	600.00
Match Dispenser, Diamond, 1 Cent	425.00
Match Dispenser, Dolphin, Iron, Cigar Cutter, 1 Cent ...	475.00
Match Dispenser, Rosebud, Northwestern, 1 Cent	250.00
Mills, Operator's Bell, 25 Cent, 1915	1900.00
Mills, Operator's Bell, Horseshoes, Spades	400.00
Movie, Caille, Cail–O–Scope, 4 Movies	3750.00
Muscle Developer, Mills, Owl Front	1200.00
Mutoscope, Hockey, Original Marquee .... 1000.00 To 1200.00	
Peanut, Advance, Big Mouth	175.00
Peanut, Advance, Hurricane Lamp Shape, 10 Cent	880.00
Peanut, Atlas, Bantam, Key, 5 Cent	150.00
Peanut, Columbus, Green Porcelain Iron, 1 Cent, 1920 .	4250.00
Peanut, Northwestern 33, Frosted Globe, Locks	350.00
Peanut, Northwestern 49er, 5 Cent, 1949	42.00
Peanut, Northwestern, 33, Red Porcelain, 1 Cent	130.00
Peanut, Pulver, Clown	380.00
Peanut, Regal, 5 Cent	110.00
Peanut, Silver King .... 85.00 To 150.00	
Peanut, Spaniard, Guitar, Glass, Iron, 1 Cent, 13 In.	132.00
Peanut, Victor Universal, Large Round Globe, 1 Cent	80.00
Peanut, Victor, 1 Cent, 1940s	50.00
Peanut, Yu–Chu	85.00
Peep Show, Exhibit Supply Co., Do You Dare	350.00
Peep Show, Mutoscope, Naughty But Nice	850.00
Perfume, Lion's Head, Iron, Wooden, 1 Cent, 20 In.	990.00
Personality Indicator, Exhibit Supply, 1 Cent	400.00
Pick–A–Pack Windmill, Baker	825.00
Picture, Caille, Cail–O–Scope, Nudie Cutie, Drop	1000.00
Picture, Rosenberg, Drop Picture	550.00
Pinball Hi–Ball, Marble, Steel Balls, 1910	500.00
Pinball, Bally, Fireball	1700.00
Pinball, Bally, Four Million B.C.	1000.00
Pinball, Genco, Baseball, 5 Cent, 1935	1200.00
Pinball, Gottlieb, Liberty Bell, 1933	450.00
Pinball, Gottlieb, Pro Football	175.00
Pinball, Japanese Pochinko Gambling	30.00
Pinball, Kentucky Derby, 5 Cent	200.00
Pinball, Northwestern, 4 Games In One	30.00
Pinball, Rock–Ola, Chicago World's Fair, 1933	1500.00
Pinball, Stoner, Beacon	350.00
Play Golf, Arcade	4950.00
Popcorn, Creator, Twin Poppers, Beveled Glass, Floor ...	5800.00
Popcorn, Movie Theater, Lights, Metal, Fringed, 1930s .	175.00
Prophylactic, Advance, Keys, 1923	50.00
Prophylactic, Harlon, Key, 1920s	65.00
Secret–In–The–Ear Communications System	1250.00
Shell Game, Automated Wizard	2200.00
Shock, Spear The Dragon	5800.00
Shooting Gallery, U.S. Marshall	522.00
Slot, 20th Century Novelty Co., Spiral, 1906	2200.00
Slot, Bally, Double Bell, 5 & 25 Cent	3000.00
Slot, Caille, Naked Lady, Jackpot, 5 Cent	2750.00

Slot, Golden Falls, 1 Dollar, Mills	1980.00
Slot, Jennings, Duchess, 1 Cent	950.00
Slot, Jennings, Dutch Boy & Girl, With Gum Vendor	200.00
Slot, Jennings, Entry Vendor, 5 Cent	1400.00
Slot, Jennings, Little Duke, 1 Cent	2200.00
Slot, Jennings, Nevada Club, 50 Cent	1500.00
Slot, Jennings, Peacock Vendor, 5 Cent	2100.00
Slot, Jennings, Rockaway, 1 Cent	1200.00
Slot, Jennings, Standard Club Chief, 50 Cent	1750.00
Slot, Jennings, Sun Chief, Brass Indian Head, 10 Cent	2000.00
Slot, Jennings, Victoria, 5 Cent	1700.00
Slot, Little Stock Broker, England	295.00
Slot, Mills, 25 Cent	1430.00
Slot, Mills, Bell Boy	3750.00
Slot, Mills, Black Cherry, 5 Cent	1400.00 To 1870.00
Slot, Mills, Bursting Cherry, 5 Cent	2900.00
Slot, Mills, Castle Front, 5 Cent	1700.00
Slot, Mills, Eleven & Field	2000.00
Slot, Mills, Hightop, 25 Cent	1200.00
Slot, Mills, Judge, Upright, 5 Cent	7000.00
Slot, Mills, Jumbo Parade	440.00 To 695.00
Slot, Mills, Lift & Dumbbell	6500.00
Slot, Mills, Little Perfection, Oak, 5–Reel Card	500.00
Slot, Mills, Mountain Man, 25 Cent	2300.00
Slot, Mills, Poinsettia, 5 Cent	2750.00
Slot, Mills, Roman Head, Gold Award & Jackpot, 1932	1175.00
Slot, Mills, Silent Mystery, 1 Cent	1650.00
Slot, Mills, Super Bell Lion, 5 Cent, 1932	1650.00
Slot, Pace, Comet All Star, 1 Cent	990.00
Slot, Royal Comet, Floor Model, 5 Cent, 1930s	2500.00
Slot, Universal, Console, Two–Way, 5 & 25 Cents, 1939	650.00
Slot, Watling, Baby Gold Seal Award	1800.00
Slot, Watling, Blue Seal, 5 Cent	2200.00
Slot, Watling, Brownie	4000.00
Slot, Watling, Lincoln DeLux, 5 Cent	1700.00
Slot, Watling, Rol–A–Top, 10 Cent	4400.00
Slot, Watling, Rol–A–Top, Cherry Front	6750.00
Slot, Watling, Treasury, 1 Cent	3850.00
Slot, Watling, Twin Jack	1400.00
Slot, Zeno, 3 Reel, Amber, Plastic, Visible Works, 3 In	. 100.00
Soccer Game, Pollard	1210.00
Stamp, 11 Cent Air Mail, 8 Cent Surface Slots	120.00
Stamp, Postage, 5 Cent	45.00
Stamp, Uncle Sam, Porcelain, 5 & 10 Cent, 1938	60.00
Stamp, Uncle Sam, Porcelain, 5 Cent, 1940	95.00
Stamping, Lord's Prayer	200.00
Strength Tester, Mercury, 1 Cent	125.00
Toy Capsules, Victor, Filled, 1950	70.00
Trade Stimulator, Baker, Pick–A–Pack	675.00
Trade Stimulator, Bluebird Target	145.00
Trade Stimulator, Buckley Horses	385.00
Trade Stimulator, Caille, 25 Reel Quinette	9500.00
Trade Stimulator, Dice King Six Jr., B.A. Withey	500.00
Trade Stimulator, Griswold, Wheel of Fortune, 5 Cent	600.00
Trade Stimulator, Indian Penny Hit The Target, Key	500.00
Trade Stimulator, Keeney, Magic Clock	375.00
Trade Stimulator, Keeney, Pick–A–Pack	400.00
Trade Stimulator, King Six Jr., Dice Game	650.00
Trade Stimulator, Puritan Bell, 1 Cent, 11 X 9 In.	688.00
Vendor, Collar Button, 10 Cent, Zeno	440.00 To 750.00
Vendor, Hot Nut, Eat 'Em Hot, Cup Dispenser, 1934	275.00
Vendor, Hot Nut, Glass Globe, Asco	175.00 To 225.00
Vendor, Jennings, Improved Century, 5 Cent	1500.00
Vendor, Jennings, Mints of Quality	1650.00

Vendor, Jennings, Peacock, 5 Cent	2100.00
Vendor, Jennings, Rockaway, 1 Cent	1200.00
Watling, Rol–A–Top, 5 Cent	3000.00
Wheel of Fortune, Griswold	770.00

Collector plates are modern plates produced in limited editions. Some will be found listed under the factory name, such as Bing & Grondahl, Royal Copenhagen, Royal Doulton, and Wedgwood. Pictures and more price information can be found in "Kovels' Price Guide for Collector Plates, Figurines, Paperweights and Other Limited Editions."

COLLECTOR PLATE, Anri, Christmas, 1985	120.00 To 165.00
Avon, Christmas, 1973	60.00
Avon, Christmas, 1973 To 1980, 8 Piece	375.00
Avon, Christmas, 1974	25.00 To 35.00
Avon, Christmas, 1983	10.00
Avon, Christmas, 1985	7.00 To 18.00
Avon, Mother's Day, 1952	3.50
Avon, Mother's Day, 1981	11.00
Avon, Mother's Day, 1985	5.00
Avon, Tenderness, 1974	10.00
Bossons, Bush Baby	32.00
Bossons, Chipmunks	32.00
Bossons, Squirrel	32.00
DeGrazia, Bronco, Apache Scout	65.00
DeGrazia, Los Ninos	1395.00
DeGrazia, White Dove	185.00
Fenton, Christmas, Church, Milk Glass, 1970	50.00
Fenton, Mother's Day, Bunny, 1982	50.00
Fenton, Mother's Day, Fawn, 1981	25.00
Ferrandiz, Mother's Day, All Hearts, Wooden	75.00
Halbert, Snow Owls	40.00
Hallmark, Christmas, Pewter, Partridge In A Pear Tree, 1977	130.00
Holly Hobbie, Christmas, 1979, 8 In.	10.00
Incolay, Antony & Cleopatra	85.00
Jean Paul Loup, Christmas, Betourne, 1973	600.00
Jean Paul Loup, Mother's Day, Champleve, Betourne, 1974	1200.00
Knowles, Bathsheba & Solomon	109.00
Knowles, Gone With The Wind, Scarlett	250.00
Knowles, Over The Rainbow, Judy Garland, 1st Edition	100.00
Knowles, Pharaoh's Daugher, Moses	60.00
Perillo, Apache Girl, 1977	270.00
Perillo, Chief Sitting Bull	485.00
Perillo, Silent Night	25.00
Perillo, Wheeler Dealer	135.00
Perillo, Young Sitting Bull	35.00
Rigolette, Alabaster, 1st Edition	50.00
Rockwell, Cobbler	119.00
Rockwell, Day After Christmas, 1979	45.00
Rockwell, John F. Kennedy	50.00
Rockwell, Light Campaign Series	150.00
Rockwell, Looking Out To Sea, Burnished Copper, R. Brown	395.00
Rockwell, Room That Light Made	63.00
Rockwell, Spring Flowers	119.00
Rockwell, Toy Maker	179.00
Skelton, Anyone For Tennis?	55.00
Skelton, Freddie's Shack	100.00
Sports, Arnold Palmer, Signed	125.00
Sports, Carl Yastrzemski, Signed	125.00
Sports, Mickey Mantle, Signed	195.00

Comic art, or cartoon art, is a relatively new field of collecting. Original comic strips, magazine covers, and even printed strips are collected. The first daily comic strip was printed in 1907. The paintings on celluloid used for movie cartoons are listed in this book under Animation Art.

COMIC ART, Krazy Kat, Sunday Page, June 10, 1917, Original Art	7000.00
Li'L Abner, Abner In Society, Original Art, 1936, 5 X 22 In.	590.00
Li'L Abner, March 22, 1940, Original Art, 6 X 22 In.	200.00
Strip, Popeye, King Features, 1931, 15 Piece	10.00
Tarzan, Sept. 10, 1933, Egyptian Scene, Original Art, 27 X 20 In.	2200.00

Commemorative items have been made to honor members of royalty and those of great national fame. World's fairs and important historical events are also remembered with commemorative pieces.

COMMEMORATIVE, see also Coronation; World's Fair

COMMEMORATIVE, Beaker, George V, Silver Jubilee, Pottery	45.00
Bowl, Victoria Diamond Jubilee, Portrait, Fluted, 6 1/2 In.	85.00
Cup & Saucer, Queen Mother, Portrait In Cup Bottom	45.00
Handkerchief, Queen Victoria Jubilee Concert, Silk, 1887	20.00
Medal, A. Lincoln, Centenary, 12 Feb. 1909, Silver, 2 In.	175.00
Mug, George V, Silver Jubilee, Pottery	45.00
Napkin Ring, King & Queen Coronation, Metal, 1937	15.00
Picture, Victoria, Jubilee, Portrait, Crocheted Flags, 9 In.	150.00
Pin Tray, Edward VII, Alfred Meakin	32.50
Plate, George V, Silver Jubilee, Pottery, 6 In.	35.00
Plate, King George VI, Square, 8 1/2 In.	45.00
Plate, Princess Anne Wedding, Aynsley, 9 1/2 In.	60.00
Plate, Queen Victoria Jubilee, Portrait, 10 In.	75.00
Plate, Queen Victoria Jubilee, Royal Worcester, 1887	195.00

A woman did not powder her face in public until after World War I. By 1920 the beauty parlor, permanent waves, and cosmetics had become acceptable. A few companies sold cake face powder in a box with a mirror and a pad or puff. Soon the compact was being designed by jewelers and made of gold, silver, and precious materials. Cosmetic companies began to sell powder in attractive compacts of less valuable metal or plastic. Collectors today search for Art Deco designs, commemorative compacts from world's fairs or political events, and unusual examples. Many were made with companion lipsticks and other fittings.

COMPACT, Acanthus Leaf Design, Sterling Silver	185.00
Baroque, Scalloped Edge, Gold Graphics, England	22.50
Black Fabric Inserts, Bakelite, 4 In.	25.00
Boston National Bank, With Pocket Mirror, Celluloid	30.00
Clair Jane, Art Deco, White Enameled, Signed, Oval	25.00
Coty, Airspun, With Lipstick Holder	20.00
Coty, Gold Metal & Fabric Pouch	7.00
Elgin, American, Engraved EEW On Back, Sterling	45.00
Elgin, American, Gold Tone, Etched Floral Spray, Red Flower	24.50
Elgin, Basket of Flowers Design, Sterling, Signed	60.00
Elgin, Bird Shape, Wings Open, Sterling Silver, Gilt, Dali, 4 In.	302.00
Elgin, Pancake, Brushed Silver Tone, Flannel, Box	48.00
Elgin, Pink & Blue, Mirrored Case	35.00
Elizabeth Arden, Scroll Design, Sifter Style, Swiss, 3 3/4 In.	50.00
Elizabeth Arden, Star Design	15.00
Estee Lauder, Hunter's Pocket Watch, With Chain, Chrome	24.50
Evans, Art Deco, Orange Enameled, Bulldog Center, Lipstick Holder	55.00
Evening In Paris, Brilliant	12.00
Evening Set, With Lipstick, Comb In Satin Case	150.00
Faberge, Enameled Metal, Logo, Extra Powder Insert, Triangular	25.00
Girl Painted On Ivory, Inlaid, Filigree Case	225.00
Gorham, Repousse Roses, Sterling, Inscribed, 3 In.	175.00
Hand Painted Ballerina, Glitter Trim, Lipstick Holder	50.00

Heart Shape, Gold Monogram, Sterling Silver	25.00
Heart Shape, Marcasites, Initial V	45.00
Horse & Rider Over Fence, Blue Leather, 1939	15.00
Houbigant, 6–Sided, Floral Basket, Compartment Flips To Mirror	38.00
Lady Vanity, Black Leather On Celluloid	22.00
Makeup & Coins, Chain, German Silver	95.00
Merle Norman, Floral Embossed, Gold Tone	18.00
Mother–of–Pearl, 1950s	40.00
Natural Pearl, Diamond, Silver & Platinum, With Lighter, 1930	5750.00
Norida Nouveau	65.00
Pattie Duette Flat Vivaudou, Necessaire, Gold Plated, Mesh Handle	45.00
Phone Dial	15.00
Pocket Watch Shape, Gold Filled	14.00
Queen Elizabeth, Round	40.00
Shield's Inc., Gold & Enameled, Embossed Stripes, Square	18.00
Silver Beaded, Art Deco, Hinged Silver Lid, 2 1/2 In.	15.00
Sterling, With Loop, Initial, 1 1/2 In.	40.00
Stratton, Enameled, Round	10.00
Volupte, Red & Clear Rhinestone Ornament	25.00
Wadsworth, Sterling	50.00
World's Fair, 1939	30.00

Consolidated Lamp and Glass Company of Coraopolis, Pennsylvania, was founded in 1894. The company made lamps, tablewares, and art glass. Collectors are particularly interested in the wares made after 1925, including black satin glass, Martele (which resembled Lalique), and colored glasswares. The company closed for the final time in 1967.

CONSOLIDATED GLASS, Compote, Martele, Birds, Yellow Frosted	50.00
Vase, Ruba Rombic, C.1928, 9 In.	2400.00
Vase, Yellow Flowers, Green Leaves, White, 9 1/2 In.	60.00

The term "contemporary glass" refers to art glass made since 1950. Some contemporary glass factories, such as Orrefors or Baccarat, are listed under their own categories.

CONTEMPORARY GLASS, Bowl, Blue, Glen Lukens, 11 1/2 In.	125.00
Bowl, Diamond Pattern, Kosta, 3 1/2 In. ¢Illus	139.00
Bowl, Vertical Air Traps, Lindstrand–Kosta, 3/14 In.	95.00
Figurine, Aerial, Blue, Clear, Dated 1973, Labino	600.00
Figurine, Breakthrough, Amber, Labino, 7 3/4 In.	725.00
Figurine, Incised Angel Fish, Jon Cerny, 3 In.	100.00
Rose Bowl, Prunts Pulled Into Flowers, Labino	950.00
Sauce, Dark Pink Grapes Cover, Handle, Sacha	27.00
Vase, 5 Pulled Leaves, Charles Lotton, 1977, 8 3/4 In.	357.50
Vase, Amber Loop, Gray Stripes, Harvey Littleton, Signed	550.00
Vase, Blue–Green Cased Festoons, Labino	650.00
Vase, Flowers, Vines, Signed Lotton, 1973, 8 1/2 In.	350.00
Vase, Orange Shades, Cobalt Blue, Labino, 5 3/4 In.	1500.00
Vase, Pulled Feather, Blue, Vandermark, 10 In.	225.00
Vase, Square Foot, Art Deco, Faceted Rim, Kosta, 10 In.	185.00

Cookbooks are collected for various reasons. Some are wanted for the recipes, some for investment, and some as examples of advertising. Cookbooks and recipe pamphlets are included in this section.

COOKBOOK, 52 Sunday Dinners, Hiller, 1915	20.00
100 Grand National Recipes, 6th Grand, 1955	6.00
Advice To Wife & Mother, P.Chavasse, New York, 1873	90.00
American Woman's Cookbook, 1947, 823 Pages	17.50
American Woman's, Blackstone, 1910	10.00
Amish Pennsylvania Dutch, 1936	9.00
Angelus Recipe Booklet	15.00
Aunt Jemima, 1928	30.00
Baker's Chocolate, Full–Color Pages, 1932	30.00

Baker's Cocoa, 1931 .... 6.00
Baker's Cocoa, Woman Holding Tray Cover, 1916 .... 55.00
Better Homes & Gardens, 1953 .... 15.00
Bisquick, Movie Star, 1935 .... 10.00
Book of Unusual Cookery, 1928, 40 Pages, 10 X 13 1/2 In. 7.50
Borden, Elsie, 1942 .... 20.00
Brer Rabbit Molasses, 1936 ....6.00 To 10.00
Calumet Baking Powder Co., English & German, 1920s, 16 Pages 10.00
Calumet Baking Powder Co., Reliable Recipes, 1920s 15.00
Ceresota Cookbook, M. Neil, Minn. 30.00
Cheek Neal Coffee Co., 1925 .... 5.00
Cyclopaedia of Practical Recipes, Cooley, 1857 .... 90.00
Elsie The Cow, Hardbound, 374 Pages 25.00
Fannie Farmer, Boston Cooking School, 1918, 656 Pages 17.50
Fannie Farmer, Boston Cooking School, 1928 .... 10.00
Frigidare, Hardback, 1929 .... 9.00
Gold Medal Flour, 1916, 72 Pages 12.00
Gold Medal Flour, Soft Cover, 1910 .... 22.00
Hilo Woman's Club, Hawaiian Recipes, 1953, 118 Pages 16.00
Home Cookery 250 Tested Recipes, Mrs. H. Howson, Pa., 1880 .... 150.00
Home Packing & Preserving The Red Wing Way 40.00
Hood's Sarsaparilla, Ladies Cooking Picture, 1880s, 32 Pages 10.00
Housewives Cookbook, Larkin Company, Pa., 1916 .... 35.00
Jack Benny, 1937 .... 10.00
Jello-O Girl Entertains, Rose O'Neill Illustrations, Kewpie 25.00
Jello-O, Jack Benny & Mary Livingston 12.00
Joy of Cooking, 1946 .... 12.00
Karo Cookbook, Hewitt, 1910, 47 Pages 5.00
Kate Smith, 1940 .... 20.00
Knox Gelatin, 1911 .... 1.00
Marion Harland, 1906 .... 35.00
Mary Dunbar, Jewel Tea, 1930s 8.00
Methodist Ladies Aid, Farmington, New Mexico, 1920, 46 Pages 9.00
Methods of Canning, H. Blits, New York, 1890 .... 60.00
Metropolitan Life Cookbook, 1925 ....5.00 To 8.00
Metropolitan Life Cookbook, 1948 .... 3.00
Michigan Federation Cookbook, Mrs. S. Weaver, 1909 .... 60.00
Modern Housewife, 1, 000 Recipes, 1857 .... 125.00
Old Dixie, Wood Cover, 1938 .... 15.00
Philadelphia Cookbook, Mrs. S. Rorer, Pa., 1914 .... 60.00
Pillsbury Bake–Off, No.3 .... 14.00
Pillsbury Bake–Off, No.6 .... 4.00
Pillsbury Cake Recipes, Kate Smith, 1st Edition, 1952 .... 8.50
Pillsbury's Balanced Recipes, Aluminum Cover, 1933 .... 40.00
Plymouth Rock Gelatin 5.00
Practical Cooking & Dinner Giving, Mrs. Henderson, 1881 .... 75.00
Presidential, 1903 .... 25.00
Prudence Penny's·Cookbook, 1930s 30.00
Ransom's Family Receipt Book, 1909 .... 3.00
Receipts In Cookery, Mary Ketteby, Leather Bound, Dated 1728 .... 300.00
Reliable, Hard Bound, 1917, 197 Pages 8.50
Rickoff's, Lima Tea Co., Lima, Oh., 1912, 128 Pages 8.00
Royal Baker & Pastry Cook, 1911 .... 8.00
Rumford, 1936, 209 Pages 10.00
Rumford, Fruit, 1927, 48 Pages 7.50
Settlement, Mrs. Simon Kander, 1951 .... 9.50
Snow White Dairy, 1955 .... 20.00
Southern Pacific Rice Cookbook, 1901 .... 15.00
U.S. Navy, 1945 .... 12.00
Victory Meal Planner, 1942 .... 8.00
Wartime Canning & Cooking Book, Pittsburg, 1943 .... 6.00
Watkins, 1933 .... 12.00
Western Recipes, 1936 .... 15.00
White House, 1916 .... 40.00

White House, Dedicated To Wives of Presidents, H.H. White, 1887 .... 30.00
White House, Photographs, 1925 .... 18.00
Woman's Home Companion, 987 Pages 15.00
World War I, Army 12.00
Yeast Foam Recipes, Victorian Children Cover 12.00
Young Woman's Book of Health, Dr. Wm. A. Alcott, 1850 .... 200.00

 Cookie jars with brightly painted designs or amusing figural shapes became popular in the mid–1930s. Many companies made them and collectors search for cookie jars either by design or by maker's name. Listed here are examples by the less common makers. Major factories are listed under their own names in other sections of the book. See also Abingdon; Brush; Hull; McCoy; Red Wing; Shawnee.

COOKIE JAR, Animal Cookies, Black Stoneware 25.00
Apple, Franciscan .... 125.00 To 190.00
Asparagus 17.00
Baker Lady, Hershey's 60.00
Balloon Lady, Pottery Guild .... 60.00 To 80.00
Barefoot Boy .... 65.00 To 175.00
Bear With Cookie, American Bisque .... 30.00 To 45.00
Bear, Avon, Red Sweater, Holding Cookie .... 45.00 To 60.00
Bear, Gilner 45.00
Bear, Metlox 35.00
Bear, Twin Winton 40.00
Beehive, Bee At Top, Moody's USA 46.00
Betsy Ross, Japan 165.00
Big Bird, Sesame Street 35.00
Black Chef, National Silver 150.00
Black Girl, Sitting, Green Dress, Treasure Craft 90.00
Black Santa Claus, Metlox .... 99.00 To 135.00
Black Topsy Girl, Red Trim, Metlox 95.00
Blackboard Bum, American Bisque 95.00
Brown Bear, With Beanie 40.00
Brown, Flowers & Dots, Mar–Crest 28.00
Casper The Ghost, Harvey .... 565.00 To 590.00
Cat On Beehive, American Bisque .... 28.00 To 36.00
Cat With Mouse On Back, Treasure Craft 30.00
Cheerleaders, American Bisque 95.00
Chef, Pearl China 225.00
Chef, Peering Out of Sack of 3 Donuts, American Bisque 55.00
Chick, Yellow, American Bisque .... 30.00 To 45.00
Chicken, Brown, Fapco 38.00
Churn, American Bisque 45.00
Cinderella, 22K Gold Trim 95.00
Circus Tent, Brayton 300.00
Clown, American Bisque .... 28.00 To 95.00
Clown, Pan American Art 45.00
Clown, Sierra Vista 48.00
Coffee Pot, Treasure Craft 35.00
Cookie Monster, California Originals 50.00
Cookie Trolley, Treasure Craft 25.00
Cookie Truck, American Bisque .... 40.00 To 55.00
Corn, Stanford 60.00
Cow Jumping Over Moon, 3–D, American Bisque 125.00
Cowboys, Porcelain, Terrace 45.00
Cream Whip, Borden's 38.00
Darth Vader, Turnabout 85.00
Donald Duck & Joe Carioca, Walt Disney 110.00
Donald Duck & Nephew, California Pottery 125.00
Donkey & Milk Wagon, American Bisque .... 55.00 To 90.00
Dutch Boy, American Bisque 25.00
Dutch Boy, Celadon 65.00
Dutch Boy, Pottery Guild .... 55.00 To 62.00
Dutch Girl, Celadon 70.00

Dutch Girl, Pottery Guild .... 55.00 To 57.00
Dutch Girl, Regal China .... 110.00 To 175.00
Ear of Corn, Stanforware .... 50.00 To 95.00
Elephant, Sitting Up, Brown American Bisque 48.00
Elephant, Sitting Up, Brown, American Bisque 44.00
Elephant, Twin Winton 45.00
Elf's School House, California Originals 50.00
Elsie The Cow, Pottery Guild .... 108.00 To 112.00
Ernie, Marked Muppets 65.00
Fancy Cat .... 20.00 To 35.00
Farmer Elephant, Treasure Craft 45.00
Flintstone's–Rubble's House 350.00
Fred Flintstone 225.00
Frog, California Originals 30.00
Fruit, Metlox 42.00
Gingerbread House, Twin Winton 38.00
Girl, Black, Topsy, Red Trim, Metlox 100.00
Goldilocks, Regal .... 90.00 To 180.00
Goodies, M.A. Hadley 25.00
Gordon's, Delivery Truck, Cover 45.00
Happy Hipp, Love Hippy, USA 40.00
Heating Stove, Black, American Bisque 25.00
Hen, Chick On Back, Rafco 45.00
Horse, Sitting, American Bisque 245.00
House, Century 21, House, Little People 275.00
Huber, The Lion 75.00
Humpty Dumpty, Red Brick Wall, Gold Trim, Regal .... 165.00 To 178.00
Ice Cream Cone .... 15.00 To 45.00
Keebler Treehouse .... 35.00 To 85.00
Kitten, Yellow, With Green Straw Hat, Bowtie, Green Dots 25.00
Koala Bear, Metlox 68.00
Kookieville Bus Co., Cardinal 45.00
Kraft Bear, Regal 125.00
Lamb, American Bisque 90.00
Li'l Red Schoolhouse 42.00
Luzianne Mammy 475.00
Majorette, American Bisque 78.00
Majorette, Gold Trim, Regal .... 110.00 To 125.00
Mammy & Chef, Pearl China, Pair 900.00
Mammy Laughing, Japan 145.00
Mammy, Blue, Large Jar, Mosaic Tile 450.00
Mammy, Mixing Bowl, Red Trim, Metlox .... 98.00 To 120.00
Mammy, Mosaic Tile Co. 450.00
Mammy, Pearl China .... 350.00 To 495.00
Mammy, USA Pottery 175.00
Mammy, Yellow, Mosaic Tile Co. 395.00
Muppets, Ernie, American Bisque 65.00
Mushrooms Canister, White, Sears 50.00
Nestle's Toll House Cookies 45.00
Noah's Ark, Brown 90.00
Nun, DeForrest of California 125.00
Old MacDonald's Farm Barn 150.00
Owl, Brown, With ABC Book, Wears Glasses, Pencil On Ear 45.00
Owl, Playing Guitar, Maurice Ceramics 35.00
Panda, Upside Down 35.00
Peaches On Front, Bark Handles 25.00
Peasant Woman, Bonnet, Flowered Apron, Brayton Laguna 270.00
Peek–A–Boo Rabbit, Van Tellingen 425.00
Pig In Diapers, Regal 125.00
Pig, American Bisque .... 25.00 To 68.00
Pig, Baby, Regal 125.00
Pig, Lady, American Bisque 40.00
Pig, Standing, Blue Overalls 38.00
Pillsbury Doughboy .... 35.00 To 40.00

Pineapple, Los Angeles Potteries	30.00
Pineapple, USA	30.00
Pink Poodle, American Bisque	40.00
Pixie In School House	30.00
Porky Pig	55.00
Quaker Oats, Regal China	75.00 To 150.00
Rabbit, Buck–Toothed	52.00
Rabbit, In Hat, American Bisque	40.00 To 45.00
Rabbit, With Patches, American Bisque	50.00
Racoon In Tree Stump	32.00
Rag Doll, Polka Dot Dress, Hands Up, Starnes, California.	70.00 To 83.00
Raggedy Ann & Andy, Tin, Ransburg	60.00
Red Riding Hood, Blue Skirt, Basket, Pottery Guild	72.00 To 85.00
Rooster, Maurice Ceramics	25.00
Rooster, Pottery Guild	30.00
Rooster, Sierra Vista	40.00
Sack of Cookies, Cardinal	35.00
Salad Chef, Regal China	175.00
Sandman Cookies, American Bisque	48.00
Santa Claus Face, American Bisque	110.00
Santa Claus Face, Empire, Plastic, Red & White	48.00
Santa Claus, Black, Metlox	110.00 To 165.00
Santa Claus, Bust, Plastic, Carolina Enterprises	35.00
School House Bell In Cupola, House of Webster	55.00
School House, American Bisque	35.00 To 50.00
Sheriff, California Originals	55.00
Shoe House, With 3 Mice, Dark Brown, Treasure Craft	50.00
Shoe, Twin Winton	30.00
Sitting Poodle, Sierra Vista	55.00
Smiling, Frowning Face, Cookie Eyes, Wooden Lid, Esmond	20.00
Snoopy	18.00
Southern Belle, Pan American Art	45.00
Spaceship, ABC	50.00
Squirrel On Pinecone, Metlox	25.00 To 40.00
Teddy Bear, Metlox	35.00
Teddy Bear, Royal Ware	26.00
Thou Shall Not Steal, Twin Winton	25.00
Thumper, Terrace Ceramics	30.00
Timmy Tortoise, Box	30.00
Toll House Cookies, Recipe Book	45.00
Toll House, Box, 1980	18.00
Transformer, Hasbro	90.00
Tree House, Keebler, 1981	35.00 To 48.00
Turn About Bear, Celadon	35.00
Turtle Standing With Sign, Take One, Japan	40.00
Umbrella Kids, ABC	145.00
Victorian House, Marked Brazil For Avon Reps.	125.00
Windmill, Blue, Fredericksburg Art Pottery	35.00 To 65.00
Winnie Pig, Terrace Ceramics	65.00
Wise Bird, Robinson Ransbottom	25.00 To 40.00
Wurlitzer Jukebox, Treasure Craft	45.00
Yogi Bear, Head	185.00
Yogi Bear, Standing	190.00

COORS U.S.A. Coors ware was made by a pottery in Golden, Colorado, owned by the Coors Beverage Company. It was produced from the turn of the century until the pottery was destroyed by fire in the 1930s. The name "Coors" is marked on the back.

COORS, Bean Pot, Rosebud, Green	48.00
Bowl, Mixing, Yellow	35.00
Cup, Orange	22.00
Dish, Fruit, Rosebud, Cobalt Blue	6.00
Dish, Fruit, Rosebud, Yellow	6.00
Jar, Drip, Rosebud	22.00

Mortar & Pestle, Small	25.00
Plate, Maroon, 9 3/4 In.	20.00
Plate, Rosebud, White, 7 In.	5.00
Plate, Rosebud, Yellow, 7 In.	5.00
Ramekin, Rosebud, Cobalt Blue Handle	18.00
Smoking Set, Lodge, Dated 1932	40.00
Vase, Buff, Ribbed, 5 In.	26.00
Vase, Green, 8 1/2 In.	75.00
Vase, Matte Orange Floral, 12 In.	50.00
Vase, Ram's Head Design, Orange, 6 In.	29.00
Vase, Ribbed, Dusty Blue, 5 In.	15.00
Vase, Tan & Turquoise, 8 1/2 In.	30.00

COPELAND SPODE ENGLAND

Josiah Spode established a pottery at Stoke–on–Trent, England, in 1770. In 1833, the firm was purchased by William Copeland and Thomas Garrett and the firm mark was changed. In 1847, Copeland became the sole owner and the mark changed again. W. T. Copeland & Sons continued until a 1976 merger when it became Royal Worcester Spode. Pieces are listed in this book under the name that appears in the mark. Copeland Spode, Copeland, and Royal Worcester have separate listings.

COPELAND SPODE, Creamer, Tower, Blue, 5 1/2 In.	55.00
Cup & Saucer, Rosalie	8.00
Cup, Tower	8.00
Figurine, Mallard, Spread Wing, Large	120.00
Gravy Boat, Buttercup	30.00
Jam Jar, Black Scene	30.00
Plate, Bopeep Center, Blue, White, Floral Border, 10 1/4 In.	55.00
Plate, Rosalie, 10 1/2 In.	13.00
Plate, Rose Briar, 10 1/2 In.	12.00
Plate, Tower, 6 1/2 In.	5.00
Plate, Tower, 8 In.	13.00
Platter, Butterfly Edge, Gold Trim, 14 1/2 X 11 In.	125.00
Platter, Tower, Blue, 12 In.	40.00
Platter, Tower, Blue, 15 In.	65.00
Platter, Tower, Pink, 12 1/2 In.	45.00
Soup, Dish, Tower, 8 In.	12.00
Sugar, Black Scene	30.00
COPELAND, Charger, Renaissance Woman, 16 1/2 In.	450.00
Cheese Keeper, Majolica, Ivory Basketweave, Wine, 12 X 10 In.	695.00
Dish, Serving, Fluted, Cover, Wild Game, Brown Transfer, 14 In.	95.00
Jug, 36 Portrait Medallions, English Kings	160.00
Plate, Rural Scenes, Black Transfer, Ironstone, 10 1/4 In., 15 Pc.	75.00
Sugar & Creamer, Milk Glass, Grape	35.00

COPPER LUSTER, see Luster, Copper

Utilitarian items, such as teakettles and cooking pans, have been handcrafted from copper in America since the days of the early colonists. Copper became a popular metal with the Arts and Crafts makers of the early 1900s and decorative pieces such as bookends and desk sets were made. Other pieces of copper may be found in the Bradley & Hubbard, Roycroft, and Kitchen categories.

COPPER, Basin, Circular, Loose Ring Handles, Footed, Continental, 1890	187.00
Bed Warmer, Engraved Floral Lid, Turned Wood Handle, 44 In.	230.00
Bed Warmer, Steel, Bulbous, Reticulated, Handle, Continental, 38 In.	440.00
Bed Warmer, Turned Maple Handle, Round, 45 In.	395.00
Bed Warmer, Wrought Iron Ferrule, Wooden Handle, Europe, 35 In.	65.00
Boiler, Hand Cover, Reticulated Interior Insert, England, 27 In.	715.00
Boiler, Oval, Cover, Inner Strainer, Mid–19th Century, 23 In.	467.00
Bowl, Silver Lining, Katharine Pratt, 2 3/4 X 6 3/4 In.	550.00
Box, Enameled Cupid & Psyche, Light Blue, Rectangular, 3 1/4 In.	490.00
Candlestick, Art Nouveau, Hammered, Benedict Studio, 4 1/2 In., Pair	125.00
Candlestick, Princess Style, Karl Kipp, C.1915, 8 In., Pair	350.00
Candlestick, Princess, Double Reeded Stem, Karl Kipp, 7 7/8 In., Pair	425.00

Candy Bowl, Cast Iron Handles, Round Bottom, 17 1/2 In.	165.00
Card Receiver, Raised Moose, Tree, Lake, Mountains, Philadelphia, 1907	38.00
Cauldron, Circular Tapered, Wrought Iron Swing Handle, 17 X 26 In.	385.00
Chamberstick, Strap Handle, Rivets, Marie Zimmermann, 16 3/4 In.	3900.00
Coffee Urn, Brass Spigot, Patent 1908	215.00
Coffeepot, Burner, Wooden Handles, Brass Spigot, Sternanware	265.00
Dipper, Tin Lined, Brass Handle, Primitive, Impressed M M, 7 In.	65.00
Dish, Chafing, Brass, Victorian, 2 Handled Lid, Benham & Sons, 18 In.	605.00
Frying Pan, Iron Handle, 43 In.	75.00
Jardiniere, Silver Band At Rim, Arthur J. Stone, Small	750.00
Kettle, Apple Butter, Large	250.00
Kettle, On Iron Stand, A & L, 27 In., 16 Gal.	300.00
Lantern, Hall, Carmel Slag Glass, C.1910, 16 X 10 1/4 In.	475.00
Measure, Haystack, Ear Handle, Anderson Brothers, Glasgow, 4 Gal.	135.00
Measure, Haystack, Ear Handle, English, Marked Gallon, 12 In.	220.00
Measure, Haystack, Front Brass Handle, Ear Handle, Marked 4 Gallon	180.00
COPPER, MOLD, see Kitchen, Mold	
Napkin Holder, Art Deco, Chase	27.00
Pen Tray, Applied Silver Band, Arthur J.Stone, 10 1/4 X 3 1/2 In.	1500.00
Pitcher, Milk, Tapered, Victorian Weights Seal, Marked 4 Gal., 14 In.	412.00
Pitcher, Water, Sterling Silver Trim, Jos. Heinrichs, 1907	75.00
Planter, Wall, Disk, Art Deco, Revere, 11 In.	15.00
Plaque, Grapes, Enameled, Sascha	65.00
Pot, Ear–Shaped Handles, 7 3/4 In.	45.00
Pot, Hammered, Dirk Van Erp, 3 1/4 X 4 In.	950.00
Pot, Irregular Diamond Shape, Lift Out Rack, 17 X 22 X 6 1/2 In.	190.00
Samovar, Charcoal Burning, Steel Lined, 22 X 16 In.	1000.00
Sauce Pan, Oval, Cover, Mid–19th Century, 11 1/2 In.	275.00
Shield, Golf Trophy, Dewar Challenge Trophy Inscribed, 36 In.	1450.00
Skillet, Cast Iron Handle, V. Olal & Sons, Phila., 7 1/2 In.	35.00
Spirit Measure, Victorian, C.1880, Stamped VR, 1 Gal., 12 In.	465.00
Still, Domed Cauldron, 2 Handles, Spigot, England, 24 X 24 In.	410.00
Still, Factory Made, 14 Gal.	75.00
Sugar, 12 Spoon Holders Around Top, Pedestal, Tin, 8 In.	65.00
Teakettle, Brass Finial, Dovetailed Construction, 6 1/2 In.	60.00
Teakettle, Dovetailed, Stamped J. Ebert, Hamilton, 8 1/2 In.	550.00
Teakettle, Gooseneck Spout, 10 1/2 In.	100.00
Teakettle, Gooseneck Spout, Acorn Finial, 9 3/4 In.	45.00
Teakettle, Gooseneck Spout, Brass Trim, 12 In.	75.00
Teakettle, Gooseneck, I. Babb, 19th Century	770.00
Tray, Hammered, Silver Strapwork, Metcalf Co., C.1907, 8 3/4 In.	250.00
Vase, Flower Shape, Fluted Sides, Marie Zimmermann, 9 7/8 X 10 In.	4400.00
Vase, Hammered, Silver Strapwork, Metcalf Co., C.1910, 10 In.	100.00
Vase, Milk Can Form, Red Patina, Dirk Van Erp, C.1915, 7 1/4 In.	2950.00
Vase, Rolled Rim, Brown Patina, Dirk Van Erp, C.1919, 8 1/2 In.	3400.00

 Coralene glass was made by firing many small colored beads on the outside of glassware. It was made in many patterns in the United States and Europe in the 1880s. Reproductions are made today.

CORALENE, JAPANESE, see Japanese Coralene

CORALENE, Pitcher, Seaweed, Shaded Rose, 9 In.	300.00
Rose Bowl, Flowers & Butterfly On Front & Sides, 5 1/2 In.	550.00
Sugar & Creamer, Florals, Melon Ribbed, Gold Outlines & Trim	95.00
Tankard, Staffordshire, 12 1/2 In.	295.00
Tumbler, Water, Yellow Beaded Allover, Blue Overlay, 3 3/4 In.	165.00
Vase, Gold, White, Green, Swastika Keramis, Handles, 8 In.	200.00
Vase, Green & Yellow Beading, 1909, 9 In.	300.00
Vase, Herringbone, Yellow To White, Allover Fleur–De–Lis, 6 In.	160.00
Vase, Pink & Lavender Iris, Cobalt & Gold Trim, 9 In.	455.00

X Boleslaw Cybis was one of the founders of the Cordey China Company in 1942 in Trenton, New Jersey. The firm produced gift shop items. In 1969 it was acquired by the Lightron Corp. and operated as the Schiller Cordey Co., manufacturers of lamps. About 1950 Boleslaw Cybis began making Cybis porcelains which are listed in their own section in this book.

CORDEY, Box, Floral On Lid, Nesting Blue Bird, Round, 7 1/4 In.	85.00
Bust, Beautiful Woman, No.8039, 16 In.	275.00
Bust, Woman, No.5054, 9 1/2 In.	75.00
Figurine, Bird On Branch, No.6004	75.00
Figurine, Bird On Stump, No.6004	95.00
Figurine, Boy, Neopolitan, No.5046	90.00
Figurine, Chinese Goddess, Roses, Medallions	135.00
Figurine, Colonial Couple, 16 1/4 In., Pair	95.00
Figurine, Colonial Man, No.5042	75.00
Figurine, Girl, Yorkshire, No.5047	90.00
Figurine, Lamb, No.6025	95.00 To 135.00
Figurine, Madame, No.5084	120.00
Figurine, Man, Flowers, Stump Base, Lace, No.4153, 14 In.	115.00
Figurine, Man, Stump With Flowers, Scroll Base, 10 1/2 In.	85.00
Figurine, Napoleon, Label, 7 3/4 In.	55.00
Lamp, Lace & Flowers, Shade	175.00
Lamp, Madame DuBarry Bust, 15 In.	250.00
Lamp, Phoenix Bird, Blue	165.00
Lamp, Woman, Upswept Hairdo, Pink Lace, Yellow Roses	150.00
Plaque, Advertising, 4 1/2 X 3 In.	100.00
Torchere, 3 Relief Roses, 4 Buds, Table	100.00
Wall Plaque, Woman, 10 In.	95.00

There has been a need for a corkscrew since the first bottle was sealed with a cork, probably in the seventeenth century. Today collectors search for the early, unusual patented examples or the figural corkscrews of recent years.

CORKSCREW, 2-Sided Man, Jigger, Bottle Opener, Spoon, Silver Plated, 1932	110.00
A-B Bottle	40.00
Anheuser-Busch, Pat. 97	60.00
Boot, Sterling Silver	85.00
Champagne, Equinox, Late 1800s	45.00
Chinnock, Crimped Top, Oval Openings, 1862	200.00
Golf Club	12.00
Green River, With Can Opener, The Whiskey Without A Headache	15.00
Kelly's Whiskey, Figural	15.00
Legs, High Button Shoes, Celluloid Handles, Germany	45.00
Listerine, Tin	8.00
Parrot, Standing, Tail Is Corkscrew, 5 1/2 In.	25.00
Peebles Whiskey, Bottle Shape	25.00
Record, Steel With Ball Bearings, Walnut Handle, C.1885	150.00
Tusk, Hand-Chased Silver Trim	550.00
Walnut & Brass, Coney's Patent, C.1884	275.00

Coronation cups have been made since the 1800s. Pottery or glass with a picture of the monarch and date have been souvenirs for many coronations. The pieces that mention King Edward VIII, the king who was never crowned, are not rare; and collectors should be sure to check values before buying.

CORONATION, see also Commemorative

CORONATION, Bank, Crown, Elizabeth II, Cast Iron	45.00
Beaker, George VI, Royal Doulton, 1937	85.00
Beaker, King & Queen, Red & White, Maddock, Square, 8 In.	28.00
Book, 24 Colored Plates, 1937, 10 X 14 In.	85.00
Book, Coloring, Elizabeth II, 1953	20.00
Bowl, George VI, Scalloped, Glass, 1937, 9 1/2 In.	55.00
Coaster, Elizabeth II, Coalport	22.00
Cup & Saucer, Edward VIII, Royal Doulton	75.00
Cup & Saucer, Elizabeth II	40.00
Cup & Saucer, George V & Mary, 1911	

Cup & Saucer, George VI, Royal Albert	48.00
Decanter, George V & Mary, Dewars, Royal Doulton, 1911	1000.00
Decanter, George V, Crown Stopper, White Portraits	250.00
Dish, Pin, Elizabeth II, Glass	15.00
Jam Jar, Edward VIII	30.00
Mug, Edward VII	30.00
Mug, Edward VIII, Profile On Red, Solian	38.00
Mug, Elizabeth II, Pictorial, Royal Winton, 1953	15.00
Pitcher, Elizabeth II, Light Blue, 1953, 5 In.	30.00
Pitcher, King & Queen Portraits, Meakin, 4 1/4 In.	48.00
Plate, Edward VII, Royal Doulton, 1902, 8 1/2 In.	125.00
Plate, Edward VIII, Profile On Blue, Myott, 8 In.	38.00
Plate, Edward VIII, Square, 1937, 8 In.	65.00
Plate, Elizabeth II, 10 1/2 In.	32.50
Plate, Elizabeth II, Colors & Sepia, 1955, 8 In.	40.00
Plate, Elizabeth II, Sepia, Staffordshire	35.00
Plate, George V & Mary, 1911, 9 1/2 In.	65.00
Plate, King & Queen Portraits, Meakin, 6 1/2 In.	38.00
Puzzle, Elizabeth II, Wooden	30.00
Spoon, Edward VII, Full Figure On Handle, Sterling, 5 3/4 In.	45.00
Teapot, George VI & Elizabeth, 1937	45.00
Tumbler, Edward VIII	28.00

Cosmos is a pressed milk glass pattern with colored flowers made from 1894 to 1915 by the Consolidated Lamp and Glass Company. Tablewares and lamps were made. A few pieces were also made of clear glass with painted decorations.

COSMOS, Butter, Cover, Pink	135.00
Butter, Cover, Pink Band	190.00 To 195.00
Castor, Pickle, Embossed, Red Jar, 10 In.	325.00
Castor, Pickle, Silver–Plated Frame, Tongs & Lid, Ruby Glass	325.00
Creamer, Pink Band	120.00
Lamp, Miniature	65.00 To 125.00
Salt & Pepper	135.00
Saltshaker, Original Lid	60.00
Spooner, Pink	130.00
Sugar & Creamer, Pink Band	220.00
Sugar, Cover, Milk Glass	35.00
Sugar, Pink Band	120.00

Linen or wool coverlets were made during the nineteenth century. Most of the coverlets date from 1800 to 1850. Four types were made: the double woven, jacquard, summer and winter, and overshot. Later coverlets were made of a variety of materials. Quilts are listed in this book in their own section.

COVERLET, Jacquard, 4 Rose Medallions, Witmer, Manor Township, 74 X 94 In.	115.00
Jacquard, Bird Border, Signed C.M. By D.I.G.1838, 76 X 84 In.	1025.00
Jacquard, Center Floral Medallion, Fruit Border, 74 X 94 In.	200.00
Jacquard, Christian & Heathen Center Design, 68 X 75 In.	450.00
Jacquard, Christian & Heathen, Peacocks, Reversible, 77 X 88 In.	475.00
Jacquard, Courthouse, Tree, Wool, Cotton, 1850s, 65 X 67 In.	330.00
Jacquard, Double Weave, Floral Design, 84 X 90 In.	175.00
Jacquard, Double Weave, Flowers, Vines, C.1900, 77 X 88 In.	425.00
Jacquard, Double Weave, Snowflake, Pine Tree Variant, 76 X 76 In.	165.00
Jacquard, Eagles, Buildings Around Edges, Dated 1843	1350.00
Jacquard, Flora Medallions, Stars, Wool, Cotton, 1845, 78 X 78 In.	1980.00
Jacquard, Floral Design, Red & Black, 90 X 94 In.	150.00
Jacquard, Floral Medallion Center, 68 X 83 In.	200.00
Jacquard, Floral Medallion, American Eagle Corners, 80 X 86 In.	100.00
Jacquard, Floral Medallions, Bird Borders, 69 X 92 In.	375.00
Jacquard, Floral Medallions, Floral Border, 72 X 86 In.	150.00
Jacquard, Floral Medallions, J. Cunningham, N.Y., 1842, 94 X 76 In.	2850.00
Jacquard, Floral Medallions, Sidney, Ohio, 1855, 80 X 94 In.	150.00
Jacquard, Floral Medallions, W., Mt. Vernon, O., 1852, 70 X 86 In.	225.00

Jacquard, Floral Pattern, Mary A. Bedell 1848, 70 X 92 In. 185.00
Jacquard, Floral, Bird Border, Samuel Meily, 1842, 72 X 88 In. 475.00
Jacquard, Floral, Peter Seibert, Easton, 1853, 74 X 88 In. 500.00
Jacquard, Floral, Wool, Blue, White, Fringed, J.G., 1836, 78 X 90 In. 800.00
Jacquard, Flower Urns, D. Cosley, 1860, 1 Piece, 80 Z 90 In. 300.00
Jacquard, Fringed, Blue & White, 90 X 90 In. 175.00
Jacquard, Geometric Pattern Within Tree Border, 166 X 140 In. 250.00
Jacquard, Hemfield Railroad Corners, Wool & Cotton, 79 X 76 In. 4400.00
Jacquard, Hemfield Railroad, Blue & White, 2 Piece 1550.00
Jacquard, Henry F. Stager, Mount Joy, Penna., 75 X 81 In. 335.00
Jacquard, Jacob Bartelemy, New Berlin, 1853 .... 525.00
Jacquard, Medallion Center, H. Stager, Mt. Joy, Penna., 70 X 82 In. 300.00
Jacquard, Memorial Hall, Centennial, 70 X 72 In. 300.00
Jacquard, Navy, Natural, Bird & Vintage, Jacob Carver, 66 X 82 In. 350.00
Jacquard, Panels, Geometric Design, Wool, Cotton, 1820, 80 X 83 In. 550.00
Jacquard, Pine Trees & Snowflake Design, 72 X 84 In. 750.00
Jacquard, Rayed Star Center, Achsah L. Shepard, 1851, 84 X 86 In. 467.50
Jacquard, Red, White, Navy & Gold, Mechanicsburg, Penna., 1839 .... 475.00
Jacquard, Star & Floral, Wool, Blue, White, Signed, 1841, 71 X 88 In. 350.00
Overshot, Floral Medallions, J. Alexander, N.Y., 1830, 80 X 98 In. 1980.00
Overshot, Geometric Pattern, Wool, Cotton, 86 X 194 In. 175.00
Overshot, Optical Design, Blue Shades, White, Fringe, 72 X 96 In. 65.00
Overshot, Plaid Pattern, Red, Blue, Yellow, 74 X 82 In., 2 Piece 200.00

Guy Cowan made pottery in Rocky River, Ohio, a suburb of Cleveland, from 1913 to 1931. The Cowan Pottery made art pottery and wares for florists. A stylized mark with the word "Cowan" was used on most pieces. A commercial, mass–produced line was marked "Lakeware." Collectors today search for the Art Deco pieces by Guy Cowan, Viktor Schreckengost, Waylande Gregory, or Thelma Frazier Winter.

COWAN, Ashtray, Seashell 22.00
Bookends, Boy & Girl 450.00
Bookends, Elephant 325.00
Bowl, Blue Luster, Marked, 8 In. 25.00
Bowl, Blue Luster, Signed, 5 1/4 X 3 In. 45.00
Cup & Saucer, Melon Design, Beige 30.00
Flower Frog, Nude, Bending Backwards, Cream 175.00
Flower Frog, Nude, Ivory, Marked, 10 In. 300.00
Holder, Pipe, Clown 100.00
Lamp, Candlestick 35.00
Tea Set, Melon Shape, Cream Color, 15 Piece 210.00
Vase, Bud, Orange Luster, 6 1/2 In. 25.00
Vase, Bulbous, Crackle Glaze, Chinese Blue, 9 1/2 In. 325.00
Vase, Chinese Orange, 7 In. 60.00
Vase, Crackle Glaze, Chinese Blue, Marked, 9 In. 200.00
Vase, Green, Fan Shape, 2 Allegorical Birds Base, 7 In. 55.00

Cracker Jack, the molasses–flavored popcorn mixture, was first made in 1896 in Chicago, Illinois. A prize was added to each box in 1912. Collectors search for the old boxes and toys and advertising materials. Many of the toys are unmarked.

CRACKER JACK, Bowl & Cup Set, Cereal 25.00
Box, 1920–30 .... 65.00
Card, Baseball, Cravath 125.00
Card, Baseball, Dugey 170.00
Card, Baseball, Magee 200.00
Card, Baseball, Murphy 200.00
Card, Baseball, Stovall 225.00
Cart, Wooden Handle, Tin 30.00
Coconut Corn Crisp, Tin 75.00
Coin, Mystery Club, President Buchanan 12.50
Doll, Box, 13 In. .... 20.00 To 30.00
Fortune Wheel, Tin, 2 Piece 25.00

Game, Midget Auto Race, Paper .... 30.00 To 35.00
Lunch Box 35.00
Number Puzzle, Envelope 43.00
Pillow 18.00
Radio, Box 35.00
Rainbow Spinner, 1940s 8.50
Watch, Pocket, Tin 20.00
Whistle 10.00

Crackle glass was originally made by the Venetians, but most of the ware found today dates from the 1800s. The glass was heated, cooled, and refired so that many small lines appeared inside the glass. It was made in many factories in the United States and Europe.

CRACKLE GLASS, Biscuit Jar, Swirl Wheel, Shell Finial, C.1880 .... 130.00
Tumbler, Clear, Set of 6 .... 100.00
Vase, Chinese Blue, Ovoid, Boch Freres, 11 In., Pair 150.00
Vase, Clear Base, Braided Stem, Cranberry Flashed, 10 In. 50.00
Vase, Puffer Fish Shape, Bulging Eyes, 9 In. 75.00

Cranberry glass is an almost transparent yellow-red glass. It resembles the color of cranberry juice. The glass has been made in Europe and America since the Civil War. It is still being made and reproductions can fool the unwary.

CRANBERRY GLASS, see also Northwood; Rubena Verde; etc.
CRANBERRY GLASS, Biscuit Jar, Allover Feather Scroll, Bear Finial 400.00
Bottle, Barber, Coin Spot, Opalescent, 7 1/4 In. 135.00
Bottle, Barber, Opalescent, Melon, Metal Stopper, 7 1/2 In. 175.00
Bowl, Opalescent, 11 In. 85.00
Bowl, Ribbon Candy Rim, Collar of Leaves, 4 1/2 In. 250.00
Box, Lift-Off Cover, 6 X 1 In. 110.00
Carafe, Diamond-Quilted & Threaded Design 135.00
Castor, Pickle, Coin Spot 475.00
Castor, Pickle, Inverted Thumbprint, Tongs 275.00
Castor, Pickle, Swirl 250.00
Celery, Chrysanthemum Base, Swirl, Opalescent, 6 3/4 In. 150.00
Condiment Set, Paneled, Plated Frame, 4 3/4 In. 255.00
Cruet, Cherry Blossoms, Bird On Branches, Gold Trim 210.00
Cruet, Enameled Flowers & Butterflies 150.00
Cruet, Flower & Bird, Gold Trim, Clear Handle 210.00
Cup & Saucer, Floral & Fern, Gold Leaf, Demitasse 110.00
Cup & Saucer, Gold Leaf Design, Polished Bottom 125.00
Decanter, Gold Leaf, Stopper, 1870, 9 3/4 In. 300.00
Decanter, White Loops, Pittsburgh, C.1880 .... 375.00
Diamond Optic, Basket, Hat, 5 In. 45.00
Dish, Cheese, Gold & White Design, Plate, 9 X 10 In. 500.00
Epergne, 3 Baskets, 4 Trumpets, Vaseline Stems, 21 1/2 In. 1850.00
Epergne, 4 Trumpets, Ruffled Base, 19 In. 225.00
Epergne, Applied Pinched Ribbons & Twisted Canes, 21 In. 1150.00
Humidor, Brass Lid, White & Blue Enamel Design, 6 In. 355.00
Jar, Knobbed Cover, Inverted Thumbprint, 5 In. 85.00
Knife Rest, Cut, Ball Ends 98.00
Lamp, Fern & Daisy, Vase Shade, Pear Font, 21 In. 295.00
Lamp, Hanging, Clear Font, 12 In. 1150.00
Lamp, Lace-Maker's, Brass Base, 19 In. 425.00
Lamp, Spiral Beaded Columns In Relief, 8 1/2 In. 395.00
Lemonade Set, Thumbprint, 7 Piece 150.00
Muffineer, Swirled Metal Top, 6 In. 125.00
Pitcher Set, Inverted Thumbprint, 2 Tumblers 150.00
Pitcher, Coin Spot, Ruffled, Clear Applied Handle, 8 1/2 In 95.00
Pitcher, Inverted Thumbprint, Applied Clear Rim 185.00
Pitcher, Puffed-Out Melon Ribs, Clear Handle, 5 1/2 In. 95.00
Pitcher, Water, Inverted Coin Spot 225.00
Pitcher, Water, Leaf Mold 350.00

Powder Jar, Cover, Opalescent 35.00
Powder Jar, Hinged Cover, Flowers, 3 Brass Ball Feet, 3 In. 210.00
Powder Jar, Knobbed Cover, Inverted Thumbprint, 4 1/2 In. 110.00
Rose Bowl, Egg Shape, Clear Swags, Berries, 4 3/4 In. 255.00
Rose Bowl, Polka Dot, 4 In. 75.00
Salt & Pepper, Enameled Flowers, Meriden Holder 195.00
Salt & Pepper, Erie Twist 95.00
Salt & Pepper, Flower Mold, Original Lids 195.00
Salt & Pepper, Rib Optic 85.00
Salt, 2 Rows of Clear Rigaree, Squatty, Round 95.00
Salt, Enameled Flowers & Border Design, English 110.00
Sugar Shaker, Parian Swirl 175.00
Sugar Shaker, Ribbed Lattice, Opalescent, Short 325.00
Sugar Shaker, Venecia 165.00
Table Set, Clear Ruffle, 4 Piece 500.00
Toothpick, Fern 250.00
Tumbler, Criss-Cross, Satin, Consolidated 150.00
Tumbler, Dot Optic, Fenton 27.00
Tumbler, Inverted Thumbprint 35.00
Vase, Diamond Optic, 5 1/2 In. 90.00
Vase, Diamond-Quilted, Crimped, Crystal Feet, 6 In. 75.00
Vase, Enameled Fish & Flowers, Bulbous, 8 1/2 In. 85.00
Vase, Frosted, White Enameled & Gilded Flowers, 6 1/4 In. 30.00
Vase, Melon, Pinched Neck, Ruffled, Bulbous, 4 3/4 In. 75.00
Vase, Ruffled Top, Footed, 8 In. 20.00
Vase, Swirl, Amber Stems, Green Leaves, Spatter, 8 In. 315.00
Water Set, Thumbprint, 7 Piece 195.00
Water Set, Thumbprint, Ruffled Pitcher, 7 Piece 250.00
Wine, Diamond Design, Cranberry To Clear, 6 3/4 In. 105.00

Creamware, or queensware, was developed by Josiah Wedgwood about 1765. It is a cream-colored earthenware that has been copied by many factories.

CREAMWARE, see also Wedgwood

CREAMWARE, Basket, Chestnut, Underplate, Cover, Mayer, 1800, 10 3/4 In. 5060.00
Coffeepot, Man & Woman, Served, Black Servant, Transfer, 1780-90 .... 300.00
Crocus Pot, Cover, Pink Luster Design, Green Trim, 7 X 8 1/2 In. 650.00
Jug, Ladies & Gentlemen In Garden, English Transfer, 1780-90 .... 330.00
Mug, Embossed Panels, Bands of Yellow, Blue Stripes, 6 In. 200.00
Pitcher, Polychrome Floral Design, 7 1/2 In. 140.00
Plate, 2 Women & Child, Marked, 9 1/8 In. 625.00
Plate, Gaudy Floral, 8 3/8 In. 45.00
Shaker, Brown Foliage Bands, Green Stripes, 4 3/4 In. 155.00
Stand, Sweetmeat, 2-Tier, Seated Figure, 10 1/4 In. 360.00
Tankard, Eagle, 12 In. 150.00
Tankard, Knop Cover, Leeds-Type, Handle, Late 18th Century 1300.00
Tea Caddy, George III, Queen Charlotte, 18th Century, 5 3/4 In. 445.00
Teapot, Acanthus Design, Ribbed Intertwined Handle, 5 1/4 In. 400.00

Cuckoo clocks sometimes need minor first aid or major repair. First try home remedies. If the clock stops, it may be because it is not level. Try shifting the clock a bit. The clock will not run correctly in a draft. Hang the clock so it is flat against the wall. Have the clock oiled every 2 years, cleaned every 4 years. Major repairs should be done by a professional.

Put your clock on the wall or on a level floor and move it as little as possible.

Teapot, Cottage Scene 550.00
Teapot, Embossed Flower Finial, Floral Design, 4 1/2 In. 700.00
Teapot, Embossed Leaf Ends, Ribbed Intertwined Handle, 4 3/8 In. 2000.00
Teapot, Embossed Ribs, Intertwined Rope Handle, Dome Lid, 9 In. 800.00
Teapot, Floral Design, Intertwined Rope Handle, 4 5/8 In. 750.00
Teapot, Lovers & Man & Dog Scenes, English Transfer, 1780–90 .... 775.00
Tureen, Green Feather Edge, 10 3/4 In. 300.00
Vase, Ethel, Weller, 9 1/2 In. 195.00
Vase, Twig Handle, Grapes, Vines, 8 3/4 In., Pair ....*Illus* 100.00

Credit cards, credit tokens, metal charge plates, and other similar collectibles are now part of the numismatic collecting hobby.

CREDIT CARD, American Express, Money Card, 6/72 .... 30.00
Ashland, Undated, Series B, White 10.00
Fina, Large Blue Fina, 6/75 .... 7.00
Mobil Gas, 1940 .... 16.00
Mobil, Tan, 5/75 .... 12.00
Shell, 11/77 .... 8.00
Sinclair, 9/72 .... 6.00

A faience factory was established at Creil, France, in 1794. The company merged with a factory in Montereau in 1819. The firm made stoneware, mocha ware, and soft paste porcelain. The name Creil appears as part of the mark on many pieces. The Creil factory closed in 1895.

CREIL, Plate, Birds, Foliage, Black, Blue, Green, Red, 8 In. 175.00
Plate, Peasants At Play Scenes, 1846, 8 Piece 950.00
Plate, Yellow Background, Flowers, 9 In. 150.00

Crown Derby is the nickname given to the works of the Royal Crown Derby factory, which began working in England in 1859. An earlier and more famous English Derby factory existed from 1750 to 1848. The two factories were not related. Most of the porcelain found today with the Derby mark is the work of the later Derby factory.

CROWN DERBY, see also Derby; Royal Crown Derby
CROWN DERBY, Cup & Saucer, Floral Design, Marked 95.00
Plate, Oak Leaf & Acorn Border, Marked, 8 3/4 In. 85.00
Plate, Oriental Design, Marked, 7 1/8 In. 35.00
Urn, Cover, Gold Design, Butterflies, Yellow Ground, 5 In. 295.00
Vase, Gold Design On Yellow Ground, 1887, 7 In. 295.00

Crown Ducal is the name used on some pieces of porcelain made by A. G. Richardson and Co., Ltd., England. The name has been used since 1916.

CROWN DUCAL, Sake Set, Tray, 4 Cups 40.00

Crown Milano glass was made by Frederick Shirley about 1890. It had a plain biscuit color with a satin finish. It was decorated with flowers and often had large gold scrolls.

CROWN MILANO, Biscuit Jar, 6 Pastel Pansies, Silver Plated Lid, 5 In. 945.00
Biscuit Jar, Allover Enameled Floral, Signed 440.00
Biscuit Jar, Butterfly Finial, Plated Lid, Marked, 5 In. 945.00
Biscuit Jar, Pale Yellow To Cream Base, Barrel Shape, 6 In. 685.00
Biscuit Jar, Pansies, Butterfly On Silverplated Cover, 5 In. 945.00
Biscuit Jar, White Hobnail, Gold Enameled Floral, Oval, Signed 725.00
Bowl, Colored Flowers All Around, Gold Outlined, 7 X 9 In. 375.00
Bowl, Flowers Outlined In Gold, Signed, 7 X 9 1/2 In. 650.00
Box, Jewelry, Silver Plated, Red Velvet Lining, 6 X 2 1/2 In. 595.00
Cracker Jar, Chrysanthemums, Gold Enamels, Signed, 9 In. 895.00
Cracker Jar, Flowers, Ruffled Rim, Plated Cover, 5 1/4 In. 495.00
Cracker Jar, Jeweled Flowers, Mottled, Pink Ground, 6 X 8 In. 975.00
Cracker Jar, Jeweled, Rose Blossoms, Thorny Stems, 5 1/2 In. 445.00
Cracker Jar, Leaves, Acorns, Gold Tracery, Silver Fittings 675.00

Cracker Jar, Peach & Amber, Rose Blossoms, Buds, 7 1/4 In.	400.00
Cracker Jar, Seaweed, Octopus Design, Signed, 6 1/2 In.	1000.00
Cracker Jar, Seaweed, Plated Bail Rim, Signed, 6 1/2 In.	1100.00
Cracker Jar, Venetian Scene	525.00
Creamer, Green Stalks, Blossoms, Handle, 3 1/2 In.	285.00
Dish, Sweetmeat, Flowers, Blown-Out Feet, Silver Top	325.00
Dish, Sweetmeat, Jeweled Starfish	1050.00
Dish, Sweetmeat, Melon Ribbed, Multicolored Flowers, 5 1/4 In.	825.00
Dish, Sweetmeat, Quilted, Enamel Design	595.00
Ewer, Spider Mum, Enameled, Mt. Washington, 1888	1800.00
Jar, Sweetmeat, Horizontal Lines, Pansies, Signed, 14 In.	550.00
Mustard, Cover, Allover Florals	575.00
Mustard, Multicolored Flowers, Gold Design, Signed	640.00
Sugar Shaker, Cylindrical, Stylized Daisies, 6 In.	435.00
Syrup, Gold Oak Branch, Lime Green Wash, Melon Ribbed	985.00
Syrup, Melon Shape, Acorns, Oak Leaves, Cover, 5 1/2 In.	475.00
Syrup, Melon Shape, Enameled & Gilded Acorns, 5 1/2 In.	525.00
Toothpick, Raised Design, Tricorner	195.00
Tray, Pansies, Gold Scrolls, Curly Edge, Signed, 9 1/2 X 12 In.	875.00
Vase, 3 Leaf Handles, Colored Pansies, Gold Trim, 8 In.	1870.00
Vase, Diamond Quilted, Peach Ground, Beaded, 4 1/2 In.	250.00
Vase, Double-Eagle Medallion, Double Scrolled Handles, 9 In.	650.00
Vase, Ferns, 24 Molded Swirls, Onion Shape, Plated Stand	385.00
Vase, Flowers, Bird On Branch, Russet & Gold, 12 In.	695.00
Vase, Geometric Designs, Earth Tones, Applied Handles, 8 In.	485.00
Vase, Jeweled, Scalloped Rim, Diamond-Quilted Body, 4 1/2 In.	275.00
Vase, Overlapping Ferns, Amber Ground, Footed, 5 3/4 In.	300.00
Vase, Pink Flamingos, Palm Fronds	1500.00
Vase, Tiny Squares of Earth Tones, , 8 In.	485.00

CROWN TUSCAN, see Cambridge

Cruets of glass or porcelain were made to hold vinegar, oil, and other condiments. They were especially popular during Victorian times but have been made in a variety of styles since the eighteenth century.

CRUET, see also Castor Set

CRUET, Blue Opalescent, Apple Blossom	110.00
Cranberry Glass, Leaf Sprig	155.00
Cranberry Glass, Ribbed, Clear Shell Handle, 7 3/4 In.	210.00
Flora, Clear, Gold, Stopper	150.00
Opalescent, Mauve Top, Stopper, Clear, Flowers, Stourbridge, 8 1/2 In.	450.00
Red Flashed, Stopper, Royal Crystal	165.00

Cup plates are small glass or china plates that held the cup while a gentleman of the mid-nineteenth century drank his coffee or tea from the saucer. The most famous cup plates were made of glass at the Boston and Sandwich factory located in Sandwich, Massachusetts. There have been many new glass cup plates made in recent years for sale to the gift shops or the limited edition collectors. These are similar to the old plates but can be identified.

CUP PLATE, Admiral Dewey, 5 1/2 In.	20.00
Anchor Center	125.00
Garfield	125.00
Harp Center	125.00
Jade Opaque Glass, 12 Hearts	450.00
Nursery Rhyme, Hey Diddle Diddle	12.00
Nursery Rhyme, Jack Be Nimble	12.00
Nursery Rhyme, Little Miss Muffett	12.00

Never throw out your plate's original box or papers. They add to the resale value. Your homeowner's insurance doesn't cover your plates or figurines. You will need a Fine Art's policy with a breakage clause.

Currier & Ives,
Champion Race, 1887,
19 X 28 In.

THE DARKTOWN OTHELLO.

I mashed her on de dangers I had passed (drivin' an army muell).

Currier & Ives, The Darktown Othello, 13 1/2 X 17 3/4 In.

Currier & Ives,
Midnight Race On The Mississippi,
9 X 13 In.

Currier & Ives made the famous American lithographs marked with their name from 1857 to 1907. The mark used on the print included the street address in New York City, and it is possible to date the year of the original issue from this information. Earlier prints were made by N. Currier and use that name from 1835 to 1847. Many reprints of the Currier or Currier & Ives prints have been made. Many collectors also buy the insurance calendars that were based on the old prints. The words large, small, or medium folio refer to size.

CURRIER & IVES, A Midnight Race On The Mississippi, Framed, 22 X 30 In. 600.00
Abraham Lincoln, Mahogany Frame, 1861, 12 1/2 X 16 1/2 In. 225.00
American Country Life, October Afternoon, Large Folio 2675.00
American Country Life, Pleasures of Winter, Large Folio 1985.00
American Field Sports, Flushed, Birds, Setters, Large Folio 995.00
American Forest Game, Turkey, Duck, Grouse, Large Folio 985.00
American Homestead, Winter, Small Folio 595.00
Among The Pines, Framed, 13 1/2 X 17 1/2 In. 100.00
Andrew Jackson, 7th President, Framed, 10 X 14 In. 125.00
Arkansas Traveler, Backwoods Scene, Small Folio 270.00
Black Duck Shooting, 14 3/4 X 18 3/4 In. 150.00
Bouquet of Roses, Old Gilt Frame, 13 1/2 X 17 1/2 In. 30.00
Bridge At The Outlet, Framed, 18 1/4 X 23 In. 275.00
Camping Out, Some of The Right Sort, Large Folio 2175.00
Celebrated Trotting Mare, Mattie Woodward, Large Folio 1775.00
Champion Race, 1887, 19 X 28 In. ....*Illus* 1320.00
Clipper Ship Dreadnought Off Sandy Hook, Large Folio 2650.00
Constitution & Guerriere, Framed, 15 1/2 X 19 1/2 In. 175.00
Crack Trotter In Harness of Period, Framed 250.00
Cutter Yacht Thistle, Framed, 15 1/2 X 18 1/2 In. 225.00
Darktown Othello, 13 1/2 X 17 3/4 In. ....*Illus* 467.50
Darktown Trial, Judge's Charge, Small Folio 70.00
Death of Tecumseh, Beveled Frame, 1841, 12 3/8 X 16 3/8 In. 75.00
Dexter, Ethan Allen & Mate, 1874, Frame, 12 5/8 X 17 1/2 In. 255.00
Express Train, C.& I., Engine, 7 Coaches, 1870, Small Folio 1250.00
Franklin Pierce, Mahogany Frame, 1852, 12 1/2 X 16 3/4 In. 75.00
Fruit Vase, Old Gilt Frame, 13 1/2 X 17 1/2 In. 25.00
Fruits of The Tropics, Small Folio 140.00
George Washington, 1st President, Framed, 10 X 14 In. 175.00
Going Against The Stream, 16 X 20 In. 35.00
Grand National American Banner, Fillmore, Donnelson, 1856 .... 275.00
Great Fire At Boston, Nov. 9th & 10th, 1872, Small Folio 295.00
Hiawatha's Wooing, Deer At Feet of Minnehaha, Large Folio 435.00
Home In The Country, Summer, Children & Women, Large Folio 595.00
James Monroe, 5th President, Framed, 10 X 14 In. 100.00
John Quincy Adams, 6th President, Seated, Small Folio 150.00
John Tyler, 10th President, Framed, 10 X 14 In. 100.00
Kiss Me Quick, Small Folio 240.00
Lake In The Woods, Buck & Doe In Clearing, Small Folio 195.00
Lawn Tennis At Darktown, Small Folio 525.00
Life of A Fireman, Fire, Large Folio 1525.00
Little Brother & Sister, Framed, 12 1/2 X 17 1/2 In. 100.00
Little May Blossom, 19 X 16 In. 75.00
Martin Van Buren, 8th President, Frame, 16 1/4 X 12 3/4 In. 100.00
Mary Ann, Framed, 14 1/2 X 18 1/2 In. 45.00
Memorial of 2 Deaths, Mahogany Frame, 16 1/2 X 12 1/2 In. 65.00
Midnight Race On The Mississippi, 9 X 13 In. ....*Illus* 358.00
Millard Fillmore, Whig, Vice Pres., 13 1/2 X 18 In. 150.00
Morning of Life, 1874, 9 3/4 X 13 1/4 In. 85.00
My Pet Bird, Young Girl Holding Dove, Large Folio 150.00
Naval Heroes of The U.S., Pine Frame, 1846, 10 X 14 In. 200.00
Noah's Ark, Framed, 11 1/2 X 15 3/4 In. 100.00
Old Ford Bridge, 9 X 12 In. 150.00
Old Mare The Best Horse, Large Folio 695.00

Old Saw Mill, Long Island, Small Folio	220.00
Past & Future, Young Mother & Daughter, Large Folio	395.00
Presidents of The United States, 16 1/2 X 12 1/2 In.	75.00
Roadside Mill, 1870, 9 X 12 In.	150.00
Roses of May, Small Folio	100.00
Soldiers Adieu, Pine Beveled Frame, 13 1/2 X 17 1/2 In.	55.00
Star Spangled Banner, Beveled Frame, 10 X 14 In.	200.00
Tomb of Washington, Mt. Vernon, Virginia, Medium Folio	260.00
View From Ft. Putnam, 9 X 12 In.	150.00
Washington's Entry Into New York, 1783, Medium Folio	595.00
William F. Johnstone, Gov. Penna, 1848, Framed, 12 X 16 In.	75.00
Woodland Gate, Framed, 17 3/8 X 21 3/8 In.	425.00

Custard glass is an opaque glass sometimes called "buttermilk glass."
It was first made in the United States after 1886 at the La Belle
Glass Works, Bridgeport, Ohio. It is being reproduced.

CUSTARD GLASS, see also Maize

CUSTARD GLASS, Argonaut Shell, Berry Bowl, Gold Design, 7 1/2 In.	145.00
Argonaut Shell, Butter, Cover, Script Signed	245.00
Argonaut Shell, Sauce	60.00
Argonaut Shell, Table Set, 4 Piece	395.00 To 440.00
Argonaut Shell, Water Set, 7 Piece	875.00
Argonaut, Cruet	200.00
Beaded Circle, Creamer	170.00
Beaded Circle, Spooner	120.00
Beaded Circle, Water Set, 5 Piece	850.00
Beaded Swag, Butter, Cover	115.00
Chrysanthemum Sprig, Berry Set, Gold Trim, Design, 7 Piece	585.00
Chrysanthemum Sprig, Butter, Cover, Blue	1000.00
Chrysanthemum Sprig, Celery Vase, Blue	1050.00
Chrysanthemum Sprig, Compote, Jelly	75.00
Chrysanthemum Sprig, Cruet	225.00
Chrysanthemum Sprig, Cruet, Blue	650.00
Chrysanthemum Sprig, Salt & Pepper	200.00
Chrysanthemum Sprig, Salt & Pepper, Blue	425.00
Chrysanthemum Sprig, Sugar, Cover, Blue, Gold Trim	575.00
Chrysanthemum Sprig, Toothpick, Blue, Gold Trim	295.00
Chrysanthemum Sprig, Toothpick, Gold Trim	235.00
Chrysanthemum Sprig, Tumbler, Blue	98.00 To 135.00
Diamond With Peg, Butter, Cover	160.00
Diamond With Peg, Creamer, Miniature	30.00
Diamond With Peg, Tumbler, Madrid, Iowa	35.00
Diamond With Peg, Wine	45.00
Everglades, Berry Set, 6 Piece	365.00
Everglades, Table Set, 4 Piece	850.00
Fan, Berry Bowl, 7 1/2 In.	200.00
Fan, Pitcher, Water	295.00
Fan, Sauce	65.00
Fluted Scroll, Water Set, Gold Trim, 5 Piece	350.00
Geneva, Butter, Cover	125.00
Geneva, Creamer, Green, Red Trim	65.00
Geneva, Cruet, Green, Gold Design	50.00 To 450.00
Geneva, Salt & Pepper, Design	165.00
Geneva, Spooner, Green & Red	60.00
Geneva, Toothpick	78.00
Georgia Gem, Butter, Cover, Enameled	135.00
Georgia Gem, Pitcher, Water, Green, Gold Trim	75.00
Georgia Gem, Spooner, Floral Design	65.00
Georgia Gem, Sugar & Creamer, Illinois State Penitentiary	85.00
Georgia Gem, Table Set, Green, Enamel Trim, 4 Piece	425.00
Georgia Gem, Toothpick, Green, Gold Trim	60.00
Georgia Gem, Tumbler	35.00
Grape & Cable, Butter, Cover, Nutmeg Stain	150.00
Grape & Thumbprint, Water Set, 7 Piece	1250.00

Grape Arbor, Hat 60.00
Grape Arbor, Tumbler, Blue Design 145.00
Intaglio, Berry Set, 7 Piece 475.00
Intaglio, Butter, Cover, Gold Trim 175.00
Intaglio, Compote, Jelly 90.00
Intaglio, Creamer ....75.00 To 100.00
Intaglio, Cruet, Green Design, Gold Trim 300.00
Intaglio, Spooner, Green, Gold Trim 110.00
Intaglio, Sugar, Green & Gold Design 125.00
Intaglio, Table Set, Blue, 4 Piece 495.00
Intaglio, Table Set, Green, Gold Trim, 4 Piece 550.00
Intaglio, Tumbler, Green Design 45.00
Intaglio, Water Set, Blue, Gold Trim, 7 Piece 475.00
Inverted Fan & Feather, Berry Bowl, 7 1/2 In. 295.00
Inverted Fan & Feather, Berry Set, 6 Piece 535.00
Inverted Fan & Feather, Butter 325.00
Inverted Fan & Feather, Creamer 115.00
Inverted Fan & Feather, Spooner 100.00
Inverted Fan & Feather, Sugar 135.00
Inverted Fan & Feather, Table Set, 4 Piece 575.00
Inverted Fan & Feather, Toothpick, Gold Trim 650.00
Inverted Fan & Feather, Tumbler, Gold Trim 35.00
    IVORINA VERDE, see Winged Scroll
Jackson, Creamer ....50.00 To 100.00
Jackson, Tumbler 20.00
    LITTLE GEM, see also Georgia Gem
Little Gem, Salt & Pepper, Souvenir 43.00
Little Gem, Toothpick, Green 45.00
Lotus & Grape, Bonbon, Nutmeg Stain 95.00
Louis XV, Butter, Cover, Gold 125.00
Louis XV, Creamer 75.00
Louis XV, Pitcher, Water, Green, Gold Trim 125.00
Louis XV, Spooner 75.00
Louis XV, Sugar, Cover 45.00
Louis XV, Table Set, Gold Trim, 4 Piece ....350.00 To 550.00
Louis XV, Tumbler, Green, Gold Trim ....50.00 To 60.00
    MAIZE, see Maize category
Maple Leaf, Banana Boat, Silver Overlay 155.00
Maple Leaf, Creamer 110.00
Maple Leaf, Spooner 110.00
Maple Leaf, Sugar 60.00
Maple Leaf, Table Set, 4 Piece ....350.00 To 450.00
Maple Leaf, Tumbler ....40.00 To 85.00
Peacock At Urn, Bowl, Ice Cream 35.00
Prayer Rug, Bonbon 30.00
Ring Band, Butter, Cover, Rose 14.00
Ring Band, Sugar, Cover, Gold & Rose ....85.00 To 110.00
Ring Band, Syrup, Gold Trim 295.00
Ring Band, Toothpick, Gold, Colorado Springs 65.00
Ring Band, Toothpick, Souvenir, Le Sueur, Minn. 75.00
Tarentum's Victoria, Butter, Cover 150.00
Thumbprint, Tumbler, Souvenir, Mankato, Minn. 55.00
Vermont, Butter, Cover, Blue Trim 150.00
Vermont, Creamer, Blue Design 100.00
Vermont, Sugar & Creamer 97.50
Vermont, Table Set, 3 Piece 180.00
Vermont, Toothpick, Blue 65.00
Winged Scroll, Ashtray 125.00
Winged Scroll, Butter, Cover 145.00
Winged Scroll, Creamer, Gold Trim 85.00
Winged Scroll, Cruet 165.00
Winged Scroll, Spooner ....55.00 To 85.00
Winged Scroll, Sugar 60.00
Winged Scroll, Toothpick, Footed 90.00

Cut glass has been made since ancient times, but the large majority of the pieces now for sale date from the brilliant period of glass design, 1880 to 1905. These pieces have elaborate geometric designs with a deep miter cut. Modern cut glass with a similar appearance is being made in England and Ireland. Chips and scratches are often difficult to notice but lower the value dramatically.

CUT GLASS, see also listings under factory name

CUT GLASS, Banana Boat, Harvard, 3 X 7 1/2 In.	68.00
Basket, Diamonds, Stars, Miters, Piecrust Edge	95.00
Basket, Hobstars, Triple Notched Handle, 6 1/4 X 7 1/4 In.	335.00
Bell, Dinner, Triple Square, Cut Handle, Clark	195.00
Bishop's Hat, 3-Footed, 6 1/2 X 13 In., Pair	2800.00
Bonbon, Russian, Scalloped, 6 In.	50.00
Bowl, Alhambra, 8 In.	1000.00
Bowl, Carolyn, Hoare, 2 X 8 1/4 In.	265.00
Bowl, Dauntless, 8 In.	225.00
Bowl, Fruit, 4 Pinwheels & Hobstar On Base, 4 X 8 In.	110.00
Bowl, Fruit, Finecut Diamond, Buzz Star, 1915, 8 1/2 In.	105.00
Bowl, Hobstar & Waffle, 8 In.	495.00
Bowl, Hobstars & Pinwheel, 8 In.	165.00
Bowl, Hobstars With Blaze Stars, Scalloped, Hobstar Base, 8 In.	125.00
Bowl, Hobstars, Fans & Crosscut Diamonds, Serrated Edge, 7 In.	175.00
Bowl, Hobstars, Fans, Diamonds, 8 In.	140.00
Bowl, Hobstars, Vesicas & Strawberry Diamond, 8 1/4 In.	225.00
Bowl, Jubilee, 10 In.	450.00
Bowl, Lotus, Egginton, 8 In.	185.00
Bowl, Marseilles, 8 In.	225.00
Bowl, Mayonnaise, 24 Ray Base, 3 X 5 In.	95.00
Bowl, Royal, Hunt, 9 In.	260.00
Bowl, Vesicas of Single Cane, Hobstars, 9 1/4 In.	230.00
Bowl, Wheat, Hoare, 4 1/2 X 10 In.	1400.00
Box, Collar, Intaglio Fruit Center Top & Bottom, 4 3/4 X 9 In.	595.00
Box, Handkerchief, Hinged Cover, Honeycomb, Cross Hatched, 7 In.	475.00
Butter Tub, Underplate, Monarch, Hoare, 3 3/4 X 6 1/2 In.	535.00
Butter, Cover, Electric, 1904, 5 X 7 3/8 In.	360.00
Butter, Cover, Hobstar, Scalloped Underplate	110.00
Butter, Cover, Orland, Bergen, 7 1/4 X 5 In.	455.00
Butter, Cover, Sterling, Straus, 5 X 8 In.	495.00
Cake Stand, Expanding Star, Hobstar Base, 8 1/2 X 12 1/4 In.	4000.00
Cake Stand, Harvard, Oblong, 9 In.	375.00
Candelabrum, Russian, 3-Light, 19 In.	600.00
Candy Dish, Russian, Crescent Shape, 7 In.	55.00
Carafe, Comet, Hoare, 5 1/2 In.	215.00
Carafe, Drape, Straus, 8 1/4 In.	205.00
Carafe, Hobstar & Pineapple, 1 Qt., Pair	60.50
Carafe, Pinwheel, Applied Handle, 17 In.	67.50
Carafe, Vertical Prisms & Punties, Sterling Neck, 9 In., Pair	2000.00
Carafe, Water, Crosscut Diamond & Fan	125.00
Carafe, Water, Lotus, Egginton, 7 X 6 1/2 In.	265.00
Casket, Metal Bands All Around, 6 Handles, Sample, 19 X 8 In.	2500.00
Celery Dish, Double Pinwheel, Notched Rayed Ends	260.00
Celery Dish, Hobstar Cross Cut, Scalloped Border, 11 1/2 In.	80.00
Celery Dish, Lotus, Egginton, 4 X 11 In.	155.00
Celery Vase, Hobstar & Diamond	185.00
Cheese Dish, Cover, Hobstars & Crosshatch, 7 1/2 X 9 In.	750.00
Cigar Jar, Marlboro, Hollow Stopper, Dorflinger, 9 X 6 In.	1750.00
Clock, Harvard, 12-Day, 8 1/4 X 5 X 10 3/4 In.	600.00
Coffeepot, Hobstars, Vesicas, Crosshatch, 10 In.	375.00
Coffeepot, Turkish Hookah Shape, Pedestal, Cut Stopper, 15 In.	2000.00
Compote, Cover, Thumbprint, Teardrop Stem & Finial, 10 1/2 In.	550.00
Compote, Cut Stem, Notched Foot, Rolled-In Top, 9 In., Pair	975.00
Compote, Drape, Flared, C.1896, 8 In.	2100.00
Compote, Hobstars, 9 1/2 In.	145.00

Compote, Hobstars, Vesicas, Cane, Serrated Stem, 10 1/2 In.	395.00
Compote, Petit Four, Adonis, Clark, 9 1/2 In.	495.00
Cooler, Champagne, Strawberry Diamonds, Plated Bail Handle	9300.00
Cream & Sugar, Pinwheel With Star	125.00
Cruet, Cornflower Cut Leaves, 24-Point Rayed Base, 7 In.	75.00
Cruet, Hobstar Strawberry Fan, Notched Handle, Rayed Base, 9 In.	90.00
Cruet, Marlboro, Dorflinger, 7 In.	450.00
Cruet, Pineapple Cut, Germany, 8 1/2 In., Pair	95.00
Cruet, Pinwheels & Notched Rays, Rayed Base, 6 3/4 In.	50.00
Decanter, Amethyst To Clear, Snowflake Style, 13 1/2 In.	475.00
Decanter, Cordial, Cranberry To Clear, Hobstars & Flutes, 11 In.	900.00
Decanter, Crosshatching & Rays, Cranberry To Clear, 15 In.	425.00
Decanter, Geometric & Abstract, 12 1/2 In., Pair	250.00
Decanter, Hobstar & Fans, Handle, 10 1/2 In.	275.00
Decanter, Hobstars, Diamond Point, 11 2/ In.	350.00
Decanter, Thumbprints & Honeycomb, Dorflinger, 14 In.	220.00
Decanter, Waffle, White Over Orange, Dorflinger, 15 1/2 In.	410.00
Decanter, Wedding Ring, Pyramid Shape, Hoare, 16 In.	1600.00
Decanter, Whiskey, Hobstars, Fans, Diamond Point, 11 1/2 In.	350.00
Dish, 4 Sections, Intricately Cut, 8 1/4 In.	350.00
Dish, Banana Split, Pedestal, Strawberry Diamond, 5 X 8 In.	295.00
Dish, Cheese, Child's, Diamond Rim, Stars, Etched Cover, 3 X 3 In.	65.00
Dish, Ice Cream, Russian With Star Buttons, 6 In., 6 Piece	550.00
Dish, Mayonnaise, Underplate, Expanding Star	225.00
Dish, Trefoil, Harvard On 3 Sides, Daisy Each Corner, 6 1/4 In.	75.00
Flask, Whiskey, Woman's, Cane, Sterling Top, Velvet Bag, 10 In.	325.00
Fruit Bowl, Intaglio, 8 In.	195.00
Fruit Bowl, Rectangular Pears & Grapes	1000.00
Goblet, St. Louis Diamond, C.1852, 6 Piece	390.00
Goblet, Water, Russian, Cut Knob Teardrop Stem, 6 3/8 In.	125.00
Hair Receiver, Sterling Lid, Double Miter Notched Bars	250.00
Humidor, Strawberry, Diamond & Fan, 6 In.	325.00
Ice Bucket, Hobstars, Hobnail, Fine Diamond, Star Base, 5 3/4 In.	595.00
Ice Bucket, Monarch, Hoare, 5 1/2 In.	295.00
Ice Tub, Underplate, Marquis, Hoare, C.1911, 8 1/4 In.	2200.00
Inkwell, Double Pyramid Form, 1900, 3 In.	55.00
Jar, Crisscross, Star Cut, Cranberry, 4 3/4 In. ¢Illus	195.00
Jar, Diagonal Crisscross, Triple Overlay, 4 3/4 In.	195.00
Jar, Dresser, Sterling Silver Lid, Monogram, 3 3/4 In.	95.00
Jug, Claret, Silver Collar, T.B. Starr, C.1900, 11 5/8 In.	1960.00
Jug, Claret, Silver-Gilt, S-Scroll Handle, Durgin Co., C.1900	7150.00
Jug, Rum, 8-Sided, Hobstars, Triple Notched Handle, 7 In.	1150.00
Jug, Whiskey, Hobstars, Fans, Cane Strawberry Diamonds, 9 1/2 In.	450.00
Knife Rest, Cross Hatching, 4 1/2 In.	50.00
Lamp, American Brilliant, 21 In.	2250.00
Lamp, Domed Shade, Hobstar Foot, Notched & Fan, 18 In.	170.00
Lamp, Mushroom Shade, Green Medallions, 40 Prisms, 21 In.	600.00
Loving Cup, Crosscut Diamonds, Strawberry Vesicas, 5 3/4 In.	525.00
Loving Cup, Diamond Point Blocks In Rows & Columns, 10 In.	950.00
Mustard, Cover, Spoon, Strawberry, Diamond & Cushion	45.00
Napkin Ring, 3 Layers, Red, White & Crystal	65.00
Nappy, Crosscut Strawberry Diamond, Chain of Hobstar	135.00
Nappy, Hobstar, Scalloped Serrated Edge	90.00
Perfume Bottle, Harvard Panels, Oval Thumbprints, Silver Collar	145.00
Perfume Caddy, Egg Shape, Brass, 4 Vials, Waterford, 8 In.	325.00
Pitcher, Cider, Pinwheel, Rayed Base, 9 In.	350.00
Pitcher, Crosscut Stars, Circles, Silver Rim, Horn Handle, 12 In.	885.00
Pitcher, Flower & Leaf, Shooting Star, Cross Diamond, 11 1/2 In.	150.00
Pitcher, Harvard, 14 3/4 In.	550.00
Pitcher, Hobstars, Pinwheels, Crosshatch, 10 In.	165.00
Pitcher, Meriden Star, Claret Shape, 11 1/4 In.	390.00
Pitcher, Russian, Rows of Oval Bull's-Eyes, 9 In.	650.00
Pitcher, Silver Trim, Stag Horn Handle, 7 In.	400.00
Pitcher, Strawberry & Diamond, Bulbous, 7 1/2 In.	225.00

Pitcher, Water, Butterfly & Daisy, 11 1/2 In. .... 185.00 To 195.00
Pitcher, Water, Flowers, Vines, Pinwheels & Zipper, 8 In. 155.00
Pitcher, Water, Intaglio Cut Sprays of Florals & Foliage, 9 In. 155.00
Pitcher, Water, Wreath & Intaglio Blossoms, 10 In. .... 158.00 To 160.00
Plate, Columbia, Blackmer, 7 In. 195.00
Plate, Strawberry & Diamond, 7 In. 60.00
Punch Bowl, Heart, Brilliant, Pitkin & Brooks, 1 Piece 1100.00
Punch Bowl, Hobstar & Fan, Flared, American Cut, 13 In. 355.00
Punch Bowl, Imperial, 24-Point Hobstar Base, Straus 1350.00
Punch Bowl, Ladle, Marlboro, Emerald Green To Clear, Dorflinger 9500.00
Relish, 4 Sections, Expanding Star, 9 In. 325.00
Relish, Pinwheels, Zipper 90.00
Relish, Royal, Hunt, 9 X 5 3/4 In. 475.00
Relish, Underplate, Sawtooth Edge, Hobstar Design, 7 X 5 In. 145.00
Rose Bowl, Pedestal, Plymouth, Meriden 285.00
Salt & Pepper, Block Cut, Cut Tops 50.00
Salt & Pepper, Zipper, Glass Top 85.00
Server, Divided, Roses, 1 1/2-In.Sterling Silver Rim, 10 In. 95.00
Serving Set, Salad, Allover Strawberry, Diamond Point, 11 1/4 In. 95.00
Spill Holder, Smocking, Sawtooth Rim, 4 1/2 In. 40.00
Sugar & Creamer, American, Brilliant, Allover Hobstars, Large 150.00
Sugar & Creamer, Beverly 155.00
Sugar & Creamer, Buzzsaws Flanked By Notched Miters, 3 3/4 In. 275.00
Sugar & Creamer, Crosscut Diamond, Notched Handles 125.00
Sugar & Creamer, Heart 365.00
Sugar & Creamer, Hobstars, Flashed Trim, 6 1/2 X 2 3/4 In. 250.00
Sugar & Creamer, Pineapple 85.00
Sugar & Creamer, Royal, Hunt .... 225.00 To 250.00
Sugar & Creamer, Tulip Leaves, Hobstars & Rays, 1900–10 .... 95.00
Sugar Shaker, Strawberry Diamond & Fan 110.00
Syrup, Intaglio Panels, Gorham Top, 5 In. 285.00
Tankard, Bands of Hobstars & Notched Cutting, 13 3/4 In. 350.00
Tankard, Bull's-Eye, Diamond Point, Hobnail, Crosscut, 11 In. 350.00
Tankard, Fern & Pinwheel, 12 1/4 In. 595.00
Tankard, Hobstars On Body, Hobstar Base, 14 In. 1700.00
Tankard, Notched Prism, Sterling Top, 12 In. 275.00
Tobacco Jar, Zipper 300.00
Toothpick, Fluted Diamonds 42.00
Tray, Fan, Crosshatch & Diamond Point, Hobstar Center, 13 In. 550.00
Tray, Hobstar Clusters, 13 1/2 In. 375.00
Tray, Hobstars, Libbey, 12 In. 650.00
Tray, Ice Cream, Alternating Hobstars, Vesicas, 13 3/4 X 9 In. 575.00
Tray, Ice Cream, Russian, Persian Buttons, 8 X 13 1/2 In. 250.00
Tray, Royal, Hunt, 12 In. 450.00
Tray, Scalloped, Russian, Persian Buttons, 11 1/2 X 5 In. 225.00
Tumbler, Cosmos & Wheat, 6 Piece 420.00
Vase, 5 Fields of Clear Button Russian, 5 of Caning, 10 In. 750.00
Vase, Alhambra, 15 3/4 In. 5000.00
Vase, Carolyn, Hoare, 6 X 8 In. 735.00
Vase, Chain of Hobstars, Divided Miters & Triangles, 8 1/2 In. 850.00
Vase, Cylindrical Shape, Pitkin & Brooks, 18 In. 525.00
Vase, Diamond & Hobstar, Quatrefoil Allover, 15 In. 3800.00
Vase, Diamond Faceted Ball Connectors, Cranberry, 7 1/2 In., Pair 325.00
Vase, Diamond Point, Cut Floral Leaf Bands Top, 9 In. 80.00
Vase, Diamond, 15 1/2 In., Pair 750.00
Vase, Florence, Hobnail Button Design, Hobstar, 21 In. 1300.00
Vase, Grape & Leaf, Diamond Point Panels, 8 1/2 In. 80.00
Vase, Hobstar, Daisy & Button, 6-Sided Zipper, Hoare, 14 In. 500.00
Vase, Hobstar, Fan & Diamond Point, Bowling Pin Shape, 12 In. 350.00
Vase, Hobstars & Stars, Flared, 8 1/2 In. 225.00
Vase, Hobstars, Bowling Pin Shape, 15 3/4 In. 1750.00
Vase, Hobstars, Fan & Cane, 2 Stepcut Handles, 12 In. 600.00
Vase, Hobstars, Fan, Crosscut Diamond, 13 In. 180.00
Vase, Montrose, Green To Clear, Dorflinger, 12 In. 1550.00

Vase, Paperweight Base, Bulbous, Dorflinger, 14 In. 6000.00
Vase, Parisian, Dorflinger, 14 1/4 In. 750.00
Vase, Rose & Leaf, Scalloped Top, Vertical Ribbing, 10 1/2 In. 150.00
Vase, Sections Joined By Center Ring, Floral Bands, 28 3/4 In. 3000.00
Vase, Silver Collar, Flowers & Leaves, Engraved 1868–1912, 15 In. 1750.00
Vase, Step Cutting From Base, Hoare, 10 In. 385.00
Vase, Strawberry Diamonds & Fans, Foliage Band, 8 1/4 In. 200.00
Vase, Strawberry Diamonds, Fans & Rays, 8 1/4 In. 200.00
Vase, Strawberry, Squat Shape, Sawtooth Rim, 5 1/2 In. 225.00
Vase, Thistles & Blossoms Overall, 15 In. 500.00
Vase, Trumpet, Marlboro, Dorflinger, 14 In. 250.00
Water Set, Cornflower, Cane Top & Bottom, Star Base, 7 Piece 375.00
Water Set, Daisy Spray, 6 Piece 375.00
Water Set, Pinwheel, 5 Piece 375.00
Wine, Strawberry Diamond, Vesicas, Teardrop Stem, 5 1/2 In., 8 Pc. 225.00
Wine, Vesicas & Fans, Knob Stem 35.00

> Glue broken china with any invisible mending cement that is waterproof.

CYBIS

Boleslaw Cybis came to the United States from Poland in 1939. He started making porcelains in Long Island, New York, in 1940. He moved to Trenton, New Jersey, in 1942 as one of the founders of Cordey China Co. and started his own Cybis Porcelains about 1950. The firm is still working. (See also Cordey.)

CYBIS, Bust, Eskimo Child, 7 1/2 In. 110.00
Bust, Indian Boy, Head Band, 1975, 10 In. 198.00
Bust, Indian Boy, Headdress, 12 In. 110.00
Figurine, Baby Brother, Duckling, 4 1/2 In. 115.00
Figurine, Baby Owl, 4 1/2 In. 85.00
Figurine, Beatrice, 12 In. 750.00
Figurine, Betty, Blue, 9 In. 200.00
Figurine, Cinderella, 7 1/2 In. 500.00
Figurine, Eskimo Mother, 10 1/2 In. 3500.00
Figurine, Goldilocks and Panda Bear, 6 In. .... 200.00 To 295.00
Figurine, In Clover, Deer Mouse, 3 1/2 In. 75.00
Figurine, Little Red Riding Hood, 6 1/2 In. 295.00
Figurine, Mr. Snowball, Bunny, 4 In. 65.00
Figurine, Nefertiti, 12 1/4 In. 2000.00
Figurine, On Cue, Ballerina, 12 1/2 In. 450.00
Figurine, On Cue, Ballerina, White, 12 1/2 In. 350.00
Figurine, Pollyanna, 7 In. 350.00
Figurine, Sebastian, Seal, 5 1/2 In. 125.00
Figurine, Sir Henry Escargot, Snail, 3 In. 165.00
Figurine, Two Colts, 1969, 8 In. 176.00
Figurine, Yankee Doodle Dandy, 9 In. 295.00

There are some collectibles that are identified by the name of the country, not a factory mark. Anything marked "Czechoslovakia" is popular today. The name, first used as a mark after the country was formed in 1918, appears on glass and porcelain and other decorative items. The name is still used in some trademarks.

CZECHOSLOVAKIA, Candlestick, Pink Blossoms, Signed Thelma, 1948, 8 3/4 In. 125.00
Creamer, Parrot, Orange & Yellow, 4 1/2 In. 25.00
Decanter, Cone Shape, Square Ruby Handle, Cut Stopper, Glass 175.00
Dresser Set, Painted, Milk Glass, 4 Piece 50.00
Figurine, Doctor, Stethoscope, Gray Hair, Full Beard, 8 In. 445.00
Figurine, Man, Beating Drum, Green Spatter Glass, 6 In. 415.00
Figurine, Smoker, Fat Pipe, Glass, 7 1/2 In. 350.00
Figurine, Watchman, With Horn, Glass, 7 1/2 In. 350.00
Flower Holder, Orange Cockatoo, Tree Trunk, 4 Holes, 9 In. 35.00
Lamp, Beaded Peacock, Pair 700.00

D'Argental, Bowl, Grapes & Vines, Amber Body, Signed, 12 1/2 In.

Paperweight, Clear Glass, Masaryk Photo Embedded, 4 In. 65.00
Perfume Bottle, Trapezoid Stopper, Cut Squares, Glass, 4 In. 110.00
Pitcher, Light Green, Green Handle, Blob Trim, Glass, 7 In. 20.00
Pitcher, Moose, 3 1/4 In. 35.00
Pitcher, Orange Luster, Bubble Design, Pottery, 7 In. 85.00
Place Card Set, Porcelain, 6 Piece 35.00
Plate, Peasant Art, Signed Mrazek, 10 In. 16.00
Vase, Art Deco, Mottled Beige Pottery, Orange, Marked 36.00
Vase, Fan, Applied Blue Threading, Glass, 9 1/2 In. 85.00
Vase, Flower Shape, Allover Spatter, Black Interior, 5 In. 45.00
Vase, Pouter Pigeons, Bracket Base, Glass, 9 3/4 In. 95.00
Vase, Purple Threading, Oil Spot Yellow, Glass, Signed, 7 In. 245.00
Vase, Yellow Enameled Striping, Red Flowers, Glass, 5 In. 28.00
Wall Pocket, Bird 15.00
Wall Pocket, Tree Limb, Figural Bird, Birdhouse, Pottery 40.00
Whiskey Set, Green Glass Decanter, Gold Trim, 6 Piece 60.00

D'argental   D'Argental is a mark used in France by the Compagnie des
Cristalleries de St. Louis. The firm made multilayered, acid–cut
cameo glass in the late nineteenth and twentieth centuries.
D'Argental is the French name for the city of Munzthal, home of
the glassworks. Later they made enameled etched glass.

D'ARGENTAL, Bowl, Grapes & Vines, Amber Body, Signed, 12 1/2 In. ....*Illus* 2750.00
Vase, Cameo, 3 Cut To Clear Window Scenes, 12 In. 5200.00
Vase, Flowering Leafy Vines, Pyriform, Signed, C.1920, 5 1/2in. 550.00
Vase, Lake, Forest, Trees, Brown & Oranges, Signed, 8 In. 1100.00
Vase, Landscape, Storks On Rooftops, Signed, C.1920, 10 1/4 In. 885.00
Vase, Red Overlay, Camel, Pyramid, Palms Scene, Cameo, 5 1/2 In. 335.00
Vase, Undulating Poppy Blossoms, Buds, Leaves, Signed, 8 1/4 In. 885.00
Vase, Wildflowers & Leaves, Signed, C.1920, 13 3/8 In. 1100.00

DAUM
NANCY
†   Jean Daum started a glassworks in Nancy, France, in 1875. The
company, now called "Cristalleries de Nancy," is still working. The
"Daum Nancy" mark has been used in many variations. The name
of the city and the artist are usually both included.

DAUM NANCY, Bowl, Buckeye Leaves, Berries, Yellow Streaks, Signed, 1910, 4 In. 1650.00
Bowl, Cameo, Footed, 11 X 9 In. ....*Illus* 3750.00

Don't put china with gold designs in the dishwasher. The gold will wash off.

Bowl, Canoe Shape, Wildflowers Sprays, Signed, C.1915, 5 3/4 In.	2100.00
Bowl, Carved & Enameled Butterfly Amid Hydrangea, 10 In.	5500.00
Bowl, Enameled Violets, Leaves, Signed, C.1910, 3 3/4 In.	1980.00
Bowl, Flowers, Naturalistic Colors, Signed, 8 3/4 In.	6050.00
Bowl, French Coin In Base, Blue, White & Red, Dated 1872, 9 In.	300.00
Bowl, Gray Walls, Jack–In–The–Pulpit Blossom, Signed, 5 1/2 In.	9075.00
Bowl, Pansies, Silver Rim & Foot, 9 In.	2250.00
Bowl, Prunus Blossoms, Hemispherical, Signed, C.1910, 3 3/8 In.	1450.00
Bowl, Quatrefoil Rim, Chartreuse Overlay, Berries, 3 1/2 In.	1750.00
Bowl, Red Fuchsias, Golden Ground, Cameo & Enameled	3950.00
Bowl, Topaz Walls, Angular Zigzags, Signed, C.1925, 14 1/2 In.	8475.00
Bowl, Trees In Autumn Colors, Signed, 5 1/2 X 2 1/2 In.	2100.00
Bowl, Wildflowers & Leaves, Gray, Signed, C.1910, 11 1/4 In.	1100.00
Box, Cover, Blossoms, Flattened Square, Signed, 6 X 3 3/8 In.	4400.00
Box, Domical Cover, Clover Blossoms, Signed, C.1910, 3 In.	3850.00
Box, Dresser, Purple Violets, Green Leaves, Gold Trim	950.00
Brush Holder, Pink Hips, Vitrified Chartreuse Leaves, 4 3/4 In.	1840.00
Ceiling Fixture, Cameo, Purple, Variegated, Grapes, Vines, 12 In.	5280.00
Chandelier, 4 Supports, Blossoms, Brandt Iron, C.1920, 31 In.	4125.00
Chandelier, Domed Shade, Knob Mounts To Chain, 1925, 15 3/4 In.	995.00
Chandelier, Sunflowers, Glass Centers, Iron Leaves, 1930, 38 In.	5775.00
Cruet, Cameo, Foliated Branch, Gold Enameled Accents, 7 1/4 In.	1750.00
Cruet, Cameos On Both Sides, Flat Sided Stopper, Sterling Frame	1750.00
Ewer, Intaglio Florets, C–Scroll Handle, Signed, 1915, 9 7/8 In.	3575.00
Figurine, Horsehead, Crystal, 5 1/2 In.	275.00
Jar, Circular Cover, Violets, Square Base, Signed, 3 In.	3300.00
Jar, Stopper, Keystone Finial, Gray, Streaked, Signed, 4 In.	6655.00
Jug, Lilies–of–The–Valley, Silver Mounted, C.1910, 4 In.	2750.00
Keg, Wine, Cameo, Berries & Leaves, Frosted, 3 X 3 In.	595.00
Lamp, Brown Leaves & Vines, Yellow Ground, 12 In.	450.00
Lamp, Calla Lily Bronze Base, Domed Shade, 16 3/4 In.	6500.00
Lamp, Cameo, Mushroom Shade, Footed Base, 10 X 18 1/2 In.	5000.00
Lamp, Iron Stork Form Base, Holds Shade, Signed, C.1910, 19 In.	1750.00
Lamp, Landscape, Iron Mounted, Signed, C.1910, 16 3/4 In.	9900.00
Paperweight, Figural, Mouse On Rock Base, Pate–De–Verre, C.1920	1100.00
Perfume Bottle, Cameo, Green, Gold, Stopper, Cylindrical, 3 In.	750.00
Perfume Bottle, Gilt Wildflowers, Silver Mounted, 5 1/2 In.	1450.00
Pitcher, Acid Cut Fuchsias, Silver Mounted	2350.00
Plate, 2 Colors, 10 1/2 In.	100.00
Shot Glass, Winter Scene, Peach Ground, Barrel Shape, 2 In.	950.00
Toothpick, Crystal, Vertical Acid Cuts Interior, Oval, 2 1/4 In.	85.00
Toothpick, Purple Flowers, Enameled Design, Urn Shape	600.00
Toothpick, Vertical Acid Cuttings, Oval, 2 X 4 In.	85.00
Tray, Summer Scene, Cameo, Rose, Triangular, 3 3/4 X 4 In.	1500.00
Tray, Winter Scene, Cameo, 5 1/4 X 5 1/4 In.	2950.00
Tumbler, Green, Mistletoe, Gold and White Enamel, 5 In.	315.00
Tumbler, Juice, Trees Reflecting In Water, Barrel Shape, 1914	850.00
Tumbler, Red & Blue Violets & Leaf Design, Signed, 4 3/4 In.	450.00
Vase, 3 Layer, Leaf & Berries, Signed, 7 In. ....*Illus*	3080.00
Vase, Alpine Lake Scene, White & Salmon Ground, Signed, 19 In.	6100.00
Vase, Amethyst, Yellow Body, Sailboats, Signed, 21 In. ....*Illus*	5600.00
Vase, Birch Trees In Winter Landscape, Signed, 1910, 13 3/4 In.	4400.00
Vase, Black Boats On Water, Orange Ground, Cameo, 2 1/2 In.	650.00
Vase, Daffodils, Green Overlay, Blue Ground, Signed, 5 3/4 In.	7150.00
Vase, Dots Over Band of Squared Os, Signed, 1925, 9 1/4 In.	3350.00
Vase, Dots Rising From Beneath Water, Signed, C.1925, 14 3/8 In.	4400.00
Vase, Enameled Summer Farm Scene, Signed, 4 1/2 In.	925.00
Vase, Etched Poppies, Green & Amber Martele, Conical, 9 1/2 In.	3800.00
Vase, Floral, 2–Tone Ground, Cameo, Signed, 4 1/2 In.	2500.00
Vase, Flowers, Scrolled Feet, Silver Base, Green & Gold, 7 In.	1450.00
Vase, Geometric Design, Iron Stand, Beaded Border, Signed, 9 In.	5250.00
Vase, Gilded Cross–Like Design, Green, Cameo, Signed, 2 7/8 In.	300.00
Vase, Green, Gold, Cameo, Ornate Silver Base, Scrolled Foot, 7 In.	1450.00
Vase, Inverted Bell, Cut Chestnut Leaves, C.1910, 13 7/8 In.	1430.00

Daum Nancy, Bowl, Cameo, Footed, 11 X 9 In.

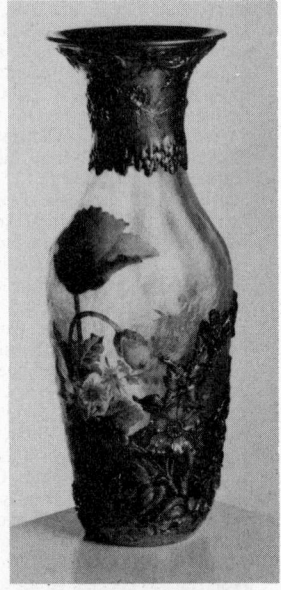

Daum Nancy, Vase, Amethyst, Yellow Body,
Sailboats, Signed, 21 In.

Daum Nancy,
Vase, Poppies,
Foliage,
Red & Green,
5 In.

Daum Nancy, Vase, Poppies, Foliage,
Silver Overlay, 12 In.

Daum Nancy, Vase, 3 Layer, Leaf & Berries,
Signed, 7 In.

Vase, Inverted Bell, Etched, Green, Signed, 5 1/4 In. 585.00
Vase, Iris, Flattened Baluster, Cameo, Signed, 6 In. 525.00
Vase, Landscape, River, Yellow Walls, Signed, C.1910, 4 1/2 In. 1200.00
Vase, Lead Overlay At Top, Mottled Green & Blue, 5 X 7 In. 450.00
Vase, Leaves & Tree Branches, Russet Brown Over Yellow, 23 In. 3025.00
Vase, Mistletoe Branches, Silver Mounts, Signed, 1910, 5 1/2 In. 1350.00
Vase, Olive Green Overlay, Cushion Form Base, C.1910, 12 In. 1650.00
Vase, Orange, Thistle Design, Silver Base, Signed, 6 In. 450.00
Vase, Overlay Trees, Grasses & Ferns Base, Cameo, 1900, 16 In. 4500.00
Vase, Poppies, Foliage, Red & Green, 5 In. ....*Illus* 1000.00
Vase, Poppies, Foliage, Silver Overlay, 12 In. ....*Illus* 6200.00
Vase, Riverside With Trees, Wildflowers, Signed, 23 In. 4950.00
Vase, Scenic, Swaying Pine Trees, 15 In. 4500.00
Vase, Stylized Fruit Pendant, Branches, Signed, 1925, 13 3/4 In. 4400.00
Vase, Trumpet Blossoms, Leaves, Signed, C.1910, 9 1/16 In. 2100.00
Vase, Upright Peacock Feathers, Blues, Signed, C.1910, 11 1/2 In. 8250.00
Vase, Wheel Carved Flowers, Red On Yellow, Signed, 19 1/2 In. 5500.00
Vase, Wild Grapes, Vines, Leaves, Signed, C.1915, 17 1/4 In. 3300.00
Vase, Windmill, Brown, Ocher, Cameo, Croix De Lorraine, 5 1/2 In. 250.00
Vase, Winter Scene, Pillow, Cameo, Signed, 4 In. 1900.00
Vase, Woodland Scene Under Snow, Amber Ground, Signed, 12 In. 3300.00
Wine Keg, Pink & Gold Cameo Berries, Frosted, Knop Cover, 3 In. 595.00

Davenport pottery and porcelain were made at the Davenport
factory in Longport, Staffordshire, England, from 1793 to 1887.
Earthenwares, creamwares, porcelains, ironstone, and other ceramics
were made. Most of the pieces are marked with a form of the word
"Davenport."

DAVENPORT, Cup & Saucer, Handleless, Floral Swags 75.00
Cup & Saucer, Imari Colors, Footed 135.00
Cup & Saucer, Japanese Pattern, 1870s 45.00
Dish, Leaf Shape, Blue Transfer, Impressed Anchor, 9 1/2 In. 175.00
Dish, Vegetable, Cover, Cousin 275.00
Plate, English Country Scene, 8 1/4 In. 80.00

Davy Crockett, the American frontiersman, was born in 1786 and
died in 1836. He became popular again in 1954 with the
introduction of a television series about his life. Coonskin caps and
buckskins became popular and hundreds of different Davy Crockett
items were made.

DAVY CROCKETT, Bag, Frontier, Walt Disney, Box 110.00
Bag, Shoulder, Walt Disney, Box 125.00
Bank, Figural, Copper Color, Metal, 5 In. 65.00
Belt & Large Buckle, 24 In. 25.00
Book, Pop-Up, Push-Outs, Box 65.00
Bow Tie 15.00
Candy Box, Picture of Fess Parker, 2 X 4 X 1 In. 45.00
Canteen 25.00
Cap Gun 25.00
Cookie Jar, Brush .... 110.00 To 135.00
Cookie Jar, Regal 165.00
Cookie Jar, Standing With Rifle, American Bisque 175.00
Costume, Bland Charnas, Shirt & Pants 75.00
Display, Complete With 12 Wallets 175.00
Doll Outfit, Vogue Dolls Inc. 45.00
Doll, Davy & Betsy, Dressed, 1950s, Pair 60.00
Doll, Stuffed, Vinyl Face, Davy On Shirt, 27 In. 85.00
Doll, Suede Outfit, 8 In. 25.00
Doll, Walker, Hard Plastic, Dressed, Madame Alexander, 8 In. 120.00
Figurine, Hartland 400.00
Game, Adventure, Fess Parker Spinner 45.00
Hat, Coonskin, Halco 40.00
Holster & Click Gun, Plastic 15.00

Holster Set, Leather, Box	55.00
Knife	20.00
Lamp Shade, Pictures Davy Crockett On Front, Oval, 9 In.	65.00
Lamp, Figural, Davy Holding Rifle	55.00
Lariat Tie, Davy Crockett Pull	15.00
Lunch Box, Thermos	75.00
Mug, Ceramic, Davy's Face	65.00
Mug, Chasing Indian In Red, White	15.00
Mug, Davy & Stagecoach, Off–White	15.00
Neckerchief, With Leather Slide	25.00
Night–Light, Box	75.00
Patch, Satin, Yellow, Brown, Felt Trim, Pictures Davy, 4 In.	15.00
Peace Pipe	15.00
Pen, Ballpoint, Giant	8.75
Pin, Sunbeam Bread	6.00
Powder Horn, Daisy, Box, 1950s	25.00
Purse, Girl's	60.00
Puzzle, 1950s	12.00
Sheet Music, Ballad of Davy Crockett, 1 Page Missing, 1954	5.00
Spoon & Fork, Stainless, Engraved Rifle, 1950s	35.00
Tumbler, Davy On Horse, Gem City Dairy	26.00

William de Morgan made art pottery in England from the 1860s to 1907. He is best known for his luster–glazed Moorish–inspired pieces. The pottery used a variety of marks.

DE MORGAN, Bowl, Silver, Blue, Copper, Ruby Luster, Leaf Design, 17 In.	7500.00
Charger, Ruby Luster, Dolphins, 1888, 14 In. ....*Illus*	3300.00
Tile, Leaves, Flowers, Green, Silver, 8 In.	275.00
Vase, Red Luster On Pink, Willow Leaves, 8 In.	550.00

De Morgan, Charger, Ruby Luster, Dolphins,
1888, 14 In.

Some repairs make the sale of an antique very difficult, if not impossible. Don't buff pewter. Don't wash ivory. Don't repaint old toys. Don't tape old paper. Don't wash oil paintings.

De Vez, Vase, Blue & Red Orange,
Yellow Ground, Peacock, 15 In.

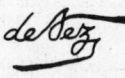 E.S. Monot founded a glass company near Paris in 1851. The company changed names many times. De Vez was a signature used on cameo glass made by this firm after 1910. Mt. Joye, another glass by this factory, is listed in its own section.

DE VEZ, Perfume Bottle, Scenic, 8 1/2 In. 795.00
Vase, Blue & Red Orange, Yellow Ground, Peacock, 15 In. ....*Illus* 3200.00
Vase, Blue, Lavender, Pink, Landscape, Bottle Form, 6 1/4 In. 660.00
Vase, Carved Butterflies, Yellow Ground, Signed 850.00
Vase, Castle & Trees, Brown & Gold On White, Signed, 14 1/2 In. 1800.00
Vase, Fern & Butterfly, Miniature 225.00
Vase, Scenic, 2 Colors, Signed, 8 In. 825.00
Vase, Scenic, 3 Cuttings, 2 Colors, Signed, 8 In. 925.00
Vase, Scenic, Birds With Fork Tails, Palm Trees, Signed, 7 1/4 In. 875.00
Vase, Scenic, Purple & Yellow, Signed, 8 In. 775.00

 Decoys are carved or turned wooden copies of birds or fish. The decoy was placed in the water or propped on the shore to lure flying birds to the pond for hunters. Some decoys are handmade, some are commercial products. Today there is a group of artists making modern decoys for display, not use in a pond.

DECOY, Black Bellied Plover 3850.00
Black Crow, Herter–Type, Composition, Full Bodied, Glass Eyes 85.00
Black Duck, Cork & Wood, Glass Eyes, 15 1/2 In. 35.00
Black Duck, Cork, Wooden Head, Glass Eyes, 19 1/4 In. 40.00
Black Duck, Crowell, 1930 .... 8250.00
Black Duck, Hollow, Glass Eyes, W. Brook, Antioch, Illinois, 15 1/4 In. 105.00
Black Duck, Madison Mitchell, Dated 1950 .... 450.00
Black Duck, Original Paint, Howard Hoadley, C.1920 .... 195.00
Black Duck, Preening Position, Crowell 6500.00
Black Duck, Preening, Standing, Ira Hudson 9350.00
Black Duck, W. Bowman 550.00

Black Mallard, St. Clair Flats Style, 15 1/2 In.	75.00
Blue Gill Duck, Willard Baldwin, Original Paint, C.1925	495.00
Blue–Winged Teal Drake, Mason, Hollow	6250.00
Blue–Winged Teal Drake, Otto Jurgenson, Hollow Body, 11 1/2 In.	95.00
Bluebill Drake, Fond Du Lac, Wisconsin, 14 In.	30.00
Bluebill Drake, Glass Eyes, 13 1/2 In.	155.00
Bluebill Drake, Glass Eyes, A. Wellington, Canada, C.1925, 14 1/2 In.	175.00
Bluebill Drake, Glass Eyes, Fond Du Lac, Wisc., 14 In.	95.00
Bluebill Drake, Glass Eyes, Frank Schmidt, Detroit, 14 1/4 In.	25.00
Bluebill Drake, Glass Eyes, Madison, Wisconsin, 13 In.	155.00
Bluebill Drake, Glass Eyes, Original Paint, Mid–20th Century, 14 In.	35.00
Bluebill Drake, Glass Eyes, Ralph Bumgartner, Michigan, 9 3/4 In.	55.00
Bluebill Drake, Glass Eyes, Turned Head, Factory Made, 13 In.	55.00
Bluebill Drake, Lake St. Clair, Glass Eyes, 13 3/4 In.	175.00
Bluebill Drake, Tack Eyes, Dodge Factory, 15 1/2 In.	30.00
Bluebill, Glass Eyes, Illinois River Area, 11 In.	40.00
Bluebill, Hollow Body, Glass Eyes, Milt Greshman, 14 In.	50.00
Bluebill, Hollow Body, Tack Eyes, 10 1/2 In.	95.00
Broadtail, Chadwick	495.00
Bufflehead, Glass Eyes, Initials, H.R.F., 9 1/2 In., Pair	170.00
Bufflehead, Tack Eyes, Harley Frieman, Canada, 10 3/4 In.	85.00
Canada Goose, Hollow Body, George Bhowker, C.1875, 23 1/2 In.	825.00
Canada Goose, Hollow Body, Jessie Birdsall, C.1918, 22 1/2 In.	1225.00
Canada Goose, Swimmer, Ghost Image, 26 1/2 In.	600.00
Canada Goose, Swimmer, Hollow Body, Carved Head, 27 In.	250.00
Canada Goose, Swimmer, Snakey Neck, Glass Eyes, 27 In.	300.00
Canvasback Drake, Balsa Body, Cast Aluminum Head, Glass Eyes, 14 In.	445.00
Canvasback Drake, Balsa Body, Pine Head, Marked F.C.H., 15 In.	75.00
Canvasback Drake, Glass Eyes, Corregated Fasteners, 15 In.	95.00
Canvasback Drake, Glass Eyes, High Head, Wisconsin, 16 1/4 In.	150.00
Canvasback Drake, Glass Eyes, Hollow Body, Henry, Illinois, 16 In.	155.00
Canvasback Drake, Glass Eyes, Lake Winnebago, Wis., Worn Paint, 17 In.	100.00
Canvasback Drake, Glass Eyes, Oshkosh, Wisconsin, 15 In.	55.00
Canvasback Drake, Glass Eyes, Paul Westervelt, Lodi, N.Y., 1920, 16 In.	20.00
Canvasback Drake, Glass Eyes, Saginaw Bay, Michigan, 14 In.	35.00
Canvasback Drake, Glass Eyes, Seneca Model, Mason, 15 3/4 In.	165.00
Canvasback Drake, Sleeper, Marked Whitefish Bay Club, 17 1/2 In.	45.00
Canvasback Drake, Tack Eyes, Swimmer, White, Dela., Worn Paint, 17 In.	55.00
Canvasback Hen, Glass Eyes, Original Paint, 17 In.	185.00
Coot, Glass Eyes, Original Paint, Wisconsin, 11 1/2 In.	65.00
Coot, Tack Eyes, Original Paint, Wisconsin, 12 1/4 In.	20.00
Crow, Glass Eyes, Black Fiber Composition, Standing, Herter, Pair	170.00
Crow, Glass Eyes, Black Paint, Wire Legs, Driftwood Base, 14 In.	400.00
Crow, Herter, Wooden, 1930s	185.00
Crow, Inset Glass Eyes, Wire Legs, Haddon Perdue, 11 1/2 In.	412.00
Crow, Wings Fold With Screw–In Fitting For Set–Up, Tin	95.00
Crown, Black Tinned Sheet Iron, Stick–Up, 6 X 16 In., Pair	175.00
Dowitcher, Boman	7150.00
Duck Call, Charley Purdew	450.00
Duck, Primitive, Black, 14 3/8 In.	85.00
Duck, William Lattin Stratford, Worn Paint, 1890	400.00
Eider Drake, Inset Head, Gus Wilson, South Portland, Maine, 14 3/4 In.	175.00
Eider, Drake, Mussel In Beak	135.00
Fish, Mickey Mouse, Black Wood Body, Wire Tail, 4 In.	675.00
Fish, Perch, Wooden Body, Metal Fins, Green Paint, Minnesota, 7 In.	10.00
Fish, Sturgeon, Metal Fins, Glass Eyes, Wooden, Neenah, Wisc., 15 In.	85.00
Fish, Sturgeon, Metal Fins, Tack Trim, Gold, Green & Blue, 27 1/4 In.	350.00
Fish, Sucker, Metal Fins, Wooden, Polychrome Paint, 9 In.	25.00
Fish, Sunfish, Copper	40.00
Frog, Kent	412.50
Golden Plover, Flattie, Crowell	2310.00
Golden Plover, Lincoln, Winter	1980.00
Goldeneye Drake, Glass Eyes, L.E. Bernard, Hale, Michigan, 15 1/2 In.	45.00
Great Horned Owl, Papier–Mache	45.00

Green–Winged Teal Drake, Glass Eyes, 11 3/4 In. 90.00
Green–Winged Teal Drake, Glass Eyes, Rinker, Original Paint, 8 In. 15.00
Green–Winged Teal Hen, Harvey Pearl, Black River, Mich., 14 3/4 In. 55.00
Green–Winged Teal Hen, Lem Ward, Hollow, Dated 1959 .... 2000.00
High Head, Old Paint, European, 12 In. 85.00
Mallard Drake, Charles Walker, Hollow 6500.00
Mallard Drake, Cork & Wood, J. Argue, Flint, 18 1/2 In. 25.00
Mallard Drake, Dodge Factory, 15 3/4 In. 95.00
Mallard Drake, Glass Eyes, Ken Snow, 17 1/4 In. 45.00
Mallard Drake, Glass Eyes, Shot Scars, Mason, 15 3/4 In. 120.00
Mallard Drake, Glass Eyes, Tim Martindale, Wolf Island, 17 1/2 In. 65.00
Mallard Drake, Hollow, Glass Eyes, London, Ontario, Canada, 11 3/4 In. 35.00
Mallard Drake, Tack Eyes, Hollow, Repaint, 13 3/4 In. 85.00
Mallard Hen, From Herter's Kit, Balsa & Pine, 16 In. 45.00
Mallard Hen, Judge Glen Cameron 7250.00
Mallard Hen, Stuffed Canvas, Printed Design, 14 In. 115.00
Mallard, Papier–Mache, Glass Eyes, Marked Victor, 14 In., Pair 20.00
Merganser, Captain Harry Jobes, Pair 250.00
Merganser, Carved Body, Glass Eyes, 14 1/4 In. 105.00
Merganser, Composition, Painted, Leather Head Tuft, T. Johnson, 10 In. 425.00
Merganser, Glass Eyes, Swimmer, Contemporary, 19 In. 95.00
Owl, Carved From Laminated Wood, White Paint, 13 In. 400.00
Partridge, Painted Metal, Repainted, C.1890, 17 In. 220.00
Pintail Drake, Glass Eyes, Hollow Body, 17 In. 140.00
Pintail Drake, Glass Eyes, Hollow Body, Original Paint, Calif., 19 In. 55.00
Pintail, Perdew, Overcoat 2200.00
Redhead Drake, Carved Back, Houghton Lake, Mich., 15 1/4 In. 55.00
Redhead Drake, Glass Eyes, Capt. Wallace Rowan, Ontario, Canada, 13 In 65.00
Redhead Drake, Glass Eyes, Carved Wings & Feathers, 13 3/4 In. 30.00
Redhead Drake, Glass Eyes, Line, Weights, 15 1/4 In. 625.00
Redhead Drake, Glass Eyes, North Shore, Lake Erie, 12 1/2 In. 45.00
Redhead Drake, Len Suzor, Pike Creek, Ontario, 13 3/4 In. 25.00
Redhead Drake, Primitive, Harris, Ontario, Canada, 14 1/2 In. 75.00
Robin Snipe, Mason 1265.00
Robin Snipe, Obediah Verity 4675.00
Rubber, Painted, Italy, Set of 4 .... 150.00
Ruddy Duck, Glass Eyes, Original Paint, 12 1/2 In. 30.00
Sandpiper, Inserted Bill, 9 1/2 In. 65.00
Shorebird, Driftwood Base, 17 1/2 In. 75.00
Shorebird, Folding, Polychrome Paint, Tin, Wooden Base, 12 In. 95.00
Shorebird, Interior Label Pat. Oct 27, 1874, Folding Tin, 9 1/2 In. 100.00
Shorebird, Sanderling Peep, Jim Slack, Original Paint, 6 3/4 In. 95.00
Shorebird, Sanderling Peep, Thomas P. Langan, Weathered, 12 1/4 In. 45.00
Shoveler Hen, Original Paint, Capt. Harry Jobes, 15 1/4 In. 25.00
Snow Goose, Ben Schmidt 6500.00
Swan, Glass Eyes, Hollow Carved, Thomas Langedon, 18 X 46 In., Pair 1320.00
Swan, Herters, Patent 1893 .... 285.00
Swan, Hollow Carved, T. Langedon, 20th Century, 18 X 46 In., Pair 1200.00
Teal Hen, Dodge Factory, 11 3/4 In. 35.00
Tern, Crowell, Oval Brand 4125.00
Trout, D.R. Hammeral, 10 In. 35.00
Widgeon Drake, Bright Paint, 14 3/4 In. 35.00
Wood Duck, Standing, Lem Ward, C.1925 .... 7150.00
Yellowlegs, Preening, A. Elmer Crowell, E. Harwich, Mass, 14 In. 8000.00

Chelsea Keramic Art Works was established in 1872 in Chelsea, Massachusetts, by members of the Robertson family. The factory closed in 1889 and was reorganized as the Chelsea Pottery U.S. in 1891. It became the Dedham Pottery of Dedham, Massachusetts, in 1895. The factory closed in 1943. It was famous for its crackleware dishes, which picture blue outlines of animals, flowers, and other natural motifs.

DEDHAM, Bowl, Rabbit, Stamped, 1920s, 8 3/4 In. 330.00
Bowl, Serving, Rabbit, Flared Rim, Stamped, 1920s, 2 1/2 X 9 1/2 In. 357.50

Cup & Saucer, Rabbit, Stamped, 1931, 4 In. 220.00
Flower Frog, Turtle, 1920s, 3 1/4 In. 385.00
Knife Rest, Rabbit, Marked, 1920s, 3 3/4 In. 412.00
Paperweight, Rabbit, 2 3/4 In. 300.00
Plate, Birds In Potted Orange Tree, Marked, 1930s, 8 1/2 In. 335.00
Plate, Butterfly, Marked, 1920s, 8 1/2 In. 525.00
Plate, Chestnut, Marked, 1920s, 6 In. 143.00
Plate, Chestnut, Maude Davenport, Stamped, 9 3/4 In. 247.50
Plate, Crab, Marked, 1920s, 8 1/4 In. 850.00
Plate, Double-Eared Rabbit, 9 3/4 In., 8 Piece 1075.00
Plate, Duck, Maude Davenport, Stamped, 6 In. 275.00
Plate, Grape, 8 1/2 In. 248.00
Plate, Horse Chestnut, Marked, Early 20th Century, 6 In. 137.50
Plate, Iris, Maude Davenport, Marked, 9 3/4 In. 220.00
Plate, Lobster, Marked, 1920s, 8 1/4 In. 525.00
Plate, Magnolia, Maude Davenport, 1920s, 10 In. 195.00
Plate, Pink Lily, Marked, Early 20th Century, 10 In. 195.00
Plate, Pond Lily Border, Chelsea Cloverleaf Mark, 10 1/4 In. 2500.00
Plate, Rabbit Border, Blue Stamp, C.1891, 10 1/4 In., 8 Piece 3385.00
Plate, Rabbit, 8 1/2 In. 660.00
Plate, Snowtree, Marked, Early 20th Century, 6 In. 170.00
Plate, Snowtree, Sticker, Marked, 1930s, 8 1/2 In. 165.00
Plate, Tercentenary, Fish Border, Molded Rim, Marked, 8 7/8 In. 2300.00
Plate, Turkey, 1920s, 8 1/4 In. 330.00
Salt & Pepper, Double-Eared Rabbit 870.00
Salt & Pepper, Rabbit, 1930s, 2 3/4 In. 275.00
Salt & Pepper, Rabbit, Signed D.P., 1930s, 3 1/2 In. 192.50
Saltshaker, Baby Elephant Border, 2 3/4 In. 625.00
Shoe, Curling Toe, Green Glaze, Chelsea, Keramic Art Works, 6 1/8 In. 385.00
Sugar & Creamer, Double-Eared Rabbit 750.00
Tile, Tea, Rabbit, Signed, 6 In. 295.00
Tray, Bacon, Rabbit, 1920s, 10 X 6 In. 302.50
Tray, Pin, Round, Central Medallion With Rabbit, 4 In. 275.00
Vase, Bulbous, Blue-Green Glaze, Signed, 6 3/4 In. 220.00
Vase, Sang De Bouf, Salmon Pink Glaze, Marked, C.1890, 5 In. 445.00

> John and Elizabeth Degenhart started the Crystal Art Glass of
> Cambridge, Ohio, in 1947. Quality paperweights and other glass
> objects were made. John died in 1964 and his wife took over
> management and production ideas. Over 145 colors of glass were
> made. In 1978, after the death of Mrs. Degenhart, the molds were
> sold. The D in a heart trademark was removed, so collectors can
> easily recognize the true Degenhart piece.

DEGENHART, Dish, Bird On Nest, Cover, Opalescent, 1970s 45.00
Figurine, Dog, Crown Tuscan 35.00
Mug, Green, Small 23.50
Owl, Tomato 85.00
Toothpick, Heart, Blue 25.00

Aerosol paint strippers are fast but need special precautions. Wear goggles, gloves, and long-sleeved shirt. The spray will float. There is no brushing and they work well on small irregular surfaces such as carvings, but large jobs are better with conventional brushed-on stripper.

Degue   Degue is a signature found acid–etched on pieces of French glass made in the early 1900s. Cameo, mold blown, and smooth glass with contrasting colored rims are the types most often found.

DEGUE, Lamp, Boudoir, Bedoin Priests, Pyramids, Palm Trees, Dessert	7200.00
Vase, Cameo, 3–Color House & Mountain Scene, Burst Finish, 5 1/4 In.	700.00
Vase, Cameo, Red Deco Flowers, Lemon–Lime, Amethyst Base, 14 In.	1250.00
Vase, Cut Flowers, Frosted Green Ground, 4 In.	450.00
Vase, Red Flowers, Amethyst, Yellow Ground, 14 In.	1350.00

DELATTE NANCY   Delatte glass is a French cameo glass made by Andre Delatte. It was first made in Nancy, France, in 1921. Lighting fixtures and opaque glassware in imitation of Bohemian opaline were made. There were many French cameo glass makers, so be sure to look in other appropriate sections.

DELATTE, Box, Flowers, Green, Yellow, 6 In.	595.00
Vase, Cameo Glass, Black Leaves, Green, Air Bubbles, Nancy, 10 In.	795.00
Vase, Landscape, Pink, Green, 8 In.	600.00
Vase, Sailboats, Green, Blue, 3 In.	450.00
DELAWARE, see Custard Glass; Pressed Glass	
DELDARE, see Buffalo Pottery Deldare	

Delft   Delft is a tin–glazed pottery that has been made since the seventeenth century. It is decorated with blue on white or with colored decorations. Most of the pieces sold today were made after 1891, and the name "Holland" appears with the Delft factory marks.

DELFT, Bottle, House Stopper	45.00
Bowl, Floral Vines, Cylindrical, England, Late 18th Century, 12 In.	1200.00
Bowl, Polychrome Floral Design, 3 1/2 In.	600.00
Canister Set, Blue, 14 Piece	245.00
Charger, Blue & White Chinoiserie Design, 11 3/4 In.	165.00
Charger, Floral Border, Center Portrait of King Charles, 13 3/4 In.	1100.00
Charger, King William Bust, Flared Lobed Form, England, 13 1/2 In.	880.00
Decanter, Dutch Girl, 10 1/2 In.	100.00
Jar, Blue, White Design of Herons, Flowers, Pines, 9 3/4 In.	650.00
Kitchen, Canister, Spice & Cruet Set, Germany, 10 Piece	265.00
Nappy, Blue Mark	45.00
Pitcher, Flowers, Sailboats, C.1830, 5 In.	125.00
Planter, Violin, Openwork On Front, English, 15 X 5 1/2 In.	125.00
Plate, Blue & White Oriental Design, Yellow Rim, 9 In.	250.00
Plate, Blue & White, Scene of Ship, Castle, 9 In.	350.00
Plate, Boat Scene, 10 1/2 In.	70.00
Plate, Polychrome Floral Design, 9 3/4 In.	350.00
Pot, Cover, 2–Handled, England, C.1800, 6 In.	575.00
Tankard, Pewter Base & Lid, Polychrome Oriental Design, 8 1/2 In.	1500.00
Tile, Cat, Mouse In Mouth, Framed, 12 1/2 X 17 1/2 In., 6 Piece	2400.00
Tile, Sailboat, Polychrome, Signed, Square, 4 1/2 In.	55.00
Tobacco Jar, French, 1763	850.00
Vase, Bird Finial On Cover, Figure of Justice, 12 1/2 In.	357.50
Vase, Creamware, Windmill Scene, 4 1/4 In.	75.00
Vase, Lion Finial On Domed Cover, Pastoral Scenes, 17 5/8 In., Pair	445.00
Vase, Marked D.W., 18th Century, 11 In.	195.00

   Dental cabinets, chairs, equipment, and other related items are listed here. Other objects may be found listed under Medical.

DENTAL, Cabinet, 2 Pull–Down Doors, 6 Shelves, 14 Drawers, Walnut, C.1890	2800.00
Cabinet, 3–Slat Rolls To Cover Shelves, Quartersawn Oak	3200.00
Cabinet, Gallery Top, 10 Foldout & Swivel Drawers, Oak	1800.00
Cabinet, Harvard, Oak, 77 X 29 In.	5000.00
Cabinet, Leaded Glass Top Compartments, Glass Pulls, Mahogany	6500.00
Case, Marble Top, Walnut, Eastlake	1795.00
Chair Unit, Ritter, Restored, 1915	2000.00
Chair, Ridder, Hydraulic, Gold & Red Upholstery, 1920	3750.00
Drill, Electric, Ritter Dental Mfg. Co., Foot Controls	165.00

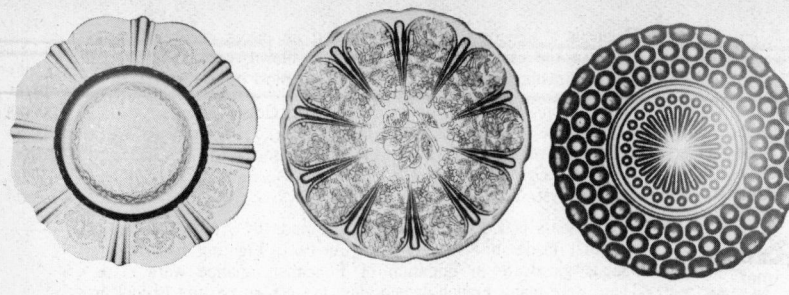

American Sweetheart   Cherry Blossom   Bubble

Jar, Embossed Dr. Hopkins Dental Paste, Glass, 1900 .... 10.00
Lamp, Cameron's Dental Lamp Vitrohm Potential Adjuster 50.00
Statement, List of Interesting Work Done, Prices, Ohio Dentist, 1906 .... 7.00
Tool Set, Stainless Steel, Mounted On Board, 39 Piece 85.00

DENVER C T & P Co   William Long of Steubenville, Ohio, founded the Lonhuda Pottery Company in 1892. In 1900 he moved to Denver, Colorado, and organized the Denver China and Pottery Company. This pottery worked until 1905 when Long moved to New Jersey and founded the Clifton Pottery. Long also worked for Weller Pottery, Roseville Pottery, and American Encaustic Tiling Company.

DENVER, Vase, Black Matte Glaze, 6 In. 175.00
Vase, Blue, White, Trees, 7 In. 475.00
Vase, Violets, Leaves, Green, Denaura, 5 3/4 In. 500.00

Depression glass was an inexpensive glass manufactured in large quantities during the 1920s and early 1930s. It was made in many colors and patterns by dozens of factories in the United States. The name "Depression glass" is a modern one. For more descriptions, history, pictures, and prices of Depression glass, see the book "Kovels' Depression Glass & American Dinnerware Price List."

DEPRESSION GLASS, Adam, Ashtray, Green 18.00
Adam, Bowl, Pink, 4 3/4 In. ....8.00 To 10.00
Adam, Butter, Cover, Pink .... 50.00 To 65.00
Adam, Cake Plate, Footed, Pink 13.50
Adam, Cup & Saucer, Green 22.00
Adam, Cup & Saucer, Pink .... 21.00 To 23.00
Adam, Grill Plate, Green 8.00
Adam, Plate, Pink, 6 In. 2.75
Adam, Plate, Pink, 9 In. 17.00
Adam, Platter, Pink, 12 In. 9.00
Adam, Salt & Pepper, Pink 39.00
Adam, Saltshaker, Pink 17.00
Adam, Sherbet, Pink 16.00
Adam, Sugar & Creamer, Pink 36.00
Adam, Sugar, Cover, Pink 28.50
Adam, Tumbler, Ice Tea, Pink 20.00
   AMERICAN BEAUTY, see English Hobnail
American Sweetheart, Bowl, Monax, 6 In. 7.00
American Sweetheart, Bowl, Pink, 9 In. .... 20.00 To 27.00
American Sweetheart, Creamer, Pink 10.50

American Sweetheart, Creamer, Red 95.00
American Sweetheart, Cup & Saucer, Pink 13.50
American Sweetheart, Cup, Red 75.00
American Sweetheart, Plate, Pink, 9 In. 14.00
American Sweetheart, Platter, Monax, 15 In. 135.00
American Sweetheart, Saltshaker, Pink 145.00
American Sweetheart, Salver, Monax, 15 In. .... 125.00 To 135.00
American Sweetheart, Saucer, Pink 2.50
American Sweetheart, Sherbet, Monax 10.00
American Sweetheart, Sherbet, Pink, 3 3/4 In. 17.00
American Sweetheart, Soup, Cream, Pink 25.00
American Sweetheart, Soup, Dish, Pink 25.00
American Sweetheart, Sugar, Pink 10.50
American Sweetheart, Tumbler, Pink, 9 Oz., 4 1/4 In. 55.00
Anniversary, Cup & Saucer, Pink 5.50
Anniversary, Soup Dish, Pink 2.50
Anniversary, Vase, Crystal, 6 1/2 In. 7.00
   APPLE BLOSSOM, see Dogwood
Aunt Polly, Pitcher, Blue 65.00
Aunt Polly, Sherbet, Blue .... 7.50 To 9.50
Aunt Polly, Sugar & Creamer, Cover, Green 148.00
Aunt Polly, Sugar, Cover, Blue 125.00
Aunt Polly, Tumbler, Blue .... 18.00 To 18.50
Aunt Polly, Vase, Blue 27.00
   AURORA, see Petalware
Avocado, Bowl, Green, Oval, 8 In. 20.00
   B PATTERN, see Dogwood
   BALLERINA, see Cameo
   BANDED CHERRY, see Cherry Blossom
   BANDED FINE RIB, see Coronation
   BANDED PETALWARE, see Petalware
   BANDED RAINBOW, see Ring
   BANDED RIBBON, see New Century
   BANDED RINGS, see Ring
Baroque, Dish, Pickle, Blue, 8 In. 23.00
Baroque, Sherbet, Blue, 3 3/4 In. 25.00
Beaded Block, Bowl, Amber, 6 1/2 In. 11.00
Beaded Block, Plate, Amber, 7 3/4 In. .... 2.50 To 6.50
   BERWICK, see Boopie
   BEVERAGE WITH SAILBOAT, see White Ship
   BIG RIB, see Manhattan
   BLOCK, see Block Optic
Block Optic, Berry Bowl, Green, 4 1/4 In. .... 4.25 To 9.00
Block Optic, Berry Bowl, Green, 8 1/2 In. 17.00
Block Optic, Bowl, Green, 5 1/4 In. 9.00
Block Optic, Bowl, Ice Tub, Pink 72.00
Block Optic, Butter, Cover, Green 32.00
Block Optic, Candlestick, Green, Pair 70.00
Block Optic, Candy Dish, Cover, Yellow, 2 1/4 In. 37.50
Block Optic, Creamer, Green, Flat 10.00
Block Optic, Cup & Saucer, Green 11.00
Block Optic, Cup, Green 3.50
Block Optic, Cup, Pink 2.50
Block Optic, Goblet, Green, 5 3/4 In. 16.00
Block Optic, Goblet, Wine, Pink 17.00
Block Optic, Grill Plate, Green 9.00
Block Optic, Ice Tub, Green 35.00
Block Optic, Mug, Green 25.00

Clean alabaster with dry cleaning fluid. It dissolves in water.

Block Optic, Sandwich Server, Pink 39.00
Block Optic, Sugar, Cover, Yellow 8.00
Block Optic, Sugar, Green, Cone 9.50
Block Optic, Tumbler, Footed, Green, 9 Oz. 15.00
Block Optic, Tumbler, Green, 5 Oz., 3 1/2 In. 13.00
Boopie, Sherbet, Green 4.50
Boopie, Tumbler, Green, 4 1/2 In. 6.00
    BOUQUET & LATTICE, see Normandie
Bowknot, Cup, Green 4.00
Bowknot, Plate, Green, 7 In. .... 5.00 To 9.00
Bowknot, Tumbler, Green, Footed, 5 In. 13.00
Bubble, Berry Bowl, Blue, 4 In. 4.00
Bubble, Berry Bowl, Blue, 8 3/8 In. 9.50
Bubble, Berry Bowl, Crystal, 8 3/8 In. 4.00
Bubble, Bowl, Blue, 5 1/4 In. .... 4.00 To 7.00
Bubble, Bowl, Flanged, Blue, 9 In. 90.00
Bubble, Creamer, Blue 24.00
Bubble, Cup & Saucer, Blue .... 3.00 To 6.50
Bubble, Cup & Saucer, Green .... 4.00 To 7.50
Bubble, Cup, Crystal 1.50
Bubble, Grill Plate, Blue .... 9.00 To 11.00
Bubble, Plate, Blue, 6 3/4 In. .... 1.50 To 2.50
Bubble, Plate, Blue, 9 3/8 In. .... 4.00 To 6.50
Bubble, Platter, Oval, Blue, 12 In. 8.50
Bubble, Platter, Oval, Crystal, 12 In. 10.00
Bubble, Saucer, Green 2.50
Bubble, Soup, Dish, Blue 7.00
Bubble, Soup, Dish, Crystal 5.00
Bubble, Sugar & Creamer, Blue .... 35.00 To 40.00
Bubble, Sugar & Creamer, Green 17.50
Bubble, Water Set, Red, 7 Piece 65.00
    BULLSEYE, see Bubble
    BUTTERFLIES & ROSES, see Flower Garden with Butterflies
    BUTTONS & BOWS, see Holiday
    CABBAGE ROSE, see Sharon
    CABBAGE ROSE WITH SINGLE ARCH, see Rosemary
Cameo, Berry Bowl, Green, 8 1/4 In. 25.00
Cameo, Bowl, Oval, Green, 10 In. 20.00
Cameo, Bowl, Oval, Yellow, 10 In. 30.00
Cameo, Cake Plate, Flat, Green 65.00
Cameo, Candy, Cover, Green, 4 In. .... 32.00 To 45.00
Cameo, Creamer, Green, 3 1/4 In. 17.50
Cameo, Cup & Saucer, Green 14.50
Cameo, Cup & Saucer, Yellow .... 8.00 To 8.50
Cameo, Decanter, Green, Stopper 115.00
Cameo, Grill Plate, Amber 8.00
Cameo, Grill Plate, Yellow .... 4.50 To 6.00
Cameo, Pitcher, Green, 5 3/4 In. 180.00
Cameo, Plate, Green, 8 In. 7.50
Cameo, Plate, Green, 9 1/2 In. .... 10.00 To 13.50
Cameo, Plate, Green, Square, 8 1/2 In. 32.50
Cameo, Plate, Yellow, 8 In. 5.00
Cameo, Platter, Green, 12 In. 17.50
Cameo, Relish, 3 Sections, Green 18.00
Cameo, Salt & Pepper, Green 65.00
Cameo, Soup, Dish, Green 27.00
Cameo, Sugar & Creamer, Pink, Tall 120.00
Cameo, Sugar, Green, 3 1/4 In. 10.50
Candlewick, Relish, Divided, 11 In. 40.00
Cape Cod, Basket, Crystal, 11 In. 125.00
Cape Cod, Cocktail, Stemmed, Red 20.00
    CAPRICE, see Cambridge Glass category
    CHAIN DAISY, see Adam

Cherry Blossom, Berry Bowl, Pink, 4 3/4 In. 13.00
Cherry Blossom, Bowl, Footed, Pink, 10 1/2 In. 38.00
Cherry Blossom, Bowl, Green, 5 3/4 In. 26.00
Cherry Blossom, Bowl, Pink, 2 Handles, 9 In. 25.00
Cherry Blossom, Cake Plate, Footed, Green 10.00
Cherry Blossom, Cake Plate, Footed, Pink .... 14.00 To 21.00
Cherry Blossom, Child's Set, Pink, Box, 14 Piece 395.00
Cherry Blossom, Coaster, Green ....7.00 To 10.00
Cherry Blossom, Coaster, Pink 15.00
Cherry Blossom, Creamer, Child's, Pink 30.00
Cherry Blossom, Creamer, Green .... 10.00 To 13.00
Cherry Blossom, Creamer, Pink 15.00
Cherry Blossom, Cup & Saucer, Child's, Pink 30.00
Cherry Blossom, Cup & Saucer, Pink .... 12.00 To 18.00
Cherry Blossom, Cup, Green 13.00
Cherry Blossom, Grill Plate, Pink, 9 In. 19.00
Cherry Blossom, Mug, Pink 225.00
Cherry Blossom, Pitcher, Flat, Green 35.00
Cherry Blossom, Plate, Green, 7 In. 16.00
Cherry Blossom, Plate, Green, 9 In. 6.00
Cherry Blossom, Plate, Pink, 7 In. .... 12.00 To 15.00
Cherry Blossom, Plate, Pink, 9 In. 15.00
Cherry Blossom, Saucer, Pink 4.00
Cherry Blossom, Sherbet, Green ....6.00 To 12.25
Cherry Blossom, Sherbet, Pink ....8.50 To 9.00
Cherry Blossom, Soup, Dish, Pink 42.50
Cherry Blossom, Sugar & Creamer, Delphite 24.00
Cherry Blossom, Sugar, Child's, Pink 30.00
Cherry Blossom, Sugar, Cover, Pink 21.00
Cherry Blossom, Tumbler, Green, 3 1/2 In. 20.00
Cherry Blossom, Tumbler, Pink, 3 1/2 In. 12.00
Cherry Blossom, Tumbler, Pink, 5 In. .... 40.00 To 41.00
CHERRY, see Cherry Blossom
CHERRY–BERRY, see also Strawberry
Cherry–Berry, Bowl, Green, 7 1/2 In. 20.00
CHINEX CLASSIC, see also Cremax
Chinex Classic, Bowl, Ivory, 5 3/4 In. 6.00
Chinex Classic, Cup & Saucer, Ivory 7.50
Chinex Classic, Plate, Ivory, 9 3/4 In. 5.50
Chinex Classic, Sherbet, Ivory 8.50
CHRISTMAS CANDY RIBBON, see Christmas Candy
Christmas Candy, Creamer, Crystal 7.50
Christmas Candy, Cup & Saucer, Teal Blue .... 14.50 To 15.00
Christmas Candy, Plate, Teal Blue, 8 1/4 In. .... 10.00 To 14.00
Christmas Candy, Soup, Dish, Teal Blue 18.00
Christmas Candy, Sugar & Creamer, Teal Blue 25.00
Christmas Candy, Sugar, Crystal 7.50
CLASSIC, see Chinex Classic
CLEO, see Cambridge Glass category
Cloverleaf, Cup, Green 5.00
Cloverleaf, Grill Plate, Green .... 10.00 To 15.00
Cloverleaf, Salt & Pepper, Green 25.00
Cloverleaf, Salt & Pepper, Yellow 75.00
Cloverleaf, Sherbet, Black 10.00
Cloverleaf, Sherbet, Green 4.00
Cloverleaf, Sherbet, Pink 4.50
Cloverleaf, Sugar & Creamer, Green 6.00
Colonial Block, Bowl, Green, 7 In. 8.00
Colonial Block, Butter, Cover, Pink 28.00
Colonial Block, Creamer, Crystal 5.00
Colonial Block, Goblet, Green ....7.00 To 8.50
Colonial, Bowl, Green, 9 In. 17.00
Colonial, Celery Vase, Crystal 50.00

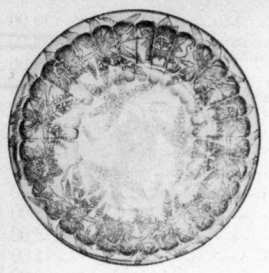

Floral

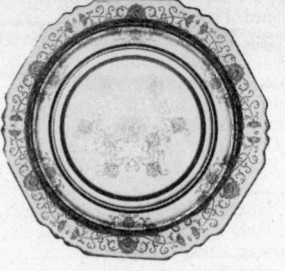

Florentine No. 1

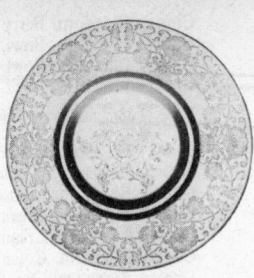

Florentine No. 2

Colonial, Plate, Green, 8 In. 6.00
Colonial, Plate, Green, 10 In. .... 38.00 To 42.00
Colonial, Sherbet, Pink, 3 In. 11.00
Colonial, Whiskey, Green 10.00
Colony, Plate, Crystal, 9 In. 20.00
Colony, Sugar, Crystal 7.00
Colony, Tumbler, Crystal, 3 5/8 In. 19.00
Coronation, Berry Set, Red, 7 Piece .... 32.00 To 35.00
Coronation, Bowl, Pink, 6 1/2 In. 3.50
Coronation, Nappy, Ruby Red, 6 1/2 In. 6.00
    CREMAX, see also Chinex Classic
Cremax, Cup, Blue 5.00
    CRISS CROSS, see X Design
    CUBE, see Cubist
Cubist, Bowl, Green, 4 1/2 In. 3.50
Cubist, Bowl, Pink, 6 1/2 In. 4.50
Cubist, Candy Jar, Cover, Green .... 22.00 To 23.00
Cubist, Creamer, Green, 3 In. 6.00
Cubist, Cup & Saucer, Green 11.00
Cubist, Plate, Green, 6 In. 3.50
Cubist, Plate, Green, 8 In. 6.00
Cubist, Salt & Pepper, Green 30.00
Cubist, Saltshaker, Green 10.00
Cubist, Saucer, Green 1.00
Cubist, Sugar & Creamer, Crystal 15.00
Cubist, Sugar, Crystal .... 3.00 To 4.00
Cubist, Sugar, Pink 3.00
    DAISY, see No. 620
    DAISY PETALS, see Petalware
    DANCING GIRL, see Cameo
    DIAMOND, see Windsor
    DIAMOND PATTERN, see Miss America
    DIAMOND POINT, see Petalware
Diamond Quilted, Bowl, Black, 7 In. 17.00
Diamond Quilted, Bowl, Blue, 7 In. 15.00
Diamond Quilted, Bowl, Pink, 7 In. 9.00
Diamond Quilted, Bowl, Red, 7 In. 20.00
Diamond Quilted, Creamer, Black 15.00
Diamond Quilted, Creamer, Pink 7.00
Diamond Quilted, Plate, Green, 6 In. 1.85
Diamond Quilted, Plate, Pink, 8 In. 5.00

Diamond Quilted, Salt & Pepper, Crystal 18.00
Diamond Quilted, Sherbet, Green 6.00
Diamond Quilted, Sugar, Blue 11.50
Diamond Quilted, Sugar, Green 6.00
Diamond Quilted, Sugar, Pink .... 4.50 To 7.00
Diana, Bowl, Amber, 11 In. 5.75
Diana, Bowl, Crystal, 11 In. 15.00
Diana, Bowl, Scalloped Edge, Crystal, 12 In. 8.00
Diana, Cup, Amber 3.00
Diana, Cup, Crystal 3.00
Diana, Salt & Pepper, Amber 75.00
Diana, Salt & Pepper, Crystal 12.50
Diana, Saucer, Crystal 1.00
Diana, Sugar & Creamer, Amber 16.00
Dogwood, Bowl, Cremax, 8 1/2 In. 20.00
Dogwood, Cake Plate, Green 68.00
Dogwood, Cup & Saucer, Pink .... 10.00 To 13.50
Dogwood, Grill Plate, Pink .... 15.00 To 16.00
Dogwood, Plate, Pink, 9 1/4 In. 16.00
Dogwood, Saucer, Pink 3.00
    DORIC & PANSY, see also Pretty Polly Party Dishes
Doric & Pansy, Saucer, Ultramarine 2.50
    DORIC WITH PANSY, see Doric & Pansy
Doric, Berry Bowl, Green, 4 1/2 In. .... 4.50 To 5.50
Doric, Berry Bowl, Green, 8 1/4 In. 15.00
Doric, Cake Plate, Green 15.50
Doric, Candy Dish, Cover, Green, 8 In. 32.00
Doric, Creamer, Green 11.00
Doric, Plate, Green, 7 In. 9.00
Doric, Plate, Pink, 6 In. 3.00
Doric, Relish, 4 Sections, Green .... 35.00 To 45.00
Doric, Salt & Pepper, Green 33.00
Doric, Salt & Pepper, Pink 28.00
Doric, Sherbet, Green 10.00
Doric, Tumbler, Green, 4 1/2 In. .... 35.00 To 45.00
    DRAPE & TASSEL, see Princess
    DUTCH ROSE, see Rosemary
    EARLY AMERICAN HOBNAIL, see Hobnail
    EARLY AMERICAN ROCK CRYSTAL, see Rock Crystal
    ELONGATED HONEYCOMB, see Colony
    ENGLISH HOBNAIL, see also Miss America
English Hobnail, Candy Dish, Cover, 3-Footed, Green 40.00
English Hobnail, Lamp, Electric, Crystal, 9 In., Pair 85.00
English Hobnail, Marmalade, Cover, Footed, Crystal 30.00
English Hobnail, Plate, Crystal, 8 In. 7.00
English Hobnail, Salt & Pepper, Crystal 30.00
English Hobnail, Tumbler, Crystal, 3 3/4 In. 10.00
    EVERGLADE, see Cambridge Glass category
    FAN & FEATHER, see Adam
    FINE RIB, see Homespun
    FIRE-KING, see also Philbe
    FIRE-KING DINNERWARE, see Philbe
Fire-King, Bowl, Mixing, Jadeite, 4 Qt. 7.00
Fire-King, Cup, Pink 3.50
Flanders, Cup, Loop Handle, Yellow 25.00
Flanders, Goblet, Water, Yellow, 8 In. 25.00
    FLAT DIAMOND, see Diamond Quilted
Floragold, Bowl, Crystal, 4 1/2 In. 3.50

Don't keep identification on your key ring. If it is lost, it is an invitation for burglars to visit.

Floragold, Creamer, Crystal	4.50
Floragold, Creamer, Pink	4.00
Floragold, Cup & Saucer, Iridescent	10.50
Floragold, Pitcher, Crystal	22.00
Floragold, Pitcher, Iridescent	24.50
Floragold, Platter, Pink, 13 1/2 In.	10.00
Floragold, Salt & Pepper, Crystal	18.00
Floragold, Salt & Pepper, Iridescent	38.50
Floragold, Sherbet, Crystal	6.00
Floragold, Sugar & Creamer, Crystal	9.00
Floral & Diamond Band, Butter, Cover, Green	70.00
FLORAL RIM, see Vitrock	
Floral, Bowl, Green, 7 1/2 In.	18.00
Floral, Creamer, Green	8.50 To 11.00
Floral, Cup & Saucer, Green	16.00
Floral, Pitcher, Pink, 8 In.	20.00
Floral, Pitcher, Pink, 10 1/4 In.	175.00
Floral, Plate, Dinner, Green, 9 In.	13.50
Floral, Salt & Pepper, Green	42.00
Floral, Saltshaker, Green	17.00
Floral, Sugar & Creamer, Cover, Green	25.00
Floral, Sugar, Cover, Green	22.00
Floral, Sugar, Pink	6.00
Florentine No.1, Ashtray, Yellow	20.00
Florentine No.1, Berry Bowl, Yellow, 8 1/2 In.	28.00
Florentine No.1, Cup, Green	5.00
Florentine No.1, Cup, Yellow	8.50
Florentine No.1, Plate, Green, 10 In.	7.00
Florentine No.1, Salt & Pepper, Green	36.00
Florentine No.1, Saltshaker, Green	15.00
Florentine No.1, Sherbet, Crystal	3.50
Florentine No.1, Sherbet, Yellow	8.50 To 10.00
Florentine No.1, Soup, Cream, Ruffled, Green	16.00
Florentine No.1, Soup, Cream, Ruffled, Pink	9.00
Florentine No.1, Sugar & Creamer, Ruffled	22.00
Florentine No.1, Sugar, Yellow	10.00
Florentine No.2, Bowl, Crystal, 5 1/2 In.	22.00
Florentine No.2, Bowl, Green, 5 1/2 In.	15.00
Florentine No.2, Butter, Cover, Crystal	55.00
Florentine No.2, Candlestick, Yellow, Pair	40.00
Florentine No.2, Gravy Boat, Amber	35.00
Florentine No.2, Pitcher, Crystal, 48 Oz., 7 1/2 In.	40.00
Florentine No.2, Plate, Green, 10 In.	9.50
Florentine No.2, Plate, Yellow, 8 1/2 In.	4.50 To 7.50
Florentine No.2, Relish, 3 Sections, Crystal	20.00
Florentine No.2, Salt & Pepper, Yellow	45.00
Florentine No.2, Sherbet, Yellow	7.50
Florentine No.2, Soup, Cream, Crystal	6.25
Florentine No.2, Sugar & Creamer, Green	11.00
Florentine No.2, Sugar & Creamer, Yellow	22.50
FLOWER & LEAF BAND, see Indiana Custard	
Flower Garden With Butterflies, Compote, Green, 7 1/4 In.	85.00
Flower Garden With Butterflies, Cup & Saucer, Green	125.00
Flower Garden With Butterflies, Plate, Green, 8 In.	22.00
Flower Garden With Butterflies, Plate, Pink, 8 In.	20.00
Flower Garden With Butterflies, Plate, Yellow, 8 In.	45.00
Flower Garden With Butterflies, Sandwich Server, Pink	70.00
Forest Green, Creamer, Square, Green	4.50
Forest Green, Cup, Green	5.00

Keep your keys on a pull apart chain so the house keys and car keys can be separated when you leave the car in a parking lot.

Forest Green, Saucer, Square, Green 1.00
Forest Green, Soup, Dish, Square, Green 6.00
Forest Green, Vase, Green, 9 In. 8.00
Fortune, Bowl, Crystal, 4 In. 4.00
Fortune, Bowl, Handle, Pink, 4 1/2 In. 5.00
Fortune, Plate, Pink, 6 In. 4.50
Fortune, Tumbler, Pink, 3 1/2 In. 5.00
Fortune, Tumbler, Pink, 4 1/2 In. 7.00
    FROSTED BLOCK, see Beaded Block
Fruits, Cup & Saucer, Green 7.00
Fruits, Saucer, Green 2.00
Georgian, Bowl, Green, 4 1/2 In. 5.50
Georgian, Creamer, Footed, Crystal, 3 In. 9.00
Georgian, Cup & Saucer, Green 8.50
Georgian, Plate, Green, 8 In. 6.50
Georgian, Sherbet, Green 9.50
Georgian, Sugar & Creamer, Green, 3 In. 20.00
Georgian, Sugar & Creamer, Green, 4 In. 30.00
Georgian, Sugar, Green, 4 In. 9.00
    GLADIOLI, see Royal Lace
    GLORIA, see Cambridge Glass category
    GRAPE, see also Woolworth
Grape, Juice Set, Crystal, 7 Piece 12.50
    HAIRPIN, see Newport
Harp, Cake Plate, Crystal .... 12.00 To 14.50
Harp, Cake Plate, Pink .... 17.50 To 22.00
Harp, Coaster Set, Crystal, Gold Trim, Box, 4 Piece 13.00
Harp, Coaster, Crystal .... 1.25 To 1.75
Harp, Plate, Crystal, Gold Trim, 7 In. 7.00
Harp, Tray, Handle, Crystal, Gold Trim, 12 3/4 In. 30.00
Harp, Vase, Crystal, Gold Trim, 7 1/2 In. 12.00
Heritage, Bowl, Crystal, 5 In. 5.00
Heritage, Bowl, Fruit, Crystal, 10 1/2 In. 9.00
Heritage, Cup, Crystal 4.00
Heritage, Plate, Crystal, 8 In. 4.50
Heritage, Saucer, Crystal .... 1.50 To 1.75
Heritage, Sugar & Creamer 33.00
    HEX OPTIC, see Hexagon Optic
Hexagon Optic, Tumbler, Green, 3 3/4 In. 2.50
    HEXAGON TRIPLE BAND, see Colony
    HINGE, see Patrician
Hobnail, Goblet, Crystal, 10 Oz. 5.00
Hobnail, Tumbler, Juice, Crystal 4.50
Hobnail, Tumbler, Wine, Footed, Crystal 4.00
Holiday, Berry Bowl, Pink, 5 1/8 In. 6.50
Holiday, Butter, Cover, Pink 30.00
Holiday, Chop Plate, Pink, 13 3/4 In. 85.00
Holiday, Console, Pink, 10 3/4 In. 95.00
Holiday, Creamer, Pink 6.50
Holiday, Cup & Saucer, Pink 10.50
Holiday, Pitcher, Green, 6 3/4 In. 25.00
Holiday, Pitcher, Pink, 4 3/4 In. .... 40.00 To 45.00
Holiday, Plate, Pink, 9 In. .... 9.00 To 12.50
Holiday, Saucer, Pink .... 1.50 To 2.50
Holiday, Sherbet, Pink .... 5.00 To 8.50
Holiday, Soup, Dish, Pink .... 32.50 To 35.00
Holiday, Sugar & Creamer, Pink 38.00
Holiday, Tray, Pink, 10 1/2 In. 9.00
Holiday, Tumbler, Flat, Pink, 10 Oz., 4 In. .... 15.50 To 20.00
Homespun, Butter, Cover, Pink 26.00
Homespun, Creamer, Pink 5.00
Homespun, Cup & Saucer, Green 8.00

Homespun, Plate, Pink, 9 1/4 In. .... 8.00 To 9.50
Homespun, Saucer, Pink .... 1.50 To 2.00
Homespun, Sugar, Green 8.00
Homespun, Sugar, Pink 5.00
Homespun, Tumbler, Footed, Pink, 5 Oz., 4 In. 4.50
    HONEYCOMB, see Hexagon Optic
    HORIZONTAL FINE RIB, see Manhattan
    HORIZONTAL RIBBED, see Manhattan
    HORIZONTAL ROUNDED BIG RIB, see Manhattan
    HORIZONTAL SHARP BIG RIB, see Manhattan
    HORSESHOE, see No. 612
Indiana Custard, Butter, Cover, Ivory 42.00
    IRIS & HERRINGBONE, see Iris
Iris, Bowl, Beaded, Iridescent, 4 1/2 In. 8.00
Iris, Bowl, Iridescent, 11 1/2 In. 6.00
Iris, Bowl, Salad, Ruffled, Crystal, 9 1/2 In. .... 8.50 To 9.00
Iris, Butter, Cover, Crystal 27.50
Iris, Candlestick, Double, Crystal, Pair 25.00
Iris, Candlestick, Iridescent, Pair 21.00
Iris, Creamer, Crystal .... 5.00 To 6.00
Iris, Goblet, Cocktail, Crystal 12.50
Iris, Goblet, Crystal, 8 Oz., 5 3/4 In. .... 14.00 To 16.00
Iris, Goblet, Wine, Iridescent, 4 In. 17.50
Iris, Goblet, Wine, Pink, 4 In. 13.00
Iris, Lamp, Crystal 30.00
Iris, Pitcher, Crystal, 9 1/2 In. 15.00
Iris, Plate, Crystal, 9 In. 25.00
Iris, Plate, Iridescent, 11 3/4 In. 16.00
Iris, Plate, Sherbet, Crystal 6.00
Iris, Saucer, Iridescent 4.00
Iris, Sugar & Creamer, Iridescent 19.00
Iris, Tumbler, Flat, Crystal, 4 In. 65.00
    IVEX, see Chinex Classic; Cremax
Jubilee, Creamer, Yellow .... 14.00 To 20.00
Jubilee, Cup & Saucer, Yellow 10.00
Jubilee, Mayonnaise Set, Yellow, 3 Piece 175.00
Jubilee, Plate, Yellow, 7 In. 7.25
Jubilee, Saucer, Yellow 3.50
Jubilee, Sugar, Yellow .... 14.00 To 16.50
Jubilee, Tray, 2 Handles, Yellow, 11 In. 32.00
June, Bowl, Footed, Yellow, 11 1/2 In. 45.00
June, Plate, Azure Blue, 7 1/2 In. 13.50
June, Salt & Pepper, Crystal 65.00
    KNIFE & FORK, see Colonial
    LACE EDGE, see also Coronation
Lace Edge, Bowl, Pink, 9 1/2 In. 12.00
Lace Edge, Bowl, Ribbed, Pink, 7 3/4 In. 42.00
Lace Edge, Butter, Cover, Pink 47.50
Lace Edge, Candy Jar, Cover, Pink .... 20.00 To 36.00
Lace Edge, Compote, Cover, Pink 35.00
Lace Edge, Cookie Jar, Cover, Pink 50.00
Lace Edge, Cup & Saucer, Pink .... 20.00 To 26.00
Lace Edge, Flower Bowl, With Frog, Pink .... 15.00 To 25.00
Lace Edge, Grill Plate, Pink .... 9.00 To 11.00
Lace Edge, Plate, 4 Sections, Pink 33.00
Lace Edge, Plate, Pink, 8 1/4 In. .... 11.00 To 14.00
Lace Edge, Plate, Pink, 8 3/4 In. 11.00
Lace Edge, Plate, Pink, 10 1/2 In. 21.00
Lace Edge, Platter, Pink, 12 3/4 In. 17.50
Lace Edge, Relish, 5 Sections, Pink 22.00
Lace Edge, Relish, Oval, 5 Sections, Pink 17.00
Lace Edge, Saucer, Pink 7.00

Lace Edge, Sherbet, Pink 70.00
Lace Edge, Tumbler, Pink, Flat, 4 1/2 In. 11.00
Laurel, Bowl, Ivory, 11 In. 22.50
Laurel, Bowl, Jade, 11 In. .... 10.50 To 27.50
Laurel, Candlestick, Jade, Pair 26.50
Laurel, Cheese Dish, Cover, Jade .... 45.00 To 50.00
Laurel, Cup, Jade 5.00
Laurel, Plate, Ivory, 9 In. 5.00
Laurel, Plate, Jade, 9 1/8 In. 7.00
Laurel, Platter, Oval, Ivory 16.00
Laurel, Sherbet, Jade 6.00
Laurel, Sugar, Jade 8.00
Laurel, Tea Set, Child's, Ivory, Red Trim, Box, 14 Piece 285.00
Leaf, Pitcher, Crystal 17.00
     LILY MEDALLION, see American Sweetheart
     LINCOLN DRAPE, see Princess
     LITTLE HOSTESS, see Moderntone Little Hostess
     LOOP, see Lace Edge
     LOUISA, see Floragold
     LOVEBIRDS, see Georgian
     LYDIA RAY, see New Century
Madrid, Butter, Cover, Amber 70.00
Madrid, Butter, Cover, Crystal .... 35.00 To 45.00
Madrid, Butter, Cover, Green .... 45.00 To 55.00
Madrid, Cookie Jar, Cover, Amber 33.00
Madrid, Creamer, Amber 7.00
Madrid, Creamer, Green .... 5.00 To 6.75
Madrid, Cup, Pink 6.50
Madrid, Jell-O Mold, Amber 8.50
Madrid, Pitcher, Amber, 8 1/2 In. .... 45.00 To 48.00
Madrid, Pitcher, Square, Blue, 8 In. .... 85.00 To 130.00
Madrid, Plate, Green, 8 7/8 In. 7.00
Madrid, Relish, Pink, 10 1/4 In. 8.50
Madrid, Salt & Pepper, Footed, Blue 135.00
Madrid, Sherbet, Amber .... 4.00 To 6.50
Madrid, Sherbet, Blue 8.00
Madrid, Sherbet, Green 9.75
Madrid, Sugar & Creamer, Amber .... 10.00 To 11.00
Madrid, Sugar, Cover, Blue 7.00
Madrid, Tumbler, Flat, Amber, 5 1/2 In. .... 14.00 To 15.00
Madrid, Tumbler, Footed, Green, 5 1/2 In. 37.50

> Feel the edges of the design of the glass. Cut glass has sharp edges; pressed-glass designs were molded into the glass.

     MAGNOLIA, see Dogwood
Manhattan, Bowl, Crystal, 9 In. 12.00
Manhattan, Bowl, Crystal, 5 1/2 In. 9.00
Manhattan, Bowl, Crystal, 9 1/2 In. .... 17.00 To 19.00
Manhattan, Candy Dish, 3-Footed, Pink, 6 1/2 In. 6.50
Manhattan, Compote, Pink 13.00
Manhattan, Pitcher, Pink, 80 Oz. 32.00
Manhattan, Plate, Crystal, 10 1/4 In. 9.00
Manhattan, Salt & Pepper, Crystal .... 14.00 To 18.00
Manhattan, Sandwich Server, Crystal, 14 In. 11.00
Manhattan, Tumbler, Crystal 9.00
Manhattan, Water Set, Pink, 7 Piece 85.00
Manhattan, Wine, Crystal 3.50
     MANY WINDOWS, see Roulette
     MAYFAIR, see Mayfair Open Rose
Mayfair Open Rose, Bowl, Cover, Pink, 10 In. 62.00
Mayfair Open Rose, Bowl, Pink, 10 In. 15.00

Mayfair Open Rose, Bowl, Pink, 12 In. 32.50
Mayfair Open Rose, Cake Plate, Handle, Pink, 12 In. 34.00
Mayfair Open Rose, Candy Dish, Cover, Pink 30.00
Mayfair Open Rose, Celery Dish, Divided, Pink 43.00
Mayfair Open Rose, Cookie Jar, Cover, Blue 100.00
Mayfair Open Rose, Cookie Jar, Cover, Pink .... 17.50 To 37.00
Mayfair Open Rose, Creamer, Pink 17.00
Mayfair Open Rose, Cup & Saucer, Blue 52.50
Mayfair Open Rose, Cup, Pink 15.00
Mayfair Open Rose, Decanter, Stopper, Pink 100.00
Mayfair Open Rose, Grill Plate, Pink 25.00
Mayfair Open Rose, Pitcher, Pink, 8 In. 30.00
Mayfair Open Rose, Plate, Pink, 8 1/2 In. 25.00
Mayfair Open Rose, Relish, 4 Sections, Crystal 8.00
Mayfair Open Rose, Saltshaker, Pink 27.50
Mayfair Open Rose, Sandwich Server, Pink, 12 In. 33.00
Mayfair Open Rose, Saucer, Cup Ring, Pink 25.00
Mayfair Open Rose, Sherbet, Pink 10.00
Mayfair Open Rose, Soup, Cream, Pink 30.00
Mayfair Open Rose, Tumbler, Pink, 3 1/2 In. 40.00
Mayfair Open Rose, Tumbler, Pink, 5 1/4 In. .... 35.00 To 37.50
Mayfair Open Rose, Vase, Sweet Pea, Blue ....53.00 To 100.00
   MEANDERING VINE, see Madrid
   MISS AMERICA, see also English Hobnail
Miss America, Bowl, Crystal, 6 1/4 In. .... 5.00 To 7.50
Miss America, Bowl, Curved In Top, Pink, 8 In. 50.00
Miss America, Butter, Cover, Pink 135.00
Miss America, Cake Plate, Crystal 15.00
Miss America, Candy Jar, Cover, Crystal 55.00
Miss America, Candy Jar, Cover, Pink 90.00
Miss America, Compote, Crystal, 5 In. 9.00
Miss America, Cup, Crystal 6.00
Miss America, Goblet, Juice, Pink, 4 3/4 In. 63.00
Miss America, Grill Plate, Crystal 9.50
Miss America, Luncheon Set, Crystal, 36 Piece 495.00
Miss America, Pitcher, Pink, 8 In. .... 88.00 To 90.00
Miss America, Platter, Oval, Pink .... 12.00 To 16.00
Miss America, Relish, 4 Sections, Pink 13.00
Miss America, Sherbet, Pink 9.00
Miss America, Tumbler, Green, 4 1/2 In. 15.00
Miss American, Candy Jar, Cover, Pink 75.00
   MODERNE ART, see Tea Room
Moderntone Little Hostess, Tea Set, Child's, Box, 16 Piece 65.00
Moderntone, Plate, Cobalt Blue, 7 3/4 In. 6.00
Moderntone, Salt & Pepper, Cobalt Blue 27.00
Moderntone, Salt & Pepper, Pink 9.00
Moderntone, Salt & Pepper, Purple 40.00
Moderntone, Salt & Pepper, Yellow 18.00
Moderntone, Sugar & Creamer, Cobalt Blue .... 14.00 To 15.00
Moondrops, Bowl, Vegetable, Oval, Amber 16.00
Moondrops, Cocktail Shaker, Pink 48.00
Moondrops, Cup, Amber 5.00
Moondrops, Decanter, Red, 11 1/4 In. 65.00
Moondrops, Plate, Amber, 9 1/2 In. 10.00
Moondrops, Platter, Oval, Amber 13.00
Moondrops, Sugar & Creamer, Red 15.00
Moondrops, Tray, Cobalt Blue, 7 1/2 In. 45.00
Moonstone, Bonbon, Heart Shape, Crystal, 6 1/2 In. 6.00
Moonstone, Bowl, Cloverleaf Shape, Crystal 11.00

> Never put anything hot in a cut glass bowl. It was not made to withstand heat, and will crack.

Moonstone, Candleholder, Crystal, Pair .... 10.00 To 17.50
Moonstone, Cigarette, Jar, Cover, Crystal 13.00
Moonstone, Creamer, Crystal .... 3.50 To 6.00
Moonstone, Cup & Saucer, Crystal 6.00
Moonstone, Goblet, Crystal .... 14.00 To 15.00
Moonstone, Perfume Bottle, Crystal 12.00
Moonstone, Plate, Crimped, Crystal, 10 In. .... 10.00 To 18.00
Moonstone, Plate, Crystal, 8 In. .... 6.00 To 8.50
Moonstone, Powder Box, Cover, Crystal .... 12.00 To 14.00
Moonstone, Relish, Divided, Crystal ....5.00 To 12.00
Moonstone, Sherbet, Crystal .... 4.00 To 8.50
Moonstone, Sugar, Crystal .... 3.50 To 6.00
Moonstone, Vase, Crystal 15.00
   MT. VERNON, see Cambridge Glass category
Navarre, Bowl, Nut, Footed, Crystal, 6 3/4 In. 26.00
Navarre, Goblet, Crystal, 7 5/8 In. 16.00

> When ordering antiques by mail, do not send cash. Keep a copy of your order.

New Century, Butter, Cover, Green 50.00
New Century, Grill Plate, Green 12.00
New Century, Salt & Pepper, Green 25.00
Newport, Berry Bowl, Cobalt Blue, 8 In. 30.00
Newport, Creamer, Cobalt Blue 11.00
Newport, Cup & Saucer, Amethyst .... 8.50 To 9.00
Newport, Plate, Amethyst, 10 In. 8.00
Newport, Salt & Pepper, Amethyst 24.00
Newport, Salt & Pepper, Cobalt Bue 45.00
Newport, Saucer, Cobalt Blue 2.50
Newport, Sherbet, Amethyst 6.50
Newport, Sherbet, Cobalt Blue 10.50
Newport, Soup, Cream, Amethyst 8.00
Newport, Sugar & Creamer, Amethyst 15.00
Newport, Sugar, Cobalt Blue 11.50
   NO. 601, see Avocado
No.610, Ice Tub, Yellow 195.00
No.612, Bowl, Green, 9 1/2 In. 26.00
No.612, Bowl, Yellow, 7 1/2 In. 19.00
No.612, Cup & Saucer, Green ....8.00 To 13.00
No.612, Cup, Green 5.50
No.612, Cup, Yellow 8.00
No.612, Pitcher, Yellow, 8 1/2 In. 225.00
No.612, Plate, Green, 8 3/8 In. .... 5.00 To 6.50
No.612, Plate, Green, 9 3/8 In. 7.00
No.612, Saucer, Green 4.00
No.612, Sherbet, Green ....8.00 To 11.00
No.612, Sherbet, Yellow 15.00
No.612, Sugar & Creamer, Yellow 8.00
No.612, Sugar, Green ....8.00 To 10.00
No.612, Tumbler, Footed, Green, 9 Oz. 16.00
No.615, Bowl, Vegetable, Oval, Green 40.00
No.615, Bowl, Yellow, 6 In. .... 35.00 To 47.50
No.615, Bowl, Yellow, 7 1/4 In. .... 38.00 To 40.00
No.615, Creamer, Yellow .... 10.00 To 12.00
No.615, Cup & Saucer, Green 13.00
No.615, Cup & Saucer, Yellow 20.00
No.615, Plate, Crystal, 8 3/8 In. 15.00
No.615, Plate, Green, 6 1/2 In. 5.50
No.615, Plate, Green, 7 3/4 In. 8.00
No.615, Plate, Green, 8 3/8 In. .... 12.00 To 13.50
No.615, Plate, Green, 10 1/4 In. 37.00
No.615, Plate, Yellow, 8 3/8 In. 15.00

No.615, Sugar & Creamer, Green 26.00
No.615, Sugar, Yellow 11.00
No.615, Tumbler, Green ....17.00 To 17.50
No.615, Tumbler, Yellow 20.00
No.620, Bowl, Amber, 6 In. 8.00
No.620, Cake Plate, Amber 8.00
No.620, Creamer, Amber 5.00
No.620, Cup & Saucer, Amber 5.00
No.620, Cup, Amber .... 3.00 To 4.50
No.620, Plate, Amber, 9 3/8 In. 5.00
No.620, Soup, Cream, Amber 6.00
No.620, Sugar, Amber 5.00
No.620, Tumbler, Amber, 9 Oz. 15.00
No.620, Tumbler, Footed, Amber, 9 Oz. 12.00
    NO. 622, see Pretzel
    NO. 624, see Christmas Candy
Normandie, Bowl, Amber, 8 1/2 In. 12.00
Normandie, Cup & Saucer, Amber 4.25
Normandie, Cup & Saucer, Pink 5.50
Normandie, Grill Plate, Iridescent 5.00
Normandie, Pitcher, Amber 40.00
Normandie, Salt & Pepper, Amber 35.00
Normandie, Sherbet, Iridescent 6.00
Normandie, Sugar & Creamer, Amber 25.00
Normandie, Sugar, Cover, Amber 60.00
Old Cafe, Bowl, Pink, 5 In. 3.00
Old Cafe, Candy Dish, Crystal 5.00
Old English, Pitcher, Green 47.00
    OLD FLORENTINE, see Florentine No. 1
    OPALESCENT HOBNAIL, see Moonstone
    OPEN LACE, see Lace Edge
    OPEN ROSE, see Mayfair Open Rose
    OPEN SCALLOP, see Lace Edge
    OPTIC DESIGN, see Raindrops
    OREGON GRAPE, see Woolworth
    ORIENTAL POPPY, see Florentine No. 2
    OXFORD, see Chinex Classic

If you discover a cache of very dirty antiques and you are not dressed in work clothes, make a temporary cover up from a plastic garbage bag.

Oyster & Pearl, Bowl, Handle, Red, 5 1/2 In. 9.50
Oyster & Pearl, Bowl, Red, 10 1/2 In. ....20.00 To 26.00
Oyster & Pearl, Relish, Pink ....7.00 To 15.00
Oyster & Pearl, Sandwich Server, Red 23.00
    PANELED ASTER, see Madrid
    PANELED CHERRY BLOSSOM, see Cherry Blossom
    PANSY & DORIC, see Doric & Pansy
    PARROT, see Sylvan
Patrician, Bowl, Green, 8 1/2 In. 25.00
Patrician, Cookie Jar, Cover, Crystal 70.00
Patrician, Creamer, Amber 5.00
Patrician, Cup, Amber 5.00
Patrician, Plate, Amber, 10 1/2 In. ....5.50 To 6.50
Patrician, Salt & Pepper, Green 65.00
Patrician, Salt & Pepper, Pink 60.00
Patrician, Sherbet, Amber ....5.25 To 8.50
Patrician, Soup, Cream, Amber 13.50
Patrician, Tumbler, Amber, 10 1/2 In. 22.00
    PEBBLE OPTIC, see Raindrops
    PETAL, see Petalware
    PETAL SWIRL, see Swirl

Petalware, Bowl, Blue, 5 3/8 In. 9.00
Petalware, Bowl, Crystal, 5 3/4 In. 2.25
Petalware, Tray, Colored Rim, Monax, 11 In. 12.00
Philbe, Sandwich Server, Blue, 10 In. 60.00
  PIE CRUST, see Cremax
  PINWHEEL, see Sierra
  POPPY NO. 1, see Florentine No. 1
  POPPY NO. 2, see Florentine No. 2
  PRETTY POLLY PARTY DISHES, see also Doric & Pansy
Pretty Polly Party Dishes, Tea Set, Ultramarine, 14 Piece 290.00
Pretzel, Berry Bowl, 9 3/8 In. 12.00
Pretzel, Celery Dish, Crystal 1.50
Pretzel, Soup, Dish, Crystal, 7 1/2 In. 7.50
  PRIMUS, see Madrid
Princess, Bowl, Hat Shape, Green, 9 1/2 In. 22.00
Princess, Bowl, Hat-Shape, Green, 9 1/2 In. 30.00
Princess, Bowl, Topaz, 5 In. 22.50
Princess, Coaster, Green 20.00
Princess, Cookie Jar, Cover, Green 35.00
Princess, Cookie Jar, Cover, Pink 40.00
Princess, Cup & Saucer, Green .... 10.00 To 13.00
Princess, Cup & Saucer, Pink .... 10.00 To 11.00
Princess, Cup & Saucer, Yellow .... 8.50 To 11.00
Princess, Grill Plate, Green 10.00
Princess, Pitcher, Green, 8 In. 28.00
Princess, Plate, Green, 9 In. 20.00
Princess, Plate, Pink, 9 In. 14.00
Princess, Plate, Yellow, 5 1/2 In. 10.00
Princess, Plate, Yellow, 9 In. 10.00
Princess, Salt & Pepper, Green 43.00
Princess, Salt & Pepper, Yellow 53.00
Princess, Sugar & Creamer, Cover, Pink 35.00
Princess, Sugar, Cover, Green 10.00
Princess, Tumbler, Footed, Green, 5 1/4 In. 16.00
Princess, Tumbler, Footed, Yellow, 5 1/4 In. .... 10.00 To 13.00

> If photographing antiques for insurance records use a Polaroid camera.
> There will be no negatives, and no one else has to see your treasures.

  PRISMATIC LINE, see Queen Mary
  PROVINCIAL, see Bubble
  PYRAMID, see No. 610
Queen Mary, Sherbet, Pink 6.00
  RAINDROPS, see also Colony
Raindrops, Cup & Saucer, Green 6.50
Raindrops, Cup, Green 4.50
  RASPBERRY BAND, see Laurel
  REX, see No. 610
  RIBBED, see Manhattan
  RIBBON CANDY, see Pretzel
Ribbon, Plate, Green, 6 1/4 In. 1.00
Ring, Cocktail Shaker, Crystal 7.50
Ring, Decanter, Stopper, Cobalt Blue 17.50
Ring, Sandwich Server, Colored Rings 16.50
Ring, Tumbler, Red, 3 1/2 In. 5.00
Rock Crystal, Cake Plate, Green, 11 In. 50.00
Rock Crystal, Champagne, Crystal 8.50
Rock Crystal, Cordial, Crystal 13.00
Rock Crystal, Finger Bowl, Red 55.00
Rock Crystal, Sherbet, Green 15.00
Rock Crystal, Vase, Amber, 11 In. 28.00
Rose Cameo, Sherbet, Green 5.00
  ROSE LACE, see Royal Lace

Rosemary, Bowl, Amber, 5 In. 4.50
Rosemary, Bowl, Oval, Amber, 10 In. 10.25
Rosemary, Creamer, Amber 8.00
Rosemary, Cup & Saucer, Amber 4.75
Rosemary, Cup & Saucer, Pink 13.50
Rosemary, Grill Plate, Amber ....5.00 To 11.00
Rosemary, Plate, Amber, 9 1/2 In. 5.25
Rosemary, Soup, Cream, Amber ....8.00 To 12.00
Rosemary, Sugar, Amber 8.00
Roulette, Tumbler, Green, 4 1/8 In. 13.00
Round Robin, Sherbet, Green ....2.00 To 4.50
Roxana, Sherbet, Yellow 1.75
Royal Lace, Bowl, Crystal, 5 In. 10.00
Royal Lace, Bowl, Pink, 5 In. 24.00
Royal Lace, Bowl, Rolled Edge, 3-Footed, Cobalt Blue, 10 In 33.00
Royal Lace, Butter, Cover, Pink 75.00
Royal Lace, Cookie Jar, Cover, Cobalt Blue 195.00
Royal Lace, Cookie Jar, Cover, Crystal 35.00
Royal Lace, Cookie Jar, Cover, Green 52.00
Royal Lace, Cookie Jar, Cover, Pink 37.50
Royal Lace, Cup & Saucer, Pink 156.50
Royal Lace, Cup, Pink 10.00
Royal Lace, Pitcher, Cobalt Blue, 48 Oz. ....90.00 To 100.00
Royal Lace, Plate, Green, 9 7/8 In. 17.00
Royal Lace, Sherbet, Metal Holder, Cobalt Blue 18.00
Royal Ruby, Cup & Saucer, Red 3.50
Royal Ruby, Goblet, Ball Stem, Red 7.00
Royal Ruby, Saucer, Red 1.00
Royal Ruby, Sherbet, Stem, Red 4.50
Royal Ruby, Snack Set, Red 22.00
Royal Ruby, Soup, Dish, Red 7.00
Royal Ruby, Tumbler, Red, 5 Oz. 4.50
Royal Ruby, Vase, 6 In. 5.00
    RUSSIAN, see Holiday
    SAIL BOAT, see White Ship
    SAILING SHIP, see White Ship
Sandwich Anchor Hocking, Bowl, Green, 6 1/2 In. 28.00
Sandwich Anchor Hocking, Pitcher, Crystal, 1/2 Gal, ... 28.00
Sandwich Anchor Hocking, Tumbler, Crystal, 3 Oz. 4.00
Sandwich Indiana, Plate, Crystal, 10 1/2 In. 12.00
Sandwich Indiana, Sugar, Crystal 5.00
    SAWTOOTH, see English Hobnail
    SAXON, see Coronation
    SCOTTIE DOG, see also Laurel
    SHAMROCK, see Cloverleaf
Sharon, Berry Bowl, Amber, 5 In. 6.50
Sharon, Berry Bowl, Green, 5 In. 11.50
Sharon, Bowl, Amber, 10 1/2 In. ....10.00 To 20.00
Sharon, Bowl, Vegetable, Oval, Pink, 9 1/2 In. 16.00
Sharon, Butter, Cover, Amber 42.50
Sharon, Butter, Cover, Green 55.00
Sharon, Butter, Cover, Pink 35.00
Sharon, Cake Stand, Amber 14.00
Sharon, Cheese Dish, Cover, Pink 550.00
Sharon, Creamer, Pink ....11.00 To 12.00
Sharon, Cup & Saucer, Pink 13.00
Sharon, Cup, Green 14.00
Sharon, Pitcher, Ice Lip, Pink 85.00
Sharon, Plate, Green, 7 1/2 In. 17.00
Sharon, Plate, Pink, 9 1/2 In. ....10.00 To 12.00
Sharon, Platter, Amber 13.50
Sharon, Salt & Pepper, Amber ....25.00 To 45.00
Sharon, Sherbet, Pink 10.00

Sharon, Soup, Cream, Pink .... 29.90 To 32.50
Sharon, Sugar & Creamer, Amber 20.00
Sharon, Sugar, Cover, Pink .... 25.00 To 33.00
Sharon, Tumbler, Thick, Pink, 9 Oz. 22.00
Sharon, Tumbler, Thick, Pink, 12 Oz. 52.50
    SHEFFIELD, see Chinex Classic
    SHELL, see Petalware
Shell, Cake Stand, Pink 18.50
Sierra, Sugar, Cover, Green 21.00
Sierra, Tray, 2 Handles, Green, 10 1/4 In. 12.00
Sierra, Tray, 2 Handles, Pink, 10 1/4 In. 9.00
    SMOCKING, see Windsor
    SNOWFLAKE, see Doric
    SPIRAL OPTIC, see Spiral
Spiral, Pitcher, Green 35.00
Spiral, Sherbet, Green 3.00
    SPOKE, see Patrician
Starlight, Cup & Saucer, Crystal 4.00
    STIPPLED ROSE BAND, see S Pattern
    STRAWBERRY, see also Cherry-Berry
Strawberry, Berry Bowl, Green, 4 In. 10.00
Strawberry, Berry Bowl, Green, 7 1/2 In. 22.00
Strawberry, Berry Bowl, Pink, 4 In. 6.00
Strawberry, Berry Bowl, Pink, 7 1/2 In. 18.00
Strawberry, Pitcher, Pink 115.00
Strawberry, Tumbler, Green 24.00
Sunflower, Cake Plate, Green, 10 In. 9.00
Sunflower, Tumbler, Pink 10.00
    SWEET PEAR, see Avocado
Swirl, Butter, Cover, Pink 140.00
Swirl, Butter, Cover, Ultramarine 150.00
Swirl, Candy Dish, Cover, Ultramarine 70.00
Swirl, Console Set, Ultramarine, 3 Piece 35.00
Swirl, Saucer, Ultramarine 3.00
Swirl, Soup, Dish, Tab Handle, Ultramarine 17.50
Swirl, Sugar & Creamer, Ultramarine 20.00
    SWIRLED BIG RIB, see Spiral
    SWIRLED SHARP RIB, see Diana
Sylvan, Berry Bowl, Green, 5 In. 20.00
Sylvan, Creamer, Green 22.00
Sylvan, Grill Plate, Amber 15.00
Sylvan, Plate, Green, 9 In. 35.00
Sylvan, Salt & Pepper, Green 200.00
Sylvan, Sherbet, Amber .... 15.00 To 16.00
Sylvan, Sherbet, Cone, Footed, Amber 9.50
Sylvan, Sherbet, Green 19.00
    TASSELL, see Princess
Tea Room, Banana Boat, Footed, Green 55.00
Tea Room, Candlestick, Green, Pair 45.00
Tea Room, Creamer, Footed, Pink, 4 1/2 In. 11.00
Tea Room, Ice Bucket, Green 120.00
Tea Room, Saltshaker, Pink 17.00
Tea Room, Sherbet, Footed, Green 28.00
Tea Room, Sugar & Creamer, Green, 4 In. 30.00
Tea Room, Sugar & Creamer, Pink, 4 In. 17.00
Tea Room, Tray, Center Handle, Green 170.00
Tea Room, Tumbler, Footed, Pink, 6 Oz. 30.00
Thistle, Cup & Saucer, Green 25.00
Thistle, Cup & Saucer, Pink 22.50
Thistle, Plate, Pink, 8 In. .... 7.00 To 8.00
    THREADING, see Old English
    THREE PARROT, see Sylvan

To be sure you have a Tiffany lamp, you must find the words "Tiffany and Co." printed on the metal base. The glass shades were also marked "L. C. Tiffany," or just with the letters "L. C. T." According to the records of the Tiffany Company, all these lamps were marked.

Tulip, Candlestick, Amethyst	50.00
Tulip, Console, Blue	45.00
Versailles, Candlestick, Blue, 3 In., Pair	45.00
VERTICAL RIBBED, see Queen Mary	
Victory, Bowl, Pink, 6 1/2 In.	9.50
Victory, Plate, Pink, 9 In.	15.00
Victory, Platter, Pink	22.00
Victory, Sandwich Server, Pink	24.00
VIVID BANDS, see Petalware	
WAFFLE, see Waterford	
Waterford, Berry Bowl, Crystal, 4 3/4 In.	3.00
Waterford, Berry Bowl, Crystal, 8 1/4 In.	5.50
Waterford, Berry Bowl, Pink, 4 3/4 In.	7.50
Waterford, Bowl, Crystal, 5 1/2 In.	13.00
Waterford, Butter, Cover, Crystal	18.00 To 19.00
Waterford, Cake Plate, Crystal	3.50
Waterford, Coaster, Crystal	1.00
Waterford, Creamer, Crystal	2.00 To 3.00
Waterford, Cup & Saucer, Crystal	4.50
Waterford, Cup & Saucer, Pink	14.00
Waterford, Lamp, Ball, Electric, 4 In.	30.00
Waterford, Pitcher, Juice, Crystal	10.00
Waterford, Pitcher, Water, Pink	110.00
Waterford, Plate, Crystal, 6 In.	1.00
Waterford, Plate, Crystal, 9 5/8 In.	4.50
Waterford, Plate, Pink, 9 5/8 In.	13.50 To 14.00
Waterford, Relish, 5 Sections, Crystal	10.00 To 15.00
Waterford, Salt & Pepper, Crystal	5.50
Waterford, Sherbet, Footed, Crystal	3.00
Waterford, Sugar & Creamer, Crystal	7.50
WEDDING BAND, see Moderntone	
WHITE SAIL, see White Ship	
White Ship, Cocktail Set, Blue, 7 Piece	50.00
White Ship, Cocktail Shaker, Blue	25.00
White Ship, Tumbler, Juice, Flat, Blue	9.00
WILD ROSE, see Dogwood	
WILDROSE WITH APPLE BLOSSOM, see Flower Garden with Butterflies	
WINDSOR DIAMOND, see Windsor	
Windsor, Bowl, Crystal, 8 In.	7.00
Windsor, Bowl, Pink, 8 In.	10.00
Windsor, Butter, Cover, Green	75.00
Windsor, Cup & Saucer, Green	10.00
Windsor, Cup, Crystal	1.75
Windsor, Cup, Pink	4.00
Windsor, Pitcher, Crystal, 4 1/2 In.	17.50
Windsor, Plate, Pink, 6 In.	2.25
Windsor, Saucer, Pink	1.25
Windsor, Sherbet, Green	4.50
Windsor, Sherbet, Pink	6.00
Windsor, Soup, Cream, Pink	18.00
WINGED MEDALLION, see Madrid	
WOOLWORTH, see also Grape	
Woolworth, Bowl, Pink, 7 1/2 In.	8.50
X Design, Reamer, Crystal	7.00

Derby porcelain was made in Derby, England, from 1756 to the present. The factory changed names and marks several times. Chelsea Derby (1770–1784), Crown Derby (1784–1811), and the modern Royal Crown Derby are some of the most famous periods of the factory.

DERBY, see also Chelsea; Crown Derby; Royal Crown Derby

DERBY, Basket, Flowers, Green, Red, Pink, 1760, 8 1/2 In. Wide	950.00
Candlestick, Boy Playing Flute, 1760,	800.00
Cup & Saucer, Embossed Spiral Ribs, Foliage, Vining, Handleless	215.00
Figurine, Boy Playing Bagpipe, Girl In Green Hat, 8 1/2 X 8 In.	1900.00
Plate, View of Chatsworth, Blue, Gold Border, 1790	850.00
Sauceboat, Leaf Molded, Green, Flowers, 7 In.	350.00
Tea Bowl & Saucer, Flowers, Pink, Yellow, Red Anchor, 1770	1500.00
Tray, Polychrome Floral Rim, Gilt, Red Crown Mark, 10 3/4 In.	65.00
Vase, Urn Shape, Handles, Scene In Center Panel, Gold, 1760, 10 1/2 In.	2000.00

The DeVilbiss Company has made atomizers of all types since 1888 but no longer makes the perfume bottle tops so popular with collectors. These were made from 1920 to 1968. The glass bottle may be by any of many manufacturers even if the atomizer says DeVilbiss.

DEVILBISS, Atomizer, Cord & Netted Bulb, Amethyst	95.00
Dresser Set, Hand Painted Flowers, Gold Trim, Signed, 7 Piece	400.00
Perfume Bottle, Amber Iridescent, Optic Ribbed, Art Glass	170.00
Perfume Bottle, Art Deco, Black & Gold, Steuben Label	525.00
Perfume Bottle, Black, 8 In.	77.50
Perfume Bottle, Black, Ribbed, Powder Box, Atomizer, 3 Piece	265.00
Perfume Bottle, Blue, Powder Box, Tray, 3 Piece	295.00
Perfume Bottle, Feather, Topaz Opalescent, Atomizer	38.00
Perfume Bottle, Light Lavender, Satin Glass, Atomizer, 2 Piece	295.00
Perfume Bottle, Pebbled Light Blue, Atomizer, 5 In.	48.00
Perfume Bottle, Purse, Sterling Silver, With Dabber	125.00
Perfume Bottle, Silver Crackle, Atomizer	45.00
Perfume Bottle, Sterling Silver Overlay, Bulbous, Stopper	295.00
Perfume Bottle, Yellow & Black Art Deco, Tassled Bulb, Cranberry	70.00
Powder Box, Lavender & Crystal	55.00

The comic strip "Dick Tracy" started in 1931. He was the hero of movies from 1937 to 1947, starred in a radio series in the 1940s and a television series in the 1950s. Memorabilia from all these activities is collected.

DICK TRACY, Badge, Crime Stopper, Brass, Red Enamel, Tracy On Front	75.00
Billfold, Crime Stoppers Member Card, Red	50.00
Book, Ace Detective	8.00
Book, Big Little Book, Dick Tracy Returns	25.00
Book, Dick Tracy Out West, 1933	20.00
Camera, 1940	70.00
Car, Riot, Friction, Box	85.00
Comic Book, Detective, 1937	125.00
Comic Section, Sunday, Daily News, May 20, 1945	15.00
Crime Stoppers, Club Kit, Box	45.00
Decal, Iron-On, Crime Stoppers, 8 X 10 In.	45.00
Detective Set, Figure Printing Outfit	80.00
Doll, Little Honeymoon, Dick's Granddaughter, Box, 1960s, 17 In.	450.00
Game, Cardboard Figures, Cards, Board, Spinner, 1960s, Selchow	45.00
Game, Crime Stopper, Ideal, Box, 1963	35.00
Game, Detective, Board, Discs, Spinner, 1933, Einson-Freeman Co.	325.00
Hand Puppet, Vinyl Head, Cloth Body, 1961	45.00
Holster, Shoulder, Tracy's Face Etched In Leather, 1930s	145.00
Iron On, Crime Stopper, Red, White, Blue, 1940s, 8 X 10 In.	45.00
Knife	22.50 To 25.00
Lunch Box	25.00
Mask, Rubber, Austin Art Studios, 1940s	125.00

Model Kit, Space Coupe, Aurora, Box, 1968	150.00
Pin, Secret Service Patrol	24.00
Plate & Cup, With Sparkle Plenty	45.00
Play Set, Original Card, 1979	22.00
Police Set, Card, 1953	65.00
Poster, Movie, 1945, 14 X 36 In.	125.00
Salt & Pepper, Dick Tracy & Junior	15.00
Siren Pistol	55.00
Soakie, Bubble Bath Container, 1960s, 10 In.	45.00
Stamp Set, Favorite Funnies, Dick, Annie & Sandy, 1935, Box	65.00
Televiewer, Color, Movies, 1973, Card	12.50
Toy, Bullet Gun, Package	10.00
Toy, Squad Car, Marx	225.00
Tumbler, Frosted Glass, Tracy On Front, 5 In.	115.00 To 125.00
Wrist Radio, 2–Way Talk, Remco, Battery Operated, Unused	25.00
Wrist Radio, 2–Way, American Doll–Toy, Box, 1961	20.00
Wristwatch, 1948, Box	325.00
Wristwatch, Digital, Pictures of Tracy, Omni	48.00

DICKENS WARE, see Royal Doulton; Weller

The Dionne quintuplets were born in Canada on May 28, 1934. The publicity about their birth and their special status as wards of the Canadian government made them famous throughout the world. Visitors could watch the girls play, reporters interviewed the girls and the staff, and thousands of special dolls and souvenirs were made picturing the quints at different ages. Emilie died in 1954, Marie in 1970. Yvonne, Annette, and Cecile still live in Canada.

DIONNE QUINTUPLETS, Book, Photos, Whitman No.937, 44 Pages	25.00
Calendar, J.L. Olson Furniture & Funeral Service, 1939	20.00
Calendar, Paper, 1936	23.00
Coloring Book, Pictures To Paint, Merrill	30.00
Composition, Painted, Wicker Basket, 7 In.	302.50
Display Card, Hair Ribbon	93.50
Doll, Composition, Stroller, Madame Alexander,	302.00 To 495.00
Doll, Emilie, Toddler, Pin, Madame Alexander, 14 In.	275.00
Doll, Pins, 8 In., 5 Piece	1300.00
Fan, School Days	18.00
Paper Doll, Cardboard Quints & Crib	65.00
Paper Doll, Let's Play House	80.00
Postcard Set, Birth, Souvenir, 7 Piece	25.00
Spoon Set, 5 Piece	150.00
Spoon, Annette	30.00

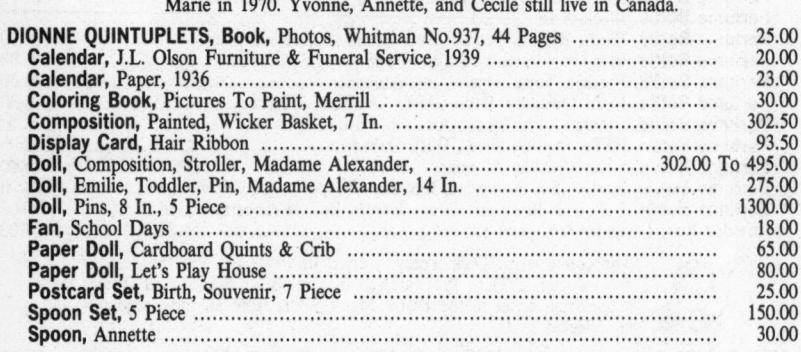

Walt Disney and his company introduced many comic characters to the world. Collectors search for examples of the work of the Disney Studios and the many commercial products modeled after his characters. These collectibles are called "Disneyana."

DISNEYANA, Alarm Clock, Mickey, Bradley	24.00
Applique, Jiminy	8.00
Ashtray Set, Donald Duck, Pressed Glass, Kemper–Thomas Co., 5 In.	125.00
Ashtray, Disneyland, Castle, Glass, 4 X 5 In.	28.00
Ashtray, Three Little Pigs, Playing Instruments, Chain, 1930s	145.00
Automaton, Dopey, Display, Speaker, Composition, 1938, 18 In.	375.00
Badge, From Easter Seals, Mickey's 60th Birthday, 3 In.	5.00
Bank, Donald Duck, Cash Register, Marx, 1950s, 4 In.	375.00
Bank, Mickey Mouse Club, Figural, Glass, Sitting Position, 7 In.	20.00
Bank, Mickey Mouse, Holding Flower, Leeds, 1940s	30.00
Bank, Mickey Mouse, Mechanical, Pride Lines, Metal, 1980, 6 1/2 In.	247.00
Bank, Pinocchio, 1939, Crown	48.00
Bank, Pinocchio, Bisque, 8 In.	195.00
Bank, Pluto, Sits On Haunches, Wooden, Disney Prod., 11 In.	50.00
Bank, Pluto, Sitting, Tongue Hanging Out, 6 1/2 In.	25.00
Barrette, Hair, Mickey, Bow With Mickey Face, 1940s	30.00
Bell, Mickey Mouse, Bicentennial, 1976, Schmid	20.00

Belt Buckle, Donald's Birthday, Brass, Donald, Chip & Dale 55.00
Belt, Utility, Mickey Mouse, Remco, Box 10.00
Blotter, Donald Duck, Sunoco, Driving, Green Car, Buy War Bonds 16.00
Book, Bango, Whitman Story Hour Series, 1958 .... 25.00
Book, Big Little Book, Donald Duck & Ghost Morgans Treasure 40.00
Book, Big Little Book, Mickey Mouse & The Bat Bandit .... • 45.00
Book, Big Little Book, Mickey Mouse Sails, Treasure Island, 1935 .... 48.00
Book, Big Little Book, Mickey Mouse, Mystery At Disneyland 4.00
Book, Big Little Book, Mickey Runs His Own Newspaper, 1937 .... 48.00
Book, Big Little Book, Silly Symphony, 1934 .... 32.00
Book, Coloring, Ferdinand The Bull, 1938 .... 22.00
Book, Coloring, Mickey Goes To Frontierland, 1957 .... 15.00
Book, Coloring, Uncle Scrooge, Dell, 1955 .... 18.00
Book, Disneyland, Souvenir, 1959 .... 30.00
Book, Donald Duck, Wise Little Hen, Linen, 1930s 85.00
Book, Donald's 50th Birthday, 50 Years of Frustration 16.00
Book, Johnny Appleseed, Whitman Story Hour Series, 1958 .... 25.00
Book, Mickey Mouse & His Friends, Linen Like, 1936, Whitman 19.00
Book, Pop–Up, Minnie Mouse, Blue Ribbon Books, 1933 .... 110.00
Book, Snow White, Jingle, Snow White Bread, 1938 .... 48.00
Book, Uncensored Mouse, Vol. 1, 1930s 80.00
Book, Uncle Scrooge, No.21, Dell–Barks 20.00
Book, Uncle Scrooge, No.30, Dell–Barks 17.00
Bottle Caps, Donald Duck Cola, 1950s, Pair 7.00
Bottle, Milk, Clarabell, Mickey's Nephew, 1930s 95.00
Bottle, Milk, Mickey Mouse, 1/2 Pt. 95.00
Bottle, Soaky, Donald Duck, Plastic, 1960s 8.00
Bottle, Soda, Mickey, National Soft Drink Asso., Donald, Goofy 45.00
Bowl & Tumbler, Mickey Mouse Club, 1950s, 2 Piece 8.50
Bowl, ABC, Mickey Mouse, Beetleware 20.00
Bowl, Cereal, Donald Duck, Pink, 5 1/4 In. 15.00
Bowl, Mickey, Lime Green, Safetyware, 1930s 22.00
Bowl, Porridge, Mickey Mouse, Silver, Mickey Handle, 1930s, 5 In. 225.00
Box, Cereal, Post, Mickey & Minnie Give A Party, 1936 .... 25.00
Box, Cereal, Post, Mickey On Ice, Donald, Pluto, 1930s 25.00
Box, Crayon, Donald Duck, Mickey Mouse, Transogram, Tin, 9 Crayons 28.00
Box, Quackers, Cheese, Donald Duck, Nabisco, 1950s, 6 Oz. 185.00
Box, Straws, Mickey Mouse 16.50
Bracelet, Donald Duck Charm, Child's, Wire 8.00
Bracelet, Jungle Book, Charms, Silver, Boy, Snake, Bear, Tiger 38.00
Breakfast Set, Lime Green, Safetyware, Donald Duck, 3 Piece 68.00
Brush, Hair, Mickey Mouse, Marked WDE 28.00
Button, Mickey Mouse, 1930s, 1 1/4 In. 42.00
Button, Mickey Mouse, 50th, Cake Logo, 1978, 3 1/2 In. 15.00
Button, Mickey's 7th Birthday, Red, Black, Celluloid, 1 1/4 In. 125.00
Button, Mickey's Official Store, Red, Yellow, Celluloid, 1 1/4 In. 145.00
Calendar, Disney World Centennial, 1981 .... 18.00
Calendar, Glow In The Dark, 1977 .... 25.00
Camera, Donald Duck, Disney 35.00
Camera, Flash, Mickey, Donald Holds Sign "Smile" 38.00
Camera, Mickey Mouse & Donald Duck, Elko, Box 100.00
Camera, Mickey Mouse's Head, 1960 .... 35.00 To 45.00
Canister, Lollipop, Mickey Mouse 28.00
Cap Pistol, Mickey Mouse, Holster, Accessories, Package, 1965 .... 65.00
Cap, Donald Duck 10.00
Car, TV, Mickey Mouse, Tin, Litho, Marx 1650.00
Card, Christmas, 101 Dalmations, Disney Studios, 1961 .... 85.00
Card, Christmas, Aristocats, Opening of Disneyworld, 1971 .... 45.00
Card, Christmas, Cartoon, Map of The New Disneyland, 1956 .... 125.00
Card, Christmas, Lady and The Tramp, Disneyland Castle, 1955 .... 145.00
Card, Christmas, Mickey Mouse Club, Bambi Centerfold, 1957 .... 125.00
Card, Christmas, Peter Pan, Disney Studios, 1953 .... 125.00
Card, Christmas, Sword In The Stone, Disney Studios, 1964 .... 85.00
Card, Christmas, The Jungle Book, Disney Studios, 1968 .... 65.00

Card, Valentine, Mickey Mouse, Mechanical, USA 28.00
DISNEYANA, CEL, see Animation Art
Chair, Beanbag, Mickey Mouse Club, No Ears 50.00
Clock, Alarm, Bugs Bunny, Animated, Ingraham 225.00
Clock, Alarm, Mickey Mouse, Bradley, Box 50.00
Clock, Alarm, Mickey Mouse, Ingersoll, Box 200.00
Clock, Alarm, Mickey Mouse, Pie–Eye, Bradley, Yellow Bells, 1970s 35.00
Clock, Alarm, Mickey, Plastic, Lorus, 4 In. 20.00
Clock, Alarm, Minnie Mouse, Travel, Phinney–Walker 40.00
Clock, Alarm, Pluto, Bayard, France, 1960s 65.00
Clock, Alarm, Snow White, Rose Colored, Bayard, France, 1964 .... 375.00
Clock, Alice In Wonderland, U.S. Time, 1970 .... 25.00
Clock, Big Bad Wolf, Ingersoll, 1934 .... 275.00
Clock, Desk, Donald Duck, Flashing LCD, Bradley, Box 15.00
Clock, Donald Duck, Ticking Head, Bayard, 1972 .... 200.00
Clock, Donald Duck, Wall, Wristwatch Shape, Bradley, 26 In. 30.00
Clock, Mickey Mouse, Bradley, 50th Birthday 175.00
Clock, Mickey Mouse, Pendulum, 1950s 95.00
Clock, Mickey Mouse, Pie–Eyed, Ticking Head, Red, 1960s, Bayard 200.00
Clock, Mickey Mouse, Pop–Up, Alarm, Lorus, Box 30.00
Clock, Mickey Mouse, Red, Electric, Wall, Elgin, Hexagonal, 15 In. 30.00
Clock, Mickey Mouse, Talking Choo Choo, Box .... 80.00 To 95.00
Clock, Mickey Mouse, Tin Litho, Steel, Bayard, 5 In. 55.00
Clock, Mickey Mouse, U.S.Time, 1947 .... 245.00
Clock, Mickey Mouse, Wall, Schoolhouse Scene, Elgin, Electric 30.00
Clock, Snow White, Tin Litho, Steel, Bayard, 5 In. 125.00
Cookie Cutter, Mickey & Minnie, Plastic, Red & Yellow Outfits 5.00
Cookie Jar, Donald Duck, Leaning On Pumpkin 115.00
Cookie Jar, Donald Duck, Nephew On Outside, Marked 125.00
Cookie Jar, Dumbo, Turnabout 95.00
Cookie Jar, Mickey & Minnie, Turnabout, Leeds, 1940s 75.00
Cookie Jar, Mickey Mouse Chef, With Rolling Pin, Marked 45.00
Cookie Jar, Pluto, Turnabout, Ceramic, 1940s 175.00
Cookie Jar, Tigger The Tiger 72.00
Cookie Jar, Tigger, Walt Disney Productions 55.00
Cookie Jar, Winnie The Pooh, Dark Yellow & Red 95.00
Cookie Jar, Winnie The Pooh, Honey Pot, Yellow, Red .... 38.00 To 95.00
Cookie Jar, Winnie The Pooh, Sitting On Honey Pot, Bee On Handle 55.00
Costume, Bambi, Mask, Ben Cooper, 1950s, Box 35.00
Costume, Cinderella, 1960s, Ben Cooper 25.00
Costume, Mickey Mouse, With Mask, 1974 .... 20.00
Costume, Sleeping Beauty, 1950s 48.00
Costume, Zorro, Walt Disney, Box 95.00
Creamer, Donald Duck, Leeds, 1940s, 6 In. 30.00
Creamer, Mickey Mouse, Light Brown, Mickey, China, 1930s, 5 In. 70.00
Creamer, White Rabbit, Regal 128.00
Cufflinks, Mickey Mouse, 1934 Disney–Hickock Dies, Gift Box 22.00
Cup & Saucer, Mickey & Minnie Dancing, Pluto On Cup, Tin 48.00
Cup, Donald & Ludwig, Embossed, Ceramic, Pair 20.00
Curtains, Peter Pan, White, Movie Characters, 60 X48 In. 20.00
Dinner Set, Cup, Saucer, Plate, Goofy, Clarabell, Donald, Tin, 3 Pc. 25.00
Dish, Child's, Feeding, Mickey Mouse, 3 Sections, 8 In. 40.00
Disneykin Play Set, Dumbo, 1960s, 6 Piece 85.00
Disneykin, Blue Fairy 22.00
Disneykin, Captain Hook 22.00
Disneykin, Doc 6.00
Disneykin, Mickey Mouse 15.00
Display Box, Gloves, Mickey & Friends, Disneyland, 8 X 12 X 3 In. 85.00
Display, Castle, Goofy, Donald, Snow White, Mickey, 15 In. 200.00
Display, Dopey, Automaton, Speaker, Movable Mouth, 1938, 18 In. 375.00
Display, Mad Hatter, Cardboard, 10 X 12 In. 38.00
Doll, Donald Duck, Autographed, Character Novelty Co., 16 In. 121.00
Doll, Donald Duck, Chalkware, Carnival 22.00
Doll, Donald Duck, Knickerbocker, 1930s, 12 In. 575.00

Doll, Donald Duck, Lenci 275.00
Doll, Donald Duck, Woolkin, 1960s, 5 In. 30.00
Doll, Dopey, Composition, Movable Arms, Marked, 9 In. 130.00
Doll, Goofy, Stuffed, Red Shirt, Yellow Vest, Blue Jeans, 12 In. .... 12.00 ·
Doll, Mary Poppins, Disney, Box 60.00
Doll, Mickey Mouse, Felt & Fabric, Long Dangling Legs, 25 In. 275.00
Doll, Mickey Mouse, Knickerbocker, 1930s, 12 In. 575.00
Doll, Mickey Mouse, Pie–Eye, Joy Toy of Australia, 1930s, 10 In. 150.00
Doll, Snow White & 7 Dwarfs, Vinyl, 1950s, 8 Piece 450.00
Doll, Snow White, Composition, Madame Alexander, 1937, 13 In. 175.00
Doll, Snow White, Madame Alexander, 1937 .... 175.00
Doll, Snow White, Painted Eyes, Composition, Knickerbocker, 13 In. 155.00
Doll, Snow White, Walt Disney Classics, Horsman, 8 In. 40.00
Doll, Tramp, Plush, Gund, Bell Inside, 1950s 30.00
Drum, Mickey, Minnie, Donald, Pluto, Tin, Ohio Art, 7 In. 175.00
Ears, Head Band, Mickey Mouse Club, Original Cardboard 12.00
Ears, Mickey Mouse Club, 1960s 8.00
Eggcup, Donald Duck Pushing Wheelbarrow, 3 In. 275.00
Eggcup, Dumbo Pulling Wagon, Crossed Eyes, 2 1/2 In. 250.00
Embroidery Set, Characters, Box, 1930s 35.00
Figurine, Alice In Wonderland, Ceramic, 1960, 5 In. 35.00
Figurine, Bambi, Disney–Shaw 68.50
Figurine, Donald Duck On Rocking Horse, Bisque, 1930s, 3 In. 150.00
Figurine, Donald Duck, Holding Bugle, Bisque, 1930s, 3 In. 150.00
Figurine, Donald Duck, Long Bill, Walking, Bisque, 1930s, 3 In. 65.00
Figurine, Donald Duck, Pushing Wheelbarrow, Porcelain, 3 In. 325.00
Figurine, Donald Duck, Standing, Bill Open, Bisque, 1930s, 3 In. 85.00
Figurine, Donald Duck, Sword, Bisque, Hagen–Renaker, 3 In. 150.00
Figurine, Dopey, Bisque, All White, 1930, 3 In. 20.00
Figurine, Dumbo, American Pottery, Marked Disney 75.00
Figurine, Dumbo, Pulling Wagon, Porcelain, 1940s, 2 1/2 X 4 In. 300.00
Figurine, Ferdinand The Bull, Bisque, 1930s, 3 In. 42.00
Figurine, Geppetto, Multi–Products, 5 1/4 In. 75.00
Figurine, Lady, From Lady & The Tramp, Hagen–Renaker, 1950s 55.00
Figurine, March Hare, Alice In Wonderland, Ceramic, 4 In. 30.00
Figurine, Mickey Mouse Riding Pluto, Bisque, 1930, 2 In. 125.00
Figurine, Mickey Mouse, Band Leader, 4 1/2 In. 65.00
Figurine, Mickey Mouse, Hands On Hip, Bisque, 1930, 2 3/4 In. 45.00
Figurine, Mickey Mouse, Waving, Bisque, Hagen–Renaker, 1 1/2 In. 85.00
Figurine, Mickie Mouse, Playing A Saxophone, Bisque, 3 1/2 In. 85.00
Figurine, Minnie Mouse, Playing The Mandolin, Bisque, 3 1/2 In. 85.00
Figurine, Sleepy, Seiberling, 5 In. 18.00
Figurine, Sneezy, Bisque, 1930s, 3 In. 25.00
Figurine, Snow White & 7 Dwarfs, Disneykins 48.00
Figurine, Snow White, American Pottery 395.00
Figurine, Snow White, Bisque, 6 In. 185.00
Figurine, Sorcerer's Apprentice, Pewter, Holding Wand, Ball 275.00
Film, Mickey Mouse, Safe–Toy, Box 25.00
Fire Truck, Mickey Driving, Donald In Back, Sun Rubber Co., 6 In. 125.00
Fire Truck, Mickey Mouse, Hard Rubber, 1930s 40.00
Flashlight, Mickey & Minnie, Usa–Lite 95.00
Fork, Jiminy Cricket, Pink Plastic Handle 10.00
Fork, Minnie Mouse, England, Nickel Plated, 4 1/2 In. 18.00
Game, Bean Bag, Dopey, Cardboard, 1938, Parker Brothers 175.00
Game, Card, Mickey Mouse, Russel Mfg.Box 12.00
Game, Cinderella, Parker Brothers, 1950, Box 45.00
Game, Dominos, Mickey Mouse, 1930s 25.00
Game, Fantasyland, Parker Bros. 25.00
Game, Ferdinand The Bull, 1938, Whitman 85.00
Game, Guess–O–Game, Ludwig Von Drake, Magic Slate, 1961 .... 20.00
Game, Mickey Mouse, Coming Home, Board, Paper Lithograph 115.00
Game, Mickey Mouse, Electric Treasure Hunt, Tudor Corp. 175.00
Game, Mickey Mouse, Starship Journey Thru Space .... 45.00 To 65.00
Game, Mickey Mouse, Treasure Hunt, Board, Tin 30.00

Game, Mickey Mouse, Tree House, Walt Disney	15.00
Game, Peter Pan Adventure, Transogram, 1953, Box	35.00
Game, Snow White & 7 Dwarfs, 1937	100.00
Game, Snow White & 7 Dwarfs, 1977	18.00
Game, Tomorrowland Rocket To The Moon	30.00
Game, Who's Afraid of Big Bad Wolf, Parker Bros., 1933	125.00
Game, Winnie The Pooh, 1964	15.00
Gum Ball Machine, Mickey Mouse, Plastic, Hasbro, 1968	15.00
Gum Card, Mickey Mouse, Movie, 24 Cards, 1930s	975.00
Hand Car, Mickey & Minnie Mouse, Track, Instructions, Lionel, Box	2500.00
Hand Puppet, Donald Duck, Cloth, Rubber Head, 1960s	15.00
Handkerchief, Cinderella & Prince Charming, White	20.00
Holder, Toothbrush, 3 Little Pigs, Bisque, 1930s, 3 3/4 In.	90.00
Holder, Toothbrush, Mickey & Minnie Mouse, Bisque, Painted	135.00
Holder, Toothbrush, Mickey Mouse & Pluto, Painted Pottery	143.00
Horn, Party, Mickey Mouse	60.00
Jar, Lollipop, Mickey, Donald & Ludwig	135.00
Jell-O Mold, Mickey, Minnie, Clarabell, Horace, Pentagon Shape	40.00
Lamp, Ceiling, Mickey Mouse & Donald Duck, Box, 1940s	295.00
Lamp, Dopey, Disney	27.00
Lamp, Snow White, Holding Up Sides of Dress, Ceramic, Leeds	110.00
Lighter, Donald, Full Figure of Donald, Gold, Zippo	25.00
Lunch Box, Disney Express	20.00
Lunch Box, Disneyland Castle	75.00
Lunch Box, Magic Kingdom, Aladdin, Thermos, Walt Disney	18.00
Lunch Box, Mickey Mouse Club	15.00
Lunch Box, Mickey Mouse, Pie-Eyed, Tin, Oval, 1930s	130.00
Lunch Box, Snow White, Ohio Art, With Spinner Game	35.00
Lunch Box, The Fox and The Hound, Aladdin	10.00
Magazine, Mickey Mouse, Vol. 5, No. 12, Pre W.D.	75.00
Magic Slate, Sleeping Beauty, Fairies, Castle, 1959	40.00
Magic Subtractor, Mickey Mouse, Box	25.00
Map, Musical, Mickey Mouse Club, Mattel	40.00
Marionette, Alice In Wonderland, Wooden, Disney, Box, Early 1950s	85.00
Marionette, Grumpy, Madame Alexander, 1938	225.00
Marionette, Minnie Mouse, Box	160.00
Mask, Minnie, Paper, Dated 1930	60.00
Mask, Pinocchio, Gillette Blue Blade Premium, 1939	15.00
Melody Maker, Tin, 1955	265.00
Menu, Tavern In Walt Disney World, Scrooge McDuck	3.00
Mirror, Bambi, Thumper & Bambi Characters, Framed, 18 X 24 In.	45.00
Mobile, Robin Hood, Unpounched, 11 Characters	25.00
Mug, Coffee, Donald & Daisy, Pepsi	8.00
Mug, Coffee, Snow White & 7 Dwarfs, Japan	185.00
Mug, Donald Duck, Heavy Glass, 1970s, 5 In.	5.00
Mug, Mickey & Donald, Tandem Bike, Beswick, 3 In.	45.00
Music Box, Goofy & Mickey's Nephew, Rudolph Red Nose Reindeer	65.00
Music Box, Mickey & Minnie, Pie-Eyed, Plays Feeling Groovy, 1978	65.00
Music Box, Mickey Mouse, Schmid, Box, 7 In.	35.00
Music Box, Mickey Mouse, With Cape, Schmid, Box, 7 In.	35.00
Music Box, Mickey, 2 Nephews, Plays Frosty The Snow Man, Schmid	65.00
Music Box, Mickey, 50th Birthday Cake, It's A Small World, 1978	75.00
Music Box, Mickey, Minnie, Ceramic, Yes Sir That's My Baby, Schmid	56.00
Neck Scarf Holder, Triple-R-Ranch, 1950s, 1 1/2 In.	35.00
Night-Light, Donald Duck, 1960s	35.00
Nodder, Donald Duck, Irwin, Box, 5 In.	65.00
Nodder, Donald Duck, Papier-Mache	95.00
Nodder, Goofy, Disney World, 8 In.	25.00
Note Paper, Envelopes, Mickey Mouse Club, Box	22.00
Ornament, Christmas, 1978 Mickey's 50th Birthday, Schmid	28.00
Ornament, Christmas, Mickey, Goofy, Donald Caroling, 3 1/4 In.	15.00
Ornament, Christmas, Winnie, Tigger, Eeyore, Piglet, Roo, 1984	20.00
Pail, 3 Little Pigs, Wolf, Ohio Art, Tin Litho, 7 In.	85.00
Pail, Donald As Police Officer, Ohio Art, 5 In.	65.00

Paint Book, Snow White, 1938	20.00
Paint Box, Donald Duck, England, 1940s	28.00
Paint Box, Donald Duck, Mickey & Minnie, English, Tin	40.00
Paint Box, Dumbo, Metal, 24 Paints	25.00
Paper Doll, Annette, Mousketeer, Walt Disney Productions, Uncut	28.00
Paper Doll, Snow White & 7 Dwarfs, Whitman, 8 Stands, 1938	75.00
Paperweight, Snow Dome, Snow White, Dopey, Magic Kingdom, 3 In.	25.00
Patch, Baseball, Mickey At Bat, 1940s, 2 In.	6.50
Patch, Mickey Mouse, Black & White, Embroidered, Cloth, 5 1/2 In.	35.00
Pencil Box, Mickey Mouse, 1930s	75.00
Pencil Box, Mickey, Minnie, Long Billed Donald	175.00
Pencil Box, Peter Pan, Covers Peter Looking In Treasure Chest	35.00
Pencil Sharpener, Donald Duck, Red, Round, 1930s	20.00
Pencil Sharpener, Mickey Mouse, Plastic, Rectangular, 1 In.	40.00
Pencil, Coloring, Mickey Mouse, Disney Enterprises, Box	75.00
Pencil, Inkograph, Mickey Mouse, Decal, 1930s,	165.00
Perfume Bottle, Mickey Mouse & Donald Duck, Pair	22.00
Perfume Bottle, Mickey Mouse, Figural	850.00
Phonograph, Mickey Mouse, Battery Operated, 1950s	38.00
Phonograph, Mickey Mouse, White, 45 RPM, Shelcore	15.00
Phonograph, Mickey Mouse, White, Aqua, G.E.	15.00
Picture, Mickey, Minnie Mouse, Enamel On Glass, Framed, 1930s, Pair	120.00
Picture, Winken–Blinken–Nod, Glow In Dark, Framed, 1940, 8 X 10 In	. 38.00
Pillow Cover, Mickey & Minnie, Vogue, 1931	165.00
Pillow, Throw, Minnie & Mickey	30.00
Pincushion, Tinkerbell, Clear Plastic Case	75.00
Pitcher, Donald Duck, Ceramic, Leeds	50.00
Pitcher, Donald, Ceramic, 1940s, 6 In.	50.00
Pitcher, Dumbo, Trunk Spout, 1950s, 6 In.	45.00
Planter, 7 Dwarfs, Ceramic, 5 1/2 In.	18.00
Planter, Donald Duck, Ceramic, Leeds, 1940s	28.00 To 30.00
Planter, Happy Dwarf, Ceramic	18.00
Planter, Pluto, Leeds, 1940s	40.00
Planter, Snow White, Pastels, Leeds, 1940s	30.00
Planter, Thumper, Ceramic, Leeds, 1940s	25.00
Plate, 3 Little Pigs, Patriot China, 1938	60.00
Plate, Mickey & Minnie Mouse, Enameled, Germany, 7 In.	44.00
Plate, Mickey & Pluto, Pie–Eyed, 7 In.	45.00
Poster, Cinderella, Belgian	23.00
Poster, Donald Duck, Walt Disney, 1943, 12 X 19 In.	35.00
Poster, Mickey's Jubilee, Belgian	23.00
Poster, Symposium of Popular Songs, Ludwig Von Drake, 1962	45.00
Poster, Wonderful World of Disney, NBC–TV, 1980, 2 X 3 Ft.	10.00
Powder Jar, Bambi, Deer On Cover, Iridized Marigold	22.00
Projector, Keystone, Mickey Mouse, Green	175.00
Puppet, Cinderella, Hand, Gund	10.00
Puppet, Mickey Mouse, Hand, Cloth, Rubber Head, 1958	8.00
Puppet, Mickey, Monkeys, Finger, Remco, 1970, 5 In.	25.00
Puppet, Paper Punch Out, Donald Duck, Bread Giveaway, 1950s	17.00
Purse, Mickey Mouse, Leather	25.00
Puzzle, 3 Little Pigs, Frame Tray, Jaymar, Jigsaw, 1950s	8.00
Puzzle, Ludwig, Pocket, Ludwig Hypnotizing Donald, Jigsaw	15.00
Puzzle, Mickey Mouse Club, Frame Tray, Jigsaw, Whitman, 1964	2.50
Puzzle, Mickey Mouse, Donald Duck, Indian, Jigsaw, Jaymar, 1960s	9.00
Puzzle, New Mickey Mouse Club, Springbok, Jigsaw, 1978, 100 Piece	17.00
Puzzle, Peter Pan, Jaymar Movie Classics, Inlaid, Jigsaw, 1970s	5.00
Puzzle, Snow White & 7 Dwarfs, 1938	18.00
Radio, Mickey Mouse, G.E., 1950–60	30.00
Radio, Mickey Mouse, Plastic, 1950s	90.00
Radio, Mickey, Pluto, Goofy, Ceramic, Box, 1960s	45.00
Radio, Shaggy Dog Movie Contest Prize, AM, Kal Kan, Box, 1959	150.00
Rattle, Mickey & Nephew On Sides, Red, White, 1930s	225.00
Record, Donald & Uncle Milty, RCA, 78 RPM	48.00
Record, Fantasia Sound Track, Story Book Set, 33 1/3 In.	20.00

Record, Lady & The Tramp, Capitol, 78 RPM, Set of 2	25.00
Record, Legend of Sleepy Hollow, LP	8.00
Record, Peter Pan, 33 1/3 RPM	18.00
Ring, Mickey Mouse, Minnie Mouse, Child's, Cloisonne	10.00
Ring, Mickey Mouse, Sterling, 1940s	75.00
Rug, Mickey, Setting Off Rocket Ship, Thumper Watches, 36 X 22 In	40.00
Salt & Pepper, Donald Duck, Ceramic, Leeds, 1940s	20.00
Salt & Pepper, Dumbo, Ceramic, 2 1/2 In.	22.00
Salt & Pepper, Mickey Mouse & Beanstalk, Ceramic, Box	12.00
Sand Set, Mickey Mouse Club, Plastic, Original Package, 1950s	25.00
Satchel, Child's, Snow White & 7 Dwarfs	75.00
Saucer, Snow White & 2 Dwarfs, 1937, 2 1/2 In.	10.00
Scissors, Donald Duck Shape, Battery Operated, Linemar	285.00
Scrapbook, Recipe, Mickey Mouse, Bread Company Giveaway	65.00
Sheet Music, A Dream Is A Wish Your Heart Makes, Cinderella	15.00
Sheet Music, Ballad of Davy Crockett, 1954	5.00
Sheet Music, Bambi Song Album, Australia, 1942	32.00
Sheet Music, Bella Notte, Lady and The Tramp, 1952	32.00
Sheet Music, Bibbidi–Bobbidi–Boo, Cinderella, 1949	15.00 To 18.00
Sheet Music, Heigh-Ho, Snow White, 1937	10.00
Sheet Music, Lavender Blue Dilly Dilly, 1948	12.00
Sheet Music, Melody Time, With Blue Shadows On The Trail, 1948	9.50
Sheet Music, Pinocchio Children's Album, British	28.00
Sheet Music, Reluctant Dragon, 1941	55.00
Sheet Music, Some Day My Prince Will Come, Snow White	10.00 To 16.00
Sheet Music, Uncle Remus Said, Song of The South, 1946	15.00
Sheet Music, When You Wish Upon A Star, Pinocchio	10.00
Sheet Music, Whistle While You Work, Snow White	10.00 To 20.00
Sheet Music, Who's Afraid of The Big Bad Wolf, 1933	25.00
Sheet Music, You Belong To My Heart, The Three Caballeros, 1943	12.00
Sheet Music, Zip-A-Dee-Doo-Dah, Song of The South, 1946	15.00
Shoe Polish, Mickey Polishing Shoes, 1950s	35.00
Shoelaces, Snow White & Dwarfs, Original Card, Marked	15.00
Silhouette, Donald Duck, Golfer, Wooden	22.00
Slipper, Cinderella, With Handkerchief, Disney	30.00
Soap Dish, Donald, Rubber, Shape of Boat, Donald In Captain's Hat	25.00
Soap Figure, Doc, 1938, 3 1/2 In.	18.00
Soap, Dumbo, Figural, 1940s	15.00
Soap, Pluto, Figural, Perfume Bottle Attached, 1930s	48.00
Soap, Snow White, Box	45.00
Song Book, Dumbo, 100 Songs, 1941	50.00
Spoon, Mickey Mouse, Silver Plate, Bradford, 1930s, 5 1/2 In.	25.00
Stationery, 3 Caballeros, Disney Studio, 1977	22.00
Stationery, Mickey Mouse Club, Walt Disney, 1970s	20.00
Tapestry, Mickey, Donald, Pluto, Dancing, Seashore, 21 X 39 In.	275.00
Target Game, Mickey As Soldier, Cardboard, 1930, 6 In.	20.00
Target Game, Mickey, Marks Bros.	75.00
Target, Rifle, Darts, Zorro, Metal Litho, Box	115.00
Tea Set, Donald Duck, Occupied Japan, 3 Piece	80.00
Tea Set, Mickey & Minnie Mouse, Dotted Borders, England, 8 Piece	110.00
Tea Set, Mickey, Minnie & Pluto, Tin, Helpmates, 12 Piece	150.00
Tin, Crayon, Donald & Mickey Flying In Rocket, 4 1/2 X 6 In.	35.00
Tool Box, Mickey Mouse	175.00
Toy, Bubble Buster, Mickey Using Gun, Metal, 1930s	135.00
Toy, Car, Donald Duck Dipsy, Windup, Tin	400.00
Toy, Car, Pull-Along, Mickey Mouse, Red Plastic, Kohner, 10 In.	22.00
Toy, Carousel, Donald Duck, Celluloid, Tin, Japan, 8 In.	9900.00
Toy, Carpet Sweeper, Donald Duck	45.00
Toy, Choo-Choo, Mickey Mouse, Pull, Fisher-Price, 8 1/2 In.	55.00
Toy, Critter, Pluto, Pop-Up	55.00
Toy, Donald Duck Choo-Choo, Fisher-Price, 1942	75.00
Toy, Donald Duck Drummer, Pull, Fisher-Price, 7 1/2 In.	143.00
Toy, Donald Duck Duet, Marx, Box	1150.00
Toy, Donald Duck, Bubble Duck, Squeeze, Morris Plastics, Box, 8 In.	44.00

Toy, Donald Duck, Celluloid, String Toy, Japan, 4 In. 66.00
Toy, Donald Duck, Drum Major, Fisher-Price, 1948 .... 100.00
Toy, Donald Duck, Duet, Mechanical, Tin Litho, Marx, 10 1/2 In. 825.00
Toy, Donald Duck, Gym, Celluloid, Linemar, 1940s 395.00
Toy, Donald Duck, Holds Umbrella, Plastic, Windup 85.00
Toy, Donald Duck, Mickey & Minnie In Crate Cart 3500.00
Toy, Donald Duck, On Motorcycle, Tin, Friction, 1950s, 3 1/2 In. 130.00
Toy, Donald Duck, Plastic, Pulls Huey, Dewey, Louie 10.00
Toy, Donald Duck, Plush, Knickerbocker, 10 In. 10.00
Toy, Donald Duck, Squeaker, Sun Rubber, 10 In. 33.00
Toy, Donald Duck, Tin, Schuco, Box, 1930s 575.00
Toy, Donald Duck, Trapeze Artist, Celluloid, Mechanical, 7 1/2 In. 110.00
Toy, Donald Duck, Windup, Schuco, Box, 6 In. 350.00
Toy, Drum, Mickey Mouse, 1930s, 11 In. 145.00
Toy, Ferris Wheel, Mickey Mouse, Chein 275.00
Toy, Fire Truck, Donald Duck, Mickey Mouse, Sun Rubber, 6 1/2 In. 65.00
Toy, Goofy, Tricycle, Red Plastic, Movable Head, Gabriel, Ind., 1977 .... 15.00
Toy, Hoppity Ball, Mickey Riding Toy, Sun Rubber 22.00
Toy, Kaleidoscope, Mickey Mouse 45.00
Toy, Mickey & Donald Speedway, Ideal, Box 125.00
Toy, Mickey & Minnie Mouse, Acrobat, Celluloid, Windup 975.00
Toy, Mickey & Minnie Mouse, Vinyl, Japan, 1970s, 10 In., Pair 135.00
Toy, Mickey Mouse In Mail Jeep, Match Box Car, 1970 .... 10.00
Toy, Mickey Mouse, Donald Duck, Goofy, Tin, Chein, 5 In. 35.00
Toy, Mickey Mouse, Puddle Jumper, 1940s, Fisher-Price 45.00
Toy, Mickey Mouse, Roller Skating, Rubber Ears & Nose, Linemar 800.00
Toy, Mickey Mouse, Stuffed, Musical, Gund 25.00
Toy, Mickey Mouse, The Unicyclist, Tin, Linemar, Box, 5 1/2 In. 1540.00
Toy, Minnie Mouse, In Rocker, Knitting, Windup, Tin 95.00
Toy, Minnie Mouse, In Rocker, Windup, Tin, Marline 400.00
Toy, Minnie Mouse, Tin, Mechanical, Action Sprung, Japan, 7 In. 160.00
Toy, Pinball, Mickey Mouse, Wolverine 25.00
Toy, Pinocchio, Walking, Mechanical, Geo.Borgfeldt, Box, 11 1/2 In. 525.00
Toy, Pluto, Plush, Knickerbocker, 1976 .... 10.00
Toy, Pluto, Pop-Up Kritter, Blue Paddle, Fisher-Price 45.00
Toy, Pluto, Wooden, Jointed, Walt Disney Prod. 250.00
Toy, Print Shop, Mickey Mouse, Box, Fulton Company 175.00
Toy, Refrigerator, Snow White, Wolverine 25.00
Toy, Rifle, Flintlock, Johnny Tremain, Fires Cap, 1950s, 42 In. 50.00
Toy, Ring Toss, Donald Duck, Plastic, Illco, 9 1/2 In. 5.00
Toy, Roly Poly, Mickey Mouse, Plastic, 4 1/2 In. 12.00
Toy, Santa's Little Helper, Mickey, Pride Lines, Box, 1982, 12 In. 330.00
Toy, Sleeping Beauty, Rubber, 6 In. 33.00
Toy, Soaky, Bambi 13.00
Toy, Soaky, Dopey 12.00
Toy, Soaky, Jiminy Cricket 25.00
Toy, Soaky, Pinocchio 18.00
Toy, Soaky, Porky Pig 12.00
Toy, Speedway, Mickey Mouse, Ideal, 1950s, Box 75.00
Toy, Steamboat Willie, Incline, Walt Disney Ent., 3 1/4 In. 75.00
Toy, Tiddly Winks, Mickey, Donald, Goofy, Pluto, Whitman, 1963 .... 35.00
Toy, Tricky Trike, Mickey Mouse 18.50
Toy, Tug Boat, Donald Duck, Rubber, Sponge, Knickerbocker 20.00
Toy, Washing Machine, Mickey Mouse, Walt Disney Ent., 1930s 600.00
Toy, Xylophone, Donald Duck & Newphews, 9 1/2 In. 20.00
Toy, Xylophone, Donald Duck, Fisher-Price 200.00
Toy, Xylophone, Mickey Mouse, Tudor Metal, Box 150.00
Toy, Yo-Yo, White, Mickey Mouse Club 15.00
Train, Circus, Mickey Mouse, Lionel 1500.00
Train, Mickey Mouse Meteor, Engine & 3 Cars, Marx, 1950 .... 825.00
Tray, Peter Pan, Surrounded By Mermaids, 7 X 15 In. 15.00
Trivet, Bambi & Thumper, Ceramic, Square, 1940s 22.00
Tumbler, All Star, Duck Family, Daisy, 1939 .... 22.00
Tumbler, America On Parade 15.00

Doll, A.M. 240/1, Sleep Eyes, Jointed, 20 In.

Doll, A.M., Bisque, Sleep Eyes, Jointed, 21 In.

Doll, Bebe Brevete, French, Swivel Head,
Kid Body, C.1870, 20 In.

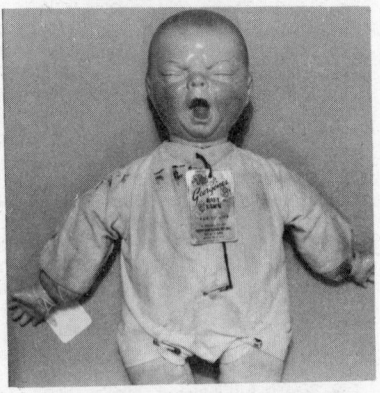

Doll, Georgene Averill, Baby Yawn,
Cloth Body, C.1918, 18 In.

Doll, Handwerck, Girl, German, Bisque,
Pierced Ears, 20 In.

Doll, Lenci, Girl, Brown Painted Eyes,
Pursed Mouth, 12 In.

Tumbler, Bashful, Orange, Libbey, 1930s, 4 3/8 In. 17.00
Tumbler, Cinderella, 1950s, 5 1/4 In. 12.00
Tumbler, Doc, Green, Libbey, 1930s, 4 3/4 In. 17.00
Tumbler, Donald Duck, Libbey, 4 5/8 In. 30.00
Tumbler, Dopey, Brown, Libbey, 4 3/8 In. 25.00
Tumbler, Pinocchio, Red, Libbey, 1940s, 4 5/8 In. 17.00
Tumbler, Snow White, Blue Dress, Libbey, 1930s, 4 5/8 In. .... 20.00 To 30.00
Umbrella, Mickey Mouse 45.00
Viewer, Mickey, Red Plastic, Craftsmen's Guild, 15 Films 185.00
Wall Pocket, Bambi & Thumper, Leeds 25.00
Watch Fob, Mickey Mouse, Ingersoll, For Pocket Watch 45.00
Watch, Mickey Mouse, Bradley, 50th Commemorative, Box, 1978 .... 175.00
Watch, Pocket, Mickey Mouse, Ingersoll, Watch Fob, 1933 .... 775.00
Watering Can, Donald Duck, Ohio Art, 6 In. 85.00
Wristwatch, Cinderella, U.S.Time, 1950s 35.00
Wristwatch, Daisy Duck, 1848 .... 215.00
Wristwatch, Donald Duck, 50th Anniversary, Bradley, Box 100.00
Wristwatch, Donald Duck, Quartz, Lorus, Plastic Box 25.00
Wristwatch, Mickey Mouse, Bubble, Yellow Case, Matching Band, 1973 .... 175.00
Wristwatch, Mickey Mouse, Ingersoll, Metal Band, Chrome, 1932 .... 1050.00
Wristwatch, Mickey Mouse, Ingersoll, Papers, Box, 1933 .... 990.00
Wristwatch, Mickey, Leather Band, 1930's 395.00
Wristwatch, Minnie Mouse, Bradley, 1973, Box 185.00
Wristwatch, Minnie Mouse, Ingersoll, Box 200.00
Wristwatch, Snow White, Purple Hands & Band, 1940s, 14 In. 60.00
Wristwatch, Woody Woodpecker, 1950 .... 215.00
Xylophone, Mickey Mouse, Tin Litho 175.00
DOCTOR, see Medical; Dental

Doll entries are listed by marks printed or incised on the doll, if possible. If there are no marks, the doll is listed by the name of the subject or country.

DOLL, .A.M.1894, Fully Jointed, 8 In. 325.00
A.B.G., Bisque, Parian Type, Molded Hair, Closed Mouth, 17 In. 500.00
A.M. 14, Bisque Head, Marked, 32 In. 900.00
A.M. 231, Fanny, All Original, 17 In. 5700.00
A.M. 233, Baby, 16 1/2 In. 500.00
A.M. 240/1, Sleep Eyes, Jointed, 20 In. ....*Illus* 285.00
A.M. 253, Nobbi Kid, Flirty Sleep Eyes, Dressed, 7 1/2 In. 475.00
A.M. 254, Googly, Intaglio Eyes, Molded Brown Hair, 6 1/2 In. 200.00
A.M. 254, Intaglio Eyes, Watermelon Mouth, 6 1/2 In. 365.00
A.M. 310 8/0, Bisque, Painted, C.1925, 8 1/2 In. 450.00
A.M. 341, Black Baby, Composition Body, Chemise, 12 In. 350.00
A.M. 351, Dream Baby, Bisque, Christening Gown, 12 In. 275.00
A.M. 353, Oriental Baby, 13 In. 675.00
A.M. 370, Bisque, Kid Body, 24 In. 500.00
A.M. 370, Sleep Eyes, Dark Blond Braids, Kid Body, 20 In. 265.00
A.M. 390, Ball–Jointed, 18 In. 275.00
A.M. 390, Silk Oriental Costume, 18 In. 375.00
A.M. 518, Baby, 25 In. 850.00
A.M. 700, Character, Pouty Child, Sleep Eyes, Wood, Composition, 12 In. 4500.00
A.M. 985, Baby, 15 In. 300.00
A.M. 990, Baby, Movable Tongue, Bisque, Sleep Eyes, 16 In. 250.00
A.M., Baby, Character, Bisque Socket Head, 5–Piece Body, 2 Teeth, 10 In. 99.00
A.M., Baby, Painted Eyes, 6 In. 100.00
A.M., Ball–Jointed Body, Straight Wrist, Set Eyes, Dressed, 13 In. 325.00
A.M., Bisque Head, Dressed, 24 In. 275.00
A.M., Bisque, 26 In. 350.00
A.M., Bisque, Blue Eyes, Brown Wig, Dressed, 30 In. 525.00
A.M., Bisque, Sleep Eyes, Jointed, 21 In. ....*Illus* 220.00
A.M., Boy, Patriotic, 10 In. 295.00
A.M., Child, Bisque, Blond Mohair, Brown Eyes, Stick Legs, 36 In. 1175.00
A.M., Columbia, Columbian Exposition, Kid Body, Stationary Eyes, 15 In. 195.00
A.M., Dream Baby, Bisque, 14 In. 225.00

A.M., Dream Baby, Sleep Eyes, Celluloid Hands, 8 1/2 In.	195.00
A.M., Floradora, 20 In.	250.00
A.M., Florodora, 13 In.	150.00
A.M., Florodora, Bisque, Sleep Eyes, Jointed, Germany, 15 In.	121.00
A.M., Girl, Kid Body, Jointed, 27 In.	350.00
A.M., Mabel, Human Hair Wig, Sleep Eyes, 19 In.	220.00
A.M., Queen Louise, Ball–Jointed Body, 20 In.	325.00
A.M., Queen Louise, Bisque Head, Jointed Body, Dressed, 22 In.	395.00
Advertising, 7–Up Freddie, Vinyl	35.00
Advertising, Aunt Jemima, Oilcloth, 12 In.	25.00
Advertising, Bell Telephone, Woman, Box	35.00
Advertising, Betty Crocker	40.00
Advertising, Bonnie Blue Ribbon, Marquette Meat, Box, 18 In.	55.00
Advertising, Bugs Bunny, Arby's, Posed, Warner Bros., 1987, 2 In.	2.00
Advertising, Burger King, 1972	6.00
Advertising, C & H Sugar, 1971	10.00
Advertising, Capt. Crunch, 15 In.	9.00
Advertising, Charlie Tuna, Vinyl	15.00
Advertising, Chicken of The Sea, Cloth	5.00
Advertising, Chiquita Banana	12.50
Advertising, Cream of Wheat, Cloth	90.00
Advertising, Dairy Queen Nell, 1974	10.00
Advertising, Dutch Boy Paint	10.00
Advertising, Eskimo Pie, Cloth	6.50 To 8.00
Advertising, Hey Culligan Man, Blond Hair, Blue Dress, 1960s, 18 In.	24.00
Advertising, Jack Frost Sugar, 18 In.	27.00
Advertising, Kellogg's Dandy Duck, Cloth, Uncut	50.00
Advertising, Levis Denim, Rag, Knickerbocker, 1974, 17 In.	9.50
Advertising, Little Green Sprout, Vinyl	8.00
Advertising, Little Sprout, Green Giant, Records Voice, 14 In.	35.00
Advertising, Miss Korn Krisp, Uncut Cloth, Dated 1899, 28 In.	295.00
Advertising, Miss Revlon, Ideal, 1955, 14 In.	79.00
Advertising, Mr.Salty Pretzel, Cloth	12.50
Advertising, Munsingwear, Twins, Tin, 1910	1800.00
Advertising, Northern Tissue, Box	20.00
Advertising, Pillsbury Doughboy, 7 In.	5.00
Advertising, Pillsbury, Poppin' Fresh, Box, Playthings, 7 In.	25.00
Advertising, Pillsbury, Poppin' Fresh, Knit Velour	16.00
Advertising, Quaker Puffed Wheat, Rag Stuffed	18.00
Advertising, RCA, Majorette, Wooden, 1920s	650.00
Advertising, RCA, Radio Tubes For Heads, Pair	950.00
Advertising, Ronald McDonald, Inflatable	35.00
Advertising, Ronald McDonald, Whistle Blowing	25.00
Advertising, Shasta Girl, Redhead, Box	150.00
Advertising, Tommy, Mohawk Carpet, 1970, 16 In.	18.00
Advertising, Vermont Maid Syrup, Vinyl, Jointed, 15 In.	35.00 To 45.00
DOLL, ALEXANDER, see Doll, Madame Alexander	
American Character, Butterball, Watermelon Smile, Big Eyes, 19 In.	110.00
American Character, Toodle–Loo, 18 In.	95.00
Apple Head, Granny, 1920–30s	30.00
DOLL, ARMAND MARSEILLE, see Doll, A. M.	
Arranbee, My Angel, 1957, 36 In.	50.00
Arranbee, Rosie, Composition, Cloth Body, 1935, 19 In.	90.00
Automaton, Tambourine Player, Original Clothes, Turning Head, 18 In.	3750.00
Automaton, Violin Player Boy, Wooden Arms, Push Stomach, 14 In.	2000.00
Baby Dimples, Composition, Original Clothes, 21 In.	250.00
Baby Tiny Tears, Character, Nude, 15 In.	50.00
Babyland, Twins, In Basket	300.00
Bahr & Proschild, Character, Toddler Body, 26 In.	1300.00
Bahr & Proschild, Toddler, White Lace Dress, 29 In.	1450.00
DOLL, BARBIE, see Doll, Mattel, Barbie	
Bebe Brevete, French, Swivel Head, Kid Body, C.1870, 20 In.	*Illus* 5225.00
Bebe, Paperweight Eyes, Blond Human Hair Wig, Closed Mouth, 24 1/2 In.	3500.00
DOLL, BERGMANN, see also Doll, S & H; Doll, Simon & Halbig	

Bergmann, Bisque, Ball–Jointed, Open Mouth, 24 In. 425.00
Bergmann, Sleep Brown Eyes, Pierced Ears, Mohair Wig, 31 In. 975.00
Betsy McCall, Cotillion Gown, 8 In. 125.00
Betsy Ross, Bicentennial, 1976 .... 14.00
Biedermeier, China, Braided Wig, 12 In. 695.00
Biedermeier, Reader, Nun's Winged Hair Style, 11 In. 1295.00
Bindi, Aborigine, Black, Full Battle Costume, Face Paint, 14 In. 128.00
Bisque, Blond Hair, Jointed Arms, Japan, 1930–40, 3 In. 10.00
Bisque, Character Baby, Closed Mouth, Outfit, Cap, England, 12 In. 200.00
Bisque, Head & Shoulder, Stuffed Body, Kid Arms, Fixed Eyes, 19 In. 467.50
Bisque, Socket Head, Black Pupilless Eyes, Open Mouth, Germany, 8 In. 77.00
Bobby Orr, Hockey Player, Box 65.00
Borgfeldt, Three Little Pigs, Box, Set 1100.00
Boy, Chinese, Bisque, Jointed, Silk Suit, Queue, 3 In. 25.00
Bradley, Pouty Boy & Girl, Box, 13 In., Pair 130.00
Bridesmaid, Plastic, 1950s, 7 1/2 In. 30.00
Brooke Shields, Box .... 30.00 To 60.00
Bru Jne, No.4, Composition Body, 12 1/2 In. 8500.00
Bruckner, Topsy–Turvy .... 145.00 To 300.00
Buddy Lee, Railroad Engineer, Compositon, Complete Outfit 145.00
Buffy, With Mrs. Beasley, Talking, Sealed Box, 1968 .... 175.00
Bugs Bunny, Stuffed, Pull-Toy, Talks 20.00
Bye–Lo, Baby, Bisque Head, Blue Glass Sleep Eyes, Cloth Body, 12 In. 275.00
Bye–Lo, Baby, Bisque Head, Blue Sleep Eyes, Celluloid Hands, 10 1/2 In. 375.00
Bye–Lo, Baby, Brown Eyes, Original Dress & Tag, Marked, 10 In. 495.00
Bye–Lo, Bisque, Blue Sleep Eyes, Closed Mouth, Painted Hair, Nude, 8 In. 82.50
Bye–Lo, Bisque, Brown Eyes, Tagged Gown 950.00
Bye–Lo, Bisque, Sleep Eyes, Molded Pink Shoes, 6 1/2 In. 395.00
Bye–Lo, Cloth Body, Celluloid Hands, Sleep Eyes, Dressed 450.00
Bye–Lo, Oily Bisque, Celluloid Hands, Dressed, Rattle, 11 In. 395.00
Cabbage Patch Kids, Astronaut, Box 35.00
Cameo, Babymine, Sleep Eyes, 18 In. 95.00
Cameo, Bride & Groom, Kewpies, 16 In. 90.00
Cameo, Kewpie, 14 In. 55.00
Cameo, Miss Peep, 18 In. 55.00
Celluloid, Boy, Kid Body, Cloth, Turtle Mark, 15 In. 125.00
Celluloid, Windup, Tin, Original Clothes, On Tricycle 125.00
Chad Valley, Boy, Brown Curly Mohair Wig 195.00
Chad Valley, Girl, Glass Eyes, 1930s, 19 In. 385.00
Chad Valley, Glass Eyes, Mohair Rabbit Slippers, Silk Pajamas, 20 In. 335.00
Chase, Baby, Painted Cloth & Stockinette, 24 In. 715.00
Chase, Boy, Hospital, Stockinette Body, Jointed 900.00
Chase, Boy, Marked, 29 In. 695.00
Chase, Boy, Molded Hair, Dressed, 16 In. 700.00
Chase, Girl, Molded Hair, Dressed, 16 In. 700.00
Chatty Cathy, Extra Outfit, Box 110.00
Chinese, Cloth, Braided Silk Hair, Painted Face, Silk Clothes, 9 In. 35.00
Cinderella, Wrist Tag, 1950, 14 In. 350.00
Cissy, Bride, 21 In. 350.00
Cissy, Satin Dress & Coat, 21 In. 325.00
Connie Lynn, 19 In. 250.00
Count Dracula, Coffin Box, 18 In. 35.00
Daddy Bear, Kellogg's, Cloth, Lithograph 65.00
Dakin, Barney, Jointed, Vinyl, 7 In. 35.00
Darth Vader, Cape, Helmet, 15 In. 65.00
Deanna Durbin, Original Clothes, Button, 24 In. 425.00
DEP, Bisque, Bathing, Germany, 7 In. 375.00
DEP, Bisque, Blue Paperweight Eyes, 21 In. 1200.00
Dolly Parton, Box 25.00
Door of Hope, Bride, Carved Hair Ornaments, Headpiece, 11 In. 550.00
Dressel & Kister, Half Doll, Nude, 5 In. 1000.00
Dressel, Bathing Beauty, Nude, Braided Hair Around Ears, Signed, 8 In. 800.00
Dressel, Bisque, Sleep Eyes, Ball–Jointed Body, 24 In. 375.00
Eegee, Georgette, Rooted Red Braids, Green Eyes, Freckles, 1971, 22 In. 35.00

Effanbee, Age of Elegance, Tag 100.00
Effanbee, Anne Shirley, Human Hair Wig, Bracelet, Clothes, Shoes 165.00
Effanbee, Art Carney, Ed Norton From Honeymooners, Box, 1986 .... 155.00
Effanbee, Baby Dainty, Sleep Eyes, Cloth Body, Dressed, 14 In. 80.00
Effanbee, Baby Dimples, Original Clothes, Bib, 1928 .... 235.00
Effanbee, Baby Lisa, In Wicker Basket, Box 100.00
Effanbee, Baby Tinyette, Nude 210.00
Effanbee, Bobbsey Twins, Tag 140.00
Effanbee, Brownie Scout, 8 1/2 In. 35.00
Effanbee, Bubbles, Composition, 22 In. 190.00
Effanbee, Butterball, Box, 1969 .... 47.50
Effanbee, Cristina, Hagara 135.00
Effanbee, Dy–Dee Baby, Hard Plastic & Vinyl, Accessories, Box 250.00
Effanbee, Girl Scout, Dated 1965, Box 25.00
Effanbee, Groucho Marx 55.00
Effanbee, Harry Truman 68.00
Effanbee, Honey, 16 In. 150.00
Effanbee, Huckleberry Finn .... 52.00 To 62.50
Effanbee, Humphrey Bogart 70.00
Effanbee, Jacqueline Kennedy 150.00
Effanbee, James Cagney 70.00
Effanbee, John Wayne, Cowboy, Box 85.00
Effanbee, Larry, Boy, Vinyl, Jan Hagara, 17 In. 80.00
Effanbee, Liberace 325.00
Effanbee, Little Lady, Composition, Dressed, Box, 21 In. 195.00
Effanbee, Louis Armstrong, Box 85.00
Effanbee, Lovums, Christmas Box, 1928 .... 168.00
Effanbee, Lucille Ball 150.00
Effanbee, Majorette, Hard Plastic, Original Clothes, 19 In. 175.00
Effanbee, Marille, Black, Composition, Black Fur Wig, 1925, 24 In. 176.00
Effanbee, Mary Jane, Flirty Eyes, Vinyl, 30 In. 135.00
Effanbee, Muhammad Ali 80.00
Effanbee, Patricia, Extra Dress 315.00
Effanbee, Patsy Tinyette, Composition, Straight Legs, Tags, 8 In. 225.00
Effanbee, Patsy, Original Clothes, Bracelet, 9 In. 135.00
Effanbee, Princess Diana, Box 120.00
Effanbee, Puppet, Clown 95.00
Effanbee, Puppet, Girl 75.00
Effanbee, Queen Elizabeth, Box 80.00
Effanbee, Sherlock Holmes, Box 55.00
Effanbee, Skippy, Sailor Suit, Cloth Body, Molded Hair & Boots, 14 In. 199.00
Effanbee, Susie Sunshine 30.00
Effanbee, Suzanne, Composition, Molded Hair, All Original, 9 In. 145.00
Effanbee, Suzette, Composition, Bridal Dress, 14 In. 85.00
Effanbee, Thomas Jefferson .... 68.00 To 80.00
Effanbee, W.C.Fields, Box 200.00
Effanbee, Winston Churchill, Box 85.00
Elise Ballerina, Vinyl 60.00
Emma Clear, Martha & George Washington, Pair 595.00
Eugene, Bride, Lovable Lorie, Box, 1960s, 20 In. 40.00
Eugene, Lorie, 1966, 24 In. 12.00
F.G., Bisque Head, Cotton Eyelet Trim Dress, Straw Bonnet, 23 1/2 In. 2800.00
F.G., Fashion, Bisque, Stationary Eyes, Long Curls, Kid Body, 17 In. 1495.00
F.G., Fashion, Trunk of Clothes & Accessories, 11 In. 2000.00
Faith Wick, Santa Claus, Box 80.00
Fashion, Gusseted Kid Body, Dark Wig, Silk Antique Costume, 13 In. 1600.00
Felix The Cat, Jointed Arms, Glass Eyes, Straw Stuffed, 12 In. 225.00
Franz Schmidt, Breather Baby, Bald Head, Sleep Eyes, Repainted, 25 In. 650.00
Fred Flintstone, Vinyl, 1961 .... 25.00
Freddy Krueger, Talking 50.00
French, Fashion, Bisque Arms, Black Dress, 17 In. 3500.00
French, Fashion, Leather Body, Dressed, 13 1/2 In. 1600.00
French, Fashion, Papier–Mache, 1850s, 12 In. 925.00
French, Fashion, Smiling, All Original, Incised D, 15 In. 6500.00

French, Fashion, Swivel Head, Kid Body, 2 Outfits, Trunk, 15 In. 2195.00
French, Man & Woman, Papier–Mache, 8 In., Pair 475.00
French, Papier–Mache Head, Glass Eyes, Kid Body, Silk Clothes, 21 In. 950.00
French, Papier–Mache, Bamboo Teeth, 23 In. 950.00
French, Toddler Boy, Glass Eyes, Celluloid, 18 In. 170.00
Frozen Charlie, 12 In. 575.00
Frozen Charlotte, 16 In. 650.00
Frozen Charlotte, Black, Red Mouth, White Eyes, 2 In. 25.00
Frozen Charlotte, Blond Hair, Stone Bisque, 3 In. 15.00
Frozen Charlotte, China, 4 3/4 In. 38.50
Frozen Charlotte, In Bathtub, Reclining, Bent Knees, 3 In. 250.00
Fulper, Baby, Bisque Socket Head, 5–Piece Body, Set Eyes, 21 In. 335.00
Fulper, Character Baby, Bisque Head, Ball–Jointed, 18 In. 495.00
Fulper, Toddler, Bisque, 21 In. 350.00
Furga, Lucy, Clothes, Original Trunk, 8 In. 110.00
G.I. Joe, Action Soldier, Hasbro, Box, 1964 .... 275.00 To 325.00
G.I. Joe, Airman, Red Hair, Orange Jumpsuit, Blue Cap ....:........ 100.00
G.I. Joe, Army Radio Man, Green Fatigues, 45 With Holster, Map Case 65.00
G.I. Joe, Boots, Scar Painted Hair, 1964, 11 1/2 In. 125.00
G.I. Joe, Combat Joe No.1, Takara, Box 85.00
G.I. Joe, Combat Joe No.5, Swat Officer, Takara, Box 85.00
G.I. Joe, Commander, Talking 40.00
G.I. Joe, Deck Commander, 1964 .... 200.00
G.I. Joe, Flocked Hair, Beard, No Boots, 1965, 11 1/2 In. 75.00
G.I. Joe, Japan 400.00
G.I. Joe, Man of Action, Hasbro, Box 100.00
G.I. Joe, Marine Clothes, Lifelike Hair, Holding U.S.Flag 60.00
G.I. Joe, Medic, Camouflage Fatigues, Helmet, Action Figure 50.00
G.I. Joe, Mr. Action, Fatigues, Carbine Grenades, Mess Kit, 10 Cards 70.00
G.I. Joe, Painted Blond Hair, Boots, Pants, MP Cap, Hasbro, 12 In. 65.00
G.I. Joe, Painted Red Hair, Pants, Jacket, Boots, Hasbro, 12 In. 65.00
G.I. Joe, Painted Red Hair, Sailor Suit, Hasbro, 12 In. 125.00
G.I. Joe, Secret Agent, Flocked Hair & Beard 50.00
G.I. Joe, Spy Outfit, Black Rubber Hat & Sweater, 1966 .... 125.00
G.I. Joe, Talking Man of Action, Fatigues, Hat, Rifle 100.00
G.I. Joe, Talking Soldier, Hasbro, Foreign, Box 900.00
Gebruder Heubach, Baby, Socket Head, Composition Body, Dressed, 9 In. 900.00
Gebruder Heubach, Croquette, 13 In. 700.00
Gebruder Heubach, Dimples, Marked, 18 In. 1800.00
Georgene Averill, Baby Yawn, Cloth Body, C.1918, 18 In. ....*Illus* 145.00
Gerber Baby, Christening, White, 1983 .... 180.00
Gerber Baby, Flirty Eyes, 1979, 17 In. 45.00
Goebel, Billy Bumps, Blue Pajamas, Mozart's Lullaby, 12 In. 60.00
Goebel, Billy Bumps, Sailor Suit, Row Your Boat, 14 In. 95.00
Goebel, Character Baby, 5–Piece, Bent Limbs, Old Baby Clothes, 28 In. 1795.00
Goebel, Dolly Dingle, Pink Bow, White Eyelet Dress, 20 In. 195.00
Goebel, Dolly Dingle, Sailor Suit, Over The Waves, 14 In. 95.00
Goebel, Googly, Bisque, Brown Eyes, Composition Body, 6 1/2 In. 295.00
Goldberger, Dolly Parton, Red Jumpsuit, Box, 12 In. 45.00
Goldberger, Prince Charles & Lady Di's Wedding, 12 In., Pair 60.00
Gotz, Walker–Talker, 24 In. 165.00
Greiner 58, Old Body, Replaced Arms, Old Clothes, 23 In. 475.00
Greiner 72, Blond, Label, 25 In. 250.00
Halbig, Bisque, Sleep Eyes, Composition, Jointed, Teeth, 13 In. 220.00
Half, Papier–Mache, Nude, Hands On Hips, Wig, Germany, 5 1/2 In. 40.00
Half, Porcelain, Bobbed Hair, Hand On Hip, Whisk Broom, Germany, 3 In. 15.00
Handwerck 109, Almond Eyes, Feathered Brows, Ball–Jointed, 7 1/2 In. 500.00
Handwerck 283–28, Composition, Jointed Body, 24 In. 500.00
Handwerck, Bisque, Ball–Jointed Body, Old Clothes, 12 In. 275.00
Handwerck, Child, Bisque, Socket Head, Ball–Jointed Body, 30 In. 895.00
Handwerck, Girl, German, Bisque, Pierced Ears, 20 In. ....*Illus* 825.00
Hendren, Baby, Composition Limbs, Cloth Body, Christening Dress, 18 In. 250.00
Hendren, Boy, Celluloid Head, Cloth Body, Velvet Suit, Hat, 19 In. 265.00
Hertel & Schwab 142, Character Baby, Brushstroke Hair, Dressed, 11 In. 325.00

Hertel & Schwab, Baby, Dressed, 22 In. 650.00
Hertel & Schwab, Googly, Large 9750.00
Heubach & Koppelsdorf, Baby, Blond, Blue Sleep Eyes, 2 Teeth, 12 In. 176.00
Heubach 275, Kid Body, Composition Arms, 17 1/2 In. 160.00
Heubach 300, Character Baby, 16 In. 345.00
Heubach 320, Character, Pierced Nostrils, Ball–Jointed, 20 In. 385.00
Heubach 342, Baby, Bisque, Painted, 16 In. 185.00
Heubach 399, Black, 13 In. 450.00
Heubach Koppelsdorf 300, Baby, 25 In. 675.00
Heubach Koppelsdorf 312, Houndstooth Coat & Hat, 23 In. 375.00
Heubach Koppelsdorf, Baby, Breather, 12 In. 275.00
Heubach, Baby Chin Chin, Bisque, Label, 4 In. 225.00
Heubach, Bisque, Molded Ribbon In Hair, 19 In. 850.00
Heubach, Boy, Bisque, Intaglio Eyes, Checkered Shirt & Pants, 16 In. 795.00
Heubach, Girl, Kid Body, Sleep Eyes, Open Mouth, 17 In. 250.00
Heubach, Just Me, Sleep Eyes, 5–Piece Body, 9 In. 700.00
Heubach, Laughing Boy, Composition Body, 15 In. 800.00
Heubach, Porcelain, Glass Eyes, 1930s, 7 1/2 In. 310.00
Heubach, Scowling Indian, 8 1/2 In. 150.00
Horsman, Baby, Knit Outfit, 13 In. 25.00
Horsman, Billiken, 12 In. 50.00
Horsman, Black, Kinky Braids, 16 In. 25.00
Horsman, Ella Cinders, 18 In. .... 53.50 To 62.50
Horsman, Gold Medal Prize Baby, 1911 .... 450.00
Horsman, Hee Bee & She Bee, Molded Clothes, Booties, Blue, Pink, Pair 57.50
Horsman, Hee Bee & She Bee, Molded Undies, Oversized Booties, Pair 62.50
Horsman, Mama, Composition, 16 In. 175.00
Horsman, Mary Poppins, Box, 1965 .... 95.00
Horsman, Police Woman, Box, 8 In. 40.00
Horsman, Puppet, Simon Sez, 30 In. 40.00
Horsman, Ronald Reagan, 17 In. 55.00
Horsman, Rosebud, Brown Mohair Wig, Tin Eyes, Dressed, 20 In. 150.00
Ideal, Action Boy, Composition, Blue & Silver Body Suit, Helmet, 1968 .... 750.00
Ideal, Andy Gibb, Box, 6 In. 55.00
Ideal, Baby Sandy, Composition, Sleep Eyes, Molded Hair, 1930s, 16 In. 235.00
Ideal, Baby, Amber Eyes, Composition & Cloth Body, 1940s, 22 In. 100.00
Ideal, Bam Bam, Box, 1962, 17 In. 175.00
Ideal, Bam Bam, Hard Body, Rubber Face, Caveman Shorts, 12 In. 45.00
Ideal, Belly Button Baby, Black 15.00
Ideal, Betsy Wetsy, Sleep Eyes, Crocheted Bonnet, Dress, C.1950, 14 In. 45.00
Ideal, Betty Big Girl, 30 In. 90.00
Ideal, Captain Action, Hat, Gun, Sword, Boots, 12 In. 225.00
Ideal, Cry Baby, Cloth Body, Molded Hair, Dressed, 18 In. 25.00
Ideal, Dr. Evil, 12 In. 295.00
Ideal, Kissy, Deluxe, Hands Together & Will Kiss, Redressed, 22 In. 50.00
Ideal, Luke Skywalker, Box, 12 In. 225.00
Ideal, Pebbles, Flintstones, Box, 1963 .... 175.00
Ideal, Pebbles, Stuffed, Rubber Hands, Bone In Ear, 14 In. 45.00
Ideal, Peter Playpal, Original Clothing, 38 In. 195.00
Ideal, Pinocchio, 8 In. 90.00
Ideal, Princess Leia, Box, 12 In. 150.00
Ideal, Saucy Walker, 16 In. 80.00
Ideal, Saucy Walker, Plastic, Blond, Flirty Sleep Eyes, 1952, 22 In. 69.50
Ideal, Soldier Boy, Hat & Tag 150.00
Ideal, Tiny Tears, Hard Plastic Head, Rubber Body 65.00
Ideal, Tiny Tears, Porcelain, Box 100.00
Ideal, Tippy Toes, Rides Trike, C.1960, 17 In. 35.00
    DOLL, INDIAN, see Indian, Doll
Ives, Automaton, Creeping Baby, Wax Over Papier–Mache, Box, 11 In. 1045.00
    DOLL, J.D.K., see also Doll, Kestner
J.D.K.211, Baby, Lamb Wig, Life Size 1900.00
J.D.K.247, Baby, Hilda's Sister, 13 In. 1100.00
J.D.K.257, Baby, Bisque, Sleep Eyes, Bent Limbs, Baby Clothes, 31 In. 235.00
J.D.K.260, Toddler, Flirty Eyes, 17 In. 1650.00

Jane Withers, 21 In.	1050.00
Japanese, Samurai, 1809–29, 20 In.	5800.00
Japanese, Samurai, 1830–47, 17 In.	3900.00
Japanese, Samurai, 1854–63, 11 1/2 In.	1800.00
Jerri, Denise	320.00
Jerri, Emily, Box	800.00
Jerri, Goose Girl	450.00
Jerri, Janice	320.00
Jerri, Meredith	365.00
Jerri, Robin	300.00
Jester, Painted Face, Oilcloth, C.1870, 26 In.	325.00
Johnny West, Poseable, Painted Hair, 12 In.	85.00
Johnson, Remco, Box	25.00
Julia, Black Nurse, Box	65.00
Jumeau, Bisque Head, Molded Teeth, Gold Dress & Bonnet, 32 In.	2595.00
Jumeau, Brown Eyes, Original Clothing, Repainted Body, 12 In.	3200.00
Jumeau, Girl, Bisque Head, Paperweight Eyes, Jointed, C.1880, 29 In.	5100.00
Jumeau, Human Hair Wig, Cork Pate, 1907, 25 In.	2250.00
Jumeau, Open Mouth, Jointed Body, Jointed Wrists, Satin Dress, 34 In.	2800.00
Jumeau, Petite, Original Outfit, Box, 14 In.	4250.00
Jumeau, Portrait, Bisque Socket Head, Human Hair Wig, C.1880, 16 In.	4500.00
Jumeau, Portrait, Fashion, Silk, All Original, 18 In.	4400.00
Just Me, Bisque, White Rabbit Coat & Hat, 15 In.	1950.00
Jutta, Baby, Bent Leg, Christening Dress, Marked, 22 In.	800.00
Jutta, Character Baby, Bent Limb, Jointed Hands, 16 In.	500.00
K * R 101, Boy, 21 In.	3500.00
K * R 117, Character Child, 24 In.	725.00
K * R 117N, Flirty Eyes, 32 In.	2900.00
K * R 117N, Flirty Eyes, Ball–Jointed, 18 In.	895.00
K * R 121, Baby Body, Bent Limb, Sleep Eyes, Long Dress, 26 In.	2000.00
K * R 121, Ball–Jointed Body, 20 In.	1000.00
K * R 126, Baby, Tremble Tongue, Fur Wig, 29 In.	1800.00
K * R 126, Boy, Teeth, Curly Wig, Jointed Body, Toddler Outfit, 33 In.	2750.00
K * R 126, Character Child, Gleeful Expression, Leather Shoes, 24 In.	725.00
K * R 126, Flirty Eyes, Double Row of Teeth, Tremble Tongue, 34 In.	3200.00
K * R 126, Fur Wig, Tremble Tongue, Sailor Suit, 30 In.	1850.00
K * R 126, Toddler, 25 In.	1050.00
K * R 126, Toddler, 5–Piece Body, Sleep Eyes, 12 In.	450.00
K * R 127, Character Boy, Molded Hair, Ball–Jointed Body, 20 In.	1395.00
K * R 128, Bisque, 22 In.	950.00
K * R 192, Open Mouth, 17 In.	650.00
K * R 255, Celluloid, Kid Body	250.00
K * R 403, Bisque, Walker, Brown Braids, Antique Dress, 24 In.	675.00
K * R 717, Character Child, Flirty Eyes, Celluloid Head, 24 In.	365.00
K * R 728/5/0, Boy, Glass Eyes, Celluloid, Tyrolean Costume, 19 In.	225.00
K * R, Bent Limb, Human Hair Wig, Sleep Eyes, 25 In.	950.00
K * R, Bisque, Sleep Eyes, Composition Body, Antique Clothes, 6 In.	125.00
K * R, Character Baby, 12 In.	295.00
Kammer & Reinhardt, 117N, Character Child, Mein Liebling, 21 In.	750.00
Kammer & Reinhardt, Gretchen, Original Clothes, 9 In.	2600.00
Karl Hartmann, Bisque Head, Joint Body, Old Clothes, 23 In.	250.00
Kathe Kruse, Boy, 17 In.	900.00
Kathe Kruse, Boy, Cloth, C.1930, 18 In.	2200.00
Kathe Kruse, Girl, Celluloid, Wrist Tag, 14 In.	550.00
Kathe Kruse, Girl, U.S. Zone, Germany, 18 In.	450.00
Kathe Kruse, Soldier, Dressed, 17 In.	1100.00
Kenner, Indiana Jones, Box, 12 In.	120.00
Kenner, Shaun Cassidy, 1978, Box, 12 In.	45.00
Kenner, Shaun Cassidy, Hardy Boys Movie, 1979, Box, 12 In.	36.00
DOLL, KESTNER, see also Doll, J.D.K.	
Kestner 129, Excelsior Body, Curly Wig, Original Clothing, 21 In.	700.00
Kestner 142, Composition Ball–Jointed Body, Sleep Eyes, 35 In.	1795.00
Kestner 143, Plaster Pate, Ball–Jointed, 14 1/2 In.	795.00
Kestner 146, Child, Blond Mohair Wig, 30 In.	1150.00

Kestner 146, Plaster Pate, Signed Excelsior Body, Dressed, 30 In. 950.00
Kestner 152, Socket Head, Ball–Jointed, 21 In. 412.50
Kestner 154, Bisque, Brown Sleep Eyes, Human Hair Wig, 14 In. 225.00
Kestner 154, Blond Hair, Blue Eyes, Open Mouth, 26 In. 595.00
Kestner 154, Pale Bisque, Brown Sleep Eyes, Human Hair, 14 In. 250.00
Kestner 164, Brown Eyes, Excelsior Body, Original Clothing, 28 In. 900.00
Kestner 164, Chubby Ball–Jointed Body, Human Hair, Sleep Eyes, 26 In. 825.00
Kestner 167, Bisque, Brown Sleep Eyes, Original Clothes, 15 1/2 In. 850.00
Kestner 167, Blue Sleep Eyes, Antique Clothes, 17 In. 850.00
Kestner 167, Child, Bisque Head, Ball–Jointed Body, 14 In. 410.00
Kestner 169, Closed Mouth, Brown Eyes, Composition Body, 27 In. 2400.00
Kestner 171, Brown Eyes, Excelsior Body, Dressed, 26 In. 800.00
Kestner 171, Daisy, Ball–Jointed Body, 24 In. 525.00
Kestner 171, Daisy, Ball–Jointed Body, 29 In. 600.00
Kestner 171, Daisy, Ball–Jointed Body, Set Eyes, 19 In. 475.00
Kestner 171, Daisy, Blond, 30 In. 850.00
Kestner 172/7, Gibson Girl, 20 In. 3150.00
Kestner 208, Bisque, Sleep Brown Eyes, Curly Wig, 9 In. 400.00
Kestner 211, Baby, Bisque, Original Clothes, 11 In. 400.00
Kestner 247, Baby, 13 In. 1100.00
Kestner 247, Toddler, 28 In. 3500.00
Kestner 257, Baby, Bisque, Ball–Jointed Body, 28 In. 1875.00
Kestner 257, Baby, Bisque, Christening Gown, 24 In. 1400.00
Kestner 980, Character Baby, Original Clothes, 19 In. 495.00
Kestner, Baby, Bisque Head, Kid Body, Composition Arms, 20 In. 1925.00
Kestner, Ball–Jointed Body, Blonde Curly Wig, Old Clothes, 26 In. 495.00
Kestner, Bisque, Jointed Head, Arms & Legs, Molded Boots, 9 In. 985.00
Kestner, Bisque, Jointed Head, Sleep Eyes, Pink Boots, 1880s, 9 In. 775.00
Kestner, Bisque, Swivel Head, Closed Mouth, 9 In. 710.00
Kestner, Character Baby, Bisque, 13 In. 195.00
Kestner, Girl, Bisque, Sleep Eyes, Blond, Open Mouth, Jointed, 5 1/2 In. 38.50
Kestner, Girl, Bisque, Sleep Eyes, Blond, Open–Close Mouth, 7 In. 132.00
Kestner, Hilda, Sleep Eyes, C.1914, 22 In. 4510.00
Kestner, Open Mouth, Molded Teeth, Sleep Eyes, Bisque, 9 In. 1250.00
Kestner, Papier–Mache Head, Cloth Body, Leather Arms, 22 In. 475.00
Kestner, Solid Dome, Original Clothes, 12 In. 185.00
Kestner, Somber Face, Closed Mouth, Sleep Eyes, Blond Wig, 22 In. 3600.00
DOLL, KEWPIE, see Kewpie, Doll
Kley & Hahn 9, Walker, 21 In. 425.00
Kley & Hahn 160, Toddler, Banner Mark, 21 In. 700.00
Kley & Hahn 161, Character Baby, Molded Tongue, 10 In. 325.00
Kley & Hahn 169, Toddler, Closed Mouth 1650.00
Kley & Hahn 282, Girl, 30 In. 875.00
Kley & Hahn, Baby, 2 Faces, 12 In. 2400.00
Kley & Hahn, Child, Long Curled Hair, Antique Clothes, 31 In. 950.00
Kley & Hahn, Child, Sleep Eyes, Ball–Jointed, Underclothes, 7 In. 225.00
Kley & Hahn, Florodora, Fur Eyebrows, 21 In. 265.00
Knickerbocker, Bam Bam, Cloth, Black & Orange Outfit, 7 In. 4.00
Knickerbocker, Boo Boo Bear, Brown, Orange & Green Cloth, 1971, 7 In. 4.00
Knickerbocker, Dwarf, Composition, Dressed, 10 In. 150.00
Knickerbocker, Fred Flintstone, Cloth, 1961, 17 In. 65.00
Knickerbocker, Mr.Spock, 12 In. 45.00
Knickerbocker, Raggedy Ann & Andy, 39 In., Pair 55.00
Knickerbocker, Raggedy Ann, 19 In. 14.00
Lenci, Blond Hair, Brown Blouse, Checkered Skirt, C.1940, 10 1/4 In. 1870.00
Lenci, Clown, C.1920, 15 In. 295.00
Lenci, Felt, Holding Chicken, 10 In. 35.00
Lenci, Felt, Peasant, Painted Blue Eyes, Blonde, 14 In. 550.00
Lenci, Girl, Brown Painted Eyes, Pursed Mouth, 12 In. ....*Illus* 440.00
Lenci, Girl, Loretta, 13 In. .... 125.00 To 295.00
Lenci, Girl, Surprised Look, Bee On Skirt, Tagged, 9 In. 275.00
Lenci, Marlene Dietrich, Smoking, C.1927, 26 In. 1400.00
Lenci, Mascotte Girl, Floppy Hat, 10 In. 105.00
Lenci, Painted Blue Eyes, Black Mohair Wig, 15 In. 40.00

Lenci, Pouty, Russian Costume, High Boots, 18 In. 950.00
Little Lulu, Rag, Oilcloth Face, 1944 .... 250.00
Little Miss Seamstress, Sewing Machine, Accessories, Hasbro, Box 65.00
Madame Alexander, Agatha, 21 In. 275.00
Madame Alexander, Amish Boy, 8 In. 530.00
Madame Alexander, Amish Girl, 8 In. 530.00
Madame Alexander, Betty, Composition, 1935, 14 In. 250.00
Madame Alexander, Brigetta, 14 In. 150.00
Madame Alexander, Chatty Cathy, Black, 1969, 18 In. 95.00
Madame Alexander, Cinderella, Blue Dress, 1986, Box, 12 In. 69.00
Madame Alexander, Cissette, Brown Hair, Jointed Knees, Straw Hat, 9 In. 195.00
Madame Alexander, Cissy, Plastic, Heeled Shoes, Taffeta Dress, 20 In. 400.00
Madame Alexander, Cissy, Velvet Pants, Lace Blouse, 1956, 20 In. 140.00
Madame Alexander, Cousin Grace, Walker, Bent Knee, 1956, 8 In. 680.00
Madame Alexander, Cowgirl, 8 In. 350.00
Madame Alexander, Dutch, 1950s, 8 In. 52.00
Madame Alexander, Elise, Ballerina, Box, 17 In. 200.00
Madame Alexander, Elise, Bride, Box, 18 In. 195.00
Madame Alexander, Elise, Bridesmaid, Pink, 17 In. 250.00
Madame Alexander, Fairy Godmother, 14 In. 100.00
Madame Alexander, I Am Buttercup, Brunette, 15 In. 40.00
Madame Alexander, Ireland, Box, 8 In. 45.00
Madame Alexander, Jacqueline, White Leather Coat, 10 In. 450.00
Madame Alexander, Jane Withers, Composition, 1937, 12 In. 650.00
Madame Alexander, Jenny Lind, 1969, Box 995.00
Madame Alexander, Jenny, Walker, Open Mouth, Composition, 14 In. 250.00
Madame Alexander, Kitten, 1965, 21 In. 55.00
Madame Alexander, Korea, Maggie Face, 8 In. 275.00
Madame Alexander, Lady Hamilton & Lord Nelson, 1976 .... 200.00
Madame Alexander, Little Women, Meg, Box, 15 In. 125.00
Madame Alexander, Madame Pompadour, 1970s, 21 In. 850.00
Madame Alexander, Madame, Pink Gown, Box, 21 In. .... 325.00 To 485.00
Madame Alexander, Madeleine De Bains, 17 In. 295.00
Madame Alexander, Magnolia, Box, 21 In. 150.00
Madame Alexander, Manet, 21 In. 255.00
Madame Alexander, Maria, 17 In. 225.00
Madame Alexander, Marie Antoinette, Multicolored Gown, 21 In. 225.00
Madame Alexander, Mary Ellen, Walker, 32 In. 450.00
Madame Alexander, Mary Martin, Sailor Suit, 17 In. 165.00
Madame Alexander, Mary Queen of Scots, Regal Gown, 21 In. 249.95
Madame Alexander, Marybel, Get Well, Case, 16 In. 275.00
Madame Alexander, McGuffey Ana, Braids, 1937, 15 In. .... 275.00 To 325.00
Madame Alexander, McGuffey Ana, Red Tartan Dress, Rickrack, 6 1/2 In. 45.00
Madame Alexander, Miss America, 1940, 14 In. 440.00
Madame Alexander, Mon Cheri, Paris, 20 In. 575.00
Madame Alexander, Napoleon & Josephine, Box, 12 In., Pair 150.00
Madame Alexander, Natasha, Box, 21 In. 260.00
Madame Alexander, Peter Pan, 14 In. 150.00
Madame Alexander, Polly Pigtails, 14 In. 250.00
Madame Alexander, Prince Philip, Hard Plastic, 18 In. 475.00
Madame Alexander, Princess Elizabeth, Long Gown, Purse, 18 In. 145.00
Madame Alexander, Renoir, Pink Lace, 13 In. 250.00
Madame Alexander, Sarah Bernhardt, Rust Gown, 21 In. 225.00
Madame Alexander, Scarlett O'Hara, Dated 1960, 21 In. 650.00
Madame Alexander, Scarlett, Rosebuds On White Dress, Straw Hat, 8 In. 480.00
Madame Alexander, Sonja Henie, Ski Outfit, 14 In. 365.00
Madame Alexander, Sweden, Bent Knee, 8 In. 65.00
Madame Alexander, Thailand, 1950s, 8 In. 52.00
Madame Alexander, Toddler, Composition, Sleep Eyes, 11 1/2 In. 82.50
Madame Alexander, Tyrolean Girl & Boy, 8 In., Pair 115.00
Madame Alexander, Victoria, Christening Gown, 14 In. 50.00
Madame Alexander, Vietnam, Maggie Face, 8 In. 275.00
Madame Alexander, W.A.A.C., 14 In. 350.00
Madame Alexander, W.A.V.E., 14 In. 350.00

Madame Alexander, Wendy Ann, Composition, Marked, 13 In.	600.00
Madame Alexander, Wendy, Bent Knee, 8 In.	240.00
Madame Alexander, Wendy, Bride, 21 In.	375.00
Madame Hendren, Boy, Celluloid Head, Cloth Body, Composition, 19 In.	185.00
Majestic, Bisque, Ball–Jointed, White Coat, Hat, Muff, 36 In.	1375.00
Man, Wax, Closed Mouth, Tuxedo, High Top Beaver Hat, 21 In.	950.00
Marionette, Alice In Wonderland, Peter Puppets, 1953	125.00 To 150.00
Marionette, Black Minstrel, Box, Painted Wood, C.1920, 7 In.	98.00
Marionette, Clown, Plastic Head & Arms, Wooden Legs, Hazelle, 15 In.	110.00
Marionette, Jiminy Cricket, Gund	65.00
Marionette, Princess, Summerfallwinterspring, Bead Eyes, 14 In.	245.00
Marionette, Princess, Summerfallwinterspring, Painted Eyes, 14 In.	145.00
Martha Chase, Boy, Stockinette, 16 In.	550.00
Martha Chase, Redressed, Pre–1920, 16 In.	425.00
Mattel, Baby Go Bye Bye, With Bumper Buggy, 1969	50.00
Mattel, Baby, Pouts Or Smiles, 1965	45.00
Mattel, Baby, With Crib, Box	50.00
Mattel, Barbie, 1962	425.00
Mattel, Barbie, 6 Ft.	1600.00
Mattel, Barbie, Astronaut	20.00
Mattel, Barbie, Ballerina, White Tutu, Case, Stand	35.00
Mattel, Barbie, Bendable Knees, Box	210.00
Mattel, Barbie, Bendable Leg, Dutchboy Hair, 1965	155.00
Mattel, Barbie, Benefit Performance, Porcelain	190.00
Mattel, Barbie, Billy Boy, Box, 1985	135.00
Mattel, Barbie, Brunette, No.4	125.00
Mattel, Barbie, Bubble Cut	58.00 To 60.00
Mattel, Barbie, Bubble Cut, Brunette, Gold Brocade Outfit	130.00
Mattel, Barbie, Bubble Cut, Red Hair, Barbie Wrist Tag, Box	175.00
Mattel, Barbie, Bubble Cut, Stewardess Outfit	165.00
Mattel, Barbie, Case of Outfits & Shoes	300.00
Mattel, Barbie, Enchanted Evening, Porcelain	250.00
Mattel, Barbie, Eskimo, Box	95.00 To 110.00
Mattel, Barbie, Fashion Model, Box, 1964	60.00
Mattel, Barbie, Fashion Queen, Molded Hair, 1963, 12 In.	85.00
Mattel, Barbie, Feelin' Good, Billy Boy, Box	85.00
Mattel, Barbie, Feelin' Groovy	55.00 To 75.00
Mattel, Barbie, German, Box	30.00
Mattel, Barbie, Giggles	135.00
Mattel, Barbie, Happy Holidays	75.00
Mattel, Barbie, Hawaiian, Box	50.00
Mattel, Barbie, Hispanic Dream Glo	20.00
Mattel, Barbie, Holiday, Box, 1988	85.00
Mattel, Barbie, India	100.00
Mattel, Barbie, Italian, Box	150.00 To 195.00
Mattel, Barbie, Japanese, Box	40.00
Mattel, Barbie, Kissing, Box	35.00
Mattel, Barbie, Machiko	315.00
Mattel, Barbie, Makimura	315.00
Mattel, Barbie, Mardi Gras	25.50 To 40.00
Mattel, Barbie, No.1, Handmade Costume, Mohair Wig	600.00
Mattel, Barbie, No.3, 5 Complete Outfits	270.00
Mattel, Barbie, Olympic	40.00
Mattel, Barbie, Oriental, Box	95.00 To 120.00
Mattel, Barbie, Parisian, Box	200.00
Mattel, Barbie, Peru	22.00
Mattel, Barbie, Russian	18.50
Mattel, Barbie, Scottish, Box	120.00 To 150.00
Mattel, Barbie, Sears 100th Birthday	60.00
Mattel, Barbie, Skipper, Box	65.00
Mattel, Barbie, Spanish, Box	65.00
Mattel, Barbie, Sun Gold, Malibu	8.00
Mattel, Barbie, Sweet Rose, PJ	12.00
Mattel, Barbie, Talking, 19 In.	18.00

Mattel, Barbie, Talking, Original Outfit, Mute, 1968	75.00
Mattel, Barbie, Teen Age Fashion Model, 1962	145.00
Mattel, Barbie, Timi	225.00
Mattel, Barbie, Twist 'N Turn, 1966	50.00
Mattel, Barbie, Twist 'N Turn, Bendable Knees, Painted Lashes, 1967	60.00
Mattel, Barbie, UNICEF	23.95
Mattel, Barbie, Wal-Mart's 25th Anniversary	50.00
Mattel, Barbie, Walk Lively	50.00
Mattel, Barbie, Ward's Anniversary, 1972	150.00
Mattel, Barbie, White, Holiday	47.00
Mattel, Buffy	46.00
Mattel, Chatty Patty, Box, 16 1/2 In.	30.00
Mattel, Debbie Boone, 1978, 12 In.	35.00
Mattel, Grizzly Adams, Box	45.00
Mattel, Ken, 1960	45.00
Mattel, Ken, Bendable Knee, 1968	25.00
Mattel, Ken, Bendable Legs, Box, 1964	60.00
Mattel, Ken, Campus Hero	140.00
Mattel, Ken, Flock Hair, Box	140.00
Mattel, Ken, Island Fun	15.00
Mattel, Ken, Malibu, 1971	15.00
Mattel, Ken, No.3, Clothes, Box, 1961	45.00
Mattel, Ken, Saturday Night Date Outfit	155.00
Mattel, Mindy, Box, 9 In.	30.00
Mattel, Sister Belle, 1961	25.00
Mattel, Spaceman, 1978	12.00
Mattel, That-A-Way Crawler, 1974	35.00
Mattel, Tippy Toes, Trike, All Original, 1967, 17 In.	35.00
McCall, Sandy, 36 In.	320.00
Mego, Kristy McNichol, 1975, 8 In.	50.00
Mego, Our Gang Buckwheat, Package, 1975, 8 In.	75.00
Mego, Sonny & Cher, 1976, 12 In., Pair	35.00
Mego, Spiderman, 1978, Large	30.00
Mego, Starsky & Hutch, 1976, 8 In., Pair	17.00
Mego, Wicked Witch, Wizard of Oz, Box, 8 In.	100.00
Mego, Wonder Woman, Box	35.00
Mein Liebling 117N, Flirty Eyes, Bisque, 30 In.	2700.00
Mein Liebling, Antique White Dress, Bonnet, 28 In.	8000.00
Michael Jackson, Box, 12 In.	25.00
Milliner's Model, Leather Body, 1830s, 18 In.	2800.00
Milliner's Model, Papier-Mache Head, Kid Body, Wood Limbs, 8 In.	220.00
Milliner's Model, Papier-Mache Head, Kid Body, Wood Limbs, 12 In.	185.00
Minerva, Tin Head, Excelsior Stuffed, Wooden Spoon In Hand, 19 In.	165.00
Moon Mullins, 1920s	120.00
Morimura, Baby, Bent Limb, Composition Body, Sleep Eyes, 13 In.	215.00
Morimura, Baby, Bisque Socket Head, Painted Eyes, Open Mouth, 8 In.	38.50
Morimura, Character Baby, 1915, 17 In.	250.00
Motschmann, Boy, China, Pink Tinge, Twill Extensions, 9 In.	3300.00
Mr. Pott, Dick Van Dyke, Talking, But Mute, 1967, 24 In.	55.00
Munic Art, Boy, Red Hair, Painted Eyes, Composition, Dressed, 19 In.	2400.00
Nancy Ann Storybook, Bride, Bisque, Box	30.00
Nancy Ann Storybook, Little Joan, Box	25.00
Nancy Ann Storybook, Silks & Satins, Box	30.00
Nippon, Baby, Sleep Eyes, Wobbly Tongue, 24 In.	335.00
Nippon, Bisque, Leather Body, 21 In.	550.00
Nippon, Character Baby, Antique Gown, Sweater, 18 In.	450.00
Norah Wellings, Dutch Girl, 8 In.	65.00
Norah Wellings, Jack Tar, Sailor, Cloth, Marked, 11 In.	40.00
Oscar Goldman, With Exploding Suitcase, Box	20.00
Our Fairy, Bisque, Brown Sleep Eyes, Open Close Mouth, 1914, 7 In.	110.00
DOLL, PAPER, see Paper Doll	
Papier-Mache, Glass Eyes, Antique Dress, Germany, 19th Century, 28 In.	550.00
Parian, Girl, Blond Ringlets, Molded Blue Ribbon, Cloth Body, 22 In.	550.00
Parian, Lady, With Fancy Hair, 20 In.	450.00

Paris Bebe, Closed Mouth, Brown Paperweight Eyes, Blond Wig, 24 In. 3500.00
Patty Duke, 1965, Box 115.00
Paul Stanley, Kiss, Box 75.00
Peasant, Cloth, Stitched Faces, Italian, 15 In.& 17 In., Pr. 85.00
Penny, Wooden, Carved, Enameled Shoulder Head, Original Outfit, C.1840 .... 150.00
Penny, Wooden, Carved, Jointed Limbs, C.1840 .... 150.00
Penny, Wooden, Original, 7 In., Pair 350.00
    DOLL, PINCUSHION, see Pincushion Doll
Poor Pitiful Pearl, 13 In. 60.00
Princess Diana & Prince Charles, Flower Girl, Wedding, 1981, 3 Piece 625.00
Princess Diana & Prince Charles, Wedding Clothes, Box, 12 In., Pair 95.00
Princess Summerfallwinterspring, 7 1/2 In. 25.00
Puppet, 3 Stooges, Vinyl, 1960s 135.00
Puppet, Bozo The Clown, Knickerbocker, 12 In. 15.00
Puppet, Dennis The Menace 145.00
Puppet, Marie Osmohd, Box 24.00
Puppet, Monkees, Finger, 4 Piece 65.00
Puppet, Mr.Bluster, Cardboard 12.00
Puppet, Pelham, Girl, Box, 1950s 35.00
Puppet, Pelham, Wolf 75.00
Puppet, Possy, Squirrel, Button & Tag, Steiff 45.00
Queen Anne, Pupilless Glass Eyes, Original Clothes, 1790, 12 In. 2500.00
R.John Wright, No.382, Christopher Robin & Pooh, Signed 685.00
Rag, Little Lulu, Oilcloth Face, 1944 .... 250.00
Rag, Yarn Hair, Button Eyes, Print Dress, 18 In. 2.00
Raggedy Ann, Mollye, 16 In. 275.00
Ravca, Harry Lawder, 13 In. 120.00
Recknagel, Girl, Composition Body, Molded Painted Shoes & Socks, 8 In. 150.00
Reinhardt 117H, Flirty, 33 In. 975.00
Remco, Goldwater, Box 25.00
Remco, Johnson, Box 25.00
Remco, Lurch 150.00
Rex Harrison, Dr. Doolittle, Painted Eyes, Open Closed Mouth, 21 In. 85.00
Royal Doulton, Nisbet, Newborn 199.00
    DOLL, S & H, see also Doll, Bergmann; Doll, Simon & Halbig
S & H 121, Baby, Bisque, Mohair Wig, Christening Dress, 20 In. 800.00
S & H 949, Bisque, Swivel Head, 14 In. 1430.00
S & H 1249, Santa Claus, Bisque, 18 In. 700.00
S & H, Baby, Bisque Socket Head, 5–Piece Body, Lace Bonnet, 9 In. 176.00
S & H, Child, Original Clothing, 29 In. 800.00
S.F.B.J. 10, Silk Store Dress & Hat, 36 In. 2500.00
S.F.B.J. 14, Paris, 30 In. 2250.00
S.F.B.J. 60, Boy, All Original, 10 In. 375.00
S.F.B.J. 235, Boy, 14 In. 1300.00
S.F.B.J. 236, Bisque, Open–Close Mouth, Nursing Gown, Cap, 20 1/2 In. 18850.00
S.F.B.J. 251, Toddler, 23 In. 2450.00
S.F.B.J. 252, Pouty, Brown Hair, Ball–Jointed, Blue Dress, 11 1/2 In. 4500.00
S.F.B.J. 301, Labeled Au Nain Bleu Outfit, 15 In. 625.00
Schoenau & Hoffmeister 1909, 23 In. 475.00
Schoenau & Hoffmeister, 24 In. 425.00
Schoenau & Hoffmeister, Ball–Jointed Body, 26 In. 495.00
Schoenau & Hoffmeister, My Cherub, 24 In. 350.00
Schoenhut 301, Pouty Girl, Closed Mouth, 16 In. 950.00
Schoenhut, Barney Google 450.00
Schoenhut, Blond Wig, Original Clothes, Plaid Dress, 14 1/2 In. 895.00
Schoenhut, Brown Decal Eyes, Facial Paint, Checked Dress, 17 In. 325.00
Schoenhut, Brown Raincoat, Hat, Human Hair, 1911, 17 In. 485.00
Schoenhut, Carved Hair, Original Dress & Underwear, 14 1/2 In. 1850.00
Schoenhut, Character, Intaglio Eyes, 2–Hole Shoes, Stand, 15 In. 850.00
Schoenhut, Clown ....95.00 To 145.00
Schoenhut, Girl, Open–Close Mouth, 4 Painted Teeth, 16 In. 495.00
Schoenhut, Girl, Painted Teeth, Replaced Wig, 16 In. 395.00
Schoenhut, Girl, Sad Eyes, 14 In. 1870.00
Schoenhut, Girl, Spring Jointed, Carved Hair, 16 In. 400.00

Schoenhut, Hobo, Circus 185.00
Schoenhut, Kid Body, Blond Hair, Bisque Arms & Hands, 16 In. 225.00
Schoenhut, Mannequin, Man, 19 In. 3800.00
Schoenhut, Mary Had A Little Lamb, Bell 600.00
Schoenhut, Pouty Boy, 19 In. 600.00
Schoenhut, Pouty Boy, Sailor Suit 1150.00
Schoenhut, Pouty Girl, Brown Intaglio Eyes, 16 In. 950.00
Schoenhut, Sleep Eyes, Wooden Body, Bisque Arms & Hands, 21 In. 225.00
Schoenhut, Toddler, Baby Face, 1911, 17 In. 650.00
Schoenhut, Toddler, Intaglio Eyes, Mohair Wig, Dress & Stand, 16 In. 580.00
Schoenhut, Wooden Head, Painted Features, Spring-Jointed Body, 12 In. 1100.00
Schuco, Perfume, Money, Bellhop 125.00
Scotchman, Blue Eyes, Open Mouth, Cardboard Body, Mohair, 12 In. 150.00
Scottish Lass, Tartan Costume, Bisque Socket Head, Germany, 7 In. 82.50
Shindana, Flip Wilson-Geraldine, Not Talking, Box, 1970 .... 35.00
Shindana, O.J.Simpson, 1976, Box, 10 In. 40.00
 DOLL, SHIRLEY TEMPLE, see Shirley Temple
 DOLL, SIMON & HALBIG, see also Doll, Bergmann; Doll, S & H
Simon & Halbig 3, Glazed Eyes, Open Mouth, Shoes, Pantaloons, 22 In. 1295.00
Simon & Halbig 540, 21 In. 425.00
Simon & Halbig 550, 22 In. 480.00
Simon & Halbig 909, Bisque, Closed Mouth, Old Clothes, 16 In. 2600.00
Simon & Halbig 949, Bisque, Long Curls, Jointed, Silk Dress, 12 In. 1295.00
Simon & Halbig 1009, Sleep Eyes, Straight Wrist, Jointed Body, 17 In. 485.00
Simon & Halbig 1079, 25 In. 395.00
Simon & Halbig 1079, 42 In. 2900.00
Simon & Halbig 1079, Child, Bisque Head, Jointed Body, 12 In. 225.00
Simon & Halbig 1159, Lady, Bisque, Ball-Jointed Body, 24 In. 2450.00
Simon & Halbig 1159, Lady, Blue Eyes, 17 In. 1800.00
Simon & Halbig 1199, Oriental, 15 In. 2300.00
Simon & Halbig 1299, Baby, Open Mouth, Gray Eyes, Blond, 11 In. 350.00
Simon & Halbig, Baby Blanche, Dresser, 23 In. 650.00
Simon & Halbig, Bisque Socket Head, Jointed Composition, Wood, 17 In. 412.00
Simon & Halbig, Bisque, Googly, Jointed Arms & Legs, 6 In. 325.00
Simon & Halbig, Mabel, 21 In. 250.00
Simon & Halbig, Open Mouth, Long Curls, Ball-Jointed Body, 32 In. 1150.00
Simon & Halbig, Oriental, Bisque, Silk Costume 1750.00
Simon & Halbig, Stationary Eyes, Composition Body, 26 In. 695.00
Skeezix, Oilcloth 35.00
Skippy, Composition, Original Wool Sailor Suit, 1942, 14 In. 375.00
Skookum, Brave & Squaw, With Papoose, Bully Good, 17 In., Pair 315.00
Skookum, Papoose On Back, Indian Blanket, Wooden Feet 30.00
Skookum, Squaw, With Papoose, 12 In. 55.00
Skookum, Squaw, With Papoose, Label, Dated 1914 .... 30.00
Sluggo, Comic Strip 20.00
Snoopy, Astronaut, 1969 .... 20.00
Star Wars, IG-88, Box 375.00
Steiff, Andreas 345.00
Steiff, Coiled Bun, Turquoise Eyes, Old Clothes, 1840s, 11 In. 565.00
Steiff, Dog, Waldili Dachshund, Dressed As Hunter, Gun, 9 1/2 In. 350.00
Steiff, Mimi 345.00
Steiff, Piroschko 345.00
Steiff, Santa Claus, Victorian 160.00
Steiff, Ulla 375.00
Steiner, Baby, Bisque Head, Cloth Body, Composition Hands, 8 1/2 In. 75.00
Steiner, Baby, Kicking, Crying, Bisque Head, Kid & Cardboard, 20 In. 1545.00
Steiner, Baby, Kicking, Crying, Paperweight Eyes, 18 In. 1850.00
Steiner, Bisque, Papier-Mache Body, Feathered Brows, Mohair Wig, 12 In. 2200.00
Steiner, Factory Frock, 12 In. 2200.00
Steiner, Jules, Bebe, A-Series, Lace Trimmed Dress, 24 In. 4800.00
Steiner, Kicking, Crying, 23 In. 2000.00
Steiner, Open Mouth, Teeth, Composition Body, 18 In. .... 2000.00 To 2300.00
Stocking, Embroidered Face, 15 In. 95.00
Suntan Tuesday Taylor 35.00

Susan Stroller, Plastic, Rooted Hair, Sleep Eyes, 1955, 21 In.	45.00
Swaine, Lori, Baby, 23 In.	2500.00
Teaching Set, Pregnant, 1930s, 3 Piece	150.00
Terri Lee, 10 In.	75.00
Terri Lee, 16 In.	110.00
Terri Lee, Baby Sister, Linda, Soft Rubber	80.00
Terri Lee, Extra Clothes, In Trunk	290.00
Terri Lee, Formal Gown, Box	225.00
Terri Lee, Tiny Terri	155.00
Tete Jumeau, Bisque, Closed Mouth, Red Wool Middy Dress, Hat, 20 In.	4400.00
Tete Jumeau, Closed Mouth, Original Wig & Clothing, 17 In.	2400.00
Tete Jumeau, Girl, Bisque Head, Paperweight Eyes, Pierced Ears, 29 In.	5100.00
Tiffany Taylor, Model, Fashion, Changing Color Hair, 18 In.	25.00
Tin Head, Boy, 20 In.	150.00
Tin Head, Glass Eyes, 18 In.	95.00
Tiny Tears, American Character, Fur Wig, Original Dress, Bonnet, 13 In.	39.00
Tiny Tears, Original Clothes, Pacifier, 13 In.	56.00
Toddler, Celluloid, Flirty Eyes, French, 16 In.	260.00
Topsy Turvy, Goldilocks, Lift Skirt To Find 3 Bears, 1960s, 18 In.	75.00
Tristar, Grace Kelly, Box, 11 1/2 In.	75.00
Tristar, Liz Taylor, White Dress, Box, 11 1/2 In.	75.00
Tristar, Marilyn Monroe, Box, 11 1/2 In.	75.00
Tuckcomb, Wooden, 17 In.	3500.00
U.S.Navy, Celluloid Head, Stuffed Body, 4 3/4 In.	10.00
Unis 301, Boy, Composition Body, Painted Shoes & Sox, 7 In.	125.00
Unis, Bisque, Silk Dress, Shoes, Box, 28 In.	1400.00
Unis, Mulatto, Fixed Eyes, 5-Piece Papier-Mache Body, Dressed	200.00
Unis, Open-Close Eyes, Open Mouth, 8 In.	275.00
United Features, Sally & Linus, Cloth, Printed, 1952, 7 In., Pair	10.00
Ventriloquist, Jerry Mahoney, 1956, Box	165.00
Vlasta, Amelia, Pat Thompson	2400.00
Vogue, Baby Dear, 1 Tuft of Hair, 18 In.	110.00
Vogue, Baby Dear, Black, 11 In.	25.00
Vogue, Baby Patsyette, 9 In.	140.00
Vogue, Blond, Twisted Waist, Tagged Clothes, 10 In.	45.00
Vogue, Ginny, African, 1972	30.00
Vogue, Ginny, Ballet Dancer, Box	300.00
Vogue, Ginny, Brickette, 1960, 22 In.	100.00
Vogue, Ginny, Coronation Queen	1150.00
Vogue, Ginny, Cowboy, 1950	775.00
Vogue, Ginny, Crib Crowd	495.00
Vogue, Ginny, First Corsage, Box	375.00
Vogue, Ginny, Gretel, Box	275.00
Vogue, Ginny, John Alden, Box	425.00
Vogue, Ginny, Poodle Cut, Plaid Dress, Kindergarten Series	700.00 To 850.00
Vogue, Ginny, Priscilla, Box	325.00
Vogue, Ginny, Scottish Girl, Box	425.00
Vogue, Ginny, Sleep Eyes, Sweater, Red Hair, 8 In.	65.00
Vogue, Ginny, Tagged Dress, Bonnet, Red Shoes	160.00
Vogue, Jeff, Swim Trunks, 10 In.	25.00
Vogue, Littlest Angel, 15 In.	38.00
Vogue, Toodles, 8 In.	100.00
Vogue, Toodles, Composition, 1940, 7 In.	154.00
Walker, Bisque, Sleep Eyes, Teeth, Jointed, Mechanical, 16 In.	416.00
Wanda, Walking, Hard Plastic, Box	75.00
Wendy Ann, Bride, 14 In.	150.00
Wernicke, Sleep Eyes, Human Hair Wig, Original Clothes, 39 In.	2100.00
Wernicke, Sleep Eyes, Jointed Leather Body, 23 1/2 In.	700.00
Woman, Wax Over Papier-Mache, 19 In.	265.00
Wonder Woman, D.C.Comics	35.00
Wooden, Articulated Arms & Legs, 17 1/2 In.	250.00
Wooden, Articulated Limbs, Carved Face, Cloth Costume, 13 In.	400.00
World, Ginger Rogers & Fred Astaire, Box, 19 In., Pair	250.00
World, Mammy, Gone With The Wind, Box, 12 In.	40.00

World, Mammy, Gone With The Wind, Red Petticoat, 18 In. 47.00
World, Marilyn Monroe, Red Dress, Box, 18 In. ....65.00 To 125.00
World, Rhett & Scarlett, Gone With The Wind, Box, 21 In., Pair 250.00
World, Rhett, Gone With The Wind, Smoking Jacket, Box, 12 In. 35.00
World, Scarlett, Gone With The Wind, Red, Box, 12 In. 35.00
World, Scarlett, Green Print Dress, Box, 19 In. 50.00
Xavier Roberts, Aerobic Girl, Amethyst, Signed 120.00
    DONALD DUCK, see Disneyana

 Iron doorstops have been made in all types of designs. The vast
majority of the doorstops sold today are cast iron and were made
from about 1890 to 1930. Most of them are shaped like people,
animals, flowers, or ships.

DOORSTOP, 2 Footmen, Signed Fish, 9 1/8 In. 1275.00
  3 Geese, Fred Everett .... 175.00 To 260.00
  3 Sailing Ships 58.00
  Abraham Lincoln, Cast Iron, 6 1/2 In. 40.00
  Apple Blossoms, Bradley & Hubbard 110.00
  Basket of Flowers, Cast Iron, Painted, 9 7/8 In. 60.00
  Bellhop, Black 1000.00
  Bird & Trellis, Cast Iron 200.00
  Black Man's Head, Polychrome Repaint, Cast Iron, 6 1/2 In. 75.00
  Bullfrog, Cast Iron 45.00
  Cape Cod House, Red Chimney, Green, Orange, Iron, 6 In. .... 100.00 To 125.00
  Cat, Black Repainted, Cast Iron 50.00
  Cat, Black, Cast Iron 225.00
  Cat, Eastern Specialty Co., Cast Iron 522.50
  Cat, Hubley, Cast Iron ....80.00 To 125.00
  Cat, Hunched, Green Eyes, Raised Tail, Cast Iron 175.00
  Cat, Reclining, White Paint, Hubley, 10 1/2 In. 150.00
  Cat, Ribbon At Neck, Brass, 7 In. 40.00
  Cat, Seated, Black Paint, Opalescent Glass Eyes, 10 1/4 In. 125.00
  Cat, Seated, Hubley, Cast Iron, Original Paint, 9 1/2 In. 170.00
  Cat, Striped Tabby, Shades of Gray, Cement, 4 1/2 X 7 In. 40.00
  Cat, White Persian, Green Eyes, Hubley 150.00
  Chicken, Bradley & Hubbard 245.00
  Chief Sitting Bull On Horse, Cast Iron 150.00
  Child, Yawning, 1931 .... 800.00
  Coastal Patrol Man, The Patrol, Repainted, Iron, 8 1/2 In. 440.00
  Colonial Woman, Cast Iron 150.00
  Conestoga Wagon, Cast Iron, 11 1/2 X 8 1/2 In. 145.00
  Cornucopia of Roses, Polychrome Paint, Cast Iron, 10 1/4 In. 85.00
  Cottage, Red Roof, Trees, Cast Iron 125.00
  Covered Wagon, Man & Woman Driving, Cast Iron 125.00
  Deer, Art Deco, Marked, Cast Iron, 9 7/8 In. 150.00
  Dog, 2 Scottys 85.00
  Dog, 3 Singing Dogs, Cast Iron, 4 3/4 In. 40.00
  Dog, Beagle Pup, Cast Iron 225.00
  Dog, Bulldog, Black Satin Glass 475.00
  Dog, Bulldog, Cast Iron 85.00
  Dog, Bulldog, Hanely's Ale, Cast Iron 550.00
  Dog, English Setter, Brown & Cream, Cast Iron, 8 1/2 X 15 In. 140.00
  Dog, Fox Terrier, Hubley 260.00
  Dog, French Poodle, Full Figure, Bronze 100.00
  Dog, German Shepherd, Cast Iron 98.00
  Dog, Russian Wolfhound, Morton Studios 75.00
  Dog, Scotty, Standing, Red Collar, Painted 120.00
  Dog, Seated, Full Figure, Cast Iron, Open Front Legs, 5 1/4 In. 105.00
  Dog, Setter, Bank, Brass 225.00
  Dog, Spuds Type, Wooden, Black & White, Die Cut 22.00
  Dog, St.Bernard, Cast Iron, 8 In. 150.00
  Dog, Terrier, Bradley & Hubbard 495.00
  Dog, Terrier, Cast Iron, 7 1/2 X 6 1/2 In. 145.00
  Dog, Wire–Haired Terrier, Cast Iron 120.00

Donkey, Bronze, Rear Feet Up 118.00
Duck, Facing Right, Cast Iron, Signed, 10 In. 350.00
Ducks, Hubley, Cast Iron 250.00
Dutch Girl, Oversized Wooden Shoes, Cast Iron, 10 In. 10.00
Dutch Girl, Oversized Wooden Shoes, Cast Iron, 8 3/4 In. 30.00
Eagle, Full Wingspread, Lacy Iron Base, Iron, 6 X 10 In. 250.00
Eagle, Hamilton Foundry, Cast Iron 95.00
Elephant, Cast Iron 150.00
Elephant, Cast Iron, Bradley & Hubbard, Worn Paint, 10 1/2 In. 175.00
Elephant, Tan Paint, Metal 100.00
Elephant, Walking, Curled Trunk, Cast Iron 80.00
Fireplace, Grand Gas Range 50.00
Fisherman & Boat, Cast Iron 250.00
Fisherman, In Raincoat, Cast Iron 65.00
Fisherman, Southwester, Coil of Net In Hands, Iron, 11 In. 330.00
Flower Basket, Albany Foundry 225.00
Flower Basket, Bradley & Hubbard 165.00
Fox's Head 250.00
Frog, Cast Iron .... 30.00 To 65.00
Frog, Collar & Neck Ornament, Bronze, 8 1/2 In. 225.00
Frog, Mouth Open, Cast Iron 50.00
Fruit Bowl, Hubley, Original Paint 95.00
Frying Pan, Cast Iron 125.00
Gettysburg Eternal Light, Cast Iron, 1939 .... 125.00
Gettysburg Eternal Light, Cast Iron, Dated 1934, Signed 68.00
Girl, Feather In Bonnet, Original Paint, Cast Iron 125.00
Girl, Short Dress, Back Turned, Leaning On Wall, Iron, 6 1/8 In. 100.00
Gnome With Keys, Cast Iron 200.00
Goose, Wings Out 175.00
Heron, Red, Black & White, Fred Everett 85.00
High Button Shoe, Cast Iron 110.00
Horse, Circus, Prancing, Cast Iron, 10 X 10 1/2 In. 220.00
Horse, Hubley, Cast Iron 140.00
Horse, King's Genius, Brass 165.00
Horse, Prancing, Painted, Cast Iron, Wood Base, 11 In. 275.00
Horses, Pulling Coach, Cast Iron 65.00
Iris, Hubley 225.00
Jockey On Horse Jumping Fence, Brass Finish, 5 X 5 In. 65.00
Lincoln Head, Cast Iron 60.00
Lion's Head, Yellow, Blue, Cast Iron, 7 1/2 In. 125.00
Lion, Full Bodied, Silver Paint, Cast Iron, Coin Slot Added, 7 In. 75.00
Lion, Reclining, Crossed Front Paws, Cast Iron, 2 1/2 X 7 In. 40.00
Little Red Riding Hood, Cast Iron 155.00
London Royal Mail Coach, Cast Iron 85.00
Major Domo, Cast Iron 285.00
Mammy, Bottle, Cardboard Stopper, Cream, Red Print Dress .... 110.00 To 195.00
Man In Waist Coat, Cast Iron, 8 In. 75.00
Man of The Sea, Cast Iron 70.00
Man With Tankard, Cast Iron, 9 3/4 In. 55.00
Masonic, Cast Iron, 19th Century 155.00
Monkey, Full Figure, Polychrome, Cast Iron, Coin Slot Added, 8 In. 260.00
Nude, Art Deco, Joe Wagner Realty Co., Cast Iron 85.00
Outline of Ohio, Cast Iron, 1803–1953, 6 1/2 In. 25.00
Pansy Bowl, Hubley 85.00
Parrot, In Medallion, Cast Iron 85.00
Parrot, Tree Stump Base, Cast Iron, 7 1/2 In. 50.00
Peacock, Cast Iron .... 125.00 To 150.00
Penguin, Full Figure, Black & White Paint, Cast Iron, 10 1/4 In. 120.00
Pheasant, Cast Iron, Original Paint 250.00
Pineapple, Cast Brass, 13 In. 115.00
Poinsettia, Cast Iron 225.00
Puppies In Basket, Cocker Spaniels, Cast Iron 185.00
Quail, Hubley, Cast Iron 250.00
Ram, Cast Iron, 6 3/4 In. 85.00

Rooster, Flat Back, Painted	135.00
Sailor, Art Deco, Cast Iron	525.00
Sheep, Salt Glaze, Cobalt Blue Detail	775.00
Ship, Mayflower, Schoefield's Iron Works, 10 X 11 In.	50.00
Ship, Polychrome Paint, Cast Iron, 11 In.	40.00
Ship, Santa Maria, Cast Iron	90.00
Southern Belle, Cast Iron	75.00
Southern Belle, Cast Iron, 4 1/2 In.	8.00
Southern Belle, Cast Iron, 8 In.	15.00
Stagecoach, Cast Iron	75.00
Uncle Sam, Cast Iron, 16 In.	285.00
Vase of Flowers, Cast Iron	67.50
White Horse, Pedestal, Cast Iron	125.00
White Knight, Cast Iron	95.00
Windmill, National, Cast Iron	85.00
Woman, Seated, Victorian, Harp At Side, Cast Metal, 9 X 8 1/2 In.	75.00

Doulton pottery and porcelain were made by Doulton and Co. of Burslem, England, after 1882. The name "Royal Doulton" appeared on their wares after 1902. Other pottery by Doulton is listed under Royal Doulton.

DOULTON, Biscuit Barrel, Tapestry, Lambeth	135.00
Biscuit Jar, Arundel Pattern, 1892 Mark	165.00
Bowl, Silver Plated Rim, Burslem, 10 In.	55.00
Box, Cover, Iris & Daisy Design, Burslem, Beige, Square, 6 In.	32.00
Ewer, Beaded Roundels, Burslem, C.1872, 8 In.	220.00
Gravy Boat, Oriel, Burslem	32.00
Humidor, Room For One, Motor	750.00
Inkwell, Bibelot, Molded As Grumpy Old Lady, Hinged Head, 3 1/4 In.	475.00
Jar, Feather-Type Design, Embossed Gilt, Lambeth, 3 7/8 In.	50.00
Jug, Flambe, Sterling Rim, Cobalt Blue & Red	195.00
Match Holder, Gentlemen, Dogs, Lambeth	65.00
Mug, Flared, Golfers In Relief, Lambeth	2200.00
Pitcher, Applied Flowers, Lambeth, C.1890	150.00
Plate, Floral Center, Gold Tracery Edge, Burslem, 8 3/4 In.	115.00
Plate, Floral On Irregular Rim, Floral Center, Burslem, 9 1/4 In.	95.00
Plate, Henry At Hampton, Historic England	75.00
Plate, Oxford, Burslem, 1890–92, 10 1/2 In.	50.00
Plate, Shakespeare's Country, 10 1/2 In.	75.00
Teapot, Pump, Blue & White Floral, Burslem	95.00
Vase, Multicolored Flowers Outlined In Gold, Burslem, 5 1/2 In.	100.00
Vase, Multicolored Flowers, Outlined In Gold, Burslem, 11 1/2 In.	230.00
Vase, Night Watchman, Square, 8 In.	135.00
Vase, Pastel Florals Vining On Tan, Burslem, 6 In.	135.00
Vase, Pastel Florals, Sleigh Mouth, Burslem, C.1885, 6 In.	110.00
Vase, Siliconware, Coffee Color, Blue & White Flowers, 6 In.	70.00

DR. SYNTAX, see Adams; Staffordshire

Moriage is a type of decoration on Japanese pottery. Raised white designs are applied to the ware. Dragonware is a form of moriage pottery. White dragons are the major raised decorations. The background color is gray and white, orange and lavender, or orange and brown. It is a twentieth-century ware.

DRAGONWARE, Pitcher, 1 3/4 In.	12.00
Sugar & Creamer	28.00
Tea Set, Pastel, 11 Piece	95.00
Vase, 4 In.	28.00

Dresden china is any china made in the town of Dresden, Germany. The most famous factory in Dresden is the Meissen factory. Figurines of eighteenth-century ladies and gentlemen, animal groups, or cherubs and other mythological subjects were popular. One special type of figurine was made with skirts of porcelain-dipped lace. Do not make the mistake of thinking that all pieces marked "Dresden" are from the Meissen factory. The Meissen pieces usually have crossed swords marks, and are listed under Meissen.

DRESDEN, Basket, Applied Flowers, 19th Century, 8 In.	55.00
Bathroom Set, Semi–Porcelain, 5 Piece	285.00
Bowl, Floral Design, Gold Trim, Open Lattice Work, 8 1/2 In.	350.00
Bowl, Floral Interior, Applied Flowers, Boat Shape, 7 1/2 X 17 In.	325.00
Bowl, Floral Interior, Applied Outer Flowers, 4–Footed, 9 In.	175.00
Bowl, Fruit, Reticulated, 4–Footed, Painted Floral Inside, 9 1/2 In.	225.00
Candelabrum, Figural Cupids, Flowers, 11 X 9 1/2 In., Pair	500.00
Candlestick, Florals On White, Gold Trim, Crown Mark, 5 3/4 In.	68.00
Candlestick, Small Florals, White, Crown Mark, 5 3/4 In.	75.00
Clock, Tall Case, Flowers In Relief, Metal Serpents, Mirror Back	825.00
Compote, 3 Figures At Base, Applied Flowers, C.1900, 19 In.	305.00
Figurine, Ballerina, 4–Tiered Lace Skirt, Applied Roses, 7 1/2 In.	125.00
Figurine, Ballerina, Crinoline Dress, Red Bodice, Marked, 6 1/2 In.	250.00
Figurine, Chess Game, 6 1/2 X 5 1/2 In.	450.00
Figurine, Dancing Couple, 6 X 5 In.	325.00
Figurine, Napolean On Horseback, 14 In.	125.00
Figurine, Spanish Dancer	350.00
Figurine, Women, Seated, Book & Basket of Flowers, 10 X 12 In.	950.00
Group, 2 Gentleman Attempt To Win 2 Ladies, Marked, 11 In.	610.00
Group, 3 Dancing Children, Victorian, 6 1/2 X 9 In.	150.00
Group, Girl, Crinoline Dress, Boy Seated At Side, 7 X 9 In.	550.00
Group, Lady & Man, Holding Hands, Flower Pedestal, Marked, 5 In.	195.00
Group, Man With Violin, Woman & Man Seated, Piano, 9 1/2 X 11 In.	1050.00
Group, Ring Around The Rosy, 3 Girls, Arms Entwined, 8 1/4 In.	550.00
Group, Tea Party, 2 Women, Lace Dresses, Set Table, 8 X 12 In.	950.00
Half–Doll, Ballerina, 3 In., Pair	100.00
Jar, Beef Malt, Figural Steer's Head, 5 1/2 X 9 In.	95.00
Lemonade Set, Grapes & Leaves, Mugs, Purple & Green, 5 Piece	135.00
Loving Cup, 3 Gold Handles, Scene of Nymphs In Woodland, 6 1/2in.	350.00
Plaque, Old Man Smoking Pipe, Baroque Frame, 3 1/2 X 2 1/2 In.	305.00
Plaque, Queen Louise, Carved Baroque Frame, 3 1/2 X 2 1/2 In.	305.00
Plate, Classical Scene, 1880s, 10 In.	145.00
Plate, Comic Man & Woman On Path & Grass, Signed, 8 1/2 In.	50.00
Plate, Floral Sprays, Scalloped Border, C.1900, 8 1/2 In., 10 Piece	220.00
Salt & Pepper, Pink Roses, Signed	50.00
Vase, Cobalt Blue, Victorian Lovers Medallion, Raised Gold, 8 In.	295.00
Vase, Multicolored Florals, White, Gold Trim, 11 1/4 In.	160.00

Duncan & Miller is a term used by collectors when referring to glass made by the George A. Duncan and Sons Company or the Duncan and Miller Glass Company. These companies worked from 1893 to 1955, when the use of the name "Duncan" was discontinued and the firm became part of the United States Glass Company. Early patterns may be listed under Pressed Glass.

DUNCAN & MILLER, Bagware, Cruet Set, Amber Panels, Holder, 5 Piece	90.00 To 110.00
Beaded Swirl, Table Set, Green, Gold Trim, 4 Piece	400.00
Button Panel, Butter, Cover, Gold Trim	62.50
Button Panel, Water Set, Ruby Flash, 6 Piece	435.00
Canterbury, Ashtray, 3 In.	5.00
Canterbury, Bowl, 10 In.	13.00
Canterbury, Candle Block, Pair	25.00
Canterbury, Candy Dish, Cover	17.00
Canterbury, Cocktail Pitcher	28.00
Canterbury, Dish, Pickle, Handles, Crystal	12.00
Canterbury, Goblet, 8 Oz.	8.00
Canterbury, Plate, Chartreuse, 7 1/2 In.	5.00
Canterbury, Relish, Cover, 15 In.	80.00
Canterbury, Tumbler, 8 Oz.	8.00
Canterbury, Vase, 8 1/2 In.	50.00
Canterbury, Vase, Crimped, Opalescent Hob, 8 In.	38.00

Cape Cod, Vase, 4 1/2 In.	30.00
Caribbean, Bowl, Handles, Footed, Blue, 8 In.	30.00
Caribbean, Candlestick, Prisms, Crystal, 7 1/2 In., Pair	20.00
Caribbean, Punch Set, Blue, Underplate, 12 Piece	425.00
Caribbean, Relish, 5 Sections, Blue, 12 3/4 In.	75.00
Caribbean, Syrup, 4 1/2 In.	43.00 To 55.00
Chicken, Salt & Pepper, Metal Heads	500.00
Cloverleaf, Dish, 6 In.	20.00
Cornucopia, Vase, Yellow Opalescent, 8 1/2 In., Pair	150.00
First Love, Bowl, Fluted, 9 In.	48.00
First Love, Candy Dish, 3 Sections, Etched Canterbury	88.00
First Love, Candy Dish, Cover, 3 Sections	88.00
First Love, Decanter, Stopper	165.00
First Love, Goblet, 10 Oz.	14.00 To 20.00
First Love, Mug, Ruby Handle	12.00
First Love, Plate, 7 3/4 In.	6.00
First Love, Sugar, Creamer & Tray	45.00
First Love, Vase, Bud, 9 In.	28.00
Georgian, Claret, Ruby, 4 1/2 Oz.	18.00
Georgian, Cup & Saucer	17.00
Georgian, Sherbet, Green	9.00
Georgian, Sugar & Creamer	35.00
Heart Shape, Bonbon, 6 In.	12.00
Heron, Figurine, Sticker	85.00
Hobnail, Hat, Crystal, 10 In.	65.00
Hobnail, Vase, Flared, Blue, 8 In.	65.00
Hobnail, Vase, Ruffled, Pink, 7 In.	75.00
Indian Tree, Fruit Bowl, Fluted	55.00
Mardi Gras, Claret, 4 Oz.	18.50
Mardi Gras, Cordial, 1 Oz.	38.00
Mardi Gras, Hat, Blue Opalescent	20.00
Mardi Gras, Nappy, 4 1/2 In.	12.00
Mardi Gras, Urn, Cigarette, Steel Body, 3 1/2 In.	28.00
Mardi Gras, Wine	15.00
Radiance, Pitcher, Blown, Sapphire Blue, 1/2 Gal.	95.00
Radiance, Vase, Black, 9 In.	65.00
Sandwich, Banana Boat, Label	215.00
Sandwich, Basket, 11 1/2 In.	70.00
Sandwich, Bowl, 10 In.	35.00
Sandwich, Butter Pat	10.00
Sandwich, Cake Stand	45.00
Sandwich, Coaster, Rayed, 4 1/2 In.	10.00
Sandwich, Compote, Footed, 5 1/2 In.	12.00
Sandwich, Cup	5.00
Sandwich, Epergne, 15 In.	125.00
Sandwich, Finger Bowl	8.00
Sandwich, Ice Cream, 5 Oz.	8.00
Sandwich, Parfait	12.00
Sandwich, Pitcher, Ice Lip, Crystal	90.00
Sandwich, Plate, 8 In.	6.00
Sandwich, Plate, 13 In.	30.00
Sandwich, Plate, Deviled Egg, 12 In.	65.00
Sandwich, Plate, Torte, 12 In.	25.00
Sandwich, Sugar, Creamer & Tray	35.00
Sandwich, Syrup	45.00
Sandwich, Wine, Stemmed	8.00
Sanibel, Plate, Pink Opalescent, 9 1/2 In.	20.00
Spiral Flutes, Bowl, Baked Apple, 7 1/2 In.	12.00
Spiral Flutes, Bowl, Green, 4 1/2 In.	4.00
Spiral Flutes, Bowl, Green, 6 1/2 In.	8.00
Swan, Chartreuse, 7 In.	25.00
Swan, Forest Green, 5 1/2 In.	20.00
Swan, Green, Clear Neck, 12 In.	55.00
Swan, Ruby, 7 In.	15.00

Swan, Ruby, Large	55.00
Swan, Spread Wings, Blue, 11 In.	135.00
Swan, Spread Wings, Opalescent Green	135.00
Teardrop, Ashtray, 3 1/4 In.	35.00
Teardrop, Bowl, 12 In.	32.50
Teardrop, Celery, Crystal	12.00
Teardrop, Cocktail, Liquor	6.00
Teardrop, Cruet, Stopper	18.00
Teardrop, Cup & Saucer	8.00
Teardrop, Plate, 10 1/2 In.	23.00
Teardrop, Plate, Cheese & Cracker	38.00
Teardrop, Plate, Handles, 8 In.	12.50
Teardrop, Relish, 3 Sections, 3 Handles, Cloverleaf Shape	15.00
Teardrop, Relish, Heart Shape	18.00
Teardrop, Salt & Pepper, 3 1/2 In.	18.50

Durand, Vase, Crackle Glass, Spherical Ball, Amber, Opal,
9 1/2 In.

Durand, Vase, 3 Green Arches, Floral, Crystal,
5 1/2 In.

Durand, Vase, Blossoms, Gold Interior, Signed,
6 1/4 In.

Durand, Vase, Crackle Glass, Green, Amber,
Opal, 9 In.

Durand, Vase, King Tut, Silver, Blue,
White Swirls, 7 In.

Durand, Vase, Feather Design, Applied Thread,
Gold, 8 1/2 In., Pair

Durand, Vase, Blue–Green Design, White,
10 In., Pair

Teardrop, Sugar & Creamer	17.00
Teardrop, Sugar, Cover, 6 Oz.	6.00
Teardrop, Sugar, Cover, 8 Oz.	8.00
Teardrop, Tumbler, Footed	10.00

Durand glass was made by Victor Durand from 1879 to 1935 at several factories. Most of the iridescent Durand glass was made by Victor Durand, Jr., from 1912 to 1924 at the Durand Art Glass Works in Vineland, New Jersey.

DURAND, Ashtray, Green, Hat Shape, Match Holder, 5 In.	750.00
Compote, Pale Lime Green Stem & Foot, Blue, Feather Design, 8 In.	725.00
Lamp, Brilliant Blue, Applied Threading, 2 Socket, 24 In.	795.00
Lamp, Mantel, Gold Threading, Green Feather Trim, 13 In., Pair	1200.00
Lamp, Pulled Feathers, Threaded, Table	450.00
Vase, 3 Green Arches, Floral, Crystal, 5 1/2 In. ....*Illus*	330.00
Vase, 3 Pulled Heart–Shaped Blossoms, Signed, 6 1/4 In.	665.00
Vase, Allover Gold King Tut Design, Flared & Ruffled, 4 1/2 In.	875.00
Vase, Allover Undulating Lines, Amber Interior, C.1910, 10 5/8 In.	990.00
Vase, Baluster, Heart & Vine, Everted Lip, Signed, 8 1/4 In.	800.00
Vase, Blossoms, Gold Interior, Signed, 6 1/4 In. ....*Illus*	660.00
Vase, Blue, Colorless Iridized Base, Marked, 12 In.	940.00
Vase, Blue, Wavy Iridescent Band, Ovoid, 5 In.	335.00
Vase, Blue–Green Design, White, 10 In., Pair ....*Illus*	715.00
Vase, Blue–Green, Pulled Arches, Floral Medallions, 5 1/2 In.	335.00
Vase, Burnt Orange Luster, Signed, 6 In.	370.00
Vase, Crackle Glass, Green, Amber, Opal, 9 In. ....*Illus*	500.00
Vase, Crackle Glass, Spherical Ball, Amber, Opal, 9 1/2 In. ....*Illus*	440.00
Vase, Cushion–Form Body, Pale Blue, Signed, C.1920, 10 In.	1045.00
Vase, Egyptian, Green & White Feather Design, Crackle, 8 3/4 In.	960.00
Vase, Feather Design, Applied Thread, Gold, 8 1/2 In., Pair ....*Illus*	1540.00
Vase, Feather Design, Gold Threading, 9 1/2 In.	895.00
Vase, Heart & Vine, Iridescent Blue & White, Signed, 7 1/2 In.	450.00
Vase, Heart & Vine, Orange, Blue Foot, Baluster, 8 1/4 In.	800.00
Vase, Horizontally Hooked & Pulled King Tut, Signed, 8 1/2 In.	1320.00
Vase, King Tut, Silver, Blue, White Swirls, 7 In. ....*Illus*	100.00
Vase, King Tut, Teal, Green, Gold, 8 In.	925.00
Vase, Lady Gay Rose, Shocking Pink, King Tut Pattern, 6 1/2 In.	1575.00
Vase, Pristine Burnt Orange, Signed, 1722, 6 In.	375.00
Vase, Pulled Feather, Allover Applied Thread, Gold, 8 1/2 In.	1540.00
Vase, Spherical Amber Ball, Crackled & Textured, 9 1/2 In.	445.00
Vase, Threaded, Flared Ruffled Rim, Trumpet Shape, 10 In.	305.00
Vase, Trumpet, Threading, Blue Foot, Gold Ground, Signed, 14 In.	800.00
Vase, White & Silver Heart & Vine, Flared Rim, Signed, 6 1/2 In.	1050.00

Elfinware was made from about 1918 to 1940. It is a Dresden–like porcelain that was sold in dime stores and gift shops. Many pieces were decorated with raised flowers. The small pieces are marked with the name "Elfinware" or with a crown and M mark. The words "Germany" or "Made in Germany" also appear on some pieces.

ELFINWARE, Box, Brass, Hinged Cover, China Roses & Daisies, Oval, 4 X 3 In.	75.00
Box, Cover, Florals, 1 1/2 X 2 1/4 In.	35.00
Box, Floral Cover, Violets, Green Leaves, Handles, 2 3/4 X 2 In.	30.00
Box, Flowers On Cover, 2 1/2 X 1 3/4 In.	35.00
Box, Pin, Green Luster, Encrusted Pink Roses, 1 X 1 X 4 In.	25.00
Perfume Bottle, Green Luster, Encrusted Pink Roses, 81/2 In.	75.00
Powder Box, Green Luster, Encrusted Pink Roses, 4 1/2 In.	25.00
Salt & Pepper	35.00
Vase, Allover Floral, 3 1/2 In.	40.00

Elvis Presley, the famous singer, lived from 1935 to 1977. He became famous by 1956. Elvis appeared on television, starred in twenty-seven movies, and performed in Las Vegas. Memorabilia from any of the Presley shows, his records, and even memorials made after his death are collected.

When buying a table, study the bottom. Look underneath the top and see if the legs are original, if the top seems to be in one piece, if there are any unexpected screw or nail holes that indicate changes in the use of the wood.

ELVIS PRESLEY, Bracelet, Ankle, Dog Tag, Wrapper, 1956 .... 22.50
   Card, Gum, Unopened Box, 1978, 36 Packs 23.00
   Card, Playing, 54 Full Color Photos, Box .... 15.00 To 20.00
   Card, Window, Viva Las Vegas 35.00
   Collage, Colorful, Lithograph, Artist, 1978, 21 X 26 In. 5.00
   Decanter, McCormick, No.2 .... 30.00
   Doll, Costume, Eugene, 1984, 12 In. 30.00
   Doll, Graceland, White Suit, Box, 1984, 12 In. 50.00
   Doll, On Music Base, Cassette Hounddog, Box, Vinyl, 21 In. 165.00
   Doll, White, Box, World, 1984 .... 145.00
   Doll, World, 21 In. 95.00
   Figurine, 10 In. 15.00
   Figurine, Porcelain, Avon 25.00
   Game, Welcomes You To His World, Boxcar Enterprises, 1978 .... 100.00
   Hat, Sunburst 125.00
   Hat, Tag, 1956 .... 45.00
   Kimono, Karate 4675.00
   Knife, Pocket, Blue & Red 2.50
   Paper Doll, 1982 .... 25.00
   Paper Doll, Elvis & Priscilla, Outfits From Movies, Uncut 40.00
   Photograph, Autograph, 8 X 10 In. 285.00
   Postcard Set, 1st Concert, Buffalo, N.Y., 1957, 12 Piece 10.00
   Poster, Easy Come, Easy Go, Belgian, 14 X 21 In 25.00
   Poster, Paradise Hawaiian Style, 13 X 30 In 35.00
   Poster, Trouble With Girls, 1969, 14 X 36 In. 50.00
   Poster, Trouble With Girls, 1969, 30 X 40 In. 50.00
   Radio, 8 In. Elvis On Top, Box 45.00
   Radio, Elvis, Box 35.00
   Rug Square, From Graceland, With Certificate, 1 In. 20.00
   Sheet Music, Doncha' Think It's Time?, 1958 .... 30.00
   Sheet Music, Love Me Tender 20.00
   Sheet Music, Shoppin Around, G.I. Blues 15.00
   Toothpick 18.00
   Watch, Pocket .... 30.00 To 35.00

In the eighteenth and nineteenth centuries, workmen from Russia, France, England, and other countries made small boxes and table pieces of enamel on metal. One form of English enamel is called "Battersea" and is listed under that name. There was a revival of interest in enameling in the thirties and a new style evolved.

ENAMEL, Bowl, Silver, Copper Insert, 4 In. 150.00
   Case, Cigarette, Black, Envelope Style, Red Stone 15.00
   Cup & Saucer, Flowers, Brown Panels, Twisted Handle, Germany, Octagon 25.00
   Koosch, Silver, Russia 300.00
   Pitcher, Floral, Amethyst, Fluted Top, Tall 220.00
   Salt, On Silver Gilt, Ball Feet, Multicolor, Russian, Spoon, 1 3/8 In. 450.00
   Salt, Raised Wire Work, 3 Ball Feet, Marked 84, Russian 325.00
   Sedan, Beveled Glass Windows, Procede Brevete, French, 6 3/4 In. 475.00

Shot Glass, Flowers, Leaves & Dots, 5–Color, Russian, 1 1/4 In.	350.00
Shot Glass, New Orleans, Black	10.00
Spoon, Seashore Top, Ornate, Allover Enameled	75.00
Sugar Basket, Creamer, Silver–Gilt, 1910, Russian, 3 5/8 In., 2 Pc.	8500.00
Teapot, Iron, Oval, Decorated Pewter & Copper Handle, 8 X 10 In.	295.00
Vase, Cover, Blue & White Geometric Design, Camille Faure, 13 In.	4400.00

ES Germany porcelain was made at the factory of Erdmann Schlegelmilch from 1861 to 1925 in Suhl, Germany. The porcelain was sold decorated or undecorated. Other pieces were made at the factory in Saxony, Prussia, and are marked "ES Prussia." Reinhold Schlegelmilch, a brother, made the famous wares marked "RS Germany."

ES GERMANY, Celery, Bird On Vines, 12 In.	55.00
Chocolate Set, Pink & Yellow Mums, Royal Saxe Mark, 11 Piece	325.00
Plate, Portrait, Cobalt Border, 11 1/4 In.	225.00
Plate, Portrait, Gold Tracery, Mother–of–Pearl Ground, 11 In.	197.50
Plate, Woman With Black Feathered Hat In Center, 9 1/2 In.	35.00
Tray, Dresser, Woman, Holly Crown, Red Ground, 8 In.	70.00
Tray, Pin, Indian Portrait of Spotted Horse, 4 In.	75.00
Vase, Lady With Peacock, Marked, 8 In.	395.00
Vase, Woman Holding Flowers, Green Pearlized Ground, 12 In.	165.00

All types of Eskimo artifacts are collected. Carvings of whale or walrus teeth are listed under Scrimshaw. Baskets are in the Basket category. All other types of Eskimo art are listed here.

ESKIMO, Awl, Bone, Polished, Etched Lines, 10 In.	125.00
Cribbage Board, Walrus Tusk, Ivory, 8 1/2 In.	110.00
Doll, Feathers, Fur, 8 In.	15.00
Effigy, Fish, Carved Bone, 4 1/8 In.	30.00
Figure, 3 Seals, Green Stone, Signed Thomassie Toak, '74, 12 In.	325.00
Figure, Eskimo & Child, Carved Stone, 2 3/4 In.	117.50
Harpoon, 1 Barb, Bone, Hole For Attachment, 8 1/2 In.	500.00
Harpoon, Bone, Wooden Handle & Sheath, 12 3/4 In.	90.00
Kayak, Ivory, Eskimo & Seal, Signed Paul Nattanguk, 6 1/2 In.	75.00
Lamp, Stone, Finial Handle, 5 1/2 In.	45.00
Mittens, Fur, Leather, 9 3/4 In., Pair	15.00
Napkin Ring, Ivory, Relief Carving, 1920s	35.00
Pendant, Ivory, 4 Etched Lines, Drilled Hole, 3 1/4 In.	50.00
Photograph, Eskimo, Spear, In Christmas Card, Nome, Framed, 5 X 10 In.	25.00
Saw, Serrated Edge, Drilled Hole, 8 In.	100.00
Toy, Sled, From Jaw Bone, Baleen Strips, 12 1/2 In.	40.00
Tusk, Walrus, Dog Sled & 5 Huskies, 12 3/8 In.	225.00
Whistle, Bone, 2 3/4 In.	75.00

ФАБЕРЖЕ **КФ** Faberge was a firm of jewelers and goldsmiths founded in St. Petersburg, Russia, in 1842, by Gustav Faberge. Peter Carl Faberge, his son, was jeweler to the Russian Imperial Court from about 1870 to 1914.

FABERGE, Frame, Gold Enameled, Rose Diamond, Floral, C.1900	7700.00
Kovsh, Enameled, Silver, 4 In.	3500.00
Liqueur Decanter, Enameled	1500.00

Definitions of the words differentiating the types of pottery and porcelain are difficult because there is so much overlapping of meaning. Faience is tin–glazed earthenware, especially the wares made in France, Germany, and Scandinavia. It is also correct to say that faience is the same as majolica or Delft, although usually the term refers only to the tin–glazed pottery of the three regions mentioned.

Don't store alcoholic beverages or perfume in silver. It will cause damage.

If you want to use a valuable Chinese export punch bowl at a party, try this: Buy a piece of lightweight clear plastic hose at a hardware store. Slit the hose and use it to protect the rim of the bowl from the punch ladle.

Faience, Vase, Mermaid, Yellow To Brown, Marked, C.1905, 12 1/2 In.

FAIENCE, Candlestick, Rampant Lions, Shield & Helmet Socket, 11 In., Pair	650.00
Charger, Polychrome Scene of Mounted Figure, French, 13 In.	110.00
Compote, Swan Ends, Boat Shape, 8 1/4 In.	25.00
Cruet, Pear Shape, Floral Design, C.1750, 5 In., Pair	137.50
Figurine, Bird, Red & Blue, Gilt Trim, French, 7 1/4 In.	25.00
Figurine, Courting Couple, J.D'Aste, 15 In.	209.00
Figurine, Lion, Seated, Open Mouths, Oriental Style, 11 X 11 In., Pr.	1760.00
Inkwell, Polychrome Flowers, C.1750, 5 In.	330.00
Jar, Tin Glaze, Drilled & Fitted As Lamp, 23 In.	15.00
Jug, Floral Spray, Pewter Hinged Lid & Foot, German, 13 In.	121.00
Plaque, Old Foley, Oliver Twist, Bowl In Hand, 1892, 12 1/2 In.	250.00
Plate, Cupid & Psyche Polychrome, Marked France, 12 3/8 In.	95.00
Plate, Floral Bird Design, Off-White, 16 In.	150.00
Platter, Central Flowers, Banded Rim, Polychrome, C.1750, 18 In.	445.00
Platter, Stylized Design, Fluted Surface, Berain, C.1730, 15 In.	495.00
Sauceboat, Double Lipped, Shell & Flower Design, 8 1/2 In.	165.00
Tile, Coat of Arms, Lion, Flint	75.00
Trivet, Stylized Floral Border, Rouen, C.1750, 10 In.	385.00
Vase, Alligatored Blue Matte Glaze, Calif., 5 In.	160.00
Vase, Cylinder, Applied Floral Design, C.1880, 8 In.	350.00
Vase, Mermaid, Yellow To Brown, Marked, C.1905, 12 1/2 In. ......*Illus*	300.00

 Fairings are small souvenir china boxes and figurines that were sold at country fairs during the nineteenth century. Most were made in Germany. Reproductions of fairings are being made, especially of the famous "twelve months of marriage" series.

FAIRING, Box, Man Married, Trouble Begins	125.00
Box, Who Said Rats?	95.50
Figurine, Cats, Leave A Drop	135.00 To 150.00
Figurine, Man Married, Trouble Begins	115.00
Figurine, Who Said Rats?	95.50
Trinket Box, Boy Holding Grapes, Germany, Marked	40.00 To 75.00
Trinket Box, Little Red Riding Hood & Wolf	60.00
Trinket Box, Little Red Riding Hood & Wolf, Worn Paint	60.00
FAMILLE ROSE, see Chinese Export	

Fans have been used for cooling since the days of the ancients. By the eighteenth century, the fan was an accessory for the lady of fashion and very elaborate and expensive fans were made. Sticks were made of ivory or wood, set with jewels or carved. The fans were made of painted silk or paper. Inexpensive paper fans printed with advertising were giveaways in the late nineteenth and early twentieth centuries. Electric fans were introduced in 1882.

FAN, Advertising, Artic Ice Cream, Paper	18.00
Advertising, Bell Telephone Co., Baseball Shape	125.00
Advertising, Dr Pepper	48.00
Advertising, Havana Cuba, Wood & Paper, 4 X 8 In.	75.00

Advertising, Miss Liberty 1 Side, Gas Station Ad On Other Side 30.00
Advertising, Patriotic Girl, Soda, Cardboard 9.00
Advertising, Putnam Dyes, Nouveau Style Butterfly, Pastel 12.00
Advertising, Putnam Dyes, Peacock 14.00
Advertising, RCA Radio, Shape of Antenna, Die Cut, Baseball Player 165.00
Advertising, Shoe, Cowgirl, Annie Oakley Type, 1908 .... 22.00
Advertising, Visit Carranza's Fan Store, Habana, Wood, Paper, 8 In. 115.00
Blue Satin, Embroidered Red Roses, Blue & White Handles, Large 65.00
Electric, A.C.Gilbert, Polar Club, No.6 .... 70.00
Electric, Bank Teller's, Copper Cage, 3 Speeds, 9 In. 475.00
Electric, Ceiling, Airplane, Chicago Arrow, Restored 1750.00
Electric, Ceiling, Fan–O–Plane, Art Deco Airplane 525.00
Electric, Ceiling, Porcelain Housing 85.00
Electric, Polar Cub, 8 In. 25.00
Electric, Ribbonaire, Safety 295.00
Electric, Star Rite, 10 In. 15.00
Electric, Upright Dome, Brass Cage 450.00
Electric, Westinghouse, Brass Guard & Blades, Oscillating, 13 In. 50.00
Hand Painted Flowers, Satin 50.00
Hassock, Art Deco 55.00
Haynes Motor Cars, Paper, Flag, Cigar 10.00
Hot Air, Air From Kerosene Lamp 3190.00
Hot Air, Lake Breeze, 21 In.–Blades 2500.00
Hot Air, Lake Breeze, Fuel Burner, Brass Blade, Wm. Strong Mfg. Co. 3500.00
Hot Air, Lake Breeze, Table Model, Stein Co., Brass, Restored, 15 In. 550.00
Ivory & Lace, Framed, C.1890 .... 125.00
Ivory Blades, Painted Court Figures, Ivory Faces, Box, C.1900, 11 In. 275.00
Ivory, Sheer Silk With Flowers, Wide Lace, 14 X 26 In. 50.00
Knapp, Model B, Battery Operated 375.00
New York, Theater, 3 Panels, 1910 .... 8.00
Oilcloth Circle Fold, Red Snowflake 23.00
Oriental, Silk Floral, Bamboo Handle, Silk Tassel 7.00
Ostrich Feathers, Black Carved Wooden Sticks, 11 X 23 In. .... 85.00 To 95.00
Ostrich, Floral Embossed Sticks, Flapper–Type 55.00
Painted Court Figures, Ivory Faces, Chinese Lacquer & Silk, C.1900 .... 135.00
Painting of Birds & Flowers, Tortoiseshell Blades, Silk, 12 In. 65.00
Polar Cub, Iron, Decals, 6 In. 75.00
Silk, Children's Tea, Peacocks, Doves, Garden, Wooden, 25 1/2 X 13 In. 127.50
Steam Powered, Brass Cage, Table Model, Restored, 16 In. 975.00
Water Powered, Brass, 9 In. 350.00
Whalebone, Wooden Handle, 1820, 14 1/2 In. 2530.00
White Goose Feather, Flat 8.50

> Federzeichnung is the very strange German name for a pattern of
> mother–of–pearl satin glass. The pattern had irregularly shaped
> sections of brown glass covered with a pattern of gold squiggle lines.
> It was first made in the late nineteenth century.

FEDERZEICHNUNG, Vase, Gold Enamel, Maze of Air Traps, 7 In. 1215.00
Vase, Mother–of–Pearl, Gold Tracery, L5 X 5 1/2 In. 1875.00

> Fenton Art Glass Company, founded in Martins Ferry, Ohio, by
> Frank L. Fenton, is now located in Williamstown, West Virginia. It
> is noted for early carnival glass produced between 1907 and 1920.
> Many other types of glass were also made.

FENTON, Alley Cat, Red Carnival 75.00
Amber Crest, Bonbon, Tricorner, 5 1/2 In. 14.00
Amber Crest, Plate, 8 1/2 In. 30.00
Apple Blossom, Compote, Footed, Low 40.00
Aqua Crest, Bonbon, 6 In. 12.00
Aqua Crest, Bowl, 7 1/2 In. 25.00
Aqua Crest, Bowl, 10 In. 65.00
Aqua Crest, Bowl, 11 1/2 In. .... 75.00 To 85.00
Aqua Crest, Cake Plate 55.00
Aqua Crest, Candleholder Vase, 4 1/2 In. 18.00

Aqua Crest, Server, 2 Tiers	42.50
Aqua Crest, Vase, 4 1/2 In.	13.00
Aqua Crest, Vase, Crimped, 5 In.	25.00
Aqua Crest, Vase, Tricorner, 5 1/2 In.	24.00
Aqua Crest, Vase, Tricorner, 6 1/2 In.	40.00
Aqua Crest, Vase, Tulip, 8 1/2 In.	35.00
Beaded Melon, Creamer, Handle, Green, 4 In.	22.00
Beaded Melon, Jug, Green Overlay, Handle	45.00
Beaded Melon, Vase, Green Overlay, 9 In.	28.00
Beaded Melon, Vase, Green, 3 1/2 In.	17.00
Beaded Melon, Vase, Tulip, Rose Overlay	45.00
Beaded Melon, Vase, Tulip, Yellow Inside, White Outside, 6 1/2 In.	45.00
Blue Dogwood, Lamp, Hurricane, Candle	45.00
Bubble Optic, Vase, Apple Green, 11 1/2 In.	275.00
Bubble Optic, Vase, Windows, Gold Overlay, 11 1/2 In.	145.00
Burmese, Box, Candy, Ogee, Cover, On Base, Blue	140.00
Burmese, Candy Box, Ogee, Blue, 3 Piece	130.00
Burmese, Creamer, Maple Leaf	35.00
Burmese, Figurine, Fawn	22.50
Burmese, Lamp, Fairy, Rose, 2 Piece	50.00
Burmese, Mug, Butterfly	75.00
Burmese, Rose Bowl	30.00
Burmese, Vase, Rose, 5 In.	50.00
Burmese, Vase, Rose, 10 In.	90.00
Burmese, Vase, Rose, Bowknot Tulip, Made For Levay, 8 In.	95.00
Burmese, Vase, Roses, 7 In.	42.00
Butterfly & Berry, Bonbon, Blue	42.00
Butterfly, Bonbon, Lime Green	20.00
Caprice, Vase, Mulberry, 7 In.	30.00
Chinese, Bowl, Cupped, Yellow, 6 1/2 In.	40.00
Coin Dot, Basket, Cranberry, 7 In.	85.00 To 125.00
Coin Dot, Bowl, Blue Opalescent, 10 In.	80.00
Coin Dot, Bowl, Cranberry, 10 In.	120.00
Coin Dot, Bowl, Green, 6 In.	75.00
Coin Dot, Bowl, Lime Green, 6 In.	75.00
Coin Dot, Bowl, Topaz, 7 In.	58.00
Coin Dot, Creamer, Blue Opalescent, Handle	24.00
Coin Dot, Creamer, Logo, Persian Blue	30.00
Coin Dot, Lamp, Boudoir, Cranberry Opalescent, Pearlized, Pair	275.00
Coin Dot, Lamp, Cranberry, 20 In.	180.00
Coin Dot, Top Hat, Blue Opalescent	20.00
Coin Dot, Tumbler, Cranberry, Footed, 5 1.4 In.	30.00
Coin Dot, Vase, Blue, 10 In.	75.00
Coin Dot, Vase, Cranberry, 5 In.	85.00
Coin Dot, Vase, Cranberry, 7 In.	60.00 To 95.00
Coin Dot, Vase, Cranberry, 10 In.	135.00
Coin Dot, Vase, Flared, Cranberry, 6 In.	125.00
Coin Dot, Vase, French, Opalescent, 4 In.	25.00
Coin Dot, Vase, Lime Green, 8 1/2 In.	200.00
Coin Dot, Vase, Ruffled, Cranberry, 5 In.	45.00
Coin Dot, Vase, Tulip, Blue, 10 1/2 In.	37.50
Crystal Crest, Bowl, 10 In.	50.00
Crystal Crest, Plate, 10 1/4 In.	18.00
Crystal Crest, Tray, Tidbit, 2 Tiers, Crystal	30.00
Daisy & Button, Bowl, Peking Blue, Oval	38.00
Daisy & Button, Cup & Saucer, Amber	20.00
Daisy & Fern, Iced Tea Set, Cranberry, 7 Piece	565.00
Daisy & Fern, Pitcher, Water, Cranberry	250.00
Daisy & Fern, Pitcher, Water, Opalescent	250.00
Diamond Lace, Console Set, Blue Opalescent, 3 Piece	108.00
Diamond Lace, Epergne, Blue Opalescent, 4 Piece	60.00
Diamond Optic, Compote, Ruby, Dolphin Handle	45.00
Diamond Optic, Jug, Ruby Overlay, Handle, 8 In.	70.00
Dolphin Handle, Candy Dish, Pink Stretch, 9 In.	60.00

Dolphin, Bowl, Jade, Footed, 11 In. 35.00
Dot Optic, Basket, Cranberry, Medium 95.00
Dot Optic, Bowl, Ruby, 7 X 3 In. 35.00
Dot Optic, Bride's Basket, Cranberry 80.00
Dot Optic, Creamer, Cranberry, Tall .... 75.00 To 80.00
Dot Optic, Lamp, Hurricane, Blue Opalescent 90.00
Dot Optic, Pitcher, Blue, 9 In. 125.00
Dot Optic, Pitcher, Cranberry 125.00
Dot Optic, Pitcher, Green, 9 In. 125.00
Dot Optic, Vase, Cranberry, 8 3/4 In. 120.00
Ebony, Vase, Pedestal, Crimped, Label, 8 1/4 In. 30.00
Emerald Crest, Cruet, Oil 20.00
Emerald Crest, Flowerpot, With Liner 60.00
Emerald Crest, Mayonnaise Set, 3 Piece 45.00
Emerald Crest, Server, Tidbit, 2-Tier 55.00
Emerald Crest, Vase, 3 1/2 In. 13.00
Fern Optic, Fairy Light, Blue Opalescent 70.00
Florentine, Candlestick, Green, Pair 200.00
Georgian, Cup & Saucer, Ruby 17.00
Georgian, Sugar & Creamer, Ruby 35.00
Gold Crest, Top Hat, Crimped 12.00
Gold Crest, Vase, Triangle, 8 In. 20.00
Gone With The Wind, Lamp, Blue Satin Glass, 24 In. 225.00
Grape & Cable, Bowl, Orange, Footed 95.00
Hobnail, Banana Bowl, Pink, 12 In. 38.00
Hobnail, Basket, Cranberry Opalescent, 7 In. 45.00
Hobnail, Basket, French Opalescent, 7 In. 30.00
Hobnail, Basket, Green, 7 1/2 In. 95.00
Hobnail, Basket, Ruffled, Milk Glass, 11 In. 25.00
Hobnail, Bonbon, Triangular, Blue, 6 In. 15.00
Hobnail, Bottle, Blue, 4 1/2 In. 35.00
Hobnail, Bowl, French Opalescent, Footed, 11 In. 55.00
Hobnail, Bowl, Light Blue, Crimped, Opalescent, 7 In. 18.00
Hobnail, Bowl, Ruffled & Crimped, Cranberry, 10 In. 45.00
Hobnail, Candleholder, Cornucopia, Blue Opalescent 12.00
Hobnail, Candleholder, Topaz, Opalescent 60.00
Hobnail, Compote, Milk Glass, 8 In. 27.00
Hobnail, Compote, Topaz Opalescent, Footed, 6 1/2 In. 40.00
Hobnail, Cornucopia, French Opalescent, Miniature 15.00
Hobnail, Creamer, Amber, Miniature 10.00
Hobnail, Creamer, Footed, French Opalescent 10.00
Hobnail, Cruet, Bulbous, Cranberry 90.00
Hobnail, Cruet, Cranberry Opalescent 40.00
Hobnail, Epergne, Jack-In-The-Pulpit, Pink, 10 In., 4 Piece 60.00
Hobnail, Epergne, Plum Opalescent, 4 Piece 135.00
Hobnail, Fairy Lamp, Blue 15.00
Hobnail, Goblet, Milk Glass, 6 In. 15.00
Hobnail, Jug, Cranberry, Handle, 4 1/2 In. .... 50.00 To 85.00
Hobnail, Lamp, 2-Light, Cranberry, 27 In. 600.00
Hobnail, Lamp, Courting, Amber 45.00
Hobnail, Lamp, Cranberry Opalescent 135.00
Hobnail, Pitcher, Ice Lip, Large 45.00
Hobnail, Relish, Milk Glass, Chrome Handle 18.00
Hobnail, Relish, Milk Glass, Divided, Oval, 12 In. 28.00
Hobnail, Salt & Pepper, Cranberry 75.00
Hobnail, Spooner, Flat 35.00
Hobnail, Sugar & Creamer, Blue Opalescent, Miniature 20.00
Hobnail, Syrup, Cranberry Opalescent, 5 1/2 In. 58.00
Hobnail, Syrup, Cranberry, 5 1/2 In. 85.00
Hobnail, Vanity Set, French Opalescent, 3 Piece 65.00
Hobnail, Vase, Blue Opalescent, 6 In. 30.00
Hobnail, Vase, Cranberry Opalescent, 5 1/2 In. 58.00
Hobnail, Vase, Crimped Top, Cranberry Red, 12 In. 75.00
Hobnail, Vase, Flared, Cranberry, 8 1/2 In. 165.00

Hobnail, Vase, French Opalescent, 5 1/2 In.	35.00
Hobnail, Vase, Medium Green, Opalescent, 6 1/2 In.	60.00
Hobnail, Vase, Topaz Opalescent, Squatty, 5 1/2 In.	75.00
Honeycomb & Clover, Butter, Cover	275.00
Honeycomb & Clover, Water Set, 7 Piece	695.00
Inverted Thumbprint, Cruet	65.00
Inverted Thumbprint, Syrup	55.00
Ivory Crest, Vase, Violet, Square, 5 In.	28.00
Ivy, Basket, Green	250.00
Jamestown, Vase, Blue, 12 In.	88.00
Leaf Tiers, Rose Bowl, French Opalescent, Footed, Large	90.00
Lincoln Inn, Compote, Dark Green	65.00
Lincoln Inn, Cup & Saucer, Pink	22.50
Lincoln Inn, Cup & Saucer, Royal Blue	25.00
Lincoln Inn, Goblet, Water, Dark Green	20.00
Lincoln Inn, Match Holder, Ribbed, Blue	20.00
Lincoln Inn, Nut, Handle, Pink	35.00
Lincoln Inn, Plate, Aqua, 6 In.	10.00
Lincoln Inn, Plate, Red, 8 In.	8.00
Lincoln Inn, Salt, Black	125.00
Lincoln Inn, Saucer, Fruit, Pink, 5 In.	45.00
Lincoln Inn, Shaker, Black, Pair	250.00
Lincoln Inn, Tumbler, Cream	6.00
Lincoln Inn, Tumbler, Ruby, Footed, 7 Oz.	10.00
Lincoln Inn, Vase, Jade, 10 In.	175.00
Lincoln Inn, Water Set, Amethyst Carnival, 7 Piece	165.00
Moss Rose, Pitcher, Milk	60.00
Moss Rose, Sugar Shaker	38.00
Orange Tree, Mug, Marigold	30.00
Panther, Berry Bowl, Marigold	55.00
Peach Crest, Basket, Tall	90.00
Peach Crest, Bowl, 10 In.	68.00
Peach Crest, Jug, Beaded Melon, White Handle, 6 In.	48.00
Peach Crest, Jug, Beaded Melon, White Handle, 7 In.	60.00
Peach Crest, Jug, Handle, 8 1/2 In.	55.00
Peach Crest, Rose Bowl, 3 1/2 In.	37.00
Peach Crest, Vase, 6 1/2 In.	45.00
Peach Crest, Vase, 8 In.	58.00
Peach Crest, Vase, Beaded Melon, 6 In.	48.00
Peach Crest, Vase, Crimped, 6 In.	30.00
Peach Crest, Vase, Double Crimp, 6 1/4 In.	20.00
Peach Crest, Vase, Tulip, 9 In.	45.00
Peacock, Vase, Custard, 8 In.	40.00
Peacock, Vase, Mongolian Green, 7 1/2 In.	150.00
Peacock, Vase, Topaz, Flared	38.00
Persian Medallion, Basket, Blue	35.00
Persian Medallion, Basket, Lime Green	28.00
Persian Medallion, Compote, Blue Opalescent	16.00
Persian Medallion, Compote, Lime Green	18.00
Persian Medallion, Lamp, Fairy	45.00
Persian Medallion, Plate, Iridescent, 9 In.	35.00
Plum, Decanter, Hobnail	235.00
Plymouth, Champagne, Red	10.00 To 12.50
Plymouth, Goblet, Water, Ruby, 9 Oz.	8.00 To 17.50
Plymouth, Goblet, Wine	14.00
Plymouth, Ice Tea, Red, 6 In.	15.00
Plymouth, Juice, Flat, Red	15.00
Prayer Rug, Plate, Custard	20.00
Rosalene, Bird, Small	25.00
Rosalene, Bonbon, Butterfly	26.00
Rosalene, Candleholder, Pair	60.00
Rosalene, Epergne, 3 Lilies, Center Bowl, 13 In.	395.00
Rosalene, Epergne, 4 Lilies, Large	250.00
Rose Bowl, Peachblow	30.00

Rose Crest, Jug, Handle, 9 In.	45.00
Silver Crest, Banana Bowl, Footed	25.00
Silver Crest, Basket, Handle, 6 1/2 In.	25.00
Silver Crest, Basket, Paisley, 8 In.	28.00
Silver Crest, Bowl, Footed, 8 1/4 In.	18.00
Silver Crest, Cake Plate, 13 In.	28.00
Silver Crest, Cake Stand, Footed, Spanish Lace, 11 In.	25.00
Silver Crest, Candleholder, 6 In.	15.00
Silver Crest, Compote, Ruffled, 4 In.	10.00
Silver Crest, Compote, Square, 9 In.	35.00
Silver Crest, Epergne, 12 X 14 In., 5 Piece	45.00
Silver Crest, Plate, 8 1/2 In.	12.00
Silver Crest, Plate, 15 In.	38.00
Silver Crest, Relish, Heart Shape	28.00
Silver Crest, Tidbit, 2–Tier, 6 In.	22.50
Silver Crest, Tidbit, 2–Tier, 8 In.	45.00
Silver Crest, Tidbit, 3–Tier	45.00
Silver Crest, Top Hat	25.00
Silver Crest, Tray, Sandwich, Chrome Holder	28.00
Silver Crest, Vase, Hat, 4 In.	18.00
Silver Crest, Vase, Spanish Lace, Label, 8 In.	20.00
Snow Crest, Compote, Green, 6 In.	65.00
Snow Crest, Lamp, Hurricane, Dark Green, 2 Piece	85.00
Snow Crest, Vase, Amber Swirl, 5 In.	50.00
Snow Crest, Vase, Spiral Optic, Cranberry Opalescent, 8 3/4 In.	90.00
Snowflake, Rose Bowl, Cobalt Blue	48.00
Sophisticated Ladies, Vase, Black, Limited Edition, 11 In.	175.00
Spanish Lace, Pitcher, Water, Pearl Iridescent	48.00
Spiral Optic, Basket, Blue Opalescent, Ribbed, 7 In.	32.00
Spiral Optic, Vase, French Opalescent, Flared, 1939, 7 In.	40.00
Swan & Cattails, Vase, Topaz	28.00
Swan, Mug, Topaz	29.00
Swirl, Pitcher, Water, Amber, Peach	65.00
Swirl, Vase, Hat, Blue Opalescent	50.00
Swirled Rib, Vase, Emerald Green, White Trim Ruffled Top, 7 1/2 In.	45.00
Teardrop, Salt & Pepper, Green	20.00
Velva Rose, Vase, Stretch, 5 In.	35.00
Vintage, Vase, Hand Painted	8.00
Waterlily & Cattails, Pitcher, Water, Blue	395.00
Waterlily & Cattails, Rose Bowl, Amethyst Opalescent, Large	60.00
Waterlily, Cake Plate, Crystal	35.00
Waterlily, Compote, Cupped, Ruby	35.00
Waterlily, Compote, Footed, Lime Green	20.00
Waterlily, Pitcher, Lime Green	25.00

fiesta

Fiesta, the colorful dinnerware, was introduced in 1936 by the Homer Laughlin China Co., redesigned in 1969, and withdrawn in 1973. The simple design was characterized by a band of concentric circles, beginning at the rim. Cups had full–circle handles until 1969, when partial–circle handles were made. Harlequin and Riviera were related wares. For more information and prices of American dinnerware, see the book "Kovels' Depression Glass & American Dinnerware Price List."

FIESTA, Ashtray, Rose	45.00
Ashtray, Yellow	30.00
Bowl, Dessert, Light Green, 6 In.	18.00
Bowl, Fruit, Light Green, 11 3/4 In.	75.00
Bowl, Fruit, Medium Green, 5 1/2 In.	50.00
Bowl, Fruit, Turquoise, 11 3/4 In.	90.00
Bowl, Mixing, Cobalt Blue, 11 1/2 In.	135.00
Bowl, Mixing, No.3, Cobalt Blue, 7 In.	55.00
Bowl, Mixing, No.3, Red, 7 In.	55.00
Bowl, Mixing, No.4, Yellow, 8 In.	48.50
Bowl, Mixing, No.5, Red, 9 In.	70.00

Bowl, Salad, Individual, Turquoise, 5 1/8 In.	30.00
Bowl, Salad, Individual, Yellow, 7 5/8 In.	42.00
Bowl, Salad, Yellow, Footed	150.00
Cake Plate, Green, Kitchen Kraft	25.00
Candleholder, Bulb, Light Green, Pair	35.00 To 45.00
Candleholder, Bulb, Red, Pair	45.00
Candleholder, Bulb, Yellow, Pair	26.50
Candleholder, Yellow, Tripod, Pair	150.00
Carafe, Light Green	95.00 To 100.00
Carafe, Red	125.00
Carafe, Turquoise	110.00
Casserole, Cobalt Blue, Cover	100.00
Casserole, Kitchen Kraft, Green, Individual	125.00
Casserole, Kitchen Kraft, Red, Individual	135.00
Casserole, Kitchen Kraft, Yellow, Individual	125.00
Casserole, Medium Green, Cover	265.00
Casserole, Red, Cover	30.00
Casserole, Turquoise, Cover	85.00
Chop Plate, Chartreuse, 15 In.	40.00
Chop Plate, Light Green, 13 In.	16.00
Chop Plate, Old Ivory, 15 In.	26.00
Chop Plate, Red, 13 In.	20.00 To 25.00
Chop Plate, Red, 15 In.	30.00
Chop Plate, Rose, 13 In.	40.00
Chop Plate, Turkey Design, 15 In.	120.00
Chop Plate, Yellow, 15 In.	21.50
Coffee Server, Gold, Marmalade	30.00
Coffee Server, Marmalade, Gold, Ironstone	30.00
Coffeepot, Cobalt Blue	80.00
Coffeepot, Light Green, After Dinner	100.00
Coffeepot, Old Ivory, After Dinner	45.00
Coffeepot, Red, After Dinner	125.00
Coffeepot, Yellow	90.00
Compote, Fruit, Cobalt Blue, 12 In.	65.00
Compote, Fruit, Red, Footed, 12 In.	75.00
Compote, Fruit, Yellow, Footed, 12 In.	55.00
Compote, Sweet, Light Green	30.00
Compote, Sweet, Yellow	33.00
Creamer, Forest Green	20.00
Creamer, Medium Green	30.00
Creamer, Rose	20.00
Creamer, Stick Handle, Light Green	16.00 To 24.00
Creamer, Stick Handle, Yellow	24.00
Cup & Saucer, Chartreuse	16.00
Cup & Saucer, Ivory, After Dinner	37.00
Cup & Saucer, Light Green, After Dinner	25.00
Cup & Saucer, Medium Green	30.00
Cup & Saucer, Red	18.00
Cup & Saucer, Rose	16.00
Cup & Saucer, Yellow	28.00
Cup, Cobalt Blue	10.00
Cup, Medium Green	35.00
Eggcup, Chartreuse	40.00 To 45.00
Eggcup, Cobalt Blue	45.00
Eggcup, Red	25.00 To 45.00
Gravy Boat, Gray	35.00
Gravy Boat, Light Green	18.00
Gravy Boat, Old Ivory	18.00
Gravy Boat, Red	35.00 To 40.00
Jar, Light Green, Cover, Kitchen Kraft, Large	375.00
Jar, Yellow, Cover, Kitchen Kraft, Medium	275.00
Jug, Cobalt Blue, 2 Pt.	55.00
Jug, Gray, 2 Pt.	65.00
Mug, Chartreuse	30.00

Mug, Medium Green	78.00
Mug, Old Ivory	45.00
Mug, Rose	55.00
Mug, Yellow	27.00
Mustard, Light Green	85.00
Mustard, Red	100.00
Nappy, Yellow, 8 1/2 In.	12.00
Pie Plate, Cobalt Blue, 10 In.	30.00
Pie Plate, Yellow, Kitchen Kraft, 10 In.	18.00 To 25.00
Pitcher, Disc, Forest Green	145.00
Pitcher, Disc, Juice, Red, 30 Oz.	90.00 To 150.00
Pitcher, Disc, Juice, Yellow, 30 Oz.	40.00
Pitcher, Disc, Turquoise, 2 Qt.	35.00
Pitcher, Disc, Water, Navy	30.00
Plate, Chartreuse, 7 In.	12.00
Plate, Chartreuse, 9 In.	15.00 To 17.00
Plate, Chartreuse, 10 In.	20.00
Plate, Cobalt Blue, 6 In.	5.00
Plate, Cobalt Blue, 9 In.	7.00
Plate, Cobalt Blue, 10 In.	18.00
Plate, Forest Green, 6 In.	8.00
Plate, Forest Green, 9 In.	17.00
Plate, Forest Green, 10 In.	35.00
Plate, Gray, 10 In.	30.00
Plate, Light Green, 9 In.	5.00
Plate, Light Green, 10 In.	14.00
Plate, Medium Green, 6 In.	12.00
Plate, Medium Green, 9 In.	20.00 To 30.00
Plate, Rose, 6 In.	8.00
Plate, Rose, 9 In.	17.00
Plate, Turquoise, 9 In.	5.00
Plate, Yellow, 7 In.	6.00
Plate, Yellow, 9 In.	9.00
Plate, Yellow, 10 In.	18.00
Platter, Chartreuse, Oval, 12 In.	35.00
Platter, Gray, Oval, 12 In.	32.00
Platter, Light Green, Oval, 12 In.	28.00
Platter, Red, Oval, 12 In.	30.00
Platter, Rose, Oval, 12 In.	20.00
Platter, Turquoise, Oval, 12 In.	12.00
Relish, Light Green, 5 Multicolored Inserts	95.00
Relish, Red, 5 Multicolored Inserts	105.00
Relish, Turquoise, 5 Multicolored Inserts	90.00
Salt & Pepper, Red, Kitchen Kraft	95.00
Salt & Pepper, Yellow	10.00 To 12.00
Sauceboat, Forest Green	35.00
Saucer, Gray	4.00
Saucer, Red	8.00
Saucer, Turquoise	6.00
Soup, Cream, Cobalt Blue	21.00
Soup, Cream, Old Ivory	32.00
Soup, Cream, Rose	21.00
Soup, Onion, Light Green, Cover	285.00
Soup, Onion, Red, Cover	475.00
Soup, Onion, Yellow, Cover	140.00
Stack Set, Yellow, Kitchen Kraft, 4 Piece	125.00
Sugar & Creamer, Figure 8 Tray, Yellow, Individual	125.00
Sugar & Creamer, Red, Cover	45.00
Sugar & Creamer, Rose	20.00
Sugar, Chartreuse, Open	15.00
Sugar, Cobalt Blue	12.00
Sugar, Medium Green, Cover	20.00
Sugar, Red, Cover	26.00
Sugar, Turquoise, Cover	7.00

Sugar, Yellow, Cover	7.00
Syrup, Cobalt Blue	175.00
Syrup, Light Green	100.00
Syrup, Yellow, Metal Top, Yellow Bakelite Handle	150.00
Teapot, Light Green, Small	65.00
Teapot, Old Ivory, Small	75.00
Teapot, Red, Large	125.00
Teapot, Turquoise, Large	58.00
Tom & Jerry Set, Bowl & 6 Mugs	150.00
Tumbler, Cobalt Blue, 8 Oz.	30.00
Tumbler, Light Green, 5 Oz.	16.00
Tumbler, Old Ivory, 8 Oz.	40.00
Tumbler, Red, 8 Oz.	35.00
Vase, Bud, Turquoise	35.00
Vase, Light Green, 10 In.	385.00
Vase, Light Green, 12 In.	300.00
Vase, Old Ivory, 12 In.	400.00
Vase, Red, 8 In.	475.00
Vase, Yellow, 8 In.	295.00
Vase, Yellow, 10 In.	350.00 To 375.00

Findlay, or onyx, glass was made using three layers of glass. It was manufactured by the Dalzell Gilmore Leighton Company about 1889 in Findlay, Ohio. The platinum, ruby, or black pattern was molded into the glass. The glass came in several colors, but was usually white or ruby.

FINDLAY ONYX, Dish, Cover, Platinum–Colored Design	985.00
Muffineer, Platinum Blossom & Top, 5 3/4 In.	385.00
Pitcher, Water, Silver Luster, 8 X 6 In.	1185.00
Sugar Shaker	350.00
Syrup	700.00

It is said that every little boy wanted to be a fireman or a train engineer 75 years ago and the collectors today reflect this interest. All types of firefighting equipment are wanted, from fire marks to uniforms to toy fire trucks.

FIREFIGHTING, Alarm Box, Brass Bell, Oak	175.00
Alarm Box, Chicago, House Shape	150.00
Alarm Box, Clockworks & Door Key	90.00
Alarm Box, Gamewell, 15 In.–Brass Bell, C.1871	3000.00
Alarm Box, Gamewell, Glass Door, 12 Volts	3000.00
Alarm Box, House Shape, Chicago, 1924	275.00
Alarm Box, Oak, Electrical Supply & Construction, 18 X 7 In.	187.00
Alarm Box, Porcelain, 1920s	75.00
Alarm, Silver Embossed Letters, Red Metal	50.00
Ax, Parade, Viking Style	150.00
Badge, Chief, Air Force	40.00
Badge, Kearney & Trecker Fire Brigade, Celluloid, 2 1/4 In.	15.00
Bell, Chief's, Oak Base, 9 1/2 X 5 1/2 In.	165.00
Bell, Fire Truck, 10 In.Diam.	300.00
Bell, Gamewell, Chicago, 1871	3000.00
Bell, Walnut, United States Electric Fire Signal, 18 In.	825.00
Bell, Warden's, Muffin, 5 In.	250.00
Belt, Parade, 1st Assistant, Leather	75.00
Book, Rules, Sheboygan Fire Dept., Leather, 1901	12.00
Book, Wis. Paid Firemen's Association Convention, 1922	5.00
Bucket, Canvas, Traces of Eagle, 10 1/2 In.	250.00
Bucket, D.Kimball, 1822, Repainted, Pair	2310.00
Bucket, Leather, Amos Arnold No.2, 1821, No Handle	200.00
Bucket, Leather, Banner Inscribed Freeman Coffin, 1836, 12 In.	275.00
Bucket, Leather, Floral, Swing Handle, 1829, 12 1/8 In.	825.00
Bucket, Leather, Nantucket, Painted, Dated 1897	1200.00
Bucket, Leather, Painted, Joined Hands, Banners, 11 1/2 In.	1900.00
Bucket, Leather, Thomas Macy, Nantucket Island, 1847, 12 In.	1320.00

Bucket, Red, Banner Says A. Edwards, No.1, 1835, Handle, 4 In. 6500.00
Button, Jefferson Co.Vol.Firemen's Assoc.1898, 1 1/4 In. 30.00
Cabinet, Fire Bell, Gamewell, Oak, Glass Window Top, 16 X 8 In. 440.00
Cap & Badge, Clermont, New York, Leather Visor, C.1890 .... 65.00
Cards, Playing, Eureka Fire Hose 25.00
Certificate, Fireman's, New York City, Engraved, 1852 .... 45.00
Extinguisher, Richmond, Instruction Sheet 28.00
Fire Card, Fire Equipment, Paper, Color, 1880, 2 X 3 7/8 In. 6.00
Fire Mark, Man, With Torch & Horn, Fire Banner, Oval, 10 In. 100.00
Gong, Station, Wood Cased 2200.00
Grenade, Blue Quilted, Patent 1883, 6 In. 75.00
Grenade, Harden Hand, Blue Glass, 6 1/2 In. 45.00
Grenade, Harden, Diamond Pattern, Footed 45.00
Grenade, Harden, Quilted, Turquoise, Sled Foot, 1 Pt. 175.00
Grenade, Harden, Turquoise 75.00
Grenade, Hayward, 2nd Size, Aqua 150.00
Grenade, Hayward, Diamond Panel, Honey Amber, 1 Pt. .... 195.00 To 225.00
Grenade, Hayward, Diamond Panel, Turquoise, 1 Pt. 425.00
Grenade, Hayward, Pleated, Aqua, 1 Pt. 150.00
Grenade, Hayward, Pleated, Clear, 1 Pt. 195.00
Grenade, Hayward, Round Panel, Cobalt Blue, 1 Pt. 225.00
Grenade, Marvel–Kil–Fyr, Glass 40.00
Grenade, Red Comet, Box, 6 Piece 125.00
Grenade, Red Comet, Glass, Carrying Case .... 75.00 To 85.00
Hat, Fireman's, Leather, Brass Fireman Finial 190.00
Hat, Leather, Brass Eagle Head, Shield, F.C.F.D. 1, 13 1/2 In. 115.00
Helmet, Fireman's, U.S.Navy 65.00
Helmet, Leather Inside, Brass, English 100.00
Helmet, Leather, Neptune SFD, Salem, 9 X 14 1/2 X 9 1/2 In. 825.00
Lantern, Dietz King, Fire Dept., Restored 185.00
Lantern, Dietz, Fire King, Brass 175.00
Lantern, Dietz, Fire King, Holder Bracket 225.00
Mark, Pumper & U.F., Oval, Cast Iron, 9 X 11 1/2 In. 135.00
Nozzle, Brass 110.00
Nozzle, Brass, 12 In. 35.00
Nozzle, Brass, Copper, 30 In. 115.00
Nozzle, Copper, Brass, Boston Woven Hose & Rubber, 31 In. 40.00
Parade Belt, Hose Type Buckle, Cutout Letters 175.00
Postcard, Fire Engine Photo, 4 Men, 2 Horse, Unused 20.00
Postcard, Horse Drawn Fire Truck No.1, Providence, R.I. 20.00
Rattle, Alarm, Wooden 75.00
Rattle, Fireman's, Primitive 110.00
Sheet Music, I'M Fireman's Love 25.00
Torch, Parade, Wooden Handle, Tin Font, Pair 220.00
Truck, Seagrave, Pumper, 1958 .... 3750.00
Trumpet, Fireman's Presentation, Middletown, NY, 19 In. 1450.00
Trumpet, Goodwill Hose Co., No.2, Milton, Penna., Etched Eagles 1850.00
Trumpet, Speaking, 3 Dimensionsl Helmets At Side 1450.00
Trumpet, Speaking, Brass, 9 In. 225.00
Trumpet, Speaking, Silver, Gilt Inside, To Chief 2250.00

The fireplace was used to cook and to heat the American home in past centuries. Many types of tools and equipment were used. Andirons held the logs in place, firebacks reflected the heat into the room, and tongs were used to move either fuel or food. Many types of spits and roasting jacks were made and are listed under Kitchen.

FIREPLACE, Andirons, Bell Metal, Sitting Cat, 1860s 550.00
Andirons, Brass & Iron, Urn Finials, Butterfly Feet, 18 1/2 In. 775.00
Andirons, Brass Finials, Wrought Iron, Penny Feet, 20 1/2 In. 340.00

Andirons, Brass, Acorn Finial, Arched Spurred Legs, 16 In. 250.00
Andirons, Brass, Acorn Finial, Arched Supports, C.1800, 18 In. 655.00
Andirons, Brass, Acorn Finial, Square Plinth, C.1800, 14 1/2 In. 440.00
Andirons, Brass, Acorn Top, Penny Foot, Late 18th Century, Pair 1045.00
Andirons, Brass, Arched Supports, Stepped Firedogs, 19 1/4 In. 385.00
Andirons, Brass, Asymmetrical Foliate Scroll, With Fender, 16 In. 250.00
Andirons, Brass, Ball Top, 17 3/4 In. 1600.00
Andirons, Brass, Beaded Urn Finials, C.1800, 15 In. 385.00
Andirons, Brass, Beehive Finial, Wrought Iron 1980.00
Andirons, Brass, Belted Ball Finials, Log Stops, C.1800, 16 In. 495.00
Andirons, Brass, Boston Style, 19th Century, 18 1/2x 17 1/2 In. 575.00
Andirons, Brass, Dachshund, Character Heads, 24 3/4 In. 1430.00
Andirons, Brass, Double Lemon Finials, Iron Shaft, 19 In. 510.00
Andirons, Brass, Dutch Baroque, Iron, Reticulated Scroll, 28 In. 495.00
Andirons, Brass, Early 1900s, 24 In. 200.00
Andirons, Brass, Lemon Finials, Fire Dog Posts, 17 1/2 In. 250.00
Andirons, Brass, Mushroom Finial, Iron Shafts & Hooks, 29 In. 935.00
Andirons, Copper & Brass, Prairie School Design, 19 X 30 In. 1900.00
Andirons, Dolphin, Brass, Foliate Base, 24 In. 1200.00
Andirons, Iron, Baroque, Basket Top, Twist Pedestal, 25 In. 110.00
Andirons, Iron, Baseball Player 3500.00
Andirons, Iron, Basket Top, Spit Holders, 1700, 28 In. 250.00
Andirons, Iron, Faceted Finials, Gooseneck Shafts, 22 1/2 In. 275.00
Andirons, Iron, George Washington On Pedestal 115.00
Andirons, Iron, George Washington, Modified, No Rails, 1920s 125.00
Andirons, Iron, Gilded Eagle Finial, Early 19th Century, 12 In. 150.00
Andirons, Iron, Hessian Soldiers 375.00
Andirons, Iron, Horseshoe Top, Wrought Iron Coiled Snakes, 45 In. 4675.00
Andirons, Iron, Owls, Glass Eyes, American, 15 N. 275.00
Andirons, Iron, Ratchet Posts, Spit Holders, 18 In. 200.00
Andirons, Iron, Scrolled Finials, Penny Feet, 18 3/4 In. 250.00
Andirons, Iron, Seated Dogs, Scrolled Base, 13 In. 100.00
Andirons, Iron, Square Top, Banded Neck, Angled Feet, 18 1/2 In. 330.00
Andirons, Iron, Sun Face, Bradley & Hubbard 1925.00
Andirons, Iron, Twisted, Knobs, 32 X 32 In. 850.00
Andirons, Silver Plated, Cannonball, 17 In. 375.00
Bellows, Brass Spout, Carved, 18 In. 85.00
Bellows, Freehand Floral Design, Yellow, Brass Nozzle, 18 In. 275.00
Bellows, National Distillers Advertising 20.00
Bellows, Smoked Paint, Fruit, Foliage Design, Brass Nozzle, 18 In. 175.00
Bellows, Stenciled & Freehand Floral Design, 1840s, 17 1/2 In. 100.00
Bellows, Stenciled Fruit & Foliage, Leather, 16 1/2 In. 265.00
Bellows, Turtle Back, Dark Green Paint, Floral Stencil, 18 In. 55.00
Bellows, Turtle Back, Floral Design, Brass Nozzle, 17 In. 550.00
Bench, Curved Back & Seat, English, Oak, 55 1/2 X 48 In. 1150.00
Broiler, Wrought Iron, 2 X 11 1/2 In. 110.00
Bucket, Coal, Copper, Swing & Side Handles, Germany, 12 X 10 In. 77.00
Bucket, Log, Copper, Swing Handle, Circular, Continental, 12 In. 385.00
Carrier, Colas, Wooden Handle, Sheet Iron, 19 In. 45.00
Chenet, Louis XVI, Gilt Bronze, Lion Standard, 15 X 15 In., Pair 900.00
Chenet, Louis XVI–Style, Figural, Poodle & Cat, Pair 2850.00
Coal Bin, Double Loose Ring Handles, Brass, 19th Century, English 210.00
Coal Hod, Cover, Embossed Ships, Hammered Brass, 20 In. 75.00
Coal Scuttle, Scoop, Brass, Floral Repousse, Victorian, 7 In. 110.00
Coal Tongs, Wrought Iron, Accordian Type, 19 In. 65.00
Crane, Curved Brace, 18th Century, Hand Forged Iron, 18th Century 150.00
Fan, Brass, Folding, Griffin Design, 38 X 25 In. 65.00
Fender, Brass Rail & Oval Finials, Woven Wire Screen, 56 In. 2200.00
Fender, Brass Top Rail, Iron With Wire Grill, 20 X 20 3/4 In. 275.00
Fender, Brass, Federal, Wire Gallery, 19th Century, 15 X 55 In. 2400.00
Fender, Brass, Fluted Rails, Leafy Supports, Victorian, 49 In. 440.00
Fender, Brass, Vinyl Upholstered, 17 1/2 X 55 In. 260.00
Fender, Iron, Intricate Design, Late–19th Century, 32 In. 150.00
Fender, Pierced Brass, Stylized Floral Design, 11 X 40 1/2 In. 275.00

Fender, Steel, Brass Floral, Victorian, Bar Top, 58 In. 302.00
Fender, Urn Finials, Sheet Iron Floor, 3 Ball Feet, 41 1/2 In. 110.00
Fender, Wrought Iron Frame, Wire Grill, Brass Rail, 13 1/2 In. 725.00
Fire Guard, Art Deco, Iron, Marble, 1925, Paul Kiss–Type, 8 Ft. 1500.00
Fire Machine, Georgian, Oak, Brass, Funnel, Crank Handle, 28 In. 385.00
Fireback, Crest Over Panels With Soldiers, Cast Iron, 22 1/2 In. 470.00
Fireback, Grapevine Border, Knight On Horseback, Iron, 23 In. 275.00
Fireback, Seated Monkey & Cat, Iron, 23 X 17 1/2 In. 250.00
Mantel, Carved Oak, Large 350.00
Screen, Adjustable, Walnut, Needlepoint, 1870 .... 485.00
Screen, Brass Frame & Handles, 3 Section 95.00
Screen, Cluster of Musical Instruments, Brass, 31 In. 1045.00
Screen, Diamond Design Ground, Iron, 32 X 25 1/4 In. 2420.00
Screen, Eastlake, Ebonized, Gilt, American, C.1875, 42 1/2 In. 395.00
Screen, Embroidered Panel, Oval Satinwood Frame, 51 In. 335.00
Screen, Landscape, Stained Glass, Jacques Gruber, 1910, 45 3/4 In. 6050.00
Screen, Lyre Form Hinged Panels, Swans' Heads, Eagles, 47 In. 2100.00
Screen, Painted Birds, Grapes, Leaves, Tin Panel, Carved Frame 850.00
Screen, Shield Shape, Needlepoint, 44 1/2 X 25 In. 135.00
Screen, Stained Glass, Landscape, Jacques Gruber, 1910 .... 5000.00
Shovel & Fork, Baroque Revival, Bronze, Steel, Reticulated, 43 In. 302.00
Spit, Salter & Co., Brass 125.00
Tea Kettle, Tipping Lever, Cast Iron, 18th Century, 8 1/2 In. 2750.00
Tile, Leaves, Vines, Framed For Mounting On Opening, 45 X 33 In. 550.00
Tinder Box, Friction Wheel, Tin & Iron, Ives Patent 495.00
Toaster, Heart Handle, Cast Iron, 18th Century, 14 In. 315.00
Wafer Iron, Star & Cryptic Design, Dated 1802, Iron, 5 X 27 In. 325.00
Wafer Iron, Strawberry Design, Long Handle, Iron, 30 In. 400.00

MF Porcelain was made in Herend, Hungary, by Moritz Fischer. The factory was founded in 1839 and continued working into the twentieth century. The wares are sometimes referred to as "Herend" porcelain.

FISCHER, Bowl, Gilt Birds, Cobalt, Gilt Bronze Mounted, Porcelain, 7 1/2 In. 665.00
Bowl, Shell Shape, Green Paint On Gilt, Scroll Feet, 15 1/2 In., Pr. 465.00
Figurine, Dancing Girl, No.3486 .... 185.00
Figurine, Kneeling Lady, No.5604, Dated 1939 .... 175.00
Figurine, Owl 65.00
Figurine, Peasant Woman With Fish 200.00
Mug, Blue, Red, Gold Flowers 125.00
Plate, Apponyi Vert, Green, Gold Trim, 8 In. 37.50
Tea Caddy, Butterflies & Birds, Basketweave Border, 5 1/2 In. 100.00
Vase, Hand Painted Bird & Flowers, 7 In. 125.00
Vase, Multicolored Flowers, Panels of Gold & Brown, 7 In. 130.00

Fishing reels of brass or nickel were made in the United States by 1810. Bamboo fly rods were sold by 1860, often marked with the maker's name. Metal lures, then wooden and metal lures were made in the nineteenth century. Plastic lures were made by the 1930s. All fishing material is collected today and even equipment of the past thirty years is of interest if in good condition with original box.

FISHING, Basket, Wicker, Canvas Lid, Trap Door, England, 1900, 13 X 17 In. 357.00
Cabinet, Tackle, Glass Top, Drawers, Painted Green Oak, 16 X 12 In. 160.00
Case, Fly, 100 Salmon Flies 800.00
Chair, Folding, Rattan, Leather Covered Legs, 27 In. ....*Illus* 550.00
Chest, Fly, D.M.C., Lock, Oak, 9 1/2 X 13 X 8 1/2 In. ....*Illus* 1155.00
Creel, Narrow Weave, 1920s 25.00
Creel, Wicker, Leather Trim, Carrying Strap 65.00
Creel, Woven Reed, Leather Strap 65.00
Creepers, Ice, Forged Iron, Pair 25.00
Float, Glass Ball, Logo of Fishing Fleet, Japanese, 13 In. 125.00
Float, Hinckley's Phantom, 1897 .... 16.00
Fly Rod, Brass Trim, Protage Atlas, Cork Covered Handle, 106 In. 125.00
Fly Rod, Montague, With Reel, Split Bamboo 48.00

Fishing, Chest, Fly, D.M.C., Lock, Oak,
9 1/2 X 13 X 8 1/2 In.

Fishing, Chair, Folding, Rattan,
Leather Covered Legs, 27 In.

Fishing, Lure, Fly Rod, Bucktail Body, Leather Ears, 1 1/2 In.

Fishing, Reel, Trout, C.F.Orvis,
Patent 1874, 2 7/8 In.

Fishing, Reel, Tarpon, Seamaster,
Mark III, Left–Hand Wind, 3 3/4 In.

Fishing, Lure, Shad, Lewis W.Reno, Glass Eyes, C.1978, 6 In.

Fishing, Lure, Shiner, Lem B.Harsen, C.1940, 5 1/2 In.

Fishing, Lure, Chubb, Lewis W.Reno, C.1978, 6 In.

Fly Rod, Shakespeare, Metal Tubes, Canvas Case, 108 In. 160.00
Fly Rod, Victor Granger, Case & Tube, 1938 .... 500.00
Knife, Trout, Ka-Bar 90.00
License, Minnesota, Non-Resident, Pinback, 1927 .... 25.00
License, Wisconsin, Non-Resident, 1931 .... 48.00
Line Drier, Double Spool, Abercrombie & Fitch, Mahogany, 18 1/2 In. 250.00
Lure, Chubb, Lewis W.Reno, C.1978, 6 In. ....*Illus* 77.00
Lure, Fly Rod, Bucktail Body, Leather Ears, 1 1/2 In. ....*Illus* 182.00
Lure, Frog, Bass Mac, Box, 1940s 25.00
Lure, Keeling, Pat.1922 .... 25.00
Lure, Metal Fins, 5 Barb Hooks, Polychrome Paint, 11 1/2 In. 30.00
Lure, Minnow, Heddon, Box 220.00
Lure, Minnow, R. Haskell, Painesville, Ohio, 1859, 4 1/2 In. 8500.00
Lure, Multi-Wobbler No.9204, Winchester 195.00
Lure, Multi-Wobbler No.9206, Winchester 185.00
Lure, Musky, Squirrel, Glass Eyes, Swivel Hinged Tail, 15 1/2 In. 200.00
Lure, Oscar Peterson, Perch, Fat Body, 9 In. 4500.00
Lure, Oscar William Peterson, Brook Trout, Tack Eyes, 8 In. 550.00
Lure, Polly-Wog, Moonlight Bait & Novelty Works, 1920s, 4 In. 200.00
Lure, Shad, Lewis W.Reno, Glass Eyes, C.1978, 6 In. ....*Illus* 110.00
Lure, Shiner, Lem B.Harsen, C.1940, 5 1/2 In. ....*Illus* 55.00
Lure, Spin Diver, Heddon, Wooden, Glass Eyes 75.00
Lure, Winchester, Multi-Wobbler, Original Paint 170.00
Lure, Wm. Renkel, Mud Minnow, Carved Tail & Mouth, C.1915, 3 1/2 In. 325.00
Minnow Trap, Camp, Blue Glass 50.00
Pole, 3 Sections, Dewey's Get Um, Brass, 4 Ft. 225.00
Pole, Bamboo, Nickel Over Brass Reel 65.00
Reel, Abbey & Imbrie, German Silver Parts, Click Switch, 2 3/4 In. 375.00
Reel, Atlas Portage 20.00
Reel, Baby Bogdan 1870.00
Reel, Bogdan 2860.00
Reel, Braiding, Line of Horsehair, Bone Handle, Iron Screw 450.00
Reel, D.Whitehead, No.EG 221-005A, Presentation.2 Piece, 8 Ft.9 In. 2750.00
Reel, Gayle 9350.00
Reel, H.L.Leonard, Marbelized 9350.00
Reel, Horn Handle, G.E.Murray, Brass, 4 1/4 In. 145.00
Reel, J.C. Higgins, Box, Unused, 1940s 8.00
Reel, Julius Vom Hofe, Marked Tiny, Click Switch, 2 1/4 In. 175.00
Reel, Lakeside Quad 15.00
Reel, Pfleuger Supreme, Bait Casting 50.00
Reel, Pflueger, Casting, 1944 .... 22.00
Reel, Pflueger, No.1355 .... 15.00
Reel, Pflueger, No.1960, Box 40.00
Reel, Pflueger, Skilcast, No.1953 .... 50.00
Reel, President 20.00
Reel, Rev-O-Noc 25.00
Reel, Seamaster 2640.00
Reel, Shakespeare, Ocean City 12.50
Reel, South Bend No.550, Box 25.00
Reel, Talbot 7820.00
Reel, Tarpon, Seamaster, Mark III, Left-Hand Wind, 3 3/4 In. ....*Illus* 2310.00
Reel, Tri-Part, Free Spool, 1904 .... 65.00
Reel, Trout, C.F.Orvis, Patent 1874, 2 7/8 In. ....*Illus* 165.00
Reel, Walker, TR-3, German Silver, Polished Aluminum, Rubber, 3 In. 1100.00
Reel, Winasigo 15.00
Rod & Reel, Hardy, Spinning, Neo Cane-Blen Rinzil, 7 Ft. 130.00
Rod, Abbey & Imbrie, German Silver Fittings, 10 1/2 Ft. 250.00
Rod, Dickerson 9900.00
Rod, Edwards 1540.00
Rod, F.E. Thomas, Bangor Rod, Red Wraps, 8 1/2 Ft. 325.00
Rod, F.E. Thomas, Dirigo, 2 Tip, 9 Ft. 110.00
Rod, Foster Bros., Ashbourne Champion, 8 Ft. 50.00
Rod, Garrison, 8 Ft. 6050.00
Rod, Halstead 8800.00

Rod, Hardy, C.C. DeFrance, Spiked Ferrules, 8 Ft. 375.00
Rod, Hardy, Hollokona–Salmon DeLuxe, 9 1/2 Ft. 250.00
Rod, Heddon Pal, Case, 1930s 45.00
Rod, Heddon, Black Beauty, No.17, 7 1/2 Ft. 225.00
Rod, Heddon, Deluxe President No.50 Model, 1940s, 8 Ft. 1050.00
Rod, Leonard, 7 Ft. 3080.00
Rod, Payne, 7 1/2 Ft. 1155.00
Rod, Payne, Canoe, 9 Ft. 1100.00
Rod, Rocky Mountain Fly & Spinning, Orvis, Set 6050.00
Rod, Simmons Royale, Steel 40.00
Rod, Thomas Classic, 8 Ft. 770.00
Rod, Young, 8 Ft. 1485.00
Sign, Trade, Fish Shape, Chain For Hanging, Maryland, 1900 .... 1450.00
Spear, Eel, Smith Made, J.W. Fordham, 16 In. 75.00
Spear, Wrought Iron, J. Rusher, 11 1/2 In. 30.00
Trap, Gabriel 210.00
Trap, Minnow, 3 Hole, Glass 37.50
Trolling Spoon, Feathered Treble Hook, Skinner 15.00
Trophy, Sail Fish, Mounted On Plaque, 84 In. 225.00
    FLAG, see Textile, Flag

Flash Gordon appeared in the Sunday comics in 1934. The daily strip started in 1940. The hero was also in comic books from 1930 to 1970, in books from 1936, in movies from 1938, on the radio in the 1930s and 1940s, and on television from 1953 to 1954. All sorts of memorabilia are collected, but the ray guns and rocket ships are the most popular.

FLASH GORDON, Action Suit, Ideal 85.00
Belt, Yellow Plastic, Gray Spaceship Buckle, 1950s 10.00
Book, Better Little Book, Flash & Power Men of Mongo, 1943 .... 30.00
Book, Big Little Book, Tyrant of Mongo Better, 1938 .... 40.00
Book, Coloring 10.00
Book, Flash Gordon In Caverns of Mongo, 1936 .... 66.00
Book, Pop–Up 450.00
Compass, Wrist 35.00
Doll, Defenders of The Earth, Package, 5 1/2 In. 12.00
Drawing, Pen & Ink, Signed Alex Raymond, 7 1/2 X 10 In. 65.00
Game, Adventures On The Moons of Mongo, Box 25.00
Game, Gem Co., 1966 .... 35.00
Gun, Razer Ray, Sparking, Friction 12.00
Ornament, Christmas, Silver Bell, Flash Decal, 1940s 35.00
Pencil Box, 1935 .... 15.00
Pistol, Signal, Decal 75.00
Play Set, Mego, Box 100.00
Puzzle Set, Milton Bradley, 1951, 2 Piece 50.00
Record, City of Sea Caves, Disc, Record Guild of America, 1948 .... 40.00
Space Outfit, 1952 .... 20.00
Space Outfit, Esquire Novelty Co., 1952, Box 175.00
Toy, Rocket Fighter Ship, Windup, Marx 450.00
Toy, Rocket Fighter, Windup 285.00
Toy, Space Vehicle, Computized, Box 30.00
Toy, Spaceship, Inflatable, Box 40.00
TV, With 4 Films On Card 25.00

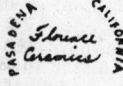

Florence Ceramics were made in Pasadena, California, from World War II to 1977. Florence Ward created many colorful figurines, boxes, candleholders, and other items for the giftshop trade. Each piece was marked with an ink stamp that included the name Florence Ceramics Co. The company was sold in 1964 and although the name remained the same the products were very different. Mugs, cups, and trays were made.

FLORENCE CERAMICS, Conch Shell, Pink Luster 25.00
Figurine, Ava .... 85.00 To 88.00
Figurine, Blue Boy, 12 In. 230.00

Figurine, Camille ....85.00 To 100.00	
Figurine, Carol, Open Handle, 10 In.	175.00
Figurine, Charmaine, 8 1/2 In.	75.00
Figurine, Clasissa	85.00
Figurine, Delia	45.00
Figurine, Delores, Pink	135.00
Figurine, Edward	95.00
Figurine, Elaine, Gold Trim, 6 In.	95.00
Figurine, Elaine, Pink & Gold, 6 In.	40.00
Figurine, Elizabeth, On Settee, Teal Blue, Gray	210.00
Figurine, Grace, 7 1/2 In.	70.00
Figurine, Her Majesty, White	150.00
Figurine, Irene ....30.00 To 50.00	
Figurine, Jeanette, 8 1/2 In.	75.00
Figurine, Jim, Gray Suit, 5 In.	45.00
Figurine, Lavon, Open Hands, 8 1/2 In.	140.00
Figurine, Lillian	35.00
Figurine, Linda Lou, Pink	125.00
Figurine, Louis XV, White & Green	250.00
Figurine, Louis XVI & Marie Antoinette	400.00
Figurine, Louis XVI, Gold & White	215.00
Figurine, Louise, Gray & Gold, 7 1/2 In.	60.00
Figurine, Marcie	70.00
Figurine, Matilda, Beige & Green, 8 1/2 In. ....75.00 To 125.00	
Figurine, Melanie, 8 In. ....75.00 To 125.00	
Figurine, Melanie, Pink, 7 1/2 In. .... 80.00 To 87.00	
Figurine, Nancy, Gray, 7 In.	50.00
Figurine, Oriental Couple, 8 1/4 In.	48.00
Figurine, Oriental Man & Woman, Pair	75.00
Figurine, Pinkie, 12 In.	230.00
Figurine, Prom Boy	75.00
Figurine, Rhett Butler	135.00
Figurine, Sarah, Pink	95.00
Figurine, Scarlett, Green, 8 1/2 In.	75.00
Figurine, Scarlett, Pink & Gold	120.00
Figurine, Sherry, 9 In.	75.00
Figurine, Victoria, Seated	250.00
Figurine, Vivian, Green Dress, 9 3/4 In.	125.00
Figurine, Woman, Light Green Suit & Bonnet, 7 1/2 In.	65.00
Flower Frog, Oriental Boy	30.00
Flower Frog, Oriental Couple	65.00
Flower Frog, Swiss Girl	40.00
Frame, Floral	90.00
Head Vase, Camille	85.00
Wall Pocket, Girl's Bust, Green, Gold, Coat, Bonnet, 7 In.	45.00

Flow blue, or flo blue, was made in England about 1830 to 1900. The plates were printed with designs using a cobalt blue coloring. The color flowed from the design to the white plate so that the finished plate has a smeared blue design. The plates were usually made of ironstone china.

FLOW BLUE, Bone Dish, Fleur-De-Lis	20.00
Bone Dish, Touraine, Stanley	38.00
Bowl, Abbey, Geo.Jones, 11 In.	68.00
Bowl, Albany, Grindley, 2 Handles, 9 1/4 In.	84.50
Bowl, Albion, B.W.M. Co., 6 1/2 In.	30.00
Bowl, Conway, 9 In.	40.00
Bowl, Eagle Border, Fairmount Near Philadelphia, 13 In.	5610.00
Bowl, Fairy Villas, 10 In. .... 58.00 To 68.00	
Bowl, Florida, Grindley, 7 1/2 In.	20.00
Bowl, Gainsborough, Ridgway, Large	75.00
Bowl, Hampton Spray, Gold Trim, Grindley, 6 In.	30.00
Bowl, Hofburg, Cover, Oval	130.00
Bowl, Hong Kong, 12 Sides, 10 1/2 In.	275.00

Bowl, Italia, Cover, 10 X 12 In. 70.00
Bowl, Kyber, 9 In. 75.00
Bowl, La Belle, Scalloped, 12 In. 125.00
Bowl, Manhattan, 8 In. 48.00
Bowl, Marechel Niel, Cover 275.00
Bowl, Millais, 9 In. 30.00
Bowl, Nonpareil, Cover 295.00
Bowl, Oregon, Cover 395.00
Bowl, Paris, 7 In. 35.00
Bowl, Pelew, Challinor, 9 1/2 In. 65.00
Bowl, Poppy, Bennett, 8 1/2 In. 50.00
Bowl, Portman, Grindley, Cover, Oval, 12 In. 205.00
Bowl, Raleigh, 8 In. 40.00
Bowl, Regent, Cover, 12 In. 185.00
Bowl, Shanghai, Grindley, 9 In. 95.00
Bowl, Timor, 3 X 6 In. 20.00
Bowl, Touraine, Stanley, Oval, 9 In. 85.00
Bowl, Touraine, Tab Handle, Stanley, Round, 10 1/2 In. 75.00
Bowl, Waldorf, Grindley, Cover, 7 3/4 In. 180.00
Bowl, Watteau, Oval, 10 In. 50.00
Breakfast Set, Abbey, George Jones, 30 Piece 1295.00
Butter Chip, Argyle, Grindley 27.00
Butter Chip, Burleigh 22.00
Butter Chip, Clover .... 22.00 To 24.00
Butter Chip, Fairy Villas, Adams 25.00
Butter Chip, Grace 30.00
Butter Chip, Lorne 28.00
Butter Chip, Lugano 22.00
Butter Chip, Osborne, Ridgway 24.00
Butter, Cover, Burleigh, Liner 165.00
Butter, Cover, Watteau, Liner 165.00
Cake Stand, Poppea 165.00
Casserole, Raleigh, Cover, Burgess & Leigh 225.00
Casserole, Turin, Cover, Johnson Bros., 11 In. 152.50
Celery Dish, La Belle 225.00
Charger, Tyrolean, Ridgway, 12 1/4 In. 160.00
Cheese Dish, Melbourne 575.00
Child's Set, Wagon Wheel, Blue, 3 Piece 550.00
Chocolate Pot, Cashmere, Morley 850.00
Coffeepot, Lafayette At Franklin's Tomb 900.00
Coffeepot, Shell 235.00
Compote, Chusan, Morley, Handles, 6 1/4 X 10 In. 550.00
Compote, Windsor Wreath, Pedestal 225.00
Creamer, Amoy 175.00
Creamer, Floral, 4 In. 65.00
Creamer, Shell 250.00
Creamer, Togo 85.00
Cup & Saucer, Chapoo, Handleless 125.00
Cup & Saucer, La Francais 15.00
Cup & Saucer, Lancaster 60.00
Cup & Saucer, Lotus 50.00
Cup & Saucer, Marquis, Grindley 65.00
Cup & Saucer, Martha Washington 55.00
Cup & Saucer, Morea, Handleless 45.00
Cup & Saucer, Raleigh, Burgess & Leigh 37.50
Cup & Saucer, Spinach 75.00
Cup & Saucer, Stanley 45.00
Cup & Saucer, Stick Spatter, Handleless 65.00
Cup & Saucer, Temple, Handleless 78.00
Cup & Saucer, Touraine, Stanley 60.00
Cup Plate, Amoy 95.00
Cup Plate, Hindustan 95.00
Cup Plate, Scinde 85.00
Cup Plate, Tivoli, T. Furnival, C.1850 .... 55.00

Cup, Sabraon, Handleless	43.00
Demitasse Set, Watteau, Doulton	50.00
Dinner Set, Geneva, Service For 8, C.1890, 53 Piece	2000.00
Dinner Set, Georgia, Johnson Bros., 114 Piece	6500.00
Dinner Set, Jewel, Johnson Bros., 38 Piece	1260.00
Dinner Set, Melbourne, Service For 8, 37 Piece	875.00
Dinner Set, Touraine, 109 Piece	4800.00
Dish, Commodore MacDonnough's Victory, Leaf Shape	5610.00
Eggcup, Denton	40.00
Eggcup, Royal Blue, Burgess & Campbell	65.00
Fruit Basket, Canal Scene, 12 1/4 In.	665.00
Game Set, Turkey, Ridgway, 4 Piece	475.00
Gravy Boat, Argyle	78.00 To 125.00
Gravy Boat, Carlton, Underplate	135.00
Gravy Boat, Douglas	85.00
Gravy Boat, Kenworth, Underplate, Johnson Bros.	75.00
Gravy Boat, Poppy	85.00
Gravy Boat, Rose, Underplate	120.00
Gravy Boat, Savoy	105.00
Pickle Dish, Verona, Ridgway, 5 X 8 1/2 In.	50.00
Pin Tray, La Belle	95.00
Pitcher & Bowl, Gingham Flower	595.00
Pitcher & Bowl, Kyber, J.Meir & Son	2100.00
Pitcher, Campion, Bulbous, 12 In.	245.00
Pitcher, Chusan, Wedgwood, 7 1/2 In.	295.00
Pitcher, Cows, 12 In.	225.00
Pitcher, Fairy Villas, 7 3/4 In.	295.00
Pitcher, Madras, Doulton, 8 In.	365.00
Pitcher, Milk, Amoy, Davenport, 7 In.	250.00
Pitcher, Milk, Le Pavot, 2 Qt.	265.00
Pitcher, Milk, Rhine, Dimmock	240.00
Pitcher, Milk, Scinde, Alcock, 8 In.	100.00
Pitcher, Milk, Wind Flower, Grindley, 5 1/2 In.	85.00
Pitcher, Nankin, Doulton, 7 1/2 In.	175.00
Pitcher, Temple, 8 In.	295.00
Pitcher, Togo, 5 In.	85.00
Pitcher, Touraine, 8 In.	450.00
Pitcher, Tulip, 6 In.	225.00
Plate, Alaska, 8 In.	38.00
Plate, Amoy, Davenport, 1844, 10 1/2 In.	90.00
Plate, Arabic, Grindley, 8 In.	17.50
Plate, Argyle, Grindley, 8 In.	50.00
Plate, Argyle, Grindley, 10 In.	70.00
Plate, Baltic, 10 In.	79.00
Plate, Beauties of China, 8 1/2 In.	75.00
Plate, Begonia, Johnson Bros., 9 In.	25.00
Plate, Brazil, 9 In.	45.00
Plate, Candia, 7 In.	30.00 To 45.00
Plate, Canton, Ashworth, 10 In.	65.00
Plate, Carlton, Alcock, 9 1/2 In.	60.00
Plate, Cashmere, Morley, 10 5/8 In.	130.00
Plate, Celtic, 7 In.	25.00
Plate, Chapoo, 8 1/4 In.	65.00
Plate, Chen–Si, 8 In.	65.00
Plate, Chen–Si, 8 3/4 In.	80.00
Plate, Chusan, Podmore & Walker, 7 1/4 In., 8 Piece	145.00
Plate, Constance, 9 In.	15.00
Plate, Conway, 10 In.	60.00
Plate, Cows, 10 In.	65.00
Plate, Fairy Villas, 8 In.	35.00
Plate, Fairy Villas, 10 1/4 In.	75.00
Plate, Fisherman's Island, 9 1/4 In.	110.00
Plate, Florida, 7 In.	40.00
Plate, Florida, 9 In.	45.00

Plate, Florida, Grindley, 10 In. .... 40.00 To 75.00
Plate, Florida, Johnson Bros., 10 In. 50.00
Plate, Gironde, Grindley, 7 In. 27.00
Plate, Grenada, 9 In. 28.00
Plate, Hamilton, 10 1/2 In. 75.00
Plate, Hampton Spray, Grindley, 6 In. 30.00
Plate, Holland, 8 In. 55.00
Plate, Hong Kong, 9 In. 45.00
Plate, Hong Kong, 10 1/2 In. .... 100.00 To 135.00
Plate, Independence Hall Center, 4 Scene Border, 9 In. 24.00
Plate, Ivanhoe, Wedgwood, 10 1/4 In. 75.00
Plate, Japan, Fell, 1860, 9 1/4 In. 70.00
Plate, Jewel, 8 In. 32.00
Plate, Knox, 8 In. 25.00
Plate, Kyber, Adams, 8 In. 35.00
Plate, Kyber, Adams, 10 In. 50.00
Plate, La Belle, 10 In. 100.00
Plate, Lancaster, 9 In. .... 45.00 To 55.00
Plate, Lancaster, 10 In. 48.00
Plate, Landing of General Lafayette, Clews, 10 In. 175.00
Plate, Lorne, Grindley, 10 In. .... 45.00 To 65.00
Plate, Lotus, 9 In. 45.00
Plate, Lugano, 8 In. 65.00
Plate, Lugano, 10 In. 85.00
Plate, Madras, 7 1/2 In. 25.00
Plate, Madras, 10 In. 50.00
Plate, Mandarin, 10 In. 58.00
Plate, Manila, 9 3/4 In. 110.00
Plate, Marlborough, Grindley, 9 In. 45.00
Plate, Marquis, 6 In. 25.00
Plate, Millais, 9 In. 32.00
Plate, Ning PO, 9 1/2 In. 95.00
Plate, Nonpareil, 9 In. 55.00
Plate, Ophir, 9 In. 15.00
Plate, Osborne, 10 In. .... 35.00 To 45.00
Plate, Oxford, Johnson Bros., 6 3/4 In. 20.00
Plate, Oxford, Johnson Bros., 9 In. 30.00
Plate, Paris, 9 In. 49.50
Plate, Paris, 10 In. 79.00
Plate, Pelew, 9 1/4 In. 95.00
Plate, Penang, Ridgway, 1840, 9 1/4 In. 70.00
Plate, Portman, Grindley, 8 In. 45.00
Plate, Quebec, 9 In. 160.00
Plate, Raleigh, Burgess & Leigh, 9 1/2 In. 42.50
Plate, Rhone, 7 In. 39.00
Plate, Rock, 7 1/2 In. 65.00
Plate, Royston, 10 In. 40.00
Plate, Sancho, Priest & Barber, 7 1/2 In. 78.00
Plate, Scinde, 9 1/4 In. 75.00
Plate, Scinde, 10 1/2 In. 110.00
Plate, Shanghai, Adams, 9 In. 70.00
Plate, Spinach, 7 1/4 In. 50.00
Plate, Stanley, 9 In. 30.00
Plate, Temple, Podmore & Walker, 8 3/4 In. .... 45.00 To 75.00
Plate, Temple, Podmore & Walker, 9 3/4 In. 110.00
Plate, Tonquin, 7 1/2 In. 60.00
Plate, Tonquin, 9 1/2 In. 95.00
Plate, Touraine, 9 In. 60.00
Plate, Touraine, 10 In. 75.00
Plate, Troy, Meigh, 1845, 8 1/4 In. 45.00
Plate, Turin, Johnson Bros., 9 In. 34.50
Plate, Turin, Johnson Bros., 10 In. 45.00
Plate, Venue, Walker, Light Blue, 1845, 8 In. 18.00
Plate, Vermont, 10 In. 48.00

Plate, Verona, 10 In. 60.00
Plate, Victoria, 8 In. 30.00
Plate, Wagon Wheel, 5 1/5 In. 40.00
Plate, Waldorf, 10 In. .... 60.00 To 65.00
Plate, Waldorf, New Wharf, 9 In. 38.00
Plate, Warwick, Gold Rim, 8 1/4 In. 25.00
Plate, Washington Praying 69.00
Plate, Watteau, 8 In. 30.00
Plate, Watteau, 10 In. 45.00
Plate, Watteau, Doulton, 10 1/2 In. 55.00
Plate, Whampoa, Mellor & Venables, 7 1/2 In. 55.00
Platter, Arabesque, Mayer, 13 In. 125.00
Platter, Argyle, Grindley, 17 1/2 X 12 In. 160.00
Platter, Arms of Delaware, 17 In. 3190.00
Platter, Ashburton, 20 X 15 In. 250.00
Platter, Cambridge, Meakin, 14 In. 185.00
Platter, Castle Scene, Floral Rim, 1828–59, Dimmock 295.00
Platter, Claremont, Johnson Bros., 16 1/4 X 11 1/4 In. 195.00
Platter, Denton, 14 In. 105.00
Platter, English Cathedral Scene, 19 In. 225.00
Platter, Formosa, Mayer, 13 1/4 In. 285.00
Platter, Formosa, Ridgway, 13 X 18 In. 300.00
Platter, Georgia, Johnson Bros., 10 1/2 X 14 In. 140.00
Platter, Gladys, 11 In. 68.00
Platter, Grace, Grindley, 21 In. 335.00
Platter, Holland, 12 In. .... 85.00 To 115.00
Platter, Idris, Grindley, 12 In. 65.00
Platter, Indian, Pratt, 13 1/4 X 10 1/4 In. 225.00
Platter, Keele, Grindley, 9 In. 115.00
Platter, Kelmscott 225.00
Platter, Kenworth, Johnson Bros., 12 X 9 1/2 In. 75.00
Platter, Kyber, Adams, Hexagonal, 14 1/2 X 11 In. 235.00
Platter, La Belle, 20 In. 295.00
Platter, La Belle, Gold Rim, 12 In. 85.00
Platter, La Francais, 12 1/2 X 9 1/2 In. 60.00
Platter, Lakewood, 12 1/4 In. 90.00
Platter, Lorne, 14 X 10 In. 110.00
Platter, Manila, 16 In. .... 325.00 To 395.00
Platter, Marguerite, Grindley, 1891, 18 In. 120.00
Platter, Marie, 16 In. 150.00
Platter, Melbourne, Grindley, 11 In. 122.50
Platter, Melbourne, Grindley, 18 In. 245.00
Platter, Mongolia, Johnson Bros., 12 In. 60.00
Platter, Oatland, Surrey, Stevenson, 16 3/4 In. 245.00
Platter, Oregon, Mayer, 13 1/2 In. 250.00
Platter, Oriental Garden, 11 3/4 In. 150.00
Platter, Osborne, Grindley, 10 1/4 X 14 In. 165.00
Platter, Osborne, Ridgway, 15 1/2 X 12 In. 150.00
Platter, Oxford, Johnson Bros., 14 In. 187.50
Platter, Paris, New Wharf, 14 1/2 In. 17.50
Platter, Petunia, T. Rathbone & Co., 10 X 14 In. 75.00
Platter, Princess, Booth, 8 X 6 In. 25.00
Platter, Raleigh, Burgess & Leigh, 17 1/2 X 14 In. 195.00
Platter, Renown, 15 In. 75.00
Platter, Sydney, 14 In. 150.00
Platter, Temple, 12 1/2 In. 295.00
Platter, Touraine, 15 X 11 1/2 In. 250.00
Platter, Touraine, Stanley, 12 1/2 In. 95.00
Platter, Turin, Johnson Bros., 12 X 16 In. 149.50
Platter, Waldorf, 10 1/2 X 7 1/2 In. .... 75.00 To 90.00
Platter, Waldorf, 18 In. 300.00
Platter, Watteau, 17 In. 175.00
Punch Bowl, Watteau, Doulton 1095.00
Relish, Colonial, Meakin, C.1891 .... 65.00

Relish, Gironde, Grindley 45.00
Relish, Jeddo, Adams, 5 X 7 1/2 In. 50.00
Relish, Shell 235.00
Sauce Ladle, Bleeding Heart 275.00
Sauce Ladle, Hamilton 75.00
Sauce, Gironde 15.00
Sauce, Lorne 22.00
Sauce, Nonpareil 22.00
Sauce, Normandy, 6 In. 35.00
Sauce, Oxford, Johnson Bros. 20.00
Saucer, Florida, Johnson Bros. 10.00
Server, Loop Handle, La Belle 250.00
Soup, Dish, Argyle, Grindley, 7 1/2 In. 55.00
Soup, Dish, Clarence, 8 Piece 240.00
Soup, Dish, Elephant, 9 1/2 In. 95.00
Soup, Dish, Lugano, 9 In. 65.00
Soup, Dish, Marechal Niel, 8 1/2 In. 58.00
Soup, Dish, Oregon, Mayer, 9 1/2 In. 100.00
Soup, Dish, Raleigh, Burgess & Leigh, 9 In. 27.50
Soup, Dish, Scinde, Alcock, 10 1/2 In. 100.00
Soup, Dish, Tonquin, 9 1/2 In. 100.00
Soup, Dish, Tonquin, Heath, 10 1/2 In. 125.00
Soup, Dish, Tulip, 9 In. 65.00
Soup, Dish, Vermont, 9 In. 45.00
Sugar & Creamer, Butter, Spooner, Melbourne, 4 Piece 425.00
Sugar & Creamer, Mongolia, Johnson Bros. 225.00
Sugar & Creamer, Oxford 145.00
Sugar & Creamer, Royal Blue 225.00
Sugar, Burleigh, Wedgwood, Cover 125.00
Sugar, Muriel, Cover 135.00
Sugar, Nonpareil, Cover 175.00
Sugar, Oregon, Mayer, Cover 225.00
Sugar, Pelew 250.00
Sugar, Savoy, Cover 115.00
Sugar, Shell 65.00
Sugar, Temple, Cover, 8 In. 250.00
Sugar, Togo, Cover 105.00
Tankard, Clarmont Groups, 6 3/4 In. 325.00
Tea Tile, Warwick, Raised Gold Gadroon Border, 7 In. 110.00
Teapot, Amoy, Davenport 375.00
Teapot, Chapoo 340.00
Teapot, Leaping Stag, 5 3/4 In. 135.00
Teapot, Manhattan, Henry Alcock, 7 1/2 In. 200.00
Teapot, Marechal Niel 325.00
Teapot, Oregon 495.00
Teapot, Sugar & Creamer, Muriel 650.00
Teapot, Temple 450.00
Toothbrush Holder, Cyprus 250.00
Toothbrush Holder, Kyber, Adams 335.00
Tureen, Ashburton, Cover 225.00
Tureen, Burleigh, Cover, 10 In. 145.00
Tureen, Crumlin, Myott, Cover, 12 In. 265.00
Tureen, Duchess, Grindley, 8 In. 110.00
Tureen, Fleur–De–Lis, Cover, Tray 250.00
Tureen, Haughton Hall, Norfolk, 16 In. 65.00
Tureen, Idris, Cover 115.00
Tureen, Kyber, Dover, Octagonal 185.00
Tureen, Louise, Cover 187.00
Tureen, Lugano, Cover, 11 1/2 In. 275.00
Tureen, Madras, Doulton, Cover, Oblong 65.00
Tureen, Marechal Niel, Grindley, Ladle 295.00
Tureen, May, Grindley, Cover, 8 1/2 In. 110.00
Tureen, Oriental, Cover 225.00
Tureen, Pelew, Challinor, Cover, 6 1/2 X 10 In. 280.00

Tureen, Savoy 90.00
Tureen, Watteau, Doulton, Cover, Tray 550.00
Vase, Huron, 5 In. .... 65.00 To 75.00
Waste Bowl, Burleigh 80.00
Waste Bowl, Clayton 65.00
Waste Bowl, Manila 150.00
Waste Bowl, Temple 175.00
Waste Bowl, Whampoa, Mellor & Venables 175.00
    FLYING PHOENIX, see Phoenix Bird

Folk art is listed in many sections of the book under the actual name of the object. See categories such as Box; Cigar Store Figure; Weather Vane; Wooden; etc.

FOLK ART, Airplane, Model, William Owens, North Carolina, Wood, Metal, 34 In. 75.00
Biplane, Black Alligatored Paint, 23 In. 80.00
Birdhouse, Agee Hog Frame, Wooden, White & Blue Paint, Large 65.00
Black Mammy, Made of Bottle Caps, 12 In. 14.00
Black Man, With Walking Stick, 20th Century, 10 1/2 In. 95.00
Box, Applied Heart & Star Designs, Poplar, 17 In. 65.00
Box, Comb, Incised Star In Circle, 1802, Nailed, 6 X 3 X 7 In. 180.00
Box, Heart & Star Designs, Wire Nail Construction, Poplar, 17 In. 65.00
Box, Lift Top, Hinged Sides, Pyramid Shape, 6 X 9 In. 65.00
Box, Pierced Compass Stars & Circles Sides, Pine, 6 1/2 X12 In. 45.00
Bust, Black Man, Well Dressed, C.1890, 21 1/2 In. 1200.00
Candelabrum, Reindeer Antler, Etched, Lapland, 1900s 45.00
Carousel Horse, White, Blacksmith-Made Rockers, 19th Century 4800.00
Cat, Fence Post, Red & Mustard Paint, 13 In. 450.00
Curlew, Root, Green Paint, Yellow Eye, 14 In. 100.00
Dancer, Black Man, Articulated, Wood & Fiberboard, 12 In. 35.00
Dancer, Black Man, Metal Rod, Wood & Tin.14 1/2 In. 50.00
Dancer, Black Woman, Original Red Paint, Wooden Rod, 9 1/4 In. 35.00
Dancer, Doll, Man & Woman, Articulated, Carved & Painted, 41 In. 1650.00
Dancer, Man, Articulated Legs, Wire Rod, Wooden Handle, Tin, 15 In. 95.00
Deer, Black Polka Dots, Morris Bober, New York, 18 3/4 In. 45.00
Diorama, English Country Church, Wood Case, 13 X 14 X 15 In. 225.00
Doll, Rag, Drawn Face, Felt & Cotton Tuxedo, Felt Hat, 13 In. 15.00
Eagle, Gold Paint, Initialed P.L., 1920s, 30 1/4 In. 375.00
Eagle, Thomas Bieck, Lancaster, Penna., Pine, Wingspread 14 In. 775.00
Farm, Working Model, Tractor, Threshing Machine, Barn, House, 1920s 8000.00
Figure, Amusement Park Fun House, W.D. Harris, 72 In., Pair 2050.00
Figure, Ball & Serpent, Sandstone Carving, Gray, Signed, 11 In. 85.00
Figure, Bellhop, Black Paint, 1930 .... 5500.00
Figure, Dog, Redstone Carved, Will Vickers, Jan.20th, 1889, 3 In. 65.00
Figure, Eagle, Plaster Over Tin, 19 In. 302.00
Figure, Eagle, Rider, Sandstone Carving, Beige, Signed, 10 1/2 In. 150.00
Figure, Man, Articulated Arms & Legs, Carved Hat & Face, 12 In. 75.00
Figure, Man, Wearing Top Hat, Smoking Long Handled Pipe 467.50
Figure, Nude, Wood, 21 1/2 In. .... *Illus* 468.00
Figure, Paul Bunyan & Babe, B. Smith, Youngstown, 1979, 12 3/4 In. 25.00
Figure, Pig Family, Black Spotted, 20th Century, 3 Pigs 2750.00
Figure, Policeman, Maine, Signed & Dated 1921, 16 In. 275.00
Figure, Woman, Standing, Maine, 3/4 Size 1600.00
Footstool, Inlaid Walnut, Skirt, Plank Ends, 18 X 6 3/4 X 7 In. 950.00
Group, Diver Embraces Mermaid, Wood, 10 In. .... *Illus* 275.00
Hen On Nest, Mechanical, Boiled Egg Pops Out 4800.00
Horse, Appalachian, Wooden, 44 X 42 In. 2200.00
Horse, Mahogany, Carved, 8 In. 200.00
Horse, Plow, Farmer, Wife, Polychrome Paint, Evan Dicker, 41 1/2 In. 525.00
Log Cabin, Wood, 18 In. .... *Illus* 385.00
Mailbox, Pull Handle, Wing Flies Up For Mailman, Dr. Clark's 550.00
Mask, Dance, Devil & Tiger, Painted, Mexican, 28 1/2 In. 105.00
Owl, Glass Eyes, Wooden, 14 1/4 In. 75.00
Painting On Board, Buxom Woman, Wearing Towel Over Red Underwear 95.00
Painting On Tin, Virgin Mary, Mexico, Tooled Tin Frame 275.00

Folk Art, Tobacco Humidor, 2 Figures, Wood, 10 In.

Folk Art, Figure, Nude, Wood, 21 1/2 In.

Folk Art, Log Cabin, Wood, 18 In.

Folk Art, Group, Diver Embraces Mermaid, Wood, 10 In.

Panel, Geometric Design, Black, Red, Framed, 14 X 25 In.	75.00
Plaque, Genre Scene, Oak, Log Cabin Frame, Bechtel, 1904	6500.00
Quail, Polychrome Paint, Cement, 20th Century, 10 1/4 In.	45.00
Retablo, Embossed Tin, Lithographic Design, 4 X 6 In.	17.50
Retablo, Oil On Canvas Scroll, Wood Trim, Mexican, 16 X 22 In.	95.00
Retablo, Paint On Tin, Gold Frame, Mexican, 12 1/4 X 16 1/4 In.	80.00
Retablo, Painted Design, Carved Pine, Mexican, 11 X 16 1/2 In.	155.00
Retablo, Painted Tin, Paper Trim, Mexican, 9 1/2 X 13 1/2 In.	175.00
Retablo, Printed Paper, Tin Frame, Mexican, 4 7/8 X 7 5/8 In.	15.00
Rooster, Carved, Pine, Polychrome Paint, Wooden Base, 11 1/4 In.	4000.00
Santo, Gentleman, Standing, Rectangular Plinth, 14 In.	130.00
Santo, Male Saint, Pierced Nimbus, Glass Eyes, 39 In.	1100.00
Santo, Nun, Standing, Rectangular Base, 11 In.	190.00
Santo, Saint, Standing, Contemporary Square Plinth, 11 1/2 In.	105.00
Santo, Saint, Standing, Raised Circular Base, 11 1/2 In.	110.00
Santo, Saint, Standing, Raised Sphere, Cylindrical Base, 14 In.	130.00
Santo, Saint, Standing, Raised Sphere, Rectangular Plinth, 12 In.	115.00
Santo, Saint, Standing, Sphere Base, Domed Plinth, 11 1/4 In.	125.00
Santo, Saint, Standing, Square Plinth, 12 In.	75.00
Santo, Saint, Standing, Square, Base, 11 1/4 In.	100.00
Santo, Saint, Standing, Stepped Rectangular Plinth, 10 In.	100.00
Santos, Madonna & Child, Angels, Demon, 27 1/2 In.	600.00
Santos, Madonna & Child, Standing, 9 1/2 In.	130.00
Sawmill Diorama, WPA, 1936	2350.00
Serpent, Gourd, Faces With Names, Howard Finster, 45 In.	200.00
Serpent, Gourd, Minnie L. Black, 2–12–8–, 24 In.	45.00
Shelf, Diamond & Heart Cutouts, Birds Flanking, 7 X 11 X 3 In.	275.00
Shelf, Hanging, Brown Finish, Carved Detail, 21 1/2 In.	230.00
Ship, Great Republic, New England, C.1920, 4 1/2 X 5 Ft.	2500.00
Spoon Rack, 3 Tiers, Painted Baskets of Flowers, Black, 9 X 15 In.	325.00
Spoon, Figural, Dan, Liberia, 17 In.	55.00
Stand, Poplar, Brown Finish, 1 Board Base Shelf & Top, 30 In.	175.00
Steamship, Wood & Tin, C.1920	950.00
Swan, 2 Piece Neck & Head, Glass Eyes, Solid Body, 28 In.	225.00
Table, Birch & Slate, 4 Tepee Legs	245.00
Tie Rack, Staghorn	53.00
Tobacco Humidor, 2 Figures, Wood, 10 In. ....*Illus*	305.00
Watch Hutch, 1 Drawer, Carved, French War Prisoner, 1800, 12 In.	1475.00
Water Witch, Wooden, Primitive	35.00
Whirligig, 2 Men Sawing Wood, Weathered Wood, Painted, 39 In.	115.00
Whirligig, Cowboy & Bronco	95.00
Whirligig, Fisherman	140.00
Whirligig, Man On Tricycle, Warner Pearson, Ashtabula, Ohio, 43 In.	500.00
Whirligig, Minstrel	225.00
Whirligig, Mule, Kicking, Metal Fittings, Wood & Metal, 28 In.	50.00
Whirligig, Sailor	2200.00
Whirligig, Sprinkling Sambo, Firestone Rubber Products	150.00
Whirligig, Thresher	495.00

Whirligig, Woman Churning & Child, 22 1/2 In.	115.00
Whirligig, Woodpecker	45.00
Wreath, American Seed, Gilt Edged Shadowbox Frame, 1860	395.00

Cold feet have been a problem for generations. Our ancestors had many ingenious ways to warm feet with portable foot warmers. Some warmers held charcoal, others held hot water. Pottery, tin, and soapstone were the favored materials to conduct the heat. The warmer was kept under the feet, then the legs and feet were tucked into a blanket, providing welcome warmth in a cold carriage or church.

FOOT WARMER, Beige Pottery, Stopper, Marked 1 1/2, Europe	50.00
Bennington	300.00
Blue Stoneware	160.00
Charcoal, Drawer, Tin	22.00
Circle Punched Design, Mortise & Tendon Frame, Tin Box	140.00
Drilled Holes, Tin Pierced Heart Design	250.00
Hardwood Case, Punched Diamonds & Circles, Tin, 5 3/4 In.	145.00
Henderson, Stoneware	75.00
Logan, Ohio, Stoneware	200.00
Pierced Tin, Wooden Frame, Wire Handle, Coal Pan, 9 X 7 X 5 In.	500.00
Pottery, Scotland	40.00
Punched Tin Hearts, Wire Bail, Coal Pan, Cherry Case	285.00
Punched Tin, Cherry Frame, Circles & Diamonds, 7 1/2 In.	375.00
Punched Tin, Mortised Cherry Frame, Turned Posts, 9 1/2 In.	150.00
Soapstone, Bail	25.00
Tinned Iron Cube, Wooden, Hinged Door, Mid–19th Century, 7 In.	500.00
Wooden, Tin Star Cutouts, No Tray	175.00

Fostoria glass was made in Fostoria, Ohio, from 1887 to 1891. The factory was moved to Moundsville, West Virginia, and most of the glass seen in shops today is a twentieth–century product. The company was sold in 1983; and new items will be easily identifiable, according to the new owners, Lancaster Colony Corporation.

FOSTORIA, see also Milk Glass	
FOSTORIA, Alexis, Cup	50.00
Alexis, Toothpick	35.00
American Lady, Champagne	11.00
American Lady, Goblet, Amethyst, 6 Oz.	15.00
American Lady, Goblet, Water	13.00
American Lady, Sherbet	7.50
American Lady, Shrimp Cocktail	11.00
American, Appetizer Set, 7 Piece	250.00
American, Ashtray, Square, 5 In.	20.00
American, Basket, Reed Handle, 13 X 9 In.	150.00
American, Bonbon, 3–Footed	10.00
American, Bottle, Bitters, Chrome Holder, Pair	98.00
American, Bottle, Bitters, Chrome Rack	170.00
American, Bottle, Condiment	125.00
American, Bowl, 10 In.	30.00
American, Bowl, Floating Garden, 11 1/2 In.	40.00
American, Bowl, Footed, Tricornered, 11 In.	40.00
American, Bowl, Handle, 4 1/2 In.	5.00
American, Bowl, Red, 11 In.	40.00
American, Bowl, Triangular, 3–Footed, 11 In.	30.00
American, Bowl, Trophy Cup, Footed, 2 Handles, 8 In.	75.00
American, Bread Plate, 6 In.	6.00
American, Butter, Cover, Round	90.00 To 105.00
American, Butter, Domed Cover	80.00 To 125.00
American, Cake Plate, 3–Footed	35.00
American, Cake Plate, Pedestal, Square	65.00
American, Candleholder, Low, Pair	18.00
American, Candlestick, Double, 4 1/2 In., Pair	50.00 To 53.00
American, Candlestick, Hurricane, Pair	150.00

American, Candlestick, Step, Pair 110.00
American, Candy Dish, Cover, 3 Sections 65.00
American, Candy Dish, Pedestal, Cover, 7 1/2 In. 35.00
American, Celery, Handle 20.00
American, Cheese & Cracker Set 52.00
American, Claret 15.00
American, Coaster, 3 3/4 In., 4 Piece 20.00
American, Compote, Jelly, Cover, 5 In. .... 25.00 To 30.00
American, Cookie Jar .... 285.00 To 325.00
American, Cruet 25.00
American, Cruet, Clear Stopper, 7 In. 20.00
American, Cup 4.00
American, Cup & Saucer ....5.00 To 10.00
American, Decanter, Stopper, 24 Oz., 9 In. 75.00
American, Decanter, Whiskey, Stopper 55.00
American, Dinner Set, Service For 6, 48 Piece 400.00
American, Goblet, 4 3/8 In. 9.00
American, Goblet, Water 12.00
American, Ice Tub 45.00
American, Iced Tea, Flared, Flat 22.00
American, Lemon Dish, Cover 25.00
American, Napkin Ring, 12 Piece 60.00
American, Nappy 7.00
American, Pitcher 58.00
American, Pitcher, Footed, 8 In. 55.00
American, Pitcher, Ice Lip, 6 1/2 In. 25.00
American, Pitcher, Ice Lip, Flat Bottom, 8 1/2 In. 65.00
American, Plate, 6 In. 6.75
American, Plate, 7 1/2 In. ....6.00 To 8.50
American, Plate, 8 1/2 In. 12.00
American, Plate, 9 1/2 In. 15.00
American, Plate, Olive, 12 In. 22.50
American, Plate, Salad, Crescent Shape, 7 1/2 In. 45.00
American, Plate, Torte, 14 In. 32.00
American, Platter, Oval, 12 In. 45.00
American, Punch Bowl, Footed 95.00
American, Punch Cup 9.00
American, Punch Set, 12 Cups 275.00
American, Relish, 3 Sections 32.50
American, Relish, 3 Sections, Oval, 10 1/4 In. .... 40.00 To 48.00
American, Relish, 4 Sections, Square, 11 In. 110.00
American, Relish, Divided, 12 In. .... 16.00 To 18.00
American, Salt Dip 4.00
American, Saltshaker, 3 1/2 In. 5.00
American, Sandwich Plate, Center Handle, 12 In. 45.00
American, Sherbet, Flared, 5 Oz. 5.00
American, Sign, Store, With Label, Glass, 4 In. 35.00
American, Syrup, Chrome Top .... 30.00 To 35.00
American, Syrup, Drip–Proof Top 25.00
American, Toothpick, Hat Shape .... 22.00 To 25.00
American, Tray, Round, 12 In. ....70.00 To 100.00
American, Tray, Sandwich, Center Handle 27.00
American, Tray, Torte, 13 1/2 In. 45.00
American, Tumbler, Footed, 4 1/4 In. 6.00
American, Tumbler, Footed, 5 1/2 In. 10.00
American, Underplate, Round, 14 In. 55.00
American, Vase, 10 In. 90.00
American, Vase, 11 3/4 In. 68.00
American, Vase, Flared, 9 1/2 In. 60.00
American, Vase, Straight Sides, 8 In. 35.00
Arcady, Champagne 12.00
Arcady, Tumbler, Footed, 9 Oz. 17.00
Arcady, Tumbler, Iced Tea 15.00
Aurora, Tumbler, 12 Oz. 10.00

Baroque, Bonbon, 3–Footed, 5 1/2 In. 20.00
Baroque, Bonbon, Yellow, 3–Footed, 6 In. 24.00
Baroque, Bowl, Flared, 12 In. 22.00
Baroque, Bowl, Gold, 11 In. 30.00
Baroque, Bowl, Yellow, 11 3/4 In., 2 Piece 11.50
Baroque, Bowl, Yellow, Flared, 11 1/2 In. 30.00
Baroque, Candelabrum, 4 X 8 In., Pair 34.00
Baroque, Candlestick, Gold 35.00
Baroque, Candlestick, Trindle, Yellow 32.50
Baroque, Candy Dish, Cover, Topaz 35.00
Baroque, Creamer 10.00
Baroque, Cruet, Topaz .... 155.00 To 185.00
Baroque, Cup & Saucer 15.25
Baroque, Dish, Pickle, Blue, 8 In. 23.00
Baroque, Goblet, Blue, 6 1/4 In. 24.00
Baroque, Ice Tub, Yellow 65.00
Baroque, Plate, 9 In. 17.00
Baroque, Plate, Yellow, 9 In. 45.00
Baroque, Punch Bowl, Footed, Blue 1250.00
Baroque, Relish, Square, Yellow, 2 Sections, 6 In. 22.00
Baroque, Salt & Pepper, Yellow 90.00
Baroque, Sherbet, Blue, 5 Oz. 25.00
Baroque, Sugar & Creamer, Yellow .... 22.50 To 25.00
Baroque, Sugar, Individual, Yellow 13.00
Baroque, Tidbit, 3–Footed, Flat 18.00
Baroque, Tumbler, Yellow, Footed, 5 1/2 In. 45.00
Baroque, Vase, Yellow, 7 3/4 In. 48.00
Beverly, Celery, Green 23.00
Beverly, Pitcher, Green, Footed 210.00
Beverly, Plate, Amber, 8 1/2 In. 7.50
Beverly, Soup, Cream, Amber 8.00
Beverly, Tumbler, Amber, Footed, 12 Oz. 15.00
Bookends, Lyre, Crystal 60.00
Bookends, Owl, Crystal 275.00
Bookends, Rearing Horse, Amber 195.00
Bouquet, Bowl, Flared, Footed, 10 3/4 In. 40.00
Bouquet, Candy Jar, Open 25.00
Bouquet, Plate, 9 1/4 In. 30.00
Bouquet, Salver, Footed, 12 1/4 In. 35.00
Brazilian, Cracker Jar 90.00
Brazilian, Finger Bowl 20.00
Buttercup, Candlestick, Trindle 40.00
Buttercup, Creamer 13.00
Camellia, Bowl, Lily Pond, 11 1/4 In. 33.00
Camellia, Plate, Lunch 8.00
Camellia, Sugar & Creamer, Tray 30.00
Century, Bowl, Vegetable, Oval, 9 1/2 In. 30.00
Century, Butter, 1/4 Lb. 18.00
Century, Candy Dish, Cover 30.00
Century, Cruet, Stopper 38.00
Century, Dish, Pickle, 8 1/2 In. 15.00
Century, Mayonnaise Set, 3 Piece 25.00
Century, Mustard, Ladle 28.00
Century, Plate, Footed, 8 In. 10.00
Century, Relish, 3 Sections, 11 In. .... 25.00 To 27.00
Century, Sugar & Creamer, Heather Etch 15.00
Century, Sugar & Creamer, Individual 20.00
Century, Sugar & Creamer, Tray 22.50
Century, Sugar & Creamer, Tray, Individual 32.00
Century, Sugar, Footed 9.00
Century, Tray, Tidbit, 2–Tier 35.00
Chintz, Bonbon, 3–Footed 22.00
Chintz, Cake Plate, Handle, 10 1/2 In. 25.00
Chintz, Cocktail, Stem, 4 Oz. 18.00

Chintz, Creamer, Individual, Footed 15.00
Chintz, Dish, Pickle, 8 In. 18.00
Chintz, Goblet, Water, 9 Oz. 18.00
Chintz, Mayonnaise Set, 3 Piece 55.00
Chintz, Plate, Cupped Rim, 13 3/4 In. 25.00
Chintz, Sherbet, Low, 4 3/8 In. 19.00
Chintz, Sugar 15.00
Chintz, Tumbler, Footed, 6 In. 22.75
Chintz, Wine, Claret, 4 1/2 Oz. 18.00
Classic, Champagne, Green 8.00
Coin, Ashtray, Red 28.00
Coin, Bowl, Blue 70.00
Coin, Bowl, Flat, 7 In. 30.00
Coin, Bowl, Footed, Amber, 8 In. .... 40.00 To 45.00
Coin, Bowl, Oval, Red, 9 In. 65.00
Coin, Bride's Bowl, Ruby 25.00
Coin, Cake Plate, Pedestal 65.00
Coin, Cake Stand, Frosted, 7 In. 85.00
Coin, Cake Stand, Pedestal 55.00
Coin, Candlestick, 8 In. 20.00
Coin, Candlestick, Amber, 8 In., Pair 35.00
Coin, Candy Dish, Cover, Green 65.00
Coin, Candy Dish, Cover, Red, 6 5/16 In. 70.00
Coin, Candy Dish, Cover, Red, 13 In. 120.00
Coin, Candy Jar, Cover 28.50
Coin, Compote, Amber 40.00
Coin, Compote, Cover, Red, 5 In. 55.00
Coin, Compote, Jelly, Footed, 4 In. 15.00
Coin, Compote, Open, 8 1/2 In. 50.00
Coin, Console Set, Olive Green, 3 Piece 115.00
Coin, Cruet .... 39.00 To 65.00
Coin, Decanter, Amber 39.00
Coin, Dish, Jelly 12.50
Coin, Dish, Red, Oval, 9 In. 65.00
Coin, Nappy, Frosted, Handle, Blue 25.00
Coin, Pitcher, Frosted, Avocado, 6 In. 18.00
Coin, Punch Set, 12 Piece 225.00
Coin, Salt & Pepper 20.00
Coin, Salt & Pepper, Blue 22.50
Coin, Sugar & Creamer, Avocado Green 45.00
Coin, Sugar & Creamer, Cover, Amber 35.00
Coin, Vase, 8 In. 25.00
Coin, Wedding Bowl, Cover .... 45.00 To 50.00
Coin, Wedding Bowl, Cover, Red .... 80.00 To 85.00
Colonial Dame, Goblet, Green, 12 Oz. 11.00
Colony, Bowl, 5 In. 18.00
Colony, Bowl, 6 1/4 In. 22.00
Colony, Bowl, Flared, 11 In. 32.00
Colony, Bowl, Mayonnaise, 2 Piece 28.00
Colony, Candlestick, 9 In., Pair 75.00
Colony, Compote, Cheese 18.00
Colony, Plate, 7 In. 5.00
Colony, Relish, 2 Sections, 7 In. 18.00
Colony, Saucer 2.50
Colony, Server, Center Handle 28.00
Colony, Tray, Muffin, Handles 22.50
Colony, Tumbler, Juice, 5 Oz. 18.00
Colony, Vase, Flared, 7 1/2 In. 35.00
Colony, Wine .... 14.00 To 18.00
Contour, Sugar & Creamer 10.00
Coronet, Bonbon, 3–Footed, 7 1/4 In. 8.00
Coronet, Bowl, Fruit, 13 In. 15.00
Coronet, Compote 12.50
Coronet, Plate, 8 1/2 In. 3.75

Corsage, Cake Plate, Handle	25.00
Corsage, Cup & Saucer	18.00
Corsage, Saucer	4.50
Corsage, Sherbet	10.00
Fairfax, Bowl, 4–Footed, Green, 10 3/4 In.	22.50
Fairfax, Butter, Cover, Green	50.00
Fairfax, Butter, Cover, Topaz	85.00
Fairfax, Console Set, Blue, 11–In. Bowl, 3 Piece	60.00
Fairfax, Cup & Saucer	10.00
Fairfax, Cup & Saucer, Blue	15.00
Fairfax, Plate, Blue, 7 In.	7.50
Fairfax, Plate, Pink, 9 1/2 In.	8.00
Fairfax, Relish, Footed, Blue	12.00
Fairfax, Tumbler, Water, Blue	18.00
Fairfax, Wine, Blue, 3 Oz.	25.00
Fern, Bonbon, Handle	12.00
Fern, Dish, Lemon	11.00
Figurine, Cardinal Head, Cranberry, Label, 1950s, 6 1/2 In.	750.00
Figurine, Mermaid	85.00
Heather, Compote	20.00
Heather, Goblet	18.00
Heather, Pitcher, Ice Lip, Crystal, 7 1/2 In.	90.00
Heather, Relish, 3 Sections	35.00
Heather, Sherbet	14.00
Heather, Sugar & Creamer, Tray	30.00
Heirloom, Bonbon, Blue	25.00
Heirloom, Bowl, Oblong, Yellow, 14 1/2 In.	45.00
Heirloom, Bowl, Pink, 12 In.	65.00
Heirloom, Bowl, Yellow, 13 In.	60.00
Heirloom, Epergne, Green, 15 In.	50.00
Holly, Goblet	15.00
Jamestown, Goblet, Amber, 8 Oz.	8.00
Jamestown, Goblet, Blue, 8 Oz.	10.00
Jamestown, Goblet, Brown, 9 1/2 Oz.	8.00
Jamestown, Plate, Ruby, 8 In.	15.00
Jamestown, Sherbet, Green	10.00
Jamestown, Tumbler, Blue, 11 Oz.	11.00
Jamestown, Tumbler, Footed, Green, 11 Oz.	8.00
Jamestown, Tumbler, Iced Tea, Footed, Green, 6 In.	12.00
Jamestown, Tumbler, Iced Tea, Ruby	20.00
Jenny Lind, Box, Dresser, Pink, Square, 5 1/2 In.	58.00
Jenny Lind, Pitcher, Milk, 8 1/4 In.	95.00 To 125.00
Jenny Lind, Pomade Jar, Cover, Milk Glass	25.00
June, Bowl, Pink, Handle	65.00
June, Candlestick, 3 In.	18.00
June, Candlestick, Mushroom, Yellow, 5 1/2 In., Pair	50.00
June, Champagne	18.50
June, Compote, Pink, 12 In.	48.00
June, Compote, Yellow, 5 In.	35.00
June, Cup & Saucer, Yellow	28.00
June, Dish, Lemon, Pink	24.00
June, Goblet, 8 1/4 In.	25.50
June, Goblet, Cocktail, 5 1/4 In.	27.00
June, Plate, 10 1/4 In.	30.00
June, Plate, Blue, 7 1/2 In.	13.50
June, Plate, Pink, 6 In.	5.00
June, Plate, Pink, 8 3/4 In.	12.00
June, Plate, Yellow, 7 1/2 In.	8.00
June, Plate, Yellow, 8 3/4 In.	12.00
June, Plate, Yellow, 10 1/4 In.	60.00
June, Platter, 12 In.	35.00
June, Salt & Pepper, Footed	65.00
June, Sherbet, Yellow, Low, 4 1/4 In.	22.00
June, Soup, Cream, Yellow	45.00

June, Sugar, Yellow	23.00
June, Wine, Topaz	30.00
Kashmir, Cup & Saucer, Green	22.00
Kashmir, Tumbler, Yellow, 8 In.	22.00
Lido, Cake Plate	25.00
Lido, Goblet	12.00
Lido, Sherbet	9.00
Lido, Sugar & Creamer	25.00
Lyre, Candleholder, 2–Light, 8 In.	27.50
Mardi Gras, Vase, 7 1/4 In.	88.00
Mayfair, Plate, Topaz, 8 1/4 In.	10.00
Mayfair, Platter, Topaz, Oval, 12 In.	18.00
Meadow Rose, Candlestick, Pair	65.00
Meadow Rose, Candy Jar, Cover, Tall	90.00
Meadow Rose, Cocktail, Oyster	22.00
Meadow Rose, Creamer	15.00
Meadow Rose, Goblet, 5 1/4 In.	30.00
Meadow Rose, Mayonnaise, 2 Piece	38.00
Meadow Rose, Nappy, Triangular, 4 1/2 In.	30.00
Meadow Rose, Plate, 7 In.	7.00
Meadow Rose, Plate, Torte, 14 In.	45.00
Meadow Rose, Relish, 3 Sections	60.00
Meadow Rose, Rose Bowl, 12 In.	35.00
Meadow Rose, Sherbet, 4 3/8 In.	18.00
Meadow Rose, Sugar & Creamer	42.00
Meadow Rose, Tumbler, Footed, 4 5/8 In.	18.00
Meadow Rose, Vase, 5 In.	45.00
Meadow Rose, Wine	33.00
Melrose, Champagne	8.00
Melrose, Wine	11.00
Midnight Rose, Cake Plate	24.00
Midnight Rose, Celery, 11 1/2 In.	28.00
Midnight Rose, Plate, 6 1/2 In.	4.50
Midnight Rose, Plate, Torte, 13 In.	32.00
Morning Glory, Candlestick, Pair	30.00
Myriad, Console Set, 3 Piece	28.00
Navarre, Bowl, Cobalt Blue, Footed, 9 In.	90.00
Navarre, Bowl, Handle, 4–Footed, 10 In.	30.00
Navarre, Cake Plate, Handles, 10 In.	30.00
Navarre, Candlestick, Double Stem, Pair	65.00
Navarre, Champagne	15.00
Navarre, Cocktail, 3 1/2 Oz., 5 1/4 In.	25.00
Navarre, Creamer	16.00
Navarre, Cup & Saucer	19.50
Navarre, Goblet, 10 Oz.	15.00
Navarre, Goblet, Blue, 7 5/8 In.	32.00
Navarre, Nappy, Tricornered, Handle, 4 5/ 8 In.	8.00
Navarre, Salt & Pepper, Flat	50.00
Navarre, Sugar	16.00
Navarre, Tumbler, Blue, 13 Oz., 5 7/8 In.	30.00
Navarre, Wine, 4 1/2 Oz.	28.00
Pioneer, Bouillon, Amber	10.00
Pioneer, Plate, Amber, 6 In.	2.00
Priscilla, Butter, Cover, Green, Gold Trim	65.00
Priscilla, Jug, Amber, Footed	90.00
Priscilla, Pitcher, Amber	50.00
Priscilla, Sugar, Green, Gold Trim	45.00
Rambler, Sauce, Oval, 6 1/2 In.	22.00
Rambler, Tray, Oval, 8 1/2 In.	22.00
Rhapsody, Sherbet, Turquoise	8.00
Rhapsody, Tumbler, Iced Tea, Turquoise	10.00
Rogene, Vase, Rolled Top, 9 In.	85.00
Romance, Bowl, 12 In.	42.50
Romance, Compote, Cream	26.00

Romance, Sherbet 12.00
Romance, Wine .... 25.00 To 28.00
Rose, Tumbler, Footed, 12 Oz. 20.00
Royal, Sherbet, Footed, Green 15.00
Royal, Tumbler, Footed, Green 27.00
Seville, Plate, Amber, 14 In. ....7.00 To 15.00
Shirley, Cocktail 10.00
Shirley, Goblet 15.00
Shirley, Tumbler, Footed, 9 Oz. 10.00
Sunray, Console Set, 3 Piece 47.00
Sunray, Mayonnaise Set, 3 Piece 25.00
Sunray, Mustard, Spoon 20.00
Sydney, Pitcher, 4 1/2 In. 15.00
Thistle, Cocktail 14.00
Thistle, Sherbet 12.00
Thistle, Tumbler, Juice 12.00
Trojan, Bowl, Dessert, Pink 65.00
Trojan, Bowl, Topaz, 11 1/2 In. 30.00
Trojan, Bucket, Sugar Cube, Topaz 67.50
Trojan, Candlestick, Yellow, 5 In., Pair 45.00
Trojan, Creamer, Yellow, Footed 18.00
Trojan, Cup & Saucer, Yellow 22.00
Trojan, Goblet, Water, Yellow, 10 Oz. 27.00
Trojan, Goblet, Yellow ....22.50 To 26.00
Trojan, Ice Tub, Pink 65.00
Trojan, Ice Tub, Topaz 65.00
Trojan, Ice Tub, Yellow, Tongs 80.00
Trojan, Mayonnaise Set, Topaz, 3 Piece 50.00
Trojan, Parfait, Topaz 37.00
Trojan, Plate, Yellow, 6 In. 5.00
Trojan, Plate, Yellow, 9 1/2 In. 18.00
Trojan, Platter, Yellow, 12 In. 65.00
Trojan, Relish, Divided, Yellow, 8 1/2 In. 30.00
Trojan, Sherbet, Yellow, Stemmed 20.00
Trojan, Sugar, Yellow, Footed 18.00
Trojan, Tray, Center Handle, Topaz, 11 1/2 In. 32.00
Trojan, Tumbler, Footed, Yellow, 9 Oz. 16.00
Versailles, Bowl, Centerpiece, Green, 12 In. 48.00
Versailles, Candleholder, Yellow, 5 1/2 In., Pair 26.00
Versailles, Candlestick, Yellow, 3 In. 20.00
Versailles, Champagne, Yellow 16.00
Versailles, Cocktail, Topaz 15.00
Versailles, Creamer, Pink 23.00
Versailles, Cup & Saucer, Blue 25.00
Versailles, Dish, Yellow 18.00
Versailles, Goblet, Water, Blue, 8 1/4 In. 40.00
Versailles, Goblet, Yellow Bowl, Footed 30.00
Versailles, Ice Tub, Pink 90.00
Versailles, Jug, Green, Footed 400.00
Versailles, Plate, Blue, 6 In. 7.00
Versailles, Plate, Pink, 7 1/2 In. 8.00
Versailles, Platter, Pink, 15 In. 125.00
Versailles, Sauce, Pink 125.00
Versailles, Saucer, Blue 6.00
Versailles, Shaker, Pink 50.00
Versailles, Sherbet, Blue, Stem, 6 In. 28.00
Versailles, Sugar & Creamer, Topaz 38.00
Versailles, Sugar Pail, Green 100.00
Versailles, Tumbler, Pink, Footed, 9 Oz., 5 1/4 In. 22.00
Versailles, Tumbler, Yellow Foot, 5 1/4 In. 15.00
Versailles, Wine, Smoky, Signed, 6 Piece 36.00
Vesper, Bowl, Grapefruit, Liner 60.00
Vesper, Candy Dish, Cover, Green, 3 Sections 85.00
Vesper, Cocktail, Oyster, Footed, Amber 15.00

Vesper, Compote, Amber	45.00
Vesper, Creamer, Amber	15.00
Vesper, Cup & Saucer, Green	12.00
Vesper, Demitasse Set, Amber	30.00
Vesper, Goblet, Water, Amber	22.50
Vesper, Ice Tub, Amber	57.50
Vesper, Parfait	25.00
Vesper, Plate, Amber, 10 1/2 In.	30.00
Vesper, Plate, Luncheon, 8 1/2 In.	7.50
Vesper, Sherbet	10.00
Vesper, Sherbet, Amber	15.00
Vesper, Sugar, Amber	17.50
Vesper, Water Set, Footed, Amber, 7 Piece	285.00
Victoria, Relish, 8 In.	10.00
Victoria, Relish, Canoe, Crystal, 8 In.	35.00
Virginia, Pitcher	70.00
Willow, Cruet	28.00
Windsor, Chalice, Cover, Footed, Topaz	75.00
Wistar, Goblet, 1940	26.00

FOVAL, see Fry Foval
FRAME, PICTURE, see Furniture, Frame

Gladding, McBean and Company started in 1875. They made sewer pipes, floor tiles, dinnerwares, and art pottery with a variety of trademarks. In 1934 dinnerware and art pottery were sold under the name Franciscan Ware. The plant was closed in 1984 but a few of the patterns are still being made.

FRANCISCAN, Bowl, Cereal, Desert Rose	8.00
Bowl, Coronado, Yellow	7.00
Butter, Cover, Desert Rose, 1/4 Lb.	27.00
Casserole, Coronado, Coral	25.00
Casserole, Yellow Rose, Cover, Large	45.00
Creamer, Coronado, Yellow	5.00
Cup & Saucer, El Patio, Desert Rose	10.00
Gravy Boat, Desert Rose, Stand	25.00
Gravy Boat, Pink, Liner	15.00
Plaque, Dealer's	55.00
Plate, Apple, 6 In.	4.00
Plate, Desert Rose, 10 1/2 In.	12.00
Plate, Dinner, Apple	9.00
Platter, Apple, 12 1/2 In.	20.00
Salt & Pepper, Desert Rose	18.00
Sauce Boat, Coronado, Turquoise	10.00
Sugar & Creamer, Desert Rose	25.00

Francisware is a named glassware made by Hobbs, Brockunier and Company of Wheeling, West Virginia, in the 1880s. It is a clear or frosted hobnail or swirl pattern glass with amber-stained rim. Some pieces were made by a pressed glass method, others were mold blown.

FRANCISWARE, Berry Bowl, Master	75.00
Cookie Jar, Desert Rose	125.00
Creamer	65.00
Ice Cream Set, Frosted Hobnail, On Plate, 9 Piece	395.00
Pitcher, Milk, Hobnail	215.00
Toothpick, Opalescent Hobs, 2 1/2 In.	50.00

Frankart, Inc., New York, New York, mass-produced nude "dancing-lady" lamps, ashtrays, and other decorative Art Deco items in the 1920s and 1930s. They were made of white lead composition and spray-painted. "Frankart Inc." and the patent number and year were stamped on the base.

FRANKART, Ashtray Stand, Arms Stretched Over Head Support Tray, Signed	600.00
Ashtray, Ballerina Center, Onyx Tray, Round, 9 In.	265.00

Ashtray, Fighting Rams	25.00
Ashtray, Floor Model	150.00
Ashtray, Golfer	85.00
Ashtray, Nude	595.00
Ashtray, Snowbird, Black Insert	35.00
Bookends, Double Horse	50.00
Bookends, Dutch Boy & Girl	140.00
Bookends, Horse, Art Deco	85.00
Bookends, Horsehead, Hugo	20.00
Bookends, Scotty	150.00
Bookends, Scotty, Full–Bodied	50.00
Candleholder, Nude, Upraised Arms Hold Holder, 12 1/2 In., Pair	375.00
Figurine, Nude, Knee In Air, Holds Tray At Side, 10 In.	265.00
Lamp, 2 Horseheads, 16 X 12 In.	150.00
Lamp, Circus Elephant, Green	145.00
Lamp, Nude Holding Frosted Disc, Green, 8 1/2 In.	850.00
Lamp, Nude, Double, Green Shade	535.00
Lamp, Shriner's Head, 1927	175.00
Plaque, Art Deco Woman's Face, Silver Colored, 7 X 10 In.	235.00

Frankoma Pottery was originally known as The Frank Potteries when John F. Frank opened shop in 1933. The factory is now working in Sapulpa, Oklahoma. Early wares were made from a light cream–colored clay, but in 1956 the company switched to a red burning clay. The firm makes dinnerwares, utilitarian and decorative kitchen wares, figurines, flowerpots, and limited edition and commemorative pieces.

FRANKOMA, Ashtray, Arrowhead, Green & Brown	10.00
Bookends, Clydesdale Horses	125.00
Bookends, Mountain Girl, Green	175.00
Bookends, Women, Green	150.00
Candleholder, Green, Leopard Mark	50.00
Candleholder, Oral Roberts, Tulsa, 1971, Pair	25.00
Casserole, Cover, Wagon Wheel	35.00
Cookie Jar, Barrel, Green	38.00
Cookie Jar, Barrel, White	35.00
Figurine, Fan Dancer, Green	185.00
Figurine, Mallard	10.00
Figurine, Panther, Stalking, Green	165.00
Figurine, Squirrel, Tan Clay, 6 In.	18.00
Figurine, Woman, Seated, No.425	95.00
Honey, Beehive Shape	15.00
Mask, Comedy & Tragedy, Green, Pair	55.00 To 58.00
Mug, Elephant, Bush, Quayle, 1989	5.50
Mug, Elephant, GOP, Brown Satin, White Interior, 1979	15.00
Mug, Elephant, Nixon–Agnew, 1973	18.50
Mug, Elephant, Red, 1969	28.00
Mug, Elephant, White, 1968	85.00
Mug, GOP, 1968	40.00
Mug, Mayan, Aqua	25.00
Pitcher, Sugar, Creamer, Salt & Pepper, Wagon Wheel	150.00
Planter, Madonna of Grace	50.00
Plaque, Mask, Tragedy, Black Glaze, Paper Label, Large	20.00
Plate, Christmas, 1970	7.50
Plate, Easter, 1972	15.00
Plate, Teenagers of The Bible, 1973–1977, 7 Piece	40.00
Salt & Pepper, Animals, Mottled Green	20.00
Salt & Pepper, Figural, Elephant	40.00
Salt & Pepper, Tan	12.00
Teapot, Mayan–Aztec, 2 Cup	15.00
Teapot, Wagon Wheel, 2 Cup	40.00
Trivet, Cherokee, Alphabet	12.00
Trivet, Oklahoma Diamond Jubilee, 1982	22.00
Vase, Bottle Shape, Blue, 12 In.	26.00 To 30.00

Vase, Green, Large 85.00
Vase, Green, Stepped, Small 40.00
Wall Pocket, Acorn 20.00

 The Fraternal section lists objects that are related to the many different fraternal organizations in the United States. The Elks, Masons, Odd Fellows, and others are included. Furniture is listed in the Furniture section.

FRATERNAL, see also Shaving Mug
FRATERNAL, B.P.O.E., Book, Elks, Constitution & Statutes, 1940 .... 1.50
B.P.O.E., Bread Plate, Clock, Cervus Alces, Floral Border, Frosted 125.00
B.P.O.E., Flask, Figural, Goofus Glass 85.00
B.P.O.E., Hatpin 20.00
B.P.O.E., Stickpin, Elk Head, Gold Filled 45.00
B.P.O.E., Watch Fob, Card Holder, Membership, Sterling 70.00
Eagles, Match Holder, Nickel Plated, Brass 22.00
Eagles, Shaving Mug, Lodge, No.1009, Liberty, Truth, Etc., Gold 130.00
Eastern Star, Book, 1910 .... 5.00
Eastern Star, Kit, Mending, Contents 20.00
Eastern Star, Pin, 20 Point Diamond, Gold Gavel, Chain Attached 125.00
Elks, Shaving Mug 200.00
F.O.E., Earrings, Ceramic 7.00
F.O.E., Shaving Mug 300.00
Knights of Columbus, Match Holder, 1919 .... 20.00
Knights of Columbus, Sword & Scabbard, 1840–60 .... 50.00
Knights of Pythias, Shaving Mug, Gold Name, Limoges 115.00
Knights Templar, Medal, 1925 .... 25.00
Knights Templar, Ribbon, Troy, Oh., Silk, Red, Ivory, 1883, 3 X 8 In. 22.00
Knights Templar, Shaving Mug 300.00
Masonic, Apron, Blue Printed Design, 16 X 17 In. 10.00
Masonic, Apron, Leather, Painted Designs, 15 1/4 X 15 1/4 In. 185.00
Masonic, Apron, Red Fringe, Painted Insignia, 17 X 18 In. 45.00
Masonic, Bible, Leather Binding, 22K Gold Stamped, 1931, 1200 Pg. 50.00
Masonic, Book, History of Free Masonry, Stillson & Hughan, 1909 .... 35.00
Masonic, Certificate, Parchment, King Hirams Lodge, C.1790 .... 3000.00
Masonic, Clock, Seth Thomas Movement, Wooden, Emblem, Striking 150.00
Masonic, Cup & Saucer, Los Angeles, 1908 ....98.00 To 145.00
Masonic, Gavel, Ivory, Silver, Presented To Father, Son, 1910, Case 175.00
Masonic, Lamp, Bulb, Symbol As Filament, 7 1/2 In. 30.00
Masonic, Loving Cup, Melita Chapter No.284, 7 1/2 In. 85.00
Masonic, Match Holder, Wall, Symbols, Walnut, 11 In. 65.00
Masonic, Medal, 14K Solid Gold 300.00
Masonic, Mug, Chief Saratoga, Pittsburgh, Sword Handle, 1903 .... 85.00
Masonic, Mug, Rising Star Lodge, Blue–Green, 1903 .... 40.00
Masonic, Paperweight, Emblems 45.00
Masonic, Picture, Cincinnati Band In Uniform, World War I Era 35.00
Masonic, Pin, Lady's, Gold & Pearl, Enameled, 1880 .... 25.00
Masonic, Salt & Pepper, Bavarian, Masonic Emblem 20.00
Masonic, Shaving Mug, Blue Lodge, Symbol, Glowing Eye, Gold Name 95.00
Masonic, Spoon, Masonic Temple, Chicago, Indian Handle, Sterling 35.00
Masonic, Spoon, Memphis 10.00
Masonic, Stein, Camels, Riders, Cobalt Blue Design, Gray Stoneware 235.00
Masonic, Wallet, Man's, Black Leather, Embossed Leaf Pattern 2.00
Masonic, Watch Fob 15.00
Odd Fellows, Charm, Watch, Enameled, Gold, 1920 .... 20.00
Odd Fellows, Invitation, Chicken Fry Luncheon, Sept. 29, 1902 .... 4.50
Odd Fellows, Shaving Mug 325.00
Odd Fellows, Shaving Mug, 3 Link Chain, Black Script Name 85.00
Odd Fellows, Spoon, Symbols, Chain For Hanging, 4 In. 130.00
Odd Fellows, Watch Fob, 94th Anniversary, April 12, 1913 .... 25.00
Order of Moose, Ashtray, Figural 10.00
Shriner, Champagne, Louisiana, Alligators Other Side, Iridescent 65.00
Shriner, Champagne, Syria Mosque, Pittsburgh & Rochester, 1911 .... 85.00

Shriner, Cup & Saucer, Los Angeles, 1906	70.00
Shriner, Hatpin, Jerusalem Shrine	35.00
Shriner, Medal, Silver	38.00
Shriner, Mug, Atlantic City, 1904	65.00
Shriner, Mug, Syria Temple, Pittsburgh, 1895, Nantasket Beach, Gold	110.00
Shriner, Plate, Camel Border, Shenango Pottery	85.00
Shriner, Tumbler, Detroit Moslem Temple	7.50
Shriner, Tumbler, Minneapolis, 3–Sided, Photo, Names, Date, 1917	85.00
Shriner, Tumbler, Pittsburgh Temple, 4–Sided, Milk Glass, 1917	125.00

Fry glass was made by the H. C. Fry Glass Company of Rochester, Pennsylvania. The company, founded in 1901, first made cut glass and other types of fine glasswares. In 1922, they patented a heat-resistant glass called "Pearl Oven glass." For two years, 1926–27, the company made Fry Foval, an opal ware decorated with colored trim. Reproductions of this glass have been made. The company also made Depression glass.

FRY FOVAL, Candlestick, Blue Threading, Pair	195.00
Plate, Center Blue Handle, 6 1/4 In.	160.00
Sugar & Creamer, Signed	140.00
Tea Set, Blue Spout, Finial & Handles, Teapot & 6 Cups & Saucers	525.00
Vase, Goblet, Large	125.00
Vase, Jack–In–The–Pulpit, Cobalt Blue Trim, Marked, 11 In.	170.00
FRY, Bowl, Cover, 8 1/2 In.	20.00
Casserole, Cover, Metal Holder, 8 1/2 In.	28.00
Custard Cup, 3 1/2 In.	6.00
Goblet, Crackle Glass, Clear, Applied Green Base, 6 Piece	120.00
Grill Plate, 3 Sections, 10 1/2 In.	25.00
Juicer, Opalescent Pearl	40.00
Pitcher, Opalescent, Cover	200.00
Platter, Oval, 13 In.	17.00
Reamer, Opalescent, 1967	35.00
Tray, Cut Glass, Hobstars & Pinwheels, Leaf Shape, 13 In.	750.00
Tray, Cut Glass, Sciota Pattern, Signed, 2 3/4 X 13 3/4 X 10 1/4 In.	1350.00

Fulper is the mark used by the American Pottery Company of Flemington, New Jersey. The art pottery was made from 1910 to 1929. The firm had been making bottles, jugs, and housewares from 1805. Doll heads were made about 1928. The firm became Stangl Pottery in 1929. Fulper art pottery is admired for its attractive glazes and simple shapes.

FULPER, Bowl, Blue Flambe Over Mustard, 10 In.	100.00
Bowl, Flared Rim, Handles, Brown To Tan, Oval, 11 3/4 In.	65.00
Bowl, Handles, Blue, 8 In.	95.00
Bowl, Lily, Blue, 6 1/2 In.	80.00
Bowl, Lily, Mirror Flambe, 9 In.	95.00
Bowl, Rectangle Suspended By 2 Arms, C.1915, 6 X 10 1/4 In.	192.00
Candlestick, 2 Handles, Pink & Green, 4 In.	75.00
Chamberstick, Hooded	45.00
Flower Frog, Nude, Sitting In Field Of Grass & Daisies, 6 In.	165.00
Flower Frog, Toad	40.00
Jug, Musical, Brown Flambe	95.00
Lamp, Ballerina, Bisque	185.00
Lamp, Parrot	700.00
Lamp, Perfume, Ballerina	425.00
Lamp, Perfume, Bisque Ballerina, Signed Stangl	200.00
Lamp, Perfume, Orange Deco Lady	165.00
Lantern, Candle, Colored Glass Inserts, Signed, C.1912, 10 3/4 In.	1815.00
Mug, Green Crystalline, Initials	58.00
Perfume Burner, Standing Woman, Large	950.00
Planter, Dogwood	20.00
Pot, Round Collar, Mirror Black, 5 In.	145.00
Rose Bowl, Mirror Flambe, 9 In.	85.00
Sugar & Creamer, Yellow	70.00

Tile, Moravian, Figural, 3 Piece 150.00
Urn, Blue, Handles, 7 In. 85.00
Vase, Angled Shoulder, 3 Tab Handles, Signed, C.1915, 6 1/2 In. 275.00
Vase, Baluster Form, Blue–Green Drip Glaze Over Buff, 16 1/4 In. 2000.00
Vase, Blue Crystalline, 3 3/4 In. 50.00
Vase, Blue Crystalline, 6 1/2 In. 275.00
Vase, Brown & Black Drip Glaze Over Blue–Green, Marked, 11 1/2 In. 3030.00
Vase, Brown & Copper Drip Glaze, Marked, C.1915, 4 5/8 In. 192.00
Vase, Chinese Blue, 6 In. 275.00
Vase, Conical, Mustard Glaze, Drapery Overglaze, 12 1/4 In. 2175.00
Vase, Flared Neck, Violet, Blue & Green Glaze, Marked, 15 1/4 In. 1350.00
Vase, Green & Rose, 10 In. 375.00
Vase, Green Over Blue, 3 1/2 In. 95.00
Vase, Green, Blue, 3 Buttresses, 13 1/2 In. 1875.00
Vase, Jade Green, 16 1/2 In. 950.00
Vase, Matte Brown, 2 Angled Handles, Marked, C.1915, 7 1/2 In. 360.00
Vase, Plum & Gray High Glaze, 2 Handles, 8 In. 165.00
Vase, Red & Gray Streak Glaze, 2 Handled, 9 In. 185.00
Vase, Spherical Form, Blue Drip Glaze Over White, 1915, 7 1/2 In. 65.00
Wall Pocket, Bird, Double 225.00
Wall Pocket, Bird, Single 125.00

All types of furniture are listed in this section. Examples dating from the seventeenth century to the 1950s are included. Prices for furniture vary in different parts of the country. Oak furniture is most expensive in the West; large pieces over eight feet high are sold for the most money in the South where high ceilings are found in the old homes. Condition is very important when determining prices. These are NOT average prices but rather reports of unique sales. If the description includes the word "style," the piece resembles the old furniture style but was made at a later time. It is not a period piece.

Furniture, Armoire, Louisiana, Mahogany, Inlaid, Cabriole Legs

FURNITURE, Armchair, see also Furniture, Chair
FURNITURE, Armchair, American Rococo Revival, Rosewood, Print Upholstery 395.00
Armchair, Centennial Chippendale, Mahogany, Ornate, Pair 1540.00
Armchair, Child's, Red, Black Graining, Yellow Striping, 21 In. 85.00
Armchair, Chinese, Lacquered, Carved, Gilt Design, Square Seat 990.00
Armchair, Chippendale, Mahogany, Square Back, Slip Seat 935.00
Armchair, Fauteuil, French Empire, Upholstered, C.1875, Pair 2090.00
Armchair, Flemish Style, Dark Finish, Cane Seat & Back 125.00
Armchair, George II, Walnut, Carved, Upholstered Seat 8500.00
Armchair, George III, Mahogany, Upholstered, Pair 1700.00
Armchair, Gothic Revival, Oak, Pierced Back, Plank Seat, England 247.00
Armchair, Jacobean Revival, Painted Leather Back & Seat, Pair 110.00
Armchair, Ladder Back, Oak, Plank Seat, Worn Dark Finish, England 95.00
Armchair, Mahogany, Chinese Dragon Design, Needlepoint, Pair 1300.00
Armchair, Oak, Turned Legs, Posts, Carved, Wainscot Back, Europe 1200.00
Armchair, Oscillating, Palmer Plastics, Pat. May 3, 1870 .... 650.00
Armchair, Queen Anne, Maple, Cherry Colored Finish, Rush Seat 1850.00
Armchair, Regency, Mahogany, Adjustable Book Stand, Upholstered 2650.00
Armchair, Sheraton, Dark Paint, Gold Striping, Turned Legs 200.00
Armchair, Sheraton, Painted, Bamboo Spindles, Rush Seat, Pair 880.00
Armchair, Shield Back, Upholstered Seat 450.00
Armchair, William & Mary, Dark Finish, Velvet Brocade Upholstery 500.00
Armoire, 2 Doors, Curved Top, Drawer Below, Stripped Pine 925.00
Armoire, Louis XV, Fruitwood, Parquetry, Cornice, 2 Doors, 90 In. 1450.00
Armoire, Louisiana, Mahogany, Inlaid, Cabriole Legs ....*Illus* 6000.00
Armoire, Oak, France, 1800, 62 X 90 X 21 In. 1500.00
Armoire, Raised Panels On 4 Doors, 2 Drawers, Walnut, 87 In. 5500.00
Basinette, Edwardian, Brass, Knotted Rope Basket, 35 X 43 In. 1000.00
Bed, 2–Color Stenciled Design Over Black, Red Graining, 3/4 Size 1250.00
Bed, Angled Rectangular Panels, French, Rosewood, 1930, 80 In. 4800.00
Bed, Arched Crest Rail, Oak, Mission, Twin, Pair 775.00
Bed, Baby's, Painted White, Iron 200.00
Bed, Cannonball, Rope, Cherry Trim, Maple, 58 X 70 In. 325.00
Bed, Cannonball, Rope, Cherry, Turned Posts, 60 3/4 In. 1200.00
Bed, Cannonball, Rope, Scrolled Headboard, 54 X 74 In. 650.00
Bed, Cannonball, Rope, Scrolled Headboard, Poplar, 52 1/2 X 70 In. 175.00
Bed, Chippendale Style, Four–Poster, Queen Size 695.00
Bed, Day, Curly Maple, Cherry, Scrolled Posts, 26 X 79 In. 975.00
Bed, Empire, Mahogany, Pineapple Finials 1350.00
Bed, Four–Poster, Rope Spring, 1880s, 3/4 Size 800.00
Bed, French Restoration, Rosewood, Inlaid, C.1830 .... 880.00
Bed, Half–Canopy, Carved Flowers, Rosewood, Double 3300.00
Bed, Half–Canopy, Oval Panel Headboard, Mahogany, Double 2800.00
Bed, High Back, Walnut, Applied Fruit, Victorian 2800.00
Bed, Inlaid Blossoms & Leaves, Rosewood Parquetry, French, C.1925 .... 715.00
Bed, Jenny Lind, 3/4 Size 80.00
Bed, L. & J. Stickley, 1 Wide, 6 Narrow Slats, C.1910, Double 9700.00
Bed, Louis XVI, Plaque of Cherub, Foliate, Fluted Columns, Double 1550.00
Bed, Mission, 12 Slat, Stickley, Double Size 2000.00
Bed, Pencil Post, Federal, Maple, 74 X 48 X 72 In. 2200.00
Bed, Rope, Acorn Finials, Pine & Poplar, 52 1/2 X 69 3/4 In. 75.00
Bed, Rope, Cherry Head & Footboards, Goblet Finials, 50 1/2 In. 325.00
Bed, Rope, Maple Posts, Curved Canopy Frame, 66 X 50 1/2 In. 350.00
Bed, Rope, Maple, Cherry Head & Footboards, 53 X 69 3/4 In. 395.00
Bed, Rope, Mennonite, Walnut & Poplar, Red Paint 600.00
Bed, Rope, Pineapple Finials, Mahogany Head & Footboards, 60 In. 650.00
Bed, Rope, Poplar, Turned Legs, Molded Rails, 50 X 70 X 38 In. 65.00
Bed, Rope, Scrolled Headboard, Raised Panels, 48 1/2 In. 1850.00
Bed, Rope, Softwood, Turned Posts, Mushroom Finial, 52 In. 125.00
Bed, Rope, Turned Posts, High Legs, Red Paint, 54 X 75 X 41 In. 225.00
Bed, Rope, Turned Posts, Poplar & Pine, 47 1/2 X 70 3/4 In. 50.00
Bed, Shaker, Pine, Cherry & Maple, Wooden Wheels, 34 X 81 In. 1760.00
Bed, Sled, Painted, Maj. Delmar, Single 200.00
Bed, Sleigh, Black Walnut, Complete, Twin, Pair 900.00

Furniture, Bench, Iron, Rustic, 19th Century,
34 1/2 In.

Furniture, Bench,
Wood & Perot Makers Philad., Cast Iron

Furniture, Bench, Windsor, Knuckle Arms, Black Paint, 87 1/2 In.

Bed, Tall Post, Federal, New England, Cherry, C.1820, 76 In.	1550.00
Bed, Tester, Pencil Posts, Birch, 75 X 53 X 75 In.	7500.00
Bed, Tester, Rosewood, Mahogany Frame, 1850	5500.00
Bed, Tester, Tiger Maple Posts, Bird's–Eye Maple Headboard	2000.00
Bed, Trundle, Rope Strung, Red Paint, Poplar	500.00
Bed, Trundle, Rope, Turned Posts, Knob, Poplar, 42 X 59 X 16 In.	325.00
Bed, Tubular Chromed Steel, Ebonized Wood, Germany, 1935, Pair	550.00
Bedroom Set, Art Deco, Blond, Dresser With Mirror, 3 Piece	400.00
Bedroom Set, Cherry, 6 1/2–Ft. Headboard, Commode, 3 Piece	3850.00
Bedroom Set, Classical, Burl Veneer, Marquetry, French, 3 Piece	700.00
Bedroom Set, Curly Maple, Applied Carvings, 3 Pc.	1400.00
Bedroom Set, French Style, Ivory, Floral, Contemporary, 5 Piece	1050.00
Bedroom Set, Lillian Russell, Walnut, 4 Piece	4250.00
Bedroom Set, Linen Press, Dresser, Twin Beds, Mahogany, C.1920	950.00
Bedroom Set, Louis XVI, Carved Oak Leaves, Plume Finials, 4 Piece	500.00
Bedroom Set, Walnut, 8–Ft. Headboard, Dresser, Marble Washstand	1750.00
Bench, Brown Stain, Poplar, 23 1/2 X 58 1/2 In.	75.00
Bench, Bucket, 3 Upper Drawers, 2 Base Doors, High Back	5500.00
Bench, Bucket, Gray Green Paint, Scalloped Side, Softwood, 36 In.	830.00
Bench, Bucket, Mortised Top & Gallery, Blue Paint, Softwood	1650.00
Bench, Carved Apron, Fluted Legs, Caned Seat, Gilded Finish	335.00
Bench, Chapel, Shelf Under Seat, English, Oak, 58 1/2 In.	200.00
Bench, Deacon's, Half Spindle, White Paint, Arms, 5 Ft.	200.00
Bench, English Elm, Ash, Rough Hewn Base, 16 X 54 X 14 In.	770.00
Bench, English Oak, Splayed Legs, Stretcher, 19 X 48 X 8 In.	550.00
Bench, Fern Pattern, Cast Iron	1695.00
Bench, Fireside, Carved Apron, Upholstered Seat, 23 1/2 In.	825.00
Bench, George III, Ebonized & Parcel Gilt, Square	4125.00
Bench, Hepplewhite, Mahogany, Slip Seat, Carved Arms, Shield Back	950.00
Bench, Hinged Lids In Seat, Shaped Arms, English, Oak, 70 In.	450.00
Bench, Hitchcock, Stenciled Design, Black Paint, Cane Seat, 76 In.	800.00
Bench, Iron, Rustic, 19th Century, 34 1/2 In. ....*Illus*	650.00

Bench, Jacobean, Paw Feet, Lion Head Scroll Arms, 43 1/2 In. 775.00
Bench, Kneeling, Green Paint, 7 1/2 X 28 In. 85.00
Bench, Kneeling, St. Thomas Church, Underhill, Vermont, C.1874 .... 25.00
Bench, Kneeling, Walnut, Worn Dark Finish, 39 In. 45.00
Bench, Lift Top, Eastlake, Ebonized & Gilt, American, 18 X 20 In. 425.00
Bench, Lift Top, Eastlake, Upholstered Seat, Walnut, C.1875, 17 In. 325.00
Bench, Mammy's, Arrow Back, Red & Black Flame, 28 In. 3100.00
Bench, Oak, 4 Cutout Squares, Triangular Legs, Charles P. Limbert 8475.00
Bench, Oak, 4 Splayed Legs, England, 18th Century, 17 X 84 In. 225.00
Bench, Paneled Back, Converts To Bed, Canadian, 1840s 600.00
Bench, Piano, Gustav Stickley 3500.00
Bench, Prayer, Baroque Style, Carved Gilded Medallions 55.00
Bench, School, Amish 565.00
Bench, Scrolled Arms, Flat Slat Back, Lift Lid Seat, 68 In. 400.00
Bench, Spindle Back, New England, Pine, Curved Arms, 45 1/2 In. 660.00
Bench, Walnut, Dovetailed Case, 2 Hinged Lids, 58 1/2 In. 2100.00
Bench, Watchmaker's, 7 Drawers, Pine, 37 X 34 In. 335.00
Bench, Water, 2 Mortised Shelves, Decorative Top, 49 1/2 In. 500.00
Bench, Water, Bootjack Feet, Pine, 44 X 27 1/2 In. 350.00
Bench, Water, Brown Paint, Gallery, Pine, 30 X 36 In. 45.00
Bench, Water, Metal Liner & Drain, Oak Molding, Poplar, 72 3/4 In. 425.00
Bench, Water, Poplar, Brown Varnish, Olive Gray, 25 1/2 In. 500.00
Bench, White Oak, Splayed Base, Bulbous Turned Legs, 16 In. 400.00
Bench, Windsor, Knuckle Arms, Black Paint, 87 1/2 In. ....*Illus* 3000.00
Bench, Windsor, Stretcher Base, Splayed Turned Legs, 87 X 15 In. 3000.00
Bench, Wood & Perot Makers Philad., Cast Iron ....*Illus* 2310.00
Bench, Wrought Iron, Eastlake Style 700.00
Bin, Seed, 18 Drawers, Oak, Small 825.00
Bin, Slant Top, Traces of Red, Iron Hasp, Poplar, 27 X 21 In. 100.00
Bookcase, 7 Sections, Oak, C.1900 .... 1100.00
Bookcase, Adjustable Shelves, 3 Glazed Doors, Walnut, 87 X 81 In. 2200.00
Bookcase, Animal Feet, Oak, 3 Glass Doors 1850.00
Bookcase, Burl Drawers & Trim, 3 Sections 1900.00
Bookcase, Carved Lion's Heads, 2 Doors, Chestnut & Walnut, 9 Ft. 2250.00
Bookcase, Eastlake, 2 Doors, Ebonized, Lower Drawers, 1875, 75 In. 1650.00
Bookcase, Georgian, Mahogany, Cornice, 6 Glazed Doors, 115 In. 8250.00
Bookcase, Gothic Revival, Rosewood, C.1830, 86 In. 3520.00
Bookcase, Gustav Stickley, 2 Glazed Doors, Oak, C.1909, 56 In. 7260.00
Bookcase, Gustav Stickley, Model 717, 2 Doors, Miter Mullioned 7000.00
Bookcase, Gustav Stickley, No.716, Leaded, 2 Doors, C.1907, 55 In. 2200.00
Bookcase, L. & G. Stickley, 1 Door, 16 Panes, C.1912, 55 In. 2640.00
Bookcase, L. & J.G. Stickley, 3 Doors 3750.00
Bookcase, L. & J.G. Stickley, Double Door 4675.00
Bookcase, L. & J.G. Stickley, No.643, One Door, 16 Panes, C.1907 .... 2200.00
Bookcase, Louis XV Style, Marble Top, 3 Shelves, Tulipwood, 40 In. 660.00
Bookcase, Mullioned Doors, Lead Glazed, Oak, C.1915, 56 In. 995.00
Bookcase, Oak, 3 Glass Doors, Place For 7 Guns, 60 X 37 X 13 In. 3000.00
Bookcase, Open, Top Bronze Plaque, Walnut, C.1860, 57 X 68 In. 1450.00
Bookcase, William IV, Mahogany, Marble Top, 1835 .... 3600.00
Box, Blanket, Bracket Base, Curly Walnut, Miniature 1650.00
Box, Blanket, Lift Lid, Cutout Ends, Painted, 24 X 44 1/4 In. 275.00
Box, Blanket, Sponged Design, Poplar, C.1800 .... 247.00
Box, Blanket, Till Under Lift Top, Graining, Pine, 41 1/2 In. 250.00
Box, Blanket, Vase, Flowers & Date, Gray Ground, 1832 .... 4000.00
Breakfront, 4 Glazed Doors, Shelves, Mahogany, 10 Ft.6 In. 6600.00
Breakfront, 5 Glazed Doors, 5 Drawers, Japanned, 84 In. 775.00
Breakfront, Cherry, Pine, Bird's-Eye Maple, Shell Design, 4 Doors 4400.00
Breakfront, William IV, Mahogany, Henredon, Grate Doors, 65 In. 770.00
Buffet, Frieze Drawer Over Doors, Oak, C.1900, 37 1/2 X 43 In. 935.00
Buffet, Nakashima, 1960 .... 5000.00
Buffet, Renaissance Revival, Marble Top, Walnut 4200.00
Buffet, Renaissance Revival, Oak, 3 Drawers, Lion Masks, 81 In. 715.00
Bureau, Bowfront, 4 Drawers, Mahogany, C.1820, 38 1/4 X 40 In. 775.00

Bureau, Case of Beaded Drawers, Painted Pine, C.1810, 44 In. 445.00
Bureau, Chippendale, 4 Graduated Drawers, Cherry, C.1780, 41 In. 2100.00
Bureau, Empire, 4 Graduated Veneered Drawers, Brass Pulls, 44 In. 450.00
Bureau, Federal, 4 Drawers, Cherry, C.1820, 47 X 40 1/2 In. 1545.00
Bureau, George III, Cylinder Front, Yew & Fruitwood, 37 In. 4125.00
Bureau, Goddard Style, Nutting, No.979, Mahogany ....*Illus* 4400.00
Bureau, Hepplewhite, 4 Drawers, Mahogany Veneer, Inlaid, 1790 .... 2450.00
Bureau, Hepplewhite, Swell Front, Tiger Maple Facings, Birch Top 1600.00
Bureau, Queen Anne, Fall Front, Walnut, Crossbanded, Inlaid, 40 In. 3750.00
Bureau, Swivel Mirror, Prairie School Style, H. Dorsett, 87 In. 1750.00
Bureau, Tooled Leather Top, 1 Drawer, Painted, 29 X 39 In. 440.00
Cabinet, Amboyna & Walnut, J. & J. Martel, C.1930, 5 Ft.10 In. 7700.00
Cabinet, Apothecary, 38 Drawers, Floor Model 850.00
Cabinet, Biedermeier Style, Fruitwood, 2 Doors, Pair 9500.00
Cabinet, Blanket, Fold Down Top, 3 Drawers, Korean, 35 X 36 In. 825.00
Cabinet, Blueprint, Oak, 13 Drawers, Early 1900s 325.00
Cabinet, Bombe Vitrine, Domed, 2 Glazed Doors, Marquetry, 77 In. 1325.00
Cabinet, Chinoiserie, Foo Lion, Landscape, 72 X 54 X 20 In. 2200.00
Cabinet, Chrome, Painted Mirror, J. Leleu, 1930, 5 Ft.9 In. 3025.00
Cabinet, Cockleshell Doors, Brass Strapwork, Mahogany, 54 In. 357.00
Cabinet, Convex Doors, Amboyna & Ivory, C.1925, 4 Ft.6 3/4 In. 7150.00
Cabinet, Corner, Blind Door, Cherry 1850.00
Cabinet, Corner, Floral Inlay, Kingwood, 35 X 23 In. 2200.00
Cabinet, Corner, Walnut, 2 Drawers, Penna., Walnut, 85 In., 2 Part 8800.00
Cabinet, Crouching Lions' Feet, C.1900, 80 X 50 In. ....*Illus* 2500.00
Cabinet, Curio, Art Deco, Inlaid, 1 Drawer, Dome Shape, 63 X 29 In. 345.00
Cabinet, Curio, Serpentine, Mahogany, England, 1900 .... 1300.00
Cabinet, D-Shaped Top, 2 Doors, Shelved, French, C.1930, 30 In. 2400.00
Cabinet, Display, Wrought Iron & Brass, French, 91 X 55 In. 4950.00
Cabinet, Dressing, Bruno Paul, Walnut, C.1930, 5 Ft. 9 5/8 In. 4675.00
Cabinet, Eastlake Style, 3 Drawers, Parcel Gilt, Walnut, C.1875 .... 2300.00
Cabinet, Etched Glass, Burlwood, English, C.1937, 4 Ft.8 3/4 In. 3650.00
Cabinet, Filing, 72 Drawers, Oak 600.00
Cabinet, Filing, 9 Drawers, Tiger Oak, C.1900 .... 1400.00
Cabinet, French Provincial, Hanging, Oak, Carved, 1 Door 950.00
Cabinet, Gadrooned Top, 1 Drawer, 2 Doors, Mahogany, 31 1/2 In. 600.00
Cabinet, Gothic, Raised Shelf On Top, 2 Drawers, Oak, 53 1/4 In. 275.00
Cabinet, Hoosier, Oak, McDougall, Ind., Tin Cutting Top 375.00
Cabinet, Hoosier, Zinc Top, Flour Box, Lebanon, Indiana, Oak 550.00
Cabinet, Kitchen, Poplar, Flat Wall, 2 Glass Doors 300.00
Cabinet, Library's Card File, 72 Drawers, Oak, 47 X 54 X 13 In. 1510.00
Cabinet, Library, Dutch Empire, Marquetry 4700.00

Furniture, Bureau, Goddard Style, Nutting,
No.979, Mahogany

Furniture, Cabinet,
Crouching Lions'
Feet, C.1900,
80 X 50 In.

Furniture,
Candlestand,
Wallace Nutting,
No.644,
Inlaid Mahogany

Cabinet, Maiden Medallions, Inlaid Satinwood, 34 In., Pair 7700.00
Cabinet, Marquetry, Marble Top, Kingwood, Mahogany, 47 1/2 In., Pr. 3450.00
Cabinet, Mother-of-Pearl Inlay, Various Woods, C.1915, 4 Ft.8 In. 4800.00
Cabinet, Music, 3-Sided Gallery, American, Walnut, C.1875, 41 In. 625.00
Cabinet, Music, Glazed Door, 3 Shelves, Charles P. Limbert, 56 In. 4840.00
Cabinet, Nut & Bolt, On Stand, 112 Drawers, Square, Oak 950.00
Cabinet, Nut & Bolt, Pedestal, 140 Drawers, Pine 1500.00
Cabinet, On Chest, William & Mary, Marquetry, Walnut & Olive, 1700 .... 5225.00
Cabinet, On Stand, Cornice Over Mullioned Doors, 64 1/2 X 37 In. 775.00
Cabinet, Parlor, Renaissance Revival, Walnut, Mirror, Carved 1500.00
Cabinet, Parlor, S Rolltop, Raised Panels, Oak, Complete Interior 1900.00
Cabinet, Regency, Rosewood, Brass, Inlaid, Marble, 1820, 30 X 14 In. 3750.00
Cabinet, Smoker's, G. Stickley, 1 Drawer, Lower Cabinet, C.1907 .... 1650.00
Cabinet, Smoker's, G. Stickley, Fitted Interior, Oak, C.1906 .... 3635.00
Cabinet, Step Back, Poplar, Ash, 4 Doors, 2 Drawers, Square Nail 950.00
Cabinet, Telephone, Renaissance Revival, Brass, Marble, 48 In. 350.00
Cabinet, Trompe L'Oeil, Fruits, Meat, Bottle, Pine, 7 Ft.4 In. 5225.00
Cabinet, Urn & Garland, 2 Doors, Carved Ram's Heads, 36 In. 425.00
Cabinet, Wall, Eastlake, 4 Shelves At Side, Walnut, C.1875, 23 In. 325.00
Cabinet, Walnut, Carved, Italy, 17th Century, 77 X 54 In. 9000.00
Cabinet, Wine, Georgian, Mahogany, Plinth Base, Paneled, 39 X 24 In 175.00
Candlestand, , Birch & Cherry, 16-Sided Top, 17 1/2 In. 150.00
Candlestand, Black Graining, Brown Ground, Tripod Base, 25 3/8 In 300.00
Candlestand, Cabriole Legs Base, Cherry, 18th Century, 27 In 650.00
Candlestand, Center Inlaid Eagle Top, 3 Spade Feet, Ct. Valley 6200.00
Candlestand, Cherry, 1 Board Dish Top, 27 In. 400.00
Candlestand, Cherry, Red Paint On Base, Tripod Base, 26 1/2 In. 400.00
Candlestand, Cherry, Snake Foot, Chapin 2400.00
Candlestand, Chippendale, Swelled Post, Maple, New England, C.1780 .... 715.00
Candlestand, Country Hepplewhite, Spider Legs, Birch, 26 3/4 In. 400.00
Candlestand, Dish Top Birdcage, Walnut, C.1780 .... 8800.00
Candlestand, Dish Top, Birdcage & Snake Feet, Walnut 2600.00
Candlestand, Elm, Circular, Turned Pedestal, 3 Legs, 26 X 13 In. 935.00
Candlestand, Empire, Tilt Top, Curly Maple, 2 Board, 19 X 26 In. 550.00
Candlestand, Federal, Cherry Inlaid, Stringing, 1790, 26 In. 2600.00
Candlestand, Federal, Oval Top, Pad Feet, Mahogany, 1790, 28 In. 3100.00
Candlestand, Hepplewhite, Cherry, Dark Finish, Spider Legs, 28 In. 1100.00
Candlestand, Oak, Whittled Legs, Octagonal Top, 24 In. 650.00
Candlestand, Octagonal, 1 Board Top, Cherry, 28 1/2 In. 300.00
Candlestand, Queen Anne, Slipper Feet, Cherry, 1740, 25 1/4 In. 1350.00
Candlestand, Regency, Octagonal Top, Mahogany, 23 1/2 In. 300.00
Candlestand, Screw-Off Top, Walnut, 29 1/2 In. 200.00
Candlestand, Scrolled Adjusting Device, Iron, 51 1/2 In. 1450.00
Candlestand, Snake Feet, 2 Board Top, Old Red, Cherry, 27 In. 375.00
Candlestand, Snake Feet, Black Paint 935.00
Candlestand, Square Top, 3 Snake Feet, 14 1/2 X 15 1/8 In. 990.00
Candlestand, Tiger Maple, 3 Scrolled Legs, C.1840, 28 In. 275.00
Candlestand, Tilt Top, Acanthus Carved, Mahogany Top 1550.00
Candlestand, Tilt Top, Chip Carved Base, Mahogany 1000.00
Candlestand, Tilt Top, Chippendale, Mahogany, Tripod Base, 28 In. 4200.00
Candlestand, Tilt Top, Mahogany, Acanthus, Birdcage, 18 X 24 In. 1540.00
Candlestand, Tilt Top, Maple Pedestal, Cherry Top 1250.00
Candlestand, Tripod Base, Adjustable Arm, Splint Holder, 35 In. 675.00
Candlestand, Tripod Base, Adjustable Candle Arm, 48 In. 1100.00
Candlestand, Tripod Base, Round Top, Brown Finish, 27 3/4 In. 700.00
Candlestand, Wallace Nutting, No.644, Inlaid Mahogany .... *Illus* 660.00
Canterbury, Divided Top, 1 Drawer, Mahogany, C.1825, 23 1/2 In. 1100.00
Canterbury, Regency, Rosewood, Lattice Form, 21 In. .... *Illus* 1100.00
Canterbury, Rosewood, Carved, Victorian, 1 Bottom Drawer 2000.00
Canterbury, Shelf Above Slotted Base, English, Walnut, 35 In. 2250.00
Canterbury, Shelves, Fretwork Sidewalls, Walnut, C.1875, 22 In. 395.00
Cellarette, 4 Decanters, 12 Glasses, Brass Stripe Inlay, Black 375.00

Furniture, Cellarette, Mahogany,
Lift Top, Paw Feet, 22 X 18 In.

Furniture, Canterbury, Regency,
Rosewood, Lattice Form, 21 In.

Furniture, Cellarette, Edwardian,
Inlaid Satinwood, 25 In.

Cellarette, Edwardian, Inlaid Satinwood, 25 In. ....*Illus*   2000.00
Cellarette, Hinged Lid, Brass Florette, Ring Handles, Mahogany 2425.00
Cellarette, Mahogany, Lift Top, Paw Feet, 22 X 18 In. ....*Illus*   1600.00
Chair Set, Arched Crest Rail, 6 Slats, Oak, C.1910, 4 ....   715.00
Chair Set, Bentwood, J.J. Kohn, Austrian, 39 In., 4 ....   357.00
Chair Set, Chippendale, Ribbonback, Upholstered Seat, 1 Arm, 5 ....   7500.00
Chair Set, Classical, Mahogany, Black Leather Slip Seat, 6 ....   1500.00
Chair Set, Dining, 2 Arm, 6 Side, Acanthus Leaves, Mahogany, 8 ....   7700.00
Chair Set, Dining, Chippendale Style, 2 Arm, 8 Sides, Mahogany, 10 ....   3000.00
Chair Set, Dining, Circular Back, French, Mahogany, C.1930, 6 ....   3630.00
Chair Set, Dining, Empire, Mahogany, 6 ....*Illus*   450.00
Chair Set, Dining, George III Style, 2 Arm, 6 Side, Mahogany, 8 ....   1650.00
Chair Set, Dining, L. & J.G. Stickley, 2 Arm, 4 Side, Oak, C.1912, 6 ....   1650.00
Chair Set, Dining, Maple, Cherry, Medallion Splat, 1830, 6 ....   770.00
Chair Set, Dining, Medallion Back, Needlepoint Seat, Fruitwood, 4 ....   665.00
Chair Set, Dining, Medallion Back, Upholstered, Walnut, 4 In. 4185.00
Chair Set, Dining, Mission Style, Oak, 4 ....   550.00
Chair Set, Dining, Regency, Silver Veneered, 6 ....   6500.00
Chair Set, Dining, Renaissance, Carved Oak, 8 ....   4200.00
Chair Set, Dining, Tiger Maple, Cane Seat, 6 ....   3800.00
Chair Set, Eastlake, Walnut & Walnut Burl, Upholstered, C.1875, 4 ....   575.00
Chair Set, Empire, Flame Veneer, Mahogany, Slip Seat, 3 ....   325.00
Chair Set, Empire, Rococo, Mahogany & Flame Mahogany, C.1845, 4 ....   800.00
Chair Set, George II, Upholstered Back & Seat, Walnut, 6 ....   3300.00
Chair Set, George III, Hoop–Shaped Back, Mahogany, 2 Arm, 10 Side 4400.00
Chair Set, George III, Ladder Back, Upholstered Seat, Mahogany, 12 ....   6600.00
Chair Set, Gustav Stickley, Vertical Slat, Slip Seat, 1905, 4 ....   1900.00
Chair Set, Hitchcock, Gold Stenciled Design, Graining, 4 ....   300.00
Chair Set, L.& J.G.Stickley, 3 Vertical Slats, C.1910, 4 ....   935.00
Chair Set, Ladder Back, Rabbit Ear, Woven Tape Seat, 4 ....   75.00
Chair Set, Ladder Back, Stephen E. White & Co., 1780, 6 ....   2900.00
Chair Set, Louis Philippe, Ladder Back, Fruitwood, 1850–75, 6 ....   550.00
Chair Set, Louis XV Style, Caned Back & Seat, Arms, 4 ....   1100.00
Chair Set, Parlor, Victorian, Red & Moss Green Upholstery, 4 ....   375.00
Chair Set, Pennsylvania, Green, C.1840, 6 ....   1800.00
Chair Set, Pennsylvania, Painted, Adam Banney, C.1877, 6 ....   2600.00
Chair Set, Plank Seat, Green Paint, Gold & Black Striped, 6 ....   2300.00
Chair Set, Pressed Back, Cane, 5 ....   275.00
Chair Set, Pressed Back, Man In North Wind, Oak, Cane Seat, 6 ....   1450.00
Chair Set, Queen Anne, Wallace Nutting, Mahogany, 4 ....*Illus*   2090.00
Chair Set, Rabbit Ear, Hitchcock, Stenciled, 6 ....*Illus*   2400.00
Chair Set, Regency, Mahogany, Needlepoint Seat, 6 ....   2250.00

Furniture, Chair, Comb Back,
Wallace Nutting, No.419, Maple

Furniture, Chair, William & Mary,
Wallace Nutting, Maple, Arms

Furniture, Chair, Wallace Nutting,
Maple, Arms, 20th Century

Furniture, Chair, Chinese,
Rosewood, Phoenix, 4 Dragons

Furniture, Chair, Chippendale,
Wingback, Mahogany

Furniture, Chair, George III Style,
Gadrooned Seat Rail, Mahogany

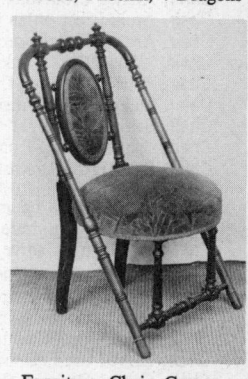

Furniture, Chair, George
Hunzinger, Walnut,
March 30, 1869

Furniture, Chair,
Hitchcock, Stenciled
Design, Pair

Chair Set, Regency, Pierced Carved Crest Rail, Mahogany, 4 .... 1100.00
Chair Set, Rosewood, Bobbin Turned, Wales, 1860s, 6 .... 2250.00
Chair Set, Shaker Style, Ladder Back, Acorn Finial, Cane Seats, 4 .... 700.00
Chair Set, Sheraton, Black Paint, Rush Seat, 2 Arm, 2 Side 200.00
Chair Set, Sheraton, New York City, Fancy, 1825, 8 .... 9000.00
Chair Set, Spindle Back, Original Red, Black Graining, 6 .... 1350.00
Chair Set, Stephen E. White & Co., Heart & Crown, 4 .... 3200.00
Chair Set, Stickley Brothers, Quaint, 6 .... 1000.00
Chair Set, T Back, Oak, Leather Seat, 4 .... 225.00
Chair Set, Thumb Back, Freehand Painted Back, Yellow, 6 .... 7500.00
Chair Set, Thumb-Arrow, Spindle Back, Painted, Stenciled, Penna., 6 .... 9500.00
Chair Set, Vase Shaped Splat, Needlepoint Seat, Mahogany, 6 .... 4950.00
Chair Set, Windsor, American Step Down, Early 19th Century, 4 .... 1200.00
Chair Set, Windsor, Birdcage, Bamboo Turnings, Pine, Maple, 6 .... 2750.00
Chair Set, Windsor, English, Yew Wood, 4 .... 1000.00
Chair Set, Windsor, Nakashima, 1960, 6 .... 3800.00
Chair Set, Windsor, Step Down, Bamboo Turnings, New England, 6 .... 6800.00
Chair Set, Windsor, Step Down, Painted, 6 .... 7500.00
Chair Set, Yellow-Green Paint, Saber Legs, Cane Seat, 4 .... 665.00
Chair Set, Zoar, Carved, Oak, 6 .... 1800.00
Chair, 3 Vertical Slats, Spring Cushion, Arms, C.1910, 37 1/2 In. 357.50
Chair, Arched Crest Rail, Padded Back & Seat, Hoof Feet, Arms, Pr. 1750.00
Chair, Arched Serpentine Crest & Seat Rail, Elm, 41 In. 600.00
Chair, Arched Upholstered Back, Louis Sue & Andre Mare, 1923 .... 6050.00
Chair, Arrow Back, Plank Bottom, Stenciled Fruit, Light Brown 47.50
Chair, Artist's, Folding, Original Paint 125.00
Chair, Balloon Back, Finger-Roll Frame, Tufted Brocade, Arms 175.00
Chair, Banister Back, BT Incised Over Banisters, Painted, 46 In. 1650.00
Chair, Banister Back, Painted & Carved, Rush Seat, 48 In. 3850.00
Chair, Banister Back, Rush Seat, Maple & Hardwood 275.00
Chair, Banister Back, Rush Seat, Maple & Other Woods, Pair 2400.00
Chair, Belter, Pierced & Carved Back, Rosewood, C.1860 .... 4675.00
Chair, Belter, Rosalie, Without Grapes, Pair 4235.00
Chair, Billiard, George W. Palmer, Oak 6000.00
Chair, Black Lacquer, Gilded Design, Arms, 1880s 400.00
Chair, Booster, Tom Thumb 25.00
Chair, Bow Back, Windsor, Saddle Seat, 7 Spindle Back, 17 1/2 In. 1250.00
Chair, Cameo Back, Painted Plume Design, Arms, Fruitwood, Pair 825.00
Chair, Carved Crest, Upholstered Back & Arms, Beechwood, Pair 1435.00
Chair, Carved Dragons, Gargoyle Faces, Teakwood, 19th Century 1250.00
Chair, Cast Iron, Signed Graff Studios, Louisville, Kentucky, Pr. 450.00
Chair, Chamfered Crest, 4 Banisters, Rush Seat, Brown Stain 2750.00
Chair, Child's, 4 Spindle, Painted, Arched Open Back, 1900 .... 55.00
Chair, Child's, Adirondack, Black Paint, 21 1/2 In. 115.00
Chair, Child's, Bentwood, Stenciled Girl, Butterflies, Floral Seat 100.00
Chair, Child's, Black Paint, Woven Diamond Pattern Seat 907.50
Chair, Child's, Black, Yellow, & Gold Paint, Pair 1250.00
Chair, Child's, Cane Seat, Late 18th Century, 31 In. 275.00
Chair, Child's, Captain's, Black Paint, Arms, C.1870 .... 260.00
Chair, Child's, Carpet, Folding, Victorian 95.00
Chair, Child's, G. Stickley, No.342, Upholstered Seat, C.1906, Pair 192.50
Chair, Child's, Gustav Stickley, Leather Seat, Arms, Oak, C.1907 .... 840.00
Chair, Child's, Gustav Stickley, No.342, C.1907, 23 1/2 In., Pair 357.50
Chair, Child's, Ladder Back, Woven Splint Seat, 18 1/4 In. 95.00
Chair, Child's, Lyre Back, Plank Bottom, Black, Yellow Striping 60.00
Chair, Child's, Morris Type, Wicker, Reclining Back, Victorian 900.00
Chair, Child's, Red, Plank Seat, 2 Spindles, Black Stenciled 50.00
Chair, Child's, Rush Seat & Back 37.50
Chair, Child's, Sack Back, 7 Spindle, Saddle Seat, C.1800 .... 5500.00
Chair, Child's, Twig, Red Paint 68.00
Chair, Child's, Windsor, 4-Arrow Back, Plank Seat, 1820s 260.00
Chair, Child's, Windsor, Painted, 3 Spindles, Open Arms, England 88.00
Chair, Child's, Wingback, Heart Cutout, Pine, 17 1/2 In. 150.00
Chair, Child's, Woven Back, Arms, Hickory, 1930s, 24 1/2 In., Pair 195.00

Chair, Chinese, Rosewood, Phoenix, 4 Dragons ....*Illus*   500.00
Chair, Chippendale, Carved Mahogany Frame, Open Arms, Mahogany 400.00
Chair, Chippendale, Cherry Finish, Upholstered Slip Seat 700.00
Chair, Chippendale, Cherry, Splat, Star Flower Design, Crest 1275.00
Chair, Chippendale, Mahogany, Black Leather, Pair 600.00
Chair, Chippendale, Maple, Square Legs, Beaded Crest, Carved Ears 1100.00
Chair, Chippendale, Spanish Feet, 1750–80 .... 1150.00
Chair, Chippendale, Wingback, Mahogany ....*Illus* 1900.00
Chair, Club, Duck Upholstered, Skirted, Henredon, Pair 1870.00
Chair, Comb Back, Wallace Nutting, No.419, Maple ....*Illus*   770.00
Chair, Continental Baroque, Mahogany, Vasiform Splat, Slip Seat 2450.00
Chair, Continental, Carved, Red Paint, Rush Seat, Pair 200.00
Chair, Corner, Carved Designs, Hardwood, Slip Seat, 32 3/4 In. 325.00
Chair, Corner, Eastlake, Upholstered Arm & Seat, Walnut, C.1870 ....   425.00
Chair, Corner, Pierced Splat, England, 1780, Pair 2950.00
Chair, Corner, Queen Anne, Cabriole Legs, Pad Feet, Mahogany 7500.00
Chair, Corner, Vase Form Splats, Green Leather Seat 1100.00
Chair, Country Chippendale, Pierced Splat, Upholstered Seat 675.00
Chair, Delaware, 3 Banister Back, Rush Seat, Arms, Maple 1200.00
Chair, Desk, Leather Seat, Oak 95.00
Chair, Dining, Circular, Crossbanded In Satinwood 2200.00
Chair, Drake Carved Feet, Gothic Back Splats, Walnut 6050.00
Chair, Dutch Neoclassical, Marquetry, Arms, C.1830, 32 In., Pair 1430.00
Chair, Eastlake, Upholstered Seat & Back, Carved Supports, Walnut 2800.00
Chair, Empire Style, Cane Seat, Turned Legs, Knob Feet, Crest 90.00
Chair, Empire, Carved Ram's Heads, Gilt & White Finish, Pair 935.00
Chair, Empire, Fauteuil, Mahogany, Brass Mounted, Arms, Pair 8500.00
Chair, Empire, Saber Legs, Upholstered Slip Seat, Mahogany, Pair 70.00
Chair, Fanback, Brace Back, 6 Spindle, Painted, C.1780, 36 1/4 In. 2000.00
Chair, Federal, Masonic, Mahogany, Masonic Splat, 1790–1800 .... 3900.00
Chair, Federal, Saber Leg, Carved Slat, Slip Seat, Mahogany 500.00
Chair, Floral & Musical Crest, Ram's Head Arms 995.00
Chair, Floral Crest Rail, Serpentine Seat Rail, Beechwood 445.00
Chair, Floral Embroidered Seat & Back, Arms, Painted, 35 1/2 In. 175.00
Chair, French, Upholstered, Painted & Gilt Wood, C.1920 ....   845.00
Chair, French, Walnut, Upholstered Curved Back, C.1925 .... 1650.00
Chair, Full–Sized Carved Bear Back, Swiss, C.1900 .... 2600.00
Chair, G. Stickey, 3 Pewter Inlaid Vertical Slts, Arms, 1903 .... 9680.00
Chair, G. Stickley, 16 Spindle Sides, 15 Spindle Back, Oak, 1908 .... 9685.00
Chair, G. Stickley, 3 Slat Back, No.370A, Open Arms, C.1906 ....   385.00
Chair, G. Stickley, Fixed Back, 6 Vertical Slats, Arms, C.1907 ....   880.00
Chair, George Hunzinger, Walnut, March 30, 1869 ....*Illus*   990.00
Chair, George II, Tub, Mahogany Frame, Leather Back & Sides, Pair 2860.00
Chair, George III Style, Gadrooned Seat Rail, Mahogany ....*Illus* 2400.00
Chair, George III, Arms, Damask Seat, Spade Feet, Inlaid Mahogany 665.00
Chair, George III, Pierced, Interlaced Splat, Mahogany, C.1800, Pr. 825.00
Chair, Gothic Revival Style, Walnut, Pair 750.00
Chair, Great, Turned Back Posts & Finials, Brown Paint, C.1780 ....   825.00
Chair, Green Paint, Striping, Angel Wing Design, Penna., Pair 320.00
Chair, Grotto, Silver Inlay, Italian, Leaf Pine, Pair 3200.00
Chair, Gustav Stickley, High Back, 9 Spindles, Oak, 1907, 49 In. 6000.00
Chair, Gustav Stickley, No.356, Leather 1320.00
Chair, Half Spindle, Plank Bottom, Brown Ground, 19th Century 650.00
Chair, Hepplewhite, Upholstered Seat, 3 Slats, Oval Pattern 625.00
Chair, Hexagonal Back & Seat, Oak, Frank Lloyd Wright, C.1916, Pr. 6650.00
Chair, Hip Rests, Floral Needlepoint Seat, Carved, Victorian 185.00
Chair, Hitchcock Style, Red, Black Graining, Rush Seat 150.00
Chair, Hitchcock, Painted Design, Writing Arm 1000.00
Chair, Hitchcock, Stenciled Design, Pair ....*Illus*   575.00
Chair, Horn, American, Hearts, Dots, Circles, C.1890 .... 1100.00
Chair, Horn, Victorian 2200.00
Chair, Ice Cream, Heart Shape 25.00
Chair, Iron, Ornate, Upholstered, Revolving Pedestal Base 4200.00
Chair, Iron, Renaissance, Cross Legged Base, Pair 357.00

Chair, Jockey's, For Weighing In, Leather Seat & Back, C.1870 .... 6000.00
Chair, John & Joseph Meeks, Upholstered Seat, 1845 .... 550.00
Chair, Kneeling, Carved Back, Velvet Upholstery 250.00
Chair, Ladder Back, 3 Arched Slats, Paper Rush Seats, Pair 500.00
Chair, Ladder Back, 3 Curved Slats, Nipple Finials, Splint Seat 35.00
Chair, Ladder Back, 3 Curved Slats, Tape Seat, Red Paint 225.00
Chair, Ladder Back, 3 Slats, Yellow Striping, Black, Rush Seat 25.00
Chair, Ladder Back, 4 Curved Slats, Shaped Arms, Splint Seat 205.00
Chair, Ladder Back, 4 Slats, Rush Seat, Painted Black, C.1880 .... 1300.00
Chair, Ladder Back, 5 Graduated Slats, Shaped Arms, English 150.00
Chair, Ladder Back, 5 Slats, Flat Arms, Wooden Seat, English 200.00
Chair, Ladder Back, 5 Slats, Maple, Turned Legs, Pair 1100.00
Chair, Ladder Back, 5 Slats, Shaped Arms, Rush Seat, English 70.00
Chair, Ladder Back, 6 Graduated Slats, English, Shaped Arms 200.00
Chair, Ladder Back, Arms, Splint Seat, Maple 350.00
Chair, Ladder Back, Bluish Green Paint, Turned Feet, Arms 275.00
Chair, Ladder Back, G. Stickley, No.306 1/2, 3 Back Slats, 1904 .... 137.50
Chair, Ladder Back, Rabbit Ear, Red Repaint, Black Stenciling 65.00
Chair, Ladder Back, Rounded Finials, Rush Seat, Ash & Maple 137.50
Chair, Laminated & Bentwood, C.1936, 5 Ft. 2 In. 660.00
Chair, Laminated, Rosewood, C.1860, 34 3/4 In. 400.00
Chair, Library, Mahogany, English Regency, Reeded, Cane Seat, 1820 .... 6500.00
Chair, Lobed & Carved Crest, Scrolled Arms, Beech, 35 1/4 In. 525.00
Chair, Lolling, Federal, Upholstered Back, Shaped Arms, 1790 .... 8800.00
Chair, Lolling, Stephen Badlam, Dorchester, Mass., C.1795 .... 5500.00
Chair, Louis XV Style, Carved, Open Arms, 38 In., Pair 775.00
Chair, Louis XV Style, Serpentine Rail, Upholstered, 36 In., Pair 935.00
Chair, Louis XV Style, Shield Back, Pair 285.00
Chair, Louis XV Style, Shield Back, Velvet Upholstery, Pair 1320.00
Chair, Louis XVI Style, Floral & Ribbon Crest, Walnut, Pair 610.00
Chair, Louis XVI Style, Gilt Wood, Upholstered, Cane Seat, Pair 187.00
Chair, Louis XVI Style, Laurel Crest, Blue Velvet 400.00
Chair, Louis XVI Style, Oval Back, Upholstered, 37 In., Pair 350.00
Chair, Lounge, Cruise Ship, Folding, Wood, C.1900 .... 250.00
Chair, Lounge, Leather, Wood, Sweden, C.1936, 40 X 59 In. ....*Illus* 1200.00
Chair, Morris, Adjustable Back, Quaint Furniture Co., Label, 1907 .... 1200.00
Chair, Morris, Back Slats, Shaped Open Arms, C.1906, 40 In. 1050.00
Chair, Morris, Flat Open Arms, Rope Frame, Cushions, C.1907 .... 445.00
Chair, Morris, G. Stickley, No.367, Drop Arm, Slatted Sides, 1909 .... 7260.00
Chair, Morris, Gustav Stickley, Flat Arms 4675.00
Chair, Morris, Gustav Stickley, Slant Arm, New Leather Cushions 7975.00
Chair, Morris, Gustav Stickley, Spindle, Flat Arm, C.1906 .... 7000.00
Chair, Mother-of-Pearl Design, Chinoiserie, Oval Back, English 182.50
Chair, Multicolored Paint Design, Reddish Brown Ground 210.00
Chair, Oak, Tapestry Padded Seat, Curved Back, Victorian 45.00
Chair, Office, High Back, Maple, Bentwood Arms 375.00
Chair, Office, Pressed Back, Oak, High 175.00
Chair, Office, Upholstered Back, Open Arms, Cushion Seat, C.1912 .... 165.00
Chair, Painted, Landscape Painted On Back Rail, H Stretcher 175.00
Chair, Peaked Crest, Onondago, No.626, Oak, 1905, 37 In. 302.00
Chair, Pierced Back Splat, Carved Crest Rail, Leather, Large 9350.00
Chair, Plank Set, Vase Splat, Brownish Yellow, Crest, Pair 3550.00
Chair, Porter's, Beveled Glass Over Seat, Leather Upholstered 1550.00
Chair, Pressed Back, Spindle, Cane Seat 95.00
Chair, Pub, English, Yew Wood, Plank Bottom, Set of 4 .... 800.00
Chair, Queen Anne, Bulbous Front Stretcher, Rush Seat, Maple 700.00
Chair, Queen Anne, Cabriole Legs, Upholstered Seat & Back, Walnut 150.00
Chair, Queen Anne, Hard & Soft Woods, Posts, Yoke-Shaped Crest 300.00
Chair, Queen Anne, Mahogany, Wallace Nutting, Set of 4 .... 2090.00
Chair, Queen Anne, Painted Maple, Urn Splat, Rush Seat, New Eng. 2000.00
Chair, Queen Anne, Rush Seat, Spanish Feet, Arms 4500.00
Chair, Queen Anne, Shaped Crest, Slip Seat, Mahogany, Pair 1870.00
Chair, Queen Anne, Spanish Feet, Rush Seat, Maple 750.00
Chair, Queen Anne, Vase Splat, Yoke Shaped Crest, Rush Seat, Maple 1250.00

Chair, Queen Anne, Wallace Nutting, Arms 1025.00
Chair, Queen Anne, Walnut, Arched Crest, C.1750 .... 5775.00
Chair, Queen Anne, Walnut, Slip Seat, Duck Feet, Cabriole Legs 1850.00
Chair, Reeded Seat Frame, Leather Seat, Scrolled Arms, Mahogany 600.00
Chair, Revolving, Wire Spindle Back, Glossy Black Paint, 1920 .... 3200.00
    FURNITURE, Chair, Rocker, see Furniture, Rocker
Chair, Rococo, Laminated, Rosewood, C.1860, 33 3/4 In. 425.00
Chair, Roycroft, 4–Slat Back, Adjustable Back, Arms 2500.00
Chair, Russian Leather Upholstered, England, 17th Century, 34 In. 225.00
Chair, Russian Neoclassical, Brass Inlaid, Mahogany, Pair 5500.00
Chair, Scrolled & Floral Carved Crest Rail, Caned Back & Seat 250.00
Chair, Scrolled & Floral Carved Seat, Beechwood, 33 X 31 In. 450.00
Chair, Scrolled Ears Over Raked Stiles, Mahogany, C.1770 .... 665.00
Chair, Serpentine Carved Crest & Seat Rails, Painted, 42 In. 310.00
Chair, Serpentine Crest Rail, Mahogany, C.1760, 36 3/4 In. 550.00
Chair, Serpentine Crest, Shaped Wings & Arms, C.1810, 50 In. 2200.00
Chair, Shaker, Maple, Original Red Finish, Tilters, Taped Seat 1100.00
Chair, Shaker, Tilter, Lebanon 1815.00
Chair, Sheraton, Black Paint, Yellow Striping, Floral, Cane Seat 50.00
Chair, Sheraton, Hitchcock Style, Eagle Crest, Foliage, Rush Seat 425.00
Chair, Sheraton, Red, Black Graining, Balloon Shape Seat, Pair 350.00
Chair, Sheraton, Shaped Crest Rail, Pierced Vasiform Splat 425.00
Chair, Shoeshine, Heart Design 275.00
Chair, Slat Back, Painted, Arms, Late 17th Century, 46 1/2 In. 1950.00
Chair, Slipper Arm, Brown Paint, Virginia 325.00
Chair, Spanish Renaissance, Rampant Lion Crest, Leather Legs 165.00
Chair, Spindle Back, Plank Seat, Red & Black Graining, Striping 125.00
Chair, Stickley Bros., Leather Seat 125.00
Chair, Stylized Carved Shield Back, Upholstered Seat, Walnut, Pr. 525.00
Chair, Throne, Carved Phoenix Back, Rosewood, 19th Century, 61 In. 935.00
Chair, Throne, Carved, Mahogany 1295.00
Chair, Transitional, Spanish Feet, Painted Black, 18th Century 445.00
Chair, Turned Posts, Urn Finials, 4 Banisters, Spool Rails, Cherry 1650.00
Chair, Velvet Covering, Walnut & Walnut Burl, Cushion, C.1865 .... 495.00
Chair, Wallace Nutting, Maple, Arms, 20th Century ....*Illus* 715.00
Chair, Walnut, Walnut Burl & Gilt, Arms, Upholstered, C.1865, Pair 750.00
Chair, Wicker, Flared Solid Back, Arms, C.1900, 41 1/2 In. 250.00
Chair, Wicker, Leather Upholstered, Arms, Heywood–Wakefield, 1900 .... 425.00
Chair, William & Mary, Wallace Nutting, Maple, Arms ....*Illus* 935.00
Chair, Windsor, 7 Spindles, Splayed Legs, Pennsylvania 1275.00
Chair, Windsor, 7 Spindles, Vase Supports, Ash & Maple, C.1790 .... 1750.00
Chair, Windsor, Bamboo Turnings .... 250.00 To 300.00
Chair, Windsor, Bamboo, Scrolled Mahogany Arms, 17 1/4 In. 275.00
Chair, Windsor, Birdcage Back, Shaped Seat, Bamboo 210.00
Chair, Windsor, Birdcage, Old Black Paint 1210.00
Chair, Windsor, Bow Back, 7 Bamboo Turned Spindles, Shaped Arms 1650.00
Chair, Windsor, Bow Back, 8 Spindles, Brace Back, Green, C.1780 .... 935.00
Chair, Windsor, Bow Back, 9 Spindles, Bamboo, Splayed Base 375.00
Chair, Windsor, Bow Back, 9 Spindles, Bamboo, E. Tracy, Pair 2700.00
Chair, Windsor, Bow Back, Ash, Maple, 1760 .... 1600.00
Chair, Windsor, Bow Back, Bamboo Turnings, Saddle Seat, 17 In. 550.00
Chair, Windsor, Bow Back, Black Paint, 31 In. 375.00
Chair, Windsor, Bow Back, Oval Seat, Knuckle Arms, Red Paint 475.00
Chair, Windsor, Bow Back, Saddle Seat, Arms 850.00
Chair, Windsor, Bow Back, Saddle Seat, Spindle Back, 16 1/2 In. 925.00
Chair, Windsor, Bow Back, Shaped Oval Seat, Knuckle Arms 500.00
Chair, Windsor, Brace Back, Marked T.C., 18 1/4 In. 125.00
Chair, Windsor, Brace Back, Splayed, H Stretcher, Black Repaint 400.00
Chair, Windsor, Child's, Bamboo Turnings, Spindle Back & Arms 300.00
Chair, Windsor, Comb Back, Crest, Oval Shaped Seat 1700.00
Chair, Windsor, Comb Back, Splayed Base, Bulbous Turned Legs 700.00
Chair, Windsor, Comb Back, Splayed, Bamboo Turnings, Arms 450.00
Chair, Windsor, Continuous Arm, Bamboo Turnings, Shaped Seat 375.00
Chair, Windsor, Continuous Arm, Saddle Seat, Black 6500.00

Chair, Windsor, Convex Crest Rail, 5 Spindles, Painted, 34 3/4 In. 385.00
Chair, Windsor, Fanback, 7 Spindles, Saddle Seat 250.00
Chair, Windsor, Fanback, 8 Spindles, Bamboo, Saddle Seat 550.00
Chair, Windsor, Fanback, 8 Spindles, Saddle Seat 200.00
Chair, Windsor, Fanback, 9 Spindles, Plank Seat, Arms 3300.00
Chair, Windsor, Fanback, Brace Back, Varnish Over Blue–Green 2700.00
Chair, Windsor, Fanback, New England, Maple & Ash, C.1810 .... 660.00
Chair, Windsor, Fanback, Saddle Seat, Back Posts 400.00
Chair, Windsor, Fanback, Splayed, Saddle Seat, Monogram L.B., Pair 1200.00
Chair, Windsor, Ladder Back, Daniel Trotter, 1780–1800 .... 5500.00
Chair, Windsor, Low Back, Trace of Red Paint 350.00
Chair, Windsor, Sack Back, Arms, 7 Spindles, Ash & Chestnut, 1790s 335.00
Chair, Windsor, Sack Back, Black Paint, Thomas Blackford 1210.00
Chair, Windsor, Wide Shaped Seat, Arm Supports, Carved Ears 2000.00
Chair, Wing, Georgian, Leather Upholstery, Swivel Base 660.00
Chair, Wing, Louis XV, Velvet Upholstered 3500.00
Chair, Wing, Peaked Back, Upholstered Seat, Oak, C.1910 .... 450.00
Chair, Wing, Queen Anne, Damask Upholstery, Mahogany, 45 In. 1985.00
Chair, Writing, Hitchcock, Original Paint Design 1050.00
Chair, Wrought Iron, White Paint, Openwork Back, Circular Seat 132.00
Chaise, Carved Irises, Plumet & Selmersheim, Walnut, 1900 .... 4500.00
Chaise, Thonet, Adjustable Back & Seat, 69 In. .... *Illus* 1100.00
Chaise, Wicker, Magazine Holders Each Side, 1900, 54 In. 550.00
Chest, 2 Drawers, Poplar Secondary Wood, Walnut, 31 X 32 3/8 In. 1900.00
Chest, 2 Small Over 3 Long Drawers, Dovetailed Case, Red Finish 3500.00
Chest, 6 Board, Blue–Green Paint, New England, Pine, 25 1/2 In. 995.00
Chest, 6 Board, Paneled, Original Red Paint, Oak & Pine, 24 In. 9350.00
Chest, 6 Board, Straight Skirt, Brown Paint, Pine, 21 X 36 1/2 In. 350.00
Chest, 6 Drawers, Curly Maple Inlay, Carved Pilasters, 47 In. 2250.00
Chest, Apothecary, 70 Drawers, Green Paint, Yellow Pine, C.1900 .... 575.00
Chest, Apothecary, Green Over Red, 19th Century, 30 In. 1975.00
Chest, Arabian Camel, 18th Century 1250.00
Chest, Bachelor's, Hinged Top, Fitted Case, Mahogany, C.1750 .... 1980.00
Chest, Biedermeier, Maple, Architectural Form, Stepped Top 8500.00
Chest, Blanket, 1 Drawer, Brown Grain Painted, 1825, 43 1/2 In. 715.00
Chest, Blanket, 2 Drawers, Iron Strap Hinges, Pine, 46 3/4 In. 1350.00
Chest, Blanket, 2 Drawers, Painted Black, Hearts, 1820, 50 7/8 In. 6650.00
Chest, Blanket, Amish, David D. Trover, Sugar Creek, Ohio, Label 8000.00
Chest, Blanket, Brown Graining, 2–Part Interior, 24 1/2 In. 400.00
Chest, Blanket, Brown Graining, Till, Stripes, 25 1/2 X 46 In. 1200.00
Chest, Blanket, Brown Sponged, Till, Dated 1821, 49 X 22 X 24 In. 4500.00
Chest, Blanket, Charles II, Lift Top, 3 Drawers, Oak, 31 1/2 In. 775.00
Chest, Blanket, Cherry, Curly Maple Panels, Till, 38 X 17 X 20 In. 325.00
Chest, Blanket, Dovetailed Case, Yellow Ground, 25 3/4 In. 2500.00
Chest, Blanket, Flame Graining, 1 Drawer, English, Pine, 37 1/4 In. 250.00
Chest, Blanket, Flame Painted, Top Opening, 2 Drawers Below, 1790 .... 2500.00
Chest, Blanket, Grained Pine, Basket of Flowers On Deep Drawer 8800.00
Chest, Blanket, Grained, Ball Footed, 1840–60 .... 1495.00

Furniture, Chair, Lounge, Leather, Wood,
Sweden, C.1936, 40 X 59 In.

Furniture, Chaise Longue, Thonet,
Bentwood, 69 In.

Chest, Blanket, Green, Painted Oval Scene 467.00
Chest, Blanket, Iron Handles & Escutcheon, Pine, 19 1/2 X 56 In. 300.00
Chest, Blanket, Jacobean, 3 Carved Panels, Oak, 25 1/4 X 49 In. 385.00
Chest, Blanket, Lift Lid, Painted Mauve, Massachusetts, C.1780 .... 1400.00
Chest, Blanket, Original Blue Paint, Till, Pine, 40 3/4 In. 375.00
Chest, Blanket, Penna. German, Green, Floral, 1793, 52 X 23 In. 2600.00
Chest, Blanket, Pine, Brown Graining, Yellow Ground, 26 In. 950.00
Chest, Blanket, Pine, Design, Chester Co., Stamped Hinges 695.00
Chest, Blanket, Pine, Red Graining, Yellow Striping, 28 1/2 In. 1200.00
Chest, Blanket, Pine, Tiger Maple, Miniature, 20 X 28 In. 1700.00
Chest, Blanket, Pine, Till, 3 Small Drawers, Ball Feet 250.00
Chest, Blanket, Pine, Till, Secret Drawer, Red Graining, 43 3/4 In. 950.00
Chest, Blanket, Poplar, Money Till, 2 Small Drawers, Iron Handles 395.00
Chest, Blanket, Poplar, Yellow Graining, 25 X 47 3/4 In. 200.00
Chest, Blanket, Red & Black Paint, Stenciled Birds On Feet, 1863 .... 8000.00
Chest, Blanket, Reddish Brown Graining, Dovetailed Case, 26 In. 325.00
Chest, Blanket, Strap Hinges, 2 Interior Drawers, Walnut, 24 In. 2750.00
Chest, Blanket, Thumb Molded Edge, Maple, 1760–90, 23 X 47 1/2 In. 1650.00
Chest, Blanket, Walnut, Dovetailed, Strap Hinges, 2 Base Drawers 4200.00
Chest, Bombe, Dutch, Walnut, Oak, 3 Graduated Drawers, 18th Century 7500.00
Chest, Bombe, Marble Top, Drawers, Mahogany & Burled Wood, 51 In. 3500.00
Chest, Bookcase Top, 2 Glazed Doors, Inlaid, Walnut, 90 3/4 In. 6000.00
Chest, Bowfront, Flamed Mahogany, String Inlay, Baltimore, 39 In. 3500.00
Chest, Bowfront, Hepplewhite, Mahogany, Crossbanded, French Feet 6000.00
Chest, Bowfront, Splayed Bracket Feet, Mahogany, C.1880, 39 In. 4400.00
Chest, Brass Bound, Brass Carrying Handle, China, Camphor, 20 In. 525.00
Chest, Butler's, 4 Drawers, Desk Section, Glass Pulls, Mahogany 3500.00
Chest, Carved & Beaded Drawer Fronts, Continental, C.1650 .... 450.00
Chest, Cedar, Lane, Veneer Inserts Top & Front 85.00
Chest, Cherry & Pine, 5 Graduated Drawers, C.1800, 47 1/4 In. 1980.00
Chest, Cherry, 2 Upper Divided Drawers, 3 Lower, 42 X 43 1/2 In. 1100.00
Chest, Cherry, 4 Drawers, Miniature 1900.00
Chest, Cherry, 4 Drawers, Pennsylvania, 1845 .... 1300.00
Chest, Cherry, 4 Drawers, Scalloped Apron, 37 X 40 In. 1000.00
Chest, Cherry, 7 Drawers, Chippendale, Fluted Corners, 49 1/4 In. 1650.00
Chest, Cherry, 9 Drawers, Fluted Quarter Columns, 1800, 37 1/2 In. 9975.00
Chest, Cherry, Reeded Column, 5 Graduated, 3 Short Top Drawers 4675.00
Chest, Chestnut, 3 Drawers, Square Nail Construction, Miniature 200.00
Chest, Child's, Empire, Sleigh Front, Walnut, 19th Century, 26 In. 750.00
Chest, Chippendale, 4 Drawers, Maple, 1760–1800, 42 X 41 1/2 In. 3500.00
Chest, Chippendale, Cherry, 45 X 49 1/2 In. ....*Illus* 1650.00
Chest, Chippendale, Graduated Drawers, Maple, 1760–90, 48 1/4 In. 3850.00
Chest, Chippendale, Poplar, Reddish Paint, Bracket Feet, 49 In. 6500.00
Chest, Country French, Cherry, 4 Drawers, Widdicomb, 27 X 34 In. 325.00
Chest, Country, 4 Dovetailed Drawers, Turned Feet, 42 1/2 In. 800.00
Chest, Country, Sheraton, 4 Drawers, Brasses, Cherry, 41 3/4 In. 1300.00
Chest, Country, Sheraton, 5 Drawers, Cherry, 47 1/4 X 39 3/4 In. 1000.00
Chest, Curved Top, Handwrought Ironwork, Key, Norway, Dated 1826 .... 3700.00
Chest, Eastlake, Mirror, Shelves, 5 Drawers, Walnut, 68 1/2 In. 1350.00
Chest, Eastlake, Raised Gallery, Walnut, 68 1/2 In. ....*Illus* 1200.00
Chest, Empire, 4 Drawers, Burl Ornaments, Cherry, 46 X 42 1/2 In. 450.00
Chest, Empire, Cherry, 4 Drawers, Rope Trim 270.00
Chest, Empire, Mahogany, Figured Veneer, 4 Drawers, 47 X 46 In. 425.00
Chest, Empire, Red Flame Graining, 6 Drawers, Poplar, 47 1/2 In. 350.00
Chest, Empire, Reproduction By Boher, 20 3/4 X 14 3/4 X 26 In. 175.00
Chest, Empire, Tiger Stripes, 1830 .... 550.00
Chest, Federal, Bowfront, 4 Drawers, Inlaid Mahogany, 1790, 35 In. 3550.00
Chest, Federal, Bowfront, 4 Drawers, Mahogany, 1815, 41 1/2 In. 2650.00
Chest, Federal, Duncan Phyfe, 1 Drawer, Brass Ball Feet, 1810–20 .... 1900.00
Chest, G. Stickley, 2 Short Over 3 Long Drawers, 1903, 42 1/2 In. 7850.00
Chest, Gentleman's, 8 Drawers, Quarter Oak Interior, Mahogany 2800.00
Chest, George II, Walnut Veneer, Oak, 4 Drawers, C.1890 .... 675.00
Chest, George III, Bowfront, 2 Short, 3 Long Drawers, Mahogany 775.00
Chest, George III, Mahogany, Molded Top, 2 Over 3 Drawers, 39 In. 1750.00

Furniture, Chest,
Chippendale, Cherry,
45 X 49 1/2 In.

Furniture, Chest,
Side Lock, Carved,
Walnut, C.1870

Furniture, Chest,
Tansu, Japanese, 3 Parts,
46 1/2 X 66 In.

Furniture, Chest,
Eastlake, Raised
Gallery, Walnut,
68 1/2 In.

Chest, George III, Serpentine Top, 4 Drawers, Mahogany, 34 1/2 In.	885.00
Chest, Glove & Handkerchief Drawers, Marble Top	400.00
Chest, Hepplewhite, 4 Cockbeaded Drawers, Walnut, 40 X 38 In.	875.00
Chest, Hepplewhite, 4 Drawers, Brass Escutcheons, Walnut, 44 In.	1300.00
Chest, Hepplewhite, Bowfront, 4 Drawers, Fan Inlays	6250.00
Chest, Hepplewhite, Bowfront, Mahogany, 4 Drawers, 39 X 21 In.	3500.00
Chest, Hepplewhite, Inlaid Walnut, 5 Drawers, French Feet, 35 In.	1000.00
Chest, Immigrant's, Pine, Ellen M. Buy 1877, 36 1/4 In.	300.00
Chest, Inlaid Diamonds, 5 Drawers, Cherry, C.1800, 43 3/4 In.	1215.00
Chest, Map, Bird's-Eye Maple, 12 Drawers	1500.00
Chest, Mule, Flame Graining, 2 Drawers, Ivory Escutcheons, Pine	275.00
Chest, Mule, Lift Top, 2 Lower Doors, North Carolina	595.00
Chest, Mule, Lift Top, Butternut, 2 Lower Drawers	2200.00
Chest, Mule, Maple, 2 Drawers Overlapping, Lift Top, 40 1/4 In.	2450.00
Chest, Mule, Red Flame Graining, Drawers, Lift Lid, Pine, 42 In.	2250.00
Chest, Mule, Refinished Pine, 2 Drawers, Lid, 38 X 18 X 39 In.	350.00
Chest, Oak, Turned Bun Feet, 4 Drawers, English, 41 X 21 X 39 In.	1000.00
Chest, Oriental, Red Over Black Lacquer, 2 Top, 2 Base Doors, Pr.	8000.00
Chest, Oxbow, 3 Reverse Serpentine Drawers, Cherry, C.1780, 35 In.	1650.00
Chest, Painted Poppy Design, Brown, Red, & Gold, 28 X 30 In.	395.00
Chest, Pine, 3 Dovetailed Drawers, Red Stain, 35 3/4 X 37 1/2 In.	200.00
Chest, Pine, 3 Drawers, Marbelized Top, Europe, 37 1/2 X 47 In.	150.00
Chest, Pine, 3 Drawers, Vinegar Graining, 34 X 41 1/2 In.	550.00
Chest, Pine, Green Paint, Dovetailed Case, Lock, Handled, 18 In.	150.00
Chest, Pine, Maple, 4 Graduated Drawers, Teardrop Brasses, 40 In.	3635.00
Chest, Pine, Orange Tan Glaze, White Ground, 5 Drawers, 13 In.	450.00
Chest, Pine, Poplar, Painted Design, Curly Maple, 38 3/4 In.	2000.00
Chest, Poplar, 3 Drawers, 32 1/4 X 31 3/4 In.	325.00
Chest, Queen Anne, 4 Graduated Drawers, Pine, New England, 1760–80	2900.00
Chest, Red Flame Graining, Rupp of York, Penn., Poplar, 48 3/4 In.	200.00
Chest, Red, Sky Blue Painted Side Panels, 6 Drawers, Norway	625.00
Chest, Reeded Stiles, Cherry, 19th Century, Miniature	2300.00
Chest, Rope Carved Columns, 4 Drawers, Brass Pulls, 51 1/2 In.	600.00
Chest, Shaving, Designed Oak, Mirror, 2 Drawers, 5 Ft.4 In.	1000.00
Chest, Sheraton, 4 Figured Maple Drawer Fronts	1200.00
Chest, Sheraton, Bowfront, Birch, Bird's-Eye Maple, Mahogany, 1810	4500.00
Chest, Sheraton, Corner Posts, 4 Drawers, Cherry, 39 3/4 X 39 In.	1000.00
Chest, Sheraton, Mahogany Veneer Front, Walnut, 47 1/2 In.	900.00
Chest, Sheraton, Walnut, Cherry, 6 Drawers, Turned Legs, 24 1/4 In.	2700.00
Chest, Side Lock, Carved, Walnut, C.1870 ....*Illus*	825.00
Chest, Sugar, Dovetailed Drawer, Paneled Sides, Cherry, 36 1/2 In.	300.00
Chest, Sugar, Holly Inlay, Walnut, Virginia, C.1785	5170.00
Chest, Tansu, Japanese, 3 Parts, 46 1/2 X 66 In. ....*Illus*	300.00
Chest, Tiger Maple, 3 Over 3 Drawer, Original Brass, 1800, 46 In.	5100.00
Chest, Top Pinwheel Drawer, 4 Drawers, Walnut, Maple, 1770, 83 In.	4650.00
Chest, Victorian, Walnut, 3 Drawers, Plinth Base, 32 X 41 X 19 In.	198.00
Chest, Wainscot, Drawer, Painted Black, Oak & Pine, 17th Century	4675.00
Chest, Walnut, 3 Inlaid Drawers, On Frame, North Carolina	3995.00

Chest, Walnut, 4 Drawers, Wooden Pulls, 44 X 39 3/4 In.	1400.00
Chest–On–Chest, Biedermeier, Walnut, 5 Long Drawers Over 2	335.00
Chest–On–Chest, Chippendale, Pullout Desk, Walnut, Veneer, 65 In.	1400.00
Chest–On–Chest, English, Mahogany	6995.00
Chest–On–Chest, George III, Mahogany, C.1780, 6 Ft.	7150.00
Chest–On–Chest, Georgian, Mahogany, Rosewood Nails, 1870	5200.00
Chest–On–Stand, Chippendale, 2 Top & 4 Graduated Drawers	4950.00
Chest–On–Stand, Lacquer, Gilt Landscape Panels, Korea, 41 In.	2850.00
Chiffonier, Marble Top, Mahogany & Rosewood, C.1930, 4 Ft.3 In.	1350.00
China Cabinet, Curved Glass Sides, Oak Lion's Heads, Oak, 72 In.	2175.00
China Cabinet, Design At Top, Claw Feet, Curved Glass, Oak	800.00
China Cabinet, G. Stickley, 2 Doors, 12 Panes Each, 1912, 64 In.	3300.00
China Cabinet, G. Stickley, Glazed Door, C.1913, 61 1/2 In.	965.00
China Cabinet, G.Stickley, Glazed Door, C.1913, 61 1/2 In.	965.00
China Cabinet, L. & J.G. Stickley, Single Door	4070.00
China Cabinet, L.& J.G.Stickley, Single Door	4070.00
China Cabinet, Limbert, Oak	1550.00
China Cabinet, Oak, Mirror Top & Back, Woman's Head, 5 Ft.10 In.	2250.00
China Cabinet, Stickley, Leaded Glass Panels Top of 2 Doors	8800.00
China Closet, Gustav Stickley, Exposed Tenons, C.1909, 64 1/2 In.	7860.00
China Closet, L. & J.G. Stickley, 2 Doors, Black, Onondago, 69 In.	7000.00
China Closet, L. & J.G. Stickley, 2 Full–Length Doors, C.1906	1325.00
China Closet, Lifetime Co., 2 Doors, Mullioned, 1910, 55 1/4 In.	2420.00
Coffer, Carved Front & Ends, Iron Hinges, 40 X 25 1/2 In.	250.00
Coffer, On Frame, Rope Turned Legs, Panels, 38 3/4 In.	800.00
Coffer, Relief Carved Facade, English, Oak, 44 1/2 In.	1600.00
Commode, 3 Drawers, Biedermeier, Fruitwood	1800.00
Commode, 3 Drawers, Fluted Skirt, Walnut, C.1880, 32 1/2 In.	8000.00
Commode, 3 Drawers, Lion's Head Handles, France, Light Mahogany	6000.00
Commode, Gentleman's, Mahogany, 38 X 26 In.	1200.00
Commode, Louis XV, Figural Mounts, Marble Top, 44 In.	750.00
Commode, Louis XVI, Marquetry, Rosewood, Kingwood, 5 Drawer, 37 In.	9000.00
Console, Rococo, Wall–Mounted, Marble Top	5500.00
Costumer, G. Stickley, No.192, 6 Iron Hooks, C.1910, 72 In.	2450.00
Costumer, J. & J.G. Stickley, No.82, C–Scroll Hooks, C.1910, 6 Ft.	1200.00
Cot, Child's, Elm, 4 High Sides, Sweden, C.1860	570.00
Couch, Empire, Tufted Sides, Camel Back, Mahogany Trim	1000.00
Couch, Fainting, Eastlake, Oak	225.00
Couch, Fainting, Folds Out To Large Bed	160.00
Counter, Tailor's, Shaker, Old Red Wash, 3 Graduated Drawers	1000.00
Cradle, Amish, Heart Cutouts At Each End, Blue–Green Paint	220.00
Cradle, Arched Hood, Hard & Soft Wood, 42 In.	225.00
Cradle, Federal, Mahogany, Rectangular Frame, 1800, 30 X 42 In.	330.00
Cradle, Heart Cutouts, Folding Blanket Guard, Grain Painted	200.00
Cradle, Heart Cutouts, Original Red Paint	575.00
Cradle, Renaissance Revival, Burled Walnut, Victorian, Spindles	1000.00
Cradle, Wicker, 1900s	1150.00
Crib, Pine, Open Mortise–Tenon, New Mexico, 1875	350.00
Cupboard, 12 Panels, 1 Piece, Walnut, C.1820, Small	2900.00
Cupboard, 3 Doors, Raised Panel, H Hinges, Pine, 76 X 37 In.	3800.00
Cupboard, 4 Doors, Porcelain Pulls, Pigeonholes, Pine, 64 1/2 In.	1100.00
Cupboard, Amish, Drop Front Dough Board, Lower Doors	535.00
Cupboard, Baker's, Ash, 8 Center Top Drawers, Glass Doors, Bin	700.00
Cupboard, Base Door, Iron Latch, Porcelain Knob, Pine, 66 In.	375.00
Cupboard, Beaded Frame, Iron Thumb Latch, Red, Poplar, 36 1/2 In.	775.00
Cupboard, Beaded Sides, 2 Shelves, Pine, 19th Century, 40 1/2 In.	365.00
Cupboard, Board & Batten Door, Open Shelves, Pine, 74 3/4 In.	550.00
Cupboard, Cherry, 2 Doors, Wisconsin, 1850–60	2800.00
Cupboard, Chimney, Pennsylvania, Olive Green, 1 Door	1250.00
Cupboard, Corner, 12 Panes In Top Door, Pine & Poplar, 88 1/2 In.	8250.00
Cupboard, Corner, 12 Panes of Glass In Single Door, Green	1150.00
Cupboard, Corner, 12 Panes Paneled Door, Walnut, 87 1/4 In.	3700.00
Cupboard, Corner, 12 Panes, Bracket Base, Softwood, Red Paint	8600.00
Cupboard, Corner, 16 Panes, Walnut Raised Panels, Cherry	4200.00

Cupboard, Corner, 2 Glaze Doors, Over 2 Doors, Walnut, 1810, 89 In. 2850.00
Cupboard, Corner, 2 Glazed Doors, 2 Doors, Walnut, 1810, 89 In. 2850.00
Cupboard, Corner, Beveled Cathedral Doors 1100.00
Cupboard, Corner, Bowfront, Danish, 4 Painted Panel Doors, 1839 .... 5800.00
Cupboard, Corner, Carved Rosettes, Arcaded Door, Drawer, Cherry 8250.00
Cupboard, Corner, Cherry & Maple, C.1800, 79 In. 1430.00
Cupboard, Corner, Cherry, Basket Weave Top, Glass Doors, 8 X 4 In. 850.00
Cupboard, Corner, Cherry, Stacked Panel, 1 Dovetailed Drawer 2800.00
Cupboard, Corner, Chippendale, Mahogany, 19th Century, 85 In. 850.00
Cupboard, Corner, Georgian, Walnut, 18th Century, 7 Ft., 2 Part 3500.00
Cupboard, Corner, H Hinges, Butterfly Shelves, Poplar, 63 In. 900.00
Cupboard, Corner, Hanging, Curved Shelves, Oak & Mahogany 985.00
Cupboard, Corner, Hanging, Knife Blade Hinges, Pink, 39 1/2 In. 700.00
Cupboard, Corner, Hanging, Pintle Hinges, English, 23 In. 400.00
Cupboard, Corner, Hanging, Walnut & Pine, 15 1/2 X 11 1/2 In. 170.00
Cupboard, Corner, Harmonist, Raised Panel Doors, Blue Inside, 1810 .... 3650.00
Cupboard, Corner, Hepplewhite, Cherry, Glass Door, Skirt, 2 Piece 2400.00
Cupboard, Corner, Mullions In Top Doors, English, 76 3/4 In. 775.00
Cupboard, Corner, Mullions Supporting Glass, Panes, Cherry, 1810 .... 3650.00
Cupboard, Corner, Pine, 2 Doors, Raised Panels, 81 3/8 In. 6400.00
Cupboard, Corner, Poplar, Red Cherry, Paneled Doors, 87 In. 1800.00
Cupboard, Corner, Poplar, Red Paint, 1 Piece, Paneled Doors, 76 In. 2650.00
Cupboard, Corner, Raised Panels, Pennsylvania, Walnut, 1810 .... 3400.00
Cupboard, Corner, Red Interior, Iron H Hinges, Pine, 78 1/2 In. 650.00
Cupboard, Corner, Step Back, 12 Panes, Cherry, 2 Piece 3200.00
Cupboard, Corner, Tombstone Arch, Shelves, Pine, 38 3/4 In. 400.00
Cupboard, Corner, Walnut, Bracket Feet, 1840, 2 Blind Panel Doors 1000.00
Cupboard, Court, Oak, 1 Base & 2 Top Doors, England, 1739, 68 In. 1300.00
Cupboard, Diamond–Point Panel, Salmon Paint, 2 Doors, Canada 5525.00
Cupboard, Double Doors In Base, Open Shelves, Poplar, 82 1/2 In. 900.00
Cupboard, Dutch, 2 Doors, Glass Panes Above, Curly Maple 5200.00
Cupboard, Dutch, Walnut, C.1830, 6 Ft.7 In.X 48 In. 5800.00
Cupboard, English Oak, 2 Base Doors, Miniature, 21 1/2 In. 250.00
Cupboard, English, Ornate Iron Hinges, Pine, 17 1/2 X 16 1/4 In. 250.00
Cupboard, Flat Wall, 9 Panes, Red Paint, Window Mullions 3700.00
Cupboard, Flat Wall, 12 Panes, Walnut, Cherry & Poplar, F. Kissel 2375.00
Cupboard, Flat Wall, Oyster White, 19th Century 6800.00
Cupboard, George III, Oak, Welsh, 81 X 72 In. 5500.00
Cupboard, Glazed Doors, 2 Shelves, Walnut Glaze, C.1810, 85 In. 3575.00
Cupboard, Hanging, 1 Shelf, 6 Panes, Mustard Paint, 39 X 26 In. 465.00
Cupboard, Hanging, Cherry, Dark Finish, 1 Door, 6 Panes, 32 In. 450.00
Cupboard, Hanging, Paneled Door, Iron Latch, Poplar, 36 1/2 In. 775.00
Cupboard, Hanging, Pine, Yellow Paint, Board, Batten Door, 42 In. 350.00
Cupboard, Hanging, Raised Panel Door, Chestnut, 17 X 15 1/2 In. 225.00
Cupboard, Hanging, Red Finish, Pine, 23 3/4 X 15 3/4 In. 450.00
Cupboard, Hanging, Rosewood Grained, Pine, Poplar, 34 1/2 In. 200.00
Cupboard, Hanging, Vertical Paneled Board Ends, Pine, 35 1/2 In. 325.00
Cupboard, Hoosier, Green & Yellow, 1920s 850.00
Cupboard, Inside Drawer, Sonnenberg, Green Paint, Cherry 3675.00
Cupboard, Jelly, 2 Doors, Porcelain Knob, Red Paint, Pine, 49 In. 650.00
Cupboard, Jelly, Green–Gray Paint, 2 Doors, Blind Door 700.00
Cupboard, Jelly, Iron & Brass Latch, Pine, 48 1/4 X 44 1/2 In. 375.00
Cupboard, Jelly, Paneled Doors, Gray Paint, Walnut, 66 1/4 In. 450.00
Cupboard, Jelly, Poplar, Penna., 1 Drawer, 28 X 18 X 63 In. 1500.00
Cupboard, Jelly, Walnut, Dovetailed Case, Cutout Feet, 54 In. 4900.00
Cupboard, Lower Doors, Walnut, 3 Drawers, 2 Piece, 84 In. 6250.00
Cupboard, Paneled Doors In Base, Open Top Shelves, 77 X 60 In. 800.00
Cupboard, Paneled Doors, 3 Drawers, Red Paint, 52 1/2 In. 700.00
Cupboard, Paneled Doors, Drawer, Step Back Top, Walnut, 64 In. 1000.00
Cupboard, Pennsylvania, Walnut Glazed, 1810 .... 3250.00
Cupboard, Pewter, Doors, Step Back Shelves, Pine, 90 1/2 In. 450.00
Cupboard, Pewter, Mustard & Traces of Green & Red Paint, 77 In. 1550.00
Cupboard, Pewter, Open Top, Brown Paint, 73 X 32 X 15 In. 950.00
Cupboard, Pewter, Open, 1 Drawer, Pine, Poplar & Walnut, 75 In. 600.00

Cupboard, Pewter, Paneled Doors, 2 Drawers, English, Pine, 78 In. 1100.00
Cupboard, Pie Shelf, 2 Drawers, Cherry & Maple, 80 1/2 In. 2600.00
Cupboard, Pine, Mustard Paint, Open Top, Plank Door, Southern, 1840 .... 400.00
Cupboard, Poplar, 4 Paneled Doors, 3 Middle Drawers, 55 In., 2 Pc. 2600.00
Cupboard, Poplar, Dark Red, 4 Doors, 48 X 18 X 84 In., 1 Piece 950.00
Cupboard, Poplar, Red Flame Graining, 2 Board Top, 30 1/4 In. 650.00
Cupboard, Poplar, Red Wash Paint, C.1850, 2 Piece 7200.00
Cupboard, Raised Panel Doors, Iron Latches, Poplar, 31 In. 200.00
Cupboard, Renaissance Revival, Oak, 3 Sections, 45 X 19 X 87 In. 600.00
Cupboard, Shaker, Watervliet, N.Y., Walnut, 89 1/2 X 49 1/2 In. 1900.00
Cupboard, Spice, Cherry, Walnut, 10 Drawers, T. Fisher, 1880, 15 In. 8000.00
Cupboard, Step Back, Blind Door, Gray Paint, 6 Ft., 2 Piece 250.00
Cupboard, Step Back, Butternut, Paint Decorated, 2 Piece 475.00
Cupboard, Step Back, Cherry, 4 Door, 2 Drawers, Penna., C.1800 .... 4100.00
Cupboard, Step Back, Chippendale Ogee Feet, St. Johns River 2585.00
Cupboard, Step Back, Open Top, Pine 295.00
Cupboard, Step Back, Pumpkin Pine, 2 Blind Doors Base 800.00
Cupboard, Trapezoidal Storage Area, Oak, 54 X 39 1/2 In. 1325.00
Cupboard, Wall, Paneled Doors, Walnut, 83 X 41 1/4 In. 800.00
Cupboard, Wall, Poplar, Brown Graining, 2 Drawers, 84 In., 2 Piece 2700.00
Cupboard, Walnut, 2 Blind Doors Over 2 Drawers, Doors, 8 1/2 Ft 675.00
Cupboard, Walnut, Raised Panel Doors, Wood Peg Construction 925.00
Cupboard, Walnut, Scalloped Apron, 72 In., 1 Piece 1950.00
Cupboard, Walnut, Sliding Center Glass Section 8250.00
Cupboard, Welsh, 3 Overlapping Drawers, Oak, 83 1/2 X 71 In. 1500.00
Cupboard, Welsh, Oak, 2 Drawers, Open Top, Molded Cornice, 74 In. 1900.00
Cupboard, Welsh, Open Bottom Section, 3 Drawers, Pine, 84 3/4 In. 900.00
Cupboard, Welsh, Plate Racks, Cubbyholes, 2 Drawers, 81 X 72 In. 5500.00
Cupboard, William & Mary, Walnut, Painted Scenes, Cornice, 80 In. 600.00
Daybed, L. & J.G. Stickley, Vertical Slats At Head & Foot, 1912 .... 610.00
Daybed, Limbert, Shaped Headrest, Spring Cushions, Oak, C.1910 .... 550.00
Daybed, Louis XVI, Painted, Cane Sides & Seat, 70 In. 55.00
Daybed, Turned Legs & Rungs, Plaid Upholstered, 74 In. 75.00
Demi–Cabinet, Galleried Marble Top, 3 Open Shelves, 45 1/2 In. 550.00
Desk Bookcase, Barrister's, Oak 495.00
Desk Bookcase, Mahogany, Original Brass, N.Y., Late 1780s, 89 In. 6900.00
Desk Box, Table Top, Carved Designs, R. Wood, 1708, 19 1/2 In. 600.00
Desk, American Gothic, Rosewood, Satinwood Interior 3750.00
Desk, Book Matched Veneer, Fitted, Galleries, 41 X 23 In. 550.00
Desk, Boulle, Louis XV Style 1500.00
Desk, Butler's, Empire, Top Hinged Drawer, Mahogany, C.1850, 43 In. 715.00
Desk, Child's, Fold Down Top, 3 Drawers, Swivel Chair, 2 Piece 75.00
Desk, Child's, Lift Top, 1 Drawer, Oak, 1820, 33 In. 1050.00
Desk, Child's, Oak, Spindle Back Chair, 1900, 2 Piece 225.00
Desk, Child's, Roll Top, Chair, 2 Piece 300.00
Desk, Child's, Roll Top, Pressed Trim On Backboard & Desk, Oak 275.00
Desk, Chippendale, Maple, Wallace Nutting, 39 X 36 In. ....*Illus* 3520.00
Desk, Chippendale, Slant Front, 4 Drawers, Mahogany, 40 1/4 In. 3000.00
Desk, Chippendale, Slant Front, Cherry, Bracket Feet, 45 1/2 In. 6000.00
Desk, Chippendale, Slant Front, Walnut, 4 Drawers, Bracket Feet 4900.00
Desk, Chippendale, Slant Lid, Birch, C.1770, 39 1/2 In. ....*Illus* 4620.00
Desk, Counter, Pine, Dovetailed, Lift Top, With Drawer 450.00
Desk, Cylinder, Marble Top, 2 Drawers, French, Walnut, 29 In. 1045.00
Desk, Davenport, Cylinder Top, Eastlake, 46 X 29 In. 1300.00
Desk, Desk, Slant Front, Chippendale, Fitted Interior, Cherry 6000.00
Desk, Drop Front, Brass Hinges, C.Rohlfs, Oak, C.1907, 50 1/2 In. 2640.00
Desk, Drop Front, Chestnut Lid, G. Stickley, C.1912, 42 1/2 In. 935.00
Desk, Drop Front, Ebenezer Felton, Maple, 3 Graduated Drawers 9575.00
Desk, Drop Front, Empire, Mahogany Veneer, Cypress & Pine, C.1850 .... 350.00
Desk, Drop Front, Gustav Stickley, 2 Short, 2 Long Drawers, 43 In. 3850.00
Desk, Drop Front, Larkin, Oak, Shaped & Beveled Mirror 365.00
Desk, Drop Front, Stickley, C.1912, 35 1/4 X 31 1/2 In. ....*Illus* 850.00
Desk, Executive, Marlborough Feet, Burl Walnut 1800.00
Desk, Federal, Tambour Front, Bottle Drawers, French Feet, 50 In. 3400.00

Furniture, Desk, Chippendale,
Slant Lid, Birch, C.1770,
39 1/2 In.

Furniture, Desk, Chippendale,
Maple, Wallace Nutting,
39 X 36 In.

Furniture, Desk, Drop Front,
Stickley, C.1912, 35 1/4 X
31 1/2 In.

Furniture, Desk, Ladies', Writing, Art Nouveau

Furniture, Desk, George III, Mahogany,
31 X 48 X 31 In.

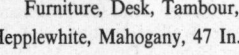

Furniture, Desk, Rotary, Lawyer's,
Oak, C.1875

Furniture, Desk, Tambour,
Hepplewhite, Mahogany, 47 In.

Desk, Flat Top, 8–Legged, Gustav Stickley, No.712, C.1912, 36 In.	2550.00
Desk, G. Stickley, Letter Rack, Iron Hardware, 1902	1430.00
Desk, Gateleg Drop Front, 2 Drawers, L. & J.G. Stickley, 1912	935.00
Desk, George I, Kneehole, Inlaid Burl Walnut, C.1710, 30 1/2 In.	9950.00
Desk, George III, Mahogany, 31 X 48 X 31 In. ....*Illus*	2600.00
Desk, Georgian Style, Kidney Shape, Leather Top, Burled Walnut	885.00
Desk, Gustav Stickley, No.708	3400.00
Desk, Hepplewhite, 4 Drawers, Fitted Interior, Figured Walnut	2500.00
Desk, Inlaid Slant Lid, 4 Drawers, Mahogany, C.1810, 41 1/2 In.	1985.00
Desk, Kneehole, Georgian, Mahogany, Leather Insert, Plinth Base	4840.00
Desk, Lap, Brass Bound, Walnut Burl Veneer, Camphorwood, 8 1/2 In.	900.00
Desk, Lap, Leather Surface, Secret Compartment, Rosewood	350.00
Desk, Lap, Papier–Mache, Gold Design, Mother-of-Pearl Inlay, China	125.00
Desk, Lap, Rosewood, Brass, Cut Glass, Fitted Interior, English	350.00
Desk, Long Drawer, Open Lower Shelf, Oak, C.1910, 45 5/8 In.	1100.00

Desk, Louis XV, Mahogany, Marquetry, Cylinder, Bombe, Dutch, 1770 .... 8500.00
Desk, Oak, 11–Stack, Fold Down , Fitted.6 X 1 1/2 Ft. 1800.00
Desk, Officer's Field, Walnut, Fold Out Surface, Compartments 290.00
Desk, Partners', Faux Tortoiseshell, Leather Surface, 5 Ft.3 In. 3575.00
Desk, Partners', Limbert, Drawers On 1 Side 3190.00
Desk, Partners', Mahogany, Winged Griffin Supports, Carved 7200.00
Desk, Partners', Pedestal, 6 Drawers, Mahogany, 5 Ft. 2850.00
Desk, Pedestal, Fruitwood & Ebony Marquetry, Mahogany, 31 1/2 In. 4450.00
Desk, Pedestal, Kidney Shape, 7 Drawers, Oak, 28 1/2 X 57 1/2 In. 725.00
Desk, Pedestal, Leather Surface, 3 Drawers, Mahogany, 4 Ft.5 In. 1350.00
Desk, Pine, Poplar, Hinged Top, Ovolo Corners, 1 Drawer, 31 In. 225.00
Desk, Plantation, Slant Front, 3 Drawers, Fitted Interior, Cherry 1600.00
Desk, Post Office, Drop Front, Poplar, Pine, Pigeonholes, 3 Drawers 550.00
Desk, Queen Anne, Pine, Hardwood, 1 Dovetailed Drawer, 38 In. 2000.00
Desk, Queen Anne, Secretary Top, Maple, Tombstone Shaped Doors 8250.00
Desk, Raised Panels, Hand Carved Pulls, Quarter Sawn Oak, 66 In. 2700.00
Desk, Regency, Mahogany, Galleried Leather Inset, Trestle Base 385.00
Desk, Roll Top, Built–In Glass Door Bookcase, Oak 3500.00
Desk, Roll Top, C Roll, Oak, 72 In. 1900.00
Desk, Roll Top, Raised Panels, Chair, Mahogany, 66 In. 2500.00
Desk, Roll Top, Right Fold Out, 57 Interior Drawers, Oak, 76 In. 6500.00
Desk, Roll Top, S Roll, 22 Interior Drawers, Oak, 54 X 30 In. 1400.00
Desk, Roll Top, S Roll, 23 Pigeonholes, Swivel Chair, 55 In. 2100.00
Desk, Roll Top, S Roll, 25 Interior Drawers, Oak, 66 In. 3500.00
Desk, Roll Top, S Roll, Bird's–Eye Maple Drawer Fronts, 60 In. 3850.00
Desk, Roll Top, S Roll, Flat Panels, Quarter Sawn Oak, 60 In. 1600.00
Desk, Roll Top, S Roll, Oak, 56 X 28 X 47 In. 2000.00
Desk, Roll Top, S Roll, Oak, Indianapolis Cabinet Co. 850.00
Desk, Roll Top, S Roll, Quarter Sawn Oak, 60 X 35 In. 2650.00
Desk, Roll Top, S Roll, Raised Panels, Quarter Sawn Oak, 54 In. 1600.00
Desk, Rotary, Lawyer's, Oak, C.1875 ....*Illus* 3300.00
Desk, Rotary, Raised Burl Walnut Panels, Full Gallery 4500.00
Desk, School, Attached Bench, Seating For 3 Pupils 300.00
Desk, School, Lift Top, Oak, C.1870 .... 185.00
Desk, School, Sheraton, Turned Legs 950.00
Desk, School, Slant Lift Top, Pine, 33 X 62 In. 300.00
Desk, Schoolmaster's, Slanted Hinged Lid, Pine, 7 Drawers, 36 In. 325.00
Desk, Schoolmaster's, Slanted Lift Top, 2 Drawers, Maple 230.00
Desk, Schoolteacher's, Lift Top, Pine 145.00
Desk, Schoolteacher's, Oak 1500.00
Desk, Slant Front, Arts & Crafts, Oak, Bracket Legs, 30 X 15 In. 440.00
Desk, Slant Front, Dutch Rococo, Rosewood 2400.00
Desk, Slant Front, Fitted Interior, 7 Drawers, Cherry, 40 3/8 In. 2100.00
Desk, Slant Front, Gold Chinoiserie Design, Red Lacquer, 43 In. 5250.00
Desk, Slant Front, Hepplewhite, Tiger Maple, C.1810, 35 In. 4125.00
Desk, Slant Front, Hepplewhite, Walnut, C.1800, 42 In. 3400.00
Desk, Slant Front, Larkin, Beveled Mirror, Oak 140.00
Desk, Slant Front, Queen Anne, Inlaid Walnut, 39 In. 3850.00
Desk, Slant Front, Serpentine Interior, Walnut, C.1800, 34 1/2 In. 9500.00
Desk, Slant Front, Sliding Lid Writing Board, Tiger Maple, C.1790 .... 7100.00
Desk, Slant Front, Tiger Maple Banding, Cherry, C.1800, 35 1/4 In. 3200.00
Desk, Slant Front, Wallace Nutting, Mahogany 625.00
Desk, Slant Front, Wallace Nutting, Maple, 39 X 36 In. 3520.00
Desk, Slant Front, Walnut, Serpentine, Fitted, French, 41 X 39 In. 2500.00
Desk, Slant Hinged Lid, Maple & Birch, C.1800, 44 X 41 In. 1760.00
Desk, Slant Lid, Matching Secretary Top, Tiger Maple 7000.00
Desk, Slant Top, 4 Graduated Drawers, 1780s 5700.00
Desk, Slant Top, On Frame, Red Graining, Lift Lid, 52 1/4 In. 950.00
Desk, Slant, English Oak, Geometric & Floral, 11 X 31 X 17 In. 495.00
Desk, Stand Up, Walnut, 1840 .... 2400.00
Desk, Table Top, Iron Nail Construction, Pine, 11 X 15 3/4 In. 575.00
Desk, Tambour, Hepplewhite, Mahogany, 47 In. ....*Illus* 1100.00
Desk, Telegraph, Roll Top, S Roll, Hidden Side Drawer, Oak, C.1890 .... 950.00
Desk, Victorian, Drop Front, Walnut 650.00

Desk, William & Mary, Slant Front, Walnut, Seaweed Marquetry 6500.00
Desk, Woman's, Art Nouveau, Mahogany, 1900–10 ....*Illus* 5500.00
Desk, Woman's, Art Nouveau, Mahogany, Bow Front, American, 1900–10 .... 225.00
Desk, Woman's, Chinese, Huang Hua–Li Wood, Bronze Mounts 1400.00
Desk, Woman's, Ebonized, Marked Diehi, Paris 3350.00
Desk, Woman's, Etagere, Thomas Brooks, Ivory Pulls, Satinwood 7700.00
Desk, Woman's, French Style, Marble Top, 1 Drawer 165.00
Desk, Woman's, Victorian, Drop Front, Walnut, High Back, 2 Piece 650.00
Desk, Wooton, Walnut, Flat Top 1750.00
Dining Set, Buffet, Hutch, Black Walnut, 8 Chairs 3500.00
Dining Set, French Provincial, Antique White & Gold, 10 Piece 2500.00
Dining Set, Jacobean, Burl Veneer, Oak, 9 Piece 650.00
Dining Set, Jacobean, Table Draw Leaves, Sideboard, 1925, 6 Chairs 1295.00
Dining Set, Mahogany, 54–In. Round Table, Seats 12, 1900s, 9 Piece 1800.00
Dining Set, Oriental Mahogany, Server, 1950s, 6 Piece 695.00
Dining Set, Queen Anne, Detachable Leaves Table, Hutch, 9 Piece 8500.00
Dining Set, Sideboard, Table, Carved Mahogany, 12 Chairs 8500.00
Dresser, 2 Side Mirrors & Center, Handkerchief Drawer, Walnut 675.00
Dresser, Bamboo Turned Maple, C.1870 .... 1400.00
Dresser, Cherry, High Ornate Mirror, Lamp Shelves, Marble, Large 1525.00
Dresser, Chinese, Rosewood, Carved Dragons, 84 In. ....*Illus* 2600.00
Dresser, Eastlake Style, Walnut, Marble Top, C.1885, Miniature 350.00
Dresser, Empire, Walnut, C.1850 .... 325.00
Dresser, G. Stickley, 2 Short Over 3 Long Drawers, C.1906, Oak 7865.00
Dresser, Handkerchief Drawers, Flame Veneer, Butternut 275.00
Dresser, Marble Top, Glove Boxes, Teardrop Pulls, Walnut 475.00
Dresser, Princess, Full Length Beveled Swivel Mirror, Oak, 4 Ft. 750.00
Dresser, Quarter Sawn Oak, Serpentine, Beveled Mirror 325.00
Dresser, Queen Anne, Red Oak, Oval Mirror, 1875 .... 350.00
Dresser, Victorian, Walnut, High Mirror, Marble, Original Pulls 2500.00
Dry Sink, High Back, Mustard Paint, 2 Doors, 3 Top Small Drawers 185.00
Dry Sink, Paneled Doors, Pink, 38 1/2 X 43 1/2 In. 1350.00
Dry Sink, Pine, 2 Walnut Drawer Fronts, Nailed, 43 X 20 X 58 In. 525.00
Dry Sink, Pine, High Back, 4 Side Base Drawers, 4 Doors, 1875 .... 2850.00
Dry Sink, Shenandoah Valley, C.1840 .... 875.00
Dumbwaiter, George III, 3 Graduated Tiers, Mahogany, 4 Ft. 1100.00
Easel, 1880s, 5 Ft. 100.00
Easel, Adirondack Style, Applied Acorns, Twig Stars, 86 In. 550.00
Easel, Black Walnut, Aesthetic Movement, Gilt Incised 5000.00
Easel, Eastlake, Gallery of Turned Spindles, C.1875, 70 In. 675.00
Etagere, Rosewood, Mirror, Marble Top, C.1850–1860 ....*Illus* 4750.00
Etagere, Victorian, Mirror Back, Openwork Design, 87 X 51 In. 1500.00

Furniture, Dresser, Chinese, Rosewood,
Carved Dragons, 84 In.

Furniture, Etagere, Rosewood, Mirror,
Marble Top, C.1850–1860

Feeding Chair–Walker–Cradle, Child's, Grained, Wis.Invented, 1870 .... 585.00
Footstool, Bootjack Legs, Pine, 6 1/2 X 15 1/2 In. 110.00
Footstool, Carved Apron, Fluted Legs, Gilded, 7 X 13 In., Pair 715.00
Footstool, Chip Carved Stars On Top & Skirt, Pine, 8 1/2 In. 110.00
Footstool, Curly Maple, Red Finish, 20 In., Pair 300.00
Footstool, Cushion Fits Into Frame, 20th Century, 17 X 20 In. 195.00
Footstool, Eastlake, Ring Turned Legs, American, Walnut, C.1875 .... 165.00
Footstool, Gothic Revival, Oak, 16 1/2 X 29 1/2 In. 4125.00
Footstool, Green Paint, White Striping, Floral Design, 8 3/4 In. 500.00
Footstool, Gustav Stickley, Spindle Sided, Upholstered, C.1907 .... 4100.00
Footstool, Handmade, Walnut, 10 X 6 3/4 X 22 1/2 In. 25.00
Footstool, L. & J.G. Stickley, Upholstered, C.1912, 16 In. 412.50
Footstool, Leather Top, Early 20th Century, 14 X 19 1/2 In. 165.00
Footstool, Louis XV Style, Carved Walnut, 14 1/2 In. 187.50
Footstool, Monk's, Leather Top, Decal, Gustav Sitckley, C.1907, Oak 550.00
Footstool, Needlepoint Seat, Burled & Walnut 110.00
Footstool, Needlepoint Seat, Painted Skirt, Cast Iron, 14 In., Pr. 275.00
Footstool, Oak, Primitive, Worn Dark, Gothic, 23 1/2 X 21 1/2 In. 200.00
Footstool, Pine, Brown Finish, Cutout Legs, Apron, 9 In. 175.00
Footstool, Pine, Green Paint, 16 In. 65.00
Footstool, Pine, Plank Ends, Removable Key Stretcher, 20 X 11 In. 65.00
Footstool, Poplar, Brown, Cabriole Legs, Scalloped Apron, 6 In. 400.00
Footstool, Poplar, Cutout Feet, Paneled End, 1 Drawer, 11 In. 350.00
Footstool, Roycroft, Needlepoint Cover, Logo, C.1910, 10 In. 412.00
Footstool, Shaker, Red Stain, 7 X 36 In. 165.00
Footstool, Splayed Legs, Scrubbed Pine, 7 1/2 X 8 In. 45.00
Footstool, Upholstered Top, Walnut, American, C.1860, 6 1/2 In. 165.00
Footstool, Windsor, Dark Finish, 8 X 8 1/4 X 6 In. 65.00
Frame, Beveled, Curly Maple Veneer On Poplar, 22 X 16 In. 75.00
Frame, Oak, Carved, Arthur Jones, 28 1/2 X 24 In. 125.00
Frame, Shadowbox, Gilded Liner, Olive Wood, 34 1/4 X 39 In. 325.00
Frame, Walnut, Architectural Detail, Carved Hinges, 23 X 25 In. 175.00
Garden Seat, Barrel Back, Terra–Cotta 825.00
Garden Seat, Elephant, Chinese Pottery 110.00
Garden Set, 2 Armchairs, 2 Side Chairs, Curved Bench, Cast Iron 3000.00
Garden Set, Victorian, Iron, White Paint, Settee, Chair, 2 Piece 3100.00
Glider, Basket Weave Settee, T–Floor Frame, Hickory, 62 In. 995.00
Gong, Eastlake, Oak Stand, Bronze Gong, American, C.1885, 38 In. 650.00
Hall Stand, 8 Wooden Pegs Around Mirror, Drawer, Walnut, C.1860 .... 950.00
Hall Stand, Inset Mirror, Cast Iron, White Paint 1045.00
Hall Stand, Mirror, 4 Metal Hooks, Umbrella Holders, Eastlake 370.00
Hall Stand, Mirror, Oak, 4 Cast Iron Hooks, Umbrella Stand 225.00
Hall Stand, Mirror, Umbrella Holders, Iron, Ohillon, C.1925 .... 7150.00
Hall Stand, Oval Mirror, Umbrella Stand, Iron, 75 In. ....*Illus* 615.00
Hall Tree, Bear Form, 8 Ft. ....*Illus* 2640.00
Hall Tree, Bear, Female, Cub In Branches, Walnut, 77 In. ....*Illus* 3150.00
Hall Tree, Carved Cub In Branches, Black Forest, 80 In. 4500.00
Hall Tree, Griffins, Cast Iron 210.00

Furniture, Hall Tree, Bear, Female,   Furniture, Hall Tree,   Furniture, Hall Stand, Oval Mirror,
Cub In Branches, Walnut, 77 In.   Bear Form, 8 Ft.   Umbrella Stand, Iron, 75 In.

Furniture, Mirror,
Swedish, Neoclassical,
Fruits, Sphinxes, 5 Ft.

Furniture, Mirror, Walnut, American,
C.1850–1860, 48 1/2 X 42 In.

Hall Tree, Walnut, Marble Top, Large	2050.00
Hall Tree, Walnut, Orante, C. Blacke, Pat.1870	1200.00
High Chair Stroller, Oak	425.00
High Chair, 2 Slats, Rush Seat, Maple, 18th Century, 35 1/2 In.	1550.00
High Chair, Floral, Blue & Yellow Striping, 32 1/2 In.	125.00
High Chair, Folds To Stroller, Cane Seat, Back, Walnut, Victorian	395.00
High Chair, Footrest, Arrow Back, Dark Green Paint, 19th Century	750.00
High Chair, Mission, Oak, Original Tray	80.00
High Chair, Pressed Back, Full Figure Santa Claus, Toys On Back	850.00
High Chair, Slat Back, Splay–Legged	2750.00
High Chair, Thonet	475.00
High Chair, U–Shaped Crest, Turned Spindles, Dark Brown, Striped	225.00
High Chair, Victorian, Cane Seat	632.50
High Chair, Wooden, Tapered Pencil Post Legs, Plank Seat, 33 In.	500.00
Highboy, 1 Drawer Over 3 Short Drawers, Maple, C.1760, 36 1/4 In.	1550.00
Highboy, 6 Drawers, Cherry & Curly Maple	1050.00
Highboy, Broken Arch Top, Drake Feet, Tiger Maple	8000.00
Highboy, Chippendale, 3 Over 2, Over 3 Drawers, Walnut, 2 Piece	1600.00
Highboy, Flat Top, Cutout Skirt, Maple	8500.00
Highboy, George I, Figures, Green Japanned, C.1720, 5 Ft.4 In.	7150.00
Highboy, Oak, 5 Graduated Drawers, Mirror, Casters, Brass Handles	375.00
Highboy, Oak, Mirror, Old Man of North Brass Pulls	460.00
Highboy, Queen Anne, 18th Century Top, Mahogany, C.1880	4500.00
Highboy, Queen Anne, Cherry, Cabriole Legs, Duck Feet, 71 1/4 In.	5500.00
Highboy, Queen Anne, Curly Maple, C.1750, 67 1/2 In.	7700.00
Highboy, Queen Anne, Flat Top, Walnut	8000.00
Highboy, Queen Anne, Scrolled Apron, 71 1/4 In.	5500.00
Highboy, Queen Anne, Top 6 Drawers, Acorn Drops, Maple, 70 3/4 In.	5250.00
Hutch–Table, Lift Lid Seat, Storage Compartment, Pumpkin Pine	575.00
Ice Cream Set, Child's, American, 1920s, 3 Piece	295.00
Ice Cream Set, Child's, Iron, 3 Piece	125.00
Kas, Raised Panel Doors, Cherry, 58 1/4 X 76 1/2 In.	4000.00
Kas, Walnut, Dovetailed Case, Paneled Door, Pintle Hinges, 76 In.	1000.00
Library Steps, George III, Mahogany, 46 In.	209.00
Linen Press, 2 Doors, 2 Shelves, 4 Drawers, Cherry, C.1780, 78 In.	4075.00
Linen Press, Eagle Brass, C.1800, Cherry, 82 X 46 1/2 In.	3300.00
Linen Press, George III, Paneled Doors, 2 Drawers, Mahogany, 6 Ft.	4950.00
Linen Press, Inlaid Walnut, Mid–19th Century, 86 X 51 X 22 In.	5800.00
Linen Press, William IV, Beaded Rim, Mahogany, 7 Ft.8 1/2 In.	1650.00
Love Seat, Belter, Rosalie Without Grapes	7000.00
Love Seat, J. & J. Meeks, Rosewood	7150.00
Love Seat, Jenny Lind, Walnut	275.00

Lowboy, Chippendale, Stylized, 2 Drawers 550.00
Lowboy, Wallace Nutting, 20th Century, 29 1/2 X 36 In. 2090.00
Meridienne, Eastlake, Upholstered Step Down Back, C.1875 .... 525.00
Mirror, Acanthus Leaf Cluster, Vines, Gilded, 44 X 38 In. 255.00
Mirror, Architectural, 2–Part, Pine, Oval Medallion, 11 X 21 In. 410.00
Mirror, Architectural, Child, Blue Suit, Medallion, 23 X 40 In. 450.00
Mirror, Architectural, Oak, Red, Brown, Natural Finish, 8 X 12 In. 400.00
Mirror, Architectural, Pine, Houses, Grass, 2–Piece, 13 X 24 In. 375.00
Mirror, Bacchanalian Scene, Tapestry Drapery Border, 57 X 40 In. 2100.00
Mirror, Beveled Glass, Oak Frame, 26 1/2 X 26 1/2 In. 45.00
Mirror, Black & Gold Paint, Reverse Painting, 15 X 28 1/2 In. 100.00
Mirror, Bound Reed Frame, 20th Century, 54 X 33 In. 300.00
Mirror, Bradley & Hubbard, Beveled, Bronze Finish, 9 1/2 X 14 In. 125.00
Mirror, Brass Rosettes, Reverse Glass, 23 1/2 X 11 1/4 In. 250.00
Mirror, Carved & Gilded Urn Crest, Beveled, 48 X 29 In. 180.00
Mirror, Carved Floral Crest, Pine, 14 1/4 X 9 3/4 In. 100.00
Mirror, Carved Flowers, Parcel Gilt, Mahogany, 43 X 32 In. 3575.00
Mirror, Charles II, Faux Tortoiseshell Frame, 56 X 44 In. 3600.00
Mirror, Cheval, Floor, Hinged Panels, 3–Way, 1910, 82 X 75 In. 550.00
Mirror, Cheval, Victorian, Mahogany, Scroll Feet, Floral Cartouche 3000.00
Mirror, Chippendale, Mahogany Frame, 17 1/4 X 11 1/2 In. 275.00
Mirror, Chippendale, Mahogany, Gold Leaf, Broken Arch 4180.00
Mirror, Chippendale, Molded Liner, Mahogany, 1800, 27 X 14 1/2 In. 357.50
Mirror, Chippendale, Scroll, Cherry Finish, 13 X 18 1/2 In. 250.00
Mirror, Chippendale, Scroll, Mahogany, Pine, Frame, 22 X 44 In. 1700.00
Mirror, Continental, Brass, Reeded, 19th Century, 63 X 35 In. 1100.00
Mirror, Continental, Scroll & Floral Border, Gilt Wood 1210.00
Mirror, Convex, Gesso & Wood Frame, Seahorse Top, 34 1/2 X 22 In. 2900.00
Mirror, Courting, Etched Plate, 18th Century, 15 1/2 X 11 In. 1100.00
Mirror, Courting, Pine, Applied Moldings, Brown, 12 X 17 In. 600.00
Mirror, Courting, Reverse Painted Strips, Dutch, 26 X 14 In. 665.00
Mirror, Dressing Table, Victorian, Oval, Gilded Metal, 15 X 11 In. 145.00
Mirror, Dressing, American Empire, Scrolled Supports, 24 In. 80.00
Mirror, Dressing, Cheval, White Metal, Victorian, 15 In. 400.00
Mirror, Dressing, Gilt Wood, Pierced Flowers, Chinese, 20 X 15 In. 175.00
Mirror, Dressing, Silver, Gadrooned, England, Oval, 9 3/4 X 8 In. 275.00
Mirror, Dressing, Stand, George III, Crossbanded, Mahogany, 37 In. 4500.00
Mirror, Eagle Finial, Convex, Gilt Frame, 29 1/2 X 21 In. 55.00
Mirror, Eastlake, Chestnut, Gilt & Ebonized, C.1875, 21 X 15 In. 135.00
Mirror, Ebonized, Silver Bronze Frame, A. Cheuret, 1925, 28 In. 6600.00
Mirror, Empire, Acanthus Carved, Mount Vernon, 39 1/2 In. 125.00
Mirror, Empire, Brass Rosettes, 2 Part, Black, Gold Paint, 27 In. 300.00
Mirror, Empire, Half Columns, Mahogany Veneer, 33 X 17 In. 200.00
Mirror, Empire, Reverse Painting, House & Bridge, 24 X 14 In. 250.00
Mirror, English Stump Work, King, Queen, Castle, Birds, 17 X 19 In. 3250.00
Mirror, Etched, Arched Frame, 19th Century, 18 1/4 X 13 5/8 In. 165.00
Mirror, Faux Tortoiseshell Lacquer, 18th Century, 20 1/2 In. 2200.00
Mirror, Federal, Eglomise & Panel, Gilt Wood, 35 1/2 X 22 In. 1045.00
Mirror, Floral Crest, Garlands, Foliate Designs, 41 In. 1045.00
Mirror, Flowers & Cherubs, Porcelain Frame, 10 X 12 1/2 In. 50.00
Mirror, Folk Art Carved Walnut Frame, 15 1/2 X 21 In. 850.00
Mirror, G. Stickley, 3 Panels, 4 Coat Hooks, Oak, 1909 42 1/2 In. 5080.00
Mirror, G. Stickley, Iron Hooks & Chain, C.1905, 28 5/8 In. 1695.00
Mirror, George I, Ribbon Carved Border, Gilt Wood, 41 X 25 In. 4125.00
Mirror, George III Style, Divided Plate, Parcel Gilt, 54 X 23 In. 425.00
Mirror, George III, Carved Acanthus Leaves, Gilt Wood, 4 Ft.3 In. 8800.00
Mirror, George III, Carved C–Scroll Frame, Gilt Wood, 56 X 29 In. 665.00
Mirror, Gilt Wood & Eglomise Panel, Ships, 1800, 35 1/2 X 22 In. 950.00
Mirror, Girandole, Federal, Gilt Wood, Eagle Crest Top, 26 In. 450.00
Mirror, Girandole, Floral Crest, 26 X 15 1/2 X 15 1/2 In. 385.00
Mirror, Girandole, Spread Eagle Top, Gilt Wood, 53 X 27 1/2 In. 825.00
Mirror, Hall, Walnut, Marble Shelf, 8 Ft.5 In., 31 In. 1500.00
Mirror, Held By Eagle, Glass Eyes, Crescent Shape, 17 X 14 In. 395.00
Mirror, Hepplewhite, Framed By Rosettes & Husks, 45 X 22 In. 225.00

Mirror, Iron Frame, Coiling Tendrils, French, C.1925, 17 1/4 In. 1765.00
Mirror, Italian Rococo, C Scroll & Leafage Frame, 54 X 42 In. 1700.00
Mirror, Italian Rococo, Gilt Wood, Serpentine Shape, 43 X 29 In. 2250.00
Mirror, Italian Rococo, Polychrome, Candleholders, 27 In., Pair 995.00
Mirror, Limbert Co., Beveled Glass, C.1910, 40 1/2 X 21 1/2 In. 605.00
Mirror, Louis XVI, Ribbon Molded Frame, Gilt Wood, 50 X 50 In. 4670.00
Mirror, Mantel, 3–Part, Ebonized Gilt Wood, 5 Ft.3 In. 2200.00
Mirror, Mantel, Classical, Gilt Wood, Eagle, 1840–60, 33 X 51 In. 6000.00
Mirror, Mantel, George II, Beveled, Mahogany, 18 X 61 In. 8800.00
Mirror, Neoclassical, Urn Crest, Scandinavian, Gilt Wood, 26 In. 445.00
Mirror, Oak Frame, Beveled, Coat Hook Each Corner 85.00
Mirror, Pier, Continental Neoclassical, Gilt Wood, 39 X 63 In. 2200.00
Mirror, Pier, Cornice, Walnut, C.1875, 48 1/2 X 24 1/2 In. 325.00
Mirror, Pier, Louis XV, Marble Top, Carved & Gilded, 96 In. 610.00
Mirror, Pier, Marble Base, Dated 1834, 90 In.Mirror, 19 In. Base 2500.00
Mirror, Pier, Pendant Acorns, Gilt Wood, C.1830, 40 X 24 In. 885.00
Mirror, Pine Frame, Scrolled Crest, Beveled Glass, 17 X 33 In. 400.00
Mirror, Plateau, Double Beveled, Beaded, Plated Frame, 8 1/2 In. 70.00
Mirror, Plateau, Ram's Head Feet, 11 3/4 In. 185.00
Mirror, Plateau, Victorian, Notched Beveled Mirror, 16 In. 85.00
Mirror, Plateau, Wide Floral Feet, Double Bevel, 16 In. 115.00
Mirror, Pyrographic Design, Mythical Serpents, Round, 21 In. 110.00
Mirror, Queen Anne, 2–Part Plate, Bouquet of Ferns, 36 In. 2300.00
Mirror, Queen Anne, Figured Walnut Veneer, 16 X 9 3/4 In. 450.00
Mirror, Queen Anne, Scalloped Crest, Walnut, 19 X 10 5/8 In. 125.00
Mirror, Queen Anne, Shaped Crest, Frame, England, 16 1/2 In. 825.00
Mirror, Queen Anne, Walnut Veneer, 1730–45, 43 1/2 X 17 1/4 In. 5280.00
Mirror, Queen Anne, Walnut, Gilt Wood C.1780, 54 3/4 X 21 1/4 In. 4650.00
Mirror, Regency Style, Greek Women, Stepped Cornice, 38 X 18 In. 1100.00
Mirror, Regency, Convex, Candle Arms, Gilt Wood, C.1820, 4 Ft.3 In. 4675.00
Mirror, Regency, Convex, Gilt Wood & Ebonized, 36 X 26 In. 2750.00
Mirror, Reverse Glass, Knight On Horse, Frame, 24 1/2 In. 200.00
Mirror, Reverse Painted, Blue & Gold, Gilt Finish, 32 1/2 In. 165.00
Mirror, Reverse Painted, House, Garden, 2 Part, 27 1/2 X 12 In. 175.00
Mirror, Reverse Painted, Ship At Top, Mahogany, 25 3/4 In. 95.00
Mirror, Reverse Painted, Woman Charming Snake, 32 X 17 In. 110.00
Mirror, Rope Twist Pilasters, Gilded Wood & Gesso, 33 X 21 In. 350.00
Mirror, Scroll Work, Mahogany, 30 1/2 X 18 In. 200.00
Mirror, Scroll, Mahogany, 19th Century, 16 1/4 X 10 1/4 In. 225.00
Mirror, Shaving, Bow Front, Mahogany Veneer On Pine, 20 In. 125.00
Mirror, Shaving, Horseshoe Shaped Frame, 16 3/4 In. 375.00
Mirror, Shaving, Horseshoe Shaped Frame, Good Luck, 24 1/2 In. 225.00
Mirror, Shaving, Milk Glass, Metal, Art Nouveau, Swivels, 14 In. 195.00
Mirror, Shell Over Bow & Floral Clusters, Gilded, 63 In. 1760.00
Mirror, Shield, Candle Arms, Mahogany, Gilt, Europe, 23 X 40 In. 375.00
Mirror, Silver Plated, Flanked By 2–Light Candelabra, 20 In. 1700.00
Mirror, String Inlay, Gilt Liner, Mahogany, 30 X 16 3/4 In. 465.00
Mirror, Stump Work Scenes, 17 X 18 3/4 In. 3250.00
Mirror, Swan's Neck Pediment, Gilt Wood & Mahogany, 55 1/2 In. 5280.00
Mirror, Swedish, Neoclassical, Fruits, Sphinxes, 5 Ft. ....*Illus* 4675.00
Mirror, Travel, Folding, Victorian, Oak, Beveled, Tin Panels, 1890 .... 125.00
Mirror, Turned Pilasters, Corner Blocks, Black & Gold, 25 3/4 In. 85.00
Mirror, Walnut Veneer On Pine Frame, 15 7/8 X 9 3/8 In. 450.00
Mirror, Walnut, American, C.1850–1860, 48 1/2 X 42 In. ....*Illus* 2800.00
Nightstand, Sheraton, Tiger Maple, Splayed Legs, Cut Corners 650.00
Ottoman, Victorian, Needlework Upholstered, 14 1/2 X 40 In. 2000.00
Parlor Set, Bronze Dore, Sphinx Decorations, Mahogany, 5 Piece 8000.00
Parlor Set, Eastlake, Settee, 2 Chairs, Upholstered 350.00
Parlor Set, Egyptian Revival, Settee, 4 Chairs, Tapestry Covered 4500.00
Parlor Set, Love Seat, Pull–Up Chair, Armchair, Carved Feet, 1850 .... 3250.00
Parlor Set, Renaissance Revival, Sofa & Armchair, C.1870, 2 Pc. 3250.00
Parlor Set, Renaissance Revival, Walnut, 6 Piece 1200.00
Parlor Set, Victorian, Sofa, 2 Chairs, Winged Nudes, Mahogany 5000.00
Pedestal, Eastlake, Inlaid Bands, Cherry, C.1880, 40 1/2 In. 925.00

Pedestal, Female Figure, Mahogany, 39 1/2 In. 1600.00
Pedestal, Folk Art, Pine, 2 Tone Inlay, 32 In. 105.00
Pedestal, Gaillard, Marble Insets In Shafts, C.1901, 51 1/2 In. 4950.00
Pedestal, J.Leleu, Bronze Banding, Rosewood, C.1925, 45 3/8 In. 3300.00
Pedestal, Limbert, 3 Tiers, Tapered 5225.00
Pedestal, Magazine, Roycroft, Exposed Key Tenons, 5 Shelves, Black 7500.00
Pedestal, Stickley Bros., Arched Apron, 4 Angled Legs, 34 In. 1600.00
Pie Safe, 12 Tins, Old Red Paint 775.00
Pie Safe, 3 Doors, 15 Original Tins, 2 Top Drawers 3200.00
Pie Safe, 3 Punched Tin Panels, 2 Drawers, 54 X 41 X 17 In. 1500.00
Pie Safe, 4 Punched Tins, 2 Drawers, 1869 .... 475.00
Pie Safe, 5 Punched Tins, Wooden, 3 Shelves, 36 X 22 X 34 In. 475.00
Pie Safe, 6 Tins, Pierced In Circle Design, Lower Drawer, Walnut 360.00
Pie Safe, Walnut, 12 Tins, 2 Dovetailed Drawers Top, N. Carolina 1195.00
Pie Safe, Yellow Graining, Red Door Panels, Poplar, 54 In. 1500.00
Pie Shelf, Hanging, Punched Tin, Mustard Paint, Lancaster County 690.00
Play Pen, Green Paint, Spool Turned Spindles, Pine, 13 X 22 In. 55.00
Porch Set, Wicker, White Paint, Sofa & 2 Armchairs, 1920s 2200.00
Porch Swing, 2 Section Back, Vertical Slats, Oak, Chains, C.1910 .... 1550.00
Rack, Baker's, Open Dowel Rod Shelves, English, Hardwood, 44 In. 175.00
Rack, Book, Limbert, No.369, 3 Open Shelves, 1910, 28 In. 715.00
Rack, Coat, 3 Scrolling Arms, Fluted Finial, Bronze & Steel, 1930 .... 7865.00
Rack, Coat, Victorian, Spool Turned, Oval Mirror Top 350.00
Rack, Drying, 3 Sections, Poplar, 60 X 24 In. 200.00
Rack, Drying, Mortised & Pinned Bars, Pine, 53 1/2 In. .... 150.00 To 175.00
Rack, Magazine, Black Wood, Hanging, Cottage, Duck Scene Front 38.00
Rack, Magazine, Eastlake, Walnut, Pierced Sides, 26 In. 130.00
Rack, Plate, Charles Rohlfs, 4 Shelves, Oak, 1901, 54 X 30 In. 3140.00
Rack, Quilt, Primitive, Shoe Type Feet, 2 Rails, Nailed, 25 X 38 In. 135.00
Rack, Quilt, Scroll Shoe Feet, Walnut, C.1820, 34 1/2 X 33 1/4 In. 225.00
Rack, Spoon, Dark Finish, Hardwood, 26 1/2 X 9 1/2 In. 130.00
Rack, Towel, Bird Head Brackets, 20th Century, 15 In. 50.00
Rack, Towel, Folding, Poplar, Dark Finish, Shoe Feet, 32 In. 400.00
Rack, Towel, Oval Mirror, Carved Frame, Walnut, C.1860, 20 1/2 In. 195.00
Rack, Towel, Pierced & Carved Pediment, Mirror, C.1865, 25 1/2 In. 175.00
Rack, Utensil, Scalloped Top, Carved Stars, Iron Knobs, 65 In. 350.00
Rocker, Arrow–Back, Sheraton, Rush Seat 75.00
Rocker, Balloon Back, Brown Paint, Striping, Gilt Design, Arms 375.00
Rocker, Bentwood, Caned Seat, Elongated S–Form Arms 2200.00
Rocker, Bentwood, New England, Arms, Cane Seat, 1825 .... 3500.00
Rocker, Cane Back & Seat, Arms 195.00
Rocker, Child's, 4 Spindle, Plank Bottom, Scrolled Arms, Brown 300.00
Rocker, Child's, Bamboo Turnings, Cutout Seat, W. Miller 75.00
Rocker, Child's, Bent Twig 65.00
Rocker, Child's, Bentwood Arms 75.00
Rocker, Child's, Captain's 125.00
Rocker, Child's, Gustav Stickley, Oak, 3 Back Slats, Decal, C.1905 .... 3385.00
Rocker, Child's, Ladder Back, Traces of Old Red, Splint Seat 150.00
Rocker, Child's, Oak Craft, Ramsey Alton, Portland, Michgan 150.00
Rocker, Child's, Original Stained Finish, Cane Seat 165.00
Rocker, Child's, Pressed Back, Oak, 30 In. 145.00
Rocker, Child's, Pressed Back, Victorian 145.00
Rocker, Child's, Red Paint, Yellow Striping, 17 3/4 In. 45.00
Rocker, Child's, Shaker, Arms 225.00
Rocker, Child's, Shaker, No.1, Mt. Lebanon 2900.00
Rocker, Child's, Shaker, No.1, Tape Seat 1800.00
Rocker, Child's, Wicker 125.00
Rocker, Child's, Wooden, Turned Rungs 120.00
Rocker, Country, Wing Back, Upholstered, Linsey–Woolsey Quilt 1350.00
Rocker, Curved Arms, Mahogany, American, C.1885, 35 In. 450.00
Rocker, Dewey's Fleet On Crest Rail, Spindle, Oak, 19th Century 82.50
Rocker, G. Stickley, 9 Spindle Sides, 11 Spindle Back, Oak, 1907 .... 5810.00
Rocker, Grained & Hand Painted Design, Pennsylvania 150.00
Rocker, Gustav Stickley, 3 Back Slats, Slip Rush Seat, Oak, C.1907 .... 1200.00

Rocker, Gustav Stickley, No.317 .... 2475.00
Rocker, Gustav Stickley, Square Nail Trim, Paper Label, Oak 1800.00
Rocker, Gustav Stickley, V Back, Oak, Leather Seat, C.1909, 34 In. 900.00
Rocker, L. & J.G. Stickley, 4 Slats Fitting Into 2 Lower Slats 470.00
Rocker, L. & J.G. Stickley, Crest, 6 Vertical Back Slats, 1912 .... 1100.00
Rocker, L. & J.G. Stickley, Morris, Slat Sided 2310.00
Rocker, Ladder Back, 4 Slats, Turned Arms, Rabbit Ear Posts 225.00
Rocker, Ladder Back, Maple, Hickory Seat 300.00
Rocker, Ladder Back, Shaped Arms, 4 Arched Slats, Tape Seat 200.00
Rocker, Ladder Back, Shaped Arms, 5 Arched Slats, Maple 275.00
Rocker, Mission Style, Oak, 5 Slat Back 400.00
Rocker, Platform, Casters, Walnut, American, C.1875, 29 In. 325.00
Rocker, Platform, Eastlake Style, Burl Walnut, Needlepoint 550.00
Rocker, Platform, Victorian, Walnut, Burl Trim 275.00
Rocker, Platform, Wicker, Scrolled Interwoven Back, 46 1/2 In. 145.00
Rocker, Polychrome Stenciled Designs, Figural Splat 125.00
Rocker, Red Flame Graining, Black & Gold Striping 400.00
Rocker, Sewing, Gustav Stickley, No.337, 3 Slat Back, Decal 265.00
Rocker, Shaker Style, Black 198.00
Rocker, Shaker, Ladder Back, Shawl Bar, Mt. Lebanon, Refinished 375.00
Rocker, Shaker, No.3, Tape Seat & Back, Acorn Finials 310.00
Rocker, Shaker, No.7 .... 1600.00
Rocker, Shaker, Woven Splint Seat 1000.00
Rocker, Sloping Arms, 7 Spindles, Saddle Seat, Painted, C.1820 .... 335.00
Rocker, Stickley, Oak, Square Slat Back & Arms 275.00
Rocker, Thonet, Bentwood, Cane Seat, 1880 .... 275.00
Rocker, Wicker, Painted, American, 1900 .... 88.00
Rocker, Wicker, Pyramid–Shaped Back, Tight Woven Seat, Open Skirt 65.00
Rocker, Windsor, 9 Spindles, Hoop Back 85.00
Rocker, Windsor, Bamboo Turning, Oval Seat, Arms, Natural Finish 400.00
Rocker, Windsor, Brown Paint, Yellow Striping, Floral Design 1500.00
Rocker, Windsor, Comb Back, Continuous Arm 825.00
Rocker, Wingback, Linsey–Woolsey Quilt Upholstered 1350.00
Rocker, Wrought Iron & Brass, Scrolled Stiles, Leather Cushion 4675.00
Rocker, Youth's, Lincoln, Cane Seat & Back 150.00
Schrank, Pennsylvania, 2 Large Doors 4100.00
Screen, 3–Panel, Folding, Brass, Oak, American, C.1890, 68 In. 625.00
Screen, 3–Panel, Landscape Reserve, 46 X 51 In. 225.00
Screen, 3–Panel, Portrait Bust, Floral, 17th Century, 69 X 63 In. 950.00
Screen, 3–Panel, Relief Carvings, Upholstered Top Panels, 66 In. 315.00
Screen, 3–Panel, Technology, Skyscraper, Carved Wood, 48 X 30 In. 1295.00
Screen, 4–Panel, Coromandel, Birds, Trees, Chinese, 72 X 16 In. 550.00
Screen, 4–Panel, Coromandel, Incised Design, Gold Ground, Chinese 525.00
Screen, 4–Panel, Coromandel, Woman In Palace Garden, 72 X 64 In. 165.00
Screen, 4–Panel, Embroidered Black Silk, Landscape Reverse 412.00
Screen, 4–Panel, English Gothic, Ebonized Castles, T.H. Gibbs 9500.00
Screen, 4–Panel, Oriental Female Figures, Rosewood, 74 In. 2100.00
Screen, 4–Panel, Painted Birds, Flowering Trees, Mahogany, 6 Ft. 650.00
Screen, 4–Panel, Semiprecious Stones, Lacquer, Chinese, 69 In. 3100.00
Screen, 4–Panel, Village & Landscape, Canvas, 62 1/2 In. 5000.00
Screen, 6–Panel, Cobalt Paint On Siver Mica, Japanese, 1700s 3750.00
Screen, 6–Panel, Gold Landscape, Reddish Ground, 72 X 108 In. 225.00
Screen, 6–Panel, Palace & Street Scenes, Lacquer Frame, 68 In. 3100.00
Screen, 8–Panel, Coromandel, Battle Scenes, Trees Reverse 2090.00
Screen, 8–Panel, Coromandel, Black, 7 Ft. 2400.00
Screen, 12–Panel, Coromandel, 8 Ft. 4750.00
Screen, Chinese, Rosewood, Ivory, Emperor, 32 X 30 In. 725.00
Screen, Ivory Inlays of Birds, Flowers, Japanese, 60 X 72 In. 775.00
Screen, Pole, Crewel Embroidery, Mahogany Frame, 56 In. 240.00
Screen, Pole, Hepplewhite, Mahogany 1250.00
Secretary Bookcase, Butler's, William IV, Mahogany 3800.00
Secretary Bookcase, Cylinder, Spoon Carving, 1 Door, 7 Ft.10 In. 2995.00
Secretary Bookcase, Drop Front, Cherry, 72 X 40 In. 1500.00
Secretary Bookcase, Fitted Interior, Slant Front, Oak, 85 In. 2860.00

Secretary Bookcase, Lattice Glazed Doors, Mahogany, 82 In. 550.00
Secretary Bookcase, Mission–Style, Glass Door, Drop Front, Oak 250.00
Secretary Bureau, 2 Glass Doors Over Drop–Front Desk, Walnut 1000.00
Secretary Desk, Chinoiserie Design, 18th Century 4500.00
Secretary Desk, Fold–Down, Fitted Interior, Walnut, 84 In. 3750.00
Secretary, Butler's, American Hepplewhite, Cherry & Mahogany 4500.00
Secretary, Child's, Compartmented Drawer, Maple, 1910 .... 975.00
Secretary, Chinese Chippendale, Chinoiserie, 82 X 34 X 17 In. 350.00
Secretary, Cylinder Top, Hidden Drawers, Cherry, C.1850 .... 3650.00
Secretary, Drop Front, Rosewood, 2 Door, Strauss 2400.00
Secretary, Drop Front, Sheraton, Mahogany, Poplar, 19th Century 2500.00
Secretary, Glazed Doors, Small Drawers, Mahogany, 78 In. 1875.00
Secretary, Hepplewhite, Paneled Doors, Flame Veneer, Cherry, 49 In 375.00
Secretary, Inlaid, Biggs, Va., 80 In. 725.00
Secretary, Stepped Base, Drop Front, 3 Drawers, Mahogany, 64 In. 5900.00
Secretary, Victorian, Liberty Head, Walnut 5000.00
Secretary, Woman's, Thomas Brooks, Cylinder, Rosewood 7700.00
Server, 3 Short Drawers, 1 Long Drawer, Mahogany, 1810, 34 3/4 In. 4400.00
Server, 3 Tiers, English, Mahogany, 40 1/2 X 29 3/4 In. 300.00
Server, Curly Maple, New York, C.1835 .... 2300.00
Server, G. Stickley, 3 Drawers, Splashboard, No.818, C.1907, 39 In. 2750.00
Server, G. Stickley, Medial Shelf, 4 Drawers, Oak, C.1910, 39 In. 3600.00
Server, Limbert Co., Drawers, Gallery Top, Oak, 47 X 44 In. 605.00
Server, Mahogany, English Style, Early 20th Century, 38 X 31 In. 250.00
Server, Sheraton, Cherry, Bird's–Eye Veneer Drawers, 35 In. 1600.00
Server, Sheraton, New York Label, 3 Short & 1 Long Drawers, Shelf 6000.00
Settee, Arrow–Back, C.1830 .... 1500.00
Settee, Camelback, Scrolled Knuckle, Upholstered Seat, 55 In. 1545.00
Settee, Dutch Rococo, Floral Marquetry, Triple Chair, Mahogany 2200.00
Settee, Dutch, Double Chair Back, Mahogany, Marquetry ....*Illus* 1900.00
Settee, Eastlake, Ebonized & Gilt, C.1875, 33 In. 1100.00
Settee, G.Walton, Wedge–Shaped Back, D–Shaped Seats, Ash, C.1890 .... 1540.00
Settee, George III, Tapered Reeded Legs, Upholstered, 68 In. 935.00
Settee, J. Hoffmann, Curved Upholstered Backrest, Beach, C.1905 .... 4675.00
Settee, Jacobean, Carved, Lions, Dogs & Monkeys, 70 In. ....*Illus* 1500.00
Settee, Leaf Tip Carved Ribbon Frame, Painted, 4 Ft. 10 In. 2750.00
Settee, Lobed Crest, Bay State Chair Co., C.1900, 41 In. 715.00
Settee, Louis XVI, Fluted Legs, Gilt Wood, 50 In. ....*Illus* 425.00
Settee, Neoclassical Style, Gilded Rope Turned Tufted Back 5000.00
Settee, Oak, Cherubs, Acanthus, 68 In. ....*Illus* 700.00
Settee, Queen Anne, Canted Corners, Walnut, C.1770 .... 7200.00
Settee, Queen Anne, Foliate Painted Design, 6 Ft.4 In. 2500.00
Settee, Queen Anne, Walnut, Needlepoint, Cabriole Legs, 47 In. 8000.00
Settee, Reanaissance, Paneled Back, Carved Oak, 67 In. 1000.00
Settee, Renaissance, Paneled Back, Carved Oak, 67 In. 1000.00
Settee, Rococo, Serpentine Rail, Padded Back & Seat, Walnut 2300.00
Settee, Satinwood Inlay On Crest, Arms, Upholstered, Mahogany 1375.00
Settee, Scrolled Arms, Acanthus Supports, C.1900, 82 In. 715.00
Settee, Triple Back, Mother–of–Pearl Inlay, China, C.1900, 73 In. 550.00
Settee, Windsor, Arrow–Back Spindles, Painted, C.1840, 74 In. 665.00
Settee, Windsor, Rod Back, Mustard Yellow Paint, Stencil Design 1300.00
Settle, 14 Vertical Slats, 4 Slats At Sides, Oak, C.1910, 78 In. 1045.00
Settle, Arrow–Back, 78 In. 65.00
Settle, Arrow–Back, Black, Gold Striping, 72 In. 400.00
Settle, Arrow–Back, Plank Seat, Curved Arms, Brown, 90 In. 600.00
Settle, Bamboo Turned Legs, Plank Seat, Black Paint, 156 In. 225.00
Settle, Black, Wood Pegged, Hand Painted Design, 19th Century 700.00
Settle, Gustav Stickley, New Leather Upholstery, 1910 .... 9900.00
Settle, Gustav Stickley, No.205, Original Black Finish 5500.00
Settle, Hinged Seat, Fruit & Leaf Design, Pine, 55 X 47 In. 3300.00
Settle, L. & J.G. Stickley, 5 Wide Side Slats, Even Arms, C.1912 .... 2530.00
Settle, Maple, Poplar, Refinished, Turned Legs, Plank Seat, 77 In. 55.00
Settle, Plail Bros., Upholstered Seat 4000.00
Settle, Straight Crest Rail Over Vertical Slats, 32 In. 775.00

Furniture, Table, Sewing, Roycroft,
C.1910, 29 X 30 X 16 1/2 In.

Furniture, Sideboard, Scandinavian,
Carved, Inlaid, C.1925

Shelf, Book, Mission Style, Oak, Slat Sides & Back 125.00
Shelf, Corner, Eastlake, Facet–Cut Shelf, C.1875, 17 1/2 X 12 In. 85.00
Shelf, Corner, Walnut, Tan Paint, Floral Cutouts, 18 3/4 In. 200.00
Shelf, Crock, 4 Tiers, Semicircular, Gray Paint, 42 X 47 1/2 In. 75.00
Shelf, Crock, Grain Painted, 18 X 12 In. 92.50
Shelf, Cutout Brackets, Pine, 14 X 10 X 33 In. 160.00
Shelf, Hanging, 3 Shelves, Pine, Brown, Scrolled Sides, 25 In. 800.00
Shelf, Hanging, Carved Rayed Back, Pine, Brown Finish, 12 1/2 In. 425.00
Shelf, Hanging, Corner, Grayish Finish, Dovetailed Corner, 9 In. 350.00
Shelf, Hanging, Oval Carved Indian Head, Oak, 18 X 18 In. 85.00

Furniture, Settee, Jacobean, Carved, Lions,
Dogs & Monkeys, 70 In.

Furniture, Settee, Louis XVI,
Fluted Legs, Gilt Wood, 50 In.

Furniture, Settee, Dutch, Double Chair Back,
Mahogany, Marquetry

Furniture, Settee, Oak, Cherubs,
Acanthus, 68 In.

Shelf, Hanging, Scalloped Ends, Green Paint On White, 20 1/2 In. 135.00
Shelf, Knickknack, Cutout Sides, Deer Antlers 55.00
Shelf, Pine, 3 Shelves, Canted, Tapered Ends, Cutout Feet, 46 In. 800.00
Shelf, Poplar, Dark Finish, Open, 4 Shelves, Bootjack Feet, 72 In. 900.00
Shelf, Wall Bracket, Low Gallery, Poplar, Brown Graining, 7 In. 95.00
Shelf, Wall, 3 Half-Round Shelves, Fretwork, C.1860, 22 X 14 In. 95.00
Shelf, Wall, Eastlake, Ebonized, Scalloped Valance, C.1875, 9 In. 75.00
Shelf, Wall, Ebonized, Walnut, C.1875, 24 X 12 1/2 In. 175.00
Sideboard, 2 Doors, 5 Drawers, Mahogany, 41 X 58 In. 2100.00
Sideboard, 2 Glazed Doors, Drawers, Marble Top, Walnut, 81 1/2 In. 550.00
Sideboard, 3 Drawers, Black Lacquer & Chrome, C.1975, 72 In. 110.00
Sideboard, 4 Drawers, Mask Head Lion Pulls, Mahogany, C.1810 .... 8000.00
Sideboard, Bowfront, Cabinet At Sides, Drawer, Mahogany, 69 In. 5500.00
Sideboard, Breakfront Top, Beveled Glass Doors, Oak, 75 In. 1350.00
Sideboard, Carved Backboard, Mahogany, English, 1850s 950.00
Sideboard, Cincinnati Crafters, 4 Drawers, Inlay Design, 57 In. 5440.00
Sideboard, Demilune, False Tambour, Mahogany, 5 Ft.6 In. 5400.00
Sideboard, Dovetailed Gallery, Linen & Bottle Drawer, Mahogany 5500.00
Sideboard, Empire, 3 Drawers, Chimney Splash, Claw Feet, 66 In. 725.00
Sideboard, English Tudor, Oak, Carved, Iron Hardware, 83 X 41 In. 250.00
Sideboard, G. Stickley, Plate Rail, 2 Doors, 3 Drawers, C.1905 .... 4000.00
Sideboard, G. Stickley, Plate Rail, 2 Doors, Drawers, 1907, 48 In. 1200.00
Sideboard, Gargoyle Heads, Lion Feet, 1850s, 78 X 26 X 38 In. 2500.00
Sideboard, George III, Mahogany, 44 X 87 In. 5000.00
Sideboard, Gustav Stickley, 3 Drawers, 2 Doors, Oak, C.1912, 56 In. 2665.00
Sideboard, Gustav Stickley, Oak, No.814 .... 2800.00
Sideboard, Hepplewhite, Compartmented Drawer, Milk Glass Knobs 625.00
Sideboard, Lion Masks On Doors, 3 Figural Columns, Oak, 72 In. 2425.00
Sideboard, Louis Marjorelle 2000.00
Sideboard, Marble Top, Carved Mahogany, C.1830 .... 2310.00
Sideboard, Scandinavian, Carved, Inlaid, C.1925 ....*Illus* 1210.00
Sideboard, Serpentine Top, Satinwood Inlay, Mahogany, 67 In. 4620.00
Sofa & Rocker Set, Stickley-Fayetteville, Cherry, 1930s, 2 Piece 2500.00
Sofa, 3-Section Back, Inlaid Medallions, Stylized Hoofed Feet 2400.00
Sofa, Bow Back, Wicker, Painted White 770.00
Sofa, Country Empire, Cherry Frame, Scrolled Arms, 89 In. 2100.00
Sofa, Empire, Carved, Mahogany, 19th Century, 90 In. 2450.00
Sofa, Empire, Mahogany Frame, Carved Cornucopias, Brocade, 83 In. 1500.00
Sofa, English Chipppendale, Camelback 8100.00
Sofa, Fainting, Arched Rail, Velvet Cover, Walnut, C.1875, 73 In. 850.00
Sofa, Federal, Mahogany, Satinwood Inlay 900.00
Sofa, French Empire, Swan Arms, Velvet Covered, Mahogany, 1830 .... 9000.00
Sofa, George III, Gilt Wood, Needlepoint Tableau Cover 2450.00
Sofa, Henredon, Linen Duck Upholstered, Skirted, 88 In., Pair 3410.00
Sofa, Marquetry Inlaid Frame, Floral Alternating With Birds 3500.00
Sofa, Pine, Spool Arms & Back, Upholstered Seat, Mid-1800s 1500.00
Sofa, Red Paint, Blue Upholstered Frame, Maple, C.1840, 75 In. 1320.00
Sofa, Regency Style, Scrolled Arms, Rosewood, 74 In. 715.00
Sofa, Rosalie, John Belter, 3-Backed 6325.00
Sofa, Sheraton, Mahogany, Slip Seat, Removable Back, 66 In. 1450.00
Sofa, Victorian, Carved, Striped Upholstered, 3 Rounded Back 1100.00
Sofa-Daybed, Tubular Chromed Steel & Leather, C.1935, 6 Ft.7 In. 1750.00
Stand, 1 Drawer, 1 Board Top, Breadboard Ends, Oak, 28 1/4 In. 250.00
Stand, 1 Drawer, New England, Cherry, Tapered Legs, 1815 .... 825.00
Stand, 1 Drawer, Snake Feet, Ring Turned Corners, Maple, 26 In. 325.00
Stand, 1 Drawer, Splay Legged, Tiger Maple Top 350.00
Stand, 1 Drawer, Tiger Maple, Turned & Reeded Legs, 19th Century 550.00
Stand, 1 Drawer, Yellow & Brown Feather Painted 3200.00
Stand, 2 Drawers, Bird's-Eye Maple, Cherry, 20 In. Top 600.00
Stand, 2 Drawers, Edge Beading, Cherry, 29 X 18 X 18 1/2 In. 350.00
Stand, 2-Tier, Burmese, Carved Hardwood, 19th Century 330.00
Stand, 3-Tier, 2 Drawers At Base, Mahogany, 52 In. 1045.00
Stand, Adam Style, Painted Design, 32 1/2 In. 145.00

Stand, Adirondack, Black Paint, Silver Daubs, 29 In. 45.00
Stand, Ashtray, Bronze, Dished, Reticulated Column, Chinese, 19 In. 247.00
Stand, Bible, Black Walnut 55.00
Stand, Book, L. & J.G. Stickley, No.46 .... 2475.00
Stand, Bowed Drawer Front, 1–Board Top, Walnut 250.00
Stand, Cherry, 1 Dovetailed Drawer, 29 In. 350.00
Stand, Cherry, Curly Maple, Dovetailed Drawer, 29 In. 1950.00
Stand, Cherry, Dovetailed Drawer, 1 Board Top, 28 1/4 In. 800.00
Stand, Cherry, Varnish Finish, Dovetailed Drawer, 28 3/4 In. 400.00
Stand, Cherry, Walnut, 3 Drawers, Ohio, 1874, 19 X 21 X 29 In. 1600.00
Stand, Chippendale, Arched Cabriole Legs, Mahogany, 1760, 27 In. 3300.00
Stand, Desk, Sheraton, Mahogany, 2 Drawers 1980.00
Stand, Dovetailed Drawer, 1 Board Top, Cherry, 30 X 19 X 17 In. 375.00
Stand, Drawer, New England, Tiger Maple & Pine, 1820, 28 In. 825.00
Stand, Eastlake, Aesthetic Movement, Ebonized, Gilt, C.1875, 35 In. 650.00
Stand, Ebonized, C.1895 .... 825.00
Stand, Empire, Drawer, Rounded Front, Cherry, 28 7/8 In. 200.00
Stand, Fabric Covered Top, Cherry, American, C.1885, 31 In. 250.00
Stand, Federal, 1 Drawer, Mahogany, 1790–1810, 28 1/4 In. 3550.00
Stand, Federal, Scrolled Legs, Drawer, Line Inlay, 29 3/8 In. 200.00
Stand, Fern, Chinese, Carved Hardwood, Marble Top 330.00
Stand, Foliage, Soapstone Insert In Top, Chinese, Teak, 35 1/2 In. 350.00
Stand, Folk Art, Walnut, Round 2 Board Top, 20 3/4 X 28 3 /4 In. 250.00
Stand, Henry A. Fairchild, Maple, 1 Drawer, New York, 1842 .... 700.00
Stand, Hepplewhite, 1 Board Top, Cherry, 28 3/4 In. 175.00
Stand, Hepplewhite, 1 Board Top, Drawer, Mahogany, 28 1/4 In. 450.00
Stand, Hepplewhite, 1 Board Top, Molded Edge, Birch, 26 3/4 In. 525.00
Stand, Hepplewhite, 1 Dovetailed Overlapping Drawer, 25 3/4 In. 550.00
Stand, Hepplewhite, 1 Drawer, 1 Board Top, Curly Maple, 28 1/2 In. 2700.00
Stand, Hepplewhite, 1 Drawer, Cherry, Square Legs, 30 1/4 In. 400.00
Stand, Hepplewhite, 1 Drawer, Glass Pulls, Hardwood, 27 1/2 In. 395.00
Stand, Hepplewhite, Cherry, Refinished, Splayed Legs, 29 In. 250.00
Stand, Hepplewhite, Stenciled Tulip & Hearts, Chip Carved 425.00
Stand, Hepplewhite, Walnut Top, Various Hardwoods, 30 In. 150.00
Stand, Legs Joined To Lower Shelves, Ebonized, C.1880, 32 In. 195.00
Stand, Magazine, 5 Graduated Shelves, Stickley Bros., C.1910 .... 935.00
Stand, Magazine, G. Stickley, Leather & Tack Edges, 44 1/4 In. 3380.00
Stand, Magazine, G. Stickley, No.79, Cutout Sides, 1912, 39 1/2 In. 2910.00
Stand, Magazine, Gustav Stickley, Oak, 4 Shelves, Handles, 39 In. 2200.00
Stand, Magazine, Gustav Stickley, Toby, 4 Open Shelves, C.1904 .... 660.00
Stand, Magazine, Roycroft, 3 Shelves, Marked, 37 In. 2800.00
Stand, Mahogany Veneered Drawer & Apron, Cherry, 28 3/4 In. 200.00
Stand, Mahogany, Inlaid, Pierced Handholds, 32 X 14 In. 750.00
Stand, Marble Top, Lozenge Shaped Top, Chinese, Rosewood, 21 In. 445.00
Stand, Mirror Flanked By Knobs, Marble Top, French, C.1930, 6 Ft. 2120.00
Stand, Music, Bentwood Support Arms, Thonet, C.1900, 60 In. 2200.00
Stand, Music, Double Sided, Pierced, Walnut, C.1875, 67 1/2 In. 995.00
Stand, Music, Eastlake, 3 Dividers, 2 Lower Drawers, C.1875, 43 In. 525.00
Stand, Music, Regency, Rosewood, Adjustable, Candle Arms, 50 In. 2530.00
Stand, Painted Compass Star Center Top, Walnut, 30 1/2 In. 350.00
Stand, Plant, 12 Saucers For Pots, Cast Iron, 42 1/4 In. 250.00
Stand, Plant, Adirondack, Red Paint, 33 In. 55.00
Stand, Plant, Cast Iron, 3–Footed, White 950.00
Stand, Plant, Cast Iron, Copper Pan Inserts 2000.00
Stand, Plant, Dark Pine, 2 Scalloped Front Tiers, Bootjack Ends 325.00
Stand, Plant, Hammered Copper, Joseph Maria Olbrich, 1880s, 29 In. 1750.00
Stand, Plant, White Paint, Folds Flat, Wire, 37 X 31 In. 85.00
Stand, Plant, Wrought Iron, Ring Handles, Copper Planter, 38 In. 66.00
Stand, Renaissance Revival, Carved, Gilded, Metal Cherub 2450.00
Stand, Rope Carved Legs, 2 Drawers, Cherry, Curly Maple Veneer 625.00
Stand, Sewing, 2 Drawers, Drop Leaves, Victorian 300.00
Stand, Sewing, 2 Drawers, Square Top, 29 X 17 In. 6600.00
Stand, Sewing, Chinoiserie, Mother-of-Pearl Inlay, 32 X 22 In. 2530.00
Stand, Sewing, Martha Washington Style, Original Finish 75.00

Stand, Sewing, Victorian, Bamboo, Rattan, Hinged, 30 X 15 X 15 In. 143.00
Stand, Sewing, Walnut Veneer, Flip Top 70.00
Stand, Shaving, Eastlake, Walnut, Veneer, 2 Drawers, Marble Top 410.00
Stand, Sheraton, 1 Dovetailed Drawer, Birch, Dark Finish, 28 In. 525.00
Stand, Sheraton, 1 Dovetailed Drawer, Cherry, Maple Legs, 27 In. 550.00
Stand, Sheraton, 1 Dovetailed Drawer, Curly Maple, Splayed, 1840 .... 600.00
Stand, Sheraton, 1 Drawer, Cherry, Dark Finish, 20 X 20 X 28 In. 300.00
Stand, Sheraton, 1 Drawer, Curly & Bird's-Eye Maple, C.1850, 18 In 575.00
Stand, Sheraton, 1 Drawer, Wood Pulls, 24 X 20 X 28 In. 280.00
Stand, Shoeshine, Oak Chairs, 2-Man 650.00
Stand, Smoking, Adirondack, Log Cabin Shape Top Box, 30 1/2 In. 65.00
Stand, Smoking, Art Nouveau, Cast Steel Frame, Copper Insert 35.00
Stand, Soapstone Insert In Top, 5 Legs, Teak, 18 3/4 In. 125.00
Stand, Somerset, 2 Drawers, Gray Paint 3100.00
Stand, Telephone, Gustav Stickley 1600.00
Stand, Tiger Maple, Splayed Legs, Conn., Small 6050.00
Stand, Tilt Top, Lacquered Scene, 3-Footed Pedestal 450.00
Stand, Tubular Skirt, Bamboo, Early 20th Century, 30 1/2 In. 250.00
Stand, Umbrella, Bear, Carved Walnut, Germany 3200.00
Stand, Umbrella, Bear, Victorian 2000.00
Stand, Umbrella, Enameled, Floral & Birds, Chinese, 26 1/2 In. 505.00
Stand, Umbrella, G. Stickley, Copper Drip Pan, Label, 1910, 33 In. 1150.00
Stand, Umbrella, Gustav Stickley, 4 Tapering Posts, Oak, C.1907 .... 275.00
Stand, Umbrella, Roycroft, Square Posts, Oak, C.1910 .... 500.00 To 550.00
Stand, Umbrella, Victorian, Carved Bear, C.1860 .... 2200.00
Stand, Walnut, Birch, Cherry, 1 Board Top, Turned Legs, 21 In. 200.00
Stand, Walnut, Delaware Valley, 2 Board Top, 38 3/4 In. 350.00
Stand, Wash, Corner, Drawer, Cutout For Accessories, Cherry 300.00
Stand, Wash, Georgian, Mahogany, Galleried Shelf, 47 X 18 X 18 In. 935.00
Stand, Wig, Turned Legs, Maple, Square Base, 10 3/4 In. 45.00
Stand, Yellow Graining Over Red, Brass Pull, Cherry, 27 1/4 In. 550.00
Stepladder, Folding, S Curve Uprights, All Wooden, 45 In. 55.00
Steps, Bedside, Victorian, 2 Lift Lids, Vase & Ring Feet, 25 In. 1435.00
Stool, Adjustable, Walnut, Needlepoint Cover, American, C.1870 .... 425.00
Stool, Country Windsor, Red Over Black, 29 3/4 In. 175.00
Stool, Ebonized, Cushion Seat, American, C.1860, 15 In. 325.00
Stool, Egyptian Type, High Back, Carved Walnut 1100.00
Stool, Empire Revival, Upholstered Seat, Mahogany, C.1920, 15 In. 225.00
Stool, George I, Carved Legs, Upholstered Seat, Walnut, C.1730 .... 2400.00
Stool, Gout 55.00
Stool, Lift Top, Needlepoint, Walnut, American, C.1865, 18 In. 325.00
Stool, Milking, Burl, 3 Mortised Legs Into Seat, 10 3/4 X 14 In. 400.00
Stool, Mitered Frame, Needlepoint Pad, Tiger Maple, 12 In. 220.00
Stool, Oak, Primitive, Carved Design, 26 1/4 X 19 1/4 In. 450.00
Stool, Oval Top, Hardwood, 21 In. 55.00
Stool, Piano, Adjustable, Walnut & Stained Maple, C.1878, 19 In. 3350.00
Stool, Piano, J.H. Belter, Rosewood, C.1850 .... *Illus* 4675.00
Stool, Prayer, Walnut, Inlaid, 5 Drawers, Spindle Columns, 1800s 2600.00
Stool, Pressed Back, High Back, Brass & Glass Feet 120.00
Stool, Upholstered Seat, Folding Iron Legs, 32 1/2 In. 940.00
Stool, Windsor, Oak, 19 1/2 In. 55.00
Stool, Windsor, Splayed Turned Legs, Hardwood, 16 1/4 In. 150.00
Table Desk, Louis XV, Leather, Tulipwood, Bacchante, 32 X 59 In. 3700.00
Table En Chiffoniere, Louis XV, Gilt Bronze, Parquetry Kingwood 5500.00
Table Set, Card, Child's, Folding, 1950s, 5 Piece 50.00
Table Set, Crossbuck, 2 High Back Benches, White, 72-In. Table 65.00
Table, 2 Hinged Leaves, Mahogany, C.1830, 4 Ft.2 In. 2200.00
Table, 2 Tiers, Galleried Top Set Wtih Gray Marble, 36 In. 335.00
Table, 3 Tiers, George III, Mahogany, 41 X 24 In. .... *Illus* 750.00
Table, 3-Lobed Top, Drawers, Slippered Feet, Mahogany, 24 1/4 In. 155.00
Table, 3-Tier, George III, Mahogany, 41 X 24 In. .... *Illus* 750.00
Table, American Victorian, Mahogany, 28 1/4 X 33 X 17 1/2 .... 1450.00
Table, Banquet, 8 Legs, Pullout Frame, 4 Leaves, Pine, 99 1/2 In. 1550.00
Table, Banquet, Banded & Line Inlay, Walnut, 28 1/2 X 42 In. 350.00

Table, Banquet, Cherry, D Ends, 20–In. Leaves, 21 X 46 1/2 In., Pr. 1250.00
Table, Banquet, Drop Leaf Section, Ebony Inlay, C.1790 .... 5750.00
Table, Banquet, Reeded Legs, Mahogany, Early 19th Century, 2 Part 2450.00
Table, Blackamoor, Polychrome, Italian ....*Illus* 990.00
Table, Book, L. & J.G. Stickley, Slat Sides, C.1912, 29 In. 3300.00
Table, Brass Galleried Marble Top, 2 Drawers, Fruitwood, 28 In. 335.00
Table, Breakfast, Drop Leaf, Claw Foot Pedestal, Mahogany 650.00
Table, Breakfast, Drop Leaf, Rococo, Secret Drawer 475.00
Table, Breakfast, Federal Style, Rectangular, Mahogany 9000.00
Table, Butler's Tray, Circular, Mahogany, 22 3/4 X 35 1/2 In. 775.00
Table, Butler's Tray, Mahogany, Victorian 700.00
Table, Butterfly, Wallace Nutting, No.624, 39 1/2 In. 605.00
Table, Cabriole Legs, Golden Oak, 24 X 24 In. 65.00
Table, Card, American Empire, Animal Legs, Pedestal, Mahogany 1250.00
Table, Card, Chippendale, Hinged Top, Mahogany, 1770–90, 28 In. 1540.00
Table, Card, Demilune, Curly Veneer, Inlaid Fan In Top, 29 3/8 In. 1200.00
Table, Card, Federal, Serpentine Front, Cherry 9500.00
Table, Card, Figured Wood Top, Swing Leg, Walnut & Poplar, 29 In. 2700.00
Table, Card, Floral Marquetry Inlaid, Dutch, D Shape, Rosewood 1900.00
Table, Card, Hepplewhite, Mahogany, Bird's–Eye Maple & Rosewood 6600.00
Table, Card, Rectangular, Water Leaf Pedestal, Mahogany, 1815 .... 3300.00
Table, Card, S. McIntire, Carved Acorns Under Rim 2530.00
Table, Card, Serpentine Hinged Top, Mahogany & Cherry, 1790–1810 .... 4400.00
Table, Card, Sheraton, Serpentine Front, Line Inlay, C.1830, 36 In. 1500.00
Table, Card, Victorian, Rosewood 700.00
Table, Carved Medallions, Square, Oak, 1930s, 30 1/4 In. 715.00
Table, Center, Art Nouveau, Walnut, 4 Women Dancers Base, 30 In. 825.00
Table, Center, Carved Walnut, Marble Top 415.00
Table, Center, G. Stickley, Round Top, Decal, C.1903, 40 In. 5080.00
Table, Center, Mahogany, Winged Griffin Supports 3900.00
Table, Charles X, Mahogany, Marble Top, 29 In. ....*Illus* 8800.00
Table, Cherry, Pine, Dovetailed Drawer, Breadboard Top, 26 1/2 In. 400.00
Table, Child's, Walnut, 1 Dovetailed Drawer, 15 3/4 In. 400.00
Table, Chinese, Rosewood, Dragon Base, 25 X 32 In. 600.00
Table, Chippendale, Child's, Swing Leg, Cherry, Late 1700s 1095.00
Table, Chippendale, Tilt Top, Birdcage, Dish Turned, 34 In.Diam. 900.00
Table, Circular Top, Molded Rim, 3 Legs, French, Rosewood, C.1925 .... 1815.00
Table, Cocktail, Paolozzi & Hartman, Brass, Glass, 1948 .... 2900.00
Table, Coffee, Chinese Chippendale, Mahogany, Fretted Apron, 46 In 275.00
Table, Coffee, Wicker, 1920s, 37 In. 325.00
Table, Console, Demilune, Spanish, Walnut, 2 Triangles, 89 In., Pair 3250.00
Table, Console, Hepplewhite, Mahogany, Inlaid, Demilune, 36 In., Pr. 1650.00
Table, Console, Louis XV, Carved, Painted, Shaped Marble Top, 34 In 385.00
Table, Console, Marquetry, Serpentine Supports, Burled Walnut 665.00
Table, Console, Wrought Iron, Demilune Marble, 32 X 39 X 14 In. 165.00
Table, Continental, Foliate Carved Apron, Walnut, C.1830, 32 In. 610.00
Table, Continental, Porcelain, Roman Emperor, 30 In. 2400.00
Table, Country Chippendale, Pine, Grained, Ocher Paint, Gallery 850.00
Table, Country Hepplewhite, Drop Leaf, Swing Legs, Cherry, 41 In. 275.00
Table, Cricket, Shelf In Base, Drawer In Apron, Pine, 28 3/4 In. 170.00
Table, Cricket, Tripod Base With Shelf, Pine, 24 3/4 X 25 In. 325.00
Table, Cushman Co., Beveled Edge, Square Skirt, C.1915, 30 In. 275.00
Table, Demilune Green Marble Top, Painted Green, 36 X 35 In. 415.00
Table, Dining, 3 Pedestal, Line Inlay, Brass Paw Feet, Mahogany 1000.00
Table, Dining, Adnet & Hermes, Leather & Glass, 84 X 48 1/2 In. 1700.00
Table, Dining, Chippendale, Drop Leaves, Cherry, C.1890, 49 1/2 In. 1000.00
Table, Dining, Duncan Phyfe, Self-Storing Leaf, 40 X 62 In. 225.00
Table, Dining, Frank Lloyd Wright, Round, Oak, C.1955, 54 In. 1000.00
Table, Dining, G. Nakashima, 2 Leaves, Rosewood & Walnut, C.1960 .... 8500.00
Table, Dining, George III, 3 Pedestal, Mahogany, 75 In. 7000.00
Table, Dining, George III, Drop Leaf, Oak, 29 X 89 In. 1200.00
Table, Dining, Gustav Stickley, 5 Legs, No.634, C.1907, 28 1/2 In. 5775.00
Table, Dining, Gustav Stickley, Round Top, 6 Leaves, C.1912, 54 In. 9680.00
Table, Dining, Jacobean, Mahogany, Drop Leaf, 1 Drawer, 36 X 16 In. 525.00

Table, Dining, M. Dufet, Mahogany & Nickeled Bronze, 1931, 72 In. 7250.00
Table, Dining, Matamorphic, Folding Surface, Mahogany, 64 1/2 In. 3200.00
Table, Dining, Oak, Ball & Claw Footed, 1900s 4950.00
Table, Dining, Queen Anne, Cherry, Square Hinged Leaves, 1770 .... 9500.00
Table, Dining, Ram's Heads & Hoof Feet, 5 Leaves, 66 In. 550.00
Table, Dining, Regency, 2 Urn Pedestals, Mahogany, 7 Ft.5 In. 1320.00
Table, Dining, Regency, Drop Leaf, Mahogany 5200.00
Table, Dining, Roycroft, Round, 4 Vertical Posts, C.1910, 48 In. 2300.00
Table, Dining, Shaped Apron, Parquetry, 2 Leaves, Oak, 43 X 65 In. 1545.00
Table, Dining, Sheraton, Drop Leaf, 6 Legs, Cherry, 48 In. 175.00
Table, Dining, Stickley Brothers, Quaint 5500.00
Table, Dining, Victorian, Mahogany, 7 Leaves, Opens To 12 Ft. 2800.00
Table, Draftsman's, Swiveling Drawer Holder, Iron Base 385.00
Table, Dressing, 3 Drawers, Edge Beading, Mahogany, 30 1/4 In. 350.00
Table, Dressing, Adam Style, Satinwood 900.00
Table, Dressing, Georgian Revival, Mahogany, C.1880, 27 3/4 In. 610.00
Table, Dressing, Inner Mirror, Marble Top, Drawer, Mahogany, C.1900 .... 1000.00
Table, Dressing, Ivory Floral & Geometric Design, Persian Monks 8500.00
Table, Dressing, L. Majorelle, Bronze Mounted, Mahogany, C.1900 .... 9350.00
Table, Dressing, Lift Lid, Mirror, Jewelry Tray, Mahogany, 1850s 1325.00
Table, Dressing, Lift Top, Interior Mirror, Walnut, C.1860, 24 In. 250.00
Table, Dressing, Louis XV, Mahogany, Dore Mount, 3 Drawers, 51 In. 8500.00
Table, Dressing, Sheraton, Shield Inlaid 3000.00
Table, Drop Leaf, 1 Drawer, Walnut, 28 X 42 In. 155.00
Table, Drop Leaf, 2 Board Top, Castors, Maple, 28 X 47 1/4 In. 500.00
Table, Drop Leaf, Applied Skirt Cutout Ends, Pine, 26 X 36 In. 200.00
Table, Drop Leaf, Birch Base, Curly Maple Top, Turned Legs, 27 In. 750.00
Table, Drop Leaf, Brass Capped Casters, Mahogany, 30 X 33 In. 775.00
Table, Drop Leaf, Butterfly Supports, Pine, C.1820, 26 1/2 In. 1650.00
Table, Drop Leaf, Country, Hepplewhite, Pine Top, 19 X 36 In. 1500.00
Table, Drop Leaf, Federal, Curly Maple, C.1810, 53 In. 1760.00
Table, Drop Leaf, George III, Mahogany, End Drawer, X Stretcher 412.00
Table, Drop Leaf, George III, Mahogany, Square Legs, 43 X 19 In. 1210.00
Table, Drop Leaf, Gustav Stickley, Oak, Label, C.1912, 28 In. 1935.00
Table, Drop Leaf, Hepplewhite, Banded Inlay, Walnut, 45 3/4 In. 250.00
Table, Drop Leaf, Mahogany, 1 Dovetailed Drawer, 28 In. 350.00
Table, Drop Leaf, Mahogany, 1 Frieze Drawer, Turned Legs, 38 In. 665.00
Table, Drop Leaf, Mahogany, American, Victorian ....*Illus* 715.00
Table, Drop Leaf, New England, Tiger Maple, 1830 .... 3500.00
Table, Drop Leaf, Queen Anne, Mahogany, Pad Feet, 18th Century 885.00
Table, Drop Leaf, Queen Anne, Maple, Oval Top, C.1760, 27 X 48 In. 7265.00
Table, Drop Leaf, Queen Anne, Santo Domingo Mahogany 8500.00
Table, Drop Leaf, Queen Anne, Swing Leg, Mahogany, 44 1/2 In. 1650.00
Table, Drop Leaf, Queen Anne, Tiger Maple, 1760 .... 6600.00
Table, Drop Leaf, Queen Anne, Walnut, Cabriole Legs, 11 X 38 In. 1800.00
Table, Drop Leaf, Red Flame Graining, Pine, 29 3/4 X 42 In. 475.00
Table, Drop Leaf, Regency Style, Rosewood, 2 Drawers, 36 In. 1320.00
Table, Drop Leaf, Rounded Leaves, Brass Casters, Mahogany, 39 In. 75.00
Table, Drop Leaf, Shaker, Red Wash, Enfield, Conn. 1200.00
Table, Drop Leaf, Sheraton, 2 D Form, Bird's-Eye Maple, 29 In. 165.00
Table, Drop Leaf, Sheraton, Cherry, C.1815, 48 X 64 In. 985.00
Table, Drop Leaf, Sheraton, Walnut, 42 X 39 In. 325.00
Table, Drop Leaf, Sheraton, Walnut, Turned Legs, 40 X 49 In. 225.00
Table, Drop Leaf, Swing Leg, Cherry, 29 1/2 In. 325.00
Table, Drop Leaf, Swing Leg, Trifid Feet, Walnut, 28 1/4 In. 1400.00
Table, Drop Leaf, Swing Legs, Maple, 28 1/4 X 48 In. 350.00
Table, Drop Leaf, Trifid Feet, Walnut, 18th Century 9075.00
Table, Drum, Mahogany, Baltimore, 1820, Small 3300.00
Table, Eagle Attacking Serpent, 4 Lion Feet, Indian ....*Illus* 700.00
Table, Eastlake, 1 Wide Drawer, Lower Shelf, Cherry, C.1880, 30 In. 425.00
Table, Eastlake, Ebonized Finish, American, 1875-90, 27 1/2 In. 425.00
Table, Eastlake, Marble Top, Walnut & Walnut Burl, C.1875, 30 In. 625.00
Table, Eastlake, Walnut & Maple Marquetry Inlay, C.1875, 29 In. 625.00
Table, Empire, Leaf Carved Feet, Mahogany ....*Illus* 935.00

Table, Empire, Ormolu Mounted, Gilt Paw Feet, Mahogany, 29 1/2 In. 775.00
Table, Farm, Cherry, Pegged, 1830, 11 Ft. 3300.00
Table, Farm, Drawers, White Paint Over Red, Softwood, 29 X 48 In. 1800.00
Table, Federal, Cherry, Frieze Drawer, Square Legs, 27 X 19 In. 385.00
Table, Federal, Maple, 2 Drawers, 19th Century, 20 X 17 X 28 In. 525.00
Table, Galle, Commemorative, 2 Tiers, Inlaid Mahogany, 30 In. 2800.00
Table, Galle, Signed In Marquetry 1550.00
Table, Game, & Reading Stand, Adjustable, Rosewood, 28 1/4 In. 8800.00
Table, Game, Baker Furniture, 1 Drawer, Oak, 30 X 34 In. 615.00
Table, Game, Desk Top, Leather Insert Over Backgammon Board 2640.00
Table, Game, George III, Baize Lined Top, Mahogany, 28 1/2 In. 1980.00
Table, Gateleg, 1 Drawer, Pine, English, 29 1/2 X 39 3/4 In. 950.00
Table, Gateleg, 1 Frieze Drawer, Walnut, C.1870, 28 1/2 In. 305.00
Table, Gateleg, 2 Drawers, Oval Top, English, Oak, 28 1/2 In. 650.00
Table, Gateleg, Drop Leaf, Drawer, Oak, Leaves, 28 3/4 In. 300.00
Table, Gateleg, Jacobean, Demilune Drop Leaf, Oval, Oak, 89 1/2 In. 1800.00
Table, Gateleg, Oval Drop Leaf, Oak, 27 X 24 In. 330.00
Table, Gateleg, Painted Black Base, Spanish Feet, Maple, 28 In. 2900.00
Table, Gateleg, Painted Black, Walnut & Maple, 27 1/2 X 40 In. 1350.00
Table, Gateleg, Spanish Feet, Walnut & Mahogany, 28 1/2 In. 6875.00
Table, Gateleg, William & Mary, Drop Leaves, Oak, 28 In. ....*Illus* 3800.00
Table, Gateleg, William & Mary, Pierced Apron, Oak, 64 1/4 In. 495.00
Table, George I, Gilt Gesso, Marble Top, 18th Century 2900.00
Table, George III, 1 Drawer, Mahogany, Gallery, Bamboo Legs, 20 In. 198.00
Table, George III, Tripod, Hinged, Pedestal, 3 Arched Legs, 29 In. 990.00
Table, Glass Top, 4 Supports, Nickeled Bronze, 1935, 49 3/8 In. 8350.00
Table, Glass Top, Baluster Form Steel Legs, 17 14 X 50 1/4 In. 475.00
Table, Glass Top, Eastlake, Ebonized, Medial Shelf, C.1880, 31 In. 750.00
Table, Glass Top, U–Form Support, Rosewood, C.1925, 34 3/4 In. 5500.00
Table, Gustav Stickley, No.632, 4 Leaves, 48 In.Diam. 5225.00
Table, Gustav Stickley, Round, Cross Stretcher, 1910, 29 X 30 In. 1300.00
Table, Hall, George III, Fruitwood, 2 Drawers, 30 X 42 X 12 In. 605.00
Table, Hall, George III, Mahogany, 2 Drawers, Square Tapered Legs 330.00
Table, Hall, Mahogany, Carved Legs, Ball & Claw Feet 70.00
Table, Harvest, Hardwood Top, 78 In. 6800.00
Table, Harvest, Pegged, H Stretcher, Turned Legs, 64 X 38 X 30 In. 525.00
Table, Hoffmann, Fabric Top, 4 Paired Columnar Legs, 1902, 31 In. 3080.00
Table, Hunt, Georgian, Mahogany, D Drop Leaf, Square Legs, 143 In. 3740.00
Table, Hutch, Hinged Lid Seat, Pine, 30 X 39 1/2 X 52 In. 1450.00
Table, Hutch, Iron Butterfly Hinges, Oak, 31 X 39 1/2 In. 475.00
Table, Hutch, Removable Seat, Pine, 30 1/4 X 43 1/2 In. 650.00
Table, Ice Cream, Swing Out Stools, Display Case Top, Iron 2000.00
Table, Indian Bone Inlay, Stylized Elephant Legs, 23 3/4 In. 1750.00
Table, J. Leleu, Lacquered, Mahogany & Gilt Bronze, C.1925 .... 2325.00
Table, Kitchen, Breadboard Under Ends, Drawers, Flour Drawer 450.00
Table, Lamp, Marble Top, Walnut 275.00
Table, Leather, Kingwood, Walnut, Marquetry, 69 In. 5225.00
Table, Library, Claw Feet, Walnut, Large 2500.00
Table, Library, Federal, 2 Drop Leaves, Mahogany, 1815, 57 3/4 In. 3850.00
Table, Library, G. Stickley, 2 Drawers, Copper Pulls, 1905, 54 In. 4235.00
Table, Library, Gustav Stickley, Leather Top 4675.00
Table, Library, Gustav Stickley, Spindled Sides 7150.00
Table, Library, L. & J.G. Stickley, No.567, 2 Drawers, 1910, 48 In. 1045.00
Table, Library, Limbert, Cutout Sides, Small 5200.00
Table, Library, Louis XV, Carved Walnut, French 1750.00
Table, Library, Regency, 8 Drawers, Mahogany, Leather, 96 In. 4850.00
Table, Library, Trestle Base, Lower Shelf, C.1910, 29 1/2 X 48 In. 335.00
Table, Limbert, Double Oval, No.158, Cutouts, Oval, 1907 .... 4675.00
Table, Lions' Heads & Masks Border, Oak, 27 X 51 In. 825.00
Table, Louis XV, Marquetry, Apricot Marble Top, 26 1/2 In., Pair 1850.00
Table, Louis XV, Rosewood, Portrait Plaques, 24 In. ....*Illus* 300.00
Table, Louis XV, Rosewood, Satinwood, Mahogany, Brass, 1850 .... 2000.00
Table, Marble Top, Carved Grapes & Leaves On Curved Legs 1350.00
Table, Marble Top, Inset Onyx, Gilt Bronze, French, C.1925, 31 In. 6955.00

Furniture, Stool, Piano,
J.H. Belter, Rosewood,
C.1850

Furniture, Table, Blackamoor,
Polychrome, Italian

Furniture, Table, Louis XV,
Rosewood, Portrait Plaques,
24 In.

Table, Marble Top, Scrolled Panels, Iron, 1925, 38 1/2 In.	2725.00
Table, Marble Top, Walnut, Brass Galleried, 2 Drawers, 20 X 30 In.	522.50
Table, Mixing, White Marble Insert, Curly Maple, 27 1/2 In.	1000.00
Table, Napoleon III, Ebonized, Frieze Drawer, C.1870, 28 1/4 In.	175.00
Table, Nesting, Banded Tops, Inlaid, Mahogany, 28 X 29 In., 4 Piece	425.00
Table, Nesting, Chinese Export, Lacquer, 27 X 17 X 10 1/2 In.	825.00
Table, Nesting, Galle, Art Nouveau, Inlaid Marquetry, 4 Piece	7500.00
Table, Nesting, Inlaid Paterae, Mahogany, 30 X 17 1/2 In., 3 Piece	235.00
Table, O. Wytrlik, Pullout Extension Each End, Ash, C.1905	1980.00
Table, Occasional, Rosewood, Hexagonal Crossbanded, 1890, 40 In.	600.00
Table, Painted Classical Portrait, Marble Top, Gilded, 28 In.	850.00
Table, Papier-Mache, Checkerboard Top, English	4510.00
Table, Pembroke, 1 Drawer, 3 Rings Over Reeded Leg, Pennsylvania	1650.00
Table, Pembroke, 1 Drawer, Diamond Shaped Inlays, Mahogany, 28 In.	5500.00
Table, Pembroke, Drop Leaf, 1 Drawer, Cherry, 28 3/4 In.	375.00
Table, Pembroke, Drop Leaf, Cherry, Button Feet, 26 1/2 In.	1500.00
Table, Pembroke, English Mahogany & Satinwood, 1820	2000.00
Table, Pembroke, Federal, Serpentine Leaves, Cherry, C.1800, 28 In.	1200.00
Table, Pembroke, George III, Inlaid Mahogany	5500.00
Table, Pembroke, Georgian, Sycamore, C.1790	8800.00
Table, Pembroke, Hepplewhite, Drop Leaf, Mahogany, 1 Drawer	1000.00
Table, Pembroke, Hepplewhite, Mahogany, 32 In. ....*Illus*	850.00
Table, Pembroke, Hepplewhite, Mahogany, Dovetailed Drawer, 28 In.	900.00
Table, Pembroke, Oval Drop Leaf Top, 1 Drawer, Mahogany, 29 In.	2300.00
Table, Pembroke, Round Drop Leaves, Inlaid Legs, Mahogany, C.1790	4675.00
Table, Pembroke, Sheraton, Drop Leaf, Faux Drawer, 35 X 19 In.	880.00
Table, Phone, Pullout Pivoting Stool, Oak, 30 X 18 In.	335.00
Table, Pier, Federal, Marble Top	1250.00
Table, Pier, Gilt Stenciled, Ormolu Mounted, New York	4925.00
Table, Pier, Marble Top, Front Columns, Glass Capitals, Mahogany	3850.00
Table, Pine, Bluish Green Paint, Square Legs, 31 1/2 In.	550.00
Table, Pub, Mahogany Top, 3 Legs, Cast Iron, C.1900, 29 In., Pair	665.00
Table, Radiating Veneer Design, Tripod Supports, French, C.1925	2475.00
Table, Refectory, Oak, Molded Top, Square Legs, 31 X 108 X 34 In.	1650.00
Table, Refectory, Walnut, Fluted Apron, Paw Feet, C.1885, 3 Ft.	1000.00
Table, Rococo Revival, Drop Finial At Corners, Walnut, C.1850	350.00
Table, Rococo Revival, Marble Top, Walnut, American, C.1855, 29 In.	1100.00
Table, Sawbuck, 2 Board Top, Birch, 29 X 21 3/4 X 36 In.	100.00
Table, Sawbuck, Green Paint On Base, 3 Board Top, Yellow Pine	2250.00
Table, Sawbuck, Pine, 1 Board Top, Branded Dean, 29 X 25 X 54 In.	300.00
Table, Sawbuck, Scrub Top, Old Red Painted Legs	1600.00
Table, Scalloped Apron, Notched Corner Top, Tiger Maple, C.1800	2100.00

Table, Sewing, Carved Walnut Pedestal Base, Bird's–Eye Maple 4100.00
Table, Sewing, Federal, Satinwood Veneer, Banded Edge, 26 1/2 In. 4400.00
Table, Sewing, Lift Top, Tambour Door, Mahogany, C.1805 .... 4600.00
Table, Sewing, Roycroft, 3 Drawers, Hinged Baskets, C.1910, 29 In. 1775.00
Table, Sewing, Roycroft, C.1910, 29 X 30 X 16 1/2 In. ....*Illus* 1600.00
Table, Sewing, Sheraton, With Bag, Maple & Bird's–Eye Maple 4000.00
Table, Shaker, 1 Drawer, Butternut Hickory, Pine, 25 1/2 X 28 In. 575.00
Table, Sheraton, Mahogany, C.1800, 23 In. 2300.00
Table, Shoe Feet, Round 2 Board Top, 28 1/2 In. 450.00
Table, Side, Louis XV, Inlaid Wood, Marble Top, 3 Drawers, Pair 550.00
Table, Sofa, Regency, Rosewood, Brass Inlaid, D Leaves, To 59 In. 3500.00
Table, Sofa, Regency, Rosewood, C.1810, 36 In. ....*Illus* 3500.00
Table, Southwestern, Blue Paint, Scalloped Apron, 1890 .... 1850.00
Table, Square Column, Dark Bluish Paint, Pine, 24 3/4 In 30 In. 110.00
Table, Stickley, Mahogany, Square Legs, X Form Stretcher, 41 In. 660.00
Table, Table, Hunt, Jacobean, Oak, 2 Drawers, 95 X 64 In. 2600.00
Table, Tavern, 1 Drawer, Dark Finish, Oak, 26 X 35 3/4 In. 500.00
Table, Tavern, 2 Board Pine Top, 27 X 28 1/2 X 42 In. 300.00
Table, Tavern, Hardwood, Pine, Button Feet, Beaded Edge, 26 1/2 In. 2100.00
Table, Tavern, Maple, Birch, Splayed, 1795–1820, 36 X 27–In. Top 3300.00
Table, Tavern, Oval Top, Painted, 18th Century, 24 1/2 In. 4125.00
Table, Tavern, Pine & Maple, 36 X 25 In. 770.00
Table, Tavern, Red Painted Base, Scrubbed Top, 27 1/4 In. 1350.00
Table, Tavern, Ring Turned Legs, Maple & Pine, New England, 24 In. 1980.00
Table, Tea, Birdcage, Snake Feet, Mahogany, C.1780, 27 3/4 In. 995.00
Table, Tea, Chippendale, Birdcage, Mahogany, 1760–80, 27 1/2 In. 3500.00
Table, Tea, Chippendale, Mahogany, Late 18th Century 1600.00
Table, Tea, Chippendale, Piecrust Rim, Walnut, Miniature 800.00
Table, Tea, Chippendale, Piecrust, Mahogany, 28 1/2 In. 550.00
Table, Tea, Chippendale, Tilt Top, Birdcage, Mahogany, 28 X 23 In. 1870.00
Table, Tea, Chippendale, Tilt Top, Tiger Maple, C.1780, 28 In. 1045.00
Table, Tea, Country, Dovetailed Cleats, Walnut, C.1830, 48 In. 850.00
Table, Tea, Dutch Rococo, Marquetry, Walnut, 18th Century, 29 In. 5775.00
Table, Tea, George I, Mahogany, Paintbrush Feet 6050.00
Table, Tea, George II, Scroll Carved Legs, Mahogany, 28 In. 4675.00
Table, Tea, George II, Shell Carved Legs, Mahogany, 28 1/2 In. 4400.00
Table, Tea, George III, Vase & Ring Pedestal, Oak, 18th Century 335.00
Table, Tea, Oval Top, Maple & Pine, 25 1/2 X 33 X 25 1/2 In. 1325.00
Table, Tea, Oval Top, Painted, 18th Centuryt, 27 3/4 In. 1540.00
Table, Tea, Oval Top, Painted, Pine & Maple, C.1800, 26 1/2 In. 2640.00
Table, Tea, Queen Anne, Maple, Birch & Oak, Maine, C.1770 .... 2200.00
Table, Tea, Tilt Top, 3 Board Top, Oak, 29 1/2 X 32 1/4 In. 175.00
Table, Tea, Tilt Top, Birdcage, Mahogany, Tripod Base, 27 In. 2000.00
Table, Tea, Tilt Top, Boston, Serpentine 5500.00
Table, Tea, Tilt Top, Cherry, 4 Board Top, Tripod Base, 27 In. 350.00
Table, Tea, Tilt Top, Cherry, Snake Feet, Tripod Base, 27 In. 800.00
Table, Tea, Tilt Top, Chippendale, Birdcage, Mahogany, 23 X 32 In. 6050.00
Table, Tea, Tilt Top, Chippendale, Tiger Maple, 29 In. 3200.00
Table, Tea, Tilt Top, Mahogany, Serpentine Sides, Boston, 1780 .... 3190.00
Table, Tea, Tilt Top, Stephen Badlam, Mass., 1800–10 .... 8800.00
Table, Tea, Tilt Top, Tripod Arched Legs, 1765–85, 27 3/4 In. 2420.00
Table, Tea, Tilt Top, Wallace Nutting, Mahogany, 33 In. 3960.00
Table, Tea, Windsor, Scrubbed Top, Conn., 1750 .... 8250.00
Table, Tilt Top, Black Painted & Parcel Gilt, C.1885, 27 1/4 In. 935.00
Table, Tilt Top, Burmese, Carved Hardwood, 19th Century 360.00
Table, Tilt Top, Clover–Shaped Top, Mahogany, 1810, 28 1/4 In. 5500.00
Table, Tilt Top, Floral Inlay, Walnut, English, 26 X 23 In. 625.00
Table, Tilt Top, George III, Mahogany, Birdcage, Tripod, 25 In. 50.00
Table, Tilt Top, George III, Piecrust, Mahogany, Acanthus Legs 440.00
Table, Tilt Top, Painted Scene, Mahogany, Oval, Brass Beaded, 1900 .... 800.00
Table, Tilt Top, Regency, Inlaid Brass, Mahogany, 28 1/2 In. 3575.00
Table, Tilt Top, Scimitar Legs, Sunburst Inlay, Walnut, 29 1/2 In. 300.00
Table, Trestle, 3 Board Top, Pine, 30 3/4 X 73 In. 110.00
Table, Trestle, Breadboard Top, 7 Turned Columns, Walnut, C.1790 .... 2550.00

Table, Trestle, Child's, Gustav Stickley, C.1907, C.1907.22 In.	525.00
Table, Trestle, Double Chimera Supports, Oak, C.1880, 76 1/2 In.	2200.00
Table, Trestle, Oak, C.1880, 30 X 76 1/2 X 32 In.	2000.00
Table, Trestle, Oak, Shoe Feet, 29 X 59 1/2 In.	550.00
Table, Trestle, White Oak, Early 18th Century, England, 31 1/2 In.	550.00
Table, Tuck–A–Way, Shoe Foot, Walnut Edge, Pine, 38 1/2 In.	1000.00
Table, Victorian, Carved Rosewood, Marble Turtle Top	2300.00
Table, Victorian, Walnut, Apron, 3 Leaves, Round	1500.00
Table, Victorian, White Marble Top, 48 X 32 X 36 In.	6000.00
Table, Vitrine, Glass Top Opens To Velvet Interior, Mahogany	1210.00
Table, Walnut, Box Stretcher, North Carolina	975.00
Table, Work, 1 Drawer, Ovolo Corners, Mahogany, C.1800, 29 1/2 In.	885.00
Table, Work, 2 Board Top, Hardwood Legs, Pine, 26 X 39 1/2 In.	250.00
Table, Work, 2 Drawers, Pullout Workbag, Mahogany, 28 3/4 In.	505.00
Table, Work, 3 Board Top, Square Legs, Cherry, 28 X 42 In.	350.00
Table, Work, Alligatored Black Paint, Poplar, 29 3/4 X 42 In.	150.00
Table, Work, American Empire, 2 Drawers, Mahogany, Turned Legs	220.00
Table, Work, Beaded Rim, Divided Drawer, Pine, 27 1/2 X 33 1/2 In.	150.00
Table, Work, Bird's–Eye Maple Veneer, Mahogany, Philadelphia	1150.00
Table, Work, Contenental, Marquetry Inlaid	2550.00
Table, Work, Drop Leaf, 2 Drawers, Mahogany, C.1835	350.00
Table, Work, E. Avril, Fruitwood, 1830s	3950.00
Table, Work, Federal, 2 Drawers, Pine & Birch, C.1820, 29 3/4 In.	825.00
Table, Work, Federal, Mahogany, Rosewood, Drawer Has Writing Board	3100.00
Table, Work, Fitted Compartments, Bag Drawer, Chinese, C.1870	880.00
Table, Work, Hepplewhite, 2 Board Top, Red Paint, Pine, 28 In.	375.00
Table, Work, Hepplewhite, Ivory Knobs, Satinwood, Line Inlay	6650.00
Table, Work, Hepplewhite, Square Legs, Pine, 29 1/2 X 61 In.	350.00
Table, Work, Pine Breadboard Top, Hardwood Base, 28 1/4 X 50 In.	800.00
Table, Work, Pine Frame, Pine Breadboard Top, 44 1/2 X 29 In.	250.00
Table, Work, Sawbuck Base, Poplar Top, Round Corners, 28 X 42 In.	225.00
Table, Work, Sheraton, 2 Short, 1 Long Drawer, Curly Maple, C.1850	1595.00
Table, Work, Sheraton, Curly Maple, C.1850	1595.00
Table, Work, Walnut, 3 Drawers, Removable 3 Board Top, 29 In.	2600.00
Table, Work, Walnut, Removable 3 Board Top, Duck Feet, 29 1/2 In.	8300.00
Table, Writing, J. & J.W. Meeks, Rosewood, C.1860, 30 In.	1760.00
Table, Writing, Marquetry, Leather Top, Kingwood & Walnut, 69 In.	5225.00
Table, Writing, Pullout Drawer, Leather Inset, Mahogany, 1775	4675.00
Table, Writing, Regency, Inlaid Rosewood, C.1830	5500.00
Table, Writing, Tooled Leather Surface, Inlaid Ebony, Fruitwood	4950.00
Table, Wrought Iron, White Paint, Marble Square Top, Shelf, 31 In.	187.00
Table, Zodiac, Pedestal, Wrought Iron	1900.00
Tabouret, Roycroft, Square Top, Splay Legs, Oak, C.1910, 18 1/2 In.	725.00
Tea Cart, 1 Drawer, Removable Glass Tray, Cherry	200.00
Tea Cart, Wicker, Original Paint	440.00
Tray, Flying Cranes, Gold & Red Lacquer, 15 1/2 X 23 1/2 In.	935.00
Tray, Galle, 2 Shepherds On Camels, Marquetry, C.1900, 19 In.	1540.00
Tray, Galle, Fruitwood Marquetry, Dragon Handles, 6 Sides	1700.00
Tray, Galle, Owl Mask Handles, Marquetry, Forest, 23 1/2 In.	1100.00
Tray, Galle, Thistle Spray, Inlaid Woods, Handles, 24 X 16 In.	550.00
Tray, Galle, Thistle Spray, Spreading Leaves, 24 X 16 In.	550.00
Tray, On Stand, Chinese Export, Rosewood Stand, Brass Tray, 25 In.	650.00
Tray, Pine, Original Green Paint, Red Striping, 4 1/4 In.	200.00
Tray, Tea, Whalebone Gallery, Mahogany Veneer, Pine, 19th Century	4950.00
Urn, Garden, W. Kent, Cast Stone, Leaf Molded Cover, 98 In., Pair	8000.00
Vanity, Bombe, Kneehole, 6 Side & 1 Top Drawers	795.00
Vanity, Opens To Mirrored & Valanced Interior, Mahogany, 30 In.	495.00
Vitrine, Queen Anne, 2 Beveled Glass Doors, 69 X 42 In.	1045.00
Wagon Seat, Ladder Back, Windsor, Black Painted, Splint Seat	1150.00
Wall Pocket, Chip Carved, Walnut, C.1860, 24 1/2 X 17 In.	165.00
Wall Pocket, Chromolith Panel, Walnut, C.1875, 23 X 13 1/2 In.	195.00
Wall Pocket, Eastlake, Tole Panel, C.1880, 5 1/2 X 19 1/2 In.	115.00
Wall Pocket, Pierced Fretwork, Walnut, C.1860, 26 1/2 X 16 In.	175.00
Wardrobe, 1 Shelf, Iron Hooks, Pine & Poplar, 87 In.	275.00

Furniture, Table, Charles X, Mahogany,
Marble Top, 29 In.

Furniture, Table, Gateleg, William & Mary,
Drop Leaves, Oak, 28 In.

Furniture, Table, Sofa, Regency,
Rosewood, C.1810, 36 In.

Furniture, Table, Pembroke, Hepplewhite,
Mahogany, 32 In.

Furniture, Table, Drop Leaf, Mahogany,
American, Victorian

Furniture, Table, Eagle Attacking
Serpent, 4 Lion Feet, Indian

Furniture, Table, Empire, Leaf Carved Feet, Mahogany

Wardrobe, 2 Drawers, Beveled Mirror In Door, Mahogany, 86 1/2 In.	600.00
Wardrobe, Amish, Original Pegs, Lock & Key, Trace of Red Paint	2200.00
Wardrobe, Burl Walnut, Beveled Mirror, 7 Ft.9 In.X 46 In.	1850.00
Wardrobe, Continental, Oak, Paneled Doors, Ian Mogven 1760, 76 In.	850.00
Wardrobe, English Oak, Center Mirrored Door, Over Drawer, 78 In.	176.00
Wardrobe, Mahogany, Ebony, Satinwood, Inlaid Crust, C.1920	2495.00
Wardrobe, Mahogany, Interior Drawers, Shaving Mirror, 65 In.	700.00
Wardrobe, Quarter Sawn Oak, Tilt Mirror In Door, Rack, 61 In.	1100.00
Wardrobe, Victorian, Walnut, Dated 1884	1000.00
Washstand, 1 Dovetailed Drawer, Birch, Pine, Turned Feet, 26 In.	300.00
Washstand, 1 Drawer, Scalloped Shelf, Pine & Poplar, 28 1/4 In.	70.00
Washstand, 2 Drawers, Wooden Pulls, Mahogany & Veneer, C.1810	495.00
Washstand, Black Marble Top, Emerald Backsplash, 2 Drawers, Oak	375.00
Washstand, Candle Shelves, Pullout Towel Rack, Walnut	250.00
Washstand, Corner, George III, Medial Shelf, Mahogany, 46 3/4 In.	250.00
Washstand, Dovetailed Drawer In Base, Gallery, Red Finish, Poplar	575.00
Washstand, Eastlake, 1 Drawer, Over 2 Drawers & Door, Walnut	125.00
Washstand, George II Style, Shelves, Mahogany, 32 In.	800.00
Washstand, Man's, 3 Drawers, Mahogany Veneer, Container	935.00
Washstand, Marble Backsplash, Candleholders, Fruit Pulls, Walnut	475.00
Washstand, Marble Top & Splashback, 1 Drawer Over 2 Drawers	370.00
Washstand, Pine, 1 Drawer, White Porcelain Knob, 29 X 16 X 27 In.	170.00
Washstand, Regency, 3 Wells, Fitted Compartment, Mahogany, 37 In.	385.00
Washstand, Scrolling Frieze, Medial Shelf, Mahogany, 31 3/4 In.	165.00
Washstand, Victorian, Pine, Painted Daisies, Splashboard, 30 In.	110.00
Washstand, Victorian, Walnut, Backsplash, Shelf, 2 Towel Bars	130.00
Whatnot, Carved Fans Over 3 Shelves, Mahogany, 47 1/2 In.	4675.00
Whatnot, Corner, Eastlake, 5 Shelves, Bamboo, C.1875, 65 In.	450.00
Whatnot, Hanging, Eastlake Style, Oak, Mirror	75.00
Whatnot, Rosewood, Reticulated Gallery, Shelf, 1 Drawer, 1860	1320.00
Whatnot, Walnut, 2 Tiers	75.00
Window Seat, Brass Inlay, Mahogany, 1815	4510.00
Window Seat, Corner, English Regency, 67 In.	357.50
Window Seat, G. Stickley, No.178, Leather Seat, C.1903, 35 1/2 In.	5800.00
Wine Cooler, George III, Hinged Top, Lead Lined, Mahogany, C.1800	1870.00
Wine Cooler, George III, Mahogany, Lift Top, Opens To Well, 26 In.	1000.00
Wine Cooler, William IV, Domed Hinged Top, Mahogany, C.1835	1650.00

A porcelain works was started in Furstenberg, Germany, in 1747. It is still working. Many of the modern products are made in the old molds.

FURSTENBERG, Candleholder, Double, Applied Roses, Marked, 5 X 7 In., Pair	250.00

G-ARGY-ROUSSEAU   Gabriel Argy-Rousseau, born in 1885, was a French glass artist who produced a variety of objects in the Art Deco style. His mark, "G. Argy-Rousseau," was usually impressed.

G.ARGY-ROUSSEAU, Vase, Aqua & Purple Flowers, Center Banding, 4 1/4 In.	3750.00
Vase, Aqua & Purple Flowers, Pate-De-Verre, 4 1/4 In.	4050.00

Emile Galle, the famous French designer, made ceramics after 1874. The pieces were marked with the initials "E.G." impressed, "Em. Galle Faiencerie de Nancy," or a version of his signature. Galle is best known for his glass, listed in the next section.

GALLE POTTERY, Basket, Egyptian Design, Peacock Headdress, 7 In. ....*Illus*	2700.00
Basket, Openwork All Around, Medallion Center, Signed, 10 In.	676.00
Boat, Harbor Scene, Flowers, Brown, 13 3/4 In.	975.00
Bonbon, Christmas Cracker Shape, Signed, C.1890, 13 In.	2860.00
Candlestick, Lion Rampant Holding Tower, C.1880, 16 In., Pair	1350.00
Dish, Turtle's Shell Shape, Head Handle, Signed, 1880, 11 In.	1000.00
Figurine, Cat, Seated, Hearts, Spots, Signed, 1900, 13 3/8 In.	1430.00
Flask, Birds, Floral, Butterflies, Turquoise, Signed, 10 In.	445.00
Flask, Pilgrim, Aqua Ground, Signed, 10 In.	440.00
Pitcher, Black, Brown & Blue Moth, Raised Dots, 3 1/4 In.	550.00
Vase, Berries, Brown Ground, Inverted Fan, 12 In. ....*Illus*	2800.00

Galle Pottery, Basket,
Design, Peacock Headdress,
Egyptian, 7 In.

Galle, Vase, Bleeding Hearts,
Foliage, Deep Red, 8 In.

Galle, Vase, Floral, Etched, Enamel,
Insects, Carmel Ground, 8 In.

Vase, Impressionistic Landscape, C.1890, 7 3/16 In., Pair 1870.00

Galle was a designer who made glass, pottery, furniture, and other Art Nouveau items. Emile Galle founded his factory in France in 1874. After Galle's death in 1904, the firm continued to make glass and furniture until 1931. The name "Galle" was used as a mark, but it was often hidden in the design of the object. Galle Pottery is listed above and his furniture is listed in the Furniture section.

GALLE, Basket, White Ground, Blue Flowers, 4 Curved Feet, Signed, 10 X 6 In. 575.00
Boat, Harbor Scene 1 Side, Flowers On Other, Signed, 13 3/4 In. 975.00
Boat, Pink & Green Flowers, White & Pink Ground, Cameo, 10 In. 3500.00
Boat, Violet, Deep Green & Pink Floral, White, Cameo, 4 1/2 X 10 In. 3500.00
Bottle, Unusual Shape, Stopper, Cameo, 10 3/4 In. 5800.00
Bowl, 4-Petaled Blossoms, Leaves, Signed, C.1900, 7 1/4 In. 2750.00
Bowl, Boat Shape, Amethyst Trumpet Vine, Cameo, Signed, 4 1/4 In. 880.00
Bowl, Canoe Shape, Cut Pyracantha Berries, Leaves, Signed, 1920, 16 In. 9900.00
Bowl, Enameled Snails & Shells, Trefoil, Green, 3 1/4 In. 1100.00
Bowl, Grasshopper On Flowering Branches, Signed, C.1890, 5 3/4 In. 3575.00
Bowl, Green Seed Pods, Fronds, White, Pinched, Cameo, Star Mark, 10 In. 2200.00
Bowl, Nasturtium Blossoms, Hexagonal Rim, Signed, C.1890, 3 3/4 In. 4535.00
Bowl, Red Chrysanthemums, Foliage, Cameo, Signed, Label, 5 In. 935.00
Bowl, Ruffled Lip, Salmon Overlay, Poppy Blossoms, Signed, 8 3/4 In. 1815.00
Bowl, Scalloped, Prunus Blossoms, Buds, Leaves, Signed, 1900, 6 1/4 In. 1700.00
Bowl, Sprays of Wild Flowers, Pods, Silver Mounts, C.1900, 7 In. 1330.00
Bowl, Wavy Scrolls, Thistles, Leaves, Signed, C.1900, 8 In. 2665.00
Box, Burgundy Fern Leaves & Flowers, Tapered Ends, 3 X 7 In. 3500.00

Maroon and yellowish chrome green were never used during the eighteenth century. Almost all the eighteenth-century figures had brown eyes.

Galle Pottery, Vase, Berries, Brown Ground,
Inverted Fan, 12 In.

Box, Crocuses On Blue Ground, Footed, 3 1/2 In.	3800.00
Box, Frosted, Purple Cut To Leaf & Berry Design, Signed, 2 1/2 In.	1650.00
Box, Gold, Burgundy Fern Leaves & Flowers, Tapered Ends, 7 X 3 In.	3150.00
Chalice, Floral, Tan, Pink & Yellow Overlay, Cameo, Signed, 7 In.	1760.00
Compote, Pink, Green Cut To Maple Leaf Design, Signed, 4 In.	1650.00
Cruet, Stopper, Scroll Handle, Wild Flowers, Signed, C.1880, 5 1/2 In.	2400.00
Cup & Saucer, Crystal, Enameled	850.00
Dish, Cover, Landscape, Dragonflies In Flight, Lily Pond, Signed, 7 In.	6500.00
Dish, Cover, Landscape, Kidney Form, Lotus Blossoms, Signed, 7 1/4 In.	7900.00
Dish, Handle, 2 Ladybugs & Dragonfly, Signed, C.1900, 16 1/2 In.	2550.00
Lamp, Base, Cut Full–Blown Roses, Buds, Signed, C.1900, 14 1/2 In.	2860.00
Lamp, Clematis, Shade, Bronze Fittings, Signed, C.1910, 14 1/8 In.	8800.00
Lamp, Flowers & Leaves, 3–Color, Brass Base, Signed, 10 1/4 In.	2000.00
Liqueur Set, Twisted Tree Form Stand, Enameled, Signed, 1900, 13 In.	6050.00
Perfume Bottle, Red Overlay, Yellow, Bell Flowers, Cameo, 5 In.	1100.00
Sherbet, Red Cherries, Gold Chain Design, Pedestal, Amber, 2 3/4 In.	675.00
Tray, Frosted Pink, Green Cut To Leaf Design, Rolled Edges, Signed	715.00
Vase, Amethyst Flowers, Foliage On Frosted Ground, Signed, 3 1/2 In.	650.00
Vase, Amethyst, Enameled, Pear Shape, Flea Rim, 7 1/2 In.	900.00
Vase, Berry Branches, Vines, Trumpet Neck, Signed, 1900, 14 In.	2640.00
Vase, Berry–Laden Branches, Signed, C.1900, 4 3/4 In.	880.00
Vase, Bleeding Hearts, Foliage, Deep Red, 8 In. ....*Illus*	7000.00
Vase, Bleeding Hearts, White Frosted Ground, Signed, 10 In.	3850.00
Vase, Blue Trees, Frosted Ground, Cameo, Signed, 13 In.	357.00
Vase, Bud, Blue & Red, 7 In.	700.00
Vase, Bud, Dragonfly Over Lily Pond, Signed, C.1900, 6 5/8 In.	1760.00
Vase, Bud, Landscape, Leafy Trees, Signed, C.1900, 6 3/4 In.	1760.00
Vase, Butterflies, Ferns, Green & Aubergine, Ovoid, Cameo, 3 1/4 In.	1000.00
Vase, Clusters of Crocus Blossoms, Buds, Signed, C.1925, 8 1/2 In.	8800.00
Vase, Daisies, Lime Ground, 6 Sides, Cameo, 11 1/2 In.	4500.00
Vase, Dark Brown Carving On Blue–Gray Ground, Signed, 6 1/4 In.	850.00
Vase, Deep Maroon Cut To Floral Design, Frosted White, Signed, 6 In.	1430.00
Vase, Dragonfly, Gray Walls, Amber Overlay, Signed, C.1910, 24 3/4 In.	8850.00
Vase, Enameled Dahlias, Compressed Form, Signed, 8 In.	220.00
Vase, Enameled Spider Chrysanthemum Blossoms, Signed, 1890, 5 3/4 In.	3325.00
Vase, Etched Day Lilies, Flared Neck, Signed, 11 1/4 In.	3300.00
Vase, Floral, Allover Lines, Yellow, 8 1/4 X 5 1/2 In.	5800.00
Vase, Floral, Etched, Enamel, Insects, Carmel Ground, 8 In. ....*Illus*	775.00
Vase, Floral, Gray To Apple Green, Paneled Ovoid, Signed, 6 In.	1100.00
Vase, Floral, Pink & Green To Opaque, Cylindrical, Cameo, 15 In.	3080.00
Vase, Flowering Branches, Inverted Pyriform, Signed, 1900, 5 1/2 In.	665.00
Vase, Flowering Branches, Spherical, Signed, C.1900, 4 In.	2750.00
Vase, Flowering Irises, Honeydew Green Ground, Signed, 18 3/4 In.	5280.00
Vase, Flowers, Foliage & Butterflies, Etched, Signed, 23 1/2 In.	8250.00
Vase, Flowers, Pods, Frosted Ground, Shaded To Pink At Top, 24 1/2 In.	6800.00
Vase, Frosted Green Cut To Floral Design, Signed, 8 In.	1500.00
Vase, Fuchsia Blossoms, Yellow Ground, Signed, 17 In.	6700.00
Vase, Full–Blown Roses, Leaves, Thorny Branches, Signed, 1900, 10 In.	5500.00
Vase, Grape Clusters, Gold, Short Flared Collar, Round, 4 1/2 In.	3000.00
Vase, Green Thistles Over Yellow, Frosted White, Bulbous, 2 3/4 In.	675.00
Vase, Green, Cut As Fronds On Satin Ground, 2 1/2 In.	375.00
Vase, Hydrangea Blossoms, Double Overlay, Signed, 29 1/4 In.	6650.00
Vase, Hydrangea Blossoms, Inverted Rim, Signed, 25 1/2 In.	7150.00
Vase, Hydrangea, Frosted Pink Ground, Signed, 13 In.	4950.00
Vase, Hydrangea, Lavender, 18 1/2 In.	5000.00
Vase, Intaglio Leaves, Twisted Body, Ruffled Rim, Amber, 12 1/2 In.	3750.00
Vase, Iris Buds, Purple Overlay, White, Cameo, Signed, 3 1/4 In.	665.00
Vase, Japan Style, Stick Neck, Bulbous, Allover Cameo Floral, 23 In.	4500.00
Vase, Lavender Overlay, Lilies, Pink, Signed, 5 1/4 In.	550.00
Vase, Leaf & Berry Design, Burgundy, Signed, 3 3/4 In.	375.00
Vase, Maroon Cut To Floral Design, Pink, 4 3/4 In.	775.00
Vase, Morning Glory Blossoms, Foliage, Signed, 15 1/4 In.	6000.00
Vase, Mountain Landscape, Signed, C.1900, 9 In.	4950.00
Vase, Pinecone Design, Frosted, Brown, Signed, 12 In.	2090.00

Vase, Pinecones, Branches, Carved Pine Needles, Citron, Signed, 8 In. 1495.00
Vase, Plum Pip, Leafy Branches, Signed, C.1925, 9 5/8 In. 9900.00
Vase, Pulled Into 3 Sections, Rope Handle, Signed, C.1890, 7 1/2 In. 8770.00
Vase, Purple Floral Design, Frosted Yellow, Signed, 3 1/2 In. 375.00
Vase, Purple Irises, Gold & Frosted Ground, Cameo, 18 1/2 In. 5175.00
Vase, Red Leaves With Ladybug, Frosted Ground, Corset Shape, 5 In. 900.00
Vase, Red Sailboats, Lake & Trees, Frosted Ground, 5 1/2 In. 2500.00
Vase, Red Wild Orchids, Gold Ground, Bowling Pin Shape, 7 3/4 In. 1850.00
Vase, Sailboats, People, Mountains, Pale Gray Top, 4 1/4 X 2 1/4 In. 450.00
Vase, Shaded Green Floral, Coral & White Frosted, Signed, 6 7/8 In. 1450.00
Vase, Single Amber & Mauve Iris, Irregular Lip, Signed, 5 3/4 In. 2250.00
Vase, Spider Chrysanthemums, Leaves, Signed, C.1900, 5 1/2 In. 3300.00
Vase, Spiky Flowers, Serrated Leaves, Signed, C.1910, 3 In. 995.00
Vase, Spray of Thistles, Thorny Leaves, Pyriform, Signed, 9 7/8 In. 2620.00
Vase, Squash Blossom, Young Fruits, Vines, Signed, C.1925, 7 1/4 In. 7700.00
Vase, Stick, Brown Pinecones, Over Blue–Gray, 3 3/4 X 2 In. 675.00
Vase, Stick, Chartreuse Leaf Design, Frosted Ground, 13 In. 975.00
Vase, Tangerine Flowers, White Ground, Upright Neck, 4 In. 595.00
Vase, Trumpet Blossoms, Dark Green Ground, Signed, 8 3/4 In. 1900.00
Vase, Various Types of Ferns, Lime Green Ground, Signed, 23 1/2 In. 7150.00
Vase, Vines, Flowers, Leaves, Yellowish–Green, Signed, 5 1/2 In. 800.00
Vase, White Shasta Daisies, Leaves, Green Ground, Signed, 11 1/2 In. 4500.00
Vase, Wooded Lake Scene, Mottled Ground, Signed, 13 In. 5500.00
Vase, Wooded Lake Scene, Mottled Ground, Signed, 14 In. 9900.00
Vase, Wreath of Roses, Thorny Branches, Signed, C.1900, 7 1/8 In. 6600.00

Game plates are plates of any make decorated with pictures of birds, animals, or fish. The game plates usually came in sets consisting of twelve dishes and a serving platter. These sets were most popular during the 1880s.

GAME PLATE, Coronet, Signed G. Rosier, 13 In. 150.00
 Large Bird, Gold Rim, Pierced For Hanging, Limoges, 10 1/2 In. 75.00
GAME SET, Deer In Forest Glade Setting, Platter & 9 Plates, 9 In. 85.00

Children's games of all sorts are collected. Of special interest are any board games or card games. Other games may be found listed under Toy, Card, or the name of the character or celebrity featured in the game.

GAME, 12 O'Clock High, Robert Lansing Pictured, Ideal, 1965 .... 45.00
 77 Sunset Strip, Board, 1960 .... 45.00
 007 Electric Drawing Set 45.00
 20, 000 Leagues Under The Sea 35.00
 6 Million Dollar Man, Porta–Communicator Transmits Your Voice 10.00
 Across America, 4 Tootsietoy Zephyr Pieces 45.00
 Addams Family, Card 20.00
 Addams Family, Ideal, 1964 .... 55.00
 Advertureland, Metal Boats, 1957 .... 25.00
 Aerial Contest, Metal Markers, Lithographed Paper, Board, 15 1/2 In. 85.00
 Alabama Coon Game 350.00
 Alice In Wonderland, Cadaco 35.00
 All In The Family, Board, Milton Bradley 6.00
 All–American Football Game, Cadaco, 1960s 25.00
 All–Star, Basketball, Metal Court, Booklet, 1960s 40.00
 Allen Game, Kenner, Box, 1979 .... 15.00
 Alley Oop, Royal Toy, 1937 .... 28.00 To 35.00
 Amazing Magic Robot, 1950s 75.00
 Amazing Magic Robot, Merit, U.K., 1953 .... 30.00
 Amos 'N Andy, Card Party, 1930 .... 60.00
 Anagrams, Fairchild 17.00
 Annie Oakley, Milton Bradley 25.00
 Army Jeep, Board 10.00
 Around The World Fliers, Wolverine, Box 135.00
 Arrest & Trial, 1963 .... 20.00
 Art Linkletter's House Party, 1968 .... 21.00

Atom Ant, Complete, 1966	38.00
Aviation Aerial Tactics, Lithographed Cardboard, Board, H.P. Gibson	35.00
Barnabas Collins	35.00 To 50.00
Barney Google & Spark Plug, Board, Box, 1923	70.00
Baseball, Game of The Week, Hasbro, 1969	25.00
Baseball, Hustler, Mechanical	125.00
Baseball, Official Carl Yastrzemski, Metal Field, Pressman	135.00
Baseball, Parker Bros.	12.00
Basketball, Baldwin, Tin	65.00
Bat Masterson, 1958, Lowell	45.00
Battlestar Galactica, Parker Bros.	12.00
Beany & Cecil Skill Ball Game, Tin, Box, 1961	225.00
Beany & Cecil, Jumping Dishonest John Action Game, Mattel	40.00
Bear Hunt, Milton Bradley, 1920	70.00
Beat The Clock, Bud Collyer, Board, 1954, Lowell	15.00
Beetle Bailey, Board, 1963	40.00
Ben Casey, 1961	20.00
Beverly Hillbillies, Standard Toycraft	45.00
Bewitched, 1965, Game Gems	65.00
Big League Baseball, 3m, Box, 1966	10.00
Bionic Crisis, Sealed Package	10.00
Bionic Woman, Board, Box	10.00
Bird, Swinging, Target, 1930s	30.00
Board, Corner Fans, Checkerboard, Backgammon, Pine, 15 3/4 X 7 3/4 In.	425.00
Board, Cribbage, Box, 1925	18.00
Board, Dominoes, Western Pictures, 1960	15.00
Board, For Pinocchio Pin The Nose, Graphics, 1939, 17 X 14 1/2 In.	80.00
Board, Handmade, Conservation Corps Worker, 3–Color Wood Inlay	55.00
Board, Painted Red & Green, Pine, 25 X 29 In.	75.00
Board, Parcheesi	715.00
Board, Parcheesi, Original Yellow, Red & Blue, 20 7/8 X 20 7/8 In.	1950.00
Board, Red, Black Background, Green Striping, 19 X 19 In.	365.00
Bobbsey Twins, Board	25.00
Bring Em' Back Alive Map & Game, 36 Cards, Animal Puzzles, Box	145.00
Buc–A–Roo, Kilgore, Cast Iron, Box	30.00
Bughouse	20.00
Bull In A China Shop, Milton Bradley, 1930	25.00
Bullseye–You Shoot, Marble, Box	12.50
Bullwinkle, Target, 1961	35.00
Burke's Law, The Game of Who Killed, Transogram	45.00
Busy Andy, Marble, Box	45.00
Cage, Chuck–A–Luck	295.00
Calling All Cars, Board, 1966	25.00
Calling All Cars, Parker Bros., 1930s	25.00
Calling Superman	135.00
Camelot, Board, Parker Bros., 1930	25.00
Candyland, Milton Bradley, 1965, Box	32.00
Captain Kangaroo, Milton Bradley, 1954	15.00
Captain Video, 1950	65.00 To 95.00
Car 54 Where Are You, Board, 1961	30.00
Card, Authors, Whitman	10.00
Card, Beverly Hillbillies, 1963	35.00
Cardino, 1970	15.00
Cards, Saddle Shape, Instructions, Box, 1950	185.00
Casper Glow In The Dark, 1974	12.00
Casper The Ghost, 1959, Box	12.00
Catchword Crossword, Whitman	8.00
Chance, Punch & Judy	165.00
Charge Account, Jan Murray's TV Word Game	22.00
Charlie Chan Detective, Milton Bradley	70.00
Charlie's Angels, Board, 1978, Milton Bradley	12.00
Checkerboard Outside, Backgammon Inside, Book Shape, Box, 13 1/2 In.	25.00
Checkerboard, 3 Tongue & Groove Pine Boards, 16 3/4 X 23 3/4 In.	85.00
Checkerboard, Blue & Black, Reverse Has Concentric Circles, Pine	230.00

Checkerboard, Decoupage & Reverse Painted Glass, 20 1/2 In.	50.00
Checkerboard, Folding, Walnut, Inlaid, Opens To 16 X 16 In.	60.00
Checkerboard, Green & Black Squares	250.00
Checkerboard, Handmade, Slide Covered Bins 2 Ends, 2 Painted Sides	50.00
Checkerboard, Inlaid Walnut, Pine, 16 X 16 In.	90.00
Checkerboard, Multicolored Veneer, 12 1/4 X 12 3/8 In.	115.00
Checkerboard, Primitive, Poplar, Red & Black Paint, 15 3/4 X 17 In.	195.00
Checkerboard, Primitive, Wooden, Black & White Paint, 17 X 27 1/2 In.	225.00
Checkerboard, Red & Black Paint, Varnished Areas, 16 1/2 X 24 In.	225.00
Checkerboard, Red, Black, New England, 19th Century, 24 X 19 3/4 In.	3500.00
Checkerboard, Reverse On Glass, Framed, 17 1/2x 17 3/4 In.	100.00
Checkerboard, Reverse Painted Glass, Framed, 17 1/2 X 17 1/2 In.	100.00
Checkerboard, Reverse Painted Glass, Framed, 19 1/2 X 19 1/2 In.	95.00
Checkerboard, Reverse Painted Glass, Walnut Frame, 23 X 23 In.	65.00
Checkerboard, Star Design On Back, Mahogany, Walnut, 13 1/4 In.	135.00
Checkerborad, Black & Ocher Squares, Red Striping, 25 X 19 In.	165.00
Chinee Checkers, Ohio Art, Tin, Box	10.00
Chinese Checkers, Board, Polychrome Paint, Plywood, Square, 16 3/4 In.	10.00
Chinese Checkers, Board, San Loo, Northwestern	24.00
Chinese Checkers, Chen Check, American Toy Words	3.00
Ching Cong Oriental Checkers, Sam Gabriel	17.00
Chivalry, Board, C.1888	20.00
Chuggedy Chug, Jerry Mahoney, Paul Winchell, Milton Bradley	65.00
Chutes & Ladders, Board, 1943	25.00
Cimarron Strip, 1967, Board, Ideal	45.00
Cinderella, Parker Bros., Box, 1895	80.00
Close Encounters of Third Kind	15.00
Combat, Cards, Playing Pieces, Ideal, 1963	45.00
Coming Home Game, Board, C.1934	85.00
Concentration, 1959, Milton Bradley	20.00
Coney Island, Plastic, Windup Cars, Technofix, 21 X 15 In.	80.00
Conflict, Land, Sea & Air, Parker Bros., 1940s	12.00
Contack, Parker Bros., 1939	25.00
Cootie, 1949	10.00 To 25.00
Countdown Space Game, Transogram	20.00
Cow, Carnival Shooting Gallery, Leather Ears, Pine, 46 X 47 In.	345.00
Cowboy Roundup, Board	26.00
Cowboys & Indians, Card, 1949	15.00
Crazy Traveler, Parker Bros., 1908	12.00
Cricket Table, Pine, Dark Finish, English, Round Top, Shelf, 25 In.	325.00
Crossword Lexicorn, 1931, Parker Bros	15.00
Dai Jobi, Parker Bros.	8.00
Dating Game, Hasbro	20.00
Dead Or Alive, Target, Marx, Box	150.00
Dealers Choice, Parker	12.00
Dexterity, Drop 2 Atom Bombs On Japan, Gilbert, 4 1/4 In.	30.00
Dick Van Dyke Show, Board, 1964, Standard Toycraft	75.00
Dixieland, Black, Card, 1895	40.00
Doc Holiday	15.00
Dominoes, Catalin, Set	25.00
Dominoes, Handmade, Ivory Top, 1890s, Box	72.50
Dominoes, Ivory, In Heart–Shaped Birch Box, 3 1/2 X 3 1/2 In., Set	260.00
Dominoes, Super Heroes	8.00
Dominoes, Union	20.00
Dominoes, Wooden, 6 3/4 In.Tin Box, 33 In.	10.00
Donald Duck, Card, Box, 1941	25.00
Donkey Shooting, Mechanical, Tin Litho, Cork Gun, Strauss, 15 1/2 In.	770.00
Dr. Busby, St. Nicholas Series, Ottman, 1910	35.00
Dr. Kildare, Ideal, 1962	35.00 To 45.00
Dr. No, Role Playing, Victory Games, 1961	6.00
Dragnet, Radar Action, Magnets, Cars, Motorcycles, Knickerbocker, 1955	65.00
Dragnet, Target, Box	135.00
Dukes of Hazzard, 1981, Ideal	6.00
Easy Money, Board, Pieces, Bradley, 1930s	35.00

Ed Wynn Fire Chief	20.00
Ella Cinders, Wooden Playing Pieces, 1944, Milton Bradley	125.00
Elsie, Board	6.50
Emergency, Milton Bradley, 1973	10.00
F Troop, Board, Ideal	45.00
F Troop, Card	15.00
Fantastic Voyage, 1968	20.00
Fantasy, Card, Disney	45.00
Fibber McGee & Molly, Wistful Vista Mystery Game, 1940	24.00 To 45.00
Fiddle Tennis, Schoenhut, Box, Dated 1938	48.00
Fish Pond, McLaughlin, Magnetic, Standup Board, 2 Poles	55.00
Fish Pond, McLoughlin, Magnetic, Standup Board, 2 Poles	65.00
Flinch, Card, Box, 1934	12.00
Flintstones, 1971, Milton Bradley	10.00
Flintstones, Storage, 1961	25.00
Flying Nun, Board, Milton Bradley, 1968	15.00
Flying Star Craft & Space Game, Star Bug, Early 1960s, Box	45.00
Football, Johnny Unitas, Board	12.00
Football, Tom Hamilton's Pigskin Game, 1935	65.00
Forty–Niners, Board	25.00
Fox Hunt, Lowe	38.00
Funky Phantom, Board	20.00
G.I. Joe, Let's Go Joe, Board, Hasbro, 1966	150.00
Game Wheel, Carnival, Oak Box	140.00
Geronimo Skillball, Nabisco Shredded Wheat Premium	10.00
Golden Egg, McLoughlin, Instructions, Wooden Box	200.00
Golf, Arnold Palmer, Box	25.00
Gomer Pyle, Board, Transogram	25.00
Government, Milton Bradley, Capitol Picture, 1939	10.00
Grand Slam	15.00
Green Ghost, Box	25.00
Green Hornet, Board, 1966, Milton Bradley	30.00
Gunsmoke Official Target Set, Matt Dillon, Box	150.00
Gunsmoke, Board	40.00
Have Gun Will Travel, Board, 1959, Parker Brothers	50.00
Hawaiian Eye, Cards, Board, Lowell, 1963	65.00
Head of The Class, Board	15.00
Henry Rings The Bell, Carl Anderson Graphics, Parker Bros., 1934	425.00
Hitchhiker, Fat Black Women Hitchhiking	100.00
Hockey, Katzenjammer Kids, Box, 1948	22.00
Home Fish Pond Game, 1890, Box	85.00
Honey West, Board, Ideal	85.00
Horserace, Tin, Wolverine	55.00
Horserace, Tru–Action, Electric, 1959	35.00
Huckleberry Hound, 1962	50.00
Huckleberry Hound, 1981, Milton Bradley	4.00
Hullabaloo, Musical Quiz, Battery, Right–Wrong Detector, Board, 1965	35.00
I Spy, Card, Sealed, 1965	30.00
Incredible Hulk, Box, 1978	24.00
Jack Straws, Milton Bradley, Box	12.50
James Bond 007, 1964	22.00
James Bond 007, Tarot, 1973	15.00
James Bond, Target, Unused	18.00
Jan Murray's Charge Account	22.00
Jan Murray, TV, Board	25.00
Jetsons Game, Milton Bradley, Box	10.00
John C. Swayze, 1954	30.00
Junior Scrabble, 1958	15.00
Jury Box	20.00
Kangadoodles, Captain Kangaroo, 1956	55.00
Kargo, Gold, England, Box	135.00
Kentucky Derby, 1963	25.00
King Kong, 1976	20.00
Kreskin's ESP	25.00

Kukla, Fran & Ollie, Parker Bros., 1962 .... 35.00
Land of The Lost 12.00
Las Vegas Wild Board 25.00
Laverne & Shirley, Board, Parker Brothers, 1977 .... 7.00
Li'L Abner, His Game, Milton Bradley, 1946 .... 45.00
Little Black Sambo .... 60.00 To 65.00
Little Black Sambo, Dart, Tin 95.00
Little Rascals Clubhouse Bingo, Gabriel, 1958 .... 60.00
Load Game, Remington, 1923 .... 110.00
Loop, Marble, Tin, Red & Green Paint 40.00
Lost Heir, Milton Bradley, 1905 .... 50.00
Lost In Space, Board, 1965 .... 65.00
Lotto, McLoughlin 32.00
M.A.S.H., Board, Milton Bradley, Box, 1981 .... 10.00
Mah Jong Junior, 1000 Wonders, 1923 .... 50.00
Mah Jong, Bamboo & Ivory, Instruction Book, Wooden Box, 1923 .... 750.00
Mah Jong, Rosewood Brass–Trimmed Box 65.00
Mah Jong, Teak, Ivory, Chinese, 1920s 650.00
Mah Jong, Trays, Tiles, Tokens, Sealed 18.00
Major League Baseball, Dart, Tin Litho, 1940s 95.00
Mandrake The Magician, Transogram, 1966 .... 25.00
Marble, Gone With The Wind, Board 28.00
Marble, Tic Tac Toe, 1940s 5.00
Margie, The Game of Whoopee, Milton Bradley, 1961 .... 45.00
Match Game, Milton Bradley, 1968 .... 10.00
McDonald's Farm, Board, Sel–Right, Box, 1965 .... 20.00
McHale's Navy, Board, Transogram 25.00
McKeever & The Colonel, Bamboozle, Board, 1962, Milton Bradley 35.00
Meet The Presidents, Board, Selchow & Righter, Box, 1950 .... 30.00
Meet The Presidents, Selchow & Righter, 1940s 30.00
Merry Milkman, 1955 .... 25.00
Messenger Boy, Lithography, McLoughlin Bros. 200.00
Mighty Mouse Skill Game, Original Card, 1950s 55.00
Mission Impossible, Ideal, 1965 .... 45.00
Monopoly, 1936 .... 40.00
Moon Mullins, Milton Bradley, 1930 .... 110.00
Mork & Mindy, Parker Brothers, 1979 .... 10.00 To 15.00
Mosaic Marble, Ball, Box 80.00
Mother Hen Target, Tin Litho, Gun, Hit Target, Eggs Fall In Basket, Box 60.00
Mr. Ed, The Talking Horse, Parker Bros., 1962 .... 25.00
Mr. Magoo, 1978 .... 27.00
Mr. Novak, Transogram 35.00
Munster & Monsters, Dracula, Board, Box 65.00
Mystery Date, Milton Bradley, 1965 .... 18.00 To 22.00
Mystic Skull, Game of Voodoo, Ideal, 1964 .... 35.00
Mystic, 1939 .... 12.00
Name That Tune, With Record, 1957, Milton Bradley 20.00
Nancy & Sluggo, Board, Milton Bradley, 1944 .... 125.00
Nancy Drew Mystery 20.00
NBC News, Board, Huntley, 1962, Dadan 35.00
New Adventures of Gilligan, Milton Bradley 10.00
New York World's Fair, Box, 1964 .... 25.00
Newlywed, Board, 1969 .... 7.00 To 15.00
Old King Cole, Card, McLoughlin, 1888 .... 22.00
Overland Limited, Bradley, Cowboy Waving On Cover 38.00
Pacman, Milton Bradley 6.00
Paladin, Have Gun Will Travel, Checkers, Ideal, 1960 .... 98.00
Parlor Baseball, Wood Board With Pegs, American Play Games, 1940 .... 90.00
Partridge Family, Board, Milton Bradley, Box, 1971 .... 20.00 To 35.00
Patty Duke, Milton Bradley, 1963 .... 25.00 To 28.00
Perry Mason, Board, 1959 .... 50.00
Petticoat Junction, Standard Tycraft 45.00
Photo–Electric Football, 1941 .... 50.00
Pick Up Sticks, Schoenhut 12.00

Pikes Peak Or Bust, Board 65.00
Pin The Tail On The Donkey, Box, 1923 .... 12.00 To 17.00
Pinball, Air Raid 71.50
Pinball, Big Broadcast 275.00
Pinball, Blastoff, Electric, Box, 1950s 50.00
Pinball, World Series 330.00
Pinball, Wrigley's Flashball, 1940s 48.00
Pipe Toss, Popeye, Box, 1935 .... 95.00
Pit, Box, 1919 .... 18.00
Planet of The Apes, Board, Milton Bradley, Box, 1974 .... 12.00 To 20.00
Poker Chips, Holder, Wooden 25.00
Poker Chips, Inlaid Maple Case, Bakelite, 200 Piece 40.00
Poker Set, Traveling, Count Rite, Bakelite, Art Deco 90.00
Pollyanna, Parker Bros., 1940 .... 38.00
Pony Express, 1947 .... 25.00
Pop The Bird, Target, Cork Gun 28.00
Power Barons, Milton Bradley, Box 7.00
Puss N' Boots 350.00
Puzzle Set, Green Hornet, 1966, Whitman, 8 X 10 In. 65.00
Puzzle, 007 Goldfinger 18.00
Puzzle, A Shady Nook, Mayfair Jig, Cardboard, 15 X 12 In. 5.00
Puzzle, Advertising, Hood Sarsaparilla, Rainy Day, 9 X 9 In. 15.00
Puzzle, Badminton Hunt, Wooden, Noninterlocking, 8 X 16 In. 25.00
Puzzle, Ben Casey, With Poster 20.00
Puzzle, Beverly Hillbillies, Granny & Ellie May, 1963 .... 15.00
Puzzle, Captain Kangaroo 10.00
Puzzle, Child's Own Clock, Paper Litho On Wood, Box, 9 In. 125.00
Puzzle, Cisco Kid 17.00
Puzzle, Cottage By River, Wooden, 9 X 12 In. 10.00
Puzzle, Cottage With Geese, Wooden, 9 X 12 In. 12.00
Puzzle, Dad's Puzzler, 1926 .... 10.00
Puzzle, David Cassidy, 1972 .... 10.00
Puzzle, Dutch Girls In Meadow, Wooden, 12 X 16 In. 30.00
Puzzle, Family Portrait, Steiff, 1902–03, Unopened, 1000 Piece 18.00
Puzzle, Fishing For Sailfish, Wooden, 8 X 9 In. 5.00
Puzzle, Flower Girl, Wooden, 9 X 12 In. 20.00
Puzzle, Franklin Park, Postcard, 1910, Cardboard, 18 Pcs., 3 X 5 In. 10.00
Puzzle, Garfield, 1978 .... 5.00
Puzzle, Girl Washing Dishes, Jessie Wilcox Smith 50.00
Puzzle, Goldfinger, James Bond 30.00
Puzzle, Humpty Dumpty, Hartley 12.00
Puzzle, Jetsons, Mini 35.00
Puzzle, Little Lulu 25.00
Puzzle, Mediterranean Harbor, Wooden, 13 X 11 In. 20.00
Puzzle, Military Take–A–Part, Box 45.00
Puzzle, Nude, Wooden, Noninterlocking, 6 X 8 In. 10.00
Puzzle, Old King Cole, C.M. Burd, 1929, 8 1/2 X 10 In. 20.00
Puzzle, Panama Cone Disc, Wooden, Box 15.00
Puzzle, Paul Jones At Constitutional Convention, Wooden 18.00
Puzzle, Planet of The Apes, 1967 .... 25.00
Puzzle, Queen Mary 24.00
Puzzle, Red Riding Hood, 17 Pcs., Masonite, 9 X 12 In. 15.00
Puzzle, Rootie Kazootie 10.00
Puzzle, Rubic Cube, Wooden, 19th Century, 4 1/4 X 4 1/4 X 7 3/4 In. 65.00
Puzzle, Shoving Off, Wooden, 9 X 12 In. 25.00
Puzzle, Silent Teacher, 64 Pcs., Sherwin–Williams, Wooden, 12 X 15 In. 95.00
Puzzle, Snake Charmer, Wooden, 14 X 10 In. 20.00
Puzzle, Space Patrol, Illustrated Envelope 75.00
Puzzle, Spiro Agnew, Friend of Silent Majority, Superman Dress, 1970 ...... 15.00
Puzzle, Star Trek 10.00
Puzzle, The Hunt, Wooden, 6 X 8 In. 12.00
Puzzle, Thirsty Cows, Wooden, 9 X 12 In. 20.00
Puzzle, Three Little Pigs, McLoughlin, Wooden Box, 9 X 11 In. 95.00
Puzzle, Thunderball Jigsaw, Box 65.00

Puzzle, U.S.A. Map, 64 Pcs., Milton Bradley, 1885, Wooden, 15 X 22 In.	90.00
Puzzle, Victor Talking Machine Co., Record Shape, 1908	98.00
Puzzle, Waterfall, Cardboard, 9 X 11 In.	6.00
Puzzle, Winding Road, Wooden, 12 X 16 In.	25.00
Puzzle, Wonder Woman, Box	15.00
Puzzle, Wyatt Earp	17.00
Puzzle, Zorro	17.00
Quick Draw McGraw, Milton Bradley	25.00
Quiz Me, Game of Riddles, Milton Bradley, 1940s	7.00
Race, Champion Spark Plug, Board, 1934	22.00
Raggedy Ann's Magic Pebble, Milton Bradley, 1940s	60.00
Raiders of Lost Ark	10.00
Rescue At Dunkirk, HO Scale Model Kit, 48 Piece	10.00
Rifleman	40.00
Rin Tin Tin Skillball	10.00
Ring Toss, Popeye, 1937	65.00
Risky, Box, 1959	15.00
Road Runner, 1969	25.00
Roll 'Em, Dice, Spinners	26.00
Roller Coaster, Chein	125.00
Roulette Wheel, Traveling, 1900s	195.00
Rube Goldberg	40.00
Secret Agent 007, Milton Bradley, 1965	25.00
Sergeant Preston	15.00
Set of Dice, 1890s	4.00
Shari Lewis Party Game, Balloons, Prizes, Picture Record, Lowell	45.00
Shari Lewis Pic–A–Pix, Go Fish Game, Peerless Playthings	35.00
Sherlock Holmes, Card, Parker Bros., Box, Instructions	15.00
Shoot A Crow, Target, Rifle, Box	25.00
Shoot Peters Shells, Tin	35.00
Shrunken Head Apple Sculpture, Unused, Box, 1975	40.00
Skip & Fox & Geese, McLoughlin Bros, 1905	145.00
Snake Eyes, Black Dice Game, Selchow & Righter, 1930s	65.00
Snake Eyes, Selchow & Righter, Box, Missing Separator	38.00
Snakes & Ladders, Board	12.00
Snoopy Pound–A–Ball, Box	20.00
Snuffy Smith's Bug Derby, King Features, 1940	35.00
Soccer, Pinball, Wooden, Steel Balls, England, 1930s	95.00
Soldier of Fortune, Target, Tin Soldiers, Cork Gun & Bullets, Marx	250.00
Soupy Sales, Cards, 1965, Ideal	25.00
Space Target, Rocket Plane Gun, 3 Rubber Projectiles, Box, 1950s	150.00
Speed Boat Race, Milton Bradley, 1920	45.00
Spider's Web, McLoughlin Bros., 1900	195.00
Spoof, Bradley, 1918	18.00
Spot–A–Car, Hasbro, 1940s	30.00
Stampede, Board, 1956	20.00
Star Trek, Ideal, 1967	35.00
Starsky & Hutch Detective Game, Milton Bradley, 1977	10.00
Steeple Chase, Parker Brothers, 1890	60.00
Steve Canyon, Cock Pit, Box	65.00
Stock Market Game, Sam Gabriel, 1955	20.00
Straight Arrow	45.00
Strawberry Shortcake, Parker	12.00
Surf Side 6, Troy Donahue Star, Lowell	65.00
Swords & Shields, 1970, Milton Bradley	6.00
Table Tennis, Spears, Box	32.00
Tarzan To The Rescue, Milton Bradley, 1977	10.00
Taxi In Parlor, Board	6.50
Taxi, Board, Car Playing Pieces, Complete	25.00
Telegraph Boy, Wooden Box, Metal Figures, 1888	175.00
Tell It To The Judge, Eddie Cantor	28.00
Three Little Pigs, 1933	40.00
Thunderball, Milton Bradley, 1964	30.00
Thunderbirds Game, Waddinton's, 1965	30.00

Tic–Tac–Dough, Jack Barry, NBC	22.00
Tiddly Winks, McDonald, Japan	35.00
To The North Pole By Airship, McLoughlin Bros., Box, 19 1/2 In.	225.00
Tomorrow Land & Rocket To Moon, Parker Brothers, Board, Spinner	28.00
Touring Automobile, 1926, Parker Bros.	12.00
Touring Automobile, Cards, 1965, Parker Bros.	6.00
Touring, Cards, 1910	20.00
Touring, Cards, Box, 1926	20.00
Touring, Cards, Box, 1947	16.00
Trolley, Cards, Box, 1904	20.00
Turn Over, Steel Ball Cylinder, Target Board, Box, Milton Bradley, 1902	60.00
Twelve O'Clock High, Card, Milton Bradley, 1965	15.00
U.S. History, Card, Parker Bros., Instructions	16.00
Uncle Jim's Question Bee, NBC	20.00
Uncle Sam's Mail, McLoughlin Bros., 1894	70.00
Uncle Wiggily, Milton Bradley, 1949	25.00 To 35.00
Undersea World of Jacques Cousteau, Parker Brothers, 1968	20.00
Untouchables, 1961	25.00
Voyage Around The World, Picture Blimp, Board	65.00
Voyage To The Bottom of The Sea, Milton Bradley, 1964	30.00
W.C. Fields, Cards	30.00
Waltons	10.00
Wat D'Ye Buy, Lithograph Box of Store Scene, McLoughlin Bros., 1887	65.00
Welcome Back Kotter, Board, Box	40.00
Wells Fargo, Milton Bradley, 1969	20.00 To 22.00
Wheel, Carnival, 1910s	240.00
Which Witch	8.00
Whirli–Crow, Red Ryder, Box	65.00
White Fleet, U.S. Navy Armada, Curtis, Playing Cards, 1908, Box	110.00
Wild West, Board	65.00
Willow Game, Box	35.00
Winnie The Pooh, Board, 1933	55.00
Wistful Vista, Fibber McGee	35.00
Wizard of Oz, 1930s	450.00
Wizard of Oz, 1974	14.00 To 21.00
Wolverine Olympic Runners, Tin, Litho, Box	175.00
Wonder Woman, 1978	10.00
Wooden Donkey, Toss, Box	22.00
Wyatt Earp, Water Color Set	65.00
Yale–Harvard Football Game, McLoughlin, 1895	395.00
Yogi Bear Go Fly A Kite, 1961	40.00
Yogi Bear, 1971	15.00
You Bet Your Life, Board, Lowell, 1955	35.00
Zorro, Board, Whitman, 1958	45.00
Zorro, Parker, 1966	35.00

ГАРДНЕРЪ   The Gardner porcelain works was founded in Verbiki, outside Moscow, by the English–born Francis Gardner in 1766. Gardner made porcelain tablewares, figurines, and faience.

GARDNER, Cup & Saucer, Floral Reserves, Cobalt Blue, Porcelain, 19th Century	95.00

Gaudy Dutch pottery was made in England for America from about 1810 to 1820. It is a white earthenware with Imari–style decorations of red, blue, green, yellow, and black. Only sixteen patterns of Gaudy Dutch were made: Butterfly, Carnation, Dahlia, Double Rose, Dove, Grape, Leaf, Oyster, Primrose, Single Rose, Strawflower, Sunflower, Urn, War Bonnet, Zinnia, and No Name. Other similar wares are called "Gaudy Ironstone" and "Gaudy Welsh."

GAUDY DUTCH, Coffee Server, Single Rose	4200.00
Cup & Saucer, Handleless, War Bonnet	500.00
Cup & Saucer, Single Rose	375.00
Jug, Milk, Double Rose	875.00
Plate, Oyster, 6 In.	98.00

Plate, War Bonnet, 5 1/4 In.	400.00
Teapot, War Bonnet, 5 7/8 In.	750.00
Waste Bowl, Butterfly	765.00

Some collectors have named the ironstone wares with the bright Gaudy Dutchlike patterns "Gaudy Ironstone." There may be other examples found in the listing for Ironstone or under the name of the ceramic factory.

GAUDY IRONSTONE, Charger, Floral, Stick Spatter, 16 1/4 In.	200.00
Cup & Saucer, Handleless, Polychrome Floral	150.00
Dish, Vegetable, Blue Floral Transfer, Marked, 10 In.	55.00
Plate, Imari, Mason's, 8 In.	175.00
Plate, Pinwheel	165.00
Plate, Urn, 8 3/4 In., Pair	300.00
Platter, Morning Glory, 14 1/4 In.	165.00
Platter, Polychrome Enameling, Black Transfer, 17 In.	205.00
Platter, Polychrome Enameling, Blue Underglaze, 15 In.	300.00
Platter, Rose, Red, Blue, Green & Black, 13 1/4 In.	75.00
Tray, Condiment, Leaf Shape, Handles, 11 In.	160.00
Vase, Winged Serpent Handles, Pagoda Cover ....*Illus*	1500.00

Gaudy Welsh is an Imari–decorated earthenware with red, blue, green, and gold decorations. It was made after 1820.

GAUDY WELSH, Creamer, 3 In.	95.00
Creamer, Oyster, 4 In.	40.00
Cup & Saucer	15.00
Cup & Saucer, Oyster	35.00
Cup & Saucer, Pink & White Luster, Gilt Trim	33.50
Loving Cup, Impressed Allerton, 1 3/4 In.	75.00
Mug, 2 3/4 In.	65.00
Mug, Purple Luster, 1 7/8 In.	35.00
Pitcher, Rust & Cobalt, Large	145.00
Pitcher, Water, Worm Handle, Allerton	90.00
Tea Set, Floral, 13 Piece	290.00
Tea Set, Pinwheel, 17 Piece	650.00
Teapot, Floral, Underglaze Blue, Purple Luster, 7 In.	400.00
Teapot, Pearlware, Enamel & Pink Luster, 7 In.	325.00

In the late nineteenth century Geisha Girl porcelain was made in Japan for export. It was an inexpensive porcelain often sold in dime stores or used as free premiums. Pieces are sometimes marked with the name of a store. Japanese ladies in kimonos are pictured on the

Gouda, Vase, Amphora, 18 In.

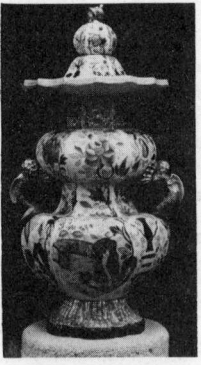

Gaudy Ironstone,
Vase, Winged
Serpent Handles,
Pagoda Cover

Gustavsberg, Bowl, Inverted Bell
Form, Geometric Design, 8 In.

dishes. There are over 125 recorded patterns. Borders of red, blue, green, gold, brown, or several of these colors were used. Modern reproductions are being made.

GEISHA GIRL, Bowl, Cobalt, Gold Ruffle, 10 In.	25.00
Chocolate Set, Red Trim, Nippon, 6 Piece	135.00
Cup & Saucer, Gold Bursts, Demitasse	10.00
Cup & Saucer, Rust, Green, Cobalt Design Inside Cup, 8 Piece	45.00
Hatpin Holder	25.00
Nut Set, Orange & Gold, Footed, 7 Piece	50.00
Tea Set, Lithophane, Kutani, 18 Piece	50.00
Teapot, 5 1/2 In.	40.00

Gene Autry was born in 1907. He began his career as the "Singing Cowboy" in 1928. His first movie appearance was in 1934, his last in 1958.

GENE AUTRY, Belt, Leather	75.00
Bicycle Horn, Box	85.00
Book, Arapaho War Drums, 1957	4.00
Book, Big Valley Grab, Dust Cover, 1952	8.00 To 15.00
Book, Cowboy Detective, Big Little Book, 1946	12.00
Book, Redwood Pirates, 1946	15.00
Booklet, Songs & Scenes, 1940	35.00
Boots, Rubber, Box	125.00
Cap Gun, Cast Iron	45.00
Cap Pistol	27.50 To 27.50
Coloring Book	12.00
Coloring Book, 1941, Large	35.00
Coloring Book, 1949, Large	25.00
Comic Book, Dell, No.10, November–December	12.50
Comic Book, Dell, No.17	12.00
Comic Book, Gene Autry's Champion, Dell	5.00
Figure, Blowup For Pool	250.00
Film, South of Texas	29.00
Flashlight	42.00
Flyer, Gene Autry Rodeo, Illustrated, Mailer	20.00
Game, Bandit Trail, Kenton, 1939	225.00
Guitar, Emenee, Box	120.00
Guitar, Melody Ranch, Wooden	200.00
Guitar, Souvenir Songbook, 1950s, Box	200.00
Guitar, Standard, Case	75.00
Guitar, Wood	45.00
Gun & Holster	80.00
Holster, Double	85.00
Lunch Box, Thermos	85.00
Paper Doll, 1950	30.00 To 35.00
Paper Doll, Melody Ranch, Cut	22.00
Pinback Button, Sunbeam Bread	20.00
Pistol, CI	80.00
Pistol, Kenton	70.00
Pistol, Secret Agent Junior, Hamilton	32.00
Popgun, 1950s	8.00
Puzzle, Frame Inlay, Color, Sleeve, 1948, Large	40.00
Ring, Horseshoe Nail, Autry's Signature, Display Card	85.00
Ring, Molded Picture Top, Horseshoe Side, Rope Hat	65.00
Scarf, Silk	110.00
Sheet Music, Red River Valley	25.00
Sheet Music, Rudolph The Red–Nosed Reindeer, 1949	7.00
Sheet Music, Sioux City Sue	35.00
Sheet Music, Trail That Follows The Stars	10.00
Song Folio, Deluxe	30.00
Songbook, 1938	12.00
Songbook, Gene & Champion On Cover	8.00
Songbook, Photographs, 1942, 51 Pages	25.00

Spurs, Box	125.00
Suspenders	75.00
Viewmaster, 1950	7.00
Wristwatch, 1948	200.00
Wristwatch, Box	125.00

Black and blue decorated Gibson Girl plates were made in the early 1900s. Twenty–four different 10 1/2–inch plates were made by the Royal Doulton Pottery at Lambeth, England. These pictured scenes from the book "A Widow and Her Friends" by Charles Dana Gibson. Another set of twelve 9–inch plates featuring pictures of the heads of Gibson Girls had all–blue decoration. Many other items also pictured the famous Gibson Girl.

GIBSON GIRL, Chocolate Pot	600.00
Paperweight, Pear, Iridescent Green	22.00
Pitcher, Water, Gold Medallions	195.00
Plate, Blue & White, Complete Set, 24 Piece	2450.00
Plate, Calendar, 1909, Advertising	50.00
Plate, Message From The Outside World	120.00
Plate, Portrait, Hearts & Bows Border, 9 In.	95.00
Plate, She Contemplates The Cloister, 10 1/2 In.	75.00
Plate, She Goes Into Colors, 10 1/2 In.	75.00
Plate, She Looks For Relief Among Old Ones, 10 1/2 I	85.00 To 90.00
Plate, They Go Fishing	115.00
Plate, Winning New Friends	135.00
Powder Jar	23.00

GILLINDER

Gillinder pressed glass was first made by William T. Gillinder of Philadelphia in 1863. The company had a working factory on the grounds at the Centennial and made small, marked pieces of glass for sale as souvenirs. They made a variety of decorative glass pieces and tablewares.

GILLINDER, Bust, Lincoln, Frosted Glass, 1876 Centennial	375.00
Dish, Blue Opalescent, Fluted, Small	15.00
Dish, Blue Opalescent, Pedestal	18.00
Mug, Ruth The Gleaner	135.00
Toothpick, Just Out, Frosted	65.00

The Girl Scout movement started in 1912, two years after the Boy Scouts. It began under Juliette Gordon Low of Savannah, Georgia. The first Girl Scout cookies were sold in 1928. Collectors search for anything pertaining to the Girl Scouts, including uniforms, publications, and old cookie boxes.

GIRL SCOUT, Bracelet, Bakelite	25.00
Catalog, Girl Scouts, Inc., National Equipment Service, 1940	23.00
Doll, Effanbee, 1966, 11 In.	40.00
Dress, Doll's, For Ginny Doll	10.00
Handbook, 1929	27.50
Lunch Box	40.00
Mess Kit, Box	20.00
GLASS, CONTEMPORARY, see Contemporary Glass	

Eyeglasses, or spectacles, were mentioned in a manuscript in 1289 and have been used ever since. The first glasses with rigid side pieces were made in London in 1727. Bifocals were invented by Benjamin Franklin in 1785. Lorgnettes were popular in late Victorian times.

GLASSES, Lorgnette, Retractable Lens, 14K Gold, 4 1/4 In.	395.00
Lorgnette, Silver Gilt, Unger Bros.	950.00
Opera, Bakelite, Rhinestone, Leather Case	25.00
Opera, Mother–of–Pearl Handle	95.00
Opera, Mother–of–Pearl, Brass	50.00
Opera, With Case	20.00
Pince–Nez, Hairpin	15.00

Spectacles, Black Tin Case	8.00
Wire Frame, C.F. Kappes Optometrist, Case	20.00

Goebel

W. Goebel Porzellanfabrik of Oeslau, Germany, now Rodental, West Germany, has made many types of figurines and dishes. The firm is still working. The pieces marked "Goebel Hummel" are listed under Hummel in this book.

GOEBEL, Bell, 1978	45.00
Breakfast Set, Meridian, Bavaria W. Germany, 19 Piece	50.00
Bust, Queen Nefertiti, Sister To Nefeteri, Stylized, Multicolored	95.00
Creamer, George Washington	25.00
Creamer, Monk, 2 1/2 In.	20.00
Creamer, Monk, Stylized Bee	20.00
Cup, Santa Claus, Full Bee	85.00
Egg Timer, 2 Monks	42.00
Egg Timer, Friar Tuck .... 25.00 To 45.00
Figurine, Bathing Beauty, Seated On Scallop Shell, Marked, 3 In.	130.00
Figurine, Cat, Mitzi, 1963	100.00
Figurine, Center Court, 1903	35.00
Figurine, Cheer Up, Nurse With Child, BYJ 50	48.00
Figurine, Gnome Girl	35.00
Figurine, Madonna & Child, Sitting, Full Bee, 5 In.	95.00
Figurine, Madonna & Child, Standing, Full Bee, 7 In.	95.00
Figurine, Peacock, Black Body, Colored Feathers, 11 X 16 In.	90.00
Lamp, Perfume, Woman With Cape	295.00
Match Holder, Silver	75.00
Mustard, Cardinal Tuck	75.00
Pincushion Doll, Pierette, Blue Skullcap	125.00
Pitcher, Clown, 7 1/2 In.	45.00
Pitcher, Fish, Marked, Small	23.00
Pitcher, Friar Tuck, 8 1/4 In.	92.00
Plaque, Awakening	90.00
Plaque, Morning Concert, Ed. No. 11	98.00
Plaque, Smiling Through, Club Ed. No.2, 6 In.	55.00
Plate, 12 Tribes of Israel, Ispanky, 1978	250.00
Plate, Lusitano	20.00
Plate, Oldenburger	20.00
Salt & Pepper, Flower, Disney	250.00
Salt & Pepper, Friar Tuck, Full Bee	30.00
Sugar & Creamer, Salt & Pepper, Monk, Red Clothes, 4 Piece	60.00

Goldscheider Wien

Porcelain has been made by three branches of the Goldscheider family. The family left Vienna in 1938 and started factories in England and in Trenton, New Jersey. The New Jersey factory started in 1940 as Goldscheider–U.S.A. In 1941 it became Goldscheider–Everlast Corporation. From 1947 to 1953 it was Goldcrest Ceramics Corporation. In 1950 the Vienna plant was returned to Mr. Goldscheider and the company continues in business. The Trenton, New Jersey, business is now Goldscheider of Vienna and imports all of the pieces.

GOLDSCHEIDER, Bust, Madonna, 5 In.	32.00
Bust, Marquess & Marquis, Signed, 10 In., Pair	125.00
Bust, Putti, 4 In.	48.00
Figurine, April Showers, Woman In Pink, Umbrella, 6/12 In.	70.00
Figurine, Butterfly Girl, Marked, C.1930, 11 5/8 In.	1540.00
Figurine, Dog, Spaniel, Reclining	65.00
Figurine, Madonna & Child, 7 1/2 In.	200.00
Figurine, Madonna, 5 1/4 In.	27.50
Figurine, Salome, Posed With Harp, Stamped, C.1900, 41 1/2 In.	1870.00
Figurine, Southern Belle, 8 In. .... 60.00 To 65.00
Figurine, Woman Holding Basket of Flowers, 7 1/2 In.	55.00
Lamp, Spanish Dancer, Artist Lorenzl	750.00
Mask, Wall, Terra–Cotta, Silver Curls	750.00
GOLF, see Sports	

Lawton Gonder opened Gonder Ceramic Arts, Inc., in 1941. He worked in the old Peters and Reed pottery in Zanesville, Ohio. Gonder pieces include lamp bases marked "Eglee" and many wares with Oriental–type glazes.

GONDER, Ewer, High Matte Green, 7 1/2 In.	20.00
Figurine, Madonna, Gray & Pink, Paper Label	10.00
Vase, Marbelized, Handles, 9 1/4 In., Pair	50.00

Goofus glass was made from about 1900 to 1920 by many American factories. It was originally painted gold, red, green, bronze, pink, purple, or other bright colors. Many pieces are found today with flaking paint and this lowers the value.

GOOFUS GLASS, Bowl, Gold On Green, 4 1/2 X 5 In.	15.00
Bowl, Reindeer Center	18.00
Butter, Cover, Blue, Scroll	85.00
Plate, Roses, 11 In.	25.00
Powder Box, Puffy, Rose, Painted, 3 X 4 In.	45.00
Relish, Flowers, Gold Trim, Handles, 9 1/2 In.	12.00
Tray, Dresser, Heart Shape, Roses	55.00
Tumbler, Crackle, Gold, Painted Grapes, 4 In.	40.00
Vase, Bird & Grapes, 9 In.	21.00
Vase, Painted Irises, 12 In.	65.00
Vase, Roses, Gold Trim, 12 In.	40.00

Goss china has been made since 1858. English potter William Henry Goss first made it at the Falcon Pottery in Stoke–on–Trent. The factory name was changed to Goss China Company in 1934 when it was taken over by Cauldon Potteries. Production ceased in 1940. Goss china resembles Irish Belleek in both body and glaze. The company also made popular souvenir china, usually marked with local crests and names.

W. H. COSS

GOSS, Box, Pin, Child On Cushion, 3 In.	300.00
Bust, Wordsworth, Parian, 6 In.	300.00
Ewer, Allied Flags, 2 In.	30.00
Figure, Shakespeare Cottage, Signed, 3 1/4 X 7 1/4 In.	135.00
House, Thomas Hardy, 4 In. Long	400.00
Tumbler, Raised Lincoln Imp	100.00

Pottery has been made in Gouda, Holland, since the seventeenth century. Two firms, the Zenith pottery, established in the eighteenth century, and the Zuid–Hollandsche pottery, made the brightly colored wares marked "Gouda" from 1880 to about 1940. Many pieces featured Art Nouveau or Art Deco designs.

GOUDA, Basket, Regina, Black, Multicolored, 6 1/2 In.	135.00
Candlestick, Drip Pan, Multicolored, Marked, 12 X 5 1/4 In.	125.00
Decanter, Musical, You Are A Jolly Good Fellow	45.00
Dish, Crocus, Footed, 2 X 3 In.	37.50
Dutch Shoe, Astra, Multicolored, 7 1/2 In.	69.00
Ewer, Multigreen, Purple, High Glaze, Zuid–Holland, 14 In., Pair	450.00
Flask, Fisherman	65.00
Inkwell, Damascus, Multicolored, Black Base, 8 1/2 X 5 1/2 In.	110.00
Inkwell, Double, Floral Ivora, High Glaze White Ground, Stand, 9 In.	250.00
Jar, Cover, Arco	55.00
Jar, Cover, Bertina Royal Zuid	55.00
Jar, Dutch Windmill Scene On Lid, Zuid, 4 In.	75.00
Jar, Ginger, Stylized Irises, Glossy, 10 In.	550.00
Pitcher, Signed, 9 In.	125.00
Pitcher, Teal, Brown & Lavender Florals, Gloria Royal, 8 1/2 In.	295.00
Vase, Amphora, 18 In. ....*Illus*	225.00
Vase, Damascus III, C.1885, 10 In.	300.00
Vase, Flowers, Gray Ground, Marked, 7 1/4 In.	75.00
Vase, Leaf & Band Design, Flared Wide Rim, Signed, C.1910, 6 X 6 In.	75.00
Vase, Regina, Black Base & Interior, Multicolored, 8 1/2 In.	140.00

 Graniteware is an enameled tinware that has been used in the kitchen from the late nineteenth century to the present. Earlier graniteware was green or turquoise blue, with white spatters. The later ware was gray with white spatters. Reproductions are being made in all colors.

GRANITEWARE, Beaker, Mormon, Utah, 1850 .... 100.00
  Bedpan, Cover, Speckled Gray & White 30.00
  Bedpan, Hospital, Blue 90.00
  Bowl, Green & White, 8 In. 78.00
  Bowl, Red, 6 In. 15.00
  Bucket & Strainer, Majestic, Brown 60.00
  Bucket, Brown & White Swirl, Bail, Wooden Turned Handle, 2 Gal. 38.00
  Bucket, Gray, Bail Handle 18.00
  Butter, Cover, Cream, Round 145.00
  Butter, Cover, White, Round 125.00
  Cake Pan, Angel Food, Blue & White 55.00
  Cake Pan, Blue & White, 8 Sides, Mottled 135.00
  Cake Pan, Blue & White, Handles, 9 X 12 In. 25.00
  Can, Cream, Brown 25.00
  Canister Set, Aqua, 4 Piece 140.00
  Coffee Boiler, Blue & White Swirl .... 80.00 To 87.50
  Coffee Boiler, Columbian Swirl, Blue 95.00
  Coffee Boiler, Gray, Bail Handle, Large 35.00
  Coffee Boiler, Turquoise, Speckled, Cobalt Blue Handle 40.00
  Coffeepot, Blue & White, Large .... 50.00 To 85.00
  Coffeepot, Blue Delft Design, Windmill, White, 8 1/2 In. 85.00
  Coffeepot, Buff, Green 12.50
  Coffeepot, Flamingo–Type Bird, White, Pewter Handle 195.00
  Coffeepot, Gray, Wire Handle, Side Pouring Handle, Large 25.00
  Coffeepot, Green & White Swirl, 10 In. 165.00
  Coffeepot, Lighthouse, Pewter Band, Scalloped Top 198.00
  Coffeepot, Red, Gooseneck 300.00
  Coffeepot, Sky Blue, 4 Cup 50.00
  Coffeepot, Stork, Rushes, Short Spout, Straight Sides, 11 In. 198.00
  Coffeepot, White Ground, Castle Scene, Pewter Scalloped Top 198.00
  Coffeepot, White Ground, Colored Foliage, Pewter Band 197.00
  Coffeepot, White, 4 Cup 30.00
  Coffeepot, White, Chateau Scene, Pewter Handle 250.00
  Colander, Blue & White 55.00
  Colander, Blue & White Swirl 68.00
  Colander, Blue & White, Handle 85.00
  Colander, Gray.Handleless, Holes In Bottom Only 47.00
  Colander, Mottled Brown 35.00
  Colander, White, Red Trim, Footed 22.50
  Cup, Gray 12.00
  Cup, Green & White Swirl, 3 1/2 In. 42.00
  Cup, Green & White, 3 1/2 In. 35.00
  Cup, Turquoise Swirl 12.00
  Cup, Yellow 10.00
  Dishpan, Blue Swirl 38.00
  Dishpan, Cream, Green Trim 40.00
  Dishpan, Gray, Rectangular 75.00
  Dough Bowl, Blue, Large 30.00
  Dough Riser, Cover, Blue & White 125.00
  Dough Riser, Tin Cover, Blue & White Mottled 295.00
  Egg Poacher, Mottled Gray 58.00
  Eggcup, Blue 34.00
  Feeding Dish, Child's, Nursery Rhyme, Green, Ivory 54.00
  Fish Poacher, Gray 95.00
  Flask, Gray, 1917 .... 35.00
  Flask, Hip, Blue, Large 60.00
  Font, Holy Water, Blue, 2 Piece 250.00

Funnel, Blue & White 45.00
Funnel, Elliptical, Gray 38.00
Funnel, Gray, Short Spout, 3 3/4 In. 40.00
Grater, Blue 48.00
Hot Plate, Electric, Green Spatter 150.00
Kettle, Preserving, Cover, Wire Handle, Mottled Blue, 6 Qt. 55.00
Ladle, Blue & White Enameled 16.00
Ladle, Cobalt Blue Swirl 45.00
Ladle, Gray, 14 In. 10.00
Lunch Box, Cup Top, Bail Handle 35.00
Measure, Gray, 1 Pt. 95.00
Measure, Gray, 1 Qt. 75.00
Milk Pail, White & Black, Wire Handle, Lock Top, 9 In. 32.00
Milk Pan, Blue & White 42.00
Mixing Bowl, Red & White Swirl, 7 In. 75.00
Mold, Jell-O, Buff, Green, Cream City Ware, Milwaukee, Oval, 12 In 50.00
Muffin Pan, Dark Blue, 8 Cup 25.00
Muffin Pan, Gray, 8 Cup 15.00
Muffin Pan, Turk's Head, 6 Hole, Gray 75.00
Muffin Pan, Turk's Head, 8 Hole, Gray 55.00
Pail, Tin Lid, Mottled Gray, 6 1/2 In. .... 45.00 To 65.00
Pan, Double Boiler, Green, Small 100.00
Pan, Jelly Roll, Blue Swirl 28.00
Pie Plate, Gray .... 6.50 To 10.00
Pitcher, Milk, Painted Vines & Flowers, White Shaded To Blue 35.00
Pitcher, Water, Gray, Ice Lip, 11 In. 38.00
Plate, Colored Scene of Child Picking Apples, Germany, 7 In. 55.00
Plate, Fish, Blue & White 135.00
Platter, Cobalt Blue Swirl, Oval, 14 In. 120.00
Potty, Cobalt Blue 180.00
Potty, Gray, Cover 45.00
Potty, White 20.00
Rack, Utensil, Shaded Orange, 3 Utensils 145.00
Rack, Utensil, White, 3 Utensils 85.00
Rack, Wall, Gray 135.00
Roaster, Blue & White, 6 1/2 X 13 In. 42.50
Roaster, Cobalt Blue Speckled, Label, 18 X 13 X 9 In. 50.00
Roaster, Gray, Nesco 27.50
Roaster, Green, Large 250.00
Roaster, Inside Tray, Oval, Blue & White 55.00
Salt Box, White 50.00
Saucepan, Blue, Cover, Heart Shape 135.00
Saucer, Blue & White 49.00
Scoop, White, Marked Bavaria, 3 In. 95.00
Soap Dish, Strainer, Cobalt Blue & White 60.00
Spatula, Mottled Gray 85.00
Spittoon, Blue 58.00
Spittoon, Blue & White Swirl 165.00
Spittoon, Green, Black Trim, 2 Piece 30.00
Spittoon, United States Stamping Co., West Virginia, Sample 750.00
Spittoon, Woman's, Blue 45.00
Strainer, Handle, Blue & White 50.00
Sugar & Creamer, Blue, White Speckled 35.00
Sugar, Blue & White, Checkered 225.00
Syrup, Brown, Pewter Trim, Dated 1872 .... 125.00
Tea Set, Child's, White, Red Flowers, Green Trim, 10 Piece 165.00
Tea Strainer, Sky Blue 35.00
Teakettle, Blue & White, Gooseneck 75.00
Teakettle, Cookstove, Red 68.00
Teakettle, Gray, Squatty, Label 65.00
Teakettle, Solid Cobalt Blue 12.00
Teapot, Child's, Flower Design In Band, Black & White, Elite 100.00
Teapot, Fastener In Spout, Gray, Flat 62.50
Teapot, Gray, 8 In. 42.00

Teapot, Gray, Pewter Trim	250.00
Teapot, Manning–Bowman, Pewter Trim	110.00
Teapot, Nickel Plated Cover, Flower Design, Metal Thumb Rest	160.00
Teapot, Turquoise	95.00
Teapot, White, 1 Cup	20.00
Tray, Gray, Oval, 10 X 12 In.	45.00
Tray, Gray, Square, 12 In.	115.00
Tray, Refrigerator, White, Black	7.00
Washboard, Cobalt Blue	45.00 To 110.00
Washboard, Dovetailed Wooden Frame	285.00

 Greentown glass was made by the Indiana Tumbler and Goblet Company of Greentown, Indiana, from 1894 to 1903. In 1899, the factory name was changed to National Glass Company. A variety of pressed, milk, and chocolate glass was made.

GREENTOWN, see also Chocolate Glass; Custard Glass; Holly Amber; Milk Glass; Pressed Glass

GREENTOWN, Bowl, 6 Flutes, Chocolate	160.00
Bowl, Cord Drapery, Green, Fluted	75.00
Butter, Austrian, Canary	275.00
Butter, Cover, Chrysanthemum, Gold Trim	165.00
Butter, Cover, Cord Drapery	65.00
Butter, Cover, Dewey, Canary	80.00
Butter, Cover, Leaf Bracket	50.00
Cake Stand, Herringbone Buttress	190.00
Cake Stand, Shuttle, 10 1/4 In.	115.00
Compote, Austrian	75.00
Compote, Cover, Cord Drapery, 4 1/4 In.	55.00
Compote, Jelly, Ruby Edge	25.00
Compote, Teardrop & Tassel	275.00
Creamer, Overall Lattice	23.00
Creamer, Teardrop & Tassel	100.00
Cruet, Dewey, Amber	125.00 To 145.00
Cruet, Dewey, Vaseline	165.00
Cruet, Serenade	85.00
Cup, Open Lattice, Ruby Edge, Pedestal	30.00
Custard, Serenade	75.00
Dish, Cat In Hamper Cover	125.00 To 250.00
Dish, Dewey, Amber, Round Ribbed Base	230.00
Dish, Hen On Nest Cover, Amber	135.00
Dish, Hen On Nest Cover, Green	165.00
Dish, Pickle, Cord Drapery, Amber	90.00
Dish, Rabbit Cover, Amber	135.00
Lamp, Oil, Sultan Font, Chocolate Glass Base, 9 In.	550.00
Mug, Serenade, Blue	30.00
Pitcher, Austrian, Canary	110.00
Pitcher, Dewey, Amber	85.00
Pitcher, Diamond Prism	250.00
Pitcher, Diamond, Gold Flashed	55.00
Pitcher, Heron	450.00
Pitcher, Ruffled Eye, Amber	100.00
Pitcher, Teardrop & Tassel	62.00
Pitcher, Water, Cord Drapery, Green	135.00
Pitcher, Water, Deer & Oak Tree	100.00
Pitcher, Water, Teardrop & Tassel	55.00
Plate, Pattern Ll, Square	55.00
Plate, Serenade, Milk Glass	55.00
Punch Cup, Austrian	16.00
Punch Cup, Shuttle	10.00
Relish, Dewey, Amber	38.00
Relish, Dewey, Serpentine, Amber	38.00
Salt, Wheelbarrow, Chartreuse	225.00
Saltshaker, Pleat Band, Blue	50.00
Saltshaker, Pleat Band, Crystal	18.00

Sauce, Austrian, Red Paint, Gold Flashed	65.00
Sauce, Herringbone Buttress	37.50
Sauce, Strawberry	495.00
Sauce, Teardrop & Tassel, Blue	32.50
Stein, Indoor Drinking Scene, Green, 5 In.	145.00
Stein, Outdoor Drinking Scene, Nile Green, 4 3/8 In.	135.00
Sugar, Brazen Shield	47.50
Toothpick, Amber	245.00
Tumbler, Austrian	35.00
Tumbler, Austrian, Topaz	235.00
Tumbler, Cattails & Water Lily	250.00
Tumbler, Dewey, Amber	45.00
Tumbler, Dewey, Vaseline	30.00
Tumbler, Teardrop & Tassel, Nile Green	275.00
Wheelbarrow, Nile Green	75.00
Wine, Shuttle	28.00
Wine, Shuttle, Small	10.00

Grueby Faience Company of Boston, Massachusetts, was incorporated in 1897 by William H. Grueby. Garden statuary, art pottery, and architectural tiles were made until 1920. The company developed a matte green glaze that was so popular it was copied by many other factories making a less expensive type of pottery. This eventually led to the financial problems of the pottery.

GRUEBY, Bowl, Pinched Rim, Matte Green Leaves, Signed, C.1905, 5 3/4 In.	525.00
Tile, 2 Geese Intertwined Under Trees, Square, 4 In.	365.00
Tile, Landscape Design, Artist M.D., Label, 1905, 6 In.	875.00
Tile, Spanish Galleon, Full Sail, Signed, C.1905, 8 In.	467.50
Tile, Stylized Figure, Brick Red Ground, C.1910, 6 In.	115.00
Vase, 3 Leaves, Dark Green, Signed, 8 In.	1600.00
Vase, Broad Leaves Alternating With Buds, C.1905, 4 1/2 In.	475.00
Vase, Bud, Pale Blue, C.1910, Marked, 4 In.	225.00
Vase, Buds Alternating, Leaves, Long Neck, Bulbous, 1905, 7 5/8 In.	1800.00
Vase, Divided By Vertical Lines, Marked, C.1905, 5 In.	225.00
Vase, Flared Rim, Bulbous Form, Overlapping Leaves, 1905, 9 In.	600.00
Vase, Flared Rim, Green Matte Glaze, Marked, C.1910, 5 In.	195.00
Vase, Green Glaze, Compressed Form, 6 In.	385.00
Vase, Impressed Lines & Leaves, 18 In.	9000.00
Vase, Leaves & Floral Buds, Yellow Glaze, Stamped, 7 1/2 In.	1695.00
Vase, Leaves About Body, Florals At Neck, Stamped, 7 In.	3870.00
Vase, Leaves On Angled Shoulder, C.1906, 12 3/4 In.	3600.00
Vase, Relief of Leaves, Stamped, Artist E.R., 10 In.	1455.00
Vase, Spherical, Short Neck, Paper Label, C.1905, 4 1/2 In.	525.00
Vase, Vase, 9 Leaves On Angled Shoulder, RE, 1904, 12 3/4 In.	8000.00
Vase, Vertical Stems & Arches, Marked, C.1905, 7 3/4 In.	775.00

Included in this category are shotguns, pistols, and other antique firearms. Rifles are listed in their own section. Be very careful when buying or selling guns because there are special laws governing the sale and ownership. A collector's gun should be displayed in a safe manner, probably with the barrel filled or a part missing to be sure it cannot be accidentally fired.

GUN, BB, Daisy, Buzz Barton	100.00
BB, Daisy, Buzz Barton No.103, 1000 Shot	85.00
BB, Daisy, Model H	100.00
BB, Daisy, No. 26	70.00
BB, Daisy, No. 36	35.00
BB, Daisy, No. 96	45.00
BB, Daisy, No.101, Model 35	37.00
BB, Daisy, No.102	75.00
BB, Daisy, No.111, Red Ryder	75.00
BB, Daisy, Red Ryder, Model 1938	25.00
BB, Daisy, Red Ryder, Wooden Stock	35.00
BB, Daisy, Scope	20.00

BB, Hellapin, 1893	250.00
BB, King	215.00
Blunderbuss, Flintlock, Grenade Launcher, Dutch, C.1780	3575.00
Line Throwing, Shoulder Type, Harrington & Richardson Arms Co., 1900	475.00
Missile, Red Fox, Hubley, Box	150.00
Musket, Cap & Ball, British Army	450.00
Musket, Flintlock, J.P. Moore, Walnut Full Stock, 56 In.	425.00
Musket, Flintlock, U.S. Federal Contract	3520.00
Nambu, 8 Mm, Japanese, World War II	175.00
Pellet, Winchester, Split Shot, Paper Tubes	65.00
Percussion, Allen Patented Bar Hammer	235.00
Percussion, Belgium, Boot	235.00
Pistol, Air, Daisy, No.118, Targeteer	25.00
Pistol, American Arms Co., Patent Oct. 31, 1866	275.00
Pistol, Army, Springfield Armory, 5 In. Barrel, 1911	800.00
Pistol, Blunderbuss, Walnut, 3/4 Stock With Checkered Wrist, 7 1/2 In.	2400.00
Pistol, Cap & Ball, 41 Caliber, Bone Handle	45.00
Pistol, Cutlass, Elgin, Navy's South Sea Expedition, 1838–43	6600.00
Pistol, CVA, Navy, Muzzle Loading, 36 Caliber, Box	75.00
Pistol, Derringer, National Arms, Civil War, 1863	325.00
Pistol, Double Barrel Flintlock, Engraved Steel, 14 In.	500.00
Pistol, Dunhill Tinder	75.00
Pistol, Luger, American Eagle, Marked Germany	1705.00
Pistol, Mauser, Broom Handled, Serrated Wooden Grips	1540.00
Pistol, Morgan & Clapp, New Haven, Conn.	225.00
Pistol, Navy, Luger, 1906	1925.00
Pistol, Pellet, Hyscore	175.00
Pistol, Pump Air, Benjamin Franklin, No.130, 1930s	130.00
Pistol, Remington, Civil War, Box of Shells	895.00
Pistol, Smith & Wesson, Model 27, Engraved, Pair	6600.00
Pistol, Smith & Wesson, Pocket	260.00
Revolver, Ruger Bearcat, 22 Caliber	125.00
Revolver, Smith & Wesson, No.1 1/2, Civil War, Rosewood Grips	90.00
Revolver, Smith & Wesson, Presentation, Pearl Finish, 10 In.Barrel	3080.00
Shotgun, Double Barrel Percussion, Engraved Steel Plate, 52 In.	250.00
Shotgun, Double Barrel, Muzzle Loading, 410 Gauge	325.00
Shotgun, Ithaca, 20 Gauge, Double Barrel, Hammerless Damascus Barrel	175.00
Shotgun, Parker Brothers, 12 Gauge, Engraved Hunting Dogs & Plumage	900.00
Shotgun, Remington Ringmaster, Model 870, 12 Gauge	215.00
Shotgun, Savage No.410, Over & Under	200.00
Shotgun, Westley Richard, Over Under, 27 5/8 In. Barrel	3960.00
Skeet, Air, Daisy, Unused, 1960	100.00
Skeet, Black Powder, 12 Gauge, Motteram & Sons, English	90.00
Split Shot, Daisy, Winchester, In Paper Tube	120.00
Winchester, Pellet, Model 423	115.00

Gunderson glass was made at the Gunderson–Pairpoint Glass Works of New Bedford, Massachusetts, from 1952 to 1957. Gunderson Peachblow is especially famous.

GUNDERSON, Powder Box, Peachblow, Finial On Lid, Brass Bindings, 7 In.	250.00
Toothpick, Peachblow, Fluted, 2 In.	125.00
Tumbler, Peachblow, 3 1/2 In.	125.00
Vase, Peachblow, Crimped, 6 1/2 In.	135.00

The Gustavsberg ceramics factory was founded in 1827 near Stockholm, Sweden. It is best known to collectors for its twentieth-century art wares, especially a green stoneware with silver inlay.

GUSTAVSBERG, Bowl, Inverted Bell Form, Geometric Design, 8 In. ....*Illus*	325.00
Charger, 3 Concentric Rings, Mermaid, Fish, 1935, 13 3/8 In.	825.00
Charger, Dragon, Silver Bands In Rim, C.1935, 12 3/8 In.	1550.00
Charger, School of Fish Amid Bubbles, C.1935, 14 1/2 In.	865.00
Plate, Geometric Grid, Maiden In Grasses, 1935, 8 1/2 In., Pair	615.00
Tray, Steamship, Swedish American Line, Silver Overlay, 6 In.	55.00
Vase, 2 Swimming Fish, Bubbles, Sea Green, C.1935, 6 3/4 In.	1320.00

Vase, Floral Bouquet, Sea Green, Silver Overlay, 1935, 6 In. 360.00
Vase, Frolicking Mermaid, Eel, Sea Green, C.1935, 7 7/8 In. 1765.00
Vase, Mottled Green, Silver Overlay, Argenta, Square, 2 In. 350.00
Vase, White Flowers, Black Glaze, Dated 1907 .... 350.00

Gutta-percha was one of the first plastic materials. It was made from a mixture of resins from Malaysian trees. It was molded and used for daguerreotype cases, toilet articles, and picture frames in the nineteenth century.

GUTTA–PERCHA, Case, Cannon, Cannonballs, 13–Star U.S. Flag, 2 1/2 X 3 In. 50.00
Case, Photograph, Brown, 1890s Man, Mustache, Screw–On Top 65.00
Crucifix, Nickel Silver, Civil War, 3 In. 45.00
Snuffbox, Shoe Shape 85.00

Haeger Potteries, Inc., Dundee, Illinois, started making commercial art wares in 1914. Early pieces were marked with the name "Haeger" written over an "H." About 1938, the mark "Royal Haeger" was used. The firm is still making florist wares and lamp bases.

HAEGER, Ewer, Orange Fusing, Black Ground, Signed, 18 3/4 In. 95.00
Figurine, Swan, Label, 8 In. 8.00
Planter, Figural, Rooster, 13 1/4 In. 35.00

Hall China Company started in East Liverpool, Ohio, in 1903. The firm made all types of wares. Collectors search for the Hall teapots made from the 1920s to the 1950s. The dinnerwares of the same period, especially Autumn Leaf pattern, are also popular. The Hall China Company is still working. Autumn Leaf pattern dishes are listed in their own category in this book.

HALL, Bean Pot, Blue Blossom, No.4 .... 125.00
Bowl Set, Gold Label, Box, 3 Piece 60.00
Bowl, Blossom, Blue, 6 In. 30.00
Bowl, Butterfly, White, Gold Trim 50.00
Bowl, Cover, Red Poppy, 5 1/2 In. 12.00
Bowl, Orchid, Pink Base, Light Yellow Top, Paper Label, 9 1/2 In. 120.00
Bowl, Vegetable, Cover, Jewel Tea 45.00
Butter, Crocus, Zephyr, 1 Lb. 575.00
Butter, Yellow, Westinghouse 20.00
Candy Container, Urn Shape, Butterfly, White, Gold Trim 30.00
Casserole, Blue & Gold Stars 16.00
Casserole, Corn King 40.00
Casserole, Cover, Rose White 36.00
Casserole, Goldspot, Handle 25.00
Casserole, Jewel Tea .... 25.00 To 40.00
Casserole, Red Poppy 18.00
Casserole, Tulip, Big Lip, Sunken Handle 28.00
Casserole, White Rose 18.00
Casserole, Yellow Rose 18.00
Child's Set, Eva Ziesel, 12 Piece 65.00
Coffeepot, Crocus 30.00
Coffeepot, Globe, Dripless, Gray, Gold Trim 45.00
Coffeepot, Jewel Tea 250.00
Coffeepot, Norse 35.00
Cookie Jar, Blossom Sundial, Blue 215.00
Cookie Jar, Cookie Time 45.00
Cookie Jar, Gold Label, Box 60.00
Cookie Jar, Orange Poppy, Pretzel Handle 48.00
Cookie Jar, Windshield 18.00
Creamer, Bopeep, Child's 32.50
Creamer, Lipton, Black 7.50
Creamer, Rose Parade 8.50
Cup & Saucer, Crocus 13.00
Custard, Yellow Rose 4.00

Dish, Cover, Red Poppy, 5 1/2 In.	17.00
Dish, Refrigerator, Cover, Yellow, Large	27.00
Drip–O–Lator, Rounded Terrace, Large	30.00
Drip–O–Lator, Target	22.00
Ewer, Butterfly, White, Pink, 13 1/2 In.	110.00
Grill Plate, Cattail	10.00
Jar, Pretzel, Monk	75.00
Jar, Zeisel, Gold Label, Yellow	70.00
Leftover, Hotpoint, Square, Green Luster	20.00
Mixing Bowl, Yellow Rose, 9 In.	10.00
Mug, Crocus	20.00
Mug, Monk Flagon, 10 Oz., 6 Piece	175.00
Pitcher, Chinese Red, 5 In.	20.00
Pitcher, Cover, Petit Point Rose	23.00
Pitcher, Norris, Turquoise	30.00
Pitcher, Radiance, Red Poppy	16.00
Pitcher, Utility, Red, 5 1/2 In.	14.00
Plate, American Airlines, Hand Painted, 4 1/16 In.	18.00
Plate, Crocus, 9 In.	13.00
Punch Set, Old Crow, 12 Piece	155.00
Salt & Pepper, Rose Parade	30.00
Salt & Pepper, Yellow Rose	18.00
Soup, Cream, Bird Nest, Paper Label	25.00
Soup, Onion, Yellow Rose	22.00
Spittoon, Green, White	25.00
Stack Set, Jewel Tea, 4 Piece	65.00
Sugar, Cover, Jewel Tea	9.00
Sugar, Cover, Serenade, Pink	35.00
Tea Set, Hollywood, Maroon, 7 Piece	22.50
Teapot, Aladdin, Infuser, Dark Green, Gold Trim	40.00
Teapot, Aladdin, Morning Glory	45.00
Teapot, Aladdin, Yellow, Gold Trim, Infuser, 6 Cup	30.00
Teapot, Alma, Navy	45.00
Teapot, Art Deco Pattern, Gold Trim, Brown	80.00
Teapot, Automobile, Cobalt Blue & Platinum	475.00
Teapot, Birdcage, Maroon & Gold	195.00
Teapot, Birdcage, Red	350.00
Teapot, Boston, Blue, Gold, 6 Cup	21.50
Teapot, Boston, Crocus, Metal Lid & Dripper	65.00
Teapot, Doughnut, Indian Red	250.00
Teapot, Doughnut, Orange Poppy	155.00
Teapot, French, Maroon, Gold	9.00
Teapot, Globe, Dripless, Blue & Gold	68.00
Teapot, Globe, Dripless, Yellow Gold	55.00
Teapot, Gold Flowers, Cobalt Blue	35.00
Teapot, Gray, Gold Trim	45.00
Teapot, Hollywood, Pink, 8 Cup	25.00
Teapot, Hook, Cover, Blue, Gold	25.00
Teapot, Hook, Cover, Chinese Red	47.00
Teapot, Ivory, Gold Decal	18.00
Teapot, Jewel Tea, Insert	46.00
Teapot, Lipton, Maroon	35.00
Teapot, Medallion	26.50
Teapot, Nautilus, Cobalt Blue	100.00
Teapot, New York, Gold Trim, 2 Cup	30.00
Teapot, New York, Green	12.00
Teapot, New York, Lattice & Flowers	78.00
Teapot, New York, Pink, Gold Flowers	18.00
Teapot, Norse, Yellow Rose	40.00
Teapot, Parade, Canary	22.50 To 25.00
Teapot, Philadelphia, Delphinium, Gold	30.00
Teapot, Rhythm, Cobalt	75.00
Teapot, Ronald Reagan	35.00 To 65.00
Teapot, Rose Parade	45.00

Teapot, Rose, Dripless 85.00
Teapot, Rutherford, Red Dot On White Eggshell 50.00
Teapot, Salada, Green, 6 Cup 30.00
Teapot, Serenade, Pink 90.00
Teapot, Streamline, Blue Blossom 125.00
Teapot, Streamline, Orange Poppy 75.00
Teapot, Streamline, Taverne 85.00
Teapot, Sundial, Yellow 42.00
Teapot, Surfside, Yellow & Gold Design 75.00
Teapot, Teataster, Cadet Blue 58.00
Teapot, World's Fair, 1939 .... 295.00
Teapot, Zeisel, Tri–Tone 79.50
Tray, Jewel Tea, Tin, Oval 55.00
Tumbler, Red Poppy 8.00
Vase, Butterfly, White, Gold Trim 30.00
Vase, Cornucopia, Woodland, Light Green Base, Yellow Top, 6 1/2 In. 50.00
Vase, Magnolia, Blue, Green, Pink Top, Pale Yellow, 12 1/2 In. 135.00
Vase, Magnolia, Pale Blue Base, Pink Top, 4 3/4 In. 35.00
Vase, Magnolia, Pale Blue Base, Pink Top, 8 1/2 In. 85.00
Vase, Open Rose, Blue, Green Base, Pink Top, 8 1/2 In. 90.00
Vase, Wildflower, Light Blue Base, Pink Top, 9 1/2 In. 75.00
Window Box, Butterfly, White, Gold Trim 35.00

Halloween is an ancient holiday that has been changed in the last 200 years. The jack–o'–lantern, witches on broomsticks, and orange decorations seem to be twentieth–century creations. Collectors started to become serious about collecting Halloween–related items in the late 1970s. The papier–mache decorations, now replaced by plastic, and old costumes are in demand.

HALLOWEEN, Candle, Cat In Witch's Costume, Black & Orange, 4 In. 5.00
   Candle, Cat, Label, Small 8.80
   Candy Container, Black Cat, Pumpkin Creature On Back, 4 1/2 In. 200.00
   Candy Container, Jack–O'–Lantern, 2 1/2 In. 22.00
   Candy Container, Jack–O'–Lantern, E & A, No.349 .... 85.00
   Candy Container, Jack–O'–Lantern, Slant Eyes, Blue Tint, No Bail 100.00
   Candy Container, Jack–O'–Lantern, Slanted Eyes, Original Bail 200.00
   Candy Container, Mr. Pumpkin–Policeman, On Box, 4 1/2 In. 165.00
   Candy Container, Pipe & Horn, Mouthpiece Pumpkin Faces, Germany 38.00
   Candy Container, Standing Cat, Germany 175.00
   Candy Container, Witch, Red Dress, Black Hat, Broom, Germany, 4 In. 195.00
   Cat, Black, Grinning, Pumpkin Critter On Back, 4 In. 140.00
   Cat, Black, Papier–Mache, 20 In. 30.00
   Cat, Black, Winking, On Honeycomb Pumpkin 10.00
   Clacker, Cat, Scary, Pan Shape, Wood 12.00
   Clacker, Head of Black Cat, Crepe Trim, Wood, German 78.00
   Cookie Cutter, Pumpkin, Inset Eyes & Mouth, Brass, 4 X 2 7/8 In. 150.00
   Costume, Annie Oakley, Dress & Vest 60.00
   Costume, Aquaman Cap'T Action Suit, Ideal 85.00
   Costume, Archie, Ben Cooper, 1969 .... 15.00
   Costume, Bat Masterson, Ben Cooper 85.00
   Costume, Bewitched, Box 45.00
   Costume, Bride, Cooper, Box 9.00
   Costume, Cap'T America Action Suit, Ideal 85.00
   Costume, Casper The Ghost, Box 15.00
   Costume, Clown, Child's, 1920s 30.00
   Costume, Dale Evans, Queen of The West, Box 110.00
   Costume, Dracula, Box, 1964 .... 95.00
   Costume, Elephant, Gray, Orange Ruffles, Box 25.00
   Costume, Farmer Alfalfa, Box 22.00
   Costume, Flintstones, 1973 .... 25.00
   Costume, Flipper, Cooper, 1964, Box 48.00
   Costume, Frankenstein, Box 15.00
   Costume, G.I. Joe, Soldier, Box, 1964 .... 65.00
   Costume, Girl From U.N.C.L.E., Box 100.00

Costume, Indian, Leggings, Shirt & Headband 45.00
Costume, Johnny Astro, Helco 30.00
Costume, Lucy & Peanuts, Hanna Barbera, Box, 1966 .... 15.00
Costume, Mr. Ed 40.00
Costume, Mr. Spock, 1976 .... 45.00
Costume, Old–Fashioned Girl, 1930s 12.00
Costume, Phantom Cap'T Action Suit, Ideal 85.00
Costume, Popeye 95.00
Costume, Snoopy, Box 15.00
Costume, Tonto, Box, 1950 .... 130.00
Costume, Witch, Box, 1920–30s 12.00
Costume, Wolfman, Box 15.00
Costume, Woman's, Dress, Moon Face On Chest, Cat On Skirt, 1920s 100.00
Doll, Pumpkin, Black Felt Hat, Dungarees, 1970s 14.00
Game, Crystal Fortunes 9.00
Game, Pie, Stunt & Fortune, Orange & Brown 8.00
Horn, Blowout, Cat, Dennison, 1940s 22.00
Horn, Party, Porcelain Mouthpiece 15.00
Jack–O'–Lantern, Accordion, Orange Papier–Mache, Germany, 10 In. 210.00
Jack–O'–Lantern, Black Cutout, Orange Tissue, 4 Sides, 2 X 6 In. 54.00
Jack–O'–Lantern, Built–In Light, Papier–Mache, 1940s 45.00
Jack–O'–Lantern, Cat Face, Papier–Mache 10.00
Jack–O'–Lantern, Inset Face, Papier–Mache, 5 In. 48.00
Jack–O'–Lantern, Mr. Pickle's Pumpkin Accordion, Pumpkin Head 420.00
Jack–O'–Lantern, Orange, Original Insert, 5 In. 27.00
Jack–O'–Lantern, Orange, Wire Bail, Pulp, 4 In. 27.00
Jack–O'–Lantern, Papier–Mache, 4 1/2 In. 47.50
Jack–O'–Lantern, Papier–Mache, 6 1/2 In. 55.00
Jack–O'–Lantern, Watermelon, Red Nose, Wire Bail, Germany 350.00
Lantern, Accordion, Metal Candleholder, 13 In. 65.00
Lantern, Bats Over Moon 85.00
Lantern, Cat, Cardboard 68.00
Lantern, Cat, Germany 85.00
Lantern, Cat, Gray Tones, Orange Eyes 58.00
Lantern, Cats 85.00
Lantern, Devils 85.00
Lantern, Orange Glass Top, Black Base, Battery 37.00
Lantern, Owl, Frosted Glass .... 32.00 To 35.00
Lantern, Pumpkin, Glass 45.00
Lantern, Pumpkins 85.00
Lantern, Skull, Milk Glass Head, Battery Operated, 4 1/2 In. 45.00
Lantern, Witches 85.00
Mask, Clown Face, Papier–Mache, 5 1/2 X 8 In. 45.00
Mask, Little Lulu 60.00
Noisemaker, 2 Wooden Clappers, Metal, Square 15.00
Noisemaker, 5 Girls Dancing & Singing, Metal, Wooden Handle 15.00
Noisemaker, Cats, Bars, Cylinder Shape, Wooden Handle 10.00
Noisemaker, Cats, Witches, Ghosts, Wooden Handle 10.00
Noisemaker, Clown & Dancing Girl, Metal, Wooden Handle 8.00
Noisemaker, Clowns Playing Drums, Metal 10.00
Noisemaker, Pipe, Wrapped In Jack–O'–Lantern Paper 55.00
Noisemaker, Racket Maker Inside, Saucer Shape, Round 6.00
Noisemaker, Scene of Children At Fair, 1928 .... 17.00
Noisemaker, Witch Cooking In Kettle, Frying Pan Shape, Metal 10.00
Noisemaker, Witch's Face, Orange & Black, Round, 4 1/2 In. 10.00
Noisemaker, Witch, Metal 10.00
Nut Cup, Jack–O'–Lantern, Papier–Mache 32.50
Nut Cup, Witch's Cauldron 6.00
Owl, Yellow Eyes, Dark Gray & Brown, 13 In. 60.00
Postcard Set, Children Playing, 5 Piece 20.00
Postcard Set, Children, Pumpkins, Black Cats, 6 Different Scenes 35.00
Postcard, Children At Party 5.00
Postcard, Girl, Pumpkin, Halloween, International Art, B. Wall 6.50
Postcard, Milkmaid, Frightened By Cow, Pumpkins On Horns, J. Bein 8.00

Postcard, Witch, Pumpkin Cauldron, Elf, Gibson Art Co. 4.50
Postcard, Woman & Man Bobbing For Apples, F. Lounsbury 7.50
Pumpkin Girl, Painted Bisque, Cotton Stuffed, 4 1/2 In. 33.00
Pumpkin, Black Face, Pressed Cardboard, Germany, 1930s .... 75.00 To 85.00
Pumpkin, Crepe Paper, Dennison 38.00
Rattle, Bell 5.00
Rattle, Chicken 5.00
Skeleton, Cardboard, 23 X 23 In. 12.00
Skeleton, Metal Riveted Joints, Cardboard, 23 X 23 In. 12.00
Sparkler, Plunger Type, Tin Lithograph, Chein, 1930s 85.00
Tambourine, Costumed Children Dancing Around Pumpkin, Tin 45.00
Tambourine, Orange, Arched Black Cat 28.00
Tambourine, Plain 15.00
Wall Decoration, Black, Green Eyes, 12 In. 10.00
Wall Decoration, Hobo Scarecrow, Crepe Arms, Jointed Neck, 30 In. 15.00
Wall Decoration, Mr.Bones 5.00
Witch & Rocket, Honeycomb Crepe Paper 18.00
Witch, Accordion, Printed Cardboard, 22 In. 28.00

Hampshire pottery was made in Keene, New Hampshire, between 1871 and 1923. Hampshire developed a line of colored glazed wares as early as 1883, including a Royal Worcester–type pink, olive green, blue, and mahogany. Pieces are marked with the printed mark or the impressed name "Hampshire Pottery" or "J.S.T. & Co., Keene, N.H." Many pieces wre marked with city names and sold as souvenirs.

HAMPSHIRE, Bowl, Mottled Green, 5 3/4 In. 55.00
Jar, Cover, Loop Handles, 9 X 10 In. 250.00
Lamp Base, Textured Blue Glaze, Metal Base, C.1910, 22 In. 440.00
Lamp, Lobed Sides, Dark Green Matte Glaze, 11 1/4 In., Pair 880.00
Pin Tray, Transfer, 6 3/4 In. 28.00
Pitcher, Transfer, 7 1/2 In. 45.00
Sugar & Creamer, Cover 45.00
Vase, Double Handled, Matte Green, 5 In. 125.00
Vase, Majolica Glaze, Molded Floral Design, 8 In. 125.00
Vase, Molded Leaves, Handle, 8 In. 85.00

Philip Handel worked in Meriden, Connecticut, from 1885 and in New York City from 1893 to 1933. His firm made art glass and other types of lamps. Handel shades were made not only of leaded glass in a style reminiscent of Tiffany but also of reverse painted glass. Handel also made vases and other glass objects.

HANDEL, Globe, Parrot In Branch, Signed, 10 In. ....*Illus* 3600.00
Humidor, Knobbed Cover, Smiling Monk On Front, Marked, 7 1/2 In. 550.00
Humidor, Moistener Band In Cover, Owl, Gilt Rim, Marked, 5 In. 412.50
Lamp, 3–Light, Green Slag Panels, Geometric Edge, Marked, 18 1/2 In. 1320.00
Lamp, Art Nouveau Ribbed Design, Boudoir Model 195.00
Lamp, Bamboo Domed Shade, Acid Cut, Signed Brown Handel, 18 In. 3520.00
Lamp, Birds, Trees, Domed Shade, Artist Signed 3200.00
Lamp, Boudoir, Blossoms, Birds On Branches, Domed Shade, 14 In. 1540.00
Lamp, Boudoir, Desert Caravan 2300.00
Lamp, Boudoir, Landscape, Lakes, Mountains, Conical Shade, 14 In. 1650.00
Lamp, Boudoir, Quince Blossoms, Leaves, Butterflies, Signed, 14 In. 1550.00
Lamp, Boudoir, Reverse Painted Landscape Shade, Signed, 14 In. 1985.00
Lamp, Boudoir, Reverse Painted Shade, Cottage, Trees, 7 In. 475.00
Lamp, Bridge Scene, Teroma Shade, Signed, 24 In. ....*Illus* 5500.00
Lamp, Buttercup, With Shade, No.6191, 14 In. 3800.00
Lamp, Desk, Bell Harp, Adjustable Swing Socket, Signed, 18 In. 445.00
Lamp, Desk, Filigree Metal Shade, Marked, C.1920, 18 3/8 In. 2090.00
Lamp, Desk, Moonlight, Reverse Painted Pine Forest Shade, Signed 1750.00
Lamp, Desk, Reverse Painted Scenic Shade, Bronze Base 1800.00
Lamp, Desk, Tropical Sunset Overlay 2800.00
Lamp, Electric, Reverse Painted Tropical Island Scene 850.00
Lamp, Finger, Oval, Miniature 2860.00

Lamp, Floral, No.2542 .... 250.00
Lamp, Hanging, Craquelle Parrot Shade 200.00
Lamp, Hanging, Domed Shade, 6 Panels of Yellow Slag, Filigree Frame 650.00
Lamp, Hemispherical Shade, Floral Borders, Circular Base, 13 7/8 In. 1320.00
Lamp, Marine Scenic, Sailboat, Palm Trees, Sunset Sky, 15 In. 5500.00
Lamp, Music, Adjustable, Metal Shade 850.00
Lamp, Pine Tree, Reverse Painted Shade, No.6517, 18 In. 3400.00
Lamp, Red Roses On Green Domed Shade, Patinated Base, 21 In. 2750.00
Lamp, Reverse Painted Roses, Yellow Ground, Signed, 15 In. 5800.00
Lamp, Reverse Painted Scenic Domed Shade, Signed, C.1920, 21 In. 2645.00
Lamp, Reverse Painted Shade, Band of Poppy Blossoms, Pods, 23 In. 5225.00
Lamp, Reverse Painted, Autumn Landscape, Patinated Base, 18 In. 9900.00
Lamp, Reverse Painted, Sun Setting, Trees, River, Domed Shade, 18 In. 3100.00
Lamp, Reverse Painted, Tree Trunk, Domed Landscape Shade, 16 In. 3850.00
Lamp, Reverse Painted, Windmills, Domed Shade, Bronze, 14 In. 2100.00
Lamp, Scenic Landscape, Teroma Shade, 3–Light, Signed, 21 In. 4400.00
Lamp, Table, 8–Sided Slag Shade 1900.00
Lamp, Table, Scenic Shade, No.6957, 18 In. 3600.00
Lamp, Tam–O–Shanter, Hand Painted Shade, Art Nouveau 325.00
Lamp, Teroma Chipped Ice Shade, No.1521, Signed, 14 In. 6000.00
Lamp, Tropical Seascape, Reverse Painted Scene, 2–Light, 22 In. 4125.00
Lamp, Tropical Sunset, Lagoon, Domed Shade, Signed, 23 1/2 In. 3850.00
Lamp, Winter Scene, Brown Tones, 16 In. Shade, 23 In. 5220.00
Lamp, Winter Scene, Snow, Stars, Signed, 23 In. 4500.00
Lamp, Wooded Landscape, Domed Shade, Signed, 18 In. ....*Illus* 5600.00
Lamp, Yellow Slag Glass Panels, Domed Shade, 14 In. 650.00
Light, Hall, Brown Vase, Foliate, Translucent White, 10 In. ....*Illus* 4100.00
Shade, Geometric Blue & White Leaded, 18 X 11 In. 1500.00
Shade, Inward Curving Lip, Daisies, Brown Leaves, Marked, 1925, 18 In. 8525.00
Shade, Wisteria Flowers, Foliage, Bamboo, Signed, 24 In. ....*Illus* 4300.00
Toothpick, Buffalo Head 95.00
Vase, Cameo Glass, Acid Etch, 11 1/8 In. 3775.00

Handel, Lamp, Bridge
Scene, Teroma Shade,
Signed, 24 In.

Handel, Lamp, Wooded
Landscape, Domed Shade,
Signed, 18 In.

Handel, Light, Hall,
Brown Vase, Foliate,
Translucent White, 10 In.

Handel, Globe, Parrot In Branch,
Signed, 10 In.

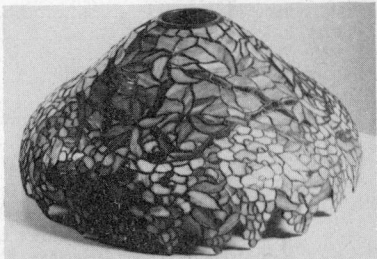

Handel, Shade, Wisteria Flowers, Foliage,
Bamboo, Signed, 24 In.

HARDWARE, see Architectural

Harker Pottery Company of East Liverpool, Ohio, was founded by Benjamin Harker in 1840. The company made many types of pottery but by the Civil War was making quantities of yellowware from native clays. They also made Rockingham–type brown–glazed pottery and whiteware. The plant was moved to Chester, West Virginia, in 1931. Dinnerwares were made and sold nationally. In 1971 the company was sold to Jeanette Glass Company and all operations ceased in 1972.

HARKER, Bean Pot, Floral, Individual	4.00
Cake Server, Amy	13.00
Casserole, Cover, Crazed	18.50
Jug, Batter, Cover, Cameoware	30.00
Mixing Bowl, Cherry, 9 In.	12.00
Pie Plate, Cameoware, 10 In.	20.00
Plate, Cameoware, 6 In.	2.00
Plate, Cameoware, 7 In.	3.00
Plate, Cameoware, 9 In.	6.00
Platter, Cameoware, 12 In.	15.00
Platter, Cameoware, 13 In.	24.00
Rolling Pin, Amy	60.00
Teapot, Cameoware	25.00

Harlequin dinnerware was produced by the Homer Laughlin Company from 1938 to 1964, and sold without trademark by the F.W. Woolworth Co. It has a concentric ring design like Fiesta, but the rings are separated from the rim by a plain margin. Cup handles are triangular in shape.

HARLEQUIN, Ashtray, Basket Weave, Turquoise	32.00
Butter, Cover, Yellow	12.00
Casserole, Cover, Rose	32.50
Casserole, Rose	75.00
Creamer, Maroon, Novelty	22.00
Creamer, Medium Green	22.00
Creamer, Spruce Green, Individual	11.00
Creamer, Turquoise, Novelty	7.00
Eggcup, Yellow	15.00
Figurine, Duck, Spruce	65.00
Figurine, Duck, Yellow, Gold Trim	50.00
Figurine, Fish, Yellow	65.00
Figurine, Maverick, Ivory, Blue Tuxedo Design	20.00
Figurine, Penguin, Yellow	65.00
Gravy Boat, Medium Green	42.00
Jug, Ball, Rose	20.00
Jug, Yellow, 22 Oz.	25.00
Mixing Bowl, Mauve, 8 In.	65.00
Nappy, Medium Green, 8 1/2 In.	45.00
Nut Dish, Yellow, 4 Piece	12.00
Pitcher, Water, Red	40.00
Plate, Spruce, Maroon, 9 In.	9.00
Platter, Rose, 11 In.	8.25
Platter, Yellow, 13 In.	8.25
Saucer Ashtray, Turquoise	35.00
Spoon Rest, Turquoise	85.00
Teapot, Chartreuse	55.00
Teapot, Mauve	60.00
Teapot, Spruce	75.00

Hatpins were fashionable from 1860 to 1920 when the large, heavy hat required special long–shanked pins to hold the hat in place. Naturally, hatpin holders were made during the same years. The hatpin holder resembles a large saltshaker, but it often has no opening at the bottom as a shaker does. Hatpin holders were made of all types of ceramics and metal. Look for other prices under the names of specific manufacturers.

HATPIN HOLDER, Art Deco 90.00
    Wide Rimmed Hat Shape, Gold Ribbon At Base, Cone Crown 110.00

Hatpins were popular from 1860 to 1920. The long pin, often over four inches, was used to hold the hat in place on the hair. The tops of the pins were made of all materials from solid gold and real gemstones to ceramics and glass. Be careful to buy original hatpins and not recent pieces made by altering old buttons.

HATPIN, 1–In. Jet Faceted Teardop, 11 In. 135.00
    Arrow, Pave Rhinestones 32.50
    Diamond Head Brass Filigree, Rhinestones, 12 In. 37.00
    Garnets, Gold Filled Bar 55.00
    Gold Club, Sterling Silver 28.00
    Marbelized, Rhinestones, Brown & Cream .... 35.00 To 53.00
    Rhinestone, Large, Pair 20.00
    Scarab, Brass .... 18.00 To 25.00
    Stylized Celluloid With Rhinestones, Suspended Blue Crystal 12.50
    Woman's Head, Art Nouveau, Sterling, Round, 1 In. 80.00
    Zircon, Blue Stone, Large 30.00

HAVILAND & CO.
Haviland china has been made in Limoges, France, since 1842. The factory was started by the Haviland Brothers of New York City. Pieces are marked H & Co., Haviland & Co., or Theodore Haviland. It is possible to match existing sets of dishes through dealers who specialize in Haviland china. Other factories worked in the town of Limoges making a similar chinaware. These porcelains are listed in this book under "Limoges."

HAVILAND, Bottle, Wine, Chantilly 50.00
    Bowl, Vegetable, Cover, Princess 35.00
    Charger, Blue Peacocks, Ireland, 13 1/2 In. 90.00
    Chocolate Set, Pink Roses, 11 1/4–In. Pot, 11 Piece 325.00
    Chocolate Set, Pink Roses, 11 1/4–In. Pot, 6 Piece 350.00
    Coffeepot, Pear Shape, White Porcelain 125.00
    Demitasse Set, Princess, 7 Piece 325.00
    Dinner Set, Bird of Paradise, Extra Pieces, Service For 12, C.1915 .... 2500.00
    Dish, Vegetable, Cover, Yale 35.00
    Eggcup, Baltimore Rose 45.00
    Game Platter, Marsh & Sky, Long–Necked Birds, 18 1/2 X 12 1/2 In. 450.00
    Gravy Boat, Autumn Leaf 35.00
    Oyster Plate, Allover Floral, Pink, Green, Scalloped, 3 Wells 55.00
    Oyster Plate, Seaweed & Fish, 5 Wells, Scalloped Rim, 8 3/4 In. 45.00
    Pancake Server, Baltimore Rose 135.00
    Pitcher, Sandoz Goose 165.00
    Platter, Pink Flowers On White, Gold Stalks, 11 1/4 In. 55.00
    Platter, Yellow Roses, Gold Trim, C.1890, 12 In. 75.00
    Sauce Boat, Attached Tray, Cover, Pink Roses 65.00
    Service For 12, Bavaria, 85 Piece 350.00
    Sign, Store, Theo. Haviland China, Made In America 150.00
    Sugar & Creamer, Autumn Leaf, Cover 40.00
    Tray, Scalloped, Flowers Around Rim, 1877 Mark, 12 1/2 X 8 1/2 In. 45.00
    Tureen, Chowder, Baltimore Rose 285.00
    Vase, Birds, Flowers, Lozenge Shape, 16 In., Pair ....*Illus* 3600.00

T. G. Hawkes & Company of Corning, New York, was founded in 1880. The firm cut glass blanks made at other glassworks until 1962. Many pieces are marked with the trademark, a trefoil ring enclosing a fleur–de–lis and two hawks. Cut glass by other manufacturers is listed under either the factory name or the general category "Cut Glass."

HAWKES, Basket, Panel Pattern, Clear Blank, 12 X 11 3/4 In. 5000.00

Bookends, Floral Intaglio, Hollow Shape, 7 X 6 6/7 In. 625.00
Bowl, 20 Bouquets In Panels, Bows Underneath, Notched, 8 1/2 In. 225.00
Bowl, Brunswick, 9 1/4 In. .... 425.00 To 450.00
Bowl, Chrysanthemum, 10 In. 825.00
Bowl, Chrysanthemum, Signed, 4 X 9 In. 575.00
Bowl, Crossed Ovals, Hobstars, Crosshatched, Diamonds, Low, 9 In. 210.00
Bowl, Cut Cobalt Blue & Crystal, Signed, 12 In. 500.00
Bowl, Grecian, 10 In. 650.00
Bowl, Grecian, 4 1/4 X 10 In. 1100.00
Bowl, Grecian, Signed, 8 3/4 In. 1400.00
Bowl, Madeline, Footed, Signed, 9 3/4 In. 900.00
Bowl, Nautilus, Signed, C.1896, 7 1/2 In. 1500.00
Bowl, Panel, Signed, 4 X 8 In. 2200.00
Bowl, Venetian, 3 X 8 In. 285.00
Candlestick, Gravic Iris, Teardrop Stem, Signed, 9 In. 495.00
Carafe, Gladys, Honeycomb Neck, Signed 160.00
Chamberstick, Signed, 3 X 5 1/2 In. 1250.00
Cocktail Server, Gold Trim, Signed, 8 1/2 In. 125.00
Cocktail Shaker, Foliate Garland, Sterling Silver Top, 19 In. 165.00
Cocktail Shaker, Sterling Top .... 140.00 To 195.00
Compote, Clear Cut Bowl, Birds, Sterling Silver Base, 7 1/2 In. 115.00
Compote, Rows of Step Cut Diamonds, Teardrop Stem, Signed, 6 1/8 In. 350.00
Cruet, Silver Top 60.00
Decanter Set, Signed, 4 Shot Glasses 550.00
Decanter, Brilliant, Oval Rose Stopper, Signed, 12 In. 335.00
Dish, Hatched Fan & Star Design, Signed, 9 In. 120.00
Dish, Ice Cream, Strawberries & Fans 50.00
Finger Bowl, Grecian, C.1887, 5 In., Pair 700.00
Flask, Harvard, Silver Holder 145.00
Ice Bucket, Etched, Sterling Handle & Mounts 295.00
Ice Tub, Cut Flowers, Bail Handle 175.00
Jam Jar, Underplate, Hand Painted Fruit 185.00
Lamp, Water, Grapevine With Leaves, Fruits, 11 1/2 In. 200.00
Loving Cup, Block Pattern, 10 In. 750.00
Nappy, 5 Large Hobstars, Rayed Star Bottom 95.00
Perfume Bottle, Sterling Cap, Lock & Key, 4 1/4 In. 85.00
Pitcher Set, Flower Pattern, 7 1/2 In., 5 Piece 295.00
Pitcher, Brunswick, 6 In. 450.00
Pitcher, Brunswick, Triple Notched Handle 425.00
Pitcher, Panel, Honeycomb Handle, Star Base, Signed, 7 3/4 In. 4750.00
Plate, Albany, Signed, 10 1/2 In. 975.00
Plate, Flowers & Leaves, 16 Point Star Center, 9 1/2 In. 95.00
Plate, Fruits & Leaves, 8 1/4 In. 40.00
Tray, 3 Leaf Clover, Hobstar, Salesman's Sample, Signed, 2 1/2 In. 125.00
Tray, Ice Cream, Devonshire, 9 X 13 In. 500.00
Tumbler, Brunswick, Signed, 3 3/4 In. 95.00
Tumbler, Hobstar, Diamond Point, Fan, Flared, 6 Piece 225.00
Tumbler, Queen, Signed 135.00
Vase, Brunswick, 12 In. 325.00
Vase, Copper Wheel of Grape Vines, Ovid Form, Signed, 11 In. 255.00
Vase, Coralene Design of Japanese Trees, Signed, 6 1/2 In. 215.00
Vase, Cut, Etched Flower Garlands, Gravic, Marked, 11 3/4 In. 255.00
Vase, Engraved Bird, Blue Flash, 10 In. 110.00
Vase, Fan, Crystal, Etched, Green Footed, 7 1/4 In. 185.00
Vase, Gravic Iris, Sterling Silver Base, 9 In. 275.00
Vase, Trumpet, Comet, Signed, 10 In. 450.00
Vase, Trumpet, Navarre, 16 1/2 In. 975.00
Water Set, Queen's, Signed, 7 Piece 1500.00
Whiskey Set, Geometric, Signed, 7 1/2 In., 5 Piece 935.00

Figural vases, generally showing a woman from the shoulders up,
were used by florists primarily in the 1950s and 1960s. Head vases,
made in a variety of sizes and often decorated with imitation jewelry

and other life–like accessories, were manufactured in Japan and the U.S. Less elaborate examples were made as early as the 1930s. Religious themes, babies, and animals are also common subjects.

HEAD VASE, African Woman, Turban, 5 1/4 In.	15.00
Amaco, 7 3/4 In.	155.00
Art Deco, Woman	9.00
Beckey, Ceramic Arts	50.00
Black Hair, Openwork Edge, Ruffled Sleeve, 1960, 8 1/2 In.	15.00
Black Native Man, Gold Trim	20.00
Black Picture Hat, Pink & White Frilled Bodice, Large	5.00
Blackamoor Man, Gray Turban	20.00
Blond, Eyes Shut, Green Dress, Hand Up, 4 1/2 In.	7.50
Brown Streaked Hair, Eyes Open, Green Dress, Bow On Shoulder, 7 In.	12.00
Brown Streaked Hair, Teal Dress, Pearl & White Brooch, 8 1/2 In.	14.00
Cupid, 5 In.	22.00
Golden Dogwood, Norcrest	50.00
Jamaican, Pair	35.00
Madonna	17.50
Mei–Ling	10.00
Pearl Earrings, Jade Brooch	18.00
Royal Copley	20.00
Tahitian Woman, Pair	37.50
Tony, Royal Copley	45.00
Woman, Black Dress & Hat	15.00
Woman, Brimmed Hat, White, Art Deco, USA, 9 X 8 1/2 In.	65.00
Woman, Gold Trim, Lefton	8.00
Woman, Grecian, Milk Glass, 5 In.	20.00
Woman, Oriental Luster, Large	14.00
Woman, Rose Covered Bonnet & Muff, Wall, 6 1/4 In.	15.00
Woman, Wall Pocket	30.00
Woman, Yellow Hat	15.00
Young Girl, With Umbrella	20.00

Heintz Art Metal shop made jewelry, copper, silver, and brass in Buffalo, New York, from 1906 to 1935. The most popular items with collectors today are the copper desk sets and vases made with applied silver designs.

HEINTZ ART, Box, Celtic Sterling Overlay, Green Patina	125.00
Desk Organizer, Compartments, Matchbox Holder, Silver On Bronze	70.00
Holder, Calendar, Silver On Bronze	50.00
Holder, Letter, Birds In Flight, Sterling On Bronze, 7 In.	85.00
Holder, Letter, Sterling Silver Deco	50.00
Inkwell, Double, Pen Tray, Sterling On Bronze, Marked	325.00
Urn, Bronze, Silver Overlay, 2 Handles, 8 1/4 In.	125.00

When repairing furniture, replace hardware nails. Keep track of nails and screws as they are removed, so each will be returned to the same hole. Often they are different sizes.

Heisey glass was made from 1896 to 1957 in Newark, Ohio, by A. H. Heisey and Co., Inc. The Imperial Glass Company of Bellaire, Ohio, bought some of the molds and the rights to the trademark. Some Heisey patterns have been made by Imperial since 1960. After 1968, they stopped using the "H" trademark. Heisey used romantic names for colors such as "Sahara." Do not confuse color and pattern names.

> When replacing lost hardware with matching new pieces, put the new handles on the lowest drawers. The difference in patina will be less visible.

HEISEY, see also Custard Glass; Ruby Glass

HEISEY, Adam, Wine, Pink, 3 1/2 Oz.	90.00 To 100.00
Albemarie, Champagne, Saucer, Chateau Cut	27.50
Albemarie, Goblet, Amber Bowl & Foot	14.00
Albemarle, Champagne, Cut Crystal	25.00
Albemarle, Cocktail, Oyster, Orchid Etch	37.00
Albemarle, Cup & Saucer, Orchid Etch	55.00
Albemarle, Sherbet, Low, Orchid Etch	25.00
Albemarle, Tumbler	10.00
Banded Flute, Champagne, Marked	20.00
Banded Flute, Jar, Mustard	35.00
Banded Flute, Plate, Marked, 5 In.	15.00
Banded Flute, Salt & Pepper	85.00
Beaded Panel & Sunburst, Cake Stand	110.00
Beaded Panel & Sunburst, Celery, Tall	47.50
Beaded Panel & Sunburst, Punch Bowl, Opalescent Milk Glass	825.00
Beaded Swag, Butter, Cover, Milk Glass, Enameled Trim	110.00
Beaded Swag, Butter, Cover, Ruby Flash	115.00
Beaded Swag, Butter, Opalescent	95.00
Beaded Swag, Pitcher	100.00
Beaded Swag, Pitcher, Ruby Stained	100.00
Beaded Swag, Spooner	30.00 To 35.00
Beaded Swag, Table Set, Gold Trim, 4 Piece	110.00 To 250.00
Beaded Swag, Toothpick	50.00
Blown Glass, Salt, Cover	12.00
Bob White, Goblet, Balboa Cutting	45.00
Bookends, Fish, Pair	75.00 To 195.00
Bookends, Horsehead	150.00
Bottle, Bitters, Tally Ho Etch	150.00
Cabachon, Goblet, Southwind Cut, 10 Oz.	29.50
Candy Dish, Glass Flower On Cover	35.00
Cape Cod, Bottle, Bar, Stopper	125.00
Cape Cod, Bowl, Cupped, 14 In.	43.50
Cape Cod, Cruet, Green	36.00
Cape Cod, Ice Bucket, Tongs, Reed Handle	135.00
Caprice, Cup & Saucer, Blue	100.00
Carcassone, Champagne, Etched	15.00
Carcassone, Cigarette Holder, Cobalt Blue	95.00
Carcassone, Flagon, Sahara, Optic, Footed, 16 Oz.	75.00
Carcassone, Goblet, Etched	20.00
Carcassone, Sherbet, Sahara	15.00
Cascade, Candelabrum, 3–Light	60.00
Cascade, Candlestick, 3–Light, Orchid Etch	135.00
Celery, Marigold, No.407	50.00
Cherries In A Wreath, Table Set, Marked, Amethyst, 4 Piece	750.00
Coarse Rib, Celery, Amber, 12 In.	59.00
Colonial Star, Relish, Scalloped, Alexandrite, 3 1/2 X 9 In.	135.00
Colonial, Goblet, 7 Oz.	25.00
Colonial, Humidor, Decagon Base, Dated 1908, 9 3/4 X 6 1/2 In.	135.00
Colonial, Parfait, Signed, 5 In., Set of 4	95.00
Colonial, Pitcher, Water	70.00
Colonial, Punch Cup, 12 Piece	60.00
Colonial, Sugar & Creamer, Scalloped, Individual	35.00
Colonial, Tray, 10 In.	25.00
Colony, Cup & Saucer, Crystal	12.00
Columbia, Bowl, Crystal, 13 In.	37.50
Compote, Victorian, Moongleam, Signed	18.00
Cone, Mustard, Pink	35.00
Continental, Pitcher, Water, Ruby Stained	95.00

Continental, Toothpick .... 37.50 To 47.50
Continental, Tumbler, 8 Oz. 15.00
Coronation, Pitcher, Martini, 12-In. Glass Stirrer, 14 In. 90.00
Creole, Goblet, 11 Oz. 165.00
Cross Lined Flute, Cruet 95.00
Crystolite, Bowl, 4 1/2 X 7 In. 17.00
Crystolite, Box, Cigarette 20.00
Crystolite, Cake Plate, Footed, Crystal 400.00
Crystolite, Cake Stand, 12 In. 395.00
Crystolite, Candleblock, 1–Light, Round, Pair 20.00
Crystolite, Candleblock, 2 1/2 In., Pair 40.00
Crystolite, Cruet .... 35.00 To 42.00
Crystolite, Cup & Saucer, Set of 8 .... 18.00
Crystolite, Dish, Nut, Leaf, Individual 14.00
Crystolite, Ice Bucket, Clear, Silver Plated Handle 75.00
Crystolite, Jam Pot, Cover & Spoon 45.00
Crystolite, Jar, Preserve, Cover, 2 Handles, 6 In. 50.00
Crystolite, Lamp, Hurricane, Cutting On 9–In. Shade, Pair 325.00
Crystolite, Mustard .... 10.00 To 18.00
Crystolite, Pitcher 80.00
Crystolite, Plate, 10 In. 40.00
Crystolite, Punch Set, Tray, Ladle, 12 Cups 225.00
Crystolite, Relish, 3 Sections, 12 In. 35.00
Crystolite, Relish, 5 Sections, Shell Shape 45.00
Crystolite, Sugar & Creamer .... 29.50 To 40.00
Crystolite, Syrup 70.00
Daisy & Leaves, Basket 145.00
Diamond Optic, Cocktail, Flamingo, 3 1/2 Oz. 18.00
Diamond Point, Salt, Marked 50.00
Diamond With Peg, Creamer, Custard 75.00
Diamond With Peg, Sugar, Cover, Custard 165.00
Diamond With Peg, Wine, Custard 45.00
Duquesne, Cocktail, Tangerine 125.00
Duquesne, Cocktail, Tangerine, Optic, 3 Oz. 185.00
Duquesne, Goblet, Iced Tea, Chintz Etch 20.00
Empress, Ashtray, Cobalt Blue, Marked 385.00
Empress, Ashtray, Flamingo, Marked 125.00
Empress, Ashtray, Moongleam, Marked 375.00
Empress, Bowl, Apple Green, 3–Footed, Small 20.00
Empress, Bowl, Dolphin Footed, Sahara, 11 In. .... 50.00 To 70.00
Empress, Bowl, Nasturtium, Dolphin Footed, Sahara, 7 1/2 In. 75.00
Empress, Bowl, Yellow, 3 In. .... 40.00 To 45.00
Empress, Candlestick, Alexandrite, Pair .... 500.00 To 575.00
Empress, Candlestick, Dolphin, Moongleam, Footed, Pair 550.00
Empress, Candy Dish, Dolphin Footed, Flamingo 27.50
Empress, Cruet, Sahara 100.00
Empress, Ice Bucket, Sterling Overlay 55.00
Empress, Plate, 8 1/4 In. 6.00
Empress, Plate, Dinner, Chintz Etch, 10 In. 110.00
Empress, Plate, Phoenix Bird, Etching, 8 1/4 In. 200.00
Empress, Plate, Sahara, 7 1/2 In. .... 12.00 To 15.00
Empress, Plate, Sahara, 8 In. 12.00
Empress, Plate, Salad, Floral Cut, Sahara, 8 In. 12.00
Empress, Tray, Sandwich, Center Handle, Moongleam, Square, 12 In. 50.00
Empress, Tray, Sterling Overlay, 13 In. 38.00
Empress, Tumbler, Sahara, 8 Oz. 10.00
Fairacre, Goblet, 10 Oz. 18.00
Fancy Loop, Cracker Jar, Cover, 10 In. 225.00
Fancy Loop, Cruet 55.00
Fancy Loop, Spooner 40.00
Fancy Loop, Tankard, Silver Plated Lip & Collar, Crystal, 1 1/2 Qt. 150.00
Fancy Loop, Toothpick 60.00
Fandango, Rose Bowl, 4 In. .... 55.00 To 65.00
Fandango, Toothpick 55.00

Figurine, Airedale 400.00
Figurine, Asiatic Pheasant .... 200.00 To 325.00
Figurine, Bull, Black 800.00
Figurine, Bull, Verde Green 1000.00
Figurine, Clydesdale, 7 In. .... 225.00 To 365.00
Figurine, Clydesdale, Salmon 800.00
Figurine, Colt, Balking .... 165.00 To 225.00
Figurine, Colt, Kicking .... 25.00 To 165.00
Figurine, Colt, Kicking, Yellow 350.00
Figurine, Colt, Standing .... 60.00 To 115.00
Figurine, Colt, Standing, Amber, Honey 550.00
Figurine, Colt, Standing, Crystal, Marked 100.00
Figurine, Cygnet 250.00
Figurine, Donkey 375.00
Figurine, Duckling, Floating 190.00
Figurine, Duckling, Standing 190.00
Figurine, Elephant, Large .... 325.00 To 375.00
Figurine, Elephant, Medium 160.00
Figurine, Elephant, Small 210.00
Figurine, Flying Mare, Amber 1200.00
Figurine, Gazelle 1295.00
Figurine, Giraffe, Head Back 225.00
Figurine, Giraffe, Head Back, Amber 175.00
Figurine, Goose, Wings Down 450.00
Figurine, Goose, Wings Halfway .... 65.00 To 105.00
Figurine, Goose, Wings Up .... 50.00 To 95.00
Figurine, Hen, Yellow 600.00
Figurine, Horse, Amber 650.00
Figurine, Mallard, Wings Down 185.00
Figurine, Mallard, Wings Halfway Up 150.00
Figurine, Mallard, Wings Up .... 165.00 To 175.00
Figurine, Piglets 75.00
Figurine, Plug Horse, Standing 80.00
Figurine, Pouter Pigeon .... 535.00 To 600.00
Figurine, Rabbit, Paperweight 165.00
Figurine, Ringneck Pheasant 125.00
Figurine, Rooster, Fighting, Pink 500.00
Figurine, Scotty .... 95.00 To 145.00
Figurine, Show Horse .... 750.00 To 1000.00
Figurine, Show Horse, Amber 800.00
Figurine, Sow, Red 600.00
Figurine, Sparrow 105.00
Figurine, Tiger, Paperweight 600.00
Flamingo, Ice Tub, Octagon 55.00
Flamingo, Ladle, Mayonnaise 35.00
Flamingo, Nut Cup 20.00
Floral Block, Kingfisher, Moongleam 165.00
Gascony, Bowl, Fruit, Footed, Cobalt Blue, 10 In. 525.00
Georgia Gem, Powder Jar, Souvenir Grove City, Minn., Custard 54.00
Georgian, Candlestick, 11 In., Pair 295.00
Giant Flute, Cordial, 5 Piece 180.00
Glenford, Tumbler, Footed, 8 Oz. 60.00
Greek Key, Banana Boat, Footed 29.00
Greek Key, Butter, Cover 250.00
Greek Key, Celery, Large Spoon, 6 1/2 In. 190.00
Greek Key, Compote, 6 In. 135.00
Greek Key, Cruet, 6 Oz. 125.00
Greek Key, Cruet, Oil, Pressed Stopper, 4 Oz. 124.00
Greek Key, Cruet, Silver Overlay, 4 Oz. 95.00
Greek Key, Cup, Signed 10.00
Greek Key, Dish, Almond, Cover, 5 In. 195.00
Greek Key, Dish, Banana Split, Pedestal 38.00
Greek Key, Eggcup 60.00
Greek Key, Ice Tub, 7–In. Underliner, 2 Piece 180.00

Greek Key, Ice Tub, Hotel, Large	335.00
Greek Key, Jar, Straw, Small Spoon, 4 1/2 In.	140.00
Greek Key, Jug, 3 Pt.	175.00
Greek Key, Nappy, Shallow, 4 1/2 In.	24.00
Greek Key, Nut Cup, Individual, Set of 6	155.00
Greek Key, Punch Cup	12.00 To 15.00
Greek Key, Punch Set, Stand, 6 Cups, Flamingo	800.00
Greek Key, Soda, 5 Oz.	45.00
Greek Key, Tray, French Bread	99.50
Greek Key, Tray, Oblong, Marked, 13 X 10 In.	125.00
Greek Key, Tumbler, 8 Oz.	65.00
Groove & Slash, Cake Stand, 12 In.	195.00
Groundhog, Caramel Slag	40.00
Heron & Lighthouse, Salt & Pepper	67.50
Horn of Plenty, Compote, Cover, Amber, 10 In.	110.00
Horsehead, Box, Cigarette, Blue Stain	48.00
Ipswich, Bowl, Floral, 11 In.	32.00
Ipswich, Centerpiece, Footed, Cobalt, H Prisms	750.00
Ipswich, Champagne, 4 Oz.	10.00
Ipswich, Cocktail, Oyster, 4 Oz.	8.00
Ipswich, Console Set, With Candlesticks, A Prisms, Crystal, 4 Piece	325.00
Ipswich, Goblet, 10 Oz.	13.00
Ipswich, Lustre, With Candleholder	65.00
Ipswich, Plate, Square, 7 In.	10.00 To 12.00
Ipswich, Sherbet	12.00
Ipswich, Soda, Footed, 8 Oz.	12.00
Ipswich, Tumbler, Footed, 8 Oz.	10.00
Ipswich, Tumbler, Juice	12.00
Iris With Meander, Bowl, Blue, 8 In.	90.00
Jamestown, Goblet, Narcissus, 9 Oz.	25.00
Jubilee, Cup & Saucer, Yellow	16.00
Kalonyal, Butter, Cover	265.00
Kohinoor, Smoke Set, Cigarette Holder & 4 Ashtrays, Marked, Box	350.00
Lariat, Basket, Bonbon, Marked	55.00
Lariat, Bowl, 12 In.	30.00
Lariat, Candleholder, 3–Light	35.00
Lariat, Candlestick, 3–Light, Pair	110.00
Lariat, Candy Dish, Cover	45.00
Lariat, Coaster	8.00
Lariat, Cruet, Oil, Double Spout, Stopper	90.00
Lariat, Cup & Saucer	35.00
Lariat, Goblet, Moonglo Cut, 10 Oz.	21.50
Lariat, Mayonnaise Set, 3 Piece	25.00
Lariat, Punch Set, 7 Piece	225.00
Lariat, Punch Set, 16 Piece	350.00
Lariat, Punch Set, Ladle, 14 Piece	275.00
Lariat, Punch Set, Underplate, 12 Cups, Ladle	350.00
Lariat, Relish, 3 Sections, Handle	40.00
Lariat, Sugar & Creamer, Marked	25.00
Lariat, Vase	26.00
Liberty, Candleholder, Moongleam, 3 In.	20.00
Locket On Chain, Shade, Electric, No.160	135.00
Lodestar, Candleholder, Dawn, Pair	225.00
Memphis, Creamer, Green, Gold	35.00
Mercury, Candleholder, Flamingo, 9 In., Pair	375.00
Minuet, Candleholder, Double Etch, Pair	92.00
Minuet, Sugar & Creamer, Etch	80.00
Moon & Star, Bowl, Collared Base, 8 In.	38.00
Moongleam, Bowl, Footed, 11 In.	75.00
Moonstone, Powder Box	15.00
Narrow Flute, Cruet, Oil, 2 Oz.	60.00
Narrow Flute, Jug, 3 Pt.	75.00
Narrow Flute, Jug, Bulbous	20.00
Narrow Flute, Parfait	60.00

Narrow Flute, Tray, 4 Sections For Condiment Set, Oval, 10 In.	45.00
Narrow Flute, Water Set, 8 Piece	145.00
Narrow Rib, Relish, Oval, Marked, 9 In.	15.00
New Era, Candelabrum, 2–Light, Prisms, Pair	135.00
New Era, Candlestick, Cut Bobeches, Pair	115.00
New Era, Cordial, 1 Oz.	25.00
Nude Stem, Ashtray, Blue	230.00
Octagon, Creamer, Flamingo	20.00
Old Cafe, Dish, Handle, Pink, 8 1/2 In.	5.00
Old Colony, Goblet, Etch, Sahara	25.00
Old Colony, Plate, Etch, Sahara, 6 In.	18.00
Old Colony, Sugar & Creamer, Yellow	40.00
Old Dominion, Soda, Footed, Old Colony Etch	15.00
Old Dominion, Wine, Pink, 2 1/2 Oz.	20.00
Old Sandwich, Ashtray	10.00
Old Sandwich, Candlestick, Cobalt Blue, Pair	450.00
Old Sandwich, Candlestick, Sahara, Pair	225.00
Old Sandwich, Jug, Sahara, 1/2 Gal.	140.00
Old Sandwich, Pitcher, Ice Lip, Marked	65.00
Old Sandwich, Pitcher, Yellow, 1/2 Gal.	155.00
Old Sandwich, Tumbler, Bar, 4 Oz.	25.00
Old Williamsburg, Candelabrum, 2–Light, 10 1/2 In., Pair	225.00
Old Williamsburg, Candelabrum, 20–Light, 10 1/2 In., Pair	260.00
Old Williamsburg, Candelabrum, 3–Light, Prisms, 10 1/4 In.	175.00
Old Williamsburg, Candlestick, 7 In.	35.00
Old Williamsburg, Candlestick, 9 In.	40.00
Old Williamsburg, Candlestick, 11 In., Pair	250.00 To 295.00
Old Williamsburg, Jug, 1/2 Gal.	30.00
Old Williamsburg, Pitcher, Milk, 1 Pt.	110.00
Old Williamsburg, Tumbler, Iced Tea	20.00
Orchid Etch, Butter, Cover, Horse Finial	145.00
Orchid Etch, Compote, Waverly, 6 1/2 In.	38.00
Orchid Etch, Mayonnaise Set, 3 Piece	45.00
Orchid Etch, Plate, 7 In.	15.00
Orchid, Bowl, Crimped, 12 In.	56.25
Orchid, Butter, Cover, 6 In.	175.00
Orchid, Cigarette Holder, Cover	135.00
Orchid, Compote, Low, 6 1/2 In.	55.00
Orchid, Goblet, 10 Oz.	38.00
Orchid, Mayonnaise, Ladle, Underplate, Yellow	10.00
Orchid, Pitcher, 73 Oz.	375.00
Orchid, Plate, 13 1/2 In.	55.00
Orchid, Tray, Handles, 12 In.	45.00
Orchid, Tumbler, Iced Tea, 12 Oz.	60.00
Orchid, Vase, Yellow, 12 In.	200.00
Oxford, Goblet	7.00
Oxford, Sherbet	5.00
Paneled Colonial, Celery	20.00
Paneled Colonial, Pitcher, 7 X 6 In.	45.00
Peerless, Berry Set, Gold Trim, 7 Piece	135.00
Peerless, Goblet, 8 Oz.	14.00
Peerless, Jar, Horseradish	48.00
Peerless, Toothpick	20.00
Peerless, Toothpick, Gold Trim	28.00
Petticoat Dolphin, Compote, Moongleam Top	150.00
Pied Piper Etch, Plate, 6 In.	7.00
Pied Piper Etch, Plate, 8 In.	12.00
Pillows, Punch Bowl, With Base, Marked	220.00
Pillows, Punch Cup, Marked	30.00
Pillows, Rose Bowl, 7 In.	125.00
Pillows, Spooner	95.00
Pineapple & Fan, Butter	25.00
Pineapple & Fan, Creamer, Green, Gold Trim	40.00
Pineapple & Fan, Saltshaker, Green	24.50

Pineapple & Fan, Toothpick, Clear, Gold 85.00
Pineapple & Fan, Toothpick, Green 125.00
Pinwheel & Fan, Punch Bowl, Footed, 14 In. 275.00
Pinwheel & Fan, Punch Cup 25.00
Pinwheel & Fan, Sugar & Creamer .... 70.00 To 75.00
Plain Band, Toothpick, Marigold 38.00
Plain Panel, Nappy, Marked, 8 In. 42.50
Plantation, Bowl, Floral 85.00
Plantation, Butter, Cover, 1/4 Lb. 65.00
Plantation, Candlestick, Triple, Pair 190.00
Plantation, Celery 22.00
Plantation, Compote, Green, 5 In. 90.00
Plantation, Goblet, 9 Oz. 29.00
Plantation, Mayonnaise Set, Ivy Etch, 3 Piece 35.00
Plantation, Punch Cup 20.00
Plantation, Relish, 3 Sections 65.00
Plantation, Relish, 5 Sections, 13 In. 150.00
Plantation, Spooner 27.50
Plantation, Syrup, Cover 85.00
Plantation, Syrup, Cut Top 55.00
Pleat & Pane, Cup & Saucer, Flamingo 32.50
Pleat & Panel, Cruet, Flamingo 40.00
Pleat & Panel, Plate, Flamingo, 7 In. 6.00
Pleat & Panel, Sugar & Creamer, Flamingo 28.00
Prince of Wales Plumes, Pitcher, Tankard, Ruby 175.00
Prince of Wales Plumes, Punch Cup .... 14.50 To 20.00
Prince of Wales Plumes, Toothpick, Gold Trim .... 85.00 To 130.00
Prince of Wales Plumes, Tumbler, Water, Ruby 50.00
Priscilla, Jug, 3 Pt. 40.00
Priscilla, Toothpick, Silver Deposit 28.00
Prison Stripe, Toothpick .... 175.00 To 250.00
Provincial, Compote, Cover 60.00
Provincial, Cruet, 4 Oz. 10.00
Provincial, Goblet, 10 Oz. 12.00
Provincial, Mayonnaise, Limelight, 3 Handles 140.00
Provincial, Sugar, Creamer & Tray, Individual 68.00
Punty & Diamond Point, Cracker Jar, Cover 295.00
Punty & Diamond Point, Punch Cup 25.00
Punty & Diamond Point, Saltshaker 22.00
Punty Band, Compote, 9 In. 35.00
Punty Band, Creamer, Custard, Individual 25.00
Punty Band, Toothpick, Ruby Stained 55.00
Puritan, Jug, 1 1/2 Qt. 85.00
Puritan, Sauce, 3 1/2 In. 7.50
Quator, Sugar & Creamer, Flamingo 65.00
Queen Ann, Candlestick, Orchid Etch, Pair 225.00
Queen Ann, Compote, Everglade Cut, Oval, 7 In. 35.00
Queen Ann, Compote, Jelly, Orchid Etch, 6 In. 30.00
Queen Ann, Decanter, Sterling Stopper, 1 Pt. 240.00
Queen Ann, Ice Bucket, Cutting, Silver Overlay, Dolphin Footed 75.00
Queen Ann, Ice Bucket, Handle 195.00
Recessed Panels, Compote 115.00
Revere, Cocktail Shaker, Chrome Top, Nimrod Etch 400.00
Ridgeleigh Star, Mustard, Cover 29.00
Ridgeleigh Star, Relish 23.00
Ridgeleigh Star, Sugar & Creamer 22.00
Ridgeleigh, Ashtray Set, Bridge 40.00
Ridgeleigh, Ashtray Set, Zircon, 4 Ashtrays 275.00
Ridgeleigh, Ashtray, 2 3/4 In. 3.00
Ridgeleigh, Bottle, Oil, 3 Oz. 65.00
Ridgeleigh, Bottle, Rock & Rye, Stopper 195.00
Ridgeleigh, Candleholder, Prisms, 10 In., Pair 195.00
Ridgeleigh, Champagne, 5 Oz. 30.00
Ridgeleigh, Coaster, Sahara, 3 1/2 In. 18.00

Ridgeleigh, Mustard, Lid, No.10 Paddle	55.00
Ridgeleigh, Nut Cup	18.00
Ridgeleigh, Shot Glass	22.50
Ridgeleigh, Sugar & Creamer	33.00
Ridgeleigh, Sugar, Creamer & Tray, Individual	37.50
Ridgeleigh, Vase, Zircon, 8 In.	125.00
Ring Band, Butter, Cover, Custard	150.00
Ring Band, Creamer, Custard	70.00
Ring Band, Tumbler, Boardwalk, Atlantic City	40.00
Ring Band, Tumbler, Custard	45.00
Ring Band, Water Set, 7 Piece	500.00
Ring Band, Water Set, Marked, 7 Piece	475.00
Rococo, Sugar & Creamer	90.00 To 95.00
Rooster, Cocktail Shaker	65.00 To 75.00
Rose Etch, Cruet, Seaweed Stopper	160.00
Rose, Champagne, Gold Bowl, Nude Stem	55.00
Rose, Goblet, 9 Oz.	39.50
Rose, Plate, Center Handle, 14 In.	65.00
Rose, Platter, 14 In.	54.00
Rose, Sherbet, 6 Oz.	30.00
Rose, Sugar & Creamer	50.00
Sahara, Cutter Chip	10.00
Sahara, Sugar & Creamer, Half Circle	85.00
Sandwich, Pitcher, Ice Lip	65.00
Satellite, Bowl, Cut, 13 In.	55.00
Saturn, Candleblock, 2–Light, Crystal, Pair	150.00
Saturn, Condiment Set, Sterling Tops, Cherry Holder, 5 Piece	210.00
Saturn, Cruet, 2 Oz.	35.00
Saturn, Sugar & Creamer, Marked	32.50
Sawtooth Band, Sherbet	32.50
Sawtooth Band, Spooner	27.50
Seneca Loop, Celery, Pedestal	25.00
Skirted Panel, Candlestick, 7 In., Pair	55.00
Spiral Optic, Vase, Moongleam	65.00
Square In Diamond Point, Cruet, Original Stopper	70.00
Stanhope, Cocktail, Rooster Stem	45.00
Stanhope, Cup & Saucer	22.00
Stanhope, Goblet	15.00
Stanhope, Goblet, Maytime Etch	45.00
Suez, Goblet, Iced Tea, Belvidere Cut, Marked	20.00
Suez, Punch Cup, Cut, Belvidere Cut, Marked	20.00
Sunburst, Berry Set, 7 Piece	155.00
Sunburst, Butter, Cover	100.00
Sunburst, Jelly, Footed, 5 In.	62.00
Sunburst, Punch Bowl, Stand	175.00
Symphone, Goblet, Minuet Etch	25.00
Syrup, Ivorina Verde, Gold Trim	225.00
Tally Ho, Decanter, Crystal	225.00
Tally Ho, Decanter, Whiskey Set, 9 Piece	750.00
Tally Ho, Mug, Beer, Etched, 16 Oz.	150.00
Tally Ho, Wine, Etched Hunt Scene	9.00
Town & Country, Bowl, Zircon, Underplate, 11 In.	300.00
Trident, Candlestick, Gold Etched, Pair	100.00
Trojan, Champagne, Flamingo	25.00
Trojan, Wine, Flamingo	40.00
Trophy, Candleholder, 6 In., Pair	145.00
Twentieth Century, Sherbet, Sahara, Footed, 4 Oz.	20.00
Twist, Bonbon, Moongleam	20.00
Twist, Bowl, Nut, Green, Individual	45.00
Twist, Bowl, Sahara, 12 In.	65.00
Twist, Celery, Green	47.00
Twist, Console Bowl, Gold Bird Border, Moongleam, 12 1/2 In.	60.00
Twist, Ice Bucket, Moongleam	40.00
Twist, Ice Tub, Moongleam	77.50

Twist, Mustard, Moongleam	67.50
Twist, Pickle, Green	34.00
Twist, Plate, Moongleam, 4 1/2 In.	10.00
Twist, Relish, Marigold, 7 In.	30.00
Twist, Tumbler, Flamingo	18.00
Versailles, Champagne, Blue	25.00
Victorian, Cocktail, Old–Fashioned, 8 Oz.	120.00
Victorian, Goblet	12.50
Victorian, Punch Cup	17.00
Victorian, Relish, 3 Sections, 11 In.	42.00
Victorian, Sherbet	10.00
Victorian, Sugar & Creamer	35.00 To 39.50
Victorian, Vase, 9 In.	69.50
Wabash, Goblet, Frontenac Etch, Marked, 6 Piece	150.00
Wabash, Goblet, Iced Tea, Handle, Pied Piper Etch, Marked	35.00
Wabash, Sherbet, Pied Piper Etch, Marked	15.00
Wabash, Tumbler, Frontenac Etch, 10 Oz.	32.00
Waldorf Astoria, Toothpick	135.00
Wampum, Cigarette Set, Crystal, Box & 4 Ashtrays	55.00
Warwick, Candleblock, 2 1/2 In., Pair	35.00
Warwick, Vase, Cornucopia, Cobalt Blue, Large	245.00
Warwick, Vase, Horn of Plenty, Cobalt Blue, 9 In.	195.00 To 300.00
Warwick, Vase, Sahara, 9 In.	175.00
Waverly, Bowl, Seahorse, Footed, Rose Etch	165.00
Waverly, Butter, Orchid Etch, Square, 6 In.	140.00
Waverly, Butter, Rose Etch, Square, 6 In.	145.00
Waverly, Candlestick, 2–Light, Orchid Etch	70.00
Waverly, Candy Dish, Cover, Bowtie Etch, Marked	165.00
Waverly, Candy Dish, Cover, Bowtie Finial, Marked	65.00
Waverly, Candy Dish, Cover, Footed, 5 In.	95.00
Waverly, Candy Dish, Seahorse Handle, 6 In.	175.00
Waverly, Compote, Jelly, 6 1/2 In.	40.00
Waverly, Compote, Oval, Marked, 7 In.	95.00 To 140.00
Waverly, Cup & Saucer	35.00
Waverly, Cup & Saucer, Marked	60.00
Waverly, Mayonnaise Set, Orchid Etch, 3 Piece	60.00
Waverly, Plate, 8 In.	32.50
Waverly, Plate, 10 1/2 In.	45.00
Waverly, Plate, Sandwich, Gardenia Etch, 14 In.	30.00
Waverly, Relish, 3 Sections, Oblong, Orchid Etch, 11 In.	70.00
Waverly, Relish, 3 Sections, Round, 7 In.	47.50
Waverly, Salt & Pepper	75.00
Waverly, Sugar	14.00
Waverly, Sugar & Creamer, Footed, Orchid Etch	55.00
Wheat & Barley, Sugar, Cover	35.00
Whirlpool, Candleblock, Round, 2 1/2 In., Pair	40.00
Whirlpool, Candy Dish, 3 Handles, Cover	80.00
Whirlpool, Cruet, 4 Oz.	10.00
Whirlpool, Goblet, Lime	55.00
Whirlpool, Sugar & Creamer, Individual	50.00
Williamsburg, Bowl, Oblong	18.50
Windsor, Lamp, Candle, 9 In.	350.00
Winged Scroll, Butter, Custard	100.00
Winged Scroll, Cruet	210.00
Winged Scroll, Salt & Pepper	225.00
Winged Scroll, Spooner, Custard	65.00
Winged Scroll, Spooner, Green, Gold Trim	150.00
Winged Scroll, Table Set, Green, 3 Piece	275.00
World, Candlestick, Pair	295.00
World, Lamp, Candlestick, Portable, Pair	235.00
Yeoman, Cruet, Flamingo	48.00
Yeoman, Cruet, Sahara	32.00
Yeoman, Cup & Saucer, After Dinner, Empress Etch	65.00
Yeoman, Cup & Saucer, Moongleam	18.00

Yeoman, Cup, Green	35.00
Yeoman, Goblet, 5 1/4 In.	15.00
Yeoman, Plate, 10 1/2 In.	25.00
Yeoman, Plate, Center Handle, Hawthorne, 10 1/2 In.	38.00
Yeoman, Saucer, Green	10.00
Yeoman, Tray, Cream	8.00
Yeoman, Tray, Decanter, Nimrod Etch, 17 In.	250.00
Yeoman, Tray, Sandwich, Cut Roses	85.00
Yeoman, Tray, Sandwich, Nimrod Etch, 15 In.	195.00
Yeoman, Tumbler, Soda, Sahara, 8 Oz.	18.00
Zodiac, Champagne, Saucer, 5 Oz.	17.00

HEREND, see Fischer

Gebruder Heubach, a firm working in Lichten, Germany, from 1820 to 1925, is best known for bisque dolls and doll heads, their principal products. They also manufactured bisque figurines, including piano babies, beginning in the 1880s, and glazed figurines in the 1900s. Dolls are not listed here, but are listed in the Doll section. Another factory, Ernst Heubach, working in Koppelsdorf, Germany, also made porcelain and dolls.

HEUBACH, Box, Trinket, Figural Clown Head On Cover, 3 1/2 X 2 1/2 In.	150.00
Candy Container, Child, Snow Covered Log, Blue Pants, 6 1/2 In.	350.00
Candy Container, Snowball, Girl On Top, Mica Covered, 6 1/2 In.	350.00

HEUBACH, DOLL, see Doll, Gebruder Heubach

Figurine, Boy & Girl Playing Dress–Up, 10 In., Pair	730.00
Figurine, Boy, Dutch, Standing, Tan Hat, Pants, Blue Shirt, 6 1/2 In.	110.00
Figurine, Dancing Girl, Smiling, Multicolored, 11 1/2 In.	505.00
Figurine, Dog In Child's Bonnet, 5 X 4 In.	225.00
Figurine, Dog, Sitting, Bib, Bonnet With Blue Ribbons, Bisque, 6 In.	275.00
Figurine, Girl, Blond Hair, Holding Up Ends of Skirt, 6 1/4 In.	120.00
Figurine, Girl, Dancing, Tan Ruffled Dress, Lace Collar, 6 1/2 In.	88.00
Figurine, Girl, Holding Bird, 11 In.	300.00
Figurine, Girl, Seated, Large Orange Hat, Pulling Off Socks, 5 In.	200.00
Figurine, Little Girl At Beach, Ruffled Pantaloons, 16 In.	855.00
Figurine, Man With Ax, Woman Holding Baby, 12 In., Pair	720.00
Figurine, Puppy, Bisque, Wearing Baby Bonnet & Bib, Blue Ribbons	265.00
Planter, Peasant Girl Herding Sheep, Signed	185.00
Tray, Jasperware, Indian	65.00
Vase, Figurine, Girl, Castle, Deer, 10 In.	425.00

Higbee glass was made by the J. B. Higbee Company of Bridgeville, Pennsylvania, about 1900. Tablewares were made and it is possible to assemble a full set of dishes and goblets in some Higbee patterns. Most of the glass was clear, not colored.

HIGBEE, see also Pressed Glass

HIGBEE, Butter, Cover, Child's, Fine Cut Star & Fan	40.00
Cake Stand, Paneled Thistle, Marked, 10 In.	34.00
Child's Set, Covered Butter, Sugar & Creamer, Pink	95.00
Sugar & Creamer, Thistle & Fern	95.00
Toothpick, Hawaiian Lei, Clear	25.00

HISTORIC BLUE, see Adams; Clews; Ridgway; Staffordshire

Hobnail glass is a pattern of glass with bumps in an allover pattern. Dozens of hobnail patterns and variants have been made. Clear, colored, and opalescent hobnail have been made and are being reproduced. Other pieces of hobnail are also listed under Carnival Glass, Hobnail.

HOBNAIL, see also Fenton; Francisware

HOBNAIL, Basket, Blue Opalescent, Large	60.00
Basket, French Opalescent, 10 In.	75.00
Basket, Milk Glass, 7 In.	45.00
Basket, Milk Glass, 12 In.	35.00
Berry Bowl, Cranberry, Hobbs Brockunier	195.00
Bowl, Blue Opalescent, Ruffled, 9 1/2 In.	62.50

Bowl, Milk Glass, Footed, 10 In.	25.00
Candleholder, Milk Glass, Low, Pair	10.00
Candy Dish, Milk Glass, Cover	10.00
Candy Dish, Plum Opalescent, Footed	88.00
Candy Jar, Milk Glass	30.00
Creamer, Child's	15.00
Jug, Milk Glass, 80 Oz.	75.00
Lamp, Dresser, Blue Opalescent	97.50
Mug, Blue	15.00
Mug, Child's	10.00
Pitcher, Thumbprint Base, Amber	45.00
Pitcher, Water, Rubena, Frosted	350.00
Pitcher, White Opalescent, Crimped Top	250.00
Planter, Milk Glass, 9 1/2 In.	30.00
Plate, Frosted, Hobbs	55.00
Plate, Pink, Shallow	80.00
Punch Set, Green Opalescent, Clear Ladle, 14 Piece	270.00
Relish, Heart Shape, Blue Marble	30.00
Relish, Milk Glass, Divided, 12 In.	18.00
Salt & Pepper, French Opalescent	35.00
Salt & Pepper, Milk Glass, Kitchen	25.00
Salt & Pepper, Westmoreland	16.00
Sugar & Creamer, Blue Opalescent	40.00
Sugar & Creamer, Milk Glass	25.00
Tankard, Cranberry, 48 Oz.	325.00
Toothpick, Canary Opalescent	55.00
Toothpick, Hat, Blue Opalescent	33.50
Tumbler, Blue	30.00
Tumbler, Milk Glass, 12 Oz.	10.00
Tumbler, Vaseline	28.50
Vase, Blue Opalescent	12.00
Vase, Blue, 4 1/2 In.	17.50
Vase, Cranberry Opalescsent, Ruffled, 6 X 7 1/2 In.	325.00
Vase, Cranberry, Ruffled, Small	42.50
Vase, Milk Glass, 8 In.	18.00
Vase, Vaseline, Large	27.50
Waste Bowl, Blue	35.00

Hochst, or Hoechst, porcelain was made in Germany from 1746 to 1796. It was marked with a six–spoke wheel. Be careful when buying Hochst; many other firms have used a very similar wheel–shaped mark.

HOCHST, Bust, Shakespeare, C.1775, 6 In.	285.00
Group, 2 Children, Blue Vest, Striped Breeches, Floral Dress, 6 In.	335.00
Group, Lovers, Dog At Man's Side, Floral Oval Base, 6 3/4 In.	440.00

Holly amber, or golden agate, glass was made by the Indiana Tumbler and Goblet Company of Greentown, Indiana, from January 1, 1903, to June 13, 1903. It is a pressed glass pattern featuring holly leaves in the amber–shaded glass. The glass was made with shadings that range from creamy opalescent to brown–amber.

HOLLY AMBER, Cake Plate, Clear Pedestal	1250.00
Compote, 4 1/2 In.	625.00 To 850.00
Compote, Cover, 7 1/2 In.	975.00 To 1285.00
Creamer, 4 1/2 In.	425.00 To 700.00
Mug, Handle, 4 1/2 In.	375.00
Parfait	550.00 To 625.00
Pitcher Set, Water, 4 Tumblers	2900.00
Sauce, Strawberry, Clear	550.00
Spooner, 4 In.	485.00
Toothpick	95.00
Tumbler	325.00 To 375.00

Hopalong Cassidy was named William Lawrence Boyd when he was born in Cambridge, Ohio, in 1895. His first movie appearance was in 1919, but the first Hopalong Cassidy film was not until 1934. Sixty-six films were made. In 1948, William Boyd purchased the television rights to the movies, then later made fifty-two new programs. In the 1950s, Hopalong Cassidy and his horse, named "Topper," were seen in comics, records, toys, and other products. Boyd died in 1972.

HOPALONG CASSIDY, Album, Record–Reader, 1950	35.00
Badge, Foreman, Hoppy Savings Club	60.00
Badge, Sheriff's	20.00
Badge, Sheriff's, Brass, 6 Points	30.00
Bandanna & Slide	75.00
Bank, Bust of Hopalong, Blue, Plastic, Topper Toys, 5 In.	85.00
Banner, Hoppy On Topper, Felt, Black, White, 1950	15.00
Bath Mat, Topper Design, 24 X 46 In,	145.00
Bedspread, Bar–20, Double Bed Size	250.00
Bedspread, Twin Size	135.00
Billfold, Gold Front	65.00
Binoculars	35.00
Book Cover, Hoppy Bond Bread	10.00
Book, 1951, Clarence E. Mulford	80.00
Book, Coloring, Hoppy & Topper Cover, 1950	18.00
Book, Punchout, Cardboard, 1950, Whitman	145.00
Bottle, Milk, Enameled, Small	30.00 To 32.00
Branding Iron, Round, Post's Grape-nuts Flakes, 1950s	145.00
Breakfast Set, Graphic, Porcelain, 3 Piece	150.00
Camera, Box	140.00
Canasta Set, Western Theme Cards, Plastic Saddle Holder	125.00
Cap Gun	30.00
Cap Gun, Metal Trigger, Leather Holster, Wyandotte	650.00
Cap Pistol, Gold	85.00
Chair, Director's	225.00
Chair, TV, Wooden, Leather Seat, Picture of Hopalong	125.00
Clock, Alarm	595.00
Coloring Outfit, Crayons, Paints, Stencils, Transogram	65.00
Comic Book	10.00
Compass, Hat Ring	185.00
Cookie Jar, Cookie Corral	240.00 To 475.00
Cookie Jar, Hopalong Cassidy Corral	285.00
Crayon & Stencil Set, 18 Hoppy Crayons	65.00
Cuff Links, Watch Fob, & Gun Tie Clasp, Box, 3 Piece	145.00
Cup	12.00
Dental Kit, Dr. West's, Mirror, Toothbrush, Toothpaste	225.00
Earmuffs	65.00 To 75.00
Film, Border Justice	65.00
Film, Heart of The West	65.00
Frontier Town, Box	200.00
Game, Board, 1950	50.00 To 65.00
Game, Canasta, Box	125.00
Game, Dominoes, Western Style, Box, 1950	155.00
Game, Hopalong Cassidy Lasso, Transogram Co., 1950	60.00
Game, Snap–Card, 40 Cards, Chad Valley Co., Ltd, England	65.00
Gum Wrapper	50.00
Gun & Holster	225.00
Gun Set, Box	275.00
Gun, Zoomerang, Box	195.00
Hat, Compass Ring	185.00
Horseshoe, Good Luck	20.00
Ice Cream Box, Front Panel, Dairylea Ice Cream, 3 X 4 In.	8.00
Jacket, Jean, Blue Bell	110.00
Knife, Pocket, Hoppy On Topper, Black Plastic, 3 1/2 In.	30.00
Lamp, Revolving Waterfall	395.00

Lunch Box 60.00
Lunch Box, Blue, William Boyd, 1950 .... 90.00
Lunch Box, With Thermos, 1954 .... 165.00 To 250.00
Milk Carton 5.00
Money Clip 25.00
Mug, Hopalong Black Drawing, White 25.00
Napkin, Package, 32 Piece 18.00
Neckerchief, Hoppy On Horse Picture, 1950 .... 10.00
Night–Light, Gun & Holster, Alacite, Aladdin .... 145.00 To 195.00
Night–Light, Revolving 350.00
Outfit, Cowgirl, With Clicker Pistol ....95.00 To 120.00
Pen, Ballpoint 70.00
Pen, Hoppy 23.00
Pen, Ink 190.00
Pencil Sharpener 35.00
Pillow Cover, Satin, Picture of Hopalong, Yellow Fringe 75.00
Pin .... 15.00 To 20.00
Pistol, Flashlight 95.00
Place Mat 25.00
Plate, On Horse, Gun Drawn, W.S. George .... 45.00 To 55.00
Poster, Hoppy's Movie, 1948 .... 45.00
Pressbook, Universal Studios, Photos of Hopalong 25.00
Puppet, Hand 125.00
Puzzle Set, Milton Bradley, Box, 3 Puzzles 50.00
Puzzle, Sleeve 45.00
Radio .... 250.00 To 300.00
Record Album, Hopalong Cassidy & Singing Bandit, 1950 .... 50.00
Record, Legend of Phantom Scout Pass, 78 RPM, Capitol 45.00
Ring, Club, Metal 50.00
Ring, Hat, Compass 185.00
Rocker, Child's, Steel, Vinyl Seat, Decal, Comfort Lines 250.00
Rocking Horse, Topper, Rich Toy, 26 X 36 In. 200.00
Rocking Horse, Windup, Marx 275.00
Rug 75.00
Sheet Music 25.00
Shooting Gallery 120.00
Shooting Gallery, Mechanical, Box .... 150.00 To 295.00
Sign, Bond Bread, Hoppy's Favorite, Red 85.00
Socks, Pair 70.00
Sparkler 95.00
Stationery Set, Album, 1950, 8 1/2 X 11 In. 75.00
Suspenders, On Original Card, Hoppy Shape 150.00
Sweater 125.00
Television, Windup, 4 Strips, Automatic Toy Co. .... 250.00 To 325.00
Tin, Hopalong Cassidy Popcorn 75.00
Tin, Potato 200.00
Topper, Hoppy's Horse, Blow–Up 80.00
Tumbler, Milk Glass 18.00
Tumbler, Picture 34.00
Viewmaster, 1950 .... 7.00
Viewmaster, Reel, Cattle Rustler, Wm. Boyd, Cover Sleeve 12.00
Wallet, Box 175.00
Watch, U.S. Time, 1950 .... 65.00 To 75.00
Wristwatch, Saddle Watch, 1950, Box .... 265.00 To 360.00

Howdy Doody and Buffalo Bob were the main characters in a
children's series televised from 1947 to 1960. Howdy was a
redheaded puppet. The series became popular with college students
in the late 1970s when Buffalo Bob began to lecture on the
campuses.

HOWDY DOODY, Album, American History, Bread Booklet, End Labels, 8 Pages 45.00
Bank, Clarabell 20.00
Bank, Howdy, Clarabell & Bluster, Flocked, OSS, 3 Piece 35.00
Book, Clarabell 10.00

Book, Coloring, Robert E. Smith Copyright, 1950	20.00
Book, Follow The Dots, Whitman, No.1410, 1955	20.00
Book, Howdy Doody Fun, Whitman, 1951	25.00
Book, Howdy Doody's Circus, Little Golden Book	9.00 To 10.00
Book, Punchout, Make Howdy Puppet, 1952, Whitman	125.00
Box, Shoe Polish	45.00
Bracelet	140.00
Brush, Zippered Case, Leather	15.00
Bubble Pipe, On Card	58.00
Chair	175.00
Cookie Jar	100.00 To 425.00
Cookie-Go-Round, Howdy, Clarabell, Tin, Litho, Red Lid, 8 In.	145.00
Costume, Ben Cooper, Box, 1976	75.00
Costume, Princess, Box	95.00
Cutout, Cardboard	30.00
Doll, Effanbee, 19 In.	300.00
Doll, Summerfall Winterspring, Plastic, Beehler Arts, 7 In.	225.00
Doll, Ventriloquist, Goldberger	35.00
Flag, Howdy's Smiling Face In Center, 8 X 10 In.	35.00
Game, 1950s, 8-In. Plastic Figure, 16 X 10 In.	120.00
Game, Adventure, Spinner, Board, Milton Bradley	65.00
Game, Bowling, Parker Bros.	40.00
Game, Kagran, TV Characters, 1950s	15.00
Game, Ring Toss, Flub-A-Dub, Box	30.00 To 45.00
Handkerchief, Howdy On Horse, Dilly Dally, Flub-A-Dub, 8 In.	15.00
Lamp, Full Figure, 1950s	360.00
Lamp, Large Head	45.00
Laundry Bag, Clarabell Hug-Me-Toy, Fabric, Hair, Instruction	125.00
Lunch Box, Plastic, With Thermos, 1977	13.00
Lunch Box, Tin	60.00 To 80.00
Marionette, Flub-A-Dub, Wooden, Composition, Crazed, 12 In.	302.50
Marionette, Howdy, Painted Composition, Wooden, 17 In.	242.00
Marionette, Peter Playthings	225.00
Mask, Rubber	165.00
Night-Light, Jointed Figure, 1950	75.00 To 95.00
Picture, Royal Puddings, Unopened	10.00
Place Setting, China, 3 Piece	90.00
Poster, Store, Twin Pops, Howdy Holding Pop, 7 X 14 In.	25.00
Puppet, Hand, Clarabelle, Flub-A-Dub, Mr.Bluster, Princess, 4 Pc.	49.00
Puppet, NBC Eegee, 27 In.	55.00
Ring, Flashlight	95.00
Salt & Pepper	15.00
Sign, Store, Ice Cream Bar, Howdy & Ice Cream Bar, 9 X 12 In.	25.00
Slide Set, Howdy Doody, Tru View, 3-D Slides, Set of 3	25.00
Slippers, Heads On Slippers, 1950	150.00
T-Shirt	50.00
Toy, Howdy, Figural, Sheriff's Outfit, Squeeze, Squeaks, 12 In.	125.00
Toy, Howdy, Standing, Hands In Pocket, Squeaks, 9 In.	125.00
Toy, Mechanical, Tin Litho, Unique Art, 8 1/2 In.	935.00
Toy, Wall, Hands Flap, 9 In.	35.00
Tumbler, Welch, 1950s	10.00 To 20.00
Umbrella, Plastic, Tags	75.00
Wrapper, Howdy Doody Fudge Bar, Early 1950s, 3 1/4 X 6 In.	3.00
Wristwatch, Moving Eyes, 1954, Box	460.00

Hull pottery was made in Crooksville, Ohio, from 1905. Addis E. Hull bought the Acme Pottery Company and started making ceramic wares. In 1917, A. E. Hull Pottery began making art pottery as well as the commercial wares. For a short time, 1921 to 1929, the firm also sold pottery imported from Europe. The dinnerwares of the 1940s, including the Little Red Riding Hood line, the high gloss artwares of the 1950s, and the matte wares of the 1940s, are all popular with collectors. The firm officially closed in March 1986.

HULL, Art Deco, Woman, 9 1/2 In.	90.00
Ashtray, Butterfly	18.00
Ashtray, Tropicana	89.50
Bank, Little Red Riding Hood, Standing	160.00
Bank, Porky Pig	40.00
Bank, Porky Pig, Brown & Blue Drip, Original Cork	25.00
Bank, Porky Pig, Pastel	22.00
Basket, Blue To Pink, 7 In.	85.00
Basket, Bow-Knot, 10 1/2 In.	225.00
Basket, Bow-Knot, Pink, 10 1/2 In.	285.00
Basket, Bow-Knot, Small	90.00
Basket, Magnolia, Glossy, 10 1/2 In.	68.00
Basket, Parchment & Pine, 16 1/2 In.	25.00 To 65.00
Basket, Rosella	72.00
Basket, Serenade, Pink, 7 In.	35.00
Basket, Sun Glow, Pumpkin Shape	22.00
Basket, Tokay	20.00 To 40.00
Basket, Tropicana	295.00
Basket, Wildflower, Pink & Blue, 10 1/2 In.	250.00
Basket, Wildflower, Pink, 7 In.	75.00
Basket, Woodland, 8 3/4 In.	50.00
Basket, Woodland, Glaze, 10 1/2 In.	55.00
Basket, Woodland, Green, 10 1/2 In.	55.00
Basket, Woodland, Peach, 10 1/2 In.	75.00
Bowl, 2-Tone Green, Fluted	15.00
Bowl, Butterfly, 3 Feet, 12 In.	23.00
Bowl, Magnolia, 12 1/2 In.	35.00
Bowl, Open Rose, Pink & Blue, 12 In.	150.00
Bowl, Woodland, 5 1/2 In.	25.00
Butter, Cover, Little Red Riding Hood	150.00 To 195.00
Candleholder, Iris, Pink, 5 In., Pair	50.00
Candleholder, Water Lily	22.50
Casserole, NuLine, Salmon, 7 1/2 In.	22.00
Console Set, Parchment & Pine, 3 Piece	35.00
Console, Butterfly, 3 Footed, 12 In.	35.00
Console, Water Lily	45.00
Cookie Jar, Apple	30.00
Cookie Jar, Apple, Red	25.00
Cookie Jar, Gingerbread Man	65.00
Cookie Jar, Gingerbread Man, Brown	30.00
Cookie Jar, Little Red Riding Hood, Green Basket	50.00 To 185.00
Cookie Jar, Little Red Riding Hood, Open Basket	75.00 To 85.00
Cornucopia, Bow-Knot	38.00 To 50.00
Cornucopia, Magnolia, 8 1/2 In.	40.00 To 60.00
Cornucopia, Open Rose, Pink & Blue, 8 1/2 In.	50.00
Cornucopia, Parchment & Pine	16.00
Cornucopia, Parchment & Pine, Green	25.00
Cornucopia, Tokay, Cornucopia, Green	25.00
Cornucopia, Water Lily, Double	50.00 To 60.00
Cornucopia, Water Lily, Matte, 6 1/2 In.	45.00
Cornucopia, Wildflower, 7 1/2 In.	28.00
Cornucopia, Wildflower, 8 1/2 In.	57.00
Cornucopia, Woodland, 11 In.	30.00
Cornucopia, Woodland, Double	225.00
Cornucopia, Woodland, Glossy, 11 In.	45.00
Cornucopia, Yellow & Brown, 7 1/2 In.	40.00
Cracker Jar, Little Red Riding Hood	140.00
Creamer, Open Rose, 5 In.	45.00
Creamer, Serenade, Blue	15.00
Creamer, Woodland, Pink	22.00
Cup & Saucer, Sunglow	23.00
Ewer, Butterfly, White, 13 1/2 In.	95.00
Ewer, Dogwood, 8 1/2 In.	48.00
Ewer, Dogwood, Peach, 11 1/2 In.	110.00

Ewer, Dogwood, Yellow, Green, 8 1/2 In.	55.00
Ewer, Magnolia, 13 1/2 In.	110.00 To 135.00
Ewer, Magnolia, 15 In.	125.00
Ewer, Serenade, Pink	30.00
Ewer, Tropicana, 12 1/2 In.	250.00
Ewer, Tulip, 8 In.	75.00
Ewer, Tulip, Blue, 8 In.	70.00
Ewer, Water Lily, 5 1/2 In.	25.00
Ewer, Wildflower, 7 1/4 In.	60.00
Ewer, Wildflower, Matte, 8 1/2 In.	80.00
Flowerpot, Bow Knot	45.00
Flowerpot, Bow-Knot	45.00
Flowerpot, Woodland, 5 1/4 In.	70.00
Jar, Batter, Little Red Riding Hood	95.00
Jar, Little Red Riding Hood, Cover, 9 In.	110.00
Jardiniere, Bow-Knot, 9 3/4 In.	495.00
Jardiniere, Iris, Pink, 5 1/2 In.	45.00
Jardiniere, Tulip, 7 In.	77.00
Jardiniere, Tulip, Pink, 5 In.	30.00
Jardiniere, Tulip, Pink, Blue	110.00 To 125.00
Jardiniere, Water Lily, 5 1/2 In.	25.00
Jardiniere, Water Lily, 8 1/2 In.	85.00
Jardiniere, Woodland, 9 1/2 In.	320.00
Jardiniere, Woodland, Matte, 5 1/2 In.	70.00
Jardiniere, Woodland, Peach, 5 1/2 In.	20.00
Lamp, Bow-Knot, Blue	225.00
Lamp, Little Red Riding Hood	750.00
Lamp, Poppy	295.00
Lamp, Sueno Tulip, 2 Socket Pull Chains, No Shade	120.00
Mustard, Little Red Riding Hood	105.00
Mustard, Little Red Riding Hood, Spoon	175.00
Pitcher, Art, Blue Flowers, Gold, 5 1/2 In.	45.00
Pitcher, Blossom Flite, Pitcher	25.00
Pitcher, Bow-Knot	75.00
Pitcher, Little Red Riding Hood, Side Pour, 6 3/4 In.	135.00
Pitcher, Milk, Little Red Riding Hood	70.00
Pitcher, Satin Florette, Pink, 7 In.	250.00
Pitcher, Sunglow, 24 Oz.	30.00
Pitcher, Water, Magnolia	30.00
Planter, Fluffy Pink Cat	16.00
Planter, Geese	20.00
Planter, Giraffe, Green	18.00
Planter, Lamb, Paper Label	18.00
Planter, Parchment & Pine	25.00
Planter, Poodle	14.00
Planter, Siamese Cat & Kitten, 11 In.	32.00
Planter, Smilin' Duck	23.00
Plate, Bow-Knot, Matte Blue, 1949	750.00
Plate, Bow-Knot, Pink	650.00
Plate, Butterfly	65.00
Rose Bowl, Iris, Peach, 7 In.	40.00 To 50.00
Rose Bowl, Iris, Pink, Blue, 7 In.	48.00
Salt & Pepper, Little Red Riding Hood, Large	30.00 To 33.00
Salt & Pepper, Little Red Riding Hood, Medium	160.00
Salt & Pepper, Little Red Riding Hood, Small	15.00
Stein, American Legion	25.00
String Holder, Little Red Riding Hood	700.00
Sugar & Creamer, Cover, Butterfly	25.00
Sugar & Creamer, Little Red Riding Hood, Open	60.00
Sugar & Creamer, Little Red Riding Hood, Pour Through Head	175.00
Sugar & Creamer, Magnolia, Matte	45.00
Sugar & Creamer, Woodland	37.00
Sugar, Cover, Butterfly	18.00
Sugar, Cover, Woodland, Pink	22.00

Sugar, Little Red Riding Hood 30.00
Sugar, Magnolia, 3 3/4 In. 28.00
Tea Set, Blossom Flite, 3 Piece 100.00
Tea Set, Magnolia, 3 Piece .... 110.00 To 175.00
Tea Set, Magnolia, Pink & Blue, Gold Trim, 3 Piece 60.00
Tea Set, Water Lily, 3 Piece 175.00
Tea Set, Woodland, Green, 3 Piece 70.00
Teapot, Butterfly 60.00
Teapot, Ebb Tide, Red 70.00
Teapot, Little Red Riding Hood 85.00
Teapot, Magnolia, Matte .... 35.00 To 45.00
Teapot, Serenade, Blue 60.00
Teapot, Serenade, Cream 40.00
Teapot, Serenade, Pink 95.00
Teapot, Water Lily, 5 1/2 In. 26.00
Teapot, Woodland 60.00
Teapot, Woodland, Matte Cream 150.00
Teapot, Woodland, Peach 38.00
Vase, Bow–Knot, 6 1/2 In. .... 40.00 To 65.00
Vase, Bow–Knot, 7 1/2 In. 75.00
Vase, Bow–Knot, 8 1/2 In. .... 40.00 To 125.00
Vase, Bow–Knot, 9 In. 45.00
Vase, Bow–Knot, Blue, 10 1/2 In. 150.00
Vase, Bow–Knot, Pink, 5 3/4 In. 45.00
Vase, Calla Lily, 6 1/2 In. 45.00
Vase, Calla Lily, 7 1/2 In. 75.00
Vase, Calla Lily, 8 In. 55.00
Vase, Calla Lily, 10 In. 70.00
Vase, Calla Lily, Green, 8 In. 50.00
Vase, Dogwood, 6 1/2 In. .... 25.00 To 45.00
Vase, Dogwood, Beige, 7 1/2 In. 40.00
Vase, Iris, 7 1/2 In. 28.00
Vase, Iris, 8 1/2 In. 65.00
Vase, Iris, 10 1/2 In. .... 90.00 To 125.00
Vase, Iris, Peach, 4 3/4 In. 20.00
Vase, Magnolia, 6 1/4 In. .... 26.00 To 38.00
Vase, Magnolia, 8 1/2 In. 65.00
Vase, Magnolia, 10 1/2 In. 75.00
Vase, Magnolia, 12 1/2 In. .... 75.00 To 125.00
Vase, Magnolia, Blue & Pink, 7 In. 95.00
Vase, Magnolia, Blue, 12 1/2 In. 80.00
Vase, Magnolia, Matte Brown, 8 1/2 In. 50.00
Vase, Magnolia, Matte, Pink, Yellow 20.00
Vase, Magnolia, Pink & Blue, 12 1/2 In. 50.00
Vase, Magnolia, Pink & Blue, 15 In. 125.00
Vase, Magnolia, Pink, 5 1/2 In. 20.00
Vase, Magnolia, Pink, Yellow, Matte 20.00
Vase, Mardi Gras, 9 In. 17.00
Vase, Morning Glory, White 2000.00
Vase, Open Rose, 7 In. 95.00
Vase, Open Rose, 8 1/2 In. 45.00
Vase, Open Rose, Swan, 6 1/2 In. .... 28.50 To 65.00
Vase, Orchid, 10 1/2 In. 125.00
Vase, Orchid, Fan, Blue, 6 1/2 In. 48.00
Vase, Orchid, Handles, 6 1/2 In. 45.00
Vase, Orchid, Pink, 9 1/2 In. 65.00
Vase, Parchment & Pine, 10 1/2 In. 30.00
Vase, Pink Floral, 6 In. 18.00
Vase, Rose To Peach, 8 1/2 In. 60.00
Vase, Rosella, 6 1/2 In. 35.00
Vase, Serenade, 11 In. 32.00
Vase, Sueno Tulip, Blue, 6 In. 45.00
Vase, Sueno Tulip, Pink & Blue, 6 In. .... 35.00 To 38.00
Vase, Sunglow, 6 1/2 In. 12.00

Vase, Sunglow, Yellow	18.00
Vase, Thistle, 6 1/2 In. .... 28.00 To	40.00
Vase, Tokay	20.00
Vase, Tulip, Matte, 10 In.	95.00
Vase, Tuscany, 10 In.	40.00
Vase, Unicorn	20.00
Vase, Water Lily, 8 1/2 In. .... 35.00 To	45.00
Vase, Water Lily, Matte, 5 1/2 In.	20.00
Vase, Water Lily, Matte, 6 1/2 In.	40.00
Vase, Wildflower, 5 1/2 In. .... 20.00 To	30.00
Vase, Wildflower, 6 1/2 In. .... 28.00 To	45.00
Vase, Wildflower, 7 1/2 In. .... 35.00 To	40.00
Vase, Wildflower, 8 1/2 In.	65.00
Vase, Wildflower, 9 1/2 In. .... 50.00 To	75.00
Vase, Wildflower, 10 1/2 In. .... 65.00 To	85.00
Vase, Wildflower, 12 1/2 In.	85.00
Vase, Wildflower, Fan, Pink, 10 1/2 In.	55.00
Vase, Wildflower, Yellow, 12 1/2 In.	70.00
Vase, Woodland, 5 1/2 In.	25.00
Vase, Woodland, 7 1/2 In. .... 28.00 To	30.00
Vase, Woodland, 8 1/2 In. .... 45.00 To	70.00
Vase, Woodland, Double	35.00
Wall Pocket, Bow–Knot, Whiskbroom, 1 Pink, 1 Blue, Pair	110.00
Wall Pocket, Cup & Saucer, Pink	95.00
Wall Pocket, Irons	28.00
Wall Pocket, Little Red Riding Hood .... 160.00 To	275.00
Wall Pocket, Open Rose, Pink & Blue	115.00
Wall Pocket, Sunglow	28.00
Wall Pocket, Sunglow, 1/2 Pitcher	20.00
Wall Pocket, Sunglow, Broom, Pink	25.00
Wall Pocket, Sunglow, Whiskbroom, Pink	22.00
Wall Pocket, Woodland, Pink & Apricot, 7 1/2 In.	55.00
Window Box, Pink, 10 1/2 In.	60.00
Window Box, Woodland, Yellow & Green, 10 In.	45.00

 Hummel figurines, based on the drawings of Berta Hummel, are made by the W. Goebel Porzellanfabrik of Oeslau, Germany, now Rodenthal, West Germany. They were first made in 1934. The mark has changed through the years. The following are the approximate dates for each of the marks: "Crown" mark, 1935 to 1949; "U. S. Zone, Germany," 1946 to 1948; "West Germany," after 1949; "full bee," with variations, 1950 to 1959; "stylized bee," 1960 to 1972; "three line mark," 1968 to 1979; "vee over gee," 1972 to 1979; "new mark," 1979 to present.

HUMMEL, Ashtray, Happy Pastime	60.00
Bookends, Bookworm, Stylized Bee	475.00
Bookends, Umbrella Boy & Girl, Stylized Bee	1450.00
Bust, Sister Hummel, White Bisque	135.00
Calendar, 1974	7.00
Calendar, 1980	7.00
Calendar, 1981	6.00
Candleholder, Christmas Angel, Full Bee, Pair	450.00
Doll, Goose Girl, Vinyl, Doll Stand	60.00
Doll, Stitch In Time, Vinyl, Doll Stand	60.00
Figurine, No. 1, Happy Days, Three Line Mark	850.00
Figurine, No. 1, Prayer Before Battle, Three Line Mark	500.00
Figurine, No. 1, Puppy Love, Three Line Mark	140.00
Figurine, No. 3/I, Bookworm, New Mark	110.00
Figurine, No. 3/II, Bookworm, V Over G	600.00
Figurine, No. 3/III, Book Worm, 9 In.	570.00
Figurine, No. 4, Little Fiddler, New Mark	110.00
Figurine, No. 5, Happy Traveler, Three Line Mark	260.00
Figurine, No. 5, School Boys, Three Line Mark	1350.00
Figurine, No. 5, School Girls, Three Line Mark	1350.00

Figurine, No. 6/0, Sensitive Hunter, Incised Corn 290.00
Figurine, No. 6/0, Sensitive Hunter, New Mark 115.00
Figurine, No. 6/II, Sensitive Hunter, Three Line Mark 350.00
Figurine, No. 10, Flower Madonna, Full Bee 800.00
Figurine, No. 10/II, Blue Madonna, Stylized Bee, 11 1/2 In. 325.00
Figurine, No. 12/I, Chimney Sweep, Full Bee 175.00
Figurine, No. 12/I, Chimney Sweep, V Over G 94.00
Figurine, No. 13/0, Meditation, Three Line Mark 90.00
Figurine, No. 13/II, Meditation, V Over G 245.00
Figurine, No. 13/V, Meditation, Three Line Mark 500.00
Figurine, No. 15/0, Hear Ye, Full Bee 195.00
Figurine, No. 16, Little Hiker, Stylized Bee, 1 Line Mark, 4 In. 60.00
Figurine, No. 17/0, Congratulations, Straight Hair, Stylized 150.00
Figurine, No. 21, Heavenly Angel, Large 195.00
Figurine, No. 21/0, Heavenly Angel, 4 3/4 In. 42.00
Figurine, No. 23, Adoration, Full Bee .... 290.00 To 320.00
Figurine, No. 24/III, Lullaby, V Over G 425.00
Figurine, No. 33, Joyful Ashtray, V Over G 80.00
Figurine, No. 45/O, Madonna, With White Halo, V Over G 42.00
Figurine, No. 47/0, Goose Girl, Blade of Grass, Full Bee 225.00
Figurine, No. 47/3/0, Goose Girl, 4 In. 65.00
Figurine, No. 47/II, Goose Girl, Stylized Bee 275.00
Figurine, No. 50/2/0, Volunteers 120.00
Figurine, No. 50/2/0, Volunteers, Stylized Bee 155.00
Figurine, No. 50/2/0, Volunteers, V Over G 120.00
Figurine, No. 50/I, Volunteers, V Over G 340.00
Figurine, No. 52/I, Going To Grandma's, 1979, V Over G 340.00
Figurine, No. 56, Culprits, Stylized Bee 170.00
Figurine, No. 56A, Culprits, Full Bee .... 360.00 To 360.00
Figurine, No. 58/0, Playmates, Crown 296.00
Figurine, No. 59, Skier, Wooden Poles, Fiber Disks, Stylized Bee 150.00
Figurine, No. 63, Singing Lesson, Stylized Bee 75.00
Figurine, No. 65, Farewell, Full Bee 190.00
Figurine, No. 66, Farm Boy, Full Bee 260.00
Figurine, No. 66, Farm Boy, Stylized 145.00
Figurine, No. 66, Farm Boy, Three Line Mark 145.00
Figurine, No. 67, Doll Mother, Full Bee 258.00
Figurine, No. 71, Stormy Weather, Stylized Bee 440.00
Figurine, No. 71/I/0, Stormy Weather 105.00
Figurine, No. 72, Spring Cheer, Full Bee 273.00
Figurine, No. 81/0, School Girl, Three Line Mark 425.00
Figurine, No. 82 2/0, School Boy, Three Line Mark 55.00
Figurine, No. 82/2/0, School Boy, Full Bee 70.00
Figurine, No. 85/II, Serenade, V Over G 200.00
Figurine, No. 86, Happiness, Full Bee, 4 3/4 In. 125.00
Figurine, No. 89/II, Little Cellist, V Over G 220.00
Figurine, No. 91B, Angel At Prayer 65.00
Figurine, No. 94/3/0, Surprise, Full Bee 125.00
Figurine, No. 94/3/0, Surprise, Three Line Mark 95.00
Figurine, No. 95, Brother, Crown Mark, 5 1/2 In. 360.00
Figurine, No. 98, Sister, Full Bee 165.00
Figurine, No.109/II, Happy Traveler, Stylized Bee 325.00
Figurine, No.109/II, Happy Traveler, V Over G 275.00
Figurine, No.111/3/0, Wayside Harmony, Full Bee 100.00
Figurine, No.112/I, Just Resting 110.00
Figurine, No.119, Postman, Full Bee .... 173.00 To 199.00
Figurine, No.119, Postman, New Mark 100.00
Figurine, No.123, Max & Moritz, Full Bee 125.00
Figurine, No.124/I, Hello, V Over G 175.00
Figurine, No.127, Doctor, Full Bee 100.00
Figurine, No.128, Baker, Full Bee 160.00
Figurine, No.129, Bandleader, Stylized Bee 170.00
Figurine, No.132, Star Gazer, Stylized Bee 139.00
Figurine, No.135, Soloist, Stylized Bee 125.00

Figurine, No.136/V, Friends, V Over G 500.00
Figurine, No.141/3/0, Apple Tree Girl, Full Bee 125.00
Figurine, No.141/I, Apple Tree Girl, Stylized 165.00
Figurine, No.141/V, Apple Tree Girl, 10 In. 500.00
Figurine, No.142/I, Apple Tree Boy, V Over G 118.00
Figurine, No.142/V, Apple Tree Boy, 10 In. 500.00
Figurine, No.143, Boots, Full Bee 258.00
Figurine, No.143/0, Boots 88.00
Figurine, No.143/0, Boots, Full Bee 150.00
Figurine, No.143/9, Boots, V Over G 88.00
Figurine, No.143/I, Boots, V Over G 145.00
Figurine, No.151, Madonna, 1952, 12 In. 300.00
Figurine, No.152/A/0, Umbrella Boy, New Mark 300.00
Figurine, No.152/A/II, Umbrella Boy, 8 In. 590.00
Figurine, No.152/B/0, Umbrella Girl, New Mark 300.00
Figurine, No.153/I, Auf Wiedersehen, V Over G 176.00
Figurine, No.154/0, Waiter 100.00
Figurine, No.154/0, Waiter, V Over G 100.00
Figurine, No.163, Whitsuntide, 7 In. 120.00
Figurine, No.165, Swaying Lullaby, Full Bee 400.00
Figurine, No.170, School Boys, Three Line Mark 1100.00
Figurine, No.170/III, School Boys, TMK5 .... 1350.00
Figurine, No.170/III, School Boys, V Over G .... 1200.00 To 1395.00
Figurine, No.173/0, Festival Harmony, Flute, Three Line Mark 150.00
Figurine, No.174, She Loves Me, Open Eyes, Three Line Mark 150.00
Figurine, No.174, She Loves, She Loves Me Not, Full Bee 225.00
Figurine, No.176/0, Happy Birthday 110.00
Figurine, No.177/I, School Girls, 7 1/2 In. 480.00
Figurine, No.177/III, School Girls 1200.00
Figurine, No.177/III, School Girls, V Over G 1200.00
Figurine, No.178, Photographer, Stylized Bee 140.00
Figurine, No.179, Coquettes, V Over G 120.00
Figurine, No.182, Good Friends, Stylized Bee 140.00
Figurine, No.184, Latest News, Full Bee 395.00
Figurine, No.184, Latest News, Stylized Bee 300.00
Figurine, No.184, Latest News, Three Line Mark 170.00
Figurine, No.184/0, Latest News, Stylized Bee 170.00
Figurine, No.185, Accordion Boy, Stylized Bee 165.00
Figurine, No.195/2/0, Barnyard Hero, Stylized Bee 125.00
Figurine, No.196/0, Telling Her Secret, Three Line Mark 175.00
Figurine, No.196/I, Telling Her Secret, V Over G 340.00
Figurine, No.197/2/0, Be Patient 95.00
Figurine, No.197/I, Be Patient, 6 1/4 In. 108.00
Figurine, No.198/2/0, Home From Market, Full Bee 125.00
Figurine, No.198/I, Home From Market 82.00
Figurine, No.199/I, Feeding Time 200.00
Figurine, No.200/0, Little Goat Herder 95.00
Figurine, No.200/0, Little Goat Herder 95.00
Figurine, No.200/0, Little Goat Herder, Full Bee, Donut Base 240.00
Figurine, No.200/0, Little Goat Herder, Three Line Mark 130.00
Figurine, No.200/0, Little Goat Herder, V Over G 95.00
Figurine, No.201/I, Retreat To Safety 150.00
Figurine, No.201/I, Retreat To Safety, V Over G 150.00
Figurine, No.203, Signs of Spring, Full Bee 325.00
Figurine, No.203/I, Signs of Spring 110.00
Figurine, No.214/L/O, King Standing 110.00
Figurine, No.214E, We Congratulate 55.00
Figurine, No.240, Little Drummer, Three Line Mark 55.00
Figurine, No.240, Little Drummer, V Over G 55.00
Figurine, No.255/4/0, Stitch In Time 65.00
Figurine, No.304, Artist 95.00
Figurine, No.314, Confidentially, V Over G 98.00
Figurine, No.319.Doll Bath, Stylized Bee 300.00
Figurine, No.322, Little Pharmacist, V Over G 110.00

Figurine, No.328, Carnival, V Over G	98.00
Figurine, No.331, Crossroads, 6 3/4 In.	175.00
Figurine, No.333, Blessed Event, Three Line Mark	378.00
Figurine, No.340, Letter To Santa, V Over G	150.00
Figurine, No.353/I, Spring Dance	385.00
Figurine, No.363, Big Housecleaning, V Over G	150.00
Figurine, No.367, Busy Student, 4 1/4 In.	69.00
Figurine, No.369, Follow The Leader	420.00
Figurine, No.369, Follow The Leader, Full Bee	615.00
Figurine, No.383, Going Home	119.00
Figurine, No.383, Going Home, 4 1/2 In.	120.00
Figurine, No.387, Valentine Gift	350.00
Figurine, No.387, Valentine Gift, V Over G	225.00
Figurine, No.396/I, Ride Into Christmas, 5 3/4 In.	175.00
Figurine, No.399, Boy, Valentine Joy, Collector Club	150.00
Figurine, No.412, Bath Time	300.00
Figurine, No.418, What's New?	200.00
Figurine, No.423, Horse Trainer	155.00
Figurine, No.424, Sleep Tight	155.00
Figurine, No.439, A Gentle Glow	75.00
Font, No. SP067	30.00
Inkwell, With Loving Greetings, Blue	135.00
Lamp, No. 44A, Culprits, Crown Mark	325.00
Lamp, No. 44B, Out of Danger, Full Bee	235.00
Lamp, No.228, Full Bee	350.00
Music Box, Chick Girl	239.00
Music Box, Ride	240.00
Plaque, No. 93, Little Fiddler, Three Line Mark	400.00
Plaque, No.126, Retreat To Safety	100.00
Plaque, No.168, Standing Boy, Three Line Mark	125.00
Plaque, No.187, Dealer, V Over G, 1976	125.00
Plaque, No.690, Smiling Through, Goebel Club ....67.00 To 105.00
Plate, Anniversary, 1974	125.00
Plate, Anniversary, 1980	125.00
Plate, Annual, 1971, Box	545.00
Plate, Annual, 1972	75.00
Plate, Annual, 1973 ....75.00 To 90.00
Plate, Annual, 1974	45.00
Plate, Annual, 1978	55.00
Plate, Annual, 1984	40.00
Plate, Annual, 1986	110.00
Plate, No.735, Collector Club, It's Cold, Box, 1989	60.00
Plate, No.741, 1985, Goebel	73.00
Salt & Pepper, Monk, Full Bee	30.00
Sugar & Creamer, Monk, Full Bee	50.00

LORENZ
HUTSCHEN REUTER   Hutschenreuther Porcelain Company of Selb, Germany, was
established in 1814 and is still working. The company makes fine
quality porcelain dinnerwares and figurines. The mark has changed
HR   through the years, but the name and the lion insignia appear in
GERMANY   most versions.

HUTSCHENREUTHER, Bowl, 3 Baroque Feet, Blue Ground, Silver, Flowers, 7 In.	150.00
Cup & Saucer, Demitasse, Blue Onion	20.00
Figurine, 2 Brown Bears, Playing, Base, Tutter	125.00
Figurine, 2 Horses, Running, White, Signed, 11 1/4 X 15 In.	500.00
Figurine, 3 Birds	200.00
Figurine, Angel With Harp	85.00
Figurine, Angel's Concert	83.00
Figurine, Bird, Holding Worm	45.00
Figurine, Boys Boxing, U.S. Zone	160.00
Figurine, Cat, Holding Ball, Lying, White, Achtziger, 6 In.	165.00
Figurine, Cherub Holding Mask, White, 5 In.	70.00
Figurine, Dachshund, Standing On Hind Legs, White, 7 In.	175.00
Figurine, Elfin Flutist, Sitting On Tray, Pastel, Tutter	135.00

Figurine, Musician of Brenos	225.00
Figurine, Nude, Throwing Gold Ball, 1920s, 10 In.	425.00
Figurine, Polar Bear, On Ball, White, Gold Trim, 4 In.	95.00
Group, Male Dancer & Female, Signed, 8 1/4 In.	345.00
Love For All Seasons, 1 Through 6	110.00
Plate, 22K Gold Leaf Design, Selb Bavaria, 10 3/4 In.	20.00
Plate, Fruit Center, Marked, 8 1/2 In.	25.00
Plate, Parsifal	120.00
Plate, Roses of Redoute, 24K Gold Trim, 6 1/4 In., 8 Piece	260.00
Plate, Roses of Redoute, Box, 8 Piece	260.00
Plate, Tristan & Isolde	125.00
Platter, Kensington, 15 X 11 In.	80.00
Sugar, Creamer & Teapot, Thistle	60.00
Vase, Parrot On Branch, White Bisque, 9 In.	150.00

An icon is a special, revered picture of Jesus, Mary, or a saint. These are usually Russian or Byzantine. The small icons collected today are made of wood and tin or precious metals. Many modern copies have been made in the old style and are being sold to unsuspecting tourists in Russia and Europe.

ICON, Christ Pantocrator, Cloisonne, Moscow, 1895, 12 X 10 In.	4180.00
Life of St.Ilya, Russia, 19th Century, Wood Panel, 14 3/4 X 17 5/8 In.	2500.00
Madonna & Child, Silver Over Copper, Russian, C.1850, 10 X 12 In.	1800.00
Madonna & Child, Silver Over Copper, Russian, C.1870, 10 X 12 In.	2400.00
Saints & Angels, Russian, 19th Century	450.00
Saints, Angels Looking From Heaven, Pewter On Copper, 1842, 11 1/2 In.	1800.00
Scenes of Life & Death of Jesus, Russian, Brass, Traveling	800.00
St. Nicholas, Silver Over Copper, Russian, C.1880	2600.00
Young Christ, Raised Enamel Design, Russian, Silver Gilt, 19th Century	1800.00

Imari patterns are named for the Japanese ware decorated with orange and blue stylized flowers. The design on the Japanese ware became so characteristic that the name "Imari" has come to mean any pattern of this type. It was copied by the European factories of the eighteenth and early nineteenth centuries.

IMARI, Bowl, Basket of Flowers, 9 In.	150.00
Bowl, Blue Floral, Celadon Ground, 3 3/4 X 11 3/4 In.	125.00
Bowl, Fish, Figural Design, China, 16 In., Pair	1100.00
Bowl, Flower, C.1820, 5 1/2 X 6 3/4 In.	250.00
Bowl, Pinched & Scalloped Rim, Bird & Floral Panels, 11 In.	405.00
Bowl, Polychrome Design, 6 1/4 X 17 1/2 In.	250.00
Bowl, Polychrome Design, Scalloped Rim, 8 5/8 In.	85.00
Bowl, Square, C.1800, 5 1/4 In.	3000.00
Charger, 4 Medallions, Diapering, Scalloped, Mid–18th Century, 12 In.	285.00
Charger, 6 Medallions, Floral Center, White Rim, 1760, 12 In.	330.00
Charger, Ikebana Center, 18th Century, 17 In.	1760.00
Charger, Leaf Veining, Scalloped, Burnt Orange, Gold, 1760, 12 1/2 In.	475.00
Charger, Multicolored Enamels, Central Medallion, 15 3/4 In.	315.00
Chrysanthemum Cup, C.1800, 2 1/4 In.	225.00
Compote, Polychrome, Gilt Initials J.N.C., 9 In.	150.00
Cup, Maple Design, C.1820, 2 1/2 In.	225.00
Daisy Cup, C.1820, 2 1/2 In.	225.00
Dish, Boat Shape, Enamel, Panels, Blue & Gilt Ground, 13 1/2 In.	525.00
Dish, Shell, Pedestal, Red & Blue, Signed, C.1800	225.00
Jar, Cover, Cavorting Lion Cubs, Flowers, 19th Century, 11 In., Pair	687.50
Jar, Temple, Cover, Children Scenes, Flying Phoenix, 18 1/2 In.	825.00
Jardiniere, Fluted, Floral Design, Footed, 6 1/2 In.	330.00
Plate, Central Landscape, Floral Panels, 9 1/4 In., 6 Piece	550.00
Plate, Polychrome Design, Scalloped Rim, 8 1/2 In.	75.00
Plate, Scenes In Rectangles, White Ground, Marked, 8 1/2 In.	50.00
Punch Bowl, Flying Phoenix, Leafy Vines Field, 7 1/2 X 15 In.	3960.00
Punch Bowl, Ribbed, Scalloped, Cartouche Design, 13 1/2 In.	990.00
Tankard, Blue Floral Design, Peach Accents, Allover Gilt, 6 In.	825.00
Toothpick, Sterling Rim, 1 3/4 In.	25.00

Urn, Domed Cover, Lion Finial, Fluted Body, Flowers, 20 In.	655.00
Urn, Temple, Floral Design, Overglaze Enamels, Japanese, 36 In., Pair'	3300.00
Vase, Baluster, Pomegranate Handles, 24 In.	220.00
Vase, Floral, Underglaze Blue & Overglaze Rust, Fluted, 8 In.	305.00
Vase, Fluted, Floral Ground, Fukugawa, 11 1/2 In., Pair	2700.00
Vase, Gold Scroll Pattern, Barrel Form, 19th Century, 12 In., Pair	825.00
Vase, Overall Paneled Floral, Fluted, 10 1/4 In.	302.50
Vase, Polychrome, 6 1/4 In.	90.00

⊢IM⊤PE⊣
⊢RI⊥AL⊣

Imperial Glass Corporation was founded in Bellaire, Ohio, in 1901. It became a division of Lenox, Inc., in 1977 and was sold to Arthur R. Lorch in 1981. It was sold again in 1982. It went bankrupt in 1982 and some of the molds and assets have been offered to other companies. The Imperial glass preferred by the collector is stretch glass, art glass, carnival glass, and the top–quality tablewares.

IMPERIAL, Candlewick, Ashtray, Eagle	50.00
Candlewick, Bowl, Blue, 11 In.	100.00
Candlewick, Bowl, Float, 11 In.	30.00
Candlewick, Bowl, Heart, Handle, 6 1/2 In.	18.00
Candlewick, Bowl, Vegetable, 8 In.	35.00
Candlewick, Box, Cutting On Cover	60.00
Candlewick, Butter, Cover	7.00
Candlewick, Cake Plate, Birthday	225.00
Candlewick, Cake Stand, Floral Cut	77.00
Candlewick, Cake Stand, Footed, Floral & Leaf Cutting	20.00
Candlewick, Candlestick	14.00
Candlewick, Clock, Boudoir	250.00
Candlewick, Compote, 5 1/2 In.	18.00
Candlewick, Cup & Saucer	2.00
Candlewick, Dish, Divided	28.00
Candlewick, Eggcup	29.50
Candlewick, Goblet, Water	15.00
Candlewick, Ice Bucket, Handles, 7 In.	200.00
Candlewick, Icer, Seafood	70.00
Candlewick, Jam Jar, Spoon	25.00
Candlewick, Mayonnaise Set, 3 Piece	22.00
Candlewick, Mayonnaise Set, Etched Stars, 2 Piece	30.00
Candlewick, Mayonnaise, Farberware Chrome Underplate, Ladle, Box	50.00
Candlewick, Mayonnaise, Underplate, Etched	23.00
Candlewick, Nappy, Gold Beaded	30.00
Candlewick, Pickle, Oval	9.50
Candlewick, Pitcher, 80 Oz.	85.00
Candlewick, Pitcher, Manhattan	205.00
Candlewick, Plate, 6 In.	6.50
Candlewick, Plate, 7 In.	7.00
Candlewick, Plate, 8 In.	8.00
Candlewick, Plate, Black, 2 Handles	60.00
Candlewick, Platter, 13 In.	60.00
Candlewick, Relish, 10 In.	20.00
Candlewick, Relish, 13 In.	55.00
Candlewick, Relish, 2 Sections, 8 In.	15.00
Candlewick, Relish, 4 Sections, 8 In.	16.00 To 18.00
Candlewick, Relish, 5 Sections, 10 1/2 In.	25.00
Candlewick, Relish, 5 Sections, 14 X 9 In.	32.50
Candlewick, Salad Set, 3 Piece	50.00
Candlewick, Salt & Pepper	22.00
Candlewick, Server, Deviled Eggs, Handle	60.00
Candlewick, Shaker, Pair	9.75
Candlewick, Sugar & Creamer, Beaded Foot	45.00
Candlewick, Sugar, Ruby Flashed	65.00
Candlewick, Tidbit, 2 Tiers	35.00
Candlewick, Tray, 5 1/4 X 9 1/4 In.	40.00
Candlewick, Tray, Center Handle, 8 1/2 In.	29.00
Candlewick, Tray, Deviled Egg	75.00 To 87.50

Candlewick, Tray, Handle, 8 In. 28.00
Candlewick, Tray, Lemon, Handle, 5 1/2 In. 30.00
Candlewick, Vase, Crimped, 2 Handles, Star Cut, 8 In. 35.00
Cape Cod, Bowl, 11 1/2 In. 80.00
Cape Cod, Bowl, Footed, 10 In. 42.00
Cape Cod, Cake Plate, Footed 17.00
Cape Cod, Celery, Oval, 10 1/2 In. 45.00
Cape Cod, Cocktail 20.00
Cape Cod, Condiment Set, 5 Piece 45.00
Cape Cod, Cookie Jar, Amber 15.00
Cape Cod, Creamer 9.00
Cape Cod, Cruet, Olive Green 35.00
Cape Cod, Cup & Saucer 2.00
Cape Cod, Dish, Baked Apple 6.00
Cape Cod, Goblet, 8 Oz. 5.00
Cape Cod, Jam Jar, 4 Piece 25.00
Cape Cod, Plate, 2 Handles 26.00
Cape Cod, Plate, Handle, 8 In. 13.00
Cape Cod, Plate, Torte, Large 30.00
Cape Cod, Relish, 3 Sections .... 15.00 To 17.00
Cape Cod, Salt & Pepper 22.00
Cape Cod, Salt & Pepper Mill 25.00
Cape Cod, Salt & Pepper, Chrome Tops 16.00
Cape Cod, Salt & Pepper, Footed 40.00
Cape Cod, Salt & Pepper, Yellow 35.00
Cape Cod, Tray, 16 1/2 In. 45.00
Cape Cod, Tray, For Sugar & Creamer 8.00
Cape Cod, Tumbler, Water, Footed, Label, 9 Oz. 6.00
Cape Cod, Vase, Bud 35.00
Cathay, Dragon Dish, Virginia B.Evans, Clear Frosted, 6 In. 15.00
Colonial, Cruet, Pink 35.00
Fernery, Clear, Luster, Iron Cross Mark 30.00
Figurine, Show Horse, Amber 650.00
Grape, Nappy, Milk Glass, 4 In. 5.00
Heather, Goblet, 10 Oz. 17.00
Loganberry, Vase, White Carnival, Large 40.00
Mayflower, Water Set, Smoke, 7 Piece 165.00
Molly, Luncheon Set, Red, 15 Piece 150.00
Mt. Vernon, Cocktail 2.50
Mt. Vernon, Creamer 42.00
Mt. Vernon, Sherbet 2.50
Nuart, Vase, Cylindrical, 7 1/2 In. 125.00
Open Rose, Butter, Cover, Helio Green 45.00
Orange & Dark Blue Luster, Vase, Pulled Drape, 8 1/2 In. 245.00
Orange Luster, Vase, Thin Tapered Neck, 10 1/4 In. 110.00
Paperweight, Pair of Bunnies 16.00
Paperweight, Rabbit 18.00
Plate, Waverly, Label, 8 In. 6.00
Red Panel, Cake Stand 18.00
Tradition, Goblet, Water, Blue 10.00
Tradition, Plate, 8 In. 6.00

 Indian Tree is a china pattern that was popular during the last half of the nineteenth century. It was copied from earlier Indian textile patterns that were very similar. The pattern includes the crooked branch of a tree and a partial landscape with exotic flowers and leaves. Green, blue, pink, and orange were the favored colors used in the design.

INDIAN TREE, Creamer, Johnson Brothers, ... 15.00
Cup & Saucer, Copeland Spode 25.00
Plate, Coalport, 9 In. 15.00
Plate, Soup, Maddock 17.50
Platter, Hancock & Sons, 11 1/2 In. 45.00
Teapot, Gold Trim, English, 1/4 Gal. 200.00

Indian art from North America has attracted the collector for many years. Each tribe has its own distinctive designs and techniques. Baskets, jewelry, pottery, and leatherwork are of greatest collector interest. Eskimo art is listed in another section in this book.

INDIAN, Apron, Yurok, Woman's, Wrapped & Plaited Bear Grass, Trade Beads	3850.00
Awl Case, Apache	1100.00
Bag, Chippewa, Bandolier, Bead Fringe, Floral Design, 13 X 39 In.	700.00
Bag, Great Lakes, Bandolier, Beaded, Velvet Trim, C.1880	1650.00
Bag, Shot, Iroquois, Bearskin & Claw, C.1880	175.00
Bag, Sioux, Bladder, Leather, Bead Trim, Sinew Sewn, White River, S.D.	925.00
Bag, Taos, Child's, Ceremonial, Fringed & Beaded Buckskin	66.00
Bag, Yakima, Beaded, Red Wool, Easter Design, Leather Strap, 8 X 8 In.	105.00
Ball Club, Sioux, Hide & Sinew, 1860	395.00
Basket, Apache, Figures Printed On Sides	3300.00
Basket, Apache, Humans, Crosses & Dogs In Whirlwind Pattern	7700.00
Basket, Apache, Purple Triangles, Maroon Double Triangles, 17 In.	350.00
Basket, Apache, Tray, 1930	450.00
Basket, Burden, Apache, 10 In.	75.00
Basket, Burden, Paiute, Cone Shaped Lattice Work, 27 In.	145.00
Basket, Cherokee, River Cane, Geometric Design, 1940s, 14 In.	165.00
Basket, Gambling, Tray Form	550.00
Basket, Iroquois, Splint, Cover Attached To Bentwood Handle	95.00
Basket, Klamath, 3–Toned Horizontal Stripes	132.00
Basket, Klikitat, 1 1/2 In.	65.00
Basket, Northeast Woodland, Splint, Wall, 2–Pocket, Painted, 26 In.	225.00
Basket, Northeastern, Stamped & Freehand Design, 9 X 10 1/2 In.	195.00
Basket, Northwest, Pointed Top On Cover, Zigzag Design, 5 1/2 In.	90.00
Basket, Ojibwa, Bark, 10 1/2 X 4 1/2 In.	25.00
Basket, Paiute, 6 X 4 In.	175.00
Basket, Papago, Faded Key–Like Design, 9 1/4 X 5 1/4 In.	65.00
Basket, Papago, Figures & Animals, 7 X 7 3/4 X 4 In.	215.00
Basket, Papago, Geometric Design, Lizards, 16 X 10 In.	275.00
Basket, Papago, Geometric, Oval, 7 X 9 In.	30.00
Basket, Papago, Saguaro Cactus & Whirlwind Designs, 4 Colors	95.00
Basket, Penobscot, Cover, Sweet Grass & Birch Bark, C.1912	65.00
Basket, Seminole, Cover, Ceremonial, Palmetto & Swamp Grass	65.00
Basket, Tarahumara, Cover, 10 In.	20.00
Basket, Woodland, Lid, Swivel Handle, Red, Blue & Natural, 10 1/2 In.	135.00
Basket, Woodland, Woven Splint & Sweet Grass, 3 3/4 X 9 1/2 In.	25.00
Basket, Woodland, Woven Splint, 3 Colors, Oblong, 12 1/4 X 16 1/2 In.	175.00
Basket, Woodland, Woven Splint, Natural Design, Handle, 8 X 11 In.	30.00
Basket, Woodland, Woven Splint, Red, Black & Natural Design, 21 In.	825.00
Belt, Navajo, 13 Conchos, Silver Buckle, Turquoise, Early 19th C.	250.00
Belt, Navajo, Concho, 6 Butterflies, Silver, Turquoise Nuggets, 45 In.	375.00
Belt, Sioux, Beaded, Double Beaded Fringes, 45 In.	165.00
Blanket, Navajo, Brown, 4 X 6 Ft.	413.00
Blanket, Navajo, Child's, Red Field, Germantown	6050.00
Blanket, Navajo, Child's, Red, White & Black Crosses, 1860–80	7700.00
Blanket, Navajo, Diamond Medallion, 5 X 7 Ft.	550.00
Blanket, Navajo, Saddle, Double, Germantown	2750.00
Blanket, Navajo, Saddle, Red, Orange, Gray, Brown, White, 29 X 30 In.	150.00
Blanket, Navajo, Storm Pattern, Gray, Red & White, 1930s	200.00
Blanket, Serape, Blue, Black, Natural, Eagle Medallion, 53 X 74 In.	100.00
Bonnet, Northern Plains, Baby's, Beaded	1100.00
Bow Case & Quiver, Plains, Buffalo Hide, Sinew–Sewn, 10 Arrows	4400.00
Bowl, Apache, Basketry, Central Star	660.00
Bowl, Dough, Santo Domingo, White Slip, Red, Black, 14 1/4 X 8 In.	475.00
Bowl, Dough, Santo Domingo, White Slip, Red, Black, Signed, 11 X 5 In.	200.00
Bowl, Glossy & Matte Black, Marie Santano, 7 X 6 In.	350.00
Bowl, Hopi, Black & White, On Pink Slip, Signed E.M.Lalo, 4 3/4 In.	30.00
Bowl, Hopi, Smoked White Slip, Red, Black, 6 X 2 1/4 In.	250.00
Bowl, Hopi, White Slip, Red, Black, 5 1/2 X 1 7/8 In.	475.00
Bowl, Hopi, White Slip, Red, Black, 6 3/4 X 3 3/4 In.	65.00

Bowl, Sioux, Pine Tree, Pottery, 3 3/4 In.	22.00
Bowl, Sioux, U Curve, Sinew Back, 4 Original Arrows	800.00
Box, Birchbark, Laced Seams, Yellow Ocher Painted Design, 8 1/2 In.	125.00
Box, Canoe, Bentwood, Painted Designs, Cord Wraps	500.00
Box, Cartridge, Leather, Brass Trim, Indian Wars, 1870s Pat.7 1/2 In.	40.00
Box, Cigarette, Navajo, Turquoise Mounted, Hinged Cover, 4 5/8 In.	385.00
Box, Micmac, Quilted Birchbark, Oval, Cover	4950.00
Bracelet, Hopi, Silver On Black Ground, Signed R.Jr.	90.00
Bracelet, Navajo, Center Nugget, Silver, Nellie Baca	100.00
Bracelet, Navajo, Silver, 5 Turquoise, Silver, Floral	110.00
Breastplate, Sioux, Woman's, Hair-Pipe, Beaded Neckpiece	1100.00
Canteen, Hopi, White Slip, Red, Black, Moki Is., 3 In.	225.00
Cape, Plains, Dance, Bright Blue Beaded	3300.00
Carrier, Papoose, Apache, Yellow Beadwork & Fetishes	150.00
Charger, San Ildefonso, Marie & Santan, Black On Black	1430.00
Club, Nootka, Whalebone, Carved Heads & Incised Designs	2000.00
Coat, Crow, Man's, Beaded Front, Back & Sleeves, 32 In.	3400.00
Cradle Board, Santo Domingo, Pendleton Blanket, 11 X 29 In.	35.00
Cradle, Osage, C.1890	1200.00
Doll, Blackfoot, Ceremonial Dress, Leather, 7 1/2 In.	95.00
Doll, Papoose, 1940s, 9 In.	15.00
Doll, Rag, Beaded Face, Horsehair Wig, Leather Clothes, Feather, 9 In.	355.00
Doll, Seminole, 5 In.	15.00
Doll, Seminole, Rag, Embroidered Face, Glass Beads, Costume, 11 In.	60.00
Doll, Sioux, Beaded, 1940, 8 In.	40.00
Dress, Cheyenne, Beaded Hide, Fringed, Turquoise Ground, Gold Bars	7700.00
Dress, Plateau, Deer Tail Style, Fringed Hide, Pony Beaded	3950.00
Dress, Sioux, Doll's, Beaded Homespun, Rawhide Tassels, 14 In.	475.00
Dress, Southern Plains, Child's, Leggings, Fringed Hide, 19th Century	4950.00
Dress, Umatilla, Wing, Ribbon, Beads, Sequins & Shells, 1865	4500.00
Harness, Braided Horsehair, Bit & Quirt	225.00
Jacket, Sioux, Child's, Pictorial Beaded	4200.00
Jar, Acoma, Brown & White, 9 1/2 In. ....*Illus*	770.00
Jar, Acoma, White Slip, Red, Black, 5 In.	125.00
Jar, Acoma, White Slip, Red, Black, 6 1/4 In.	115.00
Jar, Acoma, White Slip, Red, Black, J.M.Chavez, 6 In.	150.00
Jar, Apache, Basketry, Geometric, 10 1/2 In.	375.00
Jar, Blackware, 2-Tone Design, Manuel Royer, 5 1/2 In.	150.00
Jar, Fish Effigy, Casas Grande, Polychrome, 5 1/4 In.	75.00
Jar, Hopi, Polychrome, 3 Frogs, 5 In. ....*Illus*	220.00

Indian, Vase, Northwestern,
Geometric Design, 11 In.

Indian, Plate, Cocle, Polychrome, Birds, 8 3/8 In.

Indian, Jar, Hopi, Polychrome, 3 Frogs, 5 In.

Indian, Jar, Acoma, Brown & White, 9 1/2 In.

Kachina, Hopi, Carved Wood, Polychromed, Leather, Yarn, Rubber, 21 In.	325.00
Kachina, Hopi, Maiden, Early 1900s	1500.00
Knife, Apache, Brass Tacks, Iron Blade	200.00
Knife, Nootka, Bone & Metal, Incised Designs	1430.00
Leggings, Assiniboin, Silk Ribbonwork, Yellow Beading, C.1885	1875.00
Leggings, Boy's, Red Trade Cloth	165.00
Martingale, Crow, Cochineal–Dyed Trade Cloth, Beaded, C.1875	1750.00
Moccasins, Blackfoot, Beaded	660.00
Moccasins, Cherokee, Beaded, 1920	350.00
Moccasins, Iroquois, Beaded, 9 1/2 In.	45.00
Moccasins, Plains, Comanche Beaded	1540.00
Moccasins, Plains, Quilled, Red–Dyed Hide, Forked Tongue, Tin Cone	3300.00
Moccasins, Santee Sioux, Beaded Red Silk Trim	675.00
Moccasins, Woodland, Child's	105.00
Necklace, Navajo, Squash Blossom, Silver, Tooled Pendant	375.00
Necklace, Navajo, Squash Blossom, Turquoise, V.Spencer	275.00
Necklace, Plains, Blue Bead Ends, Rope, 64 In.	10.00
Olla, Apache, 1900s	3850.00
Olla, Apache, Basketry, 20 Deer & Horse Figures, Tall	7150.00
Ornament, Dance, Lake Titicaca Region, Feather Mosaic, 1920	800.00
Painting, Over Cloth Board, Indian In War Regalia	65.00
Photogravure, Indian, National Art Co., Framed, 1909, 8 1/2 X 10 In.	12.50
Pipe Bag, Sioux, Beaded, 1880–90s	895.00
Pipe, Catlinite, Beaded Reed Stem, Small	145.00
Pipe, Great Lakes, Woodlands, Carved Catlinite, Corkscrew Stem	3430.00
Pipe, Sioux, Catlinite, T–Bowl, Black Designed Stem, Hair Drop	1150.00
Plate, Cocle, Polychrome, Birds, 8 3/8 In. ....*Illus*	192.00
Postcard, Indian War Dance Roundup, Pendleton, Oregon, 1911, Framed	5.00
Pot, Cooking, Tarahumara, Red & White Design, Rawhide Lacing, 12 In.	125.00
Pot, Santo Dominigo, 8 X 10 In.	175.00
Pot, Zia, Stylized Bird, Flowers, 18 In.	7150.00
Pot, Zuni, Heart–Line Deer Design, C.1880	7500.00
Pouch, Apache, Ceremonial, Religious	5280.00
Pouch, Beaded Wool, Finger–Like Fringe, 10 X 18 In.	900.00
Pouch, Iroquois, Beaded, 5 1/2 X 5 1/2 In.	125.00
Pouch, Plains, Beaded Leather, Tin Cones, Horsehair, 7 X 11 In.	300.00
Pouch, Plains, Beaded, Leather, Cross 1 Side, Lizard Other, 4 1/2 In.	55.00
Pouch, Sioux, Leather, Flags, White Ground, 5 3/4 In.	235.00
Rattle, Dance, Apache, Deer Toe, Pair	125.00
Rattle, Dance, Sioux, Turtle	165.00
Rattle, Nootka, Carved Wood	2860.00
Rattle, Northwest Coast, LaValle	500.00
Ring, Navajo, Green Turquoise, Size 9	35.00
Ring, Navajo, Silver, Large Oval Turquoise	25.00
Rug, Chimayo, Gray, Black, White, Green, 51 X 90 In.	425.00
Rug, Navajo, 5 Central Stepped Medallions, 3 Ft. X 6 Ft.5 In.	137.00
Rug, Navajo, Diamonds, Crosses, Swastikas, Red Ground, 42 X 61 In.	250.00
Rug, Navajo, Diamonds, Sawtooth Band, 3 Ft.8 1/2 In. X 5 Ft.6 In.	335.00
Rug, Navajo, Germantown Red, Black, White, 61 X 87 In.	1250.00
Rug, Navajo, Pastels, 1930s, 2 X 3 Ft.	195.00
Rug, Navajo, Red, Black, Gray, Natural, 2 Ft.10 In.X 5 Ft.2 In.	250.00
Rug, Navajo, Red, Black, White, Grayish Brown Ground, 34 X 55 In.	300.00
Rug, Navajo, Serrated Designs, Red Ground, 35 X 53 In.	250.00
Rug, Navajo, Stepped Design, Crenulated Border, 8 Ft. X 4 Ft.5 In.	700.00
Rug, Navajo, Triangular Design, White, Gray, Black, Yellow, 37 X 68 In.	160.00
Rug, Navajo, White, Black, Red, Gray Ground, 35 X 63 In.	325.00
Rug, Navajo, Yei, 22 X 23 In.	125.00
Rug, Navajo, Zigzag Pattern, 20th Century, 4 Ft.5 In. X 6 Ft.8 In.	310.00
Saddle & Blanket, Chippewa, Embroidered & Tooled	4620.00
Saddle, Eastern Plains, Woman's, Tacked, Fringed, Sinew–Sewn Rawhide	2200.00
Sheath, Knife, Northern Plains, Quilled	1760.00
Shield, Cochiti, Buffalo Hide	7480.00
Skirt, Seminole, Rickrack, Orange Silk, Colored Bands, 37 In.	65.00
Throw, Navajo, Gray, Gold, White, Reddish Black, 20 X 30 In.	20.00

Totem Pole, Polychrome, Raven Totem, Wrangell, Ak., 1931, 16 3/4 In. 225.00
Toy, Canoe, Walpole, Bark, Painted Wallaceburg, Canada, 1917, 17 In. 105.00
Tray, Gambling, Shasta, Bear Grass, Tule & Hamp, C.1890 .... 1870.00
Tray, Pima, 16 In. 320.00
Vase, Black On Black, San Ildefonso, Signed Marie & Julian 850.00
Vase, Isleta, White Slip, Red, Black, 4 1/2 In. 25.00
Vase, Northwestern, Geometric Design, 11 In. ....*Illus* 2100.00
Vessel, Effigy, Mississippi Valley, Pottery 300.00
Vessel, Sioux, Beaded, Leather Over Birchbark, Polychrome, 8 In. 125.00
Vest, Sioux, Man's, Hide, Fully Beaded, Geometric Design, 22 In. 3100.00
Wall Pocket, Woodlands, Silk Beaded, Prince of Wales Feathers, 1860 .... 1400.00
War Shirt, Plains, Fringed & Beaded Hide, Tufts of Hair 8500.00
War Shirt, Plains, Fringed, Beaded Hide, With Shoulder Medicine Bag 8500.00

An inkstand was made to be placed on a desk. It held some type of container for ink, and possibly a sander, a pen tray, a pen, a holder for pounce, and even a candle to melt the sealing wax. Inkstands date to the eighteenth century and have been made of silver, copper, ceramics, and glass.

INKSTAND, 3 Cherub Legs, Fish Design, Rocker Blotter, Brass 150.00
Davis, Dated 1926 .... 18.00
Figural, Lioness, Crouching, Bronze, Green Marble, 14 In. 8000.00
Figural, Smiling Nude Harem Maiden, Bronze, Carl Kauba, 9 5/8 In. 715.00
Silver On Copper, 2 Cut Glass Wells, Holder, Gallery, 5 X 7 X 2 In. 70.00

Inkwells, of course, held ink. Ready-made ink was first made about 1836 and was sold in bottles. The desk inkwell had a narrow hole so the pen would not slip inside. Pottery, glass, pewter, silver, and other materials were used to make inkwells. Look in other sections for more listings of inkwells.

INKWELL, 3-Mold, Blown, Olive Green, 2 3/8 In. 200.00
Art Nouveau, Pen Tray, Nude, Pierced Foliage, Silver Plate 395.00
Blackamoor, Bronze, Glass Eyes 750.00
Blown Glass, Blue, 3-Mold, 2 1/4 X 1 3/4 In. 5200.00
Blown Glass, Dark Olive, 3-Mold, G II-18, 2 3/4 In. 95.00
Brass, Ceramic Insert, Hinged, Square, 5 In. 45.00
Brown Flame Graining, Stenciled Hearts, Wooden, 3 5/8 In. 75.00
Camel, Metal, Austria 135.00
Chandelier, Hard Rubber Top, Dated 60.00
Cut Glass, Onyx Base, 2 Pens 135.00
Daisy & Button, Sapphire Blue, Square, 2 In. 85.00
Deer Foot, Hinged Silver Cover 65.00
Diamond Shape, Pierced Border, Glass Panel Ends, Pewter, 1776, 4 In. 2450.00
Double Snail, Glass 155.00
Double, Porcelain Inserts, Brass, Gesch 65.00
Easterbrook Dip-Less, Black Bakelite & Glass 25.00
Ebonized, Brass & Ivory Trim, Lid Is Riding Cap, 3 1/4 In. 125.00
Enameled, Brass & Onyx, French 140.00
Figural, Bathing Beauty, Set In Seashell, German Souvenir, 5 In. 145.00
Figural, Lion, Rolled Up, Head Hinged, Painted Iron, 10 X 7 In. 225.00
Gilt Bronze, Double, Michelangelo's The Thinker On Top 270.00
Glass Turtle, J. & I.E.M., Aqua 50.00
Glass, Turtle, J. & I.E.M., Aqua 85.00
Green To Clear, Hinged Top, Square, 2 X 3 In. 70.00
Hockey Puck Shape, Gray Stoneware, C.1860 .... 50.00
Horseshoe-Shaped Pen Rack, Iron & Glass 95.00
Lap Desk, Milk Glass, Scroll, Fired Florals, 4 X 3 X 1 5/8 In. 75.00
Lion & Unicorn, Brass Fittings, Polychrome Flowers.3 3/4 In. 65.00
Louis XVI, Putto Drummer Between Drum Wells, Bronze 895.00
Mahogany, 3 Interior Inks, Brass Trim, 12 1/2 In. 175.00
Metropolitan Life Insurance Building, Metal 45.00
Panels & Miter Cut, Hinged Cut Top, 3 1/2 X 3 In. 45.00
Pewter Top, Embossed Capstan, Anchor, Rope Edge, For Ship, 4 In. 60.00
Pewter, Hinged Cover, Blue Insert, 6 X 10 In. 60.00

Porcelain, Woman's, Flower Transfer, White 35.00
Rotates From Black To Red Wells, Porcelain & Brass 55.00
Silver Cattail Inlay, Verdigris Finish, Bronze, Oval, 4 In. 75.00
Silver Mounted Horse Hoof, Hinged Lid, WN, London, 1869, 5 3/8 In. 522.00
Skull & Crossbones, Pot Metal, Cream Enameled, 2 1/4 X 3 In. 85.00
Standing Lion In Center, 2 Glass Wells, Marble, 7 X 12 In. 90.00
Swirl Glass, Wooden Base, Horseshoe Pen Holder, 19th Century 125.00
Traveling, Arrow Shape, Brass 22.50
Treen, Glass Insert, Brown Stained, Gold Stenciled, 3 5/8 In. 55.00
Washing Machine, Crank Style, White Lily Washer Co., Iron, Glass 165.00

Insulators of glass or pottery have been made for use on telegraph or telephone poles since 1844. Thousands of different styles of insulators have been made. Most common are those of clear or aqua glass, most desirable are the threadless types made from 1850 to 1870.

INSULATOR, Agee, Medium Purple 10.00
American Tel. & Tel., Aqua, Sharp Drips 100.00
B.G.M.Co., Dark Purple 175.00
Brookfield, Backward 5 Crown, Aqua 5.00
Brookfield, Backward 6 Crown, Aqua 5.00
Brookfield, Dark Aqua, Sirt Embossed 6.00
Brookfield, Dark Green 65.00
Cable, Dark Aqua, Bubbles 30.00
California, Sage 10.00
Canadian Pacific Ry., Royal Purple 30.00
Columbia, 1891, Dark Aqua 40.00
Columbia, No.2, Green 150.00
Diamond, 102, Mustard Yellow 70.00
Diamond, Deep Strawberry 30.00
Diamond, Olive Amber 20.00
Duquesne Glass Co., Cornflower 50.00
Duquesne, Aqua, Crude Dome 15.00
Dwight, Pattern, Blue 5.00
E.C.& M. Co., Dark Blue Aqua 65.00
H.G.Co., Jade, Tiny Bubbles, Pat.May 2, 1893 .... 25.00
Hemingray, 8, Aqua, Wide Flared Skirt 25.00
Hemingray, 12, Green 7.00
Hemingray, 69, Green, Amber Swirling 32.00
Hemingray, 128, Dark Yellow 100.00
Hemingray, 128, Light Green 10.00
Isorex, 35/5, Green 20.00
Jumbo, Blue Aqua, Milky Swirl, Unembossed 140.00
K.C.G.W., Dark Green Aqua 9.00
Knowles, Prism, 1890, Blue Aqua, Cable 10.00
Lynchburg, Yellow Green 5.00
M/H. G. Co., Petticoat, Aqua 10.00
Manhattan, Aqua, Dated 15.00
McLaughlin, Olive Amber 6.00
McLaughlin, White Milk Glass 20.00
NEGM, Aqua 10.00
NEGM, Blue Aqua, Straight Side 50.00
Pyrex, CD 234, Carnival 25.00
Sombrero, Carnival Glass, 10 In. 25.00
Universal, No.1003, Ceramic 20.00
W.F.G. Co., Medium Dark Purple 30.00
W.G.M. Co., Light Purple 10.00
W.G.M., Royal Purple 18.00
Whitall Tatum, Amethyst 8.00
Whitall Tatum, No.3, Crystal 2.50
   IRISH BELLEEK, see Belleek

 Iron is a metal that has been used by man since prehistoric times. It is a popular metal for tools and decorative items like doorstops that need as much weight as possible. Items are listed here or under other appropriate headings such as Bookends, Doorstop, Kitchen, or Tool. The tool that is used for ironing clothes, an iron, is listed under Kitchen, Iron; or Kitchen, Sadiron.

IRON, Armillary Sphere, Standing Man, Pedestal	1400.00
Ashtray, Sea Gull, Opens Bottle, Painted	28.50
Bed Warmer, Primitive, Brass Lid, 37 In.	450.00
Boot Jack, Naughty Nellie, Polychrome Repaint, 10 In.	25.00
Boot Scraper, 2 Dogs, On Hind Legs, Hold Scraper, 6 5/8 X 5 1/4 In.	100.00
Boot Scraper, 2 Quail Each End, Under Pan, 7 X 15 3/4 In.	275.00
Boot Scraper, Figural, Dachshund, Painted Green, 21 In.	260.00
Boot Scraper, Figure of Horse Each End, Painted, 14 1/2 X 19 In.	1320.00
Boot Scraper, Knob Finials, Worn Marble Block, 14 In.	65.00
Boot Scraper, Ram's Horn Scrolls, In Marble Block	115.00
Boot Scraper, Salem Witch On Broom, 19th Century	375.00
Boot Scraper, Sausage Dog, Red Paint	65.00
Boot Scraper, Scrolled Ends, 7 1/2 X 10 1/4 In.	65.00
Boot Scraper, Scrolled Finials, 7 X 11 1/2 In.	20.00
Boot Scraper, Terrier, Silhouette, Inscription	95.00
Boot Scraper, Urn Shape	40.00
Boot Scraper, Woodpecker, Pecking On Ground, 1850, 12 1/2 In.	125.00
Bootjack, Cricket, 10 3/4 In.	20.00
Bootjack, Folds To Become Pistol	75.00
Bootjack, Naughty Nellie, Alton, Illinois Foundry	85.00
Bowl, Fruit, Pedestal, Black, 9 1/2 X 6 1/2 In.	15.00
Bracket, Shelf, Black Painted, Lettered	30.00
Can Opener, Fish, C.1865	130.00
Candleholder, Sticking Tommy, 9 1/2 In.	70.00 To 125.00
Candlesnuffer, Hand Wrought, Scissor Type, 6 In.	85.00
Candlestand, Tripod Base, Penny Feet, 2 Sockets, 23 In.	275.00
Candlestick, Hog Scraper, Push–Up, Lip Hanger, 7 1/8 In.	125.00
Candlestick, Hog Scraper, Push–Up, Lip Hanger, 7 7/8 In.	145.00
Candlestick, Hog Scraper, Push–Up, Marked Shaws, 7 In.	175.00
Candlestick, Spiral Push–Up, Wooden Base, 7 1/2 In.	225.00
Carriage Step, Fancy Wrought Iron	10.00 To 15.00
Cornice, Goddess of Plenty, 1840–50, 43 X 20 In.	4000.00
Cutter, Buzz Saw Tobacco, Die–Cut Saw Blades Each Side	850.00
Cutter, Tobacco, Wrought Iron, Wooden Block Base, 6 1/2 X 16 In.	25.00
Dish, Art Nouveau, Bronze Plated Poppy Leaves, Seminude, 9 X 8 In.	145.00
Door Knocker, American Eagle, 1800s	32.00
Door Knocker, Parrot	65.00
Door Knocker, Parrot, Painted	55.00
Door Knocker, Wolf, 9 X 13 In.	600.00
Door Knocker, Woman's Hand, Cast Iron, Lace Cuff, Holding Ball, 6 In.	95.00
Door Pull, Cast Iron, Bear, 1800s	85.00
Eagle, Removable Base, 9 1/2 In.	200.00
Figurine, Fly, Boughton's Star Screens, Large	125.00
Figurine, Frog, Mouth Open, Green Paint, 4 3/4 In.	65.00
Figurine, Lao Tzu, Riding Ox, Chinese, 19th Century, 12 1/2 X 13 In.	195.00
Figurine, Woman, Classical Clothes, 29 1/2 In.	900.00
Finials, Horse Head, Hitching Post, 13 In., Pair	100.00
Frame, Picture, Door Closes To Cover Picture, 6 1/2 X 9 1/2 In.	125.00
Hinges, Gothic Style, Late 19th Century, 12 In., Pair	20.00
Hitching Post, Black Jockey, 41 In.	1400.00
Hitching Post, Boy Standing On Cotton Bale	1430.00
Hitching Post, Horse Head, Fluted Stem, Foliage, 69 1/2 In.	475.00
Hitching Post, Horse Head, Victorian	800.00
Holder, Utensil	660.00
Kufa, Hand Wrought, Cover, Scandinavian, Dated 1845, 23 X 16 X 10 In.	795.00
Lamp, Bracket, Coal Oil, Victorian, Wall Mount, Pair	30.00
Lighting Stand, Crescent Type, Twisted Stem, Tripod, 32 In.	45.00

Lighting Stand, Tripod Base, Adjustable Arm, Candle Socket, 41 In. 650.00
Mailbox, Griswold 35.00
    IRON, MATCH HOLDER, see Match Holder
Mortar & Pestle, Marked IP, 5 In. 65.00
Ornament, Garden, Black Man, Top Hat, Outstretched Hand, 30 In. 245.00
Ornament, Garden, Jockey, Outstretched Hand, Hole For Lantern, 25 In. 85.00
Ornament, Garden, Jockey, Polychrome Paint, 26 In. 175.00
Orrery, Cast Brass & Iron, Sun, Earth & Moon Relationship 1100.00
Plant Hook, Mermaid 28.00
Rush Light Holder, Candle Socket, Adjustable Trammel, 27 1/2 In. 1075.00
Rush Light Holder, Tripod Base, Candle Socket, 21 1/2 In. 350.00
Rush Light, Hog Scraper Base, 5 1/4 In. 135.00
Safe, Black, Gold Letters, 2 Doors, Key Lock Inside, Lock Box, Restored 575.00
Safe, Door Design, Arthur R. Curtis Co., Boston, C.1880, 28 1/2 In. 305.50
Scissors, Hand Wrought, Incised Design, 10 1/2 In. 90.00
Snow Bird, Eagles, Cast Iron, 9 X 6 1/2 In., Pair 50.00
Stove Damper 8.00
String Holder, Beehive 35.00
String Holder, Beehive, With Spool 55.00
Target, Shooting Gallery, Bear 110.00
Target, Shooting Gallery, Donkey 175.00
Target, Shooting Gallery, Rhinoceros 195.00
Target, Shooting, 2 Roosters On Spring Bar, Hand Set, 8 X 10 In. 85.00
Tongs, Coal 20.00
Tongs, Ember, Scissor Shape, Hand Forged, 18th Century, 11 1/2 In. 150.00
Tray, Card, Cupped Hands, 1860s 75.00
Trivet, Three Penny Feet, 2 1/4 In. 55.00
Urn, Garden, C–Scroll Lip, Fluted Stem, 1920s, 33 1/2 In., Pair 885.00
Urn, Garden, Flower Body, Masks, Nude Female Figure Handles, 41 In. 5250.00
Urn, Stylized Leaf Frieze, Foliate Handles, Kramer Bros., 42 X 21 In. 775.00
Wig Stand, Victorian 48.00
Windmill Weight, Bobtail Horse 195.00
Windmill Weight, Boss Bull 550.00
Windmill Weight, Boss Bull, Trace of Red Paint 1200.00
Windmill Weight, Buffalo, Painted Red, Black Horns, Hoofs & Ears 3200.00
Windmill Weight, Bull, Salmon Paint 1050.00
Windmill Weight, Crescent Moon, No.417 .... 90.00
Windmill Weight, Eclipse, 813, Wooden Base, 10 1/2 In. 175.00
Windmill Weight, Eclipse, Wooden Base, 10 3/4 In. 120.00
Windmill Weight, Horse, Black, 16 3/4 X 17 3/4 In. 350.00
Windmill Weight, Horse, Dempster, Bobtailed, 17 X 16 In. 250.00
Windmill Weight, Horse, Long Tail .... 375.00 To 750.00
Windmill Weight, Horse, Short Tail .... 150.00 To 400.00
Windmill Weight, Mogul, Woodmanse, 80 Lb. 425.00
Windmill Weight, Moon, Eclipse 275.00
Windmill Weight, Rooster, Elgin 1000.00
Windmill Weight, Rooster, Mogul 3900.00
Windmill Weight, Rooster, On Ball, Hummer 500.00
Windmill Weight, Rooster, Original Blue Paint, Hummer 1050.00
Windmill Weight, Rooster, Original Paint, 18 X 15 1/2 In. 400.00
Windmill Weight, Rooster, U.S. Naval Academy 1400.00
Windmill Weight, Rooster, Woodmanse, Large 650.00
Windmill Weight, Star, Traces of White Paint 1100.00
Windmill Weight, Woodmanse, Small 475.00

Ironstone china was first made in 1813. It gained its greatest
popularity during the mid–nineteenth century. The heavy, durable,
off–white pottery was made in white or was decorated with any of
hundreds of patterns. Much flow blue pottery was made of
ironstone. Some of the decorations were raised. Many pieces of
ironstone are unmarked but some English and American factories
included the word "Ironstone" in their marks.

**IRONSTONE, see also Chelsea Grape; Chelsea Sprig; Gaudy Ironstone;
Moss Rose; Staffordshire**

IRONSTONE, Baker, Hebe Shape, White, Alcock 35.00
Bowl & Pitcher, Blue Dragon Transfer, Mason's, 16 X 11 1/2 In. 325.00
Bowl, Blue Stick Spatter Rim, White, 4 X 7 3/8 In. 45.00
Cachepot, French, Green, 10 In. 65.00
Chocolate Pot, Hexagonal, Raised Leaf, Tall 195.00
Compote, Gothic, White, Pedestal, 10 Sides 95.00
Creamer, Cable, White 35.00
Creamer, Child's, White, Full Ribbed 50.00
Creamer, Dark Green, Shenango, Individual 2.50
Crock, Blue, Shell Border, 1 Gal. 65.00
Cup & Saucer, Manchu, Mason's 10.00
Cup & Saucer, Wheat, White, Handleless 27.00
Cup & Saucer, White, Ceres, Elsmore & Forster 45.00
Gravy Boat, Elsmore & Forster 40.00
Gravy Boat, Fuchsia 25.00
Holder, Toothbrush, Birds & Flowers, Malkin, 1879 .... 18.00
Holder, Toothbrush, Taylor & Davis Advertising, Gold Bands 23.00
Holder, Toothbrush, Wheat & Blackberry, White, Horizontal 70.00
Holder, Toothbrush, White, With Drain, Maddock 20.00
Hot Plate, Blue & White, No Spout Plugs, 11 X 2 1/2 In. 115.00
Inkwell, Brass Lid, Blue Enamel Stripes, 4 7/8 In. 75.00
Jar, Apothecary, Polychrome, Libal, Polvo De Opio, 9 3/4 In. 145.00
Mold, Man, Milking Cow, Oval, Large 175.00
Mug, Golfer, Robinson & Clay 225.00
Mug, Monk 135.00
Mug, Polychrome Floral Enameling, Copper Luster Rim, Oversize 65.00
Mug, Windy City 195.00
Mustache Cup, White 30.00
Pitcher, Blackberry & Wheat, 9 In. 68.00
Pitcher, Blue Stick Spatter Design, W.M. Co., 12 In. 90.00
Pitcher, Double Panel Scenic, Fish Handle, 6 In. 125.00
Pitcher, Hunting Scene, Tree Trunk Handle, Mason's, 1891, 8 In. 75.00
Pitcher, Imari Design, Blue Transfer, Enameled, Mason's, 5 In. 45.00
Pitcher, Ribbed, Square, Powell & Bishop, 1876 .... 38.50
Pitcher, Wheat & Blackberry, Meakin, 11 3/4 In. 125.00
Pitcher, Windy City 325.00
Plate, Acropolis, Purple, 8 In. 40.00
Plate, Indian Bridge, Oriental Design, Blue Transfer, 9 1/2 In. 55.00
Plate, Manchu, Green, Mason's, 9 1/2 In. 10.00
Plate, Manchu, Mason's, 7 1/2 In. 4.00
Plate, Mason's, 9 1/4 In. 55.00
Plate, Rooster & Foliage, French, Pexonne, 4 Piece 60.00
Platter, White, 16 In. 2.00
Sauce Bowl, Blue Floral Transfer, Lion, Unicorn Mark, 4 In. 25.00
Shaving Mug, Berlin Swirl 70.00
Soap Dish, Blue & White, Gridley 20.00
Soap Dish, Gold Trim, Taylor & Davis, 2 Piece 22.00
Soup, Dish, Ceres, Elsmore & Forster, Large 40.00
Spittoon, Double Eagle Vents 42.00
Sugar & Creamer, Child's, White, Boote's, 1851, Octagon 100.00
     IRONSTONE, TEA LEAF, see Tea Leaf Ironstone
Tea Set, Child's, White, Art Nouveau Handles, 15 Piece 145.00
Teapot, Ceres, White, Turner Goddard 225.00
Teapot, Paneled, Purple Transfer, Rose, 9 1/8 In. 75.00
Teapot, White, Prairie Shape, Clementson 125.00
Tureen, Amherst Japan Pattern, Cover, 14 In. 400.00
Tureen, Open, Attached Platter, Leaf Handles 18.00
Tureen, Sauce, Cover, Columbia Shape, White 110.00
Tureen, Sauce, Wheat & Blackberry, Meakin 69.00
Tureen, Vegetable, Cover, Boote's, 1851 .... 85.00
Tureen, Vegetable, Cover, Ivy Wreath, White, Meir 70.00
Tureen, Vegetable, Cover, White, Sydenham, T & R Boote 150.00
Tureen, Vegetable, Fruit Finial, Mason's, C.1800, 9 1/2 In. 245.00
Warmer, Spoon, Nautilus Shell, White 395.00

To preserve leather bound books, first dust. Then apply a light application of leather protector (potassium lactate) with a soft cloth. After it drys, apply a little leather dressing (lanolin and neetsfoot oil). This will de-acidify the leather and keep it from becoming brittle. In an urban home repeat this every other year.

 The tusk of an elephant is ivory and to many that is the only true ivory. To most collectors, the term "ivory" also includes such natural materials as walrus, hippopotamus, or whale teeth or tusks, and some of the vegetable materials that are of similar texture and density. Other ivory items are listed under Scrimshaw or Netsuke. Collectors should be aware of the recent laws concerning the buying and selling of ivory.

IVORY, Baton, Carved, Presentation, Silver Handle, 1914	145.00
Beads, Graduated Sizes, Ivory Clasp, American	40.00
Beads, Openwork, Chinese	85.00
Billiard Ball, Cue	75.00
Billiard Ball, Red	42.00
Bottle, Snuff, Painted Lord & Lady, Carved, 3 In., 2 Piece	200.00
Box, Dovetailed, Ivory Latch, 5 3/8 In.	250.00
Brooch, Carved Rose, 1 5/8 X 2 In.	7.50
Button, Carved Seal, 4 Piece	110.00
Cigarette Holder, Carved	50.00
Cigarette Holder, Dragon	40.00
Cribbage Board, Engraved Foliage & 2 Seals, 3 Pegs, 5 1/4 In.	100.00
Doctor's Lady, Nude, Reclining, Wooden Couch, 4 In.	75.00
Easel, Inlaid, Oak, Stylized Vine, Floral, Medallion, 1875, 77 X 26 In.	715.00
Figurine, 3 Grecian Nude Women Embracing, Erotic, G.R., 7 In.	85.00
Figurine, Chick, Hatching	85.00
Figurine, Devils Climbing On Conch Shell, Shumei, 3 1/2 In.	1705.00
Figurine, Horse, Other Animals, Wooden Stand, Oriental, 5 In.	475.00
Figurine, Immortals, Each Holding Attribute, 1930s, 4 1/2 In.	850.00
Figurine, Kwannon, 15 In.	605.00
Figurine, Mounted Knight, Sterling, Gold Wash, Glass Jewels, 12 In.	3300.00
Figurine, Nude Woman, Standing Before Shell, C.1925, 11 In.	1980.00
Figurine, Oriental Man & Woman, Dragon Throne, Stand, 3 3/8 In., Pair	215.00
Figurine, Oriental Woman, Holding Basket, 9 1/2 In.	450.00
Figurine, Penguin, 2 3/4 In.	95.00
Figurine, Wise Monkeys, See, Speak, Hear No Evil, 3 Piece	60.00
Flute, Dan Tribe, Carved, 12 In.	165.00
Glove Stretcher, Gold Monogram	45.00
Jagging Wheel, Whale Tooth, Heart Handle, Mid–19th Century, 4 3/4 In.	1870.00
Jagging Wheel, Whale, Tortoiseshell, Silver	2310.00
Letter Opener Paperweight, Art Nouveau, 14 1/2 In.	350.00
Lord's Prayer, Stanhope, France, Miniature	12.00
Mystery Ball, 6 Layers, 3 Elephants Hold Ball On Trunk Tips, 4 In.	80.00
Page Slicer, Solid, 12 In.	80.00
Pendant, Dragons, Ivory Bead Slide, Silk Cord, C.1915	125.00
Pendant, Oriental Lady, Holding Flowers, Cutout Design, 2 1/4 In.	75.00
Plaque, Robed Woman, Surrounded By Putti, Shadow Box, 14 1/4 In.	2750.00
Rosary, Silver	65.00
Shoehorn, Gold Monogram	40.00
Snuff Jar, Figures, Dragon Handles, Stand, 3 In.	45.00
Snuff Jar, Florals, Vining Scrolls, Stand, 3 1/2 In.	265.00
Snuff Jar, Oriental Executioner, Head & Sword, 2 3/8 In.	40.00
Teapot, Dragon Spout, Handle, Squirrel, Pine Tree Lid, China, 4 X 5 In.	225.00

Toggle, 2 Barrel–Shaped Dominoes	45.00
Tusk, Elephant, 2 X 33 In.	175.00
Tusk, Narwhal, Full, Canadian Arctic, 1932	2860.00

Jack Armstrong, the all–American boy, was the hero of a radio serial from 1933 to 1951. Premiums were offered to the listeners until the mid–1940s. Jack Armstrong's best–known endorsement is for Wheaties.

JACK ARMSTRONG, Airplanes, Paper, Box	35.00
Brooch, Gardenia, Betty's, Premium	375.00
Flashlight, Blue	20.00
Flashlight, Bullet, 1939	30.00 To 40.00
Football Game, Bernie Bierman's Big 10, Wheaties, 1936	110.00
Gun, 2 Propeller, Box	95.00 To 110.00
Hike–O–Meter	12.00
Model, Pre–Flight Trainer, Wheaties, Punches, Unused, 1945	95.00
Pedometer	20.00 To 45.00
Ring, Crocodile	395.00
Ring, Egyptian, Silver	45.00 To 90.00
Telescope	20.00 To 22.00
Telescope, Explorer's, 1937	50.00
Whistle, Secret	75.00

Jack–in–the–pulpit vases were named for their odd trumpetlike shape that resembles the wild plant called jack–in–the–pulpit. The design originated in the late Victorian years. Vases in the jack–in–the–pulpit shape were made of ceramic or glass.

JACK–IN–THE–PULPIT, Vase, Aurene, Gold Iridescent, 6 1/4 In.	775.00
Vase, Blue Opalescent, 8 Petal, Enameled Inside, 13 In.	255.00
Vase, Bulbous, Rainbow Star At Upper Rim, 5 In.	250.00
Vase, Crystal Petal Feet, Green, 6 7/8 In.	88,.00
Vase, Dimpled Body, Lemon To White, 7 X 5 In.	65.00
Vase, Hand Painted, Ruby, Pairpoint	100.00
Vase, Ribbed, 7 X 7 1/2 In.	98.00
Vase, Ruffled, Opalescent Maroon, 7 In.	60.00
Vase, Spatter Glass, 8 1/2 In., Pair	28.00

Jackfield ware was originally a black glazed pottery made in Jackfield, England, from 1750 to 1775. A yellow glazed ware has also been called Jackfield ware. Most of the pieces referred to as "Jackfield" today are black–glazed, red–clay wares made at the Jackfield Pottery in Shropshire, England, in Victorian times.

JACKFIELD, Coffeepot, Girl Blowing Bubbles, Rolling Hoop, Gold Trim, 8 In.	245.00
Creamer, Cow, Black, Gilt Trim, 5 X 7 In.	55.00
Pitcher, Gold & Blue Trim, 5 In.	20.00
Pitcher, Milk, Cow	65.00
Teapot, 7 1/2 In. Handle To Spout, 5 1/2 In.	25.00
Teapot, Red Clay, Black Glaze	35.00

Two different minerals, nephrite and jadeite, are called jade. Nephrite is the mineral used for most early Oriental carvings. Jade is a very tough stone that is found in many colors from dark green to pale lavender. Jade carvings are still being made in the old styles, so collectors must be careful not to be fooled by recent pieces. Jade jewelry is found in this book under Jewelry.

JADE, Bowl, Carved, Black & White Speckled, Chinese, C.1900, 3 In.	90.00
Dish, Spinach, Octagonal, 5 1/2 In.	135.00
Figurine, Bird, Flower On Back, Rosewood Stand, 3 1/4 In., Pair	310.00
Figurine, Cast, Tang Han, 1 3/8 X 2 3/4 In.	2000.00
Figurine, Fish With Man On Its Back, Stand, 1 3/4 X 2 1/4 In.	550.00
Figurine, Rooster, 4 In.	115.00
Figurine, Sitting Dog, 3 X 2 1/2 In.	7000.00
Figurine, Woman Holding Flower, 6 1/2 In.	775.00
Holder, Cigarette, Zeppelin, C.1930, 3 In.	75.00

Sauceboat, Quing Dynasty, 19th Century, 4 1/2 In.	220.00
Snuff Bottle, Coral Stopper, No Spoon, 19th Century, 2 1/2 In.	850.00
Snuff Bottle, Reticulated, Gold Engraved, Fitted Case, 1 7/8 In.	9000.00
Urn, Chinese Temple Lion On Lid, Lion Face Ring Handles, 6 1/8 In.	165.00

Japanese Coralene is a ceramic decorated with small raised beads and dots. It was first made in the nineteenth century. Later wares made to imitate coralene had dots of enamel. There is also another type of coralene that is made with small glass beads on glass containers.

JAPANESE CORALENE, Vase, Green, Cobalt Blue Borders, Beaded, 8 1/2 In.	295.00

There are two types of jasperware. Some pieces are made from colored clay with raised designs of the same or contrasting colored clay. Other pieces are made by decorating the raised portions with a glaze.

JASPERWARE, see also various art potteries; Wedgwood

JASPERWARE, Bowl, Flowers, 3 1/2 X 2 In.	25.00
Box, Black, Cover, Classical Figures, Cylindrical, 4 1/2 In.	65.00
Box, Dancing Cherubs On Cover, Blue, 4 1/2 X 3 In.	55.00
Box, Light Blue, Grapes, Vines, Cover, Round, 5 In.	58.00
Box, Stamp, Woman, Cherub & Flowers, Round, 4 1/2 In.	65.00
Cheese Dish, Blue, White, C.1880–1890	225.00
Cheese Keeper, Light Blue, 10 In.	425.00
Hair Receiver, Relief Flowers, Light Green Base, Cover, Marked	55.00
Jardiniere, White Swags, Lion's Heads, Grecian Figures, 10 In.	500.00
Jug, Cream, Putti, Musical Instruments, Brown, White, 1882, 6 In.	112.00
Pitcher, Green, Design	225.00
Plaque, Cherub With Umbrella	25.00
Plaque, Indian, Broken Arm, Sioux Chief, White On Green	115.00
Tray, Cupid, Man & Woman, 4 1/2 In.	30.00
Vase, Dark Blue, Beaker Type, Classical Figures, 3 1/2 In.	75.00

Jewelry, if made from gold and precious gems or plastic and colored glass, is still popular with collectors. Values are determined by the intrinsic value of the stones and metal and by the skill of the craftsmen and designers. Victorian and older jewelry has been popular since the 1950s. More recent interests are Art Deco and Edwardian styles, Mexican and Danish silver jewelry, and beads of all kinds. Copies of almost all styles are being made.

JEWELRY, Bar Pin, 12 Seed Pearls, 14K Gold	40.00
Bar Pin, Geometric Design, Sterling Overlay, Heintz, 2 1/4 In.	65.00
Beads, Black Jet, 2 Strand, Victorian, Black Cameo Clasp	65.00
Beads, Ivory, Graduated Sizes, Ivory Clasp, 24 In.	50.00
Bracelet & Earrings, Rhinestone, Joseph Mazer	65.00
Bracelet & Earrings, Turquoise Rhinestone, Carnegie	195.00
Bracelet, 11 Gold Slides, Each With Diamond, 14K Gold	1175.00
Bracelet, 11 Oval Opals, Mexican, 14K Gold Mounting	225.00
Bracelet, 204 Small Diamonds, Flexible 14K Gold Mount	1800.00
Bracelet, 69 Sapphires, Round Diamonds, Silver Mounting	1435.00
Bracelet, Abalone Links, Mexican Silver	25.00
Bracelet, Bakelite, Red–Brown Marbled	30.00
Bracelet, Bangle, 6 Marquise Cut Emeralds, 10 Diamonds, 14K Gold	360.00
Bracelet, Bangle, Foliate Design, 14K Gold	310.00
Bracelet, Bangle, Silver & Gilt Mounts, Pair	175.00
Bracelet, Bangle, Sterling Silver, Art Deco, Rubellite Stone	145.00
Bracelet, Buckle, Victorian, 15K Gold	1350.00
Bracelet, Carnelian, 14K Gold Beads	30.00
Bracelet, Carved Jadeite, Pearls, Gold Over Sterling, C.1915	200.00
Bracelet, Cocktail, Drinks & Recipe Charms, Sterling Silver	45.00
Bracelet, Cultured Pearls All Around, 14K Gold	135.00
Bracelet, Curb Links, 18K Rose Gold	610.00
Bracelet, Flexible, 5 3/4 Carat Diamonds	4740.00
Bracelet, Gold Filled Mesh, Victorian	55.00

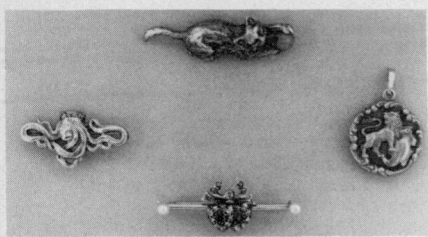

Jewelry, Pin, Cat, Reclining, Jadeite,
Jade Bead, 18K Gold

Jewelry, Pin, Woman's Head, 5 Diamonds,
Art Nouveau, 14K Gold

Jewelry, Locket, Lion, Victorian, 14K Gold

Jewelry, Pin, Double Heart, Victorian, Ruby,
Sapphire & Pearls

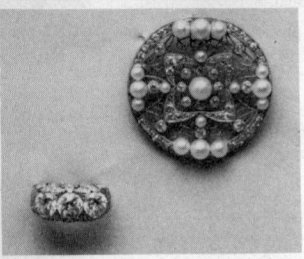

Jewelry, Ring, Diamonds, 3, European
Cut, C.1910   Jewelry, Pin, Circle,
Platinum & Diamond

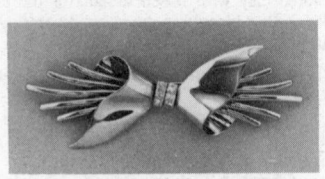

Jewelry, Pin, Bow, 6 Diamonds, Bicolor,
14K Gold, C.1940

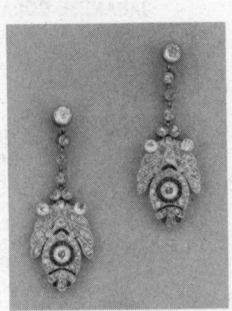

Jewelry, Earrings, Emerald
& Diamonds, Platinum
Mounted, C.1915

Jewelry, Parure, Carved Coral,
Victorian, Floral, 14K Gold, 3 Pc.

Jewerly, Watch Bracelet, Diamond Sash, Platinum, 7 Carat

Bracelet, Green Enameled Links, Gold Bars	5250.00
Bracelet, I.D., Marine Corps Insignia	20.00
Bracelet, Indian Style, Pewter, Georg Jensen	40.00
Bracelet, Jade Beads, 14K Gold	30.00
Bracelet, Lily-of-The-Valley, Whiting, 1885	45.00
Bracelet, Link, Art Deco Bead Design, Kalo Shop, 7 In.	395.00
Bracelet, Man's, Spratling	600.00
Bracelet, Mourning, Hollow Tube of Woven Hair, Gold Mounts, 1840	265.00
Bracelet, Red Celluloid Chain, Hanging Berries	30.00
Bracelet, Rhinestone Bows, Pearl Centers, Hobe, 1/8 In. Wide	55.00
Bracelet, Rhinestone, 6 Rows Wide, Weiss	30.00
Bracelet, Rhinestone, Art Deco, Pave	25.00
Bracelet, Rose & Flat Cut Diamonds, Openwork Florals, C.1905	450.00
Bracelet, Scenic Cameo, Sterling Silver	275.00
Bracelet, Schiaparelli, 7 Oval Faceted Unfoiled Stones	75.00

Bracelet, Silver & Chalcedony, Birds, Leaves, G. Jensen, 7 In. 990.00
Bracelet, Silver, Inlaid Mother-of-Pearl & Abalone, Mexico 65.00
Bracelet, Silver, Whiting & Davis, Ornate 40.00
Bracelet, Snake, Wraparound, Whiting & Davis 55.00
Bracelet, Spring Clamp, Golden Double Rams Heads, Kenneth Lane 80.00
Bracelet, Square Rhinestones, Bakelite, Hinge Closing 200.00
Bracelet, Straight Line, Platinum, 45 Round Diamonds 7250.00
Bracelet, Tennis, 28 Diamonds, 18K Gold 2310.00
Bracelet, With 23 Charms, Silver, 1940s 95.00
Buckle, American Silver & Rhinestone, Box, J. Anthony, Pair 250.00
Buckle, Homeric, Round & Rectangular, Shiebler, 1885, 2 1/8 X 3 In. 1750.00
Buckle, Leaf Shape, Spider, Fly & Bee, F.M.Whiting, C.1885, 3 1/8 In. 465.00
Buckle, Mounted Cabochons, Leaves, Lavender Glass, 2 3/4 In. 180.00
Buckle, Shoe, Marked ID, Silver, C.1700, 2 1/2 X 2 7/8 In., Pair 150.00
Buckle, Shoe, Steel Beads, French, C.1900, Pair 45.00
Buckle, Shoe, Steel Cut, Marked France, Pair 30.00
Chain, Anchor Link, 18K Gold, 24 In. 435.00
Chain, Cobra, 18K Gold, 20 In. 90.00
Chain, Human Hair, Locket Fob 35.00
Chain, Watch, Change Holder, IOOF, Goat, Brass 20.00
Chain, Watch, Human Hair, Victorian, 9 In. 95.00
Chain, Watch, Man's, With Charm, 14K Gold 135.00
Chain, Watch, Slide, Carved, Red Cameo, Fob, 1895 .... 125.00
Chain, Watch, Sterling Silver, Very Heavy, 1840 .... 110.00
Chain, Watch, With Slide, 48 In. 85.00
Charm, Bunny Key, 14K Yellow Gold, Signed Milagros 38.00
Charm, Cowboy Hat, Sterling 25.00
Charm, Fan, 14K Yellow Gold, With 9 Blue & Red Ribs 55.00
Charm, House, Opens, Sterling 100.00
Charm, Ivory Dice In Sterling Cage, 1920 .... 65.00
Charm, Luxury Line, 14K Yellow Gold 48.00
Charm, Pineapple, 14K Yellow Gold 35.00
Charm, Seahorse, Sterling 45.00
Chatelaine, Book, Pencil & Bottle 325.00
Chatelaine, Writing Pad & Pencil Case, Silver Chain, Art Nouveau 25.00
Choker, Silver Mesh, 1930s, 1/2 X 15 In. 45.00
Clip, Hand Shape, With Ring, Sterling Silver, Coro Craft 65.00
Coin Carrier, Chatelaine, Silver, Locket Type, Chain 55.00
Cross, Marcasite & Sterling, Sterling Silver Chain 125.00
Cross, Woven Hair Over Solid Core, Gold Fittings, 1870, 1 In. 95.00
Cuff Links, 1 Bear, 1 Bull, Yellow Gold 350.00
Cuff Links, 10K Gold 40.00
Cuff Links, Art Deco, Fish, Georg Jensen 60.00
Cuff Links, Galloping Horses, Gold Finish, Japanese, 1 1/4 In. 25.00
Cuff Links, Gold, Tiger Eye 10.00
Cuff Links, Monogram In Shield, 14K Yellow Gold, Box 45.00
Cuff Links, Sea Dragons, Roaring, Gold, Philadelphia, Oval 6500.00
Cuff Links, Silver, Abraham Schuyler, Albany, 18th Century 850.00
Dog Collar, Baroque Pearl, Seed Pearl, Rose Diamond, Edwardian 3575.00
Earrings, Bezel, Carnelians, Round Silver Beaded Rim, Clip, Freirich 20.00
Earrings, Cameo, 14K Yellow Gold, 1930 .... 40.00
Earrings, Cameo, Silver Mounting, Screw Type 55.00
Earrings, Emerald & Diamonds, Platinum Mounted, C.1915 ....*Illus* 4500.00
Earrings, Fetsui Jade, Seed Pearls 250.00
Earrings, Gold Filled, Coral, Pierced Drop, Victorian 75.00
Earrings, Gold Washed, Sterling, Pierced Garnet Solitaire, Victoria .... n 95.00
Earrings, Ladybug, Silver, Stone, Spratling, Mexican 150.00
Earrings, Leaf & Beaded Spray, Tiffany, 14K Gold 150.00
Earrings, Rhinestones, Crescent Shape, Clip, Kenneth Lane, 2 In. 55.00
Earrings, Shell Design, 14K Gold 115.00
    JEWELRY, HATPIN, see Hatpin
Holder, Chatelaine, Silver Plated 95.00
    JEWELRY, INDIAN, see Indian
Lavaliere, Garnet, 14K Gold 20.00

Locket, Chatelaine, Silver Plated 40.00
Locket, Gold Cameo Cover, Gold Tone, Firenza, Large 18.00
Locket, Heart Shape, Sterling Silver, U.S. Navy Inscription 15.00
Locket, Heart, LG, Unger, 1 3/4 X 1 1/2 In. 675.00
Locket, Lion, Victorian, 14K Gold ....*Illus* 250.00
Locket, Victorian, Gold Filled, Engraved, 1 5/8 In. 40.00
Magnifying Glass, Chatelaine, Silver Plated 35.00
Mirror, Chatelaine, Silver Plated, Round, Art Nouveau 40.00
Money Clip, Kalo, Initial 140.00
Necklace & Earring Set, Iridescent Red Rhinestones, Kramer 35.00
Necklace & Earrings, Purple Jet, 7 Strands, Hattie Carnegie 100.00
Necklace, 15 Graduated Elephants, Ivory, 1930s 125.00
Necklace, 33 Graduated & Faceted Amber Beads 100.00
Necklace, Adventurine Beads, Red Bead Spacers, 25 In. 35.00
Necklace, Amber Beads, Oval, Graduated, Largest 3 1/2 In., 34 In. 350.00
Necklace, Amethyst Glass Beads, Faceted, Czechoslovakian, 30 In. 35.00
Necklace, Black Onyx, Rhinestone Rondels, Double Strand, 22 In. 25.00
Necklace, Blue Lavaliere Drops, Victorian 160.00
Necklace, Carnelian, Graduated Beads, 14K Gold, 33 In. 70.00
Necklace, Carved Yellow Bakelite Rose, Chain 20.00
Necklace, Choker, Graduated Opal Beads, Faceted Crystal Rondells 1650.00
Necklace, Choker, Seed Pearl Ornament, 3 Chain, 14K Gold, C.1900 .... 250.00
Necklace, Eagle Medallion, Haskell 55.00
Necklace, Feldspar, Yellow Glass Spacers, Metal Accents, 26 In. 35.00
Necklace, Floral Link, 18K Gold, 18 In. 455.00
Necklace, Freshwater Pearls, 1 Strand, 30 In. 20.00
Necklace, Garnet, 350 Stones 295.00
Necklace, Garnets, Amethysts, Peridots, & Topaz, 14K Gold, 24 In. 340.00
Necklace, Green & White Rhinestones, Bogoff, Box 80.00
Necklace, Green Marbled Bakelite, Large Beads, 12 In. 55.00
Necklace, Ivory, Graduated Beads, Ivory Clasp, 1930s, 24 In. 65.00
Necklace, Jade & Carnelian, 2-In. Jade Disc Pendant, 28 In. 150.00
Necklace, Ojimi Bead, 36 In. 350.00
Necklace, Pear-Shaped Sapphires, Baguette & Round Diamonds 1650.00
Necklace, Pearl Slide, Rope Chain, 14K Yellow Gold, C.1890, 41 In. 280.00
Necklace, Pearl, Sapphire Pearl Clasp, 34 In. 975.00
Necklace, Pendant, Edwardian, Amethyst & Diamond, 15-In. Chain 6750.00
Necklace, Pin & Earrings, Small Baguette, Rhinestones, Weiss, 1950s 65.00
Necklace, Pink & Lavender Crystals, 4 Strands, Miriam Haskell 75.00
Necklace, Red Porcelain, 18K Gold Leaf, Leather Cord, 17 1/2 In. 55.00
Necklace, Rhinestone, Alice Caviness 45.00
Necklace, Rhinestone, Trifari 55.00
Necklace, Rhinestone, Weiss 40.00
Necklace, Seed Pearl, Coral, Tassel, C.1915 .... 2200.00
Necklace, Silver & Chalcedony, Birds, Leafage, G.Jensen, 15 3/8 In. 2750.00
Necklace, Victorian, 14K Yellow Gold, Turquoise, Freshwater Pearls 175.00
Necklace, With Agate Pendant, Anne Klein, 16 In. 30.00
Note Pad, With Pencil, Chatelaine, Silver Plated 75.00
Parure, Carved Coral, Victorian, Floral, 14K Gold, 3 Pc. ....*Illus* 1700.00
Pendant & Earrings, Sapphire & Diamond, 14K Gold, Chain 395.00
Pendant, 3 Rubies, Filigree, 14K Gold 95.00
Pendant, Applied Copper Seagull, Hammered, Karl F. Leinonen, 2 In. 175.00
Pendant, Blister Pearl, Sterling, Arts & Crafts Styling 195.00
Pendant, Cameo, Ivory Madonna, Platinum Mounting, Chain, S. Vernon 650.00
Pendant, Cameo, Sterling Silver 20.00
Pendant, Cluster of Fruit, Carved Amethyst, Chinese 78.50
Pendant, Cross, Carnelian 70.00
Pendant, Cross, Tiger Eye 55.00
Pendant, Fire Opal & Diamonds, White Gold 2640.00
Pendant, Mother-of-Pearl, Merchant, Maid, Persian, 1 1/2 X 2 1/2 In. 145.00
Pin & Earrings, Gold Tone, Purple Stones, Hobe 75.00
Pin & Earrings, Red Aurora Borealis, 3 In. 35.00
Pin, 4 Leaf Cloverleaf, Diamond Center, 14K Yellow Gold 85.00
Pin, Anchor, USN, Sterling 40.00

Pin, Art Deco, Beige Mirror, Rhinestone Trim	35.00
Pin, Billiken, On Original Card, 1928	75.00
Pin, Blossom, 3–Dimensional, Georg Jensen	195.00
Pin, Blue Flowers, Gold Rim, Porcelain, 1 3/4 In.	55.00
Pin, Bow, 6 Diamonds, Bicolor, 14K Gold, C.1940 ....*Illus*	750.00
Pin, Bow, Diamond & Ruby, Yellow & White Gold, 2 1/4 In.	3500.00
Pin, Bow, Diamond & Sapphire, 14K Gold & Silver, Victorian	4400.00
Pin, Bow, Pearl & Diamond, Platinum, French, Edwardian	7500.00
Pin, Bow, Victorian, Seed Pearls, 12K Gold	115.00
Pin, Butterfly, Marcasite & Sterling Silver	60.00
Pin, Cameo, 3 Graces, Silver	45.00
Pin, Cameo, Diana The Huntress, Black Ground, Sterling Silver Frame	125.00
Pin, Cameo, Head & Shoulder, 14K Gold Frame, 2 1/8 In.	175.00
Pin, Cameo, Profile of Woman, Foliate 14K Gold Frame	250.00
Pin, Cameo, Rebecca At The Well, Oval	85.00
Pin, Carved Ivory, Victorian Rose	30.00
Pin, Cat, Reclining, Jadeite, Jade Bead, 18K Gold ....*Illus*	600.00
Pin, Center Star Sapphire, Enamel Plique–A–Jour Petals	6000.00
Pin, Cherub, Wings Around Face, Ivory	440.00
Pin, Circle, Bird, With Flower, Art Deco, Platinum Mounting	8500.00
Pin, Circle, Platinum & Diamond, 15 Pearls ....*Illus*	2300.00
Pin, Citrine, Navette Opal, 18K Yellow Gold, Art Nouveau	880.00
Pin, Clown, Jointed, Bakelite	185.00
Pin, Coro Craft, Poppy, Pink Enamel, 2 1/2 In.	20.00
Pin, Deer, Georg Jensen, Sterling Silver	225.00
Pin, Diamond, Coral, Onyx & Emerald Circle, Bird, On Flower, Art Deco	9350.00
Pin, Diamond, Foliate Design, 14K Gold, Victorian	1000.00
Pin, Diamond, Openwork, Mine & Round Cut, C.1910	3000.00
Pin, Double Heart, Victorian, Ruby, Sapphire & Pearls ....*Illus*	700.00
Pin, Dragonflies In Flight, Fuchsia Foil Insert, Lalique, 1932	2000.00
Pin, Elephant, Rhinestone Trim, Carnegie, 2 1/4 In.	45.00
Pin, Faux Coral, Victorian, Large	12.00
Pin, Feather, Sterling	20.00
Pin, Fish Design, Triangular, Georg Jensen	380.00
Pin, Flower, Figural, Diamond Center	90.00
Pin, Flower, Unfoiled Blue Stone, Rhinestones, Trifari	75.00
Pin, Flying Dragon, Metal, 3 1/2 In.	20.00
Pin, Foil Dragon, Cloisonne	48.50
Pin, Garnet, 14k Pink Gold, 2 Seed Pearls, Victorian	75.00
Pin, Gavel, 10K Gold	20.00
Pin, Golf Club, Sterlng Silver, 1959	50.00
Pin, Hammered Brass, Peacocks Head To Head, G.W. Frost, 2 1/4 In.	245.00
Pin, Horse, Sterling Silver, Japanese, 2 In.	35.00
Pin, Insect, Rhinestone Trim, Spring Wings, Hattie Carnegie, 2 In.	60.00
Pin, Jabot, Rose Cut Diamond Arrow, Cartier	3080.00
Pin, Leaf Design, 6 Graduated Pearls, 14k Gold	175.00
Pin, Lizard, Garnet & Diamond, Edwardian, Firestone & Parson	8250.00
Pin, Maltese Cross, Pink, Weiss, 2 1/2 In.	45.00
Pin, Nude, Reclining, Brass Ocean, Sails, White Celluloid, Art Deco	50.00
Pin, Pendant, Cross Shape, Rhinestone, Alice Caviness	35.00
Pin, Pierced Copper, Sterling Overlay, Center Cabochon, 3 In.	225.00
Pin, Pierced Jadeite Plaque, Yellow Gold Mounting	135.00
Pin, Pink Enameled Poppy, Coro Craft, 2 1/2 In.	20.00
Pin, Pink Shells Mounted In Silver, C.1875, 1 1/4 In.	95.00
Pin, Pottery & Copper, Copper Border, England, C.1910, 2 1/2 In	110.00
Pin, Queen Wilhelmina, Framed In Seed Pearls, Box	350.00
Pin, Reverse Crystal Intaglio, Cat, Gold Banded Frame	5250.00
Pin, Scrubwoman, Eisenberg	300.00
Pin, Seagull, Sterling	12.00
Pin, Starfish, 14K Gold, 25 Point Diamond, Seed Pearls	375.00
Pin, Starfish, Seed Pearls, Diamond, 14K Gold	375.00
Pin, Striated Green Cabochon, Free Form, George W.Frost	250.00
Pin, Swan, Ruby Eye, 9 Pearls, 18K Gold	175.00
Pin, Swordfish, Sterling	25.00

Pin, Turtle, Napier 20.00
Pin, Wedgwood, Twisted Wire Detail, 18K Gold 1200.00
Pin, Woman's Head, 5 Diamonds, Art Nouveau, 14K Gold ....*Illus* 425.00
Ring, Amethyst Center, Design On Shank, Kalo Shop 795.00
Ring, Amethyst, Claw Set, Enameling, 14K Yellow Gold, C.1880 .... 165.00
Ring, Amethyst, Filigree, 14K Gold 125.00
Ring, Amethyst, Oval, Surrounded By Marcasites, Sterling Silver 160.00
Ring, Black Center Stone, Marcasite & Sterling Silver 35.00
Ring, Bloodstone, 10K Gold, Victorian 90.00
Ring, Blue Topaz, 14K White Gold 550.00
Ring, Blue Topaz, 14K White Gold, Tiffany Setting, 1940s 450.00
Ring, Cameo, Pink, 14K Yellow Gold 155.00
Ring, Chrysoprase, 18K Gold 135.00
Ring, Class, 14K Gold, Mitchell, S.D., 1915 .... 75.00
Ring, Dangle, Fleur–De–Lis 65.00
Ring, Diamond & Ruby Bee, 1 Pear–Shaped Diamond, 18K Yellow Gold 335.00
Ring, Diamond Center, Flanked By Marquise Diamonds, Woman's 7250.00
Ring, Diamond Cluster, 14K White & Yellow Gold, C.1915 .... 180.00
Ring, Diamond Spinner, Circle of Diamonds 595.00
Ring, Diamond, 18K Gold, 1910 .... 150.00
Ring, Diamond, Solitaire, 14K Yellow Gold Mount 2000.00
Ring, Diamonds, 3, European Cut, C.1910 ....*Illus* 4700.00
Ring, Diamonds, Sapphire, Shield Shape, 18K White Gold, C.1910 .... 195.00
Ring, Dinner, 3 Diamonds, Sapphire Baguette Each Side 425.00
Ring, Dinner, 7 Diamonds, Filigree, 14K Yellow Gold 265.00
Ring, Dinner, Round Diamond, 14K Yellow Gold 445.00
Ring, Double Heart, Bow Top, Rose Cut Diamond, 1840 .... 6000.00
Ring, Emerald, Seed Pearls, Diamonds, 14K Yellow Gold, C.1890 .... 750.00
Ring, Filigree, .44 Carat White Diamond, 18K White Gold 395.00
Ring, Garnet, 10K Gold, Round 80.00
Ring, Havana Cigar Band, Enameled Design, Tiffany Mark, Size 6 .... 175.00
Ring, Intaglio, Onyx, Pink Gold 95.00
Ring, Jade Carved, 14K Yellow Gold, Man's, Size* 295.00
Ring, Jade, Elongated, Jadeite Plaque, 14K Yellow Gold Mounting 175.00
Ring, Masonic, 1/4 Carat Diamond ....:............... 225.00
Ring, Masonic, 3/4 Carat Diamond, 10K Gold 750.00
Ring, Masonic, Black Onyx Insert 75.00
Ring, Medusa, Sterling Silver 95.00
Ring, Moonstone, Carved, Pink Gold 90.00
Ring, Nugget, Seven 2 1/2 Point Diamonds, 14K Gold 95.00
Ring, Onxy, Black, Diamond In Center, 14K Yellow Gold, Size 6 1/2 .... 60.00
Ring, Opal, Oval, Surrounded By 22 Diamonds, 14K Gold 2250.00
Ring, Opal, Pear Shape, Surrounding Diamonds, 14K Gold 375.00
Ring, Pearl Baroque, Flower & Leaf Form, 14K Gold, Kalo Shop 2250.00
Ring, Pearl, 3 White Sapphires, 14K Gold 50.00
Ring, Peridot & 2 Diamonds, 14K Gold 95.00
Ring, Princess, Opals & Garnets, 14K Gold 75.00
Ring, Rows of Channel Set Emeralds & Diamonds, Platinum Mount 1435.00
Ring, Ruby, Surrounded By Seed Pearls, Victorian 85.00
Ring, Sapphire & Seed Pearl, 14K Gold 80.00
Ring, Sapphire Center, Flanked By 2 Sapphires, 18K Yellow Gold 880.00
Ring, Sapphire, Yellow, 14K Gold Filigree 125.00
Ring, Sterling & Marcasite, Large Cut Onyx 85.00
Ring, Turquoise, Oval Center, Encircled By Tiny Turquoise, 14K Gold 165.00
Ring, Twirler, Cameo, Reverses To Onyx & Diamond 300.00
Ring, Woven Gold & Brown Hair Band, Woman's 125.00
Rope, Amber Nuggets, 72 In. 65.00
Shoe Clip, Blue & White Rhinestones, Art Deco, Pair 27.00
Shoe Clip, Gold & Clear, Pair 30.00
Shoe Clip, Rhinestones, Bakelite, Gray, Pair 35.00
Silver, Butterfly, Mexico, 3 1/4 In. 45.00
Slide, Woman's Head, Art Nouveau, With Chain 75.00
Stickpin, Aquamarine, 14K Gold 45.00
Stickpin, Case, Eagle On Globe 22.00

Stickpin, Doe–Wah–Jack, Indian, Advertising .... 20.00 To 30.00
Stickpin, Eagle & Globe, Case Knives, Advertising 105.00
Stickpin, Fireman's Ax, Advertising 20.00
Stickpin, Sapphire, Art Deco, 14K Gold 115.00
Stickpin, Shield Shape, Center Oval Cabochon, James T. Winn 650.00
Stickpin, Yellow Kid, Full Body 100.00
Stud Set, Silver & Enamel, Elk's Tooth Center 125.00
Tie Bar & Cuff Links, Golfer, Set 70.00
Tie Bar, Sterling Silver, G. Jensen 75.00
Tie Clip, Central Oval, 1930s Styling, Kalo Shop, 1 3/4 In. 125.00
Tie Tack, Galloping Horses, Menuki Design, Gold Finish, 1 1/4 In. 15.00
Tie Tack, Masonic, Diamond Chips, Gold 18.00
Tie Tack, Northrup X–15, 1940s 28.00
 JEWELRY, WATCH, see Watch
Watch Bracelet, Diamond Sash, Platinum, 7 Carat ....*Illus* 7400.00
Watch Key, Victorian, 14K Gold, 1 1/2 In. 145.00

John Rogers statues were made from 1859 to 1892. The originals were bronze, but the thousands of copies made by the Rogers factory were of painted plaster. Eighty different figures were made. Similar painted plaster figures were made by some other factories. Never repaint a Rogers figure because this lowers the value to collectors.

JOHN ROGERS, Group, Going For The Cows 325.00
Group, John Alden & Priscilla, 1855, 22 In. 600.00
Group, John Alden & Priscilla, Signed, 1855, 22 In. 665.00

Any memorabilia that refers to the Jews or the Jewish religion is collected. Interests range from newspaper clippings that mention eighteenth– and nineteenth–century Jewish Americans to religious objects, such as menorahs or spice boxes. Age, condition, and the intrinsic value of the material, as well as the historic and artistic importance, determine the value.

JUDAICA, Bible, Torah Nevi'Im Ukethuvim, Verses Numbered, 4 Volumes 1335.00
Box, Etrog, Foliate Legs, Gilt Interior, German Silver, 5 1/4 In. 335.00
Menorah, 8 Sockets, Acanthus Base, Brass, 9 1/2 In., Pair 75.00

Jugtown Pottery refers to pottery made in North Carolina as far back as the 1750s. In 1915, Juliana and Jacques Busbee set up a training and sales organization for what they named "Jugtown Pottery." In 1921, they built a shop at Jugtown, North Carolina, and hired Ben Owen as a potter in 1923. The Busbees moved the village store where the pottery was sold and promoted to New York City. Juliana Busbee sold the New York store in 1926 and moved into a log cabin near the Jugtown Pottery. The pottery closed in 1958. It reopened and is still working near Seagrove, North Carolina.

JUGTOWN, Candleholder, Green, Drip Catcher, Ben Owen, 9 1/2 In. 200.00
Cup, Brown 15.00
Jar, Cover, Green Frogskin, 6 In. 85.00
Jug, Cobalt Blue Peacock, Marked 395.00
Pitcher, 2 Incised Bands, Black & Green, 5 In. 50.00
Pitcher, Gray, 3 1/2 In. 15.00
Pitcher, Moss Green, 4 In. 55.00
Plate, Signed, 7 In. 24.00
Vase, Chinese Blue, Ben Owen 400.00
Vase, Chinese White, Small 55.00
Vase, Cover, Frogskin Glaze 95.00
Vase, Handles, Chinese Blue Over Red, 9 1/2 X 9 In. 425.00
Vase, Turquoise, 5 1/4 In. 125.00

Kate Greenaway, who was a famous illustrator of children's books, drew pictures of children in high-waisted Empire dresses. She lived from 1846 to 1901. Her designs appear on china, glass, and other pieces. Figural napkin rings depicting the Greenaway children are also to be found listed under Napkin Ring, Figural.

KATE GREENAWAY, Napkin Clip, Silver Plate, Tufts 250.00
Pitcher, Scenes Front & Back, Marked 1880, 5 3/4 In. 95.00
Planter, Wall, Medallion of 6 Girls, Partially Open Book 295.00
Print, Broomstick Ride, From Under The Window, 8 X 6 In. 30.00
Salt & Pepper, Tan Coats, Hats, 4 1/2 In. 90.00
Saltshaker, Boy, Beige Coat, 4 In. 40.00
Toothpick, Girl, Silver Plate 120.00

"Kauffmann" refers to the type of work done by Angelica Kauffmann, a painter and decorative artist for Adam Brothers in England between 1766 and 1781. She designed small-scale pictorial subjects in the neoclassic manner. Most porcelains signed "Kauffmann" were made in the 1800s. She did not do the artwork on all pieces signed with her name.

KAUFFMANN, Bowl, 2 Maidens & Child, Signed, 9 1/2 In. 65.00
Bowl, Cupid & 3 Muses, Signed, 6 In. 35.00
Bowl, Maidens, Signed, 9 1/2 In. 65.00
Box, 2 Maidens & Child On Cover, Allover Lilacs, 4 1/2 In. 85.00
Plate, Lady, Standing, Knight, Sitting, With Shield, 13 In. 63.00
Plate, Portrait, Blue, Beehive, 10 In. 58.00
    KAYSERZINN, see Pewter

KELVA

Kelva glassware was made by the C. F. Monroe Company of Meriden, Connecticut, about 1904. It is a pale, pastel-painted glass decorated with flowers, designs, or scenes. Kelva resembles Nakara and Wave Crest, two other glasswares made by the same company.

KELVA, Biscuit Jar, Orange Poppies, Blue Ground, Handle, 10 In. 925.00
Bowl, Octagonal, Sterling Ormolu, 5 1/2 In. 750.00
Box, Batik-Type Ground, Pink Flowers, Sterling Fittings, Signed 6 In. 650.00
Box, Blownout Rose, Blue, Round, 3 In. 450.00
Box, Blue-Gray Flowers, Lined, Crown Mold, 4 1/2 X 6 1/4 In. 860.00
Box, Crown Mold, Pink Flowers, Green Ground, Wave Crest, 6 1/2 In. 675.00
Box, Dresser, Cover, Pink, 3 1/2 X 6 X 5 In. 600.00
Box, Orchids On Cover, Pink, Signed, 5 In. 420.00
Box, Pastel Pink Blossoms, Green Ground, 8 In. 595.00
Box, Pink Flowers, Green, 4 In. 275.00
Dish, Pin, Dogwood Blossoms, Ormolu Mounting 95.00
Humidor, Large 500.00
Napkin Ring, Pink Flowers, Blue Ground 475.00
Salt, Ormolu Handles, Design, Signed 325.00
Tray, Mirror, Pink Flowers, Blue Ground, 6 1/4 X 2 1/4 X 3 In. 500.00
Tray, Pin, Ormolu Handles, Marked 180.00
Vase, Pink Flowers, Green Ground, Silver Plated Base, Handles, 19 In. 925.00

To hang copper molds in your kitchen, try this method: Mount a solid brass or wooden curtain rod across the top of the hanging area. Molds can then be hung by hooks and easily moved when new ones are added.

XEW-BLAS

Kew Blas is the name used by the Union Glass Company of Somerville, Massachusetts. The name refers to an iridescent golden glass made from the 1890s to 1924. The iridescent glass was reminiscent of the Tiffany glass of the period.

KEW BLAS, Compote, Folded Rim, Silvery Pink & Blue Luster, 4 X 5 3/4 In.	600.00
Goblet, Champagne, Iridized Gold Inside & Out, Signed, 5 In.	110.00
Vase, 3 Green Pulled Feathers Outlined In Gold, Signed, 8 1/2 In.	770.00
Vase, Amber Walls, White Overlay, Feathering, Marked, C.1910, 6 In.	1870.00
Vase, Gold Pulled Feather, Turned–Over Rim, Orange, 7 1/2 In.	775.00

Kewpies, designed by Rose O'Neill, were first pictured in the "Ladies' Home Journal." The pixielike figures were a success, and Kewpie dolls started appearing in 1911. Kewpie pictures and other items soon followed. Collectors search for all items that picture the little winged people.

KEWPIE, Bank, 6 Kewpies, 1 Holds K Flag, Koin Keeper, R. O'Neill, Jasperware	450.00
Bell, Brass, Small	65.00
Book, Sing–A–Song of Safety, Rose O'Neill	22.00
Bowl, Cereal, Wheaties, 3 Kewpies In Bottom	48.00
Boy, Green Coat, Pink Pants, Black Shoes, Celluloid, 5 1/2 In.	45.00
Button, Action, Bisque, Label	195.00
Cake Top, Plaster	10.00
Calendar, 1974, Paper	10.00
Candy Container, Glass Kewpie By Barrel, Partly Painted, Red	110.00
Card Holder	125.00
Card, Rolling Eyes	6.00
Clock, Blue Jasperware, Rose O'Neill	325.00
Creamer, 7 Kewpies, Blue Jasperware, Rose O'Neill	165.00
Doll, Angel, Masquerade Costume, Cameo, 12 In.	25.00
Doll, Bean Bag, Box, 9 In.	35.00
Doll, Bisque, Blue Wings, Jointed Arms, Eyes To Right, O'Neill, 7 In.	80.00
Doll, Bisque, Heart Label, Box, 5 1/2 In.	275.00
Doll, Boy, Black, Party Outfit, Cameo, 8 In.	16.00
Doll, Bride & Groom, Box, 16 In., Pair	120.00
Doll, Bride & Groom, Dressed, 4 1/2 In., Pair	295.00
Doll, Brother & Sister, Black, School Outfit, Cameo, 12 In., Pair	52.00
Doll, Cameo, Little Devil, Movable Head, 6 1/2 In.	30.00
Doll, Composition, Rose O'Neill, 13 In. ....79.00 To 100.00	
Doll, Crawling, O Mouth, Signed O'Neill, 3 1/4 In.	950.00
Doll, Girl, 14 In.	75.00
Doll, Girl, Cameo, 1972 ....16.00 To 22.00	
Doll, Groom, Composition, 9 In.	80.00
Doll, Hard Plastic, Fully Jointed, Sleep Eyes, 1950s, 13 In.	300.00
Doll, Heart–Shaped Crocheted Pincushion, Signed O'Neill, 1 1/4 In.	300.00
Doll, Heubach Koppelsdorf, Painted Shoes & Socks, 5 1/4 In.	325.00
Doll, Holding Book, O'Neill, 1 3/4 In.	125.00
Doll, Hugger, Bisque, Rose O'Neill, 4 In.	150.00
Doll, Hugger, Crepe Paper Clothes, O'Neill, 4 In.	145.00
Doll, Little Traveler, Bisque, Signed O'Neill	225.00
Doll, Original Sticker, 5 In.	125.00
Doll, Santa Claus, 28 In.	375.00
Doll, Side Glancing Eyes, Signed O'Neill, 12 In.	3850.00
Doll, Vinyl, Jesco, Box, 25 In.	125.00
Doll, Vinyl, Red Dress, Box, 27 In.	100.00
Doll, With Turkey, Bisque, O'Neil, 2 In.	250.00
Figurine, Brass, 8 In.	85.00
Figurine, Full Figure, Button On Back, Label, Rose O'Neill, 2 In.	245.00
Figurine, Jointed Arms, Germany, 4 1/2 In.	98.00
Figurine, Nurse, Bisque, 4 In.	25.00
Figurine, Thinker, O'Neill, 4 In.	80.00
Figurine, Thinker, Signed Rose O'Neill	25.00
Greeting Card, Unused, 1974, 20 Piece	20.00
Holder, Pocket Watch, Pewter	80.00

Holding Teddy Bear, Next To Blue Bud Vase, Signed O'Neill	1100.00
Letter Opener, Figural Handle	59.00
Music Box, Bisque	85.00
Pincushion, Pewter	50.00
Plaque, Kewpie With Turtle, 4 In. Diam.	45.00
Plaque, Kewpies Center, Heart Shape, Signed R.O'Neill, 4 X 3 1/2 In.	265.00
Plate, 3 Sitting On Bench, 4 Around Edge, Rose O'Neill Wilson, 7 In.	75.00
Plate, Christmas, 1973, 8 In.	22.00
Postcard, Kewpie Doll, Holding Santa Claus Mask, Rose O'Neill, 1900s	35.00
Print, Baseball Kewpie, Eating Ice Cream, Advertising, 8 X 11 In.	35.00
Purse, Child's, Kewpieville	18.00
Ring Holder	75.00
Salt & Pepper, Figural, Silver Plated, Paye & Baker, C.1910	145.00
Salt & Pepper, Sterling Silver	185.00 To 195.00
Sand Pail, Coney Island, 5 1/2 In.	150.00
Shaker, Powder, 7 In.	95.00
Sign, Made–Rite Ice Cream, 2 Kewpies, Rose O'Neill, Cardboard, 36 In.	240.00
Talcum Powder Holder, Shaker In Head, Rose O'Neill Label, 1913	225.00
Tea Set, Green Luster On White, Action, O'Neill, Service For 6	1500.00
Tea Set, Porcelain	25.00
Thimble, Metal, Marked Kewpie	49.00
Tie Tack	18.00
Toy, Squeeze, Pink Dotted	10.00
Whistle, Brass	35.00

KIMBALL, see Cluthra
KING'S ROSE, see Soft Paste

 All types of kitchen utensils, from eggbeaters to bowls, are collected today. Handmade wooden and metal items, like ladles and apple peelers, were made in the early nineteenth century. Mass–produced pieces, like iron apple peelers and graniteware, were made in the nineteenth century. Other kitchen wares are listed under manufacturers' names or under Iron; Advertising; Tool; or Wooden.

KITCHEN, Apple Corer, Box	24.00
Apple Corer, Tin, Tubular Handle, 6 1/8 In.	25.00
Apple Drier, Wooden, E. Berry, Pierced Tin Base, 13 X 9 X 4 In.	250.00
Bacon Dryer, Wire, 12 Prongs	24.00
Baking Center, Flour, Sugar Compartment, Sifter, Side Canisters, Tin	850.00
Beater, A & J, Dated 1923	7.00
Blender, Knapp–Monarch Liquidizer, Art Deco, 1940s	45.00
Blender, Knapp–Monarch Liquidizer, Instructions & Recipes	65.00
Blender, Oster, 1950s	3.00
Board, Bread, Attached Tin Rolling Pin, Wooden Handles, 22 X 22 In.	250.00
Board, Bread, Crested Ends, American, Late 18th Century, 23 In.	275.00
Board, Cutting, Drilled Holes At Sides, 11 X 17 5/8 In.	65.00
Board, Cutting, Land 'O Lakes	8.50
Board, Noodle, Stand, Pine	120.00
Board, Pastry, Wooden, Finger Groove, 19 3/4 X 17 3/4 In.	25.00
Board, Slaw, Heart Cutout, Refinished, 7 3/8 X 21 3/4 In.	125.00
Board, Slaw, Mustard Paint, Dovetailed Box, Replaced Handle	160.00
Bootjack, Pistol, American Bulldog	95.00
Bottle Corker, Yankee, Ornate	90.00
Bowl, Wooden, Stenciled Fruit Interior, Oblong, 12 1/2 X 22 In.	210.00
Bowl, Wooden, Trough–Like, 20 X 40 In.	130.00
Box, Pantry, Beveled Lap, Pinned Bottom & Top, 5 1/4 In.	150.00
Box, Pantry, Copper Nails, Monogram On Top, 6 1/2 In.	125.00
Box, Pantry, Green, Tin, 12 In.	35.00
Brazier, Kettle, Cast Iron, Heart Grid Design, 10 5/8 X 7 1/2 In.	275.00
Bread Box, Green & White, Speckled, 11 1/2 In.	50.00
Bread Box, Tin, Slant Front, 2 Drop Doors, 23 X 13 In.	55.00
Bread Raiser, Cover, Tin	30.00
Broiler, Royal Blue, Cover, 1920, Savory, 12 X 18 In.	18.00
Broom, Corn, American, 19th Century, 43 In.	55.00
Broom, Oven, Birch Splint, Hole For Hanging, 1830, 10 1/2 In.	30.00

A choice collection of Spanish-American related memorabilia, but it should be displayed on shelves away from small children. Some of the pieces could cause injury. Courtesy Len Rosenberg

HEALTHY ANTIQUES
A Guide to the Safe Use and Care of Your Antiques and Collectibles

Grandma's Victorian desk looks great in the den and Uncle Jim's sixty-year-old crib is in the nursery. The painted chair has been stripped to a natural maple glow. Fiesta plates, copper molds, and crocks, all flea market finds, are in the kitchen. Antiques add to a home's charm, but collectors must be sure the finds are safe to use with modern conveniences or modern cleaning chemicals.

Ceramics With Lead-Based Glazes

Colorful Mexican dinnerware is attractive, but some, old or new, is dangerous. The Food & Drug Administration has been monitoring the lead content in dishes since 1971. Some dishes made before that time may be safe for display only. Lead may leach out into acidic foods served in lead-glazed pitchers or pots. A few collectors, who used this pottery,

Only one of these plates may be danger-ous. Check on the origins of any orange-red pottery. These Riviera dishes do not have high lead content or radioactive glaze.

Copper pots should be tin-lined if they are to be used for cooking. Our ancestors knew this when they made these nine-teenth-century pots. Courtesy Biltmore House, Asheville, North Carolina

have been gradually poisoned. Do not store orange juice, wine, or other acidic liquids in lead-glazed dishes. Display the plates, but don't use them each day. Small scratches made by a knife cutting the food, or the acid of tomato sauce, could release lead. You can test dishes for lead content. But don't be too afraid; almost no United States-made dishes have this problem.

Rumor has it that red-orange glazed Fiesta dishes made by Homer Laughlin China Company from 1936 to 1973 are radioactive and dan-gerous. Orange glaze was made with uranium in the 1930s, but recent reproduction pieces are made with absolutely safe glazes. There is little danger from orange dishes but the rumor persists.

Cooking and Eating Utensils

Never use a copper pot to cook or store acidic foods. Copperware should be tin-lined. Don't use early redware when serving acidic foods. There are many unsafe old cooking practices.

Butcher blocks, wooden salad bowls, and other utensils should be treated with an edible oil. Use walnut oil for this purpose. All wooden cooking utensils and cutting boards should be washed regularly with hot, even boiling, water. Raw chicken, fish, and eggs carry salmonella and viruses that cause food poisoning. These illnesses can be passed on via a dirty wooden container.

Glasses were decorated with black and gold enameled designs in the 1950s. These motifs were sometimes made with lead-based enamel that deteriorates if washed in a dishwasher. This deterioration is easily noticed because the decoration has a gray, chalky look. Never use a glass with this problem.

Bottles and Jugs

In 1912 the Radium Ore Revigator Company sold a "cure" for numerous diseases, from hemorrhoids to cancer. They marketed a large tan crock that was lined with radium. You were to fill it with water, then drink the treated water six times a day. Unfortunately, these jugs are still radioactive. It is unsafe to keep them in the house. The radioactivity can cause cancer and is especially dangerous for children and pregnant women. The biggest problem is how to get the Revigator out of the house. It is illegal to dump nuclear wastes in any but approved sites.

Bottle and advertising collectors should be careful of partially filled old bottles and boxes. Many pills, potions, and drinks used in the past were made from ingredients we now know are dangerous, lethal, or addictive. Drugs deteriorate with time and may become stronger or change. One collector we know found a cache of old Oriental medicine bottles filled with opium and heroin mixtures. Be sure to empty old medical containers. Like old refrigerators, they seem safe, but a curious child may experiment and die. If you find old drugs, call your local police for help. You may pollute the area if you dispose of the drugs incorrectly.

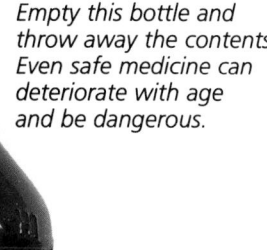

Empty this bottle and throw away the contents. Even safe medicine can deteriorate with age and be dangerous.

A sketch of the Revigator marking.

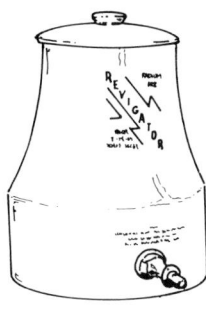

Stoneware jugs like these are attractive, safe decorations for a home. Only the "radium" jugs are a problem. Courtesy State Museum of Pennsylvania, Harrisburg, Pennsylvania

Furniture

A ntique furniture adds to the individual look of a home. But some types should be avoided by families with young children. The colonial baby was swaddled in blankets and restrained in the cradle. Never keep an infant in a cradle where the baby can roll over. The sides are too low to prevent a fall. Slats on an old crib should be no more than 2⅜ inches apart. A baby can put its head through the bars and not be able to get it out again. Some serious accidents have been caused by incorrectly spaced bars. Be sure there is no space between the end of the mattress and the foot of the bed. Pre-1950 painted furniture should be checked for poisonous lead-based paint.

Antique high chairs may be easy to tip. Watch out for an active child in an old chair. Windsor-type chairs have backs that tempt a child's curiosity. Be sure the spacing between the spindles is safe.

Although this was sold as an eighteenth-century high chair it seems dangerous to use. The spindles are widely spaced and an active child could climb over the top rail. But this early nineteenth-century Windsor chair is safe to use, even in a home with young children. It is unpainted, sturdy, and the spindles are close together.

Old painted furniture is very collectible, but be sure there is no way for a crawling infant to chew on knobs or feet. Many of the old paints contained lead.

Explosives

All war souvenirs, guns, grenades, and bullets are dangerous. They were made to explode and with careless handling they can. If you have an antique or souvenir gun, be sure it contains no bullets. If possible, fill the barrel with plaster so the gun can never fire. An antique gun is just as dangerous as a new one and all the usual precautions are necessary. If you find an old grenade or box of shells, call your local fire department. Deteriorated gunpowder could suddenly explode. It takes an expert to remove these items.

Wiring

Old lamps or electric clocks with silk-wrapped cord or cracked rubber cords are fire hazards. Have old lamps rewired. Collectible appliances such as toasters and waffle irons should be checked by an electrician. If you have a TV set that is over five years old, ask the repairman to remove the instant-on feature. It includes a light bulb that can explode and cause a fire.

Antique Fire Extinguishers

The cone-shaped metal fire extinguishers made before 1950, and the older glass ball extinguishers, may be dangerous. Many contain carbon tetrachloride or other dangerous chemicals. The chemicals can cause medical problems if eaten, inhaled, or just absorbed through the skin. If a glass "grenade" fire extinguisher accidently breaks, the liquid inside vaporizes and contaminates the surrounding area.

If one of these old Harden's Hand Grenade glass fire extinguishers breaks, leave the room. Not only have you lost a valued collectible, but you have contaminated the room.

Always rewire an old lamp. The frayed cord is a fire hazard.

Flammable Plastics

Most collectors know old nitrate movie film is dangerous. If it is stored for a long time, it can deteriorate and burst into flames. Home movies from the 1930s and 1940s are dangerous. Have them transferred to new film or videotape. Ask your local fire department about the dangers and disposal of old film.

Celluloid was made from cellulose nitrate. It too is flammable if heated for a long time. It is not safe to store celluloid toys or dresser sets in a hot attic. Deteriorating celluloid smells like acid. Rub an old piece vigorously and it has an acid smell. Once the decomposition starts, there is no way to reverse it and the piece should be destroyed.

Radioactive Jewelry

Costume jewelry made from old watches has become popular. Be sure your jewelry doesn't have a luminous old watch dial. Radium made them glow. There was little danger because the glass acted as a shield. Dismantled watches are more dangerous and must be avoided. Jewelers who assemble new jewelry from old parts are most at risk.

In 1983 the government announced that some Chinese cloisonné jewelry is radioactive. It is dangerous if it touches the skin for fifty hours a week. Be careful of pendants and pierced earrings.

Celluloid toys like these will burn if stored in a very hot attic. Rub the toy with a cloth. If it has an acid smell it is decomposing and is dangerous.

Most cloisonné is safe to own, but recently some radioactive cloisonné jewelry has been identified. This covered pot was made before that was a danger.

Toys

Our government has many agencies that try to keep us from harm. The staff of OSHA (Occupational Safety and Health Administration) checks on hazards in the factory, the EPA (Environmental Protection Agency) reports dangerous pollution, and the Consumer Product Safety Commission and other agencies warn us if consumer products are unsafe. Old toys can be dangerous as playthings for young children. Keep your collectibles on high shelves to be admired. Don't let children play with them. Tin toys that were made in Japan from about 1920 to 1960 were often made with razor-sharp edges that could cause deep cuts. Spring-wound toys sometimes have sharp edges on the springs. Miniature steam toys may explode. Painted wooden toys are no danger unless a young child decides to chew on the lead-based paint. Early teddy bears and other stuffed animals were made with eyes held in place by a long pointed wire. Few children can resist the temptation to pry out the eyes. Replace the eyes so they cannot be removed. Be sure pull toys have cords less than 12 inches long. A long cord could become wrapped around a child's neck.

Metal parts, small wheels, and sharp edges are found on some old toys.

Lovable but lethal, this early 1900s teddy bear has dangerous eyes. A curious child can pull out an eye and the long pointed metal wire holding it. Never give a young child a toy with this type of eye. Dolls' eyes are usually safe and secure. Courtesy Christies

Artist and Do-It-Yourself Chemicals

L earn the hazards of chemicals. Arsenic, antimony, cadmium, chromium, lead, manganese, mercury, toluene, uranium, methylene chloride, methanol, benzene, trichlorethylene, turpentine, paraffin, and asbestos are found in paints, ceramic glazes, cleaners, demolition dust, polishes, and glassmaking products.

Always work in a well-ventilated room when painting or working with chemicals. For some jobs, like stripping plaster or removing insulation, it is important to have an exhaust system, face mask, and goggles. Wear long sleeves, long pants legs, and a high neck to cover as much skin as possible. For most jobs wear gloves. Remove your clothes when the job is done and wash them separately. Don't walk inside with shoes that might have picked up chemical-laden dust. Don't eat or smoke near any refinishing job. You could swallow some dust from your fingers. Clean, wet-mop, and vacuum often and put all trash in closed garbage containers. Never allow pregnant women, children, or pets near chemicals.

Early American glassblowers did not realize that arsenic in the glass mixture could be dangerous. These blown amber pieces were made in Zanesville, Ohio. Courtesy Western Reserve Historical Society, Cleveland, Ohio

If you handpaint china, be careful not to lick the paintbrush. Wash your hands before you eat. Some of the chemicals are dangerous if ingested.

Arsenic poisoning has been a problem for glassblowers for centuries. This American Victorian bowl may have been hazardous to make, but is safe to own. Courtesy Biltmore House, Asheville, North Carolina

When George Ohr made this vase around the year 1900, he did not worry about the clay dust. But he worked in an open shed with ample ventilation. Courtesy David Rago Arts & Crafts, Trenton, New Jersey

If you restore a stained glass window, be cautious in cutting the lead strips. The dust is dangerous. Do the job away from children, pets, pregnant women, and food.

Rags and Refinishing

When rags soaked with oil, paint thinner, turpentine, tung oil, and other refinishing products are bunched in a corner there may be a case of spontaneous combustion and a fire. Always clean the cloths as soon as possible. Keep them in a cool place, preferably a closed, fireproof metal can.

Legal Problems

There are some new laws about buying, selling, and even owning certain types of antiques that can cause problems for a collector. If you own an antique gun and sell it without the required permits, you might be responsible for any acts involving that gun. If there is a murder or a robbery, you may be criminally liable.

Some antiques cannot be legally sold or owned. Local police or federal law enforcement officers can confiscate your illegal antiques and even charge you with a crime. In some states it is illegal to sell liquor without

In some states it is illegal to sell figural decanters like this 1972 Cyrus Noble bottle if they are filled with liquor.

All sorts of dangerous, perhaps lethal ingredients could lurk in the bottles and cans in this old store collection. Never eat or drink anything in cans and bottles this old.

a license. This includes liquor in decorative decanters, so be sure to buy or sell only *empty* whiskey containers. In some states it is illegal to own a slot machine, even if it is old and kept for your own entertainment. It can be confiscated or destroyed or you could be charged with illegal possession.

Avoid buying or selling anything that contains drugs such as cocaine or morphine. These are sometimes found in old medicine, and even if you are interested only in the bottle, the law says you are responsible for the contents too.

In all states it is illegal to sell endangered species. (There are a few exceptions to these rules based on the age of the antique.) Be very careful not to buy or sell stuffed migratory birds, eagle feathers, elephant ivory, rare tortoise shells or furniture with shell inlay, mounted heads or skins of wild tigers and other exotic, endangered animals. It is illegal and also in poor taste to buy or sell American Indian religious items, body parts (such as skeletons or shrunken heads), tombstones, or statuary from graveyards.

Don't

S tress while bidding at auction, tired feet from tramping around flea markets, or sleepless nights from dreaming about a missed antique are common collector ailments. There are more serious dangers in collecting that damage both the collector and the collection. Here is a list of warnings of the common dangers.

WARNING!
(Dangerous for antiques.)

Don't try to clean an oil painting. You may remove too much of the varnish and paint and destroy the value.

Don't wash ivory. The yellow color is preferred and newly washed ivory has a much lower value.

Don't clean coins. Collectors want coins with the patina unchanged.

Never wash ivory. This is an ivory eighteenth-century French wedding chest.

Don't retouch gold-leaf picture frames or other gold-leaf trim with anything but real gold leaf. Gold paint and other less expensive substitutes will eventually discolor.

Don't use the old mixture of boiled linseed oil, turpentine, and white vinegar on your wood furniture. Experts claim that the mixture crystallizes into a finish that cannot be removed. It makes the wood appear dark and will lower the value of the piece.

Don't put crazed pottery or porcelain in the dishwasher and don't try to bleach it clean.

Don't put china or glass with gold designs in the dishwasher. The gold will wash off in time.

Don't display glass bottles, paperweights, or other objects in a sunny window. The glass could discolor, fracture from the heat, or magnify the rays and start a fire.

Do not use the old favorite furniture polish made with boiled linseed oil, turpentine, and white vinegar. It permanently darkens wood.

Never retouch a gold-leaf frame with anything but real gold leaf.

This window display is often suggested in decorating magazines, but remember old glass may discolor or break from the heat. It is best to keep treasured glass away from direct sunlight.

Beware! The overglaze flowers on this pitcher wash off in the dishwasher. So will the gold trim on this Minton set.

Don't try to remove dents from silver or pewter yourself. This is a job for an expert.

Don't use a mechanical buffer to clean old silver, pewter, or other metals. The heat might change the color of the metal.

Don't repaint old metal toys, banks, iron bottle openers, doorstops, bookends, or other small iron or tin items. It lowers the value.

Don't replate eighteenth-century Sheffield silver. Wares from the nineteenth and twentieth centuries that were originally electroplated can be replated without a loss in value.

Don't repaint old iron bookends like these. It lowers the value.

WARNING!
(Dangerous to collectors.)

Don't clean badly tarnished pewter with lye unless you are aware of the physical dangers involved.

Don't use old electrical collectibles (such as lamps, toasters, radios, or fans) before changing the old cords. Rewire anything over fifteen years old. The old cords may have cracked and are fire hazards.

Don't use an old stove before it is inspected by a local stove expert. Fire or fumes could kill you.

Don't use paint or varnish strippers made from methylene chloride. The fumes are very dangerous. We understand that a few people have died from heart attacks after inhaling the fumes. Heavy smokers and people with heart conditions are in the greatest danger. It is also a suspected carcinogen. If you do use a paint stripper with methylene chloride, always wear eye protection. The mixture can cause corneal scarring and permanently impair your vision. If the mixture hits your skin, wash it off immediately; it can burn.

Never buff pewter.

Dents should be removed from a silver teapot as soon as possible because continuous cleaning over a dent may eventually cause a hole in the silver. Have an expert do the repair.

Don't use products for stripping paint or refinishing furniture that contain methanol, benzene, or toluene without great precautions. Always have good ventilation, safety goggles, and gloves. Many products can cause headaches, leukemia, damage to the liver, kidneys, and bone marrow, and much more.

Don't strip off lead-based paints (many were in use before 1950) without the proper safeguards. Heated paint can give off dangerous fumes. Ingested paint can cause other troubles.

Don't allow children, pregnant women, elderly people, or pets near any job where you are using strong chemicals or paint strippers.

Don't store old paint rags; they may ignite spontaneously.

Don't do jobs that bring you in contact with asbestos dust. This may happen if you are restoring a stove or heating pipes.

Don't store old nitrate-based film; it may ignite.

Don't use epoxy compounds without taking the precaution of covering eyes, hands, and arms. Work in a well-ventilated room. The fumes can cause liver or kidney damage and nasal and eye irritation.

Don't use paraffin (found in waxes and varnish) or fungicides without proper precautions. Cover your skin and work in a well-ventilated room; consider using a face mask.

Don't work without proper protective equipment. It is possible to buy face masks, goggles, respirators, safety gloves, shoes, and many other products that will make large do-it-yourself projects safer.

Don't keep military memorabilia (such as bullets or hand grenades), filled old bottles or boxes of medicine that might contain drugs, or still-full fire extinguishers in the house. Your local fire department will help you remove the dangerous ingredients. Explosives and drugs change with age and can become very dangerous.

Don't ever try to fire an old weapon before an expert has checked it.

A Final Word

Don't let all of this frighten or discourage you from using and enjoying your antiques.

Do follow these guidelines for a long, happy, and enriched life with your antiques and collectibles.

Old stoves were sometimes made with asbestos parts and should be disassembled or repaired with great care. Courtesy Minnesota Historical Society

Butter Curler, Crimped Steel, Wooden Handle, 7 In.	65.00

KITCHEN, BUTTER MOLD, see Kitchen, Mold, Butter

Butter Paddle, Burl, 10 In.	900.00
Butter Paddle, Curly Maple, 9 1/2 In.	45.00
Butter Paddle, Notched Handle	17.50
Butter Paddle, Scrubbed, Hook Handle, 9 In.	75.00
Butter Paddle, Worn Into Irregular Shape, 10 1/2 In.	35.00
Butter Press, Galleried Table, Arm & Handle Post, 64 In.	150.00
Butter Stamp, 2–Part, Floral Design, Copper Sheathing, 3 X 5 In.	35.00
Butter Stamp, 4–Part Leaf, Inserted Handle, 3 1/4 In.	45.00
Butter Stamp, Acorn, Leaf & Floral Spray In 2 Squares	95.00
Butter Stamp, Acorns & Leaves, Knob Handle, 3 1/8 X 1 1/2 In.	150.00
Butter Stamp, Apple & Leaves, Hand Carved, C.1800, 3 In.	350.00
Butter Stamp, Bird On Water, Carved Border, Lollipop	225.00
Butter Stamp, Bowtie & Leaves Over Heart, C.1830, 2 5/8 In.	220.00
Butter Stamp, Cow & Tree, Screw–In Handle, 4 In.	325.00
Butter Stamp, Cow, Flower, Turned Handle, 4 5/8 In.	175.00
Butter Stamp, Cow, Tree & Foliage, Turned Handle, 4 1/2 In.	325.00
Butter Stamp, Cow, Turned Handle, 4 1/4 In.	150.00
Butter Stamp, Eagle & Star, Turned Handle, 7 1/2 X 3 1/4 In.	95.00
Butter Stamp, Eagle With Shield & Stars, 4 1/2 In.	200.00
Butter Stamp, Eagle, Round, C.1850, 3 In.	350.00
Butter Stamp, Federal Eagle, C.1800	145.00
Butter Stamp, Fish Design, Lollipop, 7 1/4 In.	150.00
Butter Stamp, Floral Design, Round, 1 Piece Turned Handle, 4 In.	55.00
Butter Stamp, Floral Design, Stylized, With Tulip, 7 5/8 In.	100.00
Butter Stamp, Floral, Stylized, Wooden, Round, 4 In.	25.00
Butter Stamp, Flower, Strawberry & Sheaf, Pewter Bands, 3 3/4 In.	150.00
Butter Stamp, Flower, Stylized, Handle, Round, 4 In.	125.00
Butter Stamp, Heart Design, Stylized, Knob Handle, 4 In.	350.00
Butter Stamp, Lollipop, Carved Coggle Edge, Maple, 9 3/4 In.	950.00
Butter Stamp, Lollipop, Carved Scrolls, Dark Finish, 7 In.	205.00
Butter Stamp, Lollipop, Double Design, Side Handle, 8 1/2 In.	250.00
Butter Stamp, Lollipop, Single Flower, 6 1/4 In.	200.00
Butter Stamp, Pineapple, Crosshatched, Knob Handle, 3 7/8 In.	95.00
Butter Stamp, Pineapple, Leaves, Knob Handle, 1850s, 3 7/8 In.	130.00
Butter Stamp, Pomegranate, Flowering, 1 Piece Turned Handle, 4 In.	105.00
Butter Stamp, Rooster, Hand Carved, 2 3/4 In.	70.00
Butter Stamp, Roses, 1 Piece of Maple, 5 X 8 In.	145.00
Butter Stamp, Sheaf of Wheat, Round, 4 1/2 In.Diam.	130.00
Butter Stamp, Sheaf, Semicircular, 6 1/4 In.	60.00
Butter Stamp, Ship's Anchor & Rope Pattern	270.00
Butter Stamp, Star Center, Tree & Star Between Points, 1800s, 7 In.	395.00
Butter Stamp, Star Flower, Octagonal, Pine, C.1820, 4 3/4 X 5 In.	140.00
Butter Stamp, Starflower, C.1840, 4 3/4 X 5 In.	140.00
Butter Stamp, Starflower, Octagonal, Pine.C.1820, 4 3/4 X 5 In.	140.00
Butter Stamp, Strawberry, Cased, 1 1/2 In.	65.00
Butter Stamp, Swan, Plunger, C.1830	220.00
Butter Stamp, Thistle Design, Turned Handle, 2 1/2 In.	45.00
Butter Stamp, Thistle, Carved, Beveled Handle, 18th Century, 4 In.	295.00
Butter Stamp, Thistles, Intertwining, Turned Handle, 5 X 3 In.	95.00
Butter Stamp, Tulip, Round, 4 In.	205.00
Butter Stamp, Tulip, Stylized, Mushroom Knob Handle, 4 In.	350.00
Cake Pan, Funnel, Star Shape, Tin	22.00
Can Opener, Adjustable, Anderson Store, Milaga, Minn.	12.00
Can Opener, Keen Kutter, Cast Iron	15.00
Can Opener, With Wheel, Wooden Handles, USA	15.00
Candleholder Set, Cake Decoration, Cowboys, Indians, Plastic, 12 Pc.	9.00
Cheese Cutter, True Cut, White Porcelain, Brass	49.00
Cheese Ladder & Drainer, Windsor, 6 1/2 X 13 X 22 In.	220.00
Cheese Preserver, Maytac Dairy Farms, Newton, Iowa, 6 X 7 1/2 In.	42.50
Cherry Pitter, Cast Iron, Hand Crank, Patent 1863, 8 1/2 In.	55.00
Cherry Pitter, Enterprise, Double	35.00
Cherry Pitter, Enterprise, No.1, Cast Iron	21.00 To 45.00

Cherry Pitter, Goodell, 2 Prong 35.00
Cherry Pitter, Rollman, No.3, Cast Iron .... 35.00 To 45.00
Chopper, Food, 6 Blades, Cast Iron Handle 20.00
Chopper, Food, B. Denton, Primitive 28.00
Chopper, Food, Foley 8.00
Chopper, Food, Iron, Scalloped Edge Blade, Wooden Handle, 7 In. 275.00
Chopper, Food, Keen Kutter 30.00
Chopper, Nut, Hazel Atlas 8.00
Chopper, Onion, Lorraine Metal Co., New York City, Tin Lid 12.50
Churn, Bentwood, Union, 1875 .... 110.00
Churn, Crank Type, Cylinder, Iron Hoop Banded, Red Paint 125.00
Churn, Dazey, 2 Qt. 185.00
Churn, Dazey, 4 Qt. .... 40.00 To 45.00
Churn, Dazey, 6 Qt. .... 125.00 To 175.00
Churn, Dazey, Embossed, 1 Qt. 495.00
Churn, Dazey, Glass Bottom, 8 Qt. 150.00
Churn, Dazey, No. 4, Red Top 65.00
Churn, Dazey, No.10 .... 800.00
Churn, Dazey, Wooden Paddles, 1 Qt. 500.00
Churn, Monmouth, Maple Leaf Mark, 3 Gal. 80.00
Churn, Red With Black Combed Graining, Green Trim, Hinged Cover 110.00
Churn, Square, Red Wash, Black Feet 275.00
Churn, Stave Constructed, Lid & Dasher, Stave Handle, 12 1/2 In. 325.00
Churn, Stoneware, Mechanical, Signed & Dated 195.00
Churn, Table, Wooden, Round 147.50
Churn, Tabletop, J.B. Varick, Crank Turned, 13 X 14 In. 185.00
KITCHEN, COFFEE GRINDER, see Coffee Grinder
Coffeepot, Steam, Copper, French, 1904, Large 125.00
Colander, Aluminum, 3–Footed, 8 In. 9.00
Colander, Punched Star Design, Copper, 3 X 10 3/4 In. 65.00
Cookie Board, 12 Segments, Each Different, Metal, 4 5/8 X 7 1/2 In. 65.00
Cookie Board, 15 Designs, Walnut, Fellmeth's Bakery, 6 1/4 X 10 In. 375.00
Cookie Board, 5 Carved Designs, Geometric Floral, 4 X 9 In. 210.00
Cookie Board, Beech, Flower Basket, 1 Side, Grapes, 10 X 16 In. 300.00
Cookie Board, Cherry, Basket of Flowers, 1 Side Tulips, 6 X 7 In. 495.00
Cookie Board, Fish, Oval Floral Design, 3 3/8 X 11 1/2 In. 100.00
Cookie Board, Gray Paint, Pine, Stenciled Date, 1902, 28 3/4 In. 100.00
Cookie Board, Handle, Round, 16 X 19 1/2 In. 25.00
Cookie Board, Oak, Brown Patina, Man & Woman, 6 3/4 In. 250.00
Cookie Board, Pine, Friesian, Carved Design, 11 X 12 In. 205.00
Cookie Board, Pumpkin, Round, Pine, 23 X 30 1/2 In. 175.00
Cookie Board, Rooster, 2 Men & Woman Other Side, 3 X 4 In. 440.00
Cookie Board, Rooster, John Fellmeth's Bakery, N.J., 3 3/8 X 4 In. 325.00
Cookie Board, Springerle, 6 Designs In 6–In. Wreaths, 8 X 5 In. 300.00
Cookie Board, Springerle, 6 Designs, C.1830, 7 X 3 1/2 In. 295.00
Cookie Board, Springerle, 8 Designs, Wooden, 4 3/8 X 8 3/8 In. 310.00
Cookie Board, Springerle, 24 Carved Designs, Wooden, 5 X 8 1/2 In. 225.00
Cookie Board, Springerle, 6 Patterns, 3 1/4 X 7 In. 295.00
Cookie Board, Springerle, Flower, Walnut, 2 1/2 X 4 In. 250.00
Cookie Board, Urn of Fruit, 4 X 7 In. .... 25.00 To 25.00
Cookie Cutter, American Eagle, Tin, 5 X 6 In. 55.00
Cookie Cutter, Basket, Handle, Tin, 6 7/8 In. 95.00
Cookie Cutter, Bear 16.00
Cookie Cutter, Bobtailed Pony, Prancing, Tin, Flat Back, 6 1/2 In. 195.00
Cookie Cutter, Charlie Brown, Plastic, 1952 .... 6.50
Cookie Cutter, Christmas, Ateco Cookie Maker, Box, Many Discs 15.00
Cookie Cutter, Comical Horse, With Inset Eye, Handle, Tin, 5 5/8 In. 20.00
Cookie Cutter, Country Woman, Tin, Handle 50.00
Cookie Cutter, Crow, Tin 28.00
Cookie Cutter, Dog, Tin, Handle 45.00
Cookie Cutter, Dripolator Advertising 3.50
Cookie Cutter, Duck, Tin, Handle 18.00
Cookie Cutter, Father Christmas, Strap Handle, Tin, 10 1/2 X 5 In. 595.00
Cookie Cutter, Fish, Crimped Fins, Strap Handle, Tin, 7 1/4 In. 250.00

Cookie Cutter, Foley, Wheel Type 10.00
Cookie Cutter, Goose, Tin 15.00
Cookie Cutter, Goose, Tin, Handle 30.00
Cookie Cutter, Hatchet, 5 1/2 X 9 In. 75.00
Cookie Cutter, Heart Shape, Handle, Tin 20.00
Cookie Cutter, Horse 18.00
Cookie Cutter, Jockey, On Horseback, Tin, 6 1/2 X 7 In. 100.00
Cookie Cutter, Lion 16.00
Cookie Cutter, Little Red Riding Hood 150.00
Cookie Cutter, Lucy, Plastic, 1952 .... 6.50
Cookie Cutter, Maid Marion, From Robin Hood 3.50
Cookie Cutter, Man, 16 In. 325.00
Cookie Cutter, Mr. Peanut, Set 20.00
Cookie Cutter, Prancing Horse, Bobtail, Flat Back, 6 X 7 1/2 In. 250.00
Cookie Cutter, Rabbit, Tin, Large 35.00
Cookie Cutter, Reindeer, Tin, 6 3/8 X 6 1/8 In. 110.00
Cookie Cutter, Rhinoceros, Tin, 7 7/8 X 4 3/4 In. 110.00
Cookie Cutter, Robin Hood Flour, 5 Piece 45.00
Cookie Cutter, Rooster, Tin, 6 In. 85.00
Cookie Cutter, Rumford 8.00
Cookie Cutter, Santa Claus, Tin 7.00
Cookie Cutter, Scotty Dog, Bakelite 4.50
Cookie Cutter, Small Hand 350.00
Cookie Cutter, Snoopy, Plastic, 1952 .... 6.50
Cookie Cutter, Star, Tin, Handle 50.00
Cookie Cutter, Stylized Figure, Tin, 8 1/2 In. 95.00
Cookie Cutter, Wheelbarrow 350.00
Cookie Cutter, Wheelbarrow, Tin, 8 3/4 X 5 1/4 In. 360.00
Cookie Cutter, Woman, Shaped Hair & Apron, Strap Handle, Tin, 8 In. 550.00
Cookie Press, Tin Cylinder, Cutter Blades, 1870 .... 20.00
Cookie Press, Tin, Maple, Early 1900s 65.00
Corn Popper, Mazola Oil 65.00
Corn Sheller, Blackhawk, Cast Iron 40.00
Corn Sheller, Little Giant, Cast Iron 30.00
Crock, Heinz Pickle 30.00
Cup, Measuring, 3 Spout, Kellogg's, Pink 25.00
Cup, Measuring, Hazel Atlas, Green, 16 Oz. 25.00
Cup, Measuring, Jadite, Sunflower, 2 Cup 12.00
Cup, Measuring, Kellogg, 3 Spouts, Pink .... 20.00 To 24.00
Curtain Stretcher, For Lace, Oak Frame 23.00
Cutter, Asparagus, Keen Edge, Ward 45.00
Cutter, Biscuit, Rumford 12.00
Cutter, Biscuit, Rumford, Tall 12.00
Cutter, Cabbage, Keen Kutter 45.00
Cutter, Cabbage, Octagonal Hopper, Poplar & Oak, 26 1/2 In. 95.00
Cutter, Cabbage, Tombstone Crest, Walnut, 21 X 8 In. 40.00
Cutter, Doughnut, Maple Mushroom Handle, Elongated 130.00
Cutter, Doughnut, Rumford 25.00
Cutter, Ice Cube, Coolerator, Copper 65.00
Cutter, Pastry, Rolling, French 18.00
Cutter, Truffle, In Tin Cylindrical Canister, C.1850, 11 Piece 30.00
Dipper, 1 Piece Ash, Burl, 6 X 8 1/2 In. 160.00
Dipper, Bird Head Handle, Maple, 9 1/2 In. 65.00
Dipper, Bird Head Handle, Maple, 12 5/8 In. 85.00
Dipper, Burl, Hole In Handle, 4 3/4 X 3 1/2 In. 230.00
Dipper, Ice Cream Sandwich, Mayer 165.00
Dipper, Relief Carved Fish, Irregular Shape, Burl, 5 1/2 In. 60.00
Dipper, Wooden, Crooked Handle, 17 1/2 In. 115.00
Dipper, Wooden, Curved Hook Handle, 11 In. 55.00
Dough Scraper, Half-Round Steel Blade, Copper, C.1800 .... 95.00
Dough Trough, Lift Top, Red Paint, Pine, 47 X 23 1/2 In. 700.00
Drying Rack, Expandable, Hanging 42.50
Drying Rack, For Gloves, Hanging, Maple, Pine 295.00
Duster, Mahogany, Turned Spout & Handle, Plunger, 8 X 7 1/2 In. 10.00

Dutch Oven, American, 18th Century, Cast Iron, 6 X 7 In.	610.00
Dutch Oven, Cover, No.8, Griswold	52.00
Dutch Oven, Cover, No.9, Trivet, Griswold	55.00
Dutch Oven, No.18, Griswold	35.00
Egg Basket, Wire, Opens Into Flower	39.00
Egg Slicer, Superwich, Metal, Hand	9.00
Egg Whip, Twisted Wire, Early 1900s	10.00
Eggbeater, A&J, Tin, Wood Handle, Pat. 1923	18.00
Eggbeater, Aluminum	1.00
Eggbeater, Dover, 1903	21.00
Eggbeater, Taplins Improved, Cast Iron, 1903	17.00
Eggbeater, Ullman	9.00
Featherbed Tick Smoother, Hickory, 62 In.	175.00
Firkin, Wooden, Original Yellow Paint, Red Stripe	95.00
Flatware, Steel, Inlaid Pewter, 8 Knives, 8 Forks, American Cutlery	75.00
Flatware, Yellow Bakelite Handle, Universal Stainless, 6 Place Set	65.00
Flour Dredger, Brown Japanned Tin, Handle, Pierced Dome	25.00
Flue Cover, Blond Girl, Pink Dress, Victorian, 8 1/4 In.	38.00
Flue Cover, Victorian Woman	20.00
Flue Cover, Woods & Stream Picture, 1930s	8.00
Food Warmer, Cover, Hammered Argenta Silver, Berries Handle, 7 In.	10.00
Fork, Meat, Wrought Iron, 2 Tines, Heart Cutout Handle, 19 1/4 In.	510.00
Fork, Shaped Shaft, Knob Handle, Wooden, 18 In.	130.00
Fork, Wrought Iron, 11 3/8 In.	55.00
Freezer, Ice Cream, Triple Motion White Mountain, 1 Qt.	125.00
Freezer, Ice Cream, White Mountain, 6 Qt.	65.00
Funnel, Canning, Crystal	6.00
Funnel, Maple Sap, Turned & Carved, Wooden, 3 1/2 X 4 In.	120.00
Glove Stretcher, Canalletta Wood, 11 1/2 In.	15.00
Grater, Cream City, Round, Handle	9.00
Grater, Hand Forged Iron Frame, Arched Handle, Brass, 15 1/2 In.	295.00
Grater, Heart Shape, Handle, Tin	18.00
Grater, Nutmeg, Crank Style, Late 1800s	75.00
Grater, Nutmeg, Edgar	85.00
Grater, Nutmeg, Edgar, Stoneware, '91	45.00
Grater, Nutmeg, Iron, Bellow Shape, Mechanical, Pat. June 7, 1870	250.00
Grater, Nutmeg, Tin & Iron, Wooden Handle, 7 In.	65.00
Grater, Nutmeg, Tin, Maple, Dated 1877	75.00
Grater, Nutmeg, Turned Wooden Handle, Tin, 5 1/4 In.	40.00
Grater, Soap, Fels–Naptha	10.00
Griddle, Child's, Bail Handle, Wagner Ware, 1920s, 4 1/2 In.	40.00
Griddle, Griswold, No.9, Round	25.00
Grinder, Food, Glass, Tin Top, 1930s	15.00
Grinder, Food, Griswold, No.1110	20.00
Grinder, Food, Russian, No.1, Iron, Patent March 4, 1902	13.00
Grinder, Food, Universal, No.0	10.00
Grinder, Herb, Boat Mill, 18th Century, 14 X 2 X 5 In.	595.00
Grinder, Meat, Cast Iron, 1892	35.00
Grinder, Meat, Climax	12.50
Grinder, Poppyseed, Brass & Iron	35.00
Grinder, Sausage, Miles	25.00
Hot Plate, Manning–Bowman, Kerosene	20.00
Ice Cream Freezer, Triple Motion, White Mountain, 1 Qt.	125.00
Ice Cream Freezer, White Mountain, 6 Qt.	65.00
Ice Pick, Winchester, Wooden Handle	25.00
Icebox, 3 Doors, Ash	400.00
Icebox, 3 Doors, Brass Hardware, Golden Oak	600.00
Icebox, Galvanized Metal Rotating Shelves, Round	200.00
Icebox, Lift Top, Oak	425.00
Icebox, Lig–O–Nier, Commercial, 7 Doors, 6 Ft.3 In. X 7 Ft.3 In.	2500.00
Iron, Boudoir, Dover, Electric, 1920s	35.00
Iron, Box Pressing, Brass, Iron, Ornate, Scotland, 1860s	650.00
Iron, Charcoal, Wooden Handle	65.00
Iron, Curling, Duro, Celluloid Thumb Guard, Wooden Handle, 1930s	12.50

Iron , Electric, Child's, 1940s 18.00
Iron , Electric, General Electric, Art Deco, Box, 1930s 25.00
Iron , Electric, General Electric, Box, 1930s 45.00
Iron , Electric, General Electric, Thumb At Side of Handle, 1940s 12.00
Iron , Electric, Steemco Pacemaker 15.00
Iron , Electric, Sunbeam, Metal Box, 1940s .... 45.00 To 85.00
Iron , Fluting, American Machine Co. 7.50
Iron , Fluting, Crown, Cast Iron 40.00
Iron , Gas, Coleman, Blue Enamel 37.00
Iron , Matching Cathedral Swan Trivet 175.00
Iron , Pleater, Shephard Hardware, Buffalo, N.Y.., 1873–1880 .... 95.00
Iron , Smoothing, Keyhole Strap Handle 35.00
Iron , Tailor's, Cast Iron, Extra Bottom, Sensible No.6 .... 40.00
Iron , Wafer, Geometric Floral Design, Brass, Iron Handles, 17 In. 65.00
Ironing Board, Handmade, Refinished 70.00
Ironing Board, Necktie, Ty–Press Appliance Co. 47.50
Jar Lifter, Green Handle 8.00
Jar Wrench, Perfecto 6.00
Jelly Mold, Victorian, Copper, Sept.15, 1864, 5 In., 4 Piece 825.00
Juicer, Sunkist, Electric 35.00
Kettle Brazier, Heart Design Grid, Bail Handle, Iron 275.00
Kettle, Cast Iron, Slide Lid, Big 18.00
Kettle, Gypsy, Griswold, 3–Legged 40.00
Kettle, O'Brien, Cast Iron, Cover 32.00
Kettle, Swing Handle, 3–Footed, Marked B.M.& Co., Iron, 7 1/2 In. 250.00
Knife Sharpener, Brass Sword Handle 7.50
Knife Sharpener, Stag Handles, Alligator, Glass Eyes, 14 In. 12.50
Knife, Bread, Keen Kutter 25.00
Ladle, Burl, 8 1/2 In. 65.00
Ladle, Butter, Ash Burl, 9 In. 350.00
Ladle, Curly Maple, 5 3/4 X 49 In. 370.00
Ladle, Pierced, Tin, 17 In. 20.00
Ladle, Wooden, Primitive, Pot Hook Handle, 15 In. 45.00
Ladle, Wrought Iron, Small Bowl, 13 In. 40.00
Ladle, Wrought Iron, Tooled Handle, 16 In. 105.00
Ladle, Wrought Iron, Wooden Handle, 10 1/2 In. 135.00
Lemon Squeezer, 2 Part, 3 X 3 X 20 In. 95.00
Lemon Squeezer, Cast Iron, Signed 52.50
Lemon Squeezer, Hardwood, Primitive 45.00
Lemon Squeezer, Maple 47.50
Lid Lifter, Queen Stove, Cast Iron 18.00
        KITCHEN, MATCH SAFE, see Match Safe
Meat Hook, 4 Hanging Hooks 345.00
Milk Shake Machine, Albert Pick & Co., Marble Base 375.00
Milk Shake Machine, Arnold 75.00
Milk Shake Machine, Gilchrist, 1923 .... 55.00
Milk Shake Machine, Gilchrist, No.22 .... 75.00
Milk Shake Machine, Gilchrist, No.55 .... 50.00
Milk Shake Machine, Hamilton Beach, 2 Speed, 1950s .... 120.00 To 175.00
Milk Shake Machine, Hamilton Beach, Green 85.00
Milk Shake Machine, Hamilton Beach, Single Head 45.00
Milk Shake Machine, Hamilton Beach, Triple Head, 3 Speeds ..... 150.00 To 265.00
Milk Shake Machine, Hamilton Beech, Green 35.00
Milk Shake Machine, Holwick, All Nickel 95.00
Milk Shake Machine, National Dairy 16.00
Milk Shake Machine, Nyers Bullit, Green 85.00
Mixer, Bread Dough, Directions On Lid, 1904, 2 Gal. 60.00
Mixer, Green, 1923, 1 Qt. 38.00
Mixer, Horlick's Malt, Metal Insert, Staffordshire Advertising 85.00
        KITCHEN, MOLD, see also Pewter, Mold; Tinware, Mold
Mold, Butter, Eagle, Handle, Carved, 4 3/8 In. 240.00
Mold, Butter, Fleur–De–Lis, Glass 45.00
Mold, Butter, Fleur–De–Lis, Plunger Type, Glass, Wooden Handle 50.00
Mold, Butter, House, Removable Roof, 4 Hinged Sections, Norway 75.00

Mold, Butter, Leaves 75.00
Mold, Butter, Pineapple With Leaves, Plunger Type, 1 Lb. 95.00
Mold, Butter, Removable Board, 8 Carved Designs, 5 1/2 X 11 In. 175.00
Mold, Butter, Rooster Pattern, Oak, Round 125.00
Mold, Butter, Rose, Bud, Leaves, Plunger Type, 4 In. 90.00
Mold, Butter, Sheaf of Wheat, Plunger Type, 1 Lb. 85.00
Mold, Butter, Strawberries & Large Leaf, Plunger Type, 1 Lb. 85.00
Mold, Butter, Swan Pattern, Case, Plunger, Round, 1 Lb. .... 125.00 To 220.00
Mold, Butter, Thistle Design, Carved Wood, 4 1/2 X 3 3/8 In. 80.00
Mold, Cake, Bell, Aluminum 12.50
Mold, Cake, Elf Shape, Pewter, 12 In. 160.00
Mold, Cake, Lamb, Cast Aluminum, 2 Piece 40.00
Mold, Cake, Lamb, Cast Iron, 12 1/2 In. 35.00
Mold, Cake, Lamb, Griswold 125.00
Mold, Cake, Rabbit, Griswold .... 195.00 To 250.00
Mold, Cake, Rooster, Cast Iron 45.00
Mold, Cake, Santa Claus, Griswold 395.00
Mold, Cake, Santa In Chimney, 2 Piece 15.00
KITCHEN, MOLD, CANDLE, see Tinware, Mold, Candle
Mold, Candy, 60 Cat Wafers, Tin Plated Steel, 10 3/4 X 16 3/4 In. 25.00
Mold, Candy, Birds, 2 Part, Wooden, 4 X 12 In. 135.00
Mold, Candy, Fish, Pine, 8 1/2 In. 25.00
Mold, Candy, Rabbit Pushing Bunny Carriage, 10 3/8 In. 295.00
Mold, Candy, Santa Claus, 8 1/4 In. 245.00
Mold, Candy, Valentines, 10 1/4 In. 245.00
Mold, Cheese, Pierced Tin, Heart Shape, Footed, 2 Handles, 5 X 4 In. 775.00
Mold, Chocolate, 2 Sitting Rabbits 75.00
Mold, Chocolate, 6 Sitting Bear Cubs, Carved, 1 1/2 X 12 In., 2 Pc. 130.00
Mold, Chocolate, Baby, Finger In Mouth, Round Belly, Kunzig, 12 In. 125.00
Mold, Chocolate, Belsnickel Type Santa, Cast Aluminum, 8 1/4 In. 35.00
Mold, Chocolate, Boy Scout 65.00
Mold, Chocolate, Bunny, Sitting, 9 1/2 In. 72.00
Mold, Chocolate, Bunny, Sitting, Hinged, 5 In. 75.00
Mold, Chocolate, Bunny, Standing, 9 1/2 In. 72.00
Mold, Chocolate, Champagne Bottle 59.00
Mold, Chocolate, Dolly Dingle 165.00
Mold, Chocolate, Fat Chicken, On Nest, 6 1/2 In. 72.00
Mold, Chocolate, Kewpie Doll, Finger In Mouth 135.00
Mold, Chocolate, Lamb, Tin 75.00
Mold, Chocolate, Rabbit Pulls Easter Egg Cart, Tin, 3 1/2 X 7 In. 50.00
Mold, Chocolate, Rabbit, Standing, 3 X 6 In. 75.00
Mold, Chocolate, Saint Nicholas, On Horse, Tin, 6 X 8 In. 225.00
Mold, Chocolate, Santa Standing, Tin, 8 X 5 In. 75.00
Mold, Chocolate, Santa, 2 Reindeer, 6–Sided 50.00
Mold, Chocolate, Sitting Rabbits, 6 In. 60.00
Mold, Chocolate, Small Rabbit On Larger Rabbit, Tin, 6 1/2 In. 50.00
Mold, Cookie, Crowing Rooster, Pine, 7 X 9 In. 125.00
Mold, Cookie, Greeks Running, Flowers, Ribbed, Iron, 2 3/4 X 4 In. 175.00
Mold, Food, 3 Fruits, Fluted, Tin–Lined Copper, 2 1/2 X 7 In. 40.00
Mold, Food, 4 Rows of Gadrooning, Lead, Copper Covering, 13 1/2 In. 30.00
Mold, Food, Artichoke, Copper, 4 X 8 In. 40.00
Mold, Food, Eagle, Oval, Tin & Copper, 5 3/4 In. 105.00
Mold, Food, Fish, Figural, Tin, Hanging Ring 65.00
Mold, Food, Fish, Porcelain, Germany 35.00
Mold, Food, Fish, Tin–Lined Copper, 3 1/2 In. 40.00
Mold, Food, Melon Shape, Kreamer, Tin 27.50
Mold, Food, Pear, Tin–Lined Copper, 3 1/2 In. 40.00
Mold, Food, Rabbit, Cast Iron 125.00
Mold, Food, Round, Copper, 7 In.Diam. 85.00
Mold, Food, Seashell, Curved, Hook, Tin–Lined Copper, 5 In. 45.00
Mold, Food, Shell, Tin–Lined Copper, 3 1/2 In. 40.00
Mold, Food, Squirrel, Copper, 4 X 8 In. 40.00
Mold, Food, Starflowers, Tin–Lined Copper, 4 In. 40.00
Mold, Food, Tin, Copper Pineapple Design Base, Oval 95.00

Mold, Food, Turtle Design, Tin, Oval, 3 1/4 X 4 1/2 In. 165.00
Mold, Food, Turtle Design, Wooden, 3 1/2 X 8 1/2 In. 50.00
    KITCHEN, MOLD, ICE CREAM, see Pewter, Mold, Ice Cream
Mold, Maple Sugar, Heart Shape 9.00
Mold, Maple Sugar, Star Shape 7.00
Mold, Maple Sugar, Tin, 10 Qt. 4.00
Mold, Patty, Griswold, Box 15.00
Mold, Patty, Griswold, Heart 15.00
Mold, Patty, Griswold, No.2, Box 37.50
Mold, Pudding, Cantaloupe Shape, Bail Handles, Kreamer, Tin 28.00
Mold, Pudding, Melon Shape, Top Handles, Tin, 2 Part 35.00
Mold, Ring, Copper, England, 3 X 3 In. 45.00
Mold, Ring, Copper, England, 4 X 4 In. 65.00
Mold, Sponge Cake, Heart Shape, Tin, 2 Side Lifters, 2 3/4 X 12 In. 240.00
Mold, Turk's Head, Geometric Design, Copper, 10 In., Piar 110.00
Mortar & Pestle, Burl, 5 1/4 In. 95.00
Mortar & Pestle, Lignum Vitae, 6 3/8 In. 85.00
Mortar & Pestle, Turned Brass Pedestal Base, 6 In. 175.00
Mortar & Pestle, Walnut, Turned, 7 1/2 In. 85.00
Mortar, Burl, 6 1/4 In. 65.00
Nut Pick Set, F & B, Ornate, 6 Piece 75.00
Nut Pick, Silver Handle, Box, 1910, 6 Piece 20.00
Pan, Copper, Cast Iron Handle, 7 1/4 In. 35.00
Pan, Corn Bread, Griswold, Iron, Miniature 40.00
Pan, Corn Bread, Wagner Ware, 1920 .... 15.00
Pan, Corn Fritter, Iron, Pat. July 6, 1920 .... 17.50
Pan, Cornstick Miracle Maize, Glass 10.00
Pan, Cornstick, Griswold, No.954, Iron 28.00
Pan, Heart Shape, Lockwood Co., Cincinnati, Ohio, Tin, 12 Cup 75.00
Pan, Iron Handle, Dovetailed Copper, 8 3/4 X 11 In. 65.00
Pan, Lady Finger, Tin 22.00
Pan, Muffin, 6 Turk's-Head Sections, Buff Clay, 8 3/4 X 12 3/3 In. 125.00
Pan, Muffin, Griswold, 6 Cup, Cast Iron 30.00
Pan, Muffin, Turk's Head, 12 Cup 150.00
Pan, Popover, Griswold, No. 2 .... 30.00
Pan, Popover, Griswold, No.10 .... 60.00
Pan, Tart, Fluted, Scalloped, Cast Iron, 6 Holes 16.50
Pancake Turner, Rumford 20.00
Pastry Wheel, Wooden, 1800s 85.00
Pea Sheller, Holmes 40.00
Peel, Dark Brown Patina, Short Handled, Wooden, 13 1/2 In. 55.00
Peel, Hole For Hanging, 17 In. 75.00
Peel, Oven, Tombstone Shaped Paddle, Pine, C.1800, 42 In. 220.00
Peel, Ram's Horn Finial, Iron, 28 In. 105.00
Peel, Ram's Horn Handle, Iron, 37 1/4 In. 85.00
Peeler, Apple, C.E. Husson, Patent 1882 .... 60.00
Peeler, Apple, Goodell Co., Iron 22.50
Peeler, Apple, Hand Crank, Red Varnish Finish, Wooden, 15 1/2 In. 65.00
Peeler, Apple, Keen Kutter ....50.00 To 110.00
Peeler, Apple, Little Star 85.00
Peeler, Apple, Little Star, Cast Iron, 1885 .... 90.00
Peeler, Apple, Lockley-Howland, Cast Iron, Dated 1856 .... 55.00
Peeler, Apple, Ornate Iron, Sinclair Scott Co., Baltimore 45.00
Peeler, Apple, Reading Hardware, Hand Cranked 45.00
Peeler, Apple, Rival, Hand Cranked, Cast Iron, Commercial 170.00
Peeler, Apple, Sargent & Foster, Mechanical, Cast Iron, 1847 .... 130.00
Peeler, Apple, Turntable, No.98 .... 75.00
Peeler, Apple, White Mountain ....15.00 To 45.00
Peeler, Peach, Sinclair Scott 100.00
Pie Bird, Ammy 40.00
Pie Bird, Benny The Baker 35.00
Pie Bird, Black Chef, Blue 68.00
Pie Bird, Canary, Yellow 15.00
Pie Bird, Chef, Black 95.00

Pie Bird, Chef, White 45.00
Pie Bird, Elephant, White, Trunk Over Shoulder 47.00
Pie Bird, Mammy, Red Trim 52.00
Pie Bird, Owl On Stump, Brown 45.00
Pie Bird, Pink Pillsbury Twin 17.00
Pie Crimper, Brass, Wooden Handle 20.00
Pie Crimper, Crimped Wheel, All Wooden, 8 In. 85.00
Pie Crimper, Crimped Wheel, Turned Handle, Ivory, 8 In. 135.00
Pie Divider, Wire 30.00
Pie Lifter, Detachable Twisted Handle 5.00
Pie Pan, Evenslice 6.50
Plate Rack, Floor Standing, White Paint, Iron, English, 42 In. 75.00
Pleater, Accordion, Brass Cylinders, Wooden Handle, 8 X 7 X 10 In. 30.00
Pleater, Hand Cranked, Bronze Ribbed Rollers, Cast Iron 130.00
Plunger, Wash, Hebbard 6.00
Porringer, Pierced Handle, Kenrich & Co., Iron, 1/2 Pt., 4 3/4 In. 90.00
Pot Holder, Twisted Wire, Early 1900s 10.00
Pot, Copper, Iron Handles, Handmade, Gaillard, Paris, 1 Gal. 300.00
Pot, Footed, Iron, 18th Century, 10 In. 24.50
Pot, Stew, Cast Iron, Bail Handle, Cover, No.8 .... 60.00
Potato Masher, Wooden 15.00
Potato Ricer, Green Handle, Metal 12.00
Potato Ricer, Iron Handle 18.00
Press, Apple Cider, Ornate Metal Casting, Red, Green & Black, 1872 .... 800.00
Press, Fruit & Lard, Griswold, No.2 .... 60.00
Pressing Board, Maple, Pine 20.00
Raisin Seeder, Wet Your Raisins, Patent 1895 .... 40.00
Reamer, Federal, Green, F On Tab Handle 18.00
Reamer, Grapefruit, Yellow Opaque Glass 135.00
Reamer, Jennyware, Ultramarine 60.00
Roaster, Chestnut, Pierced Design, Treen Handle, Copper 160.00
Roaster, Coffee Bean, Slide Tin Cover, Wooden Handle, 42 In. 295.00
Roller, Cookie, Carved Wood, Handle, Lamb, Banner, 2 X 8 In. 375.00
Rolling Pin, Amber Glass, 14 1/2 In. 55.00
Rolling Pin, Baker's, Lignum Vitae, 6 Lbs. 65.00
Rolling Pin, Blue Band Pottery .... 150.00 To 175.00
Rolling Pin, C.P. Corneliussen & Co., Alta, Iowa, Milk Glass 110.00
Rolling Pin, Calico Tulip, Harker Pottery 50.00
Rolling Pin, Cameo, Harker 55.00
Rolling Pin, Clear Glass, Zinc Closure, 16 In. 15.00
Rolling Pin, Cobalt Blue Glass, Dated 1841 .... 40.00
Rolling Pin, Curly Maple, 20 In. 175.00
Rolling Pin, Double Bar, Cherry & Maple 295.00
Rolling Pin, Early Pennsylvania, 14 In. 195.00
Rolling Pin, Glass, Tin Screw Cap At One End, Hollow, Aqua 65.00
Rolling Pin, Green & Co., Blue & White Striped 150.00
Rolling Pin, Imperial, Mild Glass, 1921 .... 55.00
Rolling Pin, Jadite 350.00
Rolling Pin, Maple, 12 In. 7.00
Rolling Pin, Milk Glass 85.00
Rolling Pin, Noodle, Wooden, Small 48.00
Rolling Pin, Pioneer Store Co., Story City, Iowa, Crockery 225.00
Rolling Pin, Pottery, Blue Bands, Advertising 225.00
Rolling Pin, Pottery, Central Block Grocery, Decorah, Iowa 225.00
Rolling Pin, Pottery, J.P.Sweeny Gen.Merchandise, Holy Cross 225.00
Rolling Pin, Pottery, Story City, Iowa, Handles 225.00
Rolling Pin, Pottery, T.L.Greer & Co., Canton's New Dry Goods 225.00
Rolling Pin, Ravioli 45.00
Rolling Pin, Springerle, 12 Designs, Cookie Recipes 18.00
Rolling Pin, Springerle, Birds, Flowers & Fruit, 13 1/4 In. 40.00
Rolling Pin, Tiger Maple, Tapered Handles, 17 1/2 In. 75.00
Rolling Pin, Vinegar Promotional Bottle, Glass, 1920s 18.00
Rolling Pin, Wildflower, Stoneware, Blue & White .... 225.00 To 295.00
Rolling Pin, Wizard, Milk Glass .... 40.00 To 45.00

Rug Beater, Twisted Wire 16.00
Sadiron, Child's, Dover, No.912 .... 27.50
Sadiron, Grand Union Tea Co., Detachable Walnut Handle, 8 In. 35.00
Sadiron, Mrs. Potts, Wooden Handle 20.00
Sadiron, Rest, I Want U, Strauss Gas Co. 50.00
Sadiron, Sensible, No.5 .... 35.00
Sadiron, Wilton, Child's, With Trivet 45.00
    KITCHEN, SALT & PEPPER, see Salt & Pepper
Saucepan, Carmichael Wilks Range Co., Iron Handle, Copper, 9 In. 65.00
Sausage Stuffer & Press, 6 Qt. 45.00
Sausage Stuffer, Simmons Hardware 60.00
Sausage Stuffer, Wagner, Commercial, Cast Iron, 36 In. 495.00
Scoop, Apple Butter, Open D Handle, 8 1/2 In. 260.00
Scoop, Cast Aluminum, Hedges Ever Ready Chocolate 7.50
Scoop, Cranberry, Galvanized Sheet Metal, Tin Teeth, 18 1/2 In. 85.00
Scoop, Flour, Heart of Value Emblem 15.00
Scoop, Flour, Puritan, Button On Handle, Tin, 7 In. 40.00
Scoop, Flour, Red Top, Tin 37.50
Scoop, Gilchrist No.31 .... 30.00
Scoop, Ice Cream Cone, KW 45.00
Scoop, Ice Cream Sandwich 200.00
Scoop, Ice Cream, 2–Way, Dover 70.00
Scoop, Ice Cream, Clipper, Giles & Nielson, Side Thumb Flip, 10 In. 248.00
Scoop, Ice Cream, Cold Dog 595.00
Scoop, Ice Cream, Conical, Wooden Handle, Nickel Over Brass, 11 In. 182.00
Scoop, Ice Cream, Dover No.10, Back & Forth Mechanism, 11 In. 60.00
Scoop, Ice Cream, Dover No.24, Double Action 85.00
Scoop, Ice Cream, Ergos, Deplated 150.00
Scoop, Ice Cream, Erie, Round, 1908, Size 16 .... 85.00
Scoop, Ice Cream, F.S., Cone, Size 10 .... 195.00
Scoop, Ice Cream, F.S., Round, Size 30 .... 75.00
Scoop, Ice Cream, Gem, Brass, Wooden Handle, 11 In. 28.00
Scoop, Ice Cream, Gilchrist No.30 .... 18.00
Scoop, Ice Cream, Gilchrist No.31 .... 35.00
Scoop, Ice Cream, Gilchrist No.31, Size 40 .... 110.00
Scoop, Ice Cream, Gilchrist No.31, Wooden Handle, Thumb Flip, 11 In 28.00
Scoop, Ice Cream, Gilchrist No.8 .... 35.00
Scoop, Ice Cream, Gilchrist, Wooden Handle, 10 1/2 In. 20.00
Scoop, Ice Cream, Hamilton Beach, Chrome Plated, Wooden, Box, 10 In. 41.00
Scoop, Ice Cream, Hamilton Beach, Model 67, 3 Sizes 43.00
Scoop, Ice Cream, Icypi, Sandwich Style, Wooden Handle, 10 .... 195.00 To 265.00
Scoop, Ice Cream, Indestructo No.3 .... 50.00
Scoop, Ice Cream, Indestructo No.3, Round, Size 16 .... 78.00
Scoop, Ice Cream, Indestructo No.4 .... 35.00 To 48.00
Scoop, Ice Cream, Jiffy Dispenser, I.C. 200.00
Scoop, Ice Cream, Kingery, Squeeze Handle .... 200.00 To 210.00
Scoop, Ice Cream, Mayer 200.00
Scoop, Ice Cream, Naylor, Tin 65.00
Scoop, Ice Cream, No Pak No.31 .... 75.00
Scoop, Ice Cream, Philcone, Deplated 55.00
Scoop, Ice Cream, Probst, Aluminum 10.00
Scoop, Ice Cream, Square Cube, 1 1/2 In. 150.00
Scoop, Ice Cream, Victor, Pat. Date 1908 .... 30.00
Scoop, Ice Creamer, Clipper Disher 165.00
Scoop, Meal, Primitive, 1870s 68.00
Scoop, Raisin, Woven Splint, Mrs. E.G. Phillips, 5 X 6 1/2 In. 65.00
Scoop, Stylized Bird Head Handle, 7 1/2 In. 55.00
Scrubbing Stick, Primitive, 18th Century 95.00
Sieve, Bentwood Frame, Laced Seams, Horsehair, 15 In. 130.00
Sieve, Cheese, Wooden Stave, Iron Band, 39 In. 15.00
Sieve, Horsehair, Stenciled 5, Bentwood, 14 In. 90.00
Sieve, Wooden Finger–Lapped Hoop 38.00
Sifter, Child's, Hunter, Pat. 1874, Tin 35.00
Sifter, Flour, Green Handle, Bromwell 15.00

Sifter, Flour, Majestic Range Advertising 20.00
Sifter, Flour, Majestic Stoves 9.00
Sifter, Flour, Omega 6.00
Sifter, Flour, Shaker Sifter Co., Buffalo & Chicago, Tin 28.00
Sifter, Flour, Sift–Chine ....9.00 To 12.00
Skillet, Child's, Griswold, No.0 .... 40.00 To 75.00
Skillet, Child's, Wagner Ware, 1920s, 4 1/2 In. 40.00
Skillet, Copper, Cast Iron Handle, Marked Solari, 9 In. 55.00
Skillet, Griswold, No. 3 .... 20.00
Skillet, Griswold, No. 6 .... 8.00
Skillet, Griswold, No. 7, Cover 48.00
Skillet, Griswold, No. 8 .... 12.00
Skillet, Griswold, No.129, Square 20.00
Skillet, Iron Handle, Copper, Marked NN, 12 1/4 In. 75.00
Skillet, Wagner, No.8 .... 20.00
Skimmer, Cream, Self–Handle, Tin 20.00
Skimmer, Cream, Thin, Wooden, Early 1800s, 6 X 6 1/4 In. 95.00
Skimmer, Pierced Brass Bowl, Iron Handle 59.00
Slicer, French Fries, Maid–of–Honor 15.00
Smoothing Block, Floral & Star, Sawtooth Border, 3 1/2 X 6 In. 775.00
Smoothing Board, Inlaid Herringbone Border, B.St., 1894, 23 X 6 In. 150.00
Snack Server, Pyrex Glass Inserts, Instructions, Recipes, Electric 185.00
Soap Dish, Twisted Wire, Early 1900s 10.00
Spatula, Log Cabin Syrup 50.00
Spatula, Wrought Iron, 14 1/2 In. 255.00
Spatula, Wrought Iron, Blade, 1 3/4 X 13 1/4 In. 85.00
Spice Box, 6 Round Tins, Painted, Red, 6 1/4 X 8 In. 65.00
Spice Box, 9 Drawers, Labels, Cherry, 14 1/2 X 12 In. 550.00
Spice Box, Hanging, Divided, 2–Part Interior, Pine, 14 In. 400.00
Spice Box, Slant Top Lid, 1 Drawer, Dovetailed, 11 1/2 X 15 In. 325.00
Spice Box, Tin Edging, 8 Canisters, Round Bentwood, 9 1/2 In. 150.00
Spice Cabinet, 8 Drawers, Stenciled 165.00
Spice Cabinet, Hanging, Black Transfer Labels, Poplar, 16 1/2 In. 225.00
Spice Chest, 18 Drawers, Mahogany & Pine, 14 3/4 X 11 In. 200.00
Spice Chest, 6 Round Tins, Brass Handle & Hasp 65.00
Spice Set, Red Lid, Wooden Rack, Griffith, Set of 18 .... 25.00
Spider, Cast Iron, Rattail Handle, 3 Footed, 18th Century, 6 In. 160.00
Spittoon, White Enameled, Iron 50.00
Spittoon, Woman's, Bennington Type 20.00
Spoon, Chip Carved Handle, Wooden, 19 1/2 In. 40.00
Spoon, Pierced, Rumford, Wholesome Baking Powder 20.00
Spreader, Cheese, Springtime, 1847 .... 8.00
Sprinkler, Clothes, Chinese Washerman 17.50
Sprinkler, Elephant 20.00
Strainer, Cottage Cheese, Footed, Tin 70.00
String Holder, 2 Birds On Branch 38.00
String Holder, 7–Up, Double Sided, Metal 225.00
String Holder, Apple, Chalkware ....8.00 To 17.00
String Holder, Beehive, 3–Footed, Screws To Counter, Cast Iron 35.00
String Holder, Beehive, Cast Iron, Dome Shaped, 5 1/2 X 6 1/2 In. 65.00
String Holder, Beehive, Screw–Down Counter Type, Cast Iron 45.00
String Holder, Black & White Dog 50.00
String Holder, Black Bellhop, Fredericksburg .... 125.00 To 145.00
String Holder, Brass, Footed, Victorian 95.00
String Holder, Cat With Yarn, Bisque 18.00
String Holder, Cat, Wooden 12.00
String Holder, Court Jester, Chalkware 40.00
String Holder, Double–Eyed Face, Wilton 35.00
String Holder, Dutch Boy 22.50
String Holder, Dutch Head, Chalkware 15.00
String Holder, French Chef 20.00
String Holder, Gigolo, Chalkware 28.00
String Holder, Mammy, Chalkware 165.00
String Holder, Mexican Man 17.00

String Holder, Mexican Woman	17.00
String Holder, Scotty Dog	37.50
String Holder, Soldier With Pipe	35.00
String Holder, Spanish Lady, Chalkware	20.00
String Holder, Sumo Wrestler, Benihana	17.00
String Holder, Tomato Face	50.00
String Holder, Top Snuff, Shape of Toy Top, Cast Iron	875.00
String Holder, Woman, Blue Blouse	35.00
String Holder, Woman, Brown Blouse	35.00
Sweeper, Bissell, Hand	10.00
Tamper, Sauerkraut, Primitive	3.00
Tea Cozy, Russian Doll	65.00
Tea Mill, Cast Iron, Small	275.00
Tea Strainer, Faultless, Tin	7.00
Teakettle, Gooseneck, Dovetailed, Strap Handle	325.00
Teakettle, Iron, Brass Cover & Finial, Wrought Handle, 8 In.	45.00
Teakettle, Iron, Gooseneck Spout, Brass Cover & Handle, 8 Pt.	75.00
Teakettle, Wagner	35.00
Teakettle, Wrought Iron Handle, Alkiry, No.1, Cast Iron, 7 In.	175.00
Teapot, Iron, Enameled, Dogwood Flower & Vine, Pewter Fittings	295.00
Tester, Kwik–Set Jel, For Jellies & Jams	6.00
Thermos Jug, Acme Water Cooler, 1880	30.00
Toaster, Berstead	20.00
Toaster, Chrome, Art Deco	35.00
Toaster, Dominion Lady	18.00
Toaster, Flip Side, Dominion, Electric, 1961	10.00
Toaster, Hotpoint	40.00 To 60.00
Toaster, Kenmore, No.307–6314	17.50
Toaster, Knapp–Monarch, Art Deco, Aluminum	12.00
Toaster, Kwickway	14.00
Toaster, Slant Side, 2 Slice, Tin	22.00
Toaster, Star–Rite Reversible, Box	75.00
Toaster, Star–Rite, Electric, Box, 1920	45.00
Toaster, Sun–Chief, Art Deco	17.00
Toaster, Sun–Chief, Flip–Down	7.00
Toaster, Sun–Chief, Flip–Down, Chrome	12.00
Toaster, Sun–Chief, Tag, Box	55.00
Toaster, Unique, Universal	18.00
Toaster, Universal, 2 Flip Sides	45.00
Toaster, Universal, E7312A	17.50
Toaster, Universal, E79312	17.50
Toaster, Universal, Pat.Date 1915	28.00
Toaster, Westinghouse, Turn Over	30.00
Toaster, Wolverine	16.00
Toaster, Wrought Iron, 7 1/2 In.	350.00
Tumbler Holder, Twisted Wire, Early 1900s	10.00
Utensil Rack, 7 Hooks, 2 Tiers, Floral Design, Iron, 25 1/2 In.	300.00
Vacuum Cleaner, Doty, Early 1900s	200.00
Vacuum Cleaner, Push Type, Doty	100.00
Wafer Iron, Stylized Flower, Star, Cast Iron, 15 1/2 In. Handle	75.00
Waffle Iron, C.1860	50.00
Waffle Iron, Child's, Griswold, Hearts	10.00
Waffle Iron, Child's, Griswold, Star	10.00
Waffle Iron, Double, Griswold, Wooden Handles	100.00
Waffle Iron, Griswold, 1908	38.50
Waffle Iron, Griswold, Heart & Vine, Stand	65.00
Waffle Iron, Pennsylvania, Signed	165.00
Waffle Iron, Wagner Ware, Wooden Handles, Stand	50.00
Waffle Iron, Wagner, Sidney, Ohio, Wooden Handles, Feb.11, 1910, 4 In.	95.00
Washboard, Cobalt Blue Graniteware	18.00
Washboard, Columbus, Wooden, Red & Blue Letters	20.00
Washboard, Corrugated, Hand Carved, 18th Century, 8 X 25 In., 1 Pc.	75.00
Washboard, George Washington Portrait, Wood	20.00

Washboard, Lingerie, Zing King	20.00
Washboard, National No.801, Wooden Frame, Brass Corrugated Insert	20.00
Washboard, National, Zinc	12.00
Washboard, Pearl Graniteware	70.00
Washboard, Pearl, Enameled	125.00
Washboard, Silk Hosiery, 18 In.	17.50
Washboard, Standard Carolina, Family Size, Large	9.00
Washboard, Two–In–One Carolina, Small	10.00
Washboard, Wooden Rollers	95.00
Washing Machine, Favorite Edwards, Wooden	200.00
Washing Machine, Rocker Type	55.00
Washing Machine, Round Top	30.00
Wine Press, Oasis, No.20	85.00

In the 1960s, the United States government passed a law that required knife manufacturers to mark their knives with the country of origin. This seemed to encourage the collectors, and knife collecting became an interest of a large group of people. All types of knives are collected, from top quality twentieth–century examples to old bone– or pearl–handled knives in excellent condition.

KNIFE, Bullet, Remington, Repro, 1983	150.00
Case, XX	25.00
Dagger, Brass & Silver Sheath, Turkish	225.00
Dagger, Ivory Hilt, India	200.00
Dagger, Middle Eastern, Brass Sheath, Tooled Silver Trim, 16 In.	65.00
Dagger, Philippines	175.00
Dagger, Spanish, Etched Blade, Leather & Metal Scabbard, 1920s	75.00
Dagger, Wooden, Black Paint, Drilled Hole, Metal, Brass	55.00
Draw, Folding Handle	32.00
Draw, Jennings & Griffin, Wooden Handle	25.00
Draw, Jennings, Folding, 8 In.	22.00
Fruit, Coin Silver, Cameo Type Head	30.00
Gurka, Pearl Inlaid, Leather Sheaf, 13 In.	25.00
Hoof, Farrier's, T.J. Pope, Pat.Sept.12, 1899	16.00
Horse Hoof, Burdizzo, Italian	10.00
Jack, Figural, Woman's Shoe, Lenox Cutlery Co.	27.50
Jack, Kamp–King	25.00
Keen Kutter, 711SC	60.00
Kinfolk, Sheath, Leather Handle, 4–In. Blade	35.00
Machete, Case	110.00
Melon Tester, Case	12.00
Patriot Shoe	55.00
Pen, Sterling Silver, Gorham	42.50
Pocket, A. Kaster & Co., Germany	150.00
Pocket, Case Bros., No.6250, Sunfish	125.00
Pocket, Diplomat Whiskey	40.00
Pocket, Dixon Co., Old–Fashioned Woman's Shoe	45.00
Pocket, Eze Suredge, Pearl Handle	18.00
Pocket, Figural, Auto	65.00
Pocket, Pen, Case	14.00
Pocket, Remington, No.2403, Bone Handle, 5 In.	500.00
Pocket, Sausage, Cudhy Packing Co., Pearl Handle	25.00
Pocket, Winchester, No.2681	85.00
Pruning, Say It With Flowers, Pocket	25.00
Purina	12.00
Putty, Keen Kutter	25.00
Remington, Curtiss Candy Bars, Baby Ruth	125.00
Remington, Lock Back, Scrimshaw Bone Handle	60.00
Remington, R683	175.00
Schrade, Push Button, 6/6/16	65.00
Schrade, Uncle Henry, Sheath, Box	40.00
Sharpener, Denver Fur Co., Advertising, Est.1868	18.00
Siren Rocketship, Pocket, 1950s	35.00

Sow Belly, Remington, R4283, 3 3/4 In.	1500.00
Star Brand Shoes, Case	58.00
Victorinox, Swiss Army, Champion Model	20.00
Winchester, Barlow	195.00
Woman's, Boot Shape, Sample	12.00

KNOWLES, TAYLOR & KNOWLES, see KTK; Lotus Ware

KOCH   The name "Koch" is signed on the front of a series of plates decorated with fruit, vegetables, animals, or birds. The dishes date from the 1910 to 1930 period and were probably decorated in Germany.

KOCH, Bowl, Apples Over Water, 8 In.	150.00
Chop Plate, Grapes, Brown & Yellow Ground, 12 In.	150.00
Dish, Pancake, Apples	150.00
Plate, Apples, Dark Ground, 8 1/2 In.	42.00
Plate, Apples, Sprigs, White Ground, 6 1/4 In.	20.00
Plate, Purple & Green Grapes, Leaves, Signed, 8 1/2 In.	50.00

KOREAN WARE, see Sumida

KPM

X.P.M

Most dealers and collectors use the term "KPM" to refer to Berlin porcelain, but the same initials were used alone and in combination with other symbols by several German porcelain makers. They include the Konigliche Porzellan Manufaktur of Berlin, initials used in mark, 1823–47; Meissen, 1723–24 only; Krister Porzellan Manufaktur in Waldenburg, after 1831; Kranichfelder Porzellan Manufaktur in Kranichfeld, after 1903; and the Kister Porzellan Manufaktur in Scheibe, after 1838.

KPM, Bread Plate, Acorns & Leaves, Green To Ivory Ground	48.00
Bust, Young Boy, Cobalt Blue Base, Gold Trim	180.00
Dish, 3 Sections, Gold Scrolls, Flowers, Marked, 5 X 11 1/2 In.	145.00
Dish, Oval, 10 1/2 In.	250.00
Figurine, Carriage & Horse, Woman Inside, Man On Seat, 6 X 13 In.	175.00
Figurine, Harlequin, Scepter Mark, 4 1/2 In.	275.00
Figurine, Poor Boy, Winter, Red Orb Mark, 6 1/4 In.	165.00
Figurine, Stag	450.00
Figurine, Tea Time, Man & Woman, Dog, Blue & White, Marked, 7 X 11 In.	150.00
Jardiniere, Grecian Style, Gold, Handle, 5 1/2 X 10 In.	65.00

KPM, LITHOPHANE, see also Lithophane

Lithophane, Seated Woman, Holding Book, Framed, 10 1/4 X 8 In.	525.00
Plaque, Magdalena, Poised Over Scripture, Framed, 6 X 8 1/2 In.	900.00
Plaque, Woman Reading Letter By Window, 8 1/4 X 6 In.	4500.00
Plate, Black Mother, Child, Design, Porcelain	117.00
Plate, Serving, 4 Shells, Handle, Gold Flowers, 12 In.	95.00
Salt, Figural, Double, Child Behind Oval Bowls, Orb Mark, 5 In.	195.00
Tile, Tea, Portrait	40.00
Tile, Young Woman, Erbluht, 5 X 3 3/4 In.	1600.00
Tray, Dresden Flowers, Oval	65.00
Vase, Cover, Leafy Garlands, Central Medallions, Marked, 9 3/4 In.	390.00

K.T.&K.
CHINA

KTK are the initials of the Knowles, Taylor & Knowles Company of East Liverpool, Ohio, founded by Isaac W. Knowles in 1853. The company made many types of utilitarian wares, hotel china, and dinnerwares. They made the fine bone china known as Lotus Ware from 1891 to 1896. The company merged with American Ceramic Corporation in 1928. It closed in 1934. Lotus Ware is listed in its own category in this book.

KTK, Chamber Set, Girl With Sheep, Green, Gold Trim, 7 Piece	750.00
Soap Dish, Yellow Roses, Gold Trim, 3 Piece	25.00
Spittoon, White, Marked	35.00
Wash Set, Green, Pastoral Scene, Ornate, 7 Piece	750.00

KKK   Any items relating to the Ku Klux Klan are now collected because of their historic importance. Literature, robes, and memorabilia are available. The Klan is still in existence, so new material is found.

KU KLUX KLAN, Book, Historical Romance, 1st Edition, 1904 .... 60.00
Booklet, Constitution, Women of The Klan, 1923, 72 Pages 25.00
Constitution, Laws Booklet 20.00
Documents, Presque Isle, Maine, 1929, 10 Piece 30.00
Knife, Pocket, Box 75.00
Mirror, Propaganda, Leather Pouch, Pocket 10.00
Newspaper, Front Page, Office, Chicago Klan Paper Bombed, 1933 .... 9.00
Tumbler, Etched Cross, 4 In. 65.00

Kutani ware is a Japanese porcelain made after the mid-seventeenth century. Most of the pieces found today are nineteenth century. Collectors often use the term "kutani" to refer to just the later, colorful pieces decorated with red, gold, and black pictures of warriors, animals, and birds.

KUTANI, Ashtray & Lighter, Birds & Flowers, 6 1/2 In., 2 Piece 85.00
Figurine, Buddha, Green Robe, Phoenix & Dragons, 13 In. 115.00
Mustard Pot, Attached Plate, Signed 20.00
Nut Set, Bird Scene, Bowl & 4 Cups 95.00
Plate, Allover Polychrome Chrysanthemums, Gold Border, C.1850, 7 In. 115.00
Vase, Ochre, Gold, Geishas In Garden, 13 1/4 In., Pair 300.00

Lacquer is a type of varnish. Collectors are most interested in the Chinese and Japanese lacquer wares made from the Japanese varnish tree. Lacquer wares are made from wood coated with many coats of lacquer. Sometimes the piece is carved or decorated with ivory or metal inlay.

LACQUER, Box, Black Cut To Red, Brass Stud, Ivory Button Trim, 9 1/2 In. 120.00
Box, Chinoiserie Design, Fitted Drawer, Oriental, 14 In. 1575.00
Box, Red, Sections, Storks 15.00
Cocktail Shaker, Maroon, Silver Morning Glories, Maruni, 11 1/2 In. 75.00
Screen, Pagoda-Style Cornice, Diamond Pattern, Chinese, 73 In. 995.00
LADY HEAD VASE, see Head Vase

Lalique glass was made by Rene Lalique in Paris, France, between the 1890s and his death in 1945. The glass was molded, pressed, and engraved in Art Nouveau and Art Deco styles. Pieces were marked with the signature "R. Lalique." Lalique glass is still being made. Pieces made after 1945 bear the mark "Lalique."

LALIQUE, Bookends, Dove Form, Crystal, Engraved Signed, 6 1/2 In., Pair 192.00
Bowl, Armentieres, 10 1/2 In. 137.00
Bowl, Chicoree, Frosted, 9 1/2 In. 555.00
Bowl, Chicoree, Opalescent, No.3213, 9 1/2 In. 595.00
Bowl, Cut Leaves Radiate From Center, Gray Wash, Signed, 9 1/4 In. 450.00
Bowl, Dahlia, Opalescent, 9 5/8 In. 192.00
Bowl, Flora Bella, Pointed Petal Rows, Signed, C.1932, 15 3/8 In. 8800.00
Bowl, Martigues, Scrolling Fish, Amber, Signed, C.1932, 14 1/2 In. 4535.00
Bowl, Radiating Fish, Raised Block Signature, 8 1/4 In. 275.00
Bowl, Raised Roses On Outside, Square, 9 3/4 In. 445.00
Bowl, Raised Roses, Frosted To Clear, Square, 9 In. 450.00
Bowl, Songbirds, Nestled Among Ferns, 9 1/4 In. 121.00
Bowl, Swimming Fish, Signed, 8 In. 1550.00
Box, Clear Cover, Spiraling Plumes, Signed, 1 1/2 X 5 1/4 In. 600.00
Box, Cover, Angel Faces Amid Feathered Wings, Signed, 3 In. 665.00
Box, Florets In Handle On Cover, Frosted, Signed, 6 1/4 In. 850.00
Box, Mesanges, Birds In Flight, Opalescent Glass, Cover, 7 In. 445.00
Box, Swallows, Cover, Engraved, Signed, 4 In. 150.00
Chandelier, Bowl, Chrysanthemum Beech Leaves, Clear, Frosted, 12 In. 3400.00
Chandelier, Camellias & Leaves, Glass Mounts, C.1925, 12 1/4 In. 4500.00
Chandelier, Overlapping Arcs, Yellow, Signed, C.1932, 14 3/4 In. 3330.00
Cigarette Holder, Figural, Lion, Matching Lighter 200.00
Clock, Deux Figurines, 2 Women In Robes, Bronze Base, C.1932, 14 In. 3550.00
Console Set, 4-Light, Bowl, Bird, Sienna Stain, Signed 1950.00
Dish, Caviar, Cover, Bosses In Concentric Circles On Rim, 7 1/2 In. 1200.00
Dish, Trinket, 2 Lovebirds, Signed, 4 In. 95.00

Figurine, 2 Leaping Fish, 11 1/2 In.	600.00
Figurine, 2 Nude Women Dancers, Engraved Lalique, 9 1/2 In.	600.00
Figurine, Bacchantes, Glass, Signed, 8 1/2 In.	467.00
Figurine, Lovers, Signed, 10 In.	800.00
Figurine, Madonna & Child, 14 1/2 In.	1700.00
Figurine, Sirene, Nude, Signed, 4 1/8 In.	2500.00
Finger Bowl, Frosted Cherry Tree Design	135.00
Goblet, 6 Female Figures, Flared Form, Signed, 7 In.	950.00
Hood Ornament, Coq Nain	875.00
Hood Ornament, Eagle's Head, Clear & Frosted	600.00
Hood Ornament, Fish, Perch	3300.00
Hood Ornament, Grande Libellule, Dragonfly, Signed, 14 1/4 In.	4450.00
Hood Ornament, Nude, Vitesse, Frosted Glass	5170.00
Hood Ornament, Rooster, Blue	750.00
Inkwell, Aigle, Eagle On Square Frosted Base, Signed, 9 In.	2750.00
Inkwell, Trois Papillons, Overlapping Butterflies, Signed, C.1932	995.00
Jar, Cover, Molded Nude On Horseback, Frosted	190.00 To 250.00
Medallion, Orphelinat Des Armees, Pair	95.00
Orangeade Set, Bahia Design, Golden Amber, Signed, Tray, 7 Piece	1900.00
Paperweight, Bison, Frosted & Colorless, Signed, 4 X 4 3/4 In.	115.00
Paperweight, Football Shape, Clear & Frosted, 4 In.	95.00
Paperweight, Owl	75.00
Pepper Mill, Leafage, Brown Wash, Marked, C.1932, 3 1/2 In.	1430.00
Perfume Bottle, Beau Treillis, Amber Wash	895.00
Perfume Bottle, Brown Woman's Head, Houbigant, Box, 1 5/8 X 4 In.	1800.00
Perfume Bottle, Butterscotch, Lemon Yellow To Amber, C.1932, 6 In.	1500.00
Perfume Bottle, Center Circle, Jointed By Braids, C.1932, 3 1/2 In.	1100.00
Perfume Bottle, Epines, Spines	395.00
Perfume Bottle, Frosted, Heart Stopper, Blue Patina, 4 1/4 In.	6000.00
Perfume Bottle, Muguet, Lilies of The Valley	125.00
Perfume Bottle, Nina Ricci, Double Dove	100.00 To 115.00
Perfume Bottle, Perles, Overlapping Pearls, C.1932, 8 1/4 In.	715.00
Perfume Bottle, Set In Matching Tray, Dot Pattern, Signed, 3 Piece	775.00
Plate, 4 Chinese Dragons On Reverse, Marked, 14 In.	225.00
Plate, Annual, Dream Rose, Signed, 1966, Box	300.00
Plate, Annual, Fish Ballet, Signed, 1967, Box	175.00
Plate, Coquilles, Signed, 9 In.	335.00
Plate, Nude Floating In Flowers, Signed, Amber, 6 3/4 In.	295.00
Plate, Opalescent Feathers, Clear, 11 In.	395.00
Plate, Pilgrim Bust Center, Grape Vines Rim, Marked, 8 In., Pair	575.00
Plate, Tree of Life, Black, 8 In.	90.00
Powder Box, 3 Dancing Nudes On Cover, 3 3/4 In.	500.00
Powder Box, Emiliane	245.00
Powder Box, Flowers On Top, Frosted, 3 1/2 X 1 1/4 In.	375.00
Powder Box, Men On Horses, 4 X 4 In.	275.00
Powder Box, Vaucluse	395.00
Swan, Signed, 10 In., Pair	3500.00
Tray, Raised Blossoms, 2 Sections, Signed, 3 1/2 X 4 1/2 In.	250.00

Lalique, Vase, Amber, Leaf Design, Signed, 11 1/4 In.

Lalique, Vase, Esterel, Blue Wash, Leaves, Signed, 6 In.

Lalique, Vase, Gui, Foliate & Berry Design, Signed, 6 3/4 In.

Lalique, Vase, 6 Female Figures, Brown Wash, Signed, 7 1/2 In.

Tray, Ring, Frosted Lovebirds, Signed 100.00
Tray, Ring, Frosted Nude, Flowing Hair 140.00
Tumbler, Setubal Pattern, Fruit In Middle, 4 1/2 In. 325.00
Vase, 2 Lions, Recumbent, Octagonal, 6 1/2 In. 165.00
Vase, 2 Nude Women Holding Garlands To Form Handles, 4 3/4 In. 3100.00
Vase, 3 Fish Form Base, Sea Waves On Body, Signed, 7 1/2 In. 450.00
Vase, 6 Female Figures, Brown Wash, Signed, 7 1/2 In. ....*Illus* 960.00
Vase, Actina, Serrated Wavy Lines, Signed, C.1932, 8 5/8 In. 1650.00
Vase, Amber, Leaf Design, Signed, 11 1/4 In. ....*Illus* 7200.00
Vase, Antilopes, Rows of Hemispheres, Signed, C.1932, 11 In. 2250.00
Vase, Aras, Birds In Berried Branches, Marked, C.1932, 9 In. 2300.00
Vase, Archers, Nude Males, Swooping Birds, Signed, C.1932, 10 1/4 In. 8800.00
Vase, Archers, Ovoid, Amber, Signed, C.1932, 10 1/4 In. 9600.00
Vase, Avallon, Birds In Cherry Tree, Marked, 5 3/4 In. 330.00
Vase, Avallon, Etched Signed, 5 3/4 In. 220.00
Vase, Bacchantes, Maidens In Various Poses, C.1932, 9 5/8 In. 3850.00
Vase, Baies, Berries & Brambles, Black Enameled, Signed, 10 1/4 In. 9900.00
Vase, Birds & Berries, Signed, C.1950 .... 425.00
Vase, Bleuets, Blue Wash, Incised Block Signed, 6 1/4 In. 550.00
Vase, Bleuets, Sloping Sides, Marked, C.1932, 6 1/4 In. 880.00
Vase, Ceylon, Pairs of Lovebirds, Signed, C.1932, 9 1/2 In. 4950.00
Vase, Chardons, 4 Double Panels, Marked, C.1932, 7 In. 1100.00
Vase, Dampierre Pattern, Footed, 5 In. 82.00
Vase, Druides, Berry-Laden Branches, Signed, C.1932, 7 In. 880.00
Vase, Esterel, Blue Wash, Leaves, Signed, 6 In. ....*Illus* 660.00
Vase, Farandole, Dancing Cherubs, Signed, 7 In. 3080.00
Vase, Formose, Swimming Fish, Signed, 1932, 6 5/8 In. 1450.00
Vase, Formose, Swimming Fish, Yellow, Signed.C.1932, 6 3/4 In. 7150.00
Vase, Gros Palmes, C.1932, 11 1/2 In. 1200.00
Vase, Gros Scarabees, Allover Pattern, Signed, C, 1932, 11 1/2 In. 3630.00
Vase, Gui, Foliate & Berry Design, Signed, 6 3/4 In. ....*Illus* 550.00
Vase, Lierre, Ivy, Clear Light Blue Wash, Signed, 6 3/4 In. 220.00
Vase, Malesherbes, Teardrop Form, Amber, Signed, C.1930, 9 In. 2725.00
Vase, Milan, Spade-Form Leaves, Signed, C.1932, 11 In. 4800.00
Vase, Moissac, Leaves, Flowerpot Shape, 5 In. 2750.00
Vase, Moissac, Leaves, Signed, C.1932, 5 1/8 In. 885.00
Vase, Nude Dancing Women, Frosted & Plain Panels, Signed, 8 1/2 In 700.00
Vase, Perruches, Pairs of Lovebirds, Branches, Signed, C.1932, 10 In. 7750.00
Vase, Pierrefonds, Scrolling Handles, Signed, C.1932, 6 1/4 In. 7565.00
Vase, Poissons, Fish, Spherical, Signed, C.1932, 9 1/2 In. 9075.00
Vase, Raised Roosters, Berries, Frosted Glass, Signed, 6 In. 850.00
Vase, Raisins, Grape Clusters, Vines, Signed, 6 1/4 In. 1100.00
Vase, Resting Gazelles At Base, Studded Ground, Signed, 1935, 8 In. 1200.00
Vase, Serpent, Coiling, Amber, Signed, C.1932, 9 7/8 In. 6655.00
Vase, St.Francois, 6 3/4 In. 150.00
Vase, St.Francois, Signed, 7 In. 850.00
Vase, Tourbillons, Yellow Walls, Signed, C.1932, 7 7/8 In. 7200.00
Vase, Vertical Panels, Rose Heads, Frosted, Signed, 9 1/2 In. 750.00
Water Set, Serving Tray, Orangeade, Amber, 7 Piece 1985.00

Interest is strong in lamps of every type, from the early oil-burning Betty and Phoebe lamps to the recent electric lamps with glass or beaded shades. Fuels used in lamps changed through the years; whale oil (1800-40), camphene (1828), Argand (1830), lard (1833-63), turpentine and alcohol (1840s), gas (1850-79), kerosene (1860), and electricity (1879) are the most common. Other lamps are listed by manufacturer or type of material.

LAMP, Aladdin, B- 25, Victoria 350.00
  Aladdin, B- 26, Simplicity 165.00
  Aladdin, B- 40, Washington Drape, Clear Chimney, Green Base, 9 In. 110.00
  Aladdin, B- 75, Lincoln Drape, Red, Unused 365.00
  Aladdin, B- 76, Lincoln Drape, Cobalt Blue, Tall 495.00
  Aladdin, B- 76, Simplicity, White 68.00
  Aladdin, B- 81, Beehive, Green 57.50

Aladdin, B– 86, White Moonstone Bowl, Black Moonstone Base 155.00
Aladdin, B–102, Corinthian, Green 70.00
Aladdin, B–106, Hobnail, Amber 47.00
Aladdin, B–115, Moonstone, Jade 80.00
Aladdin, Electric, Camphor Shade 150.00
Aladdin, Figural, Cupid, Peach, 1950 .... 85.00
Aladdin, G–271, Alacite 33.00
Aladdin, Kerosene, Beehive 35.00
Aladdin, Lily–of–The–Valley, Alacite 29.00
Aladdin, No. 4, Boudoir, Reverse Painted Shade, Signed 325.00
Aladdin, No. 6, Burner & Spider 60.00
Aladdin, No. 6, Nickel, 301 Shade 150.00
Aladdin, No. 7, 401 Shade 325.00
Aladdin, No. 11, Burner & Spider .... 65.00 To 85.00
Aladdin, No.1214N, Hanging, Plain Shade 125.00
Aladdin, Shield & Stars 90.00
Aladdin, White Leaves, Pink Ground, Alacite, Finial 68.00
Alcohol, Watchmaker's 15.00
Amronlite, Desk, Brass, Green Overlay Shade, 1917, 17 1/2 In. 110.00
Argand, Bronze, Cut & Frosted Glass, C.1825 ....*Illus* 1100.00
Argand, Mantel, Frosted Cut To Clear Shade, Electrified, 14 In., Pair 750.00
Argand, Regency, Bronze, Double 210.00
Argand, Wall, Pair 2700.00
Astral, Victorian, Brass, Marble, Prisms 1650.00
Banquet, Blown–Out Lion, Desert Scenes, Electrified, 22 In. 1295.00
Banquet, Cherub, Floral Ball Shade, 36 In. 250.00
Banquet, Elite Princess, Pink, Miniature, Pair 425.00
Banquet, Enameled Flowers, Brass Square Column, 15 In. 135.00
Banquet, Removable Font, Frosted Ball Shade, Brass Plated 125.00
Banquet, Satin Glass Font & Stem, Frosted Shade, Brass Base, 26 In. 1465.00
Betty, Bird Finial, Wrought Iron, 4 1/2 In. 95.00
Betty, Hook & Wick Pick, Wrought Iron, Brass, 1 1/4 In. 750.00
Betty, Iron Hanger, Pick 170.00
Betty, Pick & Hanger, 6 X 7 X 4 In. 150.00
Betty, Tin, 1810 .... 240.00
Betty, With Hanger, Wick Pick, Stamped H. & R. Boker, Wrought Iron 250.00
Betty, Wooden, Adjustable Shelf, 7 3/4 In. 225.00
Bicycle, Carbide, Brass, Auto–Lite, 3 3/4 In. 25.00
LAMP, BRADLEY & HUBBARD, see Bradley & Hubbard, Lamp
Brass, Blown & Cut Shade, Prisms, Cox, 35 1/2 In. 4500.00
Bronze, Gold Painted, Bearded Rug Merchant Unfurling Rug, 19 1/8 In. 1650.00
Camphene, Twin Burner, Pewter Pedestal Base, C.1830, 7 1/2 In. 250.00

Lamp, Electric, Duffner & Kimberly, Leaded Glass Shade, 23 In.

Lamp, Electric, Moe Bridges, Summer Landscape, 21 1/2 In.

Lamp, Palm Tree Pattern, Blue & Green Panels, 16 In.

Candle, Inverted Dome Base, Tin, Brass, Mahogany, 1883, 5 1/2 In. 715.00
Candle, Louis XVI Style, Draped Woman, Marble Pedestal, 3–Light 495.00
Candle, Mirror, Drummond, C.1846 .... 250.00
Chandelier, 4–Light, Carved Flying Griffins, Oak, 3 Ft. 6000.00
Chandelier, 4–Light, Chain Link Trammel, Iron, 11 X 17 In. 500.00
Chandelier, 4–Light, Mission Oak, Wooden Chains, Cutouts 800.00
Chandelier, 4–Light, Prairie Style, Wooden Chains, Oak, Square 1000.00
Chandelier, 4–Light, Scrolled, Silk Cords, Bronze, 1920, 37 1/4 In. 2300.00
Chandelier, 5–Light, Bronze, Crystal, Electrified, 1900, 21 In. 1320.00
Chandelier, 5–Light, French Bronze, 1850, 30 In. X 4 Ft. 4500.00
Chandelier, 5–Light, Louis XV Style, Bud Shaped Drop, 11 In. 470.00
Chandelier, 5–Light, Wedgwood, Blue & White, Brass Arms, C.1910, 17 In. 565.00
Chandelier, 6–Light, Empire, Brass & Crystal, Prisms, 24 X 21 In. 85.00
Chandelier, 6–Light, Glass Leaves, Cut Glass & Brass, 19 In. 775.00
Chandelier, 8–Light, Art Glass, Bronze, Blue Shades, 1915, 23 X 48 In. 2300.00
Chandelier, 8–Light, Empire, Gilt Bronze, Tole, Chain, 27 X 45 In. 2500.00
Chandelier, 8–Light, Louis XV Style, Silver Plate, 34 In. 995.00
Chandelier, 10–Light, Louis XVI, Glass Stem, 6 Tiers, 40 In. 770.00
Chandelier, 12–Light, Crystal Prisms, Gilt Metal, C.1910, 3 X 5 Ft. 4800.00
Chandelier, 12–Light, Rococo, Bronze, Cornucopia Base, 1900, 40 In. 2750.00
Chandelier, 12–Light, Venetian, Gilt Metal, Amethyst & Glass, 36 In. 467.00
Chandelier, 12–Sided Marble Cap, 4 Supports, Bronze, C.1925, 33 In. 2540.00
Chandelier, Leaded Domed Shade, Quartersawn Oak, Wooden Chains 2000.00
Coach, Bordens, Marked 15.00
Coach, Georgian, Brass, Iron Bracket, Painted, 1800, 24 In. 176.00
Crusie, Double, European, Hanger, Iron, 6 1/2 In. 85.00
Crusie, Double, Sheet Iron, Tin Plate, Twisted Hanger, 8 3/4 In. 55.00
Electric, 2 African Scholars, Tented Mosque, Cold Painted Bronze, 1900 .... 1430.00
Electric, Airplane, Art Deco 175.00
Electric, Alabaster, Woman, Art Nouveau, Stands Before Column, 20 In. 220.00
Electric, Arab On Rug, Bronze, Amber Lantern, Art Deco, 16 1/2 In. 395.00
Electric, Architect's, Emeralite, Daylite Screen .... 275.00 To 425.00
Electric, Arts & Crafts, Cast Metal, Tin & Mica Floral Shade, 67 In. 286.00
Electric, Astral, Scroll & Leaf Column, Prisms, Floral Design, 28 In. 465.00
Electric, Bigalow–Kennard, Pinecone Shade, Red–Amber, 70 In. ....*Illus* 9350.00
Electric, Black Panther, Art Deco, 20 In. 30.00
Electric, Bronze, Camel, Holding Gold Crackle Glass Shade 65.00
Electric, Bronze, Exotic Dancer, 20 In. 145.00
Electric, Bronze, Hawaiian Hula 150.00
Electric, Bulb Behind Peacock & Foliage, Cast Iron 85.00
Electric, Charlie Tuna, Figural 55.00
Electric, Cockatoo, Orange Head, Blue, Metal Band Around Base 185.00
Electric, Coin Dot, Blue Opalescent, Handle, 1875–85 .... 495.00
Electric, Coppercraft, Mission 4400.00
Electric, Dancer, Onyx Base, Crystal Globe, Art Deco 250.00
Electric, Desk, Reverse Painted Glass, Oblong Floral 395.00
Electric, Duffner & Kimberly, Leaded Glass Shade, 23 In. ....*Illus* 2970.00
Electric, Econolite, Model T/Stutz, 1957 .... 65.00
Electric, Econolite, TV, Action, General & John Bull Locomotives, 1956 .... 65.00
Electric, Elsie & Beauregard, No Shade, Label 45.00
Electric, Emeralite, For Rolltop Desk 350.00
Electric, Falstaff Beer, Tin, 1910, 24 In. 375.00
Electric, Female Descending Step, Patinated Metal, C.1925, 17 1/2 In. 885.00
Electric, Flared Glass Lined Brass Shade, Oak Stem & Base, 24 In. 330.00
Electric, Floor, Painted Cloth Shade, Geese On Pond Scene, 1930 .... 90.00
Electric, G. Stickley, 3–Light, Silk–Lined Shade, C.1907, 22 In. 6655.00
Electric, G. Stickley, 6 Amber Glass Panels, Iron, C.1906, 33 In. 9600.00
Electric, Gustav Stickley, Desk, Arched Support, C.1907, 16 1/4 In. 8475.00
Electric, Gustav Stickley, Desk, Harp, No.501 .... 7700.00
Electric, H. Robus, Stylized Nude Females, Bronze, C.1930, 18 3/8 In. 1650.00
Electric, H.G. Cleaveland, Box Turtle Shell Arm & Shade, 9·1/2 In. 6665.00
Electric, Hanging, Heilmann Beer, Electric 21.00
Electric, Harlequin, Millefiori Glass Shade, Marble Base, Art Deco 450.00
Electric, Jefferson, Boudoir, Red Oriental Poppy, Yellow Ground, 7 In. 750.00

Electric, Kopperkraft, Hammered Copper, Mica Shade 3800.00
Electric, Leaded Glass, Wisteria, Tree Trunk Base, Shade, 18 In. 4500.00
Electric, Loie, Betty, Miner's, Iron Hook, Slide Cover 95.00
Electric, Marble, Cupids, Grapes, Vines, Marble Shade, 12 In. 1025.00
Electric, Metal Urn Shape Within Ram's Head, Painted, 21 In. 44.00
Electric, Mica Paneled Shade, D. Van Erp, C.1911, 17 1/2 In. 8475.00
Electric, Miller, 2–Light, 22 In. 110.00
Electric, Miller, Slag Glass, 8–Panel, Double Socket, Signed 250.00
Electric, Moe Bridges, 2–Light, 24 In. 145.00
Electric, Moe Bridges, 2–Light, Reverse Painted Woodland Scene, 24 In. 2200.00
Electric, Moe Bridges, Art Deco, Bronze 300.00
Electric, Moe Bridges, Chrysanthemum, Domed Shade, Paw Feet, 23 In. 4950.00
Electric, Moe Bridges, Hand Painted Interior, Landscape, 21 1/2 In. 2200.00
Electric, Moe Bridges, Hanging, 5–Light 165.00
Electric, Moe Bridges, Reverse Painted, Forest Scene, River, 14 In. 1430.00
Electric, Moe Bridges, Summer Landscape, 21 1/2 In. ....*Illus* 2200.00
Electric, Moe Bridges, Table, Country Road 1650.00
Electric, Moe Bridges, Trees, Riverside, Autumn, 16 In. 1050.00
Electric, Mother–of–Pearl, Shell, Bronze, 3–Light, Trileaf Base, 17 In. 1450.00
Electric, Newel–Post, Brass, Cherub, Opalescent Swirl Shade 750.00
Electric, Nude, Arms Behind Back, Jadite Base, Art Deco, 11 1/2 In. 175.00
Electric, Nursery, Merry–Go–Round Shade, Standing Clown, 7 In. 225.00
Electric, Palm Tree, Art Glass, Octagonal Shade, Bronze, 16 In. 275.00
Electric, Pink Flamingo, Black Pedestal Base, Ceramic, Art Deco, Pair 275.00
Electric, Pittsburgh, Reverse Painted, Call of The Wild, 18 In. 1430.00
Electric, Pittsburgh, Reverse Painted, Forest, Bronze Base, 16 In. 825.00
Electric, Pittsburgh, Reverse Painted, Winter Forest Shade, 16 In. 650.00
Electric, Pyramid Shade, Patinated Iron, Slag Glass, 21 In. 170.00
Electric, Red Satin Glass, Swirl, Petal Floral, 3–Way, 23 In. 550.00
Electric, Rembrandt, Woman Holding Lamp On Head, Tortoise Ball Shade 125.00
Electric, Silver Overlay Flowers, Green Patina Shade, 11 1/2 In. 1200.00
Electric, Slag Glass, Oak Base, 4–Light, Cutout Hipped Shade, 25 In. 1900.00
Electric, Stag, Light In Base, Bronze & Alabaster, 17 1/2 In. 6050.00
Electric, Steer Horn, Horn Shade, Table 250.00
Electric, Sunbonnet Baby, Polychrome, Iron, Shade, 12 3/4 In. 85.00
Electric, Swan, Shade, Burgundy, Art Deco, 1940s 30.00
Electric, Table, 2 Storks, Metal, Multicolored Globe 85.00
Electric, Table, Wicker, White 145.00
Electric, TV, Cardinals, Mauve, 1940s 22.00
Electric, TV, Ship, Black, 1940s 22.00
Electric, Verdelite, Desk, Cased Shade, Nickel 295.00
Electric, Verdelite, Desk, Double Knuckle, Cased Shade 325.00
Electric, Wall, Revival Style, Iron, White Ball Shades, 12 In., Pair 200.00
Electric, Weco, Empire State Building, White Plastic, Upright, 38 In. 45.00
Electric, Woman Dancer, Stage Canopy, Bronze, Art Deco 375.00
Fairy, Acid Burmese Dome Shade, Matching Base, Marked, Hanging Frame 750.00
Fairy, Ann Hathaway, 1880s 650.00
Fairy, Blue Glass, Crown Shade, Queen Victoria's Jubilee, 1887, 4 In. 165.00
Fairy, Burmese Shade, Pink To Yellow, Clarke Pyramid Base, 4 In. 500.00
Fairy, Cobwebbed Shade, Brass & Jewels 165.00
Fairy, Diamond Point Shade, Clarke Insert, Amber, 4 In. 185.00
Fairy, Embossed Mold, Shaded Blue Satin Finish, 6 1/2 In. 475.00
Fairy, Frosted Cranberry, Verre Moire, Clear Insert, Candle Cup, 5 In. 425.00
Fairy, Lighthouse Shape, Ivory Ring Handle, Marked Pantin, 8 1/4 In. 330.00
Fairy, Pink Cased To White, Hand Painted Floral, Clear Insert, England 355.00
Fairy, Ruffled Base, Verre Moire, Clarke Inset, Cranberry, 5 1/2 In. 495.00
Fairy, Tudor Cottage, 1880s 650.00
Finger, Diamond & Fan, Amber 125.00
Finger, Lyre, Pewter Pin, Flint 95.00
Finger, Nutmeg, Brass Ring Frame, Clear Chimney 150.00
Finger, Nutmeg, Cobalt Blue Glass, Brass Holder, Marked 80.00
Finger, Pink & Lavender, Crystal Handle, Spatter Glass, 4 1/2 In. 165.00
Finger, Prince Edward, Emerald Green 185.00
Fluid, Pressed Glass, Sawtooth, 10 1/2 In. ....*Illus* 70.00

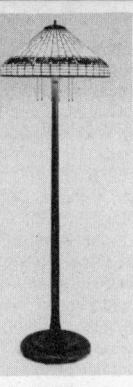

Lamp, Argand, Bronze, Cut & Frosted Glass,
C.1825

Lamp, Electric,
Bigalow–Kennard,
Pinecone Shade,
Red–Amber, 70 In.

Lamp, Fluid,
Pressed Glass,
Sawtooth,
10 1/2 In.

Fluid, Star & Punty, Flint, Brass Collar, Pewter, 6 3/4 In.	170.00
Fuller, Woman, Swirling Fabrics Over Head	7250.00
Gas, Coralene, Diamond Quilted, Satin, Brass Fitter Rim	175.00
Gas, Double, Hanging, Wellsbach	325.00
Gas, Student, St. Germain Kleeman, Single, 1879, Pat. CFA Hinrichs	195.00
Girandole, Wall Sconce, 2–Light, Mirror, Stylized Flower, 17 In., Pair	1000.00
Gone With The Wind, Beaded Crinkle	200.00
Gone With The Wind, Grape	750.00
Gone With The Wind, Hand Painted, Large	1150.00
Gone With The Wind, Red Satin Glass, Dancing Girls, 10 In.	900.00
Gone With The Wind, Regal Iris, Red Satin Glass	750.00
Gone With The Wind, Stag On Shade, Forest Scene Base	1000.00
Gone With The Wind, White Relief Florals, Green Ground, Phoenix	750.00
Grease, Single Spout, Hanger, Iron, 6 1/2 In.	55.00
Hall, Hobnail, Pear Shape, Cranberry	475.00
LAMP, HANDEL, see Handel, Lamp	
Hanging, Kittens Playing With Mouse, Bristol Shade	575.00
Hanging, Victorian, Gilded Metal Frame, Hand Painted Floral Shade	350.00
Iron, Twisted Shaft & Hook, Tooled Body, Upright Shaft, 18th Century	260.00
Kerosene, Atterbury, Chapman Font, Milk Glass, 10 1/2 In.	120.00
Kerosene, Chapman With Diamonds, Crystal Font, Brass Connector	140.00
Kerosene, Coreopsis, Miniature	275.00
Kerosene, Cosmos, Flowered, Shade, Crystal, 8 In.	35.00
Kerosene, Crucifix, Glass, 12 In.	275.00
Kerosene, Dolphin, Pink Glass	525.00
Kerosene, Findlay, Pillow Encircled Pattern	95.00
Kerosene, Finger, Blue, Inside Ribbing, Flat Base, Ring, 4 1/2 In.	140.00
Kerosene, Finger, Bull's–Eye, Green	105.00
Kerosene, Finger, Zipper Loop, Clear, 8 1/2 In.	55.00
Kerosene, Free Blown, Applied Base & Stem, Flint, 6 In.	75.00
Kerosene, Hanging, Brass, Pink Etched Dome Shade, Prisms, 1880, 13 In.	2400.00
Kerosene, Hobbs Coin Dot, White Opalescent	450.00
Kerosene, Iron Base, Bohemian Glass	180.00
Kerosene, Leaf & Jewel, Coin Dot, White Opalescent	265.00
Kerosene, Man's Double Figurehead, Bronze Stem, Frosted Font, 12 In.	105.00
Kerosene, Millefiori Shade, Satin Glass Trim	95.00
Kerosene, Nickel Plated, Single Spout Burner, 4 In.	115.00
Kerosene, Peanut Pattern, Beaded Scalloped Chimney, 8 1/2 In.	55.00
Kerosene, Pedestal Base, Bull's–Eye Safety Handle, Pair	260.00
Kerosene, Piano, Hand Painted Red Globe, Brass Reservoir	320.00
Kerosene, Piano, Royal Bonn China Shade, Dragon Design, 6 Ft.	3900.00
Kerosene, Pink Dolphin	525.00

Kerosene, Princess Feather, Blue, Complete Burner, Globe 125.00
Kerosene, Queen of Hearts, Green Stem & Base, Frosted Hearts, Flowers 525.00
Kerosene, Raindrop & Teardrop, Blue, 12 In. 165.00
Kerosene, Ram's Head Base, Drop–In Font, Nicholas Muller & Son 575.00
Kerosene, Rayo, Chimney, White Shade, Nickel 125.00
Kerosene, Rayo, Green Cased Shade, Miniature 225.00
Kerosene, Rayo, Original Shade 125.00
Kerosene, Ripley, Double Handle 80.00
Kerosene, Riverside Panel, Green Font 135.00
Kerosene, Star & Shield, Brass Stem, Marble Base 65.00
Kerosene, Thumbprint, Intricate Glass, Brass, Dated 1873 .... 165.00
Kerosene, Tin, Reflector, Green Paint, 11 In. 85.00
Kerosene, Vertical Coin Dot, Blue Opalescent 525.00
Kerosene, Wagon, Dietz, No.30, 16 X 12 In. 275.00
Kerosene, Wellsbach, No.2, Brass, Green Glass 125.00
Kerosene, White Swirl, Sheldon, Light Blue, Clear Pedestal 525.00
Kerosene, Yellow Cased Glass, Clear Overlay, Shell Feet, Miniature 535.00
Kettle, Pennsylvania, Iron & Brass, Copper Wick Support, 8 3/8 In. 125.00
Lard, Blue Japanning, Tin, 6 1/2 In. 50.00
Lard, Solar, Astral, Shade, Prisms 700.00
Leaded Shade, Wilkinson, Floral, Trailing Vine, 18 In. 1320.00
Leaded Shade, Wilkinson, Roses & Foliage, 22 1/2 In. 2420.00
Library, Castle, Deer Design, Amber Cut To Clear, Amber Prisms 1250.00
Library, Hanging, Prisms, White Splatter Glass Shade, Brass Frame 800.00
Miner's, Carbide, Kohler 30.00
Miner's, Chicken Finial, Hanger, 7 3/4 In. 125.00
Miner's, Geo. Anton, Penn. 85.00
Miner's, Hanger, Wrought Iron, 4 1/4 In. 95.00
Miner's, Tin Spout, Hook, Brass Collar, 3 In. 22.00
Oil, Apolla, Pressed Glass, 7 In. 60.00
Oil, Boudoir, 3 Female Heads Topping Legs, Cranberry Shade, 15 In. 1100.00
Oil, Bull's–Eye Band, Pressed Glass, 9 In. 125.00
Oil, Chicken Brooder, Tin 15.00
Oil, Conquistador, 12 1/2 In. 375.00
Oil, Cranberry Opalescent Glass, Coin Dot, Large, 1875–85 .... 850.00
Oil, Custard Glass, Sculptured Green Dogwood Flowers, 11 In. 75.00
Oil, Drilled & Electrified, Opaque White Base, Amethyst Font, 22 In. 95.00
Oil, Empress, Pressed Glass, Green, 10 1/2 In. .... 125.00 To 195.00
Oil, Feather, Clear Satin Glass, Matching Shade 500.00
Oil, Geranium, Satin Glass, Matching Shade 850.00
Oil, Greentown Glass Co., Clear Blown Sultan Font, C.1890, 8 1/2 In. 550.00
Oil, Hamilton, Clear Leaf, Flint 210.00
Oil, Hand, Blown Glass, Frosted, Serrated Loops, Flowers, C.1905, 3 In 60.00
Oil, Hitchcock, Mechanical 125.00
Oil, Hurricane, Pittsburgh Glass, 1820–40, Pair 1400.00
Oil, Ice Skaters, Dated 1864–67 .... 500.00
Oil, Kettle, Brass, Copper & Iron, Peter Derr, 1843, 10 3/4 In. 2400.00
Oil, Papier–Mache, C.1875 .... 275.00
Oil, Peacock Feathers, Pressed Glass 85.00
Oil, Peacock Feathers, Pressed Glass, Amber, 10 In. 350.00
Oil, Pewter, Single Spout, Brass, Pewter Burner, Handle, 3 3/8 In. 175.00
Oil, Pottery, Black Glazed, Raised Design 45.00
Oil, Prince Edward, Pink Cased, Clear Base 645.00
Oil, Princess Feather, Pressed Glass, Cobalt Blue, Tall 395.00
Oil, Princess Feather, Tall Stem 68.00
Oil, Quartered Block, Pressed Glass, 9 In. 55.00
Oil, Ribbed Bellflower, Clear 225.00
Oil, Sheldon Swirl, Clear Stem, Cranberry & White Swirl Font, 10 In. 395.00
Oil, Square Panes, Pressed Glass, Etched, 5 1/4–In. Collar 125.00
Oil, Sweetheart, Pressed Glass 195.00
Oil, Table, Cranberry Glass, Sheldon Swirl, Spatter, 1875–85 .... 450.00
Oil, Time Indicating, Pride of America, Beehive Globe, 7 In. 260.00
Oil, Tin, Conical Font On Saucer Base, Lift–Out Font, 7 1/2 In. 25.00
Oil, Veronica, 10 In. 110.00

Oil, Veronica, 11 In. 135.00
Oil, Waffle & Thumbprint, 11 In. 135.00
Oil, Wheat In Shield, Pressed Glass, 10 1/4 In. 155.00
Organ, Engraved Brass 465.00
Organ, Floor 225.00
    LAMP, PAIRPOINT, see Pairpoint, Lamp
Palm Tree Pattern, Blue & Green Panels, 16 In. ....*Illus* 275.00
Parker, Banquet, Windmills, Sailboats, Ornate Metal, Electrified, 29 In. 985.00
Peg, Double, Lemon Satin Overlay, Ruffled Shade, Electric, 24 In., Pair 650.00
Peg, Frosted Orange Peel Surface, Leaves, Violets, French, Pair 300.00
Peg, Mother-of-Pearl, Blue Swirl, Ruffled Shade, 16 1/2 In. 760.00
Peg, Pulled Feather, Gold Outlined, Durand Shade, 15 1/2 In., Pair 650.00
Peg, Satin Glass Shade, Embossed Font, Brass Base, 15 In., Pair 1470.00
Peg, Shaded Deep To Light Pink, White Interior, Brass, 16 In., Pair 1640.00
Peg, Tin Drop Burner, 2 1/2 In. 350.00
Peg, Yellow Overlay Glass, Mushroom Shade, Brass Candlestick, 15 In. 495.00
Phoebe, Hook, 3 In., 3 Piece 150.00
Piano, Brass, Floor, Adjustable, Hand Painted Shade 800.00
Piano, Floor, Hand Painted Shade, Adjustable, 56 In. To 76 In. 800.00
Porch, Owl, Glass Eyes, Patinated Sheet Metal, 3 Chains, 24 1/2 In 825.00
Rushlight, Candle Socket, Counterbalance, Twisted Stem, Iron, 12 In. ... 325.00
Rushlight, Stand, Adjustable Spring Clip, Socket, Iron, 33 In. 400.00
Rushlight, Stand, Carved Stem, Iron, 29 3/4 In. 150.00
Rushlight, Stand, Socket, Adjustable Clip, Iron, 42 3/4 In. 575.00
Rushlight, Wrought Iron, Fruitwood 200.00
S. Vellin, Sunburst Pattern, Twisted Shaft, 8-Panel Shade, 21 1/2 In. 6600.00
Sconce, 1-Light, Brass, Ram Horn Shape, England, 18 In., Pair 425.00
Sconce, 2-Light, Gilded Rococo, Spread Winged Eagle, 44 In., Pair 1760.00
Sconce, 3-Light, Renaissance Revival, Brass, C.1900, 11 1/2 In., Pair 385.00
Sconce, 4-Light, Italian Gilt Wood, Bowl Shape, Mirror Back, 42 In., Pr. 4075.00
Sconce, 6-Light, Ram's Head Center, Bronze, 19 In., Pair 1760.00
Sconce, Basketwork, Porcelain Figure, Bronze, 17 In., Pair 470.00
Sconce, Beveled Mirror Back, Satyr Head Crest, Brass, 16 In., Pair 170.00
Sconce, Candle, Circular Crest, 14 In., Pair 300.00
Sconce, Candle, Scalloped Rim Hood, Crimped Finial, 15 In., Pair 150.00
Sconce, Candle, Tassels, Crystal Drops, Electric, 18 In., Pair 150.00
Sconce, Crimped Crest, Round Reflector, Tin, 10 In. 200.00
Sconce, Cupid Rising From Tapered Base, Gold Plated, 22 In., Pair 150.00
Sconce, Lobed Backplates, Tin, 19th Century, 13 1/2 In., Pair 605.00
Sconce, Lyre Back, Ormolu & Crystal, French, C.1840, Pair 5000.00
Sconce, Mirrored, Tin & Glass, 9 1/4 In., Pair 900.00
Sconce, Neoclassical, Mirrored Backplate, Cut Glass, 17 In., Pair 610.00
Sconce, Tin, Electrified, American, 19th Century 45.00
Sconce, Tooled Back, Ribbed Crest, Tin, 9 1/2 In., Pair 900.00
Sconce, Whalebone, American, 19th Century, 8 3/4 In. 725.00
Skater's, Brass, Clear Globe, 6 7/8 In. 35.00
Solar, Gothic, Signed Cornelius 1760.00
Street, Double, Upright, Acorn-Style Globe, Cast Iron, 1900s, 22 In. 1650.00
Student, Brass, 2 Green Glass Globes 90.00
Student, C.A. Kleemann, Opaque White Shade, Brass, 20 3/4 In. 150.00
Student, Double, Opaque White Shades, Brass, 23 1/2 In. 225.00
Student, Green Cased Shade, Electrified, Berlin, Brass, 20 1/2 In. 200.00
Student, Green Ribbed Shade, Electrified, Brass, 26 In. 250.00
Student, Kaiser, Complete 325.00
Student, Miller, Art Glass Shade 295.00
    LAMP, TIFFANY, see Tiffany, Lamp
Tin, Conical Base, Handle, Open Font, Center Wick Support, 4 3/8 In. 475.00
Tin, Saucer Base, Handle, Removable Font, Central Wick Support, 4 In. ... 500.00
Torch, Scenic, Pittsburgh, Pair 150.00
Torchere, 5-Light, Double Column Supports, Gilt, Paw Feet, 79 In., Pair 1050.00
Torchere, Alabaster Domed Shade, Iron Spandrels, C. Kiss, 1925 .... 5775.00
Torchere, Greyhound Supports, Green Patinated Bronze, 43 In., Pair 6650.00
Torchere, Nickeled Bronze, Eben-De-Nacassarmc, 1930, 5 Ft. 7 1/2 In. 3025.00
Torchere, Red Veined Marble Shade, Iron Supports, French, 1930, 6 Ft. 2720.00

Trammel, Sawtooth, Twisted Rod, Star Design At Ratchet, Iron, 47 In. 125.00
Vapo–Cresolene, Milk Glass Chimney, 1898 .... 60.00
Whale Oil, Block & Thumbprint, Flint, 10 1/4 In. 95.00
Whale Oil, Cardan, Time Indicating, Pewter, C.1750 .... 875.00
Whale Oil, Double Bull's–Eye, No.10/3, Pewter, C.1820 .... 895.00
Whale Oil, Double Burner, Confederate Hospital, Vicksburg, 7 1/4 In. 210.00
Whale Oil, Folding Handle, Tin 125.00
Whale Oil, Gimbal, Brass, 6 In. 85.00
Whale Oil, Guest Room, 3–Tube Burner, Amber Japanning 550.00
Whale Oil, Jeweler's, Flame Infuser, Brass Drop, M. Roy, 2 1/2 In. 40.00
Whale Oil, Milk Warming, Tin, Stencil Design 250.00
Whale Oil, Peg, Brass, Tin Burner, 3 In. 315.00
Whale Oil, Pewter, Magnifying Lenses, Roswell Gleason, 1822–71, 8 In. 1800.00
Whale Oil, Sandwich, Yellow 425.00
Whale Oil, Student, Brass 290.00
Whale Oil, Tin & Glass, Signed & Dated, Star Tumbler, 1871 .... 395.00
Whale Oil, Weighted Base, Acorn Font, Tin, 8 In. 55.00
Wrought Iron, Angled Arms Supporting Paneled Mica Shade, 17 1/2 In. 1760.00

A lantern is a special type of lighting device. It has a light source, usually a candle, totally hidden inside the walls of the lantern. Light is seen through holes or glass sections.

LANTERN, Barn, Glass Sides, Hinged Door, Tin Socket, Vent Top, Wooden, 14 In. 225.00
Barn, Hinged Door, Pine, Hardwood, Red, Wire Bail, Tin Guard, 10 In. 350.00
Barn, Hinged Door, Tin Vent, Glass Sides, Pine, 18 In. 155.00
Barn, Pine, Glass Sides, Hinged Door, 10 1/4 In. 325.00
Candle, Crown Top, 10 In. 185.00
Candle, Punched Tin, Revere Type, Ring Handle, 13 1/2 In. 65.00
Candle, Punched Tin, Revere Type, Ring Handle, 14 In. 55.00
Candle, Red, Green Paint, Ring Handle, Wood, Tin, 15 In. 425.00
Clear Blown Globe, Pierced Vent, Whale Oil Burner, Tin, 12 1/4 In. 350.00
Dewey Mill, Tin, Tubular, Brass Label 35.00
Dietz Junior, Kerosene, Brass, Clear Globe, 12 In. 75.00
Dietz Sport, Tin, Clear Globe Marked Dietz Scout, 7 5/8 In. 55.00
Dietz, Signal, Red Globe, Northwestern Public Service 45.00
Domed Top, Finials At Corners, Sheet Iron & Glass, 14 In. 495.00
English Railway, Copper, G. Polkey, Square, Beveled, 1897, 13 In. 605.00
Glass Sides, Pyramidal Top, Pierced Star, Ray Vents, Tin, 11 1/2 In. 175.00
Hall, Hexagonal, Regency, Starburst Glass Panels, 43 In., Pair 247.00
Hall, Hipped Roof, Caramel Slag Glass, Copper Frame, 1910, 16 In. 522.00
Interior Chamberstick, Punch Tin, Ring Handle, 12 1/2 In. 55.00
Kerosene, Hanging, Built–In Reflector, Brass & Copper, 14 In. 135.00
Kerosene, Nier No.270, Pre–1940, Germany 45.00
Kerosene, Tin, 5 1/2 In. 75.00
Newel–Post, Frosted Glass, Copper, G. Stickley, C.1905, 17 1/2 In. 6000.00
Pierced, Glass Font, Pierced Door, C.1810, 15 In. 295.00
Pony Trap, Victorian, Brass, Late 19th Century 88.00
Revere Type, Punched Tin, Handmade, Black, 9 1/2 In. 55.00
Revere Type, Punched Tin, Ring Handle, 13 In. 45.00
Skater's, Brass 65.00
Skater's, Tin 50.00
Tin Conical Paneled Top, Glass Body, Ring Handle, 18 In. 110.00
Tin, With Reflector, 19th Century, 22 In. 75.00
Utility, Portable, Winchester .... 48.00 To 65.00
Vulcan, Dietz, Clear Marked Globe, 5 3/8 In. 90.00
Whale Oil, Glass Globe, Embossed Bull's–Eye, 8 In. 425.00
Whale Oil, Tin, Star & Diamond Shaped Holes, Clear Globe, 11 In. 85.00
Wooden, Barn, Beech, Oak, Pine, Glass Sides, Hinged Door, 11 In. 225.00

Le Verre Francais is one of the many types of cameo glass made in France. The glass was made by the C. Schneider factory in Epinay–sur–Seine from 1920 to 1933. It is a mottled glass, usually decorated with floral designs, and bears the incised signature "Le Verre Francais."

LE VERRE FRANCAIS, Bowl, Symmetrical Florals, Mottled, Signed, 3 3/4 In.	315.00
Compote, Cameo, Geometric, Pink & Aqua, Frosted, 4 1/2 In.	595.00
Lamp, Chrysanthemums, Mauve & Purple	4200.00
Lamp, Deco Flowers, Leaf Styled Hardware, Signed, 14 In.	1145.00
Lamp, Frieze of Cats, Iron Mounts, 1918–22, 17 1/2 In.	4400.00
Vase, Art Deco Style, Signed, 21 In.	1200.00
Vase, Art Deco, Urn Shape, 21 In.	1200.00
Vase, Birds, Fruiting Branches, Charder, 1925, 11 1/2 In.	665.00
Vase, Blue, Orange Overlay, Flowers, 12 In.	900.00
Vase, Cameo, Purples, White, 13 In.	680.00
Vase, Cameo, Stylized Floral, Mottled Yellow, 15 1/2 In.	995.00
Vase, Cameo, Stylized Floral, Orange, Yellow, Footed, 9 In.	445.00
Vase, Exotic Blossoms On Stems, Charder, C.1925, 35 In.	4125.00
Vase, Frieze of Beetles, Signed, C.1925, 17 1/2 In.	3410.00
Vase, Inverted Pyriform, Berried Blossoms, 1925.17 In.	2090.00
Vase, Luna Moths, Brickwork Cut Neck, Signed, 1925, 29 In.	4125.00
Vase, Purple To Gray To White, Charder, 7 1/2 In.	750.00
Vase, Red Leaves Up To Yellow Top, Signed, 11 2/ In.	1800.00
Vase, Red Overlay, Pink Mushroom, Signed, 9 In.	900.00
Vase, Squared–Off Flowers, Tricolor, 3 X 3 In.	625.00
Vase, Stylized Blossoms, Signed, C.1925, 22 3/4 In.	995.00
Vase, Stylized Fern Fronds, Signed, C.1925, 23 1/4 In.	1325.00

Leather is tanned animal hide and it has been used to make decorative and useful objects for centuries. Leather objects must be carefully preserved with proper humidity and oiling or the leather will deteriorate and crack. This damage cannot be repaired.

LEATHER, Apron, Blacksmith's, Buckles On Legs	45.00
Bag, Marked Marbles	18.00
Belt, Cowboy's, Hand Tooled	25.00
Belt, Motorcycle, Kidney, Wing Design	48.00
Boots, Cowboy, Pictorial, Applique, Polychrome	550.00
Boots, Riding, Handmade, English, With Stretchers, C.1900, Size 8	600.00
Box, Document	75.00
Case, Jewelry & Cosmetic, Victorian, Tooled, Brown, 14 X 10 X 7 In.	245.00
Gloves, Kidskin, Wrist Cutouts	7.50
Helmet, Motorcycle	10.00
Lariat, 43 In.	90.00
Panel, Madonna, Child, Angel, Embossed Leather, Continental, 52 In.	660.00
Pillow, Tribal Design, Africa, Camel Skin, C.1925	40.00
Robe, Sleigh, Horsehide	95.00
Saddle Flask, Glass, 10 In.	132.00
Saddle, Child's, Silver Mounted, 1940	4000.00
Saddle, McCullen, Army, Stirrups	85.00
Shoes, Colonial Style, Wood Soles & Heels, Brass & Iron Nails, 1840	325.00
Travel Case, Art Deco, Hand Mirror, Jars	20.00
Travel Case, Man's, Accessories, Alligator, 1940s	16.00

LEEDS POTTERY. Leeds pottery was made at Leeds, Yorkshire, England, from 1774 to 1878. Most Leeds ware was not marked. Early Leeds pieces had distinctive twisted handles with a greenish glaze on part of the creamy ware. Later ware often had blue borders on the creamy pottery.

LEEDS, Bowl, Peafowl, Green Sponge Spatter Trees, 4 1/2 In.	175.00
Coffeepot, Dome Top, Floral Design, Black, 3 Colors, 11 In.	200.00
Creamer, Blue, White Gaudy Floral Design, 3 1/4 In.	200.00
Creamer, Blue, White Oriental Design, 1 3/8 In.	250.00
Creamer, Floral Design, 3 7/8 In.	95.00
Jug, Puzzle, Creamware, Gentlemen Come Try Your Skill, 6 3/4 In.	225.00
Mug, Floral Design, Boy Fishing Scene, 5 3/4 In.	400.00
Pitcher, Blue, White Oriental Design, 5 7/8 In.	185.00
Pitcher, Blue, White, Gaudy Floral Design, 4 7/8 In.	125.00
Pitcher, Paragon, Silver Stripes, Roses, 3 1/2 In.	45.00
Pitcher, Polychrome Design of Flowers, 6 Sides, 7 1/2 In.	500.00

Plate, Blue, White Oriental Design, Feather Edge, 10 In.	225.00
Plate, Scalloped Green Feather Rim, Pierced Border, 6 1/4 In., 6 Pc.	715.00
Soup, Dish, Blue Feather Rim, Blue & White, 10 In.	100.00
Sugar, Blue, White Oriental Design, 2 7/8 In.	100.00
Sugar, Blue, White Oriental Design, Spout & Lid, 6 In.	150.00
Teapot, Floral Design, 4 Colors, Cover, 4 1/8 In.	65.00
Teapot, House Design, 4 Colors, 7 1/4 In.	275.00
Teapot, Oriental Design, 3 Colors, 5 3/4 In.	65.00

The Geo. Zoltan Lefton Company has imported porcelains to be sold in America since 1940. The pieces are often marked with the Lefton name. The firm is still in business. The company mark has changed through the years and objects can be dated accurately by the shape of the mark.

LEFTON, Ewer, Applied Apples, Flowers, Gold Scroll Handle, 6 In.	14.00
Figurine, Blue Boy, Gold Label	75.00
Figurine, Dainty Lace, No.4934, 13 1/4 In.	24.00
Figurine, Owl, Marked, 6 1/8 & 7 1/8 In., Pair	16.00
Planter, Elephant, Bisque	15.00
Planter, Pink Gingham Pig	15.00
Planter, Rabbit In Garden	22.00
Plaque, Hand Painted Country Scene, Shield Shape, 8 X 6 In.	18.00
Salt & Pepper, Blue Cat	9.00
Salt & Pepper, Mr. & Mrs. Claus, 1957	25.00
Sugar & Creamer, Fruit Design, Gold Handles	20.00
Sugar, Creamer & Teapot, Gold On White	42.00
Tray, Hand Painted Roses, 2 Tiers, Green	18.00

Legras was founded in 1864 by Auguste Legras at St. Denis, France. It is best known for cameo glass and enamel-decorated glass with Art Nouveau designs. Legras merged with Pantin in 1920 and became the Verreries et Cristalleries de St. Denis et de Pantin Reunies.

LEGRAS, Rose Bowl, Enameled Flowers, Yellow & Frost Interior, 7 X 5 3/4 In.	325.00
Vase, Allover Marbelized Pattern, Signed, 8 1/4 In.	425.00
Vase, Bottle Form, Enameled Landscape, 6 1/4 In.	425.00
Vase, Cameo, Enameled Coral & Water Plants, Ecru Ground, 6 1/4 In.	357.00
Vase, Cameo, Marbelized Band Around Center, Yellow, Brown, 8 1/4 In.	425.00
Vase, Carved Leaves & Branches, Maroon, Frosted, 9 In.	450.00
Vase, Cut Back Flowers, Chipped Ice Ground, Signed, 7 In.	345.00
Vase, Enameled Blue & Yellow Flowers, Frosted Ground, Signed, 7 In.	275.00
Vase, Gold Wash Leaves, Woodbine Berries, Signed, 7 1/2 In.	475.00
Vase, Hand Painted Design, Bulbous, 12 In.	1000.00
Vase, Landscape, Sleepy Town, Signed, C.1920, 4 3/4 In.	660.00
Vase, Mosaics, Gold Aventurine Cased, Amber Exterior, 10 1/2 In.	570.00
Vase, Scenic, Bulbous, 7 1/4 In.	75.00

Walter Scott Lenox and Jonathan Cox founded the Ceramic Art Company in Trenton, New Jersey, in 1889. In 1906, Lenox left and started his own company. The company makes a porcelain that is similar to Irish Belleek. The marks used by the firm have changed through the years and collectors prefer the earlier examples.

LENOX, see also Ceramic Art Co.

LENOX, Basket, Bracelet, Green, 7 In.	65.00
Bowl, Canoe Shape, Pink Exterior	20.00
Buttermilk Set, Grapes, Marked, 14 Piece	500.00
Charger, Allover Grapes, Leaves In Relief, Gold Rim, 13 In.	85.00
Coaster, Cobalt Blue, Sterling Overlay, Gold Wash	50.00
Coffee Set, Silver Overlay, Blue Wreath, 3 Piece	165.00
Compote, Autumn, 3 X 6 3/4 In.	45.00
Cup, Chocolate, Ivory, Acid-Etched Gold Rims, Green Wreath, Pair	25.00
Dish, Leaf, 2 Sections, Center Handle, Gold, Green Mark, 10 1/2 In.	45.00
Figurine, Llama, White	210.00
Figurine, Swan, 9 X 6 1/2 In.	125.00

Figurine, Woman With Fan, White Bisque, Signed	225.00
Honey Jar, Cover, Beehive Shape, Ribbed Ivory Body, Gold Bees	85.00
Jar, Apothecary, Ball Finial, Petty Drugs, Ribbed, Lettered, Green Mark	160.00
Pitcher, Golfing Scene, 14 1/2 In.	8250.00
Pitcher, Mask Spout, Hammered Effect, Coral Body, Marked, 7 1/4 In.	175.00
Plate, Dinner, Classic Rose	25.00
Plate, Southern Gardens, 7 In.	15.00
Platter, Classic Rose, 13 1/2 In.	40.00
Salt & Pepper, Nipper	35.00
Salt & Pepper, Yellow Bird, Green Wreath	35.00
Salt, Figural, Swan, 6 Piece	100.00
Saltshaker & Pepper Mill, Flying Pheasants	30.00
Sign, Dealer, Lantana, 6 In.	35.00
Soup, Dish, Classic Rose	25.00
Soup, Dish, Golden Wreath	12.00
Sugar & Creamer, Shell Pattern, Gold Mark	37.50
Sugar & Creamer, Washington, Commemorative, C.1932	100.00
Swan, Ivory, Old Style, Green Wreath, 4 1/2 In.	25.00
Tea Set, Silver Overlay, Cobalt Blue, 4 Piece	745.00
Tea Set, Silver Overlay, Marked, 3 Piece	365.00
Toby Jug, William Penn Treaty, 7 In.	155.00 To 185.00
Vase, Aorta, 8 1/2 In., Pair	130.00
Vase, Birds of Love	45.00
Vase, Fawn Brown, Pate–Sur–Pate Flowers, Green Mark, 7 In.	195.00
Vase, Roses, Gold Trim, W.H. Moreley, 6 In., Pair	650.00
Vase, Seahorses & Seaweed, Gold & Black, 11 1/2 In.	85.00
Vase, Stick Neck, 8 In.	35.00

Letter openers have been used since the eighteenth century. Ivory and silver were favored by the well-to-do. In the late nineteenth century, the letter opener was popular as an advertising giveaway and many were made of metal or celluloid. Brass openers with figural handles were also popular.

LETTER OPENER, Capital National Bank, Indianapolis, Celluloid	6.00
Crimped Edges, Brass, Forest Craft Guild, 6 3/4 In.	75.00
Eagle Claw Holding Ball, Engraved Blade, Bronze	50.00
Etched On Scabbard, Compiments of Capt. Fred K. Rogers	25.00
Figural, Fuller Brush Man	10.00
Green Marbled Celluloid, Philadelphia Centennial, 1926	20.00
Gulf Oil	10.00
Hawco Fishing Tackle, Celluloid	80.00
Iron City Coal & Coke, Pittsburgh, Pa.	20.00
Jade Handle, Chinese	18.50
Sterling Silver, Mother–of–Pearl Blade, Fancy	50.00
Victor Chemical Works, Chicago	18.00
Zenith Furnace Co.	50.00

The Libbey Glass Company has made glass of many types since 1888. Libbey made cut glass and tablewares that are collected today. The stemwares of the 1930s and 1940s are once again in style. The Toledo, Ohio, firm was purchased by Owens–Illinois in 1935 and is still working under the name "Libbey" as a division of that company.

LIBBEY, see also Amberina; Cut Glass; Maize

LIBBEY, Banana Boat, Cutting On Blown Blank, 11 1/2 X 6 3/4 In.	450.00
Bowl, Alternating Fan & Files Center, Cut Glass, Brilliant, 8 In.	245.00
Bowl, Anita, Cut Glass, 8 In.	210.00
Bowl, Aztec Pattern, Signed, C.1910, 9 1/4 In.	2000.00
Bowl, Button Hobstar Cluster, Cane & Strawberry Diamond, 10 In.	1200.00
Bowl, Colonna, Cut Glass, Low, 9 In.	215.00
Bowl, Comet Pattern, Signed, 1910, 10 In.	1000.00
Bowl, Empress, Cut Glass, 9 In.	225.00
Bowl, Hobstars, Strawberry Diamonds, Stars & Prisms, Scalloped, 8 In.	325.00
Bowl, Ice, Sultana Pattern, Double Handles, Signed, C.1901, 9 1/2 In.	850.00

Bowl, Laurent, Cut Glass, 8 In. 325.00
Bowl, Lorraine Pattern, Signed, 3 X 8 1/2 In. 1675.00
Bowl, Lovebirds Pattern, Square, 8 In. 350.00
Bowl, Marcella Pattern, Tricornered, Signed, 10 In. 1600.00
Bowl, Radiant, Cut Glass, Low, 9 In. 225.00
Bowl, Regis Pattern, Signed, 4 1/2 X 9 In. 450.00
Bowl, Teardrop In Knob, Hobstar Base, Signed, C.1895, 8 1/2 In. 2400.00
Butterfly & Cattails, Pitcher, 5 Tumblers 560.00
Candlestick, Cut Sconces & Base, Twisted, C.1920, 8 In., Pair 195.00
Candlestick, Engraved, Twisted Stem, 10 In., Pair 300.00
Celery Tray, Signed 160.00
Champagne, Figural, Squirrel 75.00
Cocktail, Frosted Kangaroo Stem, Signed 85.00
Compote, Amberina, Flared Fuchsia Rim, Colorless Bowl, 8 In. 750.00
Compote, Toledo Pattern, Paperweight Base, Signed, 4 3/4 X 7 1/4 In. 485.00
Compote, Trailing Vine, Leaves, Flowers Around Rim, Signed, 6 1/2 In. 95.00
Cup & Saucer, Frosted, Pansy Design, Columbian Exposition, 1893 .... 175.00
Cup & Saucer, Vaseline Flower, Columbian Exposition, 1893 .... 85.00
Decanter, Cut Glass, Hobstars, Diamond Point, Fan, Handle, 6 In. 175.00
Decanter, Prism Pattern, Triple Ring Neck, Signed, C.1896, 14 1/2 In. 1900.00
Decanter, Whiskey, Green Overlay Cut To Clear, 1910 .... 445.00
Lamp, Cut Glass, Mushroom–Type Shade 545.00
Mayonnaise Set, Colonna, 3 Piece 160.00
Nappy, Anita, Cut Glass, 6 In. 85.00
Nappy, Radiant, Cut Glass, Handle, 6 In. 90.00
Pitcher, Allover Green Loops, Clear Loop Handle, Nash, 8 In. 285.00
Pitcher, Ellsmere Pattern, Signed, 7 1/2 In. 1250.00
Pitcher, Harvard, Cut Handle 355.00
Pitcher, Somerset Pattern, Signed, 8 3/4 In. 535.00
Pitcher, Zelda, Bulbous, Signed 450.00
Rose Bowl, Harvard Pattern, Footed, 4 1/2 X 6 In. 350.00
Salt & Pepper, Lay Down Egg, Blue, Columbian Exposition, 1893 .... 240.00
Toothpick, Little Lobe, Flower, Rim Dots, White Satin Glass 75.00
Toothpick, Little Lobe, Flowers & Leaves, White Satin Glass 95.00
Tray, Prism Pattern, Signed, 11 3/4 X 7 3/4 In. 1650.00
Tray, Spillane, Marked, 11 1/2 In. 1250.00
Tray, Variation of Star & Feather Pattern, 12 In. 500.00
Tumbler, Anita, Signed 210.00
Vase, Amberina, 7 7/8 In. 245.00
Vase, Amberina, 12 In. 585.00
Vase, Amberina, Art Glass, Honey Hollow Stem, Bulbous Cup, 11 1/4 In. 1000.00
Vase, Amberina, Fuchsia Shaded To Amber, 1917, 12 In. 585.00
Vase, Bud, Floral Cut & Engraved, 12 In. 160.00
Vase, Corinthian, Signed, 1896, 7 In. 195.00
Vase, Cut Glass, Hobstars, Fans & Diamond Point, Bowling Pin, 12 In. 350.00
Vase, Inverted Thumbprint, Signed, 14 In. 275.00
Vase, Trumpet, Harvard Pattern, Amethyst To Clear, 14 1/2 In. 225.00

Cigarettes became popular in the late nineteenth century and with the cigarette came matches and cigarette lighters. All types of lighters are collected, from solid gold to the first of the recent disposable lighters. Most examples found were made after 1940.

LIGHTER, Cigar, Attached Wick & Chain Cover, M. Stochelberg Co., Sterling 90.00
Cigar, Brass, Iron Base, Frosted Globe, 11 In. 225.00
Cigar, Bulldog, Figural, Cast Iron 45.00
Cigar, Counter, Bulldog, Cast Iron, 4 1/2 In. 85.00
Cigar, Laughing Horse, Figural 22.50
Cigar, Midland Jump Spark 425.00
Cigar, Neo–Greque, Anthemion Handle, Wick In Spout, Gorham, 1881 .... 440.00
Cigar, Rose Tiente, Baccarat, Sterling Top 125.00
Cigar, Telephone, Figural, Occupied Japan 95.00
Cigar, Tilt, W.C. Fields 175.00
Cigarette & Holder, Cowboy Boots, Both Right Feet, Pocket 30.00
Cigarette, 2 Pictures, University of Syracuse Medallion 35.00

Cigarette, Airplane, Chrome	70.00
Cigarette, Ambassador, Tank, Chrome, Pat. 1912	45.00
Cigarette, ASR, Cup, Tray, Table Set	30.00
Cigarette, ASR, Rhodium Plated, Cup, Table Set	20.00
Cigarette, Augusta, Light–O–Matic, 8 Colored Stones, Brass Sleeve	25.00
Cigarette, Baltimore Orioles, Gas Light, Pictures Bird	15.00
Cigarette, Barclay, Chrome, Green Alligator, England, Table	27.50
Cigarette, Beacon Parker, Watch On Side, German Silver	75.00
Cigarette, Beney, ICI Dyestuffs Division, Silver Plate, Table	30.00
Cigarette, Bowling Pin, Plastic	75.00
Cigarette, Braun, Matte Chrome, Germany, Pocket	20.00
Cigarette, Butane, Porsche Design	25.00
Cigarette, Camera Shape, Occupied Japan, Box	25.00
Cigarette, Canary, Musical, Smoke Gets In Your Eyes, Japan	15.00
Cigarette, Cartier, Oval, 20 Microns, Gas, France	125.00
Cigarette, Cartier, Silver Plate, Gas, Japan, Pocket	65.00
Cigarette, Chase, Brass Top, Black Plastic Base, USA, Table	35.00
Cigarette, CMC, Chrome, Blue & White Bird, Japan, Pocket	2.00
Cigarette, Colibri, Firebird Flipper, Green, Starburst Design, Japan	8.50
Cigarette, Colibri, Knife, Tortoise, Box, Japan	22.50
Cigarette, Colibri, Pendant On Chain, Gas, Japan	9.50
Cigarette, Cygnus, Pan American World Airlines, Japan, Table	20.00
Cigarette, Dimmer, Aluminum, Hexagonal, Pocket	9.50
Cigarette, Dunhill, Auto Rollalite, Sterling Silver	55.00
Cigarette, Dunhill, Rollalite, Silver Plate, Swiss	55.00
Cigarette, Dunhill, Service, Black Enameled, USA	15.00
Cigarette, Dunhill, Silent Flame, Chrome Airplane, Battery Operated	250.00
Cigarette, Dunhill, Silvered Metal, 1930s	80.00
Cigarette, Dunhill, Talldoby, England, Table	175.00
Cigarette, Dupont, 20 Microns, Gas, France, Pocket	150.00
Cigarette, Dupont, Gas, Short, Initialed, Pocket	125.00
Cigarette, Dur–O–Liter, Windproof, Aluminum, Black Plastic	17.50
Cigarette, Durolite, Gold Aluminum, Brown Plastic Bottom, Pocket	3.50
Cigarette, Elgin, Skier Picture, USA, Pocket	20.00
Cigarette, Elgin–American, Pocket, Silver Plate, Intials	12.50
Cigarette, Evans, Art Deco	12.00
Cigarette, Evans, Baron, Nickel Plated	8.50
Cigarette, Evans, Brushed Chrome, White Marble Base	8.50
Cigarette, Evans, Built Into Case	8.00
Cigarette, Evans, Clipper	12.00
Cigarette, Evans, Gold Plated, China Base, Ivory Color, Table	8.00
Cigarette, Evans, Gold Plated, Pearl Strips Around Body, Pocket	7.50
Cigarette, Evans, Musical, Anniversary Waltz, Chrome Over Brass, USA	25.00
Cigarette, Evans, Strips of Mother–of–Pearl, Pocket	8.50
Cigarette, Eveready, Nickel Plate, 8 Shields, Germany, Pocket	27.50
Cigarette, Fumulax, Flashlight, Chrome, Battery, Box, Germany	10.00
Cigarette, Gold Golf Bag & Clubs	35.00
Cigarette, Goldenwheel, Tank, Chrome, Painted, Pat. 1928, USA	12.50
Cigarette, Hamilton, Knight, Chrome, 8 1/2 In.	25.00
Cigarette, Helicopter, Twin Rotors Fold Up, 7 1/2 In.	45.00
Cigarette, Heliocopter, Art Deco Style	30.00
Cigarette, Horsehead, Figural	12.00
Cigarette, Hot Lips, Signed, Table	350.00
Cigarette, Ivory Walrus Tusk, Figure On Front, Round	125.00
Cigarette, Klik, Touchwand, Chrome, Auto Spring, France	100.00
Cigarette, Knight, Penciliter, Chrome, Auto Spring Action, Japan	40.00
Cigarette, Kreisler, Butane, Visible Fuel Supply, Crystal	27.50
Cigarette, Little Billboard, Chrome, Blue Sunoco, Japan, Pocket	8.50
Cigarette, Made From Bullet, Plastic Base	15.00
Cigarette, Man Bowling, Figural, Porcelain, Aamco Import, 1962	75.00
Cigarette, Marathon, Comb–Compact, Cream Enameled, Puppies, USA	40.00
Cigarette, Monte Carlo, Roulette Game, Chrome, Japan	17.50
Cigarette, Musical, When Smoke Gets In Yur Eyes, Pocket	150.00
Cigarette, Negbaur, Cannon, Cast Metal, Bronze Color	37.50

Cigarette, Park, Cancer Sign, Sterling Silver 35.00
Cigarette, Park, Sherman Tank, Black Trim, Table 22.50
Cigarette, Parker Flaminaire, Parker Pen Co. 75.00
Cigarette, Penguin, Chrome, Windshield, Sterling Band, Pocket 12.00
Cigarette, Penguin, Machine Gun, Chrome, Gas, F.N. Browning 42.50
Cigarette, Perfect, Camera, Leica, On Tripod, Chrome, Japan 35.00
Cigarette, Perky, Engraved Japanese Scene, Silver, Gold Band, Pocket 10.00
Cigarette, Phillip Morris 8.00
Cigarette, Pistol, Figural, Abalone Grip, Occupied Japan 45.00
Cigarette, Pres-A-Lite, Brown Bakelite, Attaches In Car, USA 55.00
Cigarette, Queen Mary, Figural, Silver Plated, 10 In. 220.00
Cigarette, Reliance, Chrome, Baier's Amoco, Korea, Pocket 2.00
Cigarette, Remco, Aluminum, USA, Pocket 4.00
Cigarette, Ritepoint, Chrome, Black Plastic, Chesterfield, Pocket 17.50
Cigarette, Rolstar, Chrome Plated, Blue Aluminum Base, 3 Legs, Table 12.50
Cigarette, Ronson, Blue Enamel, Carrying Case, Box 42.00
Cigarette, Ronson, Chrome, Brown, Art Metal Works 18.00
Cigarette, Ronson, Colonial, Silver Plated 65.00
Cigarette, Ronson, Crown, Silver Plate 9.50
Cigarette, Ronson, Custom Comb, Chrome, Black Enamel, 1930s 65.00
Cigarette, Ronson, De-Light, Chrome, Brown Leather, Pat. Jan.17, 1928 .... 20.00
Cigarette, Ronson, Deco-Comb, Chrome, Black Enameled, Initial S 30.00
Cigarette, Ronson, Georgian, Silver Plated, USA 15.00
Cigarette, Ronson, Hound Dog, Figural, Chrome, Art Metal Works, 1935 .... 150.00
Cigarette, Ronson, Mayfair, Gold Plated 20.00
Cigarette, Ronson, Mayfair, Table 25.00
Cigarette, Ronson, Nude Top Half, Heads I Win, Pocket 15.00
Cigarette, Ronson, Penciliter, Box 95.00
Cigarette, Ronson, Penciliter, Chrome Top, USA 22.50
Cigarette, Ronson, Penciliter, Rhodium, Blue Velvet Case, USA 37.50
Cigarette, Ronson, Table 45.00
Cigarette, Ronson, Table, Queen Anne, 1940s 8.00
Cigarette, Ronson, With 2 Ashtrays 150.00
Cigarette, Rowenta, Nickel Plated, Black, Dragon, Germany, Table 37.50
Cigarette, Sir Douglas Haig, World War I 45.00
Cigarette, Stratoflame, Butane Cartridge, Label, Pocket 8.50
Cigarette, Stratoflame, Chrome, Butane, Pocket 8.50
Cigarette, Tall-Boy, Chrome, Auto Spring Action, Japan, Table 35.00
Cigarette, Thorens, Art Deco, Orange Enamel, 1930s 150.00
Cigarette, Thorens, Chrome Auto Spring Action, Swiss, Pocket 7.00
Cigarette, Win, Electronic, Gas, 12 Volt Battery, Japan 18.50
Cigarette, World War II, Okinawa, Sterling Silver 20.00
Cigarette, Zippo, 50th Anniversary, Dell 35.00
Cigarette, Zippo, Chrome, G.G. Blaisdel, 40th Anniversary, 1972 .... 50.00
Cigarette, Zippo, Kendall Gasoline 12.00
Cigarette, Zippo, Skelly Gasoline 15.00
Cigarette, Zippo, Slim, USA 8.50
Cigarette, Zippo, Standard, Chrome, 1950 .... 4.00
Cigarette, Zippo, Venetian, Engraved Design, 1978 .... 8.00

> Lightning rod balls are collected for their variety of shape and color.
> These glass balls were at the center of the rod that was attached to
> the roof of a house or barn to avoid lightning damage.

LIGHTNING ROD, Ball, Milk Glass, Amethyst 17.50
Ball, Sun-Colored Amethyst 15.00
Blue Ball, Arrow, Tin Cow, Black, 52 1/2 In. 150.00
Blue Insulator Ball, Vane Arrow, Zinc Cow, 38 1/2 In. 195.00
Hearts & Balls, Red Leaded Glass, Ball Front Frame 165.00
Reyburn Hunter Kite Tail, Daisy Pattern, Red Glass 160.00
Shooting Star, Glass Tail 105.00
Star In Diamond, Brass Embossed Kretzer Frame 240.00
Vane Arrow, Blue Insulator Ball, Zinc Roadster, 59 In. 50.00

Limoges porcelain has been made in Limoges, France, since the mid–nineteenth century. Fine porcelains were made by many factories including Haviland, Ahrenfeldt, Guerin, Pouyat, Elite, and others. Modern porcelains are being made at Limoges and the word "Limoges" as part of the mark is not an indication of age. Haviland is listed as a separate category in this book.

LIMOGES, Biscuit Jar, Anchor Shape, Rope Handle	55.00
Bowl, Art Nouveau Design, 4 Corner Panels, 8 3/4 X 9 3/4 In.	24.00
Bowl, Cover, Blue Asters, Gold, 4–Footed, 2 Handles, 1895, 12 X 7 In.	55.00
Bowl, Multicolor Flowers, Light Blue Ground, Gold Trim, 10 In.	150.00
Bowl, Pink Roses, Hand Painted, Green, Oblong, 13 1/2 In.	45.00
Box, Cigarette, Hinged Cover, Matchbox Holder, Gold Bird, 5 1/2 In.	75.00
Box, Molded Florals, Butterfly, Hinged Cover, Oval, Marked, 3 1/2 In.	95.00
Brooch, Beautiful Woman, C.1900	125.00
Butter, Cover, Floral Rose Spray, 3 Piece	45.00
Cache Pot, Male & Female Pheasants On Front, Gold Handles, 9 In.	225.00
Cake Plate, Hand Painted Gold Flowers, 10 In.	40.00
Cake Plate, Pine Needles, Oak Leaves & Acorns, Green, 11 In.	45.00
Cake Plate, Pink Roses, Dark Green Ground	55.00
Cake Plate, Pink, Yellow & Purple Mums, Signed, 15 X 13 In.	115.00
Celery Dish, Strawberries, Gold Trim	48.00
Charger, Daisies, Hand Painted, Pale Green, 12 1/2 In.	35.00
Charger, Egyptian, Gold, 13 1/2 In.	185.00
Charger, Multicolor Flowers, Signed, 13 In.	115.00
Charger, Pink & Yellow Roses, Gold Border	70.00
Chocolate Pot, Embossed Lily–of–The–Valley, 12 In.	195.00
Chocolate Pot, Purple Violets, Green Leaves, Cream, Signed, 13 In.	325.00
Chocolate Set, Allover Roses & Gold, 5 Cups & Saucers	275.00
Chocolate Set, Coronet, Ribbon Handle, 5 Piece	365.00
Chocolate Set, White, Pink Roses, 11 1/4 In. Pot, 11 Piece	315.00
Compote, Floral, Sterling Overlay, 4 1/2 In.	38.00
Cracker Jar, Violets, Green, Gold Band	40.00
Cup & Saucer, Bouillon, Pink Flowers, 2 Handles, 6 Piece	45.00
Dresser Set, Butterflies, Gold Webbing, Hand Painted, 1895, 6 Piece	175.00
Dresser Set, Pink Roses, Tray, Cologne & Hair Receiver	95.00
Dresser Set, Roses, Perfume Bottle, Powder & Pin Box, 4 Piece	95.00
Fish Plate, Gold Rococo, Scalloped Rim, Signed, 9 1/2 In.	60.00
Game Plate, Pheasants, Quail, Woodland Background, 10 1/2 In., Pair	350.00
Game Set, Golden Pheasant On Tray, Birds In Forest, 7 Piece	610.00
Game Set, Pheasants, Gilt Rims, Platter 17 X 11 In., 13 Piece	600.00
Jam Jar, White, Gold Trim	125.00
Jardiniere, Yellow Rose, Purple Flowers, 4 Baroque Feet, 5 X 9 In.	275.00
Mug, 2–Color Grapes & Leaves, Multicolor Ground, 5 In.	85.00
Mug, Cherries, Large	48.00
Mug, Indian Portrait	300.00
Mustache Cup, Autumn Leaves, Berries	65.00
Oyster Plate, Lavender, White & Gold, 8 1/4 In.	125.00
Oyster Plate, Pink, White & Gold, 8 1/4 In.	145.00
Pitcher, Art Deco, Hand Painted	43.00
Pitcher, Cherries & Branches, Hand Painted, 5 In.	65.00
Pitcher, Floral, 2 Mugs	395.00
Pitcher, Roses, Hand Painted, Gilded Handle, 10 In.	140.00
Plaque, Country Scene, Framed, M.H. Bechter, Green Mark, 8 X 11 In.	600.00
Plaque, Dancing Couple, Scalloped & Gold Rim, Signed, 12 1/2 In.	225.00
Plaque, Fish, Gold Rococo Trim, Signed, 10 1/4 In., Pair	125.00
Plaque, Game, Pheasants, Scalloped, Artist Signed, 10 In.	65.00 To 85.00
Plaque, Grapes & Watermelon, Hand Painted, Gold Rim, 11 In.	75.00
Plaque, Portrait of Girl, Artist Signed, 13 3/4 In.	225.00
Plaque, Portrait, French Girl, Feathered Hat, A. Dussou, 15 In.	650.00
Plate, Birds, Hand Painted, Brown Tones, Art Deco, 4 Piece	100.00
Plate, Castle & Moat Scene Center, Scalloped, 9 1/2 In.	125.00
Plate, Cherry Clusters, Branches, Gold Scalloped, 9 1/4 In.	30.00
Plate, D'Arceau	18.00

Plate, Deer & Doe, Scalloped Edge, Coronet, 10 In.	100.00
Plate, Elite, Flowers Transfer, Gold, Pierced Handles	35.00
Plate, Fish, Hand Painted, Rococo Gold Rim, 9 1/4 In.	30.00
Plate, Fox & 2 Birds, Gold Rococo Scalloped, Signed, 12 1/2 In.	175.00
Plate, Fox, Birds In Snow, Gold Rococo, Artist, 12 1/2 In.	175.00
Plate, Game Bird Center, Gold Rococo Border, 12 1/2 In.	225.00
Plate, Game Bird, Scalloped, Embossed, 10 In.	65.00
Plate, Gold Band, Scroll, Teal, Ruffled, 1890, 9 In., 12 Pc.	375.00
Plate, Gold Flowers & Leaves, Handles, 10 In.	52.00
Plate, Hunting Dog Scene	900.00
Plate, Mallard Duck, Rococo Edge, 16 In.	185.00
Plate, Neoclassical Greek Center Medallion, Yellow, C.1900, Piar	75.00
Plate, Pale Pink Roses, White Ground, Reticulated, 8 1/2 In.	30.00
Plate, Pheasant, 10 In.	75.00
Plate, Pink Roses On White, Reticulated, 8 1/2 In.	30.00
Plate, Roses, Waterfall, Coronet	500.00
Plate, Wood Scene, Brown Bird, Vines, Scalloped, 19th Century	50.00
Punch Bowl, Pink Flowers, White Ground, Gold Tracery, 14 1/4 In.	295.00
Punch Bowl, Yellow Birds, Blue Flowers, Gold Band, 1915, 12 1/2 In.	350.00
Relish, Pearlized Woman's Bust, Pastel Ground, GDA, 9 1/2 In.	40.00
Sauceboat, Underplate, Gold Rococo, Signed	65.00
Shaving Mug, Hand Painted Portrait	65.00
Sugar & Creamer, Roses, Gold, EAP In Script, Pedestal, 7 1/2 In.	95.00
Tankard, Grape Clusters, Hand Painted, Signed Ariez, 1909, 15 In.	450.00
Tankard, Iris, Signed, 13 1/2 In.	225.00
Tankard, Monk, Glasses On Tip of Nose, Wine Bottle, 14 1/2 In.	245.00
Tea Caddy, Portrait	98.00
Tea Set, Pink Roses, Gold Handles & Trim, 3 Piece	95.00
Teapot, Baskets of Red Flowers, Gold Handle & Spout	55.00
Teapot, Floral	29.00
Teapot, Old Abbey	45.00
Tray, Clover, Round, 12 In.	100.00
Tray, Dresser, Allover Gold, White Ground, 9 1/2 In.	35.00
Tray, Dresser, Rose, Pale Green, Artist, 11 X 7 In.	110.00
Tray, Pheasant, Hand Painted, 9 X 14 1/2 In.	185.00
Tureen, Cover, Floral Sprays, Gold Handles	75.00
Vase, Enameled Full-Blown Roses, On Copper, C.1920, 12 In.	5225.00
Vase, Iris, 2 Women, Watching Swans, Blue, 24 In.	900.00
Vase, Magnolias, Hand Painted, Green & Gold Handles, 12 1/2 In.	225.00

In 1927, Charles Lindbergh, the aviator, became the first man to make a nonstop solo flight across the Atlantic Ocean. He was a national hero. In 1932, his son was kidnapped and murdered, and Lindbergh was again the center of public interest. He died in 1974. All types of Lindbergh memorabilia are collected.

LINDBERGH, Bookends, Bronzed Washed Iron	87.00
Bookmark, Woven Silk	40.00
Box, Pencil, Picture of Airplane, Lucky Lindy, Red Tin	65.00
Coin, Souvenir, Lucky Lindbergh, 1927, 1 1/4 In.	30.00
Medallion, First Flight, Anniversary, Bronze	12.00
Newspaper, Cincinnati Times-Star, Fly Pacific, 1931	9.00
Perfume Bottle, Label, Plane, Lucky Lindy, 2 1/4 In.	15.00
Photograph, Lindbergh's Plane, Silver Colored Frame, 9 X 11 In.	18.00
Postcard, Airplane Carried By Horse, Wagon, St.Louis, 1927, Unused	25.00
Print, Lindbergh & Plane	5.00
Tapestry, New York To Paris, France, 1929	300.00
Watch Fob, New York To Paris	75.00

Lithophanes are porcelain pictures made by casting clay in layers of various thicknesses. When a piece is held to the light, a picture of light and shadow is seen through it. Most lithophanes date from the 1825-75 period. A few are still being made. Many lithophanes sold today were originally panels for lampshades.

LITHOPHANE, Boy Photographer, Taking Picture of Girl, 4 1/4 X 5 1/8 In.	135.00

Candle Shield, Woman, Carrying Basket, 6 1/8 X 5 1/8 In.	225.00
Cup & Saucer, Dragon, Oriental	12.50
Cup, Gold Painted Leaves, Tyrolean Man With Zither	65.00
Dreaming of Her Wedding, Bridal Dress, 4 1/4 X 5 1/8 In.	135.00
Farm Woman, Goat At Side, Rake Over Shoulder, 4 3/8 X 5 1/4 In.	135.00
Girl Held By Gentleman On Edge of Stream, 4 1/4 X 5 In.	135.00
Night–Light, Teapot Shape, Scrolled Feet, Boy & Girl, Chicken	1050.00
Ornament, Christmas, Santa Claus, Conical, Inside Light	95.00
Panel, Clegyman Preaching To Children, Electrified, 12 X 12 In.	95.00
Panel, Man & Trees In Foreground, Framed, 8 5/8 X 10 In.	245.00
Panel, Men Looking At Maiden In Hammock, Framed, 8 X 7 In.	230.00
Panel, Reflections In Lake, Mountains, Forest, 6 X 7 1/2 In.	135.00
Panel, Romeo & Juliet, Balcony, Stained Glass Frame, 11 X 9 In.	300.00
Panel, Woman, Instructing Girl In Sewing, 7 1/4 X 6 In.	95.00
Panel, Woman, Seated At Desk, Eagle, Framed, 8 1/4 X 7 1/4 In.	225.00
Panel, Woman, Seated On Porch, Under Arbor, 6 X 4 3/4 In.	140.00
Panel, Woman, Seated, Girl At Her Knee, Framed, 7 3/4 X 7 In.	200.00
Shade, Children & Animals, 5 Panels, Signed, 1860s, 3 X 3 X 6 In.	575.00
Stein, Munich Child, Radishes, 1/4 Liter	400.00
Stein, Porcelain, Enameled Crest, Germany, 9 1/2 In.	522.00
Tea Warmer, 4 Panels, Color	495.00

Liverpool, England, was the site of several pottery and porcelain factories from 1716 to 1785. Some earthenware was made with transfer decorations. Sadler and Green made print–decorated wares from 1756. Many of the pieces were made for the American market and feature patriotic emblems, such as eagles, flags, and other special–interest motifs.

LIVERPOOL, Mug, Black Transfer, George Washington, 5 7/8 In.	2200.00
Mug, Black Transfer, Soldier & Young Woman, Verse, C.1800, 6 In.	330.00
Mug, Jenny's Farewell, Song of Robin, Black Transfer	265.00
Mug, Masonic, Verse, 5 In.	125.00
Picture, American Eagle On Cannon, Flag, Creamware, 7 3/4 In.	1500.00
Pitcher, Union of French & American Republics, 9 1/4 In.	5170.00

LLADRÓ®

Juan, Jose, and Vicente Lladro opened a ceramics workshop in Almacera, Spain, in 1951. They soon began making figurines in a distinctive, elongated style. In 1958 the factory moved to Tabernes Blanques, Spain. The company makes stoneware and porcelain vases and figurines in limited and nonlimited editions.

LLADRO, Figurine, Anniversary Waltz, No.1372	290.00
Figurine, Bride & Groom, 7 1/4 In.	185.00

 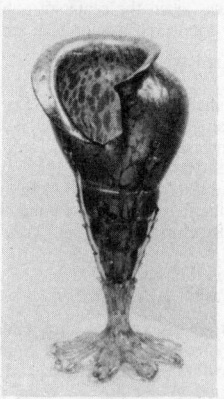 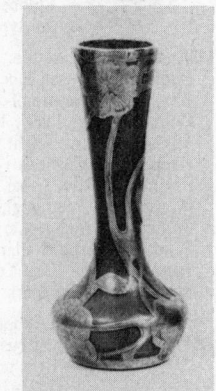

Loetz, Vase, Opalescent Design, Blue–Green, 9 In.

Loetz, Vase, Shell, Blue Oil Spot Design, Green, 12 1/2 In.

Loetz, Vase, Variegated Blue, Floral, Silver Overlay, 6 1/4 In.

Figurine, Chrysanthemum, No.4990	168.00
Figurine, Court Jester	450.00
Figurine, Girl, Manicuring Nails, 7 3/4 In.	125.00
Figurine, Nude, No.J 22 N, 19 In.	600.00
Figurine, Oriental Spring, No.4988	168.00
Figurine, Pretty Pickings, No.5222	70.00
Figurine, Woman & Chickens	85.00

Locke Art is a trademark found on glass of the early twentieth century. Joseph Locke worked at many English and American firms. He designed and etched his own glass in Pittsburgh, Pennsylvania, starting in the 1880s. Some pieces were marked "Joe Locke," but most were marked with the words "Locke Art." The mark is hidden in the pattern on the glass.

LOCKE ART, Vase, Etched Grapes, Leaves, Vines, Vaseline, 9 In.	125.00
Vase, Poppies, Flared & Ruffled, 7 1/2 In.	185.00

Johann Loetz bought a glassworks in Austria in 1840. He died in 1848 and his widow ran the company; then in 1879, his grandson took over. Loetz glass was varied. Most collectors recognize the iridescent gold glass similar to Tiffany, but many other types were made. The firm closed during World War II.

LOETZ, Bottle, Iridescent Red, Pinched Form, Metal Rim, 4 1/2 In.	50.00
Bowl, Green Iridescent, Ruffled, 8 In.	85.00
Bowl, Green Iridescent, Ruffled, Pewter Stand, 9 In.	172.00
Bowl, Green, Lobed, Dimpled Bark, 6 1/2 In.	88.00
Bowl, Purple Iridescent, Black & White Webbed, Floral, 10 1/2 In.	335.00
Bowl, Shell Form, Variegated Red & Gold, 10 In.	165.00
Bowl, Variegated Red & Iridescent Gold, Lobed Shell, Ruffled, 10 In.	165.00
Cornucopia, Floral, Silver Pedestal Base, Green Iridescent, 8 In.	250.00
Dish, Nut, Green Iridescent	90.00
Inkwell, Blue Iridescent, Random Lava Design, 5 1/2 X 2 1/4 In.	550.00
Jar, Green Opalescent Webbing, Silver Plated, 5 In.	85.00
Lamp, Peg, Green Iridescent Font, Enameled, Ruffled Shade, 12 1/2 In.	350.00
Loving Cup, Rainbow Pink, Yellow, Silver Overlay, 3 Handles, 4 1/4 In.	1750.00
Loving Cup, Silver Overlay, 4 1/4 In.	1750.00
Pitcher, Syrup, Green, Threaded Design	100.00
Plate, Gold Iridescent, Signed, 9 1/2 In.	375.00
Urn, Metal Thistle Leaves, Metal Mount	695.00
Vase, Amethyst Iridescent Ground, Gold & Purple, 14 1/2 In.	550.00
Vase, Amethyst Iridescent, Barklike Texture, Metal Rim, Signed, 8 In.	60.00
Vase, Art Glass, Fall Colors Marquety, Green, Quatrefoil, 5 1/2 In.	300.00
Vase, Black Webbed, Frosted Ground, Bulbous, Tall Neck, 8 In.	132.00
Vase, Blue Oil Spot, Green, Applied Ribbing, Star Foot, 12 1/2 In.	2145.00
Vase, Blue–Green, Floral Design, Sterling, 6 1/4 In.	990.00
Vase, Blue–Green, Gold & Purple, Amethyst Ground, Signed, 14 1/2 In.	550.00
Vase, Bottle Shape, Random Threading, Green, 9 3/4 In.	250.00
Vase, Brown Oil Spot Iridescent, Signed, 7 In.	375.00
Vase, Conch Shell Form, Domed Base, Emerald Green, C.1900, 9 In.	2550.00
Vase, Corset, Spider Web, Peacock, Green Iridescent, 14 In.	335.00
Vase, Dimpled Base, Scalloped Neck, Green & Purple, 7 1/2 In.	195.00
Vase, Flaring Rim, Bulbous Base, Green Iridescent, 8 3/4 In.	375.00
Vase, Flower Shape, Green, Art Glass, Iridized, 9 1/2 In.	150.00
Vase, Gold Iridescent, 6 In.	200.00
Vase, Gold, Oil Spot Iridescent, Art Glass, 4 1/8 In.	65.00
Vase, Green Iridescent, Applied Metal Rim, Art Glass, 6 3/4 In.	60.00
Vase, Green Iridescent, Purple Threaded, Art Glass, Pinched, 10 In.	365.00
Vase, Green Iridescent, Silver Overlay, 5 In.	450.00
Vase, Green Iridescent, Web–Like, Tall Neck, Compressed Form, 9 In.	80.00
Vase, Green Spot, Silver Leaves, 3 In.	275.00
Vase, Green, Applied Trails, Flared, Art Glass, 4 1/2 In.	110.00
Vase, Green, Rust, Orange, Brown Marquetry Inlay, 5 1/2 In.	300.00
Vase, Iridescent Feather Pull, Salmon Ground, 13 1/4 In.	5000.00
Vase, Iridescent, Signed, 4 1/2 In.	150.00

Vase, Iridescent, Threaded, 6 In. 175.00
Vase, Iridized, Rubena Verde, Art Glass, 9 In. 95.00
Vase, Jack–In–The–Pulpit, Red Iridescent, Silver Swirls, 14 In. 1750.00
Vase, Jack–In–The–Pulpit, Threaded, Signed, 8 In. 1200.00
Vase, Oil Spot, Art Deco, Gold Tracery, 6 In. 525.00
Vase, Opalescent Design, Blue–Green, 9 In. ....*Illus* 200.00
Vase, Opalescent, Pull Design, Blue–Green, Ruffled, Waisted 200.00
Vase, Overlay of Mulberry, Tulip Tree, Signed, C.1900, 13 3/4 In. 1980.00
Vase, Pinch Design, Blue & Brown, Signed, 7 In. 3000.00
Vase, Purple Iridescent, Dimpled, 7 In. 40.00
Vase, Rainbow Hues, Signed, 13 1/2 In. 750.00
Vase, Red Crackle, 9 1/4 In. 850.00
Vase, Ruby, Pinched Tricorner, Art Glass, Iridescent, 7 In. 95.00
Vase, Shell, Blue Oil Spot Design, Green, 12 1/2 In. ....*Illus* 2145.00
Vase, Stick Form, Gourd Top, Amber Base, Zigzag Lines, Signed, 12 In. 2600.00
Vase, Threaded Prunts, Silver Overlay, Signed, 6 In. 250.00
Vase, Trumpet, Green, Cream, Bulbous Cup, Everted Lip, 11 1/4 In. 125.00
Vase, Twisted, 12 1/2 In. 295.00
Vase, Variegated Blue, Floral, Silver Overlay, 6 1/4 In. ....*Illus* 990.00

 The Lone Ranger is a fictional character introduced on the radio in 1932. Over three thousand shows were produced before the series ended in 1954. In 1938, the first Lone Ranger movie was made. Television shows were started in 1949 and are still seen on some stations. The Lone Ranger appears on many products and was even the name of a restaurant chain for several years.

LONE RANGER, 2 Holsters, With Gun Belt 8.00
Badge Set, Display Card, Japan, 1950s, 12 Badges 75.00
Badge, Secret Compartment 30.00
Badge, With Gun, Die Cast, Red Ribbon, 1950s 30.00
Bandana 75.00
Belt Buckle 8.00
Belt, Glow In Dark, Instructions, Box 275.00
Blackout Kit, Mailer 75.00
Blotter, Bond Bread, 1939 .... 20.00
Book Bag, National Leather Mfg. Co. 46.00
Book, Menace of Murder Valley, Big Little Book, 1937 .... 20.00
Book, Secret Weapon, Big Little Book 16.50
Book, Tattoo Picture, Japan, 1960s 5.00
Box, Cutout Off 9.50
Bullet, Compass In Bottom 39.50
Chair, Inflatable 25.00
Coloring Book 12.00
Comic Book, Dell, Vol.1, No.114, Dec. 1957 .... 10.00
Comic Book, Disguise, 1958 .... 15.00
Comic Book, Story of Silver, Cheerios Premium, 16 Page, 1954 .... 15.00
Comic Book, Tonto, 1954 .... 10.00
Cup, Photo, Silver 15.00
Deputy Kit 12.00
Display, Little Silver, Advertising Cobakco Bread, 11 X 14 In. 145.00
Doll, & Horse, Silver, Box, 1975 .... 65.00
Doll, Tonto, Clothes, Moccasins, 1973 .... 35.00
Figure, Hartland 24.00
Figure, Lone Ranger, On Silver, 1970, Large 85.00
Figurine, Chalkware, Carnival .... 40.00 To 45.00
Flashlight Ring 65.00
Flashlight, Box 100.00
Flashlight, Signal, Siren, Tin Litho, Usalite, 1950s 125.00
Game, Box, 1938 .... 20.00
Game, Guarding Mail Train, Tin 35.00
Game, Hi Yo Silver, Parker Bros., 1938 .... 65.00
Game, Legend of Lone Ranger, Milton Bradley, 1980 .... 15.00 To 25.00
Game, Target, Tin, Metal Dart Gun, Square, 9 1/2 In. 55.00
Gauntlets 25.00

Globe, Snow 50.00
Glove Box, Yankiboy Playclothers, 1947, 11 X 10 X 5 In. 95.00
Guitar, Box 100.00
Holder, Toothbrush, 1938 .... 95.00
Jail Keys, Esquire Toy, Metal, 1950s 65.00
Kit, Lone Ranger & Silver, Plastic Figures, 1974, Box 23.50
Knife, Pocket 65.00
Lantern 48.00
Lunch Box, Legend of Lone Ranger .... 15.00 To 20.00
Lunch Box, Thermos, 1980 .... 25.00
March of Comics, No. 208, Giveaway, Clayton Moore Cover, 1960 .... 45.00
Mask, Belt, Silver Bullet, Jail Keys & Badge On Original Card 195.00
Model, Tonto, Comic Story, 3–D Mural, Aurora, Sealted, 1974 .... 40.00
Movie Set, Acme 40.00
Mystery Box No. 1, Wheaties Panel 45.00
Mystery Box, No. 6, Wheaties Panel 45.00
Mystery Box, No.10, Wheaties Panel 45.00
Outfit, Official, 1939 .... 88.00
Paperweight, Roundup 40.00
Pedometer .... 15.50 To 25.00
Pedometer, Box 60.00
Pen & Pencil, Progressive Products, Standing Figure With Gun 350.00
Pencil, Bubble 22.00
Pencil, Bullet, Metal 10.00
Penknife, Silver Bullet 45.00
Photograph, Lone Ranger, Christmas, Gimbels, 1938 .... 12.00
Photograph, Marked Warner Bros., Publicity 9.00
Pistol, Clicker 25.00
Pistol, Smoking, Click, Gray Plastic, Marx, 1950s 125.00
Poster, 1966 .... 10.00
Print, Lone Ranger Inc., Color Litho, 1947, 3 1/4 X 5 1/4 In. 10.00
Puppet, Push–Up, Lone Ranger On Silver, Kohner 95.00
Record Player, Wooden 185.00
Record, Adventures of Lone Ranger, Decca, 1951 .... 18.00
Ribbon & Horseshoe 35.00
Rifle, Click, Marx 85.00
Ring Toss, Lone Ranger Rocks On Silver, Rosebud Art, 1946 .... 325.00
Ring, Atom Bomb .... 45.00 To 80.00
Ring, Cheerios Premium, Six–Shooter, 1940s 55.00
Ring, Filmstrip, Film, Instructions & Box 175.00
Ring, Flashlight, Complete With Battery & Instructions 85.00
Ring, Secret Compartment, No Pictures 185.00
Rocking Horse, Vinyl, Stuffed, Marked Hi Yo Silver, 16 In. 185.00
Scarf, Black 25.00
School Satchel, 1940 .... 48.00
Silver Bullet, Secret Compartment .... 12.00 To 35.00
Skirt, Girl's 30.00
Snow Globe, Lone Ranger Roping Calf, Green Base, 1939 .... 65.00
Spoon, Silver, Lone Ranger & Silver At Top, 1938 .... 35.00
Suspenders, Tonto, Silver Guns 450.00
Target Game, Marx, Box 125.00
Target Gun Set, Lone Ranger & Tonto, Package, 1985 .... 5.00
Target Set, Bull's Eye On 1 Side, Ranger On Other, 1938 .... 125.00
Tattoo Transfers, Bubble Gum Wrappers, 1960s, Set of 4 .... 25.00
Tie & Slide 45.00
Tin, First Aid, 1938 .... 25.00
Toy, Ranger On Trigger, Marx, Windup, Box 750.00
Vest & Chaps, Official Outfit, Box 125.00
Wallet, 1940s 40.00
Watch Fob, Holster 15.00
Watch, Box, 1940 .... 40.00
Watch, Mask, Badge Set, Japan, 1950s 70.00
Wrapper, Bread, Wax, Cabako, Pioneer, 1930s, 3 X 19 In. 85.00
Wristwatch, 1939 .... 245.00

The Longwy Workshop of Longwy, France, first made ceramic wares in 1798. The workshop is still in business. Most of the ceramic pieces found today are glazed with many colors to resemble cloisonne or other enameled metal. The factory used a variety of marks.

LONGWY, Box, 4 In. 250.00
  Plate, Enameled Floral, 9 In. 95.00
  Tray, Enameled, 11 1/2 In. 85.00

The Lonhuda Pottery Company of Steubenville, Ohio, was organized in 1892 by William Long, W. H. Hunter, and Alfred Day. Brown underglaze slip–decorated pottery was made. The firm closed in 1896. The company used many marks; the earliest included the letters "LPCO."

LONHUDA, Vase, Green Leaves, 8 1/2 In. 175.00

Lotus Ware was made by the Knowles, Taylor & Knowles Company of East Liverpool, Ohio, from 1890 to 1900. Lotus Ware is a thin, Belleek–like porcelain. It was sometimes decorated outside the factory. Other types of ceramics that were made by the Knowles, Taylor & Knowles Company are listed under "KTK."

LOTUS WARE, Dish, Shell, Gold Enameled, Signed, 5 In. 1250.00
  Vase, Dark Green, 2 Scroll Handles 2800.00

Low art tiles were made by the J. and J. G. Low Art Tile Works of Chelsea, Massachusetts, from 1877 to 1902. A variety of art and other tiles were made. Some of the tiles were made by a process called "natural," some were hand–modeled, and some made mechanically.

LOW, Tile, Abe Lincoln, No Beard, George Washington, Green Glaze, 4 X 6 In. 185.00
  Tile, Greek Profile, Framed, Pair 150.00

The Lowestoft factory in Suffolk, England, worked from 1757 to 1802. They made many commemorative gift pieces and small, dated, inscribed pieces of soft paste porcelain.

    LOWESTOFT, see also Chinese Export
LOWESTOFT, Basket, Blue, White, Flowers, Border, 1770, 5 1/2 In. 1200.00
  Creamer, Fluted, C.1780, 4 In. 1000.00
  Cup & Saucer, Chinese Style Transfer Decoration, 1780 .... 450.00
  Cup, Blue Decoration, House, Tree, Handle, 1790 .... 150.00
    LOY–NEL–ART, see McCoy

Lunch pails and lunch boxes have been used to carry lunches to school or work since the nineteenth century. Today, most collectors want either early tobacco advertising boxes or children's lunch boxes made since the 1930s. The original Thermos bottle must be inside the children's boxes for the collector to consider them complete.

LUNCH BOX, 6 Million Dollar Man, 1974 .... 5.00 To 7.00
  A Team, Thermos 23.00
  Adam–12, Thermos, 1972 .... 35.00 To 50.00
  Addams Family 35.00
  Addams Family, Thermos 55.00
  Alice In Wonderland, Thermos 35.00
  Annie Oakley, Thermos, 1955 .... 40.00
  Astronaut, Thermos, Steel Dome, 1960s .... 65.00 To 100.00
  Atom Ant, Thermos 100.00
  Bagley's Wild Fruit Tobacco .... 110.00 To 125.00
  Barbie & Francie 45.00
  Barbie, 1962 .... 75.00
  Batman 60.00
  Beverly Hillbillies .... 20.00 To 75.00
  Bionic Woman 25.00
  Blondie, 1969 .... 65.00

Bonanza .... 20.00 To 50.00
Burley Boy Tobacco 1750.00
Campus Queen, 1967 .... 55.00
Canadian Pacific Railroad .... 30.00 To 40.00
Casey Jones 45.00
Central Union Cut Plug 20.00
Central Union Tobacco, Round Corners .... 45.00 To 50.00
Charlie's Angels, 1978 .... 15.00 To 25.00
Circus Wagon 20.00
Circus, Tin, Oval, 1930s 60.00
Close Encounters 25.00
Cracker Jack .... 20.00 To 30.00
Daniel Boone, Fess Parker, 1965 .... 35.00 To 55.00
Disneyland Castle 80.00
Disneyland Monorail 95.00
Dixie Kid Cut Plug, Black Baby, Blue, Bail, 8 X 5 1/2 In. 220.00
Dixie Queen, Basket Weave 35.00
Dixie Queen, Portrait 125.00
Donnie & Marie 50.00
Dr. Doolittle .... 25.00 To 30.00
Dr. Seuss 40.00
Dukes of Hazzard 17.50
E.T. 15.00
Emergency, Round Top 8.00
Empire Strikes Back 25.00
Evel Knievel .... 25.00 To 35.00
Fall Guy, 1981 .... 15.00
Family Affair, 1969 .... 30.00 To 55.00
Fashion Tobacco, Pictures Society Couple, Tin 150.00
Fast Mail Tobacco 155.00
Fat Albert & Cosby Kids 45.00
Firefighters 15.00
Flintstones 30.00
Flipper 30.00
Flying Nun 40.00
G.I. Joe, 1967 .... 20.00 To 65.00
Galactica 40.00
Gentle Ben 45.00
George Washington Bust, Tobacco, Wire Bale Handle, 7 1/2 In. 44.00
Green Hornet .... 50.00 To 75.00
Gremlins, Metal, Aladdin .... 12.00 To 20.00
Grizzly Adams, Dome Top, 1977 .... 35.00 To 50.00
Gunsmoke, 1972 .... 60.00
Gunsmoke, 1973 .... 35.00
Happy Days, Fonz .... 12.00 To 25.00
Hardy Boys Mysteries 20.00
Harlem Globetrotters 35.00
He–Man & Masters of Universe 15.00
Holly Hobbie, 1979 .... 5.00 To 10.00
Hoot Gibson 40.00
How The West Was Won, 1979 .... 25.00 To 45.00
Hulk Hogan & Hustler 10.00
Indiana Jones 20.00
Julia 35.00
Kiss .... 20.00 To 55.00
Knight Rider .... 10.00 To 15.00
Kung Fu, 1974 .... 6.00 To 25.00
Land of Giants 65.00
Land of The Lost 35.00
Laugh–In, 1968 .... 30.00
Lil Miss Teenager, Train Case, Vinyl 100.00
Little House On The Prairie 30.00
Loonie Tunes 80.00
Magic of Lassie .... 15.00 To 30.00

Mary Poppins .... 40.00 To 65.00
Masters of The Universe, 1983 .... 5.00 To 15.00
Mayo's Tobacco .... 25.00 To 85.00
McDonalds Gulch 12.00
Mork & Mindy .... 10.00 To 20.00
Muppet Babies, Thermos 12.00
Nancy Drew 16.00
NFL, 1976 .... 45.00
NFL, 1978 .... 15.00
North Pole Cut Plug 150.00
Northeastern Railway, Willow Ware Design 35.00
Partridge Family, 1971 .... 20.00
Partridge Family, 1973 .... 4.00
Peanuts, Charlie Brown 7.00
Peanuts, Snoopy, Yellow Vinyl 75.00
Peanuts, White 50.00
Pebbles 45.00
Pedro Tobacco 150.00
Pet–N–Pals, 1962 .... 20.00
Pete's Dragon 25.00
Pigs In Space, Muppets, Metal .... 10.00 To 20.00
Pink Panther & Sons 12.00
Pinocchio, Red, Tin .... 45.00 To 65.00
Planet of The Apes 35.00
Porky's Lunch Wagon & Firehouse, Pair 100.00
Racing Wheels 20.00
Raggedy Ann & Andy 20.00
Rat Patrol, 1967 .... 45.00 To 85.00
Red Barn, Open Doors, 1958–60 .... 35.00
Red Baron, Dome 35.00
Return of The Jedi, 1983 .... 6.00 To 15.00
Robin Hood 25.00
Ronald McDonald, Sheriff .... 17.50 To 18.00
Santa Claus, Nursery Rhymes, Small 120.00
School Bus, Disney .... 25.00 To 28.00
Scooby Doo .... 25.00 To 30.00
Secret Agent .... 25.00 To 60.00
Sesame Street, Orange .... 20.00 To 40.00
Smokey Bear 45.00
Snoopy, Domed Cover .... 10.00 To 18.00
Snow White 15.00
Space 1999, 1975 .... 12.00 To 35.00
Space Cadet, Red 150.00
Space Capsule, 1963 .... 65.00
Star Wars .... 10.00 To 20.00
Steve Canyon 35.00
Strawberry Shortcake 5.00
Submarine, 1960 .... 85.00
Sunshine Biscuit, America The Beautiful, Octagonal 25.00
Swat, Plastic, 1975 .... 3.00
Sweet Cuba Tobacco 45.00
Tarzan .... 25.00 To 55.00
Tiger Chewing Tobacco, Red & Black Basket Weave .... 60.00 To 65.00
Tiger Tobacco, Blue 90.00
Tom Corbett .... 45.00 To 55.00
Train, Tin, Red, Silver, Blue, Oval, 1930 .... 60.00
U.S. Mail, Dome .... 25.00 To 35.00
U.S. Marine Tobacco 135.00
UFO, Thermos 45.00
Union Leader Plug, Tin Litho, 5 In. 11.00
Union Leader, Basket Weave 60.00
Universal Monsters 25.00
Wild Bill Hickok & Jingles, 1955 .... 40.00
Wild, Wild West, 1969 .... 20.00 To 50.00

Winner Tobacco, Car, Wire Bale, Tin Clip, 8 X 5 In. .... 44.00 To 65.00
Wonder Woman, Blue Vinyl .... 40.00 To 55.00
Worker Tobacco 60.00
Yankee Doodle 8.00
Ziggy's Munch Box, Vinyl .... 35.00 To 40.00
Zorro, Black 50.00
LUNCH PAIL, Gray Granite, Tin Top 40.00
Happiness, Animals In Car, 1 Lb. 200.00
Joe Palooka, 1948 .... 50.00
Just Suits 35.00
Kandies For The Kiddies, Animal People In Woods 200.00
Niggerhair Tobacco 195.00
Nursery Candies, Animals Dancing To Castle, 1 Lb. 200.00
Patterson Tobacco, Tin .... 30.00 To 38.00
Pedro Tobacco 145.00
Peter Rabbit On Parade, Oval 300.00
Tiger Chewing Tobacco 30.00
United Happiness, Elephant People, 1 Lb. 250.00

Luneville, a French faience factory, was established in 1731 by Jacques Chambrette. It is best known for its fine biscuit figures and groups and for large faience dogs and lions. The early pieces were unmarked. The firm was acquired by Keller and Guerin and is still working.

LUNEVILLE, Pitcher, Dragonflies, Flowers, Wading Bird, Rope Handle, 7 1/2 In. 165.00
Plate, Floral, 9 In. 35.00

Lusterware was meant to resemble copper, silver, or gold. It has been used since the sixteenth century. Most of the luster found today was made during the nineteenth century. The metallic glazes are applied on pottery. The finished color depends on the combination of the clay color and the glaze.

LUSTER CANARY, Pitcher, Floral Design, Silver Transfer, 4 1/2 In. 100.00
LUSTER, Blue, Tea Set, Child's, Service For 6 .... 65.00
Canary, Charger, Fleur–De–Lis Center, Spanish, 16 In. 275.00
Canary, Cup & Saucer, Handleless, Sewell, Miniature 200.00
Canary, Flowerpot, Embossed Lion Heads, Copper Trim, 3 3/4 In. 300.00
Canary, Mug, Child's, Black Transfer, Mary, Leaf Handle, 2 1/2 In. 425.00
Canary, Mug, Child's, Brown Transfer, A Trifle For James, Silver Rim 400.00
Canary, Mug, Child's, Red Transfer, A Nightingale For Eliza 350.00
Canary, Mug, Child's, Red Transfer, Horse, Man, Woman & Dog, Pink Rim 100.00
Canary, Mug, Embossed Frowning & Smiling Faces, 2 3/8 In. 100.00
Canary, Pitcher, Black Transfer, 5 1/4 In. 100.00
Canary, Pitcher, Black Transfer, A Free Born Englishman, 5 1/4 In. 525.00
Canary, Pitcher, Embossed Castleford Type Transfer, 6 1/8 In. 425.00
Canary, Pitcher, Enameled Design, 5 5/8 In. 275.00
Canary, Pitcher, Floral Design, Silver Deposit, 4 1/2 In. 75.00
Canary, Pitcher, Red Enamel, Silver Luster, 5 3/4 In. 400.00
Canary, Plate, Black Stripes, Transfer of Castle, French, 4 3/8 In. 155.00
Canary, Plate, Black Transfer of Puss 'N Boots, 8 5/8 In. 100.00
Canary, Plate, Black Transfer Scene, Floral Border, 8 1/2 In. 55.00
Canary, Plate, Tan Transfer Landscape, Floral Edge, 8 1/4 In. 175.00
Canary, Salt, Embossed Design, 1 3/4 In. 105.00
Copper, Bowl, Cover, Floral, Orange Band, 6 3/4 X 6 1/4 In. 200.00
Copper, Bust, Plato, 8 1/2 In. 75.00
Copper, Creamer, Blue & Yellow Bands 58.00
Copper, Creamer, Polychrome Floral Band, 3 3/4 In. 65.00
Copper, Figurine, Dog, Seated, 7 1/2 In. 175.00
Copper, Figurine, Dog, Whippet, Raised Front Leg, 7 1/2 In., Pair 360.00
Copper, Figurine, Dog, With Chain, Staffordshire, 12 1/2 In., Pair 775.00
Copper, Flowerpot, Birds & Flowers, Lion Head Handles, 5 7/8 In., Pr. 230.00
Copper, Flowerpot, Saucer, White Classical Scenes, Pink, 3 1/2 In. 350.00
Copper, Goblet, Flowers 32.00
Copper, Goblet, Pink Transfer, Faith & Hope, 4 1/2 In. 95.00

Copper, Goblet, Sunderland Insets, Double Bands, 4 1/2 In.	40.00
Copper, Inkwell, Flower & Vine, 5 Quill Holders, 3 3/4 X 3 In.	295.00
Copper, Lamp, Whale Oil, 5 1/8 In.	310.00
Copper, Mug, Tan Band, White Portrait Busts, Purple Floral, 3 1/8 In.	75.00
Copper, Mug, White Floral Design, Pink Luster Band, 4 7/8 In.	200.00
Copper, Pitcher, 2 Blue Bands, Ocher Dots & Leaves, 3 3/8 In.	55.00
Copper, Pitcher, Black Transfer, Masonic Designs, 1819, 9 In.	375.00
Copper, Pitcher, Blue Band Bottom, Molded Garden Scene, 5 3/4 In.	95.00
Copper, Pitcher, Blue Band, 4 1/2 In.	39.00
Copper, Pitcher, Dark Brown, Tan Band, Basket of Fruit, 4 1/2 In.	55.00
Copper, Pitcher, Embossed Reindeer, England, 6 In.	48.00
Copper, Pitcher, Embossed Stag & Deer, 6 In.	65.00
Copper, Pitcher, Fallow Deer Pattern, Allover Landscape, Wedgwood	75.00
Copper, Pitcher, Floral Design, Blue Bands, 9 In.	325.00
Copper, Pitcher, General Jackson Hero of New Orleans, 8 1/2 In.	1375.00
Copper, Pitcher, Lafayette, Cornwallis, Fruit, Canary Band, 7 1/4 In.	675.00
Copper, Pitcher, Ocher, Blue Band, Footed, Ornate Handle, 4 3/4 In.	140.00
Copper, Pitcher, Paneled Side, Blue Lines Handle, 7 1/4 In.	65.00
Copper, Pitcher, Polychrome Floral Design, Green Band, 5 5/8 In.	200.00
Copper, Pitcher, Stag, Dog, Lion Handle, Pink Luster, Enameled, 6 In.	150.00
Copper, Pitcher, Woman & Child Playing Badminton, 8 In.	125.00
LUSTER, COPPER, TEA LEAF, see Tea Leaf Ironstone	
Copper, Teapot, Enameled Floral Design, 7 1/2 In.	175.00
Copper, Teapot, Floral Rim	65.00
Copper, Teapot, Green Band, Floral, 4 7/8 In.	55.00
Copper, Tumbler, Green Floral Design, White Band, 2 5/8 In.	65.00
Copper, Tumbler, Pink Luster Rim, Blue Top Band With Flowers, Leaves	175.00
Copper, Vase, Embossed Floral Design, Orange Band, 5 1/2 In., Pair	125.00
Copper, Vase, Holes For Bulbs In Lid, 5 3/4 In.	150.00
LUSTER, FAIRYLAND, see Wedgwood	
Moonlight, Wall Pocket, Shell Shape, 10 1/4 In., Pair	400.00
Pink, Bust, John Locke, Silver Deposit On Base, 8 1/4 In.	175.00
Pink, Cup & Saucer, Demitasse	85.00
Pink, Pitcher, Purple Transfer of Landscape, 5 5/8 In.	95.00
Pink, Pitcher, Vintage Design	350.00
Pink, Plaque, Profile Bust of Queen Caroline, 4 1/2 X 5 3/8 In.	325.00
Pink, Teapot	87.50
Pink, Toothpick, Portrait of Queen Louise, Gold Beaded	69.50
Pink, Tureen, Sauce, Cover, Cattle Scenes	95.00
Purple, Teapot, Vintage Design, Green Enameling, 6 1/4 In.	165.00
Silver, Creamer, Ribbed Loop Base, Incised Top Band, 5 In.	85.00
Silver, Cuspidor, Lady's, 5 1/4 In.	85.00
Silver, Figurine, Britannia With Lion, 9 5/8 In.	500.00
Silver, Figurine, Lion, 8 3/4 X 12 In.	250.00
Silver, Figurine, Woman, Child & Dolphin, 6 3/4 In.	85.00
Silver, Jug, Puzzle, Bust In Central Void, 11 1/4 In.	400.00
Silver, Jug, Puzzle, Reticulated Sides, Impressed Inscription, 6 In.	350.00
Silver, Mug, Fly Fishing Scene, Arthur Wood, England, 5 In.	225.00
Silver, Pitcher, Birds, Flowers, William Heale, 1811, 5 3/8 In.	175.00
Silver, Pitcher, Floral Design, 7 3/8 In.	450.00
Silver, Pitcher, Floral Design, White Interior, 6 1/4 In.	225.00
Silver, Pitcher, Flowers & Bird, 5 1/8 In.	25.00
Silver, Pitcher, Vintage Floral Band, 6 1/2 In.	120.00
Silver, Pot, Bough, Cover, River Scene, Fisherman, 7 X 8 1/2 In.	300.00
Silver, Shaker, Toby, 5 In.	85.00
Silver, Teapot, Pedestal, Legs	55.00
Silver, Watch Hutch, Embossed Classical Design, 8 In.	300.00
LUSTER, SUNDERLAND, see Sunderland	

Lustre Art Glass Company was founded in Long Island, New York, in 1920 by Conrad Vahlsing and Paul Frank. The company made lampshades and globes that are almost indistinguishable from those made by Quezal. Most of the shades made by the company were unmarked.

LUSTRE ART, Feather On Gold, Gold Threading, Scalloped, 5 1/4 In., Pair 300.00
   Shade, Marigold Iridescent, 7 1/2 In. 125.00

> Lustres are mantel decorations, or pedestal vases, with many hanging glass prisms. The name really refers to the prisms, and it is proper to refer to a single glass prism as a lustre. Either spelling, luster or lustre, is correct.

LUSTRES, Cranberry, White Overlay, Chrysantheum Prisms, 11 1/2 In., Pr. 550.00
   Cream Satin, 16 1/2 In., Pair 850.00
   Cut Enamel, 2–Color, Baluster Form, Floral Sprays, 13 1/4 In., Pair 440.00
   Emerald Green, Mary Gregory, Pair 450.00
   Ruby Glass, Painted Gold Design, Prisms 425.00
   Ruffled Rim, 8 Cut Glass Prisms, 8 1/2 In. 235.00
   Spear Prisms, White To Blue, Pair 180.00

> Nicolas Lutz worked at the Boston and Sandwich Glass Company from 1869 to 1888. He made delicate and intricate threaded glass of several colors. Other similar wares made by other makers are now known by the generic name "Lutz."

LUTZ, Finger Bowl, Threaded, Clambroth Opalescent 65.00

> Petrus Regout established the De Sphinx pottery in Maastricht, Holland, in 1836. The firm was noted for its transfer–printed earthenware. Many factories in Maastricht are still making ceramics.

MAASTRICHT, Bowl, Oriental Scene, 7 3/4 In. 18.00
   Pitcher, Transfer of Rooster, Iris, Leaves, Red Shades, 5 In. 65.00
   Plate, Blue & White Floral, 8 1/2 In. 20.00
   Plate, Elvire, 8 In. 25.00
   Plate, Green Leaves, Gold Spatter Flowers, Sectioned, 11 In. 65.00
   Plate, Liberation, 1944, 8 In. 15.00
   Tray, Gaudy Polychrome Florals, 11 1/2 In. 28.50

> Maize glass was made by W. L. Libbey & Son Company of Toledo, Ohio, after 1889. The glass resembled an ear of corn. The leaves were usually green, but some pieces were made with blue or red leaves. The kernels of "corn" were light yellow, white, or light green.

MAIZE, Carafe, Water, Gold Leaves, Libbey 275.00
   Pitcher, Green Leaves, Strap Handle, White, Libbey, 9 In. 65.00
   Pitcher, Water, Green Leaves, Opaque White 450.00
   Tumbler, Green Leaves, Gold Trim, Libbey 155.00
   Tumbler, Yellow Leaves 125.00
   Tumbler, Yellow Leaves, Custard 120.00

> Majolica is a general term for any pottery glazed with an opaque tin enamel that conceals the color of the clay body. It has been made since the fourteenth century. Today's collector is most likely to find Victorian majolica. The heavy, colorful ware is rarely marked. Some famous makers include Wedgwood; Minton; Griffen, Smith and Hill (marked "Etruscan"); and Chesapeake Pottery (marked "Avalon" or "Clifton").

MAJOLICA, Ashtray, Frog On Pond 20.00
   Basket, Turquoise, 15 In. 225.00
   Bell, Cat 65.00
   Bowl, Artichoke, Cover 475.00
   Bowl, Flowers & Leaves, 2 Handles, Footed, 3 1/2 X 10 1/2 In. 135.00
   Bowl, Gondola Shape, Neptune Heads On Ends, 1890s, 10 In. 375.00
   Bowl, Sunfish Shape, Scales, Fins, Sarreguimines, 8 In. 65.00
   Butter Chip, Pansy 20.00
   Butter, Cover, Cabbage 82.50
   Cake Plate, Hummingbird 250.00
   Cake Stand, Baker's Cocoa 425.00
   Cake Stand, Maple Leaf, Etruscan .... 85.00 To 160.00
   Cake Stand, Pond Lily, 3 Cranes On Pedestal 250.00
   Cake Stand, Pond Lily, Small Lily Pads At Base, 9 In. 195.00

Candlestick, Boy & Girl, Pair	55.00
Charger, Green, Brown, Floral, 15 In.	450.00
Charger, Mother Alligator With 2 Babies, Grassy Ground	295.00
Charger, Satyr, Nymphs, 23 1/2 In.	475.00
Coffeepot, Fielding's Fan	225.00
Compote, 3 Storks Support Base	1200.00
Compote, Green, Gold Trim On Ivory, Marked, 9 In.	155.00
Creamer, Rose & Basketweave, Leaf Spout	125.00
Creamer, Shell & Seaweed, Albino	45.00
Crock, Word Salt In Raised Letters, Corn Pattern	375.00
Cup & Saucer, Breakfast	45.00
Cup & Saucer, Cauliflower, Griffen, Smith & Hill	350.00
Cup & Saucer, Cottage Pattern	60.00
Cup & Saucer, Pineapple, Lavender Interior	155.00
Cup & Saucer, Ribbed Top Band, Strawberries, Vines, Leaves	150.00
Cup & Saucer, Shell & Seaweed, Griffen, Smith & Hill	225.00
Cuspidor, Shell & Seaweed, Etruscan, 7 In.	550.00
Dish, Begonia Leaf, Aqua	57.00
Dish, Begonia Leaf, Brown, Green	32.00
Dish, Cheese, Green, Brown	275.00
Dish, Fern, Brown With Yellow	65.00
Dish, Leaf Shape, Koala Bears Handle	145.00
Ewer, Leaves, Peas At Edge, Gold Handle, 7 X 13 In.	225.00
Figurine, Birds At Well, 24 In.	625.00
Figurine, Shoe, Rose, Brown & Green, French, 11 1/4 In.	125.00
Flower Frog, Bird On Stump, 8 1/2 In.	70.00
Flower Frog, Green Turtle	50.00
Humidor, Blown-Out Lions, Earth Tones	110.00
Humidor, Figural, Elephant Seated, Pink Jacket, Smoking Pipe	95.00
Jar, Apothecary, Cherubs, Mask Handles, C.1750, 8 In., Pair	610.00
Jar, Syrup, Sunflower, Pewter Lid	300.00
Jardiniere, Foliage, C Scrolls, Shaped Pedestal, 33 X 16 In.	302.00
Lamp, 2-Light, From Vase, 4-Dolphin Footed, Italy, 9 3/4 In.	500.00
Match Holder, Figural, Dwarf, Sitting On Crate, Germany, 6 In.	145.00
Match Holder, Sleeping Drunk Holding Barrel	65.00
Match Safe, Tray, Striker, Black Boy	210.00
Match Striker, Wedgwood, 5 In.	175.00
Mug, Child's, Tom Thumb Picture	18.00
Mug, Pink Flowers, Green Leaves, Brown	80.00
Oyster Plate, 9 In.	195.00
Oyster Plate, Shell Design, Turquoise, Minton	195.00
Pedestal, Standing Bear, Green & Purple, 40 In.	2200.00
Pitcher, 2 Scenes of Children, Satyr On Lip, French	150.00
Pitcher, 2-Faced, Happy, Scowling, Tree Leaves, 9 In.	110.00
Pitcher, Avalon, 5 1/2 In.	50.00
Pitcher, Avalon, 6 1/2 In.	50.00
Pitcher, Bamboo, Wardle, 8 In.	145.00
Pitcher, Barrel Shape, Violet Interior, 4 1/2 In.	125.00
Pitcher, Baseball & Soccer Scene, Yellow, Relief, 7 1/2 In.	300.00
Pitcher, Basket Weave Center, Flowers, Yellow Fence Base, 6 In.	100.00
Pitcher, Brown Flowers On Aqua, Brown Handle, 6 In.	75.00 To 95.00
Pitcher, Bull & Matador, Double Rope Handle, 13 1/2 In.	250.00
Pitcher, Figural Chanticleer, Pours Through Mouth, 7 1/4 In.	35.00
Pitcher, Figural Duck, Beak Pouring Spout, 13 In.	135.00
Pitcher, Figural Owl, 12 In.	90.00
Pitcher, Figural Parrot, 6 In.	175.00
Pitcher, Figural, Goose, 10 In.	90.00
Pitcher, Figural, Owl, 10 1/2 In.	175.00
Pitcher, Figural, Ram, 10 In.	145.00
Pitcher, Figural, Spaniel, 10 In.	350.00
Pitcher, Fish, 10 In.	125.00
Pitcher, Floral Medallion, Raised Flowers & Leaves, 12 1/2 In.	125.00
Pitcher, Floral, 4 In.	60.00
Pitcher, Flowers, Heart-Shaped Leaves, 6 In.	95.00

Pitcher, Fruit On Sides, Rose, Yellow, Gold & White, 7 In. 145.00
Pitcher, Green Leaves On Tan Bark, 6 In. 45.00
Pitcher, Green Leaves, Brown Bark Ground, 7 In. 90.00
Pitcher, King of Corn, 10 In. 125.00
Pitcher, Pineapple Mark, 4 1/2 In. 75.00
Pitcher, Scalloped, Birds & Flowers, Branch Handle, 8 In. 95.00
Pitcher, Scowling Face 1 Side, Happy Face Other, Pink, 8 1/2 In. 125.00
Pitcher, Sports Scene, Yellow, 7 1/2 In. 300.00
Pitcher, Stork, Dark Colors, 9 In. 150.00
Pitcher, Swirling Florals, Stems, Pewter Lid, 10 In. 250.00
Pitcher, Water, Sunflower & Classical Urn, 10 In. 285.00
Pitcher, Wild Rose, Etruscan, 4 1/2 In. 90.00
Plaque, Facing Birds Center, Openwork, Pierced, 13 In., Pair 600.00
Plate, 3 Lily Pads, Pink Flower, Englsh, 1878, 9 In. 50.00
Plate, Begonia Leaf, 7 1/2 In. 40.00
Plate, Bird & Cherry, Multicolor, 8 In. 65.00
Plate, Blackberries, Cherries, Basket Weave, Zell, 7 In. 55.00
Plate, Blackberries, Cherries, Basket Weave, Zell, 8 In. 60.00
Plate, Cauliflower, 9 In. 65.00
Plate, Cauliflower, Etruscan, 8 In. 45.00
Plate, Cauliflower, Etruscan, 9 In. 120.00
Plate, Dandelion, Zell, 9 In. 45.00
Plate, Dandelions, Turquoise, Ground, 7 1/2 In. 35.00
Plate, Dog & Doghouse, C.1890, 11 In. 125.00
Plate, Double Begonia, Green, Wedgwood, 8 In. 65.00
Plate, Fan & Bird, Wedgwood, 1872, 10 In. 100.00
Plate, Floral & Leaf, 8 In. 75.00
Plate, Green Leaf, Cream Ground, 8 In. 35.00
Plate, Leaf, Etruscan, 9 In. 85.00
Plate, Leaves & Fruit, Blue–Green, 9 In. 55.00
Plate, Lily, Green & Yellow, Germany, 9 In. 65.00
Plate, Maple Leaf, 9 In. 45.00
Plate, Napkin, Green & Yellow, White Ground, 9 1/4 In. 75.00
Plate, Napkin, White, Pink Ground, 6 In. 25.00
Plate, Overlapping Begonia Leaves, 8 1/2 In. 85.00
Plate, Pond Lily, Yellow Petal Rim, 7 In. 160.00
Plate, Sculptured Blackberries, Ivory Basket Weave, 9 1/2 In. 45.00
Plate, Strawberries, Plums & Grapes, Sarreguemines, 12 In. 95.00
Platter, Dog & Doghouse, Scalloped, 11 In. 145.00
Salt & Pepper, Cabbage Leaf 30.00
Salt & Pepper, Strawberries 30.00
Server, Asparagus, VBS Mark 300.00
Spittoon, Bamboo 120.00
Spooner, Bird & Iris 85.00
Spooner, Seashell, Handle, Etruscan, Marked 325.00
Stein, African Smoking Pipe, Gold Earrings, 6 3/4 In. 295.00
Sugar & Creamer, Bamboo, Etruscan 165.00
Sugar, Cauliflower, Etruscan 35.00
Sugar, Flowers, Avalon, 5 1/2 In. 60.00
Syrup, Bow & Flowers 95.00
Syrup, Pewter Lid, Sunflowers 140.00
Syrup, Sunflower .... 185.00 To 375.00
Tankard, Alligator Around Monster, Tail Handle, C.1870, 21 In. 495.00
Tankard, Sea Creatures, Serpent Handle, Cream, 1870 .... 425.00
Teapot, Cauliflower, Etruscan 300.00
Teapot, Cauliflower, Marked 335.00
Teapot, Seashell, Etruscan 270.00
Teapot, Shell & Seaweed, Griffen, Smith & Hill 550.00
Teapot, Strawberry & Bow 295.00
Teapot, Water Lily, 5 1/2 In. .... 195.00 To 295.00
Tobacco Humidor, Pipe On Lid, 5 1/4 In. 130.00
Tobacco Jar, Elephant, In Pink Jacket 95.00
Tobacco Jar, Frog 225.00
Tobacco Jar, Frog, Crouching, In Pink Jacket 95.00

Tobacco Jar, Groundhog	125.00
Tobacco Jar, Hooded Monk	135.00
Tobacco Jar, Teal & Fan Design, Wedgwood	350.00
Tray, Leaf, Etruscan, 12 In.	225.00
Umbrella Holder, Raised Flowers, Vines, Pierced Top, 22 In.	235.00
Umbrella Stand, Black & Yellow	250.00
Vase, 2 Panels of Molded Iris, 10 1/2 In.	160.00
Vase, Blue & White, Landscape, Italy, 12 1/2 In.	900.00
Vase, Boy Holding Flowerpot Next To Vase, 6 In.	95.00
Vase, Bud, Figural, Woman, Mandolin, 2 Tree Trunks, Double, 8 In.	110.00
Vase, Bust of Woman, Baluster Shape, Griffin Handles, 6 In.	75.00
Vase, Figural, Lady With Fan, By Tree Trunk, 8 In.	245.00
Vase, Iris Handles, 6 3/4 In., Pair	250.00
Vase, Relief Floral Design On Green, 18 In.	35.00
Vase, Stylized Parrot Handle	185.00

Maps of all types have been collected for centuries. The earliest known printed maps were made in 1478. The first printed street map showed London in 1559. The first road maps for use by drivers of automobiles were made in 1901. Collectors buy maps that were pages of old books, as well as the multifolded road maps popular in this century.

MAP, Alaska, Gold Coast & Coal Fields, Steamer Routes, 1889, 35 X 40 In.	35.00
Amos 'N Andy, Weber City	17.00
Atlas, LaSalle County, Illinois, 106 Drawings, 1876, 16 X 19 In.	300.00
Atlas, Road, Firestone, Bicentennial, 1975	15.00
Auto Guide, Ohio & Kentucky, King, 500 Pages, 1915	15.00
Boston, New York, Engraved, Colored, Framed, 18 3/4 X 16 1/4 In., Pair	210.00
California, Mitchell's Atlas, 1881, 15 X 22 In.	25.00
China, J.H. Colton & Co., 1855, 17 X 14 In.	24.00
Cincinnati, Ohio, City, Colored, McNally, 11 X 14 In.	9.00
City of Baltimore, Mitchell's Atlas, 1881, 11 1/2 X 15 In.	15.00
City of Chicago, Mitchell's Atlas, 1881, 15 X 22 In.	25.00
City of New York, Broadway Central Hotel, 1880s	25.00
Coal Mining, Pennsylvania, 1.C & N. Co., Shaft No.3, 1885–86	20.00
Delaware & Maryland, Full Color, Colton, 1857, 13 X 16 In.	50.00
England & Wales, Brussels Tapestry, Fragment, 18th Century	525.00
Esso, World War II, 3 Different, Original Folder	5.00
Europe, Vellum, Maria S. Rossiter, Framed, 17 X 21 In.	137.50
Freightways System, Authority Routes, 1967, 26 1/2 X 39 1/2 In.	30.00
Globe, Andrews & Co., On Floor Stand	1540.00
Globe, Celestial & Terrestrial, Tripod Supports, Newton, 20 In., Pair	450.00
Globe, Eastlake, Floor Model, Walnut	1525.00
Globe, Terrestrial, Dated 1893, Metal Tripod Base	300.00
Gram's Universal, Geographical, Astronomical & Historical, 1897	20.00
Guide, Brooklyn–Manhattan Transit Corp, 1916, 16 X 12 In.	7.50
Holland, 1721, 22 X 18 In.	30.00
Idaho, Indian Territories, U.S. Land Offices, I.P. Bertong, 33 X 46 In.	35.00
Illinois, Geographical Pub., Governors, Population, 1906	20.00
Iowa & Nebraska, Johnson	20.00
Ireland, J. Fielding, Pater Noster Row, Folds, 1782, 12 3/4 X 15 In.	40.00
Maine, Johnsons, Color, 1860, 18 X 14 In.	20.00
Mine Sites, From Lake Gogebic, Mich., To Mellen, Wisc., 1887, 19 X 25 In.	4.00
Minnesota, Johnson	20.00
Missouri, Texaco, 1960	9.00
Mitchell's Ancient World, Hand Colored, 1861, 12 Piece	60.00
North American, Thos. Couder, Published 1768, 23 X 24 1/2 In.	450.00
Nova Belgica, Hand Colored, Engraved, 22 1/2 X 27 In.	325.00
Ohio, Geological Survey, Shales & Surface Clay, Bulletin 39, 1938	12.50
Oregon & Washington, Johnson	20.00
Oregon, Its Resources & Opportunities, 1910	10.00
Palestine, Mitchell's Atlas, 1881, 11 1/2 X 15 In.	12.00
Prohibition, Chicago Business Center, Location, Saloons, Breweries, 1893	10.00
Railroad, Oak Case, 1902–04	850.00

Marble Carving, Bust, Woman, Rose Garland, 1876, 28 In.

Marble Carving, Birth of Venus, Italian, C.1900, 45 In.

Route 66, Auto Club Trip, Oklahoma City To St. Louis, 1940s	10.00
South America, Copperplate Engraved, Hand Colored, 1835, 8 X 10 In.	15.00
St. Louis, City Guide, Gross, 1951, 1916–17	5.00
Survey, Mines In Breckenridge, Colorado	75.00
Texas, Centennial, 1936	35.00
U.S. Coast Survey, Alaska & E. Siberia, 1890, 24 X 30 In.	50.00
U.S. Coast Survey, Beauford N.C. Harbor, 1862, 19 1/2 X 21 1/2 In.	20.00
U.S. Coast Survey, Chesapeake Bay, 1837, Folds, 9 X 9 1/2 In.	20.00
U.S. Coast Survey, Pensacola Harbor, 1841, 9 1/2 X 11 3/4 In.	20.00
United States, 1902, 58 X 40 In.	75.00
United States, J. Fielding, Pater Noster Row, 1783, 8 1/2 X 10 In.	95.00
United States, Kindergarten, 1880	95.00
Washington, D.C., City, Colored, McNally, 11 X 14 In.	9.00
World Atlas, Engraved, Vineyard Borders, American Cities, Mitchell, 1868	550.00
World Atlas, Hammonda Ambassador, All States & Foreign Countries	25.00
Yellowstone & Missouri Rivers, Canvas, Fold-Up, 1860	75.00
Yukon Territory, Sergeant Preston of The Yukon, Color, Quaker, 1955	45.00

 Marble is used in many ways on antiques. Marble tops are popular for tables because they resist stains and damage. Listed here are marble carvings, large or small figurines, and groups of people or animals that have been a special art form since the time of the ancient Greeks. Reproductions, especially of large Victorian groups, are being made of a mixture using marble dust. These are very difficult to detect and collectors should be careful. Other carvings are listed under Alabaster.

MARBLE CARVING, Basin, Ormolu Mounted, Italy, 36 1/2 X 27 X 12 3/4 In.	7750.00
Bench, Garden, Lion Supports For Arms, Italian, White, Pair	6000.00
Birth of Venus, Italian, C.1900, 45 In. ....*Illus*	6500.00
Bust, Beethoven	900.00
Bust, David, Cast Stone Plinth, 19th Century, 20 In.	1900.00
Bust, Man, Henry Dexter, 1850s	880.00
Bust, Woman, Rose Garland, 1876, 28 In. ....*Illus*	2300.00
Bust, Woman, With Fruit & Flowers, Plinth, Art Deco, 13 In.	600.00
Classical Female Torso, White, Gle Pecoraro, 1874, 30 In.	935.00
George Washington, In Time of Peace, 42 In.	5100.00
Group, 3 Children, With Birds	1320.00
Guardian Lion, Seated On Draped Plinth, Chinese, 32 In., Pr.	665.00
Head of Aphrodite, Wood & Marble Sockle, 13 In.	365.00
Lion, Italian, Pair	3700.00
Lion, Leaning Against Shield, Italian, 46 In., Pair	4075.00
Panel, Last Supper, C.1900, 35 X 67 In.	550.00

Pedestal, Verde Antico, C.1875	3750.00
Urn, Campagna Form, White, Acanthus, 27 In., Pair	5100.00
Urn, Neoclassical, Cover, Acanthus Leaf Knop, Italy, Pair	6500.00
Venus, Crouching Nude, Octagonal Plinth, Continental, 34 In.	5000.00

The game of marbles has been popular since the days of the ancient Romans. American children were able to buy marbles by the mid-eighteenth century. Dutch glazed clay marbles were least expensive. Glazed pottery marbles, attributed to the Bennington potteries in Vermont, were of a better quality. Marbles made of pink marble were also available by the 1830s. Glass marbles seem to have been made later. By 1880, Samuel C. Dyke of South Akron, Ohio, was making clay marbles and The National Onyx Marble Company was making marbles of onyx. The Navarre Glass Marble Company of Navarre, Ohio, and M. B. Mishler of Ravenna, Ohio, made the glass marbles. Ohio remained the center of the marble industry and the Akron-made Akro Agate brand became nationally known. The most expensive marbles collected today are the sulfides. These are glass marbles with frosted white figures in the center.

MARBLE, Albino, Raccoon, Crystal, 2 In.	600.00
Clambroth, Light Blue Core, Cobalt Blue Lines, 11/16 In.	170.00
Clambroth, White, Fine Green Lines	155.00
Cloisonne, 1 1/2 In.	400.00
Indian Swirl, Bands of Butterscotch, Red & Orange, 3/4 In.	45.00
Latticinio Core, White, 6 Red, White & Blue Outer Bands, 1 7/8 In.	125.00
Latticinio Core, Yellow, 2 Sets of 3 Bands, 3 Layers, 2 1/8 In.	175.00
Latticinio Core, Yellow, 4 Outer Bands, 2 1/8 In.	200.00
Latticinio Core, Yellow, 6 Outer Bands, Blue, 2 1/4 In.	150.00
Latticinio Swirl, Center Bands, 4 Sets of Outer Strands, 2 In.	150.00
Latticinio Swirl, Central Bands, 4 Sets of Outer Bands, 1 3/4 In.	100.00
Latticinio, 3 Transparent Red Bands, 3 Blue Bands, 1 1/8 In.	36.00
Latticinio, Triple Swirl, Red, Blue & Aqua Bands, 13/16 In.	48.00
Latticinio, Yellow Thread In Core, White Outer Bands, 15/16 In.	24.00
Lutz, Banded Clearie, Orange, 19/32	120.00
Lutz, Banded Clearie, Purple, 19/32	120.00
Lutz, Clear, Red Lines, 7/8 In.	117.00
Lutz, Lavender Bands, Crystal, 11/16 In.	125.00
Lutz, Onionskin, Rainbow Color, 5/8 In.	150.00
Lutz, Ribbon Core, 3/4 In.	175.00
Lutz, Yellow Bands, 1 1/2 In.	1000.00
Lutz, Yellow Lines, Clear Glass, 11/16 In.	108.00
Mica, Amber, 9/16 In.	18.00
Mica, Blue, 3/4 In.	30.00
Mica, Emerald Green, Large Flakes, 1 In.	112.00
Onionskin, 2 In.	300.00
Onionskin, 2 Red Panels, L Panel of Turquoise & Dark Blue, 3/4 In.	85.00
Onionskin, 3/4 In.	45.00
Onionskin, 4 Colors, Wet, 13/16 In.	55.00
Onionskin, 4 Lobes, Green & Yellow, Pink & White Panels, 1 5/8 In.	135.00
Onionskin, 4 Panels, 2 1/4 In.	175.00
Onionskin, Blue, Orange & White, 5/8 In.	60.00
Onionskin, Pink & White, With Mica, 11/16 In.	72.00
Onionskin, Red, Green, Blue & White, With Mica, 1 5/8 In.	1100.00
Onionskin, Red, White & Blue, With Mica, 2 1/4 In.	450.00
Onionskin, With Mica, 1 1/2 In.	100.00
Opaque Swirl, Pink, 11/16 In.	45.00
Opaque Swirl, Reddish-Maroon Surface Bands, 11/16 In.	100.00
Opaque, Pink, 11/16	85.00
Peppermint, 1 Red Line, 13/16 In.	130.00
Peppermint, 19/32 In.	75.00
Peppermint, 3 Red Lines, 3/4 In.	81.00
Red, White & Blue, Solid Core, 3/16 In.	280.00
Ribbon Core, Pink & White Ribbon Core, 3/4 In.	80.00
Ribbon Core, Ribbon Swirl, Green Stripe, Outer Stripes, 7/8 In.	44.00

Sulfide, Aardvark, 1 3/8 In. 120.00
Sulfide, Bear, 1 1/2 In. 85.00
Sulfide, Bear, Standing, 2 1/4 In. 250.00
Sulfide, Dog, 1 1/2 In. 85.00
Sulfide, Dog, Setter, 1 1/4 In. 70.00
Sulfide, Dog, Standing, 2 In. 175.00
Sulfide, Elephant 170.00
Sulfide, Figure of Boy Praying, 1 5/8 In. 175.00
Sulfide, Fish, 1 1/2 In. 80.00
Sulfide, Fish, 1 5/8 In. 375.00
Sulfide, Goat, Standing, 2 1/4 In. 200.00
Sulfide, Indian, 5/8 In. 35.00
Sulfide, Jackal, 1 In. 150.00
Sulfide, Lion, 1 1/2 In. 100.00
Sulfide, Lion, 2 In. 135.00
Sulfide, Lippinzaner Pony, Rearing, 1 1/2 In. 175.00
Sulfide, Little Boy, Sailboat, Polished, 11/16 In. 425.00
Sulfide, Little Girl Crawling, 2 1/4 In. 850.00
Sulfide, Pig, 1 1/4 In. 60.00
Sulfide, Rabbit, 2 1/4 In. 195.00
Sulfide, Saint Bernard, 1 1/4 In. 70.00
Sulfide, Sheep, 1 11/16 In. 75.00
Sulfide, Squirrel, 1 1/4 In. .... 70.00 To 85.00
Sulfide, Squirrel, 2 In. 300.00
Sulfide, Squirrel, Eating Nut, 1 7/8 In. 150.00
Sulfide, Standing Dog, 2 In. 135.00
Sulfide, Water Spaniel, 1 11/16 In. 90.00
Sulfide, Wild Boar, 1 1/2 In. 65.00
Sulfide, Woman Holding Basket, Dog Next To Her, 1 7/8 In. 850.00
Swirl, 3 Ribbons, Alternating Colored Outer Threads, 1 In. 32.00
Swirl, Indian, Black, 3/4 In. 65.00
Swirl, Orange & Yellow Inner Ribbons, 1 3/8 In. 40.00
Swirl, Powder Blue, White, Joseph A. Rice, 2 In. 100.00
Swirl, Solid White Core, Lobed, Blue Outer Ribbons, 15/16 In. 24.00
Swirl, Solid White Core, Thin Yellow Outer Threads, 13/16 In. 28.00

The Marblehead Pottery was founded in 1905 by Dr. J. Hall as a rehabilitative program for the patients of a Marblehead, Massachusetts, sanitarium. Two years later it was separated from the sanitarium and it continued operations until 1936. Many of the pieces were decorated with marine motifs.

MARBLEHEAD, Bowl, Gray & Blue, 5 In. 185.00
Bowl, Green Flowers, Brown Band, Yellow, 7 1/2 In. 650.00
Bowl, Lavender Interior, White, 4 1/2 In. 125.00
Bowl, Petaled Flowers, Brown Band, C.1905, 7 1/2 In. 715.00
Tile, White Clipper Ship, Blue Ground, 5 In. 220.00
Vase, Band of Dogwood Blossoms, 20th Century, 5 1/4 In. 665.00
Vase, Blue, 5 In. 105.00
Vase, Dark Blue, 6 In. 285.00
Vase, Matte Blue, 6 In. 350.00
Vase, Stylized Trees, 6 1/4 In. 2575.00

Martinware is a salt-glazed stoneware made by the Martin Brothers of Middlesex, England, between 1873 and 1915. Many figural jugs and vases were made by the three brothers. Of special interest are the fanciful birds, usually made with removable heads.

MARTIN BROTHERS, Head, Bojum, Pottery 100.00
Pitcher, 5 1/2 In. 450.00

Mary Gregory glass is identified by a characteristic white figure painted on dark glass. It was made from 1870 to 1910. The name refers to any glass decorated with a white silhouette figure and not just to the Sandwich glass originally painted by Miss Mary Gregory. Many reproductions have been made and there are new pieces being sold in gift shops today.

MARY GREGORY, Bottle, Barber, Girl, Amethyst, 8 3/4 In.	235.00
Bottle, Barber, Tennis Scene, 8 1/2 In., Pair	350.00
Box, Girl Holding Basket of Flowers On Lid, 5 1/4 In.	630.00
Box, Hinged Lid, Girl Holding Bouquet, Cobalt Blue, 3 3/4 In.	395.00
Box, Ruby, Boy Carrying Bouquet Top, Gilt Brass Frame, 4 In.	625.00
Boy, Girl, Flying Birds, Wine, Olive Green, 5 In., 12 Piece	360.00
Candy Dish, Girl With Sprays, Thorn Handle, Emerald, 5 1/2 In.	235.00
Cruet, Cranberry	125.00
Cruet, Girl & Tree, Cranberry	225.00
Decanter, Cobalt Blue	250.00
Decanter, Girl Beside Swan In Water, Cranberry, 9 1/2 In.	415.00
Decanter, Seated Girl, Handle, Blown Stopper, Green, 1870, 9 In.	300.00
Decanter, Woman Standing, Brown Stopper, Amber, 14 In.	345.00
Decanter, Young Boy, Green, Blown Stopper, 9 In.	250.00
Finger Bowl, Dark Green, 4 1/2 In.	85.00
Jar, Twisted Handle On Lid, Walking Girl, Cranberry, 6 In.	345.00
Lamp, Girl Fishing Stem, Flowers On Shade, Blue, 16 1/4 In.	1260.00
Lamp, Heater, 4 Different Scenes, Square, 4 Footed	450.00
Lamp, Kerosene Stem, Girl, White Dot Design, 13 In.	750.00
Lamp, Kerosene, Black Amethyst, Pair	1450.00
Paperweight, Boys In Colonial Dress, Black Glass, 4 In.	235.00
Perfume Bottle, Atomizer, Base, Emerald Green	90.00
Perfume Bottle, Girl Next To Tree, Birds, Dragonfly, Crystal	135.00
Perfume Bottle, Girl, Faceted Crystal Stopper, 4 In.	250.00
Perfume Bottle, Teal, Tulip Shaped Stopper, Square, 8 1/2 In.	445.00
Pin Dish, Facing Boy & Girl, Cobalt Blue, 3 In., Pair	190.00
Pitcher, Boy Standing In Tree, Peeking In Birdhouse, Amber	295.00
Pitcher, Boy, Sailboat, Sapphire Blue, 6 In.	220.00
Pitcher, Girl Feeding Bird, Clear, Swirl, Ribbed Handle, 9 In.	225.00
Pitcher, Girl Holding Leaf, Blue, 2 In.	225.00
Pitcher, Girl, Sapphire Blue, 2 In.	225.00
Pitcher, Green, White Boy With Bird, Trees, 7 X 9 In.	250.00
Pitcher, Pewter Lid, Woman Holding Flowers, Blue, 15 In.	275.00
Powder Jar, Lady, With Harp, Allover Gold Leaves, Green, Large	145.00
Rose Bowl, Boy & Dove, Yellow Enameling, Green, 5 In.	165.00
Salt & Pepper, Amber, White Boy & Girl, Holder, 5 3/4 X 6 In.	985.00
Stein, Children, Electric Blue, Cover, Pair	670.00
Stein, Cobalt Blue, Cover, Large, Pair	940.00
Tankard, Pewter Lid, Tinted Face & Hands, Blue, 14 1/2 In.	275.00
Tile, Blue, 5 In.	75.00
Tray, Dresser, Cranberry	245.00
Tumble–Up, Blue, 2 Piece	175.00
Tumbler, Clear, 3 1/2 In.	75.00
Tumbler, Girl Holding Flower, Emerald Green	67.50
Tumbler, Little Girl Dancing, Floral Ground, Crystal	50.00
Tumbler, Young Girl, Blue, 3 3/4 In.	85.00
Vase, Ballet Dancer, Cobalt Blue, 7 In.	48.00
Vase, Boy With Rod, Girl With Spoon & Dish, Blue, 7 In.	275.00
Vase, Cobalt Blue, Enamel Design, Fluted, 7 In.	150.00
Vase, Cylinder, Green, 6 In.	95.00
Vase, Facing Pair, Pink Overlay, White Lining, 9 1/2 In., Pair	325.00
Vase, Girl Handing Bird's Nest To Boy, Metal Legs, 16 3/4 In.	1000.00
Vase, Girl Holding Book, Cranberry, 4 1/8 In.	145.00
Vase, Girl In Hat, Sapphire Blue, 7 5/8 In., Pair	335.00
Vase, Herons In Flight Over Pond, Sapphire Blue, 11 In., Pair	475.00
Vase, Man & Woman, Playing Tennis, Cranberry, Stepped Foot, Pr.	295.00
Vase, Picking Grapes, Pouring From Jug, Amethyst, 15 In., Pair	1570.00
Vase, Shy Child, Stick, 7 1/4 In.	75.00
Vase, White Girl, Green, 10 1/4 In.	115.00
Vase, Woman & Man, Emerald Green, 11 In., Pair	375.00

Vase, Woman Carrying Hat, Man With Rifle, Green, 10 In., Pair	325.00
Watch Holder, Children	1200.00
Water Set, Fluted Edge, Gold Trim, Cranberry, 7 Piece	475.00

MASONIC, see Fraternal

J. Massier fils

Massier pottery is iridescent French art pottery made by Clement Massier in Golfe–Juan, France, in the late nineteenth and early twentieth centuries. It has an iridescent metallic luster glaze that resembles the Weller Sicard pottery glaze. Most pieces are marked "J. Massier."

MASSIER, Tile, Flowers, Embossed Ground, Jerome Massier, Square, 6 In.	75.00
Vase, Birds, Gold, Iridescent, 8 In.	300.00

Large wooden matches were used in the nineteenth and twentieth centuries for a variety of purposes. The kitchen stove and the fireplace or furnace had to be lit regularly. One type of match holder was made to hang on the wall, another was designed to be kept on a tabletop. Of special interest today are match holders that have advertisements as part of the design.

MATCH HOLDER, Art Nouveau Design, Iron	85.00
Berber Soldier, Holding Flag, Bugle, French, 5 1/4 In.	95.00
Bible, Blue, Milk Glass	34.00
Birds Support Holder, Fruit, Tufts	50.00
Bisque, Boy & Girl, Heads Protruding, Hats, Striker Below	225.00
Black Boy, , Sitting On Log, Bisque	125.00
Black Jester, Opaque, Dated	85.00
Black Man, Yellow Robe, Green Jacket, Basket, Metal	95.00
Bliss Native Herbs	95.00
Bode & Larson Good Shoes	70.00
Boy, Black, Glazed Ceramic, Germany, 3 /4 In.	65.00
Boy, Iron	75.00
Bulldog	30.00
Ceramic, Hand Painted, Taylor–Tunnicluffe & Co., 1875–98	325.00
Cloisonne	40.00
Columbus, Iron, Painted	95.00
DeLaval Cream Separator, Tin, 6 1/2 X 4 In.	260.00
Devil's Head, Chalkware, Leering Eyes, 7 X 6 In.	45.00
Dog & Stump	65.00
Dr. Pepper	65.00
Dr. Shoop's Health Coffee	95.00
Dr. Shoop's Laxettes	85.00
Dutch Boy, Hand Painted, 1890s	40.00
Fireplace, Lid, Cast Iron	45.00
Florals, Gold Trim, Signed MWB, Striker, Square, 3 1/4 In.	75.00
Fly, Brass	35.00
Foxy Grandpa, Flesh Colored, Germany, 3 1/2 In.	40.00
Fuller & Johnson Mfg. Farm Implements & Gasoline Engine	125.00
G.E. Refrigerator, Cast Iron	90.00
Hanging, Game Pouches, Leaves At Top, Black, Iron, 8 1/2 In.	130.00
Happy Hooligan, Policeman	40.00
Head of Devil, Grapes & Leaves, Brass, 4 X 6 In.	82.00
Horizontal Pipe Attached, Milk Glass, 2 X 4 In.	75.00
John Hauck Brewing Co., Cinn., Plated Brass	38.00
Judson, J.G. Stevens	95.00
Judson, Man, Woman & Child Fireside Scene, Tin, 5 X 3 1/2 In.	127.00
Knees To Waist Bloomers, Underwear Striker, 3 In.	135.00
Kook	19.00
Man With Barrel, Wooden	20.00
Man, Juicy Fruit	60.00
Matches Are Cheaper Than Gas, Cast Iron, Double, 1899	65.00
Michigan Stoves, Nickel Plated Iron, 8 X 4 1/2 In.	143.00
Milwaukee Binders & Mowers	65.00
Moxie, Die–Cut Bottle .... 115.00 To 300.00
New Process Gas Range, Saves Time & Gas, Tin	85.00

Old Man, With Basket, Blue Milk Glass, Portieux 55.00
Pabst, 1930 .... 26.00
R.L. Mosher Boots & Shoes 35.00
Rabbit, Thumbprint, Crystal 30.00
Scratcher, 2 Pockets, Flowers Around Each Pocket, Cast Iron 65.00
Sharples Separator Co., Pet of The Dairy, Tin 78.00
Sharples, Woman, Girl, Cream Separator, Tin, 6 1/2 X 2 1/2 In. 165.00
Solarine Metal Polish, Tin, 5 X 3 1/2 In. 116.00
Soldier Boy, White Uniform, Sword, Striker, 5 1/4 In. 85.00
Soldier Holding Flag & Bugle, 5 1/4 In. 75.00
Stultz Bros. Bitters 75.00
Table, Kangaroo, Pouch Holds Matches, Brass 22.00
Tree Trunk, Owl & Squirrel, White Metal, 5 X 6 In. 75.00
Urn, Metal, Occupied Japan 22.00
Vulcan Plows, Die-Cut Tin 575.00
Wall, Boot, Amber Glass 25.00
Wall, Rabbit, Duck & Acorn, Cast Iron, 1870, 9 In. 125.00
Wall, Scrolls, Cast Iron 30.00
Wall, Woman, Pink, Tin 25.00
William Tell Flour, Knights On Horses, Tin, 5 X 3 In. 154.00
Woman's Boot, Striker Base, Wilton, Cast Iron 35.00
Woman's Head, Columbia, Hanging, Clear Glass, 1876, 4 1/2 In. 75.00

Early matches were made with phosphorus and could ignite unexpectedly. Match safes were designed to be carried in the pocket. The matches were safely stored in the tightly closed container. Examples were made in sterling silver, plated silver, or other metals. The English call these "vesta boxes."

MATCH SAFE, A.M. Smith, Minneapolis, California Wine Depot, Silver Plate 65.00
Arm & Hammer, Gutta-Percha 60.00
Art Nouveau Woman, Campfire, Lewis & Co. Clothiers, Champagne 95.00
Baby With Rattle, Figural 75.00
Blatz Beer, Sterling Silver 25.00
Blatz Brewing Co., Nickel 150.00
Blue Union, Label, Celluloid, Nickel 72.00
Chick Hatching From Egg, Figural, Hinged Top, Brass 85.00
Cigar Makers Union, Living Wages Not Child Labor 45.00
Compliments of Barthomey's Brewing Co., 2 In. 121.00
Design On Front, Clouds, Sea, Owls On Back, Silver, Unger 875.00
Dockash Stove Factory, Tin 50.00
Dog & Quail In Relief, Silver Plate 22.00
Dr. Shoop's, Literature, Tin 95.00
Flowers & Scroll Design, Shield Shape, Double Pocket, 6 1/2 In. 75.00
Garlock Packing Co., Palmyra, New York, Brass, Stamps, Matches 95.00
Golf Bag & Clubs, Sterling Silver, 1910 .... 300.00
Gunmetal 35.00
Hot Springs, Arkansas 50.00
Hunter Baltimore Rye, Celluloid Wrap Around 45.00
Indianapolis Brewing Company 45.00
Inlaid Pearls 22.00
Inlaid Pewter, Lacquer 22.00
International Taylor Co., Nickel 60.00
Judson Whiskey 65.00
Laxets, Tin 60.00
Lennox Furnaces & Ranges, Marshalltown, Iowa 57.50
Old Reliable Ellwood Steel Fences, Tin 50.00
Pabst Chemical, 2-Way Face 28.00
Pig, Figural, Head Opens, Striker On Bottom, 1 X 1 3/4 In. 43.00
Playing Cards, Revolving Hands Keep Score, Silver Plate 135.00
Punch, Brass, Striker, 2 1/4 In. 150.00
Rainier Beer 80.00
Rectangular, Rounded Corners, Patterned, Silver, Unger 450.00
Redman Improved Order of Nickel, Brass 60.00
Ring of Flowers, Cast Iron, 2 Pockets, 4 In. 65.00

San Felice Cigars, Man & Woman Picture, 1912 .... 65.00
Scalloped Border, Ornate Front, Silver, Unger 350.00
Souvenir 1st National Bank, Fond Du Lac, Wis., Pocket, 1908 .... 30.00
Souvenir, Colorado Springs, Floral, Sterling Silver 48.00
St. Louis Fair, Striker & Cigar Cutter, 1904 .... 55.00
Stove, Economy Stove Co., Cleveland, Cast Iron 185.00
Table Model, 2 Upright Open Pockets, Scratch Surface, Tin, Blue 85.00
White Ribbon, Temperance Beverage Co., Chicago Glass 30.00

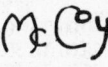

Matsu–no–ke was a type of applied decoration for glass patented by Frederick Carder in 1922. There is clear evidence that pieces were made before that date at the Steuben glassworks. Stevens & Williams of England also made an applied decoration by the same name.

MATSU–NO–KE, Applied Blue Design Forms Handles, Crystal 550.00
Basket, Trefoil Top, 3 Thorned Handles, Stevens & Williams 535.00
Rose Bowl, 6–Crimp Top, Rigaree Center, Cranberry, 4 3/4 In. 550.00
Rose Bowl, Crystal Trails Down At Thorned Stems, 4 3/4 In. 885.00
Toothpick 75.00

McCoy pottery is made in Roseville, Ohio. The J. W. McCoy Pottery was founded in 1899. It became the Brush McCoy Pottery Company in 1911. The name changed to the Brush Pottery in 1925. The word "Brush" was usually included in the mark on their pieces. The Nelson McCoy Sanitary and Stoneware Company, a different firm, was founded in Roseville, Ohio, in 1910. The firm made art pottery after 1926. In 1933 it became the Nelson McCoy Pottery. Pieces marked "McCoy" were made by the Nelson McCoy Company.

MCCOY COOKIE JAR, Kittens On Basket Weave 65.00
MCCOY, Bank, Immigrant Industrial Savings 18.00
Bank, Seaman's For Savings 6.00
Bank, Woodsy Owl 95.00
Coffee Server, El Rancho Bar–B–Que 40.00
Cookie Jar, Apollo Age 300.00
Cookie Jar, Apple, Aqua 30.00
Cookie Jar, Apple, Yellow .... 25.00 To 30.00
Cookie Jar, Asparagus 25.00
Cookie Jar, Ball Shape, Honeycomb Design 20.00
Cookie Jar, Bananas 75.00
Cookie Jar, Barn, Cow In Door 120.00
Cookie Jar, Barnum's Animals, Nabisco .... 65.00 To 150.00
Cookie Jar, Barrel, Large 25.00
Cookie Jar, Basket of Eggs 40.00
Cookie Jar, Basket of Potatoes 35.00
Cookie Jar, Bean Pot, Black, Floral 35.00
Cookie Jar, Bear and Beehive 32.00
Cookie Jar, Bear, Cookie In Vest 30.00
Cookie Jar, Bear, Upside Down 40.00
Cookie Jar, Bobby Baker .... 21.00 To 40.00
Cookie Jar, Boy On Football 85.00
Cookie Jar, Burlap Bag, Half Circle Finial 35.00
Cookie Jar, Caboose 65.00
Cookie Jar, Chef .... 75.00 To 90.00
Cookie Jar, Chilly Willy Penguin 35.00
Cookie Jar, Christmas Tree .... 365.00 To 450.00
Cookie Jar, Circus Horse, Black .... 58.00 To 160.00
Cookie Jar, Clown In Barrel, Pink .... 55.00 To 110.00

For emergency repairs to chipped pottery, try coloring the spot with a wax crayon or oil paint. It will look a little better.

Cookie Jar, Clown, Bust	50.00
Cookie Jar, Coalby Cat	140.00 To 155.00
Cookie Jar, Coffee Grinder	17.00 To 35.00
Cookie Jar, Cookie Bell, Orange Lettering	65.00
Cookie Jar, Cookie Boy, Blue	50.00
Cookie Jar, Cookie Boy, Yellow	125.00
Cookie Jar, Cookie Cabin	28.00
Cookie Jar, Cookie Churn, Brown	24.00
Cookie Jar, Cookie Jug, Molded Letters, Ceramic Cork	30.00
Cookie Jar, Cookie Log, Squirrel Finial	30.00
Cookie Jar, Cookie Pot, White, Dutch Decal	40.00
Cookie Jar, Cookstove, Black	25.00
Cookie Jar, Cookstove, White	25.00 To 35.00
Cookie Jar, Covered Wagon	35.00 To 75.00
Cookie Jar, Drum, Red, White Cover	65.00
Cookie Jar, Duck	75.00
Cookie Jar, Duck On Basket Weave	50.00
Cookie Jar, Dutch Boy	35.00
Cookie Jar, Dutch Girl	60.00
Cookie Jar, Dutch Treat Barn	45.00
Cookie Jar, Elephant	95.00
Cookie Jar, Engine, Black	98.00
Cookie Jar, Engine, Yellow	175.00
Cookie Jar, Forbidden Fruit	60.00 To 70.00
Cookie Jar, Fortune Cookies	20.00 To 50.00
Cookie Jar, Frontier Family	35.00 To 55.00
Cookie Jar, Globe	95.00 To 185.00
Cookie Jar, Granny	60.00 To 115.00
Cookie Jar, Green Pepper	20.00
Cookie Jar, Have A Happy Day	20.00 To 30.00
Cookie Jar, Hen On Nest	50.00
Cookie Jar, Hobby Horse	85.00 To 150.00
Cookie Jar, Honey Bear	45.00 To 65.00
Cookie Jar, Hot Air Balloon	22.00 To 25.00
Cookie Jar, House	80.00 To 95.00
Cookie Jar, Ice Cream Cone	25.00 To 35.00
Cookie Jar, Indian	212.00 To 230.00
Cookie Jar, Jack-O'-Lantern	450.00
Cookie Jar, Kangaroo, Blue	125.00
Cookie Jar, Kangaroo, Tan	195.00 To 240.00
Cookie Jar, Keebler Tree	35.00
Cookie Jar, Kettle, Stationary Bail	30.00
Cookie Jar, Kitten On Basket Weave	45.00
Cookie Jar, Koala Bear	95.00
Cookie Jar, Kookie Kettle	18.00
Cookie Jar, Lamb On Basket Weave	50.00
Cookie Jar, Lamb On Basketweave	50.00
Cookie Jar, Lemon	30.00
Cookie Jar, Lollipops	40.00
Cookie Jar, Lunch Bucket	25.00 To 28.00
Cookie Jar, Mac Dog	52.00 To 60.00
Cookie Jar, Mammy	65.00 To 140.00
Cookie Jar, Mammy, With Cauliflower	375.00
Cookie Jar, Milk Can, Spirit of '76, Eagle Design	40.00
Cookie Jar, Monk	28.00
Cookie Jar, Monkey On Stump	17.00
Cookie Jar, Mr. & Mrs. Owl	23.00 To 65.00
Cookie Jar, Nibble Kettle, Black	115.00
Cookie Jar, Oaken Bucket	20.00 To 25.00
Cookie Jar, Owl, Brown	35.00
Cookie Jar, Penguin, White	60.00
Cookie Jar, Picnic Basket	40.00
Cookie Jar, Pineapple	30.00 To 50.00
Cookie Jar, Puppy, Holding Sign, Brown	44.00 To 52.00

Cookie Jar, Puppy, Thinking 40.00
Cookie Jar, Quaker Oats 135.00
Cookie Jar, Raggedy Ann .... 35.00 To 55.00
Cookie Jar, Rocking Chair With Dalmatians .... 175.00 To 325.00
Cookie Jar, Rooster, Black Spray 60.00
Cookie Jar, Sack of Cookies, Gold Trim 35.00
Cookie Jar, Snoopy On Doghouse .... 75.00 To 125.00
Cookie Jar, Spaceship, Friendship 7 .... 175.00
Cookie Jar, Stagecoach 500.00
Cookie Jar, Strawberry, Red 35.00
Cookie Jar, Teakettle, Black 12.50
Cookie Jar, Tepee 300.00
Cookie Jar, Time For Cookies, Mouse Finial 35.00
Cookie Jar, Timmy Tortoise 40.00
Cookie Jar, Touring Car .... 30.00 To 75.00
Cookie Jar, Turkey 200.00
Cookie Jar, W.C.Fields .... 95.00 To 200.00
Cookie Jar, Windmill 45.00
Cookie Jar, Wishing Well .... 32.00 To 45.00
Cookie Jar, Woodsy Owl 60.00
Cookie Jar, Wren House .... 88.00 To 125.00
Cookie Jar, Yosemite Sam .... 40.00 To 75.00
Creamer, Ivy 10.00
Dish, Tortoise & Hare, 13 X 13 In. 45.00
Flowerpot, Basket Weave 8.00
Jardiniere, Lion, Lioness, Black Outlined, Art Pottery, 1920, 10 In. 250.00
Jug, Green Onyx, Stopper, Music Box 125.00
Mug, Trellis, Green 15.00
Pitcher, Blue Willow 40.00
Pitcher, Nassau County Republican Committee, 6 3/4 In. 20.00
Pitcher, W.C. Fields 45.00
Planter, Alligator 22.00
Planter, Bird Dog 50.00
Planter, Bull, Brown 9.00
Planter, Flower Frog, Green, Pair 15.00
Planter, Frog, Green, 8 1/2 In. 30.00
Planter, Green, Yellow Birds In Center, Square, Pair 25.00
Planter, Parrot, Pink, Marked, 8 In. 25.00
Planter, Squirrel 6.00
Planter, Squirrel, Gray 18.00
Planter, Triple Lily 18.00
Spoon Rest, Butterfly 25.00
Sugar & Creamer, Pine Cone, Green & Brown 15.00
Teapot, Evergreen, Art Deco Shape, 4 Cup 25.00
Teapot, Ivy 40.00
Teapot, Pine Cone 20.00
Teapot, Yellow .... 10.00 To 20.00
Tureen, Sombrero, El Rancho, Set 65.00
Umbrella Stand, Basket Weave, 20 1/2 In. 325.00
Umbrella Stand, Cherries, Loy–Nel–Art 440.00
Vase, Birds In Relief, Green, 8 In. 22.50
Vase, Grapes & Leaves, Rust, Ivory & Teal, 9 In. 60.00
Vase, Inverted Keyhole Shape, Pink, Dogwood, Square Top, 7 In. 38.00
Vase, Loy–Nel–Art, 12 3/4 In. 295.00
Vase, Tulip, 7 1/2 In. 25.00
Wall Pocket, Apple 12.00
Wall Pocket, Clock 15.00
Wall Pocket, Fan, Aqua 12.00
Wall Pocket, Fan, Sunburst, Gold 11.00
Wall Pocket, Umbrella, Yellow 15.00
Water Cooler, Cowboys & Bucking Broncos 125.00
Wren House, Pink Bird 70.00

PRESCUT The McKee name has been associated with various glass enterprises in the United States since 1836, including J. & F. McKee (1850), Bryce, McKee & Co. (1850 to 1854), McKee and Brothers (1865), and National Glass Co. (1899). In 1903, the McKee Glass Company was formed in Jeanette, Pennsylvania. It became McKee Division of the Thatcher Glass Co. in 1951 and was bought out by the Jeanette Corporation in 1961. Pressed glass, kitchenwares, and tablewares were produced.

MCKEE, see also Custard Glass

MCKEE, Bowl, Laurel, French Ivory, 11 In.	17.50
Box, Dresser, Heart Shape, Milk Glass, Painted	30.00
Bread Plate, Star Rosettes, Motto	30.00
Butter, Wiltee Swirl, Cover, Frosted	50.00
Candlestick, Laurel, Green, Pair	45.00
Clock, Tambour, Blue	225.00
Clock, Tambour, Pink	400.00
Cocktail, Rock Crystal, Footed, 3 1/2 Oz.	10.00
Compote, Prism, Flint, 7 3/4 In.	45.00
Compote, Puritan, 9 In.	32.00 To 38.00
Compote, Sunshine, 5 In.	20.00
Cup, Tom & Jerry, Opaque Yellow	15.00
Custard, Jadite	5.00 To 25.00
Dish, Cheese, Cover, Laurel, Jade	25.00
Dish, Dove Cover, Round, Topaz, Signed	350.00
Dish, Jade, Laurel, Cover, 5 X 9 In.	40.00
Dish, Rabbit Cover, White	65.00
Figure, Bird House, Wren's Honeymoon Hut, Green	75.00
Goblet, Balder, Clear, Gold	28.00
Goblet, Rock Crystal, Footed, Flared, Amber, 5 1/2 In.	10.00
Measuring Cup, Jade, 4 Cup	35.00
Mug, Bottoms Down, Seville Yellow	150.00
Mug, Troubador, Opaque Blue	65.00
Pepper Shaker, Jadite	10.00
Pitcher, Prescut, 9 1/2 In.	40.00
Pitcher, Ray, 5 3/4 In.	30.00
Plate, Laurel, Dinner, Green	7.00
Plate, Rock Crystal, Ruby, 9 1/2 In.	35.00
Relish, Stippled Bars	32.00
Relish, Union	32.00
Salt & Pepper, Black Amethyst	25.00
Salt & Pepper, Seville Yellow	20.00
Salt & Pepper, Ships	6.00
Saltshaker, Jadite, Square	9.00
Shot Glass, Bottoms Up, Custard Glass	48.00
Spooner, Vulcan, Sahara	35.00
Sugar, Rock Crystal, Cover	75.00
Tom & Jerry Set, Custard Glass, 5 Piece	35.00
Toothpick, Colonial, Apple Green	45.00
Vase, Jade, Art Glass, Nude Triangular, 8 1/2 In.	60.00
Vase, Jade, Nude, 8 In.	65.00
Vase, Lone Star, Emerald, 8 In.	25.00
Vase, Rock Crystal, Cream, 11 In.	38.00
Wine, Liberty	18.50
Wine, Rock Cyrstal, Red, 2 Oz.	45.00

MECHANICAL BANK, see Bank, Mechanical

 All types of equipment used by doctors or hospitals are included in this section. Medical office furniture, operating tools, microscopes, thermometers, and other paraphernalia used by doctors are included. Medicine bottles are listed under Bottle. There are related collectibles listed under Dental.

MEDICAL, Air Compressor, Beveled Glass On 3 Sides, Iron Feet	500.00
Apothecary Drawers, Seed Counter, Pulls Dated 1889, 38 In. 10 Ft.	1800.00

Bag, Doctor's, Cowhide, Upjohn Co.	75.00
Bedpan, Jones Relax	6.00
Bleeder, 3 Blades, Brass Holder	55.00
Bleeder, Horn Handle	75.00
Bleeder, Snowden, Single Steel Blade, Brass	225.00
Book, Antique Medical Instruments, Elisabeth Bennion, 355 Pages	75.00
Booklet, Bell–Cap–Sic Jingles, B–C–S Plasters, Creased, 1880s	25.00
Bottle, Urine Specimen, Embossed Lettering, Numbers	20.00
Breast Pump, Glass	9.00
Bunion Remover, Doctor Scholl's, 1913	20.00 To 35.00
Cabinet, Doctor's, Oak, Swing–Out Units, Locks, 1850–75, 70 In.	1800.00
Cabinet, Label, Apothecary's, 49 Compartments, Rolls of Labels	395.00
Cabinet, Veterinary Medicine, Oak, Tin Horse's Head, 16 In.	255.00
Case, Veterinarian, Dr. Daniel's Label	95.00
Case, Veterinarian, Humphrey's Label	95.00
Chair, Optometrist's, Porcelain	175.00
Corker, Bottle, Pharmacy, Hinged Middle With Plunger, C.1890	45.00
Device, Violet Ray Type, Sears & Roebuck, Box	40.00
Dilators, Rectal, Dr. Young's, Bakelite, Box	30.00
Dose Timer, Milk Glass, Metal Indicator, Pat. Applied For Base	35.00
Electric Belt, Addison, Box	35.00
Eye Chart, 19th Century	160.00
Eyecup, 2 Embossed Eyes, Dated 1937	12.00
Eyecup, 8 Panels, Amber, 2 1/2 In.	25.00
Eyecup, 8 Panels, Cobalt Blue, Marked M In Circle, 2 3/8 In.	15.00
Eyecup, Cobalt Blue, Elder Flower Lotion	24.00
Eyecup, Cobalt Blue, Pedestal	12.00
Eyecup, Embossed Optrex Sight, Safeguard, 1 1/4 In.	22.00
Eyecup, John Bull, 2 5/8 In.	25.00
Eyecup, Milk Glass	10.00 To 12.00
File Box, Drugstore, Drugpak Label, 7 X 10 In.	8.00
Fleam, 2 Blades, Borwick, Brass Shield 3 In.	85.00
Fleam, 3 Blades, Brass Casing	35.00
Fleam, 3 Heart–Shaped Blades, Brass Handle, Sheffield	75.00
Fleam, 4 Blades, Brass Case, Marked London	62.50
Fleam, 5 Blades, Brass, Varying Sizes, 18th Century	75.00
Hearing Kit, Dr. Guy Clifford Powel, Case	65.00
Inhaler, Improved Inspirator, Hard Rubber, 4 1/2 X 2 1/4 X 5/8 In.	175.00
Invalid Feeder, Gold Rim	15.00
Invalid Feeder, White Graniteware	22.00
Kit, First Aid, Bell Telephone, Hinged Tin Chest, Pocket	25.00
Kit, Tool, Optician's, Wall & Oschs Opticians, Phila., Wooden Case	60.00
Kit, Travel, Surgical Instruments, Frye's	48.00
Lancet, Spring, Brass Case, Steel Lever Release, Leather Case	145.00
Lenses, Optician's, Attachments, Set	70.00
Machine, Davis & Kidder's Magneto, Nervous Disorders, Case	245.00
Machine, Heart Defibrilator, U.S.	50.00
Machine, Ultraviolet Ray, Sun Kraft Therapy Lamp, Timer, 1946	22.00
Mask, Ether, Hinged For Holding Gauze, 20th Century	35.00
Massager, Foot, Dr. Scholl's, Chrome Base, Plastic Footrest, 6 In.	40.00
Measure, Julius Greyer Apothecary, Cincinnati	22.50
Measure, Sauk Center, Minn., Glass	8.50
Mold, Suppository, Thumbscrew Closure, Brass, 19th Century	65.00
Mortar & Pestle, Bell Metal, 18th Century, 6 1/2 In.	605.00
Notebook & Calender, Dr. Pierce's Ladies, Medicinal Promo, 1902	17.00
Oxydonor Victory, Electrode To Device, Dr. Her. Sanche, 1890	95.00
Pump, Stomach, Brass, Ebony & Ivory Fittings, Wooden Case	395.00
Scalpel, Spear Shape, Bone Handle, Case, C.1850	30.00
Shot Glass, Measure, Adlerika Natural Bowel Cleanser	8.00
Sign, Eyes Examined, Light–Up Globe, Reverse On Glass	950.00
Sign, Measles Quarantine, Board of Health, 1940s	20.00 To 25.00
Sign, Optician, Neon Glass With Eyes In Background, 8 X 24 In.	80.00
Skeleton, Doctor's, In Coffin, 1860s	1300.00
Skull, Human, Cranium Cut In Half, 19th–Century Teaching Aid	225.00

Speculum, Bivalve, Nickel Plated Brass Blades, Ebony Handle	120.00
Splint, Right Forearm, Lee's Pat. Sept. 25, 1888, Perforated Metal	75.00
Spoon, Medicine, Folding, Sterling Silver, Gorham, Case	75.00
Systoscope, Case, Accessories	22.00
Trephine, Skull Surgery, Brass, Sharp & Smith, 4 1/4 X 4 In.	110.00
Urinal, Female, White Enamel	11.00
Urinal, Male, Glass	12.00
Vaporizer, Simplex Lamp Co., Cylindrical Holder, 7 1/2 In.	60.00
Vaporizer, Vapo–Cresolene, Electric	20.00
Water Bottle, Davol, Rubber	20.00

Meerschaum pipes and other pieces of carved meerschaum, a soft mineral, date from the nineteenth century to the present.

MEERSCHAUM, Cheroot Holder, Carved Playing Dogs	58.00
Cigar Holder, Carved, Amber Mouthpiece & Trim, 4 In.	25.00
Pipe, Bearded Man, 6 In.	40.00
Pipe, Carved Horse, Case	58.00
Pipe, Carved Lion's Head, 6 1/2 In.	75.00
Pipe, Carved Man's Head	40.00
Pipe, Carved, Leather Case	60.00
Pipe, Cottage & Horse, Dated 1816	175.00
Pipe, Horse, Man's Face Match Safe, Cigar Cutter, 3 Piece	195.00
Pipe, Roman Head Bowl	50.00
Pipe, Sultan's Head, Amber Mouthpiece	60.00

Meissen is a town in Germany where porcelain has been made since 1710. Any china made in the town can be called Meissen, although the famous Meissen factory made the finest porcelains of the area. The crossed swords mark of the great Meissen factory has been copied by many other firms in Germany and other parts of the world.

MEISSEN, Bowl, In–Cut Corners, Serpentine Shape, 19th Century, 7 In.	120.00
Bowl, Raised Gold Leaves, Hand Painted Fruit Center, Marked, 10 In.	250.00
Bowl, Reticulated Border, White & Gold, 14 X 9 In.	550.00
Bowl, Reticulated, Gold & White, Trim, Marked, 10 X 14 In.	355.00
Bowl, Yellow, White & Gold, 14 X 10 In.	395.00
Box, Blue Flowers, 4 In.	94.00
Box, Easter Egg, Hand Painted Flower In & Out, 7 1/2 X 5 X 4 In.	475.00
Box, Floral Enameled, Gilt All Sides, Marked, Oval, 3 In.	325.00
Breakfast Set, Orange Floral Sprays, Basket Weave Ground, 6 Piece	412.50
Bust, Child, Grapes & Vines Draping On Shoulders, Head, 10 In.	1450.00
Butter Chip, Gold Border, Multicolored Flower Center	45.00
Candelabrum, 3–Light, Woman Figure Base, Pair	1000.00
Candelabrum, 4–Light, Vines of Flowers, Fruit, Children, 10 3/4 In.	3500.00
Candelabrum, 4–Light, Vines of Flowers, Marked, 19 3/4 In., Pair	325.00
Candelabrum, 7–Light, Vines, Children Base, Crossed Swords, 22 In.	2045.00
Centerpiece, Woman Knop, 3 Tiers, Crossed Swords, 21 In.	1100.00
Coffee Set, Mocca, 1830s, 30 Piece	2500.00
Compote, Deutschenblumen, Swirl Base, Marked, C.1870, 8 1/2 In.	475.00
Compote, Floral Center, Gold Tracery, Signed, 7 X 9 In.	245.00
Compote, Floral Relief Edge, Gold Trim, Marked, 6 1/2 X 12 In.	450.00
Compote, Fruit, Beading, Floral Edge, Gold Trim, Marked, 12 In.	450.00
Cup & Saucer, Quatrefoil, Hand Painted Harbor Scenes, Blue AR	275.00
Dish, Gold Foliage, Center Floral, Royal Blue Ground, 12 In.	125.00
Dish, Sweetmeat, Reclining Man, Floral Jacket, Marked, 8 In.	125.00
Ewer, Allegorical, 13 In.	1200.00
Figurine, Barefoot Girl, Basket of Flowers, 5 In.	550.00
Figurine, Child, Large Reticulated Birdcage, Crossed Swords, 5 In.	825.00
Figurine, Court Tailor, Riding On Goat, Crossed Swords, 16 X 14 In.	5300.00
Figurine, Cupid, Holding Wheat & Scythe, Crossed Swords, 5 1/4 In.	450.00
Figurine, Girl, Stool, Blue Pillow, Book, Crossed Swords, 5 1/2 In.	825.00

Figurine, Housekeeper, Contemporary Costume, Marked, 6 1/4 In. 1650.00
Figurine, Man, Collecting Kindling, Crossed Swords, 1870, 7 1/2 In. 610.00
Figurine, Nude, Holding Flower Garland, Crossed Swords, 5 3/4 In. 995.00
Figurine, Nude, Standing, Over Cage, Crossed Swords, 4 1/2 In. 525.00
Figurine, Silenus On A Donkey, Marked, 19th Century, 8 In. 1450.00
Figurine, Winter, Bearded Man, Naked, Pink Cloak, 10 In. 880.00
Figurine, Winter, Man, Naked, Fur Lined Cloak, 1755, 8 In. 1320.00
Figurine, Woman With Plumed Hat, Basket of Flowers, 5 1/2 In. 665.00
Figurine, Woman, Cat, Stepped Circular Base, Crossed Swords, 9 In. 1550.00
Figurine, Woman, Colonial, Dog At Feet, Marked, 6 In. 275.00
Figurine, Woman, In Shell Chariot, 1890, Crossed Swords, 7 In. 1100.00
Figurine, Woman, With Cat, Floral Housecoat, C.1870, 9 In. 1400.00
Figurine, Young Girl With Basket of Flowers, 5 In. 412.50
Group, 2 Nude Cupids, Marbelized Base, 1910 .... 995.00
Group, 2 Women, 1 Man, Gardener, Marked, 8 1/4 In. 1650.00
Group, 3 Putti, Folio Under Arm, Blue, Violet, Green, 8 In. 950.00
Group, 3 Roman Warriors Riding An Elephant 3100.00
Group, Allegorical Fire, Maiden & Cupid, Marked, 14 1/2 In. 3000.00
Group, Apple Pickers, Crossed Swords, 10 1/4 In. 1100.00
Group, Boy & Girl, Garland of Flowers, Marked, 3 In. 475.00
Group, Boy & Girl, Playing Lute & Violin, Marked, 4 In., Pair 40.00
Group, Cherub Studying, Teacher Behind, Females, 11 1/2 In. 2500.00
Group, Cow, Girl, Boy, Crossed Swords, 6 1/2 X 8 In. 600.00
Group, Cupids, Seated, Holding Sword, Marked, 5 5/8 In. 1100.00
Group, Cybele, Wearing Crown, On Lion, Surrounded By Putti, 9 In. 1550.00
Group, Lovers, Lamb In Woman's Lap, Crossed Swords, 9 In. 665.00
Group, Sea Goddess, Shell Shaped Throne, Baby Triton, Putti, 9 In. 1765.00
Group, Woman, Reading Under Tree, Mude Boy At Feet, 10 1/4 In. 550.00
Group, Young Man Toasts His Lady, Marked, 8 1/2 In. 715.00
Jug, Young Boy Saws Limbs From Tree, Another Prunes, 4 In., Pair 825.00
Pitcher, Lovers' Scene, Hand Painted Reserves, Blue, Marked, 5 In. 110.00
Plate Set, Different Center Flowers, Set of 4 .... 175.00
Plate, Flowers, Basket Weave Border, Marked, 9 1/2 In., Pair 175.00
Plate, Foliate Sprays, Basket Weave Border, 9 1/4 In., 8 Piece 465.00
Plate, Gold Rococo Border, Pink & White Lacy Pattern, 8 In. 175.00
Plate, Pink & White Center Design, Gold Rococo Rim, 8 1/2 In. 175.00
Salt, Figural, Double, Boy, Black Hat, Striped Breeches, Marked, 5 In. 525.00
Tea Set, Gold & White, Marked, Tray 16 X 16 In., 4 Piece 175.00
Tureen, Flowers, Cherubs Cover, 15 In. 2000.00
Vase, Empire Style, Entwined Snake Handles, Gold Border, 10 1/2 In. 250.00
Vase, Tapestry, 7 In. 300.00
Vase, Watteau Scenes of Lovers, Cover, Blue AR, 12 3/8 In. 335.00

Mercury, or silvered, glass was first made in the 1850s. It lost favor
for a while but became popular again about 1910. It looks like a
piece of silver.

MERCURY GLASS, Candlestick, 12 In., Pair 10.00
Figurine, Apple, 3 1/8 In. 45.00
Sugar & Creamer 65.00
Vase, Floral Design, 8 1/2 In. 18.00
Vase, Floral, 8 In., Pair 250.00
Vase, White Floral, 12 In. 50.00
Wine, Gold, Figural Nude Stem, Frosted 50.00

The Merrimac Pottery Company was founded by Thomas Nickerson
in Newburyport, Massachusetts, in 1902. The company made art
pottery, garden pottery, and reproductions of Roman pottery. The
pottery burned to the ground in 1908.

MERRIMAC, Chamberstick, Loop Handle, Dish Base, 6 In. 357.00
Mug, Flared, Mottled Green Glaze, 6 3/4 In. 137.00
Mug, Loop Handle, Green & Charcoal Glaze 77.00

Mettlach, Germany, is a city where the Villeroy and Boch factories worked. Steins from the firm are known as Mettlach steins. They date from about 1842. PUG means "painted under glaze." The steins can be dated from the marks on the bottom which include a date–number code. Other pieces may be listed in the Villeroy & Boch category.

METTLACH, Beaker, Hires Root Beer, Handle	100.00
Pitcher, No.7023, Mythological Figures, 17 In.	2750.00
Plaque, No.1769, Battle Scene, Arnold Von Winkelried, 15 In.	650.00
Plaque, No.2187, Knight, House of Hohenzollern, 17 1/2 In.	2600.00
Plaque, No.2188, Knight, House of Hapsburg, 17 1/2 In.	2600.00
Plaque, No.7045, Man & Woman, Garden, 15 1/2 X 8 In.	715.00
Stein, No.1452, 1/2 Liter, Foliage, Domed Pewter Cover	250.00
Stein, No.1467, 1/2 Liter, Harvest Scene	175.00 To 350.00
Stein, No.1526, 1/2 Liter, Woman, Foliage, Stag	225.00
Stein, No.1527, 1 Liter, 4 Men Drinking, Inlaid Lid, Etched	465.00
Stein, No.1690, 4 1/2 Liter, Man & Woman Riding Horses	2000.00
Stein, No.1695, 1/2 Liter, Hunting Scenes	240.00
Stein, No.1995, 1/2 Liter, Fat Man Drinking	120.00
Stein, No.1998, 1/2 Liter, Martin Moehn Brewery	500.00
Stein, No.2001A, 1/2 Liter, Book, Law	475.00
Stein, No.2002, 1/2 Liter, Munich	325.00
Stein, No.2038, 3 4/5 Liter, Rodenstein, 16 1/2 In.	2500.00
Stein, No.2090, 1 Liter, Man Smoking Pipe	475.00
Stein, No.2093, 1/2 Liter, Playing Cards	595.00
Stein, No.2206, 3 Liter, Tavern Scene, 1905, 16 3/4 In.	715.00
Stein, No.2211, 3/10 Liter, Tavern Scene, Pewter Bowling Pin Lift	225.00
Stein, No.2271, Tavern Scene	150.00
Stein, No.2402, 1/2 Liter, Courting of Siegfried	780.00
Stein, No.2403, 1/2 Liter, Wartburg, Etched Lid	490.00
Stein, No.2757, 2 3/10 Liter, Musical Scenes	1425.00
Stein, No.2765, 1/2 Liter, Knight On White Horse, Etched	2600.00
Stein, No.2796, 3 Liter, Scene of Heidelberg, 15 1/2 In.	650.00
Stein, No.2900, 1/2 Liter, Argentina Brewery, 1904	395.00
Stein, No.3089, 1 Liter, Diogenes	950.00
Vase, No.1537, Cherubs As 4 Seasons, Marked, 14 In., Pair	650.00
Vase, No.1897, Geometric, Blue, 11 In.	345.00

Milk glass was named for its milky–white color. It was first made in England during the 1700s. The height of its popularity in the United States was from 1870 to 1880. It is now correct to refer to some colored glass as blue milk glass, black milk glass, etc. Reproductions of milk glass are being made and sold in many stores.

MILK GLASS, see also Cosmos; Vallerysthal

MILK GLASS, Banana Stand, Old Quilt, Footed, Westmoreland	70.00
Basket, Swan, Closed Neck	50.00
Bell, Smoke, 7 X 8 In.	65.00
Bonbon, Hobnail	10.00
Bottle, Grant's Tomb, Domed Stopper	375.00
Bottle, Yellow, Pinched, Mushroom Stopper, 9 1/2 In.	450.00
Bowl, Cupped, Paneled Grape, 8 In.	37.50
Bowl, Doeskin, Crimped, Rose	12.00
Bowl, Hobnail, Ruffled, 11 In.	28.00
Bowl, Ivy, Panel Grape, Footed	45.00
Bowl, Violet, 2 1/4 In.	12.00
Box, Candy, Heart, Gold Cover, 3 Sections, Consolidated, 1950s	45.00
Bread Plate, Wheat & Barley	60.00
Butter, Cover, Ball & Claw, Crossed Ferns, Snowflake Ice Insert	95.00
Butter, Cover, King Crown Basket Weave, Black	65.00
Butter, Cover, Lamb, Child's	90.00
Butter, Cover, Paneled Grape, Westmoreland, 1/4 Lb.	15.00
Butter, Cover, Scroll, Blue	165.00
Candleholder, Doeskin, Rose	8.00

Candleholder, Hobnail, 6 In., Pair	20.00
Candy, Dolphin Cover, Westmoreland	35.00
Compote, Atlas, Large	85.00
Compote, Blue Lattice Edge	50.00
Compote, Blue, Embossed Dahlia, Hexagon Base, 4 1/2 X 2 1/2 In.	35.00
Compote, Jenny Lind, Woman Supports Bowl	95.00
Compote, Open Latticework, Apple Blossoms, Leaves, 7 In.	85.00
Condiment Set, Fan, 3 Bottles, Black & Pink Paint	45.00
Cookie Jar, Cherry & Cable, Westmoreland	52.00
Cookie Jar, Grape & Cable	50.00
Creamer, Blackberry	30.00
Creamer, Cane & Scroll	30.00
Creamer, Owl	95.00
Creamer, Owl, Blue	50.00
Creamer, Sawtooth	25.00
Creamer, Tassel With Holly	65.00
Cruet, Hobnail, 7 Oz.	28.00
Cruet, Netted Oak	38.00
Cup, Nursery Rhymes	16.00
Dish, Admiral Dewey On Battleship Cover, C.1900	75.00
Dish, Battleship Olympia Cover	85.00
Dish, Cat Cover, White Head, Oval, Blue, 4 1/4 In.	60.00
Dish, Cat On Drum Cover, Portieux	60.00
Dish, Chick In Egg Cover, On Sleigh	70.00
Dish, Chicken Cover, Glass Eyes	45.00
Dish, Covered Wagon	80.00
Dish, Dog Cover, White Head, Blue	68.00
Dish, Elephant With Rider Cover, Blue	275.00
Dish, Fish Shape	16.00
Dish, Football Cover, C.1920, 6 In.	125.00
Dish, Frosted Duck, Diamond Diapered Base	100.00
Dish, Hen Cover, Basket Weave Base, Challinor Taylor, 7 In.	55.00
Dish, Hen On Nest Cover, Blue Head	60.00
Dish, Log Cabin Cover	65.00
Dish, Lovebirds On Nest, Mother-of-Pearl, Westmoreland	48.00
Dish, Ocean Liner Cover	45.00
Dish, Rooster Cover, Basket Weave Base, Challinor Taylor, 7 In.	55.00
Dish, Rooster Cover, Blue Head, Coarse Rib Base	72.50
Dish, Squirrel On Acorn Cover	125.00
Dish, Swan On Basket Cover, Closed Neck	50.00
Dish, Turkey Cover, Full-Bodied, White, Signed Imperial, 8 In.	65.00
Eggcup, Birch Leaf, Flint	42.50
Eggcup, Chicken	10.00
Epergne, 4-Light, Blue Trim	375.00
Figurine, Scotty Dog, L.E. Smith, 1930s, Large	80.00
Fish Platter Set, Atterbury, Patent Dated, 5 Piece	200.00
Goblet, Blackberry	20.00
Gravy, Underplate, Paneled Grape, Westmoreland	48.00
Jar, Cover, Queen Victoria	195.00
Jardiniere, Hobnail, 6 In.	12.00
Jardiniere, Paneled Grape, Westmoreland	17.50
Juice Set, Hobnail, 7 Piece	68.00
Lamp, Conical Shade, Goddess of Liberty, Electrified, 20 In.	335.00
Lamp, Cube, Scotty On Top, White Metal	30.00
Lamp, Dancing Couple	45.00
Lamp, Jenny Lind	150.00
Lamp, Student, Pink Roses & Crest	325.00
Lighter, Cigarette, Hobnail, 2 1/4 In.	18.00
Mug, Liberty Bell, Child's	50.00
Mug, Westward Ho, 2 1/2 In.	175.00
Mustard, Bull's Head Cover	115.00
Mustard, Hobnail	8.00
Perfume Bottle, Beaded Rib, 10 1/2 In.	125.00
Perfume Bottle, Stopper, Jenny Lind, Fostoria	85.00

Pineapple & Fan, Syrup	165.00
Pitcher, Block	125.00
Pitcher, Indiana Sandwich	100.00
Pitcher, Old Quilt, Blue, 1 Qt.	50.00
Pitcher, Owl, 7 1/4 In.	155.00
Pitcher, Paneled Grape, Westmoreland, 1 Pt.	27.50
Pitcher, Water, Curtain, Gold Flecks	225.00
Pitcher, Water, Dart Bar	75.00
Pitcher, Water, Guttate, Cranberry	295.00
Pitcher, Water, Oval Panels	75.00
Pitcher, Water, Royal Oak, Fired-On Colors, Gold	200.00
Planter, Crescent, Hobnail, 10 In.	21.00
Plaque, Easel, Blue Enameled Flowers, Rococo, Attached Stand	45.00
Plate, Admiral William Sampson	38.00
Plate, Backward C, Jefferson Davis Center	50.00
Plate, Battleship Maine	20.00
Plate, Chickens, No Easter Without Us, 6 1/4 In.	55.00
Plate, Gothic, 9 In.	25.00
Plate, Hand Painted Floral, Lattice Edge, Trumpet Vines, 10 In.	140.00
Plate, Iowa Capitol	18.50
Plate, McKinley	96.00
Plate, Niagara Falls	25.00
Plate, Open Latticework, Apple Blossoms, 10 In.	55.00
Plate, Owl	40.00
Plate, Roger Williams	95.00
Plate, Serenade, 6 In.	35.00
Plate, Three Bears, 7 1/2 In.	30.00
Plate, Three Kittens	25.00
Plate, Three Puppies, Gold Paint	95.00
Platter, Bread, Basket Weave, Motto, Pat. Date	55.00
Platter, Hobnail, 10 In.	26.00
Platter, John Hancock Signature, Twig Handles	260.00
Platter, Rock of Ages, Oval, Atterbury, Nov.23, 1875	150.00
Powder Box, Paneled Grape, Westmorelnad	16.00
Punch Set, Pineapple & Grape, Ladle, 14 Piece	225.00 To 285.00
Punch Set, White Rose, Lemon Stained, 7 Piece	200.00
Refrigerator Set, G.E. Seal	55.00
Relish, Fish, Dated 1871	25.00
Relish, Heart Shape, Hobnail	18.00
Rolling Pin, Maple Handles	55.00
Rolling Pin, Wooden Handle, Dated 1921	87.50
Salt & Pepper, Blue, Leaf Cornered Base	55.00
Salt & Pepper, God Bless America, Great To Be American, 4 In.	22.00
Salt & Pepper, Hobnail, Footed	12.00
Salt, Basket Weave, Blue	20.00
Salt, Chick	8.00
Salt, Goose	35.00
Salt, Rabbit & Chickens, Moon & Star Top	30.00
Salt, Rabbits, Mt. Washington, Bulbous	30.00
Salt, Turtle, Hobbs	40.00
Sherbet, Rooster	10.00
Soap Dish, Paneled Grape	37.50
Spooner, Netted Oak	37.50
Spooner, Panel Grape Band	45.00
Spooner, Paneled Wheat	25.00 To 39.00
Spooner, Sawtooth	25.00
Sugar & Creamer, Cherry & Cable, Westmoreland	40.00
Sugar & Creamer, Della Robbia	20.00
Sugar & Creamer, Hobnail	12.00 To 18.00
Sugar & Creamer, Swan, Westmoreland	70.00
Sugar Shaker, Pewter Top, Blue	25.00
Sugar, Cord Drapery	425.00
Sugar, Cover, Blackberry	47.50
Sugar, Cover, King Crown Basket Weave, Black	65.00

Minton, Plate, Leda & Swan,
Herringbone Border, C.1900, 20 In.

Mocha, Pitcher, Blue Bands,
White Worming, 7 In.

Mt.Joye, Console Set,
Poppy Pods, Red Crystal,
Signed, 11 3/4 In.

Sugar, Cover, Princess Feather, Flint	125.00
Sugar, Cover, Tree of Life	75.00
Syrup, Alba, Enamel Design	45.00
Syrup, Cover, Large Raised Rose Under Spout, Painted	45.00
Syrup, Fishnet & Poppies	65.00
Table Set, Beaded Drape, Gold Trim, 4 Piece	350.00
Table Set, Guttate, White, Gold Trim, 3 Piece	200.00
Toothpick, Clown Head, Brown Hair	100.00
Toothpick, Horseshoe & Clover	30.00
Toothpick, Owl	45.00
Toothpick, Palm Leaf, Footed	40.00
Toothpick, Tramp's Shoe, Left	440.00
Tray, Card, Hatch Dove	210.00
Tumbler, Apple Blossom	60.00
Tumbler, Hobnail, 12 Oz.	11.00
Vase, 5 Red Flamingos, Leaves, Bulb Shape, 9 In.	25.00
Vase, Bud, Paneled Grape, Westmoreland	10.00
Vase, Cabbage Roses, 6 X 5 1/2 In.	10.00
Vase, Hand Holding Vase, 9 X 2 3/8 In.	95.00
Vase, Paneled Grape, Westmoreland, 14 In., Pair	120.00
Vase, Paneled Grape, Westmoreland, 9 In.	28.00
Vase, Ruby, 8 In.	75.00
Window Box, Embossed Dancing Nudes, L.E. Smith, 7 3/4 In.	25.00
Window Box, Paneled Grape	35.00

Millefiori means, literally, a thousand flowers. It is a type of glasswork popular in paperweights. Many small flowerlike pieces of glass are grouped together to form a design.

MILLEFIORI, Dish, 8 Sides, Blue & White, 5 In.	125.00
Vase, Multicolored, Hand Blown, 7 In.	145.00

Minton china has been made in the Staffordshire region of England from 1793 to the present. The firm became part of the Royal Doulton Tableware Group in 1968, but the wares continued to be marked "Minton." Many marks have been used. The one shown dates from about 1873 to 1891, when the word "England" was added.

MINTON, Butter Chip, Indian Tree	45.00
Centerpiece & Candlesticks, Napoleon & Josephine, Aqua, White, 3 Pc.	1375.00
Cup & Saucer, Enameled Flowers, Maroon, Gold Rim, Marked	50.00
Figurine, Nude Woman On Back of Lion, Parian	660.00

Flask, Blue Willow	375.00
Gravy, Vermont	50.00
Pitcher, Cobalt Blue, White Ivy, Embossed Mark, 1845, 9 In.	450.00
Pitcher, Green On Green, Fuchsia, Leaves, Embossed Mark, 6 1/2 In.	265.00
Plate, Bird, Fruit Branches, Gold Rim, 1880, 9 In.	125.00
Plate, Leda & Swan, Herringbone Border, C.1900, 20 In. ....*Illus*	1400.00
Platter, Vermont, 15 In.	115.00
Soap Dish, Green & Yellow, 3 Piece	35.00
Teapot, Underplate, White On White, Geometric, Metal Cover, 1820–50	175.00
Tile, Green Leaf Design, 6 X 6 In.	17.00

MIRROR, see Furniture, Mirror

Mochaware is an English–made product that was sold in America during the early 1800s. It is a heavy pottery with pale coffee–and–cream coloring. Designs of blue, brown, green, orange, black, or white were added to the pottery.

MOCHA, Bowl, Black & White Checkerboard Rim, Embossed Ribs, 4 1/4 In.	425.00
Bowl, Brown Bands, 5 X 10 1/2 In.	75.00
Bowl, Cover, Embossed Geometric, Stripes of Brown, Orange, Tan, 6 In.	2000.00
Bowl, Earthworm, 6 1/2 In.	525.00
Bowl, Gray Band, 2 Interwoven Rows of Earthworm Design, 6 1/4 In.	800.00
Bowl, Marbelized, 8 In.	725.00
Bowl, Waste, Gray Band, Black Rim, Earthworm Design, 4 5/8 In.	325.00
Bowl, Waste, Multicolored Dots, Black & White Rim Design, 5 1/2 In.	700.00
Creamer, Blue & White Stripes, 4 In.	20.00
Creamer, Marbelized Medallions, Embossed Leaf Handles, 4 1/4 In.	775.00
Creamer, Multicolored Earthworm Design, Leaf Handle, 3 3/8 In.	550.00
Creamer, Strainer Spout, Marbelized Design, Red, Brown, Blue, 4 7/8 In.	1000.00
Mug, Black Bands, Brown & Blue, 5 In.	160.00
Mug, Black Seaweed Design, Stripes, Leaf Handle, 3 5/8 In.	250.00
Mug, Black Seaweed On Pink Band, Marked Pint, 4 7/8 In.	75.00
Mug, Blue Stripes, Mustard Yellow Bands, Leaf Handle, 2 5/8 In.	225.00
Mug, Brown & Sand Bands, 3 In.	190.00
Mug, Chocolate Brown, Black Rim, Seaweed Design, Embossed Leaf, 4 In.	400.00
Mug, Earthworm Design, Embossed Leaf Handle, 4 3/4 In.	475.00
Mug, Earthworm, 6 In.	1600.00
Mug, Embossed Blue Band, Gray Band, Seaweed Design, 6 In.	325.00
Mug, Inlaid Agate, England, 1840	750.00
Mug, Marbelized Design, Green Bands, 5 7/8 In.	925.00
Mug, Marbelized Design, Leaf Handle, Green Rim, 3 3/4 In.	600.00
Mug, Marbelized, Blue Band, Leaf Handle, 3 7/8 In.	775.00
Mug, Marbelized, Checkerboard Band, 6 1/8 In.	900.00
Mug, Marbelized, Green Bands, 5 7/8 In.	925.00
Mug, Marbelized, Leaf Handle, Green Rim, 3 3/4 In.	600.00
Mug, Mustard Yellow, Brown Polka Dot Rim Band, 6 In.	250.00
Mug, Seaweed Design, Yellow Band, Brown Stripes, 2 1/2 In.	200.00
Mug, Tan Band, Brown Seaweed Design, Leaf Handle, 3 5/8 In.	350.00
Mug, Tree, 6 In.	750.00
Mug, White & Black Stripes, Gray, Leaf Handle, 3 5/8 In.	25.00
Mustard, Pale Blue, Black Stripes, 2 1/8 In.	85.00
Pepper Pot	975.00
Pitcher, Blue & Black Stripes, Tan Band, Leaf Handle, 7 In.	600.00
Pitcher, Blue Bands, White Worming, 7 In. ....*Illus*	660.00
Pitcher, Blue Seaweed Design, John M. Derby, Oct.13, 1846, 11 In.	3500.00
Pitcher, Cat's–Eye & Earthworm Design, Banded, 7 In.	900.00
Pitcher, Earthworm & Polka Dot Design, Gray & Blue Bands, 6 7/8 In.	800.00
Pitcher, Earthworm Design, Leaf Handle, Barrel Shape, 6 1/2 In.	250.00
Pitcher, Earthworm Design, White Trim, 8 In.	350.00
Pitcher, Leaf Emblems, Worm Band, Rust, Baluster, 6 In.	1400.00
Pitcher, Orange & Brown Stripes, Black Seaweed On Green Band, 5 In.	275.00
Pitcher, Seaweed Design, Stripes, Olive Band, 4 3/4 In.	150.00
Pitcher, Tan Bands, Black & White Stripes, Black Seaweed, 8 In.	450.00
Pot, Marbelized Brown & Yellow, Green Band, Ovoid, 2 3/4 In.	350.00
Salt, Green Enameled, Worm Band, Blue Ground, England, 2 1/4 In.	600.00

Salt, Seaweed, Pedestal 115.00
Shaker, Blue & Brown Stripes, Footed, 2 7/8 In. 160.00
Shaker, Earthworm & Cat's-Eye Design, Blue, White & Black, 5 In. 700.00
Shaker, Gray Band, Black Stripes, Seaweed Design, 4 1/2 In. 260.00
Shaker, Green Band & Dome, Seaweed Design, 4 In. 350.00
Tankard, Earthworm 1325.00
Tankard, Scroddled 1400.00

Monmouth Pottery Company started working in Monmouth, Illinois, in 1892. The pottery made a variety of utilitarian wares. They became part of Western Stoneware Company in 1906. The maple leaf mark was used until 1930. If the word "Co." appears as part of the mark, the piece was made before 1906.

MONMOUTH, Cookie Jar, Beanpot, Ears, W.S.C., 5 Qt. 18.00
   Cookie Jar, Jug Shape, Marked 30.00
   Crock, Salt Glaze, 1 Gal. 30.00
   Crock, Salt, Pierced At Sides For Hanging, 5 1/2 X 4 1/4 In. 95.00
   Jug, Beehive, 5 Gal. 150.00
   Pitcher, Children, Windmills, Blue & Gray, 7 1/2 In. 175.00
   Pitcher, Ribbed, Green 30.00
   Syrup, 1/2 Gal. 28.00
   Vase, Gothic, Matte Gray & Green, 10 In. 65.00
   Vase, Rust, Handle, 8 In. 19.00
   MONT JOYE, see Mt. Joye

William Moorcroft managed the art pottery department for James MacIntyre & Company of England from 1898 to 1913. In 1913, he started his own company, Moorcroft Pottery, in Burslem, England. He died in 1945, but the company continues. The earlier wares are similar to those made today, but color and marking will help indicate the age.

MOORCROFT, Bowl, Hibiscus, Signed, 7 In. 65.00
   Bowl, Landscape, 11 In. 1375.00
   Bowl, Tiger Lily, 1965, 12 In. 295.00
   Box, Cover, Spring Flowers, Small 285.00
   Compote, Pink & Green Flowers, Green Ground, 7 In. 135.00
   Cup & Saucer, Pomegranate, Green Mark, Demitasse 50.00
   Dish, Display Sign 70.00
   Jardiniere, Cornflower Blue, Yellow Flowers, 7 1/2 In. ....*Illus* 1000.00
   Lamp, Fruit, Leaves, Blue, Impressed Blue Mark, 11 In. 390.00
   Vase, Anemone, 12 In. .... 265.00 To 275.00
   Vase, Art Deco, Rose, 10 In. 225.00
   Vase, Blue Dragon, 7 In. 135.00
   Vase, Blue Floral, 5 In. 70.00
   Vase, Blue Hibiscus, 10 In. 190.00
   Vase, Claremont, Toadstool Design, Marked, C.1918, 10 In. 495.00
   Vase, Dragon, Blue, 7 In. 130.00
   Vase, Grape & Leaf, Paper Label, 3 3/4 In. 325.00
   Vase, Green & Gold Design of Tulips, MacIntyre, 1903, 7 1/4 In. 1000.00
   Vase, Hibiscus, Blue, 10 In. 180.00
   Vase, Orchid Design, Mottled Green Ground, Signed, 7 1/4 In. 350.00
   Vase, Pomegranate, Green Mark, 6 In. 325.00
   Vase, Red Tulip, 7 In. .... 120.00 To 125.00
   Vase, Rose, Art Deco, 10 In. .... 200.00 To 215.00
   Vase, Tulip, Yellow, 10 In. 190.00
   Vase, Wattle Flowers, 12 In. 125.00
   Vase, White Columbines, Artist Signed, 5 1/2 In. 130.00

Some types of Japanese pottery and porcelain are decorated with a special type of raised decoration known as moriage. Sometimes pieces of clay were shaped by hand and applied to the item; sometimes the clay was squeezed from a tube in the way we apply cake frosting. One type of moriage is called dragonware and is listed under that name.

MORIAGE, Bowl, Roses In Medallions, Scalloped Rim, Beaded Inside, 10 1/2 In. 60.00
  Cake Plate, Lake Scene, Pierced Handles 110.00
  Dish, Nut, Desert Scene, Footed 120.00
  Ewer, 6 Marbelized Panels, Jeweled, 7 3/4 In. ....225.00 To 245.00
  Ewer, Cover, Pink & Green, Green Ground, Snake Handle, Signed, 8 In. 225.00
  Ewer, Floral Design, Raised Enamel, Beaded, Panels of Roses, 6 In. 225.00
  Fernery, Dragon, Jewel Eyes, Footed, Signed 140.00
  Jam Jar, Underplate, Applied White Trim, Green, 7 In. 300.00
  Pitcher, Pink & Red Florals, Green Design, 7 1/2 In. 295.00
  Planter, Poppies, Brown Trim, 3–Footed, Ruffled Top, 5 In. 80.00
  Relish, Nippon 50.00
  Sugar & Creamer, Chicago Buildings, Green 90.00
  Tankard, Magenta, Pink & Blue Design, White, 13 In. 585.00
  Teapot & Cup, Dragonware 55.00
  Vase, Center Scenic Strip, Floral Bands, Pretzel Handles, 13 In. 325.00
  Vase, Dragon, Floral Designs, Allover Gold, 14 In. 275.00
  Vase, Iris Design, Oval, Handles, 7 In. 170.00

The Mosaic Tile Company of Zanesville, Ohio, was started by Karl Langerbeck and Herman Mueller in 1894. Many types of plain and ornamental tiles were made until 1959. The company closed in 1967. The company also made some ashtrays, bookends, and related gift wares. Most pieces are marked with the entwined MTC monogram.

MOSAIC TILE CO., Cookie Jar, Mammy ....225.00 To 350.00
  Figurine, Black Bear 105.00
  Figurine, German Shepherd, Tan, 9 X 8 In. 85.00
  Figurine, Police Dog, Reclining, Gray 130.00
  Figurine, Terrier, 3–Color 110.00
  Paperweight, William Penn, Blue, White, Dated 30.00
  Tile, Figural, Bear, 6 X 9 In. 115.00

Moser glass is made by Ludwig Moser und Sohne, a Bohemian glasshouse founded in 1857. Art Nouveau–type glassware and iridescent glassware were made. The most famous Moser glass is decorated with heavy enameling in gold and bright colors. The firm is still working in Czechoslovakia. Few pieces of Moser glass are marked.

MOSER, Bowl, Underplate, Allover Gold, Amethyst To Clear, 4 1/2 In. 175.00
  Box, Amethyst, Cut Glass, Cover, Bronze Art Nouveau Mounts, 6 1/2 In. 385.00
  Box, Medallion, Blown Out, Cranberry, 5 In. 300.00
  Centerpiece, Cranberry, Gold Leaves, White Branches, Unusual Shape 195.00
  Cruet, Bird & Leaf, Ruby Cut To Clear, 6 In. 135.00
  Cruet, Bird In Natural Foliage, Blue Handle 875.00
  Cruet, Multicolored Grape Leaves, Gold Vines, Wasp, Marked, 9 In. 1415.00
  Decanter Set, Lake & Hills, Girl & Boy Lovers, Signed, 7 Piece 750.00
  Decanter, Crystal, Emerald Green Top, Stopper, 10 1/2 In. 850.00
  Decanter, Gold & Silver Design, Grape Clusters, Emerald Green 475.00
  Decanter, Hand Painted Flowers, Gold Butterflies, Acorns, 10 1/2 In. 600.00

Moorcroft, Jardiniere, Cornflower Blue,
Yellow Flowers, 7 1/2 In.

Ewer, Acorn & Oak Leaf, Gold Leaf Overlay, Emerald, 14 In. ....*Illus*   880.00
Ewer, Enameled Flowers, Multicolored Beads, Signed, 11 1/2 In. 710.00
Jar, Dresser, Amber, Cut, Encrusted Gold Band, Signed, 4 1/2 In. 65.00
Lamp, Gone With The Wind, Enameled Flowers, Orange, Signed 1100.00
Nut Dish, Cranberry To Clear, Sawtooth Edge, Filigree Flowers 585.00
Nut Dish, Underplate, Cranberry To Clear, Gold Band, Sawtooth 585.00
Perfume Bottle, Allover Gold Design, Cranberry, 8 In. 230.00
Perfume Bottle, Amber, Cut, Encrusted Gold Band, Stopper, 4 1/4 In. 155.00
Perfume Bottle, Smoky, Cut Glass, Signed 135.00
Pitcher, Coin Dot, Enameled Forget–Me–Nots, Signed, 8 In. 250.00
Pitcher, Enameled Cranberry Crackle Glass, Signed 325.00
Salt & Pepper, Alexandrite, 5 In. 75.00
Salt, Sapphire Blue, White Enameled Leaves Interior, 3 1/8 In. 285.00
Tazza, Acid Cut Ship Medallions, Amber 250.00
Tea Caddy, Cranberry, 4–Color Enamel Flowers, 6 X 7 1/2 In. 375.00
Tea Caddy, Cranberry, Enamel Flowers, Paw Feet, Signed, 7 In. 375.00
Tumbler, Juice, Emerald, Yellow & Gold Russian Pattern, 3 3/4 In. 120.00
Vase, 10 Panels, Classically Dressed Women Frieze, Signed, 8 1/4 In. 475.00
Vase, Amber Flashed, Diamond Shape, Enameled, Gilded, 4 3/8 In. 45.00
Vase, Amethyst, Gold Etched Band, 7 1/2 In. 300.00
Vase, Applied Goldfish, Allover Enameling, Sapphire Blue, 8 In. 425.00
Vase, Bee, Snail Handles, Orchids, Gold Overlay, 5 1/2 In. ....*Illus*   660.00
Vase, Bud, Gold Design, Clear To Green 295.00
Vase, Cameo Cut, Elephants, Jungle Scene, Gold Overlay, Signed, 4 In. 1550.00
Vase, Cranberry Glass, Enameled Paisley Design, Gold, Signed, 12 In. 1000.00
Vase, Elephant Exhibition, 24K Gold Leaf, Signed, 13 In. 2750.00
Vase, Enameled Fish, 2 Applied Pickerel Handles, Green, Signed, 11 In. 900.00
Vase, Enameled Iris, Cobalt Blue, Signed, 10 1/2 In. 375.00
Vase, Fantasy Bird, Tropical Flowers, Ball Feet, 11 1/2 In. 2100.00
Vase, Fish, Heliolith, Enameled Carp, Seaweed, 4 1/2 In. ....*Illus*   550.00
Vase, Flowers, Gold Ground, Tapered Square, Brass Holder, 7 In., Pair 275.00
Vase, Gold Leaf Design, Blue To Amber, 9 In. ....*Illus*   1210.00

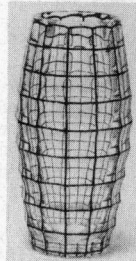

Moser, Ewer, Acorn & Oak Leaf,
Gold Leaf Overlay, Emerald, 14 In.

Moser, Vase, Bee, Snail Handles, Orchids,
Gold Overlay, 5 1/2 In.

Moser, Vase, Parrot, Red Enamel,
Etched Feathers, Green, 6 1/2 In.

Moser, Vase, Gold Leaf Design,
Blue To Amber, 9 In.

Moser, Vase, Fish,
Heliolith, Enameled Carp,
Seaweed, 4 1/2 In.

Moser, Vase, Women
With Weapons Band,
Blue, Signed, 8 1/4 In.

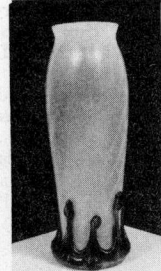

Moser, Vase, Iridescent Green, 11 In.

Vase, Green & Gold Raised Cameo Flowers, Signed, 7 In. 1250.00
Vase, Iridescent Green, 11 In. 215.00
Vase, Iridescent Green, 11 In. .... *Illus* 215.00
Vase, Jeweled Overall, Raspberries, Blossoms, 11 1/2 In. 1400.00
Vase, Lavender, Jewels, 7 1/4 In. 325.00
Vase, Malachite, Seminude Woman At Corners, 4–Sided, 10 In. 650.00
Vase, Parrot, Red Enamel, Etched Feathers, Green, 6 1/2 In. .... *Illus* 770.00
Vase, Portrait On Medallion, 7 In. 435.00
Vase, Red & Yellow Poppies, Gold Leaves & Branches, 10 1/2 In. 350.00
Vase, White Spatter, Aqua Rim, Pointed, Flowers & Insects, 12 1/2 In. 600.00
Vase, Women With Weapons Band, Blue, Signed, 8 1/4 In. .... *Illus* 475.00
Wine, Art Nouveau Design, Chipped Ice Ground, 6 In. 225.00
Wine, Light Green Bowl, Intaglio Cut, Hollow Stem, 8 Piece 475.00

Moss rose china was made by many firms from 1808 to 1900. It has a typical moss rose pictured as the design. The plant is not as popular now as it was in Victorian gardens, so the fuzz–covered bud is unfamiliar to most collectors. The dishes were usually decorated with pink and green flowers.

MOSS ROSE, Creamer, 3 In. 9.00
Eggcup 10.00
Pitcher & Bowl, Moss Rose, Meakin, Ironstone 225.00
Plate, Meakin, 6 In. 20.00

Mother–of–pearl glass, or pearl satin glass, was first made in the 1850s in England and in Massachusetts. It was a special type of mold–blown satin glass with air bubbles in the glass, giving it a pearlized color. It has been reproduced. Mother–of–pearl shell objects are listed under Pearl.

MOTHER–OF–PEARL, Basket, Pink, White Interior, Wishbone Handle, 5 1/2 In. 315.00
Biscuit Jar, Diamond–Quilted, Plated Fittings, 8 3/4 In. 735.00
Dish, Sweetmeat, Stationary Handle, Pink, Quilted, 7 1/2 In. 485.00
Mustard, Hand Painted Design, Pewter Hinged Top, 3 In. 350.00
Pitcher, Herringbone, Rainbow Satin, 8 1/2 In. 110.00
    MOTHER–OF–PEARL, SATIN GLASS, see also Satin Glass; Smith Brothers; etc.
Tumbler, Blue Cornflowers, Pink Diamond–Quilted 335.00
Tumbler, Cranberry, Quilted Satin Glass, White Lining 85.00
Tumbler, Diamond–Quilted, Apricot 95.00
Vase, Diamond–Quilted, Butterscotch To White, 9 In. 525.00
Vase, Diamond–Quilted, Pink, Satin, Bulbous, 7 In. 95.00
Vase, Ruffled Top, White Lining, Blue, 6 In., Pair 325.00
Vase, White, Peacock Eye, Ladybugs, Square Mouth, 6 3/4 In. 1245.00
Vase, Yellow Satin Glass, 11 1/2 In. 225.00
    MOUSTACHE CUP, see Mustache Cup

Mt. Joye is an enameled cameo glass made in the late nineteenth and the twentieth centuries by Saint–Hilaire Touvier de Varraux and Co. of Pantin, France. This same company made De Vez glass. Pieces were usually decorated with enameling. Most pieces are not marked.

MT.JOYE, Console Set, Poppy Pods, Red Crystal, Signed, 11 3/4 In. .... *Illus* 2900.00
Rose Bowl, Enameled Violets, Gold Leaves, Frosted Ground, 4 In. 425.00
Vase, Cameo, Enameled Flowers, Frosted Light Green Ground, 5 In. 395.00
Vase, Cameo, Green & Gold Foliage, Pale Amethyst Ground, 9 In. 275.00
Vase, Enameled Flowers, Acid Green, Gold Outlining, Signed, 20 In. 1250.00
Vase, Frosted Cameo, Sycamore Leaves, Seed Pods, 24 In. 1950.00
Vase, Frosted, Gold Enameling, 5 In. 225.00
Vase, Open Flower, Buds, Leaves, Gold Outline, Amber, 12 1/4 In. 250.00
Vase, Raised Gold On Green, Frosted Ground, Enameled Flowers, 6 In. 350.00
Vase, Spider Chrysanthemums, Leaves, C.1920, 9 3/4 In., Pair 880.00

Mt.Washington,
Biscuit Jar, Floral, Jeweled,
Signed, 6 In.

Mt.Washington, Sugar & Creamer, Lusterless,
Floral, 4 1/2 In.

Mt.Washington, Vase, Peachblow, Lily,
Trumpet Form, 8 3/4 In.

Mt.Washington, Vase, Peachblow, Dusty Rose,
3 1/2 In.

If you put camphor (mothballs) in with the silver to prevent tarnish, don't let it touch the silver. Put the camphor in a waxed paper cup.

The Mt. Washington Glass Works started in 1837 in South Boston, Massachusetts. In 1869 the company moved to New Bedford, Massachusetts. Many types of art glass were made there to the 1890s. These included Burmese, Crown Milano, Royal Flemish, and others.

MT.WASHINGTON, Bellows, Burmese, Rigaree, Handles, 11 1/2 In.	1980.00
Biscuit Jar, Double Ring Top, Bottom, Pink & White, 8 1/2 In.	450.00
Biscuit Jar, Floral, Jeweled, Signed, 6 In. ....*Illus*	750.00
Biscuit Jar, Queen's Design	625.00
Biscuit Jar, Shaded Peach, Silver Plated Lid & Bail, 9 In.	510.00
Bowl, Burmese, Ruffled, 6 In.	275.00
Box, Glove, Embossed Pink Border, Silver & Gold Flowers	575.00
Box, Shell Design, Lined, Lusterless White, Round, 3 In.	210.00
Bride's Basket, Pink Hobnail, Blue Rim, Silver Holder, 14 In.	550.00
Bride's Bowl, Enameled Bird & Foliage, Blue Satin	95.00
Compote, Fireglow, Indians & Buffalo, Metal Holder	300.00
Cracker Jar, Jeweled Florals, Pink Mottled Ground	1050.00
Creamer, Peachblow, Wishbone Feet, 4 1/2 In.	750.00
Cruet, Inverted Thumbprint, Amber Stopper	350.00
Cup & Saucer, Burmese, Thin Walled	385.00
Decanter, Amphora, Cherubs, Lions, Dragons, Stopper, 16 In.	5500.00
Ewer, Mother-of-Pearl, Twisted Rope Handle, Pedestal, 13 In.	775.00
Flask, Girl In Colonial Dress, Enameled Panel	350.00
Flower Frog, Mushroom Shape, Painted Roses	125.00
Jar, Potpourri, Cover, Flowers, Gold Tracery, 5 3/4 In.	380.00
Lamp, Fluid, Bird & Scrolling Urn Design, Marked, 11 In.	357.50
Perfume Bottle, Atomizer, Melon Shape, Enameled Pansies	145.00
Perfume Bottle, Double Gourd Shape, 4 In.	410.00
Pickle Castor, Diamond-Quilted, Rose To Pale Pink, 12 In.	505.00
Pitcher, Hand Painted Florals, Beading, Lusterless Satin	650.00
Pitcher, Lemonade, Burmese	225.00

Rose Bowl, Gold, Mother-of-Pearl, Quilted, Crimped, 6 In.	475.00
Salt & Pepper, Amberina	160.00
Salt & Pepper, Chicks, Silver Plated Heads, Label	320.00
Salt & Pepper, Tomato, Satin Glass, Enameled Flowers	375.00
Salt, Egg	50.00
Salt, Open, Orange Flowers	45.00
Saltshaker, Cockleshell, Enameled Flowers & Foliage	295.00
Saltshaker, Egg, Welcome Happy Morn In Gold	35.00
Saltshaker, Figural, Chicken, Chrysanthemum Blossoms	185.00
Sugar & Creamer, Lusterless, Floral, 4 1/2 In. _Illus_	1210.00
Sugar Shaker, Tomato, Yellow & Blue Daisies, Embossed Top	185.00
Sweetmeat, Cover, Glossy White, Raised Rib & Shell Design	345.00
Toothpick, Burmese, Enameled Shasta Daisy, Square Mouth	395.00
Toothpick, Leaves, Bouquets of Enameled Flowers	375.00
Toothpick, Parallel Greek Key	250.00
Tumbler, Burmese, Prunus Blossom Design	885.00
Tumbler, Burmese, Yellow Band At Base	335.00
Tumbler, Mother-of-Pearl, Herringbone, White & Blue	75.00
Tumbler, Verona, Green Leaves, Gold Trim, 3 3/4 In.	98.00
Tumbler, Verona, Iris, Green Leaves, 3 3/4 In.	98.00
Tumbler, Whiskey, Diamond Quilted, 2 3/4 In.	195.00
Vase Lava Glass, Asymmetrical Design, 8 In., Pair	3850.00
Vase, Blush Pink, Enameled Birds, Pairpoint Holder, 7 In., Pr.	250.00
Vase, Burmese, 2 Reeded Handles, Square Mouth, 4 1/2 In.	375.00
Vase, Burmese, Bowling Pin Shape, Trefoil Top, 12 1/2 In.	685.00
Vase, Burmese, Bulbous, Ruffled, 4 In.	225.00
Vase, Burmese, Elongated, Bulbous, 8 In., Pair	175.00
Vase, Burmese, Enameled Foliage, 11 In.	250.00
Vase, Burmese, Gourd Shape, 11 3/4 In., Pair	357.50
Vase, Burmese, Lily Shape, Floral Enameled Design, 4 1/4 In.	165.00
Vase, Burmese, Lily, 18 1/2 In.	885.00
Vase, Burmese, Whaling Scene, Polar Bear, 4 1/2 In.	495.00
Vase, Cherry Blossom Branches, Maroon Ground, 12 1/4 In.	250.00
Vase, Jack-In-The-Pulpit, Crimped, Wafer Base, 9 3/4 In.	750.00
Vase, Lava Glass, Jet, Colors Outlined In White, 3 3/4 In.	1750.00
Vase, Lava Glass, Segments of Colored Glass, 3 1/2 In.	935.00
Vase, Lily, Fuchsia Shading To Amber, 9 In.	350.00
Vase, Lily, Lusterless, 7 1/2 In.	85.00
Vase, Lily, Rose Amber, Fuchsia, Amber, 9 In.	350.00
Vase, Peachblow, Dusty Rose, 3 1/2 In. _Illus_	1765.00
Vase, Peachblow, Lily, Trumpet Form, 8 3/4 In. _Illus_	1435.00
Vase, Peachblow, Trefoil Rim, Trumpet Shape, 8 3/4 In.	1435.00
Vase, Satin Burmese, Bulbous, Ruffles, 4 In.	225.00
Vase, Spider Web, Blue On Green, 4 In.	335.00
Vase, Verona, Enameled Sunflowers, Gold Veins, 12 In., Pair	700.00
Vase, Wing Guardian & Dolphin, Green, 13 1/2 In.	2640.00
Vase, Wishbone Quatrefoil Feet, Berry Prunt, 3 1/2 In.	1765.00
Wine, Diamond & Star, Barrel Shape, 4 Piece	240.00

Mud figures are small Chinese pottery figures made in the twentieth century. The figures usually represent workers, scholars, farmers, or merchants. Other pieces are trees, houses, and similar parts of the landscape. The figures have unglazed faces and hands but glazed clothing. They were originally made for fish tanks or planters. Mud figures were of little interest and brought low prices until the 1980s. When the prices rose, reproductions appeared.

MUD FIGURE, 2 Chinese Men, Seated	95.00
Bust, Mandarin	125.00
Chinese Man, 9 In.	24.00
Elder, Seated, Paintbrush In Hand, Robe, Sandals	50.00
Elder, Sitting, Fishing, Mud Fish On Line, 4 In.	75.00
Elder, Sitting, Holding Gourd & Flute, Green & Blue Robe	75.00
Elder, Standing, Fish In Hand, Brown Robe	50.00
Elder, Standing, Holding Blue Jar	50.00

Elder, With Basket, 6 In. 22.00
Man, Holding Fish, Seal Mark, 10 In. 40.00
Man, Seated, Holding Fish Next To Basket 52.50
Parrot 25.00
Priest, Holding Cup, China, 6 1/2 In. 45.00
Woman, 8 In. 85.00
Woman, Seated, Tinted Face & Hair, 3 In. 20.00
Woman, Seated, White Robe, Holding Flower 60.00

Mulberry ware was made in the Staffordshire district of England from about 1850 to 1860. The dishes were decorated with a transfer design of a reddish brown, now called "mulberry." Many of the patterns are similar to those used for flow blue and other Staffordshire transfer wares.

MULBERRY, Bowl, Vegetable, Tonquin, Heath, 8 X 6 1/2 In. 75.00
Creamer, Corean 135.00
Creamer, Cyprus 150.00
Creamer, Washington Vase 175.00
Cup & Saucer, Handleless, Calcutta 45.00
Cup & Saucer, Handleless, Japonica, 4 Sets 130.00
Cup & Saucer, Handleless, Washington Vase 65.00
Cup Plate, Corean, 4 Piece 110.00
Cup Plate, Cyprus 60.00
Cup Plate, Jeddo 40.00
Plate Set, Corean, 9 In., 3 Piece 90.00
Plate, Dinner, Athens, 10 Piece 435.00
Plate, Dora, 9 In. 40.00
Plate, Dresden, 7 1/4 In. 15.00
Plate, Jeddo, 7 3/4 In. 35.00
Plate, Jeddo, Black, 9 3/8 In. 45.00
Plate, Neva, 9 In. 40.00
Plate, Rhone, 7 1/2 In. 45.00
Plate, Temple, Walker, 7 In. 22.00
Plate, Venus, Podmore & Walker, 8 In. 48.00
Platter, Aurora, 15 In. 80.00
Platter, Bochara, 14 1/2 In. 100.00
Platter, Corean, 15 1/2 In. 165.00
Platter, Leipzig, 1850, 14 X 10 In. 75.00
Platter, Tonquin, Heath, 10 3/4 In. 95.00
Sugar, Cover, Tonquin, Heath 175.00
Sugar, Cover, Washington Vase, Black 225.00
Sugar, Cover, Washington Vase, Lion Head Handles 175.00
Sugar, Pelow 45.00
Teapot, Rhone Scenery 225.00
Tile, Tea, Temple, P & W 75.00
Tureen, 7 X 11 In. 65.00
Tureen, Sauce, Bochara, 8–Sided, Cover, Elevated Undertray 250.00
Wash Bowl, Ning PO 125.00
Wash Bowl, Savoy 125.00
Waste Bowl, Shapoo 95.00

Muller Freres, French for Muller Brothers, made cameo and other glass from the early 1900s to the late 1930s. Their factory was first located in Luneville, then in nearby Croismaire, France. Pieces were usually marked with the company name.

MULLER FRERES, Bowl, Dutch Landscape, Purple Overlay, Signed, 1920, 6 3/4 In. 1210.00
Lamp, Boudoir, Cameo, Double Overlay 6500.00
Shade, Birds, Flowers, Frosted & Crystal, Signed, 6 X 6 In. 175.00
Vase River Landscape, Rooftops, Trees, Signed, C.1920, 9 In. 1320.00
Vase, Mountainous Landscape, Conifers, Signed, 1920, 9 3/8 In. 2750.00
Vase, Opalescent Body, Blue, Orange, Purple, Yellow, 11 In. 725.00
Vase, Poppy, Blue Shades, Gold Ground, Luneville, 10 1/2 In. 6500.00

The Muncie Clay Products Company was established by Charles
Benham in Muncie, Indiana, in 1922. The company made pottery
for the florist and gift shop trade. The company closed by 1939.
Pieces are marked with the name "Muncie" or just with a system of
numbers and letters like "1A."

MUNCIE, Bowl, Cubist, Purple & Green, 8 In.		75.00
Vase, Black, Rust Glaze, Flared, 6 In.		35.00
Vase, Pillow, Lavender, Green, Ribbed, 6 In.		30.00

Glass was made on Murano Island in Italy from 1291. The output
dwindled in the late seventeenth century, but began to flourish again
in the 1850s. Some of the old techniques of glassmaking were
revived and firms today make traditional designs and original
modern glass. Collectors have recently become interested in the Art
Deco and fifties designs.

MURANO, Paperweight, Concentric Rings, Brown, Gold & Clear, 3 3/4 X 3 In. 225.00

Music boxes and musical instruments are listed in this section.
Phonograph records, jukeboxes, phonographs, and sheet music are
listed in other sections in this book.

MUSIC, Accordion, Harmony, Case		60.00
Accordion, Mother-of-Pearl Inlay, Italian, Case		125.00
Accordion, Trafficanty, Mother-of-Pearl Inlay, Italy	125.00 To	135.00
Accordion, Zenith, Case On Wheels		75.00
Automaton, 2 Birds In Cage, Mechanical		1850.00
Automaton, Box, Birdcage, 2 Birds Move Up & Down, 2 Tunes		850.00
Automaton, Gypsy Girl Magician, Trick, Bisque, Reuge Movement, 1895		6100.00
Automaton, Mammy, Holding Child, Glass Eyes, Early 1800s, 9 In.		395.00
Automaton, Singing, 2 Birds In Cage, Mechanical		2850.00
Automaton, Singing, 2 Birds, French		1050.00
Automaton, Singing, Bird In Cage, Feathered, French, 11 In.		522.50
Automaton, Singing, Bird In Cage, Oriental Scenes, Case, 14 In.		7500.00
Autophone, Musical Casket, 6 Paper Rolls		1100.00
Banjo, Alvares, 5 String		450.00
Banjo, B & D, Silver Bells		375.00
Banjo, G. Barratt, 5 String, Friction Pegs, 10 In.		125.00
Banjo, Gibson, 24 In.		295.00
Banjo, Ludwich, Tenor		275.00
Baton, Orange Paint, Black Design, Wooden		75.00
Baton, Silver Presentation, Carved Ivory, 1914		145.00
Box, Bottle, Golfer		125.00

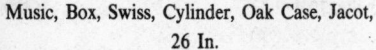

Music, Box, Swiss, Cylinder, Oak Case, Jacot,
26 In.

Music, Piano, Brinsmead, Spinet, Ivory,
Burl Veneer, 48 X 51 In.

Box, Capital, Cuff, Style A, Oak 3000.00
Box, Capitol, Violin Pipes, A Rolls, F.G. Otto & Sons 7500.00
Box, Celesta, Walnut, Zinc, Single Comb, Hand Painted, 10 Discs, 15 In. 2500.00
Box, Columbia, BF, 2 Cylinders, Original Horn 1100.00
Box, Euphonia, Wide Metal Discs 2850.00
Box, Harmonia, 10 Discs 5000.00
Box, Lecoultre, 6 Tunes, Key Wind, Tune Card, 11-In. Cylinder 1700.00
Box, Lloyd Kelley, Dancing Dolls, Coin-Operated, Disc 15 1/2 In. 2500.00
Box, Mermod Freres, 4 Interchangeable Cylinders 6800.00
Box, Mermod Freres, 10 Tunes, Coin-Operated, 1 Cent 1400.00
Box, Mermod Freres, 12 Tunes, Oak, C.1895 .... 2000.00
Box, Mermod Freres, Mira, Floor Model 8300.00
Box, Muller Freres, Mira, Floor Model, 40 8-In. Discs 8600.00
Box, Paillard, 10 Tunes, Inlaid Case 1400.00
Box, Polyphon, Black Case, 15 1/2 In. 1850.00
Box, Regina, Coin-Operated, Cherry Cabinet, 14 Discs, 15 1/2 In. 3550.00
Box, Regina, Coin-Operated, Oak, Double Comb, 8 Discs 3500.00
Box, Regina, Coin-Operated, Single Comb, Mahogany, 6 Discs 3000.00
Box, Regina, Dancing Dolls, Coin-Operated 2500.00
Box, Regina, No.20, 18 Discs, 11-In. Cylinder 2500.00
Box, Regina, No.50, Banjo Attachment, African Striped Mahogany 6500.00
Box, Regina, Single Comb, Oak, 15 1/2-In. Discs 2800.00
Box, Singing Bird, Enamel Over Sterling, Swiss, Cover, 4 X 3 In. 3500.00
Box, Swiss, Cylinder, Oak Case, Jacot, 26 In. ....*Illus* 1100.00
Box, Swiss, Grand, Carved Vines & Leaves, 31 Discs, Mahogany, 28 In. 3800.00
Box, Swiss, Zither & Piccolo, 8 Tunes, Tune Card, 21 In. 2000.00
Box, Symphonion, Coin-Operated, Double Comb, 83 X 34 In. 7500.00
Bugle, Brass & Copper, English, Late 19th Century 135.00
Calliope, Tangley, Model 43A, Hand Or Roll Play .... 7500.00 To 8000.00
Castanets, Theater 200.00
Chimes, Tubular, With Keyboard, 26 Notes 500.00
Clarinet, Bundy, Case 45.00
Concertina, 20 Buttons, Instruction Book 95.00
Concertina, Germany, 1890s 59.00
Concertina, Octagon, 20 Keys 125.00
Drum, Bass, Theater, 1 Beater, 32 In. 600.00
Drum, Kettle & Bass, Theater, 3 Beaters 600.00
Drum, Military, Civil War Style, 135th New York Volunteers 1800.00
Drum, Military, Civil War, Patrick Gilmore's 5000.00
Drum, Snare, Roll & Tap 400.00
Fife, Rosewood, Nickel Ferrels, Early 19th Century, 16 7/8 In. 77.00
Glockenspiel, Aeolian, 49 Note 1800.00
Guitar, Martin, Model F55 .... 600.00
Guitar, National, Resonator, 1932 .... 795.00
Harmonica, European Brass Band, 10 Single Holes, 1890s 55.00
Harmonica, Hohner, Aero Brand, Double-Sided, Metal Jacket, Germany 125.00
Harmonica, Hohner, Goliath 40.00
Harmonica, Hohner, Herb Shriner, Hoosier Boy 65.00
Harmonica, Hohner, No.1896, Marine Band, Box 22.00
Harmonica, Songbird, Colorful Box 40.00
Hurdy-Gurdy, 10 Tunes, Louis Casali, Spain, 1881 .... 5500.00
Mandolin, Gibson, Model A2, Hard Case 25.00
Mandolin, Harp, American, Mahogany Case, Patent 1899 ....   85.00
Mandolin, Potato Bug Style 95.00
Marimba, Deacon, 37 Notes 1800.00
Melodeon, Octagon Legs, Stool, Rosewood, 1850 .... 500.00
Nickelodeon, Capitol, Viola Pipes, Plays A Rolls 7500.00
Nickelodeon, Cremona, Leaded Glass, 10 Tunes, A Roll, Mission Oak 6000.00
Nickelodeon, Empress, Stained Glass Front, 24 Bar Bells, Electric 3600.00
Nickelodeon, Leaded Glass, Oak, 9 Instruments, 20 Rolls 7000.00
Nickelodeon, Peerless, Model D .... 6500.00 To 8500.00
Nickelodeon, Regal, 2 Rolls, 1929 .... 4500.00
Nickelodeon, Seeburg, Model A, Mandolin & Orchestion Bells, Oak 7500.00
Nickelodeon, Seeburg, Model E, Xylophone, Oak 7200.00

Nickelodeon, Seeburg, Modela, Mandolin & Orchestrion Bells, Oak 7500.00
Nickelodeon, Western Electric, Mascot .... 7500.00 To 8500.00
Orchestrion, Coinola Midget Orchestra, Cabinet Style, Restored 3000.00
Orchestrion, Othello, Art Nouveau, Popper & Co., Leipzig, 1912 .... 8600.00
Orchestrion, Regina, Mandolin, Spring Powered, 2 Rolls 6250.00
Organ, Aeolian, Pipe, Rosewood, 1893 .... 3200.00
Organ, Capitol, Pipe, Violin Pipes, Plays A Rolls 7500.00
Organ, Estey, Eastlake, Pump, 70 In. 1200.00
Organ, Estey, No.483975, Chaplain's, Folding, Instructions 475.00
Organ, Estey, Pump Medium Oak Finish, C.1800 .... 800.00
Organ, Farrand, Pump, Chapel Model, Oak 1500.00
Organ, Gavioli, Monkey, Harmoniflute–Trombone, 38 Keys 4500.00
Organ, Gem, Roller, Cobb Music Organ, Hand Crank, 3 Cobbs, Dated 1887 .... 575.00
Organ, Mason & Hamlin, Baby, 39 Keys, C.1885 .... 900.00
Organ, Molinari, Barrel, 35 Keys, 98 Pipes, 45 In. 7500.00
Organ, Molinari, Barrel, 35 Keys, 98 Pipes, Inlay, 45 In. 7500.00
Organ, Moller, Theater, 1939 .... 5000.00
Organ, Regina, No. 10, Cupola 5000.00
Organ, Regina, No. 11 .... 3200.00
Organ, Regina, No.155, Horn 4500.00
Organ, Riemer, Barrel, 184 Pipes, 61 Keys, 5 1/2 Ft. 9500.00
Organ, Wurlitzer, Double Keyboard, Electric, Footboard & Bench 500.00
Piano, Apollo, Baby Grand, Reproducing, Art Carved, Bench, 30 Rolls 5000.00
Piano, Baldwin, Baby Grand, Mahogany Case, 55 3/4 X 65 In. 1500.00
Piano, Baldwin, Player, Monarch/Chicago, 75–100 Rolls, 1926 .... 1500.00
Piano, Bechstein, Baby Grand, Gold Oak 5000.00
Piano, Brinsmead, Spinet, Ivory, Burl Veneer, 48 X 51 In. ....*Illus* 850.00
Piano, Broadwood, Square, Mahogany, Satinwood, 4 Octaves, 1793, 62 In. 4800.00
Piano, Chickering, Console, 1941 .... 1500.00
Piano, Collard & Collard, Upright, Walnut, 1843 .... 750.00
Piano, Estey, 2 Manual Full Pedal Board, Suction Blower, Bench 950.00
Piano, Estey, Upright, Rosewood, Restored, 1889 .... 3000.00
Piano, Fischer, Ampico, Reproducing, Studio Upright 9200.00
Piano, Haines Bros., Ampico, Grand 1700.00
Piano, Knabe Ampico, Reproducing, Grand 3500.00
Piano, Marshall & Wendell, Ampico A, Baby Grand, 1925 .... 1500.00
Piano, Marshall & Wendell, Player, Ampico, Restored, 200 Rolls 4500.00
Piano, Marshall & Wendell, Reproducing, Ampico B, Grand 4800.00
Piano, Mason & Hamlin, Grand, Mahogany, 1950, 5 Ft. 6000.00
Piano, Mills, Player, Single Violano Virtuoso, 14 Rolls, Mahogany 9500.00
Piano, Poppers Konzertist, Player, 39 Rolls .... 1500.00 To 2500.00
Piano, Push–Up Player, 100 Rolls 500.00
Piano, Steck, Ampico, Reproducing, Spinet 3800.00
Piano, Steck, Duo–Art, Reproducing, Grand 2500.00
Piano, Steinway, Duo–Art, Model XR, Reproducing, Grand, Walnut, 1928 .... 9050.00
Piano, Steinway, Duo–Art, Reproducing, Mahogany, 36 Rolls, 1914 .... 3400.00
Piano, Steinway, Grand, Carved Rosewood Legs, Square 975.00
Piano, Steinway, Grand, Square, 1871 .... 2500.00
Piano, Steinway, Model L, Grand, Ebonized Case 1400.00
Piano, Story & Clark, Art Deco, Bench 2900.00
Piano, Stroud, Duo Art, Upright 600.00
Piano, Stroud, Duo–Art, Reproducing, Grand 2200.00
Piano, Telektra, Player, 88–Note Brass Rolls 6500.00
Piano, Weber, Grand Concert, Ebonized Rosewood, 1875 .... 4500.00
Piano, Weber, Player, Grand 5000.00
Piano, Welte, Cabinet Style, Oak 2900.00
Piano, Welte, Grand, Schiller Art Case 2600.00
Piano, Wheelock, Duo–Art, Reproducing, Upright 1500.00
Piccolo, Cadet 100.00
Pipe Organ, Concertina, Duo–Art 5500.00
Ukelele, Tenor, Washburn 100.00
Ukelin, 16 Strings 75.00
Viola, Joseph Horvath, Cleveland, Orange Varnish, 1973, 16 1/8 In. 1540.00
Violano–Virtuoso, Mills, Mahogany Case 9500.00

Violin, Bow, J. Voirin A Paris, Nickel Mounted, Ebony Frog, Pearl Eye	495.00
Violin, Carolus Helmer In Prag, Brown Varnish, 19th Century, 14 In.	137.00
Violin, Heend Arobiac, Budapest, Aug., 1790	600.00
Violin, John Juzek, 22 In.	50.00
Violin, John Juzek, Bow & Case, 24 In.	85.00
Violin, Stainer, Case & Bow	110.00
Xylophone, Deayon, No.1729, 26 Bars	60.00
Zither, Jubalton	20.00
Zither, St. Louis, 1904	235.00

The mustache cup was popular from 1850 to 1900 when the large, flowing mustache was in style. A ledge of china or silver held the hair out of the liquid in the cup. This kept the mustache tidy and also kept the mustache wax from melting. Left–handed mustache cups are rare but are being reproduced.

MUSTACHE CUP, 4 Iris, Yellow & Pink Roses, Blue Ground, RSP, Germany	295.00
Floral, Saucer	35.00
Hand Holding 4 Playing Cards, Lucky Spots, C.1910	22.00
Hand Painted Flowers, Blue, Pink, Ivory	20.00

MZ Austria

"MZ Austria" is the wording on a mark used by Moritz Zdekauer on porcelains made at his works from about 1900. The firm worked in the town of Alt–Rohlau, Austria. The pieces were decorated with lavish floral patterns and overglaze gold decoration. Full sets of dishes were made as well as vases, toilet sets, and other wares.

MZ AUSTRIA, Bowl, Open Red Roses, Gold Ground, Scalloped, 10 1/2 In.	77.00
Butter Chip, Rose & Gold	5.00
Creamer, Hand Painted Violets, Gold Handles, Dated 1911	20.00
Platter, Florals, Multicolored, Signed, 14 1/2 X 10 1/2 In.	125.00

Nailsea glass was made in the Bristol district in England from 1788 to 1873. It was made by many different factories, not just the Nailsea Glass House. Many pieces were made with loopings of either white or colored glass as decoration.

NAILSEA, Basket, Trail Grass, Flint Liner	200.00
Bell, Chocolate Swirl, White, Wooden Handle, 11 In.	150.00
Bottle, Laydown, Blown Drape, Cranberry Opalescent	135.00
Dish, Sweetmeat, Pink & Yellow Pull–Up Design, 3 3/4 X 5 1/4 In.	475.00
Flask, Pink Loopings	140.00
Flask, White Loopings, Blue	65.00
Flask, White, Pink Loopings	142.00
Lamp, Fairy, Crimped Base, Clarke Insert, Blue & White	395.00
Perfume Flask, Cobalt Blue	140.00
Pipe, Red Looping On White, 18 In.	275.00
Pitcher, White Loopings	150.00
Shade, Blue & White, 8 In.	275.00
Vase, Trumpet, Pink Loopings On White, 16 In.	215.00

NAKARA Nakara is a trade name for a white glassware made about 1900 by the C. F. Monroe Company of Meriden, Connecticut. It was decorated in pastel colors. The glass was very similar to another glass made by the company called "Wave Crest." The company closed in 1916. Boxes for use on a dressing table are the most commonly found Nakara pieces. The mark is not found on every piece.

NAKARA, Basket, Hand Painted Florals, Blue, 3 1/4 In.	325.00
Box, Bishop's Hat Shape, Footed	450.00
Box, Blue & Pink Flowers, Cream Ground, Signed, 4 1/2 In.	425.00
Box, Cherubs, Pink Flowers, Beading, Lined, Round, 8 In.	775.00
Box, Cupids, Green, Round, 4 In.	225.00
Box, Greenaway Type Girls Having Tea, Lined, Square, 4 1/4 In.	605.00
Box, Iris On Cover, Bishop's Hat Shape, 6 In.	400.00
Box, Pink Dogwood	195.00
Box, Pink Flowers, Blue Ground, 6 In.	280.00

Box, Ring, Enameled Cover & Base, Rose Design, Green Ground 325.00
Box, Ring, Original Lining, Signed 280.00
Box, St. Andrews Cross, Blue, Flowers, Beaded, Mirror In Top, 8 In. 950.00
Box, Yellow Flowers, Pink Center, Octagonal, 4 1/2 X 6 1/4 In. 1050.00
Hair Receiver, Green, Ormolu Rosettes, 4 In. 350.00
Humidor, Cigar, Indian 850.00
Match Holder, Footed, Blue 275.00
Napkin Holder, Blue, Pair 750.00
Pin Tray, Pink, Yellow Trim, White Dots, 4 3/4 In. 255.00
Tray, Jewel, Blue Apple Blossom Design 145.00
Tray, Mirror, Flowers, Pink Interior, Green To Pink, Square, 4 1/4 In. 590.00
Vase, Indian Portrait, Black Mark, 5 1/2 In. 355.00

Nanking is a type of blue–and–white porcelain made in Canton, China, since the late eighteenth century. It is very similar to Canton, which is listed under its own name in this book. Both Nanking and Canton are part of a larger group now called "Chinese Export" porcelain. Nanking has a spear–and–post border and may have gold decoration.

NANKING, Plate, Blue & White, 9 1/2 In. 175.00
Platter, Center Pagoda, Floral Border, C.1800, 12 3/4 X 16 In. 350.00
Tea Caddy, Blue & White, 4 1/4 In. 350.00
Tureen, Cover, Blue, White, C.1800, 14 In. ....*Illus*   350.00

Napkin rings were in fashion from 1869 to about 1900. They were made of silver, porcelain, wood, and other materials. They are still being made today. The most popular rings with collectors are the figural napkin rings of silver plate. Small, realistic figures were made to hold the ring. Good and poor reproductions of the more expensive rings are now being made and collectors must be very careful, especially when buying any of the Kate Greenaway rings.

NAPKIN RING, Figural, 2 Birds On Wishbone 45.00
Figural, 2 Children, On Either Side Of Butterfly, Porcelain 60.00
Figural, Arab, Seated 110.00
Figural, Bakelite 6.00
Figural, Bird On Leaf, Silver, Meriden 220.00
Figural, Boy Clown, Kate Greenaway 125.00
Figural, Boy On Footstool, Ring On Back, Kate Greenaway 125.00
Figural, Cat & Mouse 195.00
Figural, Cherub, 3–Wheeled Cart, Wheels Revolve .... 295.00 To 360.00
Figural, Cherub, No Wings, Rides On Ring, Butterfly On Flower 295.00
Figural, Chick On Wishbone, Best Wishes, Derby, Silver Plate 50.00
Figural, Chicken Pulling Cart, Pair 350.00
Figural, Child Riding Turtle 175.00
Figural, Cockatoo On Stem Of Leaf Base, Flower In Front 198.00
Figural, Cupid Pulling Sled, Meriden 225.00
Figural, Dog Pulling Ring On Wheels, Girl, Sterling Silver 185.00
Figural, Etched Dogwood Branch, 1 3/4 In. 20.00
Figural, Fawn Pulling Cart, Wheels Revolve 295.00
Figural, Giraffe 350.00
Figural, Girl, Muff, Etched Holly, Kate Greenaway 125.00
Figural, Goat, Pulling Cart, Wheels Turn 275.00
Figural, Horse On Top, Ford & Topper, Sterling Silver 225.00
Figural, Horse Pulling Car, Wheels Revolve, Large 350.00
Figural, Horse Pulling Surrey, Sterling Silver 175.00
Figural, Horse, Next To Fence 195.00
Figural, Horseshoe Over Ring, Ball Footed, Bonheur, Tufts 105.00
Figural, Kitten Next To Ring 125.00
Figural, Leaf Base, Fluted Ring, With Flower, Stem Handle, Glass 50.00
Figural, Lion, Pulling Cart, Wheels Revolve 295.00
Figural, Long Tailed Bird On Veined Leaf, Sterling Silver 155.00
Figural, Ostrich, Standing, Chased Leaves, Silver Plate 45.00
Figural, Prancing Horse, Pulls Caisson, Silver Plate 235.00
Figural, Pumpkin, Vine 35.00

Figural, Rabbit Pulling Cart, Wheels Revolve 300.00
Figural, Reindeer Pulling Cart, Large 350.00
Figural, Sailor Boy 125.00
Figural, Sailor, Anchor & Cable, Bud Vase Attached To Ring 275.00
Figural, Star Ring, On Back 125.00
Figural, Winged Cherubs, Reed & Barton 225.00
Figurine, Chick On Wishbone, Best Wishes, Derby, Silver Plate 38.00
Sterling, Raised Flowers, Initial, 3 1/2 In. 60.00

NASH   Nash glass was made in Corona, New York, after 1919 by Arthur Nash and his sons. He worked at the Webb factory in England and for the Tiffany Glassworks in the United States.

NASH, Candleholder, Chintz, Pair 650.00
Compote, Chintz, Scalloped Rim, Zigzag Line Around, 4 In. Diam. 110.00
Compote, Spiral Chintz Inlay, Green Foot & Bowl, Red Rim, 4 1/2 In. 485.00
Platter, Chintz, Allover Pattern, Zipper Stripes, Signed, 8 1/4 In. 125.00
Vase, Allover Gold Pattern, Dark Blue, Signed, 8 1/2 In. 675.00
Vase, Impressed Pattern, Scalloped, Signed, 4 1/4 In. 300.00
Vase, White Mouth, Full–Bodied At Waist, 16 In. 355.00

Nautical antiques are listed in this section. Any of the many objects that were made or used by the seafaring trade, including ship parts, models, and tools, are included. Other pieces may be found listed under Scrimshaw.

NAUTICAL, Adze, Curved Handle, Douglas Axe, 1867 .... 38.00
Anchor, Great Lakes Ore Carrier, Steel Chain, 1900–10, 6 Ft.6 In. 1000.00
Ashtray, Bronze, Panama Mail Spanish Americas Steamship Co., 5 In 75.00
Ashtray, Matson, Monterey, Lurline, 4 Piece 20.00
Auger, Shipbuilder's, 1 Brace, 4 Piece 65.00
Azorian, Whale Boat, Whalebone Fittings, Case, 26 In. 3600.00
Basket, Nantucket Lightship, Ivory Whale Top, Reyes, 6 3/4 In. 1750.00
Bell, Ship's, Bronze, Clapper, U.S. In Raised Letters, 13 X 15 In. 1800.00
Bevel, Carpenter's, Rosewood, Brass Blades, J. Rabone & Sons 75.00
Binnacle Compass, Brass 3080.00
Binnacle, Brass 500.00
Binnacle, Brass, Domed Lid, Glazed Inspection Hatch, Compass, 16 In 465.00
Binnacle, Compass, Mahogany, Brass, Bronze, E.S. Ritchie, 49 In. 700.00
Binnacle, With Compass, Brass, Bergen Nautik, 11 1/2 In. 175.00
Booklet, S.S. Leviathan Souvenir, Ship's Photo, 5 Pages, 1943 .... 8.00
Butter Chip, Northwest, Duluth, Sterling Silver, Ship Center 30.00
Candleholder, Victorian, Silver Plated, Late 19th Century, 11 In. 154.00
Card Tray, Pewter 22.00
Cards, Playing, Eastern Steamship 8.00
Catalog, Leviathan Steamship, U.S. Lines, 80 Pages, 1922 .... 25.00
Cheese Board, U.S.S. Oldendorf 5.00
Chronometer, 21 Jewels, Up & Down Indicator, Longines 1050.00
Chronometer, Fusee Movement, Up & Down Indicator 750.00
Clock, Banjo, U.S. Lighthouse Establishment 2970.00
Clock, Chelsea, Black, 12–Hour Dial, U.S. Navy 150.00
Clock, Chrome Sails, Wooden 75.00
Clock, Chronometer, John Poole, 8–Day 687.00
Clock, Seth Thomas, 15–Day, Black Dial, Brass Case 200.00
Clock, Ship's Deck, London, Chrome Over Brass Case, 10 3/4 In. 450.00
Coffee Set, White Porcelain, Gold Trim, Cunard Line, 4 Piece 225.00
Communicator, Pilot House Engine Room, Iron, Chadburnes, 14 X 7 In 150.00
Compass, Brass & Iron, 7 In. 55.00
Desk, Chart, Pine, Lift Top, 4 Drawers, 37 X 30 X 24 In. 1075.00
Ditty Bag, Knife, Needles, Maine Schooner 25.00
Figurehead, Mermaid, Carved, Original Paint, 17 In. 2000.00
Figurehead, Ship's, Gentleman's Top Body, Weathered Paint, 30 In. 4450.00
Flag, American Whaler's Name, Niger 1750.00
Fog Horn, Brass 125.00
Fog Horn, Oak, Leather Foot Operated Bellows, Brass Horn, 28 In. 300.00
Fog Horn, Pump Type, Brass 150.00

Girondole, 7–Arm, Brass, Lyre Form Back, Prisms, 45 In., Pair 1045.00
Gun, Harpoon, Brand No.2 Model, Original Bomb 1870.00
Harpoon, Arctic, Double Flue 358.00
Horn, Tugboat, Brass 300.00
Lamp, Ship's, Copper, Red Lens, Nonsweating Adlake Lamp, 19 In. 105.00
Lamp, Signal, Black, Metal 20.00
Lance, Wahling 413.00
Lantern, Brass, Schaefer Brass & Mfg. Co., 15 In. 85.00
Lantern, Copper, English, Pair 325.00
Lantern, Griffiths & Sons, Birmingham, Clear Lens, Brass Labels 150.00
Lantern, Lighthouse, Seascape Painting On Lower Half 265.00
Lantern, Night Watch, To Warn Ships On Great Lakes, Red 65.00
Lantern, Port & Starboard, Iron Case, N. Tufts, 21 1/2 In., Pair 1100.00
Lantern, Ventilated Metal Cone, Red Glass, Wire Cage, Perkins 165.00
Light, Bow, Riverboat, Copper Back, Jeweled Inserts, 20 In. 450.00
Light, Masthead 100.00
Menu, Andrea Doria 15.00
Menu, Hamburg America Line, Girls On Cover 8.00
Menu, Queen Mary, 1954, 8 Piece 25.00
Model, 2–Gun Brig, Long Planked, Cased, 31 In. 1980.00
Model, 26–Gun, Oliver Cromwell, U.S. Colonial, Case, 41 1/2 In. 9500.00
Model, 44–Gun Frigate, Running & Standing Lines, Case, 28 In. 2950.00
Model, Alert, Harbor Tug, Case, 12 In. 1200.00
Model, America, Schooner Yacht, Basswood Hull, 24 In. 1600.00
Model, American Clipper Brig, Half–Hull, C.1840, 62 In. 1320.00
Model, Andromeda, Sloop, Self–Steering Vane, 56 X 37 In. 900.00
Model, Black Hawk, Clipper, Copper Bottom, Case, 36 In. 5500.00
Model, Bluenose, Fishing Schooner, Plexiglas Case, 36 In. 3800.00
Model, Bounty Launch, 18 Crewmen, Case, 15 In. 2200.00
Model, Charles W. Morgan, Whaling Bark, Case, 34 1/2 In. 6200.00
Model, Childers, 12 Swivel Guns, Ebony Wales, Case, 24 In. 9800.00
Model, City of New York, Tugboat, Glass Case, 35 1/2 In. 1545.00
Model, Clipper Ship, Aryan, F.D. Roosevelt, Large 2970.00
Model, Clipper Ship, Columbia, Cased, 37 In. 1430.00
Model, Collier Brig, Fully Rigged, Case, 27 In. 4200.00
Model, Colonial Bark, Merchant & Fishing, Case, 20 In. 1800.00
Model, Dash, Revenue Cutter, Mahogany Hull, Case, 15 In. 1200.00
Model, English Cutter, Bone Ivory Plinth, Case, 8 In. 3850.00
Model, Fat Fanny, Sloop, Self–Steering Vane, Stand, 94 X 52 In. 1200.00
Model, Flying Cloud, Canvas Sails, Wooden 30.00
Model, Fox, Naval Schooner, Opposed Slave Trade, Case, 28 In. 2400.00
Model, Gaspe Trader, Schooner, Eugene Leclerc, 1930 .... 687.00
Model, Ketch Courier, Plank On Frame, Late 19th Century, 49 In. 3300.00
Model, Lighthouse, Wooden, Brown, Mustard & Gold Paint, 29 In. 165.00
Model, Luhu, Rice Boat, Linen Rigging, Case, 13 In. 1200.00
Model, Marco Polo, Packet, Copper Sheathed Bottom, Case, 15 1/2 In. 8500.00
Model, Mauretania 11, Passenger, Troop Transport, Case, 19 In. 1350.00
Model, Mount Washington, Steamboat, Clifford LeCocq, 1978–80 .... 1200.00
Model, Nantucket, Excursion Steamer, 3 Ft. 2375.00
Model, New Bedford, Whale Boat, Folding Mast Step, Case, 21 In. 2600.00
Model, Nonsuch, Ketch, Brass Case, 28 In. 4500.00
Model, Robert E. Lee, C.1900 .... 265.00
Model, Rowboat, Wooden, Brown & White Paint, Oars, 34 1/2 In. 325.00
Model, Ship In Bottle, Town, Church, Lighthouse, 11 1/2 In. 35.00
Model, Washington, Revenue Cutter, Case, 1837, 20 1/2 In. 6800.00
Model, Young America, Clipper, Lift Hull, Case, 43 1/4 In. 6500.00
Model, Young America, Clipper, With The Wind, Brass Trim, 26 In. 5600.00
Painting, On Board, 2 American Sailing Ships, Primitive, S.W. Beal 1600.00
Painting, On Canvas, Portrait, Captain Richard I. Smith 1700.00
Painting, On Canvas, Seascape, Orrin Augustine White 900.00
Passenger List, Cunard Queen Mary, Etched, 8 Pages, 1930s 15.00
Pipe, Boatswain's, Hand Woven Lanyard, 5 1/4 In. 85.00
Pipe, Boatswain's, Sterling 20.00
Pitcher, Cunard Line 16.00

Porthole, Brass, 6 In. 45.00
Porthole, Hinged Cover, Bronze, 15 In. 195.00
Pulley, Double, Wooden Sleeves, C.1890 .... 23.00
Razo, S.S. St. Louis 50.00
Sea Chest, Green Paint, Pin & Eye Hinges, H. Sherburne, 1771, 26 In 880.00
Searchlight, Brass, Electric, 11 X 15 In. 70.00
Searchlight, Brass, Electric, 8 1/2 X 14 In. 85.00
Searchlight, Tugboat, Brass 75.00
Sextant, Brass, Hand Grip, Interchangeable Lenses, Mahagony Case 250.00
Sextant, Brass, Portable, A.B. Topping & Co., Mahagony Case, 4 In. 135.00
Sextant, C. Plath, Hamburg, Brass, Walnut Box, C.1870 .... 500.00
Sign, Broadside, Eben Pierce Co., Guns & Lances, Framed, 12 X 5 In. 330.00
Sign, Gladys Wood Real Estate, Whaling Scene, Map, Wood, 51 X 42 In 192.00
Spade, Cutting & Flensing 193.00
Spade, Cutting & Flensing Whale 193.00
Speed Indicator, Brass 275.00
Spoon, Serving, Furness Steamship Lines 9.00
Spyglass 35.00
Stamp, Whale Shape, Pine, For Log Book, 19th Century, 2 In. 335.00
Swift, Ivory, Whalebone & Tortoise Inlaid 665.00
Syrup, Anchor Line, Crystal & Silver Plate 60.00
Tea Set, Tuscan, Cunard Steamship Co., 4 Piece 75.00
Telephone, Deck, Glass Housing, On Stand, 40 In. 425.00
Telescope, Benjamin Pike & Sons, Mahogany Tripod, 1850–67, 63 In. 2200.00
Telescope, Complex Tripod, London Maker, Large 4125.00
Thermometer, On Walrus Tusk 440.00
Tool, Sailmaker's, Seam Rubber, Scrimshaw, Rope Type Handle, 5 Ft. 2860.00
Traverse Board, Navigational Instrument, 1714–40, 8 In. 1265.00
U.S. Constitution, On Stand, 1787, 17 X 25 In. 1600.00
U.S. Frigate, Glass & Enameled Case, C.1810, 24 7/8 In. 1600.00
Water Cask, Whale Ivory Whale Figure, For Small Boat, 8 X 5 In. 330.00
Wheel, Ship's, Brass 150.00
Wheel, Ship's, Mahogany, Brass, 8 Turned Spokes, England, 50 In. 385.00
Whistle, Boatswain's, Hand Woven Cord, Silver 25.00
Whistle, Boatswain's, Silver 30.00
Whistle, Steam Engine, Brass, Bronze, 13 In. 75.00

Small ivory, wood, metal, or porcelain pieces were used as buttons on the end of the cord that held a Japanese money pouch. These were called "netsuke." The earliest date from the sixteenth century. Many are miniature, carved works of art.

NETSUKE, Cloisonne, Paulownia Mon & Chrysanthemums, White Ground 330.00
Iron, 2 Holy Men Watching A Third On Horseback, 18th Century 247.50
Ivory, 2 Comical Warriors, Moritoshi Kosai 665.00
Ivory, 2 Shishi, 18th Century 2800.00
Ivory, 8 Noh Theater Masks, I'Sshu 1750.00
Ivory, Ama & Octopus, Mitsuyuki, 19th Century 2200.00
Ivory, Child With Net, Empty Fishing Basket, Minkoky II 335.00
Ivory, Cicadas, Dragonfly & Other Insects, Masakazu 412.50
Ivory, Cyclops Eating Rice Cakes, Tomotsugu 550.00
Ivory, Daikofu With Treasure Sack & Bales of Rice 550.00
Ivory, Daikoky & Benten, Gyokuyosai, 19th Century 2000.00
Ivory, Dancing Demon Just Emerged From Egg, Yoshikiku 550.00
Ivory, Dragon, Coiled Tail, 2 In. 50.00
Ivory, Dragon, Coiled Tail, Signed, 2 In. 75.00
Ivory, Dragons, Inlaid Silver, Shibuichi 225.00
Ivory, Ebisu Catching A Fish, Masakage 577.50
Ivory, Frog, 1 1/2 In. 18.00
Ivory, God of Good Fortune, With Turtle 302.50
Ivory, Goldfish 900.00
Ivory, Holy Man Dancing On Straw Hat 467.50
Ivory, Holy Man Holding Begging Bowl 385.00
Ivory, Hotei & Attendant With Tree In Background, Tsunenao 440.00
Ivory, Hotei With Attendants In Bamboo Grove 467.50

Ivory, Mountain Village In Landscape, C.1780	775.00
Ivory, Noh Theater Actor, Gyokuryu	900.00
Ivory, Okame Watching 2 Fleeing Devils, Kojitsu	660.00
Ivory, Old Man, Carrying Giant Toad On Head, Inlaid Eyes, 2 1/2 In.	275.00
Ivory, Openwork Design of Flowers, Byuku	907.50
Ivory, Oriental Woman, Rotating Head, Smile Is Yes, Frown Is No	22.00
Ivory, Pine Tree & Frog, Gold & Shakudo Inset, Openwork	1430.00
Ivory, Rat Holding Peapod While Scratching Itself, Okatomo	5720.00
Ivory, Rats In Bean Field	412.50
Ivory, Saddled Shishi Running Amid Openwork Waves	825.00
Ivory, Seal, With Foo Dog, 1 3/4 In.	135.00
Ivory, Shishi Running In Poppy Field	852.50
Ivory, Squirrels On Grapevine	440.00
Ivory, Symbols of Gods of Good Fortune	715.00
Ivory, Table Form With Shishi, Rensai	715.00
Ivory, Turning Face, 2 In.	38.00
Ivory, Water Lily, Mouse With Tusk–Like Shape, 5 1/4 In.	100.00
Ivory, Young Man Dancing, Horyu	247.50
Jade, Preening Swan	50.00
Silver & Gold, Crane Mon	220.00
Silver, Samurai, Seated On Bell, Woman Hiding In End, Ryuichi	8500.00
Staghorn, Straw Hat With Blossoming Cherry Branch	605.00
Wood, 3 Children In Procession, Hojitsu	715.00
Wood, Coiled Snake	675.00
Wood, Daruma, Masayuki, 19th Century	3000.00
Wood, Devil Striking A Mokugyo Bell, Masatoshi	1017.50
Wood, Man Feeding Horse, Carrying Woman & Child, Itsumin	1210.00
Wood, Mask of Old Man, 20th Century	225.00
Wood, Mask of Woman, Red Hair, Lacquered, 20th Century	385.00
Wood, Masks of Demon & Okame	302.50
Wood, Mythical Being, Looking Into Fish Trap, Coral & Ivory Inlay	2310.00
Wood, Shinto Priest	75.00
Wood, Shinto Priests, Double Figure	125.00
Wood, Shoki Leading Devil With Rope	445.00

New Hall Porcelain Manufactory was started at Newhall, Shelton, Staffordshire, England, in 1782. Simple decorated wares were made. Between 1810 and 1825, the factory made a glassy bone porcelain sometimes marked with the factory name. Do not confuse New Hall porcelain with the pieces made by the New Hall Pottery Company, Ltd., a twentieth–century firm.

NEW HALL, Bowl, Floral Design, Shallow, Porcelain, 8 1/8 In.	125.00
Bowl, Polychrome Floral Design, Red Transfer, Porcelain, 7 3/4 In.	250.00

The New Martinsville Glass Manufacturing Company was established in 1901 in New Martinsville, West Virginia. It was bought and renamed the Viking Glass Company in 1944 and is still producing fine glasswares.

NEW MARTINSVILLE, Berry Set, Carnation Pattern, Giltware, 6 Piece	75.00
Bookends, Cornucopia	40.00
Bookends, Elephant	150.00
Bookends, Police Dog	78.00
Bookends, Woman's Head	195.00 To 255.00
Bowl, Janice, 11 In.	14.00
Bowl, Prelude, 13 In.	28.00
Bowl, Ruffled, Etched	28.00
Bowl, Sunglow, 5 In.	50.00 To 53.00
Bride's Bowl, Candy Ribbon Ruffled Edge, 11 In.	100.00
Butter, Cover, Poppy, Yellow	120.00
Cake Stand, Etched	30.00
Cake Stand, Prelude	30.00
Candy Dish, Divided	16.00
Candy Dish, Radiance, Amber	14.00
Compote, Gazebo, Ball Stem, Crystal	40.00

Newcomb, Jar,
Live Oaks, 1910–15

Newcomb, Tyg,
Drinking Cup, Motto,
C.1908

Ohr, Pitcher,
Molded Figures, Flowers,
Cranberry, C.1895, 7 In.

Orrefors, Ice Bucket,
Sapphire Blue, Signed,
7 3/4 X 8 1/2 In.

Compote, Radiance, Green, 8 In.	24.00
Console Set, 3 Piece	62.00
Console Set, Flower Basket, 3 Piece	62.00
Decanter, Moondrops, Amethyst, Two 2–Oz. Tumblers	65.00
Figurine, Bear, Baby, Crystal	35.00
Figurine, Eagle, Crystal	55.00
Figurine, Elephant	90.00
Figurine, Police Dog	40.00 To 42.00
Figurine, Rooster, Curved Tail	65.00
Figurine, Seal, With Ball, 7 In.	45.00
Figurine, Swan, Red, 9 In.	32.00
Figurine, Swan, Red, 11 In.	30.00
Figurine, Wolfhound	65.00
Fruit Bowl, Bow Knot, Crystal, 12 In.	40.00
Jam Jar, Rosepoint	145.00
Liquor Set, Bow Knot, Amber, 7 Piece	70.00
Pitcher, Oscar, Amber, 2 Tumblers	47.00
Pitcher, Prelude, Crystal	95.00
Plate, Amber, 8 In.	7.00
Plate, Moondrops, Amber, 8 1/2 In.	7.00
Plate, Prelude, 11 1/2 In.	12.00
Punch Cup, Radiance, Blue	11.00
Shot Glass, Moondrops, Red, Handle	10.00 To 12.00
Toothpick, Hat, Yellow To Rust, Threaded Hat Band	250.00
Tray, Center Handle, Crystal	40.00
Tumbler, Radiance, Red	16.00
Vase, Crimped Flip Top, 8 In.	70.00
Vase, Radiance, Crystal	12.00
Vase, Radiance, Ruffled, Black, 12 In.	275.00
Water Set, Georgian, 7 Piece	185.00
Water Set, Wildflower, Amber, 7 Piece	115.00
Wine, Raindrops	18.00

Newcomb Pottery was founded by Ellsworth and William Woodward at Sophie Newcomb College, New Orleans, Louisiana, in 1896. The work continued through the 1940s. Pieces of this art pottery are marked with the printed letters "NC" and often have the incised initials of the artist as well. Most pieces have a matte glaze and incised decoration.

NEWCOMB, Candlestick, Matte Green, C.1900, 7 In.	395.00
Cup, Matte Glaze & High Glaze, 3 Handles, 4 In.	2970.00
Jar, Live Oaks, 1910–15 ....*Illus*	2530.00
Mug, High Glaze	1650.00
Pitcher, Loop Handle, Matte Gun Metal Over Brown, C.1907, 6 In.	195.00
Tyg, Drinking Cup, Motto, C.1908 ....*Illus*	1320.00
Vase, 12 Carved Daffodils, 4–Color, Signed A.M., 4 1/2 In.	725.00
Vase, Carved Daffodils, Henrietta Bailey, 1921, 8 In.	750.00
Vase, Carved Floral Design, Pink & Green, C.1931, 8 1/2 In.	2860.00

Vase, Daffodil Design, Sculptured, Simpson, 1911, 9 1/2 In.	1700.00
Vase, Floral, 4 X 3 1/2 In.	575.00
Vase, Floral, Carved Pink & Green Flowers, Signed, C.1926, 5 In.	2310.00
Vase, Floral, Raised Poppies At Base, Signed, C.1912, 4 In.	660.00
Vase, Flower, Jewel–Like, High Glaze, Amelie Roman, 1903, 6 1/2 In.	8250.00
Vase, Incised Pomegranate Design, Oviform, Marked, 1903, 6 1/2 In.	9075.00
Vase, Moss & Moon, S. Irvine, 8 In.	2500.00
Vase, Spanish Moss, Marked, C.1919, 4 X 4 In.	605.00
Vase, Woodland Scene, Artist AFS, 8 1/2 In.	1550.00

Niloak Pottery (Kaolin spelled backward) was made at the Hyten Brothers Pottery in Benton, Arkansas, between 1909 and 1946. Although the factory did make cast and molded wares, collectors are most interested in the marbelized art pottery line made of colored swirls of clay. It was called "Mission Ware."

NILOAK, Bowl, Marbelized, 3 In.	30.00
Ewer, Eagle, Matte Green, 10 In.	20.00
Match Holder, Cannon	35.00
Planter, Duckling, White Bottom, Signed, 4 In., Pair	20.00
Planter, Rabbit, Yellow	10.00
Tumbler, Marbelized, 3 3/4 In., 4 Piece	255.00
Vase, 5 1/2 X 6 In.	70.00
Vase, Marbelized, 4 1/2 In., Pair	95.00
Vase, Marbelized, 5 1/2 X 6 In.	55.00
Vase, Marbelized, 8 In.	95.00
Vase, Swan, Green, 9 In.	75.00

Nippon–marked porcelain was made in Japan from 1891 to 1921. "Nippon" is the Japanese word for "Japan." A few firms continued to use the word "Nippon" on ceramics after 1921 as a part of the company name more than as an identification of the country of origin. More pieces marked Nippon will be found in the Dragonware, Moriage, and Noritake sections.

NIPPON, Ashtray, Attached Matchbox Holder, Tree In Meadow	95.00
Ashtray, Boat & Windmill Scene, 4 3/4 In.	75.00
Ashtray, Dog In Relief	65.00
Ashtray, Kingfisher On Rim, 6 1/2 In.	60.00
Asparagus Set, Blue Borders, Hand Painted, Green Mark, 7 Piece	350.00
Basket, Boating Scene, Gold Handles, Rising Sun Mark, 8 In.	90.00
Basket, Multicolored Flowers, Rust & Brown Ground, 6 1/2 In.	115.00
Berry Set, Art Nouveau Flowers, 5 Piece	85.00
Berry Set, Pink Roses, 7 Piece	135.00
Biscuit Jar, Plate, Yellow, Beige, Pink Roses, Gold Trim, Marked, 10 In	. 130.00
Bonbon, Pierced Handles, Rosebuds, Raised Gold Border	12.00
Bowl, Floral, Ruffled, Cutout Handles, 7 1/4 In.	65.00
Bowl, Florals, Hand Painted, Gold Ground, 8 1/2 In.	120.00
Bowl, Fruit, Water Chestnut, Handle, 9 1/2 In.	130.00
Bowl, Gold Enameled Roses & Foliage, Scalloped, 10 In.	95.00
Bowl, Nut, Blown Out, Handles, Green Mark, 6 1/2 In.	195.00
Bowl, Roses, Gold, Cobalt Blue Trim, 3 Ball Feet, 9 1/2 In.	110.00
Bowl, Scenic, Windmill, Chocolate Beading, Marked, 9 In.	45.00
Bowl, Vegetable, Cover, Moriage Beading, Marked, 12 In.	225.00
Bowl, Walnuts, Blown Out, Browns, Green, Yellow, Scalloped, 7 In.	125.00
Cake Set, Moriage Dragon, Dark Gray Matte Ground, 4 Piece	195.00
Candleholder, Bluebird, Gold Design, 6 In., Pair	75.00
Candy Dish, Hunt Scene	250.00
Celery Set, Magenta, M In Wreath, 7 Piece	115.00
Celery Vase, Pink Flowers, Gold, M In Wreath, 13 1/4 In.	75.00
Chocolate Pot, White, Blue Trim	87.50
Chocolate Set, Hand Painted Flowers, Green, 5 Piece	75.00
Coffeepot, Phoenix Bird Design, Blue & White	85.00
Cookie Jar, Flowers, Footed, Cobalt Blue	400.00
Cookie Jar, Orchid Mums, White, Cobalt Blue Cover & Feet, Beaded	395.00
Cracker Jar, Geometric Design, Green & White, Gold Trim, Marked	160.00

Cracker Jar, Hunt Scene	395.00
Cracker Jar, Swans, Footed, Cobalt Blue, Gold & White	375.00
Cracker Jar, Tropical Scene, Sailboats, Cobalt Blue, Gold Trim	175.00
Cup & Saucer, Beverly Pattern, Blue, Pink Roses, Gold Rim, Marked	130.00
Decanter, Pink Roses, Blue & Pink Ground, 8 In.	115.00
Dish, Blue, Dogwood, Gold Trim, Handles, 4 Sections, Marked, 8 In.	85.00
Dish, Stylized Butterfly Shape, Cottage Scene, Marked, 8 In.	95.00
Egg Warmer, Blue Forget–Me–Nots	115.00
Eggcup, Floral, Green Mark	30.00
Fernery, 4–Lobed, Allover Moriage, 2 Scenes	65.00
Fernery, Egyptian Hieroglyphic Figures, Blown–Out Faces, 6 5/8 In.	450.00
Fernery, Pink Roses, Gold Ground, 6 1/2 In.	72.00
Fernery, Roses, Maple Leaf Mark, 5 In.	75.00
Hair Receiver, 2 Shades of Pink Roses, Black Trim, Blue Maple Leaf	85.00
Hair Receiver, Pink Roses, Gold Tracery, Cobalt Blue Trim	35.00 To 45.00
Hair Receiver, Pink Roses, Green, Gold, Rectangular, 3 In.	75.00
Hatpin Holder, Allover Florals	45.00
Hatpin Holder, Attached Underplate, Allover Roses, Gold Trim	50.00
Holder, Condensed Milk, Underplate, Roses, Gold Trim	175.00
Humidor, Camel Driver, Blown Out	1200.00
Humidor, Cottage Scene, Jewels, Green Wreath, 4 1/2 In.	265.00
Humidor, Dogs, Blown Out, Moriage Trim, Brown	950.00
Humidor, Forest Scene	300.00
Humidor, Indians & Horses	450.00
Humidor, Playing Card Design, Marked, 6 In.	495.00
Jar, Dresser, Art Deco, Windmill Scene, Footed, 6 In. Diam.	52.50
Lamp, Columbine Flowers, Muted Gold Ground, 22 1/2 In.	285.00
Lemonade Set, Apricot Roses, Leaves, Gold Trim, Marked, 5 Piece	150.00
Lemonade Set, Camel & Rider, 6 Piece	200.00
Lemonade Set, Violets, Marked, 6 Piece	135.00
Mayonnaise Set, Windmill Scene, Blue & Black, Green Mark, 3 Piece	75.00
Mug, Monk, Reading Newspaper, Green, Beaded	250.00
Mug, Sampan Scene, Rounded Sides, 5 In.	195.00
Nappy, Portrait, Gold Ring Handles, 4 1/2 In.	90.00
Pitcher, Cover, White, Pink Roses	120.00
Pitcher, Floral, Green, Maple Leaf Mark, 8 1/2 In.	350.00
Pitcher, Milk, Green, Gold Trim	225.00
Pitcher, Milk, Underplate, Roses, Gold Design	175.00
Plaque, Autumn Scene, Trees, House, 10 In.	175.00
Plaque, Dead Game, Oval, Marked	1150.00
Plaque, Dog, Calico Hound, Leaping Over Fence, 8 7/8 In.	165.00
Plaque, Farm Scene, 10 In.	110.00
Plaque, Indian & Rider, 10 In.	725.00
Plaque, Lion & Lioness, 10 In.	550.00
Plaque, Stag, Raised Leaves, Beaded Border, Blue Mark, 10 In.	295.00
Plaque, Sunset & Sailboats, 8 In.	95.00
Plaque, Windmill Scene, 10 In.	128.00
Plaque, Winter Scene, Blue & White, 10 In.	275.00
Plate, Ovals of Roses, Gold, Turquoise Ground, 10 In.	125.00
Plate, Woodland, 7 1/2 In.	60.00
Punch Bowl, Pedestal, Swan Scene	360.00
Relish Set, Butterflies, Gold Trim, Green Wreath, 7 Piece	85.00
Rose Bowl, Moriage, Floral Medallion, Green Ground, 3–Footed	295.00
Salt & Pepper, Windmill, Gold Trim	28.00
Sauce Dish, Hand Painted Roses, Gold Fluted, 5 1/2 In.	85.00
Shoe, Hand Painted Windmill Scene	75.00
Sugar & Creamer, Blue Matte, Gold Beading, Marked	145.00
Sugar & Creamer, Egyptian Sailboats, Palm Trees, Jeweled, 4 In.	125.00
Sugar & Creamer, Gold Flowers, Green Mark	35.00
Sugar Shaker, Floral, Green, Pink & Yellow Bands, Gold Trim, 5 In.	88.00
Tankard, Forest Scene	145.00
Tankard, Pink Flowers, Gold Beaded, 11 1/4 In.	175.00
Tankard, Scene With Ducks, Gold, Black & Aqua Design, 10 3/4 In.	190.00
Tea Set, Children, Clowns, Rabbit, Rising Sun, 7 Piece	85.00

Tea Set, Roses, Green, Wine, Blue Maple Leaf, 5 Piece 250.00
Tea Set, White Swan On Pink & Green Lily Pads, 3 Piece 145.00
Teapot, Trees, House, Water Scene, Green Mark, 4 1/2 In. 55.00
Tile, Tea, Pink Floral, Octagon, Green M In Wreath 22.00
Tray, Calling Card, Pinched Sides, Blue Flowers, Gold Beading, 4 In. 40.00
Tray, Gold & Red Medallions Inside Gold Rim, Gold Handles, 11 In. 160.00
Urn, Flowers Outlined In Gold, Gold Overlay, 9 1/2 In. 295.00
Urn, Nishiki, 18 In. 250.00
Urn, Scenic, Blue Roses, Bisque, 8 1/2 In., Pair 315.00
Vase, Basket, 11 In. 225.00
Vase, Coralene Rose & Foliage, Gold Beaded Handles, 5 In. 190.00
Vase, Dogwood, Pale Green, Beading, Gold Loop Handles, Ovoid, 6 In. 85.00
Vase, Enameled Glaze, Design, Bulbous, 8 1/2 In. 275.00
Vase, Flower Design, Cobalt Blue, Gold Accents, 6 In. 135.00
Vase, Flower Sprays, Double Handle, Green, Gold Trim, 7 1/2 In. 48.00
Vase, Flowers, Gold Floral Bands, Cobalt Blue, 2 Handles, 11 In. 275.00
Vase, Gray, Boat Scene, Gold Trim, Marked, 10 In. 235.00
Vase, Green, Rustic Scene, Gold Trim, Marked, 10 In. 180.00
Vase, Indian Design, 13 In. 255.00
Vase, Lady Portrait, Gold, No.1366, 11 1/2 In. 395.00
Vase, Moriage Flying Bats, 20 In. 1200.00
Vase, Multicolored Flowers, 2 Handles, 13 In. 80.00
Vase, Nishiki, 18 In. 250.00
Vase, Orange Flowers, Bulbous Top, Aqua, Green Mark, 6 1/2 In. 75.00
Vase, Orchid, Beaded, Gold Design, Handle, Marked 195.00
Vase, Palms, Lake, Geometrics, Bisque, 13 1/2 In. 175.00
Vase, Pink Flowers, Gold Beading, Pale Green, Blue Mark, 11 3/4 In. 400.00
Vase, Portrait, Gold Trim, 7 In. 295.00
Vase, Roses In Medallion, Cobalt Blue, Blue Maple Leaf Mark, 7 In. 195.00
Vase, Ruins Scene, 6 Sides, 10 In. 295.00
Vase, Scenic Center, Gold Ring Pretzel Handles, 12 1/2 In. 325.00
Vase, Scenic, Floral, Bisque & Glossy, 12 In. 175.00
Vase, Scenic, Gold Leaves & Vines, Velvet Finish, 10 In. 115.00
Vase, Swallows In Willows, Orange, Lavender, Moriage, 11 In. 295.00
Vase, Swans, Lake, Trees, Hexagonal, Wreath Mark, 11 1/2 In. 250.00
Vase, White Flowers, Pink Buds, Gold Beading, Green Mark, 8 In. 200.00

Nodders, or nodding figures, or pagods, are porcelain figures with heads and hands that are attached to wires. Any slight movement causes the parts to move up and down. They were made in many countries during the eighteenth and nineteenth centuries. A few Art Deco designs are also known. Copies are being made.

NODDER, Alligator, Bisque 25.00
Alphonse, Painted, Cast Iron, 6 1/4 In. 220.00
Andy Gump, Bisque 65.00
Ashtray, Bathing Beauty, Naughty, Bathtub, Leg Nodder 100.00
Bank, Cat, Emerald Eyes, Tall 45.00
Bear, Blue Military Clothes, Papier–Mache, Germany 55.00
Bear, Blue Suit, Gray Cavalry Hat, Brown Pants, Germany, 6 1/2 In. 75.00
Black Boy, Sitting, Holding Watermelon, Plastic, 3 3/4 In. 100.00
Boy, Bowling 14.00
Boy, With Cigar, Metal 185.00
Cat, Black, Red Ribbon, Porcelain 95.00
Choir Boy & Girl, Pair 75.00
Clown, Grinning, Grotesque, Composition, Germany 65.00
Cup, Girl, With Nodder Breasts 40.00
Denny Dimwit, Box 200.00
Dog, Mouth Opens & Closes, Inset Eyes, Hard Plastic 28.00
Doll, Hank Aaron, 8 In. 45.00
Donkey, 2 Baskets, Skin Cover, Germany, 3 1/2 In. 43.00
Donkey, Celluloid, Occupied Japan, 9 In. 40.00
Donkey, Pulls Wood Cart, Fur Felt Covered, Glass Eyes, 14 In. 425.00
Elephant, Bisque, 12 In. 135.00
German Shepherd, England, 9 In. 65.00

Golfer, Golf Ball Head, 1900, 6 1/2 In.	195.00
Harold Lloyd, Papier-Mache, Germany, 8 In.	95.00
Irishman, Green Suit, White Vest, Gray Hat, Pipe, 8 1/2 In.	115.00
Lord Plushbottom	98.00
Mama Katzenjammer, Bisque, Seated, 5 In.	225.00
Mammy & Pappy Yokum, Pair	60.00
Man, Black, Playing Trumpet, Germany	120.00
Moon Mullins, Bisque, Germany, Small	125.00
Musicians, Wooden	8.00
Mutt & Jeff, Bisque, Germany	200.00
Oriental Kissing Couple	12.00
Oriental Lord & Lady, Bisque, 6 1/2 In., Pair	50.00
Oriental Man, Spread Fan Behind Head, Bisque	285.00
Puppy, Composition, Plush, 6 X 9 In.	15.00
Rabbit, Haircloth, Fur Tail, Glass Eyes, 9 1/2 In.	295.00
Salt & Pepper, Deer, Lying Down, 1 Brown, 1 Yellow, White Base	24.00
Salt & Pepper, Indian Chief & Squaw, White Base	26.00
Salt & Pepper, Pheasant	15.00
Shriner, Papier-Mache	15.00
Snoopy	10.00
Tiger, Papier-Mache	45.00
Victorian Couple, Dressed In Christmas Colors, Germany, 3 1/4 In.	125.00
Witch, Airbrushed, Plaster Wash Over Cardboard, 10 1/2 In.	325.00
Woman In Bathtub, Lower Part Moves, Porcelain, Germany	55.00

 Noritake-marked porcelain was made in Japan after 1904 by Nippon Toki Kaisha. The best-known Noritake pieces are marked with the M in a wreath for the Morimura Brothers, a New York City distributing company. This mark was used until 1941. Another famous Noritake china was made for the Larkin Soap Company from 1916 through the 1930s. This dinnerware, decorated with azaleas, was sold or given away as a premium. There may be some helpful price information in the Nippon category since prices are comparable.

NORITAKE, Basket, Azalea, 3 In.	125.00
Basket, Gold Twig Handle, Woman In Red Skirt, Pearlized Inside	195.00
Basket, Tree In Meadow	28.00 To 60.00
Bowl, Cloverleaf, Woodland Scene, Gold Rim, 9 In.	65.00
Bowl, Marigold, Small	15.00
Bowl, Navarre, 10 In.	15.00
Bowl, Salad, Blue Luster, Underplate, Tomatoes, Lettuce, 7 1/2 In.	75.00
Box, Dresser, Figural Pierrot Cover, Pointed Hat, Marked	225.00
Box, Trinket, Bird of Paradise, Blue Luster, 2 1/4 In.	110.00
Breakfast Set, Pale Yellow, Light Blue, 20 Piece	85.00
Butter, Cover, Tree In Meadow, 5 1/4 In.	20.00
Cake Plate, Azalea, 9 3/4 In.	35.00 To 50.00
Cake Plate, Tree In Meadow, Handle	25.00
Candy Dish, Art Deco	165.00
Casserole, Cover, Azalea	65.00
Celery Set, Luster, Celery Stalks, 7 Piece	30.00
Coffeepot, Tree In Meadow	185.00
Condiment Set, Azalea, 5 Piece	35.00
Creamer, Peter Rabbit	15.00
Creamer, Tree In Meadow, Tall	15.00
Cup Plate, Tree In Meadow	25.00
Cup, Peter Rabbit	10.00
Dish, Cheese & Cracker, Cover, Figure of Girl, Blue, 9 1/2 In.	185.00
Dish, Ice Cream, Oriental Girl, Art Deco, Individual	45.00
Dish, Lemon, Azalea	18.00
Dish, Serving, Pheasant Figural Center, Blue Luster, Divided, 8 In.	125.00
Jam Jar, Azalea, Matching Ladle	125.00
Mayonnaise Set, Azalea, 3 Piece	32.00
Napkin Ring, Man, Art Deco	25.00
Place Setting, Frank Lloyd Wright, Circles, 1922, 6 Piece	5800.00

Plate, Azalea, 7 1/2 In.	9.00
Plate, Nerrisa, Narrow Brown Flower Band, 10 1/4 In.	20.00
Platter, Chaumont, 14 In.	15.00
Powder Box, Art Deco Woman With Fan On Cover, Signed	75.00
Powder Box, Art Deco Woman, Tricorner Hat, Puffed–Out Dress	110.00
Powder Box, Cover, Art Nouveau Florals, 3 3/4 In.	110.00
Relish, Tree In Meadow, 2 Sections, 8 Sides	28.00
Soup, Dish, Azalea, 7 1/8 In.	20.00
Spoon Holder, Hand Painted, Gold Handle Both Ends, Florals	45.00
Sugar & Creamer, Azalea	30.00 To 35.00
Sugar Shaker & Creamer, Tree In Meadow	45.00 To 65.00
Sugar, Azalea, Gold Finial On Cover	10.00
Sugar, Azalea, Rising Sun Mark	22.00
Teapot, Art Deco, Gold Luster, Rust Flowers, Arch Type Finial	20.00
Teapot, Peter Rabbit	20.00
Teapot, Tree In Meadow, Gold Finial	160.00
Tile, Art Deco Design, Green Mark, 6 In.	20.00
Tile, Tea, Azalea	35.00
Toothpick, Azalea	100.00
Tray, Candy, Swan On Lake Scene	12.00
Vase, Art Deco Hand Painted Design, Blue Luster, 7 In.	130.00
Wall Pocket, House Scene, Luster	28.00

The Norse Pottery Company started in Edgerton, Wisconsin, in 1903. In 1904 the company moved to Rockford, Illinois. The company made a black pottery which resembled early bronze relics of the Scandinavian countries. The firm went out of business in 1913.

NORSE, Bowl, Dragon Handles, Sun	135.00
Vase, Black With Incised Geometric Design,	125.00
Vase, Slende, 10 In.	85.00

The North Dakota School of Mines was established in 1892 at the University of North Dakota. A ceramic course was included and pieces were made from the clays found in the region. Students at the university made pieces from 1909 to 1949. Although very early pieces were marked "U.N.D.," most pieces were stamped with the university seal.

NORTH DAKOTA SCHOOL OF MINES, Ashtray, Flossie The Fish, M. Cable	165.00
Bowl, Fruit, Miller, 1941, 8 In.	650.00
Bowl, Incised Mushrooms, White, 1949, 9 In.	510.00
Bowl, Ox Cart, M. Cable, 4 In.	400.00
Bowl, Red Clay, Myrdal, 1939, 4 X 4 In.	650.00
Jardiniere, Aqua To Green, Marked, 5 In.	45.00
Jardiniere, Shaded Green, Marked, 4 In.	35.00
Lamp, Cutouts of Cowboys & Horses	500.00
Pin Tray, Raised Indian Bust, Green, 5 In.	165.00
Plaque, Stockwell, 3 X 5 In.	165.00
Plate, Flowers, J. Mattson, 1949, 10 1/2 In.	225.00
Tile, Flowers, 5–Color, 1949, 5 In.	110.00
Vase, Blue & Violet, Signed, 1942, 4 X 7 In.	175.00
Vase, Huck & Mattson, 3 1/2 In.	90.00
Vase, Matte Olive Green, U.N.D., 5 In.	185.00
Vase, Painted Under Blue Glaze, 1910, 7 In.	1800.00
Vase, Ringed Top, Cobalt Blue, 8 1/2 In.	225.00
Vase, Sgraffito, 1937, 6 1/2 In.	950.00
Vase, Signed King Tut, 8 In.	495.00
Vase, Tan & Green, Signed, 1942, 5 1/2 In.	150.00
Vase, Yellow Matte, 1911, 3 In.	110.00

The Harry Northwood Glass Company was founded by Harry Northwood, a glassmaker who worked for Hobbs, Brockunier and Company, La Belle Glass Company, and Buckeye Glass Company before founding his own firm. He opened one factory in Sinclaire,

Pennsylvania, in 1896, and another in Wheeling, West Virginia, in 1902. Northwood closed when Mr. Northwood died in 1923. Many types of glass were made, including carnival, custard, goofus, and pressed. The underlined N mark was used on some pieces.

NORTHWOOD, Banana Boat, Grape & Cable, Crystal, With Cranberry Flash & Gold	90.00
Banana Dish, Argonaut Shell, White Opalescent	45.00
Basket, Aqua Opalescent	400.00
Berry Bowl, Argonaut Shell, Signed	50.00
Bowl, Grape & Cable, Stippled	275.00
Bowl, Greek Key, Green, Footed	37.50
Bowl, Stippled Rays, 4 X 7 In.	50.00
Butter, Cover, Lion Head	125.00
Candy Dish, Holly, Green Carnival Glass	58.00
Compote, Basket Weave, Twisted Stem, Red	175.00
Creamer, Lion Head	75.00
Creamer, Reverse Swirl, Vaseline Opalescent	100.00
Lamp, Bracket, Leaf Umbrella, Cranberry	395.00
Pitcher, Water, Drape, Blue, Gold Trim	295.00
Rose Bowl, Beaded Cable, Opaque Custard, Nutmeg, Footed	135.00
Spooner, Cut Log	70.00
Spooner, Shell, Green	85.00
Sugar & Creamer, Cut Log	125.00
Sugar, Fluted Scrolls, Enameled, Vaseline Opalescent	85.00
Table Set, Grape & Cable, Marigold, 3 Piece	300.00
Table Set, Inverted Fan & Feather, Blue, 4 Piece	895.00
Table Set, Louis XV, 4 Piece	110.00
Table Set, Nestor, Amethyst, Gold Trim, Tray, 4 Piece	425.00
Toothpick, Leaf Mold, Vaseline & Cranberry	165.00
Tumbler, Interior Poinsettia, Deep Marigold, Signed	350.00
Tumbler, Juice, Grape & Cable	16.00
Tumbler, Regency, Emerald Green, Gold Trim	75.00
Vase, Pump & Trough, Opalescent	125.00
Vase, Ribbed, Aqua Opalescent, Footed, 11 In.	200.00
Vase, Tree Trunk, Marigold, 7 In.	17.50
Water Set, Drape, 5 Piece	175.00
Water Set, Intaglio, Green, Gold Trim, 7 Piece	500.00
Water Set, Maple Leaf, Cobalt Blue, 7 Piece	200.00
Water Set, Singing Birds, 6 Piece	425.00

(NU-ART) Nu-Art was a trademark registered by the Imperial Glass Company of Bellaire, Ohio, about 1920.

NU-ART, Lamp, Seated Women, Shade	195.00
Plate, Homestead, Green, Helios	395.00
Vase, Cylindrical, Crackle Glass, Purple, 7 1/2 In.	110.00

Nutcrackers of many types have been used through the centuries. At first the nutcracker was a fancy hammer; but by the nineteenth century, many elaborate and ingenious types were made. Levers, screws, and hammer adaptations were the most popular. Because nutcrackers are still useful, they are still being made, some in the old styles.

NUTCRACKER, Alligator, Brass	28.00
Alligator, Cast Iron, FM Co.	16.00
Bird Shape, All Wood, 7 1/4 In.	105.00
Crocodile, Brass	14.00
Dog, Althoff, Makers of Headlights, Cast Iron	60.00
Dog, Black & White Porcelain Over Cast Iron	250.00
Dog, Iron	225.00
Dog, With Small Squirrel Between Legs	135.00
Eagle, Brass, 5 1/2 In.	10.00
Gnome With Strong Teeth, Carved Wood, 8 1/2 In.	65.00
Man's Head, With Walrus Mustache, Carved Wood	105.00
Monkey Head, Cast Aluminum	20.00

Monkey, Sitting, Carved Wood, Signed Gosler, 8 In.	45.00
Perfection, 1914	25.00
Rooster, Brass	20.00

The Nymphenburg porcelain factory was established at Neudeck–ob–der–Au, Germany, in 1753 and moved to Nymphenburg in 1761. The company is still in existence. Modern marks include a checkered shield topped by a crown, and a crowned "CT" with the year and a contemporary shield mark on reproductions of eighteenth–century porcelain.

NYMPHENBURG, Figurine, Cherub, Carrying Flowers, White, 1925, 6 1/2 In.	175.00
Group, Minuet Dancers, Yellow Gown, Purple Breeches, 7 In.	220.00
Urn, Baluster, Figures Mounted On Handles, Floral, 14 In.	357.00

The words "Occupied Japan" were used on pottery, porcelain, toys, and other goods made during the American occupation of Japan after World War II, from 1945 to 1952. Collectors now search for these pieces. The items were made for export.

OCCUPIED JAPAN, Basket, Raised Roses, Handle, Porcelain, Tiny, Pair	25.00
Bookends, Scotty, Ceramic, Pair	26.00
Cup & Saucer, Floral, Marked	22.50
Demitasse Set, Scenic, Blue & White, 15 Piece	125.00
Figurine, Black Accordion Player, Black Mark	20.00
Figurine, Chinese Children, Lying On Stomach, Legs Raised	16.00
Figurine, Colonial Woman, Tambourine, Blue, White, 5 1/2 In.	18.00
Figurine, Girl, Large Bonnet, Side Baskets, 6 In.	25.00
Figurine, Sulky, Marked Paulux, 9 X 7 In.	125.00
Figurine, Woman & Man, Standing Against Fence, Pair	22.00
Pitcher, Figural, Corn, 7 In.	50.00
Planter, Cat, With Slipper, 2 1/2 X 5 1/4 In.	10.00
Planter, Girl Sitting On Shoe, 5 X 6 In.	9.00
Plaque, Colonial Man & Woman, Bisque, Square, 4 In., Pair	40.00
Shelf Sitter, Boy With Straw Hat, 3 In.	10.00
Shoes, Figural, Porcelain, Pair	15.00

George E. Ohr, a true eccentric, made pottery in Biloxi, Mississippi, between 1883 and 1918. The pottery was made of very thin clay that was twisted, folded, and dented into odd, graceful shapes. Some pieces were lifelike models of hats, animal heads, or even a potato. Some pieces were decorated with folded clay "snakes." Although reproductions would be almost impossible to make, there have been some reworked pieces appearing on the market. These have been reglazed, or snakes and other embellishments have been added.

OHR, Bird Feeder, Unglazed, Large	575.00
Creamer, Folded, Black Glaze	950.00
Inkwell, Figural, Bizarre, On Artist's Palette, Coiled Snake, 6 3/4 In.	495.00
Mug, Puzzle	885.00
Pitcher, Molded Figures, Flowers, Cranberry, C.1895, 7 In. ....*Illus*	1300.00
Pitcher, Orange Glaze, Black Splotches	1000.00
Salt, Dish, Master, Mottled Green, Signed, 3 In.	185.00
Tile, Country Home, Inscribed Moore's, JP, 6 X 6 In.	300.00
Vase, Olive Green & Brown, Raised Bubbling, Marked, 4 In.	395.00
Vase, Pear Shape, Ruffled Skirt, Pinched Rim, 2 7/8 In.	1700.00

OLD IVORY 84

Old Ivory china was made in Silesia, Germany, at the end of the nineteenth century. It is often marked with a crown and the word "Silesia." Some pieces are also marked with the words "Old Ivory." The pattern numbers appear on the base of each piece.

OLD IVORY, Berry Bowl, No.69, 10 In.	135.00
Berry Set, No.16, Silesia, 7 Piece	225.00
Berry Set, No.19, 5 Piece	90.00
Berry Set, No.75, 4 Piece	165.00
Berry Set, No.82, Silesia, 5 Piece	325.00
Biscuit Jar, No.16	375.00

Bowl, 5 3/4 In. 23.00
Bowl, No. 75, Silesia, 9 1/2 In. 85.00
Bowl, No. 82, Silesia, 5 1/2 In. 55.00
Bowl, No.10, Scalloped, Handles, 9 1/2 In. 60.00
Bowl, No.15, Footed, Oval, 8 X 11 In. 205.00
Bowl, No.200, 9 1/2 In. 175.00
Cake Plate, No.15, Silesia 125.00
Cake Set, No.84, Silesia, Pierced Handles, 7 Piece 225.00
Chocolate Pot, No.84, 2 Cup 300.00
Chocolate Set, No.15, 5 Piece .... 750.00 To 785.00
Cracker Jar, No.16, Silesia 375.00
Cup & Saucer, Chocolate, No.10 .... 55.00
Cup & Saucer, No.200, Silesia, Demitasse .....' 60.00
Cup & Saucer, No.202, Silesia 60.00
Pancake Warmer, Thistle 235.00
Plate, No.10, 6 1/4 In. 28.00
Plate, No.11, 8 In. 72.00
Plate, No.16, 8 1/2 In. 72.00
Plate, No.16, Silesia, 7 3/4 In. 20.00
Plate, No.16, Silesia, 8 1/2 In. 25.00
Plate, No.19, Gold Trim, 8 In. 72.00
Plate, No.82, Coupe Shape, 8 3/4 In. 145.00
Plate, No.84, 9 1/2 In. 150.00
Relish, No.16, 6 1/2 X 4 3/4 In. 40.00
Relish, No.200, Rectangular 38.00
Salt & Pepper, No.122, Silesia 95.00
Sugar & Creamer, No.10 .... 45.00
Sugar & Creamer, No.84, Silesia 150.00
Tile, Tea, No.16, Silesia 65.00
OLD SLEEPY EYE, see Sleepy Eye

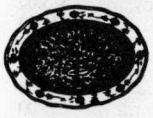

Onion pattern, originally named "bulb pattern," is a white ware decorated with cobalt blue or pink. Although it is commonly associated with Meissen, other companies made the pattern in the late nineteenth and the twentieth centuries. A rare type is called "red bud" because there are added red accents on the blue and white dishes.

ONION, Canister, Cover, Reis 75.00
Cheese Board, Black Printed Verse Center, Germany, 5 3/4 X 8 3/4 In. 225.00
Chop Plate, Meissen, 12 In. 185.00
Cup & Saucer, Meissen, 19th Century 65.00
Cup & Saucer, Meissen, Small 50.00
Eggcup, Meakin, Signed 15.00
Feeder, Invalid 40.00
Funnel 70.00
Grater, Cheese 250.00
Grater, Rectangular 128.00
Lamp, Oil, Miniature, 8 1/2 In. 45.00
Meat Tenderizer, Embossed 120.00
Platter, Oval, 17 In. 295.00
Potato Masher .... 165.00 To 185.00
Rolling Pin 225.00
Salt Box 85.00
Salt Box, Hanging, High Back, Openwork 98.00
Salt Box, Wooden Lid, Germany 165.00
Spoon Holder, Wall Mount 275.00
Spoon Rack, Side Mount, For 12 Spoons 298.00
Strainer, Cone Shape 118.00
Sugar & Creamer, Meissen 125.00
Teapot, Rose Finial, Meissen 150.00
Teapot, Rosebud Finial, Gilt Design, Meissen 160.00

Opalescent glass is translucent glass that has the tones of the opal gemstone. It originated in England in the 1870s and is often found in pressed glassware made in Victorian times. Opalescent glass was first made in America in 1897 at the Northwood glassworks in Indiana, Pennsylvania. Some dealers use the terms "opaline" and "opalescent" for any of these translucent wares.

OPALESCENT, see also Northwood; Pressed Glass; Spanish Lace

OPALESCENT, Basket, Contessa, Amber, English, 4 1/4 X 7 In.	100.00
Basket, Ruffled, Thorny Handle, Pink, 5 1/2 X 7 1/2 In.	195.00
Berry Bowl, Intaglio, Blue, Master	145.00
Berry Bowl, Jeweled Heart, Crystal, Master	30.00
Berry Set, Fluted Scrolls, Vaseline, 7 Piece	250.00
Berry Set, Scroll With Acanthus, White, 8 Piece	95.00
Berry Set, Seaweed, Cranberry, 5 Piece	295.00
Berry Set, Wreath & Shell, Vaseline, 6 Piece	245.00
Bonbon, Honeycomb & Clover, 2 Handles, Green	28.00
Bottle, Barber, Seaweed, Cranberry	175.00
Bottle, Barber, Stars & Stripes, Cranberry	250.00
Bottle, Water, Ribbed Coin Spot, Cranberry	195.00
Bowl, Barbells, Blue	25.00
Bowl, Fluted Scrolls, Custard Glass, Footed, 7 In.	33.00
Bowl, Jefferson Wheel, Green, 9 In.	43.00
Bowl, Jolly Bear, White, Ruffled, 9 In.	78.00
Bowl, Ribbed Spiral, Canary, 6 1/2 In.	28.00
Bowl, Ribbed Spiral, Ruffled, Canary, 8 In.	25.00
Bowl, Vintage, 9 In.	55.00
Bowl, Waterlily With Cattails, Amethyst, 10 1/2 In.	45.00
Bowl, Wheel & Block, Green, 8 In.	30.00
Breakfast Set, William & Mary, Vaseline, 2 Piece	130.00
Butter, Cover, Alaska, Vaseline	325.00
Butter, Cover, Double Greek Key, Blue	235.00
Butter, Cover, Fluted Scrolls, Vaseline	175.00
Butter, Cover, Hobnail, Hobbs, Vaseline	135.00
Butter, Cover, Jewel & Flower, Blue, Gold Trim	215.00
Celery, Beatty Rib, Blue	55.00
Celery, Swirl, White	38.50
Compote, Chippendale, Fluted, Canary, 8 1/2 X 7 In.	230.00
Compote, Jelly, Iris With Meander, Blue	60.00 To 70.00
Compote, Jelly, Swag With Brackets, Blue	45.00
Compote, Jelly, Swag With Brackets, Vaseline	45.00
Creamer, Alaska, Vaseline	50.00 To 60.00
Creamer, Argonaut Shell, Blue	120.00
Creamer, Child's, Hobnail, White	30.00
Creamer, Fluted Scrolls, Blue	45.00
Creamer, Fluted Scrolls, Enamel Flowers	45.00
Creamer, Fluted Scrolls, Vaseline	50.00
Creamer, Hobnail, Handle, Vaseline, 4 1/4 In.	225.00
Creamer, Seaweed, Cranberry	195.00
Creamer, Shells, Blue	75.00
Creamer, Sunburst–On–Shield, Blue	28.00
Creamer, Twist, Blue	45.00
Creamer, Wreathed Cherry, Blue	75.00
Cruet, Alaska, Vaseline	195.00 To 250.00
Cruet, Daisy & Fern, Blue	135.00
Cruet, Flora, Canary, Original Stopper	400.00
Cruet, Fluted Scrolls, Blue	150.00
Cruet, Jackson, Blue	125.00 To 150.00
Cruet, Jackson, Vaseline	120.00
Cruet, Ribbed, Opal Lattice, Cranberry	325.00
Cruet, Swag With Brackets, Green	285.00
Cruet, Swag With Brackets, Vaseline	190.00
Cruet, Tokyo, Blue	80.00 To 160.00
Cruet, Wild Bouquet, Blue, Pair	235.00 To 250.00

Cruet, Windows, Cranberry 142.00
Cruet, Windows, Swirled, Cranberry 275.00
Cuspidor, Woman's, Wreath & Shell, Vaseline 95.00
Jar, Sweetmeat, Cover, Spanish Lace, Cranberry, Silver Plate, Bail 395.00
Lamp, Finger, Coin Dot, Blue, P A A Burner, Pat.1883 & 1897 .... 325.00
Lamp, Hanging, Coin Spot, Vaseline 385.00
Lamp, Snowflake, Cranberry, Hobb 395.00
Mug, Beads In Relief, Blue, 2 1/4 In. 40.00
Mug, Stork & Rushes, Marigold 30.00
Mustard, Double Greek Key, Blue 110.00
Nappy, Sea Spray, Green 25.00
Pitcher, Buttons & Braids, Blue 70.00
Pitcher, Buttons & Braids, Green .... 125.00 To 145.00
Pitcher, Daisy & Fern, Cranberry .... 135.00 To 285.00
Pitcher, Lemonade, Vintage, Bulbous 65.00
Pitcher, Water, Alaska, Blue 395.00
Pitcher, Water, Alaska, Vaseline 325.00
Pitcher, Water, Daisy & Fern, Cranberry 165.00
Pitcher, Water, Daisy In Criss–Cross, Cranberry 600.00
Pitcher, Water, Iris With Meander, Vaseline 195.00
Pitcher, Water, Jackson, Blue 195.00
Pitcher, Water, Poinsettia, Blue 250.00
Pitcher, Water, Poinsettia, White 125.00
Pitcher, Water, Reverse Swirl, Cranberry 425.00
Pitcher, Water, Stripe, Vaseline 150.00
Pitcher, Water, Swirl, Blue 145.00
Pitcher, Water, Swirl, White 110.00
Pitcher, Water, Waterlily With Cattails, Amethyst 375.00
Plate, Jewelled Heart, White, 6 1/2 In. 33.00
Plate, Spoke & Wheels, Green, 9 In. .... 28.00 To 33.00
Rose Bowl, Beaded Fleur–De–Lis, Green 45.00
Rose Bowl, Fine Cut & Roses, Blue 250.00
Rose Bowl, Inverted Fan & Feather, White 48.00
Rose Bowl, Leaf & Beads, Blue .... 250.00 To 350.00
Rose Bowl, Palisades, Blue 33.00
Salt & Pepper, Beatty Honeycomb, Blue 85.00
Salt & Pepper, Jewelled Heart, Blue 185.00
Saltshaker, Jackson, Blue 35.00
Saltshaker, Ribbed Opal Lattice, White 42.50
Spooner, Alaska, Vaseline 60.00
Spooner, Diamond Spearhead, Green 35.00
Spooner, Drapery, Northwood, Blue 50.00
Spooner, Fluted Scrolls, Blue .... 40.00 To 70.00
Spooner, Gonterman Swirl, Blue 75.00
Spooner, Hobnail & Panelled Thumbprint, Vaseline 35.00
Spooner, Jewel & Flower, Vaseline 75.00
Spooner, Scroll With Acanthus, Vaseline 50.00
Spooner, Seaweed, Cranberry 110.00
Spooner, Shell, Blue 95.00
Spooner, Swag With Brackets, Blue 65.00
Spooner, Tokyo, Blue 95.00
Spooner, Waterlily With Cattails, Amethyst 65.00
Sugar & Creamer, Alaska, Green 90.00
Sugar & Creamer, Hobnail, Green 75.00
Sugar Shaker, Cover, Daisy and Fern, Blue, ... 90.00
Sugar Shaker, Daisy In Criss–Cross, Cranberry 395.00
Sugar, Cover, Alaska, Vaseline 150.00
Sugar, Cover, Flora, White 68.00
Sugar, Cover, Fluted Scrolls, Vaseline 125.00
Sugar, Cover, Jewel & Flower, White, Gold Trim 35.00
Sugar, Cover, Ribbed Spiral, Blue 95.00
Sugar, Dolly Madison, Green 85.00
Syrup, Big Windows, Swirl, Blue 185.00
Syrup, Coinspot & Swirl, Blue 165.00

Syrup, Daisy & Fern, Cranberry 495.00
Syrup, Daisy & Fern, Silver Plated Lid 148.00
Syrup, Diamond Spearhead, Green 245.00
Table Set, Alaska, Vaseline, Enamel Leaves, 4 Piece .... 550.00 To 595.00
Table Set, Diamond Spearhead, Green, 4 Piece 595.00
Table Set, Drapery, Northwood, White, 4 Piece 375.00
Table Set, Everglades, Blue 475.00
Table Set, Fluted Scrolls, Vaseline, 4 Piece 350.00
Table Set, Palm Beach, Vaseline, 4 Piece 595.00
Table Set, Regal, Blue, 4 Piece 550.00
Table Set, Swag With Brackets, Blue, 4 Piece 450.00
Table Set, Tokyo, Green, 4 Piece .... 400.00 To 445.00
Table Set, Wreath & Shell, Blue, 4 Piece 435.00
Table Set, Wreath & Shell, Flowers, White, 4 Piece 400.00
Toothpick, Beatty Honeycomb, Blue .... 38.00 To 43.00
Toothpick, Diamond Spearhead, Blue ....90.00 To 110.00
Toothpick, Diamond Spearhead, Vaseline 33.00
Toothpick, Gonterman Swirl, Blue, Amber Top 140.00
Toothpick, Iris With Meander, Blue 75.00
Toothpick, Iris With Meander, Green 60.00
Toothpick, Ribbed Spiral, Blue 75.00
Toothpick, Swag With Bracket, Green 35.00
Toothpick, Windows, Swirled, Cranberry 210.00
Toothpick, Wreath & Shell, White 125.00
Tray, Richelieu, Blue, Oval, 11 X 8 3/4 In. 115.00
Tumbler, Coinspot, Blue 35.00
Tumbler, Everglades, Blue 60.00
Tumbler, Fluted Scrolls, Blue 50.00
Tumbler, Iris With Meander, Blue .... 50.00 To 75.00
Tumbler, Jewel & Flower, White 35.00
Tumbler, Reverse Swirl, White 25.00
Tumbler, Richelieu, Blue 58.00
Vase, Cabbage Leaf, Green 68.00
Vase, Cape Cod, Blue, 4 1/2 In. 30.00
Vase, Chain Design, Floral, Bee Interior, Folded, 12 1/2 In. 450.00
Vase, Coin Dot, Cranberry, 8 1/2 In. 110.00
Vase, Corn Vase, Vaseline 80.00
Vase, Polka Dot, Flared, Blue, Label, 10 In. 110.00
Vase, Pump & Trough, Figural, Blue, 7 In. 65.00
Vase, Swirl, Ruffled, Cranberry, 10 In. 100.00
Water Set, Daisy & Fern, Cranberry, 7 Piece 650.00
Water Set, Hobnail, Pink, 7 Piece 95.00
Water Set, Jewelled Heart, Crystal, 7 Piece 250.00
Water Set, Jewelled Heart, Green, 6 Piece 575.00
Water Set, Palm Beach, Canary, 7 Piece 750.00
Water Set, Poinsettia, Blue, 7 Piece 450.00
Water Set, Swag With Brackets, Blue, 7 Piece .... 395.00 To 575.00
Water Set, Tokyo, Green, 7 Piece 695.00

> Opaline, or opal glass, was made in white, green, and other colors.
> The glass had a matte surface and a lack of transparency. It was
> often gilded or painted. It was a popular mid–nineteenth–century
> European glassware.

OPALINE, Biscuit Jar, Pink Streamers, Enameled Violets, Class of '95 .... 225.00
   Vase, Amaryllis Design, 3 Glass Footed, Custard, 7 1/2 In. 200.00

The stage is a long way from some of the seats at a play or an
opera, so the patrons sometimes carried special opera glasses in the
nineteenth and early twentieth centuries. Mother–of–pearl was a
popular decoration.

OPERA GLASSES, Allegorical Landscape, Enameled, French 800.00
   Chevalier 25.00
   LeMaire, Mother–of–Pearl, Brass Trim, French, 1890 .... 65.00
   Mother–of–Pearl Handle, Velvet Case 35.00

Mother-of-Pearl, Case	175.00
Mother-of-Pearl, Lamayre, Paris	70.00
Mother-of-Pearl, Late 19th Century	65.00

Little Orphan Annie first appeared in the comics in 1924. The redheaded girl and her friends have been on the radio and are still on the comic pages. A Broadway musical show and a movie in the 1980s made Annie popular again and many toys, dishes, and other memorabilia are being made.

ORPHAN ANNIE, Badge, Decoder	28.00
Bank	65.00
Bank, Annie & Sandy, Applause, 1982	10.00
Book, Life & Hard Times of Little Orphan Annie, 1935-45, 1970	22.00
Book, Little Orphan Annie & The Ghost Gang, Big Little Book	40.00
Book, Little Orphan Annie With The Circus, Big Little Book	40.00
Book, Little Orphan Annie, A Willing Helper, 1932	15.00
Book, Pop-Up Little Orphan Annie, 3 Pop-Up Pictures, 9 In.	132.00
Bracelet, Identification	14.00 To 20.00
Card, Christmas, H. Gray	35.00
Compass & Sundial, Secret Egyptian, 1938	30.00
Decoder, 1936	30.00
Doll, 50th Year, Box, 7 In.	12.00
Doll, Cloth, 36 In.	50.00
Doll, Composition Face & Hands, Cloth, Famous Artists Syn.	60.00
Doll, Knickerbocker, 1982, 6 In.	7.00
Doll, Knickerbocker, Extra Clothes, Box, 11 1/2 In.	15.00
Doll, Stuffed, 16 In.	110.00
Game, Annie, Box, 1981	18.00
Game, Orphan Annie To The Rescue, Board	48.00
Game, Treasure Hunt, Board	25.00
Lunch Box, Thermos	12.00 To 15.00
Manual, 1939	50.00
Mug, Beetleware	12.00 To 30.00
Mug, Ovaltine, Treasure Hunt, Cover, 1933	35.00 To 45.00
Nodder, Germany	60.00
Radio, Annie & Sandy, Box	22.00
Ring, Face	35.00
Secret Society Booklet & Decoder, Mailer	125.00
Sheet Music, Radio, Ovaltine, Contest Letter, Envelope, 1931	50.00
Sheetmusic, Radio, Ovaltine, Contest Letter Envelope, 1931	47.50
Stove, Child's	69.00
Stove, Electric	28.50
Toothpick	18.00
Toy, Annie Skipping Rope, Mechanical, Tin Litho, Marx, 5 In.	535.00
Toy, Annie, Skipping Rope, Windup	605.00
Toy, Goofy Circus Set, Original Mailer	60.00
Toy, Limousine, Box, Fits 7-In. Doll	22.00
Toy, Pull, Annie & Sandy, Toy-Trix, 1930s	115.00
Toy, Sandy, Annie's Dog, Plush, 1930, 10 1/2 In.	60.00
Toy, Shado-Ettes	75.00
Watch, New Haven Co., Box	247.00
Wings, Little Orphan Annie Glow	195.00
Wristwatch, 1948, Box	325.00

The Orrefors Glassworks, located in the Swedish province of Smaaland, was established in 1898. The company is still making glass for use on the table or as decorations. There is renewed interest in the glass made in the modern styles of the 1940s and 1950s. Most vases and decorative pieces are signed with the etched name.

ORREFORS, Basket, 36 Point, Hobstar, Pineapple, Thumbprint Diaper, Handle	55.00
Bowl, Frosted Pink, White Outlined, Oval, 13 1/2 In.	65.00
Candleholder, Eden, Pair	47.50
Champagne, Cut Glass, Signed, Label	50.00

Decanter, Nude Woman Picking Flowers, Signed, 9 3/4 In.	995.00
Dish, Clover Shape, Venetian, Amber, Bubbles, Petal Laid Over	35.00
Figurine, Fish, Hollow, Random Bubbles, Signed, 8 In.	125.00
Figurine, Horse, Crystal, Scalloped Mane, Red Eyes	50.00
Goblet, Etched Spur Desigh, Sven Palquist, Signed, 6 1/2 In.	350.00
Ice Bucket, Pulled & Applied Handle Openings, Labeled, 7 3/4 In.	135.00
Ice Bucket, Sapphire Blue, Signed, 7 3/4 X 8 1/2 In. ....*Illus*	135.00
Vase, 2 Dancing Girls, Signed Orrefors Palmquist 2941, 10 In.	500.00
Vase, 4 Cut Panels, Engraved Flowers, Clear, Signed, 4 3/8 In.	30.00
Vase, Art Deco, Swirl Design, 8 In.	135.00
Vase, Black Outlined Fish, In Green Seaweed, Artist, 6 1/2 In.	600.00
Vase, Clear Sides, Figure of Nude Woman, Signed, C.1935, 13 3/4 In.	1430.00
Vase, Clear, Art Glass, Engraved Woman With Ball, 2 1/2 In.	26.00
Vase, Crystal, 2 Dancing Girls, Flared Rectangular, 10 1/2 X 5 In.	500.00
Vase, Crystal, Teardrop Shape, 2 Deep Thumbprints, 11 In.	225.00
Vase, Figure of Muscular Nude Man, Diving, Signed, C.1935, 11 In.	1100.00
Vase, Flygfors, Pigeon, Black & White Swirls, Signed, 1958, 6 In.	180.00
Vase, Graal, Herd of Horses, Orange, Ovoid, Signed, C.1970, 6 3/8 In.	1750.00
Vase, Internal Female Busts, Aqua Ground, Signed, C.1956, 8 In.	4950.00
Vase, Smoky, Flared, Ruffled, 6 In.	90.00
Vase, Teardrop Shape, Thumbprints, Signed, 11 In.	225.00
Vase, Young Girl, Flowers, Frosted On Clear, Signed, 6 1/4 In.	95.00
Whiskey, Clear, Engraved Art Deco Style Fish, Square, Indented	24.00

Ott & Brewer Company operated the Etruria Pottery at Trenton, New Jersey, from 1863 to 1893. They started making belleek in 1882. The firm used a variety of marks that incorporated the initials O & B.

OTT & BREWER, Bowl, Leaf Shape, C.1865	450.00
Mustard, Multicolored Floral & Gold Paste Design	385.00
Rose Bowl, Gold Flowers, Gold Brushmarks, 4 In.	295.00

The four Overbeck sisters started a pottery in Cambridge City, Indiana, in 1911. They made all types of vases, each one-of-a-kind. Small, hand-modeled figurines are the most popular pieces with today's collectors. The factory continued until 1955 when the last of the four sisters died.

OVERBECK, Figurine, 3 Baby Birds	575.00

Owens Pottery was made in Zanesville, Ohio, from 1891 to 1928. The first art pottery was made after 1896. Utopian Ware, Cyrano, Navarre, Feroza, and Henri Deux were made. Pieces were usually marked with a form of the name "Owens." About 1907, the firm began to make tile and discontinued the art pottery wares.

OWENS, Ewer, Browns, Greens, 6 In.	20.00
Ewer, Greens, Marked Seagrove, No. Carolina, 6 In.	22.00
Humidor, Utopian, Applied Cigar & Matches	350.00
Jug, Corn, Utopian	110.00
Mug, Cherry, Utopian Type, 1908 ....85.00 To	135.00
Tankard, Utopian, 12 In. ....200.00 To	225.00
Umbrella Stand, Lotus Blossoms, 17 In.	925.00
Urn, Cover, Brown, Lavender, 12 In.	195.00
Vase, Bottle Shape, Painted Flowers, Brown To Green, Marked	125.00
Vase, Bullet, Hand Painted Pansies	195.00
Vase, Cyrano, Long-Necked, 8 In.	225.00
Vase, Floral, Silver Deposit, Artist I.S., 5 X 4 In.	1275.00
Vase, Green, 4 1/2 In.	110.00
Vase, Sunburst, Woodvine, Bottle Shape, 13 In.	350.00
Vase, Utopian, 6 3/4 In.	110.00
Vase, Utopian, 10 In.	125.00
Vase, Utopian, Lion, Artist M.T., 15 1/2 In.	5000.00
Vase, Utopian, Widemouth, 6 1/4 In.	75.00

Oyster plates were popular from the 1880s. Each course at dinner was served in a special dish. The oyster plate had indentations shaped like oysters. Usually six oysters were held on a plate. There is no greater value to a plate with more oysters although that myth continues to haunt antiques dealers. There are other plates for shellfish including cockle plates and whelk plates. The appropriately shaped indentations are part of the design of these dishes.

OYSTER PLATE, Baby Center, Encircling My Friends, Limoges, 9 In. 50.00
  Blue & Pink Floral, Haviland, 9 In. 80.00
  Center Butterfly, Scenic, 6 Wells, French 150.00
  Pastel Blue, 9 1/2 In. 75.00
  Pink, 9 1/2 In. 75.00
  Pres. Rutherford B. Hayes, Haviland, 1880, 8 3/4 In. 600.00
  Quimper, 9 1/4 In. 90.00
  Ribbed Mold, Cream & Yellow, 6 Wells, 8 In. 85.00
  Shell Shape, Black Trim On Shells, Seaweed, UPW, 1881 .... 60.00
  White, 9 1/2 In. 75.00

Paden City Glass Manufacturing Company was established in 1916 at Paden City, West Virginia. It is best known for glasswares but also produced a pottery line. The firm closed in 1951.

PADEN CITY, Compote, Ruby 35.00
  Cordial, Penny Line, Ruby 15.00
  Cup & Saucer, Crow's Foot, Ruby 16.00
  Figurine, Chinese Pheasant, Blue 75.00
  Figurine, Polar Bear 45.00
  Pitcher, Juice, Cover, 2 Tumblers, Amber, 9 1/2 In. 28.00
  Soup, Cream, Crow's Foot, Ruby, Liner 22.00
  Vase, Flower Design, Crow's Foot, Milk Glass, 10 In. 65.00
  Vase, Peacock & Rose, 10 In. 85.00
  Wine, Penny Line, Ruby 9.00

The paintings listed in this book are not works by major artists but rather decorative paintings on ivory, board, or glass that would be of interest to the average collector. To learn the value of an oil painting by a listed artist you must contact an expert in that area.

PAINTING, On Board, 2 Hunting Dogs, Primitive, E.M. Fritz, '24, 19 X 23 In. 175.00
  On Board, Autumn Morning, F.J. Girardin, 1856, 12 X 18 In. 425.00
  On Board, Clown Portrait, L. Spiegel, Framed, 20 X 16 In. 75.00
  On Board, Fields Before Country Barn, 6 X 8 1/2 In. 440.00
  On Board, Impressionistic Village, F. Burgdorff, 1917, 10 X 8 In. 400.00
  On Board, Landscape, Water, Boats, Trees, Cabin, Framed, 14 X 18 In. 425.00
  On Board, Mediterranean Landscape, Fernando, 12 1/2 X 14 1/2 In. 90.00
  On Board, Peconic Bay, Henry Prellwitz, Framed, 12 X 18 In. 3500.00
  On Board, Primitive Landscape, 19 X 26 In. 275.00
  On Board, Small Boats, Rough Sea, 13 3/4 X 23 1/4 In. 125.00
  On Canvas, 2 Oxen Resting, Yokes, Gilt Frame, 20 1/2 X 22 3/4 In. 350.00
  On Canvas, Bateau Au Port, Martha Thibaut, 1880s, 18 X 15 In. 275.00
  On Canvas, European Landscape, Oval, Framed, 23 X 28 3/4 In. 375.00
  On Canvas, Falls On Llugwy, A.A. Glendening, 27 1/2 X 31 1/2 In. 1625.00
  On Canvas, Farmhouse In Illinois, Gilt Frame, 20 X 26 In. 1100.00
  On Canvas, Gentleman Seated At Table, Gilt Frame, 29 3/4 X 24 In. 400.00
  On Canvas, Hunting Scene, Camel, Man, Rifle, Woman, 18 X 26 In. 200.00
  On Canvas, Impressionistic Landscape, A.E.B. '19, 22 X 29 In. 265.00
  On Canvas, Indian Overlooking Niagara, Framed, 24 X 28 In. 450.00
  On Canvas, Landscape, Cabin, Rose Tardriff, Framed, 25 X 29 In. 55.00
  On Canvas, Landscape, Corn Shocks, G. Scott, Frame, 12 X 20 In. 200.00
  On Canvas, Landscape, Cove, Boats, Building, Trees, 18 X 24 In. 300.00
  On Canvas, Landscape, Signed Mader, Framed, 23 X 31 In. 35.00
  On Canvas, Madonna & Child, European School, 18 X 15 In. 1450.00
  On Canvas, Mother & 3 Children At Supper, C. Bouter, 20 X 24 In. 4200.00
  On Canvas, Mother Nursing Baby, J.S. Hendrik Kever, 11 X 14 In. 1750.00
  On Canvas, Mountain Landscape, Falls, 2 Indians, 29 X 43 In. 500.00

On Canvas, Mountainous Landscape, People, 22 X 35 In. 400.00
On Canvas, Old Woman, White Bonnet, 30 X 25 In. 450.00
On Canvas, Primitive Landscape, Horse Drawn Wagon, 25 X 31 In. 775.00
On Canvas, Seated Gentleman, Pipe, Pewter Tankard, 37 X 30 In. 6100.00
On Canvas, Shellfishers On Beach, Evert Pieters 2250.00
On Canvas, Soldier At Sentry, Gilt Frame, 12 3/4 X 16 1/2 In. 325.00
On Canvas, Stylized Landscape, M.L. O'Kelley, 1973, 12 X 16 In. 375.00
On Canvas, Woman Beside Open Window, Frame, 30 3/4 X 25 In. 500.00
On Canvas, Young Man With Frock Coat, Frame, 30 1/2 X 26 In. 1500.00
On Copper, Dutch Interior, Gilt Frame, 14 1/4 X 8 1/2 In. 800.00
On Ivory, Harvest Scene, Mosaic Frame, 7 1/2 X 5 1/2 In. 95.00
On Ivory, Madame Pompadour, Miniature 165.00
On Ivory, Military Officer, Dress Uniform, Lenz, 3 1/2 X 2 1/2 In. 137.50
On Ivory, Mr.Broadquill, Powdered Wig, Bracelet Slide Frame, 2 In. 6500.00
On Ivory, Napoleon, Laurel Crown, Gerard, 3 1/2 X 2 1/2 In. 357.50
On Ivory, Officer, White Uniform, Lock of Hair In Back, 2 In. 495.00
On Ivory, Portrait of Officer, C.1800, Miniature 160.00
On Ivory, Portrait, Man, 3 1/2 In. 55.00
On Ivory, Snowflake, Harvest Scene, Persian, 7 1/2 X 5 1/2 In. 95.00
On Ivory, Woman In Elaborate Gown, Frame, India, 11 X 8 In. 155.00
On Ivory, Woman, Large Feathered Hat, 3 1/2 X 2 1/2 In. 55.00
On Ivory, Yound Girl, J.F. Sharpe, Frame, 1837 .... 137.00
On Ivory, Young Girl, Bobbed Blond Hair, 2 3/4 X 3 1/2 In. 325.00
On Ivory, Young Girl, P. Artotos, 3 X 2 1/2 In. 220.00
On Ivory, Young Woman, Framed, Signed Shumway, 1808–84, 4 X 5 In. 1500.00
On Ivory, Young Woman, Regnal, Gilded Frame, 5 1/2 X 4 In. 235.00
On Masonite, Seascape, Clarence W. Snyder, 1939, 25 X 30 In. 200.00
On Masonite, Stagecoach Scene, Hotel Back Bar, 48 X 117 1/2 In. 550.00
On Panel, Black Girl, Holding An Orange 3900.00
On Paper, Beach Coast, Watercolor, Geo. Howell Gay, 10 X 19 In. 325.00
On Paper, Compote of Fruit, Watercolor, 25 1/2 X 23 1/4 In. 1200.00
On Paper, Family Scene, Watercolor, Frame, 15 X 17 3/4 In. 250.00
On Paper, Feast Day, Blanket Woman Series, D. Roberts, 32 X 48 In. 5500.00
On Paper, Gray Tiger Cat, Watercolor, Cherry Frame, 9 X 10 In. 175.00
On Paper, Mt. Hood Sunset, B. Robbins, Frame, 17 3/4 X 20 3/4 In. 55.00
On Paper, Rival Roses, Watercolor, 1841, 12 1/2 X 10 3/4 In. 775.00
On Silk Scroll, 2 Tigers, Japan, Signed, 42 X 16 1/2 In. 132.00
On Silk, Ancestral Portrait, Chinese, 35 X 22 In. ....*Illus* 200.00
On Silk, Geishas, Black Bamboo Frame, 17 X 21 In., Pair 170.00
On Silk, Merchant Ship, Mountains, H. Shimidzu, 1923, 20 X 14 In. 450.00
On Textile, Hunt & Harvest Scene, Sepia, Gerard Copou, 41 X 68 In. 176.00
On Tin, Cavaliers, Interior Scene, European, Signed, 7 1/2 X 6 In. 235.00

Painting, On Silk, Ancestral
Portrait, Chinese,
35 X 22 In.

Paper, Fraktur, Martin
Detweiler, Pen, Ink,
1808, 6 X 7 3/4 In.

Paper, Fraktur, Joel
Griest, April 21st,
1839, 2 3/4 X 5 3/8 In.

Paper, Fraktur, Phillip
Dedrich, Cornelia
Harder, 1817, 9 X 11 In.

Painting, Reverse On
Glass, Bearded Man,
Monk With Child, Pair

Paper, Cutout, Heart
& Foliage, J.S.M.,
6 1/4 X 7 In.

On Velvet, Basket of Pansies, Frame, 23 3/4 X 23 3/4 In.	70.00
On Velvet, Theorem, 2 Puppies, Grained Frame, 15 1/2 X 19 1/2 In.	450.00
On Velvet, Theorem, Silk Flower & Fruit Filled Cornucopia, C.1870	410.00
On Wood Panel, Spanish Lady, Signed Lucas, Framed, 9 3/4 X 7 In.	650.00
Reverse On Glass, 4 Figures, Chinese, Framed, 22 1/8 X 16 1/4 In.	495.00
Reverse On Glass, Bearded Man, Monk With Child, Pair ....*Illus*	650.00
Reverse On Glass, Court Women With Children, Chinese, 23 X 35 In.	148.00
Reverse On Glass, Crucifixion Scene, Framed, 12 X 9 In.	55.00
Reverse On Glass, Emperor & Attendants, Chinese, 31 1/2 X 21 In.	2550.00
Reverse On Glass, Napoleon, Framed, 12 3/4 X 8 1/2 In.	45.00
Reverse On Glass, Titanic & Iceberg, 30 X 20 In.	195.00
Reverse On Glass, Woman At Rest, Chinese, 28 X 20 In.	198.50

 The Pairpoint Manufacturing Company started in 1880 in New Bedford, Massachusetts. It soon joined with the glassworks nearby and made glass, silver plated pieces, and lamps. Reverse–painted glass shades and molded shades known as "puffies" were part of the production until the 1930s. The company reorganized and changed its name several times but is still working today. Items listed here are glass or glass and metal. Silver–plated pieces are listed under Silver Plate.

PAIRPOINT, Barrel, Biscuit, Silver–Plated Lid & Handle, Azalea	300.00
Bowl, Bryden Burmese, 5 In.	95.00
Bowl, Flattened Rim, Oval Pedestal, Cobalt Blue, 14 1/4 In.	300.00
Bowl, Hand Painted Interior Florals & Ladybug, Signed, 9 In.	275.00
Bowl, Nude Holding Flower At Sides, Pierced Handles, 13 X 9 In.	465.00
Bowl, Vintage Engraving, Footed, Amber, 10 In.	85.00
Box, Dresser, Hinged Cover, Scalloped Rim, Gold Floral, 7 1/4 In.	375.00
Box, Glove, Gold Enameled Flowers, Pink Embossed, 9 1/2 In.	645.00
Box, Opalescent Glass, White Ground, Pink Borders, 9 X 4 In.	675.00
Box, Scrolls & Vines On Hinged Lid, Aqua Base, Logo, 6 3/4 In.	660.00
Bride's Basket, Ruffled, Pink & White	325.00
Candlestick, Arts & Crafts, Metal, 8 In., Pair	90.00
Coffee Server, Gooseneck, Hinged Lid, Floral Design	85.00
Coffeepot, Serpent Spout	275.00
Compote, Allover Rose Garlands, Rose To Clear, 7 1/2 In.	180.00
Compote, Butterflies In Spider Web, Green Cut, Flared, 12 X 5 In.	95.00
Compote, Cut Glass, Metal Base, 7 In.	160.00
Cup & Saucer, Green, Fluted, Gold Floral Design, Set of 6	121.00
Figurine, Swan, Opalescent, 4 In.	125.00
Lamp, Boudoir, Puffy, Pink, Yellow Flowers, Lobed Shades, 7 In., Pr.	550.00
Lamp, Cased Hummingbird & Roses, 14 In.	9500.00
Lamp, Directoire Shade, Ocean Scene, Signed, Table	3965.00
Lamp, Floral Design, Shade, Amber, Signed, 23 In.	1650.00
Lamp, Frosted Glass, Nautilus Shade, Glass Prisms, 19 In.	9350.00
Lamp, Gold Floral Shade, Brown Border, Bronze, Marble Base	2500.00
Lamp, Harbor Scene, 3 Dolphin Base, 14 In.	4995.00
Lamp, Lily Pad Scene, Art Deco, Signed, 16 In.Diam.	2800.00
Lamp, Mushroom Shade, 40 Prisms, 2–Light, 24 In.	3700.00
Lamp, New Bedford Scenic, Carlisle Shade	4500.00
Lamp, Peacock, 16 In.	6500.00
Lamp, Pink & Yellow Flowers, Silver Base, 7 In., Pair ....*Illus*	5500.00
Lamp, Puffy, Boudoir, Pink, Yellow Flowers, Lobed Shade, 7 In., Pair	550.00
Lamp, Puffy, Boudoir, Tulip, Signed, 14 In.	4295.00
Lamp, Puffy, Lilac & Trellis, Pisa Shade, Signed	6150.00
Lamp, Puffy, Peony Design, Square Shade, Pairpoint Base, 18 In.	6000.00
Lamp, Puffy, Rose Bouquet, White Roses, Green Ground, Signed	95.00
Lamp, Red Poppies, Green Ground, 14 X 14 In. ....*Illus*	6500.00
Lamp, Reverse Painted Shade, 3–Light, Signed, 23 In.	1650.00
Lamp, Reverse Painted Shade, Ball On Marble Base, Signed	3250.00
Lamp, Reverse Painted Shade, Bird of Paradise, 22 In.	4500.00
Lamp, Reverse Painted Shade, Farm Scene	1100.00
Lamp, Reverse Painted Shade, Jefferson, Scenic, 16 In.	1800.00
Lamp, Reverse Painted Shade, Poppy Design, Pair	1500.00

Pairpoint, Lamp, Pink & Yellow Flowers,
Silver Base, 7 In., Pair

Pairpoint, Lamp, Red Poppies, Green Ground,
14 X 14 In.

Lamp, Reverse Painted Shade, Silver Base, Signed, 16 In.	2700.00
Lamp, Reverse Painted Shade, Viking Ship, Signed, 14 1/2 In.	1760.00
Lamp, Rose Bouquet, Green, Signed	9500.00
Lamp, Silvered Metal Base, Frosted Glass Nautilus Shade, 19 In.	9350.00
Lamp, Textured Ice Chip Finish, Metal Base, Marked	3150.00
Lamp, Venetian Harbor Scene	2000.00
Perfume Bottle, Berwick, Hobstars, 6 1/2 X 4 1/2 In.	350.00
Shade, Butterflies, Flowers, Domed, 14 In.	450.00
Vase, Aurora, Grape Cutting, Loop Handles, 9 In.	105.00
Vase, Flred, Clear Bubble Stem, Ruby, 13 In.	140.00
Vase, Turned-Down Collar, Bubbles In Stem, Ruby, 8 1/2 In.	200.00

PALMER COX, BROWNIES, see Brownies

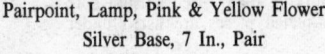

The first paper dolls were probably the pantins, or jumping jacks, made in eighteenth–century Europe. By the 1880s, sheets of printed paper dolls and clothes were being made. The first paper doll books were made in the 1920s. Collectors prefer uncut sheets or books or boxed sets of paper dolls. Prices are about half as much if the pages have been cut.

PAPER DOLL, Alice In Wonderland, Characters, Saalfield, 1934	225.00
Amos 'N Andy, Pepsodent Advertising, Framed	195.00
Around The World With Bob & Barbara, Lilja Co.	35.00
Ava Gardner, 1953	45.00
Baby Sandy	185.00
Baby Sparkle, 1948	25.00
Ballet, 5 Little Girls, Costumes & Accessories, 1964	12.00
Barbie & Ken, Box, 1974	18.00
Barbie, Folder, 1970, Cut	7.50
Barbie, Midge & Skipper, 1965, Cut	10.00
Barney The Sandpaper Bear, 4 Outfits, Uncut	35.00
Berry Hutton & Daughters	40.00
Betty Bonnet, Christmas Party, 1916, Uncut	55.00
Betty Grable	48.00
Blondie, Whitman, Uncut	85.00
Boots & Her Buddies, Uncut	50.00
Brenda Lee, Lowe, 1961	45.00
Bridal Party, 1953	16.00 To 18.00
Captain Marvel, Flying Family, Unpunched Doll	20.00
Carmen Miranda, 1942, Uncut	250.00
Charlie's Angels, Jill, 5 Outfits	7.00
Charlie's Angels, Kelly, 9 Outfits, 1977	9.00
Charming Chatty, 1964	14.00 To 25.00

Cindy & Mindy, Whitman, 1960, Uncut	7.50
Cleopatra, Costumes, Statuette, Blaise Publishing, Box	15.00
Clothes Make A Lady, 1944, Uncut	25.00
Colonial Dolls of Early American History, Platt & Munk, Box	25.00
Darkie Doll, Uncut	180.00
Deanna Durbin	170.00
Dennison's Crepe Paper Doll Outfit, 3 Jointed Dolls, Complete	100.00
Dolls From Storyland, 7 Dolls, Colorful Clothes, 1963	35.00
Dolly Dingle	20.00
Dolly Dingle, 1920s	18.00
Doris Day, Whitman, Clothes In Folder	25.00
Dresses Worn By First Ladies of White House, Cut	25.00
Dutch Boy & Girl, Drayton, Cut	8.00
Elizabeth Taylor, 1949	55.00
Elizabeth Taylor, 1952	85.00
Elizabeth Taylor, 1953	45.00
Esther Williams, Merrill, 1950, Uncut	105.00 To 150.00
Felt–O–Gram, 1932	68.00
Flying Nun, 5 Dolls, 4 Nuns, 1969	8.00
Four Dancing Dolls, Whitman, Uncut	25.00
Freckles & Sniffles, Whitman, 1972	5.00
Gone With The Wind, Merrill, 1940, Uncut	1000.00
Hedy Lamar, Uncut	75.00
Here Comes The Bride, Groom, Punch–Out Clothes, 1967, Uncut	15.00
I Love Lucy, 1953	40.00
Jane Russell, 3 Dolls, Clothes, Saalfield, 1955, Uncut	45.00
Jane Withers, 1 Adult Doll, Outfits, Whitman, 1941, Cut	75.00
Jetsons, Cut	15.00
Jolly Jane, Woman's Home Companion, Feb. 1923, Page, 10 X 13 In.	12.50
Judy Garland, 1940, Cut	35.00
June Allison, Uncut	22.00
Lennon Sisters, Uncut	45.00
Lettie Lane's Around The World Party, 1911, Uncut	15.00
Little Lulu	15.00
Little Miss America, Cut	25.00
Little Women, 5 Dolls, Saalfield, Uncut	20.00
Ludwig Von Drake, Golden Press, 1961	25.00
Magic Mary, Magnetic, Set	25.00
Margaret O'Brien, Uncut	120.00
Marilyn Monroe	60.00
Mary Hartline, 1952	45.00
Mary Martin, 1943	35.00
Mary Poppins Characters, Jane & Michael, Watkins Stratmore	35.00
Mary Poppins, Whitman, 1964	40.00
Mary Poppins, Whitman, 1973, Uncut	20.00
Munsingwear, Clothes, Uncut	18.00
Nanny & Professor, Uncut	15.00 To 25.00
National Velvet, Whitman, 1962	35.00
Nurses, Cut	18.00
Paper Playmates, Jan & Jimmy, 6 Pages, 1955, Uncut	5.00
Partridge Family, 6 Dolls, Box, Saalfield, 1973	48.00
Paulette Goddard, 1941, Uncut	400.00
Peggy Pryde's Cousin Carrie, 3 Dresses, Cut	8.00
Pillsbury, Forbes, 1895, Uncut	45.00
Pinup Girls, Saalfield, 1945, Uncut	18.00
Princess Diana's Wedding, 1982	10.00
Princess Diana, Whitman, 1985	8.50
Raggedy Ann & Raggedy Andy, Uncut	100.00
Rickey Nelson, Whitman, Uncut	28.00
Robin Hood & Maid Marion, 1956, Uncut	18.00
Rock Hudson, Whitman, Uncut	60.00
Saturday Night Barn Dance, 4 Dolls, Costumes For Dance, Uncut	25.00
Shirley Mason, Silent Screen Star	15.00
Six Reely Trooly Dolls, Cloth Mounted, Then Cut, Box	45.00

Skipper Scott, Box	8.00
Slumber Party, 4 Teenage Dolls, High Fashion Outfits, 1964, Cut	8.00
Snow White, Spanish	12.00
Sonja Henie, Merrill, 1941, Uncut	65.00
Sparkle Plenty, Saalfield, 1948	40.00
Starletts, Whitman, 1951	38.00
Teddy Bear Family, 1980	6.50
Teddy Bear, 5 Suits, Early 1900s, 10 In.	175.00
That Girl .... 20.00 To	25.00
This Is Margie, Whitman, 1939	45.00
Tillie The Toiler, 1942, Uncut	200.00
Tuesday Weld, Box, Saalfield, 1960, Uncut	48.00
United We Stand, 6 Dolls In Uniform, Uncut .... 68.00 To	80.00
Waltons, Uncut	18.00
Wedding, Uncut	25.00
Welcome Back Kotter, Box	7.00
Wendy's Wardrobe, Pattern Papers For Outfits, 1965, Cut	10.00
Wishniks, Whitman, 1965	12.00
Wizard of Oz, Showboat Theater, 1950s, Uncut	17.50
World's Fair Model, Punch–Out, Rides, Helicopter, Main Mall, 1964	35.00

Paper collectibles, including almanacs, catalogs, children's books, stock certificates, and other paper ephemera, are listed here. Paper calendars are listed separately under Calendar Paper.

PAPER, Almanac, Cultivator, Pictorial, 1851, 32 Pages	3.00
Almanac, Farmers, R.B. Thomas, 1849, 52 Pages	20.00
Almanac, Piso's Cough Remedy, Pocket	10.00
Book, Bible, Hexaglot, 6 Languages, 1906, 10 X 12 In., Set of 6	135.00
Book, Big Little Book, Buck Jones, 25th Century A.D.	35.00
Book, Big Little Book, Man From U.N.C.L.E., The Calcutta Affair	35.00
Book, Coloring, Green Hornet	20.00
Book, Coloring, Katzenjammer Kids, Saalfield, 1917	25.00
Book, Coloring, R.C.A. TV, Stars of NBC TV, 1950s	10.00
Book, Dictionary, Red Goose Shoes, Hardcover, 246 Pages	17.50
Book, Games, Kelloggs, 1931, 8 X 10 In.	16.00
Book, Indian Chiefs, Krug Bakery, Colorful, 1930s	25.00
Book, Sinclair Dinosaur, 1934	25.00
Book, Song, Kellogg's, Vernon Grant, Illustrations	10.00
Book, Swimming & Diving, Kellogg's, 1934	10.00
Catalog, Abercrombie & Fitch, Christmas, 1938	15.00
Catalog, Advance Packing & Supply Co., Chicago, 1898, 318 Pages	38.00
Catalog, Aldens, 1964	100.00
Catalog, Bear Brand Crocheted & Knitted Sport Tams & Hats, 1927	9.00
Catalog, Bindley Hardware Co., Price List For Holidays, 1895, 8 Pages	19.00
Catalog, Buerger Bros. Barber Supply, 1910	250.00
Catalog, Builders' Reliable Estimator & Contractors' Guide, 1915	26.00
Catalog, Cary MFG Co., N.Y., 1910, 36 Pages	16.00
Catalog, Case Machinery, Automobile, 84 Pages	35.00
Catalog, Champion Iron Co., Arches, Fences, C.1889, 32 Pages	50.00
Catalog, Charles Williams Stoves, 1925, 548 Pages	35.00
Catalog, Charles Williams Stoves, Fall & Winter, 1922	75.00
Catalog, Concentrated Food Co., For Animals, 1881, 18 Pages	16.00
Catalog, Conn. Military Band Instruments, Illustrated, 1880s	68.00
Catalog, Cyphers Poultry Incubator, 1907	20.00
Catalog, Domestic Sewing Machine Co., N.Y., C.1882, 10 Pages	28.00
Catalog, Dy–O–La Dye Co., Tinting, Dyeing, Art Craft, 1929, 32 Pages	13.00
Catalog, Engineering News Record, Hardcover, 1928, 180 Pages	13.00
Catalog, F. Bissell Co., Toledo, Oh., Hardcover, 1923, 887 Pages	23.00
Catalog, F.A.O. Schwarz, 1953	60.00
Catalog, F.A.O. Schwarz, 1965	60.00
Catalog, F.E. Myers & Bros. Co., Repair No.R27, 1927, 196 Pages	18.00
Catalog, F.M. VanEtten & Son, Buffalo, N.Y., 1903, 32 Pages	16.00
Catalog, Farwell Hardware, Illustrated, 1930, 4, 814 Pages	80.00
Catalog, Framingham Nurseries, Plantings, Hedges, 1922, 46 Pages	11.00

Catalog, Franklin Simon & Co., N.Y., 1923, 132 Pages, 10 X 7 3/4 In. 34.00
Catalog, Geo. E. Watson Co., Painter's Supplies, 1934, 64 Pages 21.00
Catalog, Gilbert Toys, Original Mailer, 1934 .... 38.00
Catalog, Gimbels, 1st Christmas Catalog, 1940 .... 22.00
Catalog, Gimbels, Christmas, 1920 .... 22.00
Catalog, Gum Lumber Mfg., Methods, 1916, 16 Pages 10.00
Catalog, Harlow Hardware Co., Corry, Pa., 1906, 252 Pages 30.00
Catalog, Harris Wholesale Millwork, 1940 .... 25.00
Catalog, Illinois Electrical Co., Chicago, Hardcover, 1911, 256 Pages 33.00
Catalog, J. Wiss & Sons Co., Newark, N.J., 1929, 83 Pages 23.00
Catalog, John Deere Spreader Works, E. Moline, 1927, 22 Pages 12.00
Catalog, Libbey Glass Hotel, Cafe No–Nik, 1927 .... 22.00
Catalog, Macy's, Christmas, 1940 .... 25.00
Catalog, May–Stern's Toy Sale, 1957, 32 Pages, 7 1/2 X 10 In. 38.00
Catalog, Merritt Elliot Co., Shoes, Rubbers, Slippers, 1903, 64 Pages 35.00
Catalog, Montgomery Ward & Co., 1881, Chicago, Fall & Winter, 20 Pages 120.00
Catalog, Montgomery Ward, 1904, Wearing Apparel For Women, 76 Pages 25.00
Catalog, Montgomery Ward, 1923–24, 721 Pages 50.00
Catalog, Montgomery Ward, 1941–42, 1, 182 Pages 35.00
Catalog, Montgomery Ward, 1945 .... 55.00
Catalog, Montgomery Ward, 1957 .... 55.00
Catalog, N.C.R., 1910 .... 600.00
Catalog, National Cloak & Suit Co., 1919, 424 Pages 30.00
Catalog, National Lightning Protection Co., 1937, 100 Pages 50.00
Catalog, Oldsmobile, Fold–Out, Futurama, 11 Models, 1948, 24 X 30 In. 20.00
Catalog, Parks Woodworking Co., Cincinnati, Oh., 1922, 48 Pages 11.00
Catalog, Puritan Oil Heating Stoves, 1895 .... 9.00
Catalog, Radio Corporation of America, 1924, 22 Pages 26.00
Catalog, RCA–Victor Co., Inc., 1930, 5 X 7 1/4 In. 8.00
Catalog, Remington Typewriter Co., New York, 1910, 8 Pages, Wrapping 13.00
Catalog, Ridleys Fashion Magazine, Fall & Winter, New York, 1894–95 .... 25.00
Catalog, Russell Burdsall & Ward Bolt & Nut Co., 1911, 174 Pages 12.00
Catalog, S.S. Kresge Co., Detroit, Mi., 1930, 5 1/4 X 7 3/4 In. 15.00
Catalog, S.S. White Dental Mfg.Co., Philadelphia, Pa., 1925, 167 Pgs. 44.00
Catalog, Sears, Roebuck & Co., 1908 .... 12.00
Catalog, Sears, Roebuck & Co., 1911, Chicago, Sept.Oct., 50 Pages 23.00
Catalog, Sears, Roebuck & Co., 1912, 1, 457 Pages 75.00
Catalog, Sears, Roebuck & Co., 1922, 981 Pages 55.00
Catalog, Sears, Roebuck & Co., 1924, Philadelphia, 56 Pages 8.00
Catalog, Sears, Roebuck & Co., 1931, Boston, Spring & Summer, 980 Pgs. 32.00
Catalog, Sears, Roebuck & Co., 1936, Chicago, 23 Pages, 8 X 10 3/4 In. 29.00
Catalog, Sears, Roebuck & Co., 1937, Boston, Lighting, 34 Pages 30.00
Catalog, Sears, Roebuck & Co., 1956 .... 55.00
Catalog, Sears, Roebuck & Co., 1969 .... 50.00
Catalog, South Side Lumber, Wholesale Lumber, Lath, 1901, 48 Pages 13.00
Catalog, Stark Bros. Nurseries & Orchards Co., 1941, 72 Pages 43.00
Catalog, Stoeger, The Shooter's Bible, 1948 .... 25.00
Catalog, The Stanley Works, New Britain, Conn., 1919, 34 Pages 15.00
Catalog, Tuttle & Bailey Mfg. Co., Radiator Enclosures, 1929 .... 14.00
Catalog, Violin Family, Stringed Instruments, 1909, 140 Pages 75.00
Cutout, Floral Design, Tulips, Birds, Maple Framed, 10 X10 In. 250.00
Cutout, Heart & Foliage, J.S.M., 6 1/4 X 7 In. ....*Illus* 650.00
Deed, Parchment, England, Hand Written, Framed, 16 1/2 X 23 In. 250.00
Document, Indenture, Tobias Davis, Josiah Woodberry, Salem, 1805 .... 18.50
Envelope, Dupont Powder, Color, 1933 .... 75.00
Fraktur, Birds, Floral Design, Orange, Red, Green, Framed, 7 X 12 In. 425.00
Fraktur, Birds, Flowers, German Inscription, Framed, 1829, 7 X 6 In. 650.00
Fraktur, Birth Record, Lancaster County, Penna., Framed, 1847 .... 1700.00
Fraktur, Birth, Baptism, Chester Co., Penn., 1831, 19 1/2 X 16 3/4 In. 150.00
Fraktur, Birth, Eulert Family, Central Heart Design, 1793, 14 X 12 In. 500.00
Fraktur, Birth, Geburts Und Taufschein, 1827, 13 X 16 In. 625.00
Fraktur, Birth, Geburts Und Taufschein, 1838, 15 X 19 In. 325.00
Fraktur, Birth, Geburts Und Taufschein, 1862, Framed, 14 X 17 In. 45.00
Fraktur, Birth, Pennsylvania German, Floral, 1809, 16 3/8 X 20 1/8 In. 1000.00

Fraktur, Birth, Pennsylvania German, Taufschein, 1814, 17 1/2 In. 400.00
Fraktur, Birth, Salomon Walbert, Penna., 1808, Frame, 14 X 17 In. 2650.00
Fraktur, Birth, Susanna Arnold, 1827, Facing Angels, Frame, 13 X 16 In. 190.00
Fraktur, Family Record, Watercolor, Ink, 1817, Framed, 9 X 11 1/8 In. 650.00
Fraktur, Family, Johannes Hornung, 1755–1788, Framed, 11 X 15 In. 1000.00
Fraktur, Floral Border Design, Watercolor, Ink, 1808, Framed, 8 X 9 In. 1550.00
Fraktur, Haus Segen, Handcolored, Black Frame, 15 1/2 X 19 1/2 In. 300.00
Fraktur, Joel Griest, April 21st, 1839, 2 3/4 X 5 3/8 In. ....*Illus* 400.00
Fraktur, Martin Detweiler, Pen, Ink, 1808, 6 X 7 3/4 In. ....*Illus* 1150.00
Fraktur, Paths of Heaven & Hell, Peters, Penna., 14 1/2 X 18 In. 105.00
Fraktur, Phillip Dedrich, Cornelia Harder, 1817, 9 X 11 In. ....*Illus* 650.00
Fraktur, Rev. W.E. Schlung, Wisconsin, Dated 1889, Framed 2500.00
Fraktur, Sakrament Der Firmung, Meadville, Penna., 1889, 11 X 16 In. 100.00
Fraktur, Springfield Township, Angels & Birds, 1843, 15 X 12 In. 900.00
Fraktur, Taufschein, Watercolor, Ink, Framed, 18 1/4 X 20 3/4 In. 3000.00
Fraktur, Woven Paper, Watercolor, Ink, Red, Yellow, Black, 5 X 7 5/8 In. 400.00
Label, Buffalo, Canadian Apples, 1930s, 9 X 10 1/2 In. 9.00
Label, Firkin Preserved Strawberries, New York, 1880, 8 X 10 In. 22.00
Label, Santa, Lemon, 1928, 9 X 12 In. 3.00
Menu, Antoines, Centennial Year, 4 Pages, 1940, 9 X 11 1/2 In. 5.00
Menu, Broadmoor Hotel, Parrish 250.00
Program, Folies Bergere, 1930 .... 40.00
Program, Olympic, Written In German, 96 Pages, 1936, 10 X 14 In. 50.00
Program, Skating, Sonia Henie, 1947 .... 15.00
Program, Tournament of Roses, 1969 .... 20.00
Record, Court of Common Pleas, Cincinnati, Ohio, 1795, 12 3/8 In. 55.00
Record, Court of Common Pleas, Steubenville, Ohio, 1799, 10 3/4 In. 115.00
Seals, Christmas, TB, Full Sheet, 1937, 100 Piece 8.00
TV Guide, Lucille Ball Cover, Sept. 29, 1962 .... 9.00
Wheel of Knowledge, Kellogg's, Boxes of Cereal Illustrated, 1938 .... 8.00

Paperweights must have first appeared along with paper in ancient Egypt. Today's collectors search for every type from the very expensive French weights of the nineteenth century to the modern artist weights or advertising pieces. The glass tops of the paperweights sometimes have been nicked or scratched and this type of damage can be removed by polishing. Some serious collectors think this type of repair is an alteration and will not buy a repolished weight; others think it is an acceptable technique of restoration that does not change the value. Baccarat paperweights are listed separately under Baccarat.

PAPERWEIGHT, Advertising, 100 Years of Studebaker, Revolving, Brass 95.00
Advertising, Aetna Insurance, Mirror 30.00
Advertising, Austin & Son Refiners, Assayers, Glass, 1882 .... 30.00
Advertising, Bell System Telephone Co., Bell, Blue Glass 75.00
Advertising, Bicycle, Glass 25.00
Advertising, Des Moines Stove Repair Co., Since 1869, Iron 10.00
Advertising, Electric Motor, Figural, Cast Iron 25.00
Advertising, Ferratin Quinine, Cocaine 145.00
Advertising, Hayes Equipment, 3 Monkeys 45.00
Advertising, Home Sewing Machine 55.00
Advertising, Huylins Candy, Gibson Girl, 4 In. 118.00
Advertising, Logan Bros., Kansas City, Turtle, Metal, Celluloid 45.00
Advertising, New Holland Steamship Line, New Amsterdam Logo 60.00
Advertising, New York Telephone Co., Blue Glass 75.00
Advertising, O'Neill Richardson, Agent–Val. Blatz Beer, Glass 125.00
Advertising, Parker Vises, Bear Shape, Iron 90.00
Advertising, Quick Service Express, Glass, Mirror, 4 X 2 In. 30.00
Advertising, Smith & Welker Hardware, Pennsylvania, Glass 20.00
Advertising, Southern–Western Telegraph & Telephone Co. 75.00
Advertising, Strick Truck Trailer 40.00
Advertising, Strobl Pottery, Cincinnati, Ohio 95.00
Advertising, Texaco Station, Anvil Shape 12.00
Advertising, Ward's Bread 39.00

Advertising, Winchester 41.00
Baseball, Milk Glass 29.00
Bear, On Marble 20.00
Black, Blue, Veined, Yellow Hearts, Signed 185.00
Calendar, 1912, Ruby Flash 45.00
Cat, Arched Back, Cast Iron, 2 X 3 1/2 X 3 1/2 In. 130.00
Cat, Stylized Floral Design, Porcelain, 4 3/8 In. 25.00
Clasped Hands, Parian 40.00
Clichy, 1 Pink & White Flower 3100.00
Clichy, Concentric, Ruby, 4 Loops Alternating Canes, 3 1/4 In. 1400.00
Clichy, Faceted Mushroom Type 2300.00
Clichy, Floral Bouquet, Flat 1100.00
Clichy, Scatterd Millefiori, Clear Ground, Center Rose 900.00
Clichy, Stave Basket 3410.00
Concentric, Blue & White Canes, Basket, Bohemian, 2 5/8 In. 485.00
Dog, Floppy Eared, Cast Iron 20.00
Garfield Memorial, Cleveland, Ohio, Glass 20.00
Gentile, 2 Green Striped Snakes, 2 Ladybugs 450.00
Grubb, Stylized Pink Rose, 2 Buds, Clear 230.00
Indian Head, Pawhuska, Oklahoma, 2 3/4 In. 30.00
Interior Gold Ball, Bubbles, FM Konstglas, Egg Shape, 5 In. 48.00
Ireland, 40 Shades of Green 50.00
Kaziun, Mauve & White Striped Clematis, Yellow Ground 1200.00
Kaziun, Pansy, Red Star Cane Center, 2 1/8 In. 775.00
Kaziun, Rose, Turquoise Field, Low Pedestal, Signed, 1 1/4 In. 525.00
Lincoln, Portrait, Clear & Partially Frosted, C.1876 .... 250.00
Lindbergh, 6 Punties, Cobalt Ground, Sulfide 185.00
Lundberg, Clematis & Butterfly, Shaded Purple Flower, 3 In. 250.00
Lundberg, Comet, Iridescent, Stars, Comet Trail, 3 In. 90.00
Lundberg, World, Blue & White, Clear Ground, 3 In. 125.00
Millefiori, Heart Silhouettes 475.00
Millefiori, Pinwheel, Red, White & Blue, American Faceted 8300.00
New England, Freestanding, Apple 1000.00
New England, Fruit, Latticinio Basket, 2 3/4 In. 650.00
New England, Upright Bouquet, Sodden Snow Ground 4000.00
Owl On Book, Bronzed 29.00
Perthshire, Forget–Me–Not, Signed & Dated 1976 .... 200.00
Plymouth Rock, Inscription On Bottom 75.00
Rosenfeld, Stylized Roses, Clematis & Bellflowers, Clear 400.00
Sandwich, Initialed Striped Flower 4000.00
Sepia Picture of Government Building, Kansas City, Mo. 20.00
Snow Dome, Atlantic City, Seaweed & 3 Fish 28.00
Snow Dome, Pan American Expo, Nouveau Women, N. & S. America 25.00
Snow Dome, Rudolph 13.00
St. Louis, 4 Color Crown 5850.00
St. Louis, Blue Clematis On Red & White Japser 1100.00
St. Louis, Cane Bouquet, Star–Cut Base 900.00
St. Louis, Clematis, Deep Aventurine Green Ground 2400.00
St. Louis, Concentric Millefiori 3550.00
St. Louis, Concentric Millefiori, Dancing Woman Silhouette 1700.00
St. Louis, Crown, 4 Colors 5830.00
Stankard, Magnum Environment, Flowers, Vines, Signed, 4 1/8 In. 2500.00
Trabucco, Open Red Flower, White Blossoms, Clear 300.00
Vandermark, Blue, Green & Purple, Frosty White, Egg Shape, 1983 .... 65.00
Whitefriars, Concentric 250.00
Ysart, Spotted Red Snake On Green Ground 750.00

 Papier–mache is made from paper mixed with glue, chalk, and other ingredients, then molded and baked. It becomes very hard and can be painted. Boxes, trays, and furniture were made of papier–mache. Some of the nineteenth–century pieces were decorated with mother–of–pearl.

PAPIER–MACHE, see also Furniture
PAPIER–MACHE, Bowl, Chinoiserie, 8 In. 65.00

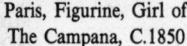

Paris, Figurine, Girl of
The Campana, C.1850

Paris, Figurine, Turkish, Room Scenters, C.1850, Pair

Box, Bird & Flower, Black, Lacquered, 3 1/2 X 10 1/2 In.	35.00
Desk, Lap, Black, Mother–of–Pearl, Victoria's Seal, 1850	225.00
Figure, George Washington, On Horse, Germany, 4 1/2 In.	170.00
Letter Rack, Chinoiserie	45.00
Tea Board, Black, Stylized Pineapples, England, 32 X 23 In.	1500.00
Tray, Mahogany Stand, Floral & Scroll Design, 29 X 36 1/2 In.	1100.00
Tray, Stand, Scrolling Gilt Design, Spanish Moss, 24 1/2 In.	1760.00

PARASOL, see Umbrella

Parian is a fine–grained, hard–paste porcelain named for the marble it resembles. It was first made in England in 1846 and gained in favor in the United States about 1860. Figures, tea sets, vases, and other items were made of Parian at many English and American factories.

PARIAN, Box, 3–D Racing, Saddled Horse On Cover, Oval, 5 X 4 In.	98.00
Bust, Garfield, 8 In.	125.00
Figurine, Mary & Lamb, 11 In., Pair	125.00
Figurine, Tramp Eating, 4 3/4 In.	25.00
Figurine, Woman, Pastel Enameling & Gilt, 12 5/8 In.	15.00
Lamp, Table, 2 Winged Caryatids Form, 16 In.	265.00
Medallion, George Washington, French, Brass Frame, 2 5/8 In.	70.00
Pitcher, Classical Woman, Cherub, Angels, Scalloped, Handle, 6 1/2 In.	115.00
Pitcher, Embossed Ivy, C.1870	60.00
Pitcher, Water, Silver, Cranberry	250.00
Vase, Relief Panels, Songbird, Swing, Foliage, 6 1/2 In.	45.00

Vieux Paris, or Old Paris, is porcelain ware that is known to have been made in Paris in the eighteenth or early nineteenth century. These porcelains have no identifying mark but can be identified by the whiteness of the porcelain and the lines and decorations.

PARIS, Bottle, Figural, Young Woman, Late 19th Century, 10 In., Pair	198.00
Cup, Napoleonic Battlefied Scene, Pedestal, 19th Century	90.00
Desk Set, Figural, 3 Young Girls, Over Inkwell & Sander, 8 In.	330.00
Figurine, Girl of The Campana, C.1850 ....*Illus*	330.00
Figurine, Turkish, Room Scenters, C.1850, Pair ....*Illus*	650.00
Jardiniere, Gold Leaves, Corinthian Column, Pedestal, 30 3/4 In.	555.00
Scenter, Turkish Figures, C.1850, Pair	850.00
Tea Set, Ovoid Form, Twist Handles, C.1900, 14 Piece	357.50
Tete–A–Tete Set, Tray, Coffeepot, Sugar & Creamer, 2 Cups	350.00
Tureen, Cauliflower Finial, Leaf Handles, Gold Banding, 8 In.	65.00
Urn, Applied Flowers & Cherubs, City View, C.1840, 60 1/2 In., Pair	1650.00
Vase, Rose Painted, Pair	990.00

Pate–de–verre is an ancient technique in which glass is made by blending and refining powdered glass of different colors into molds. The process was revived by French glassmakers, especially Galle, around the end of the nineteenth century.

PATE–DE–VERRE, Bust, Henri Cros, Signed, 4 In.	750.00
Figurine, 2 Golden Women, On Bench, Grecian Style, 8 In.	2950.00
Figurine, Grecian Woman, Standing, Noel Daum, 1905, 10 In.	2750.00
Figurine, Nude Woman, Gold, Green Tinted Base, 8 1/2 In.	4250.00
Paperweight, Nude Female, Daum Nancy, C.1910, 6 3/4 In.	4845.00
Plaque, Cherub Reading, Signed, 2 1/2 In.	300.00
Vase, Mottled Colors, Signed, Daum Nancy, 4 1/2 In.	400.00

Pate–sur–pate means paste on paste. The design was made by painting layers of slip on the ceramic piece until a relief decoration was formed. The method was developed at the Sevres factory in France about 1850. It became even more famous at the English Minton factory about 1870. It has since been used by many potters to make both pottery and porcelain wares.

PATE–SUR–PATE, Box, Cobalt Blue, White, Round, Limoges	175.00
Urn, Floral, Ovoid, Made For Lights, 26 In., Pair	880.00
Vase, Cupid Chasing Butterfly, G. Jones, 6 In.	395.00 To 525.00
Vase, Etched Green Tulips, Yellow Green Ground, 5 In.	1540.00
Vase, Green Ground, White Classic Scene, Ring Handles, Schenk	1250.00
Vase, White Lotus, Prunus, Birds, Celadon, Green Wreath, 9 In.	165.00
Wall Pocket, 2 Figures, George Jones, 9 In.	850.00

Paul Revere pottery was made at several locations in and around Boston, Massachusetts, between 1906 and 1942. The pottery was operated as a settlement house program for teen-aged girls. Many pieces were signed "S.E.G." for Saturday Evening Girls. The artists concentrated on children's dishes and tiles. Decorations were outlined in black and filled with color.

PAUL REVERE POTTERY, Bookends, Owl, Sitting On Branch, SEG, 4 X 5 In.	220.00
Bowl, Blue & Green Tree Landscape, SEG, Galner, 4 In.	1150.00
Bowl, Interior Colored Bands, SEG, 1912, 10 3/4 In.	1045.00
Bowl, Stylized Lotus Flower Band, 1926, 10 1/2 In.	200.00
Bowl, Tree Landscape, SEG, 1912, 10 3/4 In.	950.00
Bowl, Turquoise, 6 In.	28.00
Cup & Saucer, Brown Landscape Band, SEG, 1920s, 2 Sets	250.00
Cup & Saucer, Butterscotch	28.00
Paperweight, Revere On Horse, Signed, 3 In.	325.00
Pitcher, Blue & Green Landscape, SEG, C.1919, 4 1/4 In.	165.00
Plate, Butterscotch, 6 1/2 In.	28.00
Teapot, Blue Repeating Rabbit Band, White, 1928, 4 In.	275.00
Tile, Ship, Full Sail, Turquoise, SEG, 1923, 5 3/4 In.	195.00
Tumbler, White Lotus Flower Band, SEG, 1914, 3 3/4 In.	192.00
Vase, Cylindrical, Mirror Black Glaze, SEG, 13 In.	165.00

Peachblow glass originated about 1883 at Hobbs, Brockunier and Company of Wheeling, West Virginia. It is a glass that shades from yellow to peach. It was lined with white glass. New England peachblow is a one-layer glass shading from red to white. Mt. Washington peachblow shades from pink to blue. Reproductions of all types of peachblow have been made. Some are poor and easy to identify as copies, others are very accurate reproductions and could fool the unwary.

PEACHBLOW, Castor, Pickle, Enamel Floral Design, Silver Plated Holder	585.00
Castor, Pickle, Silver Plated Holder, Signed	585.00
Creamer, Mahogany Shaded To Cream, Square Top, Wheeling, 4 1/2 In	965.00
Creamer, Square Top, 4 1/2 In.	965.00
Cruet, Stopper, 7 1/2 In.	165.00
Darner, Handle, C.1890	245.00
Ewer, 10 1/2 In.	2000.00

PEACHBLOW, GUNDERSON, see Gunderson

Hat, 1939, 5 X 5 In.	55.00
Lamp, Diamond–Quilted, Clear Frosted Base, 1880, 16 X 10 In.	3000.00
Lamp, Fairy, Floral Design On Base & Shade, Clarke Cup, 5 3/4 In.	1115.00
Mustard, Hand Painted Prunus, Gold Trim, 2 1/2 In.	395.00
Mustard, Wheeling	295.00
Pitcher, Milk, Shaded To White Base, New England, 6 1/4 In.	1185.00
Pitcher, Red To Pink, Square Mouth, Handle, Wheeling, 8 1/2 In.	400.00
Punch Cup, New England, Reeded Handle, 2 3/4 In.	385.00
Rose Bowl, Ribbed, Pink Shaded To White At Base, 2 1/2 X 3 In.	185.00
Rose Bowl, World's Fair, 1893, 2 1/2 In.	95.00
Salt & Pepper, Wheeling	450.00
Saltshaker, New England, Blush On Upper Portion, 3 3/4 In.	485.00
Saltshaker, Shades To Cream Lower, New England, 3 3/4 In.	485.00
Sugar & Creamer, White Handles	700.00
Sugar Shaker, Wheeling, Original Lid	495.00
Toothpick, New England, Raspberry Pink, Tricon Rim, 2 1/4 In.	385.00
Toothpick, Square Top, Shiny Finish	400.00
Tumbler, Wheeling, Alberta Peach Color & Texture	485.00
Vase, 5 Gargoyles, Fuchsia To Opal White, 10 In.	825.00
Vase, Coralene, Pink To White, Blue Seaweed Design, 5 In.	250.00
Vase, Enameled Red Cherries, Straight Sides, 10 In., Pair	550.00
Vase, Wheeling, Fuchsia Amberina, Frosted Amber Holder, 10 In.	825.00
Vase, Wheeling, Square Mouth, 7 X 8 1/2 In.	1150.00

PEACHBLOW, WEBB, see Webb Peachblow

Listed under Pearl are items made of the natural mother–of–pearl from shells. The glassware known as mother–of–pearl is listed by that name. Opera glasses made with natural pearl shell are listed under Opera Glasses. Natural pearl has been used to decorate furniture and small utilitarian objects for centuries.

PEARL, Calling Card Case, Checkered Pattern, English	75.00
Fruit Set, 8 Knives and Forks, Case	75.00
Manicure Set, Case, 8 Tools	25.00
Serving Fork, Carved Handle, Sterling Tines, Victorian	65.00

Peking glass is a Chinese cameo glass first made popular in the eighteenth century. The Chinese have continued to make this layered glass in the old manner, and many new pieces are now available that could confuse the average buyer.

PEKING GLASS, Snuff Bottle, Elephant, Head Turned, Incised Howdah, 1800	4000.00
Vase, Cameo, Chinese Red Tropical Fish, Lotus, White, 13 In.	850.00
Vase, Leaves & Berries, Chinese Red On White, C.1920, 9 In.	550.00
Vase, Red Cut To White, Ducks, Lotus Flowers, 8 1/2 In., Pair	375.00
Vase, Tropical Fish Amid Lotus, C.1900, 13 In.	900.00

Peloton glass is a European glass with small threads of colored glass rolled onto the surface of clear or colored glass. It is sometimes called spaghetti, or shredded coconut, glass. Most pieces found today were made in the nineteenth century.

PELOTON, Lamp, Finger	1200.00
Rose Bowl, 6 Crimp Top, Strings In White, Pink & Yellow, 3 In.	225.00
Sugar Shaker, Strings, Green Cased, Silver–Plated Top, 5 3/4 In.	88.00
Vase, Pink & Crystal Crackle, 7 1/2 In.	130.00
Water Set, Amber, Multicolored Threads, 6 Piece	650.00

The first steel pen point was made in England in 1780 to replace the hand–cut quill as a writing instrument. It was 100 years before the commercial pen was a common item. The fountain pen was invented in the 1830s but was not made in quantity until the 1880s. All types of old pens are collected.

PEN & PENCIL, Arpege, Art Deco, 14K Gold	45.00
C. Parkston, Ivory & Black Marbelized	15.00
Eversharp, 14K Gold, 1945	550.00

Eversharp, Doric, Art Deco Box	40.00
Parker, No.51, 1950, Case	25.00
Shaeffer, 14K Gold, Alligator Skin Box	45.00
Sheaffer, Lenox, Green Mark	38.00
Sheaffer, Snorkel	35.00
Waterman, Ideal, Woman's, Sterling Overlay	165.00
PEN, Carved Bird, Leaves & Flower In Pearl Handle	35.00
Conklin, Crescent Filler, 1918	50.00 To 95.00
Conklin, Desk, Marbled	11.50
Cross, Gold Filled, Box	30.00
Desk, 14K Gold Point, Orange & Black	6.00
Esterbrook, Dip, In Holder	4.00
Esterbrook, Fountain, Holder	12.00
Eversharp, Skyline, Black, Striped Cap	12.50
Eversharp, Skyline, Gold Filled Caps	30.00
Keystone, Light Green Marbelized, Box	35.00
Kraker, 1917	59.00
Mable Todd & Co., Dip, Gold & Black, Wooden Handle	25.00
Majestic, Green Ribbon, Gold	35.00
Merlin, 14K Bold Nib, European	150.00
Moore CHR, Retractable, ED	21.50
Moore, L–84, Terra–Cotta, 1926	45.00
Morgan, Blue Marbelized	15.00
Parker, Big Red, Hard Rubber	250.00
Parker, Blue Diamond, Inlay	20.00
Parker, Blue Diamond, No.51, Black, 14K Gold Clip, 1946	199.00
Parker, Blue Dot	45.00
Parker, Challenger, 1945	45.00
Parker, Challenger, Emerald Pearl, 1938	89.00
Parker, Debutante, Blue Diamond Vacumatic, Silver Pearl, 1941	59.00
Parker, Duofold Jr., Desk, Mandarin Yellow, 1929, 6 X 3 3/4 In. Base	295.00
Parker, Duofold Jr., Green Jade, 1931	95.00
Parker, Duofold Sr., Big Red	150.00
Parker, Duofold Sr., Button Filled, 1925	185.00
Parker, Duofold, Lucky Curve	12.00
Parker, Duofold, Red, Black, Coverless, Large	50.00
Parker, Flighter, No.51, Stainless Steel, 1951	179.00
Parker, Golf, Burgundy Marble, Gold Filled	45.00
Parker, Lucky Curve, Duofold, Orange, Patent 9/15/16	95.00
Parker, Lucky Curve, No.33, Gold Filigree, 1911	1995.00
Parker, Lucky Curve, Red, 1911	200.00
Parker, No.51	25.00
Parker, No.61, Blue Diamond, Self–Filling	25.00
Parker, Parkette, Black Barrel, Silvertone Cap	15.00
Parker, Parkette, Black Barrel, Silvetone Cap	15.00
Parker, Signet, No.611960	125.00
Parker, Vacumatic, Brown Pearl, Black	30.00
Rocket Ship, Captain Video, 1950s	20.00
Sheaffer, Admiral Snorkel, Black, 1954	29.00
Sheaffer, Craftsman, Brown, 1950	29.00
Sheaffer, Desk Set, Brown, White Dot Lifetime, Onyx Base, Case	40.00
Sheaffer, Desk, 14K Gold Tip, Chicago Title & Trust, Marble Stand	95.00
Sheaffer, Desk, Black Onyx Holder, Barometer, 14K Gold Nib	25.00
Sheaffer, Desk, White Dot, Onyx Base	50.00
Sheaffer, Lifetime, 14K Gold Nib	20.00
Sheaffer, Lifetime, Extra Large	125.00
Sheaffer, Lifetime, Green Jade, 14K Gold Clip & Band, 1926	275.00
Sheaffer, Lifetime, Man's, Duofold, Black & Pearl Stripe, Gold Trim	75.00
Sheaffer, Lifetime, Triumph, Emerald Pearl, 1942	89.00
Sheaffer, No.2, Black Chased, 1914	12.00
Sheaffer, No.500, Feathertouch, Gold Pearl, 1948	42.00
Sheaffer, Roots 100th Anniversary, Connersville, Ind.	3.00
Sheaffer, Snorkel	12.00
Swan, Self–Filling, 1921	49.00

Wahl, Woman's, Gold Filled, Pair 40.00
Wahl–Eversharp, Command Performance, 14K Solid Gold, 1943 .... 795.00
Wahl–Eversharp, Coral Marble, 1929 .... 70.00
Wahl–Eversharp, Equipoise, Green Jade, 1931 .... 159.00
Wahl–Eversharp, Fountain, Dark Green, Marbelized, 14K Gold Point 45.00
Wahl–Eversharp, Gold Filled, Ribbon Ring 12.00
Waterman, 16 PSF, Large 175.00
Waterman, Fountain 35.00
Waterman, Ideal, Sterling Vines, Dated 1905 .... 110.00
Waterman, Lady Patricia, Onyx, Red–Cream, 1932 .... 65.00
Waterman, No.2, Crescent 95.00
Waterman, No.55 .... 130.00
Welsharp, Marble 15.00
Woman's, Pear Handle, Gold Ferrule 20.00

The pencil was invented, so it is said, in 1565. The eraser was not added to the pencil until 1858. The automatic pencil was invented in 1863. Collectors today want advertising pencils or automatic pencils of unusual design. Boxes and sharpeners for pencils are also collected.

PENCIL SHARPENER, 3 Caballeros, Celluloid 25.00
Airplane Shape, Celluloid, 1920s 35.00
Black Face, Blade In Mouth 85.00
Charlie Tuna 25.00
Dandy Automatic Pencil Sharpener Co. 50.00
E.S. Webster, Patent 1892 .... 125.00
Folding Camera Shape, Miniature 25.00
Howard Hunt Pen Co., Celluloid Container, 4 X 4 In. 17.50
Old Wizard 25.00
Revolver Shape, Metal, Top Lifts To Empty Shavings 25.00
Scotty, Red Bakelite 35.00
Sewing Machine Shape, Miniature 25.00
Smokey Bear 6.00
Snoopy 15.00
Texaco, Mechanical 28.00
U.S. Army Plane, Green Bakelite, 1940s 18.00
PENCIL, Baseball, Mechanical, 100th Anniversary, Louisville Slugger .... 25.00 To 30.00
Bullet, Allis Chalmers, Marshalltown, Iowa .... 4.00 To 5.00
Bullet, John Deere, Macomb, Ill. 15.00
Champlin Oil Co., Mechanical, Bubble Top 15.00
Chevrolet, Mechanical, 1920s 15.00
CHR, Chicago Great Western Railroad 20.00
Citrine Top, Retractable, Loop For Chain, 14K Gold 135.00
Conklin, 4B, Rolled Gold, 1920 .... 35.00
Eversharp, Gold 12.00
Eversharp, Mechanical, 14K Gold, Dated 1919 .... 200.00
Eversharp, Skyline, Gold, 1945 .... 12.00
Eversharp, Sterling Silver, 1921 .... 20.00
Hawaiian Prints, 1942, Pair 85.00
Hires Root Beer 18.00
Indian Cycles, Mechanical 20.00
Masterpiece, Orange, 14K Gold Nib 35.00
Mickey Mantle, Picture, Signature, Unused 10.00
Morrison, Gold Naval Insignia, Mechanical 1.00
Parker, Duofold, Striped 15.00
Parker, Jr., Orange, Gold Filled Trim 15.00
Poll Parrot, Leather Shoes For Boys & Girls, Mechanical 13.50
Schorr–Kolkschneider Brewing Co., St. Louis, Mo., Mechanical 27.50
Sheaffer, Balance, Pearl, Black, 1929 .... 149.00
Sheaffer, Black & Pearl, 1930s 10.00
Sheaffer, Gold, Emerald Pearl, Black, 1932 .... 59.00
Sheaffer, Jr., Silver–Red, 1934 .... 25.00
Sheaffer, No.600, Gold Pearl, 1948 .... 29.00
Sheaffer, Tuckaway, Emerald Pearl, 1943 .... 39.00

Spaceman In Spaceship, Stand–Up	10.00
Superrite, Gold Filled	6.50
Wahl, Manifold	10.00
Wahl, Vine & Flower, Sterling, 5 1/4 In.	45.00
Wahl–Eversharp, 1921	32.00
Wahl–Eversharp, Black Lines, 1922	20.00
Wahl–Eversharp, Black, 1926	49.00
Wahl–Eversharp, Gold–Filled Grecian Border, C.1919	20.00
Wahl–Eversharp, Skyliner, Green	10.00
Waterman, 100 Year, Green, 1939	165.00
Waterman, Stateleigh, Gray, 1945	32.00
Waterman, Wood Grain, No.52 1/2	35.00
Wearever, Green, Black, Mechanical	8.00

Pennsbury Pottery The Pennsbury Pottery worked in Morrisville, Pennsylvania, from 1950 to 1971. Full sets of dinnerware were made as well as many decorative items. Pieces are marked with the name of the factory.

PENNSBURY, Ashtray, Fidelity Insurance Co.	20.00
Ashtray, Kissing Couple	18.00
Bowl, Sweet Adeline, 12 In.	35.00
Cake Stand, Amish Couple	35.00
Canister, Tea	100.00
Dish, Pretzel, Eagle	30.00
Dish, Pretzel, Sweet Adeline, 11 In.	35.00
Figurine, Nuthatch	65.00 To 75.00
Figurine, Rooster & Hen, Blue & White, Pair	185.00
Mug, Beer, Red Rooster	27.50
Mug, Fishermen	25.00
Mug, Pretzel, Amish	25.00 To 27.00
Pan, Apple Pie	85.00
Pitcher, 6 In.	28.00
Pitcher, Eagle	20.00
Pitcher, Rooster, 4 1/2 In.	15.00
Pitcher, Rooster, 7 1/2 In.	32.00
Plaque, Amish Farmer & Family, Barn, 8 In.	22.00
Plate, Hanging	18.00
Plate, Yuletide, 1st Edition, 1970	28.00
Salt & Pepper, Amish	25.00
Tile, Round	15.00
Wall Pocket, Rooster	30.00

PEPSI-COLA Pepsi–Cola, the drink and the name, was invented in 1898 but was not trademarked until 1903. The logo was changed from an elaborate script to the modern block letters in the 1970 Pepsi label. All types of advertising memorabilia are collected and reproductions are being made.

PEPSI–COLA, Banner, A Hardee Happy Birthday To Mickey, 50th Birthday, Large	75.00
Blackboard, Tin	20.00
Bottle Carrier, Wooden, 6 Pack, 1930s	60.00
Bottle Opener, Box	25.00
Cake Carrier, Tin	50.00
Calendar, 1945	37.00
Carrier, 6 Pack	50.00
Clock, 1940s	85.00
Clock, Lights Up, 1950s	50.00
Coin–Operated Machine, Jacob No.56	450.00
Dispenser, Syrup	350.00
Figurine, Gnome, Signed	30.00
Figurine, Snowman, Signed	30.00
Matchbook Cover, Disney & World War II Insignia	6.00
Poster, Counterspy, Paper, 8 X 19 In.	18.00
Radio, Bottle Shape, 1939, 26 In.	300.00
Radio, Vending Machine	95.00
Sign, Black Couple, Tin, Oval, 1960s, Small	60.00

Sign, Bottle Cap, Yellow Ground, 1950s, 15 X 15 In.	75.00
Stationery, 1930s	12.00
Thermometer, 1930s	55.00
Thermometer, 27 X 7 In.	23.00
Thermometer, Drink Pepsi–Cola Ice Cold, Round, 12 In.	85.00
Thermometer, Say Pepsi Please, Tin, 1960s, 8 X 8 In.	30.00
Tip Tray, Woman, In Front of Soda Fountain	1250.00
Toy, Mickey Mouse Santa, Stuffed, 3 Ft.	95.00
Toy, Truck, 18–Wheeler, 1/16 Scale, Box	100.00
Tray, Woman, Large Hat, Holding Glass, Oval, 13 1/2 In.	1265.00
Tumbler	15.00 To 17.00
Tumbler Set, Collector Series, 1976, 6 Piece	12.00

Cut glass, pressed glass, art glass, silver, metal, enamel, and even plastic or porcelain perfume bottles have been made. Although the small bottle to hold perfume was first made before the time of ancient Egypt, it is the nineteenth– and twentieth–century examples that interest today's collector. Examples with the atomizer top marked "DeVilbiss" are listed under that name. Glass or porcelain examples will be found under the appropriate name such as Lalique, Czechoslovakia, etc.

PERFUME BOTTLE, Art Deco, Green	20.00
Basketweave, Flared Lip, Pontil, 3 In.	65.00
Black Amethyst, Gold, Floral, Footed, Atomizer, 7 1/2 In.	85.00
Black, Crystal Dabber, Czechoslovakia	65.00
Blue & White Opalescent, Art Glass, Czechoslovakia	210.00
Crackle Glass, Pink, Embossed Gold Top, Jewel, Atomizer	27.00
Cranberry Glass, Allover Gold Design	180.00
Cranberry Glass, Enameled	165.00
Cranberry Opalescent, Fenton	50.00
Cranberry, Mica Flakes, Lay Down, England, 1884, 8 In.	375.00
Cut Amethyst, Sterling Top, Glass Stopper, Lay Down, 4 In.	270.00
Cut Glass, Amethyst, Czechoslovakia	99.00
Cut Glass, Fan, Forsythe, Czechoslovakia, 3 In.	99.00
Cut Glass, Lay Down, Sterling Top	165.00
Cut Glass, Vaseline, Czechoslovakia, 7 In.	99.00
Enameled Green Branches, Blue Floral, Silver Top, 4 1/4 In.	225.00
Evening In Paris, Blue	5.50
Evening In Paris, Cobalt Blue, 6 Piece, Box	42.00
Fenton, Blue Overlay	26.00
Figural, Dice, Bakelite, France, 1 In.	25.00
Flowers, Aqua, Sheared Lip, 5 1/2 In.	45.00
For Chatelaine, Silver, Green & Blue Floral, France, 3 In.	260.00
Geometric Cutting, Gold Flip Top, Rectangular, Crystal	295.00
Golliwog	225.00 To 375.00
Green Glass, Gold, Rhinestones	18.00
Hobnail, Bulbous Bottom, Fenton, 7 In.	22.00
Holder, Robert, Rhinestones, Pearls	45.00
Hula Dancer, Bisque, Seminude, Scalp Over Cork, 5 1/2 In.	43.00
Jester Cologne, Figural, Dog Between Legs, Butterfly, 7 In.	60.00
Kaziun, Double, Paperweight, Lily Stopper, 3 1/8 In.	935.00
Kosta, Pear Shape, Clear, Emerald Lining, 4 In.	125.00
Lalique, Dans La Nuit, Blue, Box	65.00
Larkin Soap Co., Buffalo, Green, 3 In.	475.00
Le Debut Vert, Gold Stopper, Jade Green	18.00
Limoges, Enameled Black & Gold Victorian Couple, White	35.00
Maderas De Oriente, Myrurgia, Wooden Case	95.00
Marcel Franck, Brass	25.00
Marinot, Lines & Crosses, 1925, 7 1/8 In.	4400.00
Mt. Vernon Glassworks	1300.00
Myrtis, Delettrez, Pink Silk Box	125.00
Narcisse, Reindeer, Glass, Label, 2 In.	30.00
Nude Stopper, Czechoslovakia, Signed	175.00
Orloff, Brass Top, Winged Sides, Russia, 3 Oz.	18.00

Peacock, Light Purple, 4 In.	20.00
Royal, Cobalt, White, Atomizer, Bavaria	25.00
Shalimar, Cut Glass, Blue Stopper, 3 In.	35.00
Shocking, Schiaparelli, Box, 2 1/2 Oz.	25.00
Sterling Silver, Engraved, 2 1/2 In.	54.00
Swirled Candy Cane Around, Brass Top, C.1820, 3 3/4 In.	225.00
Teardrop Shape, Engraved Gold, Lay Down, Flip Top, 4 3/8 In.	495.00
Vigny, Golliwog, Sealskin Head	195.00
Woman, Figural	25.00

Peters & Reed Pottery Company of Zanesville, Ohio, was founded by John D. Peters and Adam Reed in 1897. Chromal, Landsun, Montene, Pereco, and Persian are some of the art lines that were made. The company became Zane Pottery in 1920, Gonder Pottery in 1941, and closed in 1957. Peters & Reed was unmarked.

PETERS & REED, Ewer, Raised Grapes, Orange & Yellow, 11 In.	40.00
Flower Frog, Lily Pad, Blue	15.00
Jardiniere, Moss Aztec	65.00
Spittoon, Moss Aztec, Stylized Rose	45.00
Vase, Moss Aztec, 11 1/2 In.	55.00
Vase, Pinched Neck, Garlands & Cherubs, 13 1/2 In.	60.00
Vase, Pinched Neck, Loop Handle, Squat, 4 1/2 In.	28.00
Wall Pocket, Mirror Back	35.00
Window Box, Liner, Ferrell, 6 X 11 In.	125.00
PETRUS REGOUT, see Maastricht	

The Pewabic Pottery was founded by Mary Chase Perry Stratton in 1903 in Detroit, Michigan. The company made many types of art pottery including pieces with matte green glaze and an iridescent crystalline glaze. The company continued working until the death of Mary Stratton in 1961. It was reactivated by Michigan State University in 1968.

PEWABIC, Ashtray	175.00
Bowl, Label, Signed, 6 In.	375.00
Bowl, Orange, 5 In.	150.00
Bowl, Robin's–Egg Blue, Bulbous, 7 1/4 X 4 In.	325.00
Box, Deer, Green, Yellow Glaze, 5 X 4 X 2 In.	400.00
Paperweight, Incised 1931	115.00
Paperweight, Organization Promotion, 1935	180.00
Plaque, Scene From Children's Story, 4 3/4 X 7 In.	375.00
Tile, Aries, Octagonal	325.00
Tile, Horse	250.00
Tile, Pisces	295.00
Tile, Scorpio, Zodiac, Large	175.00
Vase, Blue, 7 In.	260.00
Vase, Design, 10 X 14 In.	925.00
Vase, Floral Design, Mary Chase Stratton, Green, C.1905	2800.00
Vase, Folded–In Top, Green Overglaze, 2 1/2 In.	200.00
Vase, Mottled Greens, 3 X 4 In.	225.00
Vase, Red, Dripping Gray, 9 In.	95.00

Pewter is a metal alloy of tin and lead. Some of the pewter made after 1840 has a slightly different composition and is called "Britannia metal." This later type of pewter was worked by machine; the earlier pieces were made by hand. In the 1920s pewter came back into fashion and pieces were often marked "Genuine Pewter."

PEWTER, Basin, Continental, 7 7/8 In.	25.00
Basin, Richard Austin, Boston, 1792–1817	200.00
Basin, Townsend, 10 1/2 In.	125.00
Bowl, Cover, Marked Woodbury, 7 1/2 X 9 1/4 In.	225.00
Candelabrum, 2 Nozzles, Silberzinn, E. Hueck, C.1902, 14 1/2 In., Pr.	9900.00
Candlesnuffer, Figural, Liberty Bell	20.00

Candlestick, Charles II, Octagonal Drip Tray, C.1680, 5 3/4 In., Pr. 8200.00
Candlestick, Continental, Domed Base, 18th Century, 7 1/4 In., Pair 1435.00
Candlestick, Continental, Domed Base, Marked B.R., 7 In., Pair 825.00
Candlestick, Detachable Rim, Fuller & Smith, 6 7/8 In., Pair 460.00
Candlestick, Liberty, Hand Hammered, Pair 195.00
Candlestick, Octagonal Base, 18th Century, 6 3/4 In. 137.50
Candlestick, Push–Up, 7 7/8 In., Pair 230.00
Candlestick, Queen Anne Style, 19th Century, 10 In., Pair 95.00
Candlestick, Removable Bobeche, 9 1/4 In., Pair 125.00
Centerpiece, Thumb–Molded Rim, Sprigs, Kayserzinn, 1900, 17 1/2 In. 1650.00
Chalice, Communion, James Dixon & Son, Pair 250.00
Chalice, William Calder, 1792–1856, 6 1/8 In. 275.00
Charger, B & Co., R.B., England, 16 1/4 In. 275.00
Charger, England, 14 3/4 In. 175.00
Charger, England, 16 1/2 In. 175.00
Charger, English, Townsend & Compton, 13 1/2 In. 195.00
Charger, Hand Holding Grapes, Engraved Initials, A.P., 12 In. 85.00
Charger, Initials H B On Rim, 13 7/8 In. 200.00
Charger, J. Wylie, Glasgow, 14 3/4 In. 50.00
Charger, London Touchmark, H.M., 14 3/4 In. 200.00
Charger, Townsend & Compton, 13 1/2 In. 165.00
Cup, Christening, Garlands & Bows, June 19, 1895 .... 75.00
Flagon, Beefeater, Lid, Twin Cusp Thumbpiece, C.1670, 10 3/4 In. 4050.00
Flagon, Charles I, Bun Lid, Strap Handle, 1630–35, 10 1/2 In. 5500.00
Flagon, Charles I, Richard Glover, C.1625, 13 1/4 In. 5500.00
Flagon, Communion, Heart Shaped End At Handle Base, 12 3/4 In. 150.00
Flagon, Communion, James Dixon & Son, 12 3/4 In. 375.00
Flagon, Communion, Meeting House, Robinson Lane, Sunderland, 1766 .... 1250.00
Flagon, Communion, Reed & Barton, 14 1/2 In. 45.00
Flagon, James I, Erect Thumbpiece, C.1615, 11 1/2 In. 3900.00
Funnel, 4 1/4 X 5 1/8 In. 25.00
Inkwell, Diamond Shape, Pierced Border, Abel Gilbert, 1776, 2 3/8 In. 2200.00
Invalid Feeder, Marked F.H.1800 & Dent, 5 In. 20.00
Knife Rest, Boar 55.00
Knife Rest, Fox 55.00
Lamp, Brass Collar, Copen & Molineux, N.Y., 10 In. 150.00
Measure Set, England, 1 3/4 To 6 In. 225.00
Measure, Ale, Capacity Mark, Clarke, Fox, Twickenham, 1 Gal. 1250.00
Measure, Bellied, Touchmark, 5 1/4 In. 45.00
Measure, Dry, Graduated In Ounces, 19th Century, 4 1/2 In. 430.00
Measure, James Yates, 1 Qt. 92.00
Measure, Tankard, Birmingham, 4 1/2 In. 50.00
Mold, Ice Cream, 13 Star Flag 52.00
Mold, Ice Cream, Banana 15.00
Mold, Ice Cream, Boy On 2–Wheel Bicycle 145.00
Mold, Ice Cream, Easter Lily, 3 Part 55.00
Mold, Ice Cream, Father Knickerbocker, 3 Part 135.00
Mold, Ice Cream, Fire Steamer 95.00
Mold, Ice Cream, Fireman 95.00
Mold, Ice Cream, Flower 40.00
Mold, Ice Cream, Football 52.00
Mold, Ice Cream, Grape Cluster 35.00
Mold, Ice Cream, Grapes 15.00
Mold, Ice Cream, House, 2 3/4 In. 30.00
Mold, Ice Cream, Kewpie, Dated 1913 .... 135.00
Mold, Ice Cream, Palmer Cox Brownie, Dated 1894 .... 85.00
Mold, Ice Cream, President Grant 115.00
Mold, Ice Cream, Shamrock 20.00
Mold, Ice Cream, Star In Circle 35.00
Mold, Ice Cream, Uncle Sam With Cannon, 5 1/2 In. 100.00
Mold, Ice Cream, Yellow Kid 250.00
Mug, Barrel Shape, Samuel Turner, C.1810, 4 3/4 In. 445.00
Mug, Danforth, 1825–37, 1 Pt. 2100.00
Mug, Danforth, Incised Banding Center, 1825–37 .... 2600.00

Mug, English, 19th Century, 3 5/8 In. 165.00
Mug, Fox Handle, English 25.00
Mug, Straight Sides, Molded Handle, James Yates, C.1840, 8 Piece 385.00
Mustard, Urn Shape, 5 1/4 In. 125.00
Pitcher, Flagg, Homan, C.1842 .... 325.00
Pitcher, L.H. Vaughn, Footed, C.1842 .... 325.00
Pitcher, Mephistopheles, Kayserzinn, 13 In. 295.00
Pitcher, Water, Domed Cover, Varied Ring Design, T. Danforth, 11 In. 522.50
Plaque, German Warship Aegir, Sea Gods, Kayserzinn, 20 In. 925.00
Plate, A.F.P.1732 Engraved Design Rim, England, 9 1/4 In. 95.00
Plate, John Townsend, 8 1/4 In. 75.00
Plate, Joseph Danforth, 8 In. 240.00
Plate, Lawrence Langworthy, 1731–39, 8 1/4 In. 1000.00
Plate, Marriage, Wriggle Work, England, 18th Century, 9 In. 665.00
Plate, Reeded Scalloped Rim, Block Zinn Klinging, 9 3/4 In. 195.00
Plate, Scalloped, Continental, 9 1/2 In. 45.00
Plate, Single Reed Rim, John Dolbeare, Marked, 9 1/2 In. 375.00
Plate, Stamped F.B., 8 1/2 In. 35.00
Plate, Thomas Templeton, C.1680, 8 1/2 In. 485.00
Plate, Townsend & Compton, London, 8 In. 85.00
Platter, Oval, Marked London, 16 In. 90.00
Porringer, Cast Handle, Marked F, 4 3/4 In. 75.00
Porringer, Crown Handle, Nathaniel Austin, 4 1/2 In. 600.00
Porringer, Thomas & Sherman Boardman, C.1829 .... 1045.00
Pot, Spout, Danforth Touchmark, No.1, 11 In. 245.00
Punch Bowl, Kayserzinn .... 275.00 To 295.00
Salt & Pepper, 1880 .... 35.00
Salt, Bulbous, 18th Century, 1 1/2 In. 195.00
Salt, Bulbous, C, 1740, 1 3/5 In. 210.00
Soap Dish, Swirl, Pedestal, 3 1/2 X 2 1/2 In. 25.00
Sugar & Creamer, Flagg & Homan 95.00
Sugar & Creamer, International 35.00
Sundial, Roman Numerals, Compass Directions, Fecit/1717, 9 3/8 In. 275.00
Sundial, Roman Numerals, Geometric Design, 1800s 175.00
Syrup, Acorn Finial, Footed, Hinged Lid, 5 3/4 In. 400.00
Syrup, American Woman, Cincinnati, Ohio 975.00
Tankard, Bellied, Hinged Cover, J. Moyer, Edin., 1/2 Pt. 125.00
Tankard, George I, Domed Lid, Richard Going, Bristol, 28 Oz. 2725.00
Tankard, Yates Birch & Co., England, 1/2 Pt., 4 In. 45.00
Tea Set, Royal Holland, Wood Handles & Finials, 3 Piece 135.00
Teapot, Israel Trusk, Beverly, Mass., C.1807 .... 2125.00
Tray, Art Nouveau, Relief Flowers & Butterfly, 11 3/4 X 8 1/4 In. 70.00
Tray, Card, Woman & Harp, Archibald Knox 300.00
Tray, Card, Woman In Center On Ladder, Apple Tree, 4 1/2 X 6 In. 68.00
Tray, Gadroon Border, James Dixon & Sons, 9 In. 35.00
Urn, Tea, Ball Finial, Paw Feet, Cylindrical, Spigot, England, 21 In. 121.00
Vase, Art Nouveau, 3 Base Handles, Kayserzinn, 4 3/4 In. 80.00
Vase, Bust of Bismarck, Sea Monster, Kayserzinn, 12 In. .... 455.00 To 545.00
Vase, Fish & Flowers, 3–Footed, Kayserzinn, 7 In. 55.00
Vase, German Naval Cruiser Aegir, Sea God, Kayzersinn, 20 In. 695.00
Whistle, Dog's Head, C.1830, 1 1/4 In. 85.00
Wine Pot, Reverse Painted Erotic Panels, Chinese, 12 In. 925.00

 Phoenix Bird, or Flying Phoenix, is the name given to a blue–and–white kitchenware popular between 1900 and World War II. A variant is known as Flying Turkey. Most of this dinnerware was made in Japan for sale in the dime stores in America. It is still being made.

PHOENIX BIRD, Bowl, Vegetable, Blue & White 85.00
Cup & Saucer, ... 8.00 To 11.50
Dish, Vegetable, Cover, Blue & White 85.00
Plate, 6 In. 3.00
Plate, 9 3/4 In. 8.00
Salt & Pepper 24.50

Saucer	1.00
Sugar & Creamer, Cover	20.00
Tea Strainer	15.00
Teapot, Turkey, Blue & White, 5 In.	40.00

Phoenix Glass Company was founded in 1880 in Pennsylvania. The firm made commercial products such as lampshades, bottles, and glassware. Collectors today are interested in the sculptured glassware made by the company from the 1930s until the mid-1950s. The company is still working.

PHOENIX, Box, Floral Cover, Blue Frosted	100.00
Figurine, Madonna, Pink, 10 In.	225.00
Lamp, Blue Peonies, White Ground	300.00
Lamp, Fern, Iridescent Blue	85.00
Lamp, Floral Relief, 20th Century, 11 1/2 In., Pair	110.00
Lamp, Sculptured Bluebells	110.00
Vase, Allover Blue Flowers, Tan Stems, Baluster, 7 X 11 In.	350.00
Vase, Blown-Out Fern Fronds, Leaves, Label, 7 1/2 In.	250.00
Vase, Dance of The Seven Veils, 12 In.	300.00
Vase, Freesia, White Flowers, Blue Ground, 8 1/2 In.	165.00
Vase, Goldfish, Ormolu Footed Frame, Porcelain Cameo, 10 1/4 In.	250.00
Vase, Lovebirds On Branch, White Ground, 6 1/2 In.	95.00
Vase, Madonna, Cream	135.00
Vase, Morning Glory Vines, Frosted Ground, 7 In.	45.00
Vase, Pan & Nymphs, Full Frieze, Yellow Ground, 11 1/4 In.	82.50
Vase, Pillow Shape, Pearlized White Geese, Red Ground, Label, Large	250.00
Vase, Pillow, Frosted White Flying Geese, 9 1/2 X 11 In.	125.00
Vase, Pillow, Wild Geese, Mother-of-Pearl On White, 10 X 12 In.	120.00
Vase, Raised Green & Brown Pinecones On Branches, 7 In.	130.00
Vase, Red Nymphs & Satyrs, Cream Ground, 12 In.	375.00
Vase, Sea Gulls, Turquoise, White High Relief, 11 In.	195.00
Vase, White Raised Leaves, Red, Sticker, 11 1/2 In.	145.00
Vase, Wild Rose, Blue & Crystal, 11 In.	175.00

The tin cases that held phonograph needles are collected today by music and phonograph enthusiasts and advertising addicts. The tins are very small, about 2 inches across, and often have attractive graphic designs lithographed on the tin.

PHONOGRAPH NEEDLE, RCA Victor	25.00
Songster	8.50
Tin, British Masterpiece, Admiral Picture Cover	15.00
Tin, Cockfight, Picture On Lid, Contents	12.50
Tin, Columbia Loud Tone, Paper Covered, Contents	12.00
Tin, Victor Talking Machine, Tungstone Needles, Contents	12.50

The phonograph, invented by Thomas Edison in the 1880s, has been made by many firms. This section also includes other items associated with the phonograph. Records are listed in their own section.

PHONOGRAPH, Brunswick Panatrope Exponential, Model 15-8	350.00
Brunswick Parisians, Collapsible Cardboard Horn	420.00
Busy Bee, Key Wind Cylinder	225.00
Busy Bee, Morning Glory Horn	250.00
Carron, Model 1000, Child's, Plays 78s, Dated 1953	40.00
Columbia AU, 78 RPM, With Horn	390.00
Columbia, AH, Graphophone	1150.00
Columbia, Graphophone, Cylinder & Horn, 2 Minutes	350.00
Columbia, Graphophone, Horn, 2 & 4 Minutes	650.00
Columbia, Graphopone, With Cylinder, Horn, 2 Minutes	350.00
Columbia, Victory	600.00
Dancing Doll, Black Boxers	165.00
Dancing Doll, Black Rastus	165.00
Dancing Doll, Siam Soo	650.00
Dictaphone, For Wax Cylinder Records, Floor Model, 1919	425.00

Phonograph, Jukebox, Rock–Ola, Model 1426,   Phonograph, Perfectone, Wicker,
Colored Glass, 59 In.   Haywood Wakefield, 43 In.

Doll, Talking	550.00
Edison, Amberola 25, Inside Horn	225.00
Edison, Amberola, Wax Cylinder	750.00
Edison, Ebonized, Console No.4, 70 Discs, Original Bill of Sale	1200.00
Edison, Fireside	850.00
Edison, Fireside, Cygnet Horn	775.00 To 850.00
Edison, Gem	375.00
Edison, Gem, Cylinder, Oak Case, Brass & Paint Bell	350.00
Edison, Gem, Model B, Crane Supported Horn, 4 Minutes	450.00
Edison, Home, Nickel Horn, Crane	650.00
Edison, Language	650.00
Edison, Morning Glory Horn	800.00
Edison, Roll Player, Model C2356, 25 Rolls	4620.00
Edison, Standard Cylinder, Large Morning Glory Horn	400.00
Edison, Standard Model D, Cylinder, Small Horn	325.00
Edison, Standard, 14–In. Brass Bell Horn	525.00
Edison, Standard, Stand	550.00
Edison, Table Model, Square, Cylinder	300.00
Edison, Triumph A, Cygnet Horn, 6 Drawer Record Cabinet, Oak	1850.00
Edison, Triumph, Flowered Horn	1250.00
Edison, Triumph, Horn	950.00
Edison, Triumph, Model B, Oak Case, 10 Panel Cygnet Horn	1500.00
Gramophone, Portable, Case, Handle, Detachable Horn, 9 X 12 In.	80.00
Graphophone, Horn, 1906	795.00
Harmony, Oak, Morning Glory Horn	425.00
Haywood Wakefield, Perfectone, Wicker, 43 In. ....*Illus*	600.00
Haywood Wakefield, Wicker, Original	1200.00
Jukebox, Capehart, 5 Cent, Walnut Cabinet	995.00
Jukebox, Electramuse, 1929	4200.00
Jukebox, Music Mite, Williams, Stand	1500.00
Jukebox, Paces, Races	5250.00
Jukebox, Peerless, Model D, Nickelodeon, Restored	8500.00
Jukebox, Ristaucrat, Countertop	775.00 To 900.00
Jukebox, Rock–Ola, Model 1422	3500.00 To 4900.00
Jukebox, Rock–Ola, Model 1426, Colored Glass, 59 In. ....*Illus*	3200.00
Jukebox, Rock–Ola, Model 1438	1650.00
Jukebox, Seeburg, Model 100, Wall–O–Magic	95.00
Jukebox, Seeburg, Model 100C	1650.00
Jukebox, Seeburg, Model B	2250.00
Jukebox, Seeburg, Model C	1075.00 To 4450.00
Jukebox, Seeburg, Model VL200	2000.00
Jukebox, Wurlitzer, Model 24	2250.00

Jukebox, Wurlitzer, Model 1015 .... 4295.00
Jukebox, Wurlitzer, Model 1015, Coin Gear 8500.00
Jukebox, Wurlitzer, Model 1100 .... 3000.00 To 5500.00
Jukebox, Wurlitzer, Model 1400 .... 1800.00
Jukebox, Wurlitzer, Model 1500, Plays 45 & 78 Records, 1952 .... 3000.00
Jukebox, Wurlitzer, Model 1650 .... 800.00
Jukebox, Wurlitzer, Model 1700 .... 2000.00
Jukebox, Wurlitzer, Model 2500, Wall, 200 Selections 950.00
Jukebox, Wurlitzer, Model 3020, Wall 24 Selections 450.00
Jukebox, Wurlitzer, Model APP, Style 1, Nickelodeon, Restored 8500.00
Kalamazoo Multiphon, Cylinder, Square Case 6500.00
RCA, Table Top, 18 Records 225.00
Regina, Mandolin Piano Orchestra, Spring Wound, Oak Cabinet 6000.00
Rockola Model 1434, 78 RPM 1500.00
Super Hero, Superman, Wonder Woman, Batman & Robin, 1978 .... 25.00
Victor, Horn, Pre–Dog 1200.00
Victor, II, Oak Horn, 14 X 14 In. 1760.00
Victor, Mahogany 1000.00
Victor, Microsynchroneus, With Radio 150.00
Victor, Model V 1850.00
Victor, Model VI 250.00
Victor, Monarch 900.00
Victor, Orthophonic, Granada 195.00
Victor, Orthophonic, Model 4–40 .... 345.00
Victor, Type E, Brass Horn, Oak, Windup, Black Paint, 11 X 11 In. 688.00
Victor, Victrola VI 250.00
Victor, VV–IV, Table Top, Oak 150.00
Walnut Cabinet, 1906 .... 450.00

The first photograph was a view from a window in France taken in 1826. The commercially successful photograph started with the daguerreotype introduced in 1839. Today all sorts of photographs and photographic equipment are collected. Albums were popular in Victorian times. Cartes de visite, popular after 1854, were mounted on 2 1/2– by 4–inch cardboard. Cabinet cards were introduced in 1866. These were mounted on cards 4 1/4 x 6 1/2 inches. Stereo views are listed under Stereo Card.

PHOTOGRAPHY, Album, 62 Scenic Mounted Photos, 1901, 14 X 10 In. 100.00
Ambrotype, 4 Children Standing On Doorstep 20.00
Ambrotype, Young Boy Seated On Fringe Covered Organ Stool 20.00
Board, Trimming, Eastman Kodak, No.1 .... 25.00
Board, Trimming, Kodak, No.2 .... 25.00
Cabinet Card, 2 Seated Indians, Little Sioux, Iowa 35.00
Cabinet Card, 6 Horvath Midgets, 1880, 4 X 6 1/2 In. 33.50
Cabinet Card, Elephant Bazaar, Coney Island, 1884 .... 20.00
Cabinet Card, Etta Reed, Oval, Wendt, 1885, 6 1/2 X 4 In. 20.00
Cabinet Card, Man & Woman, In Watkins Glen, N.Y., 1885 .... 18.50
Cabinet Card, Man, Snow, Sleigh, 1885, 4 X 6 1/2 In. 17.50
Cabinet Card, Williams Studio, Honolulu, 1888, 6 1/2 X 4 In. 12.50
Camera, Ansco, Build Craftsman, Original Box, 1950s 65.00
Camera, Argus, C–3, Flash, Carrying Case, 1940 .... 30.00
Camera, Autographic Kodak, No.3, Booklet, Box 35.00
Camera, Box, Anniversary, Brown, With Seal In Chrome, 1930 .... 25.00
Camera, Brownie, 2A 75.00
Camera, Brownie, Box, No.116 .... 10.00
Camera, Brownie, Starmite, Box 8.00
Camera, Calypso UW 375.00
Camera, Century, C.1902, 8 X 10 In. 425.00
Camera, Clik–N–Pop, Dart, Metal, Target, 1950 .... 35.00
Camera, Cycle Poco, No.2, Leather Case 200.00
Camera, Eastman, Brownie, Pictures Brownies 65.00
Camera, Fotron Electronic, Leather Case, 1963 .... 30.00
Camera, Graflex, Restored, 4 X 5 In. 395.00
Camera, Graflex, Revolving Back Auto, 24 Shutter Speeds 175.00

Camera, Kodak, Autographic Folding Cartridge, Model B, 1920s 75.00
Camera, Kodak, Model B, Best–Pocket, Black 35.00
Camera, Kodak, No.1, Pocket Junior, Brown, Black Bellows, Case 25.00
Camera, Kodak, No.616 .... 35.00
Camera, Kodak, Pony 828, Carrying Case, Box 20.00
Camera, Marvel 45.00
Camera, Minetta, Pigskin Case, Miniature 29.00
Camera, Pony Primo, No.15, Rochester Optical, C.1900, 4 X 5 In. 95.00
Camera, Primo B, C.1900, 4 X 5 In. 125.00
Camera, Secret Service Spy, 1904 .... 200.00
Carte De Visite, A. Lincoln, Death Notice, Framed, 5 X 9 In. 125.00
Carte De Visite, Civil War Generals, 88 Piece 150.00
Carte De Visite, Collage of Presidents, Washington To Grant 17.00
Carte De Visite, Com. Nutt, Minnie Warren, 1870, 2 X 3 3/4 In. 18.50
Carte De Visite, Confederate Ship Sterling Price, Commander 500.00
Carte De Visite, General A. Burnsides, Bust 8.00
Carte De Visite, General Wigfall, With Book of His Life 75.00
Carte De Visite, Tom Thumb Wedding Attendants, Commodore Nutt 35.00
Chair, Adjustable Seat, Set In Middle of Seat 450.00
Daguerreotype, Woman, Sitting, Civil War, Union Case, 2 X 3 In. 40.00
Magic Lantern, 63 Glass Slides 165.00
Magic Lantern, Germany, Box 150.00
Photograph, Apollo XI Crew, Neil Armstrong Signature, Color 95.00
Photograph, Arkansas Cotton Gin, People, Blue, White, 7 X 9 In. 11.50
Photograph, Bohemian Grove, Men, Redwood, 1930, 3 1/2 X 5 In. 7.50
Photograph, Chinese Family, San Francisco, 1920s, 8 X 10 In. 27.50
Photograph, Fisherman, Catch, San Francisco, 1935, 7 X 11 In. 15.00
Photograph, Ft.Fairfield, Ma., View, 1893, 13 X 20 In. 175.00
Photograph, Hardware Store, Woman In Door, 1890, 7 X 9 In. 22.50
Photograph, Ophir Mine, Utah, 1942, 6 1/2 X 8 1/2 In. 7.50
Photograph, Pine Ridge Chief Short Bull, 1900, 9 X 12 In. 4.00
Photograph, Pope Benedict XV, Signed & Dated August 30, 1917 .... 750.00
Photograph, Rudolph Valentino, As Russian Cossack, 6 X 8 In. 230.00
Photograph, Schoolchildren, San Francisco, 1884, 5 X 8 1/2 In. 15.00
Photograph, Street, Horse Carriages, People, 1890, 8 X 10 In. 40.00
Photograph, Woman Taking Photo of Child, Kodak, Framed, 1920s 75.00
Photogravure, Boy Smoking Cigar, 2 Views, J.G.Brown, 10 X 13 In 50.00
Photogravure, Pabst Brewing Co., Plant, 1892, 5 X 7 1/2 In. 35.00
Projector, Silver Movie 275.00
Timer, Kodak, Spring Driven, Cast Iron 22.00
Tintype, Black Child, 2 1/2 X 3 In. 50.00
Tintype, Blacksmith In Shop, 4 X 5 In. 75.00
Tintype, Civil War Encampment, 3 X 4 In. 175.00
Tintype, Woman, Oval, 1870, 2 1/2 X 4 In. .... -7.50
Tintype, Young Man In Gray Uniform, Brass Buttons 150.00
Tripod, Kodak, Collapsible, 1903 .... 95.00

 About 1880, the well–decorated home had a shawl on the piano. Bisque piano babies were designed to help hold the shawl in place. They range in size from 6 to 18 inches. Most of the figures were made in Germany. Reproductions are being made. Other piano babies are listed under manufacturers' names.

PIANO BABY, Bisque, Lying On Stomach, Nightie & Bonnet, Green Ties, 8 In. 225.00
Boy & Girl, Bisque, Andrea, 12 In. 400.00
Crawling, Gebruder Heubach 250.00
Girl, Sitting, 1 Foot In Air, Blond, Bisque, Germany 1200.00
Holding Basket On Knee, Pair 500.00
Leans On Elbow, Holds Ball, 1 Leg Up, Bisque, 11 In. 85.00
Lying On Back, Playing With Toes, Gown & Bonnet, Heubach, 7 In. 350.00
Lying On Stomach, Black & White Kitten, Molded Hair, 11 In. 300.00
Lying On Stomach, With Dog 75.00
Seated, Blond, Flowered Dress, Red, No.23/110 .... 100.00
Seated, Intaglio Eyes, Molded Wind–Blown Hair, Germany, Large 450.00
Sitting, Arms Raised, 4 1/2 In. 65.00

Pickard China Company was started in 1898 by Wilder Pickard. Hand–painted designs were used on china purchased from other sources. In the 1930s, the company began to make its own china wares in Chicago, Illinois. The company now makes many types of porcelains including a successful line of limited edition collector plates.

PICKARD, Bonbon, Scenic & Rose Garden, 9 In.	155.00
Bowl, Green & Gold Design, Gold Rim, 7 In.	40.00
Bowl, Inside Gold Band, Water Lilies, Leaves, Signed, 7 1/8 In.	165.00
Bowl, Plum Design, Signed, 10 In.	125.00
Bowl, Scenic, Open Handles, 1922, 7 1/4 In.	75.00
Candy Dish, Leaf Shape, Violets, Gold Inner Handles, 1905–10, 8 In.	75.00
Candy Dish, Royal Enameled, Gold Daisies, Handles, Signed, 8 1/2 In.	110.00
Candy Dish, Scenic, Gold Tabs, Floral & Foliage Ground, 6 In.	120.00
Coffeepot, Sugar & Creamer, Aura Argenta Linear, 10 3/4 In.	750.00
Dish, Women, Dutch Scene, Handle, 9 In.	95.00
Figurine, Dog, Beagle Type, Pheasant In Mouth, 9 In	45.00
Jardiniere, Overlapping Leaves, Fluted, Marked, 5 1/2 In.	275.00
Pitcher, Allover Roses, Gold Trim, 11 In.	395.00
Pitcher, Violets, Signed Marker, 6 In.	185.00
Pitcher, Water, Gold, Band of Water Lilies, Marked, 6 Sides, 8 In.	265.00
Plate, Art Deco, Gold Leaf Design	38.00
Plate, Bellflowers, Buds, White, Yellow, Vobor, 1912–19, 7 3/4 In.	110.00
Plate, Deserted Garden, Octagonal, Marked, 11 In.	175.00 To 200.00
Plate, Floral Design, Gold Wheat Mark, 6 1/2 In.	48.00
Plate, Gold & Red Tracery, Outlined, Pink Floral, 1912–19, 7 3/4 In.	115.00
Plate, Nut Design, Beige & Browns, Signed, 8 1/2 In.	90.00
Plate, Purple Plums, Gold Border, 8 5/8 In.	95.00
Plate, Tree & Leaf Scene, Pastel, Cutout Handles, 1895, 10 1/2 In.	225.00
Plate, Tulips, Buds, Burgundy Tracery, Gold Band, Signed, 6 1/4 In.	45.00
Platter, Peacock, 11 1/2 In.	165.00
Relish, Multicolored Flowers, Brick Wall, 12 1/2 In.	155.00
Salt & Pepper, Shadow Leaves	24.00
Soup, Cream, Gold Wishbone Handle, Turquoise & Gold	45.00
Sugar & Cover, Deserted Garden, Gold, Art Deco, Signed Vokral	210.00
Sugar & Creamer, Allover Gold	48.00
Sugar & Creamer, Bavaria, Maple Leaf	65.00
Sugar & Creamer, Scenic	295.00
Sugar Shaker, Aura Argenta Linear, Signed Richter, 1910	195.00
Tankard, Apple Design, Gold Trim, Signed Leon, C.1895, 13 In.	895.00
Vase, Forest, Trees, Moon, Matte Finish, E. Challinor, 9 In.	395.00
Vase, Palm Trees Beside Moonlit Water, Signed, 6 1/2 In.	305.00
Vase, Peacock, 1/2 Gold, 1/2 Black, Signed, 10 In.	440.00
Vase, Pines, Moonlight, Gold Band Rim, Matte, E. Challinor, 8 In.	495.00
Vase, Scenic, Forest, Trees, Moon, E. Challinor, Matte Finish, 9 In.	395.00
Vase, Trees, Gray, Green & Lavender, Matte Finish, 8 In.	465.00

PICTURE FRAME, see Furniture, Frame

Silhouettes and small decorative pictures are listed here. Some other types of pictures are listed under Print or Painting.

PICTURE, Batik, Cloth Panel, Zebras, Running, Brown, White, Framed, 26 X 33 In.	65.00
Calligraphy, Family Record, Spencerian Pen & Ink, 1895, 21 X 30 In.	65.00
Calligraphy, Spencerian Exercise, Matted, Gilt Frame, 11 X 12 In.	65.00
Diorama, Gilt Metal Relief, Horsemen, Oxen, Framed, 20 X 23 In., Pair	176.00
Embroidered, American Eagle, Silk, Framed, 23 3/4 X 27 3/4 In.	160.00
Hair Wreath, Hair Basket Center, Woven, Framed Shadow Box	185.00
Hair Wreath, Victorian, Human Hair, Center Flower, Shadow Box	50.00
Needlework, Berlin Motto, Amer. Eagle, 1776–1876, Framed, 22 X 9 In.	75.00
Needlework, Berlin Motto, June 1852, Framed, 9 5/8 X 9 1/4 In.	65.00
Needlework, Cat & Dog On Pillow, Bird's-Eye Maple Frame	2200.00
Needlework, Hawking Party, Gilt Wood, Frame, 59 X 75 In.	700.00
Needlework, Map, Silk, England & Wales, 18 X 15 In. _Illus_	525.00

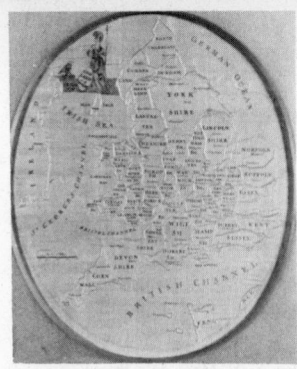

Picture, Needlework, Map, Silk,
England & Wales, 18 X 15 In.

Poster, McNamee's Minstrels,
America's Finest, 80 X 40 In.

Punched Paper, Stepladder Pattern, Board, 1885, 7 X 7 In. 37.50
Scissor Cut, Altar Type Design, Crucifix, Lamb, Framed, 9 X 13 In. 165.00
Scissor Cut, Valentine, Heart Design, Inscribed, Framed, 12 X 10 In. 110.00
Scissor Cut, Valentine, Heart, Birds, Black Fabric, Framed, 4 X 6 In. 90.00
Silhouette, 2 Facing Adults, Child Between, 11 1/2 X 13 1/2 In. 4240.00
Silhouette, Boy, Hollow Cut, Gilt Frame, 4 1/8 X 3 5/8 In. 135.00
Silhouette, Caleb Bates, American, 19th Century 275.00
Silhouette, DeWitt Clinton, Kellogg 85.00
Silhouette, Gentleman, Aqua Ground, J.F. Hanover, Penciled Details 220.00
Silhouette, Gentleman, Full–Length, Top Hat, Ships Ground, Hubbard 880.00
Silhouette, Gentleman, Full–Length, White Paper, Framed, 9 X 12 In. 350.00
Silhouette, Girl, Caroline Rudbury, Gilt Frame, 1839, 5 X 4 1/4 In. 30.00
Silhouette, Girl, Wood Block Printed Torso, Red Frame, 5 X 6 In. 250.00
Silhouette, Henry Clay, Kellogg 85.00
Silhouette, Man & Woman, Hollow Cut, Cloth Backing, Round, 5 1/4 In. 300.00
Silhouette, Man In Top Hat, Gilt Frame, 5 1/8 X 3 1/2 In. 75.00
Silhouette, Man, Woman, Hollow Cut, Framed, 4 3/4 X 5 3/4 In., Pair 400.00
Silhouette, Officer, Ink, Watercolor, Lacquered Frame, 5 X 6 In. 200.00
Silhouette, Woman In Bonnet, White Highlights, Framed, 5 X 6 In. 250.00
Silhouette, Woman, Full–Length, Blue & White Wash, Hubbard 990.00
Silhouette, Woman, Hollow Cut, Gold Frame, 5 1/4 X 4 1/4 In. 75.00
Silhouette, Woman, Hollow Cut, Pine Frame, 7 X 7 1/2 In. 125.00
Silhouette, Woman, Mr. W. Seville, Framed, 6 1/4 X 5 1/8 In. 200.00
Silhouette, Woman, Pen & Ink Detail, Brass Frame, 4 1/2 X 5 1/4 In. 105.00
Silhouette, Woman, Pen & Ink Detail, Doyle, Brass Frame, 5 X 6 In. 395.00
Silhouette, Young Man, Ink On Paper, Reeded Frame, 5 X 6 1/4 In. 175.00
Silhouette, Young Woman, Cut, Black On Black, Gilt, 5 X 6 In. 275.00
Tinsel, Reverse Painted Floral, Bird In Polychrome Colors, 15 In. 20.00
Tinsel, Reverse Painted, Basket of Flowers, 7 X 8 1/4 In. 125.00
Wax, Mrs.Josiah Wedgwood Portrait, 1762, Shadow Box Frame, 8 X 6 In. 900.00
Woven Silk, Betsy Ross Making Flag, Anderson Bros., 9 X 5 1/2 In. 45.00

The Pigeon Forge Pottery was started in Pigeon Forge, Tennessee, in 1946. Red clay found near the pottery was used to make the pieces. Molded or thrown pottery with matte glaze and slip decoration was made. The pottery is still working.

PIGEON FORGE, Mug, Pine Trees, Green, Brown, 5 In. 18.00
Pitcher, Art Deco, Yellow Stars, Brown 10.00
Vase, Dogwood Branch, 6 In. 30.00

The Pilkington Tile and Pottery Company was established in 1892 in England. The company made small pottery wares like buttons and hatpin heads but soon started decorating vases purchased from other potteries. By 1903, the company had discovered an opalescent glaze that became popular on the Lancastrian pottery line. The manufacture of pottery ended in 1937 but decorating continued until 1948.

PILKINGTON, Tile, Circus Horse, Female Trainer, C.1940	65.00
Tile, Outdoor Scene, Hand Painted	35.00

The pincushion doll is not really a doll and often was not even a pincushion. The top half of the doll was made of porcelain. The edge of the half-doll was made with several small holes for thread, and the doll was stitched to a fabric body with a voluminous skirt. The finished figure was used to cover a hot pot of tea, a powder box, a pincushion, a whiskbroom, or a lamp. They were made in sizes from less than an inch to over 9 inches high. Most date from the early 1900s to the 1950s.

PINCUSHION DOLL, Arms Up & Out, Germany	85.00
Baby, Arms Out	80.00
Baby, With Yellow Bonnet, Germany	100.00
Bisque, Box	30.00
Blond Wig, 1920s, 12 In.	38.00
Both Arms Away, Holding Letter, 3 1/4 In.	75.00
Camisole, Blue Ribbon In Hair	75.00
Child, Dutch, Object In Crook of Arm, Germany	50.00
Child, Jointed, Bisque	115.00
Cloche Hat, Pin-Striped Skirt, Germany	98.00
Cloche Hat, Tall	30.00
Colonial Woman, Flower In Cleavage, Bent Arm To Hair	40.00
Colonial Woman, Gray Hair, Bent Arm To Head	35.00
Flapper Girl, 2 1/2 In.	38.00
Flapper, Blue Cloche & Dress, Germany	60.00
Flapper, Hat, Luster Blue & Yellow	95.00
Flapper, Holding Mirror, 2 1/4 In.	75.00
Flapper, With Tennis Racket, Germany	35.00
Girl, Red Hat, Blue Feather Plume, Fan To Side, 3 In.	40.00
Green Trimmed Dress	45.00
Hand To Body, Germany	40.00
Hands Away From Body, Kister Mark, Germany	150.00
Holding Yarn, Dutch, 5 In.	100.00
Madame Pompadour, Green Dress, Brimmed Work Cap, 6 1/4 In.	125.00
Madame Pompadour, Porcelain, Green, White, Germany, 6 In.	95.00
Metal Frame For Hoopskirt, Germany	35.00
Mohair Hair, Germany	45.00
Nancy Pert	45.00
Nude Flapper, String of Beads, Marked 5445	225.00
Nude, Extended Arms, Pink Bandana	600.00
Pharaoh Man, Karl Scheider, 5 In.	350.00
Pierrette, Blue Skullcap	125.00
Pierrette, Lying On Stomach, Puff Holds Leg, Germany	250.00
Woman, 1 Arm Partially Extended, Hand Near Breast, Germany	60.00
Woman, Eyes Cast Down, Brown Mohair Wig	325.00
Woman, Flapper Hat, Orange, Blue & Yellow, 4 In.	60.00
Woman, Pink Satin Hat & Dress	30.00
Woman, Reading Letter	75.00
Woman, Roaring '20s Costume, 9 In.	70.00
Woman, With Fan, Hands Out	175.00
Woman, With Mirror	75.00
Yellow Outfit, Hand Extended, 12 In.	125.00
PINK SLAG, see Slag, Pink	

Pipes have been popular since tobacco was introduced to Europe by Sir Walter Raleigh. Meerschaum pipes are listed under Meerschaum.

PIPE, Black Stone Bowl, Inlaid Pewter, Catlinite, Leather Trim, 8 In.	500.00
Blue & White Enamel Design, Red Clay, Louis Bouchez, 10 1/4 In.	30.00
Briar, Carved Bear, Foliage	45.00
Briar, Growling Dog, Carved	90.00
Briar, MacDull, Sterling Band	15.00
Burl, Silver & Horn Trim, Czechoslovakia, 12 In.	12.50
Carved, Dog & Deer	135.00
Castello, Small Bulldog, Sea Rock Briar, KKKK, Banded Splint Shank	40.00
Corncob, Edgeworth Tobacco	20.00
Deer Antler Stem, Etched Moose Head On Wooden Bowl, 7 In.	30.00
Dog Bowl, Woman's, Case	55.00
Hand Carved Head of Indian, Monkey On His Back, Wooden	35.00
Hookah, Egyptian Brass, 22 In.	75.00
Ivory, Woman's Hand Holding Bowl	60.00
Man's Head, Gouda	125.00
Opium, 3 Pieces On Short Chain, Metal	65.00
Opium, With Tools, Brass, 15 3/4 In.	90.00
Porcelain, Hand Painted Scene of Knight & Lady, 16 In.	95.00
Rack, Hand Carved, 4 Fishermen Heads	65.00
Savinelli, Series 4, Sandblast, Square Shank	50.00
Savinelli, Series 5, Flame Grain, Smooth, Large Bowl, Freehand	110.00
Savinelli, Series 5, Straight Grain, Smooth, Large Bowl, Square Shank	1000.00
Stand, Double, Dunhill, Ceramic	25.00
Sterling Silver Overlay, Black	30.00

Pirkenhammer is a porcelain manufactory started in 1802 by Friedrich Holke and J. G. Lilst. It was located in Bohemia, now Brezova, Czechoslovakia. The company made tablewares usually decorated with views and flowers. Lithophanes were also made. The mark of the crossed hammers is easy to remember as the Pirkenhammer symbol.

PIRKENHAMMER, Plate, Gaudy Polychrome Flow Blue, Openwork, 9 1/2 In.	150.00

Pisgah pottery pieces that are marked "Pisgah Forest Pottery" were made in North Carolina from 1926. The pottery was started by Walter R. Stephen in 1914, and after his death in 1941, the pottery continued in operation. The most famous types of Pisgah Forest ware are the cameo type with designs made of raised glaze and the turquoise crackle glaze wares.

PISGAH FOREST, Bowl, Christmas Dinner, Stephen, Blue	650.00
Creamer, Hunting Scene, Pine Tree, Arden, N.C.	210.00
Jug, Turquoise, 1948, 6 In.	85.00
Mug, Flemish Monk, Blue & White	65.00
Pitcher, Milk, Wagon Scene, Pine Tree, Arden, N.C.	125.00 To 350.00
Teapot, Cameo, Knob Cover	355.00
Vase, Brushed On Brown Glaze, 6 In.	50.00
Vase, Dancing Couples, Blue	575.00
Vase, Gray–Red Glaze, 9 In.	295.00
Vase, Multicolor Crystalline, 5 In.	130.00
Vase, Pink Interior, Green Exterior, 3 1/4 In.	75.00
Vase, Purple & Turquoise, 1938, 9 In.	85.00
Vase, Turquoise, Pink Interior, 1942, 8 In.	110.00
Vase, Yellow, Semicrystalline, 5 In.	100.00

Planters Nut and Chocolate Company was started in Wilkes–Barre, Pennsylvania, in 1906. The Mr. Peanut figure was adopted as a trademark in 1916. National advertising for Planters Peanuts started in 1918. The company was acquired by Standard Brands, Inc., in 1961. Some of the Mr. Peanut jars and other memorabilia have been reproduced and, of course, new items are being made.

PLANTERS PEANUTS, Ashtray, Anniversary, 1956	25.00

Ashtray, Figural, Brass Plated, 1956	35.00
Bank, Dispenser, Plastic, 12 X 6 In.	25.00
Bank, Mr. Peanut, Cast Iron	95.00
Bank, Mr. Peanut, Dispenser, Hard Plastic, 12 X 6 In.	25.00
Bank, Mr. Peanut, Figural, Red Plastic	12.00
Blotter, Planters Peanut Butter, Peanut Shape, Paper	12.00
Book, Mr. Peanut Story & Paint Book, 1935	10.00
Bottle Opener, Mr. Peanut, Wall Mount, Black Top Hat	127.00
Canister, Tin, 2 Red Diamonds, 10 Lb.	435.00
Canister, Yellow Letters, Keep Jar Covered, 9 X 7 In.	50.00
Case Cutter, Mr. Peanut	10.00
Container, Papier–Mache	45.00
Cookbook, Giveaway, 1948	5.00
Doll, Cloth, 19 In.	13.00
Doll, Mr. Peanut	20.00
Doll, Mr. Peanut, Cloth, 19 In.	11.00 To 12.50
Jar, Barrel Shape, Embossed Label, Knopped Cover, 13 In.	209.00
Jar, Barrel Shape, Embossed Label, Peanut Cover, 13 In.	270.00
Jar, Barrel Shape, Running Mr. Peanut, 12 X 28 In.	225.00
Jar, Blown–Out Peanuts	175.00
Jar, Fishbowl, Label, Embossed Peanut Cover, 13 In.	182.00
Jar, Football, Peanut Top, 9 In.	280.00
Jar, Peanut Lid, 8 Sides, 10 1/2 In.	94.00 To 150.00
Jar, Red & White Lettering	35.00
Jar, Red, Yellow, Blue, Round, Large	45.00
Jar, Store, 4 Corners Planters Peanuts	250.00
Jar, Streamline, Tin Cover, 10 In.	72.00
Jar, Yellow Letters, 6 Sides, Cover	70.00 To 90.00
Knife, Mr. Peanut For President, 1976	6.00
Knife, Plastic Handle, Foldout	9.00
Lighter, Bic	20.00
Lighter, Cigarette, Bic, Blue	18.00
Lighter, Cigarette, Bic, Mr. Peanut	20.00
Lunch Box, Plastic Thermos, 1965	22.00
Lunch Box, Tin Thermos, 1959	38.00
Nut Set, Tin, 4 Small Bowls, 5 Piece	15.00
Ornament, Whistle, Mr. Peanut, Christmas Tree	45.00
Peanut Butter Maker, Mr. Peanut	18.00 To 40.00
Pencil, Mechanical, Blue, Figural Top, Box	20.00
Pencil, Mechanical, Mr. Peanut, Figural	18.00
Pencil, Mechanical, Mr. Peanut, Original Cellophane	8.50
Radio, Peanut Can	45.00
Salt & Pepper, Mr. Peanut	20.00
Salt & Pepper, Mr. Peanut, 14 In.	18.00
Salt & Pepper, Mr. Peanut, Blue Plastic, 3 In.	8.00
Scale, No.14	500.00
Sign, Standup, Cardboard, 48 In.	18.00
Spoon, Gold, Mr. Peanut	12.00
Spoon, Mr. Peanut Figural Handle, Gold Finish	16.00
Spoon, Silver, Original Wrapper	28.00
Vending Machine, Blue Plastic, Mr. Peanut	40.00

Plated amberina was patented June 15, 1886, by Edward D. Libbey and made by the New England Glass Works. It is similar in color to amberina, but is characterized by a cream colored or chartreuse lining (never white) and small ridges or ribs on the outside.

PLATED AMBERINA, Tumbler, Thin Walls, Optic Ribs	1550.00

Plique–a–jour is an enameling process. The enamel is laid between thin raised metal lines and heated. The finished piece has transparent enamel held between the thin metal wires. It is different from cloisonne because it is transparent.

PLIQUE–A–JOUR, Spoon	45.00
Tea Strainer, Transparent Colored Enamel Flowers, Marked	650.00

All types of political memorabilia are collected, from buttons to banners. Items related to presidential candidates are the most popular, but collectors also search for material related to state and local offices. Many reproductions have been made.

POLITICAL, Badge, Lincoln, Ferrotype, 5/8 In.	125.00
Badge, Teddy Roosevelt, My Hat Is In The Ring, Hat	435.00
Bandana, Harrison & Morton	125.00
Bandana, Ike, Printed Cotton, Red Ground, 26 1/2 X 27 In.	55.00
Bandana, McKinley, Protection, Sound Money, Silk, 18 X 18 In.	45.00
Bandana, Roosevelt, Fairbanks, 1904	75.00
Bandana, Silk, Flags of No. & So. America, 1899, 23 X 24 In.	100.00
Bandana, TR, Teddy Roosevelt, Cotton, 19 3/4 X 20 1/2 In.	95.00
Bank, F.D. Roosevelt New Deal, Painted Cast Iron, Kenton, 5 In.	49.50
Banner, Dewey, Warren, Cloth, 36 X 42 In.	400.00
Banner, Republican Convention, City Delegate's, 7 In.	40.00
Banner, Smith For President, Large	495.00
Banner, Thomas Dewey	29.00
Banner, Willkie For President, 12 X 16 In.	85.00
Beanie, Harding–Coolidge, Red, White & Blue	50.00
Belt, Washington–Harrison, 1889, Leather	130.00
Book, Coloring, Watergate, Satire, 1973	6.00
Book, Life of Woodrow Wilson	10.50
Bottle, Humphrey–Muskie, Donkey, Green, Wheaton, 1968	17.50
Bottle, Nixon–Agnew, Elephant, Amber, Wheaton, 1968	17.50
Box, Cigar, Teddy Roosevelt, Square Deal, Picture	40.00
Bread Plate, Teddy Roosevelt, Dancing Bears	95.00 To 140.00
Bubble Gum, Cigars, Nixon, Win With Dick, 1968, Box of 24	35.00
Bumper Sticker, McCarthy, Yellow & Green, 4 X 6 In.	8.50
Bumper Sticker, Reagan, Wallace, '76, 2 3/4 X 7 1/2 In.	7.00
Bust, McKinley, Cast Iron, 9 In.	50.00
Bust, McKinley, Robinson Leadbetter, Bisque, 8 In.	145.00
Button, A Gallant Leader, F.D.R.	4.00
Button, Alf Landon, Flying In Airplane, Land On Washington	2000.00
Button, Alfred Smith, Elect For Governor, Words Only	7.00
Button, America Wants Willkie	9.00
Button, Bryan & Stevenson, 1900	35.00
Button, Bryan, Sewall, Beetle With Spring–Out Wings	200.00
Button, Charles Evans Hughes, Picture, Red Border, 7/8 In.	500.00
Button, Cleaver For President, Picture, Black On Green	10.00
Button, Cleaver For President, Picture, Black On White	2.00
Button, Coolidge, Elephant	25.00
Button, Cox For President, Picture, 1 1/4 In.	625.00
Button, Cox, Rooster	15.00
Button, Davis & Bryan	6.00
Button, Every "Buddy" For Willkie, Celluloid, 1 In.	120.00
Button, Farmers For McGovern	7.00
Button, Franklin Delano Roosevelt, Figural Donkey, Celluloid	30.00
Button, Gary Hart	3.00
Button, Gillette, Roosevelt, Wallace	5.00
Button, Goldwater, Band Wagon Is Rolling Along, Hop On, 3 1/2 In.	75.00
Button, Goldwater, Best Man For Job, 3 In.	4.00
Button, Hoover, Enameled Elephant, GOP, Pinback	80.00
Button, Huey Long, Every Man A King	28.50
Button, I Want Roosevelt Again	5.00
Button, Ike & Dick–There For You	6.00
Button, Independent Vote, F.D.R.	9.00
Button, Indiana Willkie Clubs	7.00
Button, J.S.W. Beckham For Governor, 1896	8.00
Button, John F. Kennedy Inauguration, Full Color	20.00
Button, Kennedy Inauguration Day	9.50
Button, Landon & Knox	4.00 To 12.00
Button, Landon, Knox, Elephant Center	4.00

Button, Let's Make Ronald Reagan Governor 15.00
Button, McKinley & Roosevelt, Full Dinner Bucket 85.00
Button, McKinley Eclipse, 1 1/4 In. 1200.00
Button, McKinley Eclipse, With Rays, Sepia 2013.00
Button, McKinley, 1 1/4 In. 40.00
Button, No Third Term, F.D.R. .... 5.65 To 8.50
Button, Nuts To Carter 3.00
Button, President McKinley Memoriam 22.00
Button, Reagan, Bush, '84, 13/14 In. .... .75
Button, Reagan, You Ain'T Seen Nothin' Yet, 3 In. 2.00
Button, Stand By The President, Wilson, With Ribbon, 1 1/4 In. 950.00
Button, Steel Workers For Mondale 2.00
Button, Stevenson, Kefauver, Straight Democratic Ticket, Pictures 95.00
Button, Taft, From Chicago To Washington, Elephant, Cartoon 1257.00
Button, Taft, National Republican College League, Sepia, 3/4 In. 30.00
Button, Teddy Bear, Roosevelt, Tin Lithograph 50.00
Button, Wallace, 1968 .... 7.50
Button, Warren G. Harding For President, 7/8 In. 18.00
Button, We R For Rockefeller 4.00
Button, William Henry Harrison, Log Cabin, 1840 .... 175.00
Button, William J. Bryan, 1896, 1 1/4 In. 20.00
Button, William Jennings Bryan, Celluloid 35.00
Button, William Taft, 1 3/8 In. 50.00
Button, Willkie & McNary .... 5.00 To 12.00
Button, Willkie, Wings For America 4.00
Button, Wilson Inauguration, Sepia, Celluloid, 1913, 1 1/4 In. 45.00
Button, Wilson, 8 Hours, 3/4 In. 30.00
Campaign Torch, Tin, Gimbal Font, D. Linn Inscription, 79 In. 35.00
Candy Cantainer, Elephant, GOP, Original Candy 225.00
Cane, McKinley, Whistle Handle, Slogans, Winfield Mfg.Co., 33 In. 45.00
Card, Birthday, Cartoon, Nixon On Front 9.50
Cartoon, Straw Vote Hat, Harding, 1924, Signed, 7 1/4 X 9 1/4 In. 25.00
Cigar, Bubble Gum, Nixon, Win With Dick, Box of 24 .... 35.00
Clock, Roosevelt, N.R.A., The Spirit of 1933 .... 85.00
Clock, Roosevelt, Spirit of U.S.A. 85.00
Coin Set, U.S.Presidents, Washington To Nixon, Copper, Eagle Case 100.00
Compact, Thomas Dewey, Photograph On Celluloid, 3 In. 200.00
Decal, I Like Ike, Picture 8.50
Doll, Soap, My Papa Will Vote For McKinley, 4 In. 110.00
Earring, Tie Tack, Pin & Key Chain, Eisenhower, 4 Piece 22.00
Egg, Wooden, Mechanical, I Crow For Harrison, Rooster Pops Out 775.00
Envelope, James Buchanan, White House Seal In Wax, 1856 .... 500.00
Fan, Taft, Word On Each Fan Section 14.50
Ferrotype, Andrew Johnson, Lincoln, Dated April 2, 1861 .... 3200.00
Figurine, Jimmy Carter, Walking Peanut, Box, 5 In. 25.00
Game, Al Smith For President 100.00
Hat, Adlai, Democratic Convention, Turquoise, Cardboard, 1956 .... 22.00
Hat, John F. Kennedy, Convention, Campaign 65.00
Hat, Stevenson, Paper 18.50
Hatchet, Washington's Inauguration, Cast Iron, 1879 .... 85.00
Letter, James K. Polk, Commenting On Zachary Taylor's Victory 8000.00
License Plate, Landon, Knox 40.00
Milk Bottle Cap, Chester A. Arthur, 1950s 2.00
Mirror, Coolidge, Dupont, Robinson, Pocket 400.00
Mirror, Roosevelt For President, Hershey For Governor, Pocket 75.00
Mug, Bobby For President, Caricature, 1960's 12.50
Mug, Figural, Ike & Mamie, Set 65.00
Necktie, Eisenhower, Profile 35.00
Necktie, Willkie, Profile 35.00
Pack, Cigarettes, I Like Ike 20.00
Pamphlet, John Glenn Autograph 16.50
Paperweight, McKinley Bust, Flat, Bronze, 3 In. 25.00
Pencil, Hoover For President, 1928 .... 20.00
Penknife, Reagan, Bush, 1980 .... 12.00

Pennant, Dewey, Warren, Blue & White, 16 1/2 In. 30.00
Pennant, Mrs. Wilson Picture, 26 In. 50.00
Pennant, Woodrow Wilson, Bust, Felt, Silk Screen, 19 X 25 1/2 In. 135.00
Pin, Label, Hoover, Brass 15.00
Pin, Lapel, Franklin D. Roosevelt 20.00
Pin, McKinley, Gold Bug, Mechanical 250.00
Pipe, Figure of Bryan, Clay, 2 X 2 1/2 In. 95.00
Pitcher, Ben. Harrison, Engraved Log Cabin, Barrel, Hawkes, 16 In. 1275.00
Pitcher, Campaign, William Harrison 1100.00
Plaque, John F. Kennedy, Profile, Bronze, Mahogany, 1964, Life Size 125.00
Plate, Gerald Ford, Inaugural, M. Kaufman & F. Eliscu, 1974 .... 495.00
Plate, Inaugural, Nixon–Agnew, Gilroy Roberts, 1973 .... 495.00
Plate, Mamie & Ike, 7 In. 8.00
Plate, Nixon, Vernon Kilns 30.00
Plate, Republican Convention, San Francisco, G. Knight, 14 In. 55.00
Plate, Roosevelt Bear, Verse, San Juan Hill, 5 3/4 In. 48.00
Postcard Set, Women's Right To Vote, Comical, 9 Piece 55.00
Postcard, Anti John F. Kennedy 10.00
Postcard, Bryan, Kern, Foldout of White House 75.00
Postcard, J.F. Kennedy, Ask Not What Your Country Can Do 2.00
Postcard, Landon Photo, Black & White 12.00
Postcard, Ronald Reagan & George Bush, Chrome, 1980 .... 4.00
Postcard, Taft, Sherman 10.00
Postcard, Teddy Roosevelt Billiken, In Africa, 1910, Unused 22.50
Postcard, Teddy Roosevelt, Picture 25.00
Postcard, Warren G. Harding, Color, 1920 .... 5.00
Postcard, Woodrow Wilson & Wife 8.00
Postcard, Woodrow Wilson, Visit To Paris, 1918, 9 Piece 40.00
Poster, Curtis, Keep Him On The Job, Portrait, 22 X 16 1/8 In. 50.00
Poster, Decision '80, NBC–TV, Brinkley & Chancellor, 2 X 3 Ft. 8.00
Poster, Earl Warren, Portrait, Cardboard, 24 1/4 X 18 In. 45.00
Poster, Elect Congressman Nixon U.S. Senator, 14 X 11 In. 120.00
Poster, For Governor, Ronald Reagan, 1966, 34 1/2 X 23 In. 90.00
Poster, Hoover, Curtis, Keep Them On The Job, Photos, 22 X 16 In. 65.00
Poster, Hoover, Keep Him On The Job, Portrait, 22 X 16 1/8 In. 55.00
Poster, Thomas E. Dewey, Portrait, Blue, 24 1/4 X 18 In. 75.00
Poster, Truman For Senator, FDR For President, 1940, 11 X 14 In. 80.00
Print, James Monroe, Kellogg, Walnut Frame, 12 1/2 X 15 1/2 In. 100.00
Print, John Quincy Adams, Kellogg, Pine Frame, 13 1/2 X 16 In. 65.00
Print, Reagan, Jelly Beans, Color, 1981, 8 1/2 X 11 In. 9.00
Puppet, Hand, Nixon & Agnew, Pair 35.00
Record, Franklin Roosevelt's Address To Congress, Dec. 8, 1941 .... 75.00
Ribbon Badge, Eisenhower, Flasher, Inaugural 1953 .... 15.00
Ribbon, Governor Arthur James, Picture Pin On Ribbon, 1 3/4 In. 20.00
Ribbon, Harrison & Morton 70.00
Ribbon, Nixon, Lodge, Pictures, Eagle 4.50
Ring, Alfred E. Smith, Campaign, 1928 .... 150.00
Sheet Music, Cleveland's Campaign 45.00
Sheet Music, Roosevelt March 35.00
Sticker, Window, Forward With Stevenson, 3 X 7 1/2 In. 8.00
Sticker, Window, Kennedy Johnson, 3 X 6 In. 3.00
Sticker, Window, Vote For Davis, 1924 Campaign, 6 X 10 In. 32.00
Sword, Dewey For President, Embossed On Blade 145.00
Ticket, Admission, Eisenhower Rally, Madison Square Garden, 1956 .... 10.00
Ticket, Convention, Democratic, Philadelphia, FDR Nominated, 1936 .... 20.00
Ticket, Convention, Republican, Cow Palace, San Francisco, 1964 .... 12.00
Tie Bar, Gerald Ford, Presidential Seal 15.00
Tie, All The Way Adlai, Red 15.00
Tie, Roosevelt, Garner, Picture, Blue 150.00
Tie, Willkie Woven To Make A Stripe, Campaign, 1940 .... 25.00
Tile, KcKinley 45.00
Top Hat, Harrison, Glass, He's All Right, The Same Old Hat, 2 In. 55.00
Top Hat, With Parade Torch, Tin, Copper Band 825.00
Toy, Yo–Yo, Jimmy Carter, Inaugural 15.00

If you buy an Art Deco bronze and ivory figure, be very careful to examine the ivory. Even slight cracks or damage lower the value.

Don't clean rooms near bronzes with bleaching cleansing powders or disinfectant floor washing products that have chlorine; chlorine harms bronzes.

Tray, McKinley, Metal, Lithographed, Painted, 16 In.	115.00
Tray, William McKinley, Oval, 16 In.	125.00
Tumbler, J.F. Kennedy, 1963	20.00
Tumbler, McKinley, Theodore Roosevelt, Prosperity, Protection	70.00
Watch Fob, Our Next President, William H. Taft	40.00
Watch Fob, Our Next President, William J. Bryan	40.00
Watch Fob, Roosevelt & Fairbanks, 1904	135.00
Watch Fob, Taft & Sherman	40.00
Watch Fob, Taft For President	75.00
Watch, Dan Quayle, Cartoon, Jumbled Numerals, Necktie Hands	45.00
Whistle, McKinley, "Sound" Music, Brass	125.00
Wristwatch, Spiro Agnew	50.00
Wristwatch, Tricky Dick	40.00

Pomona glass is a clear glass with a soft amber border decorated with pale blue or rose–colored flowers and leaves. The colors are very, very pale. The background of the glass is covered with a network of fine lines. It was made from 1885 to 1888 by the New England Glass Company. First grind was made from April 1885 to June 1886. It was made by cutting a wax surface on the glass, then dipping it in acid. Second grind was a less expensive method of acid etching that was then developed.

POMONA, Bowl, Cornflower, 2nd Grind, 10 In.	415.00
Bowl, Ruffled Amber Edge, 1st Grind, 2 3/4 In.	62.00
Butter, Acanthus Leaf Cover, 1st Grind	530.00
Castor, Pickle, Cornflower, 2nd Grind, 12 In.	395.00
Celery Vase, Ruffled Rim, Cornflower, 1st Grind, 6 1/4 In.	350.00
Cracker Jar, Chrysanthemum, 2nd Grind, 9 In.	260.00
Cruet, 1st Grind	150.00
Cruet, Amber Stopper, Petal Base, Band of Blue Flowers, 1st Grind	495.00
Cruet, Cornflower, Amber Stained, Cut Glass Stopper	396.00
Finger Bowl, Blueberry, 2nd Grind	75.00
Finger Bowl, Cornflower, 2nd Grind	75.00
Finger Bowl, Crimped Top, 1st Grind	150.00
Goblet, Cornflower, 2nd Grind, 6 In.	395.00
Pitcher, Cornflower Design, Square Top, 1st Grind, 6 1/4 In.	395.00
Toothpick, Enameled	115.00
Toothpick, Fan Shape, Amber Stained, Ruffled, 1st Grind	145.00
Toothpick, Rigaree	95.00
Tumbler, Water, Cornflower, 2nd Grind, 3 3/4 In.	135.00
Vase, Lily, Silver Base, 2nd Grind	145.00
Vase, Ruffled Design, 1st Grind, 4 In.	275.00

PONTYPOOL, see Tole

Popeye was introduced to the Thimble Theater comic strip in 1929. The character became a favorite of readers. In 1932, an animated cartoon featuring Popeye was made by Paramount Studios. The cartoon series continued and became even more popular when the old movies were used on television starting in the 1950s. The full–length movie with Robin Williams as Popeye was made in 1980.

POPEYE, Advertisement, Green, Black, Popeye On Doorknob, 1930s, 9 In. 65.00
Bank, Daily Dime, 1950s 60.00
Bank, Dime Register, 1929 .... 32.00
Bank, Mechanical, Popeye Knockout, Tin Litho, Straits Mfg., 3 1/2 In. 385.00
Bank, Rally, Pressed Paper 85.00
Book, Big Little Book, 1980 .... 2.50
Book, Cartoon, Linen, 1936, 9 1/2 X 13 In. 35.00
Book, Popeye & Pirates, Pop–Up .... 165.00 To 195.00
Book, Popeye The Sailor Man 32.00
Bowl, Child's, Sailor's Yarn, 5 1/4 In. 195.00
Box, Chalk, No Contents, 1953 .... 18.00
Box, Crayon 24.00
Card, Club Application, Capitol Theater Popeye Club, 3 X 6 In. 15.00
Card, Playing, 1934 .... 25.00
Charm, Celluloid, 1930s ....7.50 To 15.00
Cookie Jar, American Bisque 295.00
Costume, Box 35.00
Doll, Cloth Body, Composition Arms & Head, 15 In. 25.00
Doll, Hard Plastic, Vinyl, King Features, 8 In. 15.00
Doll, Jointed, Wood, 5 1/2 In. 75.00
Doll, Jointed, Wood, With Pipe, 6 In. .... 45.00 To 75.00
Doll, Olive Oyl, Ballerina, Linemar 375.00
Doll, Popeye, In Spinach Can, Mattel 75.00
Doll, Rag, Homemade, 18 In. 50.00
Doll, Wooden Jointed, Pipe, 6 In. 75.00
Eraser, Pencil Top, Package, 1975, 3 Piece 3.00
Game, Juggler, Ball Game, Tin Lithograph, 1929 .... 55.00
Game, Pipe Toss, Rosebud Art, 1935 .... 40.00 To 65.00
Game, Popeye To The Rescue, 1930s 30.00
Game, Popeye's Game, Parker Brothers, 1940 .... 75.00
Game, Ring Toss, Colored Figures, Box, 10 1/2 In. 95.00
Game, Shipwreck, Einson–Freeman Co., 1933 .... 225.00
Game, Skeetshoot, 1950s 85.00
Game, Skooz–It, Pick A Picture, Olive Oyl, 1963 .... 22.00
Game, Sling Dart, Transogram Co., Package 50.00
Game, Target Set, Roly Poly, 1950s 85.00
Gumball Machine, Plastic, 1968 .... 12.00
Harmonica, Plastic, 1970s, 5 In. 3.00
Light Bulb, Mounted In Ceramic Socket, 5 In. 70.00
Lunch Box, Thermos, 1964 ....70.00 To 85.00
Lunch Box, Yellow, Red, 1980 .... 10.00 To 15.00
Overhead Puncher, Tin Litho, Celluloid Bag, Chien, 9 1/2 In. 6820.00
Paint Set, Popeye, Olive Oyl & Swee' Pea, Tin, American Crayon 18.00
Pen, Fountain, Bladder Type 45.00
Pencil Box, C.1929, 10 In. 23.00
Pencil, Automatic, Tin, Box, 1929 .... 75.00
Pencil, Lead, Eagle Pencil Co., 1929, 11 In. 85.00
Pencil, Mechanical, King Features, 10 In. 17.00
Pin, Popeye, 1950s 30.00
Puppet, Olive Oyl, C.1950, 12 In. 75.00
Puppet, Popeye, C.1950, 12 In. 75.00
Puzzle, Jigsaw, A Fight To The Finish, 1961, Box 25.00
Radio, Box 75.00
Record Player 25.00
Ring, Post Cereal 15.00
Saltshaker, Olive Oyl 12.00
Shirt, Size 10 .... 200.00
Soap, On Rope, Unused, Box .... 30.00 To 35.00
Tile, Wall, Olive Oyl 45.00
Tile, Wall, Wimpy 45.00

Tin, Popcorn, Purity Mills, Unused	16.00
Toy, Airplane, Popeye, Windup, Marx, 8 1/2 In.	1000.00
Toy, In Barrel, Windup, 1932	475.00
Toy, Muscle Builder, Package, 1980	5.00
Toy, Olive Oyl Ballet Dancer, Tin Litho, Friction, Linemar, 5 1/2 In.	385.00
Toy, Pluto On Tricycle, Tin Litho, Mechanical, Linemar, 4 In.	490.00
Toy, Pool Table, Package, 1984	5.00
Toy, Popeye Express, Box	1475.00
Toy, Popeye Express, Mechanical, Tin Litho, 9 In.	247.50 To 440.00
Toy, Popeye, At Punching Bag, Chein	1300.00
Toy, Popeye, Dancer, Mechanical, Tin Litho, Marx, 9 In.	550.00 To 577.50
Toy, Popeye, On Roof, Tin Litho, Mechanical, Marx, 9 In.	495.00
Toy, Popeye, The Pilot, Mechanical, Tin Litho, Marx, 7 In.	357.50
Toy, Popeye, Walker, Mechanical, Tin Litho, 8 1/4 In.	187.00
Toy, Spinach Can	19.50
Toy, Train, Popeye Express, Marx, Box	1475.00
Toy, Walker, Celluloid, Irwin, 5 In.	165.00
Tumbler, Wimpy Picture	81.00
Watch, Pocket, First Version	900.00
Watch, Pocket, USA, Stained Face	357.00
Wristwatch	250.00
Wristwatch, 1934	550.00

Major porcelain factories are listed in this book under the factory name. This section lists pieces that are by the less well-known factories.

PORCELAIN, Bowl, Blue & White Leaf Panels Interior, 17th Century, 15 In.	880.00
Bowl, Cover, Chestnuts Sticking Out, French, 9 In.	150.00
Bowl, Dancing Couple Center, Painted Pink, Square, Austria, 10 In.	35.00
Bowl, Floral Enameling, Dragon & Bat On Rim, Marked, 3 3/4 In.	75.00
Bowl, Iridescent Lappets, Yellow, Bell Form, Chinese, 8 1/4 In.	110.00
Bowl, Oriental Design, Underglaze Blue, Red Enamel, Gilt, 2 In.	200.00
Box, Blackheath Golfer, Gilt Design, French	935.00
Brush Pot, Orange & Green Dog, Oriental, 4 1/4 In.	20.00
Bust, Napoleon, Medals, Gray Cloak, Schiefe Alsbach, 10 1/2 In.	250.00
Butter, Domed Lid, Enameled Brown Stripes, Nickel Frame, 6 In.	125.00
Cachepot, Gold Drape, Leaf & Banded, Flared, Continental, 8 In.	121.00
Cachepot, Peony, Blue & White, Hexagonal, Chinese, Pair	60.00
Cachepot, Underliner, Grisaille Design of Peony, 9 In.	105.00
Cachepot, With Underliners, Peonies & Dahlia, 9 In.	305.00
Candelabrum, 5 Arms, 2 Putti, Floral Base, Germany, 23 In., Pair	165.00
Centerpiece, Oval Bowl, Figural Panel, Landscape, C.1900, 13 In.	2310.00
Charger, Boys Before Pavilion, Polychrome, Ming Mark, 14 In.	145.00
Charger, Center of Young Woman, Gilt Border, Austrian, 12 1/2in.	335.00
Charger, Enameled Floral & Leaf, Gold, 1900, Chinese, 18 In.	250.00
Charger, Mahogany Stand, Chinese, 25 1/2 In.	3850.00
Chocolate Pot, Black Cat, Coat of Arms, New Quay, Arcadian, 1880	75.00
Compote, Figural, Boy, Girl, Each Holds Basket, Germany, 8 In., Pair	198.00
Cottage, Paper Incense Burner, Brameld, 1826, 11 In.	3500.00
Cracker Jar, Floral Panels, Germany, 7 1/2 In.	250.00
Creamer, Blue Ground, Gilt Rimmed White, Floral Design, 4 In.	65.00
Creamer, Figural, Moose, Austrian	32.00
Cup & Saucer, Floral Decoration, Gilt, Handleless	500.00
Cup, Footed, Gilded Relief Design, Green Ground, 5 1/8 In.	250.00
Dish, Dragon Design, Jianjing Mark, 19th Century, 10 1/2 In.	5250.00
Dish, Polychrome Floral & Fruit Enameling, 6 X 7 3/4 In.	35.00
Dish, Rose Medallion Design, C.1860, 10 3/4 In.	465.00
Dish, Serving, Lobster Handle, Divided, Large	50.00
Egg, Branch of Dogwood, Christ Is Risen, Russian, 1900, 5 1/4 In.	715.00
Egg, Dove In Rayed Surround, Imperial Russia, C.1880, 2 7/8 In.	275.00
Egg, Intersecting Foliage & Strapwork, Russian, C.1900, 3 5/8 In.	467.00
Figurine, 2 Horses Running, Erphila, 6 In.	58.00
Figurine, Apple Pickers, Man On Ladder, Girl, Sitzendorf, 9 In.	650.00
Figurine, Bear, Standing, Cream, H & C In House, 4 In.	75.00

Figurine, Boy, Holding Vase of Flowers, Chinese, 11 In.	35.00
Figurine, Buddha, Seated, 5 Climbing Children, Chinese, 14 In.	325.00
Figurine, Buddha, Seated, Children Climbing Around, Marked, 12 In.	325.00
Figurine, Cavalier, Holding Hat, & Lady, Standing, 18 In.	450.00
Figurine, Cherub, Candlestick, Flowered Base, Sitzendorf, 15 In.	350.00
Figurine, Couple With Russian Wolfhounds, Sitzendorf, 9 X 10 In.	850.00
Figurine, Elephant, Gray Enameling, 5 7/8 In.	40.00
Figurine, Monkey Band, 9 Piece, Germany	950.00
Figurine, Napoleon's Coronation Preparation, Schiefe-Alsbach	950.00
Figurine, Othello, Seated Girl, Schiebe-Alsbach, 10 1/2 X 15 In.	1350.00
Figurine, Parrot, Continental, 12 In., Pair	412.00
Figurine, Quan Yin, Flowing Robes, Lotus Base, Box, 13 1/2 In.	110.00
Figurine, Sculptress, Mallet, Chisel In Hand, Bust, Germany, 8 In.	275.00
Figurine, Serenading Couple, Floral Dress, Sitzendorf, 9 In.	750.00
Figurine, Turkey, Blue Head, Brown Feathers, C.1875, 21 In.	2475.00
Flower Frog, Nude Woman, Yellow & Orange Floral Rope, Germany	130.00
Flowerpot, Court Scenes, Chinese, 19th Century, 7 1/2 In., Pair	660.00
Garden Seat, Blue & White, Birds, Amid, Foliage, Chinese, 19 In.	198.00
Ginger Jar, Enameled Floral, Dark Blue Ground, 9 3/4 In., Pair	110.00
Ginger Jar, Painted Enamels, Good Luck Symbols, 8 In., Pair	715.00
Group, Musical, Woman In Floral Dress, Man In Coat, 8 1/4 In.	250.00
Group, Slave Trade, Roman Noble & 2 Dogs, Sitzendorf, 9 X 17 In.	1250.00
Jar, Enameled Scene of Ship, American Flag, 8 1/4 In.	150.00
Jar, Tobacco, Indianhead, Pastel Feather Headdress, Germany	95.00
Jardiniere, Black Ship, Flanked By Scenes, Japanese, 21 In.	1430.00
Jardiniere, Coral Dragon, Black Ground, Chinese, 14 In.	121.00 To 121.00
Jardiniere, Sang De Boeuf, China, 18 In., Pair	935.00
Jug, Monkey, Lion & Unicorn Mark, 9 1/2 In.	215.00
Mug, Black Transfer Design, King of Prussia, Gabriel, 4 3/4 In.	550.00
Mug, Child's, Black Transfer, Horse & Elephant, 1 5/8 In.	85.00
Pillow, Cat, Oriental Blue Designs, Thailand, 8 1/2 In.	30.00
Pitcher, Cider, Grapes, Autumn Leaves, Azure, 5 1/2 X 8 1/2 In.	65.00
Pitcher, Dolphins, Fish & Shell, 7 1/4 In.	135.00
Plaque, Portrait, Framed, Round, 4 3/4 In.	45.00
Plaque, Recumbent Winged Putto, Birds, C.1890, 7 3/4 X 4 7/8 In.	4125.00
Plaque, Virgin & Child, Signed, Framed, 7 1/4 X 8 1/4 In.	150.00
Plate, Central Cartouche, Mandarin Figures, 8 In., 4 Piece	412.50
Plate, Dragon of Sea Mist, Japanese, C.1850, 17 1/2 In.	615.00
Plate, English, Octagonal, Blue, White Oriental Design, 7 In.	350.00
Plate, Floral, Lobed Basket Weave Border, Ludwigsburg, 10 In.	165.00
Plate, Oriental Design, Embossed Floral Rim, 8 1/2 In.	225.00
Plate, Serving, Fruit, Floral, Iridescent, Handles, Germany, 10 In.	25.00
Platter, Animal Trophies & Fruit Reserves, Russian, 15 1/4 In.	720.00
Platter, Floral, Lobed Basket Weave Border, Ludwigsburg, 16 In.	770.00
Salt Dip, Double, Cactus Flower	60.00
Sauceboat, Embossed Floral Design, Blue, 7 3/4 In.	175.00
Stand, Wig, Pierced, Foo Lions Among Waves, Chinese, 10 3/4 In.	250.00
Sugar, Flower Finial, Black Transfer Design, Flags, 4 7/8 In.	250.00
Tankard, Fisherman, Blue Transfer, 1780, 5 3/8 In.	275.00
Tea Set, Handleless Cups, Floral, England, 19th Century, 25 Piece	475.00
Teapot, Blue Floral Transfer, Polychrome Enamel, Gilt, 6 In.	105.00
Teapot, Floral Design, Polychrome Enamel, Applied Flower, 6 In.	550.00
Teapot, Floral Enamel, Underglaze, Blue Bands, Gilding, 6 In.	150.00
Teapot, Oriental Design, Underglaze Blue, Red Enamel, 7 In.	700.00
Teapot, Oriental Scenes, Gilded Trim, Polychrome Enamel, 6 In.	375.00
Teapot, Oriental, Applied Flower Cover, 5 5/8 In.	400.00 To 700.00
Teapot, Polychrome Enamel, Oriental Design, 6 1/2 In.	650.00
Tray, Desk, Rose, Gold Floral, Footed, Feather Handles, French	58.00
Tureen, Undertray, Chinese Export Style, French, 9 X 15 1/4 In.	415.00
Urn, Eagle Finial, Domed Body, Greek Key, For Lamp, France, 28 In.	825.00
Urn, Putti & Maiden Reserves, Rust, Baluster, France, 22 In., Pair	565.00
Vase, Birds Amid Foliage, Baluster, China, 23 In., Pair	440.00
Vase, Birds On Branches, F. Gardoy, 1878, 16 1/2 In.	1300.00
Vase, Castle Scene, Bird On Limb, French, 6 X 6 In.	95.00

Vase, Clair De Lune, Flaring Neck, Chinese, 8 3/4 In.	440.00
Vase, Flying Dragons, Wave–Patterned Ground, Chinese, 14 In., Pair	475.00
Vase, Gilt Cream Reserves, Navy, 2 Scroll Handles, Chinese, 10 In.	935.00
Vase, Gilt Floral, Cobalt Blue, White Enameled, French, 9 1/4 In.	45.00
Vase, Iris, Pearlware, 5 3/4 In., Pair	67.50
Vase, Peony Design, Bottle, Polychrome, Chinese, 13 1/2 In., Pair	130.00
Vase, Polychrome Floral Design, Dark Blue, Oriental, 22 1/4 In.	100.00
Vase, Polychrome Floral Design, Yellow, 11 3/4 In., Pair	130.00
Vase, Portrait, Bohemian Girl, Blue Floral, Austria, 12 In.	275.00
Vase, With Nude Cherub 1 Side, Globe Shape, Sitzendorf, 5 1/2 In.	150.00
Waste Bowl, Black Transfer, Oriental Scene, Orange, Green, 2 In.	135.00

Postcards were first legally permitted in Austria on October 1, 1869. The United States passed postal regulations allowing the card in 1872. Most of the picture postcards collected today date after 1910. The amount of postage can help to date a card. The years the rates changed and the rates are: 1872 (1 cent), 1917 (2 cents), 1919 (1 cent), 1925 (2 cents), 1928 (1 cent), 1952 (2 cents), 1959 (3 cents), 1963 (4 cents), 1968 (5 cents), 1973 (8 cents), 1975 (7 cents), 1976 (9 cents), 1978 (10 cents), 1981 (12 cents), 1981 (13 cents), 1985 (14 cents), 1988 (15 cents).

POSTCARD, Album, Moe, N.J., 1918	7.50
Album, World War II, Hitler, Prewar Views, German Surrender	75.00
Astronauts On Moon, 3–D	6.00
Billy Sunday, Leaning On Pulpit, Photograph Type	15.00
Boileau, Miss America, No. 208	15.00
Chain Letter, 1911	8.00
Chicago World's Fair, 1933, 55 Piece	35.00
Christmas, Man On Elephant, George Goodheart	9.00
Circus, Emil Ritter's Midgets, Color, 1900s	5.00
Cotton States International Expo, Women's Building, Unused, 1895	25.00
Deep Blue Sea, M. Morris, Tuck, Set of 6, Original Package	40.00
Easter, Red Padded Silk, Rabbit, Dated 1910, 3 1/2 X 5 1/2 In.	175.00
Enrico Caruso Memorial, 1921	10.00 To 15.00
European, Germany, 1900, 100 Piece	75.00
Floral, C. Kline, 4 Piece	22.50
Foxy Grandpa, Leather	18.00
France, Pre–1920, 150 Piece	65.00
Hold To Light, Artist C. Dleine, Florals	25.00
Hudson Fulton Celebration, 1909	12.00
Indians, Leather, 1906	18.00
Jack Dempsey's Broadway Restaurant	4.00
Jamestown Exposition, 1907, 8 Piece	16.00
Leather, 1909	12.00
Lovers, Sitting On Crescent Moon, Girl Photo Oval, Wooden, 1906	5.00
Manchester, New Hampshire, Illuminated Window, 5 Piece	18.00
McClelland Casket Hardware, 1941–50	1.25
New Year's, Pre–1920, 262 Piece	145.00
Orchestra of Cats Serenading Bride & Groom	15.00
Parrish, 1929	40.00
President & Mrs. Wilson, Waiting For Parade	6.00
President Wilson, Court of Honor, 1917	8.00
Red Rose Tea, Rockwell, 1958	6.00
Ringling Residence	8.00
Roller Coaster, 1909	21.00
Santa Claus, 1920s	4.00
St. Louis World's Fair, 1904, 10 Piece	55.00
State Capitol, Topeka, Kansas, Aluminum, Early 1900s	5.00
Stroh's Baseball Team, Photograph, 1910	75.00
Sunbonnet Babies, Ullman, Friday Postmark, 1907	8.00
Ted Williams, Perez–Steele	35.00
Teddy Bear, Victorian, 3 Piece	45.00
Thanksgiving, Leather, 1906	11.00
Time–Life, World's Fair, 1964, 25 Piece	15.00

Posters have informed the public about news and entertainment events since ancient times. Nineteenth–century advertising or theatrical posters and twentieth–century movie and war posters are of special interest today. The price is determined by the artist, the condition, and the rarity. Other posters are listed under World War I and World War II.

POSTER, 3 Stooges, Go Around The World In A Daze, 1963, 14 X 36 In. 75.00
  7–Up, Family Watching TV, Cardboard, 12 X 16 In. 28.00
  Air Cruise Into History, Exploits Around World, 1936 .... 265.00
  American Graffiti 6.00
  Barnum & Bailey, New Free Street Parade, 39 X 29 In. 425.00
  Black Cat Firecrackers, 24 X 36 In. 65.00
  Blind Bargain, Lon Chaney, 14 X 22 In. 400.00
  Bond Bread, Uncle Don, Seated At Piano, WOR Radio, 1933, 12 X 18 In. 15.00
  Carroll Rye & Morvilles Whiskey, Victorian Maid, 22 X 27 1/2 In. 505.00
  Cleveland Community Fund, 21st Year, 1939, 20 X 14 In. 12.00
  Coors Beer, Pretty Girl, Greetings 1904, 19 X 14 In. 800.00
  Empire State Carousel, Gloria Scheib, 20 X 28 In. 10.00
  Fighting Vigilantes, Lash Larue, 1948, 14 X 36 In. 45.00
  Henderson 4 Cylinder Motorcycle, 10 X 14 In. 65.00
  Jack Sprat, Maxfield Parrish, 1919, 20 X 15 In. 325.00
  John Huston, The Man, The Movies, The Maverick, 26 X 38 In. 20.00
  Join The Red Cross, Walter W. Seaton, 1915, 30 X 30 In. 154.00
  Laurel & Hardy, A Haunting We Will Go, 20 X 28 In. 48.00
  Libeled Lady, Jean Harlow, William Powell, 1936, 27 X 41 In. 825.00
  Magic, Gouache Design, Thurston, 24 Pages, 14 X 25 In. 192.50
  McNamee's Minstrels, America's Finest, 80 X 40 In. ....*Illus* 165.00
  Red Man Chewing Tobacco, Indian, Color, 20 X 60 In. 50.00
  Room Service, Marx Brothers, 22 X 28 In. 500.00
  Rudy Bros., Circus, Pictures Animals, 1930s, 22 X 14 In. 20.00
  Silver Springs Brewery, Fireman, Mug of Beer, Found, 16 In. 30.00
  Son of Billy The Kid, Lash Larue, 1949, 14 X 36 In. 40.00
  Sunset Boulevard, Noir Tour–De–Force, 14 X 36 In. 700.00
  Tavern Permit, Orange Cardboard, 1903, 22 X 28 In. 65.00
  Thunder Road, Robert Mitchum, 1956, 14 X 36 In. 60.00
  Tiger Bills Wild West, Bucking Horse, 1910, 14 X 36 In. 450.00
  Travelers Insurance Co., C.G.C. Plummer, Agent, Framed, 26 X 20 In. 1000.00
  Where The Boys Are, 14 X 36 In. 6.00
  White Parrot, Shoson, Japanese Woodblock, 1927, 15 1/4 X 10 1/4 In. 425.00
  World War I, Columbia Calls, F. Halstead, 30 X 40 In. 125.00

A potlid is just that, a lid for a pot. Transfer–printed potlids had their heyday from the 1840s to the early 1900s. The English Staffordshire potteries made ceramic containers with decorative lids for bear's grease, shrimp or meat paste, cold cream, and toothpaste. Printed advertising and pictures of historical events, portraits of famous people, or scenic views were designed in black and white or color. Reproductions have been made. The most famous potlids were made by Pratt and are listed in that section.

POTLID, Independence Hall, Philadelphia, Worsley 625.00
  No By Heaven I Exclaimed 120.00
  Pegwell Bay 145.00
  Strathfieldsaye, Seat of Duke of Wellington, C.1850 .... 275.00
  Tam O'Shanter & Souter Johnny 225.00

Pottery and porcelain are different. Pottery is opaque; you can't see through it. Porcelain is translucent. If you hold a porcelain dish in front of a strong light you will see the light through the dish. Porcelain is colder to the touch. Pottery is softer and easier to break and will stain more easily because it is porous. Porcelain is thinner, lighter, and more durable. Majolica, faience, and stoneware are all pottery. Many types of pottery are listed in this book under the factory name.

POTTERY, Ashtray, Hyde Park, Mottled Gold 18.00
  Ashtray, Kidney Shape, Sasha Brastoff 35.00
  Billiken, Embossed Atlanta, Ga. 55.00
  Birdbath, Blue & White, Marked Blue Ribbon Brand, Buckeye Pottery 1600.00
  Biscuit Jar, Tapestry Ground, Tunnecliffe & Sons, 6 3/4 In. 125.00
  Bottle, Book, Bennington Type, Green Splashes, 5 1/2 In. 225.00
  Bowl, Black Glaze, Asymmetrical Shape, Italy, 13 1/2 In. 80.00
  Bowl, Blue, Alamo, 15 In. 40.00
  Bowl, Combware, Oval, England, Mid–19th Century, 10 In. 77.00
  Bowl, Soup, Veterans Admin., White, Blue VA Seal, Shenango, 1930 .... 5.00
  Candlestick, Green & Amber Running Glaze, 6 In., Pair 60.00
  Canister, Spice & Cruet Set, Cover, Pearlescent, Germany, 14 Piece 245.00
  Chocolate Pot, Rose Marie, Blue Ridge 120.00
  Cup & Saucer, Greens, Chester Nicodemus 15.00
  Dish, Shell Shape, Kay Finch, 9 In. 14.00
  Figurine, 3 Victorian Gentlemen At Bar, Brayton, 7 X 8 In. 65.00
  Figurine, Airedale 125.00
  Figurine, Alphabet Bear, Kay Finch 45.00
  Figurine, Angel, Kay Finch, 4 1/2 In. 35.00
  Figurine, Baby Flower Skunk, American Pottery 55.00
  Figurine, Bear, Kay Finch, 9 In. 65.00
  Figurine, Camel, Kay Finch 40.00
  Figurine, Chinese Kids, Ceramic Arts Studio 20.50
  Figurine, Cleanser Girl, Clemison Pottery 20.00
  Figurine, Dog, Seated, Round Base, Greenish Brown Glaze, 9 1/2 In. 700.00
  Figurine, Funerary, Chinese, Unglazed, 8 In. 175.00
  Figurine, Kitten, Kay Finch 38.00
  Figurine, Man & Woman, Kay Finch, Pair 95.00
  Figurine, Man, Holding Flower Bouquet, 9 In. 65.00
  Figurine, Oriental Woman, Kay Finch, 10 1/2 In. 60.00
  Figurine, Pedro, Brayton, 8 In. 45.00
  Figurine, Rooster, Marston, 9 In. 35.00
  Figurine, Rosita, Brayton, 8 In. 45.00
  Figurine, Spaniel, Kay Finch, Small 30.00
  Figurine, Sultan On Pillow, Ceramic Art Studio 28.50
  Figurine, Tomb, Horse, Tang Dynasty, Brown Glaze, 13 X 13 In. 8800.00
  Figurine, Tomb, Male, Hands Folded On Chest, 11 In., Pair 1875.00
  Figurine, Whippet, Reclining, John Bell 1000.00
  Hibachi, Dark Blue, Light Blue & Yellow, Japanese, C.1890, 8 In. 125.00
  Humidor, Face of Woman, Glazed Hat & Hair, Unglazed 125.00
  Humidor, Pipe Holder Base, Marzi & Remi 65.00
  Jar, Cover, Applied Cicada, Scenic, Valluris, 3 In. 40.00
  Jar, Lid, Tooled Band, Brown Glaze, 6 3/4 X 9 In. 35.00
  Jar, Storage, Loop Design,, 2 Gal. 2000.00
  Jar, Storage, Loops & C In Design, Edgefield, 3 Gal. 2600.00
  Jar, Tobacco, Figural, Red Baron, Hat, Goggles, Intaglio Eyes, 5 In. 135.00
  Jug, Bellarmine, Germany, C.1740, 10 1/2 In. 465.00
  Jug, Bellarmine, Germany, Early 18th Century, 8 3/4 In. 330.00
  Jug, Grandpa Meiers Fortified Apple Wine, Bristol Paper Label 60.00
  Jug, Tan & Brown Grapes & Leaves, Turner, 6 In. 265.00
  Pitcher Set, Tuskegee Inst., 7 Piece 200.00
  Pitcher, Alamo Pottery, Black 30.00
  Pitcher, Figural, Elephant, Hot Pink, Tusk Is Spout, English, 9 In. 40.00
  Pitcher, Hand Thrown Pinched Sides, Anton Lang, Signed 55.00
  Pitcher, Peach Blossom, Metlox, 11 In. 30.00
  Pitcher, Pinks, Chester Nicodemus 15.00
  Pitcher, Sheaf of Corn, Benjamin W. Wilson, Gold Trim, 10 In. 220.00
  Pitcher, Stein, Man's Face Spout, Cobalt Dragons, Germany, 10 In. 195.00
  Planter, Light Blue, No.770, Alamo, Oval 20.00
  Plaque, African Man, Ceramic Art Co. 85.00
  Plate, Lu–Ray, Dinner 9.00
  Plate, Yellow Slip, Coggled, 9 1/2 In. 1800.00
  Relish, Lu–Ray, Green, 4 Sections 75.00
  Spice Set, Blue & White, Cover, 5 Piece 925.00

String Holder, Dutch Girl's Head	25.00
String Holder, French Lady, In Chair	69.50
String Holder, Head, Blonde Girl	46.50
String Holder, Southern Belle	32.50
Teapot, Lu–Ray, White	15.00
Teapot, Oriental Floral, Black Transfer, South Wales Pottery, 6 In.	130.00
Toothbrush Holder, Clown, Holding Comedy Mask	35.50
Triptych, 3 Rectangular Plaques Scene, Low Relief, 8 X 17 In.	45.00
Tumbler, Blue Glaze, Inscription, Gray Interior, Germany, 4 1/2 In.	55.00
Urn, Pierced Removable Rim, Satyr Handles, Cobalt Blue, 19 1/4 In.	255.00
Urn, Portrait Medallion, Geo.& Martha Washington, 1876, 28 In., Pair	700.00
Vase, Aqua, Pink, Glidden	125.00
Vase, Art Nouveau Woman In High Relief, Rick Wisecarver, 12 In.	110.00
Vase, Blue, Mission, Bulbous, Handles, 8 X 10 In., Pair	175.00
Vase, Brown Glaze, 2 Openings, Small Center Handle, BC, 15 In.	195.00
Vase, Brown, Yellow, Twisted Handles, Chester Nicodemus, 8 In., Pair	95.00
Vase, Grotesque, Figural, Globular, Lion Head Handles, Germany, 19 In	220.00
Vase, Grueby Design, Angled Shoulder, 1905, 12 In.	2100.00
Vase, Jasperware, Bust of Washington, American Eagle, 7 1/4 In.	260.00
Vase, Rozane, Indian, Headdress, A. Williams, 17 1/4 In.	1400.00
Vase, Tan Speckles, Russet Ground, James Towne Colony, 5 1/8 In.	95.00
Watch Holder, 2 Musicians, Lions, Obadiah Sherotte, 1800, 8 In.	412.00
Water Set, Ball Pitcher, Dakota, Lavender To Pink, 7 Piece	235.00
Wren House, Pink	22.00

Powder flasks and powder horns were made to hold the gunpowder used in antique firearms. The early examples were made of horn or wood; later ones were of copper or brass.

POWDER FLASK, Cargo, Deer & Relief Design, Leather, 3 Lb.	75.00
Dogs, Leather & Copper	50.00
Eagle, Copper	75.00
Hawsley Sheffield, Embossed Copper	75.00
Neptune, Copper	75.00
POWDER HORN, Compass Star & Foliage, Initials In Wooden End, 15 In.	42.50
Curved Wooden End, Dated July 1855, Leather Strap, 12 In.	225.00
John Elliott, War Scene, Soldiers, Boston Harbor, Compass, 1775	8475.00
Maken Bement of Hartford, Geometric Carvings, 1762	6050.00
New York Map, Hudson, Niagara, 16 In.	2640.00
Overall Engraving, Double Waisted, Copper, English, C.1845	210.00
Raised Hanging Game, Brass, American, C.1840	210.00

PRATT
FENTON

Pratt ware means two different things. It was an early Staffordshire pottery, cream–colored with colored decorations, made by Felix Pratt during the late eighteenth century. There was also Pratt ware made with transfer designs during the mid–nineteenth century in Fenton, England. Reproductions of the transfer–printed Pratt are being made.

PRATT, Creamer, Embossed Foliage Design, Sailor's Farewell & Return, 5 In.	250.00
Figurine Set, Four Seasons, 4 Piece	1870.00
Figurine, Blind Fiddler, 12 X 9 In.	155.00
Jar, Victor Emmanuel & Caribal, 4 1/8 In.	105.00
Lid, Sportsman & Game Bag, Mounted As Wall Plaques, Square, 5 1/2 In.	110.00
Pitcher, Heart Medallions, Children At Play, 5 Colors, 4 7/8 In.	325.00
Pitcher, Hunting & Drinking Figures, 7 1/2 X 7 In.	200.00
Pitcher, Red Flowers, Polychrome Enamel, Soft Paste, 5 1/4 In.	450.00
Pitcher, Satyr Heads, Canary & Silver Luster, 5 In.	150.00
Pitcher, Scenes of Couple Parting, Reuniting, 5 Colors, 7 1/4 In.	700.00
Plate, Persuasion	53.00
Plate, Village Wedding	53.00
Potlid, Card Players, Walnut Frame, Pair	275.00
Potlid, Cries of London, 4 1/8 In.	10.00
Sauceboat, Figural, Duck, Molded Feathers, C.1800, 4 3/4 In.	445.00
Syrup, Seashell Transfer, Beige Ground, Pewter Lid, 7 1/4 In.	155.00
Teapot, Embossed Design, Dolphin Finial, 7 In.	550.00

Teapot, Embossed Design, Vintage Panels, 7 In.	850.00
Tray, Blind Fiddler, Double Handled, Oval, 12 1/2 In.	360.00
Wall Pocket, Cornucopia Shape, Child With Bunch of Grapes, 9 In.	665.00

Pressed glass was first made in the United States in the 1820s after the invention of glass pressing machines. Hundreds of patterns of pressed glass were made in complete table settings. Although the Boston and Sandwich Works was the most famous of the pressed glass factories, there were about sixteen other factories making pressed glass from 1830 to 1850, and still more from 1850 to 1900, when pressed glass reached its greatest popularity. It is now being widely reproduced. The pattern names used in this listing are based on the information in the book "Pressed Glass in America" by John and Elizabeth Welker. There may be pieces of pressed glass listed in this book in other sections. See Lamp, Ruby, Sandwich, and Souvenir.

PRESSED GLASS

    1000–EYE, see Thousand Eye
    101, see One–Hundred–One
    8–0–8, see Eight–0–Eight
    ACANTHUS, see Ribbed Palm
    ACME, see Butterfly With Spray
    ACORN MEDALLION, BEADED, see Beaded Acorn Medallion

Acorn, Table Set, Child's, 4 Piece	535.00
Actress, Butter, Cover	130.00
Actress, Celery Vase	170.00
Actress, Compote, 7 In.	70.00
Actress, Creamer	55.00 To 75.00
Actress, Dish, Cheese, Cover	155.00
Actress, Goblet	55.00
Actress, Spooner	70.00 To 75.00
Actress, Tray, Oval, 11 In.	80.00
Ada, Saltshaker, Yellow	27.50
ADMIRAL DEWEY, see Spanish American	
Adonis, Creamer	22.50
Adonis, Relish	9.50
Adonis, Saltshaker	27.50
Aegis, Pitcher, Water	60.00
Alabama, Cake Stand, 8 In.	57.50
Alabama, Castor Set, 4 Bottles	100.00
Alabama, Creamer	45.00
Alabama, Pitcher	150.00
Alabama, Sugar, Cover, Child's	48.00
Alabama, Table Set, Clear, 4 Piece	225.00
Alaska, Berry Bowl, Green, White Enameled Square, Master	135.00
Alaska, Creamer, Green	27.50
Alaska, Pitcher, Water, Vaseline	280.00 To 375.00
Alaska, Pitcher, Water, Vaseline, Design	375.00
Alaska, Saltshaker, Blue	25.00
Alaska, Spooner, Blue	50.00
Alaska, Sugar, Cover, Enameled Flowers	145.00
Alaska, Tumbler, Vaseline, Design	75.00
Albany, Cracker Jar	45.00
Alhambra, Cup & Saucer, Bouillon, 2 Handles	58.00
Amazon, Butter, Cover	125.00
Amazon, Champagne	25.00
Amazon, Creamer	27.50 To 37.50
Amazon, Creamer, Child's	10.00
Amberette, Bread Tray, Frosted, 10 In.	85.00
Amberette, Butter Chip	35.00
Amberette, Celery Vase	130.00

Amberette, Goblet 165.00
Amberette, Salt & Pepper, Frosted 225.00
Amberette, Table Set, 4 Piece 285.00
Amberette, Vase, Bud 38.00
Ambidextrous, Pitcher, 2 Handles, 2 Lips 28.00
AMERICAN BEAUTY, see La France
American Flag, Platter, 38 Stars, 15 Stripes 125.00
Anthemion, Pitcher 45.00
Anthemion, Pitcher, Water 48.00
Anthemion, Sugar, Cover 40.00
Apollo, Cake Stand, 10 In. 60.00
Apollo, Compote, 5 In. 22.50
Apollo, Goblet, Etched 30.00
Apollo, Relish 14.50
Arabesque, Wine 25.00
Arch & Forget–Me–Not Bands, Creamer 30.00
Arched Ovals, Bowl, 5 1/2 X 8 In. 17.50
Arched Ovals, Mug, Boston, Mass., Ruby Stained 25.00
Arched Ovals, Toothpick, Green, Gold Trim .... 30.00 To 35.00
Arched Ovals, Wine, Ruby Stained 24.50
Argonaut Shell, Compote 135.00
Argus, Champagne 45.00
Argus, Eggcup, Crystal 32.50
Argus, Spill 65.00
Argus, Wine, Flint 50.00
ARROWHEAD IN OVAL, see Style
Art, Banana Stand .... 65.00 To 87.50
Art, Bowl, 7 In. 26.00
Art, Butter, Cover 50.00
Art, Cake Stand .... 42.00 To 75.00
Art, Celery Vase 37.50
Art, Compote, Cover, 8 In. 87.50
Art, Sugar, Cover 35.00
Artichoke, Saltshaker, Frosted 47.50
Ashburton, Celery Vase 125.00
Ashburton, Champagne 57.00
Ashburton, Claret 50.00
Ashburton, Creamer, Thumbprint Under Spout, Flint 250.00
Ashburton, Decanter 50.00
Ashburton, Eggcup 25.00
Ashburton, Sugar & Creamer, Flint 250.00
Ashburton, Sugar, Cover 70.00
Ashburton, Vase, Hexagonal Base, Wafer Connection, 10 In. 195.00
Ashburton, Whiskey, Handle 125.00
Ashman, Compote, Cover, 13 In. 100.00
Ashman, Goblet, Etched 42.00
Ashman, Spooner 25.00
Atlanta, Compote, 5 1/4 In. 22.50
Atlanta, Compote, Etched, 4 1/2 In. 55.00
Atlanta, Creamer 43.00
Atlanta, Goblet, Square Lion's Head, Frosted 60.00
Atlanta, Toothpick, Frosted .... 38.00 To 60.00
Atlas, Creamer 22.00
Atlas, Goblet, Etched 30.00
Atlas, Toothpick 10.00
Atlas, Tumbler 26.00
Aurora, Bowl, 8 In. 23.00
Aurora, Wine 25.00
Austrian, Cordial, Canary 115.00
Austrian, Creamer 38.00
Austrian, Cup, Punch, Amber, Handle, Footed 100.00
Austrian, Dish, Rectangular, 5 1/4 X 8 In. 35.00
Austrian, Spooner 35.00
Aztec Medallion, Syrup, Sapphire Blue 295.00

Baby Face, Celery 140.00
Bag Ware, Butter, Cover, Amber 45.00
    BALDER, see Pennsylvania
    BALKY MULE, see Currier & Ives
Ball & Bar, Compote, Cover, 11 In. 55.00
Ball & Bar, Sugar & Creamer, Cover, Etched 65.00
Baltimore Pear, Cake Plate 38.00
Baltimore Pear, Creamer 30.00
Baltimore Pear, Goblet 35.00
Baltimore Pear, Pitcher 100.00
Baltimore Pear, Sauce 15.00
Baltimore Pear, Sugar & Creamer 35.00
Baltimore Pear, Table Set, 4 Piece .... 120.00 To 175.00
Banded Buckle, Spooner .... 18.00 To 30.00
    BANDED PORTLAND, when flashed with pink, is sometimes called
    "Maiden Blush."
Banded Portland, Butter, Cover 135.00
Banded Portland, Creamer, Maiden Blush 65.00
Banded Portland, Relish, 12 In. 16.00
Banded Portland, Spooner 75.00
Banded Portland, Sugar 35.00
Banded Portland, Syrup, Maiden Blush 365.00
Banded Portland, Table Set, Maiden Blush, 4 Piece 425.00
Banded Portland, Wine 30.00
Banded Stippled Star Flower, Wine 14.00
    OTHER BANDED PATTERNS, see under name of basic pattern: e.g.,
    Banded Honeycomb, see Honeycomb, Banded
Banner, Butter, Cover 85.00
    BAR & DIAMOND, see Kokomo
Barberry, Celery 22.00
Barberry, Compote, Cover, 8 In. 87.50
Barberry, Eggcup 20.00
Barberry, Pitcher, Water, Applied Handle 85.00
Barberry, Tumbler, Footed 22.00
Barberry, Wine 38.00
    BARLEY & OATS, see Wheat & Barley
    BARLEY & WHEAT, see Wheat & Barley
Barley, Bowl, Vegetable, Oval, 11 3/4 In. 24.00
Barley, Castor, Pickle, Frame 75.00
Barley, Compote, 9 In. 32.00
Barley, Creamer 27.50
Barley, Pitcher, Water .... 30.00 To 35.00
Barley, Plate, 9 3/4 In. 24.00
Barley, Salt, Wheelbarrow, Pewter Wheel 75.00
Barley, Tray, Bonbon 15.00
Barley, Wine .... 25.00 To 40.00
Barred Forget–Me–Not, Plate, Handle, 9 In. 27.50
Barred Forget–Me–Not, Relish, 9 1/2 In. 12.00
Barred Forget–Me–Not, Wine, Amber 26.00
Barred Oval, Goblet 38.00
    BARREL HONEYCOMB, see also Honeycomb
Barrel Honeycomb, Goblet, Crystal 20.00
Barrel Thumbprint, Wine 25.00
    BARRELED BLOCK, see Red Block
Basketweave, Butter Tub, Vaseline 48.00
Basketweave, Goblet, Canary 18.00
Basketweave, Tray, Water, Blue 48.00
Basketweave, Wine, Amber 24.00
Bead & Scroll, Compote, Jelly 22.00
Bead & Scroll, Cruet 38.00
Bead & Scroll, Pitcher, Water, Gold Trim 65.00

Bead & Scroll, Pitcher, Water, Green 95.00
Bead Swag, Sugar, Cover, Ruby Flashed, Gold Trim 65.00
Bead Swag, Water Set, Floral, 7 Piece 445.00
Beaded Arches, Mug, Souvenir, Ruby Stained 35.00
Beaded Block, Pitcher, Water, Ruby Stained 145.00
    BEADED BULL'S–EYE & DRAPE, see Alabama
Beaded Dart Band, Castor, Pickle, Blue, 10 In. 125.00
    BEADED DEWDROP, see Wisconsin
Beaded Fine Cut, Creamer 27.00
Beaded Fine Cut, Sugar 30.00
Beaded Grape Medallion, Compote, Cover, 8 In. 95.00
Beaded Grape Medallion, Dish, Oval, 8 1/2 In. 15.00
Beaded Grape Medallion, Eggcup .... 15.00 To 25.00
Beaded Grape Medallion, Goblet, Buttermilk 35.00
Beaded Grape Medallion, Spooner 23.00
Beaded Grape, Cruet, Green 110.00
Beaded Grape, Plate, Square, 8 In. 27.50
Beaded Grape, Salt & Pepper, Green 85.00
Beaded Grape, Spooner, Green, Gold Trim 40.00
Beaded Grape, Sugar, Open, Square 19.00
Beaded Loop, Compote, Open, 7 In. 38.00
Beaded Loop, Goblet, Gold Trim 30.00
Beaded Loop, Platter 24.00
Beaded Loop, Relish 18.00
Beaded Loop, Salt & Pepper 35.00
Beaded Mirror, Pitcher, Water 49.50
Beaded Mirror, Plate, 8 In. 27.50
Beaded Ovals In Sand, Cruet, Blue 175.00
Beaded Scroll, Compote, Blue 20.00
Beaded Swirl, Cruet, Ruby Stained .... 58.00 To 75.00
Beaded Swirl, Table Set, 4 Piece 110.00
Beaded Tulip, Wine 30.00
Beaded Tulip, Wine, Amber 55.00
    BEARDED HEAD, see Viking
    BEARDED MAN, see Queen Anne
Beatty Rib, Toothpick, Clear Opalescent 23.00
Bedford, Sugar, Gold Trim 40.00
Beehive, Platter, Be Industrious, Bird Border 95.00
Beehive, Platter, Be Industrious, Deer On Border 95.00
Belladonna, Butter, Cover, Banded, Green, Gold Trim 45.00
Bellflower, Butter, Cover, Single Vine, Flint 90.00
Bellflower, Compote, Flint, 8 In. ....55.00 To 125.00
Bellflower, Eggcup, Flint 38.00
Bellflower, Lamp, Oil, Scalloped Base, Flint, 7 In. 150.00
Bellflower, Pitcher, Water, Double Vine 300.00
Bellflower, Spooner 35.00
Bellflower, Tumbler, Water, Flint 85.00
    BENT BUCKLE, see New Hampshire
Berkeley, Cracker Jar 45.00
Bethlehem Star, Compote, Cover, 5 In. 35.00
    BEVELED DIAMOND & STAR, see Albany
Bigler, Goblet 425.50
Bigler, Plate, 6 In. 30.00
Birch Leaf, Goblet 28.50
Bird & Strawberry, Butter 20.00
Bird & Strawberry, Butter, Cover 145.00
Bird & Strawberry, Compote, Ruffled, 8 In. 72.50
Bird & Strawberry, Creamer .... 40.00 To 45.00
Bird & Strawberry, Punch Cup 12.00
Bird & Strawberry, Relish, Heart Shape 65.00
Bird & Strawberry, Tumbler 45.00

BIRD IN RING, see Grace
Birds At Fountain, Goblet 35.00
Bismarc Star, Goblet 20.00
Blackberry, Creamer 27.50
Blackberry, Goblet 30.00
Blackberry, Sugar, Cover 48.00
Blaze, Wine, Flint 47.50
Bleeding Heart, Cake Stand, 9 1/2 In. .... 65.00 To 72.50
Bleeding Heart, Goblet .... 22.00 To 30.00
Bleeding Heart, Sauce, Flat, 4 1/4 In. 17.00
Bleeding Heart, Spooner 32.00
Bleeding Heart, Sugar 25.00
Bleeding Heart, Tumbler 32.00
BLOCK & FAN, see Romeo
BLOCK & FINE CUT, see Fine Cut & Block
BLOCK & STAR, see Valencia Waffle
BLOCKED ARCHES, see Berkeley
BLUEBIRD, see Bird & Strawberry
Bohemian, Butter, Cover, Green, Gold Trim 125.00
Bohemian, Spooner, Rose Stained Flowers, Gold Trim 55.00
Bordered Ellipse, Mug, Souvenir, Ruby Stained 35.00
Bosworth, Creamer 23.00
Bowtie, Compote, 7 In. 36.00
Bowtie, Creamer 45.00
Bowtie, Salt, Clear, C.1886 .... 22.00
Bowtie, Spooner 32.00
Box-In-Box, Creamer, Enameled Flowers, Ruby Flashed 75.00
Box-In-Box, Spooner, Enameled Flowers, Ruby Flashed 75.00
Box-In-Box, Sugar, Cover, Enameled Flowers, Ruby Flashed 110.00
Box-In-Box, Toothpick 25.00
Bracelet Band, Tumbler 28.50
Branched Tree, Pitcher, Water 65.00
Brazilian, Toothpick, Green, Gold Trim 50.00
Bridle Rosettes, Plate, 7 In. 7.50
Bringing Home The Cows, Pitcher, 10 1/2 In. 275.00
British Cane, Tumbler, Amber 22.00
Broken Column, Bowl, 8 In. 35.00
Broken Column, Bowl, Rectangular, 5 1/2 X 9 In. 27.50
Broken Column, Cake Stand, 9 1/2 In. 65.00
Broken Column, Castor, Pickle, Ruby Flashed 250.00
Broken Column, Celery Vase 48.00
Broken Column, Compote, Cover, 10 1/4 In. 85.00
Broken Column, Cracker Jar .... 88.00 To 95.00
Broken Column, Goblet .... 55.00 To 63.00
Broken Column, Pitcher 98.00
Broken Column, Sauce, 4 In. 16.50
Broken Column, Spooner, Red Notches 85.00
Broken Column, Tumbler .... 30.00 To 55.00
BROUGHTON, see Pattee Cross
BRYCE, see Ribbon Candy
BUCKET, see Oaken Bucket
Buckle & Star, Celery Vase 30.00
Buckle & Star, Creamer 25.00
Buckle & Star, Wine 16.00
Buckle, Eggcup, Flint 38.00
Buckle, Goblet 32.00
Buckle, Spooner 16.00
Budded Ivy, Goblet 26.50

To loosen a silver saltshaker lid that is stuck to the glass shaker, immerse the top in white vinegar. Soak overnight.

Bulging Loops, Cruet, Pink 250.00
Bull's–Eye & Buttons, Syrup, Emerald Green, Gold Trim 195.00
Bull's–Eye & Daisy, Butter, Cover, Gold Trim 55.00
Bull's–Eye & Daisy, Sugar, Green Eyes, Gold Trim 20.00
Bull's–Eye & Daisy, Water Set, Ruby Eyes, 5 Piece 90.00
Bull's–Eye & Fan, Butter, Cover, Green, Gold Eyes 50.00
Bull's–Eye & Fan, Creamer 25.00
Bull's–Eye & Fan, Spooner 45.00
Bull's–Eye & Fan, Sugar 65.00
Bull's–Eye & Fan, Tumbler, Sapphire Blue 40.00
Bull's–Eye & Fan, Water Set, Green, 7 Piece 190.00
Bull's–Eye & Fleur–De–Lis, Goblet 80.00
Bull's–Eye Band, Bowl, 8 In. 24.50
Bull's–Eye Band, Bowl, Piecrust, 10 1/2 In. 65.00
Bull's–Eye Band, Creamer 50.00
Bull's–Eye Band, Pitcher, Water 160.00
Bull's–Eye Band, Spooner 48.00
Bull's–Eye Band, Sugar, Cover 70.00
Bull's–Eye Variant, Spooner 25.00
Bull's–Eye Variant, Wine 22.00
Bull's–Eye With Diamond Points, Goblet, Flint 125.00
Bull's–Eye With Diamond Points, Tumbler, Flint 145.00
Bull's–Eye, Goblet, Flint 40.00
Bunker Hill, Bread Plate .... 60.00 To 85.00
   BUTTERFLY & FAN, see Grace
Butterfly With Spray, Mug, Blue 40.00
Butterfly, Pitcher, Water 100.00
Butterfly, Salt, Handles, Master 25.00
Button Arches, Berry Bowl, Emerald Green, 13 Piece 125.00
Button Arches, Cake Stand, Gold Trim 45.00
Button Arches, Compote, Ruby Stained 35.00
Button Arches, Mug, Ruby Stained 30.00
Button Arches, Sugar, Cover, Ruby Stained .... 72.50 To 85.00
Button Arches, Table Set, Ruby Stained, Frosted Band, 4 Piece 245.00
Button Arches, Toothpick, Ruby Stained 27.00
Button Arches, Tumbler 16.00
Button Arches, Water Set, Ruby Frosted Band, 6 Pc. .... 225.00 To 295.00
Button Band, Cake Stand, 7 X 10 3/4 In. 100.00
Button Band, Compote, Cover ....75.00 To 145.00
Button Band, Pitcher, Water 55.00
Button Panel, Creamer, Child's, Gold Trim 35.00
Button Panel, Punch Set, 9 Piece 195.00
Button Panel, Toothpick, Gold Trim 22.00
Buttressed Loop, Sugar & Creamer, Cover 70.00
Buzz Saw, Creamer, Child's 10.00
Buzz Star, Creamer, Child's 15.00
Buzz Star, Punch Set, Child's, 6 Piece .... 55.00 To 75.00
Buzz–Star, Tumbler 20.00
Cabbage Rose, Cake Stand, 11 In. .... 55.00 To 65.00
Cabbage Rose, Compote, Cover, 7 In. 125.00
Cabbage Rose, Compote, Cover, Child's 95.00
Cabbage Rose, Spooner 22.00
Cabbage Rose, Wine 45.00
Cable, Champagne 125.00
Cable, Decanter, Ice Lip, 1 Qt. 145.00
   CALIFORNIA, see Beaded Grape
   CAMEO, see Profile & Sprig
Canadian, Compote, Cover, 8 In. 95.00
Canadian, Goblet 50.00
Canadian, Pitcher, Water 135.00
Canadian, Plate, 6 In. 32.00
Canadian, Plate, 10 In. 36.50
Canadian, Spooner 45.00

The pressed glass pattern sometimes called Candlewick is properly named Banded Raindrop. There is also a pattern called "Candlewick" which has been made by Imperial Glass Corporation since 1936. It is listed in this book under Imperial, Candlewick.

Cane & Rosette, Celery Vase	29.00
Cane, Pitcher, Water, Blue	58.00
Cane, Toddy Plate, Amber	5.00
Cape Cod, Goblet	37.00
Capitol Building, Champagne	26.00
Capitol Building, Wine	20.00
Cardinal Bird, Creamer	48.00
Cardinal Bird, Goblet	20.00
CARMEN, see Paneled Diamond & Finecut	
Cathedral, Bowl, 6 In.	14.50
Cathedral, Cake Stand, Vaseline, 10 In.	60.00
Cathedral, Goblet, Amber	40.00
Cathedral, Table Set, 3 Piece	90.00
Cathedral, Wine, Blue	60.00
Celtic Cross, Compote, Cover, 6 In.	85.00
Celtic Cross, Goblet, Etched	45.00
CENTENNIAL, see also Liberty Bell; Washington Centennial	
Centennial, Goblet	20.00 To 45.00
CERES, see Profile & Sprig	
Chain & Shield, Bread Plate, 8 1/2 X 12 In.	35.00
CHAIN WITH DIAMONDS, see Washington Centennial	
Chain, Goblet	20.00
Champion, Syrup	65.00
Champion, Toothpick	22.00
Chandelier, Celery Vase	45.00
Chandelier, Compote, Open, 6 X 10 In.	45.00
Chandelier, Tumbler	38.00
Checkerboard, Celery Vase	36.00
Checkerboard, Wine	20.00
Cherry & Cable, Cookie Jar	45.00
Cherry & Cable, Sugar & Creamer	40.00
Cherry Lattice, Pitcher, Water	75.00
Cherry Lattice, Tumbler	15.00
Cherry With Thumbprint, Butter, Cover	40.00
Chestnut Oak, Spooner	28.00
Chippendale, Sugar & Creamer, Footed, Etched	50.00
Choked Ashburton, Goblet, Flint	35.00
Chrysanthemum, Pitcher, Blue Speckled, 9 In.	350.00
CHURCH WINDOWS, see Tulip Petals	
Circle, Creamer	25.00
Circled Scroll, Creamer, Blue	60.00
Circled Scroll, Table Set, Green, 4 Piece	550.00
Civil War, Tumbler, Flint	125.00
Civil War, Whiskey, Bumper To The Flag	85.00
Classic Medallion, Creamer	20.00 To 30.00
Classic Medallion, Spooner, 1880s	10.00
Classic, Celery Vase	135.00
Classic, Compote, Cover, Log Feet, 7 In.	140.00 To 220.00
Classic, Sauce, Open, Log Feet	35.00
Classic, Spooner	125.00
Clear & Diamond Panels, Butter, Cover, Child's	35.00
Clematis, Goblet	27.00
Coachman's Cape, Goblet	18.00
Cobb, Butter, Cover	40.00
Cobb, Cruet	35.00
Cobb, Pitcher, Water, Amber	40.00
COIN SPOT, see Coin Spot Category	

Button Arches

Cabbage Rose

Cable

Colonial, Claret, Flint		45.00
Colonial, Creamer, Emerald Green, Child's		30.00
Colonial, Pitcher, Child's		10.00
Colonial, Punch Set, Child's, 7 Piece		125.00
Colonial, Toothpick, 2 Handles, Blue		25.00
Colorado, Bowl, Footed, 7 In.		25.00
Colorado, Bowl, Green, 8 In.		28.00
Colorado, Compote, 6 3/4 In.		22.50
Colorado, Creamer, Green, Gold Trim, Child's		20.00
Colorado, Punch Cup, Etched Margaret, Green, Gold Trim, Footed		20.00
Colorado, Sherbet, Green, Gold Trim		15.00
Colorado, Sugar, Green, Gold Trim, Child's		20.00
Colorado, Table Set, Green, Gold Trim, 4 Piece	195.00 To	375.00
Colorado, Toothpick, Green, Gold Trim	30.00 To	45.00
Colossus, Cake Stand, 10 In.		58.00
Colossus, Goblet		26.00
Colossus, Sugar, Cover		25.00
Columbian Coin, Table Set, Frosted, 4 Piece		310.00
Comet, Goblet, Flint		95.00
Comet, Whiskey, Flint, Large		145.00
COMPACT, see Snail		
Concave Almond, Table Set, 4 Piece		375.00
Connecticut Flute, Wine		15.00
Constitution, Bread Plate		100.00
Continental Hall, Bread Plate		60.00
Conventional Band, Goblet		38.00
Corcoran, Goblet		23.00
Cord & Tassel, Goblet	27.50 To	35.00
Cord & Tassel, Wine		18.50
Cord Drapery, Butter, Cover		40.00
Cord Drapery, Cake Plate, Footed		145.00
Cord Drapery, Compote, Fluted, Amber, 10 In.		45.00
Cord Drapery, Pitcher, Water		30.00
Cordova, Toothpick		12.00
Cordova, Toothpick, Red Flashed		85.00
Corner Medallion, Creamer, Etched		15.00
Cornucopia, Pitcher, Water		65.00
COSMOS, see Cosmos Category		
Cottage, Bowl, Oval, 9 1/4 In.		22.50
Cottage, Cake Stand, 10 In.		37.50
Cottage, Compote		21.50
Cottage, Creamer	20.00 To	35.00

Cottage, Goblet 24.50
Cottage, Plate, 10 In. 42.50
Cottage, Wine, Blue 95.00
    CRANE, see Stork
Crescent, Sugar, Cover, Ruby Stained 130.00
Croesus, Berry Bowl, Master, Green, Gold 100.00
Croesus, Berry Set, Green, Gold Trim, 7 Piece 250.00
Croesus, Celery, Green, Gold Trim 135.00
Croesus, Creamer, Amethyst 165.00
Croesus, Cruet, Green, Gold Trim .... 125.00 To 165.00
Croesus, Pitcher, Water, Green, Gold Trim 325.00
Croesus, Salt & Pepper, Green 80.00
Croesus, Spooner, Footed, 4 1/2 In. 60.00
Croesus, Spooner, Green 65.00
Croesus, Table Set, Amethyst, Gold Trim, 4 Piece 650.00
Croesus, Tumbler, Amethyst 62.00
Crowfoot, Goblet 25.00
Crowfoot, Pitcher, Milk 35.00
    CROWN JEWELS, see Chandelier; Queen's Necklace
Crystal Wedding, Cake Stand, 9 In. 75.00
Crystal Wedding, Pitcher, Water .... 60.00 To 95.00
Crystal Wedding, Relish, Frosted, 4 X 7 1/2 In. 45.00
Crystal Wedding, Salt, Master 35.00
    CUBE WITH FAN, see Pineapple & Fan
    CUPID & PSYCHE, see Psyche & Cupid
Cupid & Venus, Bowl, 8 In. 38.00
Cupid & Venus, Celery Vase .... 32.00 To 42.00
Cupid & Venus, Creamer .... 25.00 To 36.50
Cupid & Venus, Pitcher, Milk .... 45.00 To 68.00
Cupid & Venus, Plate, Handle, 10 1/2 In. 43.00
Cupid & Venus, Wine 72.50
Cupid's Hunt, Compote, 4 1/4 In. 15.00
Cupid's Hunt, Compote, 8 In. 55.00
Cupid's Hunt, Relish 25.00
Currant, Butter, Cover 67.50
Currant, Cake Stand, 11 In. .... 47.50 To 58.00
Currant, Goblet .... 20.00 To 35.00
Currier & Ives, Cup & Saucer 45.00
Currier & Ives, Goblet, Amber 95.00
Currier & Ives, Pitcher, Water .... 48.00 To 55.00
Currier & Ives, Salt & Pepper 65.00
Currier & Ives, Tumbler, Footed 45.00
Currier & Ives, Wine, Cobalt Blue 95.00
Curtain Tieback, Creamer 30.00
Cut Log, Bowl, 8 In. 45.00
Cut Log, Cake Stand, 9 In. .... 40.00 To 63.00
Cut Log, Compote, Cover, 5 1/2 X 7 1/2 In. .... 30.00 To 45.00
Cut Log, Cruet .... 33.00 To 50.00
Czarina, Castor, Pickle 145.00
Czarina, Wine 17.50
    DAISIES IN OVAL PANELS, see Bull's-Eye & Fan
    DAISY & BUTTON, see also Paneled Daisy & Button
Daisy & Button With Crossbar, Butter, Cover, Vaseline 65.00
Daisy & Button With Crossbar, Celery Vase, Footed, Amber 40.00
Daisy & Button With Crossbar, Sugar & Creamer, Cover, Amber 85.00
Daisy & Button With Crossbar, Wine .... 16.00 To 20.00
Daisy & Button With Finecut Panels, Pitcher, Water 65.00
Daisy & Button With Narcissus, Wine 15.00
    DAISY & BUTTON WITH OVAL PANELS, see Hartley
Daisy & Button With Thumbprint Panels, Goblet, Blue 70.00
Daisy & Button With V–Ornament, Bowl, Blue, 8 In. 40.00
Daisy & Button With V–Ornament, Butter Chip, Blue 18.50
Daisy & Button With V–Ornament, Tumbler, Amber 25.00
Daisy & Button, Banana Boat, Amber 48.00

Daisy & Button, Berry Set, Amber Panels, 6 Piece 110.00
Daisy & Button, Berry Set, Amber Panels, 10 Piece 150.00
Daisy & Button, Celery Vase 45.00
Daisy & Button, Cruet, Blue, 8 In. 95.00
Daisy & Button, Plate, Blue, Scalloped 30.00
Daisy & Button, Sugar, Cover, Oval 30.00
Daisy & Button, Toothpick, Amber 70.00
Daisy & Button, Toothpick, Hat Shape, Blue 55.00
Daisy & Button, Toothpick, Square, Blue 25.00
Daisy & Button, Toothpick, Urn Shape 20.00
Dakota, Butter, Cover .... 40.00 To 55.00
Dakota, Cake Stand, Domed Cover 295.00
Dakota, Cake Stand, Fern & Berry Design, 10 1/4 In. 65.00
Dakota, Celery Vase, Etched 45.00
Dakota, Compote, Cover, 6 In. 95.00
Dakota, Creamer, Etched .... 45.00 To 60.00
Dakota, Sugar, Cover .... 45.00 To 55.00
Dakota, Tankard, Wine 125.00
Dakota, Tumbler .... 22.00 To 35.00
Dakota, Wine 22.00
Deer & Doe With Lily of The Valley, Goblet 75.00
Deer & Dog, Celery 110.00
Deer & Dog, Goblet, Etched .... 45.00 To 60.00
Deer & Dog, Pitcher, Water 80.00
Deer & Dog, Pitcher, Water, Etched 125.00
Deer & Oak Tree, Pitcher, Water .... 195.00 To 265.00
Deer & Pine Tree, Bread Plate, Vaseline 135.00
Deer & Pine Tree, Compote, 7 1/2 X 8 In. 60.00
Deer & Pine Tree, Goblet 45.00
Delaware, Berry Set, Boat Shape, Rose, Gold, 7 Piece .... 335.00 To 375.00
Delaware, Berry Set, Ruby Stained, 6 Piece 225.00
Delaware, Bowl, Flared, Green, 9 In. 47.50
Delaware, Butter, Cover, Green, Gold Trim 95.00
Delaware, Celery Vase, Rose, Gold Trim, 5 3/4 In. 110.00
Delaware, Saltshaker, Gold Trim 85.00
Delaware, Spooner, Green, Gold Trim .... 55.00 To 65.00
Delaware, Toothpick, Cranberry, Gold Trim 65.00
Delaware, Toothpick, Rose, Gold Trim 95.00
Delaware, Tumbler, Cranberry Stained 52.00
Delaware, Water Set, Green, 7 Piece 695.00
Dewdrop & Raindrop, Pitcher, Water 75.50
Dewdrop & Raindrop, Wine 12.00
Dewdrop In Points, Creamer 34.00
Dewdrop In Points, Pitcher, Water 48.00
Dewdrop With Sheaf of Wheat, Bread Plate, 11 In. .... 25.00 To 45.00
Dewdrop With Star, Creamer 45.00
Dewdrop With Star, Goblet 18.00
Dewdrop With Star, Plate, 6 1/2 In. 18.50
Dewdrop With Star, Wine 19.00
    DEWEY, see also Spanish American
Dewey, Cruet, Stopper, Amber 135.00
Dewey, Goblet, Green 135.00
Dewey, Pitcher, Amethyst 45.00
Diagonal Band With Fan, Sugar, Cover 30.00
Diagonal Band With Fan, Wine 15.00
Diagonal Band, Celery Vase 35.00
Diagonal Band, Compote, Large 30.00
Diagonal Band, Goblet 20.00
Diagonal Block Band, Goblet 20.00
Diamond & Sunburst, Tumbler, Ruby Stained 12.00
Diamond Block, Creamer 5.00
    DIAMOND HORSESHOE, see Aurora
Diamond Lil, Toothpick 40.00

DIAMOND MEDALLION, see Grand
Diamond Peg, Creamer, Souvenir, 6 In. 60.00
Diamond Point Band, Tumbler, Ruby Stained 18.00
Diamond Point, Butter, Cover, Ribbed, Flint 85.00
Diamond Point, Celery Vase, Flint 50.00
Diamond Point, Champagne 125.00
Diamond Point, Compote, 8 In. .... 50.00 To 80.00
DIAMOND PRISMS, see also Albany
Diamond Quilted, Compote, Vaseline, 9 X 6 1/2 In. 45.00
Diamond Quilted, Spooner, Blue 35.00
Diamond Sunburst, Spooner 18.00
Diamond Thumbprint, Bowl, Footed, Flint, 3 3/4 X 8 In. 65.00
Diamond Thumbprint, Compote, Flint, 6 1/2 X 8 In. 100.00
Diamond Thumbprint, Spooner 85.00
Dickinson, Compote, Flint, 8 1/2 In. 60.00
Divided Block With Sunburst, Mug 18.00
Divided Block With Sunburst, Tumbler, Handle 18.00
Divided Hearts, Goblet, Flint 165.00
Dolphin, Compote, Frosted, 6 In. 67.50
Dolphin, Pitcher, Water, Frosted 195.00
DORIC, see Feather
Double Beetle Band, Creamer, Amber 25.00
Double Beetle Band, Wine, Blue 35.00
Double Fan, Pitcher, Milk, Findlay 27.00
DOUBLE LOOP, see Ribbon Candy
Double Panel, Toothpick, Apple Green 45.00
Double Ribbon, Butter, Cover, Frosted 80.00
Double Ribbon, Creamer 32.00
Double Ribbon, Sugar, Cover 37.50
Double Spear, Sugar & Creamer 48.00
DOUBLE VINE, see Bellflower, Double Vine
Drapery, Creamer 30.00
Drapery, Sugar, Cover 40.00
Drum, Butter, Cover, Child's 85.00
Drum, Creamer, Child's 55.00
Duchess, Cruet, Green, Gold Trim 195.00
E PLURIBUS UNUM, see Emblem
EARL, see Spirea Band
Early Thumbprint, Cake Stand, 9 In. 50.00
Egg & Dart, Plate, Pittsburgh Music Hall, Etched, 5 1/2 In. 35.00
Egg In Sand, Bread Plate, 12 1/4 In. 20.00
Egg In Sand, Goblet 30.00
Egg In Sand, Spooner, Blue .... 27.50 To 45.00
Egg In Sand, Sugar, Cover .... 20.00 To 24.00
Egyptian, Bowl, 6 1/2 In. 15.00
Egyptian, Bread Plate, Cleopatra .... 20.00 To 52.50
Egyptian, Celery Vase .... 80.00 To 95.00
Egyptian, Creamer .... 38.00 To 48.00
Egyptian, Goblet 40.00
Egyptian, Pitcher, Water 150.00
Egyptian, Spooner, 5 In. 38.00
Egyptian, Table Set, 4 Piece 225.00
Eight-O-Eight, Plate, 5 1/2 In. 18.50
Electric, Syrup 35.00
Elephant Toes, Butter, Cover, Green 55.00
Elephant Toes, Sugar & Butter, Covers, Green Toes 145.00
Elephant Toes, Toothpick, Green Toes 65.00

Clean alabaster by dusting with a soft brush. Then use turpentine or dry-cleaning fluid. Do not use water. Polish with paste furniture wax.

EMBLEM, see also American Shield; Bullet

Emblem, Dish, Pickle	35.00
Empress, Lamp, Green, 9 3/4 In.	225.00
Empress, Pitcher, Water, Green, Gold Trim	200.00
Empress, Water Set, Green, Gold Trim, 7 Piece	575.00

ENGLISH HOBNAIL CROSS, see Amberette

Esther, Berry Set, Green, Gold Trim, 7 Piece	175.00
Esther, Compote, Cover, 12 In.	85.00
Esther, Cruet, Green, Gold Trim	165.00 To 210.00
Esther, Toothpick, Clear & Amber	90.00
Esther, Tumbler, Green, Gold	30.00

ETCHED DAKOTA, see Dakota

Everglades, Compote, Jelly, Blue, Gold Trim	47.50
Everglades, Creamer	30.00
Everglades, Sauce, Canary	25.00
Everglades, Spooner, Blue	75.00
Everglades, Table Set, Vaseline, 4 Piece	550.00
Excelsior Variant, Eggcup, Flint	37.50
Excelsior With Maltese Cross, Tumbler	42.00
Excelsior, Creamer, Flint	275.00
Eyewinker, Compote, 8 In.	45.00
Eyewinker, Sauce, 4 In.	38.00
Eyewinker, Spooner	45.00
Eyewinker, Sugar, Cover, Green	25.00
Falcon Strawberry, Toothpick	45.00
Fan & Flute, Cake Stand, Ruby Stained	165.00
Fan & Flute, Creamer, Ruby Stained	40.00
Fan & Flute, Pitcher, Water	150.00
Fan & Flute, Spooner	38.00

FAN WITH DIAMOND, see Shell

Fancy Arches, Syrup, Green	175.00
Fancy Arches, Table Set, 4 Piece	85.00
Fancy Cut, Butter, Cover, Child's, Teal	195.00
Fancy Cut, Punch Cup, Child's	25.00
Fashion, Tumbler	17.00
Feather Duster, Pitcher, Water, Green	50.00
Feather Duster, Plate, 7 1/4 In.	22.50
Feather Duster, Tumbler, Green	38.00
Feather, Butter, Cover	48.00 To 55.00
Feather, Cake Stand, 8 In.	25.00 To 36.50

Columbian Coin   Daisy & Button with   Deer & Dog
                         Thumbprint

Feather, Cake Stand, Green .... 150.00 To 195.00
Feather, Compote, Jelly 23.50
Feather, Pitcher 50.00
Feather, Spooner 22.00
Feather, Sugar, Green 55.00
Feather, Tumbler, Flint 45.00
Feather, Wine, Straight Border 25.00
Fernland, Creamer 15.00
Fernland, Creamer, Child's 35.00
Fernland, Sugar, Cover 18.00
    FESTOON & GRAPE, see Grape & Festoon
Festoon, Bowl, Rectangular, 9 1/4 In. 19.50
Festoon, Cake Stand, 9 In. .... 35.00 To 42.00
Festoon, Creamer .... 25.00 To 35.00
Festoon, Spooner 30.00
Festoon, Sugar, Cover .... 45.00 To 85.00
Festoon, Water Set, Tray, 8 Piece 195.00
Fickle Block, Cordial, 3 In. 12.00
Fickle Block, Goblet 20.00
Fine Cut & Block, Creamer, Crystal, Amber 65.00
Fine Cut & Block, Creamer, Pink 60.00
Fine Cut & Block, Cup, Blue 35.00
Fine Cut & Block, Sauce, Amber, Footed 14.00
    FINE CUT & FEATHER, see Feather
Fine Cut & Panel, Creamer, Amber 42.50
Fine Cut & Panel, Goblet, Vaseline 30.00
Fine Cut & Panel, Wine, Amber 25.00
Fine Cut & Panel, Wine, Vaseline 28.50
Fine Cut & Roses, Candy Dish 190.00
Fine Cut, Cruet 65.00
Fine Cut, Plate, 7 3/8 In. 11.00
Fine Diamond Point, Spooner, Pedestal 30.00
Fine Rib, Sugar, Cover, Flint 145.00
Fish Scale, Cake Stand, 9 In. 28.00
Fish Scale, Pitcher, Water 35.00
Flamingo Habitat, Goblet 35.00
Flamingo Habitat, Pitcher, Water 125.00
Flamingo Habitat, Wine 24.50
Flat Diamond & Panel, Claret 125.00
Flatiron, Butter, Cover, Amber 65.00
Flattened Diamond & Sunburst, Punch Set, Child's 50.00
Flattened Sawtooth, Spooner 28.00
Fleur–De–Lis, Butter, Cover, Amethyst, Gold Trim 85.00
Fleur–De–Lis, Goblet 14.00
Fleur–De–Lis, Goblet, Flint 75.00
Flora, Butter, Cover, Green, Gold Trim 75.00
Flora, Spooner 30.00
Flora, Tumbler, Green, Gold Trim 30.00
Florida Palm, Wine 23.00
Flower Band, Pitcher, Water, Frosted 155.00
Flower Band, Saltshaker 57.00
      FLOWER FLANGE, see Dewey
      FLOWER PANELED CANE, see Cane & Rosette
Flower Pot, Creamer 22.50
Flower Pot, Sauce, 4–Footed, 4 In. 22.50
Flute, Celery Vase 20.00
Flute, Goblet 25.00
Flute, Punch Cup 6.00
Flute, Tumbler, Flint 25.00
Fluted Scrolls, Berry Set, Blue, 7 Piece 200.00
Fluted Scrolls, Table Set, Vaseline, 3 Piece 445.00
Fluted Scrolls, Water Set, 7 Piece 695.00

Flying Birds, Toothpick 60.00
FLYING ROBIN, see Hummingbird
Flying Stork, Castor, Pickle 150.00
Flying Stork, Spooner, Etched 60.00
Fox & Crow, Pitcher 125.00
FROSTED PATTERNS, see also under name of main pattern
Frosted Circle, Berry Bowl, Master 20.00
Frosted Circle, Butter, Cover 35.00
Frosted Circle, Cake Stand 45.00
Frosted Circle, Cruet 50.00
FROSTED CRANE, see Frosted Stork
Frosted Eagle, Creamer, Etched 45.00
Frosted Eagle, Sugar 38.00
Frosted Fruits, Pitcher, Water 175.00
Frosted Leaf, Goblet, Buttermilk, Flint 55.00
Frosted Leaf, Goblet, Lady's, Flint 150.00
FROSTED LION, see Lion, Frosted
FROSTED RIBBON, see Ribbon, Frosted
FROSTED ROMAN KEY, see Roman Key, Frosted
Frosted Stork, Bread Plate, 11 1/2 In. 65.00
Frosted Stork, Compote, 8 In. 45.00
Frosted Stork, Creamer 50.00
Frosted Stork, Spooner 45.00
Frosted Stork, Tray, Water 105.00
FROSTED WAFFLE, see Hidalgo
Gaelic, Creamer, Gold Trim 25.00
Galloway, Cake Stand 60.00
Galloway, Compote, 6 In. 55.00
Galloway, Compote, 10 In. 85.00
Galloway, Creamer 35.00
Galloway, Pitcher 55.00
Galloway, Saucer, Gold Trim 15.00
Galloway, Sherbet, Footed 21.50
Galloway, Sugar & Creamer, Cover 50.00
Galloway, Toothpick, Crystal 18.00
Galloway, Vase, Green, 10 In. 52.50
GARDEN OF EDEN, see also Lotus & Serpent
Garden of Eden, Bread Plate, Give Us This Day, 12 1/2 In. 35.00
Garden of Eden, Butter, Cover, Scalloped Base, Serpent 85.00
Garfield Drape, Cake Stand 65.00
Garfield Drape, Creamer 38.00
Garfield Drape, Goblet .... 30.00 To 38.00
Garfield Drape, Spooner 25.00
Garfield Memorial, Bread Plate 35.00
Garfield Stars, Bread Plate, Frosted Bust, 6 In. 30.00
Gem Star, Compote 25.00
George Peabody, Saucer 62.50
George Washington, Platter 45.00
Giant Prism With Thumbprint Band, Celery Vase, Pedestal 65.00
Giant Prism, Pitcher, Water 130.00
Giant Sawtooth, Goblet 100.00
Gibson Girl, Tumbler 75.00
Gloria, Berry Set, Ruby Stained, 6 Piece 195.00
Goat's Head, Sugar 65.00
Golden Rule, Bread Plate 65.00
Gonterman Swirl, Creamer 75.00
Gonterman Swirl, Sugar, Cover, Frosted 135.00
Gonterman Swirl, Toothpick 165.00
GOOD LUCK, see Horseshoe
Gooseberry, Creamer 40.00
Gooseberry, Mug, Handle 45.00
Grace, Butter, Cover 65.00
Grace, Creamer .... 32.00 To 38.00

Grace, Spooner 75.00
Grace, Sugar, Cover 50.00
Grand, Goblet .... 21.50 To 35.00
Grant, U.S., Bread Plate, Let Us Have Peace 40.00
Grant, U.S., Bread Plate, Patriot & Soldier 20.00
GRAPE & CABLE, see Northwood's Grape
Grape & Festoon With Shield, Compote, Cover, 10 3/4 In. 65.00
Grape & Festoon With Shield, Mug, Cobalt Blue 35.00
Grape & Festoon, Goblet .... 20.00 To 27.00
Grape & Festoon, Spooner .... 28.00 To 32.00
Grape & Gothic Arches, Sugar & Creamer, Cover, Gold Trim 65.00
Grape Vine & Ovals, Spooner, Child's 65.00
Grape With Thumbprint, Wine 14.00
GRAPE, see also Beaded Grape; Beaded Grape Medallion; Magnet &
Grape; Magnet & Grape with Frosted Leaf; Paneled Grape; Paneled Grape
Band
Grape, Bowl, Cover, 8 1/2 In. 50.00
Grape, Bread Plate, It Is Pleasant To Labor, 12 1/2 In. 55.00
Grape, Sugar & Creamer, Cover, Westmoreland 55.00
Grapevine With Ovals, Child's, Mug 21.00
Grasshopper With Insect, Goblet 27.00
Grasshopper, Butter, Cover, Etched 70.00
Grasshopper, Compote, Cover, 8 In. 65.00
Grasshopper, Plate, 9 In. 20.00
Grasshopper, Salt, Master 40.00
Grasshopper, Spooner 50.00
Gridley, Pitcher .... 75.00 To 125.00
Hairpin, Berry Set, Amethyst, 7 Piece 85.00
Halley's Comet, Goblet 35.00
Halley's Comet, Tankard, Etched 125.00
Halley's Comet, Wine, Etched 16.00
HAMILTON WITH CLEAR LEAF, see Hamilton with Leaf
Hamilton With Frosted Leaf, Goblet, Flint 50.00
Hamilton With Leaf, Creamer, Flint 55.00
Hamilton, Butter, Cover, Flint .... 60.00 To 70.00
Hamilton, Goblet, Flint 40.00
Hamilton, Spooner, Flint 30.00
Hamilton, Sugar, Cover 50.00
Hand, Compote, Scalloped Rim, 9 X 7 1/2 In. 45.00
Hand, Jam Jar 95.00
Hand, Wine 75.00
Hanging Basket, Celery Vase 35.00
Harp, Goblet, Flared, Flint 950.00
Hartley, Pitcher, Milk, Amber 35.00
Harvard Yard, Butter, Cover 28.00
Harvard Yard, Creamer 22.00
Harvard Yard, Spooner 20.00
Hawaiian Lei, Compote, 8 In. 35.00
Hawaiian Lei, Creamer 10.00
Hawaiian Lei, Table Set, Child's, 4 Piece 95.00
Hawaiian Lei, Wine .... 10.00 To 22.00
Heart & Thumbprint, Creamer 20.00
Heart Stem, Celery Vase, Etched 38.00
Heart Stem, Compote, Cover, 7 In. 95.00
Heart With Thumbprint, Cruet 58.00
Heart With Thumbprint, Goblet 65.00
Heart With Thumbprint, Ice Bucket 60.00
Heart With Thumbprint, Jam Jar, Handles, Green 25.00
Heart With Thumbprint, Plate, 6 1/2 In. 20.00
Heart With Thumbprint, Rose Bowl 50.00
Heart With Thumbprint, Sauce, Large 8.00
Heart, Toothpick, Opaque Pink 57.50
HEARTS OF LOCH LAVEN, see Shuttle

Heavy Fine Cut, Table Set, Amber, 4 Piece 185.00
Heavy Gothic, Creamer 50.00
Hero, Butter, Cover 45.00
Heron, Pitcher 140.00
Heron, Pitcher, Blue 95.00
Herringbone Buttress, Cruet, Green, Gold Trim 275.00
Herringbone, Bowl, Green, 9 In. 25.00
Herringbone, Compote, Jelly, Green .... 20.00 To 38.00
Herringbone, Creamer, Green 35.00
Herringbone, Pitcher, Green .... 75.00 To 85.00
Herringbone, Pitcher, Water, Green .... 55.00 To 65.00
Herringbone, Spooner, Green 35.00
Herringbone, Tumbler, Green 20.00
Hexagon Block, Spooner, Blue, Amber Stained, Etched 35.00
Hexagon Block, Table Set, Ruby Stained, 4 Piece 325.00
Hickman, Cake Stand 38.00
Hickman, Compote, Cover, 7 In. 85.00
Hickman, Cup, Green 18.50
Hickman, Toothpick 45.00
Hidalgo, Goblet, Frosted 25.00
Hidalgo, Sugar, Cover 55.00
    HOBNAIL, see Hobnail category
    HOBNAIL & BARS, see Barred Hobnail
Hobnail With Thumbprint Base, Butter, Cover, Blue 55.00
Hobnail With Thumbprint Base, Sugar & Creamer, Amber 60.00
Holland, Sugar & Creamer 55.00
Holly, Cake Stand 125.00
Holly, Compote, Cover, 9 X 14 In. 145.00
Homestead, Banana Boat, Rolled Edge 24.00
    HONEYCOMB, see also Barrel Honeycomb; Loop & Honeycomb; Vernon
    Honeycomb
Honeycomb, Compote, Flint, 8 In. 42.00
Honeycomb, Decanter, Stopper, Flint, Pair 90.00
Honeycomb, Goblet, Flint 40.00
Honeycomb, Pitcher, Water, Flint 195.00
Honeycomb, Spooner 32.00
Honeycomb, Tumbler 38.00
Horizontal Threads, Butter, Cover, Child's 110.00
Horn of Plenty, Celery Vase 145.00
Horn of Plenty, Compote, Flint, 7 1/4 X 8 In. 65.00

Double Ribbon   Early Thumbprint   Egg in Sand

Horn of Plenty, Eggcup, Flint 50.00
Horn of Plenty, Plate, Flint, 6 In. 57.50
Horn of Plenty, Salt, Flat, Oval 125.00
Horn of Plenty, Whiskey, Handle 195.00
Horse Mint, Wine 10.00
Horsehead Medallion, Celery Vase 78.00
Horseshoe Daisy, Saucer, Ruby Stained 150.00
Horseshoe Medallion, Pitcher, Water, 7 5/8 In. 165.00
Horseshoe Stem, Creamer 50.00
Horseshoe, Bowl, 6 X 9 In. 28.00
Horseshoe, Bread Plate .... 55.00 To 75.00
Horseshoe, Cake Stand .... 45.00 To 55.00
Horseshoe, Celery Vase .... 35.00 To 65.00
Horseshoe, Dish, Cheese 270.00
Horseshoe, Goblet 32.50
Horseshoe, Pitcher, Water 145.00
Horseshoe, Plate, 10 In. .... 65.00 To 75.00
   HUCKLE, see Feather Duster
Hummingbird, Creamer 55.00
Hummingbird, Goblet, Amber .... 45.00 To 55.00
Hummingbird, Pitcher .... 75.00 To 100.00
Hummingbird, Pitcher, Water, Amber 110.00
Hummingbird, Wine 75.00
Icicle With Loops, Wine, Flint 27.50
   IDA, see Sheraton
Idyll, Butter, Cover, Apple Green, Gold Trim 45.00
Illinois, Pitcher, Water, Footed, Square 75.00
Illinois, Saltshaker 18.00
Illinois, Tankard, Water 125.00
Illinois, Toothpick 18.00
   INDIANA SWIRL, see Feather
Intaglio Sunflower, Table Set, Red Trim, 4 Piece 200.00
Intaglio, Compote, Jelly, Blue 40.00
Intaglio, Compote, Jelly, Green, Gold Trim 38.00
Interlocked Hearts, Butter 35.00
Interlocked Hearts, Creamer 20.00
Interlocked Hearts, Wine 16.00
Inverted Fan & Feather, Butter, Gold Trim 55.00
Inverted Fan & Feather, Tumbler, Green, Gold Trim 15.00
Inverted Fern, Eggcup, Flint 25.00
Inverted Fern, Goblet, Flint .... 22.00 To 37.00
Inverted Thumbprint & Star, Goblet 30.00
Inverted Thumbprint, Creamer, Vaseline 40.00
Inverted Thumbprint, Cruet, Blue 40.00
Inverted Thumbprint, Tumbler, Cranberry 35.00
Inverted Thumbprint, Vase, 10 In. 85.00
Inverted Thumbprint, Vase, Enamel Design, Cranberry, 6 In. 175.00
Inverted Thumbprint, Water Set, Blue, 3 Piece 170.00
Iowa, Cruet 65.00
Iowa, Cruet, Pink 35.00
Iowa, Toothpick 12.00
Iowa, Wine, Gold Trim 35.00
Iris With Meander, Spooner, Vaseline 75.00
Iris With Meander, Toothpick, Blue, Gold Trim 35.00
Iris With Meander, Toothpick, Green Opalescent 37.50
Iris With Meander, Tumbler, Blue 30.00
Ivy In Snow, Wine 35.00
Ivy Leaves, Cup & Saucer 45.00
Ivy, Cruet, Cranberry 160.00
Jacob's Ladder, Creamer 35.00
Jacob's Ladder, Goblet .... 35.00 To 65.00
Jacob's Ladder, Pitcher, Water 145.00
Jacob's Ladder, Relish, 2 Handles, 10 In. 12.00
Jacob's Ladder, Wine 32.00

Jefferson's Optic, Toothpick, Grand Forks, North Dakota, Blue 57.50
Jefferson's Optic, Toothpick, Peach & White Enamel Trim 35.00
Jenny Lind, Bread Plate 85.00
Jewel & Dewdrop, Butter, Cover 85.00
Jewel & Dewdrop, Goblet 50.00
Jewel & Dewdrop, Pitcher, Water 45.00
Jewel & Dewdrop, Toothpick .... 45.00 To 55.00
Jewel & Dewdrop, Wine 55.00
    JEWEL & FESTOON, see Loop & Jewel
Jewel & Flower, Spooner, Vaseline 75.00
Jewel Band, Creamer 19.00
Jewel Band, Wine 15.00
Jeweled Heart, Berry, Green Opalescent 48.00
Jeweled Heart, Tumbler, Blue, Gold Trim 22.00
Jeweled Heart, Water Set, Green, Gold Trim, 7 Piece 350.00
    JEWELED MOON & STAR, see Moon & Star Variant; Moon & Star
    JOB'S TEARS, see Art
    JUBILEE, see Hickman
Jumbo & Barnum, Butter, Cover, Round 400.00
Jumbo & Barnum, Sugar, Cover .... 325.00 To 425.00
Jumbo, Spoon Rack 400.00
Kalbach, Goblet 8.00
    KAMONI, see Pennsylvania
    KANSAS, see Jewel & Dewdrop
Kayak, Bread Plate, 11 In. 20.00
Kentucky, Punch Cup, Green .... 15.00 To 20.00
Kentucky, Toothpick 30.00
Kentucky, Toothpick, Green 110.00
Kentucky, Wine, Green .... 25.00 To 35.00
King Arthur, Pitcher, Water 75.00
King Arthur, Tumbler 15.00
King's 500, Bowl, 8 In. 165.00
King's 500, Butter, Cover, Blue 135.00
King's 500, Punch Cup, Cobalt Blue, Gold Trim 22.00
King's 500, Sauce, Cobalt Blue 25.00
King's Crown, Cake Stand, 9 In. 67.50
King's Crown, Celery Vase, Etched 60.00
King's Crown, Compote, Cover, 8 X 11 1/2 In. .... 145.00 To 165.00
King's Crown, Compote, Footed, Ruby Stained, 15 In. 45.00
King's Crown, Condiment Set, Holder, 4 Piece 170.00
King's Crown, Creamer 25.00
King's Crown, Goblet .... 20.00 To 42.00
King's Crown, Goblet, Ruby Stained 10.00
King's Crown, Mug, Grapevine, Child's 20.00
King's Crown, Mustard, Cover 60.00
King's Crown, Pitcher, Milk, Ruby Stained 95.00
King's Crown, Plate, Sandwich, Red Stained, 14 In. 30.00
King's Crown, Salt, Individual 38.00
King's Crown, Toothpick, World's Fair, 1893 .... 50.00
King's Crown, Tumbler, Large 12.00
King's Crown, Wine, Etched 50.00
    KLONDIKE, see Amberette
Knights of Labor, Bread Plate, Blue, C.1889 .... 200.00
Knights of Labor, Mug 60.00
Knobby Bull's–Eye, Creamer, Gold Trim 20.00
Kokomo, Compote, Cover, Low, 8 In. 25.00
Kokomo, Goblet 35.00
Kokomo, Rose Bowl, Green 16.00
Lacy Daisy, Butter, Cover 46.50
Lacy Daisy, Creamer .... 20.00 To 41.50
Lacy Daisy, Sugar 36.50
    LACY MEDALLION, see also Princess Feather

LACY SPIRAL, see Colossus
Ladder With Diamond, Cruet 30.00
Ladder With Diamond, Toothpick 20.00
Ladders & Diamond With Star, Wine, Ruby Stained, Tarentum 38.00
Lamb, Butter, Cover, Child's 50.00
Lamb, Creamer, Child's 30.00
Lamb, Sugar, Cover, Child's 125.00
Lamb, Table Set, Child's, 4 Piece 695.00
Late Block, Creamer, Individual 25.00
Late Butterfly, Bowl 28.00
Late Butterfly, Pitcher, Milk 75.00
Late Butterfly, Sugar, Cover 32.00
LATTICE & OVAL PANELS, see Flat Diamond & Panel
Lattice, Goblet 20.00
Leaf & Dart, Salt, Cover 95.00
Leaf & Dart, Sugar, Cover 42.50
Leaf & Dart, Tumbler, Footed 22.00
Leaf & Rib, Pitcher, Water, Amber 68.00
Leaf Bracket, Tumbler, Green, Gold Trim 45.00
Leaf Medallion, Berry Bowl, Master 75.00
Leaf Medallion, Compote, Jelly, Cobalt Blue, Gold Trim 145.00
Leaf Medallion, Creamer, Cobalt Blue, Gold Trim 95.00
Leaf Medallion, Sugar, Cover, Amethyst, Gold Trim 155.00
Leaf Medallion, Table Set, Amethyst, Gold Trim, 4 Piece 395.00
Liberty Bell, Bread Plate 85.00
Liberty Bell, Butter, Cover .... 75.00 To 140.00
Liberty Bell, Creamer .... 128.00 To 138.00
Liberty Bell, Relish, Twig Handles, Oval 44.00
Liberty Bell, Saltshaker, Pewter Cover 110.00
Liberty Bell, Spooner .... 55.00 To 65.00
Liberty Bell, Sugar, Cover 100.00
Liberty Bell, Table Set, 4 Piece .... 375.00 To 395.00
Lily-of-The-Valley, Compote, Cover, 8 In. 135.00
Lily-of-The-Valley, Sugar 32.50
Lincoln Drape With Tassle, Goblet, Flint 165.00
Lincoln Drape, Eggcup, Flint 65.00
Lincoln Drape, Salt, Beaded Rim, Master 125.00
Lion With Cable, Celery Vase, Etched 80.00
Lion With Cable, Compote, Cover, 10 1/2 X 7 In. 135.00
Lion With Cable, Sugar, Cover 40.00
LION'S LEG, see Alaska
Lion, Butter, Cover, Cranberry, Rampant Lion Finial 125.00
Lion, Compote, Open, Oval 52.00
Lion, Creamer, Child's 55.00
Lion, Cup & Saucer, Child's .... 45.00 To 65.00
Lion, Frosted, Bread Plate, Lion Handles, Oval .... 65.00 To 85.00
Lion, Frosted, Butter, Cover 140.00
Lion, Frosted, Celery Vase 75.00
Lion, Frosted, Compote, Oval, 8 In. 70.00
Lion, Frosted, Eggcup 55.00
Lion, Frosted, Goblet .... 55.00 To 70.00
Lion, Frosted, Spooner .... 45.00 To 60.00
Lion, Frosted, Table Set, Child's 375.00
Lion, Sugar, Cover, Child's 95.00
Locket On Chain, Cake Stand 145.00
Locket On Chain, Wine 65.00
Log Cabin, Compote, Cover, 5 X 7 In. 320.00
Log Cabin, Creamer 115.00
Log Cabin, Sugar 95.00
Loop & Block, Butter, Cover, Ruby Flashed 50.00

Loop & Block, Creamer, Ruby Flashed 65.00
Loop & Block, Spooner, Ruby Flashed 65.00
Loop & Block, Sugar, Cover, Ruby Flashed 85.00
Loop & Block, Sugar, Ruby Flashed 55.00
Loop & Dart With Round Ornaments, Salt 45.00
Loop & Dart, Butter Chip 15.00
Loop & Dart, Eggcup 25.00
Loop & Jewel, Relish 17.00
Loop & Pyramid, Cracker Jar 55.00
Loop With Dewdrop, Creamer 30.00
    LOOP WITH STIPPLED PANELS, see Texas
    LOOP, see also Seneca Loop; Yuma Loop
Loop, Spooner 18.00
    LOOPS & DROPS, see New Jersey
Lotus & Serpent, Pitcher, 5 In. 47.50
Louis XV, Creamer, Green 95.00
Louis XV, Spooner, Green 95.00
Louis XV, Table Set, Green, Gold Trim, 4 Piece 425.00
Louisiana, Bowl, Square 24.00
Louisiana, Compote, 7 In. 95.00
Louisiana, Mug 25.00
Louisiana, Tumbler 25.00
Madison, Sugar, Cover 150.00
Magnet & Grape With American Shield, Goblet .... 250.00 To 300.00
Magnet & Grape With Frosted Leaf, Goblet 75.00
Magnet & Grape, Salt, Master 20.00
    MAIDEN BLUSH, see Banded Portland
Maine, Compote, Green, 7 In. 52.00
Maine, Pitcher 95.00
Man's Head, Creamer 45.00
Manhattan, Bowl, Gold Trim, 8 In. 35.00
Manhattan, Cake Stand, 8 In. 48.00
Manhattan, Sugar & Creamer 30.00
Manhattan, Sugar & Creamer, Gold Trim 50.00
Maple Leaf, Bowl, Log Feet, Oval, 7 X 11 In. 45.00
Maple Leaf, Bread Plate, Oval, Vaseline, 9 1/2 X 13 In. 45.00
Maple Leaf, Compote, 8 X 10 1/2 In. 65.00
Maple Leaf, Creamer, Log Feet, Vaseline 65.00
Maple Leaf, Goblet 20.00
Maple Leaf, Plate, 10 7/8 In. 30.00
Maple Leaf, Spooner, Log Feet, Vaseline 65.00
Mardi Gras, Cordial 10.00
Mardi Gras, Jam Jar, Cover 25.00
Mardi Gras, Punch Cup 7.00
Marquisette, Celery Vase 45.00
Marquisette, Compote, Open 35.00
Marquisette, Goblet 30.00
Marsh Fern, Cake Stand 47.50
Marsh Fern, Compote, Cover, 7 In. 85.00
Marsh Fern, Goblet 42.50
Martyrs, Mug, Child's 85.00
Martyrs, Mug, Lincoln, Garfield 60.00
Maryland, Compote, Jelly, Cover 30.00
Maryland, Platter, Oval, 11 X 8 In. 20.00
Maryland, Sauce, 6 Piece 55.00
Maryland, Wine 30.00
Mascotte, Apothecary Jar, Dated 65.00
Mascotte, Butter, Cover, Leaf Etching 55.00
Mascotte, Sauce, Footed 7.50
Mascotte, Spooner 28.00
Mascotte, Sugar, Cover, Leaf Etching 45.00
Mascotte, Table Set, 4 Piece 165.00
Massachusetts, Jug, Rum .... 90.00 To 110.00
Massachusetts, Mug, Gold Trim 12.00

Frosted Circle

Frosted Eagle

Garfield Drape

Massachusetts, Plate, 8 In.	25.00
Massachusetts, Sauce, 4 Piece	58.00
Massachusetts, Sugar & Creamer	35.00
Massachusetts, Wine	45.00
McKinley, Bread Plate, 7 1/4 In.	35.00
McKinley, Cup, Cover	42.00
Medallion Sprig, Butter, Cover, Amethyst To Clear	85.00
Medallion Sprig, Cruet, Stopper, Clear To Green	295.00
Medallion Sprig, Saltshaker, Blue To Clear	85.00
Medallion, Goblet, Blue	35.00
Memphis, Table Set, Gold Trim, 4 Piece	250.00
Memphis, Tumbler, Gold Trim	26.00
Memphis, Tumbler, Green	20.00
Menagerie, Creamer, Amber, Child's	70.00
Menagerie, Creamer, Owl	65.00
Menagerie, Spooner, Fish, Child's	100.00
Michigan, Bowl, 10 In.	35.00
Michigan, Compote, Open, 10 In.	65.00
Michigan, Goblet, Amber	25.00
Michigan, Salt & Pepper	50.00
Michigan, Toothpick, Blue Stained Top, Yellow Enameled Dots	65.00
Mikado Fan, Goblet, 6 Piece	115.00
Mikado Fan, Pitcher, Water	42.00
Milton, Goblet	15.00
Minerva, Bowl, 4 1/2 X 7 In.	35.00
Minerva, Bowl, Footed, Cover, 7 In.	75.00
Minerva, Bread Plate	60.00
Minerva, Cake Stand	80.00 To 125.00
Minerva, Creamer	45.00
Minerva, Goblet	80.00 To 95.00
Minerva, Pitcher, Water	135.00 To 225.00
Minerva, Plate, 8 In.	72.50
Minerva, Sauce, Footed	18.50 To 24.00
Minerva, Spooner	32.00
Minerva, Sugar, Cover	75.00
Minnesota, Bowl, 8 In.	40.00 To 50.00
Minnesota, Bowl, Ruby Stained, 8 1/2 In.	100.00
Minnesota, Celery Vase, 6 X 13 In.	30.00
Minnesota, Compote, 9 In.	50.00
Minnesota, Cruet	25.00 To 35.00
Minnesota, Relish, 5 X 7 1/4 In.	10.00
Minnesota, Toothpick	40.00 To 45.00

Minnesota, Wine .... 15.00 To 20.00
Mirror Star, Table Set, 4 Piece 90.00
Missouri, Berry Bowl, Green, 8 3/4 In. 45.00
Missouri, Cake Stand 28.00
Missouri, Doughnut Stand 27.50
Missouri, Pitcher, Water, Green 75.00
Missouri, Syrup 70.00
Mitered Bars, Wine 14.00
   MITERED DIAMOND POINTS, see Mitered Bars
Mitered Diamond, Tumbler, Blue 32.00
Mitered Prisms, Creamer 5.00
Monkey, Mug, Tail Handle, Amethyst 195.00
Moon & Star Variant, Banana Boat, 10 1/2 X 8 In. 34.00
Moon & Star Variant, Bowl, Amber Stars, 7 In. 15.00
Moon & Star Variant, Spooner 45.00
Moon & Star, Compote, Cover, Clear & Frosted, 11 1/2 X 7 In. 70.00
Moon & Star, Cruet .... 40.00 To 55.00
Moon & Star, Sherbet 27.50
Moon & Star, Spooner, Frosted 45.00
Moon & Star, Sugar & Creamer 100.00
Moon & Star, Sugar, Cover, Flint 60.00
Moon & Star, Tumbler, Cranberry Stained 35.00
   MOON & STORK, see Ostrich Looking At The Moon
Morning Glory, Eggcup, Flint 225.00
Morning Glory, Wine 100.00
My Lady's Workbox, Wine 25.00
Nail, Compote, Ruby Stained, 7 1/2 In. 125.00
Nail, Creamer, Etched 32.00
Nail, Syrup 50.00
Nailhead, Butter, Cover 46.50
Nailhead, Celery Vase 45.00
Nailhead, Plate, 9 In. .... 12.00 To 18.50
Napoleon, Berry Bowl, 8 1/4 In. 18.00
Narcissus, Spooner, Leaf Etching 35.00
Narrow Swirl, Creamer 25.00
   NAUTILUS, see Argonaut Shell
   NEBRASKA, see Bismarc Star
Nellie Bly, Bread Plate 150.00
Nestor, Berry Bowl, Amethyst, Gold Trim, Small 22.00
Nestor, Berry Bowl, Green, White Enamel, Master 65.00
Nestor, Berry Set, 9 Piece 195.00
Nestor, Butter, Cover 48.00
Nestor, Creamer, Green, Enamel & Gold Trim 40.00
Nestor, Saltshaker, Amethyst 47.50
Nestor, Spooner, Blue, Gold Trim, White Enamel 55.00
Nestor, Sugar, Cover 60.00
Nestor, Water Set, Blue, Gold Trim, 7 Piece 445.00
New England Pineapple, Compote, Flint, 9 In. 145.00
New England Pineapple, Decanter, Flint, 1 1/2 Pt. 275.00
New England Pineapple, Eggcup 65.00
New England Pineapple, Pitcher, Water 310.00
New Hampshire, Creamer, Individual 25.00
New Hampshire, Creamer, Ruby & Clear 65.00
New Hampshire, Saltshaker, Maiden Blush 37.50
New Hampshire, Sugar & Creamer 35.00
New Hampshire, Toothpick, Maiden Blush Stained Top 50.00
New Jersey, Berry Set, Gold Trim, Footed, 7 Piece 135.00
New Jersey, Butter, Cover, Gold Trim 73.00
New Jersey, Dish, Pickle, 7 X 4 3/4 In. 12.00
New Jersey, Goblet, Gold Trim 36.50
New Jersey, Pitcher, Water 40.00
New Jersey, Toothpick, Gold Trim 44.00
New Jersey, Tumbler .... 15.00 To 28.50
New Jersey, Wine, Gold Trim 25.00

New York Honeycomb, Pitcher, Water, Bulbous 105.00
New York Honeycomb, Shot Glass, Handle 55.00
Notched Oval, Pitcher, Water, Gold Trim 47.50
Nova Scotia Starflower, Cake Stand 50.00
Nursery Tales, Bowl, Child's 75.00
Nursery Tales, Butter, Cover, Child's .... 45.00 To 75.00
Nursery Tales, Creamer, Child's .... 30.00 To 45.00
Nursery Tales, Pitcher, Child's 95.00
Nursery Tales, Punch Set, Child's, 7 Piece 150.00
Nursery Tales, Tumbler, Child's 15.00
O'Hara No.82, Compote, Cover, 8 In. 75.00
O'Hara's Diamond, Cruet, Ruby Stained .... 165.00 To 175.00
O'Hara's Diamond, Spooner, Ruby Stained, Etched 67.50
Oak Leaf Band, Goblet 25.00
Oaken Bucket, Butter, Cover, Amber .... 45.00 To 65.00
Oaken Bucket, Pitcher, Water .... 30.00 To 40.00
Oaken Bucket, Spooner, Blue 25.00
Oaken Bucket, Sugar, Cover 35.00
Oaken Bucket, Table Set, Blue, 4 Piece 250.00
Oaken Bucket, Toothpick, Wire Bail, Blue 20.00
Odd Fellows, Goblet 35.00
     OLD ABE, see Frosted Eagle
Old Quilt, Goblet 14.00
Old Quilt, Tumbler, 8 Oz. 8.00
One–Hundred–One, Bread Plate, Herons & Rushes 40.00
One–Hundred–One, Goblet .... 32.00 To 45.00
One–Hundred–One, Tray, Etched Girl, Basket, Flowers 52.00
     ONE–O–ONE, see One–Hundred–One
     ONE–THOUSAND EYE, see Thousand Eye
Oneata, Spooner & Creamer, Child's 50.00
Open Rose, Eggcup 25.00
Open Rose, Tumbler, Footed 25.00
Opposing Drops, Cruet 15.00
Opposing Pyramids, Compote, Scalloped, 10 X 7 In. 45.00
Opposing Pyramids, Goblet 24.50
Orange Peel, Goblet 18.00
     OREGON, see also Beaded Loop; Skilton
Oregon, Berry Set, 7 Piece 35.00
Oregon, Butter, Cover .... 45.00 To 63.00
Oregon, Cake Stand, 8 3/4 In. .... 35.00 To 45.00
Oregon, Pitcher, Milk 35.00
Oregon, Pitcher, Milk, Ruby Stained, 6 1/2 In. 100.00
Oregon, Pitcher, Water 45.00
Oregon, Salt & Pepper 35.00
Oregon, Sugar, Cover .... 30.00 To 45.00
Oregon, Wine 38.00
Orinda, Creamer 20.00
     ORION, see Cathedral
     OVAL LOOP, see Question Mark
Oval Star, Butter, Child's 30.00
Oval Star, Butter, Cover, Sugar & Spooner, Child's 45.00
Oval Star, Pitcher, Child's 25.00
Oval Star, Spooner, Child's, 2 Handles 15.00
     OWL, see Bull's–Eye with Diamond Points
Owl & Possum, Goblet 80.00
Owl In Horseshoe, Goblet 145.00
Oxford, Berry Bowl, 9 1/2 In. 20.00
Paddle Wheel, Toothpick, Gold Trim 35.00
Palm & Scroll, Table Set, 4 Piece 195.00
Palm Beach, Butter, Cover 180.00
Palm Beach, Spooner, Vaseline 70.00
Palm Beach, Table Set, Blue, 4 Piece 515.00
Palm Beach, Tumbler 42.50

Panama, Pitcher	30.00
Paneled 44, Butter, Rose Flashed	95.00
Paneled 44, Goblet, Gold Trim	35.00
Paneled 44, Plate, Amethyst, Gold Trim	45.00
Paneled 44, Tankard, Footed, Rose, Gold Trim	65.00
Paneled Cherry, Goblet	20.00
Paneled Daisy & Button, Salt, Amber	25.00
Paneled Daisy, Celery Vase	35.00 To 45.00
Paneled Daisy, Compote, Cover, 9 In.	40.00
Paneled Daisy, Relish, 8 1/4 In.	12.00
Paneled Diamond & Finecut, Butter, Cover	38.00
Paneled Diamond & Finecut, Cup, 6 Piece	58.00
Paneled Diamond & Finecut, Spooner	25.00
Paneled Dogwood, Butter, Cover, Footed	60.00
Paneled Finecut, Wine, Blue	32.50
Paneled Forget-Me-Not, Compote, Cover, 8 In.	65.00
Paneled Forget-Me-Not, Creamer	28.00
Paneled Forget-Me-Not, Relish	12.00 To 15.00
Paneled Forget-Me-Not, Spooner	25.00 To 30.00
Paneled Grape Band, Eggcup, Flint	35.00
Paneled Grape, Bowl, Footed, 9 In.	40.00
Paneled Grape, Box, Chocolate, Large	38.00
Paneled Grape, Butter, Cover	35.00
Paneled Grape, Cake Stand	45.00
Paneled Grape, Candleholder, 4 In.	8.00
Paneled Grape, Compote, Cover, 7 In.	20.00
Paneled Grape, Cup & Saucer	8.00
Paneled Grape, Dresser Set, 4 Piece	120.00
Paneled Grape, Epergne, Westmoreland, 12 In.	110.00
Paneled Grape, Pitcher, Footed, 1 Qt.	28.00
Paneled Grape, Plate, Dinner	15.00
Paneled Grape, Spooner, Flint	24.00
Paneled Grape, Sugar & Creamer	10.00
Paneled Grape, Tumbler, Flat	11.00
Paneled Grape, Vase, 5 1/2 In.	9.00
Paneled Heather, Goblet	32.00
Paneled Holly, Creamer, Blue	70.00
Paneled Iris, Wine	12.00
Paneled Nightshade, Wine	20.00
Paneled Palm, Creamer	20.00
Paneled Smocking, Sugar & Creamer	32.00
Paneled Sprig, Jam Jar, Cranberry, Plated Rim, Bail & Lid	175.00
Paneled Star & Button, Wine	14.50
Paneled Star & Button, Wine, Blue	85.00
Paneled Strawberry, Water Set, Creamer, Butter, Sauce, 10 Pc.	275.00

Hildalgo

Holly

Horn of Plenty

Inverted Fern

Paneled Sunflower, Toothpick	37.00
Paneled Thistle, Dish, Honey, Bee Mark, Cover, Square	55.00
Paneled Thistle, Vase, Oval, 9 1/2 In.	35.00
Pansy, Toothpick, Pink Cased	60.00
Parrot & Fan, Goblet	28.00
Pattee Cross, Creamer, Individual	23.00
Pattee Cross, Cruet	18.00
Pattee Cross, Pitcher	35.00
Pattee Cross, Tumbler, Child's	75.00
Pavonia, Goblet, Etched	38.00
Pavonia, Pitcher, Water, Etched	50.00 To 60.00
Pavonia, Salt & Pepper, Etched	55.00
Pavonia, Tumbler, Maple Leaf Etch	30.00
Pavonia, Water Set, 6 Piece	150.00
Pavonia, Wine	25.00 To 30.00
Peabody, Mug	50.00
Peacock Feathers, Compote, Footed, 6 In.	19.00
PEACOCK'S EYE, see Peacock Feathers	
Peacock, Compote, Open	18.00
Peacock, Cruet	38.00
Peacock, Nappy, Triangular	28.00
Peacock, Sugar	35.00
Pearl, Table Set, Ruby Flower, 4 Piece	425.00
Peerless, Goblet	25.00
Pennsylvania, Bowl, 8 1/2 In.	24.50
Pennsylvania, Butter, Cover, Gold Trim	45.00
Pennsylvania, Cup, Gold Trim	18.50
Pennsylvania, Goblet	12.00
Pennsylvania, Spooner	15.00 To 30.00
Pennsylvania, Sugar, Cover, Child's	35.00
Pennsylvania, Wine	15.00 To 17.00
Pennsylvania, Wine, Green, Gold Trim	45.00
Pequot, Jam Jar	65.00
Persian, Creamer	17.00
Persian, Mug, Blue	45.00
Persian, Relish	16.00
Persian, Spooner	15.00
Petal & Loop, Bowl, Flat, Flint, 8 In.	85.00
Petal & Loop, Compote, Flint, 8 In., Pair	90.00
Petticoat, Berry Bowl, Vaseline, 8 In.	67.50
Petticoat, Syrup, Gold Trim, Vaseline	55.00
Petticoat, Table Set, Vaseline, Gold Trim, 4 Piece	475.00
Philadelphia Centennial, Goblet	32.00 To 45.00
Picket, Compote, Cover, 6 In.	80.00
Picket, Creamer	45.00
PILLAR & BULL'S–EYE, see Thistle	
Pillar, Celery Vase, Flint	155.00
Pillow Encircled, Tumbler	25.00
PINAFORE, see Actress	
Pineapple & Fan, Mug, Green	35.00
Pineapple & Fan, Salt & Pepper	42.50
Pioneer, Celery Vase	45.00
Pleat & Panel, Celery Vase	45.00
Pleat & Panel, Compote, Cover, 8 In.	95.00
Pleat & Panel, Creamer	25.00
Pleat & Panel, Plate, 7 In.	20.00
Pleating, Table Set, Ruby Stained, 4 Piece	235.00
Plume, Butter, Cover, Etched, Red Flashed	135.00
Plume, Celery Vase	20.00 To 25.00

If you use plate hangers to display your plates, be sure they are not too tight. The clips should be covered with a soft material.

Plume, Compote, 6 1/2 In. .... 30.00 To 40.00
Plume, Spooner, Etched, Red Flashed 55.00
Plume, Sugar, Etched, Red Flashed 25.00
Pogo Stick, Creamer .... 18.00 To 25.00
Pogo Stick, Spooner 25.00
Pogo Stick, Sugar, Cover 30.00
Poinsettia, Tumbler, Blue 50.00
    POINTED PANEL DAISY & BUTTON, see Paneled , Daisy & Button
Polar Bear, Goblet, Frosted ....72.00 To 150.00
Polar Bear, Tray, Water, Frosted .... 50.00 To 95.00
Popcorn, Cake Stand, 11 In. .... 44.00 To 68.00
Popcorn, Goblet 29.00
Popcorn, Wine .... 20.00 To 30.00
    PORTLAND WITH DIAMOND POINT BAND, see Banded Portland
Portland, Compote, Cover, 8 X 10 1/2 In. 65.00
Portland, Plate, Warrior, Frosted 95.00
Portland, Sauce, Gold Flashed 7.50
Portland, Tumbler, Gold Trim 12.00
Posies & Pods, Butter, Cover, Green 125.00
    POTTED PLANT, see Flower Pot
Powder & Shot, Creamer, Applied Handle, Flint 95.00
Powder & Shot, Eggcup .... 45.00 To 50.00
Powder & Shot, Goblet .... 55.00 To 60.00
Powder & Shot, Spooner 35.00
    PRAYER RUG, see Horseshoe
Prescott Stark, Bread Tray 100.00
Pressed Diamond, Cruet, Vaseline 85.00
Pressed Diamond, Saltshaker, Green 38.00
Pressed Diamond, Tumbler, Amber 22.00
Pressed Leaf, Butter, Cover 60.00
Pressed Leaf, Pitcher, Flint, 9 1/2 In. 25.00
Pretty Maid, Toothpick 60.00
Primrose, Plate, Amber, 4 1/2 In. 12.00
Primrose, Plate, Amber, 7 In. 17.00
Primrose, Sugar, Cover 35.00
Prince of Wales Plumes, Toothpick, Ruby Stained 130.00
Princess Feather, Butter, Cover 75.00
Princess Feather, Celery Vase 41.50
Princess Feather, Goblet .... 35.00 To 42.00
Princess Feather, Spooner 18.00
Printed Hobnail, Butter, Cover, Round 48.00
Priscilla, Compote, Straight–Edge 45.00
Priscilla, Syrup, Pewter Top, Findlay 75.00
Priscilla, Wine 35.00
Prism & Clear Panels, Wine 16.00
Prism & Daisy Bar, Goblet 20.00
Prism & Sawtooth, Spooner, Scalloped Top, Flint 25.00
Prism Band, Wine 5.00
Prism With Diamond Points, Cruet 87.50
Prism, Bowl, Flint, 8 In. 43.00
Prize, Berry Bowl, 8 In. 47.50
Prize, Celery Vase, Green, Gold Trim 65.00
Prize, Creamer, Green, Gold Trim 40.00
Prize, Creamer, Ruby Stained .... 67.50 To 72.50
Prize, Spooner, Ruby Stained 52.50
Prize, Wine, Green, Gold Trim 55.00
Profile & Sprig, Spooner 35.00
Profile & Sprig, Sugar, Cover 24.00
Psyche & Cupid, Creamer 60.00
Psyche & Cupid, Goblet .... 30.00 To 35.00
Psyche & Cupid, Pitcher, Water 75.00
Quaker Lady, Compote, Open 65.00
Quartered Block, Toothpick, Gold 28.00

Queen Anne, Butter, Cover .... 35.00 To 38.00
Queen Anne, Celery Vase 36.00
Queen Anne, Creamer .... 36.00 To 48.00
Queen Anne, Nappy, 4 1/2 In. 30.00
Queen Anne, Spooner 32.00
Queen's Necklace, Toothpick, Footed 95.00
Queen's Necklace, Toothpick, Stem, C.1895 .... 95.00
Queen's Necklace, Vase, Footed, 9 In. 30.00
    QUEEN, see also Paneled, Daisy & Button
Queen, Pitcher, Water, Amber 60.00
Question Mark, Sugar Shaker 25.00
Quilted Phlox, Sugar & Creamer, Plated Tops & Handles, Pink 150.00
Racing Deer, Pitcher .... 165.00 To 175.00
Radiant Daisy, Spooner, Ruby Stained 35.00
Red Block, Butter, Cover 85.00
Red Block, Creamer, Handle 95.00
Red Block, Pitcher, Water, Ruby Stained 145.00
Red Block, Spooner, Handle 48.00
    REGENT, see Leaf Medallion
Remember The Maine, Tumbler 22.00
Reverse Swirl, Tankard, Blue Opalescent, 10 In. 350.00
    REVERSE TORPEDO, see Bull's-Eye Band
Rex, Creamer, Child's 10.00
Rib & Bead, Compote, Jelly, Ruby Stained 80.00
Rib & Bead, Creamer, Ruby Stained 55.00
Ribbed Droplet Band, Table Set, Laurel Leaf Etching, 4 Piece 375.00
Ribbed Forget-Me-Not, Creamer 25.00
Ribbed Forget-Me-Not, Creamer, Child's 45.00
Ribbed Ivy, Compote, Flint, 8 1/2 In. .... 75.00 To 95.00
Ribbed Ivy, Salt, Master, Ball Rim 55.00
    RIBBED OPAL, see Beatty Rib
Ribbed Palm, Celery Vase, Flint 75.00
Ribbed Palm, Pitcher, Water 245.00
Ribbed Palm, Tumbler, Flint 110.00
Ribbed Thumbprint, Compote, Jelly, Enameled 48.00
Ribbon Candy, Butter, Cover 25.00
Ribbon Candy, Cake Plate, Green 37.50
Ribbon Candy, Creamer 28.00
Ribbon Candy, Wine 75.00
Ribbon, Compote, Dolphin Base, Frosted, 7 X 8 1/2 In. 265.00
Ribbon, Frosted, Butter, Cover, Collared Base 65.00
Ribbon, Frosted, Spooner 18.00
Ring Band, Butter, Cover, Rose Enamel 165.00
Ring Band, Spooner, Rose Enamel 50.00
Ring Band, Sugar, Rose Enamel 120.00
Rising Sun, Butter, Cover, Green, Gold Trim 85.00
Rising Sun, Goblet, Gold Trim 25.00
Rising Sun, Toothpick 35.00
Rising Sun, Water Set, Green Sun, 5 Piece 125.00
Riverside's Victoria, Sugar, Cover, Ruby Stained 130.00
    ROCHELLE, see Princess Feather
Rock of Ages, Bread Plate, Milk Glass Center .... 115.00 To 150.00
Roman Key, Dish, Honey, Flint, 3 1/2 In. 15.00
Roman Key, Frosted, Celery Vase, Footed 75.00
Roman Key, Wine, Flint, Crystal & Frosted 45.00
Roman Rosette, Cake Stand, 10 1/2 In. 40.00
Roman Rosette, Creamer 21.00
Roman Rosette, Pitcher, Water 85.00
Roman Rosette, Sugar, Cover 40.00
Romeo, Cruet 30.00
Rooster, Butter, Cover, Dog Finial, Child's 145.00

Liberty Bell   Lily-of-the-Valley

Rooster, Creamer, Child's	125.00
Rope & Ribs, Sugar, Cover, Vaseline	45.00
Rope & Thumbprint, Candy Dish, Cover, Amber	75.00
Rope & Thumbprint, Sugar Shaker, Blue	65.00
Rope & Thumbprint, Syrup, Amber	85.00
Rose In Snow, Butter, Cover	50.00
Rose In Snow, Compote, 6 In.	30.00
Rose In Snow, Compote, 8 In.	45.00
Rose In Snow, Compote, Cover, 7 X 8 In.	80.00
Rose In Snow, Goblet, Amber	25.00 To 45.00
Rose In Snow, Plate, 6 In.	32.00
Rose In Snow, Plate, 7 In.	32.00
Rose In Snow, Relish	19.50
Rose In Snow, Spooner	35.00
Rose Sprig, Cake Stand	65.00
Rose Sprig, Cake Stand, Blue	85.00
Rose Sprig, Celery Vase, Amber	43.00
Rose Sprig, Compote, Open	32.00
Rose Sprig, Pitcher, Water, Amber	68.00
Rose Sprig, Relish, Blue, Boat Shape	38.00
Rosette & Palms, Wine	16.00
ROSETTE MEDALLION, see Feather Duster	
Rosette, Cake Stand	30.00
Rosette, Pitcher, Milk	50.00
Royal Ivy, Cruet, Cranberry, Frosted	250.00
Royal Ivy, Pitcher, Water, Frosted, Cranberry	225.00 To 250.00
Royal Ivy, Syrup, Cranberry	300.00 To 450.00
Royal Ivy, Table Set, Cranberry & Frosted, 4 Piece	750.00
Royal Ivy, Toothpick, Frosted, Cranberry	100.00
Royal Ivy, Tumbler, Cranberry	72.50
Royal Ivy, Tumbler, Frosted, Cranberry	75.00
Royal Lady, Celery Vase	50.00
Royal Lady, Compote, Cover, 8 In.	80.00
Royal Oak, Butter, Cover, Cranberry, Frosted	165.00
Royal Oak, Pitcher, Square Top, Frosted	85.00
Royal Oak, Saltshaker, Cranberry	55.00
Royal Oak, Sugar Shaker, Frosted	65.00
Royal Oak, Toothpick, Rubina	100.00
RUBY ROSETTE, see Hero	
RUBY THUMBPRINT, see King's Crown	
Rustic, Sugar, Cover	30.00

S–Repeat, Butter, Cover, Green, Gold Trim 125.00
S–Repeat, Toothpick, Blue 37.50
S–Repeat, Tumbler, Blue .... 40.00 To 65.00
    SANDWICH LOOP, see also Hairpin
    SAWTOOTH BAND, see Amazon
Sawtooth, Butter, Cover 55.00
Sawtooth, Butter, Cover, Child's 25.00
Sawtooth, Cake Stand 35.00
Sawtooth, Compote, Cover, 14 1/2 In. 350.00
Sawtooth, Spill 46.50
Sawtooth, Spooner .... 25.00 To 45.00
Saxon, Wine, Etched 16.50
Scalloped Prism, Wine 18.00
Scalloped Swirl, Table Set, 4 Piece 250.00
    SCALLOPED TAPE, see Jewel Band
Scarab, Champagne, Flint 375.00
Scroll Medallion, Sugar, Cover 30.00
Scroll With Cane Band, Butter, Cover, Amber Stained 125.00
Scroll With Flowers, Sandwich Server 35.00
Scroll With Flowers, Wine, Green 65.00
    SEDAN, see Paneled Star & Button
Seed Pod, Butter, Cover, Blue, Gold Trim 150.00
Seed Pod, Celery Vase 65.00
Seed Pod, Creamer, Blue, Gold Trim 65.00
Seed Pod, Pitcher, Blue, Gold Trim 125.00
Seed Pod, Sugar, Cover 65.00
Seneca Loop, Compote, Scalloped, Flint 65.00
Seneca Loop, Cordial, 2 5/8 In. 35.00
Sequoia, Butter, Cover 50.00
Sequoia, Platter, 8 1/2 X 13 In. 35.00
Serrated Prism, Toothpick, Tarentum 38.00
    SHEAF OF WHEAT, see Wheat Sheaf
Shell & Jewel, Pitcher, Water 40.00
Shell & Jewel, Water Set, Blue, 3 Piece 95.00
Shell & Tassel, Bowl, Amber, Oval, 10 In. 105.00
Shell & Tassel, Bread Tray, 8 X 12 In. 57.50
Shell & Tassel, Butter, Cover, Dog Finial 95.00
Shell & Tassel, Compote, 7 1/2 In. 55.00
Shell & Tassel, Compote, 9 1/2 In. 82.00
Shell & Tassel, Pitcher, Water, Square 225.00
Shell & Tassel, Salt & Pepper 225.00
Shell & Tassel, Table Set, 4 Piece 260.00
Shell & Tassel, Vase, Copper Wheel Engraving, 7 1/2 In. 110.00
Shell, Pitcher, Water 50.00
Shell, Spooner 16.00
Sheraton, Goblet 18.00
Shield & Anchor, Goblet 75.00
Shields, Spooner 22.00
    SHOSHONE, see Victor
Shrine, Pitcher, Water 37.50
Shuttle, Creamer 20.00
Shuttle, Spooner 20.00
Shuttle, Wine 18.00
Six Panel Finecut, Pitcher, Amber 65.00
Skilton, Butter, Cover, Ruby Stained 97.50
Skilton, Compote, Ruby Stained, 7 In. 67.50
Skilton, Sauce, Footed, 4 In. 8.00
Skilton, Spooner, Ruby Stained 44.50
Skilton, Sugar, Cover, Ruby Stained 82.50
Skilton, Tumbler, Ruby 40.00
Slewed Horseshoe, Butter, Cover 95.00
Slewed Horseshoe, Cruet 35.00
Snail, Bowl, 8 In. 50.00

Snail, Bowl, 9 In. 54.00
Snail, Bowl, Oval, 5 1/4 X 8 In. 30.00
Snail, Butter, Cover .... 40.00 To 72.50
Snail, Cake Stand, 10 In. 130.00
Snail, Rose Bowl, 3 In. 55.00
Snail, Salt & Pepper, Square 48.00
Snail, Spooner .... 34.50 To 60.00
Snake Drape, Goblet 18.00
Snowflake & Sunburst, Pitcher 50.00
Spanish American, Pitcher, Dewey, Battleship Olympia, Flags 65.00
Spanish American, Pitcher, Water .... 42.50 To 45.00
Spanish American, Plate, Manilla, 1898 .... 70.00
Spanish American, Water Set, 7 Piece .... 350.00 To 400.00
    SPANISH COIN, see Columbian Coin
Spearpoint Band, Toothpick, Ruby Stained 82.50
Spearpoint, Sugar 20.00
Spirea Band, Cake Stand, Blue 95.00
Spirea Band, Goblet, Amber 32.50
Spirea Band, Goblet, Blue 20.00
Spirea Band, Sugar, Cover, Etched 35.00
Sprig, Butter, Cover 65.00
Sprig, Cake Stand, 8 1/2 In. 35.00
Sprig, Cake Stand, 9 1/2 In. 40.00
Sprig, Compote, Cover, High Standard, 8 In. 60.00
Sprig, Compote, Cover, Low Standard, 6 In. 50.00
Sprig, Spooner 25.00
Sprig, Wine .... 30.00 To 45.00
Square Fuchsia, Creamer 25.00
Square Fuchsia, Pitcher, Water, Amber 90.00
Square Fuchsia, Salt, Cover, Pink 21.00
Square Fuchsia, Wine, Amber 95.00
Square Panes, Compote, Cover, 8 In. 85.00
Square Panes, Goblet, Etched 35.00
Square Panes, Salt, Apple Green, Individual 45.00
Squared Ashburton, Tumbler, Footed, Flint 47.50
Squat Pineapple, Berry Bowl, Green, 10 In. 50.00
Squat Pineapple, Bowl, Green, 9 In. 33.00
Squirrel With Nut, Pitcher, Water 150.00
Squirrel, Pitcher, Water .... 110.00 To 150.00
Squirrel, Sauce, Footed, Scalloped, 4 1/2 In. 55.00
Star & Feather, Plate, 7 In. 40.00
    STAR & PUNTY, see Moon & Star
    STAR BAND, see Bosworth
Star In Bull's–Eye, Toothpick 15.00
Star Whorl, Goblet 16.00
Stars & Stripes, Cruet, Blue 65.00
    STATES, see The States
    STAYMAN, see Rustic
Stedman, Wine, Flint 50.00
Stippled Arrow, Mug, Child's 12.00
Stippled Chain, Goblet 15.00
Stippled Chain, Spooner 25.00
Stippled Cherry, Pitcher, Water 35.00
Stippled Double Loop, Creamer 30.00
Stippled Double Loop, Goblet 47.50
Stippled Fleur–De–Lis, Goblet 35.00
Stippled Forget–Me–Not, Plate, Baby In Tub, 7 In. 47.50
Stippled Forget–Me–Not, Spooner, Child's 16.50
Stippled Forget–Me–Not, Tumbler 20.00
Stippled Grape & Festoon, Spooner, Stippled Leaf 25.00
Stippled Grape & Festoon, Water Set, Clear Leaf, 7 Piece 135.00
    STIPPLED PANELED FLOWER, see Maine

STIPPLED SCROLL, see Scroll

Stork, Goblet	55.00
Stork, Spooner	37.50
Strawberry & Currant, Goblet	20.00 To 25.00
Strawberry, Plate, Child's, Blue	35.00
Strawberry, Spooner	18.50
Strawberry, Sugar	35.00
Strawberry, Water Set, 7 Piece	235.00
Style, Compote, Open, Child's	20.00
Style, Pitcher, Water	40.00
Style, Sauce, Footed	14.00
Style, Table Set, Child's, 4 Piece	75.00 To 85.00
Style, Toothpick	25.00
Summit, Creamer, Ruby Flashed	65.00
Summit, Spooner, Ruby Flashed	65.00
Sunflower, Cake Plate, Green	9.00
Sunk Buttons, Sauce, Amber	5.00
Sunk Daisy, Wine	18.50
Sunk Honeycomb, Cake Stand, Ruby Stained	125.00
Sunk Honeycomb, Goblet, Etched	35.00

SUNRISE, see Rising Sun

Swag Block, Bowl, Amber Blocks, Engraved, 8 1/4 In.	35.00
Swag Bracket, Table Set, Amethyst, Gold Trim, 4 Piece	450.00
Swag With Brackets, Berry Bowl, Blue Opal, 8 In.	58.00
Swag With Brackets, Pitcher, Water, Vaseline	175.00
Swag With Brackets, Saltshaker, Amethyst, Gold Trim	45.00
Swag With Brackets, Spooner, Blue	50.00
Swag With Brackets, Sugar, Vaseline	75.00
Swag With Brackets, Table Set, Green, 4 Piece	275.00
Swag With Brackets, Toothpick, Green, Gold Trim	65.00
Swan, Pitcher, Water	145.00 To 160.00
Swan, Sugar, Blue	45.00
Sweetheart, Sugar & Creamer, Spooner, Cover, Child's	40.00
Sweetheart, Table Set, Child's, 4 Piece	85.00
Swirl & Panel, Toothpick	14.00
Swirl Diamond, Pitcher, Water, Ruby Stained	195.00
Swirl, Berry Set, Frosted, Amber, 7 Piece	245.00
Swirl, Celery Vase	30.00
Swirl, Pitcher, Water	90.00
Sylvan, Toothpick	28.00
Tacoma, Plate, Amber Flashed	60.00
Tacoma, Punch Cup, Amber Stained	40.00
Tacoma, Table Set, 4 Piece	245.00
Tacoma, Tumbler, Ruby Stained	42.50
Tandem Bicycle, Goblet	18.00

TAPE MEASURE, see Shields

Tappan, Spooner, Child's, Amber	15.00
Tappan, Sugar & Creamer, Cover, Child's, Amber	25.00
Tappan, Table Set, Child's, 4 Piece	65.00
Tarentum Thumbprint, Toothpick, Green Opaque, Souvenir	30.00
Tarentum's Atlanta, Syrup	48.00
Tarentum's Atlanta, Table Set, Ruby Stained	245.00
Tarentum's Atlanta, Wine	48.00

TEARDROP, see Teardrop & Thumbprint

Teardrop & Tassel, Pitcher, Water	65.00 To 75.00
Teardrop & Tassel, Tumbler, Blue	45.00 To 50.00
Teardrop & Thumbprint, Butter, Cover, Blue	60.00
Teardrop & Thumbprint, Goblet	24.00
Tennessee, Bowl, 8 1/2 In.	25.00
Tennessee, Cake Stand	45.00 To 48.00
Tennessee, Relish	26.00

Teutonic, Plate, 7 In. 9.50
    TEXAS BULL'S–EYE, see Bull's–Eye Variant
Texas Star, Butter 45.00
Texas, Toothpick 14.00
Texas, Toothpick, Gold Trim .... 20.00 To 27.00
The States, Creamer, 3 In. .... 25.00 To 30.00
The States, Cruet, Stopper 55.00
The States, Punch Bowl & Base, 2 Piece 95.00
The States, Salt & Pepper 50.00
The States, Spooner, 5 1/2 In. 25.00
The States, Wine 20.00
Theodore Roosevelt, Bread Plate, Dancing Bears 140.00
Thistle, Celery Vase 45.00
Thistle, Pitcher, Water, 6 1/2 In. 125.00
Thousand Eye, Bread Plate, Folded Corners, 10 In. 22.50
Thousand Eye, Cake Stand, Blue, 10 In. .... 75.00 To 100.00
Thousand Eye, Celery Vase .... 32.00 To 35.00
Thousand Eye, Compote, Blue, Square 85.00
Thousand Eye, Goblet, Amber .... 20.00 To 25.00
Thousand Eye, Mug, Amber 8.00
Thousand Eye, Mug, Blue .... 15.00 To 20.00
Thousand Eye, Pitcher, Milk, Amber, 6 3/4 In. 65.00
Thousand Eye, Plate, Folded Corners, Blue, 6 In. 10.00
Thousand Eye, Plate, Folded Corners, Blue, 10 In. 20.00
Thousand Eye, Plate, Vaseline, 8 In. 32.00
Thousand Eye, Platter, Amber, 8 X 11 In. 30.00
Thousand Eye, Salt & Pepper, Amber, Blue Band 10.00
Thousand Eye, Sauce, 3–Knob Stem, Vaseline, 4 1/2 In. 10.00
Thousand Eye, Spooner, 3–Knob Stem, Blue, 5 1/2 In. 20.00
Thousand Eye, Toothpick, Vaseline 30.00
Three Birds, Flowerpot 45.00
Three Birds, Pitcher, Water 135.00
Three Face, Butter, Cover 170.00
Three Face, Cake Stand, 10 1/2 In. 195.00
Three Face, Cake Stand, Clear & Frosted, 9 X 7 1/2 IIN. 125.00
Three Face, Claret 165.00
Three Face, Compote, Cover, 8 In. 125.00
Three Face, Pitcher, Water, Clear & Frosted 450.00
Three Face, Spooner 65.00
    THREE GRACES, see also Three Face
Three Graces, Bread Plate, Faith, Hope & Charity, 11 1/2 In. 45.00
Three Panel, Creamer 21.00

Mitered Diamond

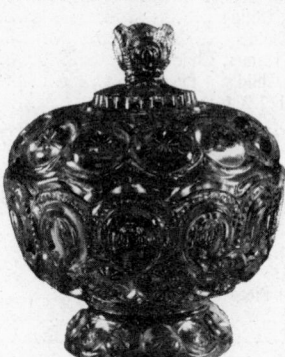

Moon & Star

New England Pineapple

Three Panel, Goblet, Amber 30.00
Three Panel, Spooner 23.00
Three Panel, Table Set, Blue, 4 Piece 235.00
Three Presidents, Bread Plate .... 35.00 To 75.00
Three Presidents, Goblet 275.00
    THREE SISTERS, see Three Face
Thumbprint, Celery Vase, Flint 125.00
Thumbprint, Celery Vase, Ruby Stained 125.00
Thumbprint, Compote, Ruby Stained, 7 1/4 X 7 In. 145.00
Thumbprint, Decanter 50.00
Thumbprint, Pitcher, Water 250.00
Thumbprint, Toothpick, Ruby Stained, Engraved 36.50
    TIDY, see Rustic
Tiny Lion, Celery Vase, Etched .... 27.50 To 40.00
Tiny Lion, Compote, Cover, 7 1/2 In. 95.00
    TOBIN, see Leaf & Star
Togo, Goblet 20.00
Togo, Sugar & Creamer 35.00
Toltec, Tumbler 18.50
Torpedo, Bowl, 8 1/4 In. 16.00
Torpedo, Butter, Cover 46.00
Torpedo, Compote, Fluted Rim 145.00
Torpedo, Goblet .... 45.00 To 50.00
Torpedo, Pitcher, Milk, Ruby Stained 125.00
Torpedo, Spooner 32.00
Torpedo, Tankard, Milk, Ruby Stained 175.00
Torpedo, Tumbler 28.50
Tree of Life With Hand, Compote 166.00
Tree of Life, Celery Vase, Silver-Plated Holder 135.00
Tree of Life, Pitcher, Water, Pittsburgh 68.00
Tree of Life, Portland, Compote, Meriden Metal Holder 185.00
Tree of Life, Portland, Creamer, Blue, Silver-Plated Holder 225.00
Tree of Life, Portland, Sugar & Creamer, Cover, Silver Holder 125.00
Trilby, Goblet 90.00
Trilby, Pitcher 125.00
Triple Band, Pitcher, Water, Hinged Pewter Lid 85.00
Triple Triangle, Cordial, Ruby Stained 20.00
Triple Triangle, Goblet, Ruby Stained 34.50
Triple Triangle, Wine 35.00
Trophy, Toothpick, Ruby Stain 25.00
Truncated Cube, Table Set, Ruby Stained, 4 Piece 200.00
Truncated Cube, Toothpick, Ruby Stained 30.00
Tulip & Honeycomb, Punch Set, Child's 55.00
Tulip & Honeycomb, Spooner, Child's 10.00
Tulip & Honeycomb, Sugar & Creamer, Child's 25.00
Tulip & Honeycomb, Table Set, Child's, 4 Piece .... 85.00 To 125.00
Tulip Band, Compote, Cover, 7 1/2 X 6 In. 30.00
Tulip Petals, Toothpick 22.00
Tulip With Sawtooth, Decanter, Stopper, Flint, 11 1/2 In. 90.00
Tulip With Sawtooth, Spooner 28.00
Tulip With Sawtooth, Toothpick 40.00
Twin Snowshoes, Creamer, Child's 15.00
Twin Snowshoes, Sugar, Cover, Child's 65.00
Twin Teardrops, Butter, Cover 25.00
    TWINKLE STAR, see Utah
Twist, Table Set, Blue, Frosted, 4 Piece 150.00
Twisted Hobnail, Toothpick 15.00
Two Band, Creamer 28.00
Two Panel, Celery Vase, Vaseline 45.00
Two Panel, Goblet 15.00
Two Panel, Spooner 35.00
Two Panel, Wine, Amber 18.00
U.S. Coin, Celery Vase, Frosted, 6 1/4 In. 350.00

U.S. Coin, Dish, Frosted Coins, 7 1/2 In. 235.00
U.S. Coin, Dish, Pickle, 10 Half Dollars, Frosted, 8 In. 395.00
U.S. Coin, Goblet, Dimes, Frosted 325.00
U.S. Coin, Relish, Frosted 90.00
U.S. Coin, Salt & Pepper 25.00
U.S. Coin, Toothpick 125.00
U.S. Coin, Toothpick, Frosted Silver Dollars 75.00
U.S. Coin, Tumbler, Dimes Frosted 235.00
U.S.Coin, Cake Stand, Frosted Dollars 550.00
Utah, Compote, Cover, 5 In. 28.00
Utah, Pitcher, 9 1/4 In. .... 25.00 To 35.00
Utah, Pitcher, Water .... 40.00 To 45.00
V–In–Heart, Banana Stand 35.00
Valencia Waffle, Butter, Cover, Green 60.00
Valencia Waffle, Celery Vase 30.00
    VALENTINE, see Trilby
Vermont, Berry Set, Green, 5 Piece 65.00
Vermont, Goblet, Green, Gold Trim 45.00
Vermont, Toothpick, Green, Gold Trim .... 55.00 To 65.00
Vermont, Tumbler, Green, Gold Trim .... 24.00 To 60.00
Victor, Butter, Cover, Gold Trim 62.50
Victor, Cake Stand, Green 45.00
Victor, Cruet, Green 70.00
Victor, Sugar, Cover, Ruby Stained 85.00
Victor, Table Set, Ruby Stained, 3 Piece 265.00
Victor, Toothpick, Ruby Trim 53.00
Viking, Butter, Cover .... 45.00 To 85.00
Viking, Celery Vase 42.00
Viking, Creamer 35.00
Viking, Jar, Apothecary, Stopper 65.00
Viking, Jar, Pickle, Ground Stopper 55.00
Viking, Pitcher, Water, Large 65.00
Viking, Sauce, Footed .... 12.25 To 30.00
Viking, Sugar & Creamer 85.00
    VIRGINIA, see also Galloway
Virginia, Butter, Cover 140.00
Waffle & Thumbprint, Spill, Flint 40.00
Waffle & Thumbprint, Sugar, Cover 195.00
Waffle & Thumbprint, Wine, Flint 48.00
Waffle, Celery Vase 50.00
Waffle, Creamer, Flint, 6 3/4 In. 77.50
Waffle, Vase, Flint, 9 In. 35.00

Parrot & Fan

Pennsylvania

Pleat & Panel

Ribbon Candy   Roman Rosette   Romeo

Waffle, Wine	95.00
Warrior, Bread Plate, 11 In.	75.00
Washboard, Soap Dish, Amber	75.00
Washboard, Sugar, Cover	35.00
Washington Centennial, Eggcup, Pedestal	37.50
Washington Centennial, Relish, Paw Handles, Oval, Dated	45.00
Washington Centennial, Syrup, Dated Pewter Lid	165.00
Washington Centennial, Wine	48.00
Washington, Celery Vase	85.00
Washington, Sugar, Cover, Clear & Frosted, Enamel Design	55.00
Washington, Sugar, Cover, Pink & Frosted Flowers	45.00
Wedding Bells, Cruet	48.50
Wee Branches, Cup & Saucer, Child's	35.00 To 50.00
Wee Branches, Sugar, Child's	25.00
Wellington, Water Set, Ruby Stained, 5 Piece	195.00
Westward Ho, Compote, 8 1/2 In.	150.00
Westward Ho, Compote, 9 1/2 In.	95.00
Westward Ho, Compote, 11 X 6 In.	190.00
Westward Ho, Creamer	130.00
Westward Ho, Goblet	30.00 To 60.00
Westward Ho, Nested Bowls, 6 1/2 To 12 In., 5 Piece	645.00
Westward Ho, Sugar, Cover, Footed	140.00
Wheat & Barley, Bread Plate, 9 In.	20.00
Wheat & Barley, Butter, Cover	45.00
Wheat & Barley, Cake Stand, 11 In.	45.00
Wheat & Barley, Goblet, Blue	25.00
Wheat & Barley, Mug, Amber	28.00
Wheat & Barley, Pitcher, Milk	40.00
Wheat & Barley, Pitcher, Water	50.00
Wheat & Barley, Tumbler, Amber	55.00
Wheat Sheaf, Bread Plate	60.00
Wheat Sheaf, Pitcher, Water	30.00 To 52.00
Wheat Sheaf, Punch Bowl, Child's	35.00
WHIRLIGIG, see Buzz Star	
Whirlwind, Tumbler	15.00
Wild Bouquet, Spooner, Blue	55.00
Wild Fern, Goblet	27.00
Wild Rose With Bowknot, Pitcher, Water, Frosted	20.00
Wild Rose, Toothpick, Scrolling, Gold Trim	110.00
Wildflower, Creamer, Blue	35.00
Wildflower, Drinking Set, Amber, 7 Piece	110.00
Wildflower, Goblet, Amber	18.00
Wildflower, Goblet, Canary	35.00
Wildflower, Pitcher, Water, Apple Green	95.00
Wildflower, Spooner, Amber	32.00
Wildflower, Sugar & Creamer	60.00
Wildflower, Syrup, Pewter Top, Amber	125.00 To 135.00

Wildflower, Tumbler, Vaseline 30.00
Wildflower, Wine, Amber 20.00
Willow Oak, Bread Plate 25.00
Willow Oak, Butter, Cover, Amber 55.00
Willow Oak, Cake Stand, Blue, 9 In. 55.00
Willow Oak, Celery Vase, Pedestal, 8 In. 75.00
Willow Oak, Creamer, Amber .... 38.00 To 45.00
Willow Oak, Creamer, Blue 55.00
Willow Oak, Goblet .... 30.00 To 35.00
Willow Oak, Goblet, Amber .... 35.00 To 40.00
Willow Oak, Plate, Amber, 9 In. 35.00
Willow Oak, Plate, Blue, 9 In. 35.00
Willow Oak, Salt & Pepper 65.00
Willow Oak, Sauce, Footed 10.00
Willow Oak, Wine, Amber 28.00
Windflower, Butter, Cover, Thistle Finial 42.00
Windflower, Goblet 45.00
Winged Scrolls, Box, Trinket, Cover, Green, Gold Trim, 3 In. 62.50
Winged Scrolls, Saltshaker 72.50
Wisconsin, Banana Stand, Pedestal 72.00
Wisconsin, Butter, Cover 95.00
Wisconsin, Cake Stand .... 35.00 To 45.00
Wisconsin, Punch Cup 18.00
Wisconsin, Saltshaker 55.00
   WOODEN PAIL, see Oaken Bucket
Wreath & Bars, Goblet 21.00
Wreath & Shell, Berry Set, Vaseline, 7 Piece 245.00
Wreath & Shell, Creamer, Blue 95.00
Wreath & Shell, Rose Bowl, Vaseline 85.00
Wreath & Shell, Salt, Blue Opalescent 58.00
Wreath & Shell, Table Set, Blue, 4 Piece 495.00
Wreathed Cherry, Sugar & Creamer, Amber 20.00
Wyoming, Butter, Cover .... 50.00 To 100.00
Wyoming, Syrup, Cover .... 75.00 To 85.00
X–Ray, Bottle, Water, Green 35.00
X–Ray, Butter, Cover, Green, Gold Trim 95.00
X–Ray, Sugar, Cover, Green, Gold Trim 65.00
X–Ray, Table Set, Green, Gold Trim, 4 Piece 300.00
X–Ray, Toothpick, Green, Gold Trim 45.00
X–Ray, Water Set, Green, Gold Trim, 5 Piece .... 215.00 To 230.00
   YALE, see Crowfoot
Yoked Loop, Goblet 18.00
York Herringbone, Tumbler .... 15.00 To 20.00
York Herringbone, Tumbler, Ruby Flashed 28.00
York, Champagne, Etched 58.00
Yuma Loop, Goblet, Buttermilk, Flint 32.50
Zanesville, Butter, Cover 67.50
Zipper Slash, Creamer, Ruby Flashed 65.00
Zipper Slash, Sugar, Ruby Flashed 60.00
Zipper Slash, Toothpick 25.00

Tree of Life

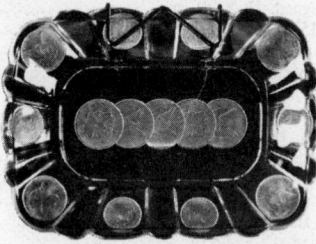

U.S. Coin

Waffle & Thumbprint

Washington Centennial

Westward Ho

Print, in this listing, means any of many printed images produced on paper by one of the more common methods, such as lithography. The prints listed here are of interest primarily to the antiques collector, not the fine arts collector. Many of these prints were originally part of books. Other prints will be found in the sections headed Currier & Ives, Advertising, and Poster.

PRINT, Armstrong, Black Lace, 16 X 20 In.	25.00
Armstrong, Double Orange, 20 X 20 In.	25.00
Armstrong, Dream Girl, 16 X 20 In.	25.00
Armstrong, June, Framed, 16 X 20 In.	160.00

Audubon bird prints were originally issued as part of books printed from 1826 to 1854. They were issued in two sizes, 26 1/2 in. by 39 1/2 in. and 11 in. by 7 in. The quadrupeds were issued in 28 in. by 22 in. size prints. Later editions of the Audubon books were done in many sizes and reprints of the books in the original size were also made. The bird pictures have been so popular they have been copied in myriad sizes by both old and new printing methods. This list includes originals and later copies because Audubon prints of all ages are sold in antiques shops.

Audubon, Boat–Tailed Grackle, Elephant Portfolio	5400.00
Audubon, Goldfinch, No.37, Reprint, Framed	165.00
Audubon, Wood Warbler, No.16, Reprint	165.00
Breed, Woodcut, Terra Intermina, Lakes, Mountains, 47 1/2 X 18 1/2 In.	125.00
Brown & Bigelow, G. Washington, G. Stuart, Framed, 21 X 18 In.	75.00
Cupid Awake, Cupid Asleep, Sepia, Copyright 1897, 6 X 8 In., Pair	22.00
Davidson, Hearthside Comfort, Framed, 5 X 7 1/2 In.	45.00
Davidson, Lambs May Feast, Framed, 12 In.	60.00
Drew, Winter Landscape, Signed, 16 X 20 In.	650.00
Elvgren, French Dressing, 15 X 20 In.	20.00
Elvgren, Man's Best Friend	35.00
Fisher, Chief Interest, Oval Metal Frame, 5 X 7 In.	22.00
Fisher, Indian Maid, Signed, 1906, 11 X 10 In.	35.00
Fisher, Lady With Umbrella, Signed, 1906, 11 X 10 In.	35.00
Fisher, Opera Night, Framed, 1910, 12 X 14 In.	75.00
Fisher, Sweetheart, Signed, 1907, 11 X 10 In.	35.00
Fox, A May Day, Sheep Scene, Framed, 1908, 19 1/2 X 15 1/2 In.	75.00
Fox, Blossom Time	35.00
Fox, Clipper Ship, 15 X 19 In.	50.00
Fox, Cottage Flowers, Framed, 15 X 12 In.	60.00
Fox, Dawn, 8 X 14 In.	28.00
Fox, Dreamland, Framed, 21 1/2 X 13 1/2 In.	65.00

Fox, Fallen Monarch	45.00
Fox, Garden Fence, Trees, Framed	45.00
Fox, Garden of Happiness, 14 X 22 In.	95.00
Fox, Garden of Romance, 25 X 17 In.	80.00
Fox, Garden Path, Mountains, Framed, 16 X 22 In.	75.00
Fox, Good Shepherd, 12 X 20 In.	50.00
Fox, Heart's Desire	125.00
Fox, Homeward Bound, Man On Horseback, Child Riding Cow, 16 X 19 In.	140.00
Fox, Landscape, Lake, Signed, 20 X 16 In.	1200.00
Fox, Love's Paradise, Framed, 18 1/2 X 11 In.	48.50
Fox, Love's Paradise, Large	125.00
Fox, Mount Hood	45.00
Fox, Nature's Beauty	70.00
Fox, Poppies, Framed, 15 X 20 In.	68.00
Fox, Seascape, 1908, 14 1/2 X 5 In.	25.00
Fox, Three Moose, 15 X 12 In.	95.00
Fuller, Golf Scene	175.00
Gemmell, In The Woods, Framed, 13 1/4 X 7 1/4 In.	35.00
Godey, 5 Women & Child, February 1879, Matted, 8 1/2 X 10 In.	30.00
Goodwin, Through Dangerous Waters, 16 X 20 In.	75.00
Gould, Pair of Ducks, Hand Colored, 14 X 20 In.	145.00
Gutmann, A Little Bit of Heaven, Framed, 21 In. .... 60.00 To 75.00
Gutmann, Awakening, Original Frame	50.00
Gutmann, Bride & Groom, Framed	125.00
Gutmann, Butterfly	150.00
Gutmann, Contentment, 4 X 7 1/2 In.	50.00
Gutmann, Cupid With Butterfly, 12 X 15 In.	95.00
Gutmann, Daddy's Coming	240.00
Gutmann, Good Morning, 8 1/2 X 11 1/2 In.	125.00
Gutmann, Lovebirds, Framed, 12 X 16 In.	95.00
Gutmann, Miss Flirt, 12 1/2 X 15 1/2 In.	60.00
Gutmann, New Love, 13 X 16 In.	40.00
Gutmann, On Dreamland's Border, Round Frame	175.00
Gutmann, On The Up & Up, Boy, Dog, Crawling Upstairs ...	48.00
Gutmann, Sweet Innocence, Oval, 14 1/2 In.	85.00
Gutmann, Sympathy, 21 X 14 In.	50.00
Hare, Jr., Pretty Woman, Red Hat, Metal Oval Frame, 1912, 8 X 10 In.	25.00
Howe, Sioux Mourning Rider, Indian On Horse, 23 X 18 3/4 In.	100.00
Humphrey, Snowballing Summer, Gold Frame, 11 3/4 X 15 1/2 In.	100.00
Humphrey, Snowballing Winter, Gold Frame, 11 3/4 X 15 1/2 In.	195.00
Icart, After The Raid, Signed, C.1917, 15 1/4 X 19 17/18 In.	995.00
Icart, Apple Girl	175.00
Icart, Blue Alcove, Oval Frame, Signed, 10 3/4 X 13 1/4 In.	1550.00
Icart, Bountiful Harvest, Drypoint	1500.00
Icart, Casanova, 1928, 14 X 21 In.	1400.00
Icart, Casanova, Signed, Copyright 1928, 20 3/4 X 13 3/4 In.	1450.00
Icart, Chestnut Vendor, Signed, 1928, 19 1/2 X 14 1/2 In.	1650.00
Icart, Cinderella, Signed, 1927, 15 1/2 X 19 In.	1760.00
Icart, Colored, 2 Girls & 2 Swans, Framed, 1937, 29 X 25 In.	7250.00
Icart, Colored, Young Woman, With Peaches, 1924, 25 X 20 In.	1300.00
Icart, Coursing II, Signed, 1929, Framed, 15 3/4 X 25 1/2 In.	5500.00
Icart, Dollar, Etching of Dog, Framed	3575.00
Icart, Don Juan, Framed	1850.00
Icart, Hydrangeas, Signed, 1929, 16 3/4 X 21 In.	1650.00
Icart, Kiss of The Motherland, Signed, C.1917, 19 1/2 X 11 1/2 In.	3575.00
Icart, Kittens, Etched	1000.00
Icart, La Lettre, Gold Frame, 1928, 15 1/2 X 19 In.	295.00
Icart, Les Chats	1200.00
Icart, Louise, Signed, 1927, 21 X 14 In.	1750.00
Icart, Love's Blossom .... 6500.00 To 8500.00
Icart, Lovers, Signed, 1930, 21 X 14 1/8 In.	1450.00
Icart, Madame Bovary, 1929, 20 X 16 In.	850.00
Icart, Message In The Tree	1850.00
Icart, Parasol	1200.00

Tips on framing paper documents and prints: No glue, scotch tape, rubber cement. No scissors—don't trim anything. No pencils or pens, don't try to rewrite an autograph. No staples or clips. No extremes of temperature or humidity. No direct sunlight—it fades the ink.

Print, Kurz & Allison, Siege of Vicksburg,
17 1/2 X 24 3/4 In.

Icart, Perfect Harmony, Signed, Framed, 13 1/4 X 17 1/4 In.		4450.00
Icart, Pierrette, By Moonlight, Signed, 1927, 21 1/8 X 14 1/4 In.		1450.00
Icart, Spanish Shawl, Signed, C.1922, 15 3/4 X 12 3/4 In.		2100.00
Icart, Winter, Framed, 10 1/2 X 7 1/2 In.		1100.00

Japanese woodblock prints are listed as follows: Print, Japanese, name of artist, title or description, type, and size. Dealers use the following terms: Tate–e is a vertical composition. Yoko–e is a horizontal composition. The words Aiban (13 by 9 inches), Chuban (10 by 7 1/2 inches), Hosoban (12 by 6 inches), Oban (15 by 10 inches), and Koban (7 by 4 inches) denote size. Modern versions of some of these prints have been made.

Japanese, Chikanobu, 2 Women, Color, 14 X 9 3/8 In.		110.00
Japanese, Eisen, Olso, Courtesan Motozue, C.1838, 14 1/4 X 9 3/4 In.		2400.00
Japanese, Hiroshige, Hodogaya, C.1833, 9 1/4 X 14 In.		4000.00
Japanese, Hiroshige, Hodogaya, C.1842, 8 3/4 X 13 1/2 In.		2400.00
Japanese, Hiroshige, Kawasaki, C.1850, 9 X 14 1/4 In.		1800.00
Japanese, Hiroshige, Numazu, C.1833, 9 3/4 X 14 1/2 In.		6000.00
Japanese, Kiyochika, Steam Engine Crossing Rice Paddy, 1880		1750.00
Japanese, Koryusai, Carp, C.1770, 27 X 4 1/2 In.		9000.00
Japanese, Koryusai, Young Couple, C.1770, 27 X 4 3/4 In.		7000.00
Japanese, Kunichika, Triptych, 19th Century, 14 X 9 In.		302.00
Japanese, Kuniyoshi, Hara Mototoki, C.1847, 14 1/2 X 10 In.		900.00
Japanese, Kuniyoshi, Rori Hakucho Chojun, C.1827, 15 1/4 X 10 1/4 In.		2500.00
Japanese, Kuniyoshi, Soga Brothers, 1852, 14 1/4 X 9 3/4 In.		800.00
Japanese, Toyokuni I, Kabuki Actor, C.1815, 14 X 10 In.		1500.00
Japanese, Toyokuni III, Kabuki Actor, 14 1/2 X 10 In.		650.00
Japanese, Toyokuni III, Man's Portrait, 1852–53, 14 X 9 5/8 In.		143.00
Japanese, Utamaro, 2 Woman After A Bath, C.1802, 15 1/2 X 10 1/2 In.		7500.00
Japanese, Utamaro, Act X, C.1802, 13 3/4 X 9 In.		7500.00
Japanese, Utamaro, Courtesan Ashidome, C.1805, 15 X 10 1/4 In.		9000.00
Japanese, Utamaro, Plum Blossoms, C.1802, 14 X 9 In.		9000.00
Japanese, Yoshitoshi, Heron Maiden, 14 X 9 1/2 In.		3800.00
Japanese, Yoshitoshi, Omari & A Demon, 14 X 9 1/2 In.		2400.00
Japanese, Yoshitoshi, Sadanobu & The Demon, 14 X 9 1/2 In.		2400.00
Japanese, Yoshitoshi, Seigen's Ghost, 14 X 9 1/2 In.		2400.00
Kellogg & Comstock, My Little Pet, Framed, 16 X 12 1/4 In.		15.00
Kellogg & Comstock, Washington, Framed, 22 1/2 X 18 1/2 In.		90.00
Kellogg, Abraham Lincoln, 16th Pres., 9 X 12 3/4 In.		150.00
Kellogg, James Buchanan, Democrat Candidate, 15th Pres., 13 X 17 In.		100.00
Kellogg, Lieutenant General Ulysses S. Grant, 16 X 12 In.		45.00
Kellogg, Silhouette of Levi Woodbury, Framed, 12 1/2 X 16 3/4 In.		25.00

Kurz & Allison, Battle of Champion Hills, 1887, 22 X 28 In.	155.00
Kurz & Allison, Battle of Champion Hills, Miss., 17 1/2 X 25 In.	190.00
Kurz & Allison, Battle of Corinth, Miss., 17 1/2 X 25 In.	200.00
Kurz & Allison, Battle of Kenesaw Mountain, 17 1/2 X 25 In.	250.00
Kurz & Allison, Battle of New Orleans, 17 1/2 X 25 In.	250.00
Kurz & Allison, Capture of Fort Fisher, 17 1/2 X 25 In.	250.00
Kurz & Allison, Declaration of Independence, 16 X 22 In.	170.00
Kurz & Allison, Siege of Vicksburg, 17 1/2 X 24 3/4 In. ....*Illus*	247.00
Kurz & Allison, Storming Stony Point, 14 1/2 X 21 In.	40.00
Kurz & Allison, Yosemite Waterfalls, California, Sepia, Large Folio	170.00
Livemont, Biscuits Et Chocolat Delacre	6600.00
Lozowick, Under The El, Signed, Dated 1929, Framed, 7 1/2 X 11 1/8 In.	9000.00
Luckeray, Humorous Hunting Design, Framed, 1925	50.00
McKenny & Hall, Black Hoof, Shawnee Chief, 1838, 14 X 20 In.	180.00
McKenny & Hall, Katawabeda, Chippewa Chief, 1841, 14 X 20 In.	190.00
McKenny & Hall, Little Crow, Sioux Chief, 1838, 14 X 20 In.	140.00
McKenny & Hall, Makaska The Younger, Iowa Chief, 1838, 14 X 20 In.	170.00
McKenny & Hall, Mistippee, Creek Chief, 1833, 14 X 20 In.	220.00
McKenny & Hall, Snake Skin, Winnebago Chief, 1841, 14 X 20 In.	198.00
McKenny & Hall, Waapashaw, Sioux Chief, 1836, 14 X 20 In.	170.00
Moran, Where Silence Reigns, Framed, 11 X 8 3/4 In.	60.00
Moses, Forest, Signed, 15 X 20 In.	250.00
Moses, Mountain Landscape, Signed, 14 X 22 In.	350.00
Mozert, My Dream Girl, 22 X 28 In.	30.00
Nast, Santa Claus's Mail, Harper's Weekly, 1871	25.00
Nicholson, Wood Block, Sarah Bernhardt, Matted, Framed, 16 X 16 In.	125.00

> Wallace Nutting is known for his pictures, furniture, and books. Nutting "prints" are actually hand–colored photographs issued from 1900 to 1941. There are over 10,000 different titles.

Nutting, A Cold Day, 14 X 16 In.	275.00
Nutting, A Garden of Larkspur, Framed, 1914, 17 1/2 X 21 1/2 In.	65.00
Nutting, A Lake Shore Oak	55.00
Nutting, A Literary Damsel	632.00
Nutting, A Little River, Framed, Matted, 17 X 21 In.	75.00
Nutting, A Warm Spring Day	352.00
Nutting, Afternoon Tea	121.00
Nutting, Among October Birches, 14 X 17 In.	75.00
Nutting, At The Well, Sorrento	475.00
Nutting, Book Scene, Framed, 9 1/2 X 7 1/2 In.	37.50
Nutting, Comfort & The Cat, 14 X 16 In.	285.00
Nutting, Coming Out of Rosa, 14 X 16 In.	135.00
Nutting, Drying Apples	770.00
Nutting, Face of The Fall	440.00
Nutting, Four O'Clock, Cow Scene	1430.00
Nutting, Garden Steps, 20 X 16 In.	150.00
Nutting, Guardian Mother	4500.00
Nutting, Headwaters, Framed, 14 X 18 In.	95.00
Nutting, Heart of New England	220.00
Nutting, Helping Mother	352.00
Nutting, Holyhock Cottage, 18 X 22 In.	185.00
Nutting, Honeymoon Cottage, Framed, 21 X 11 1/2 In.	70.00
Nutting, Italian Spring	66.00
Nutting, Life of The Golden Age	297.00
Nutting, Little River, 14 X 20 In.	150.00
Nutting, Meeting Place	2750.00
Nutting, Memory of Childhood, 15 In.	105.00
Nutting, On Dress Parade, Framed, 17 X 11 In.	85.00
Nutting, Pasture Dell	1182.00
Nutting, Red, White & Blue, Label On Back, 1942	125.00
Nutting, Rural Sweetness, Framed, 18 X 15 In.	75.00
Nutting, Shadowy Orchard Curves, 10 X 12 In.	95.00
Nutting, Snow Scene	292.00
Nutting, Stony Brook Bloom	231.00

Nutting, Swirling Seas 412.50
Nutting, Time of Roses, Framed 75.00
Nutting, Turning The Flapjack 242.00

> Maxfield Frederick Parrish was an illustrator who lived from 1870 to 1966. He is best known as a designer of magazine covers, posters, calendars, and advertisements. All Parrish prints are wanted by collectors.

Parrish, Air Castles .... 135.00 To 145.00
Parrish, Canyon, 17 X 14 In. .... 135.00 To 165.00
Parrish, Cassim In The Cave of 40 Thieves, Collier's Full Page, 1906 .... 35.00
Parrish, Cleopatra, Framed, 15 X 16 In. .... 180.00 To 220.00
Parrish, Contentment, Original Frame 575.00
Parrish, Daybreak, Framed, 10 1/2 X 6 1/2 In. .... 60.00 To 75.00
Parrish, Daybreak, Gesso, Duro Craft Frame, 6 X 10 In. 120.00
Parrish, Daybreak, Large .... 250.00 To 290.00
Parrish, Daybreak, Medium .... 125.00 To 150.00
Parrish, Dinkey Bird, 13 X 15 In. 145.00
Parrish, Dreamlight, 25 X 35 1/2 In. 75.00
Parrish, Garden of Allah, Framed, 9 X 18 In. 85.00
Parrish, Golden Hours 550.00
Parrish, Golden Treasury of Song 115.00
Parrish, Hilltop, 34 X 23 In. 500.00
Parrish, Lute Players, Large 625.00
Parrish, Morning, 17 X 14 In. .... 155.00 To 165.00
Parrish, Old King Cole 675.00
Parrish, Prometheus, 23 3/4 X 35 1/2 In. 75.00
Parrish, Quiet Solitude, 11 X 14 In. 30.00
Parrish, Quiet Solitude, 16 X 19 In. 55.00
Parrish, Reveries .... 450.00 To 550.00
Parrish, Romance 650.00
Parrish, Royal Gorge .... 350.00 To 400.00
Parrish, Sheltering Oaks, 16 X 19 In. 55.00
Parrish, Thy Templed Hills, Framed, 12 X 16 In. 110.00
Parrish, Twilight, 16 X 19 In. 55.00
Parrish, Twilight, Matted, 1920, 6 X 6 1/2 In. 25.00
Parrish, Under Summer Skies, 11 X 14 In. 30.00
Parrish, Under Summer Skies, 16 X 19 In. 55.00
Remington, Last Lull In The Fight, Harper's Weekly, Mar. 30, 1889 .... 55.00
Robinson, Dogs Representing Different Countries, Framed, 1915 .... 75.00
Sawyer, Echo Lake, Framed, 14 X 17 In. 20.00
Silkscreen, S. Chang, San Francisco Bay, Matted, 1938, 5 X 7 1/2 In. 35.00
Silkscreen, S. Hayes, Coit Tower, Matted, 1938, 4 1/2 X 7 In. 37.50
Silkscreen, Wilkins, Girl, With 2 Fawns, Matted, 8 X 11 In. 18.50
Smith, Baby Jesus, Blue Frame, 8 X 10 In. 25.00
Smith, Ring-A-Round-A-Rosie, 11 1/2 X 13 1/2 In. 35.00
Swinnerton, Down To The Fields We Go, Matted, 1926, 11 X 7 In. 15.00
Swinnerton, Woodpecker Pecks With Ne'Er A Stop, 1926, 11 X 7 In. 15.00
Vargas, Scheherazade, Framed 275.00
Virginia Gruppe, Farm Landscape, Signed, 12 X 16 In. 200.00
Weekes, Botanical, Viola Tricolor, 1860, Matted, 3 1/4 X 7 In. 27.50
Weir, Dog, Anxious Moments, Black & White, 1880, Matted, 6 X 5 In. 15.00
Wolf, Landscape, Signed, 22 X 30 In. 400.00
Zorn, The Two, Signed, Framed, 1916, 7 3/4 X 5 3/4 In. 800.00

> How to carry a handkerchief and lipstick is a problem today for every woman, including the Queen of England. The purse has been recognizable since the eighteenth century. Leather and needlework purses were preferred. Beaded purses became popular in the nineteenth century, went out of style, but are again in use. Mesh purses date from the 1880s and are still being made.

PURSE, Alligator, Brown, 1950-60, Unused 250.00
Beaded, Beveled Mirror Inside, Small 25.00
Beaded, Change, Fringed, 2 3/4 In. 35.00

Beaded, Crewel Design, Flowers, Vines, Fringed, Chain Handle, 14 In. 150.00
Beaded, Faceted & Smooth Gold & Silver Beads, Double Chain, France 60.00
Beaded, Flapper Fringe All Around, Red, Wide Strap 125.00
Beaded, Floral, Ivory Ground, Ornate Silver-Plated Frame, 8 X 13 In. 145.00
Beaded, Floral, Nez Perce, C.1915 .... 175.00
Beaded, Gilt Frame, Gold & Silver, Long Fringe, France 35.00
Beaded, Handle, Zipper, Czechoslovakia, 5 In. 20.00
Beaded, Jet, Walborg 30.00
Beaded, Mesh, France 10.00
Beaded, Pouch, Metal Clasp, Beaded Wrist Strap 40.00
Beaded, Red 45.00
Beaded, Silver Plated Frame, Medium Blue, 6 X 8 In. 55.00
Change, Compact-Type, Long-Haired Lady, Metal Top, Steel Beads, 1898 .... 65.00
Change, Enameled, Gold Foil Design, Floral, England, 3 X 2 In. 175.00
Child's, Beany & Cecil, Vinyl 35.00
Child's, Leather, Dog Design, Early 1900s 24.00
Chrome, Basket Weave, Box Style 25.00
Clutch, Mustard Leather, Blue Chevron, Andrew Geller 12.00
Clutch, Rhinestones, Lucite, Clear, 1950s .... 17.50 To 25.00
Coin, Cut Steel Beads, Bottom Clasp, Fringe, 1847, 2 1/2 X 3 1/2 In. 65.00
Coin, Green Mushroom On Silver Ground, Beaded, 3 1/2 In. 20.00
Coin, Pouch, Beaded Fabric, Silver Plated Cover 45.00
Coin, Silver Plate On Brass, Caddy Figure, 1910 .... 245.00
Coin, With Compact, Sterling Mesh, Strap, 14K Yellow Gold, Elgin 85.00
Cornhusk 65.00
Cosmetic, Gold Mesh, Whiting & Davis, 3 X 4 In. 15.00
Crocheted, Petit Point Floral Design, Art Deco, Handmade 20.00
Crocheted, Silver Beaded, Navy Blue, Tassel At Bottom, 8 In. 45.00
Elephant Hide, Vietnam 16.00
Flapper, Accordion Neck, Marcasite Design, Black, 4 1/2 In. 45.00
Flapper, Beaded, Multicolored Flowers, Fringe, Plated Frame, Chain 65.00
Flapper, Drawstring Design, Silver Mesh 50.00
Leather, Hand Tooled, Envelope Style, 1950s, 6 X 10 1/2 In. 20.00
Leather, Velvet, Silk Cord, Victorian 15.00
Lizard, Embossed, Baby Blue 10.00
Lucite, Amber, Applied Design, 1950s 25.00
Lucite, Pearlized, Lunch Box Clasp, Twisted Handle 17.50
Lucite, White Pearlized 20.00
Lucite, White, Rhinestones 22.00
Mesh, 14K Gold, 3 Diamonds, 4 Sapphires, Emerald, 7 Plus Oz. 5500.00
Mesh, Art Deco, Floral, 8 X 9 In. 90.00
Mesh, Art Deco, Purple, Green, Large 55.00
Mesh, Coin, 14K Yellow Gold, 2 1/4 X 2 1/4 In. 375.00
Mesh, Elizabeth Kinports, Large 850.00
Mesh, Floral Enameled Frame, Jeweled Clasp, Whiting & Davis 75.00
Mesh, Geometric, Art Deco, Whiting & Davis 50.00
Mesh, German Silver Repousse Clasp, Kid Lining 80.00
Mesh, Gold, 3-In. Fringe, France 70.00
Mesh, Gold, Evening, Whiting & Davis, Rhinestone Clasp 65.00
Mesh, Gold, Rhinestone Clasp, Whiting & Davis 55.00
Mesh, Gold, Whiting & Davis .... 16.00 To 44.00
Mesh, Gold, Whiting & Davis, Silver Leather Strap, 3 X 3 1/2 In. 50.00
Mesh, Hand Painted, Whiting & Davis 40.00
Mesh, Mandalian, Blue & Mauve Geometric Design, Teardrop Fringed 80.00
Mesh, Mandalian, Blue Enameled, 7 In. 55.00
Mesh, Mandalian, Filigree Frame, Painted Design, 8 1/2 X 6 In. 125.00
Mesh, Silver, Kid Lining, Germany 95.00
Mesh, Steel, Expanding Sterling Top, Paste Sapphires On Lid 65.00
Mesh, Sterling, Chanel, 1920 .... 950.00
Mesh, Whiting & Davis, Blue Points In Clasp 50.00
Mesh, Whiting & Davis, Gold, Jewel Closing 65.00
Mesh, With Bakelite Compact, Bead Handle, Chain 35.00
Metal Mesh, Whiting & Davis 65.00
Ostrich, White, Gold Shoulder Chain, Jos. Magnin, Small 14.00

Pearl, Evening, Allover, 1930s	40.00
Petit Point, Evening, Austrian, Handmade, 5 3/4 X 6 3/4	75.00
Pouch, Accordion Top, Silvery Beading & Tassel	45.00
Satin, Beaded	15.00
Sequins, Silver & Seed Pearl Design, Rhinestone Clasp, Belgium	30.00
Silk, Black Silk, Rhinestones Around Frame	18.00
Snake, Simulated, Black Leather, France	12.00
Sterling Silver, Black Suede, L.C. Tiffany	650.00
Tapestry, Brass Frame, Hand Painted Flowers, Lined, Braided Strap	15.00
Velvet, Red, Satin Poppies, Box	20.00

Quezal

Quezal glass was made from 1901 to 1920 by Martin Bach, Sr., in Brooklyn, New York. Other glassware by other firms, such as Loetz, Steuben, and Tiffany, resembles this gold–colored iridescent glass. After Martin Bach's death in 1920, his son continued the manufacture of a similar glass under the name "Lustre Art Glass."

QUEZAL, Creamer, Gold, 2 1/2 In.	545.00
Finger Bowl, Underplate, Gold, Iridescent, Onionskin Edge, Signed	275.00
Finger Bowl, Underplate, Gold, Stretched Edges On Plates, Signed	550.00
Fixture, Ceiling, Large Center Globe, 3 Small Shades, 13 1/2 In.	4900.00
Lamp, Aurene, Paneled Shade & Base, Marked Twilight, 10 In.	950.00
Plate, Optic Rib, Scalloped Rim, Gold, Signed, 7 In.	295.00
Shade, 10–Ribbed, Bell Form, Amber With Gold, Signed, 5 1/4 In., 3 Pc.	300.00
Shade, Gold Feather, On Calcite, Pair	290.00
Shade, Gold Iridescent, Bell Shape, Marked, 4 1/4 In., Pair	150.00
Shade, Gold Ribbed, 5 In.	85.00
Shade, Gold Ribbing, Banding, Gold Lined	125.00
Shade, Green Feather, Gold Iridescent	145.00
Shade, Green Pulled Feather, Gold Rim & Lining, 5 In.	115.00
Shade, Iridescent Gold Hearts, Pair	500.00
Shade, Pulled Feather, White, Gold Interior, 5 1/2 In., Pair	325.00
Shade, Pulled Feather, White, Green & Gold, 5 In., Pair	225.00
Vase, Blue Iridescent, Signed, 6 1/2 In.	675.00
Vase, Blue Swirl Design, Gold, Signed, 6 1/2 In.	1000.00
Vase, Bud, Orange & Gold Iridescent, Scalloped Top, Signed, 12 In.	425.00
Vase, Crimped Sides, Gold Iridescent, 3 In.	375.00
Vase, Gold In Ribbed Lily Blossom, Pulled Leaf, Signed, 5 1/2 In.	660.00
Vase, Gold Iridescent, Baluster, Footed, Signed, 8 In.	357.00
Vase, Green Pulled Feather Design, 8 In.	500.00
Vase, Heart & Random Thread, White, Baluster, Signed, 8 1/2 In.	665.00
Vase, Hearts, Threading, White, Signed, 8 1/2 In.	660.00
Vase, Jack–In–The–Pulpit, 8 In.	3800.00
Vase, King Tut Pattern, Art Glass, 6 3/8 In.	125.00
Vase, Ruffled Top, Gold Iridescent, 12 In.	400.00
Vase, Trefoil Rim, Green & Gold Pulled Leaf & Feather, Signed, 6 In.	715.00
Vase, Trumpet, Gold Circular Font, Signed, 6 In.	500.00

Quilts have been made since the seventeenth century. Early textiles were very precious and every scrap was saved to be reused. A quilt is a combination of fabrics joined to a filler and a backing by small stitched designs known as quilting. An appliqued quilt has pieces stitched to the top of a large piece of background fabric. A patchwork, or pieced, quilt is made of many small pieces stitched together. Embroidery can be added to either type.

QUILT, Amish, Lone Star, Red, Yellow, Blue Ground, Sadie Miller, 76 X 84 In.	475.00
Appliqued, 1903 Ford, 1915 Buick, 1917 Stutz Bearcat, 72 X 90 In.	350.00
Appliqued, 4 Cherry Trees, Berried Branches, Cotton, 76 X 67 In.	3600.00
Appliqued, 8–Point Star, Red & White, Muslin Back, 1920s, 61 X 74 In.	300.00
Appliqued, 9 Stylized Floral Medallion, 79 X 80 In.	125.00
Appliqued, Autograph, Massachusetts, C.1860, 83 X 77 In.	225.00
Appliqued, Autumn Leaf, Colored Leaves, 78 X 88 In.	35.00
Appliqued, Basket of Flowers, Cotton, 19th Century, 80 X 86 In.	2850.00
Appliqued, Colonial Girl, 84 X 99 In.	365.00
Appliqued, Double Tumbling Block, Dark Colors, 1920s, 66 X 70 In.	135.00

Appliqued, Dresden Plate, Apple Green, New Red Back, 78 X 104 In. 145.00
Appliqued, Ducks & Ducklings, Reds, Blues, 60 X 80 In. 150.00
Appliqued, Dutch Girl, Embroidered, Hand Quilted, 58 X 86 In. 225.00
Appliqued, Feathered Star, 1880s, 84 X 86 In. 225.00
Appliqued, Floral Wreath Center, Sarah R. Russell, 1853, 82 X 82 In. 105.00
Appliqued, Floral Wreath With Roses, 76 X 92 In. 225.00
Appliqued, Floral Wreath, Embroidery, 72 X 86 In. 115.00
Appliqued, Floral, Undulating Vine Border, American, 89 X 84 1/2 In. 1100.00
Appliqued, Flower Basket, Unused, 1936, 77 X 86 In. 475.00
Appliqued, Flowerpot, Pink & Green, White, Striped Border, 80 X 62 In. 550.00
Appliqued, Flowerpot, Pink, Green, White Striped Border, 80 X 62 In. 550.00
Appliqued, Flying Geese, 76 X 65 In. 65.00
Appliqued, God Bless Our Home, M. Kreyenhangen, 1945, 84 X 102 In. 3300.00
Appliqued, Kittens In Basket, 56 X 88 In. 300.00
Appliqued, Log Cabin, Silk, Victorian, Crib 195.00
Appliqued, Lone Star, Amish, Bright Colors, Black Ground, Crib, 1965 .... 150.00
Appliqued, Lone Star, White Ground, 78 X 78 In. 400.00
Appliqued, Many Stars, Yellow Ground, 70 X 78 In. 100.00
Appliqued, Mennonite, 12 Maroon Flowers, White Ground, 70 X 90 In. 200.00
Appliqued, Mrs. Hoover's Colonial, Turkey Red, White, 76 X 88 In. 495.00
Appliqued, Overall Boy, Printed Blue Shirts, C.1890, 71 X 74 In. 200.00
Appliqued, Princess Feather, Red & Green, Cotton, 102 X 102 In. 2860.00
Appliqued, Princess Feather, Red, Green On White, C.1860, 98 X 95 In. 1195.00
Appliqued, Puffed Medallions, Feather Quilted Wreaths, 66 X 82 In. 605.00
Appliqued, Red, Yellow, White & Green, Muslin, 1840, Crib 1395.00
Appliqued, Rose of Sharon, Cotton, 82 X 80 In. 825.00
Appliqued, Stylized Feather, Red, Green, E. Driggs, 1861, 97 X 106 In. 65.00
Appliqued, Stylized Flowers, Meandering Red Border, 90 X 92 In. 475.00
Appliqued, Sunbonnet Babies, Crib, 49 X 61 In. 350.00
Appliqued, Sunbonnet Sue, 87 X 85 1/2 In. 165.00
Appliqued, Swing In The Center, Blue, Pink, Green, 1900s, 67 X 81 In. 400.00
Appliqued, Trip Around The World, Pastels, 78 X 73 In. 125.00
Appliqued, Tulips, Red, Green, White Ground, Border, 96 X 112 In. 350.00
Appliqued, Wedding Quilt, John Riale, Annie Riale, 1869, 86 X 88 In. 610.00
Appliqued, Whig Rose, Polly Ann Pepples, C.1850, 85 X 109 In. 1100.00
Appliqued, Yo–Yo, Blocks, Outlined In Yellow, 85 X 56 In. 95.00
Appliqued, Yo–Yo, Pastels, Crib 75.00
Patchwork, 18 Red & White Baskets, Lined, C.1860, 33 1/2 X 43 In. 650.00
Patchwork, 25 Star Medallions, 80 X 83 In. 125.00
Patchwork, 42 Blocks, Calico 8 Pointed Stars, 106 X 90 In. 1760.00
Patchwork, 6–Point Star, Red Print Back, 68 X 72 In. 185.00
Patchwork, Axehead, Machine Stitched, Multicolored, 66 X 72 In. 85.00
Patchwork, Basket Design, Red & White Calico, 74 X 76 In. 450.00
Patchwork, Bear's Claw, Red & Green, White Ground, Border, 63 X 84 In. 650.00
Patchwork, Blue & White Country Design, Stripes, 60 X 76 In. 200.00
Patchwork, Bowtie, Calico & Prints, Signed Tape Labels, 68 X 80 In. 200.00
Patchwork, Bowtie, Multicolored Prints, Calico Border, 80 X 80 In. 300.00
Patchwork, Bowtie, Multicolored, 69 X 80 In. 300.00
Patchwork, Broken Dish Pattern, Shell Quilting, American, 92 X 88 In. 935.00
Patchwork, Carolina Lily, Cream, Yellow & Brown, 74 X 84 In. 95.00
Patchwork, Circle I Square, Multicolored Prints, 72 X 78 In. 175.00
Patchwork, Crazy, 36 X 55 In. 110.00
Patchwork, Crazy, Dark Velvet, 70 X 78 In. 95.00
Patchwork, Crazy, Embroidered Allover, 55 X 60 In. 165.00
Patchwork, Crazy, Embroidered Silk & Velvet, 64 X 72 In. 4000.00
Patchwork, Crazy, Embroidered, Wool, Lancaster Cnty., 1922, 82 X 82 In. 8000.00
Patchwork, Crazy, Gooch's Best Flour, 70 X 76 In. 85.00
Patchwork, Crazy, Heavy Beaded, Signed, Crib 150.00
Patchwork, Crazy, Patterns & Stripes, Initialed In Gold, 56 X 69 In. 135.00
Patchwork, Crazy, Velvet, Silks, Tobacco Cloths, 64 X 84 In. 80.00
Patchwork, Cross & Crown, Multicolored On White, 62 X 78 In. 165.00
Patchwork, Dahlia, 78 X 92 In. 250.00
Patchwork, Diamond–In–The–Square, Wool, 1900, 75 X 75 In. 1045.00
Patchwork, Doll's, Brown, Lavender, Blue, Floral Border, 26 X 14 In. 85.00

Patchwork, Double Irish Chain, 19th Century, 77 X 72 In. 225.00
Patchwork, Double Irish Chain, Mennonite, Cotton Quilted, 1890 .... 3200.00
Patchwork, Double Wedding Ring, 92 X 84 In. 350.00
Patchwork, Double Wedding Ring, Blue Centers, 65 X 89 In. 350.00
Patchwork, Double Wedding Ring, Calico, Scalloped Edge, Double Bed 475.00
Patchwork, Double Wedding Ring, Multicolored Pastels, 72 X 96 In. 325.00
Patchwork, Double Wedding Ring, Multicolored, 74 X 76 In. 315.00
Patchwork, Double Wedding Ring, Square, 1930s, 92 In. 495.00
Patchwork, Dove At Window, Multicolored, 62 X 72 In. 175.00
Patchwork, Dresden Plate, Khaki & Yellow, 72 X 82 In. 300.00
Patchwork, Dresden Plate, Peach Sashes, 63 X 81 In. 95.00
Patchwork, Drunkards' Path, Red Border Frames, Red Path, 83 X 83 In. 775.00
Patchwork, Embroidered Floral Basket, 1928, 72 X 82 In. 300.00
Patchwork, Evening Star, Multicolored Stars, Brown, 62 X 72 In. 200.00
Patchwork, Fan Pattern, Hand Quilted, 83 X 87 1/2 In. 165.00
Patchwork, Floral Pattern, Chintz, Brown, Green, Crib, 35 X 11 In. 75.00
Patchwork, Flower Garden, 88 X 102 In. 450.00
Patchwork, Four Patch, Greens, Reds, 60 X 72 In. 135.00
Patchwork, Friendship Star, 72 X 82 In. 120.00
Patchwork, Friendship, Red & Yellow Named Squares, Green, 82 X 96 In. 525.00
Patchwork, Grandmother's Flower Garden, 74 X 72 In. 325.00
Patchwork, Grandmother's Flower Garden, Cotton, 72 X 80 In. 385.00
Patchwork, Hearts & Gizzards, Multicolored, 72 X 74 In. 165.00
Patchwork, Hourglass, Multicolored, 72 X 88 In. 125.00
Patchwork, Inverted Nine Patch, C.1900, 74 X 94 In. 150.00
Patchwork, Irish Chain, Blue & White, 72 X 72 In. 150.00
Patchwork, Irish Chain, Red & White, 76 X 78 In. 220.00
Patchwork, King's X, Reds, 72 X 74 In. 120.00
Patchwork, Lemoyne Star, Each Star Same Fabric, 62 X 74 In. 250.00
Patchwork, Lightning, Pink & White, 66 X 84 In. 195.00
Patchwork, Log Cabin, Alternating Bright & Dark Colors, 83 X 83 In. 400.00
Patchwork, Log Cabin, Brown, White, Blue, 78 X 66 In. 400.00
Patchwork, Log Cabin, Satin, 39 X 68 In. 500.00
Patchwork, Log Cabin, Silk, Velvet & Other Fabrics, 60 X 60 In. 100.00
Patchwork, Log Cabin, Velvet & Silk, 1920s, 42 X 56 In. 150.00
Patchwork, Log Cabin, Yellow Hearth Block, 1940s, 72 X 82 In. 185.00
Patchwork, Lone Star, Prints, 88 X 88 In. 275.00
Patchwork, Maple Leaf, C.1930, 78 X 86 In. 350.00
Patchwork, Mill Wheel, Multicolored Pastels, 72 X 90 In. 225.00
Patchwork, Monkey Wrench, Prints, Reds, Blues & Green, 65 X 72 In. 85.00
Patchwork, Mosaic, Pastel Colors, 2316 Triangles, 70 X 94 In. 325.00
Patchwork, Navy & White Checked Ground, 87 X 70 In. 95.00
Patchwork, New Schoolhouse, 95 X 108 In. 400.00
Patchwork, Nine Patch Diamonds, Zigzag Border, 36 X 50 In. 150.00
Patchwork, Nine Patch With Lattice, Red & White, 76 X 76 In. 150.00
Patchwork, Nine Patch, Multicolored Prints, 80 X 80 In. 45.00
Patchwork, Nine Patch, Variant, 78 1/2 X 75 1/2 In. 125.00
Patchwork, Nine Patch, Zigzag Borders, Youth, 56 X 56 In. 200.00
Patchwork, Ocean Waves, Burgundy & Rose, 80 X 82 In. 220.00
Patchwork, Ohio Log Cabin, 80 X 82 In. 215.00
Patchwork, Orange Peel, Multicolored Prints, 70 X 72 In. 225.00
Patchwork, Patience Corner, Reversible To String, 68 X 76 In. 185.00
Patchwork, Pickle Dish, 80 X 96 In. 250.00
Patchwork, Pickle Dish, Dark Green, 62 X 76 In. 260.00
Patchwork, Pineapple Pattern, Wool, 68 X 86 In. 2090.00
Patchwork, Pink Calico, Prints, 15 1/2 X 23 In. 25.00
Patchwork, Pink Flowers, White Ground, 74 X 74 In. 225.00
Patchwork, Pinwheel Designs, Multicolored Prints, 68 X 80 In. 135.00
Patchwork, Pinwheel Variant, Blue Border, White Ground, 76 X 76 In. 700.00
Patchwork, Pinwheel, 1900, Crib 195.00
Patchwork, Pioneer Patch, Mauve, Burgundy, 86 X 94 In. 175.00
Patchwork, Postage Stamp, 1885, Crib 240.00
Patchwork, Prickly Pear, Tan, Red & Mustard, 66 X 72 In. 450.00
Patchwork, Puzzle, Reversible To Bowtie, 72 X 78 In. 175.00

Patchwork, Red & White, 78 X 79 In. 500.00
Patchwork, Red & Yellow Calico, 73 X 75 In. 125.00
Patchwork, Road To California, Brown, Purple, Wool, 1920s, 68 X 80 In. 1800.00
Patchwork, Rocky Road To Kansas, Multicolored Pastels, 72 X 80 In. 165.00
Patchwork, Rose of Sharon, Pinks, Greens, 74 X 82 In. 450.00
Patchwork, Seven Sisters, 87 1/2 X 102 In. 275.00
Patchwork, Shoofly Variant, Red, Black, Pale Green Ground, 43 X 44 In. 400.00
Patchwork, Shoofly, 70 X 86 In. 175.00
Patchwork, Smocked Squares of Prints, 76 X 90 In. 150.00
Patchwork, Smoothing Iron, Pumpkin & Reds, 60 X 76 In. 140.00
Patchwork, Snowball, Hand-Stitched, 1920s, 69 X 80 In. 550.00
Patchwork, Springtime Blossoms, Orchid & White, 103 X94 In. 525.00
Patchwork, Square & Swallow, Tan & Red, 60 X 76 In. 165.00
Patchwork, Square In Square, Yellow & Brown, 72 X 90 In. 125.00
Patchwork, Star Design, 38 X 39 In. 100.00
Patchwork, Star Design, Multicolor Prints, 84 X 96 In. 300.00
Patchwork, Star Design, Multicolored Prints, 68 X 88 In. 130.00
Patchwork, Star Design, Prints & Solids, 20th Century, 78 X 96 In. 850.00
Patchwork, Star, Calico, Red, Yellow, Green Ground, 82 X 84 In. 300.00
Patchwork, Star, Unbleached Muslin Back, 66 X 102 In. 145.00
Patchwork, Stars, Red, Goldenrod, White Ground, Stripes, 74 X 78 In. 325.00
Patchwork, Swinging In Corner, Pink & Yellow, 68 X 80 In. 135.00
Patchwork, Tree Pattern, Prints, Sawtooth Border, 76 X 92 1/2 In. 175.00
Patchwork, Tree, Squares, Triangles, Sawtooth Border, 76 X 76 In. 850.00
Patchwork, Tumbling Block Variation, Calico, 72 X 74 In. 185.00
Patchwork, Tumbling Block, Star Center, 68 X 84 In. 625.00
Patchwork, Wedding Ring, Scalloped Border, Blue Ground, 77 X 93 In. 200.00
Patchwork, Windmill, Reds, 72 X 80 In. 175.00
Patchwork, Woven Cane, Sawtooth Edge, Green & White, 90 X 100 In. 250.00
Patchwork, Yellow & Gold Flowers, Cotton, 1925, 78 X 88 In. 2090.00

HR.
Quimper

Tin-glazed, hand-painted pottery has been made in Quimper, France, since the late seventeenth century. The earliest firm, founded in 1685 by Jean Baptiste Bousquet, was known as HB Quimper. Another firm, founded in 1772 by Francois Eloury, was known as Porquier. The third firm, founded by Guillaume Dumaine in 1778, was known as HR or Henriot Quimper. All three firms made similar pottery decorated with designs of Breton peasants and sea and flower motifs. The Eloury (Porquier) and Dumaine (Henriot) firms merged in 1913. Bousquet (HB) merged with the others in 1968. The group was sold to a United States family in 1984. The American holding company is Quimper Faience Inc., located in Stonington, Connecticut. The French firm has been called Societe Nouvelle des Faienceries de Quimper HB Henriot since March 1984.

QUIMPER, Bonbon, Footed, Square, 3 1/2 In. 52.00
Cache Pot, Peasant Woman, Scalloped Rim, 4 1/2 X 5 In. 135.00
Candlestick, Flowers, Female Figure, Marked, 5 1/2 In. 225.00
Charger, Scene of 2 Women, Spinning Wheel, 6 Sides, 16 In. 500.00
Cup & Saucer, Cobalt Blue & Tan, Demitasse 35.00
Eggcup, Chick, Attached Saucer 30.00
Figure, Swan, With 6 Eggcups, Marked 1475.00
Figurine, Dancers, Double, Signed, 9 1/2 In. 225.00
Figurine, St. Anne, With Child, 9 1/2 In. 185.00
Figurine, St. Anne, With Child, P.C.F.No.463, 5 3/4 In. 125.00
Figurine, St. Vierge, Marked, 3 1/2 In. ....85.00 To 115.00
Jardiniere, Music Scene, Dragon Handles 4950.00
Mug, Peasant, Herriot Mark, 5 1/2 In. 85.00
Oyster Plate, Signed, 9 1/4 In. 85.00
Pitcher, 4 In. 38.00
Pitcher, Girl Holding Flower, Pinched Spout, C.1930, 8 1/2 In. 175.00
Plate, Female Figure, Yellow, Blue Band 38.00
Plate, Line Drawings of Young Women, C.1960, 9 In., Pair 60.00
Plate, Male Figure, Yellow, Blue Band 38.00
Plate, Man, Orange Edge, Blue Lines, Signed, 8 1/4 In. 60.00

Salt Dip, Seated Peasant	210.00
Salt, Swan, Double, Woman, Flowers, Deep Blue, France	85.00
Shoe, Pair, Small	48.00
Snuffbox, Bagpipe, Artist	295.00
Vase, 5 Finger, Gold & Enameled, Signed, 7 In.	125.00
Wall Pocket, Woman, Miniature	150.00
Warmer, Butter, 6 In., Pair	150.00

RADURA. Radford pottery was made by Alfred Radford in Broadway, Virginia, Tiffin and Zanesville, Ohio, and Clarksburg, West Virginia, from 1891 until 1912. Jasperware, Ruko, Thera, Radera, and Velvety Art Ware were made. The jasperware resembles the famous Wedgwood ware of the same name.

RADFORD, Jardiniere, Pedestal, Birds, Leaves, Green, 35 In.	650.00
Jardiniere, Tulips, Ruko, 9 In.	175.00
Vase, Cherubs, Jasperware, No.14, 6 1/4 In.	175.00
Vase, Flowers, Green, 12 In.	450.00

The first radio broadcast receiving sets were sold in New York City in 1910. They were used to pick up the experimental broadcasts of the day. The first commercial radios were made by Westinghouse Company for listeners of the experimental shows on KDKA Pittsburgh in 1920. Collectors today are interested in all early radios, especially those made of Bakelite plastic or decorated with blue mirrors.

RADIO, 1960, Cadillac	55.00
2–Color, Russian, 1960s	85.00
Addison, Red & Butterscotch, Bakelite, 1940s	200.00
Airline, Black, 84–HA–1527	10.00
Arvin, Red, Metal	175.00
Atwater Kent, Cathedral, Model 944	200.00
Atwater Kent, Model 10C	400.00
Atwater Kent, Model 20, Speaker, Wood Cabinet	150.00
Atwater Kent, Model 30, Pooley Cabinet	275.00
Atwater Kent, Model 35, 1 Dial	110.00
Atwater Kent, Model 40, Outside Speaker	95.00
Atwater Kent, Model 55, Console, 1930	80.00
Bendix, Model 526	400.00
Bendix, Super Heterodyne, Model III, Bakelite	45.00
Big Bird, Head Only, 2–Dimensional	20.00
Blabbermouth, Talking Lips	25.00
Bulova, Art Deco, Cream Color	45.00
Catalin, Sentinel, Yellow	750.00
Charlie Brown & Snoopy, Box	50.00
Coin–Operated, Hotel	85.00
Concertone, Motel, 25 Cent	295.00
Coradio, Coin–Operated	35.00
Crackerjack, Box	35.00
Crebe Synchrophase, 16–In. Remote Speaker, Earphones, Dated 1918	125.00
Crosley, Ace V	150.00
Crosley, Clock–Radio, Chartreuse, 1950s	75.00
Crosley, Grandmother's Clock	435.00
Crosley, Green	60.00
Crosley, Model 52	75.00
Crosley, Model 58TW, White	67.00
Crosley, Model 10–137, Bakelite, Green	40.00
Crosley, Model 11–114V	35.00
Crosley, Model 124, Playtime Grandfather Clock, 1931	375.00
Crosley, Model D25WE, White Bakelite	200.00
Crosley, Model XJ	185.00
Crosley, Super Regenerative Trirdyn Special, 3 Tubes	265.00
Crosley, Tombstone	75.00
Crosley, Transister, Book, 1950	65.00
Crosley, White Plastic	30.00

Dalbert, Pillow Speakers, Mouse On Headboard, Coin–Operated 175.00
DeForest, D–12 .... 125.00
Dr Pepper, Box 35.00
E.H. Scott, Metropolitan, No.16 A 525.00
Eggship, Mork, Box .... 18.00 To 35.00
Emerson, Brown, 1940s 125.00
Emerson, Miracle Wand Handle, Maroon & Beige Plastic .... 10.00 To 18.00
Emerson, Model 520, Green & Yellow Marbelized Bakelite 125.00
Emerson, Model 541 .... 8.00
Emerson, Model 544, Wooden .... 20.00 To 25.00
Emerson, Model 561, Brown & Gold Bakelite 35.00
Emerson, Tombstone, Yellow 750.00
Fada, 6 Tubes, Battery 225.00
Fada, Bakelite, Streamliner, 1941 Mode 115.00
Fada, Battery & Electric, Ivory Bakelite 195.00
Fada, Bullet, Model 1000, Blue, Yellow Trim 1650.00
Falstaff, Hand 25.00
Farnsworth, Bakelite, 2–Color .... 195.00 To 250.00
Firestone, 4–A–89, White 10.00
Firestone, 4–D–86, Green 20.00
Firestone, Air Chief, White 39.00
Firestone, Portable, Plastic, 1950s 20.00
Firestone, Portable, Plastic, Carrying Strap, 1940s 35.00
Firestone, Roamer, Battery, Wicker Covered 37.50
Fonz Jukebox, Box .... 30.00 To 45.00
Freshman Masterpiece, Box 250.00
G.I. Joe .... 15.00 To 20.00
General Electric, AM–FM, Brown Bakelite 25.00
General Electric, Catalin, Maroon Body, Yellow Inset Grill & Knobs 750.00
General Electric, Catalin, Yellow Body, Maroon Grill 850.00
General Electric, Cathedral, Model K52 .... 160.00
General Electric, Head of Mickey Mouse On Front, 1960s 95.00
General Electric, Ivory, 1940s 65.00
General Electric, Maroon, Bakelite, 1940s 65.00
General Electric, Model G.D., Brown, Bakelite 45.00
General Electric, Model KL300 .... 5500.00
General Electric, Tombstone, Wooden 85.00
Getty Gas Pump, AM–FM 30.00
Glad Sandwich Bag 36.00
Graetz, Shortwave, AM–FM, Chocolate & Ivory Bakelite, Germany, 1950s 165.00
Gramophone 18.00
Green Giant Little Sprout 40.00
Grundig, AM–FM, Short Wave, Ivory Bakelite, Germany, 1950s 95.00
Grunow, Tombstone, Nickel, 13 X 14 In. 125.00
Gumby & Pokey, Box 30.00
Hamburger Helper 30.00
Hamburger Helper, Box 35.00
Hamm's Beer Can 20.00
Hawaiian Punch, Punchy, Box 45.00
Heinz Catsup, Bottle 35.00
Hulk, 1978, Box 35.00
Jet Gas, Pump 30.00
John Player, Special Race Car, Box 30.00
Kellogg, Tony The Tiger, Orange, Black, White, 1980 .... 40.00
Kiel, Table, Octagonal Top Opens 175.00
Knight Rider, Kit Radio 25.00
Kolster, Console, 1928 .... 90.00
Ladybug .... 20.00 To 25.00
Majestic, Art Deco, Bakelite, Table Model, 1940s 55.00
Majestic, Book Form 75.00
Meck, Trail Blazer, 1949 .... 45.00 To 50.00
Michael Jackson .... 20.00 To 25.00
Mississippi 1860s Firepumper 35.00
Mitchell, Lullaby, Bed Lamp 65.00

Mitchell, With Lamp, Clip To Headboard, Brown Bakelite, 1930s	150.00
Motorola Model C186, 2–Tone Green, Blue, 1950s	22.00
Motorola, Model 5A5, Bakelite & Metal, Portable	50.00
Motorola, Model AIR23, Red, 1950s	35.00
Mountain Dew Can	20.00
Music Master, Wooden, Horn Speaker, 14 In.	195.00
Musicaire, Model MD–16, Red Catalan	300.00
Mustang Car Radio, Transister, 1950–60	75.00
National, Model SW–35, Shortwave, Metal Case, 1946	35.00
Night–Light, Sesame Street, Box	55.00
Norelco, Battery Operated, Box, 1967	35.00
Official Baseball League Trophy	750.00
Opera	175.00
Oreo Cookie	25.00 To 30.00
Peanut, Jimmy Carter	45.00
Philco, Art Deco, Tabletop, Push Button, Wooden	90.00
Philco, Jr., Cathedral	150.00
Philco, Jr., Round Top	100.00
Philco, Model 3–PT–95	10.00
Philco, Model 37–60, Cathedral	125.00
Philco, Model 461201	65.00
Philco, Model 60, Cathedral	175.00
Philco, Model 80	95.00
Philco, Model H765, Art Deco, 1950s	35.00
Philco, No.48–412	12.00
Philco, Predicta, 1959	450.00
Philco, PT–19	30.00
Philco, Table Model, Yellow Plastic, 1940s	65.00
Philco, Table, 1934	150.00
Philco, Transitone 5 Tubes, Wood & Bakelite	15.00
Philco, With Phonograph, 1938	75.00
Philco, Wood & Plastic, Art Deco	45.00
Philmore Blackbird, Crystal	95.00
Philmore, Crystal, No.7001, Box	32.50
Pink Panther Gramophone, United Artists, Box	25.00
Poppin Fresh, Walking Radio, AM–FM	35.00
Popular Mechanics, C.1920	125.00
Radiola, Model 8, Portable	175.00
Radiola, Model 17, Speaker	100.00
Radiola, Model 17, Walnut Case	55.00
Radiola, Model 25	150.00
Radioman Radio, Unfolds Into Robot, With Weapon	20.00
Raggedy Ann & Andy	25.00
Raisin Man, Box	35.00
RCA Model 94BT1, Battery	20.00
RCA Victor, Table	15.00
RCA, Art Deco, Bakelite, Table Model, 1940s	85.00
RCA, Model 94BY1, Battery	20.00
Rocketship, Crystal, Box	95.00
Roller Skate	25.00
Santa Claus Doll	15.00
Scooby Doo, Box	40.00
Sentinel, Bakelite	45.00
Silvertone, Wooden, Police & Foreign Bands, 1920s	15.00
Sinclair Gas Pump, With Case	20.00
Smurf, 1982, Box	40.00
Snoopy, Box	50.00
Sparton, Black	38.00 To 40.00
Sparton, Blue Glass Mirror, Table, Chrome, Broadcast Band, Short Wave	3200.00
Sparton, Blue Mirror, Chrome Bands, C.1936, 14 1/2 In. *Illus*	2100.00
Sparton, Blue Mirror, Model 517, 3 Knob, 1936	1250.00
Sparton, Blue Mirror, Teague Design, 1936	1850.00 To 2850.00
Stack of One Dollar Bills, Total Five Dollars	25.00
Stewart Warner, 2–Tone	35.00

Radio, Sparton, Blue Mirror, Chrome Bands, C.1936, 14 1/2 In.

Radio, Zenith, Model 6D311, Brown Bakelite, Window Dial, C.1938

Strawberry Shortcake, Box	35.00
Stromberg–Carlson, Model 1500, Brown Bakelite, Beige Knobs, Art Deco	40.00
Sylvania, Ivory, 1940s	65.00
Tom & Jerry	35.00
Transistor, Figural, Head of Donald Duck, 7 In.	42.50
Transistor, Gramophone, Figural	25.00
Tube Tester, Hickok, Instructions	35.00
Tube Tester, Instructions, Box	25.00
Tube, Tester, Oak Case, 1940	45.00
Tucker, Car	1750.00
Upright, Motel, 10 Cent	135.00
Victoria, 1960s	30.00
Vitatone, Zaneygill, Cathedral, Burled Cabinet	150.00
Westinghouse, Model H77616a, Pink, Charcoal, 1950s	24.00
Westinghouse, Reddish Brown Plastic, 1950s .... 25.00 To 35.00
Westinghouse, Refrigerator	85.00
Winston Cigarette Package	35.00
Wood Transitone, Wooden, 1940s, Small	18.00
Zenith, Bakelite, Yellow	45.00
Zenith, Black, Gold Front	25.00
Zenith, Brown Bakelite, AM–FM	40.00
Zenith, Green, Plug–In Or Battery Operated	40.00
Zenith, Magic Eye, Floor Model, Black Round Dial, 1937	350.00
Zenith, Model 5R216, Black Dial	120.00
Zenith, Model 6D311, Brown Bakelite, Window Dial, C.1938 ....*Illus*	400.00
Zenith, Model 8514 F, Blue Bakelite	300.00
Zenith, Model H511, Brown	25.00
Zenith, No.514, Gray, 1950s	20.00
Zenith, Pop–Up Dial, Leather Case, 1940s	60.00
Zenith, Portable Shortwave, Flip Top Front, 1940s	40.00
Zenith, Royal 500, 1950s	45.00
Zenith, Royal 500, Transistor, Bag, Case, 1957–58	125.00
Zenith, Shortwave, Push Button	55.00
Zenith, Tombstone, 16 X 22 In.	225.00
Zenith, Trans–Oceanic, Model 8G005	100.00
Zenith, Transistor, Case	35.00
Zenith, Wavemagnet, Portable	35.00
Zenith, Yellow Bakelite	40.00

Railroad enthusiasts collect any train memorabilia. Everything is wanted, from oilcans to whole train cars. The Chessie system has a store that sells many reproductions of their old dinnerware and uniforms.

RAILROAD, Ashtray, Clinchfield R.R., Southern Potteries	10.00
Ashtray, Pacific R.R., Blue Glass	12.00
Ashtray, Peoria Gateway Line	125.00
Ashtray, Union Pacific	4.00
Badge, Conductor's, Octagon	80.00

Bell, Locomotive, Marked NP, Pat.1868, 11 1/2 In. Diam. 750.00
Bell, Locomotive, On Stand, Marked MCRR 560.00
Bell, New York Central Railway, Brass 50.00
Bell, Steam Locomotive, Yoke & Cradle, Bronze, 17 In. .... 675.00 To 695.00
Bill Clip, Soo Line 8.00
Book, Grand Trunk Railway Rules, July 1, 1898, 115 Pages 8.00
Bottle, Milk, Missouri Pacific Lines, Original Cap 20.00
Bouillon Cup, Western Pacific Feather River Route 35.00
Box, Emergency, Santa Fe, Red Steel 25.00
Bucket, Coal, D & RG R.R. Embossed Initials 25.00
Bucket, Fire, From Steam Engine, NYC R.R., Black, Embossed 42.00
Butter Chip, Baltimore & Ohio, Blue Centenary, 1827–1927 .... 15.00
Cabinet, Depot, Mississippi R.R., 28 Pigeon Holes, Mixed Woods 150.00
Calendar, 1962, C & O 20.00
Card, Luncheon Special, Burlington Route 5.00
Chime, Locomotive, 2 Ft. 375.00
Clipboard, Atlantic Coastal, Wooden, Copper R.R. Logo & Clip 49.00
Coffeepot, Santa Fe, Silver Plated, 1910 .... 120.00
Comic Book, Railroads Deliver The Goods, 1956 .... 12.00
Comic Book, Ride The High Iron, 1955 .... 12.00
Compote, Santa Fe 65.00
Cover, Headrest, Seaboard Coast One Railroad, Palm Trees, Gold 6.25
Creamer, B & O, Blue Centenary, 1827–1927, 12 Oz. .... 65.00 To 75.00
Creamer, New North Western R.R. Depot, Chicago, Bavaria, 1890's 35.00
Creamer, Southern Pacific Lines Railway 35.00
Creamer, Southern Pacific, 2 In. 10.00
Cup & Saucer, B & O, Blue Centenary, 1827–1927 .... 65.00
Cup & Saucer, B & O, Capital 4.00
Cup & Saucer, B & O, Scammells Laberton, Demitasse 95.00
Cup & Saucer, Berry Bowl, UP Streamliner, 3 Piece 35.00
Cup & Saucer, Chicago, Milwaukee, St. Paul, Olympian, Lenox 85.00
Cup & Saucer, George Washington, Illinois Central 190.00
Cup & Saucer, Southern Pacific, Prairie Wildflowers 65.00
Cup, B & O, Blue & White 40.00
Cup, Bouillon, Wabash, Banner 65.00
Cup, Pennsylvania Lines, Tin 50.00
Date Machine, Northern Pacific, Cast Iron 50.00
Eggcup, B & O, Blue Centenary, 1827–1927, Double 45.00
Eggcup, Northwestern Logo 12.00
Fixture, Dining Car, Pullman, Signed 1100.00
Gate, Court of Two Sisters, Illinois Central 680.00
Hat, Agent's, Burlington Route 95.00
Hatchet, Claw Head, Rock Island Lines 45.00
Hatchet, KCS RY 38.00
Hatchet, Wabash, Marked 32.00
Jug, Deodorizer, Pullman, Stoneware, 1/2 Gal. 98.00
Jug, St.L. & S.F. Railway Co., Western Stoneware, Brown, White 135.00
Lamp, Caboose, Kerosene, 4–Sided, 4 Colored Lenses 100.00
Lamp, Red Shade, Rock Island 35.00
Lamp, Switch, Dressel, New York & Chicago Railway 80.00
Lamp, Switch, Dressel, New York Central 125.00
Lamp, Tin Fuel Reservoir, Glass Chimney, Handlan, St. Louis, 9 In. 45.00
Lantern, Adams, C & NW, Cast Tall Globe 70.00
Lantern, Adlake, Rock Island, Red Globe, 10 In. 45.00
Lantern, B & M 35.00
Lantern, B & M, Bell Bottom, Cast 200.00
Lantern, B & O, Keystone, Casey, Clear Globe 120.00
Lantern, Caboose, Lehigh Valley, Marked 95.00
Lantern, Conductor's, Brass 300.00
Lantern, Conductor's, Presentation 450.00
Lantern, Dietz, No.6, Red Globe 60.00
Lantern, DL & W, Cast, Red, Tall 100.00
Lantern, DW & P, Blue Embossed Globe 495.00
Lantern, Handlan, Bell Bottom, CCC & St.L 70.00

Lantern, Handlan, Mopac, Cast Globe	85.00
Lantern, Handlan, Mopac, Red Etched Globe	50.00
Lantern, Missouri–Pacific	37.50
Lantern, P & R, Cast, Green, Bell Bottom	600.00
Lantern, P.R.R., Amber Globe	80.00
Lantern, PB & W, Cast, Tall	175.00
Lantern, Rock Island Lines	150.00
Lantern, Switch, Adlake, Kerosene, 1920s	185.00
Lantern, Switch, Dressel, Kerosene, 2 Green, 2 Red Lenses, 17 In.	125.00
Lantern, Trainman's, Dietz, Amber Globe, 10 In.	35.00
Lantern, Universal Spinning Co., Brass, Tall	200.00
Lantern, V & M, Fixed Globe, 1850	350.00
Lantern, Watchman's, Copper Clad, Bull's–Eye Lens	45.00
License, Engineer's, Louisville & Nashville	99.00
Lock, Canadian National Railway	20.00
Mail Pouch, Southern, Leather	100.00
Mail Pouch, Vice President's, Southern, Leather	99.00
Manual, Poor's Railroad, 1882	144.00
Manual, Poor's Railroad, 1898	99.00
Map, Canadian National Railways, C.1925	35.00
Map, Hoover Dam, Union Pacific, 1931, 32 X 18 In.	10.00
Map, U.S., 1945, 37 X 57 In.	40.00
Map, Wall, Atchison, Topeka & Santa Fe, 1945, 37 X 57 In.	85.00
Maps, Oak Case, Dated 1902–04	850.00
Matchbook, Pennsylvania, 1940s	10.00
Matchbook, Union Pacific, Photographs, No Matches, 1950, 7 Pc.	19.00
Monkey Wrench, Union Pacific, J.M. Williams, Iron	28.00
Negatives, Maine Central Trains, 1918, 3 X 5 In., 9 Glass Plate	60.00
Oil Can, C & El	30.00
Padlock, Michigan Central, Brass, Key	30.00
Paperweight, Cast Iron	50.00
Pencil, Nickel Plate, Unused, 3 Piece	15.00
Pencil, Rock Island	1.00
Pint, Chessie, Chesapeake & Ohio, 1937, 14 1/2 X 12 In., 3 Pc.	125.00
Plate, B & O, Harpers Ferry, 1927	90.00
Plate, Canadian National Systems, 6 In.	35.00
Plate, Capitol, 6 1/2 In.	60.00
Plate, Chicago, Indianapolis & Louisville, 7 1/4 In.	125.00
Plate, Delano Clock, Railroad Scene	26.00
Plate, Missouri Pacific, State Flower	250.00
Plate, Missouri Pacific, Steam Engine, State Flower	200.00
Plate, MKT, Alamo In Center, Beige, Blue Band, 10 1/2 In.	360.00
Plate, Mountain Laurel, Pennsylvania R.R., 6 In.	15.00
Plate, Mountain Laurel, Pennsylvania R.R., 7 In.	20.00
Plate, Mountain Laurel, Pennsylvania R.R., 9 1/2 In.	30.00
Plate, New York Central Lines, 7 3/4 In.	35.00
Plate, Service, George Washington, Illinois Central	480.00
Plate, Union Pacific, 9 In.	38.00
Plate, Western Pacific Feather River Route, 5 1/2 In.	55.00
Platter, Bread, Union Pacific	80.00
Platter, Cumberland Narrows, Shenango, Blue & White, 11 X 8 In.	155.00
Platter, Pennsylvania R.R., Emblem, Syracuse China, 9 1/2 In.	55.00
Platter, Union Pacific, Blue, Stamped, 15 In.	125.00
Platter, UP Challenger, 8 In.	40.00
Platter, UP Overland, Silver	45.00
Platter, Western Pacific Feather River, Oval, 7 1/4 In.	65.00
Poster, Amer. Express Flier, Glacier Nat'L Park, 1920s, 9 X 12 In.	17.50
Poster, Great Northern, Christmas Vacation, 1930s, 9 X 13 In.	25.00
Poster, Pennsylvania R.R., Trip To Atlantic City, 1920s	950.00
Print, Mt. St. Helens, Scenic Northern Pacific Logo	125.00
Punch, Ticket, Louisville & Nashville	48.00
Puzzle, Jigsaw, Santa Fe Railroad Diesel Streamliner, 1948	12.00
Relish, Santa Fe, 1926	110.00
Rule, Surveyor's, V & M	95.00

Saucer, Northern Pacific Railway	30.00
Saucer, Pacific Lines	32.50
Sign, Railway Express Agency, Black Letters, 12 In.	125.00
Sign, Rock Island Railroad, 28 X 20 In.	85.00
Soup, Dish, New York Central	24.00
Soup, Dish, Pennsylvania System, 9 In.	35.00
Spittoon, Pullman Co.	50.00
Spoon, Soup, Norfolk & Western Railway, Silver Plate	20.00
Stock Certificate, Sioux City & Pacific R.R. Co., Unused, 1860s	35.00
Tablecloth, Interwoven California Zephyr, Oval, 36 X 42 In.	15.00
Tablecloth, Interwoven Rio Grande, White, 36 X 42 In.	12.50
Teapot, New York Central, Silver Plate	30.00
Teapot, Santa Fe R.R., Silver Plate, 1910	50.00
Telegraph Transmitter	75.00
Telephone, PRR, Oak	130.00
Ticket Punch, Conductor's	10.00
Tie Level, Brass Top, 62 In.	265.00
Tie Pin, Southern Pacific, Sterling Silver	12.50
Timetable, Alaska, Mt. McKinley, Photos, 1931, 9 X 8 In.	15.00
Timetable, Canadian National, 1950, 32 Pages	6.00
Timetable, Chicago Surface Lines, Century of Progress, 1933	6.00
Timetable, Southern Railway, 1945	7.00
Towel, Burlington Route Logos, Safety Slogans, 18 X 16 In., Pair	15.00
Towel, Interwoven UPRR, Red Stripe, 16 X 16 In.	7.00
Towel, Pullman, Marked	6.00
Towel, Tea, Pullman, Blue & White, 1930	18.00
Tray, B & O, Blue, Cumberland Gap, Oval, Porcelain	11.00
Tray, Traveler, C.M.S.T.P., Pink Geese	55.00
Tumbler, B & O	195.00
Watch Fob, Brotherhood of Locomotive Engineers, Enamel	25.00
Watch Fob, Brotherhood Railroad Trainmen, Enameled	42.50
Watch Fob, M.K.T.	60.00
Watch Fob, Northwestern Railroad	27.00
Whistle, B & O, Brass	35.00

The razor was used in ancient Egypt and subsequently wherever shaving was in fashion. The metal razor used in America until about 1870 was made in Sheffield, England. After 1870, machine–made hollow–ground razors were made in Germany or America. Plastic or bone handles were popular. The razor was often sold in a set of seven, one for each day of the week. The set was often kept by the barber who shaved the well–to–do man each day in the shop.

RAZOR, American Line Steamship, St. Louis, Etched Blade	50.00
Dispenser, Figural, Elephant, Listerine	9.00
Eveready, Blade Marked	30.00
Gem, Junior, Case, Dated 1901	18.00
Gem, Junior, Set, Box	6.00
Gem, Leather Case	45.00
Gem, With Holder, Metal Case, Velvet Lined	18.00
Gillette, Break–Down, Velvet Lined Case, Brass, 4 X 2 In.	27.50
Gillette, Debutante, Double–Edge, Brass, Box	40.00
Hone, American Hone Co., Box	15.00
Keen Kutter, Cardboard Box	20.00
Moreley Corn	28.00
Remington, Electric, Case, World's Fair, 1939	95.00
Remington, World's Fair, 1939, Box	135.00
Rolls, Box	12.50 To 20.00
Safety, Burham, Tin	45.00
Safety, Dime, Painted Black & Gold Tin Tube, Instructions	75.00
Safety, Keen Kutter, Junior, Blades, Box	35.00
Safety, Keen Kutter, Original Case	17.50
Safety, Tin Lithograph Box, 1888	32.00
Safety, Valet	5.00
Safety, Winchester, Box	50.00

Schick, Electric, Leather Case	25.00
Schick, Red Bakelite Case	14.00
Schick, Repeating, Blades	25.00
Sharpener, Blade, Aloxite, Box	12.00
Sharpener, Kriss Kross, Box	7.00
Sharpener, Kriss Kross, Mechanical, 4 In.	45.00
Sharpener, Twinplex	7.00
Straight, Bamboo Design, Celluloid	6.75
Straight, Bengall, England, Box	14.00
Straight, Black Handle, 1910s	30.00
Straight, Buck Shoe, Indian Head Picture, Pinkerton Tobacco Co.	65.00
Straight, Castle & Co., Sheffield, Black Handle, Box	10.00
Straight, Diamond Steel, Germany, Box	14.00
Straight, Double Duck, Box	8.00
Straight, Florals, Mottled Yellow & Brown	10.00
Straight, Herms, Germany, Box	13.00
Straight, Hesson Bruch, Bear on Handle	30.00
Straight, James H. Flagg, The 2 For 1 Razor, Case	45.00
Straight, Keen Kutter, No.K1150	15.00
Straight, Liberty Bell, Hand–Forged Silver Steel, Germany, Box	14.00
Straight, Nude Woman Handle	50.00
Straight, Old Faithful, England, Box	14.00
Straight, Peacock Handle	60.00
Straight, Primble, Box	8.00
Straight, Red Point, Germany, Box	14.00
Straight, Rolls Razor The Traveler, Sharpener, Box	23.00
Straight, Sextoblade	6.00
Straight, St. Louis Gem, Germany, Box	14.00
Straight, Winchester	60.00
Strop, Brass & Rosewood, 1889	40.00
Strop, Civil War	25.00
Strop, Illinois	35.00
Strop, Kriss Kross, Box, 1930	22.50
Strop, Sharpener, Kriss Kross, Box	23.00
Strop, Twinplex, 1920s	10.00
Strop, Winchester, No.8370	55.00
Wade & Butcher, Cardboard Box, Civil War	20.00
Wade & Butcher, Civil War	35.00
Wade & Butcher, Wooden Box	35.00
Wilkerson, Blades Marked For Days of Week, Stainless Case	65.00
Winchester, Instructions, Marked Blade	65.00

Reamers, or juice squeezers, have been known since 1767, although most of those collected today date from the twentieth century. Figural reamers are among the most prized.

REAMER, Baby, Scotty Dog Holding Sign	50.00
Boat	75.00
Clown's Head, With Pitcher, Hand Painted, Mirori, 7 In., 2 Piece	65.00
Clown, Juice, Pitcher Base	37.50
Elephant	100.00
Englishman's Head, Miniature	110.00
Federal, Pink	14.00
Hanging, Tea Strainer, Combination, Japan	24.00
Hazel Atlas, Pink	90.00
Lemon, Long Handle, Ribbed Pierced Cover, Knob Finial, 11 In.	55.00
Lemon, Silver Plate	65.00
Pink, Federal	14.00
Sunkist Fruit Growers, Los Angeles, Clear	27.50
Sunkist, Black	450.00
Sunkist, Chocolate	225.00
Sunkist, Green, Depression Glass	43.50 To 55.00
Sunkist, McKee	37.50
Sunkist, Milk Glass	9.00
Sunkist, White	25.00

The cylinder–shaped phonograph record for use with the early Edison phonograph was made about 1889. Disc records were first made by 1894; the double–sided disc by 1904. The high–fidelity records were first issued in 1944, the first vinyl disc in 1946, the first stereo record in 1958. The 78 RPM became the standard in 1926 but was discontinued in 1957. In 1932, the first 33 1/3 RPM was made but was not sold commercially until 1948. In 1949, the 45 RPM was introduced.

RECORD, Album, 1st Family, Vaughn Meader 25.00
Album, Child's, Foodini's Goes A Huntin', Story On Back, 1953 .... 20.00
Album, Child's, Happy Mother Goose, Kukla, Fran & Ollie 20.00
Album, Child's, I Like People, Yankee Doodle Bunny, Jimmy Durante 20.00
Album, Liberace, Autographed, 2 Records 200.00
Babes In Toyland, 1961 .... 9.50
Be–Bop Baby, Ricky Nelson, Imperial, 78 RPM 12.00
Bing Crosby & Bob Hope, Advertising Minnesota 13.00
Dinah Shore, Chevrolet, 1950 .... 10.00
I Am A Lion, On Lion Shape Cutout Talking Book, 1918 .... 55.00
Ivory Joe Hunter, 78 RPM 7.00
Little Red Riding Hood, Child's, 1949 .... 10.00
Mr. Sears & Mr. Roebuck, Dorothy Shay, 78 RPM, Columbia 10.00
Roy Milton, 78 RPM 7.00
Sparkle Plenty, 78 RPM, Illustrated 45.00
Suzy Snowflake, Little Red Riding Hood, Columbia, 45 RPM 5.00
Terry & The Pirates, Picture Record 30.00

The Red Wing Pottery of Red Wing, Minnesota, was a firm started in 1878. The company first made utilitarian pottery. In the 1920s art pottery was made. Many dinner sets and vases were made before the company closed in 1967. Rumrill pottery was made for George Rumrill by the Red Wing Pottery and other firms. It was sold in the 1930s.

RED WING, Ashtray, Donkey, Green 42.00
Ashtray, Fish 45.00
Baker, Yellow 75.00
Bean Pot, Cover, Bail, Brown & White, 1 Qt. 65.00
Bean Pot, Peterson Co. 120.00
Beater Jar, Blue & White 175.00
Beater Jar, Blue Band, Advertising On Both Sides 140.00
Beater Jar, Cream, Blue Lines 50.00
Beater Jar, Gray Line ....70.00 To 150.00
Bowl, Blue Band 48.00
Bowl, Blue Shoulder, 5 In. 85.00
Bowl, Paneled Rust & Blue, Large 75.00
Bowl, Saffron Spatter, 6 1/2 In. 50.00
Bowl, Vegetable, Divided 17.00
Bowl, Waddington, Geneva, Iowa, Blue, Rust & Cream, 7 In. 125.00
Bowl, White, 13 In. 65.00
Butter, Bobwhite 22.00
Butter, Cover, Bobwhite 35.00
Butter, Cover, Fondoso, Green 20.00
Cake Stand, Tampico, Pedestal 55.00
Casserole, Cover, Bobwhite, Long Handles 30.00
Casserole, Cover, Gray Line, 7 In. 150.00
Casserole, Cover, Leaf & Fruit 25.00
Celery, Country Garden 22.00
Chamber Pot, Cover, Lily 98.00
Chop Plate 9.00
Churn, Birch Leaf 150.00
Churn, Butterfly, 8 Gal. 975.00
Churn, Union Stoneware, 3 Gal. 48.00
Clock, Aunt Jemima 75.00

Clock, Mammy 85.00
Coffee Server, Cover, Fondoso, Green 30.00
Coffeepot, Blue Shadows 28.00
Console, Fawn Flower Frog, 16 X 10 In. 22.00
Cookie Jar, Badger, On Football, 1939 .... 95.00
Cookie Jar, Baker, Beige 50.00
Cookie Jar, Baker, Yellow & Brown 35.00
Cookie Jar, Bobwhite .... 55.00 To 60.00
Cookie Jar, Bunch of Grapes .... 55.00 To 58.00
Cookie Jar, Carousel, Colored Animals .... 250.00 To 280.00
Cookie Jar, Cattail 95.00
Cookie Jar, Chef .... 45.00 To 60.00
Cookie Jar, Dancing Dutch 40.00
Cookie Jar, Dutch Girl .... 39.00 To 40.00
Cookie Jar, Dutch People 50.00
Cookie Jar, Gopher, On Football, 1939 .... 95.00
Cookie Jar, Katrina 50.00
Cookie Jar, King of Tarts, Pink .... 165.00 To 225.00
Cookie Jar, Monk .... 35.00 To 60.00
Cooler, Buttermilk 3800.00
Cooler, Spigot, Iron Handles, 2 Gal. 50.00
Crock, Blue Target, Minnesota Stoneware, Salt Glazed, 2 Gal. ... 110.00
Crock, Elephant Ear, Signed, 5 Gal. 120.00
Crock, Large Wing, 1 Gal. 345.00
Crock, Large Wing, 6 Gal. 40.00
Crock, Milk, Spongeware 38.00
Crock, No.2, 2 Gal. 165.00
Crock, No.4 .... 35.00
Crock, Wire & Wooden Handles, 10 Gal. 69.00
Cup & Saucer, Bobwhite 15.00
Cup & Saucer, Iris 4.50
Custard, Gray Line, 3 In. .... 175.00 To 190.00
Dish, Iris, 10 1/2 In. 7.00
Figurine, Gopher, Football, Dated 1937 .... 110.00
Figurine, Gopher, Football, Dated 1939, Signed 120.00
Gravy Boat, Pepe 38.00
Hors D'Oeuvre, Bird, Bobwhite 35.00
Jar, Butter, Blue Banded, 3 Lb. 95.00
Jar, Fruit, Dome Top, Blue Shield, 1 Qt. 950.00
Jar, Fruit, Mason, Black Lettering, 1/2 Gal. 185.00
Jar, Fruit, Union, Mason, 1899, 1 Qt. 95.00
Jar, Pantry, No.3 .... 425.00
Jar, Refrigerator, Bail Handle & Cover, Blue & White 185.00
Jar, Refrigerator, Middle Size 95.00
Jar, Sand, Stag, Doe, Forest Scene, Pinecone Border, 5 Gal. ... 1200.00
Jug, Abel, Old Whiskies, Chicago, 1/2 Gal. 285.00
Jug, Aledo Vinegar, Milwaukee, 4 Oz. 165.00
Jug, Beehive, Salt Glaze, 2 Gal. 125.00
Jug, Beehive, Salt Glaze, 3 Gal. 135.00
Jug, Beehive, Salt Glaze, 5 Gal. 215.00
Jug, Blue & White Spongeware, Excelsior Spring Mineral Water ... 2000.00
Jug, Paper Label, Miniature 65.00
Jug, Petty's Hog Tonic, 2 Gal. 400.00
Jug, Phoenix Club Whiskey, Chicago, 8 Oz. 195.00
Jug, Signed, 1899, 1/2 Pt. 125.00
Jug, The Fair Store, Redwood Falls, Minn., 1/8 Pint 225.00
Jug, Turkey Eye Drippings, Salt Glaze, 1 Gal. 285.00
Jug, Vancouver, Victoria, B.C., Advertising, 5 Gal. 560.00
Jug, White, 1/2 Gal. 45.00
Jug, Wide Mouth, 1 Qt. 45.00
Monk, Blue 80.00
Mortar Bowl, C.Ph.A. Saskatoon, Miniature 75.00
Mug, N.D.F.A. Convention, Mandan, North Dakota, 1934 .... 145.00
Mug, Verse 590.00

Good tips for care of Bauer pottery—and, probably, for Fiesta and any other heavy, color-glazed dishes of the 1930s. Bauer is oven safe for baking—up to 350 degrees. Do not use in a microwave. Do not use on a direct flame. Do not wash in an automatic dishwasher. The detergent may discolor the glaze. Do not scour. Store with felt between stacked plates to avoid scratching. Early 1930 to 1942 dishes used a lead in the glazing, so do not use scratched dishes with acidic foods. Lead poisoning is possible with prolonged use.

Pepper Mill, Bobwhite	275.00
Pitcher, Blue, White, Lily	275.00
Pitcher, Bobwhite, 12 In.	25.00
Pitcher, Cherry Band, Blue, Advertising	140.00
Pitcher, Cherry Band, Small	135.00
Pitcher, Gray Line, 7 1/2 In.	165.00
Pitcher, Gray Matte Flowers In Relief, No.1012, 7 1/2 In.	28.00
Pitcher, Jeff's Dairy, Marshall, Minn., Saffron, Small	85.00
Pitcher, Lexington Rose, 17 In.	29.00
Pitcher, Lily	175.00
Pitcher, Water, Bobwhite	27.00
Planter, Wall, Green, 13 1/4 In.	15.00
Plate, Lexington Rose, 10 1/2 In.	6.50
Plate, Luncheon, Tempo	3.50
Plate, Round Up, 7 In.	20.00
Platter, Capistrano, 15 In.	13.00
Platter, Lotus, 13 In.	26.00
Reamer, Gray Line	695.00
Salt & Pepper, Bobwhite	12.00 To 28.00
Salt & Pepper, Hamm	130.00
Server, 3–Tier, Blackbird & Fruit	25.00
Snack Tray, With Cup, Lotus	18.00
Soup, Cream, Iris	4.00
Spittoon, Blue & White	135.00
Stein, Indian Head On Handle, Bushy Trees & Wigwam, Brown	450.00
Stein, Pewter Lid, Wheel Cut, Blue Bands	70.00
Sugar & Creamer, Blue Shadows	12.00
Teapot, Blue Shadows	16.00
Tray, 3 Sections, White	25.00
Tray, Hors D'Oeuvre, Bobwhite	74.00
Trivet, Bobwhite	49.50 To 140.00
Trivet, Capistrano	75.00
Trivet, Centennial	60.00
Vase, 8 1/4 In.	18.00
Vase, Brushware, Flower Design, 7 In.	20.00
Vase, Green, Squatty	28.00
Vase, Green, Yellow	12.00
Vase, Horseshoe Design, Green, 3–Prong Top	18.50
Vase, King Tut, Blue	40.00
Vase, Peacock, Art Pottery, 6 In.	100.00
Vase, Wall, Cornucopia, Yellow, Label, Pair	22.00
Water Cooler, Commemorative	65.00
Water Cooler, Cover, 15 Gal.	125.00

Redware is a hard, red stoneware that originated in the late 1600s and continues to be made. The term is also used to describe any common clay pottery that is reddish in color.

REDWARE, Bank, Apple	75.00

Bank, Black Cat 15.00
Bank, Figural, Orange, Textured, 3 1/2 X 3 1/2 In. 175.00
Bank, Globular, Incised Band Design, Knob Finial, 3 5/8 In. 100.00
Bank, Mottled Brown, Amber Glaze, Knob Finial, 3 7/8 In. 125.00
Bank, Ovoid, Unglazed, 3 5/8 In. 50.00
Bank, Ring Top Handle, 2 1/2 In. 38.00
Basket, Yellow Slip Leaves, Twisted Handle, Brown Glaze, 4 3/4 In. 475.00
Basket, Yellow Slip, Applied Vining Foliage, Braided Handle, 7 In. 200.00
Bean Pot, Advertising .... 20.00 To 68.50
Bean Pot, Applied Handle, Cover 80.00
Bottle, Manganese Glaze, 4 7/8 In. 75.00
Bowl, Brown Glazed Interior, 5 7/8 In. 70.00
Bowl, Bulbous Lip, Running Brown Glaze, 4 3/4 In. 105.00
Bowl, Floral Design, White Slip, Floral Enameling, 10 1/2 In. 25.00
Bowl, Greenish Mottled Glaze, 10 1/4 In. 55.00
Bowl, Milk, White Slip, Rim Stripes, Floral, 14 In. 55.00
Bowl, Milk, Yellow Slip Design, Green & Brown Glaze, 11 X 3 In. 65.00
Bowl, Milk, Yellow Slip Interior, 14 In. 65.00
Bowl, Molded Crimp Rim, Spotted Glaze, 9 In. 175.00
Bowl, Stylized Floral Design, Yellow Slip, Marked Ana, 9 1/4 In. 20.00
Bowl, With Spout, Glazed Interior, Incised Design, Large 75.00
Charger, Coggled Rim, 3 Line Yellow Slip Design, 13 1/4 In. 300.00
Charger, Coggled Rim, 3 Line Yellow Slip Pinwheel, 13 In. 550.00
Charger, Coggled Rim, Yellow Slip Design, 12 1/4 In. .... 300.00 To 325.00
Charger, Coggled Rim, Yellow Slipdesign, 13 In. 350.00
Creamer, Ribbed Strap Handle, Running Glaze, Streaked, 4 7/8 In. 125.00
Crock, Cheese, Koehler & Hinrichs, Gray, Blue 135.00
Crock, Cover, 8 In. 110.00
Crock, Ears, Ovoid, 3 Gal. 65.00
Crock, Glazed Interior, Incised Design, 4 1/8 X 3 3/8 In. 25.00
Cup, Strap Handle, Dark Brown Glaze, 3 3/4 In. 35.00
Cup, White Slip, Sgraffito Design, Greenish Glaze, 2 1/2 In. 500.00
Dish, 2 Line Yellow Slip Design, 7 1/2 In. 240.00
Dish, 3 Sets of Wavy Lines, Yellow Slip, 7 3/8 In. 25.00
Dish, Brown Fleck Glaze, 6 3/4 In. 65.00
Dish, Brown Fleck Glaze, 7 In. 35.00
Dish, Coggled Rim, Yellow Slip, 5 1/4 In. 195.00
Dish, Crimped, 3 Yellow Wavy Lines, Slipware, 14 In. 1300.00
Dish, Yellow Slip Design, Brown Fleck Glaze, 7 1/4 In. 165.00
Figurine, Dog, Seated, Hand Molded, Brown Sponging, 4 In. 300.00
Figurine, Frog, Clear, Greenish Glaze, 4 3/4 In. 85.00
Flask, Allover Manganese Glaze, 8 5/8 In. 475.00
Flask, Brown Glaze, Greenish Tint, 6 1/8 In. 45.00
Flask, Manganese Glaze, 6 3/8 In. 110.00
Flask, Ring, Green Mottled Glaze, Handle, 10 1/4 In. 550.00
Flowerpot, Attached Saucer, White Slip, Brown Glaze, 6 1/8 In. 225.00
Foot Warmer, Hot Water, Brown, Green, Yellow, Top Hole, 5 X 11 In. 395.00
Jar, Amber Glaze, Orange Spots, 9 3/4 In. 95.00
Jar, Brown Fleck Glaze, Ovoid, 4 5/8 In. 25.00
Jar, Canning, Cover, Green Glaze, Orange Spots 110.00
Jar, Clear Glaze, Brown Spots, Strap Handle, 5 1/2 In. 165.00
Jar, Cover, Gleason, Miniature 850.00
Jar, Cover, Jugtown Ware 25.00
Jar, Dark Brown Glaze, Greenish Amber Spots, 6 3/4 In. 75.00
Jar, Ear Handles, Orange Interior Glaze, Impressed 1, 4 1/4 In. 30.00
Jar, Greenish Glaze, Brown Splotches, Strap Handle, 5 3/4 In. 50.00
Jar, John Bell, Waynesboro, Pa., Ovoid, 1/2 Gal. 145.00
Jar, Orange Glaze, Manganese Blotches, Flared, 7 In. 170.00
Jar, Ovoid, Ear Handles, Black Manganese Splotches, 8 1/2 In. 275.00
Jar, Pickle, Crolius 1225.00
Jar, Preserve, Rust Glaze, Black Splotching, C.1810, 6 1/2 In. 220.00
Jar, Ribbed Strap Handle, Tooled Lines, Brown Splotches, 5 5/8 In. 200.00
Jar, Storage, Glazed Interior, Bulbous, 9 In. 45.00
Jar, Tiered Finial, Strap Handles, Ovoid, 12 In. 450.00

Jar, Tooled Lip, Yellow Glaze, 9 1/2 In.	15.00
Jar, Wilcox, Heart–Shaped Ears, Brown Glaze, 9 1/2 In.	260.00
Jug, Dark Brown Glaze, Ribbed Strap Handle, 7 3/8 In.	25.00
Jug, Dark Brown Glaze, Ribbed Strap Handle, 8 1/4 In.	100.00
Jug, Deep Red Glaze, Black Splotches, Ribbed Strap Handle, 6 In.	225.00
Jug, Mottled Amber Glaze, Spots, Strap Handle, 12 3/4 In.	90.00
Jug, Mottled Orange Glaze, Ribbed Strap Handle, 8 3/4 In.	135.00
Jug, Stylized Floral Design, Yellow Slip, Strap Handle, 3 1/4 In.	30.00
Jug, Tiger Eye Glaze, Ovoid, Handle, 18th Century, 1 Gal.	220.00
Jug, Tiger Eye, Brown Glaze, Ovoid, 11 In.	295.00
Lamp, Orange Glaze, Ribbed Strap Handle, 5 3/8 In.	250.00
Loaf Pan, Coggeled Rim, 3 Line Yellow Slip Design, 15 3/8 In.	475.00
Loaf Pan, Coggled Rim, 3 Line Yellow Slip Design, 15 3/8 In.	475.00
Mold, Fluted, Brown Glaze, 4 5/8 X 1 7/8 In.	75.00
Mold, Fluted, Orange Glaze, Manganese Mottled Rim, 4 1/4 In. Diam.	95.00
Mold, Food, Fish Shape, Clear Glaze, Brown, 12 1/2 In.	170.00
Mold, Food, Fish Shape, Dark Brown Glaze, 14 In.	105.00
Mold, Food, Turk's Head, Clear Glaze, Brown Sponging, 9 1/2 In.	75.00
Mold, Food, Turk's Head, Scalloped Rim, 6 1/2 In.	35.00
Mold, Food, Turk's Head, Swirled Flute Design, 8 1/2 In.	45.00
Mold, Round, Orange Glaze, Pinwheel Design, Rosette, 9 3/8 In. Diam.	160.00
Mold, Turk's Head, Orange Glaze, Manganese Mottled, 10 7/8 In.	350.00
Mold, Turk's Head, Scalloped Rim, Brown Sponging, 9 1/4 In.	20.00
Mold, Turk's Head, Scalloped Rim, Swirled Flutes, 9 In.	55.00
Mold, Turk's Head, White Slip, Wavy Vertical Lines, 7 5/8 In.	100.00
Mug, 2 Tooled Lines At Rim, Ribbed Strap Handle, 4 In.	95.00
Mug, Marbelized Glaze, White Slip, Green, Brown, Strap Handle, 6 In.	500.00
Mug, Pitcher Shaped, Brown Bands, Ribbed Strap Handle, 3 In.	175.00
Mug, Shiny Glaze, Dark Brown, 4 3/4 In.	125.00
Mug, Splotches of White Slip, Brown, Green, 4 1/2 In.	135.00
Mug, Yellow Slip, Marbelized Design, 4 1/2 In.	95.00
Pan, Coggled Rim, Combed Yellow Slip Design, 12 1/2 X 15 3/4 In.	495.00
Pan, Loaf, Coggled Edge, 3 Line Yellow Slip Design, 9 1/4 X 13 In.	425.00
Pan, Loaf, Coggled Edge, 4 Line Yellow Slip Design, 10 X 13 In.	900.00
Pan, Loaf, Coggled Edge, Wavy Yellow Slip Design, 17 1/2 In.	185.00
Pan, Loaf, Coggled Rim, Yellow Slip Design, 9 X 13 In.	675.00
Pan, Loaf, White Slip Design, English, 12 X 14 3/4 In.	40.00
Pie Plate, Coggled Rim, 3 Line Yellow Slip Design, 12 In.	175.00
Pie Plate, Coggled Rim, 3 Line Yellow Slip Design, 7 1/4 In.	375.00
Pie Plate, Coggled Rim, 3 Line Yellow Slip Design, 8 In.	250.00
Pie Plate, Coggled Rim, 3 Line Yellow Slip Design, 9 In.	65.00
Pie Plate, Coggled Rim, 4 Line Yellow Slip Design, 8 In.	115.00
Pie Plate, Coggled Rim, Crow's Foot Design, 8 In.	150.00
Pie Plate, Coggled Rim, Spots & Dashes of Yellow Slip, 10 7/8 In.	325.00
Pie Plate, Yellow Slip Design, Deep Orange Glazed Clay, 8 In.	275.00
Pie Plate, Yellow Zigzag, 10 1/2 In.	250.00
Pitcher, Brown Running Glaze, 7 3/4 In.	200.00
Pitcher, Brown, Amber Ground, Strap Handle, 10 1/4 In.	500.00
Pitcher, Cover, Orange, Manganese Mottle, Incised Band, Handle, 5 In.	425.00
Pitcher, Mottled Green, Orange, Galena, 10 1/4 In.	185.00
Pitcher, Mug Shape, Brown Splotch Glaze, 4 3/48 In.	95.00
Pitcher, Mug Shape, Dark Glaze, 4 1/8 In.	45.00
Pitcher, Pineapple, 4 Applied Leaves & Handle, 5 In.	45.00
Pitcher, Sponged Brown Design, Ribbed Strap Handle, 9 1/8 In.	320.00
Pitcher, Spout, Dark Glaze, Strap Handle, Ezra Clark, 5 3/4 In.	25.00
Pitcher, Yellow, Green & Brown, Virginia, 19th Century, 6 In.	1775.00
Planter, Tree Trunk, 5 In.	28.00
Plate, Coggled Rim, 3 Line Slip Design, 9 In.	250.00
Plate, Coggled Rim, 3 Line Yellow Slip Design, 6 3/4 In.	85.00
Plate, Coggled Rim, 3 Line Yellow Slip Design, 9 In.	300.00
Plate, Coggled Rim, Yellow 4 Quill Slip, Orange Glaze, 11 1/2 In.	1025.00
Plate, Coggled Rim, Yellow Slip Flourish, 11 In.	275.00
Plate, Quill Yellow Slip, Orange Glaze, 7 1/4 In.	380.00
Plate, Sgraffito, Floral Design, Border Inscription, 1809, 9 3/4 In.	700.00

Plate, Yellow Slip Crow's Foot, Brown Glaze, 6 5/8 In. 140.00
Plate, Yellow Slip Design, 8 1/2 In. 175.00
Pot, Brown Metallic Glaze, England, 9 3/4 In. 40.00
Pot, Strap Handle, Side Spout, Greenish Glaze, 4 3/8 In. 200.00
Rooster, Signed, Dated 1973, 3 1/4 In. 35.00
Salt, Green Glaze, White Slip Floral, Word Salt On Rim, 11 3/4 In. 65.00
Salt, Hanging, Word Salt In Applied Letters, Green Slip 140.00
Soap Dish, Manganese Striped, Orange Glaze, 5 3/8 X 4 X 1 1/4 In. 675.00
Soup, Dish, Vertical Finger Loop Handle, Interior Glaze 60.00
Tankard, Pewter Lid, Reddish Glaze, Floral Design, 10 1/4 In. 4600.00
Teapot, Embossed Beading, Dark Brown Glaze, 4 In. 55.00
Tile, Goat Design, Unglazed, 4 1/8 X 4 X 1/2 In. 55.00
Toddy, Coggled Edge, 3 Line Yellow Design, 5 1/8 In. 325.00
Whistle, Horse & Rider, 2 Notes, C.1850, 4 X 4 1/8 In. 950.00
Window Prop, Lion, Greenish Glaze, 4 1/2 In., Pair 125.00
    REGOUT, see Maastricht

Richard "Richard" was the mark used on acid–etched cameo glass vases, bowls, night–lights, and lamps made in Lorraine, France, during the 1920s. The pieces were very similar to the other French cameo glasswares made by Daum, Galle, and others.

RICHARD, Perfume Bottle, Dark Blue Flowers, Moth On Lemon, Signed, 7 3/4 In. ... 625.00
Vase, Aubergine On Orange, Signed, 11 3/4 In. 440.00
Vase, Aubergine, Orange, Stylized Floral, Butterfly, 11 3/4 In. 440.00
Vase, Grapevine, Frosted, Mahogany & Yellow, Signed, 8 1/2 In. 875.00
Vase, Orange Overlay In Brown, Signed 275.00
Vase, Trees, Cottage, Lake & Mountains, Yellow Interior, 13 3/4 In. 1500.00

Ridgway pottery has been made in the Staffordshire district in England since 1808 by a series of companies with the name Ridgway. The transfer–design dinner sets are the most widely known product. They are still being made. Other pieces of Ridgway are listed under Flow Blue.

RIDGWAY, Biscuit Jar, Coaching Days, Rattan Handle, Brown, 6 1/2 In. 230.00
Bowl, Staughton's Church, 8 1/4 In. 375.00
Bowl, Waste, Oriental, Blue 35.00
Bowl, Willow, 9 1/2 In. 25.00
Creamer, Oriental, Blue 75.00
Mug, Bull On Front, Silver Luster Handle & Rim, Brown Ground 25.00
Mug, Coaching Days, Black Transfer, Amber Glaze, 4 3/4 In. 25.00
Plaque, Coaching Days, In A Snow Drift, 12 In. 130.00
Plaque, Robert Burns' Cottage, Gold Luster Highlights, 9 1/2 In. 70.00
Plate, Two Strings To Her Bow 45.00
Platter, Bachelor Watches Nell & Grandfather, 13 X 10 1/2 In. 120.00
Sugar & Creamer, Cobalt Blue Design, Flowers On White 35.00
Tea Caddy, Brown, Square, 5 3/4 X 4 1/4 In. 150.00
Tea Caddy, Coaching Days, Brown, Square, 5 3/4 X 4 1/4 In. 150.00
Tea Set, Child's, Chintz, Black On White, 12 Piece 435.00
Teapot, Brown, 5 1/2 In. 165.00
Teapot, Oriental, Blue 175.00
Tray, Pickwick Design, Silver Luster Trim, Open Handles, 9 1/2 In. 45.00

A rifle is a firearm that has a rifled bore and that is intended to be fired from the shoulder. Other firearms are listed under Gun.

RIFLE, Air, Atlas 165.00
Air, Winchester No.422 .... 110.00
Air, Winchester, No.422 .... 115.00
American Colonial Flint Fowler, Brass Mountings, C.1760, 43 In. 495.00
Benjamin, Air, Model 312, 1930s 50.00
Benjamin, Air, Model E, Nickel Plated Barrel 150.00
Bolt Action, 22 Caliber, Savage 40.00
E. James & Co., Muzzle, Double Barrel, Tiger Maple Stock 150.00
Flintlock, Art Octagonal Round Barrel, 42 In. 880.00
Fox CE 2200.00

Plates made prior to 1850 often have an unglazed foot.

French, Needle, Fire Chase Pot, Bayonet, 1867	275.00
G & H, 7mm	2750.00
Half Stock, Ohio Percussion, Marked Riddle, Patch Box, 51 In.	575.00
Hollis, Engraved, 500 Nitro	5500.00
Hopkins & Allen, 22 Rim Fire Junior	120.00
Hopkins & Allen, 22 Rim Fire, Hexagonal Barrel	120.00
Hopkins & Allen, Single Lever Action, 22 Caliber	60.00
Kentucky, Flintlock, J. Henry, Brass Fittings, 57 In.	5060.00
Kentucky, Henry Parker, Double Set Triggers, N. Moll	2900.00
Kentucky, Percussion Lock, Maple Full Stock, 54 In.	400.00
Kentucky, Percussion Lock, Maple Half Stock, 53 In.	400.00
Military, No.7, World War II, Japanese	95.00
Mississippi, 54 Caliber, Civil War	850.00
Percussion, Brass Patch Box, Curly Maple Half Stock, 53 In.	250.00
Percussion, Brass Patch Box, Silver Inlays, 40 1/2 In.	1100.00
Percussion, Brass Patch Box, Tiger Stripe Finish, 46 1/2 In.	325.00
Percussion, Brass Patch Ox, 7 Silver Inlays, Maple Stock, 52 In.	425.00
Percussion, Curly Maple Full Stock, 65 In.	200.00
Percussion, Half Stock, 45 Caliber, W. Barnhart, 34 In.	375.00
Roper, 52 Caliber	1200.00
Sharps, 4 Barrel, Pepper Box, Brass Frame, Gutta–Percha Grips	375.00
Springfield, Trap Door, Strap, Bayonet, Scabbard	395.00
Trap Door, Swiss, 36 1/2 In. Barrel, Plum Blue Finish	1100.00
Wheelock, Gray Patina, Octagonal Barrel, I. Georg, Munich	3520.00
Winchester 1892, 32–20	450.00
Winchester, Air, Model 416	90.00 To 95.00
Winchester, Air, Model 422	115.00
Winchester, Carbine, Grade 270, Box	4125.00
Winchester, Carbine, Type 3	1500.00
Winchester, Model 70s, 250–3000	4400.00
Winchester, Model 1873, 32–20 Special, 1/2 Sight, Blue	1495.00
Winchester, Model 1890, Blue	795.00
Winchester, Model 1892, 25–20 NRA	850.00
Winchester, Model 1906, Pump, Round Barrel	110.00
Wurfflein, Philadelphia, 1877	455.00

Riviera dinnerware was made by the Homer Laughlin Co. of Newell, West Virginia, from 1938 to 1950. The pattern was similar in coloring and in mood to Fiesta and Harlequin. The Riviera plates and cup handles were square.

RIVIERA, Baker, Green, Oval	10.00
Bowl, Red, 9 In.	14.00
Bowl, Vegetable, Green, 8 In.	10.00
Cup, Mauve	6.00
Jug, Batter, Green, Cover	58.00
Pitcher, Batter, Green	100.00
Plate, Red, 9 In.	12.00
Platter, Yellow, Closed Handle, 11 1/2 In.	10.00
Teapot, Ivory	65.00
Tumbler, 1 Yellow Band, 5 In.	10.00

Rockingham, in the United States, is a brown glazed pottery with a tortoiseshell–like glaze. It was made from 1840 to 1900 by many American potteries. Mottled brown Rockingham wares were first made in England at the Rockingham factory. Other types of ceramics were also made by the English firm.

ROCKINGHAM, Bank, Bear	65.00
Bottle, Corked Hole, Bureau Shape, 5 In.	85.00

Bottle, High Laced Shoe, 7 3/4 In.	125.00
Bottle, Toby	650.00
Bowl, 2 3/8 X 9 3/8 In.	35.00
Bowl, 4 1/2 In.	65.00
Bowl, Embossed Exterior, 4 X 9 In.	35.00
Bowl, Embossed Exterior, 8 1/4 In.	35.00
Bowl, Embossed Rim, 9 X 9 In.	45.00
Bowl, Mixing, 6 3/4 In.	175.00
Bowl, Pouring Spout, Embossed Exterior, 9 3/4 In.	85.00
Bowl, Shallow, 3 3/8 In.	65.00
Creamer, 3 7/8 In.	25.00
Creamer, Figural, Cover, 9 1/2 In.	125.00
Creamer, Ribbed Strap Handle, 4 1/8 In.	90.00
Crock, Embossed Peacocks, Cover, 5 In.	65.00
Cuspidor, Embossed Design, 7 In.	12.50
Cuspidor, Embossed Ribs, 8 1/4 In.	10.00
Cuspidor, Embossed Shells, 8 In.	35.00
Dish, Side Handle, Cover, 6 1/2 In.	75.00
Figurine, Dog, 9 1/2 In.	750.00
Figurine, Dog, Seated, 10 1/2 In.	325.00
Flask, Embossed Morning Glory, Eagle, Flag, 7 1/4 In.	100.00
Frame, Ornate Embossed Design, Mirror Glass, 9 3/4 X 11 1/4 In.	550.00
Jar, Cover, 9 1/4 In.	150.00
Jar, Paneled, Embossed Handle, Cover, 9 1/4 In.	175.00
Mug, 2 5/8 In.	15.00
Mug, 3 3/8 In.	45.00
Mug, Embossed Beaded Bands, 3 1/4 In.	35.00
Mug, Ribbed Strap Handle, 3 7/8 In.	70.00
Pie Plate, 10 In.	65.00 To 85.00
Pie Plate, 7 3/4 In.	65.00
Pie Plate, Dark Glaze, 9 1/2 In.	40.00
Pitcher, Bennington Mold, Glazed, 11 3/4 In.	425.00
Pitcher, Bust of Washington In Wreath, 8 In.	90.00
Pitcher, Cover, Solid Brown Glaze, 9 3/4 In.	30.00
Pitcher, Embossed Flutes, Corseted Band, 5 1/2 In.	205.00
Pitcher, Embossed Hanging Game, 8 1/2 In.	150.00
Pitcher, Embossed Rim Design, 8 In.	55.00
Pitcher, Embossed Vantage & Thistles, 9 In.	45.00
Pitcher, Horsehead Handle, Hunting Scene, Marked, 8 In.	125.00
Pitcher, Hound Handle, Embossed Hunt Scene, 9 3/4 In.	750.00
Pitcher, Hound Handle, Nichols & Alford	150.00
Pitcher, Hound Handle, Rope Border, Marked XXX/ALE, 9 3/4 In.	165.00
Pitcher, Hunter, Game, Dog	135.00
Pitcher, Paneled With Leaf Type Design, 9 7/8 In.	65.00
Shaving Mug, Embossed Scene, Cherubs Milking Goat, 3 7/8 In.	115.00
Soap Dish, Leaves On Rim, Paneled Bottom	100.00
Soap Dish, Paneled, Oval, Side Drain, 6 X 4 In.	75.00
Spittoon, Gothic Arch, Side Vent, 6 1/2 In.	20.00
Spittoon, Gothic Arch, Side Vent, 7 1/2 In.	30.00
Teapot, Applied Floral Vines, 7 In.	350.00
Teapot, Embossed Ribs, Acanthus Leaves, 7 3/4 In.	120.00
Teapot, Paneled, Embossed Leaf Design, 5 1/8 In.	75.00
Teapot, Rebecca At The Well, 6 In.	65.00
Teapot, Rebecca At The Well, Brown, 8 In.	65.00
Window Prop, Female Busts, 4 1/2 In., Pair	390.00

ROGERS, see John Rogers

Rookwood pottery was made in Cincinnati, Ohio, from 1880 to 1960. All of this art pottery is marked, most with the famous flame mark. The R is reversed and placed back to back with the letter P. Flames surround the letters. After 1900, a Roman numeral was added to the mark to indicate the year. The name and some of the molds were purchased in 1984; new items will be clearly marked.

ROOKWOOD, Ashtray, Alligator On Side, Mottled Glaze, Dated 1922 .... 125.00

Ashtray, Embossed Figure, Columbia University, 7 In.	22.00
Ashtray, Italian Blue	40.00
Ashtray, Molded Fish, Lime Green	95.00
Ashtray, Raven	45.00
Ashtray, White Fish	42.00
Bookends, Girl, Hoop Skirt & Fan, Pink	195.00
Bookends, Owl On Book, Brown, Signed, 1924, 6 1/2 In.	75.00
Bookends, Rooks, High Glaze, Green	135.00 To 140.00
Bookends, Rooks, Ivory, 1941	200.00
Bookends, Water Lilies, Shaded Ocher, 1941, Pair	145.00
Bowl, Bulb, Vellum, Art Deco, Incised Pattern, Aqua	120.00
Bowl, Cream, Band Initial P, Pink Interior, 1916, 3 1/2 X 9 1/2 In.	110.00
Bowl, Purple Exterior, Blue Interior, 13 In.	80.00
Box, Embossed Man's Head On Lid, Flowers, Lions, 4 In.	175.00
Candleholder, Attached Saucer Base, Finger Handles, Rose, Pair	85.00
Candleholder, Dusty Rose, 3 Wild Rose Panels, 1920, 5 X 1 1/2 In.	40.00
Candleholder, Pink Matte Glaze, 1920	40.00
Candlestick, Cylindrical Stem, Glossy Blue, 10 1/4 In., Pair	165.00
Candlestick, Italian Green, 5 In.	50.00
Candlestick, Lily Pad, 1921, Pair	65.00
Candlestick, Pond Lily, Gold, 1921, Pair	50.00
Charger, Scenic, Moonlit Night, Joe Jefferson, 1902, 18 1/2 In.	1400.00
Chocolate Pot, Cover, Signed S.T., 1888	375.00
Dish, Almond, 1890	145.00
Ewer, 4 Swimming Fish, Sea-Green Glaze, 1900, 7 In.	1570.00
Ewer, Trefoil Lip, Dragon, Sea-Green Glaze, 1897, 9 In.	2300.00
Figurine, Pelican, No.6149, Open Beak, Yellow High Glaze, 1948	90.00
Figurine, Seal, Brown, 1929, 4 1/2 In.	135.00
Flower Frog, Bird, Black, Dated 1923, 6 In.	200.00
Flower Holder, Glossy Blue, 1928, 4 1/2 X 5 1/2 In.	95.00
Jar, Cover, Jewel, Triangles & Flowers, Pink, Blue, 6 In.	*Illus* 650.00
Jar, Knobbed Domical Top, Triangles & Flowers, 1930, 6 In.	725.00
Jar, Sage Green, 7 1/2 In.	95.00
Jug, Dragonfly, 1883, 4 1/2 In.	420.00
Jug, Hattie Horton, 1883, 4 3/4 In.	450.00
Jug, Honey, Blue Butterfly, 4 3/4 In.	550.00
Jug, Honey, Incised Clover & Flowers	315.00
Jug, Light Blue, Handle, 1947, 5 1/4 In.	95.00
Jug, Whiskey, Corn Design	625.00
Lamp Base, Shoreline Scene, Blues, Gray & Peach, 9 1/2 In.	425.00
Lamp, Blue, High Glaze, 1920	195.00
Lamp, Vellum, Scenic, Signed Lenore Asbury, Dated 1917	7500.00
Mug, Louis Desmant	175.00
Paperweight, Miss Duck, 1963	125.00
Paperweight, Potter At Wheel, 1935	58.50
Pitcher, 3 Spouts, Matte Green, 1927, 5 1/2 In.	125.00
Pitcher, Pale Green	18.00
Plaque, After The Storm, Schmidt, 1915	3575.00
Plaque, Connecticut River, 1912, 10 1/2 X 8 1/2 In.	4840.00
Plaque, Evening Glow, Schmidt, 1915	2090.00
Plaque, Summer Landscape, Levinda Epply, 8 1/4 X 10 1/2 In.	3700.00
Plate, Butterfly, 1884	225.00
Plate, Cameoware, 1888, 8 In.	165.00
Spoon Rest, Green, Pair	40.00
Sugar & Creamer, Salmon Color, 1891	475.00
Teapot, Glossy Blue, 1915	165.00 To 195.00
Tile, Lakeside Mountainous Landscape, 11 3/4 In.	1690.00
Tile, Stylized Landscape, Framed, C.A. Duell	2860.00
Tile, Tennis Player, 6 In.	150.00
Tray, Card, Flapping Rook, 1954	85.00
Trivet, Geometric Design, Brown, 1954	40.00
Trivet, Sea Gulls, Hand Painted	150.00
Umbrella Stand, Blended	185.00
Vase, 1st Scientific Assembly, 1949, 7 In.	75.00

Vase, 2 Turtles, Tiger Eye Glaze, 1898, 5 1/8 In. 965.00
Vase, 4 Fish, Flora, Fauna, Coral, Hurley, 1904, 7 In. 3500.00
Vase, 4 Nude Women, Birds, Burnt Orange, Jens Jensen, 12 1/4 In. 4800.00
Vase, Apple Blossoms, Pink, Marked XXIX, 6 In. 265.00
Vase, Applied Flowers, Barbotine Style, E.G., 9 1/2 In. 450.00
Vase, Arabia, 11 In. 165.00
Vase, Art Deco, Beige, Flared, 1947, 10 1/2 X 8 1/4 In. 125.00
Vase, Arts & Crafts Design, Teco Green, Buds, 1910, 6 1/2 In. 110.00
Vase, Autumn Leaves, Brown–Red & Green, 6 In. 75.00
Vase, Baluster Form, Continuous Landscape Scene, 12 3/4 In. 1800.00
Vase, Band of Holly Leaf & Berry, Blue Matte, 1916, 9 1/4 In. 125.00
Vase, Blackbird Under Pine Boughs, 1906, 8 1/2 In. 2170.00
Vase, Blue Flowers On Green Branches, Blue Wax Matte, 1922, 11 In. 485.00
Vase, Branch Spouting Flowers Around Neck, 1885, 7 1/2 In. 425.00
Vase, Butterfat, 17 In. 1800.00
Vase, Butterflies, Bamboo, 1883, 12 In. .... *Illus* 1150.00
Vase, Carved Matte Floral, 1929, 12 In. 2800.00
Vase, Cherry Blossoms Band, Vellum, 8 In. 550.00
Vase, Daffodils, Constance Baker, Shape No.9050, 1903 .... 696.00
Vase, Daisies In Relief, 1934, 5 In. 40.00
Vase, Delalerche, 8 1/2 In. 550.00
Vase, Dog, Trees Under Glaze, 5 1/2 In. 85.00
Vase, Dogwood Blossoms, Stream, Shoulder Handles, 1885, 8 3/4 In. 550.00
Vase, Dragon Around Neck, Tiger Eye Glaze, 1894, 5 7/8 In. 2175.00
Vase, Embossed Water Lilies, Yellow, 6 1/4 In. 52.00
Vase, Fan, Art Deco, Yellow, 5 In. 85.00
Vase, Fish, Sea Green, 1904, 7 In. 1700.00
Vase, Fish, Vellum, Blue–Green Sea, 1909, 11 1/2 In. .... *Illus* 1870.00
Vase, Floral, Vellum, Daffodils, Pink Ground, 1912, 8 3/4 In. 445.00
Vase, Floral, Yellow Base, Olive, M.A. Daly, 1901, 5 1/2 In. 475.00
Vase, Flowers, Yellow Wax Matte, Signed, 1927, 17 1/4 In. 1540.00
Vase, Frolicking Oriental Goldfish, 1885, 6 3/4 In. 1575.00
Vase, Glossy Light Brown, 1958, 4 1/2 In. 55.00
Vase, Green, Henchel, Carved Wax Matte, 1913, 6 X 4 1/2 In. 350.00
Vase, Hawthorne, Flowers, Vellum, 1909, 8 In. 715.00
Vase, Hawthorne, Flowers, Vellum, 1909, 8 In. .... *Illus* 715.00
Vase, Horned Dragon, Tiger Eye Glaze, Marked, 1885, 6 3/8 In. 1100.00
Vase, Hunting Scene, Vellum, F. Rotherbusch, 1917, 8 In. 1100.00
Vase, Intaglio Branch Snakes, Flowers, Caramel, 7 1/2 In. 500.00
Vase, Iris Glaze, Shirayamadani, 9 1/2 In. 600.00
Vase, Iris, Carl Schmidt, 1905, 10 1/2 In. 2750.00

Rookwood, Jar, Cover, Jewel,
Triangles & Flowers, Pink,
Blue, 6 In.

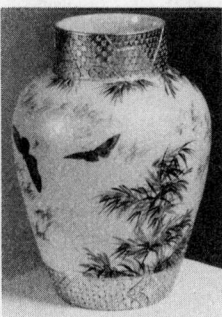

Rookwood, Vase, Butterflies,
Bamboo, 1883, 12 In.

Rookwood, Vase,
Red Flowers,
Rose Ground,
1927, 6 In.

Rookwood, Vase,
Tulip, Pink Ground,
Wax Matte, 1937

Vase, K.S., Crystalline, 7 In.	95.00
Vase, Leaves, Yellow & Green Ground, Hurley, 1926, 12 X 9 1/2 In.	1600.00
Vase, Matte Slate Blue, 1919, 9 In.	225.00
Vase, Mauve Glaze, 1925, 5 5/8 In.	125.00
Vase, Melon Ribbed, Matte Rose & Deep Green, 1931, 4 1/2 In.	55.00
Vase, Modeled Vellum, No.2143, 1918, 7 1/4 In.	245.00
Vase, Molded Floral Spray, Trophy Cup Shape, White, 1936, 6 3/4 In.	110.00
Vase, Molded Fruit, Black & Turquoise, 1928, 6 1/2 X 7 In.	125.00
Vase, Molded Gooseberries, 1921, 5 In.	150.00
Vase, Oriental Poppies, Marked, 1899, 19 In.	2665.00
Vase, Outward Rolled Rim, Double Handles, Blue, Dated 1929, 8 In.	37.50
Vase, Pillow, Olga Reed, 7 In.	350.00
Vase, Pink To Gray, Rooks & Branches	85.00
Vase, Pink, Wax Matte, 6 In.	395.00
Vase, Poppy Flowers & Buds, Rose & Green, L.N.L., 1928, 11 In.	365.00
Vase, Puce Clover, 12 In.	95.00
Vase, Raised Flowers, Matte Rose, 5 In.	65.00
Vase, Red Flowers, Rose Ground, 1927, 6 In. ....*Illus*	350.00
Vase, Rooks & Branches, Pink To Gray	85.00
Vase, Sampans In Harbor, Marked, 1924, 10 1/2 In.	3145.00
Vase, Scenic, Vellum Glaze, Lenore Ashbury, 1921, 8 1/4 In.	665.00
Vase, Scenic, Vellum, Cylindrical Form, L. Ashbury, 1914, 8 In.	797.50
Vase, Scenic, Vellum, Sally E. Coyne, 1922, Shape No.913	1950.00
Vase, Silver Bands, Iris Glaze Floral, 1901, 5 1/2 In.	3000.00
Vase, Silver Overlay, Sally Coyne, 1902, 7 In.	2750.00
Vase, Sprigs of Foliage, Urn Shape, Tan, 7 In.	85.00
Vase, Starkville, Blue, 1963, 12 In.	145.00
Vase, Stylized Band of Design, Turquoise Ground, 1919, 21 1/2 In.	600.00
Vase, Stylized Flower Stalks, Blue, C.1965, 12 3/8 In.	225.00
Vase, Stylized Leaves, White, Caroline Stegner, 1945, 5 1/4 In.	350.00
Vase, Stylized Trees, Maroon & Green, 8 In.	125.00
Vase, Swallows In Flight, White Blooms, Marked, 1883, 24 In.	3875.00
Vase, Tropical Leaves, Waves, Green Matte, Mary Nourse, 1904, 9 In.	825.00
Vase, Tulip, Pink Ground, Wax Matte, 1937 ....*Illus*	550.00
Vase, Vellum Finish, Sea Green, 1921, 6 1/2 In.	65.00
Vase, Vellum Florals, Signed L.A., 1929, 10 In.	6000.00
Vase, Vellum Glaze, Blue & Green Shades, Sunset, 1915, 7 1/2 In.	1080.00
Vase, Vellum, Flowers, Upper Blue Band, 1905, 7 1/2 In.	357.50
Vase, Vines & Flowers, M. McDonald, 1918, 7 In.	495.00
Vase, Wax Resist, Grapes & Leaves, 1930, 6 In.	495.00
Vase, White Poppies, Iris Glaze, 1907, 10 In.	3145.00
Wall Pocket, Green Matte, 7 1/2 In.	160.00
Wall Pocket, No.2008, Green Matte, 1930, 7 1/2 In., Pair	160.00

ROSALINE, see Steuben

Rose bowls were popular during the 1880s. Rose petals were kept in the open bowl to add fragrance to a room, a popular idea in a time of limited personal hygiene. The glass bowls were made with crimped tops, which kept the petals inside. Many types of Victorian art glass were made into rose bowls.

ROSE BOWL, Beaded Opalescent	38.00
Blue Opalescent, Open	35.00
Lace Opalescent Design, 4 In.	45.00
Satin Glass, Blue	85.00
Satin Glass, Green, Painted Lavender Flowers	45.00
Satin Glass, Pale To Dark Blue, Enameled Flowers, 5 1/2 X 6 In.	225.00
Satin Glass, Pink, Shell & Seaweed, Small	65.00
Satin Glass, Shaded Pink, 8–Crimp, 3 X 3 3/4 In.	65.00
Satin Glass, Yellow	75.00

Rose Canton china is similar to Rose Medallion, except no people are pictured in the decoration. It was made during the nineteenth and twentieth centuries in greens, pinks, and other colors.

ROSE CANTON, Bouillon, Saucer, Cover, Handles	65.00

Bowl, Vegetable, Cover, Oval, Berry Finial, Orange Peel Glaze 175.00

> Rose Medallion china was made in China during the nineteenth and twentieth centuries. It is a distinctive design picturing people, flowers, birds, and butterflies. Pieces are colored in greens, pinks, and other colors.

ROSE MEDALLION, Bouillon, Saucer, Cover .... 20.00 To 35.00
Bowl, Rice, Cover, 4 1/2 In. 95.00
Bowl, Underplate, Reticulated 1100.00
Bowl, Vegetable, Cover 235.00
Bowl, Vegetable, Cover, Acorn Finial, 7 1/2 X 9 In. 310.00
Bowl, Vegetable, Cover, Alternating Figural & Floral, 11 In. 220.00
Bowl, Vegetable, Diamond Shape, Cover 325.00
Brush Pot 225.00
Chamber Pot, Cover, Button Finial, Loop Handle, 7 3/4 In. 385.00
Chocolate Pot 450.00
Cup, Syllabub, Twisted Handle 225.00
Dish, Cover, Almond Shape, 8 In. 85.00
Dish, Serving, Oval, Handles, Domed Cover 450.00
Dish, Translucent, Marked, 5 In. 20.00
Flask, Moon, Gold, Dragon Ears 4950.00
Fruit Basket, Pierced Sides, Left Handles, 10 1/2 In. 495.00
Jar, Cover, Cylindrical, 3 1/2 In. 235.00
Jardiniere, Design Surrounding Exterior, 10 X 8 3/4 In. 715.00
Jardiniere, Lion Finial On Lid, C.1890, 20 In. 1200.00
Lamp, Carcel, Pair 3520.00
Plate, 19th Century, 9 1/2 In., 5 Piece 475.00
Plate, Blue Spiral, Reticulated Edge, 7 In. 350.00
Plate, Dinner, 3 Flute Rim 45.00
Plate, Monogram B, Bidwell Estate 200.00
Platter, Fruit, Footed, Oval, 12 X 15 1/4 In. 665.00
Platter, Marked, 15 In. 225.00
Punch Bowl, 6 3/8 In. 900.00
Punch Bowl, Design On Interior & Exterior, 16 In. 2975.00
Punch Bowl, Panels of Birds & Butterflies, 12 3/4 In. 1430.00
Sauceboat, Twisted Handle 275.00
Saucer, Center Duck Design, Demitasse 165.00
Tea Set, Traveling, Lined Reed Basket 270.00
Teapot, C.1840, 10 In. 850.00
Teapot, Inverted Cone, Elongated Cover 450.00
Teapot, Wicker Handle, 5 In. 195.00
Umbrella Stand, Floral & Figural Scenes, 24 In. 1435.00
Umbrella Stand, Fluted Body, Floral, Figural Scenes, 24 In. 1300.00
Vase, Baluster, Applied Handles, 18 In. 1100.00
Vase, Figural & Floral Panels, Butterflies, Roses, 12 In. 825.00
Vase, Gilt Dragons At Shoulders, 14 3/4 In. 150.00
   ROSE O'NEILL, see Kewpie

> Rose Tapestry porcelain was made by the Royal Bayreuth factory of Tettau, Germany, during the late nineteenth century. The surface of the porcelain was pressed against a coarse fabric while it was still damp, and the impressions remained on the finished porcelain. It looks and feels like a textured cloth. Very skillful reproductions are being made that even include a variation of the Royal Bayreuth mark, so be careful when buying.

ROSE TAPESTRY, Bell, Pink & Yellow Roses, White Ground, Royal Bayreuth 495.00
Box, Dresser, Cover, Kidney Shape, 4 3/4 X 3 7/8 In. 365.00
Box, Fan Shape, Royal Bayreuth, Green Mark, 2 X 3 1/2 In. 210.00
Box, Hatpin Holder, Royal Bayreuth, Blue, Mark, 4 X 4 In. 395.00
Box, Ring, Lovers Scene On Cover, Royal Bayreuth 225.00
Creamer, Pinched Spout, 3–Color Roses 140.00
Creamer, Pinched Spout, Beige Roses, Royal Bayreuth 295.00
Creamer, Pinched Spout, Blue Mark, 3 1/2 In. 225.00
Creamer, Pink Roses, 3 1/2 In. 205.00

Creamer, Royal Bayreuth, 3 1/4 In. 190.00
Ewer, Roses, Daisies, Leaves, Gold Handle & Trim, 2 1/2 In. 395.00
Fernery, Gold Handle, 3–Color Roses 225.00
Flowerpot, Bulbous Base, Interior Drainer, Blue Mark, 4 In. 550.00
Hair Receiver, Goats Grazing, Blue Mark 225.00
Hatpin Holder, 3–Color, Royal Bayreuth 285.00
Hatpin Holder, Blue Mark 450.00
Hatpin Holder, Courting Couple, Cutout Base, Blue Mark 395.00
Hatpin Holder, Pink Roses 305.00
Jardiniere, Cows, Water, Sunset Scene 250.00
Match Holder, Wall, Royal Bayreuth 400.00
Pitcher, Alligator Spout, Royal Bayreuth 400.00
Pitcher, Court Lady, Cavalier In Formal Garden, Blue Mark 425.00
Pitcher, Goat, Pinched Spout, Blue Mark 235.00
Pitcher, Milk, Scenic, Blue Mark 285.00
Plate, Ornate Rim, Blue Mark, 7 1/2 In. 250.00
Powder Box, Blue Mark .... 225.00 To 250.00
Salt & Pepper, 3–Color Roses, Blue Mark 425.00
Spooner, Blue Mark 275.00
Tray, 3–Color Roses, Blue Mark, 8 X 11 In. 450.00
Tray, Dresser, Blue Mark, 8 X 11 In. 325.00
Tumbler, Royal Bayreuth 160.00
Vase, 3–Color Roses, Gold Edge, Blue Mark, 6 1/2 In. 425.00
Vase, Chateau Scene, Blue Mark, 4 In. 225.00
Vase, Rows of Colored Roses, Ferns & Leaves, 5 1/2 In. 350.00
Vase, Scenic, Colonial Couple In Forest, 4 1/2 In. 230.00
Vase, Scenic, Deer In Forest, Royal Bayreuth, 5 1/2 In. 350.00

MARKE   Rosenthal porcelain was made at the factory established in Selb,
Bavaria, in 1880. The factory is still making fine–quality tablewares
Rosenthal   and figurines. A series of Christmas plates was made from 1910.
Other limited edition plates have been made since 1971.

ROSENTHAL, Compote, Figural Handles, Gold, 9 1/4 X 4 3/4 In. 275.00
Dish, Hand Painted, Gold Handles, Oval, 4 X 9 In. 45.00
Figurine, Ballerina, 12 In. 500.00
Figurine, Black Hat & Cape, Arm Over Face, Paper Label, 7 1/4 In. 75.00
Figurine, Bremen Musicians, Horse, Dog, Cat, Rooster, All White 225.00
Figurine, Cat, Reclining, No.1907, F. Heidenreigh, 5 1/2 In. 110.00
Figurine, Child, With Cat, Signed Claire Weiss 125.00
Figurine, Dachshund, Begging, Karner, 9 In. 375.00
Figurine, Deer, Sitting, 4 In. 150.00
Figurine, Dog, Boston Terrier, Seated 350.00
Figurine, Duckling, 9 In. 225.00
Figurine, Fairy Queen, L. Freidrich–Granau, 10 In. 350.00
Figurine, Girl, 1930, 7 In. 90.00
Figurine, Nude, Kneeling, A. Caasmann, 5 1/2 In. 325.00
Figurine, Parrot, Large 250.00
Figurine, Pheasant, Miniature 75.00
Figurine, Princess & Frog, No.7333 .... 275.00
Figurine, Princess & Frog, White, Gold, Pastel, 11 In. 375.00
Figurine, Princess, Kneeling By Goose, Egg In Hand, F. Liebermann 225.00
Figurine, Sitting Dachshund Puppy, Brown, 6 In. 200.00
Hatpin Holder, Yellow, Gold Top, 5 In. 60.00
Lamp, Hand Painted Yellow & White Daisies, 9 1/2 In. 85.00
Plate, Christmas, 1913 .... 130.00
Plate, Empire, 10 In. 12.00
Plate, Pink Roses, Leaves, Gold Border, Signed, 18 In. 25.00
Plate, Serving, Ivory, Gold F & Cobalt Blue Borders, 12 Piece 450.00
Plate, Wiinblad Christmas, 1971 .... 499.00
Plate, Wiinblad Christmas, 1973 .... 245.00
Plate, Wiinblad Christmas, 1974 .... 225.00
Platter, Empire, 15 In. 25.00
Platter, Sterling Rim, Roses, Ivory Ground, 12 In. 85.00
Powder Jar, Cover, Large Rose, Pale Green, Gold Trim, Puff, Artist 85.00

Sugar, Cover, Green Floral	20.00
Teapot, Floral, Tilt Trim, Twig Handle	45.00
Vase, Cameo, Greek God, Violet, Cream–Gold Bead, 1930, 7 In., Pair	95.00

The Roseville Pottery Company was organized in Roseville, Ohio, in 1890. Another plant was opened in Zanesville, Ohio, in 1898. Many types of pottery were made until 1954. Early wares include sgraffito, Olympic, and Rozane. Later lines were often made with molded decorations, especially flowers and fruit. Pieces are marked "Roseville."

Roseville
U.S.A.

ROSEVILLE, Ashtray & Box, Cigarette, Hyde Park	45.00
Ashtray, Donatello, Green	95.00
Ashtray, Hyde Park	30.00
Ashtray, Magnolia, Green	45.00
Ashtray, Pine Cone, Blue, 3 In.	50.00 To 65.00
Ashtray, Pine Cone, Brown, Triangular	95.00
Ashtray, Snowberry, Blue	35.00
Ashtray, Snowberry, Green	55.00
Bank, Apple	65.00
Bank, Frog, Green	95.00
Bank, Pig, 1900s	100.00 To 110.00
Basket, Apple Blossom, Green	75.00
Basket, Apple Blossom, Green, 9 In.	95.00
Basket, Blackberry, 6 In.	525.00
Basket, Blackberry, 7 In.	475.00
Basket, Bushberry, Blue, 10 In.	100.00
Basket, Bushberry, Brown, 12 In.	145.00
Basket, Clematis, Blue, 7 In.	75.00
Basket, Clematis, Orange, 10 In.	125.00
Basket, Columbine, Pink, 10 In.	135.00
Basket, Dogwood, 9 In.	40.00
Basket, Florentine, Hanging	48.00
Basket, Foxglove, Blue, 8 In.	65.00
Basket, Freesia, Brown	74.00
Basket, Freesia, Green, 7 In.	60.00
Basket, Fuchsia, Blue, 10 In.	190.00 To 195.00
Basket, Gardenia, Brown, 8 In.	75.00
Basket, Gardenia, Brown, 10 In.	85.00
Basket, Hanging, Clematis, Green	95.00
Basket, Hanging, Columbine	110.00
Basket, Hanging, Dahlrose, 7 In.	75.00 To 150.00
Basket, Hanging, Futura, 5 1/4 X 8 In.	295.00 To 350.00
Basket, Hanging, Imperial I	150.00
Basket, Hanging, Jonquil	225.00
Basket, Hanging, Ming Tree, Green, 14 In.	185.00
Basket, Hanging, Peony, Green	100.00
Basket, Hanging, Pine Cone, Blue	250.00
Basket, Hanging, Roxanne, White	75.00
Basket, Hanging, Silhouette, Brown	80.00
Basket, Hanging, Water Lily, Blue	110.00
Basket, Hanging, Zephyr Lily, Blue	75.00
Basket, Hanging, Zephyr Lily, Brown	110.00
Basket, Lustre, Pink, 9 1/2 In.	100.00
Basket, Ming Tree, Blue, 12 In.	160.00
Basket, Ming Tree, Green, 12 In.	110.00 To 140.00
Basket, Ming Tree, Green, Hanging	125.00
Basket, Peony, Gold, 8 In.	75.00
Basket, Peony, Pink	85.00
Basket, Pine Cone, Green, Sharp Mold	210.00
Basket, Rozane, Creamware, 1917	60.00
Basket, Silhouette, Turquoise	59.00
Basket, Silhouette, White, 6 In.	45.00
Basket, Snowberry, Blue, 8 In.	75.00
Basket, Thorn Apple, Pink, 10 In.	165.00

Basket, Vista, 12 In.	450.00
Basket, Wincraft, Chartreuse, Brown, 8 In.	75.00
Basket, Windsor, Rust, 10 In.	225.00
Bookends, Bittersweet	85.00
Bookends, Bleeding Heart, Blue	35.00
Bookends, Foxglove, Blue	95.00
Bookends, Freesia, Blue	80.00
Bookends, Magnolia, Brown	85.00
Bookends, Magnolia, Green	70.00 To 85.00
Bookends, Ming Tree	155.00
Bookends, Peony, Tan	70.00
Bookends, Pine Cone, Brown	200.00 To 225.00
Bookends, Pine Cone, Green	175.00
Bookends, Snowberry, Pink	50.00 To 80.00
Bookends, Wincraft, Turquoise	45.00
Bookends, Zephyr Lily, Brown	50.00 To 85.00
Bowl, Apple Blossom, Green, 8 In.	32.00
Bowl, Apple Blossom, Pink, 6 In.	36.00
Bowl, Apple Blossom, Twig Handles, Blue, 6 In.	90.00
Bowl, Blackberry, 3 X 6 In.	140.00
Bowl, Bushberry, Blue, 4 In.	40.00
Bowl, Bushberry, Blue, 5 In.	50.00
Bowl, Capri, Green, 8 In.	18.00
Bowl, Carnelian I, Blue Drip Over Pink, 10 1/2 In.	65.00
Bowl, Carnelian I, Green, 12 In.	275.00
Bowl, Carnelian II, Rose, Turquoise, 9 X 12 1/2 In.	70.00
Bowl, Cherry Blossom, Pink, 9 1/2 In.	175.00
Bowl, Corinthian, 3 In.	30.00
Bowl, Cremona, Green, 10 In.	95.00
Bowl, Dahlrose, Brown, 10 In.	45.00
Bowl, Dawn, Rose	65.00
Bowl, Donatello, 3 X 9 In.	60.00
Bowl, Falline, Brown, 11 In.	135.00
Bowl, Falline, Tan, 9 In.	200.00
Bowl, Ferella, Turquoise, Red, Oval, 13 In.	210.00
Bowl, Florentine, Flat Handles, Low	30.00
Bowl, Freesia, Blue–Green, 14 In.	62.00
Bowl, Fuchsia, Brown, 5 In.	55.00
Bowl, Gardenia, Brown, 14 In.	150.00
Bowl, Iris, Blue, 8 In.	85.00
Bowl, Luffa, 14 In.	75.00
Bowl, Magnolia, Blue, 3 1/4 X 11 In.	65.00
Bowl, Moss, Blue, 11 In.	60.00
Bowl, Mostique, 6 In.	75.00
Bowl, Mostique, 7 In.	28.00 To 55.00
Bowl, Mostique, 8 In.	22.50 To 65.00
Bowl, Peony, 4 In.	25.00
Bowl, Pine Cone, Brown, 4 In.	95.00
Bowl, Pine Cone, Brown, 8 In.	85.00
Bowl, Pine Cone, Brown, 12 In.	150.00
Bowl, Rabbit, 5 In.	55.00
Bowl, Rosecraft, Black, 8 In.	30.00
Bowl, Rosecraft, Brown, Hexagonal, 4 In.	200.00
Bowl, Royal Capri, Gold, 7 In.	125.00
Bowl, Sunflower, 4 In.	135.00
Bowl, Tourmaline, Blue & Gold, 8 In.	49.00
Bowl, Tourmaline, Blue & Tan, 4 1/2in.	40.00
Bowl, Tourmaline, Blue & Yellow, 8 In.	48.00
Bowl, Tuscany, Console, Flat, Pink, 11 In.	75.00
Bowl, Tuscany, Pink, 11 In.	35.00
Bowl, Venetian, 9 In.	45.00
Bowl, Vista, 7 In.	55.00
Bowl, Wisteria, Brown, 4 In.	135.00
Bowl, Zephyr Lily, Green, 14 In.	50.00

Box, Apple Blossom, Pink, 12 In. 45.00
Bulb Bowl, Zephyr Lily, Green, 6 1/2 In. .... 58.00 To 82.50
Candleholder, Apple Blossom, Green, 2 In., Pair 45.00
Candleholder, Bushberry, 5 In., Pair 40.00
Candleholder, Cherry Blossom, 4 In., Pair 195.00
Candleholder, Earlam, 3 In. 45.00
Candleholder, Florentine, 2 1/2 In. 25.00
Candleholder, Freesia, 2 In., Pair 35.00
Candleholder, Freesia, Green, 2 In., Pair 40.00
Candleholder, Futura, Pair 250.00
Candleholder, Gold Traced, 10 In. 300.00
Candleholder, Goodnight 325.00
Candleholder, Iris, Brown, 4 1/2 In. 50.00
Candleholder, Luffa, 5 In. 120.00
Candleholder, Magnolia, Green, Pair 45.00
Candleholder, Ming Tree, White .... 28.00 To 55.00
Candleholder, Pine Cone, Green, 2 1/2 In. 45.00
Candleholder, Snowberry, 3 In. 50.00
Candleholder, Velmoss II, Rose, 4 1/2 In., Pair 70.00
Candleholder, Water Lily, Brown, 2 In., Pair 65.00
Candleholder, Zephyr Lily, 2 In., Pair 20.00
Candleholder, Zephyr Lily, 4 1/2 In., Pair 42.00
Chamber Pot, Dutch, 11 X 13 In. 300.00
Cigarette Holder, Pine Cone, Blue 55.00
Console Set, Clematis 70.00
Console Set, Ferrella, Boat Shape, Red, 3 Piece 575.00
Console Set, Freesia, Brown, 3 Piece 95.00
Console Set, Pine Cone, Brown, 3 Piece 225.00
Console Set, Tuscany, 2 Handles, Pink, 3 Piece 48.00
Console, Donatello 25.00
Console, Pine Cone, Brown 125.00
Cookie Jar, Apple Blossom 145.00
Cookie Jar, Clematis .... 125.00 To 135.00
Cookie Jar, Freesia .... 125.00 To 140.00
Cookie Jar, Magnolia, Blue 195.00
Cookie Jar, Magnolia, Green 180.00
Cookie Jar, Water Lily, Blue .... 160.00 To 165.00
Cookie Jar, Water Lily, Brown, 8 In. 255.00
Cookie Jar, Water Lily, Rose 195.00
Cornucopia, Bushberry, Rust, 8 In. 55.00
Cornucopia, Gardenia, Aqua, 6 In. 40.00
Cornucopia, Horizon, 8 In. 65.00
Cornucopia, Mock Orange, Pink, 6 In. 50.00
Cornucopia, Peony, Pair 110.00
Cornucopia, Pine Cone, Brown, 6 In., Pair 145.00
Cornucopia, Rozane, Blue, 8 In. 175.00
Cornucopia, Snowberry, Pink, 8 In. 45.00
Creamer, Duck, Hat, 3 1/2 In. 55.00
Creamer, Juvenile, Rabbit, 2 1/2 In. 65.00
Creamer, Medallion 22.00
Cup & Plate, Juvenile, Chick 60.00
Cup & Saucer, Raymor, Brown 15.00
Cup & Saucer, Raymor, Green 15.00
Cup, Rose Point 25.00
Cuspidor, Donatello 110.00
Ewer, Apple Blossom, Green, 15 In. 175.00
Ewer, Bleeding Heart, Blue, 6 In. 70.00
Ewer, Bushberry, Blue, 6 In. 55.00
Ewer, Bushberry, Green, 6 In. 35.00
Ewer, Clematis, Blue, 10 In. .... 65.00 To 75.00
Ewer, Clematis, Green, 15 In. 110.00
Ewer, Columbine, Blue, 7 In. 55.00
Ewer, Magnolia, Brown, 15 In. 195.00
Ewer, Ming Tree, White, 10 In. 80.00

Ewer, Pine Cone, Green, 5 In.	240.00
Ewer, Pine Cone, Green, 18 In.	950.00
Ewer, Silhouette, 10 In.	40.00
Ewer, Snowberry, Pink, 15 In.	185.00
Ewer, Water Lily, Pink, 15 In.	185.00
Ewer, Zephyr Lily, Green, Burnt Orange, 15 In.	150.00
Figurine, Dog, Ivory	195.00
Flower Frog, Clematis, Blue	20.00
Flower Frog, Columbine, Pink	40.00
Flower Frog, Dahlrose, Green, 4 In.	37.50
Flower Frog, Donatello	15.00
Flower Frog, Peony, Green	30.00
Flower Frog, Pine Cone, Brown	185.00
Flower Frog, Tuscany, Pink, 5 In.	65.00
Flower Frog, White Rose, Green	20.00
Flowerpot, Apple Blossom, Blue	150.00
Flowerpot, Apple Blossom, Pink	125.00
Flowerpot, Crocus, Saucer	295.00
Flowerpot, Dahlrose, Saucer, 5 1/2 In.	165.00
Flowerpot, Freesia, 5 In.	33.00
Flowerpot, Fuchsia, Green, Saucer	120.00
Flowerpot, Jonquil	125.00
Flowerpot, Peony, Saucer	65.00
Flowerpot, Pine Cone, Brown	65.00
Flowerpot, Pine Cone, Brown, Saucer	115.00
Flowerpot, Thorn Apple	50.00
Iced Tea Set, Pine Cone, Green, 7 Piece	1500.00
Inkwell, Rozane, Egypto, Seal	250.00
Jar, Baneda, Green, 4 In.	125.00
Jar, Dahlrose, Pedestal, 25 In.	550.00
Jar, Ginger, Cover, Rosecraft, 8 In.	200.00
Jardiniere, Antique Matte Green, 4 In.	65.00
Jardiniere, Baneda, Green, 4 In.	125.00
Jardiniere, Baneda, Pink, 4 In.	120.00
Jardiniere, Bittersweet, Gray, Pedestal, 8 In.	650.00
Jardiniere, Blackberry, 4 In.	95.00
Jardiniere, Blackberry, 5 In.	165.00
Jardiniere, Blackberry, 6 In.	320.00
Jardiniere, Blackberry, 7 X 10 In.	275.00
Jardiniere, Blackberry, Pedestal, 1930s, 28 In.	1900.00
Jardiniere, Bushberry, Brown, Pedestal, 8 In.	600.00
Jardiniere, Cameo, 8 In.	1140.00
Jardiniere, Cherry Blossom, 5 1/4 In.	110.00
Jardiniere, Clematis, Blue, Pedestal, 24 1/2 In.	475.00
Jardiniere, Columbine, Pink, 3 In.	38.00
Jardiniere, Columbine, Pink, 8 In.	250.00
Jardiniere, Dahlrose, 6 In.	70.00 To 75.00
Jardiniere, Dahlrose, 8 In.	115.00
Jardiniere, Donatello, 6 In.	35.00
Jardiniere, Donatello, 11 X 10 In.	90.00 To 95.00
Jardiniere, Florentine	125.00
Jardiniere, Freesia, 8 In.	90.00
Jardiniere, Futura, 8 In.	250.00
Jardiniere, Futura, Gray, Pedestal, 28 In.	1450.00
Jardiniere, Futura, Orange, Green, 6 In.	160.00 To 225.00
Jardiniere, Futura, Pink & Purple Leaves, Handles	600.00
Jardiniere, Gardenias, Brown, 10 In.	300.00
Jardiniere, Ixia, Green, 8 In.	175.00
Jardiniere, Jonquil, 4 In.	65.00
Jardiniere, Jonquil, 8 In.	250.00
Jardiniere, Luffa, 5 In.	45.00
Jardiniere, Magnolia, Blue, 6 In.	80.00
Jardiniere, Magnolia, Brown, Pedestal, 8 In.	175.00 To 400.00
Jardiniere, Magnolia, Green, Pedestal	600.00

Jardiniere, Maroon, 6 In.	60.00
Jardiniere, Mostique, Pedestal, 1930s, 28 In., Pair	610.00
Jardiniere, Normandie, Pedestal	800.00
Jardiniere, Pine Cone, Blue, Twig Handles, 3 In.	55.00
Jardiniere, Pine Cone, Brown, Pedestal, 25 In.	395.00
Jardiniere, Poppy, Green, 3 In.	25.00
Jardiniere, Poppy, Green, 6 1/2 In.	35.00
Jardiniere, Snowberry, Green, Pedestal, 25 In.	775.00
Jardiniere, Stepped Buttresses, Pedestal, 1930s, 24 X 11 1/2 In.	402.50
Jardiniere, Wisteria, Blue, 5 In.	225.00
Jardiniere, Wisteria, Green, 4 In.	85.00
Jardiniere, Zephyr Lily, Pedestal, 25 In.	750.00
Jug, Blackberry	120.00
Jug, Juvenile, Duck With Untied Shoes	65.00
Lamp, Banquet, White Rose, Cranberry Flash, Thumbprint, 7 X 5 In.	200.00
Lamp, Carnelian II, Sticker, Mottled Glaze	135.00
Lamp, Cherry Blossom, Brown	650.00
Lamp, Persian, Original Shade, Pair	760.00
Match Holder, Pine Cone, Green	78.50
Mixing Bowl, Rhythm, Chartreuse, 10 In.	85.00
Mug, Chicks, Juvenile, Bulbous Top, Narrow Bottom	78.00
Mug, Knights of Pythias, 4 Piece	245.00
Mug, Knights of Pythias, Pair	375.00
Mug, Masonic, Osman Temple, 1916	145.00
Mug, Pine Cone, Brown, 4 In.	100.00
Mug, Quaker, Creamware	125.00
Mug, Rozane, Cherry, Silver Deposit, 6 In.	750.00
Nut Dish, Tourmaline	25.00
Pitcher, Acanthus, Tan	100.00
Pitcher, Bleeding Heart, Green, 10 In.	140.00
Pitcher, Bleeding Heart, Pink	175.00
Pitcher, Cider, Magnolia, Blue	95.00 To 160.00
Pitcher, Cow, Pre-1916	185.00
Pitcher, Cows & Trees, Milk	200.00
Pitcher, Freesia, Blue, 10 In.	90.00
Pitcher, Ideal, Rose	65.00
Pitcher, Magnolia, Ice Lip, Green	125.00
Pitcher, Pine Cone, Blue, 10 In.	425.00
Pitcher, Pine Cone, Brown, 9 In.	325.00
Pitcher, Pine Cone, Brown, 10 In.	385.00
Pitcher, Silhouette, White, 6 In.	60.00
Pitcher, Tulip	75.00
Pitcher, Water, Raymor, Brown	85.00
Pitcher, Wisteria	75.00
Planter, Artwood, Green	45.00
Planter, Egypto, White, 8 In.	20.00
Planter, Futura, 15 In.	250.00
Planter, Gardenia, 8 In.	27.50
Planter, Hanging, Bittersweet	135.00
Planter, Laurel, Red	85.00
Planter, Magnolia, Brown, 6 In.	35.00
Planter, Ming Tree, White	25.00
Planter, Peony, Blue	25.00
Planter, Persian, 6 X 13 In.	165.00
Planter, Pine Cone, Brown, Base, 5 1/4 X 4 1/2 In.	95.00
Planter, Pine Cone, Green, 5 In.	65.00
Planter, Silhouette, Red	34.00
Planter, Silhouette, White	23.00
Plate & Creamer, Juvenile, Rabbits	95.00
Plate, Juvenile, Duck With Boots & Hat, Rolled Rim	85.00
Plate, Juvenile, Rabbit	50.00
Plate, Juvenile, Rabbits, Rolled Edge, 7 3/4 In.	75.00
Plate, Rabbit, Ears Back, 8 In.	75.00
Plate, Raymor, 12 In.	15.00

Plate, Sunbonnet Girl, Rolled	78.50
Powder Jar, Donatello	240.00
Rose Bowl, Columbine, Pink	48.00
Sconce, Choloron, 3 Light, Olive	950.00
Shelf, Wall, Pine Cone	425.00
Smoke Set, Indian, Creamware	310.00
Soap Dish, Donatello	140.00
Soup, Dish, Donatello	140.00
Sugar & Creamer, Apple Blossom	45.00
Sugar & Creamer, Bittersweet, Yellow	55.00
Sugar & Creamer, Magnolia	55.00 To 60.00
Sugar & Creamer, Snowberry, Rose	70.00
Sugar & Creamer, Zephyr Lily	65.00
Sugar, Landscape, Cover	55.00
Sugar, Raymor, Brown	45.00
Sugar, Snowberry, Pink	20.00
Tankard Set, Elk, Creamware, 7 Piece	400.00
Tankard, Dutch, 11 In.	135.00
Tankard, Holland	120.00
Tankard, Snowberry, Green, 15 In.	220.00
Tea Set, Apple Blossom, Green	165.00
Tea Set, Clematis, Brown	125.00
Teapot, Apple Blossom	77.00
Teapot, Snowberry, Green	85.00
Teapot, Wincraft, Lime	60.00
Tray, Foxglove, Blue, 8 1/2 In.	48.00
Tray, Foxglove, Pink, 12 In.	85.00
Tray, Foxglove, Pink, 15 In.	125.00
Umbrella Stand, Corinthian	450.00
Umbrella Stand, Cosmos, Blue, 18 In.	395.00
Umbrella Stand, Dogwood, 1924–28	450.00
Umbrella Stand, Florentine, Ivory	275.00
Umbrella Stand, La Rose, 20 In.	435.00
Urn, Bushberry, Green, 32 In.	595.00
Urn, Cherries, Pink, 15 In.	160.00
Urn, Cherry Blossom, Pink, Blue, 4 In.	120.00
Urn, Florentine, Ivory	275.00
Urn, Freesia, Green, 8 In.	68.00
Urn, Snowberry, Pink, 15 In.	150.00
Urn, Velmoss II, Green	65.00
Vase, Apple Blossom, Blue, 10 In.	165.00
Vase, Apple Blossom, Green, 7 In.	35.00
Vase, Apple Blossom, Green, 12 In.	95.00
Vase, Artwood, Green, 8 In.	42.00
Vase, Ball, Sunflower, 4 In.	110.00
Vase, Baneda, Green, 4 In.	80.00 To 100.00
Vase, Baneda, Green, 8 In.	225.00
Vase, Baneda, Open Handles, Base, 8 1/2 In.	150.00
Vase, Bittersweet, Gold, 8 In.	55.00
Vase, Blackberry, 4 In.	95.00 To 160.00
Vase, Blackberry, 5 In.	130.00 To 150.00
Vase, Blackberry, 6 In.	350.00
Vase, Blackberry, 8 In.	275.00 To 325.00
Vase, Blackberry, 10 In.	320.00
Vase, Blackberry, 12 1/2 In.	595.00
Vase, Bleeding Heart, Green, 9 In.	85.00
Vase, Bushberry, 2 Handles, Blue, 3 1/4 In.	35.00
Vase, Bushberry, Blue, 5 In.	40.00
Vase, Bushberry, Blue, 6 In.	40.00
Vase, Bushberry, Blue, 7 In.	60.00
Vase, Bushberry, Double Bud, Green, 4 3/4 In.	45.00
Vase, Bushberry, Green, 7 In.	65.00
Vase, Bushberry, Green, 10 In.	70.00
Vase, Bushberry, Green, 12 In.	150.00

Vase, Bushberry, Green, 14 In.	175.00
Vase, Bushberry, Green, 15 In.	195.00
Vase, Bushberry, Rust, 6 In.	12.00
Vase, Carnelian II, 9 In.	100.00
Vase, Carnelian II, Pillow, Rose, 5 In.	110.00
Vase, Carnelian II, Pink & Purple, 9 In.	100.00
Vase, Cherry Blossom, Blue, Pink, 7 In.	160.00
Vase, Cherry Blossom, Brown, 5 1/2 In.	195.00
Vase, Cherry Blossom, Pink, 7 1/2 In.	195.00
Vase, Clematis, Blue, 6 In.	35.00
Vase, Cosmos, Blue, Green, Tan, 12 In.	100.00
Vase, Cremona, 10 1/2 In.	100.00
Vase, Dahlrose, Bud, Buttress Handle	65.00
Vase, Dahlrose, Oval, 10 In.	65.00
Vase, Dawn, Yellow, 7 In.	42.00
Vase, Donatello, Bud, 7 In.	35.00
Vase, Egypto, 11 1/2 In.	1375.00
Vase, Falline, Blue, 6 In.	200.00
Vase, Falline, Blue, 7 1/2 In.	340.00
Vase, Falline, Handles, Brown, 8 In.	450.00
Vase, Ferrella, 4 1/2 In.	165.00
Vase, Ferrella, Brown, 8 In.	300.00
Vase, Ferrella, Brown, 9 In.	300.00
Vase, Ferrella, Brown, 10 In.	390.00
Vase, Ferrella, Pink, 8 In.	290.00
Vase, Ferrella, Red, 8 In.	250.00
Vase, Florentine, Double Bud, 6 1/4 In.	35.00
Vase, Foxglove, Blue, 14 1/2 In.	125.00
Vase, Freesia, Blue, 10 In.	125.00
Vase, Freesia, Double Handles, 6 In.	40.00
Vase, Fuchsia, Blue, 7 In.	125.00
Vase, Fuchsia, Brown, 7 In.	60.00
Vase, Fuchsia, Green, 6 In.	47.00
Vase, Futura, 5 In.	450.00
Vase, Futura, 6 In.	175.00
Vase, Futura, Green, High Gloss, 9 In.	595.00
Vase, Gardenia, Green, 6 In.	65.00
Vase, Gardenia, Rust, 10 In.	105.00
Vase, Imperial II, 5 In.	120.00
Vase, Imperial, 1916, 10 In.	175.00
Vase, Iris, Pink, 9 In.	125.00
Vase, Jonquil, 4 In.	85.00 To 95.00
Vase, Jonquil, 6 In.	165.00
Vase, Jonquil, 7 In.	150.00
Vase, Jonquil, 8 In.	95.00 To 98.00
Vase, Jonquil, 12 In.	250.00
Vase, La Rose, 7 1/2 In.	68.00
Vase, La Rose, 9 In.	85.00
Vase, Laurel, Brown, 9 In.	90.00
Vase, Laurel, Red, 10 In.	180.00
Vase, Laurel, Yellow, 7 In.	125.00
Vase, Laurel, Yellow, 8 1/2 In.	125.00
Vase, Luffa, Brown, 6 In.	45.00
Vase, Luffa, Brown, 6 1/2 In.	75.00
Vase, Luffa, Brown, 7 In.	80.00
Vase, Magnolia, Brown, Pedestal, 8 In.	175.00
Vase, Magnolia, Green, 6 In.	48.00
Vase, Ming Tree, Blue, 6 In.	42.00
Vase, Ming Tree, Green, 6 In.	40.00
Vase, Ming Tree, White, 8 In.	60.00
Vase, Mock Orange, Pink, 12 In.	100.00
Vase, Monticello, Blue, 5 In.	65.00
Vase, Monticello, Brown, 5 In.	80.00 To 95.00
Vase, Monticello, Green, 6 In.	95.00

Vase, Morning Glory, 4 1/4 X 11 1/2 In. 295.00
Vase, Morning Glory, White, 6 In. 100.00
Vase, Moss, Blue, 6 In. 58.00
Vase, Mostique, 10 In. 50.00
Vase, Mostique, Arrow Design, 12 In. 65.00
Vase, Orian, Blue, 10 In. .... 110.00 To 125.00
Vase, Panel, Nude, 6 In. 275.00
Vase, Panel, Nude, Blue, 12 In. 475.00
Vase, Peony, 6 In. 40.00
Vase, Peony, Gold, 2 Handles, 10 In. 115.00
Vase, Peony, Yellow, 12 In. 110.00
Vase, Pillow, Iris, Pink, 8 In. 110.00
Vase, Pillow, Teasel, Rose, 8 In. 95.00
Vase, Pine Cone, Blue, 7 In. .... 175.00 To 200.00
Vase, Pine Cone, Blue, 18 In. 950.00
Vase, Pine Cone, Brown, 12 In. 190.00
Vase, Pine Cone, Brown, Double Handles, 10 In. 155.00
Vase, Pine Cone, Green, 7 In. 75.00
Vase, Pine Cone, Green, 12 In. 200.00
Vase, Pine Cone, Green, Double, 8 In. 70.00
Vase, Pine Cone, Orange, 9 In. 155.00
Vase, Pine Cone, Wincraft, Tan, 8 In. 35.00
Vase, Primrose, Tan, 6 In. .... 55.00 To 65.00
Vase, Rosecraft, Black, 7 In. 110.00
Vase, Rosecraft, Bud, Black, 8 In. 55.00
Vase, Rosecraft, Bud, Blue, 13 1/2 In. 185.00
Vase, Royal Lancaster, 7 In. 38.00
Vase, Rozane, Brown, Orange Flowers, Cylinder 175.00
Vase, Rozane, Portrait of Wanstall, Leffler, Dated 1901 .... 6000.00
Vase, Russco, Blue, 7 In. .... 40.00 To 65.00
Vase, Russco, Green Crystalline, 8 In. 125.00
Vase, Saline, Brown, 8 In. 200.00
Vase, Silhouette, Nude, Fan, Blue, 7 In. 135.00
Vase, Silhouette, Nude, White, 8 In. 195.00
Vase, Silhouette, Turquoise, Plant Design 75.00
Vase, Snowberry, Pink, 18 In. 275.00
Vase, Snowberry, Red, 7 In. 60.00
Vase, Sunflower, 5 In. 95.00
Vase, Teasel, Blue, 15 In. 425.00
Vase, Teasel, Brown, 9 In. 45.00
Vase, Thorn Apple, 2 Handles, 6 In. 45.00
Vase, Thorn Apple, 9 In. 47.50
Vase, Thorn Apple, Blue, 9 In. 110.00
Vase, Thorn Apple, Blue, Green, White, 6 In. 34.00
Vase, Topeo, Blue, 14 In. 325.00
Vase, Topeo, Red, 8 In. 225.00
Vase, Tourmaline, Blue, 5 In. 80.00
Vase, Tourmaline, Blue, 6 In. 65.00
Vase, Tourmaline, Double Handles, Blue, 6 In. 50.00
Vase, Tourmaline, Mottled, Blue Ball, 5 In. 65.00
Vase, Tuscany, Gray, Bulbous, 9 1/4 In. 40.00
Vase, Velmoss, Blue, 10 In. 100.00
Vase, Velmoss, Red, 7 In. 60.00
Vase, Vista, 10 In. 175.00
Vase, Water Lily, Blue, 5 In. 55.00
Vase, Water Lily, Brown, 6 In. 45.00
Vase, Water Lily, Brown, 12 In. 95.00
Vase, Water Lily, Brown, Blue, 4 In. 48.00
Vase, Water Lily, Pink 70.00
Vase, Water Lily, Pink, Green, 6 In. 47.50
Vase, White Rose, Blue, 9 In. 80.00
Vase, Wincraft, Blue, 10 In. 65.00
Vase, Wincraft, Blue, 6 In. 35.00
Vase, Wincraft, Blue, Handle, 14 1/2 In. 145.00

Vase, Wincraft, Green, 15 In.	150.00
Vase, Windsor, 5 In.	110.00
Vase, Windsor, Ferns, Handle, 7 In.	200.00
Vase, Wisteria, Blue, 4 In.	175.00
Vase, Wisteria, Brown, 6 In.	85.00
Vase, Wisteria, Brown, 10 In.	330.00
Vase, Woodland, 10 In.	370.00
Vase, Zephyr Lily, Blue, 9 In.	85.00
Vase, Zephyr Lily, Green, 9 In.	75.00
Wall Pocket, Apple Blossom, Blue	65.00
Wall Pocket, Apple Blossom, Green	145.00
Wall Pocket, Apple Blossom, Pink	95.00
Wall Pocket, Baneda, Green	900.00
Wall Pocket, Bittersweet	95.00
Wall Pocket, Burmese, Green	160.00
Wall Pocket, Bushberry, Blue	125.00
Wall Pocket, Bushberry, Brown	145.00
Wall Pocket, Carnelian I, Blue, 8 In.	65.00
Wall Pocket, Carnelian II, Pink	125.00
Wall Pocket, Cherry Blossom	350.00
Wall Pocket, Clematis	50.00 To 75.00
Wall Pocket, Corinthian, 9 1/2 In.	110.00
Wall Pocket, Cornelian, Pink, Blue Drip, 8 1/2 In.	75.00
Wall Pocket, Dahlrose, 10 In.	125.00 To 150.00
Wall Pocket, Donatello, 9 In.	125.00
Wall Pocket, Donatello, 11 1/2 In.	125.00
Wall Pocket, Earlam, 5 1/2 In.	95.00
Wall Pocket, Florentine, 9 In.	80.00 To 95.00
Wall Pocket, Florentine, Brown, 12 1/2 In.	165.00
Wall Pocket, Foxglove, Pink	135.00
Wall Pocket, Freesia, Blue, 8 In.	70.00
Wall Pocket, Freesia, Brown	110.00 To 135.00
Wall Pocket, Futura	295.00
Wall Pocket, Gardenia, Green	95.00
Wall Pocket, Jonquil	250.00
Wall Pocket, La Rose, 7 1/2 In.	75.00
Wall Pocket, La Rose, 9 In.	70.00
Wall Pocket, Lombardy, Blue Glaze, 8 In.	125.00 To 165.00
Wall Pocket, Ming Tree, Blue, 8 In.	180.00
Wall Pocket, Mostique, 9 1/2 In.	125.00
Wall Pocket, Mostique, 10 In.	70.00
Wall Pocket, Orian, Brown	425.00
Wall Pocket, Panel, Nude, Brown, 6 In.	250.00
Wall Pocket, Panel, Nude, Green, 8 In.	295.00
Wall Pocket, Pine Cone, Brown	295.00
Wall Pocket, Pine Cone, Green, Double	185.00
Wall Pocket, Pine Cone, Orange, Tan, Double	295.00
Wall Pocket, Primrose, Blue, 8 1/2 In.	125.00
Wall Pocket, Primrose, Brown, 8 1/2 In.	140.00
Wall Pocket, Silhouette, Green, Floral	85.00
Wall Pocket, Silhouette, Red	95.00
Wall Pocket, Silhouette, Turquoise	87.00
Wall Pocket, Snowberry, Green	40.00
Wall Pocket, Sunflower	495.00
Wall Pocket, Tuscany, Gray	150.00
Wall Pocket, Tuscany, Pink	68.00
Wall Pocket, Wincraft, 5 In.	80.00
Wall Pocket, Wincraft, 5 1/2 In.	70.00
Wall Pocket, Wisteria	595.00
Wall Pocket, Zephyr Lily, Brown	65.00
Window Box, Apple Blossom, Green, 12 In.	65.00
Window Box, Bushberry, Blue, 12 In.	135.00
Window Box, Bushberry, Brown, 8 In.	50.00
Window Box, Ming Tree, Blue, 11 1/2 In.	70.00

Window Box, Pine Cone, Green, 15 In. 60.00
Window Box, Sunflower 160.00
Window Box, Zephyr Lily, Blue 45.00

Rowland & Marsellus Company is a mark which appears on historical Staffordshire dating from the late nineteenth and early twentieth centuries. Rowland & Marsellus is believed to be the mark used by the British Anchor Pottery Co. of Longton, England, for some pieces made for export to a New York firm. Many American views were made. Of special interest to collectors are the rolled edge, blue and white plates.

ROWLAND & MARSELLUS, Cup & Saucer, Niagara Falls 60.00
Grill Plate, Willow 18.00
Plate, Albany, Rolled Edge 45.00
Plate, Cleveland, Ohio, Rolled Edge, 10 In. 55.00
Plate, George Washington, Brown, 9 In. 35.00
Plate, Grand Rapids 17.50
Plate, Lewis & Clark Centennial, Rolled Edge 55.00
Plate, Philadelphia, Rolled Edge 45.00
Plate, San Francisco, Blue, White, 10 In. 75.00
Plate, Saratoga, New York, 10 1/2 In. 50.00

Roy Rogers was born in 1911 in Cincinnati, Ohio. In the 1930s, he made a living as a singer; and in 1935, his group started work at a Los Angeles radio station. He appeared in his first movie in 1937. From 1952 to 1957, he made 101 television shows. Roy Rogers memorabilia is collected, including items from the Roy Rogers restaurants.

ROY ROGERS, Archery Set, With Son Dusty, Box, 4 Ft. 165.00
Badge, Roy & Trigger, 1 1/2 In. 15.00
Bank, Boot, Metal 35.00
Bank, Ceramic 75.00
Belt, Double Holster, Leather 75.00
Billfold 35.00
Binoculars 32.00
Book, Activity & Coloring, Double–R Ranch, Whitman 25.00
Book, Comic, Dale Evans, 1958 .... 68.00
Book, Enchanted Canyon, 1954 .... 32.00
Book, Gopher Creek Gunman, 1940, Coca–Cola Book Cover 25.00
Book, Outlaws of Sundown Valley, 1950 .... 15.00
Book, Raiders of Sawtooth Ridge, 1946 ....8.50 To 10.00
Book, Roy Rogers & The Rimrod Renegades 5.00
Book, Tall Tales For Little Folks, Gabby Hayes, Connie Lowe 35.00
Bookbag 28.00
Button, Grape–Nuts, Roy's Boots, Roy's Brand 7.50
Camera ....25.00 To 95.00
Card, Mutescope, 1943, 5 X 3 In. 8.50
Chaps, Leather 45.00
Chaps, Vinyl ....20.00 To 30.00
Clock, Alarm, Prairie Scene, Trigger, Roy ....95.00 To 110.00
Clock, Animated Alarm, Box 345.00
Cowboy Band Set 350.00
Cup ....20.00 To 25.00
Cup, F & F, Signed 10.00
Curtain 45.00
Figurine Set, Hartland 185.00
Figurine, Bullet, Roy's Dog, Hartland, Plastic, 4 In. 65.00
Fishing Pole, Gabby Hayes, Tin 100.00
Flashlight ....32.00 To 65.00
Game, Rodeo, 4 Games In 1, 15 Playing Pieces, Rogden Co., 1949 .... 225.00
Guitar, Box ....55.00 To 85.00
Gun & Holster Set, Atomite, Hat Band, Miniature ....65.00 To 70.00
Gun & Holster Set, Box 425.00
Gun & Holster Set, Double 175.00

Gun, Cap .... 35.00 To 55.00
Gun, Leather Holster, Wooden Bullets, Box, 1955 .... 110.00
Gun, Shootin' Iron, Classy, On Card, 5 In. 65.00
Gun, Tuck–A–Way, Flintlock, Cap, Original Display, 2 1/2 In. 25.00
Gun, Tuck–Away 17.50
Harmonica, Reed Toys 50.00
Harmonica, Riders, Silver, Embossed Roy's Face, Reed Toys 65.00
Hat, Cowboy, Felt 30.00
Hat, Quick Shooter, Box 135.00
Horseshoe Set .... 35.00 To 70.00
Jeans, Sears 100.00
Lamp, Figural, Plaster, 12 1/2 In. .... 150.00 To 175.00
Lamp, Figural, Roy & Trigger, Plastic, 1950s, 15 In. 185.00
Lantern, Box .... 30.00 To 85.00
Lantern, Horseshoe Style, Lithographed Tin, Handle, 12 In. 55.00
Life Magazine Cover, 1943 .... 18.00
Lucky Horseshoe .... 7.50 To 25.00
Lunch Box, Chuck Wagon, 1956–61 .... 30.00 To 80.00
Lunch Box, Dale Evans & Roy, Double R Bar Ranch 66.00
Lunch Box, Saddlebag, Tan 50.00
Mug, Figural, Roy's Head, Quaker Oats, 1950s .... 15.00 To 30.00
Neckerchief, King of The Cowboys, 1950s, 26 X 26 In. 50.00
Neckerchief, Red, White, Square, Trigger, Roy, 18 In. 45.00
Outfit, Official Cowboy, Yankiboy, Box 175.00
Paper Doll, Folder, Clothes, Composition, 1953 .... 65.00
Paper Doll, With Dale Evans, Whitman, 1957, Uncut 125.00
Patch, Iron–On 10.00
Photograph, Autographed, 8 X 10 In. 25.00
Pistol, Cap, Disc, Chrome Finish, Kilgore, 11 In. 500.00
Puppet, Dale Evans, Washcloth, Terrycloth 45.00
Puzzle, Tray, Frame, Roy Working On Anvil, Horseshoe, 9 X 11 In. 25.00
Record, Album, Cowboy Songs, 64 Pages, Wrappings, 1941 .... 25.00
Record, Album, Songs From 8 Movies, Souvenir, Large 45.00
Rifle, Clicker 60.00
Ring, Branding, With Cap 125.00
Scarf 30.00
Scarf Tie 35.00
Sheet Music, Corral In The Sky, Dale Evans 25.00
Sheet Music, I'M Gonna Have A Cowboy Wedding 75.00
Sheet Music, Roy On Cover, 1952 .... 10.00
Sheet Music, Think of Me 25.00
Shirt, Boy's .... 25.00 To 40.00
Spats, Vinyl 65.00
Suit, Pair 72.50
T–Shirt 25.00
Tent, Canvas .... 125.00 To 250.00
Tent, Child's, Box 375.00
Tie, Scarf .... 32.00 To 35.00
Toothbrush, With Medallion 15.00
Toy, Jeep & Trailer, Nellie Bell 30.00
Toy, Rodeo 135.00
Toy, Roy, Stagecoach, 2 Horses, Plastic, 9 In. 50.00
Toy, Trigger, Blow–Up For Pool, Plastic 150.00
Toy, Trigger, Bullet Hobby Horse, Hill Brass Co., Box 300.00
Toy, Truck, Van, Box 290.00
Toy, Yo–Yo, Roy & Trigger 40.00
Vest & Chaps, Cowhide 60.00
Vest, Cloth .... 58.00 To 75.00
Viewmaster Pack, 3 Reels, Adventure Roundup, Sawyers, 1956 .... 45.00
Wallet, Brown, Roy & Trigger Picture 10.00
Wood Burning Set, Picture of Roy & Trigger, Box 33.00
Wristwatch .... 100.00 To 150.00
Wristwatch, Dale Evans, Flasher, 3–D Box Scene, 1956 .... 410.00
Wristwatch, Goldtone Case, Matching Band, 1951, Box 300.00

The Royal Bayreuth factory was founded in Tettau, Bavaria, in 1794. It has continued to modern times. The marks have changed through the years. A stylized crest, the name "Royal Bayreuth," and the word "Bavaria" appear in slightly different forms from 1870 to about 1919. Later dishes may include the words "U.S. Zone," the year of the issue, or the word "Germany" instead of "Bavaria."

ROYAL BAYREUTH, see also Rose Tapestry; Sand Babies; Snow Babies; Sunbonnet Babies

ROYAL BAYREUTH, Ashtray, Elk ....85.00 To 135.00
Ashtray, Sparrow	395.00
Bell, Beach Babies, Blue Mark	295.00
Bell, Dutch Boy & Girl, Standing On Dock, 3 1/2 In.	180.00
Bowl, Lobster, 5 X 7 1/2 In.	80.00
Bowl, Lobster, Cover, 5 X 5 In.	68.00
Bowl, Oyster & Pearl, Signed	60.00
Bowl, Roses, Fan Mold, Gold Tracery, Blue Mark, 10 1/2 In.	187.50
Box, Cover, Little Bopeep, Kidney Shape	115.00
Box, Dresser, Little Jack Horner, Kidney Shape	125.00
Box, Trinket, Phoenician, Kidney Shape, 3 In.	45.00
Cake Plate, Multicolor Florals, Blue Mark, Large	85.00
Candleholder, Elks Scene, 4 In.	65.00
Candleholder, Farmer, Chicken Scene, Shield Back	195.00
Candleholder, Little Bopeep, Shield Back, 5 In., Pair	275.00
Candleholder, Little Jack Horner, Shield Back, Blue Mark	140.00
Candy Dish, Devil & Cards, 7 In.	125.00
Chamberstick, Corinthian, Matte Black, Marked, 5 1/2 In.	65.00
Chamberstick, Devil & Cards, Sigend	325.00
Chamberstick, Elk, Blue Mark, 7 3/4 In.	175.00
Chamberstick, Pansy	445.00
Chamberstick, Portrait Beautiful Lady, Shield, Blue Mark	125.00
Clown, Candleholder On Top, Holding Match Holder At Bottom	550.00
Cracker Jar, Poppy, Pearlized Luster	325.00
Cracker Jar, Red Poppy, Blue Mark	650.00
Cracker Jar, Tomato, Cover, 3 1/2 In.	20.00
Cracker, Jar, Red Poppy, Green Stem Handles	275.00
Creamer, Apple	45.00
Creamer, Apple, Blue Mark	95.00
Creamer, Bear	575.00
Creamer, Britanny Girl	75.00
Creamer, Bull, Black	145.00
Creamer, Bull, Red	140.00
Creamer, Butterfly, Open Wing	265.00
Creamer, Butterfly, Signed	265.00
Creamer, Butterfly.Closed Wing	475.00
Creamer, Cat, Black, Yellow & Black Eyes, Blue Mark, 5 In.	110.00
Creamer, Cavaliers	60.00
Creamer, Chimpanzee	425.00
Creamer, Clown, Black Buttons	100.00
Creamer, Clown, Green	395.00
Creamer, Clown, Pearlized	325.00
Creamer, Clown, Red, Black Buttons, Blue Mark, 3 3/4 In.	125.00
Creamer, Coachman	295.00
Creamer, Coachman, Blue Mark	185.00
Creamer, Corinthian, Blue Mark	35.00
Creamer, Corinthian, Yellow	75.00
Creamer, Cow Head, Brown, Blue Mark, 4 In.	75.00
Creamer, Crow, 5 In. ....65.00 To 135.00
Creamer, Crow, Black, Tan Beak, Blue Mark	195.00
Creamer, Dachshund, Gray & Dark Liver	195.00
Creamer, Dog, St. Bernard	145.00
Creamer, Duck, Marked	125.00
Creamer, Elk ....35.00 To 60.00
Creamer, Fish, Open Mouth, Blue Mark	160.00

Creamer, Fisherman	75.00
Creamer, French Poodle, Black, Signed	205.00
Creamer, French Poodle, Orange Detail	205.00
Creamer, Frog, Green, Bulging Eyes	185.00
Creamer, Grape, Pearlized	65.00
Creamer, Lamplighter, Signed	215.00
Creamer, Little Boy Blue	75.00 To 85.00
Creamer, Maple Leaf, Blue Mark	125.00
Creamer, Melon	80.00
Creamer, Milk, Oak Leaf, Pearlized	245.00
Creamer, Monkey	250.00 To 285.00
Creamer, Mother-of-Pearl, White	90.00
Creamer, Murex Shell, Blue Mark	40.00
Creamer, Oak Leaf	125.00
Creamer, Old Man of The Mountain	60.00
Creamer, Owl	375.00
Creamer, Oyster & Pearl, Signed	165.00
Creamer, Pansy	135.00
Creamer, Pear	175.00
Creamer, Penguin	395.00
Creamer, Poppy, Red.Blue Mark	85.00
Creamer, Robin, Blue Mark	130.00
Creamer, Roses, Pink, 3 1/2 In.	205.00 To 395.00
Creamer, Seal, Pink, Blue Mark	250.00
Creamer, Sheep, Grazing, Pinched Spout, Blue Mark, 4 In.	90.00
Creamer, Shell, Green Mark, 4 1/2 In.	50.00
Creamer, St. Bernard, Black Mark	240.00
Creamer, St. Bernard, Blue Mark	190.00
Creamer, St. Bernard, White, Gray, Black & Cinnamon	235.00
Creamer, Trout, Blue Mark, 4 In.	165.00
Creamer, Turtle	250.00
Creamer, Washerwoman	65.00
Creamer, Water Buffalo, Blue Mark	95.00
Creamer, Water Buffalo, Red	170.00
Cup, Elk, Miniature	125.00
Cup, Jack & The Beanstalk	60.00
Dish, Child's, Feeding, Little Boy Blue	70.00 To 135.00
Dish, Child's, Feeding, Little Jack Horner, Blue Mark	125.00
Dish, Child's, Feeding, Sand Babies, 7 1/4 In.	150.00
Dish, Fishing Scene, Red Beading, Gray, Handles, 5 1/2 In.	40.00
Dish, Lemon, Yellow Flowers, Green Ground, Handle, 6 3/4 In.	48.00
Dish, Mint, Clam Shell, Blue Mark, Murex, Souvenir	65.00
Gravy Boat, Tomato, Leaf Underplate, Signed	90.00
Hair Receiver, Goose Girl, Blue Mark	125.00
Hair Receiver, Oyster & Pearl	125.00
Hatpin Holder, Dachshund, 4 3/4 In.	225.00 To 495.00
Hatpin Holder, Penguin, Blue Mark	650.00
Hatpin Holder, Red Poppy, Blue Mark	275.00
Hatpin Holder, Tapestry, Courting Couple, Blue Mark	235.00
Humidor, Red Girl, Blue Mark	495.00
Humidor, Sailboat	250.00
Inkwell, Elk, Signed	185.00
Jardiniere, Corinthian, Blue Mark, 8 X 7 In.	125.00
Match Holder, Devil & Cards, Signed	200.00
Match Holder, Eagle, Wall, Blue Mark	110.00
Match Holder, Murex Shell, Hanging	50.00
Mug, Little Jack Horner	65.00
Mug, Little Jack Horner, Blue Mark	125.00
Mustard, Grape, Yellow & White, Blue Mark	80.00
Mustard, Lobster, Blue Mark	125.00
Mustard, Lobster, Spoon	105.00
Mustard, Poppy, Blue Mark	65.00
Mustard, Tomato, Spoon	70.00
Pipe Holder, Clown	375.00

Pitcher, Bellringer, 6 1/2 In. 995.00
Pitcher, Devil & Cards, 4 1/2 In. 185.00
Pitcher, Devil & Cards, Blue Mark 325.00
Pitcher, Devil & Cards, Green Mark, 6 1/2 In. 500.00
Pitcher, Devil & Cards, Left-Hand, 7 In. 425.00
Pitcher, Fisherman In Boat, Gold Handle, 3 1/2 In. 25.00
Pitcher, Gray Cat, Blue Mark, 4 1/2 In. 325.00
Pitcher, Jack & The Beanstalk, 4 1/2 In. 85.00
Pitcher, Lemon, Blue Mark, 6 1/2 In. 300.00
Pitcher, Little Boy Blue, 4 1/2 In. 85.00
Pitcher, Lobster, Blue Mark, 6 1/2 In. 425.00
Pitcher, Musicians, 4 3/4 In. 85.00
Pitcher, Parrot, Niagara Falls, 5 In. 33.00
Pitcher, Shell, Boot Shape, Blue Mark, 6 1/2 In. 395.00
Pitcher, Shell, Murex, Blue Mark, 6 1/2 In. 375.00
Pitcher, St. Bernard, 4 1/2 In. 235.00
Pitcher, Strawberry, 4 1/2 In. 185.00
Plaque, Tapestry, 9 1/2 In. 515.00
Plate, 2 Men In Rowboat, Black Mark, 5 1/2 In. 60.00
Plate, Boy, 2 Donkeys, Farmhouse, Blue Mark, 12 3/4 In. 145.00
Plate, Hunting Scene, 10 1/2 In. 165.00
Plate, Jack & Jill, 4 1/2 In. 30.00
Plate, Lettuce Leaf, Blue Mark, 7 In. 50.00
Plate, Little Boy Blue, 6 1/2 In. 70.00
Plate, Nursery Rhyme, Jack & The Beanstalk, 6 1/2 In. 145.00
Plate, Shell, Tinted Gray, 8 1/4 In. 25.00
Plate, Shell, Tinted Green, 8 1/4 In. 25.00
Rose Bowl, Little Miss Muffet 110.00
Salt & Pepper, Jewel & Flower 185.00
Salt & Pepper, Radishes 195.00
Saltshaker, Figural, Bellringer 235.00
Shaving Mug, Divided, 2 Donkeys & Farm Boy, Marked 225.00
Shaving Mug, Elk 265.00
Shoe, High Top, Woman's, Brown, 3 1/2 X 4 3/4 In. 90.00
Stirrup Cup, Moose 395.00
Sugar & Creamer, Apple, Yellow 379.00
Sugar & Creamer, Cover, Conchshell, Pearlized 85.00
Sugar & Creamer, Lobster, Blue Mark 90.00
Sugar & Creamer, Murex Shell 100.00
Sugar & Creamer, Musicians 105.00
Sugar & Creamer, Pearlized Grapes 180.00
Sugar & Creamer, Tomato, Blue Mark 80.00
Sugar & Creamer, Yellow Apple, Blue Mark 375.00
Sugar, Desert Scene 30.00
Syrup, Smiling Pear 95.00
Teapot, Swans On Lake, Blue, Gold Trim, 5 1/4 In. 165.00
Teapot, Tomato, 5 In. 95.00
Tobacco Jar, Pink Roses, Light Blue 125.00
Toothpick, Cavalier, 4-Footed 60.00
Toothpick, Goats Grazing, Blue Mark 35.00
Toothpick, Little Bopeep 95.00
Toothpick, Scuttle Shape, Hunt Scene 95.00
Tray, Cucumber, 12 1/2 X 5 1/2 In. 145.00
Tray, Dresser, Devil & Cards, Marked 350.00
Tray, Dresser, Roses, Blue Mark, 7 X 10 In. 55.00
Vase, Bearded Fisherman In Wooden Boat, 6 1/4 In. 145.00
Vase, Brown-Haired Women Busts, Band of Roses, 4 1/2 In. 85.00
Vase, Castle Scene, Blue Mark, 4 1/2 In. 130.00
Vase, Dutch Children Playing Jump Rope, 3 1/4 In. 70.00
Vase, Girl With Candle, Cylindrical, Blue Mark, 5 In. 65.00
Vase, Man Lighting Pipe, Cylindrical, Blue Mark, 5 In. 75.00
Vase, Portrait, Pink, Green & Gold, 5 In. 65.00
Vase, Tavern Scene, Jerusalem, Capt. No.3, RAM, 1906, 6 In. 110.00
Vase, Violet Tapestry, Blue Mark, 4 1/4 In. 325.00

Royal Bonn is the nineteenth– and twentieth–century trade name for the Bonn China Manufactory. It was established in 1755 in Bonn, Germany. A general line of porcelain was made. Many marks were used, most including the name "Bonn," the initials "FM," and a crown.

ROYAL BONN, Biscuit Jar, Flowers, Beige, Silver Plated Fittings, 7 In.	118.00
Charger, Burgermeister Delft Portrait, 13 1/2 In.	145.00
Chocolate Set, Multicolored Roses, Gold Handles & Tracery	165.00
Dish, Cheese, Florals, Green Castle Mark, 8 X 8 X 9 In.	87.50
Dish, Cheese, Pink Roses, Dark Green	60.00
Vase, 2 Dutch Women, Scenic, Pedestal Base, 5 3/4 In.	135.00
Vase, Allover Flowers, Outlined In Gold, Marked, 15 In.	100.00
Vase, Animal Head Handles, Rose & Leaf, Marked, 1890, 14 In.	350.00
Vase, Blown–Out Flowers, Leaves & Flowers Ground, 5 1/2 In.	180.00
Vase, Blown–Out Mold, Gold Flowers, 5 1/2 In.	135.00
Vase, Hand Painted Bust of Woman, Flowers, Mountains, 8 X 7 In.	200.00
Vase, Hand Painted Iris, Spherical Shape, Signed, 11 3/4 In.	550.00
Vase, Scenic, 2 Dutch Women, Pedestal Base, 5 3/4 In.	135.00
Vase, Seaman, Looking Out To Sea, Marked, 8 7/8 In.	450.00

Royal Copenhagen porcelain and pottery have been made in Denmark since 1772. The Christmas plate series started in 1908. The figurines with pale blue and gray glazes have remained popular in this century and are still being made. Many other old and new style porcelains are made today.

ROYAL COPENHAGEN, Candlestick, Bisque Lion Heads, Garlands, 9 In., Pair	150.00
Coffeepot, Blue Flower, Basket Weave Border	145.00
Cup & Saucer, Blue Flower, Basket Weave Border	38.00
Cup & Saucer, Flora Danica, Wood Stand, 2 1/2 In., 11 Pc.	1100.00
Figurine, Amager Girl, No.1315	135.00
Figurine, Ballet Dancer, No.4075, Overglaze	575.00
Figurine, Boy With Broom, No.3250	60.00
Figurine, Boy, Blue Coat, Umbrella, No.3556, 7 1/4 In.	140.00
Figurine, Boy, No.3556	125.00
Figurine, Boy, White Coat, Brown Umbrella, 6 1/2 In.	110.00
Figurine, Bulldog, Sitting, 5 In.	185.00
Figurine, Cairn Terrier, Standing, No.11149	145.00
Figurine, Cocker Spaniel, Standing, 6 In.	135.00
Figurine, Collie, Lying, 11 In.	450.00
Figurine, Elk, Reclining, No.2813	525.00
Figurine, Emperor's Clothes, Triple	795.00
Figurine, Faun On Stump, No.01738, 3 3/4 In.	165.00
Figurine, Fish, 8 In.	35.00
Figurine, Girl, Long Dress	45.00
Figurine, Goose Girl, 9 1/4 In.	210.00
Figurine, Hans Clodhopper, No.1228	415.00
Figurine, Little Skaters, Blue Plate, 7 In.	35.00
Figurine, Lovebirds, No.402	115.00
Figurine, Man & Woman, Signed, 17 In.	1050.00
Figurine, Mermaid, No.2444	190.00
Figurine, Mermaid, No.4027	120.00
Figurine, Mermaid, No.4431, 9 1/2 In.	190.00
Figurine, Nude Woman, Sitting On Rock, 5 3/4 In.	175.00
Figurine, Pair of Owls, No.00834, 3 1/4 In.	125.00
Figurine, Robin, No.2266	60.00 To 65.00
Figurine, Scotch Terrier, Standing, 5 1/2 In.	175.00
Figurine, Shepherd Dog, Lying, 10 1/4 In.	474.00
Figurine, Sitting Dachshund Puppy, Gray, Turned Ear, 8 In.	300.00
Figurine, White Poodle, No.4638	195.00
Plaque, San Francisco, Blue & White, 1915, 10 In.	250.00
Plate, 1912	109.00
Plate, Christmas, 1924	75.00

Plate, Christmas, 1944	149.00
Plate, Christmas, 1946	125.00
Plate, Christmas, 1951	175.00
Plate, Christmas, 1961	170.00
Plate, Christmas, 1962	159.00
Plate, Christmas, 1969	35.00
Plate, Christmas, 1971	30.00 To 35.00
Plate, Christmas, 1981	23.00
Plate, Mother's Day, 1977	8.00
Plate, Statue of Liberty	22.00
Teapot, Blue Flower, Basket Weave Border	135.00
Tureen, Soup, Cover & Stand, Botanical Specimen, 16 In.	3950.00
Tureen, Soup, Cover, Flora Danica, 13 5/8 In.	1750.00
Vase, Floral, Crackle Glaze, 6 In.	175.00
Vase, Flowering Tree, 6 1/2 In.	195.00
Vase, Summer River Landscape, Signed, C.1900, 29 In.	1650.00
Vase, Teardrop, Peony Blossoms, Signed, C.1900, 28 3/4 In.	2090.00

Royal Copley china was made by the Spaulding China Company of Sebring, Ohio, from 1939 to 1960. The figural planters and the small figurines, especially those with Art Deco designs, are of great collector interest.

ROYAL COPLEY, Bank, Piggy, Porky	20.00
Figurine, Dog & Mailbox	15.00
Planter, Bear With Mandolin	30.00
Planter, Cat, By Tub	14.00
Planter, Cocker Spaniel	15.00
Planter, Dog Next To Mailbox	15.00
Planter, Fruit Plate Plaque	7.50
Planter, Teddy Bear, Brown, 6 1/4 In.	20.00
Vase, Floral Elegance, Green, 8 In.	15.00
Vase, Head, Oriental Girl, 7 1/2 In.	12.00
Wall Pocket, Blackamoor, Pair	25.00

Royal Crown Derby Company, Ltd., was established in England in 1876. There is a complex family tree that includes the Derby, Crown Derby, Worcester, and Royal Crown Derby porcelains. The Royal Crown Derby mark includes the name and a crown. The words "Made in England" were used after 1921.

ROYAL CROWN DERBY, Creamer, Imari	150.00
Cup & Saucer, Imari	100.00
Cup & Saucer, Old Avesburg	12.00
Dinner Set, Lombardy, 5 Piece Setting, 60 Piece	1500.00
Ewer, Raised Gold Floral, Arabesque, C.1880, 7 1/2 In.	195.00
Ewer, Yellow Gold Design, 14 In.	350.00
Plate, Gold Medallion, 10 In.	150.00
Plate, Imari, 7 In.	75.00
Plate, Imari, Footed, Marked, 9 In., Pair	330.00
Plate, Red Waves, 8 In.	25.00
Platter, Tree of Life, Red, 19 X 16 In., Pair	900.00
Sugar, Imari	175.00
Tureen, Soup, Underplate, Imari, 9 X 12 In.	525.00
Vase, Imari, Marked, Miniature	45.00

"Royal Doulton" is the name used on Doulton and Company pottery made from 1902 to the present. Doulton and Company of England was founded in 1853. Pieces made before 1902 are listed in this book under Doulton. Royal Doulton collectors search for the out-of-production figurines, character jugs, and series wares.

ROYAL DOULTON, Animal, Chatcull Nyala Antelope, HN 2664	75.00
Animal, Chestnut Mare & Foal, HN 2522	750.00
Animal, Drake, HN 807	80.00
Animal, French Poodle, HN 2631	95.00
Animal, Hare, HN 2594	68.00

Animal, Scotch Terrier, Albourne Arthur, HN 1015 .... 225.00
Animal, Scotch Terrier, K 10 .... 125.00
Animal, Siamese Cat, HN 2660 .... 110.00
Animal, Spaniel With Pheasant, HN 1029 .... 100.00
Ash Pot, Auld Mac 125.00
Ash Pot, Old Charley, A Mark 135.00
Bank, Bunnykins, 1934 .... 50.00
Bottle, Dewars Whiskey, Uncle Sam 395.00
Bowl, Canterbury Pilgrims, 10 In. 195.00
Bowl, Child's, Bunnykins 15.00
Bowl, Gaffers, 8 1/2 X 11 In. 125.00
Box, Nursery Rhyme, Cow Jumped Over The Moon 200.00
Candlestick, Woodlands, 6 1/2 In. 90.00

> Character jugs are the modeled head and shoulders of the subject.
> They are made in four sizes: large, 5 1/4 to 7 inches; small, 3 1/4
> to 4 inches; miniature, 2 1/4 to 2 1/2 inches; and tiny, 1 1/4
> inches. Toby jugs depict a seated, full figure.

Character Jug, 'Ard of 'Earing, Miniature ....900.00 To 1100.00
Character Jug, 'Arriet, Tiny 180.00
Character Jug, 'Arry, A Mark, Miniature 81.00
Character Jug, Anne Boleyn, Large 45.00
Character Jug, Anne Boleyn, Small 32.00
Character Jug, Apothecary, Large 80.00
Character Jug, Apothecary, Miniature 50.00
Character Jug, Apothecary, Small 60.00
Character Jug, Aramis, Large 55.00
Character Jug, Athos, Large ....52.00 To 55.00
Character Jug, Auld Mac, Large 75.00
Character Jug, Auld Mac, Small 75.00
Character Jug, Auld Mac, Tiny ....175.00 To 200.00
Character Jug, Bacchus, Small 32.00
Character Jug, Beefeater, Large 55.00
Character Jug, Beefeater, Small 55.00
Character Jug, Beefeaters, Small 65.00
Character Jug, Blacksmith, Large 80.00
Character Jug, Blacksmith, Small 60.00
Character Jug, Bootmaker, Large 80.00
Character Jug, Bootmaker, Miniature 50.00
Character Jug, Bootmaker, Small 60.00
Character Jug, Cap'N Cuttle, A Mark, Small ....85.00 To 110.00
Character Jug, Cardinal, A Mark, Miniature 45.00
Character Jug, Cardinal, Large ....110.00 To 135.00
Character Jug, Cardinal, Small 75.00
Character Jug, Cardinal, Tiny 210.00
Character Jug, Cavalier, Large 130.00
Character Jug, Cavalier, Small 85.00
Character Jug, Clown, White Hair, Large 950.00
Character Jug, Dick Turpin, Gun Handle, Large 110.00
Character Jug, Dick Turpin, Gun Handle, Miniature 54.00
Character Jug, Dick Turpin, Small 75.00
Character Jug, Dick Whittington, Large 375.00
Character Jug, Don Quixote, Large 75.00
Character Jug, Don Quixote, Miniature 25.00
Character Jug, Doultonville Town Crier, Tiny 35.00
Character Jug, Drake, Large ....89.00 To 110.00
Character Jug, Falstaff, Large 75.00
Character Jug, Farmer John, Large 135.00
Character Jug, Farmer John, Small 65.00
Character Jug, Fat Boy, Miniature 55.00
Character Jug, Fat Boy, Tiny ....80.00 To 100.00
Character Jug, Fortune Teller, Large 425.00
Character Jug, Fortune Teller, Miniature ....265.00 To 300.00
Character Jug, Friar Tuck, Large 345.00

Character Jug, Gardener, Large 175.00
Character Jug, Gardener, Small 70.00
Character Jug, Gladiator, Miniature 275.00
Character Jug, Gone Away, Large 80.00
Character Jug, Gone Away, Miniature 35.00
Character Jug, Gone Away, Small .... 35.00 To 60.00
Character Jug, Granny Toothless, Large 675.00
Character Jug, Granny, A Mark, Large .... 70.00 To 76.00
Character Jug, Granny, Small 45.00
Character Jug, Grant & Lee, Large 225.00
Character Jug, Gunsmith, Large 80.00
Character Jug, Gunsmith, Miniature 50.00
Character Jug, Gunsmith, Small 60.00
Character Jug, Henry V, Large 155.00
Character Jug, Henry VIII, Miniature 25.00
Character Jug, Henry VIII, Small 32.00
Character Jug, Jane Seymour, Large 45.00
Character Jug, Jarge, Large 300.00
Character Jug, Jarge, Small 175.00
Character Jug, Jockey, Large 200.00
Character Jug, John Barleycorn, Large .... 120.00 To 135.00
Character Jug, John Barleycorn, Miniature 50.00
Character Jug, John Barleycorn, Small 55.00
Character Jug, John Doulton, Small 50.00
Character Jug, John Peel, A Mark, Miniature .... 55.00 To 65.00
Character Jug, John Peel, A Mark, Small 45.00
Character Jug, John Peel, Tiny .... 185.00 To 215.00
Character Jug, Johnny Appleseed, Large 300.00
Character Jug, Lawyer, Miniature 25.00
Character Jug, Lawyer, Small 32.00
Character Jug, Lobster Man, Miniature 25.00
Character Jug, Lobster Man, Small 32.00
Character Jug, Long John Silver, Small 45.00
Character Jug, Lord Nelson, Large 385.00
Character Jug, Lumberjack, Large 95.00
Character Jug, Macbeth, Large 55.00
Character Jug, Mad Hatter, Miniature 50.00
Character Jug, Mad Hatter, Small .... 50.00 To 75.00
Character Jug, Merlin, Miniature 25.00
Character Jug, Mr. Bumble, Tiny 35.00
Character Jug, Mr. Micawber, Miniature 48.00
Character Jug, Mr. Micawber, Small 75.00
Character Jug, Mr. Micawber, Tiny .... 100.00 To 150.00
Character Jug, Mr. Pickwick, Tiny 145.00
Character Jug, Night Watchman, Miniature 50.00
Character Jug, North American Indian, Large 60.00
Character Jug, North American Indian, Small 45.00
Character Jug, Old Charley, A Mark, Miniature .... 27.00 To 38.00
Character Jug, Old Charley, Tiny .... 75.00 To 95.00
Character Jug, Old King Cole, Large .... 210.00 To 280.00
Character Jug, Old Salt, Large 65.00
Character Jug, Old Salt, Miniature 25.00
Character Jug, Oliver Twist, Tiny 35.00
Character Jug, Paddy, A Mark, Miniature .... 40.00 To 45.00
Character Jug, Paddy, A Mark, Small 45.00
Character Jug, Paddy, Tiny .... 70.00 To 90.00
Character Jug, Pied Piper, Miniature 50.00
Character Jug, Poacher, Small 32.00
Character Jug, Regency Beau, Miniature 700.00
Character Jug, Rip Van Winkle, Miniature 25.00
Character Jug, Robinson Crusoe, Large 80.00
Character Jug, Robinson Crusoe, Miniature 40.00
Character Jug, Sairey Gamp, A Mark, Large 75.00
Character Jug, Sairey Gamp, A Mark, Miniature 40.00

Character Jug, Sairey Gamp, Large 50.00
Character Jug, Sairey Gamp, Tiny .... 75.00 To 85.00
Character Jug, Sam Johnson, Large 225.00
Character Jug, Sam Weller, A Mark, Miniature 50.00
Character Jug, Sam Weller, Miniature .... 45.00 To 49.00
Character Jug, Sam Weller, Small 60.00
Character Jug, Sam Weller, Tiny 90.00
Character Jug, Sancho Panza, Large 95.00
Character Jug, Sancho Panza, Small 60.00
Character Jug, Simon The Cellarer, Large .... 115.00 To 126.00
Character Jug, Simon The Cellarer, Small .... 55.00 To 85.00
Character Jug, Simple Simon, Large 550.00
Character Jug, Sleuth, Small 45.00
Character Jug, Smuggler, Large .... 35.00 To 85.00
Character Jug, Smuggler, Small .... 50.00 To 60.00
Character Jug, Tam O'Shanter, Large 75.00
Character Jug, Toby Philpots, Miniature .... 40.00 To 45.00
Character Jug, Toby Philpots, Small 45.00
Character Jug, Town Crier, Large .... 175.00 To 195.00
Character Jug, Trapper, Canadian Centennial, Large 360.00
Character Jug, Trapper, Large .... 80.00 To 95.00
Character Jug, Trapper, Small 45.00
Character Jug, Ugly Duchess, Large 395.00
Character Jug, Uncle Tom Cobbleigh, Large .... 315.00 To 425.00
Character Jug, Veteran Motorist, Miniature 50.00
Character Jug, Veteran Motorist, Small 45.00
Character Jug, Vicar of Bray, A Mark, Large 175.00
Character Jug, Vicar of Bray, Large 125.00
Character Jug, Viking, Large 150.00
Character Jug, W.C. Fields, Large 100.00
Character Jug, Yachtsman, Large .... 50.00 To 100.00
Charger, Falstaff, 10 In. 125.00
Chocolate Pot, Enameled, Burgundy, Pink, Blue, Gold, Marked 125.00
Chocolate Pot, Pink, Rose & Ivory, Gold Trim, 1880s 155.00
Cup & Saucer, Chrysanthemums, Gold Trim, Burslem, Miniature 95.00
Cup & Saucer, Welsh Ladies 110.00
Dinner Set, Pomeroy, Service For 8, 4 Serving Pieces 600.00
Ewer, Dainty Floral, Burslem 125.00
Figurine, Abdullah, HN 1410 .... 775.00
Figurine, Abdullah, HN 2104 .... 450.00
Figurine, Affection, HN 2236 .... 80.00
Figurine, Afternoon Tea, HN 1747 .... 180.00 To 300.00
Figurine, Ajax, HN 2908 .... 500.00
Figurine, Alchemist, HN 1282 .... 1000.00
Figurine, All Aboard, HN 2940 .... 150.00
Figurine, Angela, HN 2389 .... 75.00
Figurine, As Good As New, HN 2971 .... 75.00
Figurine, At Ease, HN 2473 .... 200.00
Figurine, Autumn Breezes, HN 1934 .... 140.00 To 195.00
Figurine, Balinese Dancer, HN 2808 .... 690.00
Figurine, Ballerina, HN 2116 .... 225.00 To 250.00
Figurine, Balloon Man, HN 1954 .... 135.00 To 245.00
Figurine, Balloon Seller, HN 583 .... 300.00 To 600.00
Figurine, Beachcomber, HN 2487 .... 140.00 To 240.00
Figurine, Beat You To It, HN 2871 .... 300.00
Figurine, Bedtime Story, HN 2059 .... 135.00 To 246.00
Figurine, Bedtime, HN 1978 .... 50.00 To 85.00
Figurine, Beggar, HN 526 .... 675.00
Figurine, Belle, HN 2340 .... 95.00
Figurine, Bernice, HN 2071 .... 850.00
Figurine, Bess, HN 2002 .... 235.00
Figurine, Betsy, HN 2111 .... 200.00
Figurine, Biddy Penny Farthing, HN 1843 .... 135.00 To 245.00
Figurine, Blacksmith of Williamsburg, HN 2240 .... 150.00 To 165.00

Figurine, Blithe Morning, HN 2021 .... 200.00
Figurine, Bluebeard, HN 2105 .... 225.00 To 295.00
Figurine, Bo–Peep, HN 1810 .... 275.00
Figurine, Bo–Peep, HN 1811 .... 90.00
Figurine, Boatman, HN 2417 .... 100.00 To 120.00
Figurine, Bon Appetit, HN 2444 .... 155.00
Figurine, Bonnie Lassie, HN 1626 .... 280.00
Figurine, Boudoir, HN 2542 .... 400.00
Figurine, Breton Dancer, HN 2383 .... 675.00
Figurine, Bride, HN 2166 .... 175.00 To 225.00
Figurine, Bridget, HN 2070 .... 210.00
Figurine, Broken Lance, HN 2041 .... 400.00
Figurine, Bunny, HN 2214 .... 130.00
Figurine, Buttercup, HN 2309 .... 125.00 To 140.00
Figurine, Calumet, HN 1689 .... 600.00 To 700.00
Figurine, Camilla, HN 1711 .... 400.00
Figurine, Camille, HN 1586 .... 400.00
Figurine, Capt.MacHeath, HN 464 .... 695.00
Figurine, Captain Cook, HN 2889 .... 265.00
Figurine, Captain, HN 2260 .... 135.00 To 180.00
Figurine, Carmen, HN 2545 .... 200.00
Figurine, Carolyn, HN 2112 .... 200.00 To 315.00
Figurine, Carpet Seller, HN 1464 .... 225.00
Figurine, Cavalier, HN 2716 .... 170.00
Figurine, Celeste, HN 2237 .... 200.00
Figurine, Centurion, HN 2726 .... 180.00
Figurine, Charley's Aunt, HN 35 .... 500.00
Figurine, Charmian, HN 1569 .... 725.00
Figurine, Chief, HN 2892 .... 155.00
Figurine, China Repairer, HN 2943 .... 120.00 To 150.00
Figurine, Chinese Dancer, HN 2840 .... 475.00 To 650.00
Figurine, Choice, HN 1959 .... 1800.00
Figurine, Christmas Morn, HN 1992 .... 100.00
Figurine, Christmas Parcels, HN 2851 .... 180.00
Figurine, Christmas Time, HN 2110 .... 300.00
Figurine, Cicely, HN 1516 .... 595.00
Figurine, Cissie, HN 1809 .... 88.00
Figurine, Clarissa, HN 2345 .... 135.00
Figurine, Cleopatra, HN 2868 .... 1000.00
Figurine, Clockmaker, HN 2279 .... 250.00
Figurine, Clown, HN 2890 .... 195.00 To 240.00
Figurine, Coachman, HN 2282 .... 495.00
Figurine, Cobbler, HN 1706 .... 190.00
Figurine, Collinette, HN 1999 .... 550.00
Figurine, Columbine, HN 2185 .... 225.00
Figurine, Constance, HN 1511 .... 975.00
Figurine, Coralie, HN 2307 .... 85.00
Figurine, Country Lass, HN 1991A .... 110.00 To 135.00
Figurine, Cup of Tea, HN 2322 .... 120.00
Figurine, Curly Knob, HN 1627 .... 575.00
Figurine, Curtsey, HN 57B 1750.00
Figurine, Daffy Down Dilly, HN 1712 .... 250.00 To 325.00
Figurine, Daisy, HN 1575 .... 375.00
Figurine, Damaris, HN 2079 .... 1800.00
Figurine, Darling, HN 1319 .... 175.00
Figurine, Darling, HN 1985 .... 55.00 To 85.00
Figurine, Daydreams, HN 1731 .... 155.00
Figurine, Debbie, HN 2385 .... 110.00
Figurine, Debbie, HN 2400 .... 75.00
Figurine, Debutante, HN 2210 .... 300.00
Figurine, Delight, HN 1772 .... 145.00 To 245.00
Figurine, Denise, HN 2273 .... 235.00 To 275.00
Figurine, Detective, HN 2359 .... 160.00
Figurine, Dinky Do, HN 2120 .... 50.00

Figurine, Dorcas, HN 1558 .... 260.00
Figurine, Dreamweaver, HN 2283 .... 225.00
Figurine, Drummer Boy, HN 2679 .... 325.00
Figurine, Duke of Edinburgh, HN 2386 .... 425.00
Figurine, Dulcie, HN 2305 .... 130.00
Figurine, Dulcinea, HN 1419 .... 1595.00
Figurine, Easter Day, HN 1976 .... 415.00
Figurine, Easter Day, HN 2039 .... 225.00 To 275.00
Figurine, Elegance, HN 2264 .... 125.00 To 165.00
Figurine, Elyse, HN 2429 .... 180.00
Figurine, Ermine Coat, HN 1981 .... 225.00
Figurine, Eve, HN 2466 .... 500.00
Figurine, Evelyn, HN 1622 .... 850.00 To 1200.00
Figurine, Fair Lady, HN 2193 .... 100.00
Figurine, Fair Maiden, HN 2211 .... 85.00 To 110.00
Figurine, Fairy, HN 1376 .... 400.00
Figurine, Falstaff, HN 2054 .... 150.00
Figurine, Farmer's Boy, HN 2520 .... 1800.00
Figurine, Favourite, HN 2249 .... 235.00
Figurine, Fiddler, HN 2171 .... 700.00
Figurine, Fiona, HN 2694 .... 135.00
Figurine, First Dance, HN 2803 .... 170.00
Figurine, Flora, HN 2349 .... 250.00
Figurine, Flower Seller's Children, HN 1342 .... 350.00
Figurine, Foaming Quart, HN 2162 .... 175.00
Figurine, Fortune Teller, HN 2159 .... 375.00
Figurine, Forty Winks, HN 1974 .... 210.00
Figurine, Francine, HN 2422 .... 120.00
Figurine, Gaffer, HN 2053 .... 275.00
Figurine, General Washington At Prayer, HN 2861 .... 1500.00
Figurine, Genie, HN 2989 .... 75.00 To 95.00
Figurine, Georgiana, HN 2093 .... 995.00
Figurine, Gillian, HN 1670 .... 450.00
Figurine, Gollywog, HN 1979 .... 235.00
Figurine, Good Catch, HN 2258 .... 175.00
Figurine, Good King Wenceslas, HN 2118 .... 350.00
Figurine, Goody Two Shoes, HN 2037 .... 85.00 To 135.00
Figurine, Gossips, HN 2025 .... 280.00
Figurine, Grace, HN 2318 .... 125.00
Figurine, Granny's Heritage, HN 2031 .... 300.00
Figurine, Greta, HN 1485 .... 225.00
Figurine, Griselda, HN 1993 .... 500.00
Figurine, Gypsy Dance, HN 2230 .... 250.00
Figurine, Harlequin, HN 2186 .... 225.00
Figurine, He Loves Me, HN 2046 .... 144.00
Figurine, Helen of Troy, HN 2387 .... 800.00
Figurine, Helmsman, HN 2499 .... 165.00
Figurine, Hermione, HN 2058 .... 1600.00
Figurine, Highwayman, HN 527 .... 675.00
Figurine, Hilary, HN 2335 .... 135.00
Figurine, Hinged Parasol, HN 1578 .... 375.00
Figurine, Honey, HN 1909 .... 300.00 To 375.00
Figurine, Hornpipe, HN 2161 .... 495.00
Figurine, Huntsman, HN 2492 .... 165.00
Figurine, Irene, HN 1621 .... 315.00
Figurine, Jacqueline, HN 2001 .... 425.00
Figurine, Jane, HN 2806 .... 125.00
Figurine, Janet, HN 1537 .... 110.00
Figurine, Janice, HN 2165 .... 410.00
Figurine, Janine, HN 2461 .... 170.00
Figurine, Jean, HN 1878 .... 375.00
Figurine, Jester, HN 2016 .... 150.00 To 195.00
Figurine, Jolly Sailor, HN 2172 .... 450.00
Figurine, Jovial Monk, HN 2144 .... 170.00

Figurine, Judith, HN 2089 .... 300.00
Figurine, June, HN 1691 .... 300.00
Figurine, Juno & The Peacock, HN 2827 .... 1500.00
Figurine, Kate Hardcastle, HN 1719 .... 375.00
Figurine, Kate Hardcastle, HN 2028 .... 550.00
Figurine, Kathleen, HN 1252 .... 550.00
Figurine, Kurdish Dancer, HN 2867 .... 625.00
Figurine, La Sylphide, HN 2138 .... 325.00
Figurine, Lady April, HN 1958 .... 285.00
Figurine, Lady Charmian, HN 1949 .... 210.00
Figurine, Lady Clare, HN 1465 .... 650.00
Figurine, Lady Pamela, HN 2718 .... 200.00
Figurine, Lambing Time, HN 1890 .... 135.00
Figurine, Last Waltz, HN 2315 .... 150.00
Figurine, Leisure Hour, HN 2055 .... 295.00 To 440.00
Figurine, Lido Lady, HN 1220 .... 800.00 To 900.00
Figurine, Lights Out, HN 2262 .... 195.00
Figurine, Lily, HN 1798 .... 200.00
Figurine, Lion On Rock, HN 2641 .... 650.00
Figurine, Lisa, HN 2310 .... 125.00
Figurine, Little Lady Make Believe, HN 1870 .... 380.00
Figurine, Little Mistress, HN 1449 .... 295.00
Figurine, Loretta, HN 2337 .... 125.00
Figurine, Love Letters, HN 2149 .... 300.00
Figurine, Lucrezia Borgia, HN 2342 .... 675.00
Figurine, Lucy Lockett, HN 524 .... 525.00
Figurine, Lunchtime, HN 2485 .... 165.00
Figurine, Lynne, HN 2329 .... 125.00
Figurine, Margaret, HN 1989 .... 225.00
Figurine, Marguerite, HN 1928 .... 500.00
Figurine, Marie, HN 1370 .... 50.00 To 95.00
Figurine, Marietta, HN 1699 .... 525.00
Figurine, Market Day, HN 1991 .... 265.00
Figurine, Mary Jane, HN 1990 .... 325.00
Figurine, Masque, HN 2554 .... 200.00
Figurine, Masquerade, HN 600 .... 600.00
Figurine, Master, HN 2325 .... 150.00 To 200.00
Figurine, Maureen, HN 1770 .... 215.00 To 325.00
Figurine, Maureen, M 85 .... 275.00
Figurine, Mayor, HN 2280 .... 225.00
Figurine, Memories, HN 2030 .... 325.00
Figurine, Mendicant, HN 1365 .... 175.00
Figurine, Mephistopheles & Marguerite, HN 755 .... 1600.00
Figurine, Mexican Dancer, HN 2866 .... 650.00
Figurine, Midinette, HN 2090 .... 225.00
Figurine, Midsummer Noon, HN 2033 .... 450.00
Figurine, Milkmaid, HN 2057A 110.00
Figurine, Mirabel, HN 1744 .... 800.00
Figurine, Miss Muffet, HN 1936 .... 139.00
Figurine, Modena, HN 1846 .... 1195.00
Figurine, Monica, HN 1467 .... 100.00
Figurine, Mr. Pickwick, HN 556 .... 300.00
Figurine, Mr. Pickwick, M 41 .... 60.00
Figurine, Negligee, HN 1219 .... 750.00
Figurine, Newsboy, HN 2244 .... 375.00
Figurine, News vendor, HN 2891 .... 185.00
Figurine, Nicola, HN 2839 .... 280.00
Figurine, Noelle, HN 2179 .... 280.00
Figurine, Officer of The Line, HN 2733 .... 140.00 To 200.00
Figurine, Old Balloon Seller, HN 1315 .... 145.00
Figurine, Old King, HN 2134 .... 395.00
Figurine, Old Lavender Seller, HN 1492 .... 675.00
Figurine, Old Meg, HN 2494 .... 210.00
Figurine, Orange Lady, HN 1759 .... 225.00

Figurine, Orange Lady, HN 1953 .... 160.00
Figurine, Organ Grinder, HN 2173 .... 475.00
Figurine, Owd Willum, HN 2042 .... 195.00
Figurine, Painting, HN 3012 .... 775.00
Figurine, Paisley Shawl, HN 1392 .... 400.00
Figurine, Paisley Shawl, HN 1987 .... 275.00 To 325.00
Figurine, Pantalettes, HN 1362 .... 295.00
Figurine, Parisian, HN 2445 .... 150.00
Figurine, Parson's Daughter, HN 2018 .... 400.00
Figurine, Patchwork Quilt, HN 1984 .... 250.00
Figurine, Paula, HN 2906 .... 135.00
Figurine, Pearly Girl, HN 2036 .... 335.00
Figurine, Pecksniff, HN 1891 .... 300.00
Figurine, Peggy, HN 2038 .... 80.00
Figurine, Penelope, HN 1901 .... 225.00
Figurine, Pensive Moments, HN 2704 .... 155.00
Figurine, Perfect Pair, HN 581 .... 795.00
Figurine, Picnic, HN 2308 .... 110.00
Figurine, Pierrette, HN 644 .... 475.00 To 900.00
Figurine, Poacher, HN 2043 .... 275.00
Figurine, Polish Dancer, HN 2836 .... 685.00
Figurine, Polly Peachum, HN 550 .... 300.00
Figurine, Potter, HN 1493 .... 145.00 To 300.00
Figurine, Premiere, HN 2343 .... 215.00
Figurine, Pretty Polly, HN 2768 .... 90.00
Figurine, Prince of Wales, HN 2883 .... 375.00
Figurine, Princess of Wales, HN 2885 .... 425.00
Figurine, Printemps, HN 3066 .... 575.00
Figurine, Priscilla, HN 1340 .... 300.00
Figurine, Private, Mass.Reg., 1778, HN 2760 .... 600.00
Figurine, Prized Possessions, HN 2942 .... 495.00 To 525.00
Figurine, Professor, HN 2281 .... 135.00 To 155.00
Figurine, Punch & Judy Man, HN 2765 .... 245.00
Figurine, Puppetmaker, HN 2253 .... 385.00 To 500.00
Figurine, Queen Elizabeth II, HN 2878 .... 375.00
Figurine, Queen Mother, HN 2882 .... 825.00
Figurine, Queen of Sheba, HN 2328 .... 675.00 To 800.00
Figurine, Queen of The Ice, HN 2435 .... 175.00
Figurine, Rag Doll, HN 2142 .... 60.00 To 75.00
Figurine, Regal Lady, HN 2709 .... 165.00
Figurine, Rendezvous, HN 2212 .... 275.00 To 335.00
Figurine, Romance, HN 2430 .... 120.00
Figurine, Rose, HN 2123 .... 50.00 To 85.00
Figurine, Roseanna, HN 1921 .... 300.00
Figurine, Royal Governor's Cook, HN 2233 .... 395.00
Figurine, Sailor's Holiday, HN 2442 .... 145.00 To 275.00
Figurine, Sairey Gamp, HN 2100 .... 295.00
Figurine, Schoolmarm, HN 2223 .... 125.00 To 185.00
Figurine, Scribe, HN 1235 .... 595.00
Figurine, Sea Harvest, HN 2257 .... 145.00
Figurine, Sea Sprite, HN 2191 .... 400.00
Figurine, Seafarer, HN 2455 .... 155.00
Figurine, Seashore, HN 2263 .... 195.00
Figurine, Secret Thoughts, HN 2382 .... 180.00
Figurine, Serenade, HN 2753 .... 150.00
Figurine, Shadow Play, HN 3526 .... 125.00
Figurine, She Loves Me Not, HN 2045 .... 144.00
Figurine, Shepherd, HN 1975 .... 150.00
Figurine, Shepherdess, HN 750 .... 995.00
Figurine, Shore Leave, HN 2254 .... 175.00
Figurine, Shy Anne, HN 64 .... 2500.00
Figurine, Sibell, HN 1668 .... 500.00
Figurine, Sleepy Darling, HN 2953 .... 225.00
Figurine, Smiling Buddha, HN 454 .... 1300.00 To 1400.00

Figurine, Southern Belle, HN 2229 .... 168.00
Figurine, Spanish Flamenco Dancer, HN 2831 .... 1500.00
Figurine, Spring Flowers, HN 1807 .... 250.00
Figurine, Spring Morning, HN 1922 .... 165.00 To 235.00
Figurine, St.George, HN 2051 .... 395.00
Figurine, St.George, HN 2067 .... 2500.00
Figurine, Stephanie, HN 2807 .... 135.00
Figurine, Stitch In Time, HN 2352 .... 120.00 To 145.00
Figurine, Stop Press, HN 2683 .... 135.00 To 170.00
Figurine, Suitor, HN 2132 .... 325.00
Figurine, Sunday Best, HN 2206 .... 170.00 To 250.00
Figurine, Susanna, HN 1233 .... 900.00
Figurine, Suzette, HN 2026 .... 225.00 To 325.00
Figurine, Sweet & Twenty, HN 1549 .... 475.00
Figurine, Sweet Anne, HN 1318 .... 215.00
Figurine, Sweet Anne, HN 1330 .... 225.00
Figurine, Sweet Anne, M 5 .... 250.00
Figurine, Sweet Maid, HN 1504 .... 650.00
Figurine, Sweet Seventeen, HN 2734 .... 175.00
Figurine, Sweet Suzy, HN 1918 .... 775.00
Figurine, Taking Things Easy, HN 2677 .... 150.00 To 215.00
Figurine, Thanks Doc, HN 2731 .... 125.00
Figurine, This Little Pig, HN 1793 .... 55.00
Figurine, Tinker Bell, HN 1677 .... 75.00
Figurine, Tinsmith, HN 2146 .... 550.00
Figurine, To Bed, HN 1805 .... 175.00
Figurine, Top O' The Hill, HN 1833 .... 175.00
Figurine, Top O' The Hill, HN 1834 .... 150.00
Figurine, Town Crier, HN 2119 .... 200.00 To 275.00
Figurine, Toymaker, HN 2250 .... 300.00
Figurine, Twilight, HN 2256 .... 170.00
Figurine, Uncle Ned, HN 2094 .... 375.00
Figurine, Uriah Heep, HN 554 .... 300.00
Figurine, Verena, HN 1835 .... 1000.00
Figurine, Veronica, HN 1517 .... 255.00
Figurine, Victoria, HN 2471 .... 165.00
Figurine, Virginia, HN 1693 .... 695.00
Figurine, Vivienne, HN 2073 .... 325.00
Figurine, Votes For Women, HN 2816 .... 170.00
Figurine, Wardrobe Mistress, HN 2145 .... 365.00
Figurine, Wee Willie Winkie, HN 2050 .... 255.00 To 350.00
Figurine, West Indian Dancer, HN 2384 .... 690.00
Figurine, Wigmaker of Williamsburg, HN 2239 .... 185.00
Figurine, Willy–Won't He, HN 2150 .... 395.00
Figurine, Windflower, HN 2029 .... 375.00
Figurine, Winter, HN 2088 .... 275.00
Figurine, Young Love, HN 2735 .... 275.00
Figurine, Young Master, HN 2872 .... 195.00
Figurine, Young Miss Nightingale, HN 2010 .... 495.00
Humidor, New Cavaliers, Better Do It Than Wish It Done 100.00
Inkwell, Owl, Faience, No.1876 .... 235.00
Jardiniere, Tapestry, Lambeth Mark, 7 X 7 1/2 In. 200.00
Lamp, Owl, 1885 .... 750.00
Lighter, Cigarette, Poacher 78.00
Loving Cup, Charles Dickens 550.00
Loving Cup, Lord Nelson 950.00
Loving Cup, Pilgrim Fathers 550.00
Loving Cup, Pottery In Past 220.00
Mustard, Raised Pink Grapes, Blue Leaves, Marked 90.00
Pitcher & Bowl, Flowers, Dark Blue & White, Burslem 100.00
Pitcher, Aldin's Dogs, Smoking Pipe, C.1930, 9 X 7 In. 245.00
Pitcher, Authors & Inns, Goldsmith 85.00
Pitcher, Blue Willow, 6 In. 85.00
Pitcher, Floral, Gold Tracery, Turquoise Jewel, Burslem, 5 In. 200.00

Lusterware requires special handling because it can wear away if it is improperly washed. The ware should be washed in warm water with a mild soap or detergent. Do not rub too hard, or you will remove the luster glaze.

Pitcher, Jackdaw of Rheims, 5 In.	145.00
Pitcher, Old Curiosity Shop, Square	150.00
Pitcher, Old Peggotty, Square	335.00
Plaque, Wall, Dr.Johnson At Cheshire Cheese, 13 1/2 In.	145.00
Plate, Bookworm	195.00
Plate, Cardinal Wolsey, Large	185.00
Plate, Coaching Days, 6 3/4 In.	60.00
Plate, Coaching Days, 7 3/4 In.	65.00
Plate, Coaching Days, Scalloped Rim, 8 3/4 In.	80.00
Plate, Gallant Fishers, 10 1/2 In.	40.00
Plate, Jackdaw of Rheims, 10 In.	95.00
Plate, Nursery Rhyme, Tommy Tucker	35.00
Plate, Poor Jo, 10 1/2 In.	45.00
Plate, Sampler, D 3749	85.00
Plate, Tonkin, 10 In.	10.00
Plate, Valentine, 1976	15.00
Plate, Valentine, 1977	8.00
Platter, Penelope, Grape Clusters	80.00
Sugar, Sairey Gamp, Miniature	550.00 To 575.00
Tankard, Dickens Ware, Oliver	200.00
Tea Set, Bayeau Tapestry, 3 Piece	150.00
Tea Set, Old Trentham Sprays, 3 Piece	165.00
Teapot, Old Charley	2700.00
Teapot, Tony Weller	2700.00
Tobacco Jar, Old Charley	2750.00
Toby Jug, Winston Churchill, Seated, Medium	175.00
Toothpick, Dickens Ware, Mr. Pickwick	125.00
Toothpick, Sunset Scene	85.00
Tray, Cottage Scene, Flambe, Noke, C.1936, 5 1/2 In.	95.00
Vase, Babes In Woods, C.1901, 14 In.	395.00
Vase, Country Cottage Scene, Flambe, 7 In.	185.00
Vase, Dutch, Handle, 5 In.	110.00
Vase, Green Floral, Blue, Bulbous Base, 11 1/4 In., Pair	450.00
Vase, Lace, Cobalt Blue Interior, Stick Neck, Slater, 10 In.	95.00
Vase, Portrait of Children, Gold Ground, Burslem, 10 1/4 In.	250.00
Vase, Scenic, Harlech Castle, 5 1/2 In.	325.00
Vase, Shakespeare, Ophelia, 7 In.	155.00

The Duxer Porzellanmanufaktur was founded in Dux, Bohemia, in 1860 by E. Eichler. By the turn of the century, the firm specialized in porcelain statuary and busts of Art Nouveau–style maidens, large porcelain figures, and ornate vases with three-dimensional figures climbing on the sides. The firm is still in business.

ROYAL DUX, Bowl, Centerpiece, Maidens Holding Up Shell, 22 In.	1000.00
Bust, Woman, Art Deco, Spanish Hat, Matte & Shiny, 6 1/2 In.	225.00
Chess Set, Porcelain, 4 1/2–In.King, Each Piece Marked	895.00
Compote, Maiden, Cherubs, Holding Up Shell, 20 In.	1150.00 To 1250.00
Figurine, Bird, Marked, 5 3/4 In.	10.00

Figurine, Boy With Dog, 24 In.	325.00
Figurine, Bulldog	45.00
Figurine, Children, Basket, Pink Triangle Mark, 8 1/2 In.	395.00
Figurine, Cockatoo, 12 In.	335.00
Figurine, Deer & Wolf	165.00
Figurine, Deer, Resting	125.00 To 150.00
Figurine, Dog, German Shepherd, 16 In.	135.00
Figurine, Elephant, 14 X 20 In.	575.00
Figurine, Harvester & Wife, Gold Trim, Cobalt Blue, Marked, 21 In.	850.00
Figurine, Hippopotamus	45.00
Figurine, Horse, Triangle Mark, 14 In.	675.00
Figurine, Hunting Dog	195.00
Figurine, Lady On Conch Shell, Gold, Tan, Off–White, 13 1/2 In.	400.00
Figurine, Little Girl Holding Little Sister, Marked, 15 X 12 In.	775.00
Figurine, Maiden, With Tambourine, 14 In.	225.00
Figurine, Man, With Scythe, Girl, With Apron, 11 3/8 In., Pair	550.00
Figurine, Mother, Holding Child, Next To Basket, Marked	395.00
Figurine, Nude, Kneeling On Rock, Pool, Marked, 11 X 9 In.	495.00
Figurine, Nude, Sitting, Butterfly On Knee, Pink Mark, 8 In.	120.00
Figurine, Nude, Standing, Towel, 9 1/2 In.	185.00
Figurine, Parrot.12 In.	325.00
Figurine, Peacock, White, Art Deco, Marked, 11 In.	95.00
Figurine, Rhinoceros Beetles, Marked, Pair	250.00
Figurine, Spanish Lady, Cobalt Blue, White, Art Deco, 9 In.	350.00
Figurine, Tiger	365.00
Figurine, Tom Sawyer, Fishing Pole, Dog, Marked, C.1925, 14 In.	195.00
Figurine, Woman, Cobalt Blue Gown, 9 In.	160.00
Figurine, Woman, Deco, Dress, Tam, Gloves, Windblown Skirt, 10 In.	275.00
Group, Mother Feeding Baby, Father Drinking, 1860, 8 X 13 In.	550.00
Group, Romantic Couple, Seated, Outstretched Arms, Marked, 8 In.	375.00
Humidor, Pipe On Lid, Pre–1918	245.00
Tray, Dresser, Satin Glass, French	65.00
Urn, Cover, Ovoid Finial, Rams' Heads At Shoulder, 12 1/4 In.	305.00
Vase, Art Nouveau, Green Dolphin Handles, 5 1/2 X 13 In.	195.00
Vase, Pink & Green Floral, Hourglass Shape, 9 In.	110.00
Vase, Woman Emerging From Vase, Playing Harp, Marked, 14 1/2 In.	450.00

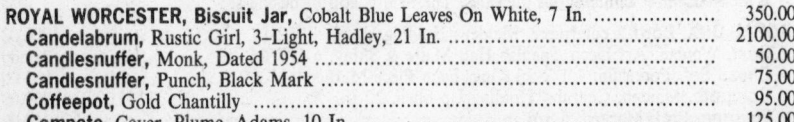

Royal Flemish glass was made during the late 1880s in New Bedford, Massachusetts, by the Mt. Washington Glass Works. It is a colored satin glass decorated with dark colors and raised gold designs. The glass was patented in 1894. It was supposed to resemble stained glass windows.

ROYAL FLEMISH, Jar, Flowers, Frosted Glass, 6 In.	850.00
Vase, Jeweled, Ring Handles, Blossoms, Thorny Stems, 9 In.	1545.00
Vase, Signed, 9 1/2 In.	1995.00

ROYAL HAEGER, see Haeger
ROYAL IVY, see Pressed Glass, Royal Ivy
ROYAL OAK, see Pressed Glass, Royal Oak
ROYAL RUDOLSTADT, see Rudolstadt
ROYAL VIENNA, see Beehive

Worcester porcelains were made in Worcester, England, from about 1751. The firm went through many different periods and name changes. It became the Worcester Royal Porcelain Company, Ltd., in 1862. Today collectors call the porcelains made after 1862 "Royal Worcester." In 1976, the firm merged with W. T. Copeland to become Royal Worcester Spode. Some early products of the factory are listed under Worcester.

ROYAL WORCESTER, Biscuit Jar, Cobalt Blue Leaves On White, 7 In.	350.00
Candelabrum, Rustic Girl, 3–Light, Hadley, 21 In.	2100.00
Candlesnuffer, Monk, Dated 1954	50.00
Candlesnuffer, Punch, Black Mark	75.00
Coffeepot, Gold Chantilly	95.00
Compote, Cover, Plume, Adams, 10 In.	125.00

Creamer, Gold Chantilly	40.00
Cup & Saucer, Chelsea	30.00
Cup & Saucer, Doreen	25.00
Cup & Saucer, Gnomes Working, C.1904	165.00
Cup & Saucer, Gold Chantilly	30.00
Egg Coddler, Blackberry, Box	20.00
Ewer, Empress, Pink & White Dogwood, C.1893, 12 In.	350.00
Figurine, A Merry New Song, No.3252	250.00
Figurine, Babes In The Wood, No.3302	195.00 To 225.00
Figurine, Boy With Parakeet, No.3087, Dated 1950	150.00
Figurine, Bringaree Indians, No.1243, Pair	750.00
Figurine, Burmah, No.3068, 5 In.	115.00
Figurine, Cairo Water Carrier, Male, No.1250	295.00
Figurine, Dachshund, 4 1/2 In.	35.00
Figurine, Duchess's Dress, No.3106	300.00
Figurine, First Cuckoo, No.3082	195.00
Figurine, Fortune Teller, No.2924	300.00
Figurine, Grandmother's Dress, Green, No.3081	170.00
Figurine, Johnnie, No.3433	200.00
Figurine, Mother Machree, No.2924	300.00
Figurine, October, No.3417	155.00
Figurine, Palomino Stallion, No.160, 9 IIN.	300.00
Figurine, Sealyham, No.2932, On Plinth	250.00
Figurine, Water Baby, No.3151	200.00
Figurine, Wind, No.2617	185.00
Figurine, Woodland Dance, No.3076	300.00
Gravy Boat, Gold Chantilly, Underplate	85.00
Jug, Owl On Branch, Serpent Handle, Gold, 1885, 11 1/4 In.	925.00
Mug, Monday's Child	85.00
Mug, Sabbath Day's Child	85.00
Patch Box, Reticulated Lid, Granger Mark, 3 In.	225.00
Pitcher, Cream, Purple & Gold Flower, Gold Handle, 10 In.	250.00
Pitcher, Gold Encrusted Flowers, C.1899, 9 In.	290.00
Pitcher, Gold Foliage On Red Satin Ground, 7 In.	225.00
Pitcher, Salamander, 6 1/2 In.	325.00
Plate, Currier & Ives, The Road, Winter, Pewter, 1974	30.00
Plate, Independence, 1976	50.00
Platter, Boston, Blue & White, 12 1/2 In.	78.00
Ring Tree, Pink & Yellow Flowers, C.1898, 4 1/2 In.	145.00
Sugar & Creamer, Scalloped Neck, Serpent Handle, Marked	195.00
Sugar, Cover, Gold Chantilly	55.00
Teapot, Kashmir, Large	75.00
Tureen, Soup, Elephant Handles, Small	90.00
Vase, Black–Faced Sheep, Scrolled Base, C.1891, 6 1/2 In.	275.00
Vase, Cover, Potpourri, Butterflies, Head Handles, 13 In.	895.00
Vase, Flowers On Front, Gold Handles, Marked, 8 In.	250.00
Vase, Handles, 1883, 12 1/2 In.	275.00
Vase, Nautilus Shell, Gold Trim, Marked, 8 1/2 In.	450.00
Vase, Pate–Sur–Pate Birds, Turquoise, Green & Gold, 10 In.	295.00
Vase, Pedestal, Nautilus Shell Shape, 4 In.	225.00
Vase, Pheasant, Signed, 8 3/4 In.	475.00
Vase, Turquoise Stone Rows, Gold Design, Ivory, 5 1/8 In.	655.00
Vase, Tusk, Poppies, Butterfly, Fuchsias, Tan, 1890, 9 In.	365.00

Roycroft products were made by the Roycrofter community of East Aurora, New York, in the late nineteenth and early twentieth centuries. The community was founded by Elbert Hubbard, famous philosopher, writer, and artist. The workshops owned by the community made furniture, metalwork, leatherwork, embroidery, and jewelry. A printshop produced many signs, books, and the magazines that promoted the sayings of Elbert Hubbard. Furniture by the Roycroft community is listed in the furniture section.

ROYCROFT, Bookends, Bent To Scroll Side, Logo, C.1910, 5 1/4 In.	275.00
Bookends, Hammered Copper, Poppy Flowers	185.00

Bookends, Raised Flower, Copper, 5 1/4 X 8 1/4 In.	175.00
Bookends, Ship	120.00
Bookrack, Table Top, No.0116, Logo, C.1910, 15 In.	275.00
Bowl, Nut, Spoon, Hammered Silver On Copper, 6 Crimp, 2 1/4 X 6 In.	225.00
Bowl, Wide Mouth, Flared, Logo, C.1910, 5 1/2 X 5 In.	220.00
Candlestick, Hammered Copper, Spiral, Signed, Pair	600.00
Candlestick, Princess, Double Stem, C.1910, 7 3/4 In., Pair	412.50
Desk Set, Hammered Copper, Perpetual Calendar, Bookends, 4 Piece	595.00
Frame, Leather, 8 X 4 In.	250.00
Honey Pot	12.00
Inkwell, Hammered Copper, Cover, Original Glass Insert, 3 1/2 In.	125.00
Jug, Brown, 5 In.	22.00
Lamp, Flame Finial, Parchment Shade, C.1920, 22 1/2 In.	605.00
Lamp, Scrolled Shaft, Pink & Gold Steuben Shade, Copper, 15 In.	5800.00
Letter Holder, Hammered Copper	15.00
Tray, Loop Handles, Logo, Round, C.1910, 15 3/4 In.	357.00
Vase, American Beauty, Riveted Strapwork, Signed, C.1910, 19 In.	995.00
Vase, Hammered Copper, Flaring Cylindrical Neck, C.1910, 18 In.	990.00
Vase, Riveted Strapwork, Copper, Signed, 19 In.	900.00
Vase, Roosevelt Bears, Tin Plate, 1907	85.00

ROZANE, see Roseville

RRP is the mark used by the firm of Robinson–Ransbottom. It is not a mark of the more famous Roseville Pottery. The Ransbottom brothers started a pottery in 1900 in Ironspot, Ohio. In 1920, they merged with the Robinson Clay Product Company of Akron, Ohio, to become Robinson–Ransbottom. The factory is still working.

RRP, Bowl, Blue, 5 In.	22.00
Cookie Jar, Ball Shape, Off White, Peach Design	40.00
Cookie Jar, Chef	25.00
Cookie Jar, Oscar	20.00
Cookie Jar, Wise Bird	30.00
Jardiniere, Pedestal, Basket Weave, Tan, Brown, Gold Designs	100.00
Mug, Windy City	95.00
Pitcher, Dancing Girl Design, Blue	225.00
Vase, Leaves, White, 10 In.	12.00

The RS Germany mark was used on porcelain made at the factory of Reinhold Schlegelmilch from about 1910 to 1956 in Tillowitz, Germany. It was sold decorated and undecorated. The Schlegelmilch family made porcelains marked in many ways. Each type is listed separately. See also ES Germany, RS Poland, RS Prussia, RS Suhl, and RS Tillowitz.

RS GERMANY, Biscuit Jar, Floral & Blue Dot	95.00
Bowl, Cabbage Leaf, Flowers, Shaded Green Iridescent, Mold 12	250.00
Bowl, Cottages, Trees, Ruffled, Green Mark, 9 1/2 In.	100.00
Bowl, White Tulips, Marked, 10 1/4 In.	48.00
Cake Plate, Pink, Yellow & Salmon Flowers, Handles, 10 In.	70.00
Cake Set, Fuchsia Design, Pierced Handles, 7 Piece	195.00
Chocolate Set, Cotton Plant Design, 7 Piece	275.00
Coffeepot, Cover, Floral, Puffed, Stippled, Mold 525	215.00
Cookie Jar, Tulip Spray, Leaves, Gold Rim, Marked	85.00
Cracker Jar, White Tulips, Blue Gray, Satin Finish	175.00
Cup & Saucer, Cotton Plant, Large	65.00
Cup & Saucer, White Open Rose, Pale Green, 2 X 3 1/2 In.	50.00
Dish, Bird On Floral Limb, Handle, 7 1/2 In.	95.00
Dresser Set, Pink Roses, Powder Jar, Green Mark, 4 Piece	275.00
Hatpin Holder, Art Deco, Line Design On Greens, Rose Panels	95.00
Hatpin Holder, Florals	60.00
Hatpin Holder, Poppies	65.00
Hatpin Holder, Single Calla Lily, Marked	60.00
Hatpin Holder, Yellow & Pink Roses, Green Mark	65.00
Holder, Condensed Milk, Floral, Gold Bands, White, Cover, 5 In.	145.00
Holder, Toothbrush, Wall Mount, Pink Rose, Thorn, Leaves	85.00

Pin Dish, White Lilies, 6 X 4 1/2 In. 60.00
Pitcher, Milk, Fruit Design, 5 X 6 1/2 In. 300.00
Plaque, Friederike Von Gumpenberg, Porcelain, 1900, 7 X 9 In. 265.00
Plate, Cotton Plant, Blue Mark, 8 1/4 In. 85.00
Plate, Dogwood Blossoms, Maroon, 8 In., 6 Piece 100.00
Plate, Snowballs, Wide Gold Border, Marked, 6 In., 5 Piece 40.00
Relish, Bowl of Flowers, Gold Mark, 12 1/2 In. 65.00
Salad Set, Cabbage Bowl, 7 Piece 295.00
Tea Set, Blue Band, Flowers, Ivory, Gold Handles, 3 Piece 145.00
Toothpick, Hand Painted Roses Around Rim, Pearlized, 2 1/2 In. 40.00
Toothpick, White Rose 55.00
Tray, Dresser, Floral Center, Gold Border, Marked, 11 1/4 X 7 In. 145.00
Tray, Snowbirds, Open Handles, 15 1/4 X 5 1/4 In. 325.00
Vase, Apple Blossom, 3 In. 30.00
Vase, Bud, Pink Rose, Leaves, Shaded Ground, 6 In. 55.00
Vase, Night Watch, Red, Gold Trim, Green Mark, 6 1/2 In. 350.00

The RS Poland (German) mark was used by the Reinhold Schlegelmilch factory at Tillowitz from about 1945 to 1956. This is one of many of the RS marks used. See also ES Germany, RS Germany, RS Prussia, RS Silesia, RS Suhl, and RS Tillowitz.

RS POLAND, Candlestick, Roses, Brown Trim, 6 1/4 In., Pair 195.00
Planter, Band of Pink Flowers, Gold Trim, Pedestal, 6 3/4 In. 230.00
Sugar Shaker, Red Mark 150.00
Vase, Crowned Crane, 3 1/2 In. 800.00
Vase, Night Watch Scene, 4 Men & A Woman, 4 In. 300.00
Vase, Pink Roses, Cobalt Blue, 8 1/4 In., Pair 225.00
Vase, White Poppies, Cream To Brown Ground, 12 In., Pair 750.00
Vase, Yellow Roses, Tan Ground, 3 5/8 In. 105.00

"RS Prussia" is a mark that appears on porcelain made at the factory of Reinhold Schlegelmilch from the late 1870s to 1914 in Tillowitz, Germany, or on items made at the Erdmann Schlegelmilch factory in Suhl, Germany, from about 1910 to 1956. It was sold decorated or undecorated. The factories were owned by brothers. See also ES Germany, RS Germany, RS Poland, RS Suhl, and RS Tillowitz.

RS PRUSSIA, Berry Bowl, Cottage Scene, Browns, 5 1/2 In. 50.00
Berry Set, Blown-Out Iris, Pink Poppies, Red Mark, 7 Piece 500.00
Berry Set, Gold-Beaded Scalloped Edge, Red Mark, 5 Piece 225.00
Berry Set, Icicle Mold, 7 Piece 900.00
Berry Set, Pink Flowers, Carnation Mold, Red Mark, 5 Piece 650.00
Biscuit Jar, Swallow & Water Lilies, Lavender To Caramel 375.00
Bowl, 3 Pink Rose Clusters, Lavender, Cream, Pleating, Red Mark 295.00
Bowl, 4 Carnations, Dark Green, Fuchsia, Marked, 10 1/2 In. 395.00
Bowl, 5 Cupped Medallions, Tapestry Type Ground, Marked, 11 In. 325.00
Bowl, 6 Medallions, Floral Design, 10 1/2 In. 250.00
Bowl, Bluebird & Swans, Pearlized Finish, 11 In. 450.00
Bowl, Cherubs In Medallions, Red Mark, 10 1/4 In. 600.00
Bowl, Cobalt Blue, 6 Blown-Out Sections, 11 In. 475.00
Bowl, Countess Anna Potocka, 10 In. 1450.00
Bowl, Countess Catherine Litta Portrait, Scalloped, 9 In. 350.00
Bowl, Crowned Crane, 10 In. 1900.00
Bowl, Diana The Huntress, Red Mark, 10 In. 1650.00
Bowl, Floral Center, Cobalt Blue, 3 X 10 1/2 In. 595.00
Bowl, Floral Design, Square In Square 185.00
Bowl, Floral Medallion Mold, 3 Victorian Ladies, Lions, 9 In. 900.00
Bowl, Floral, Blown-Out Iris Mold, Red Mark, 10 In. 195.00
Bowl, Floral, Turquoise To Nile, Plume Mold, Red Mark, 10 3/4 In. 255.00
Bowl, Hanging Basket of Flowers, Red Mark, 11 In. 165.00
Bowl, Lady, Reclining, 10 In. 2000.00
Bowl, Leaf Mold, Self-Handle, Red Mark, 6 1/2 In. 155.00
Bowl, Lebrun Portraits, 5 Medallion Mold, Red Mark, 11 In. 895.00
Bowl, Man In Mountain, Red Mark, 11 1/2 In. 795.00

Bowl, Masted Ship Scene, Oval, 9 X 13 In. 910.00
Bowl, Multicolored Flowers Inside & Out, Blown–Out Mold, 8 In. 135.00
Bowl, Peach Roses, Gold Tracery, Black Border, 10 1/2 In. 235.00
Bowl, Peafowl, 10 In. 1495.00
Bowl, Pink & White Roses, Green Shading, Red Mark, 7 In. 75.00
Bowl, Pink Roses, Green, Gold, Red Mark, 10 In. 145.00
Bowl, Pink Roses, White, Green, Gold, Satin, 3 X 10 3/4 In. 430.00
Bowl, Reflected Poppies & Daisies, 3–Footed, 6 X 3 1/4 In. 395.00
Bowl, Roses, Green Piecrust Border, Ivory Ground, 9 1/2 In. 110.00
Bowl, Roses, White Lilies, Gold Trim, Luster, Red Mark, 10 X 3 In. 160.00
Bowl, Satin Roses Inside & Outside, Gold Inside, 7 X 9 In. 325.00
Bowl, Sheepherder Scene, Marked, 10 In. 750.00
Bowl, Snowball, Pink Roses, 10 3/4 In. 325.00
Bowl, Stag, 11 In. 1500.00
Bowl, Swan Scene, Red Mark, 10 1/2 In. 350.00
Bowl, Yellow Roses, Beaded Scalloped Rim, Red Mark, 10 1/2 In. 175.00
Box, Dresser, Gazelle, 5 In. 3100.00
Butter, Cover, Double Portrait, 7 3/4 In 600.00
Cake Plate, Barnyard Scene, Open Handles, 10 In. 1000.00
Cake Plate, Basket of Roses, Pearl Luster, Marked, 10 1/2 In. 275.00
Cake Plate, Bluebird & Cottage 325.00
Cake Plate, Easter Lily, Cobalt Blue, Gold Trim, 6 In. 75.00
Cake Plate, Fall Season 850.00
Cake Plate, Floral, Domes, Jewels, Gold Tracery, Red Mark, 11 In. 265.00
Cake Plate, Florals, Iris Mold, 11 In. 195.00
Cake Plate, Jonquils, Cobalt Blue, 10 1/2 In. 295.00
Cake Plate, Medallions, Pastel, Flower Basket, Signed, 10 1/2 In. 235.00
Cake Plate, Mill Scene, Open Handles, Red Mark 500.00
Cake Plate, Quiet Cove, Medallion Mold 395.00
Cake Plate, Snowbirds, Icicle Mold 1000.00
Cake Plate, Summer Season 1400.00
Cake Plate, Winter Season, Satin 950.00
Candy Dish, Green, Pedestal 55.00
Candy Dish, White Roses, Ruffled, Clover Shape 45.00
Celery, 4 Jewels 225.00
Celery, Cobalt Blue, Gold Beaded Rim 295.00
Celery, Dogwood Blossoms 100.00
Celery, Iris Mold, Roses, Pierced Handles, 12 In. 150.00
Celery, Old Man In Mountain 425.00
Centerpiece, Diana The Huntress, 10 1/2 In. 475.00
Centerpiece, Pink Poppies, Blue, Carnation Mold, 11 1/2 In. 400.00
Chocolate Pot, Bird of Paradise 4000.00
Chocolate Pot, Chinese Pheasant 275.00
Chocolate Pot, Hummingbird 4000.00
Chocolate Pot, Iris Mold, Spring Season 2150.00
Chocolate Pot, Pink Roses, Red Mark, 11 In. 175.00
Chocolate Pot, Summer Season, 10 1/2 In. 1600.00
Chocolate Pot, Swan, Raspberry Mold, Berry Finial, 9 In. 495.00
Chocolate Set, Brown Hops Plant, Satin, Cream, Red Mark, 13 Piece 600.00
Chocolate Set, Flowers, 12 In.Scalloped Pot, 9 Piece 575.00
Chocolate Set, Gold Beaded, Double Handle, 9 Piece 575.00
Chocolate Set, Gold Beading At Neck, Signed, 6 Piece 575.00
Chocolate Set, Leaves, Clusters of Flowers, Red Mark, 6 Piece 1150.00
Chocolate Set, Mill Scene, 7 Piece 2000.00
Chocolate Set, Pink Roses, Ivory, Pedestal, Red Mark, 5 Piece 495.00
Chocolate Set, Swan & Pine Trees, 7 Piece 2400.00
Coffeepot, Roses, Green Ground, Pedestal, Signed, 6 1/2 In. 210.00
Cookie Jar, Fleur–De–Lis, Mother-of-Pearl, Handles, Red Mark 300.00
Cookie Jar, Varied Fruit Design, Red Mark, Large 350.00
Cracker Jar, Buttercup Finial, Floral, Gold Outlined, Red Mark 325.00
Cracker Jar, Embossed Leaves, Mauve & Yellow Floral, Gold Pods 250.00
Cracker Jar, Leaves, Cluster of Flowers, Blown–Out Sides, Marked 395.00
Cracker Jar, Melon Eaters 1300.00
Cracker Jar, Pleat Mold, Lavender, Roses, 2 Handles, Red Mark 400.00

Creamer, Applied Flower Spout, Countess Anna Potocka, Gold, Red 170.00
Creamer, Cover, White Floral, Red Mark, 4 In. 120.00
Creamer, Mill Scene 225.00
Cup & Saucer, Castle Scene, Browns 195.00
Cup & Saucer, Floral, Red Mark, Demitasse, 12 Piece 685.00
Cup & Saucer, Fuchsia Roses, Gold Branches, Footed, Demitasse 98.50
Cup & Saucer, Iris, Red Mark 75.00
Cup & Saucer, Pink Satin Swan, Demitasse 135.00
Cup & Saucer, Shadow Flowers, Red Mark 75.00
Cup, Roses Inside & Out, Gold Trim, 4–Footed 40.00
Demitasse Pot, Poppies, Lily-of-The-Valley, Red Mark, 9 1/2 In. 385.00
Dessert Service, Rose & Snowball, 9 Piece 1000.00
Dish, Asters, Daisies, Shadowed Flowers, Pink, Green, Loop Handle 85.00
Dish, Stag & Holly, Footed, Pink, 11 In. 44.00
Dish, Underplate, Leaf Mold, Dogwood, Gold Tracery 250.00
Ewer, Swan Scene 275.00
Fernery, Floral, Satin Finish, Red Mark 185.00
Hair Receiver, Roses, Gold, Signed 125.00
Hatpin Holder, Basket of Roses, Signed, 4 1/2 In. 145.00
Hatpin Holder, Floral, Footed, Red Mark 170.00
Hatpin Holder, Hanging Basket Design, Attached Cover & Tray 275.00
Hatpin Holder, Lavender Floral, 3 Handles, Red Mark 325.00
Mustache Cup, Blue Water Lily, Red Mark 175.00
Mustache Cup, Pheasants, Evergreens, White, Red Mark 265.00
Mustard, Holly & Berry Design, Ladle 175.00
Mustard, Pink & White Roses, Red Mark, 3 1/2 In. 175.00
Nut Set, Peach Roses, Footed, 5 3/4 In. Bowl, 7 Piece 450.00
Pitcher, Lemonade, Pink Shaded Roses, Melon Shape, Red Mark 300.00
Pitcher, Milk, Farmyard Scene, Ducks, Duckling, Swans, Blue 285.00
Plaque, Mill Scene, 11 1/4 In. 495.00
Plaque, Mill Scene, Green Ground, Lavender Rim, 11 1/4 In. 710.00
Plate, Castle Scene, Iris Mold, Pastel Colors, 9 1/2 In. 600.00
Plate, Dice Player, Jeweled 950.00
Plate, Flowers, Jewels, Red Star, Green Wreath, 9 In. 300.00
Plate, Flowers, Raised Gold, Icicle Mold, Red Mark, 11 In. 355.00
Plate, Girl, Apple Basket, Keyhole Mold, 8 In. 1600.00
Plate, House By Lake, Red Mark 1250.00
Plate, Masted Schooner, Gold Trim, Red Mark, 11 In. 350.00
Plate, Melon Boy, Keyhole Mold, Red Mark, 6 In. .... 450.00 To 550.00
Plate, Melon Eater, Keyhole Mold, 6 In. 450.00
Plate, Pink Flowers, Blue Ground, 2 Handles, 11 In. 225.00
Plate, Pink Roses, Pearlized, Signed, 8 In. 85.00
Plate, Scenic Portrait, Pan, Putti, St.Killian, 10 In. 175.00
Plate, Snowbirds, Icicle Mold, 10 1/4 In. 650.00
Plate, Spring Portrait, Gold Trim 750.00
Plate, Stippled Flower, Castle, Hanging Tabs, 6 In. 135.00
Plate, Tiger, 8 1/2 In. 2000.00
Plate, Winter Season, Keyhole Mold 1100.00
Pot, Demitasse, Glossy White, Gold Garlands, Roses, Red Mark 250.00
Powder Jar, Swans, Gold, Pedestal, Scenic Cover, Red Mark, 5 In. 400.00
Relish, Gold Tracery, Turquoise, Yellow Ground, Iris Mold, 12 In. 245.00
Relish, Peacock, Icicle Mold, Red Mark 225.00
Relish, Roses, Red Mark, 10 In. 98.00
Relish, Swan, Evergreen 135.00
Relish, Woman, Watering Flowers 650.00
Shaving Mug, Hand Painted Roses, Blown–Out Iris Mold 195.00
Shaving Mug, Melon Eaters, Footed 775.00
Shaving Mug, Pheasant, Evergreen Trees, White, Red Mark 395.00
Shaving Mug, Pink Florals, Green 295.00
Shaving Mug, Red Roses, Blown–Out Iris Mold, Blue Ground 195.00
Shaving Mug, Red Roses, Carnation Mold, Red Mark 175.00
Sugar & Creamer, Dogwood, Red Mark 145.00
Sugar & Creamer, Fall Portrait, Violet Ground 950.00
Sugar & Creamer, Gold Design 395.00

Sugar & Creamer, Lilac, Red Mark 145.00
Sugar & Creamer, Purple & Gray Flowers, Ivory Ground, Gold Trim 95.00
Sugar, Cover, Florals, Footed, Red Mark 50.00
Sugar, Pink Roses, Shaded Lavender, Blue Ground 97.50
Syrup, Pink Roses, White Ground, Gold Trim 75.00
Tankard, Fall Season, 14 In. 2200.00
Tankard, Fruit Design, 13 In. 1000.00
Tankard, Hanging Basket of Flowers, Roses, Marked, 9 1/2 In. 560.00
Tankard, Summer Season, Carnation Mold, 13 In. 5750.00
Tea Set, Child's, Bluebirds, Castle & Cottage Scenes 1500.00
Teapot, Brown Cottage Scene, Red Mark 450.00
Teapot, Cabbage Roses, Red Mark 160.00
Teapot, Carnations, Red Mark 60.00
Teapot, Gold Roses, Fleur–De–Lis Mold, Green 295.00
Teapot, Hidden Images 395.00
Toothpick, Pink & Red Roses, Green Leaves, Gold Trim 165.00
Tray, Blue Flowers, Lily Mold, 11 3/4 In. 215.00
Tray, Bun, 4 Portraits, Cobalt Blue, Medallion Mold, 14 X 6 In. 875.00
Tray, Bun, Fall Season 8000.00
Tray, Carnation Mold, Open Handles, Red Mark, 11 X 7 1/2 In. 265.00
Tray, Dresser, Spring Season, 12 In. 1500.00
Tray, Swan, Swag & Tassel Mold, 11 X 7 In. 475.00
Vase, Blue Flowers, Gold Trim, Red Mark, 4 7/8 In. 300.00
Vase, Castle Scene, Green Tints, 8 1/4 In. 635.00
Vase, Courting Scene, 10 In. 2000.00
Vase, Dice Players, 9 In. 695.00
Vase, Fall Season, 3 Handles, 7 In. 4000.00
Vase, Fall Season, Portrait, Red Mark, 10 In. 2900.00
Vase, Golden Pheasant, Marked, 4 In. 300.00
Vase, Lebrun, Triple Handles, Greek Key Design, 9 In. 625.00
Vase, Lion, 11 In. 1650.00
Vase, Lion, Handle, 14 1/2 In. 8000.00
Vase, Madame Henriette As Flora, Handles, 7 In. 175.00
Vase, Ostrich, 9 In. 1200.00
Vase, Red Chinese Pheasant, 8 In. 350.00
Vase, Turkey, Chicken, Swallows, Barnyard Scene, 11 1/2 In. 950.00
Vase, Turkeys, Ducks, Swallows & Pheasant, 2 Handles, 14 In. 2800.00

RS Suhl was a mark used by the Erdmann Schlegelmilch factory in Suhl, Germany, from c.1900 to the mid–1920s. The factory worked from 1861 to 1925. The Schlegelmilch family made porcelains in many places. See also ES Germany, RS Germany, RS Poland, RS Prussia, and RS Tillowitz.

RS SUHL, Bowl, Fall Hunt Scene, Men On Horseback, Green, Marked, 8 1/2 In. 295.00
Coffee Set, Scenes On Each Piece, Marked Kauffmann, 9 Piece 1675.00
Cup & Saucer, Scenes, Demitasse 60.00
Pin Tray, Bird Mark 40.00
Salt & Pepper, Floral 30.00
Vase, Farm Women Feeding Chickens, Winding Flax, 6 1/2 In. 495.00
Vase, Melon Eaters, 9 In. 810.00
Vase, Night Watch, Handles, 6 In. 150.00

The RS Tillowitz mark was used by the Reinhold Schlegelmilch factory at Tillowitz, near Silesia, from about 1920 to the mid–1930s. Table services and ornamental pieces were made. See also ES Germany, RS Germany, RS Poland, RS Prussia, RS Silesia, and RS Suhl.

RS TILLOWITZ, Bowl, Game Birds, Flowers, 9 1/4 In. 245.00

Rubena Verde is a Victorian glassware that was shaded from red to green. It was first made by Hobbs, Brockunier and Company of Wheeling, West Virginia, about 1890.

RUBENA VERDE, Epergne, 1–Light, Applied Rigaree, 15 In. 285.00
  Finger Bowl, Inverted Thumbprint 90.00
  Pitcher, Inverted Thumbprint 300.00
  Tumbler, Hobnail 150.00
  Vase, Colonial Man, Reverse Woman, Gold Handles, 8 In. 385.00
  Vase, Jack–In–The–Pulpit, Spirals Around Stem, 13 3/4 In. 265.00

Rubena is a glassware that shades from red to clear. It was first made by George Duncan and Sons of Pittsburgh, Pennsylvania, about 1885. This coloring was used on many types of glassware. The pressed glass patterns of Royal Ivy and Royal Oak are listed under Pressed Glass.

RUBENA, Biscuit Jar, Diamond Pattern, Silver Plate, 7 1/4 In. 360.00
  Castor, Pickle, Diamond, Floral Design, 4 1/2 In. 165.00
  Castor, Pickle, Paneled Sprig, Gilded Top, Ribbed, 4 1/4 In. 130.00
  Cruet, Medallion Sprig 245.00
  Sugar Shaker, Cut Panels, Silver Plated Screw, 5 1/2 In. 65.00
  Toothpick, Pedestal, Ruffled Rim, Gold & Orange Flowers, 3 In. 350.00
  Tumbler, Hobnail, Verde 115.00
  Vase, Threaded, 4 Lobed, Straight Sides, Crystal Feet, 10 1/2 In., Pr. 450.00
  Vase, Trumpet, Gold Colored Enameling, 10 In. 110.00

Ruby glass is the dark red color of the precious gemstone known as a ruby. It was a popular Victorian color that never went completely out of style. The glass was shaped by many different processes to make many different types of ruby glass. There was a revival of interest in the 1940s when modern shaped ruby table glassware became fashionable. Sometimes the red color is added to clear glass by a process called flashing or staining. Flashed glass is clear glass dipped in a colored glass, then pressed or cut. Stained glass has color painted on a clear glass. Then it is refired so the stain fuses with the glass. Pieces of glass colored in this way are indicated by the word "stained" in the description.

RUBY GLASS, see also Cranberry Glass; Pressed Glass; Souvenir
RUBY GLASS, Celery Vase, Heavy Gothic, Clear 65.00
  Decanter Set, Enameled, Gilded, Stopper, 3 1/2 In. Wines, 7 Piece 75.00
  Decanter, Bohemian Deer & Castle 75.00
  Decanter, Bulging Loops, 8 In. 48.00
  Flower Band, Salt & Pepper 85.00
  Flower Holder, Scalloped, Circular 12.00
  Punch Set, Child's, Westmoreland, 7 Piece 65.00
  Sugar, Insect Form, Silver Plated Mounts, 6 In. 88.00
  Sugar, Prescut Pattern, Scalloped, Large 15.00
  Syrup, Venecia, Enameled Design 575.00
  Table Set, Co–Op's Royal, Clear 350.00
  Tumbler, Anchor Hocking, Paper Label, 6 Piece 32.00
  Vase, Flowers Cut To Clear, Flashed, 10 1/2 In. 39.00

Rudolstadt was a faience factory in the Thuringia region of Germany from 1720 to about 1791. In 1854, Ernst Bohne began working in the area. From about 1887 to 1918, the New York and Rudolstadt Pottery made decorated porcelain marked with the RW and crown familiar to collectors. This porcelain was imported by Lewis Straus and Sons of New York, which later became Nathan Straus and Sons. The word "Royal" was included in their import mark. Collectors often call it "Royal Rudolstadt." Late nineteenth- and early twentieth–century pieces are most commonly found today.

RUDOLSTADT, see also Kewpie
RUDOLSTADT, Brooch, Queen Louise, Porcelain 100.00

Rug, Chinese, Center Dragons, C.1910,
7 Ft.10 In. X 7 Ft.1 In.

Rug, Kazak, Prayer, Hexagonal Design, Navy,
4 Ft. X 3 Ft.8 In.

Rug, Tekke, Geometric Design, Reds,
7 X 4 Ft.

Hanging textiles should be given a rest from time to time. The weight of the hanging causes strain on the threads. If the textile is taken down and stored for a few months the threads regain some strength.

Never store a rug in a plastic bag. The fibers need to breathe. Wrap the rug in a clean sheet. Don't store rugs in a hot attic.

Bust, Indian Chief	175.00
Creamer, 4 Kewpies, 3 3/4 In.	175.00
Creamer, Goat	95.00
Ewer, Floral Design, Reticulated, Bulbous, 15 In.	385.00
Figurine, Begger Girl, Tambourine, C.1905, 5 1/2 In.	95.00 To 150.00
Figurine, Girl, Holding Fish, White Dress, 14 In.	85.00
Group, Girl, Boy, On Bench, Castle, Cream, Beige, Gold, 7 In.	195.00
Lamp, Ewer Shape, Pebbly Ground, Floral, 11 In.	310.00
Lamp, Lady Playing Lyre, 14 In.	325.00
Lamp, Oil, Cherubs In Relief, Chimney, 20 In.	250.00
Pitcher, Floral Design, Cream, 5 1/2 In.	50.00
Pitcher, Red Flower, Gold Highlighted Leaf, Signed RW, 7 1/2 In.	30.00
Plate, George Washington Portrait, Gold Rim, 8 1/2 In.	45.00
Plate, Hand Painted Roses, 6 In.	180.00
Plate, Poppy, 8 1/2 In.	55.00
Sugar & Creamer, Floral, Signed Hahn	65.00
Sugar & Creamer, Pale Pink Roses	80.00
Sugar, Creamer & Teapot, Orange Luster, 3 Piece	45.50
Tea Set, Happifats, 8 Piece	325.00
Teapot, Hanging Pink Roses, Gold Handle, Marked	115.00
Tray, New York's Astor Hotel, 5 In.	65.00
Urn, White & Gold Flowers, Gold Outlining, Blue, 13 In., Pair	575.00
Vase, Enameled Flowers, Cream Ground, Ornate Handles, 12 X 6 In.	60.00
Vase, Enameled Flowers, Raised Gold Ground, 6 1/2 In.	175.00
Vase, Florals, Double Gold Handles, 16 In.	125.00
Vase, Florals, Drilled For Lamp, 16 In.	95.00

Rugs have been used in the American home since the seventeenth century. The Oriental rug of that time was often used on a table, not on the floor. Rag rugs, hooked rugs, and braided rugs were made by housewives from scraps of material.

RUG, Afghan Bokhara, 3 Ft.8 In. X 5 Ft.10 In.	375.00
Afghan, Concentric Hexagonal Medallion, 7 Ft. X 4 Ft.3 In.	275.00
Afshar, 2 Diamond Medallions, Blue Field, 5 Ft. X 4 Ft.2 In.	1870.00
American, Art Deco, Brown Swirls & Sprinkles, C.1930, 47 X 59 In.	385.00
American, Art Deco, Stylized Figures, Wool, C.1930, 5 Ft.4 In. X 4 Ft.	880.00
American, Geometric Design, Wool, C.1930, 13 Ft. X 8 Ft.2 In.	385.00
Amish, Hall Runner, Woven, 20 X 62 In.	135.00
Anatolian, Memling Gul Octagons, 6 Ft.6 In. X 5 Ft.6 In.	3960.00
Anatolian, Tulip Cross Panel, Mihrab Rests, 5 Ft.2 In. X 3 Ft.8 In.	110.00
Aubusson, Floral Medallion, Wine Field, 9 Ft.7 In. X 8 Ft.3 In.	9075.00
Bahktiari, Diamond Lattice Overall, 12 Ft.8 In. X 4 Ft.	445.00
Bahktiari, Floral Vases & Birds, 1900–01, 22 X 14 Ft.	4675.00
Bakshaish, Overall Herati Design, C.1920, 8 Ft.6 In. X 3 Ft.	770.00
Baluch, Aubergine Center Field, Flower Heads, 8 Ft.4 In. X 3 Ft.5 In.	445.00
Baluch, Mina Khani Floral Lattice, 6 Ft.5 In. X 4 Ft.5 In.	495.00
Baluch, Rust Field, Hooked Design, 5 Ft.11 In. X 3 Ft.6 In.	137.50
Bergama, Geometric, Tomato Red Ground, 1880s, 7 Ft.2 In. X 6 Ft.4 In.	2600.00
Bergama, Madder Field, 4 Small Medallions, 5 Ft. X 5 Ft.7 In.	4400.00
Beshir Chuval, Hexagon Columns, Zigzag Stripes, 5 Ft. X 3 Ft.2 In.	1100.00
Bidjar, Hexagonal Navy Medallion, Red, 12 Ft.3 In. X 9 Ft.6 In.	1760.00
Bidjar, Overall Flowering Shrubs, 11 Ft.2 In. X 9 Ft.10 In.	9350.00
Bidjar, Scalloped Diamond Medallion, Pendants, 9 Ft.6 In. X 4 Ft.7 In.	1045.00
Bokhara, 2 Ft.9 In. X 4 Ft.10 In.	300.00
Bokhara, 2 Rows Navy & Orange Guls, Burgundy, 3 Ft.5 In. X 2 Ft.1 In.	55.00
Bokhara, Cream & Black Guls In Squares, Red, 6 Ft.5 In. X 3 Ft.9 In.	200.00
Braided, Blue & Brown, 42 X 56 In.	125.00
Braided, Blue, Gray & Red, 32 X 48 In.	65.00
Caucasian, Diagonally Striped Field, C.1920, 7 Ft. X 3 Ft.3 In.	2100.00
Caucasian, Lesghi Stars In Compartment Field, 6 Ft.5 In. X 3 Ft.8 In.	2425.00
Caucasian, Oriental, Woven, Camel Hair, 4 Ft.6 In. X 5 Ft.10 In.	300.00
Caucasian, Prayer, Oriental, 4 Ft. X 4 Ft.9 In.	500.00
Chichi, 4 Ft.3 In. X 3 Ft.2 In.	3300.00
Chinese, Allover Floral & Butterfly, Magenta, 11 Ft.8 In. X 8 Ft.8 In.	1350.00

Chinese, Art Deco, Flower Urn, Brown–Purple, 9 Ft.7 In. X 7 Ft.11 In. 725.00
Chinese, Art Deco, Padgoda Pavillion, Navy, 17 Ft.2 In. X 10 Ft.3 In. 165.00
Chinese, Birds, Vines, C.1910, 7 Ft.10 In. X 4 Ft.1 In. 1300.00
Chinese, Center Dragons, C.1910, 7 Ft.10 In. X 7 Ft.1 In. ....*Illus* 1700.00
Chinese, Center Medallion, Floral Border, 9 X 12 Ft. 700.00
Chinese, Clover–Form Medallion, Butterflies, 11 Ft.4 In. X 8 Ft.9 In. 1750.00
Chinese, Floral Design, Royal Blue Ground, 9 X 12 Ft. 725.00
Chinese, Foo Dogs, Dragons, Bats, Blue Ground, 12 Ft. X 16 Ft.3 In. 300.00
Chinese, Gold, Center, Florals, Butterflies, 7 Ft.9 In. X 5 Ft.6 In. 550.00
Chinese, Lotus Blossom, Flanked By Vases, 9 Ft.1 In. X 6 Ft.4 In. 4950.00
Chinese, Oval Medallion & Flowers, Blue Ground, 10 X 14 In. 885.00
Chinese, Runner, Rice Design, C.1900, 16 Ft.7 In. X 2 Ft. 4950.00
Daghestan, Stylized Blossoming Plants, 4 Ft.5 In. X 3 Ft.6 In. 1325.00
Drugget, India, Nile Pattern, C.1910, 138 Ft. X 112 In. 1300.00
Ersari, 3 Columns of Chuval Guls, Hooked Diamonds, 4 Ft.9 In. X 4 Ft. 665.00
Ersari, Stylized Blossoms, Prayer Arch, 5 Ft.7 In. X 3 Ft.3 In. 2970.00
Garden, Oriental, Wool, Urns, Birds, Floral, Navy, 18 Ft.9 In. X 5 Ft. 600.00
Geometric Design, Birds, 3 Ft.6 In. X 4 Ft.10 In. 3700.00
Hamadan, Allover Boteh Field, 10 Ft. X 4 Ft.11 In. 2425.00
Hamadan, Herati Designs, Blue Field, 6 Ft.8 In. X 4 Ft. 825.00
Hamadan, Medallion & Anchor Design, 6 Ft.2 In. X 4 Ft. 665.00
Hamadan, Stylized Florals, Flower Head Border, 6 Ft.6 In. X 4 Ft.2 In. 275.00
Hereke, Silk, Blue Floral Border, 2 Ft.6 In. X 4 Ft.6 In. 2100.00
Heriz, Center Medallion Inset With Rosettes, 4 Ft.1 In. X 3 Ft.8 In. 2200.00
Heriz, Center Medallion, Palmette Pendants, 4 Ft.3 In. X 3 Ft. 5 In. 995.00
Heriz, Foliate Design, Medium Red Ground, 1930, 9 Ft.5 In. X 6 Ft.8 In. 3250.00
Heriz, Gabled Medallion, Rose Field, 11 Ft.8 In. X 8 Ft. 2850.00
Heriz, Gabled Square Medallion, Red Field, 12 Ft.6 In. X 9 Ft. 1325.00
Heriz, Kaleidoscopic Diamond Medallion, 8 Ft.2 In. X 8 Ft. 2250.00
Heriz, Stepped Medallion, Rust Field, 10 Ft.4 In. X 8 Ft. 2200.00
Hooked, American Shield Center, Drum Shape, 20 X 31 In. 50.00
Hooked, Barn Scene, House, Farm, Horse, White, Wine Border, 17 X 33 In. 85.00
Hooked, Basket of Flowers Center, 20 X 33 In. 450.00
Hooked, Central Floral Medallion, Foliate Border, 71 1/2 X 54 In. 225.00
Hooked, Colorful Stripes, Alternating Squares, 27 X 36 In. 110.00
Hooked, Compass Star, Round, 39 In. 400.00
Hooked, Family & Conestoga Wagon, Pioneer Family, 12 1/2 X 30 1/2 In. 65.00
Hooked, Farm Buildings, Horses In Pasture, 27 X 42 1/2 In. 687.50
Hooked, Floral Center, Black On Variegated Ground, 22 X 51 In. 600.00
Hooked, Floral Design, Bluish Gray Ground, 33 X 58 In. 275.00
Hooked, Floral Design, Red, Green, Pale Blue Border, 20 X 32 In. 125.00
Hooked, Floral, Beige Ground, 31 X 54 1/2 In. 200.00
Hooked, Floral, Black Border, 2 X 4 Ft. 68.00
Hooked, Floral, Crocheted String Edge, Yarn, Rag, 1894, 27 1/2 X 40 In. 150.00
Hooked, Floral, Geometric Squares, Black, Purple, Blue, 7 Ft. X 9 Ft.5 In 450.00
Hooked, Floral, Gray Ground, 24 X 38 In. 45.00
Hooked, Floral, Pink Ground, Black Border, 18 1/2 X 30 1/2 In. 50.00
Hooked, Floral, Tulips, Border, Dated 1905 .... 345.00
Hooked, Floral, With Roses & Chains, Braided Border, 21 1/2 X 41 In. 25.00
Hooked, Flowering Tree, Beige Ground, Rag, 36 X 59 In. 100.00
Hooked, Flowers, Black Cat, Yarn, 19 X 34 In. 125.00
Hooked, Foliage Design, Black Border, 91 X 118 In. 325.00
Hooked, Folk Art Landscape With Wishing Well, Yarn, 21 1/2 X 35 In. 40.00
Hooked, Folk Art Scene, Black Horse, Greenish Gray Ground, 17 X 34 In. 950.00
Hooked, Geometric Star Design, 26 X 103 In. 500.00
Hooked, Gray Cat, Green Stripe Ground, Black, Maroon, 24 X 47 In. 275.00
Hooked, Hand Sewn Yarn Shag, Random Pattern, Ticking Back, 25 X 43 In. 85.00
Hooked, Horse & Buggy, Black, White, 2 Shades of Green, Yarn, 23 X 36 In. 100.00
Hooked, Horse & Buggy, Dog & Flying Goose, In Oval, 36 X 66 In. 500.00
Hooked, House, Trees, 29 X 43 In. 55.00
Hooked, Hunt Scene, Pink–Coated Rider, 7 Ft.2 In. X 3 Ft.10 In. 995.00
Hooked, Mat, Eagle, Yellow On Blue Ground, Rag, 14 1/2 In. 95.00
Hooked, Medallions, Black Grid, 31 X 38 In. 175.00
Hooked, Oriental Pattern, 36 X 59 In. 300.00

Hooked, Oval Medallion, Chain–Like Border, Wool, 77 X 37 1/2 In.	175.00
Hooked, Penny Design, Multicolors, Gray Ground, 27 X 72 In.	1175.00
Hooked, Polka Dots, Light Ground, 23 X 35 In.	175.00
Hooked, Roses, Red Shades, Green Stripe Ground, 14 X 24 In.	55.00
Hooked, Runner, Floral Design, Multicolor Border, 2 Ft.3 In. X 25 Ft.	365.00
Hooked, Stripes, Alternating Blocks, Black, 32 X 68 In.	175.00
Hooked, Stripes, Beige, Yellow Green Border, 26 X 40 In.	55.00
Hooked, Stripes, Rag, Pennsylvania, 10 Ft. X 14 Ft.3 In.	220.00
Hooked, Stripes, Vivid Solid Colors, 33 X 72 In.	300.00
Hooked, Stripes, White, Brown, Red, Blue, 31 X 39 In.	50.00
Hooked, Stylized Florals, 24 X 79 In.	75.00
Hooked, Stylized Horse, Beige Ground, 18 X 30 In.	150.00
Hooked, Stylized House Design, 34 1/2 X 27 1/2 In.	355.00
Hooked, Stylized Maple Leaves, Variegated Ground, 105 X 178 In.	825.00
Hooked, Stylized Rooster, Salmon Ground, 32 X 32 In.	300.00
Hooked, Stylized Tulip Design, Stripes, 29 X 49 1/2 In.	175.00
Hooked, Sun Ray, Maroon Border, Ivory Center, Floral, 1880, Hearth Size	115.00
Hooked, Swans, Floral Border, 25 1/2 X 39 In.	25.00
Hooked, Tree, Animals, Mustard Ground, New York, 1900, 32 X 65 In.	3250.00
Hooked, Woven, Blue, Gold Homespun, Rag, 2 Ft.9 In. X 13 Ft.	300.00
Hooked, Woven, Browns, Blues, Beige, Rag, 22 X 21 In.	55.00
Hooked, Woven, Stripes, Beige, Blue, Rag, 2 Ft.10 In. X 11 Ft.6 In.	45.00
Hungarian, Savonnerie Style, Center Medallion, Floral Border, 9 X 8 Ft.	465.00
India, Overlapping Squares, C.1915, 9 Ft.3 In. X 8 Ft.6 In.	495.00
Indian Oriental, Savonnerie Style, Oval Medallion Center, 9 X 12 Ft.	385.00
Indian, Chenille, 48 X 66 In.	670.00
Iranian, Runner, Oriental, 2 Ft.9 In. X 7 Ft.	225.00
Isfahan, 16 Ft.10 In. X 12 X 1 In.	3850.00
Isfahan, 9 Ft.6 In. X 13 Ft.6 In.	1700.00
Isfahan, Allover Palmette, Navy, Borders, 6 Ft.7 In. X 9 Ft.8 In.	2200.00
Isfahan, Multilobed Medallion Center, 6 Ft.2 In. X 4 Ft.	825.00
Isfahan, Pea Green Floral, Medallion, Navy, 11 Ft.5 In. X 7 Ft.11 In.	2850.00
Karabagh, Floral Medallion, Bouquets, 7 Ft.5 In. X 4 Ft.11 In.	3850.00
Karabagh, Sunburst Medallions, Stars, Rose Field, 9 Ft.3 In. X 4 Ft.	550.00
Karagashli, Dated 1329, 7 Ft.3 In. X 4 Ft.2 In.	9350.00
Kashan, Lobed Circular Medallion, 18 Ft.6 In. X 10 Ft.4 In.	6700.00
Kazak, 3 Hooked Medallions, Geometric Border, 3 Ft.5 In. X 6 Ft.5 In.	275.00
Kazak, 4 Hooked Diamonds, Animal Designs, 3 Ft.1 In. X 6 Ft.2 In.	1210.00
Kazak, Angular Medallion, 6 Ft.10 In. X 4 Ft.11 In.	3850.00
Kazak, Cloud Band, C.1900, 8 Ft.3 In. X 5 Ft.	5500.00
Kazak, Divided Center Field, Floral Border, 7 Ft.8 In. X 4 Ft.3 In.	1435.00
Kazak, Hexagonal Medallions, Red Field, 4 Ft.3 In. X 3 Ft.8 In.	1550.00
Kazak, Linked Medallions, Stylized Birds, 6 Ft.8 In. X 4 Ft.7 In.	610.00
Kazak, Octagonal Memling Guls, Red Field, 6 Ft.4 In. X 4 Ft.4 In.	995.00
Kazak, Prayer, 5 Ft.6 In. X 4 Ft.	8850.00
Kazak, Prayer, Hexagonal Design, Navy, 4 Ft. X 3 Ft.8 In.	1400.00
Kazak, Square Medallion, Geometric Designs, 4 Ft.9 In. X 3 Ft.2 In.	7150.00
Kazak, Tile Design, Latch–Hooked Diamonds, 6 Ft.3 In. X 3 Ft.11 In.	3300.00
Kazak, Turtleback Medallion, Green, Red, Blue, 4 X 7 Ft.	3300.00
Kerman, Center Lobed Medallion, Red Field, 11 Ft.10 In. X 8 Ft.10 In.	2500.00
Kerman, Scalloped Medallion, Gold Border, 17 Ft.6 In. X 11 Ft.8 In.	775.00
Khorasson, Tree of Life, Navy, Borders, 16 Ft.10 In. X 11 Ft.5 In.	1870.00
Kirman, Floral Central Medallion, Rose Red Field, 9 X 12 Ft.	6500.00
Kirman, Floral Design, Blue & Red On Ivory, 6 Ft.10 In. X 2 Ft.7 In.	715.00
Kirman, Overall Birds, Trees, Foliage, C.1900, 11 Ft.4 In. X 17 Ft.4 In.	5285.00
Kis Ghiordes, Diamond & Medallion Field, 6 Ft. X 4 Ft.7 In.	3850.00
Knotted, Geometric Design, Stylized Waves, Bruhns, 121 X 72 1/2 In.	6100.00
Konagkend, Allover Ivy Trellis, 4 Ft.4 In X 3 Ft.	7800.00
Kuba, Cornflower Blue Field, Flowering Vines, 8 Ft.4 In. X 3 Ft.5 In.	2250.00
Kuba, Polychrome Flower Heads, 4 Ft.5 In. X 3 Ft.5 In.	6050.00
Kuba, Seichour Design, Blue Field, 8 Ft. X 3 Ft.2 In.	1100.00
Kuba, Shield Medallions, Blue Field, 5 Ft.2 In X 10 Ft.7 In.	1545.00
Kuba, Starflowers & Gul, 4 Ft.4 In. X 4 Ft.1 In.	9995.00
Kurdish Afshan Design, Pumpkin Field, 9 Ft.10 In. X 4 Ft.	2300.00

Kurdish, Floral Field, Geometric Border, 13 Ft.9 In. X 3 Ft.2 In. 550.00
Kurdish, Geometric Grid, Floral Borders, 9 X 3 Ft. 600.00
Kurdish, Stars Inside Octagonal Lozenges, 7 Ft.11 In. X 3 Ft.6 In. 615.00
Luri, Center Jagged Keyhole, Leaf & Bird Poles, 7 Ft. X 4 Ft.5 In. 465.00
Luri, Persia, 1900, 4 Ft.8 In. X 6 Ft.10 In. 5500.00
Mahal, Floral On Wine Red, 2 Ft.7 In. X 5 Ft. 100.00
Mahal, Tree, Urn & Floral Design, Rose, 11 Ft.9 In.X 8 Ft.9 In. 300.00
Malayer, Flowering Shrubs, 6 Ft.7 In. X 4 Ft.3 In. 3800.00
Malayer, Overall Boteh Design, Navy, Borders, 5 Ft.10 In. X 4 Ft.4 In. 275.00
Mickey Mouse, 20 Characters, 1950s, 6 X 8 Ft. 2750.00
Moud, Blue Circular Medallion, Ivory, Rosettes, 7 Ft.1 In. X 6 Ft.7 In. 1650.00
Needlepoint, Portuguese, 8 Ft.10 In. X 5 Ft.9 In. 2475.00
Ninghsia, Peony Medallion, 6 Ft.6 In. X 4 Ft.7 In. 4950.00
Oushak, 14 Ft.8 In. X 12 Ft.10 In. 5600.00
Penny, Wool Medallions, Maroon Circles, Ivory Ground, 51 1/2 X 58 In. 400.00
Perepedil, Stylized Birds Around Rosettes, 5 Ft.6 In. X 4 Ft. 2420.00
Persian, Hooked Floral Medallion, Black Border, 11 Ft. X 6 Ft.8 In. 885.00
Princess Bokhara, 6 Ft.4 In. X 9 Ft.12 In. 800.00
Qashqa'l, 11 Ft.3 In. X 5 Ft.2 In. 7150.00
Qashqa'l, Geometric Design, 7 Ft.2 In. X 6 Ft.4 In. 6650.00
Qum, Silk, Geometric Medallion, Sand Field, 3 Ft.6 In. X 2 Ft.5 In. 3500.00
Qum, Wool & Silk, 6 Ft.5 In. X 4 Ft.3 In. 1430.00
Sarouk, Detached Floral Sprays, 6 Ft.7 In. X 4 Ft.3 In. 825.00
Sarouk, Floral Sprays, Palmettes, Blue Field, 10 Ft.6 In. X 7 Ft. 3600.00
Sarouk, Oval Floral Medallion, Floral Sprays, 9 Ft.9 In. X 7 Ft.9 In. 1765.00
Savonnerie, Center Floral Medallion, Ribbon–Tied Branches, 18 X 14 Ft. 7000.00
Senneh, Diamond–Shaped Medallion, 6 Ft.8 In. X 4 Ft.4 In. 3500.00
Senneh, Rosettes & Leaves, Vine Border, 6 Ft.3 In. X 4 Ft.3 In. 1050.00
Senneh, Stylized Boteh, 5 Ft.6 In. X 4 Ft.5 In. 2000.00
Serapi, 13 Ft.5 In. X 10 Ft.6 In. 1550.00
Serebend, Oriental, 5 Ft.4 In. X 10 Ft.4 In. 1050.00
Seychour, Macrame Fringe, 6 Ft.3 In. X 3 Ft.5 In. 8800.00
Shiraz, Prayer, 3 Ft.3 In. X 4 Ft.6 In. 225.00
Shirvan, 3 Lesghi Stars, Ivory Star Border, 4 Ft.4 In. X 3 Ft.2 In. 885.00
Shirvan, 3 Lesghi Stars, Scattered Florals, 4 Ft.5 In. X 3 Ft.5 In. 2535.00
Shirvan, 3 Lesghi Stars, Small Florals, 4 Ft.2 In. X 3 Ft.8 In. 2475.00
Shirvan, 5 Lesghi Stars, Kufic Border, 5 Ft.11 In. X 4 Ft. 2425.00
Shirvan, Browns, C.1875, 4 Ft.2 In. X 3 Ft.4 In. 7750.00
Shirvan, Columns of Geometric Design, 19th Century, 4 Ft.3 In. X 3 Ft. 330.00
Shirvan, Diagonal Rows of Colored Snowflakes, 6 Ft. X 3 Ft.9 In. 550.00
Shirvan, Hexagonal Stepped Lozenge, 6 Ft.8 In. X 3 Ft.9 In. 4125.00
Shirvan, Polychrome Stepped Diamonds, 6 Ft.2 In. X 3 Ft.6 In. 7750.00
Shirvan, Stepped Diamond Medallions, 9 Ft.10 In. X 5 Ft.10 In. 4500.00
Soumak, 4 Medallions, Brick Red Field, 11 Ft.4 In. X 9 Ft.9 In. 6100.00
Soumak, Bidjov–Style Palmettes, Blue Field, 10 Ft.8 In. X 7 Ft. 7150.00
Tabriz, Anatolian Type, 1900s, 9 X 12 Ft. 4600.00
Tabriz, Blossom & Leaf Medallions, 5 Ft.4 In. X 4 Ft. 2860.00
Tabriz, C.1940, 9 Ft.10 In. X 7 Ft.9 In. 880.00
Tabriz, Floral Design, Oriental, Black Ground, 4 Ft.2 In. X 6 Ft.6 In. 2500.00
Tabriz, Floral Medallion, Blue Field, 12 Ft.5 In. X 9 Ft. 1650.00
Tabriz, Foliate Medallion, Red Field, 17 Ft.4 In. X 12 Ft.3 In. 8000.00
Tabriz, Ivory Reserves, Center Flowers, Red, 11 Ft.6 In. X 2 Ft.3 In. 88.00
Tabriz, Medallion Center, Cream Field, 11 Ft.8 In. X 8 Ft.3 In. 1200.00
Tabriz, Overall Floral, Blue Field, 8 Ft. X 9 Ft.7 In. 2650.00
Tabriz, Synthetic Dye, 10 1/2 X 21 Ft. 5700.00
Talish, Mid–19th Century, 8 Ft.3 In. X 3 Ft.6 In. 9000.00
Tekke, 3 Columns of Blue, Apricot & Ivory, 5 Ft.3 In. X 3 Ft.6 In. 775.00
Tekke, 5 Columns of Guls, 9 Ft.10 In. X 7 Ft.6 In. 2250.00
Tekke, 5 Columns of Guls, Red Field, 8 Ft.6 In. X 6 Ft.8 In. 2755.00
Tekke, Geometric Design, Reds, 7 X 4 Ft. ....*Illus* 775.00
Tekke, Rows of Tekke Guls, Red Field, 7 Ft.3 In. X 6 Ft.7 In. 5500.00
Tekke, Salar–Style Guls, C.1880, 4 Ft.3 In. X 2 Ft.6 In. 1000.00
Tibetan, Stylized Tiger Stripes, C.1930, 5 Ft.3 In. X 2 Ft.9 In. 4500.00

Turkish, Prayer, Silk, C.1850, 4 Ft.9 In. X 7 Ft. ....*Illus*   600.00
Turkish, Tribal, Woven With Goat Hair, 7 Ft.5 In. X 3 Ft.10 In. 260.00
Uzbek, Continuous Diamond Pattern, 4 Ft.10 In. X 2 Ft.9 In. 2100.00
Uzbek, Memling Guls, Brick Red Field, 6 Ft.10 In. X 5 Ft.10 In. 665.00
Yarn, Pastel Floral, Ivory Ground, 8 Ft.6 In. X 11 Ft.8 In. 325.00
Yomud, Latch Hooked Design, C.1875, 5 Ft.3 In. X 5 Ft. 3100.00

Rumrill Pottery was designed by George Rumrill of Little Rock, Arkansas. From 1930 to 1933, it was produced by the Red Wing Pottery of Red Wing, Minnesota. In 1938, production was transferred to the Shawnee Pottery in Zanesville, Ohio. Production ceased in the 1940s.

RUMRILL, Pitcher, Cream, 2 Qt. 20.00
Pitcher, Tilt, Blue 20.00
Pitcher, Tilt, Ice Lip, Blue 40.00
Pitcher, Tilt, Ice Lip, Orange 40.00
Planter, Acorn 18.00
Vase, Bone & Aqua, 8 1/2 In. 20.00
Vase, Double Cornucopia, Aqua 40.00
Vase, Handles, Pink, 9 In. 25.00
Vase, Ivory 15.00
Vase, Off-White, 9 In. 12.00
Vase, Off-White, Swan Handles, 5 X 7 In. 15.00
Vase, White, Handles, Urn Shape, 7 3/4 In. 30.00

Russel Wright designed dinnerwares in modern shapes for four companies. Iroquois China Company, Harker China Company, Steubenville Pottery, and Justin Therod and Sons made dishes marked "Russel Wright." The Steubenville wares, first made in 1938, are the most common today. This section lists the dinnerwares and other pieces by Wright. He was a designer of domestic and industrial wares, including furniture, aluminum, radios, interiors, and glassware.

RUSSEL WRIGHT, Bowl, Vegetable, American Modern, Coral 15.00
Bowl, Vegetable, American Modern, Seafoam 16.00
Bowl, Vegetable, Divided, Iroquois, White 18.00
Butter, Cover, Iroquois 45.00
Carafe, Wine, Iroquois 60.00
Carafe, Wine, Yellow 68.00
Casserole, American Modern, Coral, Stick Handle 30.00
Casserole, Cover, Iroquois, Divided, Avocado 35.00
Celery, American Modern, Chartreuse .... 12.00 To   20.00
Chop Plate, American Modern, Gray 20.00
Clock 60.00
Coaster, American Modern, Coral 11.00
Creamer, American Modern, Black Chutney 9.00
Creamer, American Modern, Cedar Green 7.00
Creamer, American Modern, Chartreuse 8.00
Creamer, American Modern, Coral 10.00
Creamer, American Modern, Gray 8.00
Creamer, Iroquois, Nutmeg 9.00
Cup & Saucer, American Modern, Coral 9.00
Cup & Saucer, American Modern, Coral, Demitasse 20.00
Cup & Saucer, American Modern, Demitasse 20.00
Cup & Saucer, Seafoam 22.00
Cup, American Modern, Black Chutney 7.00
Cup, American Modern, Coral 7.00
Cup, Iroquois, Avocado 5.50

Dinner Set, Iroquois, White, Service For 6 .... 160.00
Mug, Iroquois, Blue 25.00
Mug, Iroquois, Lettuce Green 37.50
Pitcher, Water, American Modern, Chartreuse 25.00
Pitcher, Water, American Modern, Coral 60.00
Pitcher, Water, American Modern, Seafoam .... 38.00 To 45.00
Plate, Dinner, American Modern, Coral 6.00
Plate, Dinner, Iroquois, Avocado 4.50
Platter, Iroquois, White, 14 In. 10.00
Relish, Divided, American Modern, Coral 40.00
Salt & Pepper, American Modern, Coral 13.00
Salt & Pepper, Clover 25.00
Soup, Dish, American Modern, Lug, Coral 11.00
Sugar, Cover, American Modern, Coral 9.00
Teapot, American Modern, Chartreuse 24.00
Teapot, American Modern, Seafoam 35.00
Teapot, Iroquois, Casual, Pink 50.00
Teapot, Iroquois, Yellow 35.00
Tumbler, American Modern, Cedar Green 47.00
Tumbler, American Modern, Coral 45.00

SABINO FRANCE

Sabino France

Sabino glass was made in the 1920s and 1930s in Paris, France. Founded by Marius–Ernest Sabino, the firm was noted for Art Deco lamps, vases, figurines, and animals in clear, colored, and opalescent glass. Production stopped during World War II but resumed in the 1960s with the manufacture of nude figurines and small opalescent glass animals. The new pieces are a slightly different color and can be recognized.

SABINO, Figurine, Butterfly 35.00
Figurine, Dragonfly 150.00
Figurine, Fish, 4 1/2 In. 145.00
Figurine, Fish, Amber, Signed, 4 In. 225.00
Figurine, Gazelle, 4 1/2 In. 100.00
Figurine, Hen 25.00
Figurine, Sparrow, In Flight 60.00
Oyster Plate, 7 3/4 In. 200.00
Perfume Bottle, Nudes All Around, 6 In. 145.00

Salopian ware was made by the Caughley factory of England during the eighteenth century. The early pieces were blue and white with some colored decorations. Another ware called "Salopian" today is a tableware decorated with color transfers. This ware was made during the late nineteenth century.

SALOPIAN, Jardiniere, Hand Painted Flowers, 7 1/2 X 10 In. 275.00
Teapot, Embossed Ribs, Floral Design, Underglaze Blue, Gilt, 6 In. 475.00

Matched sets of salt and pepper shakers were first used in the nineteenth century. Collectors are primarily interested in figural examples made after World War I. Huggies are pairs of shakers which appear to embrace each other. Many salt and pepper shakers are listed in other categories and can be located through the index at the back of this book.

SALT & PEPPER, Acorn, Peachblow 95.00
Anchor Hocking, Pink Bakelite Tops 10.00
Angel Fish, 1 Pink, 1 Yellow 7.00
Ballglove & Bat, Miniature 10.00
Banana Guys, Reclining, Green Pants 10.00
Barbarossa Beer, Paper Label 25.00
Bear Cubs, 1 White, 1 Tan, In Lined Basket 8.50
Bear, Huggies, Brown, Van Tellingen 13.00
Bear, Huggies, Pink, Van Telligen 8.00
Bear, Huggies, Yellow, Van Tellingen 12.50
Bear, Sitting, In Hollowed Out Tree Trunk, Bone China 12.00
Bee & Flower, Miniature 10.00

Beer Bottle, Schlitz Label, Brown Glass, 4 In. ....8.00 To 15.00
Binoculars & Case, Black Binoculars, Brown Case 8.00
Black Cat, 10 In. 5.00
Black Cat, Tail Forms Ring, 10 1/2 In. 12.00
Black Notes, Hanging On Black & White Music Rack, 3 Piece 12.50
Blossom Top, Blue Ridge 16.50
Bluebirds, Blue & Cream, On Ceramic Branch, 3 Piece 12.50
Borden's Elsie & Elmer, Ceramic 55.00
Boxing Glove & Punching Bag, Brown 12.00
Boy & Dog, Huggies, Van Tellingen 25.00
Boy & Girl, Occupied Japan 14.00
Bride & Groom, Before & After, Turnabout, 10 Years Later 14.00
Briefcase & Fedora 6.50
Bunny, Huggies, White, Van Tellingen 13.00
Bunny, Huggies, Yellow, Van Tellingen 13.00
Bye–Lo, Grace S.Putnam, Sticker 650.00
Carrot People, Frilly Collars 10.00
Cats, 1 Sitting, 1 Lying, Black 7.50
Century of Progress Towers, 1933 .... 35.00
Chelsea Cow, Straw Hats, Blue Bows 8.50
Chicken 16.00
Chicken, Ceramic Arts 16.00
Clematis With Scroll, Original Stopper 18.00
Clown, Red & Yellow Trim, Black & White Metal 22.00
County Courthouse, Catskills, N.Y., Deep Blue, White Top 50.00
Courting Frogs, On Lily Pad Tray, Green 9.50
Dairy Queen Maid 8.00
Dressed Pigs, Playing Violins, Gold Trim, Occupied Japan 16.00
Duck, Huggies, Van Telligen 20.00
Dumbo, Large 45.00
Dutch Boy & Girl, Huggies, Van Tellingen .... 17.00 To 22.00
Dutch Couple, Ceramic Arts Studio, 3 In. 16.00
Falstaff Beer 15.00
Fifi & Fido, Ken–L–Ration ....8.00 To 15.00
Fish, Rosemeade 18.00
Fish, Standing On Tail, Ceramic Arts Studio 26.00
Flat Tire, Hand Pump, Gray & Brown 14.00
Flying Turkey 22.00
Gas Pump, 1950s Convertible 10.00
Gas Pump, Texaco Gasoline, 1940s 25.00
GE Refrigerator Shape, Milk Glass 70.00
Golf Clubs, Yellow, In Brown Gold Bag, 3 Piece 12.00
Hat Rack 8.00
Heart Shape, Blue Opaque 50.00
Humpty–Dumpty, Plastic 12.00
Idaho & Potato, Parkcraft 18.00
Jazzmen 95.00
John F.Kennedy, In Rocking Chair 22.00
July & Fire Cracker, Parkcraft 25.00
July & Firecracker, Parkcraft 25.00
Kermit & Miss Piggy, Ceramic 10.00
Kissing Bride & Groom, On Bench 5.00
Lampost, Plastic, Box 15.00
Leprechauns, Traditional Dress, Rosy Cheeked 18.00
Lil' Stinker, Black & White Skunk, 10 In. 12.00
Little Sprout 15.00
Love Bug, Bendel 8.00
Love Bug, Huggies, Van Tellingen 35.00
Mammy & Pappy, Wooden 12.00
Man & Woman, Souvenir of Mexico 30.00
Mary & Lamb, Huggies, Van Tellingen .... 20.00 To 25.00
Mason Jar, Ball, Box 25.00
Milk Can, On Base With Wooden Napkin Holder 13.50
Milk Glass, Purple Floral, Avon 18.00

Millie & Willie, Penguins ....8.00 To 14.00
Monkeys 24.00
Mouse & Cheese, Ceramic Arts Co. 15.00
Nebraska & Cowboy Boot, Parkcraft 18.00
Nelson Dairy Milk Bottles 35.00
New Era Potato Chip Can 27.00
Nipper, Dog & Phonograph, Plastic, Box 22.00
Nodder, Fish 30.00
Owl, Glass Eyes, Silver Plate 85.00
Peek–A–Boo, Rabbit, Van Tellingen 425.00
Pheasant, Rosemeade ....6.50 To 10.00
Pop–Up Toaster, Box 7.00
Poppin' Fresh, Ceramic 10.00
Poppin' Fresh, Plastic 12.50
Rabbit, Huggies, Van Telligen 12.00
Range, With Coffeepots, Celluloid, 1950s 10.00
RCA Nipper ....8.50 To 30.00
Red Lobster 15.00
Rose Petals, Pink Satin Glass 300.00
Sailor & Mermaid, Huggies, Van Tellingen .... 38.00 To 65.00
Santa Claus 7.00
Santa Claus, Winking 15.00
Scottish Couple 5.00
Scotty 5.00
Sea Urchins, White Bone China, Pink Roses On Top 17.50
Secretary's Special, Black Desk, Purple Typewriter 13.00
Silent Sam, Comic Strip, Adamson, 1922 .... 22.00
Skunks, Madison Art Ceramics 22.00
Sled & Skates, Miniature 10.00
Smiling Jack–O'Lantern & Black Cat 12.50
Smokey The Bear 35.00
Snap & Pop, Kellogg 12.50
Steve & Eydie Dinosaur, Interlocking Necks, Green & Pink 14.50
Strawberry, Hangs On Silver Plated Frame 15.00
Suitcase & Valise, Old Fashioned, Black & White Metal 7.00
Swan, Pink Rosettes, White Bone China 17.50
Tappan Chef, Yellow & Blue Glass 15.00
Telephone, Pink, Plastic 8.00
Theatrical Masks, Comedy & Tragedy, White, Brown & Black 14.00
Thermos & Lunch Box 12.50
Thimble & Thread 12.50
Tivoli Beer 20.00
Toaster & Bread 12.50
Top Hat & Gloves 6.50
Tweedledee, Disney 23.00
Umpire & Baseball Player, Porcelain, 1940s 75.00
Victor RCA, Lenox 35.00
Victorian House, On Hill, Blue & White, Brown & White 12.50
Westinghouse, Laundry Twins, Pink 15.00
Wringer Washer, Celluloid, 1950s 10.00

Salt glaze has a grayish-white, pitted, orange-peel-textured surface. It is a method of decoration that has been used since the eighteenth century. Salt-glazed pieces are still being made.

SALT GLAZE, Bottle, Impressed HH, Miltisided, Blue Around Top 7250.00
Charger, Border of Stars & Dots, Diaper Rim, English, 15 3/8 In. 445.00
Cookie Jar, Cookies, Cattail, Brown 145.00
Crock, 2 Gal. 20.00
Crock, Blue Grapevines Around, M.Friedman & Co., 8 X 5 In. 185.00
Crock, Butter, Apricot 195.00
Crock, Butter, Draped Windows 225.00
Crock, No.4, Cobalt Blue Line, 4 Gal. 85.00

Jar, Storage, 2 1/2 Gal.	65.00
Jug, F & Co., St.Louis, Blue 2, Leaf Design, 2 Gal.	320.00
Jug, F.T. Wright & Co., Taunton, Mass., Floral, 2 Gal.	340.00
Jug, Hamilton & Jones, Small	65.00
Jug, Leaves & Berries, Handle	850.00
Jug, Marked C & Co., Mounted As Lamp	95.00
Jug, S.S. Wandell, West Troy, Ovoid, 1 Gal.	200.00
Jug, Universe, Wreathed Medallion, People & Animals, 9 5/8 In.	295.00
Pitcher, Enameled Landscape Scene, Flowers, Trees, 9 In.	1600.00
Plate, Allover Embossed Design, Reticulated Rim, 10 In.	800.00
Plate, Embossed Scalloped Rim, 9 1/2 In.	300.00
Plate, Embossed Scalloped Rim, 12 In.	450.00
Salt, Daisy & Honeycomb	210.00
Spittoon, Blue & White	55.00
Syrup, Embossed Scenes, Figures, Gothic Arches, Pewter Lid, 6 In.	155.00
Teapot, Camel Shape, Embossed Detail, 5 1/4 In.	6100.00
Teapot, Embossed Classical Design, Blue Striping, 5 5/8 In.	800.00
Teapot, Embossed Designs On Panels, Animal Finial, 5 3/8 In.	2250.00
Teapot, Embossed Floral Design, Green Enamel, Swan Finial, 6 In.	1500.00
Teapot, White, Dark Brown Medallions, Oriental Design, 6 1/2 In.	200.00
Tenderizer, Meat, Oak Handle, 1877	75.00

Samplers were made in America from the early 1700s. The best examples were made from 1790 to 1840. Long, narrow samplers are usually older than square ones. Early samplers just had stitching or alphabets. The later examples had numerals, borders, and pictorial decorations. Those with mottoes are mid–Victorian.

SAMPLER, Alphabet Border 3 Sides, Peacock, Floral, Linen, Framed, 10 X 11 In.	725.00
Alphabet, Florals, Dog, Turned–Up Tail, 1800, 9 1/4 X 8 1/4 In.	175.00
Alphabet, Flowers, Anna Lindemuth, 1853, Framed, 21 1/4 X 23 In.	400.00
Alphabet, Flowers, Crowns, Linen Homespun, Framed, 18 3/4 X 12 In.	425.00
Alphabet, Ink Inscription, Sarah Breck, 1750, 13 X 8 1/4 In.	1600.00
Alphabet, Numerals, Ellen Smith, 1844, Oak Frame, 12 X 17 In.	450.00
Alphabet, Stripes, Gold, Black, White, Homespun, Framed, 9 X 8 In.	150.00
Alphabet, Stylized Flowers, Linen, Gold, Blue, Homespun, 14 X 18 In.	450.00
Alphabet, Verse, Elizabeth Mary Wilson, 1834, 18 1/2 X 19 1/2 In.	325.00
Alphabet, Verse, Signed, Dated 1843, 8 X 19 In.	375.00
Alphabet, Vine Border, Stylized Flowers, Trees, Birds, 16 X 13 In.	400.00
Alphabet, Vining Strawberry Border, Homespun, Flowers, 13 X 17 In.	1100.00
Animals, Trees, Hannah —Ton, April 28, 1824, 12 1/2 X 12 1/2 In.	435.00
Bees & Dogs Over Basket of Flowers, Framed, 9 3/4 X 6 3/4 In.	195.00
Bird, Butterfly, Charlotte Crowder, Framed, Square, 15 1/2 In.	595.00
Buildings, Stylized, People, Verse, Sarah Nash, 1845, 17 3/4 X 15 In.	700.00
Family Record, Collins Family, Gilt Frame, 17 3/4 X 17 3/4 In.	150.00
Family Record, Mary Howlet Aged 12, Born 1819, 20 X 27 3/4 In.	125.00
Family Record, Titsworth, 1784 Through 1866, Framed, 24 X 28 In.	300.00
Floral Border, Elisa Carlton, Age 9, July 6, 1826, 13 1/2 X 16 In.	350.00
Floral, Admonition, Catherine A. Pader, A.D.1824, 18 X 18 In.	205.00
Floral, Mary P.Herring, In 11th Year, 1803, 18 3/8 X 14 3/4 In.	1325.00
Flowers, Stylized, Sarah Ann Brown, 1831, 18 X 11 3/4 In.	775.00
Hymnal, 1822	275.00
Memorial To Edward & Molley Peers, 1870, 31 1/4 X 29 In.	105.00
Pious Verse, Silk Threads, Elizabeth Shepard, 1769, 15 X 12 1/2 In.	250.00
Verse, Mary Baxter, Scott Peebles, February 1816, 16 1/2 X 16 In.	600.00
Vine Border, Architectural Design, Homespun, 23 X 19 1/2 In.	700.00

Samson and Company, a French firm specializing in the reproduction of collectible wares of many countries and periods, was founded in Paris in the early nineteenth century. Chelsea, Meissen, Famille Verte, and Chinese Export porcelain are some of the wares that have been reproduced by the company. The firm uses a variety of marks on the reproductions. It is still in operation.

SAMSON, Bowl, Punch, Chinese Export Style, Blue, Gold, Coat of Arms	450.00
Box, Polychrome Floral, 4 X 4 In.	350.00

Clock, Imari Decoration, 21 In.	3000.00
Figurine, Man With Helmet, Sword, Floral Base, Chelsea Style, 11 In.	400.00
Plate, Famille Rose, Pierced Border, 9 1/2 In., 12 Piece	1650.00
Tea Caddy, Flowers, Pink, Green, Chinese Export Style, 6 In.	175.00
Urn, Cover, Sevres Style, 14 In.	4000.00

Sand Babies were used as decorations on a line of children's dishes made by the Royal Bayreuth China Company. The children are playing at the seaside. Collectors use the names "Sand Babies" and "Beach Babies" interchangeably.

SAND BABIES, Vase, Brown Ground, 3 1/4 In.	100.00

Sandwich glass is any one of the myriad types of glass made by the Boston and Sandwich Glass Works in Sandwich, Massachusetts, between 1825 and 1888. It is often very difficult to be sure whether a piece was really made at the Sandwich factory because so many types were made there and similar pieces were made at other glass factories.

SANDWICH GLASS, see also Pressed Glass, etc.

SANDWICH GLASS, Bottle, Ink, Pale Blue, 3 Mold, McK–GIII–25, Disc Mouth	5200.00
Bowl, Fruit, Clear, Footed, Scalloped	125.00
Bride's Bowl, Inverted Hobnail, Pink Cased, Square, 9 In.	250.00
Candlestick, Clambroth, C.1840, 7 1/2 In., Pair ....*Illus*	385.00
Candlestick, Columnar, Clambroth, Pair	675.00
Candlestick, Dolphin, Canary, Pair	950.00
Candlestick, Hexagonal Baluster, Clambroth, 7 1/2 In., Pair	385.00
Compote, Nectarine, 5 X 8 In.	650.00
Cup Plate, Hearts & Vines	32.00
Cup Plate, Scalloped	45.00
Decanter, Baroque Style, Sapphire Blue, Stopper	3750.00
Decanter, Sunburst With Concentric Ring Band, 1 Pt.	300.00
Decanter, Sunburst, Solid Rayed Stopper, 1 Pt.	275.00
Dish, Clear & Frosted Pheasant Cover	115.00
Dish, Spaniel Cover, Lattice On Sides of Base, White	395.00
Flatiron, Child's, Green	900.00
Jam Jar, Gold Snake Entwined On Cover, Underplate	275.00
Lamp, Atlantic Cable Pattern, No Shade, 11 1/2 In.	110.00
Lamp, Canary, Looped Fonts, Flint, Pair	1800.00
Lamp, Oil, Medium Blue, Pair	2200.00
Lamp, Quatrefoil, Double Overlay, Pink Over White, Clear	850.00
Lamp, Waterfall, 4 In.	295.00
Lamp, Whale Oil, Diamond–Quilted, Matching Spill	225.00
Paperweight, Blue Poinsettia, Green, Red & White Ground	850.00
Perfume Bottle, Geometric Vertical & Horizontal Ribbing	195.00
Perfume Bottle, Gilded Amber, Lily Stopper	395.00
Pitcher, Electric Blue, Blown, Enameled Floral, Gauffered	390.00
Pitcher, Enameled Floral, Electric Blue	390.00
Pitcher, Overshot	135.00
Plate, Beaded Daisy, Green, 5 In.	130.00
Plate, Circle, 13 Hearts	95.00
Punch Cup, Pink Overshot, Clear Handle, 8 Piece	245.00
Relish, Rayed Peacock Eye, Lacy	78.00
Rose Bowl, Applied Pink Flowers	185.00
Salt, Cover, Lacy	800.00
Saltshaker, Christmas, Amber	60.00
Shaker, Pepper, Barrel Shape, Vaseline, Pewter Top	50.00
Spillholder, Star, Blue, 1840–60, 5 1/2 In. ....*Illus*	900.00
Sugar, Acanthus & Shield, Cover, Marbled White	4100.00
Sugar, Gothic Arch, Cover	250.00
Tumbler, Inverted Thumbprint, Cranberry Spatter, Pair	125.00
Tumbler, Threaded, Polished Pontil	110.00
Vase, Bud, Cranberry, Threaded	75.00
Vase, Clambroth, Cobalt Snake, 10 In., Pair	360.00

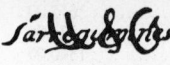

Utzschneider and Company, a porcelain factory, made ceramics in Sarreguemines, Lorraine, France, from 1770. Transfer-printed wares and majolica were made in the nineteenth century. The nineteenth-century pieces, most often found today, usually had colorful transfer-printed decorations showing peasants in local costumes.

SARREGUEMINES, Pitcher, Flowers, Handle	62.50
Plate, Figure of Oriental Man, 9 In.	20.00
Plate, Majolica, Plums, Green Leaf Ground, 7 1/2 In.	35.00
Toothpick, Figural, Swan	25.00
Tray, French Peasants, 10 X 5 In.	150.00
Vase, Holes At Shoulder, Satyr Head Handles, Pink, 8 5/8 In.	200.00
Wall Pocket, Beetle, Blue, Green, Brown, 4 X 9 In.	200.00

Satin glass is a late nineteenth-century art glass. It has a dull finish that is caused by a hydrofluoric acid vapor treatment. Satin glass was made in many colors and sometimes had applied decorations. Satin glass is also listed by factory name or in the mother-of-pearl category in this book.

SATIN GLASS, Basket, Herringbone, Mother-of-Pearl, Blue Interior, 5 3/4 In.	315.00
Basket, Vaseline, Base, 2 Piece	95.00
Candlestick, Rebecca At The Well, Sky Blue, Signed, 10 In.	95.00
Condiment Set, Ribbon Mother-of-Pearl, Red, Holder, 6 In.	835.00
Cracker Jar, Red, Florette, Silver Plated Cover	225.00
Cracker Jar, Shell & Seaweed, Pink	250.00
Cruet, Florette, Pink	250.00
Decanter, Wine, Blown-Out Grape Clusters, Leaves	75.00
Epergne, Blue Quilted Mother-of-Pearl, 3 Lilies, Large	450.00
Epergne, Blue, Applied Red Glass Apples	475.00
Epergne, Victorian, Blue, Ruffled, 19 In., 5 Piece	375.00
Ewer, Blue To Pale Blue Shades, Camphor Handle, 9 In.	145.00
Ewer, Dark To Light Blue, Herringbone, Thorn Handle, 10 1/2 In.	250.00
Holder, Calling Card, Diamond-Quilted, Metal Frame, 9 1/2 In.	915.00
Lamp, Blown-Out Roses Top & Bottom, Prisms, 20 In.	325.00
Lamp, Diamond-Quilted, Mother-of-Pearl, Ruffled Shade, 8 In.	165.00
Pitcher Set, Diamond-Quilted, Apricot To White, 7 Piece	1275.00
Pitcher, Pink, Diamond-Quilted	350.00
Pitcher, Water, Cranberry, Speckled Reverse Swirl	350.00
Pitcher, Water, Florette, Pink	225.00
Pitcher, Water, Leaf Umbrella, Blue	350.00
Rose Bowl, Butterflies, Flowers, 4-Crimp, 6 3/4 X 4 In.	15.00
Rose Bowl, Dark To Light Pink, Enameled Leaves & Stems, 6 In.	250.00
Rose Bowl, Pale Green, Pink Floral Design, Green Leaves, 6 In.	180.00
Rose Bowl, Peacock Eye, Red, Mother-of-Pearl Interior, 3 In.	900.00
Sugar & Creamer, Mother-of-Pearl, Pale To Bright Yellow	225.00
Tumbler, Frosted White Shaded To Rose, White Lattice Stripes	85.00
Vase, Birds, Diamond-Quilted, Ruffled Turned-Down Rim, 9 In.	2530.00
Vase, Coralene Seawood Design, Blue To Off-White, 6 1/2 In.	295.00
Vase, Diamond-Quilted, Pink, Mother-of-Pearl, Ruffled, 7 In.	135.00
Vase, Enameled Flowers, Brown Branches, Lavender, 9 1/2 In.	225.00
Vase, Folded Rim, Gold & Green Flower, Gold Leaves, Blue, 12 In.	750.00
Vase, Ribbon Mother-of-Pearl, Gold Flowers, Red, 3 In.	500.00
Vase, Wave Or Ripple, Ruffled Edge, Apricot, 6 1/4 In., Pair	450.00
SATIN GLASS, WEBB, see Webb	

Satsuma is a Japanese pottery with a distinctive creamy beige crackled glaze. Most of the pieces were decorated with blue, red, green, orange, or gold. Almost all the Satsuma found today was made after 1860. During World War I, Americans could not buy undecorated European porcelains. Women who liked to make hand-painted porcelains at home began to decorate plain Satsuma. These pieces are known today as "American Satsuma."

SATSUMA, Berry Set, Gentleman, Lily Pads, Gold, 3 Piece	150.00
Bowl, Dragons, Figures, 1890s, 6 In.	100.00

Bowl, Interior Scene Medallion, Gilt, Flowers, 1910, 4 3/4 In. 295.00
Bowl, Landscapes, Villagers, Water View Interior, 4 7/8 In. 615.00
Box, Cover, Procession Theme, Interior Ceremonial Scenes, 3 7/8 In. 825.00
Cup & Saucer, Gilt-Painted Cup, Silver Stem, 10 1/4 In., Pair 1540.00
Ewer, Enameled White Mums, Red On Lower Half, Yellow Top, 1870 .... 105.00
Jar, Cover, Court Scene, Scene of Artisans, Paper Label, 2 1/2 In. 825.00
Jar, Parade Scene, Gilt, Wooden Stand, 7 In. 675.00
Lamp, Jeweltone Flowers, Raw Silk Shade, Filigree Finial, 35 In. 325.00
Plate, Figure Flanked By Deities, 19th Century, 7 1/4 In. 445.00
Plate, Lohan, Crimped Rim, Shimazu Crest, Marked, 7 1/2 In. 115.00
Plate, Man, Scene, 7 In. 16.00
Plate, Shimazu Crest, Scenes, Scalloped, 1900, 6 3/8 In., Pair 275.00
Pot, Cover, Alternating Floral & Landscape Panels, 2 In. 385.00
Salt Dip, Floral, Marked 29.00
Tea Set, Child's, Service For 6 .... 150.00
Teapot, Flowers, Woven Swing Handle 95.00
Teapot, Inverted Cover, Women Allover, Rattan Handle, 2 1/4 In. 525.00
Teapot, Lohan Design, Lizard Handle, Spout & Finial, 4 In. 335.00
Teapot, Overall Design of Lohans, Dragon, Globular Shape, 4 In. 225.00
Tray, Quatrefoil Lobed, Attendants, Dragon, Marked, C.1910, 8 1/2 In. 385.00
Urn, Battle Scene, Florals, Dragon Handles, 30 1/4 In. 135.00
Urn, Rooster Handle, Gold, Raised, 1890-1900, 9 In. 245.00
Urn, Samurai Warriors, Rooster Handles, 18 X 9 In. 345.00
Urn, Samurai, Geisha, Blue Ground, 8 1/2 In. 400.00
Vase, Allover Lohans, Attendants & Dragon, Bulbous, C.1900, 9 In. 85.00
Vase, Allover Warrior Design, Elephant Handles, 16 In. 330.00
Vase, Arahats With Haloes & Kwannon, 1920, 9 1/2 In. 250.00
Vase, Butterflies, Japanese Lilies, Bamboo Design, 10 1/2 In., Pair 325.00
Vase, Cartouches, Birds, Floral Sprays, Bottle Shape, 5 3/4 In. 1210.00
Vase, Floral, Enameled, C.1900, 14 X 8 In. 525.00
Vase, Large Phoenix, Mounted As Lamp, 18 In. 165.00
Vase, Lohan, Attendants & Dragon, Signed, Late 19th Century, 6 In. 445.00
Vase, Panels of Flowers, Warriors & Courtesans, 11 3/4 In. 775.00
Vase, Panels, People & Other Scenes, Gold, 4 In. 195.00
Vase, Peacocks, Floral, 6 In. 35.00
Vase, Portrait, Beading, Gold Trim, 9 1/4 In. 175.00
Vase, Relief Sea Life Design, Kyoto, 15 X 8 In. 395.00
Vase, Scholar, Children, Tassel Handles, 12 In., Pair 600.00
Vase, Scholars & Courtesans Panels, Marked, 5 In., Pair 275.00
Vase, Tiered, Panels of Courtesans & Lohans, C.1900, 3 3/4 In., Pair 365.00
Water Pail, Scholar, Arahat Figures, Border, 14 1/2 In. 650.00
Wig Stand, Florals & Bird, Cylindrical, Late 19th Century, Pair 210.00

Special scales have been made to weigh everything from babies to
gold. Collectors search for all types. Most popular are small gold-
dust scales and special grocery scales.

SCALE, Apothecary, Brass, Mahogany, 2 Pans, Drawers In Base, England, 25 In. 225.00
Apothecary, Set, Original Wooden Carrying Case, Mid-19th Century 45.00
Apothecary, Triple Beam Agate, C.1900 .... 190.00
Arosia, Kitchen, Brass Dial, Weighs To 20 Lbs. 95.00
Baby's, Balance, Cast Iron Base, 1930s 50.00
Baby's, Pocket, Pat.Feb.3, 1912, Weighs 16 Lbs. 40.00
Baby's, Weighs To 24 Lbs., Ounces, Red 42.00
Balance, 2 Pans, Brass On Walnut Base, 26 In. 225.00
Barber Shop 995.00
Buffalo Hide 125.00
Buffalo, Brass Tray, Cast Iron Bottom 245.00
Buffalo, Brass, Cast Iron 17.50
Buggy, Weights, Walnut 1200.00
Chatillon, Hanging, Spring, 0 To 80 Lbs. 30.00
Chatillon, Milk, Brass 90.00
Christian Becker, Glass Door, Oak Case, 18 X 15 In. 185.00
Confectionary, Spring, Brass Tray, Tin, 1899 .... 45.00
Drugstore, Balance, Porcelain Top 65.00

Fairbanks & Greenleaf, Grain, Iron Fittings, Brass 45.00
Fairbanks, Balance, Iron & Brass, Fitted Wood Box, 13 In. 150.00
Fairbanks, Cast Iron, Red Paint 45.00
Fairbanks, Gold Dust, Red Paint, Iron & Brass, Dated 1878 .... 275.00
Fairbanks, Gold Miner's, Patent 1878 .... 150.00
Fairbanks, Grain, Brass 125.00
Fairbanks, Postal, Brass 70.00
Fairbanks, Produce, Scoop & Weights, Double Beams 58.00
Forschner, Pan, Brass 98.00
Frary's, Brass 15.00
Glass & Marble Top, Oak Case, 7 1/2 X 13 In. 275.00
Gold Miner's, Balance, Trays, Brass, Germany, 3 In.Diam. 35.00
Gold Miner's, Iron, Small 150.00
Gold Miner's, With Weights, Original Case 80.00
H. Troemner, Carved Pine, Marble, Weights, Victorian, 6 X 22 X 10 In. 121.00
H. Troemner, Drugstore, Marble On Base, Weight Wheel On Shaft 150.00
Hanging, Brass Face, Green Paint, 100 Lb. 25.00
Hanson, Penny Counter, Case 40.00
Hanson, Postal, C.1925 .... 30.00
Hanson, Postal, Dated 1963 .... 12.00
Howe, Store, Cast Iron 80.00
Jacobs, Candy, Pedestal, Weights 145.00
Jennings, Lollipop ....550.00 To 1050.00
Jiffyway, Egg, Brass 18.00
Kitchen, With Weights 18.00
Lander's, Hanging, Improved Balance No.2, Brass Front, 50 Lbs.Maximum 14.00
Lollipop, White Porcelain, 1 Cent 995.00
Meat, Brass, Pat.1867 .... 55.00
Meat, Portable, Brass, Germany 45.00
National, Novelty 550.00
Oakes Co., Egg, Tipton, Indiana 12.50
Ohaus, Grain, White Brass, 1 Qt. 250.00
Ohaus, Triple Beam, To 2610 Grams 65.00
Pacific Scale Works, Platform, Made For 1893 World's Fair, 6 Ft. 1000.00
Peerless, Lollipop, Blue Porcelain 850.00
Pelouze Dairy, White Enameled 65.00
Pelouze Princess, Postal, Quadruple Plate, 1899 .... 75.00
Pelouze Victor, Postal, 1898, 4 1/2 In. 28.00
Pelouze, Postal, Scroll Panels, Nickel Plate, Patent 1895 .... 35.00
Pennsylvania Scales, To 20 Pounds 150.00
Philadelphia Scoop & Scale Co., Brass Scoop 135.00
Royal Springs, Hanging, Brass Face 28.00
Standard, Computer, Gold, Glass Tray, 32 In. 99.00
Steel Yard, Iron, Hooks, Beam & Balance Weights, 0 To 50 Lbs. 19.00
Store, Beam–Type 70.00
Toledo, Candy, Brass Pan 115.00
Toledo, Counting, Large 100.00
Triner, Postal, Air Mail, 1946 .... 30.00
Universal, Penny, 5 1/2 In. 425.00
Watling, President Lollipop Style, Fortune, Coin 1900.00
Wrigley Jr., Candy, Rotary Type 425.00
Wrigley's Spearmint Pepsin Gum, Brass Frame & Scoop 225.00

Schafer & Vater, makers of small ceramic items, are best known for their amusing figurals. The factory was located in Volkstedt-Rudolstadt, Germany, from 1890 to 1962. Some pieces are marked with the crown and R mark, but many are unmarked.

SCHAFER & VATER, Ash Holder, Fat Naked Cupid, 3 In. 100.00
Ashtray, Bald Man, Open Mouth, Keep Your Hair On, 5 1/4 In. 145.00
Bottle, Old Scotch, Little Scotch, 5 1/2 In. 130.00
Box, 2 Googly–Eyed Boys In Oval Tub, Marked, 3 X 2 3/4 In. 135.00
Creamer, Bear 125.00
Figurine, Boy & Girl, Sitting Together, 4 X 3 1/2 In. 70.00
Figurine, Boy, Googly–Eyes, Brown Dog At Side, Marked, 3 In. 110.00

Figurine, Boy, Whispering In Girl's Ear, Marked, 4 1/8 In.	85.00
Figurine, Girl, Googly-Eyes, On Brick Stoop, Reading, 4 In.	110.00
Figurine, Girl, Holding 2 Large Slippers, Marked, 4 3/8 In.	110.00
Hatpin Holder, Art Nouveau	225.00
Hatpin Holder, Classic White Figures On Green Bisque	45.00
Hatpin Holder, Oriental Woman, Jasperware, Gold Trim	195.00
Jar, Figural, Pig, 5 1/2 In.	95.00
Match Holder, Mustached Man Points To Tongue	60.00
Matchbox, Boy & Fat Man, Bisque, Marked, 3 1/2 X 4 1/2 In.	95.00
Mustard, Embossed, Classical Figures, Bisque	42.00
Nodder, Goblin, Green, 4 In.	185.00
Nodder, Monkey, 4 In.	195.00
Pitcher, Black Woman, Huge Eyes, Mouth, Marked, 5 In.	165.00
Pitcher, Chinese Man With Baboon On Back, 5 In.	110.00
Pitcher, Dutch Boy's Head, Blue & White, Marked, 4 In.	108.00
Pitcher, Grinning Chinaman Holding Bird, 3 1/8 In.	95.00
Pitcher, Milkmaid With Keys	65.00
Planter, Girl, Goose, Basket	115.00
Powder Box, Woman's Face On Lid, Pink Bisque, 3 3/4 In.	105.00
Skeleton, Poison On Robe, With Tray & 2 Shot Glasses	225.00
Striker, Cat & Kitten, Don'T Scratch Me, Scratch Mother	100.00
Vase, 4 Cupid Musicians, Colored Jewels, 5 In.	55.00

Schneider

Schneider Glassworks was founded in 1903 at Epinay-sur-Seine, France, by Charles and Ernest Schneider. Art glass was made between 1903 and 1930. The company still produces clear crystal glass.

SCHNEIDER, Christmas Tree, Clear, Signed, 8 In.	95.00 To 150.00
Compote, Blue & Mottled Orange, Amethyst Stem, Metal Base, 9 In.	595.00
Compote, Mottled Red, Purple Freeform Design Interior, 4 1/2 In.	750.00
Compote, Peach Bowl, Amethyst Base & Stem, 7 1/2 X 6 1/4 In.	380.00
Lamp, Domed Shade, Stylized Floral, Yellow, 19 1/2 In.	4400.00
Night-Light, Felines On Shade, 3 Bronze Feet, Signed, 7 1/4 In.	3300.00
Vase, Amethyst, Art Glass, Swirled Pink, Footed, Ovoid, 17 In.	550.00
Vase, Band of Squares & Dashes, Marked, C.1925, 14 1/4 In.	1980.00
Vase, Coiled Stringing, Inverted Form, Signed, C.1925, 10 1/4 In.	1450.00
Vase, Frieze of Flowers, Mottled Foot, Signed, C.1925, 24 2/3 In.	885.00
Vase, Fruit-Filled Compote, Square Bands, Signed, C.1925, 14 In.	2250.00
Vase, Numerous Butterflies, White Ground, Signed, 19 1/2 In.	4500.00
Vase, Orange & White Glass, Black Handles, 17 In.	1100.00
Vase, Swirled Yellow With Dark Amethyst, Signed, 11 In.	1400.00
Vase, Violet Design, Peach & Mauve Ground, Signed, 12 1/4 In.	3350.00

Scrimshaw is bone or ivory or whale's teeth carved by sailors and others for entertainment during the sailing-ship days. Some scrimshaw was carved as early as 1800. There are modern scrimshanders making pieces today on bone, ivory, or plastic.

SCRIMSHAW, see also Ivory, Nautical

SCRIMSHAW, Basket, Swing Handle, Oval, Late 19th Century, 9 3/4 X 7 1/8 In.	8250.00
Bed, Doll's, Mahogany & Whale Ivory, 1845	4500.00
Bodkin, Whale, Tortoiseshell Inlay, Tapered Shape, 3 15/16 In.	1335.00
Box, Ditty	3850.00
Box, Ditty, Shake Type, Abalone, Mid-19th Century, 4 5/8 In.	3850.00
Box, Puzzle, Whale, Tortoiseshell Star, 19th Century, 2 5/8 In.	3025.00
Bracelet, Walrus Tusk, Carved, Eskimo	25.00
Cane, Cherry, Whale, Baleen Inlaid, 1835, 35 3/4 In.	1100.00
Cane, Spiral Whalebone Shaft, Island Wood Top, 34 3/4 In.	1375.00
Cane, Top Third Section Mermaid, Wooden, 19th Century, 35 1/4 In.	880.00
Capt.J. Weeks 1 Side, Whaling Scene Other, 6 3/4 In.	75.00
Corset Busk, Whaling Scene, Mid-19th Century, 14 In.	1925.00
Cribbage Board, Ivory, Marked	350.00
Figure, Narwhal, Ivory Tusk, Wooden, White Coral Mount, 18 In.	445.00
Flask, Whale Ivory, Mahogany, Brass Hoops, 1850, 1/2 Pt., 5 In.	4125.00
Jagging Wheel, Erotic, Female Body, Fork From Pelvic, 8 5/8 In.	4400.00

Knife & Fork Set, Carved Whalebone 110.00
Letter Opener, Whale & Horn, 2 Clasped Hands Handle, 8 1/2 In. 1375.00
Measure, Whale, 19th Century, 10 7/8 In. 82.50
Mold, Butter, American Flag Shield, In Wreath, 1860, 2 3/8 In. 3025.00
Pie Crimper, 6 Wheels, Tortoiseshell, Cupid's Arrows, 7 In. 4400.00
Razor, Straight, Engraved Erotic Ivory Handle, 1850, 6 1/8 In. 1760.00
Rolling Pin, Engraved Stars & Whales 950.00
Rolling Pin, Rows of Stars & Whales On Handles, 10 In. 1045.00
Rolling Pin, Whale Ivory Ends, Wooden Roller, 10 In. 770.00
Seam Rubber, Ropework, Whale, 3 Baleen Separators, 4 7/8 In. 2860.00
Thimble, Ivory, Ship, Flowers 15.00
Tooth, Whale, American Ship, Eagle, Mid–19th Century, 6 1/2 In. 7150.00
Tooth, Whale, Bath, Me., Harbor, 7 In. 3100.00
Tooth, Whale, Full Figure Woman, Mid–19th Century, 8 1/8 In. 4450.00
Tooth, Whale, Ship, Clouds, Gulls, 2 1/4 In. 32.00
Tooth, Whale, Whaling Scene, Signed P.In Sky, Wm.Perry, 6 1/2 In. 1150.00
Toothpick, Nude Woman, Fold Between Legs, Ivory, Bone, 2 1/4 In. 250.00
Tumbler, Horn, Sam'L Beateman, Hunters On Horses, 1836, 4 1/2 In. 650.00
Twister, 2 Whalebone Handles, Rope, Used As Handcuff, 11 1/4 In. 335.00
Walking Stick, Narwhal Tusk, Mahogany Tip, Head, Primitive, 32 In. 1550.00
Walrus Tusk, Whaling Ship, Whales, Men In Boats, 1842, 23 1/2 In. 1000.00

Prescott W. Baston made the first Sebastian miniatures in 1938 in
Marblehead, Massachusetts. More than 400 different designs have
Prescott W. Baston been made and the collectors search for the out–of–production
models. The mark may say "Copr. P. W. Baston U.S.A.," or "P. W.
Baston, U.S.A.," or "Prescott W. Baston." Sometimes a paper label
was used.

SEBASTIAN MINIATURES, Aunty Betsy Trotwood .... 50.00 To 65.00
Becky Thatcher, 1948 .... 50.00
Ben Franklin At The Printing Press, Marblehead 89.00
Betsy Ross 45.00
Clown 30.00
Colonial Kitchen 35.00
Coronado's Senora 90.00
David & Dora Copperfield .... 52.00 To 70.00
Diedrich Knickerbocker 59.00
Doctor 97.00
Family Fishing 25.00
Family Sing 70.00
Fisherman, Dahl 80.00
Ichabod Crane 59.00
Jean LaFitte 90.00
Jim, 1948 .... 65.00
John & Priscilla Alden .... 25.00 To 75.00
John Alden 75.00
Lacemaker, Blue Label 20.00
Little Mother 60.00
Mr.& Mrs. Beacon Hill 200.00
Oliver Twist & Parish Beadle 65.00
Parade Rest, Green Label 30.00
Pecksniff 65.00
Plaque, Collector Society, Yellow 20.00
Plate, In The Candy Store 40.00
Priscilla, Spinning Wheel 75.00
Rip Van Winkle, Marblehead Sticker, Box 70.00
Sairey Gamp 50.00
Scrooge 32.00
Sidewalk Days, Boy & Girl, Box, 1978 .... 70.00 To 75.00
Sidewalk Days, Boy, Green 25.00
Sidewalk Days, Girl, Green 25.00
Thomas Jefferson 50.00
Tom Sawyer, 1948 .... 40.00 To 75.00
Town Crier 125.00

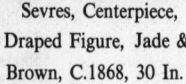

Sevres, Centerpiece, Draped Figure, Jade & Brown, C.1868, 30 In.

Sevres, Clock, Lion Handles, Lovers, Landscape, 18 In.

Sevres, Urn, Cherubs, Garden Setting, 24 In., Pair

Williamsburg Couple	175.00
Williamsburg Lady	75.00 To 115.00
Yankee Sea Captain, 1940	35.00
SEG, see Paul Revere Pottery	

Sevres porcelain has been made in Sevres, France, since 1769. Many copies of the famous ware have been made. The name originally referred to the works of the Royal Porcelain factory. The name now includes any of the wares made in the town of Sevres, France. The entwined lines with a center letter used as the mark is one of the most forged marks in antiques. Be very careful to identify Sevres by quality, not just by mark.

SEVRES, Bowl, Floral Sprig, Cobalt Blue, 6 1/4 In.	850.00
Bowl, Gilt Floral Sprig, Cobalt Blue, Rim Foot, 6 1/4 In.	850.00
Bowl, Lady & Gentleman In Garden, Satyr Mask Handles, Gilt Bronze	1200.00
Box, 2 Lovers On Hinged Top, Garden Scene, Marked, C.1880, 12 1/2 In.	1875.00
Box, Dresser, Scenic Panel, Figures In Garden, 16 X 10 In.	1500.00
Box, Hand Painted, DuBarry, Signed, 1848	950.00
Box, Hinged Top, Figural Panel, Gilt-Metal Mounted, Marked, 15 In.	3300.00
Box, Polychrome Enameled Floral, Oblong, 2 1/4 In.	150.00
Box, Polychrome Enameled Landscapes, Gilt, 3 1/4 In.	300.00
Cake Plate, Mottled Blue & Aqua, Bronze Ormolu Rims & Feet	250.00
Centerpiece, Draped Figure, Jade & Brown, C.1868, 30 In. ....*Illus*	1600.00
Clock, Lion Handles, Lovers, Landscape, 18 In. ....*Illus*	1900.00
Dish, Sauce, Birds & Flowers, Dore Mounts As Compote	120.00
Figurine, Woman, Flowing Robes, Bouquet At Breast, 1930, 20 1/2 In.	610.00
Perfume Bottle, Floral Enameled, Brass, 4 1/8 In.	125.00
Plaque, 2 Courting Couples, C.1900, 6 X 4 1/2 In., Pair	225.00
Plate, Cabinet, Classical Figures, Cobalt Blue & Gold Border, 11 In.	300.00
Plate, Center Flowers, Shaped Rim, Blue Acanthus, 10 In., 18 Piece	1200.00
Plate, Crowns & Bees, Blue Gilt Rim, C.1885, 9 1/4 In., 12 Piece	95.00
Plate, Madame De Lavalliere, Gold Trim, Signed, 9 1/2 In.	135.00
Plate, Portrait, Debrie, Chateau Mark	135.00
Plate, Service, Armorial Crest, Peach Border Floral Vine, 8 1/4 In.	357.00
Plate, Woman On Each Plate, Gilt Rim, Poithevain, 1844, 12 Piece	415.00
Tete-A-Tete, Tray, Teapot, Sugar, Cup & Saucer, Chateau, 19th Century	3300.00
Urn, Cherubs, Garden Setting, Bellflowers, 24 In., Pair ....*Illus*	5500.00
Urn, Cover, Couple In Grotto, Ormolu Mounts, 14 1/2 In.	225.99
Urn, Cover, Lady In Period Dress, Dark Green, Ormolu Mounts, 8 In.	350.00
Urn, Cover, Napoleon On Horseback, Gilt-Bronze Mounts, 41 In.	8250.00
Urn, Figures In Salon, Landscapes, Mask Handles, 11 1/2 In., Pair	2200.00
Urn, Floral Garlands, White, Gilt, Plinth Base, Handles, 15 In., Pair	1800.00

Urn, Lavender Luster, Gold Pebbled Design, Signed, 15 In.	1275.00
Urn, Musician & Lady, Hand Painted Mask Handles, C.1900, 27 In.	1540.00
Vase, Amber Grapes & Vine, Amber Ground, 5 1/2 In.	425.00
Vase, Cameo of Orchid On Frosted Gray, Signed, 7 1/2 In.	250.00
Vase, Cover, Frieze of Lovers, Gilt-Bronze Mounted, C.1900, 31 In.	2475.00
Vase, Dark Blue At Base, Shading Up To Mottled Lighter Blue, 12 In.	250.00

Sewer tile figures were made by workers at the sewer tile and pipe factories in the Ohio area during the late nineteenth and early twentieth centuries. Figurines, small vases, and cemetery vases were favored. Often the finished vase was a piece of the original pipe with added decorations and markings. All types of sewer tile work are now considered folk art by collectors.

SEWER TILE, Canoe, Signed Carl Funk, 36 In.	375.00
Cat, Seated, Bow, 5 3/4 In.	200.00
Cat, Tooled Detail, 13 1/4 In.	500.00
Dog, Mottled Brown Glaze, 8 In.	170.00
Dog, Rectangular Base, 7 1/2 In.	450.00
Dog, Seated, Black Paint, 10 1/4 In.	175.00
Dog, Seated, Flat Back, 10 1/2 In.	450.00
Dog, Seated, Mottled Brownish Amber Glaze, 9 In.	50.00
Dog, Smoked 2-Tone Tan Glaze, Curled Tail, 7 1/2 In.	275.00
Football, 7 1/4 In.	75.00
Frog, 8 In.	150.00
Frog, Tooled Detail, Silver Paint, 7 3/4 In.	85.00
House Number, 27, 8 X 11 In.	55.00
Iowa Goldfish, What Cheer, 3 1/2 X 6 In.	75.00
Jar, Applied Leaf Ornaments, 30 In.	225.00
Lion, 8 1/2 In.	50.00
Lion, Doorstop, 3 1/2 X 6 X 16 In.	280.00
Lion, Tiered Base With Tooled Design, 7 In.	350.00
Owl, 3 3/4 In.	35.00
Paperweight, Man's Head, 2 7/8 In.	75.00
Pig, Open Legs, Embossed Floral Design On Back, 6 3/4 In.	300.00
Pitcher, Impressed Mark, 10 1/2 In.	25.00
Pitcher, U.S. Stoneware, Akron, Ohio, Large	110.00
Planter, Dutch Wooden Shoe, 11 In.	50.00
Planter, Tree Stump With Vine, 12 In.	45.00
Planter, Tree Stump, 2 Owls, 4 1/8 In.	50.00
Shoe, 5 In.	25.00

All types of sewing equipment are collected, from sewing birds that held the cloth to old wooden spools.

SEWING, Awl, Unger Bros., 6 In.	40.00
Basket, Darning, Woven Wood, 3 X 8 In.	5.00
Bird, Blue Stone, Heart Cutout, Brass	165.00
Bird, Cast Iron	48.00
Bird, Ivory	58.00
Bird, Patent Feb. 15, 1853	245.00
Bird, Pincushion Top, Table Clamp, 5 1/4 In.	55.00
Bird, Spring Operated, Screw, Table Clamp, Steel, C.1820	220.00
Bird, Table Clamp, Iron, 1840	285.00
Bird, Table Clamp, Wrought Iron, Jacquard Pincushion Top, 1780	235.00
Box, 2 Drawers, 3 Tiers, Pincushion, Thread Compartment, 19th Century	95.00
Box, Federal, Painted, Phoenix Bird Top, Ball Feet, Side Panels	1250.00
Box, Heart Shape, Wooden, 8 In.	34.00
Box, Inlaid Wood, Cover, 10 X 17 In.	1375.00
Box, Mahogany, Applied Jigsaw Work, Pincushion On Lid, 8 1/2 In.	85.00
Box, Mahogany, Central Medallion, Printed Scene Cover, Octagonal	1210.00
Box, Regency, Rosewood, Brass Inlay, English, C.1830	250.00
Box, Treen Ware, Pedestal	110.00
Caddy, 3 Tiers, Pincushion Top, Mahogany, 11 3/4 In.	65.00
Case, Thimble & Needle, Acorn Shape, Wooden	25.00

Case, Thimble, Brass, Walnut 20.00
Case, Thimble, Sweet Grass 25.00
Crayons, Tailor's 8.00
Crochet Hook, Mother–of–Pearl Handle 20.00
Egg, Handle, Black Wood, 6 In. 5.00
Egg, Hollow Handle Holds Needles, Wooden 10.00
Egg, Wooden 7.50
Footstool, Holding Sewing Box, Walnut Trim, Tapestry Top 15.00
Hem Marker, Brass, Pat.Dated 1874 .... 45.00
Hoop, Embroidery, Table Clamps, Brass Hardware, Wooden Bolts, 15 In. 230.00
Kit, Celluloid, Red Striped 8.00
Kit, Contents, Bakelite, France 16.00
Kit, For Mending Silk Stockings, Real Silk, Girlie Leg Front, 1930s 4.00
Kit, Mending, Blue & White Bakelite, Footed, Contents 18.00
Kit, Mending, Tube, Eastern Star 15.00
Kit, Screw–On Thimble 25.00
Lamp, Table Clamp, Wooden Screws, Ball Finials, Walnut & Maple, 5 In. 85.00
Loom, Black Walnut & Wormy Chestnut, Early 1800s, Large 1500.00
Machine, Child's, Singer, Black 115.00
Machine, Jones 200.00
Machine, New Home, Treadle, Oak Case 30.00
Machine, New National, Table Model, Hand Crank, Gold Trim 125.00
Machine, Singer, Brown & Tan Metal, Electric, Cover, 5 1/2 X 11 In. 72.00
Machine, Singer, Featherweight, Model 221, Case .... 210.00 To 275.00
Machine, Singer, Featherweight, Model 221K, Black, Case 165.00
Machine, Union Special, Table Top, 12 X 13 In. 65.00
Machine, White, Treadle, Tiger Oak, 3 Drawers Each Side, Iron Base 200.00
Mannequin, Simplicity, Composition, Patterns, Box 125.00
Needle Book, Pastel Sketch of Girl & Flowers 4.00
Needle Book, Woolworth 5 & 10, Woolworth Building, 1940s 10.00
Needle Book, World Progress 5.00
Needle Case, Bromo–Seltzer, Bottle Shape, 50 Count 18.00
Needle Case, Closed Parasol Shape, Red & Green, Bakelite 38.00
Needle Case, Petitpoint, On Brass, Germany 4.00
Needle Case, Pop–Up, Children & Dolls Picture, 1930s 12.00
Needle Case, Silver Ribbed, 2 1/2 In. 15.00
Needle Case, Sterling Silver, 3/8 In. 38.00
Needle Case, Tole, 9 In. 65.00
Pincushion & Tape Measure, Black Cat 14.00
Pincushion & Tape Measure, Lamp Shape, Fringed, Pulls From Base 12.00
Pincushion & Tape Measure, Pressing Iron Shape 14.00
     SEWING, PINCUSHION DOLL, see Pincushion Doll
Pincushion, Coin Shape, Pins Fit Into Rim, Unger 185.00
Pincushion, Elephant, Bisque 20.00
Pincushion, Fish, Bisque 15.00
Pincushion, Flying Fish, Beaded, Pink & Green, 4 X 7 1/2 In. 85.00
Pincushion, Googly–Eyed Polka Dot Dog, Porcelain 17.00
Pincushion, Half–Doll, On Bisque, Original Box 30.00
Pincushion, Heart Shape, Beaded, Multicolored 32.00
Pincushion, Kewpie, Metal 25.00
Pincushion, Lady's Shoe, Brown Velvet, Embroidered, 6 1/4 In. 10.00
Pincushion, Monkey, Brass 10.00
Pincushion, Shoe, Patterned Metal 5.00
Pincushion, Swan, Silver Plated, Padded Top 15.00
Pincushion, Table Clamp, Heart Shaped Thumb Screw, Initials X.B. 35.00
Pincushion, Tinkerbell, Container 75.00
Pincushion, Woman, 1 Hand At Throat, 1 At Waist, 4 3/4 In. 60.00
Razor Blade, Folding, Silver, Advertising 10.00
Rule, Hemming, Sterling Top 50.00
Scissors Holder, Embroidered, Sweet Grass, Germany 25.00
Scissors, Buttonhole, Keen Kutter 22.00
Scissors, Buttonhole, Winchester 50.00
Scissors, Crane Shape 17.00
Scissors, Pinking, Wiss, 11 In. 15.00

Scissors, Sweet Grass, Case	37.50
Shuttle, Tatting, Sterling Silver, 1912	65.00
Shuttle, Textile Mill, With Filled Bobbin, 16 In.	8.00
Spool Cabinet, Clark's ONT, Foil–Backed Glass Inserts	110.00
Spool Cabinet, Eastlake, Walnut	995.00
Spool Cabinet, J.P. Coats, 3 Drawers	145.00
Spool Cabinet, Merrick, Curved Glass, Oval	1400.00
Spool Holder, Center Pincushion, 2 Tiers, Redwood, C.1910, 8 1/4 In.	55.00
Tape Measure, Allentown Dairy Co., Perfectly Pasteurized Milk	20.00
Tape Measure, Atkins, IA Savings Bank	15.00
Tape Measure, Babcock Carriages, Pretty Girl, Celluloid	75.00
Tape Measure, Cat In Shoe, Celluloid	35.00
Tape Measure, Causton Ostrich Farm	55.00
Tape Measure, Clock, Roman Numeral Face, Hands Move As Tape Pulled	95.00
Tape Measure, Coffee Grinder	85.00
Tape Measure, Cracker Jack	38.00
Tape Measure, Dog, Plush	30.00
Tape Measure, Eastern Clay Goods, Pictures Stoneware Jug, Celluloid	75.00
Tape Measure, Farmer's & Mechanic's Trust Co., Bath, N.Y.	17.00
Tape Measure, Frigidaire, Celluloid	40.00
Tape Measure, Fruit Basket, Painted, 1930s, 2 In.	30.00
Tape Measure, G.E. Refrigerator	19.00
Tape Measure, Gulf Fuel Oil	25.00
Tape Measure, Gulf Oil	20.00
Tape Measure, Hoover Vacuum	18.00
Tape Measure, International Harvester	10.00
Tape Measure, John Deere, 1919	55.00
Tape Measure, Kangaroo, Celluloid	10.00
Tape Measure, Lewis Lye, Celluloid	15.00
Tape Measure, Liberty Bell, Clapper Pulls Tape, Philadelphia	75.00
Tape Measure, Lydia Pinkham Medicines	40.00
Tape Measure, Pincushion, Black Baby On Top, Movable Limbs	75.00
Tape Measure, Plum, Celluloid	46.00
Tape Measure, Pot of Holly Leaves, Berries, Spins As Tape Moves	18.50
Tape Measure, Red Apple, Leaf Pull	22.50
Tape Measure, Sears Plows & Cultivators	20.00
Tape Measure, Sioux City, Iowa	22.00
Tape Measure, Stromberg Carburetor	25.00
Tape Measure, Turtle	95.00
Tape Measure, Turtle, Embossed Scene, Battleship, 2 1/4 In.	45.00
Thimble Holder, Vegetable Ivory	135.00
Thimble, 14K Gold, Victorian, Engraved	90.00
Thimble, Aluminum, Advertising, Enameled	9.00
Thimble, Hudson's Soap, Brass	40.00
Thimble, Sterling Silver, Narrow Engraved Band	20.00
Thread Case, J.P. Coats, Wooden, 17 1/4 In.	175.00
Thread Winder, Clamp, 1915	40.00

 Shaker–produced items are characterized by simplicity, functionalism, and orderliness. There were many Shaker communities in America from the eighteenth century to the present day. The religious order made furniture, small wooden pieces, and packaged medicines, herbs, and jellies to sell to "outsiders." Other useful objects were made for use by members of the community. Shaker furniture is listed in this book under Furniture.

SHAKER, Almanac	50.00
Basket, Cane, Woven, Reed, Hinged Lid, Laced Handle, 8 In.	55.00
Basket, Picnic, Sliding Lid, Brass Nails	200.00
Basket, Splint, Side Splints, Painted Splint At Top, 7 1/2 X 11 In.	150.00
Basket, Work, Woven Splint Sides, Woven Bottom, Side Handles, 16 In.	137.50
Basket, Woven Cane, Handle, 7 X 9 X 13 In.	25.00
Bean Sorter, Wooden, Slotted, Wing Nut Adjuster, Label	220.00
Boot Jack, Wooden, Watervliet	198.00
Box, 3–Finger, Copper Tacks, Red On Lid, Oval, 12 In.	550.00

Box, 3–Finger, Natural Finish, 12 In. 400.00
Box, 4–Finger, 1 Finger Lid, Copper Tacks, Oval, 13 1/2 In. 875.00
Box, 5–Finger, Fitted Lid, 19th Century, 5 1/2 X 13 1/2 In. 995.00
Box, Candle, Dovetailed, Walnut, 1850s 695.00
Box, Cover, Yellow Paint, Oval, 10 1/2 In. 7700.00
Box, Document, Ivory Keyhole, Bird's–Eye Maple, 13 X 11 In. 795.00
Box, Knife, Bentwood, Turned Handle, Mustard Yellow, 8 1/4 X 13 In. 300.00
Box, Seed, Label, Mount Lebanon, Paper Label, 11 1/4 X 24 In. 375.00
Box, Seed, Shaker Seed Co., 6 Compartments, Hinged Cover 5610.00
Box, Seed, Shaker Seeds, Black & White Interior Label, Hinged Cover 1870.00
Box, Sewing, 3–Finger, Lined, Lillian Barlow, Oval, 9 1/4 X 6 In. 495.00
Box, Sewing, 3–Finger, Pincushion Top, Copper Tacks, C.1830, 3 5/8 In. 8000.00
Box, Sewing, 4–Finger, Oval, Bentwood, 3 3/8 In. 425.00
Box, Sewing, Handle, Oval, Lined, Sabbathday Lake, Maine, 8 In. 950.00
Box, Wooden, Cover, Blue Paint, 6 1/4 X 5 X 2 3/8 In. 175.00
Box, Wooden, Cover, Nailed, Oval, 5 X 4 1/4 X 2 1/2 In. 200.00
Box, Wooden, Cover, Oval, 7 1/8 X 4 3/4 X 1 5/8 In. 175.00
Broom, Corn, Maple Handle, Hand–Tied, New Lebanon, C.1870, 56 In. 250.00
Brush, Pastry, Maple 85.00
Carrier, Butternut, Swing Handle, Canterbury, N.H., 1840, Square, 6 In. 4000.00
Carrier, Maple, Pine, Hickory Handle, 3–Finger, C.1840, 11 In. 2200.00
Circular, Harvard North Family, J. Orsment As Agent, 1863, 6 X 4 In. 77.00
Clothespin, 13 Piece 82.50
Coffeepot, Tin, Short & Squat, 8 In. 150.00
Counter, Tailoring 1100.00
Dipper, Brass Bands, Bentwood Handle, Large Bowl, 11 1/2 In. 70.00
Dustpan, Blue 95.00
Flax Wheel, Frances Winker, Canterbury 1200.00
           SHAKER, FURNITURE, see Furniture
Glove Stretcher, Adjustable Thumb, Right Hand, Wooden, 6 1/2 In. 295.00
Hanger, Clothes, 16 In., Pair 110.00
Hanger, Clothes, Turned Wood, 17 3/4 In., Pair 50.00
Measure, Bentwood, Turned Handle, 8 In. 100.00
Mold, Doll's Bonnet, 3 Piece 605.00
Oven, Fireplace 95.00
Pail, Wire & Wood Handle, Good Boy, Horse & Stars, 4 3/4 In. 650.00
Rack, 4 Pegs, Stamped Shaker Society, Sabbathday Lake, 13 1/2 In. 95.00
Rack, 4 Pegs, Stamped Shaker Society, Sabbathday Lake, 23 In. 145.00
Rack, 6 Pegs, Stamped Shaker Society, Sabbathday Lake, 36 In. 225.00
Rack, Herb Drying, Pine & Black Ash, Watervliet, C.1830, 7 Ft.2 In. 1150.00
Scoop & Butter Curler, Maple, Hand Carved, Miniature 175.00
Sewing Kit, Unusual Style 58.00
Stool, Milking, Butternut, Pine, Arched Base, Varnish, 17 X 16 X 7 In. 2600.00
Stretcher, Embroidery, Maple, 18th Century, 31 X 26 In. 675.00
Sunbonnet, Woven, Poplar, Paper Label, 7 In. 225.00
Textile, Iridescent Silk & Wool, 2 Piece 275.00
Tray, Collection, Green Velvet Over Metal, 3 X 14 In. 250.00

Shaving mugs were popular from 1860 to 1900. Many types were made, including occupational mugs featuring pictures of men's jobs. There were scuttle mugs, silver plated mugs, glass–lined mugs, and others.

SHAVING MUG, Black Man 250.00
Embossed Busts of Mr. & Mrs. Garfield, Milk Glass 110.00
Flowers, 3 1/2 In. 6.00
Freedom, Charity, Friendship, Eagle Medallion, Name In Gold 125.00
Golden Knights Advertising 40.00
Horses, 3 1/2 In. 28.00
Occupational, Artist 275.00
Occupational, Artist, Palette & Brushes, Gold Initials 210.00
Occupational, Barber, Pair of Hair Clippers, Name 125.00
Occupational, Bartender, J.M. Long 350.00
Occupational, Bartender, Scene With 2 Customers, Gold Trim 200.00
Occupational, Bicycle, Ed Yowse 450.00

Occupational, Blacksmith, Shoeing Horse 125.00
Occupational, Boat Scene 250.00
Occupational, Bridge Builder 425.00
Occupational, Bridge Inspector, Rowboat, Stone Bridge 175.00
Occupational, Butcher .... 200.00 To 275.00
Occupational, Butcher, Multicolored, 3 3/4 In. 1430.00
Occupational, Butcher, Steer's Head, Butcher's Tools, Gold Name 185.00
Occupational, Carpenter 400.00
Occupational, Deer Hunter 200.00
Occupational, Dentist 195.00
Occupational, Drayman, Name 200.00
Occupational, Drayman, Top Hat, Driving Horse Drawn Wagon 450.00
Occupational, Druggest, Mortar & Pestle 50.00
Occupational, Engineer, Stationary Steam Engine, Gold Name 190.00
Occupational, Farrier 300.00
Occupational, Fireman, 3 Horses, 4 Firemen 850.00
Occupational, Grocer, Wagon 350.00
Occupational, Horse & Carriage 275.00
Occupational, Horse, Running 225.00
Occupational, Horseman, Horse's Head, Gold Design & Name 165.00
Occupational, Hunter 350.00
Occupational, Iceman 45.00
Occupational, Iceman, 3 1/2 In. 11.00
Occupational, Interior Decorator, Draperies, Floral Vase 475.00
Occupational, Mason 800.00
Occupational, Meat Cutter 175.00
Occupational, Mortician, Pink Floral, Yellow Band 125.00
Occupational, Printer, At Cabinet, Gold Trim 200.00
Occupational, Railroad Engineer 200.00
Occupational, Rancher 350.00
Occupational, Rod & Gun Club 450.00
Occupational, Stationary Engineer, Workhorse 350.00
Occupational, Tailor, Callahan, Gold Medallion, Ironstone 235.00
Occupational, Tavern Owner 500.00
Occupational, Teacher 135.00
Occupational, Telegrapher, Hand With Key Set 350.00
Occupational, Train Engine 375.00
Occupational, Train Engine, R.G. Rackley 65.00
Occupational, Trolley Car Operator, Meriden Electric R.R. 650.00
Occupational, United Mine Workers 150.00
Occupational, Waiter, Serving A Couple 1870.00
Scuttle, Figural, Chinese Man, Queue Handle, Bavaria, 3 3/4 In. 165.00
Scuttle, Figural, Dog's Head, Tan & White, Gold Trim, 3 5/8 In. 110.00
Scuttle, Figural, Monkey, White & Pink, Brown Hair, 3 3/4 In. 135.00
Tonique Liquid Headrest, Germany 35.00
U.S. Vermont, Eagle, Stars & Stripes, Limoges, 4 In. 176.00
Victorian, Bell Shaped Mirror Center, 3 3/4 In. 60.00
Victorian, Round Beveled Mirror Center, 3 In. 55.00

Shawnee USA   The Shawnee Pottery was started in Zanesville, Ohio, in 1935. The company made vases, novelty ware, flowerpots, figurines, dinnerwares, and cookie jars. Shawnee produced pottery for George Rumrill during the late 1930s. The company stopped working in 1961.

SHAWNEE, Bank, Winnie Pig, Chocolate Base 125.00
Basket 12.00
Bookends, Geese, Black 12.00
Bowl, Corn King, No.6 .... 20.00
Butter, Corn King, Cover .... 30.00 To 42.50
Casserole, Corn King 35.00
Cookie Jar, Corn King 105.00
Cookie Jar, Drummer Boy .... 85.00 To 88.00
Cookie Jar, Dutch Boy .... 45.00 To 60.00
Cookie Jar, Dutch Boy, Stripes .... 55.00 To 125.00

Cookie Jar, Dutch Girl, Tulip .... 60.00 To 78.00
Cookie Jar, Farmer Pig 50.00
Cookie Jar, Farmer Pig, Shamrock 85.00
Cookie Jar, Jug, Blue 45.00
Cookie Jar, Lucky Elephant, Gold .... 110.00 To 160.00
Cookie Jar, Lucky Elephant, Pink, White Collar .... 25.00 To 45.00
Cookie Jar, Mugsy Dog, Flower, Gold Trim 210.00
Cookie Jar, Puss 'N Boots .... 50.00 To 80.00
Cookie Jar, Puss 'N Boots, Flower, Gold Trim .... 115.00 To 145.00
Cookie Jar, Sailor Boy, Gold Trim 125.00
Cookie Jar, Smiley Pig, Blue Scarf .... 65.00 To 70.00
Cookie Jar, Smiley Pig, Red Scarf, Daisies 65.00
Cookie Jar, Winking Owl .... 65.00 To 105.00
Cookie Jar, Winking Owl, Gold Trim .... 82.00 To 120.00
Cookie Jar, Winnie Pig, Blue Collar, Gold Trim .... 119.00 To 145.00
Creamer, Lucky Elephant .... 10.00 To 20.00
Creamer, Pig, Gold Trim 45.00
Creamer, Puss 'N Boots .... 15.00 To 21.00
Creamer, Puss 'N Boots, Gold 50.00
Creamer, Puss 'N Boots, White 20.00
Creamer, Winnie Pig, Pink .... 12.50 To 18.00
Cup & Saucer, Corn Queen 20.00
Cup, Corn King, 5 Oz. 18.00
Figurine, Lamb, 6 In. 25.00
Flowerpot, Owl 10.00
Flowerpot, Puss 'N Boots 10.00
Flowerpot, Wheelbarrow 10.00
Pitcher, Bopeep, 8 In. .... 35.00 To 37.00
Pitcher, Chanticleer Rooster .... 25.00 To 35.00
Pitcher, Corn King, 8 In. 38.00
Pitcher, Corn King, Gold Trim, 1 Qt. 60.00
Pitcher, Corn Queen .... 22.00 To 30.00
Pitcher, Elephant, Gold 45.00
Pitcher, Milk, Bopeep 38.00
Pitcher, Puss 'N Boots 20.00
Pitcher, Smiley Pig, Red Bib 12.00
Pitcher, Smiley Pig, Red Flowers 40.00
Pitcher, Water, Chanticleer Rooster 40.00
Planter, Bicycle For Two 20.00
Planter, Bull, Brown 9.00
Planter, Chihuahua 15.00
Planter, Giraffe 20.00
Planter, Globe, 7 In. 20.00
Planter, Pig 15.00
Planter, Polynesian Girl, 6 In. 16.00
Planter, Squirrel 8.00
Planter, Squirrel, Pulling Acorn 25.00
Planter, Teddy Bear, With Cart 25.00
Planter, Three Pigs 4.00
Planter, Truck, 2 Piece 12.50
Planter, Wishing Well 25.00
Planter, Woman, Seated, With Flowers 18.00
Plate, Corn King 15.00
Relish, Corn King .... 14.00 To 20.00
Salt & Pepper, Baker 15.00
Salt & Pepper, Chanticleer Rooster, Large .... 18.00 To 20.00
Salt & Pepper, Chef 16.00
Salt & Pepper, Corn .... 12.50 To 28.50
Salt & Pepper, Dog 15.00
Salt & Pepper, Duck 15.00
Salt & Pepper, Dutch Boy & Girl, Gold Trim .... 12.00 To 15.00
Salt & Pepper, Falstaff Beer, 4 1/4 In. 25.00
Salt & Pepper, Kittens 12.00
Salt & Pepper, Mammy & Mose 10.00

Salt & Pepper, Milk Can	10.00 To 12.00
Salt & Pepper, Mugsy	16.00
Salt & Pepper, Mugsy, Large	22.50
Salt & Pepper, Owl	6.50 To 9.00
Salt & Pepper, Owl, Gold Trim	18.00 To 25.00
Salt & Pepper, Puss 'N Boots	6.50
Salt & Pepper, Puss 'N Boots, Small	10.00
Salt & Pepper, Sailor	15.00
Salt & Pepper, Smiley Pig, Green Bib, Large	35.00
Salt & Pepper, Smiley Pig, Peach Bib	15.00
Salt & Pepper, Smiley Pig, Red Bib	45.00
Shaker, Corn King	15.00
Sugar & Creamer, Corn King	45.00
Sugar, Corn King, Cover	20.00
Teapot, Black Engine	35.00
Teapot, Cookie House	250.00
Teapot, Corn King	75.00 To 80.00
Teapot, Elephant, Yellow	45.00
Teapot, Granny Ann	30.00 To 45.00
Teapot, Granny Ann, Gold Trim	60.00
Teapot, Tom, Tom, The Piper's Son, White	25.00 To 45.00
Vase, Doe In Shadowbox, Gray	18.00
Vase, Gray, 7 In.	15.00

The Shearwater pottery is a family business started by Mr. and Mrs. G. W. Anderson, Sr., and their three sons. The local Ocean Springs, Mississippi, clays were used to make the wares in the 1930s. The company is still in business.

SHEARWATER, Bowl, High Glaze Turquoise, 4 1/2 X 9 In.	60.00
Figurine, Black Mammy, Basket On Head, 6 In.	120.00
Figurine, Black Rider On Horse, 6 In.	120.00
Figurine, Cat, Gunmetal Green, 4 X 5 In.	90.00
Figurine, Pirate, Multicolor High Glaze, 6 In.	65.00
Vase, Glossy Turquoise, 8 3/4 In.	45.00
Vase, Green Matte, Double Handles, 5 1/2 In.	60.00
Vase, Green, Brown, Bottle Shape, 6 In.	25.00
Vase, High Gloss, 6 X 7 In.	50.00

Sheet music from the past centuries is now collected. The favorites are examples with covers featuring artistic or historic pictures. Early sheet music covers were lithographed but by the 1900s photographic reproductions were used. The early music was larger than more recent sheets and you must watch out for examples that were trimmed to fit in a twentieth-century piano bench.

SHEET MUSIC, Ain't Got No Use For Sleep, Black Cover	5.00
All Shook Up, Photograph of Elvis Presley	36.00
Apple Jack Rag	20.00
Army Bonds Today, Irving Berlin, 1941	7.50
As Time Goes By, Ingrid Bergman, Humphrey Bogart	20.00
Babes In Arms	12.00
Barney Google, 1923	22.00
Beautiful Isle Somewhere, McKinley's Picture, E. Excell, 1901	8.00
Beeswax Rag, 1911	15.00
Big Brown Bear, 1919	15.95
Bromo–Seltzer, Guard The Flag March, 1899, 14 In.	12.50
Bromo–Seltzer, Manila Quickstep, 1899, 4 Pages	20.00
Can't Help Falling In Love, 1961	20.00
Carolina Mammy, Aunt Jemima Photo Cover, 1923	12.50
Chili Sauce Rag, Heinz Sauce	15.00
Copper Colored Gal	10.00
Darktown Strutters Ball	16.00
Day At The Races, Marx Brothers, Groucho, Chico & Harpo	25.00
Did I Remember, Jean Harlow	20.00
Dinah, Eddie Cantor In Blackface, 1931	14.00

Down In Jungletown, Madden, Morse, Monkey Ditty, 1908	8.00
Dreams of Long Ago, Composed & Recorded By Caruso	12.00
Four Little Blackberries	16.00
Good–By–Boys, Al Jolson, The Honeymoon Express, Dated 1918	16.00
Henry's Made A Lady Out of Lizzie, Henry Ford, 1928	10.00
Horse Feathers, Marx Brothers, 4 Brothers On Cartoon Horse	25.00
Huckleberry Finn Cake Walk, Brennan, 1900	15.00
I'm Following You, Duncan Sisters	10.00
I'm On My Way To Dublin Bay, Murphy, 1905	8.00
In The City Where Nobody Cares, Street Scene	5.00
Inky Dinks	16.00
Is It True What They Say About Dixie, Blackface Jolson	10.00
Johnny Guitar, Joan Crawford	45.00
Just A Little Fond Affection, Kate Smith, 1934	7.50
Just As The Ship Went Down, Titanic	25.00
Let's All Be Americans Now, Irving Berlin, World War I	10.00
Lindy's Triumphant March	12.00
Little Cotton Pickers, Children, Mammy On Cover, 1944	20.00
Lusitania March & 2 Step, Drawing of Ship, 1908	20.00
Mary's A Grand Old Name, Photograph of James Cagney Dancing	12.00
My Darling, My Darling, Where's Charley, Ray Bolger, 1948	10.00
My Sugar Coated Chocolate Boy, 1919	10.00
Old Gray Mare, 1817	6.00
Over There, Rockwell Cover	35.00
Ragpicker Rag, Blacks	20.00
River of No Return, Marilyn Monroe	25.00
Rock Around The Clock, Photograph of Bill Haley & The Comets	25.00
San Francisco, Clark Gable & Jeanette MacDonald	12.00
Shoo–Shoo Baby, 3 Cheers For The Boys, Andrews Sisters, 1943	8.50
Short'Nin' Bread, Hawaiian Guitar Solo, 1939	10.00
Silk & Rags, Blacks	28.00
Sippin Cider Thru A Straw, Fatty Arbuckle Picture, 1919	18.00
Song For The Union, F. Scott, Folded, 1850	25.00
Songs of Safety, Rose O'Neill Illustrated, 1937	35.00
Southern Military Music, A.E. Blackmar, New Orleans, 1863	40.00
Stars & Stripes Forever, John P. Sousa, 1897	8.50
Stormy Weather, Lena Horne, 1933	12.50
Surrey With The Fringe On Top	10.00
Thanks For The Memory, Big Broadcast of 1938	15.00
The White Wash Man, Black Cover	5.00
There's Nothing Half So Nice As Big Slice of Ham, Blacks	5.00
They Made It Twice As Nice, Paradise, Dixieland, Blacks, 1916	15.00
They're On Their Way To Mexico, Soldiers, I. Berlin, 1914	10.00
Trottin' At The Cotton Pickin' Ball	10.00
Uncle Tom's Cabin Rag, 1911	15.00
Underneath The Harlem Moon, 1942	9.00
Volga Boatman Song, Xavier Cugat Cover, 1938	5.00
Washington & Lee Swing, 1920	5.00
When It's Circus Day Back Home, 1917	35.00
When That Midnight Choo Choo Leaves For Alabam, Train Cover	5.00
Whistle While You Work, 1937	20.00
White Christmas, I. Berlin, 1943	7.50
Wizard of Oz, Heads of Stars Cover, 1939	40.00
Wreck of Titanic	25.00
Younger Than Springtime, South Pacific, Mary Martin, 1949	10.00

SHEFFIELD, see Silver–English; Silver Plate

The name Shelley first appeared on English ceramics about 1912. The Foley China Works started in England in 1860. Joseph Ball Shelley joined the company in 1862 and became a partner in 1872. Percy Shelley joined the firm in 1881. The company went through a series of name changes and in 1910 the then Foley China Company became Shelley China. In 1929 it became Shelley Potteries. The

company was acquired in 1966 by Allied English Potteries, then
merged with the Doulton group in 1971. The name Shelley was put
into use again in 1980.

SHELLEY, Ashtray, Blue Rock	30.00
Bowl, Vegetable, Cover, Dainty Blue	225.00
Bread Plate, Dainty Blue	20.00
Breakfast Set, Rose Spray, 7 Piece	490.00
Cake Plate, Rosebud, Handle, 8 In.	48.00
Coffeepot, Pansy, White & Gold	48.00
Coffeepot, Sugar & Creamer, Begonia, 3 Piece	185.00
Creamer, Blue Rock	25.00
Cup & Saucer, Begonia	38.50
Cup & Saucer, Blue Dot	40.00
Cup & Saucer, Bridal Rose	32.00
Cup & Saucer, Dainty Blue	38.50
Cup & Saucer, Pansy, Yellow Edge	45.00
Cup & Saucer, Primrose	32.00
Cup & Saucer, Rose Spray, Demitasse	95.00
Cup & Saucer, Rosebud	30.00 To 38.50
Dish, Pancake, Cover, Blue Dot, 7 1/2 In.	60.00
Eggcup, Blue Dot	40.00
Eggcup, White Shell	25.00
Figurine, Armored Car, Crest	75.00
Figurine, Speedboat, Crest	50.00
Gravy Boat, Dainty Blue	125.00
Mustard, Underplate, Rosebud	55.00
Plate, Begonia, 8 In.	30.00
Plate, Dainty Blue, 8 In.	40.00
Plate, Rose Spray, 8 In.	30.00
Plate, Rosebud, 5 1/2 In.	18.00
Plate, Rosebud, 10 In.	85.00
Plate, Violet, 8 In.	38.00
Platter, Dainty Blue, 13 In.	95.00
Saucer, Begonia	7.00
Saucer, Daffodils	7.00
Soup, Dish, Rosebud, Rimmed, 8 In.	30.00
Sugar & Creamer, Rose Spray	65.00
Sugar & Creamer, Tray, White, Fluted, 3 Piece	48.00
Teapot, Rosebud, Small	140.00
Vase, Gray, Pink, 3 1/4 In.	37.50
Vase, Memorial Scene	12.00

Shirley Temple, the famous movie star, was born in 1928. She made
her first movie in 1932. Thousands of items picturing Shirley have
been and still are being made. Shirley Temple dolls were first made
in 1934 by Ideal Toy Company. Millions of Shirley Temple cobalt
blue glass dishes were made by Hazel Atlas Glass Company and
U.S. Glass Company from 1934 to 1942. They were given away as
premiums for Wheaties and Bisquick. A bowl, mug, and pitcher
were made as a breakfast set. Some pieces were decorated with the
picture of a very young Shirley, others used a picture of Shirley in
her 1936 "Captain January" costume. Although collectors refer to a
cobalt creamer it is actually the 4 1/2 inch high milk pitcher from
the breakfast set. Many of these items are being reproduced today.

SHIRLEY TEMPLE, Book, 1933	40.00
Book, Dimples	20.00
Book, Sing Along With Shirley Temple Song Album, 1935	35.00
Book, Susannah of The Mounties, 1936	20.00 To 35.00
Book, Through The Day	15.00
Carriage, Wicker	450.00
Doll, 1957, 19 In.	300.00
Doll, Composition, Plaid Dress, Ideal, 18 In.	375.00
Doll, Effanbee, Hawaiian, 13 In.	475.00

Doll, Ideal, 36 In.	795.00
Doll, Ideal, C.1935, 22 In.	550.00
Doll, Jointed Wrists, Ideal, 1950s, 35 In.	950.00
Doll, Little Colonel, Composition, 17 In.	700.00
Doll, Music, 18 In.	395.00
Doll, Original Wig & Clothes, Button, Ideal, 20 In.	450.00
Doll, Original Wig, Blue Sunsuit, Polka Dots, 1930s, 18 In.	250.00
Doll, Sleep Eyes, Composition, Crazed Paint, 12 In.	143.00
Doll, Vinyl, Tagged Slip, Pin, Box, 1958, 12 In.	210.00
Dress, Cinderella, Red Velvet, White Nylon, Size 4	15.00
Magazine, Now I Am Eight	15.00
Mirror, Hand, 1934	10.00
Mirror, Pocket, Advertising, Set of 4	11.00
Mug, Cobalt Blue	30.00 To 35.00
Paper Doll, 5 Outfits, 34 In.	125.00
Paper Doll, Box	15.00
Paper Doll, Masquerade Costumes	185.00
Paper Doll, Saalfield, 1936, Life Size	90.00
Pin, Cloisonne, From Baby Takes A Bow	9.00
Pin, Cloisonne, Sailor Girl	11.00
Pitcher, Cobalt Blue	47.50
Poster Stamp, Little Princess, With Doll, 1939	5.00
Poster, Adventure In Baltimore, 1949	85.00
Program, Movie, Since You Went Away	25.00
Sewing Cards, Box	65.00
Sheet Music, At The Codfish Ball, Captain January, 1936	15.00
Sheet Music, I'Ll Be Seeing You, Movie, Rogers, Cotten, 1948	12.50
Sheet Music, On The Good Ship Lollipop, 1934	12.50 To 15.50
Sheet Music, Stowaway	18.50
Sheet Music, That's What I Want For Christmas, 1935, 6 Pg.	19.00
Sign, Puffed Wheat, Spends Her Vacation, 1937, 13 X 15 In.	10.00
Table Set, Cobalt Blue, 3 Piece	110.00 To 135.00
Television Theater	65.00
Wristwatch	35.00

SHRINER, see Fraternal

Silver deposit glass was made during the late nineteenth and early twentieth centuries. Solid sterling silver was applied to the glass by a chemical method so that a cutout design of silver metal appeared against a clear or colored glass. It is sometimes called silver overlay.

SILVER DEPOSIT, Mayonnaise, Underplate, Daisy Centers, Darts, Feather Points	36.00
Pitcher, Flowers, Tendrils, Pedestal, Bulbous, 7 1/2 In.	40.00
Vase, Duncan & Miller, Black, 9 In.	155.00

Listed in this section are many of the current and out–of–production silver and silver plated flatware patterns made in the past eighty years. Other silver is listed under Silver–American, Silver–English, etc. Most silver flatware sets that are missing a few pieces can be completed through the help of one of the many silver matching services listed in "The Kovels' Collectors' Source Book."

SILVER FLATWARE PLATED, Adoration, Butter Knife, Master, 1847 Rogers	6.00
Adoration, Teaspoon, 1847 Rogers	3.00 To 3.50
Bird of Paradise, Salad Fork, Community	5.00
Bird of Paradise, Sugar & Creamer, Community	45.00
Charter Oak, Cocktail Fork	18.00
Charter Oak, Grapefruit Spoon	18.00
Charter Oak, Spreader, Individual	16.00
Columbia, Salad Fork, 1847 Rogers	35.00
Columbia, Sugar Tongs, 1847 Rogers	45.00
Columbia, Tomato Server, 1847 Rogers	65.00
Daffodil, Baby Fork, 1847 Rogers	10.00
Daffodil, Butter Spreader, 1847 Rogers	12.50
Daffodil, Cocktail Fork, 1847 Rogers	12.50

Daffodil, Dinner Fork, 1847 Rogers 9.00
Daffodil, Dinner Knife, 1847 Rogers 10.00
Daffodil, Gravy Ladle, 1847 Rogers 30.00
Daffodil, Soup Ladle, 1847 Rogers 125.00
Daffodil, Sugar Tongs, 1847 Rogers .... 30.00 To 38.00
Daffodil, Teaspoon, 1847 Rogers 4.50
Daffodil, Vegetable Spoon, 1847 Rogers 50.00
Eternally Yours, Dinner Knife, 1847 Rogers 8.00
Eternally Yours, Fruit Spoon, 1847 Rogers 12.50
Eternally Yours, Iced Tea Spoon, 1847 Rogers 12.50
Evening Star, Teaspoon, Community 3.00
First Love, Carving Set, 1847 Rogers 100.00
First Love, Dinner Knife, 1847 Rogers 8.00
First Love, Pastry Server, 1847 Rogers 40.00
First Love, Sugar Tongs, 1847 Rogers 40.00
First Love, Teaspoon, 1847 Rogers 3.50
Hampton Court, Service For 6, Community, 49 Piece 225.00
Heraldic, Iced Tea Spoon, 1847 Rogers 12.50
Heraldic, Salad Fork, 1847 Rogers 5.00
Heritage, Dinner Fork, 1847 Rogers 7.00
Heritage, Salad Fork, 1847 Rogers 8.00
Leilani, Demitasse Spoon, 1847 Rogers 10.00
Morning Star, Tablespoon, Community 8.00
Morning Star, Teaspoon, Community 3.00
New Elegance, Dinner Knife, Gorham 8.00
New Elegance, Gravy Ladle, Gorham 12.00
New Elegance, Salad Fork, Gorham 6.00
Newport, Gravy Ladle, 1847 Rogers 25.00
Old Colony, Cocktail Fork, 1847 Rogers 10.00
Old Colony, Ice Cream Fork, 1847 Rogers 30.00
Old Colony, Iced Tea Spoon, 1847 Rogers 20.00
Orchid, Salad Serving Fork, Rogers 40.00
Remembrance, Carving Set, 1847 Rogers, 2 Piece 65.00
Remembrance, Dinner Fork, 1847 Rogers 4.00
Remembrance, Salad Fork, 1847 Rogers 7.00
Remembrance, Teaspoon, 1847 Rogers .... 3.00 To 3.50
Sheraton, Pie Fork, Community 12.00
Treasure, Berry Spoon, Wm. Rogers 12.00
Treasure, Gravy Ladle, Wm. Rogers 12.00
Treasure, Service For 8, Wm. Rogers, 1940, 61 Piece 275.00
Vintage, Cocktail Fork, 1847 Rogers 15.00
Vintage, Oyster Ladle, 1847 Rogers 15.00
Vintage, Pie Server, 1847 Rogers 135.00
Vintage, Salad Fork, 1847 Rogers 40.00
Vintage, Service For 12, 1847 Rogers, 135 Piece 1620.00
Vintage, Sugar Tongs, 1847 Rogers 50.00
SILVER FLATWARE STERLING, 1776, Bouillon Spoon, Dominick & Haff 15.00
1776, Teaspoon, Dominick & Haff 13.00
Adam, Lemon Fork, Whiting 12.00
Adam, Pie Server, Whiting 195.00
American Chippendale, Fork, F. Smith 15.00
Aristocrat, Iced Tea Spoon, Towle 16.00
Aristocrat, Pickle Fork, Towle 15.00
Aristocrat, Tablespoon, Towle 25.00
Arlington, Dessert Spoon, Towle 21.00
Armor, Jelly Spoon, Whiting 45.00
Avalon, Salad Set, International 325.00
Avon, Sugar Spoon, Fessenden 27.00
Baronial, Sardine Tongs, Gorham 45.00
Bead, Tablespoon, Durgin 27.00
Benjamin Franklin, Butter Knife, Towle 15.00
Betsy Patterson, Pickle Fork, Stieff 18.00
Blossom Time, Cream Soup Spoon, International 35.00
Bridal Rose, Cold Meat Fork, Alvin 235.00

Bridal Rose, Teaspoon, Alvin	10.00
Buckingham, Sugar Spoon, Gorham	19.00
Burgundy, Dinner Knife, Reed & Barton	30.00
Buttercup, Asparagus Server, Gorham	395.00
Buttercup, Fish Fork, Gorham	35.00
Buttercup, Ice Cream Fork, Gorham	28.00
Buttercup, Salad Serving Spoon, Gorham	125.00
Buttercup, Seafood Fork, Gold Wash, Gorham	35.00
Buttercup, Sugar Tongs, Gorham	38.00
Cambridge, Asparagus Fork, Gorham	245.00
Cambridge, Chocolate Muddler, Gorham	65.00
Cambridge, Fork, Gorham	18.00
Cambridge, Sugar Shell, Gorham	24.00
Cambridge, Teaspoon, Gorham	11.00
Candlelight, Cold Meat Fork, Towle	36.00
Canterbury, Mustard Ladle, Towle	85.00
Canterbury, Serving Berry Spoon, Towle	60.00
Carrollton, Cheese Scoop, Stieff	48.00
Cascade, Cold Meat Fork, Towle, 8 In.	40.00
Cat Tails, Lemon Fork, Durgin	75.00
Celeste, Service For 8, Gorham, 48 Piece	1040.00
Chantilly, Butter Fork, Gorham	45.00
Chantilly, Carving Fork, Gorham	19.99
Chantilly, Fruit Spoon, Gorham	18.00
Chantilly, Lettuce Spoon, Gorham	150.00
Chantilly, Nut Spoon, Gorham	24.00
Chantilly, Salad Set, Gorham	180.00
Chantilly, Teaspoon, Gorham	8.00
Chantilly, Tomato Server, Gorham	58.00
Chapel Bells, Service For 8, Alvin, 48 Piece	650.00
Charles II, Claret Ladle, Dominick & Haff	175.00
Charles II, Ice Cream Knife, Dominick & Haff	335.00
Chateau Rose, Service For 8, Alvin, 48 Piece	975.00
Chippendale, Bonbon Spoon, Lunt	24.00
Chrysanthemum, Butter Pick, Gold Wash, Durgin	110.00
Chrysanthemum, Fork, Durgin, 7 In.	39.00
Chrysanthemum, Sugar Spoon, Durgin	60.00
Clermont, Lemon Fork, Gorham	16.00
Cloeta, Bonbon Spoon, International	45.00
Cloeta, Gravy Ladle, International	145.00
Cloeta, Luncheon Knife, International	40.00
Cloeta, Soup Ladle, Intenational	375.00
Clover, Salad Set, Towle, Dated 1887	225.00
Colfax, Service For 8, Durgin, 32 Piece	640.00
Colonnade, Cream Soup Spoon, Manchester	12.00
Colonnade, Luncheon Fork, Manchester	17.00
Cordova, Cream Soup Ladle, Towle	30.00
Crown Princess, Knife, International, 9 1/4 In.	16.00
Cupid, Tablespoon, Dominick & Haff	50.00
Damask Rose, Luncheon Setting, Oneida, 4 Piece	48.00
Damask Rose, Sauce Ladle, Oneida	30.00
Decor, Punch Ladle, Gorham	495.00
Decor, Salt Spoon, Gorham	14.00
Devon, Bouillon Spoon, Reed & Barton	10.00
Dorothy Bradford, Sauce Ladle, Towle	28.00
Dorothy Vernon, Cold Meat Fork, Whiting	90.00
Dorothy Vernon, Dessert Spoon, Whiting	35.00
Duke of York, Asparagus Fork, Monogram, Whiting	250.00
Duke of York, Bouillon Spoon, Whiting	16.00
Duke of York, Food Pusher, Whiting	55.00
Eloquence, Luncheon Setting, Lunt, 4 Piece	90.00
Eloquence, Pierced Tablespoon, Lunt	95.00
Empire, Fruit Spoon, Whiting	18.00
Empire, Salad Fork, Towle	15.00

English Gadroon, Place Setting, Gorham, 4 Piece	65.00
Etruscan, Bonbon, Gorham	25.00
Etruscan, Butter Knife, Master, Gorham	16.00 To 18.00
Etruscan, Chocolate Spoon, Gorham	12.00
Etruscan, Jelly Spreader, Gorham	14.00
Etruscan, Service For 12, Gorham, 60 Piece	1320.00
Etruscan, Tablespoon, Gorham	32.00
Fairfax, Beef Fork, Durgin	55.00
Fairfax, Cream Soup Spoon, Gorham	16.00
Fairfax, Ice Tongs, Durgin	195.00
Fairfield, Mustard Ladle, Whiting	35.00
Federal Cotillion, Butter Knife, Frank Smith	18.00
Federal Cotillion, Soup Spoon, Frank Smith	22.00
Florentine, Fish Fork, Gorham	45.00
Florentine, Fish Knife, Gorham	60.00
Florentine, Iced Tea Spoon, Gorham	55.00
Fontaine, Pie Server, International	27.00
Fontaine, Sugar Spoon, International	21.00
Fontaine, Teaspooon, International	12.00
Fontainebleau, Jelly Trowel, Gorham	195.00
Francis I, Baby Set, Reed & Barton	45.00
Francis I, Lemon Fork, Reed & Barton	55.00
Francis I, Place Setting, Reed & Barton, 4 Piece	105.00
Francis I, Soup Ladle, Reed & Barton	210.00
Francis I, Sugar Spoon, Reed & Barton	25.00
Francis I, Tomato Server, Reed & Barton	375.00
Frontenac, Fork, International, 7 1/8 In.	22.00
Frontenac, Jelly Trowel, International	135.00
Gainsborough, Vegetable Spoon, Alvin, 9 In.	80.00
Georgian, Butter Pick, Towle	110.00
Georgian, Cheese Server, Towle	235.00
Georgian, Place Setting, Towle, 4 Piece	198.00
Georgian, Sugar Spoon, Towle	38.00
Georgian, Teaspoon, Towle	23.00
Governor Winthrop, Iced Tea Spoon, Whiting	14.00
Governor Winthrop, Spoon, Oval, Whiting	15.00
Grande Baroque, Cake Fork, 3 Prong, Wallace	27.50
Grande Baroque, Cream Soup Spoon, Wallace	40.00
Grande Baroque, Pie Fork, Wallace	75.00
Grande Baroque, Punch Ladle, Wallace	225.00 To 450.00
Grecian, Ice Cream Server, Gorham	150.00
Grecian, Pudding Spoon, Gorham	150.00
Grecian, Sugar Sifter, Gorham	165.00
Greenbrier, Cream Soup Spoon, Gorham	14.00
Greenbrier, Place Setting, Gorham, 4 Piece	68.00
Greenbrier, Teaspoon, Gorham	13.00
Guildhall, Place Setting, Reed & Barton, 4 Piece	85.00
Hamilton, Gravy Ladle, Alvin	55.00
Heiress, Luncheon Setting, Oneida, 4 Piece	55.00
Heraldic, Preserve Spoon, Whiting	48.00
Heraldic, Salad Set, Whiting, 2 Piece	595.00
Hunt Club, Cream Spoon, Gorham	16.00
Hunt Club, Place Setting, Gorham, 4 Piece	95.00
Imperial Queen, Pie Server, Gold Wash, Whiting	165.00
Imperial Queen, Punch Ladle, Whiting	400.00
Imperial Queen, Serving Salad Fork, Whiting	95.00
Imperial Queen, Strawberry Fork, Whiting	30.00
Imperial Queen, Youth Fork, Whiting	18.00
Intermezzo, Cream Soup Spoon, National	14.00
Intermezzo, Salad Fork, National	17.00
Iris, Fruit Spoon, Durgin	75.00
Ivy, Berry Spoon, Gorham	145.00
Ivy, Sugar Sifter, Gorham	120.00 To 275.00
Joan of Arc, Place Setting, International, 4 Pc.	70.00

Josephine, Dinner Fork, Gorham 38.00
Josephine, Soup Ladle, Gorham 275.00
Kensington, Toast Fork, Gorham 135.00
King Albert, Ice Tongs, Whiting 225.00
King Cedric, Gravy Ladle, Oneida 48.00
King Edward, Dinner Fork, Whiting 45.00
King Edward, Ice Cream Fork, Gorham 28.00
King Edward, Ice Tongs, Whiting 350.00
King Edward, Mustard Ladle, Whiting 195.00
King Edward, Salad Fork, Gorham 25.00
King Edward, Salad Fork, Whiting 50.00
King George, Sugar Sifter, Enameled, Gorham 185.00
King Richard, Baked Potato Fork, Towle 55.00
Kings, Bonbon Spoon, Pierced, Towle 23.00
Kings, Soup Spoon, Towle 30.00
La Parisienne, Bonbon Spoon, Reed & Barton 55.00
La Parisienne, Luncheon Fork, Reed & Barton 18.00
La Parisienne, Teaspoon, Reed & Barton 18.00
La Reine, Cheese Scoop, Reed & Barton 70.00
La Reine, Strawberry Fork, Reed & Barton 40.00
La Splendide, Sugar Tongs, Reed & Barton 46.00
Lace Point, Luncheon Setting, Lunt, 4 Piece 55.00
Lady Baltimore, Baby Food Pusher, Whiting 15.00
Lady Constance, Ice Cream Fork, Towle 20.00
Lady Diane, Service For 12, Towle, 48 Piece 960.00
Lafayette, Steak Set, Towle, 2 Piece 75.00
Lancaster, Beef Fork, Gorham 55.00
Lancaster, Chocolate Spoon, Gorham 25.00
Lancaster, Cold Meat Fork, Gorham 65.00
Lancaster, Crumber, Gorham .... 165.00 To 225.00
Lancaster, Dinner Knife, Gorham .... 45.00 To 70.00
Lancaster, Fish Fork, Gorham, 6 Piece 360.00
Lancaster, Fried Oyster Server, Gorham 375.00
Lancaster, Lettuce Fork, Gorham 65.00
Lancaster, Meat Fork, Gold Wash, Gorham, 9 In. 65.00
Lancaster, Olive Spoon, Gorham 65.00
Lancaster, Sardine Fork, Gorham 52.00
Lancaster, Soup Ladle, Gold Wash, Gorham 375.00
Lancaster, Waffle Server, Gorham 75.00
Lenore, Butter Knife, Master, Manchester 13.00
Lenore, Tablespoon, Manchester 32.00
Les Cinq Fleurs, Butter Pick, Reed & Barton 110.00
Les Cinq Fleurs, Gravy Ladle, Reed & Barton 135.00
Les Cinq Fleurs, Orange Spoon, Reed & Barton 30.00
Les Cinq Fleurs, Sugar Tongs, Reed & Barton 55.00
Lily of The Valley, Sauce Ladle, Whiting 85.00
Lily, Teaspoon, Whiting 30.00
Louis XV, Asparagus Fork, Whiting 225.00
Louis XV, Service For 6, Whiting, 36 Piece 1950.00
Louis XV, Sugar Tongs, Whiting 42.00
Love Disarmed, Teaspoon, Reed & Barton 65.00
Lucerne, Butter Pick, Wallace 35.00
Lucerne, Ice Cream Spoon, Wallace 30.00
Lucerne, Teaspoon, Wallace 20.00
Luxembourg, Cherry Fork, Gorham 35.00
Luxembourg, Cracked Ice Spoon, Gorham 495.00
Luxembourg, Horseradish Spoon, Gorham 75.00
Luxembourg, Sardine Fork, Gorham 48.00
Lyric, Buillon Spoon, Monogram, Gorham 14.00
Madame Jumel, Cocktail Fork, Whiting 28.00
Madame Jumel, Demitasse Spoon, Whiting 55.00
Madame Royale, Egg Spoon, Durgin 25.00
Madame Royale, Serving Spoon, Durgin 40.00
Madrigal, Place Setting, Luncheon, Lunt, 4 Piece 58.00

Madrigal, Service For 8, Lunt, 32 Piece 696.00
Majestic, Cucumber Server, Alvin 95.00
Majestic, Sardine Fork, Alvin 48.00
Manchester, Cream Ladle, Manchester 35.00
Mandarin, Place Setting, Luncheon, Towle, 4 Piece 75.00
Marcell, Sugar Shell, International 24.00
Marechal Niel, Cold Meat Fork, Durgin 225.00
Marechal Niel, Lemon Fork, Durgin 35.00
Margaret Rose, Dinner Fork, National 21.00
Margaret Rose, Salad Fork, National 12.00
Margaret, Mustard Ladle, National 40.00
Marie Antoinette, Sugar Shell, Dominick & Haff 22.00
Martinique, Teaspoon, Oneida 12.00
Mary Chilton, Fork, Towle, 7 1/4 In. 19.00
Mary Chilton, Jelly Spoon, Towle 45.00
Mary Chilton, Tablespoon, Towle 32.00
Mazarin, Dessert Spoon, Dominick & Haff 23.00
Mazarin, Strawberry Fork, Dominick & Haff 28.00
Mazarin, Sugar Sifter, Dominick & Haff 65.00
Mazarin, Tablespoon, Dominick & Haff 35.00
Medallion, Sugar Tongs, Gorham .... 85.00 To 95.00
Medici, Place Setting, Luncheon, Gorham, 4 Piece 88.00
Melrose, Sugar Shell, Alvin 30.00
Mount Vernon, Fruit Spoon, Lunt 35.00
Napoleon, Sugar Shell, International 22.00
New Art, Berry Spoon, Gold Wash, Durgin 394.00
New King, Butter, Master, Dominick & Haff 85.00
New King, Gravy Ladle, Dominick & Haff 115.00
Newbury, Relish Spoon, Large, Towle 95.00
Newport Shell, Pickle Fork, Frank Smith 22.00
Norfolk, Chocolate Spoon, Gorham, 6 Piece 90.00
Northern Lights, Gravy Ladle, International 42.00
Oak, Sugar Shell, Frank Smith 45.00
Old Colonial, Butter Knife, Towle 25.00
Old Colonial, Steak Knife, Towle 28.00
Old Colonial, Sugar Spoon, Towle 40.00
Old English, Fork, Towle, 7 1/2 In. 19.00
Old English, Olive Fork, Towle 15.00
Old English, Teaspoon, Towle 8.00
Old King, Gravy Ladle, Whiting 65.00
Old King, Sugar Shell, Whiting 40.00
Old Lace, Butter Knife, Towle 9.00
Old Lace, Sugar Spoon, Towle 17.00
Old Maryland, Cream Soup Spoon, Kirk 28.00
Old Maryland, Ice Tongs, Kirk 115.00
Old Maryland, Jelly Spoon, Kirk 22.00
Old Maryland, Meat Fork, Kirk 90.00
Old Maryland, Sugar Sifter, Kirk 85.00
Old Master, Teaspoon, Towle 15.00
Old Mirror, Berry Spoon, Towle 105.00
Old Mirror, Jelly Spoon, Towle 30.00
Old Mirror, Sauce Ladle, Towle 60.00
Old Newbury, Luncheon Fork, Towle 12.00
Old Newbury, Salad Fork, Towle 25.00
Old Newbury, Sauce Ladle, Towle 45.00
Old Newbury, Tablespoon, Towle 25.00
Orange Blossom, Ladle, Alvin, 13 1/2 In. 450.00
Orange Blossom, Teaspoon, Alvin 25.00
Orient, Teaspoon, Alvin 15.00
Park Avenue, Pickle Fork, Manchester 14.00
Park Avenue, Teaspoon, Manchester 13.00
Patrician, Ice Cream Slice, Gorham 195.00
Plymouth, Cream Soup Spoon, Manchester 14.00
Plymouth, Gumbo Soup Spoon, Manchester 15.00

Pomona, Salt, Master, Gold Wash, Towle	45.00
Pomona, Tablespoon, Towle	28.00
Pompadour, Fork, Whiting, 6 7/8 In.	30.00
Poppy, Berry Spoon, Gorham	85.00
Poppy, Butter Knife, Gorham	16.00
Poppy, Cake Knife, Gorham	125.00
Poppy, Tongs, Gorham, 4 1/2 In.	22.00
Quadrille, Salad Fork, Kirk	40.00
Radiant, Luncheon Fork, Whiting	25.00
Raleigh, Butter Pick, Alvin	60.00
Raleigh, Ice Tongs, Alvin	195.00
Raleigh, Sugar Tongs, Alvin	36.00
Rambler Rose, Butter, Towle	12.00
Rambler Rose, Teaspoon, Towle	12.00
Rambler, Sugar Spoon, Towle	14.00
Raphael, Berry Spoon, Gorham	85.00
Raphael, Oyster Ladle, Gorham	325.00
Regent, Sugar Spoon, Alvin	12.00
Regent, Tablespoon, Alvin	28.00
Repousse, Cake Trowel, Kirk	195.00
Repousse, Carving Set, Kirk, 2 Piece	295.00
Repousse, Pickle Fork, Kirk	20.00
Repousse, Service For 8, Kirk, 32 Piece	825.00
Repousse, Sugar Shell, Kirk	55.00
Repousse, Tomato Server, Kirk	145.00
Repousse, Tongs, Kirk, 6 1/8 In.	70.00
Revere, Ice Cream Fork, International	65.00
Rococo, Bonbon Spoon, Dominick & Haff	55.00
Rococo, Tea Strainer, Dominick & Haff	225.00
Romance of The Sea, Butter Fork, Wallace	43.00
Romance of The Sea, Butter Knife, Wallace	22.00
Romance of The Sea, Olive Fork, Wallace	30.00
Romance of The Sea, Sugar Spoon, Wallace	42.00
Romantique, Cream Soup Spoon, Alvin	14.00 To 15.00
Romantique, Tablespoon, Alvin	37.00
Romantique, Teaspoon, Alvin	12.00
Rondo, Baked Potato Server, Gorham	35.00
Rose Point, Gravy Ladle, Wallace	75.00
Royal Danish, Carving Set, International	275.00
Royal Danish, Cold Meat Fork, International	95.00
Royal Danish, Jelly Spoon, International	22.00
Sea Rose, Gravy Ladle, Gorham	48.00
Sea Rose, Teaspoon, Gorham	13.00
Serenity, Pickle Fork, International	13.00
Silverstream, Coffee Spoon, Manchester	12.00
Silverstream, Gumbo Soup Spoon, Manchester	15.00
Sir Christopher, Butter Fork, Wallace	21.00
Sir Christopher, Luncheon Setting, Wallace, 4 Pc.	95.00
Sir Christopher, Serving Spoon, Wallace	55.00
Southern Charm, Cream Soup Spoon, Alvin	17.00
Southern Charm, Pie Server, Alvin	26.00
Southern Rose, Bouillon Spoon, Manchester	35.00
Southern Rose, Demitasse Spoon, Manchester	25.00
Spanish Baroque, Cake Breaker, Reed & Barton	42.00
Spanish Baroque, Teaspoon, Reed & Barton	14.00
Spanish Lace, Service For 12, Wallace, 72 Piece	1296.00
Spanish Lace, Wedding Cake Knife, Wallace	48.00
Spring Serenade, Sugar Spoon, Lunt	18.00
St. Cloud, Jelly Spoon, Gorham	125.00
Stanton Hall, Service For 8, Oneida, 48 Piece	1144.00
Strasbourg, Butter Knife, Master, Gorham	26.00
Strasbourg, Macaroni Server, Gorham	450.00
Strasbourg, Mayonnaise Ladle, Gorham	55.00
Strasbourg, Saltshaker, Gorham	30.00

Strasbourg, Stuffing Spoon, Gorham 495.00
Stratford, Sugar Tongs, International 44.00
Swiss, Pickle Fork, Gorham 35.00
Swiss, Pie Knife, Flat Handle, Gorham 125.00
Tara, Tomato Server, Reed & Barton 95.00
Tulip, Sardine Fork, Fessenden 50.00
Venetian Scroll, Salad Fork, Oneida 18.00
Versailles, Bouillon Spoon, Gorham 25.00
Versailles, Dessert Spoon, Gorham 25.00
Versailles, Fork, Gorham, 6 3/4 In. 28.00
Versailles, Ice Cream Knife, Gorham 350.00
Versailles, Iced Tea Spoon, Gorham 75.00
Versailles, Pastry Fork, Gold Wash, Gorham 70.00
Versailles, Place Setting, Gorham, 4 Piece 250.00
Versailles, Tablespoon, Gorham 57.00
Versailles, Teaspoon, Gorham 19.00
Versailles, Waffle Server, Round, Gorham 595.00
Vespera, Place Setting, Luncheon, Towle, 4 Piece 60.00
Victoria, Cake Knife, Dominick & Haff 450.00
Victoria, Ice Cream Slice, Dominick & Haff 575.00
Violet, Butter Knife, Wallace 22.00
Violet, Chocolate Spoon, Wallace 45.00
Violet, Cocktail Fork, Whiting 22.00
Violet, Place Setting, Wallace, 4 Piece 95.00
Violet, Strawberry Fork, Wallace 35.00
Violet, Sugar Tongs, Whiting 48.00
Virginia, Lettuce Set, Dominick & Haff 145.00
Virginian, Pie Server, Oneida 20.00
Virginian, Service For 12, Oneida, 72 Piece 1428.00
Virginian, Teaspoon, Oneida .... 11.00 To 13.00
Watteau, Demitasse Spoon, Durgin 25.00
Watteau, Soup Ladle, Durgin 425.00
Waverly, Demitasse Spoon, Wallace 20.00
Waverly, Salt, Master, Wallace 30.00
William & Mary, Knife, Lunt, 9 In. 17.00
William & Mary, Lemon Fork, Lunt 11.00
William & Mary, Sugar Spoon, Lunt 18.00
William & Mary, Tablespoon, Lunt 32.00
Willow, Baby Spoon, Gorham 14.00
Willow, Sugar Spoon, Gorham 15.00
Willow, Teaspoon, Gorham 13.00
Woodlily, Pie Knife, Flat Handle, Frank Smith 160.00
Woodlily, Soup Spoon, Frank Smith, Set of 6 .... 190.00

Ⓔ Ⓟ 🜍 Ⓝ Ⓢ   Silver plate is not solid silver. It is a ware made of a metal, such as nickel or copper, that is covered with a thin coating of silver. The letters "EPNS" are often found on American and English silver plated wares. Sheffield silver is a type of silver plate.

SILVER PLATE, Basket, Cake, Swing Handle, Tufts 55.00
Basket, Floral, Repousse Design, 1976–84 .... 185.00
Basket, Victorian Flowers, Butterflies, J.W. Tufts, 10 1/2 In. 95.00
Bowl, Spring Garden, 8 X 12 In. 70.00
Box, American Golfing Society, Prize, 1922, Large 175.00
Box, Collar Button, Figural, Pairpoint 20.00
Box, Embossed Foliage, 2 Portrait Medallions, 8 1/2 In. 160.00
Bread Tray, Argosy 95.00
Bread Tray, Daffodil 95.00
Bucket, Wine, Rococo, English, C.1860, Pair 1320.00
Butter, Dome Cover, Cartouches, Scrolls Band, Gorham, C.1865 .... 990.00
Butter, Dome Cover, Knife Rest, Floral, Vanbergh Co. 35.00
Cake Basket, Bail Handle, Geometric Pattern, Rogers, 9 1/2 In. 220.00
Candelabrum, 1–Light, Intertwining Arms, Bobeches, 12 1/2 In. 125.00
Candelabrum, 2–Light, Sheffield, Fluted Design, 15 1/2 In., Pr. 975.00
Candelabrum, 2–Light, Stepped Beaded Base, 20 1/2 In., Pair 660.00

Candelabrum, 3–Light, Lion Mask Supports, European, 26 1/2 In. 495.00
Candelabrum, 3–Light, Matthew Boulton, C.1810, 19 3/4 In., Pair 770.00
Candelabrum, 3–Light, Open Lyre Column, Sheffield, 12 In., Pair 415.00
Candelabrum, 3–Light, Renaissance, Reed & Barton, 17 In., Pair 512.00
Candlestick, Repousse Scene, Figures, Dutch, 11 1/2 In., Pair 95.00
Case, Cigar, Scrollwork With Leaves, For 3 Cigars, 5 In. 35.00
Castor Set, 6 Bottles, Blown–Out Stoppers, Toothpick In Frame 135.00
Castor, Pickle, Colonial Silver 75.00
Castor, Sugar, Cranberry 200.00
Cocktail Shaker, Enameled Golfer On Front 350.00
Cocktail Shaker, Penguin Shape, Napier, 12 1/4 In. 1760.00
Coffee Set, Alpaca, Wood Finials, C.1930, 3 Piece 1100.00
Coffee Set, Her Majesty, 3 Piece 195.00
Coffeepot, Argosy 115.00
Coffeepot, Domed Lid, Flame Finial, Roger Williams, 11 1/4 In. 385.00
Coffeepot, Remembrance 135.00
Condiment Set, Squirrel Eating Nut Finial Handle, 4 1/2 In. 165.00
Cup, Cover, Bud Finial, Ram's Head Mask, 9 1/2 In., Pair 525.00
Dish, Entree, Hot Water Base, 2 Handles, Odiat, 1830, 4 X 14 In. 412.00
Dish, Vegetable, Chased Rose Design Cover, Oval, 12 In. 95.00
Dresser Set, Head of Maiden, Whiplash Hair, C.1900, 17 Piece 1430.00
Eggcup, Leaf Design, Stand, 6 Piece 75.00
Epergne, 1 Large Bowl, 4 Small Surrounding, England 1430.00
Epergne, Clear Waterford Bowls, M. Boulton, 1815, 17 3/4 In. 900.00
Flask, Double, Canvas Carrying Case, England, 10 In. 44.00
Frame, Draped Lady, Reaching, Flowers, Art Nouveau, 11 X 7 In. 60.00
Hatpin, Golf Club Shape 35.00
Holder, Calling Card, Figural Kate Greenaway Girl & Dog 225.00
Humidor, Boy Lying On Lid, Holding Top Hat Match Holder 250.00
Inkstand, Chamberstick At Side, 2 Wells, Sheffield, C.1820 .... 775.00
Inkwell, Elephant's Head, Monkey Opens To Well, Meriden 660.00
Knife Rest, 2 Steers 35.00
Knife Rest, Dolphin, Pairpoint 35.00
Letter Opener, Figural, Horsehead Handle, Reed & Barton 85.00
Match Safe, Dog & Quail 22.00
Mirror, Plateau, Beveled, Cut Rosettes In Circle, 18 In. 185.00
Mirror, Plateau, Scrolled, Openwork Sides, Victorian, 8 In. 70.00
Mustard, Cover, Cobalt Blue Glass Liner, English, C.1880 .... 165.00

SILVER PLATE, NAPKIN RING, see Napkin Ring

Pickle Fork Set, Orange Blossom, 1910, 6 Piece 30.00
Pitcher, Everted Rim, Beaded Moldings, Whiting, C.1870, 12 In. 1540.00
Pitcher, Medallion, Greek Key Band, Gorham, C.1865, 9 3/8 In. 880.00
Pitcher, Water, Eternally Yours 225.00
Pitcher, Water, First Love 235.00
Pitcher, Water, Silver Artistry, Ice Guard 95.00
Pitcher, Water, Squared Handle, Randahl Shop, 8 1/2 In. 1210.00
Plaque, Bust of Art Nouveau Woman Center, Marked WMF, 20 In. 950.00
Plaque, Leda & Swan, Pierced Border, Marked WMF, 14 X 9 In. 385.00
Plate, Engraved Floral Clusters, Gorham, 10 In. 105.00
Platter, Baroque, Wall & Tree, Footed, 20 In. 175.00
Salt & Pepper, Baroque 75.00
Salt, Ornate, Cobalt Blue Ruffle Top, Liner, Master 25.00
Saltcellar, Cauldron Form, Gorham, 1872, 3 X 2 1/4 In. 660.00
Scissors, Wick, With Tray, Floral, Hallmark, 10 1/4 In., 2 Piece 85.00

SILVER PLATE, SPOON, SOUVENIR, see Souvenir, Spoon, Silver Plate

Sugar & Creamer, Argosy 85.00
Sugar & Creamer, Skyline 75.00
Sugar, With Spoon Holder, Bird Lid, Pedestal 95.00
Syrup, Deer Heads, Hoof Feet, Simpson, Hall & Miller 65.00
Tankard, Ice Water, Lined, Woodman Cook Co., 13 1/2 In. 195.00
Tantalus Set, 2 Decanters, Silver Plated Frame 195.00
Tea & Coffee Set, Gourd Form, Raffia Handles, 1955, 5 Piece 1650.00
Tea Set, Etched Floral Design, C.1930, Indian, 3 Piece 57.00
Tea Strainer, Wooden Handle, Hallmarked, 1917 .... 30.00

Tea Urn, Leaf Handles, Repousse Leaves, Bailey & Kitchen, 1833 .... 3100.00
Teapot, Stand With Burner, Lozenge Design, German, 13 1/4 In. 1200.00
Teapot, Stand, Georgian, English 265.00
Toast Rack, Sheffield 42.00
Toothpick, Aurora, Barrel Shape 15.00
Toothpick, Chinese Man Carrying Box, Aurora, 4 In. .... 105.00 To 148.00
Tray, Anniversary, Handles, 19 X 11 1/2 In. 115.00
Tray, Ballard, 24 X 13 In. 165.00
Tray, Floral & Acanthus Leaf Handles, 26 X 21 In. 385.00
Tray, Open Handles, Oval, Scrolled Foliage, Gorham, 1874, 35 In. 715.00
Tray, Oyster Shell Shape, Flute–Playing Frog, German, 9 In. 1100.00
Trophy, Bicycle, Linscott Road Race, May 13, '93, 7 In. 77.00
Tureen, Cover, Beaded Handles, Maple & Co., London 885.00
Tureen, Cover, Greek Key Band, W. Gale, Jr., 1860, 16 1/4 In. 8250.00
Tureen, Cow's Handle & Finial, Reed & Barton 500.00
Tureen, Loop Handles, Shell Design Ladle, Gorham, C.1900 .... 415.00
Tureen, Soup, Neoclassical, Walker, Knowles & Co., 12 X 16 In. 950.00
Urn, Hot Water, Pear Shape, Figural Handles, Gorham, 14 3/8 In. 137.50
Urn, Tea, Georgian, Domed Cover, Foliate Finial, 1900, 19 In. 775.00
Urn, Water, Georgian, Acorn & Oak Leaf Handles, 1830, 15 In. 1100.00
Watch Stand, Boy Holding Staff, Hook Holds Watch, Tufts 155.00

SILVER, SHEFFIELD, see Silver Plate; Silver–English

 The silver listed in this book is subdivided by country. Silver–American is the first listing, followed by Silver–Austrian, Silver–Canadian, Silver–Chinese, Silver–Danish, etc. There are also other pieces of silver and silver plate listed under special categories, such as Napkin Ring or Tiffany, and under Silver Flatware.

SILVER–AMERICAN, see also Tiffany Silver; Silver–Sterling

SILVER–AMERICAN, Ashtray, Leaf Form, Whiting, 3 1/2 In., 16 Piece 105.00
Basket, Fluted, Beaded Border, Towle, 7 In. 75.00
Basket, Leaf Form, Copper Fly, Shiebler, C.1885, 10 1/2 In. 6100.00
Basket, Nut, Arts & Crafts, Arthur Stone 4450.00
Basket, Nut, Frieze of Lilies & Leaves, A.J. Stone, 5 In. 4845.00
Bonbon Spoon, Pierced & Chased Design, Arthur J. Stone 250.00
Bowl, 5 Fluted Sections, Arthus J. Stone, C.1924, 9 3/4 In. 1100.00
Bowl, Blossom–Shaped Sides, James T. Woolley, 4 1/4 In. 300.00
Bowl, Cover, Pointed Flanges, Mulholland Bros., 12 1/4 In. 1500.00
Bowl, Curved Rim, Scroll Handles, Allan Adler, 14 1/4 In. 1200.00
Bowl, Cyma Border With Acanthus, Whiting, 11 In. 125.00
Bowl, Flowers & Foliage On Matte Ground, Kirk & Son, 9 In. 990.00
Bowl, Fruit, Embossed, With Nut Spoon, Kirk & Son, 5 1/8 In. 40.00
Bowl, Hammered, Arts & Crafts, Novick, Lobed, 1900, 9 In. 825.00
Bowl, Hammered, Border, Marshall Field, 10 In. 700.00
Bowl, Irises & Dragonfly, Footed, Whiting, C.1885, 8 1/2 In. 7150.00
Bowl, Lion's Paw Feet, Grapes, M.A. Fuller, C.1900, 14 In. 1210.00
Bowl, Melon Form, Chrysanthemum & Leaf, Kalo, 14 In. 5445.00
Bowl, Mint, Chased Lines of Flower, Gebelein, 3 In. 215.00
Bowl, Notched Rim, Norse Line, Kalo, 1938, 6 5/8 In. 445.00
Bowl, Peter Muller Munk, N.Y.C., C.1935, 15 In. 9900.00
Bowl, Ribbed Sides, Barbed Rim, Frank M.Whiting, 16 1/2 In. 1320.00
Bowl, Square, Rounded Corners, Arthur J. Stone, 7 5/8 In. 625.00
Box, Cigarette, Van Erp, 11 In. 350.00
Box, Stamp, Angel Draping Reclining Nude, Blackinton 225.00
Bread Tray, Chased Flowers, Gorham, 1898, 2 X 15 In. 3300.00
Bread Tray, Pierced Repousse Border, Shiebler 1295.00
Butter Knife, Ball, Black & Co., C.1851, 7 1/2 In., 4 Piece 320.00
Butter Knife, Buffalo, P.Dubois, C.1842, 7 1/2 In. 38.00
Butter Knife, Master, Bright Cut, Zahm & Jackson, C.1850 .... 55.00
Butter Knife, Olive Pattern, C.E. Bacon, 1859, 7 3/4 In. 55.00

Buttonhook, Repousse, Kirk	85.00
Candelabrum, 3–Light, Mandalian, 1930s, 13 1/4 In., Pair	465.00
Candelabrum, 3–Light, Turned Supports, 15 In.	467.00
Candlestick, 4–Arm, Shreve & Co., 23 In., Pair ....*Illus*	4400.00
Candlestick, Detachable Nozzles, Gorham, 1917, 16 In., Pair	885.00
Candlestick, Golden Repousse, Kirk, 4 Piece	250.00
Candlestick, Lenox Inserts, Gorham, 1912, 10 1/4 In., Pair	650.00
Candlestick, Reeded Bands, Drip Pan, 1940, 9 3/4 In., 4 Pc.	775.00
Candlestick, Shreve & Co., Engraved, C.1900, 12 In., Pair	4400.00
Candlestick, Spring Load, Reticulated Shades, Gorham, 8 Pc.	280.00
Case, Cigarette, Dancing Nudes, Clouds, Gorham	225.00
Case, Cigarette, Kentucky Long Rifle, 6 In.	125.00
Centerpiece, Repousse Border, Insert, Frank Whiting, 13 In.	2500.00
Chalice, Chased Florals, Stebbins & Co., 6 1/8 In., Pair	570.00
Chalice, Vermeil, Gilt Bowl, Garnet Stem, 9 1/2 In.	412.00
Coaster, Chased Design, Stylized Snowflake, Kalo Shop	150.00
Cocktail Shaker, Royal Danish, International	395.00
Coffee Set, Pear Form, Scroll Supports, Poole, 3 Piece	605.00
Coffee Urn, Repousse, Bell Shape, Spigot, Schofield	8995.00
Compote, Inscribed, Kalo Shop, Dated 1914	2300.00
Condiment Ladle, Ivy, Gorham, C.1870, 7 1/4 In.	132.00
Crumber, Foliate Design On Blade, Lowell & Senter, C.1830	295.00
Cup, Arlington Handicap, Spaulding & Co., 1956, 12 In.	2100.00
Cup, Presentation, Cylindrical, Coin	195.00
Cup, Presentation, Footed, Coin, C.1850–1855	125.00
Cup, Presentation, Paneled Gothic, Coin, C.1850	275.00
Curler, Hair, Collapsible Travel Stand, Unger	625.00
Dish, 4 Sections, Strap Handle, Lebolt & Co., 10 1/4 In.	1750.00
Dish, High Relief Flower Design, Arthur J.Stone, 3 5/8 In.	650.00
Dish, Oyster Shell, Clamshell Feet, Gorham, 4 X 4 1/2 In.	275.00
Dish, Sweetmeat, Pulled Handles, Mulholland Bros., 11 In.	605.00
Dish, Vegetable, Hammered, Divided, Lebolt, 1910, 9 In.	412.00
Dish, Virginia Carvel, Towle, 10 In.	105.00
Epergne, Repousse Acorn, Large Oval, 4 Bowl, Gorham, 12 In.	9900.00
Ewer, Cover, Floral Repousse, Running Dog, S.Kirk, 13 In.	4180.00
Figurine, German Shepherd, Kirk & Son, 3 In.	185.00
Fish Knife, Hyde & Goodrich	660.00
Fish Server, Scrolled Leaves, Albert Coles, 1850, Pair	550.00
Fish Slice, Davis, Palmer & Co., C.1841, 12 5/8 In.	275.00
Fish Slice, Prince Albert, J.& W. Moir, C.1850	275.00
Fish Slice, Twisted Handle, J.E. Caldwell & Co., C.1848	295.00
Flask, Bombe Shape, Monogram, Unger, 4 1/2 X 2 3/4 In.	750.00
Flower Basket, Boat Form, David & Galt, C.1900, 13 3/4 In.	1045.00
Flower Frog, Shape of Opening Water Lily, Wallace	200.00
Food Pusher, FNR, Unger, 3 7/8 In.	325.00
Fork, Beaded Edge, Crane & Co., C.1842, 7 7/8 In.	45.00
Fork, Josephine, Robert Ratt, Patent 1855, 7 In.	35.00
Fork, Prince Albert, Lincoln & Reed, C.1835, 7 3/4 In.	45.00
Fork, Prince Albert, N.Harding & Co., C.1830, 7 5/8 In.	65.00
Fork, Serving, Beaded, Twist Handle, A.Coles, C.1850	175.00
Fruit Knife, Bird, T & W, Arm & Hammer, C.1850	18.00
Glove Stretcher, Engraved, Gorham	85.00
Goblet, Flared Bowl, S.Kirk & Son, 6 3/4 In., 8 Piece	825.00
Goblet, Leaf & Vine, Boston Watch To Cap'T. Barrett, 1854	425.00
Goblet, Monogrammed S, Reed & Barton, 6 1/4 In., 12 Pc.	450.00
Gravy Boat, Hammered, Robert R. Jarvis, 2 1/8 X 6 3/4 In.	3600.00
Handle, Cane, Unger, 1 5/8 In.	425.00
Jug, Cream, Repousse, T.E.& Co., Coin, C.1858	120.00
Julep Cup, Hyde & Goodrich	495.00
Julep Cup, R.E.Smith, Louisville	425.00
Kettle, On Stand With Burner, Arthur J.Stone, 12 1/4 In.	3250.00
Ladle, Bouillon, Olive Pattern, A.Skinner & Co., C.1850	175.00
Ladle, Condiment, Basket of Flowers, G.Boyce, C.1820	220.00
Ladle, Condiment, Fiddle, EE & SC Bailey, C.1825, 4 7/8 In.	45.00

Ladle, Condiment, Mayflower, H.Hotchkiss, C.1850, 5 3/8 In.	45.00
Ladle, Gravy, Hammered, Lebolt & Co., 6 7/8 In.	125.00
Ladle, Gravy, Palmer & Bachelders, C.1850, 7 3/8 In.	95.00
Ladle, Gravy, Putney, Sacketts Harbor	35.00
Ladle, Onslow Style, Arthur J.Stone, 5 5/8 In.	245.00
Ladle, Sauce, Fiddle, J.H. Cheadell, C.1827, 6 1/8 In.	48.00
Ladle, Sauce, W.C. Defriez, C.1848, 6 1/4 In.	68.00
Ladle, Soup, Coffin-End, William G. Forbes, C.1800, 14 In.	550.00
Ladle, Soup, Fiddle Thread, Hyde & Goodrich, C.1840, 14 In.	625.00
Ladle, Soup, Flowers, C.Johnson, Albany, C.1824, 8 7/8 In.	475.00
Ladle, Soup, Fruit Pattern, E.A.Tyler, C.1860	275.00
Ladle, Soup, Gothic, Koehler & Ritter, C.1870	250.00
Ladle, Soup, J.Lownes, Philadelphia, C.1780	750.00
Ladle, Soup, King's Pattern, Gale & Moseley, C.1828	595.00
Ladle, Soup, MUH, New Orleans, C.1822, 13 In.	675.00
Ladle, Soup, Pinched Fiddle, E.Jaccard & Co., C.1852, 13 In.	395.00
Ladle, Soup, Smith & Chamber, 11 In.	210.00
Ladle, Toddy, Chance & Son, C.1820, 11 3/4 In.	850.00
Letter Opener, Ivory Cutter, Unger	250.00
Letter Opener, Rounded End, Arthur J.Stone, 7 3/4 In.	250.00
Mug, Child's, C.1915, 3 X 2 7/8 In.	535.00
Mug, Robert & Wm. Wilson, 1825-46, 3 In.	350.00
Mug, Square Handle, Newell Harding, Boston, 1820, 4 1/2 In.	470.00
Mustard Pot, Spoon, Golden Repousse, Kirk	45.00
Pillbox, Hanging, Lapel Clasp, Unger	325.00 To 375.00
Pillbox, Hinged Lid, Arthur J. Stone, C.1910, 2 1/2 In.	495.00
Pitcher, Grape Design, Tucker	2000.00
Pitcher, Hammered, Intertwined Monogram, Kalo, 14 3/4 In.	4700.00
Pitcher, Milk & Cereal Bowl, Arthur J.Stone	850.00
Pitcher, Repousse Floral & Scroll, Baluster, Theo.B.Starr	440.00
Pitcher, Rose, Footed, Stieff, 1935	2420.00
Pitcher, Water, Art Deco, Old Newbury Crafters	1495.00

Silver-American, Bowl, Peter Muller Munk,
N.Y.C., C.1935, 15 In.

Silver-American, Candlestick, 4-Arm,
Shreve & Co., 23 In., Pair

Silver-American, Tea & Coffee Set, C.Kuchler,
5 Piece

Pitcher, Water, Baltimore Silversmiths, C.1903, 8 3/4 In.	550.00
Pitcher, Water, Hammered, Black, Starr & Frost, 8 1/4 In.	412.00
Pitcher, Water, Oyster Shells, Whiting, 7 1/8 In.	3850.00
Plate, Hammered, Orange Blossoms, Friedell, 11 3/8 In.	3385.00
Platter, Chased Flowers, Foliage, S.Kirk & Son, 13 1/2 In.	660.00
Platter, Woolsey Style, Arthur J.Stone, 18 X 13 In.	2950.00
Porringer, Keyhole Handle, John Hancock, C.1750, 8 1/4 In.	2420.00
Porringer, Keyhole Handle, William Simpkins, C.1730, 8 In.	1980.00
Porringer, Mushroom-Shaped Handles, Kalo Shop, 5 1/2 In.	975.00
Porringer, Pierced Handle, Jonathan Otis, C.1750, 8 In.	2860.00
Punch Bowl, Repousse, Stieff	2860.00
Rattle, Bells On Ring, Wood & Hughes, C.1880	125.00
Rattle, Mother Goose, Unger Brothers	275.00
Salt & Pepper, Bulbous, Ball Feet, Allan Adler, 2 3/4 In.	265.00
Salt & Pepper, Teardrop, Allan Adler, 3 1/2 & 4 1/2 In.	265.00
Salt Shovel, B.Pitman, New Bedford, Mass., C.1840	21.00
Saltcellar, Oval Boat Shape, Swing Handles, A.J. Stone	375.00
Salver, Gregg & Hayden, C.1850	975.00
Scoop, Berry, Olive Pattern, Wood & Hughts, C.1850, 8 In.	325.00
Scoop, Marrow, Twisted Arms, Gale & Willis, 1840, 10 3/8 In.	1430.00
Scoop, Nut, Duvaine, Unger	85.00
Server, Pastry, Olive, Haddock, Lincoln & Foss, C.1860	175.00
Shears, Poultry, Repousse, Kirk	95.00
Silver Caddy, Festoon & Tessel Banding, C.Aldrige, London	2530.00
Spoon, Dessert, Alexander & Riker, N.Y.C., C.1797	125.00
Spoon, Dessert, Fiddle Tip, W.Kendrick, C.1840, 7 1/8 In.	65.00
Spoon, Dessert, J.Avery, Preston, Conn., C.1760	495.00
Spoon, Dessert, Swallow, Caldwell, 8 3/4 In.	85.00
Spoon, Dessert, Van Voorhis & Schenck, C.1790	75.00
Spoon, Dressing, Gregg & Hayden & Co., C.1846, 12 In.	275.00
Spoon, Mustard, Fiddle, F.Marquend, C.1820, 4 3/8 In.	65.00
Spoon, Nut, Stemmed Leaf Shape, Katharine Pratt, 4 In.	150.00
Spoon, Salt, Basket of Flowers, J.B. Jones, C.1838, 4 In.	75.00
Spoon, Salt, Farrington & Hunnewell, Boston, C.1850, Pair	42.00
Spoon, Salt, Fiddle, Steele & Crocker, C.1853, 3 7/8 In.	27.00
Spoon, Salt, Flared Handle, Bacon & Smith, C.1845, 3 3/4 In.	32.00
Spoon, Salt, Grecian, H.Hebbard	21.00
Spoon, Salt, Shell Shape, A.W. Cram	25.00
Spoon, Salt, Shoemaker, Philadelphia, C.1790	75.00
Spoon, Serving, Homeric, Flared Handle, Shiebler, C.1885	462.00
Spoon, Serving, Joel Sayre, C.1798, 9 3/4 In., 6 Piece	1700.00
Spoon, Stuffing, Bright Cut, Mudge & Co., New York, C.1850	325.00
Sugar & Creamer, Hammered, Kalo Shop, 3 5/8 In.	675.00
Sugar & Creamer, Waste Bowl, Repousse, Oval, Knowles, 3 Pc.	1800.00
Sugar Shell, Coin, Ornate Handle, J.Gray	55.00
Sugar Shell, Fiddle Tip, B.Pitman, C.1848, 6 5/8 In.	55.00
Sugar Shell, Fiddle, A.Coles, C.1840	35.00
Sugar Shell, Fiddle, H.L.Webster & Co., Providence	35.00
Sugar Shell, Oval Tip, A.Sanborn, C.1849, 6 1/8 In.	48.00
Sugar Sifter, Bright Cut, Moseley, Boston	60.00
Sugar Sifter, Lancaster, Gorham	95.00
Sugar Spoon, Hammered, Lebolt & Co., 5 3/8 In.	85.00
Sugar Tongs, Acorn Tips, I & S, C.1795, 5 3/4 In.	195.00
Sugar Tongs, Bright Cut, C.Wiltburger, C.1790, 6 1/4 In.	385.00
Sugar Tongs, Fiddle, Stevens & Lakeman, C.1830, 5 3/8 In.	75.00
Sugar Tongs, Hammered, Lebolt & Co., 4 In.	75.00
Sugar Tongs, Scalloped Fiddle, Barzillai Benjamin, C.1814	195.00
Sugar, Cover, Flower Finial, A.E.Warner, Jr., C.1865	475.00
Sugar, Cover, Pedestal, Daniel Dupey, C.1775, 6 In.	4620.00
Sugar, Creamer & Tray, Key Pattern, C.1940	2310.00
Tablespoon, Bright Cut, A.Dubois, Philadelphia, C.1790	160.00
Tablespoon, F & H Clark, Memphis	75.00
Tablespoon, G.Haverstick, Lancaster, Penn., C.1805, 6 Piece	925.00
Tablespoon, J.Brevoort, N.Y.C., C.1750	225.00

Tablespoon, J.Loring, Boston, C.1790	165.00
Tablespoon, J.Moulton II, Newburyport, Mass., C.1760	325.00
Tablespoon, J.R.Reynolds, Hagerstown, Maryland	95.00
Tablespoon, J.Sayre, New York, C.1790	175.00
Tablespoon, Jenny Lind, Freeman & Bennett, C.1853, 6 Piece	300.00
Tablespoon, P.Lupp, New Brunswick, N.J., C.1760	70.00
Tablespoon, P.Vergereau, New York City, C.1740	295.00
Tablespoon, Pinched Fiddle, H.Hudson, C.1841, 8 3/4 In.	38.00
Tablespoon, S.Haley, C.1750	395.00
Tablespoon, Upturned Front, P.Syng, Jr., C.1760	70.00
Tablespoon, Upturned Front, R.Humphreys, C.1765	375.00
Tablespoon, W.Homes, Boston, C.1750	325.00
Talcum Shaker, Gorham	115.00
Tea & Coffee Set, Buckingham, Whiting, 5 Piece	3300.00
Tea & Coffee Set, C.Kuchler, 5 Piece ....*Illus*	6600.00
Tea & Coffee Set, Floral Design, Alvin	1650.00
Tea & Coffee Set, Floral, Wood & Hughes, C.1875, 5 Pc.	5500.00
Tea & Coffee Set, Ivory Mounts, Kalo, C.1914, 6 Piece	7865.00
Tea & Coffee Set, Pear-Shaped Bodies, Arthur Stone, 6 Pc.	7750.00
Tea & Coffee Set, S.Hoyt, New York, C.1840, 4 Piece	1540.00
Tea Set, Buttercup, Gorham, 6 Piece	2300.00
Tea Set, Claw & Ball Feet, Fletcher & Gardner, 1812, 3 Pc.	4250.00
Tea Set, Floral Cartouches, S.Kirk & Son, C.1860, 5 Piece	2420.00
Tea Set, Hammered, Ebony Flame Finial, Handles, Kalo, 10 Pc.	1815.00
Teapot, Full Form, Hammered, Palick Novick, 6 1/2 In.	2500.00
Teapot, Hinged Cover, Finial, Arthur J. Stone, 6 3/8 In.	1500.00
Teapot, Oval Form, Chased Design, A.J. Stone, 6 3/8 In.	1500.00
Teaspoon, A. & C. Brandt, Philadelphia, C.1800	40.00
Teaspoon, B. Wenman, New York City, C.1790	75.00
Teaspoon, Basket of Flowers, A. Fellows, C.1837, 4 Piece	170.00
Teaspoon, Birdback, W. Haverstick, Lancaster, Penna., C.1790	85.00
Teaspoon, Bright Cut, Van Voorhis	40.00
Teaspoon, C.A. Burnett, D.C. & Virginia, C.1820	30.00
Teaspoon, Downing & Phelps, Newark, N.J., C.1820	22.00
Teaspoon, E.Brasher, New York City, C.1790	75.00
Teaspoon, Fiddle, JA & SS Virgin, C.1834, 5 7/8 In.	65.00
Teaspoon, Front Mid-Rib, R. Humphreys, C.1765, 6 Piece	2100.00
Teaspoon, J. Bedford, Fishkill, N.Y., C.1790	75.00
Teaspoon, J. Moulton, Newburyport, Mass., C.1790	65.00
Teaspoon, J.& N. Richardson, Philadelphia, C.1785	75.00
Teaspoon, J.Howell & J.W. Gethen, Philadelphia, C.1810	45.00
Teaspoon, J.Richardson, Sr., Philadelphia, C.1740	275.00
Teaspoon, J.Standiford, Connecticut, C.1790	65.00
Teaspoon, J.Trott, Boston, C.1760	175.00
Teaspoon, Oval End, E.Garretson, C.1795, 5 3/4 In.	250.00
Teaspoon, P. Jones, Wilmington, Delaware, C.1840	55.00
Teaspoon, P.Jones, Wilmington, Delaware, C.1840	40.00
Teaspoon, R.Fairchild, Connecticut & New York, C.1760	175.00
Teaspoon, S.Pancoast, Philadelphia, C.1780, Pair	150.00
Teaspoon, S.Richards, Philadelphia, Penna., C.1790	100.00
Teaspoon, Sheaf of Wheat, American Sheffield	65.00
Teaspoon, Sheaf of Wheat, Higbie & Crosby, C.1825, 6 In.	17.00
Teaspoon, Shell On Back, A.G.Storm, C.1830, 5 3/4 In.	25.00
Teaspoon, T.Hammersley, N.Y.C., C.1760	175.00
Teaspoon, W.Kittle, Newburyport, Mass., C.1760	175.00
Tongs, Asparagus, Jenny Lind, Q.E.Warner, Baltimore	695.00
Tongs, Fiddle Shell, Wm.Thomson, N.Y.C., C.1825	175.00
Tongs, Howe & Guion, New York City, C.1840	65.00
Tongs, J.Sayre, Southampton & New York, C.1810	125.00
Tongs, Jones, Lowe & Ball, Boston, C.1835	65.00
Tray, Buttercup & Dandelion, Martele, Gorham, 6 3/4 In.	385.00
Tray, Central Monogram, Hammered Surface, Randahl, 12 In.	475.00
Tray, Engraved On Flange, Arthur J.Stone, 7 In.	395.00
Tray, Floral Rim, Baroque Pearl Inset, Kalo, 1914, 8 1/4 In.	4600.00

Tray, Light Hammering, Karl F. Leinonen, 11 7/8 In.	950.00
Tray, Riveted Copper Border, Oak Center, 27 In.	5080.00
Tray, Spiral Border, Foliate Feet, Ball, Black, 12 In.	110.00
Tray, Squiggles & Circles, Arthur J.Stone, 11 In.	1250.00
Tray, Well–and–Tree, Kent, M. Fred Hirsch, 20 In.	550.00
Urn, Water, Domed Cover, Handles, J.Lownes, 1800, 15 1/4 In.	3600.00
Vase Holder, Stylized Foliate Design, 7 In.	137.00
Vase, Auto, Unger, 6 1/8 In.	325.00
Vase, Flaring Outward At Top, Marie Zimmermann, 7 In.	1975.00
Yo–Yo, Scrolled Design, Gorham	119.00 To 125.00
SILVER–AUSTRIAN, Bowl, Baptismal, Fluted Interior, Inscription, 14 3/4 In.	625.00
Candelabrum, 2–Light, Rococo Stepped Base, 12 1/2 In., Pair	3500.00
Candlestick, Campana Form Sconce, 1870s, 13 3/4 In., Pair	770.00
Castor, Inverted Pear Form, Fluted Foot, Vienna, 1817, 7 In.	550.00
Coffeepot, Hot Milk Jug, Tray, Covers, C.1930, E.Bachmann	4800.00
Kettle, On Stand, Franz Tuma, Vienna, 1840, 12 5/8 In.	1045.00
SILVER–BELGIAN, Coffee Set, Stylized Organic Design, P.Wolfers, 1896, 3 Pc.	5500.00
SILVER–CHINESE, Box, Floral Filigree, Wooden Liner, 4 X 3 In.	125.00
Box, Incense, Gourd Shape, Enameled Flowers, 3 1/4 In.	175.00
Castor, Campana Form, Gadroon Rim, Bud Finial, 4 In., Pair	665.00
Mug, Relief Hunting Scene, Dragon Handle, C.1880, 4 1/2 In.	1600.00
Tea Strainer, Animals, Jade Handle, C.1920, 6 In.	195.00 To 250.00
SILVER–CONTINENTAL, Basket, Repousse, Double Loop Handles, 14 In.	775.00
Candelabrum, 5–Light, Urn Form Sconces, 22 1/2 In., Pair	4675.00
Case, Cigarette, Enameled Sides & Cover, 1920, 4 3/4 In.	1100.00
Creamer, Urn Shape, Floral Mid–Band, Beaded, 8 3/4 In.	400.00
Decanter, Floral Cut, Amber, Initial, 11 In.	110.00
Figurine, Elk, Chased Body, Removable Head, 1900, 10 In.	1100.00
SILVER–DANISH, Bonbon, Georg Jensen	125.00
Bottle Opener, Acorn, Georg Jensen	45.00
Bowl, Berry Design, Footed, Georg Jensen, 7 1/2 In.	2800.00
Bowl, Notched Scalloped Rim, Georg Jensen, C.1912, 8 In.	6050.00
Bowl, Solid Central Foot, Georg Jensen, 11 In.	3300.00
Bowl, Support Column, Vine Design, G.Jensen, C.1925, 7 1/2 In.	2420.00
Box, Cigarette, Domed Lid, Rectangular, Wood Lining, 6 In.	330.00
Box, Cigarette, Hinged Cover, Georg Jensen, 1933, 6 3/8 In.	600.00
Candelabrum, Berries Finial, Georg Jensen, 1925, 8 7/8 In.	7150.00
Carving Set, Acanthus, Georg Jensen	395.00
Centerpiece, Leaf, Berry Design, 1930, Jensen, 14 In.	6600.00
Champagne, Art Deco, Hand Hammered, Georg Jensen	650.00
Cocktail Shaker, Loop Handles, Georg Jensen, 1930, 10 5/8 In.	1325.00
Cup, Cover, Openwork & Bead Stem, G. Jensen, 1945, 6 1/2 In.	1650.00
Dish, Applied Shell Handles, Georg Jensen, 6 1/4 In.	176.00
Fish Server, Pierced Blade, R. Jorgensen, 1936, 6 7/8 In., Pr.	525.00
Food Pusher, Georg Jensen	95.00
Fork, Ice Cream, Acorn, Jensen	125.00
Fork, Lemon, Acorn, Georg Jensen	48.00
Fork, Salad, Acorn, Georg Jensen	35.00
Ladle, Gravy, Georg Jensen	275.00
Mustard Pot, Pepper Shaker, Open Salt, Georg Jensen	695.00
Pitcher, Cluster of Grapes, Ebony Handle, G.Jensen, 8 3/4 In.	3350.00
Pitcher, Stylized Leaves, Bone Handle, G.Jensen, 11 3/8 In.	4450.00
Pitcher, Water, Ebony Handle, Georg Jensen, 17 Oz.	1900.00
Scoop, Nut, Shovel Shape, Curved Handle, Georg Jensen, 6 In.	75.00
Server, Pie, Acorn, Hollow Handle, Georg Jensen	495.00
Service For 4, Cactus, Georg Jensen, 20 Piece	1750.00
Serving Set, Pyramid, Georg Jensen	250.00
Spoon, Berry, Acorn, Georg Jensen	300.00
Spoon, Cream Soup, Acorn, Jensen	125.00
Spoon, Serving, Hollow Handle, Georg Jensen	395.00
Spoon, Serving, Squash Blossom, Georg Jensen, 6 3/4 In.	335.00
Sugar & Creamer, Inverted Lobed Pear Form, Georg Jensen	1100.00
Sugar Nippers, Acorn, Jensen	50.00
Sugar, Cover, 3 Bird–Form Supports, Georg Jensen, 1919, 6 In.	3300.00

Tea Caddy, Amber Finial, Georg Jensen, C.1915, 5 1/4 In.	1870.00
Tea Strainer, Acorn, Georg Jensen	125.00
Tongs, Grapes In Heart Shape, Spring Handle, G.Jensen, 4 In.	250.00
Tray, Leaf Handles, Georg Jensen, 15 3/8 In.	2500.00
SILVER–DUTCH, Candlestick, Scalloped Shell Rising To Stem, C.1733, Pair	9500.00
Pillbox, Tricorner Hat Shape	225.00

English silver is marked with a series of four or five small hallmarks. The standing lion mark is the most commonly seen sterling quality mark. The other marks indicate the city of origin, the maker, and the year of manufacture. These dates can be verified in many good books on silver.

SILVER–ENGLISH, Basket, Pierced, 4 Acanthus Feet, Swing Handle, 10 In.	600.00
Basket, Reticulated, Flared Top, Handle, 4 1/2 In.	60.00
Beaker, Fitted Case, Hester Bateman, 1788, 3 In.	660.00
Beaker, Gothic Foliage, Omar Ramsden, 1921, 10 In.	2300.00
Bun Warmer, Folding, C.1860, Sheffield	650.00
Buttonhook & Shoehorn, Leather Case	100.00
Cake Basket, George II, Peter Taylor, 1743	9750.00
Cake Basket, Serrated Rectangle, I.L., 1774, 14 1/8 In.	2640.00
Candlesnuffer & Tray, Sheffield, 1830, 2 Piece	275.00
Candlestick, George V, Mappin & Webb, 1934–35, 9 In., Pair	1110.00
Castor Set, Openwork Sides, 6 Bottle, R.Hennell, 1774	605.00
Castor, Sugar, Cylindrical, Handle, Sheffield, 1902, 6 In.	154.00
Coaster, Bottle, On Copper, Wooden Base, Sheffield, 4 1/4 In.	105.00
Coffeepot, George II, Repousse Cartouche, Pear Shape, 11 In.	1760.00
Coffeepot, Shellwork Border, Thomas Wallis, 1774, 9 5/8 In.	1540.00
Creamer, Footed, 18th Century, 3 1/4 In.	465.00
Cup, Campana Form, 2 Handles, C.& G. Cowles, 1768, 11 1/4 In.	1430.00
Cup, Cover, Fruit Finial, Handles, James Dixon, 18 3/4 In.	2545.00
Demitasse Set, Bright Cut, Leatherette Case, 1896, 13 Piece	245.00
Fish Knife, Crighton Bros., 1912	600.00
Flask, Gilt Interior, Rawlings & Summers, 1874, 9 3/4 In.	825.00
Flask, Travel, Cut Glass, Leather Case, Sheffield, 1923, 8 In.	275.00
Frame, Curvilinear Shape, Flowers & Leaves, 1904, 13 1/4 In.	1980.00
Frame, Picture, 2 Putti At Top, L.K./H.K., 1894, 15 In.	2310.00
Frame, Young Woman & Sheep, 1904, 8 3/4 In., Pair	3850.00
Funnel, Wine, Georgian, Sheffield, James Young & Sons, 1788	375.00
Holder, Place Card, Owl, Glass Eyes	110.00
Inkstand, Galleried Walls, 2 Wells, CTF/GF, 1852, 9 7/8 In.	1540.00
Loving Cup, Leaf Design, Birmingham, 1916, 5 1/2 In., Pair	360.00
Mirror, Hand, Beaten Circular, Monogram, 1883, 6 In.Diam.	110.00
Mug, Double Scroll Handle, Francis Crump, 1759, 5 1/8 In.	715.00
Mug, Molded Borders, Shoulder Band, Nathaniel Lock, 1712	990.00
Porringer, Queen Anne, Flat, Wm. Gamble, 1709, 6 3/4 In.	2750.00
Salt, Gardrooned Rim, Hoof Feet, Dorothy Mills, 1762, Pair	400.00
Salver, 4 Scroll Feet, Charles S. Harris, 1930, 8 1/2 In.	440.00
Salver, George III, Leaf-Capped Feet, Paul Storr, 11 7/8 In.	1200.00
Snuffbox, Book Form, Hinged Cover, 2 X 2 In.	275.00
Spoon, Serving, Williams, Ely & Fearn, 1814	65.00
Sugar Sifter, Georgian, Marked WE/WF, C.1797	145.00
Sugar Tongs, Bright Cut, Monogram, 1805–06, 5 1/2 In.	205.00
Tankard, Flowers, Shell Rim, Robin Albin Cox, 1756, 7 7/8 In.	1650.00
Tea Caddy, George II, Edward Gibben, 1724, 4 3/4 In.	770.00
Tea Set, Lobed Bodies, E.J. & W. Barnard, 1847, 7 Piece	3630.00
Teapot, Bright Cut Crests, Ivory Finial, A. Folgelert, 1801	1100.00
Teapot, Georgian Style, Ovoid, Wood Handle, 7 1/2 In.	135.00
Teapot, Wooden Handle & Finial, W. Hutton & Son, 5 1/4 In.	120.00
Toast Rack, 1916	185.00
Tray, 2 Coats of Arms, Edward Wakelin, 1754, 13 1/2 In.	675.00
Tray, Tea, John Crouch & Thomas Hannam, 1809, 19 In.	4200.00
Tureen, Cover, Shells, Leaves, C.1820, 15 3/4 In.	2310.00
Waiter, Cyma Edge, Rectangular, CA, London, 1929, 24 In.	1595.00
Waiter, George II, Engraved Coat of Arms, 1730, 6 In., Pair	4800.00

SILVER–FRENCH, Beaker, Tulip Shape, Beaded Collar, Jean Despres, 3 7/8 In.	850.00
Box, Cigarette, Enamel & Lapis Lazuli, 1927, 6 1/4 In.	4675.00
Candlestick, Charles X, C.1835, Pair	3575.00
Candlestick, Empire, C.1825.Pair	3025.00
Candlestick, Louis XVI, Ormolu, Pair	1750.00
Chalice, Applied Medallion, 12 Apostles At Base, 1879	3500.00
Chocolate Pot, Louis XVI, Treen Handle, Limoges, 9 1/2 In.	5000.00
Jug, Claret, Bacchus & Grapevines, C.1880, 12 1/2 In., Pair	3100.00
Jug, Claret, Pear Shape, Swirl Body, 10 In.	1050.00
Tea & Coffee Set, Sandoz, Paris, 1930, 3 Pcs.	3850.00
Wine Taster, Louis XVI, Snake Loop Handle, C.1775, 4 1/4 In.	1210.00
SILVER–GERMAN, Bowl, Floral & Bird Design, Cutout, Chased, 1890, 6 X 5 In.	450.00
Bowl, Pierced, Scrolled, Center Putti, Oval, 5 Oz., 9 1/2 In.	66.00
Bowl, Repousse, Masks With Wings, 6 In., Pair	2800.00
Box, Peasant Drinking, Dancing On Sides, C.1900, 10 7/8 In.	2750.00
Box, Rococo Style, Scroll Reserves of Putti, C.1900, 9 In.	2850.00
Box, Singing Bird, Oval Lid Opens To Reveal Bird, C.1880	1650.00
Bread Basket, Latticework Sides, C.1900, 12 1/4 In.	445.00
Coffeepot & Teapot, Bombe, Flat Cover & Rim, C.1930	1650.00
Cordial, Footed, Crest	25.00
Figurine, Knight, British Arms, 1928, 7 In., Pair	3520.00
Kettle, On Stand With Burner, Fruit & Foliage, 18 3/4 In.	1760.00
Nef, Nersheimer, Sailors, Cannons, Dolphin, 22 In.	6875.00
Pillbox, Flying Squirrel On Cover, Foliage, Round, 2 In.	18.00
Salt, Cover, Gilt Inner Compartment, C.1745, 2 1/4 In.	1540.00
Sauceboat, Stand, Gilt Interior, Elimeyer, C.1900, 11 7/8 In.	825.00
Spoon, Art Nouveau Design, Late 19th Century, 7 Oz., 6 Piece	100.00
Tankard, Coins & Foliage, Paul Kerfack, C.1870, 5 1/8 In.	1210.00
Teapot, Bamboo Shape Spout & Finial, C.1870, 5 3/8 In.	1320.00
Vase, Trumpet, Glass, Green Repousse Figural Base, 14 In.	110.00
Wager Cup, Bearded Man, Woman, 10 In., Pair	4675.00
SILVER–INDIA, Box, Elephant, Tooled Design, 7 7/8 In.	115.00
SILVER–IRISH, Bowl, Waste, Swirling Flutes, Dublin, 18th Century, 6 3/8 In.	825.00
Spoon, Dessert, Michael Keating, Dublin, C.1790	75.00
Sugar & Creamer, Alex Barry, Newcastle, 1820, 5 In.	1100.00
SILVER–ITALIAN, Garniture, Fighting Cock, Chased Plumage, 8 1/2 In., Pair	1000.00
SILVER–MEXICAN, Bowl, Scalloped, 3 Ball Feet, 6 3/4 In.	125.00
Box, Inlaid Abalone Top & Sides, Wood Lined, 7 1/4 X 4 In.	295.00
Nut Spoon, Duck Handle, 3 Dimensional Head, W. Spratling	395.00
Pitcher, Ice Lip, Melon Ribs, Myers, 11 1/2 In.	400.00
Pitcher, Strap Handle, Pear Shape, 8 3/4 In.	295.00
Pitcher, Water, Cover Set Into Neck, W. Spratling, 7 3/4 In.	4500.00
Plate, Gadroon Border, Hecho HNOS, 8 5/8 In., 6 Piece	950.00
Tea Set, Pear Form, Scroll Supports, Stand, 11 1/4 In.	660.00
Tray, Scroll Handles, Oval, 25 1/4 In.	715.00
SILVER–NORWEGIAN, Bowl, Fish Center, David Andersen, C.1940, 14 3/8 In.	2175.00
Jug, Claret, Presentation	1430.00
SILVER–PERUVIAN, Candelabrum, 3–Light, Urn Shape Sconces, 6 5/8 In., Pair	330.00
Candelabrum, 5–Light, Scroll & Floral Rim, 11 1/2 In., Pair	495.00
Salt Dip, Llama	79.00
Tea & Coffee Set, Tray, Scroll & Shell Rims, 7 Piece	825.00
SILVER–PORTUGUESE, Coffee & Tea Set, Round Bodies, Tray, 3 Piece	6600.00

T6 88
+R

Russian silver is marked with the cyrillic, or Russian, alphabet. The numbers 84, 88, or 91 indicate the silver content. Russian silver may be higher or lower than sterling standard. Other marks indicate maker, assayer, or city of manufacture. Many pieces of silver made in Russia are decorated with enamel.

SILVER–RUSSIAN, Box, Tobacco, Niello Landscape, Patterned Ground, 4 1/2 In.	225.00
Candlestick, Fluted Stem, 1861, 12 1/4 In., Pair ....*Illus*	1050.00
Cup, Vodka, Engraved E, 19th Century	330.00
Egg, Sbitnev	3850.00
Flask, Wildlife & Religious Scene, 1852, 17 In. ....*Illus*	880.00
Glass Holder, Enamel Trim, Fedor Ruckart	4400.00

Napkin Ring, Engraved, Marked 84d895 .... 125.00
Salt, Boat Form, Sail & Oar 500.00
SILVER-SCOTTISH, Spoon, Serving, Wm. Jameson, 1932 .... 165.00
SILVER-SPANISH, Casket, Jewelry, Cover, Metal Lined, Paw Feet, 10 1/4 In. 1435.00
Pail, Bombe Form, Cherub Heads On Handles, 18th Century 5000.00

> Sterling silver is made with 925 parts silver out of 1,000 parts of metal. The word "sterling" is a quality guarantee used in the United States after about 1860. The word was used much earlier in England and Ireland. Pieces listed here are not identified by country. Other pieces of sterling quality silver are listed under Silver–American, Silver–English, etc.

SILVER-STERLING, Basket, Reticulated, Monogramed Handle, 6 3/4 X 10 1/2 In. 150.00
Bowl, Ivy Pattern, Hammered, G.Andersen, 13 X 8 3/8 In. 895.00
Bowl, Oviform, Flared Rim, Kalo, 11 5/8 In. 1210.00
Bowl, Poppies, Alvin, 10 In. 300.00
Box, Heart Scene, Round, No.800 .... 45.00
Box, Heart, Chased, Monogram, Sheafer & Lloyd, 1891, 4 In. 155.00
Brush, Bonnet, Art Nouveau, Relief Floral, 6 1/2 In. 75.00
Buckle, Belt, Man's, Vertical Stripes, 1 1/4 In. 25.00
Candlesnuffer, Walnut Handle, 10 In. 28.00
Candlestick, Leaf On 1, Floral On Other, 10 1/8 In., Pair 600.00
Candlestick, Removable Bobeches, R.Sturm, 12 In., Pair 1330.00
Case, Card, Hinged Lid, Cherubs On Lid, Scrolls, Marked 800 .... 165.00
Case, Spectacles, Velvet Lined 85.00
Castor, Egg, 4 Eggcups, 4 Spoons, Gold Wash Interior 275.00
Chatelaine, C.1870 .... 1200.00
Coffee Set, Countess Chantilly, Bachelor, 1904, 3 Piece 1400.00
Coin Holder, Compact Shape 45.00
Curling Iron, Mustache, Nacre Button, Release Lever, 6 In. 65.00
Cutter, Cigar, With Chain, 9 In. 75.00
Dish, Serving, Art Nouveau, Poppies, 15 In. 485.00
Food Pusher, Stork Handle, Dated 1937 .... 85.00
Frame, Oval, 3 1/2 X 4 1/2 In. 25.00
Frame, Purse, Chain & Chatelaine Hook, Cherubs, C.1900 .... 200.00
Funnel, Perfume 25.00
Hair Brush, Child's 15.00
Handle, Umbrella, 12 In. 65.00
Ice Bucket, Ribbed Finial, Cartier, 1930s, 11 5/8 In. 935.00
Inkwell, Jade Bowl, Medallion On Lid, E.F. Farmer, 4 In. 1950.00
Mirror, Hand, Beveled Glass, C.1915, 16 In. 150.00
Mirror, Hand, Double, Opens To Compact, Art Deco, 5 1/4 In. 125.00

Silver–Russian, Candlestick, Fluted Stem, 1861,
12 1/4 In., Pair

Silver–Russian, Flask,
Wildlife & Religious Scene, 1852, 17 In.

Muffineer, Chased Roses, Monogram, 6 1/4 In. 175.00
Nut Set, 6–In. Dish On Pedestal, Hammered, 7 Piece 145.00
Pad, Memo, Cartier, 2 1/2 In. 135.00
Piercer, Cigar, 2 3/4 In. 55.00
Rattle, Teddy Bear, Victorian, Marked 130.00
Salad Serving Set, George C. Erickson, 8 3/4 In., 2 Piece 310.00
Salt & Pepper Castors, Currier & Roby, C.1940, 4 7/8 In. 125.00
Sauce, Fluted Flower Form, Joel F. Jewes, 4 1/4 In. 125.00
Shears, Grape, Victorian, 1860–80 .... 150.00
Shoebutton & Shoehorn, Art Deco, Handle 50.00
Snuffbox, Rectangular, Book Form, Hinged Cover, 3 X 2 In. 275.00
    SILVER–STERLING, SPOON, SOUVENIR, see Souvenir, Spoon, Sterling
    Silver
Tatting Shuttle, Marked 1912 .... 65.00
Tea Ball, Octagonal Teapot Shape, Silver Chain 85.00
Tea Ball, Repousse Floral 64.00
Tea Strainer, Footed, Glass Bowl, Sterling Rim 75.00
Thimble, Engraved Mother, 1900s, Marked 85.00
Tray, Foliage Scroll Rim, Marked, 6 3/4 In. 100.00
Watering Can, Gold Wash, Miniature 118.00

Sinclaire cut glass was made by H.P. Sinclaire and Company of Corning, New York, between 1905 and 1929. He cut glass made at other factories until 1920. Pieces were made of crystal as well as amber, blue, green, or ruby glass. Only a small percentage of Sinclaire glass is marked with the S in a wreath.

SINCLAIRE, Candlestick, Black Glass, Hanging Lustres, Signed, 9 In., Pair 135.00
Candlestick, Black Jade, White Rim, Signed, 9 In. 90.00
Inkwell, Etched 115.00
Nappy, Crossed Ovals, Hobstars & Fans, 6 1/2 In. 55.00
Tray, Holly, 11 X 6 In. 700.00
Vase, Diamond, 1 Band of Hobstars Near Pedestal, 13 1/2 In. 375.00
    SKIING, see Sports

Slag glass resembles a marble cake. It can be streaked with different colors. There were many types made from about 1880. Pink slag was an American Victorian product of unknown origin. Purple and blue slag were made in American and English factories. Red slag is a very late–Victorian and twentieth–century glass. Other colors are known but are of less importance to the collector.

SLAG, Blue, Dish, Owl On Nest Cover 30.00
Blue, Dish, Turkey On Nest Cover 30.00
Blue, Figurine, Bear Cub 25.00
Blue, Figurine, Butterfly, On Stand 25.00
Blue, Figurine, Girl 50.00
Blue, Rabbit, Atterbury 55.00
Blue, Shade, Hanging, Paneled Round Dome, Beaded Rim, 28 In. 610.00
    SLAG, CARAMEL, see Chocolate Glass
Pink, Cruet, Inverted Fan & Feather 950.00
Pink, Dish, Jelly 375.00
Pink, Lamp, Wrought Iron Base & Frame, Black, Pink, Clear, Green, 20 In. 250.00
Pink, Toothpick, Inverted Fan & Feather 575.00
Pink, Tumbler .... 125.00 To 175.00
Pink, Tumbler, Inverted Fan & Feather 350.00
Purple, Candy Dish, Cover, Hoffman 40.00
Purple, Celery Dish, Flute 90.00
Purple, Creamer, Oak Leaf 30.00
Purple, Creamer, Sunflower .... 15.00 To 30.00
Purple, Dish, Hen On Nest Cover, Basket Weave Bottom, 7 1/8 In. 65.00
Purple, Dish, Lion On Nest Cover, Lacy Base 85.00
Purple, Dish, Rooster On Nest Cover, Lacy Base 85.00
Purple, Figurine, Cow, 6 In. 26.00
Purple, Figurine, Duck, White Head, Atterbury 55.00
Purple, Jam Jar, Dome Cover, Straight Sided 100.00

Purple, Match Holder, Flute	35.00
Purple, Mug, Intaglio Cat In Bottom, Birds & Nests In Relief	125.00
Purple, Pitcher, Embossed Cherries.4 1/2 In.	85.00
Purple, Spooner, Crossbar & Flute	65.00
Purple, Spooner, Flower Panel	65.00
Purple, Spooner, Flute	65.00
Purple, Sugar & Creamer	35.00
Purple, Toothpick, British Boot	40.00
Purple, Toothpick, S–Repeat	25.00
Purple, Tumbler, Bottom Marked 1/2 Pt.	55.00
Purple, Vase, Floral, Sowerby, 4 In.	75.00
Red, Bowl, Black Glass Pedestal, Fenton, C.1930, 9 1/2 In.	175.00
Red, Candy Dish, Herringbone	38.00
Red, Cruet	38.00
Red, Pitcher, Windmill, 1 Pt.	65.00
Red, Plate, White Leaf	40.00
Red, Vase, Nudes	75.00

Sleepy Eye collectors look for anything bearing the image of the 19th–century Indian chief with the drooping eyelid. The Sleepy Eye Milling Co., Sleepy Eye, Minnesota, used his portrait in advertising from 1883 to 1921. It offered many premiums, including stoneware and pottery steins, crocks, bowls, mugs, and pitchers, all decorated with the famous profile of the Indian. The pottery was popular and was made by Western Stoneware and other potteries long after the flour mill went out of business in 1921. Reproductions of the pitchers are being made today. The original pitchers came in only five sizes: 4 in., 5 1/4 in., 6 1/2 in., 8 in., and 9 in. The Sleepy Eye image was also used by companies unrelated to the flour mill.

SLEEPY EYE, Calendar, 1904, Imitation Leather	200.00
Cookbook, Loaf of Bread	50.00
Cookbook, Square	120.00
Crock, Butter .... 500.00 To 750.00
Crock, Salt, Blue & Gray .... 270.00 To 495.00
Flour Sack	110.00
Flour Sack, Printed In Spanish, James J. Broich, Minnesota	205.00
Hot Plate, Blue On White	1900.00
Label, Barrel, Framed	315.00
Letterhead	10.00
Match Holder, Brown & Silver Paint, 5 1/2 In.	1100.00
Mug, Blue & Gray	420.00
Mug, Blue & White .... 150.00 To 175.00
Pillow Top .... 450.00 To 695.00
Pitcher Set, Blue & White, 5 Piece	1500.00
Pitcher, No.1, Blue & White .... 110.00 To 145.00
Pitcher, No.2, Blue & White .... 60.00 To 175.00
Pitcher, No.3, Blue & Gray	300.00
Pitcher, No.3, Blue & White .... 165.00 To 250.00
Pitcher, No.4, Blue & Gray	175.00
Pitcher, No.4, Blue & White .... 275.00 To 440.00
Pitcher, No.5, Blue & Gray	205.00
Pitcher, No.5, Green	300.00
Pitcher, Swan, Blue & White	350.00
Pitcher, War Head Indian, Blue & White	375.00
Postcard	17.50
Scraper, Bread Board	625.00
Spoon, Indian .... 115.00 To 130.00
Stein, Blue	585.00
Stein, Blue & Gray	550.00
Stein, Blue & White	350.00
Stein, Board of Directors, 1968	185.00
Stein, Board of Directors, 1973	130.00
Stein, Brown & Yellow .... 650.00 To 900.00
Stein, Brown & Yellow, 7 3/4 In. .... 650.00 To 1000.00

Stein, Brown, 1952	300.00 To 500.00
Stein, Green & White	700.00
Sugar, Blue & White	510.00
Trivet, Stoneware	1775.00
Vase, Cattails, Blue & White	350.00
Vase, Cattails, Brown & Yellow	750.00
Vase, Cylindrical, Indian & Iris, Blue Glaze, 8 1/2 In.	325.00

> Slip is a thin mixture of clay and water, about the consistency of sour cream, that is applied to pottery for decoration. It is a very old method of making pottery and is still in use.

SLIPWARE, Box, Money, Birds On Top & At Shoulders, Staffordshire	660.00
Chamberstick, England, 17th Century, 5 In.	715.00
Dish, Loaf, Coggled Rim, England, 18th Century, 17 In.	885.00
Dish, Loaf, Rectangular, Eastern Connecticut, 12 X 10 In.	2400.00
Figurine, Cat, England, Early 19th Century, 5 3/4 In.	995.00
Jug, England, 18th Century, 8 1/2 In.	440.00
Jug, Initialed HRB, England, 18th Century, 8 In.	385.00
Jug, Initialed T.P., England, 18th Century, 6 1/2 In.	355.00
Jug, Puzzle, Incised A. Higgs, Dated 1665, 8 1/2 In.	1875.00
Mug, England, 18th Century, 2 1/4 In.	935.00
Porringer, England, 18th Century, 2 In.	300.00
Pot, Applied Handle, England, 18th Century, 5 In.	775.00
Pot, Cover, Applied Handles, 18th Century, 7 1/2 In.	1435.00
Pot, Double–Handled, England, 18th Century, 6 In.	1985.00

SLOT MACHINE, see Coin–Operated Machine

Smith Bros. Co.   Smith Brothers glass was made after 1878. Alfred and Harry Smith had worked for the Mt. Washington Glass Company in New Bedford, Massachusetts, for seven years before going into their own shop. They made many pieces with enamel decoration.

SMITH BROTHERS, Biscuit Jar, Barrel, Enameled Daisies, Plated Cover & Bail	695.00
Bowl, Beaded Rim, Gold Scrollwork, Signed, 9 In.	325.00
Bowl, Melon Ribbed, Beaded Rim, Pink Pansies, 2 1/2 X 3 In.	200.00
Bowl, Melon Ribbed, Beaded Rim, Yellow Pansies, 3 In.	200.00
Bowl, Melon Ribbed, Enameled Beaded, Raised Flowers, 9 In.	325.00
Bowl, Melon Ribbed, Shasta Daisies & Foliage, 9 In.	115.00
Bowl, Opalescent, Blue Lace, Yellow Flowers, 4 X 2 1/2 In.	235.00
Box, Cover, Melon Shape, Blue Pansy, Marked, 3 In.	110.00 To 120.00
Butter, Sugar & Creamer, Amberina	25.00
Figurine, Goose Girl, Frosted, Sculpted Base, 6 In.	25.00
Sweetmeat, Blue Flowers, Ribbed Glass Lid, Handle, 5 1/4 In.	635.00
Sweetmeat, Pink Carnations, Cream, Melon Shape, 5 1/2 In.	685.00
Vase, Conical, Body Rings, Bird On Branch, 6 In.	125.00
Vase, Enameled Birds On Branch, Moon & Sun, 12 In.	195.00
Vase, Heron In The Rushes, 1890s, 4 1/4 In.	45.00
Vase, Heron In The Rushes, 1890s, 5 3/4 In.	95.00
Vase, Pilgrim, Wisteria Traced In Gold, Double, 7 1/4 In.	1215.00

Most shaving mug reproductions are imaginative copies of old mugs that would not fool a serious collector. There is often no space for the owner's name. Some examples are marked Brandenburg. Copies include designs such as Currier and Ives prints, a hearse drawn by horses, and trade names such as Peddler, Fireman, or Painter.

Snow Babies, made from bisque and spattered with glitter sand, were first manufactured in 1864 by Hertwig and Company of Thuringia. Other German and Japanese companies copied the Hertwig designs. Originally, Snow Babies were made of candy and used as Christmas decorations. There are also Snow Babies tablewares made by Royal Bayreuth. Copies of the small Snow Babies figurines are being made today and can easily confuse the collector.

SNOW BABIES, Holding Camera, 1 3/4 In.	130.00
Plate, Sledding With Dog	110.00
Seated, Germany, 2 In.	200.00
Standing, Germany, 2 1/2 In.	200.00
Vase, Brown Ground, Royal Bayreuth, 3 1/4 In.	100.00
Vase, Royal Bayreuth, 5 1/2 In.	145.00
SNUFF BOTTLE, see Bottle, Snuff	

Taking snuff was popular long before cigarettes became available. The snuff was kept in a small box. The gentleman or lady would take a small pinch of the ground tobacco or snuff in the fingers, then sniff it and sneeze. Snuffboxes were made of many materials, including gold, silver, enameled metal, and wood. Most snuffboxes date from the late eighteenth or early nineteenth centuries.

SNUFFBOX, Burl, 2 3/4 X 3 3/4 In.	150.00
Burl, Shell Lining	85.00
Burl, Tortoiseshell Lining, Push-Up Lid	125.00
Inlaid Mother-of-Pearl, Black Lacquer	85.00
Maple Burl, Hinged Lid, C.1810, 2 X 3 In.	130.00
Pewter, Pocket Watch Shape, Lid Opens On Face, C.1775	125.00
Pine, Wooden Pinned Hinged Top, 1830, 1 1/2 X 3 In.	17.00
Silver, Engine-Turned Design, A. Coles, 1870, 3 1/2 X 2 1/2 In.	225.00
Silver, Portrait of George Washington, Scrolls, 2 1/8 X 3 1/8 In.	200.00

Soapstone is a mineral that was used for foot warmers or griddles because of its heat-retaining properties. Soapstone was carved into figurines and bowls in many countries in the nineteenth and twentieth centuries. Most of the soapstone seen today is from China or Japan. It is still being carved in the old styles.

SOAPSTONE, Figurine, Foo Dog, Standing On Tomb, Hand Carved, 7 1/2 In.	120.00
Figurine, Head, Oriental, Green, 4 In.	35.00
Figurine, Shou Lao, Mounted As Lamp, Gilded Base	82.50
Lamp, Pierced Raised Base of Birds & Flowers, Silk Shade, 41 In.	600.00
Toothpick, Bird, Double	18.00
Toothpick, Flowers	18.00
Toothpick, Monkey	25.00
Vase, Cutout Chrysanthemums, Birds, C.1900, 8 1/2 In.	195.00
Vase, Dragon, Oriental, Greenish Gray, 6 In.	125.00

Soft paste is a name for a type of pottery. Although it looks very much like porcelain, it is a chemically different material. Most of the soft-paste wares were made in the early nineteenth century. Other pieces may be listed under Gaudy Dutch or Leeds.

SOFT PASTE, Bowl, Cows, Blue Transfer, 7 1/2 X 3 In.	125.00
Bowl, Floral Design, 5 Colors, 4 1/2 In.	1575.00
Bowl, Waste, King's Rose, Solid Border, 2 3/4 In.	175.00
Coffeepot, Dome Top, Black Transfer, Landscape Scene, 9 3/4 In.	200.00
Coffeepot, Dome Top, King's Rose, 11 3/4 In.	950.00
Coffeepot, Dome Top, Yellow Band, Brown Striping, 5 5/8 In.	300.00
Creamer, Embossed Ribs, Intertwined Handle, Blue, 4 3/4 In.	300.00
Creamer, King's Rose, Embossed Shell, Vine Border, 4 1/4 In.	350.00
Creamer, King's Rose, Solid Border, 4 1/2 In.	450.00
Cup & Saucer, Embossed Reeding, Floral Design, Yellow Ocher	105.00
Cup & Saucer, Embossed Reeding, Scalloped Rims, Handleless	55.00

Cup & Saucer, King's Rose, Oyster	225.00
Cup & Saucer, King's Rose, Solid Border	250.00
Cup & Saucer, King's Rose, Vine Border	200.00
Cup & Saucer, Pink, Purple Luster Church Design, Handleless	95.00
Cup & Saucer, Polychrome Floral Design, Handleless	65.00
Cup & Saucer, Strawberry, Line Border, Handleless	85.00
Cup Plate, King's Rose, Vine Border, 3 1/2 In.	90.00
Cup, Sprig, Handleless	25.00
Figurine, Lovers Rendezvous, Marked, 8 X 7 In.	450.00
Mug, Beige, White Bands, Black Stripes, Embossed Leaf, 3 In.	275.00
Mug, Child's, Primitive Horse Scene	140.00
Mug, Panther, Blue Transfer, 2 3/8 In.	95.00
Pitcher, Black Transfer, Oriental Design, 5 3/4 In.	100.00
Pitcher, Floral Decoration, 5 Colors, 9 In.	425.00
Plate, A Present For Ann, Polychrome Floral, 6 3/4 In.	250.00
Plate, Embossed Feather, Leaf Rims, Blue, White, 9 3/4 In.	250.00
Plate, King's Rose, Sectional Border, 9 3/4 In.	325.00
Plate, King's Rose, Solid Border, 10 In.	325.00
Platter, Light Blue Transfer, 16 3/4 In.	200.00
Soup, Dish, King's Rose, Solid Border, 9 7/8 In.	325.00
Sugar, Blue, White Floral Design, Lion Heads Handles, 5 1/4 In.	135.00
Sugar, King's Rose, Embossed Shell, Solid Border, 5 5/8 In.	200.00
Teapot, Blue Granite Glaze, Embossed Geometric Bands, 8 In.	700.00
Teapot, Embossed Designs, Polychrome Enamel, 5 5/8 In.	650.00
Teapot, Embossed S, Acorn Finial, Floral Design, 6 1/8 In.	180.00
Teapot, Embossed S, Zigzag Border, Swan Finial, 6 1/4 In.	350.00
Teapot, Floral Design, Brown, Blue, Yellow, Orange, 6 In.	145.00
Teapot, Floral Design, Red, Green Enameling, 6 In.	225.00
Teapot, Floral Design, Underglaze Blue, Red Enameling, 5 In.	475.00
Teapot, Floral Design, Underglaze Blue, Yellow Ocher, 6 In.	500.00
Teapot, Floral Enameling, 5 3/8 In.	45.00
Teapot, King's Rose, Embossed Shell, Solid Border, 5 3/8 In.	50.00
Teapot, King's Rose, Sectional Border, 5 7/8 In.	400.00
Teapot, Polychrome Floral Design, 5 7/8 In.	400.00
Teapot, Strawberry Design, Purple Luster Trim, 5 5/8 In.	150.00
Vase, Shaded Green Ground, Handles, Austrian, 8 3/4 In., Pair	225.00

What could be more fun than to bring home a souvenir of a trip? Our ancestors enjoyed the same thing and souvenirs were made for almost every location. Most of the souvenir pottery and porcelain pieces of the nineteenth century were made in England or Germany, even if the picture showed a North American scene. In the twentieth century, the souvenir china business seems to have gone to the manufacturers in Japan, Taiwan, Hong Kong, England, and America. Another popular souvenir item is the souvenir spoon, made of sterling or silver plate. These are usually made in the country pictured on the spoon.

SOUVENIR, see also Coronation; World's Fair

SOUVENIR, Ashtray, Holophane Co.	28.00
Ashtray, Tennis, Cartoon Encased In Glass, Gary Patterson, 7 In.	45.00
Bell, Atlantic City, Ruby, 1903	45.00
Boomerang, Greetings From Australia, Wooden	12.00
Bottle, Hot Water, Jane Mansfield	175.00
Box, Ice Cream, Bing Crosby, Picture, 1953, 1 Pt.	6.00
Box, Jewelry, Salt Lake City, Art Nouveau	18.00
Bread Plate, Independence Hall, Glass	38.00
Bread Plate, Iowa City, Be Virtuous, Off-Center Style	125.00
Cigarette Case, Bradford, Pa., Silver, 1919	28.00
Cup, Custard Glass, Sithee, Wisconsin	30.00
Cup, St.Louis Exposition, Red, Clear Handle & Bottom, 1897	30.00
Glass, Kentucky Derby, 1954	31.00
Goblet, Sparta, Wisconsin	27.50
Handkerchief, Ft. Mills, Corregidor, P.I. Island, Silk Embroidered	7.50
Handkerchief, Minnesota Territorial Centennial	10.00

Heart, U.S. Naval Fleet, 1908 .... 20.00
Mirror, Graf Zeppelin Over N. & S. America, 2 1/2 In. 100.00
Mirror, Mardi Gras, Red, New Orleans, Carnival, 1899, 7 In. 59.00
Mug, Knights of Labor, Glass, 6 In. 50.00
Mug, New York, Nude Woman Handle, Ceramic 32.00
Mug, Vassar College, 1948 .... 12.00
Mug, Victorian Woman, Plumber's Convention, 1907 .... 35.00
Panties, Seattle, Remember Pearl Harbor, Silk, Miniature 9.00
Pennant, Tacoma, Washington, School, School Photo, Felt, 4 X 18 In. 10.00
Pillow Cover, Lackland Air Force Base, Silk 6.00
Pin, Columbia University, Sterling, Enameled, 1903 .... 15.00
Pitcher, Reading, Penna. 12.00
Plate, Cedar Falls, Iowa, Early 1900s 20.00
Plate, Ephrata, Penna., 10 In. 10.00
Plate, Golden Gate Exposition, 1939 .... 85.00
Plate, Lititz, Penna, 10 In. 10.00
Purse, Leather, Steeple Chase Island, Doll Size 18.00
Ribbon, Labor Day, Color, 1918 .... 15.00
Spoon, Daniel Boone, Gold Washed, Orange Bowl 49.00
Spoon, Silver Plate, Battleship Maine 10.00
Spoon, Silver Plate, Olympics, Box, 1980 .... 6.00
Spoon, Silver Plate, Rifle Musket, G.A.R., Pittsburg, 1894 .... 65.00
Spoon, Silver Plate, U.S. of America, Eagle, Wheat, Wm. Rogers, 1916 .... 18.00
Spoon, Sterling Silver, Actors Fund Fair, Gorham .... 165.00 To 170.00
Spoon, Sterling Silver, Alexandria, Va., Christ Church, Demitasse 30.00
Spoon, Sterling Silver, Art Palace, Columbian Exposition 65.00
Spoon, Sterling Silver, Battle Monument, Trenton, New Jersey 20.00
Spoon, Sterling Silver, Birmingham, Alabama, Factory .... 15.00 To 30.00
Spoon, Sterling Silver, Cedar Falls, Iowa, Script In Bowl 40.00
Spoon, Sterling Silver, Charleston, S.C., Round Bowl 119.00
Spoon, Sterling Silver, Cleveland, Ohio, Beaded Handle 15.00
Spoon, Sterling Silver, Colorado, Gold Miner & Pike's Peak 45.00
Spoon, Sterling Silver, Colorado, Scenic Handle 30.00
Spoon, Sterling Silver, Cornell University, Art Nouveau Woman 50.00
Spoon, Sterling Silver, Covington, Oregon, Roses In Bowl 22.00
Spoon, Sterling Silver, Devil's Lake, N.D., Indian Head Handle 35.00
Spoon, Sterling Silver, Eastern Star, Masonic Home, Boone, Iowa 35.00
Spoon, Sterling Silver, Eureka, California 5.00
Spoon, Sterling Silver, Excelsior Springs, Woman's Head 30.00
Spoon, Sterling Silver, Famous Loop, Colorado 20.00
Spoon, Sterling Silver, Ft. Worth, Ribbons Entwined Handle 30.00
Spoon, Sterling Silver, Garner Church, Initial On Handle 15.00
Spoon, Sterling Silver, Golden Gate Bridge, Demitasse 10.00
Spoon, Sterling Silver, High School, Lawrenceville, Illinois 35.00
Spoon, Sterling Silver, Home of N.C.R., Dayton 35.00
Spoon, Sterling Silver, Hudson-Fulton Celebration, Ornate 50.00
Spoon, Sterling Silver, Idaho Seal, Embossed Eagle 35.00
Spoon, Sterling Silver, Illinois, Ears of Corn, Scrolls On Handle 18.00
Spoon, Sterling Silver, Indian Chief, Old Man of The Mountain 40.00
Spoon, Sterling Silver, Iowa Flag Bearer, Indian 30.00
Spoon, Sterling Silver, Maplewood Farm, Hillsboro Center, N.H. 28.00
Spoon, Sterling Silver, Maryland, Eagle Handle 20.00
Spoon, Sterling Silver, Monument Park, Ohio, Moses Cleaveland 30.00
Spoon, Sterling Silver, Morrisonville, Ill. 25.00
Spoon, Sterling Silver, Morrow Castle, Cuba 40.00
Spoon, Sterling Silver, Mt. Hood, Portland, Oregon .... 10.00 To 20.00
Spoon, Sterling Silver, Nevada Falls, Yosemite Valley, Demitasse 30.00
Spoon, Sterling Silver, New Cliff House, San Francisco 18.00
Spoon, Sterling Silver, New Mexico Eagles, Farmington Bowl 30.00
Spoon, Sterling Silver, New York City, Cutout Empire State Bldg. 12.00
Spoon, Sterling Silver, Niagara Falls, Flowers On Handle 15.00
Spoon, Sterling Silver, Niagara Falls, Indian & Buffalo Handle 40.00
Spoon, Sterling Silver, Ostrich Farm, South Pasadena 20.00
Spoon, Sterling Silver, Pacific Grove, California, Roses 28.00

Spoon, Sterling Silver, Pan American Exposition Tower, 1901	13.50
Spoon, Sterling Silver, Paul Revere, Bunker Hill	25.00
Spoon, Sterling Silver, Peoria, Ill.	25.00
Spoon, Sterling Silver, Phoenix, Ariz., Figural Cactus Handle	38.00
Spoon, Sterling Silver, Pomona, California, 3 Buildings	30.00
Spoon, Sterling Silver, Ponca City, Oilwell Cutout Handle	35.00
Spoon, Sterling Silver, Portland, Me., Longfellow's Home, Demitasse	30.00
Spoon, Sterling Silver, Post Office, Milwaukee, Wisc.	35.00
Spoon, Sterling Silver, San Gabriel Mission, Building On Handle	18.00
Spoon, Sterling Silver, Santa Barbara, Calif., Cutout Scene	22.50
Spoon, Sterling Silver, Seattle, Washington, Fish Handle	30.00
Spoon, Sterling Silver, St. Paul's, Halifax, Nova Scotia, 1898	16.00
Spoon, Sterling Silver, State Capitol, Des Moines, Iowa	45.00
Spoon, Sterling Silver, State House, Boston, Beans On Handle	10.00
Spoon, Sterling Silver, State Normal School, Cedar Falls, Iowa	45.00
Spoon, Sterling Silver, Statue of Liberty, Tiffany	60.00
Spoon, Sterling Silver, Summit, Pike's Peak, Colorado	36.00
Spoon, Sterling Silver, Switzerland, Demitasse	10.00
Spoon, Sterling Silver, Tampa, Fla., Figural Pineapple Handle	38.50
Spoon, Sterling Silver, Tipton, Iowa, Corn, Eagle On Handle	18.00
Spoon, Sterling Silver, Wisconsin Dells, Fish Handle	30.00
Spoon, Sterling Silver, Wisconsin Seal, Tree & Fruit	30.00
Toothpick, Glen Ullen, North Dakota, Ruby Glass	22.00
Tumbler, Kentucky Derby, 1963	16.00

Spangle glass is multicolored glass made from odds and ends of colored glass rods. It includes metallic flakes of mica covered with gold, silver, nickel, or copper. Spangle glass is usually cased with a thin layer of clear glass over the multicolored layer.

SPANGLE GLASS, see also Vasa Murrhina

SPANGLE GLASS, Basket, Pin, Gold, Thorn Handle, 6 X 6 1/2 In.	225.00
Bowl, Mica Flecks, Flower & Leaf, Silver-Plated Stand, 16 In.	450.00
Bride's Basket, Mica Flakes, Pink Interior, 6 X 6 1/2 In.	225.00
Lighter, Cigarette, Controlled Bubbles, Gold, Mica, 6 In.	45.00
Tumbler, Gold, Amber	80.00
Tumbler, Silver, Blues, Pinks, Yellows, Cased White Interior	95.00
Vase, Gold Mica, Applied Cherries, Ruffled, Handle, 8 In., Pair	550.00
Vase, Melon Sections, Colored Mica, Ruffled, 14 1/2 In.	250.00

Spanish lace is a type of Victorian glass that has a white lace design. Blue, yellow, cranberry, or clear glass was made with this distinctive white pattern. It was made in England and the United States after 1885. Copies are being made.

SPANISH LACE, Bottle, Water, Bulbous, Cranberry, 8 1/2 In.	395.00
Castor, Pickle, Bulbous Insert, Frame & Tongs, Cranberry	450.00
Cracker Jar, Cranberry Glass	560.00
Lamp, Clear Chimney, Cranberry, Miniature	225.00
Pitcher, Water, Blue	175.00
Rose Bowl, Vaseline, 4 In.	45.00
Syrup, Blue	225.00
Vase, Ruffled Top, Yellow Opalescent, 6 In.	20.00

Spatter glass is a multicolored glass made from many small pieces of different colored glass. It is sometimes called "End-Of-Day" glass. It is still being made.

SPATTER GLASS, Ashtray, Morning Glory Shape	10.00
Basket, Cased, Thorn Handle, Large	175.00
Basket, Gold Aventurine On Cranberry, Amber, 6 1/2 In.	350.00
Basket, Pink, Aqua, Brown, White, Clear Thorn Handle, 8 In.	245.00
Basket, Twisted Thorn Handle.White Interior, 4 1/2 X 6 In.	195.00
Berry Bowl, Leaf Mold, Master, Amber, Cased Cranberry	100.00
Bowl, Brown, Wall Lake, Iowa, Blue, Rust, Cream, 6 1/2 In.	85.00
Pitcher, Reeded Handle, Cased White, 9 In.	135.00
Vase, Cupped Goblet Neck, Swirl Pattern, 10 In., Pair	250.00

Vase, Girl Bending, Powder Blue, 5 In. 325.00
Vase, Pastel, Thorn Handles, 9 In. 75.00
Vase, Rainbow Colors, Thorn Handles, 9 In. 85.00
Vase, Shaded Pink, White & Yellow, White Lining, Pontil, 7 In. 45.00
Whimsey, Pig, Vaseline Outside, Red & White Inside, 3 1/2 In. 125.00

The creamware or soft–paste dinnerware decorated with spatter designs in color is called, of course, spatterware. The earliest pieces were made in the late eighteenth century, but most of the spatterware found today was made from about 1800 to 1850 or is a late nineteenth– and twentieth–century form of kitchen crockery that has added spatter designs. The early spatterware was made in the Staffordshire district of England for sale in America. The later kitchen type is an American product.

SPATTERWARE, Band Black Leaves, Dark Green Stripes, 8 1/2 In. 15.00
Bowl, Blue & Tan Sponge, Cream Ground, 4 1/8 X 7 In. 55.00
Bowl, Blue & White Sponge, 3 3/8 X 7 5/8 In. 65.00
Bowl, Blue & White Sponge, 6 X 13 3/4 In. 275.00
Bowl, Blue & White Sponge, 9 3/4 In. 65.00
Bowl, Embossed Exterior, Blue & White, 10 1/4 In. 45.00
Bowl, Green, Brown & Cream, 8 In. 45.00
Bowl, Waste, Peafowl, Red, 3 X 6 In. 375.00
Chamber Pot, Blue & White Design, 4 3/4 X 8 1/2 In. 15.00
Chamber Pot, Embossed Florals, Blue & White Sponge, 9 In. 20.00
Collander, Dark Blue & White, Handle 22.00
Creamer, Blue, Tulip In Red, Green, Blue & Black, 3 1/2 In. 100.00
Creamer, House Design, 3 5/8 In. 550.00
Creamer, Red & Blue, 5 1/2 In. 265.00
Creamer, Rose In Red, Green, Black & 4 1/4 In. 150.00
Crock, Salt, Embossed Label, Swastikas, Blue & White, 6 In. 35.00
Cup & Saucer, Columbine, Green Daisies Border, Harvey 260.00
Cup & Saucer, Handleless, 4–Part Flower Center, Black 55.00
Cup & Saucer, Handleless, Blue 45.00
Cup & Saucer, Handleless, Peafowl 130.00
Cup & Saucer, Handleless, Rooster, Blue 725.00
Cup & Saucer, Handleless, Thistle, Brown 250.00
Cup & Saucer, Pansy, Blue Flower–Head Border 210.00
Cup & Saucer, Pink Bowknot, Blue Striping 85.00
Cup & Saucer, Red Flower Head Border 100.00
Cup Plate, Peafowl, Red, 3 3/8 In. 45.00
Cup, Handleless, Marbelized Blue & Green 55.00
Cup, Purple, Acorn Design, Green, Yellow Ocher, Black 355.00
Cuspidor, Blue Stripes, Blue & White, 5 X 7 1/2 In. 65.00
Mug, Purple, 2 3/4 In. 225.00
Pie Plate, Yellow, Brown, 10 1/2 In. 185.00
Pitcher & Bowl, Blue & White Sponge, 11 X 14 In. 150.00
Pitcher, 3 Sponged Bands, Blue & White, 10 5/8 In. 105.00
Pitcher, Barrel Shape, Blue & White Sponge, 10 In. 150.00
Pitcher, Blue & White Sponge, 8 1/2 In. 175.00
Pitcher, Blue & White Sponge, 9 5/8 In. .... 200.00 To 425.00
Pitcher, Blue & White Sponge, 10 1/4 In. 175.00
Pitcher, Co–Op, Grain & Product Co., Ringsted, Iowa, 4 1/2 In. 75.00
Pitcher, Embossed Floral Design, Blue & White Sponge, 9 In. 225.00
Pitcher, Ovoid, Blue & White Sponge, 10 3/4 In. 190.00
Pitcher, Rainbow, Embossed Handle, Stripes, Green, Black, 9 In. 750.00
Pitcher, Red, Parrot In Red, Green, Black, Paneled, 7 3/4 In. 1050.00
Pitcher, Red, Peafowl In Blue, Yellow, Green, Black, 5 3/8 In. 250.00
Plate, 8–Petaled Purple Flower, Red Border, 8 3/4 In. 140.00
Plate, Blue & Purple, 9 1/2 In. 125.00
Plate, Blue Feather Edge, Peafowl In Red, 9 7/8 In. 450.00
Plate, Columbine, Green Daisies Border, 6 1/2 In. 65.00
Plate, Columbine, Green Daisies Border, 8 1/2 In. 80.00
Plate, Columbine, Red Daisies Border, 9 3/4 In. 110.00
Plate, Dogwood, Purple Bowknot Border, T.W. Barlow, 8 5/8 In. 55.00

Plate, Fort Pattern, Blue, 8 3/4 In. 150.00
Plate, Green, Peafowl In Blue, Red, Black, 7 3/4 In. 1075.00
Plate, Marbelized Blue & Green, 6 1/4 In. 65.00
Plate, Marbelized Blue & Green, 8 3/8 In. 50.00
Plate, Pansy, Blue Flower–Head Border, 5 5/8 In. 200.00
Plate, Pansy, Green Flower–Head Border, Blue Band, 7 5/8 In. 65.00
Plate, Pansy, Red Flower–Head Border, 8 5/8 In. 85.00
Plate, Peafowl In Red, Blue, Yellow Ocher, Black, 7 3/4 In. 180.00
Plate, Peafowl, Blue, 9 1/2 In. 400.00
Plate, Purple Floral Transfer, T. Walker, Flora, 10 In. 125.00
Plate, Rabbit, 10 In. 850.00
Plate, Rainbow, 6 7/8 In. 75.00
Plate, Red & Black Star Design, 8 3/4 In. 75.00
Plate, Thistle, Green No–Center Daisies Border, 6 1/2 In. 50.00
Plate, Thistle, Red Bowknot Border, 8 5/8 In. 100.00
Platter, Blue, Rose In Red, Blue & Black, 13 1/2 In. 325.00
Platter, Thistle, Red Smoke–Ring Border, 13 3/8 X 10 1/8 In. 300.00
Pot, Handle, Pouring Spout, Blue & White Sponge, 5 In. 70.00
Sauce, Thistle, Red Smoke–Ring Border, 5 1/4 In. 180.00
Slop Jar, Blue & White Sponge, Initials A.W. On Handle, 11 In. 50.00
Sugar, Black Oriental Scene, Paneled, Blue, 5 1/8 In. 50.00
Sugar, Blue, 5 1/4 In. 650.00
Sugar, Cover, Acorn, Green, Brown, Black, 4 1/2 In. 600.00
Sugar, Cover, Red, Blue & Green Dahlia, 4 1/2 In. 90.00
Teapot, Blue & Purple, 10 In. 175.00
Teapot, Red, Peafowl In Blue, Green, Yellow, Black, 6 7/8 In. 350.00
Teapot, Thistle, Red, 9 1/4 In. 1000.00

Spelter is a synonym for a zinc alloy. Figurines, candlesticks, and other pieces were made of spelter and given a bronze or painted finish. The metal has been used since about the 1860s to make statues, tablewares, and lamps that resemble bronze. Spelter is soft and breaks easily. To test for spelter, scratch the base of the piece. Bronze is solid; spelter will show a silvery scratch.

SPELTER, Bust, Art Nouveau Woman, L'Hiver & Tifflano, 8 In. 138.00
Figurine, Horse, Cheval De Marly, France, Pair 325.00
Figurine, Jockey, Horse, Hurdle, Hunter's Blended Whiskey, 12 In. 475.00
Lamp, Classical Woman With Book, White Shade, 28 In. 75.00
Lamp, Maiden, Arm Holds 5–Light Candelabrum, Electric, 44 In. 275.00
Lamp, Torchere, Warrior, Victorian, C.1885 .... 850.00
Statue, Navy, Fighting Sailor .... 150.00 To 180.00

The old spinning wheel in the corner has been the symbol of earlier times for the past 100 years. Although spinning wheels date back to medieval times, the ones found today are rarely more than 200 years old. Because the style of the spinning wheel changed very little, it is often impossible to place an exact date on a wheel.

SPINNING WHEEL, Flax, Castle, 2–Color Design, Chip Carved, 36 In. 395.00
Flax, Signed M. Wise, Oak 350.00
Flax, Walnut 450.00
Hardwood, 31 1/2 In. 65.00
Oak & Maple, 38 In. 200.00
Oak, Hardwood, Chip Carved Block With A. Knox, 36 In. 200.00
Shaker, Signed 150.00
Various Hardwood, 35 In. 135.00
Walking 425.00
Wood, Flax Holder, With Flax, 6–In. Wheel, 11 1/2 In. 135.00
Wool, Bobbin Assembly, Oak, 58 X 43 1/2 In. 135.00

Spode pottery, porcelain, and bone china were made by the Stoke-on-Trent factory of England founded by Josiah Spode about 1770. The firm became Copeland and Garrett from 1833 to 1847, then W.T. Copeland or W.T. Copeland and Sons until 1976. It then became Royal Worcester Spode Ltd. The word "Spode" appears on many pieces made by the factories. Most collectors include all the wares under the more familiar name of Spode. Porcelains are listed in this book by the name that appears on the piece.

SPODE, see also Copeland; Copeland Spode

SPODE, Bread Plate, Camilla, Pink	20.00
Bread Plate, Florence	12.00
Butter Chip, Wickerdale	8.00
Chop Plate, Tower, Pink, 12 In.	45.00
Coffeepot, Camilla, Pink	150.00
Cup & Saucer, Billingsley Rose	25.00
Cup & Saucer, Camilla, Pink	35.00
Dinner Set, Buttercup, Service For 8	350.00
Jug, Lilies of The Valley, Long Leaves, Stippled Ground, Parian, 6 In.	55.00
Plate, Billingsley Rose, 9 In.	18.00
Plate, Billingsley Rose, 10 In.	20.00
Plate, Delaware, Black & White Tercentenary Celebration, 1938, 6 Pc.	85.00
Plate, Florence, 10 In.	20.00
Plate, Tower, Blue, 5 1/4 In.	15.00
Soup, Cream, Billingsley Rose	30.00
Soup, Dish, Tower, Blue	20.00
Vase, Oriental Garden, 967 Pattern, Blue, Red, 1810, 10 In.	2925.00

Spongeware is very similar to spatterware in appearance. The designs are applied to the ceramics by daubing the color on with a sponge or cloth. Many collectors do not differentiate between spongeware and spatterware and use the names interchangeably. Modern pottery is being made to resemble the old spongeware, but careful examination will show it is new.

SPONGEWARE, Bean Pot, Blue & White	625.00
Bowl, A.B.C., Little Girl & Boy Doctor Transfer, L8 1/2 In.	70.00
Bowl, Batter, Blue & White, Large	285.00
Bowl, Black & Yellow Sponge Diamond & Square Band, 9 1/4 In.	100.00
Bowl, Blue & White, 5 1/4 X 10 3/4 In.	195.00
Bowl, Blue On Cream, 7 In.	35.00
Bowl, Blue, Bulbous, 7 In.	140.00
Bowl, Camellia, Red Border, Footed, 4 3/4 In.	55.00
Bowl, Dark Blue, C.1820, 6 X 8 1/2 In.	225.00
Bowl, Footed, Blue Diamond Design, Baker & Co., 7 5/8 In.	90.00
Bowl, Vegetable, Blue, Scalloped, 7 3/4 X 2 5/8 In.	95.00
Bowl, Vegetable, Blue, Scalloped, Square, 7 1/4 In.	180.00
Bowl, Wedding Ring, Blue & White, 8 1/2 In.	95.00
Cake Plate, Scroll Design, Blue, Open Handles, 10 X 10 1/2 In.	170.00
Carpet Ball, Black Florets, 3 1/4 In.	65.00
Carpet Ball, Red Florets, 3 1/2 In.	220.00
Carpet Ball, Yellow Florets, 4 In.	140.00
Casserole, Cover, Blue, Rust, Cream	45.00
Chamber Pot, Cover, Blue, White	165.00
Creamer, Maynard, Minnesota	45.00
Crock, Butter, Cover, Blue, 3 Lb.	60.00
Cup & Saucer, Deer, Blue	425.00
Cup & Saucer, Handleless, Blue	210.00
Cup & Saucer, Mush, 8 1/2–In. Saucer	115.00
Cup & Saucer, Red Band & Black Leaf Bands, Blue Stripe	200.00
Cuspidor, Blue & White	250.00
Cuspidor, Embossed Grapes, Blue & White	145.00
Cuspidor, Yellow & Brown	65.00
Custard Cup, Green & Brown Paneled, 3 Piece	36.00
Dish, Blue, 9 3/4 X 8 1/4 In.	275.00
Dish, Cheese, Cover, Moira	100.00
Holder, Toothbrush, Blue, 4 3/8 In.	240.00
Mug, Child's, Purple Scroll Design	150.00
Pitcher, Allover Blue & White, 9 3/4 In.	225.00
Pitcher, Blue & White, 8 7/8 In.	325.00

Pitcher, Blue & White, Blue Stripes, 12 In. 200.00
Pitcher, Blue Florets Band, Green Leaves Band, 10 5/8 In. 190.00
Pitcher, Blue, 2 3/8 In. 170.00
Pitcher, Cobalt Blue & White, C.1870, 6 1/2 In. 335.00
Pitcher, Floral, Blue & White, 9 3/4 In. 235.00
Pitcher, Milk, Blue & White, Ovoid 150.00
Pitcher, Scroll, Blue, 7 1/2 In. 160.00
Pitcher, Tankard Shape, Blue, 8 1/2 In. 165.00
Pitcher, Water, Relief Fern Design, Yellow & Green 85.00
Plate, Blue, 6 5/8 In. 80.00
Plate, Blue, 7 1/4 In. 100.00
Plate, Blue, E.L.B., Burford Bros., 7 In. 85.00
Plate, Camellia, Blue Border, 7 3/8 In. 85.00
Plate, Camellia, Purple Border, Blue Florets, 8 3/4 In. 95.00
Platter, Blue, 13 1/2 X 10 In. 275.00
Platter, Camellia, Red Border, 17 X 12 1/2 In. 260.00
Platter, Scroll, Blue, 15 X 10 3/4 In. 260.00
Rolling Pin, George W. Radcliff, Buckingham, Pa. 350.00
Soap Dish, Blue Diamond Band, 4 1/2 X 3 3/8 In. 80.00
Soap Dish, Blue, Cream 58.00
Soup, Dish, Blue & White, 9 1/2 In. 190.00
Soup, Dish, Pink Peony, Green Leaves, 8 1/4 In. 105.00
Syrup, Pewter Spring Lid, Knowles, Taylor & Knowles, Dated 1872 .... 350.00
Teapot, Blue & White 425.00
Wash Bowl & Pitcher, Scroll, Cobalt Blue, 2 Piece 270.00

Sporting goods, equipment, brochures, and related items are listed
here. Other sections of interest are Bicycle, Fishing, Gun, Rifle,
Sword, Toy, and Weapons.

SPORTS, Badge, Hunting License, Nebraska, 1942 .... 20.00
Ball, Target, Bogardus, Amber 225.00
Ball, Target, Parker, Amber 65.00
Ball, Target, Parker, Cobalt Blue 95.00
Baseball Bat, Joe Sewell, Autographed, Official Model 80.00
Baseball Bat, Louisville Slugger, Jackie Robinson, 1940s 25.00
Baseball Bat, Louisville Slugger, Original Decal of Honus Wagner 600.00
Baseball Box, Mitt Shape, Joe Gordon 65.00
Baseball Glove, Gordon's, Fielder, Box, 1939 .... 50.00
Baseball Guide, Spalding, Major League, 1923 .... 48.00
Baseball Patch, Official, 1983 World Series 11.00
Baseball, Bob Gibson Autograph 12.00
Baseball, Bobby Thompson Autograph 20.00
Baseball, Brooklyn Dodgers, 17 Signatures, World Champion, 1955 .... 1597.00
Baseball, Brooks Robinson Autograph 20.00
Baseball, George Brett Autograph 20.00
Baseball, Monte Irvin Autograph 20.00
Baseball, New York Yankees World Series, Signed, 1958 .... 750.00
Baseball, Ted Williams Autograph 65.00
Billiard Cue, 1890 .... 9.00
Billiard Table, Brunswick–Balke–Collender 7700.00
Boxing Gloves, Leather, 1920s 49.00
Boxing Program, Larry Holmes Vs. Leon Spinks, 1980 .... 49.00
Boxing Program, Max Baer Vs. Paulino Uzcudun, 1931 .... 45.00
Boxing Program, Muhammad Ali Vs. Brian London, 1976 .... 33.50
Caddy Stand, George Bussey, 1895 .... 1150.00
Clay Pigeon Dispenser, Remington Arms, Cast Iron, Spring–Powered 90.00
Coin, Babe Ruth, 3–D Picture of Babe, 1955 .... 11.00
Cross Bow, Arrows 125.00
Crow Call, Charles Perdew 125.00
Crow Call, Higgins, Box 35.00
Crow Call, Perdue 125.00
Crow Call, Royd Martin, Tube 55.00
Duck Call, Allen 100.00
Duck Call, Bean Lake 50.00

Football Program, All Star, All–Americans, Green Bay Packers, 1937	55.00
Football Program, NFL, Green Bay Packers, Dallas Cowboys, 1967	61.00
Football Program, World, Baltimore Colts, New York Giants, 1959	151.00
Glasses, Souvenir, Kentucky Derby, 1953	21.95
Glasses, Souvenir, Kentucky Derby, 1956	19.95
Glasses, Souvenir, Kentucky Derby, 1969	4.95
Glasses, Souvenir, Kentucky Derby, 1974, Golden Anniversary	11.95
Glasses, Souvenir, Kentucky Derby, 1983	2.95
Golf Ball, Gutties, Box, 12 Piece	2640.00
Golf Ball, Rubber Core, Post–1900s	50.00
Golf Ball, Rubber Wound, Haskell	264.00
Golf Ball, Spalding Black Domino, C.1912, Box, 12 Piece	1650.00
Golf Club, Putter, Otto Hackbarth	605.00
Golf Club, Putter, Philip	2420.00
Golf Club, Putter, Tom Morris	2585.00
Golf Club, Sand Iron, Walter Hagen, Concave	506.00
Goose Call, Olt, Box	10.00
Ice Skates, Ace of Spades, Clamp On Shoe Style	9.50
Ice Skates, Curled Ends, Steel Blades, Wooden, Leather Straps	250.00
Ice Skates, Kees Mfg., Iron, Box	20.00
Ice Skates, Man's, Winchester	30.00
Ice Skates, Rogers & Co., Blondin, Engraved Brass, 1860	500.00
Ice Skates, Sonja Henie, Signed, White, Box, 1938	200.00
Ice Skates, Union Hardware, May 1860	35.00
Ice Skates, Webster City, Iowa, Patent 1902	37.50
Ice Skates, Winchester, Boxed Clamp	25.00
Ice Skates, Winchester, No.6121	20.00
Ice Skates, Wrought Iron Blades, Front Curve, 12 3/4 In.	150.00
Lamp, Figural, Baseball, Bat On Shoulder, Batter On Shade	365.00
License, Deer, New York, 1936	12.00
License, Hunting, Illinois, Linen Canvas, Red, 1907	350.00
License, Trapping, New York, 1917	85.00
Photograph, Babe Ruth, With Autograph	550.00
Pin, Angels Baseball Team, 25th Anniversary, 1961–1985	6.00
Pin, Dodgers, Beat Twins 4 Games To 3, 1965 World Series, 3 In.	3.00
Pin, Ducks Unlimited, 1947	80.00
Pin, Ducks Unlimited, 1948	80.00
Pin, Press, Brooklyn Dodger, 1953	466.00
Pin, Yogi Berra, Topps, 1956	75.00
Plate, Lou Gehrig, N.Y. Yankees Old–Timers Day, Commemorative, 1953	1980.00
Pool Table, 4 Slate, Leather Pocket, Piano–Type Legs, 1865	4500.00
Pool Table, Brunswick, Iron Lion's Head Base, Civil War Period	7200.00
Pool Table, Brunswick, Mahogany, 3 Piece Slate, 1910, 10 Ft.	3500.00
Pool Table, Brunswick, Medalist, 1928	7500.00
Pool Table, Brunswick, Monarch, Cast Iron Lion Head Base	6300.00
Pool Table, Rosewood Rails, Ivory Diamonds, Oak, C.1900, 9 Ft.	2900.00
Poster, Football, Swarthmore–Bucknell, 1930s	75.00
Program, Joe Louis Vs. Harry Thomas, Chicago, April 1, 1938	35.00
Puck, Hockey, Winchester	190.00
Record, Babe Ruth, Lou Gehrig, Home Run Twins, 78 RPM	25.00
Roller Skates, Winchester, 1925	35.00
Silks, Turkey Red Tobacco, 1911, 15 Piece	225.00
Sled, Walnut, Oak, Iron Runners, 72 In.	110.00
Snooker Table, Pearl Inlay, Walnut, 1920s, 5 X 10 Ft.	850.00
Snowshoes, Ash Frame, Rawhide Filled, Maine	60.00
Tennis Racket, Wright & Ditson	35.00
Thrower, Clay Pigeon, Remington Arms, Cast Iron, Spring–Powered	90.00
Ticket Stub & Program, World Series, Game 3, 1932	1485.00
Turkey Call, Roger Latham, True Tone	20.00
Yearbook, Dodgers, 1963	20.00
Yearbook, Green Bay Packers, 1967	37.00
Yearbook, Mets, 1975	12.00
Yearbook, New York Jets, 1969	30.00

Pottery and porcelain have been made in the Staffordshire district in England since the 1700s. Hundreds of kilns are still working in the area. Thousands of types of pottery and porcelain have been made in the many factories that worked and still work in the area. Some of the most famous factories have been listed separately, such as Adams, Davenport, Ridgway, Rowland & Marsellus, Royal Doulton, Royal Worcester, Spode, Wedgwood, and others. Some Staffordshire pieces are listed under sections like Fairing, Flow Blue, Shaving Mug, etc.

STAFFORDSHIRE, see also Flow Blue; Mulberry

STAFFORDSHIRE, Bank, Cottage, Man & Woman, Standing On Either Side 650.00
Bowl, Railway Scene, Brown Transfer, 1830, 6 3/4 In. 110.00
Bowl, Red & Blue Stick Flowers, Pedestal, 5 In. 42.00
Box, Trinket, Held By Hand 85.00
Chamber Pot, Genevese, Green Transfer 85.00
Chimney Piece, Boy & Cow, Crazed, 9 In. 135.00
Chimney Piece, Equestrian Scotsmen, 14 1/2 X 14 3/4 In., Pr. 600.00
Chimney Piece, Figural, Man, Enameled, 16 In. 350.00
Chimney Piece, Sheep, Marked, 4 3/4 In. 80.00
Clock, 2 Girls & Dog, 9 1/2 In. 340.00
Clock, Dancing Couple, Painted, 11 1/2 In. 300.00
Coffeepot, Dome Cover, Sprig Design, Blue, Red, Green, 12 In. 85.00
Coffeepot, Man Sitting Under Tree, 13 In. 400.00
Creamer, 3 Color Swag Design, Leaf Handle, 4 1/4 In. 45.00
Creamer, Cow 625.00
Creamer, Cow, Milkmaid 175.00
Cup & Saucer, Floral Reserves On Powder Blue, 11 Sets 275.00
Cup & Saucer, Handleless, Basket of Flowers 95.00
Cup & Saucer, Handleless, Birds & Flowers 35.00
Cup & Saucer, Handleless, Floral Design, Purple Luster 55.00
Cup Plate, Aurora, Light Blue Transfer, C.1850 .... 25.00
Cup Plate, Blue Transfer, English Country House, 3 3/4 In. 75.00
Cup Plate, Blue Willow Transfer, Hackwood, 3 3/8 In. 25.00
Cup Plate, Fakeer's Rock 95.00
Cup Plate, Longport, Blue 45.00
Dish, Hen On Cover, Basket Base, White, 7 In. 225.00
Dish, Hen On Cover, Basket Weave Nest, 3 1/2 X 3 1/2 In. 75.00
Dish, Hen On Cover, Black & Brown, Orange Basket Base 250.00
Dish, Hen On Cover, Black, Gold Eggs, 8 In. 250.00
Dish, Hen On Cover, White, Light Brown Basket, 10 In. 325.00
Dish, Vegetable, Cover, Olmypian, Purple Transfer, 12 In. 150.00
Dish, Vegetable, Cover, Valle Crucis Abbey, Wales, 12 1/4 In. 325.00
Figurine, Blue Hawks, M. Doubell Miller, 8 1/2 In., Pair 195.00
Figurine, Cat, On Haunches, Sarah & James, 9 3/4 In., Pair 935.00
Figurine, Cat, Polychrome Enamel, 7 1/4 In., Pair 210.00
Figurine, Country Couple, 10 In. 275.00
Figurine, Dog, Brown, White, Gilt, Glass Eyes, 13 1/4 In. 85.00
Figurine, Dog, Copper Luster Spots, 9 1/4 In., Pair 360.00
Figurine, Dog, Puppy, Brown & White, 1840, 3 1/2 In. 50.00
Figurine, Dog, Red & White, Basket In Mouth, 7 1/2 In., Pair 800.00
Figurine, Dog, Red & White, Gilt Trim, 12 1/2 To 13 In., Pair 370.00
Figurine, Dog, Seated, Black & White Enamel, Gold, 14 In. 300.00
Figurine, Dog, Seated, Purple Luster Basket, 3 1/8 In. 95.00
Figurine, Dog, Seated, Red & White, 5 1/4 In. 105.00
Figurine, Dog, Spaniel, Black & White, Miniature 60.00
Figurine, Dog, White, Gold Luster Spots, Pair 235.00
Figurine, Lamb, Tree, Polychrome Enamel, Marked, 4 3/4 In. 45.00
Figurine, Lion, Mottled Brown, Glass Eyes, 11 In. 175.00
Figurine, Lion, Paw On Ball, Bocage, Walton, 5 In. 302.00
Figurine, Man With Sheaf of Wheat, Woman With Ewer, 10 In. 265.00
Figurine, Mother & Child, Enameled, Pink Luster, 6 3/8 In. 200.00
Figurine, Poodle, Coleslaw Coat, Polychrome Enamel, 4 In., Pr. 170.00
Figurine, Prince Albert, Standing, With Flag, 1850, 16 In. 467.00

Figurine, Prince Albert, With Unicorn & Lion, 6 3/4 In. 300.00
Figurine, Prince Frederick William, On Horse, Prussia, 14 In. 660.00
Figurine, Prince Frederick William, Prussia, 12 1/2 In. 710.00
Figurine, Prodigal's Return, 13 3/4 In. 300.00
Figurine, Robbie Burns & Highland Mary, 14 1/2 In. 325.00
Figurine, Soldier's Dream, 1 Legged, 10 1/4 In. 425.00
Figurine, Spaniel, King Charles, 1850–60 .... 285.00
Figurine, Woman With Mandolin, 6 1/2 In. 245.00
Figurine, Woman, Child's Coffin, Spaniel, Pillow, 9 In. 725.00
Figurine, Woman, Sheaf, Personifying Autumn, 8 3/4 In. 275.00
Figurine, Zebra, Rocky Base, 8 1/2 In., Pair 885.00
Group, 2 British Sailors, Cannon, 10 1/2 In. 660.00
Group, 2 Girls, Polychrome Enamel, 9 3/4 In. 105.00
Group, 2 Lovers Beneath Arbor, 13 In. 198.00
Group, Pig Tithing, C.1800 .... 1350.00
Group, Woman, Leading Goat, 5 1/2 In. 385.00
Inkwell, Figural, Bird's Nest 120.00
Jug, Wide Band Top & Bottom, Handle, Spout, 5 1/2 In. 110.00
Mug, 2 Frogs, Hunt Scene, George Lowbridge, 1851, 5 1/2 In. 275.00
Mug, A Trifle For Eliza, Yellow, 2 In. 275.00
Mug, Child's, Gleaners, Girl With Sheaf of Wheat 110.00
Mug, D For Dog, Red Transfer, 3 In. 125.00
Mug, Farmer, Wife, Cows, 4 In. 45.00
Mug, Frog, Drinking Scenes, 2 Handles, 5 1/2 In. 170.00
Mug, Silver Resist Medallion, Yellow Glaze, 2 In. 185.00
Mug, Zebra & Cat With Dish, Black Transfer, 3 1/2 In. 115.00
Pitcher, Black Transfer, European Scene, 10 3/4 In. 95.00
Pitcher, Embossed Scenes of Stags & Hunt, 6 3/4 In. 75.00
Pitcher, Floral Enameling, Underglaze Blue, 7 1/2 In. 55.00
Pitcher, Genovese, Medium Blue, 5 1/2 In. 75.00
Pitcher, Mask Spout, Black Floral Transfer, 5 1/4 In. 95.00
Pitcher, Polychrome Spray On Peach Ground, C.1805, 6 1/8 In. 295.00
Pitcher, Purple Transfer, King & Constitution, 6 1/4 In. 225.00
Pitcher, Purple Transfer, Landscape Scene, 9 In. 100.00
Pitcher, Seal of The United States, 6 1/2 In. 7040.00
Pitcher, Virginia, Black Transfer, 11 In. 135.00
Plate, Adam's Rose, 9 1/2 In. 95.00
Plate, Albion & C, Blue Transfer, Pair 20.00
Plate, Alphabet, Dr. Franklin Transfer, 7 In. 135.00
Plate, American Villa, Dark Blue, Foliage Edge, 7 1/2 In. 75.00
Plate, Boston Mails, Black Transfer, 9 In. 98.00
Plate, Capitol, Washington, Dark Blue, R & W Stevenson 575.00
Plate, Columbus, Center Indians, Buffalo Edge, 1830s, 12 In. 225.00
Plate, Dam & Water Works, Henshall, 10 In. 400.00
Plate, Entrance of Erie Canal Into Hudson, 10 1/4 In. 450.00
Plate, Floral, Red, Blue, Green & Black, 8 7/8 In. 95.00
Plate, Harvard College, Stevens, 10 In. 475.00
Plate, King's Cottage Windsor Park, Blue, 7 In., 4 Piece 220.00
Plate, Landing of Cadmus, 10 In. 275.00
Plate, McDonough's Victory, 10 In. 302.50
Plate, Medallion of Lafayette The Nation's Guest, 7 1/2 In. 2200.00
Plate, Nahant Hotel Near Boston, 8 1/2 In. 185.00
Plate, Oriental Scene, 9 1/4 In. 115.00
Plate, Oriental Scene, Clews, 8 3/4 In. 85.00
Plate, Oriental Scenery, Purple Transfer, 10 1/2 In. 45.00
Plate, Queen's Rose, 7 1/2 In. 135.00
Plate, Red Transfer, Italian Villas, 10 3/8 In. 85.00
Plate, Toddy, Green Transfer, Keep Within Compass, 5 1/4 In. 90.00
Plate, Toddy, Hospital Near Poissy, France, 6 1/8 In. 65.00
Plate, View of Transylvania University, 9 1/4 In., Pair 305.50
Plate, Warleigh House, Somersetshire, 8 1/4 In. .... 55.00 To 85.00
Plate, Welcome To The Land of Liberty, Lafayette, 6 3/4 In. 195.00
Plate, William Penn's Treaty, Brown Transfer, 7 1/2 In. 155.00
Platter, Hunting Scene, Clews, 18 1/2 In. 500.00

Platter, Landing of General Lafayette, Clews, 15 1/4 In. 450.00
Platter, Peach & Plenty, Clews, 17 In. 275.00
Platter, Post Office Dublin, 17 In. 350.00
Platter, R. Hall's Select Views, Vienna, Dark Blue, 19 In. 250.00
Platter, View, Christianburg, Danish Settlement, 18 1/2 In. 3410.00
Pot, Purple Transfer, Garden Scenery, Mayer, 11 3/4 In. 95.00
Sauceboat, Fruit & Flowers, 7 3/4 In. 135.00
Soup, Dish, Apple Blossom, C.1838 .... 25.00
Soup, Dish, Biddulph Castle, Staffordshire, 10 In. .... 55.00 To 90.00
Sugar Basin, Visit of Lafayette Vist America, 1824, Luster 450.00
Sugar Shaker & Creamer, Toby, Robust Man, Red Coat, 5 1/4 In. 195.00
Sugar, Lafayette At Franklin's Tomb, 4 3/4 In. 85.00
Tea Bowl, Scudder's American Museum, Staunton's Church Cup 95.00
Tea Set, Child With Dog & Cat, Brown Transfer, 8 Piece 65.00
Tea Set, Painted Pink Roses, Ivory Ground, Crown, 21 Piece 154.00
Teapot, Birds & Flowers, Medium Blue, 5 5/8 In. 85.00
Teapot, Medium Blue Transfer, Floral, 6 3/4 In. 175.00
Teapot, Purple Transfer, Persian, 6 In. 145.00
Teapot, Red, Green, Enameled Polka Dot Flowers, 7 In. 115.00
Teapot, Toby, Handle & Spout Are Legs, 10 1/2 X 7 In. 265.00
STAFFORDSHIRE, TOBY JUG, see Toby Jug
Tureen, Sauce, Tray, R. Hall's Select Views, 6 In. 375.00
Tureen, Turk With Camel, Blue & White, 12 In. 850.00
Vase, Cherub, With Lily–Like Bowl, Enameled, 9 1/4 In. 150.00
Vase, Marbled Glaze, Wilkinson, Late 19th Century, 8 1/4 In. 55.00
Vase, Spill, Stag & Hound, 11 1/4 In., Pair 925.00
Watch Holder, Castle Form, 12 In. 385.00
Watch Holder, Figural, Colonial Man, Sitting On Grass, 13 In. 165.00
Whistle, Child, Holding Rabbit On Lap, 2 In. 45.00
Whistle, Hen, Sitting On Brown Nest, 3 X 2 In. 45.00

The Fulper Pottery had a long history that entwined with the Stangl Pottery in 1910 when Johann Martin Stangl started work. He bought into the firm in 1913, became president in 1926, and in 1929 changed the company name to Stangl Pottery. The pottery made dinnerwares and a line of limited–edition bird figurines. The company went out of business in 1972.

STANGL, Ashtray, Flying Bird, 10 1/2 X 8 In. 15.00
Ashtray, Quail, Oval, 4 In. 30.00
Basket, Caribbean, Double 12.00
Bird, Bird of Paradise, No.3408 .... 85.00
Bird, Bluebird, No.3276 .... 58.00
Bird, Broadtail Hummingbird, No.3629 .... 110.00
Bird, Canaries, No.3746, No.3747, Pair .... 325.00 To 375.00
Bird, Cardinal, No.3444 .... 55.00 To 75.00
Bird, Cardinal, No.3596 .... 40.00 To 65.00
Bird, Carolina Wren, No. 590 .... 95.00
Bird, Cerulean Warbler, No.3456 .... 35.00 To 45.00
Bird, Chickadee, Group, No.3581 .... 100.00 To 140.00
Bird, Cock Pheasant, No.3492 .... 150.00
Bird, Cockatoo, No.3405 .... 40.00 To 55.00
Bird, Cockatoo, No.3580 .... 275.00
Bird, Cockatoos, Double, No.3405D .... 110.00 To 135.00
Bird, Cockatoos, No.3405D .... 110.00 To 135.00
Bird, Duck, Feeding, No.3250–C 30.00
Bird, Duck, No.3432 .... 225.00
Bird, Duck, No.3443 .... 225.00 To 275.00
Bird, Evening Grosbeak, No.3813 .... 85.00
Bird, Golden–Crowned Kinglet, No.3848 .... 85.00
Bird, Hen Pheasant, No.3491 .... 150.00
Bird, Hummingbird, No.3626 .... 70.00
Bird, Hummingbird, No.3627 .... 80.00
Bird, Hummingbird, No.3634 .... 48.00
Bird, Hummingbirds, No.3599D .... 130.00 To 250.00

Bird, Key West Quail Dove, No.3454	195.00
Bird, Kingfisher, No.3406	45.00
Bird, Oriole, No.3402	35.00
Bird, Orioles, No.3402D	75.00
Bird, Parakeets, No.3582D	95.00
Bird, Pheasant, No.3491, 12 In.	75.00
Bird, Prothontary Warbler, No.3447	70.00
Bird, Redstarts, No.3490D	175.00
Bird, Rooster, No.3445	175.00
Bird, Rufous Hummingbird, No.3585	50.00
Bird, Titmouse, No.3592	40.00 To 42.50
Bird, Western Tanager, No.3749	225.00
Bird, Woodpecker, No.3752D	250.00
Bird, Wrens, No.3401D	85.00
Bowl, Holly, Green & Tan, 10 In.	35.00
Candlestick, Gold	7.00
Candy Dish, Granada Gold	12.00
Coffeepot, Fruits	30.00
Coffeepot, Magnolia	25.00
Coffeepot, Town & Country, Spatter Design, Green	45.00
Creamer, Tiger Lily	5.00
Creamer, Wild Rose	5.00
Cup & Saucer, Fruit	16.00
Cup & Saucer, Orchard Song	7.00
Dinner Set, Garden Flower, 1950, 45 Piece	350.00
Dinner Set, Thistle, 57 Piece	225.00
Dish, Cover, Corn, 7 In.	35.00
Figurine, Dog, Brown & White, 5 In.	225.00
Figurine, Dog, Seated, Brown & Blue, 5 1/2 In.	225.00
Jug, Orange Rib	30.00
Juvenile Set, Mug & Divided Plate, Box	95.00
Match Holder, Donkey, Yellow	40.00
Pie Plate, Fruit	2.00
Pitcher, Terra Rose Fruit, 4 In.	7.00
Plate, Dessert, Country Garden With Well, Cup, 6 Sets	30.00
Plate, Fruit, Flowers, 10 In.	10.00
Plate, Gold Rim, Gold, Gray, Blue & Green Allover, 14 1/2 In.	25.00
Plate, Gold, Teal, Tan & Blue, 14 In.	20.00
Plate, Rose Tulip, 9 1/2 In.	12.00
Plate, Star Flower, Green, Yellow & White, 14 In.	15.00
Plate, Tulip, 14 In.	35.00
Relish, Magnolia	12.00
Salt & Pepper, Rooster & Hen	120.00
Sign, Granada Pottery	65.00
Sugar & Creamer, Magnolia	10.00
Vase, Terra Rose, 7 1/4 In.	35.00

Figurines are often damaged. Examine the fingers, toes, and other protruding parts for damage or repairs.

Steins have been used by beer and ale drinkers for over 500 years. They have been made of ivory, porcelain, stoneware, faience, silver, pewter, wood, or glass in sizes up to nine gallons. Although some were made by Meissen, Capo–di–Monte, and other famous factories, most were made in Germany. The words "Geschutz" or "Musterschutz" on a stein are the German words for patented or registered design, not company names. Steins are still being made in the old styles.

STEIN, ABC Brewery, King of Bottle Beers, Germany, 3 Liter 2500.00
   Bardwells Embossed In Blue, Stoneware, Pewter Lid 500.00
   Blown Glass, 15 In. 485.00
   Budweiser, Chicago Skyline 95.00
   Budweiser, Eagle Logo, Gray & White 100.00
   Budweiser, Figural Bud Man 252.00
   Budweiser, Holiday, 1981 .... 200.00
   Budweiser, Holiday, 1982 .... 80.00
   Budweiser, Olympics, 1984 .... 30.00
   Bulbous, Open, Pottery, Marzi & Remi, 6 In. 45.00
   Embossed Head & Florals, Glass Encased In French Pewter, 18 1/4 In. 550.00
   Enameled Shield, Armor & Animals, Germany, Green, 15 In. 495.00
   Hamm's Rathskeller 50.00
   Hand Painted Hunting Scene, 1890 .... 295.00
   Knight & Lady, With Falcon & Dog, Soldier, Cobalt Blue & Brown, 1890 .... 300.00
   Loving Couple, Cherub, Pewter Lid, Germany, 866 In Triangle, 4 Liter 225.00
     STEIN, METTLACH, see Mettlach, Stein
   Meunchner Kindel, Red On Tan Pottery, Pewter Lid, 1/2 Liter 165.00
   Monk, Stoneware, Gray & Cobalt Blue, Pewter Lid, 7 1/4 In. 165.00
   Moriage, Cover 175.00
   Munich Maid, Branch of Fruit, Prunts, Pewter Lid, Amber, 14 1/2 In. 495.00
   Munich, Child, Figure Holding Turnip, 1902, 1/2 Liter 200.00
   Pewter, Bicycle & Rider On Lid, 18 In. 285.00
   Regimental, 2nd Guard Ulan, Berlin, 1903–1904, Pottery 600.00
   Regimental, Nude Woman Lithophane, German 55.00
   Stein, Monk, Stoneware, Brown Beard, Hood Over Head, 6 7/8 In. 165.00
   Twisted Twig Handle, Open, Occupied Japan 15.00
   Usinger's Sausage, Milwaukee, Elves, Stoneware 15.00
   Woman's Head, Pigtail, Hat, Gold Beads Around Neck, Musterschutz 695.00
   Yowling Cat On Book, 1/2 Liter 1900.00

Stereo cards that were made for stereopticon viewers became popular after 1840. Two almost identical pictures were mounted on a stiff cardboard backing so that, when viewed through a stereoscope, a three–dimensional picture could be seen. Value is determined by maker and by the subject. These cards were made in quantity through the 1930s.

STEREO CARD, Black Woman Nursing White Child, Log Cabin, 1894 .... 90.00
   Blackfoot Indian Village, Tepees, Squaws, Montana 8.50
   Bofe Arms Full & Dat Rooster Beggin' To Be Took Along, 1904 .... 70.00
   Canton, China, Street Scene, 1900 .... 5.00
   Capitol of Old Dominion, Elevated View, Richmond, Va. 5.00
   Hindenburg, Black & White, Exterior & Interior View 275.00
   Hunting & Fishing Scene 12.00
   Kids Playing Marbles 60.00
   Moon, 4 Different Views, 4 Piece 32.00
   Motor Test Room, Detroit Auto Plant 7.50
   Mule–Drawn Trolley Wagon, Washington, D.C., 1870s 25.00
   S.S. Leviathan, Tugboats 10.00
   Views of 1889 Johnstown Flood, R.K. Bonine, 11 Piece 100.00
   We're Helpin' Dis Mule Plow Dis Stump Patch, 1909 .... 60.00
   Yosemite Valley, Bierstadt, 4 Different Views, 4 Piece 32.00

The stereoscope, or stereopticon, was used for viewing stereo cards. The hand viewer was invented by Oliver Wendell Holmes, although more complicated table models were used before his was produced in 1859.

STEREOSCOPE, Double, Folding, C.1860, 23 In. 200.00
   Free Standing, Cast Iron Base, 600 Around The World Views 600.00
   Mills, Floor Model, Oak 650.00

Monarch, 20 View Cards 75.00
STERLING SILVER, see Silver–Sterling

Steuben glass was made at the Steuben Glass Works of Corning, New York. The factory, founded by Frederick Carder and T. C. Hawkes, Sr., was purchased by the Corning Glass Company. They continued to make glass called "Steuben." Many types of art glass were made at Steuben. The firm is still making exceptional quality glass but it is clear, modern–style glass.

STEUBEN, see also Aurene

STEUBEN, Basket, Woven Pomona Green Crystal, Rod Handles, 8 In. 195.00
  Bonbon, Cover, Stylized Long–Horned Llama Head, Signed, 5 1/4 In. 220.00
  Bonbon, Rosaline, Alabaster Pedestal, Ruffled, Signed, 2 1/2 X 5 In. 125.00
  Bowl, 2 Rows of Light Blue Jade, Signed, Clear, 5 In. 125.00
  Bowl, Alabaster, Green Jade, Triangle Paper Label, 12 In. 375.00
  Bowl, Applied Scrolled Feet, Signed, Clear, 11 In. 255.00
  Bowl, Bristol Yellow Swirl Ribbed, Green Pedestal, 4 1/4 In. 120.00
  Bowl, Center, Yellow, Paneled Sides, Signature, 14 1/2 In. 130.00
  Bowl, Crystal, 8 In. 165.00
  Bowl, Flared, 1940, 11 In. 400.00
  Bowl, Flared, Petaled Floroform Foot, Signed, C.1925, 12 1/4 In. 770.00
  Bowl, Fleur–De–Lis, Mark Clear, 10 1/2 In. 195.00
  Bowl, Green Bowl, Amber Pedestal, Signed, 5 1/2 X 12 In. 195.00
  Bowl, Green Jade On Alabaster, Sticker Label, 12 In. 375.00
  Bowl, Grotesque, Amethyst, Rim Shaded To Clear, 6 In. 225.00
  Bowl, Rosaline, 8 1/2 In. 225.00
  Bowl, Rouge Flambe, 14 In. 6000.00
  Bowl, Silverina, Amethyst, 11 In. 850.00
  Bowl, Swirl, 6 Sides, Rosa Circular Foot, 6 In. 395.00
  Bunch of Grapes, Crystal, 7 1/2 In. 325.00
  Candleholder, Red, Ribbed, Hollow Stem, Floral Engraved, 7 In. 275.00
  Candlestick, Celeste Blue, 11 1/2 In. 150.00
  Candlestick, Green Jade, Alabaster, Baluster, 9 In. 220.00
  Candlestick, Hearts & Flowers, Green & Crystal, 4 X 5 In., Pair 125.00
  Candlestick, Twisted, Green, 10 In., Pair 250.00
  Candy Dish, Mica Fleck, Applied Green Leaves, Crystal, 5 1/2 In. 375.00
  Candy Dish, Underplate, Rosaline & Alabaster 170.00
  Centerpiece, Green, Swirled, Applied Leaves At Base, Footed 121.00
  Cigarette Holder, Alabaster, 4 1/2 In. 190.00
  Cocktail Set, Teardrop, Shaker & 6 Glasses 600.00
  Compote, Cover, Optic Rib, Pear Finial With Green Leaf, 8 3/4 In. 900.00
  Compote, Jelly, Underplate, Pear Finial 145.00
  Compote, Rosaline, Alabaster, Paper Label, 7 In., Pair 580.00
  Compote, Spiral Stem, Applied Prunts, Signed, 1905, 7 1/2 In. 1760.00
  Console Set, Mica Flakes, Glass Prunts, Topaz & Green, 3 Piece 1900.00
  Cracker Jar, Rosaline, Acorn Shape, 9 In. 350.00
  Decanter, Ship 500.00
  Figurine, Buddha, Alabaster Flower Holder, 7 In. 750.00
  Figurine, Buddha, Quan Yin, Alabaster, Flower Holder, 7 In. 750.00
  Figurine, Buddha, Quan Yin, Green, Stepped Black Glass, 8 1/2 In. 975.00
  Figurine, Elephant, Trumpeting, Upturned Trunk, Signed, 7 1/2 In. 675.00
  Figurine, Fisherman, Sterling Silver Eskimo, Box, 6 1/2 In. 2200.00
  Figurine, Gazelle 325.00
  Figurine, Owl, Signed, 5 1/2 In. 395.00
  Figurine, Penguin, Signed, Crystal 200.00
  Figurine, Snail, Signed, Crystal 175.00
  Figurine, Songbird, No.8112, Crystal, Signed, 4 1/2 In. 250.00
  Goblet, Ribbed Blue Crystal, Swirl Stem, 8 1/2 In. 95.00
  Goblet, Rosaline, Alabaster Twist Stem 325.00
  Goblet, Swirled Stem, Green Jade & Alabaster, Signed, 8 1/2 In. 155.00
  Goblet, Water, Cylindrical, Octagonal Base, 5 1/2 In., 15 Piece 415.00
  Jar, Chinese Style, Floral, Medallions, Pink On White, Lamp, 6 In. 225.00
  Jar, Ginger, Oriental Medallion, Leaves All Around, Black, 8 In. 1800.00
  Lamp, Acid Cut Back, Bristol Design, Green Jade, 20 In. 1100.00

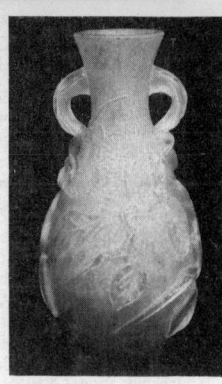

Steuben, Vase, Cluthra, Purple, Fleur–De–Lis, Signed, 8 In.

Steuben, Vase, Fan, Oriental Poppy, Pink, Green Foot, 8 1/2 In.

Steuben, Vase, Matsu–No–Ke, Rose Quartz, Frosted, 11 In.

Lamp, Acorn Design, Acid Cut Back, Crystal, 20 In.	650.00
Lamp, Chinese Pattern, 3 Arms, Gold Aurene Shades, Signed, 28 In.	1400.00
Lamp, Floor, Aurene, Intarsia Bordered Shade, Green, 58 In.	4000.00
Lamp, Green, 10 In.Intarsia Border Shade, Harp Aurene Base, 58 In.	3600.00
Lamp, Organic Leaf & Pod Design, Gold Aurene To Black, 32 In.	1650.00
Lamp, Plum Jade Acid Cut Back, Gold Aurene Shade	1450.00
Lamp, Sculptured Design, Acid Cut Back, Yellow Jade, 21 In.	1400.00
Lamp, Torchere, Brass & Iron Illuminating Mount, 6–Footed, 68 In.	1650.00
Lamp, Yellow Jade, Blue Aurene Design, 4 Cherubs Support, 24 In.	2395.00
Muddler, Twisted Rope Design, Clear, 1941, 4 3/8 In.	30.00
Ornament, Stylized Fish, Signed, Crystal, C.1935, 10 1/2 In., Pair	1200.00
Paperweight, Bird, Signed	200.00
Paperweight, Cane Twist, 3 In.	295.00
Paperweight, Frog, Signed	140.00
Paperweight, Snail, Signed	195.00
Parfait, Rosaline, Alabaster, 6 1/2 In.	150.00
Perfume Bottle, Lobed Teardrop Stopper, 8–Lobed Bottle, 4 1/2 In.	525.00
Perfume Bottle, Ribbed, Flower Top, Amber Stem, Bubbles, 12 3/4 In.	850.00
Pitcher, Silver Flowers Overlay, 8 1/2 In.	87.00
Plate, Amber, Aquamarine Gilded Edge, Signed, 8 3/4 In., 9 Piece	305.50
Plate, Opalescent, Red Edged, 8 1/2 In.	175.00
Plate, Rosaline, 8 1/2 In.	100.00
Shade, Gold Drape On Calcite	250.00
Shade, Gold Leaf & Vine On Calcite, Gold, Lining, Signed, 4 1/2 In.	155.00
Shade, Green Drape, Gold Edge On Calcite, Gold Lining, 5 In.	165.00
Sherbet, Celeste Blue, Amethyst, Mica Fleck Foot, 3 1/2 In.	165.00
Sherbet, Jade, White Base	100.00
Sherbet, Sterling Deposit, 6 Piece	420.00
Sherbet, Underplate, Jade Green, Alabaster, Signed, 4 X 6 1/4 In.	120.00
Sugar, Green Reeding At Top, Footed, 3 3/4 X 4 In.	85.00
Tazza, Calcite, Gold Interior, 6 1/2 X 2 In.	135.00
Vase, Alabaster, 6 In.	135.00
Vase, Alabaster, Green Jade, Signed, 8 In.	325.00
Vase, Applied Design, Cerise & Ruby, Silver Deposit, 3 In.	295.00
Vase, Bouquet, George Thompson Design, 6 1/4 X 5 In.	180.00
Vase, Bristol Swirl, 12 In.	395.00
Vase, Bubbly Body, Pink Reeded Top, Art Deco Shape, Signed, 8 In.	170.00
Vase, Bud, Black Amethyst, Fleur–De–Lis Mark, 16 In.	110.00
Vase, Cameo Design In Medieval Pattern, Black, 9 In.	3000.00
Vase, Chinese Rouleau, Green Overlay Landscape Panels, Lamp, 12 In.	710.00
Vase, Cluthra, Purple, Fleur–De–Lis, Signed, 8 In. ....*Illus*	1760.00
Vase, Crystal Floral Body, Blue Foot, 10 In.	100.00

Vase, Diamond Optic, Black Threading, Signed, 6 1/2 In. 145.00
Vase, Diamond, Green Threading, 13 In. 225.00
Vase, Dragon & Cloud, Black, Signed, 9 In. 1760.00
Vase, Fan, Amber, 8 1/2 In. 85.00
Vase, Fan, Oriental Poppy, Pink, Emerald Green Foot, 8 1/2 In. 2000.00
Vase, Fan, Oriental Poppy, Pink, Green Foot, 8 1/2 In. ....*Illus* 2200.00
Vase, Fan, Ribbed Topaz Crystal, Pedestal Foot, 8 1/2 In. 385.00
Vase, Flared Top Cover, Black Glass Threads, Bristol Yellow, 3 In. 150.00
Vase, Flared, Prunt On Each Side, Crystal, 4 3/4 X 6 1/2 In. 85.00
Vase, Fleur–De–Lis, Green Threaded, Clear, 5–In. Wide Top, 4 In. 185.00
Vase, Florida Pattern, Acid Cut Back, Black & White, 15 In. 3800.00
Vase, Green Jade, Diagonal Ribbed, Alabaster Lion's Heads, 7 In. 200.00
Vase, Green Jade, Diagonal Ribbed, Signed, 5 1/2 In. 150.00
Vase, Green Silverina, 6 3/4 In. 525.00
Vase, Green Swirl, 6 Sides, Amber Foot, 7 1/2 X 9 1/2 In. 325.00
Vase, Grotesque, 4 Sided, Clear To Green Shaded, Signed 375.00
Vase, Ivory Glass, Chinese Ovoid Shape, 8 In. 385.00
Vase, Ivory, Ribbed Base, Flared, Corset Shape, 5 X 5 In. 135.00
Vase, Jack–In–The–Pulpit, Ivrene, 6 1/2 In. 595.00
Vase, Matsu–No–Ke, Rose Quartz, Frosted, 11 In. ....*Illus* 5250.00
Vase, Oriental Poppy, Gold Dore Tiffany Mount, 19 In. 1950.00
Vase, Paperweight, Floral, 8 In. 2000.00
Vase, Pedestal Foot, Turned–Out Rim, Amethyst, Signed, 5 In. 120.00
Vase, Plum Jade & Amethyst, Paper Label, 10 In. 925.00
Vase, Ribbed Pedestal, Celeste Blue, 6 In. 100.00
Vase, Rosaline, 6 In. 700.00
Vase, Selenium Ruby Swirled, Signed, 7 In. 200.00
Vase, Silverina Air–Trap, Signed, 36 X 12 In. 700.00
Vase, Tree Trunk, Thorny, 6 1/8 In. 195.00
Vase, Tricornered, Ivory, 8 In. 185.00
Vase, Trumpet, Amber, Ribbed, 12 In. 80.00
Wine, Iridescent Red Base, Blue Bowl, Fleur–De–Lis, 6 In., 6 Pc. 300.00
Wine, Ribbed Crystal, Purple Swirl, Purple Plate, Signed, 5 1/2 In. 110.00
Wine, Rosaline, Cut Back To Alabaster, Pair 1250.00
Wine, Signed 75.00

Stevengraphs are woven pictures made like fancy ribbons. They were manufactured by Thomas Stevens of Coventry, England, and became popular in 1862. Most are marked "Woven in silk by Thomas Stevens" or were mounted on a cardboard that tells the story of the Stevengraph. Other similar ribbon pictures have been made in England and Germany.

STEVENGRAPH, Bookmark, Disraeli 75.00
Bookmark, Garibaldi 110.00
Bookmark, George Washington, 1876 Centennial ....85.00 To 125.00
Bookmark, With Kind Wishes For The New Year, Flowers 40.00
Present Time, Double–Sided 425.00
The Good Old Days, Framed 145.00

Stevens & Williams of Stourbridge, England, made many types of glass, including layered, etched, cameo, and art glass, between the 1830s and 1930s. Some pieces are signed "S & W." Many pieces are decorated with flowers, leaves, and other designs based on nature.

STEVENS & WILLIAMS, Basket, Butterflies, Thorn Handle, Stand, 8 3/4 In. 960.00
Basket, Robin's–Egg Blue, Amber Thorn Legs, 11 In. 750.00
Biscuit Jar, Ruffled Leaves, Pink Lined, 7 3/4 In. 275.00
Bottle, Scent, Blue Swirl Design, Enameled, 13 In. 325.00
Bowl, Floral, Crimped, White, Blue Inside, 6 X 7 1/2 In. 325.00
Bowl, Ruffled, Orange, 2 1/2 X 3 3/4 In. 145.00
Bride's Basket, Lime Green, Rose Mica Flakes, Marked 275.00
Bride's Bowl, Triangular 375.00
Jar, Cover, Alabaster Trim, Violet, 6 In. 225.00
Plate, Jewel, Threaded, Marked, 7 In. 65.00
Rose Bowl, Arabesque, Crimped Top, Crackle Surface 235.00

Rose Bowl, Box Pleated Top, Blue To White, 4 In.	225.00
Rose Bowl, Box Pleated Top, Brown & Gold, 4 1/8 In.	225.00
Rose Bowl, Box Pleated Top, Swirled, Aqua, 4 3/8 In.	195.00
Rose Bowl, Green & Amber, 2 3/4 In.	165.00
Rose Bowl, Pink & White Cased In Crystal, 3 In.	100.00
Rose Bowl, Thumbprint, Blue, 2 3/4 In.	175.00
Rose Bowl, Yellow & White Cased In Crystal, 2 1/4 In.	100.00
Rose Bowl, Yellow Amber, 2 3/4 In.	165.00
Shade, Peach, Ruffled, Clear Applied Flowers	165.00
Sherbet, Underplate, Royal Blue, Intaglio Cut, 5 In.	295.00
Sweetmeat, Blue Ribbon Swirl, Ribbed	265.00
Toothpick, Arabesque, Cranberry & White, Pair	125.00
Vase, 3 Panels of Flowers, Leaves, Green & Clear, 10 In.	815.00
Vase, Applied Flowers & Vines, 8 In.	350.00
Vase, Applied Leaves & Acorns, 7 In.	85.00
Vase, Arabesque, 5 In.	125.00
Vase, Crimped Top, Cranberry, 4 In.	175.00
Vase, Flowering Branches, Marked, C.1890, 13 1/2 In.	4675.00
Vase, Folded Top, Flowers, Amber Vine Feet, 11 In.	550.00
Vase, Golden Amber Interior, White, Exterior, 14 In.	125.00
Vase, Jack–In–The–Pulpit, Flowers, Amber & Pink	135.00
Vase, Layered In White, Vine Design, Amethyst	3200.00
Vase, Nasturtium Vines, Beetle At Side, Signed, 6 In.	3520.00
Vase, Rainbow Threaded, 8 In.	200.00
Vase, Sweetpea Shape, Emerald Green, 6 1/2 In.	225.00
Vase, Tan, Yellow, Blue Swirl, Floral, Pear Shape, 13 In.	275.00
Vase, White, Crystal Stripes, Center Dimples, 7 1/2 In.	340.00

Henry William Stiegel, a colorful immigrant to the colonies, started his first factory in Pennsylvania in 1763. He remained in business until 1774. Glassware was made in a style popular in Europe at that time and was similar to the glass of many other makers. It was made of clear or colored glass and was decorated with enamel colors, mold blown designs, or etching. It is almost impossible to be sure a piece was made by Stiegel, so the knowing collector now refers to this glass as Stiegel type.

STIEGEL TYPE, Flip, Engraved, Flint, Large	145.00
Vase, Tulip, Blue, 1939, 4 In.	85.00

Stoneware is a coarse, glazed, and fired potter's ceramic that is used to make crocks, jugs, bowls, etc. It is often decorated with cobalt blue decorations. Stoneware is still being made.

STONEWARE, Batter Jar, Robert Lohmann, Wheatland, Iowa	68.00
Bean Pot, Blue & Gray	395.00
Bean Pot, Blue & White	230.00
Bean Pot, Robin's–Egg Blue, Cobalt Blue Design	25.00
Beater Jar, 1/2–In.Cobalt Stripe Around Middle	40.00
Beater Jar, Blue Stripe	20.00
Beater Jar, Wesson Oil	75.00
Berry Bowl, 2 Cherries, Tan & Green, 7 3/8 In.	57.50
Bird Bath, Birds, Blue Ribbon, Blue & White	650.00
Bird House, 1890s	85.00
Bird Whistle, Yellow & Green Glaze, 4 In.	250.00
Bottle, Doughnut Shape, 9 In.	200.00
Bottle, E. Schmidt	40.00
Bottle, G & Co., Blue Highlights, 9 3/8 In.	30.00
Bottle, G.H. Winn, Blue, 9 3/4 In.	10.00
Bottle, Marked M. Moran	10.00
Bottle, Paul Pohl, Chicago	65.00
Bottle, Sake, Tamba, 10 In.	110.00

Bottle, Smith White Root Beer, Patent July 17, 1866, 9 7/8 In. 55.00
Bottle, Walters Whiskey, Cincinnati, Ohio, 11 In. 65.00
Bowl, Apricot & Honeycomb, 9 In. 125.00
Bowl, Apricot, 8 In. 60.00
Bowl, Apricot, 9 1/2 In. 75.00
Bowl, Apricot, Blue & White, 9 In. 95.00
Bowl, Blue Sawtooth, Ruckles Pottery 50.00
Bowl, Cobalt Blue Leaf, Spout, Impressed 1, 10 7/8 In. 325.00
Bowl, Cobalt Blue Slip, Label Johanns Bros., 4 4/8 X 8 1/2 In. 150.00
Bowl, Colonial, Blue Trim, 8 In. 50.00
Bowl, Daisy & Waffle, 9 1/2 In. 80.00
Bowl, Daisy & Waffle, 10 1/4 In. 80.00
Bowl, Dough, McNerney, 136 .... 275.00
Bowl, Dough, White & Blue Stripes, Robinson Clay Products, 14 In. 85.00
Bowl, Geneva, Iowa, Advertising, Blue, Rust & Cream Spatter, 7 In. 125.00
Bowl, Greek Key, Blue & White, Large 95.00
Bowl, Milk, Rim Spout, Applied Handles, Foliage Design, 4 1/2 In. 425.00
Bowl, Milk, Spout, Cobalt Blue Rim Foliage, 4 In. 300.00
Bowl, Mixing, Dark Blue, Raised Design, Small 15.00
Bowl, Reverse Pyramids, Reverse Picket Fence, Ruckels, 10 1/2 In. 100.00
Bowl, Swirl, Blue & White, Large 150.00
Bowl, Three Brushed Cobalt Blue Stripes, 3 7/8 In. 425.00
Bowl, Wedding Ring, Blue & White, 5 In. .... 50.00 To 55.00
Bowl, Wedding Ring, Blue & White, 7 In. 60.00
Brick, Architectural, 2–Rayed Rosette Design, 8 1/2 X 4 X 2 In. 75.00
Brick, Architectural, Fleur–De–Lis, Star In Circle, 8 1/2 X 4 In. 130.00
Butter Carrier, Swastika, Wire Bail, Wood Handle, 6 In. 150.00
Butter, Cover, Apple Blossom .... 160.00 To 200.00
Butter, Cover, Butterfly, Blue & White .... 90.00 To 95.00
Butter, Cover, Cows & Columns 175.00
Butter, Cover, Eagle, Blue & White 475.00
Butter, Cover, Grapes & Leaves, 8 In. 135.00
Butter, Cows & Columns, Blue & White 245.00
Butter, Daisy On Waffle 75.00
Butter, Good Luck 65.00
Butter, Wildflower, Blue & White 250.00
Canister, Rice, Blue & White 175.00
Canister, Snowflake, Blue & White 100.00
Canister, Snowflake, Blue & White, 6 Piece 575.00
Canteen, Embossed Design, String Handle, 3 In. 500.00
Casserole, Cover, Sawtooth, Ruckles, Blue 55.00
Chamber Pot, Beaded Rose 110.00
Chamber Pot, Blue & White, Applied Handle 100.00
Churn, A.D. Ruckles, White Hall, Ill., Albany Glazed, 6 Gal. 75.00
Churn, Blue Floral, N. Clark, Athens, N.Y. 575.00
Churn, Brushed Cobalt Blue, Foliage Design, 19 1/2 In. 175.00
Churn, Burger, Shore Bird, 5 Gal. 2600.00
Churn, Butter, Slip Design, W.A. Macquid, 1863, 15 In. 550.00
Churn, Butter, Swan & States 375.00
Churn, Davis Bros., Blue Bands, Wooden Lid 45.00
Churn, E & LP Norton, Bird On Dotted Leaf Spray, 2 Gal. 1600.00
Churn, Eagle Pottery, Benton, Ark, 10 Gal. 85.00
Churn, John Burger, Sunflower, Ribbed Leaves, Dotted Bird, 4 Gal. 2000.00
Churn, M.C. Ward Stoneware Depot, Zanesville, 5 Gal. 245.00
Churn, Western Stoneware Co., Wooden Lid & Dasher, 10 Gal. 87.50
Churn, Western, Bail Handle, 3 Gal. 120.00
Churn, White & Wood, Blue Floral & Leaf, 8 Gal. 4800.00
Churn, White's, Binghamton, Stylized Urn of Flowers, 6 Gal. 420.00
Cider Set, Pitcher & 8 Mugs, Barrel Shape 125.00
Coffee Pail, Home Brand, Biggs, Cooper, Bail Handle, 5 Lb. 35.00
Colander, Straight Sides, Dated July 4, 1895 .... 1300.00
Cooler, Blue & White, Western Stoneware, Chain, 16 In. 795.00
Cooler, Cover, Robinson Clay Products, Ohio, Blue & Gray 350.00
Cooler, J. Fisher & Co., Bird On Branch, Sponge Bands, 6 Gal. 2500.00

Cooler, Polar Bear, Blue & White	525.00
Cooler, Rebecca At The Well	275.00
Cooler, Revigator, Uranium Lined, Dangerous	120.00
Cooler, T. Crafts & Co., Pouring Holds Front & Back, 4 Gal.	750.00
Cooler, Water, Cobalt Blue Clover, 2 Handles, Spigot, 13 5/8 In.	425.00
Cooler, Weeks, Akron, Ohio, Sponge Design	170.00
Cooler, Wm. M.L. Bruney, Eagle Medallion, 4 Gal.	3750.00
Creamer, Swirl Handle, Black Chain Link Bands, Gray	60.00
Crock, 2 Blue Bands, 2 Qt.	38.00
Crock, 2 Freehand Flowers, No. 8, 8 Gal.	195.00
Crock, A.J. Burger Jr., Dotted Bird Standing On Leaves, 3 Gal.	2400.00
Crock, A.W. Eddy, McComb, Ill., 6 Gal.	100.00
Crock, Applied Half–Moon Handles, Cobalt Rose, 3 Gal.	350.00
Crock, B.G. Chace, Somerset, Cobalt Blue Design, 17 1/2 In.	137.00
Crock, Beige & Brown, 6 Gal.	22.50
Crock, Bird On Branch, Cobalt Blue Slip, 8 In.	250.00
Crock, Blue Band, Bail Handles, Round Mark, 6 Gal.	75.00
Crock, Blue Rearing Horse, Palatine Pottery Co., 2 Gal.	750.00
Crock, Blue Ribbed, Freestanding Handles, Ovoid, 1 Gal.	2500.00
Crock, Blue Rooster, J.A. & C.W. Underwood, Fort Edward, 3 Gal.	2750.00
Crock, Bouquet of Flowers, Cobalt Blue, 6 X 12 In.	495.00
Crock, Bread In Relief, Trees All Around, Blue, Cream, 11 X 13 In.	295.00
Crock, Brushed Cobalt Blue Leaf, Norton, 6 Gal.	475.00
Crock, Butter, Blue & White Sponge Spatter, 4 X 10 In.	100.00
Crock, Butter, Cobalt Blue Foliage, 6 X 9 1/2 In.	250.00
Crock, Butter, Cobalt Blue Scroll, 8 1/2 X 5 1/4 In.	225.00
Crock, Butter, Cover, Applied Handles, Brushed Cobalt Blue, 7 In.	725.00
Crock, Butter, Cover, Maple Leaves, White's Pottery, Bail Handle	175.00
Crock, C. Hadle & Co., Triple Flowers On Blue, 2G, 2 Gal.	100.00
Crock, Cake, Blue Floral From Top To Bottom & Around, 3 Gal.	500.00
Crock, Cala Lilies, Cobalt Blue, 2 Gal.	58.00
Crock, Cheese, Koehler & Hinrichs, Gray & Blue	135.00
Crock, Chicken' Pickin' Corn, New York State, 2 Gal.	695.00
Crock, Child Life Shoes, Blue Lettering, 3 1/2 In.	30.00
Crock, Cluster of Grapes, Cowden & Wilcox, 4 Gal.	625.00
Crock, Cobalt Blue 6 & Floral Design, Handles, 6 Gal.	320.00
Crock, Cobalt Blue Bird On Branch, 5 Gal.	750.00
Crock, Cobalt Blue Bird On Tree Stump, C.1850, 6 Gal.	247.50
Crock, Cobalt Blue Bird, No.2, 2 Gal.	100.00
Crock, Cobalt Blue Maple Leaf, 3 Gal.	42.00
Crock, Cobalt Blue Quill Work, No.3, West Troy, N.Y., 10 3/4 In.	250.00
Crock, Cobalt Blue Slip Design, No.2, Double X's, 10 1/4 In.	250.00
Crock, Cobalt Blue Tulip, Cowden & Wilcox, Harrisburg, 8 In.	260.00
Crock, Cobalt Blue, Floral Design, Large 5, 12 3/4 In.	150.00
Crock, Cobalt Blue, No.4, 11 3/4 In.	275.00
Crock, Cobalt Flowers, 1 Gal.	58.00
Crock, Cobalt Starburst, T. Harrington, Lyons, Ovoid, 5 Gal.	4500.00
Crock, Cover, Blue Wildflowers, Word Butter On Side, 9 In.	150.00
Crock, Cream, Cobalt Wreath, Nathan Clark, C.1813	435.00
Crock, Floral Design, E. Norton & Co., 12 1/2 In.	225.00
Crock, Ft. Dodge, Iowa, Brown Glaze, 4 Gal.	85.00
Crock, James Hamilton, 1 Gal.	185.00
Crock, Leaf Design, Fisher & Co., Lyons, N.Y., No.2, 9 In.	105.00
Crock, Macomb, Ill., Satin Glaze, Ears, 12 Gal.	65.00
Crock, Minnesota, Brown Lined Salt Glaze, 1 Gal.	40.00
Crock, No.3 & Cobalt Blue Quill Work, 10 1/2 In.	95.00
Crock, Pecking Chicken, Athens	525.00
Crock, Pickle, Vent Holes In Lid, 2 Gal.	185.00
Crock, Pittsburgh Pottery, 4 Gal.	45.00
Crock, Reclining Dog, Tree & Fence, J & E Norton, 2 Gal.	1600.00
Crock, Robin On Branch, New York Stoneware Co., 1870–90, 2 Gal.	137.50
Crock, Salt Glaze Design, Maxfield, C.1854, 2 Gal.	750.00
Crock, Salt Glazed, Galesburg, Illinois, 12 Gal.	225.00
Crock, Salt, Butterfly, Blue & White	150.00

Crock, Salt, Hanging, Wildflower, All Around Pattern 195.00
Crock, Salt, Peacock, Blue & White 165.00
Crock, Swan Design, 6 Gal. 110.00
Crock, Western Stoneware Co., Brown & White, 1 Gal. 19.00
Crock, White, Sawtooth, 1 Pt. 30.00
Crock, White, Sawtooth, 1 Qt. 32.00
Crock, Wilkinson Fleming, Shinston, W.Va., 1 Gal. 275.00
Cup, Bowtie, Bird Transfer, Blue & White 75.00
Cup, Bowtie, Rose Decal 65.00
Cuspidor, 5 1/8 X 2 3/8 In. 60.00
Cuspidor, Beaded Rose, Blue & White 115.00
Cuspidor, Blue & White 100.00
Cuspidor, Blue Leaves 275.00
Cuspidor, Brown Albany Slip Interior, Blue Design, 6 3/4 In. 70.00
Cuspidor, Peacock, Blue & White 300.00
Cuspidor, Revolving Leaf Design 110.00
Flagon, Pewter Lid, Incised Foliage, 11 In. 55.00
Flask, Cobalt Blue Band Rim, 8 In. 65.00
Flask, Ovoid, Gray & Tan, 8 1/2 In. 95.00
Holder, Toothbrush, Roses & Bows 75.00
Humidor, What Cheer, Dog Finial 135.00
Ink Bottle, Conical, Cobalt Blue Zigzag Line, 2 3/8 In. 350.00
Inkwell, Quill Holder, Mustard Green Glaze, 4 In. 190.00
Jar, Applied Handle, Cobalt Blue Floral, 12 In. 350.00
Jar, Applied Handles, Floral, 11 1/2 In. 325.00
Jar, Applied Handles, Impressed Label, Wreath, Cobalt Blue, 12 In. 550.00
Jar, Blue Foliage, S. Bell & Son, Strasburg, No.2, 12 3/4 In. 150.00
Jar, Brushed Cobalt Blue Floral, Handles, Ovoid, 11 1/2 In. 160.00
Jar, Brushed Cobalt Blue Flower, Ovoid, 8 3/4 In. 235.00
Jar, Brushed Cobalt Blue Stripes, 6 1/2 In. .... 150.00 To 175.00
Jar, Brushed Cobalt Blue Stripes, Wavy Line, 6 3/4 In. 150.00
Jar, Brushed Floral Design & 5, Ovoid, 16 In. 600.00
Jar, Canning, 4 Stenciled Stars, 6 1/4 In. 450.00
Jar, Canning, Cobalt Blue Floral Band, 10 1/4 In. 145.00
Jar, Canning, Cobalt Blue, Flowers, 8 3/8 In. 125.00
Jar, Canning, Cobalt Blue, Foliage, 8 1/8 In. .... 100.00 To 110.00
Jar, Canning, Dark Brown Albany Slip, 5 5/8 In. 90.00
Jar, Canning, Freehand Label, Hamilton & Jones, 10 In. 50.00
Jar, Canning, G. Husher, Brazeil, Indiana, 19th Century 170.00
Jar, Canning, Large Mouth, Minnesota Stoneware, Tall 42.00
Jar, Canning, Peoria Pottery 20.00
Jar, Canning, Stenciled 1 & Dot Design, 9 1/2 In. 50.00
Jar, Canning, T.F. Reppert, Greensboro, Pa., Cobalt Stenciled 225.00
Jar, Canning, Zinc Lid, Macomb Pottery, 2 Qt. 62.00
Jar, Cobalt Blue Design, Open Handles, R.H., 8 3/4 In. 200.00
Jar, Cobalt Blue Floral & 3, Gray Salt Glaze, 14 1/2 In. 175.00
Jar, Cobalt Blue Floral Design, Open Handles, 8 5/8 In. 175.00
Jar, Cobalt Blue Floral, Ovoid, 10 1/4 In. 175.00
Jar, Cobalt Blue Flower, Ovoid, 6 5/8 In. 150.00
Jar, Cobalt Blue Flower, Red Interior, Golden Highlights, 11 In. 250.00
Jar, Cobalt Blue Greek Key, Dated 1886, 1/2 Gal. 115.00
Jar, Cobalt Blue Quill, 7 3/8 In. 375.00
Jar, Cobalt Blue Slip, No.3, Stylized Foliage, Ovoid 200.00
Jar, Cobalt Blue Stenciled & Freehand Label, 14 1/2 In. 200.00
Jar, Cobalt Blue, No.12, Ovoid, 21 3/4 In. 95.00
Jar, Cover, Buff Clay & Brown Glaze, Incised 10 .... 65.00
Jar, Cover, Pantry, Banded, Blue & White 275.00
Jar, Crolius, Blue Stars On Either Side 800.00
Jar, Diagonal Stenciled Label, Cobalt Blue, 6 1/4 In. 250.00
Jar, Dotted Chain & Flower, Morgan, 4 Gal. 1100.00
Jar, E.N. Ballard, Burlington, Vt., 2, Quill Work Floral, 10 In. 300.00
Jar, Eagle, Words T.F. Reppert, Eagle Pottery, 16 Gal. 2100.00
Jar, Floral, Brushed Blue Cobalt, 15 In. 200.00
Jar, Flowers, Stenciled & Free Hand, Hamilton & Jones, 13 3/4 In. 275.00

Jar, Flowers, Stenciled & Freehand, Hamilton & Jones, 13 3/4 In. 275.00
Jar, Hamilton & Jones, Greensboro, Pennsylvania, 13 1/2 In. 150.00
Jar, Hamilton & Jones, No.4, Stenciled, Freehand Label, 14 3/4 In. 175.00
Jar, Impressed 1, Band of Florals At Shoulder, 10 3/4 In. 225.00
Jar, Impressed Label, Cobalt Blue Slip, Polka Dot Bird, 9 3/4 In. 550.00
Jar, Impressed Label, Foliage, Cobalt Blue, 20 In. 350.00
Jar, Lid, Moon, Green, 1 Qt. 50.00
Jar, Lid, Stars, Green, 2 Qt. 50.00
Jar, Polka Dot Floral, Cobalt Blue Slip, 10 1/4 In. 475.00
Jar, Preserving, Cobalt Blue Brushed Leaf Design, 8 3/8 In. 95.00
Jar, Red Clay, Gray Salt Glaze, Ovoid, 13 1/2 In. 40.00
Jar, Refrigerator, Cover, Bail Handle, Blue & White 185.00
Jar, Refrigerator, Nebraska Advertising 165.00
Jar, S. Purdy, Daubs of Cobalt Blue, 14 1/2 In. 100.00
Jar, Salt–Glazed, Lug Handles, Cowden & Wilcox, 2 Gal. 2800.00
Jar, Stag Between 2 Fences, Trees, J & E Norton, 3 Gal. 2250.00
Jar, Stenciled, Freehand Label, 11 3/4 In. 105.00
Jar, Storage, Cobalt Blue 2 and R.P. Williams, 11 5/8 In. 150.00
Jar, Swan, Brushed Cobalt Blue, 8 In. 550.00
Jug, Allover Cobalt Blue Sponging, 1 Gal. 250.00
Jug, Batter, Cobalt Floral, Evans R. Jones, No.4, Wire, 8 7/8 In. 525.00
Jug, Beehive, Buckeye, 5 Gal. 75.00
Jug, Bird On Branch, Cobalt Blue Slip, Impressed Label, 7 In. 300.00
Jug, Bird On Branch, Cobalt Blue Slip, Impressed Label, 13 In. 400.00
Jug, Bird On Branch, Norton & Co., 14 In. 400.00
Jug, Bird Perched On Branch, E. & I.P. Norton, C.1861, 3 Gal. 400.00
Jug, Blue Band, Straight Mark, 1 Gal. 47.50
Jug, Blue Horse Head, W. Hart, Ogdensburg, 5 Gal. 3100.00
Jug, Brown & Gray Mottled Salt Glaze, Circle Designs, 11 1/4 In. 45.00
Jug, Brown Glaze, Black Slip Floral Design, 1 Gal. 175.00
Jug, Brown Slip Design, Flower, Foliage, Impressed Label, 11 In. 500.00
Jug, Brushed Cobalt Blue Design, 1840, 12 In. 300.00
Jug, Brushed Cobalt Blue Leaf Design, 12 In. 65.00
Jug, Brushed Floral Design, Lyman & Clair, Gardiner, 12 1/2 In. 485.00
Jug, Cobalt Blue At Handle, Ribbed, Impressed Label, 12 In. 175.00
Jug, Cobalt Blue Brushed Design, Stripe & Commas, 9 1/2 In. 210.00
Jug, Cobalt Blue Daisy & Lazy Eight, Double Fisted, 8 Gal. 1250.00
Jug, Cobalt Blue Floral Design, Double Ear Handle, 17 In. 450.00
Jug, Cobalt Blue Floral Design, Impressed 3, 14 3/4 In. 200.00
Jug, Cobalt Blue Floral Design, No.3, Ovoid, 14 1/4 In. 225.00
Jug, Cobalt Blue Floral, Label 2, Ovoid, 14 3/4 In. 225.00
Jug, Cobalt Blue Flower, No.2, Gray Salt Glaze, 11 3/4 In. 225.00
Jug, Cobalt Blue Flower, Shenfelder, Reading, Pa., 1 Gal. 525.00
Jug, Cobalt Blue Foliage Design, 11 In. 175.00
Jug, Cobalt Blue Foliage, Ovoid, 10 In. 145.00
Jug, Cobalt Blue Illinois Map, 2 Gal. 42.00
Jug, Cobalt Blue Medallion, H. Cowden, Harrisburg, 1 Gal. 150.00
Jug, Cobalt Blue Pumpkin–Head Man, Leaves, 13 3/4 In. 550.00
Jug, Cobalt Blue Slip Flowers, C. Hart, Sherburne, No.2, 13 In. 175.00
Jug, Cobalt Blue Stenciled Label, Hamilton & Jones, 12 1/2 In. 125.00
Jug, Cobalt Blue Tulip, Cowden & Wilcox, 1870–81, 2 Gal. 325.00
Jug, Cobalt Blue, Floral Wreath, Stenciled, Freehand Label, 11 In. 500.00
Jug, Cobalt Leaf, A.J. Buttler, No.3, Squatty, Wooden Plug, 3 Gal. 270.00
Jug, Dash Marks In Cobalt Blue Slip, 1840, 12 In. 325.00
Jug, Floral Design, Cobalt Blue Quill, Impressed Label, 11 In. 200.00
Jug, Floral Design, Cobalt Blue Slip, Impressed Label, 16 In. 650.00
Jug, Floral Design, Impressed 1, Ovoid, 11 In. 75.00
Jug, Floral Design, Seymour, Troy Factory, No.2, 12 1/2 In. 80.00
Jug, Floral, Stylized, E. & L.P. Norton, No.2, 14 1/2 In. 225.00
Jug, Flower & 2 In Quillwork, Burger & Lang, 14 1/2 In. 300.00
Jug, Flowering Fruit Tree, J. & E. Norton, Handle, C.1850, 2 Gal. 550.00
Jug, Freehand Litha Spring Water, Londonberry, N.H., 3 Gal. 375.00
Jug, Gray Salt Glaze, Brown Highlights, 7 1/2 In. 250.00
Jug, Hear Design, Burley & Winter, Crooksville, Ohio, 5 Gal. 60.00

Jug, Impressed Bird, Brushed Blue, 12 In. 200.00
Jug, Impressed Flower In Deep Cobalt Blue Quill, 14 In. 1750.00
Jug, Incised Stylized Tulip, Cobalt Blue, Ribbed Handle, 14 In. 90.00
Jug, Lip Spout, Brown Albany Slip Glaze, Molasses Label, 10 In. 40.00
Jug, Lip Spout, Brown Albany Slip, E. & L.P. Norton, 9 1/4 In. 55.00
Jug, Lovebirds, Branch, Cobalt Blue Quill, Impressed Label, 11 In. 625.00
Jug, Minnesota Stoneware Co., 1 Pt. 275.00
Jug, Mottled Brown Highlights, Cobalt Blue Under Label, 11 In. 125.00
Jug, Mottled Salt Glaze, H. Purdy Label, 11 1/2 In. 150.00
Jug, National Pickel & Canning Co., 1 Gal. 68.00
Jug, Ovoid, Dark Gray Glaze, Handle, C.1830, 6 In. 150.00
Jug, Ovoid, H. Tyler, Albany, No.2, 13 1/4 In. 125.00
Jug, Ovoid, I. Seymour & Co., Troy, 14 1/2 In. 75.00
Jug, Ovoid, J. Swank & Co., Johnston, Pa., 10 In. 300.00
Jug, Ovoid, Stedman Seymour, New Haven, Tooled Lines, 16 In. 180.00
Jug, Ovoid, Swaine, Albany Slip, Tooled Neck, 3 Gal. 50.00
Jug, Parrot On Branch, Cobalt Blue Slip, Impressed Label, 12 In. 925.00
Jug, Parrot On Branch, J. Norton & Co., 10 3/4 In. 450.00
Jug, Petty's Tonic, Sioux City, Iowa, Pig Front, 3 Gal. 185.00
Jug, Platt Valley, Straight Corn Whiskey, 1 Pt. 45.00
Jug, Polka Dot Bird, Branch, Cobalt Blue, Impressed Label, 14 In. 825.00
Jug, Poppy Flower, Roberts, Binghamton, 1 Gal. 190.00
Jug, Poppy, Leaves, Honesdale, Penna., Blue & Gray, 2 Gal. 350.00
Jug, Rock Island Line, Blue Letters, 1 Gal. 165.00
Jug, S. Hart, Marked Jaud In Blue Script, 1 Gal. 75.00
Jug, Satterlee & Mory, 4 Gal. 975.00
Jug, Stylized Floral Design, Cobalt Blue Quill, 13 3/4 In. 375.00
Jug, Tin Lid, Spout Cap, Wooden Handle, Wire Bail, 8 1/4 In. 1350.00
Jug, Triple Budded Flower, Lewis & Caddy, 2 Gal. 175.00
Jug, When Empty Return To A.P. Grizzard, 1 Gal. 55.00
Jug, White, Large Bird, 5 Gal. 800.00
Jug, Wine, Labeled His Master's Breath, Blue Dog 50.00
Jug, Woven Basket of Flowers, James Power, Wine Merchant, 4 Gal. 750.00
Measure Set, Handle, Graduated, 4 Piece 495.00
Mug, 2 Incised Bands, Cobalt Blue, 4 1/4 In. 55.00
Mug, Auld Lang Syne, Bearded Man Handle 45.00
Mug, Bardwells Root Beer, Embossed Scene In Blue 100.00
Mug, Barrel Shape, Blue, Set of 6 .... 45.00
Mug, Battleship Maine 55.00
Mug, Belfast Root Beer 12.00
Mug, Blue Scroll Design, N. White, Utica 190.00
Mug, Bowtie, Hot Water, Transfer of Roses 65.00
Mug, Cobalt Blue & Manganese Design, Germany, 4 1/8 In. 170.00
Mug, Embossed Bands, Cobalt Blue, 5 In. 25.00
Mug, Embossed Bands, Marked Hausmann, N.Y., 5 In. 25.00
Mug, Embossed Blue Vintage & Prosit, 4 7/8 In. 10.00
Mug, Flying Bird, Blue & White ....95.00 To 185.00
Mug, Incised Floral, Cobalt Blue Bands, 6 In. 110.00
Mug, Incised Lines, Cobalt Blue Floral Design, 5 In. 110.00
Mug, Old Milwaukee, Windmill, Cabins, Lake, Brown 35.00
Mug, White, Brown Transfer, Gesundheit, Lane Co, Cleveland, 6 In. 35.00
Mug, Wildflower, Blue & White 95.00
Pan, Milk, Diamond Point, Blue & White 55.00
Pitcher & Bowl Set, Fishscale & Wild Rose, 5 Piece 600.00
Pitcher & Bowl, Basket Weave, Blue & White 220.00
Pitcher & Bowl, Fishscale & Wild Rose, Blue & White ....225.00 To 250.00
Pitcher, ABC Incised On Each Side, Miniature 600.00
Pitcher, Apricot Pattern, Blue & White, 8 In. 245.00
Pitcher, Avenue of Trees, Blue & White, 8 In. 300.00
Pitcher, Banded Scroll, Blue & White, 7 In. 115.00
Pitcher, Basket Weave With Flower, Blue & White, 8 In. 155.00
Pitcher, Basket Weave, Large Flower Each Side, Brown, 7 In. 95.00
Pitcher, Blue Bands, Christel's Cash Store, Brillion, Wisc., 8 In. 210.00
Pitcher, Blue Cow, Alkaline Glaze, 9 1/2 In. ....175.00 To 325.00

Pitcher, Blue Flower, Germany, 1 1/2 Liter	185.00
Pitcher, Bluebird, Blue & White, 9 In.	275.00
Pitcher, Bow & Knot, Blue & White, 8 In.	100.00
Pitcher, Bowtie, Blue & White, 9 In.	145.00
Pitcher, Brushed Cobalt Blue, Stylized Leaf Design, 13 1/4 In.	375.00
Pitcher, Butterfly, Blue & White, 9 In.	295.00
Pitcher, Cattail, Blue & White, 7 In.	105.00
Pitcher, Cattails, Blue & White, 8 In.	125.00
Pitcher, Cherry Band, Advertising, 7 In.	220.00
Pitcher, Cherry Band, Blue & White, 7 In.	125.00
Pitcher, Cosmos, Blue & White, 7 In.	165.00
Pitcher, Cows, Blue & White, 8 In.	160.00
Pitcher, Cows, Dark & Pale Blue, 9 In.	185.00
Pitcher, Cows, Yellow & Green, 7 In.	90.00
Pitcher, Deer Leaping, Blue & White, 9 In.	175.00
Pitcher, Doe & Fawn, Blue & White, 9 In.	150.00
Pitcher, Doe & Fawn, Solid Blue, 9 In.	115.00
Pitcher, Double Cherry Band, Blue & White, 8 In.	145.00
Pitcher, Dragonfly, Blue & White, 8 In.	165.00
Pitcher, Dutch Boy & Girl Kissing, 7 In.	125.00 To 175.00
Pitcher, Dutch Landscape Scene, Blue & White, 7 In.	165.00
Pitcher, Edelweiss, Blue & White, 8 In.	125.00
Pitcher, Elk Standing, Blue & White, 10 In.	325.00
Pitcher, Embossed Blue & Black Designs, Germany, 9 1/8 In.	25.00
Pitcher, Embossed Grapes, Blue & White, 7 3/4 In.	95.00
Pitcher, Fishscale & Wild Rose, Blue & White, 7 In.	70.00
Pitcher, Fishscale & Wild Rose, Blue & White, 10 In.	135.00
Pitcher, Floral Design, Brushed Cobalt Blue, 12 1/4 In.	150.00
Pitcher, Flying Birds, 3 Birds, Blue & White, 9 In.	200.00 To 260.00
Pitcher, Good Luck, 8 In.	190.00
Pitcher, Grape & Lattice, Blue & White, 7 In.	100.00
Pitcher, Grape Arbor, Blue & White, 7 In.	120.00
Pitcher, Grape Arbor, Blue & White, 10 In.	150.00
Pitcher, Grape Cluster, Blue & White, 7 In.	155.00
Pitcher, Grapes & Shield, Green, 7 1/2 In.	65.00
Pitcher, Grapes & Waffle, Blue & White, 8 In.	165.00
Pitcher, Gray Salt Glaze, Floral Design, Cobalt Blue, 9 1/4 In.	55.00
Pitcher, Indian Boy & Girl, Blue, White, 8 In.	230.00
Pitcher, Indian Head In Relief, Brown Glaze, 8 1/2 In.	75.00
Pitcher, Indian In War Bonnet, Blue & White, 8 In.	195.00 To 225.00
Pitcher, Indian With Headdress, Green & Cream, 8 1/2 In.	145.00
Pitcher, Indian, Good Luck, Blue & White, 8 In.	115.00
Pitcher, Lovebirds, Blue & White, 9 1/2 In.	195.00 To 325.00
Pitcher, Morning Glory, Basket Weave, Blue & White, 8 In.	150.00
Pitcher, Old Men With Canes, Dogs' Heads, Fish Handle, 10 1/2 In.	175.00
Pitcher, Poinsettia, Blue & White, 10 1/2 In.	245.00
Pitcher, Rose & Basket Weave, Blue & White, 8 In.	135.00
Pitcher, Rose On Trellis, Spatter Over Pattern, 8 In.	150.00
Pitcher, Rose On Trellis, Tan, 8 In.	95.00
Pitcher, Spongeware, Blue, White, Square Handle, 6 1/2 In.	245.00
Pitcher, Stag, Blue & White, 9 1/2 In.	275.00 To 295.00
Pitcher, Swan, Blue & White, 8 In.	185.00 To 295.00
Pitcher, Swirl, Blue & White, 10 1/2 In.	280.00
Pitcher, Tavern Scenes, Flemish Jugs, Blue & White, 8 3/4 In.	125.00
Pitcher, Wild Rose, Blue & White, 10 In.	275.00 To 350.00
Pitcher, Wildflower, Blue & White, 10 In.	295.00
Pitcher, Windmill & Tulip, Blue & White, 8 1/2 In.	165.00
Punch Set, Cover, Castle Scenes, Gerz, 7 Piece	295.00
Rock, R.T. Williams, New Geneva, Penna., 20 Gal.	550.00
Rolling Pin, Decorah, Iowa	200.00
Rolling Pin, Holy Cross, Iowa	200.00
Rolling Pin, Jos. A. Huber, Ft. Atkinson, Iowa	225.00
Rolling Pin, Orange Band	200.00
Rolling Pin, Wildflower, Advertising	210.00

Rolling Pin, Wildflower, Blue & White .... 170.00 To 300.00
Salt Box, Blue & White, Flying Birds 95.00
Salt Box, Blue, Gray, Crazed 67.50
Salt Box, Butterfly 125.00
Salt Box, Chick On Nest 150.00
Salt Box, Cover, Good Luck, Blue & White 175.00
Salt Box, Flying Bird, Blue & White 225.00
Salt Box, Indian Good Luck, Blue & White 75.00
Salt Box, Lid, Daisy, Word Salt, Blue & White 105.00
Salt Box, Lid, Embossed Basket Weave Design, 6 3/4 X 6 1/2 In. 55.00
Salt Box, Oak Leaf 85.00
Salt Box, Peacock 300.00
Salt Box, Wooden Lid, Blackberry, Blue & White 125.00
Sandwich Server, Gold, Brown Rim, Canonsburg Pottery, 14 In. 27.50
Slop Jar, Basket Weave, Blue & White 150.00
Slop Jar, Bowtie 75.00
Smoking Stand, Sponging, Robinson Clay Products, 1910, 8 In. 80.00
Soap Dish, Beaded Medallion 100.00
Soap Dish, Bowknot, Blue & White 110.00
Soap Dish, Cat, Blue & White 100.00
Soap Dish, Drain, Goodwin Bros. 15.00
Soap Dish, Fishscale & Wild Rose, Blue & White 90.00
Soap Dish, Lion, Blue & White 165.00
Syrup, Peoria Pottery 150.00
Syrup, Rich Fruit, Brown & White, Paper Label, 1 Gal. 145.00
Syrup, Whites, Utica, Blue Slip Daffodils & Lily, 6 1/2 In. 190.00
Tankard, Brown & White, Silver Lid, Applied Design, Trees, 11 In. 250.00
Tankard, Scrolled Border, Green Cows Each Side, 2 Qt. 125.00
Teapot, Morning Glory, Blue & White 115.00
Teapot, Wild Boars & Flowers, Blue & White 250.00
Tray, Green Glaze, Lug Feet, R. Kitaoji, C.1930 .... 1320.00
Umbrella Holder, White 100.00
Urn, Cobalt Blue, Conrad, 1 Gal. 80.00
Vase, 2 Handles, Gray, Cobalt Trim, 7 In. 245.00
Vase, Cemetery Icicle, White 40.00
Vase, Nicodemus, Columbus, Ohio, 8 1/8 In. 85.00
Vase, Silver Overlaid, Silver Coiling Snake, W. Kage, C.1935 .... 2500.00
Waste Pail, Fishscale & Rose 225.00
Whiskey Barrel, 6 Raised Bands, Tan Glaze, 14 X 21 In. 395.00

Most items found in an old store are listed under advertising in this book. Store fixtures, cases, cutters, and other items that have no advertising as part of the decoration are listed here.

STORE, Backbar, Light Oak, Refinished, 1890s, 18 Ft. 4500.00
Backbar, Rococo Style, 11 Beveled Mirrors, Mahogany 3750.00
Barber Shop, Oak, 3 Sections, 11-Ft. Mirrored Backbar 1700.00
Bin, Seed, Oak, 14 1/2 Ft. 4000.00
Box, Cabinet, Pearl Button, Cardboard 20.00
Box, Coffee, Red Cardboard, Floor Size 20.00
Cabinet, Bolt, Revolving, Octagonal, Hardware Store Type 450.00
Cabinet, Display, Adjustable Shelves, Oak, 6 Ft.2 In. X 10 Ft. 4250.00
Cabinet, Drugstore, Pine, Crown Top, 2 Glass Doors, 2 Sliding Doors 1250.00
Cabinet, Hardware, Revolving, 98 Drawers 1350.00
Cabinet, Nuts & Bolts, 98 Drawers, Revolving, 30 X 64 In. 1075.00
Cabinet, Nuts & Bolts, Revolving, 6 Sides 750.00
Cabinet, Pine, 9 X 9 Ft. 575.00
Cabinet, Ribbon, Oak, 4 Pull Down Glass Doors, 26 1/2 X 28 X 7 In. 468.00
Cabinet, Tobacco, Mahogany, 8 X 8 Ft. 895.00
Carrier, Milk Bottle, Wooden Handle 20.00
Case, Cigar, Glass Top, Marble Base, Water Trays, Tin Lined 240.00
Case, Collar, 5 Glass Sides, Oak, Collar Tin Clips, 25 X 14 X 9 In. 385.00
Case, Collar, Holds 6 Collars Vertically 650.00
Case, Display, Oak, Marble Base, Glass All Sides, 24 Ft. X 36 X 36 In. 578.00
Case, Hand Carved, Glass Doors, Black, French 2000.00

Case, Mahogany, Cornice, 2 Glazed Doors, England, 59 X 44 In.	412.00
Case, Oak, Floor, Mirrored Sliding Back Doors, 42 X 49 X 27 In.	468.00
Cash Drawer, Oak, Indiana, Serial 191832	35.00
Change Dispensing Machine, Penny Arcade, Wooden	65.00
Check Perforator, B.F. Cummins Co., Cast Iron, Pat.July 29, 1890	65.00
Check Writer, Rotary, Nickel Plated	75.00
Check Writer, Wesley, 1897	90.00
Cheese Cutter, Cast Iron	95.00
Cigar Cutter, Harvard, Keywind, Works	300.00
Cigarette Machine, Counter, Rotary	125.00
Clothes Rack, Metal, Circular	90.00
Counter, Bank, Art Deco, Walnut, Black Marble, 2 Windows, 1920s, 10 Ft.	300.00
Counter, Bean Or Macaroni, Oak, 18 Drawers, 89 X 34 X 28 In.	1100.00
Counter, Coffee Display, Oak, 4 Glass Front Bins, 48 X 47 X 17 In.	660.00
Counter, Golden Oak, Flat Panels, 10 Ft. X 34 X 20 In.	330.00
Counter, Oak, 12 Back Drawers & Front Glass Display Drawers	1895.00
Counter, Walnut Top, Pine Bottom, 8 Drawers, 35 In. X 15 Ft.	600.00
Cutter, Oilcloth, Iron	50.00
Figure, Twinkle, Clown, Eyes Roll, Nose Lights, Mechanical, 19 X 12 In.	295.00
Grain Bin, Slant Lid, Hand–Planed, Ohio	485.00
Holder & Cutter, Wrapping Paper, 30 In.	10.00
Ice Cream Cone Holder, Glass, Dated July 1916	275.00
Icebox, Commercial, 7 Doors, Lig–O–Nier, 6 Ft.3 In. X 7 Ft.3 In.	2500.00
Lighter, Cigar, Ruby Globe, Y & B, 20 In.	900.00
Peanut Machine, Star Peanut, Clown On Top	675.00
Pie Rack, Grocery Store, Holds 8 Pies, Nickel Plated, 1930s	65.00
Popcorn & Peanut Machine, From Movie House, 70 X 26 X 29 In.	2600.00
Potato Chip Stand, Wall Style, Blue	15.00
Rack, Oak, Floor, 4 Adjustable Shelves, Step Type, 4 Ft.	335.00
Receipt Writer, National, Autographic	750.00
Safe, Black, Gold Letters, Key Lock Inside 2 Doors, Lock Box, 1920s	575.00
Seed Counter, Sherer, Display Windows, 31 Drawers, Label Handles	1750.00
Shoe Fitter, X–Ray, Wooden Base, 1927	150.00
String Holder, Ball of String, Cast Iron	42.00
String Holder, Beehive, Cobalt Blue Glass, 1880	225.00
String Holder, Mexican Hat Man	22.00
Till, Shopkeeper's, Mahogany, Victorian, 2 6–Tiered Banks, 17 X 25 In.	405.00
Tobacco Cutter, Buzz Saw, Small Saw Blades On Sides	325.00
Workbench, Jeweler's, Drawers	360.00

Stoves have been used in America for heating since the eighteenth century and for cooking since the nineteenth century. Most types of wood, coal, gas, kerosene, and even some electric stoves are collected.

STOVE, Cook, Home Comfort	650.00
Cook, Kalamazoo, Wood Burning, Turquoise & Cream, Queen Anne Legs	950.00
Cook, Roper, Cream & Green Enameled, Oven, 4 Burners	100.00
Demilune, Iron, Brass, Pierced Panels, Victorian, Ring Handles, 37 In.	770.00
Parlor, Art Westminster, Troy, N.Y., Dated 1885, Lowe Art Tiles	5500.00
Parlor, Atlantic, Model 214, Cast Iron, Dated 1901, 56 X 19 X 19 In.	176.00
Parlor, National Arcana, Cast Iron, 40 In.	165.00
Pot Belly, Dandy, No.11	250.00
Pot Belly, King, No.30	250.00
Pot Belly, Leader Globe No.128	150.00
Pot Belly, Mt. Penn, No.11	250.00
Pot Belly, Victory, No.16	500.00

STRAWBERRY, see Soft Paste

Stretch glass is named for the strange stretch marks in the glass. It was made by many glass companies in the United States from about 1900 to the 1920s. It is iridescent. Most American stretch glass is molded; most European pieces are blown and may have a pontil mark.

STRETCH GLASS, Bowl, Topaz, Fenton, 1921, 10 In.	35.00

Ring Tree, Vaseline 34.00

Sumida, or Sumida Gawa, is a Japanese pottery. The pieces collected by that name today were made about 1895 to 1970. There has been much confusion about the name of this ware, and it is often called "Korean Pottery" or "Poo ware." Most pieces have a very heavy orange–red, blue, or green glaze, with raised three-dimensional figures as decorations.

SUMIDA, Bowl, 5 Oriental Figures At Top, Nest of Eggs, Symbols, 8 1/2 In. 225.00
   Bowl, Creatures On Rim, Seal Mark, 7 In. 95.00
   Brush Pot, Applied Monkeys, Seal Mark, 4 In. 90.00
   Brush Pot, Child's, Seal Mark, 4 In. 90.00
   Pitcher & Mugs, Various Scenes of People, Cartouche, 7 Piece 825.00
   Tankard Set, With 3 Mugs, 12 1/2 In. 825.00
   Tankard, Orange Tigers On Ledge, Ribbed Body, Drip Glaze, 12 1/2 In. 350.00
   Vase, 4 Oriental Boys, Glossy Mottled Gray, Blue & Brown, 9 1/2 In. 165.00
   Vase, 4 Relief Oriental Children On Front, Brown Glaze, 9 5/8 In. 195.00
   Vase, Battle Scenes, 7 3/4 In., Pair 25.00
   Vase, Oriental Children On Front, Letters On Back, 11 5/8 In. 245.00

 Sunbonnet Babies were first introduced in 1902 in the "Sunbonnet Babies Primer." The stories were by Eulalie Osgood Grover, illustrated by Bertha Corbett. The children's faces were completely hidden by the sunbonnets. The children had been pictured in black and white before this time, but the color pictures in the book were immediately successful. The Royal Bayreuth China Company made a full line of children's dishes decorated with the Sunbonnet Babies. Some Sunbonnet Babies plates have been reproduced but are clearly marked.

SUNBONNET BABIES, Bell, Fishing, Wooden Clapper, Royal Bayreuth 450.00
   Book, 7 Color Plates of Days of Week, Hardcover, 1907 .... 45.00
   Box, Stamp, Cover, Washing & Ironing, 2 3/4 X 2 In. 295.00
   Box, Trinket, Cleaning, Scrolled Rim, Blue Mark, 4 In. 350.00
   Cake Plate .... 380.00 To 380.00
   Candleholder, Cleaning, Shield Back 350.00
   Candlestick, Blue Mark, 4 In. 145.00
   Candlestick, Cleaning, Blue Mark 210.00
   Candlestick, Washing, Blue Mark 210.00
   Compote, Cleaning, Blue Mark, 3 X 5 3/4 In. 395.00
   Creamer, Bulbous, Gold Handle, Royal Bayreuth 195.00
   Cup & Saucer, Washing & Ironing 90.00
   Dish, Child's, Feeding, Mending, Blue Mark 225.00
   Dish, Child's, Feeding, Underwood's High Chair, 1912 .... 85.00
   Dish, Trinket, Fishing, Club Shape, Blue Mark 235.00
   Fernery, Washing, Ironing, Mending, Sweeping, 5 3/4 In. 795.00
   Hair Receiver, Sweeping, 3 Gold Feet, Blue Mark 450.00
   Hair Receiver, Washing, Scalloped Base 525.00
   Jug, Cleaning, Blue Mark, 4 1/4 In. 235.00
   Mush Set, Ironing, Underplate, 3 Piece 775.00
   Nappy, Royal Bayreuth 300.00
   Plate, 3 Groupings, Sewing, Gold Trim, 7 1/2 In. 90.00
   Plate, Days of The Week, Royal Bayreuth, 7 Piece 950.00
   Plate, Fishing, Royal Bayreuth, 6 In. 60.00
   Postcard, 12 Months of The Year, Dated 1908, Set 130.00
   Postcard, 7 Days of The Week, Dated 1908, Ullman, 7 Piece 98.00
   Postcard, Being Kissed, Bliss, R. Behrendt, 1902 .... 6.50
   Postcard, December 9.00
   Postcard, Twins, Tuesday 9.00
   Print, 7 Days of The Week, Complete Set 25.00
   Relish, Open Handle, Royal Bayreuth, 8 In. 125.00
   Toothpick, 3 Square Handles Out of Rim, Blue Mark 375.00
   Toothpick, Cleaning, Sterling Rim, Royal Bayreuth 395.00
   Toothpick, Mending, Coal Hod Shape 325.00
   Tray, Dresser, Royal Bayreuth, 9 3/4 In. 340.00

Tray, Handles, Oval, Blue Mark, 7 3/4 X 4 1/4 In.	195.00
Tray, Ironing, Blue Mark, 7 X 10 In.	275.00

Sunderland luster is a name given to a special type of pink luster made by Leeds, Newcastle, and other English firms during the nineteenth century. The luster glaze is metallic and glossy and appears to have bubbles in it.

SUNDERLAND, Bowl, Black Transfer, Scenes, Sailor's Farewell, 10 1/8 In.	570.00
Bust, Shakespeare, Pearlware, Pink Luster Base, 8 1/2 In.	325.00
Chamber Pot, Black Transfer, Bridge, Marriage Verse, 8 1/2 In.	550.00
Creamer, Blue Band, Enameled Floral Design, 3 5/8 In.	135.00
Cup & Saucer, Handleless, Miniature	45.00
Figurine, Allegorical, 4 Seasons, Pink Luster, 8 1/2 To 9 In.	3000.00
Jar, Cover, Black Transfer, Pink Luster, Enameling, 4 1/2 In.	100.00
Jug, Dickens Characters, Pink Cloud Luster, 8 In.	175.00
Jug, Puzzle, Gaudy Welsh Floral, 7 In.	300.00
Mug, 2 3/4 In.	55.00
Mug, Black Transfer, Sailor's Farewell, 5 In.	225.00
Mug, Seashells, Pink & White Inside & Out	47.50
Pitcher, Bride, Verse, Man Doom'D To Sail, 7 1/4 In.	375.00
Pitcher, Mariner's Arms, Word Game Landlord Caution, 5 7/8 In.	300.00
Pitcher, Old Castle, Coach & Horses On Front, 3 In.	145.00
Pitcher, Portrait Medallions, Brown, Black, 5 3/4 In.	4550.00
Pitcher, Sailor's Tear, Ship, Florals, 5 In.	280.00
Plaque, Black Transfer, Green Stripe, 6 1/4 In.	175.00
Plaque, Black Transfer, Ship, Verse, 8 1/2 X 7 5/8 In.	250.00
Plaque, Center Portrait of William Gladstone, Spatter Rim	90.00
Plaque, May They Ever Be United, Black Transfer, 8 X 9 In.	250.00
Pot, Masonic Verse, Reverse, May They Ever Be United, 6 1/2 In.	300.00
Shaving Mug, Masonic, Inscriptions, Black, Purple, 3 3/4 In.	300.00
Tea Caddy, Black Transfer of 4 Seasons, 4 3/4 In.	15.00
Wine, Copper Luster Trim, Polychrome Floral Design, 4 In.	105.00

Superman was created by two seventeen–year–olds in 1938. The first issue of "Action" comics had the strip. Superman remains popular and became the hero of a radio show in 1940, cartoons in the 1940s, a television series, and several major movies.

SUPERMAN, Book, Return To Krypton, Annual, United Kingdom, 1960–61	25.00
Button, Official Superman Fan Club, 1966, 3 1/2 In.	20.00
Card, Playing, 1977	10.00
Dime Bank, Breaking His Chains, Tin Litho, 1940s	225.00
Doll, Mego, 1979, Box, 12 1/2 In.	35.00
Figure, Comic Action Hero, Mego, 1975, 3 3/4 In.	47.00
Figure, Flying, Inflatable, Japan, 1966	35.00
Figure, Metal Joints, Elastic Belt, Mego, 1973, Box, 8 In.	175.00
Figurine, Chalkware, Carnival	150.00
Figurine, Musical, Ceramic, Japan, 1978, 7 1/2 In.	30.00
Game, Board, Calling Superman	100.00
Game, Flying Bingo, Whitman, 1966	25.00
Game, Speed, Milton Bradley, 1941	115.00
Glasses, 1964, Large	15.00
Glasses, 1964, Small	10.00
Lunch Box, Thermos, 1967	25.00 To 125.00
Lunch Box, Thermos, 1978–80	35.00
Model Kit	15.00
Night–Light, Ceramic, Japan, 1978, Box, 7 1/2 In.	50.00
Pencil Box	35.00
Phonograph, 1978	45.00
Pinback, Superman PEP	8.00
Poncho, 1976	35.00
Puppet, Ideal, Package, 11 1/2 In.	30.00
Radio, Box, 1973	35.00 To 100.00
Record Set, 33 1/3 RPM, 1970s, 3 Piece	5.00
Ring, Crusader	200.00

Spoon, Stainless Steel, Imperial, 1966 .... 9.00
Tank, Battery Operated 600.00
Thermos, 1980 .... 4.00 To 5.00
Toy, Watch, 1976 .... 8.00
Truck, Corgi Junior, Daily Planet Ads On Side Panels, 1978 .... 12.00
Tumbler, Pepsi–Cola, 1976 .... 8.00
Turnover Airplane, Red Face, Tin Litho, Mechanical, Marx, 6 In. 1870.00
TV Guide, George Reeves & Superman, 3 Pages, Sept. 25, 1953 .... 225.00
Wallet, 1940s 50.00
Wallet, 1966 .... 25.00
Wristwatch, 1948 .... 235.00

In 1933, the Kraft Food Company began to market cheese spreads in decorated, reusable glass tumblers. These were called "Swankyswigs." They were discontinued from 1941 to 1946, then made again from 1947 to 1958. Then plain glasses were used for most of the cheese, although a few special decorated Swankyswigs have been made since that time. A complete list of prices can be found in "The Kovels' Illustrated Price Guide to Depression Glass and American Dinnerware."

SWANKYSWIG, Carnival, Orange .... 3.00 To 5.00
Cornflower, No.2 .... 3.50
Daisy 3.00
Forget–Me–Not, Red 2.00
Rooster 8.50
Star, Blue 5.00
Star, Red 5.00
Tulip, No.1, Red, 3 1/2 In. 3.00

All types of swords are of interest to collectors. The military dress sword with elaborate handle is probably the most wanted. Be sure to display swords in a safe way, out of reach of children.

SWORD, American, Polished Steel, Ivory Handle, Etched Blade & Case, 36 In. 220.00
Basket Hilt, Blade, 37 In. 2090.00
Bayonet, Brown Bess, Revolutionary War, British 65.00
Bayonet, Hauger, Scabbard & Over Shoulder Sling, Civil War 95.00
Bayonet, Remington, In Scabbard Marked Jewell, 1917 .... 80.00
Bayonnet, Brass Hilt, Steel Single Edged Blade, Pattern 1801, England 124.50
Long, Dragon Blades, Ivory Inlay On Wood, Scabbard, Japan, 75 In., Pair 4250.00
Navy, Ames, Civil War, 1833 .... 235.00
Saber, Cavalry, 1840 .... 325.00
Wakizashi, Black Lacquer Sheath, Japanese 1650.00
SYBIS, Figurine, Match Girl 195.00

SYRACUSE China Syracuse is a trademark used by the Onondaga Pottery of Syracuse, New York. The company was established in 1871. It is still working. The name became the Syracuse China Company in 1966. It is known for fine dinnerware and restaurant china.

SYRACUSE, Bowl, Cereal, Sherwood 8.00
Bread Plate 7.00
Character Jug, Herbert Hoover 75.00
Chop Plate, Bombay 85.00
Coffeepot, Apple Blossom 65.00
Coffeepot, Bombay 95.00
Coffeepot, Jefferson 95.00
Coffeepot, Monticello 25.00
Creamer, Arcadia 30.00
Creamer, Jefferson 30.00
Creamer, Marietta 7.00
Creamer, Old Cathay 6.00
Creamer, Suzanne .... 15.00 To 20.00
Cup & Saucer, Apple Blossom 27.50
Cup & Saucer, Arcadia, Demitasse 25.00
Cup & Saucer, Baroque, Gray 10.00

Cup & Saucer, Beverly	27.50
Cup & Saucer, Bracelet	12.00
Cup & Saucer, Jefferson	25.00
Cup & Saucer, Lady Louise	9.00
Cup & Saucer, Sherwood	20.00
Cup & Saucer, Suzanne	15.00 To 25.00
Gravy Boat, Arcadia	65.00
Gravy Boat, Baroque Gray	35.00
Gravy Boat, Elizabeth	15.00
Gravy Boat, Fusan	25.00
Gravy Boat, Platter, Apple Blossom	65.00
Gravy Boat, Suzanne	65.00
Match Holder, Ashtray, Flower Trim	18.00
Plaque, Easel, Oval, 4 In.	125.00
Plate, Baroque Gray, 7 1/2 In.	5.00
Plate, Bread, Beverly	15.00
Plate, Bread, Suzanne	6.00
Plate, Dinner, Apple Blossom	25.00
Plate, Dinner, Beverly	25.00
Plate, Dinner, Suzanne	15.00
Plate, Marietta, 9 1/2 In.	10.00
Plate, Royal Court, 10 3/4 In.	35.00
Plate, Salad, Beverly	16.00
Plate, Salad, Sherwood	8.00
Plate, Selma, 7 In.	7.00
Plate, Sherwood, 10 In.	10.00
Platter, Arcadia, 12 In.	45.00
Platter, Arcadia, 14 In.	55.00
Platter, Arcadia, 16 In.	65.00
Platter, Baroque Gray, 12 In.	35.00
Platter, Baroque Gray, 14 In.	45.00
Platter, Beverly, 12 In.	50.00
Platter, Bombay, 16 In.	65.00
Platter, Carvel, 14 In.	65.00
Platter, Fusan, 14 In.	35.00
Platter, Jefferson, 12 In.	65.00
Platter, Jefferson, 14 In.	75.00
Platter, Marietta, 12 In.	8.00
Platter, Pennsylvania R.R., Mountain Laurel, 7 1/2 In.	42.00
Platter, Suzanne, 12 In.	40.00
Platter, Suzanne, 14 In.	40.00
Saucer, Marietta	6.00
Soup, Cream, Monticello	15.00
Soup, Dish, Indian Tree, Bouillon	20.00
Sugar & Creamer, Apple Blossom	40.00
Sugar, Carvel	35.00
Sugar, Cover, Beverly	25.00
Sugar, Jefferson	35.00
Sugar, Old Cathay	7.00
Sugar, Suzanne	15.00 To 20.00

TANKARD, see Stein
TAPESTRY, PORCELAIN, see Rose Tapestry

 A tea caddy is a small box made to hold tea leaves. In the eighteenth century, tea was very expensive and it was stored under lock and key. The first tea caddies were made with locks. By the nineteenth century, tea was more plentiful and the tea caddy was larger. Often there were two sections, one for green tea, one for black tea.

TEA CADDY, Federal, Inlaid Satinwood, Hinged Lid, Turned Foot, 7 X 8 X 5 In.	550.00
Fruitwood, Original Brasses, Alfred Assid	195.00
George III, Burl Walnut, Lozenge Form Top, C.1801, 6 X 12 X 6 In.	2300.00
George III, Shell Inlay, English, C.1780	850.00
George III, Stained Fruitwood, Melon Shape, 18th Century, 5 In.	4000.00

Painted Fruitwood, Tudor Cottage Shape, Hinged Roof, 12 1/2 In.	3750.00
Rosewood, Rectangular, 3 Covered Sections, England, 6 X 13 In.	412.00
Silver Wire & Nacre Inlay, Rosewood Veneer, 8 1/2 In.	55.00
Tin Cap, Painted Red Fruit, Yellow Leaves, 8 1/2 In.	240.00
Tortoiseshell Cover, Sarcophagus Shape, English	2300.00
Tortoiseshell, Casket Shape, Turned Feet, 19th Century	1200.00
Yale Insignia, Blue, Gold Trim	125.00

There was a superstition that it was lucky if a whole tea leaf unfolded at the bottom of your cup. This idea was translated into the pattern of dishes known as "tea leaf." By 1850, at least twelve English factories were making this pattern; and by the 1870s, it was a popular pattern in many countries. The tea leaf was always a luster glaze on early wares, although now some pieces are made with a brown tea leaf.

TEA LEAF IRONSTONE, Bone Dish, Wilkinson	40.00
Bowl, Apple, Meakin	435.00
Bowl, Apple, Pedestal, Wilkinson	475.00
Bowl, Meakin, Square	45.00
Bowl, Mush	20.00
Bowl, Vegetable, Cover	65.00
Bread Plate, Handles, Mellor Taylor, 9 X 12 In.	50.00
Butter Chip	12.00
Butter, Cover, Bamboo, Meakin	125.00
Butter, Cover, Drainer, Fishhook	85.00
Cake Plate, Bamboo, Meakin	45.00
Creamer, Bamboo, Meakin, Large	95.00
Cup & Saucer, Morning Glory, Elsmore Forster	75.00
Cup Plate, Wilkinson	40.00
Holder, Toothbrush, Bamboo, Meakin	135.00
Mug	100.00
Pitcher & Bowl	425.00
Plate, 6 1/2 In.	8.00
Plate, 8 In.	12.00
Plate, 9 In.	20.00
Plate, 10 In.	18.00
Plate, Adams, 8 In.	20.00
Platter, Meakin, Rectangular	50.00
Platter, Pinwheel, 13 1/2 X 17 In.	65.00
Relish, Pepper Leaf	125.00
Service For 8, Walley & Livesley Powell, 44 Piece	495.00
Soap Dish, Cover, With Liner, Burgess	175.00
Soup, Dish	20.00
Sugar, Bamboo, Meakin, Large	65.00
Sugar, Cover	70.00
Tea Set, Child's, Mellor Taylor, 21 Piece	1195.00
Teapot	45.00
Teapot, Bamboo, Meakin	135.00
Teapot, Meakin	95.00
Tureen, Sauce, Underplate, Ladle	395.00
Washbowl	95.00
Washbowl & Ewer Set, Burgess	315.00
Washbowl, Lily-of-The-Valley	160.00

Teco is the mark used on the art pottery line made by the American Terra Cotta and Ceramic Company of Terra Cotta and Chicago, Illinois. The company was an offshoot of the firm founded by William D. Gates in 1881. The Teco line was first made in 1885 but was not sold commercially until 1902. It continued in production until 1922. Over 500 designs were made in a variety of colors, shapes, and glazes. The company closed in 1930.

TECO, Bookends, Gargoyle, Green	1200.00 To 1500.00
Bookends, Gargoyle, White	425.00
Bowl, 4 Columnar Legs, Green Glaze, Stamped, C.1910, 11 1/2 In.	3630.00

Teddy Bear, Steiff, On Wheels, Growler, 48 In.

If you buy an old teddy bear that had been stored in a basement, be sure to treat it for insect infestation. Put the bear in a box with a stick insecticide and seal the box for 60 hours.

Bowl, Green, 4 1/2 In.	95.00
Bowl, Ivy Design, Ribbed, Green, 2 1/4 X 9 In.	300.00
Centerpiece, Holmes Smith	3300.00
Chamberstick, 10 1/2 In.	650.00
Creamer, I.S.C., 1930	25.00
Pot, Yellow, 9 In.	1350.00
Sundial	125.00
Undertray, Green Glaze, 2 Circles, Shaped Edge, C.1910, 10 X 6 In.	137.50
Vase, 3 Handles, 3–Footed, 3 1/4 In.	350.00
Vase, 4 Buttresses, 6 In.	1320.00
Vase, 4 Square Shaft Arms, Oviform, Stamped, C.1910, 8 In.	1575.00
Vase, Amphora Form, Held In 4 V–Form Feet, Stamped, C.1910, 8 3/4 In.	3385.00
Vase, Architectural Square Top, Round Bottom, 5 In.	255.00
Vase, Art Nouveau, Brown	8000.00
Vase, Double–Handled, Matte Green, 6 X 8 In.	1350.00
Vase, Matte Green, Stamped, 5 1/2 In.	350.00
Vase, No.182, Green, 16 In.	1550.00
Vase, Terra–Cotta, Matte Green Glaze, Marked, C.1910, 6 In.	440.00
Wall Pocket, Indian, Green, 5 1/4 X 6 1/2 In.	350.00

The first teddy bear was a cuddly toy said to be inspired by a hunting trip made by Teddy Roosevelt in 1902. Morris and Rose Michtom started selling their stuffed bears as "Teddy bears" and the name stayed. The Michtoms founded the Ideal Novelty and Toy Company. The German version of the teddy bear was made about the same time by the Steiff Company. There are many types of teddy bears and all are collected. The old ones are being reproduced.

TEDDY BEAR, 2 Faces, Jointed, 3 1/2 In.	500.00
Beige Mohair, Straw Stuffed, Movable Limbs, French, 24 In.	375.00
Champagne Mohair, Germany, 1930s, 30 In.	1500.00
Clown, Blown Glass Eyes, Mohair, 12 In.	210.00
Clown, Glass Eyes, Felt Clothes, Gauze Collar, 12 In.	250.00
Curly Mohair, Jointed, 10 In.	100.00
Furga, Display, Italian, 46 In.	580.00
Gold Haircloth, Felt Paw Pads & Nose, Voice Box, 14 1/2 In.	300.00
Gold Mohair, Jointed, Germany, 12 In.	295.00
Gold Mohair, Jointed, Growler, 1920s, 22 In.	325.00
Gold Wool, Growler, Australian, 3 In.	137.50
Heather Castilli, Mink Fur, 1984, 14 In.	350.00
Hermann, Open Mouth, Jointed, 1950s, 8 In.	75.00
Hermann, Straw, Beige, 12 In.	225.00

Hermann, White, 1950, 19 In. 725.00
Ideal, Fully Jointed, Tan Plush, 1920s 350.00
Mechanical, Mohair, Jointed, Glass Eyes, 8 In. 285.00
Mohair, Electric Eye, 16 In. 235.00
Raikes, Eric 350.00
Schuco, Gold Mohair, 18 In. 54.50
Schuco, Gold Mohair, Schuco, 1930s, 4 In. 125.00
Schuco, Yes/No, 8 In. 750.00
Schuco, Yes/No, Musical, 17 1/2 In. 1995.00
Steiff, Button, 1900s, 14 In. 800.00
Steiff, Button, C.1915, 9 In. 650.00
Steiff, Chocolate, Leather Paws 85.00
Steiff, Chocolate, Straw Stuffed, Hump 650.00
Steiff, Cinnamon Mohair, Blank Button, Whole Button Eyes, 14 In. 1750.00
Steiff, Cinnamon, 1940s, 16 In. 500.00
Steiff, Curly Brown Mohair, Straw Stuffed, 30 In. 2000.00
Steiff, Curly Tan Mohair, Working Growler, Button, 1950s, 24 In. 2400.00
Steiff, Gold, 1903, 12 In. 950.00
Steiff, Jointed, Stomach Squeaker, Metal Clip, Left Ear 900.00
Steiff, Koala, Mohair, Raised Silver Button, Squeaker, 7 In. 345.00
Steiff, Mama & Baby, Box, 1981 .... 489.00
Steiff, Mohair, Button & Tag, 1950s, 24 In. 1600.00
Steiff, Mohair, Jointed, Shoe Button Eyes, 26 In. 325.00
Steiff, Mr. Cinnamon 165.00
Steiff, On Wheels, Cinnamon, Jointed Head, Button, 18 In. 2500.00
Steiff, On Wheels, Growler, 48 In. ....*Illus* 4180.00
Steiff, Raised Button, 1950s, 5 1/2 In. 250.00
Steiff, Short Hair, Squeaker In Stomach, Jointed, Ear Clip 1330.00
Steiff, White, 1905, 14 In. 1100.00
Steiff, Zotty, Button & Tag, 11 In. 260.00
Steiff, Zotty, Mohair, 12 In. 135.00
Strauss, American Bear, 1913, 16 In. 1200.00
Twyford, Jointed, Red & White Paw Pads, England, 1960s, 18 In. 40.00

 The first telephone may have been made in Havana, Cuba, in 1849, but it was not patented. The first publicly demonstrated phone was used in Frankfurt, Germany, in 1860. The phone made by Alexander Graham Bell was shown at the Centennial Exhibition in Philadelphia in 1876, but it was not until 1877 that the first private phones were installed. Collectors today want all types of old phones, phone parts, and advertising.

TELEPHONE, American Electric, Double Box, Oak, Swivel Mouth, 31 X 12 In. 1128.00
Bell, Oak, All Original 175.00
Book, Telephone Almanac, Bell System Subscribers, 1933 .... 7.50
Booth, Cast Iron, England .... 1250.00 To 2300.00
Booth, Oak 950.00
Booth, Single Door, Raised Panels, Sante Fe R.R.Station 1200.00
Booth, Stained Glass Window In Left Side, Fan & Light, Walnut 1650.00
Candlestick, American Bell, Brass, Patent 1910 .... 120.00
Candlestick, Black, Brass Receiver & Dial 395.00
Candlestick, Connecticut Telephone & Electric Co. 125.00
Candlestick, Dial, Black, 12 In. 171.00
Candlestick, Gray/Western Electric, Pay Phone, 1898–1910 .... 595.00
Candlestick, Magneto Type, 315A 150.00
Candlestick, Patent 1908 .... 110.00
Chrome Elite, Black Handset 179.00
Coin Box, For Dial Phone, Metal 140.00
Deveau, Tapered Shaft 450.00
Dial, Norwegian 15.00
Double Box, Oak, Outside Terminal Receiver, Boston, 25 X 7 In. 550.00
French Horn, Danish, 1913 .... 55.00
Generator, Ringer Box, Front Metal Bells, Oak 50.00
Kellogg, Switchboard Model 925, Desk, Art Deco, Late 1920s 110.00
Kellogg, Wooden 225.00

Kit, First Aid, Bell Telephone, Hinged Lid 15.00
Pay, 3 Slots, Half Wooden 114.00
Pay, 3 Slots, Iron .... 90.00 To 99.00
Pay, Kellogg, Wooden, 1902 .... 595.00
Pay, Wall, Wooden, Brass Lightning Arrester, 1898 .... 595.00
Siemens & Halske, Precision, Late 1870s 2640.00
Sign, Bell System Telephone, Blue & White Porcelain, 20 X 4 In. 127.00
Sign, New England Telephone & Telegraph On Base, Round, 24 In. 825.00
Sign, Says Telephone Public, Bell, Porcelain, 11 X 12 In. 165.00
Sign, Telephone, Brass, Black Recessed Letters, 30 X 4 In. 94.00
Star Kist, Advertising 145.00
Stromberg–Carlson, Metal, Wall 65.00
Stromberg–Carlson, Model 1212, Bakelite, Cradle, Late 1920s 110.00
Wall, Crank, Oak 150.00
Wall, Elk Hart, Ind., Oak 200.00
Wall, Oak 185.00
Western Electric, 1915 .... 175.00
Western Electric, Crank, Rings 95.00
Western Electric, No.202, Black Desk, 1922 .... 269.00

Although the first television transmission took place in England in 1925, collectors find few sets which pre-date 1946. The first sets had only five channels, but by 1949 the additional VHF channels were included. The first color television set became available in 1951.

TELEVISION, Arvin, Model 212–3–TM 100.00
Belmont 85.00
Crowley, 1950s 150.00
Federal, Model 58 .... 575.00
Grunow 110.00
Olympic, With Radio & Phonograph, Mirrored Wooden Case 350.00
Philco, Model 16B 275.00
Pilot, 3 In. 300.00
Predicta, Console, 1960 .... 300.00
RCA, Art Deco, Table Model, 1940s, 7 In. 900.00
RCA, Model TS–247 .... 100.00
Stromberg–Carlson, Art Deco, Oak, Table Model, 9–In. Tube, 1940s 225.00
Western Electric, Model 527W 200.00
Zenith, Table Model, Early, 1950s, 16 In. .... 100.00 To 110.00

Teplitz refers to art pottery manufactured by a number of companies in the Teplitz–Turn area of Bohemia during the late nineteenth and early twentieth centuries. The Amphora Porcelain Works and the Alexandra Works were two of these companies.

TEPLITZ, Basket, Applied Flowers, Basket Weave Design, Amphora, 9 In. 345.00
Ewer, Stylized Owl On Branch, Turquoise Lip & Handle, 10 1/2 In. 225.00
Ewer, Violets On Cream, Gold Trim, Marked 115.00
Figurine, Peasant Girl, With Baskets, Green & Gold, Amphora, 18 In. 325.00
Lamp, Kingfisher, 13 In. 195.00
Plaque, Head of Art Nouveau Woman, E. Wahliss, 13 1/4 In. 175.00
Vase, 3 Long–Beaked Birds, Amphora, C.1905, 12 3/8 In. 4125.00
Vase, 4 Handles Fuse Into Pierced Rim, Poppy Panels, 7 In. 250.00
Vase, Art Nouveau, Bronze Color, Applied Wolfhound, Imperial, 11 In. 695.00
Vase, Art Nouveau, Reticulated Rim, 16 In. 250.00
Vase, Band of Repeating Clover, Molded Panels, 8 1/4 In. 450.00
Vase, Buccaneer, 5 In. 65.00
Vase, Crane, Handles, Amphora, 5 1/2 In. 65.00
Vase, Embossed Blue Flowers, Gold Dragon Encircling Neck, 17 In. 675.00
Vase, Enameled Flower With Man's Face, 11 In. 145.00
Vase, Enameled Stylized Flowers, 2 Handles, Amphora, 12 In. 355.00
Vase, Figural, Chicken At Side, Branches, Amphora, C.1900, 16 1/4 In. 2475.00
Vase, Flowers, Hourglass Shape, 4 Jeweled Handles, 12 X 7 In. 255.00
Vase, Geometric Enameled Design, Amphora, 11 1/2 In. 275.00
Vase, Kneeling Semi–Nude, Veils, Jewels, Gold, Red, 18 In. ....*Illus* 4800.00

> If you want to remove a grease stain from silk, wool, or paper, cover it with grated chalk. Cover the chalk with a piece of a brown paper bag. Set a warm iron on the paper. Repeat if necessary. Be sure the iron is not hot enough to scorch the paper.

Teplitz, Vase, Kneeling Semi–Nude, Veils,
   Jewels, Gold, Red, 18 In.

Vase, Owls, Handles, Amphora, 9 1/2 In.	98.00
Vase, Peasant Woman, Apron, Man With Lantern, Amphora, 12 In., Pair	895.00
Vase, Thistle On Cream, Gold Reticulated Handles	120.00
Vase, Turned–Down Pierced Lip, Shoulder Handles, Amphora, 16 In.	475.00
Vase, White Flowers, Gold Serpent Entwines Neck, Marked, 17 In.	595.00
Wall Pocket, Basket Weave, Blue Band & Flowers, Amphora, 9 In.	110.00

Terra–cotta is a special type of pottery. It ranges from pale orange to dark reddish–brown in color. The color comes from the clay, which is fired but not always glazed in the finished piece.

TERRA–COTTA, Biscuit Jar, Dragon, Gold Leaf Trim	225.00
Bust, Mozart, Marked C & C, 9 In.	40.00
Figurine, Nude Woman, Curly Hair, Keramos, C.1930, 17 1/4 In.	1815.00
Figurine, Woman, Fruit Basket, Head, A. Parisse, C.1930, 26 In.	605.00
Figurine, Young Nude Woman, Keramos, C.1930, 29 1/8 In.	1450.00
Figurine, Young Woman, Seated, M. Fernandex, C.1930, 18 3/4 In.	665.00
Paperweight, Dog, N.Y. Architectural Terra–Cotta Co., 1886	75.00
Pipe Holder, Clown, High Glaze	95.00
Teapot, Embossed Foliage, Lion Finial, Hexagonal, 5 4/3 In.	5400.00
Teapot, Embossed Oriental Scenes, Boy, Tree, 3 5/8 In.	1200.00
Vase, Dragon Design, 6 In.	16.00

Textile includes many types of printed textiles, table and household linens, and clothing. Some other textiles will be found under Clothing, Coverlet, Rug, Quilt, etc.

TEXTILE, Afghan, Ripple, Browns & Gold, 50 X 72 In.	10.00
Altar Cloth, Gold Couchwork, 5–Toed Dragon, Silk, Chinese	500.00
Bag, Newsboy's, Canvas, Saturday Evening Post, Country Gentleman	12.00
Banner, Mardi Gras, 45 X 35 In.	150.00
Bedspread, Bouquet, Blue & White, Handmade, 55 X 92 In.	125.00
Bedspread, Candlewick, Blue & White, Kittens, Crib	20.00
Bedspread, Crocheted, 83 X 80 In.	175.00
Bedspread, Crocheted, Diamond Design, Popcorn Stitch, 83 X 80 In.	175.00
Bedspread, Crocheted, Ecru, 108 X 112 In.	250.00
Bedspread, Crocheted, Ecru, Fringed, 88 X 84 In.	165.00
Bedspread, Crocheted, Ecru, Wheel Pattern, Fringes, 88 X 84 In.	125.00
Bedspread, Crocheted, Popcorn & Diamond, Ecru, 68 X 96 In.	135.00
Bedspread, Crocheted, Popcorn Stitch, Ivory, Double	625.00
Bedspread, Crocheted, Wheel Pattern, Fringed, 88 X 84 In.	125.00
Bedspread, Embroidered, Multi–Drawn Center, 78 X 92 In.	450.00
Bedspread, Kiss Graphics, Faces, Cotton, Plastic Bag, 1978, Twin	60.00
Bedspread, Octagon Star Pattern, Ecru, 82 X 98 In.	175.00
Bedspread, Shams, Battenburg, 98 X 77 In., 3 Piece	500.00
Bedspread, Summer, White Cotton, 84 X 84 In.	20.00
Bell Pull, Theorem Painted, Cotton, Velvet, Silk, England, 91 In., Pr.	2860.00
Blanket, Blue & Ivory Wool, 1800s, 64 X 78 In.	125.00
Blanket, Colored Stripes, 4 Points, Hudson Bay Co., 72 X 90 In.	25.00
Blanket, Homespun, Brown Plaid, Cream Ground, 80 X 74 In.	78.50

Blanket, Linsey-Woolsey, Candlewick Star Designs, 64 X 74 In.	145.00
Blanket, Wool, Red, Blue, Yellow Embroidered, A.W., 1848, 78 X 62 In.	110.00
Case, Handkerchief, Cut-Work, White Linen	9.00
Case, Hankerchief, Silk, Floral	4.00
Casket, Floral & Animal Design, Bargello Stitch, Canvas, 10 X 7 In.	610.00
Chair Set, Crochet Filet, American Eagle, 3 Piece	20.00
Comforter, Wool Patchwork, Multicolored, Black Border, Large	90.00
Coverlet, Geometric, Red, White & Blue, Wool, 79 X 75 In.	150.00
Doily, Battenberg Lace, Many Different Stitches, White, 21 In.	35.00
Fabric, Star Wars, Brown, 4 Yds.	6.50
Flag, 31 Stars, Hand-Stitched Linen, 1851–58, 5 X 10 Ft.	125.00
Flag, 48 Stars, Cotton, 36 X 48 In.	60.00
Flag, 48 Stars, Cotton, 9 X 13 1/2 In.	25.00
Lap Robe, Bulldog Center, Florals, Wool, Lined	150.00
Lap Robe, Victorian, Heavy	35.00
Pad, Chair, Hooked, Eagle, Round	9.00
Panel, Duo Hwa, Silk Weaving Factory, Hong Kong, 1935, 8 X 28 In.	45.00
Panel, Embroidered, Silk, Butterfly, Basket of Flowers, 5 X 6 Ft.	225.00
Panel, Embroidered, Silk, Eagle, Flock of Finches, Japan, 96 In.	3400.00
Panel, Needlepoint, Oval, Woman, Goat, Wool Appliqued, 13 X 15 In.	325.00
Panel, Needlework, 2 Sheep, Herringbone Border, 22 1/4 X 17 7/8 In.	245.00
Panel, Needlework, Black Floss, White Silk, Landscape, 14 X 16 In.	550.00
Panel, Spanish Women & Men, Belgium Tapestry, 19 X 58 1/2 In.	50.00
Panel, Yarn, 3–Dimensional Floral Design, Frame, 18 X 18 1/2 In.	75.00
Pillow Sham, Embroidered, Peacock Center, 26 X 28 In., Pair	78.00
Pillow Sham, Lace Border, Red Stylized Flower, 25 X 25 In., Pair	25.00
Pillow Sham, Linen, Embroidered Catharine Musselman, 1858, Pair	100.00
Pillow Sham, Patchwork, Flying Geese, Green, Brown Checked, Pair	210.00
Pillow Sham, Victorian, Red On White, Fancy, Pair	60.00
Pillow Sham, Whore House, Black, Rose, Aqua Crochet, Satin, 5 1/2 In.	25.00
Pillowcase, Amish, Button Closure, 15 X 17 1/2 In.	15.00
Pillowcase, Linen, 1910, Pair	22.00
Pillowcase, Peter Max, Signed	35.00
Runner, Battenburg Lace, Drawnwork Center, 16 X 48 In.	125.00
Runner, Indian, Honeycomb Pattern, C.1910, 3 Ft.1 In. X 14 Ft.5 In.	1300.00
Runner, Table, Battenburg, 2 Center Panels, 15 X 34 In.	78.00
Runner, Tatted, Cream, 17 X 37 In.	115.00
Scarf, Cabbage Rose, Gold Floral Sprays, Chiffon, 15 X 55 In.	55.00
Scarf, Crewel, Multicolor On Dusky Rose, 11 1/2 X 214 In.	65.00
Scarf, Dresser, White Linen, Scalloped Edges, Victorian, 17 X 34 In.	29.00
Scarf, Piano, 32 1/2 X 68 In.	25.00
Shawl, Paisley, 64 X 66 In.	45.00
Shawl, Paisley, Black Center, Colored Border, 160 In.	135.00
Shawl, Paisley, Woven Design, 65 X 136 In.	150.00
Shawl, Paisley, Woven, 67 X 68 In.	125.00
Shawl, Piano, Art Deco, Black, Purple	145.00
Sheet, Handwork On Border, Linen, Double Bed	65.00
Sheet, Homespun, 78 X 82 In.	165.00
Sheet, Homespun, Embroidered Initials B.G., Cotton, 64 X 108 In.	40.00
Sheet, Homespun, Initials B.G., Hand Hemmed, Cotton, 82 X 122 In.	30.00
Sheet, Homespun, Initials C.F., Hand Hemmed, Cotton, 78 X 78 In.	30.00
Sheet, Homespun, Red Embroidered Initials, M.K., 72 X 76 In.	40.00
Sheet, Linen, Red Embroidered Heart & ER, 1843 Corner, 77 X 80 In.	70.00
Tablecloth, Battenburg Lace, 74 X 151 In.	250.00
Tablecloth, Battenburg Lace, Grape, Round, 60 In.	250.00
Tablecloth, Battenburg Lace, Round, 45 In.	185.00
Tablecloth, Battenburg Lace, Round, 50 In.	240.00
Tablecloth, Battenburg Lace, Round, 69 In.	425.00
Tablecloth, Beige, Lace Trim, Filigree Inserts, 6 Napkins	200.00
Tablecloth, Blue & White Plaid, 48 X 40 In.	45.00
Tablecloth, Crocheted Lace, Ecru, Square, 110 In.	160.00
Tablecloth, Crocheted, Pineapple, Oval, 59 X 78 In.	75.00
Tablecloth, Cupid Cutwork, Linen, 12 Napkins, 96 X 64 In.	185.00
Tablecloth, Damask, Geometric Border, Germany, Square, 4 Ft.5 In.	605.00

Tablecloth, Damask, Green, Irish, 6 Napkins, 92 X 70 In. 95.00
Tablecloth, Damask, Linen, 96 X 72 In. 25.00
Tablecloth, Damask, White, 1920s, 60 X 100 In. 40.00
Tablecloth, Ecru Linen, Embroidered, Italy, 8 Napkins, 84 X 62 In. 55.00
Tablecloth, Ecru, Cutwork, Linen, Filet Lace Border, 68 X 104 In. 55.00
Tablecloth, Fiesta, Light Green, Linen, 54 X 54 In. 37.50
Tablecloth, Hemstitched, 8 Napkins, 84 X 64 In. 45.00
Tablecloth, Homespun Linen, Woven Stripe Design, 44 X 62 In. 40.00
Tablecloth, Homespun, Gold & White Plaid, 70 X 76 In. 225.00
Tablecloth, Homespun, Machine Hemmed, Linen, 64 X 90 In. 35.00
Tablecloth, Linen, Red Embroidered, M H, 1826 In Corner, 46 X 76 In. 55.00
Tablecloth, Linen, Robin's–Egg Blue, Irish, 8 Napins, 64 X 82 In. 55.00
Tablecloth, Mustard & White Checked, Fringed, 30 X 30 In. 90.00
Tablecloth, Pointe Venice, 12 Napkins, Swiss Cutwork, 70 X 106 In. 395.00
Tablecloth, Pointe Venice, 1930s, 12 Napkins, 66 X 128 In. 3500.00
Tablecloth, Pointe Venice, Ecru, 68 X 104 In. 700.00
Tablecloth, Quad–Drawn Linen, Drawn Ends, Germany, 72 X 100 In. 135.00
Tablecloth, Satin Stitch Embroidery, 12 Napkins, 72 X 126 In. 60.00
Tablecloth, Shamrock, Linen, 72 X 90 In. 85.00
Tablecloth, Stripe Design, Embroidered Initials, 62 X 64 In. 5.00
Tableclotoh, Woven Floral Design, Linen, Fringe, 50 X 53 In. 95.00
Tapestry, 2 Birds, Exotic Landscape, France, 29 3/4 X 52 In. 50.00
Tapestry, 2 Boys With Rifle, Girl, Brussels, 7 Ft. X 5 Ft.3 In. 5500.00
Tapestry, 5 Men, 2 Women, Horse, Palm Trees, 5 Ft.9 In. X 4 Ft. 400.00
Tapestry, Boys With Rifles, Girl In Plumed Hat, 7 Ft. X 5 Ft.3 In. 5500.00
Tapestry, Egrets In Forest Scene, 40 X 66 In. 425.00
Tapestry, Louis XV Style, Figures In Drawing Room, 47 X 67 In. 44.00
Tapestry, Scenic, Italy.19 X 56 In. 90.00
Towel, Cutwork Band, Red Embroidery, Cadharnae Horn, 1830, 67 In. 55.00
Towel, Embroidered Stylized Flowers & Birds, 1837, 16 X 53 In. 165.00
Towel, Embroidered, Sarah Ann Renninger, 1850, 15 X 57 In. 55.00
Towel, Homespun, Knotted Warp Fringe, Open Bands, 38 1/2 X 17 In. 180.00
Towel, Linen, Drawnwork, Tree of Life, Birds, Fringe, 14 X 58 In. 350.00
Towel, Stylized Floral, Birds, Frances Mast, 1856, 19 X 47 In. 115.00
Towel, Stylized Flowers, Alphabet, 1839, 17 X 33 In. 135.00
Towel, Stylized Flowers, Elizabeth Hoffer, 1844, 20 X 54 In. 55.00

The thermometer was invented in 1731. It measures temperature of
either water or air. All kinds of thermometers are collected, but
those with advertising messages are the most popular.

THERMOMETER, 7–Up, Pam Clock Co., Round 65.00
7–Up, Porcelain, French 35.00
7–Up, Round, 12 In. 65.00
A.J. Dodge, Fitted Case, Sliding Lid, 7 1/2 X 13 3/8 In. 82.50
Arrow 77 Beer, Tin 95.00
B-1 Lemon Lime, Tin, C.1950, 28 X 12 In. 20.00
Beck Provisions, Tin, Reverse Painting On Glass, 6 X 8 In. 20.00
Bireley's, With Bottle 40.00
Black Boy, 1949 .... 53.00
Borden's Feed, 1952 .... 25.00
Brooder 9.00
Candy, Wood & Brass, C.1900 .... 20.00
Case Tractor 25.00
Clark Candy Bar, Wooden, Candy Bar Picture 325.00
Desk, Nuart, Alcohol, Round Metal Wheel, Eagle, Repainted 40.00
Desk, Taylor, Barometer, Walnut, 1930s 22.00
Dr Pepper, 25 1/2 X 6 1/4 In. 18.00
Dr Pepper, Tin, 1960s Log, 20 In. 50.00
Dr. Daniel's 125.00
Dr. Green's Nervura 95.00
Dr. Pierce's Chemical Co., Bakelite, 1931 .... 18.00
Electric Starch, Pictures Box, Woman & Iron 275.00
Eliott's, Abiline, Texas 15.00
Ex–Lax, 5 Colors, Porcelain, 8 X 36 In. 125.00

Five Roses, Porcelain, Red & White, 8 X 39 In.	120.00 To 125.00
Fleet Wing Motor Oil	15.00
Fram Oil Filters, Tin	50.00
Full-O-Pep, 1948	65.00
G & G Live Poultry	12.00
Gold Girl Cola, Sun-Drop, 4-Color, 27 X 7 1/4 In.	110.00
Headlight Stove & Range, Chicago, Bakelite	18.00
Hires Root Beer, Bottle Shape, Tin, 1920s, 29 In.	120.00
Ilium Hair Tonic & Toilet Water, Wooden, 15 In.	45.00
Independent Life Insurance Co., Capital Stock, 200, 000 Club	85.00
International Tailoring, Wooden	285.00
Jests Antacid, Porcelain, 36 In.	110.00
Jeweler, Fancy Pocket Watch, 21 In.	175.00
Kant Drack Collars, Wooden, 11 Different Collar Styles, 48 In.	475.00
Mail Pouch, Porcelain, 80 X 38 In.	95.00
Maxwell House Coffee, Round, 12 In.	35.00
Meat, Morton Salt	24.00
Meat, Taylor, Hanging, Original Box Top, 6 In.	8.50
Monroe Shock, Painted	25.00
Nesbitt	28.50
Orange Crush, Bottle Shape, Brown	45.00
Orange Crush, Wood	135.00
Peter's Shoe Thermometer, Weather Bird, 1915	375.00
Polar Bear Chewing Tobacco, Porcelain, 27 In.	2200.00
Prestone, Porcelain	45.00
R.C. Cola, 13 X 6 In.	48.00
R.C. Cola, Mirror	55.00
R.C. Cola, Tin, Red, White & Blue, 26 X 10 In.	37.00
Ramon's Brownie Pills	125.00
Ramon's Pills, Wood	250.00
RCA Victor Radio, Porcelain, Purple, Yellow, White, 8 X 38 In.	360.00
Red Goose Shoes, Porcelain	350.00
Royal Crown Cola, Red, White & Gray, 13 X 6 In.	23.00
Royal Oak Coal, Coal Fire	45.00
Standard Fruit & Steamship Co., New Orleans	15.00
Standard Oil, 12 X 2 In.	38.00
Stanford The Jeweler, Pictures Pocket Watch, Diamond Ring	265.00
Stegamier Beer, Glass Fronted, Round	43.00
Sun Crest, Bottle Shape, Tin	60.00 To 70.00
Sweet & Pure Flour, Porcelain, 27 X 7 In.	225.00
Tums For The Tummy	40.00
Tycos Maple Syrup, Copper, Wooden Box	65.00
Vaal's General Store, Mountain Scene, Calendar Back, 1957	12.00
Vanderbilt Tires	95.00
Ward's Vitamin Bread, Girl, Slice of Bread, Porcelain, 21 In.	325.00
Whitehouse Coffee	95.00

Tiffany glass was made by Louis Comfort Tiffany, the American glass designer who worked from about 1879 to 1933. His work included iridescent glass, Art Nouveau styles of design, and original contemporary styles. He was also noted for his stained glass windows, his unusual lamps, bronze work, pottery, and silver. Other types of Tiffany are listed under Tiffany Pottery, Tiffany Silver, or at the end of this section under Tiffany. The famous Tiffany lamps are under Tiffany, Lamp. Reproductions of some types of Tiffany are being made.

Louis C. Tiffany

Louis C. Tiffany Furnaces Inc Favrile

TIFFANY GLASS, Bonbon, Mint Green Top, Light Green, Ribs, 5 3/4 X 2 1/2 In.	475.00
Bottle, Dresser, Floral Form, Gold, Signed, 5 1/4 In.	990.00
Bowl, Dragonfly, 12 5/8 In.	1300.00
Bowl, Favrile, Blue, Ruffled, Ribs, Ruffled Top, Signed, 6 In.	550.00
Bowl, Favrile, Gold Iridescent, Ruffled, 6 X 2 1/2 In.	500.00
Bowl, Gold Iridescent, Ruffled, Signed, 4 1/2 In.	350.00
Bowl, Leaf Design, Aqua, Signed, 5 3/4 In.	450.00
Bowl, Ruffled, Ribbed, Violet Highlights, Signed, 4 1/2 In.	425.00

Bowl, Scalloped Rim, Stand–Out Ribs, Pastel, Signed, 8 1/2 In. 750.00
Bowl, Stretch Rim, Opalescent Star Pattern, 1855, 8 In. 760.00
Bowl, Underplate, Gold Iridescent, Round, 4 1/2 In.Bowl, 2 Pc. 650.00
Butter Pat, 8–Scalloped Rim, Blue 225.00
Butter Pat, Blue Iridescent, Pat. & Number 175.00
Butter Pat, Gold Iridescent, Scalloped, Paper Label, 4 In. 175.00
Candleholder, Cupped Bobeche Rim, Twisted Amber Body, 5 In. 310.00
Candlestick, Gold Iridescent, Diamond–Quilted, 4 In., Pair 2800.00
Candlestick, Green To White, Green Overlay, 4 In., Pair 1300.00
Candlestick, Pale Green, Ribbed, Stick, Tapered Body, 11 In. 1500.00
Candlestick, Pastel, Ribbed Bottom, Tapered, Signed, 11 In. 1500.00
Candlestick, Tapered Stem, Flared Base, Signed, 9 3/8 In., Pr. 1870.00
Compote, Favrile, Blue, Stretched Rim, Signed, 5 In. 1800.00
Compote, Favrile, Gold Iridescent, Ruffled, 3 X 2 3/4 In. 595.00
Compote, Flared Rim, Blue Iridescent, Signed, 1915, 10 1/4 In. 2090.00
Compote, Pastel, Green Top, Iridescent, Optic, Leaves, 6 In. 650.00
Compote, Pastel, Pink Top, Laurel Leaves, Pedestal, 5 3/4 In. 650.00
Compote, Pastel, Purple Top, Opalescent Optic, 6 In. 600.00
Compote, Peacock Blue Iridescent, Footed, Ruffled, 4 X 2 In. 650.00
Compote, Peacock Blue, Flower Form, Signed, 1906, 5 1/2 In. 2750.00
Compote, Raised Ruffled Edge, Cut Design, Signed, 4 1/2 In. 1200.00
Cordial, Swirl Design Center Outside, Signed, 4 1/2 In. 325.00
Creamer, Opalescent Pastel Pink, Signed, 3 In. 475.00
Cup & Saucer, Free–Form Design, Applied Handle 850.00
Cup & Saucer, Rickrack Pattern, Reeded Shell Handle, Signed 550.00
Flower Vase, Gold Dore, Heart Bottom, Tubes, Handle, 4 In. 750.00
Jar, Bronze Cover, Blue Star, Signed, 3 1/4 In. 700.00
Jar, Gold Iridescent, Intaglio Knobbed Fitted Cover, 8 In. 1500.00
Paperweight, Seal, Favrile, 3 Corners, Triangular, 1 3/4 In. 425.00
Punch Cup, Amber, Green Leaf, Handle, 3 In. .... 300.00 To 350.00
Punch Cup, Favrile, Amber, Green Leaf Design, 3 X 2 1/4 In. 350.00
Salt, Favrile, Gold Iridescent, Twists All Around, Signed 275.00
Salt, Favrile, Gold, Dimpled Sides, Signed 247.00
Salt, Footed, Signed, Gold Iridescent 195.00
Salt, Raised Twists In Glass, Silver–Blue Tones, Signed 275.00
Salt, Ruffled Edge, Gold Iridescent, Signed, 1 1/4 In. 200.00
Seal, Form of 3 Scarabs At Corners, Beaded Edge, 1 3/4 In. 425.00
Seal, Scarab 485.00
Shade, 6 Sides, Gold Iridescent, Signed, 5 X 3 3/4 In. 450.00
Sherbet, Blue Iridescent, Signed, 4 In. 325.00
Sherbet, Hollow Stem, Gold Iridescent, Signed, 3 1/4 In. 225.00
Sugar & Creamer, Favrile, Blue Highlights, Signed, 2 3/4 In. 850.00
Vase, Agate, Amber, Gold Interior, 8 In. ....*Illus* 3000.00
Vase, Applied Lily Pad, Gold Iridescent, Signed, 3 1/2 In. 895.00
Vase, Blue & Silver Highlights, Squat, Signed, 3 1/2 In. 850.00
Vase, Blue Curvilinear Design, Signed, 3 1/2 In. 4620.00
Vase, Blue Iridescent, Allover Standout Ribs, 10 3/4 In. 2100.00
Vase, Blue Iridescent, Signed, 3 In. 345.00
Vase, Blue, Gold Iridescent Top, Slim Neck, Signed, 6 In. 875.00
Vase, Bud, Favrile, Iridescent Ivory, Feather, Flared, 8 In. 650.00
Vase, Bud, Folded Rim, Green Pulled Feather, Gold, 8 In. 1210.00
Vase, Cypriot, Swirling Opalescent Ground, Signed, 5 1/8 In. 1760.00
Vase, Decanter Shape, Red–Amber Star Base, Rainbow, 5 In. 1850.00
Vase, Double Gourd, Cupped Pedestal, Signed, 12 1/4 In. 2425.00
Vase, Emerald Green Pulled Leaf, Gold Iridescent, 3 1/4 In. 750.00
Vase, Favrile, Blue, Allover Standout Ribs, 4 1/4 In. 2000.00
Vase, Favrile, Blue, Silver, Blue Base, 4 1/2 In. 1400.00
Vase, Favrile, Gold Iridescent, Flared, Ruffled, 18 In. 2500.00
Vase, Favrile, Gold, Bottle Form, Signed, 4 1/2 In. 264.00
Vase, Favrile, Paperweight Glass, 8 5/8 In. 4950.00
Vase, Favrile, Ribbed, Red Highlights, Knob Base, 8 1/4 In. 1100.00
Vase, Favrile, Stand–Out Ribs, Ruffled, Blue, Signed, 4 1/4 In. 2000.00
Vase, Feathered, Blue & Silver, Signed, 5 In. 495.00
Vase, Floriform, Amber Iridescent, Signed, C.1905, 17 3/4 In. 4950.00

Vase, Floriform, Favrile, Leaf, Vines, Signed, 9 In. ....*Illus*   1400.00
Vase, Floriform, Gold Stem, Ribbed Base, Signed, 15 1/2 In. 4620.00
Vase, Floriform, Green Feathering, Signed, 10 14/ In. 2850.00
Vase, Floriform, Opalescent, Green Feathered, 10 1/4. ....   3500.00
Vase, Floriform, Ruffled Lip, Feathering, C.1916, 4 1/2 In. 1210.00
Vase, Floriform, Shaded Gold To Green, Marked, 10 In. 2100.00
Vase, Gold Inside, Ripples Over Gold Ground, Signed, 13 In. 895.00
Vase, Gold Iridescent, Simples, Ribs, Ruffled, Squat, 3 1/2 In. 850.00
Vase, Gold Swirls, Iridescent, Marked, 3 1/4 X 4 In. 1010.00
Vase, Green Pulled Feather Design, Marked, 4 In. 2400.00
Vase, Intaglio Leaves, Grapes, Orange–Gold Iridescent, 4 In. 425.00
Vase, Iridized Oyster White, Clear Foot, Signed, 4 5/8 In. 475.00
Vase, Jack–In–The–Pulpit, Gold, 4 In. 750.00
Vase, Jack–In–The–Pulpit, Swirled, Ovoid, 6 1/2 In. 3300.00
Vase, Jack–In–The–Pulpit, Turquoise Gold Iridescent, 19 In. 9350.00
Vase, Jack–In–The–Pulpit, Undulating, Scalloped Foot, 15 In. 6600.00
Vase, Lava, Flattened Spherical Form, Label, 3 1/4 In. 7700.00
Vase, Overlaid Heart–Shaped Leaves, Signed, C.1910, 7 5/8 In. 3575.00
Vase, Ovoid Body, Ruby Red, Signed, 5 1/2 In. 3575.00
Vase, Pinched Body, Yellow Pulled Feather, Signed, 6 1/4 In. ....⋮.......   775.00
Vase, Ribbed Body, Gold Pulled Feather, 7 1/2 In. 4620.00
Vase, Ribbed, Blue Iridescent, Signed, 8 In. 950.00
Vase, Ribbed, Chocolate Stripes, Signed, C.1913, 9 1/4 In. 2750.00
Vase, Silver Hooked Feathers, Black, Signed, 4 1/2 In. 4000.00
Vase, Stand–Out Ribs, Peacock Blue, Signed, 4 1/4 In. 2000.00
Vase, Swirled Feathers, Amber Loopings, 1920, 3 5/16 In. 2310.00
Vase, Tapered Ribbed Body, Red Highlights, Signed, 8 1/4 In. 1100.00
Vase, Tree Shape, Blue–Gold Iridescent, Signed, 4 1/2 In. 1400.00
Vase, Trumpet, Trailing Vines, Gold, Bulbous Stem, 15 In. 4840.00
Vase, Urn Shape, Scrolled Handles, Gold,, Signed, 6 1/2 In. 1800.00
Vase, Vertical Stripes, Bubble Inclusions, Signed, 4 1/2 In. 2750.00
Vase, Wave & Water Optic, Amber Top, Blue Chintz, 9 1/4 In. 2300.00
TIFFANY POTTERY, Lamp Base, Raised Leaves, Signed, 1906, 12 1/2 In. 5500.00
Vase, Chocolate Brown, Glazed In & Out, 9 1/2 X 8 In. 1200.00
Vase, Glazed Purple, Black Veining, Signed, 4 1/4 In. 1500.00
Vase, Green Glaze, Green Leaves, Branches, Signed, 8 In. 2000.00
Vase, Green, Red–Brown Splatters, 6 In. 1500.00
Vase, Hanging Pods Around Center, Signed, 6 1/2 In. 2000.00
Vase, Irregular Top, Unglazed Buff, Signed, 8 3/4 In. 1500.00
Vase, Mottled Green Over Ivory, Signed, 9 In. 850.00
Vase, Purple, Green Shaded, Black Veining, 4 1/4 X 2 In. 1500.00
Vase, Raised Blossoms & Branches, Textured, Unglazed, 4 In. 450.00
Vase, Raised Leaves & Branches, Green, Signed, 8 In. 2000.00
Vase, Raised Leaves & Branches, Textured, Unglazed, 6 In. 850.00
Vase, Raised Leaves, Pods From Branches, Signed, 12 1/4 In. 1100.00
Vase, Rust, Top Design, Tel–El, Signed, 7 3/4 X 3 1/4 In. 4200.00
Vase, Shades of Green, Green Drippings, Signed, 6 In. 1500.00
Vase, Tulips In Relief, Bronze, Royal Blue Interior, 7 In. 1200.00
Vase, Unglazed, Allover Blossoms, Signed, 13 1/4 In. 1500.00
TIFFANY SILVER, Berry Spoon, Chrysanthemum, 9 1/4 In. 450.00
Berry Spoon, Salem 275.00
Bookmark, Circle & Arrow .... 40.00 To 70.00
Bowl, Chrysanthemum, C.1880, 13 1/4 In. 2975.00
Bowl, Chrysanthemums & Scrolls On Rim, 1902, 10 1/4 In. 1045.00
Bowl, Flared Rim, Ribbed Band Around Middle, 1907, 8 In. 335.00
Bowl, Flared Sides, Detachable Liner, 1907, 8 1/8 In. 775.00
Bowl, Fluted Into 6 Sections, Hammered, Signed, 8 1/2 In. 1750.00
Bowl, Wave Border, Lobed Body, Early 20th Century, 8 1/2 In. 825.00
Butter Knife, Marquise, Individual 45.00
Cake Server, Chrysanthemum 300.00
Candlestick, Queen Anne, Faceted Stem, C.1907, 55/8 In., Pair 1650.00
Castor, Salt & Pepper, Cover, Japanese Scenes, 5 In., Pr. 7500.00
Cigar Cutter, 2 In. 135.00
Coffee Set, Urn Finial, Paneled Bracket Handles, 3 Piece 1200.00

Coffeepot & Sugar, Bead Finial, Ivory Ring, 1892 .... 3550.00
Compote, Band of Mythological Figures, 6 5/8 X 9 1/4 In. 5500.00
Cream Ladle, Olympian 195.00
Creamer, Lap–Over–Edge 2495.00
Dish, Leaf Shape, 6 X 5 1/4 In. 175.00
Dish, Serving, Flower & Shell, Pierced Tray, 2 Handles 3630.00
Dish, Shell, 2 Ball Feet, 2 3/4 In. 80.00
Dish, Shell, 2 Ball Feet, 4 In., Pair 145.00
Dish, Vegetable, Cut–Card Border, Marked, 1 5/8 X 11 In. 605.00
Dressing Set, Traveling, Fitted Suitcase, C.1907, 14 Piece 1100.00
Fish Slice, English King 375.00
Fish Slice, Ram's Head On Handle, Fish Cut–Out On Blade 550.00
Flask, Pocket, Floral Engraved, Rectangular, 8 Oz. 625.00
Fork, Asparagus 850.00
Fork, Clinton, 7 1/2 In. 40.00
Fork, Cold Meat, Salem 175.00
Fork, Cucumber, English King 395.00
Fork, Steak Carving, Bamboo 70.00
Glove Stretcher, Embossed Floral Design, Pat.1875 .... 250.00
Gravy Ladle, Blackberry 395.00
Gravy Ladle, English King 185.00
Gravy Ladle, Persian .... 195.00 To 350.00
Ice Tongs, English King 575.00
Jelly Server, Olympian 250.00
Jelly Spoon, Blackberry 195.00
Ladle, Palm, 11 In. 375.00
Pipe Tamp, 3 In. 75.00
Pitcher, Water, Bands of Stylized Leaves, Flowers, 8 1/4 In. 4500.00
Pitcher, Water, Basket Weave Band, 1877–91, 7 5/8 In. 2650.00
Pitcher, Water, Flowers & Leaves, C.1886, 7 3/4 In. 7150.00
Plate, Fluted Rim, 9 In. 198.00
Post Light, Newell, Plated, Reticulated Ball, 36, 8 Piece 4400.00
Pudding Spoon, English King 425.00
Ring Tree, Figural Angel 450.00
Salad Set, Applied Insects & Plants, C.1890, 2 Piece 5500.00
Salt, 3–Footed, Open, England, 2 Oz., 1 3/4 In. 95.00
Salt, 4 Ball Feet, Square, 1 3/4 In. 75.00
Serving Spoon, Chrysanthemum, Kidney Shape 395.00
Shovel, Flamingo Heads & Flowers On Handle End 175.00
Smoking Set, Flower Head & Ribbon, Tray, 13 1/4 In. 1045.00
Soup Ladle, Olympian 750.00
Soup Spoon, Clinton, Oval 35.00
Sugar Sifter, Beekman, Large 295.00
Sugar Tongs, Palm 145.00
Tazza, Reeded Border, Pedestal, 3 1/8 X 9 In. 750.00
Teapot, Urn Shape, Swan Finial, C–Scroll Handle, 1851, 10 In. 880.00
Teaspoon, Chrysanthemum 65.00
Teaspoon, Colonial 20.00
Teaspoon, Renaissance 65.00
Teaspoon, Wave Edge 45.00
Tongs, Bird Claws, Chrysanthemum, C.1890, 3 1/2 In. 195.00
Tray, Beaded Open Handle, Greek Key Border, C.1855, 28 In. 5280.00
Tray, Flower Head & Ribbon Border, 21 1/2 In. 2860.00
Trowel, Ice Cream, Beekman 250.00
Tureen, Soup, Stag's Head Handles & Finial 4900.00
Vase, Trumpet, Applied Reeded Band, Knopped Stem, 17 In. 1600.00

Tiffany objects made from a mixture of materials, such as bronze and glass boxes, are listed here. Tiffany lamps are included in this section.

TIFFANY, Andirons, Twisted Handles, Lion's Paw Feet, Bronze & Iron, C.1900 .... 2200.00
Ash Stand, Adjustable Column, Stylized Leaves, Bronze, 26 1/2 In. 2420.00
Ashtray & Match Safe, Adam, Bronze, Gold Dore, 6 X 2 3/4 In. 250.00
Ashtray & Match Safe, Spanish, Bronze, Octagon, 7 X 1 1/2 In. 225.00

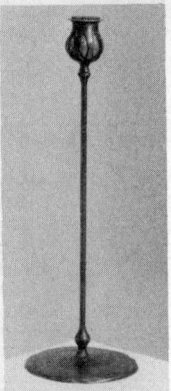

Tiffany, Candlestick, Bronze
& Glass, Signed, 18 In.

Tiffany, Clock, Garniture Set, Bronzed,
Winged Cherubs, 16 In.

Tiffany, Candleholder,   Tiffany, Lamp, Tobacco   Tiffany, Box, Pine Cone,   Tiffany, Lamp, Candlestick,
Cobra Form, Bronze,   Leaf, Acorn Shade,   Bronze, Glass, Signed,   Favrile, Ruffled Shade,
Signed, 8 In.   Bronze, Signed, 16 In.   2 3/4 X 7 3/4 In.   Signed, 14 In.

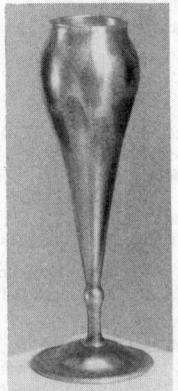

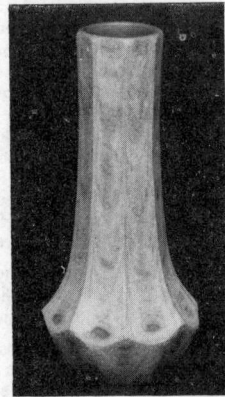

Tiffany, Lamp, Linenfold,
10 Panels, Amber,
Signed, 16 In.

Tiffany Glass, Vase, Floriform,
Favrile, Leaf, Vines, Signed, 9 In.

Tiffany Glass, Vase, Agate,
Amber, Gold Interior, 8 In.

Ashtray, Crab, Abalone & Bronze 450.00
Ashtray, Gold Dore Finish, Zodiac Symbol Center, Bronze, 4 X 3 In. 135.00
Ashtray, Match Safe, Zodiac, Bronze, Signed, 4 1/2 X 4 1/2 In. 150.00
Bill File, Octagon, Bronze, Abalone, Discs Around, Curved Arm, 8 In. 500.00
Bill File, Pine Needle, Bronze, Green Slag, 7 1/2 In. 500.00
Blotter Ends, Abalone, Bronze, Signed, 19 X 2 3/4 In., 2 Piece 350.00
Blotter Ends, Abalone, Bronze, Triangular, 4 1/2 In., 4 Piece 350.00
Blotter Ends, American Indian, Dore, 19 In. 395.00
Blotter Ends, Pine Needle, 4 Corners, Bronze .... 175.00 To 250.00
Blotter Ends, Zodiac, Bronze, 19 In., 2 Piece 215.00
Blotter, Hand Roll, Grapevine, Gold Dore, Amber, Knob, 6 X 3 In. 295.00
Bookends, Abalone, Bronze, Gold Dore, Line & Leaf Design, 5 1/2 In. 695.00
Bookends, Buddhist, Seated Deity, Bronze, Signed, 6 In. 405.00
Bookends, Grapevine, Amber Slag, Gold Dore, Bronze, 5 1/2 In. 700.00
Bookends, Spanish, Dragon In Relief, Signed, 6 X 4 1/4 In. 900.00
Bookends, Venetian, Polychrome Within Design, Signed, 6 1/4 In. 405.00
Bookends, Zodiac, Etched Design, Bronze, Signed, 6 X 5 In. 475.00
Bookrack, Abalone, Discs In Flower Design, Signed, 14 1/2 In. 1200.00
Bookrack, Grapevine, Bronze, Green Slag Glass, 14 In. 1200.00
Bookrack, Pine Needle, Bronze, Green Glass, Extends To 23 In. 1200.00
Bowl, 4 Lion Head Medallions, Bronze, Signed, 2 1/2 X 5 In. 182.50
Box, Bronze, Gold Dore, Enameled, 4 Ball Feet, 6 1/2 X 3 1/2 X 2 In. 750.00
Box, Bronze, Green Slag Inserts, 6 3/4 In. 210.00
Box, Card, Pine Needle, Bronze, Amber Slag, 2 Sections, 3 X 4 1/4 In. 475.00
Box, Chinese, Gold Dore, Bronze, Hinged Cover, Cedar Lined, 8 X 5 In. 900.00
Box, Crab, Bronze 375.00
Box, Jewelry, Bronze, Pine Needle, Green Slag, 9 1/2 X 7 X 3 In. 1500.00
Box, Jewelry, Modeled, Bronze, Hinged Cover, 4 3/4 X 3 3/4 In. 350.00
Box, Jewelry, Patterned Squares, Bronze, Signed, 3 X 3 3/4 X 8 In. 2000.00
Box, Jewelry, Pine Needle, Bronze, Green Slag Glass, 7 In.Square 950.00
Box, Jewelry, Venetian, 14K Gold Plate, Hinged Cover, 5 1/2 X 4 In. 575.00
Box, Pine Cone, Bronze, Glass, Signed, 2 3/4 X 7 3/4 In. ....Illus 248.00
Box, Pine Needle, Green Insert, 2 Sections, Cover, 4 1/4 In. 375.00
Box, Scarab, Glass 275.00
Box, Stamp, Abalone, Bronze, Hinged Cover, Tray, 4 X 2 X 1 1/4 In. 395.00
Box, Stamp, Grapevine, Gold Dore Over Amber Glass, Signed, 4 In. 350.00
Box, Zodiac, Symbols On Hinged Lid, Signed, 5 1/4 In. .... 275.00 To 350.00
Calendar, Grapevine, Green Glass, Bronze 425.00
Candelabrum, 6–Light, Bronze, Candlesnuffer Opening, Oval, 15 In. 3000.00
Candelabrum, Floral Form, Gold Dore, Stamped, 9 In. 825.00
Candleholder, Cobra Form, Bronze, Signed, 8 In. ....Illus 1650.00
Candleholder, Double, Candlesnuffer, Fleur–De–Lis Base, Bronze 1700.00
Candleholder, Jeweled Inserts, Leaf Base, Bronze, Signed, 8 In. 1650.00
Candleholder, Leaf Form Base, Jeweled Glass Inserts 1500.00
Candlestick, 2–Arm, Gold Dore, Bud Center Arm, Oval, 7 1/2 X 9 In. 1400.00
Candlestick, Bamboo Stick Shape, Bronze, Marked, 10 In. 935.00
Candlestick, Bobeche Insert, Knopped Stem, Bronze, 1928, 16 5/8 In. 1100.00
Candlestick, Bronze & Glass, Signed, 18 In. ....Illus 1400.00
Candlestick, Bronze, Apple Green Glass, Magnolia, 17 1/2 In. 2500.00
Candlestick, Bronze, Bobeches, Stick Body, 20 1/2 In., Pair 2100.00
Candlestick, Bronze, Green Glass, 3 Spread Curled Feet, 10 1/2 In. 1200.00
Candlestick, Bronze, Opaque Yellow–Green Lined Socket, 20 1/4 In. 1300.00
Candlestick, Bronze, Stick Body, Tripod Base, Green Glass, 12 In. 1500.00
Candlestick, Cobra, Bronze, Signed 275.00
Candlestick, Double, Bronze, Signed, 18 In. 2500.00
Candlestick, Green Glass Blown Into Mount, Bronze, Signed, 18 In. 3850.00
Candlestick, Magnolia, Glass & Bronze, Signed, 17 1/2 In. 2500.00
Candlestick, Stick Body, Bobeches, Bronze, Signed, 20 1/2 In., Pair 2100.00
Candlestick, Tulip Shape, Amber, Glass & Bronze, 1928, 13 3/8 In. 1980.00
Candy Dish, Phantom Luster, Insert, Bronze, Signed, 5 In. 675.00
Centerpiece, Bronze, Enameled Raised Flowers, Signed, 4 X 9 In. 1100.00
Clock, Garniture Set, Bronzed, Winged Cherubs, 16 In. ....Illus 4500.00
Clock, Line Design, Bronze & Enamel, Signed, 5 1/2 X 5 1/2 In. 975.00
Clock, Mantel, Chain Design Around Chapter Ring, Gilt Bronze, 1928 .... 3025.00

Clock, Tall, Moon Face, Hour & 1/2–Hour Strike, Mahogany 8900.00
Compote, Bronze, Gold Dore, Knob Shaped Pedestal, 4 X 6 1/4 In. 225.00
Compote, Sunburst Line Design Top, Bronze, Signed, 3 1/2 X 6 In. 195.00
Daily Memoranda, Zodiac, Bronze, Gold Dore, Top Cover, 6 X 5 In. 450.00
Desk Garniture Set, Gilt Bronze, Mother–of–Pearl, 8 Piece 2400.00
Desk Set, Abalone, 6 Piece 3000.00
Desk Set, Grapevine, Bronze & Glass, Signed, 3 Piece, 5 1/2 X 9 In. 1800.00
Desk Set, Indian, Gold Dore, Bronze, Signed & Numbered, 9 Piece 1550.00
Desk Set, Zodiac, 6 Piece .... 715.00 To 885.00
Desk Set, Zodiac, Bronze, Complete, 1899–1920, 12 Piece 1500.00
Fixture, Ceiling, Domed Shade, Openwork Rope & Bead, Copper, 12 In. 6050.00
Frame, Abalone, Leaf & Floral Design, Bronze, 7 1/3 X 9 1/4 In. 2200.00
Frame, Bronze, Grapevine, Easel, Oval Opening, 9 3/4 X 8 In. 1800.00
Frame, Calendar, Grapevine, Bronze, Amber Slag, 5 3/4 X 4 In. 400.00
Frame, Indian, Bronze, Gold Dore, 7 1/2 X 6 In. 475.00
Frame, Louis XVI, Bronze, Wreath Top, Gold Dore, 6 X 5 1/2 In. 475.00
Frame, Pine Needle, Bronze & Glass, Signed, 12 1/2 X 9 3/4 In. 2200.00
Frame, Pine Needle, Bronze, Green Slag Glass, 6 1/4 X 4 1/2 In. 350.00
Frame, Venetian, Row of Minks, 14K Gold Plate, 11 3/4 X 9 In. 1800.00
Frame, Zodiac, Bronze, 8 1/4 X 7 1/4 In. 650.00
Frame, Zodiac, Bronze, 12 X 14 In. 275.00
Globe, Hanging, Leather Line & Swirl, Bronze Holder, Signed, 13 In. 2600.00
Humidor, Bronze All Around Body, Cedar Lined, Signed, 9 X 6 In. 3500.00
Inkstand, Chinese, Bronze, Marked, 4 1/2 In. 1045.00
Inkwell, Abalone Shell, Bronze, Hinged Cover, Gold Dore, 3 1/2 In. 600.00
Inkwell, Byzantine, Bronze, Jewels, Beaded, Round, 4 1/2 X 2 3/4 In. 2000.00
Inkwell, Chinese, Double, Bronze, Gold Dore, Hinged Cover, 4 1/2 In. 550.00
Inkwell, Chinese, Gilt Bronze, 4 1/4 In. .... 550.00 To 675.00
Inkwell, Double, Venetian, Bronze Chain Latch, Signed, 3 X 2 3/4 In. 550.00
Inkwell, Glass Blown Through Openings, Bronze, Signed, 3 1/2 In. 1800.00
Inkwell, Grapevine, Bronze, Amber Slag Glass, Hinged Cover, 7 In. 750.00
Inkwell, Grapevine, Bronze, Green Slag Glass, Hinged Cover, 7 In. 750.00
Inkwell, Grecian Key, 3 1/4 X 5 1/4 In. 525.00
Inkwell, Indian, Bronze, Signed, 4 In. 495.00
Inkwell, Leaf, Bronze & Glass, 4 X 4 In. 225.00
Inkwell, Pine Needle, Bronze, Green Slag Glass, Beaded, 4 1/4 In. 550.00
Inkwell, Spanish, Gold Dore, Hinged Knobbed Cover, 4 1/2 X 6 In. 750.00
Inkwell, Zodiac, Bronze, Glass Insert, Signed, 3 1/2 X 6 3/4 In. 500.00
Inkwell, Zodiac, Gold Patina, 4 In. .... 175.00 To 300.00
Inkwell, Zodiac, Hinged Lid, Hexagonal Shape, Signed, 6 1/2 In. 395.00
Jar, Pine Needle, Bronze, Green Slag Glass, Cover, 2 1/2 X 3 3/4 In. 295.00
Lamp Base, Ribbed Standard, 3 Light Sockets, Bronze, 22 1/2 In. 3200.00
Lamp Base, Root–Like Feet, Gilt–Bronze, C.1920, Signed, 18 3/8 In. 8800.00
Lamp, 12–Sided Shade, Glass & Bronze, Signed, 1928, 11 1/4 In. 1350.00
Lamp, 3 Arms, Yellow–Green Wire Work Shade, Bronze, 14 3/4 In. 3500.00
Lamp, 6–Sided Column, Concave Platform, Bronze, 26 In. 4180.00
Lamp, Abalone Discs In Circular Design, Bronze, Signed, 9 In. 3200.00
Lamp, Acorn, Greek Urn Font, 14 In. 6000.00
Lamp, Acorn, Leaded, Bamboo Base, No.474, 10 In. 2500.00
Lamp, Adjustable, Bronze, Arrow Design, Signed, 48 To 60 In. 1800.00
Lamp, Bands of Geometric Tiles, Bronze Base, 1899–1920, 18 1/2 In. 7150.00
Lamp, Bronze, 3–Branch, Green Domed Damascene Shade, 7 In. 700.00
Lamp, Bronze, Blue–Green Ivy Leaf Shade, Stick Body, 16 In. 7500.00
Lamp, Bronze, Dark Dore, Curved Arm Holds Amber Shade, 10 In. 2300.00
Lamp, Bronze, Glass Beetle–Form Shade, 9 In. 4750.00
Lamp, Bronze, Gold Dore, Favrile, Spread Umbrella Shade, 14 In. 2300.00
Lamp, Bronze, Gold Iridescent & Emerald Green Shade, 13 In. 1800.00
Lamp, Byzantine, Bronze, Queen Ann's Lace, 17 1/2 In. 8500.00
Lamp, Candelabrum Bronze Base, Ivory Favril Shade, 22 In. 1800.00
Lamp, Candelabrum, 2–Light, Bronze Tassels & Finial, Signed, 22 In. 1800.00
Lamp, Candle, Bronze Holder, Pink Shade, Pulled Feather, 5 In. 700.00
Lamp, Candle, Gold Favrile Glass, Feather Riser, 16 In. 2150.00
Lamp, Candle, Twisted Glass Base, Feather Shades, Signed, 15 1/2 In. 2800.00
Lamp, Candle, Twisted Ribbed Body, Gold Shade, 16 1/2 In. 2200.00

Lamp, Candlestick Column, Slag Shade, Bronze 800.00
Lamp, Candlestick, Amber Swirling Ribs, Electrified, 15 3/8 In., Pr. 5225.00
Lamp, Candlestick, Bronze, Gold Dore, Tulip Shaped Shade, 14 1/2 In. 1800.00
Lamp, Candlestick, Favrile, Ruffled Shade, Signed, 14 In. ....*Illus* 1300.00
Lamp, Candlestick, Pine Needle Shade, Bronze Post, Signed, 22 In. 1800.00
Lamp, Chinese, Glass & Gilt–Bronze, Signed, C.1920, 16 1/2 In. 3080.00
Lamp, Conical Shade, Radiating Brickwork Tiles, Gilt–Bronze, 27 In. 9350.00
Lamp, Counter–Balance, Bronze Stick Body, Gold Shade, Signed, 15 In. 6000.00
Lamp, Counter–Balance, Glass & Bronze, C.1920, 4 Ft. 6 In. 6600.00
Lamp, Counter–Balance, Gold Favrile Shade, Bronze, Marked, 16 In. 4400.00
Lamp, Double Arm, Adjustable Balance Sphere, Glass Shade, 57 In. 825.00
Lamp, Double Arm, Bronze Base, Green Feather Shade, Signed, 13 In. 3800.00
Lamp, Fabrique Shade, 10 Panels, Amber Favrile, Bronze, 16 In. 3500.00
Lamp, Fleur–De–Lis, Mottled & Striated Green Shade, 21 In. 9500.00
Lamp, Geometric, Domical Shade, Striated Tiles, Bronze, 1899, 18 In. 8800.00
Lamp, Glass & Bronze, Nautilus Shell Shade, Signed, 1920, 14 1/2 In. 9075.00
Lamp, Gold Dore, Feather, Bronze, Stalactite Shade, Floor 5000.00
Lamp, Green Feather Shade, 2 Arms, Gold Dore, 13 X 14 In. 3800.00
Lamp, Hanging, Gold Iridescent, Bronze Hooks & Chain, 6 X 13 In. 2600.00
Lamp, Harp, Bronze, Favrile Glass Shade, 13 In. 2500.00
Lamp, Harp, Bronze, Green Damascened Shade, Signed, 13 1/2 In. 3410.00
Lamp, Ivy Leaf Around Shade, Bronze Urn–Shaped Body, Signed, 20 In. 9500.00
Lamp, Ivy Leaf, Bronze, Stick Body, Blue–Green Mottled Glass, 16 In. 7500.00
Lamp, Jack–In–The–Pulpit, Blossom Rim, Amber, Signed, 13 3/4 In. 6050.00
Lamp, Liberty Bell, Bronze Base, Gold Glass Ball, Signed, 14 1/2 In. 6000.00
Lamp, Lily, 3–Light, Gilded Bronze 3900.00
Lamp, Linenfold, 10 Panels, Amber, Signed, 16 In. ....*Illus* 7000.00
Lamp, Moorish, Flattened Dome Shade, Turtle–Back Tiles, 29 In. 9900.00
Lamp, Mosque, Allover Pattern, Opal Ground, Octagon Base, 9 1/2 In. 2500.00
Lamp, Nautilus, Bronze, Impressed, 13 In. 2200.00
Lamp, Plique–A–Jour, Floral Design, Bronze, Marked, 13 In. 5500.00
Lamp, Pods & Stems On Adjustable Column, Bronze, Marked, 28 In. 8250.00
Lamp, Pomegranate, Conical Urn Base, Bronze, Marked, 15 1/4 In. 8250.00
Lamp, Root With 4 Raised Shoots At Foot, Bronze, Marked, 24 In. 4400.00
Lamp, Striated Leaded Glass Shade, Bronze Base, Signed, 23 In. 8000.00
Lamp, Student, Double, Signed 750.00
Lamp, Student, Leaf Design, Bronze Supports, Glass Shade, Signed 3750.00
Lamp, Tobacco Leaf, Acorn Shade, Bronze, Signed, 16 In. ....*Illus* 3850.00
Lamp, Torch, Gold Dore, Favrile Green Leaf Shade, Signed, 57 In. 5200.00
Lamp, Trailing Leaf & Vine, Gold Favrile, 24 In. 1250.00
Lamp, Verdigris, Bell–Shaped Shade, Bronze Base, Signed, 15 In. 3795.00
Lamp, Zodiac, 2–Light, 12–Paneled Shade, Bronze, 16 1/2 In. 2400.00
Lantern, Hanging, Gold Iridescent, Favrile, Octagon Shade, 12 In. 1700.00
Letter Holder, Indian, Red Enameled Highlights 600.00
Letter Holder, Pine Needle, Green Slag Glass, Bronze, Signed 575.00
Letter Opener, Chinese, Signed, 11 In. 175.00
Letter Opener, Crab, Impressed No.1096, 9 1/4 In. 80.00
Letter Opener, Grapevine, Bronze, Green Slag Glass, 9 1/4 In. 155.00
Letter Opener, Ninth Century, 10 1/4 In. 200.00
Letter Rack, 2 Sections, Sculptured Design, Signed, 10 In. 750.00
Letter Rack, Abalone Discs, Bronze, Iridescent, 2 Sections 650.00
Letter Rack, Chinese, Bronze, 2 Sections, 9 1/2 X 6 X 2 1/2 In. 450.00
Letter Rack, Grapevine, 3 Sections, Bronze, Glass, Signed, 8 X 7 In. 650.00
Letter Rack, Pine Needle, Metal, Green Slag, 10 X 6 1/2 X 2 1/2 In. 650.00
Letter Rack, Spanish, 2 Sections, Gold Dore, 10 In. 750.00
Letter Rack, Venetian, 2 Sections, 14K Gold Plate, Signed 450.00
Letter Rack, Zodiac, Bronze, Gold Dore, 2 Sections, 9 1/2 In. 350.00
Liquor, Favrile, Gold Iridescent, Diagonal Ribbed, 4 1/2 In., Pair 875.00
Magnifying Glass, Pine Needle, Bronze, Green Slag Glass, 8 1/2 In. 650.00
Match Holder, Chinese, Dark Dore 250.00
Night–Light, Gold Iridescent Shade, Bronze, Gold Dore, 6 1/2 In. 1500.00
Night–Light, Scarab 2200.00
Paper Clip, 14K Gold, Large 110.00
Paper Clip, Zodiac, Bronze, Signed, 3 1/2 X 2 In. 225.00

Paperweight, Bulldog, Sitting, Bronze, Gold Dore, 2 1/4 X 1 1/2 In. 475.00
Paperweight, Glass & Bronze Turtle–Back Tile, 1900, 4 In. 467.00
Paperweight, Lioness, Recumbent, Bronze, Signed, 5 X 1 1/2 In. 550.00
Paperweight, Spherical, Dark Red Interior Spots, Red, 3 In. 275.00
Paperweight, Zodiac, Bronze, Signed, 3 3/4 X 2 1/4 In. 250.00
Pen Brush, Pine Needle, Bronze, Green Slag, 2 1/4 X 2 In. 250.00
Pen Tray, Abalone, Bronze, 4 Ball Feet, 8 1/2 X 2 1/2 In. 295.00
Pen Tray, Adam, Curved Sides As Handles, Signed, 9 1/2 In. 175.00
Pen Tray, Bronze, Gold Iridescent Mosaic, Curved, 7 3/4 X 3 In. 2200.00
Pen Tray, Chinese, Bronze, Signed, 12 X 3 3/4 In. 175.00
Pen Tray, Grapevine, 4 Bronze Ball Feet, 11 1/4 X 3 In. 250.00
Pen Tray, Medallion, Bronze, 1890, 8 1/2 In. 210.00
Pen Tray, Pine Needle, Green Glass Under Bronze, Signed, 9 1/2 In. 250.00
Pen Tray, Spanish, Raised Border Design, 9 3/4 X 3 3/4 In. 300.00
Pen Tray, Zodiac, Dore & Enameled 250.00
Pen Wipe, Grape 110.00
Pendant, Butterfly, Yellow Wings, Bronze & Leaded Glass, 10 In. 2420.00
Pendant, Dragonfly, Multihued Wings, Bronze & Glass, 10 In. 1760.00
Pipe Tray, Setter, Bronze 275.00
Planter, Geometric, Gold Dore, Liner, Bronze, Signed, 8 1/2 In. 450.00
Planter, Grapevine, Bronze, Amber Slag, Tapered To 10 1/4–In.Base 1500.00
Planter, Red Jewel, Bronze, Embossed Floral & Geometric, Gold Dore 550.00
Platter, Gold Dore, Center Well, Signed, 9 X 1 3/4 In. 95.00
Scale, Pine Needle, Bronze Over Amber Glass, Signed, 3 1/4 In. 575.00
Scale, Zodiac, Gold Dore, 3 1/4 X 2 3/4 X 1 1/2 In. 450.00
Sconce, Silver Dore, Bronze, 6 Shades, Electrified, 21 X 18 In., Pr. 8500.00
Shade, Black–Eyed Susan, Amber Centers, Signed, 1899–1920, 16 In. 9900.00
Shade, For Wall Sconce, Gold Favrile, 7 In., Pair 850.00
Shade, Lily, Amber–Green Feathering, Signed, 1928, 4 1/8 In. 770.00
Stamp Box, Zodiac, Gold Dore, Hinged Cover, 3 Sections, 4 X 2 In. 300.00
Thermometer, Easel Back 550.00
Toothpick, Bronze, Embossed Design 55.00
Tray, Art Nouveau Border, Blue Enameled Ground, Signed, 10 In. 325.00
Tray, Card, Double Tier Ruffle, Bronze, Signed, 5 3/4 In. 175.00
Tray, Entwined Line Design, Bronze, Signed, 8 X 10 In. 475.00
Tray, Pipe, Setter, Bronze 275.00
Tray, Serving, Bronze, Gold Dore, Twisted Rope Edge, 8 1/4 In. 150.00
Trivet, Bronze, Blue–Green Cypriote Glass Style, Square, 6 1/4 In. 850.00
Trivet, Openwork Design, Favrile Glass Inset, Marked, 6 1/2 In. 1320.00
Vase, Atomic Cloud, Allover Gold Damascene, Signed, 8 1/2 In. 1275.00
Vase, Bud, Gold Iridescent, Bronze Base, Hexagon, 16 In., 2 Piece 1850.00
Vase, Floriform, Feathering, Bronze Stem, C.1904, 17 3/16 In. 4400.00
Vase, Iridescent Feather Design, Crystal, Bronze, 1899, 15 5/8 In. 935.00
Vase, Mirrored, Peacock Blue, Dimpled Sides, Signed, 6 In. 1950.00
Vase, Trumpet, Brown Feather, Yellow & Gold, Bronze, 14 3/4 In. 1500.00
Wax Seal, 3 Scarabs On Spherical Base, Letter M, 1 3/4 In. 275.00

The Tiffin Glass Company of Tiffin, Ohio, was a subsidiary of the
United States Glass Co. of Pittsburgh, Pennsylvania, in 1892. The
U.S. Glass Co. went bankrupt in 1963, and the Tiffin plant
employees purchased the building and the inventory. They continued
running it from 1963 to 1966, when it was sold to Continental Can
Company. In 1969, it was sold to Interpace; and in 1980, it was
closed. The black satin glass, made from 1923 to 1926, and the
stemware of the last twenty years are the best–known products.

TIFFIN, Ashtray, Twilight, Cloverleaf Shape, 3 In. 20.00
Bowl, Cascade, 14 X 8 1/2 In. 35.00
Bowl, Rolled Edge, Yellow, 5 1/2 In. 35.00
Bowl, Twilight, 12 1/2 In. 145.00
Candlestick, Double, June Night 20.00
Candlestick, Green Satin, 8 1/2 In., Pair 60.00
Champagne Goblet & Plate, Clorinda, Set 75.00
Champagne, Forever Yours 12.00
Champagne, Shawl Dancer, Crystal, Green Stem 22.50

Cocktail, June Night 13.00
Compote, Black Satin, On Stand, 7 3/4 In. 85.00
Compote, Cumula, Blue Rolled Edge, 6 1/2 In. 35.00
Compote, Williamsburg, 2 Handles 20.00
Cordial, June Night 20.00
Cordial, True Lover 22.50
Creamer & Sugar, Cerise, Crystal 50.00
Dish, Swan, Red, Clear Neck & Head 45.00
Figurine, Pheasant, Blue, Pair 550.00
Goblet, Byzantine .... 12.00 To 17.00
Goblet, Forever Yours 16.00
Goblet, Green Foot, 8 3/4 In., Pair 35.00
Goblet, Hobnail, Purple, 6 In. 9.00
Goblet, Rock Crystal, 8 In., 8 Piece 60.00
Goblet, Shawl Dancer, Crystal, Green Stem 25.00
Goblet, True Love 18.00
Pitcher, Byzantine, Yellow, 64 Oz. 225.00
Pitcher, Lemonade, Hand Painted Woman Fishing, Frosted, 1930s 125.00
Plate, Byzantine, 8 In. 5.00
Plate, Cascade, 15 In. 40.00
Rose Bowl, Williamsburg, Large 25.00
Sherbet, Byzantine 9.00
Sherbet, Cherokee Rose 20.00
Sherbet, La Fleur, Yellow 16.00
Tray, Flanders, Center Handle, 10 In. 60.00
Tumbler, Byzantine, Juice, Footed, Crystal 12.00
Tumbler, Iced Tea, Cherokee Rose 20.00
Tumbler, Water, Cherokee Rose 15.00
Vase, Blown–Out Poppies, Black Satin, 5 In. 30.00
Vase, Cherokee Rose, 11 In. 30.00
Vase, Floral Coralene Beading, Black, 9 In. 50.00
Vase, Horn of Plenty, Red On Clear Base, 10 1/2 In. 150.00
Vase, Mulberry, 19 In. 65.00
Vase, Raised Florals, Black, 9 In. 75.00
Vase, Reddish, Green Foot, 9 1/4 In. 250.00
Wine, Cherokee Rose 20.00
Wine, Forever Yours 15.00

Tiles have been used in most countries of the world as a sturdy building material for floors, roofs, fireplace surrounds, and surface toppings. Many of the American tiles are listed in this book under the factory name.

TILE, 5 Colors, 8 Sides, S & S Tile Co., San Jose, California 75.00
Bird, Moravian, 4 In. 75.00
Boy & Girl, Duck, Black On White, Robertson, 4 X 4 In. 95.00
Breton Figures, Square, 4 In., Pair 185.00
Colonial Lady Spinning, Flowers, Name Priscilla, 4 X 4 In. 75.00
Dressed Koala Bear In Tree, Wheeling, Square, 4 1/4 In. 40.00
Fruit, Blue, Batchelder, 4 In. 60.00
Gleaners, Royal Doulton 48.00
Hand Painted Birds, Flowers, Leaves, Wheeling Pottery 24.00
Mission Shaped Top Rim, Carmel Kilns Co., 11 1/4 X 14 In. 85.00
Mosaic Art, Bird 24.00
Multicolor Fruit, California Faience, 6 In. 340.00
Multicolor Ship, Wheeling, 4 In. 30.00
Old Man, High Glaze, Trent Tile Co., Isaac Broome Design, 4 1/4 In. 125.00
Picture of Cat, Holland, Tin–Glazed, 18th Century, 15 1/4 X 10 1/2 In. 715.00
Roof, Pottery, Figure of Wrestler, Glazed, Chinese, 16 In. 525.00
Sailing Ship, 6 Colors, California Faience 250.00
Stylized Poppies, 4 Colors, California Faience 275.00
Tea, Boat & Windmill Scene, Marked 47 .... 85.00
Trees, Robertson, 4 In. 50.00
Viking Ship, 6 Colors, California Faience 375.00

Tin has been used to make household containers in America since the seventeenth century. The first tin utensils were brought from Europe; but by 1798, tin plate was imported and local tinsmiths made the wares. Painted tin is called "tole" and is listed separately. Some tin kitchen items may be found listed under Kitchen. The lithographed tin containers used to hold food and tobacco are listed under Advertising, Tin.

TINWARE, Case, Comb, Wall Hanger	30.00
Chamberstick, Oblong Shaped Pan, Brass Push–Up Knob, 9 3/4 In.	95.00
Chamberstick, Push–Up, Conical Snuffer On Chain, 7 1/2 In.	175.00
Chandelier, 2 Tiers, 15 Candle Arms, 24 In.	400.00
Coffeepot, Punched, Floral & Heart Design, Cone, Brass Knob, 10 In.	2800.00
Coffeepot, Punched, Tulip Design, 11 In.	1210.00
Coffeepot, Punched, Tulip Design, Black Paint, 11 In.	2600.00
Coffeepot, Wire Bail Handle, 23 In.	450.00
Dryer, Mitten, Pierced Holes In Top, Oval, 23 X 10 X 13 In.	130.00
Flask, Oval Bottom, Tapered, Screw Cap, 7 In.	100.00
Foot Warmer, Pierced, Wooden Frame, Wire Bail, Square, 10 1/2 In.	220.00
Jug, Face, B.B. Craig, Early 1940s	295.00
Mold, Candle, 2 Tube	425.00
Mold, Candle, 6 Tube, 10 1/2 In.	70.00
Mold, Candle, 8 Tube, Ribbon Handle, 9 5/8 In.	85.00
Mold, Candle, 8 Tube, Side Handle, 7 X 9 In.	230.00
Mold, Candle, 12 Tube, 10 3/4 In.	65.00
Mold, Candle, 12 Tube, 2 Strap Handles	125.00
Mold, Candle, 12 Tube, Rectangular, 11 1/2 In.	65.00
Mold, Candle, 25 Tube, 12 In.	155.00
Mold, Candle, 48 Tube, Ring Handle, 10 1/2 In.	495.00
Mold, Cheese, Pierced, Diamond Shape, Footed, 7 7/8 X 5 X 3 3/8 In.	100.00
Mold, Chocolate, 8 Easter Bunnies, 9 X 10 In.	35.00
Muffin, 12 Heart Holes, Riveted To Solid Back, Mason's, 13 X 9 In.	550.00
Sconce, Candle, Crimped Crest, Black Paint, 13 In., Pair	250.00
Sconce, Candle, Electrified, 13 In., Pair	125.00
Spittoon, Turtle, Cast Tin	425.00
Torch, Campaign, Flared Conical Font, Turned Wooden Handle, 22 In.	36.00
Torch, Campaign, Wooden Pole, Added Wire Font Frame, 48 In.	45.00
Wall Pocket, Punched, Heart Designs, 7 3/4 In.	250.00
Warmer, 1 Door, 2 Shelves, Silver Paint, 23 X 15 X 12 In.	60.00

TOBACCO CUTTER, see Advertising

Because tobacco needs special conditions of humidity and air, it has been stored in special containers since the eighteenth century. The tobacco jar is often made in fanciful shapes.

TOBACCO JAR, Blue Boar Inn, Coaching Scene, Brown Transfer On Gold	75.00
Boy's Head, Cap	60.00
Englishman, Pipe Hanging From Mouth, Red Mustache, Hat	135.00
Great War, Views of Saar, English Pottery	125.00
Head of Indian Chief, War Bonnet, 6 In.	135.00
Humidor, Aviator's Head, Leather Helmet, 6 X 5 In.	245.00
Indian, Majolica	60.00
Lady Hippo Carrying Her Purse, Austria	85.00
Monk's Head	150.00
Scotsman's Bust, Blue Tam, Gray Sideburns, 6 In.	145.00
Skull	125.00
Woman Driver In Duster & Goggles	4950.00

The toby jug is a very special form of pitcher. It is shaped like the full figure of a man or woman. A pitcher that shows just the top half of a person is not correctly called a toby. More examples of toby jugs can be found under Royal Doulton and other factory names.

TOBY JUG, Jailer, Occupied Japan, 7 In.	50.00
Man, Tricorner Hat, Porcelain, Polychrome Enameled, Gilt, 8 1/4 In.	135.00

Mustard Container, Tricorner Hat Lid, Flow Blue Base, 6 In.	245.00
Parson, Red, Occupied Japan, 8 1/2 In.	50.00
Peddler, Occupied Japan, 5 In.	35.00

 Tole is painted tin. It is sometimes called "japanned ware," "pontypool," or "toleware." Most nineteenth–century tole is painted with an orange–red or black background and multicolored decorations. Many recent versions of toleware are made and sold.

TOLE, see also Tinware

TOLE, Box, Book Shape, Orginial Black Paint, Gold Lettering, 4 3/8 X 6 In.	550.00
Box, Brown Japanning, Yellow Striping, Floral Design, 6 1/2 In.	200.00
Box, Comb, Hanging, Says American Eagle & Comb Case, Blue, 6 5/8 In.	45.00
Box, Deed, Domed Lid, Brown Japanning, Floral Design, Ring Handle, 9 In.	650.00
Box, Deed, Domed Lid, Brown Japanning, Gilt Floral Design, 4 In.	45.00
Box, Deed, Domed Lid, Brown Japanning, White Band, 9 In.	75.00
Box, Deed, Domed Lid, Japanning, White Band, Floral Design, 8 3/4 In.	60.00
Box, Deed, Yellow Paint, Black Striping, Brass Bail Handle, 10 In.	27.50
Box, Document, Flower Band, Brown, Yellow Striped, Hinged, 4 X 3 X 3 In.	225.00
Box, Pencil, Original Pencils, A.W. Faber, Castell	18.00
Box, Strawberries, Yellow Ground	467.00
Bread Tray, Crystalline Bottom, Flowers, Cream, Open Handles, 8 X 3 In.	200.00
Bread Tray, Red Plum Design, Brown, Oval, 12 3/8 X 8 X 4 In.	1200.00
Canister, Hand Painted Birds, Flowers, Hearts, 1820s, 6 In.	75.00
Chamberstick, Red Paint, Gold Lip, 2 3/8 In.	125.00
Chocolate Urn, Domed Lid, Pyriform Body, Flower Swags, 21 1/2 In.	935.00
Coal Hod, Calla Lilies, Claw Feet, Black, 20 In.	55.00
Coal Hod, Floral & Landscape, Red, 19 In., Pair	1050.00
Coal Hod, G.D.W. Mfg. Co., 24 In.	75.00
Coffeepot, Yellow Floral, Red, Gooseneck Spout, Brass Knob Lid, 10 In.	225.00
Creamer, Floral Design, Brown, Ribbon Handle, Hinged Lid, 3 X 4 In.	1200.00
Creamer, Strap Handle, Cylindrical, New England, 5 1/4 In.	4500.00
Lamp, Bulbous, Gilt Bronze Mask Head Handles, Wreaths, French, 20 In.	385.00
Lamp, Columnar, Transfer of Figures & Gardens, Yellow, 21 In.	522.50
Lamp, Orange Paint, Black Transfer Design, Glass Globe, 5 In.	225.00
Lantern, Candle, Collapses In Book Shape, Gold Trim, 6 1/8 In.	220.00
Lantern, Candle, Hinged Shutters, Brass Top, 6 3/4 In.	125.00
Mug, Pomegranate Design, Brown, Ribbon Handle, Tapered, 4 3/8 In.	550.00
Needle Case, Knitting, Red & Yellow Leaves, Brown, 19 Needles, 9 In.	200.00
Oil Can, Hinged Cover, Design, 6 In.	350.00
Plate, Portrait, Child, Anger Bakery On Back, 1905, 10 In.	70.00
Sconce, Candle, Shield Reflectors, Sailing Ship Scene, 15 1/2 In., Pair	95.00
Snuffbox, Liberty No Slavery, Black Ground, 3 3/8 In.	350.00
Snuffbox, Portrait of Commodore Isaac Chauncey, 2 1/8 X 3 In.	400.00
Sugar, Cover, Leaf Design, Brown, Loop Handle, Gallery Base, 4 X 3 In.	250.00
Tea Caddy, Floral Design On Black Ground, 4 1/4 In.	90.00
Tea Caddy, Rose Design, Blue Paint, 4 5/8 In.	85.00
Teapot, Pomegranate Design, Brown, Ribbon Handle, Hinged, 4 1/2 In.	650.00
Teapot, White, Yellow, Red & Green Floral Design, 5 In.	2300.00
Tray, Apple, Crystalline Bottom, Brown, Floral, 12 5/8 X 7 1/2 X 2 In.	750.00
Tray, Apple, Floral & Foliage Design, Yellow, White Band, 2 3/4 In.	2050.00
Tray, Apple, Floral, Foliage Design, Red, Yellow, Green, Oval, 2 3/4 In.	4450.00
Tray, Chippendale, Floral, Peacocks, Black, Gold, 19 3/4 X 26 In.	365.00
Tray, Crystalline Center, Cream Band, Tulip, Coffin Shape, 9 X 6 In.	260.00
Tray, Floral & Foliage Design, Dark Brown Ground, Crystalline Center	4450.00
Tray, Flowers & Fountain, Black, Chippendale Edge, 27 1/2 In.	325.00
Tray, Flowers In Reserves Border, Center Peacock, 30 3/4 In.	550.00
Tray, Gold Crystallized Center, White Band, Octagonal, 8 X 12 1/4 In.	1500.00
Tray, Snuffer, Peach Design, Gilt Panels, Red, 10 5/8 X 4 1/4 In.	70.00
Tray, Stenciled & Painted Peacock & Swan In Garden, 21 X 28 1/2 In.	225.00
Tray, Transfer Decorated, Allegorical Persian Scene, Oval, 30 In.	1600.00
Washbasin, Fitted Top Over Fitted Case, Stenciled Monuments, C.1860	660.00

Tom Mix was born in 1880 and died in 1940. He was the hero of over 100 silent movies from 1910 to 1929, and 25 sound films from 1929 to 1935. There was a Ralston Tom Mix radio show from 1933 to 1950, but the original Tom Mix was not in the show. Tom Mix comics were published from 1942 to 1953.

TOM MIX, Badge, Dobie County	20.00
Bird Call, Bullet	125.00
Book, Tom Mix Western Song Book, Miracle Rider Photos, 1935	50.00
Book, Trail of The Terrible Six	25.00
Book, Western Songs, Tom, Scenes From Miracle Rider, 64 Pages, 1935	50.00
Bracelet, Identification	30.00
Buckle	42.50
Button, Wash, Tony, Jane, Curly & Mike, 5 Piece	100.00
Catalog, Premium, 1936	35.00
Comic Book, No.38, February 1951	12.50
Compass & Magnifier, Brass, 1940	25.00
Compass & Magnifier, Lucite, Radio Premium	85.00
Decoder, Badge	35.00
Decoder, Pin Back, Curley	20.00
Game, Circus, Parker Bros.	165.00
Gun, Wooden	75.00
Knife, Pocket, Straight Shooter	40.00
Pencil Sharpener	45.00
Photograph, Silver Frame	60.00
Pinback, Tony	6.00
Poster, Safety	35.00
Ring, Look In & See Picture of Tom Mix & Tony, Ralston Premium	165.00
Ring, Magnet	45.00 To 60.00
Ring, Straight Shooter	60.00
Ring, Tiger Eye, Radio Premium	200.00
Shooting Gallery, Target Picturing Tom Mix, 1935, Parker Bros.	125.00
Signal Set, Postal	85.00
Spinner, Good Luck	35.00
Spurs, Glow In The Dark	40.00 To 95.00
Sun Watch	40.00 To 60.00
Telegraph Set	21.00
Telegraph, Ralston	75.00
Telescope & Whistle	35.00
Telescope & Whistle, Straight Shooter	65.00
Telescope, Bullet, With Bird Call	50.00
Telescope, Bullet, With Bird Call, Instructions, Box	150.00
Toy, Rocking Horse, Tony	275.00
Toy, Television Set, Brown	32.00

Tools of all sorts are listed here, but most are related to industry. Other tools will be found listed under Iron; Kitchen; Tinware; and Wooden.

TOOL, Abacus, Brass Trim, Wooden Ends, Walnut	25.00
Adding Machine, Calcumeter	45.00
Adding Machine, Marchant	65.00
Adze, Cooper's, Bolt Through Handle, Hickory Handle, Small	45.00
Adze, Gutter, Curved, Pointed Poll, Hand Forged, 1 1/2 In. Cut	60.00
Air Compresser, Pin Striped, Belt Driven, 1915	375.00
Angle Fence, Stanley, No.386, For Metal Joiner Planes	45.00
Auger, Hollow, Sterns, Adjustable, 3/8 To 1 In.	45.00
Ax, Broad, Aslee Bros., Hillsborough, N.H., 11 In.	55.00
Ax, Broad, Beatty & Son, Cast Steel, Wooden Blade Sheath	140.00
Ax, Broad, Oil Well Supply Co., Scene of Oil Wells, Indian's Head	850.00
Ax, Double Bitted Mortise, Head 13 In.	125.00
Ax, Goosewing, Hand Made, Holmsten–Gundsvall	100.00
Ax, Goosewing, Staller Wien, Touchmarks	225.00
Ax, Keen Kutter	12.00
Bag Stamp, J.K. Shellenberger, Carved Wood, 19 1/4 X 2 7/8 In.	30.00

Bag Stamp, Samuel Bollinger, Carved Wood, Border, 16 1/4 X 7 1/2 In.	55.00
Battery Recharger, Eveready, Alkaline	12.00
Beater, Basket Maker's, Convex, Wooden Handle, 2 3/8 X 5 1/2 In.	55.00
Bench, Cobbler's, Leather Seat, 2 Drawers, 19th Century, 45 In.	875.00
Bench, Shingle Maker's, Pine	145.00
Bench, Shoemaker's, With Tools, 4 Drawers, Colbaith's Bench	3740.00
Bench, Wooden Vise, 1 3/8 In. Poplar Boards, 10 Ft.X 26 In.	400.00
Bevel, Carpenter's, Thomas Bradburn & Sons, Rosewood & Brass	75.00
Bevel, Ship's Carpenter, J. Rabone & Sons, Rosewood & Brass	75.00
Billy Club & Tear Gas Combination, Brass, 1925	155.00
Bit Brace, Self–Acting, Robert Marples, Beech, 1848, 14 1/2 In.	250.00
Block, Keen Kutter, No.220, Japanned, 7 In.	32.50
Blow Torch, Brass, Pat.1921	18.00
Bookbinder's, Brass, Rosewood, 5 Wheels	165.00
Boot Scraper, Cat, 1920s	125.00
Bootjack, Cast Iron, Hearts & Diamonds Design, 1860–70, 16 In.	250.00
Bootjack, Naughty Nellie, Pronounced Nipples, Cast Iron	130.00
Bootjack, Wooden, Red, Hole, 4 1/2 X 11 1/2 In.	38.00
Bottle Corker, Wooden, Plunger–Type	22.00
Box, Dovetailed Wood, Hinged Lid, Iron Strap Hinges, 29 X 12 In.	45.00
Box, Machinist's, 5 Drawers, Leather Cover, H. Gerstner, 11 X 14 In.	150.00
Box, Tool, Walnut, 2 Trays	145.00
Brace, Angle, Miller Falls	25.00
Branding Iron, ABC	60.00
Bucksaw, Wooden Frame	20.00
Buggy Jack, Red Paint	30.00
Bung Start, Oak, Cooper	45.00
Burnisher, Burled Wood, Gold Foil Trim, 5 1/2 In.	55.00
Calipers, Adjustments For Legs, Brass Top, Stoddard	40.00
Calipers, Heart–Shaped Screw, Hand Wrought, Iron, 18th Century, 10 In.	95.00
Calipers, Pattern Maker's, Brass, 13 1/2 In.	65.00
Calipers, Timber, Dring & Fage, London, Boxwood Handle, Brass Joint	195.00
Candlesnuffers, Hand Forged Iron, Scissor Shape, 18th Century	45.00
Carder, Cotton	20.00
Carpet Stretcher, Iron, Wooden	18.50
Cattle Punch, Ear, Stearn's, 10 1/2 In.	27.00
Caulking, Shipwright's, 2 Mallets, 17 Irons	325.00
Check Writer, Lighting, Hand Operated, Pat.1915	20.00
Chest, Cabinet Maker's, Pine, Fitted, Painted, J. Talsma, 1889, 38 In.	425.00
Chest, Carpenter's, 2 Drawers, Poplar, 16 1/2 X 27 1/4 X 16 3/4 In.	200.00
Chisel, Corner	21.00
Chisel, Keen Kutter, Hardwood Handle, 1/4 In.	12.50
Chisel, Ripping	30.00
Chuteboard & Plane, Stanley, No.52, Mounted On Bench Jack	800.00
Cider Press, J.L. Haven, Cincinnati, Wooden, 2 16–In. Tubs, Pat. 1866	795.00
Cigarette Roller, Cigarola, Cast Iron .... 25.00 To 30.00	
Cigarette Roller, Wooden, Box	10.00
Clamp, Door, Morse Duplex, Patent 4/10/1915	16.00
Clamp, Wood Gluing, 12 In.	9.00
Cleaner, Horse Hoof, Cast Iron Handle	18.00
Cobbler's Bench, Pine, Brown, 5 Drawers, Leather Seat, 42 In.	450.00
Coffin Smoother, Casey & Co., Wooden, Iron, 7 7/8 In.	25.00
Coffin Smoother, Young McMaster, Iron, With Cover, 1838–43, 8 In.	40.00
Coin Counter, 1 To 50 Cents	50.00
Coin Sorter & Counter, Brandt Cashier Co.	400.00
Compass, Surveyor's, Pike, Philadelphia, Case	800.00
Corebox, Stanley, No.57, 1 Extension	150.00
Cork Press, Enterprise, No.2	65.00
Corn Cutter, Cast Iron, Painted, Fastens To Arm & Leg	6.00
Corn Cutter, I.Z. Merrian, Whitewater, Wisc., Straps To Shin, 1892	70.00
Corn Husker, A & O, Brass, 1862	22.00
Corn Husker, Hand, Iron, Leather Wrist	12.00
Corn Planter, Hand	20.00
Corn Planter, Janesville, Wisc.	24.00

Corn Sheller, Fulton, Iron	30.00
Cranberry Picker, Wood, Iron Tines, Large	165.00
Dado, E.C. Ring, Ringville, With Brass Side Stop, 1843–55, 1/4 In.	35.00
Detonator, Blasting Machine, Wooden Case	125.00
Dictaphone, Office	5.00
Digger, Potato, Smiley's, Engraved Patent	330.00
Dividers, Both Legs Adjustable Spring Top, 12 In.	42.00
Drawshave, Carpenter's, Striped Tiger Maple, 2 Handles, Blade, 12 In.	55.00
Drawshave, Coach Maker's, Tiger Maple, 12 In.	57.00
Drill, Breast, Millers Falls, Adjustable, Wood Handle, With Level, 1910	45.00
Drill, Pistol Shape, 3 Jaw Chuck, Ruger Corp., Bits Stored In Handle	95.00
Flashlight, Eveready, With Beveled Lens	25.00
Flashlight, Ray–O–Vac, Copper	15.00
Flashlight, White Eagle, Lantern Style, 1927	50.00
Flashlight, Winchester, Brass, Chrome, 10 In.	32.00
Flax Hackle, Wooden Board, Comb, Anne Elisabeth Bedgerin, 1794, 24 In.	120.00
Flax Hackle, Wooden Board, Punched Tin Border, Comb, 5 5/8 X 19 In.	35.00
Flax Hackle, Wooden, Brass, Name John Porterin Rose Nails, 4 X 14 In.	85.00
Fly Catcher, Aqua Glass, 1920s	30.00
Fork, Harvest, Wooden	110.00
Froe, Cooper's, Splitting Curved Staves, Iron, 15 1/2 In.	75.00
Gas Mask, Miner's, 1921	37.50
Gauge, Babcock & Wilcox	220.00
Gauge, Combustion Engineering	220.00
Gauge, Mortise, Brass Post, Ebony Head, Brass Faced	75.00
Gauge, Mortise, Stanley, Brass Plated Bar, Rosewood	50.00
Gauge, Planer & Shaper, L.S. Starrett, No.599, Label, Wooden Box	70.00
Gauge, Wire Rope, Edwards	15.00
Grinder, Cutter & Chisel, No.200, Patent 12–10–12	75.00
Grinder, Tool Post, Dumore, Model 14–011	450.00
Hacksaw & Tie Splitter, Racine, Power	300.00
Hammer, Ball Peen, Keen Kutter	20.00
Hammer, Brass Head	38.00
Hammer, Broom Maker's, 9 In.	38.00
Hammer, Claw, Round Head, Keen Kutter	35.00
Hammer, English Cobbler's	7.00
Hammer, Farrier's, Scotch Pattern, Rounded Claws, Head 4 3/4 In.	28.00
Hammer, Slater's, Stortz, Phila., Leather Handle, Head 7 3/8 In.	35.00
Hammer, Step Claw, E.C. Clark's, Patent 1897	115.00
Hammer, Tack, Hand Forged, Head–4 1/4 In.	9.00
Hammer, Upholsterer's, Osborne & Co., Rosewood Handle, France, 11 In.	55.00
Hand Beader, Windsor, 3 Cutters, Factory Box	250.00
Hand Warmer, Book Shape, Ceramic, Rooster & Motto, Amities	75.00
Harpoon, Whale	150.00
Hat Blocking Set, Wooden, 2 Piece	30.00
Hatchet, Brad Hed, Keen Kutter	30.00
Hatchet, Keen Kutter	20.00
Hatchet, Winchester	30.00
Hay Tester, Hand–Forged, Wooden Handle, 24 In.	49.00
Hook, Boot, Military, Tack Puller, Hand Forged, 4 1/4 In.	68.00
Hook, Copper's Block, Spike, 8 In.	45.00
Hoop Driver, Oak, Iron Collar, Cooper, 4 X 6 1/2 In.	15.00
Horizontal Milling Machine, Kempsmith, Power Feed, 12–In.Swivel Vise	1100.00
Hose Reeler, John Deere, 1885	175.00
Ice Tongs, Iron	30.00
Iron, Branding, QT	25.00
Jack, Furniture, Iron, Brady Furniture Jack, Pat. July 6, 1869	150.00
Jigsaw, Treadle, New Rogers	325.00
Kettle, Butchering, Farm, For Cooking Down Tallow, Medium Size	37.50
Key, Rope Bed	40.00 To 50.00
Knife Sharpener, Raw Fur, E.A. Stephens & Co.	25.00
Lard Press, Farm, On Handmade Bench	45.00
Lathe Bed, Atlas, 24–In. Centers, 12–In. Lathe	375.00
Lathe, Jeweler's, 3 1/2 X 4 1/2 In.	20.00

Lawn Mower, Punch–Type, Keen Kutter 18.00
Level & Transit, Surveyor's, Gurley, Case, Accessories, Tripod, C.1885 .... 750.00
Level, Bell Knapp, Walnut, 30 In. 20.00
Level, Cabinet Maker's, 19th Century 32.50
Level, Carpenter's, Cast Iron, Brass Mount, Cutout Heart & Star, 12 In. 330.00
Level, Davis, No.3, 7 In. 225.00
Level, Disston, Wooden 20.00
Level, Foliage Design, Adjustable Bubble Housing, Iron, 1867, 24 In. 65.00
Level, Goodell Pratt Co., Greenfield, Mass., 2 Brass Plums, 26 In. 45.00
Level, Keen Kutter, No.3 .... 15.00
Level, Keen Kutter, No.5 .... 18.00
Level, Pitch, Mahogany, 2 Blades, Plumb & Level Vials, 2 Piece 125.00
Level, Spirit, John Rabone & Sons, Brass & Rosewood, 15 In. 95.00
Level, Stanley, Adjusting Screws, Brass, Wood, Dated 1872 .... 45.00
Level, Stanley, No. 3, Brass Fittings 15.00
Level, Stanley, No.41 .... 15.00
Level, Stanley, Wooden, 1 3/16 X 28 In. 12.50
Level, Starrett, Instruction Book, Wooden Case, C.1939 .... 75.00
Level, Tarpedo, W. Marples & Son, Brass Top, Bottom Ends 25.00
Lock Box & Padlock, Tin, Handle, 12 X 6 X 5 In. 25.00
Lock, Miller & Lever 15.00
Lock, Valiant 10.00
Loom, 4 Harness, Cambridge, Reed Loom Co., Books, 1931, 45 In. 650.00
Loom, Rug, Walnut, C.1860 .... 2350.00
Mallet, Carpenter's, Burl, 12 1/2 In. 25.00
Mandrel, Butchering, Folding 12.00
Manicure Set, California Perfume Co., Tin, 1929 .... 175.00
Measure, CSCO, Pop–Up Sights, Hardwood, 28 In. 125.00
Measure, Foot, Dr. Scholl's, Wooden 30.00
Measure, Haystack, Copper, Dovetailed, Handle, 8 In. 95.00
Measure, Haystack, Copper, Dovetailed, Marked Gallon, 12 In. 135.00
Measure, Rope, John A. Roellings & Sons 175.00
Measuring Stick, Shoemaker's, Belcher Bros. & Co., 1822–77 .... 47.00
Measuring Tape, Keen Kutter, Retractable 60.00
Micrometer, Starrett, 5 Piece 100.00
Microscope, Brass Mountings, Double Lens, G. Lentmayer, Case, 17 In. 825.00
Microscope, C. Zeiss, Walnut Case, C.1880, Brass 525.00
Microscope, Corneal, Bausch & Lomb, Brass, Black Finish 225.00
Microscope, Dissecting, Bausch & Lomb, Jointed Lens, Wooden Case 85.00
Microscope, Dissecting, L.E. Knott Apparatus Co., 10–In. Stand 275.00
Microscope, Slides, Bottles, Case, 1932 .... 95.00
Mold, Ball, Pewter, Wooden Pins Hold 2 Halves, 18th Century, 2 In. 165.00
Mold, Hammer, No.4, Charles Field 55.00
Nail Holder, Lazy Susan, Cobbler's, Iron 150.00
Needle, Sail Mender's, Brass Ferrule 10.00
Niddy–Noddy, Wooden Pegged, Initial DR, 17 1/2 X 12 1/4 In. 55.00
Oilstone, Partial Label, Wooden Box 30.00
Padlock, Sargent, Brass, Key 18.00
Permanent Wave Machine, Art Deco 125.00
Picker, Blueberry, Tinned Sheet Iron, Slide Cover, 1914 .... 45.00
Picker, Mulberry 135.00
Pinking Machine, Heavy Duty 48.00
Pitch Fork, Solid Oak 90.00
Plane Set, Pattern Maker's, Aluminum, Wooden Tote, 6 Cutters, 12 In. 150.00
Plane, Barton, Dated 1832 .... 40.00
Plane, Bead, Thos. Grant 100.00
Plane, Bed Rock, Stanley, No.605 .... 29.00
Plane, Beech, Auburn Tool Co., 3/4–In. Round, 1864–93 .... 28.00
Plane, Block, Cabinet Maker's, Stanley, No.9 .... 900.00
Plane, Block, Sargent, No.206, 5 1/2 In. 18.00
Plane, Bullnose, Humped Back, Rosewood Wedge, Brass, 3 1/2 In. 125.00
Plane, Chamfer, Stanley, No.72 .... 140.00
Plane, Chariot, Steel Sole, Adjustable Mouth, Ebony & Brass, 3 1/8 In. 245.00
Plane, Circular, Bailey, No.13, Poor Japanning 75.00

Plane, Circular, Stanley, No.113, Side Gears, 1914 ....95.00 To 105.00
Plane, Combination, Stanley No.55, 51 Cutters, Early 1900s, Box 375.00
Plane, Cooper's, Iron Wedge, 54 In. 50.00
Plane, Core Box, Stanley, No.57, Marked, Patent 3-10-96 .... 295.00
Plane, Firestone Supreme, No.4 & 5, Pair 45.00
Plane, Groove, J.J. Vinall, Cleveland, Ohio 32.00
Plane, Gutter, Parker & Son, Wooden, 2 1/4 X 9 3/4 In. 45.00
Plane, Hollow, P. Brooks & Co., Pittsfield, Fully Boxed 65.00
Plane, Jack, Keen Kutter, 9 3/4 In. 47.50
Plane, Jack, Metallic Plane Co., 15 In. 125.00
Plane, Jack, Stanley, No.5 1/4, Training Manual 30.00
Plane, Jack, Winchester, No.W5-1/2 .... 110.00
Plane, Molding, Cabinet Maker's, Signed, 19th Century 22.50
Plane, Molding, Gladwin, Boston, No.5 1/2, 9 In. 25.00
Plane, New York Tool Co., Wooden, Handle, 12 X 16 In. 17.50
Plane, Nosing, Ohio Tool Co., Multiform, Beech, 1854, Box 145.00
Plane, Nosing, Ohio Tool Co., Iron, 1851, 9 1/2 In. .... 32.00 To 45.00
Plane, Panel, A. Mathieson & Son, Brass Lever Cap, 14 1/4 In 495.00
Plane, Phillipson, Narrow Round, 18th Century 75.00
Plane, Plow, A & E Baldwin, New York, Boxwood, Set of 5 Cutters 150.00
Plane, Plow, Auburn, No.90 .... 125.00
Plane, Plow, E.F. Geybold, Brass Turn Screw 95.00
Plane, Plow, Eric, London, Screw Arm, 4-In.Box 90.00
Plane, Plow, Ohio Tool, No.105, Boxwood, Screw Arm 575.00
Plane, Plow, Sandusky, No.125, Toted Applewood, Right Handed, 8 Blades 265.00
Plane, Plow, Sargent, No.1080, Original Roll, With Cutters 145.00
Plane, Rabbet & Block, Stanley, No.140 .... 80.00
Plane, Rabbet, Bullnose, Stanley, No.90, Patent 3-13-90 .... 55.00
Plane, Rabbet, Circle, Stanley, No.196 .... 1375.00
Plane, Rabbet, Israel White, Skewed 7/8 In., 1804-39 .... 45.00
Plane, Rabbet, Sargent, No.507 .... 150.00
Plane, Rabbet, Stanley, No.10 1/2, B Casting 100.00
Plane, Rabbet, Stanley, No.A78 .... 210.00
Plane, Scraper, Stanley, No.85 .... 450.00
Plane, Scrub, Sargent, No.160, Steel Body 75.00
Plane, Smoothing, Bailey, No.2 .... 195.00
Plane, Smoothing, Eclipse, No.2, Hardwood Knob & Tote, 1940 .... 125.00
Plane, Smoothing, Loughborough, No. 4, Patent 1000.00
Plane, Smoothing, Stanley, No.2, Type 16, Japanned, 1936 .... 145.00
Plane, Smoothing, Tower & Lyon, C Bottom, Wood Knob & Tote 100.00
Plane, Stanley, No. 2C 375.00
Plane, Stanley, No. 3, Bed Rock 80.00
Plane, Stanley, No. 4, Bed Rock 70.00
Plane, Stanley, No. 22 .... 20.00
Plane, Stanley, No. 45, 21 Blades 100.00
Plane, Stanley, No. 72 .... 35.00
Plane, Stanley, No.113 .... 85.00
Plane, Thumb, Violin Maker's, E. Preston & Sons, Cast Brass, 2 1/8 In. 195.00
Plane, Tongue Grooving, N. Spaulding, Handle, 11 1/2 In. 30.00
Plane, Violin Maker's, Toothing Blade, Brass, Ash Handle, 1 1/4 X 2 In. 125.00
Pliers, Winchester, No.2105, 5 1/2 In. 15.00
Plumb Bob Level, Wooden, 4 Ft. 850.00
Plumb Bob, Brass, Leather Case 15.00
Plumb Bob, Egg Shape, Brass, 18th Century 95.00
Plumb Bob, K & E 6471, Brass Top Screw & Body, 16 In. 20.00
Plumb Bob, Lufkin No.590, 6 1/2 In. 30.00
Plumb Bob, With Reel, Brass 55.00
Powder Tester, S. Nock, London 1150.00
Printing Press, Chandler, Price, Complete, 1900 .... 1000.00
Protractor, Starret Universal, Patent 1892 .... 45.00
Punch, Butchering, Hook Shaped Pole, 30 In. 85.00
Punch, Leather, Harness 7.50
Putty Knife, Keen Kutter, Unused 19.00
Rake, Hickory Handle, Iron, 74 In. 40.00

Rake, Trace of Old Red, Hickory, 71 In. 205.00
Reamer, Wheelwright's, Hooked, 23–In. Cross Handle, 2 X 24 In. 65.00
Reamer, Wood Faucets, Tapered 15.00
Roller, Paint, Graining Furniture Or Woodwork 28.50
Rule Level, Combination, Stephens, No.36, Inclinumeter, Pitch Finder 110.00
Rule, Accordion, JVA, In Circle, 96 Meters 12.00
Rule, Bench, Stanley, No.34 1/4, Brass Ends, 12 In. 20.00
Rule, Blacksmith, Rabone & Sons, No.1243, 2–Fold 25.00
Rule, Caliper, Lufkin, 372, 2 Fold, 1 Ft. 28.00
Rule, Carpenter's, Upson, No.12, Sliding, 2–Foot, 2–Fold 50.00
Rule, Combination, Level & Protractor, Rabone & Sons, No.1190 .... 100.00
Rule, Drafting, Ivory 225.00
Rule, Hat Sizing, Thomas Bradburn & Sons, Boxwood & Brass 45.00
Rule, Keen Kutter, No.K680, Brass Tips, 4 Fold 32.00
Rule, Log, Brass Disc, Steel Ferrule, Octagonal, Beech, 36 In. 45.00
Rule, Lufkin No.3851, Arch Joint, 4 Fold, 3 Ft. 30.00
Rule, Lufkin, No. 42, Brass Tips 40.00
Rule, Lufkin, No. 62, 4 Fold, 2 Ft. 30.00
Rule, Lufkin, No.1206F, 72 In. 15.00
Rule, Stanley, No.62, 4–Fold, 2 Ft. 25.00
Rule, Stanley, No.68, 4–Fold 28.00
Rule, Stanley, No.89, Ivory 350.00
Rule, Stephens & Co., No.36, Inclinometer Blade, Pat. Jan 12, 1858 .... 195.00
Saw, 2 Man, Primitive, Wooden Handles, 54 In. Blade 27.00
Saw, Bow, Beech, 13 X 24 In. 75.00
Saw, Buhl, Brass Trim, Maple, Rosewood Handle, Patent 1870 .... 155.00
Saw, Hand, Jeweler's, Adjusting Thumb Screw, Masonic Emblem 55.00
Saw, Hand, Winchester, Old Trusty 75.00
Saw, Stair, Curved Handle, Beech, 7 Teeth Per Inch, 11 3/4 In. 65.00
Scissors & Tray, Wick Trimmer, Brass, 6 1/4 In. 65.00
Scissors, Brass Fitting, Label, Iron, 13 1/4 In. 30.00
Scissors, Buttonhole, Keen Kutter 10.00
Scissors, Wallpaper, 13 In. 6.00
Scissors, Winchester, No.9045 .... 20.00
Scorp, For Chair, Closed Steel, Hickory Handle 75.00
Screwdriver, For Springfield Rifle 12.00
Screwdriver, Gunsmith's, British Brown Bess Rifle, Wood Handle 50.00
Screwdriver, Ratchet, Pistol Grip, Mahogany Handle, 9 In. 22.00
Screwdriver, Winchester 18.00
Screwdriver, Winchester, Pocket, Nickel Plated 3.50
Scribe, Lumberman's, Walnut Handle, Weiss, 6 In. 65.00
Scribe, Timer, Folds Into Brass Handle, Drag Knife, New York Knife Co. 65.00
Scribe, Wood, Long Handle 2.00
Scythe Anvil, Rubino, Marked 75.00
Seed Counter, Shearer, 52 In. 1350.00
Sharpener, Deering Harvester, Hand Crank, Stone Wheel, Cog Driven 50.00
Sharpener, Scissors, Disc, Metal 7.00
Sharpener, Scissors, Esso 8.00
Sharpener, Sickle, Hand Crank, Whetstone 24.50
Sharpener, Slate Pencil, Maple Post & Frame, 3 X 10 In. 230.00
Shears, Sheep, Keen Kutter 15.00
Shears, Tailor's, Newark, N.J., Cast Iron, 15 In. 95.00
Shovel, Swedish, Hand Hewn Tiger Maple 650.00
Shredder, Tobacco, Wooden Handle, 9 In. 40.00
Shucking Peg, Metal, Leather Strap 15.00
Sifter, Grain, Fine Mesh, Pine 32.00
Slate Remover, Roof, Bangor Slate Co., Easton, Penna., C.1850, 32 In. 55.00
Slate, School, Walnut Frame, 11 1/2 X 16 In. 85.00
Slick, Carpenter's, 3 1/2–In. Blade, Short Handle, 21 1/2 In. 65.00
Slide Rule, K & E, Leather Case 15.00
Slide Rule, Marked O.J., Leather Case 15.00
Slide Rule, Pickett 160, Leatherette Case 5.00
Socket Ratchet, Tubelox, 1/8 In. 10.00
Spoke Shave, Brass Wear Plate, William Marples & Sons, 1918, 7 1/2 In. 45.00

Spoke Shave, Brass, 3 1/4 In. 33.00
Spoke Shave, Millers Falls, Rosewood Handles, Pat. Feb.18, 1884 .... 39.00
Spoke Shave, Snell & Atherton, 2 Screw Adjust, Open Handles, 8 3/4 In. 15.00
Sprayer, Spray–Well, Insect, Amber Bowl 15.00
Spurs, Cowboy, North & Judd, 1900 .... 48.00
Square, Winchester, Beech Handle, Walton & Tousley 85.00
Stamp, Cast Iron, Black, Gold Trim, Desk Mount Type, Long Handle 32.00
Stencil, Barrel, High Grade Sweepstakes, Corn, Brass, 1875, 8 X 11 In. 65.00
Stencil, Rooster, H.A. & Co., 56 Boston, Brass, Square, 13 5/8 In. 210.00
Stool, Shoeshine, Wooden Seat, Cast Iron Feet 155.00
Stretcher, Barbed Wire 17.00
Surveying Instrument, Y Level, 21 In. Telescope 450.00
Swift, Wooden, Table Clamp, Worn Red & Black Paint, 21 In. 25.00
T Bevel, Stanley, No.18, Iron Handle, Box of 6, 6 In. 58.00
Ticker Tape, Edison, Stock, Glass Dome 5700.00
Ticker Tape, Machine, Edison, Glass Dome 5600.00
Ticker Tape, Machine, Quotation Service, Western Union 2000.00
Ticker Tape, Machine, Universal 4000.00
Ticker Tape, Western Union, Quotation 2000.00
Trammel, Sawtooth, Brass, Bird Head Ratchet, 18 In. 95.00
Trammel, Scroll Finial, Iron, 18th Century, 45 1/2 In. 295.00
Trammel, Wrought Iron, Diamond Tooling, 1785, 28 In. 350.00
Trammel, Wrought Iron, Sawtooth, Heart Cutout In Crest, 47 In. 1750.00
Vise, Carver's, Pivoting Jaws 95.00
Vise, Leather Worker's, Design, Large 65.00
Vise, Miter, Stanley, No.400 .... 60.00
Wallpaper Trimmer, Waukegan, 1910 .... 80.00
Weight Set, Brass, Graduated, Grams & Mils, Tool, Fisher Scientific, Box 45.00
Wood Plane, Auburn Tool Co., No.89 .... 75.00
Wool Card, Wooden, Handle, Incised Initials PM, Pair 17.50
Wool Carding Paddles, Wire Teeth, Pair 20.00
Wool Comb, Brass Teeth, 9 1/2 In. 50.00
Wrench, Adjustable, Wrapped Steel Handle, Acme Co., 9 1/2 In. 18.00
Wrench, Alligator, Keen Kutter 125.00
Wrench, Bed, Tightening Ropes On Bed, T Shape, 17 In. 30.00
Wrench, Double Head, Engineer's, Berylco, Size 1 1/16 & 1 1/4, 12 In. 35.00
Wrench, Keen Kutter, 10 In. 22.00
Wrench, Monkey, Bemis & Call, 12 1/2 In. 50.00
Wrench, Monkey, Bernis & Call, Metal Handle, Marked, 8 In. 15.00
Wrench, Monkey, Trimo 8, Trimont Mfg.Co., Pat.12/19/11 .... 15.00
Wrench, Monkey, Trimont Mfg. Co., Drop Forged, Pat. 12–19–11 .... 15.00
Wrench, Pipe, Winchester, 14 In. 30.00
Wrench, Winchster, 21 In. 55.00
Yarn Reel, Clock Works Counter, Floor Standing, 44 In. 55.00
Yarn Winder, Iron, Wooden 80.00
Yarn Winder, Squirrel Cage 65.00

If garage windows are painted, burglars won't be able to tell if cars are home or not. Use translucent paint to get light in the closed garage, if it has an entrance to your house.

Toothpick holders are sometimes called "toothpicks" by collectors. The variously shaped containers made to hold the small wooden toothpicks are of glass, china, or metal. Most of the toothpick holders are Victorian.

TOOTHPICK, see also other categories such as Bisque; Silver Plate; Slag; etc.

TOOTHPICK, Agata, Bulbous, Ruffled, N.E. Glass Co.	375.00
Barrel, Glenwood Springs, Iron, Hand Painted	45.00
Beatty Ribbed, Opalescent Glass, White, 1 7/8 In.	25.00
Bird, Cast Iron	85.00
Bubble Lattice, Canary Satin, Tricorner Rim, Glass	225.00
Bulldog, Porcelain	10.00
Bulldog, Standing On Footed Base, Frosted	40.00
Button & Bulge, Blue Green, Flower Decoration	38.00
Cat With Barrel, Glass	15.00
Chick On Wishbone, Triple Silver Plate	30.00
Chrysanthemum Sprig, Custard Glass, Art Deco	195.00
Coal Hod Form, Peach Blow, Rothsbay Looking West, Royal Bayreuth	145.00
Cut Glass, Flat Diamonds	50.00
Deer, Blue, Clear, Bohemian, Glass	18.00
Diamond Pyramids, Inverted Imperial, Glass	30.00
Esther, Green, Gold, Glass	70.00
Finecut, Hat, Vaseline	40.00
Florette, Opaque Turquoise Blue, Glass	95.00
Florette, Translucent Pale Pink, Thin White Interior	80.00
Forget–Me–Not, Cobalt Blue, Glass	20.00
Framed Ovals, Crystal, Gold	25.00
Francisware, Hobnail, Opalescent, 2 1/2 In.	50.00
Georgia Gem, Green Opaque, Glass	39.00
Gypsy Kettle, Ruby Stained, Gold Top Band, Metal Bail	22.00
Harvard, Custard Glass, Richville, N.Y.	25.00
Hat, Parallel Fine Line, Light Green, Glass, Souvenir	35.00
Keystone Cop, Bisque, 9 1/2 In.	75.00
Long Underwear, Figural, Crystal	145.00
Pansy, Green, Glazed	45.00
Parrot & Top Hat, Milk Glass	60.00
Pig On Railroad Car, Figural, Amber, Glass	245.00
Pink Guttate, Pink To White, Glass	110.00
Potty, Says For Your Half–Friends, Pottery	22.00
Reverse Swirl, Speckled, Blue, Glass	85.00
Rising Sun, Gold Traces, Glass	20.00
Royal Co–Op, Ruby Stained	30.00
Set, Brass, Tray, Salt	18.00
Skeleton Head, On Book, Bisque	40.00
Skirted Optic, Crystal, Enameled Deco	35.00
Skull, Green Glass Eyes, Joker Lookalike	85.00
Souvenir, Newton, Iowa, Bull's–Eye, Ruby Flashed, Crystal	20.00
Spearpoint Band, Red Flashed	80.00
Stars & Stripes, Commemorative, Night Light Safety Co., Brooklyn	30.00
Sterling Silver, Overlay Monogram, 3 Handles	175.00
Sunk Honeycomb, Crystal, Ruby, Red Pinpricks	35.00
Take Your Pick, Handle, Silver, Forbes	12.00
Teasel & Fan, Crystal, Slightly Tilted	32.00
Thousand Eye, Amber, Glass	20.00
Thumbprint, Ruby Stained, Etched	35.00
Tiny Thumbprint, Crystal, Hand Painted Rose, Niagara Falls	25.00
Trophy, Pedestal, 2 Handles, Nippon, 2 1/2 In.	20.00
Trophy, Ruby Stained	22.00
Uncle Sam's Hat, Milk Glass, Red & Blue Worn	25.00
Vermont, Custard, Blue Trim, Glass	85.00
Winged Scroll, Emerald Green, Gold Straight Sided, Heisey	225.00
Woman With Flower, Bisque	35.00
Wreath & Shell, White Opalescent, Glass,	115.00

TORQUAY

Torquay is the name given to ceramics by several potteries working near Torquay, England, from 1870 until 1962. Until about 1900, the potteries used local red clay to make classical style art pottery vases and figurines. Then they turned to making souvenir wares. Items were dipped in colored slip and decorated with painted slip and sgraffito designs. They often had mottos or proverbs, and scenes of cottages, ships, birds, or flowers. The "Scandy" design was a symmetrical arrangement of brush strokes and spots done in colored slips. Potteries included Watcombe Pottery (1870–1962); Torquay Terra–Cotta Company (1875–1905); Aller Vale (1881–1924); Torquay Pottery (1908–1940); and Longpark (1883–1957).

TORQUAY, Cracker Jar, Cottage, Wicker Handle	148.00
Cracker Jar, Ruby, Silver–Plated Collar & Bail	325.00
Creamer, Cottage, A Thing of Beauty, Dartmouth Pottery	20.00
Creamer, Cottage, Motto Ware	27.00 To 30.00
Creamer, Flower	21.00
Creamer, Ruby, Embossed Silver Rims	95.00
Creamer, Sailboats, 2 1/4 In.	30.00
Cup & Saucer, Cottage	35.00
Dish, Cheese & Biscuit, Sectioned, Black Cockerel, 8 X 8 3/4 In.	85.00
Jug, Cockerel In Color, The Devils Aya Kind Tae His Ain, 5 In.	45.00
Lamp, White, Pink, Miniature	150.00
Mug, House, Large	29.50
Pitcher, Cottage, 2 1/4 In.	15.00
Pitcher, Cover, 8 In.	50.00
Pitcher, Motto, Black Cockerel, Marked, 5 1/2 In.	125.00
Pitcher, Sailboats, 2 1/4 In.	30.00
Pitcher, Water, Ruby	175.00 To 250.00
Spooner, Ruby, Embossed Silver Rims	85.00
Teapot, Motto Ware, Dawntee Be Fraid Aut Now, Marked, 4 In.	60.00
Tile, Curling Iron Lamp, Motto, 5 X 7 1/2 In.	125.00
Toothpick, Albermarle, Loving Cup Style	40.00
Vase, Kingfisher, 6 In.	58.00

Tortoiseshell glass was made during the 1800s and after by the Sandwich Glass Works of Massachusetts and some firms in Germany. Tortoiseshell glass is, of course, named for its resemblance to real shell from a tortoise. It has been reproduced.

TORTOISESHELL GLASS, Cruet, Clear Shell Handle, 7 In.	145.00
Pitcher, Amber Handle, Bronze Prunts, Pinched, 8 In.	150.00
Tankard, Large	95.00
Tumbler, Brown, White	80.00
Vase, Tankard, 10 In.	65.00

The shell of the tortoise has been used as inlay and to make small decorative objects since the seventeenth century. Some species of tortoise are now on the endangered species list, and objects made from these shells cannot be sold legally.

TORTOISESHELL, Bowl, Warrior, Geisha, Serpent, 21 In.	300.00
Box, Bowed Body, Corner Figures, Gilt Bronze, England, 5 In.	275.00
Box, Scene of Amorous Couple, Hinged	800.00
Brush & Comb, Victorian, Sterling Silver	75.00
Comb, Back, Solid Gold Inlay	45.00
Comb, Cultured Pearls Border, 14K Gold	145.00
Mirror, Hand, Beveled	20.00
Teapot, Embossed Leaf Designs, 4 1/2 In.	1500.00
Vase, Mon Art, Large Pontil	375.00

Toys are designed to entice children; and today, they have attracted new interest among adults who are still children at heart. All types of toys are collected. Tin toys, iron toys, battery operated toys, and many others are collected by specialists. Dolls, Games, Teddy Bears, and Bicycles are listed under their own categories. Other toys may be found under company or celebrity names.

Accordion, Magnus Toy Co., 1950s	13.00
Acrobat, Aerial, 1920s, Marx	125.00
Acrobat, Gent, Bisque Head, Original Clothes, Schoenhut	375.00
Acrobat, On Horse, Clockwork, Box	40.00
Acrobat, Windup, Celluloid, C.1934	950.00
Adding Machine, Wolverine, Steel, Box	20.00 To 35.00
Adding Machine, Wolverine, Tin	25.00
Adebar Stork, Steiff, 6 In.	250.00
Aeroplane, Paper Fuselage, Metal & Fiber Trim, Henley, 6 In.	175.00
Air Pump, Joe Palooka	25.00
Airplane, Air Force, 4 Engines, Props Turn With Wheels, Friction	50.00
Airplane, American Airlines, Battery Operated, Props & Wheels Move	375.00
Airplane, Army, Combat, Windup, Wing Guns, 1930s	95.00
Airplane, Army, Flying Boxcar, Ideal, Combat Team, Box, 24–In.Wingspan	85.00
Airplane, Boeing 727, Battery Operated, Tin, Box	22.00
Airplane, Boeing 727, Friction, Box	45.00
Airplane, Boeing 727, Tin, Friction, Jet Engine Noise	45.00
Airplane, Cessna, Box.24 In.	225.00
Airplane, Circus, Lindbergh, Stick Model Kit, Box	55.00
Airplane, Double Wing, Friction, Tin, World War I, Kakar Toys, Box	95.00
Airplane, Double Wing, World War I, Friction, Tin, Box	95.00
Airplane, Flipover, Tin Pilot Head, Marx	95.00
Airplane, Folding Wings, Metal, Hubley, 6 In.	26.00
Airplane, Gyroplane, Glides On Own Power, Roars Like A Plane	65.00
Airplane, Helicopter, Highway Patrol, Tin Litho, Battery, Box, 14 1/2 In.	44.00
Airplane, Helicopter, Police Dept., Cragstan, Tin, Friction	45.00
Airplane, Helicopter, Tin Litho, Actions, Noise, Battery Operated, 10 In.	45.00
Airplane, Kenton, Cast Iron, Green	485.00
Airplane, Loop The Loop, Tin Litho, Mechanical, Japan, 3 1/2 In.	60.00
Airplane, Merry–Go–Round, Windup, Germany	125.00
Airplane, Military, Windup, Box	125.00
Airplane, Monoplane, Trimotor, Kingsbury, Cast Iron	1100.00
Airplane, P–38, Camouflage Colored, Hubley	125.00
Airplane, Pan American, 4 Props, Marx, 28 In.	265.00
Airplane, Pontoon, Chein	125.00
Airplane, Snoopy	45.00
Airplane, Spirit of St. Louis, Metal Craft	140.00
Airplane, Superjet, Boeing, Marx, Box	495.00
Airplane, Thunderbolt Fighter, Blade Rotator, Japan, 1950s	35.00
Airplane, Tin Litho, Friction, Linemar, 7 In.	77.00
Airplane, Tin Litho, Meccano, 14 In.	110.00
Airplane, Transport, Buddy L, 27 In.	350.00
Airplane, Transport, Wyandotte, 7 In.	20.00
Airplane, Windup, Tin Litho, Marx, 6 3/4 In.	110.00
Airplane, With Pilot, Windup, Strauss, Tin, 1920s, 13 In.	425.00
Airplane, Wyandotte, Steel, 13 In.	85.00
Alabama Coon Jigger, Oh My, Tin Litho, Lehmann, 10 1/4 In.	775.00
Alligator, Jungle Pete, Mechanical	75.00
Alligator, Mechanical, Windup, On 2 Wheels, Green & Yellow, 14 In.	110.00
Alligator, Schoenhut	450.00
Alligator, Steiff, 13 In.	60.00
Alphabet Board, Patent 1886, 13 1/2 In.	100.00
American Model Builder, Construction Set, Manual, Box, 1913	70.00
Arab & Camel, Windup, Tin Litho, Germany, Box, 6 In.	187.00
Arcade Shooting Gallery, Automatic, Marx	55.00
Ark, With 6 Animals, Silk Screened, Wooden, 1920s, 21 3/4 In.	165.00
Atomic Reactor Set, Battery Operated, Linemar, 1950s, Box	300.00
Attache Case, Secret Sam, Spy, Gun & Accessories, 1966	85.00
Auto Lift, Mechanical, Windup, With Tin Car, Wolverine, Box	150.00

Automaton, Drinker, Black Man In Chair, Drink In Hand, 1880s 8885.00
Autotransport, Marx, Box, 1950s 75.00
Baboon, Coco, Steiff, 4 In. 40.00
Baby, Crawling, HiHi, Windup, Box, Japan, 1950s 35.00
Badge, Bathing Suit Inspector, Metal, Embossed Roses, 3 In. 25.00
Badge, Rocky Jones, Space Ranger, Box 25.00
Badge, Wild Bill Hickok, Marshal, Card 65.00
Bake Set, Like Mother's, Mirror, Box, 17 Piece 60.00
Ball Toss, Popeye & Olive Oyl, Tin Litho, Windup, Linemar, 19 In. 1100.00
Ball, Baby's, Sawdust Stuffed, Lithographed Cloth, 8 1/2 In. 165.00
Balloon Man, Windup, Tin, Germany 150.00
Bambi, Steiff, 5 In. 125.00
Barbie's Head & 3 Wigs, 1960s 45.00
Barn Set, Wooden, Hand Painted, Red Roof, 3 Buildings, 8, 5 & 5 In. 125.00
Barn, Electric Interior Light, Plywood, 15 1/2 In. 85.00
Barn, Wooden, Painted Red Slant Roof, 17 X 24 X 18 In. 40.00
Barney Google On Spark Plug 2200.00
Barnyard Set, Animals, Metal Fence, Farmer, Lincoln 75.00
Bartender, Battery Operated, Box 40.00
Bartender, Mechanical, Box 75.00
Bartender, Revolving Eyes, Tin, Lithographed Fabric, Rosko, 11 In. 12.00
Baseball Catcher, Windup, Tin & Celluloid, Occupied Japan 125.00
Bat, Louisville Slugger, Jackie Robinson, 1950s 25.00
Battering Ram, Planet of Apes, Box 25.00
Battleship, Metal, 1940s, Tootsietoy, 8 In. 15.00
Battleship, Painted, Tin, Clockwork, Germany, 1910 .... 6300.00
Beads, Baby's, String, Wooden 15.00
    TOY, BEAR, see also Teddy Bear
Bear, Blacksmith, Tin Litho, Plush, Mechanical, Japan, 6 In. 49.50
Bear, Blinky Ben, Black, 4 In. 28.00
Bear, Circus, Kenton Overland, Cast Iron, 14 In. 525.00
Bear, Circus, Mechanical, Keywind, Germany 350.00
Bear, Cleans Glasses, Windup, Japan, 6 In. 65.00
Bear, Drinking Milk, Windup, Japan, 6 In. 70.00
Bear, Golfer, Windup, Tin 130.00
Bear, Mother, Rocking, Knitting, Battery Operated 90.00
Bear, On Wheels, German, Cast Iron, 24 In. 765.00
Bear, Pipe Smoking, Battery Operated 55.00
Bear, Pipe Smoking, Tin, Battery Operated, Japan 75.00
Bear, Playing Ball, Tin Litho, Celluloid, Battery Operated, Japan, 10 In. 181.50
Bear, Reading Book, Windup, Japan, Box 85.00
Bear, Teddy Cycle, Box, Occupied Japan 65.00
Bear, Tumbling, Windup, Box, Japan, 1950s 15.00
Bear, Tumbling, Windup, Occupied Japan, Box 50.00
Bear, Wooden Frame & Wheels, Plush Covering, Glass Eyes, Pull, 23 In. 450.00
Beatle, Crawling, Windup, Lehmann, Box 150.00
Beauty Parlor, Tin Litho, Cloth, Plastic, Battery Operated, S & E, 9 In. 605.00
Bed, Doll's, Bunk, Ladder, Maple 58.00
Bed, Doll's, Canopy, Crocheted Lace Linens 38.00
Bed, Doll's, Eastlake, Handmade 100.00
Bed, Doll's, Folding, 22 In. 50.00
Bed, Doll's, Folding, Metal 30.00
Bed, Doll's, Gold Stenciling On Red Paint, 9 X 15 In. 48.00
Bed, Doll's, High Posts, Casters, Feather Tick, Spread, Mahogany, 19 In. 285.00
Bed, Doll's, Red Paint, Painted Birds & Dog, Soft Wood, 21 1/4 In. 70.00
Bed, Doll's, Tester, Turned Wood, 1780–90, 15 X 10 X 14 In. 950.00
Bed, Doll's, Wooden, Brass Caps & Top Rail, Casters, Spring 65.00
Bedroom Set, Doll's, Art Deco 155.00
Bedroom Set, Doll's, Donna Lee, Wooden, Box 15.00
Beer Wagon, Marx 185.00
Bell Toy, Two Coons, Painted, Cast Iron, 8 1/2 In. 600.00
Bench, Tool, With Tools, Wooden 145.00
    TOY, BICYCLE, see Bicycle
Big Bedford Van, Heinz 57 Varieties, Metal, 5 1/2 In. 71.00

Big Foot, Bionic	75.00
Big Joe Chief, Windup, Box, Japan, 1950s	145.00
Big John The Chimpee Chief, Soft Rubber, Tin Litho, Alps, Box, 12 In.	6.00
Big Maze, Marx	75.00
Big Parade, Marx, Box	150.00
Big Valley, Playset, Figures, Horses, Wagon, Auburn Rubber, 1967	95.00
Billy Goat, Brown Horns, Celluloid, 6 In.	12.00
Billy Goat, On Platform, Fur Covered Papier–Mache & Wood, 11 In.	412.00
Bird, Finch, Steiff, 6 In.	205.00
Bird, In Cage, Pip–Squeak, Polychrome Paint, Tin, Windup, 3 3/8 In.	25.00
Bird, In Cage, Push Lever, Bird Goes Back & Forth, Germany, C.1910	100.00
Bird, Pecking, Windup, Tin, 1927	18.50
Bird, Pip–Squeak, Red & Green, Germany	40.00
Bison, Steiff, 6 In.	80.00
Blackboard, Foxy, Alphabet, Round	65.00
Blanket Chest, Doll's, 1800s, 24 X 12 In.	325.00
Blocks, ABC, 1 1/4 In., 27 Piece	10.00
Blocks, Bilt E.Z. Architectural Outfit, Box, 1920s	75.00
Blocks, Puzzle, Golf Scene	145.00
Blocks, Puzzle, Lithographed Paper On Wood, Farm Animals, Box, 9 In.	185.00
Blocks, Richter's Eagle, Pat. 1900, Box	200.00
Blocks, Richter, Stones, Anchor, Directions, Germany	135.00
Blondie & Dagwood, Children, Construction Set, Dated 1930, Box	120.00
Blushing Frankie, Battery, 1980	20.00
Boat, Cabin Cruiser, Tin Litho, Chein, 8 1/2 In.	35.00
Boat, Coast Guard, Tin, 8 In.	10.00
Boat, Columbus Ocean Liner, Lehmann	65.00
Boat, Destroyer, 4 Stacks, Clockwork, Painted Tin, Bing, 22 In.	2860.00
Boat, Express Cruiser, Chriscraft, Sterling, Box, 42 In.	75.00
Boat, Gunboat, Flywheel, Tin Litho, Hess, 12 In.	110.00
Boat, Johnson Outboard Motor, Marklin, Box	375.00
Boat, Ocean Liner, Carette, Clockwork	660.00
Boat, Outboard Motor, Longcraft Power Model, Box	65.00
Boat, Racing, Driver, Hand Painted, Ernst Plank, 1920s	385.00
Boat, River Queen, Paddle Wheel Steamer, Marx, Box	65.00
Boat, Riverboat, Cast Iron, Wilkins, C.1910	135.00
Boat, Submarine, Clockwork, Tin, Bing, 9 1/2 In.	302.50
Boat, Texaco Tanker, Box	120.00
Boat, Torpedo, Sparking, Mechanical, Ideal	95.00
Boat, Tug, Painted Tin, 13 1/2 In.	495.00
Boat, Windup, Tin, Chein, 14 In.	60.00
Boat, With Outboard Motor, Flarecraft, Box	120.00
Book, Wonder, Felix On Television	10.00
Borden Milk Wagon, Horse, Wooden, Rich Toys	450.00
Box, Lithographed Paper, Scene, Our Little Ones, 15 In.	165.00
Boxers, In Ring, Rap & Tap, Strauss, Windup, 1920s	475.00
Boxing Gloves, Jack Dempsey, 2 Pair	30.00
Boxing Ring, Muhammad Ali, Figures	75.00
Boy On Tricycle, Boy Jointed At Knees, Hips, Shoulders, Windup, Marx	225.00
Boy, Drinking, Tin Litho, Cloth, Mechanical, Schuco, 5 1/2 In.	71.00
Boy, On Swing, Windup, Celluloid	100.00
Brooke Shields Beauty Center	45.00
Buffalo, Black & Brown, Celluloid, 4 In.	16.00
Buffalo, Wood, Painted Eyes, Schoenhut, 7 1/2 In.	310.00 To 350.00
Building Bricks, M–I Toys, 1950, Container	45.00
Bull, With Man Holding Tail, Tin Windup, Bull Bellows	150.00
Bulldozer, Tonka, 9 In.	40.00
Bunny, Baby In Carriage, Rotating Carousel, Celluloid, Tin Base, Windup	115.00
Bunny, Cart, Metal	135.00
Bunny, Plush & Tin, Windup, 10 In.	45.00
Bus, Double–Decker, English	60.00
Bus, Double–Decker, France, S.B., 2 3/8 In.	60.00
Bus, Fageol, Cast Iron, Arcade, 8 In.	120.00
Bus, Greyhound Lines, Painted Metal, Tootsietoy, 6 In.	22.00

Bus, Greyhound Scenic Cruiser, Box 40.00
Bus, Greyhound, Arcade, Cast Iron, 10 In. 225.00
Bus, Greyhound, Buddy L 225.00
Bus, Greyhound, Friction 25.00
Bus, Greyhound, Tin Litho, Japanese, 1950s, 11 In. 90.00
Bus, Greyhound, Windup, Kingsbury 55.00
Bus, Greyhound, Wood Wheels, Tootsietoy .... 20.00 To 30.00
Bus, Greyhound, World's Fair, Arcade, 5 1/2 In. 200.00
Bus, Inter-State, Windup, Tin Litho, Strauss, 10 In. 357.50
Bus, Jackie Gleason Express 650.00
Bus, Liberty, Marx 95.00
Bus, London, Corgi, Box, 1973 .... 45.00
Bus, Nickel Plated Wheels, Cast Iron, 5 In. 60.00
Bus, Robot, Windup, Woodhaven Metal Stamping Co., 15 In. 325.00
Busy Bridge, Windup, Marx 375.00
Busy Secretary, Tin Litho, Linemar, 7 In. 132.00
Butterfly, Push Toy, Wings Flap, Tin, Chein 32.00
Butterfly, Windup 15.00
Camel, 1 Hump, Glass Eyes, Schoenhut, 8 1/2 In. .... 275.00 To 350.00
Camel, 2 Humps, Glass Eyes, Schoenhut, 7 In. .... 345.00 To 465.00
Camel, Brown & Tan, Celluloid, 3 In. 15.00
Camel, Glass Eyes, Tin Wheels, Rope Tail, Wood & Papier-Mache, 7 In. 45.00
Camel, On Wheels, Papier-Mache, Green Saddle With Dresden Trim, 7 In. 200.00
Camel, Windup, 5 X 7 In. 95.00
Camera, Brenda Starr, Box 100.00
Camera, Bugs Bunny, 1976 .... 22.25
Camera, Fred Flintstone, Original Package 55.00
Camera, Sun Magic Picture, Package, Japan 10.00
Camera, Yogi Bear, Figural 10.00
Can, Riot, Police Station, Friction 195.00
Canister Set, Doll's, Cup & Plate, Tin, Cat Design, Ohio Art, 8 Piece 120.00
Cannon, Big Bang, Cast Iron 50.00
Cannon, Brass, 17 1/4 In. 125.00
Cannon, Cap, Callen 30.00
Cannon, Cap, Kilgore 45.00
Cannon, Civil War, Iron Wheels, Cast Iron 30.00
Cannon, Red, Tin 20.00
Cannon, Shooting, Cragstan 35.00
Cap Gun, Animated, Chinese, 1879 .... 675.00
Cap Gun, Big Horn, Kilgore, Box 35.00
Cap Gun, Billy The Kid, Black Grips, Buffalo Each Side, 7 1/2 In. 30.00
Cap Gun, Buc-A-Roo, Kilgore, Cast Iron, Box 125.00
Cap Gun, Buffalo Bill, Cast Iron 95.00
Cap Gun, Colt .45, Hubley 35.00
Cap Gun, Colt Automatic, Hubley, Box 30.00
Cap Gun, Cowboy, Holster 45.00
Cap Gun, Cowboy, Jr., Hubley, Box 85.00
Cap Gun, Cowboy, Plastic Grips, Metal, Hubley, 11 1/2 In. 30.00
Cap Gun, Coyote, Hubley, Picture of U.S.A. On Box 65.00
Cap Gun, Daisy, Brown Woodgrain Grips, Gold Hammer, 9 1/2 In. 40.00
Cap Gun, Daisy, Store Premium, Box 85.00
Cap Gun, Echo, 1930 .... 30.00
Cap Gun, Fancy Bango, Box 75.00
Cap Gun, G-Boy, Box 75.00
Cap Gun, Gene Autry, With Holster, White Grips 35.00
Cap Gun, Hip, Spitfire, Nichols, Box, 9 In. 25.00
Cap Gun, Holster, Wyatt Earp, Box 80.00
Cap Gun, Hubley, Black Grips, Ric-O-Shays, 11 1/2 In. 45.00
Cap Gun, Hubley, Ivory Handles, Brown Leather Holster, 8 In. 50.00
Cap Gun, King, 1925 .... 40.00
Cap Gun, Kit Carson, Pot Metal .... 15.00 To 30.00
Cap Gun, Liberty, Patent April 22, 1973, Cast Iron 60.00
Cap Gun, Long Boy, 1922 .... 110.00
Cap Gun, Mountie, Kilgore, Box 20.00

Cap Gun, Mustang 500 .... 55.00
Cap Gun, Numatic 55.00
Cap Gun, Oh Boy, 5 1/2 In. 25.00
Cap Gun, Pal, In Fleece Holsters, Pair 70.00
Cap Gun, Paladin, Ivory Grips, Brown Circle, 2 Horseshoes, 9 In. 40.00
Cap Gun, Peacemaker, Cast Iron 55.00
Cap Gun, Pinto, Ivory Grips, Horsehead Each Side, 8 In. 35.00
Cap Gun, Pioneer, J & E Stevens, Box 20.00
Cap Gun, Pirate, Double Barrel, 9 3/4 In. 35.00
Cap Gun, Pluck .... 17.00 To 20.00
Cap Gun, Pony Boy, Ivory & Brown Grips, Horse Head Logo, 9 1/2 In. 30.00
Cap Gun, Pony, 5 1/4 In. 25.00
Cap Gun, President, Cast Iron 45.00
Cap Gun, Punch & Judy, Animated, 1880s 875.00
Cap Gun, Rodeo, Amber Handles, Hubley 25.00
Cap Gun, Ronson Repeater, Lithographed Picture On Box 35.00
Cap Gun, Saddle Rifle, Bonanza, Holster Belt, Box, 1966, 25-In. Rifle 200.00
Cap Gun, Sambo, June 17, 1890 .... 425.00
Cap Gun, Sheriff, Cast Iron, Box 65.00
Cap Gun, Stallion 32, Nichols, Box .... 40.00 To 85.00
Cap Gun, Super Defense, Metal 25.00
Cap Gun, Sure Shot, Hubley, Box 50.00
Cap Gun, Texan Jr., Hubley 10.00
Cap Gun, Texas, Cast Iron 35.00
Cap Gun, Thundergun, Marbelized Tan & Black Grips, Marx, 12 1/2 In. 50.00
Cap Gun, Trooper, Hubley .... 10.00 To 15.00
Cap Gun, Victor, 1880 .... 295.00
Cap Gun, Wagon Train 40.00
Cap Gun, Western Pioneer, Double Leather Holster, Stones, Studs, Box 35.00
Cap Gun, Western, Marbelized Grips, Maroon, Steer's Head, 8 1/2 In. 35.00
Cape Canaveral Missile Set, Marx, Box 250.00
Cape Kennedy Play Set, Marx, Tin Litho Carry-All, 1968 .... 75.00
Captain America, Windup, Remco, 1979 .... 22.00
Captain Video, Ray Gun, Secret, Instructions 95.00
Captain, Drinking, Tin Litho, Plush, Box, 13 In. 33.00
Car Carrier, 3 Cars, Painted, Nickel Plated Wheels, Iron, 12 1/2 In. 350.00
Car, Air Flow, Tin 40.00
Car, Amazamatics, Car With Brain, Hasbro, 1969, Box 50.00
Car, Ambulance, Windup, White, Red Printing On Side, Wyandotte 255.00
Car, Ambulance, World War I, 2 Horses, Driver, Elastolin, Tin 525.00
Car, Ambulance, Wyandotte 55.00
Car, Army Combat, Buddy L, Wooden 5.00
Car, Aston-Martin, James Bond, Battery Operated, Tin, Box, Gilbert, 13 In. 750.00
Car, Batmobile 170.00
Car, Beverly Hillbillies, Seated, Windup, Molded Plastic, 22 In. 360.00
Car, Borgwardt, Red & Black, Marklin, Box 82.00
Car, Buick, Coupe, Tootsietoy 65.00
Car, Buick, Tootsietoy, Black, 3 In. 65.00
Car, Buick, Tootsietoy, Tin Wheels, 3 In. 85.00
Car, Bump 'N' Go, Tin 65.00
Car, Bumper, No.8, Marx 200.00
Car, Cadillac, 1960, 18 In. 1000.00
Car, Cadillac, 1961, Convertible, Red, Japan, 17 In. 465.00
Car, Carnival, Bumper, Bouncing Girl's Head, Irwin Corp. 75.00
Car, Chevrolet Coupe, 1928, Arcade 2255.00
Car, Chevrolet, 1961, 11 In. 225.00
Car, Chevrolet, Windup, Tin, Box 100.00
Car, Coaster, Rubber Tires, Chrome Plated, 45 In. 135.00
Car, Convertible, Red & White, Marx, Tin 150.00
Car, Convertible, Yellow, Plastic Driver's Compartment, Box 50.00
Car, Corvette, Ken & Barbie's, Box, 1968 .... 55.00
Car, Corvette, Stingray, Japan, Tin, Box, 11 In. 95.00
Car, Cougar, 1967, Friction, Bandai, 10 1/2 In. 75.00
Car, Coupe, 6 Windows, Red, Cast Iron, 1920, 4 In. 175.00

Car, Crazy, Charlie McCarthy, Box 550.00
Car, Crazy, Uncle Wiggily, Marx .... 400.00 To 550.00
Car, Deluxe, Structo, No.12 .... 875.00
Car, Estate Wagon, Toytown, 21 In. 275.00
Car, Evel Knievel Funny Car, Metal, Plastic, Ideal, 1976, Box 45.00
Car, Ferrari Superfast II, Friction, Japan 85.00
Car, Fire Chief's, Coupe, Siren, Keywind, Battery, Taillights 250.00
Car, Fire Chief's, Crazy, Tin Litho, Plastic, Mechanical, Marx, 6 In. 70.00
Car, Fire Chief's, Remote Control, Box 100.00
Car, Fire Chief's, Windup, Marx 95.00
Car, Ford Ranchero, 1959 .... 375.00
Car, Ford, Coupe, Red, Gold Striping, Decals, Cast Iron, 7 In. 375.00
Car, Ford, Friction, Box, Japan, 11 1/2 In. 595.00
Car, Ford, Haji, Tin, Friction, 7 In. 45.00
Car, Ford, Model T, Coupe, Arcade, 6 1/2 In. 495.00
Car, Ford, Model T, Lever Action, Tin 75.00
Car, Ford, Model T, Woman Driver, Windup, Bing, 1920s 375.00
Car, Friction, Woody, Green, Marx 75.00
Car, Huckleberry Hound, Marx 250.00
Car, Huckleberry Hound, Tin, Friction, Box .... 150.00 To 195.00
Car, Jaguar, Doepke 400.00
Car, James Bond, Aston Martin, "262," Corgi, Box 115.00
Car, Joy Riders Whoopee Car, Windup, Marx, Tin, 1930s 250.00
Car, Krazy Kar, With Clown, Strauss, Windup, 1930s 425.00
Car, LaSalle Coupe, Silver, Tootsietoy, Tiny 121.00
Car, Leaping Lena, Mechanical, Tin Litho, Strauss, 8 In. 110.00
Car, Limousine, Tin Litho, Windup, Adjustable Front Wheel, 10 In. 660.00
Car, Lincoln, 1943, Talstoy, Metal, 7 In. 30.00
Car, Lincoln, 1960, 11 In. 225.00
Car, Milton Berle, Tin Litho, Mechanical, Marx, 5 1/2 In. 200.00
Car, Mortimer Snerd Tricky Auto, Tin, Mechanical, Marx, 7 In. 770.00
Car, Moxiemobile, Man Riding Horse In Touring Car 750.00
Car, Mystery, Tin Plated, Wolverine 250.00
Car, Nascar Pacer, Set, Ertl, Box, 1981 .... 30.00
Car, Old Jalopy, Windup, Tin Litho, Marx, 7 In. 225.00
Car, Olds, 1948, Windup, Saunders, Plastic 20.00
Car, Oldsmobile, 1958, Orange Top, Purple Body, 12 In. 1650.00
Car, Our Gang Clubhouse, Boat, Figures, Box, 1975 .... 650.00
Car, Plymouth, Plastic, Windup, Aluminum Model Toys, Inc., Box, 7 1/2 In. 66.00
Car, Police, Volkswagen, Blinking Light, Siren, Battery Operated, Tin 85.00
Car, Porsche, Silver Gray, Tekno, Box 140.00
Car, Pursuit, G–Man, Marx, Windup, 1930 .... 650.00
Car, Racing, Alfa Romeo P2, Leather Seats, Tin, Original Key, 21 In. 2420.00
Car, Racing, Dooling, Gasoline Powered 935.00
Car, Racing, Extra Bodies, Electric Motor, Keystone, 1920s 350.00
Car, Racing, Friction, Tin, Japan, 6 In. 60.00
Car, Racing, Maroon, Driver, Nose Windup, Mohawk, 1920s 165.00
Car, Racing, Midget Racer, No.7, Marx, Windup, 1930s 85.00
Car, Racing, No. 8, Penny Toy, 4 1/2 In. 45.00
Car, Racing, No.52, Windup, Red & Yellow, Chein 65.00
Car, Racing, Pull Rod Action, Tin Litho of Driver, Elnee, 1930s, 11 In. 195.00
Car, Racing, Red & Silver, No.22, Cast Iron, 7 1/2 In. 25.00
Car, Racing, Renwal, Clear Plastic 20.00
Car, Racing, Windup, Marx, 4 In. 20.00
Car, Redbug, 2 Seater, Electric, Porcelain License Plate, 1915 .... 2800.00
Car, Retractable Hard Top, Wyandotte 215.00
Car, Riding, Flintstones 300.00
Car, Roadster, 2–Seater, Bing, Clockwork, Yellow Upholstery, 9 In. 6050.00
Car, Roadster, Kingsbury 325.00
Car, Rollover, Marx, Box 85.00
Car, Rumble Seat Coupe, Arcade 100.00
Car, Scarab, Buddy L 115.00
Car, Sedan, Maroon, Tootsietoy 55.00
Car, Sedan, Nickeled Driver, Cast Iron, Arcade, 6 1/2 In. 579.50

Car, Sedan, White Rubber Tires, Tootsietoy, 5 1/2 In.	20.00
Car, Shuttling, Mechanical, Linemar, Box	325.00
Car, Silver Coupe, Buddy L	575.00
Car, Speedway Coupe, Windup, Tin, Marx, 1930s	250.00
Car, Sports, Red, Remote Control, Motion Toy Co.	75.00
Car, Sportster, Convertible, Red & Cream Tin Litho, Marx	60.00
Car, Sportster, Marx, 1950s, 20 In.	50.00
Car, Station Wagon, Fisher-Price, No.234	130.00
Car, Station Wagon, Friction, Tin, Marx	95.00
Car, Station, Aeroplane, Bing	8550.00
Car, Studebaker, Windup, Occupied Japan, Box	55.00
Car, Thunderbird, 1956, Box, 11 In.	465.00
Car, Tin Lizzie, Windup, Tin	495.00
Car, Torpedo Coup, White Rubber Wheels, Tootsietoy	38.00
Car, Torpedo Roadster, Black Wood Wheels, Tootsietoy	38.00
Car, Touring, Friction, Clark	265.00
Car, Touring, Model T, Arcade	445.00
Car, Touring, Open, Windup, Greppert & Kelch, 8 In.	650.00
Car, Touring, Tin Litho, Windup Mechanism, Bing, 9 In.	935.00
Car, Touring, With Driver, Pennytoy	175.00
Car, Turbo Jet, Ideal, Box	115.00
Car, Tut-Tut, Lehmann	875.00
Car, Volkswagen, Steel, Tonka, 9 In.	25.00
Car, Volkswagen, Tin, Battery Operated, 3 Actions, 1950s	45.00
Car, Whoopee, Marx	210.00
Car, With Rumble Seat, Pressed Steel, C.1930, 8 1/2 In.	145.00
Car, Wonder MG, Windup, Box, Japan, 1950s	250.00
Car, Yogi Bear, Tin, Friction, Box	150.00
Card Table Set, Metal, Folds, 1950s	50.00
Carousel, 2 Jockey Riders, Hand Painted, 1880s, 6 X 3 In.	385.00
Carousel, Kiddie Go Round, Windup, Unique Art, 1940s	225.00
Carousel, Moyer-Kader	2600.00
Carousel, Musical, 2 Horses, 2 Sleighs, Tin Man, Cloth Cover, 20 1/2 In.	475.00
Carpet Sweeper, Pretty Maid, Linemar	28.00
Carpet Sweeper, Sally Ann	45.00
Carriage, Doll's, All Metal, 1960	20.00
Carriage, Doll's, Blue Cloth	14.00
Carriage, Doll's, Leatherette	100.00
Carriage, Doll's, Metal & Canvas	150.00
Carriage, Doll's, Ohio Art, 4 1/2 X 5 In.	45.00
Carriage, Doll's, Parasol, Wire Spool Wheels, Cushioned Seat, Wicker	495.00
Carriage, Doll's, Shirley Temple Stamped On Hubcaps, Green	400.00
Carriage, Doll's, Silk Bonnet, Beige, Gold, Blue, Marklin, 9 X 6 1/2 In.	4850.00
Carriage, Doll's, Tin, Silk Lining	110.00
Carriage, Doll's, Victorian, Wicker	300.00
Carriage, Doll's, White Wicker, Wooden Wheels, Small	165.00
Carriage, Doll's, Wicker	100.00 To 180.00
Carriage, Doll's, Wicker, Metal Wheels	285.00
Carriage, Surrey-Type, Fringed Top	375.00
Cart, Chester Gump	400.00
Cart, Doll's, Green & Yellow Paint, 36 In.	210.00
Cart, Dump, White Horse, Merrian, Red Harness	605.00
Cart, Goat, Cast Iron, 5 In.	90.00
Cart, Horse & Bakery, Pull Toy, Original Paint, 7 1/2 In.	325.00
Cart, Orange Striping, Red & Black Trim, Wooden, 15 In.	25.00
Cart, Pull, Wicker & Metal, Collapsible, White, Lloyd	185.00
Case, Barbie, With Clothes, 1964	30.00
Cash Register, American Flyer	25.00
Cash Register, Benjamin Franklin, Linemar	15.00
Cash Register, Little Storekeeper	20.00
Cash Register, Tom Thumb	7.50 To 35.00
Cash Register, Tom Thumb, Play Money, Dated 1948	28.00
Cat, Black Mohair, Straw Filled, Steiff, 8 In.	135.00
Cat, Felix, Schoenhut, 4 In.	195.00

Cat, Gray, Bushy Tail, Steiff, Tagged, 12 In.	195.00
Cat, Lizzy, Steiff, Button, 2 1/2 In.	85.00
Cat, On Wheels, Steiff	235.00
Cat, Playful, Celluloid & Tin, Windup, Occupied Japan	50.00
Cat, Pushing Ball, Windup, Marx, 5 In.	35.00
Cat, Roll Over, Cloth Covered, Tin Ball, Windup, Japan, 1930s, 3 In.	75.00
Cat, Susi, Steiff, Button, 2 1/2 In.	65.00
Cat, Tabby, Steiff, Button, 2 1/2 In.	55.00
Cat, Topsi, Steiff, Button, 2 1/2 In.	55.00
Cavalry & Indian Set, Lead, Hand Painted, Early 1900s, 29 Piece	180.00
Cement Mixer, Battery Operated, Marx	15.00
Cement Mixer, Buddy L, 1929	675.00 To 695.00
Cement Mixer, Steel, Structo, 22 In.	120.00
Chair, Doll's, Alphabet, Paper Lithographs On Wood, Forbes Co., 12 In.	412.00
Chair, Doll's, Bentwood, Stenciled, Red	48.00
Chair, Doll's, Rush Seat, Wooden	22.00
Chair, Doll's, Wicker, Mustard Paint, 13 1/2 In.	65.00
Chair, Doll's, Windsor, Green & Red, Design On Seat	185.00
Chair, Metal, Tootsietoy	7.00
Chair, Rocker, Metal, Tootsietoy	7.00
Charlie Chimp, Windup, Box, Japan, 1950s	125.00
Charm Bracelet, Huckleberry Hound & Yogi Bear, On Card, 1959	75.00
Chemistry Set, Gilbert, 1930–40	75.00
Chemistry Set, Gilbert, No.12	65.00
Chest, Doll's, Biedermeier	1500.00
Chest, Doll's, Curly Maple, Cherry, Mahogany, 4 Drawers, Watch Holder	2650.00
Chest, Doll's, Oak, 3 Drawers	60.00
Chick, In Egg, Windup, Metal, Haji	10.00
Chick, Windup, Fur, Glass Eyes, Walks & Chirps, Original Ribbon	48.00
Chicken, Multicolored, Celluloid Feet, Rattle, 3 In.	17.00
Chicken, Pecking, Man Holding Pan, Clockwork, Tin Plate, Japan, 1920	850.00
Chickens, Pecking, Windup, Move Forward & Backward, Tin Litho	125.00
Child Beating Drum, Clockwork, Box	40.00
China Hutch, Doll's, Glass Doors	75.00
Chinaman, Spins, Dances, Windup, Tin, 6 In.	125.00
Choo–Choo Car, Tin Litho, Mechanical, Marx, 8 In.	170.00
Circus Wagon, Cage, Schoenhut	900.00
Circus Wagon, Horse Drawn, Cage, Cast Iron, Kenton, 1941	300.00
Circus Wagon, Overland, Cast Iron	145.00
Circus Wagon, Overland, Kenton	695.00
Circus Wagon, With Bear, Cast Iron, Painted, Kenton	425.00
Circus Wagon, With Giraffe, Steiff	270.00
Circus Wagon, Wood & Cast Iron, Arcade, 14 1/2 In.	55.00
Circus, Ring–A–Ling, Windup, Marx	525.00
Clicker, Frog, Tin, Red, Yellow, Green, Orange, Large	5.00
Clip–Craft Snap Action Set, Build Anything of Aluminum, 1960s	20.00
Clippo The Builder, Choo–Choo Construction Set & Train, Remco, 1965	10.00
Clock, Teaching, Fisher-Price	25.00
Clothespins, Plastic, Multicolored, 10 Piece	1.00
Clown, Artie, Box	695.00
Clown, Bear, Cone Hat, Tassle Buttons, 9 In.	550.00
Clown, Charlie, Drumming, Tin, Cloth, Cragstan, 9 In.	50.00
Clown, Highjinks Circus, Tin Litho, Plush, Cragstan, 10 In.	67.00
Clown, Jack–In–The–Box, Papier-Mache, Litho, Childhood Scenes	200.00
Clown, Juggling, Windup, Schuco, Box	85.00
Clown, On Scooter, Tin Litho, Tippco, 1930s	400.00
Clown, Papier-Mache, Windup, Germany, 6 In.	175.00
Clown, Playing Accordion, Monkey Playing Cymbals, Battery Operated	350.00
Clown, Playing Accordion, Y Co.	85.00
Clown, Playing Drum, Windup, Schuco	150.00
Clown, Roller Skating, Windup	115.00 To 135.00
Clown, With Accordion, Remote Control	75.00
Clowns, Drumming, Pull Toy, Gong Bell Manufacturing Co., Wooden, Tin	60.00
Coach, With Horse & Driver, Penny Toy, Tin Litho of Man & Woman	175.00

Coal Wagon, Red Wheels, Orange Sign, Bags of Coal, Wooden, 9 1/2 In. 85.00
Coffee Grinder, Little Tot 65.00
Colorform Set, Addams Family, Box, 1965 .... 95.00
Colorform Set, Green Hornet, 6 Page Booklet, 1966 .... 85.00
Comic Action Hero, Shazam, Mego, 8 In. 75.00
Comic Action Hero, Wonder Woman, Diana Prince Outfit, Mego, 3 3/4 In. 60.00
Conestoga Wagon, Cloth Top, Wood, Tin & Cast Iron, 18 3/4 In. 100.00
Conestoga Wagon, Polychrome Paint, Gibbs, Wood, Metal, Cloth, 18 1/2 In. 350.00
Cook 'N' Serve Set, Renwal, Complete Kitchen, 3 Figures, C.1950 .... 35.00
Cookware Set, Aluminum, Creative, Riveted Handles 125.00
Cookware Set, Revere Ware, 6 Piece 35.00
Coon Jigger, Lehmann 550.00
Couple Waltzing, Celluloid, Occupied Japan, Box 65.00
Cow, Bossy The Moo Cow, Tin, 1930s, Box 195.00
Cow, Bossy, Fisher–Price 54.00
Cow, Brown, White Spots, Celluloid, 4 In. 12.00
Cow, Elsie, Jointed, Wooden 50.00
Cow, Hide Covered, On Wheels 625.00
Cow, Walk–A–Way, Plastic, Marx, 1962, 5 In. 24.00
Cowardly Lion, Mego, 1973 .... 35.00
Cowboy, On Horse, Lasso, Windup, Marx 45.00
Cowboy, Windup, Twirls Rope Over Head, Celluloid & Tin 85.00
Cradle, Doll's, Blue Metal, 1930s, 10 In. 25.00
Cradle, Doll's, Dark Finish, Poplar, 14 In. 75.00
Cradle, Doll's, Painted Design, Brown Ground, 17 In. 95.00
Cradle, Doll's, Pine, 13 In. 40.00
Cradle, Doll's, Swinging, Wicker 65.00
Cradle, Doll's, Yellow Graining, Pine, 22 1/2 In. 130.00
Crawling Soldier, Ohio Art 125.00
Creepy Crawlers Thingmaker, Plastic Goop, Mattel, 1964 .... 50.00
Crib, Doll's, Sears Roebuck, Metal, 1940 .... 100.00
Crocodile, Native On Back, Chein, Windup 295.00
Cross Country Racer, 3 Cars, Automatic Toy Co., Box 32.00
Cupboard, Doll's, Tin 20.00
Cupboard, Stepback, Old Paint 90.00
Cyclist, Windup, Tin, Unique Art 175.00
Dairy, Toytown, Marx 140.00
Dancer, Hula, Windup, Celluloid 75.00
Dancer, Irishman, Articulated, Tin, 11 1/2 In. 150.00
Dancing Couple, Windup, Celluloid, 5 In. 32.00
Dancing Couple, Windup, Celluloid, Occupied Japan, Box 50.00
Dancing Dolls, Automaton, 6 Figure, Jigging On Music Box 1100.00
Dandy Jim, Windup, Tin Litho, Strauss, 10 3/4 In. 250.00
Dandy Periscope, Marx Bros., Box 50.00
Daniel Boone, Flintlock Wilderness Scout, Marx, 12 In. 100.00
Death Valley Days, 20 Mule Team, Tv Mail In Promo, Box 75.00
Deer, Brown, White Spots, Celluloid, Set of 5 .... 50.00
Diesel Roller, Silver Wheels, Hubley 60.00
Diggy Badger, Running, Steiff, 12 In. 225.00
Dinner Set, Chiquita, Pressman 115.00
Dishwasher & Sink, Snow White, Wolverine, 2 Piece 22.00
Dizzy Donkey, Fisher–Price 50.00
Doctor's Set, Stethoscope, Tweezers, Scissors, Rubber, Japan, 1952 .... 7.85
Dog, Airedale Terrier, Straw Stuffed, Mohair, Collar, 10 1/2 In. 28.00
Dog, Astro, Plush, Remote, Plastic, Japan, Box, 10 In. 17.00
Dog, Astro, Space Suit, Battery Operated, Tin, Walks, Barks, Amico 95.00
Dog, Basset Hound, Sitting, Steiff 795.00
Dog, Biting Man, Polychrome Paint, Wooden, 7 3/4 In. 65.00
Dog, Black Spots, Glass Eyes, Red Collar, Germany, Papier-Mache, 7 In. 150.00
Dog, Black, White Spotted, Red Collar, Papier-Mache, 7 In. 140.00
Dog, Boxing, Tin Litho, Cloth, Mechanical, Box, Japan, 5 3/4 In. 22.00
Dog, Bulldog, Brown, White Underbelly, Roly Poly, Celluloid, 3 1/2 In. 110.00
Dog, Bulldog, Pull Toy, 1920s 58.00
Dog, Bulldog, Pull, Bulging Glass Eyes, Barks & Bobs Head, Papier-Mache 1265.00

Dog, Bulldog, Schoenhut 575.00
Dog, Bulldog, Steiff, Button, 4 In. 75.00
Dog, Bulldog, Steiff, Button, Limited Edition, 1984 .... 150.00
Dog, Bulldog, Windup, Plush Covered Tin, Glass Eyes, 9 In. 85.00
Dog, Buttons, Plush, Battery Operated, Tin Litho, Marx, 12 In. 27.50
Dog, Candy Loving Canine, Tin, Rubber, Mechanical, T.P.S., Box, 5 3/4 In. 44.00
Dog, Collie, Sitting, Steiff, 9 In. 125.00
Dog, Dachshund, Barks, Steiff 150.00
Dog, Dachshund, On Wheels, Long–Haired, Russet Mohair, Steiff, 11 In. 250.00
Dog, Dalmatian, Sitting, Button & Chest Tag, Steiff, 1950s, 4 In. 75.00
Dog, Dancing, Lindstrom 30.00
Dog, Drums, Plays Cymbals, Eyes Light, Battery Operated 85.00
Dog, Foxy, Steiff, Button, 3 In. 85.00
Dog, German Shepherd, Leather Collar, My Toy, 1965, 36 In. 45.00
Dog, Hush Puppy 8.00
Dog, Klic–Klac, Schuco 250.00
Dog, Pekingese, Open Mouth, Steiff, Button, 4 In. 65.00
Dog, Pluto The Pup, Painted Wood, Bendable, 4 In. 22.00
Dog, Pointer, Brown & White, Celluloid, 5 In. 15.00
Dog, Poodle, Mohair, Tag, Steiff 45.00
Dog, Poodle, Reclining, Plush & Mohair, Glass Eyes, Button, Steiff, 15 In. 95.00
Dog, Red Dachshund, Long Hair, Sitting, Button & Tag, Steiff 250.00
Dog, Red Muzzle, Roly Poly, Celluloid, 3 1/2 In. 110.00
Dog, Rope Jumping, Tin 55.00

TOY, DOLL, see Doll

Dollhouse, 1 Story, Bungalow, Removable Roof, Schoenhut, 9 X 12 X 10 In. 125.00
Dollhouse, 2 Stories, Front Opens, Brick Wallpaper, 1920s, 16 X 14 In. 85.00
Dollhouse, 3 Stories, 3 Fireplaces, Lithograph Front, England 695.00
Dollhouse, 4 Rooms, Cindy, Open Top, Marx, Box 55.00
Dollhouse, 4 Rooms, Wooden, Wood Furniture, Composition People, 1940s 95.00
Dollhouse, 5 Rooms, Renwal Furniture, Marx, 1960s 150.00
Dollhouse, 6 Rooms, English Tudor, Wood Furniture, Rich Toys 195.00
Dollhouse, 7 Rooms, Tin, Plastic Furniture, Marx, Box 115.00
Dollhouse, Barbie's Dream House, 1963 .... 30.00
Dollhouse, Bungalow, Converse, C.1915, 15 X 19 X 19 1/2 In. 360.00
Dollhouse, Cardboard, Mansion, Tootsietoy, No.2501 .... 85.00
Dollhouse, Converse, Hinged Front, 9 X 7 In. 95.00
Dollhouse, Dress Shop, Box, 1938 .... 35.00
Dollhouse, Folding, McLaughlin, Dated 1894 .... 650.00
Dollhouse, Furniture, 2 School Desks & Baby, Renwal 25.00
Dollhouse, Furniture, 4 Rooms, Cast Iron, Arcade 2750.00
Dollhouse, Furniture, Andirons, Brass 20.00
Dollhouse, Furniture, Armchair, Strombecker, Box 20.00
Dollhouse, Furniture, Bathroom, Painted Tin, 13 1/2 In. 550.00
Dollhouse, Furniture, Crib, Ginnette, Box 45.00
Dollhouse, Furniture, Dining Set, Mahogany, Tootsietoy, 6 Piece 60.00
Dollhouse, Furniture, Dining Set, Tootsietoy, 8 Piece 55.00
Dollhouse, Furniture, High Chair, Strombecker, Box 25.00
Dollhouse, Furniture, Hutch, 2 Doors, 2 Shelves, Brass Handle, 10 In. 60.00
Dollhouse, Furniture, Iron, 5 Piece 35.00
Dollhouse, Furniture, Kitchen, Broom Closet, Wall Spice Rack, Germany 235.00
Dollhouse, Furniture, Kitchen, Green Enameled, Schoenhut, 7 Piece ... 75.00
Dollhouse, Furniture, Kitchen, Nancy Forbes 50.00
Dollhouse, Furniture, Litho On Wood, Bliss, 1900 .... 525.00
Dollhouse, Furniture, Mirror, Tynietoy 35.00
Dollhouse, Furniture, Petite Princess, Box, 36 Piece 75.00
Dollhouse, Furniture, Petite Princess, Box, Set 15.00
Dollhouse, Furniture, Radio, Console, Brown, Tootsietoy 40.00
Dollhouse, Furniture, Refrigerator, Coil Top, Green, Tootsietoy 40.00
Dollhouse, Furniture, Refrigerator, Stove, Hoosier Cabinet, Wolverine 48.00
Dollhouse, Furniture, Sink, Stove & Refrigerator, White, Wolverine ... 50.00
Dollhouse, Furniture, Stove, Alcohol Burning, Accessories, 13 3/4 In. 445.00
Dollhouse, Furniture, Stove, Kitchen, Green, Tootsietoy 40.00
Dollhouse, Furniture, Table, Chair & Couch, Wicker, 3 Piece 20.00

Dollhouse, Furniture, Table, Coffee, Strombecker, Box 25.00
Dollhouse, Furniture, Table, Corner, Strombecker, Box 20.00
Dollhouse, Furniture, Victorian Desk & Chair, Wicker 25.00
Dollhouse, Furniture, Victorian Living Room Set, Renwal, 3 Piece 25.00
Dollhouse, Glass Windows, Hinged Door, Chip Carved Trim, 8 1/4 In. 40.00
Dollhouse, Log, 3 Rooms, Battery Lighted, Wooden Furniture, 25 X 18 In. 850.00
Dollhouse, McLoughlin, Box, Unfurnished 450.00
Dollhouse, My Dolly's, Bungalow, Litho, IMS Co., 1910 .... 85.00
Dollhouse, Plantation, Long Porch, Portico, C.1920, 2 Ft.8 In. 750.00
Dollhouse, Plantation-Type, 6 Rooms, Front Porch, C.1920, 2 Ft.8 In. 750.00
Dollhouse, Red Clapboard, Wooden, Green Trim, Lima, Ohio, 1920s 675.00
Dollhouse, Tin, Marx, Miniature 40.00
Dollhouse, Tudor, Painted Wood, Hinged Front, Germany, 18 1/2 In. 1100.00
Dollhouse, Victorian, Painted Wood, Papered Interior, 12 3/4 In. 665.00
Dollhouse, Walton, Megon, Box 95.00
Dollhouse, With Custom-Made Furniture, Lights, Jos. Butcher, Eng., 1908 .... 2800.00
Dollhouse, Wooden, Cardborad, Lithographed, Unmarked Bliss 1850.00
Donkey Cart, Tin Litho, Mechanical, Marx, 8 1/2 In. 55.00
Donkey, Circus, Painted Wood, Schoenhut, 10 In. 38.00
Donkey, Cloth Covered Ears, Tail, Tin, Windup, Occupied Japan 50.00
Donkey, Wagon, Felt, Brown Glass Eyes, Bridle, Harness, Hub Wheels, 20 In. 475.00
Donkey, Windup, Moving Ears & Tail 150.00
Donny & Marie TV Show Playset 65.00
Dozer, Windup, Steel Tracks, Structo, 1920 .... 225.00
Draft Horses, Pulling Manure Spreader, McCormick Deering, Arcade 90.00
Dresser, Doll's, 2 Drawers, Tilting Mirror, White Paint 85.00
Dresser, Doll's, Oval Mirror, American Toy Co., Sticker, 1917 .... 12.50
Dressing Room, Cher 40.00
Drum Major, Mechanical, Tin Litho, Wolverine, 13 3/4 In. 77.00
Drum Major, Windup, 13 In. 135.00
Drum, Mother Goose, Tin Litho 35.00
Drum, Silk Screened Uncle Sam, Flags & Eagles, Tin, 10 1/4 In. 165.00
Drum, Soldier, Colonist, Nobel & Cooley 60.00
Drum, Tin Litho, Schlesinger, 4 1/4 In. 11.00
Drum, Tin, Ohio Art .... 22.00 To 25.00
Drum, Tin, Wooden Rims, Military Design, Painted, 9 In. 66.00
Drummer Boy, Windup, Tin Litho, Marx, Box, 9 In. 550.00
Drummer, African Native, TPS Japan 115.00
Drummer, Boy, Windup, Tin, Celluloid Head, Japan, Pre-War 350.00
Duck, Drumming, Battery Operated, Daisy 180.00
Dude, Wooden, Schoenhut 275.00
Egg, Easter, Musical, Tin, Windup, Mattel, 1953 .... 14.00
Eggbeater, Doll's 10.00
Elephant, Bubble Blowing, Tin Litho, Plush, Japan, Yone, Box, 7 In. 45.00
Elephant, Circus, Pulling 3 Clowns, Windup 35.00
Elephant, Clockwork, Moves Legs, Leather Body, Windup, 9 X 15 In. 1125.00
Elephant, Cloth Covered, Battery Operated, JSK, Japan, 6 3/4 In. 11.00
Elephant, Cloth Covered, Windup Tail, Wooden Tusks, 6 In. 135.00
Elephant, Felt, Steiff 60.00
Elephant, Gray, Celluloid, 3 In. 12.00
Elephant, Hubley, Box, 4 In. 22.50
Elephant, Juggling, Battery Operated 150.00
Elephant, Nodder, Pull, Felt Ears, Pewter Wheels, Papier-Mache, 7 1/4 In. 55.00
Elephant, On Iron Wheels, Wooden 350.00
Elephant, On Wheels, Steiff, Button, 1950 .... 425.00
Elephant, Steiff, Mechanical, C.1940 .... 1500.00
Elephant, Walking, Jumbo, Tin Litho, Schuco 165.00
Elephant, Walking, Remote Control, Magnet Nose, Linemar Toys 100.00
Elephant, Yes-No, Schuco, On Wheels 1395.00
Elf, With 12-In.Red Hat, Steiff, 15 In. 2250.00
Equestrienne, Mechanical, British, C.1900 .... 2860.00
Erector Set, Gilbert, No. 4, Cardboard Box, Unused 70.00
Erector Set, Gilbert, No. 6 1/2, Pieces On Cards .... 55.00 To 55.00
Erector Set, Gilbert, No. 7 1/2 .... 165.00 To 165.00

Erector Set, Gilbert, No. 7 1/2, Engineer's, Red Metal Case .... 110.00 To 110.00
Erector Set, Gilbert, No. 8 1/2 .... 100.00
Erector Set, Gilbert, No. 8 1/2, Metal Box, Manual, Motor 150.00
Erector Set, Gilbert, No.10021 .... 30.00
Erector Set, Gilbert, No.10072, Instruction Book, Motor, Box 95.00
Erector Set, Meccano, 1925 .... 35.00
Erector Set, Moorecraft, Manual, Box, 1937 .... 35.00
Erector Set, Wooden Box, Dated 1928 .... 195.00
Eskimo Girl, With Spear, Egee 300.00
Express Wagon, 2 Horses, Driver, Multicolored, Fallow 1980.00
Farm Animals, Fence Enclosure, Bradley, 1930s, Box, 14 Piece 75.00
Farm Set, Handmade, House, Barn, Chicken Coops, Fence, 8-In. House, 12 Pc. 250.00
Farm Set, Tractor, Mower, Mechanical, Tin Litho, Box, 11 In. 93.50
Farm Wagon, 2 Horses, Wood, Cast Iron & Tin.18 In. 65.00
Farm Wagon, Metal Wheels, Red, Cast Iron, Arcade 55.00
Farm, Steam Tractor, Threshing Machines, Working 1920 Model, 6 X 18 In. 8000.00
Farmer, On Tractor, Fisher-Price 20.00
Fawn, Steiff, Button & Tag 110.00
Felix The Cat, Composition, 13 In. 220.00
Felix The Cat, Wooden Jointed, Schoenhut, 1920s, 3 1/2 In. 150.00
Felix, Painted Wood, Sullivan, 4 In. 70.00
Ferris Wheel, Carette, Tin Litho, Manually Operated, 15 In. 2200.00
Ferris Wheel, Chein, 1950s, 16 1/2 In. .... 195.00 To 245.00
Ferris Wheel, Motor Driven, Chicago Vitrio, 23 In. 300.00
Ferris Wheel, Tin Litho, Plastic Seats, 17 In. 90.00
Field Hospital, 6 Composition Figures, Elastolin, Label 450.00
Fighting Knights, Playset, Marx, Metal Case 80.00
Figure, Chicken, Papier-Mache, White, Red Comb, Yellow Beak, Wire Feet 15.00
Filling Station, Brite Lite, Marx, Complete 180.00
Fire Engine, Pumper, Jeep, Ladder, Red, Tonka 85.00
Fire Truck, A.C. Williams, Cast Iron, 3 1/2 In. 97.00
Fire Truck, Aerial Ladder, Structo, 34 In. 175.00
Fire Truck, Barney's, Plastic, 1964 .... 55.00
Fire Truck, Driver & 4 Men, Swinging Bell, Ladder Moves, Tin, 4 In. 350.00
Fire Truck, Kenton, Cast Iron 250.00
Fire Truck, Ladder, Kingsbury 1000.00
Fire Truck, Light, Tonka, 10 In. 37.50
Fire Truck, Painted Steel, Battery Operated Lights, Keystone, 21 In. 104.00
Fire Truck, Pumper, Cast Iron 1000.00
Fire Truck, Pumper, Clark 395.00
Fire Truck, Pumper, Doepke, No.2010, 18 In. 325.00
Fire Truck, Pumper, Friendship, Double Hose, Plunger Action, Iron, 15 In. 935.00
Fire Truck, Set No.30, Hubley 375.00
Fire Truck, Texaco Products On Bottom, Tin, Wen-Mac Corp. 50.00
Fire Truck, Tin, Friction, Marx, 15 In. 187.00
Fire Truck, Weight Driven Flywheel, Rear Strip, Metal, 1921 .... 290.00
Fire Truck, Windup, Saunders, 14 In. 35.00
Fire Truck, Winky Blinky, Fisher-Price .... 40.00 To 85.00
Fire Wagon, Hook & 2 Ladders, 1 Figure, Cast Iron, 19 In. 225.00
Firehouse, With Fire Engine, Battery Operated, Tin, USA, Box 175.00
Fireman, Climbing, Marx 195.00
Fireman, Climbing, Tin Litho, Linemar, 17 In. 112.00
Fish, Billy The Ball-Blowing Magic Whale, Windup, Box, 6 In. 65.00
Fishing Fred, Windup, Tin Litho, Germany, Box, 6 In. 395.00
Flashlight, Dennis The Menace, White, Decal, 3 In. 22.00
Flashy Flickers Magic Picture, Gun, Box 50.00
Flatiron, With Trivet, 4 1/2 In. 16.00
Flute, Capt. Marvel, Magic 48.00
Flying Saucer, X-16, Tin, Japan 165.00
Football Helmet & Pants, Early 1900s 75.00
Fort Apache Play Set, Marx, 1977 .... 30.00 To 60.00
Fort Dearborn Set, Marx, Box 180.00
Frankenstein, Battery Operated, Box 225.00

Frog, Clock Movement, Windup, Tin 125.00
Frog, Windup, Green, Orange & Yellow, 4 X 2 1/2 In. 85.00
G–Man, Shoots Sparks, Makes Noise 17.00
G.I. Joe & Bouncing Jeep, Tin, Unique Art Co. 135.00
G.I. Joe & K–9 Pups, Mechanical, Tin Litho, Unique Art, 9 In. 82.50
G.I. Joe Adventure Team Headquarters 65.00
G.I. Joe Jeep, Mechanical, Tin Litho, Unique Art, 7 1/2 In. 132.00
G.I. Joe, Headquarters, Box 150.00
G.I. Joe, Jeep, Desert Patrol 500.00
G.I. Joe, Jeep, Trailer, 3 Piece 95.00
G.I. Joe, Jouncing Jeep, Tin, Windup 155.00
G.I. Joe, Scuba Tank, Accessories Pack, No.7606, Sealed, 1964 .... 35.00
    TOY, GAME, see Game
Game, The Toy, Charles Eames, Dowels, Braces, Panels, 30 In. ....*Illus* 3850.00
Garage, Keystone 35.00
Gas Station, Texaco, With Accessories, Buddy L, Metal 250.00
George The Drummer Boy, Windup, Tin, Box 250.00
Gertie The Galloping Goose, Marx, Windup, 1940s 115.00
Giraffe, Pull Toy, Tick Tock, Firestone, Wooden 40.00
Giraffe, Steiff, Late 1950s, 9 In. 1800.00
Girl, Bathing Suit, In Rocking Chair, Windup, Pre–War, Japan, Box 425.00
Gnomes Sawing Wood, Penny Toy, Germany 265.00
Goat Cart, Cast Iron, 5 In. 95.00
Goat Wagon, Cast Iron 65.00
Godzilla, With Shooting Fist 80.00
Golden Goose, Wings Up, Louis Marx 135.00
Golf Set, Mashie, Putter, 6 Obstacles, 2 Holes, Ball, Wooden, 1940s 60.00
Goodyear Blimp, Blow Up 30.00
Gorilla, Walking, Remote Control 180.00
Gun & Holster Set, Bonanza, 2 Guns .... 150.00 To 175.00
Gun & Holster Set, Ramar of Jungle, Daisy, Jon Hall, 1950s, Box .... 185.00 To 250.00
Gun & Holster Set, Tight Rope, Esquire Novelty Corp. 95.00
Gun & Holster Set, Wagon Train, 2 Guns, Box 165.00
Gun & Holster Set, Wyatt Earp, Hugh O'Brian, Esquire Novelty Co. 65.00
Gun, 2 Propellers, Jack Armstrong, Daisy, Box 110.00
Gun, Anti–Aircraft, Astra–London, Box 125.00
Gun, Anti–Aircraft, Marx, Box 150.00
Gun, Anti–Aircraft, Mechanical, Steel, Iron, Hand Crank, Langson, 12 In. 33.00
Gun, Astro Ray Space, Box 95.00
Gun, Atom, Tennessee Jeb 38.00
Gun, Atomic Disintegrator, Hubley 35.00
Gun, Clicker, P–38, Steel 35.00

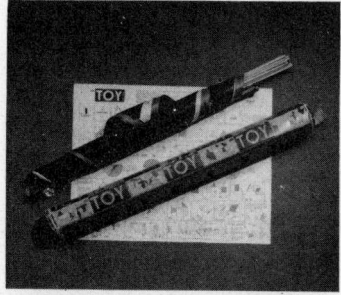

Toy, Game, The Toy, Charles Eames,
Dowels, Braces, Panels, 30 In.

Toy, Pedal Car, Pioneer, Red, Wire Wheels

Gun, Dart, Space Patrol 65.00
Gun, Dart, Space Patrol, Black, Unopened Pack 165.00
Gun, Electronic Space, Remco, Box, 1950s 35.00
Gun, G–Man Siren, Blue Metal, 1930s 145.00
Gun, G–Man Windup 30.00
Gun, Paper Popper, Box 75.00
Gun, Paper Popper, Daisy 37.50
Gun, Pop, Cork On String, Plastic, 10 In. 12.00
Gun, Pow R, Box 75.00
Gun, Pulver, Scrip, Yellow Kid 35.00
Gun, Rapid–Fire Tracer, Star Trek, On Card, 1967 .... 28.00
Gun, Ray, Secret, Captain Video 95.00
Gun, Red Fox Missile, Hubley, Box 150.00
Gun, Revolver, Breakaway, Tin, 10 In. 25.00
Gun, Rocket Dart, Daisy, 1950 .... 90.00
Gun, Rubber Band, Mechanical, H & H Novelty, Cleveland, Ohio 25.00
Gun, Set, Fanner, Mattel 125.00
Gun, Signal, Electronic, Remco 60.00
Gun, Skeet Practice, Darts, Japan, 1950s 20.00
Gun, Space, Corbett, Box 175.00
Gun, Sparkling, Combat, Windup, Marx 24.00
Gun, Squirt, Barney Rubble, Red Plastic, Durham, 1974, 6 In. 6.00
Gun, Squirt, Dennis The Menace, Box, 1954 .... 52.00
Gun, Sub–Machine, G–Man Sparkling, Plastic, Windup, Marx, 25 In. ... 145.00
Gun, Target, Kadet Officer's, Paris Mfg. Co., Pull Barrel Down, 9 In. .. 55.00
Gun, Water, Daisy, Metal 45.00
Gun, Water, Daisy, No.71 .... 25.00
Gunboat, Carette, Clockwork 550.00
Gunboat, Friction, Pressed Steel 135.00
Gunboat, Weight Driven, Tin 150.00
Ham & Sam, Strauss, Box 1350.00
Ham & Sam, Windup, Linemar, 1950s 850.00
Hamburger Chef, Tin Litho, Japan, 8 In. 45.00
Hand Car, Celluloid Tag, Wooden Frame & Seat, F.A.O. Schwarz 1750.00
Hand Car, Moon Mullins 475.00
Handcar, Felix The Cat, Windup, Tin Litho, 7 1/2 In. 467.00
Happy & Sad Clown, Tin Litho, Plush, Remote, Yone, Box, 10 In. 39.00
Happy Munching Bunny, Windup, Box, Japan, 1950s 50.00
Happy Puppy, Tin, Plush, Remote, Japan, 10 In. 8.00
Happy Santa, Tin Litho, Plush, Alps, Box, 9 In. 95.00
Happy The Clown Puppet Show, Tin Litho, Plush, Frankonia, 10 In. ... 110.00
Haunted House Play Set, Hard Plastic, Box 48.00
Hedgehog, Micki & Mecki, 1950s, Pair 50.00
Hen & Chickens, 2 Actions, Battery Operated, China 85.00
Hen, Lays Eggs, Tin, Wyandotte .... 70.00 To 95.00
Hen, Push Toy, Flaps Wings, Clucks, Tin, C.1930, 7 1/2 In. 45.00
High Chair, Doll's, Metal 18.00
High Chair, Doll's, Metal, Red, Box, 30 In. 25.00
High Chair, Doll's, Wooden, Strombecker, 8 In. 12.00
Hippo, Dark Gray, Celluloid, 3 1/2 In. 16.00
Hobbyhorse, Galloping, Steel, Mobo, Paper Sticker 395.00
Hobbyhorse, Glider, Wooden, 1890s 700.00
Hobo, Wooden, Schoenhut 250.00
Honeymoon Express, Tin Litho, Windup, Marx, 9 1/2 In. 220.00
Horse & Buggy, Polychrome Paint, Wood, Wire, Cloth, Leather, 16 In. .. 200.00
Horse & Cart, Windup, Plastic, Wolverine 125.00
Horse & Lady, Pull Toy, Tin Litho 1000.00
Horse & Sulky, Cast Iron, 7 In. 50.00
Horse & Sulky, Pedal, T & T Toys, 16 X 38 In. 1000.00
Horse & Sulky, Rider, Cast Iron, Kenton 150.00
Horse & Wagon, Borden's 250.00
Horse & Wagon, Ives, Fast Mail, Articulated Legs, Tin, Cast Iron, 17 In. .. 825.00
Horse & Wagon, Penny, Blue, Red Wheels, Brown, 4 1/2 In. 18.00
Horse & Wagon, Sand & Gravel, Cast Iron, 10 1/2 In. 165.00

Horse, Brown, Schoenhut .... 160.00 To 170.00
Horse, Fiber Coat, Fur Mane, Glass Eyes, Wood & Composition, 9 In. 95.00
Horse, Glider, Metal Frame, Gray Paint, Glass Eyes, Wooden, 35 In. 800.00
Horse, Glider, Plush Cloth Cover, Jewel Eyes, Covered Wood, 31 3/4 In. 95.00
Horse, On Wheels, Painted, Wooden, C.1930, 24 X 20 In. 680.00
Horse, On Wheels, Papier–Mache, Brown, Bridle, Iron Wheels, Germany, 6 In. 120.00
Horse, On Wheels, Removable Rockers, 1900s 750.00
Horse, Pedal, Mobo, Metal, 1930s 250.00
Horse, Pull Toy, Cloth Covered Wood, Iron Wheels, 14 In. 200.00
Horse, Pull Toy, Haircloth Covering, Glass Eyes, Wheels, 28 1/2 In. 305.00
Horse, Pull Toy, Open Cart, Gibbs, Wood, Cast Iron & Tin, 13 1/4 In. 225.00
Horse, Pull Toy, Papier–Mache, Large Enough To Ride 450.00
Horse, Pull Toy, Straw Stuffed, Haircloth Cover, Wood Frame, 22 1/2 In. 70.00
Horse, Pull Toy, Wood, Brown Haircloth Covering, Saddle, Blanket, 8 In. 250.00
Horse, Rocking, Beige, Red Rockers, Leather Saddle, Harness, 54 In. 375.00
Horse, Rocking, Dapple Gray Paint, Harness, Saddle, 32 1/2 In. 450.00
Horse, Rocking, Doll's, Seat, 5 In. 25.00
Horse, Rocking, Gabby Hayes 200.00
Horse, Rocking, Gray, Floral Design, Horsehair Tail, 21 In. 950.00
Horse, Rocking, Horsehair Mane & Tail, 1870's 2900.00
Horse, Rocking, Horsehair Tail, Leather Ears, Wooden Rockers, 54 1/2 In. 2400.00
Horse, Rocking, On Frame, Laminated Red & Black Silhouettes, 31 In. 130.00
Horse, Rocking, Platform, Papier–Mache 400.00
Horse, Tan, Saddle, Bridle, Papier–Mache, Germany, 5 X 5 In. 110.00
Horse, White, Gray Dapple, Harness, Saddle, Papier–Mache, Germany, 5 In. 80.00
Horse, White, Schoenhut .... 175.00 To 185.00
Huckleberry Hound, Windup, Linemar 135.00
Humphrey Mobile, Windup, Tin Litho, Wyandotte, Box, 8 1/2 In. .... 650.00 To 750.00
Humpty–Dumpty, No.736, Fisher–Price 10.00
Ice Snow Cone Maker, Snoopy & Charlie Brown 5.00
Iron, Lady Dover, Red Paint, Wooden Handle 35.00
Iron, Sunny Suzy, Electric, Green Wooden Handle 16.00
Ironing Board & Iron 25.00
Ironing Board, Doll's, Folding, 7 X 11 In. 15.00
Ironing Board, Metal, Bopeep & Boy Blue, Wolverine 42.00
Ironing Board, Ohio Art, Metal .... 12.00 To 28.00
Ironing Board, Sunny Miss, Metal, Ohio Art 8.00
Ironing Board, Wooden .... 48.00 To 65.00
Isometric Gym, Mickey Mantle 15.00
Jack Rabbit, Steiff, C.1960 .... 600.00
Jack–In–The–Box, Clown, Wooden Box, Children Scenes, Papier–Mache Head 65.00
Jack–In–The–Box, Curious George, Monkey Head, Marx Bros., 6 1/2 In. 85.00
Jack–In–The–Box, Curious George, Monkey Head, Marx, 6 1/2 In. 85.00
Jack–In–The–Box, Jolly–Tone Clown, Mattel, Early 1950s 12.00
Jack–In–The–Box, Papier–Mache Figure, Paper Over Wood, Germany 50.00
Jack–In–The–Box, Scarecrow, Mattel 12.00
Jacks, Iron, Suede Bag, 45 Piece 15.00
Jazzbo Jim, Jigger, Windup, Tin, Strauss, Box 750.00
Jazzbo Jim, Jigger, Windup, Tin, Unique Art, 1920s 725.00
Jeep, Anti–Aircraft Guns In Back, 2 Men, Battery Operated 75.00
Jeep, Army, Dinky 20.00
Jeep, Army, Tin, Composition Driver, Windup, 1954 .... 175.00
Jeep, Groggy, Tin, Celluloid Man, Windup 250.00
Jeep, Jumping, Windup, Tin, Marx .... 65.00 To 105.00
Jeep, Mach 4077, With Hawkeye, Box 25.00
Joe Penner Goo Goo, Mechanical, Tin Litho, Marx, 8 In. 165.00
Jolan The Pig, Steiff, 2 In. 60.00
Jolly Chimp, Battery Operated, Musical, Multi–Action, Box 35.00
Jolly Pianist, Tin Litho, Plush, Battery Operated, Box, 8 1/2 In. 88.00
Jumping Jack, Jester, Papier–Mache Head, Wooden, 11 1/4 In. 50.00
Jumping Jack, Original Paint, Thin Poplar, 33 In. 275.00
Jumping Jack, Santa Claus, Pull String, Arms & Legs Dance, 1930s, U.S.A. 35.00
Katy Kackler, Fisher–Price, No.140 .... 55.00 To 125.00
Kazoo, Wimpy's Hum–Burger, Musical 185.00

Kiddy Cyclist, Tin Litho, Mechanical, Unique Art, 8 In. .... 120.00 To 250.00
King Kong, Windup 195.00
Kit, Car, 1930 Packard Dietrick, Hubley, Metal 65.00
Kit, Car, 1932 Chevrolet Coupe, Hubley, Metal 45.00
Kit, Packard Classic Sport Phaeton, Metal 65.00
Kit, Radial Engine Airplane, Metal Craft 225.00
Kit, Spirit of St. Louis, Metal Craft, Box 175.00
Kit, Tarzan Paint & Wear Clothes, Fabric Painting, 1976 .... 15.00
Kit, Zeppelin, Metalcraft, Box 175.00
Kitty & Ball, Windup, Box, Japan, 1950s 110.00
Kitty, Rollover, Windup 45.00
Knitting Machine, Gabriel, Wooden Spoke, Makes Harness 22.00
Knockout Champs, Windup, Tin, Strauss, 1920s 275.00
Ladybug, Friction, Tin 20.00
Lamb, Lying, Steiff, 11 In. 250.00
Lamb, Organ Grinding, Arm Grinds Box 300.00
Lamb, Steiff, Button In Ear, 8 In. 40.00
Lamb, White, Tag, Bell, Steiff, C.1950, Box, 9 In. 225.00
Lamb, Wood, Papier–Mache, White Wooley Coat, Red Ribbon, Bell, 2 5/8 In. 65.00
Lawnmower, Box 20.00
Leopard, Roars, Walks, Windup, Tin & Cloth, Marx 95.00
Li'L Abner Dogpatch Band, Windup, Tin Litho, Unique Art, 8 In. 425.00
Lincoln Logs, Box, 1923 .... 20.00 To 45.00
Lincoln Tunnel, Windup, Tin Litho, Unique Art, Box 500.00
Lion, Clockwork, French, 14 In. 950.00
Lion, Pull Toy, Cloth Covered Composition, Glass Eyes, 14 In. 50.00
Lion, Pull Toy, On Wheels, Tin, Pink Celluloid 65.00
Lion, Steiff, Button & Tag, 7 In. 85.00
Lion, Wooden, Painted Eyes, Schoenhut, 8 In. 440.00
Locomotive, Whitling, Kellogg's, Premium, Box, 1950s 75.00
Logs, No.825, Halsam American, 211 Pieces 35.00
Loom, Structo, Metal, 3 Different Designs, 1930 .... 115.00
Lop–Ear Looie, Fisher-Price 135.00
Lucky Seven Dice–Throwing Monkey, Hard Plastic, Plush, Alps, Box, 10 In. 30.00
Luncheon Set, Campbell's Lunch Time, Plastic, Box, 28 Piece 35.00
Machine Gun, G–Man, Marx .... 45.00 To 50.00
Machine Gun, Turn Crank For Sound Or Fire Roll of Caps, Buddy L, 1954 .... 245.00
Maggie & Jiggs, Tin Litho, Windup, 7 In. 1265.00
Magic Kit, Mandrake The Magician, Box, 1949 .... 50.00
Magic Trick Set, Spy, Man From U.N.C.L.E 95.00
Magician, Windup, Tin, Celluloid, West Germany, 8 1/2 In. 110.00
Man, Dancing, Hollywood & Vine, Windup 250.00
Man, Eating, Hot Dog, Windup, Mr. Dan, Box 65.00
Man, Sharpening Tool, Sparks Fly, Windup, Strauss 185.00
Marionette Theater, Windup, Celluloid, Tin Litho, Box, 10 In. 313.50
Mask, Little Lulu, Paper, Kleenex, 1945 .... 25.00
Matinee Concert, Paper Litho On Tin, Mechanical, Frankreich, 6 1/2 In. 88.00
McNamara's Band Set, Soldiers, Wooden Theater, Linemar 165.00
Melody Player, Crank Box, Paper Roll, Chein, 1930s 100.00
Men, On Seesaw, Windup, Gibb 80.00
Men, Playing Pool, Windup, 1940s, 14 In. 235.00
Merry–Go–Round, 3 Women, Facing Outward, Clockwork, Tin, Germany, 16 In. 2800.00
Merry–Go–Round, Marx, 11 In. 195.00
Merry–Go–Round, Tin Litho, Hand Crank, Toyville, 5 1/2 In. 100.00
Merry–Go–Round, Unique Art 120.00
Microscope & Lab Set, Gilbert, 1960 .... 30.00
Midget, Climbing Tractor, Windup, Marx 55.00
Mighty Game–Launcher, 3 Gliders, On Card, 1981 .... 20.00
Mikado, Mechanical, Britains, Box 1300.00
Milk Bottle, Doll's, Milk Glass, Box, 1950 .... 3.50
Milk Bucket, Girl Milking Cow Picture, Marx, Tin 15.00
Millenium Flacon, Star Wars, Action Sound, Clicking Lazer Gun, 1981 .... 45.00
Minky Zotty, Steiff, 11 In. 400.00

Miss Friday The Typist, Tin Litho, Japan, 8 In. 55.00
Missile, Ballistic, Alpha–1, With Launcher, Box 95.00
Missile, Mattel, 1950 .... 45.00
Model Kit, Airplane, RAF Spitfire, Wright, World War II 12.50
Model Kit, Aurora Robin, Box, 1966 .... 00.00
Model, Austro–Daimler, Nickel Plated Brass, 12 In. 2420.00
Modeling Set, Tom Corbett, Box 75.00
Momma Dog, Feeding Baby Dog, Milk Bottle, Battery Operated, 8 In. 125.00
Monkey, Bartender, With Shaker, Tin, Windup, 7 1/2 In. 45.00
Monkey, Bell Toy, Cast Iron, 6 1/4 In. 440.00
Monkey, Bellhop, Yes–No, Schuco, 1925, 9 In. .... 400.00 To 450.00
Monkey, Bubble Blowing, Battery Operated, Eyes Light Up, Japan 30.00
Monkey, Chef, Automaton, C.1860 .... 7700.00
Monkey, Climbing, Penny Toy, Mechanical 300.00
Monkey, Crap Shooting, Battery Operated, Shakes Dice, Cragstan, Box 95.00
Monkey, Drummer, Windup, Schuco 135.00
Monkey, Eating Cone, Tin Litho, Plush, Mechanical, Japan, 7 1/2 In. 38.50
Monkey, On Stick Horse, Windup, Japan, 4 In. 25.00
Monkey, On Stick, Slides Up Over Top, C.1880, 11 1/2 In. 130.00
Monkey, On String, Fabric, 4 1/2 In. 38.50
Monkey, On Trapeze, Monkey Flips Over Bar 325.00
Monkey, Playing Banjo, Windup 75.00
Monkey, Steiff, 12 In. 85.00
Monkey, Tumbling, Windup, Box, Japan, 1950s 20.00
Monkey, Tumbling, Windup, Occupied Japan, Box 40.00
Monkey, Violinist, Windup, Schuco 135.00
Mono–Rail, Rocket Express, Marx 125.00
Monster Machine, Totocast, Gabriel 60.00
Moon Rocket, Box 110.00
Motorboat, Schuco 250.00
Motorcycle, Camouflaged, With Gun, Marx, 8 1/4 In. 425.00
Motorcycle, Champion, Blue, 7 In. 325.00
Motorcycle, Friction, Tin Litho 20.00
Motorcycle, Harley, Civilian Driver, Hubley, 6 1/4 In. 375.00
Motorcycle, Japanese Patrol, 1950s, 9 1/2 In. 320.00
Motorcycle, Mystic, Windup, Marx, Box, 1930s 235.00
Motorcycle, Police Rider, Runs On Wire Track 65.00
Motorcycle, Police, Pedal, 3 Wheels 275.00
Motorcycle, Police, With Sidecar, Marx 150.00
Motorcycle, Policeman, Marx 475.00
Motorcycle, Policeman, Windup, Marx, 4 In. 95.00
Motorcycle, Sidecar & Driver, Hubley, Cast Iron 200.00
Motorcycle, Sidecar, Police, Siren, Windup, Tin Litho, Marx, 8 1/2 In. 242.00
Motorcycle, Sparkling, Soldier, Marx, Box 395.00
Motorcycle, Technofix 135.00
Motorcycle, Tricky, Windup, Marx, Box, 1930s 235.00
Motorcycle, With Side Car, Friction, 1940s, 9 In. 48.00
Motorycle, Rider, Harley Davidson, Blue, Cast Iron, 6 In. 250.00
Mouse, Sniffles, Windup, Marx 55.00
Movie Projector, 2 Boxes of Film, Irwin, Dated 1932 .... 20.00
Movie Projector, Cragstan 50.00
Mr. & Mrs. Potato Head, 1950s 120.00
Mr. Fox The Magician, Tin Litho, Battery Operated, Cragstan, Box, 9 In. 154.00
Mr. Machine, Ideal .... 35.00 To 55.00
Mrs. Dog, Flowers & Watering Can, Battery Operated, Tin, Japan, 1960s 225.00
Mule, Balky, Lehmann 290.00
Mule, Balky, Windup, Tin Litho, Cloth, 5 X 7 1/2 In. 475.00
Mule, Bell Ringer, Painted Cast Iron, Mechanical, 8 In. 1100.00
Mule, Brown, Celluloid, 4 In. 12.00
Mule, On Paddle, String, Fisher–Price 21.00
Mule, Pulling Man In Cart, Windup, Tin, Marx 80.00
Mule, Walking, Windup, Eyes Roll, 6 In. 150.00
Music Box, Dr. Seuss, Crank, Mattel, 1970 .... 12.50
Music Box, Hand Crank, Mattel, 1963 .... 18.50

Music Box, Movie Camera, Fisher–Price, 4 Discs 15.00
Music Box, Player Piano, Schoenhut 325.00
Music Box, Pop–Up, Snoopy, Tin 17.50
Music Box, Red Baron, Wooden Aeroplane, Box 75.00
Music Box, Woody Woodpecker, 1963 .... 8.00
Native, Pango–Pango, Windup, Tin Litho 100.00
Noah's Ark, 18 Animals, Red Roof, Black Windows, White, 7 1/4 In. 225.00
Noah's Ark, 42 Animals, Cardboard, Britains No.1550 .... 6000.00
Noah's Ark, 44 Animals, 2 People, Hinged Cover, 20 In. 450.00
Noah's Ark, Noah, Wife, 2 Cows & Giraffes, Red, Wood Tone, 4 X 3 In. 35.00
Noah's Ark, Paper Litho On Wood, 38 In. 600.00
Noah's Ark, Tin, Germany 310.00
Noah's Ark, White, Red Trim, Animals, 1950s, 19 X 10 In. 125.00
Noah's Ark, Wooden, On Wheels, 1950s, 19 X 10 In., 13 Piece 125.00
Nodder, Papier–Mache Indian Woman, 4 Part, 10 In. 30.00
Nosy Rhinoceros, Steiff, 3 In. 110.00
Ocelot, Steiff, Button, 8 In. 150.00
Old Black Joe, Dances On Wooden Board, Metal Wand 75.00
Organ, Cathedral Shape, Hand Crank, Chein 50.00
Organ, Magnus, 1939 .... 45.00 To 85.00
Oven, Suzy Homemaker, Working, 1968 .... 40.00
Paddle Ball, Dr. Pepper 20.00
Pail & Shovel, Goldilocks & Three Bears, Chein 85.00
Pail, Jack & Jill, Ohio Art, 8 In. 6.00
Pail, Sand, Tin, 4 In. 26.00
Paint Box, Blondie & Dagwood, 1946 .... 25.00
Paint By Number Set, Wyatt Earp 95.00
Parrot, Red & Green Mohair, Steiff, 1910, 11 In. 850.00
Patrol Wagon, Gong, Cast Iron, 21 1/2 In. 1375.00
Pea Shooter, Metal, Cannon 15.00
Peacock, Pao–Pao, Tin Litho, Hans Eberl, 1920s, 9 In. 395.00
Pedal Car, Comet, 1950s 250.00
Pedal Car, Essex, Toledo Metal Wheel Co., 1920s 1980.00
Pedal Car, Fire Truck, 1950s 150.00
Pedal Car, Fire Truck, Anson, 1923 .... 220.00
Pedal Car, Firefighter, Unit 808, Windshield & Bell Missing, 44 In. 290.00
Pedal Car, Ford, 1934 .... 435.00
Pedal Car, Jeep, Blue 130.00
Pedal Car, Lincoln Zephyr, 1934 .... 1750.00
Pedal Car, Mercury, 1940s 475.00
Pedal Car, Murray Suburban, 1950s 250.00
Pedal Car, Murray, Suburban, Truck 575.00
Pedal Car, Mustang, 1965 .... 225.00
Pedal Car, Pioneer, Red, Wire Wheels ....*Illus* 2310.00
Pedal Car, Speedster, Garton 185.00
Pedal Car, Tractor, John Deere, Cast Aluminum .... 175.00 To 185.00
Pedal Car, Tractor, Murray, 1960s 150.00
Pedal Car, U.S. Army Airplane, Silver Paint 1000.00
Pedal Car, Western Flyer 125.00
Pelican & Fish, Tin Litho, Plush, Plastic, Drosko, Box, 9 In. 35.00
Pencil Sharpener, Snoopy, Battery, Kenner, 1968 .... 12.00
Penguin, Skier, Windup, On Leash, Box 75.00
Penguin, Tuxedo, Chein, Windup, 1940s 60.00
Penguin, Waddling, Plastic, Windup, Black & Orange, Marx 175.00
Penguin, Windup, Tin, Chein 20.00
Penny Whistle, Tin Litho, France 200.00
Periscope Firing Range, Tin Litho, Battery Operated, Cragstan, 9 In. 33.00
Phonograph, Beany & Cecil, 1961 .... 225.00
Phonograph, Crank, General Phonograph, Wooden Case, Decals, C.1920 .... 650.00
Phonograph, Merry–Go–Sound, 1945 .... 60.00
Phonograph, Windup, Floor Model, Children Painted On Door 750.00
Physics Set, Gilbert, 1960, Box 45.00
Piano & Bench, Doll's, Barbie, 1981 .... 10.00
Piano Stool, Doll's, Revolving, 9 In. 175.00

Piano, Baby Grand, 18 Keys, Fold–Down Top, Schoenhut	295.00
Piano, Bliss, Lithograph	250.00
Piano, Grand, 25 Keys, White, Schoenhut, 13 1/2 X 13 1/2 In.	75.00
Piano, Play Away, Marx	85.00 To 100.00
Piano, Player, Hubley, 1960s	30.00
Piano, Schoenhut, 8 Keys	63.00
Piano, Schoenhut, 12 Keys	68.00
Piano, Schoenhut, 17 X 10 X 10 In.	55.00
Piano, Schoenhut, 25 Keys, Bench, 1950s	75.00
Piano, Schoenhut, 25 Keys, Maple Finish, 19 X 17 X 10 In.	135.00
Piano, Schoenhut, 30 Keys, Bench	100.00
Picnic Bunny, Plush, Tin Litho, Alps, 11 In.	27.00
Pig, Pink, Black Spots, Celluloid, 4 1/2 In.	17.00
Pig, Pink, Black Spots, Papier-Mache, Germany, 2 1/2 In.	22.00
Piggy, Hopper, Windup, Tin, Marx, 4 1/2 In.	25.00
Pip–Squeak, Bird, Polychrome, Germany, 3 3/8 In.	25.00
Pistol, Flashlight, Rex Mars	45.00
Plate, Raggedy Anne & Andy, 1941	12.50
Playpen, Doll's, Renwal	18.00
Polar Bear, Steiff, 9 In.	150.00
Polar Bear, White Bisque, Wire Jointed, Germany, 3 In.	250.00
Pony Cart, Covered, Tin Litho, Mechanical, Pull Bar, Paris, 10 In.	357.00
Pony, Chime, Fisher-Price, No.138	25.00
Pony, On Wheels, Button, Steiff	565.00
Pool Players, Windup, Tin, Box, 1930s	150.00
Porky Pig, Windup, Tin, Leon Schlesinger, Dated 1939	225.00
Porter, Redcap, Mechanical, Tin Litho, Strauss, 6 1/2 In.	580.00
Post Office, Tin, Wolverine, Box, 1930s	165.00
Powerful Katrinka, Lifts Out Jimmy, Tin Litho, Mechanical, 5 1/4 In.	1100.00
President Kennedy, Reading Newspaper, Rocking, Windup, Box, 12 In.	275.00
Projector, Give–A–Show, Kenner	68.00
Projector, Give–A–Show, Kenner, 15 Hanna-Barberra Slides, 1962	48.00
Projector, Magic Lantern, 5 Slides	195.00
Pull A Tune, Fisher-Price No.870, 1964	26.00
Punching Bag, Joe Palooka, 1950s	25.00
Puppet, 3 Stooges, Vinyl, Hand, Set of 3	600.00
Puppet, Bruce Lee	30.00
Puppet, Hermann Munster, Hand	65.00
Puppet, Mighty Mouse	42.00
Puppet, Miss Piggy, 17 In.	15.00
Puppet, Odd Job, From James Bond, With Hat, Hand	100.00
Puppet, Raggedy Ann & Andy, Knickerbocker, 1970s, Pair	9.00
Puppet, Snap, Kellogg's	18.00
Puppet, Stan Laurel, Hand, 1966	25.00
Purse, Get Smart, Package, 1965	68.00
Push Cart, Doll's, Victorian, Leather Top	190.00
Rabbit, Button, Steiff, 6 In.	55.00
Rabbit, Chein	45.00
Rabbit, Dr., With Green Case, Pink Tie, Holds Cigar, Celluloid, 5 In.	45.00
Rabbit, Floppy Ear, Button, Steiff, 1940s, 8 In.	95.00
Rabbit, Hop Hop, Tin, Friction, Lehmann	17.50
Rabbit, Hopping, Windup, Tin, 1940s	25.00
Rabbit, Hoppy, Steiff, 6 In.	150.00
Rabbit, Little Girl, Child's Face, Rattle, Celluloid, 4 In.	45.00
Rabbit, Manni, Steiff, 9 In.	125.00
Rabbit, Plays Drum, Windup	40.00
Rabbit, Pulling Egg & Chicks, Windup, Occupied Japan	85.00
Rabbit, Pulls Cart, Chein	35.00
Rabbit, Runs, Stops & Sits Up, Key Wind, Pink Eyes	50.00
Rabbit, Windup, Turns Leaves In Book	65.00
Rabbit, With Cart, Wooden Wheels, Tin, Ohio Art	25.00
Rabbit, With Easter Basket, Annalee, 1982, 18 In.	57.50
Rabbits, Carriage, Tin Litho, Plush, Battery Operated, S & E, 10 In.	110.00
Radio, Wrist, Spiderman	12.00

Railroad Depot, 7 X 10 X 12 In.	95.00
Ram, White, Horns, Celluloid, 5 In.	15.00
Rattle, Felix The Cat, Celluloid	175.00
Refrigerator, Snow White, Wolverine	30.00
Refrigerator, Wizard	30.00
Reindeer, Schoenhut	600.00
Rhinoceros, Schoenhut	500.00
Rifle Set, Annie Oakley, Daisy Air Rifle, Cap Pistol, Canteen	325.00
Rifle, Daisy Pump, Buck Jones	55.00
Rifle, Paper Cracker, Buddy L, Box	48.00
Rifle, Space, Tom Corbett, Marx	100.00
Ring, Space Patrol, Hydrogen Ray Gun	145.00 To 150.00
Ring, Terry & The Pirates, Gold Ore	95.00
Ring, Tom Corbett Space Cadet, Face	165.00
Ring, Zorro	8.00
Road Grader, Hubley	55.00
Road Grader, Yellow, Doepke, No.2006	280.00
Road Roller, Wooden Front Wheel, Hubley, 1930s	125.00
Robby The Robot, Robbie, Box	4800.00
Robot Rocket, Jumping, 1950s	160.00
Robot, Atom, Friction	125.00
Robot, Attacking Martian, Tin, Japan	135.00
Robot, Captain Robot, Tin, Plastic, Box, 1960s	65.00
Robot, Durham, Battery Operated, 1960s	50.00
Robot, Electric, Morse Code On Back of Head, Red Plastic, 14 1/2 In.	300.00
Robot, Jupiter, Orange, Legs Operate Independently, Yonezawa, 13 In.	5280.00
Robot, Lost In Space, Box	125.00
Robot, Lost In Space, Gray Plastic, Stop & Go, 1977, 10 In.	132.00
Robot, Lunar, 4–Wheel Drive, Hong Kong	75.00
Robot, Magnor Magnetic, 1970, Box	85.00
Robot, Man From Mars, Mechanical, 11 In.	200.00
Robot, Mars Explorer	145.00
Robot, Mars King, Box	195.00
Robot, Mighty Robot, Key Wind, Walks, Moves Arms, Yonezawa, 9 In.	418.00
Robot, Moon Patrol Space Division, No.3	5720.00
Robot, Mr. Hustler	150.00
Robot, Mr. Mechanical, Cragstan, Walking, Windup, Tin, Box	400.00
Robot, Mr. Television, Battery Operated, 1950s	600.00
Robot, Mr. Zerox	125.00
Robot, Non–Stop Lavender, Litho Panels, Light Up Eyes, Masudaya, 14 In.	4620.00
Robot, Radicon, Gray, Remote Control, Masudaya, 1958, Box	5500.00
Robot, Rock–Em, Sock–Em, Mechanical, Boxing Ring, Marx	28.00 To 55.00
Robot, Rotate–O–Matic Astronaut, Tin Body, Box	65.00
Robot, Rotate–O–Matic, 1960s	90.00
Robot, Rotomatic Super Astronaut, Tin, Japan	165.00
Robot, Rudy, Remco, Cob	95.00
Robot, Saturn, Box	25.00
Robot, Space Explorer	105.00
Robot, Space Explorer, 1960s, Box	125.00
Robot, Sparky, Tin, Windup, Box, 1950, 8 In.	175.00
Robot, Sparky, Windup	50.00
Robot, Star Strider, Red, Gray, Hinged Doors With Guns, Horikawa, 11 In.	154.00
Robot, Star Wars, R2D2, Remote Control, Box	85.00
Robot, Sun Vulcan, God, Aiken, Box, 1982	35.00
Robot, Super Giant	395.00
Robot, Super Space, Battery–Operated, 5 Action, Box	240.00
Robot, Thunder, Brown, Cone–Shaped Head, Arms Are Firing Guns, 11 In.	9020.00
Robot, Toby, Talking	35.00
Robot, Train, Sonic, Red, Black Head, Siren Sound, Masudaya, 4 In.	4950.00
Robot, Video, Box, Japan, 1960s	195.00
Robot, Walks, Sparks Flash In Chest, Tin, Windup, Box	225.00
Robot, Wrench In Hand, Battery Operated, Tin, 1950s	100.00
Robot, X–70, Box	850.00
Robot, Zeroid	50.00

Robotrac, With Driver, Linemar, Box, 9 In. 125.00
Rocker, Doll's, Bentwood Arms, Splint Seat, Hickory, 9 1/2 In. 38.00
Rocket Fighter, Flash Gordon 495.00
Rocket Fighter, Key Wind, Marx 195.00
Rocket II, Space, Tom Corbett, Marx 485.00
Rocket Launcher, Erector, Gilbert, No.10052, Carrying Box, Literature 25.00
Rocket Launcher, Tootsietoy 35.00
Rocket Racer, Flash Gordon, Windup 425.00
Rocket, Apollo Explorer, Motorized, Remco, Box, 1969 .... 50.00
Rocket, Moon Patrol II, Top of Body Tin, Space Man In Cockpit 95.00
Rocket, Space, Solar X, Tin 135.00
Rocket, Tom Corbett Space Cadet, Marx 250.00
Rocky Mountains Express-Way, Windup, Box, Japan, 1950s 85.00
Rodeo Joe, Windup, Marx 250.00
Rodeo Joe, Windup, Unique Art 90.00
Roller Coaster, Windup, Chein 75.00
Roller Coaster, With 2 Cars, Chein 125.00
Roly Poly, Brown Dog, White Coat, Muzzle, Germany, 3 In. 90.00
Roly Poly, Bulldog, 3 In. 90.00
Roly Poly, Cat, Lop Ear, Celluloid, 3 1/2 In. 110.00
Roly Poly, Circus Clown, Windup, Box, Japan, 1950s 175.00
Roly Poly, Clown, Composition, 7 1/2 In. 47.50
Roly Poly, Clown, Papier-Mache, Germany, 14 In. 70.00
Roly Poly, Kitty, White, 2 1/2 In. 75.00
Roly Poly, Rabbit In Suit, Chein, 1930s 35.00
Rooster, Crowing, Metal, Plush, Plastic, Yone, Box, 11 In. 72.00
Sam, The City Gardener, Mechanical, Tin Litho, Plastic, Marx, Box, 8 In. 154.00
Sambo Special, Pull, Polychrome Paint, Wood & Steel, Barry Co., 13 In. 85.00
Sambo, Struttin', Black Jigger Dances On Round Stage, C.1850, 11 In. 225.00
Sambo, Struttin', Jigger, Dances On Stage, Battery Operated, Tin, 11 In. 225.00
Sambo, The Tiger, Advertising, Dakin 28.00
Sand Loader, Sandy Andy, Patent 1909 .... 55.00
Sand Mill, Chein 60.00
Sand, Tick Tock Clock, Box 90.00
Santa Claus, Battery Operated, Eyes Light Up, Rings Bell, Japan, Box 125.00
Santa Claus, Bell Ringer, Windup, Tin & Celluloid, 1940s .... 50.00 To 75.00
Santa Claus, In Sled, Friction, Japan 35.00
Santa Claus, On Reindeer, Windup, Tin, Cloth & Plastic, 5 3/4 In. 25.00
Santa Claus, Plastic, Plush, Japan, Box, 13 In. 72.00
Santa Claus, Sleigh, Windup, 1 Reindeer, Tin, Occupied Japan, 6 X 3 In. 75.00
Santa Claus, Windup, Tin Litho, Mechanical, 1920s, 11 In. 1295.00
Saucepan, Spatula, Ladle, Strainer, Spoon, Red Wooden Handles, Aluminum 10.00
Scale, Country Store, Counter Top, Cast Iron 55.00
Schoolhouse Set, Tin Litho, McLoughlin, Box 90.00
Scooter, Air Flow 250.00
Scooter, Firestone, Radial Steel Tires, 1930s 125.00
Scooter, Smitty, Marx, Windup 1800.00
Scooter, Wooden, 1930s 65.00
Scooter, Wooden, Logo 37.00
Sea Lion, Schoenhut .... 550.00 To 650.00
Sea Lion, Spins Celluloid Ball On Nose, Windup, Tin 30.00
Seal, Friction, Lehmann 235.00
Seal, Tricky, Celluloid & Tin, Windup, Occupied Japan 65.00
Seal, Wood, Painted Eyes, Schoenhut, 9 In. 350.00
Seesaw Rabbit & Boy, Windup, Box, Japan, 1950s 150.00
Seesaw, Wigwag, Pull Toy, Steiff 200.00
Service Station, Sunnyside, 2 Gas Pumps, Air Pump, Accessories, Marx 150.00
Service Station, Texaco, Buddy L, 1938 Design, 1950s 450.00
Settee & 2 Chairs, Doll's, Wicker, Rolled Backs, Natural 85.00
Sewing Basket, Doll's, On Stand, Germany, 14 In. 275.00
Sewing Kit, Uncle Sam Soldiers, Painted Wood, Box, 5 In. 100.00
Sewing Machine, Betsy Ross, Green Metal .... 28.00 To 50.00
Sewing Machine, Casige Sew-O-Matic, Tin 23.00
Sewing Machine, Casige, Metal, British Zone 55.00

Sewing Machine, Gareway Jr., 1940s 25.00
Sewing Machine, Germany, 1910–20 .... 90.00
Sewing Machine, Kay–An–Ee Sewmaster, Blue Metal, Wooden Base, Germany 48.00
Sewing Machine, Lennea, Chicago 150.00
Sewing Machine, Little Miss, Lindstrom, Box 48.00
Sewing Machine, Little Red Riding Hood 55.00
Sewing Machine, Necchi, Supernova, Red & Ivory Plastic, Sewing Kit 25.00
Sewing Machine, Sew–O–Matic, Thimble, Thread, Scissors, Metal, 6 1/2 In. 60.00
Sewing Machine, Singer ....49.00 To 115.00
Sewing Machine, Singer, Lithograph of Girls Sewing, Toys, Germany 95.00
Sewing Machine, Singer, Metal, Electric, Cover, Instructions, 11 In. 72.00
Sewing Machine, Stitch Mistress 25.00
Sewing Set, Sleeping Beauty 21.00
Sheep, On Metal Wheels, Wooden Base, Red Saddle, Germany, 7 X 6 In. 295.00
Sheep, Pull Toy, Wood, Papier–Mache & Wooly Coat, 9 1/4 In. 275.00
Sheep, White Wooley Coat, Pink Ribbons, Wood & Papier–Mache, 4 3/4 In. 60.00
Shooting Gallery, Ohio Art 25.00
Shovel, Metal, Ohio Art, 12 In. 9.50
Side–Wheeler, Pull Toy, Columbia, Painted Tin 4290.00
Sink, Pedestal, Cast Iron, Arcade 60.00
Skier, Windup, Chein, 8 In. 195.00
Skip Rope Animals, Cat, Squirrel & Bear, Windup, Japan, Box 175.00
Skunk, Steiff, Button, 4 In. 125.00
Sky Ranger, Unique Art 135.00
Sky Robot, Battery Operated, Tin, Red, Yellow, Blue, Box 85.00
Slate, Book, Agate, 1867 .... 45.00
Sled, Child's, Iron Runners, Green Paint, Gold Striping, 9 3/4 X 36 In. 150.00
Sled, Hero, Red, Yellow, Black Paint, Scalloped Board, 33 X 12 1/2 In. 660.00
Sled, Old Red Paint, Runners 37 In. 325.00
Sled, Paris, Indian Head Stencil, Blue Ground, 29 X 12 In. 303.00
Sled, Primitive, Late 1800s 300.00
Sled, Primitive, Wooden, Trace of Old Blue Paint, Bedford County, Ind. 30.00
Sled, Wooden Runners, Stencils 247.50
Sleigh, Pulled By Pony Or Dog, Wrought Iron & Wood, 53 In. 475.00
Sleigh, Rocking Horse, Slate Blue Paint, Stencil 660.00
Slo Turtle, Steiff, 7 1/4 In. 75.00
Slo Turtle, Steiff, 12 In. 125.00
Smokey Sam, Mechanical, Tin Litho, Plastic, Marx, Box, 6 1/2 In. 110.00
Smoking Grandpa, Battery Operated 150.00
Smoking Papa Bear, Tin Litho, Plush, Remote Control, Marusan Toys, 8 In. 60.00
Snobby Poodle, Steiff, Gray, 4 In. 75.00
Snoopy In The Box, Pops Up, Tin 25.00
Snoopy The Mailman, Rubber, Squeaker, United Features, 1953–66 .... 5.00
Soakie, Elmer Fudd 18.00
Soldier, American Machine Gunners, World War I, Mignot, Box, 6 Piece 121.00
Soldier, Band of Imperial Prussian Guard, Georg Heyde 1320.00
Soldier, Bedouin Arabs of The Desert, Drawn Sabers, 1905, 3 In., 5 Pc. 195.00
Soldier, British Infantry, In Action, Britain, Box, 24 Piece 297.00
Soldier, Crawling, With Rifle, Windup, Ohio Art, Box 125.00
Soldier, Fife & Drum Band of Welsh Guards 3190.00
Soldier, Horse Guard, Winter Coats, Britain, Box, 5 Piece 330.00
Soldier, Horses, Carts, Heyde, 50 Piece 275.00
Soldier, Infantry, Combat Troop, Lead, England, No.109, 6 Piece 17.50
Soldier, On Horse, Litho Paper, T. Roosevelt, 12 Roughriders, 5 1/2 In. 125.00
Soldier, Royal Canadian Mounted Police, Pewter, Box, 1905, 3 In., 5 Pc. 225.00
Soldier, U.S. Army Band, Yellow & Black Uniforms, 25 Piece 4950.00
Soldier, U.S. Army Cavalry Service, Dress Uniform, Pewter, 3 In., 5 Pc. 250.00
Soldier, U.S. Infantry, With Tank, World War II, 8 Soldiers, 1 1/4 In. 33.00
Soldier, U.S. Marine Corps Band, Summer Dress, 25 Piece 4400.00
Space Patrol Glow Belt & Decoder Buckle 350.00
Space Patrol Gun, Darts, Unopened Package 165.00
Space Ship, UFOX05, Tin, Flashes, Beeps, Battery Operated, Box, Bump & Co. 65.00
Spaceship & Launcher, ET 8.00

Spaceship Set, Captain Video, Box	105.00
Spaceship, Tom Corbett, Space Cadet, Windup, Marx	325.00
Sparkler, Archie	150.00
Sparkler, Chimney Sweep, Tin Litho, Germany, 5 In.	110.00
Sparkler, Soldier, Marx, Box	275.00
Speedboat, Clockwork, Miss America, Wood & Brass, 14 In.	195.00
Speedboat, Display Stand, Lionel, 1930s	625.00
Speedboat, Ocean, Driver, Windup, 12 In.	175.00
Speedway, Figure 8 Dual Track, Tin Litho, 2 Racers, 1940s	210.00
Spelling Board, Dated Feb.16, 1886	35.00
Spiderman, Mego, 8 In.	16.00
Spring Shoes, Kangru–Springshu, Box	35.00
Sprinkling Can, Ohio Art	21.00
Spy Detecto Writer, Sky King	105.00
Squirrel, Jumping, Windup, Box, Japan, 1950s	35.00
Squirrel, Tin, Windup, Marx	35.00
Stable, Lithograph On Painted Wood, Papier–Mache Figures, 9 1/4 In.	220.00
Stamp Set, Pinocchio	75.00
Star Wars, Emperor, Box	10.00
Steam Roller, Keystone, Painted, Decals, 20 In.	250.00
Steam Roller, Red & Black, 20 In.	325.00
Steam Shovel, Buddy L	12.00
Steam Shovel, Contractor, Lumar	90.00
Steam Shovel, Decals, Buddy L	300.00
Steam Shovel, Ride–Em, Keystone, Labels	225.00
Steam Shovel, Riding, Keystone	180.00
Steam Shovel, Rubber Tire Wheels, Tonka, 20 In.	115.00
Steam Shovel, Sheet Metal, Buddy L, 20 1/2 In.	35.00
Steam Shovel, Structo, Orange Cab, Gray Crane, Box	135.00
Steam Shovel, Tin Litho, Fricton, Linemar, 8 In.	42.00
Stool, Piano, Schoenhut, 19 1/2 In.	50.00
Stove, Camping, Gabby Hayes & Sgt. Preston, Quaker Puffed Wheat, 1952	75.00
Stove, Cast Iron & Tin, Venus	110.00
Stove, Cooking Range IXL, Iron	95.00
Stove, Daisy	40.00
Stove, Doll's, Crescent, 8 In.	20.00
Stove, Eagle, Cast Iron, On Legs	80.00
Stove, Empire, Metal	55.00
Stove, Holly Hobbie	20.00
Stove, Iron, Crown, 1800	135.00
Stove, Kitchen, Orange, Tin Litho, Pots & Pans, 1900s, 5 In.	145.00
Stove, Lady Jr., Electric	85.00
Stove, Lionel, Model 455, Electric, 1931	900.00
Stove, Little Chef, Electric	50.00
Stove, Pet, Lid Lifter, Waffle Iron, Suacepan, Kettle, 11 1/2 In.	395.00
Stove, Queen, Tin & Cast Iron	60.00
Stove, Snow White, Wolverine, 11 X 6 1/2 X 11 1/2 In.	58.00
Stove, Triumph, Cast Iron	450.00
Stove, Turner	50.00
Streetcar, Sandy Andy, Tin Litho, Wolverine, 1920s, 13 In.	395.00
Stroller, Doll's, Metal	75.00
Stroller, Doll's, Ohio Art, Tin	35.00
Stroller, Doll's, Reed & Wicker, Iron Undercarriage, Adjustable Back	950.00
Stroller, Doll's, Wire Spoke Wheels, 26 In.	110.00
Struttin' Sam, Tin Litho, Japan, 11 In.	350.00
Submarine, Diving, Windup, Germany, 11 1/2 In.	600.00
Sulky, Jockey, Composition, Windup, 1930s, Germany	250.00
Sunny Andy Fun Fair, Children On Swings	175.00
Super Circus Playset, Marx, Box	560.00
Surrey, Kenton, 12 In.	300.00
Sweeper & Dust Mop, Suzy Goose	20.00
Sweeper, Hoover, Metal, Wooden Handle & Cloth Bag	85.00
Sweeper, Little Jewel, Bissell	95.00
Sweeper, Suzy Goose, Tin, Wood, Kiddie Brush, 7 X 14 In.	60.00

Sylvester, Dakin, 1969 .... 24.00
Table, 2 Chairs, Porcelain Alphabet & Nursery Rhyme Top, Metal Base 250.00
Table, Alphabet, Graniteware 125.00
Table, Doll's, Drop Leaf, 5 In. 65.00
Talk Alarm 77, Hasbro 125.00
Tank, Anti–Aircraft, Tin Litho, Battery Operated, Cragstan, 9 In. 88.00
Tank, Flip Over, Tin, Marx 195.00
Tank, Jetson Turnover 390.00
Tank, Rollover, Marx 85.00
Tank, Rubber Treads, Marx 110.00
Tank, Turnover, Flintstone 235.00
Tank, Turnover, Superman, Windup, Tin Litho, Linemar 350.00
Tank, Windup, World War II, Marx, 3 1/2 X 5 In. 25.00
Tank, With Pop–Up Soldier, Marx 95.00
Tank, World War I, Kilgore, Cast Iron 150.00
Target Game, Tin Litho, Mangetic Dart, 1940s 65.00
Target Set, Tarzan, Jos. Schneider Inc., 1930s, 18 X 18 In. 225.00
Taub Aircraft, Penny, 2 Revolving, Germany, 1910 .... 395.00
Taxi, 7 Passenger, Arcade 795.00
Taxi, Amos 'N' Andy, Fresh Air 600.00
Taxi, Hanson, Painted, Cast Iron, Labeled Box, 15 1/2 In. 302.50
Taxi, Hubley, Cast Iron, Yellow, 8 In. 675.00
Taxi, Old Time, Tin Litho, Plastic, Battery Operated, Alps, 11 In. 49.50
Taxi, Trickey, Keywind, Silver Grill, Marx, 4 In. 50.00
Taxi, Yellow, Friction Motor, Tin, Marx 240.00
Taxi, Yellow, Windup, Marx 140.00
Taxi, Yellow, Windup, Tin Litho, Chein, 6 In. 143.00
Tea Cart, Mighty Mouse, Holds Tray Over Shoulders, On Wheels 675.00
Tea Kettle, Singing, West Bend 25.00
Tea Set, Abraham Lincoln, Box, 8 Piece 18.00
Tea Set, Applied White Cameo Design, Blue, Plastic, 30 Piece 18.00
Tea Set, Barbie's 25th Anniversary, China, Box, 1984 .... 65.00
Tea Set, Blue Willow, 15 Piece 135.00
Tea Set, Bopeep, Aluminum, 15 Piece 50.00
Tea Set, Campbell's Lunch Timebox, 28 Piece 35.00
Tea Set, Children Pictured, Germany, 9 Piece 125.00
Tea Set, Dutch Children, Figural Handles 95.00
Tea Set, Ginny, 10 Piece 17.50
Tea Set, Girl On Orange & Yellow, Ohio Art, Box, 15 Piece 125.00
Tea Set, Girl With Teddy Bears, China, Setting For 6, 6 1/2–In. Teapot 495.00
Tea Set, Girl, In Wicker Buggy, Tin Litho, Box, 10 Piece 175.00
Tea Set, Laurel, Cream, Red Trim, 13 Piece 175.00
Tea Set, Little House On The Prairie, 26 Piece 30.00
Tea Set, Old Mother Hubbard, Mary, Little Lamb, Staffordshire, 24 Piece 650.00
Tea Set, Petsy Bear, Steiff, Box, 16 Piece 70.00
Tea Set, Pink Rose Medallion, Metal Tray, Service For 6, 1940s 95.00
Tea Set, Queen of Hearts, Blue, Gold, White, Tin, Tray With Rhyme, 7 Piece 20.00
Tea Set, Red Riding Hood, Tin Litho, 7 Piece 125.00
Tea Set, Tan Luster, China, Oriental Landscape, Nagoya, 1930, 13 Piece 175.00
Tea Set, Tin Litho, 4 Canisters, 13 Piece 75.00
Tea Set, Windmill & Tree, Japan 85.00
     TOY, TEDDY BEAR, see also Teddy Bear
Teddy Bear, Rhythmical Drummer, Alps, Japan, Battery Operated, Box 45.00
Teeter–Totter, Boy & Girl, Ratchet Mechanism, 1920s 150.00
Teeter–Totter, Boy & Girl, Tin, Flip Over, Goes Again, 14 1/2 In. 285.00
Teether, Baby's, Colored Wooden Beads 10.00
Teether, Baby's, Ivory–Type, 3 In. 15.00
Telephone, Black, Dial, 1930s 14.00
Telephone, Gong Bell Co., Cowboy Design, Wall, Metal 38.00
Telephone, Mighty Mouse, Talking 25.00
Telephone, Play Phone, Gong Bell, Box 200.00
Ten Pin Set, Varnished Wood, Boxed 16.00
Terminal, Truck, Tin Litho, Marx, Large 195.00
The Buddy Miner, Marx 275.00

Theatre, Sonny & Cher, Go Round	65.00
Tidy Tim The Cleanup Man, Windup, Tin, Louis Marx	350.00
Tiger, Bengal, Sitting, Open Mouth, Steiff, 5 1/2 In.	95.00
Tiger, Button, Steiff, 30 In.	525.00
Tiptop Porter, Strauss, Box	575.00
Toaster, Flip–Open, Electric, Excel Electric, Muncie, Indiana	65.00
Tom Corbett, Playset, Marx, Box	595.00
Tony The Tiger, Cloth On Tin, Windup, Marx, 6 In.	95.00
Tool Box, Hammer, Plane, Chisel, Miter Box	95.00
Tool Chest, Boy's, Pine, Lithograph In Lid, Tools, 1890s	195.00
Tool Chest, Busy Boy's, Ohio Art	90.00
Tool Chest, Gilbert, No.3, Big Boy, 1940s	75.00
Tool Chest, Little Daisy No.11, Tools, Original Label	200.00
Tool Chest, Little Daisy, No.11, Tools, Original Label	200.00
Tool Chest, Union Boys, Oak, 7 Tools, Litho Top, 1910	115.00
Tool Kit, Handy Andy, Box	35.00
Toonerville Trolley, Tin Litho, Mechanical, Fox, 5 In.	325.00
Toonerville Trolley, Tin, Fontane Fox, 1922	675.00
Top, Spinning, Tin, Large, 1940s	22.00
Toy Peddler, Tin Litho, Mechanical, Mickey, Teddy, String, Germany, 6 In.	660.00
Tractor & Trailer, Ertl Co., Dyersville, Red, 18 In.	65.00
Tractor, Baby, Tin Litho, Self–Winding, Box, 3 1/2 In.	154.00
Tractor, Caterpillar, Windup, Marx	40.00
Tractor, Flatbed, Hubley, Red, White Tires, 13 In.	22.00
Tractor, Fordson, Arcade	65.00
Tractor, Fordson, With Driver, Cast Iron, 4 In.	225.00
Tractor, Hubley, 4 In.	145.00
Tractor, International Harvester	15.00
Tractor, International, With Trailer, Die Cast, Plastic Wheels, 3 In.	10.00
Tractor, Power House, Remote Control, Box	50.00
Tractor, Tin Litho, Self–Winding, Box, 3 1/2 In.	140.00
Tractor, Windup, Marx, Yellow & Green	40.00
Trail Kit, Sgt. Preston, Gun, Whistle, Badge, On Card	100.00
Train Set, American Flyer, Box, 1923	850.00
Train Set, American Flyer, No.10, Clockwork Engine, Tender, 2 Cars, 1922	110.00
Train Set, Army, All Tin, 1930s, Box	625.00
Train Set, Bachmann, DeWitt Clinton, HO, Electric	80.00
Train Set, Bing, Engine, 4–Wheel Tender, Clockwork, 1906	525.00
Train Set, Cragstan, Battery Operated, Box	40.00
Train Set, Engine, Baggage & Chair Cars, Signal, Cast Iron & Tin, 1924	435.00
Train Set, Engine, Track & 2 Cars, Battery Operated, Box	23.00
Train Set, Key Wind, Engine, 3 Cars, Track	70.00
Train Set, Lionel No.259E, Box	400.00
Train Set, Lionel, Passenger Car, Locomotive, Tender, 0 Gauge, Pre–War	525.00
Train Set, Marklin, Clockwork Engine, Coal Trucks, Tanker, 0 Gauge, 1895	2490.00
Train Set, Marklin, Engine, Tender, Passenger Carriage, 0 Gauge, 1930s	2290.00
Train Set, Marx, Battery Operated, 1950s, Complete	75.00
Train Set, Marx, Santa Fe Diesel, Box	150.00 To 200.00
Train Set, Unique Art, Jewel Tea, Boxcar & U Gondola Caboose	490.00
Train Station, 2 Rooms, Waiting Area, Ticket Window, Germany, C.1915	275.00
Train Station, Hyde Park, Metal	10.00
Train Station, Lionel	155.00
Train, 4 Cars, Lionel, Steam Switcher, HO, No.5741, Box	330.00
Train, Amtrak, Lionel, Box	330.00
Train, Car, Wooden, Tiny Tot By Jaymar, 10 1/2 In.	12.50
Train, Clockwork, 1 Gauge, Marklin, Box, 1910	950.00
Train, Coal Dump Car, Lionel, No.3069	40.00
Train, Diesel Switcher, 6 Cars, Lionel	385.00
Train, Electric Standard Gauge No.4, Double Motor, Lionel, 1908	8500.00
Train, Electric, Marx	130.00
Train, Engine & Coal Car, Yellow Striping, Iron Wheels, Wooden, 20 In.	350.00
Train, Engine No.400e, Passenger Cars, Lionel Blue Comet, 84 In.	8250.00
Train, Engine With Tender, Die Cast, Lionel, Early 1950s, 19 In.	150.00
Train, Fire Car, Lionel, No.52	210.00

Train, Freight, Santa Fe Diesel, Marx, 1930s, Box 150.00
Train, Honeymoon Express, Marx, Box, 1948 .... 125.00
Train, Locomotive, Lackawanna, AB Diesel, 0 Gauge, Lionel, No.2321 .... 360.00
Train, Locomotive, No.3000, Bullet–Nose, Gray, Attached Gondola Car 95.00
Train, Mystery Alpine Express, Windup, Tin, Mountains, Station, Box 125.00
Train, Passenger Car, American Flyer, Northern Pacific, No.900 .... 120.00
Train, Passenger, Windup, Girard Model Works, Joyline, Tin, 1920s 300.00
Train, Power Car, Union Pacific, Windup, 5 Coaches, Observation, 1930s 300.00
Train, Rail Car, Hand Pedal, Doepke 175.00
Train, Railroad, Men, Lead, Lincoln Log, No.30, Box, 6 Piece 17.50
Train, Santa Fe Locomotive & 3 Cars, Lionel 550.00
Train, Searchlight Car, No.3620, Lionel 20.00
Train, Smoking, Marx, Electric, Box, 6 Piece 85.00
Train, Sparky, The Locomotive, Tin Litho, Friction, Box, Japan, 13 1/2 In. 55.00
Train, Stafford Liner, Pressed Steel, 1930s, 3 Piece 95.00
Train, Steam Engine & 3 Cars, Penny Toy 225.00
Train, Steam Engine, Germany 150.00
Train, Steam Engine, Marklin, 15 In. 875.00
Train, Steam Engine, Weeden ....75.00 To 135.00
Train, Tasty Food Coffee, Engine & 3 Cars, Tin 450.00
Train, Tootsietoy, Boxcar, Southern Pacific, Fruit Growers, Metal 15.00
Train, Trolley, Electric, O Gauge, Carette 295.00
Train, Tunnel, Papier–Mache, 1940s 25.00
Train, Union Pacific Streamlined Passenger, Marx, No.10005, 3 Cars 65.00
Train, Western Special Locomotive, Battery Operated, Box 65.00
Train, Windup, Marx, Complete Track 75.00
Trick Elephant, Bell Ringer, Cast Iron, No.40, 7 X 4 3/4 In. 990.00
Trick Rope, Monty Montana, Package 75.00
Trolley, Broadway, Antennae, Tin Litho, Chein, 1920s, 8 1/4 In. 190.00
Trolley, Broadway, Battery Operated, Tin 50.00
Trolley, Horse Drawn, Converse, 25 In. 660.00
Trolley, Horse Drawn, Tin Litho, Repainted, American, 11 In. 357.00
Trolley, Morton, Wood & Leather 750.00
Trolley, Powell & Mason Streets Municipal Railway, Tin, Bell, Friction 65.00
Truck, Aerial Ladder, Tootsietoy 75.00
Truck, Allied Van Lines, Metal, Tonka, Large 85.00
Truck, Army Supply Corps, Metal Wheels, Canvas Top, Wyandotte 60.00
Truck, Bell Telephone, Hubley, Early 1950s ....95.00 To 135.00
Truck, Cab, Buddy L, International 35.00
Truck, Camper, Tonka 48.00
Truck, Car Carrier, With 4 Cars, Hubley, 10 In. 425.00
Truck, Cargo Van, Buddy L, 1932 .... 325.00
Truck, Champion Gas & Oil, Cast Iron, C.1930 .... 370.00
Truck, Coal, Mechanical, Cortland, Box 120.00
Truck, Delivery, Structo, Box 120.00
Truck, Dump, Buddy L, 1925, 24 In. 250.00
Truck, Dump, Friction, Japan, Box 75.00
Truck, Dump, Kilgore, 5 In. 100.00
Truck, Dump, Mack Bulldog, C Cab, Cast Iron, 12 In. 1750.00
Truck, Dump, Mack, Bulldog, Steelcraft 350.00
Truck, Dump, Metal Craft 55.00
Truck, Dump, Open Cab, Steel, Buddy L 522.50
Truck, Dump, Orange Tin, Rubber Tires, Marx, 18 X 8 X 7 In. 20.00
Truck, Dump, Packard, Front Crank To Dump Load, Keystone, 26 In. 475.00
Truck, Dump, Painted Steel, Clockwork, 9 In. 220.00
Truck, Dump, Painted Steel, Gear Drive, Nut & Bolt, Structo, 18 In. 550.00
Truck, Dump, Pressed Steel, Turner, 1929 License Plate 130.00
Truck, Dump, Ratchett, Buddy L 475.00
Truck, Dump, Riding, Keystone 185.00
Truck, Dump, Shovel, Structo, Box 120.00
Truck, Dump, Tip Top, Tin Litho, Windup, T.F.S. Co. 500.00
Truck, Dump, Toytown, Wooden 75.00
Truck, Dump, Turner, Original Paint, 20 In. 295.00
Truck, Dump, Wyandotte, 11 In. 25.00

Truck, Dump, Wyandotte, 17 In. 97.00
Truck, Dump, Wyandotte, Battery Operated Headlights, Red, 10 In. 55.00
Truck, EHE, Lehmann 575.00
Truck, Euclid Earth Hauler, Doepke, 27 In. 170.00
Truck, Excavating, Structo 60.00
Truck, Express Line, 6 Wheels, Screen–Type Back, Buddy L 3800.00
Truck, Express, Wyandotte 100.00
Truck, Fanny Farmer, Friction, Box 75.00
Truck, Farm, Cattle, Structo 75.00
Truck, Gas, Mack, Champion, Cast Iron, 7 In. 525.00
Truck, Gasoline, Pressed Steel, 1930s, 10 3/4 In. 95.00
Truck, Guided Missile Squadron 115.00
Truck, Hauling, Machinery, Structo, No.607 .... 20.00
Truck, Heinz 57 .... 475.00
Truck, Heinz, Metal Craft 250.00
Truck, Highway Express, Marx 125.00
Truck, Hook & Ladder, Lithographed, Wyandotte 125.00
Truck, Horse Trailer & Cab, Brown, Beige, Buddy L, Box 70.00
Truck, Hydraulic Dump, Buddy L 100.00
Truck, Ice Cream, 5 Cents, Key Wind, Tin 65.00
Truck, Ice, Mack, Arcade, Cast Iron, 6 1/2 In. .... 195.00 To 270.00
Truck, Ladder, Kingsbury, Cast Iron, 18 1/2 In. 1300.00
Truck, Ladder, White Sheet Metal, Working Headlights, Buddy L 300.00
Truck, Lieferwagen, Corgi, Box, 1978 .... 50.00
Truck, Lincoln Construction 100.00
Truck, Lint Lift, Windup, Mechanical Picks Up Load & Turns, 1950s 150.00
Truck, Log, Hubley, Box 175.00
Truck, Mack, Bulldog Hood Ornament 25.00
Truck, Mack, Red, Cast Iron, 5 In. 135.00
Truck, Mack, Red, Tootsietoy 35.00
Truck, Mack, Telephone, Hubley, 5 In. 100.00
Truck, Milk, Bowman, Tin Litho, 1955, 19 In. 175.00
Truck, Mobile Field Force, Hubley, 8 In. 40.00
Truck, Moving Van, Buddy L, Wooden, 1940, 27 1/2 In. 285.00
Truck, Moving Van, Gold Star, Marx, No.320 .... 35.00
Truck, Moving Van, Lyon, Rubber Wheels, Metal 18.00
Truck, Oil Tank, Sinclair, Tootsietoy, 6 In. 40.00
Truck, Oil, Sinclair, Wooden Wheels, Tin, 17 1/2 In. 160.00
Truck, Patrol, 2 Patrolmen, Cast Iron, 10 1/2 In. 495.00
Truck, Pickup, Tonka, 12 1/2 In. 20.00
Truck, Pickup, Tonka, 1950s 18.00
Truck, Popsicle, Buddy L, Wooden 175.00
Truck, Postal Savings, Friction, Japan, 1950s 95.00
Truck, Pull Toy, Wooden, Wooden Building Blocks, C.1930, 15 In. 45.00
Truck, Railway Express, Hubley, 5 In. 385.00
Truck, Road Grader, Adams, Doepke 265.00
Truck, Road Grader, Doepke 100.00
Truck, Semi, Transport, Structo 30.00
Truck, Semi, Wyandotte Truck Line, 1930s 80.00
Truck, Side Dump, Trailer, Friction, Box, 9 In. 85.00
Truck, Smitty Miller, Yellow Cab, Wood Bed, 1950s 65.00
Truck, Stake, Mack, Green, Cast Iron, 5 In. 225.00
Truck, Stake, Shell Oil, Buddy L 210.00
Truck, Stake, Structo, 1900s 100.00
Truck, Steel Cargo Co., Structo, Blue Cab, Red Trailer 120.00
Truck, Steel, Buddy L, 1950, 20 In. 55.00
Truck, Sunshine Biscuit Van, Buddy L, 1960s 65.00
Truck, Sunshine Biscuit, Punch Out, Assembled, 1932 .... 24.00
Truck, Telephone, Tonka 55.00
Truck, Texaco Oil Tanker, Box, Booklet, 28 In. 175.00
Truck, TV Repair, Ideal, Box, Unused 75.00
Truck, U.S. Army, White Tires, Sun Rubber, 6 In. 40.00
Truck, U.S. Mail, Keystone, 26 In. 850.00
Truck, U.S. Mobile Guided Missile Squadron, Marx 145.00

Truck, Wrecker, Ford, Arcade, Cast Iron, 10 In. 825.00
Truck, Wrecker, Red, Cast Iron, Hubley, 5 In. 155.00
Truck, Wrecker, Tootsietoy 22.00
Truck, Wrigley's Spearmint, Buddy L 625.00
Trunk, Doll's, Blue Metal, 8 X 14 In. 30.00
Trunk, Doll's, Dome, No Tray, 7 X 12 In. 25.00
Trunk, Doll's, Paper–Covered Wood, Fabric Lined, 16 In. 65.00
Trunk, Doll's, Steamer, Mini Travel Stickers, C.1932 .... 75.00
Trunk, Doll's, Tray, Doll Clothes 225.00
Turkey, Madame Alexander, 8 In. 65.00
Turtle, Friction, Japan 35.00
Turtle, Steiff, Button, 5 In. 25.00
Turtle, Tail & Head Move, Fiber Board, 5 In. 65.00
Tut–Tut, Lehmann 695.00
Tweetie Bird, Stuffed, Talks When String Pulled, Warner Bros., 1971 .... 10.00
Typewriter, Berwin Jr. Executive 35.00
Typewriter, Bing, No.2, 1926 .... 125.00
Typewriter, Dial Typewriter, Marx 30.00
Typewriter, Marx .... 15.00 To 35.00
Typewriter, Simplex, Box, 1940s .... 25.00 To 65.00
Typewriter, Tom Thumb, Metal Case 40.00
Typewriter, Unique Art, Box 65.00
Umbrella, Doll's, Lace Covered, Folding 18.00
Umbrella, Doll's, Wooden Dog Handle, 1940s, 12 In. 25.00
Umbrella, Mother Goose 15.00
Vacuum Cleaner, Raggedy Ann 12.50
Velocipede, Doll's, Cast Iron, Wooden Pedals & Seat 275.00
Vendor, Ice Cream, On 3–Wheeled Cart, Courtland Toy Co. 110.00
View–Master, 3 Discs 40.00
View–Master, Stereo, Sawyer's, Box 10.00
Violinist, Windup, Schuco 135.00
Waffle Iron, Griswold, Hearts & Stars, Wooden Handle 10.00
Wagon Train, Vinyl, Ralston Purina Co., 1975 .... 18.00
Wagon, Airflow .... 175.00 To 195.00
Wagon, Birdsell, Extra Wheels For Replacement 150.00
Wagon, Cage, Circus, Schoenhut 900.00
Wagon, Child's, Express, Iron Tipped Wooden Wheels, Red, Black Design 800.00
Wagon, Kiddie Kart, Red Wheels, K.C. White Co., Oak, 9 1/2 X 24 In. 280.00
Wagon, Milk, Trixietoy 115.00
Wagon, Radio Flyer, New York World's Fair 75.00
Wagon, Red, Wire Wheels & Rims 325.00
Wagon, Steel Frame, Wire Wheels, Tin Sides, Wooden Bottom, 22 1/2 In. 235.00
Wagon, Wooden, 4 Tin Milk Cans, Red Striping, 12 In. 175.00
Wagon, Wooden, Orange Paint, Black Trim, 13–In. Bed 20.00
Wagon, Wooden, Tin Wheel Rims, Cream With Red Striping, 12 1/2 In. 265.00
Wagon, Yellow Paint, Green Stenciled, Wooden Spokes, Beauty 675.00
Walkie–Talkie, Remco, Box, 1950s 35.00
Walkie–Talkie, Space Model QX–2, Box, 1950s .... 100.00 To 150.00
Wallet, G.I. Joe 15.00
Wallet, Space Ranger, Play Money & Identification Card 50.00
Washboard, Clothesline & Clothespins On Card, Wooden, 4–In. Washboard 7.50
Washboard, Kitchenette 9.00
Washboard, Little Helper, Tin Scrubber, 18 1/2 X 8 1/2 In. 7.00
Washing Machine, Blue & White, Wolverine 40.00
Washing Machine, Maytag, Cast Iron 400.00
Washing Machine, With Wringer, Sunny Suzy .... 40.00 To 65.00
Washtub, Doll's, Scrub Borad, Tin 22.00
Water Fountain, Steam Accessory, Hand Crank, Tin, 11 In. 75.00
Water Fountain, Tin, Mustard Yellow, Pink Flowers 275.00
Water Tower, Marx, Plastic 12.50
Water Tower, Tootsietoy, No.4653 .... 90.00
Watercolor Set, Wyatt Earp, Box 65.00
Weinermobile, Oscar Mayer, Oscar Pops Up 150.00
Wheelbarrow, Maple, Red Wheels, 14 1/2 X 44 In. 325.00

Wheelbarrow, Wooden, Fox On Each Side, S.A. Smith Mfg.Co., 34 In. 155.00
Whistle, For 17–In. Ronald McDonald Doll 2.00
Whistle, Jack Webb, Dragnet 5.00
White Mice In Cardboard Case, Animated, Moves When Cranked, 4 1/4 In. 45.00
Wild Mule Jack, Cast Iron, Bell, 8 In. 220.00
Wizard of Oz Play Set, Emerald City, Dolls & Accessories 160.00
Woman Circus Rider, Wooden, Schoenhut 225.00
Woofy Wowser, Fisher–Price 125.00
Xylophone, Pull Toy, Fisher–Price 30.00
Xylophone, Story Book 65.00
Xylophone, Tin Litho, Germany 35.00
Yo–Yo, Burger Chef 20.00
Yo–Yo, Pee Wee Herman 11.00
Yo–Yo, Spiderman, Box 20.00
Yo–Yo, Sterling Silver, Gorham 135.00
Yo–Yo, Yogi Bear, Green & Brown Plastic 3.00
Yogi Bear, Windup, Linemar 95.00
Zebra, Pulling Cart, Lehmann, Box 1300.00
Zeppelin, Steelcraft 165.00
Zicky Goat, Steiff, 4 In. 90.00
Zoo Set, Diorama, Mignot 800.00

> Tramp art is a form of folk art made since the Civil War. It is usually made from chip–carved cigar boxes. Examples range from small boxes and picture frames to full–sized pieces of furniture.

TRAMP ART, Bottle, Cross Inside 15.00
Box, 2 End Drawers, Red Pincushion Top, 10 1/2 In. 100.00
Box, 4 X 4 1/2 In. 20.00
Box, 5 Sides of Cube, Handle On Cover, 6 1/4 In. 65.00
Box, 6 1/2 X 10 In. 85.00
Box, 7 X 4 In. 20.00
Box, 9 Drawers, 11 X 7 X 16 In. 650.00
Box, Applied Heart Design, Sliding Lid, Nailed, 4 X 4 3/4 X 3 In. 75.00
Box, Cover, Pyramid Shape, Pyramid Finial 145.00
Box, Geometric, 3 Drawers Open Either Side, 8 X 11 X 20 In. 300.00
Box, Hanging, Brown Paint, Black Trim, 12 X 12 In. 45.00
Box, Hinged Cover, Dark Varnish Finish, 8 1/2 In. 55.00
Box, Hinged Cover, Pedestal, 11 In. 45.00
Box, Jewelry, Heart Design On Bottom 375.00
Box, Jewelry, Stars All Over 250.00
Box, Mirror In Lift Lid, 8 1/2 In. 75.00
Box, Mirror Inserts In Lid & 4 Sides, Lock & Key, 11 In. 100.00
Box, Sewing, Pedestal, Marked Carrie 170.00
Box, Sewing, Wallpaper Interior 90.00
Box, Sewing, York, Nebraska 295.00
Cabinet, Church Shape, C. Hicks, N.C., 77 1/2 In. 665.00
Caddy, Sewing, Chimney Pincushion, 2nd Floor Thread Holder 185.00
Chest, 3 Drawers, Scalloped Crest, 6 X 10 X 12 In. 160.00
Chest, 3 Drawers, Varnish Finish, 12 In. 95.00
Cupboard, 2 Bottom Doors, Norwegian, Dated 1869 .... 2850.00
Dresser, 3 Drawers, Gothic Arch Mirror, 22 X 10 1/2 In. 225.00
Frame, German Diploma, Philadelphia, 1915, 19 1/2 X 17 1/4 In. 45.00
Mirror, Horn Inlaid, Tramp Art Figures, New England, 1886–1900 .... 9600.00
Stand, Pedestal, Drawer, C.1900 .... 1550.00
Stand, Removable Planter Top, Diamond Sides, 30 3/8 In. 325.00
Tray, Coffee 5.00

Animal traps may be handmade. One of the most unusual is the mousetrap made so that when the mouse entered the trap, it was hit on the head with a mallet. Other traps were commercially manufactured and often are marked with the name of the manufacturer. Many traps were designed to be as humane as possible, and they would trap the live animal so it could be released in the woods.

TRAP, Alligator, No.2, Chain 110.00
  Bear, Davenport, Sure Death 75.00
  Bear, McKensie District Fur Co., No.5, Chain, Swivel & Ring 225.00
  Bear, Newhouse, No. 5, Chain, Swivel & Rings 200.00
  Bear, Newhouse, No.15, Chain & Swivel, C.1870 .... 350.00
  Bear, Oneida Newhouse, No.15, Chain With Ring, 35 In. 450.00
  Bird, Thayer 700.00
  Coyote & Fox, Verbail, Catches Animal Alive 100.00
  Coyote, Newhouse, No.2 .... 25.00
  Deer, Herter's, No.87 .... 60.00
  Fly, Blown Crystal, Pre–Civil War 45.00
  Fly, Screen, Shur–Katch Bug & Fly Trap, Nesco Co. 40.00
  Gopher, California, No.44 .... 30.00
  Gopher, Crago Clutch, No.4 .... 200.00
  Gopher, Evans, Small Size 200.00
  Kodiak Bear, Herter's, No.6, Chain & Swivel 400.00
  Minnow, Blue Glass, Galvanized Strips Carriage, Wire Hand Grip, 11 In. 40.00
  Minnow, Clear Glass, C.F. Orvis, Wire Carriage, Hand Grip, 13 1/2 In. 85.00
  Mole & Gopher, Automatic Self–Setting 40.00
  Mole, Nash 10.00
  Mouse, 4 Holes, Round 15.00
  Mouse, Copper Wire, Bread Loaf Shape, Wire Bail, 4 X 8 In. 65.00
  Mouse, Dome Shape, Ring For Hanging, 4 X 8 In. 75.00
  Mouse, Pine, 11 X 7 X 4 1/2 In. 75.00
  Mouse, Quart Jar 25.00
  Mouse, Victor, Choker, 4 Hole, Wooden 15.00
  Muskrat, Funsten Brothers, Floating 500.00
  Rabbit, Spring Operated, Iron 30.00
  Rat, Can'T Miss, 4–Way 8.00
  Rat, Gladiator 35.00
  Rat, Texas 40.00
  Rat, Wire, 15 In. 35.00
  Wildcat, Newhouse, No.3 .... 20.00
  Wolf, Newhouse, No. 14 .... 45.00
  Wolf, Newhouse, No.114, Chain & Swivel 200.00
  TREEN, see Wooden

> Trench art is a form of folk art made by soldiers. Metal casings from bullets and mortar shells were cut and decorated to form useful objects such as vases.

TRENCH ART, Coffee Set, Demitasse, 5 Piece 40.00
  Crucifix, Made From Shells, World War I 24.00
  Flask, Shot Shell, Deer Leather Design, Binding Around Top 40.00
  Letter Opener, Made From Machine Gun Bullet 12.50
  Lighter, Bullet, Ministere De Finance, Fulmer Parisien, 1918 .... 22.50
  Shell, Howitzer, Designs 85.00
  Vase, Bullet, Marked Alsace 40.00
  Vase, Floral, Verdun, 1918 .... 80.00

> Trivets are now used to hold hot dishes. Most trivets of the late nineteenth and early twentieth centuries were made to hold hot irons. Iron or brass reproductions are being made of many of the old styles.

TRIVET, 2–Heart Shape, Iron 190.00
  A Learned Man I Now Appear, But Turn Me Round, An Ass Is There 37.50
  Blacksmith, Horseshoe With Tongs, Hammer, Cast Iron, 4 X 5 In. 85.00
  Brooms, Wilton, Cast Iron 7.00
  Brown Stove, Cast Iron, 3 X 5 In. 28.00
  Campfire, Iron 45.00
  Center Lithograph, American Fence, Blue & White, 6 1/2 In. 65.00
  Cleveland Foundry Co., Cast Iron 35.00
  Colebrookdale Iron Co., Cross & Crown Cutout 19.50
  Colebrookdale Iron Co., Pottstown, Penna., Cast Iron 20.00
  Firefighting Design, Cast–Bronze 90.00

Footman, Pierced Design, Brass	32.00
George Washington, Iron	145.00
Good Luck, Iron	22.50
Griswold, No.1728	25.00
Griswold, No.1900	25.00
Handwrought Iron, Footed, Twisted Rods, Triangular, 18th Century	75.00
Heart Design, Cast Iron, 7 1/2 In.	125.00
Heart Shape, Scroll & Heart Design, Iron, Boot Feet, 4 X 10 3/4 In.	1600.00
Heart, Hand Forged Iron, Footed, 18th Century, 5 X 7 1/2 In.	250.00
Home Sweet Home, Peg Footed, Brass	75.00
Horseshoe & 1884 Center, Handle, Cast Iron, 4 X 7 1/2 In.	55.00
Jenny Lind, Iron	145.00
Long Handle, Iron, Child's	125.00
Lyre Form, Brass Top, Iron Frame, Turned Handle, 12 In.	30.00
Owner's Initials, Brass, C.1830	165.00
Pierced Fox & Tree, Brass	35.00
Reticulated Foliage Design, Brass, Iron Feet, Wooden Handle, 12 In.	155.00
Richmond, Va., Cast Iron, CSA, 1822, Large	90.00
Rooster, Brass, Israel	12.00
Sadiron, Open Circle Center, 6–Pointed Star, Brass, 8 1/2 In.	65.00
Scenic, 10 1/2 In.	150.00
Spade Feet, Turned Wooden Handle, Round, 6 1/2 X 6 1/4 In.	45.00
Stitch In Time, Iron	65.00
Stylized Tulip & Floral, Cast Iron, W.B.R., 1843 On Handle, 12 In.	160.00
Teakettle, Iron, Round Cutout Heart Top, 9 In. Diam., 15 5/8 In.	400.00
Victoria Jubilee, Iron, Dated 1887	30.00
Wrought Iron, 4–Legged, Handle, 5 1/2 X 8 1/2 In.	85.00
Wrought Iron, Nailhead Feet With Scrolled Tops, Handle, 5 X 13 In.	110.00

Trunks of many types were made. The nineteenth–century sea chest was often handmade of unpainted wood. Brass–fitted camphorwood chests were brought back from the Orient. Leather–covered trunks were popular from the late eighteenth to mid nineteenth centuries. By 1895, trunks were covered with canvas or decorated sheet metal. Embossed metal coverings were used from 1870 to 1910. By 1925, trunks were covered with vulcanized fiber or undecorated metal.

TRUNK, Camel Back, Tin Cover	95.00
Dome Top, Dark Vinegar Painted, Small	22.00
Dome Top, Hide–Bound, Brass Bale, Iron Lock, 16 In.	40.00
Dome Top, Leather Bound, Brass Bale Handle, Stud Trim, 12 1/2 In.	150.00
Dome Top, Pine, Brass, England, Early 19th Century, 11 X 32 X 16 In.	55.00
Dome Top, Pine, Impressed Tinplate Rosettes, England, 8 X 12 1/2 In.	99.00
Humpback, Pine, Large	125.00
Immigrant's, Blue Paint, Name Stenciled On Front	130.00
Immigrant's, Norwegian, Floral Painted, Dated 1868	2750.00
Scrolling Stitched Design, Red & Gilt, Pigskin, 11 1/4 X 29 1/2 In.	445.00
Stagecoach, Iron Straps, Pine, 1800s	100.00
Wallpaper Covered, C.1800, 4 X 4 X 7 1/2 In.	295.00

The Tuthill Cut Glass Company of Middletown, New York, worked from 1902 to 1923. Of special interest are the finely cut pieces of stemware and tableware.

TUTHILL, Bowl, Centerpiece, Rosemere, Ruffled, Signed	1250.00
Bowl, Cut Glass, Intaglio Fruit, Sawtooth Rim, 10 1/2 In.	265.00
Bowl, Phlox, 3 1/2 X 8 In.	225.00
Bowl, Rex Variation, 8 3/4 In.	750.00
Bowl, Thousand Eye, Signed, 9 In.	1250.00
Bowl, Whipped Cream, Lotus, Cut Glass, 8 In.	235.00
Celery, Geometric, Signed	450.00
Compote, Geometric & Intaglio, 7 1/2 In.	300.00
Compote, Vintage, Bishop Hat Shape, Signed, C.1904, 8 In., Pair	750.00
Compote, Vintage, Bishop Hat Shape, Sterling Base, Signed, 10 In.	850.00
Decanter, Whiskey, Primrose & Geometric, Signed, 9 In.	750.00
Fruit Bowl, Bishop Hat Shape, Signed	1200.00

Mayonnaise Set, Primrose & Geometric, Signed, 3 Piece	500.00
Plate, Intaglio Design, Signed, 10 In.	1100.00
Plate, Rosacea, Signed, 10 In.	1100.00
Rose Bowl, Full Pinwheel, Chalice Shape, 8 X 10 1/4 In.	1025.00
Salad Bowl, Four Fruits	725.00
Tray, Rosacea & Chain of Hobstars, Oval, Signed, 9 3/4 X 7 In.	550.00
Tray, Vintage & Geometric, 12 In.	1100.00
Tray, Vintage, Handles, Signed, 14 In.	1400.00
Vase, Intaglio & Geometric, 10 In.	450.00

The first successful typewriter was made by Sholes and Glidden in 1874. Collectors divide typewriters into two main classifications: the index machine, which has a pointer and a dial for letter selection, and the keyboard machine, most commonly seen today.

TYPEWRITER, Bing, No.2	75.00
Blickensderfer, No.5, Spare Head, Case	200.00
Corona, Folding, Case	35.00
Corona, Model B, Patent 1910, Small	47.50
Hammond Multiplex, Folding	50.00
Nikkel, 1958, Japan, 2000 Characters	630.00
Odell, Case	825.00
Odell, No.2	255.00
Oliver, No.3, Standard, Visible Writer	75.00
Rem–Sho–Bronze, 1896, American	1750.00
Simplex, Box	30.00
Simplex, Index Type, Wooden Case	70.00
Simplex, Model B	25.00
Underwood, Enameled Bronze, 1912	18.00
Underwood, Standard, Portable, Red Wood–Grain Metal, 1912	30.00

Uhl pottery was made in Evansville, Indiana, in 1854. The pottery moved to Huntingburg, Indiana, in 1908. Stoneware and glazed pottery were made until the mid–1940s.

UHL, Bowl, Tulip, Brown	35.00
Crock, Blue Acorn, 1 Gal.	50.00
Crock, Blue Acorn, 2 Gal.	70.00
Crock, Wooden Lid & Dasher, 1 1/2 Qt.	70.00
Dish, Dog	125.00
Figurine, Dog, Miniature	125.00
Jug, Acornware, Brown, White, 2 Gal.	45.00
Jug, Canteen, Miniature	90.00
Jug, Elephant, Black, Miniature	49.50
Jug, Elephant, Dark Crown	67.50
Jug, Meier Label, Miniature	85.00
Mug, 4 In.	85.00
Mug, 5 In.	100.00
Pitcher, Blue Grapes, 8 In.	125.00
Pitcher, Blue Grapes, Squat, Cover	185.00
Pitcher, Blue, 8 In.	120.00
Pitcher, Flagon, 5 Pt.	80.00
Pitcher, Grape & Trellis, Blue & White, 8 1/4 In.	120.00
Pitcher, Indian Head	350.00
Pitcher, No.197, 1/2 Gal.	110.00
Pitcher, Swan	300.00
Vase, Rose, 8 1/4 X 6 1/4 In.	45.00

The first known umbrella was owned by King Louis XIII of France in 1637. The earliest umbrellas were sunshades, not designed to be used in the rain. The umbrella was embellished and redesigned many times. In 1852, the fluted steel rib style was developed and that has remained the most useful style.

UMBRELLA, Child's, Blue & White Print	25.00
Parasol, Handle, Ivory Bust of Woman, Sterling Silver Band	135.00
Parasol, Pagoda Style, Mother–of–Pearl Inlaid Folding Handle	55.00

Parasol, Purple Silk, Silver Handle, Chinese 75.00
Parasol, Silk, Wooden Handle, Small 50.00
Parasol, White Linen 40.00

The Union Porcelain Works was established at Greenpoint, New York, in 1848 by Charles Cartlidge. The company went through a series of ownership changes and finally closed in the early 1900s. The company made a fine quality white porcelain that was often decorated in clear, bright colors.

UNION PORCELAIN WORKS, Oyster Plate, White, Gold Line, 8 1/2 In. ....65.00 To 125.00
 Sugar & Creamer, Allover Florals, Blue To White 250.00

UNIVERSITY OF NORTH DAKOTA, see North Dakota School of Mines

Val St. Lambert Cristalleries of Belgium was founded by Messieurs Kemlin and Lelievre in 1825. The company is still in operation. All types of table glassware and decorative glassware were made. Pieces were often decorated with cut designs.

VAL ST.LAMBERT, Ashtray, Shell, Gold Label, 4 Piece 18.00
 Block, Engraved Goonie Bird, Clear, Artist, 9 1/4 In. 175.00
 Bowl, Cameo, Purple Florals, Frosted, Cover, 6 1/2 In. 750.00
 Candleholder, 3–Light, Clear, Red Shadings 175.00
 Jar, Cover, Tiger Head, Clear, 3 1/4 X 2 1/2 In. ....110.00 To 150.00
 Paperweight, Impressed Frosted Eagle, Signed 50.00
 Perfume Bottle, Cobalt Blue, Atomizer, Cameo, Textured, 4 In. 275.00
 Plate, Zodiac Signs, Clear, Art Glass, Signed, 11 3/4 In. 250.00
 Tazza, Red, Clear Stem, Signed, 6 In. 137.00
 Tumble–Up, Amber To Clear 350.00
 Vase, 3 Notched Bands, Cut Glass, Signed, C.1940, 7 In. 95.00
 Vase, Art Deco, Green Cut To Clear, Signed, C.1900, 7 In. 450.00
 Vase, Berries, Frosted, Clear, Signed, 9 3/4 In. 550.00
 Vase, Clear & Cranberry, Signed, 8 In. 275.00
 Vase, Hand Painted Blossoms, Gold Thorned Branches, 10 In. 120.00

Vallerysthal Glassworks was founded in 1836 in Lorraine, France. In 1854 the firm became Klenglin et Cie. It made table and decorative glass, opaline, cameo, and art glass. A line of covered, pressed glass animal dishes was made in the nineteenth century. The firm is still working.

VALLERYSTHAL, Bowl, Cover, Blue Milk Glass, 3 Dolphin Legs, 5 1/2 In. 30.00
 Candy Dish, Cover, Seashell & Dolphin 55.00
 Compote, Branched Tree Trunk Supports Bowl, Amber, 9 In. 150.00
 Compote, Square Rim, Blue Opalescent, 6 X 6 1/4 In. 100.00
 Compote, Tree, Amber, 9 In. ....100.00 To 145.00
 Dish, Blue Robin On Nest Cover 95.00
 Dish, Hen Cover, 4 1/2 In. 35.00
 Dish, Setter Dog Cover, Opaline, Signed 65.00
 Dish, Walking Duck Cover, Signed, 6 1/2 In. 55.00
 Figurine, Dog, Blue, Flowered Base 150.00
 Figurine, Dog, On Rug, Blue Milk Glass, Signed 155.00
 Figurine, Duck, Swimming, White, Signed 95.00
 Figurine, Squirrel, On Acorn 125.00
 Figurine, Swan, Blue Milk Glass 65.00
 Plate, Thistle, 8 1/2 In. 25.00
 Vase, Spiraling Vines, Foil Patches, Signed, 1900, 13 3/8 In. 8250.00

Van Briggle Pottery was made by Artus Van Briggle in Colorado Springs, Colorado, after 1901. Van Briggle had been a decorator at the Rookwood Pottery of Cincinnati, Ohio. He died in 1904. His wares usually had modeled relief decorations and a soft, dull glaze. The pottery is still working and still making some of the original designs.

VAN BRIGGLE, Ashtray, Girl Kneading Bread, Ear of Corn 95.00
 Bookends, Indian Head, Turquoise 175.00

Bookends, Owl, Maroon	30.00
Bookends, Owl, Ming Blue	18.00
Bookends, Owl, Outspread Wings, Blue Matte	45.00
Bookends, Squirrel, Mulberry	95.00 To 110.00
Bowl & Flower Frog, Dragonflies, Maroon, 8 1/2 In.	95.00
Bowl, Blue & Pale Blue, 6 1/2 In.	95.00
Bowl, Turquoise, 4 1/2 In.	65.00
Bowl, With Flower Frog, Turquoise, 6 In.	45.00
Candleholder, Russet Leaf, Pair	25.00
Candlestick, Green, Brown Fluted Base, 1914	168.00
Candlestick, Leaf Shape, Pair	35.00
Candlestick, Oak Leaf, Green Overspray, Red, Pair	65.00
Conch Shell, White, 12 In.	40.00
Ewer, Turquoise, 11 1/2 In.	32.00
Figure, Cherub, Holding Cornucopia Vase, 9 In.	100.00
Figurine, Elephant, 3 1/2 In.	30.00
Figurine, Elephant, Dark Green, 4 1/2 X 7 In.	45.00
Figurine, Elephant, Tan, 3 X 4 In.	55.00
Figurine, Hopi Maiden	75.00
Figurine, Horse	45.00
Flower Frog, Colorado Springs	25.00
Flower Frog, Duck, Aqua	20.00
Flower Frog, Molded Leaf	45.00
Flower Frog, Turtle, Persian Rose	45.00
Lamp, Boudoir, Butterfly Pattern, Paper Labels, Pair	350.00
Lamp, Damsel of Damascus, Blue, Signed	95.00
Lamp, Damsel of Damascus, Double Marked	300.00
Lamp, Floral, Ming–Turquoise Glaze, Original Shade, 16 1/2 In.	185.00
Lamp, Lady of The Lake, Original Shade, Nellie Walker	750.00
Lamp, Natural Grasses, Butterfly Shade, 12 In.	125.00
Lamp, Rebecca At The Well, Moonglow Glaze, Shade	400.00
Paperweight, Rabbit	75.00
Pitcher, Acorn, Blue Salt Glaze	135.00
Pitcher, Grape Shield, Green On Yellow	150.00
Planter, Shell, 17 In.	50.00
Plaque, Indian, Turquoise, 4 3/4 In.	55.00
Plaque, Mermaid, 10 In.	65.00
Pot, Leaf, Honey Brown Glaze, 4 1/2 In.	250.00
Rose Bowl, Blown–Out Butterflies	40.00
Tile, Landscape Scene, Square, C.1909, 6 In.	350.00
Vase, Aqua Matte Glaze, 10 In.	95.00
Vase, Blue Over Rose, 22 In.	995.00
Vase, Brown & Green Daffodils, 9 3/4 In.	50.00
Vase, Butterfly Mold, Turquoise & Blue, 3 1/2 In.	27.50
Vase, Chocolate Brown & Green, 8 In.	45.00
Vase, Crocus, Plum, 5 In.	45.00
Vase, Florals, Tapered, Honey Brown, 1916, 6 In.	350.00
Vase, Green, 1901, 9 In.	2900.00
Vase, Green, Dated 1905, 3 1/2 In.	275.00
Vase, Heads of 3 Indian Men, 1930, 11 In.	265.00
Vase, Iris Design, C.1908, 10 In.	2530.00
Vase, Leaf Mold, Turquoise To Blue, 5 1/2 In.	27.50
Vase, Leaves & Vines, Green & Brown, 4 1/2 In.	28.00
Vase, Lorelei, Blue, 10 3/4 In.	210.00
Vase, Lorelei, Off–White, 10 1/2 In.	325.00
Vase, Ming, Stylized Flowers, Blue, Bulbous, 9 In.	125.00
Vase, Mulberry, Bulbous, Blue Outline, 4 1/2 In.	37.00
Vase, Peacock, Greenish Black Matte, 10 3/4 In.	4500.00
Vase, Persian Rose, 7 1/2 In.	60.00
Vase, Persian Rose, 8 In.	42.00
Vase, Raised Floral Design, Blue, 9 X 8 In.	85.00
Vase, Rosebud, 1914, 8 In.	210.00
Vase, Shell, Blue Green Shades, Marked, 3 3/4 X 8 In.	35.00
Vase, Stylized Flower, Turquoise, Signed & Dated 1918, 4 In.	35.00

If you are moving be sure to get special insurance coverage for damage to your antiques.

Vase, Turquoise, 3 1/2 In.	35.00
Vase, Twisted, Turquoise, 7 In.	30.00
Vase, White, Handles, 12 In.	85.00

Vasa Murrhina is the name of a glassware made by the Vasa Murrhina Art Glass Company of Sandwich, Massachusetts, about 1884. The glassware was transparent and was embedded with small pieces of colored glass and metallic flakes. Some of the pieces were cased. The same type of glass was made in England. Collectors often confuse Vasa Murrhina glass with aventurine, spatter, or spangle glass. There is much confusion about what actually was made by the Vasa Murrhina factory.

VASA MURRHINA, see also Spangle Glass

VASA MURRHINA, Basket, Autumn Orange, Handle, 11 In.	97.00
Basket, Aventurine Green, Blue, 11 In.	97.00
Basket, Ruffled, 6 1/2 X 8 In.	180.00
Bowl, Rose, 4 X 5 In.	75.00
Bowl, Scalloped, Tightly Crimped Edge, Gold Flecks, 9 1/4 In.	135.00
Bride's Bowl, Butterscotch To Opal, Crimped, V Handle, 13 In.	550.00
Creamer, Autumn Orange	65.00
Creamer, Aventurine Green	90.00
Ewer, Clear Handles, Gold Cased, 11 1/2 In., Pair	500.00
Jug, Blue	30.00
Pitcher, Water, Cranberry With Gold Mica, Ruffled	185.00
Toothpick, Gold Mica Flakes	195.00
Vase, Autumn Orange, 10 In.	138.00
Vase, Autumn Orange, 11 In.	85.00
Vase, Aventurine Diagonally Across, 14 1/2 X 7 In.	325.00
Vase, Aventurine Green, Blue 4 In.	25.00
Vase, Aventurine Green, Blue, 8 In.	45.00
Vase, Aventurine Green, Blue, 11 In.	82.00
Vase, Aventurine Green, Blue, 14 In.	95.00
Vase, Aventurine Green, Blue, Melon, 11 In.	85.00
Vase, Aventurine Green, Rose, Square, 7 In.	60.00
Vase, Blue Mist, 14 In.	90.00
Vase, Green & Blue, 4 In.	48.00
Vase, Melon, 8 In.	80.00
Vase, Ruffled Top, Mica Flecking, 9 1/2 In.	75.00
Vase, Silver Mica Exterior, Applied Rigaree, 7 1/2 In.	95.00

Vaseline glass is a greenish–yellow glassware resembling petroleum jelly. Some vaseline glass is still being made in old and new styles. Pressed glass of the 1870s was often made of vaseline–colored glass. Some pieces of vaseline glass may also be listed under Pressed Glass in this book.

VASELINE GLASS, Berry Set, Daisy & Button, Octagonal, 13 Piece	225.00
Butter, Cover, Cherry	38.50
Cake Stand, Cathedral, 10 X 4 In.	45.00
Candlestick, Dolphin, Pair	60.00
Candlestick, Petal & Loop, 7 In., Pair	300.00
Compote, Diamond–Quilted, Open, 9 X 6 1/2 In.	35.00
Compote, Fluted, 1891, 8 1/4 In.	225.00
Cruet Set, Pressed Optic, On Tray	235.00
Cruet, Column Block, Stopper	89.00
Dish, Kitten On Hamper Basket	49.00
Fruit Bowl, Rose Sprig, Pedestal, Oval	75.00
Fruit Set, Grape, Underplate, 5 Bowls	375.00
Mug, Button With V, VanDyke	36.00
Mug, Dewey, Greentown	60.00

Mustard, Cover, Hobnail, Opalescent	35.00
Pickle Jar, Cover, Pressed Diamond	45.00
Pitcher, Thumbprint, 6 In.	25.00
Salt & Pepper, Sunken Buttons, Pewter Lids	85.00
Sauce, Cathedral, 4 In.	20.00
Sauce, Pressed Diamond	14.00
Slipper, Daisy & Button	25.00
Spooner, Cathedral	50.00
Spooner, Daisy & Button	28.00
Spooner, Rope & Thumbprint	35.00
Sugar & Creamer, Hobnail, Opalescent	65.00
Sugar, Cover, Winged Scroll, Gold	35.00
Syrup, Cover, Bulging Midriff, Applied Twisted Handle	145.00
Syrup, Pilgrim Bottle	165.00
Toothpick	25.00
Tray, Daisy & Button, 10 X 12 In.	90.00
Tumbler, Diamond Point & Panels, Footed	325.00

Venetian glass has been made near Venice, Italy, from the thirteenth to the twentieth century. Thin, colored glass with applied decoration is favored, although many other types have been made.

VENETIAN GLASS, Candy Dish, Cover, Applied Rigaree, High Standard	45.00
Compote, Blue, Gold Flecked Ball Stem, Leaf Prunts, 8 In.	75.00
Figurine, Swan, Opalescent, Color, 8 In., Pair	35.00

Paolo Venini established a glass factory in Murano, Italy, in 1925. He is best known for pieces of modern design, including the famous "handkerchief" vase. The company is still working.

VENINI, Bowl, Opaque, 3 1/4 X 2 3/8 In.	85.00
Finger Bowl, Underplate, Latticinio, Pink, Pastels, 7 In.	150.00
Rose Bowl, Clear, Green Stained Top, 3 3/4 In.	90.00
Vase, Handkerchief, Latticinio, Brown–Orchid & White, 4 In.	190.00

Verlys glass was made in France after 1931. It was made in the United States from 1935 to 1951. The glass is either blown or molded. The American glass is signed with a diamond–point–scratched name, but the French pieces are marked with a molded signature. The designs resemble those used by Lalique.

VERLYS, Bowl, Bees, Large Sea Gulls, Signed, 11 1/2 In.	125.00
Bowl, Bluebird With Dragonflies, Marked, 12 In.	95.00 To 105.00
Bowl, Pine Cone, Blue, 1 1/2 X 6 In.	175.00
Bowl, Pine Cone, Frosted, 1 1/2 X 6 In.	60.00
Bowl, Tassel Pattern, Signed, 11 3/4 In.	135.00
Bowl, Wild Duck, Directoire Blue, 13 1/2 In.	270.00 To 275.00
Box, Opalescent Butterflies, Signed, Round, 7 In.	375.00
Charger, Iris, Blue Frosted, Signed, 14 In.	200.00
Charger, Poppies, Frosted, 14 In.	155.00
Charger, Water Lilies, 13 In.	95.00
Dish, Les Anemones, Scalloped, Blue, Signed, 5 1/4 In.	255.00
Figurine, Fish, Opalescent, Signed, 4 X 6 In.	75.00
Figurine, Rabbit, 9 In.	75.00
Plaque, 3 Raised Fantail Fish, Signed, 5 In.	55.00
Vase, Fan, Frosted Lovebirds, 4 1/2 X 6 1/2 In.	75.00 To 95.00
Vase, Four Seasons, Signed, Dated 1940, 8 1/2 In.	225.00
Vase, Gem, Brass Base, 6 3/4 In.	110.00
Vase, Maidens, Fruit Tree, Fire, Frosted, 8 1/2 In.	180.00

Vernon Potteries, Ltd., started in Vernon, California, in 1931. It became Vernon Kilns by 1948. The company made dinnerware and figurines until it closed in 1958. Collectors search for the brightly colored dinnerware and the pieces designed by Rockwell Kent, Walt Disney, and Don Blanding.

VERNON KILNS, Ashtray, New Mexico	20.00

Ashtray, Rhode Island, 5 1/2 In.	15.00
Bowl, Chowder, Homespun	6.00
Bowl, Flower, Light Blue	25.00
Bowl, Fluted, Blue–Gray, 12 In.	85.00
Bowl, Mixing, Organdie, 8 In.	21.00
Carafe, Cover, Organdie	25.00
Carafe, Tradewinds	10.00
Casserole, Cover, Organdie, 8 In.	25.00
Coffeepot, Hawaiian Flowers, Blue, Regular	50.00
Coffeepot, Southern Rose	45.00
Creamer, Mayflower, 4 In.	9.00
Cup & Saucer, Maroon & Blue, Demitasse	18.00
Cup & Saucer, Wheat, Demitasse	100.00
Mug, Homespun	7.00
Pitcher, Organdie, Bulbous, 1 Qt.	16.00
Plate, Baker's Chocolate, 10 1/2 In.	25.00
Plate, Clifton's, Los Angeles	7.00
Plate, Composer	20.00
Plate, Douglas MacArthur	15.00
Plate, Eisenhower	18.00
Plate, Franz Liszt	17.00
Plate, Georgia	4.50
Plate, Grand Caynon	9.00
Plate, Greetings, Austin Christmas, 10 In.	35.00
Plate, Hawaiian Flowers, Blue, 6 1/2 In.	12.50
Plate, Hawaiian Flowers, Blue, 10 1/2 In.	22.00
Plate, Holy Night, Christmas, 1975	10.00
Plate, Houston Engineers, 1951, 8 1/2 In.	30.00
Plate, Logging, 8 1/2 In.	32.00
Plate, Los Angeles	10.00
Plate, Our National Capitol, 10 In.	20.00
Plate, Remember Pearl Harbor	20.00
Plate, Republican Convention, 13 In.	59.00
Plate, Salamina, Rockwell Kent Design, 14 In.	135.00
Plate, Statue of Liberty, Bedloe's Island, Multicolor	40.00
Plate, Tulsa	8.00
Plate, Vicksburg, Miss.	4.50
Plate, Washington State, 4 3/8 In.	12.00
Plate, Will Rogers	15.00
Platter, California, Yellow, 12 1/2 In.	10.00
Platter, Flower Ballet, 14 In.	245.00
Platter, Organdie, Round, 14 In.	21.00
Salt & Pepper, Hop Low	130.00
Salt & Pepper, Maroon & Blue	18.00
Shaker, Winchester	20.00
Sugar, Cover, Casual California, Pink	10.00
Teapot, Hawaiian Flowers	65.00
Teapot, Organdie	30.00
Tidbit, Organdie, 2 Tiers	10.00
Tumbler, California, Orange, Bulb Bottom, 3 3/4 In.	18.00

 Verre de soie glass was first made by Frederick Carder at the Steuben Glass Works from about 1905 to 1930. It is an iridescent glass of soft white or very, very pale green. The name means glass of silk, and it does resemble silk. Other factories have made verre de soie, and some of the English examples were made of different colors. Verre de soie is an art glass and is not related to the iridescent, pressed, white Carnival glass mistakenly called by its name.

VERRE DE SOIE, see also Steuben

VERRE DE SOIE, Compote, Blue Trim, Teardrop Stem, 6 In., Pair	620.00
Cruet, Silver Lid, Steuben	295.00
Perfume Bottle, Bristol Yellow Trim, 10 In.	325.00
Powder Box, Bristol Yellow Trim, 8 In.	300.00

Vase, Allover Wheel Engraved Floral, Signed, 8 1/4 In.	175.00
Vase, Ruffled Rim, Stretched, Steuben, 6 1/4 In.	175.00

Vienna Art plates are round metal serving trays produced at the turn of the century. The designs, copied from Royal Vienna porcelain plates, usually featured a portrait of a woman encircled by a wide, ornate border. Many were used as advertising or promotional items and were produced in Coshocton, Ohio, by J.F. Meeks Tuscarora Advertising Co. and H.D. Beach's Standard Advertising Co.

VIENNA ART, Plate, Dr Pepper	300.00
Plate, Lady With Urn	55.00
Plate, Mythical Scenes, Pair	65.00
Plate, Nude	125.00

VIENNA, see Beehive

The Villeroy & Boch Pottery of Mettlach was founded in 1841. The firm made many types of pottery, including the famous Mettlach steins. It is confusing for the collector because although Villeroy and Boch made most of its pieces in the city of Mettlach, Germany, they also had factories in other locations. There is a dating code impressed on the bottom of most pieces that makes it possible to determine the age of the piece.

VILLEROY & BOCH, see also Mettlach

VILLEROY & BOCH, Figurine, Dante & Beatrice, Anchor Mark, Pair	125.00
Figurine, Penguin, Ivory, Paper Label, 6 In.	20.00
Pitcher, Dresden Pattern, Red Flower, Green Leaves	42.00
Pitcher, Mephistopheles, Men Playing Cards, 10 1/2 In.	85.00
Plaque, Boat Scene, Blue & White, Matte, 10 1/4 In.	85.00
Plaque, Mother's Day, 1979	85.00
Plate, Magical Fairy Tales	65.00
Plate, Snow Maiden, 6 1/2 In.	45.00
Stein Set, Four Seasons, 1 Liter, Box, 4 Piece	695.00
Sugar, Wild Onion	35.00
Tea Set, Green Floral On White, 3 Piece	45.00
Tile, Abstract Compass Design, Tan & Brown	15.00
Tray, Sandwich, Le Balloon	32.00

Volkmar pottery was made by Charles Volkmar of New York from 1879 to about 1911. He was associated with several firms, including the Volkmar Ceramic Company, Volkmar and Cory, and Charles Volkmar and Son. Volkmar had been a painter, and his designs often look like oil paintings drawn on pottery.

VOLKMAR, Plaque, Blue & White, 12 In.	250.00
Tankard, Glossy Green, 8 In.	275.00

Volkstadt was a soft-paste porcelain manufactory started in 1760 by Georg Heinrich Macheleid at Volkstadt, Thuringia. Volkstadt-Rudolstadt was a porcelain factory started at Volkstadt-Rudolstadt by Beyer and Bock in 1890. Most pieces seen in shops today are from the later factory.

VOLKSTADT, Figurine, Canova Woman, 6 In.	160.00
Figurine, Canova Woman, Girl In Print Dress, Red Hair, 6 In.	140.00
Figurine, Dachshund, 7 3/4 In.	360.00
Figurine, Man & Woman, Seated, Chess Game Table, 6 X 9 In.	950.00
Figurine, Portrait Painter, Woman With Fan, Seated Artist, 9 In.	525.00
Figurine, St. Bernard, Lying, 12 In.	165.00
Figurine, Woman, 18th-Century Clothes, C.1850, 7 3/4 In.	465.00
Group, 2 Women & 1 Man, Musical Instruments, 9 1/2 X 9 In.	1050.00
Group, Wedding March, Bride & Groom, 2 Girls, Boy, 9 X 13 In.	1250.00

WALLACE NUTTING photographs are listed under Print, Nutting. His reproduction furniture is listed under Furniture.

If the name "England" (or that of some other country) appears, the dish was made after 1891, but it may have been made as early as 1887. The words "made in England" (or some other country) indicate the piece was made after 1914.

Frederich Walrath was a potter who worked in New York City, Rochester, New York, and at the Newcomb Pottery in New Orleans, Louisiana. He died in 1920. Pieces listed here are from his Rochester period.

WALRATH, Candlestick, Brown & Green, 4 1/2 In.	250.00
Mug	25.00

WALT DISNEY, see Disneyana
WALTER, see A. Walter

Warwick china was made in Wheeling, West Virginia, in a pottery working from 1887 to 1951. Many pieces were made with hand painted or decal decorations. The most familiar Warwick has a shaded brown background. The name "Warwick" is part of the mark and sometimes the word "IOGA" is also included.

WARWICK, Ale Set, Picture of Monk With 4 Mugs, Brown & Red, 1890, 5 Piece	295.00
Cake & Ice Cream Set, Cherries On White, 7 Piece	80.00
Chocolate Set, Hibiscus, 7 Piece	275.00
Mug, Black Man, Floppy Hat, Playing Guitar	195.00
Mug, Dickens Character, IOGA, 4 1/2 In.	125.00
Mug, Friar, Brown, Flowers	115.00
Mustard, 1933	40.00
Pitcher, B.P.O.E., 10 1/2 In.	130.00
Pitcher, Blue Flowers, Cream	60.00
Pitcher, Cream, Blue Flowers, Gold Trim	70.00
Pitcher, Elk & Clock, B.P.O.E., Brown Ground, IOGA, 10 1/2 In.	195.00
Pitcher, Handle, 13 In.	95.00
Pitcher, Lemonade, Woman Decal, IOGA, 7 In.	50.00
Pitcher, Milk, Currants On Brown, Melon Ribbed, Scalloped Rim	85.00
Pitcher, Monk, Browns, Red Hat	125.00
Plate, Fish, IOGA, 8 1/2 In.	100.00
Tankard, Brown Chrysanthemums, IOGA, 11 In.	75.00
Tankard, Hooded Monk Drinking Ale, Brown, 11 In.	225.00
Tray, Pin, Poppy, 7 X 11 1/2 In.	48.00
Vase, Debutante Decal, IOGA, 10 1/2 In.	175.00
Vase, Floral Design, IOGA, 11 In.	95.00
Vase, Indian, Headdress, Shaded Brown Ground, IOGA, 12 1/4 In.	425.00
Vase, Portrait, Woman, Matte Finish, 10 In.	130.00
Vase, Portrait, Young Woman, Charcoal Ground, IOGA, 12 1/2 In.	225.00
Vase, Red Floral, Brown & White, IOGA, 10 In., Pair	275.00
Vase, Woman In Cap Decal, Bouquet Shape, Twig Handles	135.00
Vase, Woman With White Rose, Twig Handles, IOGA, 11 1/2 In.	125.00

Watch fobs were worn on watch chains. They were popular during Victorian times and after. Many styles, especially advertising designs, are still made today.

WATCH FOB, Alaska Pacific Steamship Co.	45.00
Allis Chalmers Harvester	50.00

American Bowling Congress, 1918	14.00
American Cash Register	18.00
American Chain & Cable Co., Brass	20.00
American Legion, 1937	15.00
AOUW, Enamel, Gold–Filled	65.00
Athelstan Lodge, Worcester, Mass., 1865	40.00
Aultman Tayler, Rooster, Brass	65.00
Avery, Bulldog	65.00
Avery, Tractor	65.00
Banting Machine Co., Buffalo, Pittsburgh	35.00
Bell Roasted Coffee, Strap, Brass	55.00
Billiken, Dated 1925	15.00
Billiken, Ivory, Chain	85.00
Biston's Gold Grain Coffee, Shape of Coffee Bean, Brass	95.00
Bluescher Band Instruments	28.00
Buick, Porcelain	55.00
Bull Durham, 14K Gold	35.00
Bulldog, Avery	75.00
Case, Tractor	55.00
Cody, Wyoming	10.00
Compass, Framed In 14K Yellow Gold	95.00
Connecticut, 1925	22.00
Cook Equipment Co., Caterpillar, Des Moines, Mason City	17.50
Curtis Publishing Co.	22.50
DeLaval Advertising, Leather Strap	85.00
DeLaval, Enamel	95.00
Diston Keystone Saw Works, Enameled	50.00
Dr Pepper, Billiken	115.00
DuPont, Presentation, Sterling Silver	95.00
E–Z Ola Polish, Brass	28.00
ELCAR, A Well–Built Car, Elkhart, Ind., 1916	75.00
Engman–Matthew Range, Cutout Design of Range	65.00
Euclid Bulldozer	22.00
Exchange National Bank	22.00
Fish Bros., Clinton, Iowa	45.00
Frost King Gasoline	75.00
Gallion Graders & Rollers	28.50
Gallion Roller	38.00
Gearench Mfg. Co., Forged Steel Wrench, Houston	15.00
General Warren, 1913	50.00
Geo. Miller, Engines	60.00
Gold Wash, Signet Type, C.1912	25.00
Golden Grain Rye	35.00
Green River Whiskey, Horseshoe	35.00
Green River, Strap	45.00
Habana Cigars, Bulldog Shape, With Cigar Cutter, Bronze	75.00
Harley–Davidson Motorcycle	150.00
Heinz 57, Nickel & Brass	85.00
Heydt Bakery, St. Louis	17.50
Horseshoe Charm, Red Stone, 1888, 12 In.	50.00
Illinois State Undertakers Association, Strap, 1907	30.00
Ingersoll Jackbits, Man With Jackhammer, Pewter	25.00
Inter–Southern Life Insurance Co., Louisville, Brass	25.00
International Harvester, Century of The Reaper	27.50
IOOF	25.00
J.I. Case, Oval, Eagle On Globe, Brass	125.00
Jacob Dold Hams & Bacon, Wichita, Kansas	25.00
Keck–Gonnerman, Oval, Brass	265.00
Kellogg's Toasted Corn Flakes, Cereal Box Shape	65.00
Keystone Watch Case Co., Opener, Columbian Exposition	22.50
Knights of Malta, 14K Gold, Onyx, Enamel	150.00
Knights of Pythias, Cross, Swords, Diamonds & Rubies	175.00
La Salle Extension University, Gilded	24.00
Lion's Stock Remedy, Livestock Remedy Co., Celluloid	65.00

Miles City Saddlery Co., Miles City, Montana, Leather Strap 100.00
Miller Beer, Girl On Moon, Porcelain 85.00
Moss Agate, Hinged Yellow Gold Frame 85.00
Napoleon Flour, Strap 65.00
New York Life Insurance Co., 200, 000 Club, Bronze, 1926 .... 30.00
New York State Fair, Syracuse, Sept. 12, 1921 .... 20.00
Old Dutch Cleanser, Dutch Lady In Center, Porcelain 65.00
Olds Motor Works, Car, Enameled 85.00
Pabst Brewing Co., Enameled 125.00
Paplin Orendoff Agriculture Implements, Woman & Plow, Brass 45.00
Peck Bros., Bull & Pig 35.00
Peters Weatherbird Shoes, Enameled 45.00
Philadelphia Lawn Mower Co., Golfer, Nickel Over Brass 45.00
Pierce Arrow, Enameled 95.00
Pope Pius XI, 1925 .... 38.50
Porter Hay Carrier, Carrier In Center, Scrolled Shield 140.00
Red Diamond Overalls .... 17.50 To 27.50
Red Goose Shoes, Oval, Enameled Goose 85.00
Red Owl Coal, Porcelain Owl Insert, Nickel Over Brass 85.00
San Francisco Earthquake 25.00
Savage Semi–Automatic Pistol 135.00
Scher Band Instruments, Blue 28.00
Sheep Union Stockyards 35.00
Star Ball Bearings 30.00
Sterling Mfg., Hay Loader & Rake 75.00
Travelers Insurance Co., Ticket Department, Train, Strap 75.00
Travelers Insurance, 1914 .... 24.00
Trojan Powder Co. .... 52.00 To 85.00
United Mine Workers, Enameled 55.00
Weatherbird Shoes 75.00
With Hair Watch Chain 65.00
Women's Auxiliary, Sons Veterans, 1883, Crossed Cannon, Strap 55.00
Women's Auxiliary, Sons, Veterans, 1883, Crossed Cannon, Strap 55.00

The pocket watch was important in Victorian times because it was
not until World War I that the wristwatch was used. All types of
watches are collected: silver, gold, or plated. Watches are listed by
company name or by style. Pocket watches are listed here.
Wristwatches are listed in their own category.

WATCH, Accutron, Pocket, Ohio State University On Dial, Gold Filled 150.00
Admiral, Pendant, Woman's, Gold Filled, Ornate 100.00
Alaska Air Lines 10.00
American Watch Co., Coin Silver Case, Key Wind, C.1866 .... 225.00
American Watch Co., Sterling, Roman Numerals, White Face 125.00
Ansonia, Sun, Brass 40.00
Aristocrat, Railroad Special, Train On Back 15.00
Arrow Watch Co., 17 Jewel ....80.00 To 100.00
Art Deco, Platinum & Diamond, Gebelin, 17 Jewel ....*Illus* 800.00
Atlantic, Gold–Filled, 21 Jewel, Ornate 100.00
Ball, 19 Jewel, 14K White Gold–Filled Case 200.00
Boston Watch Co., Gold–Filled Hunting Case 200.00
Breitling Laederich, Silver Hunting Case, Key Wind, Key Set 115.00
Burlington, Gold Filled, Monogrammed Case, 21 Jewel, Size 16 In. 185.00
Burlington, Railroad, 19 Jewel, Open Face, 5 Positions 150.00
Charles LeRoy, Enameled, 18K Gold, 1770–90 .... 2585.00
Child's, Kellogg's, 4 Faces, Tony, Toucan Sam, Dig Em, Poppy 35.00
Chromographe–Compteur, Horse Racing, Silver Case 125.00
Chronograph, Sandoz, Jockey Club, German Silver Case, Pat. 1890 .... 185.00
Dueber, 18K Gold, Box Hinged Case, Large, C.1890 .... 450.00
Dueber, Box Hinged Case, 10K Gold, C.1890 .... 750.00
Dueber, Engraved Coin Silver Hunting Case, 15 Jewel 95.00
Dueber, Hampden, Railroad, Size 16, 14K Gold, Pocket 400.00
E. Howard, Hunting Case, Gold Filled, 15 Jewel, 1890 .... 675.00
Edgemere, Woman's, 14K Gold, Birds & Flowers 395.00

Watch, English, Pocket,
Village Scene, Key
Wind, 18K Gold

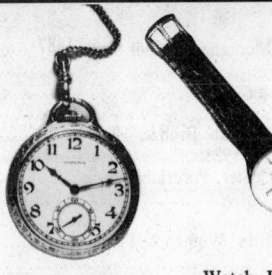

Watch, Hamilton,
Pocket, Floral Case,
19 Jewel, 1930

Watch, Patek
Philippe, 18K Gold

Watch, Art Deco, Platinum
& Diamond, Gebelin, 17 Jewel

Elgin, 15 Jewel, Multicolored Dial, Rose Gold	275.00
Elgin, 19 Jewel, Open Face, 20 Year	75.00
Elgin, 21 Jewel, Adjusted 5 Positions, 14K Gold	250.00
Elgin, Art Deco, Black, Chrome	65.00
Elgin, Clam Shell Hunter, 14K Gold	725.00
Elgin, Embossed Back, Open Face, Sterling Case	150.00
Elgin, Enameled Birds, Flowers, House Case, Gold Filled, 1888	350.00
Elgin, Engraved Bluebird, Hunting Case, 14K Gold	165.00
Elgin, Engraved Buck's Head, Gold–Filled Case	55.00
Elgin, Floral Hunting Case, Multicolored Dial, 25 Year Case	200.00
Elgin, Hunting Case, 14K Gold, Size 6	750.00
Elgin, Hunting Case, Key Wind, 9K Gold	175.00
Elgin, Hunting Case, No.1907178, 14K Gold, Size 16, 22 Jewel, 1885	1650.00
Elgin, Hunting Case, Rose Gold, 15 Jewel, Multicolor Dial	275.00
Elgin, Key Wind & Set, G.M. Wheeler, 1880	175.00
Elgin, Key Wind, Coin Silver Case	375.00
Elgin, Woman's, Hunting Case, 15 Jewel	125.00
England, Fusee, Sterling, Key Wind, Lever Set, 1862, Size 18	170.00
English, Pocket, Village Scene, Key Wind, 18K Gold ....*Illus*	320.00
Equality Watch Co., Size 16	45.00
Geneva, Railroad, Gold Filled	85.00
Gruen, 19 Jewel, Open Face, 14K Gold	275.00
Gruen, Veri Thin, Gold Filled, 25 Year Case	100.00
Gruen, Yellow Gold Filled, 17 Jewel	85.00
Hamilton, 16 Jewel, Hunting Case, Sterling Silver	1000.00
Hamilton, 16 Jewel, Hunting Case, Sterling Silver, Grade 933	975.00
Hamilton, 19 Jewel, Eagle & American Flag On Case	250.00
Hamilton, 2 Hour Dial, Star Case	135.00
Hamilton, 20 Year Model, Gold Filled	225.00
Hamilton, 21 Jewel, 5 Positions, Gold Filled	185.00
Hamilton, 23 Jewel, 14K White Gold	550.00
Hamilton, Chronometer, 21 Jewel, Adjusted To 6 Positions	550.00
Hamilton, Chronometer, 21 Jewel, Wind Indicator	550.00
Hamilton, Chronometer, 21 Jewel, Wind Indicator, 56 Hours	475.00
Hamilton, Chronometer, 6 Positions, Wind Indicator, 56 Hours	600.00
Hamilton, Model 932, Coin Silver Case	1400.00
Hamilton, Pocket, Floral Case, 19 Jewel, 1930 ....*Illus*	250.00
Hamilton, Railroad, 21 Jewel, 5 Positions, Glass Back, C.1899	165.00
Hamilton, Railroad, 21 Jewel, See–Through Glass Back	250.00
Hamilton, Railroad, 21 Jewel, Size 16	225.00
Hamilton, Railroad, Lever Set, Gold Filled, C.1917	175.00
Hamilton, Railway Special, 992B, 21 Jewel	175.00
Hampden Watch Co., Key Wind, C.1884	175.00
Hampden, 17 Jewel, Adjustable Special Railway, Gold Filled	125.00
Hampden, General Stark, 17 Jewel, Engraved Hunting Case	225.00
Hampden, Key Wind & Set, C.1884	175.00 To 200.00
Hampden, Key Wind, Open Face, Silver Case	75.00
Hampden, Lever Set, 25 Year, Train On Case, 14K Gold, C.1887	225.00

Hampden, Railroad, 14K Gold, Lever Set, Ornate Train Case, 1887 .... 225.00
Hampden, Railroad, No.105 .... 135.00
Harman, With Alarm, Swiss 115.00
Honeycomb Cereal 22.00
Howard, 15 Jewel, Gold Filled, Hunting Case, C.1890 .... 675.00
Howard, 18K Gold, Hunter Case 1800.00
Howard, Abbott Sure Time, Scenic & Floral Hunting Case 300.00
Howard, Chronometer, Series II, 21 Jewel 400.00
Howard, Engine Room, 15 Jewel, C.1900, 10 3/4 In. 950.00
Howard, G Series, Multicolor Box, Hunting Case 1500.00
Howard, Luminous Dial & Hands 165.00
Illinois, 17 Jewel, 14K White Gold–Filled Case, C.1920 ....90.00 To 125.00
Illinois, 21 Jewel, 14K White Gold–Filled, C.1920 .... 150.00
Illinois, 21 Jewel, Adjustable To 3 Positions, White Gold 135.00
Illinois, 21 Jewel, Bunn Special R.R., Lever Set, C.1909 .... 165.00
Illinois, 21 Jewel, Burlington Watch Co. 275.00
Illinois, 21 Jewel, White Gold–Filled Case, C.1920 .... 150.00
Illinois, Bunn Special, 21 Jewel 200.00
Illinois, Bunn Special, 24 Jewel, Sterling Silver 600.00
Illinois, Bunn, Ruby Jewel, Gold Case, 6 Positions 1000.00
Illinois, C.& O. Special, Silver Train Case 650.00
Illinois, Chesapeake & Ohio, 17 Jewel 600.00
Illinois, Coin Silver Hunting Case, 1876 .... 150.00 To 200.00
Illinois, Key Wind & Set, Low Serial Number, C.1872 .... 250.00
Illinois, Sangamo, 23 Jewel, Open Face 325.00
Ingersoll, New York To Paris, Airplane On Dial & Back Cover 300.00
Ingersoll, Reliance, Design On Back, Chain 100.00
Ingersoll–Trenton, 19 Jewel, See–Through Glass Back 300.00
Ingraham, Dollar, Made For Graf Zeppelin, 1931 .... 250.00
Jules Jurgensen .... 300.00 To 375.00
Lawrey's Beef Jerky 55.00
Little King 125.00
Longines, 17 Jewel, 14K Solid Gold 250.00
Lord Elgin, 10K Gold Filled, Black Face, 1930s, Box 125.00
Movado, Chronometer, Rose Gold & Enameled Case, Purse 500.00
Nathan, Bond Street, 17 Jewel 65.00
Non–Magnetic Watch Co., 15 Jewel, Paillard 250.00
Non–Magnetic Watch Co., Hunting Case, Enameled, Size 0 .... 1000.00
Omega, 15 Jewel, 20 Year Hunting Case ....90.00 To 150.00
Omega, 15 Jewel, 24 Hour Dial, Silveroid, C.1910 .... 75.00
Omega, Automatic Seamaster, Gold–Filled Case 95.00
Omega, Open Face, Gold–Filled Case, Gold–Filled Chain 225.00
P.S. Barnett, Silver, Key Wind & Set, C.1866, Size 18 .... 185.00
Packard 135.00
Patek Philippe, 18K Gold ....Illus 1700.00
Patek Philippe, Pendant, Diamond Set Clover, 18K Gold Case, C.1897 .... 4250.00
Pep Bros. 95.00
Piaget, 7 Jewel, 18K Gold, Hunter, Key Wind, Ornate 600.00
Pillsbury 54.50
Pocket, Hollister of Greenfield, Mass., Roxbury, 1862 .... 650.00
Poitevin, 21 Ruby Jewels, Exposed Ruby Pallets, 18K Gold ....900.00 To 1450.00
Railroad, Santa Fe, 21 Jewel, 1920 .... 275.00
Rockford, Key Wind, Hunting Case 295.00
Rockford, Porcelain Case 300.00
Sears , Roebuck, Special, Hunting Case 350.00
South Bend, 19 Jewel, Adjusted To 4 Positions .... 185.00 To 200.00
South Bend, 21 Jewel, 25 Year, Gold Case, C.1913 .... 150.00
South Bend, 21 Jewel, 5 Positions, 25 Year Case 225.00
South Bend, 21 Jewel, Adjusted To 5 Positions, 14K Gold 250.00
South Bend, Polaris, 14K Gold 850.00
Spaulding, Open Face, Gold Filled 110.00
Tiffany, Open Face, 18K Gold 750.00
Tremont Watch Co., Open Face Coin Silver Case 290.00
Vacheron & Constantine, 21 Jewel, Micrometer Regulator 1050.00

Waltham, 16 Jewel, Silveroid, C.1902	85.00
Waltham, 17 Jewel, Chain	100.00
Waltham, 21 Jewel, Gold Filled	100.00
Waltham, 23 Jewel, 8 Positions, 10K Gold–Filled Case	275.00
Waltham, Canadian Pacific Logo On Movement	325.00
Waltham, Coin Silver Hunting Case, Porcelain Dial, C.1898	85.00
Waltham, Pendant, Woman's, Neck Chain, C.1918	155.00
Waltham, Railroad, Lever Set, Gold Filled, C.1907	165.00
Waltham, Riverside Maximus, 23 Jewel, Gold Gear Wheels	1500.00
Waltham, Riverside, Railroad, 21 Jewel	125.00
Waltham, Size 18	35.00
Waltham, Skeletonized Movement, Train On Back	200.00
Waltham, Wm. Ellery, Open Face, 7 Jewel, Gold Filled, 1885	85.00
Waltham, Woman's, 15 Jewel, 20 Year, Gold Case	100.00
Waltham, Woman's, 5 Diamonds On Back, Half–Moon & Star	350.00
Westclox, Scotty, Metal Base, Magnet Bottom	20.00
Woman's, Gold Case, Flowers & Birds On Back, C.1890	125.00

Waterford–type glass resembles the famous glass made from 1783 to 1851 in the Waterford Glass Works in Ireland. It is a clear glass that was often decorated by cutting. Modern glass is being made again in Waterford, Ireland, and is marketed under the name "Waterford."

WATERFORD, Basket, Bright Cut Silver Mounts, Shaped Rim, 11 In.	225.00
Champagne, Eileen, 8 Piece	325.00
Cordial, Rosslore, 4 In.	20.00
Jar, Oval, Ornate Gilded Brass Frame & Lid, Marked, 7 In.	335.00
Lamp, Electric, Kerosene Style, Sticker, 27 In.	275.00
Punch Set, Diamond Cut, Wreath Border, 12–In. Bowl, 12 Cups	2300.00
Sugar & Creamer, C.1940	60.00
Tumbler, Maureen	20.00

The Watt family bought the Globe pottery of Crooksville, Ohio, in 1922. They made pottery mixing bowls and dishes of the type made by Globe. In 1935 they changed the production and made the pieces with the freehand decorations that are popular with collectors today. Apple, Starflower, Rooster, Red & Blue Tulip, and Autumn Foliage are the best–known patterns. Apple, the most popular pattern, can be dated from the leaves. Originally, the apples had three leaves; after 1958 two leaves were used. The plant closed in 1965.

WATT, Baker, Apple, No.96	18.50
Bean Pot, Apple, No.76	55.00
Bowl Set, Apple, No.5, 6, 7, 8	95.00
Bowl Set, Apple, No.63, 64, 65	100.00
Bowl, Apple, No. 5	35.00
Bowl, Apple, No. 7	35.00
Bowl, Apple, No.14	22.00
Bowl, Apple, No.64	18.00
Bowl, Apple, No.65	35.00
Bowl, Apple, No.73	40.00
Bowl, Apple, No.74, 5 1/2 In.	15.00
Bowl, Bleeding Heart, No.74, 5 1/2 In.	15.00
Bowl, Dutch Tulip, Cover, No.66	85.00
Bowl, Eagle, No.8, Maroon	55.00
Bowl, Green Band, Red Flowers & Cherries, 6 In.	20.00
Bowl, Rooster, No.8	45.00
Bowl, Spaghetti, Apple, No.39	55.00
Bowl, Spaghetti, Autumn Foliage, No.39	50.00
Bowl, Spaghetti, Pansy	45.00
Bowl, Tulip, No.65	55.00
Casserole, Apple, No.110	40.00
Casserole, Cover, Apple, No.96	35.00 To 65.00
Casserole, Cover, Starflower, No.18	35.00
Casserole, Eagle, No.601	150.00

Coffee Mug, Apple	85.00
Cookie Jar, Cover, Apple, No.76	50.00
Cookie Jar, Cover, Tulip, No.76	70.00
Creamer, Apple, No.62 .... 35.00 To 45.00
Creamer, Pennsylvania Dutch, No.62 .... 55.00 To 75.00
Creamer, Starflower, No.62	40.00
Creamer, Tulip	45.00
Ice Bucket, Apple, No.59	95.00
Ice Bucket, Cover, Rooster, No.59	125.00
Mug, Apple, No.501	100.00
Mug, Starfire, No.501	45.00
Nappy, Apple, No.7	32.00
Pie Plate, Apple, Advertising .... 65.00 To 95.00
Pitcher, Apple, No.15 .... 15.50 To 85.00
Pitcher, Apple, No.16 .... 25.00 To 45.00
Pitcher, Apple, No.17 .... 95.00 To 96.00
Pitcher, Apple, No.62 .... 15.00 To 38.00
Pitcher, Bleeding Heart, No.15 .... 18.00 To 25.00
Pitcher, Cherry, No.15	35.00
Pitcher, Dogwood, No.15	60.00
Pitcher, Morning Glory, No.96	32.00
Pitcher, Pansy, No.15	39.50
Pitcher, Pennsylvania Dutch, No.15	75.00
Pitcher, Rooster, No.15 .... 20.00 To 60.00
Pitcher, Rooster, No.16, Advertising .... 30.00 To 55.00
Pitcher, Rooster, No.62, Advertising	64.00
Pitcher, Starflower, No.15 .... 32.50 To 35.00
Pitcher, Starflower, No.16 .... 30.00 To 35.00
Pitcher, Starflower, No.17	50.00
Pitcher, Tulip, No.15	60.00
Pitcher, Tulip, No.16 .... 55.00 To 75.00
Pitcher, Tulip, No.17 ....85.00 To 110.00
Salt & Pepper, Apple .... 125.00 To 225.00
Sugar, Apple, No.98	70.00

WAVE CREST WARE

Wave Crest glass is a white glassware manufactured by the Pairpoint Manufacturing Company of New Bedford, Massachusetts, and some French factories. It was decorated by the C. F. Monroe Company of Meriden, Connecticut. The glass was painted in pastel colors and decorated with flowers. The name "Wave Crest" was used after 1898.

WAVE CREST, Ashtray, Gold Club & Ball On Rim, Blue Flowers, 4 1/4 In.	355.00
Biscuit Jar, Egg Crate, Flowers, Cover & Handle, 10 3/4 In.	475.00
Biscuit Jar, Pink & Coral Flowers, Cream Ground, Barrel Shape	325.00
Biscuit Jar, Robins, Blue Glass	300.00
Biscuit Jar, Windmills, Plated Fittings, 10 In.	750.00
Box, Cigar, Egg Crate, Large	675.00
Box, Collars & Cuffs, 7 In.	675.00
Box, Cover, Scenic, Square, 3 X 3 1/2 In.	3300.00
Box, Dresser, Double Round, Gilt Metal Mounts, 3 X 5 1/4 In.	135.00
Box, Dresser, Yellow Daisies, Pink Ground, Lavender Scrolling	120.00
Box, Egg Crate, Pink Mums, 3 X 3 In.	155.00
Box, Farm Scene Cover, Embossed, Signed, 4 1/4 In.	395.00
Box, Hinged Cover, Bachelor Buttons, Puffy Swirls, 5 1/2 In.	240.00
Box, Hinged Cover, Cigar Band, Clear	450.00
Box, Hinged Cover, Enameled Flowers, White, Brass Trim, 3 X 3 In.	325.00
Box, Holds Deck of Cards, Niagara Falls, Blue Ground	395.00
Box, Jewelry, Baroque Shell, 4 In.	325.00
Box, Lily of The Valley	150.00
Box, Quilted, Pink Flowers, Green, 3 X 3 In.	295.00
Box, Rococo Cover, Inside Mirror, Scrolling, Signed, 4 X 7 In.	875.00
Box, White Daisies, Pink Ground, Pink Lining, 3 X 5 3/4 In.	700.00
Casket, Jewelry, Open, Ormolu Trim	220.00
Dish, Florals, Handles, On Brass Stem, 5 1/2 In.	140.00

Ewer, Hand Painted Florals, Ormolu Trim, Tall	110.00
Fernery, Cut Glass, Silver-Plated Rim, Large	110.00
Fernery, Enameled Blue Daisies, Ring Handled Insert, Signed	325.00
Holder, Brush, Ormolu Mount	975.00
Holder, Cigarette & Match	675.00
Holder, Toothbrush, Tooth Powder Box, Pomade Box, Brass Lids	1250.00
Holder, Whiskbroom, Lined	725.00
Humidor, Tobacco, Blue Florals, Purple Lettering, 5 1/4 In.	550.00
Ice Bucket, Wild Roses, Blue Ground, 13 1/4 In.	1000.00
Jam Jar, Pink Apple Blossoms, Dotted White Centers	495.00
Jar, Dresser, Swirl Floral, Hinged Cover, Brass Collar, 3 In.	225.00
Jar, Pomade, Embossed Design, Small	325.00
Jardiniere, Pink & Gold Flowers, Cream, Cupid Feet, 8 1/2 In.	750.00
Letter Holder, Brass Edge, Black Mark	250.00
Match Box, Cover	395.00
Salt & Pepper, Allover Rococo Scrolls, Hand Painted Mums	160.00
Salt & Pepper, Leaf Spear	85.00
Sugar & Creamer, Cover, Bird On Fence, Blue Flowers, Pink Ground	195.00
Sugar & Creamer, Pink Rosebuds, Tan & White Swirl	635.00
Sugar Shaker, Helmschmeid Swirl	480.00
Syrup, Annie Written In Gold, Bird Finial, Pink Bottom	350.00
Syrup, Hand Painted Florals, Pewter Lid, Bird Finial, 1872	650.00
Table Set, Syrup, Spooner, Sugar & Creamer, 4 Piece	495.00
Tobacco Jar, Pink Flower, Sponge Holder In Lid, Word Tobacco	525.00
Toothpick, Enameled Daisy, Dotted Rim, Ormolu Pedestal Base	395.00
Toothpick, Floral, Ormolu Footed	215.00
Toothpick, Floral, Ormolu Footed Base, Marked	285.00
Tray, Jewel, Medallions, Shasta Daisies, Signed, 10 1/2 In.	395.00
Vase, Blue Flowers, Blush Pink, Signed, 7 In.	400.00
Vase, Blue Flowers, Pink Panels, Ormolu Base, Signed, 7 1/2 In.	400.00
Vase, Embossed Ships, Pink Ground, Footed, 12 In.	735.00
Vase, Flowers, White, Brass Throat, Handles, Black Mark, 3 1/2 In.	150.00
Vase, Orchids Allover, Green, Marked, 11 In.	600.00

 The earliest American weather vanes were used in seventeenth-century Boston. The direction of the wind was an indication of coming weather, important to the seafaring and farming communities. By the mid-ninteenth century, commercial weather vanes were made of metal. Today's collectors often consider weather vanes to be examples of folk art, even though they may not have been handmade.

WEATHER VANE, 2 Men In Boat, Sperm Whale, Carved, Metal Base, 1925, 46 In.	1870.00
3 Flying Geese, Arrow, Directionals, Wrought Iron, 36 In.	65.00
American Eagle, Full-Bodied, Outspread Wings, Copper, 14 In.	550.00
Antique Car & Driver	300.00
Cock, Copper, 19th Century, Small	2700.00
Cock, Strutting, Copper, Traces of Gold Leaf, 1830, 18 1/2 In.	4250.00
Cock, Tin Tail Feathers, Wooden, 20 In.	935.00
Cow, Gilded Copper, C.1800, 28 1/2 In.	3700.00
Cow, Silhouette, Sheet Iron, C.1890, 19 X 20 In.	350.00
Dexter, Running, Full-Bodied, Copper, 11 X 27 In.	715.00
Eagle, 36-In. Wingspread, 19th Century	1700.00
Eagle, On Globe, Outstretched Wings, Copper, 1800, 31 X 35 In.	1980.00
Eagle, On Orb, Brass Arrow, Full-Bodied, Directionals	985.00
Ethan Allen, Full-Bodied, Molded Copper, Harris, 17 X 31 In.	3200.00
Fish, Wooden, Red Paint, 31 1/2 In.	175.00
Gabriel, Blowing Horn, Cutout	1100.00
Gabriel, Sailor's Angel, Red & White, 19th Century, 41 1/2 In.	2600.00
Gamecock, On Arrow, Ball, Directionals, L.W. Cushing, 49 In.	6250.00
Grasshopper, Sheet Iron	1870.00
Hackney, Directionals & Standard, Sheet Zinc	1750.00

Horse & Sulky, Copper, 19th Century, 34 In. 1980.00
Horse, Full–Bodied, Yellow Paint, Copper, 25 X 34 In. 4950.00
Horse, Jockey, Full–Bodied, Copper, 14 1/2 X 26 1/4 In. 2640.00
Horse, Prancing, Silhouette, Sheet Iron, 19th Century, 34 In. 885.00
Horse, Running, Blackhawk, C.1880 .... 3950.00
Horse, Running, Copper, Cast Iron Head, 30 In. 1295.00
Horse, Running, Directionals, Blue Glass Ball Below 180.00
Horse, Running, Full–Bodied, Copper & Zinc, 16 X 27 1/2 In. 665.00
Horse, Running, Molded Copper, Stand 7200.00
Horse, Running, Silhouette, Galvanized Sheet Metal, 26 In. 550.00
Horse, Tin, On Iron Arrow 150.00
Horse, Trotter, Long Tail, J. Howard & Co., Index, 27 In. 5750.00
Horse, Trotter, Short Tail, J.W. Fiske & Co., 32 In. 8250.00
Horse, Trotting, Jockey, Full–Bodied, Sulky, Copper, 18 1/2 In. 885.00
Hupmobile, On Base, 20th Century, 22 In. 8500.00
Indian, Plains, On Galloping Horse, Sheet Metal 2970.00
Mermaid, Pointing, Sheet Iron, Laminated Wooden Base, 40 In. 8350.00
Pennant–Type, Iron, 48 In. 225.00
Pieman, Simple Simon & Dog, Flat, 1940s, 48 X 54 In. 770.00
Rooster, Copper, Ball & Urn Base, L.W. Cushing, 38 In. 1900.00
Rooster, Crowing, Full–Bodied, Copper, 18 In. 45.00
Rooster, On Ball, Dated 1851, 30 In. 7500.00
Rooster, Sheet Iron, Painted Silver, Wooden Stand, 21 In. 130.00
Rooster, Silhouette, Primitive, Sheet Iron, 16 1/2 In. 375.00
Rooster, Silhouette, Sheet Copper, Feathers, Wood Base, 37 In. 1000.00
Rooster, Standing, Molded, Gilt Copper, Sheet Iron Tail, 57 In. 2200.00
Salmon, Wooden Cutout Covered With Copper, Button Eye 1100.00
Seaman, Horizontal, Blowing Foghorn, Wood, Painted, 44 X 24 In. 2750.00
Sperm Whale, Carved Wood, Nantucket, Late 19th Century, 50 In. 660.00
Stag, Leaping, Flattened Full–Bodied, Gold Paint, 29 X 37 In. 610.00
Stag, Leaping, Full–Bodied, Cushing & Sons, Copper, 19 3/4 In. 9900.00
Turkey, Lead–Weighted, 24 In. 3100.00
Welsh Dragon Finial, Wood Pedestal, Iron, Copper, 78 X 38 In. 1540.00

Webb

Webb glass was made by Thomas Webb & Sons of Stourbridge, England. Many types of art and cameo glass were made by them during the Victorian era. The factory is still producing glass. Webb Burmese and Webb Peachblow are special colored glasswares of the Victorian period.

WEBB BURMESE, Biscuit Jar, Grapes, Vines & Leaves, 8 1/4 In. 1770.00
Bowl, Ivy, 8 Folded–In Scallops Around Opening, 4 1/2 In. 385.00
Centerpiece, 3 Fairy Lamps, Flower Form Vase, 6 X 8 In. 2500.00
Creamer, Yellow Handle, Fluted Top, Flower & Leaves, 2 3/4 In. 550.00
Fairy Lamp, Epergne, Clear Cups, 3 Metal Rings, 10 3/4 In. 2120.00
Fairy Lamp, Original Crimped Bottom, Acid Finish, 6 1/4 In. 675.00
Fairy Lamp, Square Folded–Over Base, Clarke Insert, 6 1/8 In. 550.00
Perfume Bottle, Purple Flowers, Sterling Top, 3 1/2 In. 690.00
Pitcher, Water, Queensware, Signed, 6 7/8 In. 675.00
Rose Bowl, 8–Crimp Top, Red Buds, Green Leaves, 2 3/8 In. 295.00
Saltshaker, Small Enameled Butterfly, Floral 550.00
Vase, Acorns, 4 1/2 In. 245.00
WEBB PEACHBLOW, Fairy Lamp, Green Leaves, Clarke Insert, 3 3/4 In. 405.00
Rose Bowl, Crimped Rim, Central Blue Blossoms, 4 1/2 In. 335.00
Rose Bowl, Gold Flowers, Butterfly, 2 1/2 In. 375.00
Vase, Bottle Shape, White Lining, Rose To Pale Pink, 9 In. 395.00
Vase, Branches, Birds, Gold Tracery, Heavy Base, 16 In. 100.00
Vase, Gold Branches & Prunus Blossoms, 9 1/2 In. 475.00
Vase, Gold Leaves, Silver Flowers, 5 In., Pair 850.00
WEBB, Cup & Saucer, Chinoiserie Garden Scene, 4 5/8 In. 2090.00
Jar, Amber, White Enameled Bird & Flowers, 5 1/2 In. 75.00
Jar, Potpourri, Flowers, Aqua Border Top, Hinged Cover, 5 1/2 In. 610.00
Lamp Shade, Green Floral, Frosted, Signed 525.00
Lamp, Florals, Butterfly, Green Ground, Brass Finger Loop, Miniature 475.00
Lamp, Kerosene, Red & White Shade, Silver Plated Fittings 6500.00

Lamp, Reverse–Painted Shade, 22 In.	1300.00
Perfume Bottle, Fringe At Neck, Gold Flowers, Silver Top, 4 1/2 In.	495.00
Perfume Bottle, Long–Billed Duck Form, Leather Case, 1884, 8 3/4 In.	3300.00
Perfume Bottle, Teardrop, Ferns, Wildflower Plants, Spring Cover	825.00
Perfume Bottle, Teardrop, Rose Blossoms, Butterfly, 8 1/2 In.	1600.00
Rose Bowl, Cameo Glass, Lime Green, Carved Raspberries, Butterfly	1435.00
Urn, Cover, White Cased, Handles, Pink Satin, 8 In.	225.00
Vase, Allover Leafy Vines, Tendrils, Berries, Signed, 6 1/2 In.	4400.00
Vase, Alternating Panels of Thumbprint, Stars & Prisms, 10 In.	195.00
Vase, Bird & Dragon Front & Reverse, Pink To White, Marked, 9 In.	825.00
Vase, Blue Layered In White, Thorny Branch, Leaves, Signed, 3 3/4 In.	665.00
Vase, Blue, White Clematis Branch, Stippled, 7 1/2 In.	3750.00
Vase, Bunches of Enameled Cherries, Gold Outlined, Blue, 8 3/8 In.	145.00
Vase, Citron, White Hibiscus Floral, Butterfly, 6 In.	1750.00
Vase, Citron, White Oak Leaves, 2 Acorns, 4 X 4 In.	100.00
Vase, Coralene, 5 In.	425.00
Vase, Deep Red, White, Lilies, Foliage, 5 1/2 In.	1200.00
Vase, Dogwood Branch, Flowers & Leaves, White, 2 1/2 X 2 In.	875.00
Vase, Dots & Dashes Form Lacy Design, Gold, Signed, 10 1/4 In.	350.00
Vase, Enameled Flowers & Buds, Off–White Lining, 6 1/8 In., Pair	395.00
Vase, Florentine, Blue Satin, White Enameled Church, 9 In.	185.00
Vase, Flowers & Leaves, Butterfly On Back, 8 1/2 In.	3900.00
Vase, Flowers, Vines, 6 Medallions of Birds & Butterflies, 8 1/4 In.	3300.00
Vase, Geraniums, Frosted Yellow, Red & White, Signed, 9 In.	2750.00
Vase, Gold Threading On Pink, Blue Trim, Marked, 9 In.	425.00
Vase, Gold, Silver & White Bird, Yellow Cased, Marked, 9 1/2 In.	410.00
Vase, Melon Rib, Molded Netting, 11 In.	235.00
Vase, Raised Bull's–Eye, Top Cut Design, Signed, 12 In.	250.00
Vase, Red, Flowers & Leaves, Butterfly, White, 8 1/2 In.	3900.00
Vase, Ruffled Top, Pink Inside, Aqua Ground, 5 X 6 In.	325.00
Vase, White Dogwood Blossoms & Branches Around, Blue, 9 1/4 In.	1950.00

WEDGWOOD   Josiah Wedgwood, although considered a cripple by his brother and forbidden to work at the family business, founded one of the world's most successful potteries. The pottery was founded in England in 1759. A large variety of wares has been made, including the well–known jasperware, basalt, creamware, and even a limited amount of porcelain. There are two kinds of jasperware. One is made from two colors of clay, the other is made from one color clay with a color dip to create the contrast in design. The firm is still in business.

WEDGWOOD, Ashtray, Jasperware, Yellow, White	30.00
Biscuit Jar, Acorn Cover, Finial, Classical Figures, Yellow, 6 In.	535.00
Biscuit Jar, Japserware, Dark Blue & White, Silver Fittings	150.00
Biscuit Jar, Jasperware, Lavender Bands, Silver Plated, 9 In.	1000.00
Biscuit Jar, Jasperware, Silver Plated Mountings, 1892, 7 1/4 In.	395.00
Biscuit Jar, Jasperware, Yellow Trellis Design, Blue, 1882, 7 In.	610.00
Biscuit Jar, Lavender Bands, Green, White Figures, 9 In.	1000.00
Bourdalou, Pearlware, Gold Line Trim, C.1872, 3 1/2 X 10 1/2 In.	285.00
Bowl & Plate, Ning PO, Flower & Leaves, Octagon Shape, 12 In.	350.00
Bowl, Acanthus Leaf & Bellflower, Tricolor, 2 3/8 X 5 In.	975.00
Bowl, Basalt, Grecian, 6 1/4 In.	80.00
Bowl, Butterfly Luster, Gold Peacocks, Red Exterior, 6 1/2 In.	375.00
Bowl, Cauliflower Pattern, 10 1/2 In.	250.00
Bowl, Fairyland Luster, Dragon, 13 In.	595.00
Bowl, Fairyland Luster, Fairies Interior, Octagonal, 9 1/2 In.	2500.00
Bowl, Fairyland Luster, Moorish, Smoke Ribbons Interior, 8 In.	2700.00
Bowl, Fairyland Luster, Orange, Birds In Flight, 10 In.	550.00
Bowl, Jasperware, Dancing Women, Yellow, 9 In.	320.00
Bowl, Ram's Head, Etruria, White, 8 1/2 In.	95.00
Bowl, Secretariat, Kentucky Derby, 1974, Large	150.00
Box, Cigarette, Basalt, White On Black	135.00
Box, Cover, Jasperware, Green, Oval, 3 X 4 1/2 In.	80.00
Box, Cover, Queensware, Berries & Vine, 4 X 5 In.	90.00
Box, Jasperware, Heart, Dark Blue, White	50.00

Box, Sardine	450.00
Butter Chip, Chinese Pattern	25.00
Butter, Cover, Shell & Fish	350.00
Cache Pot, Basalt, Black, C.1815	375.00
Cache Pot, Grapes, Lion Heads, Marked, 3 3/4 In., Pair	120.00
Cake Stand, Jasperware, White On Blue Grape, Acorn Finial Cover	500.00
Candleholder, Jasperware, White Leaf Design, Green, 4 X 2 In., Pair	35.00
Candlestick, Creamware, Fruiting Vine At Top, 10 1/2 In., 4 Piece	440.00
Candy Dish, Jasperware, Lewis & Clark Exposition, 1905	40.00
Clock, Mantel, White, Blue, Garland & Scroll, 15 1/4 In.	1050.00
Clock, Tricolored Woman, Reading, Swiss Made, Marked, 19th Century	1475.00
Compote, Moonlight Luster, Boat Shape, 5 3/8 X 11 1/2 In.	75.00
Creamer, Basalt, Black, Octagonal, C.1790	495.00
Creamer, Queensware, Pink	12.00
Cup & Saucer, Basalt, Black, C.1867, Demitasse	80.00
Cup & Saucer, Caneware, Chrysanthemum, Marked A	240.00
Cup & Saucer, Jasperware, Light Blue, Wine	35.00
Cup, Fairyland Luster, Melba, Leapfrogging Elves, 3 In.	750.00
Dish, Cover, Caneware, Duck Finial, Game & Grapevines, 10 In.	220.00
Dish, Cover, Rabbit Finial, Birds, Vines, Marked, 9 1/2 In.	445.00
Dish, Jasperware, John F. Kennedy Profile, 4 1/2 In.	35.00
Dish, Pastry, Caneware, Acanthus Leaf, C.1800, 9 X 12 In.	650.00
Dish, Potpourri, Cover, Basalt, Black, C.1815	495.00
Dish, Strawberry, Creamware, Drainer, Underplate, C.1790, 12 In.	650.00
Ewer, Basalt, Black, Triton Seated, Sea Monster, 14 1/2 In., Pair	2325.00
Feeding Set, Child's, Beatrix Potter	22.00
Figurine, Ravine, Basalt, Pair	500.00
Flowerpot, Underplate, Basalt, Black C.1795	425.00
Holder, Toothbrush, Cream, Brown Design Drain, Stoneware, 1878	20.00
Honey, Attached Underplate, Caneware, Strap Handle, 4 In.	250.00
Inkstand, Drabware, Leaf & Floral Gallery, 3 Wells, 10 1/2 In.	310.00
Jug, Hunting Scene, Under Green Majolica Glaze, Marked, 6 In.	80.00
Jug, John Peel Hunting Scene, Hound Handle, 5 In.	125.00
Lamp, Creamware, Grape Pattern, 1940–50, 29 In., Pair	250.00
Lighter, Table, Green, England	9.50
Paperweight, Jasperware, Black, White	55.00
Pitcher, Blue, Red Inside Lip, Luster, 2 In.	255.00
Pitcher, Hound Handle, Ivory, Etruria	100.00
Pitcher, Milk, Jasperware, Maidens With Peacock, Bouquet, 6 In.	150.00
Pitcher, Women & Cherubs, 3–Petal Top, Marked, 5 1/2 In.	150.00
Plaque, Egyptian King Tut, Gold On Black, 8 X 8 1/2 In.	325.00
Plaque, Fallen Deer & Doe, Winter, Marked, 12 1/8 In.	600.00
Plaque, Jasper Ovals, Gilded Frames, Marked, C.1900, 7 1/2 In., Pair	950.00
Plaque, Jasperware, Seven Graces, Blue, White, 1860, 4 X 11 5/8 In.	325.00
Plate, 125th Anniversary Marietta College, Blue, 10 In.	20.00
Plate, American Clipper Ship, 8 Piece	150.00
Plate, Christmas, 1969	135.00 To 150.00
Plate, Dinner, Ironstone, White, Fluted Pearl	13.00
Plate, Festoon, Blue Scene, Gold & Enameled Border, 10 In.	45.00
Plate, Golden Goose, 1979	12.00
Plate, Leaf, Etruscan Handle, 12 In.	195.00
Plate, Old South Church, Etruria, 1899, 9 1/4 In.	35.00
Plate, Oriental, 8 1/2 In.	90.00
Plate, Patrician, 10 1/2 In.	20.00
Plate, Queensware, Columbia University Library, 1912	38.00
Plate, Trophy, Bicentennial, 1978	450.00
Plate, U.S. Military Academy, 1952, 9 In.	18.00
Plate, Vassar College, Library, Blue, White, 10 1/4 In.	75.00
Plate, White Leaf Figures, Blue, Marked, 4 1/2 In.	15.00
Platter, White, Flower Transfer, 16 In.	45.00
Ring Tree, Jasperware, White Figures On Dark Blue, 2 3/4 In.	115.00
Soup, Dish, Laurel, Ironstone	15.00
Syrup, Jasperware, White Figures, Pewter Lid, Marked, 5 1/4 In.	145.00
Teapot, Jasperware, Grecian Scene, White Acanthus Leaf, 7 1/2 In.	350.00

Teapot, Jasperware, Light Blue, Wine	85.00
Teapot, Sugar & Creamer, Light Blue, 3 Piece	175.00
Tile, Calendar, U.S. Frigate Constitution, Battleship, 1911	30.00
Tile, Fairbanks House, Etruria, Blue, Dated 1929, 6 X 6 In.	48.00
Toothpick, Jasperware, Black, Grapevines, 1955	25.00
Tumbler, Luster, Orange, Black, Gold Creatures Interior, 1 1/4 In.	250.00
Tureen, With Ladle, Pearlware, C.1880, 4 Piece	245.00
Urn, Cover, Jasperware, White Classic Figures, Lavender, 9 1/2 In.	1190.00
Urn, Cover, Jasperware, White Figures, Blue, C.1860, 14 3/4 In.	2250.00
Urn, Dolphin Stand, Jeweled Ground, C.1895, 12 3/4 In.	1600.00
Vase, Basalt, Black, Trumpet Shape, 8 In.	95.00
Vase, Basalt, Black, Trumpet Shape, Pedestal Foot, 11 1/2 In.	525.00
Vase, Classical Figures, Blue & White	350.00
Vase, Dragon Luster, Gold Dragon, Dark Blue, 8 In.	350.00
Vase, Dragon Luster, Oriental Design, Marked, 12 3/4 In.	975.00
Vase, Fairyland Luster, Marked, 8 In.	950.00
Vase, Portland, Draped Classical Figures, 8 1/4 In.	385.00
Vase, Tray, Box, Jasperware, Green & White, 3 Piece	48.00
Vase, Victoria Ware, Classical Figures, Brown & Cream, 7 1/2 In.	395.00

LOUWELSA WELLER — Weller pottery was first made in 1873 in Fultonham, Ohio. The firm moved to Zanesville, Ohio, in 1882. Art wares were first made in 1893. Hundreds of lines of pottery were made, including Louwelsa, Eocean, Dickens, and Sicardo, before the pottery closed in 1948.

WELLER, Ashtray, Dachshund	75.00
Basket, Roba, Tan To Brown Swirls, Floral, 6 X 8 In.	55.00
Basket, Warwick, 9 In.	75.00
Basket, Waterlily, Brown, 12 In.	100.00
Bowl, Cameo, Blue, White Roses, Footed, 4 In.	35.00
Bowl, Fairfield, 4 1/2 X 9 In.	68.00
Bowl, Velva, Green, 5 In.	85.00
Candlestick, Cameo, Creamware, 11 In.	85.00
Clock, Mantel, Louwelsa	800.00 To 900.00
Console Set, Fish Flower Frog, 4 Piece	255.00
Console Set, Lavonia, 3 Piece	135.00
Console Set, Silvertone	250.00
Dish, Child's, Duckling	45.00
Dish, Child's, Feeding, Zona, Embossed Bunny & Bird On Branch	40.00
Ewer, Louwelsa, 6 In.	180.00
Ewer, Louwelsa, Corn, 12 In.	700.00
Ewer, Louwelsa, Green & Brown Leaves, 6 In.	180.00
Ewer, Wild Rose, Pink, 10 In.	30.00
Figurine, Boy Fishing	47.50
Figurine, Frog, Garden, Coppertone, 6 X 7 In.	375.00
Figurine, Frog, Opened Lotus, Coppertone, 4 In.	110.00
Figurine, Owl, Woodcraft, 16 1/2 In.	950.00
Figurine, Swan, Muskota	150.00
Flower Frog, Brighton Kingfisher, 9 In.	165.00
Flower Frog, Coppertone	95.00 To 150.00
Flower Frog, Glendale	95.00
Flower Frog, Kingfisher	195.00
Flower Frog, Lorbeek	35.00
Flower Frog, Muskota	60.00
Flower Frog, Nude Lady, Muskota	115.00
Flowerpot, Roma, Raised Fruit, 5 In.	30.00
Jar, Bonito, 3 1/2 In.	55.00
Jardiniere, Aurelian, Grape Design, Pedestal, 47 In.	4000.00
Jardiniere, Blue Drapery, 6 1/2 In.	65.00
Jardiniere, Dickens Ware, Cobalt, Devil's Face 1 Side, Marked	900.00
Jardiniere, Eocean, 7 X 9 In.	250.00
Jardiniere, Louwelsa, Artist, 11 In.	300.00
Jardiniere, Louwelsa, Floral, 11 In.	425.00
Jardiniere, Louwelsa, Marked K, 9 X 12 In.	295.00
Jardiniere, Marvo, Brown, Pedestal, 36 In.	575.00

Jardiniere, Souevo, 8 In. 85.00
Lamp Base, Roma, Candlestick, 9 1/2 In. 40.00
Lamp, Louwelsa, Glass Shade, 11 In. 290.00
Lamp, Oil, Dickens Ware, Chrysanthemums, 3–Footed, Marked 650.00
Lamp, Owl, Woodcraft, Old Shade 350.00
Mug, Etna, Shade Light To Dark Gray, 6 In. 100.00
Mug, Louwelsa, 6 In. 95.00
Pitcher, Cider, Wild Rose, White, 11 1/2 In. 32.00
Pitcher, Kitchen Gem 27.00
Pitcher, Marvo, Green, 8 In. 115.00
Pitcher, Milk, Louwelsa, Honey Glazed 135.00
Pitcher, Water, Zona, Kingfisher, Creamware 175.00
Pitcher, Woodcraft, 9 In. 32.00
Pitcher, Zona, Kingfisher, Pink, 7 In. 70.00
Planter, Dachshund, 8 1/2 In. 60.00
Planter, Forest, Tub, 3 X 5 1/2 In. 68.00
Planter, Softone, Blue, 3 X 10 1/4 In. 10.00
Planter, Woodcraft, 3 Little Foxes Peering Out of Den, 7 1/2 In. 135.00
Rose Bowl, Atlas, Blue, 4 In. 75.00
Sign, Dealer, Pink & Green, Signed, 9 In. 350.00
Stand, Umbrella, Claywood, Cream Wild Roses, Chocolate Brown, 22 In. 187.00
Syrup, Mammy 385.00
Teapot, Mammy 495.00
Urn, Chengtu, Paper Label, 5 1/2 In. 125.00
Vase, Arcola, 7 In. 75.00
Vase, Atlas, Star, Blue, 4 In. 55.00
Vase, Baldin, Blue, 7 In. 195.00
Vase, Blue Drapery, 7 In. 48.00
Vase, Blue Drapery, 8 In. 30.00
Vase, Bonito, Ornate Handles, Brown Trim, Signed, 6 In. 55.00
Vase, Bud, Woodcraft, 10 1/2 In. 35.00
Vase, Burntwood, 7 In. 175.00
Vase, Cameo, Blue & White, 6 1/2 In. 25.00
Vase, Cameo, Double Handles, Coral, 7 In. 28.00
Vase, Chengtu, 10 In. 50.00
Vase, Clarmont, Double Ring Handles, 8 In. 30.00
Vase, Clarmont, Handles, 4 1/2 In. 70.00
Vase, Cloudburst, Green, Marked, 5 In. 65.00
Vase, Coppertone Glaze, 2 Handles, 18 1/2 In. 325.00
Vase, Coppertone, 6 1/2 In. 65.00
Vase, Coppertone, 9 In. 37.50
Vase, Coppertone, 12 In. 375.00
Vase, Dickens Ware, Crackle, Cream Leaves & Floral, Brown, 10 In. 55.00
Vase, Dickens Ware, Fish Pattern, 3 Handles, 6 1/4 In. 425.00
Vase, Dickens Ware, Green Flowers, 10 In. 115.00
Vase, Dickens Ware, Indian, 7 1/2 In. 395.00
Vase, Dickens Ware, Monk, 5 X 7 In. 240.00
Vase, Dickens Ware, Mr. Weller Sr., Pickwick Papers, Green, 8 In. 750.00
Vase, Dickens Ware, Pillow, Monk 210.00
Vase, Elberta, 6 In. 50.00
Vase, Ethel, Creamware, 9 1/2 In. 195.00
Vase, Etna, Daffodils, 11 In. 160.00
Vase, Etna, Red Glaze, Frog Climbing On Side, 4 In. 150.00
Vase, Evergreen, 12 In. .... 65.00 To 75.00
Vase, Fan, Voile 55.00
Vase, Flemish, 12 1/2 In. 150.00
Vase, Forest, 8 In. 50.00
Vase, Fruitone, 9 In. 65.00
Vase, Glendale, 8 3/4 In. 285.00
Vase, Greenbriar, 6 1/2 In. 25.00
Vase, Hudson Light, Dogwood Flowers, 9 1/2 In. 165.00
Vase, Hudson Light, Jonquil Flowers, 9 3/4 In. 170.00
Vase, Hudson, Blue, Signed, 9 In. 345.00
Vase, Hudson, Iris, Blue, 11 1/2 In. 165.00

Vase, Hudson, Iris, Blue, Tapered Cylinder, 11 1/2 In. 165.00
Vase, Hudson, Pillsbury, Lilacs, 15 In. 400.00
Vase, L'Art Nouveau, 10 In. 155.00
Vase, L'Art Nouveau, Full–Figured Woman, Flower, 17 1/2 In. 525.00
Vase, L'Art Nouveau, Glossy, Marked, 15 1/2 In. 575.00
Vase, LaSa, 6 In. 140.00
Vase, LaSa, 8 1/2 In. 200.00
Vase, LaSa, Cylinder, 13 In. 375.00
Vase, LaSa, Palm Trees In Landscape, C.1915, 7 3/4 In. 165.00
Vase, LaSa, Signed, 10 1/2 In. 425.00
Vase, Louwelsa, Blue Pansies, 7 1/2 In. 500.00
Vase, Louwelsa, Chrysanthemums, Shaded Brown Glaze, 6 In. 115.00
Vase, Louwelsa, Floral, 3 X 6 In. 125.00
Vase, Louwelsa, Floral, 5 1/2 In. 175.00
Vase, Louwelsa, Floral, Blue, 6 1/2 In. 200.00
Vase, Louwelsa, Flower, Cylindrical, Artist, 6 1/2 In. 95.00
Vase, Louwelsa, Flowers, Brown Glaze, Bulbous, Artist, 5 1/2 In. 95.00
Vase, Louwelsa, Hand Painted Tulips, Long Stems, Signed, 15 In. 315.00
Vase, Louwelsa, Portrait of Chief Hollow Horn Bear, A.F. Best 3200.00
Vase, Marbelized, Octagonal, 8 In. 65.00
Vase, Mirror Black, 14 In. 100.00
Vase, Muskota, Fishing Boy, 7 In. 150.00
Vase, Neiska, Blue, 6 In. 12.00
Vase, Oak Leaf, Gray–Green, 7 1/2 In., Pair 75.00
Vase, Panella, Gold, 13 In. 60.00
Vase, Paragon, Burgundy, 7 In. 55.00
Vase, Patricia, Green, 18 In. 200.00
Vase, Pumila, 8 In. 55.00
Vase, Selma, Squirrel, 11 1/2 In. 250.00
Vase, Sicard, 15 In. 850.00
Vase, Sicard, Allover Foliate Design, Signed, Bulbous, 6 1/2 In. 445.00
Vase, Sicard, Flowers, Twisted Body, Knob Handles, C.1905, 4 1/2 In. 665.00
Vase, Sicard, Foliate Design, Signed, 6 1/2 In. 440.00
Vase, Sicard, Holly Leaves & Berries, 3 1/2 In. 925.00
Vase, Silvertone, Molded Floral Design, 7 1/2 In. 8.00
Vase, Silvertone, Pastel, Handles, Marked 1/2–Kiln Stamp, 9 1/2 In. 140.00
Vase, Woodcraft, Owl In A Tree Trunk, 13 In. 275.00
Vase, Woodcraft, Rose, 9 In. 35.50
Wall Pocket, Fairfield 95.00
Wall Pocket, Flemish, 9 1/2 In. 50.00
Wall Pocket, Glendale, 9 In. 225.00
Wall Pocket, Klyro 85.00
Wall Pocket, Pearl, 8 In. 110.00
Wall Pocket, Woodcraft, 9 1/2 In. 50.00
Wall Pocket, Woodcraft, Apple, 11 1/2 In. 68.00
Wall Pocket, Woodrose, Lavender, 6 1/2 In. 40.00
Window Box, Forest, 5 X 7 X 14 In. 250.00

Iridescent pottery such as Sicardo should be carefully cleaned. Wash in mild detergent and water. Rinse and dry by buffing vigorously with dry, fluffy towels. Then polish with a silver cloth as if it were made of metal. Buff again with a clean towel.

Whieldon was a potter in England who worked alone and with Josiah Wedgwood in eighteenth–century England. Whieldon made many pieces in natural shapes, like cauliflowers or cabbages. The tortoiseshell glazed pieces are known as "clouded ware."

WHIELDON, Bowl, Tortoise Shell, Brown, Blue, Green, Embossed Rim, 2 1/2 In.	275.00
Butter Tub, Cow Finial	9750.00
Cookie Jar	350.00
Creamer, Cow	5800.00
Creamer, Cow, With Milkmaid, 6 In.	2000.00
Creamer, Green, Brown Glaze, 2 3/4 In.	325.00
Figurine, Cow, With Calf	775.00
Figurine, Ram, Lying, 6 In.	1850.00
Pitcher, Brown Running Glaze, 5 5/8 In.	550.00
Pitcher, Embossed Pineapple, Green, Amber, 5 1/2 In.	1100.00
Plate, 10 In.	100.00
Plate, Embossed Feather Rim, Glaze, Brown, Blue, Green, 10 In.	300.00
Plate, Leaf Shape, Embossed Design, Bird, Tree, 8 X 10 In.	800.00
Plate, Octagonal Embossed Rim, Brown Glaze, Green, Blue, 9 In.	425.00
Plate, Scalloped Rim, Embossed Foliage Designs, 8 In.	300.00
Plate, Tortoise Glaze, Gray, Green, Scalloped Rim, 9 3/8 In.	350.00
Tea Set, Brown Running Glaze, 9 Piece	1600.00
Teapot, Applied Brown Running Glaze, 4 3/8 In.	850.00
Teapot, Blue, Brown, 3 Paw Feet, 4 In.	5400.00
Teapot, Embossed Cabbage Leaves, 4 3/4 In.	4150.00
Teapot, Embossed Cabbage Leaves, Rabbit Finial	4250.00
Teapot, Embossed Cauliflower Design, Green, White, 4 In.	1200.00
Teapot, Embossed Design, Fruit, Flowers, 5 In.	800.00
Teapot, Embossed Leaf Design, Spout, Handle, 4 1/2 In.	1500.00
Teapot, Oriental Design, Paneled, Green, Amber, 5 1/4 In.	4400.00

Willets Manufacturing Company of Trenton, New Jersey, worked from 1879. The company made belleek in the late 1880s and 1890s in shapes similar to those used by the Irish Belleek factory. They stopped working about 1912. Pieces were marked with a variety of marks, all including the name Willets.

WILLETS, Cup & Saucer, Gold Border, Sterling Filigree Holder & Saucer	35.00
Figurine, Swan, Cream Iridescent, Gold Breast, Neck & Head, 2 In.	50.00
Hatpin Holder, Ivory, Ribbed, 5 1/4 In.	95.00
Sugar & Creamer, Dragon Handles, Floral & Gold Paste Design	225.00
Tankard, Gold Dragon Handle & Spout, Leaves & Berries, 11 1/2 In.	250.00
Tankard, Grapes, Scrolled Handle & Base, C.1895, 14 1/4 In.	425.00
Tankard, Lafayette, Dragon Handle, 11 In.	225.00
Tankard, Rose, Ornate Handle, Band of Leaves, 11 3/4 In.	275.00
Vase, Roses, 12 1/2 In.	250.00
Vase, Swans, Art Deco, Black & Gray, 16 In.	450.00
WILLOW, see Blue Willow	

Stained glass and beveled glass windows were popular additions to houses during the late nineteenth and early twentieth centuries. The old windows became popular with collectors in the 1970s; today, old and new examples are seen.

WINDOW, Amethyst, Etched, 28 X 49 1/2 In.	400.00
Arts & Crafts, Chipped Ice Panels, Opalescent Strips, 14 X 37 In.	295.00
Arts & Crafts, Thin Opalescent Stripes Design, 14 X 37 In., Pair	325.00
Beveled Glass, Curved Pieces, 45 X 19 In.	375.00
Clairbourne Court, Illinois Central R.R.	680.00
French Quarter, Illinois Central R.R.	680.00
Golf Clubs & Ball In Center, From Golf Club, 22 X 32 In.	30.00
Jesus Praying In Garden Of Gethsemane, 12 Ft.6 In. X 10 1/2 In.	3500.00
Leaded & Jeweled, Geometric Design, Central Shell, 48 X 18 In., Pair	715.00
Leaded & Stained, Crane, Jeweled Fan, 40 X 18 In. ....*Illus*	1100.00
Leaded Prism, Luxfer, Frank Lloyd Wright	800.00
Leaded, Grape Vines, Geometric Grid, C.1910, 44 3/4 X 19 In.	1870.00

Window, Leaded & Stained, Crane,
Jeweled Fan, 40 X 18 In.

Never use commercial window cleaner on a stained glass window. It could remove the color or damage the lead.

Wooden boxes, toys, or decoys should not be kept on the fireplace mantel or nearby floor area when the fire is burning. The heat dries the wood and the paint. Unprotected wooden items on warm TV sets and stereos may also be damaged.

Leaded, Stylized Roses, Slag Glass, C.1910, 55 3/4 In., Pair	250.00
Prairie School, Bands Crossed With Metal Squares, 36 X 24 5/8 In.	1650.00
Stained Glass, Floral Pattern	55.00
Stained Glass, King & Queen, C.1885, 11 Ft., Pair	2750.00
Stained Glass, St. Catherine & St. Giles, 16th Century	9900.00

Wood carvings and wooden pieces are listed separately in this book. There are also wooden pieces found in other sections, such as Kitchen.

WOOD CARVING, Black Man & Woman, Cane, Polychrome, 6 1/2 In., Pair	380.00
Blackamoor, 1870, 7 In.	8250.00
Bracket, Cupid, Spread Wings, Shell Shelf, 12 3/4 In., Pair	605.00
Coach & Team of Horses, Polychrome Paint, 21 1/2 In.	90.00
Crucifix, Primitive, Gesso, Polychrome Repaint, 19 In.	200.00
Deer Heads, Germany, Pair	100.00
Doll, Flat Body, Painted Torso & Trousers, 16 In.	175.00
Duck, For Carnival Game, Tack Eyes, Numbers 26 & 12, 9 In., Pr.	150.00
Eagle, Carved Feathers, Gold Repaint, 11 3/4 In.	200.00
Eagle, Fully Dimensional, Carved Feather Design, 10 3/4 In.	750.00
Eagle, Green, Yellow Paint, 7 1/2 In.	275.00
Figure, Black Cellist & Guitarist, 5 1/2 In., Pair	75.00
Foo Dog, Paw On Ball, Gilded, 4 X 9 1/2 In.	85.00
Girl, Head & Face, Curls, Hanging, 4 X 4 1/2 In.	130.00
Group, Pieta, Christ In Lap, Spanish, 18th Century, 27 In.	1045.00
Horse, Inserted Legs, Horsehair Tail, Oilcloth Saddle, 31 In.	1125.00
Horse, Leather Saddle, Harness, Red, Black Detail, 8 In.	225.00
Madonna & Child, Pierced Scroll Case, Fruitwood, 18 In.	885.00
Model, Locomotive & Tender, 1907, 43 In.	6800.00
Moose, Standing, On Base	900.00
Mourning Dove, Swivel Head, 7 In.	175.00
Old Fisherman, Ivory Eyes, Rosewood, Chinese, 12 1/2 In.	23.50
Oxen, Leather Collar, 7 In.	25.00

Plate, Transylvania University, Lexington, 9 In.	335.00
Plate, View of Trenton Falls, 7 1/2 In.	400.00
Relic, Christian Saint, Netherlands, 16th Century, Pair	9500.00
Rooster, Pine, Red On Comb, 6 1/4 In.	325.00
Scoop, Bone Marrow, Hand Carved, 5 In.	30.00
Scoop, Flour, Handle Applied To Bowl, Rivets, 15 5/8 In.	50.00
Wallpaper Block, Scroll, Leaf, 19th Century, 31 X 29 In.	55.00
Watch Holder, Scroll & Column, Painted, Germany, 10 1/2 In.	110.00

Wood was used for many containers and tools used in the early home. Small wooden pieces are called "treenware" in England, but the term "woodenware" is more common in the United States.

WOODEN, see also Kitchen; Advertising; Tool

WOODEN, Barrel, Sycamore, American, 19th Century, 28 In.	95.00
Bird House, Victorian, 19th Century	625.00
Board, Sleigh, Striping, Diamond Shaped Windmill Scene, 24 In.	365.00
Board, Smoothing, Carved Horse Handles, 1822, 28 In.	775.00
Boot Jack, Pine, Primitive	25.00
Bowl, 1 Piece Poplar, 21 X 22 In.	150.00
Bowl, Almond Shape, 5 1/2 X 15 3/4 In.	200.00
Bowl, Blue–Gray Paint, American, 18th Century, 9 1/2 In.	360.00
Bowl, Burl, 1 1/2 X 4 1/2 In.	275.00
Bowl, Burl, 1 3/8 X 2 5/8 In.	250.00
Bowl, Burl, Figural, Twisted Rim, 7 X 16 In.	200.00
Bowl, Burl, Molded Rim, Incised Line Design, 3 1/2 X 9 In.	330.00
Bowl, Burl, Protruding Rim Handles, 5 1/4 X 13 1/4 In.	925.00
Bowl, Burl, Treen Ladle, American, 18th Century	365.00
Bowl, Burl, Turned Lip, 7 X 18 1/2 In.	1400.00
Bowl, Burl, Walnut, Oblong, 13 X 24 In.	185.00
Bowl, Butter, 18th Century, 14 X 15 In.	85.00
Bowl, Dark Patina, Black Paint On Exterior, 2 1/4 In.	180.00
Bowl, Elliptical Shape, 1 Piece Cherry, C.1820, 11 1/2 X 23 In.	140.00
Bowl, Maple, Mustard Paint, Round, 9 1/2 X 10 1/4 In.	75.00
Bowl, Pennsylvania, Lehnware Style	185.00
Bowl, Protruding End Handles, Oblong, 15 X 25 1/2 In.	145.00
Box, Inlaid Satin, Oval Paterae, Ebony Escutcheon, 4 1/8 In.	350.00
Box, Wall, Pine, Pieced Design, Shamrock Finial, 3 1/2 X 8 X 10 In.	220.00
Bracket, Wall, Gilded Florentine, Italy, 8 1/2 X 11 In., Pair	20.00
Bucket, Chestnut, Large	48.00
Bucket, Cover, New Jersey Preserves Label	32.50
Bucket, Maple Sugar, Square Nails, Maple	35.00
Bucket, Stave Constructed, Galvanized Iron Bands, 10 1/2 X 14 In.	20.00
Bucket, Stave Constructed, Wire Bands, Red Varnish, Oval, 8 1/4 In.	95.00
Bucket, Sugar, Cover, Stave Constructed, 14 1/2 In.	25.00
Bucket, Sugar, Stave Constructed, 2–Tone Brown Stain, 10 In.	75.00
Bucket, Sugar, Stave Constructed, Conch Grained, Label On Lid, 10 In.	125.00
Bucket, Sugar, Stave Constructed, Handle, Wire Bail, 6 1/2 In.	105.00
Bucket, Sugar, Stave Constructed, Stenciled 18XX, 9 3/4 In.	85.00
Cabinet, Screw, 72 Drawers	1100.00
Canteen, Bentwood, Wrought Iron Nails, 5 5/8 In.	225.00
Carrier, Walnut, Inlaid Shield Design, Top Handle	1800.00
Casket, Jewelry, Carved Gryphons, Unicorns, Fruitwood, C, 1840, 11 In.	2100.00
Chamberstick, Push–Up, 4 7/8 In.	185.00
Chest, Jewelry, Parquetry, Lift Top, Drawers, Japanese, 15 5/8 In.	385.00
Compote, Red Sponging, Poplar, 7 5/8 X 11 1/2 In.	375.00
Dripper, Hand Hewn, Wooden, 9 In.Bowl, Hole, 1 Piece, 25 1/2 In.	230.00
Eggcup, Traveling, Pedestal Base, Smoke Grain Design, Pair	120.00
Engraving, Man On Horseback, Comic, Framed, 14 3/4 X 12 3/4 In.	125.00
Hat Block, Solid, C.1890	25.00
Jar, Carved Floral Design, Black Paint, 6 1/4 In.	25.00
Jar, Red & Yellow Sponged Paint, Turned Poplar, 5 In.	145.00
Jar, Red Sponged, 3 1/8 In.	170.00
Jar, Red Sponged, Ivory Button On Cover, 1 7/8 In.	135.00
Jar, Tobacco, Turned, Chip Carved, Knob Finial, 5 X 7 3/4 In.	250.00

Keg, Canteen Shape, Red, 4 1/4 In.	175.00
Keg, Cover, Jar Shape, Poplar, Turned Detail, 8 In.	200.00
Ladder, 6 Steps, Pyramid Form, Old Blue Paint	195.00
Mold, Cigar, 2–Part	27.00
Mold, Cigar, Karl Hart, Mannheim, 21 In.	10.00
Pitcher, Cover, Stave Construction, Bent Sapling Bands, 12 1/2 In.	65.00
Pitcher, Noggin, English, 1798, 10 1/2 In.	125.00
Pitcher, Noggin, Maple, Handle, 1800, 1 Piece, 5 3/4 In.	250.00
Plate, Painting of Winter Landscape, 7 1/2 In.	145.00
Porringer, Cherry, Turned, 2 Tab Handles, 1810	175.00
Propeller, 90 In.	475.00
Rattle, Child's, Red Varnish Finish, 8 3/4 In.	75.00
Saltbox, Light Blue Paint, Amish, Ohio	275.00
Scoop, Seed, Winnower	170.00
Tankard, America, 18th Century, 5 1/4 In.	660.00
Torchiere, Black Paint, 41 1/2 In., Pair	55.00
Tray, Drying, Herb, Wire Nail Construction, 17 1/4 X 17 1/2 In.	45.00
Tray, Knife, Slant Sides, Arched Center, Carrying Handle, C.1830	250.00
Tray, Lazy Susan, Turned Base, 16 X 8 In.	95.00
Tray, Stenciled Scene of Children, Black Lacquer, 16 X 24 1/2 In.	45.00
Tub, Stave Constructed, Side Handles, Iron Bands, 9 X 25 In.	185.00
Tub, Stave Constructed, Side Handles, Metal Bands, 10 1/2 X 14 In.	75.00
Wastebasket, Walnut, Scalloped, Flared, Rectangular, 12 X 18 In.	110.00

Worcester porcelains were made in Worcester, England, from 1751. The firm went through many name changes and eventually, in 1862, became The Royal Worcester Porcelain Company Ltd. Collectors often refer to Dr. Wall, Barr, Flight, and other names that indicate time periods and artists at the factory. It became part of Royal Worcester Spode Ltd. in 1976.

WORCESTER, see also Royal Worcester

WORCESTER, Basket, Chestnut, Pinecone, Sprig Handle, Soft Paste, 1775, 8 In.	5500.00
Bowl, Blue, White Floral Design, Dr.Wall, Crescent Mark, 6 In.	400.00
Bowl, Blue, White Floral Design, Fruit, Vegetables, 9 3/4 In.	600.00
Bowl, Printed Underglaze, Double Rim Band, Marked, C.1780	550.00
Cup & Saucer, Blue, White Floral Design	250.00
Cup & Saucer, Underglaze Blue, Gilt, Red Rims	150.00
Dish, Embossed Spiral Fluting, Floral, Blue, Gilt, 7 In.	100.00
Dish, Fluted Scalloped Rim, Floral Polychrome, Oval, 9 X 11 In.	500.00
Plate, Blue, White Floral Design, Scalloped Rim, 7 5/8 In.	525.00
Plate, Floral Center, 3 Shell Feet, Grainger, 10 1/2 In.	750.00
Plate, Scalloped Rim, Crescent Mark, 8 In.	200.00
Teapot, Blue Oriental Transfer, Applied Flower Finial, 5 3/4 In.	300.00
Teapot, White Oriental, Embossed Floral Design, Blue, 5 In.	1700.00
Tray, Oval, Floral Design, Impressed Crown, Enameled, Gilt, 10 In.	150.00

Souvenirs of World War I and World War II are collected today. Be careful not to store anything that includes live ammunition. Your local police station will tell you how to dispose of the explosives. See also Trench Art.

WORLD WAR I, Belt, Red Cross, With Pouches	45.00
Belt, Sam Brown, Nickel & Brass Rings	15.00
Binoculars, Long Range, With Compass, Case	65.00
Binoculars, Signal Corps, Case	40.00
Book, Honor Roll, Webster County, Iowa, 240 Pages, 12 X 9 In.	30.00
Button, Lapel, American Legion, With Guard, Sterling, 1919	3.50
Canister, Metal, Film Songs, Small	7.00
Compass, U.S. Army, Brass Dated 1918	75.00
Compass, Walking, Leather Case	85.00
Helmet, Aviator's Crash, Germany	795.00
Helmet, Doughboy	40.00
Lanyard, Pistol, U.S. Cavalry	2.00
Letter Opener, 03 Rifle	12.00
Medal, Victory, British	5.00

Postcard, Draft Notice, Golen, California, Sept., 1918 .... 6.00
Poster, Beat Back The Hun, Buy Liberty Bonds .... 80.00 To 95.00
Poster, Buy War Savings Stamps, Keep Him Free, Framed 175.00
Poster, Clear The Way, Howard Chandler Christy, 30 X 20 In. 198.00
Poster, Cold Blooded Murder, Sinking of Lusitania, 40 X 25 In. 44.00
Poster, For France Pour Out Your Gold, French, J.A.Faivre 180.00
Poster, Girl, Honor Roll Liberty Loan, Christy, 39 X 27 In. 75.00
Poster, Hey Fellows, Amer. Library Assn., Sheridan, 20 X 30 In. 35.00
Poster, I Want You, J.F. Flagg 500.00
Poster, Join The Army Air Service, American Eagle, 1917 .... 200.00
Poster, Keep 'Em Smiling, Soldier, Sailor & Marine, Bracher 70.00
Poster, Oh, Boy! That's The Girl, 1918 .... 65.00
Poster, Together We Win, Flagg, 1915, 40 X 29 In. 165.00
Saddle Bags, Model M1904, U.S. Cavalry 75.00
Sheet Music, Marine Band, H.B.Pryor, Drum Major Drawing, 1923 .... 15.00
Song Book, Army, 1918 .... 12.50
Sword, Belt & Buckle, U.S.Navy 120.00
Uniform, Captain's, With Topcoat, Medical Corps 75.00
Uniform, Doughboy 75.00
Uniform, Infantry, Khaki 80.00
Uniform, U.S. Navy, Size 36 .... 125.00
WORLD WAR II, Armband, Nazi 20.00
Armband, Observer's 10.00
Badge, Swastika Center, Silver Iron Cross Design, No Pin 10.00
Banner, Nazi, 12 Ft. 55.00
Banner, Swastika, Germany, 29 X 44 1/2 In. 70.00
Binoculars, German Army, Case 55.00
Book, Ration 18.00
Book, Submarine Operations, Naval Institute, Hard Cover, Large 30.00
Booklet, Calendar, 1945, 459th Bomb Group, 15th Air Force 11.00
Buckle, Belt, Nazi SS 75.00
Buckle, Hitler Youth 20.00
Canteen, With Sling & Carrier, British 25.00
Cap, Officer's, Nazi Police, Leather Visor 325.00
Cap, Pilot's, Germany 75.00
Card, Store Punch, Let's Punch Hitler, Cardboard 10.00
Christmas Card, Sign Says To Berlin, From GI In England 5.00
Compass, Sperry Gryo, Battleship, Electrical Components 900.00
Compass, Wrist, Japanese 22.00
Dagger, Luftwaffe, Leather Scabbard 100.00
Dagger, Nazi Dress, Bullion 120.00
Dagger, Nazi, Human Shoulder Bone Handle 150.00
Ditty Bag, American Red Cross 10.00
First Aid Dial, Home–Front, Packet, 1942 .... 15.00
Flag, Red Army, Red, Yellow Hammer & Sickle, 34 X 36 In. 25.00
Flag, Red Cross 15.00
Flag, Tank, Swastika, Heavy Silk 100.00
Game, Carnival, Hitler With Breakable Nose 395.00
Hand Grenade, Kodak, Round, With Fuse 150.00
Hat, Officer's, Nazi Army, Peaked 225.00
Helmet, Police, Nazi, Decal On Each Side 135.00
Hilt, Officer's, Model 1902, German Silver, Springfield Armory 325.00
Jacket, Bomber, Size 38R 500.00
Jacket, Bomber, Size 46 .... 200.00
Jewelry, Cross, Nazi's Mothers, Gold, Ribbon, Box 145.00
Knife, Coast Guard, Rope 15.00
Knife, Forester's, Nazi 395.00
Lantern, Railroad, Nazi, Carbide, Handle 135.00
License, Pilot's 100.00
Map, Battle, Pacific 2.50
Map, Berghoff Beer, Poster Size 95.00
Medal, Marksman, Sterling Silver 21.00
Mug, Deutschland, Glass, Green Handle 485.00
Patch, Correspondent's 9.00

Petition, Mother's, Congress, No Foreign Wars, 17 In.	10.00
Pin, E Service, Sterling Silver	7.00
Postcard Set, Nazi Emblem, Wine Festival, C.1935, 45 Cards	40.00
Poster, Atlantic Charter, FDR & Churchill, 1941	15.00
Poster, Freedom of Speech, War Bonds, Rockwell, 20 X 28 In.	50.00
Poster, Hug The Ground & Live Longer, 1943	14.50
Poster, U.S. Cadet Nurse Corps, Edmundson, 20 X 27 1/2 In.	20.00
Puzzle, Victory Series, U.S., Nazi Planes, Dirigible, 1943	15.00
Sheet Music, March To Victory, Winston Churchill	17.50
Sword, Japanese	325.00
Sword, Officer's, Nazi, Holder	375.00
Valentine, Boy In Khaki, Mechanical, 9 X 6 1/2 In.	7.50
Valentine, Soldier, I'D March Million Miles, Your Smile, 5 In.	5.00
Whip, Nazi, From Concentration Camp	175.00

Souvenirs of all world's fairs are collected. The first fair was the Great Exhibition of 1851 in London. Other important exhibitions and fairs include Philadelphia, 1876 (Centennial); Chicago, 1893 (World's Columbian); Buffalo, 1901 (Pan-American); St. Louis, 1904 (Louisiana Purchase); San Francisco, 1915 (Panama-Pacific); Philadelphia, 1926 (Sesquicentennial); Chicago, 1933 (Century of Progress); Cleveland, 1936 (Great Lakes); San Francisco, 1939 (Golden Gate International); New York, 1939 (World of Tomorrow); Seattle, 1962 (Century 21); New York, 1964 (World's Fair); Montreal, 1967 (Man and His World); and Knoxville, 1982 (Energy Expo). Memorabilia of fairs include directories, pictures, fabrics, ceramics, etc.

WORLD'S FAIR, AC Spark Plug, 1933, 3/8 Tap, Original Paper	2.00
Ashtray, 1933, Chicago, Metal, Hall of Science	6.00
Ashtray, 1933, Chrysler Exhibit, Copper	8.00
Ashtray, 1934, Century of Progress, Chicago	45.00
Ashtray, 1962, Silver	15.00
Ashtray, 1974, Spokane, Silver	15.00
Bank, 1876, Crystal	500.00
Bank, 1933, American Can	30.00
Bank, 1934, Century of Progress, Tin, Canco	12.00
Bank, 1939, New York, Glass, Round	38.00
Bank, Dime, 1964, New York, Tin, Original Card	15.00
Bell, Dinner, 1893, Columbian Exposition, Frosted Swirl Handle	175.00
Book, 1893, Columbian Exposition, Color Plates, Germany	35.00
Book, 1934, Chicago, 64 Pages	45.00
Book, Flip, 1939, New York, Bromo-Seltzer Movie	60.00
Book, Pop-Up, 1964, New York	19.00
Booklet, 1939, Come Visit Cuba	15.00
Booklet, 1964, Sinclair Oil Dinosaur	10.00
Bookmark, 1893, View of Woman's Building, Silk	75.00
Bookmark, 1933, Chicago, Metal	6.00
Bottle Opener, 1933, Chicago, Nude Egyptian Maiden, Brass	55.00
Bowl, 1892, Woman's Building, Palmer Handle, Embossed, 6 In.	89.00
Bowl, 1900, Indian Handle, Women Form America Continent, 6 In.	95.00
Bowl, 1933, Logo, Nudes, Hall of Science, Deco Handle, 5 1/4 In.	49.00
Bracelet, 1933, Century of Progress, Cuff Style	12.00
Brochure, 1904, Cable Piano Co., Louisiana Expo., Ads, 30 Pgs.	12.00
Cane, 1893, Folding, Wooden Seat	55.00
Cards, Playing, 1934, Different Pictures On Each	23.50
Cards, Playing, 1939, Double Deck, Trylon & Perisphere	25.00
Case, Cigarette, 1939, Wooden Inlaid Design, T & P	40.00
Catalog, Art, 1940, New York, American & European Paintings	20.00
Chair, Cane, 1939, New York, Folding	65.00
Cigar Band, 1939, New York	10.00
Clock, 1893, Landing Scene, Columbian Exposition	250.00
Comb, 1939, Metal Case	30.00
Compact, Powder, 1939, New York	12.00
Cup & Saucer, Plate Set, 1939, New York, American Potter	48.00

Cup, 1904, Graniteware	30.00
Decanter, 1939, Milk Glass	15.00
Diary, 1904, St.Louis, 5 Week Daily Railroad Trip	50.00
Dish, 1904, St.Louis Exposition, Brass, Mule, Flowers, 3 1/2 In.	15.00
Dish, Heart, 1962, Seattle, 5 In.	8.00
Fabric Cutter, 1933, Singer Advertising, 10 In.	24.00
Flier, 1939, New York, San Fran., General Motors, 8 X 11 In.	10.00
Frame, 1893, Reverse Painting, Horticulture Building	70.00
Golf Bag, 1939, Souvenir, 3 Golf Pencils, 6 In.	40.00
Handkerchief, 1893, Chicago	10.00
Handkerchief, 1933, Japanese Silk	16.00
Handkerchief, Multicolored, 1904, St. Louis Exposition	20.00
Hatchet, 1892, Chicago Fair, Libbey	55.00
Hatchet, 1904, Glass, St.Louis	85.00
Hot Pad, 1939, Foil–Like Silver, Name, Date & Attractions	12.00
Invitation, 1939, Opening of Fair	50.00
Jacket, 1939, Trylon Shoulder Patch, Bakelite Buttons	95.00
Jacket, Dress, 1939	95.00
Key Chain, 1939, Enameled	15.00
Lamp, Kerosene, 1893, Columbus, Government Building	950.00
Letter Opener, 1933, Metal	55.00
Letter Opener, 1934, Chicago, Metal	13.00
License Plate, 1939, California World's Fair	45.00
Lighter, 1962, Seattle, Space Needle, Chrome, 10 In.	27.50
Luggage, 1964–65, Overnight, Fair Logo On Both Sides	20.00
Magazine, 1939, New York Times, Mar.5, 73 Pages	10.00
Match Safe, 1904, St. Louis, Palace of Transportation	85.00
Matchbook, 1939, Advertising, No Matches, 3 Piece	16.00
Mirror, 1893, Columbian Exposition, Admin.Bldg., Pocket	15.00
Mug, 1893, Ruby Flashed, 3 In.	30.00
Mug, 1933, Chicago, Copper	45.00
Paperweight, 1893, Columbian Exposition, Christopher Columbus	100.00
Paperweight, Havoline Oil	35.00
Parasol, 1933, Chicago, Wood Handle, Paper, Open–24 X 30 In.	100.00
Pincushion, 1898, Metal Shoe	45.00
Pitcher, 1919, Inscribed Martha, Glass, Green	20.00
Pitcher, Water, 1893, Flowers, Flags, Columbus	295.00
Plaque Set, 1876, Carved Wood, Buildings, 6 Piece	250.00
Plate, 1904, St.Louis, Festival Hall, Cascade Gardens, 7 In.	22.00
Plate, 1939, Blue & White, England	85.00
Plate, 1940, Potter's, Turquoise, Fiesta, Pair	45.00
Plate, 1940, Trylon Perisphere Center, 11 In.	48.00
Postcard, 1904, Hold To Light, Palace of Manufacturers	55.00
Postcard, 1964, New York, 12 Piece	10.00
Program, 1964, New York, Hawaii Exhibit, 8 1/2 X 11 In.	15.00
Purse, 1904, St.Louis, Leather, With Chain, Small	20.00
Record, 1964, Traveler's Insurance	15.00
Salt & Pepper, 1904, St.Louis, Glass Bladder Holds Both	145.00
Salt & Pepper, 1933, Chicago, Pitcher Shape	25.00
Salt & Pepper, 1933, Chicago, Stylized Bird, Metal	35.00
Salt & Pepper, 1940, 4 Seasons, New York, 4 Colors, HLC	200.00
Scarf, Piano, 1933	48.00
Snuffbox, 1892, Stack of Columbian Gold Coins, Hinged, Brass	145.00
Spoon, 1904, St.Louis, Cascade Garden, Sterling Silver	29.00
Spoon, 1904, St.Louis, Sterling Silver, Ornate	65.00
Spoon, 1909, Seattle, Sterling Silver	65.00
Spoon, 1933, Hall of Science, Silver	14.00
Spoon, 1939, New York	20.00
Sword & Scabbard, 1893, Columbian Exposition	150.00
Teaspoon, 1933, Century of Progress, Silver Plate, Set of 6	48.00
Thermometer, 1933, Chicago, 24K Gold Plated, Box	100.00
Thermometer, 1939	25.00
Tie Clip, 1939, New York	8.00
Tip Tray, 1904, Junket, St. Louis, 4 3/8 In.	30.00

Tip Tray, 1964, New York	6.00
Toothpick, 1893, Ruby Thumbprint	40.00
Toy, Bus, 1933, Greyhound, GMC, Chicago, Cast Iron, 11 In.	150.00
Travel Guide, 1893, B & O Railroad, 92 Pages	25.00
Tray, 1933, Impressed Aerial View, Copper, 7 X 10 In.	50.00
Tumbler, 1893, Woman's Building, Etched	40.00
Tumbler, 1962, Seattle	8.00
Tumbler, 1964, Circus, Glass	7.00
Tumbler, 1964, New York, Frosted	8.00
Umbrella, 1962, Seattle	14.95
Vase, 1933, Chicago, Dancing Girls, Black Amethyst	30.00
Walking Stick, 1933, Miniature Beer Keg Handle	35.00
Watch Fob, 1893, Opens For I.D.	40.00
Watch Fob, 1903, Each Link Engraved With Date & Building	125.00

The wristwatch came into use during World War I. Pocket watches
are listed in the watch category.

WRISTWATCH, 17 Jewels, Arabic Numbers, Platinum & Diamond, White Cord Band	247.50
Advertising, Honeycomb Cereal	22.00
Advertising, Pillsbury Doughboy	30.00
Advertising, Ritz Crackers, Crackers Indicate Hour, Steel, 1960s	690.00
Advertising, Ronald McDonald	12.00
All-Star Baseball, M. Mantle, R. Maris, W. Mays Names On Face	135.00
Angelus, Chronodate, 45 Minute Register, Month, Day, Date, 1950's	950.00
Babe Ruth, 1949	395.00
Baume & Mercier, Woman's, Diamonds, 18K White Gold	2420.00
Breitling, Chronograph, Navitimer, Stainless Steel	500.00
Breitling, Navistar, Papers, Box	650.00
Bucherer, Woman's, 18K Gold, 12 Diamonds, Brick Design Band	1500.00
Bulova, 10K Gold Filled, 21 Jewel, Arabic Numbers, 1940s	780.00
Bulova, 10K Gold, 21 Jewel, Arabic Numbers, Sub Seconds, 1940s	780.00
Bulova, 14K Yellow Gold, 17 Jewel, Classic, 1950s	800.00
Bulova, Accutron, 18K Gold, Military Time Zone, Link Band	2150.00
Bulova, Woman's, 14K White Gold, Face Diamonds, Through Band	350.00
Cartier, Quartz, Roman Numerals On Bezel, Flexible Band	335.00
Cinderella, U.S. Time, 1950s	25.00
Concord, Woman's, 17 Jewel, Diamond Set Bezel, White Gold Band	1100.00
Elgin, 14K Gold, Rectangular, 1940s	150.00
Elgin, Art Deco, 14K White Gold, Cobalt Enameled, 1920s	3900.00
Elgin, Woman's, 10K Gold, 4 Diamonds Each End	95.00
Elgin, Woman's, 14K White Gold, 8 Diamonds	155.00
Elgin, Woman's, 14K White Gold, Lady & Tiger, 1920s	2000.00
Girard Perregaux, Man's, 14K Gold, Gyromatic, Round	395.00
Girard Perregaux, Man's, Stainless Steel, 1940, Box	65.00
Girard Perregaux, Woman's, 14K Gold, 8 Diamonds	195.00
Girard Phillippe, Man's, Automatic, Date, 4 Diamonds In Case	350.00
Gruen, Curvex, 14K White Gold, 3 Diamonds On Dial, 1940s	595.00
Gruen, Doctor's, 14K Gold Filled, Swiss Movement, 1930s	2500.00
Gruen, Doctor's, Duo-Dial, 17 Jewel, 1930s	2500.00
Gruen, Woman's, 14K Gold, Diamonds On Band & Bezel	550.00
Gubelin, Platinum & Diamond, 17 Jewel ....*Illus*	800.00
Hamilton, Man's, 14K Gold, Masterpiece, Electric	500.00
Hamilton, Piping Rock, 14K White Gold, Roman, 1920s	2500.00
Hamilton, Spur, Roman Numerals, Silver Dial, 1920s	6000.00
Hamilton, Vega, Gold Filled, Converted To Quartz, 1950s	900.00
Hampden, Woman's, 15 Jewel, Yellow Gold, Grosgrain Strap	85.00
Jules Jurgensen, 19 Diamonds, 14K Gold	325.00
LeCoultre, Moonphase, 10K Yellow Gold Filled, 1950s	5300.00
LeCoultre, Mystery, 14K White Gold, Diamonds At 5 Minutes	2500.00
LeCoultre, Woman's, 19K Gold, Enameled Flowers	250.00
Longines, 14K Gold, Crackled Blue Enamel Face, Hours On Case	500.00
Longines, Aviator's, Lindbergh Design, 10K Gold Filled, 17 Jewel	4600.00
Lord Elgin, Digital, 14K Gold, Cutout For Hours, 1940	950.00
Lucian Piccard, Man's, Very Thin, 14K Gold	200.00

Mary Marvel, 1940s, Plastic Box .... 200.00 To 345.00
Mary Marvel, 1948, Plastic Box 345.00
Movado, 14K Yellow Gold, Minute Track On Outer Perimeter 2000.00
Movado, Man's, 14K Gold, 6–Sided, Thin Case, 1950 .... 1200.00
Omega, Woman's, Wide Gold Band 375.00
Patek Philippe, 18K Gold, 18 Jewel, C.1960 .... 2860.00
Patek Philippe, Calatrava, 18 Jewel, 3/4 Size, 1950s 4900.00
Patek Philippe, Man's, 18K Yellow Gold, Automatic 4200.00
Patek Philippe, Square, Gold, Black Enamel Arabic Numbers 4400.00
Patek Philippe, Woman's, 18K White Gold, 26 Diamonds 5500.00
Paul Ditisheim, Solvil, 14K Rose Gold, Arabic Numbers 1700.00
Paul Garnier, Am/Pm, Gold–Plated Bezel, 15 Jewel, 1960s 475.00
Pebbles, 1960s 45.00
Pee Wee Herman 16.00
R2d2–C3p0, Bradley, Box 35.00
Ritz Crackers, Crackers Around Face, Steel, 1960s 690.00
Rolex, 14K Gold & Stainless, Date Adjustment, Champagne Dial 1275.00
Rolex, 18K Rose Gold, 18 Jewel, Rose Colored Dial, 1940s 3100.00
Rolex, Demihunter, Hexagonal Shape, Black Enamel Numbers, 1920s 3800.00
Rolex, Oyster Perpetual, 18K Yellow Gold, 17 Jewel, 1940s 4000.00
Rolex, Stainless Steel, 3 Subsidiary Dials, Oyster Bracelet 3300.00
Seiko, Man's, Gold Nugget, 14K Gold 595.00
Smitty, 1935, Box 425.00
Snoopy, On Doghouse Roof, Aviator & Airplane Move, 1965 .... 65.00
Swiss, 17 Jewel, Train On Reverse, Colsen Incabloc 110.00
Swiss, Olympia, Stainless Steel, Moonphase, Calendar 450.00
Tavannes, 18K Yellow Gold, 17 Jewel, Elliptical Case, 1920s 4500.00
Tissot, Man's, Stainless Steel, Automatic, Waterproof, Sweep Hand 200.00
Tom & Jerry, Lincoln International, Battery Operated, Wind, Box 60.00
Tom Corbett, 1951 .... 145.00
Vacheron & Constantin, 14K Gold, 17 Jewel, Hooded Bezel, 1940s 4000.00
Vacheron & Constantin, 14K Rose Gold 1800.00
Vacheron & Constantin, 18K Gold Reeded Case, C.1943 .... 6600.00
Vulcan Cricket, Man's, Alarm 100.00
Waltham, 14K Yellow Gold, 15 Jewel, Waterproof, 1920s 2200.00
Waltham, Premier, 10K Gold Filled, Curved Lugs, 1930s 1200.00
Wittnauer, 10K Gold, Round 85.00
Wittnauer, Woman's, 10K Gold Filled, 1950s 45.00
Wonder Woman, Box 25.00

Yellowware is a heavy earthenware made of a yellowish clay. It varies in color from light yellow to orange–yellow. Many nineteenth– and twentieth–century kitchen bowls and jugs were made of yellowware. It was made in England and in the United States. Another form of pottery that is sometimes classed as yellowware is listed in this book under Mocha.

YELLOWWARE, Bank, Penny, Lion 45.00
Bottle, Embossed Bands, Label, D.Colver, 8 In. 125.00
Bottle, Figural, Man With Fiddle, 8 1/2 In. 250.00
Bowl Set, Ribbed Exterior, Blue Stripes, 5 In. To 15 In., 9 Pc. 275.00
Bowl, 2 Brown Stripes, Molded Fluting, 5 In. 35.00
Bowl, 3 Blue Bands, 8 In. 25.00
Bowl, Blue Bands, 10 In. 35.00
Bowl, Blue Bands, 11 In. 22.00
Bowl, Blue Seaweed Design, White Band, Blue Stripe, 10 In. 65.00
Bowl, Blue Seaweed, White Band, 10 X 5 In. 85.00
Bowl, Blue Stripes, Embossed Design, 6 1/2 In. 65.00
Bowl, Brown Band, 15 In. 95.00
Bowl, Brown Band, Small 18.00
Bowl, Brown Sponging, 9 1/2 In. 30.00
Bowl, Girl With Sprinkling Can, 10 In. 45.00
Bowl, Mixing, 6 1/4 In. 45.00
Bowl, Mixing, 6 3/4 In. 65.00
Bowl, Mixing, 8 1/2 In. 65.00

Bowl, Mixing, Blue & White Stripes, Embossed Ribs, 5 1/2 In. 17.50
Bowl, Mixing, Blue Bands, 11 1/2 In. 40.00
Bowl, Mixing, Brown Stripes, Blue Seaweed Design, White Band 90.00
Bowl, Ovoid, 5 1/2 X 4 1/2 In. 25.00
Bowl, Pink & Blue Stripes, 14 In. 85.00
Bowl, Reversed Picket Fence, 12 In. 50.00
Bowl, Scalloped Rim, Gilt Trim, Blue Sponge Spatter, 8 In. 95.00
Bowl, Seaweed Design, Brown Stripes, White Band, 9 In. 300.00
Bowl, White Ribs, Brown Stripes, 3 3/4 X 5 In. 65.00
Bowl, Wide Brown Stripe, 6 1/2 In. 85.00
Box, Urns of Fruit, 15 1/2 In. 200.00
Canister, Dutch Children, Windmill, Black Stenciling, 3 Piece 45.00
Casserole, Cover, Brown Sponging, 7 1/4 In. 40.00
Chamber Pot, Child's, Multi–Brown Bands, 6 X 9 1/2 In. 65.00
Chamber Pot, Green Seaweed Pattern 235.00
Chamber Pot, White Band, 2 1/8 In. 50.00
Chamber Pot, White, Blue Seaweed Design, Brown Stripes, 2 In. 95.00
Coffeepot, Floral Finial, 9 1/2 In. 50.00
Cookie Jar, Painted Cherries, Open Handles 65.00
Creamer, Brown Stripes, Cup Shape, 3 3/8 In. 25.00
Creamer, Cow 2000.00
Crock, Brown Bands, 5 1/2 In. 30.00
Crock, Butter, Cover 95.00
Crock, Butter, Elsie The Cow 125.00
Crock, Sailboat, 10 X 14 In. 150.00
Cup & Saucer, Brightly Colored Glaze 35.00
Custard, Blue Band 23.00
Desk Set, Sheep & Lion Head, With Sander 200.00
Dish, Brown Sponging, 2 X 4 3/4 In. 15.00
Dish, Cover, Seaweed Design, White Band, Brown Stripes, 4 1/4 In. 250.00
Figurine, Dog, With Keg, Amber Glaze, 7 1/2 In. 175.00
Inkstand, Recumbent Lion, 2 Inserts, Gold Trim, 1850s 275.00
Jar, Cover, Minerva Head Handles, Seaweed Design, 8 1/2 In. 450.00
Jar, Preserve, Barrel Shape 60.00
Jar, Preserve, Keg Shape, 6 In. 175.00
Jar, Preserve, Keg Shape, 7 In. 85.00
Jug, Black Stripes, 3 3/8 In. 95.00
Lamp, Grease, Blue–Green Running Glaze, Marked W, 14 1/2 In. 55.00
Meat Tenderizer, Pat.Date, Dec.25, 1877 .... 125.00
Mold, Candle, 3 Sections 70.00
Mold, Corn .... 40.00 To 85.00
Mold, Pudding, Corncob Center, 19th Century 75.00
Mold, Rabbit, Small 125.00
Mold, Sheaf of Wheat 95.00
Mug, Bluish Green Seaweed Design, White Band, Stripes, 3 In. 175.00
Mug, Flared Lip, Embossed Leaf Handle, 3 In. 105.00
Mug, Marbelized Band, Rib Handle, 3 1/4 In. 200.00
Mug, Seaweed Design, White Band, Brown Stripes, 3 In. 125.00
Mug, Seaweed Design, White Band, Dark Brown Stripes, 3 1/2 In. 225.00
Mug, White Slip Stripes, Wavy Lines, Handle, 3 7/8 In. 275.00
Mug, Yellow, 12 Oz. 25.00
Mustard, Cover, Blue Stripe Design, 3 In. 150.00
Nested Bowls, Brown Flower Stencil, 4 Piece 175.00
Nested Bowls, Brown Flower Stencil, 8 & 9 In., 2 Piece 150.00
Nested Bowls, Flower Stencil, 5 Piece 225.00
Pitcher, 3 Qt. 165.00
Pitcher, Basket Weave, Flower 135.00
Pitcher, Brown Band, Dark Brown Stripes, 8 1/2 In. 205.00
Pitcher, Buckeye 150.00
Pitcher, Mask Spout, White Design, England, 6 3/8 In. 95.00
Pitcher, Rose & Lattice 175.00
Plate, 10 In. 38.00
Rolling Pin, Turned Wooden Handle, 15 1/2 In. 250.00
Salt, Chicken On Nest 195.00

Salt, Hanging, Embossed Peacock	100.00
Salt, White Band, Blue Seaweed Design, 2 1/8 X 3 In.	155.00
Saltshaker, White Band, Blue Seaweed Design, 4 1/4 In.	375.00
Soap Dish, Open Impressed Flower	125.00
Spigot, From Akron, Ohio, Large, 2 Piece	85.00
Tieback, Curtain, Floral Design, Brown, Sponging	75.00
Toothpick, Black Stamp	185.00

ZANE WARE Zane Pottery was founded in 1921 by Adam Reed and Harry McClelland in South Zanesville, Ohio, at the old Peters and Reed Building. Zane pottery is very similar to Peters and Reed pottery, but it is usually marked. The factory was sold in 1941 to Lawton Gonder.

ZANE, Flower Frog, Turtle, Blue	25.00
Tankard Set, Lomora, Matte, 7 Piece	250.00

LA MORO The Zanesville Art Pottery was founded in 1900 by David Schmidt in Zanesville, Ohio. The firm made faience umbrella stands, jardinieres, and pedestals. The company closed in 1962. Many pieces are marked with just the words "La Moro."

ZANESVILLE, Tile, 3 Sections, 6 X 18 In., Pair	500.00
Vase, 12 In., Pair	85.00

ZSOLNAY PÉCS Zsolnay pottery was made in Hungary after 1862 and was characterized by Persian, Art Nouveau, or Hungarian motifs. A series of new Zsolnay figurines with green-gold luster finish is available in many shops today. Early Zsolnay was not marked; but by 1878, the tower trademark was used.

ZSOLNAY, Bowl, Art Nouveau Design, 3 1/2 In.	65.00
Bowl, Gold Iridescent, Blue Inclusions, Art Nouveau, 6 In.	225.00
Bowl, Iridescent Green, Steeple Mark, 3 1/2 In.	57.00
Ewer, 1906, 5 In.	95.00
Ewer, Florals, Face On Spout, Gold Trim, 12 1/2 In.	150.00
Figurine, Bird, Green, Green Touches, 4 1/2 In.	85.00
Figurine, Nude, Blue, 10 In.	175.00
Vase, 6 Floriform Straps, Iridescent, Signed, C.1900, 7 5/8 In.	3575.00
Vase, Blue, Marked, 15 In.	625.00
Vase, Double Walled, Reticulated, Marked, 6 1/2 In.	350.00
Vase, Draped Seated Woman, Flared Floral Leaf Rim, 9 1/4 In.	250.00
Vase, Flowers, Blue, Orchid, Tan, Reticulated, Square Shape, 9 1/4 In.	495.00
Vase, Flowers, Brown Tower, Reticulated, 2 Handles, Square, 4 In.	415.00
Vase, Puzzle, Pink, Art Nouveau, Gold Outline, 4 Handles, 12 In.	125.00
Vase, Stylized Landscape, Fruiting Trees, Signed, C.1900, 9 1/4 In.	3080.00

It is easy to glue pieces of broken china. Use a new fast setting but not instant glue. Position the pieces correctly, then use tape to hold the parts together. If the piece needs special support, lean it in a suitable position in a box filled with sand.

THE KOVELS' LIBRARY

Kovels' 365 Collectibles Calendar 1991

America's collecting passion! From Arts & Crafts to Art Moderne, Majolica to memorabilia, cookie jars, penny banks, and Pez. A new-old treasure is pictured everyday in a Page-A-Day™ calendar with all the right pieces.

Available wherever calendars are sold.

Workman Publishing   708 Broadway   New York, New York 10003
Page-A-Day is a trademark of Workman Publishing.

American Country Furniture 1780–1875

Over 700 close-up photographs identify styles, construction, woods, finishes, hardware, and other details. All the information you need to be an expert on American country furniture. Special sections on Pennsylvania, Shaker furniture, spool furniture and furniture construction, plus an illustrated glossary of accessories and terms.
54668X $14.95 paper

Dictionary of Marks—Pottery and Porcelain (1580–1880)

A classic in the field, the *Dictionary of Marks* is a comprehensive guide to more than 5,000 American and European pottery and porcelain marks. It shows at a glance the geographical location of the factory, family name or manufacturer's name, type of ware, color of mark, and the date the mark was used.

001411 $10.95 hardcover

Kovels' New Dictionary of Marks—Pottery and Porcelain
1850 TO THE PRESENT

Kovels' New Dictionary of Marks provides the quickest and easiest way to identify more than 3,500 American, European, and Oriental marks. The perfect companion to the Kovels' original best seller, *The Dictionary of Marks—Pottery and Porcelain,* this is the most comprehensive reference for nineteenth- and twentieth-century marks. Together, the two volumes are an indispensable guide to the porcelain and pottery marks of the last four centuries.

559145 $17.95 hardcover

Kovels' American Silver Marks

Almost everyone owns an old piece of silver. Few know the complete history of that piece. This is a simple-to-use guide to identifying marks and monograms that appear on silver. Collectors and professional dealers can quickly determine the maker of a piece of silver. Each listing includes working dates, location, mark (if known), and bibliographic references to more than 200 books and articles. Makers working from 1650 to the present are included, and over 10,000 silversmiths are listed in alphabetical order, with a cross-indexing system for monograms and pictorial marks.
568829 $40.00 hardcover

Kovels' Bottles Price List
EIGHTH EDITION

Over 10,000 current prices for hundreds of types of bottles—more than any other bottle price list on the market. More than 500 illustrations in full color and black and white. Includes old and new bottles, bitters, figurals, flasks, Avons, Beams, and a host of others. Notes on styles and manufacturers, lists of bottle magazines and clubs, and an extensive bibliography. The most definitive listing of current prices available.
566133 $12.95 paper

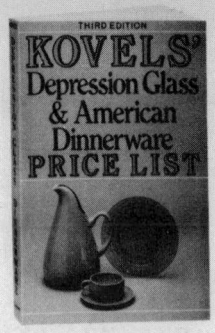

Kovels' Depression Glass & American Dinnerware Price List
THIRD EDITION

The inexpensive pastel-colored glassware that became popular from 1925 on and the ceramic dinnerware produced during the same period are now attracting collectors in great numbers. Here are the latest and most accurate prices, based on a comprehensive survey of actual sales, shows, catalogs, auctions, and other reliable sources.
568659 $12.95 paper

Kovels' Illustrated Price Guide to Royal Doulton
SECOND EDITION

Over 5,000 prices of Royal Doulton pieces, including complete listings of figurines, character jugs, limited editions, Toby jugs, dolls, as well as series ware, animals and birds, rouge flambé, and miscellaneous categories. Includes descriptions, dates of manufacture, HN listings, with a history of the Doulton factory and notes on rarities and color changes. Special section on Royal Doulton marks. Over 400 illustrations in color and black and white.
55044X $10.95 paper

Kovels' Know Your Antiques
REVISED AND UPDATED EDITION

How to recognize and evaluate any antique—large or small—like an expert. Ideal for the beginner. Detailed advice about recognition, evaluation, and care of antiques, and identification of fakes.
578069 $14.95 paper

Kovels' Know Your Collectibles

This up-to-date illustrated guide (more than 1,000 photographs and illustrations) focuses on today's most fascinating collecting trends: pottery, porcelain, silver, glass, furniture, toys, and other objects that are not old enough to be officially called "antiques" but nonetheless are rapidly increasing in value. It contains information about value, origin, availability, storage, and buying and selling, plus extensive bibliographies and charts.
536080 $18.95 hardcover

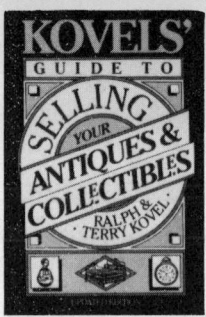

KOVELS' GUIDE TO SELLING YOUR ANTIQUES & COLLECTIBLES
UPDATED EDITION

This short, handy, pocket-size guide tells you how to sell *your* antiques and collectibles for the best possible price. What is the right market for your particular collection? Should you have your items professionally appraised? Should a dealer do the appraisal? Should you sell to a friend? What are the proper procedures for a house sale? How do you take table space at a flea market? What fees will an auction house charge? These are just some of the questions that the Kovels answer, as well as giving advice on how to sell more than seventy-five categories of collectibles—from baseball cards, beer cans, carousel figures, coins, decoys, furniture, and glass to music boxes, postcards, television sets, stamps, stocks and bonds, toys, and Western art.
58008X $9.95 paper

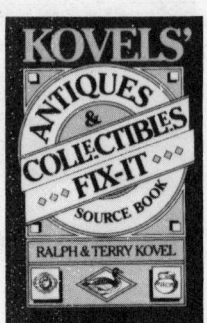

KOVELS' ANTIQUES & COLLECTIBLES FIX-IT SOURCE BOOK

This book will be a valuable companion for everyone seeking information on do-it-yourself or professional restoration and all the services and parts available for the care of your antiques.
573334 $9.95 paper

K O V E L S

SEND ORDERS & INQUIRIES TO: **Crown Publishers, Inc.**
201 East 50th Street, New York, NY 10022
ATT: SALES DEPT.

SALES & TITLE INFORMATION
1-800-733-3000

NAME _____

ADDRESS _____

CITY & STATE _____   ZIP _____

PLEASE SEND ME THE FOLLOWING BOOKS:

ITEM NO.	QTY.	TITLE		PRICE	TOTAL
580950	_____	Kovels' Antiques & Collectibles Price List 23rd Edition	PAPER	$11.95	_____
54668X	_____	American Country Furniture 1780–1875	PAPER	$14.95	_____
001411	_____	Dictionary of Marks-Pottery and Porcelain	HARDCOVER	$10.95	_____
559145	_____	Kovels' New Dictionary of Marks	HARDCOVER	$17.95	_____
568829	_____	Kovels' American Silver Marks	HARDCOVER	$40.00	_____
566133	_____	Kovels' Bottles Price List 8th Edition	PAPER	$12.95	_____
568659	_____	Kovels' Depression Glass & American Dinnerware Price List 3rd Edition	PAPER	$12.95	_____
55044X	_____	Kovels' Illustrated Price Guide to Royal Doulton 2nd Edition	PAPER	$10.95	_____
578069	_____	Kovels' Know Your Antiques Revised and Updated	PAPER	$14.95	_____
536080	_____	Kovels' Know Your Collectibles	HARDCOVER	$18.95	_____
58008X	_____	Kovels' Guide to Selling Your Antiques & Collectibles Updated Edition	PAPER	$ 9.95	_____
573334	_____	Kovels' Antiques & Collectibles Fix-It Source Book	PAPER	$ 9.95	_____

_____ TOTAL ITEMS   TOTAL RETAIL VALUE _____

CHECK OR MONEY ORDER ENCLOSED MADE PAYABLE TO
CROWN PUBLISHERS, INC., 201 East 50th Street,
New York, N.Y. 10022
or telephone 1-800-733-3000
(No cash or stamps, please)

Charge: ☐ MasterCard ☐ Visa ☐ American Express
Account Number (include all digits)   Expires MO. YR.
_____

Shipping & Handling
Charge $1.50 for one book;
50¢ for each additional book.
Please add applicable
sales tax.   _____

TOTAL AMOUNT DUE _____

Signature _____
                         Thank you for your order.

PRICES SUBJECT TO CHANGE
WITHOUT NOTICE. If a more
recent edition of a price list has
been published at the same price, it
will be sent instead of the old edition.